W9-DEU-170

Glencoe

WORLD HISTORY

Reading Essentials and Study Guide

Glencoe McGraw-Hill

New York, New York   Columbus, Ohio   Chicago, Illinois   Peoria, Illinois   Woodland Hills, California

To the Teacher

Glencoe World History Reading Essentials and Study Guide is designed to help students use recognized reading strategies to improve their reading-for-information skills. For each section of the student textbook, the students are alerted to key terms and are asked to draw from prior knowledge, organize their thoughts with a graphic organizer, and then follow a process to read and understand the text. The *Reading Essentials and Study Guide* was prepared to help your students get more from their textbook by reading with a purpose.

Glencoe/McGraw-Hill

A Division of The ***McGraw-Hill*** *Companies*

Send all inquiries to:
Glencoe/McGraw-Hill
8787 Orion Place
Columbus, OH 43240

ISBN 0-07-829442-8

Printed in the United States of America

1 2 3 4 5 6 7 8 9 10 009 08 07 06 05 04 03 02

Table of Contents

Chapter 17: Revolution and Enlightenment

Chapter 18: The French Revolution and Napoleon

Chapter 19: Industrialization and Nationalism

Chapter 20: Mass Society and Democracy

Chapter 21: The Height of Imperialism

Chapter 22: East Asia Under Challenge

Chapter 23: War and Revolution

Chapter 24: The West Between the Wars

Chapter 25: Nationalism Around the World

Chapter 26: World War II

Chapter 27: Cold War and Postwar Changes

Chapter 28: The Contemporary Western World

Chapter 29: Latin America

Chapter 30: Africa and the Middle East

Chapter 31: Asia and the Pacific

Chapter 32: Challenges and Hopes for the Future

Name ______________________ Date ______________ Class ______________

Reading Essentials and Study Guide

Chapter 1, Section 1

For use with textbook pages 19–25

EARLY HUMANS

KEY TERMS

prehistory the period in human history before writing was developed *(page 19)*

archaeology the study of past societies through an analysis of what people have left behind *(page 19)*

artifacts objects that archaeologists examine, such as tools, pottery, paintings, weapons, buildings, and household items *(page 20)*

anthropology the study of human life and culture *(page 20)*

fossils remains of humans, plants and animals *(page 20)*

australopithecines ("southern apes") the earliest humanlike creatures that lived in Africa three to four million years ago *(page 21)*

hominids humans and other creatures that walk upright *(page 21)*

Homo erectus ("upright human being") a hominid species that emerged around 1.5 million years ago and used fire and larger tools *(page 21)*

Homo sapiens ("wise human being") a hominid species that emerged around 250,000 years ago and developed into two subgroups, Neanderthals and *Homo sapiens sapiens (page 21)*

Neanderthals a subgroup of *Homo sapiens* whose remains were first found in the Neander Valley in Germany *(page 21)*

Homo sapiens sapiens ("wise, wise human beings") the first anatomically modern humans that appeared in Africa between 150,000 and 200,000 years ago *(page 22)*

Paleolithic Age ("Old Stone Age") the early period of human history (approximately 2,500,000 to 10,000 B.C.) when humans used simple stone tools *(page 22)*

nomads people who moved from place to place in search of food *(page 23)*

DRAWING FROM EXPERIENCE

Have you ever wondered about the earliest humans? How did they get their food and clothing? What did they use for shelter?

In this section, you will learn about the early stages of human development. You will also learn how scientists analyze the remains that early humans left behind and what they have learned from these remains.

Name ______________________ Date ______________________ Class ______________________

Reading Essentials and Study Guide

ORGANIZING YOUR THOUGHTS

Use the diagram below to help you take notes. Three stages in early human development are described in this section. Identify and summarize these stages.

	Stage 1	**Stage 2**	**Stage 3**
Name of hominids	**1.**	**4.**	**7.**
Time period	**2.**	**5.**	**8.**
Location(s)	**3.**	**6.**	**9.**

READ TO LEARN

• Before History *(page 19)*

Prehistory is the period of human history before writing was developed. Because there are no writings to tell us what happened during this time, scientists must study other things to learn about early humans. **Archaeology** is the study of past societies through an analysis of what people left behind. Archaeologists dig up and study the tools, pottery, paintings, weapons, buildings, and household items that people used. These objects are called **artifacts. Anthropology** is the study of human life and culture. Anthropologists use artifacts and human **fossils** (the remains of humans) to find out how early people lived.

Archaeologists and anthropologists use scientific methods to help them with their work. For example, they learn what early people ate by analyzing the bones, skins, and plant seeds that they find. They also need to determine how old the objects are. This is called *dating a find*. One method is radiocarbon dating. This method dates (determines the age of) an object by measuring the amount of radioactive carbon (C-14) left in it. This method can only be used for dating objects that are less than 50,000 years old. Another method is thermoluminescence dating. This method dates objects by measuring the light given off by electrons in the soil around the objects. This method helps scientists date objects as far back as 200,000 years ago. Scientists have also begun to use biological methods, such as DNA testing, to learn more about the lives of early people.

10. How do archaeologists and anthropologists determine the age of the objects they find?

____

____

____

____

• Early Stages of Development *(page 21)*

Archaeologists and anthropologists use their discoveries to create theories about early human history. According to the current theory, there were three stages in the development of early humans. The earliest humanlike creatures lived in Africa three to four million years ago. They were called **australopithecines** or "southern apes" by their discoverer, Donald Johanson. They lived in eastern and southern Africa. They were the first hominids to make stone tools. **Hominids** are humans and other creatures that walk upright. Archaeologists have recently discovered a skull that they think is a new form of hominid. They think it is about 3.5 million years old. It is called Kenyanthropus platyops (the flat-faced man of Kenya).

The second stage in human development is marked by the appearance of ***Homo erectus*** ("upright human being"). These hominids emerged about 1.5 million years ago in Africa. Then they moved into Europe and Asia. They used fire and made larger and more varied tools.

The third stage in human development began about 250,000 years ago. This stage is marked by the emergence of ***Homo sapiens*** ("wise human being"). Neanderthals and *Homo sapiens sapiens* both developed from Homo sapiens.

The remains of **Neanderthals** were first discovered in the Neander Valley in Germany. Remains have also been found throughout Europe and Southwest Asia. Neanderthals lived between 100,000 and 30,000 B.C. They used a variety of stone tools and buried their dead. They also made clothes from animal skins.

Homo sapiens sapiens ("wise, wise human being") appeared in Africa 150,000 to 200,000 years ago. They were the first anatomically modern humans (people who looked like us). By 30,000 B.C., they had replaced the Neanderthals. They spread gradually from Africa to other parts of the world. All humans today belong to the subspecies *Homo sapiens sapiens.*

11. What two subgroups developed from *Homo sapiens?*

____

____

____

____

____

• The Hunter-Gatherers of the Old Stone Age *(page 22)*

Early humans used tools made of stone. The period in history when humans used simple stone tools is called the **Paleolithic Age** ("Old Stone Age"). This period lasted from about 2,500,000 to 10,000 B.C. During this period, humans used hunting and gathering to get their food. They gathered wild nuts, berries, fruits, wild grains, and green plants. They hunted and ate various animals, such as buffalo, horses, reindeer, and fish. They were **nomads** (people who moved from place to place). They moved in order to find food. Both men and women were responsible for finding food. Men probably did most of the hunting of large animals. Women may have gathered berries, nuts, and grains, so that they could stay closer to their camps.

Paleolithic people found shelter in caves. They also created shelters made of wood poles or sticks covered with animals hides. They used fire to stay warm and to protect themselves from wild animals. They also used fire to cook food. Archaeologists believe that friction (rubbing two pieces of wood together) was probably the earliest method for starting fires. Fire allowed humans to survive during the Ice Ages. During the most recent Ice Age, ice covered large parts of Europe, Asia, and North America. This Ice Age lasted from about 100,000 B.C. to 8000 B.C.

Paleolithic people also created art. Cave paintings have been found in various parts of the world, including Lascaux in southwestern France and Altamira in northern Spain. Most cave paintings focused on large animals, such as lions, oxen, and panthers. According to archaeologists, these cave paintings were done between 25,000 and 12,000 B.C.

12. How did Paleolithic people get their food?

____

____

____

____

____

Name ______________________ Date ______________________ Class ______________________

Reading Essentials and Study Guide

Chapter 1, Section 2

For use with textbook pages 27–31

THE NEOLITHIC REVOLUTION AND THE RISE OF CIVILIZATION

KEY TERMS

Neolithic Revolution the revolution that occurred in the Neolithic Age, the period of human history from 10,000 to 4000 B.C. *(page 27)*

systematic agriculture the growing of food on a regular basis *(page 28)*

domestication the adaptation of animals for human use *(page 28)*

artisans skilled workers who made products such as weapons and jewelry *(page 29)*

Bronze Age the period of history from around 3000 to 1200 B.C. that was characterized by the widespread use of bronze *(page 30)*

culture the way of life of a people *(page 30)*

civilization a complex culture in which large numbers of human beings share a number of common elements *(page 30)*

monarchs kings or queens who rule a kingdom *(page 30)*

DRAWING FROM EXPERIENCE

Imagine that you are asked to make a display that is a representation of your culture. What items would you include? Why?

In the last section, you read about the early stages of human development. You also learned about the culture (way of life) of Paleolithic people. In this section, you will learn about the culture of people in the Neolithic Age. You will also learn how the Neolithic Revolution set the stage for the rise of civilization.

ORGANIZING YOUR THOUGHTS

Use the concept web below to help you take notes. A civilization has six characteristics. Name the characteristics.

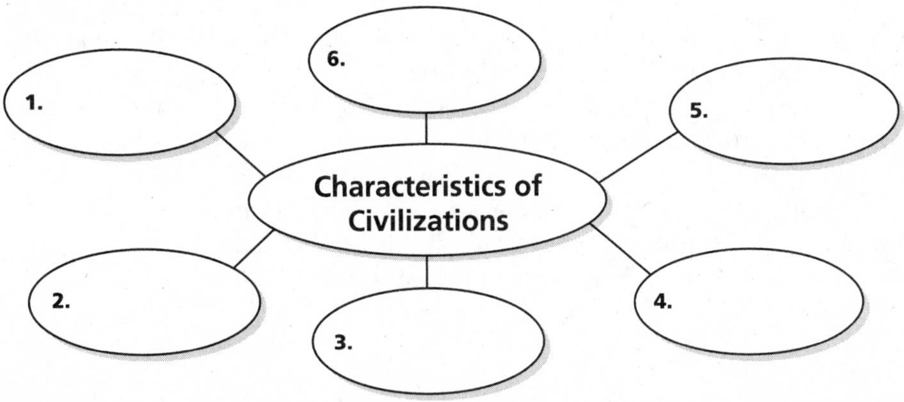

READ TO LEARN

• The Neolithic Revolution

At the end of the last Ice Age, around 8000 B.C., a major change took place. People began to plant and grow food on a regular basis—what we call **systematic agriculture.** They also began to tame and keep animals as a source of meat, milk, and wool. This adaptation of animals for human use is called **domestication.** The change from gathering food and hunting animals to planting crops and taming animals is called the **Neolithic Revolution,** because it took place in the Neolithic Age. The Neolithic Age is the period of human history from 10,000 to 4000 B.C. Some historians believe this revolution was the single most important development in human history. It gave humans greater control over their environment. It also meant that they could stop being nomads and live in settled communities.

Between 8000 and 5000 B.C., systematic agriculture developed in different parts of the world. People in Southwest Asia began to grow wheat and barley and to domesticate (tame) pigs, cows, goats, and sheep. Farming spread from southwestern Asia into Europe, Egypt, and parts of India. A different kind of farming developed in parts of Africa. Root crops, such as yams, and tree crops, such as bananas, were grown in central Africa. In Southeast Asia and in southern China, rice began to be grown. In the Western Hemisphere, Mesoamericans (people who lived in present-day Mexico and Central America) grew beans, squash, and maize (corn). They also domesticated dogs and fowl during this period.

Because people were no longer forced to move from place to place to find food, they began to live in settlements. Historians call these settlements Neolithic farming villages. Two of the largest ones were Jericho, in Palestine near the Dead Sea, and Catal Huyuk, in what is present-day Turkey. People often had more food than they needed right away. This made it possible for people to do things other than farming. For example, some people became artisans. **Artisans** were skilled workers who made items such as weapons and jewelry. These items could be traded with other people. In Catal Huyuk, shrines and statues show that religion had an important role in the lives of Neolithic people.

The Neolithic Revolution led to other changes. People began to build houses and to store food and other goods. They could trade the food and goods for other things. People began to specialize in different crafts, and a division of labor developed. Fibers from plants, such as flax and cotton, were used to make cloth. The relationship between men and women also changed. Men became more active in farming and herding animals. Women cared for the children, wove cloth, and performed other tasks that they could do in the home settlement. As a result, men began to play a more dominant role.

Name ______________ Date ______________ Class ______________

Between 4000 and 3000 B.C., people began to use metals. This allowed them to have even more control over their environments. Copper was the first metal that was used to make tools. After 4000 B.C., people in western Asia learned how to make bronze, by combining copper and tin. The period from around 3000 to 1200 B.C. is called the **Bronze Age** because of the widespread use of bronze during this time.

7. What changes took place during the Neolithic Age?

____

____

____

____

____

• The Emergence of Civilization *(page 30)*

The **culture** of a people is the way of life that they follow. Neolithic settlements developed from villages with simple cultures to large civilizations. A **civilization** is a complex culture in which large numbers of human beings share a number of common elements. Historians have identified six basic characteristics of civilizations. The characteristics are cities, government, religion, social structure, writing, and art.

In each civilization, a significant part of the population lived in cities. Governments organized armies to protect the people and made laws to regulate their lives. In the first civilizations, rulers led governments. These rulers were usually **monarchs** (kings or queens who rule a kingdom).

All of the new civilizations developed religions to explain their world. Priests performed rituals to please gods and goddesses. Rulers claimed that the gods gave their power to them. Some rulers even claimed to be gods.

New social structures developed in the new civilizations. Rulers and an upper class of priests, government officials, and warriors were at the top. Below this upper class was a large group of free people-farmers, artisans, and craftspeople. At the bottom was a slave class.

Writing was important in these new civilizations. Rulers, priests, and merchants used writing to keep accurate records. Writing also became a means of creative expression. The world's first works of literature were written. Art was also a characteristic of the new civilizations. People began to build temples as places for worship and sacrifice. They built pyramids as places to bury kings and other important people. They also began to use painting and sculpture to portray gods and goddesses or natural forces.

Reading Essentials and Study Guide

Chapter 1, Section 2 *(continued)*

8. How are civilizations different from simpler cultures?

____

____

____

____

____

Name ______________________ Date ______________________ Class ______________________

Reading Essentials and Study Guide

Chapter 2, Section 1

For use with textbook pages 37–43

CIVILIZATION BEGINS IN MESOPOTAMIA

KEY TERMS

city-state cities and the countryside around them, which were the basic units of Sumerian civilization *(page 39)*

ziggurat a massive stepped tower with a temple on top *(page 39)*

theocracy a government by divine authority *(page 39)*

empire a large political unit or state, usually under a single leader, that controls many people or territories *(page 40)*

patriarchal a form of society dominated by men *(page 41)*

polytheistic a belief in many gods *(page 42)*

cuneiform ("wedge-shaped") the Sumerian system of writing *(page 42)*

DRAWING FROM EXPERIENCE

What do you think life would be like if you did not have a system of writing? How would you communicate? What problems would result?

In this section, you will learn about the beginning of civilization in Mesopotamia. You will learn about the Sumerians, the people who invented the first writing system. You will also learn about the first empires in this region.

ORGANIZING YOUR THOUGHTS

Use the concept web below to help you take notes. Name six inventions of the Sumerians.

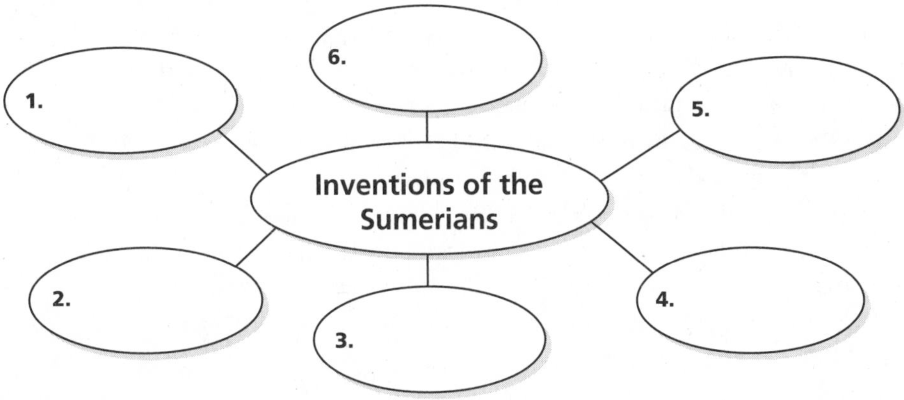

READ TO LEARN

• The Impact of Geography *(page 37)*

The valley between the Tigris and Euphrates Rivers is called Mesopotamia. Mesopotamia means the land "between the rivers." Mesopotamia was at the eastern end of the Fertile Crescent. The Fertile Crescent is an area from the Mediterranean Sea to the Persian Gulf. Early civilizations began in this area, because it had land with rich soil.

The soil in Mesopotamia was rich because of the two rivers. Each spring, the rivers overflowed their banks. The floods left layers of silt, the material deposited by the rivers. The people of Mesopotamia learned how to control the flow of the rivers. They created irrigation and drainage ditches. This made it possible for them to grow crops on a regular basis. They were able to grow an abundance of food, which allowed people to live together in cities.

Ancient Mesopotamia included three general areas: Assyria, Akkad, and Sumer. The Sumerians were the creators of the first Mesopotamian civilization.

7. Where was Mesopotamia located?

____

____

____

____

• The City-States of Ancient Mesopotamia *(page 38)*

By 3000 B.C., the Sumerians had started several cities in southern Mesopotamia. Three of these cities were Eridu, Ur, and Uruk. The cities controlled the countryside around them. These **city-states** were the basic units of Sumerian civilization. Walls made out of mud bricks surrounded the cities. The Sumerian people also used mud bricks to build their houses and other buildings. They also invented the arch and the dome.

The most important building in a Sumerian city was the temple. The temple was dedicated to the chief god or goddess of the city. The temple was often built on top of a ziggurat. A **ziggurat** is a massive stepped tower. The temples and related buildings were the center of Sumerian cities. Priests and priestesses supervised the temples, so they had a great deal of power.

The Sumerians believed that the gods ruled the cities. This made their city-states theocracies. A **theocracy** is a government by divine authority. Eventually, kings began to rule the Sumerian city-states. The Sumerians believed that kings got their power from the gods. Kings led armies and supervised building and irrigation projects.

Name ______________________ Date ____________________ Class ____________________

Reading Essentials and Study Guide

Most of the Sumerians were farmers, but the Sumerians also learned how to make metal goods, pottery, and wool cloth. The Sumerians began to trade their goods for copper, tin, and timber. The invention of the wheel around 3000 B.C. made it easier to take goods from place to place.

Sumerian city-states had three major social groups: nobles, commoners, and slaves. The nobles were the kings and priests and their families. Commoners included farmers, fishers, merchants, and craftspeople. Slaves belonged to palace and temple officials. Rich landowners also used slaves to farm their lands.

8. Which people had the most power in the Sumerian city-states?

____

____

____

____

• Empires in Ancient Mesopotamia *(page 40)*

City-states began to fight other city-states for control of land and water. Other groups also invaded city-states. The land of Mesopotamia was very flat, so it was easy to invade. To the north of the Sumerian city-states were people called the Akkadians. Their leader's name was Sargon. Around 2340 B.C., the Akkadians overran the Sumerian city-states. They set up the first empire in world history. An **empire** is a large political unit or state, usually under a single leader, that controls many peoples or territories

People from the neighboring hills eventually attacked the Akkadian Empire. It ended about 2100 B.C., and the system of warring city-states returned. In 1792 B.C., a new empire began to control much of Mesopotamia. The leadership of this empire came from Babylon, a city-state south of Akkad. The king of Babylon was Hammurabi. He gained control of Sumer and Akkad. After he died in 1750 B.C., weaker kings were unable to keep the Babylonian Empire united, and it finally fell to new invaders.

9. What two empires gained control of the Sumerian city-states?

____

____

____

____

Reading Essentials and Study Guide

• The Code of Hammurabi *(page 41)*

One of Hammurabi's most important achievements was a collection of laws. These laws are called the Code of Hammurabi. Penalties were severe, but they were different for each class of people. Lower class people (commoners) were punished more severely than upper class people (nobles). The principle of retribution ("an eye for an eye, tooth for a tooth") was the basis for many of the laws.

A large category of the laws focused on marriage and the family. Society in Mesopotamia was **patriarchal.** This means that men dominated it. Men ruled their wives and children. A woman who neglected her home could be drowned. A child who struck his father could have his hand cut off. Hammurabi's law code covered almost every aspect of people's lives.

10. What principle was the basis for many of the laws in Hammurabi's code?

____

____

____

____

____

• The Importance of Religion *(page 42)*

The climate in Mesopotamia was harsh. There were heavy rains, scorching winds, and famines. Floods were heavy and unpredictable. The people knew that they could not control these things, so they believed that supernatural forces controlled their world. They believed that there were almost three thousand gods and goddesses. Their religion is called **polytheistic,** because they believed in many gods. Human beings were supposed to obey and serve the gods. They could never be sure what the gods might do to help or hurt them.

11. Why did the people of Mesopotamia believe that supernatural forces controlled their world?

____

____

____

____

____

Name ______________________ Date ______________________ Class ______________________

• The Creativity of the Sumerians *(page 42)*

The Sumerians invented many things that still affect our lives today. Perhaps their greatest invention was their writing. Their system of writing is called **cuneiform** ("wedge-shaped"). They made wedge-shaped marks on clay tablets. The tablets were then baked or dried in the sun. These tablets could last a long time. Many of the tablets have lasted until modern times and have been found by archaeologists.

The people of Mesopotamia used writing to keep records. Cuneiform writing was taught in schools that trained scribes. The schools were in operation by 2500 B.C. Boys from wealthy families learned to be scribes as a way to start their careers. Scribes often became leaders of their cities, temples, and armies. Students learned how to write by copying the same writings over and over again.

Writing allowed people to pass knowledge from person to person and generation to generation. It also made it possible to record poems and other forms of literature. The most famous piece of Mesopotamian literature is the *Epic of Gilgamesh*. It is a poem about a legendary king named Gilgamesh.

The Sumerians also invented devices to help them in their daily lives. The wagon wheel made it easier to get people and goods from place to place. The potter's wheel, the sundial, and the arch are other examples of Sumerian inventions. The Sumerians were also the first people to make bronze out of copper and tin. They also made outstanding achievements in math and astronomy.

12. Why was writing important to the Sumerians?

____

____

____

____

____

Name ______________________ Date ______________________ Class ______________________

Reading Essentials and Study Guide

Chapter 2, Section 2

For use with textbook pages 45–53

EGYPTIAN CIVILIZATION: "THE GIFT OF THE NILE"

KEY TERMS

dynasty a family of rulers whose right to rule is passed on within the family *(page 47)*

pharaoh ("great house" or "palace") the most common title of Egyptian monarchs *(page 47)*

bureaucracy an administrative organization with officials and regular procedures *(page 48)*

vizier ("the steward of the whole land") the official in charge of the government bureaucracy in ancient Egypt *(page 48)*

mummification a process of slowly drying a dead body to prevent it from rotting *(page 48)*

hieroglyphics ("priest-carvings" or "sacred writings") the Greek name for the earliest Egyptian writing *(page 52)*

hieratic script a simplified version of hieroglyphics that was used for business transactions, record keeping, and the general needs of daily life in Egypt *(page 52)*

DRAWING FROM EXPERIENCE

What do you think of when you hear the words "ancient Egypt"? What do you think life was like in ancient Egypt?

In the last section, you learned about the early civilization of Mesopotamia. In this section, you will learn about Egyptian civilization in the Nile Valley.

ORGANIZING YOUR THOUGHTS

Use the chart below to help you take notes. Historians have divided Egyptian history into three major periods, the Old Kingdom, Middle Kingdom, and New Kingdom. List the major accomplishments and events that occurred during these periods.

Egyptian Periods	Accomplishments and Events
Old Kingdom	1.
Middle Kingdom	2.
New Kingdom	3.

Name ______________________ Date ______________ Class ______________

Reading Essentials and Study Guide

READ TO LEARN

• The Impact of Geography *(page 45)*

The Nile is the longest river in the world. It begins in Africa and empties into the Mediterranean Sea. About a hundred miles before it reaches the sea, it splits into two branches. This split forms a triangle of land, called a delta. The Nile Delta is called Lower Egypt. The land to the south is called Upper Egypt. The point where the delta splits is called the tip of the delta. The most important cities in Egypt developed at the tip of the delta.

The yearly flooding of the Nile was called the "miracle" of the Nile. Unlike the floods in Mesopotamia, the Nile floods were predictable. When the river flooded, it left a deposit of mud on both sides of the river. This created an area of rich soil. Farmers were able to grow a surplus of food in the Nile Valley. This surplus made Egypt prosperous. The Nile also made it easy to travel throughout the land.

Egypt had natural barriers that protected it from invasion. The barriers were the deserts to the west and east; the Red Sea to the east; the cataracts (rapids) to the south; and the Mediterranean Sea to the north. These barriers and the regularity of the Nile floods made the Egyptian people feel secure. They also had confidence in the stability of things.

4. How did the Nile affect life in ancient Egypt?

____

____

____

____

• The Importance of Religion *(page 46)*

Religion also made Egyptians feel secure. Like the people of Mesopotamia, they were polytheistic. Their most important gods were sun gods and land gods. They believed that the sun god had different forms and names, depending on his role. Two names for the sun god were Atum and Re. Egyptian rulers had the title Son of Re, because they were seen as earthly forms of Re.

Two of the river and land gods were Osiris and Isis. Osiris was a symbol of resurrection (coming back to life). A famous Egyptian myth says that Osiris was killed by his brother Seth, who cut his body into pieces and threw them into the Nile. Osiris's wife, Isis, found the pieces, and she and the other gods brought Osiris back to life. Egyptians believed that they could be reborn after they died, like Osiris.

Name ______________________ Date ________________ Class ________________

Reading Essentials and Study Guide

5. Which gods were most important to the Egyptians?

____

____

____

____

• The Course of Egyptian History *(page 47)*

Historians have divided Egyptian history into three major periods, known as the Old Kingdom, Middle Kingdom, and New Kingdom. These periods were times of stability. Between these periods were times of chaos and invasion, known as Intermediate periods.

Egyptian history begins around 3100 B.C., when King Menes united Upper and Lower Egypt into one kingdom. King Menes also created the first dynasty. A **dynasty** is a family of rulers whose right to rule is passed on within the family.

The Old Kingdom lasted from about 2700 to 2200 B.C. It was a time of prosperity and splendor. The monarchs of the Old Kingdom were powerful rulers. The most common title for Egyptian monarchs was **pharaoh.** The word pharaoh originally meant "great house" or "palace." The Egyptians believed that pharaohs were gods. By obeying their pharaoh, they believed that they were helping to keep their world stable. Pharaohs had unlimited power to rule their people, but they developed a bureaucracy to help them rule. A **bureaucracy** is an administrative organization with officials and regular procedures. The most important official was the **vizier** ("the steward of the whole land"). He reported directly to the pharaoh and was in charge of the government bureaucracy.

One of the greatest achievements of Egyptian civilization was the building of the pyramids. This took place during the Old Kingdom. Pyramids were tombs for the bodies of dead pharaohs. The tombs were stocked with food and other supplies. The Egyptians believed that human beings had two bodies, a physical one and a spiritual one. The spiritual body was called the *ka*. If the physical body was preserved after death and its tomb was stocked with food and supplies, the *ka* could return. To preserve the physical body after death, the Egyptians used mummification. **Mummification** is the process of slowly drying a dead body to prevent it from rotting.

The largest of the pyramids was built at Giza around 2540 B.C. It was built by King Khufu and is called the Great Pyramid. Tradition says that it took 100,000 Egyptians 20 years to build the Great Pyramid. Guarding this pyramid is a huge statue, known as the Great Sphinx. It has the body of a lion and a human head. The Great Pyramid still stands as a symbol of the power of the Egyptian pharaohs.

The Old Kingdom eventually collapsed. It was followed by a period of chaos that lasted about 150 years. Around 2050 B.C., a new dynasty gained control of Egypt. This marked the beginning of the Middle Kingdom. The Middle Kingdom lasted until 1652 B.C. and was a time of stability. During the Middle Kingdom, Egypt conquered Nubia and sent armies to Syria and Palestine. The pharaohs of the Middle Kingdom were concerned about their people. They drained the swampland in the Nile Delta to give the people more land to farm. They also dug a canal to connect the Nile and the Red Sea. This aided trade and transportation.

The Middle Kingdom ended around 1652 B.C. when the Hyksos invaded Egypt. The Hyksos were people from western Asia who used horse-drawn chariots. They ruled Egypt for almost a hundred years. The Egyptians learned some important skills from the Hyksos. They learned how to make bronze tools and weapons. They also learned how to use chariots.

Eventually a new dynasty of pharaohs used the new skills and weapons to drive out the Hyksos. The New Kingdom lasted from about 1567 to 1085 B.C. During the period of the New Kingdom, Egypt created an empire and became the most powerful state in Southwest Asia. The pharaohs of the New Kingdom built new temples. Hatshepsut, the first woman to become pharaoh, built a great temple at Deir el Bahri, near Thebes.

There were also problems during the New Kingdom. The pharaoh Amenhotep IV forced the people to worship a single god, Aton. He closed the temples of the other gods, and changed his own name to Akhenaton ("It is well with Aton"). After he died, the new pharaoh, Tutankhamen, restored the old gods. But the problems caused by Amenhotep's changes led to a loss of Egypt's empire.

Under Ramses II, the Egyptians tried to regain control of their earlier empire, but they were only partly successful. During the thirteenth century B.C., "Sea Peoples" invaded the Egyptian Empire and it came to an end. The New Kingdom itself ended in 1085 B.C.

For the next thousand years, Libyans, Nubians, Persians, and Macedonians dominated Egypt. In the first century B.C., the pharaoh Cleopatra VII tried to regain Egypt's independence. But she was defeated, and Egypt became part of the Roman empire.

6. What is mummification, and why did the Egyptians use it?

____

____

____

____

Name ______________________ Date ______________________ Class ______________________

Reading Essentials and Study Guide

• Society in Ancient Egypt *(page 51)*

Egyptian society was organized like a pyramid. The pharaoh was at the top. Under him was a small upper class of nobles and priests. Below the upper class were merchants, artisans, scribes, and tax collectors. Merchants traded goods up and down the Nile. Some of them also traded with other countries. Artisans made many different goods, such as paper, stone dishes, painted boxes, wooden furniture, linen clothes, and gold, silver and copper items.

Most of the people in Egypt were in the lower classes. They were mainly peasants who farmed the land. They paid taxes from the crops they grew, and they lived in small villages. They also served in the military and were forced to work on building projects.

7. How was Egyptian society like a pyramid?

____

____

____

____

____

• Daily Life in Ancient Egypt *(page 52)*

Ancient Egyptians had a positive attitude toward daily life. They married young, and a man normally had only one wife. If a marriage ended in divorce, the wife was compensated. Men were the masters in their houses, but women were well respected. Wives were in charge of the household and the education of children. They kept control of their property and inheritance even after they married. Some women operated businesses. Upper-class women could become priestesses, and four queens became pharaohs

Parents arranged marriages for their children. The main purpose of marriage was to produce children, especially sons. Only sons could carry on the family name. But daughters were also valued.

8. How were women treated in Ancient Egypt?

____

____

____

____

____

Name ______________________ Date ____________________ Class ____________________

• Writing and Education *(page 52)*

Writing in Egypt began around 3000 B.C. The Greeks called the earliest Egyptian writing **hieroglyphics.** Hieroglyphics means "priest-carvings" or "sacred writings." Hieroglyphics used both pictures and more abstract forms. It was complex and took a long time to learn. It was used for writing on temple walls and in tombs. A simpler version of hieroglyphics was developed. It is called **hieratic script** and was used for business and in daily life. At first, hieroglyphics were carved in stone. Later, hieratic script was written on papyrus. Papyrus was a paper made from the papyrus reed that grew along the Nile.

Egyptian scribes taught the art of writing. At the age of 10, boys from upper class families went to schools run by scribes to learn to read and write. Girls stayed at home and learned housekeeping skills from their mothers.

9. What is hieratic script?

• Achievements in Art and Science *(page 52)*

Pyramids, temples, and other monuments show the artistic ability of the Egyptians. Artists and sculptors followed particular formulas in style. This gave Egyptian art a distinctive look.

Egyptians also made advances in mathematics and science. They used geometry and learned how to calculate area and volume. This helped them build the pyramids. They also developed a 365-day calendar, and became experts in human anatomy. They used splints, bandages, and compresses to treat fractures, wounds, and disease.

10. What advances did the Egyptians make in math and science?

Name ______________________ Date ______________________ Class ______________________

Reading Essentials and Study Guide

Chapter 2, Section 3

For use with textbook pages 54–60

NEW CENTERS OF CIVILIZATION

KEY TERMS

pastoral nomads nomads who domesticated animals for food and clothing *(page 55)*

monotheistic the belief in one god *(page 59)*

DRAWING FROM EXPERIENCE

What are the Ten Commandments? When do you think they were established? What do you think was their purpose? What purpose do you think they have today?

In the last section, you learned about the civilization of Ancient Egypt. In this section, you will learn about some other early civilizations, including the Phoenicians and the Israelites. The Ten Commandments were the basis of the law of the Israelites.

ORGANIZING YOUR THOUGHTS

Use the chart below to help you take notes. The achievements of the Hittites, Phoenicians, and Israelites still affect our lives today. Identify at least one achievement of each civilization that still affects us today.

Civilization	Achievement
Hittites	**1.**
Phoenicians	**2.**
Israelites	**3.**

Reading Essentials and Study Guide

READ TO LEARN

• The Role of Nomadic Peoples *(page 54)*

On the fringes of the civilizations of Mesopotamia and Egypt, there were still nomads who survived by hunting and gathering and herding animals. **Pastoral nomads** domesticated animals for food and clothing. They moved along regular routes to find food for their animals.

The Indo-Europeans were one of the most important nomadic peoples. They probably originated somewhere in the steppe region north of the Black Sea or in Southwest Asia. Around 2000 B.C., they began to move into Europe, India, and western Asia. One group of Indo-Europeans combined with the native peoples of Asia Minor and Anatolia to form the Hittite kingdom.

Between 1600 and 1200 B.C., the Hittites created their own empire. The Hittites were the first of the Indo-Europeans to use iron. This allowed them to use weapons that were stronger and cheaper to make. The Hittites even threatened the power of the Egyptians. But around 1200 B.C., new invaders called "the Sea Peoples" destroyed the Hittite Empire.

4. What are pastoral nomads?

____

____

____

• The Phoenicians *(page 55)*

The Phoenicians lived in the area of Palestine along the Mediterranean coast. Because of their location, trade was the basis of their economy. After the downfall of the Hittites and Egyptians, they were able to expand their trade. They improved their ships and became a trade empire. They sailed into the Atlantic Oceans and even went as far as Britain and the west coast of Africa. They set up colonies in the Mediterranean. Their most famous colony was Carthage, which was located on the North African coast.

The Phoenician culture is best known for its alphabet. Phoenicians developed a system of writing that used 22 different signs to represent the sounds of their language. These signs (letters) could be used to spell all of the words in their language. This alphabet was passed on to the Greeks. The Roman alphabet that we use today is derived from this alphabet.

5. What was the basis of the Phoenician economy?

____

____

____

• The "Children of Israel" *(page 56)*

Another group of people, the Israelites, lived to the south of the Phoenicians. They played only a minor role in the politics of the region, but their religion became a major world religion. This religion, known today as Judaism, influenced the religions of Christianity and Islam. Much of the history and beliefs of the Israelites are recorded in what Christians call the Old Testament.

According to their history, the Israelites came from Mesopotamia to Palestine, which they called Canaan. Their lifestyle was based on grazing flocks and herds. Because of a drought, they moved to Egypt. In Egypt they became slaves until Moses led them out. They wandered in the desert for many years and finally returned to Palestine. They were organized in tribes. Between 1200 and 1000 B.C., the tribes formed a united kingdom known as Israel.

By the time of King Solomon, the Israelites controlled all of Palestine and made Jerusalem their capital. Solomon ruled from about 970 to 930 B.C. He expanded the government and army and encouraged trade with other countries. He is best known for building a temple in Jerusalem.

After Solomon's death, the northern and southern tribes split into two separate kingdoms. The ten northern tribes became the Kingdom of Israel. Their capital was at Samaria. The two southern tribes became the Kingdom of Judah. Their capital was Jerusalem. In 722 B.C., the Assyrians attacked the Kingdom of Israel. Many Israelites were sent to other parts of the Assyrian Empire. These Israelites merged with other peoples and lost their identity. They are called the "ten lost tribes."

The Kingdom of Judah survived the Assyrians. But the Chaldeans defeated the Assyrians and then conquered the Kingdom of Judah. Jerusalem was completely destroyed in 586 B.C. Many of the people of Judah were sent to Babylonia as captives. Finally, the Persians conquered the Chaldeans and allowed the people of Judah to return to Jerusalem. The Kingdom of Judah stayed under Persian control until the fourth century B.C. The people of Judah eventually became known as the Jews, and their religion became known as Judaism.

The Jews were **monotheistic.** This means that they believed in one God. They called him Yahweh. He was the creator of the world and everything in it. The stars, moon, rivers, wind, and other natural forces were not gods. The Jews believed that when Moses led the Israelites out of Egypt, God made a covenant, or contract, with them. To fulfill the covenant, they needed to obey the law of God, called the Ten Commandments. The Jews also believed that God sent prophets to his people to teach them and warn them. The prophets said that God wanted people to live justly and care for the poor. The Ten Commandments and the words of the prophets became the basis for modern laws and ideas of social justice.

Name ______________________ Date ______________________ Class ______________________

Reading Essentials and Study Guide

Chapter 2, Section 3 *(continued)*

The Jewish religion was unique among the religions of western Asia and Egypt. The other religions were polytheistic, and only priests had access to the gods and their wishes. In the Jewish tradition, God's wishes had been written down. No single person could claim that he alone knew God's will. This knowledge was open to anyone who could read Hebrew. Unlike most of the other peoples of Southwest Asia, the Jews would not accept the gods of their conquerors. To obey their God, they might even have to refuse to obey their conquerors.

6. How was the Jewish religion different from other religions in western Asia and Egypt?

Name ______________________________ Date ______________________ Class ______________________

Reading Essentials and Study Guide

Chapter 2, Section 4

For use with textbook pages 61–64

THE RISE OF NEW EMPIRES

KEY TERMS

satrapy a province in the Persian empire *(page 63)*

satrap ("protector of the kingdom") the governor of each province, who collected taxes, provided justice, and recruited soldiers *(page 63)*

monarchy government under the rule of a king or queen *(page 64)*

DRAWING FROM EXPERIENCE

What do you think of when you hear the word "empire"? Are there any empires today? Are "superpowers" empires? Why or why not?

In the last section, you learned about the civilizations of the Hittites, Phoenicians, and Israelites. In this section, you will learn about the empires that conquered the Israelites

ORGANIZING YOUR THOUGHTS

Use the time line below to help you take notes. List the major events in Assyrian and Persian history.

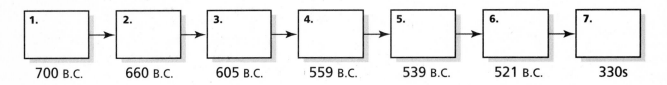

1.	2.	3.	4.	5.	6.	7.
700 B.C.	660 B.C.	605 B.C.	559 B.C.	539 B.C.	521 B.C.	330s

Reading Essentials and Study Guide

Chapter 2, Section 4 *(continued)*

READ TO LEARN

• The Assyrian Empire *(page 61)*

Assyria is located on the upper Tigris River. The Assyrians used iron weapons to conquer other people and build an empire by 700 B.C. The Assyrian Empire included Mesopotamia, parts of the Iranian Plateau, sections of Asia Minor, Syria, Palestine, and Egypt.

The Assyrian Empire was well organized. The Assyrians developed a system of communication throughout the empire. Relays of horses carried messages along a network of posts. A message could be sent to the king from anywhere in the empire and receive an answer within a week. Ashurbanipal, one of the last Assyrian kings, built one of the world's first libraries at Nineveh. The Assyrian army was large, well organized, and disciplined. It was the first large army to use iron weapons. The Assyrians treated the people they conquered cruelly.

The Assyrian Empire did not last long, however. In 605 B.C., it fell to the Chaldeans and Medes, who were people who lived in the East.

8. How did the Assyrians communicate throughout their empire?

• The Persian Empire *(page 62)*

After the fall of the Assyrian Empire, the Chaldeans made Babylonia the most important state in western Asia. The king of the Chaldeans was Nebuchadnezzar. He rebuilt Babylon as the center of his empire and made it one of the great cities of the ancient world.

In 539 B.C., Babylon fell to the Persians. The Persians were an Indo-European people who lived in what is now southwestern Iran. The Persians were nomads who were organized in groups. One family was able to unite the groups. Cyrus, who was a member of that family, created a powerful Persian empire that stretched from Asia Minor to western India.

Cyrus ruled from 559 to 530 B.C. The people of his time called Cyrus "the Great." He was an unusual ruler, who ruled with great wisdom and compassion. He allowed the Jews, who had been brought to Babylon in the sixth century B.C., to return to Jerusalem. He had a respect for other cultures. When he built his palaces, he used Assyrian, Babylonian, and Egyptian designs and methods.

Reading Essentials and Study Guide

Chapter 2, Section 4 *(continued)*

The rulers after Cyrus added to the Persian Empire. His son Cambyses invaded Egypt. Darius, who ruled from 521 to 486 B.C., added a province in India. He then moved into Europe and conquered Thrace. The Persian Empire became the largest empire that the world had ever seen.

Darius divided the empire into 20 provinces, called **satrapies.** A governor, or **satrap,** ruled each province. Satrap means "protector of the kingdom." The satraps collected taxes, provided justice, and recruited soldiers. Like the Assyrians, the Persians used a relay of horses to take messages throughout the empire. The roads were well maintained. The Royal Road went from Lydia to Susa, the chief capital of the empire.

The power of the Persian Empire depended upon the military. By the time of Darius, the Persian kings had created an army of professional soldiers. It had a cavalry of ten thousand and an infantry of ten thousand. These groups were called the Immortals because there were always ten thousand in each group. If one soldier died, he was immediately replaced.

Persians kings had many wives and children. For example, Artaxerxes II had 115 sons. The sons of the kings had no real power, so they were always plotting to gain the throne. Nine of the rulers after Darius were murdered. For example, Xerxes II reigned for only 45 days before his half-brother murdered him in bed. Over time, these struggles for the throne weakened the **monarchy** (government under the rule of a king or queen). During the 330s B.C., the Persian Empire fell to the Greek ruler Alexander the Great.

The Persians' religion was called Zoroastrianism. According to Persian tradition, Zoroaster was born in 660 B.C. His teachings were written down in the *Zend Avesta*, the sacred book of Zoroastrianism. The followers of Zoroaster were monotheistic. Their god was called Ahuramazda (the "Wise Lord"). He was the creator, but Ahriman, an evil spirit, opposed him. Zoroaster taught that humans could choose between good and evil. He also taught that there would be an end to the struggle between good and evil and that Ahuramazda would triumph.

9. Why was Cyrus called "the Great"?

Name ________________ Date ________________ Class ________________

Reading Essentials and Study Guide

Chapter 3, Section 1

For use with textbook pages 71–79

EARLY CIVILIZATION IN INDIA

KEY TERMS

monsoon a seasonal wind pattern in southern Asia *(page 72)*

Sanskrit a writing system developed by the Aryans *(page 74)*

raja an Aryan prince or leader *(page 74)*

caste system a set of rigid social categories or classes that determines a person's occupation, economic potential, and position in society *(page 75)*

caste the English term for an Indian social class *(page 75)*

Hinduism the religion of the majority of the Indian people that originated in the religious beliefs of the Aryans *(page 77)*

reincarnation the belief that the individual soul is reborn in a different form after death *(page 77)*

karma the force generated by a person's actions that determines how the person will be reborn in the next life *(page 77)*

dharma the divine law in Hinduism that requires all people to do their duty *(page 77)*

yoga ("union") a method of training designed to lead to union with Brahman *(page 77)*

ascetics people who practiced self-denial to achieve an understanding of ultimate reality *(page 78)*

nirvana ultimate reality in Buddhism (the end of the self and a reunion with the Great World Soul) *(page 78)*

Buddhism a religion founded in India in the sixth century B.C. by Siddhartha Gautama, known as the Buddha *(page 78)*

DRAWING FROM EXPERIENCE

What kind of climate do you live in? How does the climate affect the way you live?

In this section, you will learn about the early civilizations in India and how the climate of India influenced those civilizations.

ORGANIZING YOUR THOUGHTS

Use the diagram below to help you take notes. The caste system in India had five major divisions. List the five divisions, starting from the top of the social scale.

The Caste System of India
1.
2.
3.
4.
5.

READ TO LEARN

• The Land of India *(page 71)*

The Indian subcontinent is shaped like a triangle and "hangs" from the southern ridge of Asia. The geography of India is diverse. In the far north are the Himalaya, the highest mountains in the world. South of the Himalaya region is the rich valley of the Ganges River. This was one of the chief regions of Indian culture. To the west is the Indus River valley. Today it is a dry plateau, but in ancient times, it had a more moderate climate and was the cradle of Indian civilization. South of these two river valleys is the Deccan. It is a plateau that extends from the Ganges Valley to the southern tip of India. The interior of the plateau is hilly and dry. India's western and eastern coasts are lush plains. They have historically been some of the most densely populated regions of India.

The most important feature of India's climate is the monsoon. A **monsoon** is a seasonal wind pattern in southern Asia. The summer monsoon blows warm, moist air from the southwest. The winter monsoon blows cold, dry air from the northeast. The summer monsoon brings heavy rains. Indian farmers depend on these rains to grow their crops. If the rains come early or late, or if there is too much or too little rain, crops are ruined and many people starve.

6. How do monsoons affect life in India?

____

____

____

____

Reading Essentials and Study Guide

• India's First Civilization *(page 72)*

Early civilization in India began in river valleys. Between 3000 B.C. and 1500 B.C., the valleys of the Indus River had a flourishing civilization. Archaeologists have found the remains of more than a thousand settlements in this region. There were two major cities, Harappa and Mohenjo-Daro. The civilization in these cities lasted for hundreds of years. Historians call it Harappan or Indus civilization.

At its height, Harappa had 35,000 people. Mohenjo-Daro probably had around 35,000 to 40,000 people. Both cities were carefully planned. The main streets ran in a north-south direction and were crossed by smaller east-west streets. The cities were divided into large walled neighborhoods. Most buildings were made of mud bricks. Public wells provided the people with a regular supply of water. Houses had drains that were connected to a sewer system under the streets. A system of chutes took trash from houses to garbage bins.

It took a well-organized government to maintain these cities. Harappan rulers based their power on a belief in divine assistance. Religion and politics were closely linked. The palace and the temple were located in the same citadel, or fortress, at Harappa.

The Harappan economy was based on farming. The Indus River flooded each year and provided rich soil for growing crops. The chief crops were wheat, barley, and peas. The Harappans traded with city-states in Mesopotamia. Much of this trade was carried by ship through the Persian Gulf.

7. In what ways were the cities of Harappa and Mohenjo-Daro well planned?

____

____

____

____

____

• The Arrival of the Aryans *(page 74)*

Around 1500 B.C., a group of Indo-European nomads moved from central Asia into northern India. These people were known as the Aryans. They conquered the Harappans and created a new Indian society based on their own culture. They were experts in warfare. They eventually gained control of all of India.

After settling in India, the Aryans stopped being pastoral nomads and became farmers. The creation of the iron plow and the use of irrigation made it possible for them to turn the jungle along the Ganges River into farmland. The basic crops in the north were wheat, barley, and millet. Rice was grown in the river valleys. Grain and vegetables were grown in the south. Cotton and spices, such as pepper, ginger, and cinnamon, were also grown.

Around 1000 B.C., the Aryans developed a system of writing. This writing system is called Sanskrit. They used Sanskrit to write down the legends and religious rituals that had been passed down from generation to generation. The early writings of the Aryans show that the Aryans were often at war. Aryan leaders, known as **rajas** (princes), attacked each other's fortresses and seized women, cattle, and other treasures.

8. How did the Aryans change after they settled in India?

• Society in Ancient India *(page 75)*

During the time of the Aryans, a system of social classes developed in India. This system has lasted, with only minor changes, to the present day. The **caste system** was a set of rigid social categories that determined a person's occupation, economic potential, and position in society. It was based in part on skin color. There were five major divisions of Indian classes, or **castes,** in ancient times. At the top was the priestly class, whose members were known as Brahmans. The second caste was the Kshatriyas, or warriors. The third-ranked caste was the Vaisyas, or commoners. Most Vaisyas were merchants or farmers. The fourth caste was the Sudras. This was the largest group of Indian people. The Sudras were dark-skinned native people, not Aryans. Most of them were peasants or people who did other forms of manual labor. They had only limited rights in society. At the lowest level were the Untouchables. They were given degrading jobs that other Indians would not do, like collecting trash and handling dead bodies. They were not considered human. No Indian would touch or eat food handled by an Untouchable.

Life in ancient India centered on the family. The family was the basic unit in society. The ideal was an extended family, with three generations (grandparents, parents, and children) living under one roof. Indian society was patriarchal. Only men could inherit property. Women were not allowed to serve as priests, and generally, only men were educated. Upper-class young men were not supposed to marry until they completed 12 years of study. Divorce was usually not allowed. Husbands could take a second wife if the first wife could not bear children. Children were important because they were expected to take care of their parents as they grew older. When a man died, his wife was expected to follow the ritual of *suttee*. In ancient India, the dead were placed on heaps of material called pyres, which were then set on fire. Suttee required a wife to throw herself on the fire with her dead husband's body.

9. How were women treated in ancient India?

____

____

____

____

____

• Hinduism *(page 77)*

Hinduism is the religion of the majority of the Indian people. It had its origins in the religious beliefs of the Aryans. Most of our information about their religion comes from the Vedas. The Vedas were collections of hymns and other religious rituals. Early Hindus believed in the existence of a single force in the universe called *Brahman*. It was the duty of the individual self, or *atman*, to seek to know Brahman.

Hinduism contains the idea of reincarnation. **Reincarnation** is the belief that the individual soul is reborn in a different form after death. After being reincarnated a number of times, the soul reaches its final goal, which is union with Brahman. Important to this process is the idea of karma. **Karma** is the force generated by a person's actions that determines how a person will be reborn in the next life. The concept of karma is ruled by the **dharma,** or the divine law. The law requires all people to do their duty. Duties vary depending on a person's status in society. Reincarnation provided a religious basis for the caste system. It justified the privileges of the people in the higher castes. They believed that they deserved their privileges because of what they had done in earlier lives.

Hindus developed the practice of yoga. **Yoga** is a method of training designed to lead to union with Brahman. In fact, yoga means "union." Over time, the Hindu religion came to have more than 33,000 gods and goddesses. The three chief ones were Brahma the Creator, Vishnu the Preserver, and Siva the Destroyer. Many Hindus regard the gods as different expressions of Brahman. Through devotion at temples, Hindus seek not only salvation but also a way to gain the ordinary things they need in life.

10. What is reincarnation, and how does it help to justify the caste system?

___

___

___

___

• Buddhism *(page 78)*

In the sixth century B.C., a new religious doctrine appeared in northern India. It is called **Buddhism** because it was founded by Siddhartha Gautama, also known as the Buddha or "Enlightened One." Siddhartha was born around 563 B.C. in the foothills of the Himalaya. He was the son of a ruling family and appeared to have everything. But in his late twenties, he decided to spend his life seeking the cure for human suffering. At first, he followed the example of the ascetics. **Ascetics** are people who practice self-denial to achieve an understanding of ultimate reality. He later turned instead to an intense period of meditation. While meditating, Siddhartha believed that he finally reached enlightenment as to the meaning of life. He spent the rest of his life preaching what he had discovered. His teachings became the basic principles of Buddhism.

Siddhartha believed that the physical world was an illusion. Once people let go of the things of this world, pain and sorrow could be forgotten. Then comes *bodhi*, or wisdom. Achieving wisdom is a key step to achieving nirvana. **Nirvana** is the ultimate reality—the end of the self and a reunion with the Great World Soul. The core of Siddhartha's message is contained in the Four Noble Truths and the Eightfold Path. He accepted the idea of reincarnation but rejected the Hindu caste system. He taught that all human beings could reach nirvana. This made Buddhism appealing to the people at the lower end of the social scale. Siddhartha also rejected the multitude of gods in Hinduism. He forbade his followers to worship him or his image. After he died in 480 B.C., his followers spread his message throughout India. Buddhist monasteries were established to promote his teaching.

11. What parts of Hinduism did Siddhartha accept, and what parts did he reject?

___

___

___

___

___

Name ______________________ Date ______________________ Class ______________________

Reading Essentials and Study Guide

Chapter 3, Section 2

For use with textbook pages 81–86

NEW EMPIRES IN INDIA

KEY TERMS

Silk Road one of the main trade routes in the ancient world that was used to transport goods, such as silk, from China across central Asia to Mesopotamia *(page 81)*

pilgrim people who travel to religious places *(page 85)*

DRAWING FROM EXPERIENCE

Have you ever thought about the way we count? Why do we count in tens? Where did the decimal system come from?

In the last section, you learned about the early civilizations in India. In this section, you will learn about two empires that arose in India, the Mauryan and Gupta Empires. The decimal system of counting in tens was developed during the Gupta Empire.

ORGANIZING YOUR THOUGHTS

Use the diagram below to help you take notes. Trade developed between the Roman Empire, India, and China. List the items that were exported from each of these areas.

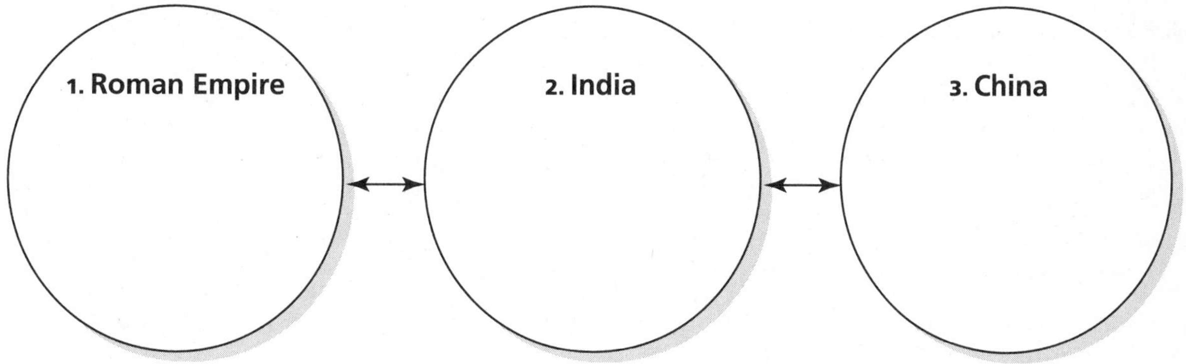

Name ______________________ Date ____________________ Class ____________________

Reading Essentials and Study Guide

READ TO LEARN

• The Mauryan Dynasty *(page 82)*

The Aryans did little to bring peace and unity to India. Between 1500 and 400 B.C., there were many wars between the Aryan rajas. After 400 B.C., India was attacked from the outside. First came Persia, which extended its empire into western India. Then came the Greeks and Macedonians. Alexander the Great had heard about the riches of India, and he invaded India in the summer of 327 B.C. But his soldiers refused to continue fighting, and they left almost as quickly as they came. This invasion, however, led to the first dynasty to control India.

Chandragupta Maurya, who ruled from 324 to 301 B.C., founded the new dynasty. He drove out the foreign forces and set up his capital at Pataliputra in northern India. He divided his empire into provinces that were ruled by governors. He had a large army and a secret police that followed his orders.

Asoka was the grandson of Chandragupta Maurya. The Mauryan Empire flourished under his rule, and he is considered to be the greatest ruler in the history of India. He converted to Buddhism and used Buddhist ideals to guide his rule. He set up hospitals for both people and animals. He had trees planted and shelters built along the roads to provide shade and rest for travelers. During the time of Asoka, India's role in trade began to expand. India became a crossroads in a trade network that extended from the Pacific to Southwest Asia and the Mediterranean Sea. After Asoka's death in 232 B.C., the Mauryan Empire began to decline. In 183 B.C., the last Mauryan ruler was killed by one of his military commanders.

4. Why is Asoka considered to be the greatest ruler in Indian history?

____

____

____

____

____

• The Kushan Kingdom and the Silk Road *(page 83)*

After the collapse of the Mauryan Empire, new kingdoms arose along the edges of India, in what is now Afghanistan. In the first century A.D., nomadic warriors seized power and established the Kushan kingdom. For the next two centuries, the Kushans spread over northern India. In the rest of India, other kingdoms fought for control.

Name ______________________ Date __________________ Class __________________

The Kushans prospered because of the trade that passed through their land. Most of the trade was between the Roman Empire and China. It was shipped along a route called the **Silk Road.** The Silk Road was about 4000 miles long and reached from the city of Changan in China across central Asia to Mesopotamia. One section of the Silk Road passed through the mountains northwest of India. The route ended at Antioch in Syria on the Mediterranean Sea. Goods were shipped from Antioch across the Mediterranean to Greece and Rome. Only luxury goods were carried on the Silk Road, because camel caravans were difficult, dangerous, and thus expensive.

Chinese merchants traded silk, spices, teas, and porcelain. Indian merchants sent ivory, textiles, precious stones, and pepper. The Romans traded woolen and linen clothes, glass, and precious stones. Silk was China's most valuable product and what the Romans particularly wanted. That is why the trade route was called the Silk Road.

5. How did the Silk Road make the Kushans prosperous?

____

____

____

____

____

• The Kingdom of the Guptas *(page 84)*

The Kushan kingdom came to an end in the third century A.D., when invaders from Persia overran it. In 320, a prince named Chandragupta created a new kingdom in the central Ganges Valley. He was not related to the earlier Chandragupta Maurya. His son Samudragupta expanded the empire into surrounding areas. The new kingdom of the Guptas became the dominant power in northern India. It also had loose control over central India. This made it the greatest state since the Mauryan Empire. The Gupta Empire had a series of good kings and created a new age of Indian civilization. Visitors from other lands admired the culture. One of these visitors was Faxian, a Buddhist monk from China who traveled to India in the fifth century. He admired the rulers, their tolerance of Buddhism, and the prosperity of the country. The Gupta Empire traded with China, Southeast Asia, and the Mediterranean. Cities were built along the main trade routes throughout India. These cities became wealthy from trade and from the pilgrims who traveled across India to visit the major religious centers. **Pilgrims** are people who travel to religious places.

Name ______________________ Date ______________________ Class ______________________

Reading Essentials and Study Guide

The Gupta Empire did not last, however. Invasions by the Huns in the late fifth century A.D. reduced the power of the empire. A military leader in the seventh century revived the empire for a while, but the empire fell apart after his death. Northern India would not be reunited for hundreds of years.

6. Why were the cities in the Gupta Empire wealthy?

____

____

____

____

____

• The World of Indian Culture *(page 85)*

The Indian culture has produced great works in literature, architecture and science. The Vedas are the earliest known works of Indian literature. These were originally passed down orally from generation to generation. After the development of Sanskrit writing, the Vedas were written down. India's great historical epics, the *Mahabharata* and the *Ramayana,* were also written down. The *Mahabharata* is the longest poem in any written language. It describes a war between cousins in Aryan society. The most famous section is the Bhagavid Gita. It is a sermon by the god Krishna before a major battle. The *Ramayana* is much shorter than the *Mahabharata*. It is the story of the fictional ruler Rama. Both the *Mahabharata* and the *Ramayana* contain religious and moral lessons. To this day, they continue to inspire the people of India. One of ancient India's most famous authors was Kalidasa, who lived during the Gupta Dynasty. One of his poems, *The Cloud Messenger*, remains one of the most popular Sanskrit poems.

India also made major achievements in architecture. Three types of structures were developed to foster the spread of Buddhism: pillars, stupas, and rock chambers. Many stone pillars were built to mark sites related to events in Buddha's life. The stupas were originally intended to hold relics of Buddha, such as a lock of hair. They were built in the form of burial mounds and became places for devotion. Rock chambers were developed to house monks and to serve as halls for religious ceremonies. The rooms were carved out of rock cliffs on the sides of mountains.

Ancient Indians also made advances in astronomy and mathematics. They charted the movements of the heavenly bodies. They knew that the Earth was round and that it rotated on its axis and revolved around the sun. Indian mathematicians introduced the concept of zero and used a symbol (0) for it. Aryabhata, the most famous Indian mathematician of the Gupta Empire, devised a decimal system of counting in tens. After Arabs conquered parts of

Name ______________________ Date ______________________ Class ______________________

Reading Essentials and Study Guide

Chapter 3, Section 2 *(continued)*

India, Arab scholars adopted the Indian number system. European traders borrowed it from the Arabs, and it spread through Europe in the 1200s. It is the system that we use today and is called the Indian-Arabic numeral system.

7. Who developed the decimal system of counting in tens?

Name ______________________ Date ______________________ Class ______________________

Reading Essentials and Study Guide

Chapter 3, Section 3

For use with textbook pages 88–97

EARLY CHINESE CIVILIZATIONS

KEY TERMS

Mandate of Heaven a belief during the Zhou dynasty that kings received their authority to command, or mandate, from Heaven *(page 91)*

Dao the proper "Way" that a king was expected to rule in order to please the gods and protect the people *(page 92)*

filial piety the duty of members of a family to subordinate their needs and desires to those of the male head of the family *(page 93)*

Confucianism a system of ideas based on the teachings of Confucius *(page 95)*

Daoism a system of ideas based on the teachings of Laozi *(page 96)*

Legalism a philosophy that stressed harsh laws and punishments *(page 97)*

DRAWING FROM EXPERIENCE

Do you think people are basically good or basically evil? Are strict laws necessary to keep order and make people obey?

In the last two sections, you learned about the early civilizations and empires of India. In this section, you will learn about early civilizations in China and the philosophies they developed.

ORGANIZING YOUR THOUGHTS

Use the diagram below to help you take notes. The Shang and Zhou dynasties had several similarities. List five similarities in the area where the two circles overlap.

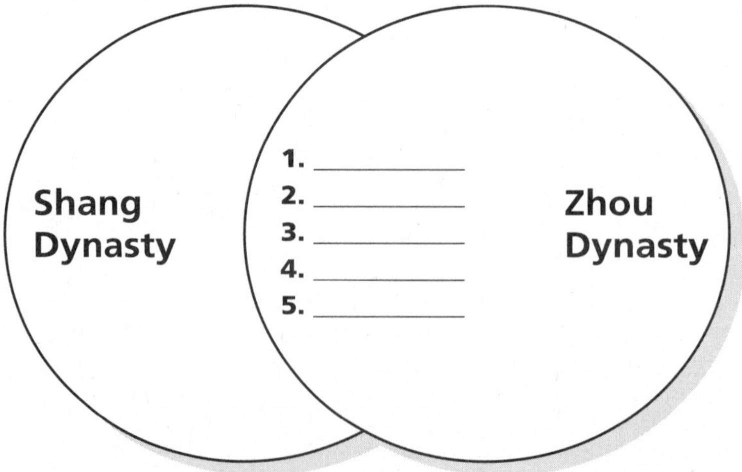

Name ______________________ Date ______________ Class ______________

Reading Essentials and Study Guide

Chapter 3, Section 3 *(continued)*

READ TO LEARN

• The Geography of China *(page 88)*

The Huang He, or Yellow River, is more than 2900 miles long. It extends from Mongolia to the Pacific Ocean. The Chang Jiang, or Yangtze River, is more than 3400 miles long. It flows across central China and empties into the Yellow Sea. The valleys of these two rivers became one of the great food-producing areas of the ancient world. Not all of China is fertile land, however. Only 12 percent of the total land is suitable for farming. Much of the rest of the land consists of mountains and deserts.

The mountains and deserts have played an important role in Chinese history. They served as barriers that separated the Chinese people from other Asian people. In the regions created by the mountains and deserts, there were peoples of Mongolian, Indo-European, and Turkish backgrounds. There were often conflicts between these groups and the Chinese.

6. What role have the mountains and deserts played in Chinese history?

____

____

____

____

____

• The Shang Dynasty *(page 89)*

Chinese civilization began with the Xia dynasty over four thousand years ago. Little is known about this dynasty. It was replaced by a second dynasty, the Shang, which lasted from about 1750 to 1122 B.C. The Shang dynasty was primarily a farming society. An aristocracy whose major concern was war ruled it. An **aristocracy** is an upper class whose wealth is based on land and whose power is passed from one generation to another.

There were large cities in Shang China. The cities had huge walls, royal palaces, and large royal tombs. The Shang king ruled from the capital city of Anyang. His kingdom was divided into territories with aristocratic warlords (military leaders) in charge of each territory. The king chose these leaders and could remove them. The king controlled large armies, which often fought on the fringes of the kingdom.

The Shang rulers believed that they could communicate with the gods to get help with their affairs. Priests scratched questions on bones to get answers from the gods. These bones were called oracle bones. The priests stuck heated metal rods into the bones, which caused the bones to crack. The priests then interpreted the cracks as answers from the gods. The Chinese had a strong belief in life after death. Humans were sacrificed to win the favor of the gods and to provide companions for the king and his family on their journey to the next world. From the belief in an afterlife came the idea of the veneration of ancestors (sometimes called "ancestor worship"). The Chinese believed that the spirits of ancestors could bring good or evil to the living members of a family. So it was important to treat the spirits well.

The king and his family were at the top of Shang society. Aristocratic families helped them. The aristocrats waged war, served as officials, and were also the chief landowners. The majority of the people were peasants who farmed the land of the aristocrats. Shang society also included a small number of merchants and artisans. The Shang are well known for their mastery of the art of bronze casting. Thousands of bronze objects from this period have survived. These are some of the most admired creations of Chinese art.

7. What were some of the religious beliefs during the Shang dynasty?

• The Zhou Dynasty *(page 91)*

In 1122 B.C., the ruler of the state of Zhou revolted against the last of the Shang rulers and established a new dynasty. The Zhou dynasty lasted for almost nine hundred years (1122 to 256 B.C.). It was the longest dynasty in Chinese history. The Zhou dynasty continued the political system of the Shang rulers. At the head of the government was the Zhou king. Like the Shang rulers, he divided the kingdom into territories governed by officials that he appointed. These officials were aristocrats. The king was in charge of defense and controlled large armies.

The Zhou kings also made some changes. The Zhou dynasty claimed that it ruled China because it had the **Mandate of Heaven.** It was believed that Heaven kept order in the world through the Zhou king. Thus, the Zhou king had a *mandate*, or authority to command, from Heaven. The king was chosen by Heaven because of his talent and virtue. He was expected to rule according to the proper "Way," called the **Dao.** It was his duty to keep the gods pleased to protect the people from bad harvests or disasters. If he failed, he could be overthrown. This gave people the "right of revolution." The king was not a divine being himself and could be replaced. The Mandate of Heaven led to a pattern of *dynastic cycles*. From the beginning of Chinese history to A.D. 1912,

Reading Essentials and Study Guide

Chapter 3, Section 3 *(continued)*

China was ruled by a series of dynasties. Each dynasty said that it ruled with the Mandate of Heaven. It established its power, ruled successfully for many years, and then began to decline. Rebellions or invasions would cause it to collapse, and a new dynasty would take over. Then the cycle would be repeated.

The Zhou dynasty followed this cycle of rise, decline, and collapse. Some of the territories in the Zhou kingdom became powerful states and challenged the Zhou ruler. In 403 B.C., civil war broke out. This began a time in Chinese history called the "Period of the Warring States." By this time, warfare in China had changed. Iron weapons were being used. Foot soldiers (the infantry) and soldiers on horseback (the cavalry) made their first appearance. The cavalry was armed with crossbows, a Chinese invention of the seventh century B.C. In 221 B.C., one of the warring states, the state of Qin, took control and created a new dynasty.

During the Zhou dynasty, peasants worked on land owned by lords (aristocrats), but they also had land of their own. A class of artisans and merchants lived in walled towns. Merchants did not operate freely but were considered the property of the lords. There was also a class of slaves. Trade consisted mainly of the exchange of local goods that were used on an everyday basis. Eventually, it increased to include goods from distant lands, such as salt, iron, cloth, and luxury items. One of the most important items that the Chinese traded was silk.

By the sixth century B.C., irrigation was in wide use. Large water projects controlled the flow of rivers and spread water evenly to the fields. The use of iron led to the development of iron plowshares. This made it possible to plow land that had not yet been used for farming. Because of these advances in farming, the population of China rose as high as fifty million people during the Zhou dynasty.

The family was the basic economic and social unit in China. The Chinese believed in the idea of **filial piety.** *Filial* refers to sons and daughters. Filial piety is the duty of members of the family to subordinate their needs and desires to those of the male head of the family. Every family member had his or her place. People needed to work together to farm the land. Children were important because they worked in the fields when they were young. Later, sons were expected to take over the physical labor on their family's land and take care of their parents as the parents got older. Men were important because they worked in the fields and provided food for their families. They were also the warriors, scholars, and government officials. Women raised the children and worked in the home.

Perhaps the most important cultural contribution of ancient China was the development of a written language. By the time of the Shang dynasty, the Chinese had developed a simple script that is the ancestor of the complex written language that the Chinese use today. It was primarily pictographic and ideographic in form. Pictographs are picture symbols, usually called characters, that form a picture of the object they represent. Ideographs are characters that combine two or more pictographs to represent an idea.

8. What was the Mandate of Heaven and how did it lead to dynastic cycles?

• The Chinese Philosophies *(page 94)*

Toward the end of the Zhou dynasty, three major schools of thought, or philosophies, developed in China. Chinese philosophers were concerned about the world in which people lived and how to create a stable order in the world. **Confucianism** is a system of ideas developed by Confucius, known to the Chinese as the First Teacher. Confucius was born in 551 B.C. He lived during a time of chaos in China. He provided a set of ideas about how to restore order to society. His interest in philosophy was ethical and political, not spiritual. His concern was with human behavior. According to Confucius, the key to proper behavior was to behave in accordance with the Dao (Way). Duty and humanity were important elements of the Dao. The concept of duty meant that all people had to subordinate their own interests to the broader needs of the family and the community. This concept of duty is often expressed as a "work ethic." If each person worked hard to fulfill his or her duties, society would prosper. The concept of humanity consisted of a sense of compassion and empathy for others. Confucius taught, "Do not do unto others what you would not wish done to yourself." Confucius believed that government should not be limited to people of noble birth, but should be open to all men. His ideas did not have much effect in his lifetime. But after his death in 479 B.C., his message spread widely throughout China. Until the twentieth century, almost every Chinese pupil studied his sayings.

Daoism was a system of ideas based on the teachings of Laozi. According to tradition, Laozi, or the Old Master, lived during the time of Confucius. Scholars do not know if Laozi actually existed. But the ideas that people associate with him became popular in the fifth and fourth centuries B.C. The main ideas of Daoism are contained in the *Tao Te Ching* (The Way of the Dao). Like Confucianism, Daoism does not concern itself with the meaning of the universe. It is concerned about proper forms of behavior. Its ideas about human behavior are very different from those of Confucius, however. Daoists believe that the true way to follow the will of Heaven is not action but inaction. The best way to act in harmony with the universe is to act spontaneously and let nature take its course by not interfering with it.

A third philosophy that became popular in China was **Legalism.** Legalists believed that human beings were evil by nature. They could only be brought to follow the correct path by harsh laws and punishments. Legalists believed that a strong ruler was needed to create an orderly society. The ruler did not need to have compassion for the needs of the people. Fear of harsh punishment would cause the people to serve the interests of the ruler. This would maintain order and stability in society.

9. What three philosophies developed in China near the end of the Zhou dynasty?

____

____

____

____

____

Name ______________________ Date ____________________ Class ____________________

Reading Essentials and Study Guide

Chapter 3, Section 4

For use with textbook pages 98–103

RISE AND FALL OF CHINESE EMPIRES

KEY TERMS

regime the government in power *(page 99)*

censorate a division of the bureaucracy in the Qin dynasty that had inspectors who checked on government officials to make sure they were doing their jobs *(page 99)*

DRAWING FROM EXPERIENCE

Have you ever applied for a job? What questions did you have to answer? What criteria do you think employers should use when choosing people for jobs?

In the last section, you learned about the early civilizations in China. In this section, you will learn about two Chinese empires, the Qin and Han dynasties. Both dynasties chose their government officials on the basis of merit rather than birth.

ORGANIZING YOUR THOUGHTS

Use the web organizer below to help you take notes. New technology added to the economic prosperity of the Han Era. List six inventions or areas of technological progress during the Han dynasty.

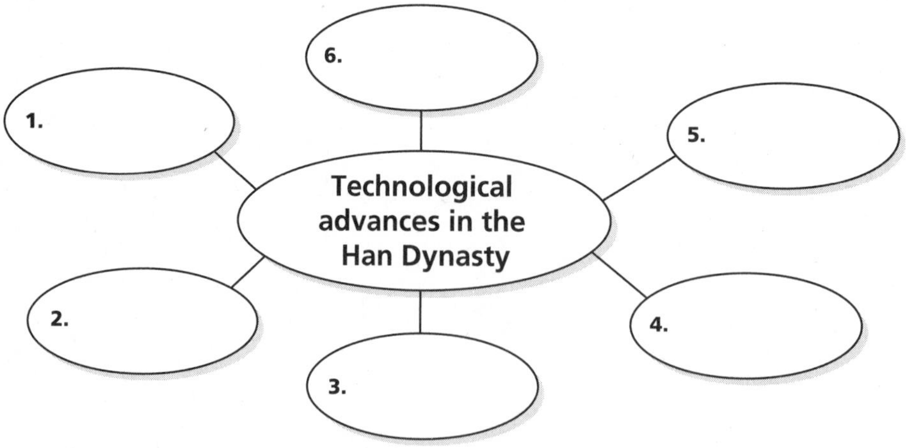

Name ______________________ Date ______________ Class ______________

READ TO LEARN

• The Qin Dynasty (221–206 B.C.) *(page 98)*

From about 400 to 200 B.C., there were civil wars in China. Powerful states fought each other and ignored the Zhou kings. The Qin state gradually defeated the other states. In 221 B.C., the Qin ruler started a new dynasty. This ruler's name was Qin Shihuangdi, which means "the First Qin Emperor." The Qin dynasty made many changes in Chinese politics. Legalism was adopted as the regime's philosophy. (A **regime** is a government in power.) Anyone who opposed the new regime was punished or executed. The Qin dynasty was a centralized state. The central bureaucracy was divided in three parts: the civil division, the military division, and the **censorate.** The censorate had inspectors (censors) who checked on government officials to make sure they were doing their jobs. Below the central government were two levels of administration—provinces and counties. Officials at these levels did not inherit their positions but were appointed by the emperor. The censors kept a close watch over these officials and reported to the emperor. If the officials were found guilty of wrongdoing, they were executed.

Qin Shihuangdi unified the Chinese world. He created a single monetary system and built a system of roads throughout the entire empire. His armies advanced to the south and extended the border of China to the edge of the Yuan River, or Red River, in modern-day Vietnam. His major concern was in the north. In the area south of the Gobi, there were people known to the Chinese as the Xiongnu. They were nomadic people and fought on horseback. The Xiongnu became a threat to the Chinese communities near the northern frontier. The Chinese began to build walls to keep them out. Qin Shihuangdi added to these walls. He linked the existing walls together to create "The Wall of Ten Thousand *Li*" (a *li* is about a third of a mile). Today this is known as the Great Wall of China. The great wall that we see today was actually built 1500 years later, however. Most of Qin Shihuangdi's walls were constructed of loose stone and sand and disappeared long ago.

Qin Shihuangdi died in 210 B.C., and his dynasty was overthrown four years later. The fall of the Qin dynasty was followed by a period of civil war. This period did not last long, and was followed by a new dynasty.

7. What changes did the Qin dynasty make in Chinese politics?

____

____

____

____

____

• The Han Dynasty (202 B.C.-A.D. 220) *(page 100)*

Liu Bang founded the Han dynasty in 202 B.C. Liu Bang was a peasant who became known by his title, Han Gaozu ("Exalted Emperor of Han"). The Han dynasty was one of the greatest and longest dynasties in Chinese history. Han Gaozu discarded the harsh policies of the Qin dynasty. Confucian principles, rather than Legalism, became the philosophy for the new government. The Han dynasty did not change all of the systems of government, however. It kept the three divisions of the central government. It also kept the system of provinces and counties. Most important, it kept the system of choosing officials on the basis of merit rather than birth. The Han dynasty introduced the civil service examination and started a school to train officials. Students were expected to learn Chinese history, law, and the teachings of Confucius. During the Han dynasty, the population increased rapidly to over sixty million people.

The Han emperors, especially Han Wudi, expanded the Chinese empire. They added the southern regions below the Chang Jiang to the empire. Part of what is now northern Vietnam became part of the empire. The Han armies went westward into central Asia and extended the Chinese boundary there. They also drove the Xiongnu back to the north. After Han Wudi's death in 87 B.C., China experienced almost 150 years of peace.

The Han period was a time of prosperity. Peasants began to suffer, however. They were forced into military service or labor of up to one month per year. The growing population eventually reduced the size of the average farm plot to about one acre per person, which was barely enough to survive. Many poor peasants were forced to sell their land and become tenant farmers. The aristocrats once again controlled the land.

Technological advances were made during the Han Era. Progress was made in textile manufacturing, water mills for grinding grain, and iron casting. Iron casting led to the invention of steel. Paper was also developed during the Han dynasty. The rudder and fore-and-aft rigging for ships were invented. Ships could sail into the wind for the first time. This led to a major expansion of trade. Trade was established with countries as far away as India and the Mediterranean.

Over time, the Han Empire began to decay. Rulers became weak, and the aristocrats forced more and more farmers to become tenants. By A.D. 170, peasant uprisings and wars caused the Han dynasty to collapse. In 189, rebel armies sacked the Han capital, Changan. In 220, a general seized control but was unable to stay in power. China plunged again into civil war, and there were new invasions by northern peoples. The next great dynasty would not arise for four hundred years.

Reading Essentials and Study Guide

Chapter 3, Section 4 *(continued)*

8. In what way was the government of the Han rulers different from the government of the Qin Emperor? In what ways was it similar?

• Culture in Qin and Han China *(page 103)*

The Qin and Han dynasties were also known for their cultural achievements. The main Confucian writings were made into a set of classics during this time. These writings became required reading for generations of Chinese schoolchildren.

Perhaps the most remarkable achievement of the Qin period was discovered in 1974. Underground pits were found about a mile east of the burial mound of the First Qin Emperor. They contained a vast army made of terra-cotta (hardened clay). Archaeologists believe it was a re-creation of Qin Shihuangdi's imperial guard and was meant to be with the emperor on his journey to the next world. There are more than six thousand figures in the first pit alone, along with horses, chariots, and seven thousand bronze weapons. The terra-cotta figures are slightly larger than life-size. The detail on the uniforms is realistic, and the heads were modeled individually to reflect the different ethnic types in the army.

9. What do archaeologists think was the purpose of the terra-cotta figures found near the burial mound of the First Qin Emperor?

Name ______________________ Date ______________________ Class ______________________

Reading Essentials and Study Guide

Chapter 4, Section 1

For use with textbook pages 109–113

THE FIRST GREEK CIVILIZATIONS

KEY TERMS

epic poem a long poem that tells the deeds of a great hero *(page 112)*

arete the Greek term for excellence, which heroes strove to attain *(page 113)*

DRAWING FROM EXPERIENCE

Do you enjoy reading poems? What kinds of literature do you like the most? Why?

In this section, you will learn about the early civilizations of Greece. You will also learn about the writings of Homer, one of the great poets of all time.

ORGANIZING YOUR THOUGHTS

Use the time line below to help you take notes. Identify five important events in the development of Greek civilization.

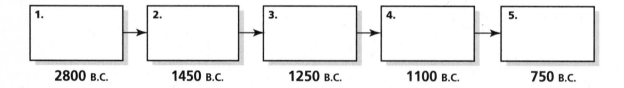

1.	→	**2.**	→	**3.**	→	**4.**	→	**5.**
2800 B.C.		**1450 B.C.**		**1250 B.C.**		**1100 B.C.**		**750 B.C.**

Reading Essentials and Study Guide

READ TO LEARN

• The Impact of Geography *(page 109)*

Compared with Mesopotamia and Egypt, Greece is small. It is a peninsula about the size of Louisiana. It is made up of small plains and river valleys surrounded by high mountains. The mountains influenced Greek history, because they separated Greeks from each other. This caused different Greek communities to develop their own ways of life. The small size of these communities encouraged people to be involved in politics. But the rivalry between the communities led to warfare. The sea also influenced Greek history. Greece has a long seacoast with many harbors, so the Greeks became seafarers. Greeks also lived on many islands off the Greek mainland. They sailed into the Aegean, the Mediterranean, and the Black Seas. They later established colonies that spread Greek civilization throughout the Mediterranean world.

6. How did the mountains and the sea influence Greek history?

• The Minoan Civilization *(page 110)*

By 2800 B.C., a Bronze Age civilization existed on the large island of Crete, southeast of the Greek mainland. It flourished between 2000 and 1450 B.C. It was called the Minoan civilization by the English archaeologist, Arthur Evans, who discovered it. He named it after Minos, the legendary king of Crete. Evans discovered a huge palace complex on Crete at Knossos. The remains of this complex revealed a rich culture. The palace contained vases, ivory figurines, and jewelry. The rooms were decorated with paintings that showed sporting events and nature scenes. Storerooms held gigantic jars of oil, wine, and grain. The Minoans were traders, and their ships took them to Egypt and southern Greece.

The Minoan civilization on Crete was suddenly destroyed around 1450 B.C. Some historians believe that a tidal wave triggered by a volcanic eruption was responsible. Most historians, however, believe that the destruction was the result of an invasion by mainland Greeks known as Mycenaeans.

7. Why is the Bronze Age civilization on Crete called the Minoan civilization?

Name ______________________ Date ______________________ Class ______________________

Reading Essentials and Study Guide

Chapter 4, Section 1 *(continued)*

• The First Greek State: Mycenae *(page 111)*

The term Mycenaean comes from Mycenae, a fortified site in Greece that was discovered by the German archaeologist Heinrich Schliemann. Mycenae was one of several centers in the Mycenaean civilization. This civilization flourished between 1600 and 1100 B.C. The Mycenaeans were part of the Indo-European peoples. Over time, they gained control of Greece and developed a civilization.

The Mycenaean civilization was made up of powerful monarchies. These monarchies were independent of each other, but they probably formed a loose alliance. Each monarch lived in a fortified palace center. These centers were built on hills and were surrounded by gigantic walls. The royal families lived within the walls. The rest of the population lived outside.

The Mycenaeans were warriors. They took pride in their heroic deeds in battle. Mycenaean paintings often show war and hunting scenes. The Mycenaeans also developed a trade network. Some historians believe that the Mycenaeans conquered Crete. Some of the Aegean islands also came under Mycenaean control. We know about some of the military adventures of the Mycenaeans through the poetry of Homer. According to Homer, Mycenaeans, led by Agamemnon, the king of Mycenae, sacked the city of Troy around 1250 B.C.

By the late thirteenth century B.C., Mycenaean Greece was in serious trouble. Mycenaean states fought one another, and major earthquakes caused widespread damage. In the twelfth century B.C., invaders moved into Greece from the north. By 1100 B.C., Mycenaean civilization had collapsed.

8. What troubles did the Mycenaean civilization have before it collapsed?

• The Greeks in a Dark Age *(page 112)*

After the collapse of Mycenaean civilization, Greece entered a period when food production dropped and population declined. Historians call this period the Dark Age, because there are few records to tell us what happened during this time. This period lasted from about 1100 to 750 B.C.

During the Dark Age, many Greeks left the mainland and sailed across the Aegean Sea to various islands. Many went to the western shores of Asia Minor. They settled in an area called Ionia, which is in modern-day Turkey.

Name ______________________ Date ______________________ Class ______________________

Reading Essentials and Study Guide

Chapter 4, Section 1 *(continued)*

Two groups settled in other parts of Greece. The Aeolian Greeks colonized the island of Lesbos and the territory near the mainland. The Dorians settled in southwestern Greece and on some of the Aegean islands, including Crete.

Some important events occurred in this Dark Age. There was a revival of trade. Iron replaced bronze as a way to make weapons. This made weapons affordable for more people. Farming tools that were made of iron helped increase food production.

In the eighth century B.C., the Greeks adopted the Phoenician alphabet. They made all of their words with a combination of twenty-four letters. This made learning to read and write simpler. Near the end of the Dark Age, the work of Homer appeared. Homer was one of the truly great poets of all time. He wrote the *Iliad* and the *Odyssey*. These were the first epic poems of early Greece. An **epic poem** is a long poem that tells the deeds of a great hero. Homer based his poems on stories that had been passed down from generation to generation. He used stories about the Trojan War to write the *Iliad* and the *Odyssey*. Homer taught values, such as courage and honor. The heroes in his poems strove for excellence, which the Greeks called **arete.** Arete is won in a struggle or contest. By fighting, the hero protects his family and friends, preserves his own honor, and earns his reputation. Homer's heroes became the ideal for Greek males. His poems were used to educate young men for generations to come.

9. Why was the period after the collapse of the Mycenaean civilization called the Dark Age?

Name ______________________ Date ______________________ Class ______________________

Reading Essentials and Study Guide

Chapter 4, Section 2

For use with textbook pages 115–120

THE GREEK CITY-STATES

KEY TERMS

polis the Greek word for a city-state *(page 115)*

acropolis a fortified area at the top of a hill in a Greek city-state *(page 115)*

agora an open area below the acropolis where people would assemble and where the market was located *(page 115)*

hoplites heavily armed infantry soldiers *(page 116)*

phalanx a rectangular formation used by hoplites to create a wall of shields *(page 116)*

democracy rule of the many *(page 118)*

oligarchy rule by the few *(page 118)*

helots people captured by the Spartans *(page 118)*

ephors a group of five men who were elected each year by the Spartans and who were responsible for the education of the youth and the conduct of all citizens *(page 119)*

DRAWING FROM EXPERIENCE

How is the city you live in (or the nearest city) arranged? Where is the center of the city? In what part of the city are most business activities carried on? Where are the city's government offices? Where are the residential areas?

In the last section, you read about the beginnings of Greek civilization. This section focuses on the culture and politics of Greek city-states.

ORGANIZING YOUR THOUGHTS

Use the chart below to help you take notes. Reform-minded aristocrats made major changes in the society and politics of early Athens. Describe the reforms of the following leaders.

Leader	Reforms
Solon	**1.**
Pisistratus	**2.**
Cleisthenes	**3.**

Name ______________________ Date ______________ Class ______________

Reading Essentials and Study Guide

Chapter 4, Section 2 *(continued)*

READ TO LEARN

• The Polis: Center of Greek Life *(page 115)*

Greek villages gradually expanded and became city-states. The Greek word for a city-state is **polis.** Our word *politics* comes from this Greek word. The polis was a town, a city, or even a village, along with its surrounding countryside. By 750 B.C., the polis became the center of Greek life. The main gathering place in the polis was usually a hill. At the top of the hill was a fortified area called an **acropolis.** The acropolis was a place of refuge during attacks. Sometimes it was also a religious center where temples were built. Below the acropolis was an **agora.** The agora was an open area where people could assemble and where the market was located.

The polis was a community of people who had a common identity and common goals. The polis consisted of three main groups: citizens with political rights (adult males), citizens with no political rights (women and children), and noncitizens (slaves and people from foreign lands). The citizens of a polis had rights, but they also had responsibilities. Citizens were expected to be loyal to the state. This loyalty had a negative side. City-states distrusted one another, and this eventually led to the downfall of Greece.

A new military system developed in Greece. In earlier times, nobles (aristocrats) on horseback had fought wars. By 700 B.C., the military system was based on hoplites. **Hoplites** were heavily armed infantry soldiers (foot soldiers). Each carried a round shield, a short sword, and a spear about nine feet long. Hoplites marched into battle in a rectangular formation called a **phalanx.** This formation created a wall of shields to protect the hoplites.

4. What three groups made up a polis?

• Greek Colonies *(page 116)*

Between 750 and 550 B.C., many Greeks moved to distant lands. The growth of trade and the need for good farmland were two reasons that people moved. Each colony that they formed became a new polis. New Greek colonies were formed in southern Italy, southern France, eastern Spain, and northern Africa. The Greeks also set up colonies in Thrace, to the north, and along the shores of the Black Sea. One important city that they established was Byzantium, which later became Constantinople (now Istanbul).

Reading Essentials and Study Guide

Chapter 4, Section 2 *(continued)*

Colonization spread the Greek culture throughout the Mediterranean. It also led to an increase in trade and industry. The Greeks exported pottery, wine and olive oil. In return, they received grains and metals from the west. They also received fish, timber, wheat, metals, and slaves from the Black Sea region.

5. What were some of the results of Greek colonization?

___

___

___

___

___

• Tyranny in the City-States *(page 117)*

The increase in trade and industry created a new group of wealthy people in many city-states. These men wanted political power, but they found it difficult to get more power because of the aristocrats. This led to the rise of tyrants in the seventh and sixth centuries B.C. Tyrants were not necessarily wicked, as our word *tyrant* implies. Greek tyrants were rulers who seized power from the aristocrats. The new group of wealthy men supported the tyrants. So did the poor peasants who were in debt to the aristocrats. Tyrants gained power by using hired soldiers. After gaining power, they built new marketplaces, temples and walls.

By the end of the sixth century B.C., the tyrants had fallen out of favor. But their rule was important in Greek history. It ended the rule of the aristocrats in many city-states. This allowed many new people to be involved in government. In some city-states, this led to the development of **democracy,** rule of the many. Other city-states remained committed to rule by the few, or **oligarchy.** The differences in these two forms of government can be seen in Sparta and Athens, the two most famous and powerful Greek city-states.

6. Why was the rule of the tyrants important in Greek history?

___

___

___

___

___

Name ______________________ Date ______________________ Class ______________________

Reading Essentials and Study Guide

• Sparta *(page 118)*

Like other Greek city-states, Sparta needed more land. But instead of starting new colonies, the Spartans conquered other Greeks. First they conquered the Laconians. Later, around 730 B.C., they conquered the Messenians. The Laconians and Messenians were captured and were forced to work for the Spartans. These captured people were known as **helots.**

Between 800 and 600 B.C., the lives of the Spartans were rigidly organized and tightly controlled. Males spent their childhood learning military discipline. At age 20, they entered the army. Even if they married, they continued to live in the military barracks until age 30. At 30, Spartan men were allowed to vote and live at home, but they stayed in the army until age 60. While their husbands lived in the barracks, Spartan women lived at home. They were expected to exercise and remain fit to bear and raise healthy children. Because of their separation from their husbands, Spartan women had greater freedom and power in the household than other women in Greece. Many Spartan women supported the strict Spartan values and expected their husbands and sons to be brave in war.

The Spartan government was an oligarchy headed by two kings. The kings led the Spartan army on its campaigns. A group of five men, who were elected each year, was responsible for the education of the youth and the conduct of all citizens. These men were known as the **ephors.** There was also a council of elders, which included the two kings and 28 citizens over the age of 60. The council of elders decided on the issues that would be presented to an assembly made up of male citizens. The assembly voted on the issues, but did not debate.

Spartans had little contact with the outside world. They were not allowed to travel abroad, except for military reasons. Foreigners were discouraged from visiting Sparta. Spartan citizens were also discouraged from studying philosophy, literature, or the arts. The art of war was the only art that was encouraged.

7. How was the Spartan government organized?

____

____

____

____

____

- **Athens** *(page 120)*

Early Athens was ruled by a king. By the seventh century B.C., however, Athens had become an oligarchy under the control of aristocrats. There was an assembly of citizens, but it did not have much power. Many Athenian farmers were sold into slavery, because they were unable to pay their debts to the aristocrats. There were cries to cancel the debts and give land to the poor. By the end of the seventh century B.C., Athens was on the verge of civil war. The aristocrats reacted to this crisis in 594 B.C. They gave full power to Solon, a reform-minded aristocrat. Solon cancelled all land debts and freed people who were slaves because of their debts. However, he did not take land from the rich and give it to the poor.

Pisistratus, an aristocrat, seized power in 560 B.C. He gave aristocrats' land to the peasants in order to please the poor. He also aided Athenian trade to please the merchants. His son succeeded him, but the Athenians rebelled against his son in 510 B.C. Two years later, Cleisthenes gained control.

Cleisthenes was a reformer and created a new council of five hundred. This council supervised foreign affairs, oversaw the treasury, and proposed laws. The Athenian assembly was given final authority to pass laws after free and open debate. The assembly was made up of all male citizens. Cleisthenes's reforms laid the foundations for Athenian democracy.

8. What was government like under Cleisthenes?

Name ______________________ Date ______________________ Class ______________________

Reading Essentials and Study Guide

Chapter 4, Section 3

For use with textbook pages 121–125

CLASSICAL GREECE

KEY TERMS

Age of Pericles the period in Greek history between 461 and 429 B.C. when Athens' power and brilliance was at its height *(page 123)*

direct democracy a democratic system in which people participate directly in government decision making through mass meetings *(page 123)*

ostracism the Athenian practice of banning a person from the city for 10 years, if at least six thousand members of the assembly wrote the person's name on pottery fragments, called *ostrakon (page 123)*

DRAWING FROM EXPERIENCE

In what areas of life, if any, do you think women today still need to achieve equality with men? Why do you think so?

In the last section, you read about Sparta and Athens. This section focuses on the triumphs and decline of the Greek city-states.

ORGANIZING YOUR THOUGHTS

Use the diagram below to help you take notes. Name three results of the Peloponnesian War.

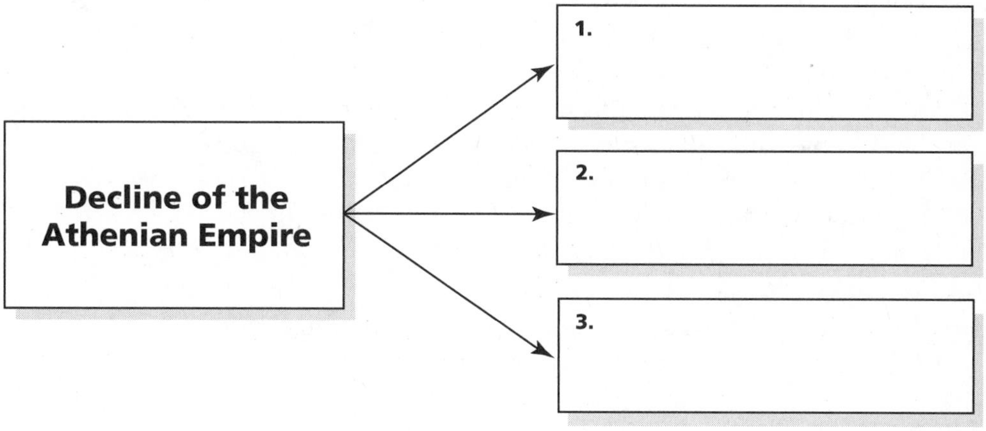

READ TO LEARN

• The Challenge of Persia *(page 121)*

As the Greeks spread throughout the Mediterranean, they came in contact with the Persian Empire. The Persians had already conquered the Ionian Greeks in Asia Minor. In 499 B.C., the Ionian cities tried to revolt against the Persians. The Athenian navy assisted them. The revolt was unsuccessful, but it led the Persian ruler Darius to seek revenge. In 490 B.C., the Persians landed on the plain of Marathon, about 26 miles from Athens. The Athenian army attacked and defeated the Persians.

After Darius died in 486 B.C., Xerxes became the new Persian ruler. Xerxes led an invasion of Greece in 480 B.C. The Athenians were forced to abandon their city, but the Greek navy managed to defeat the Persian fleet. A few months later, early in 479 B.C., the Greeks formed the largest Greek army up to that time. They defeated the Persian army at Plataea, northwest of Athens.

4. What two Persian rulers invaded Greece?

• The Growth of the Athenian Empire *(page 123)*

After the defeat of the Persians, Athens took over the leadership of the Greek world. In the winter of 478–477 B.C., the Athenians formed the Delian League. This was an alliance against the Persians. Its headquarters was on the island of Delos, but its chief officials were Athenians. The Delian League continued the attack against the Persian Empire. Eventually, it liberated nearly all of the Greek states in the Aegean that were under Persian control. In 454 B.C., the Athenians moved the treasury of the Delian League from Delos to Athens. By controlling the Delian League, Athens created an empire.

Between 461 and 429 B.C., Athens expanded its new empire. This period in Greek history is called the **Age of Pericles.** Pericles was a dominant figure in Athenian politics during this time. Democracy flourished, and Athens was at the height of its power and brilliance.

Reading Essentials and Study Guide

Chapter 4, Section 3 *(continued)*

5. What was the Delian League?

____

____

____

____

____

• The Age of Pericles *(page 123)*

In the Age of Pericles, every citizen in Athens played a role in government. The form of government was a direct democracy. A **direct democracy** is a democratic system in which people participate directly in government decision-making through mass meetings. In Athens, every male citizen over the age of 18 was a part of the assembly and voted on all major issues. Most residents of Athens were not citizens, however. Meetings of the assembly were held every 10 days on a hillside east of the Acropolis. The assembly passed all laws, elected public officials, and made final decisions on war and foreign policy. Pericles made it possible for poor citizens to take part in public affairs, by making lower class citizens eligible for public office and by paying officeholders. On a daily basis, a large body of city officials ran the government. Ten officials, known as generals, were the directors of policy. These officials were elected, so they could be reelected or removed from office. The Athenians also developed the practice of **ostracism.** If a person was considered harmful to the city, he could be banned from the city for 10 years, if at least six thousand members of the assembly wrote his name on pottery fragments (called *ostrakon*).

Under Pericles, Athens became the center of Greek culture. The Persians had destroyed much of the city during the Persian Wars. Pericles used the Delian League treasury to rebuild the city. New temples and statues were built. Art, architecture, and philosophy flourished. Athens' achievements alarmed the other Greek states, especially Sparta. This eventually led to a new war.

6. What was Athenian government like during the Age of Pericles?

____

____

____

____

____

• The Great Peloponnesian War *(page 124)*

After the defeat of the Persians, the Greek world became divided into two main parts: the Athenian Empire and Sparta. Sparta and its allies feared the Athenian Empire. A series of disputes between Athens and Sparta led to the beginning of the Great Peloponnesian War in 431 B.C. Pericles knew that the Spartan army could beat the Athenians in open battle. So the Athenians decided to stay behind the walls of their city. In the second year of the war, a plague broke out in Athens and killed more than a third of the people. Pericles himself died in 429 B.C. Despite these losses, the Athenians held out for 27 years. In 405 B.C., the Athenian navy was destroyed at Aegospotami. Within the next year, Athens surrendered. The great war was over, and the Athenian Empire was destroyed.

The Great Peloponnesian War weakened all of the Greek states. It also ruined any possibility of cooperation among them. During the next 70 years, Sparta, Athens, and Thebes struggled for control. In the process, they ignored the growing power of Macedonia. This would eventually cost them their freedom.

7. What was the basic cause of the Great Peloponnesian War?

• Daily Life in Classical Athens *(page 125)*

In the fifth century B.C., Athens had the largest population of the Greek city-states. Before the plague in 430 B.C., there were about 150,000 citizens living in Athens. About 43,000 of them were adult males who could vote. There were about 35,000 foreigners in Athens during this time. There were also about 100,000 slaves. Slavery was very common. Most people owned at least one slave. Most slaves worked in the fields or in the home as cooks or maids. Some slaves were owned by the state and worked on construction projects.

The Athenian economy was based on farming and trade. Athenians grew grains, vegetables, and fruit. Wine and oil olive were exported. The Athenians also raised sheep and goats for wool and milk. Because of its large population, Athens had to import from 50 to 80 percent of the grain it used. This made trade very important.

Women were citizens who could take part in religious festivals. Otherwise, they were excluded from public life. They could not vote or own property. They married early, at age 14 or 15. A woman was expected to bear children and take care of her family and her house. Women were strictly controlled. If they left the house, they had to have a companion. They were not given any formal education, but some still managed to learn how to read and play musical instruments.

8. What was the role of women in ancient Athens?

____

____

____

____

____

Name ______________________ Date ______________________ Class ______________________

Reading Essentials and Study Guide

Chapter 4, Section 4

For use with textbook pages 127–133

THE CULTURE OF CLASSICAL GREECE

KEY TERMS

ritual a religious ceremony or rite *(page 128)*

oracle a sacred shrine where a god or goddess revealed the future through a priest or priestess *(page 128)*

tragedy a serious play or drama *(page 129)*

philosophy ("love of wisdom") an organized system of thought *(page 130)*

Socratic method a teaching method used by Socrates in which a question and answer format leads pupils to see things for themselves by using their own reason *(page 130)*

DRAWING FROM EXPERIENCE

Do you have a philosophy, or set of ideas, about what is important for having a good life? What are your ideas? What helped you formed your ideas?

In the last section, you read about the Greek city-states. In this section, you will learn about Greek religion, philosophy, drama, and art.

ORGANIZING YOUR THOUGHTS

Use the chart below to help you take notes. Early Greek philosophers tried to explain the universe. For each of the philosophers below, summarize their basic beliefs or teachings.

Philosopher	Beliefs/Teachings
Pythagoras	**1.**
Socrates	**2.**
Plato	**3.**
Aristotle	**4.**

Name ______________________ Date ______________ Class ______________

Reading Essentials and Study Guide

Chapter 4, Section 4 *(continued)*

READ TO LEARN

• Greek Religion *(page 127)*

Religion was very important in Greek life. Temples were the major buildings in Greek cities. The Greeks thought that twelve main gods lived on Mount Olympus, the highest mountain in Greece. One of these twelve was Zeus, who was the chief god and father of the gods. Greek religion did not focus on morality. The Greeks believed that the spirits of most people went to an underworld ruled by the god Hades, regardless of what the people had done in life. Greeks performed rituals to please the gods. **Rituals** are religious ceremonies or rites. The Greek rituals combined prayers with gifts to the gods. The Greeks also held festivals to honor the gods and goddesses. Athletic games often took place at the festivals. All Greeks were invited to these games. The first games of this kind were held at the Olympic festival in 776 B.C.

The Greeks used oracles to learn the will of the gods. An **oracle** was a sacred shrine where a god or goddess revealed the future through a priest or priestess. The most famous was the oracle of the god Apollo at Delphi. A priestess at Delphi listened to questions. Her responses were thought to be inspired by Apollo and were interpreted by priests. Many people traveled to Delphi to consult the oracle of Apollo.

5. What was an oracle?

____

____

____

____

____

• Greek Drama *(page 129)*

The Greeks created drama as we know it. Plays were presented in outdoor theaters as part of religious festivals. The first Greek dramas were **tragedies** (serious plays or dramas). They were presented in a trilogy (a set of three plays) built around a common theme. The only complete trilogy that we still have today is the *Oresteia* by Aeschylus. Another great Athenian playwright was Sophocles. His most famous play was *Oedipus Rex*. A third important Athenian dramatist was Euripides. He was controversial. He questioned traditional values and portrayed war as brutal and barbaric. Greek tragedies dealt with universal themes still relevant today. They were concerned with such problems as the nature of good and evil and the rights of individuals.

Greek comedy developed later than tragedy. It was used to criticize politicians and intellectuals. It was intended both to entertain and to provoke a reaction. The plays of Aristophanes are examples of Greek comedy.

6. Why are Greek tragedies still relevant today?

____

____

____

____

____

• Greek Philosophy *(page 130)*

Philosophy is an organized system of thought. It comes from a Greek word that means "love of wisdom." Many early Greek philosophers tried to explain the universe on the basis of unifying principles. In the sixth century B.C., Pythagoras taught that the essence of the universe was in music and numbers.

Socrates was a philosopher who left no writings. We know about him from his pupils. He believed that the goal of education was to improve the individual. His teaching method is still called the **Socratic method.** He used a question-and-answer format to lead pupils to see things for themselves by using their own reason. This belief in the individual's ability to reason was an important contribution of the Greeks. Socrates questioned authority. This got him into trouble. He was accused of corrupting the youth of Athens and was sentenced to die by drinking hemlock, a poison.

Plato was one of Socrates' students. He is considered by many to be the greatest philosopher of Western civilization. Unlike Socrates, Plato wrote a great deal. His main question was: How do we know what is real? He believed that a higher world of eternal Forms has always existed. The objects that we perceive with our senses are simply reflections or shadows of the ideal Forms. Reality is found in the Forms themselves.

Plato wrote about government in a work entitled *The Republic*. Plato did not trust the workings of democracy. In Plato's ideal state, people were divided into three groups. At the top was an upper class of philosopher-kings. The second group was a class of warriors who protected society. The third group contained all the rest, the masses. Plato also believed that men and women should have the same education and equal access to all positions.

Plato established a school in Athens called the Academy. Aristotle was one of his pupils. He did not accept Plato's theory of ideal forms. He thought that by examining objects, we could perceive their form. But he did not believe that the forms existed in a separate, higher world of reality. He was interested

Reading Essentials and Study Guide

in analyzing and classifying things. He wrote about many subjects, including ethics, logic, politics, poetry, astronomy, geology, biology, and physics.

Unlike Plato, Aristotle did not try to create an ideal form of government. He tried to find the best form of government by analyzing existing governments. For his *Politics,* Aristotle looked at the constitutions of 158 states and found three good forms of government: monarchy, aristocracy, and constitutional government. He thought constitutional government was the best form for most people.

7. What is the Socratic method?

____

____

____

____

____

• The Writing of History *(page 132)*

History, as a systematic analysis of past events, was created by the Greeks. The Greek historian Herodotus wrote the *History of the Persian Wars.* This is considered to be the first real history in Western civilization. Herodotus traveled widely to get his information and was a master storyteller.

Many historians today consider Thucydides to be the greatest historian of the ancient world. Thucydides was an Athenian general who fought in the Great Peloponnesian War. A defeat in battle sent him into exile, where he wrote his *History of the Peloponnesian War.* He saw war and politics in purely human terms. He examined the causes and the course of the Peloponnesian War clearly and fairly. He placed a great emphasis on the accuracy of his facts. He also believed that the study of history is of great value in understanding the present.

8. Who were two great historians of ancient Greece?

____

____

____

____

____

Reading Essentials and Study Guide

Chapter 4, Section 4 *(continued)*

• The Classical Ideals of Greek Art *(page 132)*

Greek art has influenced the art of the Western world for centuries. Classical Greek art was concerned with expressing eternal ideals. In architecture, the most important form was the temple. The most famous temple was the Parthenon. It was built between 447 and 432 B.C. It is regarded as the greatest example of the classical Greek temple. It shows the principles of classical architecture: the search for calmness, clarity, and freedom from unnecessary detail.

Greek sculpture also developed a classical style. Greek sculptors did not try to achieve realism, but rather a standard of ideal beauty. Polyclitus, a fifth-century sculptor, wrote down rules for proportions in a work known as the *Doryphoros*. His theory said that the use of ideal proportions could produce an ideal human form.

9. What did Classical Greek sculptors try to achieve in their sculptures?

Name ______________________ Date ____________________ Class ____________________

Reading Essentials and Study Guide

Chapter 4, Section 5

For use with textbook pages 138–143

ALEXANDER AND THE HELLENISTIC KINGDOMS

KEY TERMS

Hellenistic Era the new age created by Alexander the Great, during which the Greek language and culture spread to other parts of the world *(page 141)*

Epicureanism the philosophy founded by Epicurus, including the belief that happiness is the goal of life and that the pursuit of pleasure is the means to achieve happiness *(page 143)*

Stoicism the philosophy founded by Zeno, including the belief that happiness is found when people gain inner peace by living in harmony with the will of God *(page 143)*

DRAWING FROM EXPERIENCE

Do you enjoy visiting art museums? What styles of sculptures and paintings do you enjoy looking at the most? Why are they your favorites?

In the last section, you read about Greek contributions to philosophy, drama, and art. This section focuses on the Hellenistic culture.

ORGANIZING YOUR THOUGHTS

Use the diagram below to help you take notes. The Hellenistic Era was a period of cultural accomplishment in many areas. List two accomplishments in each of the following areas.

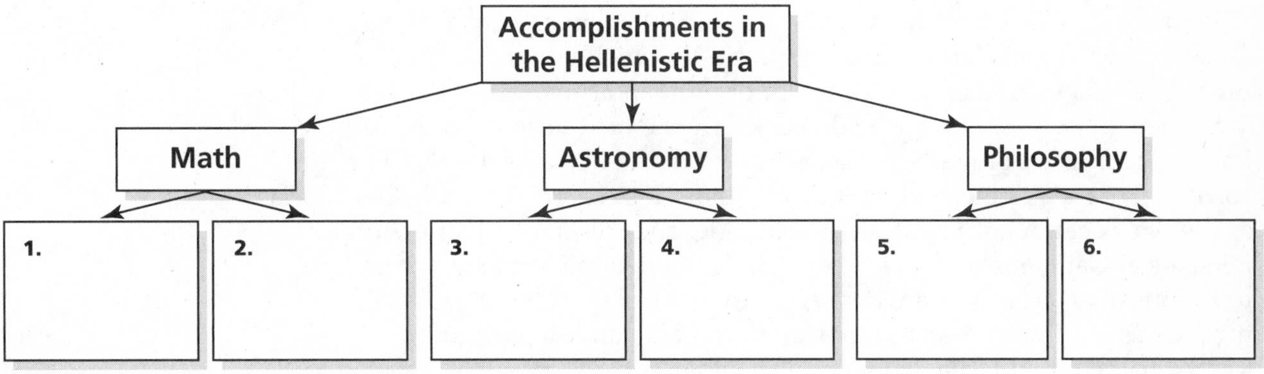

Reading Essentials and Study Guide

Chapter 4, Section 5 *(continued)*

READ TO LEARN

• The Threat of Macedonia *(page 138)*

The Greeks thought their northern neighbors, the Macedonians, were barbarians. The Macedonians were rural people who were organized in groups, not city-states. By the end of the fifth century B.C., however, Macedonia became a powerful kingdom.

In 359 B.C., Philip II became king. He built a powerful army and made Macedonia the chief power of the Greek world. The Athenians tried to stop him. They allied with other Greek states and fought the Macedonians at the Battle of Chaeronea in 338 B.C. The Macedonian army crushed the Greeks. Philip quickly gained control of all of Greece. This brought an end to the freedom of the city-states. Philip then insisted that the Greek states form a league and help him in a war with Persia. But he was assassinated before he could invade Asia.

7. What did Philip want the Greek states to do?

____

____

____

____

____

• Alexander the Great *(page 139)*

Philip's son, Alexander the Great, was only 20 when he became king of Macedonia. After his father's death, Alexander quickly invaded the Persian Empire. In 334 B.C., he entered Asia Minor with an army of thirty-seven thousand men, both Macedonians and Greeks. By the next year, he had freed the Ionian Greek cities of western Asia Minor from the Persians. By the winter of 332 B.C., Syria, Palestine, and Egypt were under his control. He built Alexandria as the Greek capital of Egypt. In 331 B.C., Alexander fought a battle with the Persians at Gaugamela, not far from Babylon. After this victory, Alexander took control of the rest of the Persian Empire. Over the next three years, he moved east and northeast, as far as modern Pakistan. By the summer of 327 B.C., he had entered India. However, his soldiers were weary and refused to go farther. Alexander returned to Babylon, where he planned more campaigns. In June 323 B.C., he died at the age of 32.

Alexander created a new age, the **Hellenistic Era.** The word *Hellenistic* is derived from a Greek word that means "to imitate Greeks." During this period in history, the Greek language and culture spread to many other parts of the world.

8. Why is the new age that was created by Alexander called the Hellenistic Era?

• The Hellenistic Kingdoms *(page 141)*

The empire that Alexander had created fell apart soon after his death. The Macedonian generals struggled for power. By 300 B.C., any hope of unity was dead. Four Hellenistic kingdoms emerged: Macedonia, Syria, the kingdom of Pergamum in western Asia Minor, and Egypt.

Many cities were founded by Alexander and by the Hellenistic rulers after him. Alexandria, the city that Alexander founded in Egypt, was the largest city in the Mediterranean region by the first century B.C. Hellenistic rulers encouraged Greek colonists to move to the new cities in Southwest Asia. Architects, engineers, dramatists, and actors were all in demand in the new cities. Many Greeks and Macedonians were happy to seek their fortunes in the new cities. The new cities of the Hellenistic Era helped to spread Greek culture throughout Asia.

9. What were the four kingdoms that emerged during the Hellenistic Era?

• Hellenistic Culture *(page 142)*

The Hellenistic Era was a period of cultural accomplishment in many areas. Alexandria became a center for poets, writers, philosophers, and scientists. The library there was the largest in ancient times. Architects and sculptors had many opportunities in the new cities. Hellenistic kings were very willing to spend their money to beautify their cities. Greek buildings, like baths, theaters and temples, soon lined the streets of the new cities. Thousands of statues were erected in towns and cities all over the Hellenistic world. Hellenistic sculptors moved away from the idealism of classical Greek art to a more realistic and emotional art.

Name ______________________ Date ______________________ Class ______________________

Reading Essentials and Study Guide

Chapter 4, Section 5 *(continued)*

Great progress was made during the Hellenistic Age in astronomy and mathematics. One astronomer, Aristarchus, developed the theory that the Sun is at the center of the universe and that Earth revolves around the Sun. Another astronomer, Eratosthenes, determined that Earth was round. He also calculated that Earth's circumference was 24,675 miles, which is within 200 miles of the actual figure. The mathematician Euclid wrote the *Elements*, a textbook on plane geometry. His work has been used up to modern times. The most famous scientist of the Hellenistic period was Archimedes. He established the value of the mathematical constant pi. He was also a practical inventor and built a number of devices to repel attackers during sieges.

Athens remained the center of philosophy in the Hellenistic world. Two new systems of thought developed in Athens during this time. Epicurus founded a school in Athens near the end of the fourth century B.C. His philosophy came to be known as **Epicureanism.** He believed that happiness was the goal of life. The means to achieving happiness was the pursuit of pleasure. Pleasure was not the same as satisfying one's physical desires. It was freedom from worry and emotional turmoil. To achieve this kind of pleasure, people had to free themselves from public activity.

Another school of thought was **Stoicism.** It became the most popular philosophy of the Hellenistic world. Stoicism was the philosophy of Zeno. Zeno had a school in Athens known as the Painted Portico. Like Epicureanism, Stoicism was concerned with helping people find happiness. The Stoics, however, took a different approach. To them, happiness could only be found when people gained inner peace by living in harmony with the will of God. Life's problems could not disturb these people. Unlike the Epicureans, the Stoics did not believe in the need to separate themselves from the world and politics. The real stoic was a good citizen and could even be a good government official.

10. What were some differences between Epicureanism and Stoicism?

Name ______________________ Date ______________ Class ______________

Reading Essentials and Study Guide

Chapter 5, Section 1

For use with textbook pages 149–154

THE RISE OF ROME

KEY TERMS

republic a form of government in which the leader is not a monarch and certain citizens have the right to vote *(page 151)*

patrician one of Rome's wealthy landowners, who became Rome's ruling class (one of two groups of Roman citizens) *(page 152)*

plebeian a member of the second and larger group of Roman citizens, who were less wealthy landowners, craftspeople, merchants, and small farmers *(page 152)*

consul an officer of the Roman Republic who ran the government and led the Roman army into battle *(page 152)*

praetor an officer of the Roman Republic who was in charge of civil law *(page 152)*

DRAWING FROM EXPERIENCE

What are the three branches of the United States government? What are the two parts of the legislative branch? Who selects the members of the legislative branch?

This section focuses on the development of the Roman Republic, including its government.

ORGANIZING YOUR THOUGHTS

Use the diagram below to help you take notes. Early Rome was divided into two groups of citizens, the patricians and the plebeians. List which offices or governing bodies each group could serve in. Include the following: consuls, praetors, tribunes, Senate, council of the plebs, centuriate assembly.

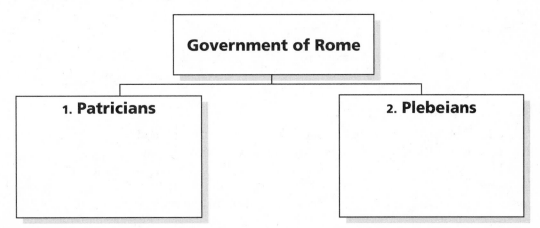

Government of Rome

1. Patricians

2. Plebeians

Reading Essentials and Study Guide

READ TO LEARN

• The Land and Peoples of Italy *(page 149)*

Italy is a peninsula that is about 750 miles long and about 120 miles wide. It is divided down the middle by a mountain range, the Apennines. These mountains are not as rugged as the mountains of Greece, however. They did not isolate communities from each other like the Greek mountains did. Italy also had more land for farming than Greece, so it could support a large population.

Rome was located on the Tiber River, about 18 miles inland. It had a way to the sea, but it was far enough inland to be safe from pirates. It was built on seven hills, so it could be easily defended. It also had a good central location in Italy. It was located at a place on the Tiber River where the river could be easily crossed. So it became a natural crossing point for people traveling from north to south.

Indo-European peoples moved into Italy during the period from about 1500 to 1000 B.C. Little is known about these peoples. We do know that one group lived in the region of Latium and spoke Latin. They were herders and farmers. About 800 B.C., other people began to move into Italy. The two most important groups were the Greeks and the Etruscans. Many Greeks came to Italy during the age of Greek colonization (750–550 B.C.). They also settled in Sicily, an island south of Italy. The Greeks had a big influence on Rome. The Romans imitated their sculpture, architecture, literature, and alphabet. The Romans also learned how to grow olives and grapes from the Greeks.

The Etruscans also influenced the Romans. The Etruscans lived north of Rome in Etruria. After 650 B.C., they controlled Rome and most of Latium. They changed Rome from a village to a city. The Romans adopted the Etruscans' clothing—the toga and short cloak. The organization of the Roman army was also borrowed from the Etruscans.

3. In what ways did the Greeks and Etruscans influence the Romans?

• The Roman Republic *(page 150)*

In 509 B.C., the Romans overthrew the last Etruscan king and formed a republic. A **republic** is a form of government in which the leader is not a monarch and certain citizens have the right to vote. For the next two hundred years, Rome was almost continually at war. By 340 B.C., Rome had crushed the Latin states in Latium. During the next 50 years, the Romans were at war with people from the Apennines. Rome was again victorious. Soon, the Romans were at war with the Greek cities in southern Italy. By 267 B.C., they had defeated the Greeks. Over the next three years, they also defeated the Etruscan states to the north. They now had control of virtually all of Italy.

To rule Italy, the Romans formed the Roman Confederation. Rome allowed some people, especially the Latins, to become Roman citizens. Most of the other communities were made allies. They were free to run their own affairs, but they had to provide soldiers for the Roman army. The Romans made it clear that loyal allies could become Roman citizens. This gave the conquered peoples a stake in Rome's success.

Why was Rome so successful? The Romans believed in duty, courage, and discipline. They were also good diplomats. They gained support by giving other people Roman citizenship and allowing them to run their own affairs. They also excelled in military matters. If they lost an army or a fleet, they did not quit. They built new armies and new fleets. As they conquered new areas, they built fortified towns and connected the towns by roads. This allowed them to move their troops quickly around the country. Finally, the Romans were practical in politics. They did not try to build an ideal government. They designed their government in response to problems, as the problems arose.

4. In what way were the Romans good diplomats?

____

____

____

____

• The Roman State *(page 152)*

Early Rome was divided into two groups or orders—the patricians and the plebeians. The **patricians** were wealthy landowners, who became Rome's ruling class. The **plebeians** were less wealthy landowners, craftspeople, merchants, and small farmers. They were also the larger group. Men in both groups were citizens and could vote, but only the patricians could be elected to government offices. Consuls and praetors headed the executive branch of the Roman government. The consuls and praetors were patricians. There were two consuls, who were elected every year. They ran the government and led the Roman army into battle. The praetors were in charge of civil law. At first, there was only one praetor, who only judged cases involving Roman citizens. Later, another praetor was added to judge cases when one or both people were noncitizens. There were also other officials with specific duties, such as supervising the treasury.

Reading Essentials and Study Guide

Chapter 5, Section 1 *(continued)*

The legislative branch included the Senate and the centuriate assembly. The Roman Senate was a group of about three hundred patricians who served for life. At first, they were only advisors to the government officials. By the third century B.C., however, their advice had the force of law. The centuriate assembly elected the chief officials, such as the consuls and praetors, and passed laws. It was made up of patricians, and the wealthiest citizens always had a majority.

There were often conflicts between the patricians and the plebeians. The plebeians resented that they were not treated equally. They could not hold government offices, and their children could not marry the children of the patricians. The conflicts between the patricians and the plebeians eventually led to the creation of an assembly for plebeians only. This assembly was called the council of the plebs and was created in 471 B.C. It elected officials, known as the tribunes, to protect the plebeians. In the fourth century B.C., plebeians were permitted to become consuls. Finally, in 287 B.C., the council of the plebs gained the right to pass laws for all Romans. All male citizens were now supposedly equal under the law. In reality, a few wealthy patrician and plebeian families dominated the political offices.

Rome's first code of laws was the Twelve Tables. It was adopted in 450 B.C. From the Twelve Tables, the Romans developed a more sophisticated system of laws. This system only applied to Roman citizens, however. As legal questions arose that involved both Romans and non-Romans, special rules were often needed. These rules formed the basis for a new group of laws, known as the Law of Nations. These laws established standards of justice that applied to all people. A person was considered innocent until proven guilty. People who were accused of crimes were allowed to defend themselves before a judge. The judge was expected to weigh the evidence carefully before making a decision. These principles are the basis of our legal system today.

5. Why did the plebeians resent the patricians?

____

____

____

____

• Rome Conquers the Mediterranean *(page 153)*

Even after they conquered Italy, the Romans continued to be at war. They had a series of wars with the state of Carthage. Carthage was located on the coast of North Africa. It was founded around 800 B.C. by the Phoenicians. It created a huge trading empire in the Mediterranean. Carthaginians settled in Sicily, an island close to Italy. The Romans were afraid of the Carthaginians.

They sent an army to Sicily in 264 B.C. The Carthaginians saw this as an act of war, because they considered Sicily part of their empire. This war is called the First Punic War. (The Latin word for Phoenician is *punicus*.) The Romans created a navy and defeated the Carthaginian navy off the coast of Sicily. The First Punic War came to an end in 241 B.C. Carthage gave up its rights to Sicily and paid a fine to the Romans. Sicily became the first Roman province.

Carthage added new lands in Spain to make up for the loss of Sicily. The Romans encouraged one of the Spanish leaders to revolt against Carthage. Hannibal, the greatest of the Carthaginian generals, struck back. This began the Second Punic War, which lasted from 218 to 201 B.C. Hannibal decided to invade Italy. He entered Spain, moved east, and crossed the Alps. He had an army of thirty to forty thousand men and six thousand horses and elephants. In 216 B.C., the Romans fought Hannibal's army at Cannae. The Romans lost an army of almost forty thousand men, but they refused to surrender. Hannibal conquered parts of Italy but was not able to attack the major cities, like Rome. The Romans gradually regained some of Italy and sent troops to Spain. By 206 B.C., they had pushed the Carthaginians out of Spain. Then Rome decided to invade Carthage. This forced the Carthaginians to bring Hannibal back from Italy. At the battle of Zama in 202 B.C., the Romans defeated Hannibals's army.

Fifty years later, the Romans fought their third and final war with Carthage. In 146 B.C., Carthage was destroyed, and the people of Carthage became slaves. Carthage became a Roman province called Africa. Rome also fought the Hellenistic states in the eastern Mediterranean. The Fourth Macedonian War ended in 148 B.C., and Macedonia became a Roman province. Two years later, Greece was placed under the control of the Roman governor of Macedonia. In 133 B.C., Pergamum became Rome's first province in Asia. Rome now controlled all of the Mediterranean.

6. What started the First Punic War?

____

____

____

____

____

Name ______________________ Date ______________ Class ______________

Reading Essentials and Study Guide

Chapter 5, Section 2

For use with textbook pages 156–162

FROM REPUBLIC TO EMPIRE

KEY TERMS

triumvirate a government by three people with equal power *(page 157)*

dictator an absolute ruler *(page 158)*

imperator commander in chief of the Roman army, a title given to Augustus by the Senate *(page 159)*

DRAWING FROM EXPERIENCE

Do you think there is any reason that people in the United States should be hungry? Should the government provide free food for anyone who needs it? Why?

In the last section, you read about the development of ancient Rome. This section focuses on the end of the Roman Republic and the beginning of the Roman Empire. Many of the Roman emperors helped the poor by giving them grain.

ORGANIZING YOUR THOUGHTS

Use the diagram below to help you take notes. List the following emperors in the order that they ruled Rome: Trajan, Tiberius, Hadrian, Marcus Aurelius, Nerva, Caligula, Antoninus Pius, Claudius, Augustus, Nero. Circle the names of the "five good emperors."

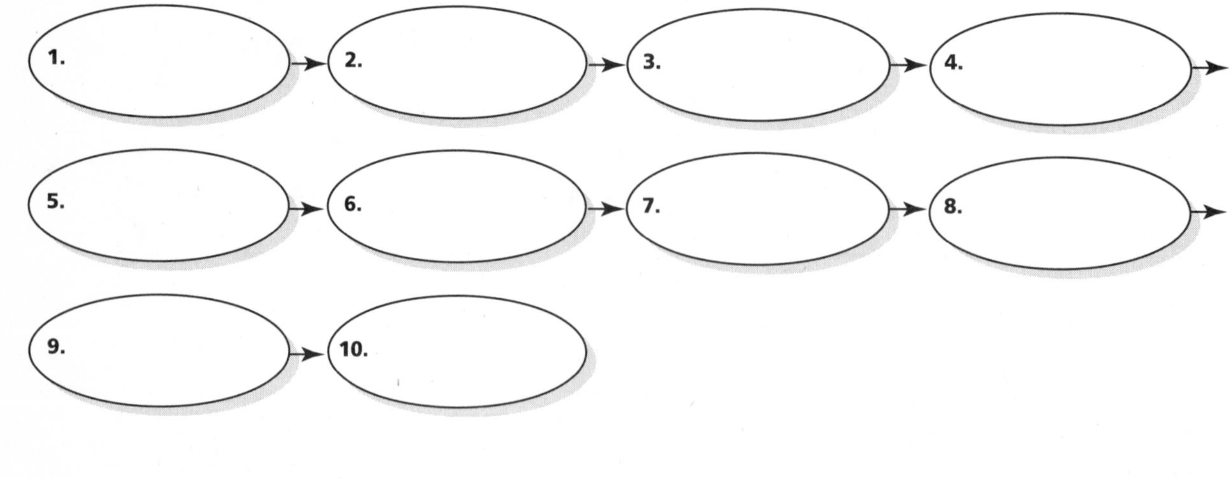

Name ______________________ Date ______________________ Class ______________________

Reading Essentials and Study Guide

Chapter 5, Section 2 *(continued)*

READ TO LEARN

• Growing Inequality and Unrest *(page 156)*

In the second century B.C., the Senate had become the real governing body in the Roman Republic. The Senate was controlled by a small group of wealthy aristocrats. These aristocrats were only a tiny minority of the Roman people. Most of the Roman people were small farmers. Over time, many of these small farmers lost their lands to the wealthy landowners. They were forced to move to the cities and formed a large class of landless poor. Two brothers, Tiberius and Gaius Gracchus, tried to solve this problem. They urged the council of the plebs to pass laws that would take back land from the large landowners and give it to the landless poor. Many senators were furious, because they were large landowners themselves. A group of senators killed the Gracchus brothers.

11. How did the Gracchus brothers try to help the poor?

• A New Role for the Army *(page 157)*

At the beginning of the first century B.C., a Roman general named Marius began to recruit his armies from the landless poor. To recruit them, he promised them land. These soldiers swore an oath of loyalty to the general himself. As a result, Marius created a new type of army that was not under government control. Generals were now forced to become involved in politics to get laws passed to provide land for their soldiers. Generals began to have a great deal of power in Rome.

The Senate gave the command of the war in Asia Minor to another general, Lucius Cornelius Sulla. The council of the plebs tried to transfer the command to Marius. A civil war broke out. Sulla won and seized Rome in 82 B.C. He conducted a reign of terror to wipe out all opposition. Then he restored power to the Senate and eliminated most of the power of the other assemblies. Future leaders would follow his example and continue to use armies to seize power.

12. How did Marius and Sulla change the role of the army in ancient Rome?

Reading Essentials and Study Guide

Chapter 5, Section 2 *(continued)*

• The Collapse of the Republic *(page 157)*

For the next fifty years (82–31 B.C.), Rome was torn by civil wars. Various men competed for power. Three men—Crassus, Pompey, and Julius Caesar—were victorious. Crassus was the richest man in Rome. Pompey and Caesar were military heroes. In 60 B.C., they formed the First Triumvirate. A **triumvirate** is a government by three people with equal power. Crassus received a command in Spain, Crassus was given a command in Syria, and Caesar received a command in Gaul (what is now France). Crassus was killed in battle in 53 B.C. This left only two leaders. Some of the senators decided that they wanted Pompey to be the only leader. They voted for Caesar to lay down his command. Caesar refused. He kept his army and marched on Rome. This led to a civil war between Caesar's army and the army of Pompey and his allies. Caesar's army defeated Pompey's army, and Caesar took complete control of the Roman government. He was officially made dictator in 47 B.C. A **dictator** is an absolute ruler. Caesar gave land to the poor and increased the number of senators to 900. This weakened the power of the Senate. In 44 B.C., a group of leading senators assassinated him.

After Caesar's death, there was a struggle for power. Three men—Octavian, Antony, and Lepidus—joined forces and formed the Second Triumvirate. Octavian was Caesar's grandnephew, Antony had been Caesar's assistant, and Lepidus had been the commander of Caesar's cavalry. Within a few years, only two of the men, Octavian and Antony, were in power. They divided the Roman world between them. Octavian took the west, and Antony took the east. Octavian and Antony soon came into conflict. Antony allied himself with the Egyptian queen Cleopatra VII. At the Battle of Actium in Greece in
31 B.C., Octavian's forces defeated the army and navy of Antony and Cleopatra. Antony and Cleopatra both committed suicide a year later.

13. What leaders formed the First and Second Triumvirates?

____

____

____

____

____

• The Age of Augustus *(page 159)*

Octavian was now the only leader of Rome. The civil wars had ended. So had the republic. In 27 B.C., Octavian proclaimed the "restoration of the Republic," but he knew that the republic could not be completely restored.

Although he gave some power to the Senate, Octavian became the first Roman emperor. The Senate gave him the title of Augustus, which means "the revered one." The period from 31 B.C. to A.D. 14 is known as the Age of Augustus.

Augustus was popular, but most of his power came from his control of the army. The Senate gave Augustus the title **imperator,** or commander in chief. Augustus had an army of 28 legions, or about 150,000 men. Only Roman citizens could be legionnaires (members of a legion). Augustus also set up a praetorian guard of 9,000 men, who guarded the emperor. Augustus conquered many new areas, but he was not able to conquer Germany. The defeats in Germany taught Augustus that Rome's power was not unlimited.

14. What two titles did the Senate give Octavian? What do the titles mean?

____

____

____

____

• The Early Empire *(page 159)*

Beginning in A.D. 14, a series of new emperors ruled Rome. This period is called the Early Empire. It ended in A.D. 180. The emperor could select his successor from his own family. The first four emperors after Augustus came from his family. They were Tiberius, Caligula, Claudius, and Nero. These emperors took away more and more of the Senate's powers. The emperors became more powerful and more corrupt. Nero, for example, had people killed if he wanted them out of the way. He even killed his own mother. The Roman legions finally revolted, and Nero committed suicide.

At the beginning of the second century, there was a series of five emperors who are called the "good emperors." They were Nerva, Trajan, Hadrian, Antoninus Pius, and Marcus Aurelius. They created a period of peace and prosperity known as the *Pax Romana* (the "Roman Peace"). This period lasted for almost a hundred years. Officials appointed by the emperor took over the running of the government. The good emperors created new programs to help the poor. They also built aqueducts, bridges, roads, and harbor facilities in Rome and throughout the provinces.

During the Early Empire, Rome expanded into new areas. Trajan extended the empire into Dacia, Mesopotamia, and the Sinai Peninsula. His successors realized that the empire was getting too large to be defended easily. Hadrian withdrew Roman forces from Mesopotamia. He strengthened the fortifications along a line connecting the Rhine and Danube Rivers. He also built a wall about 80 miles long across northern Britain to keep out the Scots. This is called Hadrian's Wall.

Name ______________________ Date ______________________ Class ______________________

Reading Essentials and Study Guide

Chapter 5, Section 2 *(continued)*

In the second century, the Roman Empire was at its height. It was one of the greatest states that the world had ever seen. It covered about three and a half million square miles and had a population of over fifty million. In A.D. 212, the emperor Caracalla gave Roman citizenship to every free person in the empire. Latin was the language of the western part of the empire. Greek was used in the east. Roman culture spread to all parts of the empire and was mixed with Greek culture. The result has been called Greco-Roman civilization.

Trade flourished during the Early Empire. Silk was imported from China. Large quantities of grain were imported from Egypt. Farming was still the main occupation of most people. Large estates, called *latifundia,* dominated farming in southern and central Italy. A huge gap separated the rich and poor. The upper classes lived in luxury. Small farmers often became dependent on the wealthy aristocrats. In the cities, poor citizens worked in shops and markets. Thousands of people depended on the emperor's handouts of grain to survive.

15. What was the *Pax Romana*?

____

____

____

____

____

____

____

Name ______________________ Date ______________________ Class ______________________

Reading Essentials and Study Guide

Chapter 5, Section 3

For use with textbook pages 163–168

CULTURE AND SOCIETY IN THE ROMAN WORLD

KEY TERMS

paterfamilias the dominant male in a Roman family *(page 165)*

insulae apartment blocks in Rome where the poor lived *(page 167)*

DRAWING FROM EXPERIENCE

What kinds of recreational facilities are available to the public in or near your community? What type of facility is your favorite? Why?

In the last section, you learned about the beginnings of the Roman Empire. In this section, you will learn about the cultural accomplishments of ancient Rome. You will also learn about daily life during this time, including the kinds of recreation and entertainment that were available to the people.

ORGANIZING YOUR THOUGHTS

Use the web organizer below to help you take notes. The Romans had major accomplishments in architecture and engineering. List three of those accomplishments.

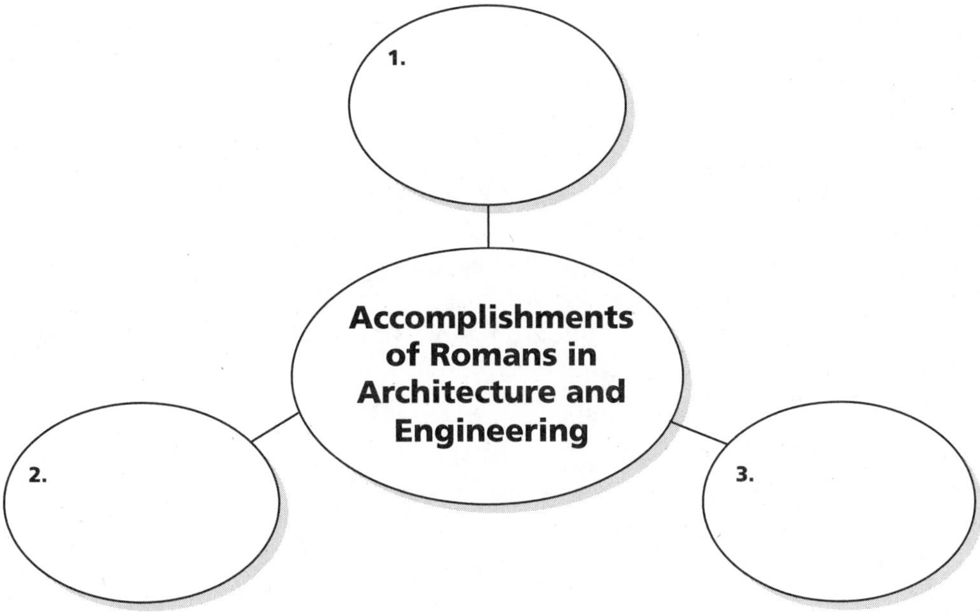

Reading Essentials and Study Guide

Chapter 5, Section 3 *(continued)*

READ TO LEARN

• Roman Art and Architecture *(page 163)*

During the third and second centuries B.C., Greek art influenced the Romans. They put Greek statues in their homes and in public buildings. Roman sculptors imitated the Greeks, but they also made some changes. They produced realistic statues that even showed unpleasant physical details, something the Greeks would never do.

The Romans excelled in architecture and engineering. They used Greek styles, such as colonnades and rectangular buildings. However, they also used forms based on curved lines, such as arches, vaults, and domes. They were also the first people to use concrete on a large scale. By using concrete and the new forms, they were able to make huge buildings undreamed of by the Greeks. They also built roads, bridges, and aqueducts. They built almost a dozen aqueducts in Rome alone. The aqueducts kept the Romans supplied with water. They built over 50,000 miles of roads to connect the different parts of the empire.

4. How was Roman sculpture different from Greek sculpture?

• Roman Literature *(page 164)*

The Age of Augustus has been called the golden age of Latin literature. The greatest poet of the Augustan Age was Virgil. He wrote his greatest work, the *Aeneid,* in honor of Augustus. Another important Augustan poet was Horace. In his *Satires,* he made fun of human weaknesses. The most famous prose writer of the golden age was Livy. He was an historian whose masterpiece was the *History of Rome.* He was good storyteller, but his stories were not always accurate. Even so, his work became the standard history of Rome for a long time.

5. What was the golden age of Latin literature?

Name ______________________________ Date ______________________ Class ______________________

• The Roman Family *(page 165)*

The family was the basic unit in Roman society. The head of the Roman family was the **paterfamilias,** the dominant male. Each household also included the wife, sons with their wives, unmarried daughters, and slaves. Unlike the Greeks, Romans raised their children at home. All upper-class children were expected to learn to read. This included the girls. Fathers were in charge of the children's education. Greek slaves were often used as teachers, because upper-class Romans had to learn Greek as well as Latin. Roman boys learned reading and writing, moral principles, law, and physical training to prepare them to be soldiers. Girls were taught by private tutors or were sent to primary schools. They did not attend secondary schools. They were usually married at that age. The minimum age for girls to marry was 12, but 14 was a more common age. For men, the minimum age was 14, but most men married later. Fathers arranged the marriages of their daughters. Marriages were meant to be for life, but divorce was introduced in the third century B.C.

By the second century A.D., changes were occurring in the Roman family. The paterfamilias no longer had absolute authority over his children and wife. Women were no longer required to have guardians. They had the right to own, inherit, and sell property. Women were not segregated from men in the home. They were viewed as enjoyable company and were at the center of household social life. Outside their homes, women could attend races, the theater, and events in the amphitheater. Women could not participate in politics, but many important women influenced politics through their husbands.

6. How did the role of Roman women change in the second century A.D.?

____

____

____

____

____

• Slavery *(page 166)*

The Romans had many slaves, especially after their victories in the Mediterranean. Many foreign people were captured in war and brought to Italy as slaves. Greek slaves were used as tutors, musicians, doctors, and artists. Slaves of all nationalities were used as household workers, such as cooks and gardeners. Slaves were also used to build roads and public buildings. They also farmed the estates of the wealthy. Conditions for the slaves were often pitiful. Some slaves revolted against their owners and even murdered them. In 73 B.C. the gladiator Spartacus led the most famous slave revolt. This revolt involved seventy thousand slaves. Spartacus defeated several Roman armies before he was captured and killed in 71 B.C. Six thousand followers of Spartacus were crucified (put to death by nailing to a cross).

7. What kinds of work did slaves do in ancient Rome?

• Daily Life in the City of Rome *(page 167)*

Rome was the capital city of the Roman Empire. It had the largest population of any city in the empire—close to one million by the time of Augustus. The city was overcrowded and noisy. Augustus organized a police force in Rome, but people were still assaulted or robbed. A huge gap separated the rich and the poor. The rich had comfortable villas. The poor lived in apartment blocks called ***insulae.*** These apartment buildings were poorly built and often collapsed. Fire was also a constant problem in the *insulae.* High rents forced entire families to live in one room. There was no plumbing or central heating. The homes were so uncomfortable that many poor Romans spent most of their time outdoors in the streets. Beginning with Augustus, emperors provided food for the city poor. About two thousand people received free grain. Even with the free grain, they barely survived.

Certain parts of Rome were magnificent, however. There were beautiful temples, baths, theaters, government buildings, and amphitheaters. Entertainment was provided on a grand scale. During the religious festivals, there were three major types of entertainment. Chariot races were held at the Circus Maximus. Dramatic performances were held in theaters. The most famous form of entertainment, however, was the gladiatorial shows.

8. What was life like for the poor of Rome?

Name ______________________ Date ______________________ Class ______________________

Reading Essentials and Study Guide

Chapter 5, Section 4

For use with textbook pages 169–174

THE DEVELOPMENT OF CHRISTIANITY

KEY TERMS

procurator a Roman official who directed the affairs of a province *(page 170)*

New Testament the second part of the Christian Bible *(page 172)*

clergy church leaders *(page 173)*

laity regular church members *(page 173)*

DRAWING FROM EXPERIENCE

What does the Golden Rule "Do to others what you would have them do to you" mean? Do you think most people follow this rule? Why or why not?

In the last section, you learned about culture and society in ancient Rome. This section focuses on the beginnings of Christianity.

ORGANIZING YOUR THOUGHTS

Use the chart below to help you take notes. Christianity developed from a persecuted religion to the state religion of Rome. Indicate how Christians were treated under each of the following Roman emperors.

Emperor	Treatment of Christians
Nero	**1.**
Diocletian	**2.**
Constantine	**3.**
Theodosius the Great	**4.**

READ TO LEARN

• Background: Roman Religion *(page 169)*

The official state religion of Rome focused on the worship of several gods and goddesses, including Jupiter, Juno, Minerva, and Mars. During the late Roman Republic, the state religion had declined. Augustus brought back traditional festivals and ceremonies to revive the state religion. The Romans believed that proper rituals by state priests brought peace and prosperity. They believed that their success in creating an empire meant that they had earned the favor of the gods. The Romans were also tolerant of other religions. They allowed the people they conquered to worship their own gods and goddesses. They even adopted many of the gods of the people they conquered. Starting with Augustus, the emperors were officially made gods by the Roman Senate. Religions from the east also began to have an impact on the Roman world.

5. What was the focus of the state religion of Rome?

• The Jewish Background *(page 170)*

By A.D. 6, the old Jewish kingdom of Judah was a Roman province. It was called Judaea and was placed under the direction of a Roman official called a *procurator*. The Jewish people were divided into different political groups. The Sadducees wanted to cooperate with the Romans. The Essenes were waiting for a Messiah (anointed one) who would save Israel from oppression and bring the kingdom of God to Earth. The Zealots wanted to overthrow the Roman rule. A Jewish revolt began in 66 A.D., but the Romans crushed it four years later. The Jewish temple in Jerusalem was destroyed, and the Romans continued to control Judaea.

6. What were three of the political groups in Judaea, and what were their goals?

Name ______________________ Date ______________________ Class ______________________

Reading Essentials and Study Guide

• The Rise of Christianity *(page 170)*

During this time of conflict in Judaea, Jesus of Nazareth began his public preaching. He taught that God's primary command was to love God and one another. He said, "Love the Lord your God with all your heart and with all your soul and with all your mind and with all your strength. This is the first commandment. The second is this: Love your neighbor as yourself." He taught that strict following of the Jewish law was not what was important. He said, "So in everything, do to others what you would have them do to you, for this sums up the Law and the Prophets." The teachings of Jesus about humility, charity, and love toward others would form the basis of the value system of medieval Western civilization.

The Judaean authorities thought Jesus was a revolutionary who might lead the Jews into another revolt against Rome. Jesus was turned over to the Roman authorities. The procurator Pontius Pilate had him crucified. This did not stop his followers. They believed that he had overcome death and come back to life. They believed that he was the Messiah, the long expected Savior of Israel.

Two prominent followers of Jesus were Simon Peter and Paul of Tarsus. Simon Peter was a Jewish fisherman. Paul of Tarsus was a highly educated Jewish Roman citizen. They and the other disciples (followers) taught that Jesus was the Savior, the Son of God, who had come to Earth to save all humans. They taught that Jesus' death made up for the sins of all humans. By accepting Jesus as Christ and Savior, people could be saved from the penalty of sin. (Christ comes from the Greek word *Christos,* which means "anointed one.") Paul followed the command of Jesus to preach the gospel to both Jews and Gentiles (non-Jews). He founded Christian communities throughout Asia Minor and along the shores of the Aegean Sea.

When people heard that Jesus had come back to life, Christianity spread quickly. Within 60 days, there were approximately ten thousand converts in the city of Jerusalem alone. The teachings of early Christianity were passed on orally at first. Between A.D. 40 and 100, the teachings of Jesus were written down as the Gospels—the "good news" about Jesus. Paul and other followers of Jesus also wrote letters, or epistles, outlining Christian beliefs for the communities they founded. These writings became the **New Testament,** the second part of the Christian Bible.

By 100, Christian churches had been established in most of the major cities of the eastern empire. Churches had also been founded in some places in the western part of the empire. At first, the Romans paid little attention to the Christians. They saw the Christians as just another sect of Judaism. As time passed, however, they came to view Christians as harmful. Christians refused to worship the state gods and the emperors because they believed that there was only one God. The Romans saw this as an act of treason, punishable by death. The Roman government began persecuting Christians during the reign of Nero. (Persecution is harassment that causes suffering.) Many Christians were put to death, often in cruel ways.

7. Why did the Roman government persecute the Christians?

• The Triumph of Christianity *(page 172)*

The persecution of Christians did nothing to stop the growth of Christianity. In fact, it did the opposite. It strengthened Christianity by forcing it to become more organized. Church leaders, called bishops, began to assume more control over Christian communities. A new structure was created in which the **clergy** (the church leaders) had distinct functions separate from the **laity** (the regular church members). Fear of persecution also meant that only the most committed individuals would choose to become Christians.

The persecution of the Christians began to decline in the second century. In the third century, some emperors began new persecutions, but they failed. The last great persecution was by Diocletian at the beginning of the fourth century. Even he had to admit that Christianity was too strong to be blotted out by force. In the fourth century, Christianity prospered when Constantine became the first Christian emperor. In 313, he issued the Edict of Milan, which proclaimed official tolerance of Christianity. Later, under Theodosius the Great, the Romans adopted Christianity as their official religion.

8. How did persecution strengthen Christianity?

Name ______________________ Date ______________________ Class ______________________

Reading Essentials and Study Guide

Chapter 5, Section 5

For use with textbook pages 175–178

DECLINE AND FALL

KEY TERMS

plague an epidemic disease *(page 176)*

inflation a rapid increase in prices *(page 177)*

DRAWING FROM EXPERIENCE

What economic problems has the United States faced during your lifetime? Have there been any recessions? Have there been any periods of inflation?

In the last section, you learned about the development of Christianity during the Roman Empire. In this section, you will learn about the decline and fall of the Roman Empire. Economic problems contributed to this decline.

ORGANIZING YOUR THOUGHTS

Use the diagram below to help you take notes. List three factors that led to the decline of the Roman Empire.

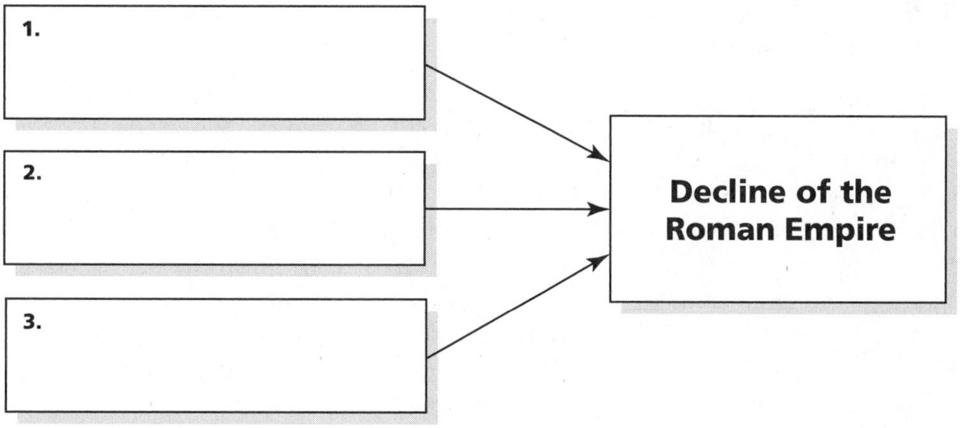

READ TO LEARN

• The Decline *(page 175)*

Marcus Aurelius, the last of the five good emperors, died in A.D. 180. A series of civil wars followed. Septimius Severus and his sons (the Severan rulers) formed a military government and restored order. After the Severan rulers, there was a period of disorder. From 235 to 284, there were 22 emperors. Twenty of them died violently. At the same time, the empire was being invaded. The Sassanid Persians invaded Roman territory in the east. Germanic tribes invaded the Balkans, Gaul, and Spain.

The invasions, civil wars, and plagues came close to causing an economic collapse of the Roman Empire in the third century. There was a decline in trade and industry. **Plagues** (epidemic diseases) created a labor shortage that affected both the military and the economy. By the mid-third century, Rome had to hire Germans to fight in the Roman army. Farm production declined, because invaders and the army destroyed fields.

Two emperors, Diocletian and Constantine, made reforms that temporarily restored the Roman Empire. The empire was changed into a new state, the Late Roman Empire. The new state had a new governmental structure, a rigid economic system, and a new state religion, Christianity. Diocletian ruled from 284 to 305. He believed that the empire was too large for a single ruler. So he divided it into four parts, each with its own ruler. Because of his military power, Diocletian still had the ultimate authority. Constantine ruled from 306 to 337. He continued and even expanded Diocletian's policies.

Both rulers increased the bureaucracy of the Roman Empire. A hierarchy of officials had control at various levels of government. The army was increased to five hundred thousand men, including German troops. More money was needed to pay for the army and the bureaucracy. The population was not growing, so the tax base could not be increased. Diocletian and Constantine created new economic policies to deal with these problems. To fight inflation, Diocletian set wage and price controls for the entire empire. (**Inflation** is a rapid increase in prices.) These controls failed to work. To ensure the tax base and keep the empire going, the emperors also forced people to remain in their jobs. Certain jobs, such as bakers and shippers, became hereditary. Many farmers lost their lands and became dependent on large landowners.

Constantine's biggest project was the construction of a new capital city in the east. It was built on the site of the Greek city of Byzantium. The city was eventually named Constantinople. It had an excellent strategic location. Constantine built a forum, large palaces, and a huge amphitheater in the new city. Constantinople would become the center of the Eastern Roman Empire and one of the great cities of the world.

4. What were some of the economic problems in the Roman Empire in the third century?

• The Fall *(page 177)*

The restored empire of Diocletian and Constantine survived for more than a century. After Constantine, the empire was divided into western and eastern parts. The capital of the Western Roman Empire was Rome. The capital of the Eastern Roman Empire was Constantinople. The Western Roman Empire had problems with invaders. The Visigoths, a Germanic people, crossed the Danube and settled in Roman territory. In 410, they sacked Rome. Another group, the Vandals, crossed into Italy from Northern Africa. In 455, they too sacked Rome. In 476, the Germanic head of the army overthrew the western emperor, Romulus Augustulus. This is usually considered the date of the fall of the Western Roman Empire. A series of German kingdoms replaced the Western Roman Empire. The Eastern Roman Empire continued to thrive, however. It was also called the Byzantine Empire.

5. What event is normally used to mark the fall of the Western Roman Empire?

Name ______________________ Date ______________ Class ______________

Reading Essentials and Study Guide

Chapter 6, Section 1

For use with textbook pages 191–194

THE RISE OF ISLAM

KEY TERMS

sheikh the ruler of an Arab tribe *(page 191)*

Quran the holy scriptures of Islam *(page 193)*

Islam ("peace through submission to the will of Allah") the religion founded by Muhammad *(page 193)*

Hijrah the journey of Muhammad and his followers to Madinah *(page 193)*

hajj a pilgrimage to Makkah, one of the Five Pillars of Islam *(page 193)*

shari'ah a set of laws followed by Muslims *(page 194)*

DRAWING FROM EXPERIENCE

Does your community have many churches? What religions do these churches represent? How do you think people decide what religion to follow?

This section focuses on the development and beliefs of Islam.

ORGANIZING YOUR THOUGHTS

Use the time line below to help you take notes. Identify five important events in the development of Islam.

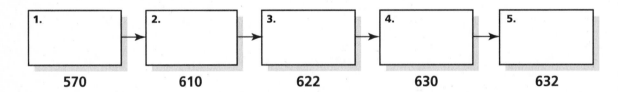

1.	→	2.	→	3.	→	4.	→	5.
570		610		622		630		632

Name ____________________ Date ____________________ Class ____________________

Reading Essentials and Study Guide

Chapter 6, Section 1 *(continued)*

READ TO LEARN

• The Arabs *(page 191)*

The Arabian Peninsula is a desert land. The early Arabs were nomads who lived in the Arabian Peninsula. They moved constantly to find water and food for their animals. They were organized into tribes to help one another. The ruler of each tribe was called a **sheikh.** A council of elders chose the sheikh from one of the leading families. At first, the Arabs made their living by shepherding or by raiding the trading caravans that passed through the desert. Eventually, they began to take part in the caravan trade themselves. They became some of the major traders in the area. A trade route developed that went through Makkah (Mecca) to present-day Yemen and then by ship across the Indian Ocean. Towns along this route prospered from the trade. But tensions developed between the wealthy merchants in the towns and the Arabs in the deserts, called Bedouins.

Most early Arabs were polytheistic—they believed in many gods. The Arabs trace their ancestors to Abraham and his son Ishmael, who were believed to have built at **Makkah** (Mecca) the Kaaba (KAH•buh), a house of worship whose cornerstone was a sacred stone, called the Black Stone. The Arabs recognized a supreme god named **Allah** (*Allah* is Arabic for "God"), but they also believed in other tribal gods. They revered the Kaaba for its association with Abraham.

The Arabian Peninsula took on a new importance when political disorder in Mesopotamia and Egypt made the usual trade routes in Southwest Asia too dangerous to travel. A safer trade route that went through Makkah to present-day Yemen and then by ship across the Indian Ocean became more popular.

Communities along this route, such as Makkah, prospered from the increased caravan trade. Tensions arose, however, as increasingly wealthy merchants showed less and less concern for the welfare of their poorer clanspeople and slaves.

6. How did the early Arabs make their living?

• The Life of Muhammad *(page 192)*

Muhammad was born in Makkah in 570 A.D. He grew up to become a caravan manager. Over time, he became concerned about the gap between the Makkans and the rich merchants in the city. He began to go the nearby hills to meditate. In 610, during one of these times of meditation, he had a vision. He heard a voice that he believed was inspired by Allah. The voice told him to recite what he was hearing. Muhammad believed that Allah had already revealed himself through Moses and Jesus. But he believed that the final revelations of Allah were now being given to him. Muhammad's revelations were eventually written down in the **Quran,** the holy scriptures of **Islam.** (The word *Islam* means "peace through submission to the will of Allah.") Those who practice Islam are called Muslims. Muslims believe that there is only one God, Allah, and that Muhammad is his prophet.

Muhammad tried to convince the people of Makkah about the truth of his revelations. Most of the people of Makkah did not accept his message, so he and his followers moved to Yathrib. Yathrib was later renamed Madinah (Medina), which means "city of the prophet." The journey of Muhammad and his followers to Madinah is known as the ***Hijrah.*** The journey took place in 622. This year became year 1 in the official calendar of Islam. Muhammad began to gain supporters in Madinah. He also had supporters in the Bedouin tribes. Muslims did not see any difference between political and religious authority. Submission to the will of Allah meant submission to his prophet, Muhammad. Muhammad soon became both a religious and a political leader. He formed a military force to defend himself and his followers. Their success soon attracted more supporters. In 630, Muhammad returned to Makkah with a force of ten thousand men. The city surrendered, and most of the people converted to Islam. In 632, Muhammad died, just as Islam was beginning to spread throughout the Arabian Peninsula.

7. What event marks the beginning of the Islamic calendar?

____

____

____

____

____

• The Teachings of Muhammad *(page 193)*

Like Christianity and Judaism, Islam is monotheistic. Muslims believe that Allah is the only God, who created the universe and everything in it. Islam offers the hope of an afterlife. Those who want life after death must submit to the will of Allah. Muslims do not believe that Muhammad was divine. He is considered a prophet, but he was also a man like other men. Muslims believe that Allah sent his final revelation through Muhammad because people rejected his earlier prophets.

Islam stresses the need to obey the will of Allah. This means following the Five Pillars of Islam. These are: (1) belief in Allah and in Muhammad as his prophet; (2) standard prayer fives times a day and public prayer on Fridays at midday; (3) giving alms, such as food and money, to the poor; (4) observance of the holy month of Ramadan, including fasting from dawn to sunset; (5) making a pilgrimage to Makkah at least once in a lifetime. This pilgrimage is called the **hajj.**

Islam is not just a set of beliefs but also a way of life. After Muhammad's death, Muslim scholars drew up a set of laws to regulate daily life. These laws are called the ***shari'ah.*** Much of the *shari'ah* is taken from the Quran. Muslims are expected to follow strict guidelines for behavior. In addition to the Five Pillars, Muslims are forbidden to gamble, eat pork, drink alcohol, or engage in dishonest behavior.

8. What is the *shari'ah?*

____

____

____

____

____

Name ______________________ Date ______________________ Class ______________________

Reading Essentials and Study Guide

Chapter 6, Section 2

For use with textbook pages 196–202

THE ARAB EMPIRE AND ITS SUCCESSORS

KEY TERMS

caliph a successor to Muhammad, or ruler of Islam *(page 197)*

jihad ("struggle in the way of God") the Arabic custom of raiding one's enemies *(page 197)*

Shiite Muslims who accept only the descendants of Ali as the true caliphs *(page 199)*

Sunni Muslims who accept only the descendants of the Umayyads as the true caliphs *(page 199)*

vizier a prime minister who advised the caliph *(page 200)*

sultan ("holder of power") the title of the Turkish leader who took command of the Arab Empire *(page 201)*

mosque a Muslim temple or house of worship *(page 202)*

DRAWING FROM EXPERIENCE

What recent world events have involved conflicts between religious groups or ethnic groups? Where have they happened? Why do you think these kinds of conflicts still happen today?

In the last section, you read about the rise of Islam. In this section, you will learn about the development of the Arab Empire.

ORGANIZING YOUR THOUGHTS

Use the time line below to help you take notes. Identify ten key events in Islamic history.

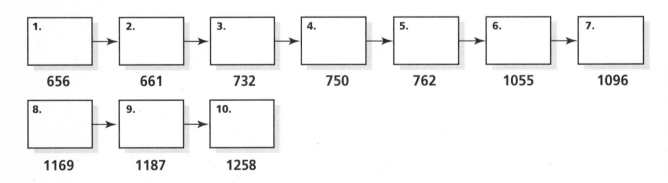

1.	2.	3.	4.	5.	6.	7.
656	661	732	750	762	1055	1096

8.	9.	10.
1169	1187	1258

Name ______________________ Date ______________________ Class ______________________

READ TO LEARN

• Creation of an Arab Empire *(page 196)*

The death of Muhammad left his followers with a problem. He had never named a successor. After his death, some of his followers chose Abu Bakr to be their leader. He was a wealthy merchant and Muhammad's father-in-law. He was named **caliph,** or successor to Muhammad. Under Abu Bakr, the Islamic movement began to grow. Abu Bakr used the Arabic custom of raiding one's enemies to expand the movement. The Quran called this activity "struggle in the way of God," or **jihad.** Muslim soldiers believed that they were assured of a place in Paradise if they died in battle. In 636, the Arab army defeated the Byzantine army. By 642, Syria, Egypt, and other areas of northern Africa had been added to the new Arab Empire. By 650, the Arabs had conquered the entire Persian Empire. Conquered people were not forced to convert to Islam. They were only required to be loyal to Muslim rule and to pay taxes.

After Abu Bakr died, it was not clear who should be his successor. The first two caliphs who ruled after his death were assassinated. In 656, Ali was chosen to be caliph. He was Muhammad's son-in-law. He too was assassinated, after ruling for five years.

11. Who was the first caliph, or successor to Muhammad?

• The Umayyads *(page 198)*

In 661, the general Mu'awiyah became caliph. He was also the governor of Syria and one of Ali's chief rivals. He only used force when absolutely necessary. He made the office of caliph, called the caliphate, hereditary. By doing this, he established the Umayyad dynasty. He also moved the capital of the Arab Empire from Madinah to Damascus, in Syria.

At the beginning of the eighth century, Arab armies conquered and converted the Berbers. The Berbers lived along the Mediterranean coast of northern Africa. Around 710, the Berbers and the Arabs invaded Spain. By 725, most of Spain had become a Muslim state. However, in 732, Arab forces were defeated at the Battle of Tours in Gaul. Arab expansion into Europe ended.

During the Umayyad dynasty, Muslims who were not Arabs, such as Persians and Byzantines, felt that they were treated unfairly. This sometimes led to revolt. Hussein, the second son of Ali, led one important revolt. This revolt was crushed, but the struggle split Islam into two groups. The Shiite Muslims accept only the descendants of Ali as the true caliphs. The Sunni Muslims accept only the descendants of the Umayyads as caliphs. This split in Islam continues today.

12. What is the difference between Shiite and Sunni Muslims?

____

____

____

____

• The Abbasid Dynasty *(page 199)*

Resentment against the Umayyads grew. In 750, Abu al-Abbas overthrew the Umayyad dynasty and set up the Abbasid dynasty. This dynasty lasted until 1258. In 762, the Abbasids built a new capital city at Baghdad, on the Tigris River. Baghdad had a good location. It was on the caravan route from the Mediterranean to central Asia. Under the Abbasids, all Muslims could hold both civil and military offices, regardless of their ethnic backgrounds. The best known of the caliphs during this time was Harun al-Rashid. His reign is called the golden age of the Abbasid caliphate. He was known for his charity. He and his son, al-Ma'mum, also supported artists and writers. This was a period of great prosperity. Baghdad became the center of a huge trade empire that included Asia, Africa, and Europe. This added to the riches of the Islamic world.

A bureaucracy helped the caliph rule the empire. A council headed by a prime minister, known as a **vizier,** advised the caliph. There was much fighting over who would be the next caliph. When Harun al-Rashid died, his two sons fought over who would succeed him. They almost destroyed the city of Baghdad. Eventually, rulers of the provinces of the Abbasid Empire began to break away and form their own dynasties. Spain established its own caliphate in 750. A new dynasty under the Fatimids was established in Egypt in 973.

13. What was the golden age of the Abbasid caliphate?

____

____

____

____

Name ______________________ Date ______________ Class ______________

Reading Essentials and Study Guide

Chapter 6, Section 2 *(continued)*

• The Seljuk Turks *(page 201)*

The Fatimid dynasty in Egypt created an army of soldiers from other countries to fight for them. One group in the army was the Seljuk Turks. They were nomads from central Asia. They converted to Islam and grew stronger as the Abbasids grew weaker. By the eleventh century, they had taken over the eastern provinces of the Abbasid Empire. In 1055, a Turkish leader captured Baghdad and took command of the empire. His title was **sultan,** or "holder of power." The Abbasid caliph was still the religious leader, but the Seljuk Turks now held the real military and political power. In 1071, the Byzantines attacked the Turks, but the Turks defeated them. The Turks then took over most of the Anatolian peninsula.

14. Who were the Seljuk Turks?

___

___

___

___

___

• The Crusades *(page 201)*

The Byzantine emperor Alexius I asked the Christian states of Europe for help against the Turks. Because the Christian states and the Islamic world feared each other, many Europeans agreed. A series of crusades began in 1096. At first, the crusaders were able to conquer areas and establish crusader states. In 1169, Saladin, a new Muslim ruler, took control of Egypt and made himself sultan. This ended the Fatimid dynasty. Saladin took control of Syria and attacked the crusader states in the area. In 1187, Saladin's army invaded Jerusalem and destroyed the Christian army there. The Crusades ended, but they led to centuries of mistrust between Muslims and Christians.

15. Why did many Europeans agree to help the Byzantine emperor?

___

___

___

___

___

• The Mongols *(page 202)*

New invaders, the Mongols, attacked the Arab Empire in the thirteenth century. The Mongols were people from the Gobi. They were destructive and cruel. Their goal was to create so much terror that people would not fight back. In 1258, the Mongols seized Persia and Mesopotamia. This brought an end to the Abbasid caliphate at Baghdad. The Mongols' leader, Hülegü, hated Islam. He decided to destroy the city of Baghdad. He burnt schools, libraries, palaces and **mosques** (Muslim houses of worship). The Mongols advanced as far as the Red Sea but were unable to conquer Egypt. With Baghdad destroyed, Cairo became the new center of Islamic civilization.

Over time, the Mongol rulers converted to Islam. They rebuilt many of the cities they had destroyed. By the fourteenth century, the Mongol Empire had begun to split into separate kingdoms. The old Islamic Empire had come to an end.

16. Why were the Mongols so destructive and cruel?

Name ______________________ Date ______________________ Class ______________________

Reading Essentials and Study Guide

Chapter 6, Section 3

For use with textbook pages 203–206

ISLAMIC CIVILIZATION

KEY TERMS

bazaar a covered market *(page 204)*

dowry in Islamic society, a gift of money or property given to a bride by her husband *(page 206)*

DRAWING FROM EXPERIENCE

Is there are a flea market or a farmers' market in or near your community? Do you ever shop there? What items do they sell?

The last two sections focused on the rise of Islam and the Arab Empire. This section focuses on Islamic civilization, including the development of a trade network and marketplaces.

ORGANIZING YOUR THOUGHTS

Use the chart below to help you take notes. An extensive trade network brought goods from many parts of the world to the Arab Empire. List the goods that were traded by the following areas.

Area	**Items Traded**
Africa south of the Sahara	**1.**
China	**2.**
Eastern Africa	**3.**
Southeast Asia and India	**4.**
Egypt	**5.**
Iraq	**6.**
Western India	**7.**

READ TO LEARN

• Prosperity in the Islamic World *(page 203)*

Overall, the period of the Arab Empire was prosperous. Trade flourished under the Abbasid dynasty. The development of banking and the use of coins made it easier to buy and sell goods. A huge variety of goods were available. From south of the Sahara came gold and slaves. China traded silk and porcelain. Gold and ivory came from eastern Africa. Sandalwood and spices came from Southeast Asia and India. Egypt traded grain, and Iraq traded linens, dates, and precious stones. India supplied textile goods.

Cities on the trade routes flourished. Baghdad, Cairo, and Damascus were three great trading cities. They were also the capital cities of their regions. Islamic cities had a distinctive appearance. The most impressive buildings were the palaces of the caliphs and the mosques. There were also buildings with fountains and courtyards, public baths, and bazaars. The **bazaar,** or covered market, was an important part of every Muslim city or town. Goods from many areas were available in the bazaars.

The Arab Empire had more cities than most other areas of the world at that time. But a majority of people still lived in the countryside. They made their living by farming or herding animals. During the early Empire, peasants owned most of the farmland. Later, wealthy landowners began to create large estates, as they did in other parts of the world.

8. What were the three main trading centers in the Arab Empire?

• Islamic Society *(page 205)*

According to Islam, all people are equal in the eyes of Allah. In reality, this was not always the case in the Arab Empire. There was an upper class of ruling families, government officials, and wealthy merchants. One group of people, in particular, was not considered equal. They were the slaves. Muslims could not be slaves, so most of their slaves came from southern Africa or from non-Islamic parts of Asia. Many slaves had been captured in war. Slaves often served in the army. Many military slaves were eventually freed. Slaves were also used as domestic servants. These slaves were sometimes able to buy their freedom. Islamic law made it clear that slaves should be treated fairly. It was also considered a good act to free them.

Women were also not considered equal. The Quran instructed men to treat women with respect. Women had the right to own and inherit property. But men were dominant in Muslim society. Women were supposed to be good mothers and wives by raising their children and caring for their husbands. Every woman had a male guardian. Parents arranged marriages for their children. The Quran allowed men to have more than one wife, but no more than four. Most men could only afford one wife, because they had to pay a **dowry** (a gift of money or property) to their brides. Arabic custom required women to stay in their homes and keep away from men outside their own families. It also required women to cover nearly all of their bodies when appearing in public. Despite these restrictions, women were better off in Islamic society than they had been in earlier times, when they had been treated like slaves.

9. What two groups were not considered equal in the Arab Empire?

Name ____________________ Date ____________________ Class ____________________

Reading Essentials and Study Guide

Chapter 6, Section 4

For use with textbook pages 207–210

THE CULTURE OF ISLAM

KEY TERMS

astrolabe an instrument used by sailors to determine their location by observing the position of stars and planets *(page 208)*

minaret a tower on a mosque *(page 209)*

muezzin a crier, who calls the faithful to prayer *(page 209)*

arabesque geometric patterns that decorated Islamic works of art *(page 210)*

DRAWING FROM EXPERIENCE

Have you ever read "Aladdin and His Lamp," "Ali Baba and the Forty Thieves," or any other stories from *The Arabian Nights?* Have you seen the movie *Aladdin?* Why do you think these stories continue to be popular?

ORGANIZING YOUR THOUGHTS

Use the concept web below to help you take notes. List at least one Islamic achievement in the areas of philosophy, math, astronomy, medicine, history, and architecture.

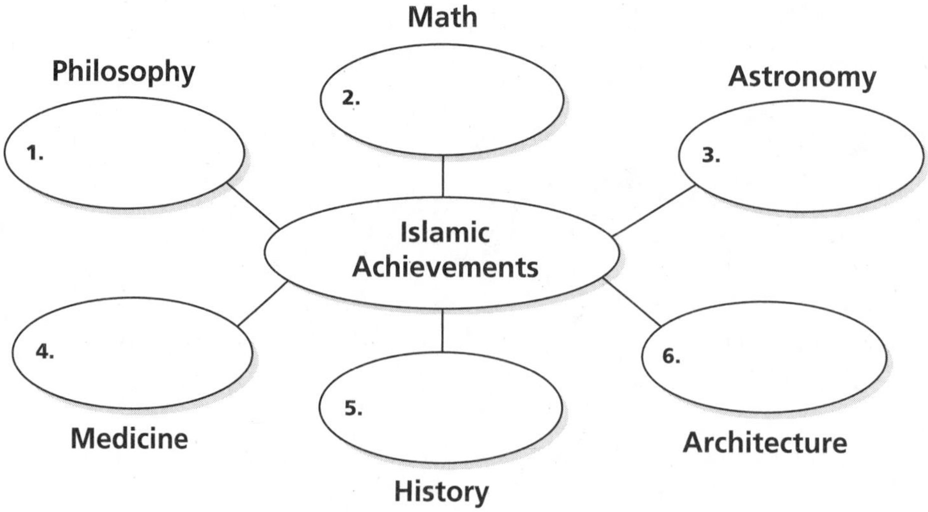

Reading Essentials and Study Guide

Chapter 6, Section 4 *(continued)*

READ TO LEARN

• Preservation of Knowledge *(page 207)*

During the Arab Empire, Arabs translated the works of Plato and Aristotle into Arabic. The translations were put in a library called the House of Wisdom in Baghdad. They were read and studied by Muslim scholars. These works were almost lost in Europe. In the twelfth century, the Arabic translations were translated into Latin. This made them available to Europeans.

Texts on mathematics were brought to Baghdad from India. Paper was brought from China in the eighth century. By the end of the century, paper factories had been established in Baghdad. The use of paper helped to preserve knowledge.

7. How did Muslim scholars preserve the writings of Plato and Aristotle?

____

____

____

____

____

• Philosophy, Science, and History *(page 208)*

Arabic philosophers did more than just translate the works of Plato and Aristotle. They also wrote commentaries. One philosopher, Ibn-Rushd, wrote a commentary on nearly all of Aristotle's works.

Islamic scholars also made great contributions in mathematics and science. The Muslims adopted and passed on the numerical system of India. In Europe, it became known as the "Arabic" system. A ninth-century Iranian mathematician created algebra. Muslims also set up an observatory at Baghdad to study the stars. They were aware that the Earth was round, and they named many stars. They also improved the **astrolabe,** an instrument used by sailors to determine their location by observing the positions of stars and planets. The astrolabe made it possible for Europeans to sail to the Americas.

Muslim scholars developed medicine as a field of scientific study. One scientist, Ibn Sina, wrote a medical encyclopedia. He stressed the contagious nature of diseases. His work became a basic medical textbook in medieval Europe. Islamic scholars also took an interest in history. The most prominent historian was Ibn-Khaldun. He wrote *Muqaddimah (Introduction to History).* He believed that civilizations go through regular cycles of birth, growth, and decay.

Reading Essentials and Study Guide

Chapter 6, Section 4 *(continued)*

8. How did the astrolabe make it possible for Europeans to sail to the Americas?

• Literature *(page 208)*

Muslims regarded the Quran as their greatest work of literature. However, other writings were still popular. Two of the most famous works of Middle Eastern literature are the *Rubaiyat* of Omar Khayyám and *The 1001 Nights* (also called *The Arabian Nights*). Omar Khayyám was a twelfth-century Persian poet, mathematician, and astronomer. He did not write down his poems. He told them orally, and they were written down later by friends or scribes. No one knows who wrote *The Arabian Nights*. Like the *Rubaiyat*, the stories in *The Arabian Nights* were told orally at first and then written down later. They are a collection of folktales, fables, and romances, including the famous story of Aladdin.

9. How were the *Rubaiyat* and *The Arabian Nights* written?

• Art and Architecture *(page 209)*

Islamic art is a blend of Arab, Turkish, and Persian traditions. The greatest examples of Islamic art and architecture are the Muslim mosques. The Great Mosque of Samarra is the largest mosque ever built. The most famous section of this mosque is its **minaret.** This is the tower from which the **muezzin,** or crier, calls the faithful to prayer five times a day. The minaret of Samarra was unusual because it had an outside spiral staircase. Palaces constructed by Islamic rulers are some other examples of Islamic art. The finest example is the fourteenth-century Alhambra in Spain. Every inch of the castle's surface is decorated with floral and abstract patterns.

Name ____________________ Date ____________________ Class ____________________

Reading Essentials and Study Guide

Chapter 6, Section 4 *(continued)*

Most decorations on all forms of Islamic art consisted of Arabic letters, abstract figures, and floral designs. These decorations were repeated over and over in geometric patterns called **arabesques.** They completely covered the surfaces of the objects. No representations of people or other living beings appear in Islamic religious art. The Quran does not forbid representational art. But the Hadith, an early collection of Muhammad's sayings, warns against any attempt to imitate God by creating pictures of living beings.

10. Why does Islamic religious art use abstract figures rather than representations of living beings?

____

____

____

____

____

Name ______________________ Date ______________________ Class ______________________

Reading Essentials and Study Guide

Chapter 7, Section 1

For use with textbook pages 223–226

THE DEVELOPMENT OF CIVILIZATIONS IN AFRICA

KEY TERMS

plateau a relatively high, flat land area *(page 225)*

savanna a broad grassland dotted with small trees and shrubs *(page 225)*

DRAWING FROM EXPERIENCE

What different climates are there in the United States? How does the climate affect the economy of different parts of the country? What is the climate where you live?

In this section, you will learn about the development of the first civilizations in Africa. Africa has several different geographical zones and four distinct climates.

ORGANIZING YOUR THOUGHTS

Use the concept web below to help you take notes. Identify the four climate zones in Africa and describe where they are located.

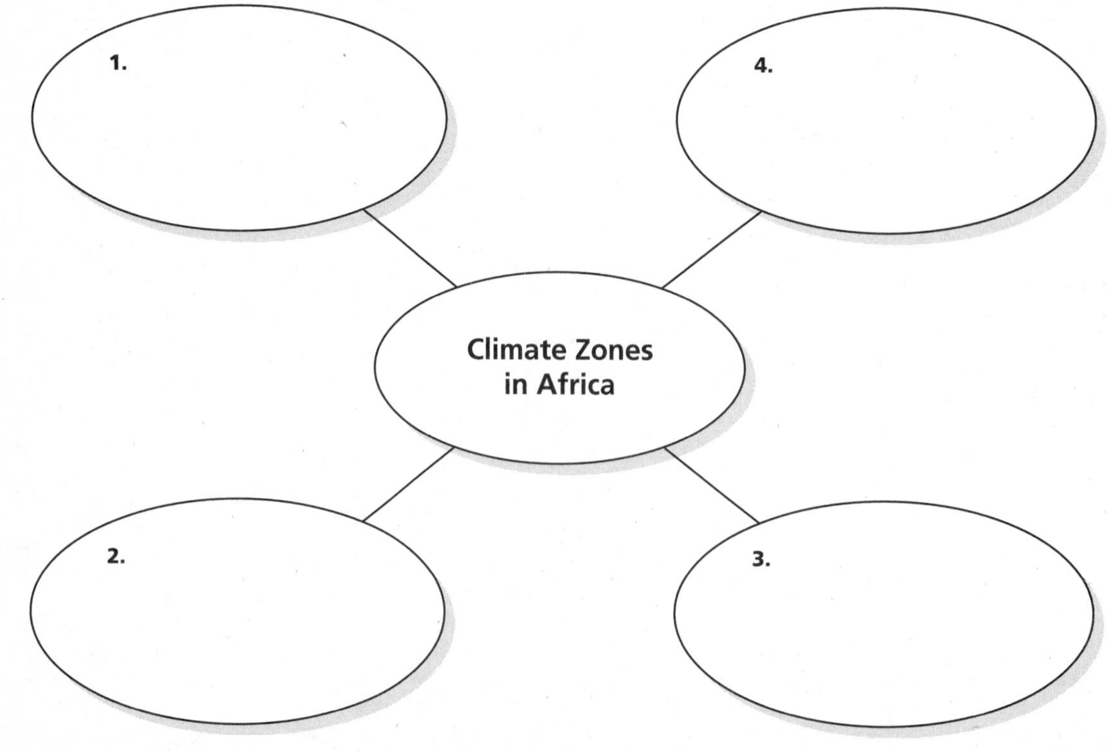

Name ______________ Date ______________ Class ______________

READ TO LEARN

• The Land of Africa *(page 223)*

Africa is the second largest continent. Its geography is very diverse. There are mountains on the northern coast. South of the mountains, there is a desert, the Sahara. This is the largest desert on Earth. South of the Sahara, there are several other regions. In the west, the desert gradually changes to grasslands and then to tropical jungles along the coast. To the east, there are snow-capped mountains, upland **plateaus** (relatively high, flat land areas), and lakes. The Great Rift Valley is in this part of Africa. It has deep canyons surrounded by mountains. Further to the south is the Congo basin, which has tropical rain forests. In the far south, the rain forest gradually changes into hills, plateaus, and deserts.

5. What are some of the different geographical features of Africa?

____

____

____

____

____

• The Climate of Africa *(page 225)*

Africa has four distinct climate zones. These different climates help to explain the different lifestyles of the peoples of Africa. Along the northern coast and the southern tip of Africa, there is a mild climate zone. In these areas, the temperature is warm, and there is moderate rainfall. Abundant crops can be grown in these areas. Deserts form another climate zone. Deserts cover about 40 percent of Africa. The two largest deserts are the Sahara in the north and the Kalahari in the south. A third climate zone is the rain forest. It is located along the equator and makes up about 10 percent of Africa. In this area, there are heavy rains and warm temperatures. This produces dense forests where farming and travel are very difficult. There are also disease-carrying insects in this area. The fourth climate zone consists of the savannas. The **savannas** are broad grasslands dotted with small trees and shrubs. The savannas are located both north and south of the rain forest and make up about 40 percent of Africa. There is usually enough rainfall in the savannas to farm and herd animals, but the rainfall is unreliable.

6. What are the two largest climate zones in Africa?

____

____

____

____

____

• Emerging Civilization and the Rise of Islam *(page 225)*

About seven or eight thousand years ago, people in Africa began to tame animals and grow crops. This led to the rise of the first civilizations in Africa. One of these early civilizations was Egypt. The other two early civilizations were Kush and Axum.

The area to the south of Egypt was originally known as Nubia. The people of Nubia had a busy trade with Egypt. They traded ivory, ebony, frankincense (a fragrant tree resin), and leopard skins. Nubia was under Egyptian control for many centuries, but it freed itself around 1000 B.C. It then became the state of Kush. In 750 B.C., Kush conquered Egypt. In 663 B.C., however, the Kushites were defeated by the Assyrians, who had iron weapons. The Kushites were driven out of Egypt and returned to their original lands.

At first, the economy of Kush was based mainly on farming. It soon became a major trading state, however. The Kushites learned how to make iron weapons and tools from the Assyrians. They traded these iron goods with the Roman Empire, Arabia, and India. They also traded ivory, gold, ebony, and slaves. They traded these goods for luxury goods, such as jewelry and silver lamps from Arabia and India. Kush flourished from about 250 B.C. to about A.D. 150. It declined because of the rise of a new power in the region. This new power was known as Axum.

Axum was located in what is now Ethiopia. Arabs founded it as a colony. It eventually became an independent state that combined Arab and African cultures. Axum was prosperous because it was on the trade route between India and the Mediterranean. It exported ivory, frankincense, myrrh (another tree resin), and slaves. It imported textiles, metal goods, wine, and olive oil. It competed with Kush for control of the ivory trade.

In the fourth century A.D., King Ezana, an Axumite ruler, invaded Kush and conquered it. In A.D. 324, King Ezana converted to Christianity. He then made Christianity the official religion of Axum.

In 641, Arab forces took control of Egypt. By the eighth century, Arabs controlled the entire coastal region of North Africa. Several Muslim trading states were established on the African coast of the Red Sea. Axum was a Christian state, but it had peaceful relations with these Muslims states for hundreds of

Reading Essentials and Study Guide

years. In the twelfth century, however, the Muslim states began to move inland. They wanted control over the trade in slaves and ivory. Axum fought back. By the fifteenth century, Axum was involved in a growing conflict with Adal, a Muslim state.

7. Why did Axum come into conflict with the Muslim trading states?

____

____

____

____

____

Name ______________________ Date ____________________ Class ____________________

Reading Essentials and Study Guide

Chapter 7, Section 2

For use with textbook pages 228–234

KINGDOMS AND STATES OF AFRICA

KEY TERMS

Bantu a family of languages spoken by peoples who migrated from the Niger River region to East Africa and the Congo River basin *(page 232)*

subsistence farming growing just enough crops for personal use, not for sale *(page 232)*

Swahili a mixed African-Arabian culture along the coastal area of East Africa (also used for the major language in this area) *(page 233)*

stateless society a group of independent villages organized by clans and led by a local ruler or clan head *(page 234)*

DRAWING FROM EXPERIENCE

Do you add salt to your food? Do you like salty snacks? Would you enjoy food as much if you did not have salt?

In the last section, you read about the development of the first African civilizations. In this section, you will learn about the growth of new kingdoms in Africa. These kingdoms prospered because of the gold and salt trade. Salt was very valuable, because it both preserved food and improved its taste.

ORGANIZING YOUR THOUGHTS

Use the chart below to help you take notes. Describe the location, government and economy of each of the kingdoms in this chart.

Kingdom	Location	Government	Economy
Ghana	**1.**	**2.**	**3.**
Mali	**4.**	**5.**	**6.**
Songhai	**7.**	**8.**	**9.**

READ TO LEARN

• The Kingdom of Ghana *(page 228)*

The kingdom of Ghana emerged in the fifth century A.D. It was located in the upper Niger River valley, between the Sahara and the tropical forests along the West African coast. (The modern state of Ghana is located in the forest region to the south.) The kings of Ghana were strong rulers who governed without any laws. They relied on an army of thousands of men to protect their kingdom and enforce their wishes.

Most of the people of Ghana were farmers. But Ghana prospered because of its abundant supply of iron ore and gold. The blacksmiths of Ghana were skilled in making tools and weapons from iron ore. Ghana's gold made it the center of a trade empire. Ghanaians traded their gold for other products. Muslim merchants from North Africa brought metal goods, textiles, horses, and salt to Ghana. Salt was very important. It was used to preserve food and to improve its taste. People also needed salt to replace what their bodies lost in the hot climate. Eventually, Ghana also traded other goods, such as ivory, ostrich feathers, hides, and slaves. The Berbers carried much of the trade across the desert. The Berbers were nomads who used camels. Camels were crucial to trade across the Sahara because they could go for days without drinking water or eating food.

The kingdom of Ghana flourished for several hundred years. Eventually, it was weakened by wars and collapsed around 1200.

10. Why was salt an important item of trade in Africa?

____

____

• The Kingdom of Mali *(page 230)*

Mali is located on the Atlantic coast, but it extends far inland to the famous city of Timbuktu. Sundiata Keita established Mali in the thirteenth century. In 1240, Sundiata defeated the Ghanaians and captured their capital. He united the people of Mali and created a strong government. Mali built its wealth and power on the gold and salt trade, but most of its people were farmers. They grew grains, such as sorghum, millet, and rice. They lived in villages with local rulers. These rulers were both religious and administrative leaders. They collected taxes and sent the taxes to the kings of Mali.

One of the richest and most powerful kings was Mansa Musa. He ruled from 1307 to 1337. He doubled the size of the kingdom of Mali and divided the kingdom into provinces ruled by governors. He was a devout Muslim and made a pilgrimage to Makkah. He took a large caravan with him and spent a huge amount of gold along the way. He brought architects back with him to build mosques and a palace. He also brought scholars and books to introduce his subjects to message of Allah. But he was the last powerful ruler of Mali. By 1359, civil war divided Mali.

11. Who was the founder of the kingdom of Mali?

• The Kingdom of Songhai *(page 231)*

The Niger River in West Africa has regular floods. It provides a rich soil for raising crops and taking care of cattle. East of Timbuktu, the river makes a wide bend. The Songhai people lived along the Niger River, south of the bend. In 1009, a ruler named Kossi converted to Islam and established the Dia dynasty. This was the first Songhai state. It prospered because of the Muslim trade routes that linked Arabia, North Africa, and West Africa.

In 1464, Sunni Ali created a new dynasty, the Sunni. Under his leadership, Songhai began to expand. Sunni Ali conquered many areas, including Timbuktu and Jenne. This gave Songhai control of the trading empire that had made Ghana and Mali so prosperous. The Songhai Empire reached the height of its power during the reign of Muhammad Ture. He overthrew the son of Sunni Ali in 1493 and created a new dynasty, the Askia. Under Muhammad Ture, the Songhai Empire continued to expand. It eventually stretched a thousand miles along the Niger River. Muhammad Ture divided Songhai into provinces, with a governor in charge of each one. He maintained peace and security with a navy and soldiers on horseback. The empire prospered because of the salt and gold trade.

After the reign of Muhammad Ture, Songhai began to decline. Near the end of the sixteenth century, the forces of the sultan of Morocco occupied much of Songhai.

12. What two leaders expanded the Songhai Empire?

• Societies in East Africa *(page 232)*

Beginning in the first millennium B.C., new peoples began to migrate into eastern Africa from the west. Farming peoples who spoke dialects of the **Bantu** family of languages began to move from the Niger River region into East Africa and the Congo River basin. The communities they built were based on **subsistence farming** (growing just enough crops for personal use, not for sale). The main crops were grains, yams, melons, and beans. They farmed with iron and stone tools. Men and women performed different tasks. Women tilled the fields and cared for the children. Men tended the herds, hunted, or took part in local trade.

The Bantu peoples gradually began to take part in the regional trade along the eastern coast of Africa. Beginning in the eighth century, Muslims from the Arabian Peninsula and the Persian Gulf began to settle at ports along the coast. They formed a string of trading ports, including Mogadishu, Mombasa, and Kilwa. Merchants in these ports became very wealthy. The city of Kilwa became one of the most beautiful cities in the world. In the fourteenth century, two huge buildings were constructed in Kilwa—the Great Mosque and the Husuni Kubwa palace. Homes near the mosque and palace were luxurious. Kilwa began to decline, however. In 1505, the Portuguese sacked the city and destroyed its major buildings.

A mixed African-Arabian culture began to emerge along the coast. This culture became known as **Swahili.** The Muslim religion and Arabic architectural styles gradually became a part of African culture in this area. The term Swahili was also applied to the major language used in the area. Swahili combined Bantu with Arabic words and phrases. It is the national language of Kenya and Tanzania today.

13. How did the arrival of Muslims affect the eastern coast of Africa?

____

____

____

• States and Stateless Societies in South Africa *(page 234)*

Until the eleventh century A.D., most of the peoples in the southern half of Africa lived in stateless societies. A **stateless society** is a group of independent villages organized by clans and led by a local ruler or clan head. Beginning in the eleventh century, these villages began to consolidate. Out of these groupings came the first states. From about 1300 to about 1450, Zimbabwe was the wealthiest and most powerful state in the region. It prospered from the gold trade. Its gold was traded as far as China. Porcelain from China has been found at the ruins of Zimbabwe's capital, the Great Zimbabwe.

14. What was the most powerful state in southern Africa in the fourteenth and fifteenth centuries?

____

____

____

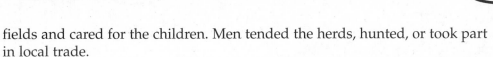

Name ______________________ Date ______________________ Class ______________________

Reading Essentials and Study Guide

Chapter 7, Section 3

For use with textbook pages 236–241

AFRICAN SOCIETY AND CULTURE

KEY TERMS

lineage group a community whose members trace their lineage (descent) from a common ancestor *(page 237)*

matrilineal a society in which descent is traced through the mother *(page 237)*

patrilineal a society in which descent is traced through the father *(page 237)*

diviner a person who believes that he or she has the power to foretell events, usually by working with supernatural forces *(page 238)*

griot a storyteller in African society *(page 241)*

DRAWING FROM EXPERIENCE

Are there stories that you were told as a child by your grandparents or other older members of your family? What makes these stories special in your family?

In the last two sections, you learned about the development of early civilizations and kingdoms in Africa. In this section, you will learn about African society, religious beliefs, and culture. Early Africans communicated knowledge about their culture and history through storytelling.

ORGANIZING YOUR THOUGHTS

Use the concept web below to help you take notes. Most African societies shared some common religious beliefs. List four traditional beliefs that were shared by many African religions.

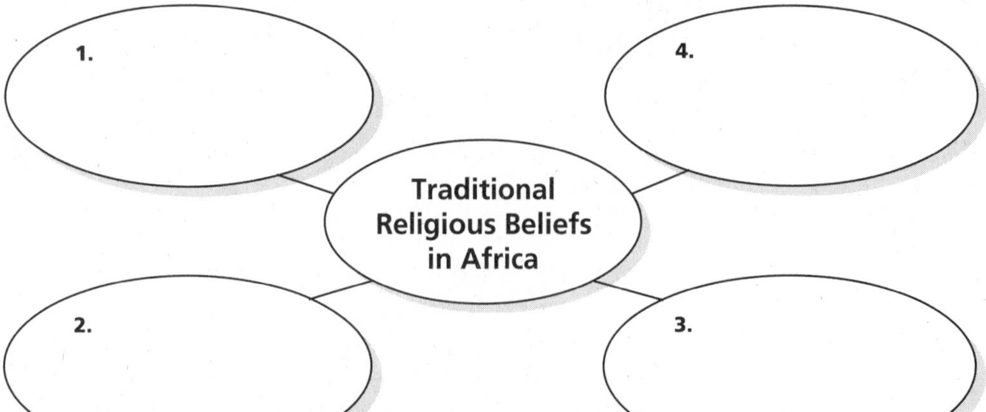

READ TO LEARN

• Aspects of African Society *(page 236)*

African towns often began as walled villages and grew into larger communities. These towns were the centers of governments. They had markets that were filled with goods from faraway places. Artisans and farmers also lived in these towns. The farmers grew crops in nearby fields.

In Africa, kings were held in high esteem, but they were not as isolated from the common people as they were in other societies. Rulers often held audiences (meetings) to allow people to voice their complaints. However, most people lived in small villages in the countryside and never had an audience with the king.

The basic level in African society was the extended family. The extended family was made up of parents, children, grandparents, and other dependents. They lived in small, round houses made of mud and topped with a thatch roof. The extended families were combined into larger communities known as **lineage groups.** All members of a lineage group could trace their lineage (descent) from a common ancestor. Members of extended families and lineage groups were expected to take care of one another.

Women were usually subordinate to men in Africa, but they were valued because of the work they could do or for having children. Women often worked in the fields, while men tended the cattle or hunted. In many African societies, lineage was based on the mother rather than the father. These societies are called **matrilineal** (societies in which descent is traced through the mother) rather than **patrilineal** (societies in which descent is traced through the father). Women were often allowed to inherit property, and the husband was often expected to move into his wife's house.

In a typical African village, there was a process for educating young people. This prepared them to become part of the community. Both boys and girls were raised by their mothers until they were six years old. From their mothers, they learned language, songs, and their family history. At six, boys and girls went different ways. Fathers took control of their sons' education. Boys learned how to hunt and fish, how to grow plants, and how to clear fields. Girls continued to learn what they needed from their mothers. This included how to take care of the home and work in the fields. As children got older, they took on more responsibility in the community. Young people reached a point where they were expected to enter the community fully. This transition occurred at the time of puberty. It was marked by an initiation ceremony.

Slavery was practiced in Africa from ancient times. Berber groups in North Africa raided farming villages south of the Sahara and took captives. The captives were then taken north and sold throughout the Mediterranean. Slavery was also common in other parts of Africa. Slaves included people captured in war, debtors, and criminals. Slaves were not necessarily seen as inferior. Many were trusted servants or were respected because of their special knowledge or talents. But life was difficult for most slaves. Those who worked on farmlands had hard, long hours. Those who worked as soldiers were sometimes better off. Slaves who worked as domestic servants usually had the best lives.

5. What was the process for educating young people in African villages?

____

____

____

____

____

• Religious Beliefs in Africa *(page 238)*

Most African societies shared some common religious ideas. One of these was a belief in a single creator god. Many people believed that that the creator god was merciful and could be appeased by proper behavior. One way to communicate with the gods was through ritual. This was carried out by a special class of **diviners** (people who believe they have the power to foretell events, usually by working with supernatural forces). Many diviners were employed by the king to guarantee a good harvest or otherwise protect the ruler and his subjects.

Ancestors were also important in African religion. Ancestors were believed to be closer to the gods and to have the power to influence the lives of their descendants. Ceremonies dedicated to ancestors were important rituals. Many African religions believed in an afterlife. Ancestral souls would live on in the afterlife as long as the lineage group continued to perform rituals in their names.

When Islam was brought to Africa, it swept rapidly across the northern coast. It was accepted more slowly in the lands south of the Sahara, but by the end of the fifteenth century, much of this area had converted to Islam. Islam had less success in the mountains of Ethiopia, where Christianity continued to win followers. Muslim merchants first brought Islam to East Africa from Arabia, but it did not win many followers there until the twelfth and thirteenth centuries.

In some ways, the beliefs of Islam were in conflict with traditional African beliefs. Islam rejected spirit worship and insisted on the separation of men and women. These ideas were contrary to the beliefs of many Africans and were often ignored. Native beliefs were combined with Islam to create a unique brand of Africanized Islam.

6. In what ways did the beliefs of Islam conflict with traditional African beliefs?

____

____

____

____

____

• African Culture *(page 240)*

In early Africa, the arts were a means of expressing religion. The earliest art forms in Africa were rock paintings. The most famous examples are in the Tassili Mountains in the central Sahara. Woodcarvings were another important art form. Wood carvers throughout Africa made masks and statues. The carvings often represented gods, spirits, or ancestral figures. Terra cotta (clay) and metal figurines and statues were also made in parts of Africa.

African music and dance often served a religious purpose too. Dances were a means of communicating with the spirits. The words to songs transmitted religious traditions, folk legends, and historical information from generation to generation. Storytelling served the same purpose. Storytelling was usually done by priests or by a special class of storytellers known as **griots.** These storytellers were also historians. Through their stories, they kept the history of their people alive.

7. In what ways did African art, music, and dance serve religious purposes?

____

____

____

____

____

Name ______________________ Date ______________________ Class ______________________

Reading Essentials and Study Guide

Chapter 8, Section 1

For use with textbook pages 247–252

CHINA REUNIFIED

KEY TERMS

scholar-gentry a class of people that replaced the landed aristocracy and became the political and economic elite of Chinese society *(page 252)*

dowry in China, a gift of money or goods given by a bride's parents to her husband *(page 252)*

DRAWING FROM EXPERIENCE

What invention do you think has changed the world the most in the last fifty years? Why do you think so? What invention is most important to your way of life? Why?

In this section, you will learn about China during the Sui, Tang, and Song dynasties, including the inventions that were developed during this time.

ORGANIZING YOUR THOUGHTS

Use the chart below to help you take notes. List the time periods, rulers, and achievements of the Sui, Tang, and Song dynasties.

Dynasty	Time Period	Achievements	Problems
Sui	**1.**	**2.**	**3.**
Tang	**4.**	**5.**	**6.**
Song	**7.**	**8.**	**9.**

Reading Essentials and Study Guide

READ TO LEARN

• The Sui Dynasty *(page 247)*

For three hundred years after the end of the Han dynasty, there was chaos and civil war in China. Then, in 581, the Sui dynasty took control of China. The Sui dynasty only lasted until 618, but it was able to reunify China.

Sui Yangdi, the second emperor of the dynasty, completed the Grand Canal. This canal linked the two great rivers of China, the Huang He (Yellow River) and the Chang Jiang (Yangtze River). This made it easier to ship rice from the south to the north. Sui Yangdi was a cruel ruler, however. He used forced labor to build the canal. He also made the people pay high taxes, while he lived extravagantly. These factors, as well as military failures, led to rebellion. Sui Yangdi was murdered, and his dynasty came to an end.

10. Why did the Chinese people rebel against Sui Yangdi?

• The Tang Dynasty *(page 248)*

The Tang dynasty soon emerged. It lasted from 618 until 907. The early Tang rulers were reformers. They restored the civil service examination, and they gave land to the peasants. They also brought peace to northwestern China and extended their control into Tibet, the area north of the Himalaya. The Tang rulers also set up trade and diplomatic relations with Southeast Asia.

The Tang dynasty had problems, however. There were struggles for control and government corruption. The Uighurs were hired to fight for the Tang dynasty. The Uighurs were a tribal group of Turkic-speaking people. But instead of fighting for him, the Uighurs overthrew the Tang ruler in 907.

11. In what ways were the Tang rulers reformers?

Name ______________________ Date ______________ Class ______________

• The Song Dynasty *(page 249)*

In 960, the Song dynasty rose to power. It lasted until 1279. During the Song dynasty, China was prosperous, and there were many cultural achievements. There were also problems, however, especially from the Uighurs in northern China. Because of the Uighurs, the Song rulers were forced to move the capital from Changan to Hangzhou, which is farther south. They also lost control of Tibet.

To stay in power, the Song rulers formed an alliance with the Mongols. This was a mistake. Within a few years, the Mongols turned on the Song dynasty. They overthrew the Song and created a new Mongol dynasty.

12. Why did the Song rulers move the capital from Changan to Hangzhou?

• Government and the Economy *(page 250)*

During the Sui, Tang, and Song dynasties, a political system emerged that was based on principles developed during the Qin and Han dynasties. The government was a monarchy with a large bureaucracy. The empire was divided into provinces, districts, and villages. The government was based on Confucian principles.

Trade and manufacturing grew dramatically, but the economy was still based on farming. The reforms of the Tang and Song dynasties put more land in the hands of the poor peasants. These reforms and improvements in farming techniques led to an abundance of food.

Technological developments created new products. During the Tang dynasty, the Chinese began to make steel. The steel was used to make swords and sickles. Cotton was also introduced. This led to new kinds of clothes. Gunpowder was also invented during the Tang dynasty. It was used to make explosives and a flamethrower called a fire-lance. Trade began to revive. It had declined after the fall of the Han dynasty and the Roman Empire. The Silk Road was renewed, and trade between China and Southwest Asia thrived. Trade also increased with regions near China. The Chinese exported tea, silk, and porcelain to the countries beyond the South China Sea. In return, they received exotic woods, precious stones, and various tropical goods.

13. How did agriculture improve during the Tang and Song dynasties?

____

____

____

____

____

____

• Chinese Society *(page 252)*

For the rich city dwellers in China, life during the Tang and Song dynasties was very enjoyable. There were new forms of entertainment, such as playing cards and chess. Block printing was invented during the eighth century and allowed people to communicate in new ways. Most of the people still lived in villages, however. They made their living by farming. Changes were taking place in the countryside, however. Previously, there had been a huge gulf between wealthy landowners and poor peasants. Now there was a more complex mixture of landowners, free peasants, sharecroppers, and landless laborers. A new class, known as the **scholar-gentry,** emerged. This group replaced the old landed aristocracy. The scholar-gentry controlled much of the land in the countryside and also produced most of the civil servants. They became the political and economic elite in Chinese society.

The status of women in China during this time was low. Female children were considered less desirable than male children. When there were famines, female infants were sometimes killed if there was not enough food for the whole family. A girl's parents were expected to provide a **dowry** (money or goods) to her husband when she married. Poor families often sold their daughters to wealthy villagers.

14. How were women treated in China during this time?

____

____

____

____

____

____

Name ______________________ Date ______________ Class ______________

Reading Essentials and Study Guide

Chapter 8, Section 2

For use with textbook pages 253–257

THE MONGOLS AND CHINA

KEY TERMS

khanates territories in the Mongol Empire, each ruled by one of the sons of Genghis Khan *(page 254)*

neo-Confucianism a new form of Confucianism that developed during the late Tang dynasty in response to Buddhism and Daoism *(page 256)*

porcelain a ceramic made of fine clay baked at very high temperatures *(page 257)*

DRAWING FROM EXPERIENCE

Have you heard of Marco Polo? How did you learn about him? Why is he famous?

In the last section, you learned about China during the Sui, Tang, and Song dynasties. In this section, you will learn about China during the time of the Mongol dynasty. It was during this time that Marco Polo visited China.

ORGANIZING YOUR THOUGHTS

Use the time line below to help you take notes. Identify seven key events in the history of the Mongols

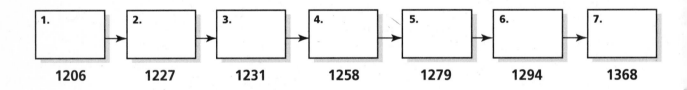

1.	→	2.	→	3.	→	4.	→	5.	→	6.	→	7.
1206		1227		1231		1258		1279		1294		1368

READ TO LEARN

• The Mongol Empire *(page 253)*

The Mongols were nomads from the region of modern-day Mongolia. They were organized into clans. Temujin unified the Mongols. In 1206, he was elected Genghis Khan ("universal ruler"). He devoted himself to conquering other lands. Mongol armies traveled both to the west and to the east. Some went as far as central Europe. The Mongols created the largest land empire in history.

After the death of Genghis Khan in 1227, his sons divided the empire into separate territories, called **khanates.** Each khanate was ruled by one of the sons. In 1231, the Mongols attacked Persia. In 1258, they defeated the Abbasids at Baghdad. In the 1260s, the Mongols attacked the Song dynasty. In China, they learned about gunpowder and the fire-lance. By the end of the thirteenth century, the fire-lance developed into the handgun and cannon.

8. What inventions did the Mongols learn about from the Chinese?

• The Mongol Dynasty in China *(page 254)*

In 1279, one of Genghis Khan's grandsons completed the conquest of China. His name was Kublai Khan. He established a new Chinese dynasty, the Yuan. He ruled China until his death in 1294. He set up his capital at Khanbaliq in northwestern China. This city would later be known as Beijing.

The Yuan (or Mongol) dynasty continued to expand the empire. The Mongols invaded Vietnam, Java, and Sumatra. Only Vietnam was conquered. The other campaigns failed. The Mongol tactics were not effective in tropical and hilly regions.

The Mongols had more success in ruling China. They adapted to the Chinese political system and used the Chinese bureaucrats. But the Mongols became a separate class with their own laws. Mongols usually held the highest positions in the bureaucracy. Many Chinese people came to respect the stability and prosperity that the Mongols brought to China. The capital at Khanbaliq was especially prosperous. Foreign visitors were impressed by its splendor. One of these foreign visitors was Marco Polo. He lived in Khanbaliq during the time of Kublai Khan.

The Mongol dynasty began to have problems. The Mongol rulers spent too much money on foreign conquests. There were also problems with internal instability and corruption at court. In 1368, a peasant named Zhu Yuanzhang put together an army and ended the Mongol dynasty. He set up a new dynasty, the Ming dynasty.

9. Why did many Chinese people respect the Mongols?

• Religion and Government *(page 255)*

By the time of the Mongols, religion in China had changed. Merchants and missionaries brought Buddhism to China from India in the first century A.D. After the collapse of the Han dynasty, both Buddhism and Daoism became popular. Early Tang rulers supported Buddhist monasteries. Buddhists and Daoists became advisors at court. Eventually, Buddhism and Daoism began to lose favor. Buddhism was criticized for being a foreign religion. Buddhist monasteries had also acquired thousands of acres of land and serfs. By the end of the Tang dynasty, Buddhism and Daoism were no longer supported by the state. The government destroyed many Buddhist temples and monasteries

The government now supported Confucianism. It was different from the Confucianism during the Han dynasty. **Neo-Confucianism,** as it was called, developed in response to Buddhism and Daoism. Neo-Confucianism teaches that the world is real, not an illusion, and that fulfillment comes from participation in the world, not from withdrawal. Neo-Confucianists divide the world into a material world and a spiritual world. Although humans live in the material world, Neo-Confucianists believe that they are also linked with the Supreme Ultimate. They believe that the goal of humans should be to move beyond the material world to reach union with the Supreme Ultimate.

10. How was Buddhism introduced in China?

• A Golden Age in Literature and Art *(page 256)*

The period from the Tang dynasty to the Ming dynasty was a great age of Chinese literature. The invention of printing during the Tang dynasty made literature more available and popular. The Tang dynasty is viewed as the great age of poetry in China. At least 48,000 poems were written by 2,200 authors. Li Bo and Duo Fu were two of the most popular poets during the Tang Era. Li Bo's poetry often focused on nature. Duo Fu was a serious Confucian. Many of his poems are concerned with social injustice and the plight of the poor.

During the Song and Mongol dynasties, landscape painting reached its high point. Daoism influenced Chinese artists. They went into the mountains to paint and find the Dao, or Way, in nature. Chinese artists tried to show the hidden forms of the landscape. Rather than depicting a realistic mountain, for example, they tried to portray the idea of "mountain." Daoism also influenced how people were portrayed. Chinese artists painted people as tiny figures, because people were viewed as insignificant in the midst of nature. Ceramics were also an important Chinese art form. Tang artisans perfected the making of porcelain. Porcelain is a ceramic made of fine clay baked at very high temperatures.

11. Which dynasty is viewed as the great age of Chinese poetry? During which dynasties did landscape painting reach its high point?

____

____

____

____

____

Reading Essentials and Study Guide

Chapter 8, Section 3

For use with textbook pages 263–267

EARLY JAPAN AND KOREA

KEY TERMS

samurai ("those who serve") Japanese warriors who protected the security and property of their employers *(page 265)*

Bushido ("the way of the warrior") the samurai's code of behavior, based on loyalty to his lord *(page 265)*

shogun a powerful military leader, or general, who had the real power in Japan *(page 265)*

shogunate a system of government in Japan, in which the emperor was the ruler in name only and the shogun exercised the actual power *(page 265)*

daimyo ("great names") heads of noble families in Japan who controlled vast landed estates *(page 265)*

Shinto ("the Sacred Way" or "the Way of the Gods") the state religion of Japan *(page 266)*

Zen a sect of Buddhism in Japan *(page 266)*

DRAWING FROM EXPERIENCE

Has anyone in your family ever served in the military? What branch of service were they in? Where were they stationed?

In the last two sections, you learned about China during the Sui, Tang, Song, and Mongol dynasties. In this section you will learn about the early history of Japan and Korea. The early Japanese were fierce warriors.

ORGANIZING YOUR THOUGHTS

Use the concept web below to help you take notes. The Chinese and the Mongols both had a major impact on Japan and Korea. Summarize the impact of the Chinese and the Mongols on these two countries.

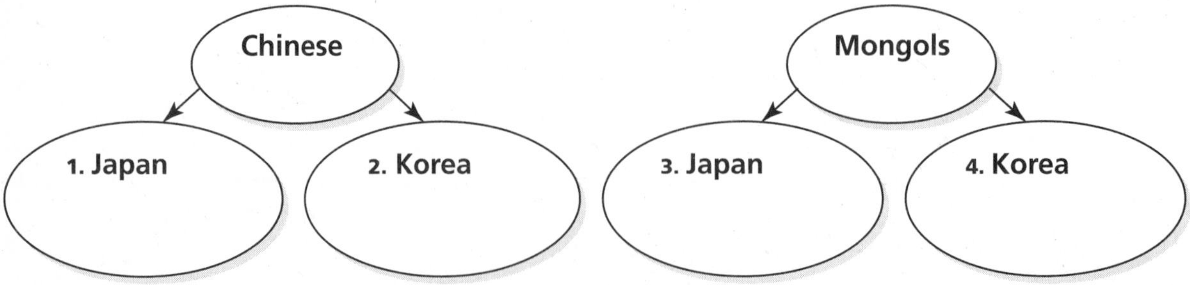

Reading Essentials and Study Guide

READ TO LEARN

• The Geography of Japan *(page 263)*

Japan is a chain of many islands. Its total land area is about 146,000 square miles. Much of Japan is mountainous. Volcanoes formed the mountains. Only about 20 percent of the total land can be farmed, but the volcanic soil is very fertile. Because of their isolation from the mainland, the Japanese developed many unique qualities. They believed that they had a destiny separate from the peoples on the mainland.

5. How did the fact that Japan is an island country affect its development?

____

____

____

____

____

• The Rise of the Japanese State *(page 264)*

The early Japanese settled in the Yamato Plain in the first centuries A.D. The Yamato Plain is near the present-day cities of Osaka and Kyoto. Japanese society was made up of clans. The people were divided between a small aristocratic class (the rulers) and a large class of rice farmers, artisans, and household servants. Eventually, one ruler of the Yamato clan became the ruler of Japan. However, other families continued to compete for power.

In the early seventh century, Shotoku Taishi tried to unify the clans to resist an invasion by the Chinese. Shotoku Taishi was a Yamato prince. He sent representatives to China to learn more about how the Chinese organized their government. Then he created a centralized system of government in Japan, based on the Chinese model. He wanted to limit the powers of the aristocrats and increase the ruler's (his own) authority. As a result, the ruler was portrayed as a divine figure and the symbol of the Japanese nation. Japan was divided into administrative districts. The village was the basic unit of government. A new tax system was set up. Now all farmland belonged to the state. Taxes were paid directly to the central government rather than to local aristocrats.

After Shotoku Taishi's death in 622, the Fujiwara family gained power. A Yamato ruler was still emperor, but he was strongly influenced by the Fujiwara clan. In 710, a new capital was established at Nara. The emperor began to use the title "son of Heaven." The aristocrats were still powerful, however. They were able to keep the taxes from the lands for themselves.

Reading Essentials and Study Guide

Chapter 8, Section 3 *(continued)*

In 794, the emperor moved the capital from Nara to Heian, on the site of present-day Kyoto. The emperor continued to rule in name, but actual power remained in the hands of the Fujiwara clan. The government was becoming more decentralized. Powerful aristocrats dominated the rural areas. These aristocrats began to take justice into their own hands. They hired warriors to protect their security and property. These warriors were called the samurai ("those who serve"). The samurai were supposed to live by a strict warrior code, known as Bushido ("the way of the warrior"). The samurai's code was based on loyalty to his lord.

By the end of the twelfth century, a powerful noble named Minamoto Yoritomo defeated several rivals and set up his power near present-day Tokyo. He created a more centralized government under a powerful military leader, known as the **shogun** (general). The emperor remained ruler in name only, and the shogun had the real power. This system of government is called the **shogunate.** The Kamakura shogunate, founded by Yoritomo, lasted from 1192 to 1333. In 1281, Kublai Khan invaded Japan. Fortunately for the Japanese, almost the entire Mongolian fleet was destroyed by a typhoon. Fighting the Mongols put a heavy strain on the government, however. In 1333, the Kamakura shogunate was overthrown by a group of powerful families led by the Ashikaga family.

The power of the aristocrats grew during the fourteenth and fifteenth centuries. Heads of noble families, called **daimyo** ("great names"), controlled vast landed estates that owed no taxes. The daimyo relied on the samurai for protection. A civil war, known as the Onin War, began in 1467 and lasted until 1477. During this war, the capital city of Kyoto was virtually destroyed. Central authority disappeared. The aristocrats seized control over large territories, which they ruled as independent lords. Their rivalries caused almost constant warfare.

6. What ideas about government did Shotoku Taishi get from the Chinese?

• Life in Early Japan *(page 266)*

The economy of early Japan was based on farming. Because of the limited amount of farmland and the abundant rainfall, the Japanese people grew wet rice (rice grown in flooded fields). Foreign trade began during the eleventh century. This trade was mainly with China and Korea. Japan traded raw materials, paintings, swords, and other manufactured items for silk, porcelain, books, and copper coins.

In early Japan, women had a certain level of equality with men. A law guaranteed the right of women to inherit property. Wives who were abandoned could divorce and remarry. However, some practices show that women were not considered equal. A husband could divorce his wife if she did not produce a male child, or if she committed adultery, talked too much, was jealous, or had a serious illness. Even if they did not possess full legal and social rights, women played an active role in society. Aristocratic women were prominent at court. Some became known for their artistic or literary talents.

The early Japanese worshipped spirits, called *kami.* They believed the *kami* lived in trees, rivers, and mountains. The Japanese also believed that their ancestors were in the air around them. These beliefs evolved into a kind of state religion, called **Shinto** ("the Sacred Way"). In time, Shinto included a belief in the divinity of the emperor and the sacredness of the Japanese nation. Shinto is still practiced today.

Monks from China brought Buddhism to Japan during the sixth century A.D. One sect of Buddhism, known as **Zen,** became the most popular. Zen beliefs became part of the samurai warrior's code of behavior. In Zen Buddhism, there are different ways to achieve enlightenment. Some believe that it can be achieved suddenly, while others believe that it can only be achieved through self-discipline, including meditation.

Many aristocratic men in Japan believed that prose fiction was "vulgar gossip" and thus beneath them. So women were the most productive writers of fiction from the ninth to the twelfth centuries. Women learned to read and write at home, and they wrote diaries, stories, and novels to pass the time. One of the world's great novels, *The Tale of the Genji,* appeared during this time. Murasaki Shikibu wrote it around the year 1000.

In Japanese art and architecture, landscape was an important means of expression. The Golden Pavilion in Kyoto was built in the fourteenth century and is one of the great treasures of the world. Its landscape plays an important part in its beauty.

7. Why were women the most productive writers of fiction from the ninth to the twelfth centuries?

• The Emergence of Korea *(page 267)*

Korea is only slightly larger than the state of Minnesota. It is relatively mountainous. Its closeness to China and Japan influenced its history. In 109 B.C., the northern part of Korea came under the control of the Chinese. The Koreans drove them out in the third century A.D. Three separate kingdoms emerged in Korea: Koguryo, Paekche, and Silla. These three kingdoms were bitter rivals from the fourth to the seventh centuries. The kingdom of Silla eventually gained control. After the king of Silla was assassinated, Korea had a period of civil war. In the tenth century, a new dynasty called Koryo arose in the north. This kingdom adopted Chinese political institutions and remained in power for four hundred years.

In the thirteenth century, the Mongols seized the northern part of Korea. By accepting Mongol authority, the Koryo dynasty was able to remain in power. Mongol rule led to much suffering for the Korean people, however. Many peasants and artisans were forced to build ships for Kublai Khan. After the end of the Mongol dynasty in China, the Koryo dynasty broke down. In 1392, Yi Song-gye, a military commander, seized power and founded the Yi dynasty.

8. How was the Koryo dynasty able to remain in power so long?

Name ______________________ Date ______________________ Class ______________________

Reading Essentials and Study Guide

Chapter 8, Section 4

For use with textbook pages 268–272

INDIA AFTER THE GUPTAS

KEY TERMS

Theravada a sect of Buddhism that sees Buddhism as a way of life, not a religion *(page 268)*

Mahayana a sect of Buddhism that sees Buddhism as a religion and believes that the Buddha is divine *(page 268)*

DRAWING FROM EXPERIENCE

How do most people acquire their religious beliefs? How important do you think religion is in the lives of people today? Why do you think so?

In the last section, you learned about the early history of Japan and Korea. In this section, you will learn about the history of India after the Guptas. During this period, new religious beliefs influenced India.

ORGANIZING YOUR THOUGHTS

Use the chart below to help you take notes. A split developed among the followers of Buddhism in India. Identify some key differences between Theravada and Mahayana Buddhism.

Type of Buddhism	Religion or Way of Life	Beliefs About the Buddha	Beliefs About Nirvana
Theravada	**1.**	**2.**	**3.**
Mahayana	**4.**	**5.**	**6.**

READ TO LEARN

• The Decline of Buddhism *(page 268)*

For hundreds of years, Buddhism remained popular with the Indian people. Over time, the teachings of the Buddha were interpreted in different ways. People did not always agree about the meaning of the Buddha's teachings. As a result, a split developed among the followers of Buddhism in India. One group called themselves the school of **Theravada** ("the teachings of the elders"). They believed that they were following the original teachings of the Buddha. They saw Buddhism as a way of life, not a religion. They believed that nirvana was a release from the "wheel of life" and could be achieved through an understanding of one's self. Another school was known as Mahayana Buddhism. To Mahayana Buddhists, Buddhism was a religion, not a philosophy. They believed that Buddha was divine, not just a wise man. They also believed that nirvana is not just a release from the wheel of life, but a true heaven. Nirvana could be achieved through devotion to the Buddha.

In the end, neither the Mahayana nor the Theravada sect of Buddhism remained popular in India. Hinduism revived, and Islam also became more popular. Despite its decline in India, monks carried Buddhism to China, Korea, Southeast Asia, and Japan. Buddhism is still practiced in all four of these areas.

7. What two religions replaced Buddhism in India?

____

____

____

____

____

• The Eastward Expansion of Islam *(page 269)*

In the early eighth century, Islam became popular in the northwestern corner of the Indian subcontinent. The impact of Islam is still visible in this region today. India is mostly Hindu, while Bangladesh and Pakistan are Islamic.

When the Arab armies reached India in the early eighth century, they only occupied the frontier regions. A new phase of Islamic expansion took place in the tenth century. Turkish people, who had formerly been slaves, founded a new Islamic state, known as Ghazni. Ghazni was located in what is now Afghanistan. When the founder of Ghazni died in 997, his son Mahmud succeeded him. Before his death in 1030, Mahmud extended his rule throughout much of northern India. Hindu warriors, known as the Rajputs, tried to resist, but they were no match for the invaders. Mahmud's successors continued their advances. By 1200, the Muslims had conquered the entire plain of northern India. They created a new Muslim state known as the Sultanate of Delhi.

8. How is the impact of Islam still visible in the Indian subcontinent today?

____

____

____

____

____

• The Impact of Timur Lenk *(page 269)*

During the latter half of the fourteenth century, the Sultanate of Delhi began to decline. Near the end of the century, a new military force crossed the Indus River from the northwest and raided the capital of Delhi. As many as 100,000 Hindu prisoners were killed. Timur Lenk (Tamerlane) led the invaders. Timur Lenk was the ruler of a Mongol state based in Samarkand. He seized power in 1369 and began a period of conquest. During the 1380s, he conquered the entire region east of the Caspian Sea and then occupied Mesopotamia. His invasion of northern India was brief. He died in 1405 in the midst of a military campaign.

9. Who was Timur Lenk?

____

____

____

____

____

• Islam and Indian Society *(page 270)*

The Muslim rulers in India saw themselves as foreign conquerors. They kept a strict separation between themselves and the mass of the Hindu population. Most Muslim rulers realized that there were too many Hindus to convert them all. They accepted the need to tolerate the Hindus' religion. However, they did impose many Islamic customs on Hindu society. Overall, the relationship between Muslims and Hindus was marked by suspicion and dislike.

10. Why did the Muslim rulers in India tolerate the Hindus' religion?

• Economy and Daily Life *(page 270)*

Between 500 and 1500, most Indians lived on the land and farmed their own tiny plots. They paid a share of their harvest each year to a landlord. The landlord then sent part of the payment to the local ruler. Many people also lived in cities. The wealthy usually lived in the cities. Agriculture was a source of wealth. So was trade. Trade within India declined during this period, because of fighting among the states. But foreign trade remained high because of India's location. Wealthy Hindu merchants carried on much of the trade, but Muslims were also involved.

11. How did most Indians make their living?

• The Wonder of Indian Culture *(page 271)*

Between 500 and 1500, Indian artists and writers made significant achievements in their fields. Architecture and literature, in particular, flourished during this time. From the eighth century on, Indian architects built monumental Hindu temples. The temples were very ornate, with huge towers. Some of the greatest examples of Hindu temple art are the temples at Khajuraho. Of the 80 temples built there in the tenth century, 20 are still standing today.

Prose literature was well developed in India by the sixth and seventh centuries. It did not develop in Japan until the tenth century or in Europe until the seventeenth century. One of the great masters of Sanskrit prose was Dandin, a seventh-century author. In his work *The Ten Princes,* he created a fantastic world, combining history and fiction.

Reading Essentials and Study Guide

Chapter 8, Section 4 *(continued)*

12. What are some of the greatest examples of Hindu temple art?

____

____

____

____

____

Name ______________________ Date ______________ Class ______________

Reading Essentials and Study Guide

Chapter 8, Section 5

For use with textbook pages 273–278

CIVILIZATION IN SOUTHEAST ASIA

KEY TERMS

archipelago a chain of islands *(page 273)*

agricultural society a society whose economy is based primarily on farming *(page 277)*

trading society a society whose economy is based primarily on trade *(page 277)*

DRAWING FROM EXPERIENCE

Do people from a variety of cultures live in your community? How are these cultures reflected in your community?

In the last section, you read about the history of India after the Guptas. In this section, you will learn about the history of various countries in Southeast Asia.

ORGANIZING YOUR THOUGHTS

Use the chart below to help you take notes. Compare the government, economy, and religion of the following areas in Southeast Asia.

	Government	Economy	Religion
Vietnam	**1.**	**2.**	**3.**
Angkor	**4.**	**5.**	**6.**
Thailand	**7.**	**8.**	**9.**
Burma	**10.**	**11.**	**12.**
Malay Peninsula and Indonesian Archipelago	**13.**	**14.**	**15.**

READ TO LEARN

• The Land and People of Southeast Asia *(page 273)*

Southeast Asia is the region between China and India. It has two major parts. One is the mainland region. It extends from the Chinese border to the tip of the Malay Peninsula. The other is a large **archipelago,** or chain of islands. Most of these islands are part of present-day Indonesia and the Philippines. Southeast Asia is a melting pot of peoples. It contains a mixture of races, cultures, and religions.

Mainland Southeast Asia has several mountain ranges. Between these ranges are several fertile river valleys. The people living in the river valleys were cut off from one another by the mountains, and they had only limited contacts with the people living in the mountains. The geographical barriers may explain why Southeast Asia was never unified under a single government. The barriers also encouraged the development of separate cultures, with different religions and languages.

16. How did geography affect the development of Southeast Asia?

• The Formation of States *(page 274)*

Between 500 and 1500, a number of states developed throughout Southeast Asia. They used China and India as models, but they adapted the models to their own needs and created their own unique states.

The Vietnamese were one of the first peoples in Southeast Asia to develop their own state. After the Chinese conquered Vietnam in 111 B.C., they tried to make Vietnam part of China. But the Vietnamese clung to their own identity. In the tenth century, they overthrew the Chinese. However, the Chinese did influence Vietnam. The Vietnamese adopted the Chinese model of centralized government. Their new state, which called itself Dai Viet (Great Viet), adopted state Confucianism. The rulers called themselves emperors and adopted Chinese court rituals. They also introduced the civil service examination. The Vietnamese state grew and expanded southward. By 1600, the Vietnamese had reached the Gulf of Siam.

Name ______________________ Date ____________________ Class ____________________

Reading Essentials and Study Guide

In the ninth century, the kingdom of Angkor arose in what is present-day Cambodia. Angkor is also called the Khmer Empire. A powerful leader named Jayavarman united the Khmer people and set up a capital at Angkor Thom. In 802, Jayavarman was crowned as the god-king of his people. For several hundred years, Angkor was the most powerful state in mainland Southeast Asia. In 1432, however, the Thai destroyed the Angkor capital. The Angkor ruling class fled to the southeast and set up a new capital near Phnom Penh. Phnom Penh is the capital of present-day Cambodia.

The Thai first appeared in the sixth century along the frontier of China. Beginning in the eleventh or twelfth century, Thai groups began moving south. They came into conflict with Angkor. They set up their own capital at Ayutthaya on the Chao Phraya River. They were a major force in the region for the next four hundred years. They converted to Buddhism and borrowed Indian political practices. But they also created a unique culture that evolved into the modern-day culture of Thailand.

The Burmans formed their own society in the valleys of the Salween and Irrawaddy Rivers. They had migrated from the highlands of Tibet in the seventh century A.D., probably to escape Chinese armies in the area. The Burmans were nomads, but they adopted farming after they arrived in Southeast Asia. In the eleventh century, they created the first Burman state, the kingdom of Pagan. Like the Thai, they converted to Buddhism and adopted Indian political institutions and culture. Pagan played an active role in the sea trade throughout the region. Attacks from the Mongols in the late thirteenth century weakened Pagan and caused it to decline.

In the Malay Peninsula and the Indonesian Archipelago, a different pattern developed. For centuries, this area had been involved in the trade that passed from East Asia to the Indian Ocean. However, the area had never been united as a single state. Two states eventually emerged in this region. In the eighth century, the state of Srivijaya dominated the trade route passing through the Strait of Malacca. At the same time, the kingdom of Sailendra emerged in eastern Java. The economy of Sailendra was based primarily on farming. Both states were influenced by Indian culture.

In the late thirteenth century, the new kingdom of Majapahit was founded. It became the greatest empire the region had ever seen. In the mid-fourteenth century, it united most of the archipelago, and perhaps part of the mainland, under a single rule. Around 1400, an Islamic state began to form in Melaka, a small town on the western coast of the Malay Peninsula. Melaka soon became the major trading port in the region and a chief rival of Majapahit. Eventually, nearly all the people of the region were converted to Islam and became part of the Sultanate of Melaka.

Name ______________________ Date ______________________ Class ______________________

Reading Essentials and Study Guide

17. In what ways did China and India influence Southeast Asia?

____

____

____

____

____

• Economic Forces *(page 277)*

The states of Southeast Asia can be divided into two groups: agricultural societies and trading societies. The economies of **agricultural societies** are based on farming, while the economies of **trading societies** are based on trade. Some states, such as Vietnam, Angkor, Pagan, and Sailendra, depended largely on farming. Others, such as Srivijaya and the Sultanate of Melaka, depended chiefly on trade. The demand for spices added to the amount of trade in the region. Merchants from India and the Arabian Peninsula sailed to the Indonesian islands to buy cloves, pepper, nutmeg, and cinnamon, as well as precious woods, like teak and sandalwood.

18. Which states in Southeast Asia were trading societies? Which were agricultural societies?

____

____

____

____

____

• Social Structures *(page 277)*

In most Southeast Asian societies, hereditary aristocrats were at the top of the social ladder. They held both political power and economic wealth. Most aristocrats lived in the major cities. Beyond the major cities lived the rest of the population, which consisted of farmers, fishers, artisans, and merchants. The majority of the people were rice farmers, who barely survived.

In most of the societies of Southeast Asia, women had more rights than they did in China and India. They worked side by side with men in the fields and were often involved in trading activities.

19. How were women treated in most of the societies of Southeast Asia?

• Culture and Religion *(page 277)*

Chinese culture made an impact on Vietnam. Indian culture influenced other areas of Southeast Asia. The most visible evidence of the Indian influence is the architecture in these areas. The temple of Angkor Wat, at Angkor Thom, is a beautiful example. It combines Indian architectural techniques with native inspiration.

Hinduism and Buddhism were introduced into Southeast Asia, but they did not entirely replace existing beliefs. Old beliefs were blended with the new faiths. Buddhism did not have much impact at first. However, after Theravada Buddhism was introduced in Burma in the eleventh century, it spread rapidly to other areas of Southeast Asia. It eventually became the religion of the masses in much of Southeast Asia. It was popular because it taught that people could seek nirvana on their own, without the need for priests or rulers. It also tolerated local gods and posed no threat to established faiths.

20. Why was Theravada Buddhism popular in Southeast Asia?

Name ______________________ Date ______________ Class ______________

Reading Essentials and Study Guide

Chapter 9, Section 1

For use with textbook pages 285–290

TRANSFORMING THE ROMAN WORLD

KEY TERMS

wergild ("money for a man") a fine paid by a wrongdoer to the family of the person he or she had injured or killed *(page 287)*

ordeal a physical trial used as a means of determining a person's guilt or innocence *(page 287)*

bishopric a group of parishes under the authority of a bishop *(page 287)*

pope the head of the Roman Catholic Church *(page 287)*

monk a man who separates himself from ordinary human society in order to pursue a life of total dedication to God *(page 288)*

monasticism the practice of living the life of a monk *(page 288)*

missionary a person sent out to carry a religious message *(page 288)*

nun a woman who withdraws from the world to dedicate herself to God *(page 288)*

abbess the head of a convent *(page 288)*

DRAWING FROM EXPERIENCE

What do you think of when you hear the word "monk"? Why do monks live in monasteries? Are there any monasteries in or near your community?

In this section, you will learn about the division of the Western Roman Empire into states ruled by German kings. In this section and those following, you will learn about the role that monks played in the development of European civilization during the period from 500 to 1500 A.D. This period is called the Middle Ages or the medieval period.

Reading Essentials and Study Guide

Chapter 9, Section 1 *(continued)*

ORGANIZING YOUR THOUGHTS

Use the concept web below to help you take notes. List five ways that monks and monasteries contributed to, or influenced, life in Europe.

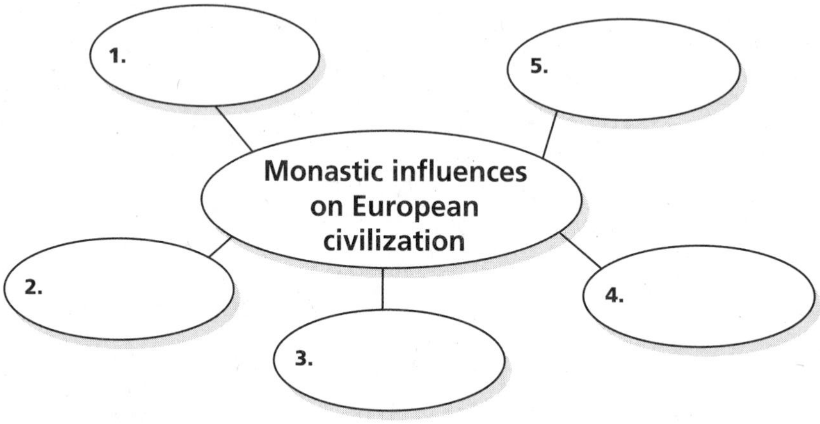

READ TO LEARN

• The New Germanic Kingdoms *(page 285)*

By 500, the Western Roman Empire had been divided into a number of states ruled by German kings. The Ostrogoths controlled Italy, and the Visigoths occupied Spain. The Ostrogoths and the Visigoths were both Germanic tribes. They continued to use the Roman structure of government, but they excluded Romans from holding power.

When the Roman armies abandoned Britain at the beginning of the fifth century, the Angles and Saxons settled there. The Angles and Saxons were Germanic tribes from Denmark and northern Germany. They eventually became the Anglo-Saxons.

By 510, Clovis had established a powerful kingdom in what is now France and western Germany. Clovis was the king of the Franks, a Germanic group. He became a Christian around 500. His conversion to Christianity gained him the support of the Christian church in Rome, which was now known as the Roman Catholic Church. After his death, his sons divided the Frankish kingdom among themselves.

Over time, Germans and Romans married one another and began to create a new society. Among the Germanic peoples, the family was very important. The concept of family included the extended family of husbands, wives, children, brothers, sisters, cousins, and grandparents. The family worked the land together and provided protection for one another. The German concept of family influenced Germanic law. Crimes were personal and could lead to feuds and bloodshed. To avoid bloodshed, a system developed that was based on a fine called wergild. **Wergild** was the amount paid by a wrongdoer to the family of the person he or she had injured or killed. Wergild means "money for a man," and was the value of a person in money. A crime against a member of nobility cost more than a crime against an ordinary person or a slave. In Germanic law, one way to determine whether a person was guilty or innocent was the ordeal. The **ordeal** was a physical trial. It was based on the idea that divine forces would not allow an innocent person to be harmed. If an accused person was unharmed after the ordeal, he or she was considered innocent.

6. Which Germanic tribes controlled Italy, Spain, Britain, and France by the sixth century?

____

____

____

• The Role of the Church *(page 287)*

By the fourth century, the Christian church had developed a system of organization. Priests led local Christian communities, called parishes. A bishop headed a group of parishes. His area of authority was called a **bishopric,** or diocese. Over time, the bishops of Rome became the heads of the Roman Catholic Church. They became known as **popes.** In the sixth century, a strong pope, Gregory I, took control of Rome and its surrounding territories. This gave the papacy (office of the pope) political power. The territories around Rome became known as the Papal States

Gregory I was also active in converting the pagan peoples (heathens or non-Christians) to Christianity. He used monks to help spread Christianity to all of Europe. A **monk** is man who separates himself from ordinary human society in order to pursue a life of total dedication to God. The practice of living the life of a monk is known as **monasticism.** English and Irish monks were especially enthusiastic **missionaries** (people sent to carry a religious message).

In the sixth century, Saint Benedict founded a community of monks. He wrote a set of rules for this community. Other monastic groups later used the Benedictine rule. It divided each day into a series of activities. The main emphasis was on prayer and manual labor. The monks ate, worked, slept, and worshiped together in a monastery. An abbot, or "father" ruled each monastery. Monasteries owned lands that allowed them to be self-supporting. They also became centers of learning.

Monks became an important force in the new European civilization. They provided schools, hospitals, and hospitality for travelers. Although the first monks were men, women also began to withdraw from the world to dedicate themselves to God. These women were called **nuns.** Nuns lived in convents headed by **abbesses.**

7. How was the Christian church organized by the fourth century?

____

____

____

____

• Charlemagne and the Carolingians *(page 289)*

During the 600s and 700s, the kings of the Frankish kingdom began to lose their power to the mayors of the palace. The mayors of the palace were the chief officers of the king's household. One of these mayors, Pepin, became king himself. Pepin was the son of Charles Martel, the leader who had defeated the Muslims at the Battle of Tours in 732. When Pepin died, his son became king. This new king became known as Charles the Great, or Charlemagne. He ruled from 768 to 814.

Charlemagne expanded the territory of the Frankish kingdom and created the Carolingian Empire. At its height, the Carolingian Empire covered much of western and central Europe. Charlemagne used his household staff and counts (German nobles) to rule his empire. The counts were the king's representatives in the local districts. Charlemagne used *missi dominici* ("messengers of the lord king") to check on the counts to make sure that they were carrying out the king's wishes. In 800, Charlemagne was given a new title—emperor of the Romans. His coronation (crowning) symbolized the coming together of the Roman, Christian, and Germanic elements of European civilization. It also shows that the idea of a Roman Empire had not died.

Although Charlemagne could not read or write, he promoted learning in his kingdom. This led to a revival of learning and culture sometimes called the Carolingian Renaissance. This revival included a renewed interest in the works of the Greeks and Romans. The monks played a central role in this revival. Monasteries had scriptoria, or writing rooms, where the monks copied manuscripts. They copied the works of ancient Roman authors, as well as the Bible and other Christian works. Most of the ancient Roman literature we have today exists because the monks copied it.

8. What were some of Charlemagne's achievements as emperor?

____

____

____

____

Name ____________________ Date ____________________ Class ____________________

Reading Essentials and Study Guide

Chapter 9, Section 2

For use with textbook pages 291–296

FEUDALISM

KEY TERMS

feudalism a political and social system in which a powerful lord offered protection to a vassal in return for military service *(page 293)*

vassal a man who served a lord in a military capacity *(page 293)*

knight a heavily armored soldier who fought on horseback *(page 293)*

fief land given to a vassal by a lord *(page 294)*

feudal contract a set of unwritten rules that determined the relationship between a lord and his vassal *(page 294)*

tournament a contest where knights could show their fighting skills *(page 295)*

chivalry a code of ethics that knights were supposed to uphold *(page 295)*

DRAWING FROM EXPERIENCE

What do you think of when you hear the word "Vikings"? Who were they? What were their contributions to the development of North America?

In the last section, you learned about the development of German kingdoms in Europe. In this section, you will learn about the invasion of Europe by other peoples, including the Vikings. These invaders threatened the safety of people throughout Europe, which led to the development of feudalism.

ORGANIZING YOUR THOUGHTS

Use the diagram below to help you take notes. Under the feudal contract, lords and vassals both had obligations to one another. Summarize some of those obligations in the boxes below.

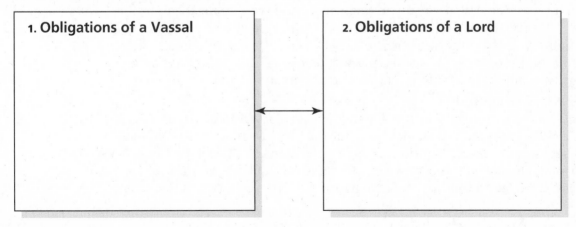

1. Obligations of a Vassal	↔	2. Obligations of a Lord

Reading Essentials and Study Guide

READ TO LEARN

• The Invaders *(page 291)*

After Charlemagne's death in 814, the Carolingian Empire began to fall apart. Within 30 years, it was divided into three major sections: the western Frankish lands, the eastern Frankish lands, and the Middle Kingdom. There were also many invasions in Europe in the ninth and tenth centuries. The Muslims attacked southern France. The Magyars, a people from western Asia, moved into central Europe and invaded Western Europe. The most far-reaching attacks came from the Norsemen of Scandinavia, also known as the Vikings. They were warriors, but they were also great shipbuilders and sailors. Their ships were long and narrow. This made it possible for the Vikings to sail up European rivers and attack places that were far inland.

Beginning in 911, the ruler of the west Frankish lands gave land at the mouth of the Seine to one band of the Vikings. This section of France became known as Normandy. By allowing the Vikings to settle in this land, the Frankish people were able to convert the Vikings to Christianity. The Vikings soon became a part of European civilization.

3. What peoples invaded Europe during the ninth and tenth centuries?

• The Development of Feudalism *(page 292)*

The Vikings and other invaders threatened the safety of people throughout Europe. People began to turn to local landed aristocrats (lords) to protect them. In return for protection, people were willing to serve the lords. This led to a new political and social system called **feudalism.** In Germanic society, warriors swore an oath of loyalty to their leaders and fought for them. In return, the leaders took care of the warriors' needs. A man who served a lord in a military capacity was known as a **vassal.** When a lord wanted men to fight for him, he gave each vassal a piece of land. The land supported the vassal and his family. By the ninth century, the gift of land to a vassal became known as a **fief.**

In feudal society, loyalty to one's lord was the chief virtue. The lord-vassal relationship was not a master-slave relationship. It was an honorable relationship between free men. Over time, a set of unwritten rules developed that determined the relationship between a lord and a vassal. These rules were known as the **feudal contract.** A vassal had to perform military service, usually about 40 days a year. The vassal could also be asked to come to the lord's court to give advice. Vassals had to make payments to the lord on certain occasions, such as the knighting of the lord's eldest son or the marriage of his eldest daughter. The lord also had responsibilities to the vassal. The lord supported the vassal by giving him land. He also had to protect the vassal. This could mean defending him militarily, or it could mean taking his side in a court of law.

The Frankish army began to change during this time. It had originally consisted of foot soldiers dressed in coats of mail (armor made of metal links or plates). In the eighth century, larger horses and the use of stirrups made it possible for horsemen to wear coats of mail, too. Armies now consisted mainly of armored cavalry (soldiers on horseback). These soldiers became known as **knights.**

4. Why did men choose to become vassals?

____

____

____

____

• The Nobility of the Middle Ages *(page 295)*

In the Middle Ages, the nobles were the kings, dukes, counts, barons, and even bishops who had large landed estates. They formed an aristocracy, or nobility, that had most of the political, economic, and social power. Knights also had social prestige. In the twelfth century, knights began to take part in tournaments. **Tournaments** were contests where knights could show their fighting skills. The joust became the main part of the tournament. The joust was an individual contest between two knights.

In the eleventh and twelfth centuries, the idea of chivalry evolved. **Chivalry** was a code of ethics that knights were supposed to follow. Knights were expected to defend the Church and defenseless people. They were also supposed to treat captives as honored guests instead of putting them in dungeons. Chivalry also implied that knights should fight for glory and not for material rewards.

5. What kinds of behavior did the code of chivalry expect from knights?

____

____

____

____

- **Aristocratic Women** *(page 296)*

During this time, women could own property, but most remained under the control of their fathers or husbands. Some aristocratic women had opportunities to play important roles, however. The lady of the castle often had to manage the estate while the lord was away at war or court. This could involve supervising many servants, taking care of the financial accounts, and overseeing the supplies, including food, for the entire household. Women were expected to be subservient to their husbands, but some strong women advised or even dominated their husbands.

6. In what ways did aristocratic women play important roles?

____

____

____

____

____

Name ______________________ Date ______________________ Class ______________________

Reading Essentials and Study Guide

Chapter 9, Section 3

For use with textbook pages 297–301

THE GROWTH OF EUROPEAN KINGDOMS

KEY TERMS

common law laws that are common to a whole kingdom, as opposed to laws that vary from place to place *(page 298)*

Magna Carta (the Great Charter) a document of rights that limited the king's power signed by King John in 1215 *(page 299)*

estate each of the three social classes in France *(page 299)*

DRAWING FROM EXPERIENCE

What rights are people in the United States guaranteed by the Constitution? Which of these rights do you think is the most important? Why?

In the last two sections, you learned about the rise of German kingdoms in Europe and the development of feudalism. In this section, you will learn about the growth of kingdoms in Europe during the High Middle Ages. You will also learn how representative government and the protection of rights developed in some of these countries.

ORGANIZING YOUR THOUGHTS

Use the chart below to help you take notes. Indicate what contributions the following rulers made to the growth of kingdoms in their countries.

Ruler	Country	Contributions
William of Normandy	**1.**	**2.**
Henry II	**3.**	**4.**
John	**5.**	**6.**
Edward I	**7.**	**8.**
Philip II Augustus	**9.**	**10.**
Philip IV	**11.**	**12.**

READ TO LEARN

• England in the High Middle Ages *(page 297)*

In the late ninth century, King Alfred the Great united the Anglo-Saxon kingdoms in England. After that time, Anglo-Saxons ruled England. On October 14, 1066, an army of knights under William of Normandy landed on the coast of England and defeated King Harold, the Anglo-Saxon king, at the Battle of Hastings. William was then crowned king of England. He took a census, known as the Domesday Book. This was the first census taken in Europe since Roman times. William also developed more fully the system of taxation and royal courts begun by the Anglo-Saxon kings. As the Norman ruling class married the Anglo-Saxon nobility, a new English culture began to develop. This culture merged Anglo-Saxon and French language and customs.

The power of the English monarchy was enlarged during the reign of Henry II. He ruled from 1154 to 1189. He increased the number of criminal cases tried in the king's court. He also made it possible for property cases to be tried in the royal courts. This expanded the power of the royal courts, as well as the king's power. Because the royal courts were now found throughout all of England, a body of **common law** (law that was common to the whole kingdom) began to replace laws that varied from place to place. Henry also believed that he had the right to try clergymen in royal courts. When Thomas à Becket, the archbishop of Canterbury, claimed that only Roman Catholic Church courts could try clerics, knights who supported the king murdered the archbishop.

Many English nobles resented the growing power of the kings. During the reign of King John, they rebelled. In 1215, they forced King John to sign a document of rights called the **Magna Carta** (Great Charter). The Magna Carta put in writing that the relationship between the king and vassals was based on mutual rights and obligations. In later years, it was used to support the idea that a king's power was limited, not absolute.

During the reign of Edward I in the thirteenth century, the English Parliament emerged. The parliament played an important role in the development of representative government. It was composed of two knights from every county, two people from every town, and all of the nobles and bishops throughout England. Eventually, the nobles and bishops formed the House of Lords, and the knights and townspeople formed the House of Commons. During the time of Edward I, the parliament passed laws and taxes.

13. What two cultures merged to form a new English culture?

____

____

____

____

Name ______________________ Date ______________________ Class ______________________

• The French Kingdom *(page 299)*

After the death of the last Carolingian king in 987, the west Frankish nobles chose Hugh Capet as the new king. This established the Capetian dynasty of French kings. The Capetians had the title of king, but they had little real power. The land that they controlled only included the area around Paris.

The reign of King Philip II Augustus was a turning point in the growth of the French monarchy. He ruled from 1180 to 1223. He waged war with England, and gained control of the French territories of Normandy, Maine, Anjou, and Aquitaine. These territories had been under English control. Adding these territories increased the income of the French monarchy and expanded its power.

Philip IV, called Philip the Fair, ruled from 1285 to 1314. He strengthened the monarchy by expanding the royal bureaucracy. He also brought a French parliament into existence by meeting with representatives of the three estates (classes). These **estates** were the clergy (first estate), the nobles (second estate), and townspeople (third estate). The meeting was held in 1302 and began the Estates-General, the first French parliament.

14. What were the three estates in France?

____

____

____

• The Holy Roman Empire *(page 300)*

In the tenth century, Saxon dukes became kings of the eastern Frankish kingdom. This kingdom became known as Germany. The best-known Saxon king of Germany was Otto I. In return for protecting the pope, Otto I was crowned emperor of the Romans in 962. This title had not been used since Charlemagne. The German kings tried to rule both German and Italian lands. Frederick I considered Italy the center of a "holy empire." This was the origin of the name Holy Roman Empire. Frederick's attempt to conquer northern Italy failed. The pope opposed him, because he was afraid that Frederick wanted to include Rome and the Papal States in his empire. The cities of northern Italy also opposed him. Together, the pope and the northern Italian cities defeated the army of Frederick I in 1176.

The struggle between popes and emperors weakened the Holy Roman Empire. The German emperors spent their time fighting in Italy. Back in Germany, powerful German lords ignored the emperors and created their own independent kingdoms. In the end, the Holy Roman Empire had no real power over either Germany or Italy. Germany and Italy continued to be made up of small, independent states. They did not develop national monarchies in the Middle Ages, like France and England did.

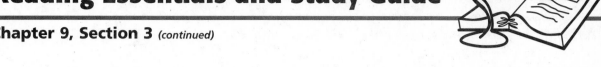

Reading Essentials and Study Guide

Chapter 9, Section 3 *(continued)*

15. What was the origin of the name Holy Roman Empire?

• Central and Eastern Europe *(page 300)*

The Slavic people were originally a single group of people in central Europe. Over time, they divided into three major groups: the western, southern, and eastern Slavs. The western Slavs formed the Polish and Bohemian kingdoms. German monks converted the Czechs in Bohemia and the Slavs in Poland to Christianity. The kingdom of Hungary was also converted. Czechs, Poles, and Hungarians all became part of the Roman Catholic Church.

The eastern and southern Slavs took a different path. Byzantine missionaries converted the eastern Slavs of Moravia to Eastern Orthodox Christianity. Most of the southern Slavs also converted to Eastern Orthodox Christianity. These peoples included the Croats, the Serbs, and the Bulgarians. By accepting Eastern Orthodox Christianity, the southern and eastern Slavs were linked to the Byzantine culture.

16. In what way did the eastern and southern Slavs take a different path from the western Slavs?

• The Development of Russia *(page 301)*

Eastern Slavic peoples had also settled in what is now Ukraine and Russia. Beginning in the eighth century, Swedish Vikings moved into their lands. The native peoples called the Viking rulers the Rus. This is the origin of the name Russia. One Viking leader, Oleg, settled in Kiev at the beginning of the tenth century. He created a Rus state known as the principality of Kiev. His successors extended their control over the eastern Slavs and expanded the principality of Kiev. The Rus married Slavic wives, and they were gradually assimilated into the Slavic population. Byzantine missionaries began to come to the principality of Kiev. One Rus ruler, Vladimir, married the Byzantine emperor's sister and accepted Eastern Orthodox Christianity in 988. Orthodox Christianity became the official religion of the state. The principality of Kiev prospered and reached its high point in the first half of the eleventh century. But civil wars and invasions brought an end to this first Russian state in 1169.

In the thirteenth century, the Mongols conquered Russia. They occupied Russian lands and made the Russian princes pay tribute to them. One of the Russian princes, Alexander Nevsky, defeated a German army in northwestern Russia in 1242. The leader of the western Mongol Empire gave Nevsky the title of grand-prince. His descendants became princes of Moscow and eventually leaders of all Russia.

17. What is the origin of the name Russia?

____

____

____

____

____

Name ______________________ Date ______________________ Class ______________________

Reading Essentials and Study Guide

Chapter 9, Section 4

For use with textbook pages 303–308

THE BYZANTINE EMPIRE AND THE CRUSADES

KEY TERMS

patriarch the head of the Eastern Orthodox Church *(page 305)*

schism the separation of Christianity into two branches, Roman Catholic and Eastern Orthodox *(page 305)*

Crusades military expeditions made by European Christians to regain the Holy Land from the Muslims *(page 306)*

infidel (unbeliever) the Crusaders' term for a Muslim *(page 306)*

DRAWING FROM EXPERIENCE

How does trade with other countries affect you? What items do you buy that are imported from other countries?

In the last section, you learned about the development of European kingdoms. In this section, you will read about the development of the Byzantine Empire. The capital of this empire, Constantinople, was the chief center of trade during the Middle Ages.

ORGANIZING YOUR THOUGHTS

Use the chart below to help you take notes. There were several key differences between the Western Roman Empire and the Eastern Roman, or Byzantine, Empire. Summarize some of those differences in the chart below.

Empire	Language	Capital	Church	Head of Church
Western Roman (refer to Chapter 5)	**1.**	**2.**	**3.**	**4.**
Eastern Roman/ Byzantine	**5.**	**6.**	**7.**	**8.**

Name ______________________ Date ______________ Class ______________

READ TO LEARN

• The Reign of Justinian *(page 303)*

Justinian became emperor of the Eastern Roman Empire in 527. He was determined to reestablish the Roman Empire in the Mediterranean. By 552, his empire included Italy, part of Spain, North Africa, Asia Minor, Palestine, and Syria.

Riots in Constantinople in 532 destroyed much of the city. Justinian rebuilt the city and gave it the appearance that it would have for almost a thousand years. Justinian also simplified Roman laws into a code of laws called *The Body of Civil Law*. This code was the basis of law in the Eastern Roman Empire and was also used in the West. It became the basis for much of the legal system of Europe.

9. What were Justinian's main accomplishments?

____

____

____

____

• From Eastern Roman Empire to Byzantine Empire *(page 304)*

Justinian's conquests left the Eastern Roman Empire with serious problems. There was too much territory to protect, an empty treasury, and new threats to the frontiers of the empire. Within three years of Justinian's death in 565, the Lombards had conquered much of Italy. Other areas were soon lost. Islamic forces defeated an army of the Eastern Roman Empire at Yarmuk in 636. As a result, the empire lost the provinces of Syria and Palestine. In 679, the Bulgars took possession of the lower Danube Valley. By the beginning of the eighth century, the Eastern Roman Empire was much smaller. It consisted only of the eastern Balkans and Asia Minor. Historians call this smaller Eastern Roman Empire the **Byzantine Empire.** This empire lasted until 1453.

The Byzantine Empire was different from the Western Roman Empire in many ways. Greek replaced Latin as the official language of the Byzantine Empire. The Christian church of the Byzantine Empire became known as the Eastern Orthodox Church. The Byzantines believed that God had commanded their state to preserve the true Christian faith. They also believed that God chose the emperor. The emperor appointed the head of the Eastern Orthodox Church, known as the **patriarch.** As a result, the emperor had control over the church as well as the state.

10. How did the emperor of the Byzantine Empire control the church as well as the state?

____

____

____

• Life in Constantinople *(page 305)*

Constantinople was the largest city in Europe during the Middle Ages. Until the twelfth century, it was also Europe's chief center of trade between West and East. Many goods from China, Southeast Asia, India, Russia, and the Balkans arrived in Constantinople and were shipped from there to the Mediterranean area and northern Europe. Raw materials were also imported and were used by local industries in Constantinople. In Justinian's reign, silkworms were smuggled from China by two Byzantine monks. A silk industry developed in Constantinople, and silk became the city's most desired product.

The city of Constantinople included an immense palace complex, hundreds of churches, and a huge arena, known as the Hippodrome. Both gladiator fights and chariot races were held in the Hippodrome. Most of these buildings had been constructed during Justinian's reign. His greatest achievement was the famous Hagia Sophia, the Church of the Holy Wisdom. Justinian also built many roads, bridges, walls, public baths, courts, and schools, as well as underground reservoirs to hold the city's water supply.

11. Why did Constantinople become a major center of trade?

____

____

____

• New Heights and New Problems *(page 305)*

From 867 to 1081, a new dynasty of emperors ruled the Byzantine Empire. They were known as the Macedonians. They expanded the empire to include Bulgaria, the islands of Crete and Cyprus, and Syria. By 1025, the Byzantine Empire was the largest it had been since the beginning of the seventh century. The Macedonians also created a time of prosperity by expanding trade with western Europe. The Macedonian dynasty restored much of the power of the Byzantine Empire during the tenth and eleventh centuries, but later rulers undid most of the gains. In the late eleventh century, there were struggles for power between military leaders and aristocratic families. This led to political and social disorder.

Reading Essentials and Study Guide

Chapter 9, Section 4 *(continued)*

During the eleventh century, there was also a split between the Eastern Orthodox Church and the Roman Catholic Church. The Eastern Orthodox Church was unwilling to accept the pope's claim that he was the sole head of the Christian faith. In 1054, Pope Leo IX and Michael Cerularius, the patriarch of the Byzantine Church, excommunicated each other. (Each took away the other's right of church membership.) This began a **schism,** or separation, between the two branches of Christianity.

In the eleventh century, the Seljuk Turks moved into Asia Minor. This threatened the Byzantine Empire, because Asia Minor was the heartland of the empire and the main source of food and workers. In 1071, a Turkish army defeated Byzantine forces at Manzikert.

12. What event started the schism between the Eastern Orthodox Church and Roman Catholic Church?

____

____

____

____

____

• The Crusades *(page 306)*

From the eleventh to the thirteenth centuries, European Christians carried out a series of military expeditions to regain the Holy Land. These expeditions are known as the **Crusades.**

The push for the Crusades began when the Byzantine emperor Alexius I asked the Europeans for help against the Seljuk Turks. Because the Seljuk Turks were Muslims, Pope Urban II agreed to help. He challenged Christians to take up weapons and join in a holy war to liberate Jerusalem and the Holy Land (Palestine) from the Muslims. The Muslims were called **infidels** (unbelievers) by the Christians.

Warriors from western Europe, particularly France, formed the first crusading army. Most of the knights who made up this army were motivated by religious fervor, but some were seeking adventure. Others saw this as an opportunity to gain territory, riches, and possibly a title. The crusading army captured Antioch in 1098. The crusaders reached Jerusalem in June 1099. They took control of the city and massacred the inhabitants. The crusaders created four crusader states. These states depended on Italian cities for supplies from Europe. As a result, some Italian port cities, such as Genoa, Pisa, and Venice, became rich and powerful.

Reading Essentials and Study Guide

Chapter 9, Section 4 *(continued)*

By the 1120s, the Muslims had begun to strike back. Saint Bernard of Clairvaux enlisted the help of King Louis VII of France and Emperor Conrad II of Germany to start a Second Crusade. This crusade was a total failure. In 1187, Jerusalem fell to Muslim forces under the command of Saladin. Three important rulers then agreed to lead a Third Crusade. These three rulers were Emperor Frederick Barbarossa of Germany, Richard I (Richard the Lionhearted) of England, and Philip II Augustus of France. The Third Crusade also failed. Richard the Lionhearted finally negotiated a settlement with Saladin. Saladin agreed to allow Christian pilgrims free access to Jerusalem.

After the death of Saladin in 1193, Pope Innocent III started the Fourth Crusade. Leaders of the Fourth Crusade from Venice saw an opportunity to eliminate their main trade competitor, Constantinople. The crusading army was sent to Constantinople and sacked the city in 1204. In 1261, a Byzantine army was able to regain the city, but the Byzantine Empire was no longer a great Mediterranean power. The empire survived for another 190 years, but the Ottoman Turks finally conquered it in 1453.

Historians disagree about the effect of the Crusades on European civilization. The Crusades helped the Italian port cities, but the Crusades also had unfortunate side effects. The first widespread attacks against Jews began during the Crusades. Many Christians believed that the Jews were the "murderers of Christ." They believed that both the Muslims and the Jews should be eliminated. Many Jews were massacred during the Middle Ages.

13. What are some of the reasons that Europeans took part in the Crusades?

Name ______________________ Date ________________ Class ________________

Reading Essentials and Study Guide

Chapter 10, Section 1

For use with textbook pages 315–322

PEASANTS, TRADE, AND CITIES

KEY TERMS

manor an agricultural estate run by a lord and worked by peasants *(page 317)*

serf a peasant legally bound to the land *(page 317)*

money economy an economic system based on money, rather than barter *(page 320)*

commercial capitalism an economic system in which people invest in trade and goods in order to make profits *(page 320)*

guild a business association, or association of craftspeople, in the Middle Ages *(page 322)*

masterpiece a finished piece in a craft that was used to judge whether a journeyman was qualified to become a master and join a guild *(page 322)*

DRAWING FROM EXPERIENCE

How does money affect your ability to get the things you need? Could you get what you need by trading with people, without using money?

In this section, you will learn about daily life during the Middle Ages. It was during this period that a money economy began to emerge in Europe.

ORGANIZING YOUR THOUGHTS

Use the diagram below to help you take notes. Several factors led to an increase in food production during the High Middle Ages. List five of those factors.

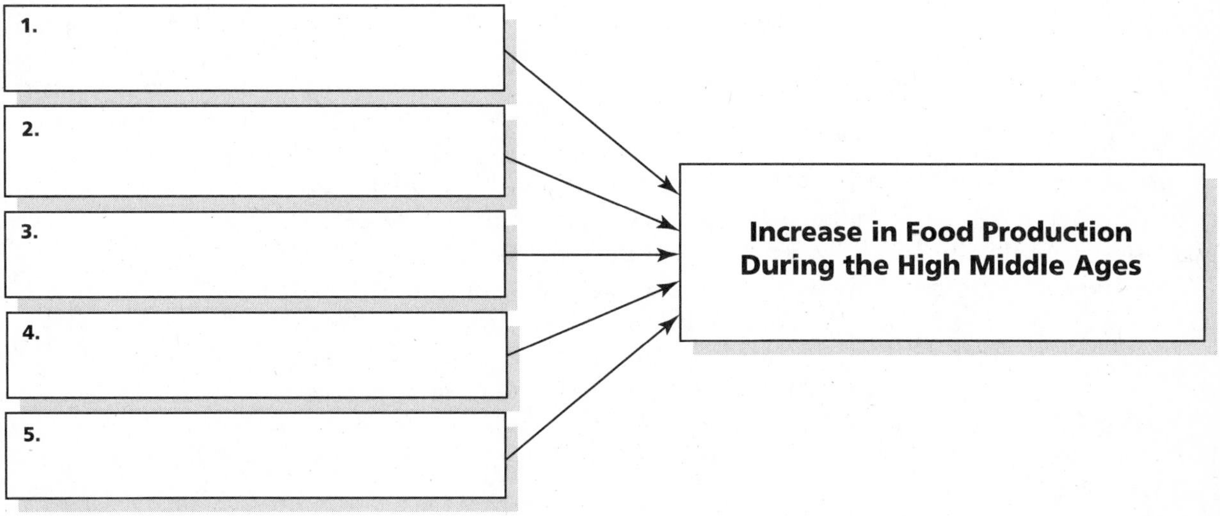

READ TO LEARN

• The New Agriculture *(page 315)*

In the early Middle Ages, Europe had a relatively small population. Between 1000 and 1300, however, the population almost doubled, from 38 million to 74 million people. This period is called the High Middle Ages. During this period, food production increased dramatically. There were several reasons for this increase. There was more peace and stability during this time, because the invasions of the early Middle Ages had stopped. There was also a change in climate during the High Middle Ages that improved growing conditions. There was also more land to farm, because peasants cut down trees and drained swamps. New inventions also helped the development of farming. Two of these inventions, the horse collar and the horseshoe, made it possible for horses to plow fields instead of oxen. Because horses were faster, this increased production. The shift from a two-field to a three-field system of crop rotation also added to the increase in food production.

Labor-saving devices were also invented during this time. The people of the Middle Ages used the power of water and wind to do jobs such as grinding grain that had previously been done by humans or animals. Iron was mined in various areas of Europe and was used to make tools for farming and building. Iron was crucial for making the *carruca*, a heavy, wheeled plow with an iron plowshare that could turn over heavy clay soils. The use of this plow led to the growth of farming villages. Plows and teams of horses were too expensive to be bought by one family, so the entire village shared the cost.

6. How did the use of the *carruca* lead to the growth of farming villages?

____

____

____

____

• The Manorial System *(page 317)*

A **manor** was an agricultural estate run by a lord and worked by peasants. Although there were free peasants, more and more peasants became serfs. **Serfs** were peasants who were legally bound to the land. Serfs had to work for the lord and pay rents, and they were subject to the lord's control. By 800, probably 60 percent of the people of western Europe were serfs. A serf's work included farming the lord's land, building barns, and digging ditches. Serfs usually worked about three days a week for their lords. The rest of the week, they worked their own land to grow food for themselves. The serfs paid rent by giving the lords a share of everything they raised.

Lords had various legal rights over their serfs. Serfs could not leave the manor, or marry anyone outside the manor, without the lord's approval. Peasants also had to pay lords for certain services, such as having their grain ground in the lords' mills. Some lords had the authority to try peasants in their own courts. But serfs were not slaves. The land assigned to serfs to support themselves could not be taken away, and their responsibilities to the lord were fairly fixed. It was also the lord's duty to protect his serfs.

7. How were serfs different from slaves?

____

____

____

____

• Daily Life of the Peasantry *(page 318)*

The life of peasants in Europe was simple. Their houses were made of wood frames surrounded by sticks. The spaces between sticks were filled with straw and then plastered over with clay. Most houses consisted of one or two rooms. The basic staple of a peasant's diet was bread. It was very nutritious because it was made of wheat, rye, barley, millet, and oats. Peasants also ate vegetables from their gardens, cheese from cow's or goat's milk, and nuts, berries and fruit. Chickens provided eggs and sometimes meat. Peasants usually ate meat only on the great feast days, like Christmas and Easter.

The seasons of the year determined most of a peasant's activities. Harvest time was in August and September. In October, peasants worked the ground for the planting of winter crops. In November, excess livestock were slaughtered. In February and March, the land was plowed for the planting of spring crops. Early summer was a fairly relaxed time, but there was still weeding and sheepshearing to be done. In every season, the serfs worked both their own land and the lords' land. They also tended gardens next to their homes. Peasants had breaks from their work, however, thanks to the feast days (holidays) of the Catholic Church. The feast days celebrated the great events of the Christian faith or the lives of Christian saints. A total of more than 50 days were holidays. The feast days, Sunday mass, baptisms, marriages, and funerals brought peasants into contact with the village church. The village priest taught the peasants the basic ideas of Christianity so that they could gain the Christians' final goal—salvation.

The role of peasant women was both important and difficult. They had to work in the fields and at the same time bear children. Their ability to manage the household could determine whether their family would starve or survive in difficult times.

Name ______________________ Date ______________________ Class ______________________

Reading Essentials and Study Guide

8. What events gave peasants a break from their work?

____

____

____

____

• The Revival of Trade *(page 319)*

The revival of trade in Europe was gradual. Cities in Italy took the lead. Venice developed a fleet of trading ships and became a major trade center by the end of the tenth century. While Venice and other Italian cities were busy trading in the Mediterranean, the towns of Flanders were doing the same in northern Europe. Flanders was the area along the coast of what is now Belgium and northern France. Its location made it an ideal center for the traders of northern Europe. Merchants from England, Scandinavia, France, and Germany met there to trade their goods for the woolen cloth made in Flanders. By the twelfth century, trade developed between Flanders and Italy. As trade increased, demand for gold and silver coins arose. A money economy slowly began to emerge. A **money economy** is an economic system based on money rather than barter. Trading companies and banking firms were set up to manage the sale of goods. All of these practices were part of the rise of **commercial capitalism,** an economic system in which people invest in trade and goods in order to make profits.

9. What two areas in Europe were major trading centers during the Middle Ages?

____

____

____

____

• The Growth of Cities *(page 320)*

The revival of trade led to a revival of cities. Merchants began to settle in the old Roman cities. They were followed by craftspeople who could make goods for the merchants to sell. Many new cities and towns were founded in northern Europe. Merchants usually built settlements near castles because the castles were located on trade routes and could offer protection. Walls were built to protect the settlements. Merchants and artisans of these cities became known as *burghers* or *bourgeoisie.* (These words come from the German word *burg,* which means "a walled enclosure.") Medieval cities were small in comparison with ancient or modern cities. A large trading city had about five thousand people.

Reading Essentials and Study Guide

Chapter 10, Section 1 *(continued)*

Most towns were dependent on the food grown in the surrounding manors. The towns were often part of the territory that belonged to a lord and were subject to his authority. But townspeople needed the freedom to trade. They also needed their own laws and were willing to pay for them. Lords and kings saw this as an opportunity to make money and were willing to sell the townspeople the rights they wanted. These included the right to buy and sell property and freedom from military service. Some new towns also received the right to govern themselves by electing their own officials and having their own courts. Over time, medieval cities developed their own governments. Only males who had been born in the city, or who had lived there for some time, were citizens. In many cities, these citizens elected a city council. The members of the city council served as judges and passed laws. Elections were usually rigged to make sure that only patricians (members of the wealthiest families) were elected.

10. What rights were townspeople willing to buy from lords and kings?

____

____

____

• Daily Life in the Medieval City *(page 321)*

Stone walls surrounded medieval towns. The walls were expensive to build, so the space inside was limited and crowded. Streets were narrow, and houses were built against one another. The second and third stories were built out over the streets. The houses were built mostly of wood, so the danger of fire was great. The cities were often dirty and smelled from animal and human waste. Air pollution and water pollution were a fact of life. Because of pollution, cities did not use the rivers for drinking water, but relied on wells instead.

There were more men than women in the medieval cities. Women were expected to supervise the household, prepare meals, raise the children, and manage the family's finances. They were often expected to help their husbands in their trades, as well. Some women developed their own trades to earn extra money. Many women became brewers, weavers, and hatmakers.

11. Why were medieval towns so crowded?

____

____

____

• Industry and Guilds *(page 322)*

From the twelfth century on, craftspeople began to organize themselves into **guilds,** or business associations. There were guilds for almost every craft. There were also guilds for groups of merchants, such as dealers in silk and wool. Craft guilds directed almost every aspect of the production process. They set the standards for the goods produced and determined the prices for the goods. They also determined the number of people who could enter a trade and what procedure they had to follow to do so. A person who wanted to learn a trade first became an apprentice, usually around the age of 10. Apprentices were not paid but received room and board from their masters. After five to seven years of service, apprentices became journeymen and worked for wages. To become masters, journeymen had to produce a **masterpiece,** a finished piece in their craft. This piece was used to judge whether a journeyman was qualified to become a master and join the guild.

12. What process did a person follow to learn a trade and join a guild?

____

____

____

____

____

Name ______________________ Date ______________________ Class ______________________

Reading Essentials and Study Guide

Chapter 10, Section 2

For use with textbook pages 323–328

CHRISTIANITY AND MEDIEVAL CIVILIZATION

KEY TERMS

lay investiture a practice in which secular (lay) rulers gave the symbols of office to church officials they had chosen *(page 324)*

interdict a command by the pope forbidding priests from giving the sacraments of the Church to a particular group of people *(page 325)*

sacraments Christian rites, such as baptism, marriage, and communion *(page 325)*

heresy the denial of basic Church doctrines *(page 326)*

Inquisition a medieval court whose job was to find and try heretics *(page 326)*

relic an object connected with a saint that was considered worthy of worship *(page 328)*

DRAWING FROM EXPERIENCE

What do you think people expect from their spiritual or religious leaders? Do you think religious leaders should be involved in government or in social issues? Why or why not?

In the last section, you learned about daily life in Europe during the Middle Ages. In this section, you will learn about the role of the Church in medieval society.

ORGANIZING YOUR THOUGHTS

Use the chart below to help you take notes. New religious orders emerged during the Middle Ages. Compare three of those orders, the Cistercians, the Franciscans, and the Dominicans, in the chart below.

Religious Order	Founder(s)	Main Emphases
Cistercians	1.	2.
Franciscans	3.	4.
Dominicans	5.	6.

Reading Essentials and Study Guide

READ TO LEARN

• The Papal Monarchy *(page 323)*

The popes of the Catholic Church were the spiritual leaders of the Church, but they also had political power. They had control of territories in central Italy that were known as the Papal States. Other church officials, such as bishops and abbots, also had political ties. When a person became a church official, he was given a ring and staff. These objects symbolized the spiritual authority that the official was granted, or *invested* with, by the Church. Secular (lay) rulers usually chose the nominees to church offices and also gave them the symbols of their office. This practice was known as **lay investiture.** Bishops and abbots were often chosen by the lay rulers for political reasons. Church officials became involved in political matters, often at the expense of their spiritual duties.

Gregory VII was elected pope in 1073. He realized the need to be free from secular involvement in the appointment of church officials. He decided to reform the Church. He claimed that his authority extended over all the Christian world, including its rulers. He also claimed that the Church had the right to appoint clergy and run its own affairs. If rulers did not accept this, the pope would remove them. These claims brought Pope Gregory into conflict with Henry IV, the king of Germany. German kings appointed high-ranking clergy as their vassals so that they could use them as administrators. Eliminating lay investiture threatened the king's ability to administer his kingdom.

In 1075, Pope Gregory issued a decree forbidding high-ranking clergy from receiving their investiture from lay leaders. Henry IV had no intention of obeying this decree. The struggle between Henry IV and Gregory VII is known as the Investiture Controversy. The struggle continued until there was a new king and a new pope. They reached an agreement in 1122 called the Concordat of Worms. Under this agreement, Church officials elected a bishop in Germany, but the new bishop paid homage to the king as his lord. The king then invested him with the symbols of a temporal (worldly) office. A representative of the pope invested the bishop with the symbols of his spiritual office.

During the papacy of Pope Innocent III in the thirteenth century, the Catholic Church reached the height of its political power. Innocent III forced the King of France, Philip Augustus, to take back his wife after Philip had tried to have his marriage annulled. The pope also forced King John of England to accept the pope's choice for the archbishop of Canterbury. Pope Innocent was able to force the kings to do what he wanted by using interdicts. An **interdict** forbids priests from giving the **sacraments** (Christian rites) to a particular group of people. The sacraments included baptism, marriage, and the Eucharist (Communion). When people were denied the sacraments, they put pressure on their rulers to do what the pope wanted.

7. How were popes able to force rulers to do what they wanted?

____

____

____

• New Religious Orders *(page 325)*

In the second half of the eleventh century and the first half of the twelfth century, more and more men and women joined religious orders. The most important new order of the early Middle Ages was the Cistercian order. It was founded in 1098 by a group of Benedictine monks who were unhappy with the lack of discipline at their own monastery. The Cistercians were strict. They ate a simple diet and each had only one robe. They spent less time at religious services and more time in prayer and manual labor. While Benedictine monks spent most of their time inside the monastery, the Cistercians took their religion to the people outside the monastery.

The number of women who joined convents grew dramatically during this time. In the High Middle Ages, most nuns were from aristocratic families. Convents were convenient for families who were unable or unwilling to find husbands for their daughters. Widows and women who did not wish to marry also joined convents. Most of the learned women of the Middle Ages were nuns. One famous example is Hildegard of Bingen. She became the abbess of a convent in western Germany. She was also one of the first important women composers. She made important contributions to the body of music known as the Gregorian chant.

In the thirteenth century, two new religious orders emerged. These orders had a strong impact on the lives of ordinary people. They were the Franciscans and the Dominicans. Saint Francis of Assisi founded the Franciscans. Although he was born to a wealthy Italian family, Saint Francis gave up his riches. His followers took vows of poverty and agreed to live by working and begging for their food. The Franciscans lived among the people, preaching repentance and simplicity and helping the poor. The Franciscans were also missionaries. They traveled throughout Italy and then to all parts of Europe and even to the Muslim world.

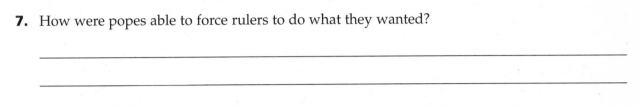

A Spanish priest, Dominic de Guzmán, founded the Dominican order. Dominic wanted to defend Church teachings from heresy. **Heresy** is the denial of basic Church doctrines. The Church's desire to deal with heretics (people who believed in heresies) led to the creation of a court called the **Inquisition.** The job of this court was to find and try heretics. The Dominicans were often the examiners of people suspected of heresy. If an accused heretic confessed, he or she was forced to repent publicly and then was physically punished, often by flogging. Beginning in 1252, people who did not confess were tor-

Reading Essentials and Study Guide

tured until they did confess. Many did not confess but were still considered guilty and were executed. The Christians of this time thought that heresy was a crime against God. They thought that using force to save souls from damnation was the right thing to do.

8. How did the Church deal with heretics during the Middle Ages?

____

____

____

• Popular Religion in the High Middle Ages *(page 327)*

The sacraments made the Church a crucial part of people's lives during the Middle Ages. The sacraments were seen as the means for receiving God's grace and were considered necessary for salvation. Only the clergy could administer the sacraments, so everyone who hoped to gain salvation depended on the clergy to help them. The veneration of saints was also important during the Middle Ages. Saints were men and women who were considered especially holy. It was believed that they had achieved a special position in heaven that allowed them to ask for favors from God for people who prayed to them. The Virgin Mary, mother of Jesus, was the most highly regarded of all the saints. A sign of Mary's importance is the number of churches all over Europe that were dedicated to her in the twelfth and thirteenth centuries. In France, these churches were named *Notre Dame* ("Our Lady"). **Relics** of the saints were often worshipped. Relics were usually bones of saints or objects connected with saints that were considered worthy of worship because they linked the earthly world and God. It was believed that relics could heal people or produce other miracles. Medieval Christians also believed that pilgrimages to holy shrines had spiritual benefits. The greatest shrine, but the most difficult to reach, was the Holy City of Jerusalem. Shrines dedicated to the Virgin Mary also became pilgrimage centers.

9. Why was the clergy so important in the lives of medieval people?

____

____

____

____

____

Name ______________________ Date ______________________ Class ______________________

Reading Essentials and Study Guide

Chapter 10, Section 3

For use with textbook pages 329–333

THE CULTURE OF THE HIGH MIDDLE AGES

KEY TERMS

theology the study of religion and God *(page 330)*

scholasticism a philosophical and theological system that tried to reconcile faith and reason *(page 330)*

vernacular the language of everyday speech in a particular region *(page 331)*

DRAWING FROM EXPERIENCE

Have you ever visited a university? Why do people attend universities? Do you plan to attend a university?

In the last section, you learned about the role of the Church in medieval life. In this section, you will learn about the role of universities and the development of literature and architecture during this period.

ORGANIZING YOUR THOUGHTS

Use the concept web below to help you take notes. Students at medieval universities began their studies with the traditional liberal arts curriculum. List the seven subjects that were studied in that curriculum.

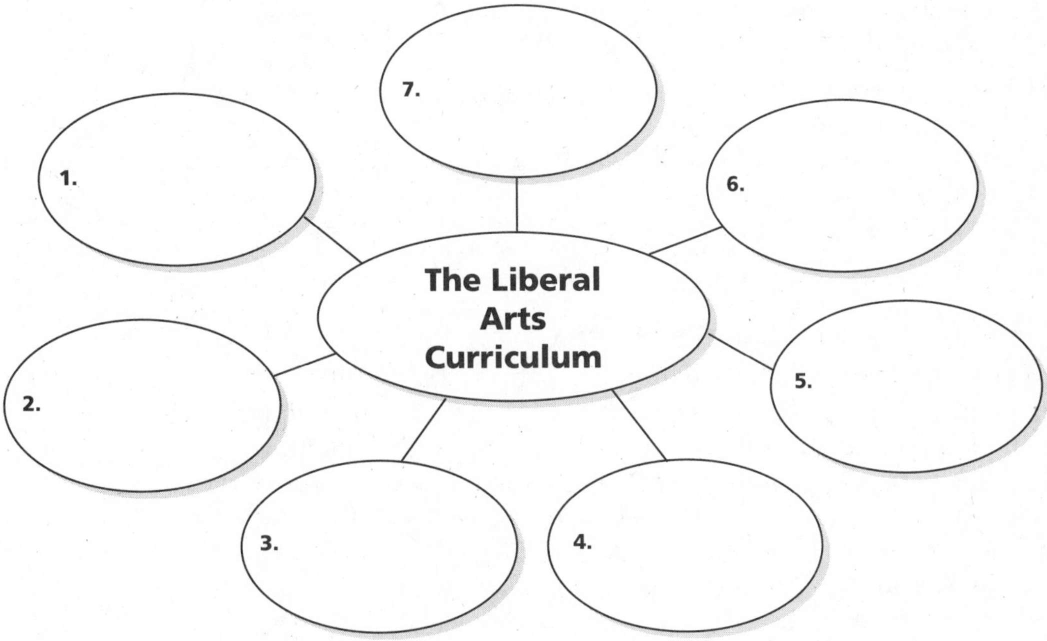

READ TO LEARN

• The Rise of Universities *(page 329)*

The university as we know it today was a product of the Middle Ages. The word *university* comes from the Latin word *universitas,* which means "corporation" or "guild." Like other guilds, universities had a product. They "produced" educated and trained people. The first European university was started in Bologna, Italy. The first university in northern Europe was the University of Paris. In the second half of the twelfth century, several students and teachers left Paris and started their own university at Oxford in England. By 1500, there were 80 universities in Europe.

Students began their studies at a medieval university with the traditional liberal arts curriculum (course of study). This curriculum consisted of grammar, rhetoric, logic, arithmetic, geometry, music, and astronomy. Teaching at medieval universities was done by a lecture method. Few students could afford books, so teachers read from a basic text and then added their own explanations. (The word *lecture* is derived from Latin and means "to read.") No exams were given until a student applied for a degree. At that time, a committee of teachers gave the student an oral examination. The first degree a student could earn was a bachelor of arts. Later, he might earn a master of arts. After completing the liberal arts curriculum, a student could go on to study law, medicine, or theology. **Theology** is the study of religion and God, and it was the most highly regarded subject at medieval universities. A student who passed his oral examinations in one of these areas was granted a doctor's degree. Those who earned doctor's degrees were able to teach, but they also pursued other careers. Universities provided the teachers, administrators, lawyers, and doctors for medieval society.

8. What was the most highly regarded subject at medieval universities?

____

____

____

• The Development of Scholasticism *(page 330)*

The study of theology was strongly influenced by scholasticism. **Scholasticism** was a philosophical and theological system that tried to reconcile faith and reason. It tried to show that what was accepted on faith was in harmony with what could be learned through reason and experience. In the twelfth century, western Europe was introduced to the works of Aristotle, and these works upset many Christian theologians. Aristotle had arrived at his conclusions by reason, not by faith, and some of his ideas contradicted the teachings of the Church. In the thirteenth century, Saint Thomas Aquinas

Reading Essentials and Study Guide

attempted to reconcile Aristotle with Christian doctrines. Thomas Aquinas is best known for his *Summa Theologica*. He tried to reconcile the Bible and other Christian writings with the knowledge learned through reason and experience. He believed that some truths were learned by reason and other truths were learned by faith and that they did not contradict each other.

9. What is scholasticism?

____

____

____

• Vernacular Literature *(page 331)*

Latin was the universal language of medieval civilization. It was used in the Church and in schools and allowed educated people to communicate anywhere in Europe. However, by the twelfth century, many works of literature were being written in the **vernacular**—the language of everyday speech in a particular region, such as Spanish, French, English, or German. One of the most popular forms of vernacular literature in the twelfth century was troubadour poetry. This poetry told of the love of a knight for a lady. Another type of vernacular literature was the chanson de geste, or heroic epic. The earliest and greatest example is the *Song of Roland*. It appeared around 1100 and was written in French. The chief events in heroic epic poems are battles and political contests.

10. What is vernacular literature?

____

____

____

• Architecture *(page 333)*

During the eleventh and twelfth centuries, there was an explosion of building in Europe, especially the building of churches. The cathedrals of the eleventh and twelfth centuries were built in the Romanesque style. The Romanesque churches had a basilica shape like the churches in the late Roman Empire. Basilicas were rectangular buildings with flat wood roofs. Romanesque builders replaced the flat roof with a stone arched structure, called a barrel vault. Stone roofs were very heavy, so Romanesque churches needed massive pillars and walls to hold them up. There was little space for windows, so Romanesque churches were very dark.

Reading Essentials and Study Guide

Chapter 10, Section 3 *(continued)*

A new style, called Gothic, appeared in the twelfth century. The Gothic cathedral was one of the greatest artistic accomplishments of the High Middle Ages. In Gothic cathedrals, the barrel vault was replaced with a combination of ribbed vaults and pointed arches. This made Gothic churches higher than Romanesque churches and created an impression of upward movement. The buildings looked as if they were reaching to God. Gothic cathedrals also used flying buttresses. A flying buttress is a heavy, arched support built onto the outside of the walls. Flying buttresses made it possible to distribute the weight of the vaulted ceilings outward and down. Heavy walls were no longer needed for support, so the walls could be filled with stained glass windows. These windows depicted religious scenes and scenes from daily life.

11. How were Gothic cathedrals different from Romanesque cathedrals?

____

____

____

____

____

Name ______________________ Date ________________ Class ________________

Reading Essentials and Study Guide

Chapter 10, Section 4

For use with textbook pages 335–340

THE LATE MIDDLE AGES

KEY TERMS

Black Death a plague that killed nearly half of the population in Europe between 1347 and 1351 *(page 335)*

anti-Semitism hostility toward Jews *(page 336)*

Great Schism the period from 1378 to 1417 when there were two popes, one in Rome and one in Avignon *(page 337)*

new monarchies monarchies, such as France, England, and Spain, that reestablished centralized power in the late fifteenth century *(page 339)*

taille an annual direct tax, usually on land or property *(page 339)*

DRAWING FROM EXPERIENCE

Have you heard of a person known as Joan of Arc? Why is she so famous?

In the last section, you learned about the culture of the High Middle Ages. In this section, you will learn about some disastrous changes that took place in the late Middle Ages.

ORGANIZING YOUR THOUGHTS

Use the diagram below to help you take notes. The Black Death killed nearly half of the European population in the late Middle Ages. In the diagram below, list five other consequences of the plague.

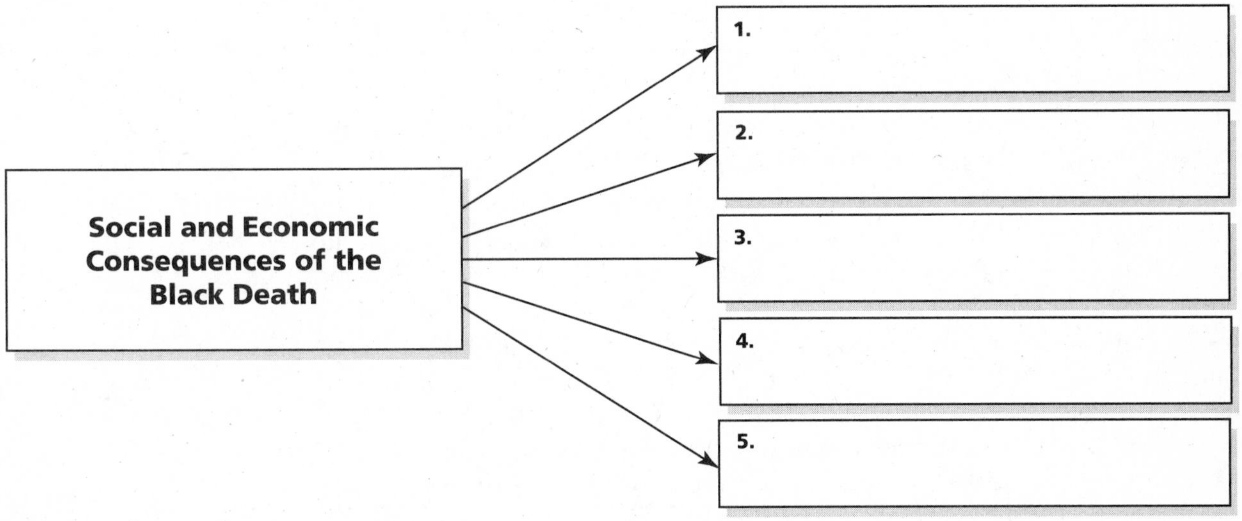

READ TO LEARN

• The Black Death *(page 335)*

The Middle Ages in Europe reached a high point in the thirteenth century. In the fourteenth century, some disastrous changes took place. The most catastrophic event was the Black Death. It was the worst natural disaster in European history. Bubonic plague was the most common form of the Black Death. Black rats infested with fleas carrying a bacterium spread it. People at the time did not know this, however. Italian merchants brought the plague with them from Caffa, on the Black Sea, to Sicily in 1347. It spread northward along the trade routes. By 1351, it had spread through Italy, Spain, France, the Low Countries, Germany, England, Scandinavia, Eastern Europe, and Russia. Out of a total European population of 75 million, as many as 38 million people died of the plague between 1347 and 1351.

Because people did not know what caused the plague, they believed that God either sent it as a punishment for their sins or that it was caused by the devil. In some towns, Jews were accused of causing the plague by poisoning town wells. This led to an outbreak of **anti-Semitism** (hostility toward Jews). The worst attacks on Jews took place in Germany. Many Jews fled eastward, especially to Poland, during this time. The death of so many people also had severe economic consequences. Trade declined, and some industries were severely affected. A shortage of workers caused the price of labor to rise. Because there were fewer people, the demand for food declined. This resulted in lower food prices. Landlords were now paying more for labor, while their incomes were declining. Some peasants bargained with their lords to pay rents instead of owing services. This change freed them from serfdom.

6. How did medieval people explain the Black Death?

____

____

____

• The Decline of Church Power *(page 337)*

In the fourteenth century, a series of problems led to a decline in the Church's power. King Philip IV of France claimed that he had a right to tax the clergy of France. However, the pope at the time, Boniface VIII, said that the clergy could not pay taxes to their ruler without the pope's consent. Boniface claimed that popes were supreme over both the Church and the state. Philip IV refused to accept the pope's claims. He sent French forces to Italy to bring Boniface to France for trial. The pope escaped but died soon afterward. Philip IV rigged the election of the next pope, so that a Frenchman was elected. This pope, Clement V, was elected in 1305 and took up residence in Avignon, in southern France. From 1305 to 1377, the popes lived in

Reading Essentials and Study Guide

Chapter 10, Section 4 *(continued)*

Avignon. But the popes were criticized for living in Avignon, rather than Rome. They were also criticized because of the splendor in which they lived.

Pope Gregory XI returned to Rome in 1377, but he died soon after his return. When the college of cardinals met to elect a new pope, the citizens of Rome said that they would kill the cardinals if they did not elect an Italian. The cardinals elected Pope Urban VI, an Italian. Five months later, a group of French cardinals declared the election invalid and chose a Frenchman as pope. This pope returned to Avignon. There were now two popes, one in Rome and one in Avignon. The **Great Schism,** as this was called, lasted from 1378 to 1417. It divided Europe. France and its allies supported the pope in Avignon. England and its allies supported the pope in Rome. The Great Schism also damaged the Catholic Church. When each line of popes said the other was the Antichrist (one who opposes Christ), people's faith in the papacy and the Church were damaged. A church council finally met at Constance, Switzerland, and ended the schism in 1417. A new pope who was acceptable to both sides was elected.

The problems in the Catholic Church led to cries for reform. A group of Czech reformers led by John Hus called for an end to the corruption of the clergy and the excessive power of the papacy. Hus was accused of heresy and burned at the stake in 1415. This angered the Czechs and led to a revolution in Bohemia. By the early 1400s, the papacy and the Catholic Church had lost much of their political power and spiritual authority.

7. How did the Great Schism damage the Catholic Church's spiritual authority?

• The Hundred Years' War *(page 337)*

In the thirteenth century, England still held one small territory in France, known as the duchy of Gascony. The English king was also the duke of Gascony. When King Philip VI of France seized Gascony in 1337, King Edward III of England declared war on Philip. This began the Hundred Years' War between France and England. It was a turning point in warfare. Peasant foot soldiers, not knights, won the chief battles of the Hundred Years' War. The English foot soldiers were armed with longbows and arrows, as well as spears. The first major battle took place in 1346 at Crécy. The arrows of the English soldiers devastated the French cavalry. At the Battle of Agincourt in 1415, the French were again defeated. The English now had control of northern France.

The French cause seemed hopeless, until a French peasant woman decided to free France. Joan of Arc was born in 1412. She was a deeply religious person who experienced visions. In February 1429, she made her way to the court of Charles, the heir to the French throne. She persuaded him to allow her to accompany a French army to Orléans. The French soldiers found a new confidence in themselves and captured Orléans. Joan of Arc herself was captured in 1430 and turned over to the English. She was tried as a witch, because her visions were thought to be inspired by the devil. She was condemned to death and burnt at the stake. Joan of Arc's achievements were important, however. The French defeated the English in Normandy and Aquitaine and the war ended in 1453.

8. How did Joan of Arc affect the outcome of the Hundred Years' War?

____

____

____

____

____

• Political Recovery *(page 339)*

In the fourteenth century, European rulers faced serious problems. Many dynasties in Europe were unable to produce male heirs. Rulers often had to fight for their positions. They also had financial problems. In the fifteenth century, however, some rulers began to reestablish the centralized power of their monarchies. Some historians call these reestablished monarchies the **new monarchies.** The term applies especially to France, England, and Spain at the end of the fifteenth century.

The Hundred Years' War left France exhausted, but it also developed a strong national spirit. The kings used this spirit to reestablish royal power. King Louis XI, in particular, helped to develop a strong French state. He ruled from 1461 to 1483. He strengthened the use of the ***taille.*** The *taille* is an annual direct tax, usually on land or property. This tax gave Louis a regular source of income, which helped him to create a strong French monarchy.

The Hundred Years' War also affected the English. The cost of the war and the losses in manpower strained the economy. After the war, groups of nobles fought to control the monarchy. These conflicts are known as the War of the Roses. They ended in 1485, when Henry VII abolished the nobles' private armies. Henry VII was the first Tudor king. He gained the support of the nobles and the middle class by not overburdening them with taxes.

Name ______________________ Date ______________ Class ______________

Reading Essentials and Study Guide

Chapter 10, Section 4 *(continued)*

In Spain, Muslims had conquered much of the country by 725. During the Middle Ages, Christian rulers in Spain had fought to regain their lands from the Muslims. Several independent Christian kingdoms had emerged. Two of the strongest kingdoms were Aragon and Castile. When Isabella of Castile married Ferdinand of Aragon in 1469, it was a major step toward unifying Spain. Ferdinand and Isabella were also strict Catholics. In 1492, they expelled all Jews from Spain. In 1502, Isabella expelled all Muslims from her kingdom. Ferdinand and Isabella created religious uniformity in Spain. Being Spanish was the same as being Catholic.

The Holy Roman Empire did not develop a strong monarchy. Germany was made up of many states. Almost all of them acted independently of the emperor. After 1438, the position of Holy Roman emperor was held by the Hapsburg dynasty. The house of Hapsburg was one of the wealthiest landholders in the empire. By the mid-fifteenth century, the Hapsburg rulers began to play an important role in European affairs.

In eastern Europe, rulers also found it difficult to centralize their states. Religious differences were part of the problem. In Poland, the nobles established the right to elect their kings. This policy severely weakened the king's authority. In Russia, the Mongols had been in control since the thirteenth century. The princes of Moscow used their close relationship to the Mongol khans to increase their wealth and power. During the reign of the great prince Ivan III, a new Russian state was created. By 1480, the Mongols no longer controlled Russia.

9. Which European countries established strong centralized monarchies during the late Middle Ages?

____

____

____

____

____

Name ______________________ Date ______________ Class ______________

Reading Essentials and Study Guide

Chapter 11, Section 1

For use with textbook pages 347–350

THE PEOPLES OF NORTH AMERICA

KEY TERMS

longhouse an Iroquois house, built of wooden poles and covered with sheets of bark, that could house about a dozen families *(page 348)*

clan a group of related families *(page 349)*

tepee a circular tent made by stretching buffalo skins over wooden poles *(page 349)*

adobe sun-dried brick used to build pueblos *(page 350)*

pueblo a multi-storied structure built by the Anasazi that could house many people *(page 350)*

DRAWING FROM EXPERIENCE

Have you ever wondered about the earliest Americans? How did they get their food and shelter? What did their towns and cities look like?

In this section, you will learn how and why the first people came to the Americas. You will also learn about the cultures of the early peoples of North America.

ORGANIZING YOUR THOUGHTS

Use the chart below to help you take notes. Identify where the following Native Americans lived, how they got their food, and what shelters and other structures they built.

Native American Group	Location	Food	Buildings
The Inuit	**1.**	**2.**	**3.**
The Hopewell People (The Mound Builders)	**4.**	**5.**	**6.**
The Iroquois	**7.**	**8.**	**9.**
The Peoples of the Great Plains	**10.**	**11.**	**12.**
The Anasazi	**13.**	**14.**	**15.**

Name ______________________ Date ________________ Class ________________

Reading Essentials and Study Guide

READ TO LEARN

• The Lands of the Americas *(page 347)*

The Americas cover an enormous land area, from the Arctic Ocean in the north to Cape Horn at the tip of South America. Over this huge area, there are many different landscapes: ice-covered lands, dense forests, fertile river valleys, coastlines, tropical forests, and hot deserts. On the western side of the Americas, there are two major mountain ranges, the Rocky Mountains in North America and the Andes in South America. There are lower mountain ranges along the eastern coasts. Between the mountain ranges there are valleys with rich farmland. Great rivers run through the valleys. The two largest are the Mississippi in North American and the Amazon in South America.

16. What are the two major mountain ranges in the Americas?

____

____

____

• The First Americans *(page 348)*

No one knows for sure when the first human beings began to live in the Americas. Scholars do know that between 100,000 and 8,000 years ago, the last Ice Age produced low sea levels. The low sea levels created a land bridge in the Bering Strait between Asia and North America. Historians believe that small groups of people from Asia crossed the Bering Strait into North America. They were probably hunters who were following herds of bison and caribou. These people became the first Americans.

17. How did the first Americans cross from Asia into North America?

____

____

____

• The Peoples of North America *(page 348)*

About 4000 B.C., a group of people called the Inuit moved into North America. They settled along the coasts of the tundra region. The tundra region is the treeless area south of the Arctic. They had to learn ways to survive in such a cold environment. They hunted seal, caribou, and fish, which they used for both food and clothing. They built homes of stone and turf. The traditional igloo was only a temporary shelter used during traveling.

Around 1000 B.C., farming villages developed in the Eastern Woodlands. This is the land in eastern North America from the Great Lakes to the Gulf of Mexico. People in the Eastern Woodlands grew crops, but they also continued to gather wild plants for food. The best known of the Eastern Woodlands peoples are the Hopewell people. They are also known as the Mound Builders. They lived in the Ohio River valley and eventually extended their culture along the Mississippi River. They built earth mounds that were used as tombs or for ceremonies. Around A.D. 700, there was a shift to full-time farming in the Mississippi River valley. The most common crops were corn, squash, and beans. Cities began to appear in this area. Between A.D. 850 and A.D. 1150, a city called Cahokia was the seat of government for much of the Mississippian culture. Near the site of Cahokia, archaeologists have found a burial mound over 98 feet high.

To the northeast of the Mississippian culture, there were peoples known as the Iroquois. The area where they lived included present-day Pennsylvania, New York, and southern Canada. The Iroquois lived in villages that consisted of longhouses. **Longhouses** were built of wooden poles covered with sheets of bark and were about 150 to 200 feet long. They could house about a dozen families. Women owned the houses, gathered wild plants, and farmed the land. They also cooked, made baskets, and took care of the children. The most important crops were corn, beans, and squash.

Iroquois men hunted deer, bear, caribou, rabbits, and beaver. They were also warriors. War was common among the Iroquois. Iroquois legend says that Deganawida, an elder of one of the Iroquois groups, and Hiawatha, a member of the Onondaga group, worked to created the Great Peace. Five groups formed an alliance called the Iroquois League. A council of representatives met regularly to settle differences within the league. This council was known as the Grand Council. The representatives were men, but the women chose them. Each Iroquois group was made up of **clans** (groups of related families). The women of each clan chose a woman to be the clan mother. It was the clan mothers' responsibility to choose the members of the Grand Council. Benjamin Franklin later used the Iroquois League as a democratic model for a Plan of Union for the British colonies.

To the west of the Mississippi were people known as the Plains Indians. They lived in the river valleys of the eastern Great Plains. They grew beans, corn, and squash. In the summer, the men hunted buffalo. The buffalo had many uses. The people ate the meat, used the skins for clothing, and made tools from the bones. They made circular tents by stretching buffalo skins over wooden poles. These tents are called **tepees.**

In the Southwest, the Anasazi civilization developed. The Southwest includes the present-day states of New Mexico, Arizona, Utah, and Colorado. This area is dry, but there is enough rain in some areas for farming. Between A.D. 500 and 1200, the Anasazi used canals and dams to turn parts of the desert into fertile gardens. They also made baskets and pottery. They used stone and **adobe** (sun-dried brick) to build pueblos. **Pueblos** were multistoried structures that could house many people. The Anasazi built large communities at Chaco Canyon in northwestern New Mexico and at Mesa Verde in southern Colorado. Droughts eventually caused them to abandon both communities, however.

18. How did the Iroquois contribute to the development of democracy?

Name ______________________ Date ________________ Class ________________

Reading Essentials and Study Guide

Chapter 11, Section 2

For use with textbook pages 352–358

EARLY CIVILIZATIONS IN MESOAMERICA

KEY TERMS

Mesoamerica the name for areas of Mexico and Central America that were civilized before the Spaniards arrived *(page 352)*

hieroglyph a picture used in a writing system *(page 354)*

tribute goods or money paid by conquered people to their conquerors *(page 356)*

DRAWING FROM EXPERIENCE

Have you ever visited an archaeological dig or the ruins of an ancient city? Do you think you would be interested in being an archeologist? Why or why not?

In the last section, you learned about the early civilizations of North America. In this section, you will learn about the early civilizations of Mesoamerica.

ORGANIZING YOUR THOUGHTS

Use the chart below to help you take notes. Identify where and when the following peoples lived, and summarize their main achievements.

People	Location	Time Period	Achievements
Olmec	**1.**	**2.**	**3.**
Maya	**4.**	**5.**	**6.**
Toltec	**7.**	**8.**	**9.**
Aztec	**10.**	**11.**	**12.**

Name ______________________________ Date ______________________ Class ______________________

Reading Essentials and Study Guide

Chapter 11, Section 2 *(continued)*

READ TO LEARN

• The Olmec and Teotihuacán *(page 352)*

The Olmec civilization appeared in Mesoamerica around 1200 B.C. **Mesoamerica** is the name for areas of Mexico and Central America that were civilized before the Spaniards arrived. The Olmec peoples lived in the hot and swampy lowlands along the coast of the Gulf of Mexico. They were farmers. They had large cities that were centers for their religious rituals. One of these cities, La Venta, had a large pyramid. The Olmec carved huge stone heads, probably to represent their gods. Around 400 B.C., the Olmec civilization declined and eventually collapsed.

The first major city in Mesoamerica was Teotihuacán. Its name means "Place of the Gods." This city was the capital of an early kingdom that existed from around 250 B.C. until about A.D. 800. It was located near what is now Mexico City. Along its main street, there were temples and palaces. There was also a huge pyramid, the Pyramid of the Sun, which was over 200 feet high.

13. What was the first major city in Mesoamerica, and what does its name mean?

____

____

____

____

• The Maya and Toltec *(page 353)*

On the Yucatán Peninsula, the civilization of the Maya flourished between A.D. 300 and 900. This civilization was one of the most sophisticated in the Americas. It eventually included much of Central America and southern Mexico. Mayan cities were built around a pyramid topped with a shrine to the gods. Other temples and palaces were built nearby. Some of these cities had a hundred thousand people. Mayan civilization was made up of city-states. These city-states were often at war with each other. Captured soldiers became slaves or were used as human sacrifices. The Maya practiced human sacrifice as a way to appease the gods. They also used human sacrifices to celebrate special occasions.

A hereditary ruling class governed each Mayan city-state. Mayan rulers claimed to be descended from the gods. Nobles and a class of scribes, who may also have been priests, assisted them. Mayan society also included artisans, merchants, and officials. Most of the Mayan people were peasant farmers. Men did the hunting and fighting, and women took care of the homes and raised the children. Women also made cornmeal, the basic food of many Mayans.

The Maya also created a sophisticated writing system based on **hieroglyphs** (pictures.). Many of the hieroglyphs recorded important events in Mayan history. The Spanish conquerors of the sixteenth century did not respect the Maya's writings. They thought the writings were evil and burned the Maya's books. The Spaniards also destroyed religious objects and, sometimes, entire cities.

The Maya developed a complicated calendar known as the Long Count. They used two different systems for measuring time. One was based on a solar calendar of 365 days. The other was based on a sacred calendar of 260 days. Only priests could read and use this calendar. They used it to foretell the future.

The Toltec controlled the upper Yucatán Peninsula for several centuries, beginning around A.D. 900. The Toltec were warriors, but they were also builders. They constructed pyramids and palaces. The center of the Toltec Empire was at Tula, which was northwest of present-day Mexico City. They extended their control into the Mayan lands of Guatemala and the northern Yucatán. In about 1200, their civilization also declined.

14. Describe the two Mayan systems for measuring time.

____

____

____

____

• The Aztec *(page 356)*

No one knows for sure where the Aztec came from. Sometime during the twelfth century A.D., they began to migrate to the Valley of Mexico. They set up their capital at Tenochtitlán, on an island in the middle of Lake Texcoco. This is the location of present-day Mexico City.

The Aztec built pyramids, temples, public buildings, and houses. They also built many roads. The Aztec were outstanding warriors. They eventually conquered much of what is now central Mexico. Their kingdom was not a centralized state. It was made up of territories ruled by local lords. The Aztec ruler supported these lords in return for tribute. **Tribute** is money or goods paid by conquered peoples to their conquerors. The Aztec ruler claimed that he was descended from the gods. A council of lords and government officials assisted him. The rest of the population was made up of commoners, indentured workers, and slaves. Indentured workers were people who did not own land but contracted to work on the nobles' estates. The slaves were people captured in war. Most people were commoners, and most commoners were farmers or merchants.

Name ______________________ Date ______________________ Class ______________________

Reading Essentials and Study Guide

Chapter 11, Section 2 *(continued)*

Women in Aztec society were not equal to men but were allowed to own and inherit property. They could also enter into contracts. Women were expected to work in the home, weave textiles, and raise children. They could also become priestesses.

The Aztec believed in many gods. Huitzilopochtli was the most important god. He was the god of the sun and of war. The Aztec religion was based on a belief in a struggle between the forces of good and evil. The Aztec believed that earthquakes would eventually destroy the world. The Aztec practiced human sacrifice. They believed that by appeasing the god Huitzilopochtli they could delay the destruction of the world. At the top of Aztec pyramids were shrines to the gods and altars for performing human sacrifices.

In 1519, a Spanish army under the command of Hernán Cortés landed at Veracruz, on the Gulf of Mexico. Cortés marched to Tenochtitlán. As he went, he made alliances with city-states that were tired of the Aztec rule. When Cortés arrived at Tenochtitlán, the Aztec ruler Montezuma, who believed that Cortés was a representative of the god Quetzalcoatl, welcomed him. Eventually, tensions arose between the Spaniards and the Aztec. In 1520, the local people revolted and drove the Spaniards from the city. However, many of the Aztec were soon infected by diseases brought by the Spaniards. In the meantime, Cortés received fresh soldiers and attacked the city. After four months, the city surrendered. The Spaniards then destroyed the city. They used the stones from the pyramids, temples, and palaces to build government buildings and churches.

15. How was the city of Tenochtitlán destroyed?

____

____

____

____

____

____

Name ______________________ Date ____________________ Class ____________________

Reading Essentials and Study Guide

Chapter 11, Section 3

For use with textbook pages 359–362

EARLY CIVILIZATIONS IN SOUTH AMERICA

KEY TERMS

maize corn *(page 360)*

quipu a system of knotted strings used by the Inca to keep records *(page 362)*

DRAWING FROM EXPERIENCE

What would your life be like if you did not have a system of writing? How would you be able to communicate? How would you be able to obtain information?

In the last two sections, you learned about the early civilizations of North America and Mesoamerica. In this section, you will learn about the early civilizations in South America. These civilizations did not develop writing systems, but they were able to keep records in other ways.

ORGANIZING YOUR THOUGHTS

Use the pyramid diagram below to help you take notes. Show the hierarchy of the Incan political structure.

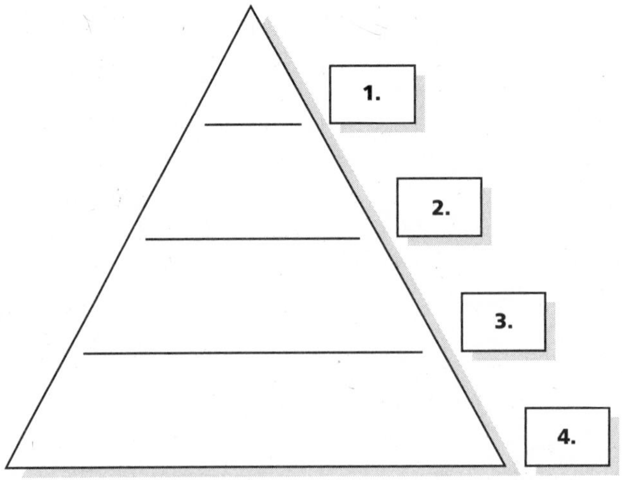

READ TO LEARN

• Early Civilizations *(page 359)*

The city of Caral was the oldest major city in the Americas. It was located in the Supe River valley of Peru. It contained buildings for officials, apartment buildings, and large homes, all built of stone. The people of Caral developed a system of irrigation by diverting a river into their fields. Caral was abandoned between 2000 and 1500 B.C.

Sometime after 1000 B.C., another civilization appeared near the Pacific coast, south of the border of present-day Ecuador. Moche was the capital of this state. It was located in the valley of the Moche River. The Moche River irrigated the fields in this area. Farmers in the area grew **maize** (corn), peanuts, potatoes, and cotton. The power of the Moche rulers extended far along the coast. The people of Moche had no written language, but their pottery tells us about them. It shows that they led lives centered around warfare. Paintings and pottery show warriors, prisoners, and human sacrifices. The Moche civilization ended around A.D. 700.

5. What was the oldest major city in the Americas and where was it located?

____

____

____

____

• The Inca *(page 360)*

About three hundred years after the end of the Moche civilization, a new power arose. This power, the kingdom of Chimor, controlled the area for about four centuries. The Inca finally destroyed it. In the late 1300s, the Inca were only a small community in the area of Cuzco. Cuzco was a city located high in the mountains of southern Peru. In the 1440s, under the leadership of the ruler Pachacuti, the Inca began to conquer the entire region. Pachacuti created a centralized state. He and his successors, Topa Inca and Huayna Inca, extended the boundaries of the Incan Empire as far as Ecuador, central Chile, and the edge of the Amazon basin. Once an area came under Incan control, the local people were taught the Quechua language. A noble was sent out to govern the new region. Local leaders could keep their posts as long as they were loyal to the Inca ruler. Pachacuti divided the empire into four quarters, each ruled by a governor. The quarters were divided into provinces, also ruled by governors. Each province was supposed to contain about ten thousand people. At the top of the system was the emperor. The people believed that he was descended from the sun god, Inti.

All young men had to serve in the Incan army. The army had two hundred thousand soldiers. Supplies were carried on llamas, because the Inca did not use the wheel. The Inca were great builders. All Incan subjects had to perform labor service, usually for several weeks each year. Laborers were moved from one part of the country to another to take part in building projects. Incan buildings and monuments were built of close-fitting stones with no mortar. This helped them to withstand the earthquakes in the area. The Inca also built roads. Their system of roads was a total of 24,800 miles long. Rest houses and storage depots were placed along the roads. Bridges of various types were built over ravines and waterways.

Incan society was very regimented. Men and women had to select a marriage partner from within their own social groups. Women were expected to care for the children and to weave cloth. Some young girls became priestesses in temples. In rural areas, most of the people were farmers. In the mountains, they used terraced farms, watered by irrigation systems. They planted corn, potatoes, and other crops. The houses of the farmers were built of stone or adobe with thatched roofs.

The Inca did not have a writing system, but they kept records using a system of knotted strings called the ***quipu.*** Even without a writing system, the Inca had many cultural achievements. They had a tradition of court theater, with both tragic and comic works. Poetry was also recited. It was often accompanied by music played on reed instruments.

The Incan Empire was still flourishing when the first Spanish expeditions arrived. In 1530, Francisco Pizarro landed on the Pacific coast of South America. The Incan Empire experienced an epidemic of smallpox. Like the Aztec, the Inca had no immunities to European diseases. Smallpox killed entire villages. Even the Incan emperor was a victim. When the emperor died, each of his two sons claimed the throne for himself. This led to civil war. One of the sons, Atahuallpa, defeated his brother's army. Pizarro then captured and killed Atahuallpa. Pizarro and his soldiers marched on Cuzco and captured the city. By 1535, Pizarro had set up a new capital at Lima for a new colony of the Spanish Empire.

6. How did the Inca keep records without a writing system?

____

____

____

____

____

Name ________________ Date ________________ Class ________________

Reading Essentials and Study Guide

Chapter 12, Section 1

For use with textbook pages 375–381

THE RENAISSANCE

KEY TERMS

urban society a society in which many of the people in cities *(page 375)*

secular worldly, rather than religious *(page 375)*

mercenary a soldier who sells his services to the highest bidder *(page 377)*

dowry in Renaissance Italy, a sum of money given by a wife's family to her husband upon marriage *(page 381)*

DRAWING FROM EXPERIENCE

What does being an individual mean to you? In what ways can a person foster his or her individuality?

In this section, you will learn about the beginnings of the Renaissance in Italy. During the Renaissance, a new view of human beings emerged that emphasized individual ability.

ORGANIZING YOUR THOUGHTS

Use the concept web below to help you take notes. Name five characteristics of the Italian Renaissance.

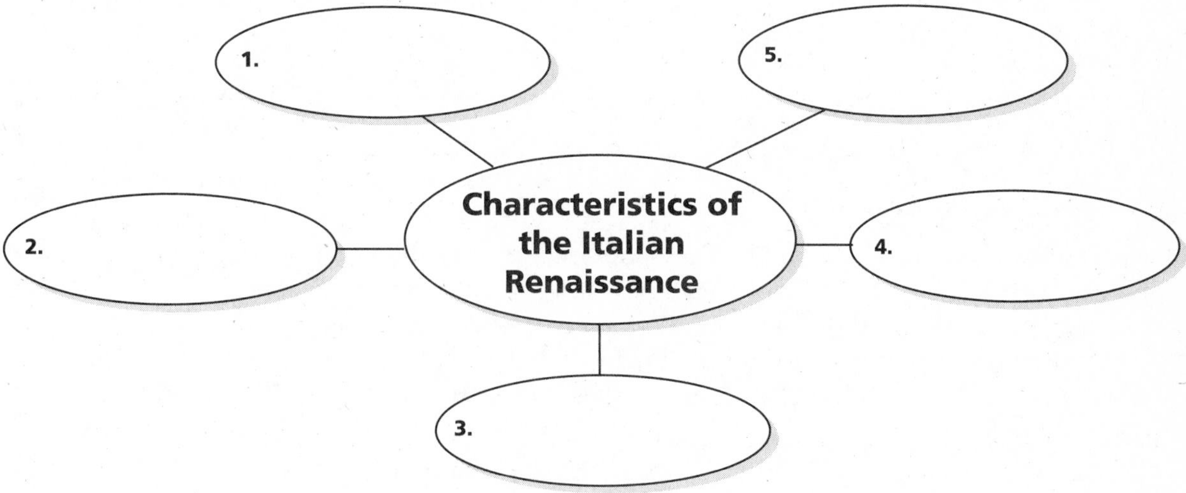

READ TO LEARN

• The Italian Renaissance *(page 375)*

The word *renaissance* means rebirth. Many people who lived in Italy between 1350 and 1550 believed that they were seeing a rebirth of the ancient Greek and Roman worlds. Historians call this period the Renaissance, or Italian Renaissance. The Renaissance began in Italy and spread to the rest of Europe. The Italian Renaissance had several important characteristics. Renaissance Italy was largely an **urban society** (that is, many of the people lived in cities). During the Middle Ages, powerful city-states had become the centers of Italian political, economic, and social life. As wealth increased, a **secular** (worldly) viewpoint developed. People became more focused on enjoying material things. The Renaissance was also an age of recovery from the problems of the fourteenth century, such as the plague, political instability, and a decline in Church power. There was a rebirth of interest in ancient culture (the culture of ancient Greece and Rome). This revival influenced both politics and art. People in the Renaissance began to emphasize what individuals could achieve. They believed that human beings could accomplish anything. A well-rounded person who had achievements in many areas was the ideal. Leonardo da Vinci, for example, was a painter, sculptor, architect, inventor, and mathematician.

6. What does the word *renaissance* mean?

• The Italian States *(page 376)*

During the Middle Ages, Italy did not develop a centralized monarchy like other countries in Europe. Without a single strong ruler, many city-states in Italy were able to remain independent. The Italian city-states prospered because of trade with other parts of the world. Three of these city-states, Milan, Venice, and Florence, played important roles in Italian politics.

Milan was located in northern Italy at the crossroads of some of the main trade routes. In the fourteenth century, members of the Visconti family became the dukes of Milan. They eventually controlled all of Lombardy. The last Visconti ruler died in 1447. Francesco Sforza then conquered Milan and became its new duke. Sforza was the leader of a group of **mercenaries** (soldiers who sold their services to the highest bidder). Both the Visconti and Sforza rulers helped to build a strong centralized state. They created a tax system that gave their governments a huge income.

Venice had developed a trade empire by trading with both Asia and Western Europe. Venice was officially a republic with an elected leader called a *Doge*. In reality, a small group of merchant-aristocrats ran the government of Venice and promoted their own interests.

Florence was located in the region of Tuscany. During the fourteenth century, a group of merchants controlled the government of Florence. They led the people of Florence in wars with their neighbors and made Florence a major city-state. In 1434, Cosimo de Medici took control of Florence. The Medici family was wealthy and controlled the government from behind the scenes. During this time, Florence was the cultural center of Italy. In the late 1400s, the economy of Florence, which was based on cloth making, began to decline. This was due mainly to competition from English and Flemish cloth makers. At the same time, a Dominican preacher named Girolamo Savonarola began to condemn the rich Medici family. Many people followed him, and the Medici family turned Florence over to him. Savonarola had regulations against gambling, horseracing, swearing, painting, music, and books. People eventually grew tired of these regulations. Savonarola also attacked the corruption of the church. In 1498, he was accused of heresy and sentenced to death. The Medici family then returned to power.

Attracted by the riches of Italy, the French king Charles VIII led an army into Italy in 1494. He occupied the kingdom of Naples in southern Italy. Northern Italian states asked the Spanish for help. The Spanish sent soldiers to Italy. For the next 30 years, the French and Spanish fought over Italy. In 1527, troops belonging to the Spanish king Charles I arrived in Rome. They had hired mercenaries from other countries. They attacked the city and destroyed many churches and palaces. They also looted much of the city and sold church officials as slaves. The sack of Rome ended the Italian wars. It also made Spain a dominant force in Italy.

7. What events started and ended the Italian wars?

____

____

____

____

____

Reading Essentials and Study Guide

Chapter 12, Section 1 *(continued)*

• Machiavelli and the New Statecraft *(page 378)*

The Italians loved political power. Niccolò Machiavelli, an Italian, wrote a book about how to acquire and keep political power. This book, *The Prince*, is one of the most important works on political power that was ever written. Before Machiavelli, many writers had stressed that a prince's activities should be based on Christian principles. Machiavelli wrote that political decisions should not be restricted by moral principles. He believed that human beings were basically self-centered and that a prince should take this into account. According to Machiavelli, a prince acts on behalf of the state and must be willing to act against his conscience if necessary. His views had a great influence on future political leaders.

8. What was Machiavelli's view of human nature?

____

____

____

____

• Renaissance Society *(page 379)*

During the fourteenth and fifteenth centuries, nobles (aristocrats) had declining incomes, but they still kept their lands and titles. By 1500, they were only 2 to 3 percent of the population in most countries, but they held important political posts and were advisers to the kings. Nobles were expected to fulfill certain ideals. Baldassare Castiglione expressed these ideals in his work *The Book of the Courtier*. According to Castiglione, a noble was born, not made. He was expected to have character, grace, and talent. A noble also had to develop two basic skills. He had to perform military and physical exercises to prepare himself as a warrior. He was also expected to have a classical education and pursue the arts. The noble also needed to follow a standard of conduct that would enable him to serve his prince in an effective and honest way.

Peasants still made up 85 to 90 percent of the population in most of Europe, but serfdom was declining. By 1500, more and more peasants had become legally free and paid rent, rather than labor, to the lords. Townspeople were the rest of the population. During the Middle Ages, townspeople had been mainly merchants and artisans. By the fifteenth century, towns and cities were more diverse. At the top of urban society were patricians. They were people who had acquired wealth through trade, industry and banking. Below them were the burghers. These were the shopkeepers, artisans, and guild members. Below the patricians and burghers were the workers, who earned pitiful wages, and the unemployed. These people made up 30 to 40 percent of the urban population. They had miserable lives.

The family was important in Renaissance Italy. Parents arranged marriages, often to strengthen business or family ties. A marriage contract sealed the agreement between families. The most important part of the agreement was the amount of the dowry. The **dowry** was a sum of money given by the wife's family to her husband when they were married. The father was the center of the Italian family. He gave the family his name, managed all finances, and made decisions that affected his children's lives. The mother's main role was to supervise the household. A father's authority over his children was absolute until he died or freed his children. Children did not become adults until their father went before a judge and formally freed them. The age of adulthood could be anywhere from the early teens to the late twenties.

9. How were towns and cities in the fifteenth century different from the Middle Ages?

____

____

____

____

____

____

Name ______________________ Date ______________________ Class ______________________

Reading Essentials and Study Guide

Chapter 12, Section 2

For use with textbook pages 382–387

THE INTELLECTUAL AND ARTISTIC RENAISSANCE

KEY TERMS

humanism an intellectual movement of the Renaissance that was based on the study of the ancient Greek and Roman classics *(page 382)*

fresco a painting done on fresh, wet plaster with water-based paints *(page 384)*

DRAWING FROM EXPERIENCE

Do you enjoy looking at paintings and sculptures? What periods or styles do you like best?

In the last section, you read about the beginnings of the Renaissance in Italy. In this section, you will learn about art, literature, and education during the Renaissance.

ORGANIZING YOUR THOUGHTS

Use the chart below to help you take notes. List some of the characteristics of the following art forms during the Renaissance.

Art Form	**Characteristics**
Architecture	**1.**
Sculpture	**2.**
Painting	**3.**

READ TO LEARN

• Italian Renaissance Humanism *(page 382)*

Secularism and an emphasis on the individual characterized the Renaissance. A key intellectual movement of the Renaissance was humanism. **Humanism** was based on the study of the classics, the literary works of ancient Greece and Rome. Humanists studied subjects like grammar, rhetoric, poetry, moral philosophy, and history. Today these subjects are called the humanities.

Petrarch has been called the father of Italian Renaissance humanism. He looked for forgotten Latin manuscripts. This began a search for these manuscripts in monasteries throughout Europe. He also began the humanist emphasis on using pure classical Latin (Latin as it was used by the ancient Romans). Humanists used the works of Cicero as a model for prose. They used the works of Virgil as a model for poetry. Early humanists, like Petrarch, described the intellectual life as a life of solitude. In the early 1400s, however, humanists began to take a new interest in civic life. They believed that it was the duty of intellectuals to live active lives. They also believed that their study of the humanities should be used to serve the state.

4. How did humanism change in the early 1400s?

____

____

• Vernacular Literature *(page 383)*

Because of the humanists' emphasis on classical Latin, scholars, lawyers, and theologians used it. However, some writers wrote in the vernacular (the language spoken in their own regions, such as Italian, French, or German). In the fourteenth century, the works of Dante and Chaucer made vernacular literature popular. Dante was an Italian author. His masterpiece is the *Divine Comedy*. It is the story of the soul's journey to salvation. Chaucer was an English author. His famous work *The Canterbury Tales* is a collection of stories told by a group of pilgrims on their way to the tomb of Saint Thomas à Becket at Canterbury. Another writer who used the vernacular was Christine de Pizan. She was a Frenchwoman who wrote works in defense of women. She argued that women could learn as well as men if they could attend the same schools.

5. What two authors made vernacular literature popular in the fourteenth century?

____

____

Name ______________________ Date ____________________ Class ____________________

Reading Essentials and Study Guide

Chapter 12, Section 2 *(continued)*

• Education in the Renaissance *(page 383)*

Renaissance humanists believed that education could change people. They wrote books on education and opened schools based on their ideas. Humanists believed that the liberal studies (what we now call the liberal arts) helped people reach their full potential. The liberal studies included history, moral philosophy, eloquence (rhetoric), letters (grammar and logic), poetry, mathematics, astronomy, and music. The purpose of the liberal studies was to produce individuals who would act with virtue and wisdom. Humanists also stressed physical education, because they believed in the Greek ideal of a sound mind in a sound body. Humanists thought that a liberal education was practical. Their goal was not to create great scholars but complete citizens.

Women normally did not attend the humanist schools. If they did, they studied the classics and history and learned how to ride, dance, sing, play the lute, and appreciate poetry. They did not study mathematics or rhetoric. Religion and morals were emphasized, so that women would become good wives and mothers.

6. According to humanists, what was the purpose of a liberal education?

____

____

• The Artistic Renaissance in Italy *(page 384)*

Renaissance artists tried to imitate nature in their works. They wanted the objects and events they portrayed to look real. These artists also developed a new worldview in which human beings became the focus of attention. The first masterpieces of early Renaissance art were the frescoes painted by Masaccio in Florence. A **fresco** is a painting done on fresh, wet plaster with water-based paints. Human figures in medieval paintings looked flat. Masaccio mastered the laws of perspective, which helped him to create the illusion of three dimensions. As a result, Masaccio's figures have depth and look real. This new style was used and adapted by other Florentine painters in the fifteenth century. They understood the laws of perspective and the organization of outdoor space and light. They also studied movement and human anatomy. One of the chief aims of Italian Renaissance art was the realistic portrayal of people, especially human nudes.

Sculptors and architects also made advances during the Renaissance. The sculptor Donatello spent time in Rome studying and copying the statues of the Greeks and Romans. He created realistic, free-standing figures. The buildings of classical Rome inspired the architect Filippo Brunelleschi. He created a new architecture in Florence. The Medici family hired him to design the church of San Lorenzo. This church does not overwhelm worshipers like Gothic cathedrals did. It was created to fit human, not divine, needs.

Name ______________________ Date ______________________ Class ______________________

Reading Essentials and Study Guide

Chapter 12, Section 2 *(continued)*

The final stage of Italian Renaissance painting is called the High Renaissance. It flourished between 1490 and 1520. Three artistic giants, Leonardo da Vinci, Raphael, and Michelangelo, are associated with this period. Leonardo mastered the art of realistic painting. He even dissected human bodies to see how they worked. He went beyond realism, however. His goal was to create idealized forms that would show the perfection of nature and the individual. Raphael also tried to achieve an ideal of beauty that surpassed reality. He is especially well-known for his madonnas (paintings of the Virgin Mary) and his frescoes in the Vatican Palace. Michelangelo was an accomplished painter, sculptor, and architect. His famous figures on the ceiling of the Sistine Chapel show an ideal type of human being with perfect proportions. The beauty of these idealized forms was meant to be a reflection of divine beauty.

7. Who are the three artists most associated with the High Renaissance?

____

____

____

• The Northern Artistic Renaissance *(page 386)*

The artists of northern Europe were also interested in portraying the world realistically. Northern artists painted illustrations for books and wooden panels for altarpieces. They had to depict each object on a small scale and became masters at painting details. The most important northern school of art in the fifteenth century was in Flanders. The Flemish painter Jan van Eyck was one of the first to use oil paint. Oil paint allowed artists to use a wide variety of colors and to create fine details. Like the Italian Renaissance painters, van Eyck tried to imitate nature. But he did this, not by using the laws of perspective, but by observing reality and portraying details as best he could. By 1500, northern artists had begun to study in Italy and were influenced by Italian artists. One German artist who was influenced by the Italians was Albrecht Dürer. He used both minute details and the laws of perspective in his works. Like the Italians, he also tried to achieve a standard of ideal beauty by carefully examining human forms.

8. How did the technique of the northern Renaissance painters differ from that of the Italian Renaissance artists?

____

____

____

Name ______________________ Date ____________________ Class ____________________

Reading Essentials and Study Guide

Chapter 12, Section 3

For use with textbook pages 389–393

THE PROTESTANT REFORMATION

KEY TERMS

Christian humanism a movement in northern Europe during the Renaissance (also called Northern Renaissance humanism) that stressed a belief in the ability of human beings to reason and improve themselves *(page 390)*

salvation acceptance into heaven *(page 390)*

indulgence a release from all or part of the punishment for sin *(page 391)*

DRAWING FROM EXPERIENCE

Have you ever attended Catholic mass? Have you ever attended a Lutheran worship service? What differences did you see?

In the last two sections, you learned about the changes and achievements during the Renaissance period. In this section, you will learn about the Protestant Reformation that took place during the end of this period.

ORGANIZING YOUR THOUGHTS

Use the chart below to help you take notes. Summarize some of the main differences between Lutheranism and Catholicism at the time of the Reformation.

	Salvation	Sacraments	Clergy and Marriage	Church Services
Lutheranism	**1.**	**2.**	**3.**	**4.**
Catholicism	**5.**	**6.**	**7.**	**8.**

READ TO LEARN

• Erasmus and Christian Humanism *(page 389)*

The Protestant Reformation is the name that is used for the reform movement that divided the western Church into Catholic and Protestant groups. Several developments set the stage for religious change. During the second half of the fifteenth century, the new classical learning that was part of Italian Renaissance humanism spread to northern Europe. A movement called **Christian humanism** (or Northern Renaissance humanism) developed. Christian humanists believed in the ability of human beings to reason and improve themselves. One of their major goals was the reform of the Catholic Church. Humanists believed that in order to change the Church and society, they needed to change individuals first. They thought that if people read the classics and the works of Christianity, they would become more pious. This would bring about a reform of the Church and society.

The best known of the Christian humanists was Desiderius Erasmus. He called his view of religion "the philosophy of Christ." He believed that Christianity should show people how to live good lives. To reform the Church, Erasmus wanted to spread the philosophy of Christ and provide education in the works of Christianity. He also criticized the abuses of the Catholic Church. He did not wish to break away from the Church, however. He sought reform within the Catholic Church. But his ideas prepared the way for the Reformation.

9. What did Christian humanists believe was the best way to reform the Church and society?

____

____

____

____

____

• Religion on the Eve of the Reformation *(page 390)*

Erasmus and others were calling for reform because of the corruption of the Catholic Church. Between 1450 and 1520, the popes were more concerned with Italian politics and worldly interests than with spiritual matters. Pope Julius II personally led armies against his enemies. This disgusted Christians because the pope was supposed to be a spiritual, not a military, leader. Many church officials were concerned with money and used their church offices to get wealthy. Parish priests were often ignorant of their spiritual duties. People wanted a meaningful religion and assurance of **salvation** (acceptance into Heaven), but many priests were unable to teach them. Collections of relics became popular as a means to salvation. According to Church practice at that time, a person could gain an **indulgence** (release from all or part of the punishment for sins) through relics. The church also sold indulgences in the form of certificates. This practice, in particular, upset many of the reformers.

10. Why did Erasmus and others think that the Catholic Church needed to be reformed?

____

____

____

____

____

• Martin Luther *(page 391)*

Martin Luther was a monk and a professor at the University of Wittenberg. Through his study of the Bible, Luther found an answer to a problem that had bothered him since he became a monk. This problem was how to be certain of salvation. Catholic teachings had stressed that both faith and good works were needed to gain salvation. Luther believed that people could never do enough good works to be saved. He came to believe that people are not saved through their goods works but through their faith in God. If a person has faith in God, God makes that person just, or worthy of salvation. God grants salvation because he is merciful, not because of a person's good works. This idea is called justification (being made right with God) by faith. It became the chief teaching of the Protestant Reformation. Because Luther had found the answer to his problem by studying the Bible alone, the Bible became the primary source of religious truth for Luther and all other Protestants.

Luther did not see himself as a rebel, but the selling of indulgences upset him. He believed that people were actually harming their chances for salvation by buying indulgences. On October 31, 1517, Luther nailed his Ninety-Five Theses on the door of the Castle Church in Wittenberg. The theses (statements) were an attack on the selling of indulgences. Thousands of copies of the Ninety-Five Theses were printed and spread to all parts of Germany. By 1520, Luther was ready to break away from the Catholic Church. He asked the German princes to establish a reformed German church. Luther also attacked the Church's system of seven sacraments. He kept only two sacraments, baptism and the Eucharist (Communion). Luther also thought that the clergy should marry. This went against the Catholic belief that the clergy should remain celibate (unmarried).

The Catholic Church excommunicated Luther in 1521. The newly elected emperor, Charles V, thought he could convince Luther to change his ideas. He summoned Luther to appear before the imperial diet (legislative assembly) of the Holy Roman Empire. But Luther refused to change his mind. By the Edict of Worms, Luther was made an outlaw in the empire. His works were supposed to be burned, and Luther was supposed to be captured and brought to the emperor. But Frederick of Saxony, Luther's ruler, sent Luther into hiding. When Luther returned to Wittenberg in 1522, Frederick protected him.

During the next few years, Luther's religious movement became a revolution. Many of the German rulers supported Luther and formed state churches. Luther set up new religious services to replace the Catholic mass. These services consisted of Bible readings, preaching of the word of God, and songs. These new churches became known as Lutheran churches, and Luther's doctrine became known as Lutheranism. Lutheranism was the first Protestant faith.

11. What were the Ninety-Five Theses?

____

____

____

____

____

• Politics in the German Reformation *(page 393)*

Charles V, the Holy Roman emperor, was also Charles I, the king of Spain. He ruled an immense empire consisting of Spain, the Austrian lands, Bohemia, Hungary, the Low Countries, the duchy of Milan, the kingdom of Naples, and Spanish territories in the New World. He wanted to keep this empire under the control of his dynasty, the Hapsburgs. He hoped to preserve his empire by keeping it Catholic. However, he had other problems at the same time. His chief political concern was his rivalry with the king of France, Francis I. Their conflicts led to a series of wars that lasted 20 years. Charles also had problems with the pope, Clement VII, who sided with the French king. At the same time, the invasion of the Ottoman Turks forced Charles to send troops to the eastern part of his empire.

Name ______________________ Date ______________________ Class ______________________

Reading Essentials and Study Guide

Chapter 12, Section 3 *(continued)*

Many of the princes of the German states supported Luther as a way to assert their own authority over the authority of Charles V. By the time Charles V was able to bring military forces to Germany, the Lutheran princes were well organized. Charles was unable to defeat them and was forced to seek peace. An end to religious warfare in Germany came in 1555 with the Peace of Augsburg. This agreement formally accepted the division of Christianity in Germany. The German states could now choose between Catholicism and Lutheranism. Lutheran states were given the same legal rights as Catholic states. The right of each German ruler to determine the religion of his subjects was recognized, but not the right of the subjects to choose their own religion.

12. What was the result of the Peace of Augsburg?

____

____

____

____

____

Name ______________________ Date ______________________ Class ______________________

Reading Essentials and Study Guide

Chapter 12, Section 4

For use with textbook pages 395–401

THE SPREAD OF PROTESTANTISM AND THE CATHOLIC RESPONSE

KEY TERMS

predestination the belief that God has determined in advance (predestined) who will be saved and who will be damned *(page 396)*

annul declare a marriage invalid *(page 397)*

DRAWING FROM EXPERIENCE

Do you think religion should ever influence a government's policies? Why or why not?

In the last section, you read about the beginnings of the Protestant Reformation in Germany. In this section, you will learn about the spread of Protestantism to other countries. You will also learn about the Catholic Reformation that took place in response to Protestantism.

ORGANIZING YOUR THOUGHTS

Use the concept web below to help you take notes. Think about the different forms of Protestantism that started in Europe as the Reformation spread. Summarize the reforms of the following Protestant leaders.

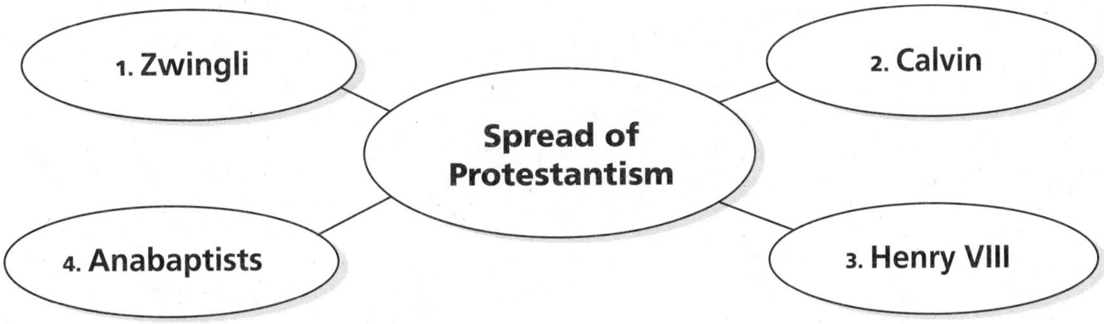

Name ______________ Date ______________ Class ______________

READ TO LEARN

• The Zwinglian Reformation *(page 395)*

Even before the Peace of Augsburg, other Protestant groups had developed. One of these new groups was in Switzerland. Huldrych Zwingli, a priest in Zürich led this movement. Due to his influence, the council of Zürich began to make religious reforms. All paintings, decorations, and relics were removed from the churches. A new church service replaced the Catholic mass. This service consisted of scripture reading, prayer, and sermons. In October 1531, war broke out in Switzerland between the Protestant and Catholic states. Zwingli was killed. The leadership of Protestantism in Switzerland passed to John Calvin.

5. Who was the leader of the first Protestant reform movement in Switzerland?

• Calvin and Calvinism *(page 396)*

John Calvin was born and educated in France. After he converted to Protestantism, he was forced to flee to Switzerland because France was still Catholic. In 1536, he published the *Institutes of the Christian Religion,* a summary of Protestant doctrines. This book made Calvin one of the new leaders of Protestantism. In many ways, Calvin's beliefs were similar to Luther's. Like Luther, he believed in the doctrine of justification by faith alone. But Calvin also emphasized the all-powerful nature of God. This caused him to believe in another doctrine, predestination. **Predestination** is the belief that God has determined in advance (predestined) who will be saved and who will be damned.

In 1536, Calvin began working to reform the city of Geneva. He created a church government that used both clergy and laity. A court was set up to oversee the moral life and religious doctrines of the people of Geneva. This court was called the Consistory. It had the right to punish people for crimes, which included dancing, drunkenness, swearing, and playing cards. Geneva became a powerful center of Protestantism. Missionaries trained in Geneva were sent to all parts of Europe. By the mid-sixteenth century, Calvinism had replaced Lutheranism as the most important form of Protestantism.

6. What religious doctrine is associated with John Calvin?

____

____

____

• The Reformation in England *(page 397)*

The Reformation in England had its beginnings in politics, not religion. King Henry VIII wanted to divorce his first wife, Catherine of Aragon, because she had not been able to have a son. Because Henry needed a male heir, he wanted to marry Anne Boleyn. Henry asked the pope to **annul** (declare invalid) his marriage to Catherine, but the pope refused. Henry then asked the church courts in England for the annulment. In 1533, Thomas Cranmer, the archbishop of Canterbury, granted the annulment, and Henry married Anne Boleyn.

The next year, Henry asked Parliament to separate the Church in England from the pope in Rome. The Parliament passed the Act of Supremacy of 1534. This act made the king the head of the Church of England. Henry used his new powers to close the monasteries and sell their land and possessions. This put more money in his treasury. It also created new supporters for the king, because the people who had bought the monks' land did not want the Catholic Church to be in power again. Despite these changes, Henry's religious beliefs were similar to those of the Catholic Church.

When Henry died in 1547, his son, Edward VI, took the throne. He was only nine years old and sickly. During Edward's reign, church officials moved the Church of England (also called the Anglican Church) in a Protestant direction. Parliament gave the clergy the right to marry and created a new Protestant church service. Many people opposed these changes. When Edward VI died in 1553, Mary, Henry's daughter by Catherine of Aragon, took the throne. She was a Catholic and wanted to restore England to Roman Catholicism. The way she went about it had the opposite effect, however. She had more than three hundred Protestants burned as heretics, which gave her the nickname "Bloody Mary." As a result, England was even more Protestant by the end of her reign than it had been at the beginning.

7. Why did England break away from the Roman Catholic Church?

____

____

____

• The Anabaptists *(page 398)*

Many of the Protestant reformers allowed the state (government) to play an important role in church affairs. Some people were against the state having this kind of power. These people were called the Anabaptists. According to the Anabaptists, the true Christian church was a voluntary community of adult believers. Believers were first reborn spiritually and then baptized. This belief in adult baptism separated Anabaptists from Catholics and also other Protestants who baptized infants. Anabaptists based many of their beliefs and practices on the accounts of the early Christian church in the New Testament. They believed that all Christians were equal. Each Anabaptist church chose its own minister (spiritual leader). Because all Christians were considered priests, any member of the community was eligible to be a minister.

Most Anabaptists believed in the complete separation of church and state. They thought that government should be kept out of religion. They even thought that government should not have any authority over real Christians. Anabaptists refused to hold political office or bear arms. Their political and religious beliefs caused the Anabaptists to be regarded as dangerous radicals. The only thing that most Protestants and Catholics could agree on was the need to persecute the Anabaptists.

8. How were the beliefs of the Anabaptists different from those of other Protestants?

____

____

____

____

• Effects on the Role of Women *(page 399)*

Protestants developed a new view of the family. They did not believe that there was anything especially holy about being celibate. They did away with monasticism and the requirement of celibacy for the clergy. Marriage and family were now emphasized. But the role of women did not change very much. Women were still subordinate to men. Women were expected to bear children and obey their husbands. Being a wife and mother was the only role that most Protestant women could play in society.

9. How did the Protestant view of marriage and family affect the clergy?

____

____

____

____

• The Catholic Reformation *(page 400)*

By the mid-sixteenth century, Protestantism was well established in many parts of Europe. The situation in Europe did not look good for the Catholic Church. However, the Catholic Church had its own reformation in the sixteenth century that gave it new strength. Three factors brought about this Catholic Reformation. These three factors were the Jesuits, reform of the papacy, and the Council of Trent.

Jesuits were also known as the Society of Jesus. Ignatius of Loyola, a Spanish nobleman, founded the Society. All Jesuits took a vow of absolute obedience to the pope. Jesuits used education to spread their message. Jesuit missionaries were very successful in restoring Catholicism to parts of Germany and eastern Europe. They also spread it to other parts of the world.

Pope Paul III saw the need for changes in the Catholic Church and appointed a Reform Commission in 1537. The commission blamed the Church's problems on the corruption of the popes. Renaissance popes had been involved in questionable financial dealings and in Italian political and military affairs. In 1545, Pope Paul III began the Council of Trent. It was made up of Church leaders and theologians. The Council met off and on for 18 years. It reaffirmed traditional Catholic teachings. According to the Council, both faith and good works were necessary for salvation. The seven sacraments, the Catholic view of the Eucharist, and celibacy were all upheld. However, the selling of indulgences was forbidden.

10. What three factors brought about a reformation of the Catholic Church in the sixteenth century?

Name ______________________ Date ______________________ Class ______________________

Reading Essentials and Study Guide

Chapter 13, Section 1

For use with textbook pages 407–413

EXPLORATION AND EXPANSION

KEY TERMS

conquistadors Spanish conquerors of the Americas *(page 412)*

colony a settlement of people living in a new territory, linked with the parent country by trade and direct government control *(page 413)*

mercantilism a set of principles that dominated economic thought in the seventeenth century, which emphasized the accumulation of bullion through government involvement in the promotion of industries and trade *(page 413)*

balance of trade the difference in value between what a nation imports and what it exports over time *(page 413)*

DRAWING FROM EXPERIENCE

What places today are unknown and still being explored? Do you think you would be interested in taking part in these explorations? Why or why not?

In this section, you will learn about early explorations by European nations, especially in the Americas.

ORGANIZING YOUR THOUGHTS

Use the chart below to help you take notes. Identify the nationality of each of the following explorers and summarize their explorations.

Explorer	Nationality	Explorations
Vasco da Gama	**1.**	**2.**
Christopher Columbus	**3.**	**4.**
John Cabot	**5.**	**6.**
Francisco Pizarro	**7.**	**8.**
Ferdinand Magellan	**9.**	**10.**

Reading Essentials and Study Guide

READ TO LEARN

• Motive and Means *(page 407)*

In the fifteenth century, Europeans began to sail all over the world. Because of conquests by the Ottoman Turks in the fourteenth century, Europeans could no longer travel by land to the East, like Marco Polo had done in the thirteenth century. This problem made them attempt to reach Asia by sea. They had three main motives for undertaking these dangerous voyages. The first motive was economic. Europeans hoped to find precious metals and to expand trade, especially for the spices of the East. The second motive was religious. Many Europeans believed that it was their duty to convert other peoples to Christianity. The third motive was a desire for glory and adventure. These three motives are sometimes referred to as "God, glory, and gold."

Not only did Europeans of the fifteenth century have motives for exploration, but they also had the means that they had not had before. By the second half of the fifteenth century, European monarchies had increased their power and their resources and were able to sponsor voyages. Europeans had also reached a level of technology that made the voyages possible.

11. What were the three main reasons that Europeans of the fifteenth century were willing to make dangerous voyages?

• The Portuguese Trading Empire *(page 409)*

Beginning in 1420, Portuguese fleets began to explore the western coast of Africa. These fleets were sponsored by Prince Henry the Navigator. In Africa, the Portuguese discovered a new source of gold. The southern coast of West Africa became known to Europeans as the Gold Coast.

Portuguese sea captains heard about a route to Indian around the southern tip of Africa. In 1488, Bartholomeu Dias rounded the tip, called the Cape of Good Hope. Later, Vasco da Gama went around the cape and cut across the Indian Ocean to the coast of India. There he took on a cargo of spices. After he returned to Portugal, he made a profit of several thousand percent. Portuguese fleets returned to the area to gain control of the spice trade, which had been controlled by the Muslims. In 1509, a Portuguese fleet defeated a fleet of Turkish and Indian ships off the coast of India. A year later, Admiral Afonso de Albuquerque set up a port at Goa, on the western coast of India. The Portuguese then began to search for the source of the spice trade. Albuquerque gained control of Melaka, which was a thriving port for the spice trade. From Melaka, the Portuguese made expeditions to China and the Spice Islands. They signed a treaty with a local ruler for the purchase and export of cloves. This treaty gave the Portuguese control of the spice trade. The Portuguese now had a trading empire, but they did not try to colonize the Asian regions.

12. How did the Portuguese gain control of the spice trade?

____

____

____

• Voyages to the Americas *(page 410)*

The Portuguese sailed eastward through the Indian Ocean to reach the source of the spice trade. The Spanish tried to reach it by sailing westward across the Atlantic Ocean. Christopher Columbus, an Italian, believed that he could reach Asia by sailing west, instead of east around Africa. He persuaded Queen Isabella of Spain to finance an expedition. In October 1492, he reached the Americas. He believed that he had reached Asia. He made three more voyages to try to find a route through the islands to the Asian mainland. In his four voyages, he reached all of the major islands of the Caribbean and Honduras in Central America. Still convinced that he was in Asia, he called the islands the Indies.

By the 1490s, both Spain and Portugal had explored new lands. Both countries were afraid that the other might claim some of its newly discovered territories. In 1494, they signed the Treaty of Tordesillas. This treaty created a line of demarcation, an imaginary line that extended from north to south through the Atlantic Ocean and the easternmost part of South America. Unexplored territories east of the line would be controlled by Portugal. Those west of the line would be controlled by Spain. The treaty gave Portugal control over its route around Africa. It gave Spain rights to almost all of the Americas.

The governments of many countries began to sponsor expeditions to the Americas. A Venetian seaman, John Cabot, explored the New England coastline for England. The Portuguese sea captain Pedro Cabral landed in South America in 1500. Amerigo Vespucci went along on several voyages and wrote letters describing what he saw. His letters led to the use of the name America for the new lands. Europeans called these lands the New World, but they were only new to the Europeans. They already had flourishing civilizations when the Europeans arrived.

13. What name did Columbus give to the islands he explored? Why?

____

____

____

• The Spanish Empire *(page 412)*

The Spanish conquerors of the Americas were known as **conquistadors.** Their weapons brought them incredible success. The forces of Hérnan Cortés took only three years to overthrow the Aztec Empire in Central America. By 1550, the Spanish had gained control of northern Mexico. In South America, an expedition led by Francisco Pizarro took control of the Inca Empire. The Portuguese took over Brazil, which fell on their side of the line of demarcation.

By 1535, the Spanish had created a system of colonial administration in the Americas. Queen Isabella declared the Native Americans to be her subjects. She granted the Spanish settlers *encomienda* (the right to use Native Americans as laborers). Spanish settlers were supposed to protect Native Americans, but few did. Instead, they put them to work on sugar plantations and in gold and silver mines. Forced labor, starvation, and disease took a terrible toll on Native American lives. The native peoples had little resistance to European diseases, and 30 to 40 percent of them died from smallpox, measles, and typhus. In the early years of the conquest, Catholic missionaries converted and baptized hundreds of thousands of native peoples. Native American social and political structures were torn apart and replaced by European systems of religion, language, culture, and government.

14. How did Spanish colonization of the Americas affect the Native American peoples?

____

____

____

• Economic Impact and Competition *(page 412)*

Wherever they went, Europeans searched for gold and silver. Gold, silver, sugar, dyes, cotton, vanilla, and hides soon flowed into Spain from the Americas. Agricultural products, such as potatoes, coffee, corn, and tobacco, were also shipped to Europe. Because of its trading posts in Asia, Portugal soon became the chief entry point for the trade in spices, jewels, silk, carpets, ivory, leather, and perfumes.

By the end of the sixteenth century, several European countries were vying for the eastern trade. Ferdinand Magellan, a Portuguese explorer who was financed by the king of Spain, sailed around the tip of South America and crossed the Pacific Ocean to the Philippine Islands. The Spanish then established a colony in the Philippines. Spanish ships carried silver from Mexico to the Philippines and returned to Mexico with silk and other luxury goods. At the beginning of the seventeenth century, an English fleet landed on the northwestern coast of India and established trade relations with the people there. The first Dutch fleet arrived in India in 1595. Shortly after, the Dutch formed the East India Company and began competing with the English and the Portuguese.

The Dutch also formed the West India Company to compete in the Americas. They established the Dutch colony of New Netherlands in the Hudson River valley. However, the English seized the colony of New Netherlands and renamed it New York. They also founded the Massachusetts Bay Colony in 1630. By 1700, the English had established a colonial empire along the eastern seaboard of North America. The French were also interested in the Americas and made Canada a French colony.

In the 1500s and 1600s, European nations established trading posts and colonies in the Americas and the East. A **colony** is a settlement of people living in a new territory, linked with the parent country by trade and direct government control. Colonies played a role in the theory of **mercantilism,** a set of principles that dominated economic thought in the seventeenth century. According to mercantilists, the prosperity of a nation depended on a large supply of bullion (gold and silver). To bring in gold and silver, nations tried to have a favorable balance of trade. The **balance of trade** is the difference in value between what a nation imports and what it exports over time. When the balance is favorable, the goods exported are of greater value than those imported. To encourage exports, governments stimulated export industries and trade. They granted subsidies, or payments, to new industries and improved transportation systems. They tried to keep foreign goods out of their own countries by placing high tariffs (taxes) on these goods. Colonies were important because they were sources of raw materials and were markets for finished goods.

15. Why were colonies important in the theory of mercantilism?

____

____

____

Name ______________________ Date ______________ Class ______________

Reading Essentials and Study Guide

Chapter 13, Section 2

For use with textbook pages 415–418

AFRICA IN AN AGE OF TRANSITION

KEY TERMS

plantations large agricultural estates that often depended on slavery to provide the labor they needed *(page 416)*

triangular trade a pattern of trade that connected Europe, Africa and Asia, and the American continents *(page 416)*

Middle Passage the journey of slaves from Africa to the Americas (the middle portion of the triangular trade route) *(page 416)*

DRAWING FROM EXPERIENCE

Have you ever read about a plantation? How did the plantation owners live? How did the workers or slaves live?

In the last section, you learned about European exploration and colonization of the Americas. In this section, you will learn how the need for labor in the new colonies led to an increase in the slave trade. You will also learn about the impact that Europeans and the slave trade had on Africa.

ORGANIZING YOUR THOUGHTS

Use the diagram below to help you take notes. List the goods that were traded by each of the three areas on the triangular trade route. Indicate which section of the triangle was the Middle Passage.

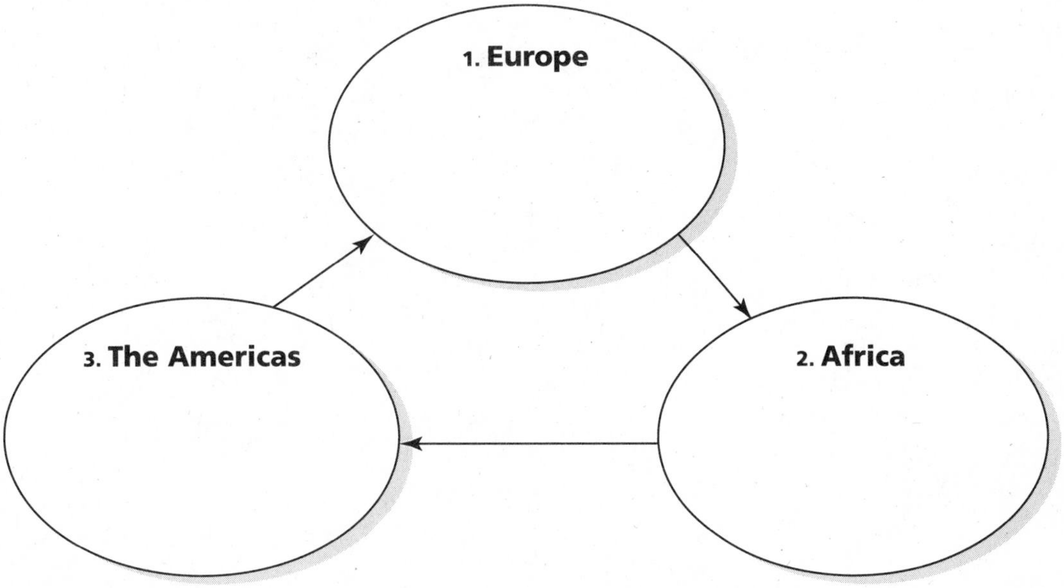

READ TO LEARN

- **The Slave Trade** *(page 415)*

Slavery had been practiced in Africa since ancient times. The primary market for slaves was Southeast Asia, where most slaves were used as domestic servants. Slavery also existed in some European countries. The demand for slaves increased dramatically with the discovery of the Americas in the 1490s. During the sixteenth century, **plantations** (large agricultural estates) that grew sugar cane were set up in Brazil and on islands in the Caribbean. Growing sugar cane requires much labor. African slaves were shipped to Brazil and the Caribbean to work on the plantations.

In 1518, a Spanish ship carried the first boatload of slaves directly from Africa to the Americas. During the next two centuries, the trade in slaves grew dramatically and became part of the **triangular trade.** In the triangular trade system, European ships carried manufactured goods, such as guns and cloth, to Africa, where they were traded for a cargo of slaves. The slaves were then shipped to the Americas and sold. Europeans then bought tobacco, molasses, sugar, and raw cotton and shipped them back to Europe. As many as ten million African slaves were brought to the Americas between the early sixteenth and the late nineteenth centuries.

The journey from Africa to the Americas became known as the **Middle Passage,** the middle portion of the triangular trade route. Many slaves died on the journey. Those who arrived often died because they had little or no immunity to diseases.

Before Europeans became involved in the slave trade, most slaves in Africa were prisoners of war. Slaves were sold at slave markets on the coasts. At first, African slave traders got their supplies of slaves from coastal areas nearby. As the demand for slaves increased, they began to move farther inland to find their victims. Many local rulers traded slaves. They viewed slaves as a source of income. Many sent raiders into defenseless villages in search of victims. Some local rulers became concerned about the impact of the slave trade on their societies, but their protests were generally ignored by Europeans and other Africans.

The slave trade led to the depopulation of some areas. It also took the youngest and strongest men and women from many communities. The need to provide a constant supply of slaves led to increased warfare in Africa. Coastal leaders increased their raids on neighboring peoples. Of course, the slave trade always had tragic effects on the lives of individual victims and their families. The slave trade also had a devastating effect on some African states. In Benin, for example, the slave trade caused the population to decline and warfare to increase. As time went on, the people of Benin lost their faith in their gods, their art deteriorated, and human sacrifice became more common.

Reading Essentials and Study Guide

4. How did the discovery of the Americas change the slave trade in Africa?

• Political and Social Structures *(page 417)*

In general, the European influence in Africa did not extend beyond the coastal regions. Only in a few areas, such as South Africa and Mozambique, were there signs of a permanent European presence. In most areas, traditional African political systems continued to exist. By the sixteenth century, monarchy had become a common form of government throughout Africa. Some kingdoms were highly centralized, but others were more like collections of small principalities, knit together by ties of kinship or other loyalties. Many Africans continued to live in small political units in which authority rested in a village leader.

Europeans were causing changes in other ways, however. In the western Sahara, trade with Europeans caused trade routes to shift toward the coast. This led to the weakening of the old Songhai trading empire. It also helped a new Moroccan dynasty to emerge in the late sixteenth century. In 1590, Moroccan forces defeated the Songhai army and then occupied the city of Timbuktu. Eventually, the Moroccans were forced to leave, but Songhai was never the same.

Foreigners also influenced African religious beliefs, but Europeans had less influence than the Islamic culture. In North Africa, Islam continued to expand. It also spread southward into the states of West Africa. The Portuguese engaged in some Christian missionary activity in Africa, but the English, Dutch and French did very little to spread the message of the gospel. The spread of Christianity was mainly limited to South Africa and Ethiopia.

5. In what ways did foreigners influence Africa?

Name ______________________ Date ____________________ Class ____________________

Reading Essentials and Study Guide

Chapter 13, Section 3

For use with textbook pages 419–422

SOUTHEAST ASIA IN THE ERA OF THE SPICE TRADE

KEY TERMS

mainland states states that are part of a continent, as distinguished from peninsulas or offshore islands *(page 421)*

bureaucracy a body of nonelective government officials *(page 422)*

DRAWING FROM EXPERIENCE

Have you ever thought what life would be like if you did not have spices for your food? What spices do you like best? How much would you be willing to pay for your favorite spices?

In the last section, you learned about the impact of Europeans and the slave trade on Africa. In this section, you will learn about the impact of Europeans and the spice trade on Southeast Asia.

ORGANIZING YOUR THOUGHTS

Use the chart below to help you take notes. There were four main styles of kingship in Southeast Asia at the time of the spice trade. Summarize those four styles of kingship in this chart.

Region	Style of Kingship
1.	2.
3.	4.
5.	6.
7.	8.

Name ______________________ Date ______________________ Class ______________________

Reading Essentials and Study Guide

READ TO LEARN

• Emerging Mainland States *(page 419)*

In 1500, mainland Southeast Asia was a relatively stable region. Kingdoms with their own ethnic, linguistic, and cultural characteristics were being formed. Conflicts eventually erupted among the emerging states. There was a bitter conflict between the Thai and the Burmese. In 1767, a Burmese army sacked the Thai capital. This forced the Thai to create a new capital at Bangkok, farther to the south. By the end of the fifteenth century, the Vietnamese had subdued the state of Champa and gradually took control of the Mekong delta from the Khmer. By 1800, the Khmer monarchy had virtually disappeared.

In the Malay Peninsula and the Indonesian Archipelago, Muslim merchants in search of spices caused changes. New states arose along the trade route created by the Muslims. In the fifteenth century, the sultanate of Melaka became the leading power in the region. It owed its power to its location and to the rapid growth of the spice trade.

9. Why did Melaka become the leading power in the region?

____

____

____

____

____

• The Arrival of Europeans *(page 420)*

In 1511, the Portuguese seized Melaka and soon occupied the Moluccas. The Moluccas were known to Europeans as the Spice Islands. They were the chief source of the spices that had attracted the Portuguese to the Indian Ocean. The Portuguese set up small settlements, which they used as trading posts. They did not have the resources to make colonies in the area. When English and Dutch traders arrived, things changed. In the early 1600s, the Dutch gradually pushed the Portuguese out of the spice trade. They took over most of the Portuguese forts along the trade route, including Melaka. The Dutch traders also drove the English traders out of the spice market. The English were left with a single port on the southern coast of Sumatra. The Dutch tried to dominate the clove trade by limiting the growing of cloves to one island. They also established a fort at Batavia on the island of Java in 1619. They gradually took control of the entire island.

The arrival of Europeans had less impact on mainland Southeast Asia. The Portuguese had limited trade relations with several mainland states, including Thailand, Burma, and Vietnam. (Mainland states are states that are part of the continent, as distinguished from peninsulas or offshore islands.) These states had strong monarchies that resisted foreign intrusion. When other European nations began to compete for trade and missionary privileges in the area, the mainland states were able to unite and drive them out.

In Vietnam, a civil war temporarily divided the country into two separate states. When the Europeans arrived in the mid-seventeenth century, they began to build trading posts and to take sides in Vietnamese politics. By the end of the seventeenth century, however, most of the trading posts were abandoned, when it became clear that the economic opportunities in this area were limited. French missionaries tried to stay, but their efforts were blocked by the Vietnamese authorities, who saw Catholicism as a threat to the prestige of the Vietnamese emperor.

10. Why did Europeans have less of an impact on mainland Southeast Asia than on non-mainland states?

____

____

____

____

____

• Religious and Political Systems *(page 422)*

Religious beliefs changed in Southeast Asia during the period from 1500 to 1800. Islam and Christianity were beginning to attract converts, especially in the non-mainland states and the Philippines. Buddhism was advancing on the mainland. It became dominant from Burma to Vietnam. Traditional beliefs still survived, however, and influenced the new religions.

The political systems in Southeast Asia evolved into four main styles of kingship: Buddhist kings, Javanese kings, Islamic sultans, and Vietnamese emperors. All of these styles adapted foreign models of government to local circumstances. The Buddhist style of kingship was the main form of government in Burma, Thailand, Laos, and Cambodia. In this style, the king was considered superior to other human beings. He served as a link between humans and the universe. The Javanese style was based on political traditions in India and was similar to the Buddhist system in many ways. Javanese kings were believed to have a sacred quality. They maintained the balance between the sacred and material worlds.

The Islamic style was found on the Malay Peninsula and in the small states on the Indonesian Archipelago. In this style, the head of state was a sultan. He was viewed as a mortal, but with some special qualities. He defended the Islamic faith and staffed his bureaucracy (a body of nonelected government officials) mainly with aristocrats.

In Vietnam, kingship followed the Chinese model. The Vietnamese emperor ruled according to the teachings of Confucius. He was seen as a mortal appointed by Heaven to rule because of his talent and virtue. He was also the intermediary between Heaven and Earth.

11. How did religious beliefs change in Southeast Asia from 1500 to 1800?

____

____

____

____

____

Name ______________________ Date ______________________ Class ______________________

Reading Essentials and Study Guide

Chapter 14, Section 1

For use with textbook pages 429–432

EUROPE IN CRISIS: THE WARS OF RELIGION

KEY TERMS

militant combative *(page 429)*

armada a fleet of warships *(page 432)*

DRAWING FROM EXPERIENCE

Do you think having a single individual with total power to govern a nation could ever be good for a nation? Why or why not?

In this section, you will learn how conflict between Catholics and Protestants led to wars in many European nations. At the same time, many European rulers increased their power and their territories.

ORGANIZING YOUR THOUGHTS

Use the chart below to help you take notes. Identify the country and religion of the following rulers, and summarize their achievements.

Ruler	Country	Religion	Achievements
Henry IV	**1.**	**2.**	**3.**
Philip II	**4.**	**5.**	**6.**
Elizabeth I	**7.**	**8.**	**9.**

Name ______________________ Date ______________________ Class ______________________

READ TO LEARN

• The French Wars of Religion *(page 429)*

By 1560, Calvinism and Catholicism had become highly **militant** (combative) religions. They both wanted to win converts and to eliminate the other's authority. This was the main cause of the religious wars in Europe in the sixteenth century, but economic, social, and political forces also played important roles.

The French Wars of Religion lasted from 1562 to 1598. The French kings persecuted Protestants, but the persecution did not stop the spread of Protestantism. French Protestants who were influenced by John Calvin were called Huguenots. The Huguenots made up only about 7 percent of the total French population, but 40 to 50 percent of the nobility were Huguenots. The conversion of so many nobles made the Huguenots a threat to the French monarchy, which was strongly Catholic. An extreme Catholic party also strongly opposed the Huguenots. They were known as the ultra-Catholics. They were able to recruit and pay for large armies. Although the main issue in the French wars was religion, other factors also played a role. Many towns and provinces had long resisted the power of French monarchy. They were willing to assist the Huguenot nobles in weakening the monarchy.

For 30 years, there were battles in France between the Catholics and Huguenots. Finally in 1589, Henry of Navarre became king of France. As king, his name was Henry IV. He was the political leader of the Huguenots and a member of the Bourbon dynasty. He realized that he would never be accepted as king by most of Catholic France, so he converted to Catholicism. To solve the religious problem, he issued the Edict of Nantes in 1598. The edict recognized Catholicism as the official religion of France, but it gave Huguenots the right to worship. It also gave them full political rights.

10. Who were the Huguenots?

____

____

____

____

____

• Philip II and Militant Catholicism *(page 430)*

The greatest supporter of militant Catholicism in the second half of the sixteenth century was King Philip II of Spain. He reigned from 1556 to 1598. His first major goal as king was to consolidate the lands he had inherited from his father, Charles V. These included Spain, the Netherlands, and possessions in

Italy and the Americas. To strengthen his control, he insisted on strict conformity to Catholicism and strong monarchical authority. The Catholic faith was important to both Philip II and the Spanish people. Spain saw itself as a nation of people chosen by God to save Catholic Christianity from the Protestant heretics.

Philip II became a champion of Catholic causes. He led a Holy League against the Turks. This resulted in a victory over the Turkish fleet in the Battle of Lepanto in 1571. He was not as successful in the Netherlands. The Spanish Netherlands consisted of 17 provinces (modern Netherlands and Belgium). It was one of the richest parts of Philip's empire. Philip tried to strengthen his control in this region. The nobles of the Netherlands strongly opposed him. Philip also tried to crush Calvinism in the Netherlands. Violence broke out in 1566 when Calvinists began to destroy statues in Catholic churches. Philip sent ten thousand troops to crush the rebellion. In the northern provinces, the Dutch, under the leadership of William the Silent, offered growing resistance. Finally, in 1609, a 12-year truce ended the war. The northern provinces began to call themselves the United Provinces of the Netherlands. They became the core of the modern Dutch state. The seventeenth century has been called the golden age of the Dutch Republic.

Philip's reign ended in 1598. At that time, Spain was the most populous empire in the world. It controlled almost all of South America and a number of settlements in Asia and Africa. To most Europeans, it seemed to be the greatest power at the time. However, its treasury was empty. Philip II had gone bankrupt from spending too much on war. The armed forces were out-of-date, and the government was inefficient. Spain continued to play the role of a great power, but real power had shifted to England.

11. Why is Philip II called the "Most Catholic King"?

• The England of Elizabeth *(page 431)*

During the reign of Elizabeth Tudor, England became the leader of the Protestant nations of Europe and laid the foundations for a world empire. Elizabeth became queen in 1558. To solve the religious problem in England, she repealed the laws favoring Catholics that had been passed under her Catholic half-sister, Mary Tudor. A new Act of Supremacy named Elizabeth as the "only supreme governor" of both church and state. The Church of

England under Elizabeth was basically Protestant, but it followed a moderate Protestantism that kept most people satisfied.

Elizabeth tried to keep Spain and France from becoming too powerful by balancing power. If one nation seemed to be getting more powerful, England would support the weaker nation. Philip II of Spain wanted to invade England, partly to overthrow Protestantism. His advisers told him that the people of England would rise against Elizabeth when the Spaniards arrived. In 1588, Philip ordered preparations for an **armada** (a fleet of warships) to invade England. But the Spanish were no match for the English. After a number of battles, the Spanish armada sailed back to Spain by a northern route around Scotland and Ireland. The ships were pounded by storms, and many sank.

12. How did Elizabeth solve the religious problem in England?

____

____

____

____

____

Name ______________________ Date ______________ Class ______________

Reading Essentials and Study Guide

Chapter 14, Section 2

For use with textbook pages 434–439

SOCIAL CRISES, WAR, AND REVOLUTION

KEY TERMS

inflation rising prices *(page 434)*

witchcraft magic performed by witches *(page 435)*

divine right of kings the belief that kings receive their power from God and are responsible only to God *(page 437)*

commonwealth a republic (used especially for the government of England from 1649 to 1660) *(page 438)*

DRAWING FROM EXPERIENCE

Are you concerned about inflation? How have you been affected by inflation? How many times has the price of a postage stamp increased in your lifetime?

In the last section, you read about the religious wars in France and other countries in the sixteenth century. In this section, you will learn how religious disputes continued in many countries and led to the Thirty Years' War in Germany. You will also learn about the revolutions in England during the seventeenth century and about the social and economic problems, such as inflation, that plagued Europe during this time.

ORGANIZING YOUR THOUGHTS

Use the diagram below to help you take notes. Identify the rulers of England after Elizabeth I and before William and Mary.

Elizabeth I → 1. → 2. →

3. → 4. → 5. →

William and Mary

Name ______________ Date ______________ Class ______________

Reading Essentials and Study Guide

Chapter 14, Section 2 *(continued)*

READ TO LEARN

• Economic and Social Crises *(page 434)*

From 1560 to 1650, Europe had severe economic and social crises. One major economic problem was **inflation,** or rising prices. The influx of gold and silver from the Americas was one cause of the inflation. There was also a growing population in the sixteenth century. This increased the demand for land and food and drove up prices for both. Spain's economy was seriously failing by the 1640s. It had grown dependent on imported silver, and the silver mines were producing less silver. Italy was the financial center of Europe in the Renaissance, but it was also declining economically.

The population in Europe increased from about 60 million in 1500 to 85 million by 1600. By 1620, the population began to level off. By 1650, it began to decline, especially in central and southern Europe. Warfare, plague, and famine all contributed to the population decline.

6. What were some of the causes of inflation in the sixteenth and early seventeenth centuries?

• The Witchcraft Trials *(page 435)*

A belief in **witchcraft,** or magic, had been part of traditional village culture for centuries. During the sixteenth and seventeenth centuries, an intense hysteria about witchcraft affected the lives of many Europeans. More than a hundred thousand people were charged with witchcraft. As more and more people were brought to trial, the fear of witches grew. So did the fear of being accused of witchcraft. Poor, common people were the ones most often accused. More than 75 percent of those accused were women. Most of them were single or widowed and over 50 years old. Under torture, accused witches usually confessed.

By 1650, the witchcraft hysteria had begun to lessen. Officials were less willing to disrupt their societies with witch trials. People were also less willing to believe in the old view of a world haunted by evil spirits.

7. Which people were most likely to be accused of witchcraft?

• The Thirty Years' War *(page 435)*

Religious disputes continued in Germany after the Peace of Augsburg in 1555. One reason for the disputes was that Calvinism had not been recognized by the peace settlement. Religion played an important role in the start of the Thirty Years' War, but there were also political and territorial motives for this war. The war began in 1618. At first, it was a struggle between Catholic forces and Protestant nobles in Bohemia. The Protestant nobles were primarily Calvinists who rebelled against the Hapsburg emperors. Soon the conflict became a political one. Denmark, Sweden, France, and Spain all entered the war. The war became a struggle between France and the rulers of Spain and the Holy Roman Empire. Most of the battles of the war were fought on German soil. For 30 years, Germany was plundered and destroyed. The Peace of Westphalia ended the war in 1648. It stated that all German states, including the Calvinist ones, could determine their own religion. The states that had made up the Holy Roman Empire were recognized as independent states. This brought an end to the Holy Roman Empire. Germany would not be united again for another two hundred years. France, on the other hand, emerged from the war as the dominant nation in Europe.

8. What was the impact of the Thirty Years' War on Germany and France?

• Revolutions in England *(page 437)*

The civil war in England is known as the English Revolution. It began as a struggle between the king and Parliament to determine what role each should play in governing England. After Queen Elizabeth died in 1603, the Tudor dynasty came to an end. The Stuart line of rulers began when Elizabeth's cousin, the king of Scotland, became James I of England. He ruled from 1603 to 1625. James believed in the **divine right of kings** (that kings receive their power from God and are responsible only to God). Parliament, on the other hand, believed that the king or queen and Parliament ruled England together.

Religion was also an issue. The **Puritans** (Protestants in England inspired by Calvinist ideas) did not like the king's strong defense of the Church of England. The Puritans were part of the Church of England, but they wanted to make it more Protestant. Many of England's wealthy landowners had become Puritans. These Puritans were an important part of the House of Commons, the lower house of Parliament.

The conflict began during the reign of James but came to a head during the reign of his son, Charles I. Charles ruled from 1625 to 1649. In 1628, Parliament passed a petition that prohibited the passing of any taxes without Parliament's consent. At first, Charles I accepted this petition, but he later changed his mind, because the petition put limits on the king's power. Charles also tried to impose more ritual on the Church of England. To the Puritans, this was a return to Catholic practices. When Charles tried to force them to accept his religious policies, thousands of Puritans went to America.

In 1642, a civil war began between the supporters of the king (the Cavaliers or Royalists) and the parliamentary forces (called the Roundheads because of their short hair). Parliament was victorious. This was due mainly to the New Model Army of Oliver Cromwell. This army was made up primarily of extreme Puritans who believed that they were doing battle for God. After the victory, Cromwell purged Parliament of any members who had not supported him. What was left of the Parliament is known as the Rump Parliament. The Rump Parliament had Charles I executed on January 30, 1649. Parliament then abolished the monarchy and the House of Lords and declared England a republic, or **commonwealth.** Cromwell found it difficult to work with the Rump Parliament and finally dispersed it by force. After destroying both the king and Parliament, Cromwell set up a military dictatorship.

Cromwell ruled from 1653 until he died in 1658. In 1660, Parliament made Charles II king. He was the son of Charles I. He ruled until his death in 1685. Parliament passed laws that made the Church of England the state religion again. The laws also took away some rights of Catholics and Puritans. Charles II was sympathetic to Catholicism. He suspended the laws that Parliament had passed, but Parliament forced him to back down.

In 1685, James II, the brother of Charles II, became king. He was an open and devout Catholic. He named Catholics to high positions in the government and military. In 1688, a group of English noblemen invited the Dutch leader, William of Orange, to invade England. William of Orange was the husband of James' daughter, Mary. William and Mary were Protestants. They raised an army and "invaded" England. James fled to France. With almost no bloodshed, England had undergone a "Glorious Revolution."

In January 1689, Parliament offered the throne to William and Mary. They accepted it, along with a Bill of Rights. The Bill of Rights set forth Parliament's right to make laws and levy taxes. It also stated that standing armies could only be raised with Parliament's consent. The rights of citizens to keep arms and have a jury trial were also confirmed. The bill laid the foundation for a limited, or constitutional, monarchy. Another important action of Parliament was the Toleration Act of 1689. This act granted Puritans, but not Catholics, the right of free public worship. Few English citizens would ever again be persecuted for religion. By deposing one king and establishing another, Parliament destroyed the divine-right theory. William was king, not by the grace of God, but by the grace of Parliament.

9. What was the "Glorious Revolution" in England?

____

____

____

____

____

Name ________________ Date ________________ Class ________________

Reading Essentials and Study Guide

Chapter 14, Section 3

For use with textbook pages 441–447

RESPONSE TO CRISIS: ABSOLUTISM

KEY TERMS

absolutism a system of government in which a ruler holds total power *(page 441)*

czar the Russian word for caesar, which became the title of the Russian rulers beginning with Ivan IV *(page 445)*

boyars the Russian nobility *(page 446)*

DRAWING FROM EXPERIENCE

What do you think is the purpose of dress codes? Do you think dress codes should be enforced in public schools? Why or why not?

In the last section, you read about the wars, revolutions, and economic problems in Europe during the seventeenth century. In this section, you will learn how monarchs in certain countries gained absolute power during this time. One of these absolute monarchs, Peter the Great, even told people how they should dress.

ORGANIZING YOUR THOUGHTS

Use the chart below to help you take notes. Identify the countries of the following monarchs and summarize their achievements.

Monarch	Country	Achievements
Louis XIV	1.	2.
Frederick William the Great Elector	3.	4.
Peter the Great	5.	6.

READ TO LEARN

• France Under Louis XIV *(page 441)*

The reign of Louis XIV has been regarded as the best example of the practice of absolutism in the seventeenth century. **Absolutism** is a system in which a ruler holds total power. In seventeenth-century Europe, absolutism was tied to the idea of the divine right of kings. Absolute monarchs had tremendous powers. They had the ability to make laws, levy taxes, administer justice, control the state's officials, and determine foreign policy.

French history for the 50 years before Louis was a period of struggle. Both Louis XIII and Louis XIV were only boys when they became kings. Royal ministers controlled the government. Cardinal Richelieu, Louis XIII's chief minister, strengthened the power of the monarchy. Because the Huguenots were seen as a threat to the king's power, Richelieu took away their political and military rights. He also set up a network of spies to uncover plots by nobles against the government. When plots were discovered, he executed the conspirators. Louis XIV came to the throne in 1643 at the age of four. Due to the king's young age, Cardinal Mazarin, the chief minister, took control of the government. During the time of Mazarin, there was a revolt led by nobles who were unhappy with the growing power of the monarchy, but the revolt was crushed. When Mazarin died in 1661, Louis XIV, now age 23, took over supreme power. He had complete authority over foreign policy, the Church, and taxes. He created a myth of himself as the Sun King—the source of light for all of his people.

Louis set up his royal court at Versailles. His court served three purposes. It was the personal household of the king. The chief offices of the state were located there, so Louis could watch over them. It was also the place where people came to find favors and offices for themselves. The royal council was the king's chief administrative body. To keep nobles and royal princes from becoming too powerful, Louis removed them from the royal council. At the same time, he invited them to court, where he could keep them busy with court life and out of politics. At the local level, however, Louis's power was limited. The nobles, local officials, and town councils had more influence than the king in the day-to-day operations of the local governments. As a result, the king bribed people in the provinces to see that his policies were carried out. Louis had an anti-Protestant policy. He ordered the destruction of Huguenot churches and closed their schools. As many as two hundred thousand Huguenots left France for England, the United Provinces, and the German states.

Louis developed a standing army of four hundred thousand. He waged four wars between 1667 and 1713. His ambitions caused many nations to form coalitions against him. Through his wars, Louis added some territory to France's northeastern frontier and set up a member of his own family on the throne of Spain. The cost of pursuing wars, building palaces, and maintaining his court made finances a crucial issue for Louis XIV. His controller-general of finances was Jean-Baptiste Colbert. Colbert followed the ideas of mercantilism. To decrease imports, he raised tariffs (taxes) on foreign goods. He also created a merchant marine to carry French goods. Nonetheless, when Louis XIV died in 1715, he left France with great debts and surrounded by enemies.

7. What is absolutism?

____

____

____

• Absolutism in Central and Eastern Europe *(page 444)*

After the Thirty Years' War, there was no German state, but over three hundred "Germanies." Two of these states, Prussia and Austria, became great powers in the seventeenth and eighteenth centuries. Frederick William the Great Elector laid the foundation for the Prussian state. He built a large and efficient standing army. To maintain the army and his own power, Frederick William set up the General War Commissariat to levy taxes for the army and oversee its growth. The Commissariat soon became an agency for civil government as well. Many of its officials were members of the Prussian aristocracy, known as the Junkers. They also served as officers in the army. In 1701, Frederick William's son officially gained the title of king. Elector Frederick III became King Frederick I.

The Austrian Hapsburgs had long played an important role in European politics as Holy Roman emperors. The Hapsburgs made a difficult transition in the seventeenth century. After the Thirty Years' War, they had lost the German Empire, but now they created a new empire in eastern and southeastern Europe. The core of the new Austrian Empire was the traditional Austrian lands in present-day Austria, the Czech Republic, and Hungary. After the defeat of the Turks in 1687, Austria took control of all of Hungary, Transylvania, Croatia, and Slovenia. By the beginning of the eighteenth century, the Austrian Hapsburgs had a new empire, but it never became a highly centralized, absolutist state. This was chiefly because it was made up of so many different national groups. Each of these areas had its own laws and political life. No common sentiment tied the regions together.

8. How was the Austrian Empire of the seventeenth and eighteenth centuries different from the old Hapsburg Empire?

____

____

____

• Russia Under Peter the Great *(page 445)*

In the sixteenth century, Ivan IV became the first ruler to take the title of **czar,** the Russian word for caesar. Ivan expanded the territories of Russia eastward. He also crushed the power of the Russian nobility, known as the **boyars.** He was known as Ivan the Terrible because of his ruthless deeds. When Ivan's dynasty came to an end in 1584, a period of anarchy known as the Time of Troubles followed. This period did not end until the Zemsky Sobor, or national assembly, chose Michael Romanov as the new czar in 1613.

The Romanov dynasty lasted until 1917. One of its most prominent members was Peter the Great. Peter became czar in 1689. He was an absolutist monarch who claimed the divine right to rule. A few years after becoming czar, Peter made a trip to the West. When he returned to Russia, he was determined to westernize Russia. He borrowed European technology, especially for the military. Under Peter the Great, Russia became a great military power. One of his first goals was to reorganize the army. He employed both Russians and Europeans as officers. He built a standing army of 210,000 men. He also formed the first Russian navy. After his trip to the West, Peter introduced Western customs, practices, and manners into Russia. He ordered the preparation of the first Russian book of etiquette to teach Western manners. Because Westerners did not wear beards or long coats, Russian beards had to be shaved and coats shortened. Because Western women mixed freely with men, Peter insisted that Russian upper-class women remove the veils that had traditionally covered their faces and move out into society. Peter also held gatherings in which both sexes could mix for conversation and dancing, a practice he had learned in the West.

Peter also wanted to "open a window to the West," an ice-free port with year-round access to Europe. This could only be achieved on the Baltic Sea. At that time, however, the Baltic coast was controlled by Sweden. Peter fought a long war with Sweden and finally acquired the lands he needed. In 1703, Peter began the construction of a new city, St. Petersburg, on the Baltic Sea. St. Petersburg was finished during his lifetime and became the Russian capital until 1917.

9. How did Peter's trip to the West change Russia?

____

____

____

Name ______________________ Date ______________ Class ______________

Reading Essentials and Study Guide

Chapter 14, Section 4

For use with textbook pages 448–451

THE WORLD OF EUROPEAN CULTURE

KEY TERMS

Mannerism a movement in art that emerged in Italy in the 1520s and 1530s, which emphasized emotions, suffering, and religious ecstasy *(page 448)*

baroque a movement in art that began in Italy in the late sixteenth century, which tried to bring together the classical ideals of Renaissance art and the spiritual feelings of the sixteenth-century religious revival *(page 449)*

natural rights rights with which humans are born, including rights to life, liberty, and property *(page 451)*

DRAWING FROM EXPERIENCE

Have you ever attended the performance of a Shakespearean play? Have you read any of Shakespeare's works? Which ones do you like best?

In the last three sections, you read about political, economic, and religious developments in Europe in the sixteenth and seventeenth centuries. In this section, you will learn about developments in art, literature, and political thought during this period. Two of the world's greatest writers, Shakespeare and Cervantes, lived during this time.

ORGANIZING YOUR THOUGHTS

Use the chart below to help you take notes. Two political thinkers, Thomas Hobbes and John Locke, both lived in England during the seventeenth century, but they developed quite different political theories. Compare and contrast their political ideas in this chart.

	Thomas Hobbes	**John Locke**
Title of political work	**1.**	**2.**
View of human nature	**3.**	**4.**
Reason given for why humans developed governments/social contracts	**5.**	**6.**
Type of government promoted	**7.**	**8.**

Name ______________ Date ______________ Class ______________

READ TO LEARN

• Mannerism *(page 448)*

A new movement called **Mannerism** emerged in Italy in the 1520s and 1530s. The religious upheavals of the Reformation caused the worldly enthusiasm of the Renaissance to decline. People were anxious and uncertain and wished for spiritual experiences. This was reflected in Mannerism. The rules of proportion were deliberately ignored. Elongated figures were used to show suffering, heightened emotions, and religious ecstasy. Mannerism spread from Italy to other parts of Europe. It reached its high point in the work of El Greco. In his paintings, El Greco used elongated and contorted figures. He portrayed them in shades of yellow and green against an eerie background of stormy grays.

9. How did Mannerism reflect the uncertainty of the Reformation period?

• The Baroque Period *(page 449)*

Mannerism was eventually replaced by a new movement—the **baroque.** This movement began in Italy in the last quarter of the sixteenth century and spread to the rest of Europe and even Latin America. Baroque artists tried to bring together the classical ideals of Renaissance art with the spiritual feelings of the sixteenth-century religious revival. The baroque painting style was known for its use of dramatic effects to arouse the emotions. Baroque art and architecture also reflected the search for power in the seventeenth century. Baroque churches and palaces were magnificent and richly detailed. Perhaps the greatest baroque artist was the Italian architect and sculptor Gian Lorenzo Bernini. He completed Saint Peter's Basilica in Rome.

10. What effect did Baroque artists try to achieve?

Name ____________ Date ____________ Class ____________

Reading Essentials and Study Guide

Chapter 14, Section 4 *(continued)*

• A Golden Age of Literature *(page 449)*

The period in England from the late sixteenth to the early seventeenth centuries is often called the Elizabethan Era, because so much of it fell within the reign of Queen Elizabeth. During this period, there were many cultural achievements. Drama, in particular, flourished during this period. Of all the dramatists, none is more famous than William Shakespeare. During the Elizabethan period, theater was a very successful business. Both the lower classes and the well-to-do enjoyed the theater. Because Elizabethan audiences varied so much, playwrights had to write works that pleased many different kinds of people. Shakespeare understood this. He was a master of the English language, but he also had a remarkable understanding of human psychology.

The theater also flourished in Spain. Every large town had a public playhouse, including Mexico City in the New World. Touring companies brought the latest Spanish plays to all parts of the Spanish Empire. Beginning in the 1580s, the standard for playwrights was set by Lope de Vega. He wrote an extraordinary number of plays, perhaps 1500 in all. He wrote his plays to please his audiences and satisfy public demand. His plays are witty, charming, action-packed, and realistic. Other forms of literature also flourished during this time. One of the greatest achievements of the golden age of Spanish literature was the work of Miguel de Cervantes. His novel Don Quixote is considered one of the greatest literary works of all time.

11. What form of literature particularly flourished in England and Spain in the late sixteenth and early seventeenth centuries?

• Political Thought *(page 451)*

Two English philosophers, Thomas Hobbes and John Locke, developed political theories in response to the English revolutions of the seventeenth century. Their theories were very different. Thomas Hobbes wrote a political work called *Leviathan*. It was published in 1651. Hobbes was alarmed by the revolutionary upheavals in England. His work tried to deal with the problem of disorder. He believed that humans were guided not by reason and moral ideals, but by a ruthless struggle for self-preservation. He believed that people made a social contract and agreed to form a state to save themselves from destroying one another. Hobbes called the state "that great Leviathan to which we owe our peace and defense." People in the state agreed to be governed by an absolute ruler who possessed unlimited power. Hobbes believed that absolute power was necessary to preserve order in society.

Reading Essentials and Study Guide

Chapter 14, Section 4 *(continued)*

John Locke wrote a political work in 1690 called *Two Treatises of Government*. Locke did not believe in the absolute rule of one person. He believed that before society was organized, humans lived in a state of equality and freedom, not a state of war. He believed that humans had certain **natural rights** (rights with which they were born). These included rights to life, liberty, and property. He believed that people agreed to establish a government to ensure the protection of their rights. The contract between people and government involved mutual obligations. Government would protect the rights of people, and people would act reasonably toward government. If a government broke the contract, people could form a new government. Locke's ideas can be found in the American Declaration of Independence and the U.S. Constitution.

12. What are "natural" rights?

____

____

____

____

____

Name ______________________ Date ______________________ Class ______________________

Reading Essentials and Study Guide

Chapter 15, Section 1

For use with textbook pages 457–463

THE OTTOMAN EMPIRE

KEY TERMS

janissary a soldier in the Ottoman sultans' elite guard *(page 458)*

pasha a local official in the Ottoman empire, who collected taxes, maintained law and order, and was directly responsible to the sultan's court *(page 459)*

gunpowder empire an empire whose success was based largely on its mastery of the technology of firearms *(page 460)*

sultan the head of the Ottoman empire *(page 460)*

harem ("sacred place") the private domain of a sultan *(page 461)*

grand vizier a chief minister who led the meetings of the imperial council in the Ottoman Empire *(page 461)*

ulema a group of religious advisers in the Ottoman Empire who administered the legal system and the schools for educating Muslims *(page 461)*

DRAWING FROM EXPERIENCE

How is religious toleration guaranteed in the United States? Why do you think some people are not tolerant of religious beliefs that are different from their own?

In this section, you will learn about the empire of the Ottoman Turks. Although the Ottomans were Sunni Muslims, they were generally tolerant of other religions in their empire.

ORGANIZING YOUR THOUGHTS

Use the chart below to help you take notes. List the areas that were conquered by the Ottoman rulers in this chart.

Ruler	Areas Conquered
Mehmet II	**1.**
Selim I	**2.**
Süleyman I	**3.**

Name ______________________ Date ________________ Class ________________

Reading Essentials and Study Guide

READ TO LEARN

• Rise of the Ottoman Turks *(page 457)*

In the late thirteenth century, a new group of Turks began to build power in the northwest corner of the Anatolian Peninsula. The name of the leader of this group of Turks was Osman. As the Seljuk Empire began to decline in the early fourteenth century, the Osman Turks began to expand. This was the beginning of the Ottoman dynasty.

The Ottomans expanded westward and eventually controlled the Bosporus and the Dardanelles. These two straits (narrow passageways) connect the Black Sea and the Aegean Sea. The Byzantine Empire had previously controlled this area. In the fourteenth century, the Ottoman Turks expanded into the Balkans. Ottoman rulers took the title of sultan and began to build a strong military by developing an elite guard called **janissaries.** The Ottomans also began to master firearms. The Ottomans defeated the Serbs at the Battle of Kosovo in 1389. Around 1400, they took over Bulgaria.

4. What steps did the Ottomans take to build a strong military?

____

____

____

____

• Expansion of the Empire *(page 458)*

Under the leadership of Mehmet II, the Ottomans moved to end the Byzantine Empire. They attacked Constantinople. The Byzantines fought for almost two months to save their city, but the Ottomans finally conquered it. The Byzantine emperor died in the final battle. The Ottomans made Constantinople their capital. It was later renamed Istanbul. The Ottomans now dominated the Balkans and the Anatolian Peninsula. From 1514 to 1517, Sultan Selim I took control of Mesopotamia, Egypt, and Arabia. He now controlled several of the holy cities of Islam, including Jerusalem, Makkah, and Madinah. He declared himself to be the new caliph, defender of the Islamic faith and successor to Muhammad. Ottoman forces then moved westward along the African coast, eventually reaching almost to the Strait of Gibraltar. Where possible, the Ottomans preferred to administer their conquered lands through local rulers. The central government appointed officials, called **pashas.** The pashas collected taxes, maintained law and order, and were responsible to the sultan's court in Constantinople.

During the reign of Süleyman I, the Ottomans attacked Europe. They advanced up the Danube and seized Belgrade. In 1526, at the Battle of Mohacs on the Danube, they won a major victory over the Hungarians. The Ottomans

Name ______________ Date ______________ Class ______________

then conquered most of Hungary, moved into Austria, and advanced as far as Vienna. They were defeated at Vienna in 1529. They also extended their power into the western Mediterranean until a large Ottoman fleet was destroyed by the Spanish at Lepanto in 1571. For the next hundred years, the Ottomans did not try to conquer any more of eastern Europe. In the second half of the seventeenth century, however, they again went on the offensive. By mid-1683, the Ottomans had marched through the Hungarian plain and attacked Vienna. But an army of Europeans forced them to retreat, and they were pushed out of Hungary. They would never again be a threat to central Europe.

5. How did the Ottomans prefer to administer their conquered territories?

• Nature of Ottoman Rule *(page 460)*

The Ottoman Empire is often called a **"gunpowder empire."** Gunpowder empires were formed by outside conquerors who unified the regions that they conquered. The success of these empires was based mainly on the use of gunpowder and firearms.

At the head of the Ottoman system was the **sultan.** He was the supreme authority in both a political and a military sense. The position of sultan was hereditary. As the empire expanded, the status and prestige of the sultan increased. The sultan controlled his bureaucracy through an imperial council that met four days a week. A chief minister, known as the **grand vizier,** led the meetings of the council. The empire was divided into provinces and districts, each governed by officials. Senior officials were given land by the sultan. They were then responsible for collecting taxes and supplying armies for the empire.

The sultan became increasingly isolated in his palace. The private domain of the sultan was called the **harem** ("sacred place"). The sultan and his wives resided here. When a son became sultan, his mother became known as the queen mother and acted as a major adviser to the throne.

6. Why is the Ottoman Empire called a "gunpowder empire"?

• Religion in the Ottoman World *(page 461)*

The Ottomans were Sunni Muslims. The Ottoman sultans had claimed the title of caliph since the early sixteenth century. In theory, they were responsible for guiding the Muslims in their empire and maintaining Islamic law. In practice, they gave their religious duties to a group of religious advisers known as the **ulema.** The ulema administered the legal system and schools for educating Muslims.

The Ottoman system was generally tolerant of non-Muslims. Non-Muslims paid a tax, but they were allowed to practice their religion or to convert to Islam. Most people in the European areas of the empire remained Christian. In some areas, such as present-day Bosnia, many people converted to the Islamic faith.

7. How did the Ottomans treat non-Muslims in their empire?

____

____

____

____

• Ottoman Society *(page 462)*

Ottomans were divided into groups by occupation. In addition to the ruling class, there were four main occupational groups: peasants, artisans, merchants, and pastoral peoples (nomadic herders). Except for the ruling class, merchants were the most privileged class in Ottoman society. They were largely exempt from government regulations and taxes and often amassed large fortunes.

Women in the Ottoman Empire had the same restrictions as women in other Muslim societies, but their position was somewhat better. Women were allowed to own and inherit property. They could not be forced into marriage. In certain cases, they were permitted to seek divorce. A few women even served as senior officials, such as governors of provinces.

8. In what ways did women in the Ottoman Empire have a better legal position than women in other Muslim societies?

____

____

____

____

• Problems in the Ottoman Empire *(page 462)*

The Ottoman Empire reached its high point under Süleyman the Magnificent, who ruled from 1520 to 1566. After the death of Süleyman, sultans became less involved in government and allowed their ministers to exercise more power. Senior positions were given to the sons or daughters of the elite. Members of the elite soon formed a privileged group seeking wealth and power. The central bureaucracy became less connected with rural areas. As a result, local officials grew corrupt, and taxes rose.

Officials and merchants began to imitate the habits and lifestyles of Europeans. They wore European clothes, bought Western furniture and art objects, and ignored Muslim rules against the drinking of alcohol. Both coffee and tobacco were introduced into Ottoman society in the sixteenth and seventeenth centuries.

9. How did the government of the Ottoman Empire change after the death of Süleyman?

• Ottoman Art *(page 463)*

During the period from Mehmet II to the early eighteenth century, the arts flourished in the Ottoman Empire. The sultans were enthusiastic patrons of the arts. By far the greatest contribution of the Ottoman Empire to world art was in architecture. The mosques of the last half of the sixteenth century were magnificent. In the mid-sixteenth century, the greatest of all Ottoman architects, Sinan, began building the first of his 81 mosques. One of Sinan's masterpieces was the Suleimaniye Mosque in Istanbul.

Textiles and rugs also flourished during the sixteenth century. Factories produced silks for wall hangings, sofa covers, and especially court costumes. Rugs were a peasant industry. The rugs were made of wool and cotton. Different regions had their own distinctive designs and color schemes.

10. What art forms flourished during the Ottoman Empire?

Name ______________________ Date ______________________ Class ______________________

Reading Essentials and Study Guide

Chapter 15, Section 2

For use with textbook pages 468–471

THE RULE OF THE SAFAVIDS

KEY TERMS

shah the title used by Safavid rulers *(page 469)*

orthodoxy conforming to traditional religious beliefs *(page 469)*

anarchy lawlessness and disorder *(page 470)*

DRAWING FROM EXPERIENCE

Have you ever seen a Persian rug? How are Persian rugs different from other rugs or carpets? Why do you think they are so valuable?

ORGANIZING YOUR THOUGHTS

Use the pyramid diagram below to help you take notes. Show the hierarchy of the Safavid political system.

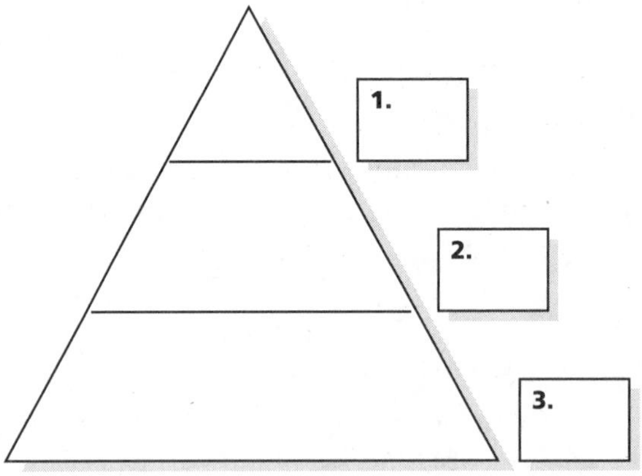

READ TO LEARN

- **Rise of the Safavid Dynasty** *(page 468)*

After the empire of Timur Lenk (Tamerlane) ended in the early fifteenth century, Persia fell into **anarchy** (lawlessness and disorder). At the beginning of the sixteenth century, a new dynasty took control. This dynasty was known as the Safavids. Ismail, who was the descendant of an earlier leader named Safi al-Din, founded it. (The word *Safavid* comes from his name.) In 1501, Ismail seized much of what is now Iran and Iraq. He then called himself the **shah,** or king, of a new Persian state.

Name ______________________ Date ______________________ Class ______________________

Reading Essentials and Study Guide

Chapter 15, Section 2 *(continued)*

The Safavids were devout Shiite Muslims. Ismail sent Shiite preachers into Anatolia to convert members of Turkish tribes in the Ottoman Empire. He also ordered the massacre of Sunni Muslims when he conquered Baghdad in 1508. The Ottoman sultan, Selim I, was alarmed and attacked the Safavids in Persia. He won a major battle near Tabriz, but a few years later, Ismail regained Tabriz. Like the Ottoman sultan, the shah claimed to be the spiritual leader of all Islam. In the 1580s, the Ottomans again attacked. They gained control of Azerbaijan and the Caspian Sea. This forced the new Safavid shah, Abbas, to sign a peace treaty in which he lost much territory.

4. Why did the Ottomans attack the Safavids?

____

____

____

____

• Glory and Decline *(page 469)*

Under Shah Abbas, who ruled from 1588 to 1629, the Safavids reached their high point. In the early seventeenth century, Shah Abbas moved against the Ottomans to regain lost territories. In 1612, a peace treaty was signed that returned Azerbaijan to the Safavids.

After the death of Shah Abbas in 1629, the Safavid dynasty gradually declined. Most of his successors did not have the same talent and political skills. The power of Shiite religious groups began to increase. The pressure to conform to traditional religious beliefs, called religious **orthodoxy,** also increased. Persian women were now forced into seclusion and were required to adopt the wearing of the veil.

During the reign of Shah Hussein in the early eighteenth century, Afghan peoples invaded and seized the capital of Isfahan. The Safavid ruling family was forced to retreat to Azerbaijan. The Turks took advantage of the situation to seize territories along the western border. Persia sank into a long period of political and social **anarchy.**

5. During what period was the Safavid dynasty at its height?

____

____

____

____

• Political and Social Structures *(page 470)*

Persia under the Safavids was a mixed society. The Safavids had come to power with the support of nomadic Turkish groups, but the majority of the people were Persian. Most of them were farmers or townspeople. The combination of Turkish and Persian elements affected nearly all aspects of Safavid society.

The Safavid political system was organized in the shape of a pyramid. The shah was at the top, the bureaucracy and landed classes were in the middle, and the common people were at the bottom.

The Safavid rulers were supported by Shiites. The Shiites believed that the founder of the empire (Shah Ismail) was a direct successor of the prophet Muhammad. The shahs declared Shiism to be the state religion. The shahs were more available to their subjects than other rulers were. Appointment to senior positions in the bureaucracy was based on merit rather than birth. To avoid competition between Turkish and non-Turkish people, Shah Abbas hired a number of foreigners for positions in his government.

The shahs played an active role in trade and manufacturing. There was also a large urban middle class involved in trade. Most goods traveled by horse or camel caravans. The government provided resting places for travelers. In times of strong rulers, the roads were kept fairly clear of thieves and bandits.

6. In what way was Persia under the Safavids a mixed society?

____

____

____

• Safavid Culture *(page 471)*

The arts flourished during the reign of Shah Abbas from 1588 to 1629. The capital of Isfahan was built by Shah Abbas. It was a planned city with wide spaces and a sense of order. Silk weaving based on new techniques also flourished. So did carpet weaving. There was a great demand for Persian carpets in the West. Persian painting during this period featured soft colors and flowing movement. Riza-i-Abbasi was the most famous artist of this period. He created beautiful works on simple subjects, such as oxen plowing, hunters, and lovers.

7. What art forms flourished in the Safavid Era?

____

____

____

Name ______________________________ Date ______________________ Class ______________________

Reading Essentials and Study Guide

Chapter 15, Section 3

For use with textbook pages 473–478

THE GRANDEUR OF THE MOGULS

KEY TERMS

zamindar a local official in the Mogul Empire *(page 474)*

suttee the Hindu custom of cremating a widow on her husband's funeral pyre *(page 475)*

DRAWING FROM EXPERIENCE

Have you ever visited Washington, D.C.? What monuments have been built there in memory of U.S. presidents? Can you think of any other famous landmarks that honor former presidents?

In the last two sections, you learned about the Ottoman and Safavid Empires. In this section, you will learn about the Mogul Empire. One of the Mogul emperors built the famous Taj Mahal in memory of his wife.

ORGANIZING YOUR THOUGHTS

Use the chart below to help you take notes. After the Akbar Era, the Mogul Empire began to decline. List five factors that contributed to this decline.

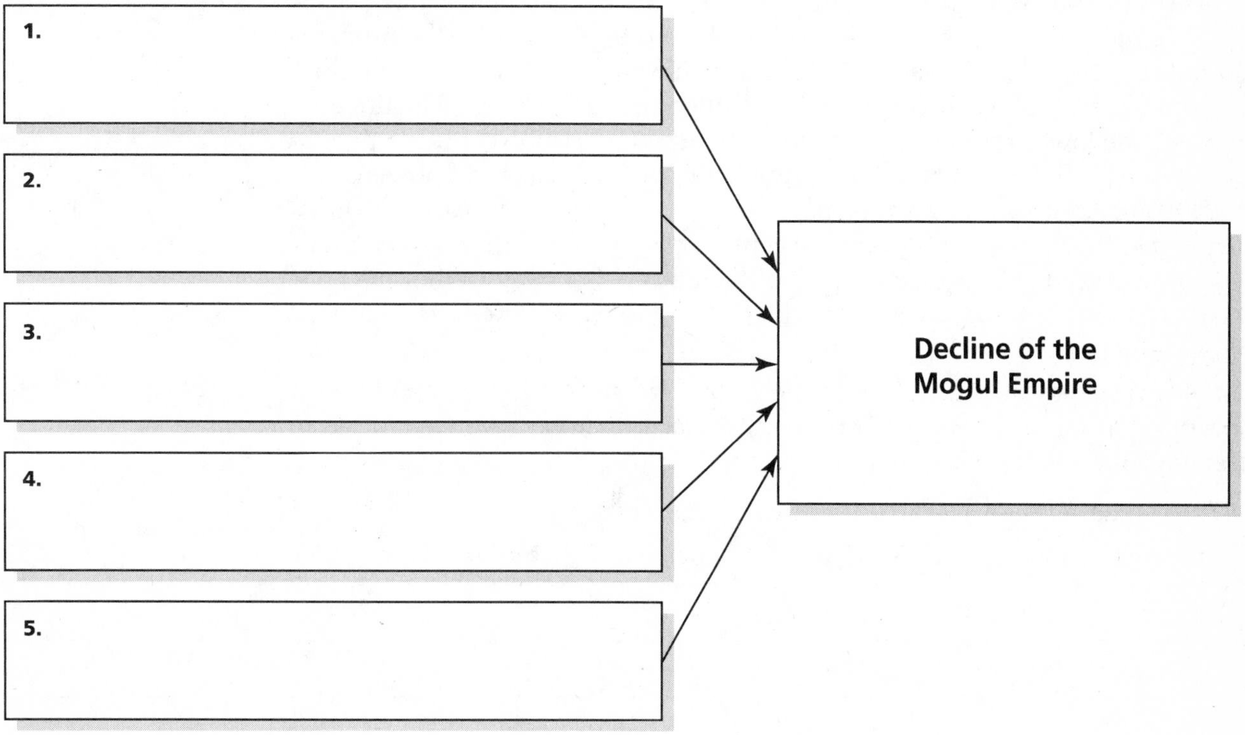

Reading Essentials and Study Guide

READ TO LEARN

• The Mogul Dynasty *(page 473)*

In 1500, the Indian subcontinent was still divided into a number of Hindu and Muslim kingdoms. However, the Moguls established a new dynasty and brought a new era of unity to the region. The founder of the Mogul dynasty was Babur. His father was descended from Timur Lenk and his mother from Genghis Khan. Babur inherited a part of Timur Lenk's empire. As a youth, he commanded a group of warriors who seized Kabul in 1504. Thirteen years later, his forces crossed the Khyber Pass to India. Babur captured Delhi and established his power in the plains of North India. He continued his conquests in North India until his death in 1530.

6. Who founded the Mogul dynasty?

____

____

____

• The Reign of Akbar *(page 474)*

Babur's grandson Akbar was only 14 when he came to the throne. By 1605, he had brought Mogul rule to most of India. His armies used heavy artillery to overpower the stone fortresses of their enemies. Akbar created the greatest Indian empire since the Mauryan dynasty. He is best known for the humane character of his rule. He was a Muslim, but he was tolerant of other religions. The upper-ranks of his government were filled with non-native Muslims, but many of the lower-ranking officials were Hindus. It became common practice to give these officials plots of farmland for their use. These local officials were known as **zamindars.** They kept a portion of the taxes as their salaries. They forwarded the rest of the taxes to the central government. All Indian peasants were required to pay about one-third of their annual harvest to the state, but the system was applied justly. When bad weather struck, taxes were reduced or even suspended.

Foreign trade was prosperous in the Akbar Era. Indian goods, including textiles, tropical food products, spices, and precious stones, were exported in exchange for gold and silver.

7. In what ways was Akbar a humane ruler?

____

____

____

Name ______________ Date ______________ Class ______________

Reading Essentials and Study Guide

Chapter 15, Section 3 *(continued)*

• Decline of the Moguls *(page 475)*

Akbar died in 1605. He was succeeded by his son Jahangir. During the early years of his reign, Jahangir continued to strengthen the central government's control of the empire. His control began to weaken when he fell under the influence of one of his wives. The empress used her position to enrich her own family. She also arranged the marriage of her niece to her husband's son, Shah Jahan.

Shah Jahan ruled from 1628 to 1658. He maintained the Mogul political system and expanded the boundaries of the empire. But he failed to deal with growing domestic problems. He had inherited a nearly empty treasury. His military campaigns and building projects put a heavy strain on the imperial finances and forced him to raise taxes, while most of the people lived in poverty.

When Shah Jahan became ill in the mid-1650s, two of his sons struggled for power. One of them, Aurangzeb, had his brother put to death and imprisoned his father. He then crowned himself emperor in 1658. He is one of the most controversial rulers in the history of India. He tried to eliminate what he thought were India's evils. He forbade both the Hindu custom of **suttee** (cremating a widow on her husband's funeral pyre) and the levying of illegal taxes. He was a devout Muslim and reversed many of the Mogul policies of religious tolerance. The building of new Hindu temples was prohibited, and Hindus were forced to convert to Islam. These policies led to Hindu protests. Revolt broke out in provinces throughout the empire. India became divided and vulnerable to attack. In 1739, Delhi was sacked by the Persians, who left it in ashes.

8. Why is Aurangzeb considered controversial?

• The British in India *(page 475)*

The arrival of the British hastened the decline of the Mogul Empire. In 1650, British trading forts had been established at Surat, Fort William, and Chennai. From Chennai, British ships carried Indian-made cotton goods to the East Indies, where they were traded for spices. The French established their own forts at Pondicherry, Surat, and in the Bay of Bengal. They even captured the British fort at Chennai. The British were eventually able to restrict the French to the fort at Pondicherry and a few other territories on the southeastern coast. This was largely due to the efforts of Sir Robert Clive. Clive became the chief representative in India of the East India Company. The East India Company had been given authority by the British crown to act on its behalf. It was Clive's job to fight any force, French or Indian, that threatened the power of the East India Company in India. In 1757, Clive led a small British force to victory over a Mogul-led army more than ten times its size. The Mogul court was then forced to give the British East India Company the power to collect taxes from lands in the area surrounding Calcutta.

In the late eighteenth century, the East India Company moved inland from the coastal cities. British expansion made many British merchants and officials rich. British officials found that they could obtain money from local rulers by selling trade privileges. The British were in India to stay.

9. How did the arrival of the British hasten the decline of the Mogul Empire?

• Society and Daily Life in Mogul India *(page 477)*

The Moguls were foreigners in India. They were Muslims but were ruling a largely Hindu population. The Mogul attitudes toward women affected Indian society. Women had long played an active role in Mogul society, and some even fought on the battlefield alongside the men. Women from aristocratic families were allowed to own land and to take part in business activities. At the same time, Moguls placed certain restrictions on women under Islamic law. The Islamic practice of isolating women was compatible with Hindu customs and was adopted by many upper-class Hindus. In other ways, Hindu practices continued despite Mogul rule. The custom of suttee continued. Child marriage also remained common.

During the Mogul era, a wealthy landed nobility and a prosperous merchant class emerged. As the Mogul Empire declined, many prominent Indians made trading ties with the British. This benefited the Indians, but only temporarily.

10. How did Mogul attitudes toward women affect Indian society?

Name ________________ Date ________________ Class ________________

Reading Essentials and Study Guide

Chapter 15, Section 3 *(continued)*

• **Mogul Culture** *(page 477)*

The Moguls brought together Persian and Indian influences in a new and beautiful architectural style. This style is best symbolized by the Taj Mahal. This building is considered to be the most beautiful in India, if not in the entire world. It was built by the emperor Shah Jahan in memory of his wife. To finance it, the government raised land taxes. This drove many Indian peasants into complete poverty.

Another major artistic achievement of the Mogul period was in painting. The "Akbar" style combined Persian and Indian elements. Akbar also encouraged his artists to imitate European art forms, including the use of perspective and lifelike portraits. The Mogul emperors were dedicated patrons of the arts. Going to India was the goal of painters, poets, and artisans from many other countries.

11. Mogul architecture and painting combined influences from what two cultures?

____

____

____

____

____

Name ______________________ Date ____________________ Class ____________________

Reading Essentials and Study Guide

Chapter 16, Section 1

For use with textbook pages 485–490

CHINA AT ITS HEIGHT

KEY TERMS

queue a pigtail worn by Chinese men during the Qing dynasty *(page 488)*

banner a Manchu military unit during the Qing dynasty *(page 489)*

DRAWING FROM EXPERIENCE

What do you think life would be like in the United States if we did not have any contact with other countries? Do you think your own life would be affected very much? Why or why not?

In this section, you will learn about China during the Ming and Qing dynasties. During the Qing dynasty, the Chinese government began to limit contacts between Europeans and Chinese.

ORGANIZING YOUR THOUGHTS

Use the concept web below to help you take notes. During the Ming dynasty, China was at the height of its power as the most magnificent civilization on Earth. List seven accomplishments during the Ming dynasty.

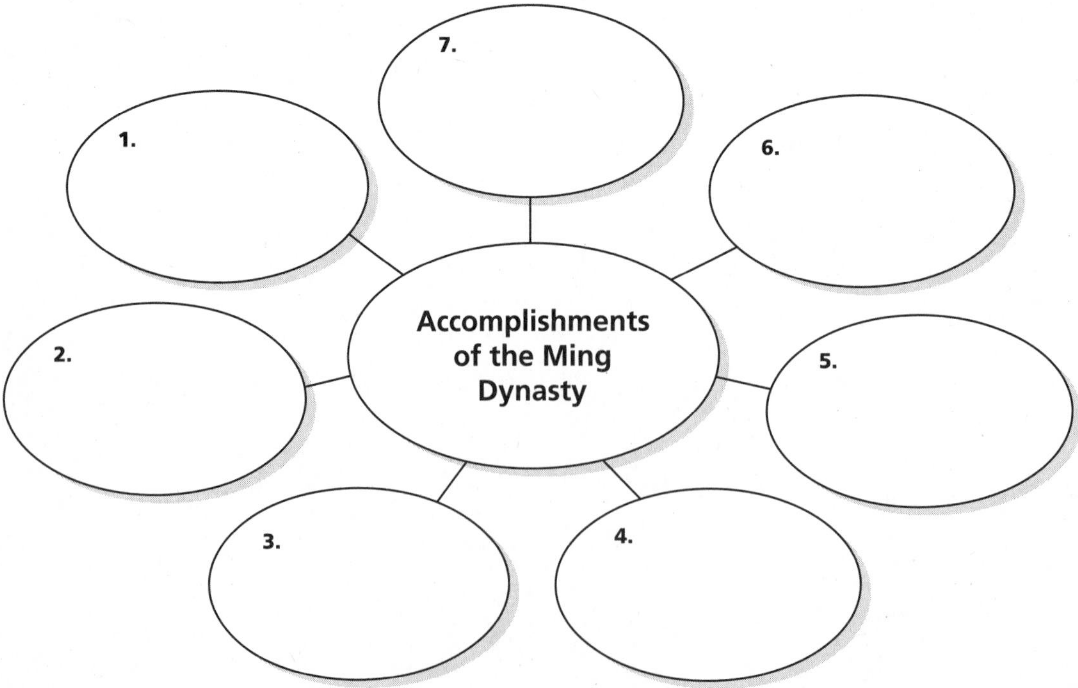

READ TO LEARN

• The Ming Dynasty *(page 485)*

The Mongol dynasty in China was overthrown in 1368. The founder of the new dynasty took the title of Ming Hong Wu (the Ming Martial Emperor). This was the beginning of the Ming dynasty, which lasted until 1644. The Ming dynasty was a time of greatness in Chinese history. The Chinese extended their rule into Mongolia and central Asia. They strengthened the Great Wall and made peace with nomadic tribes in the north. The Ming rulers had an effective government using a bureaucracy made up of officials chosen by the civil service examination system. They also set up a nationwide school system. More manufactured goods were produced in workshops and factories. New crops were introduced. These crops greatly increased food production. The Ming rulers also completed the Grand Canal. This made it possible to ship grain and other goods from southern to northern China.

Ming Hong Wu died in 1398. His son Yong Le then became emperor. Yong Le began construction of the Imperial City in Beijing in 1406. In 1421, he moved the capital from Nanjing to Beijing. For nearly 500 years, the Imperial City was the home to China's emperors. It is known today as the Forbidden City. Yong Le also built large monuments, strengthened the Great Wall, restored Chinese rule over Vietnam, and sent ships into the Indian Ocean. The ships sailed as far west as the eastern coast of Africa. The voyages were led by the court official Zheng He. The ships returned with items unknown in China and information about the outside world. The voyages also led to huge profits. Many traditionalists in the bureaucracy were upset, because they held the Confucian view that trading activities were unworthy. After Yong Le's death, the voyages were stopped and were never revived.

In 1514, a Portuguese fleet arrived off the coast of China. It was the first direct contact between the Chinese Empire and Europe since the journeys of Marco Polo. At first, the Portuguese had little impact on Chinese society. The emperor viewed Europeans as barbarians. Direct trade between Europe and China remained limited. But an exchange of ideas and cultures took place. Christian missionaries made the voyage to China on European merchant ships. They were impressed with many aspects of Chinese civilization, such as the teachings of Confucius, the printing and availability of books, and Chinese architecture. Chinese officials marveled at European inventions that were brought by the missionaries, such as clocks and eyeglasses.

During the late sixteenth century, a series of weak rulers led to a period of government corruption in China. High taxes led to peasant unrest. Crop production declined because of bad weather. In the 1630s, a major epidemic killed many people. The suffering caused by the epidemic helped spark a peasant revolt led by Li Zicheng. In 1644, Li and his forces occupied Beijing. The last Ming emperor hung himself from a tree in the palace gardens.

8. What impact did the Portuguese have in China in the sixteenth century?

____

____

____

____

____

• Qing Dynasty *(page 488)*

The overthrow of the Ming dynasty created an opening for the Manchus. The Manchus were a farming and hunting people who lived northeast of the Great Wall in the area known today as Manchuria. They defeated Li Zicheng's army and conquered Beijing. The Manchus declared the creation of a new dynasty called the Qing (meaning "pure"). This dynasty remained in power from 1644 until 1911. At first, the Chinese resisted the new rulers. Rebels seized the island of Taiwan just off the coast of China. To make it easier to identify the rebels, the government ordered all men to adopt Manchu dress and hairstyles. All Chinese men had to shave their foreheads and braid their hair into a pigtail called a **queue.** Those who refused were executed.

The Qing eventually adopted the Chinese political system and were gradually accepted as the legitimate rulers of the country. But they faced one major problem. The Manchus were ethically and culturally different from the rest of the Chinese. The Qing dealt with this in two ways. First, they tried to preserve their distinct identity within Chinese society. The Manchus were defined legally as distinct from everyone else in China. In the military, Manchus were organized into separate units, called **banners.** Second, the Qing brought Chinese people into the top ranks of the imperial administration. All important positions were shared equally by Chinese and Manchus. The Manchus' willingness to share power won the support of many Chinese.

Kangxi was perhaps the greatest emperor in Chinese history. He ruled from 1661 to 1722. He calmed the unrest along the northern and western frontiers. He was a patron of the arts and gained the support of scholars throughout the country. He was also tolerant of Christian missionaries. It is estimated that three hundred thousand Chinese became Catholics during his reign. After the death of Kangxi, however, his successor began to suppress Christian activities in China.

Qianlong was another outstanding Qing ruler. He ruled from 1736 to 1795. As he grew older, however, he fell under the influence of destructive elements at court. Corrupt officials and higher taxes led to unrest in rural areas. Growing pressure on the land due to population growth led to economic hardship for many peasants. In central China, unhappy peasants started a

Reading Essentials and Study Guide

revolt known as the White Lotus Rebellion. The revolt was suppressed, but the expenses of fighting the rebels weakened the Qing dynasty. At the same time, Europe was seeking more trade with China. At first, the Qing government sold trade privileges to the Europeans. However, to limit contacts between Europeans and Chinese, the Qing confined all Europeans to a small island outside Guangzhou. They also limited the number of Chinese firms that European traders could deal with.

By the end of the eighteenth century, British traders began to demand access to additional cities along the Chinese coast. At the same time, the Chinese government was under pressure from their own merchants to open China to British manufactured goods. In 1793, a British mission led by Lord George Macartney visited Beijing to ask for more liberal trade policies. But Emperor Qianlong wrote to King George III that China had no need of British manufactured goods.

9. How did the Qing deal with the ethnic and cultural differences in China?

____

____

____

____

____

Name ______________________ Date ______________________ Class ______________________

Reading Essentials and Study Guide

Chapter 16, Section 2

For use with textbook pages 491–494

CHINESE SOCIETY AND CULTURE

KEY TERMS

commercial capitalism private business based on profit *(page 492)*

clan a group of related families *(page 493)*

porcelain a ceramic made of fine clay baked at very high temperatures *(page 494)*

DRAWING FROM EXPERIENCE

How many people live in your home? Do any of your grandparents live with you? How often do you see your other relatives, such as aunts, uncles, and cousins?

The last section focused on politics and government during the Ming and Qing dynasties. In this section, you will learn about economic changes, cultural developments, and daily life during this period. In Chinese families, as many as three or four generations lived together under the same roof.

ORGANIZING YOUR THOUGHTS

Use the diagram below to help you take notes. During the late Ming and the early Qing dynasties, culture in China reached new heights. List at least one example of Chinese cultural achievements in the areas of literature, architecture, and decorative arts.

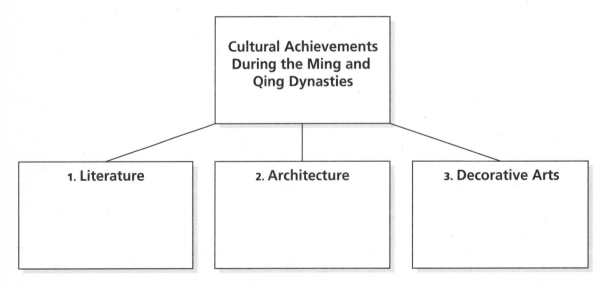

Cultural Achievements During the Ming and Qing Dynasties

1. Literature
2. Architecture
3. Decorative Arts

READ TO LEARN

• Economic Changes *(page 491)*

Between 1500 and 1800, China was a mostly agricultural society. Nearly 85 percent of the people were small farmers. But the Chinese economy was changing. The population increased to more than 300 million by the end of the 1700s. One cause of this population increase was the peace and stability under the early Qing dynasty. Another cause was the food supply. A faster growing rice from Southeast Asia increased the food supply. The population increase meant that there was less land available for each family. The emperor tried to make more land available by limiting the amount wealthy landowners could hold. By the eighteenth century, however, almost all the land that could be farmed was being farmed.

Another change in this period was a growth in trade and manufacturing. Trade in silk, porcelain, cotton goods, and other products increased. China did not develop the kind of **commercial capitalism** (private business based on profit) that was emerging in Europe, however. Trade and manufacturing in China were under the control of the government. In China, trade and manufacturing were considered inferior to farming. The government levied heavy taxes on manufacturing and trade and low taxes on farming.

4. What were two causes of the population increase in China?

• Daily Life *(page 492)*

Chinese society was organized around the family. All family members were expected to sacrifice their individual desires for the benefit of the family as a whole. The ideal family unit was the extended family. As many as three or four generations lived under the same roof. When sons married, they brought their wives to live with them in the family home. The Chinese respected the elderly. Aging parents knew that they would be cared for by their children. Beyond the extended family was the **clan.** The clan consisted of dozens, or even hundreds, of related families. The clan system made it possible for wealthier families to help poorer relatives.

Women were considered inferior to men in Chinese society. Only males could have a formal education and pursue a career in government or scholarship. Legally, a woman could not divorce her husband or inherit property. The husband, on the other hand, could divorce his wife if she did not produce sons. He could also take a second wife. One-half to two-thirds of the women in China bound their feet. The process of footbinding was begun in childhood and was very painful. But bound feet were a status symbol. Women who had bound feet were more marriageable than those who did not. Because women who had bound feet could not walk, women who worked in the fields or in occupations that required mobility did not bind their feet.

5. In what ways were women treated as inferior to men in Chinese society?

• Cultural Developments *(page 494)*

During the Ming dynasty, a new form of literature arose that eventually evolved into the modern Chinese novel. One Chinese novel, *The Golden Lotus*, is considered by many people to be the first realistic social novel. *The Dream of the Red Chamber*, by Cao Xuegin, is still considered to be China's most distinguished popular novel. It was published in 1791.

Art flourished during the Ming and early Qing dynasties. In architecture, the most outstanding example is the Imperial City in Beijing. Perhaps the most famous of all the arts of the Ming Era was blue-and-white **porcelain.** Europeans admired this porcelain and bought huge quantities of it.

6. What novel is considered to be China's most distinguished popular novel?

Name ________________ Date ________________ Class ________________

Reading Essentials and Study Guide

Chapter 16, Section 3

For use with textbook pages 496–500

TOKUGAWA JAPAN AND KOREA

KEY TERMS

daimyo heads of noble families in Japan *(page 497)*

han a separate territory or domain in Japan, each ruled by a daimyo *(page 497)*

hostage system a system that the shogunate used to control the daimyo, by forcing the families of the daimyo to stay in Edo, where the court of the shogun was located *(page 498)*

eta outcasts in Japan during the Tokugawa Era *(page 499)*

DRAWING FROM EXPERIENCE

Are some occupations valued more highly than others in the United States? Which occupations do you think are the most highly valued? Which ones do you think are considered the least desirable?

In the last two sections, you learned about China during the Ming and Qing dynasties. In this section, you will learn about Japan and Korea during the Tokugawa Era, which lasted from 1598 to 1868. During this period, Japan developed a rigid class system, based largely on occupations.

ORGANIZING YOUR THOUGHTS

Use the diagram below to help you take notes. List the four main social classes in Japan during the Tokugawa Era. Also identify the four groups that made up the first class.

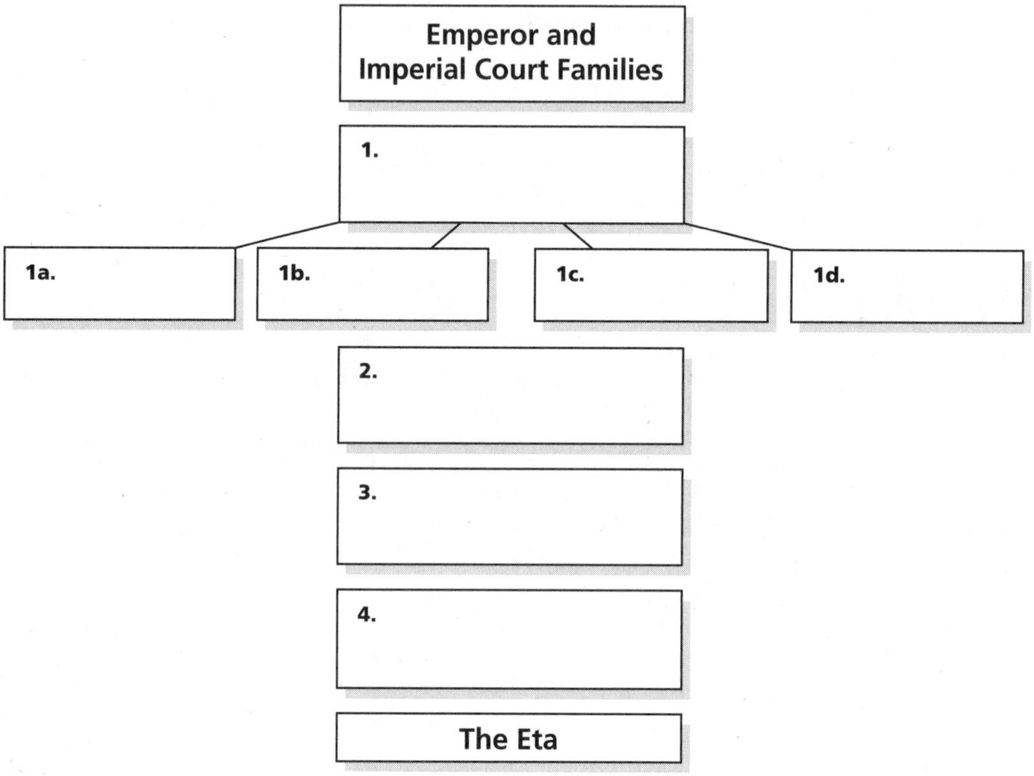

READ TO LEARN

- **The Three Great Unifiers** *(page 496)*

At the end of the fifteenth century, Japan was in chaos. The power of the shogunate had collapsed. **Daimyo** (heads of noble families) controlled their own lands and warred with their neighbors. In the mid-sixteenth century, however, Japan began to be unified. Three powerful people brought about this unification. Oda Nobunaga seized the imperial capital of Kyoto and placed the reigning shogun under his control. During the next few years, he tried to consolidate his rule throughout the central plains. He was succeeded by Toyotomi Hideyoshi. Hideyoshi was a farmer's son who became a military commander. By 1590, he had persuaded most of the daimyo to accept his authority. After Hideyoshi's death in 1598, Tokugawa Ieyasu took control of Japan. He was the powerful daimyo of Edo. In 1603, he took the title of shogun. Tokugawa shoguns remained in power until 1868. Their rule brought a long period of peace known as the "Great Peace."

Name ______________________ Date ______________ Class ______________

Reading Essentials and Study Guide

Chapter 16, Section 3 *(continued)*

5. What period in Japanese history is known as the "Great Peace"?

___

___

• Europeans in Japan *(page 497)*

Portuguese traders landed in Japan in 1543. At first, they were welcomed. The Japanese were fascinated by tobacco, clocks, eyeglasses, and other European goods. Daimyo were interested in buying all types of European weapons. In 1549, the first Jesuit missionary, Francis Xavier, arrived. By the end of the sixteenth century, thousands of Japanese had become Christians. However, the Jesuits destroyed shrines. This caused a severe reaction. In 1587, Hideyoshi issued an edict prohibiting Christian activities within his lands. At first, the edict was not strictly enforced, and Jesuits were allowed to continue their activities. Under Tokugawa Ieyasu, however, all missionaries were expelled, and Japanese Christians were persecuted. European merchants were also expelled from Japan. Only a small Dutch community in Nagasaki was allowed to remain in Japan.

6. What caused Jesuit missionaries to be expelled from Japan?

___

___

• Tokugawa Rule *(page 497)*

The Tokugawa rulers set out to establish control of the feudal system that had governed Japan for over three hundred years. The state was divided into about 250 separate territories, called **hans,** or domains. Each was ruled by a daimyo. The shogunate controlled the daimyo by a **hostage system.** In this system, the daimyo were required to maintain two residences, one in their own lands and one in Edo. Edo was the location of the shogun's court. When the daimyo was away from his residence in Edo, his family was forced to stay there. During the Tokugawa Era, the samurai who had served the daimyo gradually ceased to be a warrior class. Many of them became managers on the lands of the daimyo.

7. How did the role of the samurai change during the Tokugawa Era?

___

___

Name ______________________ Date ____________________ Class ____________________

Reading Essentials and Study Guide

• Economic and Social Changes *(page 498)*

A major economic change took place during the Tokugawa Era. Previously, trade and industry had been considered undesirable. Under the Tokugawa, trade and industry began to flourish. Banking also flourished, and paper money became the normal medium of exchange in business transactions. A Japanese merchant class emerged.

Some farm families benefited from the growing demand for cash crops (crops grown for sale). Most peasants, however, experienced both declining profits and rising costs and taxes. Many were forced to become tenants or to work as hired help. When conditions became desperate, some peasants revolted. Almost seven thousand peasant revolts and demonstrations against high taxes took place during the Tokugawa Era.

During this era, Japan's class system became rigid. There were four main classes: warriors, peasants, artisans, and merchants. The emperor and imperial court were at the very top of the political and social structure. Next came the warrior class. This class was composed of the shogun, daimyo, samurai, and ronin. The ronin were warriors without masters who traveled the countryside seeking employment. Below the warriors were the farmers (peasants). Next was the artisan class, which included craftspeople such as swordmakers and carpenters. The merchant class was at the bottom because they profited from the labor of others. Below these classes were Japan's outcasts, the **eta.** The Tokugawa had strict laws for the eta. They regulated the places of residence, the dress, and even the hairstyles of the eta.

The role of women in Tokugawa society became somewhat more restricted. Men had broad authority over property, marriage, and divorce. Parents arranged marriages, and a wife was expected to move in with her husband's family. A wife who did not meet the expectations of her husband or his family was likely to be divorced. Among the common people, women were generally valued for their roles as childbearers and homemakers. Both sexes worked in the fields.

8. Why did so many peasant revolts and demonstrations take place during the Tokugawa Era?

____

____

____

• Tokugawa Culture *(page 499)*

In the Tokugawa Era, popular literature written by and for townspeople began to appear. The best examples of the new urban fiction were the works of Ihara Saikaku. His greatest novel, *Five Women Who Loved Love*, has a tragic

Reading Essentials and Study Guide

theme, but much of the popular literature of the Tokugawa Era was lighthearted. Exquisite poetry was also written during this period. The greatest of all Japanese poets, Matsuo Basho, lived during the seventeenth century.

Kabuki theater began to appear in the cities. Kabuki dramas were full of action, music, and dramatic gestures. Early dramas dealt with the world of teahouses and dance halls. Government officials feared that these dramas could corrupt the nation's morals, so they forbade women to appear on stage. This led to the creation of a new professional class of actors who impersonated female characters.

Architecture flourished during this period because of the shogun's order that all daimyo have residences in Edo. Nobles competed to build the most magnificent mansions. Japanese art during this period was influenced by other cultures. Japanese pottery makers borrowed techniques from Korea. The Japanese studied Western medicine, astronomy, languages, and painting styles. In turn, Westerners wanted Japanese ceramics.

9. Why did architecture flourish during the Tokugawa Era?

____

____

____

• Korea: The Hermit Kingdom *(page 500)*

The Yi dynasty in Korea was founded at the end of the fourteenth century. It remained in power during the entire Tokugawa Era in Japan. Yi rulers patterned their society after Chinese society. Korean rulers tried to keep their country isolated from the outside world. Because of this, Korea was referred to as "the Hermit Kingdom." In the late sixteenth century, however, a Japanese force under Toyotomi Hideyoshi invaded Korea. The Japanese were defeated, but Korea was devastated. In the 1630s, a Manchu army invaded northern Korea and forced the Yi dynasty to become subject to China. Although Korea was not able to remain completely isolated, it was largely untouched by European merchants and missionaries.

10. What influence did Europeans have on Korea during the Tokugawa Era?

____

____

____

____

____

Name ______________________________ Date ______________________ Class ______________________

Reading Essentials and Study Guide

Chapter 17, Section 1

For use with textbook pages 511–517

THE SCIENTIFIC REVOLUTION

KEY TERMS

geocentric (Earth-centered) placing Earth at the center of the universe *(page 513)*

Ptolemaic system a model of the universe constructed by philosophers of the Middle Ages that was based on the ideas of Ptolemy, a second-century astronomer *(page 513)*

heliocentric (sun-centered) placing the Sun at the center of the universe *(page 513)*

universal law of gravitation a law of nature defined by Isaac Newton that states that every object in the universe is attracted to every other object by a force called gravity *(page 514)*

rationalism a system of thought based on the belief that reason is the chief source of knowledge *(page 517)*

scientific method a systematic procedure for collecting and analyzing evidence *(page 517)*

inductive reasoning reasoning from particular facts to general principles *(page 517)*

DRAWING FROM EXPERIENCE

What field of science do you find most interesting? What aspects of the science make it most interesting to you?

In this section, you will learn how changes in scientific thought during the sixteenth and seventeenth centuries gave Europeans a new way to view the universe and their place in the universe.

ORGANIZING YOUR THOUGHTS

Use the chart below to help you take notes. Identify the contributions that the following people made to the Scientific Revolution.

Scientist/Philosopher	Contributions to the Scientific Revolution
Copernicus	**1.**
Kepler	**2.**
Galileo	**3.**
Newton	**4.**
Bacon	**5.**

READ TO LEARN

• Background to the Revolution *(page 511)*

Medieval scientists were known as "natural philosophers." They did not make observations of the natural world. They relied on a few ancient philosophers, especially Aristotle, for their scientific knowledge. In the fifteenth and sixteenth centuries, natural philosophers began to give up their old views and develop new ones. Renaissance humanists had learned Greek and Latin. They were able to read works by Ptolemy, Archimedes, and Plato. These writings made it obvious that some ancient thinkers disagreed with Aristotle. At the same time, the invention of new instruments, such as the telescope and microscope, made new scientific discoveries possible. The printing press helped spread new ideas quickly and easily.

Mathematics played an important role in the scientific achievements of the sixteenth and seventeenth centuries. Nicholas Copernicus, Johannes Kepler, Galileo Galilei, and Isaac Newton were all great mathematicians who believed that the secrets of nature were written in the language of mathematics. After studying the ideas of the ancient mathematicians, they sometimes rejected these ideas. They developed new theories that became the foundation of the Scientific Revolution.

6. What developments in the fifteenth and sixteenth centuries caused natural philosophers to give up their old ideas and develop new ones?

____

____

____

• A Revolution in Astronomy *(page 512)*

Discoveries in astronomy were an important part of the Scientific Revolution. These discoveries changed how Westerners viewed the universe. During the Middle Ages, philosophers had created a model of the universe known as the **Ptolemaic system.** Ptolemy was the greatest astronomer of antiquity. He lived during the second century A.D. It was from his ideas and those of Aristotle that philosophers had built the Ptolemaic system. This system is called **geocentric** because it places Earth at the center of the universe. According to this system, the universe is a series of concentric spheres (spheres one inside the other). Earth is fixed, or motionless, at the center of these spheres. The rotation of these spheres makes the heavenly bodies rotate around Earth.

In 1543, Nicolas Copernicus published his famous book, *On the Revolutions of the Heavenly Spheres*. Copernicus believed in a **heliocentric,** or sun-centered, model of the universe. He believed that the Sun, not Earth, was at the center

Name ______________________ Date ______________________ Class ______________________

Reading Essentials and Study Guide

of the universe. The planets, including Earth, revolved around the Sun. Another mathematician, Johannes Kepler, used detailed astronomical data to create laws of planetary motion. His observations confirmed that the Sun was at the center of the universe. He also discovered that the orbits of the planets around the Sun were not circular, as Copernicus had thought. Instead, the orbits were elliptical (egg-shaped).

Another mathematician, Galileo Galilei, was the first European to make regular observations of the heavens with a telescope. He discovered mountains on the Moon, four moons revolving around Jupiter, and sunspots. His observations indicated that heavenly bodies were not pure orbs of light, but were composed of material substance like Earth. After Galileo published his discoveries in *The Starry Messenger* in 1610, the Catholic Church ordered him to abandon the Copernican system. The new system threatened the Church's view of the universe and seemed to contradict the Bible. In spite of the Church's position, by the 1630s and 1640s, most astronomers had come to accept the heliocentric model. However, the problem of explaining motion in the universe had not been solved.

Isaac Newton is considered the greatest genius of the Scientific Revolution. His major work, *Mathematical Principles of Natural Philosophy*, is also known as *Principia* (the first word of its Latin title). In the *Principia*, Newton defined the three laws of motion that govern both the planetary bodies and objects on Earth. The **universal law of gravitation** explains why the planetary bodies do not go off in straight lines but continue in elliptical orbits around the Sun. The law states that every object in the universe is attracted to every other object by a force called gravity. Newton's laws created a new picture of the universe. It was now seen as a huge machine that worked according to natural laws.

7. What is the main difference between the geocentric and heliocentric models of the universe?

• Breakthroughs in Medicine and Chemistry *(page 515)*

A revolution in medicine also began in the sixteenth century. In 1543, Andreas Vesalius wrote *On the Fabric of the Human Body*. In this book, he discussed what he had found when dissecting human bodies. He presented a careful and accurate examination of human organs and the general structure of the human body. In 1628, William Harvey published *On the Motion of the Heart and Blood*. His work was based on close observations and experiments.

Name ______________________ Date ______________ Class ______________

Reading Essentials and Study Guide

Chapter 17, Section 1 *(continued)*

Harvey showed that the heart was the beginning point for the circulation of blood in the body. He also proved that the same blood flowed in both veins and arteries and that it makes a complete circuit as it passes through the body. These observations disproved many of the theories of Galen, a second century Greek physician. His theories had dominated medicine in the Middle Ages.

The science of chemistry also arose in the seventeenth and eighteenth centuries. Robert Boyle was one of the first scientists to conduct controlled experiments. His work on the properties of gas led to Boyle's Law. This law states that the volume of a gas varies with the pressure exerted on it. In the eighteenth century, Antoine Lavoisier invented a system of naming the chemical elements. He is considered by many to be the founder of modern chemistry.

8. Whose theories were disproved by William Harvey's observations?

• Women and the Origins of Modern Science *(page 515)*

Women as well as men were involved in the Scientific Revolution. Margaret Cavendish was one of the most prominent female scientists of the seventeenth century. She wrote a number of works on scientific matters, including *Observations Upon Experimental Philosophy*. In her work, she was critical of the belief that humans, through science, were masters of nature. In Germany, many of the women who were involved in science were astronomers. The most famous of the female astronomers in Germany was Maria Winkelmann. She made some original contributions to astronomy, including the discovery of a comet. However, when Winkelmann applied for a position as an assistant astronomer at the Berlin Academy, she was denied the position because she was a woman, even though she was highly qualified. Women scientists often faced these kinds of obstacles because scientific work was considered to be men's work.

9. What obstacles did women scientists face in the seventeenth century?

• Descartes and Reason *(page 516)*

The Scientific Revolution strongly influenced the Western view of man. This is especially evident in the work of the seventeenth-century French philosopher René Descartes. The starting point for Descartes was doubt. In his most famous work, *Discourse on Method*, Descartes decided to set aside everything that he had learned and to begin again. One fact seemed to him to be beyond doubt—his own existence. From his first principle—"I think, therefore I am"—Descartes used his reason to arrive at a second principle, the separation of mind and matter. He argued that because "the mind cannot be doubted but the body and material world can, the two must be radically different." Descartes's idea that mind and matter were completely separate allowed scientists to view matter as something that was totally detached from themselves and that could be investigated by reason. Descartes has been called the father of modern **rationalism.** This system of thought is based on the belief that reason is the chief source of knowledge.

10. What were Descartes's first two principles?

____

____

____

____

• The Scientific Method *(page 517)*

During the Scientific Revolution, the **scientific method** was created. The scientific method is a systematic procedure for collecting and analyzing evidence. The person who developed the scientific method was Francis Bacon. He believed that instead of relying on the ideas of ancient authorities, scientists should use **inductive reasoning** to learn about nature. Scientists should proceed from the particular to the general. Systematic observations and carefully organized experiments to test hypotheses (theories) would lead to general principles. Bacon also believed that science could give humans power over nature.

11. According to Francis Bacon, how should scientists learn about nature?

____

____

____

____

Name ______________________ Date ______________________ Class ______________________

Reading Essentials and Study Guide

Chapter 17, Section 2

For use with textbook pages 518–525

THE ENLIGHTENMENT

KEY TERMS

philosophe an intellectual of the Enlightenment *(page 519)*

separation of powers the division of a government into executive, legislative, and judicial branches that limit and control each other in a system of checks and balances *(page 520)*

deism an eighteenth-century religious philosophy based on the idea that the world is a machine and that God is a mechanic who created the world and allows it to run without his interference, according to its own natural laws *(page 520)*

laissez-faire ("to let [people] do [what they want]") the belief that government should not interfere in economic matters *(page 521)*

social contract in the theories of philosophers such as Locke and Rousseau, an agreement among individuals that they will be governed by the general will *(page 522)*

salon elegant drawing rooms of the wealthy upper class, in which writers, artists, aristocrats, and government officials gathered to take part in conversations that were often centered on the ideas of the philosophes *(page 524)*

DRAWING FROM EXPERIENCE

Imagine that you are hosting a gathering of famous musicians, artists, writers, and politicians. Who would you ask to the gathering? Why?

In the last section, you read about the Scientific Revolution during the sixteenth and seventeenth centuries. In the eighteenth century, intellectuals used the ideas of the Scientific Revolution to reexamine all aspects of life. They often held gatherings to discuss these new Enlightenment ideas.

ORGANIZING YOUR THOUGHTS

Use the diagram below to help you take notes. Summarize the influence of Enlightenment ideas on government, religion, economics, and women's rights.

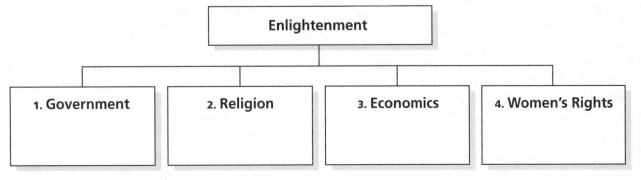

Enlightenment

1. Government	**2. Religion**	**3. Economics**	**4. Women's Rights**

READ TO LEARN

• Path to the Enlightenment *(page 518)*

The Enlightenment was an eighteenth-century philosophical movement of intellectuals who were impressed with the achievements of the Scientific Revolution. They hoped that by using the scientific method, they could make progress toward a better society. Words such as *reason, natural law, hope,* and *progress* were common words to the thinkers of the Enlightenment. The Enlightenment was especially influenced by the ideas of Isaac Newton and John Locke. To Newton, the physical world and everything in it was a giant machine. Because Newton had discovered natural laws that governed the physical world, the intellectuals of the Enlightenment thought they could discover the natural laws that governed human society. John Locke's theory of knowledge also greatly affected eighteenth-century intellectuals. Locke believed that people were born with blank minds and were molded by the experiences that came through their senses from the surrounding world. He believed that if environments were changed and people were exposed to the right influences, people could be changed and a new society could be created.

5. How did the ideas of Isaac Newton and John Locke influence the intellectuals of the Enlightenment?

____

____

____

• Philosophes and Their Ideas *(page 519)*

The intellectuals of the Enlightenment were known by the French name **philosophe.** To the philosophes, the purpose of philosophy was to change the world. A spirit of rational criticism was to be applied to everything, including religion and politics. Three French philosophers, Montesquieu, Voltaire, and Diderot, dominated Enlightenment thought. Montesquieu's most famous work, *The Spirit of the Laws*, was published in 1748. This work was a study of governments. Montesquieu tried to use the scientific method to find the natural laws that govern the social and political relationships of human beings. He identified three basic kinds of governments: republics, despotism, and monarchies. In his study of the English monarchy, he identified three branches: the executive, the legislative, and the judicial. The government functioned through a **separation of powers.** In this separation, the three branches limit and control each other in a system of checks and balances. By preventing any one person or group from gaining too much power, this system provides the greatest freedom and security for the state. Montesquieu's work was translated into English and influenced the U.S. Constitution.

Name ______________________ Date ______________________ Class ______________________

The greatest figure of the Enlightenment was François-Marie Arouet, known simply as Voltaire. He wrote many pamphlets, novels, plays, letters, essays, and histories, which brought him both fame and wealth. He was especially well known for his criticism of Christianity and his strong belief in religious tolerance. He believed in **deism,** an eighteen-century religious philosophy based on reason and natural law. Deism was built on the idea of the Newtonian world-machine. In the Deists' view, a mechanic (God) had created the universe. The universe was like a clock. God had created it, set it in motion, and allowed it to run without his interference, according to its own natural laws.

Denis Diderot was a writer who studied and read in many subjects and languages. His most famous contribution to the Enlightenment was his *Encyclopedia*. This was a 28-volume collection of knowledge that he edited. The purpose of the *Encyclopedia* was to "change the general way of thinking." Many of its articles attacked religious superstition and supported religious toleration. Other articles called for social, legal, and political improvements that could lead to a more tolerant and humane society. The *Encyclopedia* was sold to doctors, clergymen, teachers, and lawyers, and helped to spread the ideas of the Enlightenment.

6. How did the ideas of Newton affect religious beliefs in the eighteenth century?

• Toward a New Social Science *(page 521)*

The philosophes' belief that there are natural laws that govern human society led to the development of the social sciences (areas such as economics and political science). The Physiocrats and Adam Smith are considered the founders of the social science of economics. The Physiocrats believed that if individuals were free to pursue their own economic self-interest, all society would ultimately benefit. They believed that government should not interrupt the free play of natural economic forces by imposing regulations on the economy. This doctrine became known by its French name, **laissez-faire,** meaning to "let (people) do (what they want)." The best statement of laissez-faire was made by Adam Smith in his work *The Wealth of Nations*. Smith believed that government should not interfere in economic matters. He believed that government should only have three basic roles: protecting society from invasion (the army); defending citizens from injustice (the police); and keeping up certain public works, such as roads and canals.

By the eighteenth century, most European states had developed a system of courts to deal with crime. Punishments for crimes were often cruel. It was believed that extreme punishments were needed to deter crime. One philosophe proposed a new approach to justice. His name was Cesare Beccaria. He argued that punishments should not be cruel. He also opposed capital punishment. He did not believe that it stopped people from committing crimes.

7. What roles did Adam Smith believe that governments should and should not have?

____

____

• The Later Enlightenment *(page 522)*

By the late 1760s, there was a new generation of philosophes. The most famous was Jean-Jacques Rousseau. In his *Discourse on the Origins of the Inequality of Mankind,* Rousseau argued that people had adopted laws and government in order to protect their property. In the process, they had become enslaved by government. In another work, *The Social Contract,* Rousseau explained his concept of the **social contract.** Through a social contract, an entire society agrees to be governed by its general will. Individuals who wish to follow their own self-interests must be forced to abide by the general will.

Unlike many Enlightenment thinkers, Rousseau believed that emotions, as well as reason, were important to human development. He sought a balance between emotions and reason.

8. What was Rousseau's concept of the social contract?

____

____

• Rights of Women *(page 523)*

By the eighteenth century, female writers began to express their ideas about improving the condition of women. Mary Wollstonecraft is often viewed as the founder of the movement for women's rights. In her book, *A Vindication of the Rights of Women,* Wollstonecraft identified two problems with the views of many Enlightenment thinkers. She argued that if government based on the arbitrary power of monarchs was wrong, the power of men over women was equally wrong. She also argued that the Enlightenment was based on the idea of reason in all human beings. Because women have reason, they are entitled to the same rights as men.

9. What two arguments did Mary Wollstonecraft use to show that women should have equal rights?

____

____

Reading Essentials and Study Guide

• Social World of the Enlightenment *(page 523)*

The common people, especially the peasants, were mostly unaware of the Enlightenment. The Enlightenment had its greatest appeal with the aristocrats and upper classes in large cities. In the eighteenth century, publishing and reading began to grow. This was important to the spread of the Enlightenment. Many books were now directed at the new reading public of the middle classes, which included women and artisans. The development of daily newspapers and magazines for the general public began in the eighteenth century. The first daily newspaper was printed in London in 1702.

Enlightenment ideas were also spread through the **salon.** Salons were elegant drawing rooms of the wealthy upper class. Guests gathered in these salons and discussed the ideas of the philosophes. The salons brought writers and artists together with aristocrats, government officials, and wealthy middle-class people. The women who hosted the salons were in a position to sway political opinion and influence literary and artistic taste.

10. How did the salons help to spread Enlightenment ideas?

____

____

____

• Religion in the Enlightenment *(page 525)*

Although many philosophes attacked Christianity, most Europeans in the eighteenth century were still Christians. Many people sought a deeper personal devotion to God. In England, the most famous new religious movement was Methodism. This was the work of John Wesley, an Anglican minister. Wesley preached to the masses in open fields. He appealed especially to the lower classes. His sermons often caused people to have conversion experiences. Many of these converts joined Methodist societies in which they helped each other do good works. In this way, Methodism gave the lower and middle classes a sense of purpose and community. It proved that the need for spiritual experience had not been eliminated by the eighteenth-century search for reason.

11. How does Methodism prove that the need for spiritual experience had not been eliminated in the eighteenth century?

____

____

____

Name ______________________ Date ______________________ Class ______________________

Reading Essentials and Study Guide

Chapter 17, Section 3

For use with textbook pages 526–534

THE IMPACT OF THE ENLIGHTENMENT

KEY TERMS

rococco an artistic style in the eighteenth century that emphasized grace, charm, and gentle action *(page 527)*

enlightened absolutism a type of monarchy in which rulers tried to govern by Enlightenment principles, while maintaining their royal powers *(page 529)*

DRAWING FROM EXPERIENCE

Do you like classical music? Do you enjoy attending symphony performances? What composers do you like best?

In the last section, you read about the ideas of the Enlightenment. In this section, you will learn how these ideas had an impact on art, music, literature, and politics during the eighteenth century. Some of the world's greatest composers lived during this period.

ORGANIZING YOUR THOUGHTS

Use the diagram below to help you take notes. During the Seven Years' War, new alliances developed in Europe. Identify the members of the two new alliances.

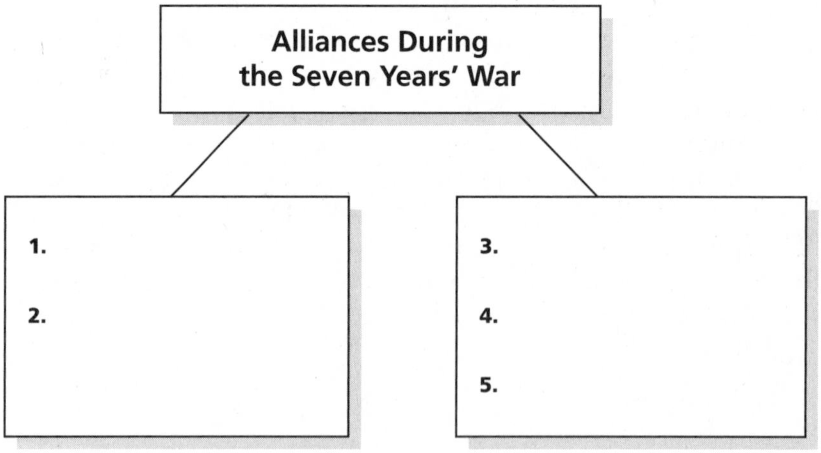

READ TO LEARN

• The Arts *(page 526)*

During the eighteenth century, important achievements were made in architecture, art, music, and literature. After Louis XIV built the palace of Versailles in the seventeenth century, other European rulers began to build elaborate palaces. Most of these palaces were modeled after the Italian baroque style of the 1500s and 1600s. One of the greatest architects of the eighteenth century was Balthasar Neumann. His two masterpieces are the Church of the Fourteen Saints in southern Germany and the Residence, the palace of the prince-bishop of Würzburg.

The baroque and neoclassical styles continued into the eighteenth century. By the 1730s, however, a new artistic style had spread all over Europe. It is known as **rococo.** Rococo emphasized grace, charm, and gentle action. It made use of delicate designs with graceful curves. Its lightness and charm spoke of the pursuit of happiness, pleasure, and love. One of the most famous rococo painters was Antoine Watteau. In his paintings, upper-class men and women are depicted in a world of pleasure and joy. Another aspect of rococo was a sense of enchantment and enthusiasm. This is especially evident in the works of Giovanni Battista Tiepolo. His masterpiece is the ceiling of the Bishop's Palace at Würzburg.

The eighteenth century was one of the greatest periods in the history of European music. Johann Sebastian Bach and George Frederick Handel were two musical geniuses who composed music during the first half of the century. They perfected the baroque musical style. During the second half of the century, two other geniuses, Franz Joseph Haydn and Wolfgang Amadeus Mozart, wrote music called classical.

The eighteenth century was also important in the development of the European novel. Middle-class readers especially enjoyed the novel. The English author Henry Fielding wrote novels about people without morals who survive by their wits. His characters reflect real types in eighteenth-century English society.

6. What four musical geniuses lived during the eighteenth century?

____

____

____

• Enlightenment and Enlightened Absolutism *(page 528)*

The philosophes believed in natural rights for all people. These rights included equality before the law; freedom of religious worship; freedom of speech; freedom of the press; and the rights to assemble, hold property, and pursue happiness. Most philosophes believed that people needed to be governed by enlightened rulers. Enlightened rulers allow religious toleration, freedom of speech and of the press, and the rights of private property. They promote the arts, sciences, and education. Above all, they obey the laws and enforce them fairly for all people. Many historians once assumed that a new type of monarchy emerged in the eighteenth century, which they called **enlightened absolutism.** In the system of enlightened absolutism, rulers tried to govern by Enlightenment principles while maintaining their royal powers. This idea has since been questioned. Of the major rulers in Europe in the eighteenth century, only Joseph II of Austria made truly radical changes based on Enlightenment ideas. Most rulers were guided primarily by a concern for the power and well-being of their states.

Two Prussian kings, Frederick William I and Frederick II, made Prussia a major European power in the eighteenth century. Frederick William I tried to maintain a highly efficient bureaucracy of civil service workers. He also doubled the size of the army. Because of its size and its reputation as one of the best armies in Europe, the army was the most important institution in Prussia. Frederick II (also called Frederick the Great) was cultured and well educated. He was well informed about the ideas of the Enlightenment. He, too, enlarged the Prussian army, and he kept a strict watch over the bureaucracy. He made some enlightened reforms. He abolished the use of torture except in treason and murder cases. He also granted limited freedom of speech and press and complete religious toleration. However, he did not abolish serfdom or the rigid social structure in Prussia.

By the beginning of the eighteenth century, the Austrian Empire had become one of the great European states. It was difficult to rule, however, because it was made up of many different nationalities, languages, religions and cultures. Empress Maria Theresa, who inherited the throne in 1740, worked to centralize the Austrian Empire and strengthen the power of the state. Her successor was Joseph II. He was determined to make changes. He abolished serfdom, eliminated the death penalty, established the principle of equality of all before the law, and enacted religious reforms. Most of his reforms failed, however. He made the nobles upset by freeing the serfs. The Catholic Church was unhappy with his religious reforms. Even the serfs were unhappy, because they were confused by the drastic changes in his policies.

In Russia, Peter the Great was followed by six weak czars. After the last of the six czars, Peter III, was murdered, his German wife became the ruler of Russia. Catherine II (also known as Catherine the Great) ruled Russia from 1762 to 1796. She was an intelligent woman who was familiar with the works of the philosophes, but she thought many of their ideas were impractical. She did consider the idea of a new law code that would recognize the equality of all people. In the end, however, she did nothing because she knew that her success depended on the support of the Russian nobility. Her policies led to worse conditions for the Russian peasants and eventually to rebellion. The rebellion spread across southern Russia, but soon collapsed. Catherine took stronger measures against the peasants. All rural reform was halted, and serfdom was expanded into newer parts of the empire. Under Catherine, Russia spread southward to the Black Sea. To the west, Russia gained about 50 percent of Poland's territory.

7. What European ruler made major changes based on Enlightenment ideas?

____

____

____

• War of the Austrian Succession *(page 531)*

In 1740, a major war broke out in connection with the succession to the Austrian throne. When the Austrian emperor Charles VI died, he was succeeded by his daughter, Maria Theresa. King Frederick II of Prussia took advantage of the situation and invaded Austrian Silesia. France then entered the war against Austria, its traditional enemy. Maria Theresa made an alliance with Great Britain. The War of Austrian Succession was fought in three parts of the world. In Europe, Prussia seized Silesia, and France occupied the Austrian Netherlands. In the Far East, France took Madras in India from the British. In North America, the British captured the French fortress of Louisbourg at the entrance to the St. Lawrence River. After seven years of war, all parties were exhausted and agreed to the Treaty of Aix-la-Chapelle in 1748. This treaty returned all occupied territories except Silesia to their original owners. Prussia's refusal to return Silesia meant another war between Prussia and Austria.

8. In what three parts of the world was the War of Austrian Succession fought?

____

____

____

• The Seven Years' War *(page 532)*

Maria Theresa refused to accept the loss of Silesia. She rebuilt her army and worked to separate Prussia from its chief ally, France. French-Austrian rivalry had been a fact of life in Europe since the late sixteenth century. However, two new rivalries now replaced the old one: the rivalry of Britain and France over colonial empires and the rivalry of Austria and Prussia over Silesia. France abandoned Prussia and allied with Austria. Russia joined the new alliance with France and Austria. In turn, Britain allied with Prussia. This diplomatic revolution led to another worldwide war. The war had three major areas of conflict: Europe, India, and North America.

There were now two major alliances in Europe: the British and Prussians against the Austrians, Russians, and French. Frederick the Great of Prussia was able to defeat the Austrian, French, and Russian armies for a time. However, his forces were eventually worn down. He faced disaster until Peter III, a new Russian czar, withdrew Russian troops from the conflict. This withdrawal created a stalemate and led to the desire for peace. The European war ended in 1763. All occupied territories were returned to their original owners, and Austria officially recognized Prussia's control of Silesia.

The struggle between Britain and France in the rest of the world had more decisive results. Known as the Great War for Empire, it was fought in India and North America. The British ultimately won in India. With the Treaty of Paris in 1763, the French withdrew and left India to the British.

By far the greatest conflicts of the Seven Years' War took place in North America. French North America (Canada and Louisiana) was run by the French government as a vast trading area. It was valuable for its fur, leather, fish and timber. British North America consisted of 13 colonies on the eastern coast of the present United States. The British and French fought over two primary areas in North America. One was the waterway of the Gulf of St. Lawrence. The other was the Ohio River Valley. The French began to establish forts in the Ohio River Valley. This threatened the ability of British settlers to expand into this area. The French were able to gain the support of the Indians, because they were traders, not settlers. At first, the French had a number of victories. The French had more troops in North America than the British, but not enough naval support. The defeat of French fleets in major naval battles gave the British an advantage. A series of British victories soon followed. In 1759, British forces defeated the French on the Plains of Abraham, outside Quebec. The British went on to seize Montreal, the Great Lakes area, and the Ohio River Valley. The French were forced to make peace. By the Treaty of Paris, they transferred Canada and the lands east of the Mississippi to England. Their ally Spain transferred Florida to British control. By 1763, Great Britain had become the world's greatest colonial power.

9. Where did the greatest conflicts of the Seven Years' War take place?

____

____

____

____

____

Reading Essentials and Study Guide

Chapter 17, Section 4

For use with textbook pages 536–540

COLONIAL EMPIRES AND THE AMERICAN REVOLUTION

KEY TERMS

mestizo the offspring of Europeans and Native Americans *(page 537)*

mulatto the offspring of Africans and Europeans *(page 537)*

federal system a system of government in which power is shared between the national, or federal, government and the state governments *(page 540)*

DRAWING FROM EXPERIENCE

What rights are guaranteed to all Americans by the Constitution? Which of these rights do you consider most important? Why?

In the last two sections, you read about the impact of Enlightenment ideas on European life during the eighteenth century. The ideas of the Enlightenment also made a strong impact on the colonies in North America, which eventually led to the American Revolution. Many of these ideas were incorporated into the Declaration of Independence and the Constitution of the United States.

ORGANIZING YOUR THOUGHTS

Use the diagram below to help you take notes. The Constitution created a federal system in which power was shared between the national and state governments. The national, or federal, government was divided into three branches. Identify and describe these three branches.

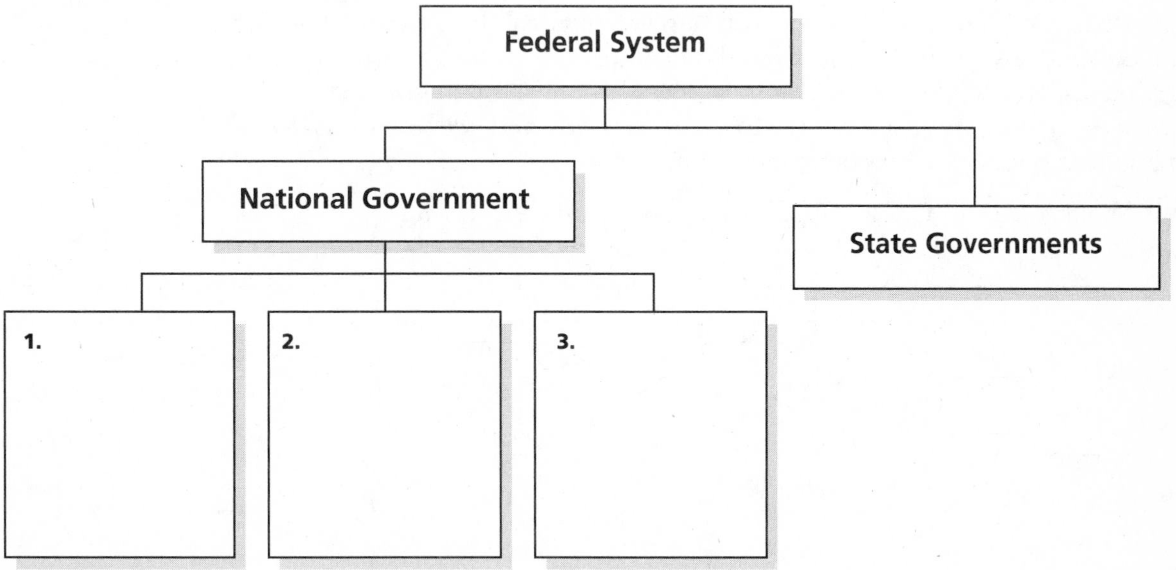

• Colonial Empires in Latin America *(page 536)*

In the sixteenth century, Portugal dominated Brazil. At the same time, Spain established an enormous colonial empire that included parts of North America, Central America, and most of South America. Within the lands of Central and South America, a new civilization arose, which we call Latin America. Latin America was a multiracial society. Spanish rulers permitted intermarriage between Europeans and Native Americans. Their offspring were known as **mestizos.** As many as 8 million African slaves were brought to Latin America to work the plantations. The offspring of Africans and Europeans were known as **mulattoes.** The society of Latin America was a combination of Europeans, Africans, Native Americans, mestizos, and mulattoes.

The Portuguese and Spanish both profited from their colonies in Latin America. The abundant supplies of gold and silver were one source of wealth. Other products that were shipped to Europe included sugar, tobacco, diamonds, and animal hides. Latin American agriculture was dominated by large landowners. Native Americans either worked on the estates of the large landowners or worked as poor farmers on marginal lands. This system of large landowners and dependent peasants has remained a lasting feature of Latin American society.

Spanish and Portuguese monarchs tried to oversee their empires, but the difficulties of communication and travel made this virtually impossible. As a result, colonial officials in Latin America had a great deal of freedom in carrying out imperial policies. Spanish and Portuguese rulers were determined to Christianize the native peoples. This policy gave the Catholic Church an important role in the Americas. Catholic missionaries went to different parts of the Spanish Empire. To make their efforts easier, the missionaries brought Native Americans together into villages, or missions, where the native peoples could be converted, taught trades, and encouraged to grow crops. The missions made it possible for the missionaries to control the lives of the Native Americans. The Catholic Church also built cathedrals, hospitals, orphanages, and schools in the colonies. The Catholic Church also allowed women who did not wish to marry to enter convents and become nuns. Many nuns worked outside their convents by running schools and hospitals.

4. What role did the Catholic Church play in Latin America?

____

____

____

____

____

Reading Essentials and Study Guide

• Britain and British North America *(page 538)*

The United Kingdom of Great Britain came into existence in 1707 when the governments of England and Scotland were united. The term *British* came to refer to both the English and the Scots. In eighteenth-century Britain, the monarch and the Parliament shared power, with the Parliament gradually gaining more power. In 1714, a new dynasty, the Hanoverians, was established when the last Stuart ruler, Queen Anne, died without an heir. The crown was offered to her nearest relatives, Protestant rulers of the German state of Hanover. The first two Hanoverian kings, George I and George II, did not know the British system very well and allowed their chief ministers to handle Parliament. Robert Walpole was the prime minister from 1721 to 1742. He pursued a peaceful foreign policy. The growing middle class favored expansion of trade and the British Empire. When William Pitt the Elder became prime minister in 1757, he expanded the British Empire by acquiring Canada and India in the Seven Years' War.

The British colonies in North America were thickly populated, containing about 1.5 million people by 1750. The colonies were supposedly run by the British Board of Trade, the Royal Council, and Parliament. But the colonies had legislatures that tended to act independently. Merchants in many cities did not want the British government to run their affairs.

5. Why did British prime ministers become more powerful in the eighteenth century?

• The American Revolution *(page 539)*

After the Seven Years' War, British leaders wanted to get new revenues from the colonies. These revenues would be used to cover war costs, as well as to pay for the expenses of maintaining an army to defend the colonies. In 1765, the Parliament imposed the Stamp Act on the colonies. Certain printed materials, such as legal documents and newspapers, had to carry a stamp showing that a tax had been paid. Opposition was widespread and often violent. The act was repealed in 1766, but the crisis was not over.

To counteract British actions, the colonies organized the First Continental Congress. It met in Philadelphia in 1774. Fighting erupted between colonists and the British army in April 1775 in Lexington and Concord, Massachusetts. The Second Continental Congress met soon afterward and formed an army, called the Continental Army. They named George Washington as commander in chief. On July 4, 1776, the Second Continental Congress approved a declaration of independence written by Thomas Jefferson. The American Revolution had formally begun.

The colonies had support from foreign countries. These countries wanted revenge for earlier defeats at the hands of the British. The French supplied arms and money to the rebels. French officers and soldiers also served in Washington's army. Spain and the Dutch Republic also entered the war against Great Britain. When the army of General Cornwallis was forced to surrender to American and French forces under Washington at Yorktown in 1781, the British decided to end the war. The Treaty of Paris, signed in 1783, recognized the independence of the American colonies. It also gave the Americans control of the western territory from the Appalachians to the Mississippi River.

6. What countries supported the American colonies in their war against the British?

____

____

____

____

____

• The Birth of a New Nation *(page 539)*

The 13 American colonies had gained their independence. They were now states, but each one was primarily concerned about its own interests. At first, the states were not enthusiastic about creating a united nation with a strong central government. The Articles of Confederation were approved in 1781. This first American constitution did not provide for a strong central government. It soon became clear that the government under the Articles lacked the power to deal with the new nation's problems. In the summer of 1787, 55 delegates met in Philadelphia to revise the Articles. The delegates decided to write a plan for an entirely new national government.

The proposed Constitution created a **federal system** in which power would be shared between the national government and the state governments. The national, or federal, government was given the power to levy taxes, raise an army, regulate trade, and create a national currency. The federal government was divided into three branches, each with some power to check the workings of the other branches. The first branch was the executive. A president served as the chief executive. The second branch was the legislative branch. It consisted of the Senate and the House of Representatives. The third branch was the judicial branch. It consisted of the Supreme Court and other courts.

Name ______________________ Date ______________________ Class ______________________

Reading Essentials and Study Guide

Chapter 17, Section 4 *(continued)*

Important to the eventual adoption of the Constitution was a promise to add a bill of rights. In 1789, the new Congress proposed 12 amendments, and the 10 that were approved by the states became known as the Bill of Rights. These amendments guaranteed freedom of religion, speech, press, petition, and assembly. They gave Americans the right to bear arms and to be protected against unreasonable searches and arrests. They guaranteed trial by jury, due process of law, and the protection of property rights. Many of the rights were derived from the natural rights proposed by the eighteenth-century philosophes.

7. How did the Articles of Confederation differ from the Constitution?

____

____

____

____

____

Name ______________________________ Date ______________________ Class ______________________

Reading Essentials and Study Guide

Chapter 18, Section 1

For use with textbook pages 547–553

THE FRENCH REVOLUTION BEGINS

KEY TERMS

estate each of the three divisions of French society *(page 548)*

relics of feudalism obligations that French peasants owed to their local landlords even though serfdom no longer existed *(page 548)*

bourgeoisie the middle class in France that included merchants, bankers, industrialists, and professional people *(page 548)*

sans-culottes ("without breeches") the name that members of the Paris Commune gave themselves *(page 553)*

DRAWING FROM EXPERIENCE

Do you think the United States is divided into social classes? If yes, what are the classes in U.S. society? If not, why not?

In this section, you will learn about the factors that contributed to the French Revolution. France's class system was one of those factors.

ORGANIZING YOUR THOUGHTS

Use the pyramid diagram below to help you take notes. French society was divided into three orders, or estates. Identify the groups that made up each estate. List some of the occupations of the people in the Third Estate.

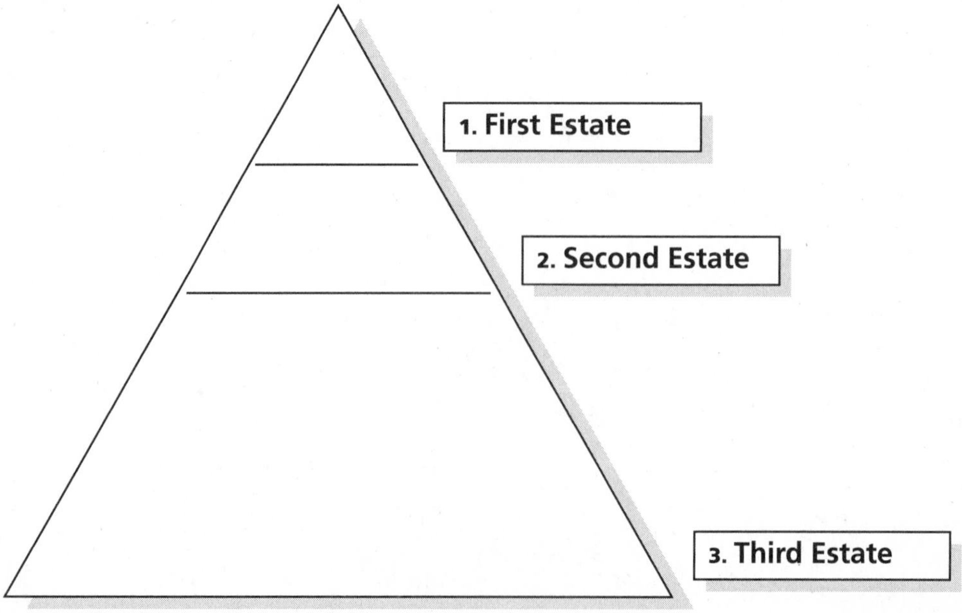

READ TO LEARN

• Background to the Revolution *(page 547)*

The French Revolution began in 1789. It was more complex, more violent, and more radical than the American Revolution. It tried to create both a new political order and a new social order. The immediate causes of the French Revolution were economic problems at the time, but there were also long-range problems that created an environment for revolution. Before the revolution, French society was based on inequality. France was divided into three orders, or **estates.** The First Estate consisted of the clergy. There were about 130,000 people in the First Estate. They owned about 10 percent of the land and were exempt from the *taille,* the main tax in France. The Second Estate was the nobility. There were about 350,000 people in this estate. They owned about 25 to 30 percent of the land. They held many of the leading positions in the government, military, courts, and the higher church offices. They were also exempt from the *taille.*

The Third Estate consisted of the commoners. This was the majority of the French population. The Third Estate was further divided by occupations and wealth. The peasants were the largest segment of the Third Estate. They were about 75 to 80 percent of the total French population. As a group, they owned about 35 to 40 percent of the land, but over half of them had little or no land on which to survive. Serfdom had been largely eliminated, but French peasants still had obligations to their local landlords. These **relics of feudalism,** or aristocratic privileges, were obligations that survived from an earlier age. The peasants deeply resented these obligations, which included fees to use village facilities, such as the flourmill, community oven, and winepress. Another part of the Third Estate consisted of skilled craftspeople, shopkeepers, and other wage earners in the cities. A rise in consumer prices that was greater than the increase in wages made it difficult for these urban groups to survive. This struggle for survival led many of these people to play an important role in the revolution. The **bourgeoisie,** or middle class, was another part of the Third Estate. This group included about 8 percent of the population, or 2.3 million people. They owned about 20 to 25 percent of the land. This group included merchants, bankers, industrialists, doctors, lawyers, and writers. Members of the middle class were unhappy with the privileges of the nobility. At the same time, they had a great deal in common with the nobility. By obtaining public offices, wealthy middle-class people could become part of the nobility. Members of the nobility and the bourgeoisie were both influenced by the new ideas of the Enlightenment. Many of the people in both of these groups were opposed to the monarchy.

The social inequality in France created the background for the French Revolution, but the immediate cause of the revolution was the near collapse of government finances. Bad harvests in 1787 and 1788 and a slowdown in manufacturing led to food shortages, rising prices for food, and unemployment in the cities. The number of poor reached crisis proportions. At the same time, the French government continued to spend enormous amounts of money on wars and luxuries. The queen, Marie Antoinette, was known for her extravagance. On the verge of a complete financial collapse, the government of Louis XVI was forced to call a meeting of the Estates-General. This was the French parliament, and it had not met since 1614.

4. What was the immediate cause of the French Revolution?

____

____

____

____

____

• From Estates-General to National Assembly *(page 549)*

The Estates-General was composed of deputies (representatives) from the three estates. The First and Second Estates had about three hundred delegates each. The Third Estate had almost six hundred delegates. In order to fix France's financial problems, most members of the Third Estate wanted to set up a constitutional government that would abolish the tax exemptions of the clergy and nobility. The meeting of the Estates-General opened at Versailles on May 5, 1789. There was an immediate dispute about voting. Traditionally, each estate had one vote. That meant that the First and Second Estates together could outvote the Third Estate two to one. The Third Estate demanded that each deputy have one vote. With the help of a few nobles and clerics, that would give the Third Estate a majority. The king, however, declared that he was in favor of the current system, in which each estate had one vote.

The Third Estate reacted quickly. On June 17, 1789, it called itself a National Assembly and decided to draft a constitution. When the deputies of the Third Estate arrived at their meeting place three days later, they found the doors locked. They moved to a nearby indoor tennis court and swore that they would continue to meet until they had produced a French constitution. The oath they swore is called the Tennis Court Oath. Louis XVI began to make plans to use force against the Third Estate. But before he could do this, a mob of Parisians stormed the Bastille, an armory and prison in Paris. They tore the Bastille apart, brick by brick. This took place on July 14. Paris soon came under the control of the rebels. Louis XVI was no longer in control. Revolutions and peasant rebellions broke out throughout France. They became part of the Great Fear, a panic that spread quickly through France in the summer of 1789. Citizens began to form militias, because they were afraid that they would be invaded by foreign troops that supported the French monarchy.

5. What event brought an end to Louis XVI's control in France?

• The Destruction of the Old Regime *(page 550)*

One of the first acts of the National Assembly was to destroy the relics of feudalism. On August 4, 1789, the National Assembly voted to abolish the rights of landlords and the financial privileges of the nobility and clergy. On August 26, the National Assembly adopted the Declaration of the Rights of Man and the Citizen. This was a charter of basic liberties that was inspired by the American Declaration of Independence and Constitution and the English Bill of Rights. It proclaimed freedom and equal rights for all men, access to public office based on talent, and an end to exemptions from taxation. All citizens were to have the right to take part in the making of laws. Freedom of speech and the press were guaranteed. The guarantee of equal rights did not include women, however. In response, Olympe de Gouges, a female author, wrote a Declaration of the Rights of Woman and the Female Citizen. In it, she insisted that women should have the same rights as men. But the National Assembly ignored her demands.

Louis XVI remained at Versailles and refused to accept the National Assembly's decrees on the abolition of feudalism and the Declaration of Rights. On October 5, thousands of Parisian women marched to Versailles. They forced the king to accept the new decrees. They insisted that the royal family return to Paris to show the king's support of the National Assembly. On October 6, the royal family moved to Paris, where they became virtual prisoners.

The Catholic Church was seen as a pillar of the old order. The National Assembly seized and sold the lands of the Church. A new Civil Constitution of the Clergy was put into effect. Bishops and priests were to be elected by the people and paid by the state. The French government now controlled the Church. As a result, many Catholics became enemies of the revolution.

The National Assembly completed a new constitution, the Constitution of 1791. It set up a limited monarchy. There was still a king, but a Legislative Assembly made the laws. This Assembly was to have 745 representatives. Although all males had the same rights, only men over 25 who paid a specified amount in taxes could vote. This ensured that only the more affluent members of society would be elected. By 1791, the old order had been destroyed, but many people opposed the new order. These included Catholic priests, nobles, lower classes hurt by a rise in the cost of living, and radicals who wanted even more drastic solutions.

Some European leaders began to fear that revolutions would spread to their countries. The rulers of Austria and Prussia tried to use force to restore Louis XVI to full power. The Legislative Assembly declared war on Austria in the spring of 1792. The French fared badly at first. Defeats in war and economic shortages at home led to new demonstrations in the spring of 1792. In August, radical political groups in Paris declared themselves a commune. Many of the members of the Paris Commune proudly called themselves the ***sans-culottes*** ("without breeches"). This meant that they were ordinary patriots without fine clothes. They attacked the royal palace and the Legislative Assembly. They took the king captive. They forced the Legislative Assembly to suspend the monarchy and call for a National Convention. This convention would be chosen on the basis of universal male suffrage. (Under universal male suffrage, all adult males had the right to vote.)

6. What groups in France in 1791 opposed the new order?

____

____

____

____

____

Name ______________________ Date ______________________ Class ______________________

Reading Essentials and Study Guide

Chapter 18, Section 2

For use with textbook pages 555–561

RADICAL REVOLUTION AND REACTION

KEY TERMS

factions dissenting groups *(page 556)*

elector an individual qualified to vote in an election *(page 561)*

coup d'état a sudden overthrow of a government *(page 561)*

DRAWING FROM EXPERIENCE

Have you ever seen or heard about the play *Les Misérables?* What is the theme of the play?

In the last section, you read about the French Revolution. In this section, you will learn how radical groups and leaders began to control the revolution and how other countries reacted to the revolution.

ORGANIZING YOUR THOUGHTS

Complete the time line below using information from this section and the last section. Identify the four governmental bodies that ruled France after the Estates-General convened in 1789 and before Napoleon seized control in 1799. Also indicate the dates (years) that each of these four bodies controlled France.

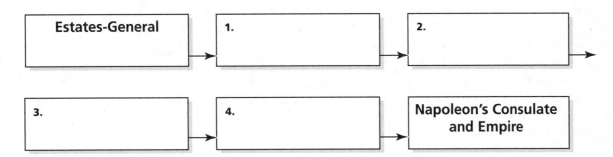

Estates-General → **1.** → **2.** →

3. → **4.** → **Napoleon's Consulate and Empire**

READ TO LEARN

• The Move to Radicalism *(page 555)*

The Paris Commune had forced the Legislative Assembly to call a National Convention. The *sans-culottes* (members of the Commune) took other steps toward a more radical revolution. They took revenge on people who had helped the king or resisted the revolution. Thousands of people were arrested and killed. New leaders, such as Jean-Paul Marat, encouraged the poor to use violence to get what they needed.

In September 1792, the newly elected National Convention began to meet. Although it had been created to draft a new constitution, it also acted as the ruling body of France. The Convention was dominated by lawyers, professionals, and property owners. Almost all of the deputies distrusted the king. The Convention's first major step was to abolish the monarchy and establish a republic, the French Republic. The Paris Commune favored radical change and put constant pressure on the National Convention to adopt more radical positions. The National Convention did not rule all of France, however. Peasants in western France and people in France's major provincial cities refused to accept the authority of the National Convention.

The members of the Convention soon split into **factions** (dissenting groups) over the fate of the king. The two most important factions were the Girondins and the Mountain. Both factions were members of the Jacobin club, a large network of political groups throughout France. The Girondins represented the provinces, the areas outside the cities. The Girondins feared the radical mobs in Paris and wanted to keep the king alive. The Mountain represented the radicals in Paris. The Mountain won at the beginning of 1793 when they convinced the National Convention to condemn Louis XVI to death. He was beheaded on the guillotine on January 21, 1793. The execution of the king outraged the royalty of most of Europe. An informal coalition of Austria, Prussia, Spain, Portugal, Britain, the Dutch Republic, and Russia took up arms against France. By the spring of 1793, they were ready to invade France. To meet this crisis, the National Convention gave broad powers to a special committee of 12 known as the Committee of Public Safety. It was dominated at first by Georges Danton, then by Maximilien Robespierre.

5. Why did the National Convention form the Committee of Public Safety?

• The Reign of Terror *(page 557)*

For a 12-month period, from 1793 to 1794, the Committee of Public Safety took control. The Committee acted to defend France from foreign enemies and rebellions at home. The Committee set in motion an effort that came to be known as the Reign of Terror. During the Reign of Terror, nearly 40,000 people were killed, many by the guillotine. Most executions were held in places that had openly rebelled against the authority of the National Convention. The Committee of Public Safety decided to make an example of the city of Lyons. 1,880 people in that city were executed. In western France, the revolutionary armies were brutal in defeating rebel armies. Perhaps the most notorious act of violence occurred in Nantes, where victims were executed by being sunk in barges in the Loire River. People from all classes were killed during the Terror. About 15 percent of the victims were from the clergy and nobility, and the rest were from the bourgeoisie and peasant classes.

The Committee of Public Safety took other steps to control France and to create a new order, called the Republic of Virtue. The Committee tried to provide some economic controls by establishing price limits on goods considered necessities, such as food, fuel, and clothing. But the controls did not work very well. The National Convention also pursued a policy of dechristianization. The word *saint* was removed from street names, churches were pillaged or closed, and priests were encouraged to marry. In November 1793, a public ceremony dedicated to the worship of reason was held in the cathedral of Notre Dame. A new calendar was also adopted. Years were no longer numbered from the birth of Christ but from September 22, 1792—the first day of the French Republic. Sundays and church holidays were eliminated. Dechristianization failed to work, however, because France was still overwhelmingly Catholic.

Women were actively involved in the revolution. Women observed sessions of the National Convention and made their demands known. In 1793, two women founded the Society for Revolutionary Republican Women. This group was made up of working-class women. They were ready to defend the new French Republic if the need arose. Many men, however, continued to believe that women should not participate in political and military affairs.

6. What steps did the National Convention take to try to dechristianize France?

____

____

____

____

____

Reading Essentials and Study Guide

• A Nation in Arms *(page 560)*

To save the republic from its foreign enemies, the Committee of Public Safety decreed a universal mobilization of the nation on August 23, 1793. In less than a year, the revolutionary government had raised an army of 650,000. By September 1794, the army numbered 1,169,000. The republic's army was the largest in European history. It pushed the allies invading France back across the Rhine and even conquered the Austrian Netherlands. The French revolutionary army was a new kind of army. It was not made up of professional soldiers. It was created by a people's government. Its wars were people's wars, not wars between rulers.

By the summer of 1794, the French had defeated most of their foreign enemies. There was less need for the Committee of Public Safety, but it continued to exist. Robespierre had become very powerful and was obsessed with ridding France of all its corrupt elements. Many deputies in the National Convention feared Robespierre and voted to execute him. He was guillotined on July 28, 1794. After his death, more moderate leaders took control, and the Reign of Terror came to an end.

7. In what ways was the French revolutionary army different from previous armies?

• The Directory *(page 560)*

The National Convention reduced the power of the Committee of Public Safety. Churches were allowed to reopen. A new constitution was created in August 1795. It established a national legislative assembly. It had two chambers: a lower house, known as the Council of 500, which initiated legislation, and an upper house, the Council of Elders, which accepted or rejected the proposed laws. The members of the two chambers were chosen by **electors** (individuals qualified to vote in an election). The electors had to be owners or renters of property worth a certain amount. This limited the number of electors to 30,000.

The Council of Elders elected five directors to act as the executive committee, or Directory. The Directory and the legislature ruled the country. The period under the government of the Directory (1795–1799) was a time of corruption. The Directory had many enemies. Both royalists and radicals were unhappy. Royalists wanted to restore the monarchy. Radicals were unhappy

Name ______________________ Date ______________________ Class ______________________

with the turn toward moderation. The Directory was unable to find a solution to the country's economic problems, and it was still carrying on wars started by the Committee of Public Safety. In 1799, a **coup d'état** (a sudden overthrow of the government) ended the Directory. The coup d'état was led by the successful and popular general Napoleon Bonaparte.

8. Why was the government of the Directory unpopular?

____

____

____

____

____

Name ______________________ Date ______________________ Class ______________________

Reading Essentials and Study Guide

Chapter 18, Section 3

For use with textbook pages 563–569

THE AGE OF NAPOLEON

KEY TERMS

consulate the French government under Napoleon before he was crowned emperor *(page 564)*

nationalism the unique cultural identity of a people based on common language, religion, and national symbols *(page 568)*

DRAWING FROM EXPERIENCE

What do you think of when you hear the name "Napoleon"? Does a particular picture of Napoleon come to mind? What do you know about Napoleon?

In the last two sections, you read about the French Revolution and its results. In this section, you will learn how Napoleon's rise to power brought an end to the French Revolution but also helped to preserve certain aspects of the revolution.

ORGANIZING YOUR THOUGHTS

Use the chart below to help you take notes. Although Napoleon is best known for his military achievements (and failures), he also had significant domestic achievements (achievements within France). List three of Napoleon's achievements in France and three of his achievements outside of France.

Napoleon's Achievements	
In France	**Outside of France**
1.	**4.**
2.	**5.**
3.	**6.**

Name ______________________ Date ______________________ Class ______________________

READ TO LEARN

• The Rise of Napoleon *(page 563)*

Napoleon was born in 1769 on the island of Corsica. His family came from Italy. As a young man, Napoleon received a scholarship to study at a military school in France. In 1785, he was commissioned as a lieutenant in the French army. He rose quickly through the ranks. By age 25, he was made a brigadier general. In 1796, he became commander of the French armies in Italy, where he won many victories. He was able to win the confidence of his men and the support of many people because of his energy, charm, and intelligence. In 1797, he returned to France as a hero. He was given the command of an army in training to invade Britain. He proposed that France strike indirectly at Britain by taking Egypt and threatening India. However, because the British controlled the seas, they were able to cut off Napoleon's army in Egypt. Napoleon abandoned his army and returned to Paris.

In Paris, Napoleon took part in the coup d'état that overthrew the government of the Directory. A new government called the **consulate** was proclaimed. As first consul, Napoleon controlled the entire government. He appointed members of the bureaucracy, controlled the army, conducted foreign affairs, and influenced the legislature. In 1802, he was made consul for life. Two years later, he had himself crowned Emperor Napoleon I.

7. How did Napoleon win the support of the French people?

____

____

____

____

____

• Napoleon's Domestic Policies *(page 565)*

One of Napoleon's first acts at home was to establish peace with the oldest enemy of the revolution, the Catholic Church. Napoleon himself had no personal religious faith, but he saw the need to restore stability to France. In 1801, Napoleon made an agreement with the pope. The agreement recognized Catholicism as the religion of a majority of the French people. In return, the pope agreed not to ask for the return of the church lands seized in the revolution. This agreement was popular both with Catholics and with people who had bought church lands during the revolution.

Napoleon's most famous domestic achievement was his codification of the laws. Before the revolution, France did not have a single set of laws but almost 300 different legal systems. Napoleon completed seven codes of law.

The most important of the codes was the Civil Code (also called the Napoleonic Code). This code preserved most of the gains of the revolution by recognizing the principle of the equality of all citizens before the law, the right of the individual to choose a profession, religious toleration, and the abolition of serfdom and feudalism. Property rights were carefully protected. The rights of women were curtailed, however. Divorce was still allowed, but it was difficult for women to get divorces. When women married, their property came under the control of their husbands. In lawsuits, they were treated as minors.

Napoleon worked hard to develop a bureaucracy of capable officials. Promotion was based on ability, not on rank or birth. This was a change that the middle class had wanted before the revolution. Napoleon also created a new aristocracy based on merit in the civil or military service. 3,263 new nobles were created between 1808 and 1814. Only 22 percent of Napoleon's aristocracy came from the nobility of the old regime. Almost 60 percent were middle class people.

Napoleon claimed that he preserved the gains of the revolution. In some respects, this was true. The Civil Code preserved the equality of all citizens. Opening government careers to more people was another gain. On the other hand, Napoleon destroyed some revolutionary ideals. Liberty was replaced by despotism. He also eliminated freedom of the press. He shut down 60 of France's 73 newspapers and required that all manuscripts be approved before they were published. Even the mail was opened by government police.

8. In what ways did Napoleon preserve the gains of the revolution? In what ways did he destroy those gains?

____

____

____

____

____

• Napoleon's Empire *(page 566)*

When Napoleon became consul in 1799, France was at war with a European coalition of Russia, Great Britain, and Austria. Napoleon achieved a peace treaty in 1802, but it did not last long. War with Britain broke out again in 1803. Britain was soon joined by Austria, Russia, and Prussia. In a series of battles, Napoleon's army defeated the Austrian, Prussian, and Russian armies.

From 1807 to 1812, Napoleon was the master of Europe. His Grand Empire was composed of three parts: the French Empire, dependent states, and allied states. The French Empire consisted of an enlarged France that extended to the Rhine in the east and included the western half of Italy north of Rome.

Dependent states were kingdoms under the rule of Napoleon's relatives. These included Spain, Holland, the kingdom of Italy, the Swiss Republic, the Grand Duchy of Warsaw, and the Confederation of the Rhine (a union of all German states except Austria and Prussia). Allied states were countries defeated by Napoleon and forced to join his struggle against Britain. They included Prussia, Austria, Russia, and Sweden. Within his empire, Napoleon tried to spread some of the principles of the French Revolution, including legal equality, religious toleration, and economic freedom. In many areas, the nobility and clergy lost their special privileges.

9. What countries were included in Napoleon's Grand Empire?

____

____

____

____

____

• The European Response *(page 567)*

Napoleon's Grand Empire collapsed almost as quickly as it had been formed. There were two main reasons for Napoleon's defeat: the survival of Great Britain and the force of nationalism. Britain's survival was due primarily to its sea power. Napoleon hoped to invade Britain, but the British navy's defeat of a combined French-Spanish fleet at Trafalgar in 1805 destroyed any idea of an invasion. Napoleon then turned to his Continental System to defeat Britain. The goal of the Continental System was to prevent British goods from reaching the European continent. Napoleon hoped to weaken the British economy by preventing the sale of British goods. But the Continental System failed. Allied states resented being told that they could not trade with the British, and some began to cheat. New markets in the Middle East and in Latin America gave Britain other outlets for its goods. By 1809–1810, British exports were at near-record highs.

The second important factor in the defeat of Napoleon was **nationalism.** Nationalism is the unique cultural identity of a people based on common language, religion, and national symbols. Napoleon's spread of the principles of the French Revolution beyond France indirectly brought a spread of nationalism as well. The French aroused nationalism in two ways. First, they were hated as oppressors. This hatred stirred the patriotism of other peoples in opposition to the French. Second, the French showed the people of Europe what nationalism was and what a nation in arms could do.

10. What were the two main factors that led to the defeat of Napoleon?

____

____

____

____

____

• The Fall of Napoleon *(page 568)*

The Russians refused to remain in the Continental System. This left Napoleon with little choice but to invade Russia. In June 1812, a Grand Army of over six hundred thousand men entered Russia. Napoleon's hopes for victory depended on a quick defeat of the Russian armies. But the Russian forces refused to fight. They retreated for hundreds of miles. As they retreated, they burned their own villages and countryside to keep Napoleon's army from finding food. When the Grand Army arrived in Moscow, they found it on fire. Without food and supplies, Napoleon abandoned Moscow and began the "Great Retreat" across Russia. Only forty thousand of the original army made it back to Poland. This military disaster led other European states to attack the French army. Paris was captured in March 1814. Napoleon was sent into exile on the island of Elba. The Bourbon monarchy was restored to France. Louis XVIII became king. He was the brother of the executed king, Louis XVI.

The new king had little support, and Napoleon was able to slip back into France. When troops were sent to capture him, they went over to his side. Napoleon entered Paris in triumph on March 20, 1815. Napoleon raised another army and moved to attack the nearest allied forces in Belgium. At Waterloo in Belgium on June 18, 1815, Napoleon met a combined British and Prussian army under the Duke of Wellington. He was defeated and exiled to St. Helena, a small island in the south Atlantic.

11. What were the consequences of Napoleon's invasion of Russia?

____

____

____

____

____

Name ________________________ Date ________________ Class ________________

Reading Essentials and Study Guide

Chapter 19, Section 1

For use with textbook pages 581–588

THE INDUSTRIAL REVOLUTION

KEY TERMS

capital money available for investment *(page 582)*

entrepreneur a person who invests in a new business or businesses in order to make profits *(page 582)*

cottage industry a production method in which individuals did the work in their rural homes *(page 582)*

puddling a process developed by Henry Cort in the 1780s that produced high quality iron by using coke to burn away impurities in crude iron *(page 583)*

industrial capitalism an economic system based on industrial production *(page 586)*

socialism a system in which society, usually in the form of the government, owns and controls the means of production *(page 588)*

DRAWING FROM EXPERIENCE

Have you ever been to a history museum? Have you seen any early inventions used in the textile industry, such as a flying shuttle, a spinning jenny, or a cotton gin? What were these inventions like?

In this section, you will learn about the Industrial Revolution and the impact that it had in Europe and North America.

ORGANIZING YOUR THOUGHTS

Use the diagram below to help you take notes. The Industrial Revolution began in Great Britain. List five factors that help to explain why the Industrial Revolution began there.

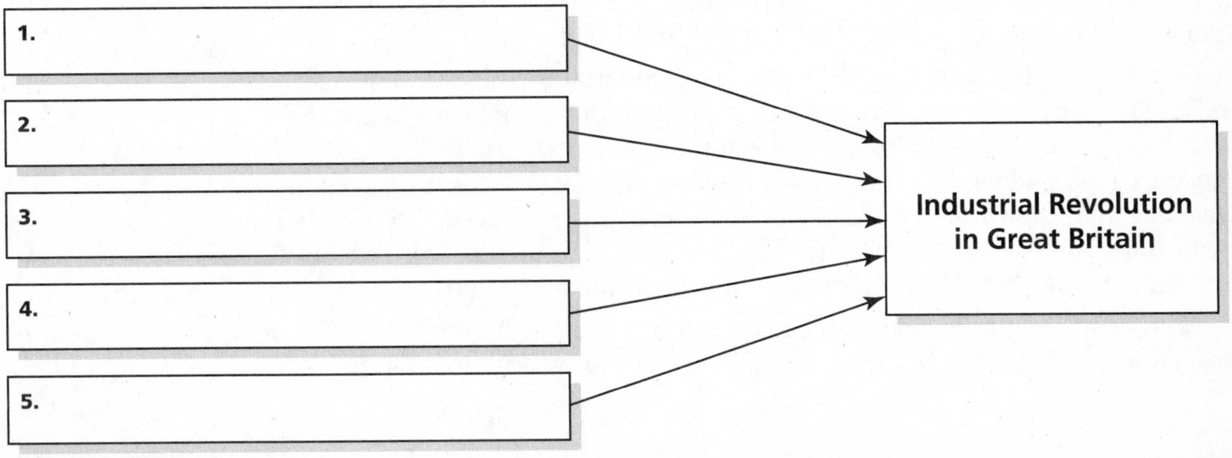

READ TO LEARN

• The Industrial Revolution in Great Britain *(page 581)*

The Industrial Revolution began in Great Britain in the 1780s. There were several reasons why it started there. First, agricultural practices in the eighteenth century had changed. More people could be fed at lower prices with less labor. Now even ordinary British families had money to buy manufactured goods. Second, with more abundant food supplies, the population grew. This increase created a large labor force to work in the new factories in Britain. Third, Britain had money to invest in the new industrial machines and factories. This money is called **capital.** Many British people were very wealthy and were interested in finding new business opportunities and new ways to make profits. These people are called **entrepreneurs.** Fourth, natural resources, such as coal and iron ore, were plentiful in Britain. Finally, Britain had a huge empire that gave the British many markets for their goods.

One of the main industries in Great Britain was the production of inexpensive cotton goods. There were two steps in the manufacture of cotton cloth—spinning (making thread) and weaving (turning the thread into cloth). Originally, the work was done by individuals in their rural homes. This production method is known as **cottage industry.** Advances in technology made cottage industry inefficient, however. The invention of the "flying shuttle" made weaving faster. Weavers now needed more thread from spinners. By 1768 James Hargreaves had invented a spinning machine called the spinning jenny, which made the spinning process faster. In fact, thread was being produced faster than weavers could use it. By 1787, Edmund Cartwright had invented a water-powered loom that made it possible for the weaving of cloth to catch up with the spinning of thread. It now became more efficient to do the work in factories, which were located near streams and rivers. The cotton industry became even more productive when the steam engine was improved by a Scottish engineer, James Watt. Watt made changes that allowed the engine to drive machinery. Steam power could now be used to spin and weave cotton. Before long, cotton mills were found all over Britain. By 1840, cotton cloth was Britain's most valuable product. British cotton goods were sold everywhere in the world and were produced mainly in factories.

The steam engine was crucial to Britain's Industrial Revolution. For fuel, the engine depended on coal. The need for coal led to an increase in coal production. The need for coal increased even more when Henry Cort developed a process called **puddling.** In this process, coke (which was derived from coal) was used to burn away impurities in crude iron. This produced a better quality of iron. The British iron industry boomed. The high-quality iron was used to build new machines, especially new means of transportation.

Railroads were particularly important to the success of the Industrial Revolution. In 1804, the first steam-powered locomotive ran on an industrial rail-line in Britain. By 1850, there were 6000 miles of railroad track across the country. Building railroads created new jobs for farm laborers and peasants. Less expensive transportation led to lower-priced goods, which created larger markets. More sales meant more factories and more machinery.

Factories created a new labor system. Factory owners wanted to use their new machines constantly. As a result, workers were forced to work in shifts to keep the machines running all day. Factory owners created a system in which employees became used to working set hours and doing the same work over and over. Adult workers were fined or fired for being late or for other misconduct. Child workers were often beaten.

6. How did factories create a new labor system?

• The Spread of Industrialization *(page 584)*

By the mid-nineteenth century, Great Britain had become the world's first and richest industrial nation. It produced one-half of the world's coal and manufactured goods. The Industrial Revolution spread to the rest of Europe at different times and speeds. The first countries to be industrialized in continental Europe were Belgium, France, and the German states. In these places, governments were very active in encouraging the development of industrialization.

An Industrial Revolution also occurred in the new nation of the United States. In 1800, six out of every seven American workers were farmers. By 1860, only 50 percent of American workers were farmers. Labor for the growing number of factories in the Northeast came mainly from the farm population. Many of the workers in the new factories were women. Women made up more than 80 percent of the workers in large textile factories.

The United States was a large country in the 1800s. A transportation system to move goods across the nation was vital. Thousands of miles of roads and canals were built to link east and west. Robert Fulton built the first paddle-wheel steamboat in 1807. By 1860, there were a thousand steamboats on the Mississippi River. The railroad was the most important part of the American transportation system. By 1860, about 30,000 miles of railroad track covered the United States.

Reading Essentials and Study Guide

7. What countries were the first to be industrialized in continental Europe? Why?

• Social Impact in Europe *(page 585)*

The Industrial Revolution drastically changed the social life of Europe and the world. By 1850, the population of Europe had almost doubled to 266 million. The key to this growth was a decline in death rates, wars, and diseases. Because of an increase in the food supply, more people were better fed and resistant to diseases. Famine disappeared from most of western Europe. Cities and towns grew dramatically in the first half of the nineteenth century. The growth was directly related to industrialization. People moved from the country to the cities to find work in factories. The rapid growth of cities led to pitiful living conditions for many people, however.

With the Industrial Revolution came the rise of **industrial capitalism,** an economic system based on industrial production. Industrial capitalism produced a new middle-class group—the industrial middle class. The new industrial middle class was made up of the people who built the factories, bought the machines, and figured out where the markets were. Their qualities included initiative, vision, ambition, and often, greed.

The Industrial Revolution also created an industrial working class. Industrial workers had terrible working conditions. Work hours ranged from 12 to 16 hours a day, six days a week, with a half-hour for lunch and dinner. The worst conditions were in the cotton mills. The mills were hot, dirty, dusty, dangerous, and unhealthy. In Britain, women and children made up two-thirds of the cotton industry's workforce by 1830. However, the number of children declined under the Factory Act of 1833, which set 9 as the minimum age for employment. As the number of children declined, women took their places. They were mostly unskilled labor and were paid half, or less than half, of what men received. Excessive working hours for women were outlawed in 1844.

The laws that limited the work hours of children and women gradually led to a new pattern of work. In cottage industry, husband, wife, and children had always worked together. Men were now expected to earn most of the family income by working outside the home. Women took over daily care of the family and performed low-paying jobs, such as laundry work, that could be done in the home.

Reading Essentials and Study Guide

In the first half of the nineteenth century, the pitiful conditions created by the Industrial Revolution gave rise to a movement known as **socialism.** Socialism is a system in which society, usually through government, owns and controls the means of production (natural resources, factories, etc.). Early socialism was primarily the idea of intellectuals who believed in the equality of all people and who wanted to replace competition with cooperation in industry. Later socialists called these early socialists utopians because they thought their ideas were impractical dreams. Robert Owen, a British cotton manufacturer, was one utopian socialist. He believed that humans would show their natural goodness if they lived in a cooperative environment. He formed two communities, one at New Lanark in Scotland and one at New Harmony, Indiana. The community at New Lanark flourished, but the one at New Harmony failed.

8. In what ways did the Industrial Revolution change the social life of Europe?

Name ______________________ Date ______________ Class ______________

Reading Essentials and Study Guide

Chapter 19, Section 2

For use with textbook pages 589–594

REACTION AND REVOLUTION

KEY TERMS

conservatism a political philosophy based on tradition and social stability *(page 590)*

principle of intervention the belief that the great powers in Europe had the right to send armies into countries where there were revolutions, in order to restore legitimate monarchs to their thrones *(page 591)*

liberalism a political philosophy based largely on Enlightenment principles that held that people should be as free as possible from government restraint and that civil liberties should be protected *(page 591)*

universal male suffrage the right of all adult men to vote *(page 592)*

DRAWING FROM EXPERIENCE

In the 1800s, liberals were people who supported ideas such as individual freedom, freedom of speech, freedom of the press, and religious freedom. Do you think you would have been a liberal in the 1800s? Why or why not?

In the last section, you read about the Industrial Revolution. In this section, you will learn how liberalism and nationalism led to changes in Europe, including the revolutions of 1848.

ORGANIZING YOUR THOUGHTS

Use the chart below to help you take notes. Compare and contrast the philosophies of conservatism and liberalism.

Political Philosophy	Views:		
	Government	**Religion**	**Civil Rights**
Conservatism	**1.**	**2.**	**3.**
Liberalism	**4.**	**5.**	**6.**

Name ______________________ Date ______________________ Class ______________________

Reading Essentials and Study Guide

READ TO LEARN

• The Congress of Vienna *(page 589)*

After the defeat of Napoleon, European rulers wanted to restore the old order. The great powers (Great Britain, Austria, Prussia, and Russia) met at the Congress of Vienna in September 1814 to arrange a final peace settlement. The leader of the congress was the Austrian foreign minister, Prince Klemens von Metternich. He claimed that he was guided by the principle of legitimacy. This meant that monarchs from the royal families that had ruled before Napoleon would be restored to their positions of power in order to keep peace and stability in Europe. The great powers rearranged territories in Europe because they believed that this would form a new balance of power. For example, to balance Russian territorial gains, new territories were given to Prussia and Austria.

7. What were the four great powers that met at the Congress of Vienna?

____

____

____

____

____

• The Conservative Order *(page 590)*

The arrangements that were worked out at the Congress of Vienna were a victory for rulers who wanted to stop the forces of change begun by the French Revolution. These rulers, like Metternich, believed in the political philosophy known as **conservatism.** Conservatism is based on tradition and social stability. Most conservatives favored obedience to political authority and believed that organized religion was crucial to order in society. Conservatives hated revolutions and were unwilling to accept demands from people who wanted either individual rights or representative governments.

To maintain the new balance of power, Great Britain, Russia, Prussia, Austria, and later France, agreed to have meetings that would maintain the peace in Europe. These meetings were called the Concert of Europe. Eventually, most of the great powers adopted a **principle of intervention.** According to this principle, the great powers had the right to send armies into countries where there were revolutions in order to restore legitimate monarchs to their thrones. Britain refused to accept the principle, arguing that the great powers should not interfere in the internal affairs of other states. But the other great powers used military force to crush revolutions in Spain and Italy.

8. What was the principle of intervention?

____

____

____

____

____

• Forces of Change *(page 591)*

Between 1815 and 1830, conservative governments tried to maintain the old order. But powerful forces for change were also at work. One of these forces was **liberalism.** Liberalism was a political philosophy based on Enlightenment principles. Liberals believed that people should be as free as possible from government restraint. They also believed in the protection of civil liberties (the basic rights of all people). Most liberals wanted religious toleration and the separation of church and state. They believed that laws should be made by a representative assembly (legislature) elected by qualified voters. Many liberals favored government ruled by a constitution. They believed that written constitutions would guarantee civil rights. Liberals did not believe in a democracy in which everyone had a right to vote, however. They feared mob rule and thought that the right to vote and hold office should be open only to men of property.

Another force for change was nationalism. Nationalism arose out of people's awareness of being part of a community with common institutions, traditions, language, and customs. This community is called a nation. After the French Revolution, nationalists came to believe that each nationality should have its own government. The Germans were separated into many different states but wanted a single German nation-state with one central government. The Hungarians were part of the Austrian Empire but wanted the right to establish their own government. Conservatives feared these changes and tried hard to repress nationalism, but many liberals supported nationalism. Most liberals believed that freedom would only be possible if people ruled themselves. So most liberals agreed with the nationalists that each people group should have its own state.

Beginning in 1830, liberalism and nationalism began to change the political order in Europe. In France, liberals overthrew the Bourbon king Charles X and established a constitutional monarchy. Louis-Philippe, a cousin of Charles X, became king. Nationalism brought changes in other countries. Belgium rebelled against the Dutch Republic and became an independent state. There were also revolutions in Poland and Italy, but they were soon crushed by the Russians and Austrians.

9. How did conservatives and liberals feel about nationalism in the early nineteenth century?

____

____

____

____

____

• The Revolutions of 1848 *(page 592)*

The forces of nationalism and liberalism erupted again in the revolutions of 1848. Beginning in 1846, there were severe economic problems in France. These problems brought suffering to the lower middle class, workers, and peasants. At the same time, the middle class demanded the right to vote, but the government of Louis-Philippe refused to make changes. In 1848, the monarchy was overthrown. A group of republicans set up a provisional (temporary) government. The republicans were people who wanted France to be a republic (a government in which leaders are elected). The provisional government called for the election of representatives to a Constituent Assembly that would draw up a new constitution. Election would be by **universal male suffrage** (that is, all adult men could vote). The new constitution was ratified on November 4, 1848. It set up a new republic, called the Second Republic. The Second Republic had a single legislature and a president who served for four years. The legislature and the president were both elected by universal male suffrage. Elections for the presidency were held in December 1848, and Charles Louis Napoleon Bonaparte (called Louis-Napoleon) won. He was the nephew of Napoleon Bonaparte.

News of the 1848 revolution in France led to revolutions in other parts of Europe. Cries for change led many German rulers to promise constitutions, a free press, and jury trials. An all-German parliament, called the Frankfurt Assembly, was held to prepare a constitution for a new united Germany. The members drafted a constitution but had no real way of forcing the German rulers to accept it. As a result, German unification was not achieved.

The Austrian Empire was a multinational state. It was a collection of different peoples, including Germans, Czechs, Magyars (Hungarians), Slovaks, Romanians, Slovenes, Poles, Croats, Serbians, and Italians. Many of these peoples wanted their own governments. In March 1848, there were demonstrations in the major cities in the Austrian Empire. In Vienna, revolutionary forces took control of the capital and demanded a liberal constitution. To appease the revolutionaries, the government gave Hungary its own legislature. In Bohemia, the Czechs demanded their own government. Austrian officials had made concessions to appease the revolutionaries, but they were determined to reestablish control. Austrian military forces crushed the Czech rebels and the rebels in Vienna. In 1849, the Hungarian revolutionaries were also defeated.

In 1848, a revolt also broke out in Lombardy and Venetia, two provinces in Italy that were part of the Austrian Empire. Revolutionaries in other Italian states also took up arms and tried to create liberal constitutions and a unified Italy. By 1849, however, the Austrians had regained complete control over Lombardy and Venetia. Italy was not unified.

10. What revolutions took place in Europe in 1848?

____

____

____

____

____

Name ______________________ Date ______________ Class ______________

Reading Essentials and Study Guide

Chapter 19, Section 3

For use with textbook pages 596–603

NATIONAL UNIFICATION AND THE NATIONAL STATE

KEY TERMS

militarism reliance on military strength *(page 598)*

kaiser the title of the emperors of the Second German Empire *(page 599)*

plebiscite popular vote on a particular issue *(page 600)*

emancipation setting people free from slavery or serfdom *(page 601)*

abolitionism a movement to end slavery *(page 602)*

secede to withdraw from a political group or nation (used especially for the withdrawal of the Southern States from the Union at the start of the U.S. Civil War) *(page 603)*

DRAWING FROM EXPERIENCE

Have you ever wondered what our country would be like today if the South had won the Civil War? Have you ever thought what it would be like if each state were its own separate country with its own government and national leaders? How would this affect your life?

In the last section, you learned how the forces of liberalism and nationalism led to changes and revolutions in Europe in the first half of the nineteenth century. In this section, you will learn how nationalism contributed to the unification of Germany and Italy. You will also learn how divisions over slavery and other issues threatened national unity in the United States and led to the U.S. Civil War.

ORGANIZING YOUR THOUGHTS

Use the chart below to help you take notes. Identify some of the causes and effects of the following wars.

Causes	War	Effects
1.	Crimean War	**2.**
3.	Franco-Prussian War	**4.**
5.	United States Civil War	**6.**

READ TO LEARN

• Breakdown of the Concert of Europe *(page 596)*

The revolutions of 1848 had not achieved unification in Germany and Italy. By 1871, however, both Germany and Italy would be unified. The changes that made this possible began with the Crimean War. This war was the result of conflicts between Russia and the Ottoman Empire. The Ottoman Empire had long controlled much of the territory in the Balkans in southeastern Europe. Russia was interested in expanding its territories into the Ottoman lands in the Balkans. In 1853, the Russians invaded the Balkan provinces of Moldavia and Walachia. In response, the Ottoman Turks declared war on Russia. Great Britain and France also declared war on Russia because they were afraid that Russia would gain control of this area. The Crimean War was poorly planned and poorly fought. Heavy losses caused the Russians to seek peace. By the Treaty of Paris in 1856, Russia agreed to allow Moldavia and Walachia to be placed under the protection of all the great powers.

The Crimean War destroyed the Concert of Europe. Austria and Russia became enemies, because Austria had its own interests in the Balkans and had refused to support Russia in the war. Russia withdrew from European affairs for 20 years. Austria was now without friends among the great powers. This new situation opened the door for the unification of Italy and Germany.

7. How did the Crimean War destroy the Concert of Europe?

____

____

____

• Italian Unification *(page 597)*

After the failure of the revolution of 1848, people began to look to the northern Italian state of Piedmont for leadership in achieving the unification of Italy. The ruler of the kingdom of Piedmont was King Victor Emmanuel II. The king named Camillo di Cavour his prime minister in 1852. Cavour knew that Piedmont's army was not strong enough to defeat the Austrians. He would need help, so he made an alliance with the French emperor Louis-Napoleon. He then provoked the Austrians into invading Piedmont in 1859. The final result of this conflict was a peace settlement that gave the French Nice and Savoy. (Cavour had promised Nice and Savoy to the French for making the alliance.) Lombardy was given to Piedmont, but Venetia was still controlled by Austria. Cavour's success caused nationalists in some other northern Italian states (Parma, Modena, and Tuscany) to overthrow their governments and join their states to Piedmont.

In southern Italy, Giuseppe Garibaldi, an Italian patriot, raised an army of a thousand volunteers. They were called Red Shirts because of the color of their uniforms. Garibaldi's forces landed in Sicily, which was ruled by France. By the end of July 1860, they controlled most of the island. In August, they crossed over to the mainland and marched up the Italian peninsula. Naples, which was ruled by France, fell in early September. Garibaldi turned over his conquests to Piedmont. On March 17, 1861, a new kingdom of Italy was proclaimed under King Victor Emmanuel II. But the task of Italian unification was not yet complete, because Venetia was still held by Austria and Rome was under the control of the pope.

The Italians gained control of Venetia as a result of the Austro-Prussian War of 1866. The kingdom of Italy was an ally of Prussia in the war. Prussia won the war and gave Venetia to the Italians. In 1870, during the Franco-Prussian War, French troops withdrew from Rome. Their withdrawal made it possible for the Italian army to annex Rome on September 20, 1870. Rome then became the capital of the united Italian state.

8. How did the Austro-Prussian and Franco-Prussian Wars contribute to the unification of Italy?

____

____

____

• German Unification *(page 598)*

After the Frankfurt Assembly was unable to achieve German unification, Germans looked to Prussia to take the lead in this cause. Prussia had become a strong and prosperous state. It was also known for its **militarism** (reliance on military strength). In the 1860s, King William I tried to enlarge the Prussian army. When the Prussian legislature refused to levy new taxes for the army, William I appointed a new prime minister, Count Otto von Bismarck. Bismarck is known for his practice of *realpolitik* ("the politics of reality")—politics based on practical matters rather than on theory or ethics. From 1862 to 1866, he governed Prussia without the approval of the parliament. He collected taxes and strengthened the army. He also followed an active foreign policy that soon led to war. Bismarck created friction with the Austrians and forced them into a war on June 14, 1866. The Austrians were no match for the Prussian army and were defeated on July 3.

Prussia now organized the German states north of the Main River into a North German Confederation. The southern German states were largely Catholic and feared Prussia. But they also feared the French and agreed to sign military alliances with Prussia for protection against the French. In 1870, Prussia and France came into conflict because a relative of the Prussian king was a candidate for the throne of Spain. Bismarck took advantage of the misunderstandings between the French and Prussians and pushed the French into declaring war on Prussia on July 15, 1870. This conflict was called the Franco-Prussian War. The French were no match for the Prussian army. The southern German states also joined the war effort against the French. On September 2, 1870, an entire French army and the French ruler, Napoleon III, were captured. France surrendered on January 28, 1871. France had to pay 5 billion franks (about $1 billion) and give up the provinces of Alsace and Lorraine to the new German state.

Even before the war ended, the southern German states had agreed to enter the North German Confederation. On January 18, 1871, William I of Prussia was proclaimed **kaiser** (emperor) of the Second German Empire. German unity had been achieved. With its industrial resources and military might, this new German state became the strongest power on the European continent.

9. How did Prussia achieve German unity?

____

____

____

• Nationalism and Reform in Europe *(page 600)*

In 1832, the British Parliament passed a bill that increased the number of male voters. The new voters were mainly members of the industrial middle class. By giving the industrial middle class an interest in ruling Britain, Britain avoided revolution in 1848. In the 1850s and 1860s, Parliament continued to make social and political reforms that helped the country to remain stable. Another reason for Britain's stability was its continuing economic growth. After 1850, the working classes began to share in the prosperity. Wages for laborers increased more than 25 percent between 1850 and 1870. The British feeling of national pride was well reflected in Queen Victoria. She ruled from 1837 to 1901—the longest reign in English history. Her sense of duty and moral responsibility reflected the attitude of her age, which is known as the Victorian Age.

In France, Louis Napoleon asked the people to restore the empire. In this **plebiscite** (popular vote), 97 percent responded with a yes vote. On December 2, 1852, Louis-Napoleon became Napoleon III, Emperor of France. The Second Empire had begun. The government of Napoleon III was authoritarian. He controlled the armed forces, police, and civil service. Only he could introduce legislation and declare war. There was a Legislative Corps that gave an appearance of representative government, but its members could not initiate legislation or affect the budget. Napoleon III completely controlled the government and limited civil liberties. Nonetheless, the first five years of his reign were a huge success. Railroads, harbors, roads, and canals were built. Iron production tripled. Napoleon III also carried out a vast rebuilding of the city of Paris. In the 1860s, however, oppositions to some of Napoleon's policies grew. In response, Napoleon III gave the legislature more power. In a plebiscite held in 1870, the French people gave Napoleon III another victory. After the French were defeated in the Franco-Prussian War, however, the Second Empire fell.

Until the Austro-Prussian War, the Austrian Empire had been able to keep the ethnic groups in its empire from gaining independence. Austria's defeat in 1866, however, forced the Austrians to make concessions to the Hungarians. The result was the Compromise of 1867. This compromise created the dual monarchy of Austria-Hungary. Austria and Hungary each had its own constitution, its own legislature, its own bureaucracy, and its own capital. The two countries shared a common army, foreign policy, and system of finances. They also had a single monarch. Francis Joseph was both Emperor of Austria and King of Hungary.

At the beginning of the nineteenth century, Russia was overwhelmingly agricultural and autocratic. After the Russians were defeated in the Crimean War. Czar Alexander II decided to make serious reforms. Serfdom was the biggest problem in czarist Russia. On March 3, 1861, Alexander issued an **emancipation** edict that freed the serfs. Peasants could now own property and marry as they chose. The government provided land for the peasants by buying it from the landlords. But there were problems with the new land system. The landowners kept the best lands for themselves, so the Russian peasants did not have enough good land to support themselves. Alexander II attempted other reforms but soon found that he could please no one. He was assassinated in 1881 by a group of radicals. His son, Alexander III, turned against reform and returned to the old methods of repression.

10. What was the Compromise of 1867?

____

____

____

• Nationalism in the United States *(page 602)*

In the United States, two factions fought over the division of power in the new government. The Federalists favored a strong central government. The Republicans wanted the federal government to be subordinate to the state governments. These early divisions ended with the War of 1812. There was a surge of national feeling. The election of Andrew Jackson as president in 1828 opened a new era in American politics. Property qualifications for voting had been dropped. The right to vote was extended to all adult white males.

By the mid-nineteenth century, national unity was again an issue. Slavery had become a threat to that unity. The economy in the southern states was based on growing cotton on plantations, using slave labor. At the same time, **abolitionism,** a movement to end slavery, arose in the North. Abolitionism challenged the southern way of life. As opinions over slavery grew more divided, compromise became less possible. After Abraham Lincoln was elected president in 1860, a South Carolina convention voted to **secede** (withdraw) from the United States. In February 1861, six more southern states did the same. A rival nation, the Confederate States of America, was formed. In April, fighting erupted between North and South—the Union and the Confederacy. The American Civil War lasted from 1861 to 1865. It was an extremely bloody war. The Union had more men and resources and gradually wore down the Confederacy. On January 1, 1863, Abraham Lincoln's Emancipation Proclamation declared that most of the nation's slaves were "forever free." The Confederate forces finally surrendered on April 9, 1865. National unity had prevailed in the United States.

11. What was the main issue that divided Federalists and Republicans in the United States before the War of 1812?

____

____

____

• Emergence of a Canadian Nation *(page 603)*

The Treaty of Paris in 1763 gave Canada to the British. By 1800, most Canadians wanted more freedom from British rule. But there were serious differences among Canadians. Upper Canada (now Ontario) was mostly English-speaking, and Lower Canada (now Quebec) was mostly French. In 1840, the British Parliament formally joined Upper and Lower Canada into the United Provinces of Canada. Canadians began to push for self-government. John Macdonald, the head of Upper Canada's Conservative Party, was a leader in this cause. The British were afraid of losing Canada to the United States and finally gave in to Canadian demands. In 1867, Parliament passed the British North American Act. This act established a Canadian nation, the Dominion of Canada. It had its own constitution, and John Macdonald became the first prime minister. Canada now had a parliamentary system and ruled itself, but foreign affairs were still in the hands of the British government.

12. What was the main difference between Upper Canada and Lower Canada?

____

____

____

Name ______________________ Date ______________ Class ______________

Reading Essentials and Study Guide

Chapter 19, Section 4

For use with textbook pages 605–609

CULTURE: ROMANTICISM AND REALISM

KEY TERMS

romanticism an intellectual movement that emphasized feelings, emotions, and imagination as sources of knowing *(page 605)*

secularization indifference or rejection of religion or religious consideration *(page 607)*

organic evolution the principle that each kind of plant and animal has evolved over a long period of time from earlier and simpler forms of life *(page 608)*

natural selection the process whereby organisms that are more adaptable to the environment survive and thrive, while those that are less adaptable do not survive *(page 608)*

realism a movement in the arts that emphasized a realistic view of the world and focused on the everyday life of ordinary people *(page 608)*

DRAWING FROM EXPERIENCE

Have you ever read the novels *A Christmas Carol*, *Oliver Twist*, or *Great Expectations*, by Charles Dickens? Perhaps you have seen the movies or plays based on these novels. What is the main theme of these novels?

In the last three sections, you read about the Industrial Revolution and other changes in Europe and North America during the nineteenth century. In this section, you will learn how the Industrial Revolution created a new interest in science, which helped produce the realist movement in the arts. Another movement, romanticism, was also important in the nineteenth century.

ORGANIZING YOUR THOUGHTS

Use the chart below to help you take notes. Summarize the main emphases and themes of romanticism and realism, and list some of the important writers and artists in these two movements.

Movement	Emphases/Themes	Important Writers	Important Artists
Romanticism	**1.**	**2.**	**3.**
Realism	**4.**	**5.**	**6.**

Name ______________________ Date ______________________ Class ______________________

Reading Essentials and Study Guide

READ TO LEARN

• Romanticism *(page 605)*

At the end of the eighteenth century, a new intellectual movement, known as **romanticism,** emerged. It was a reaction to the ideas of the Enlightenment. The Enlightenment had stressed reason as the chief means for discovering truth. The romantics emphasized feelings, emotion, and imagination as ways of knowing. Romantics also valued individualism, the belief in the uniqueness of each person. Many romantics had a strong interest in the past. They revived medieval architecture and built castles, cathedrals, and other public buildings in a style called neo-Gothic. Literature also reflected this interest in the past. For example, many of the novels of Walter Scott were set in medieval England and other historical periods and became best-sellers. The exotic and unfamiliar also attracted many romantics and gave rise to Gothic literature. Mary Shelley's *Frankenstein* and Edgar Allen Poe's short stories are examples of Gothic literature.

The romantics viewed poetry as the direct expression of the soul. Romantic poetry gave expression to one of the most important characteristics of romanticism—its love of nature. This is especially evident in the poetry of William Wordsworth. The worship of nature caused Wordsworth and other romantic poets to be critical of eighteenth-century science. They believed that science had reduced nature to a cold object of study. Many romantics were convinced that the emerging industrialization would cause people to become alienated from their inner selves and the natural world around them.

The visual arts and music were also affected by romanticism. Romantic artists abandoned classical reason for warmth and emotion. Romantic art was a reflection of the artist's inner feelings. Eugène Delacroix was one of the most famous romantic painters from France. His paintings showed two chief characteristics: a fascination with the exotic and a passion for color. To many romantics, music was the most romantic of the arts, because it enabled the composer to probe deeply into human emotions. Music historians have called the nineteenth century the age of romanticism. One of the greatest composers of all time, Ludwig van Beethoven, was the bridge between the classical and romantic periods in music. His early work was largely classical, but his music also reflected his deepest inner feelings.

7. How did many romantics view science and industrialization?

• A New Age of Science *(page 607)*

The Industrial Revolution led to an increased interest in scientific research. By the 1830s, new discoveries in science had brought many practical benefits that affected all Europeans. In biology, Louis Pasteur proposed the germ theory of disease. This was crucial to the development of modern scientific medical practices. In chemistry, Dmitri Mendeleyev classified all the material elements then known on the basis of their atomic weights. In Great Britain, Michael Faraday created a primitive generator that laid the foundation for the use of electric current.

The dramatic material benefits often provided by science and technology led Europeans to have a growing faith in science. This faith undermined the religious faith of many people. The nineteenth century was an age of increasing **secularization** (indifference or rejection of religion or religious consideration). For many people, truth was now to be found in science and the material existence of humans. Charles Darwin, in particular, created a picture of humans as material being that were simply part of the natural world. In 1859, Darwin published *On the Origin of Species by Means of Natural Selection*. The basic idea of this book was that each kind of plant and animal had evolved over a long period of time from earlier and simpler forms of life. Darwin called this principle **organic evolution.** Darwin believed that some organisms are more adaptable to the environment than others, a process that Darwin called **natural selection.** Those that are naturally selected for survival ("survival of the fittest") reproduce and thrive. The unfit do not. In the *Descent of Man*, published in 1871, Darwin argued that human beings had animal origins and were not an exception to the principle of organic evolution. Darwin's ideas created a huge controversy. Some people objected that Darwin's theory made human beings ordinary products of nature rather than unique beings. Others were bothered by his idea of life as a mere struggle for survival. Many people also condemned Darwin for denying God's role in creation. Gradually, however, many scientists and other intellectuals began to accept Darwin's theory.

8. How did achievements in science and technology contribute to secularization in the nineteenth century?

____

____

____

____

____

Reading Essentials and Study Guide

Chapter 19, Section 4 *(continued)*

• Realism *(page 608)*

After 1850, many people believed that the world should be viewed realistically. This belief was closely related to the scientific outlook. **Realism** became a movement in the literary and visual arts. Realists rejected romanticism. Realist writers wanted to write about ordinary people from real life rather than romantic heroes in exotic settings. They also tried to avoid emotional language by using precise description. They preferred novels to poems. The realist novel was perfected by the French author Gustave Flaubert. Another important realist was the British novelist Charles Dickens. His realistic novels focused on the lower and middle classes in Britain's early Industrial Age.

Realism also became dominant in art after 1850. Realist artists tried to show the everyday life of ordinary people and the world of nature with photographic realism. The French became leaders in realist painting. Gustave Courbet was the most famous artist of the realist school. One of his famous works, *The Stonebreakers,* shows two roadworkers breaking stones to build a road. To Courbet, no subject was too ordinary, too harsh, or too ugly.

9. What literary form did realist writers prefer?

____

____

____

____

____

Name ______________________ Date ______________ Class ______________

Reading Essentials and Study Guide

Chapter 20, Section 1

For use with textbook pages 615–619

THE GROWTH OF INDUSTRIAL PROSPERITY

KEY TERMS

bourgeoisie the middle class *(page 619)*

proletariat the working class *(page 619)*

dictatorship a government in which a person or group has absolute power *(page 619)*

revisionists Marxists who rejected the revolutionary approach and argued that workers must organize in mass political parties and work with other parties to gain reforms *(page 619)*

DRAWING FROM EXPERIENCE

Have you ever thought about ways to improve society? What are some areas of society that need improvement? What are your ideas for improving these areas of society?

In this section, you will learn about the Second Industrial Revolution and the changes that it brought to many European countries. You will also learn how the desire to improve working and living conditions led many industrial workers to form political parties and unions based on the theories of Karl Marx.

ORGANIZING YOUR THOUGHTS

Use the diagram below to help you take notes. By 1900, Europe was divided into two economic zones. One zone was highly industrialized, and the other was still largely agricultural. Identify the countries or regions that made up each zone.

Economic Zones in Europe (circa 1900)

Industrialized

1.
2.
3.
4.
5.
6.
7.

Agricultural

8.
9.
10.
11.
12.
13.

READ TO LEARN

• The Second Industrial Revolution *(page 615)*

Westerners in the late 1800s worshiped progress. The main reason for their belief in progress was the material growth created by what is called the Second Industrial Revolution. The first Industrial Revolution changed the production of textiles, iron, and coal. In the Second Industrial Revolution, new industries arose in steel, chemicals, electricity, and petroleum. The first major change in industry between 1870 and 1914 was the substitution of steel for iron. New methods for shaping steel made it useful in the building of lighter, smaller, and faster machines and engines. It was also used to make railways, ships, and weapons.

Electricity was a major new form of energy. It could be easily converted into other forms of energy, such as heat, light, and motion. In the 1870s, the first practical generators of electrical current were developed. The use of electricity led to a series of inventions. The light bulb was created by Thomas Edison in the United States and Joseph Swan in Great Britain. Alexander Graham Bell invented the telephone in 1876, and Guglielmo Marconi sent the first radio waves across the Atlantic in 1901. Electricity also transformed factories. Conveyor belts, cranes, and machines could all be powered by electricity. With electric lights, factories could remain open 24 hours a day.

The development of the internal combustion engine revolutionized transportation. This engine was powered by oil and gasoline. It made ocean liners, airplanes, and automobiles possible. In 1903, Orville and Wilbur Wright made the first flight in a fixed-wing plane at Kitty Hawk, North Carolina.

Industrial production grew as sales of manufactured goods increased. Europeans could afford to buy more goods for several reasons. Wages for workers increased after 1870. Prices for manufactured goods were lower because of lower transportation costs. In the cities, the first department stores began to sell new products, such as clocks, bicycles, electric lights, and typewriters.

Not all nations benefited from the Second Industrial Revolution. By 1900, Europe was divided into two economic zones. Great Britain, Belgium, France, the Netherlands, Germany, the western part of the Austro-Hungarian Empire, and northern Italy made up an advanced industrialized zone. These nations had a high standard of living and decent transportation systems. Another part of Europe was still primarily agricultural. This was the area to the south and east. It was made up southern Italy, most of Austria-Hungary, Spain, Portugal, the Balkan kingdoms, and Russia. These countries provided food and raw materials for the industrial countries.

The Second Industrial Revolution and the growth of transportation by steamship and railroad led to a true world economy. By 1900, Europeans were receiving beef and wool from Argentina and Australia, coffee from Brazil, iron

Name ______________________ Date ______________________ Class ______________________

Reading Essentials and Study Guide

ore from Algeria, and sugar from Java. Foreign countries also provided markets for the manufactured goods of Europe. With its capital, industries, and military might, Europe dominated the world economy by the beginning of the twentieth century.

14. How was the Second Industrial Revolution different from the first Industrial Revolution?

____

____

____

____

____

• Organizing the Working Classes *(page 618)*

The desire to improve their working and living conditions led many industrial workers to form Socialist political parties and trade unions. These organizations emerged after 1870, but the theory on which they were based had been developed earlier by Karl Marx. In 1848, Marx and Friedrich Engels published *The Communist Manifesto,* which they had written. They were shocked by the horrible conditions in factories. They blamed the system of industrial capitalism for these conditions. They proposed a new social system. One form of Marxist socialism was eventually called communism. Marx believed that all of world history was a "history of class struggles." One group of people, the oppressors, owned the means of production (land, raw materials, money, and so forth). This gave them the power to control government and society. The other group, the oppressed, depended on the owners of the means of production. Marx believed that industrialized societies were splitting up into two great classes. The **bourgeoisie** (the middle class) were the oppressors. The **proletariat** (the working class) were the oppressed. Marx predicted that the struggle between the two groups would finally lead to an open revolution where the proletariat would violently overthrow the bourgeoisie. After their victory, the proletariat would form a **dictatorship** (government in which a person or group has absolute power) to organize the means of production. Marx believed that the final revolution would ultimately produce a classless society.

In time, working-class leaders formed socialist parties based on Marx's ideas. Most important was the German Social Democratic Party (SPD). Once in parliament, SPD delegates worked to pass laws that would improve conditions for the working class. After the 1912 elections, it became the largest single party in Germany. Socialist parties also emerged in other European countries. In 1889, leaders of the various socialist parties joined together and formed the Second International. This was an association of national socialist

Reading Essentials and Study Guide

groups that would fight against capitalism worldwide. Marxist parties were divided over their goals. Pure Marxists wanted to overthrow capitalism by a violent revolution. Other Marxists, called **revisionists,** disagreed. They believed that workers must continue to organize in mass political parties and even work with other parties to gain reforms.

Trade unions were another socialist force working for change. In Great Britain, unions won the right to strike in the 1870s. (A strike is a work stoppage called by members of a union to pressure an employer into meeting their demands.) Workers in factories organized into trade unions so that they could use strikes to achieve reforms. By 1914, trade unions in Europe had made considerable progress in bettering the living and working conditions of the working classes.

15. What was the main difference in the beliefs of pure Marxists and revisionists?

____

____

____

____

____

Name ______________________ Date ______________________ Class ______________________

Reading Essentials and Study Guide

Chapter 20, Section 2

For use with textbook pages 621–628

THE EMERGENCE OF MASS SOCIETY

KEY TERMS

feminism the movement for women's rights *(page 625)*

literacy the ability to read *(page 627)*

DRAWING FROM EXPERIENCE

Have you ever thought what your life would be like if you were unable to read? What problems would you have? How would this affect your ability to find a job?

In the last section, you read about the Second Industrial Revolution. In this section, you will read about the mass society that emerged as a result of the industrialization of Europe. Public education and an increase in literacy were two products of the new mass society.

ORGANIZING YOUR THOUGHTS

Use the pyramid diagram below to help you take notes. List the groups or occupations that made up the elite, the middle classes, and the working classes in Europe at the end of the nineteenth century.

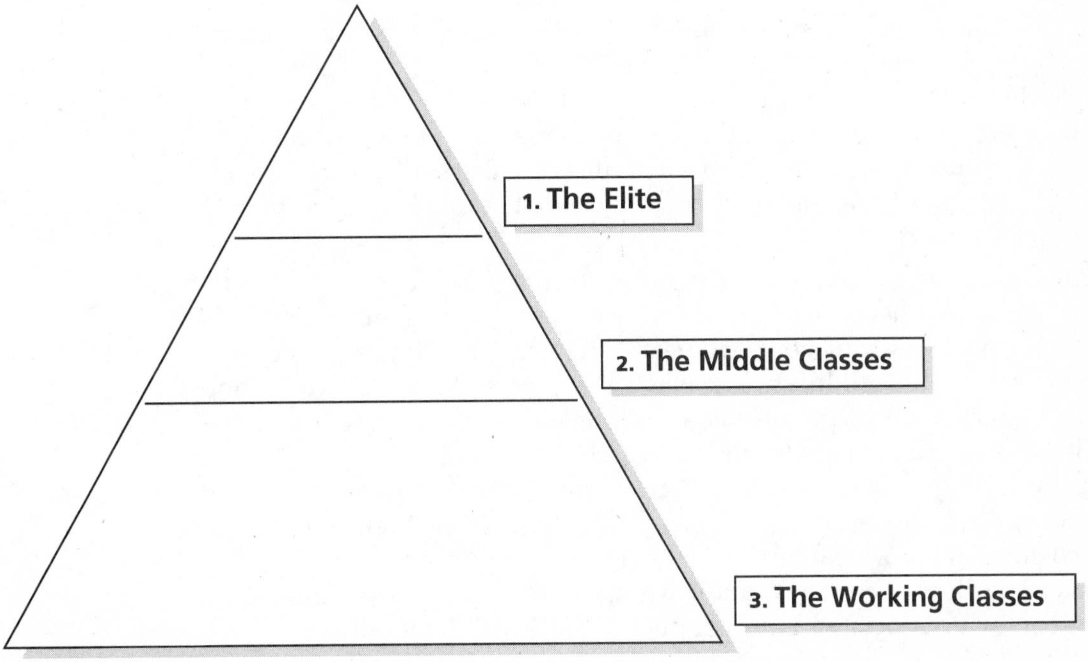

Name ______________________ Date ______________________ Class ______________________

Reading Essentials and Study Guide

READ TO LEARN

• The New Urban Environment *(page 621)*

By the end of the nineteenth century, a mass society emerged in the industrial world. In this society the concerns of the majority—the lower classes—were central. Urban populations grew rapidly because of the vast migration to cities from rural areas. In the cities, people found jobs in factories and, later, in service trades and professions. Cities also grew because living conditions improved so much that people could survive there longer. City governments created boards of health to improve the quality of housing. Dwellings were now inspected for health hazards. New building regulations required running water and drainage systems for all new buildings. The ability to bring in clean water and expel sewage was essential to the public health in cities. New systems of aqueducts, tunnels, and pipes made this possible.

4. What changes were made in cities in the nineteenth century to improve the public health?

____

____

____

____

____

• Social Structure of Mass Society *(page 622)*

After 1871, most people enjoyed an improved standard of living. Even so, great poverty remained a part of Western society. The wealthy elite were at the top of European society. This group was only 5 percent of the population but controlled 30 to 40 percent of the wealth. It was made up of the landed aristocrats and the most successful industrialists, bankers, and merchants (the wealthy upper middle class). Members of the elite became leaders in the government and military.

The middle classes consisted of a variety of groups. Below the upper middle class was a middle group that included lawyers, doctors, members of the civil service, business managers, engineers, architects, accountants, and chemists. Beneath this middle group was a lower middle class of small shopkeepers, traders, and prosperous peasants. The members of this group provided goods and services for the classes above them. The Second Industrial Revolution produced a new group of white-collar workers between the lower middle class and the lower classes. Although not highly paid, these white-collar workers were often committed to middle-class ideals. The European middle classes believed in hard work. They were also regular churchgoers who associated good conduct with Christian morality.

Below the middle classes on the social scale were the working classes. They made up almost 80 percent of the European population. Many of the members of these classes were peasants, farm laborers, and sharecroppers. The urban working class consisted of many different groups, including artisans and semi-skilled laborers. At the bottom of the urban working class were the unskilled laborers. They were the largest group of workers and included day laborers and large numbers of domestic servants. Urban workers experienced an improvement in their lives after 1870. Reforms created better living conditions in cities. As wages increased and the cost of consumer goods declined, workers could buy more than just food and housing. Workers now had money for more clothes and even leisure activities. At the same time, strikes were leading to 10-hour workdays and Saturday afternoons off.

5. In what ways did the lives of urban workers improve after 1870?

____

____

____

____

____

• The Experiences of Women *(page 624)*

During much of the nineteenth century, middle-class and working-class groups believed that women should remain at home and not be allowed in the industrial workforce. Marriage remained the only honorable and available career for most women. One important change in women's lives did occur during this time, however. The number of children born to the average woman began to decline.

Some differences existed in the lives of middle-class and working-class women. Most working-class women had to earn money to help their families. Daughters in working-class families generally worked until they married. After marriage, they often did small jobs at home to help support the family. Between 1890 and 1914, however, higher-paying jobs in heavy industry allowed many working-class families to depend on the income of husbands alone.

The Second Industrial Revolution opened the door to new jobs for women. A high demand for relatively low paid white-collar workers led many employers to hire women. Industrial plants and retail shops both needed clerks, typists, secretaries, file clerks, and salespeople. Women also took jobs in the fields of education, health, and social services.

Modern **feminism,** or the movement for women's rights, had its beginnings during the Enlightenment. In the 1830s, a number of women in the United States and Europe argued for the right of women to divorce and own property. These early efforts were not very successful, and women in Britain did not win the right to own property until 1870. The fight for property rights was only the beginning of the women's movement. Some middle-class women fought for and gained access to universities. Others tried to enter occupations dominated by men. Women generally could not train to become doctors. Some, however, entered the medical field by becoming nurses. Amalie Sieveking, Florence Nightingale, and Clara Barton were leaders in the nursing profession.

In the 1840s and 1850s, the movement for women's rights expanded as women demanded equal political rights. Many feminists believed that the right to vote was the key to improving the overall position of women. Suffragists (people who advocate the extension of political rights) had one basic aim: the right of women to full citizenship. Before World War I, however, only women in Norway and some states in the United States actually received the right to vote.

6. How did the Second Industrial Revolution open the door to new jobs for women?

____

____

____

____

____

• Universal Education *(page 626)*

Universal education was a product of the mass society of the late nineteenth and early twentieth centuries. Most Western governments began to set up state-financed primary schools. Both boys and girls between the ages of 6 and 12 were required to attend these schools. Western nations made this commitment to public education for two main reasons. One reason was industrialization. The new firms of the Second Industrial Revolution needed trained, skilled labor. Both boys and girls with an elementary education now had new job possibilities. These included white-collar jobs in railways, post offices, and the teaching and nursing fields. The chief reason for public education, however, was political. Giving more people the right to vote created a need for better-educated voters. Primary schools also instilled patriotism.

The most immediate result of public education was in increase in **literacy** (the ability to read). In western and central Europe, most adults could read by

1900. With the increase in literacy after 1870 came the rise of mass newspapers. These newspapers were all written in an easily understood style. They were also sensationalistic (that is, they provided gossip and gruesome details of crimes).

7. What were the two main reasons that Western nations made a commitment to public education?

• New Forms of Leisure *(page 628)*

The Second Industrial Revolution allowed people to pursue new forms of leisure. Leisure came to be viewed as what people do for fun after work. The industrial system gave people new times for leisure activities—evening hours, weekends, and a week or two in the summer.

Amusement parks introduced people to new experiences and technology. Team sports also developed into another form of leisure. Subways and streetcars made it possible for even the working classes to get to athletic games, amusement parks, and dance halls. Amusement parks and professional sports teams were essentially big businesses organized to make profits.

8. How did the Second Industrial Revolution allow people to pursue new forms of leisure?

Name ______________________ Date ______________________ Class ______________________

Reading Essentials and Study Guide

Chapter 20, Section 3

For use with textbook pages 629–634

THE NATIONAL STATE AND DEMOCRACY

KEY TERMS

ministerial responsibility the idea that the prime minister is responsible to the popularly elected legislative body, not to the executive officer *(page 631)*

Duma a legislative assembly in Russia during the time of Nicholas II *(page 632)*

DRAWING FROM EXPERIENCE

Have you ever thought what your life would be like if you had been born in a different country? What do you think would affect you more—the difference in economics or the difference in political systems?

In the last section, you learned about the effects of industrialization in Europe and the United States in the late nineteenth and early twentieth centuries. In this section, you will learn about the political developments during this time. Many nations in Western Europe became more democratic, but rulers in much of Central and Eastern Europe resisted change.

ORGANIZING YOUR THOUGHTS

Use the diagram below to help you take notes. By 1907, Europe was divided into two opposing camps. List the countries in each of the two alliances.

European Alliances 1907

The Triple Alliance

1.

2.

3.

The Triple Entente

4.

5.

6.

READ TO LEARN

• Western Europe and Political Democracy *(page 629)*

By the late nineteenth century, progress had been made toward establishing constitutions, parliaments, and individual liberties in the major European states. By 1871, Great Britain had a working two-party parliamentary system. Laws passed in 1867 and 1884 increased the number of adult males who could vote. By the end of World War I, all males over age 21 and women over 30 could vote. The working class supported the Liberal Party, but two developments threatened this support. First, trade unions grew, and they began to favor a more radical change of the economic system. Second, in 1900, a new party, the Labour Party, was formed. It was dedicated to the interest of workers. To keep the support of the workers, the Liberals voted for a series of social reforms. The National Insurance Act of 1911 provided benefits for workers in case of sickness and unemployment. Other laws provided a small pension for people over 70 and compensation for people injured in accidents at work.

In France, the Second Empire had collapsed. In 1875, a new constitution turned the nation into a republic—the Third Republic. The new French government had a president and a legislature made up of two houses. Members of the upper house, called the Senate, were elected indirectly. Members of the lower house, called the Chamber of Deputies, were elected by universal male suffrage. The powers of the president were not well defined by the constitution. A premier (prime minister) actually led the government. The premier and his deputies were actually responsible to the Chamber of Deputies, not to the president. This principle of **ministerial responsibility** (the idea that the prime minister is responsible to the popularly elected legislative body and not to the executive officer) is crucial for democracy. The existence of a dozen political parties forced the premier to depend on a coalition of parties to stay in power. There were frequent changes in government leadership.

By 1870, Italy was a united national state. The nation had little sense of unity, however. A huge gulf separated the poverty-stricken south from the industrialized north. Constant turmoil between labor and industry weakened the nation. Universal male suffrage was granted in 1912 but did little to stop corruption and weakness in the government.

7. What reforms did the Liberal Party make in Great Britain to keep the support of the workers?

Reading Essentials and Study Guide

Chapter 20, Section 3 *(continued)*

• Central and Eastern Europe: The Old Order *(page 631)*

The new imperial Germany begun by Otto von Bismarck in 1871 had a two-house legislature. The lower house of the German parliament, the Reichstag, was elected by universal male suffrage. Ministers of government were responsible to the emperor, not to the parliament, however. The emperor controlled the armed forces, foreign policy, and the government bureaucracy. As chancellor (prime minister), Bismarck worked to keep Germany from becoming a democracy. By the reign of William II, who was the emperor from 1888 to 1918, Germany had become the strongest military and industrial power in Europe. Demands for democracy increased. Conservative forces in Germany tried to block the movement for democracy by supporting a strong foreign policy. They believed that expansion abroad would not only increase profits but also divert people from pursuing democratic reforms.

After the creation of the dual monarchy of Austria-Hungary in 1867, Austria enacted a constitution that, in theory, set up a parliamentary system with ministerial responsibility. In reality, the emperor, Francis Joseph, ignored the system. He appointed and dismissed his own ministers and issued laws when the parliament was not in session. Austria remained troubled by conflicts between the various nationalities in the empire. Representatives of these groups in parliament worked for their freedom. This encouraged the emperor to ignore the parliament even more. On the other hand, Hungary had a parliament that worked. But it was controlled by Magyar landowners who dominated the peasants and ethnic groups.

In Russia, Nicholas II began his rule in 1894 believing that the absolute power of the czars should be preserved. Conditions in Russia were changing, however. Industrialization progressed rapidly in Russia after 1890. With industrialization came factories, an industrial working class, and pitiful working and living conditions. Socialist parties developed, but government repression forced them to go underground. Opposition to the czar finally exploded into the Revolution of 1905. On January 22, a procession of workers went to the Winter Palace in St. Petersburg to present a petition of grievances to the czar. Troops opened fire on the peaceful demonstration, killing hundreds. This "Bloody Sunday" caused workers throughout Russia to call strikes. Nicholas II was forced to grant civil liberties and create a legislative assembly, called the **Duma.** By 1907, however, the czar had already reduced the power of the Duma. He again used the army and bureaucracy to rule Russia.

8. Why did conservative forces in Germany support a strong foreign policy?

____

____

____

____

Reading Essentials and Study Guide

• The United States and Canada *(page 633)*

After the Civil War, the old South was destroyed. One-fifth of the adult male population in the South had been killed, and four million slaves had been freed. In 1865, the Thirteenth Amendment to the Constitution was passed, which abolished slavery. Later, the Fourteenth and Fifteenth Amendments gave citizenship to African Americans and the right to vote to African American males. However, new state laws in southern states soon stripped African Americans of their right to vote.

Between 1860 and 1914, the United States shifted from an agrarian to an industrial nation. Industrialization led to urbanization. By 1900, over 40 percent of Americans lived in cities. The United States had become the world's richest nation, but serious problems remained. In 1890, the richest 9 percent of Americans owned 71 percent of the wealth. Labor unrest led workers to organize unions. By the turn of the century, the American Federation of Labor had become the chief voice of labor, but it lacked real power.

At the end of the nineteenth century, the United States began to expand abroad. The Samoan Islands in the Pacific became the first important United States colony. By 1887, American settlers had gained control of the sugar industry on the Hawaiian Islands. When Queen Liliuokalani tried to strengthen the power of the Hawaiian monarchy to keep the islands under her peoples' control, the U.S. government sent military forces to the islands. The queen was deposed, and the United States annexed Hawaii in 1898. In the same year, the United States defeated Spain in the Spanish-American War. As a result, the United States acquired Puerto Rico, Guam, and the Philippines. By the beginning of the twentieth century, the United States had an empire.

At the beginning of 1870, the Dominion of Canada had four provinces: Quebec, Ontario, Nova Scotia, and New Brunswick. In 1871, two more provinces, Manitoba and British Columbia, were added. The Dominion of Canada now extended from the Atlantic to the Pacific. However, the English-speaking and French-speaking peoples of Canada distrusted each other. Wilfred Laurier, who became the first French-Canadian prime minister in 1896, was able to reconcile these two groups. During his administration, industrialization boomed. Immigrants from Europe helped to populate Canada's vast territories.

9. What provinces were added to the Dominion of Canada in 1871?

____

____

____

____

____

• International Rivalries *(page 633)*

Otto von Bismarck was afraid that France would create an anti-German alliance, so he created an alliance with Austria-Hungary in 1879. In 1882, Italy joined the alliance. The Triple Alliance of 1882 united Germany, Austria-Hungary, and Italy in a defensive alliance against France. At the same time, Bismarck had a separate treaty with Russia and tried to remain on good terms with Great Britain. In 1890, Emperor William II fired Bismarck and took control of Germany's foreign policy. He dropped the treaty with Russia. This brought France and Russia together. In 1894, they formed a military alliance. Over the next 10 years, German policies caused the British to draw closer to France. By 1907, an alliance of Great Britain, France, and Russia—known as the Triple Entente—was formed. Europe was now divided into two opposing camps that became more and more unwilling to compromise. A series of crises in the Balkans between 1908 and 1913 set the stage for World War I.

10. What sequence of events led to the formation of the Triple Entente?

____

____

____

____

____

• Crises in the Balkans *(page 634)*

During the nineteenth century, the Balkan provinces had gradually gained their freedom. By 1878, Greece, Serbia, Romania, and Montenegro had become independent states. Bulgaria did not become totally independent, but was allowed to operate under Russian protection. The Balkan territories of Bosnia and Herzegovina were placed under the protection of Austria-Hungary. In 1908, Austria-Hungary annexed Bosnia and Herzegovina. Serbia was outraged. Bosnia and Herzegovina were Slavic-speaking territories, and Serbia had hopes of creating a large Serbian kingdom that would include most of the southern Slavs. Backed by the Russians, the Serbs prepared for war against Austria-Hungary. Emperor William II of Germany demanded that the Russians accept Austria-Hungary's annexation of Bosnia and Herzegovina or face war with Germany. The Russians backed down, but two wars between Balkan states in 1912 and 1913 created more tensions between the great powers.

Reading Essentials and Study Guide

Chapter 20, Section 3 *(continued)*

The Serbians blamed Austria-Hungary for their failure to create a large Serbian kingdom. Austria-Hungary was convinced that Serbia was a threat to its empire and must be crushed. As Serbia's chief supporters, the Russians were angry and determined not to back down again. The allies of Austria-Hungary and Russia were determined to support their allies more strongly in another crisis. By the beginning of 1914, most of the countries of Europe viewed each other with suspicion.

11. What tensions existed in Europe at the beginning of 1914?

____

____

____

____

____

Name ______________________ Date ________________ Class ________________

Reading Essentials and Study Guide

Chapter 20, Section 4

For use with textbook pages 636–641

TOWARD THE MODERN CONSCIOUSNESS

KEY TERMS

psychoanalysis a method of psychotherapy developed by Freud, in which a therapist and patient probe deeply into a patient's memory *(page 637)*

pogrom an organized massacre (especially of Jews) *(page 639)*

modernism changes in the arts in the late nineteenth and early twentieth centuries involving a break with traditional literary and artistic styles and a search for new forms of expression *(page 639)*

DRAWING FROM EXPERIENCE

Do you like modern art? Who is your favorite artist? Is there a particular movement that you are especially interested in?

In the last three sections, you read about the Second Industrial Revolution and other social and political changes in the late 1800s and early 1900s. In this section, you will read about new ideas in the arts and sciences during this time.

ORGANIZING YOUR THOUGHTS

Use the diagram below to help you take notes. In the late 1800s and early 1900s, many writers and artists rebelled against traditional literary and artistic styles. List the movements in literature, painting, architecture, and music during this period. Also list some of the important writers, artists, and musicians in these movements.

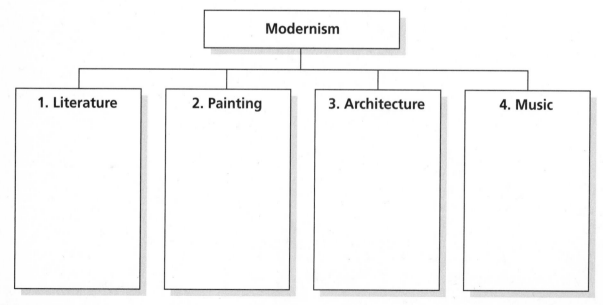

Modernism

1. Literature	2. Painting	3. Architecture	4. Music

Name ______________________ Date ______________________ Class ______________________

Reading Essentials and Study Guide

READ TO LEARN

• A New Physics *(page 636)*

In the nineteenth century, Westerners had a view of the world that was based on the ideas of Isaac Newton. The universe was viewed as a giant machine. Matter was thought to be composed of solid material bodies called atoms. Time, space, and matter were believed to be objective realities that existed independently of people observing them. These views were questioned at the end of the nineteenth century. The French scientist Marie Curie discovered that an element called radium gave off energy, or radiation, that came from the atom itself. This meant that atoms were not simply hard material bodies but were small, active worlds.

At the beginning of the twentieth century, a new view of the universe was provided by Albert Einstein. In 1905, Einstein published his special theory of relativity. It stated that space and time are not absolute but are relative to the people observing them. Matter and energy also reflect the relativity of time and space. Einstein concluded that matter is simply another form of energy. This idea led to an understanding of the vast energies contained within the atom and to the Atomic Age. To some people, however, a relative universe was a universe without certainty.

5. How did Einstein's theory of relativity change people's view of the universe?

____

____

____

____

____

• Freud and Psychoanalysis *(page 637)*

The ideas of Sigmund Freud added to the uncertainty that people felt about the world at the turn of the century. In 1900 his theories were published in *The Interpretation of Dreams*. According to Freud, human behavior was strongly determined by past experiences. Freud believed that painful experiences were repressed, or hidden, from a person's conscious awareness. But these experiences continued to influence behavior because they were part of the unconscious. Repression of these experiences began in childhood. Freud devised a method by which a therapist and patient could probe deeply into the patient's memory. This method is called **psychoanalysis.** Freud's ideas gained worldwide acceptance in the 1920s. Psychoanalysis developed into a major profession. Freudian terms, such as *unconscious* and *repression*, became standard vocabulary words.

6. What was Freud's theory concerning human behavior?

____

____

____

____

____

• Social Darwinism and Racism *(page 638)*

In the late nineteenth and early twentieth centuries, scientific theories were sometimes applied inappropriately. For example, nationalists and racists applied the theories of Charles Darwin to human society. Their ideas are known as social Darwinism. One social Darwinist, Herbert Spencer, argued that social progress came from the "struggle for survival" in which the "fit" survive. Some businessmen used social Darwinism to explain their success. They believed that they were successful because they were "fit" (strong and capable). Extreme nationalists also believed that nations were engaged in a "struggle for existence" in which only the fittest (the strongest) survived. In Germany, extreme nationalism and racism were combined. Houston Stewart Chamberlain, for example, believed that Germans were the only pure successors of the Aryans (who were the original creators of Western culture, according to Chamberlain). Chamberlain also believed that Jews were enemies who wanted to destroy the Aryan race.

7. What are some ways that Darwin's theories were applied inappropriately in the late nineteenth and early twentieth centuries?

____

____

____

____

____

• Anti-Semitism and Zionism *(page 638)*

Anti-Semitism (hostility toward and discrimination against Jews) had been a part of European civilization since the Middle Ages. In the nineteenth century, Jews were granted legal equality in many European countries. Many Jews became successful as bankers, lawyers, scientists, scholars, and journalists. Discrimination still existed, however. In 1895, Alfred Dreyfus, a French Jew, was found guilty of selling army secrets and was condemned to life imprisonment. Evidence soon showed that Dreyfus was innocent and that the real traitor was a Catholic aristocrat. But the army refused a new trial. Public outrage finally forced the government to hold a new trial and pardon Dreyfus in 1899.

In Germany and Austria-Hungary, new parties arose during the 1880s and 1890s that used anti-Semitism to win votes. The worst treatment of Jews at the turn of the century occurred in eastern Europe, where 72 percent of the world's Jews lived. Russian Jews were forced to live in certain regions of the country. Persecutions and **pogroms** (organized massacres) were widespread. Hundreds of thousands of Jews decided to emigrate (move to another country) to escape the persecution. Many went to the United States. Some went to Palestine, the land of ancient Israel. Palestine became home for a Jewish nationalist movement called Zionism. Settlement in Palestine was difficult, however, because it was part of the Ottoman Empire and the Ottomans opposed Jewish immigration.

8. Why did so many Jews decide to emigrate around the turn of the century?

• The Culture of Modernity *(page 639)*

Between 1870 and 1914, many writers and artists rebelled against traditional literary and artistic styles. The changes that they produced have since been called **modernism.** During much of the nineteenth century, literature was dominated by naturalism. Naturalists felt that literature should be realistic and address social problems. Two examples of naturalist writers are Henrik Ibsen and Émile Zola. At the beginning of the twentieth century, a group of writers known as symbolists caused a literary revolution. They were primarily interested in writing poetry and were influenced by the ideas of Freud. They believed that the external world was only a collection of symbols that reflected the true reality—the human mind.

The period from 1870 to 1914 was one of the most productive in the history of art. Impressionism was a movement that began in France in the 1870s. Impressionist artists rejected studios and went out into the countryside to paint nature directly. One important Impressionist was Claude Monet. In his paintings, he tried to capture the interplay of light, water, and sky. Other Impressionist painters include Pierre-Auguste Renoir and Berthe Morisot. In the 1880s, a new movement, known as Postimpressionism, arose in France.

Reading Essentials and Study Guide

Vincent van Gogh is one famous Postimpressionist. For van Gogh, art was a spiritual experience. He believed that artists should paint what they feel.

Realism in painting began to decline. The spread of photography was one important reason. Now, anyone could take a photograph that looked exactly like the subject. Artists began to realize that their strength was not in mirroring reality, but in creating reality. Between 1905 and 1914, artists searched for individual expression. This search created modern art. One of the most important figures in modern art was Pablo Picasso. He painted in many different styles. He also created a new style, called cubism, that used geometric designs to recreate reality in the viewer's mind. In 1910, abstract painting began. Wassily Kandinsky was one of the founders of abstract expressionism. He tried to avoid visual reality completely. He believed that art should speak directly to the soul and should use only line and color.

Modernism in the arts revolutionized architecture. A new movement in architecture, known as functionalism, developed. Functionalism was the idea that buildings should be functional, or useful. All unnecessary ornamentation should be stripped away. The United States was a leader in the new architecture. Two important pioneers were Louis H. Sullivan and Frank Lloyd Wright.

At the beginning of the twentieth century, developments in music paralleled developments in painting. The music of the Russian composer Igor Stravinsky was the first to reflect expressionist theories. His ballet *The Rite of Spring* revolutionized the world of music.

9. How did photography contribute to the decline of realism in painting?

____

____

____

____

____

Name ______________________ Date ______________________ Class ______________________

Reading Essentials and Study Guide

Chapter 21, Section 1

For use with textbook pages 647–652

COLONIAL RULE IN SOUTHEAST ASIA

KEY TERMS

imperialism the extension of a nation's power over other lands *(page 648)*

protectorate a political unit that depends on another government for its protection *(page 649)*

indirect rule a system of colonial government in which local rulers were allowed to maintain their positions of authority and status *(page 651)*

direct rule a system of colonial government in which local rulers were removed from power and replaced with a new set of officials brought from the mother country *(page 651)*

DRAWING FROM EXPERIENCE

Do you think there are any good reasons for one country to take control of another country? If so, under what circumstances do you think it would be justified? If not, why not?

In this section, you will learn about the "new imperialism" of the late nineteenth century. During this time, European nations began to acquire colonies in Asia and Africa in order to obtain raw materials and markets for their manufactured goods.

ORGANIZING YOUR THOUGHTS

Use the chart below to help you take notes. Indicate which Western power (France, Great Britain, Holland, or the United States,) controlled each of the following countries in Southeast Asia at the end of the nineteenth century. (If a country remained free of colonial rule, write "none.")

Southeast Asian Country	**Controlling Country:**
Burma	**1.**
Cambodia	**2.**
East Indies	**3.**
Laos	**4.**
Philippines	**5.**
Singapore	**6.**
Thailand	**7.**
Vietnam	**8.**

Reading Essentials and Study Guide

Chapter 21, Section 1 *(continued)*

READ TO LEARN

• The New Imperialism *(page 647)*

In the nineteenth century, a new phase of Western expansion into Asia and Africa began. Beginning in the 1880s, European nations began to compete for overseas territory. **Imperialism,** (the extension of a nation's power over other lands) was not new. But the "new imperialism" of the late nineteenth century was different. Previously, European expansion in Africa and Asia had been limited to setting up a few trading posts. Now European nations wanted direct control over vast territories.

Europeans had various motives for imperialism. There was a strong economic motive. Europeans were looking for raw materials, such as rubber, oil, and tin, for their industries. They were also looking for new markets for their manufactured goods. They wanted more direct control over the areas with the raw materials and markets. There were also political motives. European nations were rivals. They tried to acquire colonies in order to gain an advantage over their rivals. Some people believed that a nation could not be great without colonies. Imperialism was also tied to social Darwinism and racism. Racism is the belief that race determines traits and capabilities. Racists believe that particular races are superior or inferior to others. Finally, some Europeans had religious and humanitarian motives. They believed that Europeans had a moral responsibility to civilize primitive people. They called this responsibility "the white man's burden." These people believed that Western nations should help the nations of Asia and Africa. To some, this meant bringing the Christian message to these nations. To others, it meant bringing the benefits of Western capitalism and democracy to these countries.

9. How was the "new imperialism" different from earlier expansion by European nations?

• Colonial Takeover in Southeast Asia *(page 649)*

By 1900, nearly all of Southeast Asia was under Western rule. In 1819, Britain founded a new British colony on a small island at the tip of the Malay Peninsula called Singapore. Singapore soon became a major stopping point for steamships going to or from China. The next country to fall to the British was the kingdom of Burma. Britain wanted control of Burma in order to protect its possessions in India. It also wanted a land route through Burma into South China.

The French watched nervously as the British moved into Burma. France had missionaries in Vietnam. To keep the British from moving into Vietnam, the French government decided to force the Vietnamese to accept French protection. The Vietnamese ruler gave up territories in the Mekong River delta. The French also occupied the city of Saigon. During the next 30 years, the French extended their control over the rest of the country. In 1884, France seized the city of Hanoi and made the Vietnamese Empire a French **protectorate** (a political unit that depends on another government for its protection). In the 1880s, France also extended its protection over Cambodia, Annam, Tonkin, and Laos. By 1900, France included all of its new possessions in a new Union of French Indochina.

After the French conquest of Indochina, Thailand was the only remaining free state in Southeast Asia. Two remarkable rulers, King Mongkut and his son King Chulalongkorn, were able to prevent the French and British from placing Thailand under colonial rule. Both kings promoted Western learning and had friendly relations with major European powers. In 1896, Britain and France agreed to maintain Thailand as an independent buffer state between their possessions in Southeast Asia.

One more conquest took place in Southeast Asia at the end of the nineteenth century. In 1898, during the Spanish-American War, United States naval forces under Commodore George Dewey defeated the Spanish fleet in Manila Bay in the Philippines. President William McKinley decided to turn the Philippines into an American colony. The Philippine Islands gave the United States a convenient jumping-off point for trade with China. Many Americans, including President McKinley, also believed that Western nations had a moral obligation to "civilize" other parts of the world. The Filipinos did not agree. Emilio Aguinaldo was the leader of a movement for independence in the Philippines. His guerrilla forces fought against U.S. troops to gain their independence, but they were defeated.

10. How was Thailand able to remain free of colonial rule?

____

____

____

____

• Colonial Regimes in Southeast Asia *(page 650)*

Western powers ruled their new colonial empires either by indirect or direct rule. Sometimes a colonial power could accomplish its goals through cooperation with local rulers or political elites. In these cases, **indirect rule** was used. Local rulers were allowed to maintain their positions of authority and status.

Indirect rule made it easier to gain access to an area's natural resources. It also lowered the cost of government, because fewer officials had to be trained. Indirect rule also had less impact on local culture. One example of indirect rule was in the Dutch East Indies. Officials of the Dutch East India Company allowed local landed aristocrats in the Dutch East Indies to control local government. These local elites maintained law and order and collected taxes.

Indirect rule was not always possible, however. This was especially true when local rulers resisted colonial rule. In these cases, the local rulers were removed from power and replaced with a new set of officials brought from the mother country. This system is called **direct rule.** In Burma, for example, the monarchy opposed colonial rule. As a result, Great Britain abolished the monarchy and ruled the country directly through its colonial government in India.

In Indochina, France used both direct and indirect rule. It used direct rule in the southern provinces in the Mekong delta, but the northern parts of Vietnam were governed as a protectorate. The emperor still ruled but had little power. France had a similar policy in Cambodia and Laos. Local rulers were left in charge, with French advisors to counsel them.

To justify their conquests, Western nations had said they wanted to bring the blessings of Western civilization to their colonies. Many colonial powers said they wanted to teach the native peoples about the democratic process. However, many Westerners became afraid of giving native peoples political rights. They were afraid that the native peoples would want full participation in the government or even independence.

The colonial powers did not want their colonies to develop their own industries. Colonial policy stressed the export of raw materials. In many cases, this policy led to some form of plantation agriculture, in which peasants worked as wage laborers on plantations owned by foreigners. Plantation owners kept the wages at poverty levels in order to increase the owners' profits. Conditions on plantations were often so unhealthy that thousands died. Taxes were also a burden for peasants. But colonial rule did bring some benefits to Southeast Asia. Colonial governments built railroads and highways. In some countries, small growers of rubber, palm oil, coffee, tea, and spices were able to benefit from the development of an export market.

11. How are direct and indirect rule different? Why was indirect rule not always used?

____

____

____

____

____

Name ______________________ Date ______________ Class ______________

• Resistance to Colonial Rule *(page 651)*

Many people in Southeast Asia were very unhappy about being ruled by Western powers. At first, resistance came from the ruling classes. In Burma, for example, the monarch himself fought against British rule. Sometimes, resistance to Western rule took the form of peasant revolts. Many peasants were driven off the land to make way for plantations. This led to peasant uprisings. Early resistance movements failed, but a new kind of resistance began to emerge at the beginning of the twentieth century. This resistance was based on nationalism. The leaders were often part of a new class that had been created by colonial rule—westernized intellectuals in the cities. This new class had been educated in Western-style schools. They were the first generation of Asians to understand the institutions and values of the West. Many spoke Western languages. At first, many of the leaders of these movements did not focus on the idea of nationhood. They simply tried to defend the economic interests or religious beliefs of the natives. In Burma, for example, students at the University of Rangoon formed an organization to protest British lack of respect for local religious traditions. Not until the 1930s did these resistance movements begin to demand national independence.

12. What new form of resistance to colonial rule began to emerge at the beginning of the twentieth century?

____

____

____

____

____

Name ______________________ Date ______________________ Class ______________________

Reading Essentials and Study Guide

Chapter 21, Section 2

For use with textbook pages 654–660

EMPIRE BUILDING IN AFRICA

KEY TERMS

annex to incorporate a country within a state *(page 655)*

indigenous native to a region *(page 658)*

DRAWING FROM EXPERIENCE

Has anyone ever told you that your traditions and customs were wrong? How would this make you feel?

In the last section, you read about imperialism in Southeast Asia. In this section, you will learn about imperialism in Africa. Most colonial powers did not respect the local customs and traditions of the countries they controlled.

ORGANIZING YOUR THOUGHTS

Use the chart below to help you take notes. List which European nations had claims in the following parts of Africa by 1914.

African Region	European Nations With Claims in the Region
West Africa	**1.**
North Africa	**2.**
Central Africa	**3.**
East Africa	**4.**
South Africa	**5.**

Name ______________________ Date ______________ Class ______________

Reading Essentials and Study Guide

READ TO LEARN

• West Africa *(page 654)*

Between 1880 and 1900, European countries took control of nearly all of Africa. West Africa had been particularly affected by the slave trade, but that had begun to decline by 1800. By the 1890s, slavery had been abolished in all major countries of the world. As slavery declined, Europe became interested in other forms of trade. Europeans sold textiles and other manufactured goods in exchange for peanuts, timber, hides, and palm oil from West Africa. Early in the nineteenth century, the British set up settlements along the Gold Coast and in Sierra Leone.

For a long time, most African nations were able to maintain their independence. However, in 1874, Great Britain **annexed** (incorporate a country within a state) the west coastal states. They called this first British colony Gold Coast. At about the same time, Britain established a protectorate over warring groups in Nigeria. By 1900, France had added the huge area of French West Africa to its colonial empire, and Germany controlled Togo, Cameroon, and German Southwest Africa (now Namibia).

6. What forms of trade replaced the slave trade in West Africa?

____

____

____

____

• North Africa *(page 656)*

Egypt had been part of the Ottoman Empire, but Egyptians began to seek their independence as the Ottoman Empire declined. In 1805, an officer of the Ottoman army named Muhammad Ali seized power and established a separate Egyptian state. During the next 30 years, he introduced reforms to bring Egypt into the modern world.

Europeans were interested in Egypt because they wanted to build a canal east of Cairo to connect the Mediterranean and Red Seas. The Suez Canal was completed in 1869. The British were especially interested in the canal. They believed it was their "lifeline to India." In 1875, Britain bought Egypt's share in the Suez Canal. When an Egyptian army revolt against foreigners broke out in 1881, Britain suppressed the revolt. Egypt became a British protectorate in 1915. The British believed they should also control the Sudan, south of Egypt, in order to protect both Egypt and the Suez Canal. But Muslim troops under Muhammad Ahmad resisted. Not until 1898 were British troops able to seize the Sudan.

The French also had colonies in North Africa. In 1879, the French government took control of Algeria. Two years later, France imposed a protectorate on Tunisia. In 1912, France also established a protectorate over much of Morocco. In 1911, Italy invaded and seized Turkish Tripoli, which it renamed Libya.

7. Why was Egypt important to Europeans in the nineteenth century?

____

____

____

____

____

• Central Africa *(page 656)*

Explorers, such as David Livingstone, aroused Europeans' interest in the jungles of Central Africa. Livingstone arrived in 1841. For 30 years, he explored Central Africa. After Livingstone's death in 1873, Henry Stanley carried on the work of exploration. In the 1870s, Stanley explored the Congo River and sailed down it to the Atlantic Ocean. He encouraged the British to send settlers to the Congo River basin. When Britain refused, he turned to King Leopold II of Belgium. King Leopold became the real driving force behind the colonization of Central Africa. In 1876, he hired Stanley to set up Belgian settlements in the Congo. Belgium ended up with the territories south of the Congo River. France occupied the areas to the north.

8. How did Europeans become interested in Central Africa?

____

____

____

____

____

• East Africa *(page 657)*

By 1875, Britain and Germany had become the chief rivals in East Africa. At first, the German chancellor Otto von Bismarck did not think that colonies were very important. But more and more Germans wanted an empire, so Bismarck became interested in colonialism for political reasons. Germany had possessions in West Africa, but it began to seek colonies in East Africa. The British were also interested in East Africa, because control of East Africa would connect the British Empire in Africa from Egypt in the north to South Africa. Portugal and Belgium also claimed parts of East Africa. To settle these conflicting claims, the Berlin Conference was held in 1884. The conference gave official recognition to both British and German claims in East Africa. Portugal received a clear claim to Mozambique. No Africans were present at this conference, which divided up their continent.

9. What was the purpose of the Berlin Conference of 1884?

____

____

____

____

____

• South Africa *(page 658)*

By 1865, the total white population in South Africa had risen to nearly two hundred thousand. The descendants of the original Dutch settlers were called Boers or Afrikaners. They had occupied Cape Town and surrounding areas in South Africa since the seventeenth century. During the Napoleonic Wars, the British seized these lands from the Dutch. Afterward, the British encouraged settlers to come to what they called Cape Colony. In the 1830s, the Boers fled northward to the region between the Orange and Vaal Rivers and to the region north of the Vaal River. In these areas, the Boers formed two independent republics—the Orange Free State and the Transvaal (later called the South African Republic). The Boers believed that God ordained white superiority. They put many of the **indigenous** (native to a region) peoples in these areas on reservations. The Boers had frequent battles with the indigenous Zulu people. In the late 1800s, the British became involved in conflicts with the Zulu, and the Zulu were defeated.

In the 1880s, Cecil Rhodes, the prime minister of Cape Colony, set British policy in South Africa. Rhodes had founded diamond and gold companies that made him a fortune. He gained control of a territory north of the Transvaal, which he named Rhodesia after himself. In 1896, the British government forced him to resign as prime minister of Cape Colony after it was discovered that he planned to overthrow the Boer government of the South African Republic. This was too late to avoid a war between the British and the Boers, however. This war was called the Boer War and lasted from 1899 to 1902. Boer women and children were put in detention camps. Lack of food caused 26,000 deaths in the camps. Eventually, the British army won the war. In 1910, the British created an independent Union of South Africa. This new nation combined the old Cape Colony and the Boer republics. To appease the Boers, the British agreed that only whites could vote.

Name ______________________ Date ____________________ Class ____________________

10. Who were the Boers?

____

____

____

____

____

• Colonial Rule in Africa *(page 659)*

By 1914, Great Britain, France, Germany, Belgium, and Portugal had divided up Africa. Only Liberia and Ethiopia remained free states. Native peoples who tried to resist were no match for the superior military power of the Europeans. The British used indirect rule in their territories in Africa. In some areas, the British simply asked a local ruler to accept British authority and to fly the British flag over official buildings. The system of indirect rule had one good feature: it did not disrupt local customs and institutions. But the system was basically a fraud because British administrators made all major decisions. Another problem was that indirect rule kept the old African elites in power. In this way, it sowed the seeds for class and tribal tensions.

Most other European nations used a form of direct rule. This was true in the French colonies. At the top was a French official, usually known as a governor-general. He ruled with the help of a bureaucracy in the capital city of the colony. The French believed in assimilating Africans into French culture rather than preserving native traditions. Africans were eligible to run for office and even to serve in the French National Assembly in Paris. A few were appointed to high positions in the colonial administration.

11. What were the good and bad features of indirect rule?

____

____

____

____

____

• Rise of African Nationalism *(page 660)*

A new class of leaders emerged in Africa by the beginning of the twentieth century. They were educated in colonial schools or in Western nations. The members of this new class admired Western civilization and sometimes disliked the ways of their own countries. Many resented foreigners and their lack of respect for African peoples. Westerners said that they believed in democracy, equality, and political freedom, but they did not apply these values in the colonies. There were few democratic institutions. For many Africans, colonialism had meant the loss of their farmlands or terrible jobs on plantations or in sweatshops and factories. Middle-class Africans did not suffer as much as poor peasants and plantation workers, but they also had complaints. They usually qualified only for menial jobs in the government or business. Their salaries were lower than those of Europeans in similar jobs. Europeans set up segregated clubs, schools, and churches. Europeans also had a habit of addressing natives by their first names or calling an adult male "boy." For all of these reasons, educated Africans resented colonial rule and were determined to assert their own nationality. During the first part of the twentieth century, resentment turned to action. Educated African peoples began to organize political parties and movements seeking the end of foreign rule.

12. How did the new class of educated Africans feel about Western civilization and colonial rule?

Name ______________________ Date ______________ Class ______________

Reading Essentials and Study Guide

Chapter 21, Section 3

For use with textbook pages 666–670

BRITISH RULE IN INDIA

KEY TERMS

sepoy an Indian soldier serving in the British army *(page 666)*

viceroy a governor who ruled as a representative of a monarch *(page 667)*

DRAWING FROM EXPERIENCE

Have you ever read any stories or poems by the British writer Rudyard Kipling? What insights do his stories and poems give us into life in India during the Age of Imperialism?

In the last two sections, you learned about imperialism in Southeast Asia and Africa. In this section, you will learn about the British Empire in India.

ORGANIZING YOUR THOUGHTS

Use the diagram below to help you take notes. British rule in India had both benefits and costs for the Indian people. List four benefits and four costs of the British rule.

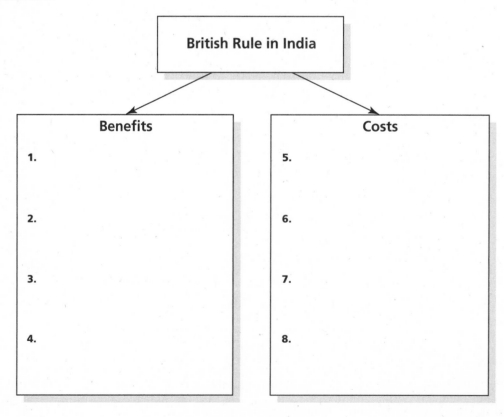

British Rule in India

Benefits	Costs
1.	5.
2.	6.
3.	7.
4.	8.

READ TO LEARN

• The Sepoy Mutiny *(page 666)*

Over the course of the eighteenth century, British power in India had increased while the power of the Mogul rulers had declined. The British East India Company was given power by the British government to rule India. The British East India Company had its own soldiers and forts. It also hired Indian soldiers, known as **sepoys,** to protect its interests.

In 1857, the Indians' distrust of the British led to a revolt. The revolt was known to the British as the Great Rebellion or the Sepoy Mutiny. Indians call it the First War of Independence. The immediate cause of the revolt was a rumor that the British were issuing their Indian troops new bullets that were greased with cow and pig fat. The cow was sacred to Hindus. The pig was taboo to Muslims. A group of sepoys refused to load their rifles with the new bullets. When the British arrested them, the sepoys went on a rampage. They killed 50 Europeans. The revolt quickly spread. The Indian troops fought bravely but were not well organized. Rivalries between Hindus and Muslims kept Indians from working together. Within a year, the revolt was crushed. As a result of the revolt, the British Parliament transferred the powers of the East India Company directly to the British government. In 1876, Queen Victoria was given the title of Empress of India.

9. What was the immediate cause of the Sepoy Mutiny?

• Colonial Rule *(page 667)*

The British government ruled India directly through a British official known as a **viceroy** (a governor who ruled as a representative of a monarch). British rule had both benefits and costs for the Indian people. There were four main benefits. British rule brought order and stability to India. It also led to a fairly honest and efficient government. A new school system was set up. Its goal was to train Indian children to serve in the government and army, but only elite, upper-class Indians could attend. Finally, the British brought railroads, the telegraph, and a postal service to India.

British rule also had costs for the Indian people. British manufactured goods destroyed local industries. For example, the introduction of British textiles put thousands of women out of work and severely damaged the Indian textile industry. In rural areas, the British sent the zamindars to collect taxes. The zamindars took advantage of their new authority and increased taxes. This forced many peasants to become tenants or lose their land entirely. The British also encouraged many farmers to switch from growing food to growing cotton. As a result, food supplies could not keep up with the growing population. Between 1800 and 1900, 30 million Indians died of starvation. Finally, British rule was degrading. The best jobs and the best housing were reserved for the British. Despite their education, the Indians were never considered equals of the British. The British were also disrespectful of India's cultural heritage.

10. Why did 30 million Indians die of starvation between 1800 and 1900?

• An Indian Nationalist Movement *(page 669)*

British racial attitudes led to the rise of an Indian nationalist movement. The first Indian nationalists were upper class and English-educated. Some were trained in British law and were members of the civil service. In 1885, a small group of Indians formed the Indian National Congress (INC). The INC did not demand immediate independence, but did call for a share in the governing process. The INC had difficulties because of religious differences. Many of its leaders were Hindu and reflected Hindu concerns. Muslims began to call for the creation of a separate Muslim League to represent the interests of the Muslims in India.

In 1915, Mohandas Gandhi brought new life to India's struggle for independence. Gandhi was born in India but studied in London. He became a lawyer and went to South Africa. After he returned to India, he became active in the independence movement. He set up a movement based on nonviolent resistance. It had two goals: to force the British to improve the lot of the poor and to gain independence for India.

11. What were the goals of Gandhi's movement?

Name ______________________ Date ____________________ Class ____________________

Chapter 21, Section 3 *(continued)*

• Colonial Indian Culture *(page 670)*

A cultural revival took place in India in the early nineteenth century. It began with the creation of a British college in Calcutta. A local publishing house was soon opened. It printed textbooks on various subjects, as well as grammars and dictionaries in the Indian languages. The revival soon spread to other regions of India. Indian novelists and poets began writing historical romances and epics. Most preferred to use their own regional languages rather than English. The most famous Indian author was Rabindranath Tagore. He was also a social reformer, spiritual leader, educator, philosopher, singer, and painter. Tagore's life mission was to promote national pride. Tagore was more than just an Indian nationalist, however. He worked for human dignity, world peace, and the mutual understanding between East and West.

12. How did the cultural revival in India in the nineteenth century begin?

____

____

____

____

____

Name ______________________ Date ______________________ Class ______________________

Reading Essentials and Study Guide

Chapter 21, Section 4

For use with textbook pages 671–677

NATION BUILDING IN LATIN AMERICA

KEY TERMS

creole a person of European descent who was born in Latin America and who lived there permanently *(page 672)*

peninsulare a Spanish or Portuguese official who resided temporarily in Latin America for political and economic gain *(page 672)*

mestizo a person of European and Indian descent *(page 672)*

Monroe Doctrine a doctrine issued by U.S. President James Monroe in which he guaranteed the independence of the new Latin American nations and warned against any European intervention in the Americas *(page 673)*

caudillo a Latin American leader who ruled chiefly by military force *(page 674)*

DRAWING FROM EXPERIENCE

Have you ever been to Texas? Did you know that Texas was once an independent country? How did Texas become a U.S. state?

In the last three sections, you read about European imperialism in Southeast Asia, Africa, and India. In this section, you will learn how most of the countries of Latin America gained their independence from Spain and Portugal in the nineteenth century.

ORGANIZING YOUR THOUGHTS

Use the time line below to help you take notes. Indicate which Latin American countries gained their independence in the following years.

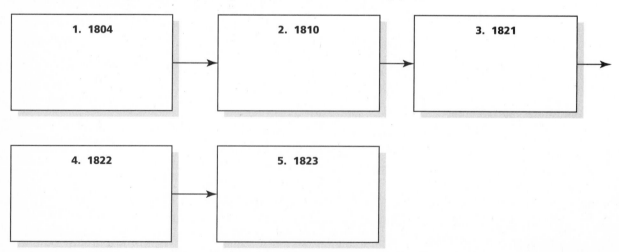

1. 1804 → **2. 1810** → **3. 1821** →

4. 1822 → **5. 1823**

Name ______________________ Date ______________________ Class ______________________

READ TO LEARN

- **Nationalist Revolts** *(page 671)*

Social classes based on privilege divided colonial Latin America. At the top were *peninsulares*, who held all of the important positions. ***Peninsulares*** were Spanish and Portuguese officials who resided temporarily in Latin America for political and economic gain and then returned to their mother countries. **Creoles** were descendants of Europeans born in Latin America and lived there permanently. They controlled land and business but were regarded as second class citizens by *peninsulares*. **Mestizos** (people of European and Indian descent) were the largest group but worked as servants or laborers.

Creoles found the principles of equality of all people, free trade, and free press very attractive. They deeply resented the *peninsulares*. The creole elites began to denounce the rule of the Spanish and Portuguese. When Napoleon overthrew the monarchies of Spain and Portugal, the authority of the Spanish and Portuguese in their colonies was weakened. Between 1807 and 1825, a series of revolts brought independence to most of Latin America.

Before these revolts, an unusual revolution took place in the French colony of Saint Domingue on the island of Hispaniola. Led by François-Dominique Toussaint-Louverture, more than a hundred thousand slaves revolted and took control of Hispaniola. On January 1, 1804, the western part of Hispaniola (now called Haiti) announced its freedom and became the first independent state in Latin America.

Beginning in 1810, Mexico also experienced a revolt. The first real hero of Mexican independence was Miguel Hidalgo, a parish priest. Hidalgo had studied the French Revolution and encouraged the local Indians and mestizos to free themselves from the Spanish. On September 16, 1810, a crowd of Indians and mestizos formed a mob army to attack the Spaniards. The revolt was crushed, and Hidalgo was sentenced to death, but September 16 is still remembered as Mexico's Independence Day. The creoles and *peninsulares* were both frightened by the Indians and mestizos. They cooperated in defeating the revolutionaries. Then the creoles and *peninsulares* decided to overthrow Spanish rule to preserve their own power. They selected a creole military leader, Agustín de Iturbide, as their leader. In 1821, Mexico declared its independence from Spain. Iturbide named himself emperor in 1822 but was deposed in 1823. Mexico then became a republic.

José de San Martín of Argentina and Simón Bolívar of Venezuela have been called the "Liberators of South America." They led revolutions throughout the continent. San Martín believed that the Spaniards must be removed from all of South America if any South American nation was to be free. By 1810, his forces had liberated Argentina. Bolívar began the struggle for independence in Venezuela and then went on to lead revolts in New Granada (Colombia) and Ecuador.

In January 1817, San Martín led his forces over the Andes to attack the Spanish in Chile. The Spanish were badly defeated at the Battle of Chacabuco on February 12, 1817. Then San Martín moved on to Peru, where he was joined by Bolívar and his forces. The last significant Spanish army was crushed at Ayacucho on December 9, 1824. By the end of 1824, Peru, Uruguay, Paraguay, Colombia, Venezuela, Argentina, Bolivia, and Chile had all become free states. Earlier, in 1822, Brazil had gained its independence from Portugal. The Central American states had become independent in 1823. In 1838 and 1839, they divided into five republics: Guatemala, El Salvador, Honduras, Costa Rica, and Nicaragua.

There was still one threat to the independence of the Latin American states. Members of the Concert of Europe wanted to use troops to restore Spanish control of Latin America. The British disagreed, because they wanted to trade with Latin America. They joined with the United States against any European moves in Latin America. In 1823, United States President James Monroe issued the **Monroe Doctrine.** He guaranteed the independence of the new Latin American nations and warned against any European intervention in the Americas.

6. Who were the "Liberators of South America"?

____

____

____

• Difficulties of Nation Building *(page 673)*

The new Latin American nations had serious problems after they gained their independence. Many people had been killed, and much livestock and property had been destroyed. The new nations were not sure of their exact boundaries and went to war with each other to settle border disputes. Poor roads, a lack of railroads, thick jungles, and mountains were also problems. They made communication, transportation, and national unity difficult.

Soon after independence, strong leaders known as **caudillos** came into power in many countries. Caudillos ruled chiefly by military force and were usually supported by large landowners. Some caudillos were modernizers who built roads, canals, ports, and schools. Others were destructive. Antonio López de Santa Anna, for example, ruled Mexico from 1829 to 1855. He misused state funds, stopped reforms, and created chaos. In 1835, American settlers in the Mexican state of Texas revolted against Santa Anna's rule. Texas gained its independence in 1836 and United States statehood in 1845. War between Mexico and the United States soon followed (1846–1848). Mexico was defeated and lost almost one-half of its territory to the United States in the Mexican War. Santa Anna's rule was followed by a period of reform from 1855 to 1876. Benito Juárez ruled Mexico during much of this time. He brought liberal reforms to Mexico, including separation of church and state, land distribution to the poor, and an educational system for all of Mexico.

Some caudillos, such as Juan Manual de Rosas in Argentina, were supported by the masses and brought about radical change. Unfortunately, the caudillo's authority depended on his personal power. When he died or lost power, civil wars for control of the country often erupted.

Great Britain now dominated the Latin American economy. British merchants moved into Latin America in large numbers. Latin America continued to serve as a source of raw materials and food for the industrial nations of Europe and the United States. Exports included wheat, tobacco, wool, sugar, coffee, and hides. Manufactured goods were imported, especially textiles. The emphasis on exporting raw materials and importing manufactured goods meant that the Latin American economy continued to be dominated by foreigners.

A fundamental problem for all of the new Latin American nations was the domination of society by large landowners. Their estates were often so large that they could not be farmed efficiently. Land was the basis of wealth, social prestige, and political power. The large landowners ran governments and controlled courts. They made huge profits by growing export crops, such as coffee. The masses had no land to grow basic food crops and experienced terrible poverty.

7. In what ways were large landowners a fundamental problem for the new Latin American nations?

____

____

____

• Political Change in Latin America *(page 676)*

After 1870, Latin American governments wrote constitutions similar to those of the United States and European democracies. However, the large landowners limited voting rights in order to keep their power.

By 1900, the United States had begun to interfere in the affairs of many Latin American nations. As a result of the Spanish-American War (1898), Cuba became a United States protectorate, and Puerto Rico was annexed to the United States. In 1903, the United States supported a rebellion that made it possible for Panama to separate itself from Colombia. In return, the United States was granted control of a strip of land 10 miles wide that ran from coast to coast in Panama. The United States built the Panama Canal there.

Americans began to invest in Latin America. Beginning in 1898, American military forces were sent to Cuba, Mexico, Guatemala, Honduras, Nicaragua,

Panama, Colombia, Haiti, and the Dominican Republic to protect American interests. Some of these troops remained for many years. Many Latin Americans began to resent U.S. interference.

In some countries, large landowners supported dictators who looked out for their interests. Porfirio Díaz, for example, ruled Mexico between 1877 and 1911. He came to power with the support of the army, foreign capitalists, large landowners, and the Catholic Church. During his reign, the wages of workers declined. 95 percent of the rural population owned no land. About a thousand families owned almost all of Mexico. After Díaz was forced from power, Emiliano Zapata aroused the landless peasants and began to seize the estates of wealthy landowners. Between 1910 and 1920, the Mexican Revolution caused great damage to the Mexican economy. Finally, a new constitution was enacted in 1917. It set up a government led by a president. It also created land-reform policies, set limits on foreign investments, and had an agenda to help the workers.

8. Why did the United States support the rebellion in Panama?

____

____

____

• Economic Change in Latin America *(page 677)*

After 1870, a period of prosperity began in Latin America. It was based to a large extent on the export of a few basic items. These included wheat and beef from Argentina, coffee from Brazil, coffee and bananas from Central America, and sugar and silver from Peru. After 1900, Latin Americans also increased their own industrialization, especially by building textile, food-processing, and construction material factories.

One result of this prosperity was growth in the middle sectors (divisions) of Latin American society. These sectors included lawyers, merchants, shopkeepers, businesspeople, schoolteachers, professors, bureaucrats, and military officers. These middle-class Latin Americans lived in the cities, believed in education, and saw the United States as a model, especially in regard to industrialization. They sought liberal reform, not revolution. Once they had the right to vote, they usually sided with the landholding elites.

9. What were some characteristics of middle-class Latin Americans?

____

____

____

Name ________________________ Date ________________ Class ________________

Reading Essentials and Study Guide

Chapter 22, Section 1

For use with textbook pages 683–689

THE DECLINE OF THE QING DYNASTY

KEY TERMS

extraterritoriality living in a foreign country without being subject to its laws *(page 685)*

self-strengthening a policy in China in the late nineteenth and early twentieth centuries that encouraged the adoption of Western technology, while keeping Confucian values and institutions *(page 686)*

spheres of influence areas in China where imperial powers had exclusive trading rights *(page 687)*

indemnity a payment for damages *(page 689)*

DRAWING FROM EXPERIENCE

Do you like change? Why do you think many people are resistant to change?

In this section, you will read about the decline of the Qing dynasty in China. As the Qing dynasty declined, some Chinese leaders pushed for reforms, but others were resistant to change.

ORGANIZING YOUR THOUGHTS

Use the diagram below to help you take notes. The decline of the Qing dynasty was the result of internal problems within China, as well as external pressures by Western countries. List four of the internal problems that caused the Qing dynasty to decline.

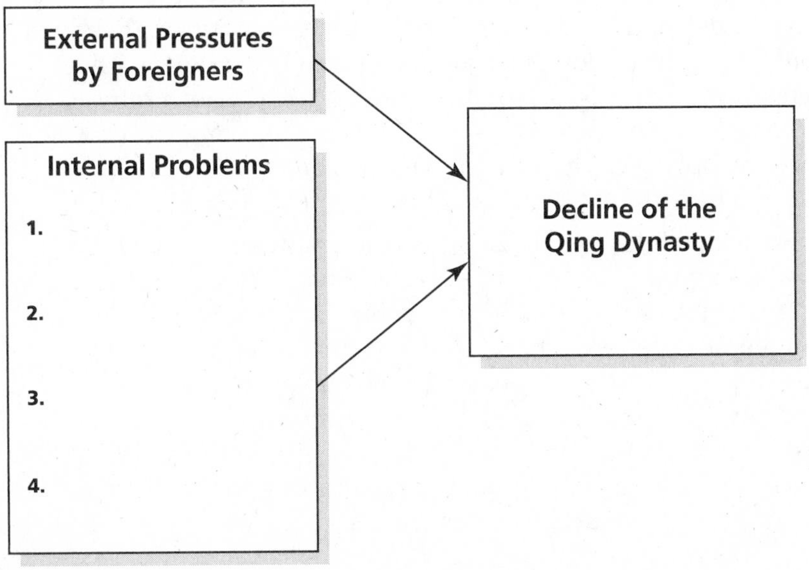

Name ______________________ Date ______________________ Class ______________________

READ TO LEARN

• Causes of Decline *(page 683)*

In 1800, the Qing dynasty was at the height of its power. During the next hundred years, however, it declined and collapsed. One important reason for the decline was external pressure from Westerners. But internal problems also played a role in its decline. The Qing dynasty began to have problems with corruption, peasant unrest, and incompetence. Population growth made things worse. By 1900, there were 400 million people in China. Population growth created a serious food shortage, and many people died of hunger.

5. How did population growth contribute to the decline of the Qing dynasty?

____

____

____

____

____

• The Opium War *(page 684)*

By 1800, Europeans had been in contact with China for more than two hundred years. But European merchants were restricted to a small trading post at Guangzhou (Canton). The British did not like this arrangement. The British also had a trade imbalance in China. Britain imported tea, silk, and porcelain from the Chinese and sent Indian cotton to China to pay for these imports. But the cotton did not cover all of the imports, and the British had to pay for more and more of the imports with silver. To improve their trade balance, the British began to trade opium with the Chinese. Opium is a highly addictive drug that was grown in northern India. The Chinese government had already seen how dangerous opium was and had made the opium trade illegal. They asked the British government to stop the opium trade, but the British refused. The Chinese government then blockaded the foreign area in Guangzhou so that they could seize the opium before it came into the country. The British responded with force, which started the first Opium War (1839–1842).

The Chinese were no match for the British. British warships destroyed Chinese forts and sailed up the Chang Jiang (Yangtze River). The Qing dynasty decided to make peace with the British. In the Treaty of Nanjing in 1842, the Chinese agreed to open five coastal ports to British trade. In these ports, Europeans lived in their own sections and were subject to their own laws, not to Chinese laws. This practice is known as **extraterritoriality.** The Chinese also agreed to limit taxes on imported British goods and to pay for the costs of the war. China also gave the island of Hong Kong to the British. Nothing was said in the treaty about the opium trade.

Reading Essentials and Study Guide

6. Why did the British begin to trade opium with China?

____

____

____

____

____

• The Tai Ping Rebellion *(page 685)*

The Chinese government was unable to deal with the economic problems at the time. This led to a peasant revolt, known as the Tai Ping Rebellion (1850–1864). Hong Xiuquan, a Christian convert, led it. He believed that God had given him the mission of destroying the Qing dynasty. He was joined by many peasants and captured the town of Yongan. He then proclaimed a new dynasty, the Heavenly Kingdom of Great Peace (Tai Ping Tianguo). The Tai Ping Rebellion had several goals. These goals included giving land to all peasants and treating women as equals of men. People were also required to give up their private possessions. Money, food, and clothing were to be shared equally by all. Hong outlawed alcohol and tobacco and the practice of binding women's feet. In March 1853, the rebels seized Nanjing and killed 25,000 people. The revolt continued for 10 more years but gradually began to fall apart. Europeans came to the aid of the Qing dynasty. In 1864, Chinese forces recaptured Nanjing and destroyed the rebel forces. By the end of the rebellion, twenty million people had been killed.

One reason that the Qing dynasty was unable to deal effectively with these internal problems was its struggle with the Western powers. In 1856, Great Britain and France began a new series of attacks against China (the second Opium War). They seized the capital, Beijing, in 1860. The Chinese government then agreed to legalize the opium trade and open new ports to foreign trade. They also gave the peninsula of Kowloon to Great Britain.

7. What were some of the goals of the Tai Ping Rebellion?

____

____

____

____

____

• Efforts at Reform *(page 686)*

By the late 1870s, the Qing dynasty was in decline. Government troops had relied on the armies of regional warlords to help fight the Tai Ping Rebellion. To pay their armies, warlords had collected taxes from local people. After the rebellion was over, many warlords continued to collect taxes for their own use.

The Qing dynasty finally began to listen to reformers. The reformers wanted a new policy that they called **"self-strengthening."** This meant that China should adopt Western technology while keeping Confucian values and institutions. This became the basis for China's foreign and domestic policy for the next 25 years. Factories were built to produce modern weapons and ships. Railroads were also built. But the traditional Chinese bureaucracy was retained, and civil service examinations were still used to select government officials.

8. What reforms did the Qing dynasty begin to make in the late 1870s?

____

____

____

____

____

• The Advance of Imperialism *(page 687)*

Russia took advantage of the Qing dynasty's weakness and forced China to give up territories north of the Amur River in Siberia. In Tibet, Russia and Great Britain struggled for control. This allowed Tibet to become free from Chinese influence.

European countries began to create **spheres of influence** in China. These were areas where the imperial powers had exclusive trading rights. After the Tai Ping Rebellion, warlords began to negotiate directly with foreign nations. In return for money, the warlords gave these nations exclusive trading rights or railroad-building or mining privileges. Britain, France, Germany, Russia, and Japan all established spheres of influence in China.

In 1894, China went to war with Japan over Japanese involvement in Korea. The Chinese were defeated. Japan demanded and received the island of Taiwan and the Liaodong Peninsula. But European powers forced Japan to give the Liaodong Peninsula back to China. In 1897, two German missionaries in China were murdered. Germany used this pretext to demand territories in the Shandong Peninsula. China gave these territories to Germany. As a result, other European nations began to make new claims on Chinese territory.

Name ____________________ Date ____________________ Class ____________________

Reading Essentials and Study Guide

Chapter 22, Section 1 *(continued)*

In the spring of 1898, the young emperor Guang Xu started a reform program based on changes in Japan. During the following weeks, known as the One Hundred Days of Reform, he issued edicts calling for major political, administrative, and educational reforms. Many conservatives opposed these reforms. The emperor's aunt, Empress Dowager Ci Xi, also opposed the reforms. With the aid of the imperial army, she was able to imprison the emperor and end his reform efforts.

9. Why did the reform efforts of Guang Xu fail?

• Opening the Door to China *(page 688)*

Great Britain and the United States became afraid that other nations would overrun China if the Chinese government collapsed. In 1899, U.S. secretary of state John Hay presented a proposal that ensured equal access to the Chinese market for all nations. It also preserved the unity of the Chinese Empire. When none of the other governments opposed the idea, Hay proclaimed that all major nations had agreed that China should have an Open Door policy.

The Open Door policy did not end the system of spheres of influence. But it did reduce the limits on foreign imports that had been imposed within each sphere. The policy also lessened fears in Britain, France, Germany, and Russia that other powers would take advantage of China's weakness and try to dominate the Chinese market.

10. What was the Open Door policy? What were some of its effects?

• The Boxer Rebellion *(page 689)*

The Open Door policy did not stop the Boxer Rebellion. *Boxer* was the popular name for members of a secret organization called the Society of the Harmonious Fists. The Boxers were upset by the foreign takeover of Chinese lands. Their slogan was "destroy the foreigner." They especially disliked Christian missionaries and Chinese converts to Christianity. At the beginning of 1900, Boxers roamed the countryside and killed missionaries and Chinese Christians. Their victims also included foreign businessmen and even the German envoy to Beijing. In response to the killings, an allied army of twenty thousand British, French, German, Russian, American, and Japanese troops attacked Beijing in August 1900. The army restored order and demanded more concessions from the Chinese government. The Chinese government was forced to pay a heavy **indemnity** (a payment for damages) to the nations that had crushed the rebellion.

11. Who were the Boxers? Why were they upset?

Name ______________________ Date ______________ Class ______________

Reading Essentials and Study Guide

Chapter 22, Section 2

For use with textbook pages 691–696

REVOLUTION IN CHINA

KEY TERMS

provincial local, as opposed to national *(page 691)*

commodity a marketable product *(page 694)*

DRAWING FROM EXPERIENCE

Have you ever read any books about China? What are some customs or traditions in China? How are they the same or different from your family's customs or traditions?

In the last section, you read about the decline of the Qing dynasty. In this section, you will learn about the fall of the Qing dynasty in the early twentieth century, and the changes in Chinese society and culture during this time.

ORGANIZING YOUR THOUGHTS

Use the diagram below to help you take notes. The coming of Westerners dramatically affected China. List three ways that the Chinese economy was affected by Westerners. Also list three ways that the West influenced Chinese culture.

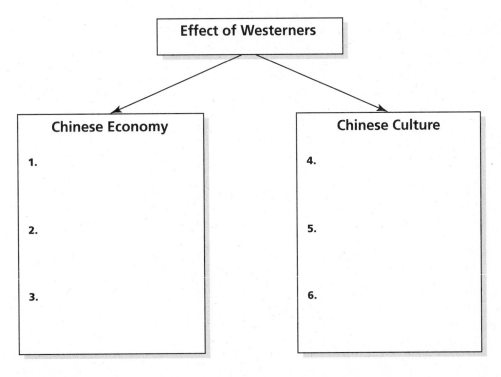

Effect of Westerners

Chinese Economy	Chinese Culture
1.	4.
2.	5.
3.	6.

READ TO LEARN

• The Fall of the Qing *(page 691)*

After the Boxer Rebellion, the Qing dynasty tried to make reforms. The civil service examination system was replaced by a new educational system based on the Western model. After 1905, legislative assemblies were formed at the **provincial** (local) level. Elections for a national assembly were held in 1910. Reformers soon became angry, however, when they discovered that the new assemblies could not pass laws but could only give advice to the ruler. The reforms also did nothing for the peasants, artisans, and miners. Their living conditions were getting worse because of tax increases. Unrest grew in the countryside.

The first signs of revolution appeared during the last decade of the nineteenth century. A young radical, Sun Yat-sen, formed the Revive China Society. Sun believed that the Qing dynasty could no longer govern the country. But he knew that the Chinese people were not ready for democracy. He developed a reform process that had three stages: a military takeover, a transitional phase in which Sun's own revolutionary party would prepare the people for democratic rule, and the final stage of a constitutional democracy. In 1905, Sun united radical groups across China and formed the Revolutionary Alliance.

In 1908, Empress Dowager Ci Xi died. The throne now passed to China's "last emperor," Henry Pu Yi, who was an infant. In October 1911, followers of Sun Yat-sen started an uprising in Central China. The Qing dynasty collapsed, but Sun's party did not have the military or political power to form a new government. The party was forced to turn to General Yuan Shigai, who controlled the army. He agreed to serve as president of a new Chinese republic.

7. What were the three stages of reform proposed by Sun Yat-sen?

____

____

____

____

____

• An Era of Civil War *(page 693)*

After the collapse of the Qing dynasty, the military took over. General Yuan Shigai ruled in a traditional way and even tried to set up a new imperial dynasty. Reformers hated him because he used murder and terror to destroy the new democratic institutions. He was hated by traditionalists for being disloyal to the Qing dynasty. He came into conflict with Sun's party, now called the Guomindang, or Nationalist Party. When Yuan dissolved the new parliament, the Nationalists started a rebellion. The rebellion failed, and Sun Yat-sen fled to Japan.

General Yuan died in 1916 and was succeeded by one of his officers. For the next several years, China slipped into civil war. Warlords seized power in the provinces. Their soldiers caused massive destruction throughout China.

8. Why was General Yuan Shigai so unpopular?

____

____

____

____

____

• Chinese Society in Transition *(page 694)*

The coming of Westerners to China affected the Chinese economy in three ways. Westerners introduced modern means of transportation and communication. They also created an export market and integrated the Chinese economy into the world economy. The growth of industry and trade was especially noticeable in the cities. A national market for **commodities** (marketable products), such as oil, copper, salt, tea, and porcelain, had developed. New crops brought in from other countries increased food production. To some, these changes were beneficial. Western influences forced the Chinese to adopt new ways of thinking and acting. But China paid a heavy price for the new ways. Its local industry was largely destroyed. Many of the profits in the new economy went to foreign countries.

After World War I, Chinese businesspeople began to develop new ventures. Shanghai, Wuhan, Tianjin, and Guangzhou became major industrial and commercial centers with a growing middle class and an industrial working class.

9. In what ways did the coming of Westerners have a negative effect on the Chinese economy?

____

____

____

____

____

• China's Changing Culture *(page 695)*

In 1800, daily life for most Chinese people was the same as it had been for centuries. Most were farmers, living in villages in rice fields and on hillsides. 125 years later, there was a different society in China. The changes were most obvious in the cities. The educated and wealthy in the cities had been affected by the presence of Westerners in the country. Confucian social ideals were declining. Radical reformers wanted to eliminate traditional culture. They wanted to create a new China that would be respected by the modern world.

The first changes in traditional culture came in the late nineteenth century. Intellectuals began to introduce Western books, paintings, music, and ideas to China. Western literature and art became popular in China, especially among the urban middle class. Most creative artists followed foreign trends, although traditionalists held on to Chinese culture. Literature in particular was influenced by foreign ideas. Most Chinese novels written after World War I dealt with Chinese subjects, but they reflected the Western tendency toward realism. Most of China's modern authors also showed a clear contempt for the past. Ba Jin was one of China's foremost writers at the turn of the century. In his trilogy, *Family, Spring,* and *Autumn,* he describes the disintegration of traditional Confucian ways as the younger members of a large family attempt to break away from their elders.

10. In what ways was Chinese literature particularly influenced by foreign ideas?

____

____

____

____

____

Name ______________________ Date ______________________ Class ______________________

Reading Essentials and Study Guide

Chapter 22, Section 3

For use with textbook pages 697–704

RISE OF MODERN JAPAN

KEY TERMS

concession a political compromise *(page 698)*

prefecture a territory in Japan during the Meiji government *(page 699)*

DRAWING FROM EXPERIENCE

What is the first thing that comes to mind when you hear the word "Japanese"? Do you think first of Japanese products, such as cars? Or do you think first of events in Japanese history, such as World War II?

In the last two sections, you learned about changes in China during the late nineteenth and early twentieth centuries. In this section, you will learn about changes in Japan during the same period.

ORGANIZING YOUR THOUGHTS

Use the diagram below to help you take notes. Under the Meiji Constitution of 1890, the Japanese government was divided into an executive branch and a legislative branch. Describe the structure of these two branches of government and how officials in each branch were appointed or elected. Circle the branch of government that had the most authority.

Political Structure Under the Meiji Constitution

Executive Branch	Legislative Branch
1.	2.

READ TO LEARN

• An End to Isolation *(page 697)*

By 1800, the Tokugawa shogunate had ruled the Japanese islands for two hundred years. It had driven out foreign traders and missionaries and isolated the country from nearly all contact with the outside world. To the Western powers, Japanese isolation was a challenge. They began to approach Japan in the hope of opening it up to foreign economic interests. The first foreign power to succeed with Japan was the United States. In the summer of 1853, an American fleet of warships under Commodore Matthew Perry arrived in Edo Bay (now Tokyo Bay). Perry brought with him a letter from President Millard Fillmore. The U.S. president asked for better treatment of sailors shipwrecked on the Japanese islands. He also requested the opening of relations between the United States and Japan.

A few months later, Perry returned to Japan for an answer. Shogunate officials had been discussing the issue. Some argued that contacts with the West would hurt Japan. Others feared the military superiority of the United States and recommended **concessions** (political compromises). Under pressure from Perry's warships, Japan agreed to the Treaty of Kanagawa. This treaty provided for the return of shipwrecked sailors, the opening of two ports to Western traders, and the establishment of a U.S. consulate in Japan. In 1858, U.S. consul Townsend Harris signed a more detailed treaty. It opened several new ports to the United States. It also provided for an exchange of ministers. Similar treaties were soon signed by Japan and several other European nations.

3. What attitude did the Tokugawa shogunate have toward the outside world prior to the nineteenth century?

____

____

____

____

____

____

• Resistance to the New Order *(page 698)*

The decision to open relations with Western nations was very unpopular in parts of Japan. Resistance was especially strong among the samurai warriors in two territories in the south, Satsuma and Choshu. Both territories had strong military traditions and had not been exposed to Western military pres-

sure. In 1863, the Sat-Cho (Satsuma-Choshu) alliance made the shogun promise to end relations with the West. In January 1868, the Sat-Cho armies attacked the shogun's palace and proclaimed that the authority of the emperor had been restored. After a few weeks, the shogun's forces collapsed. The shogunate system came to an end.

4. In what parts of Japan was the decision to open relations with the West particularly unpopular? Why?

____

____

____

____

____

____

• The Meiji Restoration *(page 698)*

The Sat-Cho leaders realized that Japan must change to survive. They began a policy of reform that turned Japan into a modern industrial nation. The symbol of the new era was the young emperor Mutsuhito. He called his reign the Meiji ("Enlightened Rule"). This period became known as the Meiji Restoration. The Sat-Cho leaders controlled the Meiji ruler, just as earlier emperors had been controlled by the shogunate. The capital was moved from Kyoto to Edo (now Tokyo). To reduce the power of the daimyo, the new leaders stripped them of the titles to their lands in 1871. As compensation, the daimyo were given government bonds and were named governors of the territories that had been under their control. The territories were now called **prefectures.**

During the next 20 years, the Meiji government studied Western political systems. The Meiji Constitution of 1890 was modeled after the constitution of Imperial Germany. The executive branch had the most authority. In theory, the emperor had all executive authority. In practice, a prime minister and his cabinet of ministers had the real executive authority. The Meiji leaders picked these ministers. The legislative branch consisted of a parliament with two houses. Members of the upper house were to be appointed, while members of the lower house were to be elected. The two houses were to have equal powers. The final result was a political system that was democratic in form, but authoritarian in practice. Power remained in the hands of the Sat-Cho leaders. The system allowed the traditional ruling class to keep its influence and economic power.

The Meiji leaders set up a new system of land ownership. A land reform program turned the traditional lands of the daimyo into private property for the peasants. The Meiji leaders also levied a new land tax. The new tax was an excellent source of revenue for the government, but it was a burden on the farmers. Under the old system, farmers had paid a tax on their harvest. In bad harvest years, they owed little or nothing. Under the new system, farmers had to pay the land tax every year, even if the harvest was bad. As a result, in bad years, many peasants were unable to pay their taxes. This forced them to sell their lands to wealthy neighbors and become tenant farmers who paid rent to the new owners. By the end of the nineteenth century, about 40 percent of all farmers were tenants.

The Meiji government encouraged the development of new industries. It gave subsidies to industries and provided training and foreign advisors. It also improved transportation and communications and started a new educational system that stressed applied science. By 1900, Japan's industrial sector was beginning to grow. Besides tea and silk, other key industries were weapons, shipbuilding, and sake (Japanese rice wine).

The Meiji reformers also focused on the military. The reformers were well aware that Japan would need a modern army to compete with the Western powers. A new imperial army was formed in 1871. It was based on compulsory military service. All Japanese men served for three years. The new army was well equipped with modern weapons.

Education also changed. The education ministry adopted the American model of elementary schools, secondary schools, and universities. It brought foreign specialists to Japan, and sent bright students to study abroad. In the schools, a great deal of emphasis was still placed on the virtues of family and community. Loyalty to the emperor was especially valued.

The Meiji Restoration had a dramatic effect on the traditional social system in Japan. Special privileges for the aristocracy were abolished. Women were allowed to seek an education. As the economy shifted from an agricultural to an industrial base, many Japanese people began to get new jobs and establish new relationships. Western fashions, dancing, and sports became popular in Japan. Japanese young people began to imitate the clothing styles, eating habits, hairstyles, and social practices of European and American young people.

The Meiji Restoration had a less attractive side. Many commoners were exploited in the coal mines and textile mills. Workers labored up to 20 hours a day, often under terrible conditions. In many areas, villagers sought new political and human rights. Women took part in this process and formed the Freedom and People's Rights Movement. This movement was demanding voting rights for women as early as 1876. However, the Constitution of 1890 only gave men the right to vote. The Civil Code of 1898 played down individual rights and placed women within the context of their family role.

5. What were some of the changes that the Meiji Restoration made in the areas of economics and education?

____

____

____

____

____

____

• Joining the Imperialist Nations *(page 702)*

The Japanese also copied Western imperialism. Japan is a small country that is densely populated and lacks resources. The Japanese felt that they needed to expand into other territories. They also believed that Western nations were wealthy and powerful because they had colonies. The Japanese began their expansion close to home. In 1874, Japan claimed control of the Ryukyu Islands. Two years later, Japan's navy forced the Koreans to open their ports to Japanese trade. During the 1880s, Chinese-Japanese rivalry over Korea grew. In 1894, Japan and China went to war. Japanese ships destroyed the Chinese fleet and seized the Manchurian city of Port Arthur. In the treaty that ended the war, China recognized the independence of Korea. They also ceded (transferred) Taiwan and the Liaodong Peninsula to Japan. The Japanese later returned the Liaodong Peninsula to China.

Russia was also interested in Korea. Rivalry over Korea led to strained relations between Japan and Russia. In 1904, Japan attacked the Russian naval base at Port Arthur, which Russia had taken from China in 1898. When Japanese forces moved into Manchuria and the Liaodong Peninsula, Russian troops were no match for them. Russia sent its Baltic fleet to Japan, but the new Japanese navy defeated the Russian fleet. Russia agreed to a peace settlement in 1905. They gave the Liaodong Peninsula back to Japan. The Japanese victory stunned the world. Japan had become one of the great powers.

The Japanese government annexed Korea in 1910. The United States was the first nation to recognize this annexation. In return, the United States asked for Japan's support for American authority in the Philippines. However, suspicion between Japan and the United States was growing. In 1907, President Theodore Roosevelt made an agreement with Japan that essentially stopped Japanese immigration to the United States.

Name ______________________ Date ______________________ Class ______________________

6. Why did the Japanese think that expansion was necessary?

____

____

____

____

____

____

• Culture in an Era of Transition *(page 703)*

Western technology and ideas were introduced to Japan in the nineteenth century and greatly altered Japanese culture. Literature was especially affected. Japanese authors began translating and imitating European literature. Japanese novels were particularly influenced by Western realism. The Japanese also copied Western artistic techniques and styles. Huge buildings of steel and concrete, with Greek columns, appeared in many Japanese cities. A national reaction to these changes began by the end of the nineteenth century. Many Japanese artists began to return to older techniques. In 1889, the Tokyo School of Fine Arts was established to promote traditional Japanese art.

The cultural exchange went both ways. Japanese art influenced Western painters. Japanese arts and crafts, porcelains, textiles, fans, folding screens, and woodblock prints became fashionable in Europe and North America. Japanese gardens became especially popular in the United States.

7. How was Japanese culture affected by Western technology and ideas?

____

____

____

____

____

____

Name ______________________ Date ______________________ Class ______________________

Reading Essentials and Study Guide

Chapter 23, Section 1

For use with textbook pages 717–720

THE ROAD TO WORLD WAR I

KEY TERMS

conscription a military draft *(page 718)*

mobilization the process of assembling troops and supplies and making them ready for war *(page 720)*

DRAWING FROM EXPERIENCE

Have you ever been given an ultimatum? How did you react to the ultimatum?

In this section, you will learn about the events that led to the start of World War I. Ultimatums played an important role in starting World War I.

ORGANIZING YOUR THOUGHTS

Use the time line below to help you take notes. Identify seven key events during the summer of 1914 that led to World War I.

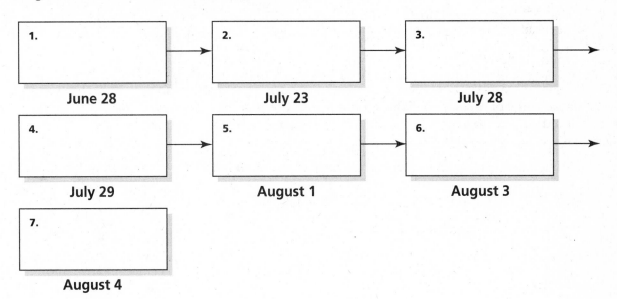

1. →	**2.** →	**3.** →
June 28	**July 23**	**July 28**
4. →	**5.** →	**6.** →
July 29	**August 1**	**August 3**
7.		
August 4		

READ TO LEARN

• Nationalism and the System of Alliances *(page 717)*

The growth of nationalism in the nineteenth century had many serious results. Competition for colonies and trade increased. Europe's great powers were soon divided into two alliances, the Triple Alliance and the Triple Entente. Crises in the Balkans between 1908 and 1913 made many European nations angry with each other. They were willing to go to war to preserve the power of their national states. Not all ethnic groups had become nations. But the growth of nationalism made the Irish, the Poles, and the Slavic peoples dream of creating their own national states.

8. What were some of the results of the growth of nationalism in the nineteenth century?

____

____

____

____

____

• Internal Dissent *(page 718)*

National desires were not the only reason for internal conflicts in the early 1900s. Socialist labor movements had become more powerful. These movements were more and more willing to use strikes to reach their goals, even if this led to violence. Some conservative leaders were afraid that their nations were on the verge of revolution. Some historians believe that the fear of revolution and the desire to suppress internal conflicts encouraged the leaders of some nations to go to war in 1914.

9. How might Socialist labor movements have contributed indirectly to the start of World War I?

____

____

____

____

____

• Militarism *(page 718)*

After 1900, the size of armies throughout Europe grew at an alarming rate. **Conscription,** a military draft, was used by most Western nations before 1914. It caused the size of European armies to double between 1890 and 1914. Militarism (preparation for war) was growing. Military leaders became more powerful. They began to draw up plans that could be used if their countries went to war. They insisted that any changes to these plans would cause chaos in the military. In the 1914 crises, this forced European political leaders to make decisions for military rather than political reasons.

10. How did the plans of military leaders affect the decisions of political leaders in 1914?

____

____

____

____

• The Outbreak of War: Summer 1914 *(page 719)*

Nationalism, internal conflicts, and militarism all played a role in the starting of World War I. But it was a crisis in the Balkans in the summer of 1914 that led directly to war. States in southeastern Europe had struggled for years to free themselves from Ottoman rule. Austria-Hungary and Russia both wanted to control these new nations. By 1914, Serbia, supported by Russia, was determined to create a large Slavic state in the Balkans. Austria-Hungary was determined that this would not happen.

On June 28, 1914, Archduke Francis Ferdinand, the heir to the throne of Austria-Hungary, visited the Bosnian city of Sarajevo. Members of the Black Hand made plans to kill him. The Black Hand was a Serbian terrorist organization that wanted Bosnia to be free of Austria-Hungary. An attempt to kill the archduke with a bomb was unsuccessful. Later in the day, however, Gavrilo Princep, a 19-year-old Bosnian Serb, shot and killed both the archduke and his wife.

The Austro-Hungarian government did not know whether the Serbian government was involved in the assassination of the archduke, but it did not care. It saw this as an opportunity to crush Serbia. Austrian leaders wanted to attack Serbia, but they feared that Russia would intervene to help Serbia. The Austrians asked their German allies for help. Emperor William II of Germany agreed to give Austria-Hungary his full support. Austrian leaders sent an ultimatum to Serbia on July 23. Many of the demands were so extreme that Serbia had no choice but to reject some of them. On July 28, Austria-Hungary declared war on Serbia.

Reading Essentials and Study Guide

Russia was determined to support Serbia. Czar Nicholas II ordered partial mobilization of the Russian army. **Mobilization** is the process of assembling troops and supplies and making them ready for war. In 1914, mobilization was seen as an act of war. Russian military leaders told the czar that they could not partially mobilize. Their mobilization plans were based on a war against both Germany and Austria-Hungary. They claimed that mobilization against only Austria-Hungary would create chaos. Based on this claim, the czar ordered full mobilization of the Russian army on July 29. The German government warned Russia that it must stop its mobilization. When Russia refused, Germany declared war on Russia on August 1.

Germany also had a military plan. One of its generals, Alfred von Schlieffen, had drawn up a plan that called for war against both Russia and France. Under the Schlieffen Plan, Germany could not go to war against Russia only. As a result, Germany declared war on France on August 3. It also issued an ultimatum to Belgium, in which it demanded the right of German troops to pass through Belgium, even though Belgium was a neutral nation.

On August 4, Great Britain declared war on Germany, officially for violating Belgian neutrality. In fact, Britain was allied with France and Russia and was concerned about maintaining its own world power. Now all of the great European powers were at war.

11. What warnings and ultimatums did European countries issue in the summer of 1914? What were the results of these ultimatums?

____

____

____

____

____

Name ______________________ Date ______________________ Class ______________________

Reading Essentials and Study Guide

Chapter 23, Section 2

For use with textbook pages 721–727

THE WAR

KEY TERMS

propaganda ideas spread to influence public opinion for or against a cause *(page 721)*

trench warfare warfare fought in trenches (ditches protected by barbed war) *(page 722)*

war of attrition a war based on wearing the other side down by constant attacks and heavy losses *(page 724)*

total war a war involving a complete mobilization of resources and people in the warring countries *(page 726)*

planned economies economic systems directed by government agencies *(page 726)*

DRAWING FROM EXPERIENCE

Have you ever read the book *All Quiet on the Western Front?* How does the book describe the fighting on the Western Front during World War I?

In the last section, you learned about the events that led to the start of World War I. In this section, you will learn about the war itself and its impact on civilians at home.

ORGANIZING YOUR THOUGHTS

Use the chart below to help you take notes. World War I was a new kind of war because of new strategies and technology. Indicate how each of the following strategies or technologies was used during the war.

War Strategy or Technology	Use During the War
Propaganda	**1.**
Trench warfare	**2.**
War of attrition	**3.**
Airplanes	**4.**
Submarines	**5.**
Planned economies	**6.**

READ TO LEARN

• 1914 to 1915: Illusions and Stalemate *(page 721)*

Before 1914, many leaders believed that war was so full of risks that it would not be worth fighting. Others believed that diplomats could control any situation and avoid war. In August 1914, these ideas were shown to be wrong.

Prior to the war, government **propaganda** (ideas spread to influence public opinion for or against a cause) had been used to stir up hatred towards other nations. When the war broke out, European governments had no trouble getting their citizens' support for the war effort. Most people were truly convinced that their nation's cause was just. Most people also believed that the war would end in a few weeks.

The German hopes for a quick end to the war rested on a military gamble. The Schlieffen Plan called for German troops to make a wide arc through Belgium into northern France. The German army would then sweep around Paris and surround most of the French army. However, the German advance was halted a short distance from Paris at the First Battle of the Marne (September 6–10). To stop the Germans, the French military leaders loaded 2,000 Parisian taxicabs with fresh troops and sent them to the front.

On this Western Front, the war turned into a stalemate, with both sides taking shelter in their trenches. Trenches were ditches protected by barbed wire. These trenches soon stretched from the English Channel to the border of Switzerland. This **trench warfare** kept both sides in virtually the same positions for four years.

The war on the Eastern Front was fought much differently. There was a great deal of movement by the various armies on this front. As the war began, Russia moved into eastern Germany but was defeated at the Battle of Tannenberg on August 30 and at the Battle of Masurian Lakes on September 15. These defeats ended the Russian threat to Germany. Germany's ally, Austria-Hungary, fared less well at first. The Austrians were defeated by the Russians in Galicia and were thrown out of Serbia. Then Italy, their other ally, betrayed them by attacking Austria in May 1915. Italy joined France, Great Britain, and Russia, who were now called the Allied Powers or Allies.

Germany came to the aid of their Austrian friends. A German-Austrian army defeated the Russians in Galicia and pushed them back into their own territory. The Russians had been almost knocked out of the war. Bulgaria joined Germany and Austria-Hungary in September 1915. They attacked and eliminated Serbia from the war. Their success in the east allowed them to focus their attention back on the Western Front.

Reading Essentials and Study Guide

7. How did the war on the Western Front turn into a stalemate?

____

____

____

____

• 1916 to 1917: The Great Slaughter *(page 723)*

By 1916, the trenches on the Western Front had become elaborate systems of defense. Barbed wire, machine-gun nests, and heavy artillery protected the trenches on both sides. The troops lived in holes in the ground. A strip of land, known as no-man's-land, separated the opposing forces. Trench warfare baffled the military leaders of both sides. Never before in the history of war had armies fought each other in this way. The leaders believed that if they could break through enemy lines, they could return to the type of fighting that they understood. These attempts to break through the lines would begin with a heavy artillery barrage that was intended to flatten the other side's barbed wire and leave them in a state of shock. Troops would then be ordered to leave their trenches and attack the other side with fixed bayonets. These attacks seldom worked, however, because the troops were fired at by the enemy's machine guns. In 1916 and 1917, millions of young men were killed in their attempts to achieve these breakthroughs. World War I had turned into a **war of attrition,** a war based on wearing the other side down by constant attacks and heavy losses.

For the first time in history, warfare was waged in the sky. Airplanes appeared over battlefields for the first time in 1915. At first, planes were only used to spot the enemy's position, but they soon began to attack ground targets. Battles began to be waged between the opposing pilots. At first, they used pistols. Later, machine guns were added to the noses of the planes.

The Germans also used their giant airships, the zeppelins, to bomb London and eastern England. The zeppelins were filled with hydrogen gas, and Germany's enemies soon found that these airships could be turned into raging infernos when hit by antiaircraft guns.

8. Why did attempts to break through enemy lines rarely work under trench warfare?

____

____

____

____

Reading Essentials and Study Guide

Chapter 23, Section 2 *(continued)*

• Widening of the War *(page 724)*

Because of the stalemate on the Western Front, both sides sought new allies. The Ottoman Empire had already joined the war on Germany's side in August 1914. Russia, Great Britain, and France declared war on the Ottoman Empire in November. The Allies tried to open a Balkan front by landing forces at Gallipoli, southwest of Constantinople, in April 1915. But Bulgaria entered the war on the side of the Central Powers (Germany, Austria-Hungary, and the Ottoman Empire). After a disastrous campaign at Gallipoli, the Allies were forced to withdraw.

By 1917, the war had truly become a world war. Italy, now on the side of the Allies, opened up a front against Austria-Hungary. In the Middle East, a British officer known as Lawrence of Arabia encouraged Arab princes to revolt against their Ottoman rulers. In 1918, British forces from Egypt destroyed the Ottoman Empire in the Middle East. The British used forces from India, Australia, and New Zealand in their Middle East campaigns. During the war, the Allies were able to seize German colonies around the world. Japan, a British ally since 1902, seized several German-held islands in the Pacific. Australia seized German New Guinea.

9. In what ways did the Allies try to widen the war from 1915 to 1918?

____

____

____

____

____

• Entry of the United States *(page 725)*

At first, the United States tried to remain neutral. However, as the war dragged on, this became increasingly difficult. The United States finally entered the war as a result of the naval war between Great Britain and Germany. As part of its war strategy, Britain used its navy to block war materials and other goods from reaching Germany by sea. Germany retaliated by setting up its own blockade of Britain. German strategy included the use of submarines. The submarines were allowed to attack not only military ships but also civilian ships, such as passenger liners.

On May 7, 1915, German forces sank the British ship *Lusitania.* 1,100 civilians were killed, including over 100 Americans. As a result of American protests, the German government stopped unrestricted submarine warfare. The German and British navies fought only one direct battle, the Battle of Jutland. This battle took place on May 31, 1916, and neither side won a conclusive victory. By January 1917, the Germans were desperate to win the war. German naval officers convinced Emperor William II that the use of unrestricted submarine warfare would starve the British into submission. They convinced the emperor that the British would starve before the United States could act.

The German naval officers were wrong. The British did not surrender. The return to unrestricted submarine warfare caused the United States to enter the war in 1917. By 1918, large numbers of American troops had arrived in Europe. The entry of the United States in the war boosted the Allies psychologically and gave them a new source of money and supplies.

10. What was the immediate cause of U.S. entry into World War I?

____

____

____

____

____

• The Home Front: The Impact of Total War *(page 726)*

World War I became a **total war,** a war involving a complete mobilization of resources and people. The war affected all of the citizens in the warring countries. As a result of the war effort, there was an increase in government powers and in the use of propaganda. Once it became clear that the war would last far longer than expected, it also became clear that many more men and supplies would be needed. Governments expanded their powers to meet these needs. Countries drafted tens of millions of young men to serve in their militaries. Wartime governments also expanded their power over their economies. Capitalism, with its free market system, was temporarily set aside. In order to mobilize all the resources of their nations for the war effort, European nations set up **planned economies**—systems directed by government agencies. Governments set up price, wage, and rent controls. They also rationed food supplies and materials, regulated imports and exports, and took over transportation systems and industries.

As the war dragged on and the casualties mounted, patriotic enthusiasm decreased. War governments fought back against the growing opposition to the war. Authoritarian governments, like those of Germany, Russia, and Austria-Hungary, used force to control their people. Soon, even democratic states expanded their police powers in order to stop opposition to the war. In Great Britain, a law was passed that allowed the government to arrest protestors as traitors. Newspapers were censored or even suspended. Governments continued to use propaganda to create enthusiasm for the war.

Because so many of the world's men were involved in fighting the war, new opportunities were opened up for women. Women were asked to take over jobs that had not been available to them before. But many of the new jobs for women proved to be only temporary when men returned to the job market. There were some lasting results, however. In Great Britain, Germany, Austria, and the United States, women were given the right to vote soon after the war ended.

11. How did World War I affect the lives of women in Western countries?

Name ______________________ Date ______________________ Class ______________________

Reading Essentials and Study Guide

Chapter 23, Section 3

For use with textbook pages 732–737

THE RUSSIAN REVOLUTION

KEY TERMS

soviets councils in Russia composed of representatives from the workers and soldiers *(page 734)*

war communism a Communist policy that was used to ensure regular supplies for the Red Army through government control of banks and industries, the seizing of grain from peasants, and the centralization of state administration under Communist control *(page 737)*

DRAWING FROM EXPERIENCE

What is communism? Have you ever thought what it would be like to live in a Communist country? How would your life be different?

In the last two sections, you read about World War I. In this section, you will learn about the Russian Revolution, which took place while the war was still going on. By 1921, the Communists were in total command of Russia.

ORGANIZING YOUR THOUGHTS

Use the time line below to help you take notes. Identify eight important events during the Russian Revolution.

1. → **2.** → **3.** →

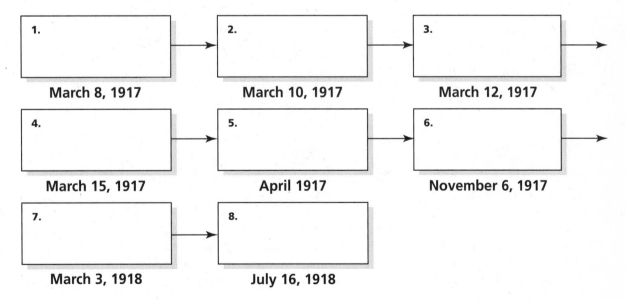

March 8, 1917 | **March 10, 1917** | **March 12, 1917**

4. → **5.** → **6.** →

March 15, 1917 | **April 1917** | **November 6, 1917**

7. → **8.**

March 3, 1918 | **July 16, 1918**

READ TO LEARN

• Background to Revolution *(page 732)*

Russia was not prepared for World War I. There were no competent military leaders in Russia. Czar Nicholas II was in charge of the armed forces, but he had no training or ability for this. Russian industry was not able to produce the weapons needed for the army. Because of these problems, the Russian army suffered heavy losses. Between 1914 and 1916, two million soldiers were killed.

While the czar was at the battlefront, his wife Alexandra made all of the important decisions. She consulted Rasputin, a Siberian peasant who claimed to be a holy man. She was influenced by him because he seemed to be able to stop the bleeding of her son Alexis, who had hemophilia. Because of his influence, Rasputin became an important power in Russia.

With such poor leadership, the Russian people suffered through a series of military and economic disasters. The people became more and more upset with the rule of the czar. Even the conservative aristocrats, who supported the czar, felt that something must be done. They assassinated Rasputin in December 1916. But even this drastic move could not save the reign of the czar.

In March 1917, working women led a series of strikes in the capital city of Petrograd (formerly St. Petersburg). The government had begun rationing bread. The same women who were working 12-hour days in the factories were now forced to wait in long lines to get bread to feed their children. On March 8, 1917, about 10,000 women marched through the city of Petrograd. Other workers soon joined them. They called for a general strike, which shut down all the factories in the city on March 10. Czar Nicholas ordered troops to break up the crowds by shooting them if necessary. But large numbers of soldiers soon joined the demonstrators and refused to fire on the crowds.

The Duma, or legislative body, which the czar had tried to dissolve, met anyway. On March 12, it set up a provisional government. This government asked the czar to step down. Because Nicholas II had no support from the army or even from the wealthy aristocrats, he did step down, on March 15. The provisional government, led by Alexander Kerensky, decided to carry on the war to preserve Russia's honor. This was a major blunder. Workers and peasants no longer supported the war. The provisional government was also faced with a challenge to its authority—the **soviets.** The soviets were councils in Russia composed of representatives from the workers and soldiers. They were largely made up of socialists. One group, the Bolsheviks, began to play a crucial role.

9. How did World War I contribute to the start of the Russian Revolution?

____

____

____

____

____

• The Rise of Lenin *(page 735)*

The Bolsheviks began as a small faction of a Marxist party called the Russian Social Democrats. Vladimir Ilyich Ulianov, better known as V.I. Lenin, led them. Lenin believed that violent revolution was the only way to destroy the capitalist system. He believed that a small group of well-disciplined revolutionaries could accomplish this. From 1900 to 1917, Lenin spent most of his time in Switzerland. When the provisional government was formed, he saw this as an opportunity for the Bolsheviks to seize power. In April 1917, German military leaders shipped Lenin back to Russia. They hoped that he would create disorder in Russia.

Lenin's arrival in Russia started a new stage of the Russian Revolution. He believed that the Bolsheviks should try to gain control of the soviets and use them to overthrow the provisional government. The Bolsheviks told the people what they wanted to hear. They promised an end to the war, the redistribution of land to the peasants, the transfer of factories from capitalists to the workers, and the transfer of government power to the soviets.

10. What promises did the Bolsheviks make to the Russian people?

____

____

____

____

____

• The Bolsheviks Seize Power *(page 736)*

By October 1917, the Bolsheviks held a slight majority in the Petrograd and Moscow soviets. The number of Bolsheviks had grown from 50,000 to 240,000. Leon Trotsky, a dedicated revolutionary, led the Petrograd soviet. This put the Bolsheviks in a position to claim power in the name of the soviets. During the night of November 6, the Bolsheviks seized the Winter Palace, where the provisional government met. The government quickly collapsed. This overthrow occurred at the same time as a meeting in Petrograd of the all-Russian Congress of Soviets. This group represented soviets from all over the country. Outwardly, Lenin turned power over to the Congress of Soviets. But the real power passed to the Council of People's Commissars, headed by Lenin.

The Bolsheviks changed their name to the Communists. Now that they were in power, they faced the difficult task of removing Russia from the war. This would mean the loss of much Russian territory, but there was no real choice. On March 3, 1918, Lenin signed the Treaty of Brest-Litovsk and gave up eastern Poland, Ukraine, Finland, and the Baltic provinces. Even with this treaty, real peace did not come, because the country soon sank into civil war.

11. Why did Lenin sign the Treaty of Brest-Litovsk?

____

____

____

____

____

• Civil War in Russia *(page 736)*

Many people were opposed to the new Communist government. These people included groups loyal to the czar, liberals, anti-Lenin socialists, and the Allies. The Allies sent troops to various parts of Russia in the hope of bringing Russia back into the war. The troops rarely fought on Russian soil, but they gave aid to anti-Communist forces. From 1918 to 1921, the Communist (Red) Army was forced to fight on many fronts against the anti-Communist (White) forces. In the early part of the civil war, the White Army had several successes. But by 1920, the major White forces had been defeated. Within a year, the Communists regained control of Ukraine, Georgia, Russian Armenia, and Azerbaijan.

The royal family was a victim of the civil war. On July 16, 1918, members of the local soviet in Ekaterinburg murdered Nicholas II and his family, where they were being held captive.

12. What was the White Army? What groups made it up?

____

____

____

____

____

- **Triumph of the Communists** *(page 736)*

The Communists had won the civil war against seemingly insurmountable odds. There were several reasons for their success. First, the Red Army was well disciplined. This was largely due to the efforts of Leon Trotsky, the commissar of war. He reinstated the draft and insisted on complete obedience. Second, the Whites were not unified. They had no common goal, and the different groups did not trust each other. The Communists, on the other hand, had a clear vision of a new socialist order. Third, the Communists implemented a policy of **war communism.** This policy was used to ensure regular supplies for the Red Army. This meant government control of banks and industries, the seizing of grain from peasants, and the centralization of state administration under Communist control. The Communists also formed a new secret police, known as the Cheka. The Cheka began a Red Terror aimed at destroying those who opposed the new regime. Finally, the presence of foreign armies on Russian soil was used to stir up Russian patriotism. The Communists were able to call on patriotic Russians to fight foreign attempts to control the country.

By 1921, the Communists had total control of Russia. Russia was now a centralized state dominated by a single party. The state was also hostile to the Allies, because the Allies had helped the Communists' enemies in the civil war.

13. Why did the Communists win the civil war in Russia?

____

____

____

____

____

Name ______________________ Date ______________________ Class ______________________

Reading Essentials and Study Guide

Chapter 23, Section 4

For use with textbook pages 739–744

END OF THE WAR

KEY TERMS

armistice a truce or an agreement to end the fighting in a war *(page 740)*

reparation a payment by a nation defeated in a war to other nations to cover the costs of the war *(page 742)*

mandate a commission from the League of Nations to a nation that allowed it to officially govern another nation or region without actually owning the territory *(page 744)*

DRAWING FROM EXPERIENCE

Have you ever heard the slogans, "the war to end all wars" and "to make the world safe for democracy"? Did you know that these slogans were used in reference to World War I?

In the last section, you read about the events that led to the Russian Revolution. In this section, you will read about the end of World War I and the efforts to restore peace after the war.

ORGANIZING YOUR THOUGHTS

Use the chart below to help you take notes. In January 1919, representatives of the victorious nations met in Paris to make a final settlement of World War I. The peace settlement with Germany was called the Treaty of Versailles. List the major provisions of the treaty as they relate to the four areas in this chart.

Major Provisions of the Treaty of Versailles	
Responsibility/costs of the war	**1.**
Military	**2.**
Territory	**3.**
Buffer zone	**4.**

READ TO LEARN

• The Last Year of the War *(page 739)*

1917 had been a very difficult year for the Allied forces. Their offensives on the Western Front had been defeated, and the Russian Revolution led to Russia's withdrawal from the War. However, the entry of the United States into the war gave the Allies a much-needed psychological boost. In 1918, fresh American troops would be crucial.

With Russia out of the war, Germany was free to concentrate entirely on the Western Front. Erich von Ludendorff, who guided German military operations, decided to make a grand offensive to break the stalemate. The German attack began in March 1918. The Germans were stopped at the Second Battle of the Marne on July 18. French, Moroccan, and American forces, supported by hundreds of tanks, threw the Germans back over the Marne. The German offensive had failed.

With the arrival of two million more American troops, the Allies began to advance toward Germany. On September 29, 1918, General Ludendorff informed the German leaders that the war was lost. He demanded that the government ask for peace. The Allies were unwilling to make peace with the present German government, so reforms were begun to create a more liberal government. However, the exhausted German people were unwilling to wait for this process to take place. On November 3, sailors in the town of Kiel mutinied. Soldiers and workers began to form councils throughout Germany. By November 9, William II was forced to leave the country. The Social Democrats under Friedrich Ebert announced the creation of a democratic republic. On November 11, the new government signed an **armistice** (a truce or an agreement to end the fighting in a war).

The war was over, but revolutionary forces had been set in motion in Germany. A group of radical socialists formed the German Communist Party in December 1918. The Communists tried to seize power in both Berlin and Munich. The new Social Democratic government used army troops to crush the rebels and murdered two of the Communist party leaders. The attempt at revolution left the German middle class with a deep fear of communism.

Austria-Hungary also experienced revolution. Ethnic groups tried harder and harder to gain their independence. By the end of the war, the Austro-Hungarian Empire no longer existed. The independent republics of Austria, Hungary, and Czechoslovakia, along with the monarchical state called Yugoslavia, replaced it.

5. What was the effect of U.S. entry into World War I?

____

____

____

____

____

• The Peace Settlements *(page 741)*

In January 1919, representatives of 27 victorious Allied nations met in Paris to make a final settlement of the war. Idealistic reasons for fighting World War I had replaced the original reasons for starting the war. Even before the end of the war, the U.S. president, Woodrow Wilson, had presented his "Fourteen Points" to the U.S. Congress. These points were his basis for a peace settlement. His proposals included reaching the peace agreements openly rather than through secret diplomacy, reducing armaments (military forces or weapons), and ensuring self-determination (the right of each people to have its own nation). He also pushed for a general association of nations that would guarantee independence for large and small nations alike.

When the delegations met at the Paris Peace Conference, it became obvious that secret treaties and agreements had been made before the war. These agreements had raised the hopes of European nations for territorial gains. These hopes could not be totally ignored, even if they were in conflict with the principle of self-determination. David Lloyd George, prime minister of Great Britain, was determined to make Germany pay for the war. Georges Clemenceau, the premier of France, was mainly concerned about national security. Clemenceau wanted Germany to be stripped of all weapons. He also wanted German **reparations** (payments to cover the costs of the war) and a separate Rhineland as a buffer zone between France and Germany.

Wilson, Lloyd George, and Clemenceau made the most important decisions at the Paris Peace Conference. Germany was not even invited to attend, and Russia could not be present because of civil war. On January 25, 1919, the conference accepted Wilson's idea of a League of Nations. In return, Wilson agreed to make compromises on territorial arrangements. He did this because he believed that the League could later fix any unfair arrangements. Clemenceau also compromised. He gave up France's wish for a separate Rhineland. Great Britain and the United States pledged to help France if Germany attacked it.

The final peace settlement consisted of five separate treaties with the defeated nations (Germany, Austria, Hungary, Bulgaria, and Turkey). The most important treaty was the Treaty of Versailles with Germany. It was signed on June 28, 1919. The treaty said that Germany and Austria were responsible for starting the war. It ordered Germany to pay reparations for the damage done to the Allied nations. Germany also had to reduce its army and navy and eliminate its air force. Alsace and Lorraine were returned to France. Parts of eastern Germany were given to a new Polish state. German land on both sides of the Rhine was made a demilitarized zone and stripped of all weapons and fortifications. It was hoped that this would prevent Germany from making advances toward France.

As a result of the war and the peace treaties, the map of Europe was redrawn. Both the German and Russian empires lost much territory. The Austro-Hungarian Empire disappeared. New nations emerged: Finland, Latvia, Estonia, Lithuania, Poland, Czechoslovakia, Austria, and Hungary. Romania acquired additional lands from Russia, Hungary, and Bulgaria. Serbia became part of a new nation, called Yugoslavia. The Paris Peace Conference was supposedly guided by the principle of self-determination, but the mixtures of peoples in Eastern Europe made it impossible to draw boundaries totally along ethnic lines. As a result, almost every eastern European country still had ethnic minorities. The problem of ethnic minorities would lead to later conflicts.

The Ottoman Empire was also broken up by the peace settlement. To gain Arab support during the war, the Allies had promised to recognize the independence of Arab states in the Ottoman Empire. After the war, however, France took control of Lebanon and Syria, and Britain took control of Iraq and Palestine. These arrangements were called **mandates.** Under the mandate system, a nation officially governed another nation as a mandate on behalf of the League of Nations but did not own the territory.

World War I had other results as well. The death of so many people undermined the idea of progress. This war had been a total war that required a complete mobilization of people and resources. As a result, the power of governments increased. The turmoil created by the war led to even more insecurity. Revolutions broke up old empires. New states were created, which led to new problems.

6. What new nations emerged as a result of the war and the peace treaties?

____

____

____

____

____

Name ______________________ Date ______________________ Class ______________________

Reading Essentials and Study Guide

Chapter 24, Section 1

For use with textbook pages 751–756

THE FUTILE SEARCH FOR STABILITY

KEY TERMS

depression a period of low economic activity and rising unemployment *(page 754)*

collective bargaining the right of unions to negotiate with employers over wages and hours *(page 755)*

deficit spending going into debt to finance government projects *(page 756)*

DRAWING FROM EXPERIENCE

Have you ever read the novel *The Grapes of Wrath*? Have you ever seen the film? What period in history is portrayed in this novel?

In this section, you will learn about events in Europe and the United States following World War I. After a brief period of peace and prosperity, the Western nations were shaken by the Great Depression.

ORGANIZING YOUR THOUGHTS

Use the diagram below to help you take notes. Identify two causes and three political effects of the Great Depression.

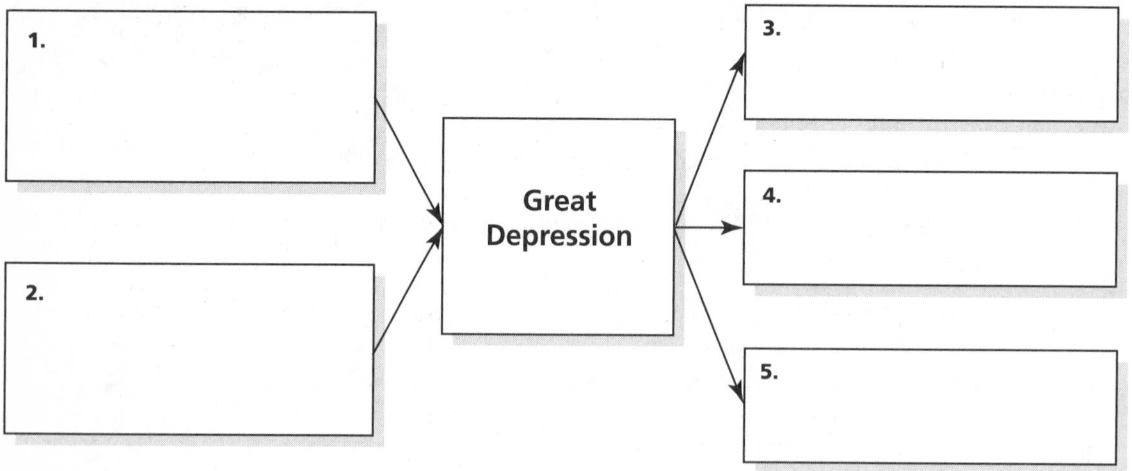

Name ______________________ Date ______________________ Class ______________________

Reading Essentials and Study Guide

Chapter 24, Section 1 *(continued)*

READ TO LEARN

• Uneasy Peace, Uncertain Security *(page 751)*

The peace settlement at the end of World War I made many nations unhappy. Some of the provisions in the settlement led to border disputes in eastern Europe. The League of Nations was not very effective in maintaining peace. This was partly because the League could not use military force. It was also due to the fact that the United States was not in the League. The U.S. Senate refused to ratify (approve) the Treaty of Versailles. This meant that the United States could not be a member of the League of Nations.

The Germans, in particular, were unhappy with the peace settlement. The French government demanded strict enforcement of the Treaty of Versailles. In April 1921, the Allied Reparations Commission determined that Germany had to pay 33 billion dollars for reparations (the payments the Germans were supposed to make for the damage they had done in the war). Germany tried to make these payments, but after one year, they announced that they could no longer afford to pay. France sent troops to occupy the Ruhr Valley, the chief industrial and mining center of Germany. The French intended to collect reparations by operating the Ruhr mines and factories. German workers resisted by going on strike. To pay the workers, the German government printed more and more paper money. This added to the inflation (rise in prices) that had already begun in Germany. The German mark (Germany's currency) soon became worthless. Workers took their weekly pay home in wheelbarrows.

The Allies could see that this situation could not continue. In August 1924, a new plan for reparations, the Dawes Plan, was produced. It reduced the total amount that Germany had to pay. It also reduced the yearly payment amount to something that Germany could afford to pay. The plan also granted a $200 million loan to Germany. This loan opened the door to American investments in Europe. There was a brief period of prosperity from 1924 to 1929.

In 1925, France and Germany signed the Treaty of Locarno. This treaty guaranteed Germany's new western borders with France and Belgium. This treaty was viewed by many as the beginning of a new era of European peace. Germany joined the League of Nations in 1926. In 1928, sixty-three nations signed the Kellogg-Briand pact. These nations pledged "to renounce war as an instrument of national policy." Unfortunately, there was no way to enforce the Kellogg-Briand pact. Most nations were unwilling to risk their national security by reducing their military forces.

Name ______________________ Date ______________________ Class ______________________

6. Why was the League of Nations not very effective in maintaining peace?

___

___

___

___

• The Great Depression *(page 754)*

The brief period of prosperity that began in 1924 ended in an economic collapse that became known as the Great Depression. A **depression** is a period of low economic activity and rising unemployment.

At least two factors played an important role in the start of the Great Depression. The first factor was a series of downturns in the economies of individual nations during the second half of the 1920s. The second factor was an international financial crisis involving the U.S. stock market. During the 1920s, the U.S. stock market was booming. American investors, who had been making loans to Germany, began to pull money out of Germany to invest it in the stock market. Then, in October 1929, the U.S. stock market crashed. U.S. investors withdrew even more money from Germany and other European markets. This weakened the banks of Germany and other European countries. By 1931, trade was slowing down, industrial production was declining, and unemployment was rising. During 1932, the worst year of the depression, 25 percent of British workers were unemployed, and 40 percent of the German workforce was without work. Governments did not know how to deal with the crisis. Traditional solutions, such as cutting costs by lowering wages, made matters worse.

The Great Depression had serious political effects. First, governments became more and more involved in the economies of their countries. Second, Communism became more popular. Marx had predicted that capitalism would eventually destroy itself through overproduction, and this seemed to be coming true. Finally, masses of people began to follow dictators who offered solutions.

7. How did the crash of the U.S. stock market affect Germany and other European countries?

___

___

___

___

• Democratic States After the War *(page 755)*

In 1919, most European countries had democratic governments. In many nations, women could now vote. In Germany, the imperial government had come to an end. A German democratic state known as the Weimar Republic was created, but it had problems. First, it had no outstanding political leaders. In 1925, Paul von Hindenburg was elected president. He was a military hero and did not fully endorse the republic that he was elected to lead. The Weimar Republic also had serious economic problems. Inflation caused fixed incomes and life savings to become worthless. This pushed the middle class toward political parties that opposed the republic. After a brief period of prosperity, the Great Depression struck and led to mass unemployment. Fear seized the country and led to the rise of extremist parties.

After the war, France became the strongest power on the European continent. Because its economy was more balanced than the economies of other nations, the French did not experience the full effects of the Great Depression until 1932. The economic problems had political effects. The government changed six times in less than two years. Finally, in 1936, a coalition of leftist parties (Communists, Socialists, and Radicals) formed the Popular Front government. This government gave workers the right to **collective bargaining,** (the right of unions to negotiate with employers over wages and hours), a 40-hour workweek, a two-week paid vacation, and a minimum wage. But the Popular Front's policies were unable to solve the problems of the depression.

During the war, Great Britain had lost many of the markets for its products to the United States and Japan. This led to a rise in unemployment. From 1925 to 1929, however, Britain had a period of prosperity. After the Great Depression struck, the Labour Party was unable to solve the country's problems and fell from power in 1931. A new government, led by the Conservatives, took credit for bringing Britain out of the worst stages of the depression.

Most of the political leaders in Britain ignored the new ideas of a British economist, John Maynard Keynes. Keynes believed that unemployment came from a decline in demand, not from overproduction. He believed that the government should increase demand by putting people back to work building highways and public buildings. He believed that governments should finance these projects even if this meant **deficit spending** (going into debt).

After Germany, no nation was more affected by the Great Depression than the United States. By 1933, over 15 million people were unemployed. Under these circumstances, Franklin Delano Roosevelt was elected to the presidency in 1932. He introduced an economic policy called the New Deal. The New Deal included an increase in government-funded public works, including the Works Progress Administration (WPA). The WPA was a government organization that employed between 2 and 3 million people. WPA workers built bridges, roads, post offices, and airports. The Roosevelt administration also introduced new legislation that began the U.S. welfare system. In 1935, the Social Security Act created old-age pensions and unemployment insurance. However, the New Deal alone could not solve the unemployment problems of the Great Depression. In 1938, 11 million Americans were still unemployed.

8. What was the New Deal?

____

____

____

____

____

____

Name ______________________ Date ________________ Class ________________

Reading Essentials and Study Guide

Chapter 24, Section 2

For use with textbook pages 758–764

THE RISE OF DICTATORIAL REGIMES

KEY TERMS

totalitarian state a government that aims to control the political, economic, social, intellectual, and cultural lives of its citizens *(page 759)*

fascism a political philosophy that glorifies the state above the individual by emphasizing the need for a strong central government led by a dictatorial ruler *(page 759)*

New Economic Policy an economic policy in Russia under Lenin that was a modified version of the old capitalist system *(page 761)*

Politburo a seven-member committee that was the leading policy-making body of the Communist Party in the Soviet Union *(page 761)*

collectivization a system in which private farms are eliminated in favor of government ownership of the land *(page 763)*

DRAWING FROM EXPERIENCE

What do you think of when you hear the word "fascist"? Why do people follow fascist leaders?

In the last section, you read about economic problems in Europe and the United States following World War I. In this section, you will learn how dictators came to power in several countries during this period. The economic problems in these countries were a major factor in the rise of these dictatorships.

ORGANIZING YOUR THOUGHTS

Use the chart below to help you take notes. List the dictator who took control in each of these countries following World War I, and describe how each dictator came to power.

Country	Dictator	How He Came to Power
Italy	1.	2.
Soviet Union	3.	4.
Spain	5.	6.

READ TO LEARN

• The Rise of Dictators *(page 758)*

The apparent triumph of democracy in Europe in 1919 was extremely short-lived. Of the major European powers, only France and Great Britain were still democratic by 1939. Italy, the Soviet Union, Germany, and many other European countries adopted dictatorships. Some of these dictatorships were totalitarian states. A **totalitarian state** is a government that aims to control the political, economic, social, intellectual, and cultural lives of its citizens. These totalitarian states wanted to control the minds and the hearts of their citizens. This goal was achieved through the use of mass propaganda techniques and modern communications. A single leader and a single party led the totalitarian states. The result was government that was no longer interested in individual freedoms but in imposing the collective will of the masses on everyone. Of course, the will of the masses was determined and organized by the dictator.

7. What is a totalitarian state?

____

____

____

____

• Fascism in Italy *(page 759)*

In the early 1920s, Benito Mussolini established the first European Fascist movement in Italy. **Fascism** is a political philosophy that glorifies the state above the individual by emphasizing the need for a strong central government led by a dictator. The government controls people, and any opposition is suppressed.

Italy, like other European countries, experienced severe economic problems following World War I. Inflation grew, and there were strikes. Socialists spoke of revolution. The middle class was afraid of a Communist takeover. In 1919, Mussolini created a new political group, the *Fascio di Combattimento* (League of Combat). The term Fascist comes from this name. In 1920 and 1921, he formed bands of armed Fascists called *squadristi* (Blackshirts). They attacked socialist offices and newspapers. They also used violence to break up strikes. By 1922, Mussolini's movement was growing rapidly. The middle-class fear of socialism, communism, and disorder made the Fascists attractive to many people. Mussolini also knew that the Italian people were angry that Italy did not receive more land in the peace settlement after the war. He won thousands of supporters by demanding more land.

Name ______________________ Date ______________________ Class ______________________

In 1922, the Fascists threatened to march on Rome if they were not given power. The king of Italy, Victor Emmanuel III, gave in and made Mussolini prime minister. Mussolini used his position to create a Fascist dictatorship. The prime minister was made head of the government, with the power to make laws by decree. The police were given unlimited power to arrest and jail people. In 1926, the Fascists outlawed all other political parties in Italy. Mussolini ruled Italy as *Il Duce,* "The Leader."

Mussolini used various means to control the Italian people. He created a secret police, known as the OVRA. He also used the mass media to spread propaganda. The Fascists used organizations to promote fascism and to control the people. For example, youth groups were formed that focused on military activities and values. The Fascists hoped to create a nation of new Italians who were fit, disciplined, and war-loving.

However, the Fascists did not completely destroy the country's old power structure. The military was able to keep most of its independence. Victor Emmanuel was retained as king. The Catholic Church was allowed to keep its territory in Rome, known as Vatican City. Mussolini also gave the Church a large grant of money and recognized Catholicism as the "sole religion of the state." In return, the Catholic Church recognized the Italian state and encouraged Italians to support the Fascist regime.

8. What is fascism?

____

____

____

____

• A New Era in the Soviet Union *(page 761)*

During the civil war in Russia, Lenin followed a policy of war communism. The government controlled most industries and took grain from peasants in order to feed the army. When the war was over, peasants began to sabotage the program by hoarding food. The situation became even worse when a great famine hit Russia between 1920 and 1922. Five million people died. Industrial collapse followed the famine.

In March 1921, Lenin gave up the policy of war communism. He began a program known as the **New Economic Policy** (NEP). It was a modified version of the old capitalist system. Peasants were allowed to sell their produce openly. Small businesses could be privately owned and operated. The NEP saved the country from economic disaster. In 1922, Lenin and the Communists formally created a new state called the Union of Soviet Socialist Republics (also known as the USSR or the Soviet Union.)

When Lenin died in 1924, there was a struggle for power within the Politburo. The **Politburo** was a seven-member committee that had become the leading policy-making body of the Communist Party. One group in the Politburo wanted to end the NEP and begin a program of rapid industrialization. Leon Trotsky led this group. This group also wanted to spread communism to other nations around the world. Another group wanted to continue the NEP and to focus on building a socialist state in Russia. This group believed that rapid industrialization would hurt the peasants.

At the same time, there was a personal rivalry in the Politburo between Trotsky and another Politburo member, Joseph Stalin. Stalin was the party general secretary and appointed regional and local party officials. He used this influential position to gain control of the Communist Party. Because he had appointed thousands of officials within the party, he had a great deal of support. By 1929, Stalin was able to establish a powerful dictatorship. Trotsky was expelled from the party and eventually murdered.

The Stalinist Era was a period of economic, social and political changes that were even more revolutionary than the revolutions of 1917. Stalin ended the NEP in 1928 and began his first Five-Year Plan. The Five-Year Plans set economic goals for five-year periods. Their purpose was to transform Russia from an agricultural country into an industrial country. The First Five-Year Plan emphasized the production of capital equipment (heavy machines that produce other goods) and weapons. This plan resulted in dramatic increases in the production of steel and oil. But the Russian people paid a terrible price for industrialization. The number of workers in the cities increased by millions, but housing actually declined. As a result, millions of people lived in pitiful conditions. Wages also declined by 43 percent between 1928 and 1940. The government also began to collectivize farms. **Collectivization** was a system in which private farms were eliminated. Instead, the government owned all of the land while the peasants worked it. By 1934, 26 million family farms had been collectivized into 250,000 units. Like industrialization, collectivization had a terrible cost. Peasants responded by hoarding food and killing livestock. This produced a widespread famine. 10 million peasants died in famines in 1932 and 1933.

Stalin's programs had other costs. Stalin's desire to make all decisions by himself led to purges (removals) of the Old Bolsheviks (people who had been involved in the early days of the revolution). Stalin also purged army officials, diplomats, union officials, party members, intellectuals, and many ordinary citizens. Eight million Russians were arrested. Millions were sent to labor camps in Siberia. Others were executed.

9. What economic changes were made during the Stalinist Era?

____

____

____

____

• Authoritarian States in the West *(page 763)*

A number of governments in the Western world were not totalitarian but were authoritarian. They had some features in common with totalitarian states, such as using police powers. But these governments did not try to create a new kind of mass society. Their main concern was preserving the old social order.

Some of these governments were in Eastern Europe. Austria, Poland, Czechoslovakia, Yugoslavia, Romania, Bulgaria, and Hungary all adopted parliamentary systems after the war. But authoritarian governments soon replaced most of these systems. Only Czechoslovakia maintained its democracy. Parliamentary systems failed for several reasons. First, these countries did not have a tradition of democracy. They were mostly rural, and many of the peasants were illiterate. Ethnic conflicts also caused problems. Powerful landowners, the churches, and even some members of the middle class were afraid of land reform, communism, and ethnic conflict. These groups supported authoritarian governments that maintained the old system.

In Spain, democracy also failed to survive. General Francisco Franco led a revolt against the democratic government in 1936. A bloody civil war began. Germany and Italy aided Franco's forces with weapons, money, and men. The Spanish republican government was aided by thousands of foreign volunteers and by trucks, planes, tanks, and advisers from the Soviet Union. The Spanish Civil War ended when Franco's forces took Madrid in 1939. Franco established a dictatorship that favored large landowners, businesspeople, and the Catholic clergy. Because it favored traditional groups and did not try to control every aspect of people's lives, his dictatorship was authoritarian, not totalitarian.

10. Why did parliamentary systems fail in many Eastern European countries?

____

____

____

____

Name ______________________ Date ______________________ Class ______________________

Reading Essentials and Study Guide

Chapter 24, Section 3

For use with textbook pages 766–771

HITLER AND NAZI GERMANY

KEY TERMS

Reichstag the German parliament *(page 767)*

concentration camp large prison camps in which members of minority groups and political dissidents are confined *(page 768)*

DRAWING FROM EXPERIENCE

Have you ever read *The Diary of Anne Frank?* What does Anne Frank describe in her diary?

In the last section, you read about the rise of dictatorial regimes in several countries in Europe. In this section, you will read about the rise of Hitler and the Nazi party in Germany.

ORGANIZING YOUR THOUGHTS

Use the chart below to help you take notes. Summarize the policies and activities of Hitler and the Nazi Party as they relate to the subjects or groups in this chart.

Nazi Policies and Activities	
Terror	**1.**
Economy	**2.**
Spectacles/organizations	**3.**
Women	**4.**
Jews	**5.**

Reading Essentials and Study Guide

READ TO LEARN

• Hitler and His Views *(page 766)*

Adolf Hitler was born in Austria in 1889. He moved to Vienna to become an artist but was rejected by the Vienna Academy of Fine Arts. While in Vienna, however, he developed his basic ideas. Racism was at the center of Hitler's ideas. Hitler was also an extreme nationalist. He believed in the need for struggle and understood how political parties could use propaganda and terror. In 1919, he joined the German Worker's Party, a right-wing extreme nationalist party in Munich. By the summer of 1921, Hitler had taken total control of the party. He renamed it the National Socialist German Workers' Party (NSDAP) or Nazi for short.

In 1923, he organized an armed uprising against the government in Munich. This uprising, called the Beer Hall Putsch, was crushed, and Hitler was put in prison. During his time in prison, Hitler wrote *Mein Kampf (My Struggle),* a book about his movement and its basic ideas. In *Mein Kampf,* extreme German nationalism, strong anti-Semitism, and anticommunism are combined with a theory of struggle. Hitler's theory emphasized the right of superior nations to gain *Lebensraum* (living space) through expansion. It also emphasized the right of superior individuals to gain authoritarian leadership over the masses.

6. What were some of the ideas expressed by Hitler in *Mein Kampf?*

____

____

____

____

____

• Rise of Nazism *(page 767)*

Hitler decided that the Nazis would have to gain power by legal means, not by a violent overthrow of the government. This meant that the Nazi Party would have to become a mass political party that could compete for votes. After his release from prison, Hitler expanded the Nazi Party to all parts of Germany. By 1932, it had 800,000 members and was the largest party in the **Reichstag** (the German parliament).

Germany's economic problems were a crucial factor in the Nazi rise to power. Unemployment had risen to 6 million by the winter of 1932. The impact of the Great Depression made extremist parties more attractive. Hitler also promised to create a new Germany. His focus on national pride, national honor, and traditional militarism appealed to his listeners.

7. How did the Great Depression contribute to the rise of Nazism in Germany?

____

____

____

• Victory of Nazism *(page 768)*

The elites of Germany looked to Hitler for leadership. He had the mass support to create a right-wing, authoritarian government that would save Germany and people in privileged positions from a Communist takeover. In 1933, President Hindenburg agreed to allow Hitler to become chancellor and create a new government. On March 23, 1993, the Reichstag passed the Enabling Act. This law gave the government the power to ignore the constitution for four years while it issued laws to deal with the country's problems. It gave Hitler's actions a legal basis. He no longer needed the Reichstag or President Hindenburg. He became a dictator appointed by the Reichstag itself.

The Nazis worked quickly to bring all institutions under Nazi control. The civil service was purged of Jews and democratic elements. Large prison camps (called **concentration camps**) were set up for people who opposed the new government. Trade unions were dissolved. All political parties except for the Nazis were abolished. When Hindenburg died in 1934, the office of president was also abolished. Hitler became the sole ruler of Germany. Public officials and soldiers were required to take an oath of loyalty to Hitler as their *Führer* ("Leader").

8. What was the Enabling Act?

____

____

____

• The Nazi State, 1933–1939 *(page 769)*

Hitler wanted to develop an Aryan racial state that would dominate Europe and possibly the world for generations to come. Nazis thought that the Germans were the true descendants and leaders of the Aryans. (They misused the term Aryan to mean the ancient Greeks and Romans and twentieth-century Germans and Scandinavians.) They believed that they could create another empire like the ancient Roman Empire. They also believed that there had been two German empires or *Reichs* (the Holy Roman Empire and the German Empire of 1871 to 1918). It was Hitler's goal to create a Third Reich, the empire of Nazi Germany.

The Nazis used terror and repression to create their totalitarian state. The *Schutzstaffeln* ("Guard Squadrons"), also known simply as the SS, played an important role. It was originally created as Hitler's bodyguard. Under the direction of Heinrich Himmler, the SS came to control both the secret police forces and the regular police in Germany. Besides the police forces, it used concentration camps, execution squads, and death camps (concentration camps where prisoners were killed).

To end the depression, Hitler created public works projects and gave money to construction firms to put people back to work. But it was a huge rearmament program that finally solved the unemployment problem. By 1937, less than 500,000 people were unemployed. The Nazis' part in bringing an end to the depression was an important reason that many Germans accepted Hitler and the Nazis. Demonstrations and spectacles were also used to make the German people accept Hitler's policies. These events created mass enthusiasm and excitement. Churches, schools, and universities were also brought under the control of the Nazis. Youth organizations were created that taught Nazi ideals.

Women were considered important in the Aryan state because they bore children. The Nazis believed that men were meant to be warriors and political leaders, while women were meant to be wives and mothers. These ideas determined employment opportunities for women. Jobs in heavy industry, university teaching, medicine, and law were considered unsuitable for women. The Nazis encouraged women to pursue other occupations, such as social work and nursing, or not to work at all.

The Nazi party reflected Hitler's anti-Semitic beliefs. In September 1935, the Nazis announced new racial laws at the annual party rally in Nuremburg. These "Nuremburg Laws" excluded Jews from German citizenship and forbade marriages between Jews and German citizens. Jews were also required to wear yellow Stars of David and to carry identification cards saying they were Jewish. A more violent phase of anti-Semitism began on the night of November 9, 1938—the *Kristallnacht* ("night of shattered glass"). Nazis burned synagogues and destroyed seven thousand Jewish businesses. Thirty thousand Jewish men were rounded up and sent to concentration camps. At least a hundred Jews were killed. After *Kristallnacht,* Jews were barred from all public transportation and public buildings, such as schools and hospitals. They were not allowed to own, manage, or work in any retail store. Jews were also encouraged to emigrate from Germany.

9. What did the Nazis mean when they used the term *Aryan?*

____

____

____

Name ______________________ Date ______________________ Class ______________________

Reading Essentials and Study Guide

Chapter 24, Section 4

For use with textbook pages 772–775

CULTURAL AND INTELLECTUAL TRENDS

KEY TERMS

photomontage a picture made of a combination of photographs *(page 774)*

surrealism an artistic movement that sought a reality beyond the material world and found it in the world of the unconscious *(page 774)*

uncertainty principle a theory of the German physicist Werner Heisenberg that suggests that all physical laws are based on uncertainty *(page 775)*

DRAWING FROM EXPERIENCE

What do you like to do with your free time? Do you go to movies and sporting events? Or do you spend most of your free time at home?

In the last three sections, you learned about economic problems and political developments in Western countries after the end of World War I. In this section, you will learn about cultural and intellectual developments during this time. New work patterns after World War I provided people with more free time to pursue leisure activities.

ORGANIZING YOUR THOUGHTS

Use the diagram below to help you take notes. The years following World War I were characterized by political, economic, and social uncertainty. Describe how this uncertainty was reflected in art, literature, and science.

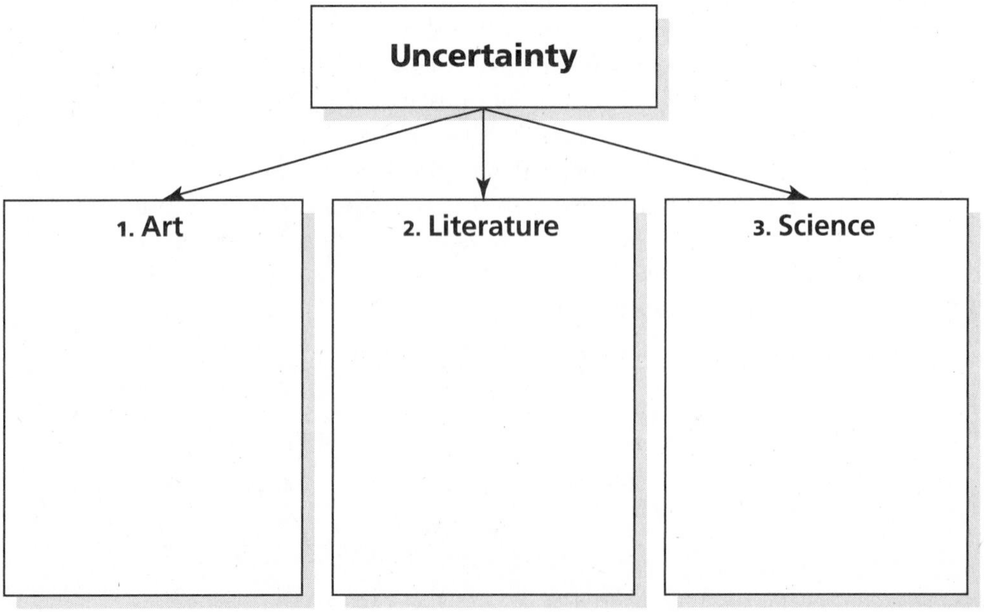

Reading Essentials and Study Guide

READ TO LEARN

• Mass Culture: Radio and Movies *(page 772)*

A series of inventions in the late nineteenth century led to a revolution in mass communications. After Marconi's discovery of wireless radio waves, broadcasting facilities were built in the United States, Europe, and Japan in 1921 and 1922. Mass production of radios also began. Although motion pictures had first appeared in the 1890s, full-length feature films did not appear until shortly after World War I. By 1939, about 40 percent of adults in the more industrialized countries were attending a movie once a week.

Radio and the movies were used for political purposes. Radio enabled leaders, like Hitler, to get their messages to the masses. The Nazi regime encouraged manufacturers to produce inexpensive radios that could be bought on an installment plan. Movies also had propaganda potential. Joseph Goebbels, the propaganda minister of Nazi Germany, created a special film division in his Propaganda Ministry. It supported the making of both documentaries (nonfiction films) and popular feature films that carried the Nazi message.

4. How were radio and the movies used for political purposes in Nazi Germany?

____

____

____

____

• Mass Leisure *(page 773)*

By 1920, the eight-hour workday had become the norm for many office and factory workers in Europe. This gave people more free time for leisure activities. Leisure activities included professional sporting events and travel. Trains, buses, and cars made trips to the beach or holiday resorts popular and affordable. Mass leisure also offered new ways for totalitarian states to control the people. The Nazis adopted a program called *Kraft durch Freude* ("Strength through Joy"). The program offered its own leisure activities, including concerts, operas, films, guided tours, and sporting events. The program's inexpensive vacations were especially popular.

5. How did the Nazis use leisure activities to control people?

____

____

____

____

• Artistic and Literary Trends *(page 774)*

World War I had left many Europeans with a sense of despair. To many people, the war meant that something was terribly wrong with Western values and that human beings were violent animals. The Great Depression and the growth of fascist movements added to the despair and uncertainty. This uncertainty was reflected in the artistic and intellectual achievements following World War I. Abstract expressionism became even more popular. There was a fascination with the absurd and the unconscious. The idea that the world did not make sense gave rise to two movements, Dadaism and surrealism. Dadaists were artists who were obsessed with the idea that life has no purpose. They tried to express the insanity of life in their art. Dada artist Hannah Höch, for example, used **photomontage** (a picture made of a combination of photographs) to comment on women's roles in the new mass culture. Another movement, **surrealism,** sought a reality beyond the material world and found it in the world of the unconscious. Surrealists portrayed fantasies, dreams, and even nightmares to show this greater reality. Salvador Dalí was one of the foremost surrealists. He painted everyday objects but separated them from their normal contexts. By placing recognizable objects in unrecognizable relationships, Dalí created a strange world in which the irrational became visible.

In the 1920s, Weimar Germany was one of the chief European centers for modern arts and sciences. Hitler and the Nazis, however, rejected modern art as "degenerate." They believed that they could create a new and genuine German art. It would glorify the strong, the healthy, and the heroic. The new German art was actually derived from nineteenth-century folk art and emphasized realistic scenes of everyday life.

The interest in the unconscious was also found in new literary techniques. "Stream of consciousness" was a technique used by writers to show the thoughts of each character. The most famous example of this technique is the novel *Ulysses* by James Joyce. The German writer Hermann Hesse dealt with the unconscious in a different way. His novels reflect the influence of both Freud's psychology and Asian religions. In *Siddhartha* and *Steppenwolf,* Hesse used Buddhist ideas to show the psychological confusion of modern existence.

6. What did Hitler and the Nazis think about modern art?

____

____

____

____

____

• The Heroic Age of Physics *(page 775)*

The revolution in physics begun by Albert Einstein continued after World War I. One physicist, Ernest Rutherford, called the 1920s the "heroic age of physics." Newton's physics had made people believe that all phenomena could be defined and predicted. In 1927, this belief was shaken when the German physicist Werner Heisenberg explained an observation that he called the **uncertainty principle.** This theory suggests that all physical laws are based on uncertainty. The foundation for the uncertainty principle is the fact that the behavior of subatomic particles is unpredictable. The theory's emphasis on randomness and uncertainty challenged Newtonian physics and represented a new worldview.

7. What scientific fact was the foundation for the uncertainty principle?

____

____

____

____

____

Reading Essentials and Study Guide

Chapter 25, Section 1

For use with textbook pages 781–785

NATIONALISM IN THE MIDDLE EAST

KEY TERMS

genocide the deliberate mass murder of a particular racial, political, or cultural group *(page 782)*

ethnic cleansing another term for genocide, used during the Bosnian War of 1993 to 1996 *(page 782)*

DRAWING FROM EXPERIENCE

What do you think of when you hear the words "genocide" and "ethnic cleansing"? Has genocide been practiced anywhere during your lifetime? In what parts of the world?

In this section, you will learn how the decline and fall of the Ottoman Empire led to the creation of the Turkish Republic. You will also learn how Persia became the modern state of Iran and how changes in the Middle East after World War I led to conflicts in that region that continue today.

ORGANIZING YOUR THOUGHTS

Use the diagram below to help you take notes. Trace the loss of territories that gradually reduced the Ottoman Empire to the area of present-day Turkey.

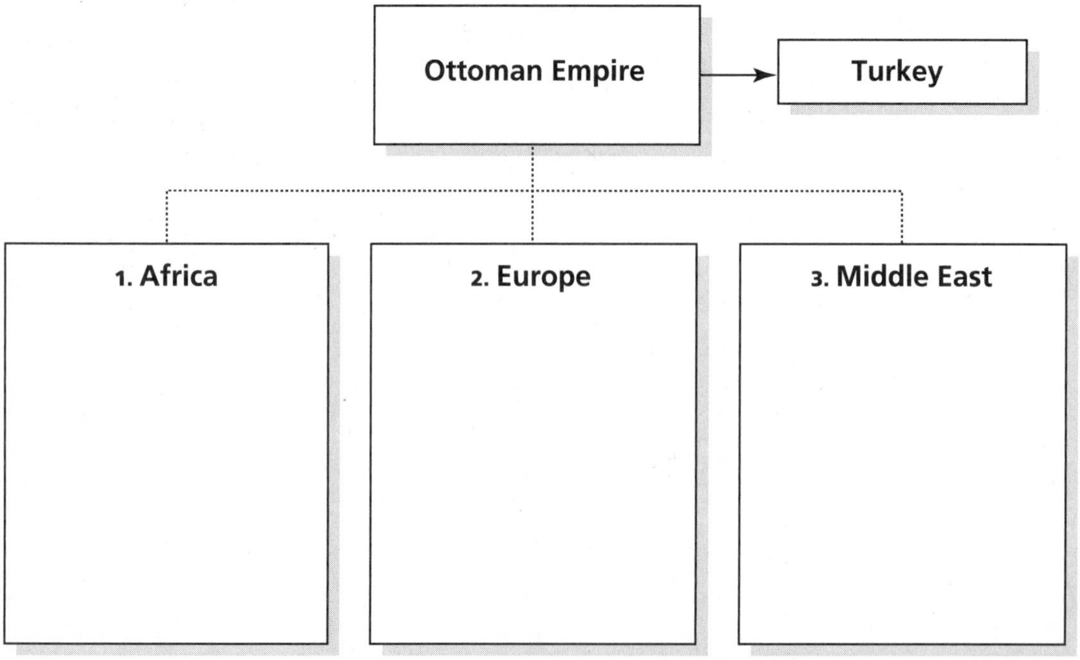

READ TO LEARN

• Decline and Fall of the Ottoman Empire *(page 781)*

The Ottoman Empire had been growing weaker since the end of the eighteenth century. Its size had decreased dramatically. In North Africa, Ottoman rule had ended in the nineteenth century when France seized Algeria and Tunisia and Great Britain took control of Egypt. Greece also declared its independence in the nineteenth century.

In 1876, reformers took control of the empire's government. They adopted a constitution with the goal of forming a legislative assembly. But the sultan they put on the throne, Abdulhamid II, suspended the new constitution. The constitution became a symbol of change to a group of reformers named the Young Turks. This group forced the restoration of the constitution in 1908. They deposed the sultan in 1909.

The Ottoman Empire came to an end during World War I. The Ottoman government allied with Germany. As a result, the British tried to undermine the Ottoman Empire by supporting Arab nationalists in the Arabian Peninsula. In 1916, the local governor of Makkah declared Arabia's independence. British troops seized Palestine.

During the war, the Ottoman Turks practiced **genocide**—the deliberate mass murder of a particular racial, political, or cultural group. (A similar practice would be called **ethnic cleansing** in the Bosnian War of 1993 to 1996.) The Christian Armenians were a minority in the Ottoman Empire. They had been demanding their independence for years. In 1915, the government reacted to an Armenian uprising by killing Armenian men and deporting (sending out of the country) women and children. By 1918, 1.4 million Armenians had been killed.

At the end of World War I, the Ottoman Empire collapsed. Great Britain and France divided up territories in the Middle East. Greece invaded Turkey and seized western parts of the Anatolian Peninsula. As a result of this invasion, Colonel Mustafa Kemal called for the creation of an elected government. His forces drove the Greeks from the Anatolian Peninsula. The Ottoman sultans fled the country, which was now declared to be the Turkish Republic. Colonel Kemal became president.

4. Why did the British support Arab nationalists during World War I?

____

____

____

____

• The Modernization of Turkey *(page 783)*

President Kemal was now known as Atatürk ("father Turk"). A democratic system was put in place. But Kemal did not allow opposition and suppressed his critics. He tried to transform Turkey into a modern state. Popular education was introduced. All Turkish citizens were forced to adopt family (last names), like Europeans. Factories were built, and a five-year plan was developed for the economy.

Atatürk also tried to break the power of the Islamic religion. He wanted to make Turkey a secular state (a state that rejects religious influence on its politics). The caliphate was abolished in 1924. Men were forbidden to wear the fez, the cap worn by Turkish Muslims. Women were forbidden to wear the veil, an Islamic custom. New laws gave women marriage and inheritance rights. In 1934, women received the right to vote. All citizens were given the right to convert to other religions.

5. In what ways did Atatürk try to break the power of Islam in Turkey?

____

____

____

____

____

• The Beginnings of Modern Iran *(page 784)*

In Persia, the Qajar dynasty (1794–1925) had not been very successful in resolving the country's problems. The discovery of oil in the country in 1908 attracted foreign interest. The presence of more and more foreigners led to the rise of a Persian nationalist movement. In 1921, Reza Khan led a military uprising that took control of Tehran, the capital. In 1925, Reza Khan made himself the shah (king) and was called Reza Shah Pahlavi. He introduced a number of reforms to modernize the government, the military, and the economic system. He did not try to destroy Islamic beliefs, but he did encourage a Western-style educational system. He also forbade women to wear the veil in public.

Persia became the modern state of Iran in 1935. To free himself from Great Britain and the Soviet Union, Reza Shah Pahlavi drew closer to Nazi Germany. The Soviet Union and Great Britain sent troops to Iran during World War II. Reza Shah Pahlavi resigned in protest and was replaced by his son, Mohammad Reza Pahlavi.

Name ______________________ Date ______________ Class ______________

6. What were some of the changes that Reza Shah Pahlavi made in Persia?

____

____

____

____

____

• Arab Nationalism *(page 784)*

World War I gave Arabs the chance to escape from Ottoman rule. The Arabs were not an actual nation, but a collection of peoples united by language and religion. Great Britain had supported Arab nationalists in 1916. The nationalists hoped that this support would continue after the war. Instead, France and Britain created mandates in the area. These mandates were territories that had previously been part of the Ottoman Empire but were now supervised by the League of Nations. Great Britain was given the right to govern Iraq and Jordan. France governed Syria and Lebanon. In most of these nations, the Europeans determined the borders and divided the peoples. In most cases, the people in each country did not identify strongly with their country. But they continued to have a sense of Arab nationalism.

In the early 1920s, a reform leader, Ibn Saud, united Arabs in the northern part of the Arabian Peninsula. Ibn Saud had a great deal of support among Arab peoples. He created the kingdom of Saudi Arabia in 1932. (The word Saudi comes from his name.) At first, Saudi Arabia was very poor. Muslim pilgrimages to Makkah and Madinah were its main source of income. During the 1930s, however, U.S. prospectors began to explore for oil. Standard Oil found oil at Dhahran on the Persian Gulf in 1938. Saudi Arabia was flooded with Western oil industries that brought the promise of wealth.

7. Who determined the borders of most of the nations in the Middle East following World War I?

____

____

____

____

____

Name ______________________ Date ____________________ Class ____________________

• The Problem of Palestine *(page 785)*

The situation in Palestine made the Middle East even more complicated. Palestine had been the home of the Jews in ancient times, but few had lived there for almost two thousand years. Palestine was mainly inhabited by Muslims. In 1917, in the Balfour Declaration, Britain supported the idea of making Palestine a national home for the Jews. This made Arab nationalists angry. They questioned how a national home for the Jews could be created in a territory that was 98 percent Muslim.

The promises of the Balfour Declaration drew Jewish settlers to Palestine. During the 1930s, tensions between the Jews and Muslims increased. At the same time, persecution of Jews in Nazi Germany caused many European Jews to flee to Palestine. By 1939, there were about 450,000 Jews in Palestine. Because of Arab protests, the British decided in 1939 that only 75,000 Jewish immigrants would be allowed into Palestine over the next five years. After that, no more Jews could enter the country. This decision would produce severe conflicts in the region.

8. What was the Balfour Declaration? What were some of its results?

____

____

____

____

____

Name ______________________ Date ______________________ Class ______________________

Reading Essentials and Study Guide

Chapter 25, Section 2

For use with textbook pages 786–791

NATIONALISM IN AFRICA AND ASIA

KEY TERMS

Pan-Africanism a movement that stressed the need for the unity of all Africans *(page 788)*

Mahatma ("Great Soul") the name given to Mohandas Gandhi by the Indian people *(page 788)*

civil disobedience refusal to obey laws considered to be unjust *(page 788)*

zaibatsu a large financial and industrial corporation in Japan *(page 789)*

DRAWING FROM EXPERIENCE

Have you ever thought that a rule was unfair? How could you protest this rule in a nonviolent way?

In the last section, you read about the end of the Ottoman Empire and the rise of nationalism in the Middle East. In this section, you will read about nationalism in Africa and Asia. In India, the followers of Mahatma Gandhi used the methods of civil disobedience to protest British laws.

ORGANIZING YOUR THOUGHTS

Use the chart below to help you take notes. Leaders of reform and independence movements in parts of Africa and Asia used various methods to protest colonial rule. Identify the countries of the following leaders and summarize the methods that they used.

Leader	Country	Methods of Protest
Harry Thuku	**1.**	**2.**
Omar Mukhtar	**3.**	**4.**
Nnamdi Azikiwe	**5.**	**6.**
Mohandas Gandhi	**7.**	**8.**
Ho Chi Minh	**9.**	**10.**

READ TO LEARN

- **Movements Toward Independence in Africa** *(page 786)*

Black Africans fought in World War I in British and French armies. Many Africans hoped that they would be rewarded with independence after the war. But the peace settlement after World War I was a big disappointment. Germany lost its African colonies, but they were given to Great Britain and France as mandates. Britain and France now controlled much of Africa.

After World War I, Africans became more active in politics. The Africans who had fought in the war had learned new ideas about freedom and nationalism. Many Africans decided to seek reforms. In Kenya, Harry Thuku organized the Young Kikuyu Association. In 1921, it protested the high taxes imposed by the British. Thuku was arrested. When an angry crowd demanded his release, government forces fired on the crowd and killed 50 people. In Libya, forces led by Omar Mukhtar used guerrilla warfare against the Italians and defeated them several times. The Italians reacted by creating concentration camps and using modern weapons against the revolt. Mukhtar's death ended the revolt. Although the colonial powers often used force against independence movements, they also began to make some reforms. But the reforms were too few and too late. By the 1930s, more and more African leaders were calling for independence, not reform.

Many of the new African leaders had been educated in Europe and the United States. They were influenced by the ideas of W.E.B. Du Bois and Marcus Garvey. Du Bois was an African American educated at Harvard University. He was the leader of a movement that tried to make all Africans aware of their cultural heritage. Garvey was a Jamaican who lived in Harlem. He stressed the need for the unity of all Africans, a movement known as **Pan-Africanism**. His *Declaration of the Rights of the Negro Peoples of the World* had a strong impact on African leaders. Jomo Kenyatta of Kenya wrote a book, *Facing Mount Kenya,* in which he argued that British rule was destroying the traditional culture of African peoples. Léopold Senghor, a poet, organized an independence movement in Senegal. Nnamdi Azikiwe of Nigeria began a newspaper, *The West African Pilot.* He believed in nonviolence as a method to gain independence. Despite the efforts of these leaders, the independence movements in Africa were not successful until after World War II.

11. How did an African American and a Jamaican in the United States influence many of the new African leaders in the 1920s and 1930s?

____

____

____

• The Movement for Indian Independence *(page 788)*

Mohandas Gandhi had become active in the movement for Indian self-rule before World War I. The Indian people began to call him India's "Great Soul," or **Mahatma.** He began to organize mass protests to achieve his goals. He believed in nonviolence and protested British laws by using the methods of **civil disobedience** (refusal to obey laws considered to be unjust). In 1919, the protests led to violence. In response, British troops killed hundreds of protesters. Gandhi was arrested for his role in the protests and spent several years in prison.

In 1935, Great Britain passed the Government of India Act. It gave Indians a greater role in the governing process. The Legislative Council became a two-house parliament. Two-thirds of its members were to be elected. Five million Indians were given the right to vote, although this was still only a small percentage of the total population.

The Indian National Congress (INC) had been founded in 1885 to try to reform Britain's government of India. Reforms were no longer enough for many of the members of the INC. Motilal Nehru, the new leader of the INC, pushed for full independence.

Gandhi was released from prison and returned to his policy of civil disobedience. Nonviolence was still at the center of his policy. Gandhi led a protest against the British salt tax. Britain had increased the tax and prohibited the Indian people from manufacturing or harvesting their own salt. In 1930, Gandhi and his supporters walked to the sea. This became known as the Salt March. When they reached the coast, Gandhi picked up a pinch of salt. Thousands of Indians did the same thing. Gandhi and many other members of the INC were arrested.

In the 1930s, there was a new leader in the Indian independence movement. Jawaharlal Nehru, the son of Motilal Nehru, was a new kind of Indian politician. He was upper class and intellectual. He had studied law in Great Britain. The independence movement now split into two paths. Gandhi's movement was religious and traditional. Nehru's movement was secular and modern. Hostility between Muslims and Hindus complicated the situation in India even further. Muslims were dissatisfied with the INC because Hindus dominated it. In 1930, the Muslim League called for the creation of a separate Muslim state, called Pakistan, in the northwest part of the country. Conflict between Muslims and Hindus grew.

12. In what ways were Gandhi's and Nehru's independence movements different?

____

____

____

• The Rise of a Militarist Japan *(page 789)*

The economic and social reforms of the Meiji Era had made Japan prosperous. A modern industrial and commercial sector had developed. In the Japanese economy, various manufacturing processes were concentrated within large financial and industrial corporations called ***zaibatsu.*** The *zaibatsu* often received government help and developed into vast companies that controlled major segments of the Japanese economy. The concentration of wealth led to economic inequalities. City workers were poorly paid and had poor housing. A rapid increase in population led to food shortages. Inflation in food prices led to food riots. When the Great Depression struck, workers and farmers suffered the most. Many Japanese people began to call for a return to traditional values. They also demanded that Japan use its strength to dominate Asia.

In the early twentieth century, Japan began to have difficulty finding sources of raw materials and foreign markets for its manufactured goods. Japan had dealt with the problem by seizing territories, such as Formosa, Korea, and southern Manchuria. The United States was concerned about Japanese expansion. In 1922, the U.S. held a conference of nations that had interests in the Pacific. The conference produced a treaty that maintained the Open Door policy in China and recognized the territorial boundaries of China. Japan accepted the treaty in return for recognition of its control of southern Manchuria. However, as the Japanese expanded into new industries, the Japanese government came under increasing pressure to find new sources of raw materials.

During the first part of the twentieth century, Japan moved toward a more democratic government. The parliament and political parties grew stronger. However, at the end of the 1920s, new problems caused militant forces to become more powerful. Some of the militants were civilians who were convinced that the government had been corrupted by Western ideas. Others were members of the military who were angered by cuts in military spending and the government's pacifist policies. In the 1930s, civilians and members of the army and navy formed extremist patriotic organizations. One group of army officers invaded Manchuria in 1931, without government permission. Within a short time, all of Manchuria was conquered.

The Japanese government opposed the conquest of Manchuria, but the Japanese people supported it. The military and other supporters of Japanese expansion soon dominated the government. Japan was put on wartime status. A military draft was started in 1938. The economy came under government control. Labor unions were disbanded. Education and culture were purged of most Western ideas. Militant leaders stressed traditional Japanese values.

13. How did industrialization in Japan lead to the rise of militarism?

____

____

____

____

____

• Nationalism and Revolution in Asia *(page 791)*

Before World War I, Marxism had no appeal for most Asians. Most Asian societies were agricultural and did not seem ready for revolution. After the revolution in Russia, the situation began to change. The Russian Revolution showed that a Marxist revolution could work even in a country that was not fully industrialized. In 1919, the Communist International, or Comintern, was formed. It was a worldwide organization of Communist parties that worked for world revolution. At its headquarters in Moscow, agents were trained and then returned to their own countries to form Marxist parties and promote revolution. By the end of the 1920s, nearly every colonial society in Asia had a Communist party.

In some countries, the Communists were able to work with nationalists to fight Western imperialism. This was true in French Indochina, where Vietnamese Communists were organized by Ho Chi Minh, who had been trained in Moscow. A strong Communist-nationalist alliance was also formed in China. In most colonial societies, however, Communist parties had little success in the 1930s.

14. What was the Comintern?

____

____

____

____

____

Name ______________________ Date ______________________ Class ______________________

Reading Essentials and Study Guide

Chapter 25, Section 3

For use with textbook pages 793–797

REVOLUTIONARY CHAOS IN CHINA

KEY TERMS

guerrilla tactics military maneuvers based on the element of surprise *(page 795)*

redistribution of wealth the shifting of wealth from a rich minority to a poor majority *(page 797)*

DRAWING FROM EXPERIENCE

What do you know about China? What kind of government does it have? What is life like for the people living there? What is the main way of making a living in China?

In the last two sections, you read about nationalism in Africa, Asia, and the Middle East. In this section, you will read about the conflict between Nationalists and Communists for control of China.

ORGANIZING YOUR THOUGHTS

Use the chart below to help you take notes. Chiang Kai-shek established a Nationalist government over China in 1928. Summarize the programs and projects of Chiang Kai-shek as they relate to the areas in this chart.

Programs and Projects of Chiang Kai-shek	
Values	**1.**
Transportation	**2.**
Economy	**3.**
Education	**4.**
Government	**5.**

READ TO LEARN

• Nationalists and Communists *(page 793)*

In 1921, a group of young radicals founded the Chinese Communist Party (CCP) in Shanghai. Comintern agents advised the new party to join with the more experienced Nationalist Party. Sun Yat-sen, the leader of the Nationalist Party, welcomed the cooperation. In 1923, the two parties formed an alliance to oppose the warlords and drive the imperialist powers out of China. For three years, the two parties worked together. They trained a revolutionary army to march north and seize control of China. This Northern Expedition began in the summer of 1926. By the following spring, revolutionary forces had taken control of all of China south of the Chang Jiang (Yangtze River).

Tensions between the two parties eventually caused problems. Sun Yat-sen died in 1925 and was succeeded by Chiang Kai-shek as head of the Nationalist Party. Chiang pretended to support the alliance with the Communists. But in April 1927, he attacked the Communists in Shanghai. Thousands were killed in what is called the Shanghai Massacre. The Communist-Nationalist alliance came to an end. In 1928, Chiang Kai-shek founded a new Chinese republic at Nanjing. During the next three years, he worked to reunify China.

6. What two parties formed an alliance in 1923 to drive the imperialist powers out of China?

____

____

____

____

____

• The Communists in Hiding *(page 794)*

After the Shanghai Massacre, most of the Communist leaders went into hiding in Shanghai. Some party members fled to Jiangxi Province. The young Communist organizer Mao Zedong led them. Mao was convinced that peasants in the countryside instead of the urban working class would lead a Chinese revolution.

Chiang Kai-shek tried to force the Communists out of hiding in Shanghai. In 1931, most Communist party leaders were forced to flee to Mao's base in Jiangxi Province. Chiang then turned his forces against Mao's base. Chiang's forces far outnumbered Mao's, but Mao made effective use of **guerrilla tactics** (using unexpected maneuvers like sabotage and subterfuge to fight the enemy.)

7. How did Mao Zedong believe that a Chinese revolution would take place?

____

____

____

____

____

• The Long March *(page 795)*

In 1933, Chiang's troops surrounded the Communist base in Jiangxi. But Mao's army, the People's Liberation Army (PLA), broke through the Nationalist lines and began its famous Long March. Mao's army traveled almost 6,000 miles on foot through mountains, marshes, and deserts. One year later, they reached safety in North China. Only nine thousand of the original ninety thousand survived the journey. In the course of the Long March, Mao Zedong had become the sole leader of the Chinese Communist Party.

8. What was the Long March?

____

____

____

____

____

• The New China of Chiang Kai-shek *(page 796)*

In the meantime, Chiang Kai-shek had been trying to build a new nation. He was committed to the plans of Sun Yat-sen, which called for a republican government. First, there would be a transitional period. Chiang announced a period of political tutelage (training) to prepare the Chinese people for constitutional government. The Nationalists also tried to carry out a land-reform program and to modernize industry.

Creating a new China was not easy, however. Most of the people who lived in the countryside were drained by warfare. The peasants were still very poor, and most of them were illiterate. Chiang Kai-shek was aware of the problem of introducing foreign ideas into a conservative population. He tried to combine modern Western innovations with traditional Confucian values of hard work, obedience, and integrity. He set up a "New Life Movement." Its goal was to promote traditional Confucian ethics. It also rejected the individualism and material greed that was associated with Western capitalism.

Reading Essentials and Study Guide

Chiang Kai-shek had other problems. His government only had total control over a few provinces in the Chang Jiang Valley. The Japanese threatened to gain control of northern China. The Great Depression was also having a negative effect on China's economy. But Chiang did have some success. He undertook a huge road-building program and added to the country's railroad system. He also set up a national bank and improved the educational system. But he was less successful in other areas. His land-reform program had little effect. Because wealthy landowners and the urban middle class supported him, he did not push for programs that would lead to a **redistribution of wealth** (the shifting of wealth from a rich minority to a poor majority). His government was also repressive. Chiang was afraid of Communist influence and suppressed all opposition and censored free expression. As a result, he alienated many intellectuals and political moderates.

9. What was the New Life Movement? What were some of its goals?

____

____

____

____

____

Name ______________________ Date ______________________ Class ______________________

Reading Essentials and Study Guide

Chapter 25, Section 4

For use with textbook pages 799–803

NATIONALISM IN LATIN AMERICA

KEY TERM

oligarchy a government where a select group of people exercises control *(page 801)*

DRAWING FROM EXPERIENCE

What goods do you use that are imported from Mexico or another Latin American country? Do you eat food grown in these countries? Do you wear clothes made in one of these countries?

In the last three sections, you read about nationalism in Africa, Asia, and the Middle East. In this section, you will read about nationalism and the rise of dictatorships in Latin America during the early twentieth century. The Latin American economy at this time was based largely on the export of food and raw materials to the United States and other countries.

ORGANIZING YOUR THOUGHTS

Use the diagram below to help you take notes. Instability caused by the Great Depression led to the creation of many military dictatorships in Latin America in the 1930s. Describe the governments in Argentina, Brazil, and Mexico during the 1930s.

Country	Government in the 1930s
Argentina	**1.**
Brazil	**2.**
Mexico	**3.**

READ TO LEARN

• The Latin American Economy *(page 799)*

At the beginning of the twentieth century, the Latin American economy was based on the export of food and raw materials. The economies of some countries depended on the export of only one or two products. Argentina exported beef and wheat; Chile, nitrates and copper; Brazil and Caribbean nations, sugar; and Central America, bananas. Although a few people made big profits, most people gained little from these exports.

Beginning in the 1920s, the United States began to replace Great Britain as the biggest investor in Latin America. U.S. investors put their funds directly into production companies and ran the companies themselves. As a result, large segments of Latin America's export industries came into U.S. hands.

Latin Americans were angry that U.S. investors controlled so many Latin American industries. Many Latin Americans viewed the United States as an imperialist power. They pointed out that profits from U.S. businesses were sometimes used to keep ruthless dictators in power. The United States had intervened militarily in Latin America for years. This was especially true in Central America and the Caribbean. In 1935, however, President Franklin Roosevelt announced the Good Neighbor policy. This policy rejected the use of U.S. military force in Latin America. Roosevelt withdrew the last U.S. marines from Haiti in 1936.

The Great Depression was a disaster for Latin America's economy. There was a decreased demand for Latin American products and raw materials, especially coffee, sugar, metals, and wheat. The countries that depended on the export of only one product were especially damaged. There was one positive effect, however. With a decline in exports, Latin American countries no longer had the money to buy imported goods. Many Latin American governments encouraged the development of new industries to produce goods that had previously been imported. Governments often invested in the new industries. This led to government-run industries in Chile, Brazil, Argentina, and Mexico.

4. What were the effects of the Great Depression on Latin America's economy?

____

____

____

____

____

• The Move to Authoritarianism *(page 801)*

Most Latin American countries had republican forms of government. In reality, however, a small group of church officials, military leaders, and large landowners dominated each country. They were kept in power by military forces. Military leaders often took control of the government. This trend toward authoritarianism increased during the 1930s, mainly because of the impact of the Great Depression. The trend was especially evident in Argentina, Brazil, and Mexico.

Argentina was controlled by an **oligarchy** (a government where a select group of people exercises control). This oligarchy of large landowners had grown wealthy from the export of beef and wheat. It did not realize the growing importance of industry and cities. It also ignored the growing middle class. The middle class reacted by forming the Radical Party in 1890. In 1916, Hipólito Irigoyen, leader of the Radical Party, was elected president of Argentina. The Radical Party was afraid of the industrial workers, who used strikes to improve their conditions. As a result, it drew closer to the large landowners and became more corrupt. The military was also concerned about the power of the industrial workers. In 1930, the Argentine army overthrew President Irigoyen and put the large landowners back in power. During World War II, military officers formed a new organization, known as the Group of United Officers (GOU). They were unhappy with the government and overthrew it in June 1943. Three years later, Juan Perón, a GOU member, seized sole power of the country.

In Brazil, the army had overthrown the monarchy in 1889 and established a republic. The republic was controlled mainly by the large landowners, who had become wealthy by growing coffee. The Great Depression devastated the coffee industry, and the landowners were no longer able to remain in power. In 1930, a military coup made Getúlio Vargas, a wealthy rancher, president of Brazil. He ruled from 1930 to 1945. He tried to win the support of workers by establishing an eight-hour workday and a minimum wage. In 1937, Vargas made himself dictator. Beginning in 1938, he established his New State. It was an authoritarian state with some Fascist-like features. Political parties were outlawed and civil rights restricted. A secret police used torture against Vargas's enemies. Vargas also encouraged new industries. The government established the Brazilian steel industry and set up a company to explore for oil.

Mexico was not an authoritarian state, but it was not truly democratic. The official political party of the Mexican Revolution, known as the Institutional Revolutionary Party (PRI), controlled the major groups in Mexican society. Party bosses of the PRI chose the party's presidential candidate, who was then elected by the people. Change began when Lázaro Cárdenas became president in 1934. He distributed 44 million acres of land to Mexican peasants. He also took a strong stand with the United States, especially over oil. After a dispute over workers' wages, the Cárdenas government seized control of the oil fields and the property of the oil companies. The U.S. oil companies were furious and asked President Roosevelt to intervene. He refused, because of the Good Neighbor policy. Eventually, the Mexican government paid the oil companies for their property. It then set up PEMEX, a national oil company.

5. What were some of the changes that Cárdenas made after he became president of Mexico?

____

____

____

____

____

• Culture in Latin America *(page 803)*

During the early twentieth century, European artistic and literary movements began to have an impact on Latin America. In major cities, the wealthy were interested in the work of modern artists. Latin American artists went abroad and brought back modern techniques. Many artists and writers used their work to promote a new national spirit. The Mexican artist Diego Rivera is one example. He used murals. His works were aimed at the masses of people, many of whom could not read. He tried to create a national art that would show Mexico's past and its festivals and folk customs. His work also had a political and social message. Rivera did not want people to forget the Mexican Revolution, which had overthrown large landowners and foreign interests.

6. What were some of the goals that Diego Rivera tried to achieve with his art?

____

____

____

____

____

Name ______________________ Date ______________________ Class ______________________

Reading Essentials and Study Guide

Chapter 26, Section 1

For use with textbook pages 809–813

PATHS TO WAR

KEY TERMS

demilitarized an area that is free of weapons or fortifications *(page 810)*

appeasement a policy of giving in to the demands of a dissatisfied power in an attempt to keep the peace *(page 810)*

sanction a restriction intended to enforce international law *(page 813)*

DRAWING FROM EXPERIENCE

How do you resolve conflicts with other people? Do you ever give in to their demands in order to avoid conflict?

In this section, you will learn about the actions of Germany and Japan that paved the way for the start of World War II. In an attempt to avoid war, some European countries initially gave in to Hitler's demands to occupy other territories.

ORGANIZING YOUR THOUGHTS

Use the time line below to help you take notes. From 1936 to 1939, Hitler became more and more aggressive and invaded more and more territories. Trace Hitler's acts of aggression during these years.

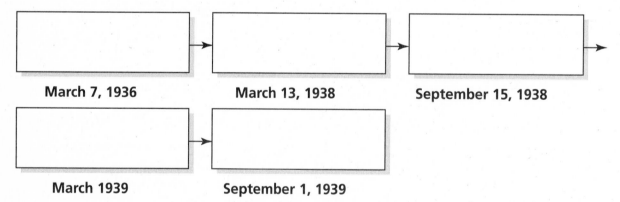

March 7, 1936 → **March 13, 1938** → **September 15, 1938** → **March 1939** → **September 1, 1939**

Reading Essentials and Study Guide

READ TO LEARN

• The German Path to War *(page 809)*

World War II had its roots in the beliefs of Adolf Hitler. He believed that Aryans were superior to other races. He believed that Germans, in particular, were superior to other people and could create a great civilization. He also believed that Germany needed more land in order to become a great power.

After World War I, the Treaty of Versailles had limited Germany's military power. At first, Hitler said that Germany wanted to revise the unfair provisions of the treaty by peaceful means. However, on March 9, 1935, Hitler announced the creation of a new air force. One week later, he began a military draft. Hitler was convinced that the Western states had no intention of using force to maintain the Treaty of Versailles. On March 7, 1936, he sent German troops into the Rhineland. The Rhineland was part of Germany, but it was a **demilitarized** area. According to the Treaty of Versailles, Germany was not permitted to have weapons or fortifications there. France had the right to use force against any violation of the demilitarized area but would not act without British support. Great Britain did not support the use of force against Germany. Great Britain began to practice a policy of **appeasement.** This policy was based on the belief that if European states satisfied the reasonable demands of dissatisfied powers, the dissatisfied powers would be content, and peace would be maintained.

Meanwhile, Hitler gained new allies. Fascist Italy invaded Ethiopia in October 1936. France and Britain were opposed to this invasion. This made Mussolini angry, and he welcomed Hitler's support. In 1936, Mussolini and Hitler made an agreement that recognized their common political and economic interests. This new alliance was known as the Rome-Berlin Axis. Germany and Japan signed the Anti-Comintern Pact, in which they promised to maintain a common front against communism.

By 1937, Hitler decided to pursue one of his goals: union with Austria, his native land. He threatened Austria with invasion. This forced the Austrian chancellor to put Austrian Nazis in charge of the government. The new government invited German troops to enter Austria. On March 13, 1938, Hitler annexed Austria to Germany.

Hitler's next goal was the destruction of Czechoslovakia. On September 15, 1938, he demanded that Germany be given the Sudetenland, an area in northwestern Czechoslovakia. Most of the people who lived in this area were Germans. Hitler said that he was willing to risk "world war" to achieve his objective. At a conference in Munich, Britain, France, Germany, and Italy reached an agreement that gave Hitler nearly all of his demands. German troops were allowed to occupy the Sudetenland. The Czechs stood by helplessly. Neville Chamberlain, the British prime minister, boasted that the agreement meant "peace for our time." Hitler had promised Chamberlain that he would make no more demands. Like many others, Chamberlain believed Hitler's promises. In fact, Hitler was more convinced than ever that the Western democracies were weak and would not fight. In March 1939, Hitler invaded and took control of Bohemia and Moravia in western Czechoslovakia.

At last, the Western nations reacted to the Nazi threat. Hitler's aggression had made clear that his promises were worthless. When Hitler began to demand the Polish port of Danzig, Great Britain offered to protect Poland in the event of war. At the same time, both France and Britain realized that they needed the Soviet Union in order to stop Nazi aggression. They began negotiations with Joseph Stalin, the Soviet dictator. Hitler was afraid that the West and the Soviet Union might make an alliance. To keep this from happening, Hitler made his own agreement with Joseph Stalin. On August 23, 1939, Germany and the Soviet Union signed the Nazi-Soviet Nonaggression Pact. In it, the two nations promised not to attack each other. To get Stalin to sign the pact, Hitler offered Stalin control of eastern Poland and the Baltic states. On September 1, 1939, German forces invaded Poland. Two days later, Britain and France declared war on Germany.

6. Why did Great Britain give in to so many of Hitler's demands?

____

____

____

____

____

• The Japanese Path to War *(page 812)*

By the mid-1930s, militants had gained control of Japanese politics. In September 1931, Japanese soldiers had seized Manchuria, because Manchuria had natural resources that Japan needed. As an excuse for seizing Manchuria, Japan pointed to a Chinese attack on a Japanese railway near the city of Mukden. In fact, Japanese soldiers disguised as Chinese had carried out the "Mukden incident." Worldwide protests led the League of Nations to send investigators to Manchuria. When the investigators issued a report condemning the seizure, Japan withdrew from the League. Over the next several years, Japan strengthened its hold on Manchuria. Japan now began to expand into North China.

Because of the threat from Communists within China, Chiang Kai-shek tried to avoid conflict with Japan. He tried to appease Japan by allowing it to govern areas in North China. When Japan began to move southward, Chiang was forced to end his military efforts against the Communists. In 1936, he formed a new united front against the Japanese. In July 1937, Chinese and Japanese forces clashed south of Beijing. Japan had not planned to declare war on China but was now involved in a major conflict. The Japanese seized the Chinese capital of Nanjing. Chiang Kai-shek refused to surrender and moved his government upriver.

Japan's military leaders had hoped to create a New Order in East Asia comprised of Japan, Manchuria, and China. Part of Japan's plan was to seize Soviet Siberia, with its rich resources. In the late 1930s, Japan began to cooperate with Nazi Germany. Japan thought the two countries would launch an attack on the Soviet Union and divide Soviet resources between them. When Germany signed the nonaggression pact with the Soviets, Japanese leaders were forced to turn to Southeast Asia to find the raw materials they needed to fuel their military machine. A move into Southeast Asia, however, would risk war with the European colonial powers and the United States. In the summer of 1940, Japan demanded the right to exploit economic resources in French Indochina. The United States objected. It warned Japan that it would apply economic **sanctions** (restrictions intended to enforce international law) unless Japan withdrew from the area. Japan badly needed the oil and scrap iron it was getting from the United States. Japan was now caught in a dilemma. To gain access to the raw materials it wanted in Southeast Asia, Japan had to risk losing raw materials from the United States. After much debate, Japan decided to launch a surprise attack on U.S. and European colonies in Southeast Asia.

7. When Germany signed the nonaggression pact with the Soviets, what dilemma did this create for Japan?

____

____

____

____

____

Name ______________________ Date ______________________ Class ______________________

Reading Essentials and Study Guide

Chapter 26, Section 2

For use with textbook pages 814–822

THE COURSE OF WORLD WAR II

KEY TERMS

blitzkrieg ("lightning war") the German method of warfare, based on panzer divisions supported by airplanes *(page 814)*

partisan a resistance fighter *(page 822)*

DRAWING FROM EXPERIENCE

Have you ever heard of D-Day, V-E Day, and V-J Day? What happened on these days?

In the last section, you read about the actions of Germany and Japan that led to the beginning of World War II. In this section, you will read about the war itself.

ORGANIZING YOUR THOUGHTS

Use the diagram below to help you take notes. During World War II, the major countries of the world were divided into two coalitions, the Grand Alliance (or Allies) and the Axis powers. Identify the three Axis powers and the three major Allies.

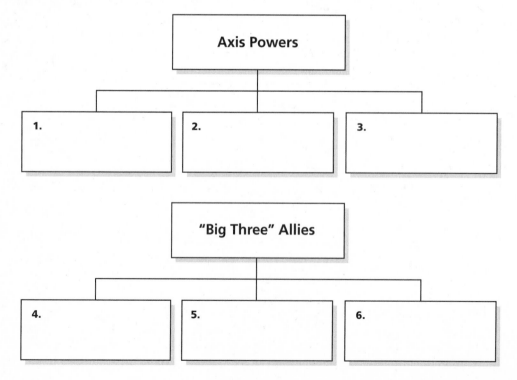

Axis Powers

1.

2.

3.

"Big Three" Allies

4.

5.

6.

Reading Essentials and Study Guide

Chapter 26, Section 2 *(continued)*

READ TO LEARN

• Europe at War *(page 814)*

Hitler stunned Europe with the speed of his attack on Poland. His **blitzkrieg,** or "lightening war," used panzer divisions, supported by airplanes. Each panzer division was a strike force of about three hundred tanks with accompanying forces and supplies. Within four weeks, Poland had surrendered. On September 28, 1939, Germany and the Soviet Union divided Poland.

Hitler attacked again on April 9, 1940, with a blitzkrieg against Denmark and Norway. On May 10, Germany launched an attack on the Netherlands, Belgium, and France. The Germans split the Allied armies, trapping French troops and the entire British army on the beaches of Dunkirk. The British managed to evacuate 338,000 Allied troops through the heroic efforts of the Royal Navy and civilians in private boats.

The French signed an armistice on June 22. German armies now occupied about three-fifths of France. An authoritarian regime under German control was set up over the rest of the country. It was known as Vichy France. It was led by an aged French hero from World War I, Marshal Henri Petain. Germany was now in control of western and central Europe, but Britain had still not been defeated. After Dunkirk, the British appealed to the United States for help.

The United States followed a strict policy of isolationism. Laws passed in the 1930s prevented the United States from taking sides or becoming involved in any European wars. President Franklin D. Roosevelt was convinced that the neutrality acts actually encouraged Axis aggression and wanted the acts repealed. The laws were gradually relaxed as the United States supplied food, ships, planes, and weapons to Britain.

Hitler realized that an invasion of Britain could only succeed if Germany gained control of the air. At the beginning of August 1940, the Luftwaffe—the German air force—launched a major offensive. German planes bombed British air and naval bases, harbors, communication centers, and war industries. The British fought back. But by the end of August, the British air force had suffered critical losses. In retaliation for a British attack on Berlin, the Luftwaffe began bombing British cities instead of military targets. Instead of demoralizing the British people, this allowed the British air force to rebuild quickly. The British were able to inflict major losses on Luftwaffe bombers. At the end of September, Hitler postponed the invasion of Britain.

Hitler became convinced that Britain was remaining in the war only because it expected Soviet support. He thought that if the Soviet Union could be smashed, Britain's last hope would be eliminated. Hitler's invasion of the Soviet Union was scheduled for the spring of 1941, but the attack was delayed because of problems in the Balkans. Mussolini's invasion of Greece had failed in 1940. To secure his southern flank, Hitler seized Greece and Yugoslavia in April 1941.

On June 22, 1941, Hitler invaded the Soviet Union. German troops advanced rapidly, capturing two million Russian soldiers. However, an early winter and fierce Soviet resistance stopped the Germans. The Germans had no winter uniforms, because they had originally planned to invade in the spring. For the first time in the war, the German armies had been stopped.

7. What prevented Roosevelt from responding to British appeals for help in 1940?

____

____

____

• Japan at War *(page 817)*

On December 7, 1941, Japanese aircraft attacked the U.S. naval base at Pearl Harbor in the Hawaiian Islands. The same day, the Japanese also began assaults on the Philippines and advanced toward the British colony of Malaya. Soon after, the Japanese invaded the Dutch East Indies and occupied a number of islands in the Pacific Ocean. By the spring of 1942, almost all of Southeast Asia and much of the western Pacific were in Japanese hands. Japan now declared the creation of a community of nations. The name given to this new "community" was the Greater East-Asia Co-prosperity Sphere. The entire region would now be under Japanese direction. Japan also announced its intention to liberate the colonial areas of Southeast Asia from Western rule. For the time being, however, Japan needed the resources of the region for its war machine, and it treated the countries under its rule as conquered lands.

Japanese leaders had hoped that their attack on American bases would destroy the U.S. fleet in the Pacific. They also thought that the Roosevelt administration would accept Japanese domination of the Pacific. But the Japanese miscalculated. The attack on Pearl Harbor unified American opinion about becoming involved in the war. The United States now joined with European nations and Nationalist China in an effort to defeat Japan. Hitler believed that American involvement in the Pacific would make the United States ineffective in Europe, so he declared war on the United States four days after Pearl Harbor. Another European conflict had turned into a global war.

8. When the Japanese attacked American bases, what did they hope to accomplish? Were their ideas correct?

____

____

____

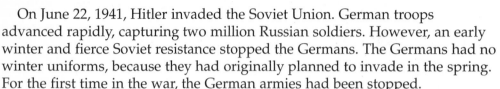

• The Allies Advance *(page 818)*

The entry of the United States into the war created a new coalition, the Grand Alliance. The three major Allies—Great Britain, the United States, and the Soviet Union—agreed to stress military operations and ignore political differences. At the beginning of 1943, the Allies agreed to fight until the Axis Powers—Germany, Italy, and Japan—surrendered unconditionally.

Defeat was far from Hitler's mind at the beginning of 1942. In North Africa, German forces under General Erwin Rommel broke through the British defenses in Egypt and advanced toward Alexandria. A new German offensive in the Soviet Union led to the capture of the entire Crimea in the spring of 1942. But by the fall of 1942, the war had turned against the Germans. In North Africa, British forces had stopped Rommel's troops at El Alamein in the summer of 1942. In November 1942, British and American forces invaded French North Africa and forced the German and Italian troops there to surrender in May 1943. On the Eastern front, against the advice of his generals, Hitler decided that Stalingrad should be taken. Between November 1942 and February 2, 1943, the Soviets launched a counterattack. German troops were stopped and then encircled. Supply lines were cut off, in frigid winter conditions. The Germans were forced to surrender at Stalingrad. The entire German Sixth Army, considered the best of the German troops, was lost.

In 1942, the tide of battle in the East also changed dramatically. In the Battle of the Coral Sea on May 7 and 8, 1942, American naval forces stopped the Japanese advance and saved Australia from the threat of invasion. The turning point of the war in Asia came on June 4, at the Battle of Midway Island. U.S. planes destroyed four Japanese aircraft carriers. The United States defeated the Japanese navy and established naval superiority in the Pacific. By the fall of 1942, Allied forces in Asia were gathering for two chief operations. One, commanded by U.S. general Douglas MacArthur, would move into South China from Burma through the islands of Indonesia. The other would move across the Pacific with a combination of U.S. Army, Marine, and Navy attacks on Japanese-held islands. The policy was to capture some Japanese-held islands and bypass others, "island hopping" up to Japan.

9. What was the turning point of the war in Asia?

____

____

• Last Years of the War *(page 821)*

By the beginning of 1943, the war had turned against Germany, Italy, and Japan. The Allies carried the war to Italy. After taking Sicily, Allied troops began an invasion of mainland Italy in September. After the fall of Sicily, German forces were forced to move in and occupy much of Italy. The Germans set up new defensive lines in the hills south of Rome. The Allied advance up the Italian Peninsula was difficult, with very heavy casualties. Rome did not fall to the Allies until June 4, 1944. By that time, the Italian war had assumed a secondary role, as the Allied forces opened their "second front" in western Europe.

On June 6, 1944, Allied forces under U.S. general Dwight D. Eisenhower landed on the Normandy beaches of France. Within three months, the Allies had landed two million men and a half-million vehicles. Allied forces then pushed inland and broke through German defensive lines. The Allied troops moved south and east. In Paris, resistance fighters rose up against the occupying Germans. The Allies liberated Paris by the end of August. In March 1945, they crossed the Rhine River and advanced into Germany. At the end of April 1945, Allied armies in northern Germany moved toward the Elbe River, where they linked up with the Soviets.

The Soviets had come a long way since the Battle of Stalingrad in 1943. In July, the Soviets defeated German forces at the Battle of Kursk, the greatest tank battle of World War II. Soviet forces now began advancing westward. They had reoccupied Ukraine by the end of 1943 and moved into the Baltic states by the beginning of 1944. In the north, Soviet troops occupied Warsaw in January 1945 and entered Berlin in April. In the south, Soviet troops swept through Hungary, Romania, and Bulgaria.

By January 1945, Adolf Hitler had moved into a bunker under the city of Berlin to direct the final stages of the war. Hitler continued to blame the Jews for the war. He committed suicide on April 30, two days after Mussolini had been shot by Italian **partisans** (resistance fighters). On May 7, 1945, German commanders surrendered. The war in Europe was finally over.

The war in Asia continued. Beginning in 1943, U.S. forces had gone on the offensive and advanced, slowly at times, across the Pacific. There was a new U.S. president, Harry S Truman, who had become president on the death of Roosevelt in April. Truman had a difficult decision to make. Should he use newly developed atomic weapons to bring the war to an end or find another way to defeat the Japanese forces? Truman decided to use the bombs. The first bomb was dropped on the Japanese city of Hiroshima on August 6, 1945. Three days later, a second bomb was dropped on Nagasaki. Both cities were leveled. Thousands of people died immediately after the bombs were dropped. Thousands more died in later months from radiation. Japan surrendered on August 14.

World War II was finally over. Seventeen million had died in battle. Perhaps twenty million civilians had died as well. Some estimates place total losses at fifty million.

10. How did President Truman bring the war to an end?

____

____

Name ______________________ Date ______________ Class ______________

Reading Essentials and Study Guide

Chapter 26, Section 3

For use with textbook pages 824–829

THE NEW ORDER AND THE HOLOCAUST

KEY TERMS

genocide the physical extermination of a racial, political, or cultural group *(page 825)*

collaborator a person who assists the enemy *(page 827)*

DRAWING FROM EXPERIENCE

Have you ever heard about the Holocaust? Have you ever been to the Holocaust Museum in Washington, D.C.? What was the Holocaust? Why did it take place?

In the last two sections, you learned about events leading to World War II and the battles of the war. In this section, you will learn about the atrocities committed by the Nazis and the Japanese against the peoples they conquered.

ORGANIZING YOUR THOUGHTS

Use the chart below to help you take notes. Describe the following policies or programs of Hitler and the Nazis.

Nazi Policy	Description
resettlement	**1.**
forced labor	**2.**
Final Solution	**3.**
Einsatzgruppen	**4.**
death camps	**5.**

READ TO LEARN

• The New Order in Europe *(page 824)*

In 1942, the Nazi regime stretched across Europe from the English Channel in the west to the outskirts of Moscow in the east. Nazi-occupied Europe was mainly organized in one of two ways. Some areas were annexed by Nazi Germany and made into German provinces. In other areas, German military or civilian officials would run the area with help from local people who were willing to collaborate with the Nazis. In the conquered lands to the east, the Nazis were especially ruthless. These lands were seen as "living space" for German expansion. Heinrich Himmler, the leader of the SS, was put in charge of German resettlement plans in the east. His job was to move the Slavic peoples out and replace them with Germans. One million Poles were forced to move to southern Poland. By 1942, two million ethnic Germans had been settled in Poland.

Labor shortages in Germany led to a policy of rounding up foreign workers for Germany. By the summer of 1944, seven million Europeans were working in Germany. Another seven million people were forced to work for the Nazis in their own countries on farms, in industries, and in military camps. In the end, the use of forced labor caused problems for Germany. Sending so many workers to Germany disrupted industrial production in the occupied countries that could have helped Germany. The brutal way that Germany recruited foreign workers led more and more people to resist the Nazi occupation forces.

6. How did the use of forced labor cause problems for Germany?

• The Holocaust *(page 825)*

No aspect of the Nazi New Order was more terrifying than the deliberate attempt to exterminate the Jews. Racial struggle was a key element in Hitler's ideas. To him, racial struggle was a clearly defined conflict of opposites. On one side were the Aryans, creators of human cultural development. On the other side were the Jews, parasites, in Hitler's view, who were trying to destroy the Aryans. Himmler and the SS shared Hitler's racial ideas. The SS was given responsibility for what the Nazis called their Final Solution to the Jewish problem. The Final Solution was **genocide** (physical extermination) of the Jewish people. Reinhard Heydrich, head of the SS's Security Service, was given the task of administering the Final Solution. Heydrich created special strike forces, called *Einsatzgruppen,* to carry out Nazi plans. After the defeat of Poland, he ordered these forces to round up all Polish Jews and put them in ghettos in a number of Polish cities. Conditions were horrible in these ghettos. Despite the suffering, the people in the ghettos tried to carry on, and some ghettos organized resistance against the Nazis. In June 1941, the strike forces were given the new job of acting as mobile killing units. These SS death squads followed the regular army's advance into the Soviet Union. Their job was to round up Jews in their villages, execute them, and bury them in mass graves. The graves were often giant pits dug by the victims themselves before they were shot.

Although these strike forces killed over one million Jews, this was not enough for the Nazi leaders. They decided to kill the European Jewish population in death camps. Beginning in 1942, Jews from occupied countries were shipped to one of six extermination centers that had been built in Poland. Auschwitz was the largest of these centers. By the spring of 1942, the death camps were in full operation.

The Germans killed between five and six million Jews, over three million of them in the death camps. Virtually 90 percent of the Jewish populations of Poland, the Baltic countries, and Germany were killed. Overall, the Holocaust was responsible for the death of nearly two-thirds of European Jews. The Nazis were also responsible for the death by shooting, starvation, or overwork of at least another nine to ten million non-Jewish people. The Nazis considered the Gypsies of Europe, like the Jews, to be a race containing alien blood. The Gypsies were rounded up for mass killing. About 40 percent of Europe's one million Gypsies were killed in the death camps. The leading citizens of the Slavic peoples—the clergy, intellectuals, civil leaders, judges, and lawyers—were arrested and killed. Another four million Poles, Ukrainians, and Belorussians lost their lives as slave laborers for Nazi Germany. Finally, at least three million to four million Soviet prisoners of war were killed in captivity.

This mass slaughter of European civilians, particularly European Jews, is known as the Holocaust. Jews in and out of the camps tried to resist the Nazis. Some were helped by friends and even strangers, hidden in villages or smuggled into safe areas. Foreign diplomats tried to save Jews by issuing exit visas. The nation of Denmark saved almost its entire Jewish population.

Some people did not believe the stories about the death camps. This was partly because the Allies in World War I had exaggerated German atrocities to create enthusiasm for the war. Other people pretended not to notice what was happening. Even worse, **collaborators** (people who assisted the enemy) helped the Nazis hunt down Jews. The Allies were aware of the concentration camps and death camps but chose to concentrate on ending the war. Not until after the war did they learn the full extent of the horror and inhumanity of the Holocaust.

Young people of all ages were also victims of World War II. Because they were unable to work, Jewish children were the first ones selected for gas chambers when they arrived in the death camps. Altogether, 1.2 million Jewish children died in the Holocaust. Many children were evacuated from cities during the war in order to avoid the bombing. Many of the children who were evacuated to the countryside never saw their parents again. In 1945, there were perhaps 13 million orphaned children in Europe. In some places, young people were expected to carry the burden of fighting the war. In the last year of the war, Hitler Youth members, often only 14 or 15 years old, could be found in the front lines.

7. Why did the Holocaust continue until the end of the war?

____

____

____

____

____

• The New Order in Asia *(page 828)*

Japanese war policy in the occupied territories in Asia was basically defensive. Japan hoped to use the occupied territories to meet its growing need for raw materials. These territories would also be a market for Japanese manufactured goods. To organize these territories, Japanese leaders included them in the Greater East-Asia Co-prosperity Sphere. The Japanese had conquered Southeast Asia under the slogan "Asia for the Asiatics." Japanese officials in occupied territories quickly made contact with anticolonialists. They promised the people that local governments would be established. Such governments were eventually set up in Burma, the Dutch East Indies, Vietnam, and the Philippines.

In fact, real power rested with Japanese military authorities in each territory. In turn, the local Japanese military command was under the authority of the Army General Staff in Tokyo. The economic resources of the colonies were used for the benefit of the Japanese war machine. The native peoples in occupied lands were recruited to serve in local military units or were forced to work on public works projects. In some cases, these policies brought severe hardships to peoples living in the occupied areas. In Vietnam, for example, local Japanese authorities forcibly took rice and shipped it abroad. This led directly to a food shortage that caused over a million Vietnamese to starve to death in 1944 and 1945.

Reading Essentials and Study Guide

At first, many Southeast Asian nationalists took Japanese promises at face value and agreed to cooperate with their new masters. Eventually, the nature of Japanese occupation policies became clear, and sentiment turned against Japan. Japanese officials provoked negative reactions by their arrogance and contempt for local customs. In the Dutch East Indies, for example, Indonesians were required to bow in the direction of Tokyo and to recognize the divinity of the Japanese emperor. In Burma, Buddhist pagodas were used as military latrines.

In construction projects to help their war effort, the Japanese made extensive use of labor forces composed of both prisoners of war and local peoples. In building the Burma-Thailand railway in 1943, for example, the Japanese used 61,000 Australian, British, and Dutch prisoners of war and almost 300,000 workers from Burma, Malaya, Thailand, and the Dutch East Indies. An inadequate diet and appalling work conditions in an unhealthy climate led to the death of 12,000 Allied prisoners of war and 90,000 workers by the time the railway was completed.

Indonesian patriots tried to have it both ways. They pretended to support Japan while actually sabotaging the Japanese administration. In French Indochina, Ho Chi Minh's Communist Party made contact with U.S. military units in South China. The Communists agreed to provide information on Japanese troop movements and to rescue downed American fliers in the area. By the end of the war, little support remained in the region for the Japanese "liberators."

8. How did the Japanese gain the support of people in occupied territories? Why did they eventually lose this support?

____

____

____

____

____

Name ______________________ Date ______________________ Class ______________________

Reading Essentials and Study Guide

Chapter 26, Section 4

For use with textbook pages 830–836

THE HOME FRONT AND THE AFTERMATH OF THE WAR

KEY TERMS

mobilization the act of assembling and preparing for war *(page 830)*

kamikaze ("divine wind") Japanese pilots who performed suicide missions against U.S. fighting ships *(page 832)*

Cold War the period of political tensions between the United States and the Soviet Union from the end of World War II until the end of the 1980s *(page 834)*

DRAWING FROM EXPERIENCE

Have you heard of the "iron curtain"? What does this describe? Who first used this term?

In the last three sections, you learned about events before and during World War II. In this section, you will learn about events immediately following the war. You will also learn how the war affected civilians in Europe, the United States, and Japan.

ORGANIZING YOUR THOUGHTS

Use the chart below to help you take notes. Describe how the populations of Germany, Japan, the Soviet Union, and the United States were mobilized for war.

Country	Mobilization
Soviet Union	**1.**
United States	**2.**
Germany	**3.**
Japan	**4.**

READ TO LEARN

• The Mobilization of Peoples: Four Examples *(page 830)*

World War II had an enormous impact on civilian life in the Soviet Union, the United States, Germany, and Japan. Even more than World War I, World War II was a total war. Fighting was much more widespread and covered most of the world. Economic **mobilization** (the act of assembling and preparing for war) was more extensive. The mobilization of women was also greater. The number of civilians killed—almost twenty million—was far higher. Many of these victims were children.

The initial defeats of the Soviet Union led to drastic emergency measures that affected the lives of the civilian population. Leningrad, for example, experienced nine hundred days of siege. Its people became so desperate for food that they ate dogs, cats, and mice. Probably 1.5 million people died in the city. As the German army advanced into Soviet territory, Soviet workers dismantled and shipped the factories in the western part of the Soviet Union to the interior. This "battle of machines" produced 78,000 tanks and 98,000 artillery pieces. Soviet women played a major role in the war effort. Women and girls worked in industries, mines, and railroads. The Soviet Union was the only country in World War II to use women in battle.

The home front in the United States was different. The United States was not fighting the war in its own territory. Eventually, the United States became the arsenal of the Allied Powers. It produced much of the military equipment the Allies needed. At the height of war production in November 1943, the country was building six ships a day and ninety-six thousand planes per year.

The mobilization of the American economy resulted in some social turmoil, however. The construction of new factories created boomtowns. Thousands of people, many of them women, came there to work but then faced a shortage of houses and schools. Widespread movements of people took place. Sixteen million men and women were enrolled in the military and moved frequently. Another sixteen million, mostly wives and girlfriends of servicemen or workers looking for jobs, also moved around the country.

Over a million African Americans moved from the rural South to the cities of the North and West, looking for jobs. The presence of African Americans in areas where they had not lived before led to racial tensions and sometimes even racial riots. One million African Americans enrolled in the military, but they were segregated in their own battle units. Angered by the way they were treated, some became militant and prepared to fight for their civil rights. Japanese Americans faced even more serious problems. On the West Coast, 110,000 Japanese Americans were moved to camps surrounded by barbed wire. They were required to take loyalty oaths, even though 65 percent of them had been born in the United States. Public officials claimed this policy was necessary for security reasons.

In Germany, Hitler was well aware of the importance of the home front. He believed that the collapse of the home front in World War I had caused Germany's defeat. In his determination to keep this from happening again, he adopted economic policies that may have cost Germany the war. To maintain morale during the first two years of the war, Hitler refused to cut consumer goods production or to increase the production of armaments. After German defeats on the Russian front and the American entry into the war, Hitler finally ordered a massive increase in armaments production and in the size of the army. Albert Speer, the minister for armaments and munitions, tripled the production of armaments between 1942 and 1943, despite Allied air raids. A total mobilization of the economy was put into effect in July 1944. Schools, theaters, and cafes were closed. By that time, though, total war mobilization was too late to save Germany from defeat.

Nazi attitudes toward women changed over the course of the war. Before the war, the Nazis had worked to keep women out of the job market. As the war progressed and more and more men were called up for military service, these attitudes changed. Nazi magazines now proclaimed, "We see the woman as the eternal mother of our people, but also as the working and fighting comrade of the man." In spite of this change, the number of women working in industry, agriculture, commerce, and domestic service increased only slightly. Many women, especially those of the middle class, did not want jobs, particularly in factories.

Wartime Japan was a highly mobilized society. To guarantee its control over all national resources, the government created a planning board to control prices, wages, labor, and resources. Citizens were encouraged to sacrifice their resources, and sometimes their lives, for the national cause. Young Japanese were encouraged to volunteer to serve as pilots in suicide missions against the American ships. These pilots were known as **kamikaze,** or "divine wind."

Japan was extremely reluctant to mobilize women on behalf of Japan's war effort. General Hideki Tojo, prime minister from 1941 to 1944, opposed female employment. Female employment increased during the war, but only in such areas as the textile industry and farming, where women had traditionally worked. Instead of using women to meet labor shortages, the Japanese government brought in Korean and Chinese laborers.

5. How were women used in the war effort in Germany, Japan, the Soviet Union, and the United States?

____

____

____

____

Name ______________________ Date ______________________ Class ______________________

• Frontline Civilians: The Bombing of Cities *(page 833)*

Bombing was used in World War II against military targets, enemy troops, and civilian populations. The bombing of civilians in World War II made the home front a dangerous place. The first sustained use of civilian bombing began in early September 1940 in Great Britain. For months, the German air force bombed London nightly. Thousands of civilians were killed or injured, and enormous damage was done. Nevertheless, Londoners' morale remained high. The blitz, as the British called the German air raids, soon became a national experience. The blitz was carried to many other British cities and towns. The ability of Londoners to maintain their morale set the standard for the rest of the British population. The theory that the bombing of civilian targets would force peace was proved wrong. The British failed to learn from their own experience, however. Churchill and his advisers believed that destroying German communities would break civilian morale and bring victory. Major bombing raids on German cities began in 1942.

Bombing raids added an element of terror to circumstances that were already difficult because of shortages of food, clothing, and fuel. Germans especially feared the incendiary bombs, which created firestorms that swept through cities. The bombing of Dresden from February 13 to 15, 1945, created a firestorm that may have killed as many as a hundred thousand people. Germany suffered enormously from the Allied bombing raids. Millions of buildings were destroyed, and possibly half a million civilians died. But the bombings did not destroy Germany's industrial capacity. Production of war materials actually increased between 1942 and 1944, despite the bombing. However, the widespread destruction of transportation systems and fuel supplies made it very difficult for the new materials to reach the German military.

In Japan, the bombing of civilians reached a new level with the use of the first atomic bomb. Japan was open to air raids toward the end of the war because its air force had almost been destroyed. Attacks on Japanese cities by the new U.S. B-29 Superfortresses had begun on November 24, 1944. By the summer of 1945, many of Japan's industries had been destroyed, along with one-fourth of its dwellings. The Japanese government decreed the mobilization of all people between the ages of 13 and 60 into a People's Volunteer Corps. Fearing high U.S. casualties in a land invasion of Japan, President Truman and his advisers decided to drop the atomic bomb on Hiroshima and Nagasaki in August of 1945.

6. What was the theory behind the bombing of civilians? Did this theory prove to be right or wrong?

____

____

____

• Peace and a New War *(page 834)*

The end of World War II was followed by a period of political tensions, known as the **Cold War.** The Cold War was primarily an ideological conflict between the United States and the Soviet Union, but it dominated world affairs until the end of the 1980s.

Stalin, Roosevelt, and Churchill were the leaders of what was called the Big Three (the Soviet Union, the United States, and Great Britain) of the Grand Alliance. They met at Tehran in November 1943 to decide the future course of the war. Their major decision concerned the final assault on Germany. Stalin and Roosevelt argued for an American-British invasion through France. This was scheduled for the spring of 1944. This plan had important consequences. It meant that Soviet and British-American forces would meet in Germany along a north-south dividing line. Soviet forces would liberate Eastern Europe. The Allies also agreed to a partition of postwar Germany.

The Big Three powers met again at Yalta in southern Russia in February 1945. By then, the defeat of Germany was obvious. The Western powers were now faced with the reality that eleven million Soviet soldiers were taking possession of Eastern and much of Central Europe. Stalin was very suspicious of the Western powers. He wanted a buffer to protect the Soviet Union from future Western aggression. This would mean establishing pro-Soviet governments along the border of the Soviet Union. Roosevelt, however, favored the idea of self-determination for Europe. He wanted to help liberated Europe create "democratic institutions of their own choice." Liberated countries would hold free elections to determine their political systems.

At Yalta, Roosevelt sought Soviet military help against Japan. Roosevelt agreed to Stalin's price for military aid against Japan. Stalin wanted Sakhalin and the Kuril Islands, which were ruled by Japan. He also wanted two warm-water ports and railroad rights in Manchuria. The creation of the United Nations was another American concern at Yalta. Roosevelt wanted the Big Three powers to pledge to be part of an international organization before difficult issues divided them into hostile camps. Both Churchill and Stalin accepted Roosevelt's plans for the establishment of a United Nations organization and set the first meeting for San Francisco in April 1945.

The decisions about Germany and Eastern Europe were less decisive. The Big Three reaffirmed that Germany must surrender unconditionally. It would be divided into four zones, which would be occupied and governed by the military forces of the United States, Great Britain, France, and the Soviet Union. A compromise was also worked out in regard to Poland. Stalin agreed to free elections in the future to determine a new government in that country. The issue of free elections in Eastern Europe caused a serious split between the Soviets and the Americans. The principle was that Eastern European governments would be freely elected, but they were also supposed to be pro-Soviet. This attempt to reconcile two irreconcilable goals was doomed to failure. This soon became evident at the next conference of the Big Three powers at Potsdam, Germany.

The Potsdam conference of July 1945 began under a cloud of mistrust. Roosevelt had died on April 12 and had been succeeded by Harry Truman. At Potsdam, Truman demanded free elections throughout Eastern Europe. Stalin objected. He wanted absolute military security. To him, this security could be gained only by the presence of Communist states in Eastern Europe. Free elections might result in governments hostile to the Soviets.

The war had ended, but a new struggle was already beginning. Many in the West thought Soviet policy was part of a worldwide Communist conspiracy. The Soviets viewed Western, and especially American, policy as nothing less than global capitalist expansionism. In March 1946, in a speech to an American audience, the former British prime minister Winston Churchill declared that "an iron curtain" had "descended across the continent," dividing Europe into two hostile camps. Stalin called Churchill's speech a "call to war with the Soviet Union." Only months after World War II had ended, the world seemed to be bitterly divided once again.

7. Why did Stalin object to free elections in Eastern Europe?

____

____

____

____

____

Name ______________________ Date ______________________ Class ______________________

Reading Essentials and Study Guide

Chapter 27, Section 1

For use with textbook pages 849–854

DEVELOPMENT OF THE COLD WAR

KEY TERMS

satellite state a state that is economically and politically dependent on a larger, more powerful state *(page 850)*

policy of containment the policy of the United States regarding the Soviet Union, with the goal of keeping communism within its existing boundaries and preventing further Soviet aggression *(page 850)*

arms race the build-up of huge arsenals of nuclear weapons and missiles by the United States and the Soviet Union *(page 851)*

domino theory the belief held by U.S. policymakers that if the Communists succeeded in South Vietnam, other countries in Asia would fall (like dominoes) to communism *(page 853)*

DRAWING FROM EXPERIENCE

Which countries of the world would you consider to be superpowers today? Why do you think so?

In this section, you will learn about the period of conflict called the Cold War that developed between the United States and the Soviet Union after the end of World War II.

ORGANIZING YOUR THOUGHTS

Use the chart below to help you take notes. During the Cold War period, new military alliances were created. Identify the members of the alliances in the chart below.

Alliance	Members
NATO	**1.**
Warsaw Pact	**2.**
SEATO	**3.**
CENTO	**4.**

READ TO LEARN

• Confrontation of the Superpowers *(page 849)*

After World War II, the United States and the Soviet Union soon became rivals. U.S. leaders still feared communism, and Stalin still feared the capitalist West. Between 1945 and 1949, the two superpowers (a country whose military power is combined with political influence) began to oppose each other. The Soviet government was not willing to give up its control of Eastern Europe. American leaders were not willing to give up the power and prestige the United States had gained throughout the world.

The United States and Great Britain believed that the nations of Eastern Europe should freely determine their own governments. Stalin opposed their plans. The Soviet army had freed Eastern Europe from the Nazis, and it stayed in these countries after the war.

Greece was another area of disagreement between the superpowers. In 1946, the Communist People's Liberation Army fought anticommunist forces for control of Greece. Great Britain supported the anticommunist forces. However, economic problems in Britain forced the British to withdraw their aid from Greece. U.S. President Harry Truman responded to the British withdrawal by issuing the Truman Doctrine. The Truman Doctrine stated that the United States would provide money to countries (such as Greece) that were threatened by Communist expansion. By 1947, the split in Europe between the United States and the Soviet Union had become a fact of life. The United States adopted a **policy of containment** to keep communism within its existing boundaries and prevent further Soviet aggression.

The European Recovery Program followed the Truman Doctrine in June 1947. It is better known as the Marshall Plan. The goal of the program was to rebuild the prosperity and stability of Europe. It included $13 billion in aid for Europe's economic recovery. The Marshall Plan was based on the belief that Communist aggression was successful in countries that had economic problems. The Marshall Plan was not meant to shut out the Soviet Union or its Eastern European **satellite states** (states that are economically and politically dependent on a larger, more powerful state). But they refused to participate. The Soviets saw the Marshall Plan as an attempt to buy the support of countries. In 1949, the Soviet Union responded to the Marshall Plan by founding the Council for Mutual Assistance (COMECON) to help the Eastern European states. COMECON largely failed, however, because the Soviet Union was unable to provide large amounts of financial aid.

Germany was also an area of disagreement between the Soviets and the West. At the end of the war, the Allied Powers had divided Germany into four zones. Each zone was occupied by one of the Allies (the United States, the Soviet Union, Great Britain, and France). Berlin was also divided into four zones. By 1948, Great Britain, France, and the United States were making plans to unify the three Western sections of Germany into a West German state. The Soviets were against this plan. They tried to prevent it by blockading the three Western zones of Berlin. Food and supplies could not get through to the 2.5 million people in these zones. To keep these people alive, the Western powers started the Berlin Air Lift. Supplies were flown in by American and British airplanes. More than 200,000 flights carried 1.5 million tons of supplies. The Soviets finally gave in and lifted the blockade in May 1949.

In September 1949, the Federal Republic of Germany (or West Germany) was created. Its capital was Bonn. A month later, a separate East German state, the German Democratic Republic, was set up by the Soviets. East Berlin was its capital.

5. What was the Marshall Plan?

____

____

____

____

• The Spread of the Cold War *(page 851)*

In 1949, Chinese Communists took control of the government of China. This added to U.S. fears about the spread of communism. The Soviet Union also exploded its first atomic bomb in 1949. The United States and the Soviet Union were soon involved in an **arms race,** in which both countries built up their armies and weapons. In 1952, the Soviet Union and the United States both developed hydrogen bombs. These bombs were even more deadly than atomic bombs. By the mid-1950s, both nations had intercontinental ballistic missiles that could send bombs anywhere in the world. Both sides believed that they needed arsenals of nuclear weapons to prevent war. They believed that neither side would launch a nuclear attack, because the other side would be able to strike back with its nuclear weapons. In 1957, the Soviets sent *Sputnik I,* the first man-made space satellite, to orbit the earth. Americans began to fear that the Soviet Union had a huge lead in building missiles.

The need for security during the Cold War led to the formation of new military alliances. The North Atlantic Treaty Organization (NATO) was formed in April 1949. Belgium, Luxembourg, France, the Netherlands, Great Britain, Italy, Denmark, Norway, Portugal, and Iceland signed a treaty with the United States and Canada. All of these nations agreed to help each other if any of them was attacked. A few years later, West Germany and Turkey joined NATO. In 1955, the Soviet Union formed an alliance with Albania, Bulgaria, Czechoslovakia, East Germany, Hungary, Poland, and Romania. This alliance was known as the Warsaw Pact. To stop Soviet aggression in the East, the United States, Great Britain, France, Pakistan, Thailand, the Philippines, Australia, and New Zealand formed the Southeast Asia Treaty Organization

Name ______________________ Date ______________ Class ______________

Reading Essentials and Study Guide

(SEATO). To prevent the Soviet Union from expanding to the south, Turkey, Iraq, Iran, Pakistan, Great Britain, and the United States formed the Central Treaty Organization (CENTO). By the mid-1950s, the United States was allied militarily with 42 states around the world.

Berlin was still divided into two parts, a reminder of the division of West and East. West Berlin was far more prosperous than East Berlin and East Germany. Many East Germans escaped their country by fleeing through West Berlin. Nikita Khrushchev, who became the leader of the Soviet Union in 1955, decided to stop the East Germans from escaping in this way. In August 1961, the East German government began to build a wall separating West Berlin from East Berlin. The Berlin Wall became a symbol of the division between the two superpowers.

6. Why did the United States and the Soviet Union become involved in an arms race?

____

____

____

____

• The Cuban Missile Crisis *(page 853)*

The Cold War intensified during the administration of U.S. President John F. Kennedy. In 1959, Fidel Castro overthrew the Cuban dictator Fulgencio Batista and set up a Communist government in Cuba. President Kennedy approved a secret plan for Cuban exiles to invade Cuba in the hope of causing a revolt against Castro. The invasion, called the Bay of Pigs, was a disaster. Many of the exiles were killed or captured.

After the Bay of Pigs, the Soviet Union sent arms and military advisers to Cuba. In 1962, Khrushchev began to place nuclear missiles in Cuba. The missiles were meant to counteract U.S. nuclear weapons that had been placed in Turkey within range of the Soviet Union. The United States was not willing to allow nuclear weapons so close to the U.S. mainland. In October 1962, Kennedy found out that Soviet ships carrying missiles were heading to Cuba. He tried to stop them by blockading Cuba. This gave the two sides time to find a peaceful solution. Khrushchev agreed to stop the ships and remove Soviet missiles from Cuba if Kennedy pledged not to invade Cuba. Kennedy quickly agreed.

The Cuban missile crisis had brought the world close to nuclear war. The realization that the world might have been destroyed had a profound influence on both sides. A hotline communications system between Moscow and Washington, D.C. was installed in 1963. The two superpowers could now communicate quickly in times of crisis.

Name ______________________ Date ______________ Class ______________

Reading Essentials and Study Guide

7. What series of events led to the Cuban missile crisis?

____

____

____

____

____

• Vietnam and the Domino Theory *(page 853)*

By 1963, the United States had been drawn into a new conflict—the Vietnam War. In 1964, under President Lyndon B. Johnson, more and more U.S. troops were sent to Vietnam. Their purpose was to keep the Communist government of North Vietnam from gaining control of South Vietnam. The United States saw the conflict in terms of a **domino theory.** According to this theory, if the Communists were able to gain control of South Vietnam, other countries in Asia would also fall (like dominoes) to communism.

The United States failed to defeat the determined North Vietnamese. The large number of American troops sent to Vietnam soon produced an antiwar movement in the United States, especially among college students. Richard Nixon was elected president by pledging to stop the war. But ending the war was not easy. Finally, in 1973, President Nixon reached an agreement with the North Vietnamese that allowed the United States to withdraw its troops. Within two years, Communist armies from the North had reunited Vietnam.

The domino theory turned out to be wrong. New nations in Southeast Asia were able to avoid Communist governments. A split between Communist China and the Soviet Union put an end to the idea that there was single form of communism directed by Moscow. Under President Nixon, American relations with China were reestablished. The Vietnam War showed that there were limits to American power. By the end of the war, a new era in American-Soviet relations had begun.

8. What was the domino theory? Was it right or wrong? Why?

____

____

____

____

____

Name ________________ Date ________________ Class ________________

Reading Essentials and Study Guide

Chapter 27, Section 2

For use with textbook pages 855–858

THE SOVIET UNION AND EASTERN EUROPE

KEY TERMS

heavy industry the manufacture of machines and equipment for factories and mines *(page 856)*

de-Stalinization the process of eliminating the more ruthless policies of Stalin *(page 856)*

DRAWING FROM EXPERIENCE

What kind of house or apartment do you live in? How many rooms does it have? Do you have your own room?

In the last section, you read about the Cold War between the United States and the Soviet Union. In this section, you will read about the Soviet Union and Eastern Europe during 1950s and 1960s. During this time, the average Russian family lived in a one-room apartment.

ORGANIZING YOUR THOUGHTS

Use the diagram below to help you take notes. After World War II, six countries in Eastern Europe became Soviet satellite states. Identify these six countries.

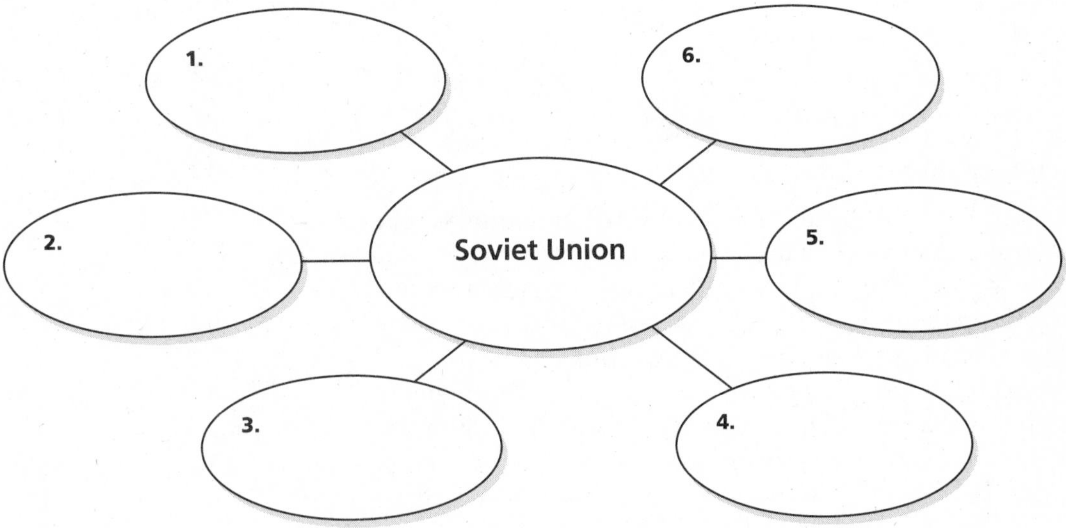

READ TO LEARN

• The Reign of Stalin *(page 855)*

World War II devastated the Soviet Union. To create a new industrial base after the war, Stalin emphasized the production of goods for export. In some respects, this led to a rapid economic recovery. By 1950, industrial production had surpassed prewar levels by 40 percent. New power plants, canals, and giant factories were built. **Heavy industry** (the manufacture of machines and equipment for factories and mines) increased, mainly for the benefit of the military. But the Soviet people did not benefit from the industrialization. The emphasis on heavy industry meant that not enough consumer goods were produced. The housing shortage was also severe. The average Russian family lived in a one-room apartment.

Stalin was still the master of the Soviet Union. He did not share power and had little respect for other Communist Party leaders. His suspicions and lack of trust caused the repression in the Soviet Union to increase. In 1946, the government decreed that all literary and scientific work had to conform to the political needs of the state.

7. How did the emphasis on heavy industry affect the Soviet people?

• The Khrushchev Era *(page 856)*

Stalin died in 1953. A group of leaders succeeded him, but Nikita Khrushchev soon emerged as the chief Soviet policy maker. Khrushchev took steps to undo some of the worst features of Stalin's regime. The process of eliminating the more ruthless policies of Stalin became known as **de-Stalinization.** Khrushchev loosened government controls on literary works. In 1962, for example, he allowed the publication of *A Day in the Life of Ivan Denisovich* by Alexander Solzhenitsyn. This book dealt with life in a Siberian forced-labor camp. Khrushchev also placed more emphasis on producing consumer goods. He also tried to increase farm production by growing corn and cultivating lands east of the Ural Mountains. The attempt to increase farm production failed. This failure and the increased military spending hurt the Soviet economy. Foreign policy failures also damaged Khrushchev's reputation. After the Cuban missile crisis, he was voted out of office and forced into retirement.

8. What changes in Soviet policy did Khrushchev make?

____

____

____

____

• Eastern Europe: Behind the Iron Curtain *(page 857)*

Between 1945 and 1947, Soviet-controlled Communist governments took control of East Germany, Bulgaria, Romania, Poland, and Hungary. In Czechoslovakia, there was a strong tradition of democracy and a multi-party system, so the Soviets did not seize control until 1948. Albania and Yugoslavia were also Communist countries, but the Soviet Union did not control them. During the war, both countries had strong Communist movements that resisted the Nazis. After the war, local Communist parties took control. In Albania, Communists set up a Stalinist-type regime that grew more and more independent of the Soviet Union. In Yugoslavia, Josip Broz, known as Tito, had been the leader of the Communist resistance movement. After the war, he worked to create an independent Communist state in Yugoslavia. Stalin hoped to gain control of Yugoslavia, but Tito refused to give in to Stalin's demands. Tito ruled Yugoslavia until his death in 1980. Yugoslavia had a Communist government, but it was not a Soviet satellite state.

Between 1948 and 1953, the Eastern European satellite states followed the example of the Soviet Union. They had five-year plans, with emphasis on heavy industry rather than consumer goods. They began to collectivize agriculture. They eliminated all noncommunist parties and set up secret police and military forces. But communism did not develop deep roots among the peoples of Eastern Europe. The Soviets exploited Eastern Europe economically and made living conditions hard for most people.

In the 1950s and 1960s, the Soviet Union made it clear that it would not allow its satellite states to become independent of Soviet control. In 1956, protests erupted in Poland. In response, the Polish Communist Party adopted a series of reforms and elected Wladyslaw Gomulka as first secretary. Gomulka declared that Poland had the right to follow its own path. But Poland compromised. It pledged to remain loyal to the Warsaw Pact.

In Hungary, economic problems and unrest led to calls for revolt. To end the rebellion, Imre Nagy, the Hungarian leader, declared that Hungary was a free nation on November 1, 1956. He also promised free elections. Three days after Nagy's declaration, the Soviet Army attacked Budapest. The Soviets reestablished control over the country. Nagy was captured by the Soviet military and executed two years later.

Reading Essentials and Study Guide

Chapter 27, Section 2 *(continued)*

In Czechoslovakia, Antonin Novotny had been placed in power in 1952 by Stalin himself. In fact, he was called "Little Stalin." By the late 1960s, Novotny had alienated many members of his own party. Czech writers especially disliked him. A writers' rebellion led to Novotny's resignation in 1967. In January 1968, Alexander Dubćek was elected first secretary of the Communist party. He began a number of reforms, including freedom of speech and press and the freedom to travel abroad. He relaxed censorship and promised to democratize the Czechoslovakian political system. A period of euphoria broke out that became known as the "Prague Spring." In response, the Soviet Army invaded Czechoslovakia in August 1968 and crushed the reform movement. Gustav Husák replaced Dubćek, did away with his reforms, and reestablished the old order.

9. Why were Albania and Yugoslavia able to remain free of Soviet control?

Name ______________________ Date ______________ Class ______________

Reading Essentials and Study Guide

Chapter 27, Section 3

For use with textbook pages 860–868

WESTERN EUROPE AND NORTH AMERICA

KEY TERMS

welfare state a state in which the government takes responsibility for providing citizens with services and a minimal standard of living *(page 862)*

bloc a group of nations with a common purpose *(page 863)*

real wages the actual purchasing power of income *(page 863)*

DRAWING FROM EXPERIENCE

How do you feel about welfare? Do you think the government has a responsibility to provide citizens with basic needs, such as food and medical care?

In the last section, you read about developments in the Soviet Union and Eastern Europe following World War II. In this section, you will read about economic, political, and social changes in Western Europe, the United States, and Canada after the war. Some countries, such as Great Britain and the United States, developed welfare systems.

ORGANIZING YOUR THOUGHTS

Use the chart below to help you take notes. In the late 1950s, six countries in Western Europe created the European Economic Community, also known as the Common Market. Identify the six original members of the Common Market.

Common Market

1.	2.
3.	4.
5.	6.

READ TO LEARN

• Western Europe: Recovery *(page 860)*

With the help of the Marshall Plan, the countries of Western Europe recovered rapidly. By 1950, industrial output in Europe was 30 percent above prewar levels. The 1950s and 1960s were a period of dramatic growth and prosperity in Western Europe. There was nearly full employment during this period.

After the war, one man, the war hero Charles de Gaulle, dominated France. In 1946, de Gaulle helped established a new government called the Fourth Republic. It had a strong parliament and a weak presidency. No party was strong enough to dominate, and the government was largely ineffective. De Gaulle was unhappy with the Fourth Republic and withdrew from politics. In 1958, French leaders asked de Gaulle to form a new government and revise the constitution. He drafted a new constitution for the Fifth Republic that increased the power of the presidency. The president would now have the right to choose the prime minister, dissolve parliament, and supervise defense and foreign policy. French voters overwhelmingly approved the new constitution. De Gaulle became the first president of the Fifth Republic.

To achieve the status of a world power, de Gaulle invested heavily in nuclear weapons. France exploded its first nuclear bomb in 1960. During de Gaulle's presidency, the French economy grew rapidly. France became a major industrial producer and exporter, especially of automobiles and weapons. But there were still problems. Large government deficits and a rise in the cost of living led to unrest. In May 1968, a series of student protests was followed by a general labor strike. De Gaulle resigned in April 1969 and died within a year.

The three Western zones of Germany were unified as the Federal Republic of Germany in 1949. From 1949 to 1963, Konrad Adenauer was chancellor (head of state). He cooperated with the United States and other Western European nations. Under Adenauer, West Germany experienced an "economic miracle." Unemployment fell from 8 percent in 1950 to 0.4 percent in 1965. Adenauer resigned in 1963. Ludwig Erhard, who continued Adenauer's policies, succeeded him. An economic downturn in the mid-1960s opened the door to the Social Democratic Party, a moderate socialist party. It became the leading party in 1969. Willy Brandt, the mayor of West Berlin, led the Social Democrats.

Great Britain had serious economic problems at the end of World War II. In elections after the war, the Labour Party defeated Churchill's Conservative Party. The Labour Party had promised many reforms, especially in the area of social welfare. The Labour government set out to create a modern **welfare state** (a state in which the government takes responsibility for providing citizens with services and a minimal standard of living). In 1946, the new government passed the National Insurance Act and the National Health Service Act. The insurance act provided government funds to help the unemployed, the sick, and the aged. The health act created a system of socialized medicine that ensured medical care for everyone. The cost of building a welfare state at home forced the British to reduce expenses abroad. This meant the end of the British Empire. Britain was forced to give in to the demands of its colonies for independence. Britain was no longer able to play the role of a world power. Economic problems brought the Conservatives back into power from 1951 to 1964. The Conservatives favored private enterprise, but they accepted the welfare state. They even added to it by starting a building program to improve British housing.

7. How did the British Empire come to an end?

• Western Europe: The Move Toward Unity *(page 862)*

In 1957, France, West Germany, Belgium, the Netherlands, Luxembourg, and Italy signed the Rome Treaty. This treaty created the European Economic Community (EEC), also known as the Common Market. The EEC was a free-trade area made up of the six member nations. These six nations agreed not to impose any tariffs (import charges) on each other's goods. As a group, they would be protected by a tariff on goods from non-EEC nations. All the member nations benefited economically. By the 1960s, the EEC had become an important trading **bloc** (a group of nations with a common purpose). With a total population of 165 million, the EEC was the world's largest exporter and purchaser of raw materials.

8. What is the Common Market?

• The United States in the 1950s *(page 863)*

The New Deal had brought basic changes to American society. These changes included an increase in the role and power of the federal government and the beginning of a welfare state. Other changes included the growth of organized labor and the realization of the need to deal fairly with the concerns of minorities, especially African Americans. The New Deal tradition continued when Democrats were elected president—Harry Truman in 1948, John Kennedy in 1960, and Lyndon Johnson in 1964. Even the election of a Republican president, Dwight Eisenhower, in 1952 and 1956 did not change the basic direction of the New Deal.

An economic boom followed World War II. A shortage of consumer goods during the war had left many Americans with extra income and the desire to buy goods after the war. The growth of labor unions brought higher wages and gave more workers the ability to buy consumer goods. Between 1945 and 1973, **real wages** (the actual purchasing power of income) grew an average of 3 percent a year.

Cold War struggles made many Americans afraid that Communists had infiltrated the United States. The threat seemed even more real when thousands of American soldiers were sent to Korea to fight against Communist aggression. This climate of fear produced a dangerous politician, Senator Joseph McCarthy. He created a "Red Scare" (fear of communist subversion) by charging that hundreds of communists were in high government positions. Several people, including intellectuals and movie stars, were questioned about Communist activities. When McCarthy attacked alleged "Communist conspirators" in the U.S. army, Congress condemned him in 1954. His anticommunist crusade soon came to an end.

9. What was the "Red Scare"?

____

____

____

____

• The United States in the 1960s *(page 864)*

The 1960s began on a youthful and optimistic note. At age 43, John F. Kennedy became the youngest elected president in U.S. history. His administration was cut short when an assassin killed him on November 22, 1963. Vice President Lyndon Johnson then became president. Johnson pursued the growth of the welfare state. His programs included health care for the elderly, various programs to combat poverty, and federal assistance for education. His other passion was the civil rights movement. This movement had its beginnings in 1954 when the U.S. Supreme Court ruled that the practice of racial segregation (separation) in public schools was illegal. In August 1963, Martin Luther King, Jr., leader of a growing movement for racial equality, led a march on Washington, D.C. King believed in the principle of passive disobedience practiced by Mohandas Gandhi. By the end of 1963, a majority of the American people called civil rights the most significant national issue. President Johnson took up the cause of civil rights. The Civil Rights Act of 1964 began the process of ending segregation and discrimination in the workplace and all public places. The Voting Rights Act of 1965 made it easier for African Americans to vote in southern states.

In the North and West, blacks had had voting rights for many years. But local patterns of segregation led to higher unemployment for blacks than for whites. In the summer of 1965, race riots broke out in the Watts district of Los Angeles. Thirty-four people were killed. In 1968, Martin Luther King, Jr., was assassinated. Riots broke out in over a hundred cities. The riots led to a "white backlash" (whites became less sympathetic to the cause of racial equality).

Antiwar protests also divided the American people. As the Vietnam War progressed, protests grew. In 1970, four students at Kent State University were killed by the Ohio National Guard during a student demonstration. Americans became less and less willing to continue the war. The riots and antiwar demonstrations caused many people to call for "law and order." Richard Nixon used this appeal when he was elected president in 1968. With his election, a shift to the right began in American politics.

10. What were some of the important events in the civil rights movement from 1954 to 1965?

____

____

____

____

• The Development of Canada *(page 866)*

Canada had always had a strong export economy based on its abundant natural resources. After World War II, it developed electronic, aircraft, nuclear, and chemical engineering industries. Much of the Canadian growth was financed by capital from the United States. This led to U.S. ownership of Canadian businesses, and many Canadians worried that the United States would dominate their country economically. Canada sought to establish its own identity in world politics. It was a founding member of the United Nations and joined the North Atlantic Treaty Organization in 1949. The Liberal Party dominated Canadian politics throughout most of this period. The Liberal government created Canada's welfare state, which included a national social security system and a national health insurance program.

11. Why did Canadians worry that the United States would dominate their country economically?

____

____

____

____

• The Emergence of a New Society *(page 866)*

After World War II, Western societies experienced rapid change. New inventions, such as televisions, computers, and jet planes altered the pace and nature of human life. Changes in the middle class were especially noticeable. The middle class had traditionally included businesspeople, lawyers, doctors, and teachers. A new group of managers and technicians now joined the ranks of the middle class. Changes also occurred in the lower classes. The number of farmers declined drastically. The number of industrial workers also began to decline, as the number of white-collar workers increased. An increase in the real wages of workers made it possible for them to imitate the buying patterns of the middle class. This led to what some people have called the consumer society (a society preoccupied with buying goods). Buying on credit became widespread in the 1950s. Workers could now buy such products as televisions, washing machines, refrigerators, vacuum cleaners, stereos, and automobiles.

Women's roles also began to change. After World War I, many governments had expressed thanks to women by granting them voting rights. Sweden, Great Britain, Germany, Poland, Hungary, Austria, and Czechoslovakia gave women the right to vote in 1918, followed by the United States in 1920. Women in France and Italy gained the right to vote in 1945. During World War II, women had entered the workforce in huge numbers. At the end of the war, many of them were let go to provide jobs for soldiers returning home. For a time, many women fell back into traditional roles. Birthrates rose, creating a "baby boom" in the late 1940s and the 1950s.

By the end of the 1950s, the birthrate began to fall, and the size of families decreased. The number of married women in the workforce increased in both Europe and the United States. These women faced an old problem. They still earned less than men for equal work. Women also tended to enter traditionally female jobs. Many faced the burden of earning income and raising a family at the same time. These inequalities led many women to rebel. In the late 1960s, there was a renewed interest in feminism, or the women's liberation movement, as it was now called. Simone de Beauvoir's book *The Second Sex* influenced the women's movements in both Europe and the United States.

Before World War II, most of the people who went to universities were from the wealthier classes. After the war, European countries began to encourage more people to get a higher education by eliminating fees. Enrollments grew dramatically as students from the middle and lower classes began to attend. There were problems, however. Many European university classrooms were overcrowded. Many professors paid little attention to their students. Growing discontent led to student protests in the late 1960s. Many of these protests were an extension of the revolts in U.S. universities. Some students wanted to reform the university system. They did not believe that universities responded to their needs or to the realities of the modern world. Student protest movements in both Europe and the United States reached a high point in 1968. At the time, many people thought that the student protests were a turning point in history. By the early 1970s, however, the movements had largely disappeared. In the 1970s and 1980s, most student rebels became middle-class professionals.

12. How did women's roles change during and after World War II?

____

____

____

____

____

Name ______________________ Date ______________________ Class ______________________

Reading Essentials and Study Guide

Chapter 28, Section 1

For use with textbook pages 875–878

DECLINE OF THE SOVIET UNION

KEY TERMS

détente a relaxation of tensions between nations, especially used for American-Soviet relations in the 1970s *(page 875)*

dissident a person who speaks out against a regime *(page 876)*

perestroika ("restructuring") the term used by Mikhail Gorbachev for economic reforms in the Soviet Union in the late 1980s *(page 877)*

DRAWING FROM EXPERIENCE

Have you heard of the "evil empire"? Who used this expression? What country was he talking about?

In this section, you will learn about changes in the Soviet Union in the 1980s and 1990s.

ORGANIZING YOUR THOUGHTS

Use the chart below to help you take notes. Identify the rulers of the Soviet Union, and later the Russian Republic, following Nikita Khrushchev.

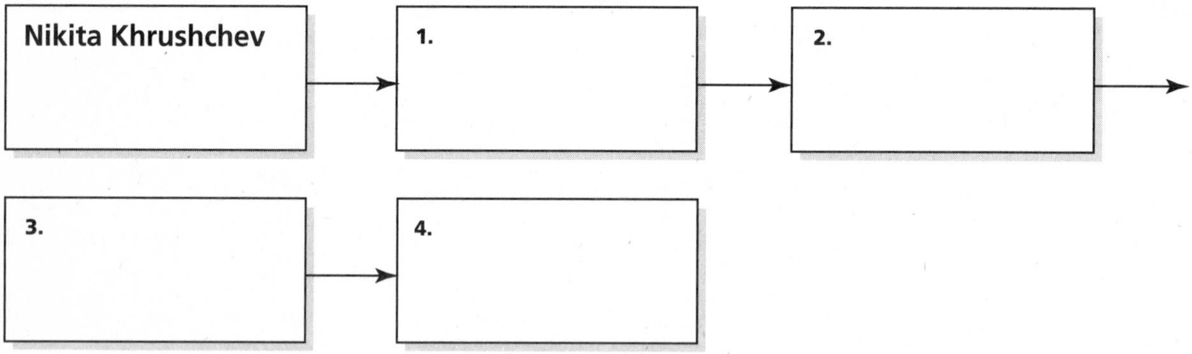

READ TO LEARN

• From Cold War to Post-Cold War *(page 875)*

In the 1970s, relations between the United States and the Soviet Union improved. This phase in U.S.-Soviet relations is called **détente** (the relaxation of tensions between nations). The United States began to sell grain and consumer goods to the Soviet Union. Détente collapsed in 1979, however, when the Soviet Union invaded Afghanistan. President Jimmy Carter stopped the shipment of grain to the Soviet Union. He also would not allow Americans to participate in the 1980 Olympic Games, which were held in Moscow.

The Cold War intensified when Ronald Reagan was elected president in 1980. Reagan called the Soviet Union an "evil empire" and began a new arms race. Reagan also gave military aid to the Afghan rebels. When Mikhail Gorbachev became the leader of the Soviet Union in 1985, changes began that eventually ended the Cold War. Gorbachev made an agreement with the United States in 1987 to eliminate intermediate-range nuclear weapons. Both sides had reasons to slow down the arms race. Gorbachev hoped to make economic and other reforms in the Soviet Union. The national debt in the United States had tripled, and the United States had moved from being a creditor nation (a nation that exports more than it imports) to being the world's biggest debtor nation. By 1990, both countries knew that their large military budgets would make it difficult to solve their domestic problems.

Gorbachev stopped giving military support to Communist governments in Eastern Europe. This opened the door to the overthrow of Communist governments in these countries. A revolutionary movement swept through Eastern Europe in 1989. Germany was reunified on October 3, 1990. In 1991, the Soviet Union was dissolved. The Cold War had come to an end.

5. Why did the United States and the Soviet Union begin to slow down the arms race?

____

____

____

____

____

• Upheaval in the Soviet Union *(page 876)*

When Nikita Khrushchev was removed from office in 1964, two men, Alexei Kosygin and Leonid Brezhnev, replaced him. Brezhnev became the dominant leader. He was determined to keep Eastern Europe in Communist hands and was not interested in reform. He insisted on the right of the Soviet Union to intervene if communism was threatened in another Communist state. This was known as the Brezhnev Doctrine. Under Brezhnev, the government did allow more access to Western styles of music, dress, and art. But dissidents (those who spoke out against the regime) were still punished.

Brezhnev continued to emphasize heavy industry. Problems weakened the Soviet economy. The government's central planning led to a huge, complex bureaucracy. This discouraged efficiency and led to indifference. Collective farmers also had no incentive to work hard. By the 1970s, Communist party leaders and leaders of the army and secret police enjoyed a high standard of living and had become corrupt. By 1980, the Soviet Union was in serious trouble, with a declining economy, a rise in infant mortality rates and alcoholism, and poor working conditions. Within the Communist Party, a small group of reformers emerged. One of these was Mikhail Gorbachev. In March 1985, he was chosen to lead the Soviet Union.

From the start, Gorbachev saw the need for radical reforms. The basis of these reforms was **perestroika** (restructuring). At first, this meant restructuring economic policy. Gorbachev wanted to start a market economy, where consumers influence what is produced. But Gorbachev soon realized that it was not possible to reform the economy without political reform. In 1988, Gorbachev established a new Soviet parliament, the Congress of People's Deputies. The members were elected and met in 1989. In 1990, Gorbachev allowed non-Communist political parties to organize. At the same time, he strengthened his own power by creating a new position—president of the Soviet Union. In March 1990, Gorbachev became the Soviet Union's first (and last) president.

As Gorbachev loosened the control of the Communist Party, ethnic tensions in the Soviet Union surfaced. Nationalist movements emerged throughout the republics of the Soviet Union. Between 1988 and 1990, there were calls for independence in Soviet Georgia, Latvia, Estonia, Moldavia, Uzbekistan, Azerbaijan, and Lithuania. By 1991, many Soviet leaders were worried. The breakup of the Soviet Union would mean an end to their privileges. On August 19, 1991, a group of conservative leaders arrested Gorbachev and tried to seize power. The attempt failed. Boris Yeltsin, president of the Russian Republic, and thousands of Russians resisted the takeover. The Soviet republics now moved for complete independence. Ukraine voted for independence on December 1, 1991. A week later, the leaders of Russia, Ukraine, and Belarus announced that the Soviet Union had "ceased to exist." Gorbachev resigned on December 25, 1991, and turned his responsibilities over to Boris Yeltsin, the new president of Russia.

Boris Yeltsin was committed to introducing a free market economy as quickly as possible, but the transition was not easy. Economic hardships were made worse by a rise in organized crime. Yeltsin also used brutal force against the Chechens, who wanted to secede from Russia and create their own republic. At the end of 1999, Yeltsin resigned and was replaced by Vladimir Putin.

Reading Essentials and Study Guide

Putin vowed to return the breakaway state of Chechnya to Russian authority. In July 2001, Putin began reforms to strengthen the Russian economy. The reforms included the free purchase and sale of land, tax cuts, and efforts to join the World Trade Organization.

6. What series of events led to the end of the Soviet Union?

____

____

____

____

____

Name ______________________ Date ______________________ Class ______________________

Reading Essentials and Study Guide

Chapter 28, Section 2

For use with textbook pages 879–882

EASTERN EUROPE

KEY TERMS

ethnic cleansing the Serb policy of killing or forcibly removing Bosnians from their lands *(page 881)*

autonomous self-governing *(page 882)*

DRAWING FROM EXPERIENCE

Have you ever seen pictures of the Berlin Wall? What did it look like? Why was it built? Why did it fall?

In the last section, you read about the fall of communism in the Soviet Union. In this section, you will read about the fall of communism in other countries in Eastern Europe.

ORGANIZING YOUR THOUGHTS

Use the chart below to help you take notes. Describe how communism ended in the countries in this chart. Also indicate some results of the revolutions in these countries.

Country	How Communism Ended	Results of Revolution
Poland	**1.**	**2.**
Czechoslovakia	**3.**	**4.**
Romania	**5.**	**6.**
East Germany	**7.**	**8.**
Yugoslavia	**9.**	**10.**

READ TO LEARN

- **Revolutions in Eastern Europe** *(page 879)*

People in Eastern Europe had not always been happy with their Soviet-style Communist governments. After Gorbachev made it clear that the Soviet Union would not intervene militarily in their countries, revolutions broke out throughout Eastern Europe.

In Poland, workers' protests led to changes. In 1980, a worker named Lech Walesa organized a national trade union known as Solidarity. Solidarity gained the support of the workers and the Roman Catholic Church. During a period of military rule in the 1980s, Walesa was arrested, but the movement continued. After more demonstrations in 1988, the Polish government agreed to free parliamentary elections—the first free elections in Eastern Europe in 40 years. A new government was elected, ending 45 years of Communist rule in Poland. In December 1990, Walesa was chosen as president. But the new path was not easy. Free-market reforms led to severe unemployment and discontent. At the end of 1995, Aleksander Kwasniewski, a former Communist, defeated Walesa and became the new president. He continued Poland's move toward a prosperous free market economy.

In Czechoslovakia, mass demonstrations took place in 1988 and 1989. In December 1989, the Communist government collapsed. At the end of December, Václav Havel became the new president. He was a writer who had played an important role in bringing down the Communist government. The new government in Czechoslovakia faced old ethnic conflicts. The two national groups, Czechs and Slovaks, agreed to a peaceful division of the country. On January 1, 1993, Czechoslovakia split into the Czech Republic and Slovakia.

In Romania, the Communist leader Nicolae Ceauşescu had set up a rigid dictatorship in 1965. He used secret police to crush all dissent. His economic policies led to a sharp drop in living standards, including food shortages and the rationing of bread, flour, and sugar. His plan for rapid urbanization also made the Romanian people angry. Entire villages were bulldozed as part of the plan. In December 1989, the secret police murdered thousands of people who were peacefully demonstrating. Finally, the army refused to support any more repression. Ceauşescu and his wife were captured and executed. A new government was quickly formed.

In East Germany, Erich Honecker became head of the Communist Party in 1971. He used the Stasi, the secret police, to rule for the next 18 years. In 1988, many East Germans began to flee their country. Mass demonstrations broke out in the summer and fall of 1989. On November 9, the Communist government gave in and opened its border with the West. Thousands of East Germans rushed across the border. Families who had not seen each other in years were reunited. People on both sides of the Berlin Wall began tearing the wall down. The government gave in again and ordered the rest of the wall torn down.

During East Germany's first free elections in March 1990, the Christian Democrats won almost 50 percent of the vote. The Christian Democrats supported reunification with West Germany. The reunification of Germany took place on October 3, 1990.

11. What series of events led to the reunification of Germany?

• The Disintegration of Yugoslavia *(page 881)*

Although Yugoslavia had a Communist government, it had never been a Soviet satellite state. After Tito died in 1980, a government composed of representatives from the six republics and two provinces of Yugoslavia kept the country under Communist rule. By 1990, new parties had emerged, and the Communist Party lost its power.

The situation in Yugoslavia was complex. In 1990, the Yugoslav republics of Slovenia, Croatia, Bosnia-Herzegovina, and Macedonia began to push for independence. Slobodan Milošević, who became the leader of Serbia in 1987, was against their plans, because the republics included Serb minorities. He wanted to redraw borders to include the Serb minorities in a new Greater Serbian state. In June 1991, Slovenia and Croatia declared their independence. In September, the Yugoslavian army began a full assault against Croatia. Serbia dominated the Yugoslavian army. Before a cease-fire was arranged, the Serbian forces captured one-third of Croatia's territory.

In 1992, the Serbs began an assault against Bosnia-Herzegovina. By mid-1993, Serbian forces had acquired 70 percent of Bosnian territory. Many Bosnians were Muslims. Toward them, the Serbs followed a policy they called **ethnic cleansing** (killing them or forcibly removing them from their lands). By 1995, 250,000 Bosnians (mostly civilians) had been killed, and two million others were homeless. In 1995, Bosnian and Croatian forces regained much of the territory that had been lost to Serbian forces. Air strikes by NATO bombers were launched in retaliation for Serb attacks on civilians. These attacks forced the Serbs to sign a peace treaty on December 14. The agreement split Bosnia into a loose union of a Serb republic and a Muslim-Croat federation. NATO sent a force of sixty thousand troops to monitor the area.

Name ______________________ Date ____________________ Class ____________________

Reading Essentials and Study Guide

Chapter 28, Section 2 *(continued)*

Peace in Bosnia did not bring peace to the region. A new war began in 1998 over Kosovo. In 1974, Tito had made Kosovo an **autonomous** (self-governing) province within Yugoslavia. Kosovo's inhabitants were mainly ethnic Albanians. In 1989, Milošević took Kosovo's autonomous status away. Groups of ethnic Albanians formed the Kosovo Liberation Army in the mid-1990s and began a campaign against Serbian rule. In response, Serb forces began to massacre ethnic Albanians. After months of negotiations, the Kosovo Albanians agreed to a peace plan in 1999 that would give them autonomy for a three-year period. When Milošević refused to sign the agreement, the United States and its NATO allies began a bombing campaign that forced the Yugoslavian government to cooperate. In the elections of 2000, Milošević was removed from power.

12. Why did Serbia oppose the other republics' plans for independence?

____

____

____

____

____

Name ______________________ Date ________________ Class ________________

Reading Essentials and Study Guide

Chapter 28, Section 3

For use with textbook pages 884–888

EUROPE AND NORTH AMERICA

KEY TERMS

Thatcherism a term for the economic policy of British Prime Minister Margaret Thatcher *(page 886)*

budget deficit spending by a government that exceeds revenues *(page 887)*

DRAWING FROM EXPERIENCE

Do you or your family have a budget? What kinds of things do you include in your budget? What happens if you spend more than your budget had allowed?

In the last two sections, you read about changes in the Soviet Union and Eastern Europe after 1970. In this section, you will read about developments in Western Europe and North America during this time. Economic issues dominated politics during much of this period.

ORGANIZING YOUR THOUGHTS

Use the chart below to help you take notes. Indicate the effect of economic issues on politics in the countries in this chart.

Effect of Economic Issues on Politics	
Canada	**1.**
France	**2.**
Germany	**3.**
Great Britain	**4.**
United States	**5.**

READ TO LEARN

• Winds of Change in Western Europe *(page 884)*

Between the early 1950s and late 1970s, Western Europe had nearly full employment. However, an economic downturn occurred in the mid-1970s and early 1980s. Inflation and unemployment rose dramatically. A dramatic increase in the price of oil after the Arab-Israeli conflict in 1973 was a major cause of the downturn. Western European economies recovered in the 1980s, but there were still problems.

The Western European nations moved toward a greater union of their economies after 1970. The European Economic Community (EEC) expanded in 1973 to include Great Britain, Ireland, and Denmark. By 1986, Spain, Portugal, and Greece had become members. Austria, Finland, and Sweden joined in 1995. The Treaty on European Union in 1994 turned the EEC into the principal organization of the new European Union (EU). One of the European Union's first goals was to establish a common European currency, the euro. Most of the EU nations gave up their currency in favor of the euro by January 1, 2002.

France's economic problems in the 1970s caused a shift to the left politically. By 1981, the Socialists had become the chief party in the National Assembly. The Socialist leader, François Mitterrand, was elected president. To help workers, Mitterrand implemented a higher minimum wage, a 39-hour work week, and higher taxes for the rich. The Socialist government also nationalized (took over) major banks, the steel industry, the space and electronics industries, and insurance firms. But most Socialist policies failed to work. In 1993, French unemployment was 10.6 percent. In the elections in March 1993, a coalition of conservative parties gained 80 percent of the seats in the National Assembly. In 1995, the conservative mayor of Paris, Jacques Chirac, was elected president.

In West Germany, the Social Democrats, a moderate socialist party, replaced the Christian Democrats as the leading party in 1969. The first Social Democratic chancellor was Willy Brandt. In March 1971, Brandt worked out the details of a treaty with East Germany that led to more cultural, personal, and economic contacts between West and East Germany. In 1982, the Christian Democratic Union of Helmut Kohl formed a new, more conservative government. When events in East Germany led to the reunification of the two Germanies in 1990, the new Germany became the leading power in Europe.

It soon became clear that rebuilding eastern Germany would take far more money than had originally been thought. Kohl's government was forced to raise taxes. The collapse of the economy in eastern Germany led to high levels of unemployment and discontent. One result was a return to power for the Social Democrats in 1998. Unemployment and economic problems caused tensions to grow between Germans and immigrant groups. Attacks against foreigners by right-wing extremists, especially young neo-Nazis, became part of German life.

Between 1964 and 1979, Great Britain's Conservative Party and Labour Party alternated in power. One problem both parties had to face was intense fighting between Catholics and Protestants in Northern Ireland. There were also economic problems and frequent labor strikes. In 1979, the Conservatives came to power under Margaret Thatcher. Thatcher pledged to limit social welfare, restrict union power, and end inflation. Although she did not eliminate the basic parts of the welfare system, she did break the power of the unions and controlled inflation. **Thatcherism,** as her economic policy was called, improved the British economic situation overall. The south of England, for example, prospered. But old industrial areas in other parts of the country had high unemployment, poverty and even violence. In 1990, Thatcher's government tried to replace local property taxes with a flat-rate tax for all adults. Antitax riots broke out. Thatcher's popularity fell to an all-time low, and she resigned as prime minister. The Conservative Party was now led by John Major. In the elections of 1997, the Labour Party won a landslide victory. Tony Blair, a moderate, became prime minister.

6. What were some of the problems faced by Germany after reunification?

____

____

____

____

____

• The U.S. Domestic Scene *(page 886)*

With the election of Richard Nixon in 1968, politics in the United States shifted to the right. In his campaign for the presidency, Nixon used "law and order" issues and a slowdown in racial desegregation to appeal to southern whites. The South, which had been a stronghold for the Democrats, began to form a new allegiance to the Republican Party. As president, Nixon used illegal methods to gain political information about his opponents. This led to the Watergate scandal. A group of men working for Nixon's reelection campaign broke into the Democratic National Headquarters in the Watergate Hotel in Washington, D.C. They were caught trying to install electronic listening devices. At first, Nixon lied about his involvement in the affair, but secret tapes of his own conversations in the White House revealed the truth. On August 9, 1974, Nixon resigned to avoid impeachment.

Vice President Gerald Ford became president when Nixon resigned. In the 1976 election, he lost to the former governor of Georgia, Jimmy Carter. By 1980, the Carter administration faced two serious problems. First, high rates of inflation and a decline in average weekly earnings were causing a drop in

Reading Essentials and Study Guide

American living standards. Second, 52 Americans were taken hostage by the Iranian government of the Ayatollah Khomeini. Carter was unable to gain the release of the hostages. The economic problems and the hostage situation contributed to Carter's loss to Ronald Reagan in the election of 1980.

The Reagan Revolution, as it has been called, sent U.S. policy in new directions. Reagan cut back on the welfare state by decreasing spending on food stamps, school lunch programs, and job programs. At the same time, he oversaw the largest peacetime military buildup in U.S. history. The spending policies of the Reagan administration produced record budget deficits. A **budget deficit** exists when a government spends more than it collects in revenues. George Bush, Reagan's vice president, succeeded him as president.

Economic problems enabled a Democrat, Bill Clinton, to defeat Bush in the presidential election in 1992. Clinton claimed to be a new Democrat—one who favored a number of the Republican policies of the 1980s. This was a clear indication that the shift to the right in American politics had not ended. An economic revival helped Clinton to be reelected. Much of his second term was overshadowed by charges of misconduct. The House of Representatives voted two articles of impeachment (formal charges of misconduct) against him. He was tried in the Senate and acquitted. But Clinton's problems helped the Republican candidate, George W. Bush, win the presidential election in 2000.

7. Why did President Nixon resign?

____

____

____

____

____

• Canada *(page 888)*

During a major recession in the early 1960s, the Liberals came into power in Canada. The most prominent Liberal government was that of Pierre Trudeau, who became prime minister in 1968. Trudeau was French-Canadian, but he was dedicated to preserving a united Canada. His government passed the Official Languages Act, which allowed both English and French to be used in the federal civil service. Trudeau also supported a vigorous program of industrialization.

An economic recession in the early 1980s brought Brian Mulroney to power in 1984. Mulroney's government tried to return some of Canada's state-run corporations to private owners. In 1993, Canada approved the North American Free Trade Agreement (NAFTA) along with the United States and Mexico. The purpose of NAFTA was to make trade easier and more profitable

Reading Essentials and Study Guide

by establishing guidelines for cooperation between the countries. Many Canadians thought the agreement was too favorable to the United States. It cost Mulroney much of his popularity. In 1993, the Liberal party came to power with Jean Chrétien as prime minister.

Debate over Quebec continued throughout this period. In the late 1960s, the Parti Québecois began to propose that Quebec secede from Canada. In 1980, the party called for a vote that would grant Quebec's independence from the rest of Canada. In 1995, voters in Quebec narrowly rejected the plan.

8. What is NAFTA? Why were many Canadians opposed to it?

____

____

____

____

____

Name ______________________ Date ______________________ Class ______________________

Reading Essentials and Study Guide

Chapter 28, Section 4

For use with textbook pages 889–894

WESTERN SOCIETY AND CULTURE

KEY TERMS

pop art an art style beginning in the early 1960s that took images of popular culture and transformed them into works of fine art *(page 892)*

postmodernism a movement in the arts beginning in the 1980s that was marked by a revival of traditional elements and techniques *(page 893)*

DRAWING FROM EXPERIENCE

Where were you when you heard about the attacks on the World Trade Center Towers? How did this event affect your life?

In the last section, you read about economic and political developments in Western Europe and North America in the late twentieth century. In this section, you will read about changes in Western society and culture during this time. The growth of terrorism has had a great impact on Western countries.

ORGANIZING YOUR THOUGHTS

Use the diagram below to help you take notes. American culture has increasingly influenced other parts of the world since the end of World War II. Indicate four ways that American culture has influenced other countries.

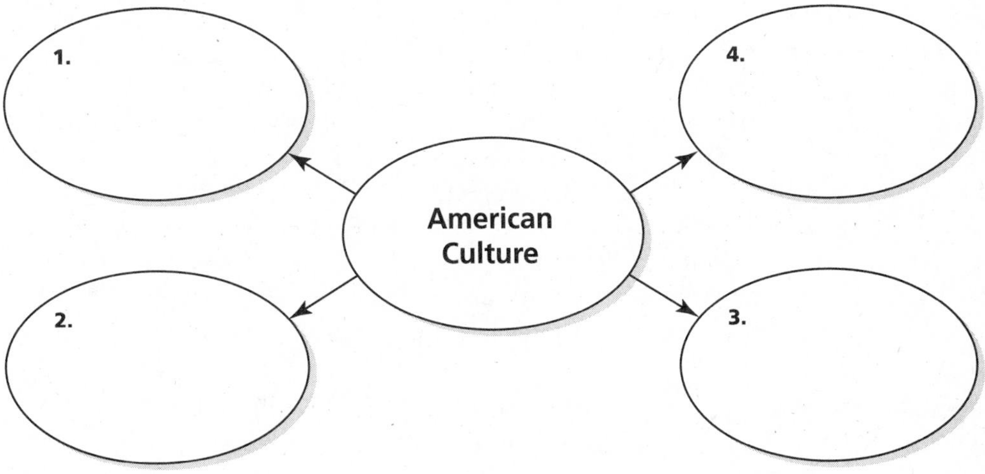

READ TO LEARN

• Changes in Women's Lives *(page 889)*

Since 1970, more and more women have entered the workforce in Western countries. However, women continue to receive lower wages than men for the same work, and they have fewer opportunities to reach top positions. In the 1960s and 1970s, some women in the women's liberation movement began to believe that women themselves must make changes in their lives. Women formed "consciousness-raising groups" to make people aware of women's issues. During this time in the United States, the Equal Pay and Sex Discrimination Acts were passed. These laws gave legal support to equal rights for women.

In the 1990s, there was a backlash against the women's movement. Some women wanted to return to traditional roles. Other women tried to redefine the term "feminism," as they struggled to balance career, family, and personal goals.

5. What laws were passed in the United States in the 1960s and 1970s that gave support to equal rights for women?

____

____

____

____

• The Growth of Terrorism *(page 890)*

Acts of terrorism have become a part of modern society. Terrorists use the killing of civilians, the taking of hostages, and the hijacking of airplanes to draw attention to their demands or to achieve their goals. Some terrorists are militant nationalists who wish to create separate states. One example is the Irish Republican Army (IRA). Its goal is to unite Northern Ireland, which is ruled by Great Britain, with the Irish Republic. Since the 1970s, IRA terrorists have been responsible for the deaths of thousands of people. State-sponsored terrorism is another form of terrorism. Some militant governments have provided support to terrorist organizations. Iraq, Syria, Cuba, and North Korea are some examples.

One of the most destructive acts of terrorism occurred on September 11, 2001. Four groups of terrorists hijacked four commercial U.S. jets. They flew two of the airplanes into the World Trade Center towers in New York City. They flew the third airplane into the Pentagon in Washington, D.C. The fourth plane was diverted by heroic passengers and crashed in an isolated area of Pennsylvania. Thousands of people were killed, including all of the people aboard the airplanes.

The U.S. government gathered evidence that indicated that the acts had been carried out by al-Qaeda, the terrorist organization of Osama bin Laden. Bin Laden had inherited a fortune and used it to train terrorists in Afghanistan. U.S. President George W. Bush vowed to wage war on terrorism. The United States developed a coalition of nations to rid the world of terrorist groups. The process began with military action against Afghanistan in October 2001. At home, President Bush established the White House Office of Homeland Security. Its purpose was to protect the United States from terrorism and to respond to any future attacks.

6. What methods do terrorists use to draw attention to their demands?

____

____

____

____

• Science and Technology *(page 891)*

Scientific and technological achievements since World War II have revolutionized people's lives. During the war, many scientists had been recruited to develop new weapons. The most famous product of wartime research was the atomic bomb. After the war, wartime technology was adapted for peacetime uses. Computers and jet airplanes are two examples. By sponsoring projects, governments and the military created a new model for scientific research. Wartime projects were complex and required large teams of scientists and huge laboratories. After the war, the new scientific establishment continued to operate. The space program is one example. Massive government funding enabled the United States to land astronauts on the Moon in 1969.

In the 1960s and 1970s, people began to worry that technological advances were having side effects that were damaging to the environment. Chemical fertilizers, for example, helped farmers grow more abundant crops, but these fertilizers also destroyed the ecological balance of streams, rivers, and woodlands.

7. How has wartime research been adapted for peacetime use?

____

____

____

____

• Religious Revival *(page 892)*

Many people were concerned about a collapse in values during the twentieth century. The revival of religion was one response to that collapse. Religion continued to play an important role in the lives of many people. This was in spite of the attempts of the Communist world to build an atheistic society and the attempts of the West to build a secular society. Christian thinkers tried to breathe new life into traditional Christian teachings. Karl Barth is one example. To Barth, the imperfect nature of human beings meant that humans could not know religious truth through reason, but only through the grace of God.

In the Catholic Church, efforts for religious renewal came from two popes, John XXIII and John Paul II. Pope John XXIII started a revival when he summoned the twenty-first ecumenical council of the Catholic Church. Known as Vatican Council II, it liberalized several Catholic practices. For example, the mass could now be celebrated in vernacular languages as well as Latin. John Paul II was the first non-Italian pope since the sixteenth century. He alienated many people by supporting traditional Catholic teachings on birth control and a ban on women in the priesthood. But John Paul II reminded Catholics of the need to balance the pursuit of materialism with spiritual concerns.

8. What efforts for religious renewal have taken place in the Catholic Church?

____

____

____

____

____

• Trends in Art *(page 892)*

The United States has dominated the art world since the end of World War II. American art is often vibrantly colored and filled with activity. In this way, it reflected the energy of the postwar United States. After 1945, New York City became the artistic center of the Western world. Abstractionism was the most popular form of modern art after World War II. The enormous canvases of Jackson Pollock, for example, are filled with the vibrant energy of abstract expressionism. In the early 1960s, pop art emerged. **Pop art** took images of popular culture and transformed them into works of fine art. Andy Warhol was the most famous of the pop artists.

In the 1980s, styles emerged that have been called *postmodern.* **Postmodernism** is marked by a revival of traditional elements and techniques. These include not only traditional painting styles, but also traditional crafts. Weavers, potters, glassmakers, metalsmiths, and furniture makers have all gained respect as postmodern artists. During the 1980s and 1990s, many artists experimented with technologies, such as digital cameras and computer programs, to create new art forms. These new art forms are often interactive and give the viewer the opportunity to influence the production of the artwork itself.

9. What new art forms and styles have emerged since the 1960s?

____

____

____

____

____

• Popular Culture *(page 893)*

The United States has been the most powerful force in shaping popular culture in the West and, to a lesser degree, the whole world. Through movies, television, and music, the United States has spread its ideals and values of material prosperity ("the American Dream") around the world. Other countries often object to the influence of American culture. It has been called "cultural imperialism."

American movies have dominated both European and American markets since the end of World War II. Television did not become available until the 1940s, but it spread quickly. By 1954, there were 32 million television sets in the United States. As television spread around the world in the 1960s, U.S. programs became popular in both European and non-Western countries.

The United States has also dominated popular music since the end of World War II. Jazz, blues, rhythm and blues, rock, and rap have been the most popular music forms in the Western world (and in much of the non-Western world) during this time. All of these music forms began in the United States, and all are rooted in African American musical traditions. American popular music inspired musicians in other countries, who then transformed music in their own way. For example, in the 1950s, American musicians such as Chuck Berry and Elvis Presley inspired the Beatles and other British musicians. The Beatles then led an "invasion" of the United States in the 1960s that inspired new American musicians. An increasing number of performers are moving beyond regional boundaries to develop international audiences. For example, in the late 1990s, Latin American artists became popular in non-Latin markets. The development of the video music channel MTV in the early 1980s has also changed the music scene, by making image as important as sound to the selling of records.

10. What is "cultural imperialism"?

• Sports, Television, Politics *(page 894)*

In the postwar years, sports became big business. Through television, sports were transformed into a worldwide experience. Many sports organizations began to receive most of their revenues from television contracts. The Olympics, for example, are now funded chiefly by American television. These funds come from advertising sponsors.

Sports have become big politics as well as big business. Soccer, for example, is a source of national pride in many countries. Unfortunately, this has sometimes led to violence. Another example of the mix of politics and sports is the Olympic Games. The Soviets used the Olympics to promote the Communist system. In 1972, at the Munich Games, a Palestinian terrorist group seized 11 Israeli athletes as hostages. All of the hostages were killed. The United States boycotted the 1980 Moscow Olympics, and the Soviets responded by refusing to participate in the Los Angeles Games in 1984.

11. What are some ways that sports and politics have been mixed?

Name ______________________ Date ______________ Class ______________

Reading Essentials and Study Guide

Chapter 29, Section 1

For use with textbook pages 901–905

GENERAL TRENDS IN LATIN AMERICA

KEY TERMS

multinational corporation a company with divisions in more than two countries *(page 902)*

magic realism a movement in Latin American literature in which realistic events are mixed with dreamlike or fantastic backgrounds *(page 905)*

DRAWING FROM EXPERIENCE

Have you ever bought anything that was grown or made in a Latin American country? If so, what?

In this section, you will learn about developments in Latin America since the end of World War II. Exporting raw materials and importing manufactured goods led to economic and political problems for many Latin American nations.

ORGANIZING YOUR THOUGHTS

Use the chart below to help you take notes. For each topic in the chart, describe its effect on the countries of Latin America.

Effect on Latin American Countries of:	
Great Depression	**1.**
multinational corporations	**2.**
borrowing from foreign countries	**3.**
debt crisis	**4.**
population growth	**5.**
Cold War	**6.**

READ TO LEARN

• Economic and Political Developments *(page 901)*

Since the nineteenth century, Latin Americans had exported raw materials and imported manufactured goods from industrialized countries. As a result of the Great Depression, exports declined, and the Latin American countries did not have the money they needed to buy imported goods. In response, many Latin American countries developed their own industries to produce goods that had been imported previously. By the 1960s, however, Latin American countries still had economic problems. They were dependent on the United States, Europe, and Japan for the technology needed for modern industries. Many Latin American countries also had problems finding markets for their manufactured goods.

In the 1960s, military governments in Chile, Brazil, and Argentina returned to export-import economies. These governments also encouraged **multinational corporations** (companies with divisions in more than two countries) to come to Latin America. Multinational corporations made these countries more dependent on industrialized nations. In the 1970s, Latin American nations became even more dependent as they tried to maintain their weak economies by borrowing money. By 1982, many Latin American economies had begun to crumble. Wages fell. Unemployment and inflation skyrocketed. To get new loans, Latin American governments were now forced to make basic reforms. During this process, many people began to believe that government had taken control of too many industries. Many people also believed that peasants should be encouraged to grow food for use within their country rather than for export. They hoped that this would stop the flow of people from the countryside to the cities.

With the debt crisis of the 1980s came a movement toward democracy. Some military leaders were unwilling to deal with the huge debt problems. Many people also began to realize that military power alone could not create a strong state. By the mid-1990s, several democratic governments had been created. But this revival of democracy was sometimes fragile. For example, in 1992, President Fujimori of Peru returned that country to an authoritarian system.

7. What is a multinational corporation?

____

____

____

____

____

Reading Essentials and Study Guide

• Latin American Society *(page 904)*

Latin America's economic problems were made worse by dramatic growth in population. By the mid-1980s, the population of Latin America had grown to 400 million. With the increase in population, there was an increase in the size of cities. By 1990, 29 Latin American cities had over a million people. Slums or shantytowns became part of many of these cities. The gap between the poor and the rich was still enormous in Latin America. Peasants and the urban poor struggled just to survive.

The international drug trade brought crime and corruption to some Latin American countries. This undermined their stability. Bolivia, Peru, and Colombia were especially big producers of cocaine and marijuana.

8. How has the international drug trade affected Latin American countries?

• The United States and Latin America *(page 904)*

The United States has always played a large role in Latin America. For years, the United States sent troops into Latin American countries to protect U.S. interests and to help dictators that were friendly to the United States. In 1948, the countries of the Western Hemisphere formed the Organization of American States (OAS). The OAS called for an end to military involvement by one state in the affairs of any other state. But the formation of the OAS did not end U.S. involvement in Latin American affairs. As the Cold War developed, the United States took action when it believed that Soviet agents were trying to establish Communist governments. The United States also provided huge amounts of military aid to anti-Communist governments.

9. What are some reasons that the United States has taken military action in Latin America?

• Latin American Culture *(page 905)*

Writers and artists in Latin America have a very high status. They are seen as people who can express the hopes of the people. In literature, Latin Americans developed a unique form of expression called **magic realism.** Magic realism brings together realistic events with dreamlike or fantastic backgrounds. Perhaps the foremost example of magic realism is *One Hundred Years of Solitude,* a novel by Gabriel García Márquez. Another important Latin American writer is the Chilean poet Gabriela Mistral. Both García Márquez and Mistral have been awarded the Nobel Prize for literature.

Latin American art and architecture were strongly influenced by international styles after World War II. In painting, abstract styles were especially important. Some of the best examples of modern architecture can be seen in Brasília, the capital city of Brazil. Latin America's greatest modern architect, Oscar Niemeyer, designed some of the major buildings in Brasília.

10. Why do writers and artists enjoy a high status in Latin America?

____

____

____

____

____

Name ______________________ Date ______________________ Class ______________________

Reading Essentials and Study Guide

Chapter 29, Section 2

For use with textbook pages 906–909

MEXICO, CUBA, AND CENTRAL AMERICA

KEY TERMS

privatization the sale of government-owned companies to private firms *(page 907)*

trade embargo prohibiting trade with a particular country *(page 907)*

contra a member of a group in Nicaragua opposed to the Sandinistas *(page 909)*

DRAWING FROM EXPERIENCE

How far is Cuba from the United States? What kind of relationship does our country have with Cuba? Have you ever bought any goods grown or made in Cuba? Why do you think this is so?

In the last section, you read about general trends in all of Latin America. In this section, you will read about economic and political crises in Mexico, Cuba, and Central America following World War II.

ORGANIZING YOUR THOUGHTS

Use the chart below to help you take notes. The United States has been involved in the affairs of many Latin American countries. Describe U.S. relations after World War II with the countries in this chart.

U.S. Relations With:	
Cuba	**1.**
El Salvador	**2.**
Nicaragua	**3.**
Panama	**4.**

Name ______________________ Date ______________ Class ______________

Reading Essentials and Study Guide

READ TO LEARN

• The Mexican Way *(page 906)*

The official political party of the Mexican Revolution was the Institutional Revolutionary Party (PRI). It came to dominate Mexico. Every six years, leaders of the PRI chose the party's presidential candidate, who was then elected by the people. During the 1950s and 1960s, economic growth led to real gains in wages for more and more people in Mexico. At the end of the 1960s, however, students began to protest the one-party system in Mexico. On October 2, 1968, university students gathered in Mexico City to protest government policies. Police forces opened fire and killed hundreds. People became concerned about the need for change. The next two presidents, Luís Echeverría and José López Portillo, made political reforms and opened the door to new political parties. Greater freedom of debate in the press and universities was allowed.

In the late 1970s, new reserves of oil were discovered in Mexico. The sale of oil abroad increased dramatically. The government became more dependent on oil revenues. When oil prices dropped in the mid-1980s, Mexico was no longer able to make payments on its foreign debt. The government was forced to adopt new economic policies. One of these policies was **privatization** (the sale of government-owned companies to private firms). The debt crisis and rising unemployment caused support for the PRI to drop. In 2000, Vicente Fox defeated the PRI candidate for the presidency.

5. What was the effect of the discovery of oil on the Mexican economy?

____

____

____

____

____

• The Cuban Revolution *(page 907)*

In the 1950s, a strong opposition movement arose in Cuba. The movement was led by Fidel Castro and overthrew the government of the dictator Fulgencio Batista in 1959. Many Cubans who disagreed with Castro fled to the United States. When Cuba began to receive aid and arms from the Soviet Union and Eastern Europe, relations with the United States deteriorated. In October 1960, the United States declared a **trade embargo** (prohibited trade with Cuba) and broke all diplomatic relations with Cuba. In April 1961, the American president, John F. Kennedy, supported an attempt to overthrow Castro's government. When the invasion at the Bay of Pigs failed, the Soviets decided to make an even greater commitment to Cuba. In December 1961,

Name ______________________ Date ______________ Class ______________

Castro declared that he was a Marxist. The Soviets began placing missiles in Cuba in 1962, which led to the Cuban missile crisis.

The Cuban missile crisis caused Castro to realize that the Soviet Union had been unreliable. Castro tried to start his own revolutionary movement in the rest of Latin America, but this failed. Castro's Marxist government continued in Cuba, but with mixed results. The Cuban people did benefit in some ways. The government provided free medical services for all citizens. Illiteracy in Cuba was nearly eliminated.

The Cuban economy relied on the production and sale of sugar. Economic problems forced Castro's government to depend on Soviet aid and the purchase of Cuban sugar by Soviet bloc countries. After the collapse of these Communist governments in 1989, Cuba lost their support. Economic conditions in Cuba have steadily declined, but Castro has managed to remain in power.

6. How did the collapse of Communist governments in Eastern Europe affect Cuba?

• Upheaval in Central America *(page 908)*

Central America includes seven countries: Costa Rica, Nicaragua, Honduras, El Salvador, Panama, Belize and Guatemala. Central America has depended on the export of bananas, coffee, and cotton. Prices for these products have varied over time. This has created economic crises at different times. A huge gulf between the wealthy elite and poor peasants in these countries has also created a climate of instability. Fear of communism has often led the United States to support repressive regimes in this area.

In El Salvador, the wealthy elite and the military controlled the government after World War II. In the late 1970s and the 1980s, El Salvador was torn apart by a bloody civil war. Marxist-led guerrillas and right-wing groups fought one another. During the presidency of Ronald Reagan, the United States provided weapons and training to the Salvadoran army to defeat the guerrillas. In 1984, José Duarte, a moderate, was elected president. But the elections did not stop the killing. By the early 1990s, the civil war had led to the deaths of at least 75,000 people. In 1992, a peace settlement finally brought the war to an end.

Reading Essentials and Study Guide

Chapter 29, Section 2 *(continued)*

In Nicaragua, the Somoza family took control of the government in 1937 and kept control for the next 42 years. The Somoza government had the support of the United States during most of this time. But the Somozas got rich at the nation's expense and used murder and torture against their opponents. By 1979, the United States was no longer willing to support the Somoza government. In that year, Marxist guerrilla forces, known as the Sandinista National Liberation Front, won a number of victories against the government forces. They gained control of the country. Soon, a group called the **contras,** who were opposed to the Sandinistas' policies, began to try to overthrow the new government. The Reagan and Bush administrations in the United States supported the contras, because they were worried about the Sandinistas' ties with the Soviet Union. The war with the contras caused the Sandinistas to lose support. In 1990, the Sandinistas agreed to free elections. They lost to a coalition headed by Violeta Barrios de Chamorro. They lost again in 2001 but remained one of the strongest parties in Nicaragua.

Panama became a nation in 1903, when it broke away from Colombia with the help of the United States. In return for this help, the United States gained control of the Panama Canal. The United States also had a great deal of influence over the government and economy of Panama. After 1968, power in Panama came into the hands of the military leaders of Panama's National Guard. One of these leaders, Manuel Noriega, took control of Panama in 1983. At first, the United States supported Noriega. But his brutality and involvement with the drug trade turned American leaders against him. In 1989, President George Bush sent U.S. troops to Panama. Noriega was arrested and sent to prison in the United States on charges of drug trafficking.

7. What are the main export products of Central America? How has the export of these products affected the Central American economies?

____

____

____

____

____

Name ______________________ Date ______________________ Class ______________________

Reading Essentials and Study Guide

Chapter 29, Section 3

For use with textbook pages 911–914

THE NATIONS OF SOUTH AMERICA

KEY TERMS

cooperative a farm organization owned by and operated for the peasants' benefit *(page 913)*

Shining Path a radical guerrilla group in Peru whose goal was to smash all authority and create a classless society *(page 913)*

DRAWING FROM EXPERIENCE

Have you ever seen the musical or movie *Evita*? Who was Evita? Why do you think a musical was written about her?

In the last section, you read about economic and political crises in Mexico, Cuba, and Central America following World War II. In this section, you will read about economic, political, and social problems in South America during the same period.

ORGANIZING YOUR THOUGHTS

Use the chart below to help you take notes. The military has played an important role in many South American countries. Describe the role of the military in each of the countries in this chart.

Role of the Military in:	
Argentina	**1.**
Brazil	**2.**
Chile	**3.**
Peru	**4.**

READ TO LEARN

- **Argentina** *(page 911)*

Argentina is Latin America's second largest country. For years, it had been ruled by a powerful oligarchy. In 1943, a group of army officials overthrew the oligarchy. Juan Perón, the labor secretary of the new military government, tried to win the support of the workers. He encouraged them to join labor unions. He also increased job benefits and the number of paid vacations and holidays. In 1944, Perón became vice president of the military government. He made sure that people knew that he was responsible for the better conditions for workers. Perón was elected president of Argentina in 1946. His main support came from labor and the urban middle class. To please them, he followed a policy of increased industrialization. He also tried to free Argentina from foreign investors. The government bought the railways and took over the banking, insurance, shipping, and communications industries. Perón's regime was authoritarian. He created Fascist gangs modeled after Hitler's Brownshirts. The gangs used violence to terrify Perón's opponents. Fearing Perón's power, the military overthrew him in September 1955. Perón went into exile in Spain. The military leaders were soon overwhelmed by problems and allowed Perón to return. He was reelected as president in 1973 but died a year later.

In 1976, the military once again took control. The new regime allowed no opposition. Perhaps 36,000 people were killed. At the same time, there were serious economic problems. To divert people's attention, the military government invaded the Falkland Islands in April 1982. The Falklands were islands off the coast of Argentina that Great Britain had controlled since the nineteenth century. Great Britain sent ships and troops and took the islands back. The loss made the military look bad. In 1983, Raúl Alfonsín was elected president and worked to restore democratic practices. In 1989, the Perónist Carlos Saúl Menem won the presidential election. This peaceful transfer of power made many people hope that Argentina was moving on a democratic path.

5. Who were Perón's main supporters? How did he gain their support?

____

____

____

- **Brazil** *(page 912)*

Like other Latin American countries, Brazil experienced severe economic problems after World War II. When democratic governments were unable to solve these problems, the military stepped in and took control in 1964. The military remained in control for the next 20 years. It set a new economic direction. It reduced government interference in the economy and stressed free market forces. Beginning in 1968, Brazil experienced an "economic miracle." Its economy grew spectacularly. But ordinary Brazilians benefited very little from this economic growth. The gulf between rich and poor grew even wider.

Rapid development led to an inflation rate of 100 percent a year. The military government was overwhelmed. This opened the door for a return to democracy in 1985. The new democratic government faced enormous problems. Brazil had a huge foreign debt, severe inflation (800 percent in 1987), and a lack of social unity. In the 1990s, a series of democratically elected presidents managed to restore some stability to Brazil's economy.

6. In what ways did Brazil experience an "economic miracle"? In what ways was it not a miracle?

____

____

____

• Chile *(page 913)*

In 1970, Salvador Allende, a Marxist, became president of Chile. He tried to create a socialist society by constitutional means. He increased the wages of industrial workers and nationalized the largest corporations. In March 1973, new elections increased the number of Allende's supporters in the Chilean congress. The Chilean army, under the direction of General Augusto Pinochet, was afraid of Allende's power. In September 1973, military forces seized the presidential palace and shot Allende. The military then set up a dictatorship.

The Pinochet dictatorship was one of the most brutal in Chile's history. Thousands of opponents were imprisoned. Others were tortured and murdered. The regime also outlawed all political parties and did away with the congress. The abuses of human rights led to unrest in the 1980s. In 1989, free presidential elections led to the defeat of Pinochet. Chile moved toward a more democratic system

7. What were some characteristics of Pinochet's regime?

____

____

____

• Peru *(page 913)*

The history of Peru has been marked by instability. Peru's dependence on exports has led to extreme ups and downs in the economy. With these ups and downs have come many changes in the government. A military takeover in 1968 brought General Juan Velasco Alvarado to power. He tried to help the peasants. His government took almost 75 percent of the nation's large landed estates and gave the land to peasant **cooperatives** (farm organizations owned by and operated for the benefit of the peasants). The government also nationalized many foreign-owned companies and kept food prices low to help urban workers. Economic problems continued, and military leaders removed General Alvarado from power in 1975.

Five years later, the military returned Peru to civilian rule. There were new problems for the civilian government. A radical guerrilla group with ties to Communist China, known as **Shining Path,** emerged. It killed mayors, missionaries, priests, and peasants. The goal of Shining Path was to smash all authority and create a classless society. In 1990, Peruvians chose Alberto Fujimori as president. Fujimori promised reforms. Two years later, he suspended the constitution and congress and became a dictator. He began a campaign against Shining Path. He was removed from power in 2000. In June 2001, Alejandro Toledo became the first freely elected president of Native American descent.

8. How has Peru's dependence on exports affected its economy and government?

____

____

____

• Colombia *(page 914)*

Colombia has had a democratic political system for a long time, but a conservative elite has dominated the government. After World War II, Marxist guerrilla groups began to organize Colombian peasants. The government responded with violence. More than two hundred thousand peasants had been killed by the mid-1960s. Peasants who lived in poverty turned to a new cash crop—coca leaves. Coca leaves are used to make cocaine. The drug trade increased. Drug lords formed cartels (groups of drug businesses). The cartels used bribes and violence to eliminate competitors and to force government cooperation. Attempts to stop the traffic in drugs had little success. The government has begun an aerial eradication program, but Colombia still supplies the majority of cocaine to the international drug market.

Colombia continues to have major economic problems. Unemployment is high (around 20 percent in 2000). Colombia's main exports, coffee and oil, often fluctuate in price, which leads to ups and downs in the economy.

9. How did the drug trade begin in Colombia? What has the government done to try to stop it?

____

____

____

Name ______________________ Date ______________________ Class ______________________

Reading Essentials and Study Guide

Chapter 30, Section 1

For use with textbook pages 921–927

INDEPENDENCE IN AFRICA

KEY TERMS

apartheid ("apartness") a system of racial segregation in South Africa *(page 922)*

Pan-Africanism the unity of all black Africans, regardless of national boundaries *(page 923)*

DRAWING FROM EXPERIENCE

Have you read any poems by Africans? Have you seen any African artwork? Have you listened to any African music? What do these art forms tell you about African culture?

In this section, you will learn about political, economic, social, and cultural developments in Africa following World War II. Most African nations achieved their independence during this period.

ORGANIZING YOUR THOUGHTS

Use the diagram below to help you take notes. Poverty is widespread in much of Africa. Identify six problems in Africa that account for much of its poverty.

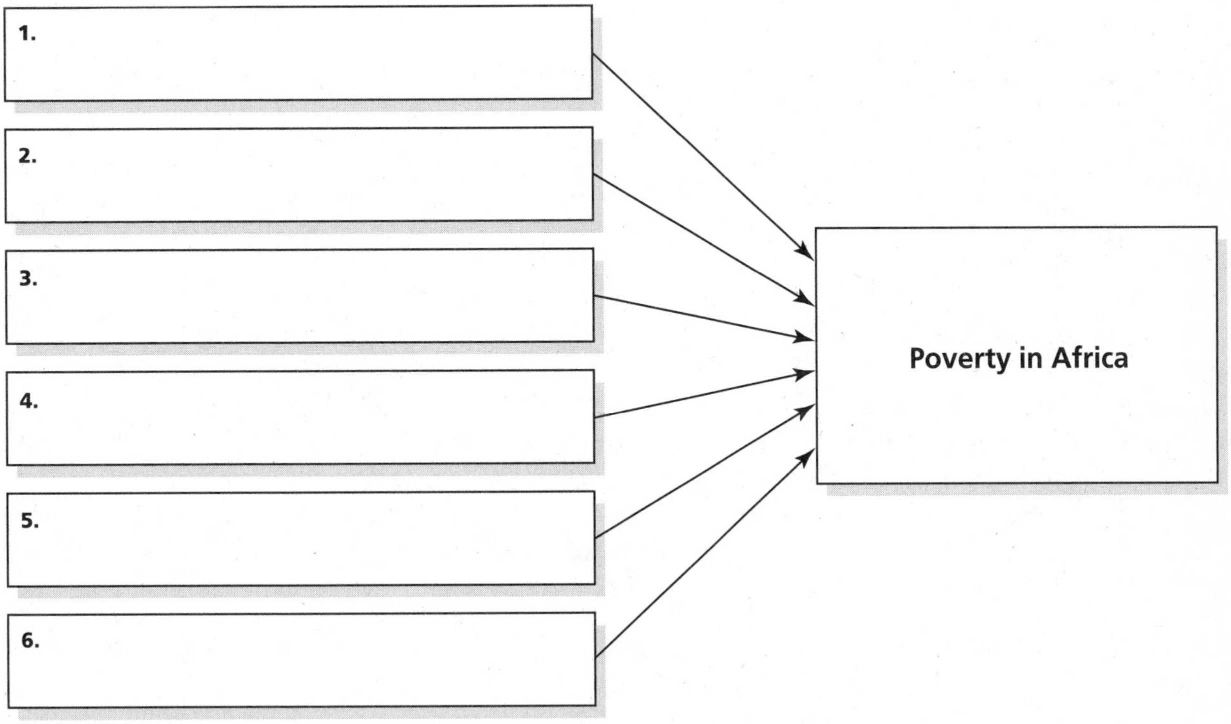

READ TO LEARN

• The Transition to Independence *(page 921)*

After World War II, Europeans realized that colonial rule would have to end. Great Britain and France both decided to let go of their colonial empires. In the 1950s and 1960s, most black African nations gained their independence. In 1957, the Gold Coast was the first former British colony to gain independence. It was renamed Ghana. Nigeria, the Belgian Congo (renamed Zaire), Kenya, and others followed. Seventeen new African nations emerged in 1960. Another 11 nations followed between 1961 and 1965. After a series of guerrilla wars, the Portuguese finally gave up their colonies of Mozambique and Angola in the 1970s. In North Africa, the French gave Morocco and Tunisia their independence in 1956. The French chose to keep control of Algeria, but independence was finally granted in 1962.

In South Africa, the situation was more complicated. By the 1950s, South African whites that were descendants of the Dutch (called Afrikaners) had laws separating whites and blacks. The result was a system of racial segregation known as **apartheid** ("apartness"). Blacks had formed the African National Congress (ANC) in 1912. Its goal was economic and political reform, but it had little success. Blacks demonstrated against the apartheid laws, but the white government brutally repressed the demonstrators. After the arrest of ANC leader Nelson Mandela in 1962, members of the ANC called for armed resistance to the white government.

7. What was apartheid?

____

____

____

____

____

• The New Nations *(page 923)*

Most of the leaders of the newly independent African nations came from the urban middle class. They had studied in either Europe or the United States. They spoke and read European languages and believed in democracy. The views of these leaders on economics were more diverse. Some believed in Western-style capitalism. Others wanted an "African form of socialism." The African form of socialism was based on African traditions of community. Ownership of the country's wealth would be put in the hands of the people. Some African leaders believed in the dream of **Pan-Africanism** (the unity of all black Africans, regardless of national boundaries). Pan-Africanism was supported by several of the new African leaders, including Léopold Senghor of Senegal, Kwame Nkrumah of Ghana, and Jomo Kenyatta of Kenya. The Organization of African Unity (OAU) was a result of the belief in Pan-Africanism. It was founded in 1963 by the leaders of 32 African nations. The OAU has contributed to African unity through such activities as settling border disputes.

Independence did not bring economic prosperity to the new African nations. Most of the countries still relied on the export of a single crop or natural resource. When prices for these exports dropped, their economies suffered. Most African nations also had to import technology and manufactured goods from the West. The new nations sometimes created their own problems. Natural resources were spent on military equipment or expensive consumer goods rather than on building the foundations for an industrial economy. Corruption and bribery became common. Population growth also kept many countries from creating modern economies. Drought conditions led to widespread hunger and starvation. Millions fled to neighboring countries in search of food. In recent years, the spread of acquired immunodeficiency syndrome (AIDS) in Africa has reached epidemic proportions. According to one estimate, one-third of the population of sub-Saharan Africa is infected with the virus that causes AIDS. As a result of all these problems, poverty is widespread in Africa. Cities have grown tremendously. They are often surrounded by slums populated by people who came to the cities looking for work. Millions live without water and electricity in their homes. At the same time, a few people enjoy lavish lifestyles. The rich in many East African countries are known as the *wabenzi* (Mercedes-Benz people).

Many people had hoped that independence would lead to stable political systems based on "one person, one vote." They were soon disappointed. Democratic governments gave way to military regimes and one-party states. Between 1957 and 1982, over 70 leaders of African countries were overthrown by violence. Within many African nations, there were warring ethnic groups. The concept of nationhood was not strong. This was the result of the way that the countries were formed. The boundaries of many African countries had been drawn arbitrarily by colonial powers. Nearly all of these countries included different ethnic, linguistic, and territorial groups. During the late 1960s, civil war tore Nigeria apart. Northerners began to kill the Ibo people, who fled to their home region in the eastern part of Nigeria. The Ibo declared the eastern region of Nigeria an independent state called Biafra. After three years of bloody civil war, Biafra finally surrendered and accepted the authority of the Nigerian government. In central Africa, fighting between the Hutu and Tutsi created unstable governments in both Burundi and Rwanda. In 1994, a Hutu rampage left five hundred thousand Tutsi dead in Rwanda.

8. What two economic systems have African leaders advocated?

- **New Hopes** *(page 925)*

In recent years, demonstrations have led to the rise of democracies in several countries. In Uganda, for example, Idi Amin had ruled by terror and repression throughout the 1970s, but he was deposed in 1979. Dictatorships also came to an end in Ethiopia, Liberia, and Somalia. In these cases, however, the fall of the dictatorships was followed by civil war.

One of the most remarkable events in recent African history was the election of Nelson Mandela to the presidency of the Republic of South Africa. Mandela had been sentenced to life imprisonment in 1962 for his activities with the ANC. He spent 27 years in prison. Bishop Desmond Tutu and others worked to free him and to end apartheid in South Africa. Worldwide pressure on the white South African government led to reforms and the end of apartheid laws. In 1990, Mandela was released from prison. In 1993, the government agreed to hold democratic elections. In 1994, Nelson Mandela became South Africa's first black president.

9. What factors contributed to the release of Nelson Mandela and the end of apartheid laws in South Africa?

- **Society and Culture in Modern Africa** *(page 926)*

Africa is a study in contrasts. Old and new, native and foreign live side by side. There is a constant tension between traditional ways and Western culture. Most African cities look like cities elsewhere in the world. They have high-rise apartments, neon lights, movie theaters, and traffic jams. Outside the major cities, where about three-quarters of the people of Africa live, modern influence has had less of an impact. Millions of people live much as their ancestors did, in thatched dwellings without modern plumbing and electricity. They farm, hunt, or raise livestock by traditional methods. They also wear traditional clothing and practice traditional beliefs. Many urban people see rural people as backward. Rural people see the cities as corrupting and destructive to traditional African values and customs.

Independence from colonial powers had an impact on women's roles in Africa. Women were allowed to vote and run for political office. Women dominate some professions, such as teaching, child care, and clerical work, but they do not have the range of career opportunities that men do. Most African women are employed in low-paid positions. In many rural areas, traditional attitudes toward women, including arranged marriages, still prevail.

Africans have kept their native artistic traditions while adapting them to foreign influences. A dilemma for many African artists is the need to balance Western techniques and training with the rich heritage of traditional African art forms. In some countries, governments make the artists' decisions for them. Artists are told to depict scenes of traditional African life. These works are designed to serve the tourist industry.

African writers have often addressed the tensions and dilemmas that modern Africans face. The conflicting demands of town versus country and native versus foreign were the themes of most of the best-known works of the 1960s and 1970s. For example, the novels of Chinua Achebe show the problems of Africans caught up in the conflict between traditional and Western values.

10. How do most of the people of Africa live?

____

____

____

____

____

Name ______________________ Date ______________ Class ______________

Reading Essentials and Study Guide

Chapter 30, Section 2

For use with textbook pages 929–934

CONFLICT IN THE MIDDLE EAST

KEY TERMS

Pan-Arabism Arab unity *(page 931)*

intifada ("uprising") a movement among PLO supporters living inside Israel *(page 932)*

DRAWING FROM EXPERIENCE

Have you ever looked at a world map to find the Middle East? The Middle Eastern countries are located on two continents. What are the two continents? Why do geographers classify countries from two different continents into the same region (the Middle East)? What do these countries have in common?

In the last section, you read about developments in Africa following World War II. In this section, you will read about developments in the Middle East during this time. There have been many armed conflicts in this region.

ORGANIZING YOUR THOUGHTS

Use the chart below to help you take notes. Identify the causes and outcomes of each conflict in this chart.

Middle East Conflict	Causes	Outcomes
Suez War of 1956	1.	2.
Six-Day War of 1967	3.	4.
Arab-Israeli War of 1973	5.	6.
Iraq-Iran War (1980s)	7.	8.
Persian Gulf War	9.	10.

Reading Essentials and Study Guide

READ TO LEARN

• The Question of Palestine *(page 929)*

In the Middle East, World War II led to the emergence of new independent states. Syria and Lebanon gained their independence near the end of World War II. Jordan achieved self-rule soon after the war. These new states were predominantly Muslim.

In the years between the two world wars, many Jews had immigrated to Palestine. Tensions between Jews and Arabs had increased during the 1930s. Great Britain governed Palestine under a United Nations mandate. It had limited Jewish immigration into the area and had rejected proposals for an independent Jewish state in Palestine. As a result of the Holocaust, sympathy for the Jewish cause grew following World War II. In 1948, a United Nations resolution divided Palestine into a Jewish state and an Arab state. The Jews in Palestine proclaimed the state of Israel on May 14, 1948. Israel's Arab neighbors saw the new state as a betrayal of the Palestinian people, most of whom were Muslim. Several Arab countries invaded Israel. The invasion failed, but the Arab states still refused to recognize Israel's right to exist. As a result of the division of Palestine, hundreds of thousands of Palestinians fled to neighboring Arab countries. Other Palestinians came under Israeli rule.

11. How did the Holocaust influence events in the Middle East?

____

____

____

• Nasser and Pan-Arabism *(page 930)*

In the early 1950s, Colonel Gamal Abdel Nasser took control of the Egyptian government. On July 26, 1956, Nasser seized the Suez Canal Company, which had been under British and French control. Great Britain and France decided to strike back. Israel quickly joined them. The three nations launched an attack on Egypt. This started the Suez War of 1956. The United States and the Soviet Union supported Nasser and forced Britain, France, and Israel to withdraw their troops from Egypt.

Nasser emerged from the conflict as a powerful leader. He now began to promote **Pan-Arabism** (Arab unity). In March 1958, Egypt united with Syria to form the United Arab Republic (UAR). Nasser was named the first president of this new state. Egypt and Syria hoped that the union would eventually include all Arab states. But many other Arab leaders were suspicious of Pan-Arabism. Oil-rich Arab states were concerned that they would have to share revenues with poorer states in the Middle East. In 1961, military leaders took over Syria and withdrew the country from its union with Egypt.

12. What is Pan-Arabism? Why were some Arab leaders suspicious of it?

____

____

____

• The Arab-Israeli Dispute *(page 931)*

During the late 1950s and 1960s, the dispute between Israel and other states in the Middle East became more heated. In 1967, Nasser imposed a blockade against Israeli shipping through the Gulf of Aqaba. He also said that he was ready to confront Israel. Fearing attack, Israel launched air strikes against Egypt and several of its Arab neighbors on June 5, 1967. Israeli planes wiped out most of the Egyptian air force. Israeli armies broke the blockade and occupied the Sinai Peninsula. Israel also seized territory on the West Bank of the Jordan River, occupied Jerusalem, and took control of the Golan Heights. During this Six-Day War, Israel tripled the size of its territory. Over the next few years, Arab states demanded the return of the occupied territories. Nasser died in 1970 and was succeeded by Anwar el-Sadat. In 1973, Arab forces led by Sadat launched a new attack against Israel. This conflict ended in 1974 by a cease-fire agreement negotiated by the UN.

The war was having indirect effects in Western nations. A number of Arab oil-producing states had formed the Organization of Petroleum Exporting Countries (OPEC) in 1960 to gain control over oil prices. During the 1973 war, some OPEC nations announced large increases in the price of oil to foreign countries. The price hikes and cuts in oil production led to oil shortages in the United States and Europe. In 1977, U.S. president Jimmy Carter began to push for a peace agreement between Arabs and Israelis. In September 1978, Carter met with President Sadat of Egypt and Israeli Prime Minister Menachem Begin at Camp David. The result was the Camp David Accords, an agreement to sign an Israeli-Egyptian peace treaty. Sadat and Begin signed the treaty in March 1979. It ended the war between Egypt and Israel.

13. Why did the United States become involved in the Arab-Israeli conflict? What was the result?

____

____

____

Name ______________________ Date ______________________ Class ______________________

• The PLO and the *Intifada* *(page 932)*

In 1964, the Egyptians took the lead in forming the Palestine Liberation Organization (PLO) to represent the interests of the Palestinians. The PLO believed that only the Palestinian peoples had the right to create a state in Palestine. A guerrilla movement called al-Fatah began to launch terrorist attacks on Israeli territory. The PLO leader Yasir Arafat headed it. During the early 1980s, Palestinian Arabs became even more militant. This militancy led to a movement called the ***intifada*** ("uprising") among PLO supporters living inside Israel.

As the 1990s began, peace talks opened between Israel and a number of its Arab neighbors. Finally, in 1993, Israel and the PLO reached an agreement calling for Palestinian autonomy in certain areas of Israel. In return, the PLO recognized the Israeli state. Yasir Arafat became the head of the semi-independent area known as the Palestinian Authority.

14. What is the PLO? What agreement did it reach with Israel in 1993?

____

____

____

• Revolution in Iran *(page 932)*

The leadership of Shah Mohammad Reza Pahlavi and revenue from oil helped Iran to become a rich country. But there was much opposition to the shah in Iran. Millions of devout Muslims looked with distaste at the new Iranian civilization. In their eyes, it was based on greed and materialism, which they identified with American influence. Leading the opposition to the shah was the Ayatollah Ruhollah Khomeini, a member of the Muslim clergy. In 1979, the shah's government collapsed and was replaced by an Islamic republic. The new government, led by Ayatollah Khomeini, began to restore Islamic law. Anti-American sentiments led to the taking of 52 American hostages from the United States embassy in Tehran. After the death of Khomeini in 1989, a new government under President Hashemi Rafsanjani, began to loosen control over personal expression and social activities. But a new wave of government repression began in the mid-1990s.

15. Why did many Muslims in Iran oppose the shah?

____

____

____

• Iraq's Aggression *(page 933)*

Iraq and Iran have had a poor relationship for a long time. Both are Muslim nations, but the Iranians are mainly Shiites, while most Iraqi leaders are Sunnis. Iran and Iraq have also had disputes over territory, especially the Strait of Hormuz, which connects the Persian Gulf and the Gulf of Oman. In 1980, President Saddam Hussein of Iraq launched an attack on Iran. Poison gas was used against civilians, and children were used to clear minefields. A ceasefire was finally arranged in 1988.

In 1990, Iraqi troops moved across the border and occupied the small neighboring country of Kuwait. This sparked what has been called the Persian Gulf War. The United States led an international force that freed Kuwait and destroyed a large part of Iraq's armed forces. The allies hoped that a revolt within Iraq would overthrow Hussein, but he remained in power.

16. Why do Iraq and Iran have a poor relationship?

____

____

____

• Afghanistan and the Taliban *(page 933)*

After World War II, the king of Afghanistan developed close ties with the Soviet Union, in order to gain economic assistance for his country. After the king was overthrown, new leaders attempted to create a Communist government, but groups wanting to create an Islamic state opposed them. One of the new leaders, Babrak Karmal asked for aid from the Soviets, who launched an invasion of Afghanistan in 1979. The Soviets occupied Afghanistan for 10 years but were forced to withdraw by anti-Communist forces supported by the United States and Pakistan. Various Islamic groups began to fight for control. One of these, the Taliban, seized Kabul, the capital, in 1996. By the fall of 1998, the Taliban controlled more than two-thirds of the country.

The Taliban was condemned for its human rights abuses and harsh social policies. It was also suspected of sheltering Osama bin Laden and his al-Qaeda organization. In 1990 and 2000, the United Nations Security Council demanded that the Taliban hand over bin Laden for trial, but it refused. In 2001, the Taliban was driven out of Kabul by rebel forces and American bombers.

17. What is the Taliban? Why has it been condemned?

____

____

____

• Society and Culture *(page 933)*

In recent years, conservative religious forces have tried to replace foreign culture and values with Islamic beliefs and behavior. This movement is called Islamic revivalism or Islamic activism. For most Muslims, the Islamic revival is a reassertion of cultural identity, religious observance, family values, and morality. In the eyes of some Islamic leaders, Western values and culture are based on materialism, greed, and immorality. The goal of Muslim extremists is to remove all Western influence in Muslim countries. The movement to return to the pure ideals of Islam began in Iran, under the Ayatollah Khomeini. In revolutionary Iran, the return to traditional Muslim beliefs affected clothing styles, social practices, and the legal system. In Egypt, militant Muslims assassinated President Sadat in 1981. The extreme and militant movements in Islam have received much media exposure, giving many people an unfavorable impression of Islam.

At the beginning of the twentieth century, women's place in Middle Eastern society had changed little for hundreds of years. In the nineteenth and twentieth centuries, many Muslim scholars argued for the need to rethink outdated practices that prevented women from realizing their potential. Until the 1970s, there was a general trend in urban areas toward a greater role for women. Beginning in the 1970s, however, there was a shift back toward more traditional roles for women. This trend was especially noticeable in Iran.

The literature and art of the Middle East since 1945 has reflected a rise in national awareness. This encouraged an interest in historical traditions. Literature is no longer reserved for the elite but is increasingly written for broader audiences. The most famous contemporary Egyptian writer is Naguib Mahfouz. He was the first writer in Arabic to win the Nobel Prize for literature. Middle Eastern artists tended to imitate Western models at first. Later, they began to experiment with national styles and returned to earlier forms for inspiration.

18. What is Islamic revivalism?

____

____

____

____

____

Name ______________________ Date ____________________ Class ______________________

Reading Essentials and Study Guide

Chapter 31, Section 1

For use with textbook pages 941–946

COMMUNIST CHINA

KEY TERMS

commune a vast collective farm in China that contained more than thirty thousand people who lived and worked together *(page 942)*

permanent revolution an atmosphere of constant revolutionary fervor *(page 942)*

per capita per person *(page 943)*

DRAWING FROM EXPERIENCE

Do you have any relatives who fought in the Korean War? What caused the war between North and South Korea?

In this section, you will learn how the Communist Party came to power in China and the effects that communism has had on China. You will also learn how Cold War tensions led to the Korean War.

ORGANIZING YOUR THOUGHTS

Use the chart below to help you take notes. Describe the Communist programs in this chart and list the outcomes of these programs.

Communist Program	Description	Outcomes
collectivization	**1.**	**2.**
Great Leap Forward	**3.**	**4.**
Cultural Revolution	**5.**	**6.**
Four Modernizations	**7.**	**8.**

READ TO LEARN

• Civil War and the Great Leap Forward *(page 941)*

By 1945, there were two Chinese governments. The Nationalist government of Chiang Kai-shek was based in southern and central China. The United States supported it. The Communist government under Mao Zedong was based in North China. In 1946, war broke out between the Nationalists and the Communists. Many peasants joined Mao's People's Liberation Army. By the spring of 1949, the People's Liberation Army had defeated the Nationalists. Chiang Kai-shek and his followers fled to the island of Taiwan.

The Communist Party now ruled China (called the People's Republic of China). In 1955, the Chinese government began a program to build a socialist society. Lands were taken from wealthy landlords and given to poor peasants. About two-thirds of the peasants received land under the new program. Most industry and commerce was nationalized. Most of the farmland was collectivized. Chinese leaders hoped that collective farms would increase food production. They hoped that this would allow more people to work in industry. But food production did not grow.

To speed up economic growth, Mao began a radical program, known as the Great Leap Forward, in 1958. Collective farms were combined into vast **communes.** Each commune contained more than thirty thousand people who lived and worked together. The Great Leap Forward was a disaster. The peasants hated the new system. Bad weather and the peasants' hatred made food production decline. As a result, almost fifteen million people died of starvation. In 1960, the government ended the communes and returned to collective farms.

9. What two governments existed in China in 1945? Who were their leaders, and where were they located?

____

____

____

____

____

• The Great Proletarian Cultural Revolution *(page 942)*

In spite of the commune failure, Mao still dreamed of the final stage of communism—a classless society. Mao believed that only **permanent revolution** (an atmosphere of constant revolutionary fervor) would make it possible for the Chinese to overcome the past and reach this final stage. In 1966, Mao launched the Great Proletarian Cultural Revolution. ("Proletarian" means the working class.) A collection of Mao's thoughts, called the *Little Red Book,* was considered the most important source of knowledge in all areas.

To promote the Cultural Revolution, the Red Guards were formed. These were revolutionary groups that were made up primarily of young people. Red Guards were sent throughout the country to eliminate the "Four Olds"—old ideas, old culture, old customs, and old habits. The Red Guard destroyed temples, books written by foreigners, and foreign music. People who had not followed Mao's plan were attacked. Intellectuals and artists accused of being pro-Western were especially open to attack. But there were groups within the country that did not share Mao's desire for permanent revolution. Many people were upset by the Red Guards' attacks and began to turn against the movement.

10. What was considered the most important source of knowledge during the Cultural Revolution?

• China After Mao *(page 943)*

In 1976, Mao Zedong died at the age of 83. A group of practical reformers seized power and brought the Cultural Revolution to an end. Deng Xiaoping led them. Under Deng, the government followed a policy called the Four Modernizations. This policy focused on four areas—industry, agriculture, technology, and national defense. China needed to catch up with the technological advances that had been taking place in the rest of the world. The government invited foreign investors to China. Thousands of students were sent to other countries to study science, technology, and modern business techniques. A new agricultural policy was also begun. Collective farms could now lease land to peasant families who paid rent to the collective. Anything produced on the land above the amount of the rent could be sold on the private market. Overall, modernization worked. Industrial output skyrocketed. **Per capita** (per person) income doubled during the 1980s. The standard of living increased for most people.

As more Chinese people began to study abroad, more information about Western society reached educated people. But the new leaders did not allow criticism of the Communist Party. People who called for democracy were often sent to prison. In the late 1980s, high inflation led to discontent, especially in the cities. Corruption and special treatment for officials also led to

Name ______________________ Date ______________________ Class ______________________

Reading Essentials and Study Guide

criticism of the government. In May 1989, students protested the corruption and demanded the resignation of China's Communist party leaders. Many people in the cities supported the students. They led mass demonstrations in Tiananmen Square in Beijing. Deng Xiaoping saw the students' desire for democracy as a demand for the end of the Communist Party. He ordered tanks and troops into Tiananmen Square to crush the demonstrators.

Throughout the 1990s, China's human rights violations and its determination to unify with Taiwan strained its relationship with the West. China's increasing military power has also caused concern in other countries.

11. How were calls for democracy treated under Deng Xiaoping?

____

____

____

____

• Chinese Society Under Communism *(page 944)*

The Chinese Communist Party wanted to create a new kind of citizen. These new citizens would be expected to contribute their utmost for the good of all. Women's roles were changed. Women were now allowed to take part in politics. In 1950, a new marriage law guaranteed women equal rights with men. The Communists also tried to destroy the influence of the traditional family. Loyalty to the family had always been an important part of the Confucian social order. The Communists thought that loyalty to family undermined loyalty to the state. During the Great Leap Forward, children were encouraged to spy on their parents. They were supposed to report any comments that their parents made that criticized the system. This continued during the Cultural Revolution.

After the death of Mao, there was a shift away from revolutionary fervor and a return to family traditions. For most people, this shift meant better living conditions. The new attitudes also were reflected in people's clothing. Under Mao, people had worn only baggy "Mao suits." After Mao's death, young Chinese people began to wear jeans, sneakers, and sweat suits.

12. What was the attitude of the Communists toward the family?

____

____

____

____

• China and the World: The Cold War in Asia *(page 945)*

Korea had been part of the Japanese Empire from 1905 until 1945. In August 1945, the Soviet Union and the United States agreed to divide Korea into two zones at the 38th parallel. The original plan was to hold elections after the end of World War II to reunify Korea. But the relationship between the United States and the Soviet Union grew worse after the war. Two separate governments were set up in Korea—a Communist one in the north and an anti-Communist one in the south.

North Korean troops invaded South Korea on June 25, 1950. U.S. President Harry Truman sent U.S. troops to fight the North Koreans. The United Nations supported this move. In September 1950, UN forces (mostly Americans) marched across the 38th parallel. Their goal was the reunification of Korea. The Chinese sent hundreds of thousands of Chinese troops into North Korea and pushed UN forces back across the 38th parallel. The fighting continued for three more years, but there was no final victory. An armistice was signed in 1953. The 38th parallel remained the dividing line between North and South Korea.

In 1950, China had signed a pact of friendship and cooperation with the Soviet Union. Some Americans and other Westerners began to worry about a Communist desire for world domination. These fears led to China's isolation from the major Western powers. China was forced to rely almost entirely on the Soviet Union for technological and economic aid. In the late 1950s, however, relations between China and the Soviet Union began to deteriorate. In the 1960s, Chinese and Soviet military forces often clashed at the border between the two countries. Chinese leaders decided to improve relations with the United States. In 1972, President Richard Nixon made a state visit to China. He was the first U.S. president to visit the People's Republic of China. In 1979, diplomatic relations were established with the United States. Chinese relations with the Soviet Union also gradually improved during the 1980s.

13. How did Korea become two countries?

Name ______________________ Date ________________ Class ________________

Reading Essentials and Study Guide

Chapter 31, Section 2

For use with textbook pages 952–956

INDEPENDENT STATES IN SOUTH AND SOUTHEAST ASIA

KEY TERMS

stalemate a situation in war in which neither side is able to make significant gains *(page 956)*

discrimination prejudice *(page 956)*

DRAWING FROM EXPERIENCE

Do you know anyone who fought in the Vietnam War? Do you know anyone who protested the war? Why did the U.S. send troops to Vietnam?

In the last section, you read about Communist China and the Korean War. In this section, you will learn how India, Pakistan, and the countries of Southeast Asia gained their independence. You will also learn about the problems these countries have faced since gaining their independence. Many of these problems have led to armed conflicts, including the Vietnam War.

ORGANIZING YOUR THOUGHTS

Use the chart below to help you take notes. For each of the countries in this chart, describe some of the challenges and conflicts that they have faced since the end of World War II.

Country	**Challenges and Conflicts**
India	**1.**
Pakistan	**2.**
Philippines	**3.**
Vietnam	**4.**

READ TO LEARN

• India Divided *(page 952)*

At the end of World War II, the leaders of India realized that India would have to be divided into two countries, one Hindu (India) and one Muslim (Pakistan). Pakistan consisted of two regions separated by India. One part, West Pakistan, was to the northwest of India. The other, East Pakistan, was to the northeast. On August 15, 1947, India and Pakistan became independent. Millions of Hindus and Muslims fled across the new borders—Hindus to India and Muslims to Pakistan. Violence broke out, and more than a million people were killed. One of those killed was Mohandas Gandhi, who was assassinated by a Hindu militant on January 30, 1948.

5. Why was India divided into two countries?

____

____

____

____

____

• The New India *(page 953)*

The Indian National Congress began to rule India. It was renamed the Congress Party. Jawaharlal Nehru was the new prime minister. He was a popular figure with strong ideas about the future of India. Nehru's vision of the new India combined a parliamentary form of government with a moderate socialist economic structure. The government took over the ownership of major industries, utilities, and transportation. Private enterprise was permitted at the local level. Farmland remained in private hands. Industrial production almost tripled between 1950 and 1965.

Nehru died in 1964. In 1966, the leaders of the Congress Party selected Nehru's daughter, Indira Gandhi, as the new prime minister. She held that position until 1984. India had many problems during this period. Its population growth was one of the most serious problems. In spite of government efforts, India was unable to control this growth. One result was poverty for many people. Millions lived in vast city slums. Another problem was ethnic and religious conflict. This conflict involved the Sikhs. The Sikhs were followers of a religion based on both Hindu and Muslim ideas. Many Sikhs lived in a province called the Punjab. Many of them wanted this province to be independent from India. Gandhi refused to allow this. In 1984, she used military force against Sikh rebels. More than 450 Sikhs were killed. Two Sikhs in Gandhi's bodyguard assassinated her in retaliation for the killings.

Reading Essentials and Study Guide

Gandhi's son Rajiv replaced his mother as prime minister. He began to move the government in new directions. Private enterprise was encouraged. Foreign investment was also encouraged. Rajiv Gandhi was prime minister from 1984 to 1989. He was assassinated in 1991 while campaigning for reelection. His successors have continued to emphasize free market enterprise and to transfer state-run industries into private hands. This has led to growth in India's middle class. The Congress Party has remained the leading party in India, but new parties have competed for control. Tensions between Hindus and Muslims continued to disturb India's stability.

6. What was Nehru's vision of the new India?

• Pakistan *(page 954)*

Pakistan was a completely new nation when it gained its independence in 1947. During its early years, there were intense conflicts within the country. The division between East and West Pakistan was a major source of conflict. The government was based in West Pakistan. Many people in East Pakistan felt that the government ignored their needs. In 1971, East Pakistan declared its independence. After a brief civil war, it became the new nation of Bangladesh.

Bangladesh and Pakistan have both had problems establishing stable governments. In both nations, military officials have often seized control of the government. Both nations are also very poor.

7. Why did East Pakistan declare its independence?

• Southeast Asia *(page 954)*

In July 1946, the United States granted total independence to the Philippines. Great Britain also ended its colonial rule in Southeast Asia. Burma became independent in 1948. Malaya became independent in 1957. The Netherlands and France were less willing to give up their colonial empires. Nationalists in Indonesia tried to set up an independent republic, but the Dutch suppressed it. The Indonesian Communist Party then tried to seize power. The United States pressured the Netherlands to grant independence to the non-Communist Nationalist Party. In 1949, the Netherlands recognized the new Republic of Indonesia.

In Vietnam, the leading force in the movement to end colonial rule was the Communist Party, led by Ho Chi Minh. In August 1945, the Vietminh seized control of most of Vietnam. The Vietminh was an alliance of forces under Communist leadership. Ho Chi Minh was elected president of a new republic in Hanoi. But France refused to accept the new government and seized the southern part of the country. France fought the Vietminh for control of Vietnam, but France was unable to regain control. In 1954, France agreed to a peace settlement. Vietnam was divided into two parts. In the north, the Communists were based in Hanoi. In the south, the non-Communists were based in Saigon. Both sides agreed to hold elections in two years to create a single government. But the conflict continued. The United States began to provide aid to South Vietnam. In spite of this aid, the Viet Cong were on the verge of seizing control of the entire country by early 1965. The Viet Cong were South Vietnamese Communist guerrillas, who were supported by military units from North Vietnam.

In 1965, President Lyndon Johnson decided to send U.S. troops to South Vietnam to prevent the Communists from taking control. By the end of the 1960s, the war had reached a **stalemate** (neither side was able to make significant gains). President Richard Nixon reached an agreement with North Vietnam in 1973 that allowed the United States to withdraw its forces. Within two years, Communist armies had reunited Vietnam under Communist control. By the end of the year, both Laos and Cambodia had Communist governments. In Cambodia, the dictator Pol Pot, leader of the Khmer Rouge, massacred more than a million Cambodians. But the Communist victories in Indochina did not lead to the "falling dominoes" that many U.S. leaders had feared.

Many of the leaders of the newly independent states in Southeast Asia hoped to form democratic, capitalist systems. By the end of the 1950s, hopes for economic growth had failed. Disputes within the new countries weakened democratic governments. This opened the door to both military and one-party regimes. In more recent years, some Southeast Asian societies have shown signs of moving toward more democratic governments. In the Philippines, Ferdinand Marcos came to power in 1965. Under Marcos, fraud and

Name ______________________ Date ______________________ Class ______________________

Reading Essentials and Study Guide

corruption were widespread. Marcos was accused of involvement in the killing of Benigno Aquino, a leader of the opposition. An uprising forced Marcos to flee the country. In 1986, Corazon Aquino, wife of the murdered leader, became president and worked for democratic reforms.

Women's roles in South and Southeast Asia have changed considerably. After independence, India's leaders tried to expand women's rights. The constitution of 1950 forbade **discrimination** (prejudicial treatment) based on gender. It also called for equal pay for equal work. Child marriage was outlawed. Women were encouraged to attend school and to get jobs. In Southeast Asia, nearly all of the newly independent states gave women full legal and political rights.

8. How have women's roles changed in South and Southeast Asia?

____

____

____

____

____

Name ______________________ Date ______________________ Class ______________________

Reading Essentials and Study Guide

Chapter 31, Section 3

For use with textbook pages 957–962

JAPAN AND THE PACIFIC

KEY TERMS

occupied a country whose lands are held and controlled by military forces *(page 957)*

state capitalism a form of capitalism in which the central government plays an active role in the economy *(page 958)*

DRAWING FROM EXPERIENCE

Do you or your family own any products that were made in Japan? What are these products?

In the last two sections, you read about changes in China, India, Pakistan, and Southeast Asia since the end of World War II. In this section, you will read about changes in Japan and other countries of the Pacific during this time. Many of these countries have created successful industrial societies.

ORGANIZING YOUR THOUGHTS

Use the diagram below to help you take notes. Japan's transformation into an economic giant since the end of World War II has been described as the "Japanese miracle." List six factors that have contributed to Japan's economic success.

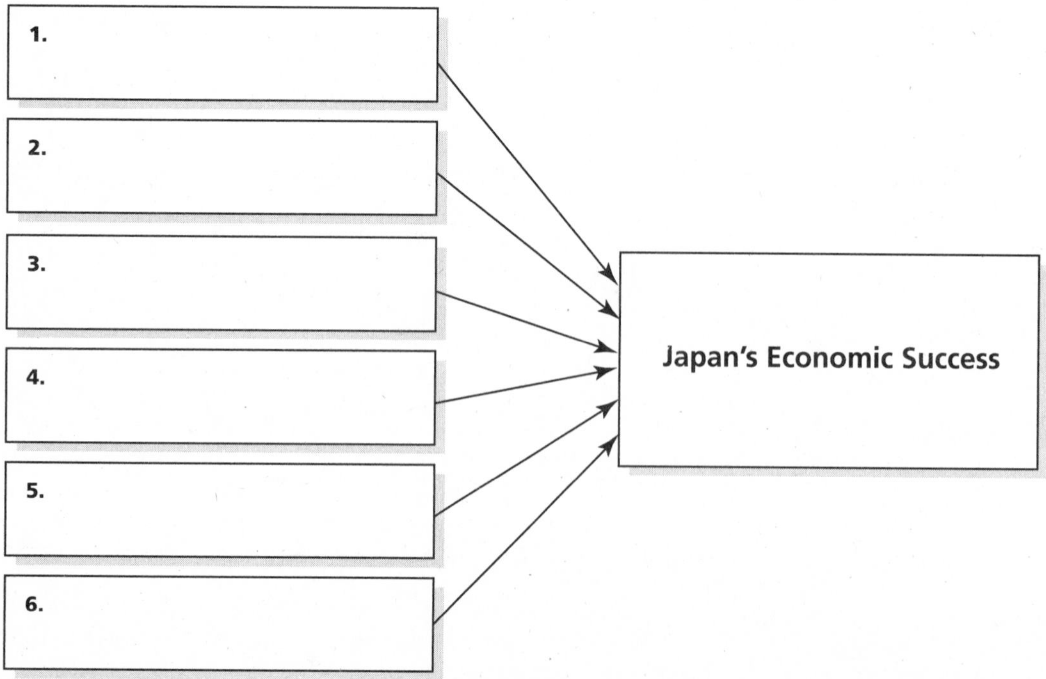

Reading Essentials and Study Guide

READ TO LEARN

• The Allied Occupation *(page 957)*

From 1945 to 1952, Japan was an **occupied** country. Its lands were held and controlled by Allied military forces. An Allied administration governed Japan. This administration was under the command of U.S. General Douglas MacArthur. A new constitution was created. In it, Japan agreed to keep its armed forces at levels that were only enough for self-defense. The new constitution also set up a parliamentary system and reduced the power of the emperor. It guaranteed basic civil rights and gave women the right to vote.

On September 8, 1951, the United States and other World War II allies signed a peace treaty that gave Japan its independence. Japan and the United States also signed an alliance in which the Japanese agreed that the United States could keep military bases in Japan.

7. What were some of the provisions of Japan's new constitution?

____

____

____

____

____

• The Japanese Miracle *(page 958)*

After World War II, Japan quickly became an economic giant. This has often been described as the "Japanese miracle." Japan made a dramatic recovery from the war. Several factors contributed to this "miracle." The government played a major role. Japan's new constitution provided for universal suffrage and a balance of power between the executive, legislative, and judicial branches of government. Today Japan is a stable democratic society. The current Japanese political system still has some of the features of Japan's political system under the Meiji. Japan has a multiparty system with two major parties, the Liberal Democrats and the Socialists. But the Liberal Democrats have dominated the government. Key decisions were made by a small group within this party. A change took place in 1993, when the Liberal Democrats were defeated. Mirohiro Hosokawa was elected prime minister and promised to clean up the political system.

The central government plays an active role in the economy. It establishes price and wage policies and subsidizes industries. The government's role in the economy is often cited as a key reason for the efficiency of Japanese industry. Japan's economic system has been described as **"state capitalism."** During the occupation of Japan, a land reform program was put in place. Under this

program, lands were sold on easy credit terms to the tenants. The reform program created a strong class of farmers. Today Japan is the greatest exporting nation in the world. Its per capita income is among the highest in the world.

Cultural factors also help to explain Japan's economic success. The Japanese are group oriented and find it easy to cooperate with one another. They are also hardworking and are inclined to save rather than to buy. These characteristics have produced high savings rates and labor productivity.

There are other, more practical reasons for Japan's success. Japan's industries were destroyed in World War II, so Japan was forced to build entirely new, modern factories. Japanese workers spend considerably more time at their jobs than workers in other countries. Corporations reward innovation and maintain good management-labor relations. Finally, some people believe that Japan uses unfair trade practices—that it sells goods at prices below cost to break into foreign markets and restricts imports from other countries.

There have been major social and cultural changes in Japan since the end of World War II. A new educational system removed all references to patriotism and loyalty to the emperor. It also stressed individualism. Women were given the right to vote and were encouraged to enter politics. But many of the distinctive characteristics of traditional Japanese society still exist. Emphasis on the work ethic is still strong. The tradition of hard work is stressed in the educational system. The subordinate position of women has not been entirely eliminated. Women are now legally protected against discrimination in employment, but very few have reached senior levels in business, education, or politics. Women now make up 50 percent of the workforce, but most are in retail or service jobs. Their average salary is only half that of men.

After the Japanese defeat in World War II, many of the writers who had been active before the war continued to write. But their writing was more sober now. Several writers committed suicide. Since the 1970s, there has been a huge production of books. In 1975, Japan produced twice as much fiction as the United States. Current Japanese authors were raised in cities and soaked up movies, television, and rock music. These writers deal with the concerns of all wealthy industrialized nations. Haruki Murakami is one of Japan's most popular authors. He was one of the first writers to give up the somber style of the postwar period.

8. What characteristics of traditional Japanese society still exist?

____

____

____

____

____

• The "Asian Tigers" *(page 961)*

South Korea, Taiwan, Singapore, and Hong Kong have imitated Japan and have created successful industrial societies. They are called the "Asian tigers."

In 1953, Korea was exhausted from three years of war. It was divided into two parts at the 38th parallel. North of this line was the People's Republic of Korea (North Korea) under the Communist leader Kim Il Sung. South of the line was the Republic of Korea (South Korea) under the dictatorial president Syngman Rhee. In South Korea, there were several years of harsh rule and government corruption. Demonstrations broke out in the capital city of Seoul in the spring of 1960. Rhee was forced to retire. Two years later, General Chung Hee Park was elected president. He began to strengthen the economy. Land was given to the peasants, and new industries were promoted. The key industries were chemicals, textiles, and shipbuilding. In the 1980s, South Korea began to move into automobile production. But South Korea was slow to develop democratic principles. Park ruled by autocratic means and suppressed protest. Many people began to demonstrate against government policies. New elections in 1992 brought Kim Young Sam to the presidency. He promised that he would make South Korea a "freer democracy."

In Taiwan, Chiang Kai-shek and his followers established a capital at Taipei. The government continued to call itself the Republic of China. Chiang Kai-shek's government maintained that it was the legitimate government of China and would eventually return to the mainland. Taiwan was protected by the American military. This made it possible for Taiwan to concentrate on economic growth. Taiwan made good use of foreign aid and the efforts of its own people. It was able to build a modern industrialized society. A land-reform program put farmland in the hands of peasants and doubled food production. With government help, local manufacturing and commerce expanded. Prosperity did not lead to democracy, however. Under Chiang Kai-shek, the government refused to allow new political parties to form. After the death of Chiang in 1975, the Republic of China slowly began to move toward a more representative form of government. By the end of the 1980s, opposition parties were allowed, and democratic elections had been held. Unification is still a major issue for Taiwan. The People's Republic of China on the mainland is still committed to eventual unification. The United States supports self-determination for the people of Taiwan.

Singapore was once a British colony and is now an independent state. Under the leadership of Prime Minister Lee Kuan Yew, Singapore developed an industrial economy based on shipbuilding, oil refineries, and electronics. Singapore has also become the banking center of the region. Singapore has an authoritarian political system. The prime minister once said that democracy was not appropriate for Singapore. But its citizens are beginning to demand more political freedoms.

Name ______________________ Date ______________________ Class ______________________

Reading Essentials and Study Guide

Chapter 31, Section 3 *(continued)*

Hong Kong has also become an industrial powerhouse with high standards of living. For over 150 years, Hong Kong was under British rule. In 1997, Great Britain returned control of Hong Kong to mainland China. China promised that it would allow the people of Hong Kong to be self-governing and to live under a capitalist system for the next 50 years.

9. What are the "Asian tigers"? Why are they called this?

____

____

____

____

____

• Australia and New Zealand *(page 962)*

Both Australia and New Zealand have identified themselves culturally and politically with Europe rather than with their Asian neighbors. Their economies resemble those of the industrialized countries of the world. Both are members of the British Commonwealth. Since the majority of the people in both Australia and New Zealand have European origins, cultural differences often hinder mutual understanding between the two countries and their Asian neighbors. However, in recent years, trends have been drawing both countries closer to Asia. Immigration from East and Southeast Asia has increased. Trade relations with Asia are also increasing. About 60 percent of Australia's export markets are now in East Asia.

10. In what ways are Australia and New Zealand more like European countries than Asian countries?

____

____

____

____

____

Name ______________________ Date ______________ Class ______________

Reading Essentials and Study Guide

Chapter 32, Section 1

For use with textbook pages 969–973

THE CHALLENGES OF OUR WORLD

KEY TERMS

ecology the study of the relationship between living things and their environment *(page 970)*

deforestation the clearing of forests *(page 970)*

ozone layer a thin layer of gas in the upper atmosphere that shields Earth from the Sun's ultra-violet rays *(page 970)*

greenhouse effect global warming caused by the buildup of carbon dioxide in the atmosphere *(page 970)*

acid rain the rainfall that results when sulfur produced by factories mixes with moisture in the air *(page 970)*

global economy an economy in which the production, distribution, and sale of goods take place on a worldwide scale *(page 972)*

DRAWING FROM EXPERIENCE

Do you or your family recycle cans and other types of containers? Are there any other things that you do to help the environment?

In this section, you will read about the environmental, economic, social, and political challenges facing the world at the end of the twentieth century.

ORGANIZING YOUR THOUGHTS

Use the diagram below to help you take notes. Hunger is a huge problem in many parts of the world. List five reasons why hunger continues to be a problem.

1.
2.
3.
4.
5.

→ **Hunger in the World**

Reading Essentials and Study Guide

Chapter 32, Section 1 *(continued)*

READ TO LEARN

• The Environmental Crisis *(page 969)*

In 1962, an American scientist, Rachel Carson, wrote a book called *Silent Spring.* In it she warned that the use of pesticides (chemicals sprayed on crops to kill insects) was having deadly results. The pesticides were killing birds, fish, and other wild animals. The pesticide residue on food was also harmful to human beings. Carson's warning alarmed many scientists. It led to a new field of science called **ecology** (the study of the relationship between living things and their environment). Many people became more aware of the dangers to the environment.

Dangers to the environment have many sources. A rapid increase in world population has led many people to fear that the Earth's resources simply cannot support the growing number of human beings. **Deforestation** (the clearing of forests) is one result of the growing population. Forests and jungles are cut down to provide farmland and firewood for people on Earth. As forests are cut down, dwelling places for plants and animals are destroyed. The destruction of tropical rain forests is a special concern. The tropical rain forests support 50 percent of the world's species of plants and animals. They are also crucial to human survival. They remove carbon dioxide from the air and return oxygen to it.

Another danger to the environment is chemical waste. Chlorofluorocarbons are a particular concern. They are the gases used in aerosol cans, refrigerators, and air conditioners. Many scientists warn that the release of chlorofluorocarbons is destroying the **ozone layer** (a thin layer of gas in the upper atmosphere that shields Earth from the Sun's ultraviolet rays). Other scientists have proposed that there is a **greenhouse effect** (global warming caused by the buildup of carbon dioxide in the atmosphere). Another problem is **acid rain** (the rainfall that results when sulfur from factories mixes with moisture in the air). Acid rain has killed forests in both North America and Europe.

Major ecological disasters have also occurred during the last 20 years. The nuclear explosion at Chernobyl in 1986 and the oil spill caused by the oil tanker *Exxon Valdez* in 1989 are two examples. These disasters made people aware of the need to deal with environmental problems. In 1987, representatives of 46 nations met in Montreal. They agreed to protect the Earth's ozone layer by reducing the use of chlorofluorocarbons. In 1992, an Earth Summit in Rio de Janeiro looked at the challenges to the environment and proposed new solutions.

6. Why are the rain forests a special environmental concern?

____

____

____

Name ______________________ Date ______________ Class ______________

Reading Essentials and Study Guide

• The Technological Revolution *(page 971)*

Modern transportation and communication systems are transforming the world. Jumbo jets, the Internet, satellites, cable television, fax machines, and cellular telephones are some examples. The exploration of space has led to many world-changing developments. In 1969, the American astronauts Neil Armstrong and Buzz Aldrin landed on the moon. Since then, space probes have increased our understanding of distant planets. Satellites provide information about weather and transmit signals for radio, television, and telephone communications.

In the field of health, new technologies have enabled doctors to perform "miracle" operations. Mechanical valves and pumps for the heart and organ transplants have allowed people to live longer lives. Technological changes in the health field have also raised new concerns. For example, genetic engineering is a new scientific field that alters the genetic information of cells to produce new variations. Some people worry that the new variations could be deadly. The overuse of antibiotics has already created "supergerms" that do not respond to treatment with available antibiotics. The issues of stem-cell research and human cloning have also created intense debates.

In agriculture, the Green Revolution has promised huge returns. The Green Revolution refers to the development of new strains of rice, corn, and other grains that have greater yields. It was promoted as the technological solution to feeding the world's growing population. But immense amounts of chemical fertilizers and pesticides are needed to grow the new strains. Many farmers cannot afford the fertilizers, and the pesticides create environmental problems.

The technological revolution has also led to the development of nuclear, biological, and chemical weapons. Although the end of the Cold War reduced the chances of a major nuclear war, there is still concern that nuclear materials (bombs or radioactive matter) will be obtained and used by terrorists. **Biowarfare** (the use of disease and poison against civilians and soldiers in wartime) is not new. Biological weapons were used in World War I. Chemical weapons were used in the Iran-Iraq War in the 1980s. Governments have made agreements to limit the research, production, and use of biological and chemical weapons. But these agreements have not prevented terrorists from practicing **bioterrorism** (the use of biological and chemical weapons in terrorist attacks).

7. What concerns have been raised by technological changes in the health field?

• Economic and Social Challenges *(page 972)*

Since World War II, the nations of the world have developed a **global economy** (an economy in which the production, distribution, and sale of goods take place on a worldwide scale). In 1995, the World Trade Organization (WTO) was established. Trade agreements are negotiated, signed, and upheld by its member nations. The WTO has been criticized for placing commercial interests above environmental and health concerns. It has also been criticized for leaving out small and developing countries.

One of the features of the global economy is the wide gap between rich and poor nations. The rich, industrialized nations are mainly in the Northern Hemisphere. These nations have well-organized industrial and agricultural systems, use advanced technologies, and have strong educational systems. The poor nations (sometimes called developing countries) are located mainly in the Southern Hemisphere and include many nations in Africa, Asia and Latin America. Developing countries are primarily farming nations with little technology. A serious problem in developing countries is population growth. The world's population is 6.2 billion today. Rapidly growing populations have caused many people to move to cities to find jobs. Millions of people in cities in developing countries live in terrible conditions.

Hunger has also become a staggering problem. Every year, over 8 million people die of hunger. Besides rapid population growth, poor soil, natural catastrophes, and economic and political factors contribute to widespread hunger. Civil wars have created severe food shortages. In Sudan, civil war broke out in the 1980s. Both sides refused to allow food to be sent to their enemies. As a result, 1.3 million people had died from starvation in Sudan by the early 1990s.

In the Western countries, the gap between men and women has been steadily decreasing. The number of women in the workforce continues to increase, along with the number of women university graduates. Many countries have passed laws that require equal pay for equal work. A number of Western countries also have laws that prohibit sex discrimination. Women in developing countries, on the other hand, often remain bound to their homes and families and are subordinate to their fathers and husbands. They continue to face problems in obtaining education, property rights, and decent jobs.

8. What are some of the main differences between rich and poor nations?

____

____

____

____

____

Name ______________________ Date ______________________ Class ______________________

• Political Challenges *(page 973)*

Within a decade of World War II, military dictatorships or one-party governments had replaced democratic systems in many developing countries. Many leaders underestimated the difficulty of building democratic political systems. Recently, there have been signs of renewed interest in democracy in various parts of the world.

Regional, ethnic, and religious differences continue to create conflict around the world. In Europe, Yugoslavia has been torn apart by ethnic divisions. In the Middle East, the conflict between Israelis and Palestinians continues to produce acts of violence. Conflicts between ethnic groups in Africa have led to massacres of hundreds of thousands of people.

9. What differences continue to create conflicts around the world?

____

____

____

____

____

Name ____________________ Date ____________________ Class ____________________

Reading Essentials and Study Guide

Chapter 32, Section 2

For use with textbook pages 974–976

GLOBAL VISIONS

KEY TERMS

peacekeeping force a military force drawn from neutral states to settle conflicts and supervise truces *(page 975)*

disarmament limiting or reducing armed forces and weapons *(page 976)*

DRAWING FROM EXPERIENCE

Have you heard the slogan "Think globally, act locally"? What do you think this slogan means? How might this slogan be carried out in your community?

In the last section, you read about global challenges at the end of the twentieth century. In this section, you will read about international organizations that have been formed to respond to these challenges. You will also read about groups led by ordinary citizens that have tried to address some of these problems.

ORGANIZING YOUR THOUGHTS

Use the chart below to help you take notes. The United Nations is one of the organizations that have tried to address global problems. List the three main parts of the United Nations and describe their functions. Also list three of the specialized agencies that are under the direction of the United Nations.

United Nations		
1.	2.	3.

4.

5.

6.

Name ______________________ Date ______________________ Class ______________________

READ TO LEARN

• The United Nations *(page 974)*

Representatives of the Allied forces founded the United Nations (UN) in 1945 in San Francisco. The United Nations had two main goals: peace and human dignity. The General Assembly of the United Nations is made up of representatives of all member nations. It has the power to discuss any question of importance to the organization and to recommend the action to be taken. The secretary-general, whose offices are located in New York City, supervises the day-to-day administrative business of the UN. The most important advisory group of the UN is the Security Council. It is made up of 5 permanent members (the United States, Russia, Great Britain, France, and China) and 10 members chosen by the General Assembly to serve limited terms. The Security Council decides what actions the UN should take to settle international disputes.

Several specialized agencies function under the direction of the United Nations. These include the United Nations Educational, Scientific, and Cultural Organization (UNESCO), the World Health Organization (WHO), and the United Nations International Children's Emergency Fund (UNICEF). All of these agencies have been successful in helping to address economic and social problems. The United Nations has also organized international conferences on important issues such as population growth and the environment. It has also provided **peacekeeping forces** (military forces drawn from neutral member states to settle conflicts and supervise truces) on various occasions.

7. What are the two main goals of the United Nations?

• New Global Visions *(page 975)*

One approach to global problems has been the development of social movements led by ordinary citizens. These movements have addressed issues such as environmental problems, women's liberation, human potential, technology, and nonviolence. "Think globally, act locally" is the slogan of such groups.

Name ____________________ Date ____________________ Class ____________________

Reading Essentials and Study Guide

Chapter 32, Section 2 *(continued)*

Nongovernmental organizations (NGOs) are another way that people have addressed global issues. NGOs include business and professional organizations, foundations, and religious, peace, and **disarmament** groups (groups that work to limit or reduce armed forces and weapons). Other examples are youth and women's organizations, environmental and human rights groups, and research institutes. These groups help to create global perspectives. Despite the efforts of these groups, global approaches to global problems continue to be hindered by political, ethnic, and religious disputes around the world.

8. What are NGOs? What are some examples?

____

____

____

____

____

Reading Essentials and Study Guide

Answer Key

Chapter 1 Section 1.1

Organizing Your Thoughts

1. australopithecines
2. three to four million years ago
3. eastern and southern Africa
4. *Homo erectus*
5. emerged around 1.5 million years ago
6. Africa, Europe, and Asia
7. *Homo sapiens* (and later Neanderthals and *Homo sapiens sapiens*)
8. emerged about 250,000 years ago
9. Africa, Europe, and Southwest Asia

Read to Learn

10. One method is radiocarbon dating. It dates an object by measuring the amount of radioactive carbon (C-14) left in it. This method can only be used for dating objects that are less than 50,000 years old. Another method is thermoluminescence dating. It dates objects by measuring the light given off by electrons in the soil around the objects. This method can be used to date objects as far back as 200,000 years ago.
11. Neanderthals and *Homo sapiens sapiens*
12. Paleolithic people used hunting and gathering to get their food. They had to move from place to place in order to find food.

Section 1.2

Organizing Your Thoughts

1. cities
2. government
3. religion
4. social structure
5. writing
6. art

Read to Learn

7. People began to plant and grow food on a regular basis (systematic agriculture). They also began to tame and keep animals as a source of meat, milk, and wool (domestication). Because they were no longer forced to move from place to place to find food, they began to live in settlements. They often had more food than they needed right away, so they were able to do things other than farming. Some people became artisans and made items such as weapons and jewelry. They began to trade the items they made and their surplus food. Division of labor occurred. Use of metals occurred.
8. Civilizations are complex cultures in which large numbers of people share a number of common elements. Civilizations have six basic characteristics: cities, governments, religion, social structure, writing, and art.

Chapter 2 Section 2.1

Organizing Your Thoughts

1–6. cuneiform writing, wagon wheel, potter's wheel, sundial, arch, first to make bronze out of copper and tin

Read to Learn

7. Mesopotamia was at the eastern end of the Fertile Crescent, between the Tigris and Euphrates Rivers.
8. the kings and the priests and priestesses (nobles)
9. the Akkadian Empire and the Babylonian Empire
10. the principle of retribution ("an eye for an eye, tooth for a tooth")
11. The climate in Mesopotamia was harsh. Floods were unpredictable. There were also heavy rains, scorching winds, and famines. The people of Mesopotamia knew that they could not control these things, so they believed that supernatural forces controlled their world.
12. Sumerians used writing to keep records. People who could write (scribes) often became leaders of their cities, temple, and armies. Writing allowed people to pass knowledge from person to person and from generation to generation. It also made it possible to record poems and other forms of literature.

Section 2.2

Organizing Your Thoughts

1. A bureaucracy was developed to help the pharaohs rule. Pyramids were built as tombs for the bodies of dead pharaohs. Mummification was used to preserve the dead bodies. The Great Pyramid was built around 2540 B.C.

2. Egypt conquered Nubia and sent armies to Syria and Palestine. The pharaohs were concerned about their people and drained the swampland in the Nile Delta to give the people more land to farm. They also dug a canal to connect the Nile and the Red Sea. The Middle Kingdom ended when the Hyksos invaded Egypt around 1652 B.C.

3. Egypt created an empire and became the most powerful state in Southwest Asia. The pharaohs built new temples. Hatshepsut, the first woman to become pharaoh, built a great temple at Deir el Bahri. The pharaoh Amenhotep IV forced the people to worship a single god, Aton. After he died, the new pharaoh, Tutankhamen, restored the old gods. The Egyptian Empire came to an end when the "Sea Peoples" invaded the empire during the thirteenth century B.C.

Read to Learn

4. When the Nile flooded, it left a deposit of mud on both sides of the river. This created an area of rich soil, so farmers were able to grow a surplus of food in the Nile Valley. The Nile also made it easy to travel throughout the land. The yearly flooding of the Nile was predictable and gave the people a feeling of security and stability.

5. The most important gods were sun gods and land gods.

6. Mummification is the process of slowly drying a dead body to prevent it from rotting. The Egyptians used mummification to preserve the physical body after death. They believed that human beings had two bodies, a physical one and a spiritual one. If the physical body was preserved after death and its tomb was stocked with food and other supplies, the spiritual body, or *ka*, could return.

7. The pharaoh was at the top. Under him was a small upper class of nobles and priests. Below the upper class was a larger group of merchants, artisans, scribes, and tax collectors. At the bottom was the largest group, the lower classes. Most of them were peasants who farmed the land.

8. Women were well respected. If a marriage ended in divorce, the wife was compensated. Wives were in charge of the household and the education of the children. They kept control of their property and inheritance even after they married. Some women operated businesses. Upper-class women could become priestesses, and four queens became pharaohs.

9. Hieratic script was a simplified version of hieroglyphics that was used for business and daily life.

10. Egyptians used geometry and learned how to calculate area and volume. This helped them build the pyramids. They also developed a 365-day calendar, and became experts in human anatomy. They used splints, bandages, and compresses to treat fractures, wounds, and disease.

Section 2.3

Organizing Your Thoughts

1. The Hittites were the first Indo-Europeans to use iron.

2. The Phoenicians developed an alphabet that was passed onto the Greeks. The Roman alphabet that we use today is derived from this alphabet.

3. The religion of the Israelites became a major world religion. It is known today as Judaism and it influenced the religions of Christianity and Islam. The Ten

Commandments and the words of the prophets became the basis for modern laws and ideas of social justice.

Read to Learn

4. Pastoral nomads were nomads who domesticated animals for food and clothing. They moved along regular routes to find food for their animals.
5. Trade was the basis of the Phoenician economy.
6. The Jewish religion was unique because it was monotheistic. The other religions of western Asia and Egypt were polytheistic, and only priests had access to the gods and their wishes. In the Jewish religion, God's wishes had been written down, so no single person could claim that he alone knew God's will. This knowledge was open to anyone who could read Hebrew.

Section 2.4

Organizing Your Thoughts

1. The Assyrian Empire is established.
2. Zoroaster is born.
3. The Assyrian Empire falls to the Chaldeans and Medes.
4. Cyrus begins to rule.
5. Babylon falls to the Persians.
6. Darius begins to rule.
7. The Persian Empire falls to Alexander the Great.

Read to Learn

8. The Assyrians used relays of horses to carry messages along a network of posts.
9. Cyrus was called "the Great" because he ruled with great wisdom and compassion. He created a powerful empire, but he respected other cultures. He allowed the Jews, who had been brought to Babylon in the sixth century B.C., to return to Jerusalem.

Chapter 3 Section 3.1

Organizing Your Thoughts

1. Brahmans or priests
2. Kshatriyas or warriors
3. Vaisyas or commoners
4. Sudras
5. Untouchables

Read to Learn

6. The summer monsoons bring heavy rains, which the farmers depend on to grow their crops. If the rains come early or late, or if there is too much or too little rain, crops are ruined and many people starve.
7. Their main streets ran in a north-south direction and were crossed by smaller east-west streets. The cities were divided into large walled neighborhoods. Public wells provided the people with a regular supply of water. Houses had drains that were connected to a sewer system under the streets. A system of chutes took trash from houses to garbage bins.
8. The Aryans stopped being pastoral nomads and became farmers.
9. Women did not have many rights in ancient India. Only men could inherit property. Women were not allowed to serve as priests, and generally, only men were educated. When a man died, his wife was expected to follow the ritual of *suttee.*
10. Reincarnation is the belief that the individual soul is reborn in a different form after death. A person's actions determine how the person will be reborn in the next life. Reincarnation justified the privileges of the people in the higher castes. They believed that they deserved their privileges because of what they had done in earlier lives.
11. Siddhartha accepted the idea of reincarnation but rejected the Hindu caste system. He taught that all human beings could reach nirvana. He also rejected the multitude of gods in Hinduism.

Reading Essentials and Study Guide

Answer Key

Section 3.2

Organizing Your Thoughts

1. Roman Empire—woolen and linen clothes, glass, and precious stones
2. India—ivory, textiles, precious stones, and pepper
3. China—silk, spices, teas, and porcelain

Read to Learn

4. Asoka used Buddhist ideals to guide his rule. He set up hospitals for both people and animals. He had trees planted and shelters built along the road to provide share and rest for travelers. India's role in trade expanded under his rule.
5. One section of the Silk Road passed through the land of the Kushans. Trade between the Roman Empire and China was shipped along this route. The Kushans prospered because of this trade.
6. The cities were built along the main trade routes throughout India. The cities became wealthy because of the trade that was shipped along these routes and because of the pilgrims who traveled across India to visit the major religious centers.
7. Aryabhata, the most famous Indian mathematician of the Gupta Empire

Section 3.3

Organizing Your Thoughts

1–5. Both kingdoms were divided into territories. Aristocratic officials appointed by the king governed these territories. The king controlled large armies. Peasants farmed the land of the aristocrats. There was also a class of artisans and merchants in both kingdoms

Read to Learn

6. The mountains and deserts served as barriers that separated the Chinese people from other Asian people. In the regions created by the mountains and deserts, there were other people groups who were often in conflict with the Chinese.
7. The Shang rulers believed that they could communicate with the gods to get help with their affairs. Priests used oracle bones to get answers from the gods. There was a strong belief in life after death. Humans were sacrificed to please the gods and to provide companions for the king and his family on their journey to the next world. The Chinese also believed that the spirits of ancestors could bring good or evil to living members of a family, so it was important to treat the spirits well.
8. The Mandate of Heaven was the belief that kings received their authority to command, or mandate, from Heaven. It was the king's duty to keep the gods pleased to protect people from bad harvest and disasters. If he failed, he could be overthrown. This gave people the "right of revolution." The king was not a divine being and could be replaced. This led to a pattern of dynastic cycles. Each dynasty said that it ruled with the Mandate of Heaven, but eventually the dynasty would decline, and a new dynasty would take over.
9. Confucianism, Daoism, and Legalism

Section 3.4

Organizing Your Thoughts

1–6. textile manufacturing, water mills for grinding grain, iron casting, the invention of steel, paper, and the rudder and fore-and-aft rigging for ships

Read to Learn

7. Legalism was adopted as the regime's philosophy. Anyone who opposed the regime was punished or executed. The Qin dynasty was a centralized state. The central bureaucracy was divided in three parts: the civil division, the military division, and the censorate. Below the central government were two levels of administration, provinces and counties.

8. The Han dynasty discarded the harsh policies of the Qin dynasty. Confucian principles, rather than Legalism, became the philosophy of the Han government. The Han dynasty kept the three divisions of the central government. It also kept the system of provinces and counties. Most important, it kept the system of choosing officials on the basis of merit rather than birth.
9. Archaeologists believe that the terra-cotta figures were a re-creation of Qin Shihuangdi's imperial guard and were meant to be with the emperor on his journey to the next world.

Chapter 4 Section 4.1

Organizing Your Thoughts

1. 2800 B.C.—The Minoan civilization is established on the island of Crete.
2. 1450 B.C.—The Minoan civilization is destroyed.
3. 1250 B.C.—The Mycenaeans sack the city of Troy.
4. 1100 B.C.—The Mycenaean civilization collapses, and the Dark Age begins.
5. 750 B.C.—The Dark Age of Greece ends.

Read to Learn

6. The mountains influenced Greek history because they separated Greeks from each other. This caused different Greek communities to develop their own ways of life. The small size of these communities encouraged people to be involved in politics. But the rivalry between the communities led to warfare. The sea also influenced Greek history. The Greeks became seafarers. They sailed into the Aegean, the Mediterranean, and the Black Seas. They later established colonies that spread Greek civilization throughout the Mediterranean world.
7. The English archaeologist Arthur Evans named the Minoan civilization after Minos, the legendary king of Crete.
8. The Mycenaean states fought one another, and major earthquakes caused widespread damage. Invaders moved into Greece from the north.
9. This period is called the Dark Age because there are few records to tell us what happened during this time. We do know that it was a period when food production dropped and population declined.

Section 4.2

Organizing Your Thoughts

1. Solon—cancelled all land debts and freed people who were slaves because of their debts.
2. Pisistratus—gave aristocrats' land to the peasants.
3. Cleisthenes—laid the foundations for Athenian democracy by creating a new council of five hundred and by giving the assembly, which was made up of all male citizens, the final authority to pass laws.

Read to Learn

4. citizens with political rights (adult males), citizens with no political rights (women and children), and noncitizens (slaves and people from foreign lands)
5. Colonization spread the Greek culture throughout the Mediterranean. It also led to an increase in trade and industry.
6. The rule of the tyrants ended the rule of the aristocrats in many city-states. This allowed many new people to be involved in government. In some city-states, this led to the development of democracy.
7. The Spartan government was an oligarchy headed by two kings. A group of five men, known as the ephors, was responsible for the education of the youth and the conduct of all citizens. There was also a council of elders, which included the two kings and 28 citizens over the age of 60. This council decided on the issues that would be presented to the assembly. The assem-

bly, which was made up of male citizens, voted on the issues but did not debate.

8. A council of five hundred supervised foreign affairs, oversaw the treasury, and proposed laws. The assembly had the final authority to pass laws after free and open debate. The assembly was made up of all male citizens.

Section 4.3

Organizing Your Thoughts

1–3. The Athenian Empire was destroyed. The war weakened all of the Greek states. It ruined any possibility of cooperation among them. (While fighting with each other, they also ignored the growing power of Macedonia, which eventually cost them their freedom.)

Read to Learn

4. Darius and Xerxes.

5. The Delian League was an alliance against the Persians. Its headquarters was on the island of Delos, but its chief officials were Athenians.

6. In the Age of Pericles, every citizen played a role in government. The form of government was a direct democracy. Every male citizen over the age of 18 was a part of the assembly and voted on all major issues. Meetings of the assembly were held every 10 days. The assembly passed all laws, elected public officials, and made final decisions on war and foreign policy. On a daily basis, a large body of city officials ran the government. Ten officials, known as generals, were the directors of policy. These officials were elected. Lower class citizens were eligible for public office, and officeholders were paid.

7. Sparta and the other Greek states feared the growing Athenian Empire. A series of disputes between Athens and Sparta led to the beginning of the war.

8. Women were citizens who could take part in religious festivals, but otherwise, they were excluded from public life. They could not vote or own property, and they received no formal education. They were expected to bear children and take care of their families and their homes. Their lives were strictly controlled. If they left the house, they had to have a companion.

Section 4.4

Organizing Your Thoughts

1. Pythagoras—taught that the essence of the universe was in music and numbers.

2. Socrates—believed that the goal of education was to improve the individual. He also believed in the individual's ability to reason and questioned authority.

3. Plato—believed that a higher world of eternal Forms has always existed and that the objects that we perceive with our senses are simply reflections or shadows of the ideal Forms. He did not trust the workings of democracy, but he believed that men and women should have the same education and equal access to all positions.

4. Aristotle—did not believe in Plato's theory of ideal forms. He believed that by examining objects, we could perceive their form. But he did not believe that the forms existed in a separate, higher world of reality. He did try to create an ideal form of government. He tried to find the best form of government by analyzing existing governments.

Read to Learn

5. An oracle was a sacred shrine where a god or goddess revealed the future through a priest or priestess.

6. Greek tragedies dealt with universal themes. They were concerned with such problems as the nature of good and evil and the rights of individuals.

7. The Socratic method is a teaching method that uses a question-and-answer format to lead pupils to see things for themselves by using their own reason. The Greek philosopher Socrates developed it.
8. Herodotus and Thucydides
9. Classical Greek sculptors did not try to achieve realism, but rather a standard of ideal beauty.

Section 4.5

Organizing Your Thoughts

1–2. Math—Euclid wrote the *Elements*, a textbook on plane geometry used for centuries. Archimedes established the value of the mathematical constant pi.
3–4. Astronomy—Aristarchus developed the theory that the Sun is at the center of the universe and that the earth revolves around the Sun. Eratosthenes determined that the earth was round and calculated its circumference within 200 miles of the actual figure.
5–6. Two new philosophies, Epicureanism and Stoicism, were developed.

Read to Learn

7. Philip wanted the Greek states to form a league and help him in a war with Persia.
8. The word *Hellenistic* is derived from a Greek word that means "to imitate Greeks." During this period in history, the Greek language and culture spread to many other parts of the world.
9. Macedonia, Syria, Pergamum, Egypt
10. Epicureans believed that the way to achieve happiness was the pursuit of pleasure. To achieve this pleasure, people had to free themselves from public activity. Stoics believed that happiness could only be found when people gained inner peace by living in harmony with the will of God. Life's problems could not disturb these people, so Stoics did not believe that people needed to separate themselves from the world and politics.

Chapter 5, Section 5.1

Organizing Your Thoughts

1. Patricians: consuls, praetors, Senate, centuriate assembly
2. Plebeians: council of the plebs (after 471 B.C.), tribunes, consuls (from the 4th century B.C.)

Read to Learn

3. The Romans imitated the Greek's sculpture, architecture, literature, and alphabet. They also learned how to grow olives and grapes from the Greeks. The Romans adopted the Etruscans' clothing—the toga and short cloak. The organization of the Roman army was also borrowed from the Etruscans.
4. They gained the support of conquered people by giving them Roman citizenship and by allowing them to run their own affairs.
5. The plebeians resented the patricians because the patricians did not treat the plebeians as equals. The plebeians could not hold government offices, and their children could not marry the children of the patricians.
6. The Romans sent an army to Sicily in 264 B.C. The Carthaginians considered this an act of war, because they considered Sicily part of their empire.

Section 5.2

Organizing Your Thoughts

1. Augustus
2. Tiberius
3. Caligula
4. Claudius
5. Nero
6. Nerva*
7. Trajan*
8. Hadrian*
9. Antoninus Pius*
10. Marcus Aurelius*
*"five good emperors"

Read to Learn

11. They urged the council of the plebs to pass laws that would take back land from the large landowners and give it to the landless poor.

12. Marius recruited soldiers by promising them land. His soldiers swore an oath of loyalty to Marius himself. This created a new type of army that was not under government control. Generals were now forced to become involved in politics to get laws passed to provide land for their soldiers. Sulla used his army to seize power. Future leaders would continue to use armies in this way.

13. Crassus, Pompey, and Julius Caesar formed the First Triumvirate. Octavian, Antony, and Lepidus formed the Second Triumvirate.

14. Augustus and imperator. *Augustus* means "the revered one." *Imperator* means commander in chief.

15. The *Pax Romana* was a period of peace and prosperity under the Roman emperors. *Pax Romana* means the "Roman Peace."

Section 5.3

Organizing Your Thoughts

1–3. The Romans were the first people to use concrete on a large scale. By using concrete and new forms based on curved lines, the Romans were able to make huge buildings. They built over 50,000 miles of roads and they also built many aqueducts, almost a dozen in Rome alone.

Read to Learn

4. The Romans made realistic statues that even showed unpleasant physical details.

5. The Age of Augustus

6. Women were no longer required to have guardians. They had the right to own, inherit, and sell property. Women were not segregated from men in the home, and they could attend races, the theater, and events in the amphitheater. Women could not participate in politics, but many important women influenced politics through their husbands.

7. Greek slaves were used as tutors, musicians, doctors, and artists. Slaves of all nationalities were used as household workers. Slaves were also used to build roads and public buildings. They also farmed the estates of the wealthy.

8. The poor lived in apartment blocks called *insulae.* These buildings were poorly built and often collapsed. High rents forced entire families to live in one room. There was no plumbing or central heating. The homes were so uncomfortable that many poor Romans spent most of their time outdoors in the streets. Many of the poor were only able to survive because they received free grain from the emperors.

Section 5.4

Organizing Your Thoughts

1. The Roman government began persecuting Christians during the reign of Nero. Many Christians were put to death, often in cruel ways.

2. The last great persecution of Christians took place under Diocletian.

3. Constantine issued the Edict of Milan, which proclaimed official tolerance of Christianity.

4. Under Theodosius the Great, the Romans adopted Christianity as their official religion.

Read to Learn

5. The official state religion of Rome focused on the worship of several gods and goddesses. The Romans believed that proper rituals by state priests brought peace and prosperity.

6. The Sadducees wanted to cooperate with the Romans. The Essenes were waiting for a Messiah who would save Israel from oppression and bring the kingdom of God to Earth. The Zealots wanted to overthrow Roman rule.
7. The Christians refused to worship the state gods and the emperors. The Romans saw this as an act of treason, punishable by death.
8. Persecution strengthened Christianity by forcing it to become more organized. Fear of persecution also meant that only the most committed individuals would choose to become Christians.

Section 5.5

Organizing Your Thoughts

1–3. invasions, civil wars, and plagues

Read to Learn

4. There was a decline in trade and industry. Plagues created a labor shortage that affected both the military and the economy. Farm production declined, because invaders and the army destroyed fields. Inflation was also a problem.
5. In 476, the Germanic head of the army overthrew the western emperor, Romulus Augustulus. This is normally considered the date of the fall of the Western Roman Empire.

Chapter 6, Section 6.1

Organizing Your Thoughts

1. Muhammad is born
2. Muhammad has his first vision
3. Muhammad and his followers journey to Madinah (the *Hijrah*)
4. Muhammad returns to Makkah with his army, and the city surrenders
5. Muhammad dies

Read to Learn

6. The early Arabs made their living by shepherding or by raiding trade caravans.
7. The *Hijrah*, the journey of Muhammad and his followers to Madinah, took place in 622. This year became year 1 in the Islamic calendar.
8. The *shari'ah* is a set of laws that regulates the daily life of Muslims. Much of the *shari'ah* is taken from the Quran.

Section 6.2

Organizing Your Thoughts

1. Ali is chosen to be caliph.
2. Mu'awiyah becomes caliph and establishes the Umayyad dynasty.
3. Arab forces are defeated at the Battle of Tours, and Arab expansion into Europe ends.
4. Abu al-Abbas overthrows the Umayyad dynasty and sets up the Abbasid dynasty.
5. The Abbasids build a new capital city at Baghdad.
6. The Seljuk Turks capture Baghdad and take control of the Abbasid Empire.
7. The Crusades begin.
8. Saladin takes control of Egypt and ends the Fatimid dynasty.
9. Saladin invades Jerusalem, defeats the Christian army, and the Crusades end.
10. The Mongols seize Persia and Mesopotamia, and the Abbasid caliphate ends.

Read to Learn

11. Abu Bakr
12. The Shiite Muslims accept only the descendants of Ali as the true caliphs. The Sunni Muslims accept only the descendants of the Umayyads as caliphs.
13. The reign of Harun al-Rashid is often described as the golden age of the Abbasid caliphate.

14. The Seljuk Turks were nomads from central Asia who converted to Islam and took control of the Abbasid Empire.
15. The Christian states of Europe and the Islamic world feared each other.
16. The Mongols were destructive and cruel because they wanted to create so much terror that people would not fight back.

Section 6.3

Organizing Your Thoughts

1. Gold and slaves
2. Silk and porcelain
3. Gold and ivory
4. Sandalwood and spices
5. Grain
6. Linens, dates, and precious stones
7. Textile goods

Read to Learn

8. Baghdad, Cairo, and Damascus
9. Slaves and women

Section 6.4

Organizing Your Thoughts

1. Arabic philosophers translated the works of Plato and Aristotle, and they also wrote commentaries.
2. Muslims adopted and passed on the numerical system of India, which became known as the "Arabic" system. An Iranian mathematician created algebra.
3. Muslims set up an observatory at Baghdad, and they named many stars. They also improved the astrolabe.
4. Muslim scholars developed medicine as a field of scientific study. Ibn Sina wrote a medical encyclopedia that became a basic medical textbook in medieval Europe.
5. Ibn-Khaldun wrote *Muqaddimah* (*Introduction to History*), in which he argued for a cyclical view of history.
6. Muslims built many mosques, including the Great Mosque at Samarra. It is famous for its tower, or minaret. Islamic rulers also built beautiful palaces, including the Alhambra in Spain.

Read to Learn

7. They translated the works of Plato and Aristotle into Arabic. They put the translations in a library called the House of Wisdom, where the translations were read and studied. In the twelfth century, the Arabic translations were translated into Latin. This made them available in Europe, where they were almost lost.
8. Sailors used the astrolabe to determine their location by observing the positions of stars and planets.
9. Both the *Rubaiyat* and *The Arabian Nights* were told orally at first and then written down later.
10. Islamic religious art does not use representations of living beings because the Hadith, a collection of Muhammad's sayings, warns against any attempt to imitate God by creating pictures of living beings.

Chapter 7, Section 7.1

Organizing Your Thoughts

1. mild climate zone, along the northern coast and southern tip of Africa
2. deserts, the Sahara in the north and the Kalahari in the south
3. rain forest, along the equator
4. savannas, both north and south of the rain forest

Read to Learn

5. mountains, deserts, grasslands, tropical jungles, upland plateaus, lakes, canyons, tropical rain forests
6. deserts and savannas (both cover about 40 percent of Africa)
7. The Muslim trading states began to move inland. They wanted control over the trade in slaves and ivory, so Axum fought back.

Section 7.2

Organizing Your Thoughts

1. The kingdom of Ghana was located in the upper Niger River valley, between the Sahara and the tropical forests along the West African coast.
2. The kings of Ghana were strong rulers who governed without any laws. They relied on an army of thousands of men to protect their kingdom and enforce their wishes.
3. Most of the people of Ghana were farmers, but Ghana prospered because of iron and gold. Blacksmiths made tools and weapons from iron ore. Ghanaians traded gold for other products.
4. Mali is located on the Atlantic coast, but it extends far inland to the city of Timbuktu.
5. The people of Mali lived in villages with local rulers. These rulers collected taxes and sent the taxes to the kings of Mali. Under the rule of Mansa Musa, the kingdom of Mali was divided into provinces ruled by governors.
6. Most of the people of Mali were farmers, but Mali built its wealth on the gold and salt trade.
7. The Songhai people lived along the Niger River, south of the bend east of Timbuktu.
8. Under Muhammad Ture, Songhai was divided into provinces, with a governor in charge of each one. Peace and security were maintained with a navy and soldiers on horseback.
9. The Songhai Empire prospered because of the salt and gold trade, but the people also raised crops and cattle.

Read to Learn

10. Salt was used to preserve food and to improve its taste. People also needed salt to replace what their bodies lost in the hot climate.
11. Sundiata Keita
12. Sunni Ali and Muhammad Ture
13. Muslims formed a string of trading ports along the eastern coast of Africa. Merchants in these ports became very wealthy. A mixed African-Arabian culture, known as Swahili, began to emerge along the coast. The Muslim religion and Arabic architectural styles gradually became a part of the culture in this area.
14. Zimbabwe

Section 7.3

Organizing Your Thoughts

1. the belief in a single creator god
2. the belief that the creator god could be appeased by proper behavior and ritual
3. the belief that ancestors were closer to the gods and had the power to influence the lives of their descendants
4. the belief in an afterlife

Read to Learn

5. Both boys and girls were raised by their mothers until they were six years old. From their mothers, they learned language, songs, and their family history. At six, boys and girls went different ways. Fathers took control of their sons' education. Boys learned how to hunt and fish, how to grow plants, and how to clear fields. Girls continued to learn from their mothers. They learned how to take care of the home and work in the fields. As children grew older, they took on more responsibility in the community.
6. Islam rejected spirit worship and insisted on the separation of men and women.
7. African art forms, such as woodcarvings, often represented gods, spirits, or ancestral figures. Dances were a means of communicating with the spirits. African songs transmitted religious traditions from generation to generation.

Chapter 8, Section 8.1

Organizing Your Thoughts

1. 581–618
2. The Sui dynasty reunified China and completed the Grand Canal.
3. Sui Yangdi used forced labor to complete the canal and made people pay high taxes. These factors, as well as military failures, led to rebellion.
4. 618–907
5. The Tang rulers restored the civil service examination and gave land to the peasants. They brought peace to northwestern China and extended their control into Tibet. They also set up trade and diplomatic relations with Southeast Asia. Steel, gunpowder, and block printing were all invented during the Tang dynasty.
6. There were struggles for control and government corruption. The Tang rulers hired the Uighurs to fight for them, but the Uighurs overthrew the Tang ruler in 907.
7. 960–1279
8. During the Song dynasty, China was prosperous, and there were many cultural achievements. The Song dynasty put more land in the hands of the poor peasants. These reforms, as well as improvements in farming techniques, led to an abundance of food.
9. There were problems with the Uighurs in northern China. The Song rulers were forced to move the capital from Changan to Hangzhou. They also lost control of Tibet. They formed an alliance with the Mongols, which was a mistake.

Read to Learn

10. Sui Yangdi was a cruel ruler. He used forced labor to build the Grand Canal. He also made the people pay high taxes, while he lived extravagantly. These factors, as well as military failures, led to rebellion.
11. The Tang rulers restored the civil service examination, and they gave land to the peasants.
12. The Song rulers were forced to move the capital from Changan to Hangzhou because of the threat from the Uighurs in northern China.
13. The reforms of the Tang and Song dynasties put more land in the hands of the poor peasants. These reforms and improvements in farming techniques led to an abundance of food.
14. The status of women in China during this time was low. Female children were considered less desirable than male children, and they were sometimes killed if there was not enough food for the whole family. A girl's parents had to pay a dowry to her husband when she married. Poor families often sold their daughters to wealthy villagers.

Section 8.2

Organizing Your Thoughts

1. 1206—Temujin is elected Genghis Khan.
2. 1227—Genghis Khan dies.
3. 1231—The Mongols attack Persia.
4. 1258—The Mongols defeat the Abbasids at Baghdad.
5. 1279—Kublai Khan completes the conquest of China.
6. 1294—Kublai Khan dies.
7. 1368—Zhu Yuanzhang defeats the Mongols and establishes the Ming dynasty.

Read to Learn

8. The Mongols learned about gunpowder and the fire-lance from the Chinese.
9. Many Chinese people respected the stability and prosperity that the Mongols brought to China. The Mongols were also willing to adapt to the Chinese political system.

10. Buddhism was brought to China in the first century A.D. by merchants and missionaries from India.
11. The Tang dynasty is viewed as the great age of poetry in China. Landscape painting reached its high point during the Song and Mongol dynasties.

Section 8.3

Organizing Your Thoughts

1. Shotoku Taishi unified the clans to resist an invasion by the Chinese. He sent representatives to China to learn about their government and then created a centralized government based on the Chinese model.
2. In 109 B.C., the northern part of Korea came under the control of the Chinese, but the Koreans drove them out in the third century A.D. The Koryo dynasty adopted Chinese political institutions and was able to remain in power for four hundred years.
3. Kublai Khan invaded Japan, although most of his fleet was destroyed by a typhoon. Fighting the Mongols put a heavy strain on the government, however, and the Kamakura shogunate was overthrown in 1333.
4. In the thirteenth century, the Mongols seized the northern part of Korea. Mongol rule led to much suffering for the Korean people. Many peasants and artisans were forced to build ships for Kublai Khan.

Read to Learn

5. Because of their isolation from the mainland, the Japanese developed many unique qualities. They also believed that they had a destiny separate from the peoples on the mainland.
6. Shotoku Taishi created a centralized system of government based on the Chinese model. Japan was divided into administrative districts. The village was the basic unit of government. A new tax system was set up, in which the taxes were paid to the central government rather than to local aristocrats.
7. Many aristocratic men in Japan believed that prose fiction was "vulgar gossip" and thus beneath them. So they left the writing of fiction to the women.
8. The Koryo dynasty adopted Chinese political institutions. After the Mongols seized the northern part of Korea, the Koryo dynasty accepted Mongol authority in order to remain in power.

Section 8.4

Organizing Your Thoughts

1. Way of life (not a religion)
2. A wise man (not divine)
3. A release from the "wheel of life," achieved through an understanding of one's self
4. Religion, not a philosophy
5. Divine, not just a wise man
6. Not just a release from the wheel of life, but a true heaven, achieved through devotion to the Buddha

Read to Learn

7. Hinduism and Islam
8. The impact of Islam is still visible in the Indian subcontinent today, because the region is divided into mostly Hindu India and two Islamic states, Pakistan and Bangladesh.
9. Timur Lenk was the ruler of a Mongol state based in Samarkand. During the 1380s, he conquered the entire region east of the Caspian Sea and then occupied Mesopotamia. He also invaded northern India and raided the capital of Delhi.
10. The Muslim rulers realized that there were too many Hindus to convert them all, so they accepted the need to tolerate the Hindus' religion.
11. Most Indians made their living by farming.
12. Some of the greatest examples of Hindu temple art are the temples at Khajuraho.

Section 8.5

Organizing Your Thoughts

1. adopted the Chinese model of centralized government
2. based largely on farming
3. adopted Confucianism as the state religion
4. a kingdom under a single powerful leader
5. based largely on farming
6. crowned their ruler god-king (a link between the people and the gods)
7. borrowed Indian political practices
8. based largely on farming
9. converted to Buddhism
10. adopted Indian political institutions
11. adopted farming after they arrived in Southeast Asia
12. converted to Buddhism
13. various states, some influenced by India
14. based on trade (Srivijaya and the Sultanate of Melaka) and farming (Sailendra)
15. Most of the region converted to Islam.

Read to Learn

16. Much of Southeast Asia consists of islands, which are separated from each other by water. The mainland region has several mountain ranges, which also separated people. These geographical barriers may explain why Southeast Asia was never unified under a single government. The barriers also encouraged the development of separate cultures, with different religions and languages.

17. The Vietnamese adopted the Chinese model of centralized government. They adopted state Confucianism. The rulers called themselves emperors and adopted Chinese court rituals. They also introduced the civil service examination. The Thai and the Burmans both adopted Indian political practices. The states of Srivijaya, Sailendra, and Angkor were also influenced by Indian culture.

18. Vietnam, Angkor, Pagan, and Sailendra were agricultural societies. Srivijaya and the Sultanate of Melaka were trading societies.

19. In most of the societies of Southeast Asia, women had more rights than they did in China and India. They worked side by side with men in the fields and were often involved in trading activities.

20. Theravada Buddhism was popular because it taught that people could seek nirvana on their own, without the need for priests or rulers. It also tolerated local gods and posed no threat to established faiths.

Chapter 9, Section 9.1

Organizing Your Thoughts

1–5. Monks provided schools, hospitals, and hospitality for travelers. Monasteries were centers of learning. Monks copied manuscripts of both Christian and Roman works, which helped to preserve these works. Monks were also missionaries and helped spread Christianity throughout Europe.

Read to Learn

6. The Ostrogoths controlled Italy, the Visigoths controlled Spain, the Angles and Saxons controlled Britain, and the Franks controlled France.

7. Priests led parishes (local Christian communities). A bishop headed a group of parishes. His area of authority was called a bishopric, or diocese. The bishops of Rome became the heads of the Roman Catholic Church and were called popes.

8. Charlemagne expanded the territory of the Frankish kingdom and created the Carolingian Empire. In 800, Charlemagne was crowned the emperor of the Romans. He promoted learning in his kingdom, which led to a revival of learning and culture called the Carolingian Renaissance.

Section 9.2

Organizing Your Thoughts

1. Vassals had to perform military service. They could also be asked to come to the lord's court to give advice. They had to make payments to the lord on certain occasions.
2. Lords supported vassals by giving them land. They also had to protect their vassals, by defending them militarily or by taking their side in court.

Read to Learn

3. The Muslims, the Magyars and the Vikings all invaded Europe during the ninth and tenth centuries.
4. Men chose to become vassals for protection and because the lords gave them land in exchange for military service.
5. Knights were expected to defend the Church and defenseless people. They were also supposed to treat captives as honored guests instead of putting them in dungeons. They were also expected to fight for glory and not for material rewards.
6. Aristocratic women often had to manage their estates while the lords were away at war or court. This could involve supervising many servants, taking care of the financial accounts, and overseeing the supplies for the entire household. Some strong women advised and even dominated their husbands.

Section 9.3

Organizing Your Thoughts

1. England
2. William of Normandy brought French language and customs to England. He took a census called the Domesday Book. He also developed more fully the system of taxation and royal courts begun by the Anglo-Saxon kings.
3. England
4. Henry II increased the number of criminal cases tried in the king's court and made it possible for property cases to be tried in the royal courts. This led to the development of common law in England.
5. England
6. He signed (was forced to sign) the Magna Carta.
7. England
8. The English Parliament emerged during the reign of Edward I.
9. France
10. Phillip II gained control of the territories of Normandy, Maine, Anjou, and Aquitaine, which had been under English control. This increased the income of the French monarchy and expanded its power.
11. France
12. Philip IV expanded the royal bureaucracy. He also brought a French parliament into existence by meeting with representatives of the three estates.

Read to Learn

13. The Anglo-Saxon and French cultures merged to form a new English culture.
14. The clergy (first estate), the nobles (second estate), and the townspeople (third estate)
15. Frederick I considered Italy the center of a "holy empire." The German kings tried to rule both German and Italian lands, which became known as the Holy Roman Empire.
16. The eastern and southern Slavs converted to Eastern Orthodox Christianity. This linked them to the Byzantine culture.
17. The native peoples in what is now Ukraine and Russia called the Viking rulers (who moved into their land) the Rus.

Section 9.4

Organizing Your Thoughts

1. Latin
2. Rome
3. Roman Catholic
4. pope

5. Greek
6. Constantinople
7. Eastern Orthodox
8. patriarch

Read to Learn

9. Justinian expanded the Eastern Roman Empire so that it included Italy, part of Spain, North Africa, Asia Minor, Palestine and Syria. He rebuilt the city of Constantinople after riots destroyed much of the city. He simplified Roman laws into a code of laws called *The Body of Civil Law*. This code became the basis for much of the legal system of Europe.
10. The Byzantine emperor appointed the head of the Eastern Orthodox Church.
11. Constantinople was located between East and West. Goods from China, Southeast Asia, India, Russia, and the Balkans arrived in Constantinople and were shipped from there to the Mediterranean area and northern Europe. Raw materials were also imported by the local industries in Constantinople. A silk industry also developed in Constantinople.
12. In 1054, the pope of the Roman Catholic Church, Leo IX, and the patriarch of the Byzantine Church, Michael Cerularius, excommunicated each other.
13. Most of them were motivated by religious fervor, but some were seeking adventure. Others saw this as an opportunity to gain territory, riches, and possibly a title.

Chapter 10, Section 10.1

Organizing Your Thoughts

1. peace and stability during this time
2. a change in climate that improved growing conditions
3. more land to farm, as peasants cut down trees and drained swamps
4. new inventions, such as the horse collar, horseshoe, and the *carruca*
5. the shift from a two-field to a three-field system of crop rotation

Read to Learn

6. The carruca was a heavy, wheeled plow with an iron plowshare. This plow and the teams of horses that pulled it were too expensive for a single family to own, so entire villages shared the cost.
7. The land assigned to serfs to support themselves could not be taken away, and the serfs' responsibilities to their lord were fairly fixed. It was also the lord's duty to protect his serfs.
8. The feast days (holidays) of the Catholic Church gave peasants a break from their work.
9. Italy and Flanders
10. Townspeople bought the right to buy and sell property and freedom from military service. Some new towns also received the right to govern themselves by electing their own officials and having their own courts.
11. Stone walls surrounded medieval towns. The walls were expensive to build, so the space inside was limited and crowded.
12. A person who wanted to learn a trade first became an apprentice, usually around the age of 10. After five to seven years of service, apprentices became journeymen. To become masters, journeymen had to produce a masterpiece. This piece was used to judge whether a journeyman was qualified to become a master and join the guild.

Section 10.2

Organizing Your Thoughts

1. a group of Benedictine monks
2. discipline and service outside the monastery
3. Saint Francis of Assisi
4. vows of poverty, preaching repentance and simplicity, helping the poor, serving as missionaries
5. Dominic de Guzmán
6. defending Church teaching from heresy

Read to Learn

7. Popes were able to force rulers to do what they wanted by using interdicts. An interdicts forbids priests from giving the sacraments to a particular group of people. When people were denied the sacraments, they put pressure on their rulers to do what the pope wanted.

8. The Church created a court called the Inquisition. The job of this court was to find and try heretics. If an accused heretic confessed, he or she was forced to repent publicly and then was physically punished. People who did not confess were tortured until they did confess. Many did not confess but were still considered guilty and were executed.

9. The sacraments were seen as the means for receiving God's grace and were considered necessary for salvation. Only the clergy could administer the sacraments, so everyone who hoped to gain salvation depended on the clergy to help them.

Section 10.3

Organizing Your Thoughts

1–7. grammar, rhetoric, logic, arithmetic, geometry, music, and astronomy

Read to Learn

8. theology

9. Scholasticism is a philosophical and theological system that tries to reconcile faith and reason.

10. Vernacular literature is literature written in the vernacular, the language of everyday speech in a particular region, as opposed to Latin.

11. In Gothic cathedrals, the barrel vault of Romanesque cathedrals was replaced by a combination of ribbed vaults and pointed arches. This made Gothic cathedrals higher than Romanesque cathedrals and created an impression of upward movement. Gothic cathedrals also used flying buttresses to distribute the weight of the vaulted ceilings outward and down. The heavy walls that had been needed for support in Romanesque cathedrals were no longer needed, so the walls in Gothic cathedrals could be filled with stained glass windows.

Section 10.4

Organizing Your Thoughts

1–5. In some towns, Jews were accused of causing the plague by poisoning town wells, which led to an outbreak of anti-Semitism. Many Jews fled eastward, especially to Poland. Trade declined, and some industries were severely affected. A shortage of workers caused the price of labor to rise. Because there were fewer people, the demand for food declined, resulting in lower food prices. Some peasants bargained with their lords to pay rents instead of owing services, which freed them from serfdom.

Read to Learn

6. Medieval people believed that the Black Death was either sent by God as a punishment for their sins or that it was caused by the devil. In some towns, Jews were accused of causing the plague.

7. During the Great Schism, there were two popes, one in Rome and one in Avignon. Each line of popes said the other was the Antichrist, which damaged people's faith in the papacy and the Church.

8. Joan of Arc convinced Charles, who was heir to the French throne, to allow her to accompany a French army to Orléans. The French soldiers found a new confidence in themselves and captured Orléans. The French later defeated the English in Normandy and Aquitaine, and the war ended in 1453.

9. France, England, and Spain established strong centralized monarchies during the late Middle Ages.

Reading Essentials and Study Guide

Answer Key

Chapter 11, Section 11.1

Organizing Your Thoughts

1. the tundra region south of the Arctic
2. hunted seal, caribou, and fish
3. built homes of stone and turf, and igloos for temporary shelter while traveling
4. the Ohio River Valley and eventually along the Mississippi River
5. grew crops (corn, squash, and beans) and gathered wild plants
6. built earth mounds that were used as tombs or for ceremonies
7. present-day Pennsylvania, New York, and southern Canada
8. grew crops (corn, beans, and squash), gathered wild plants, hunted deer, bear, caribou, rabbits, and beaver
9. built longhouses that could house a dozen families
10. west of the Mississippi, in the river valleys of the Great Plains
11. grew beans, corn, and squash and hunted buffalo
12. made tepees (circular tents made by stretching buffalo skins over wooden poles)
13. the Southwest (present-day states of New Mexico, Arizona, Utah, and Colorado)
14. farmed when there was enough rain
15. built pueblos, made of stone and adobe, that could house many people

Read to Learn

16. the Rocky Mountains in North America and the Andes in South America
17. The Last Ice Age produced low sea levels that created a land bridge in the Bering Strait between Asia and North America.
18. Five groups of the Iroquois formed an alliance called the Iroquois League. A council of representatives met regularly to settle differences within the league. Benjamin Franklin later used the Iroquois League as a democratic model for a Plan of Union for the British colonies.

Section 11.2

Organizing Your Thoughts

1. the lowlands along the coast of the Gulf of Mexico
2. around 1200–400 B.C.
3. large cities, pyramids, huge stone heads (carvings)
4. Yucatán Peninsula, eventually including much of Central America and Mexico
5. flourished between A.D. 300–900
6. cities, pyramids, temples, palaces, two calendars, a writing system based on hieroglyphs
7. upper Yucatán Peninsula
8. around A.D. 900–1200
9. pyramids and palaces
10. central Mexico
11. twelfth century-sixteenth century A.D.
12. pyramids, temples, public buildings, roads

Read to Learn

13. The first major city in Mesoamerica was Teotihuacán, which means "Place of the Gods."
14. One system was based on a solar calendar of 365 days. The other was based on a sacred calendar of 260 days.
15. A Spanish army under Hernán Cortés came to Tenochtitlán. Diseases brought by the Spaniards soon infected many of the Aztec. The Spaniards attacked the city, and after four months, the city surrendered. The Spaniards then destroyed the city.

Section 11.3

Organizing Your Thoughts

1. the emperor.
2. four quarters ruled by governors
3. provinces, also ruled by governors
4. the people, ten thousand per province

Read to Learn

5. The city of Caral was the oldest major city in the Americas. It was located in the Supe River valley of Perus.

6. They kept records using a system of knotted strings called the *quipu.*

Chapter 12, Section 12.1

Organizing Your Thoughts

1–5. an urban society, a secular viewpoint, recovery from the problems of the fourteenth century, a rebirth of interest in ancient culture, an emphasis on what individuals could achieve

Read to Learn

6. The word *renaissance* means rebirth.

7. The French king Charles VIII led an army into Italy in 1494 and occupied the kingdom of Naples. This started the Italian wars. The wars ended in 1527, when troops belonging to the Spanish king Charles I sacked Rome.

8. Machiavelli believed that human beings were basically self-centered.

9. During the Middle Ages, townspeople had been mainly merchants and artisans. In the fifteenth century, towns and cities were more diverse. They were made up of patricians, burghers, poor workers, and the unemployed.

Section 12.2

Organizing Your Thoughts

1. Classical Rome inspired Renaissance architecture. Churches were created to fit human, not divine needs. They did not overwhelm worshipers like Gothic cathedrals did.

2. Renaissance sculptors studied and copied the statues of the Greeks and Romans. They created realistic, free-standing figures.

3. Renaissance painters wanted the people, objects, and events that they painted to look real. They understood the laws of perspective, which helped them to create the illusion of three dimensions. Their paintings have depth, and they portrayed people realistically. During the High Renaissance, painters went beyond realism. They created idealized forms that showed the perfection of nature and the individual.

Read to Learn

4. Humanists began to take a new interest in civic life. They believed that it was the duty of intellectuals to live active lives. They also believed that the study of the humanities should be used to serve the state.

5. Dante and Chaucer

6. The purpose of a liberal education was to produce individuals who would act with virtue and wisdom. Humanists thought that a liberal education was practical. Their goal was not to create great scholars but complete citizens.

7. Leonardo da Vinci, Michelangelo, and Raphael

8. Northern Renaissance artists were also interested in portraying the world realistically. But they did this, not by using the laws of perspective, but by observing reality and portraying details as best they could. They became masters at painting details.

Section 12.3

Organizing Your Thoughts

1. salvation through faith in God

2. only two sacraments (baptism and Eucharist)

3. clergy could marry

4. services consisting of Bible readings, preaching, and songs

5. salvation by both faith and good works

6. seven sacraments

7. clergy had to be celibate

8. Catholic mass

Read to Learn

9. Humanists believed that in order to change the Church and society, they needed to change individuals first. They thought that if people read the classics and the works of Christianity, they would become more pious. This would bring about a reform of the Church and society.

10. They believed that the Catholic Church was corrupt. Between 1450 and 1520, popes were more concerned with Italian politics and worldly interests than with spiritual matters. Many church officials were concerned with money and used their church offices to get wealthy. Parish priests were often ignorant of their spiritual duties. The church also sold indulgences (certificates releasing people from all or part of the punishment for their sins).

11. The Ninety-Five Theses were statements written by Martin Luther. They were an attack on the selling of indulgences. Luther nailed the theses to the door of the Castle Church in Wittenberg in 1517.

12. The Peace of Augsburg ended religious warfare in Germany. It formally accepted the division of Christianity in Germany. The German states could now choose between Catholicism and Lutheranism.

Section 12.4

Organizing Your Thoughts

1. All paintings, decorations, and relics were removed from the churches in Zürich. A new church service, consisting of scripture readings, prayer, and sermons, replaced the Catholic mass.

2. Calvin created a church government that used both clergy and laity. A court, called the Consistory, was set up to oversee the moral life and religious doctrines of the people of Geneva.

3. Henry VIII asked Parliament to separate the Church in England from the pope in Rome. Parliament passed the Act of Supremacy that made the king the head of the Church of England. Henry used his new powers to close the monasteries and sell their land and possessions.

4. The Anabaptists believed in adult baptism. They also believed that all Christians were priests and were equal. Each Anabaptist church chose its own minister, and any member of the community was eligible. They also believed in the complete separation of church and state. They would not hold political office or bear arms.

Read to Learn

5. Huldrych Zwingli

6. predestination (the belief that God has determined in advance who will be saved and who will be damned)

7. England broke away from the Roman Catholic Church because of politics, not religion. Because he needed a male heir, King Henry VIII wanted to divorce his wife, Catherine of Aragon, to marry Anne Boleyn. When the pope refused to annul his marriage, Henry asked the church courts in England for the annulment. He then asked Parliament to separate the Church in England from the pope in Rome.

8. Many of the Protestant reformers allowed the state to play an important role in church affairs. The Anabaptists were against the state having this kind of power. They believed in a complete separation of church and state. They refused to hold political office or bear arms. Unlike many other Protestants, the Anabaptists also believed in adult baptism.

9. Protestants did not believe that there was anything especially holy about being celibate. They did away with monasticism and the requirement of celibacy for the clergy.

10. The Jesuits, reform of the papacy, and the Council of Trent brought about the Catholic Reformation.

Chapter 13 Section 13.1

Organizing Your Thoughts

1. Portuguese

2. sailed around the Cape of Good Hope and crossed the Indian Ocean to the coast of India.
3. Italian (but explored for Spain)
4. reached all of the major islands of the Caribbean and Honduras in Central America
5. Venetian (but explored for England)
6. explored the New England coastline of North America
7. Spanish
8. took control of the Inca Empire in South America
9. Portuguese (but explored for Spain)
10. sailed around the tip of South America and crossed the Pacific Ocean to the Philippine Islands

Read to Learn

11. The first motive was economic. Europeans hoped to find precious metals and to expand trade, especially for the spices of the East. The second motive was religious. Many Europeans believed that it was their duty to convert other peoples to Christianity. The third motive was a desire for glory and adventure. These three motives are sometimes referred to as "God, glory, and gold."
12. Admiral Afonso de Albuquerque gained control of Melaka, which was a thriving port for the spice trade. From Melaka, the Portuguese made expeditions to China and the Spice Islands. They signed a treaty with a local ruler for the purchase and export of cloves. This treaty gave the Portuguese control of the spice trade.
13. Columbus called the islands he explored the Indies, because he thought he had reached Asia.
14. Forced labor, starvation, and disease took a terrible toll on Native American lives. The native peoples had little resistance to European diseases, and 30 to 40 percent of them died from smallpox, measles, and typhus. Catholic missionaries converted and baptized hundreds of thousands of native peoples. Native American social and political structures were torn apart and replaced by European systems of religion, language, culture, and government.
15. Colonies were important in the theory of mercantilism, because they were sources of raw materials and were markets for finished goods.

Section 13.2

Organizing Your Thoughts

1. manufactured goods, such as guns and cloth
2. slaves
3. tobacco, molasses, sugar, and raw cotton (The section of the triangle between Africa and the Americas was the Middle Passage.)

Read to Learn

4. The demand for slaves increased dramatically, because plantations were set up in the Americas to grow sugar cane. Growing sugar cane requires much labor. African slaves were shipped to Brazil and the Caribbean to work on the plantations. Before Europeans became involved in the slave trade, most slaves in Africa were prisoners of war. As the demand for slaves increased, however, slave traders began to send raiders into defenseless villages in search of victims.
5. In general, the European influence in Africa did not extend beyond the coastal regions. However, trade with Europeans caused trade routes to shift toward the coast. This led to the weakening of the old Songhai trading empire. It also helped a new Moroccan dynasty to emerge in the late sixteenth century. Foreigners also influenced African religious beliefs. In North Africa, Islam continued to expand. It also spread southward into the states of West Africa. The spread of Christianity was mainly limited to South Africa and Ethiopia.

Section 13.3

Organizing Your Thoughts

1. Burma, Thailand, Laos, and Cambodia
2. Buddhist kings—were considered superior to other human beings. They served as a link between humans and the universe.
3. Java
4. Javanese kings—were believed to have a sacred quality. They maintained the balance between the sacred and material worlds. This style was based on political traditions in India.
5. Malay Peninsula and the small states on the Indonesian Archipelago
6. Islamic sultans—were viewed as mortals, but with some special qualities. They defended the Islamic faith and staffed their bureaucracies mainly with aristocrats.
7. Vietnam
8. Vietnamese emperors—followed the Chinese model. They ruled according to the teachings of Confucius. They were seen as mortals appointed by Heaven to rule because of their talent and virtue. They were also intermediaries between Heaven and Earth.

Read to Learn

9. Melaka became the leading power in the region because of its location and the rapid growth of the spice trade.
10. Mainland states had strong monarchies that resisted foreign intrusion. When European nations began to compete for trade and missionary privileges in the area, the mainland states were able to unite and drive them out.
11. Islam and Christianity began to attract converts, especially in the non-mainland states and the Philippines. Buddhism advanced on the mainland. Traditional beliefs still survived, however, and influenced the new religions.

Chapter 14 Section 14.1

Organizing Your Thoughts

1. France
2. Protestant (Huguenot) but converted to Catholicism for political reasons after he became king
3. To solve the religious problem in France, Henry IV issued the Edict of Nantes, which recognized Catholicism as the official religion of France, but gave Huguenots the right to worship and full political rights.
4. Spain
5. Catholic
6. By the end of Philip's reign, Spain was the most populous empire in the world. It controlled almost all of South America and a number of settlements in Asia and Africa. Philip also led a Holy League against the Turks that resulted in a victory over the Turkish fleet in the Battle of Lepanto in 1571.
7. England
8. Protestant (Church of England)
9. Elizabeth was named as the "only supreme governor" of both church and state in England. She was able to solve the religious problem in England by repealing laws favoring Catholics and by following a moderate form of Protestantism. She tried to keep Spain and France from becoming too powerful by balancing power. Her navy successfully defeated an invasion by the Spanish armada in 1588.

Read to Learn

10. Huguenots were French Protestants influenced by John Calvin.
11. He insisted on strict conformity to Catholicism. Philip and the Spanish people saw Spain as a nation of people chosen by God to save Catholic Christianity from the Protestant heretics. Philip became a champion of Catholic causes. He led a Holy League against the Turks. He also tried to crush Calvinism in the Netherlands.

12. She repealed the laws favoring Catholics that had been passed under her Catholic half-sister, Mary Tudor. During her reign, the Church of England was basically Protestant, but it followed a moderate Protestantism that kept most people satisfied.

Section 14.2

Organizing Your Thoughts

1. James I
2. Charles I
3. Cromwell
4. Charles II
5. James II

Read to Learn

6. The influx of gold and silver from the Americas was one cause of inflation. There was also a growing population in the sixteenth century. This increased the demand for land and food and drove up prices for both.
7. Poor, common people were the ones most often accused of witchcraft. More than 75 percent of those accused were women. Most of them were single or widowed and over 50 years old.
8. The Peace of Westphalia that ended the war stated that all German states could determine their own religion. The states that made up the Holy Roman Empire were recognized as independent states. This brought an end to the Holy Roman Empire. Germany would not be united again for another two hundred years. France emerged from the war as the dominant nation in Europe.
9. In 1688, a group of English noblemen invited the Dutch leader, William of Orange, to invade England. William and Mary raised an army and "invaded" England, with almost no bloodshed. James II fled to France, and Parliament offered the throne to William and Mary. They accepted it, along with a Bill of Rights.

Section 14.3

Organizing Your Thoughts

1. France
2. Louis XIV had complete authority over foreign policy, the Church, and taxes. He created a myth of himself as the Sun King—the source of light for all his people. He set up his royal court at Versailles, where he kept a close watch over the chief offices of the state. He developed a standing army of four hundred thousand. He waged four wars between 1667 and 1713. Through his wars, he added some territory to France's northeastern frontier and set up a member of his family on the throne of Spain.
3. Prussia
4. Frederick William the Great Elector laid the foundation for the Prussian state. He built a large and efficient standing army. He also set up the General War Commissariat to levy taxes for the army and oversee its growth. The Commissariat soon became an agency of civil government as well.
5. Russia
6. Peter the Great westernized Russia. Under his rule, Russia became a great military power. He built a standing army of 210,000 men. He also formed the first Russian navy. He wanted an ice-free port with year-round access to Europe. He fought a long war with Sweden and finally acquired the lands he needed. He then constructed a new city, St. Petersburg, that became the Russian capital.

Read to Learn

7. Absolutism is a system in which a ruler holds total power. Absolute monarchs had the ability to make laws, levy taxes, administer justice, control the state's officials, and determine foreign policy.
8. The Hapsburgs had lost the German Empire after the Thirty Years' War, but

they created a new empire in eastern and southeastern Europe. The core of the new Austrian Empire was the traditional Austrian lands in present-day Austria, the Czech Republic, and Hungary. After 1687, they also took control of all of Hungary, Transylvania, Croatia, and Slovenia. This empire never became a highly centralized, absolutist state, chiefly because it was made up of so many different national groups.

9. After Peter returned from his trip to the West, he was determined to westernize Russia. He borrowed European technology, especially for the military. He also introduced Western customs, practices, and manners into Russia. He ordered the preparation of the first Russian book of etiquette to teach Western manners. Russian beards had to be shaved and coats shortened, because Westerners did not wear beards or long coats. Peter insisted that Russian upper-class women remove the veils that had traditionally covered their faces and move out into society, like Western women. Peter also wanted to "open a window to the West," which led him to build a new city, St. Petersburg, on the Baltic Sea.

Section 14.4

Organizing Your Thoughts

1. *Leviathan*
2. *Two Treatises of Government*
3. Hobbes believed that humans were guided not by reason and moral ideals, but by a ruthless struggle for self-preservation.
4. Locke believed that before society was organized, humans lived in a state of equality and freedom, not a state of war.
5. People made a social contract and agreed to form a state to save themselves from destroying one another.
6. People agreed to establish a government to ensure the protection of their rights.
7. Absolutism—Hobbes believed that absolute power was necessary to preserve order in society.
8. A government in which there were mutual obligations—Government would protect the rights of people, and people would act reasonably toward government. If a government broke the contract, people could form a new government.

Read to Learn

9. The rules of proportion were deliberately ignored. Elongated figures were used to show suffering, heightened emotions, and religious ecstasy.
10. Baroque artists tried to bring together the classical ideals of Renaissance art with the spiritual feelings of the sixteenth-century religious revival. The baroque painting style was known for its use of dramatic effects to arouse the emotions.
11. Drama
12. Natural rights are rights with which humans are born. According to Locke, these included rights to life, liberty, and property.

Chapter 15 Section 15.1

Organizing Your Thoughts

1. Constantinople
2. Mesopotamia, Egypt, Arabia, African coastal areas as far as the Strait of Gibraltar
3. Belgrade, most of Hungary, parts of Austria

Read to Learn

4. They built a strong military by developing an elite guard called janissaries. They also began to master firearms.
5. Ottomans preferred to administer their conquered lands through local rulers. The central government appointed officials, called pashas, who collected taxes, maintained law and order, and were responsible to the sultan's court in Constantinople.

6. The Ottoman Empire is often called a "gunpowder empire," because its success was based mainly on the use of gunpowder and firearms.
7. The Ottomans were generally tolerant of non-Muslims. Non-Muslims paid a tax, but they were allowed to practice their religion or convert to Islam.
8. Women were allowed to own and inherit property. They could not be forced into marriage. In certain cases, they were permitted to seek divorce.
9. After the death of Süleyman, sultans became less involved in government and allowed their ministers to exercise more power. Senior positions were given to the sons or daughters of the elite. The central bureaucracy became less connected with rural areas, and local officials became corrupt.
10. architecture, textiles, and rugs

Section 15.2

Organizing Your Thoughts

1. the shah
2. the bureaucracy and landed classes
3. the common people

Read to Learn

4. Ismail, the leader of the Safavids, sent Shiite preachers into Anatolia to convert members of Turkish tribes in the Ottoman Empire. He also ordered the massacre of Sunni Muslims when he conquered Baghdad in 1508. The Ottoman sultan, Selim I, was alarmed and attacked the Safavids in Persia.
5. The Safavid dynasty was at its height under Shah Abbas, who ruled from 1588 to 1629.
6. The Safavids had come to power with the support of nomadic Turkish groups, but the majority of the people were Persian. Most of them were farmers or townspeople.
7. architecture, silk weaving, carpet weaving, painting

Section 15.3

Organizing Your Thoughts

1. Akbar's son, Jahangir, was influenced by one of his wives and began to lose some of his control of the empire. He also left a nearly empty treasury.
2. Shah Jaran failed to deal with domestic problems. His military campaigns and building projects put a heavy strain on the imperial finances and forced him to raise taxes, while most of the people lived in poverty.
3. When Shah Jaran became ill, two of his sons struggled for power. One of them, Aurangzeb, had his brother put to death and imprisoned his father. He then crowned himself emperor.
4. Aurangzeb reversed many of the Mogul policies of religious tolerance. The building of new Hindu temples was prohibited, and Hindus were forced to convert to Islam. These policies led to Hindu protests, and revolt broke out in provinces throughout the empire. India became divided and vulnerable to attack.
5. The arrival of the British hastened the decline of the Mogul Empire.

Read to Learn

6. Babur
7. He was a Muslim, but he was tolerant of other religions. The upper-ranks of his government were filled with non-native Muslims, but many of the lower-ranking officials were Hindus. All Indian peasants were required to pay about one-third of their annual harvest to the state, but the system was applied justly. When bad weather struck, taxes were reduced or even suspended.
8. He had his brother put to death and imprisoned his father. On the other hand, he tried to eliminate what he thought were India's evils, so he forbade the Hindu custom of suttee and the levying of illegal

taxes. However, because he was a devout Muslim, he reversed many of the Mogul policies of religious tolerance and forced Hindus to convert to Islam.

9. In 1757, Sir Robert Clive led a small British force to victory over a Mogul-led army. The Mogul court was then forced to give the British East India Company the power to collect taxes in the area surrounding Calcutta.

10. Women played an active role in Mogul society, and some even fought on the battlefield alongside men. Women from aristocratic families were allowed to own land and to take part in business activities. The Islamic practice of isolating women was compatible with Hindu customs and was adopted by many upper-class Hindus.

11. Persian and Indian

Chapter 16 Section 16.1

Organizing Your Thoughts

1. The Chinese extended their rule into Mongolia and central Asia.

2. They strengthened the Great Wall and made peace with nomadic tribes in the north.

3. The Ming rulers had an effective government using a bureaucracy made up of officials chosen by the civil service examination system.

4. They set up a nationwide school system.

5. More manufactured goods were produced in workshops and factories.

6. New crops were introduced that increased food production.

7. The Ming rulers completed the Grand Canal, which made it possible to ship grain and other goods from southern to northern China.

Read to Learn

8. At first, the Portuguese had little impact on Chinese society. The emperor viewed Europeans as barbarians. Direct trade between Europe and China remained limited. But an exchange of ideas and cultures took place. Christian missionaries brought new inventions, such as clocks and eyeglasses.

9. The Qing, who were Manchus, dealt with the ethnic and cultural differences in two ways. First, they tried to preserve their distinct identity within Chinese society. The Manchus were defined legally as distinct from everyone else in China. In the military, Manchus were organized into separate units. Second, the Qing brought Chinese people into the top ranks of the imperial administration. All important positions were shared equally by Chinese and Manchus.

Section 16.2

Organizing Your Thoughts

1. A new form of literature arose that eventually evolved into the modern Chinese novel. *The Golden Lotus* and *The Dream of the Red Chamber* are two examples of early Chinese novels.

2. The most outstanding example is the Imperial City in Beijing.

3. The most famous of the decorative arts was the blue-and-white porcelain of the Ming Era.

Read to Learn

4. One cause of the population increase was the peace and stability under the early Qing dynasty. Another cause was the food supply. A faster growing rice increased the food supply.

5. Only males could have a formal education and pursue a career in government or scholarship. Legally, a woman could not divorce her husband or inherit property. The husband, on the other hand, could divorce his wife if she did not produce sons. He could also take a second wife.

6. *The Dream of the Red Chamber*

Section 16.3

Organizing Your Thoughts

1. warrior class
1a. shogun
1b. daimyo
1c. samurai
1d. ronin
2. farmers (peasants)
3. artisans
4. merchants

Read to Learn

5. The period during the rule of the Tokugawa shoguns is known as the "Great Peace."
6. The Jesuits destroyed shrines, which caused a severe reaction and, eventually, their expulsion from Japan.
7. During the Tokugawa Era, the samurai gradually ceased to be a warrior class. Many of them became managers on the lands of the daimyo.
8. Most peasants experienced both declining profits and rising costs and taxes. Many were forced to become tenants or to work as hired help. When conditions became desperate, some peasants revolted.
9. Architecture flourished during the Tokugawa Era because of the shogun's order that all daimyo have residences in Edo. Nobles competed to build the most magnificent mansions.
10. Korea was largely untouched by European merchants and missionaries.

Chapter 17 Section 17.1

Organizing Your Thoughts

1. Copernicus believed in a heliocentric, or sun-centered, model of the universe. He wrote about this in his famous book, *On the Revolutions of the Heavenly Spheres.*
2. Kepler's observations confirmed that the Sun was at the center of the universe. He also discovered that the orbits of the planets around the Sun were elliptical, not circular.
3. Galileo was the first European to make regular observations of the heavens with a telescope. He discovered mountains on the Moon, four moons revolving around Jupiter, and sunspots. His observations indicated that heavenly bodies were not pure orbs of light, but were composed of material substance like Earth.
4. Newton defined the three laws of motion that govern both the planetary bodies and objects on Earth. The universal law of gravitation states that every object in the universe is attracted to every other object by a force called gravity. Newton created a new picture of the universe, as a huge machine that worked according to natural laws.
5. Bacon developed the scientific method. He believed that scientists should use systematic observations and inductive reasoning to learn about nature.

Read to Learn

6. Renaissance humanists had learned Greek and Latin. They were able to read works by Ptolemy, Archimedes, and Plato. These writings made it obvious that some ancient thinkers disagreed with Aristotle. At the same time, the invention of new instruments, such as the telescope and microscope, made new scientific discoveries possible.
7. The geocentric model places Earth at the center of the universe, with the heavenly bodies rotating around Earth. The heliocentric model places the Sun at the center of the universe, with the planets, including Earth, revolving around the Sun.
8. William Harvey's observations disproved many of the theories of Galen, a second century Greek physician, whose theories had dominated medicine in the Middle Ages.

9. Scientific work was considered to be men's work. Women scientists, such as Maria Winkelmann, were denied scientific positions because they were women.

10. Descartes first principle was "I think, therefore I am" (the certainty of his own existence). His second principle was the separation of mind and matter.

11. According to Bacon, scientists should use inductive reasoning to learn about nature. They should proceed from the particular to the general. Systematic observations and carefully organized experiments to test hypotheses would lead to general principles.

Section 17.2

Organizing Your Thoughts

1. Montesquieu identified three branches of government: the executive, the legislative, and the judicial. He showed that the greatest freedom and security exists when the government functions through a separation of powers, in which the three branches limit and control each other in a system of checks and balances. His ideas influenced the U.S. Constitution.

2. Voltaire and other Enlightenment thinkers were deists. Deists believe that the universe is like a clock. God created it, set it in motion, and allowed it to run without his interference.

3. The philosophes believed that there are natural laws that govern human society. This led to the development of the social sciences (areas such as economics and political science). Eighteenth-century economists, such as the Physiocrats and Adam Smith, believed that if individuals were free to pursue their own economic self-interest, all society would ultimately benefit. They believed that government should not interfere in economic matters—a doctrine know as laissez-faire.

4. An eighteenth-century woman, Mary Wollstonecraft, is often viewed as the founder of the movement for women's rights. In her book, *A Vindication of the Rights of Women,* she argued that women should have the same rights as men.

Read to Learn

5. Because Newton had discovered natural laws that governed the physical world, the intellectuals of the Enlightenment thought that they could discover natural laws that governed human society. John Locke's theory of knowledge also influenced them. Locke believed that people could be changed by changing their environments and exposing them to the right influences.

6. To Newton, the physical world and everything in it was a giant machine. This idea led to deism, an eighteenth-century religious philosophy based on reason and natural law. In the Deists' view, a mechanic (God) had created the universe. He set it in motion and then allowed it to run without his interference, according to its own natural laws.

7. Adam Smith believed that government should not interfere in economic matters. He believed that government should have only three basic roles: protecting society from invasion (the army); defending citizens from injustice (the police); and keeping up certain public works, such as roads and canals.

8. According to Rousseau, through a social contract, an entire society agrees to be governed by its general will. Individuals who wish to follow their own self-interests must be forced to abide by the general will.

9. Wollstonecraft argued that if government based on the arbitrary power of monarchs was wrong, the power of men over women was equally wrong. She also argued that the Enlightenment was based on the idea of reason in all human beings. Because women have reason, they are entitled to the same rights as men.

10. Salons were elegant drawing rooms of the wealthy upper class. Guests gathered in these salons and discussed the ideas of the philosophes. The salons brought writers and artists together with aristocrats, government officials, and wealthy middle-class people.
11. The sermons of John Wesley often caused people to have conversion experiences. Many of these converts joined Methodist societies in which they helped each other do good works. Methodism gave the lower and middle classes a sense of purpose and community and proved that the need for spiritual experience had not been eliminated in the eighteenth century.

Section 17.3

Organizing Your Thoughts

1–2. the British and Prussians
3–5. the Austrians, Russians, and French

Read to Learn

6. Johann Sebastian Bach, George Frederick Handel, Franz Joseph Haydn, and Wolfgang Amadeus Mozart
7. Joseph II of Austria
8. Europe, the Far East, and North America
9. in North America

Section 17.4

Organizing Your Thoughts

1. the executive—A president served as the chief executive.
2. the legislative—It consisted of the Senate and the House of Representatives.
3. the judicial—It consisted of the Supreme Court and other courts.

Read to Learn

4. The Catholic Church played an important role in Latin America. Spanish and Portuguese rulers were determined to Christianize the native peoples. Catholic missionaries brought Native Americans together into villages, or missions, where they could be converted, taught trades, and encouraged to grow crops. The missions made it possible for the missionaries to control the lives of the Native Americans. The Catholic Church also built cathedrals, hospitals, orphanages, and schools. The Catholic Church allowed women who did not wish to marry to enter convents and become nuns.
5. The first two Hanoverian kings, George I and George II, did not know the British system very well and allowed their chief ministers to handle Parliament.
6. France, Spain, and the Dutch Republic
7. The Articles of Confederation did not provide for a strong central government. The government under the Articles did not have much power. The Constitution created a federal system in which power was shared between the national government and the state governments. The national, or federal, government was given the power to levy taxes, raise an army, regulate trade, and create a national currency.

Chapter 18 Section 18.1

Organizing Your Thoughts

1. the clergy
2. nobility
3. commoners—peasants, skilled craftspeople, shopkeepers, other wage earners in the cities, the bourgeoisie: merchants, bankers, industrialists, doctors, lawyers, writers

Read to Learn

4. The immediate cause of the French Revolution was the economic situation at the time, including the near collapse of government finances.
5. the storming of the Bastille
6. Catholic priests, nobles, lower classes hurt by a rise in the cost of living, and radicals who wanted even more drastic solutions

Section 18.2

Organizing Your Thoughts

1. National Assembly, 1789–1791
2. Legislative Assembly, 1791–1792
3. National Convention and the Committee of Public Safety, 1792–1795
4. Directory/legislature, 1795–1799

Read to Learn

5. An informal coalition of Austria, Prussia, Spain, Portugal, Britain, the Dutch Republic, and Russia took up arms against France and were ready to invade. To meet this crisis, the National Convention gave broad powers to the Committee of Public Safety.
6. The word *saint* was removed from street names, churches were pillaged or closed, and priests were encouraged to marry. In November 1793, a public ceremony dedicated to the worship of reason was held in the cathedral of Notre Dame. A new calendar was adopted. Years were no longer numbered from the birth of Christ. Sundays and church holidays were eliminated.
7. The French revolutionary army was the largest in European history. It was not made up of professional soldiers. It was raised by a universal mobilization of the nation. It was created by a people's government. Its wars were people's wars, not wars between rulers.
8. The period under the government of the Directory was a time of corruption. Both royalists and radicals were unhappy with the Directory. The Royalists wanted to restore the monarchy. Radicals were unhappy with the turn toward moderation. The Directory was unable to find a solution to the country's economic problems, and it was still carrying on wars started by the Committee of Public Safety.

Section 18.3

Organizing Your Thoughts

1. Napoleon made peace with the Catholic Church. In 1801, he made an agreement with the pope that recognized Catholicism as the religion of the majority of the French people. In return the pope agreed not to ask for the return of the church lands seized in the revolution.
2. Napoleon completed seven codes of law. The most important of the codes was the Civil Code (also called the Napoleonic Code). This code recognized the equality of all citizens before the law, the right of the individual to choose a profession, religious toleration, and the abolition of serfdom and feudalism. Property rights were carefully protected.
3. Napoleon developed a bureaucracy of capable officials. Promotion was based on ability, not on rank or birth. He also created a new aristocracy based on merit in the civil or military service.
4. Napoleon achieved a peace treaty in 1802 (but it did not last long).
5. In a series of battles, Napoleon's army defeated the Austrian, Prussian, and Russian armies.
6. From 1807 to 1812, Napoleon was the master of Europe. His Grand Empire was composed of the French Empire, which consisted of an enlarged France that extended to the Rhine in the east and included the western half of Italy north of Rome; dependent states that were under the rule of his relatives; and allied states—countries defeated by Napoleon and forced to join his struggle against Britain.

Read to Learn

7. His victories in Italy made him popular, and his energy, charm, and intelligence gained him the support of many people.

8. The Civil Code preserved the equality of all citizens. Opening government careers to more people was another gain. But Napoleon destroyed some revolutionary ideals. Liberty was replaced with despotism. Freedom of the press was eliminated.
9. an enlarged France; dependent states: Spain, Holland, the kingdom of Italy, the Swiss Republic, the Grand Duchy of Warsaw, and the Confederation of the Rhine; allied states: Prussia, Austria, Russia, and Sweden.
10. the survival of Great Britain and the force of nationalism
11. Napoleon's invasion of Russia was a military disaster. The Russian forces refused to fight and retreated for hundreds of miles. As they retreated, they burned their own villages and countryside to keep Napoleon's army from finding food. Without food and supplies, Napoleon was forced to abandon Moscow and begin the "Great Retreat" across Russia. Only forty thousand of the original army of six hundred thousand made it back to Poland. This military disaster led other European states to attack the French army. Paris was captured in March 1814, and Napoleon was sent into exile on the island of Elba.

Chapter 19 Section 19.1

Organizing Your Thoughts

1. Agricultural practices had changed. More people could be fed at lower prices with less labor. Even ordinary British families had money to buy manufactured goods.
2. The population grew and created a large labor force to work in the new factories in Britain.
3. Britain had money (capital) to invest in the new industrial machines and factories.
4. Natural resources, such as coal and iron ore, were plentiful in Britain.
5. Britain had a huge empire that gave the British many markets for their goods.

Read to Learn

6. Factory owners wanted to use their machines constantly. As a result, workers were forced to work in shifts to keep the machines running all day. Factory owners created a system in which employees became used to working set hours and doing the same work over and over.
7. Belgium, France, and the German states were the first countries to be industrialized in continental Europe. Their governments were very active in encouraging the development of industrialization.
8. People moved from the country to the cities to find work in factories. Living conditions in the cities were pitiful for many people. Industrial capitalism produced two new classes: the industrial middle class and the industrial working class. The working class had terrible working conditions. Laws were eventually passed that limited the work hours of children and women. Men were now expected to earn most of the family income by working outside the home. This was a change from the earlier cottage industry, in which husband, wife, and children had worked together.

Section 19.2

Organizing Your Thoughts

1. favored obedience to political authority/opposed revolutions and representative government
2. believed that organized religion was crucial to society
3. unwilling to accept demands from people who wanted individual rights
4. believed that people should be as free as possible from government restraint and that laws should be made by a representative assembly/favored government ruled by a constitution, but did not believe in a democracy in which everyone had a right to vote

5. wanted religious toleration and the separation of church and state
6. believed in the protection of civil rights

Read to Learn

7. Great Britain, Austria, Prussia, and Russia
8. According to the principle of intervention, the great powers had the right to send armies into countries where there were revolutions in order to restore legitimate monarchs to their thrones.
9. Conservatives feared the changes brought by nationalism and tried to repress it, but many liberals supported nationalism. Most liberals believed that freedom would only be possible if people ruled themselves, so most liberals agreed with the nationalists that each people group should have its own state.
10. In France, the monarchy was overthrown, and a new republic (the Second Republic) was formed. In Vienna, revolutionary forces took control of the capital and demanded a liberal constitution. To appease the revolutionaries, the Austrian government gave Hungary its own legislature. In Bohemia, the Czechs demanded their own government. A revolt also took place in Lombardy and Venetia. Revolutionaries in other Italian states also took up arms and tried to create liberal constitutions and a unified Italy. By 1849, however, the Austrians had defeated the revolutionaries in Vienna, Bohemia, and Hungary and regained control of Lombardy and Venetia.

Section 19.3

Organizing Your Thoughts

1. In 1853, Russia invaded the Balkan provinces of Moldavia and Walachia. In response, the Ottoman Turks, who controlled this area, declared war on Russia. Great Britain and France also declared war on Russia because they were afraid that Russia would gain control of this area.
2. Russia agreed to allow Moldavia and Walachia to be placed under the protection of all the great powers. The Crimean War also destroyed the Concert of Europe. Russia withdrew from European affairs for the next 20 years. Austria was now without friends among the great powers. This new situation opened the door for the unification of Italy and Germany.
3. In 1870, Prussia and France came into conflict because a relative of the Prussian king was a candidate for the throne of Spain. Bismarck took advantage of the misunderstandings between the French and Prussians and pushed the French into declaring war on Prussia.
4. France had to pay 5 billion franks and give up the provinces of Alsace and Lorraine. The Second (French) Empire fell. The southern German states, which had joined the war effort against the French, agreed to enter the North German Confederation. William I of Prussia was proclaimed kaiser of the Second German Empire, and German unity was achieved. During the war, French troops withdrew from Rome, which made it possible for the Italian army to annex Rome. Rome then became the capital of the united Italian state.
5. Divisions between the southern and northern states, especially over slavery, made compromise less and less possible. After Abraham Lincoln was elected president, a South Carolina convention voted to secede from the United States. Six more southern states also seceded, and a rival nation, the Confederate States of America, was formed.
6. The Confederacy was defeated, and national unity prevailed in the United States. The Emancipation Proclamation freed the slaves.

Read to Learn

7. Great Britain and France had declared war on Russia. Austria and Russia also became enemies, because Austria had refused to support Russia in the war.

8. After the Prussians won the Austro-Prussian War, they gave Venetia to the Italians. During the Franco-Prussian War, French troops withdrew from Rome. Their withdrawal made it possible for the Italian army to annex Rome.

9. Prussia organized the German states north of the Main River into a North German Confederation. The southern German states signed military alliances with Prussia for protection against the French. During the Franco-Prussian War, the southern German states joined the war effort against the French. Even before the war ended, these states agreed to enter the North German Confederation. On January 18, 1871, William I of Prussia was proclaimed kaiser of the Second German Empire.

10. The Compromise of 1867 created the dual monarchy of Austria-Hungary. Austria and Hungary each had its own constitution, its own legislature, its own bureaucracy, and its own capital. The two states shared a single monarch and a common army, foreign policy, and system of finances. Francis Joseph was both Emperor of Austria and King of Hungary.

11. Federalists and Republicans fought over the division of power in the government. The Federalists favored a strong central government. The Republicans wanted the federal government to be subordinate to the state governments.

12. Upper Canada was mostly English-speaking, and Lower Canada was mostly French.

Section 19.4

Organizing Your Thoughts

1. emphasized feelings, emotion, and imagination as ways of knowing/valued individualism/had a strong interest in the past and in the exotic and unfamiliar/loved nature

2. Walter Scott, Mary Shelley, Edgar Allen Poe, William Wordsworth

3. Eugène Delacroix

4. rejected romanticism/focused on ordinary people from real life/avoided emotion

5. Gustave Flaubert, Charles Dickens

6. Gustave Courbet

Read to Learn

7. They believed that science had reduced nature to a cold object of study. Many also believed that industrialization would cause people to become alienated from their inner selves and the natural world around them.

8. The dramatic material benefits often provided by science and technology led Europeans to have a growing faith in science. This faith undermined the religious faith of many people, which led to secularization (indifference or rejection of religion or religious consideration). For many people, truth was now to be found in science.

9. novels (rather than poems)

Chapter 20 Section 20.1

Organizing Your Thoughts

1–7. Great Britain, Belgium, France, the Netherlands, Germany, the western part of the Austro-Hungarian Empire, northern Italy

8–13. southern Italy, most of Austria-Hungary, Spain, Portugal, the Balkan kingdoms, Russia

Read to Learn

14. The first Industrial Revolution was primarily the result of changes in the production of textiles, iron, and coal. In the Second

Industrial Revolution, steel, chemicals, electricity, and petroleum created new industries.

15. Pure Marxists thought that capitalism should be overthrown by a violent revolution. Revisionists disagreed. They believed that workers must continue to organize in mass political parties and even work with other parties to gain reforms.

Section 20.2

Organizing Your Thoughts

1. landed aristocrats and the most successful industrialists, bankers, and merchants

2. lawyers, doctors, members of the civil service, business managers, engineers, architects, accountants, chemists, shopkeepers, traders, prosperous peasants, white-collar workers

3. peasants, farm laborers, sharecroppers, artisans, semi-skilled laborers, day laborers, domestic servants

Read to Learn

4. City governments created boards of health to improve the quality of housing. Dwellings were now inspected for health hazards. New building regulations required running water and drainage systems for new buildings. New systems of aqueducts, tunnels, and pipes made it possible to bring clean water into cities and to expel sewage from cities.

5. Reforms created better living conditions in cities. A rise in wages and a decline in many consumer costs made it possible for workers to buy more than just food and housing. Workers now had money for more clothes and even leisure activities. Strikes led to 10-hour workdays and Saturday afternoons off.

6. Industrial plants and retail shops both needed white-collar workers, such as clerks, typists, secretaries, file clerks, and salespeople. A high demand for these relatively low paid jobs led many employers to hire women.

7. One reason was industrialization. The new firms of the Second Industrial Revolution needed trained, skilled labor. The chief reason, however, was political. Giving more people the right to vote created a need for better-educated voters. Primary schools also instilled patriotism.

8. The industrial system gave people new times for leisure activities. Subways and streetcars made it possible for even the working classes to get to athletic games, amusement parks, and dance halls.

Section 20.3

Organizing Your Thoughts

1–3. Germany, Austria-Hungary, Italy

4–6. Great Britain, France, Russia

Read to Learn

7. The Liberals voted for a series of social reforms. The National Insurance Act of 1911 provided benefits for workers in case of sickness and unemployment. Other laws provided a small pension for those over 70 and compensation for those injured in accidents at work.

8. Conservative forces in Germany tried to block the movement for democracy by supporting a strong foreign policy. They believed that expansion abroad would not only increase profits but also divert people from pursuing democratic reforms.

9. Manitoba and British Columbia

10. Emperor William II dropped Germany's treaty with Russia. This brought France and Russia together. In 1894, they formed a military alliance. Over the next 10 years, German policies caused the British to draw closer to France. By 1907, Great Britain, France, and Russia were allies, and the Triple Entente was formed.

11. Europe was divided into two opposing camps, the Triple Alliance and the Triple Entente. The Serbians blamed Austria-Hungary for their failure to create a large Serbian kingdom. Austria-Hungary was convinced that Serbia was a threat to its empire and must be crushed. As Serbia's chief supporters, the Russians were angry and determined not to back down again. The allies of Austria-Hungary and Russia were determined to support their respective allies more strongly in another crisis.

Section 20.4

Organizing Your Thoughts

1. naturalism (Ibsen and Zola), symbolism
2. Impressionism (Monet, Renoir, Morisot), Postimpressionism (van Gogh), cubism (Picasso), abstract expressionism (Kandinsky)
3. functionalism (Sullivan and Wright)
4. expressionism (Stravinksy)

Read to Learn

5. Before Einstein published his special theory of relativity, people thought that time, space, and matter were objective realities that existed independently of the people observing them. Matter was thought to be composed of solid material bodies called atoms. Einstein's theory stated that space and time are not absolute but are relative to the people observing them. Einstein also showed that matter is simply another form of energy. To some people, the universe now seemed to be a universe without certainty.
6. According to Freud, human behavior was strongly determined by past experiences. Freud believed that painful experiences were repressed from a person's conscious awareness, but these experiences continued to influence behavior because they were part of the unconscious.
7. Darwin's theories were applied, inappropriately, to human society by nationalists and racists. They argued that social progress came from the "struggle for survival" in which only the "fit" survive. Some businessmen used the theories of Darwin to explain their success. Extreme nationalists believed that nations were engaged in a struggle for existence in which only the fittest (the strongest) survived.
8. In Germany and Austria-Hungary, new parties used anti-Semitism to win votes. In Russia, Jews were forced to live in certain regions of the country. Persecutions and pogroms were widespread. As a result, hundreds of thousands of Jews decided to emigrate.
9. After the use of photography became widespread, anyone could take a photograph that looked exactly like the subject. Artists began to realize that their strength was not in mirroring reality, but in creating reality.

Chapter 21 Section 21.1

Organizing Your Thoughts

1. Great Britain
2. France
3. Holland
4. France
5. United States
6. Great Britain
7. none
8. France

Read to Learn

9. Earlier expansion in Africa and Asia had been limited to setting up a few trading posts. Now European nations wanted direct control over vast territories.
10. King Mongkut and his son King Chulalongkorn promoted Western learning and had friendly relations with major European powers. Great Britain and

France agreed to maintain Thailand as an independent buffer state between their possessions in Southeast Asia.

11. Under indirect rule, local rulers were allowed to maintain their positions of authority and status. Under direct rule, local rulers were removed from power and replaced with a new set of officials brought from the mother country. Indirect rule was not always possible, especially when local rulers resisted colonial rule.

12. The new form of resistance was based on nationalism. The leaders were often intellectuals in the cities who had been educated in Western-style schools.

Section 21.2

Organizing Your Thoughts

1. Great Britain, France, Germany
2. Great Britain, France, Italy
3. Belgium, France
4. Germany, Great Britain, Portugal
5. Great Britain

Read to Learn

6. Europeans sold textiles and other manufactured goods in exchange for peanuts, timber, hides, and palm oil from West Africa.

7. Europeans were interested in Egypt because they wanted to build a canal east of Cairo to connect the Mediterranean and Red Seas.

8. Explorers, such as David Livingstone, aroused Europeans' interest in the jungles of Central Africa.

9. The Berlin Conference of 1884 was held to settle the conflicting claims of European nations in East Africa.

10. The Boers were the descendants of the original Dutch settlers of South Africa.

11. The system of indirect rule had one good feature: it did not disrupt local customs and institutions. But it was basically a fraud because British administrators made all major decisions. It also kept the old African elites in power, which sowed the seeds for class and tribal tensions.

12. The new class of educated Africans admired Western civilization but resented colonial rule. They saw the lack of respect that foreigners had for African peoples and the inequality that this produced.

Section 21.3

Organizing Your Thoughts

1–4. British rule brought order and stability to India. It also led to a fairly honest and efficient government. A new school system was set up. Railroads, the telegraph, and a postal service were brought to India by the British.

5–8. British manufactured goods destroyed local industries. The British sent zamindars to collect taxes in rural areas. The zamindars increased taxes, which forced many peasants to become tenants or lose their land entirely. The British also encouraged many farmers to switch from growing food to growing cotton. As a result, food supplies could not keep up with the growing population. British rule was also degrading. The British were disrespectful of India's cultural heritage, and the Indians were never considered equals of the British.

Read to Learn

9. The immediate cause of the Sepoy Mutiny was a rumor that the British were issuing their Indian troops new bullets that were greased with cow and pig fat. A group of sepoys refused to load their rifles with the new bullets. When the British arrested them, the sepoys went on a rampage.

10. The British encouraged many farmers to switch from growing food to growing cotton. Food supplies could not keep up with the growing population, and 30 million

Indians died of starvation between 1800 and 1900.

11. Gandhi's movement had two goals: to force the British to improve the lot of the poor and to gain independence for India.

12. The cultural revival in India in the nineteenth century began with the creation of a British college in Calcutta.

Section 21.4

Organizing Your Thoughts

1. the western part of Hispaniola (now called Haiti)

2. Argentina

3. Mexico

4. Brazil

5. the Central American states

Read to Learn

6. José de San Martín and Simón Bolívar

7. Land was the basis of wealth, social prestige, and political power in Latin America. Large landowners ran governments and controlled courts. They made huge profits by growing export crops, such as coffee. The masses had no land to grow basic food crops and experienced terrible poverty.

8. The United States supported the rebellion because they wanted control of a strip of land that ran from coast to coast in Panama. The United States built the Panama Canal on this strip of land.

9. Middle-class Latin Americans lived in the cities, believed in education, and saw the United States as a model, especially in regard to industrialization. They sought liberal reform, not revolution.

Chapter 22 Section 22.1

Organizing Your Thoughts

1–4. corruption, peasant unrest, incompetence, population growth

Read to Learn

5. Population growth created a serious food shortage, and many people died of hunger.

6. The British began to trade opium with China to improve their trade balance.

7. The goals of the Tai Ping Rebellion included giving land to all peasants and treating women as equals of men. People were also required to give up their private possessions. Money, food, and clothing were to be shared equally by all. Alcohol, tobacco, and the practice of binding feet were outlawed.

8. The Qing dynasty adopted a new policy called "self-strengthening." This meant that China should adopt Western technology while keeping Confucian values and institutions. Factories were built to produce modern weapons and ships. Railroads were also built.

9. Many conservatives opposed his reforms. The emperor's aunt, Empress Dowager Ci Xi, also opposed the reforms. She was able to imprison the emperor and end his reform efforts.

10. The Open Door policy meant that all nations would have equal access to the Chinese market. It reduced the limits on foreign imports that had been imposed within the spheres of influence. It also lessened fears in Britain, France, Germany, and Russia that other powers would take advantage of China's weakness and try to dominate the Chinese market.

11. The Boxers were members of a secret organization called the Society of the Harmonious Fists. They were upset by the foreign takeover of Chinese lands. They especially disliked Christian missionaries and Chinese converts to Christianity.

Section 22.2

Organizing Your Thoughts

1–3. Westerners introduced modern means of transportation and communication to China. They also created an export market and integrated the Chinese economy into the world economy.

4–6. Confucian social ideals declined. Most creative artists followed foreign trends. Literature was particularly influenced by foreign ideas.

Read to Learn

7. a military takeover, a transitional phase in which Sun's own revolutionary party would prepare the people for democratic rule, and the final stage of a constitutional democracy

8. Reformers hated him because he used murder and terror to destroy the new democratic institutions. He was hated by traditionalists for being disloyal to the Qing dynasty.

9. China's local industry was largely destroyed. Many of the profits in the new economy went to foreign countries.

10. Most Chinese novels written after World War I reflected the Western tendency toward realism. Most of China's modern authors also showed a clear contempt for the past.

Section 22.3

Organizing Your Thoughts

1. In theory, the emperor had all executive authority. In practice, a prime minister and his cabinet of ministers had the real executive authority. The Meiji leaders picked these ministers.

2. The parliament had two houses. Members of the upper house were to be appointed, while members of the lower house were to be elected. The two houses were to have equal powers.
(The executive branch had the most authority.)

Read to Learn

3. The Tokugawa shogunate had isolated Japan from nearly all contact with the outside world. It had driven out foreign traders and missionaries.

4. The decision to open relations with the West was particularly unpopular in two territories in the south, Satsuma and Choshu, because both territories had strong military traditions and neither had been exposed to heavy Western military pressure.

5. The Meiji leaders set up a new system of land ownership. They also levied a new land tax. They encouraged the development of new industries, by giving subsidies and providing training and foreign advisors. They also improved transportation and communications and started a new educational system that stressed applied science. They adopted the American model of elementary schools, secondary schools, and universities. They brought foreign specialists to Japan and sent bright students to study abroad. Women were allowed to seek an education.

6. Japan is a small country that is densely populated and lacks resources. This made the Japanese feel that they need to expand into other territories. The Japanese also believed that Western nations were wealthy and powerful because they had colonies.

7. Literature was especially affected. Japanese authors began imitating European literature. Japanese novels were particularly influenced by Western realism. The Japanese also copied Western artistic techniques and styles. Huge buildings of steel and concrete, with Greek columns, appeared in many Japanese cities.

Chapter 23 Section 23.1

Organizing Your Thoughts

1. Archduke Francis Ferdinand is assassinated by members of the Black Hand.

2. Austrian leaders send an ultimatum to Serbia.

3. Austria-Hungary declares war on Serbia.
4. Czar Nicholas II orders full mobilization of the Russian army.
5. Germany declares war on Russia.
6. Germany declares war on France and issues an ultimatum to Belgium.
7. Great Britain declares war on Germany.

Read to Learn

8. Competition for colonies and trade increased. Europe's great powers were soon divided into two alliances. European nations were willing to go to war to preserve the power of their national states. Ethnic groups, such as the Irish, Poles, and the Slavic peoples, began to dream of creating their own national states.
9. Social labor movements were more and more willing to use strikes to reach their goals, even if this led to violence. Some conservative leaders were afraid that their nations were on the verge of revolution. Some historians believe that this fear and the desire to suppress internal conflicts encouraged the leaders of some nations to go to war.
10. Military leaders drew up plans that could be used if their countries went to war. They insisted that any changes to these plans would cause chaos in the military. This forced European political leaders to make decisions for military rather than political reasons.
11. Austrian leaders sent an ultimatum to Serbia on July 23. Many of the demands were so extreme that Serbia had no choice but to reject some of them. As a result, Austria-Hungary declared war on Serbia. The German government warned Russia to stop its mobilization. When Russia refused, Germany declared war on Russia. Germany issued an ultimatum to Belgium, in which it demanded the right of German troops to pass through Belgium. As a result, Great Britain declared war on Germany, officially for violating Belgian neutrality.

Section 23.2

Organizing Your Thoughts

1. Propaganda was used to stir up hatred towards other nations. It was used to create enthusiasm for the war.
2. Trench warfare was used on the Western Front. Trenches were ditches protected by barbed wire. Troops on both sides lived in the trenches but attempted to break through enemy lines by leaving the trenches and attacking the other side with fixed bayonets.
3. Because of trench warfare and the attempts to break through enemy lines, World War I turned into a war of attrition, a war based on wearing down the other side by constant attacks and heavy losses.
4. Airplanes were first used to spot the enemy's position, but they soon began to attack ground targets. Battles were also waged between opposing pilots.
5. Germany used submarines in its attempt to blockade Britain. The submarines were allowed to attack both military and civilian ships.
6. European nations set up planned economies in order to mobilize all the resources of their nations for the war effort. They set up price, wage, and rent controls. They also rationed food supplies and materials, regulated imports and exports, and took over transportation systems and industries.

Read to Learn

7. The war on the Western Front turned into a stalemate because of the use of trench warfare. Trench warfare kept both sides in virtually the same positions for four years.
8. Attempts to break through enemy lines rarely worked because the troops were fired at by the enemy's machine guns.
9. The Allies tried to open a Balkan front, but they were forced to withdraw. Italy opened up a front against Austria-Hungary. British

forces from Egypt destroyed the Ottoman Empire in the Middle East. The British used forces from India, Australia, and New Zealand. The Allies also seized German colonies around the world.

10. German submarines sank the British ship *Lusitania,* a civilian passenger liner. Over 100 Americans were killed in this attack. The United States protested, and the German government temporarily stopped unrestricted submarine warfare. However, Germany resumed the use of this warfare in order to starve the British into submission. This caused the United States to enter the war.

11. Because so many of the world's men were involved in fighting the war, women were asked to take over jobs that had not been available to them before. Many of the new jobs for women proved to be temporary when men returned to the job market. However, women in Great Britain, Germany, Austria, and the United States were given the right to vote after the war ended.

Section 23.3

Organizing Your Thoughts

1. 10,000 women march through the city of Petrograd in protest of bread rationing.

2. A general strike shuts down all the factories in Petrograd.

3. The Duma sets up a provisional government.

4. Nicholas II steps down as czar.

5. German military leaders ship Lenin back to Russia, in hopes that he would create disorder in Russia.

6. The Bolsheviks seize the Winter Palace, the seat of the provisional government.

7. Lenin signs the Treaty of Brest-Litovsk.

8. Nicholas II and his family are murdered.

Read to Learn

9. Because Czar Nicholas II was in charge of the armed forces, he was often away at the battlefront. In his absence, his wife Alexandra made all of the important decisions, which were often poor ones. Because Russia was not prepared for the war, the Russian army suffered heavy losses. Because of these military disasters and economic problems, the Russian people became more and more upset with the rule of the czar. This set the stage for revolution.

10. The Bolsheviks promised an end to the war, the redistribution of land to the peasants, the transfer of factories from capitalists to the workers, and the transfer of government power to the soviets.

11. Lenin signed the Treaty of Brest-Litovsk because he had promised the Russian people that he would end the war. Giving up territories was the only way to remove Russia from the war.

12. The White Army was the name given to the anti-Communist forces during the civil war. The anti-Communist forces included groups loyal to the czar, liberals, anti-Lenin socialists, and the Allies.

13. First, the Red Army was well disciplined. Second, the Communists had a clear vision of a new socialist order. The Whites, on the other hand, were not unified. Third, the Communists implemented a policy of war communism to ensure regular supplies for the Red Army. Finally, the Communists were able to use the presence of foreign armies to stir up Russian patriotism.

Section 23.4

Organizing Your Thoughts

1. The treaty said that Germany and Austria were responsible for starting the war. It ordered Germany to pay reparations for the damage done to the Allied nations.

2. Germany had to reduce its army and navy and eliminate its air force.
3. Alsace and Lorraine were returned to France. Parts of eastern Germany were given to a new Polish state.
4. German land on both sides of the Rhine was made a demilitarized zone and stripped of all weapons and fortifications. It was hoped that this would prevent Germany from making advances toward France.

Read to Learn

5. The entry of the United States into the war gave the Allies a much-needed psychological boost. With the arrival of two million American troops, the Allies began to advance toward Germany. This forced Germany to end the war.
6. Finland, Latvia, Estonia, Lithuania, Poland, Czechoslovakia, Austria, Hungary, and Yugoslavia

Chapter 24 Section 24.1

Organizing Your Thoughts

1. a series of downturns in the economies of individual nations during the second half of the 1920s
2. an international financial crisis involving the U.S. stock market
3. Governments became more and more involved in the economies of their countries.
4. Communism became more popular.
5. Masses of people began to follow dictators who offered solutions.

Read to Learn

6. The League of Nations was not very effective for at least two reasons. First, it could not use military force. Second, the United States was not in the League.
7. During the 1920s, the U.S. stock market was booming, so American investors began to pull money out of Germany to invest it in the stock market. When the stock market crashed in 1929, U.S. investors withdrew even more money from Germany and other European markets. This weakened the banks of Germany and other countries. By 1931, trade was slowing down, industrial production was declining, and unemployment was rising.
8. The New Deal was an economic policy adopted by Franklin Roosevelt in the 1930s. It increased government-funded public works, including the WPA, and introduced new legislation that began the U.S. welfare system.

Section 24.2

Organizing Your Thoughts

1. Benito Mussolini
2. In 1919, he created a new political group, the *Fascio di Combattimento.* He formed bands of armed Fascists called *squadristi.* In 1922, the Fascists threatened to march on Rome if they were not given power. The king of Italy gave in and made Mussolini prime minister. Mussolini used this position to create a Fascist dictatorship.
3. Joseph Stalin
4. He was the party general secretary and appointed regional and local party officials. He used this position to gain control of the Communist Party. Because he had appointed so many officials within the party, he had a great deal of support. By 1929, he was able to establish a powerful dictatorship.
5. Francisco Franco
6. He led a revolt against the democratic government in 1936. A bloody civil war began. Franco's forces took Madrid in 1939. This ended the civil war, and Franco established a dictatorship that favored large landowners, businesspeople, and the Catholic clergy.

Read to Learn

7. A totalitarian state is a government that aims to control the political, economic, social, intellectual, and cultural lives of its citizens. Totalitarian states want to control the minds and hearts of their citizens.

8. Fascism is a political philosophy that glorifies the state above the individual by emphasizing the need for a strong central government led by a dictator. The government controls people, and any opposition is suppressed.

9. Stalin ended the NEP and began Five-Year Plans. The Five-Year Plans set economic goals for five-year periods. Their purpose was to transform Russia from an agricultural country into an industrial country. The First Five-Year Plan emphasized the production of capital equipment and weapons. The government also began to collectivize farms. By 1934, 26 million family farms had been collectivized into 250,000 units. The Russian people paid a terrible price for industrialization and collectivization. Millions of people in the cities lived in pitiful conditions. Wages declined by 43 percent between 1928 and 1940. Millions of peasants died in famines in 1932 and 1933.

10. Parliamentary systems failed in Eastern Europe for several reasons. First, these countries did not have a tradition of democracy. They were mostly rural, and many of the peasants were illiterate. Ethnic conflicts also caused problems. Powerful landowners, the churches, and even some members of the middle class were afraid of land reform, communism, and ethnic conflict. They supported authoritarian governments that maintained the old system.

Section 24.3

Organizing Your Thoughts

1. The Nazis used terror and repression to create their totalitarian state. They created the *Schutzstaffeln* (SS). It controlled both the secret police forces and the regular police in Germany. It also used concentration camps, execution squads, and death camps to achieve its purposes.

2. To end the depression, Hitler created public works projects and gave money to construction firms to put people back to work. But it was a huge rearmament program that finally solved the unemployment problem. The Nazis' part in bringing an end to the depression was an important reason that many Germans accepted Hitler and the Nazis.

3. Demonstrations and spectacles were used to make the German people accept Hitler's policies. These events created mass enthusiasm and excitement. Churches, schools, and universities were also brought under Nazi control. Youth organizations were created that taught Nazi ideals.

4. The Nazis believed that men were meant to be warriors and leaders, while women were meant to be wives and mothers. These ideas determined employment opportunities for women. Jobs in heavy industry, university teaching, medicine, and law were considered unsuitable for women. The Nazis encouraged women to pursue other occupations, such as social work and nursing, or not to work at all.

5. The Nuremburg Laws excluded Jews from German citizenship and forbade marriages between Jews and German citizens. Jews were also required to wear yellow Stars of David and to carry identification cards saying they were Jewish. On November 9, 1938 *(Kristallnacht),* Nazis burned synagogues and destroyed thousands of Jewish businesses. Thirty thousand Jewish men were sent to concentration camps. At least a hundred Jews were killed. After *Kristallnacht,* Jews were barred from all public transportation and public buildings. They were not allowed to own, manage, or work in any retail store. They were also encouraged to emigrate from Germany.

Read to Learn

6. *Mein Kampf* combined extreme German nationalism, strong anti-Semitism, and anticommunism with a theory of struggle. It emphasized the right of superior nations to gain *Lebensraum* (living space) through expansion. It also emphasized the right of superior individuals to gain authoritarian leadership over the masses.

7. Germany's economic problems were a crucial factor in the rise of Nazism. Unemployment rose to 6 million by the winter of 1932. The impact of the Great Depression made extremist parties more attractive.

8. The Enabling Act gave the German government the power to ignore the constitution for four years while it issued laws to deal with the country's problems. It gave Hitler's actions a legal basis.

9. The Nazis misused the term *Aryan* to mean the ancient Greeks and Romans and twentieth-century Germans and Scandinavians.

Section 24.4

Organizing Your Thoughts

1. Abstract expressionism became even more popular. There was a fascination with the absurd and the unconscious. The idea that the world did not make sense gave rise to two movements, Dadaism and surrealism. Dadaists were artists who were obsessed with the idea that life has no purpose. They tried to express the insanity of life in their art. Surrealists sought a reality beyond the material world and found it in the world of the unconscious. They portrayed fantasies, dreams, and even nightmares to show this greater reality.

2. The interest in the unconscious was also found in new literary techniques. "Stream of consciousness" was a technique used by writers to show the thoughts of each character. It was used by James Joyce in his novel *Ulysses.* Hermann Hesse dealt with the unconscious in a different way. In two of his works, he used Buddhist ideas to show the psychological confusion of modern existence.

3. In 1927, the German physicist Werner Heisenberg explained an observation that he called the uncertainty principle. This theory suggests that all physical laws are based on uncertainty.

Read to Learn

4. Radio enabled leaders, like Hitler, to get their messages to the masses. The Nazi regime encouraged manufacturers to produce inexpensive radios. Movies also had propaganda potential. Joseph Goebbels created a special film division in his Propaganda Ministry. It supported the making of documentaries and popular feature films that carried the Nazi message.

5. The Nazis adopted a program called *Kraft durch Freude.* It offered its own leisure activities, including concerts, operas, films, guided tours, and sporting events. It also offered inexpensive vacations that were especially popular.

6. Hitler and the Nazis rejected modern art as "degenerate." They believed that they could create a new and genuine German art that would glorify the strong, the healthy, and the heroic.

7. The foundation for the uncertainty principle is the fact that the behavior of subatomic particles is unpredictable.

Reading Essentials and Study Guide

Answer Key

Chapter 25 Section 25.1

Organizing Your Thoughts

1. In Africa, Ottoman rule ended in the nineteenth century when France seized Algeria and Tunisia and Great Britain took control of Egypt.
2. Greece declared its independence in the nineteenth century.
3. In 1916, the local governor of Makkah declared Arabia's independence. British troops seized Palestine. After World War I, Great Britain and France divided up the other territories in the Middle East.

Read to Learn

4. During World War I, the Ottoman government allied with Germany. As a result, the British tried to undermine the Ottoman Empire by supporting Arab nationalists.
5. The caliphate was abolished in 1924. Men were forbidden to wear the fez, and women were forbidden to wear the veil. Women were given new rights, including the right to vote. All citizens had the right to convert to other religions.
6. Reza Shah Pahlavi introduced a number of reforms to modernize the government, the military and the economic system. He did not try to destroy Islamic beliefs, but he did encourage a Western-style educational system. He also forbade women to wear the veil in public.
7. Europeans determined the borders and divided the peoples in most of the nations in the Middle East.
8. In the Balfour Declaration, Britain supported the idea of making Palestine a national home for the Jews. It made Arab nationalists angry. It also drew Jewish settlers to Palestine. By 1939, there were about 450,000 Jews in Palestine.

Section 25.2

Organizing Your Thoughts

1. Kenya
2. He organized the Young Kikuyu Association, which protested high taxes imposed by the British.
3. Libya
4. His forces used guerilla warfare against the Italians.
5. Nigeria
6. He began a newspaper, *The West African Pilot,* and promoted nonviolence as a method to gain independence.
7. India
8. He organized mass protests against British laws by using the methods of civil disobedience and nonviolence.
9. Vietnam (French Indochina)
10. He organized the Vietnamese Communists and worked with nationalists against Western imperialism.

Read to Learn

11. Many of the new African leaders had been educated in Europe and the United States. They were influenced by the ideas of W.E.B. Du Bois and Marcus Garvey. Du Bois was an African American educated at Harvard University. He was the leader of a movement that tried to make all Africans aware of their cultural heritage. Garvey was a Jamaican who lived in Harlem. He stressed the need for the unity of all Africans, a movement known as Pan-Africanism. His *Declaration of the Rights of the Negro Peoples of the World* had a strong impact on African leaders.
12. Gandhi's movement was religious and traditional. Nehru's movement was secular and modern.
13. As the Japanese expanded into new industries, the Japanese government came under increasing pressure to find new sources of raw materials. The Japanese people supported expansion as a way to obtain raw materials. The military and other supporters of Japanese expansion soon dominated the government.

14. The Comintern (or Communist International) was a worldwide organization of Communist parties formed in 1919. It worked for world revolution. At its headquarters in Moscow, agents were trained and then returned to their own countries to form Marxist parties and promote revolution.

Section 25.3

Organizing Your Thoughts

1. He tried to combine modern Western innovations with traditional Confucian values of hard work, obedience, and integrity. He set up a New Life Movement to promote traditional Confucian ethics.
2. He undertook a huge road-building program and added to the country's railroad system.
3. He tried to carry out a land-reform program and to modernize industry. He also set up a national bank. But his land-reform program had little effect, and he did not push for programs that would lead to a redistribution of wealth.
4. He improved the educational system and started a training program to prepare the Chinese people for constitutional government.
5. He was committed to the plans of Sun Yat-sen, which called for a republican government. He began the transitional period of government, during which the Chinese people were to be prepared for constitutional government. But his government was repressive. Because he was afraid of the Communists, he suppressed all opposition and censored free expression.

Read to Learn

6. the Chinese Communist Party and the Nationalist Party
7. Mao believed that peasants in the countryside instead of the urban working class would lead a Chinese revolution.
8. The Long March was a march begun by Mao's army, the People's Liberation Army, in 1933. The army traveled almost 6000 miles on foot across China. The march took a year, and only nine thousand of the original ninety thousand survived the journey.
9. The New Life Movement was set up by Chiang Kai-shek to promote traditional Confucian ethics. It also rejected the individualism and material greed that was associated with Western capitalism.

Section 25.4

Organizing Your Thoughts

1. In 1930, the Argentine army overthrew President Irigoyen and put the large landowners back in power. Military officials continued to be powerful.
2. In 1930, a military coup made Getúlio Vargas, a wealthy rancher, president of Brazil. In 1937, he made himself dictator. Beginning in 1938, he established his New State. It was an authoritarian state with some Fascist-like features.
3. Mexico was not an authoritarian state, but it was not truly democratic. The PRI, the official political party of the Mexican Revolution, controlled the major groups in Mexico. Party bosses chose the party's presidential candidate, who was then elected by the people. But changes began when Lázaro Cárdenas became president in 1934.

Read to Learn

4. The Great Depression was a disaster for Latin America's economy. There was a decreased demand for Latin American products and raw materials. The countries that depended on the export of only one product were especially damaged. There was one positive effect, however. With a decline in exports, Latin American countries could no longer afford to buy imported goods. Many Latin American govern-

ments encouraged the development of new industries to produce goods that had previously been imported. Governments often invested in the new industries. This led to government-run industries in Chile, Brazil, Argentina, and Mexico.

5. Cárdenas distributed 44 million acres of land to Mexican peasants. He also took a strong stand with the United States, especially over oil. After a dispute over workers' wages, his government seized control of the oil fields and the property of the oil companies. Eventually, the Mexican government paid the oil companies for their property. It then set up PEMEX, a national oil company.

6. Rivera's works of art were aimed at the masses of people, many of whom could not read. He tried to create a national art that would show Mexico's past and its festivals and folk customs. His work also had a political and social message. He did not want people to forget the Mexican Revolution.

Chapter 26 Section 26.1

Organizing Your Thoughts

1. Hitler sent German troops into the Rhineland.
2. Hitler annexed Austria to Germany.
3. Hitler demands that Germany be given the Sudetenland.
4. Hitler invaded and took control of Bohemia and Moravia.
5. German forces invaded Poland.

Read to Learn

6. Great Britain had a policy of appeasement. This policy was based on the belief that if European states satisfied the demands of dissatisfied powers, the dissatisfied powers would be content, and peace would be maintained. When Hitler demanded the Sudetenland, he promised Chamberlain that he would make no more demands. Like many others, Chamberlain believed Hitler's promises.

7. When Germany signed the nonaggression pact with the Soviet Union, Japanese leaders had to give up their plan to get natural resources from Soviet Siberia. They were forced to turn to Southeast Asia to find the raw materials they needed. But a move into Southeast Asia would risk war with the European colonial powers and the United States. Japan badly needed the oil and scrap iron it was getting from the United States. Japan now had a dilemma. To gain access to the raw materials it wanted in Southeast Asia, it had to risk losing raw materials from the United States.

Section 26.2

Organizing Your Thoughts

1–3. Germany, Italy, Japan
4–6. Great Britain, the United States, and the Soviet Union

Read to Learn

7. The United States followed a strict policy of isolationism. Laws passed in the 1930s prevented the United States from taking sides or becoming involved in any European wars.

8. The Japanese hoped that their attack on American bases would destroy the U.S. fleet in the Pacific. They also thought that the Roosevelt administration would accept Japanese domination of the Pacific. But the Japanese miscalculated. The attack on Pearl Harbor unified American opinion about becoming involved in the war. The United States now joined with European nations and Nationalist China in an effort to defeat Japan.

9. the Battle of Midway Island on June 4, 1942

10. He dropped atomic bombs on the Japanese cities of Hiroshima and Nagasaki. Thousands of people died, and the Japanese surrendered on August 14, 1945.

Section 26.3

Organizing Your Thoughts

1. The Nazis saw the conquered lands to the east as "living space" for German expansion. Himmler was put in charge of German resettlement in the east. His job was to move the Slavic peoples out and replace them with Germans. One million Poles were forced to move to southern Poland. By 1942, two million ethnic Germans had been settled in Poland.
2. Labor shortages in Germany led to a policy of rounding up foreign workers for Germany. By the summer of 1944, seven million Europeans were working in Germany. Another seven million were forced to work for the Nazis in their own countries on farms, in industries, and in military camps.
3. The Final Solution to the "Jewish problem" was genocide (physical extermination) of the Jewish people. This was carried out through *Einsatzgruppen* and death camps.
4. *Einsatzgruppen* were special strike forces that rounded up Jews and put them in ghettos. In June 1941, the strike forces were given the new job of acting as mobile killing units. They followed the regular army's advance into the Soviet Union. Their job was to round up Jews, execute them, and bury them in mass graves.
5. The Nazi leaders decided to kill the European Jewish population in death camps. Beginning in 1942, Jews from occupied countries were shipped to one of six extermination centers that had been built in Poland. The Germans killed over three million Jews in the death camps.

Read to Learn

6. Sending so many workers to Germany disrupted industrial production in the occupied countries that could have helped Germany. The brutal way that Germany recruited foreign workers led more and more people to resist the Nazi occupation forces.
7. Some people did not believe the stories about the death camps. Other people pretended not to notice what was happening. Even worse, collaborators helped the Nazis hunt down Jews. The Allies were aware of the concentration camps and death camps but chose to concentrate on ending the war. Not until after the war did they learn the full extent of the horror and inhumanity of the Holocaust.
8. The Japanese conquered Southeast Asia under the slogan "Asia for Asiatics." Japanese officials in occupied territories quickly made contact with anticolonialists. They promised the people that local governments would be established. But real power rested with Japanese military authorities in each territory. The Japanese used the resources of these territories for their own benefit. The native peoples were recruited to serve in local military units or were forced to work on public works projects. In Vietnam, Japanese authorities took rice and shipped it abroad. This led to a food shortage and caused over a million Vietnamese to starve to death. Japanese officials also provoked negative reactions by their arrogance and contempt for local customs.

Section 26.4

Organizing Your Thoughts

1. After the initial defeats of the Soviet Union, drastic emergency measures were put into effect. As the Germany army advanced into Soviet territory, Soviet workers dismantled and shipped factories in the western part of the Soviet Union to the interior. These machines were used to produce 78,000 tanks and 98,000 artillery pieces.

2. The United States became the arsenal of the Allied Powers. It produced much of the military equipment the Allies needed. At the height of war production, the country was building six ships a day and ninety-six thousand planes per year. The mobilization of the American economy resulted in some social turmoil. The construction of new factories created boomtowns. Thousands came there to work but then faced a shortage of houses and schools. Widespread movements of people took place. 110,000 Japanese Americans were forced to move to camps surrounded by barbed wire for "security reasons."

3. Hitler believed that the collapse of the home front in World War I had caused Germany's defeat. To maintain morale on the home front, Hitler refused to cut consumer goods production or to increase the production of armaments during the first two years of the war. After German defeats on the Russian front and the American entry into the war, Hitler finally ordered a massive increase in armaments production and in the size of the army. A total mobilization of the economy was put into effect in July 1944. Schools, theaters and cafes were closed. By that time, though, total war mobilization was too late to save Germany from defeat.

4. Wartime Japan was a highly mobilized society. To guarantee its control over all natural resources, the Japanese government created a planning board to control prices, wages, labor, and resources. Citizens were encouraged to sacrifice their resources, and sometimes their lives, for the national cause.

Read to Learn

5. In Germany, the number of women working in industry, agriculture, commerce, and domestic service increased only slightly during the war. Before the war, the Nazis had worked to keep women out of the job market. As the war progressed, attitudes changed, as more and more men were called up to military service. Although Nazis now endorsed jobs for women, many women did not want jobs, particularly in factories.

Japan was extremely reluctant to mobilize women on behalf of the war effort. The prime minister was opposed to female employment. Female employment increased during the war, but only in such areas as the textile industry and farming, where women had traditionally worked. Instead of using women to meet labor shortages, the Japanese government brought in Korean and Chinese workers.

In the Soviet Union, women played a major role in the war effort. Women and girls worked in industries, mines, and railroads. The Soviet Union was the only country in World War II to use women in battle.

In the United States, both men and women were enrolled in the military. Women also worked in factories. Wives and girlfriends of servicemen moved around the country.

6. The theory was that the bombing of civilian targets would force peace. This theory was proved wrong. In the case of Great Britain, morale remained high, and the British did not give in.

7. Stalin wanted absolute military security. To him, this security could only be gained by the presence of Communist states in Eastern Europe. Free elections might result in governments hostile to the Soviets.

Chapter 27 Section 27.1

Organizing Your Thoughts

1. Belgium, Luxembourg, France, the Netherlands, Great Britain, Italy, Denmark, Norway, Portugal, Iceland, United States, Canada, West Germany, Turkey

2. Soviet Union, Albania, Bulgaria, Czechoslovakia, East Germany, Hungary, Poland, Romania
3. United States, Great Britain, France, Pakistan, Thailand, the Philippines, Australia, New Zealand
4. Turkey, Iraq, Iran, Pakistan, Great Britain, United States

Read to Learn

5. The Marshall Plan is the more common name for the European Recovery Program. The goal of the program was to rebuild the prosperity and stability of Europe after World War II. It included $13 billion in aid for Europe's economic recovery. It was based on the belief that Communist aggression was successful in countries that had economic problems.
6. Both the United States and the Soviet Union believed that they needed arsenals of nuclear weapons to prevent war. They believed that if both sides had nuclear weapons, neither side would launch a nuclear attack, because the other side would be able to strike back with its nuclear weapons.
7. In 1959, Fidel Castro set up a Communist government in Cuba. U.S. President Kennedy approved a secret plan for Cuban exiles to invade Cuba in the hope of causing a revolt against Castro. This invasion, called the Bay of Pigs, was a disaster. Many of the exiles were killed or captured. After the Bay of Pigs, the Soviet Union sent arms and military advisers to Cuba. In 1962, Khrushchev began to place nuclear missiles in Cuba. The missiles were meant to counteract U.S. nuclear weapons that had been placed in Turkey within range of the Soviet Union. The United States was not willing to allow nuclear weapons so close to the U.S. mainland. In October 1962, President Kennedy found out that Soviet ships carrying missiles were heading to Cuba. He tried to stop them by blockading Cuba.
8. According to the domino theory, if the Communists were able to gain control of South Vietnam, other countries in Asia would also fall (like dominoes) to communism. The theory turned out to be wrong. Even though Vietnam came under Communist control, other nations in Southeast Asia were able to avoid Communist governments. A split between Communist China and the Soviet Union put an end to the idea that there was a single form of communism directed by Moscow.

Section 27.2

Organizing Your Thoughts

1–6. East Germany, Bulgaria, Romania, Poland, Hungary, Czechoslovakia

Read to Learn

7. The emphasis on heavy industry meant that not enough consumer goods were produced. This hurt the Soviet people.
8. Khrushchev took steps to undo some of the worst features of Stalin's regime, a process known as de-Stalinization. He loosened government controls on literary works. He also placed more emphasis on producing consumer goods and tried to increase farm production by growing corn and cultivating lands east of the Ural Mountains.
9. Albania and Yugoslavia were Communist countries, but the Soviet Union did not control them. During the war, both countries had strong Communist movements that resisted the Nazis. After the war, local Communist parties took control in both countries and refused to give in to Stalin's demands.

Section 27.3

Organizing Your Thoughts

1–6. France, West Germany, Belgium, the Netherlands, Luxembourg, Italy

Read to Learn

7. Great Britain had serious economic problems at the end of World War II. The Labour government set out to create a welfare state. The cost of building a welfare state at home forced the British to reduce expenses abroad. This meant the end of the British Empire. Britain was forced to give in to the demands of its colonies for independence.

8. The Common Market is another name for the European Economic Community or EEC. The EEC was originally a free-trade area made up of six member nations. These six nations agreed not to impose any tariffs on each other's goods, but they were protected by a tariff on goods from non-EEC nations.

9. The Red Scare was a fear of communist subversion created by Senator Joseph McCarthy. He charged that hundreds of communists were in high government positions. Several people, including intellectuals and movie stars, were questioned about Communist activities.

10. In 1954, the U.S. Supreme Court ruled that the practice of racial segregation in public schools was illegal. In August 1963, Martin Luther King, Jr., led a march on Washington, D.C. The Civil Rights Act of 1964 began the process of ending segregation and discrimination in the workplace and all public places. The Voting Rights Act of 1965 made it easier for African Americans to vote in southern states.

11. After World War II, Canada developed electronic, aircraft, nuclear, and chemical engineering industries, but much of the growth was financed by capital from the United States. This led to U.S. ownership of Canadian businesses and caused many Canadians to worry that the United States would dominate Canada economically.

12. During World War II, women had entered the workforce in huge numbers. At the end of the war, many of them were let go to provide jobs for soldiers returning home. For a time, many women fell back into traditional roles. Birthrates rose, creating a "baby boom" in the late 1940s and 1950s. By the end of the 1950s, the birthrate began to fall, and the size of families decreased. The number of married women in the workforce increased in both Europe and the United States. But women still earned less than men for equal work. They also faced the burden of earning income and raising a family at the same time. In the late 1960s, there was a renewed interest in feminism, or the women's liberation movement.

Chapter 28 Section 28.1

Organizing Your Thoughts

1. Leonid Brezhnev
2. Mikhail Gorbachev
3. Boris Yeltsin
4. Vladimir Putin

Read to Learn

5. Gorbachev hoped to make economic and other reforms in the Soviet Union. The national debt in the United States had tripled, and the United States had moved from being a creditor nation to being the world's biggest debtor nation. Both countries knew that their large military budgets would make it difficult to solve their domestic problems.

6. In March 1985, Gorbachev was chosen to lead the Soviet Union. He saw the need for radical reforms. In 1990, Gorbachev allowed non-Communist political parties to organize. As Gorbachev loosened the control of the Communist Party, ethnic tensions in the Soviet Union surfaced. Nationalist movements emerged throughout the republics of the Soviet Union. There were calls for independence in several of the republics. In 1991, a group of conservative leaders arrested Gorbachev and tried to seize power. The attempt failed, because Boris Yeltsin, president of the Russian Republic, and thousands of Russians resisted the takeover. The Soviet republics now moved for complete independence. Ukraine voted for independence on December 1, 1991. A week later, the leaders of Russia, Ukraine, and Belarus announced that the Soviet Union had "ceased to exist."

Section 28.2

Organizing Your Thoughts

1. In Poland, a worker named Lech Walesa organized a national trade union known as Solidarity. Solidarity gained the support of the workers and the Roman Catholic Church. Walesa was arrested, but the movement continued. After more demonstrations in 1988, the Polish government agreed to free parliamentary elections. A new government was elected, ending 45 years of Communist rule in Poland.
2. Free-market reforms led to severe unemployment and discontent. At the end of 1995, Aleksander Kwasniewski, a former Communist, defeated Walesa and became the new president. He continued Poland's move toward a prosperous free market economy.
3. In Czechoslovakia, mass demonstrations took place in 1988 and 1989. In December 1989, the Communist government collapsed.
4. Václav Havel became the new president. The new government faced old ethnic conflicts. The two national groups, Czechs and Slovaks, agreed to a peaceful division of the country. On January 1, 1993, Czechoslovakia split into the Czech Republic and Slovakia.
5. In Romania, the Communist leader Ceauşescu used secret police to crush dissent. His economic policies and plans for rapid urbanization also angered many Romanians. In December 1989, the secret police murdered thousands of people who were peacefully demonstrating. The army refused to support any more repression.
6. Ceauşescu and his wife were captured and executed. A new government was quickly formed.
7. In 1988, many East Germans began to flee the country. Mass demonstrations broke out in the summer and fall of 1989. On November 9, the Communist government gave in and opened its border with the West. Thousands of East Germans rushed across the border. People on both sides of the Berlin Wall began tearing it down. The government gave in again and ordered the rest of the wall torn down.
8. The reunification of Germany took place on October 3, 1990.
9. By 1990, new parties had emerged in Yugoslavia, and the Communist Party lost its power.
10. In 1990, the Yugoslav republics of Slovenia, Croatia, Bosnia-Herzegovina, and Macedonia began to push for independence. Milošević, the leader of Serbia, opposed their plans. In June 1991, Slovenia and Croatia declared their independence. In September, the Yugoslavian army, which was dominated by Serbia, began a full assault against Croatia. In 1992, the Serbs also began an assault on Bosnia-Herzegovina. The Serbs followed a policy of ethnic cleansing toward the Muslims in Bosnia. Air strikes by NATO bombers were launched in retaliation for Serb attacks on civilians. These attacks forced the Serbs to sign a peace treaty. The agreement split Bosnia into a loose union of a Serb republic and a Muslim-Croat federation.

Read to Learn

11. In November 1989, the Communist government opened East Germany's border with the West. In March 1990, East Germany's

first free elections were held. The Christian Democrats won almost 50 percent of the vote. They supported reunification with West Germany. The reunification of Germany took place on October 3, 1990.

12. Serbia was against their plans for independence because the republics included Serb minorities. Milošević, the leader of Serbia, wanted to redraw borders to include the Serb minorities in a new Greater Serbian state.

Section 28.3

Organizing Your Thoughts

1. During a major recession in the early 1960s, the Liberals came into power in Canada. An economic recession in the early 1980s brought Brian Mulroney to power. The approval of NAFTA in 1993 cost Mulroney much of his popularity. In 1993, the Liberal party came to power again with Jean Chrétien as prime minister.

2. France's economic problems in the 1970s caused a shift to the left politically. By 1981, the Socialists had become the chief party in the National Assembly, and the Socialist leader, François Mitterrand, was elected president. But most Socialist policies failed to work. In the elections in 1993, a coalition of conservative parties gained 80 percent of the seats in the National Assembly. The conservative mayor of Paris, Jacques Chirac, was elected president in 1995.

3. Following reunification, the economy of eastern Germany collapsed. The collapse led to high levels of unemployment and discontent. One result was a return to power for the Social Democrats.

4. In 1979, the Conservatives came to power in Great Britain. Margaret Thatcher was the prime minister. She pledged to limit social welfare, restrict union power, and end inflation. Her economic policy was called Thatcherism. It improved the British economic situation overall. In 1990, Thatcher's government tried to replace local property taxes with a flat-rate tax. Antitax riots broke out. Thatcher's popularity fell to an all-time low, and she resigned as prime minister.

5. By 1980, high rates of inflation and a decline in weekly earnings were causing a drop in American living standards. This contributed to Jimmy Carter's loss to Ronald Reagan in the election of 1980. Economic problems under George Bush enabled Bill Clinton to defeat Bush in the presidential election of 1992. An economic revival helped Clinton to be reelected.

6. It soon became clear that rebuilding eastern Germany would take far more money than had originally been thought. The German government was forced to raise taxes. The collapse of the economy in eastern Germany led to high levels of unemployment and discontent. Unemployment and economic problems caused tensions to grow between Germans and immigrant groups. Attacks against foreigners by right-wing extremists, especially young neo-Nazis, became part of German life.

7. Nixon used illegal methods to gain political information about his opponents. A group of men working for Nixon's reelection campaign broke into the Democratic National Headquarters in the Watergate Hotel in Washington, D.C. They were caught trying to install electronic listening devices. At first, Nixon lied about his involvement in the affair, but secret tapes of his conversations in the White House revealed the truth. Nixon resigned to avoid impeachment.

8. NAFTA, or the North American Free Trade Agreement, was a trade agreement between Canada, the United States, and Mexico. Its purpose was to make trade easier and more profitable by establishing guidelines for cooperation between the countries. Many Canadians were opposed to it, because they thought the agreement was too favorable to the United States.

Section 28.4

Organizing Your Thoughts

1–4. art, movies, television, music

Read to Learn

5. the Equal Pay and Sex Discrimination Acts

6. Terrorists use the killing of civilians, the taking of hostages, and the hijacking of airplanes to draw attention to their demands.

7. Computers and jet airplanes are two peacetime applications of wartime technology. By sponsoring projects during the war, governments and the military created a new model for scientific research. After the war, the new scientific establishment continued to operate. The space program is one example.

8. In the Catholic Church, efforts for religious renewal came from two popes, John XXIII and John Paul II. Pope John XXIII started a revival when he summoned the twenty-first ecumenical council of the Catholic Church. Known as Vatican II, it liberalized several Catholic practices. For example, the mass could now be celebrated in vernacular languages as well as Latin. Pope John Paul II reminded Catholics to balance the pursuit of materialism with spiritual concerns.

9. pop art, postmodern styles, and new art forms that use technologies, such as digital cameras and computer programs

10. "Cultural imperialism" is the name that has been given to the influence of American culture on other countries.

11. Soccer is one example of the mix of sports and politics. Soccer is a source of national pride in many countries, but this has sometimes led to violence. Another example is the Olympic Games. The Soviets used the Olympics to promote the Communist system. In 1972, at the Munich Games, a Palestinian terrorist group seized 11 Israeli athletes as hostages. All of the hostages were killed. The United States boycotted the 1980 Moscow Olympics, and the Soviets responded by refusing to participate in the Los Angeles Games in 1984.

Chapter 29 Section 29.1

Organizing Your Thoughts

1. During the Great Depression, exports declined, and Latin American countries did not have the money they needed to buy imported goods. As a result, many Latin American countries developed their own industries to produce goods that had been imported previously.

2. Multinational corporations made Latin American countries more dependent on industrialized nations.

3. By borrowing money, Latin American nations became even more dependent on foreign countries.

4. To get new loans, Latin American governments were forced to make basic reforms. Some military leaders were unwilling to deal with the debt crisis. This led to a movement toward democracy. By the mid-1990s, several democratic governments had been created.

5. Latin America's economic problems were made worse by population growth. With the increase in population, there was an increase in the size of cities. Slums or shantytowns became part of many Latin American cities.

6. As the Cold War developed, the United States took action when it believed that Soviet agents were trying to establish governments in Latin America. The United States also provided huge amounts of military aid to anti-Communist governments.

Read to Learn

7. A multinational corporation is a company with divisions in more than two countries.
8. The international drug trade brought crime and corruption to some Latin American countries. This undermined their stability.
9. The United States sent troops into Latin American countries to protect U.S. interests and to help dictators that were friendly to the United States. The United States also took military action when it believed that Soviet agents were trying to establish Communist governments in Latin America.
10. Writers and artists in Latin America are seen as people who can express the hopes of the people.

Section 29.2

Organizing Your Thoughts

1. When Cuba began to receive aid and arms from the Soviet Union and Eastern Europe, relations with the United States deteriorated. In October 1960, the United States declared a trade embargo and broke all diplomatic relations with Cuba. During the presidency of John Kennedy, concerns over Castro's government and its ties with the Soviet Union led to the Bay of Pigs disaster and the Cuban missile crisis.
2. During the presidency of Ronald Reagan, the United States provided weapons and training to the Salvadoran army to defeat Marxist-led guerrillas.
3. The Somoza government had the support of the United States during most of the time that it was in control of Nicaragua. By 1979, however, the United States was no longer willing to support the Somoza government. After the Sandinistas took control of the country, the Reagan and Bush administrations supported the contras, a group opposed to the Sandinistas' policies.
4. Panama was able to break away from Colombia because of the help it received from the United States. In return for this help, the United States gained control of the Panama Canal. The United States also had a great deal of influence over the government and economy of Panama. When the military leader Manuel Noriega first took control of Panama, the United States supported him. But his brutality and involvement with the drug trade turned American leaders against him. In 1989, President Bush sent U.S. troops to Panama. Noriega was arrested and sent to prison in the United States on charges of drug trafficking.

Read to Learn

5. The sale of oil abroad increased dramatically. The government became more dependent on oil revenues. When oil prices dropped in the mid-1980s, Mexico was no longer able to make payments on its foreign debt. The government was forced to adopt new economic policies, including privatization.
6. Economic problems had forced Cuba to depend on Soviet aid and the purchase of Cuban sugar by Soviet bloc countries. After the collapse of these governments in 1989, Cuba lost their support. Economic conditions in Cuba have steadily declined.
7. The main export products of Central America are bananas, coffee, and cotton. Prices for these products have varied over time. This has created economic crises at different times.

Section 29.3

Organizing Your Thoughts

1. In 1943, a group of army officials overthrew the oligarchy that ruled Argentina. One of the military officials, Juan Perón, was elected president in 1946. He was overthrown by the military in 1955. The

military leaders were soon overwhelmed by problems and allowed Perón to return, but he died in 1974. In 1976, the military once again took control. But the invasion of the Falkland Islands made the military look bad, and the country was returned to civilian rule.

2. When democratic governments in Brazil were unable to solve the country's economic problems, the military stepped in and took control in 1964. The military remained in control for the next 20 years. It set a new economic direction, and Brazil experienced an "economic miracle." However, rapid development led to an inflation rate of 100 percent a year. The military government was overwhelmed, which opened the door for a return to democracy in 1985.
3. In 1970, Salvador Allende became president of Chile. The Chilean army, under the direction of General Augusto Pinochet, was afraid of President Allende's power. In 1973, military forces shot Allende. The military then set up a dictatorship. The abuse of human rights under Pinochet led to unrest in the 1980s. In 1989, Pinochet was defeated in free presidential elections.
4. A military takeover in Peru in 1968 brought General Juan Velasco Alvarado to power. He tried to help the peasants. Economic problems continued, however, and military leaders removed General Alvarado from power in 1975. Five years later, the military returned Peru to civilian rule.

Read to Learn

5. Perón's main support came from labor and the urban middle class. To win the support of workers, he encouraged them to join labor unions. He also increased job benefits and the number of paid vacations and holidays.
6. Beginning in 1968, Brazil's economy grew spectacularly, as the military reduced government interference in the economy and stressed free market forces. However, ordinary Brazilians benefited very little from this economic growth. The gulf between rich and poor grew even wider. Rapid development let to an inflation rate of 100 percent a year.
7. The Pinochet dictatorship was one of the most brutal in Chile's history. Thousands of opponents were imprisoned. Others were tortured or murdered. The regime also outlawed all political parties and did away with the congress.
8. Peru's dependence on exports has led to extreme ups and downs in the economy. With these ups and downs have come many changes in the government.
9. Peasants who lived in poverty in Colombia began to grow a new cash crop—coca leaves. Coca leaves are used to make cocaine. The drug trade increased. Drug lords formed cartels and used bribes and violence to eliminate competitors and to force government cooperation. The government has begun an aerial eradication program to try to stop the drug trade.

Chapter 30 Section 30.1

Organizing Your Thoughts

1. Most of the African countries relied on the export of a single crop or natural resource. When prices for these exports dropped, their economies suffered.
2. Natural resources were spent on military equipment or expensive consumer goods rather than on building the foundations for an industrial economy.
3. Corruption and bribery became common.
4. Population growth has kept many countries from creating modern economies.
5. Drought conditions led to widespread hunger and starvation.
6. AIDS has reached epidemic proportions in Africa.

Read to Learn

7. Apartheid was a system of racial segregation in South Africa.
8. Some leaders believed in Western-style capitalism. Others wanted an "African form of socialism." The African form of socialism was based on African traditions of community, in which ownership of the country's wealth would be put in the hands of the people.
9. Bishop Desmond Tutu and others worked to free Nelson Mandela and to end apartheid in South Africa. Worldwide pressure on the white South African government led to reforms and the end of apartheid laws. In 1990, Mandela was released from prison.
10. Most of the people of Africa live outside the major cities. They live much as their ancestors did, in thatched dwellings without modern plumbing or electricity. They farm, hunt, or raise livestock by traditional methods. They also wear traditional clothing and practice traditional beliefs.

Section 30.2

Organizing Your Thoughts

1. On July 26, 1956, Nasser seized the Suez Canal Company, which had been under British and French control. Great Britain and France decided to strike back. Together with Israel, they launched an attack on Egypt. This started the Suez War of 1956.
2. The United States and the Soviet Union supported Nasser and forced Britain, France, and Israel to withdraw their troops from Egypt. Nasser emerged as a powerful leader and began to promote Pan-Arabism.
3. In 1967, Nasser imposed a blockade against Israeli shipping through the Gulf of Aqaba. He also said that he was ready to confront Israel. Israel was afraid of attack and launched air strikes against Egypt and several of its Arab neighbors.
4. Israeli armies broke the blockade and occupied the Sinai Peninsula. Israel also seized territory on the West Bank, occupied Jerusalem, and took control of the Golan Heights. During this war, Israel tripled the size of its territory.
5. In 1973, Arab forces led by Sadat launched a new attack against Israel.
6. The war had indirect effects in Western nations. During the war, some OPEC nations announced large increases in the price of oil, which led to oil shortages in the United States and Europe. The conflict was ended by a cease-fire agreement in 1974.
7. Iraq and Iran had a poor relationship. They had religious differences and disputes over territory. In 1980, President Saddam Hussein of Iraq launched an attack on Iran.
8. Poison gas was used against civilian, and children were used to clear minefields. A ceasefire was finally arranged in 1980.
9. In 1990, Iraqi troops moved across the border and occupied Kuwait. This sparked the Persian Gulf War.
10. The United States led an international force that freed Kuwait and destroyed a large part of Iraq's armed forces.

Read to Learn

11. As a result of the Holocaust, sympathy for the Jewish cause grew following World War II. In 1948, a United Nations resolution divided Palestine into a Jewish state and an Arab state.
12. Pan-Arabism is a movement for Arab unity. Arab leaders in oil-rich states were suspicious of Pan-Arabism because they were afraid that they would have to share revenues with poorer states in the Middle East.
13. During the 1973 war, some OPEC nations announced large increases in the price of oil. The price hikes and cuts in oil production let to oil shortages in the United

States and Europe. In 1977, U.S. President Jimmy Carter began to push for a peace agreement between Arabs and Israelis. In September 1978, Carter met with Sadat of Egypt and Begin of Israel at Camp David, where they agreed to sign an Israeli-Egyptian peace treaty. The treaty was signed by Sadat and Begin in March 1979 and ended the war between Egypt and Israel.

14. The PLO, or Palestinian Liberation Organization, is an organization that represents the interests of the Palestinians. The PLO believed that only the Palestinian peoples had the right to create a state in Palestine. In 1993, Israel and the PLO reached an agreement calling for Palestinian autonomy in certain areas of Israel. In return, the PLO recognized the Israeli state.

15. Many devout Muslims in Iran opposed the shah because they did not approve of the new Iranian civilization under the shah. In their eyes, it was based on greed and materialism, which they identified with American influence.

16. Iran and Iraq have a poor relationship for two reasons. First, they have religious differences. Both are Muslim nations, but the Iranians are mainly Shiites, while most Iraqi leaders are Sunnis. Iran and Iraq have also had disputes over territory, especially the Strait of Hormuz.

17. The Taliban is an Islamic group that took control of Kabul in 1996 and eventually two-thirds of the country of Afghanistan. It has been condemned for its human rights abuses and harsh social policies. It was also suspected of sheltering Osama bin Laden and his al-Qaeda organization.

18. Conservative religious forces in Arab countries have tried to replace foreign culture and values with Islamic beliefs and behavior. This movement is called Islamic revivalism. For most Muslims, the Islamic revival is a reassertion of cultural identity, religious observance, family values, and morality. The movement began in Iran under the Ayatollah Khomeini.

Chapter 31 Section 31.1

Organizing Your Thoughts

1. Most of the farmland was collectivized. Chinese leaders hoped that collective farms would increase food production. They hoped that this would allow more people to work in industry.

2. Food production did not grow.

3. Collective farms were combined into vast communes. Each commune contained more than thirty thousand people who lived and worked together.

4. The Great Leap Forward was a disaster. The peasants hated the new system. Bad weather and the peasants' hatred made food production decline. As a result, almost fifteen million people died of starvation. In 1960, the government ended the communes and returned to collective farms.

5. The Great Proletarian Cultural Revolution was a program begun by Mao Zedong to make it possible for the Chinese to overcome the past and reach the final stage of communism (a classless society). Red Guards were sent throughout the country to eliminate the "Four Olds"—old ideas, old culture, old customs, and old habits.

6. The Red Guard destroyed temples, books written by foreigners, and foreign music. People who had not followed Mao's plan were attacked. Intellectuals and artists were especially open to attack. Many people were upset by the Red Guards' attacks and began to turn against the movement.

7. The Four Modernizations was a government policy under Deng Xiaoping. It focused on four areas—industry, agriculture, technology, and national defense. It was intended to help China catch up with the technological advances that had been taking place in the rest of the world. The government invited foreign investors to China. Thousands of students were sent to other countries to study science, technology, and modern business techniques. A new agricultural policy was also begun. Collective farms could now lease land to peasant families who paid rent to the collective. Anything produced above the amount of the rent could be sold on the private market.

8. Overall, modernization worked. Industrial output skyrocketed. Per capita income doubled during the 1980s. The standard of living increased for most people.

Read to Learn

9. The Nationalist government of Chiang Kai-shek was based in southern and central China. The Communist government under Mao Zedong was based in North China.

10. the Little Red Book, a collection of Mao's thoughts

11. People who called for democracy were often sent to prison. When students began to protest government corruption, Deng saw the students' desire for democracy as a demand for the end of the Communist Party. He ordered tanks and troops to crush the demonstrators.

12. The Communists tried to destroy the influence of the traditional family. The Communists thought that loyalty to the family undermined loyalty to the state. During the Great Leap Forward and the Cultural Revolution, children were encouraged to spy on their parents.

13. In August 1945, the Soviet Union and the United States agreed to divide Korea into two zones at the 38th parallel. The original plan was to hold elections after the end of World War II to reunify Korea. But the relationship between the United States and the Soviet Union grew worse after the war. Two separate governments were set up in Korea—a Communist one in the north and an anti-Communist one in the south. The Korean War did not reunify Korea. The 38th parallel is still the dividing line between North and South Korea.

Section 31.2

Organizing Your Thoughts

1. At the end of World War II, India was divided into two countries, one Hindu (India) and one Muslim (Pakistan). When India and Pakistan became independent in 1947, millions of Hindus and Muslims fled across the new borders. Violence broke out, and more than a million people were killed. Under Indira Gandhi, India continued to have many problems. Population growth was one of the most serious problems. It led to poverty for many people. Another problem was ethnic and religious conflict. This conflict involved the Sikhs. They lived in a province called the Punjab. Many of them wanted this province to be independent. In 1984, Indira Gandhi used military force against the Sikh rebels. More than 450 Sikhs were killed. Gandhi herself was assassinated in retaliation for the killings. Tensions between Hindus and Muslims have continued to disturb India's stability.

2. During Pakistan's early years, there were intense conflicts. The division between East and West Pakistan was a major source of conflict. In 1971, East Pakistan declared its independence. After a brief civil war, it became the nation of Bangladesh. Bangladesh and Pakistan both had problems establishing stable governments. In both nations, military officials have often seized control of the government. Both nations are also very poor.

3. In the Philippines, Ferdinand Marcos came to power in 1965. Under Marcos, fraud and corruption were widespread. Marcos was accused of involvement in the killing of Benigno Aquino, a leader of the opposition. An uprising forced Marcos to flee the country. In 1986, Corazon Aquino became president and worked for democratic reforms.

4. In August 1945, the Vietminh seized control of most of Vietnam. Ho Chi Minh was elected president, but France refused to accept the new government and seized control of the southern part of the country. France fought the Vietminh for control of Vietnam, but France was unable to regain control. In 1954, France agreed to a peace settlement, in which Vietnam was divided into two parts. Both sides agreed to hold elections in two years to create a single government, but the conflict continued. In 1965, U.S. President Johnson decided to send troops to South Vietnam to prevent the Communists from taking control. By the end of the 1960s, the war had reached a stalemate. President Nixon reached an agreement with North Vietnam in 1973 that allowed the United States to withdraw its forces. Within two years, Communist armies had reunited Vietnam under Communist control.

Read to Learn

5. India was divided because of religious differences. One country (called India) was predominantly Hindu, while the other one (called Pakistan) was predominantly Muslim.
6. Nehru's vision of the new India combined a parliamentary form of government with a moderate socialist economic structure. The government took over the ownership of major industries, utilities, and transportation. Private enterprise was permitted at the local level. Farmland remained in private hands.
7. Many people in East Pakistan felt that the government in West Pakistan ignored their needs.
8. Women's roles in South and Southeast Asia have changed considerably. After independence, India's leaders tried to expand women's rights. The constitution of 1950 forbade discrimination based on gender. It also called for equal pay for equal work. Child marriage was outlawed. Women were encouraged to attend school and to get jobs. In Southeast Asia, nearly all of the newly independent states gave women full legal and political rights.

Section 31.3

Organizing Your Thoughts

1. The central government plays an active role in the economy. It establishes price and wage policies and subsidizes industries. Japan's economic system has been described as "state capitalism."
2. During the occupation of Japan, a land reform program was put in place. Under this program, lands were sold on easy credit terms to the tenants. The reform program created a strong class of farmers.
3. Cultural factors also help to explain Japan's economic success. The Japanese are group oriented and find it easy to cooperate with one another. They are also hardworking and are inclined to save rather than to buy. These characteristics have produced high savings rates and labor productivity.
4. Japan's industries were destroyed in World War II, so Japan was forced to rebuild entirely new, modern factories.
5. Japanese workers spend considerably more time at their jobs than workers in other countries. Corporations reward innovation and maintain good management-labor relations.
6. Some people believe that Japan uses unfair trade practices—that it sells goods at prices below cost to break into foreign markets and restricts imports from other countries.

Read to Learn

7. Japan agreed to keep its armed forces at levels that were only enough for self-defense. The constitution set up a parliamentary system and reduced the power of the emperor. It also guaranteed civil rights and gave women the right to vote.
8. Emphasis on the work ethic is still strong. The tradition of hard work is stressed in the educational system. The subordinate position of women has not been entirely eliminated. Women now make up 50 percent of the workforce, but most are in retail or service jobs. Their average salary is only half that of men. Few women have reached senior levels in business, education, or politics.
9. The "Asian tigers" are South Korea, Taiwan, Singapore, and Hong Kong. They are called this because they have imitated Japan and have created successful industrial societies.
10. The majority of the people in both Australia and New Zealand have European origins. Both countries have identified themselves culturally and politically with Europe rather than with their Asian neighbors. Their economies resemble those of the industrialized countries of the world. Both are members of the British Commonwealth.

Chapter 32 Section 32.1

Organizing Your Thoughts

1-5. rapid population growth, poor soil, natural catastrophes, economic factors, and political factors, including civil wars

Read to Learn

6. Tropical rain forests support 50 percent of the world's species of plants and animals. They are also crucial to human survival. They remove carbon dioxide from the air and return oxygen to it.
7. Genetic engineering alters the genetic information of cells to produce new variations. Some people worry that the new variations could be deadly. The overuse of antibiotics has already created "supergerms" that do not respond to treatment with available antibiotics. The issues of stem-cell research and human cloning have also created intense debates.
8. The rich nations are mainly in the Northern Hemisphere. These nations have well-organized industrial and agricultural systems, use advanced technologies, and have strong educational systems. The poor nations are located mainly in the Southern Hemisphere and include many nations in Africa, Asia, and Latin America. These nations are primarily farming nations with little technology. Population growth is a serious problem in these countries.
9. Regional, ethnic, and religious differences continue to create conflict around the world.

Section 32.2

Organizing Your Thoughts

1. The General Assembly of the United Nations is made up of representatives of all member nations. It has the power to discuss any question of importance to the organization and to recommend the action to be taken.
2. The secretary-general, whose offices are located in New York City, supervises the day-to-day administrative business of the UN.
3. The Security Council is the most important advisory group of the UN. It is made up of 5 permanent members (the United States, Russia, Great Britain, France, and China) and 10 members chosen by the General Assembly to serve limited terms. It decides what actions the UN should take to settle international disputes.

4. the United Nations Educational, Scientific, and Cultural Organization (UNESCO)
5. the World Health Organization (WHO)
6. the United Nations International Childrens' Emergency Fund (UNICEF)

Read to Learn

7. The two main goals of the United Nations are peace and human dignity.
8. NGOs are nongovernmental organizations. Many of these organizations address global issues. NGOs include business and professional organizations, foundations, and religious, peace, and disarmament groups. Other examples are youth and women's organizations, environmental and human rights groups, and research institutes.

event on the timeline could be placed in more than one category. Some scholars claim that globalization has been happening for a long time, and others say as only been happening for a relatively short time. As you read through this timeline, think about how current events happening in your social world are part his larger process of global change.

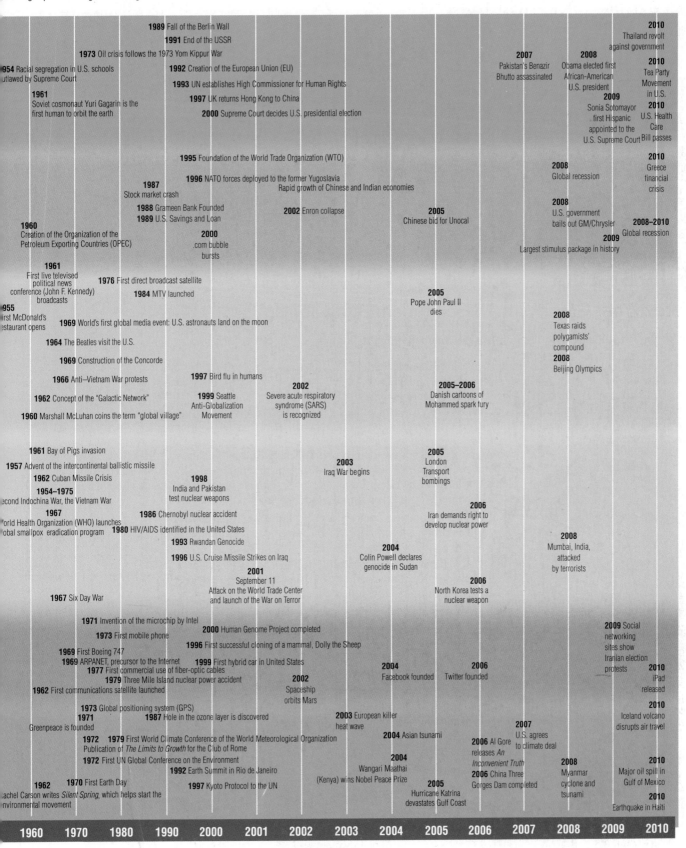

1989 Fall of the Berlin Wall
1991 End of the USSR
1973 Oil crisis follows the 1973 Yom Kippur War
954 Racial segregation in U.S. schools utlawed by Supreme Court
1992 Creation of the European Union (EU)
1993 UN establishes High Commissioner for Human Rights
1961 Soviet cosmonaut Yuri Gagarin is the first human to orbit the earth
1997 UK returns Hong Kong to China
2000 Supreme Court decides U.S. presidential election
2007 Pakistan's Benazir Bhutto assassinated
2008 Obama elected first African-American U.S. president
2009 Sonia Sotomayor first Hispanic appointed to the U.S. Supreme Court
2010 Thailand revolt against government
2010 Tea Party Movement in U.S.
2010 U.S. Health Care Bill passes

1995 Foundation of the World Trade Organization (WTO)
1996 NATO forces deployed to the former Yugoslavia
1987 Stock market crash
Rapid growth of Chinese and Indian economies
1988 Grameen Bank Founded
1989 U.S. Savings and Loan
2002 Enron collapse
1960 Creation of the Organization of the Petroleum Exporting Countries (OPEC)
2000 .com bubble bursts
2005 Chinese bid for Unocal
2008 Global recession
2008 U.S. government bails out GM/Chrysler
2009 Largest stimulus package in history
2010 Greece financial crisis
2008–2010 Global recession

1961 First live televised political news conference (John F. Kennedy) broadcasts
1976 First direct broadcast satellite
1984 MTV launched
955 irst McDonald's estaurant opens
1969 World's first global media event: U.S. astronauts land on the moon
1964 The Beatles visit the U.S.
1969 Construction of the Concorde
1966 Anti–Vietnam War protests
1962 Concept of the "Galactic Network"
1960 Marshall McLuhan coins the term "global village"
1997 Bird flu in humans
1999 Seattle Anti-Globalization Movement
2002 Severe acute respiratory syndrome (SARS) is recognized
2005 Pope John Paul II dies
2005–2006 Danish cartoons of Mohammed spark fury
2008 Texas raids polygamists' compound
2008 Beijing Olympics

1961 Bay of Pigs invasion
1957 Advent of the intercontinental ballistic missile
1962 Cuban Missile Crisis
1954–1975 econd Indochina War, the Vietnam War
1967 orld Health Organization (WHO) launches obal smallpox eradication program
1998 India and Pakistan test nuclear weapons
1986 Chernobyl nuclear accident
1980 HIV/AIDS identified in the United States
1993 Rwandan Genocide
1996 U.S. Cruise Missile Strikes on Iraq
2001 September 11 Attack on the World Trade Center and launch of the War on Terror
1967 Six Day War
2003 Iraq War begins
2004 Colin Powell declares genocide in Sudan
2005 London Transport bombings
2006 Iran demands right to develop nuclear power
2006 North Korea tests a nuclear weapon
2008 Mumbai, India, attacked by terrorists

1971 Invention of the microchip by Intel
1973 First mobile phone
2000 Human Genome Project completed
1996 First successful cloning of a mammal, Dolly the Sheep
1969 First Boeing 747
1969 ARPANET, precursor to the Internet
1999 First hybrid car in United States
1977 First commercial use of fiber-optic cables
1979 Three Mile Island nuclear power accident
1962 First communications satellite launched
2002 Spaceship orbits Mars
2004 Facebook founded
2006 Twitter founded
2009 Social networking sites show Iranian election protests
2010 iPad released

1973 Global positioning system (GPS)
1971 Greenpeace is founded
1987 Hole in the ozone layer is discovered
2003 European killer heat wave
1972 Publication of *The Limits to Growth* for the Club of Rome
1979 First World Climate Conference of the World Meteorological Organization
1972 First UN Global Conference on the Environment
1992 Earth Summit in Rio de Janeiro
1962 achel Carson writes *Silent Spring*, which helps start the nvironmental movement
1970 First Earth Day
1997 Kyoto Protocol to the UN
2004 Asian tsunami
2004 Wangari Maathai (Kenya) wins Nobel Peace Prize
2005 Hurricane Katrina devastates Gulf Coast
2006 Al Gore releases *An Inconvenient Truth*
2006 China Three Gorges Dam completed
2007 U.S. agrees to climate deal
2008 Myanmar cyclone and tsunami
2010 Iceland volcano disrupts air travel
2010 Major oil spill in Gulf of Mexico
2010 Earthquake in Haiti

1960 1970 1980 1990 2000 2001 2002 2003 2004 2005 2006 2007 2008 2009 2010

MODERN ERA

FOURTH EDITION

OUR SOCIAL WORLD

Introduction to Sociology

Jeanne H. Ballantine | Keith A. Roberts

To the Student

Improve Your Grade With These Student Study Tools!

Our praised Student Study Site at **www.sage.com/ballantine4e** features

- Updated and revised audio episodes of National Public Radio's *This American Life*
- New video links from YouTube, PBS's *Frontline*, and TED
- Updated chapter quizzes, e-flashcards, and Internet exercises
- Updated "Learning From SAGE Journal Articles" features for each chapter with related discussion questions
- New recommended readings
- and much more!

Chapter-opening visual representations of the **social world model**—now rendered with particular attention to clarity and simplicity—display the micro, meso, and macro levels for that chapter's topic, with "**Think About It**" questions to focus your thinking on key ideas and "**What's Coming in This Chapter**" to guide you through the chapter organization.

This feature, streamlined for the **fourth edition**, provides active learning opportunities to encourage you to further engage with the subject matter.

"**Thinking Sociologically**" features throughout the text challenge your understanding of core concepts and ask you to apply the material to your own life.

Thinking Sociologically

Identify several dyads, small groups, and large organiza to which you belong. Did you choose to belong, or wer born into membership in these groups? How does group influence who you are and the decisions you ma

Color bars at the end of each chapter pose important questions for you to consider and provide you with a brief look ahead to what will be covered in the next chapter.

Think About It	
Micro: Self and Inner Circle	How can sociology help me understand my own life and my sense of self?
Local Community	How can sociology help me be a more effective employee and citizen in my commu
Meso: National Institutions; Complex Organizations; Ethnic Groups	How do sociologists help us understand and even improve our lives in families, clas and health care organizations?
Macro: National Society	How do national loyalty and national policies affect my life?
Macro: Global Community	How might global events affect my life?

Chapter-ending review material includes "**What Have We Learned?**" features to ensure mastery of each chapter's core material.

Suggestions are offered for public sociology volunteer work, internships, and career possibilities in "**Contributing to Your Social World.**"

The next issue is how we gather data that inform how we understand and influence the social world. When we say we know something about society, how is it that we know? What is considered evidence in sociology, and what lens (theory) do we use to interpret the data? These are the central issues of the next chapter.

Discussion Questions

1. Think of a problem that impacts you personally (e.g., the high cost of tuition, unemployment, divorce) and explain how you would make sense of it differently if you viewed it as (a) a personal problem or (b) a public issue. How do possible solutions to the problem differ depending on whether you view it as a personal problem or a public issue?
2. How can sociology help you become a more informed ... to understand how government
4. Think of some of the ways the social institutions of government and education interconnect. Why is it in the interest of the government to support higher education? How has government support (or lack of support) impacted your college experience?
5. Imagine you would like to look at reasons behind the college dropout rate in the United States. How might your explanations differ based on whether your ... or macro level? Why?

What Have We Learned?

How can sociology help me understand my own life, who I am, and how I relate to others? This question was posed at the beginning of the chapter. Throughout this book you will find ideas and examples that will expand on the *sociological imagination*, illustrating how sociology can help you communicate more effectively and understand your interactions with others.

How do sociologists help us understand and even improve

How do national policies and global events influence my life? As the world changes, we need to be aware of global issues and how they affect us, from our job changes and lost jobs to skills demanded in the 21st century.

We live in a complex social world with many layers of interaction. If we really want to understand our own lives, we need to comprehend the levels of analysis that affect

Excerpt From Review in *Teaching Sociology*

"It is exciting to see a new offering such as Our Social World *that is innovative in its pedagogical choices. It is an exceptionally well-organized and well-written text, and as such is an exciting new option for any introductory sociology class. This text strikes us as particularly effective at engaging students. It becomes quite evident that these two award-winning coauthors understand where students are coming from and which questions are most likely to engage them and push them to think analytically."*

—Reviewed by Catherine Fobes and Laura von Wallmenich,
Alma College, in *Teaching Sociology*, Vol. 36, 2008 (April: 161–184)

Student Praise for *Our Social World*

"It's been one of my favorite textbooks to read!"

"I felt the text was speaking 'my language.'"

"I liked that it explains what careers come from sociology. I love the real-life examples to explain key words. This really helped me understand how sociology applies to life."

"I really enjoyed how it started off with a story as an example of what sociology is . . . I formed a picture in my mind that stayed there throughout the chapter."

"It helped me relate my life and personal experiences to the concepts in sociology . . . . It made me concentrate on what was happening to others instead of worrying whether I could get through all the reading. I stayed focused."

"The chapters provide a good overview of the concepts of sociology."

"The charts/diagrams are very helpful in understanding the topics."

"The 'Thinking Sociologically' questions are a great way to stop and reflect because you remember what you read so much better when you have a chance to make it personal."

"It made me become more aware of why people are the way they are and do the things they do. It taught me to view the world with a different outlook. . . . By being aware of the various social groups out there, I can become a better person."

Overall, I found this to be one of the most interesting things I have ever been forced to read, and I mean that in a good forced way."

"I really enjoy the book. It is clear to understand, funny at times, and has great examples!"

"I enjoyed how a real person's story was told at the opening of the chapters. It made sociology seem pertinent to real life."

To the Instructor

A New Intro Text for a New Generation of Students . . .
Incredibly Successful in Its First Three Editions and Now Even Better!

Written by two award-winning sociology instructors who are passionate about excellence in teaching, this textbook has been adopted at a variety of community colleges, four-year colleges, and comprehensive research universities, and these schools have used it in traditional as well as online Introduction to Sociology courses. Some of the many schools that have adopted the book include

- American River College
- Boise State University
- Buffalo State College
- Cape Cod Community College
- Capital Community College
- Capital University
- Chaffey College
- Cleveland State University
- College of Staten Island, The City University of New York
- Drexel University
- Hanover College
- Hofstra University
- Indiana University of Pennsylvania
- Ithaca College
- La Salle University
- Le Moyne College
- Long Island University
- Messiah College
- Minot State University
- Monroe County Community College
- New Mexico State University
- The Ohio State University
- Pennsylvania State University
- Quinebaug Valley Community College
- St. Cloud State University
- San Francisco State University
- Shippensburg University
- Sinclair Community College
- The State University of New York
- Stevenson University
- Tennessee State University
- Towson University
- University of Central Oklahoma
- University of Akron
- University of Maryland
- University of Nebraska
- University of Richmond
- University of Tennessee
- University of the Ozarks
- Wright State University

. . . and many, many more! We would like to say **THANK YOU** to our loyal adopters who chose *Our Social World* in its first three editions, making it such an overwhelming success. We hope you find the **fourth edition** even more exciting.

Instructor Praise for *Our Social World*

"Unlike most textbooks that I have read, the breadth and depth of coverage . . . is very impressive. This text forces the students deep into the topics covered and challenges them to see the interconnectedness of them."
—Keith Kerr, Texas A&M University

"I love the global emphasis, the applied material, and the emphasis on solutions to social problems."
—Gina Carreno, Florida Atlantic University

"So often students ask, 'What can I do with sociology?' Having this applied information interspersed in the text allows them to get answers to that question over and over again."

"Finally, a text that brings sociology to life! . . . This is so well written that I'm not sure the students will even realize they are learning theory!"
—Martha Shockey, St. Louis University

"This is an excellent textbook it has definitely made life easier, and the ancillary material is extremely helpful."
—Jamie M. Dolan, Carroll College

New to This Edition!

- Increased attention to public sociology, including description of the work of at least one public sociologist per chapter in a "Sociologists in Action" feature
- Increased attention to the sociology of disabilities, especially a feature on the deaf subculture in the United States
- Major topics listed at the start of each chapter
- New discussion questions at the end of each chapter
- Seventeen new featured essays
- Revised and new "Engaging Sociology" features, with more opportunity for data analysis by students
- Clarified and often simplified definitions in an updated glossary
- Scores of new examples
- Reorganization of the religion, education, groups and organizations, and other chapters
- Discussion of new 2012 social movements and the 2012 election
- Roughly 100 new and updated tables, more than 800 new references, more than 130 new photos, and a dozen new or updated maps
- "Contributing to Our Social World" feature including additional ideas for volunteer work, internships, and careers
- A new exercise for each chapter on public sociology, available on the web

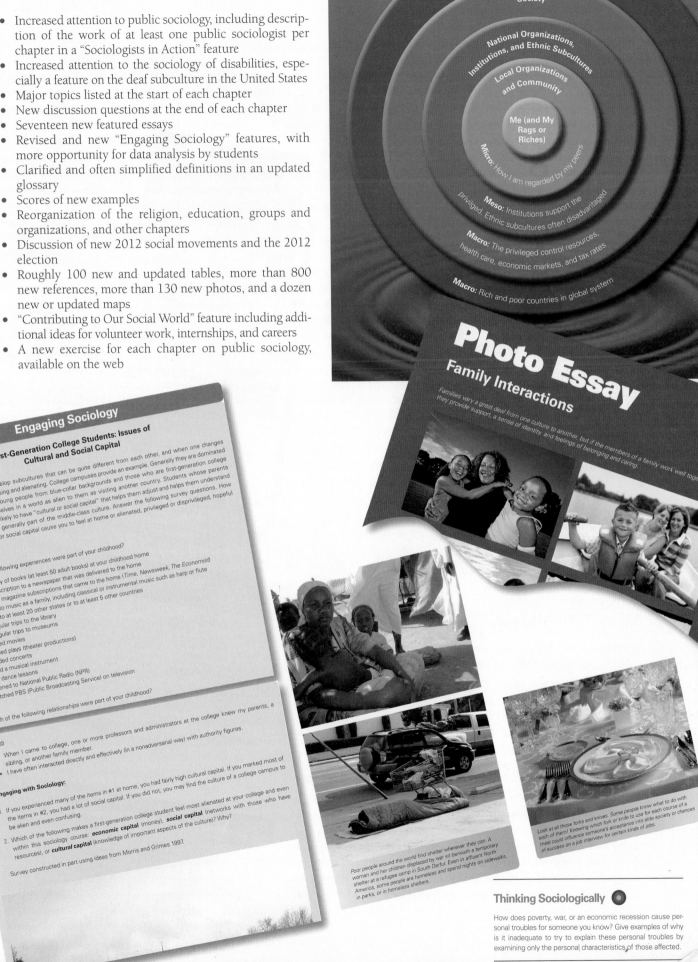

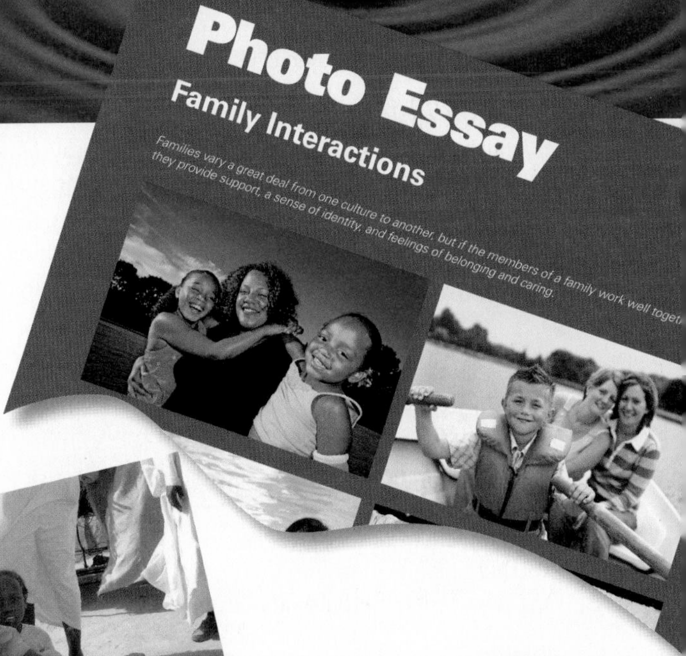
Photo Essay
Family Interactions
Families vary a great deal from one culture to another, but if the members of a family work well toget
they provide support, a sense of identity, and feelings of belonging and caring.

Engaging Sociology

First-Generation College Students: Issues of Cultural and Social Capital

...omic classes develop subcultures that can be quite different from each other, and when one changes ...es, it can be confusing and alienating. College campuses provide an example. Generally they are dominated ...-class cultures. Young people from blue-collar backgrounds and those who are first-generation college ... often find themselves in a world as alien to them as visiting another country. Students whose parents ...college are more likely to have "cultural or social capital" that helps them adjust and helps them understand ...ofessors who are generally part of the middle-class culture. Answer the following survey questions. How ...your own cultural or social capital cause you to feel at home or alienated, privileged or disprivileged, hopeful ...pairing?

A. Which of the following experiences were part of your childhood?

- Had a library of books (at least 50 adult books) at your childhood home
- Had a subscription to a newspaper that was delivered to the home
- Had news magazine subscriptions that came to the home (*Time, Newsweek, The Economist*)
- Listened to music as a family, including classical or instrumental music such as harp or flute
- Traveled to at least 20 other states or to at least 5 other countries
- Took regular trips to the library
- Took regular trips to museums
- Attended movies
- Attended plays (theater productions)
- Attended concerts
- Played a musical instrument
- Took dance lessons
- Listened to National Public Radio (NPR)
- Watched PBS (Public Broadcasting Service) on television

B. Which of the following *relationships* were part of your childhood?

(Continued)

- When I came to college, one or more professors and administrators at the college knew my parents, a sibling, or another family member.
- I have often interacted directly and effectively (in a nonadversarial way) with authority figures.

Engaging with Sociology:

1. If you experienced many of the items in #1 at home, you had fairly high cultural capital. If you marked most of the items in #2, you had a lot of social capital. If you did not, you may find the culture of a college campus to be alien and even confusing.
2. Which of the following makes a first-generation college student feel most alienated at your college and even within this sociology course: ***economic capital*** (money), ***social capital*** (networks with those who have resources), or ***cultural capital*** (knowledge of important aspects of the culture)? Why?

Survey constructed in part using ideas from Morris and Grimes 1997.

Poor people around the world find shelter wherever they can. A woman and her children displaced by war sit beneath a temporary shelter at a refugee camp in South Darfur. Even in affluent North America, some people are homeless and spend nights on sidewalks, in parks, or in homeless shelters.

Look at all those forks and knives. Some people know what to do with each of them! Knowing which fork or knife to use for each course of a meal could influence someone's acceptance into elite society or chances of success on a job interview for certain kinds of jobs.

Thinking Sociologically

How does poverty, war, or an economic recession cause personal troubles for someone you know? Give examples of why is it inadequate to try to explain these personal troubles by examining only the personal characteristics of those affected.

Finally, here is a text that engages students. *Our Social World* uses a unique, dynamic approach to focus on developing sociological skills of analysis rather than simply emphasizing memorization of basic ideas.

The text is both personal and global. It introduces sociology clearly, with the updated social world model providing a clear and cohesive framework that lends integration and clarity to the course. With the theme of globalization intertwined throughout the text and an emphasis on deep learning and the public side of sociology, *Our Social World*, now in its fourth edition, inspires both critical thinking and community participation.

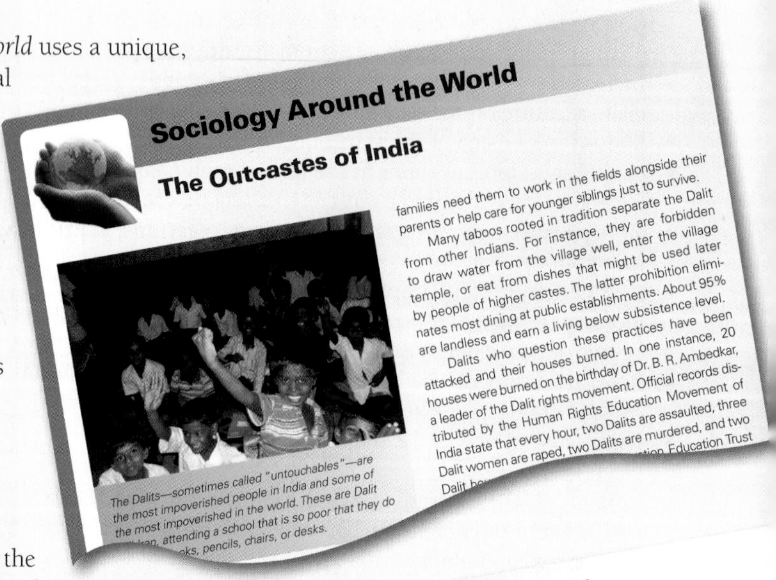
Sociology Around the World

The Outcastes of India

families need them to work in the fields alongside their parents or help care for younger siblings just to survive.

Many taboos rooted in tradition separate the Dalit from other Indians. For instance, they are forbidden to draw water from the village well, enter the village temple, or eat from dishes that might be used later by people of higher castes. The latter prohibition eliminates most dining at public establishments. About 95% are landless and earn a living below subsistence level.

Dalits who question these practices have been attacked and their houses burned. In one instance, 20 houses were burned on the birthday of Dr. B. R. Ambedkar, a leader of the Dalit rights movement. Official records distributed by the Human Rights Education Movement of India state that every hour, two Dalits are assaulted, three Dalit women are raped, two Dalits are murdered, and two

The Dalits—sometimes called "untouchables"—are the most impoverished people in India and some of the most impoverished in the world. These are Dalit ... attending a school that is so poor that they do ...oks, pencils, chairs, or desks.

Teach Students the Basics of Sociology via the Newly Simplified, Visually Compelling "Social World Model"

This model, which provides the organizing framework for the text and visually introduces each chapter, illustrates the level of analysis of each topic (from micro to meso to macro), and addresses how each topic is related.

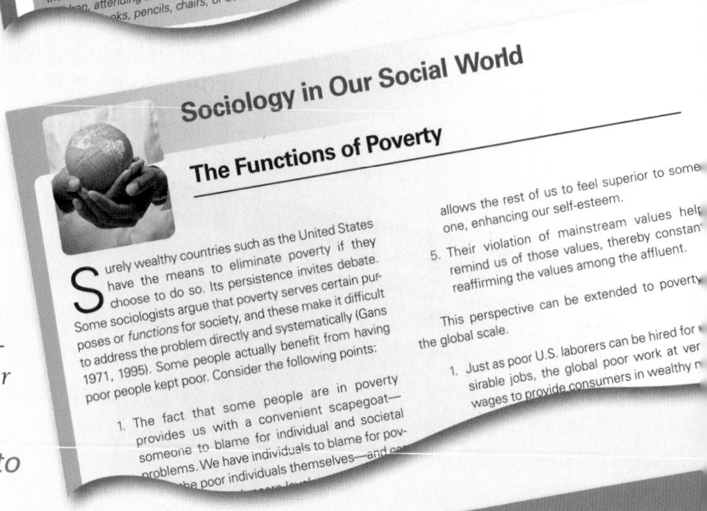
Sociology in Our Social World

The Functions of Poverty

Surely wealthy countries such as the United States have the means to eliminate poverty if they choose to do so. Its persistence invites debate. Some sociologists argue that poverty serves certain purposes or *functions* for society, and these make it difficult to address the problem directly and systematically (Gans 1971, 1995). Some people actually benefit from having poor people kept poor. Consider the following points:

1. The fact that some people are in poverty provides us with a convenient scapegoat—someone to blame for individual and societal problems. We have individuals to blame for poverty—the poor individuals themselves—and ...

allows the rest of us to feel superior to some... one, enhancing our self-esteem.

5. Their violation of mainstream values help... remind us of those values, thereby constan... reaffirming the values among the affluent.

This perspective can be extended to poverty... the global scale.

1. Just as poor U.S. laborers can be hired for ... sirable jobs, the global poor work at ver... wages to provide consumers in wealthy n...

Engage Students . . . With Engaging Sociology

Active learning exercises keep sociology fun, drawing students into an analysis of a relevant table, the application of a population pyramid to the business world, or an interactive survey on the differences in social and cultural capital for first-generation students. This feature has generated extraordinarily strong positive responses from instructors who used the third edition of *Our Social World.*

Introduce a Global Perspective, Asking Students to Be Citizens of the World

This text uniquely weaves a truly global perspective into each part of the book, challenging students to think of themselves as global citizens rather than as local citizens looking out at others in the world. "Sociology Around the World" features introduce fascinating historical or global examples of key concepts.

What Have We Learned?

The opening question in "Think About It" asked, "How do you know?" In this chapter, we have outlined the process of research that describes how sociologists and other social scientists "know." The next question asks, "Why is evidence important?" Our simple answer is that it is better to base social policies on evidence (scientifically collected facts and data) than on our untested assumptions or biased opinions. We also asked, "How do sociologists gather dependable facts?" The process of planning and carrying out a scientific study is outlined in the beginning of this chapter and provides a partial answer to this question. Finally, "How can theories help us understand social forces affecting our lives?"

What makes a discipline scientific is not the subject matter but how we conduct our research and what we consider ... The core features of a science are (1) com...

It is the fourth feature that causes us to be open to criti... and alternative interpretations. To have credible find... we always consider the possibility that we have overlo... alternative explanations of the data and alternative w... view the problem. This is one of the hardest princi... grasp, but it is one of the most important in reachi... truth. Science—including social science—is not fac... memorized. Science is a process that is made possi... social exchange of ideas, a clash of opinions, and a... ual search for truth. Knowledge in the sciences is c... vigorous debate. Rather than just memorizing the... in this book to take a test, we hope you will eng... creation of knowledge by entering into these deb...

Encourage Deep Learning and Critical Thinking With Uniquely Effective Pedagogy

"Thinking Sociologically" questions, "What Have We Learned?" end-of-chapter summaries and discussion questions, and "Sociology in Our Social World" features encourage critical thought, challenging students to reflect on how the material is relevant and applicable to their lives.

Inspire an Active Engagement in Sociology Using Motivating Chapter Features

"Contributing to Our Social World: What Can We Do?" suggestions include work and volunteer opportunities in which students can apply their newfound sociological knowledge right away. "Sociologists in Action" boxes—five of which are new to this edition—introduce students to a variety of people with sociological degrees, illuminating bachelors through PhD post-degree career options.

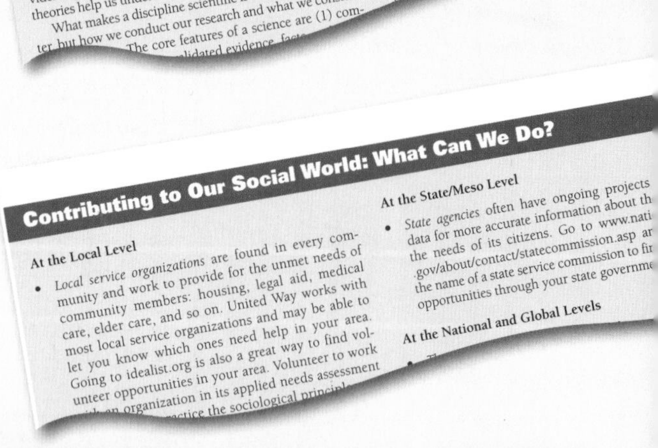
Contributing to Our Social World: What Can We Do?

At the Local Level

- *Local service organizations* are found in every community and work to provide for the unmet needs of community members: housing, legal aid, medical care, elder care, and so on. United Way works with most local service organizations and may be able to let you know which ones need help in your area. Going to idealist.org is also a great way to find volunteer opportunities in your area. Volunteer to work ... organization in its applied needs assessment ...

At the State/Meso Level

- *State agencies* often have ongoing projects ... data for more accurate information about th... the needs of its citizens. Go to www.nati... .gov/about/contact/statecommission.asp ar... the name of a state service commission to fi... opportunities through your state governme...

At the National and Global Levels

Ancillaries

Compatible With Blackboard and Other Course Management Systems

To facilitate the use of the fourth edition of *Our Social World* with Blackboard and other course management platforms, SAGE Publications provides the following teaching and learning ancillaries at **www.sage.com/ballantine4e**:

A password-protected **Instructor Teaching Site**

An open-access **Student Study Site**

Instructor Teaching Site

The Instructor Teaching Site features a variety of popular and effective teaching aids, including

Chapter Outlines: Carefully crafted outlines follow the structure of each chapter, providing an essential reference and teaching tool.

Chapter Exercises and Activities: These include lively and stimulating ideas for use both in and out of class to reinforce active learning. The activities apply to individual or group projects.

Course Syllabi: Sample syllabi—for semester, quarter, and online classes—provide suggested models for creating the syllabus for your course.

Web Resources: These links to relevant websites direct both instructors and students to additional resources for further research on important chapter topics.

Photographic Essay Projects: Unique assignments encourage students to observe and evaluate social issues in creative ways.

SAGE Journal Articles: A "Learning From SAGE Journal Articles" feature provides access to recent, relevant full-text articles from SAGE's leading research journals. Each article supports and expands on the concepts presented in the chapter. Also provided are discussion questions to focus and guide student interpretation.

Video Resources: Carefully selected, web-based video resources feature relevant interviews, lectures, personal stories, inquiries, and other content for use in independent or classroom-based explorations of key topics. Discussion questions are provided to guide interpretation of material. The site also includes new video links for YouTube and for PBS's *Frontline.*

Test Bank (Word): This Word test bank offers a diverse set of multiple-choice, true/false, short-answer, and essay test questions and answers for every chapter to aid instructors in assessing students' progress and understanding.

Test Bank (Diploma): This electronic test bank using Diploma software is available for use with a PC or Mac. The test bank offers a diverse set of multiple-choice, true/false, short-answer, and essay test questions and answers for every chapter to aid instructors in assessing students' progress and understanding.

PowerPoint Slides: Chapter-specific slide presentations offer assistance with lecture and review preparation by highlighting essential content, features, and artwork from the book.

Teaching Tips: Teaching Tips provide suggestions and resources for using the social world model for traditional and online Introduction to Sociology courses.

Additional Resource: Adopters will receive free online access to Bryant's *21st Century Sociology: A Reference Handbook* (SAGE, © 2007), to help make teaching globally even more effective. Contact Customer Care at 1-800-818-SAGE (7243) for more information on this extraordinary teaching aid.

Student Study Site

To further enhance students' understanding of and interest in the course material, we have created a Student Study Site, which includes

Podcasts and Audio Clips: Each chapter includes links to podcasts, which cover important topics and are designed to supplement key points within the text. The site also includes updated and revised audio episodes of National Public Radio's *This American Life*.

Video Resources: Carefully selected, web-based video resources feature relevant interviews, lectures, personal stories, inquiries, and other content for use in independent or classroom-based explorations of key topics. Discussion questions are provided to guide interpretation of material. The site includes new video links for YouTube and for PBS's *Frontline*.

Web Quizzes: Self-quizzes allow students to independently assess their progress in learning course material.

Web Exercises and Activities: These links direct both instructors and students to useful and current web resources, as well as creative activities to extend and reinforce learning.

E-flashcards: This study tool reinforces student understanding of key terms and concepts that have been outlined in the chapters.

SAGE Journal Articles: A "Learning From SAGE Journal Articles" feature provides access to recent, relevant full-text articles from SAGE's leading research journals. Each article supports and expands on the concepts presented in the chapter. Discussion questions focus and guide student interpretation.

Recommended Readings: Interesting and relevant supplements provide a jumping-off point for course assignments, papers, research, group work, and class discussion.

and much more!

SAGE Teaching Innovations and Professional Development Awards Fund

Partly inspired by the authors of *Our Social World*, SAGE has created this awards fund to help graduate students and pretenure faculty attend the annual American Sociological Association teaching preconference, hosted by the Section on Teaching and Learning in Sociology, with grants of $500 per recipient. In its first year, there were 13 award recipients. Since that time, 23 additional authors have joined the program as co-sponsors, and in the six years of the program, 152 recipients have benefitted from this award. In 2008, the ASA's Section on Teaching and Learning in Sociology awarded SAGE Publications a glass plaque to honor the publisher and its participating authors and editors—including the authors of *Our Social World*—for their commitment to excellence in teaching.

About the Authors

Jeanne H. Ballantine (far right) is Professor Emerita of Sociology at Wright State University, a state university of about 17,000 students in Ohio. She has also taught at several four-year colleges, including an "alternative" college and a traditionally Black college, and at international programs in universities abroad. She has been teaching introductory sociology for more than 30 years with a mission to introduce the uninitiated to the field and to help students see the usefulness and value in sociology. She has been active in the teaching movement, shaping curriculum, writing and presenting research on teaching, and offering workshops and consulting in regional, national, and international forums. She is a Fulbright Senior Scholar and serves as a Departmental Resources Group consultant and evaluator.

Jeanne has written several textbooks, all with the goal of reaching the student audience. As the original director of the Center for Teaching and Learning at Wright State University, she scoured the literature on student learning and served as a mentor to teachers in a wide variety of disciplines. Local, regional, and national organizations have honored her for her teaching and for her contributions to helping others become effective teachers. In 1986, the American Sociological Association's Section on Undergraduate Education (now called the Section on Teaching and Learning in Sociology) recognized her with the Hans O. Mauksch Award for Distinguished Contributions to Teaching of Sociology. In 2004, she was honored by the American Sociological Association with its Distinguished Contributions to Teaching Award. In 2010, the North Central Sociological Association awarded her the J. Milton Yinger Lifetime Award for a Distinguished Career in Sociology.

Keith A. Roberts (top left) is Emeritus Professor of Sociology at Hanover College, a private liberal arts college of about 1,100 students in Indiana. He has been teaching introductory sociology for more than 30 years with a passion for active learning strategies and a focus on "deep learning" by students that transforms the way they see the world. Prior to teaching at Hanover, he taught at a two-year regional campus of a large university.

He has been active in the teaching movement, writing on teaching and serving as a consultant to sociology departments across the country in his capacity as a member of the American Sociological Association Departmental Resources Group. He has written a very popular textbook in the sociology of religion, has coauthored a book on writing in the undergraduate curriculum, and annually runs workshops for high school sociology teachers. He has chaired the Selection Committee for the SAGE Teaching Innovations and Professional Development Awards since the program's inception. He has been honored for his teaching and teaching-related work at local, state, regional, and national levels. The American Sociological Association's Section on Teaching and Learning awarded him the Hans O. Mauksch Award for Distinguished Contributions to Teaching of Sociology in 2000. He was honored with the American Sociological Association's Distinguished Contributions to Teaching Award in 2010. In 2012, the North Central Sociological Association awarded Keith the J. Milton Yinger Lifetime Award for Distinguished Career in Sociology.

2004 AMERICAN SOCIOLOGICAL ASSOCIATION

DISTINGUISHED CONTRIBUTIONS TO TEACHING AWARD

2010 AMERICAN SOCIOLOGICAL ASSOCIATION

DISTINGUISHED CONTRIBUTIONS TO TEACHING AWARD

Your authors—teaching "outside the box."

OUR SOCIAL WORLD

4

Writing this book has been a labor of love,
for we are both passionate about sociology and about teaching sociology.

Still, this labor of love has sometimes come at a steep price to others we love.

Thus, we dedicate this book to two saints of patience, support, and understanding,

Hardy Ballantine

and

Judy Roberts,

our supportive and beloved spouses,
and to our children, who have shared their educational trials and triumphs,
giving us food for thought as we wrote.

OUR SOCIAL WORLD

Introduction to Sociology 4

Jeanne H. Ballantine
Wright State University

Keith A. Roberts
Hanover College

SAGE

Los Angeles | London | New Delhi
Singapore | Washington DC

SAGE

Los Angeles | London | New Delhi
Singapore | Washington DC

FOR INFORMATION:

SAGE Publications, Inc.
2455 Teller Road
Thousand Oaks, California 91320
E-mail: order@sagepub.com

SAGE Publications Ltd.
1 Oliver's Yard
55 City Road
London EC1Y 1SP
United Kingdom

SAGE Publications India Pvt. Ltd.
B 1/I 1 Mohan Cooperative Industrial Area
Mathura Road, New Delhi 110 044
India

SAGE Publications Asia-Pacific Pte. Ltd.
3 Church Street
#10-04 Samsung Hub
Singapore 049483

Acquisitions Editor: David Repetto
Editorial Assistant: Lauren Johnson
Production Editor: Brittany Bauhaus
Copy Editor: Melinda Masson
Typesetter: C&M Digitals (P) Ltd.
Proofreader: Theresa Kay
Indexer: Diggs Publication Services, Inc.
Cover Designer: Gail Buschman
Marketing Manager: Erica DeLuca
Permissions Editor: Karen Ehrmann

Printed in Canada.

Library of Congress Cataloging-in-Publication Data

A catalog record of this book is available from the Library of Congress.

9781412992466

This book is printed on acid-free paper.

13 14 15 16 17 10 9 8 7 6 5 4 3 2 1

MIX
Paper from responsible sources
FSC www.fsc.org
FSC® C011825

Brief Contents

Detailed Contents

Chapter 14 • Medicine: An Anatomy of Health and Illness 510

PART V. Social Dynamics 553

Chapter 15 • Population and Urbanization: Living on Spaceship Earth 554

Preface

To Our Readers

This book asks you to think outside the box. Why? The best way to become a more interesting person, to grow beyond the old familiar thoughts and behaviors, and to make life exciting is to explore new ways to view things. The world in which we live is intensely personal and individual in nature, with much of our social interaction occurring in intimate groups of friends and family. Our most intense emotions and most meaningful links to others are at this "micro" level of social life.

However, these intimate micro-level links in our lives are influenced by larger social structures and global trends. In the second decade of the 21st century, technological advances make it possible to connect with the farthest corners of the world. Multinational corporations cross national boundaries, form new economic and political unions, and change job opportunities of people everywhere. Some groups embrace the changes, while others try to protect their members from the rapid changes that threaten to disrupt their traditional lives. Even our most personal relationships or what we eat tonight may be shaped by events on the other side of the continent or the globe. From the news headlines to family and peer interactions, we confront sociological issues daily. The task of this book and of your instructor is to help you see world events and your personal life from a sociological perspective. Unless you learn how to look at our social world with an analytical lens, many of its most intriguing features will be missed.

The social world you face in the job markets of the 21st century is influenced by changes and forces that are easy to miss. Like the wind, which can do damage even if the air is unseen, social structures are themselves so taken for granted that it is easy to miss seeing them. However, their effects can be readily identified. Sociology provides new perspectives, helping students to understand their families, their friends, their work lives, their leisure, and their place in a diverse and changing world.

A few of you will probably become sociology majors. Others will find the subject matter of this course relevant to your personal and professional lives. Some of the reasons the authors of this book and your own professor chose to study sociology many years ago are the factors that inspire undergraduates today to choose a major in sociology: learning about the social world from a new perspective; working with people and groups; developing knowledge, inquiry, and interpersonal skills; and learning about social life, from small groups to global social systems. As the broadest of the social sciences, sociology has a never-ending array of fascinating subjects to study. This book touches only the surface of what the field has to offer and the exciting things you can do with this knowledge. These same considerations motivated us and gave us direction in writing this introductory book.

Where This Book Is Headed

A well-constructed course, like an effective essay, needs to be organized around a central question, one that spawns other subsidiary questions and intrigues the participants. The problem with introductory courses in many disciplines is that there is no central question and thus no coherence to the course. These courses have more of a flavor-of-the-week approach (a different topic each week), with no attempt at integration. We have tried to correct that problem in this text.

The Social World Model

For you to understand sociology as an integrated whole rather than a set of separate chapters in a book, we have organized the chapters in this book around the *social world model*: a conceptual model that demonstrates the relationships between individuals (micro level); organizations, institutions, and subcultures (meso level); and national societies and global structures (macro level). At the beginning of each chapter, a visual diagram of the model will illustrate this idea as it relates to the topic of that chapter, including how issues related to the topic have implications at various levels of analysis in the social world, influencing and being affected by other parts of society. No aspect of society exists in a vacuum. On the other hand, this model does not assume that everyone always gets along or that relationships are always harmonious or supportive. Sometimes, different parts of society are in competition for resources, and intense conflict and hostility may be generated.

This micro- to macro-level analysis is a central concept in the discipline of sociology. Many instructors seek first and foremost to help students develop a *sociological imagination*, an ability to see the complex links between various levels of the social system, from the micro level of close relationships to the macro level of globalization. This is a key goal of this book. Within a few months, you may not remember all the specific concepts or terms that have been introduced, but if the way you see the world has been transformed during this course, a key element of deep learning has been accomplished. Learning to see things from alternative perspectives is a precondition for critical thinking. This entire book attempts to help you recognize connections between your personal experiences and problems and larger social forces of society. Thus, you will be learning to take a new perspective on the social world in which you live.

A key element of that social world is diversity. We live in societies in which there are people who differ in a host of ways: ethnicity, socioeconomic status, religious background, political persuasion, gender, sexual orientation, and so forth. Diversity is a blessing in many ways to a society because the most productive and creative organizations and societies are those that are highly diverse. This is the case because people with different backgrounds solve problems in very different ways. When people with such divergences come together, the outcome of their problem solving can create new solutions to vexing problems. However, diversity often creates challenges as well. Misunderstanding and "we" versus "they" thinking can divide people. These issues will be explored throughout this book. We now live in a global village, and in this book, you will learn something about how people on the other side of the village live and view the world.

We hope you enjoy the book and get as enthralled with sociology as we are. It genuinely is a fascinating field of study.

Jeanne H. Ballantine

Jeanne H. Ballantine

Keith A. Roberts

Keith A. Roberts

Instructors

How to Make This Book Work for You

Special features woven throughout each chapter support the theme of the book. These will help students comprehend and apply the material and make the material more understandable and interesting. These features are also designed to facilitate deep learning, to help students move beyond rote memorization, and to increase their ability to analyze and evaluate information.

For students to understand both the comparative global theme and sociology as an integrated whole rather than as a set of separate chapters in a book, we have organized the chapters in this book around the *social world model:* a conceptual model that demonstrates the relationships between individuals (micro level); organizations, institutions, and subcultures (meso level); and societies and global structures (macro level). At the beginning of each chapter, a visual diagram of the model will illustrate this idea as it relates to the topic of that chapter, including how issues related to the topic have implications at various levels of analysis in the social world.

"Think About It"

So that students can become curious, active readers, we have posed questions at the outset of each chapter that we hope are relevant to everyday life, but that are also tied to the micro-meso-macro levels of analysis that serve as the theme of the book. The purpose is to transform students from passive readers who run their eyes across the words into curious active readers who read to answer a question and to be reflective. Active or deep reading is key to comprehension and retention of reading material (Roberts and Roberts 2008). Instructors can also use this feature to encourage students to think critically about the implications of what they have read. Instructors might want to ask students to write a paragraph about one of these questions before coming to class each day. These questions might also provide the basis for in-class discussions.

Students should be encouraged to start each chapter by reading and thinking about these questions, looking at the topics in the chapter outlined just below the "Think About It" feature, and asking some questions of their own. This will mean that they are more likely to stay focused, remember the material long-term, and be able to apply it to their own lives.

"What's Coming in This Chapter"

Each chapter begins with a simple listing of the key topic headings. Research on deep reading shows that if students begin to ask questions and become active readers at the outset, they comprehend and retain more of the material. This new feature is added in response to requests by reviewers of the text.

A Global Perspective and the Social World Model

We are part of an ever-shrinking world, a global village. What happens in distant countries is not only news the same day but also affects relatives living in other countries, the cost of goods, work and travel possibilities, and the balance of power in the world. Instead of simply including cross-cultural examples of strange and different peoples, this book incorporates a global perspective throughout. This is done so that students can see not only how others live different but rewarding lives, but also the connections between others' lives and their own. Students will need to think and relate to the world globally in future roles as workers, travelers, and global citizens. Our analysis illustrates the interconnections of the world's societies and their political and economic systems and demonstrates that what happens in one part of the world affects others. For instance, if a major company in your area moves much of its operation to another country with cheaper labor, jobs are lost, and the local economy is hurt. Likewise, this new company in a developing country of the world may contribute to deterioration of the local culture as the people adapt to the lifestyles and cultures of Western societies.

This global approach attempts to instill interest, understanding, and respect for different groups of people and their lifestyles. Race, class, and gender are an integral part of understanding the diverse social world, and these features of social life have global implications. The comparative global theme is carried throughout the book in headings and written text, in examples, and in boxes and selection of photos. As students read this book, they should continually think about how the experiences in their private world are influenced by and may influence events at other levels: the community, organizations and institutions, the nation, and the world.

Opening Vignettes

Chapters typically open with an illustration relevant to the chapter content. For instance, in Chapter 2, "Examining the Social World," the case of Hector, a Brazilian teenager living in poverty in a *favela*, is used to illustrate research methods and theory throughout the chapter. Chapter 3, "Society and Culture," begins with scenarios of mealtime scenes from around the world to illustrate the variations in human cultures. In Chapter 4, "Socialization," there is the case of Phoebe Prince, a 15-year-old immigrant from Ireland, who was so harassed and bullied by peers that she hung herself. Chapter 7 begins with a discussion of the royal wedding of Prince William and Kate Middleton. Chapter 8 begins with an actual account of trafficking in body parts, examining the ethnic implications of the practice. These vignettes are meant to interest students in the upcoming subject matter by helping them relate to a personalized story. In several cases, the vignettes serve as illustrations throughout the chapters.

"Thinking Sociologically" Questions

Following major topics, students will find questions that ask them to think critically and apply the material just read to some aspect of their lives or the social world. The purpose of this feature is to encourage students to apply the ideas and concepts in the text to their lives and to develop critical thinking skills. These questions can be the basis for in-class discussions and can be assigned as questions to start interesting conversations with friends and families to learn how the topics relate to their own lives. Note that some of these questions have a miniature icon—a small version of the chapter-opening model—signifying that these questions reinforce the theme of micro, meso, and macro levels of social influence.

"Engaging Sociology"

Perhaps the most innovative feature is called "Engaging Sociology"—and the double entendre is intentional. We want students to think of sociology as engaging and fun, and these features are designed to engage—to draw students into active analysis of a table, application of a population pyramid to the business world, taking a survey to understand why differences in social and cultural capital make first-generation students feel alienated on a college campus, and reading a map and learning to analyze the patterns. This feature offers opportunities for students to engage in some quantitative data analysis—a major new emphasis in teaching sociology.

Key Concepts, Examples, and Writing Style

Key terms that are defined and illustrated within the running narrative and that appear in the glossary appear in bold. Other terms that are defined but are of less significance are italicized. The text is rich in examples that bring sociological concepts to life for student readers. Each chapter has been student tested for readability. Both students and reviewers describe the writing style as reader friendly, often fascinating, and accessible, but not watered down.

Special Features

Although there are numerous examples throughout the book, featured inserts provide more in-depth illustrations of the usefulness of the sociological perspective to understand world situations or events with direct relevance to a student's life. There are four kinds of special features. "Sociology in Our Social World" features focus on a sociological issue or story, often with policy implications. "Sociology Around the World" takes readers to another part of the globe to explore how things are different from (or how they are the same as) what they might experience in their own lives. "Sociologists in Action" features appear in many chapters and examine profiles of public sociologists who are working in the field. This helps students grasp what sociologists can actually do with sociology.

Technology and Society

Nearly every chapter examines the issues of technology as they would be relevant to that chapter. We have especially sought out materials that have to do with the Internet and with communications technology.

Social Policy and Becoming an Active Citizen

Most chapters include discussion of some social policy issues: an effort to address the concerns about public sociology and the relevance of sociological findings to current social debates. Furthermore, because students sometimes feel helpless to know what to do about social issues that concern them at macro and meso levels, we have concluded every chapter with a few ideas about how they might become involved as active citizens, even as undergraduate students. Suggestions in the "Contributing to Your Social World: What Can We Do?" section may be assigned as service learning or term projects, or may help students find an internship opportunity or get involved on their own time as a volunteer.

Summary Sections and Discussion Questions

Each chapter ends with review material: a "What Have We Learned?" feature that includes a "Key Points" bulleted summary of the chapter's core material. The summary is followed by probing questions that ask students to go beyond memorization of terms to apply and use sociology to think about the world. Research indicates that unless four discrete sections of the brain are stimulated, the learning will be not long-term and deep but surficial and short-term (Zull 2002). These questions are carefully crafted to activate all four critical sections of the brain.

A Little (Teaching) Help From Our Friends

Whether the instructor is new to teaching or an experienced professor, there are some valuable ideas that can help invigorate and energize the classroom. A substantial literature on teaching methodology tells us that student involvement is key to the learning process. Built into this book are discussion questions and projects that students can report on in class. In addition, there are a number of teaching suggestions in the supplements and teaching aids for active learning in large or small classes.

Instructor Teaching Site

A password-protected site, available at www.sagepub.com/ballantine4e, features resources that have been designed to help instructors plan and teach their course. These resources include an extensive test bank, chapter-specific PowerPoint presentations, lecture notes, sample syllabi for semester and quarter courses, discussion questions to facilitate class discussion, class assignments, links to SAGE journal articles, recommended readings, and links to video, audio, and web resources.

Test Bank

Compatible with both PC and Mac computers, the computerized test bank allows for easy question sorting and exam creation. It includes multiple-choice, true/false, short-answer, and essay questions. In keeping with the deep learning thrust of this book, however, the test questions will have more emphasis on application skills than on rote memorization—the latter being a too common characteristic of test banks.

PowerPoint Slides

Because visuals are an important addition to classroom lectures, in recognition of the varying learning styles of students, PowerPoint slides that include lecture outlines and relevant tables, maps, diagrams, pictures, and short quotes for instructors to use in the classroom are included on the Instructor Teaching Site.

Student Study Site

A web-based study site is available at www.sagepub.com/ballantine4e. This site provides access to several study tools including eFlashcards, web quizzes, links to full-text SAGE journal articles, links to video, audio, and web resources, web exercises, recommended readings, and study questions.

What Is New in the Fourth Edition?

There are 18 new boxed features in this book. The "Applied Sociologist at Work" feature has been replaced by "Sociologists in Action"—with more emphasis on policy work in many of the new additions.

In this major revision we have reorganized several chapters and updated all data, added many new studies, and included new emphases in sociology. The addition of a discussion on deaf subcultures in the chapter on culture (Chapter 3) and the new discussions on obesity in several chapters are examples of this. Most chapters have *extensive* updates: Chapter 11, for example, has new material with 72 new citations (dozens of dated references were dropped); Chapter 12 has 87 new ones; Chapter 15 has 80. There are also 130 new photos in this edition.

New to the third edition, the section opener that more clearly frames "institutions" has been well received and has undergone minor improvements. We had discovered that our first editions—and almost all other introductory texts—had done a notoriously poor job of defining institutions. Considerable attention has also been given to clarifying and simplifying definitions throughout the book and determining what should be in the glossary. Several reviewers wanted more attention to definitions, so all defined terms are either italicized or in bold blue font. If the words are in bold, they are key vocabulary words, with the definition itself italicized and the terms appearing in the glossary. The glossary is also separate in this addition rather than an integrated glossary/index. The core elements of the book—with the unifying theme and the social world model at the beginning of every chapter—have not changed.

Finally, although we had been told that the writing was extraordinarily readable, we have tried to simplify sentence structure in a number of places. In short, we have tried to respond to what we heard from all of you—both students and instructors (and yes, we *do* hear from students)—to keep this book engaging and accessible.

A Personal Note to the Instructor

We probably share many of the same reasons for choosing sociology as our careers. Our students also share these reasons for finding sociology a fascinating and useful subject: learning about the social world from a new perspective; working with people and groups; developing a range of knowledge, inquiry, and interpersonal skills; and learning the broad and interesting subject matter of sociology, from small groups to societies. In this book, we try to share our own enthusiasm for the subject with students. The following explains what we believe to be unique features of this book and some of our goals and methods for sharing sociology. We hope you share our ideas and find this book helps you meet your teaching and learning goals.

What Is Distinctive About This Book?

What is truly distinctive about this book? This is a text that tries to break the mold of the typical textbook synthesis, the cross between an encyclopedia and a dictionary. *Our Social World* is a unique course text that is *a coherent essay on the sociological imagination—understood globally*. We attempt to radically change the feel of the introductory book by emphasizing coherence, an integrating theme, and current knowledge about learning and teaching, but we also present much traditional content. Instructors will not have to throw out the well-honed syllabus and begin from scratch, but they can refocus each unit so it stresses understanding of micro-level personal troubles within the macro-level public issues framework. Indeed, in this book, we make clear that public issues must be understood as global in nature.

Here is a text that engages students. *They* say so! From class testing, we know that the writing style, the structure of chapters and sections, the "Thinking Sociologically" features, the wealth of examples, and other instructional aids help students stay focused, think about the material, and apply it to their lives. It neither bores them nor insults their intelligence. It focuses on deep learning rather than memorization. It develops sociological skills of analysis rather than emphasizing memorization of vocabulary. Key concepts and terms are introduced but only in the service of a larger focus on the sociological imagination. The text is both personal and global. It speaks to sociology as a science as well as addressing public or applied aspects of sociology. It has a theme that provides integration of topics as it introduces the discipline. This text is an analytical essay, not a disconnected encyclopedia.

As one of our reviewers noted,

> Unlike most textbooks I have read, the breadth and depth of coverage in this one is very impressive. It challenges the student with college-level reading. Too many textbooks seem to write on a high-school level and give only passing treatment to most of the topics, writing in nugget-sized blocks. More than a single definition and a few sentences of support, the text forces the student deep into the topics covered and challenges them to see interconnections.

Normally, the global-perspective angle within textbooks, which seemed to grow in popularity in the mid- to late 1990s, was implemented by using brief and exotic examples to show differences between societies—a purely comparative approach rather than a globalization treatment. They gave, and still give to a large extent, a token nod to diversity. This textbook, however, forces the student to take a broader look at similarities and differences in social institutions around the world, and structures and processes operating in all cultures and societies.

So our focus in this book is on deep learning, especially expansion of students' ability to role-take or "perspective-take." Deep learning goes beyond the content of concepts and terms and cultivates the habits of thinking that allow one to think critically. Being able to see things from the perspective of others is essential to doing sociology, but it is also indispensible to seeing weaknesses in various theories or recognizing blind spots in a point of view. Using the sociological imagination is one dimension of role-taking because it requires a step back from the typical micro-level understanding of life's events and fosters a new comprehension of how meso- and macro-level forces—even global ones—can shape the individual's life. Enhancement of role-taking ability is at the core of this book because it is a *prerequisite* for deep learning in sociology, and it is the core competency needed to *do* sociology. One cannot do sociology unless one can see things from various positions on the social landscape.

This may sound daunting for some student audiences, but we have found that instructors at every kind of institution have had great success with the book because of the writing style and instructional tools used throughout. We have made some strategic decisions based on these principles of learning and teaching. We have focused much of the book on higher-order thinking skills rather than memorization and regurgitation. We want students to learn to think sociologically: to apply, analyze, synthesize, evaluate, and comprehend the interconnections of the world through a globally informed sociological imagination. However, we think it is also essential to do this with an understanding of how students learn.

Many introductory-level books offer several theories and then provide a critique of the theory. The idea is to teach critical thinking. We have purposefully refrained from extensive critique of theory (although some does occur) for several reasons. First, providing critique to beginning-level students does not really teach critical thinking. It trains them to memorize someone else's critique. Furthermore, it simply confuses many of them, leaving students with the feeling that sociology is really just contradictory ideas, and the discipline really does not have anything firm to offer. Teaching critical thinking needs to be done in stages, and it needs to take into account the building steps that occur before effective critique is possible. That is why we focus on the concept of deep learning. We are working toward building the foundations that are necessary for sophisticated critical thought at upper levels in the curriculum.

Therefore, in this beginning-level text, we have attempted to focus on a central higher-order or deep learning skill—synthesis. Undergraduate students need to grasp this before they can fully engage in evaluation. Deep learning involves understanding of complexity, and some aspects of complexity need to be taught at advanced levels. While students at the introductory level are often capable of synthesis, complex evaluation requires some foundational skills. Thus, we offer contrasting theories in this text, and rather than telling what is wrong with each one, we encourage students through "Thinking Sociologically" features to analyze the use of each and to focus on honing synthesis and comparison skills.

Finally, research tells us that learning becomes embedded in memory and becomes long-lasting only if it is related to something that learners already know. If they memorize terms but have no unifying framework to which they can attach those ideas, the memory will not last until the end of the course, let alone until the next higher-level course. In this text, each chapter is tied to the social world model that is core to sociological thinking. At the end of a course using this book, we believe that students will be able to explain coherently what sociology is and construct an effective essay about what they have learned from the course as a whole. Learning to develop and defend a thesis, with supporting logic and evidence, is another component of deep learning. A text that is mostly a dictionary does not enhance that kind of cognitive skill.

Organization and Coverage

Reminiscent of some packaged international tours, in which the travelers figure that "it is Day 7, so this must be Paris," many introductory courses seem to operate on the principle that it is Week 4 so this must be deviance week. Students do not sense any integration, and at the end of the course, they have trouble remembering specific topics. This book is different. A major goal of the book is to show the integration between topics in sociology and between parts of the social world. The idea is for students to grasp the concept of the interrelated world. A change in one part of the social world affects all others, sometimes in ways that are mutually supportive and sometimes in ways that create intense conflict.

Although the topics are familiar, the textbook is organized around levels of analysis, explained through the social world model. This perspective leads naturally to a comparative approach and discussions of diversity and inequality.

Each chapter represents a part of the social world structure (society, organizations and groups, and institutions) or a process in the social world (socialization, stratification, and change). Chapter order and links between chapters clarify this idea. Part I (Chapters 1 and 2) introduces the student to the sociological perspective and tools of the sociologist: theory and methods. Part II examines "Social Structure, Processes, and Control," exploring especially processes such as socialization, interaction, networks, and the *rationalization* of society. Part III covers the core issue of inequality in society, with emphasis on class, race or ethnicity, and gender. Part IV turns to the structural dimensions of society, as represented in institutions. Rather than trying to be all-encompassing, we examine family, education, religion, politics, economics, and medicine to help students understand how structures affect their lives. We do not cover sports, science, mass media, or the military in separate chapters, but aspects of emerging institutions are woven into many chapters. It was a painful decision to leave any institution out, but attention to length and cost required hard choices. Part V turns to social dynamics: how societies change. Population patterns, urbanization and environmental issues, social movements, technology, and other aspects of change are included.

As instructors and authors, we value books that provide students with a well-rounded overview of approaches to the field. Therefore, this book takes an eclectic theoretical approach, drawing on the best insights of various theories and stressing that multiple perspectives enrich our understanding. We give attention to most major theoretical perspectives in sociology: structural-functional and conflict theories at the meso and macro levels of analysis and symbolic interaction and rational choice theories at the micro to meso levels of analysis. Feminist, postmodern, and ecological theories are discussed where relevant to specific topics. Each of these is integrated into the broad social world model, which stresses development of a sociological imagination.

The book includes 16 chapters plus additional online materials, written to fit into a semester or quarter system. It allows instructors to use the chapters in order, or to alter the order, because each chapter is tied into others through the social world model. We strongly recommend that Chapter 1 be used early in the course because it introduces the integrating model and explains the theme. Also, if any institutions chapters are used, the four-page section opener on "Institutions" may be useful to include as well. Otherwise, the book has been designed for flexible use. Instructors may also want to supplement the core book with other materials, such as those suggested on the Instructor Teaching Site. Each chapter, for example, has an online exercise that helps students grasp the practical, public implications of sociology. While covering all the key topics in introductory sociology, the cost and size of a midsized book allows for this flexibility. Indeed, for a colorful introductory-level text, the cost of this book is remarkably low—roughly half the cost of some other very popular introductory texts.

A Unique Program Supporting Teaching of Sociology

There is one more way in which *Our Social World* has been unique among introductory sociology textbooks. In 2007, we teamed with SAGE to start a new program to benefit the entire discipline. Using royalties from *Our Social World,* there is a new awards program called the SAGE Teaching Innovations and Professional Development Awards. It is designed to prepare a new generation of scholars within the teaching movement in sociology. People in their early career stages (graduate students, assistant professors, newer PhDs) can be reimbursed $500 each for expenses entailed while attending the daylong American Sociological Association (ASA) Section on Teaching and Learning's preconference workshop. The workshop is the day before ASA meetings. In 2007, 13 young scholars—graduate students or untenured faculty members—received this award and benefited from an extraordinary workshop on learning and teaching. Subsequently joined by 23 other SAGE authors who support this program from textbook royalties, a total of 152 young scholars have been beneficiaries as of 2013. We are pleased to have had a hand in initiating and continuing to support this program.

We hope you find this book engaging. If you have questions or comments, please contact us.

Jeanne H. Ballantine
jeanne.ballantine@wright.edu

Keith A. Roberts
robertsk@hanover.edu

Acknowledgments

Knowledge is improved through careful, systematic, and constructive criticism. The same is true of all writing. This book is of much greater quality because we had such outstanding critics and reviewers. We, therefore, wish to honor and recognize the outstanding scholars who served in this capacity. These scholars are listed on this page and the next.

We also had people who served in a variety of other capacities: drafting language for us for special features, doing library and Internet research to find the most recent facts and figures, and reading or critiquing early manuscripts. These contributors include Khanh Nguyen, Kate Ballantine, Kelly Joyce, Justin Roberts, Kent Roberts, Susan Schultheis, and Vanessa M. Simpson. Authors of short sections within the book include Kevin Bales, Helen Berger, Jeremiah Castle, Mary Gatta, Susan Guarino-Ghezzi, Kirk Hadaway, Thomas Horejes, Melanie Hughes, Kichiro Iwamoto, David Kirk, Kathleen Korgan, Alan McEvoy, Laura McCloud, Ruth Meizen-Dick, Wendy Ng, Amy Orr, Robert Pellerin, Elise Roberts, Susan St. John, David Stadden, Brent Staples, Jay Weinstein, and five students from William Paterson University: Donna Yang, Christian Agurto, Michelle Benavides, Brianne Glogowski, Deziree Martinez, and Michele Van Hook. Scholars who helped with early drafts of some chapters include James W. Burfiend, Timothy Buzzell, Dora Lodwick, and Gregory Weiss. The religion chapter has some new approaches to denominationalism and to church polity, and David Yamane drafted early versions of much of that. Still, the most important contributor to this edition was Kathleen Korgan. She helped revise the discussion of public and applied sociology, wrote or found authors for "Sociologists in Action" features (many from her coauthored books, *Sociologists in Action* and *The Engaged Sociologist*), revised and updated "Contributing to Our Social World," wrote the discussion questions at the end of each chapter, and designed exercises that are online and involve students in thinking about and even doing public sociology.

Both of us are experienced authors, and we have worked with some excellent people at other publishing houses. However, the team at SAGE Publications was truly exceptional in support, thoroughness, and commitment to this project. Our planning meetings have been fun, intelligent, and provocative. Jerry Westby has been a sustaining member of the team as executive editor. Dave Repetto stepped into the senior acquisitions editor role seamlessly and effectively and has been a great support to us. Other folks who have meant so much to the quality production of this book include Lauren Johnson, editorial assistant; Brittany Bauhaus, production editor; Melinda Masson, copy editor extraordinaire; Sheri Gilbert, permissions editor; Erica DeLuca, senior marketing manager; Claudia Hoffman, managing editor; Scott Hooper, manufacturing manager; Ravi Balasuriya, art director; Steven Martin, vice president—production; Michele Sordi, vice president and editorial director—books acquisitions; David Horwitz, vice president—sales; and Blaise Simqu, president and chief executive officer. We have become friends and colleagues with the staff at SAGE Publications. They are all greatly appreciated.

Thanks to the following reviewers:

Sabrina Alimahomed, *University of California at Riverside*

Richard Ball, *Ferris State University*

Fred Beck, *Illinois State University*

David L. Briscoe, *University of Arkansas at Little Rock*

James A. Crone, *Hanover College*

Jamie M. Dolan, *Carroll College (MT)*

Obi N. I. Ebbe, *The University of Tennessee at Chattanooga*

Lance Erickson, *Brigham Young University*

Stephanie Funk, *Hanover College*

Loyd R. Ganey, Jr., *Western International University*

Mary Grigsby, *University of Missouri at Columbia*

Chris Hausmann, *University of Notre Dame*

Todd A. Hechtman, *Eastern Washington University*

Keith Kerr, *Blinn College*

Elaine Leeder, *Sonoma State University*

Jason J. Leiker, *Utah State University*

Stephen Lilley, *Sacred Heart University*
David A. Lopez, *California State University at Northridge*
Akbar Madhi, *Ohio Wesleyan University*
Gerardo Marti, *Davidson College*
Laura McCloud, *The Ohio State University*
Meeta Mehrotra, *Roanoke College*
Melinda S. Miceli, *University of Hartford*
Leah A. Moore, *University of Central Florida*
Katy Pinto, *California State University at Dominguez Hills*
R. Marlene Powell, *University of North Carolina at Pembroke*
Suzanne Prescott, *Central New Mexico Community College*
Olga Rowe, *Oregon State University*
Paulina Ruf, *Lenoir-Rhyne University*
Sarah Samblanet, *Kent State University*
Martha L. Shockey-Eckles, *Saint Louis University*
Toni Sims, *University of Louisiana at Lafayette*
Terry L. Smith, *Harding University*
Frank S. Stanford, *Blinn College*
Tracey Steele, *Wright State University*
Rachel Stehle, *Cuyahoga Community College*
Amy Stone, *Trinity University*
John Stone, *Boston University*
Stephen Sweet, *Ithaca College*
Ruth Thompson-Miller, *Texas A&M University*
Tim Ulrich, *Seattle Pacific University*
Thomas L. VanValey, *Western Michigan University*
Connie Veldink, *Everett Community College*
Chaim I. Waxman, *Rutgers University*
Debra Welkley, *California State University at Sacramento*
Debra Wetcher-Hendricks, *Moravian College*
Deborah J. White, *Collin County Community College*
Jake B. Wilson, *University of California at Riverside*
Laurie Winder, *Western Washington University*
Robert Wonser, *College of the Canyons*
Luis Zanartu, *Sacramento City College*
John Zipp, *University of Akron*

PART I

Understanding Our Social World

The Scientific Study of Society

Why would anyone want to study relationships with friends and family, how groups work, and where societies fit into the global system? What can we learn from scientifically studying our everyday lives? What exactly does it mean to see the world sociologically? Can sociology make our lives any better as the study of biology or chemistry does through medical advances and medications?

Those are some of the questions we hope to answer as we take a trip to a deeper level of understanding of ourselves and our social world. The first chapter of this book helps answer two questions: What is sociology, and why study it? Like your sociology professor, this book will argue that sociology is valuable because it gives us new perspectives on our personal and professional lives and because sociological insights and skills can help all of us make the world a better place. It is relevant to everything we do—enhancing our competence and our quality of life.

The second chapter addresses how sociology began and how sociologists know what they know. When sociologists make a statement about the social world, how do they know it is true? What perspective or lens might sociologists employ to make sense of their information? For example, how do sociologists know that education does not treat all children equally? Further, what can be done about it? What evidence would be considered reliable, valid, dependable, and persuasive? As we study sociology, we consider how we interact with each other; why we join groups and organizations; why some people are richer than others; why some people commit crimes; how race, class, and gender influence our positions in the social world; and many other aspects of our social world.

By the time you finish reading the first two chapters, you should have an initial understanding of what sociology is, how it can help you understand your social world, why the field is worth taking your time to explore, and how sociologists know what they know. We invite you to take a seat and come on a trip to see our social world through the fascinating lens of sociology.

CHAPTER 1

Sociology

A Unique Way to View the World

Sociology involves a transformation in the way one sees the world—learning to recognize the complex connections between our intimate personal lives, large organizations, national structures, and global events.

Our Social World Model

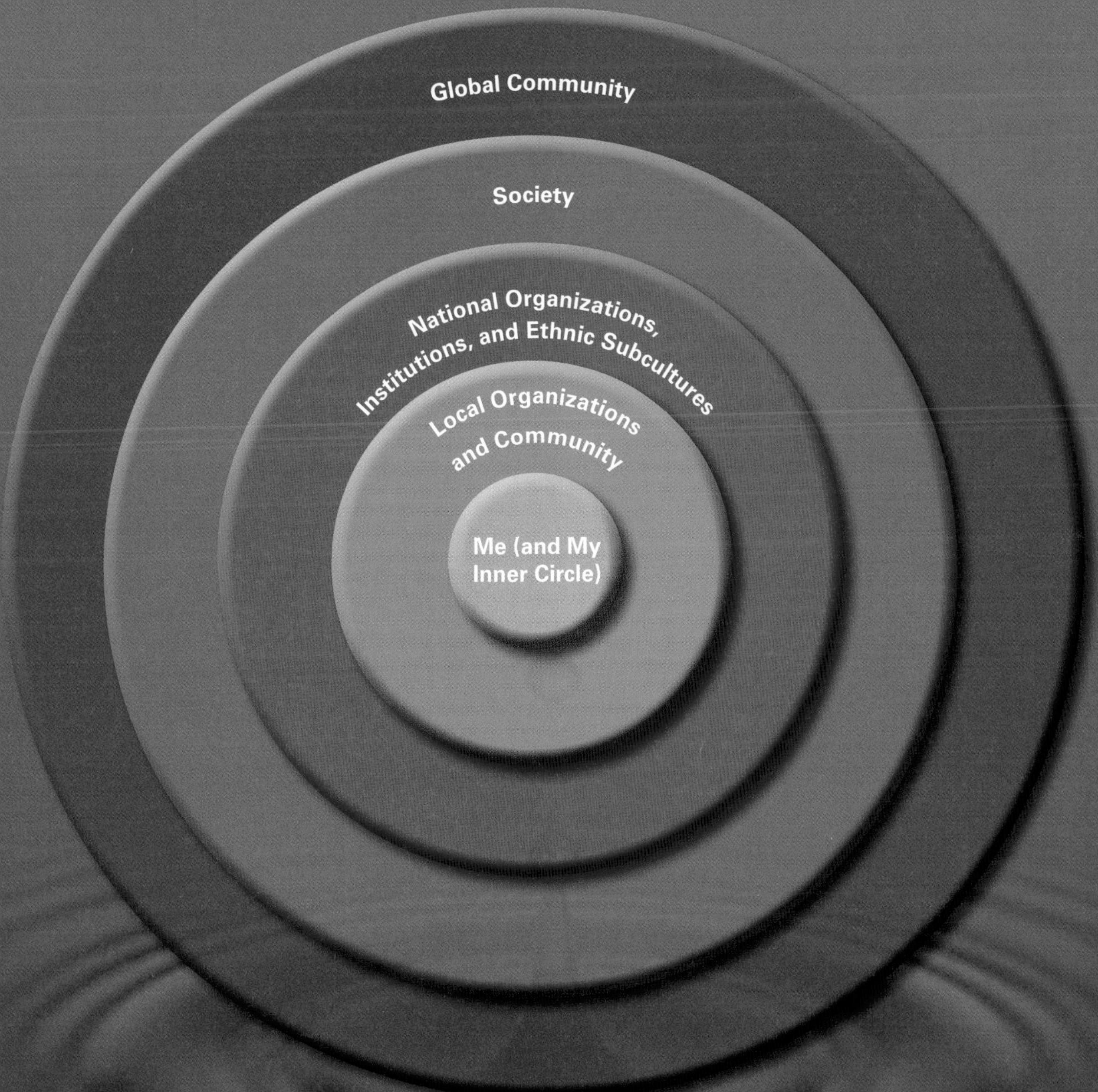

This model illustrates a core idea carried throughout the book—the way in which your own life is shaped by your family, community, society, and world, and how you influence them in return. Understanding this model can make you more aware of your social world and a more knowledgeable and effective person.

Think About It	
Micro: Self and Inner Circle	How can sociology help me understand my own life and my sense of self?
Local Community	How can sociology help me be a more effective employee and citizen in my community?
Meso: National Institutions; Complex Organizations; Ethnic Groups	How do sociologists help us understand and even improve our lives in families, classrooms, and health care organizations?
Macro: National Society	How do national loyalty and national policies affect my life?
Macro: Global Community	How might global events affect my life?

What's coming in this chapter?

"It may win the prize for the strangest place to get a back massage," but according to a recent scientific article, twins do a good deal of it in the womb (Weaver 2010). Scientists studied the movement of five pairs of twin fetuses using ultrasonography, a technique that visualizes internal body structures, and found that by the fourth month of gestation, twin fetuses begin reaching for their "womb-mates," and by 18 weeks, they spend more time touching their neighbors than themselves or the walls of the uterus. (Fetuses that have single womb occupancy also tend to touch the walls of the uterus a good deal to make contact with the mother.) Nearly 30% of the movements of twins are directed toward their companions. Movements toward the partner—such as stroking the back or the head—are more sustained and more precise than movements toward themselves—touching their own mouths or other facial features. As Castiello et al. (2010) put it, they're "wired to be social." In short, humans are innately social creatures.

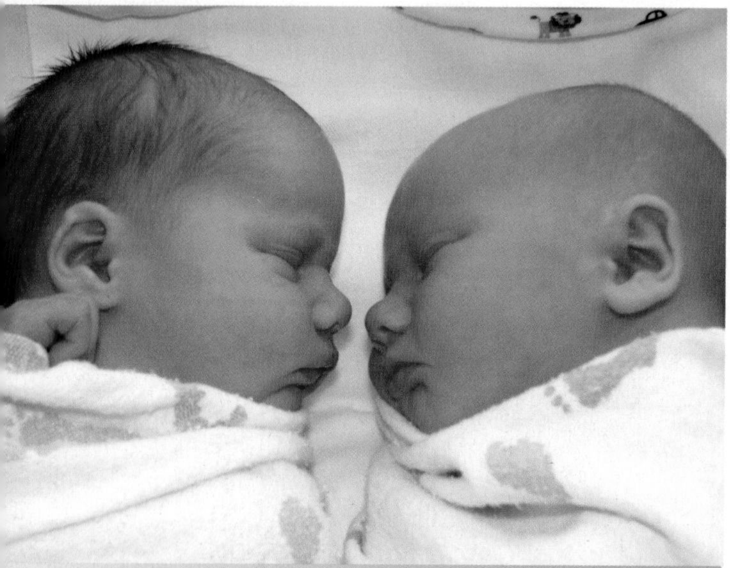

Within hours of their birth in October 2010, Jackson and Audrey Pietrykowski became highly fussy if the nurses tried to put them in separate bassinets. At one point shortly after birth they were both put in a warmer, and Jackson cried until he found Audrey, proceeding to intertwine his arms and legs with hers. Twins, like all humans, are hardwired to be social and in relationships with others.

Strange as it may seem, the social world is not merely something that exists outside us. As the story of the twins illustrates, the social world is also something we carry inside us. We are part of it, we reflect on it, and we are influenced by it, even when we are alone. The patterns of the social world engulf us in ways both subtle and obvious, with profound implications for how we create order and meaning in our lives. The point is that we need others—and that is where sociology enters.

Sometimes it takes a dramatic and shocking event for us to realize just how deeply embedded we are in our relationships in the social world that we take for granted. "It couldn't happen in the United States," read typical world newspaper accounts. "This is something you see in the Middle East, Central Africa, and other war-torn areas. . . . It's hard to imagine this happening in the economic center of the United States." Yet on September 11, 2001, shortly after 9 a.m., a commercial airliner crashed into a New York City skyscraper, followed a short while later by another pummeling into the paired tower, causing this mighty symbol of financial wealth—the World Trade Center—to collapse. After the dust settled and the rescue crews finished their gruesome work, nearly 3,000 people were dead or unaccounted for. The world as we knew it changed forever that day. This event taught U.S. citizens how integrally connected they are with the international community. More than a decade later, we still wonder why the attacks occurred.

Following the events of 9/11, the United States launched its highly publicized War on Terror, and many terrorist strongholds and training camps became targets for destruction. Still, troubling questions remain unanswered. Why did this extremist act occur? How can such actions be deterred in the future? How do the survivors recover from such a horrific event? Why was this event so completely disorienting to Americans and to the world community?

Such terrorist acts horrify people because they are unpredicted and unexpected in a normally predictable world. They violate the rules that foster our connections to one another. They also bring attention to the discontent and disconnectedness that lie under the surface in many societies—discontent that can come to the surface and express itself in hateful violence. Such discontent and hostility are likely to continue until the root causes are addressed.

Terrorist acts represent a rejection of the modern civil society we know. The terrorists themselves see their acts as justifiable, as a way they can strike out against injustices and threats to their way of life—but more on that later. Few outside the terrorists' inner circle understand their thinking and behavior. When terrorist acts occur, we struggle to fit such events into our mental picture of a just, safe, comfortable, and predictable social world. The events of 9/11 forced U.S. citizens to realize that although they may see a great diversity among themselves, people in other parts of the world view Americans as all the same. U.S. citizens are despised by some for what they represent—consumerism, individualism, freedom of religion, and tolerance of other views. The United States is a world power, yet its values challenge and threaten the views of many people around the world. For many U.S. citizens, a sense of loyalty to the nation was deeply stirred by the events of 9/11. Patriotism abounded. So, in fact, the nation's people became more connected as a reaction to an act against the common identity of U.S. citizens.

Most of the time, we live with social patterns that we take for granted as routine, ordinary, and expected. These

These signs were put up right after the 9/11 attacks on the World Trade Center by people looking for missing loved ones. The experience of New Yorkers was alarm, fear, grief, and confusion—precisely the emotions that the terrorists sought to create. Terrorism disrupts normal social life and daily routines and undermines security. It provides an effective tool for those disaffected people with no power or way of lashing out at perceived threats and injustice.

social patterns are essential in social groups. Unlike our motivations or drives, social expectations come from those around us and guide (or constrain) our behaviors and thoughts. Without shared expectations between humans about proper patterns of behavior, life would be chaotic. Our social interactions require some basic rules, and these rules create routine and safe normalcy in everyday interaction. It would be strange if someone broke the expected patterns. The point is that for the people in and around the World Trade Center on 9/11, the social rules governing everyday life broke down that awful day. How could anyone live in society if there were no rules, and can a society exist without rules?

This chapter examines the social ties that make up our social world, as well as sociology's focus on those connections. We will learn what sociology is and why it is valuable to study; how sociologists view the social world and what they do; how studying sociology can help us in our everyday life; and how the social world model is used to understand the social world and as a framework for the topics we will study throughout this book.

What Is Sociology?

According to the American Sociological Association (2009),

> ***Sociology*** *is the study of social life, social change, and the social causes and consequences of human behavior.* Sociologists investigate the structure of groups, organizations, and societies and how people interact within these contexts. Since all human behavior is social, the subject matter of sociology ranges from the intimate family to the hostile mob; from organized crime to religious traditions; from the divisions of race, gender, and social class to the shared beliefs of a common culture. (p. 5)

Sociologists conduct scientific research on social relationships and problems that range from tiny groups of two people to national societies and global social networks.

Unlike the discipline of psychology, which focuses on the attributes, motivations, and behaviors of individuals, sociology tends to focus on group patterns. Whereas a psychologist might try to explain behavior by examining the personality traits of individuals, a sociologist would examine the positions of different people within the group and how these positions influence what individuals do. Sociologists seek to analyze and explain why people interact with others and belong to groups, how groups work, who has power and who does not, how decisions are made, and how groups deal with conflict and change. From the early beginnings of sociology (discussed in Chapter 2), sociologists have asked questions about the rules that govern group behavior; about the causes of social problems, such as child abuse, crime, or poverty; and about why nations declare war and kill each other's citizens.

Two-person interactions—*dyads*—are the smallest units sociologists study. Examples of dyads include roommates discussing their classes, a professor and student going over an assignment, a husband and wife negotiating their budget, and two children playing. Next in size are small groups consisting of three or more interacting people—a family, a neighborhood or peer group, a classroom, a work group, or a street gang where most people know each other. Then come increasingly larger groups—organizations such as sports or scouting clubs, neighborhood associations, and local religious congregations. Among the largest groups contained within nations are ethnic groups and national organizations or institutions, such as the auto industry, the Republican and Democratic national political parties, and national religious organizations like the Presbyterian Church (USA). Nations themselves are still larger and can sometimes involve hundreds of millions of people. In the past several decades, social scientists have also pointed to globalization, the process by which the entire world is becoming a single interdependent entity. Of particular interest to sociologists is how these various groups are organized, how they function, why they conflict, and how they influence one another.

An athletic team teaches members to interact with teammates, cooperate with the group to succeed, develop awareness of the power of others, and deal with conflict. Here children experience ordered interaction in the competitive environment of a football game. What values, skills, attitudes, and assumptions about life and social interaction do you think these young boys are learning?

Thinking Sociologically

Identify several dyads, small groups, and large organizations to which you belong. Did you choose to belong, or were you born into membership in these groups? How does each group influence who you are and the decisions you make?

Ideas Underlying Sociology

Most people share certain ideas with others that they just take for granted: For example, heavy drinking before driving might cause an automobile accident. Sociologists also share several ideas that they take for granted about the social world. These ideas about humans and social life are supported by considerable evidence, and they are no longer matters of debate or controversy—they are assumed at this point to be true. Understanding these core assumptions helps us see how sociologists approach the study of people in groups. The idea that one action can cause something else is a core idea in all science.

People are social by nature. This means that humans seek contact with other humans, interact with one another, and influence and are influenced by the behaviors of others. Furthermore, humans need groups to survive. Although a few individuals may become socially isolated as adults, they could not have reached adulthood without sustained interactions with others. The central point here is that we become who we are because other people and groups constantly influence us.

People live much of their lives belonging to social groups. It is in social groups that we interact with family, friends, and work groups; learn to share goals and to cooperate with others in our groups; develop identities that are influenced by our group affiliations; obtain power over others—or are powerless; and have conflicts with others over resources we all want. Our individual beliefs and behaviors, our experiences, our observations, and the problems we face are derived from connections to our social groups.

Interaction between the individual and the group is a two-way process in which each influences the other. In our family or on a sports team, we can influence the shape and direction of our group, just as the group provides the rules and decides the expected behaviors for individuals.

Recurrent social patterns, ordered behavior, shared expectations, and common understandings among people characterize groups. Consider the earlier example of the chaos created by 9/11. This event was so troubling because it was unexpected and out of the normal range of expectations. Normally, a degree of continuity and recurrent behavior is present in human interactions, whether in small groups, large organizations, or society.

The processes of conflict and change are natural and inevitable features of groups and societies. No group can remain unchanged and hope to perpetuate itself. To survive, groups must adapt to changes in the social and physical environment, yet rapid change often comes at a price. It can lead to conflict within a society—between traditional and new ideas and between groups that have vested interests in particular ways of doing things. Rapid change can give rise to protest activities; changing in a controversial direction or failing to change fast enough can spark conflict, including revolution. The Arab Spring demonstrations illustrate the desire for rapid change of long-standing dictatorships, springing from citizens' discontent with corrupt or authoritarian rule. The problem is finding acceptable replacement governments to take over what has been overthrown.

The above ideas underlying sociology will be relevant in each of the topics we discuss. As you read this book, keep in mind these basic ideas that form the foundation of sociological analysis: People are social; they live and carry out activities largely in groups; interaction influences both individual and group behavior; people share common behavior patterns and expectations; and processes such as change and conflict are always present. Thus, in several important ways, sociological understandings provide new lenses for looking at our social world.

Sociology Versus Common Sense

Common sense refers to *ideas that are so completely taken for granted that they have never been seriously questioned and seem to be sensible to any reasonable person.* We all use common sense, based on our personal experiences, to process information and decide how to act. Although all of us base decisions on common sense, that does not mean it is always accurate. The difference between common sense and sociology is that sociologists use scientific methods to test the accuracy of commonsense beliefs and ideas about human behavior and the social world.

These are examples of maxims that people use as "absolute" guides to live by. They become substitutes for real analysis of situations. The fact is that all of them are accurate *at some times, some places, about some things.* Sociological thinking and analysis are about studying the conditions in which these maxims hold and do not hold (Eitzen and Zinn n.d.).

Common sense sayings

Birds of a feather flock together	←→	Opposites attract
Absence makes the heart grow fonder	←→	Out of sight, out of mind
Look before you leap	←→	He who hesitates is lost
You can't teach an old dog new tricks	←→	It's never to late to learn
Above all to thine own self be true	←→	When in Rome, do as the Romans do
Variety is the spice of life	←→	Never change horses in midstream
Two heads are better than one	←→	If you want something done right, do it yourself
You can't tell a book by its cover	←→	The clothes make the man
Haste makes waste	←→	Strike while the iron is hot
There's no place like home	←→	The grass is always greener on the other side

A Palestinian and an Israeli work together and cooperate. Although their governments are hostile to one another, the people themselves often have very different sentiments toward those on the other side of the divide.

Thinking Sociologically

What are some other commonsense sayings that you know that contradict one another? Also, take a look at the commonsense quiz online at www.pineforge.com/ballantine4e. Do some of the answers surprise you? If so, why?

Would our commonsense notions about the social world be reinforced or rejected if examined with scientifically gathered information? Some commonsense notions (above) actually contradict each other, yet all guide behavior at some time.

Human tragedy can result from false commonsense beliefs. For example, the Nazi genocide and the existence of slavery both have their roots in false beliefs about racial superiority. Often citizens interpret news stories through a "common sense" lens rather than digging deeper for better analysis.

Our beliefs and assumptions about the social world often are based on our experiences, our judgments about what our friends and family believe, what we have read or viewed on television, and common stereotypes (rigid beliefs, often untested and unfounded) about a group or a category of people. At times our views result in hostility toward others, but they can also result in our desire to understand and cooperate with those who hold different sentiments.

Social Science Findings and Commonsense Beliefs

Sometimes we hold commonsense beliefs that are a part of common knowledge. However, sometimes these beliefs are disproven by research. Here are some examples:

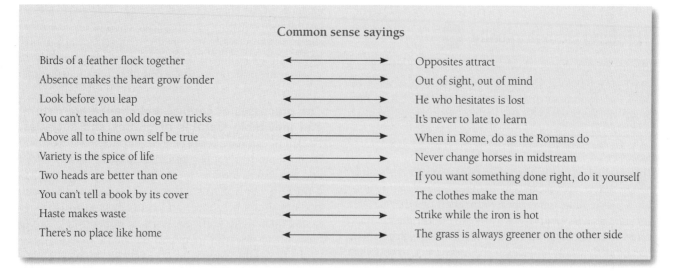

Belief: Most of the differences in the behaviors of women and men are based on "human nature"; men and women are just plain different from each other. Research shows that biological factors certainly play a part in the behaviors of men and women, but the culture (beliefs, values, rules, and way of life) that people learn as they grow up determines who does what and how biological tendencies are played out. A unique example illustrates this: In the nomadic Wodaabe tribe in Africa, women do most of the heavy work, while men adorn themselves with makeup, sip tea, and gossip (Beckwith 1983; Loftsdottir 2004). Each year the group holds a festival where men show their white teeth and the whites of their eyes to attract a marriage partner. Such dramatic variations in the behavior of men and women around the world are so great that it is impossible to attribute behavior to biology or human nature alone.

The Wodaabe society in Niger in sub-Saharan Africa illustrates that our notions of masculinity and femininity—which common sense tells us are innate and universal—are actually socially defined, variable, and learned. Wodaabe men are known for their heavy use of makeup to be attractive to women.

Belief: As developing countries modernize, the lives of their female citizens improve. This is generally false. In fact, the status of women in many developed and developing countries is getting worse. Women make up roughly 51% of the more than 7 billion people and account for two-thirds of the world's hours at work (National Geographic Society 2011). However, in no country for which data are available do they earn what men earn, and sometimes the figures show women earning less than 50% of men's earnings for similar work. Women hold many unpaid jobs in agriculture, and they own only 1% of the world's property. Furthermore, of the world's 793 million illiterate adults, two thirds are women (World Factbook 2012). Only 79.2% of the world's women over age 15 can read and write compared with 88.3% of men. Illiteracy rates for women in South Asia, sub-Saharan Africa, and the Middle East are the highest in the world, implying lack of access to education. These are only a few examples of the continuing poor status of women in many countries (World Factbook 2012; youthxchange 2007). The "common sense" idea is clearly wrong.

Belief: Given the high divorce rates in the United States and Canada, marriages are in serious trouble. The highest divorce rates in the United States are found among those below the average on education and who live in poverty. Those who are middle class or higher have extremely stable marriages (Luscombe 2010; Pew Research Center 2010). Although the overall divorce rate in North America is high, the rate of marriage is also one of the highest in the world. Moreover, even those who have been divorced tend to remarry. Despite talk about the decline of marriage and despite genuine concern about the high levels of marital failure, Americans now spend more years of their lives in marriage than at any other time in history. Divorce appears to be seen as rejection of a particular partnership rather than as a rejection of marriage itself (Coontz 2005, 2011; Wallerstein and Blakeslee 1996). The divorce rate reached a peak in the United States in 1982 and has declined modestly since that time (Newman and Grauerholz 2002).

As these examples illustrate, many of our commonsense beliefs are challenged by social scientific evidence. On examination, the social world is often more complex than our commonsense understanding of events, which is based on limited evidence. Throughout history, there are examples of beliefs that seemed obvious at one time but have been shown to be mistaken through scientific study. The point is that the discipline of sociology provides a method to assess the accuracy of our commonsense assumptions about the social world.

To improve the lives of individuals in our communities and in societies around the world, decision makers must rely on an accurate understanding of the society. Accurate information gleaned from sociological research can be the basis for more rational and just social policies—policies that better meet the needs of all groups in the social world. The sociological imagination, discussed below, helps us gain an understanding of social problems.

Thinking Sociologically

What are some of your commonsense beliefs about your new classmates? How did you develop these beliefs, and what evidence do you have to support these beliefs?

The commonsense *notion is that most children in the world, boys and girls, have equal access to education. Literacy is a major issue for societies around the globe. These Chinese children are learning to read, but in many developing countries, boys have more access to formal education than girls have; many children, especially girls, do not gain literacy.*

The Sociological Imagination

Events in our social world affect our individual lives. If we are unemployed or lack funds for our college education, we may say this is a personal problem. Yet, broader social issues are often at the root of our situation. The sociological perspective holds that we can best understand our personal experiences and problems by examining their broader social context—by looking at the big picture.

Individual problems (or private troubles) are rooted in social or public issues (what is happening in the social world outside one's personal control). C. Wright Mills (1959) called this *complex interactive relationship between micro-level individual experiences and macro-level public issues* the **sociological imagination**. For Mills, many personal experiences can and should be interpreted in the context of large-scale forces in the wider society. Consider, for example, someone you may know who has been laid off from a job. The personal trauma caused by being laid off is a common situation in today's economy due to the economic problems and high unemployment. The unemployed person often experiences feelings of inadequacy or lack of worth. This, in turn, may produce stress in a marriage or even result in divorce. These conditions not only are deeply troubling to the person most directly affected but also are related to wider political and economic forces in society. The unemployment may be due to unsound banking practices, to corporate downsizing, or to a corporation taking operations to another country where labor costs are cheaper and where there are fewer environmental regulations on companies. People may blame themselves or each other for personal troubles such as unemployment or a failed marriage, believing that they did not try hard enough. Often, they do not see the connection between their private lives and larger economic and social forces beyond their control. They fail to recognize the public issues that create private troubles.

Families also experience stress as partners have, over time, assumed increasing responsibility for their mate's and their children's emotional and physical needs. Until the second half of the 20th century, the community and the extended family unit—aunts, uncles, grandparents, and cousins—assumed more of that burden. Extended families continue to exist in countries where children settle near their parents, but in modern urban societies, both the sense of community and the connection to the extended family are greatly diminished. There are fewer intimate ties to call on for help and support. Divorce is a very personal condition for those affected, but it can be understood far more clearly when considered in conjunction with the broader social context of economics, urbanization, changing gender roles, lack of external support, and legislated family policies.

As we learn about sociology, we will come to understand how social forces shape individual lives, and this will help us understand aspects of everyday life we take for granted. In this book, we will investigate how group life influences our behaviors and interactions and why some individuals follow the rules of society and others do not. A major goal is to help us incorporate the sociological perspective into our way of understanding the social world and our place in it. Indeed, the notion of *sociological imagination*—connecting events from the global and national levels to the personal and intimate level of our own lives—is the core organizing theme of this book.

Thinking Sociologically

How does poverty, war, or an economic recession cause personal troubles for someone you know? Give examples of why is it inadequate to try to explain these personal troubles by examining only the personal characteristics of those affected.

Questions Sociologists Ask—and Don't Ask

Perhaps you have had late-night discussions over beers about the meaning of life, the existence of God, the ethical implications of stem cell research, the ethics of abortion, or the prettiest woman or coolest dude in the room—philosophical issues that sociologists, like other scientists, cannot answer. What sociologists *do* ask are questions about people in social groups and organizations—questions that can be studied scientifically. How people feel about the above issues can be determined (the percentage of people who approve of stem cell research, for example), but sociologists cannot say what are right and wrong answers to such value-driven, often controversial opinions.

Consider the following examples of questions sociologists might ask:

- *Who gets an abortion, why do they do so, and how does society as a whole view abortion?* These are matters of fact that a social scientist can explore. However, sociologists avoid making ethical judgments about whether abortion is sometimes acceptable or always wrong. The question about the morality of abortion is very important to many people, but it is based on philosophical or theological rationale and values, not on scientific analysis.
- *Who is the most beautiful or handsome person in the room?* Cultural standards of beauty affect individual popularity and social interaction, an issue that interests some social scientists. However, the sociologist would not judge which individuals are more or less attractive. Such questions are matters of aesthetics, a field of philosophy and art.
- *What are the circumstances around individuals becoming drunk and drunken behavior?* This question is often tied more to the social environment than to alcohol itself. The researcher does not make judgments about whether use of alcohol is good or bad, right or wrong, and avoids—as much as possible—opinions regarding responsibility or irresponsibility. The sociologist does, however, observe variations in the use of alcohol in social situations and the resulting behaviors. Note that a person might be very intoxicated at a fraternity party but will behave differently at a wedding reception, where the expectations for behavior are very different. An applied sociologist researching alcohol use on campus for a college or for a national fraternity may, following the research, offer advice based on that research about how to reduce the number of alcohol-related deaths or sexual assault incidents on college campuses (Sweet 2001).

What effect does holding certain ideas or adhering to certain ethical standards have on the behavior and attitudes of people? For example, are people more likely to obey rules if they believe that there are consequences for their actions or bad behavior in an afterlife? Sociologists can study whether an individual's beliefs influence her or his behavior. They focus on issues that can be studied objectively and scientifically—looking for causes or consequences.

Many sociologists carry out sociological research in order to impact society. They seek to understand society better so that they can help improve it. These sociologists fall under the umbrella of *public sociology*. Applied sociologists, public sociologists who carry out research to help organizations solve problems, agree with other sociologists that the research itself should be as objective as possible. After the research is completed, the applied sociologists might use the research findings to explore policy implications and make recommendations for change in an organization.

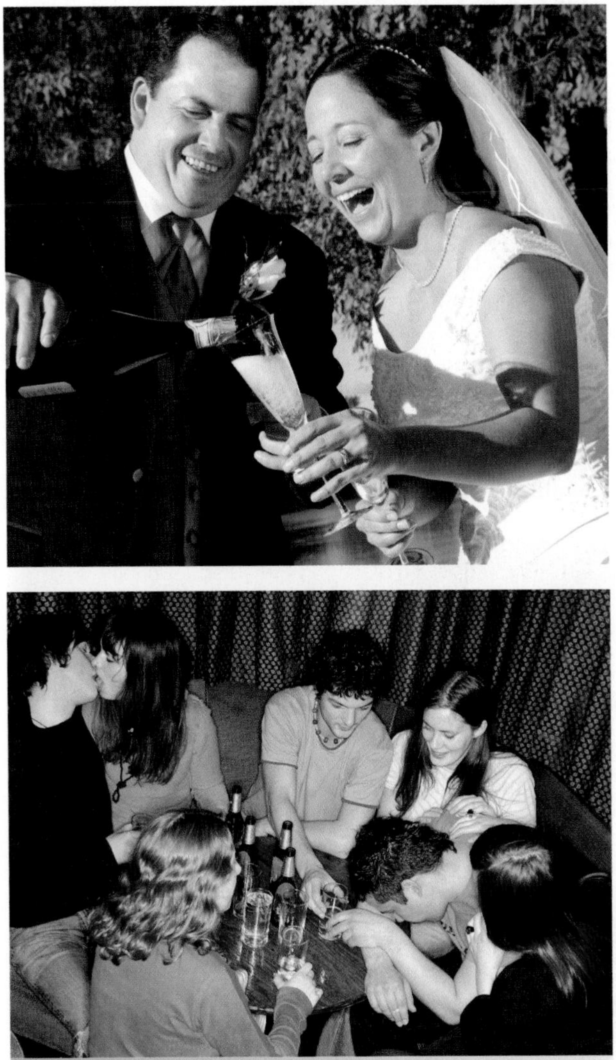

What is acceptable or unacceptable drinking behavior varies according to the social setting. Binge drinking, losing consciousness, vomiting, or engaging in sexual acts while drunk may be a source of storytelling at a college party but can be offensive at a wedding reception. Sociologists study different social settings and how the norms of acceptability vary in each, but they do not make judgments about those behaviors.

Sociologists learn techniques to avoid letting their personal opinions or values about issues influence their research designs, data gathering, and analysis. Still, complete objectivity is difficult at best, and what one chooses to study may be influenced by one's interests and concerns about injustice in society. The fact that sociologists know they will be held accountable by other scientists for the objectivity of their research is a major factor in encouraging them to be objective when they do their research.

Thinking Sociologically

Consider the information you have just read. What are some questions sociologists might ask about cohabitation or same-sex unions? What are some questions sociologists would not ask about these topics, at least while in their roles as researchers?

The Social Sciences: A Comparison

Not so long ago, our views of people and social relationships were based on stereotypes, intuition, superstitions, supernatural explanations, and traditions passed on from one generation to the next. Natural sciences first used the scientific method, a model later adopted by social sciences.

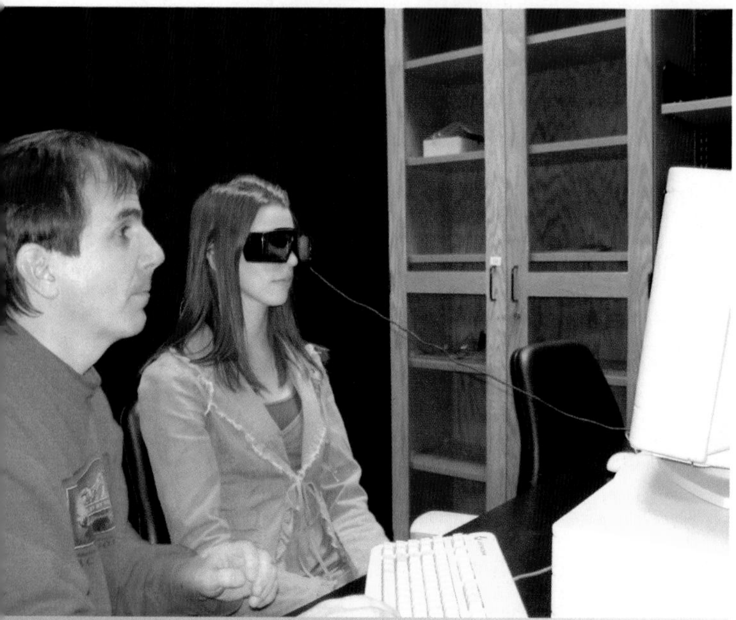

Psychology as a discipline tends to focus on individuals, including fields such as sensation, perception, memory, and thought processes. In this study, the researcher is using some equipment and a computer to measure how the eye and the brain work together to help create depth perception.

Social scientists, including anthropologists, psychologists, economists, cultural geographers, historians, and political scientists, apply the scientific method to study social relationships, to correct misleading and harmful misconceptions about human behaviors, and to guide policy decisions. Consider the following examples of specific studies various social scientists might conduct. This is followed by a brief description of the focus of sociology as a social science.

One anthropological study focusing on garbage studied what people discard to understand what kind of life they lead and foods they eat—their patterns of life. *Anthropology* is the study of humanity in its broadest context. It is closely related to sociology, and the two areas have common historical roots. There are four major subfields within anthropology: physical anthropology (which is related to biology), archaeology, linguistics, and cultural anthropology (sometimes called *ethnology*). This last field has the most in common with sociology. Cultural anthropologists study the culture, or way of life, of a society.

A psychologist wires research subjects to a machine that measures their physiological reaction to a violent film clip, then asks them questions about what they were feeling. *Psychology* is the study of individual behavior and mental processes (e.g., sensation, perception, memory, and thought processes). It differs from sociology in that it focuses on individuals rather than on groups, institutions, and societies. Although there are different branches of psychology, most psychologists are concerned with what motivates individual behavior, personality attributes, attitudes, beliefs, and perceptions. Psychologists also explore abnormal behavior, the mental disorders of individuals, and the stages of normal human development (Wallerstein 1996; Wallerstein and Blakeslee 2004).

A political scientist studies opinion poll results to predict who will win the next election, how various groups of people are likely to vote, or how elected officials will vote on proposed legislation. *Political science* is concerned with government systems and power—how they work, how they are organized, the forms of government, the relations between governments, who holds power and how they obtain it, how power is used, and who is politically active. Political science overlaps with sociology, particularly in the study of political theory and the nature and the uses of power.

An economist studies the banking system and market trends, trying to determine what will remedy the global recession. *Economists* analyze economic conditions and explore how people organize, produce, and distribute material goods. They are interested in supply and demand, inflation and taxes, prices and manufacturing output, labor organization, employment levels, and comparisons between industrial and nonindustrial nations.

What all these social sciences—sociology, anthropology, psychology, economics, political science, cultural geography, and history—have in common is that they study aspects of human behavior and social life. Social sciences share many common topics, methods, concepts, research findings, and theories, but each has a different focus or perspective on the social world. Each of these social sciences relates to topics studied by sociologists, but sociologists focus on human interaction, groups, and social structure, providing the broadest overview of the social world.

Thinking Sociologically

Consider other issues such as the condition of poverty in developing countries or homelessness in North America. What question(s) might different social sciences ask about these problems?

Why Study Sociology . . . and What Do Sociologists Do?

Why are some families close while others are estranged? Why do some groups work very productively while others are unproductive? Why are some people rich and others remain impoverished, even homeless? Why do some people engage in criminal behaviors while others conform rigidly to rules? Sociologists have the perspective and methods to search for a deeper understanding about human interaction than common sense can provide.

This unique perspective helps us be more effective as we carry out our roles as significant others, workers, friends, family members, and citizens. For example, an employee who has studied sociology may better understand how to work with groups and how the structure of the workplace affects individual behavior, how to approach problem solving, and how to collect and analyze data. Likewise, a schoolteacher trained in sociology may have a better understanding of classroom management, student motivation, the causes of poor student learning that have roots outside the school, and other variables that shape the professional life of teachers and academic success of students. Consider the example in the next "Sociology in Our Social World," on page 14 which explores how high school groups such as "jocks" and "burnouts" behave and why each high school clique's behavior might be quite logical in certain circumstances. "Burnouts and Jocks in a Public High School" explores a social environment very familiar to most of us.

Two ingredients are essential to the study of our social world: (1) a keen ability to observe what is happening in the social world and (2) a desire to find answers to the question of why it is happening. The value of sociology is that it affords us a unique perspective and provides methods to answer important questions about human interaction, group behavior, and social structure. The practical significance of the sociological perspective is that it

- fosters greater self-awareness, which can lead to opportunities to improve one's life;
- encourages a more complete understanding of social situations by looking beyond individual explanations to include group analyses of behavior;
- helps people understand and evaluate problems by enabling them to view the world systematically and objectively rather than in strictly emotional or personal terms;
- cultivates an understanding of the many diverse cultural perspectives and how cultural differences are related to behavioral patterns;
- provides a means to assess the impact of social policies;
- reveals the complexities of social life and provides methods of inquiry to study them; and
- provides useful skills in interpersonal relations, critical thinking, data collection and analysis, problem solving, and decision making.

What Sociologists Do

Your first encounter with a sociologist is probably in the classroom. About three quarters of sociologists work in higher education settings, teaching and doing research. However, sociologists are employed in a variety of other settings as well. Table 1.1 illustrates that a significant portion of sociologists work in business, government, and social

Table 1.1 **Where Sociologists Are Employed**

Places of Employment	*Percentage Employed*
College or university	75.5
Government (all positions)	7.1
Private, for-profit business	6.2
Not-for-profit public service organizations	7.6
Self-employed	0.4

Source: American Sociological Association (2006).

Sociology in Our Social World

Burnouts and Jocks in a Public High School

High schools are big organizations made up of smaller friendship networks and cliques. A careful examination can give us insight into the tensions that exist as the groups struggle for resources and power in the school.

In the high school studied by sociologist Penelope Eckert (1989), there were two familiar groups of students that exist in many high schools in North America: "burnouts" and "jocks." The burnouts defied the authorities, smoked in the restrooms, refused to use their lockers, made a public display of not eating in the school cafeteria, and wore their jackets all day. Their open and public defiance of authority infuriated the jocks—the college prep students who participated in choir, band, student council, and athletics and who held class offices. The burnouts were disgusted with the jocks. In their view, by constantly sucking up to the authorities, the jocks received special privileges, and by playing the goody-two-shoes role, they made life much more difficult for the burnouts.

Despite their animosity toward one another, the goal of both groups was to gain more autonomy from the adult authorities who constantly bossed students around. As the burnouts saw things, if the jocks would have even a slight bit of backbone and stand up for the dignity of students as adults, life would be better for everyone. The burnouts believed that school officials should earn their obedience—not just expect it because they were older or held a certain status. The burnouts maintained their dignity by affirming that they did not recognize bossy adults as authorities. Wearing coats all day was one way to emphasize the idea that "I'm just a visitor in this school."

The jocks, for their part, became irritated at the burnouts when the latter caused trouble and were belligerent with the authorities; then the administration would crack down on everyone, and no one had any freedom. The jocks found that if they did what the adults told them to do—at least while the adults were around—they got a lot more freedom. When the burnouts got defiant, however, the principal got mad and removed everyone's privileges.

Eckert found that the behavior of both groups was quite logical for their circumstances and ambitions. Expending energy as a class officer or participating in extracurricular activities is a rational behavior for college preparatory students because those leadership roles help students get into the colleges of their choice.

However, those activities do not help one get a better job in a town factory. In fact, hanging out at the bowling alley makes far more sense. For the burnouts, having friendship networks and acquaintances in the right places is more important to achieving their goals than a class office listed on their résumé.

Eckert's method of gathering information was effective in showing how the internal dynamics of schools—conflicts between student groups—were influenced by outside factors such as working- and upper-middle-class status. Recent research upholds Eckert's findings on the importance cliques play in shaping school behavior. Like Eckert, Bonnie Barber, Jacquelynne Eccles, and Margaret Stone (2001) followed various friendship cliques starting in 10th grade in a Michigan high school. The jocks in their study were the most integrated to mainstream society in adult life. The burnouts (or criminals, as they are labeled in Barber's research) were most likely to have been arrested or incarcerated, showing that the propensity to defy authority figures may carry on into adult life.

These studies show that sociological analysis can help us understand some of the ways in which connections between groups—regardless of whether they are in conflict or harmony—shape the perceptions, attitudes, and behaviors of people living in this complex social world.

service agencies (American Sociological Association 2006; Dotzler and Koppel 1999).

College graduates who seek employment immediately after college (without other graduate work) are most likely to find their first jobs in social services, administrative assistantships, or some sort of management position. The areas of first jobs of sociology majors are indicated in Figure 1.1. With a master's or a doctorate degree, graduates usually become college teachers, researchers, clinicians, and consultants.

Consider your professor. The duties of professors vary depending on the type of institution and the level of courses offered. In addition to teaching classes, activities include preparing for classes, preparing and grading exams and assignments, advising students, serving on committees, keeping abreast of new research in the field, and conducting and publishing research studies. This last "publish or perish" activity is deemed the most important activity for faculty in some universities.

Sociologists who work outside of academia, public and applied sociologists, use their knowledge and research skills to address the needs of businesses, nonprofit organizations, and government. For example, they often work in human resources departments and as consultants for businesses. In government jobs, they provide data such as population projections for education and health care planning. In social service agencies, such as police departments, they help address deviant behavior, and in health agencies, they may be concerned with doctor-patient interactions. Public and applied sociology are important aspects of the field, and some of the "Sociologists in Action" you will find featured throughout the book are applied sociologists. They provide examples of what one can do with a sociology degree. In addition, at the end of some chapters you will find a section discussing policy examples and implications related to that chapter topic.

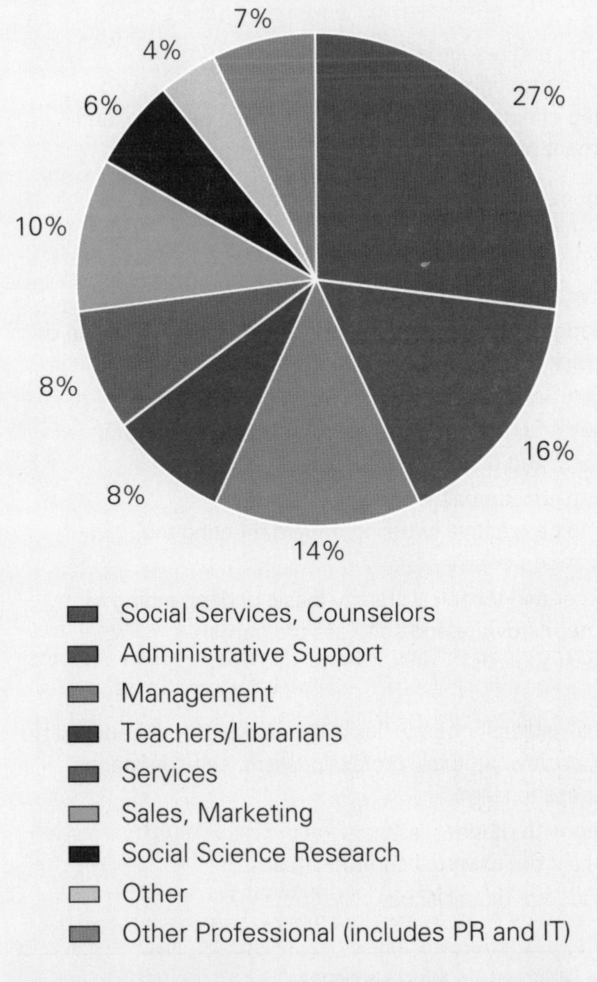

Figure 1.1 Occupational Categories for Sociology Graduates' First Jobs

Source: Based on "21st Century Careers With an Undergraduate Degree in Sociology," American Sociological Association, 2009.

Thinking Sociologically

From what you have read so far, how might sociological topics (e.g., social interaction skills and knowledge of how groups work) be useful to you in your anticipated major and career?

What Employers Want

Ask employers what they want in a new hire and the focus is likely to be on writing, speaking, and analytical skills—especially when the new employee will be faced with complex problems. In addition, understanding of diversity and other cultures, the ability to work effectively in diverse teams, and the ability to gather and interpret quantitative information are key needs. The left column in Table 1.2 on page 16 indicates what employers want from college graduates; the right column indicates the skills and competencies that are part of most sociological training. Compare the two, noting the high levels of overlap.

These competencies show that skills stressed in the sociology curriculum are also those sought by employers: the ability to understand and work with others, research and computer skills, planning and organizing, oral and written communication competency, and critical thinking skills (WorldWideLearn 2007).

We now have a general idea of what sociology is and what sociologists do. It should be apparent that sociology is a broad field of interest; sociologists study all aspects

Table 1.2 What Employers Want and What Sociology Majors Can Deliver

Employers Who Want Colleges to "Place More Emphasis" on Essential Learning Outcomes		*Traits and Knowledge That Are Developed in Most Sociological Training*
Knowledge of Human Culture	**% Seeking**	**Skills and Competencies**
1. Global issues	72	➤ Knowledge of global issues ➤ Sensitivity to diversity and differences in cultural values and traditions
2. The role of the United States in the world	60	➤ Sociological perspective on the United States and the world
3. Cultural values and traditions—U.S. and global	53	➤ Understanding diversity ➤ Working with others (ability to work toward a common goal)
Intellectual and Practical Skills	**% Seeking**	➤ Effective leadership skills (ability to take charge and make decisions)
4. Teamwork skills in diverse groups	76	➤ Interpersonal skills (working with diverse coworkers)
5. Critical thinking and analytic reasoning	73	➤ Analytical and research skills ➤ Organizing thoughts and information ➤ Planning effectively (ability to design, plan, organize, and implement projects and to be self-motivated)
6. Written and oral communication	73	➤ Communication skills (listening, verbal and written communication) ➤ Working with peers ➤ Effective interaction in group situations
7. Information literacy	70	➤ Knowledge of how to find information one needs—online or in a library
8. Creativity and innovation	70	➤ Flexibility, adaptability, and multitasking (ability to set priorities, manage multiple tasks, adapt to changing situations, and handle pressure)
9. Complex problem solving	64	➤ Ability to conceptualize and solve problems ➤ Ability to be creative (working toward meeting the organization's goals)
10. Quantitative reasoning	60	➤ Computer and technical literacy (basic understanding of computer hardware and software programs) ➤ Statistical analysis
Personal and Social Responsibility	**% Seeking**	➤ Personal values (honesty, flexibility, work ethic, dependability, loyalty, positive attitude, professionalism, self-confidence, willingness to learn)
11. Intercultural competence (teamwork in diverse groups)	76	➤ Working with others ➤ Ability to work toward a common goal
12. Intercultural knowledge (global issues)	72	➤ Knowledge of global issues

Source: American Sociological Association (2009); Hansen and Hansen (2003); WorldWideLearn (2007).

of human social behavior. The next section of this chapter shows how the parts of the social world that sociologists study relate to each other, and it outlines the model you will follow as you continue to learn about sociology. Table 1.3 provides some ideas of career paths for graduates with a degree in sociology.

Table 1.3 **What Can You Do With a Sociology Degree?**

Business or Management	*Human Services*	*Education*
Market researcher	Social worker	Teacher
Sales manager	Criminologist	Academic research
Customer relations	Gerontologist	Administration
Manufacturing representative	Hospital administrator	School counselor
Banking or loan officer	Charities administrator	Policy analyst
Data processor	Community advocate or organizer	College professor
Attorney		Dean of student life
Research	*Government*	*Public Relations*
Population analyst	Policy advisor or administrator	Publisher
Surveyor	Labor relations	Mass communications
Market researcher	Legislator	Advertising
Economic analyst	Census worker	Writer or commentator
Public opinion pollster	International agency representative	Journalist
Interviewer	City planning officer	
Policy researcher	Prison administrator	
Telecommunications researcher	Law enforcement	
	FBI agent	
	Customs agent	

Note: Surveys of college alumni with undergraduate majors in sociology indicate that this field of study prepares people for a broad range of occupations. Notice that some of these jobs require graduate or professional training. For further information, contact your department chair or the American Sociological Association in Washington, DC, for a copy of *21st Century Careers With an Undergraduate Degree in Sociology* (2009).

Source: American Sociological Association (2006).

Thinking Sociologically

Imagine that you are a mayor, legislator, police chief, or government official. You make decisions based on information gathered by social scientific research rather than on your own intuition or assumptions. What are some advantages to this decision-making method?

The Social World Model

Think about the different groups you depend on and interact with on a daily basis. You wake up to greet members of your family or your roommate. You go to a larger group—a class—that exists within an even larger organization—the college or university. Understanding sociology and the approach of this book requires a grasp of **levels of analysis**—that is, *social groups from the largest to the smallest.* It may be relatively easy to picture small groups, such as a family, a sports team, or a sorority or fraternity. It is more difficult to visualize large groups, such as corporations—the Gap, Abercrombie & Fitch, Eddie Bauer, General Motors Company, or Starbucks—or organizations such as local or state governments. The largest groups include nations or international organizations, such as the sprawling networks of the United Nations or the World Trade Organization. Groups of various sizes shape our lives. Sociological analysis relies on our understanding of these groups at various levels of analysis.

The **social world model** helps us picture *the levels of analysis in our social surroundings as an interconnected series of small groups, organizations, institutions, and societies.* Sometimes these groups are connected by mutual support and cooperation, but sometimes there are conflicts and power struggles over access to resources. What we are asking you to do here and throughout this book is to develop a sociological imagination—the basic lens used by sociologists. Picture the social world as connected levels of increasingly larger circles. To understand the units or parts of the social world model, look at the model shown on page 18 (and at the beginning of each chapter).

This social world model will be used throughout our book to illustrate how each topic fits into the big picture—our social world. No social unit stands alone, and all units fit into the model and affect each other, either because they cooperate and serve the needs of other units in the system or because of conflict and tension between units.

These men carry the supplies for a new school to be built in their local community—Korphe, Pakistan. The trek of more than 20 miles up mountainous terrain was difficult, but their commitment to neighbors and the children of the community made it worthwhile. The project was a local one (micro level), but it was also made possible by an international organization—the Central Asia Institute.

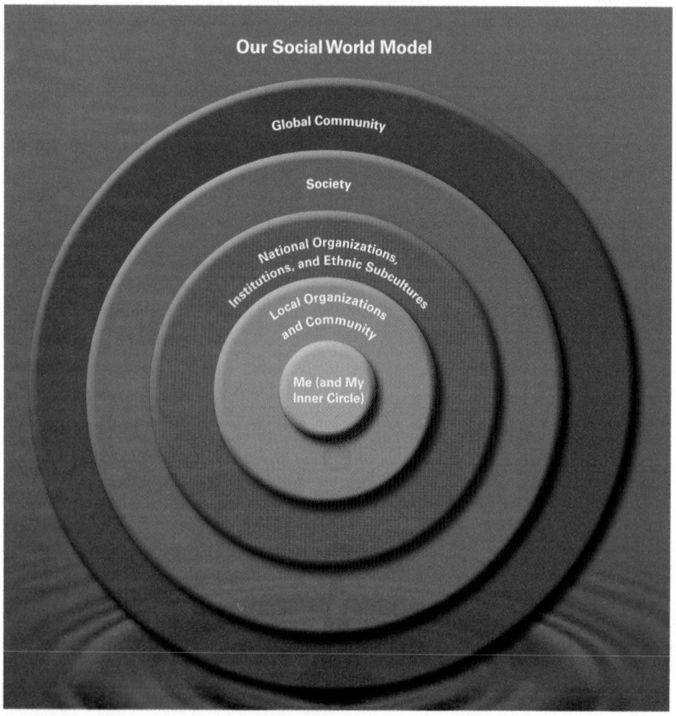

The social world is organized into two main parts that occur at each level—*social structures* and *social processes*. Now, let us take a trip through our social world.

Social Structures

The social world model is made up of a number of parts that combine to form the **social structure.** Picture the human body, held together by bones and muscles. The units that make up that body include things like the brain, heart, lungs, and kidneys, just as **social units** *connect to make the social structure in societies (or countries)*. Those social units include dyads, two people such as a husband and wife; small groups, for example the members of a family; community organizations including schools and churches; large-scale organizations such as political parties or state and national governments; and global societies such as the United Nations. All of these social units combine to make up a system that brings order to our lives. Think about these parallels between the structure that holds together the human body and the structure that holds together societies and their parts.

Sometimes, however, the units in the social structure conflict. For example, a religion that teaches that birth control is wrong may conflict with the health care system regarding how to provide care to women. This issue was controversial in the Republican primaries leading up to the U.S. presidential election of 2012.

Social institutions are *the largest units that make up every society—organized, patterned, and enduring sets of social structures that provide guidelines for behavior and help each society meet its basic survival needs.* Think about the idea that all societies have some form of family, education, religion, politics, economics, science, sports, health care, and military. These are the institutions that provide the rules, roles, and relationships to meet human needs and guide human behavior. They are the units through which organized social activities take place, and they provide the setting for activities essential to human and societal survival. For example, we cannot survive without an economic institution to provide guidelines and a structure for meeting our basic needs of food, shelter, and clothing. Likewise, we would never make it to adulthood as functioning members of society without the family, the most basic of all institutions. Most social units you can think of should fall under one of these institutions.

Like the human body, society and social groups have a structure. Our body's skeleton governs how our limbs are attached to the torso and how they move. Like the system of organs that make up our bodies—heart, lungs, kidneys, bladder—all social institutions are interrelated. Just as a change in one part of the body affects all others, a change in one institution affects the others. A heart attack affects the flow of blood to all other parts of the body. Likewise, if many people are unable to afford medical treatment, the society is less healthy, and there are consequences for families, schools, workplaces, and society as a whole.

All social institutions are interrelated, just as the parts of the body are interdependent: if the skeletal system of the body breaks down, the muscular system and nervous system are not going to be able to get the body to do what you want it to do.

The **national society**, one of the largest social units in our model, includes *a population of people, usually living within a specified geographic area, who are connected by common ideas and are subject to a particular political authority.* It also features a social structure with groups and institutions. France, Kenya, Brazil, and Laos are all national societies on separate continents, but they are linked as part of the global system of nations. In addition to having relatively permanent geographic and political boundaries, a national society has one or more languages and a unique way of life. In most cases, national societies involve countries or large regions where the inhabitants share a common identity as members. In certain other instances, such as contemporary Great Britain, a single national society may include several groups of people who consider themselves distinct nationalities (Welsh, English, Scottish, and Irish within the United Kingdom). Such multicultural societies may or may not be harmonious.

This refugee mother and child from Mozambique represent the smallest social unit, a dyad. In this case, they are trying to survive with help from larger groups such as the United Nations.

Thinking Sociologically

Think about how a major conflict or change in your family (micro level) might affect your education, economic situation, or health care. How might change in one national institution such as health care affect change in another institution (such as the family or the economy)?

Social Processes

If social structure is similar to the human body's skeletal structure, social processes are similar to what keeps the body alive—beating heart, lungs processing oxygen, stomach processing nutrients. **Social processes** *take place through actions of people in institutions and other social units or structures.* Processes keep the social world working, much as the beating heart keeps the body working. For example, the process of socialization teaches individuals how to become productive members of society. It takes place through actions in families, educational systems, religious organizations, and other social units. Socialization is essential for the continuation of any society because it teaches members the thoughts and actions needed to survive in their society. Another process, conflict, occurs between individuals or groups over money, jobs, and other needed resources. The process of change is also a continuous pattern in every social unit; change in one unit affects other units of the social world, often in a chain reaction. For instance, change in the quality of health care can affect the workforce; a beleaguered workforce can affect the economy; instability in the economy can affect families, as breadwinners lose jobs; and family economic woes can affect religious communities because devastated families cannot afford to give money to the churches, mosques, or temples.

Sociologists generally do not judge these social processes as good or bad. Rather, they try to identify, understand, and explain the processes that take place within social units. Picture these processes as overlaying and penetrating our whole social world, from small groups to societies. Social units would be lifeless without the action brought about by social processes, just as body parts would be lifeless without the processes of electrical impulses shooting from the brain to each organ or the oxygen transmitted by blood coursing through our arteries to sustain each organ.

The Environment of Our Social World

Surrounding each social unit, whether a small family group or a large corporation, is an **environment**. It includes *everything that influences the social unit, such as its physical and* *organizational surroundings and technological innovations.* This does not refer to just our physical environment, but is actually much broader. Each unit has an environment to which it must adjust, just as each individual has a unique environment, including family, friends, and other social units that make up his or her immediate environment.

Some parts of the environment are more important to the social unit than others. Your local church, synagogue, temple, or mosque is located in a community environment. That religious organization may seem autonomous and independent, but it depends on its national organization for guidelines and support, the local police force to protect the building from vandalism, and the local economy to provide jobs to members so that the members, in turn, can support the organization. If the religious education program is going to train children to understand the scriptures, local schools are needed to teach the children to read. A religious group may also be affected by other religious bodies, competing with one another for potential members from the community. These religious groups may work cooperatively—organizing a summer program for children or jointly sponsoring a holy-day celebration—or they may define one another as evil, each trying to stigmatize the other. Moreover, one local religious group may be composed primarily of professional and business people and another group mostly of laboring people. The religious groups may experience conflict in part because they each serve a different socioeconomic constituency.

The point is that to understand a social unit *or* the human body, we must consider the structure and processes within the unit as well as the interaction with the surrounding environment. No matter what social unit the sociologist studies, the unit cannot be understood without considering the interaction of that unit with its unique environment.

Perfect relationships or complete harmony between the social units is unusual. Social units, be they small groups or large organizations, are often motivated by self-interest and the need for self-preservation, with the result that they compete with other units for resources (time, money, skills, energy of members). Therefore, social units within a society are often in conflict. Whether groups are in conflict or they cooperate does not change their interrelatedness; units are interdependent. The nature of that interdependence is likely to change over time and can be studied using the scientific method.

Studying the Social World: Levels of Analysis

Picture for a moment your sociology class as a social unit in your social world. Students (individuals) make up the class, the class (small group) is offered by the sociology department, the sociology department (a large group) is part of the college or university, the university (an organization) is located in a community and follows the practices approved by the social institution (education) of which it is a part, and education is an institution located within a nation. Practices the university follows are determined by a larger accrediting agency that provides guidelines and oversight for institutions. The national society, represented by the national government, is shaped by global events—technological and economic competition between nations, natural disasters, global warming, wars, and terrorist attacks. Such events influence national policies and goals, including policies for the educational system. Thus, global tensions and conflicts may shape the content of the curriculum taught in the local classroom, from what is studied to the textbooks used.

Each of these social units—from the smallest (two students in a discussion group) to the largest (society and the global system)—is referred to as a level of analysis (see Table 1.4). These levels are illustrated in the social world model at the beginning of each chapter and relate to that chapter's content as shown through examples in the model.

MICRO-LEVEL ANALYSIS

A focus on individual or small-group interaction in specific situations is called **micro-level analysis**. This level is important because face-to-face interaction forms the basic foundation of all social groups and organizations to which we belong,

Table 1.4 **The Structure of Society and Levels of Analysis**

	Level	*Parts of Education*
Micro-level analysis	Interpersonal	Sociology class; study group cramming for an exam
	Local organizations	University; sociology department
Meso-level analysis	Organizations and institutions	State boards of education; National Education Association
	Ethnic groups within a nation	Islamic madrassas or Jewish yeshiva school systems
Macro-level analysis	Nations	Policy and laws governing education
	Global community	World literacy programs

from families to corporations to societies. We are members of many groups at the micro level.

To illustrate micro-level analysis, consider the problem of spousal abuse. Why does a person remain in an abusive relationship, knowing that each year thousands of people are killed by their lovers or mates and millions more are severely and repeatedly battered? To answer this question, several possible micro-level explanations can be considered. One view is that the abusive partner has convinced the abused person that she is powerless in the relationship or that she "deserves" the abuse. Therefore, she gives up in despair of ever being able to alter the situation. The abuse is viewed as part of the interaction—of action and reaction—and the partners come to see abuse as what comprises "normal" interaction.

Another explanation for remaining in the abusive relationship is that battering is a familiar part of the person's everyday life. However unpleasant and unnatural this may seem to outsiders, it may be seen by the abuser or by the abused as a "normal" and acceptable part of intimate relationships, especially if either partner grew up in an abusive family.

Another possibility is that an abused woman may fear that her children would be harmed or that she would be harshly judged by her family or church if she "abandoned" her mate. She may have few resources to make leaving the abusive situation possible. To study each of these possible explanations involves analysis at the micro level because each focuses on interpersonal interaction factors rather than on large society-wide trends or forces.

Now consider the meso-level analysis that leads to quite different explanations for abuse.

MESO-LEVEL ANALYSIS

Analysis of intermediate-size social units, called **meso-level analysis**, involves looking at intermediate-sized *units smaller than the nation but larger than the local community or even the region.* This level includes national institutions (such as the economy of a country, the national educational system, or the political system within a country), nationwide organizations (such as a political party, a soccer league, or a national women's rights organization), nationwide corporations (such as Ford Motor Company or IBM), and ethnic groups that have an identity as a group (such as Jews, Mexican Americans, or Native Americans in the United States). Organizations, institutions, and ethnic communities are smaller than the nation or global social forces, but they are still beyond the everyday personal experience and control of individuals. They are intermediate in the sense of being too large for members to know everyone in the group, but they are not as large as nation-states at the macro level. For example, meso-level states in the United States, provinces in Canada, prefectures in Japan, or cantons in Switzerland are more accessible and easier to change than the national bureaucracies of these countries.

Using meso-level analysis to examine changes in women's status, for example, could include study of women's legal, educational, religious, economic, political, scientific, and sports-related opportunities in society. However, meso-level changes that create new opportunities for women may also cause conflicts and even abuse within individual families at the micro level as women take advantage of expanding opportunities outside the home. In discussing micro-level analysis, we used the example of domestic violence. We must be careful not to "blame the victim"—in this case, the abused person—for getting into an abusive relationship and for failing to act in ways that stop the abuse. To avoid blaming victims for their own suffering, many social scientists look for broader explanations of spousal abuse, such as the social conditions at the meso level of society that cause the problem (Straus and Gelles 1990). When a pattern of behavior in society occurs with increasing frequency, it cannot be understood solely from the point of view of individual cases or micro-level causes. Remember the sociological imagination. For instance, sociological findings show that fluctuations in spousal or child abuse at the micro level are related to levels of unemployment at the meso and macro levels. Frustration resulting in abuse erupts within families when poor economic conditions make it nearly impossible for people to find a stable and reliable means of supporting themselves and their families. The message here is that economic issues must be addressed if violence in the home is to be lessened.

MACRO-LEVEL ANALYSIS

Studying the largest social units in the social world, called **macro-level analysis**, involves looking at *entire nations, global forces, and international social trends.* Macro-level analysis is essential to our understanding of how larger social forces, such as global events, shape our everyday lives. A natural disaster such as the 2011 earthquake and tsunami off Japan, the cold wave of the 2012 winter in Europe that killed many people, Hurricane Sandy on the East Coast of the United States in the fall of 2012 that disrupted supply chains and destroyed factories, or the frequent earthquakes around the world may change the foods we are able to serve at our family dinner table, since much of our food is now imported from other parts of the world. (Map 1.1 shows some of the most deadly natural disasters of the past few years.) Likewise, a political conflict on the other side of the planet can lead to war, which means that a member of your family may be called up on active duty and sent into harm's way more than 7,000 miles from your home. Each member of the family may experience individual stress, have trouble concentrating, and feel ill with worry. The entire globe has become an interdependent social unit. If we are to prosper and thrive in the 21st century, we need to understand connections that go beyond our local communities.

Even patterns such as domestic violence, considered as micro- and meso-level issues above, can be examined at the macro level. Violence against women (especially rape) occurs at very different rates in different societies, with some societies being completely free of rape and others having a "culture of rape" in countries such as South Africa and Kenya (Kristof and WuDunn 2009). The most consistent predictor of violence against women is a macho conception of masculine roles and personality. Societies that did not define masculinity in terms of dominance and control were virtually free of rape.

South Africa has one of the highest levels of rape in the world, with one in four men (often under 20) having raped a woman, and 46% of those more than once. The cultural beliefs support men who rape with ideas such as "don't leave a woman unsatisfied" and "raping a virgin can cure AIDS." The men show no remorse because the behavior is "accepted" by their segments of society and is considered "macho" (Lindow 2009).

This photo depicts the damage following the catastrophic earthquake that hit Haiti on January 12, 2010. This event not only changed the lives of people in Haiti—one of the poorest countries in the world—but had ripple effects on economic exchange, relief efforts around the globe, and international trade. Those, in turn, can affect the cost of various products such as the foods you put on your table.

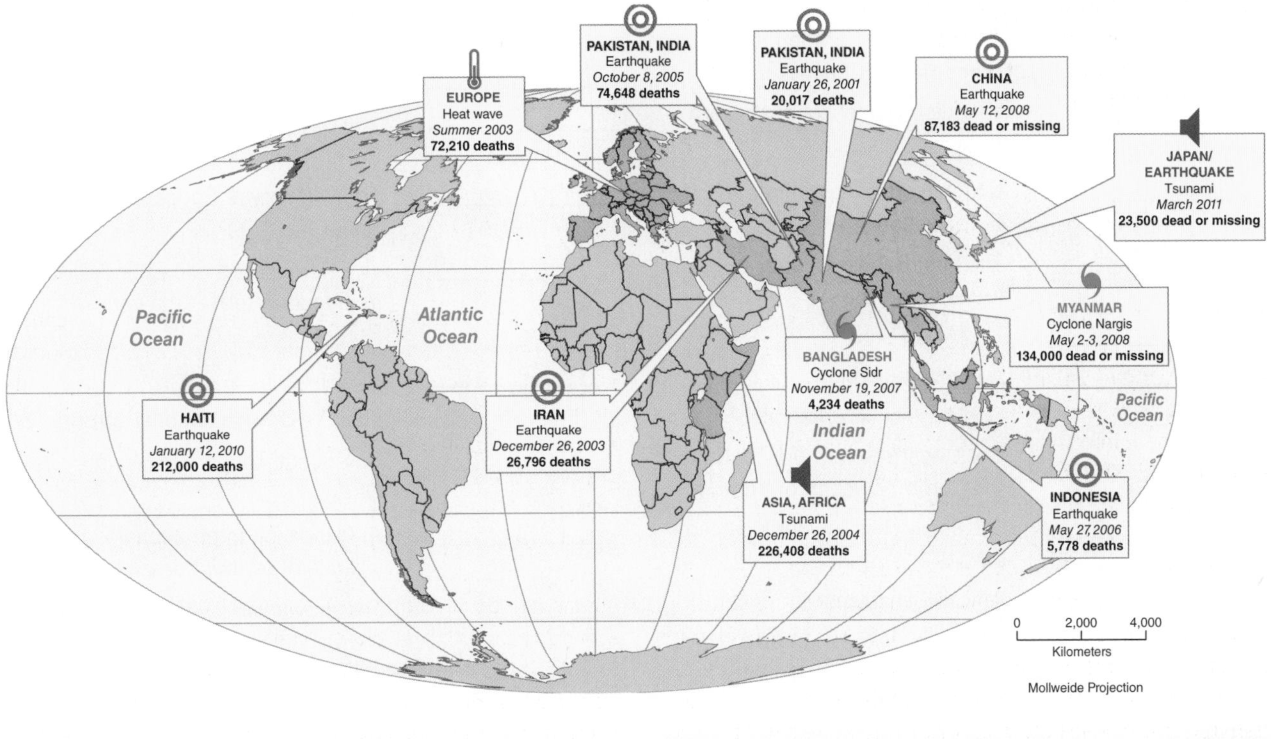

Map 1.1 The Deadliest Natural Disasters From January 2001 to June 2011

Source: EM-DAT emergency events database, Centre for Research on the Epidemiology of Disasters. Map by Anna Versluis.

Engaging Sociology

Micro-Meso-Macro

Look at the list of various groups and other social units below. Identify which level each group would belong to—(1) micro, (2) meso, or (3) macro. The definitions below should help you make your decisions. Answers are found online at www.pineforge.com/ballantine4e.

Micro-level groups: Small, local, community social units such as families and school classrooms in which everyone within the group knows everyone else or knows someone everyone else knows.

Meso-level groups: Social units of intermediate size such as state governments or ethnic groups, usually so large that many members may never have heard the names of many other members and may have little access to the leaders yet not so large as to make the leaders seem distant or unapproachable. If members do not know the leader themselves, they probably know someone who is friends with the leader.

Macro-level groups: Large social units, usually quite bureaucratic, that operate at a national or a global level, such as national governments or international organizations. Most members are unlikely to know or have communicated with the leaders personally or know someone who knows the leaders. The "business" of these groups is of international import and implication. Some research indicates that every person on the planet is within 7 degrees of relatedness to every other human being. A macro-level system is one in which most of the members are at least 5 degrees of relatedness from one another—that is, they know someone who knows someone who knows someone who knows someone who knows the person in question.

1. Micro social units | **2. Meso social units** | **3. Macro social units**

1	Your nuclear family
3	The United Nations
2	A local chapter of the Lions Club or the Rotary Club
2	Your high school baseball team
3	India
3	NATO (North Atlantic Treaty Organization)
2	The First Baptist Church in Muncie, Indiana
2	The World Bank
2	A family reunion
3	Google, Inc. (international)
3	The Department of Education for the Commonwealth of Kentucky
2	The show choir in your local high school
2	African Canadians
2	The Dineh (Navajo) people
3	Canada

2	The Republican Party in the United States
3	The World Court
2	A fraternity at your college
3	The International Monetary Fund (IMF)
3	The Ministry of Education for Spain
2	The Roman Catholic Church (with its headquarters at the Vatican in Rome)
3	Australia
3	The Chi Omega national sorority
2	Boy Scout Troop #3 in Marion, Ohio
3	Al-Qaeda (an international alliance of terrorist organizations)
3	The provincial government for the Canadian province of Ontario
3	The United States of America

Most of these fall into clear categories, but some are "on the line," and one could legitimately place them in more than one group. It should be viewed as a continuum from micro to macro social units. See how your authors rate these at www.pineforge.com/ballantine4e.

Some sociologists believe that the same pattern holds for domestic violence: A society or subgroup within society that teaches males that the finest expression of their masculinity is physical strength and domination is very likely to have battered women (Burn 2005). The point is that understanding individual human behavior often requires investigation of the larger societal beliefs that support that behavior. Worldwide patterns may tell us something about a social problem and offer new lenses for understanding that problem. Try the previous "Engaging Sociology" to test your understanding of levels of analysis and the sociological imagination.

Thinking Sociologically

What factors at each level of analysis influenced you to take this sociology class? Micro-level factors might include your advisor, your schedule, and your interest in sociology. At the meso and macro levels, what other factors influenced you?

Distinctions between each level of analysis are not always sharply delineated. The micro level shades into the meso level, and the lines between the meso level and the macro level are blurry on the continuum. Still, it is clear that in some micro-level social units, you know everyone, or at least every member of the social unit is only 2 degrees of relatedness away. That means every person in the social unit knows someone who you also know.

We all participate in meso-level social units that are smaller than the nation but that can be huge. Millions of people may belong to the same religious denomination or the same political party. We share connections with those people, and our lives are affected by people we do not even know. Consider the political activities in the United States and other countries that take place on the Internet. In political campaigns, millions of individuals join organizations such as the Tea Party movement, MoveOn.org, or the Free Syria movement; participate in dialogues online; and contribute money to political organizations. People living thousands of miles from one another united financially and in spirit to support Obama-Biden or Romney-Ryan in the 2012 U.S. presidential election. Thus, the meso level is different from the micro level, but both influence us.

The macro level is even more removed from the individual, but its impact can change our lives. Washington, DC, can seem very distant, but decisions by Congress, the president, and courts may determine whether or not your own family has health care coverage (and of what quality) and whether the price of gasoline will escalate due to the president's policies.

The social world model presented in the chapter opening illustrates the interplay of micro-, meso-, and macro-level forces, and Figure 1.2 illustrates that this micro-to-macro model should be seen as a continuum. In the next "Sociology Around the World," we examine a village in Tunisia to see how macro-level forces influence a meso-level local community and individual micro-level lives.

Building and staffing of this resort in Tunisia—which is patronized by affluent people from other continents (global)—changed the economy, the culture, the social structure (meso level), and individual lives (micro level) in the local community.

Figure 1.2 The Micro-to-Macro Continuum

Sociology Around the World

Tunisian Village Meets the Modern World

This is a story of change as macro-level innovations enter a small traditional village. It illustrates how the social units of the social world model and the three levels of analysis enter into sociological analysis. As you read, try to identify both the units and the levels of analysis being discussed and the impact of globalization on a community that cannot know what these changes will bring.

The workday began at dawn as usual in the small fishing village on the coast of Tunisia, North Africa. Men prepared their nets and boats for the day, while women prepared breakfast and dressed the young children for school. About 10 a.m., it began—the event that would change this picturesque village forever. Bulldozers arrived first, followed by trench diggers and cement mixers, to begin their overhaul of the village.

Villagers had suspected something was afoot when important-looking officials arrived two months earlier with foreign businessmen, followed by two teams of surveyors. Without their approval, the government had sold the land that the village had held communally for generations to the foreigners so that they could build a multimillion-dollar hotel and casino. When concerned citizens asked what was happening in their village, they were assured that their way of life would not change. The contractor from the capital city of Tunis said that they would still have access to the beach and ocean for fishing. He also promised them many benefits from the hotel project—jobs, help from the government to improve roads and housing, and a higher standard of living.

The contractor had set up camp in a trailer on the beach, and word soon got around that he would be hiring some men for higher hourly wages than they could make in a day or even month of fishing. Rivalries soon developed between friends over who should apply for the limited number of jobs.

As the bulldozers moved in, residents had mixed opinions about the changes taking place in their village and their lives. Some saw the changes as exciting opportunities for new jobs and recognition of their beautiful village; others viewed the changes as destroying a lifestyle that was all they and generations before them had known.

Today, the village is dwarfed by the huge hotel, and the locals are looked on as quaint curiosities by the European tourists. Fishing has become a secondary source of employment to working in the hotel and casino or selling local crafts and trinkets to souvenir-seeking visitors. Many women are now employed outside the home by the hotel, creating new family structures as grandparents, unemployed men, and other relations take over child-rearing responsibilities.

To understand the changes in this one small village and other communities facing similar change, a sociologist uses the sociological imagination. This involves understanding the global political and economic trends that are affecting this village and its inhabitants (macro-level analysis). It requires comprehension of the transformation of social institutions within the nation (meso-level analysis). Finally, sociological investigation explores how change affects the individual Tunisian villagers (micro-level analysis).

To sociologically analyze the process of change, it is important to understand what is going on in this situation. The government officials and the international business representatives negotiated a lucrative deal to benefit both Tunisia and the business corporation. The community and its powerless residents presented few obstacles to the project from the point of view of the government, and in fact, government officials reasoned that the villagers could benefit from new jobs. However, the economic and family roles of the villagers—how they earned a living and how they raised their children—changed dramatically with the disruption of their traditional ways. The process of change began with the demand of people far from Tunisia for vacation spots in the sun. Ultimately, this process reached the village's local environment, profoundly affecting the village and everyone in it. For this Tunisian village, the old ways are gone forever.

The Social World Model and This Book

The social world engulfs each of us from the moment of our birth until we die. Throughout our lives, each of us is part of a set of social relationships that provides guidelines for how we interact with others and how we see ourselves. This does not mean that human behavior is strictly determined by our links to the social world. Humans are more than mere puppets whose behavior is programmed by social structure. It does mean, however, that the individual and the larger social world influence each other. We are influenced by and we have influence on our social environment. The social world is a human creation, and we can and do change that which we create. It acts on us, and we act on it. In this sense, social units are constantly emerging and changing in the course of human interaction.

The difficulty for most of us is that we are so caught up in our daily concerns that we fail to see and understand the social forces that are at work in our personal lives. What we need are the conceptual and methodological tools to help us gain a more complete and accurate perspective on the social world. The ideas, theories, methods, and levels of analysis employed by sociologists are the very tools that will help give us that perspective. To use an analogy, each different lens of a camera gives the photographer a unique view of the world. Wide-angle lenses, close-up lenses, telephoto lenses, and special filters each serve a purpose in creating a distinctive picture or frame of the world. No one lens will provide the complete picture. Yet the combination of images produced by various lenses allows us to examine in detail aspects of the world we might ordinarily overlook. That is what the sociological perspective gives us: a unique set of tools to see the social world around us with deeper understanding. In seeing the social world from a sociological perspective, we are better able to understand who we are as social beings.

Throughout this book, the social world model will be used as the framework for understanding the social units, processes, and surrounding environment. Each social unit and process is taken out, examined, and returned to its place in the interconnected social world model so that you can comprehend the whole social world and its parts, like putting a puzzle together. Look for the model at the beginning of every chapter. You can also expect the micro-, meso-, and macro-level dimensions of issues to be explored throughout the text. Try identifying the levels of analysis in the following "Engaging Sociology."

Engaging Sociology

Micro-Meso-Macro: An Application Exercise

Imagine that there has been a major economic downturn (recession) in your local community. Identify three possible events at each level (micro, meso, and macro) that might have contributed to the economic troubles in your town.

The micro (local community) level:

1. ____________________
2. ____________________
3. ____________________

The meso (intermediate—state, organizational, or ethnic subculture) level:

1. ____________________
2. ____________________
3. ____________________

The macro (national/global) level:

1. ____________________
2. ____________________
3. ____________________

The next issue is how we gather data that inform how we understand and influence the social world. When we say we know something about society, how is it that we know? What is considered evidence in sociology, and what lens (theory) do we use to interpret the data? These are the central issues of the next chapter.

What Have We Learned?

How can sociology help me understand my own life, who I am, and how I relate to others? This question was posed at the beginning of the chapter. Throughout this book you will find ideas and examples that will expand on the *sociological imagination*, illustrating how sociology can help you communicate more effectively and understand your interactions with others.

How do sociologists help us understand and even improve our lives in families, educational systems, or health care systems? Understanding organizations and bureaucracies can make us better family members, more effective citizens, and more adept at getting along with coworkers. As citizens of democracies, we need to understand how to influence our social environments, from city councils, school boards, health care systems, and state legislatures to congressional, presidential, and other organizations.

How do national policies and global events influence my life? As the world changes, we need to be aware of global issues and how they affect us, from our job changes and lost jobs to skills demanded in the 21st century.

We live in a complex social world with many layers of interaction. If we really want to understand our own lives, we need to comprehend the levels of analysis that affect our lives and the connections between those levels. To do so wisely, we need both objective lenses for viewing this complex social world and accurate, valid information (facts) about the society. As the science of society, sociology can provide both tested empirical data and a broad, analytical perspective, as you will learn in the next chapter. Here is a summary of points from Chapter 1.

Key Points

- Humans are, at their very core, social animals—more akin to pack or herd animals than to individualistic cats. (See pp. 4–6.)
- Sociology is based on scientific findings, making it more reliable than commonsense beliefs in a particular culture. (See pp. 6–9.)
- A core idea in sociology is the sociological imagination. It requires that we see how our individual lives and personal troubles are shaped by historical and structural events outside our everyday lives. It also prods us to see how we can influence our society. (See p. 10.)
- Sociology is a social science and, therefore, uses the tools of the sciences to establish credible evidence to understand our social world. As a science, sociology is scientific and objective rather than value laden. (See pp. 10–12.)
- Sociology has pragmatic applications, including those that are essential for the job market. (See pp. 13–16.)
- Sociology focuses on social units or groups, on social structures such as institutions, on social processes that give a social unit its dynamic character, and on their environments. (See pp. 16–26.)
- The social world model is the organizing theme of this book. Using the sociological imagination, we can understand our social world best by clarifying the interconnections between micro, meso, and macro levels of the social system. Each chapter of this book will examine society at these three levels of analysis. (See p. 27.)

Discussion Questions

1. Think of a problem that impacts you personally (e.g., the high cost of tuition, unemployment, divorce) and explain how you would make sense of it differently if you viewed it as (a) a personal problem or (b) a public issue. How do possible solutions to the problem differ depending on whether you view it as a personal problem or a public issue?
2. How can sociology help you become a more informed citizen and better able to understand how government policies impact society?
3. What are three ways the sociological perspective can help you succeed in college and the workforce?
4. Think of some of the ways the social institutions of government and education interconnect. Why is it in the interest of the government to support higher education? How has government support (or lack of support) impacted your college experience?
5. Imagine you would like to look at reasons behind the college dropout rate in the United States. How might your explanations differ based on whether your analysis was on the micro, meso, or macro level? Why? Which level or levels would you focus on for your study? Why?

Contributing to Our Social World: What Can We Do?

At the end of this and all subsequent chapters, you will find suggestions for work, service learning, internships, and volunteering that encourage you to apply the ideas discussed in the chapter. Suggestions for Chapter 1 focus on student organizations for sociology majors and nonmajors.

At the Local Level

- *Student organizations and clubs* enable students to meet other students interested in sociology, carry out group activities, get to know faculty members, and attend presentations by guest speakers. These clubs are usually not limited to sociology majors. If no such organization exists, consider forming one with the help of a faculty member. Sociologists also have an undergraduate honors society, Alpha Kappa Delta (AKD). Visit the AKD website at https://sites.google.com/site/alphakappadeltainternational/ to learn more about the society and what it takes to form a chapter.

At the Regional, National, and Global Levels

- *The American Sociological Association (ASA)* is the leading professional organization of sociologists in the United States. Visit the ASA website at www.asanet.org and take a look around. You will find many programs and initiatives of special interest to students. If you are interested in becoming a sociologist, be sure to look at the links under the heading "News on the Profession." The organization also sponsors an Honors Program at the annual meeting that introduces students to the profession and gives them a heads-up on being successful in sociology. For more information go to www.asanet.org/students/honors.cfm.
- *State and regional sociological associations* are especially student-friendly and feature publications and sessions at their annual meetings specifically for undergraduates. The ASA lists organizations and their website addresses, with direct links to their home pages, at www2.asanet.org/governance/aligned.html.
- *The International Sociological Association (ISA)* serves sociologists from around the world. Every four years, they sponsor a large meeting (Yokohama, Japan, in July 2014). Specialty groups within ISA hold smaller conferences throughout the world during the other years. Check out www.isa-sociology.org.

Visit the Student Study Site at **www.sagepub.com/ballantine4e** to access additional study tools, including eFlashcards, web quizzes, video resources, audio resources, web resources, SAGE journal articles, recommended readings, and more.

CHAPTER 2

Examining the Social World

How Do We Know?

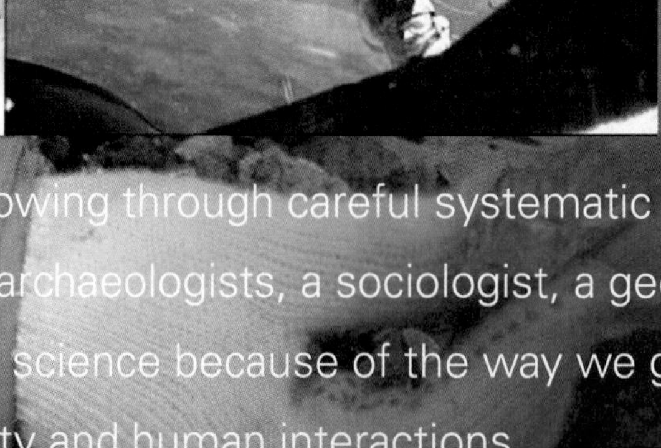

Science is about knowing through careful systematic investigation. Pictured here are scientists: archaeologists, a sociologist, a geologist, and a chemist. Sociology is a social science because of the way we gather scientific evidence to understand society and human interactions.

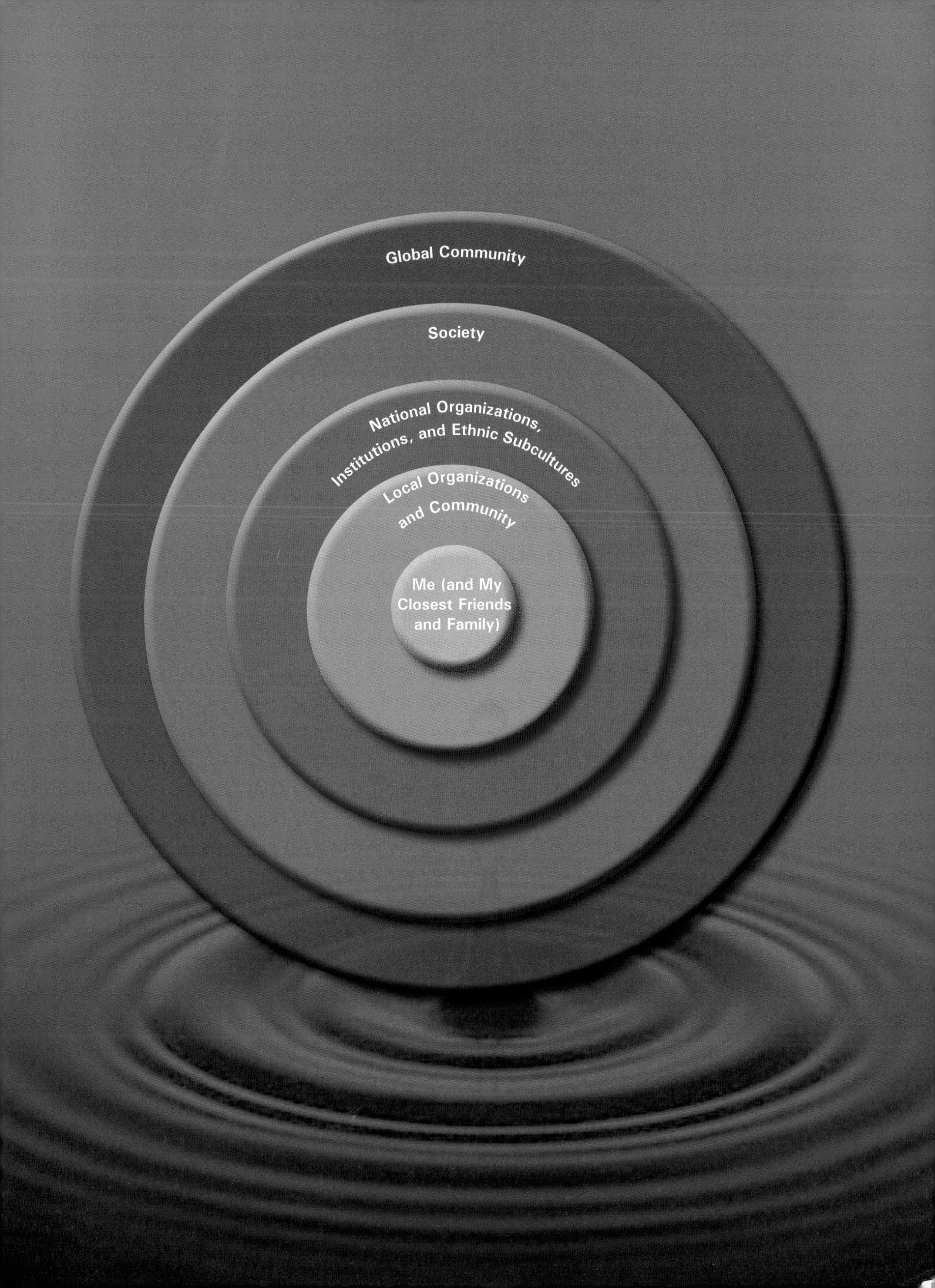
Global Community
Society
National Organizations, Institutions, and Ethnic Subcultures
Local Organizations and Community
Me (and My Closest Friends and Family)

Think About It	
Micro: Me (and My Closest Friends/Family)	When you are talking with friends and you say you know something or give an opinion, *how* do you know it?
Micro: Local Community	When you are trying to convince neighbors or people in your community to accept your opinion, why are facts and evidence important?
Meso: National Institutions; Complex Organizations; Ethnic Groups	How do sociologists gather accurate data about families, educational institutions, or ethnic groups?
Macro: National Society	How do social scientists study national societal patterns scientifically?
Macro: Global Community	How can theories about global interactions help us understand our own lives at the micro level?

What's coming in this chapter?

Ideas Underlying Science
Empirical Research and Social Theory
How Sociologists Study the Social World
The Development of Sociology as a Discipline
Sociology's Major Theoretical Perspectives
Putting Sociology to Work—Public Sociology

Let us travel to the Southern Hemisphere to meet a teenage boy, Hector. He is a 16-year-old living in a *favela* (slum) on the outskirts of São Paulo, Brazil. He is a polite, bright boy, but his chances of getting an education and a steady job in his world are limited. Like millions of other children around the world, he comes from a poor rural family that migrated to the urban area in search of a better life. However, his family ended up in a crowded slum with only a shared spigot for water and one string of electric lights along the dirt road going up the hill on which they live. The sanitary conditions in his community are appalling—open sewers, no garbage collection—which makes the people susceptible to various diseases. His family is relatively fortunate, for they have cement walls and wood flooring, although no bathroom, running water, or electricity. Many adjacent dwellings are little more than cardboard walls with corrugated metal roofs and dirt floors.

Hector wanted to stay in school but was forced to drop out to help support his family. Since leaving school, he has picked up odd jobs—deliveries, trash pickup, janitorial work, gardening—to help pay the few centavos for the family's dwelling and to buy food to support his parents and six siblings. Even when he was in school, Hector's experience was discouraging. He was not a bad student, and some teachers encouraged him to continue, but other students from the city teased the *favela* kids and made them feel unwelcome. Most of his friends dropped out before he did. Hector often missed school because of

Slum dwellers of São Paulo, Brazil. Hector lives in a neighborhood with shelters made of available materials such as boxes, no electricity or running water, and poor sanitation.

other obligations—looking for part-time work, visiting a sick relative, or taking care of a younger sibling. The immediate need to put food on the table outweighed the long-term value of staying in school. What is the bottom line for Hector and millions like him? Because of his limited education and work skills, obligations to his family, and limited opportunities, he most likely will continue to live in poverty.

Sociologists are interested in the factors that influence the social world of children like Hector: family, friends, school, community, and the place of one's nation in the global political and economic structural systems. To understand how sociologists study poverty and many other social issues, we consider the theories and methods they use to do their work. Understanding the *how* helps us see that sociology is more than guesswork or opinion. Rather, it involves the use of scientific methods based on a systematic process for expanding knowledge of the social world.

Whatever our area of study or job interests, we are likely to find ourselves asking sociological questions. All of us will face situations where conducting a research study will help our organization or community. Knowing what is involved in a good study and the tools to carry out a study will make us more effective participants. Consider some examples of questions we might ask:

Why is there binge drinking on college campuses?

Do sexually explicit videos and magazines reinforce sexist stereotypes or encourage sexual violence?

Do tough laws and longer prison sentences deter people from engaging in criminal conduct?

How do we develop our religious and political outlooks?

Do classroom teachers treat children from different social classes, races, or ethnic groups the same or differently?

How are the Internet and other technologies affecting everyday life for people around the world?

How are people's lives affected by the globalization of jobs and companies?

This chapter will introduce you to the basic tools used to plan studies and gather dependable information on topics of interest. It will help you understand how sociology approaches research questions. To this end, we will consider ideas underlying science, social research and social theory, how sociologists study the social world, the relationship between sociological theories and research methods, ethical issues, the development of sociology as a discipline, sociology's major theoretical perspectives, and putting sociology to work: practical applications and uses of sociological knowledge. We start with some ideas underlying sociology as a science.

Ideas Underlying Science

Throughout most of human history, people came to "know" the world by the traditions passed down from one generation to the next. Things were so because authoritative people in the culture said they were so. Often, there was reliance on magical or religious explanations of the forces in nature, and these explanations became part of tradition. People were interested in the natural world and observed it carefully, but with advances in the natural sciences, observations of cause-and-effect processes became more systematic and controlled. As the way of knowing about the world shifted, tradition and magic as the primary means to understand the world were challenged. It was little more than 200 years ago that people thought lightning storms were a sign of an angry god, not electricity caused by meteorological forces.

The scientific approach is based on several core ideas: First, there is a real physical and social world that can be studied scientifically. Second, there is a certain order to the world, with identifiable patterns that result from a series of causes and effects. The world is not merely a collection of unrelated random events but rather events that are systematically sequenced and patterned—that is, *causally* related. Third, the way to gain knowledge of the world is to subject it to empirical testing. **Empirical knowledge** involves *the collection of facts and observations that can be objectively observed and carefully measured using the five senses (sometimes enhanced by scientific instruments); the reality of what is being measured should be the same for all people who observe it.*

Lightning has been understood as a form of electricity rather than a message from an angry god only since 1752, thanks to an experiment by Benjamin Franklin.

For knowledge to be scientific, it must come from phenomena that can be observed and measured. Phenomena that cannot be subject to measurement are not within the realm of scientific inquiry. The existence of God, the devil, heaven, hell, and the soul cannot be observed and measured and therefore cannot be examined scientifically. While certain religious notions cannot themselves be subjects of scientific inquiry, religion can be studied in terms of the role it plays in society and our lives, its impact on our values and behavior (the sociology of religion), the historical development of specific religious traditions (the history of religion), or the emotional comfort and stability it brings to people (the psychology of religion).

Finally, science is rooted in **objectivity**—that is, *steps taken to ensure that one's personal opinions or values do not bias or contaminate data collection or analysis.* **Evidence** *refers to facts and information that are confirmed through systematic testing using our five senses, sometimes enhanced with research tools.* Scientists are obliged not to distort their research findings so as to promote a particular point of view. Scientific research is judged first on whether it relies on careful efforts to be objective.

One way to evaluate objectivity is to see whether the research does or does not support what the researcher thinks is true. For example, if we wish to study whether Hector dropped out of school because of his need to work, then we must plan the research study so that we can either support or disprove our **hypothesis** (*our educated guess or prediction*) about Hector's situation.

What factors—individual, group, institutional, national, and global—cause poverty in the developing world? This grocery store in Ethiopia is a typical illustration of poverty in parts of Africa, Latin America, and Asia. Imagine that this is the only place for miles around to buy food.

Failure to meet these standards—empirical knowledge, objectivity, and scientific evidence—means that a study is not scientific. Someone's ideas can seem plausible and logical but may still not be supported by the facts. This is why evidence is so important. Sociology is concerned with having accurate evidence, and it is important to know what is or is not considered accurate evidence. Perhaps you have seen an episode of the *CSI: Crime Scene Investigation* or *Bones* series on television. The shows in these series depict the importance of careful collection of data and commitment to objective analysis. Sociologists deal with different issues, but the same sort of concern for accuracy in gathering data guides their work.

Sociologists have come a long way from the early explanations of the social world that were based on the moral judgments of the 18th- and 19th-century social philosophers and the guesswork of social planners. Part of the excitement of sociology today comes from the challenge to improve the scientific procedures applied to the study of humans and social behavior and to base policy on carefully collected and analyzed data.

Thinking Sociologically

If you wanted to learn something about the morale of one of your university's athletic teams or in a Greek sorority or fraternity, which of the following would produce better results: (a) interviewing those who have quit the organization, (b) interviewing a wide range of campus athletes or Greek members, or (c) interviewing students who are neither athletes nor Greeks? Why? Why might some of those approaches end up with bias in the results and not give the full story?

Empirical Research and Social Theory

We all have beliefs that we take for granted about how our social world works. Social researchers use the scientific method to examine these beliefs about society. They assume that (a) there are predictable social relationships in the world, (b) social situations will recur in certain patterns, and (c) social situations have causes that can be understood. If the social world were totally chaotic, little would be gained by scientific study.

Just as individuals develop preferences for different religious or political beliefs that guide their lives, sociologists develop preferences for different explanations of the social world, called social theories. The main difference between individual beliefs and social theories is that the latter are subject to ongoing, systematic testing.

Theories are *statements or explanations regarding how and why two or more facts are related to each other and the connections between these facts.* Sociological theories try to explain social interactions, behaviors, and problems. A good theory should allow the scientist to make predictions about the social world. Different theories are useful at each level of analysis in the social world—micro, meso, and macro. Which theory a sociologist uses to study the social world depends on the level of analysis to be studied, as illustrated in Figure 2.1.

Each theory discussed in this chapter gives a perspective on the way the social world works. To study Hector's life in Brazil, researchers might focus on the micro-level interactions between Hector and his family members, peers, teachers, and employers as factors that contribute to his situation. For example, why does Hector find some activities (for example, working) more realistic or immediately rewarding than others (such as attending school)? A meso-level focus might examine the organizations and institutions—such as the business world, the schools, and the religious communities in Brazil—to see how they shape the forces that affect Hector's life. Alternatively, the focus might be on macro-level analysis—the class structure (rich to poor) of the society and the global forces, such as trade

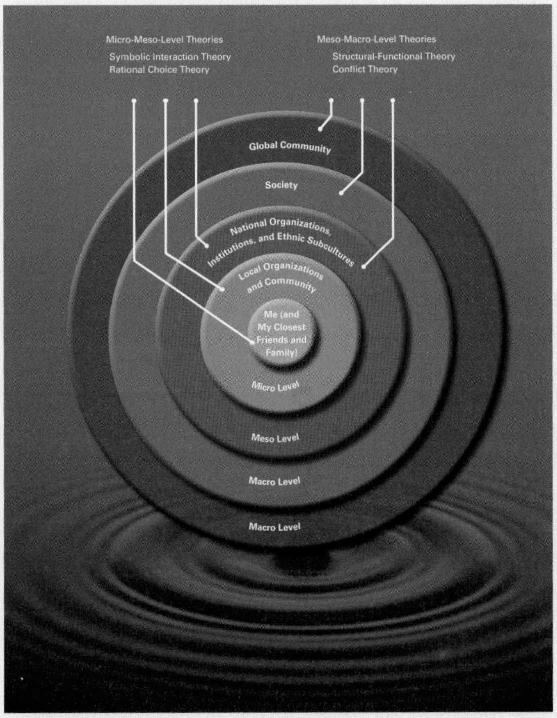

Figure 2.1 Social World Model

relations between Brazil and other countries, that influence opportunities for Brazilians who live in poverty.

Sociologists focus on group or societal explanations to understand issues such as the poverty that haunt Hector's life. Different research methods to collect data are appropriate at different levels of analysis (micro, meso, and macro) and depend on the theory being used and the question being researched.

Scientists, including sociologists, often use theories to predict why things happen and under what conditions they are likely to happen. So theory tells the researcher what to look for and what concepts or variables need to be measured. However, explanations about the relationships between social variables need to be tested. This is where research methods—the procedures one uses to gather data—are relevant. The facts (data) must be carefully gathered and are then used to assess the accuracy of the theory. If a theory is not supported by the data, it must be reformulated or discarded. Theory and research are used together and are mutually dependent. We turn first to the discussion of how we gather data.

How Sociologists Study the Social World

How do we know? Sociologists design research studies using scientific tools to answer sociological questions. What is presented here is a skeleton of the research process that sociologists and other social scientists spend years studying and perfecting. This section will begin to provide a sense of how sociologists study issues and know what they know. If you study more sociology, you will learn more about the research process. It is exciting to collect accurate information and find out answers to important, meaningful questions that can make a difference in people's lives and in your own organization or community.

A researcher follows a number of logically related steps.

A. PLANNING A RESEARCH STUDY

- *Step 1:* Define a topic or problem that can be studied scientifically.
- *Step 2:* Review existing relevant research studies and theory to refine the topic and define variables.
- *Step 3:* Formulate hypotheses or research questions and figure out how to define and measure the variables.

B. DESIGNING THE RESEARCH PLAN AND METHOD FOR COLLECTING THE DATA

- *Step 4:* Design the research plan that specifies how the data will be gathered.

- *Step 5:* Select a sample of people or groups to study.
- *Step 6:* Collect the data using appropriate research methods.

C. MAKING SENSE OF THE DATA

- *Step 7:* Analyze the data, figuring out exactly what the study says about the research question(s) from Step 3.
- *Step 8:* Draw conclusions and present the final report, including suggestions for future research. Recommendations for actions may be part of the report.

Each of these steps is very important, whether you become a professional sociologist or do a study for a local organization or your workplace. To introduce the research process, we provide a quick summary reduced to the three central issues from the outline above: planning a research study; designing the research plan and method for collecting data; and making sense of the data through analysis and drawing conclusions.

Planning a Research Study

Planning a research study involves three main steps: (1) define the topic or problem clearly, (2) review existing research to find out what is already known about the topic, and (3) formulate hypotheses (educated guesses) or research questions with clear definitions and ways to measure variables.

Gathering data—through interviews, direct observations of behavior, experiments, and other methods—is part of the science of sociological investigation.

Step 1, the most important step, is to *define a topic or problem* that can be investigated scientifically. Without a clear problem, the research will go nowhere. Specific research topics, ones that can be measured and tested, are usually posed in the form of questions. Consider the case of Hector: Why is it that, in some countries, large segments of the population live in poverty? Why are there many more women and people of color living in poverty? What causes some students—especially those in poor families—to drop out of school? Are people who are poor more vulnerable to excessive drug or alcohol use? The research question must be asked in a precise way. Otherwise, it cannot be tested empirically.

Thinking Sociologically

Pick a topic of interest to you. Now, write a research question based on your topic.

Step 2 in planning the research is *reviewing relevant existing research studies and theory* to determine what other researchers have already learned about the topic. One needs to know how the previous research was done, how terms such as *poverty* were defined, and the strengths and limitations of that research. Social scientists can then link their study to existing findings and expand what is known about the topic. This step usually involves combing through scholarly journals and books on the topic. In the case of Hector, researchers would need to identify what previous studies have said about why young people living in poverty drop out of school.

In *Step 3* (based on the review of the literature on the topic in Step 2), social scientists often *formulate hypotheses—educated guesses about how variables are related to each other, including causal relationships; the speculations do not yet have supporting data.* An example of a hypothesis to study Hector's situation might be as follows: "Poverty is a major cause of *favela* teenagers dropping out of school because they need to earn money for the family." Another hypothesis could predict the opposite—that dropping out of school leads to poverty. Again, a hypothesis provides a statement that we can then test to see if it is true.

Researchers then identify the key concepts, or ideas, in the hypothesis (e.g., poverty and dropping out of school). These concepts can be measured by collecting facts or data. **Variables** are *concepts (ideas) that can vary in frequency of occurrence from one time, place, or person to another.* Examples include levels of poverty, percentage of people living in poverty, and number of years of formal education. Variables can then be measured by collecting data to test the hypothesized relationships between variables. The process of determining how to measure concepts is called *operationalization.*

To operationalize variables, researchers link concepts such as poverty to specific measurements. Using the hypothesis above, concepts such as school dropouts and poverty can be measured by determining the number of times they occur. Dropouts, for instance, might be defined by the number of days of school missed in a designated period of time according to school records. Poverty could be defined as having an annual income that is less than half of the average income for that size of family in Brazil. Measurement of poverty could also include family assets such as ownership of property or other tangible goods such as cattle, automobiles, and indoor plumbing, as well as access to medical care, education, transportation, and other services available to citizens. It is important to be clear, precise, and consistent in how one measures poverty. This is essential so that those reading the study are clear on how the study was done and those doing follow-up studies can critique and improve on the study. Background research—including examination of previous studies of poverty—can provide guidelines or examples for how to operationalize variables.

Thinking Sociologically

Considering your research question, write a hypothesis and identify your variables in the hypothesis. How could you *operationalize* them?

The relationship between variables is central to understanding *causality*, and because use of language is so important, the elements of causal reasoning are discussed in the next "Sociology in Our Social World."

Designing the Research Method and Collecting the Data

After the researcher has carefully planned the study, *Step 4* is to *select appropriate data collection methods*. This selection depends on the levels of analysis of the research question (micro, meso, and macro) the researcher is asking. If researchers want to answer a macro-level research question, such as the effect of poverty on students dropping out of school in Brazil, they are likely to focus on large-scale social and economic data sources such as the Brazilian census. To learn about micro-level issues such as the influence of peers on an individual's decision to drop out of school, researchers will focus on small-group interactions at the micro level. Figure 2.2 illustrates the different levels of analysis.

The method selected is one of the most important decisions in the research process because the quality of the data collected is directly related to answering the research question. Accuracy in planning can mean the difference between a fruitful scientific study and data that have little meaning.

The primary methods used to collect data for research studies include surveys (both interviews and questionnaires), observation studies, controlled experiments, and use of existing materials. Our discussion cannot go into detail about how researchers use these techniques, but a brief explanation gives an idea of why they use these primary methods.

Surveys. The **survey method** *is used when sociologists want to gather information directly from a number of people regarding how they think or feel or what they do. Two forms of surveys are*

The months when ice cream is consumed the most are the same months when drownings occur. However, this is not because of a causal connection. Both variables are related to another factor—hot weather.

Sociology in Our Social World

Being Clear About Causality

Sociology as a science tries to be very careful about language—more precise than we usually are in our everyday conversations. What do we really mean when we say that something causes something else? At the heart of the research process is the effort to find causal relationships (i.e., one variable causes another one to change and not just vary together), called covariations. The following key terms are important in understanding how two variables (concepts that vary in frequency and can be measured) are related:

CORRELATION

- **Correlation** *refers to a relationship between variables (such as poverty and low levels of education), with change in one variable associated with change in another.* The hypothesis above predicts that poverty and teenagers dropping out of school are related and vary together. That is, when the poverty level is high, dropping out of school is also high. If we claim that there is a correlation, however, that is only the first step. We have not yet established that change in one variable *causes* a change in the other.

CAUSE AND EFFECT VARIABLES

- **Cause-and-effect relationships** *occur when there is a relationship between variables so that one variable stimulates a change in another.* Once we have determined that there is probably a relationship, or correlation (the fact that the two variables, such as poverty and dropping out of school, both occur in the same situation), we need to take the next step: figuring out which comes first and seeing if one variable causes change in another. The **independent variable** *is the variable in a cause-and-effect relationship that comes first in a time sequence and causes a change in another variable—the* **dependent variable.** If we hypothesize that poverty causes Hector and others to drop out of school, *poverty* is the independent variable in this hypothesis and *dropping out of school* is the dependent variable, dependent on the poverty. In determining cause and effect, the independent variable must always precede the dependent variable in time sequence if we are to say that one variable causes another.

SPURIOUS RELATIONSHIPS

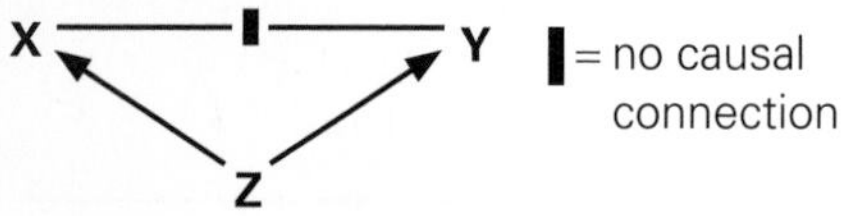

- **Spurious relationships** *occur when there is no causal relationship between the independent and dependent variables, but they vary together, often due to a third variable affecting both of them.* For example, if the quantity of ice cream consumed is highest during those weeks of the year when most drownings occur, these two events are correlated. However, eating ice cream did not cause the increase in deaths. Indeed, hot weather may have caused more people both to purchase ice cream and to go swimming, with the larger number of swimmers resulting in more drowning incidents. The connection between ice cream and drownings is a *spurious relationship.*

CONTROLS

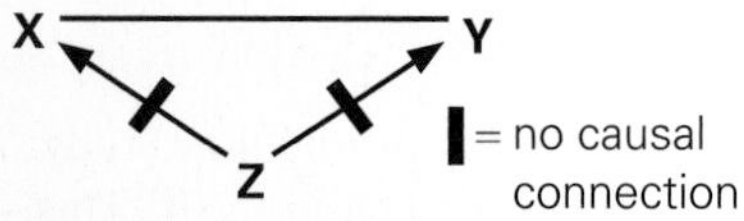

- **Controls** are *steps used by researchers to eliminate all variables except those related to the hypothesis—especially those variables that might be spurious.* Using controls helps ensure that the relationship is not spurious. Using the ice cream example, we might have studied beaches where lots of ice cream is sold and beaches where none is available in order to compare water death incidents.

Micro Level	
Individual	Hector
Small group	Hector's family and close friends
Local community	The *favela*; Hector's local school, church, neighborhood organizations
Meso Level	
Organizations	Brazilian corporations, Catholic Church, and local school system in Brazil
Institutions	Family; education; political, economic, and health systems in the region or nation of Brazil
Ethnic subcultures	Native peoples, African-Brazilians
Macro Level	
National society	Social policies, trends, and programs in Brazil
Global community of nations	Status of Brazil in global economy; trade relations with other countries; programs of international organizations or corporations

Figure 2.2 The Social World Model and Levels of Analysis

common: the interview and the questionnaire. Both involve a series of questions asked of respondents.

Interviews are conducted by talking directly with people and asking questions in person or by telephone. *Questionnaires* are written questions to which respondents reply in writing or electronically. In both cases, questions may be open-ended, allowing the respondent to say or write whatever comes to mind, or closed-ended, requiring the respondent to choose from a set of possible answers.

One method to study school dropouts is to survey teenagers about what caused them to leave school. The researcher would have to evaluate whether an interview or a questionnaire would provide the best information. Interviews are more time-consuming and labor-intensive than questionnaires but are better for gathering in-depth information. However, if the researcher wants information from a large number of teenagers, questionnaires are often more practical and less costly.

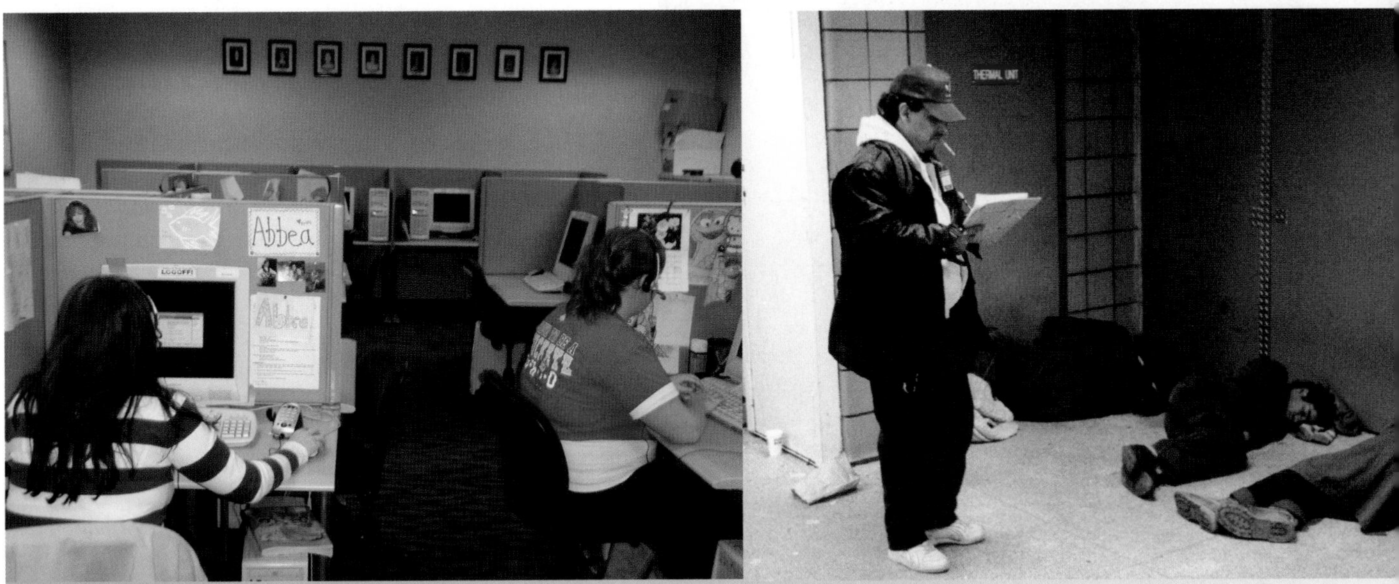

Two examples of the survey are the telephone research lab—like this one on the left at Wright State University in Ohio—and the government census. The university's lab hires out for government or business surveys. The census is taken in the United States and many other countries every 10 years. Sometimes it is difficult to gather accurate data on the entire population, as in the situation with this census worker, who is counting homeless people in Penn Station in New York City.

Thinking Sociologically

How would you word questions objectively (without bias) in a survey about the effects of peer influence on dropping out of school? How could you find out whether your questions are good ones? Would a survey be a good method of data collection to study this research question? Why or why not?

Observational Studies. **Observational studies** (also called field methods) *involve systematic, planned observation and recording of interactions or human behavior in natural settings.* They can take several forms: observations in which the researcher is not involved in group activities but observes or videotapes the activity, or observations in which the researcher actually participates in the activities of the group being studied. The important thing is for observers to avoid altering group functioning and interaction by their presence. The researcher must also be aware that interpretation of the social scene is subject to misunderstanding. Despite these potential problems, observation remains a useful way of obtaining information.

Experiments are especially effective at controlling all of the variables to be able to know which outcomes result from the independent variable. Of course, they are not as effective as observation studies in terms of being real-life situations, and they are more subject to researcher effects—that is, respondents being influenced by the researcher or the research setting.

The results from observation studies are referred to as *qualitative research* (involving the use of written or verbal language or observation to interpret the meaning of something). They provide valuable information that is rich in detail about the context, such as everyday life in the *favela* or Hector's classroom. Unlike research driven by hypotheses to be tested, this method allows the researcher to respond to new ideas that come up during the research. *Quantitative research*, on the other hand, provides hard data such as percentages or other numbers that answer the researcher's questions and can be illustrated in neat tables (Creswell 2009).

Experiments. In **controlled experiments**, *all variables except the one being studied are controlled so researchers can study the effects of the variable under study.* A controlled experiment usually requires an **experimental group**, in which *subjects in the group are exposed to the variable being studied to test the effects of that variable on human behavior,* and a **control group**, in which *the subjects are not exposed to the variable the experimenter wants to test.* The control group provides a baseline to which the experimental group can be compared. Controlled experiments are powerful because they are the most accurate test of cause and effect. By separating the sample into experimental and control groups, the researcher can see if the study's independent variable makes a difference in the behavior of people who are exposed to that variable compared to those who are not. For example, researchers may want to determine whether a new teaching method using technology might help Hector and other kids from the *favela* in their classroom achievement. The control group is exposed to the usual teaching, and the experimental group is provided with the new method or experimental technology. If there is a more positive effect on achievement in the experimental group than the control group, researchers can conclude that the new approach increases learning.

The problem is that many sociological questions cannot be studied in controlled settings because they cannot be placed in a controlled situation like the lab pictured above. For example, Hector's situation in the *favela* cannot be studied in a laboratory setting. Thus, there are many variables that social scientists cannot introduce in the laboratory.

Existing Sources. **Existing sources** refer to *materials that already exist but the researcher uses in a new way or reanalyzes to understand a different research question.* Two main approaches to using existing sources are (a) secondary analysis and (b) content analysis.

Secondary analysis *uses existing data, information that has already been collected in other studies.* Often, large data-collecting organizations such as the United Nations or a country's census bureau, the national education department, or a private research organization will make data available for use by researchers. Consider the question of the dropout rate in Brazil. Researchers can learn a great deal about the patterns of school dropouts from analysis of information gathered by ministries or departments of education. Likewise, if we want to compare modern dropout rates with the rates of an earlier time, we may find data from previous decades to be invaluable.

Secondary analysis can be an excellent way to do meso- or macro-level studies that reveal large-scale patterns in the social world.

Content analysis involves *systematic categorizing and recording of information from written or recorded sources.* With content analysis (a common method in historical research and study of organizations), sociologists can gather the data they need from printed materials—books, magazines, newspapers, laws, letters, videos, archived radio broadcasts, or even artwork. They develop a coding system to classify the source content. A researcher trying to understand shifts in Brazilian attitudes toward Hector's poverty could do a content analysis of popular magazines to see how many pages or stories were devoted to child poverty in the Brazilian media from the 1960s to 2010. Content analysis has the advantage of being relatively inexpensive and easy to do. It is also unobtrusive, meaning that the researcher does not influence the participants being investigated by having direct contact. Furthermore, using materials in historical sequence can be effective in recognizing patterns over time.

Thinking Sociologically

What methods would be appropriate to collect data on your research question? Why?

An example of historical research using existing materials to examine social patterns is illustrated in "Sociology in Our Social World" on page 42. In this case, the researcher, Virginia Kemp Fish, studied records and writings of early women sociologists in Chicago to discover their contributions to sociology and to the betterment of society.

Triangulation *refers to the utilization of two or more methods of data collection to enhance the amount of data for analysis and the accuracy of the findings.* To study Hector's situation, a research study could use macro-level quantitative data on poverty and on educational statistics in Brazil and micro-level interviews with Hector and his peers to determine their goals and their attitudes toward education. Thus, if all findings point to the same conclusion, the researcher can feel much more confident about the study results. Data collection techniques—survey, observation study, controlled experimentation, and analysis of existing sources—represent the dominant methods used to collect data for sociological research.

Social scientists aren't the only professionals who use triangulation. Journalists also consult a variety of sources including social scientists to put together news broadcasts.

Step 5 involves *selecting a sample.* It would be impossible to survey the reasons for poverty or for every teenager dropping out of school in Brazil. Researchers must select a representative group to study that will help them understand the larger group. A part of the research design is determining how to make sure the study includes people who are typical of the total group. When the research study involves a survey or field observation, sociologists need to decide who will be observed or questioned to provide responses representative of the whole. This involves careful selection of a **sample**, *a small group of systematically chosen people in survey research who represent a much larger group.* The objective of sampling is to select a group that accurately represents the characteristics of the entire group (or population) being studied. Researchers use many types of samples. A common one, the representative sample, attempts to accurately reflect the group being studied so that the sample results can be generalized or applied to the larger population. In the case of Hector's *favela*, a sample for a study could be drawn from all 13- to 16-year-olds in his region or city in Brazil.

The most common form of representative sample is the *random sample.* People from every walk of life and every group within the population have an equal chance of being selected for the study. By observing or talking with this smaller group selected from the total population under study, the researcher can get an accurate picture of the total population and have confidence that the findings apply to the larger group. Drawing a representative sample is not

Sociology in Our Social World

The Hull House Circle: Historical Content Analysis in Sociology

Jane Addams, social researcher, critic, and reformer.

Hull House was a settlement house in Chicago, one of several residences established in urban immigrant neighborhoods. Settlement houses created a sense of community for residents and offered a multitude of services to help residents and neighbors negotiate poverty. In addition to offering services, Hull House was the location for a group of women social researchers, reformers, and activists. The well-known social activist Jane Addams (1860–1935), who received a Nobel Peace Prize, was one of them. These women had obtained college degrees in some of the few fields then open to women (political science, law, economics), and because they were often excluded from full-time careers in their fields, they used their education and skills to help others and to do research on social conditions, contributing to the development of the science of sociology. Until recently, women sociologists, such as the members of the Hull House Circle, have not received much attention for their contributions to the science of sociology. Yet some of the earliest social survey research was conducted by the women connected with Hull House, sometimes employing the Hull House residents to help collect data. These women led the first systematic attempt to describe an immigrant community in an American city, a study found in *Hull House Maps and Papers* (Residents of Hull House [ca. 1895] 1970).

Historical research can be an important source of data for sociological analysis, for history can demonstrate causal events vividly. Historical circumstances help us understand why things evolved to the present state of affairs. Virginia Kemp Fish, who originated the designation Hull House Circle, researched historical literature to learn more about the lives and contributions of these women and their place in the sociological literature (Fish 1986). She examined records, letters, biographies, and other historical sources to piece together their stories. By studying their writings and their activist work, Fish showed how they supported each other's work and scholarship and provided emotional encouragement and intellectual stimulation rather than interacting in terms of an unequal power distribution. Fish also made an interesting observation about these women's professional styles as compared with the styles of men. While men often received their training and support from a mentor (an older, established, and respected man in the field), the women of Hull House operated within a network of egalitarian relationships and interactions.

According to Fish's research, the data and documents collected by their leader, Jane Addams, and other Hull House women provide baseline information that has been used as a starting point or comparison for later studies—for social researchers in the fields of immigration, ethnic relations, poverty, health care, housing, unemployment, work and occupations, delinquency and crime, war, and social movements.

always simple. In the case of Brazil, people constantly move in and out of the *favela*. Those who have just arrived may not have the same characteristics as those who have been living there a long time. Developing an effective sampling technique is often a complex process, but it is important to have a sample that represents the group being studied. If researchers wanted to know the attitudes of Brazilian teenagers toward school, they would not question only adults from the city of São Paulo, Brazil.

Step 6 involves *collecting the data*. Now that the appropriate research method for collecting data and the sample to study have been selected, the researcher's next step is to analyze the data collected and see what they say about the research questions and hypotheses.

Making Sense of the Data: Analysis

Once data are gathered, *Step 7* is to *analyze the data and evaluate the relationship of variables to each other*. Let's say we have 100 interviews from residents of Hector's *favela*, plus a notebook full of field observation notes from "hanging out" with the youth there. What do we do with them? Social researchers use multiple techniques to analyze data. First, the variables being tested must be clear: If dropout rates are high among Hector's friends, was their school achievement low? How were they treated by peers and teachers? What other factors are present? This analysis can become quite complex, but the purpose is the same—to determine the relationship between the variables being examined. Second, sociologists determine the most effective tools to analyze the relationships between variables. Sociology is not guesswork or speculation. It involves careful, objective analysis of specific data.

Discussion and criticism are an important part of science and make possible more accurate findings, new ideas and interpretations, and more sophisticated approaches to studying problems. Interpretation of data involves judgment and opinion, often based on the theory guiding the research. As such, it can be challenged by other researchers, who might interpret the results differently or challenge the methods that were used to collect and analyze the data. Sociologists grow through these critiques, as does the field of sociology itself. Because every research study should be *replicable*—capable of being repeated—enough information must be given to ensure that another researcher could repeat the study and compare the results.

Step 8 involves *discussion of results and drawing conclusions* for the analysis. A report is developed, outlining the research project and analysis of the data collected. The final section of the report presents a discussion of the results, draws conclusions as to whether or not the hypotheses were supported, interprets the results, and makes recommendations from the researcher's point of view, if appropriate. As part of the presentation and discussion of results, the report may contain tables or figures presenting summaries of data that are useful in understanding the data. The "Engaging Sociology" on page 44 provides useful tips on reading research tables found in journal articles and newspapers.

Given that social science research focuses on humans and humans are changeable, it is difficult to say that any single study has definitively proven the hypothesis or answered a research question with finality. Indeed, the word *prove* is never used to describe the interpretation of findings in the social and behavioral sciences. Rather, social scientists say that findings tend to support or reject hypotheses.

Science and Uncertainty

So why bother doing social science research if findings can be challenged, nothing seems absolute, and conclusions seem so uncertain? We can base social policy and our understanding of society on information that is as close to the truth as possible, even if we can never claim absolute truth. Systematic, scientific research brings us closer to the reality of the social world than guesswork and opinions. Having supportive findings from numerous studies, not just one, builds a stronger case to support a theory and conclusions. The search for truth is ongoing—a kind of mission in life for those of us who do research. Furthermore, as we get closer to an accurate understanding of society, our social policies can be based on the most accurate knowledge available.

What makes a discipline scientific is not the subject matter. It is how we conduct our research and what we consider valid evidence. The four core features of a science are (1) a commitment to *empirically validated evidence, facts, and information* that are confirmed through systematic processes of testing using the five senses; (2) a focus on *being convinced by the evidence* rather than by our preconceived ideas; (3) *absolute integrity and objectivity* in reporting and in conducting research; and (4) continual openness to *having our findings reexamined* and new interpretations proposed.

It is the fourth feature that causes us to be open to criticism and alternative interpretations. To have credible findings, we always consider the possibility that we have overlooked alternative explanations of the data and alternative ways to view the problem. This is one of the hardest principles to grasp, but it is one of the most important in reaching the truth. Science—including social science—is not facts to be memorized. Science is a process that is made possible by a social exchange of ideas, a clash of opinions, and a continual search for truth. Knowledge in the sciences is created by vigorous debate. Rather than just memorizing the concepts in this book to take a test, we hope you will engage in the creation of knowledge by entering into these debates.

Engaging Sociology

How to Read a Research Table

A statistical table is a researcher's labor-saving device. Quantitative data presented in tabular form are clearer and more concise than the same information presented in several written paragraphs. A good table has clear signposts to help the reader avoid confusion. For instance, Table 2.1 shows many of the main features of a table, and the list that follows explains how to read each feature.

Table 2.1 **Educational Attainment by Selected Characteristic: 2009, for Persons 25 Years Old and Over, Reported in Thousands**

	Percentage of Population—Highest Level						
Characteristic	*Population (1,000)*	*Not a High School Graduate*	*High School Graduate*	*Some College, but No Degree*	*Associate's Degree*[a]	*Bachelor's Degree*	*Advanced Degree*
Total persons	194,318	14.3	31.6	16.7	8.6	18.9	9.9
Age years:							
25–34	40,520	11.7	28.0	19.2	8.9	22.8	9.3
35–44	41,322	11.7	28.7	16.6	10.2	21.4	11.4
45–54	44,366	10.9	32.2	17.0	10.8	18.8	10.4
55–64	34,289	11.1	30.2	17.8	9.2	18.6	13.1
65–74	20,404	17.7	36.4	15.5	5.9	13.9	10.5
75 and over	17,384	26.3	36.6	13.7	4.9	11.4	7.0
Sex:							
Male	95,518	13.8	31.4	16.8	7.9	19.0	11.1
Female	102,767	12.9	30.8	17.3	10.0	19.0	10.1
Race:							
White[b]	162,079	12.9	31.2	16.9	9.1	19.3	10.7
Black[b]	22,598	15.9	35.4	20.3	9.0	12.7	6.6
Other	13,608	14.3	22.3	13.9	7.8	25.8	16.0
Hispanic origin:							
Hispanic	25,956	38.1	29.3	13.3	6.1	9.6	3.6
Non-Hispanic	172,329	9.6	31.3	17.6	9.4	20.4	11.6
Region:							
Northeast	36,572	11.8	33.3	13.1	8.6	19.9	13.3
Midwest	43,163	10.2	34.4	17.1	9.8	18.2	9.7
South	72,720	15.0	31.8	16.9	8.6	17.9	9.8
West	45,829	14.8	25.1	19.9	9.1	20.7	10.5

Source: U.S. Census Bureau (2011c).

Note: Features of the table are adapted from Broom and Selznick (1963).

a. Includes vocational degrees.

b. For persons who selected this race group only.

TITLE: The title provides information on the major topic and variables in the table.

"Educational Attainment by Selected Characteristic: 2009"

HEADNOTE (or Subtitle): Many tables will have a headnote or subtitle under the title, giving information relevant to understanding the table or units in the table.

For this table, the reader is informed that it includes all persons over the age of 25 and they will be reported in thousands.

HEADINGS AND STUBS: Tables generally have one or two levels of headings under the title and headnotes. These instruct the reader about what is in the columns below.

In this table, the headings indicate the level of education achieved so that the reader can identify the percentage with a specified level of education.

The table also has a stub: the far-left column under "Characteristic." This lists the items that are being compared according to the categories found in the headings. In this case, the stub indicates population of various characteristics: age, sex, race, Hispanic origin, and region.

MARGINAL TABS: In examining the numbers in the table, try working from the outside in. The marginals, the figures at the margins of the table, often provide summary information.

In this table, the first column of numbers is headed "Population (1,000)," indicating (by thousands) the total number of people in each category who were part of the database. The columns to the right indicate—by percentages—the level of educational attainment for each category.

CELLS: To make more detailed comparisons, examine specific cells in the body of the table. These are the boxes that hold the numbers or percentages.

In this table, the cells contain data on age, sex, racial/ethnic (white, black, Hispanic), and regional differences in education.

UNITS: Units refer to how the data are reported. Data could be in percentages, in number per 100 or 1,000, or in other units.

In this table, the data are reported first in raw number in thousands and then in percentages.

FACTS FROM THE TABLE: After reviewing all of the above information, the reader is ready to make some interpretations about what the data mean.

In this table, the reader might note that young adults are more likely to have a college education than older citizens.

Likewise, African Americans and Hispanics are less likely than whites to have college or graduate degrees, but the rate for "Other" is even higher than that for whites, probably because it includes Asian Americans. People in the Northeast and West have the highest levels of education. What other interesting patterns do you see?

FOOTNOTES: Some tables have footnotes, usually indicating something unusual about the data or where to find more complete data.

In this table, two footnotes are provided so that the reader does not make mistakes in interpretation.

SOURCE: The source note, found under the table, points out the origin of the data. It is usually identified by the label "Source."

Under this table, the source note says "U.S. Census Bureau (2011c)."

Ethical Issues in Social Research

What problems are created if a scientist conducts research that has negative impacts on the participants? It is due to this concern that most universities and other research organizations, especially those receiving public money, have human subjects review boards. The boards review the proposed research plans and methods to be used to be sure they will not hurt the subjects in some way. Of special concern are research projects in medical sciences, but social scientists must also have their research reviewed.

Sociologists and other scientists are bound by the ethical codes of conduct governing research. The American Sociological Association (ASA) code of ethics outlines standards that researchers are expected to observe when doing research, teaching, and publishing. They include points such as being objective, reporting findings and sources fully, making no promises to respondents that cannot be honored, accepting no support that requires violation of these principles, completing contracted work, and delineating responsibilities in works with multiple authors. Related to these standards are the following key ethical issues for sociologists, each a part of the ASA code of ethics:

- How will the findings from the research be used? Will the information hurt individuals, communities, or nations if it gets into the hands of "enemies"? Can it be used to aggravate hostilities? In whose interest is the research being carried out?
- How can the researcher protect the privacy and identities of respondents and informants? Is the risk to participants justified by an anticipated outcome of improved social conditions? For example, in several instances, courts have subpoenaed journalists and social scientists, forcing them to reveal confidential sources and information, and some have spent time in jail to protect the confidentiality of their respondents (Liptak and Newman 2005; Scarce 1999).
- Is there informed consent among the people being studied? How much can and should the researcher tell participants about the purpose of the research without completely biasing the outcome? Does informed consent mean only signing a release form at the beginning of a study? Is it acceptable to lie or to mislead participants so that they do not change their behavior when they are responding to the situations that the researcher has created? Will there be any harm to the participants—including injury to self-esteem or feelings of guilt and self-doubt? Consider the following study: Philip Zimbardo and colleagues conducted a well-known social psychological experiment in which he designed a mock prison and assigned students to roles of prisoners and guards (Zimbardo et al. 1973). The purpose of the study was to gauge the degree to which social roles affect attitudes and behaviors. However, the students took the roles so seriously that they no longer distinguished reality from the artificial situation, and some "guards" became violent and abusive toward the "prisoners." Given these negative reactions, the experiment was discontinued, and students were informed about the purpose of the study. Is a research project unethical if it negatively affects a participant's self-esteem? Most social scientists would say that such research is unethical.
- How much invasion of privacy is legitimate in the name of research? How much disclosure of confidential information, even in disguised form, is acceptable? For example, a researcher who studies sexual behavior and attitudes may collect data about the most intimate of relationships. How this confidential information is handled to protect respondents is of utmost importance in research ethics.

Codes of ethics provide general guidelines. In addition, most universities and organizations where research is common have human subjects review boards whose function is to ensure that human participants are not harmed by the research.

Thinking Sociologically

What might be some ethical problems in the research project you are thinking about as you read this chapter? What, for example, would be the ethical issues of studying a setting or situation but not informing those people involved that you are studying them?

The Development of Sociology as a Discipline

Throughout recorded history, humans have been curious about how and why people form groups. That should not be surprising because the groups we belong to are so central to human existence and to a sense of satisfaction in life.

Early Sociological Thought

Religion had a major influence on the way individuals thought about the world and their social relationships. Christianity dominated European thought systems during the Middle Ages, from the end of the Roman Empire to the 1500s, while Islamic beliefs were very widespread in much of the Middle East and parts of Africa. The North African Islamic scholar Ibn Khaldun (1332–1406) was the first on record to suggest a systematic approach to explain the social world. Khaldun was particularly interested in understanding the feelings of solidarity that held tribal groups together during his day, a time of great conflict and wars (Alatas 2006; Hozien n.d.). These issues interested philosophers and theologians, but they did not use scientific methods to gather data and test their theories, processes that now allow us to get closer to the facts.

Sociology has its modern roots as a scientific discipline in mostly European ideas of 19th-century social, political, and religious philosophers, who laid the groundwork for the scientific study of society. Until the 19th century, social philosophers provided the primary approach to understanding society, one that invariably had a strong moral tone. Their opinions were derived from abstract reflection about how the social world should work. Often, they advocated forms of government that they believed would be just and good, denouncing those they considered inhumane or evil. For instance, Plato's *Republic*, written around 400 BCE, outlines plans for an ideal state—complete with government, family, economic systems, class structure, and education—designed to achieve social justice. Even today, people debate the ideal communities proposed by Plato, Aristotle, Machiavelli, Thomas More, and other philosophers from the past.

Conditions Leading to Modern Sociology

Several conditions in the 19th century gave rise to the emergence of sociology. First, European nations were imperial powers that were establishing oppressive colonies in other cultures. This exposure to other cultures encouraged at least some Europeans to learn more about the people in their new colonies. Second, they sought to understand the social revolutions taking place and the changes brought about by the Industrial Revolution. Finally, advances in the natural sciences demonstrated the value of the scientific method, and some wished to apply this scientific method to understand the social world.

The social backdrop for the earliest European sociologists was the Industrial Revolution (which began around the middle of the 1700s) and the French Revolution (1789–1799). No one had clear, systematic explanations for why the old social structure, which had lasted since the early Middle Ages, was collapsing or why cities were exploding with migrants from rural areas. French society was in turmoil, members of the nobility were being executed, and new rules of justice were taking hold. Churches were subordinate to the state, equal rights under the law were established for citizens, and democratic rule emerged. These dramatic changes marked the end of the traditional monarchy and the beginning of a new social order. With no methods to collect information on the dramatic changes taking place, leaders in France had to rely on the social philosophies of the time to react to the problems that surrounded them, philosophies that were not informed by social science studies.

It was in this setting that the scientific study of society emerged. Two social thinkers, Henri Saint-Simon (1760–1825) and Auguste Comte (1798–1857), decried the lack of systematic data collection or objective analysis in social thought. These Frenchmen are considered the first to suggest that a science of society could help people understand and perhaps control the rapid changes and unsettling revolutions taking place.

Comte officially coined the term *sociology* in 1838. His basic premise was that religious or philosophical speculation about society did not provide an adequate understanding of how to solve society's problems. Just as the natural sciences provided basic facts about the physical world, so, too, there was a need to gather scientific knowledge about the social world. Only then could leaders systematically apply this scientific knowledge to improve social conditions.

Comte asked two basic questions: What holds society together and gives rise to a stable order in lieu of anarchy? Further, why and how do societies change? Comte conceptualized society as divided into two parts:(1) *Social statics* referred to aspects of society that give rise to order, stability, and harmony. (2) *Social dynamics* referred to change and evolution in society over time. Simply stated, Comte was concerned with what contemporary sociologists and the social world model in this book refer to as *structure* (social statics) and *process* (social dynamics). By understanding these aspects of the social world, Comte felt that leaders could strengthen the society and respond appropriately to change. His optimistic belief was that sociology would be the "queen of sciences," guiding leaders to construct a better social order.

Sociology continued developing as scholars contemplated further changes brought about by the Industrial Revolution. Massive social and economic changes in the 18th and 19th centuries brought about restructuring and sometimes the demise of political monarchies, aristocracies, and feudal lords. Scenes of urban squalor were common in Great Britain and other industrializing European nations. Machines replaced both agricultural workers and cottage (home) industries because they produced an abundance of goods faster, better, and cheaper. Peasants were pushed off the land by new technologies and migrated to urban areas to find work at the same time as a powerful new social class of capitalists was emerging. Industrialization brought the need for a new skilled class of laborers, putting new demands on an education system that had served only the

Industrialization had a number of positive outcomes, including the expansion of prosperity to a larger class of people, but it also had some high costs in exploitation of workers and slums in places like Paris.

The Bastille, a state prison in Paris, France, and a symbol of oppression, was seized by the common people in the French Revolution, an upheaval in society that forced social analysts to think differently about society and social stability. Today rallying points for social movements and revolutions such as Tahrir Square in Cairo, Egypt, and various parks and squares in New York City for Occupy Wall Street illustrate that uprisings of the common people are still changing societies.

elite. Families now depended on wages from their labor in the industrial sector to stay alive.

These changes stimulated other social scientists to study society and its problems. The writings of Émile Durkheim, Karl Marx, Harriet Martineau, Max Weber, W. E. B. Du Bois, and many other early sociologists set the stage for the development of sociological theories. Accompanying the development of sociological theory was the utilization of the scientific method—the systematic gathering and recording of reliable and accurate data to test ideas.

Three Approaches to the Discipline of Sociology

First, we have the situation of Hector living in poverty (research problem). Then, we have possible explanations to help us understand his situation (theories). Finally, we have methods of collecting information (data) to study his situation. Sociologists put these three parts together to carry out research. Here, we introduce three long-standing approaches to sociology that speak to the relationship between research and theory: scientific sociology, humanistic sociology, and activist public sociology (Buechler 2008). Keep in mind that all three approaches have been around for almost as long as sociology has existed. The founders of sociology sometimes combined the approaches, which lay the foundation for most modern theories we use today. Sometimes these approaches led to controversy within sociology over the proper role of sociologists, as we see below.

Scientific Sociology. One approach, strongly influenced by the ideas of Auguste Comte, Émile Durkheim, and other early sociologists, stresses *scientific sociology*—being objective and modeling the discipline after the natural sciences. For these early scholars, the net result of sociological work was pure, unbiased analysis for the purpose of scientific understanding. As they saw it, others would be left to decide how to *use* the facts. Sociology was to stick to pure science: fact-finding and testing hypotheses.

Humanistic Sociology. A second view of the discipline is called *humanistic sociology*: "When scientific sociologists do science, they emphasize the word *science*, linking it to other sciences. When humanistic sociologists do social science, they emphasize the word *social*, separating it from other sciences" (Buechler 2008:326). This tradition puts much more emphasis on the unique capacity of humans to create *meaning* in their lives—the way humans interpret their social world. However, when one is studying meaning—what does a handshake, a kiss, or a cross symbolize for people?—it is virtually impossible to produce objective quantitative data, which are often the standard of the natural sciences. Humanistic sociologists argue that studying humans is qualitatively different from research in the natural sciences, and that focusing only on rigorous methods and standards of objectivity causes researchers to miss some of the most interesting and important dimensions of human social behavior.

Public Sociology. The third view stresses the relevance of sociology to society. Most early sociologists—beginning with Lester Ward, the first president of the American Sociological Association—promoted sociology as means for improving society (Calhoun 2007). These **public sociologists** *strive to better understand how society operates and to make practical use of their sociological findings*. They use their findings to help create and advocate for social policies that they hope will make society better. Those advocating for "public sociology" want to move the focus of sociology from the classrooms and labs of universities into communities where they can have a direct impact on social change and decision making (American Sociological Association Task Force on Institutionalizing Public Sociologies 2005). In advocating for public sociology, president of the American Sociological Association Michael Burawoy wrote: "As a mirror and conscience of society, sociology must define, promote and inform public debate about deepening class and racial inequality, new gender regimes, environmental degradation, market fundamentalism, state and non-state violence" (Burawoy 2005:4). Sociology should deal with multiple groups outside the university, from the media to oppressed communities, and at all levels of analysis. The focus is typically on policy analysis or on helping social movements identify strategies of change that will be effective. The idea is to consider what *might* be and what would make a better world. We might say it is a "do something about problems out there" sociology.

One aspect of public sociology has received increased attention in recent years because there are job opportunities in this area: applied sociology. **Applied sociology** uses *sociological knowledge and research skills to address organizational needs or problems in government, education, health care settings, social service agencies, and business organizations; often the client determines the research questions*. Depending on their positions, they may be known as sociological practitioners, applied sociologists, clinical sociologists, policy analysts, program planners, or evaluation researchers, among other titles. They focus on pragmatic ways to improve organizations or society, sometimes recommending major changes and sometimes proposing modest policy proposals. Their careers take them outside of academia.

As the discipline of sociology grew from its early days and became an acknowledged "social science," some sociologists advocated for "pure" research that is disconnected from the public sphere. Throughout the history of the discipline, sociologists have debated their proper role in society. However, like physicists, chemists, and geologists, many sociologists believe that there are both important practical applications of the discipline and many policy issues that need to be informed by good science. Public sociologists—whether professors or those in a variety of professions outside academia—share a common goal: to better understand how society operates *and* to make practical use of their sociological findings (Pickard and Poole 2007).

Table 2.2 outlines the key differences between basic (pure) scientific sociology and public sociology. In most chapters, you will find a feature called "Sociologists in Action," which describes a sociologist with a bachelor's, master's, or doctoral degree working in the topic area being discussed.

In summary, the different traditions of sociology include the following:

1. *Scientific sociology*—developing theory and doing scientific research (e.g., natural sciences that simply seek to expand human knowledge)
2. *Humanistic sociology*—focusing on what is human and humane, with less concern for whether it is scientific in the same way that physics or geology is scientific
3. *Public sociology*—stressing how sociology can be practical and can make human life better

Each of the approaches to sociology is rooted in history and plays a part in sociological research. Which is most relevant to a study depends on the purpose of the study. All three approaches will be given attention in this book, for they are all part of mainstream sociology today. All three approaches use the same sociological theories, to which we turn next.

Table 2.2 **Scientific Versus Public Sociology**

	Scientific Sociology	*Public/Applied Sociology*
Orientation	Theory building, hypothesis testing	Program effects, focus on consequences of practices
Goal	Knowledge production	Knowledge utilization, problem solving
Source	Self- or discipline-generated; supported by grants	Self- or discipline-generated (public sociology) or client-generated (applied sociology)

Source: Adapted with permission from the NTL Institute (DeMartini 1982).

Sociology's Major Theoretical Perspectives

Recall the description of the social world model presented in Chapter 1. It stresses the levels of analysis—smaller units existing within larger social systems. We have mentioned that some methods of data collection are better for analyzing micro-level processes of interaction (e.g., participant observation), whereas other methods work more effectively for understanding macro-level social systems (e.g., secondary data analysis). The same is true of theoretical perspectives. Some theoretical perspectives are especially effective in understanding micro-level interactions, and others illuminate macro-level structures, although the distinctions are not absolute. Either type of theory—those most useful at the micro or macro levels—can be used at the meso level, depending on the research question being asked. To illustrate how a social problem is approached differently by these four major theoretical perspectives, we will further delve into our examination of Hector's circumstances (Ashley and Orenstein 2009). Keep in mind that sociologists use many theories, some of which will be introduced in future chapters.

Sociologists have several perspectives that can help us understand the poverty Hector experiences in São Paulo, Brazil. For example, Hector's interactions with family, peers, schoolteachers, employers, and religious leaders can be studied at the micro level of analysis. A micro analysis would stress the individual friends, small groups, and neighborhood of which he is a part.

In contrast, meso-level analysis focuses on institutions, large organizations, and ethnic communities. For instance, the policies of the city of São Paulo regarding transportation, sanitation, education, and health affect what happens to local residents in a *favela.* Migration of native Brazilians ("Indians") from rural areas into the big city of São Paulo is a meso-level issue. These ethnic communities often have little education (due to inadequate schools in the areas where they live), and residents have few job skills, but they have been displaced from their native areas due to encroachment of corporations and agribusiness in their territories. They may find themselves in urban slums where there is conflict between ethnic groups for the few jobs that do exist. This is not a global issue or a micro-level issue. It has to do with how large corporations and institutions meet the needs of ethnic groups within the nation—or fail to do so.

Macro-level analysis considers the larger social context—national and global—within which Hector and his family live. From this perspective, Hector's position in society is part of a total system in which Brazilian people in poverty constitute a reserve labor force, available to work in unskilled jobs as needed. The key is "as needed." International trade, or a change in the Brazilian economy, could have an influence on Hector's job prospects quite independent of his individual motivation to work. Macro-level theories would consider questions related to Brazilian policies as a nation and the position of Brazil in the world system.

A **theoretical perspective** is *a basic view of society that guides sociologists' research and analysis. Theoretical perspectives are the broadest theories in sociology, providing overall approaches to understanding the social world and social problems.* Sociologists draw on major theoretical perspectives at each level of analysis to guide their research and to help them understand social interactions and social organizations.

Micro-level interactions occur in classrooms every day, both among peers and between teachers and students.

Micro- to Meso-Level Theories

If we want to study Hector's interaction with his friends and their influence on him (micro level) or his school performance, successes, and failures, theories at the micro and meso levels will help guide our research. Two theories that are most often used at the micro and meso levels of analysis are discussed in this section.

Symbolic Interaction

Symbolic interaction theory (also called social construction or interpretative theory) *sees humans as active agents who create shared meanings of symbols and events and then interact on the basis of those meanings.* For example, Hector interacts with his family and friends in the *favela* in ways that he has learned are necessary for survival there. In Hector's world of poverty, the informal interactions of the street and the more formal interactions of the school carry different sets of meanings that guide Hector's behavior.

Symbolic interaction theory assumes that groups form around interacting individuals. Through these interactions, people learn to share common understandings and to learn what to expect from others. They make use of **symbols**, *actions or objects that represent something else and therefore have meaning beyond their own existence*, such as flags, wedding rings, language, or verbal and nonverbal communication (words and gestures) to interpret interactions with others. Symbolic communication (e.g., language) helps people construct a meaningful world. This implies that humans are not merely passive agents responding to their environments. Instead, they are actively engaged in creating their own meaningful social world based on their constructions and interpretations of the social world. Many people accept the social definitions and interpretations of others, saving themselves the effort of interpreting symbols and making sense of the stimuli around them (Blumer 1969; Fine 1990). Still, more than any other theory in the social sciences, symbolic interaction theory stresses *human agency*—the active role of individuals in creating their social environment.

George Herbert Mead (1863–1931) is prominently identified with the symbolic interaction perspective (Mead [1934] 1962). Mead explored the mental processes associated with how humans define or make sense of situations. He placed special emphasis on human interpretations of gestures and symbols (including language) and the meanings we attach to our actions. He also examined how we learn our social roles in society, such as mother, child, teacher, and friend, and how we learn to carry out these roles. Indeed, as we will see in Chapter 4, he insisted that our notion of who we are—our *self*—emerges from social experience and interaction with others. Language is critical to this process, for it allows us to step outside of our own experience and reflect back on how others see us. Indeed, human language is a unique and powerful human trait, as is illustrated in the next "Sociology in Our Social World."

These ideas of how we construct our individual social worlds and have some control over them come from a perspective known as the Chicago School of symbolic interaction. Another symbolic interaction approach—the Iowa School—makes an explicit link between individual identities and positions within organizations—the meso level of the social system (Kuhn 1964). If we hold several

Sociology in Our Social World

Human Language and the Marvel of a College Classroom

A college classroom is a magical place, and this is true mostly because of human language. All other species communicate with a fairly limited number of sounds they can make. We can learn to recognize when our dog is hungry, when it needs to go to the bathroom, or when it is alarmed by an unrecognized person in the yard. Human language is distinctive. Except for humans and perhaps dolphins, whales, and chimpanzees, other animals only communicate about something that is happening in the present time and location.

Humans as infants can make hundreds of sounds—perhaps as many as a thousand. Each language identifies about 50 of those sounds that come to be designated as meaningful language sounds. In English, this includes such sounds as *sss, mmm, nnn, ttt, kkk, bbb,* and *ooo.* We take these designated sounds and combine them in various ways to make words: *cat, dog, college, student.* This ability to combine sounds into words and words into sentences is called a *distinctive feature system.* A distinctive feature system allows you to say something to your instructor that she or he has never heard any other human say before. The sounds are familiar, as are the words themselves, but you may combine them in a novel way that causes a new idea to occur to your listener. This is actually the root of much humor: you say a sentence or tell a story that has such a surprising ending that it causes the listener to laugh.

Now your animal companions at home clearly have memory. They can recognize you when you get home. Your dog may well remember the other pups in his litter. However, they cannot remember together. They cannot gather to recall and share stories about good old dad the way you can recall the quirky traits of your professors with friends. Your dogs and cats cannot plan for the future—planning a litter reunion for next summer, for example.

The fact that our communication is a *distinctive feature system* allows something unique: temporal and spatial sharing. We can remember together our experiences of the past, and we can pass ideas from one person to another. We can discuss the ideas of people who have died and have perhaps been gone for more than a century. A mare cannot transmit to her colt the racing ideas of Man o' War, the great racehorse of the 1920s, let alone the experiences of horses involved in the Trojan War, or even the more recent derby winner Secretariat. However, whether in a classroom or a pub, humans can discuss the ideas of Plato, or Muhammad, or Karl Marx. Further, humans, because of words, can take other perspectives—to vicariously visit the other side of the planet or to go back in history to experience a time when an entirely different set of ideas about life were common.

When we come into a classroom, something mysterious, something amazing, happens. Language allows us to see things from a new point of view. What a remarkable gift that we can share ideas and see things through the eyes of someone different from ourselves, and it is largely because of the human *distinctive feature system* of communication. What an interesting species to study! What a marvel that we can do so in a classroom.

positions—honors student, club president, daughter, sister, student, athlete, thespian, middle-class person—those positions form a relatively stable core—our *self.* We will interpret new situations in light of our social positions, some of which are very important and anchor how we see the social world. Once a core *self* is established, it guides and shapes the way we interact with people in many situations—even new social settings (Kuhn 1964). Thus, if you are president of an organization and have the responsibility for overseeing the organization, part of your self-esteem, your view of responsible citizenship, and your attitude toward life will be shaped by that position. Thus, the Iowa School of symbolic interactionism places less emphasis on individual choice, but more on recognizing the link between the micro, meso, and macro levels of society, as we add the millions of interactions together to form large groups and societies (Carrothers and Benson 2003; Stryker 1980).

The following principles summarize the modern symbolic interaction perspective and how individual action results in groups, organizations, and institutions in societies (Ritzer 2011):

- Humans are endowed with the capacity for thought, shaped by social interaction.
- In social interaction, people learn the meanings and symbols that allow them to exercise thought and participate in human action.
- People modify the meanings and symbols as they struggle to make sense of their situations and the events they experience.
- Interpreting the situation involves seeing things from more than one perspective and choosing one course of action.
- These patterns of action and interaction make up the interactive relations that we call groups, institutions, and societies.
- Our positions or memberships in these groups, organizations, and societies may profoundly influence the way we define ourselves and may lead to fairly stable patterns of interpretation of our experiences and of social life.

To summarize, the modern symbolic interaction theory emphasizes the process each individual goes through in creating or changing his or her social reality and identity within a social setting. Without a system of shared symbols, humans cannot coordinate their actions with one another, and hence society as we understand it would not be possible.

Critique of the Symbolic Interaction Perspective. Each theory has its critics, just as each political party has critics. Although symbolic interaction theory is widely used by sociologists today, it is often criticized for neglecting the macro-level structures of society that affect human behavior. By focusing on interpersonal interactions, large-scale social forces such as an economic depression or a political revolution that shape human destinies are given less consideration. With the focus on individual *agency* and the ability of each individual to create his or her meaning in social situations, symbolic interaction has often been less attuned to important macro-level issues of social class position, social power, historical circumstances, or international conflict between societies (Meltzer, Petras, and Reynolds 1975). In addition, it is difficult to study abstract ideas like "the development of the self."

Despite these limitations, theorists from the symbolic interaction perspective have made significant contributions to understanding the development of social identities and interactions that underlie groups, organizations, and societies. Many of these studies will be discussed in chapters throughout the book.

Rational Choice (Exchange) Theory

Hector and his friends from the *favela* make decisions to stay in school or drop out. According to **rational choice theory**, *humans are fundamentally concerned with self-interests, making rational decisions based on weighing costs and rewards of the projected outcome*. Picture it as a mental balance sheet: On the plus side, staying in school may lead to future opportunities not available to the uneducated. On the minus side, school is a negative experience, and the family needs help now to feed its members, so going to school is a "waste of time." Which side will win depends on Hector's balance sheet, and on family and friends' assessment of the rewards versus costs.

Consider another example—that of women deciding whether to stay in abusive relationships based on rewards versus costs. In considering a divorce, do the rewards of escaping a conflicted, abusive marriage outweigh the costs of daily economic and emotional stress related to going it alone or the criticism of family and friends? Also, consider homosexual couples. There are potential costs of coming

Rational choice theory states that people make decisions based on a rational calculation of costs and benefits. For some women in violent relationships, the options of leaving and of living on their own without resources seems more costly than the abuse they suffer. The balance of costs and benefits must shift before they are likely to leave the situation.

out of the closet to friends, family, and employers. There may also be significant benefits: acknowledged homosexuals no longer live in hiding with constant fear of being exposed, and when applying for health insurance, coverage is available only for recognized partners. These cost-and-benefit decisions are the types of questions addressed by rational choice theorists.

Rational choice, also called exchange theory, has its roots in several disciplines—economics, behavioral psychology, anthropology, and philosophy (Cook, O'Brien, and Kollock 1990). Social behavior is seen as an exchange activity—a transaction in which resources are given and received (Blau 1964; Homans 1974). Every interaction involves an exchange of something valued—money, time, material goods, attention, sex, allegiance, and so on. People stay in relationships because they get something from the exchange, and they leave relationships that cost them without providing adequate benefits. They constantly evaluate whether there is reciprocity or balance in a relationship so that they are receiving as much benefit as they give. Simply stated, people are more likely to act if they see some reward or success coming from their behavior. The implication is that self-interest for the individual is the guiding element in human interaction.

In summary, rational choice theory involves the following key ideas:

- Human beings are mostly self-centered and are driven in their behavior by self-interest.
- Humans calculate costs and benefits (rewards) in making decisions.
- Humans are rational—not in the sense that they seek to determine meaning, but in that they weigh choices in order to maximize their own benefits and minimize costs.
- Every interaction involves exchanges entailing rewards and penalties or expenditures.
- A key element in exchanges is reciprocity—a balance in the exchange of benefits.
- People keep a mental ledger in their heads about whether they owe someone else or that person owes them.

Critique of the Rational Choice Theory. Rational choice theorists give little attention to micro-level internal mental processes, such as self-reflection. They see human conduct as self-centered, with rational behavior implying that people seek to maximize rewards and minimize costs. Charitable, unselfish, or altruistic behavior is not easily explained by this view. Why would a soldier sacrifice his or her life to save a comrade? Why would a starving person in a Nazi concentration camp share a crust of bread with another? Proponents of rational choice counter the criticism by arguing that if a person feels good about helping another, that in itself is a reward that compensates for the cost.

Sometimes acting in one's short-term self-interest can backfire. In some U.S. states and school districts, some residents voted against public school levies because they did not want to pay the extra hundred dollars or so per year in taxes. Yet the same voters have been dismayed to find when trying to sell their house that their property value has dropped by as much as $15,000 because they live in a district that does not support education (Roberts 2003). In short, acting in what seems to be our own self-interest may not always end up being the best choice.

Thinking Sociologically

How can symbolic interaction and rational choice perspectives help explain dating behavior? For example, how might a "hookup" mean something different to females as opposed to males? How would each of the micro theories above answer this question a bit differently?

Rational choice theory assumes that people act in ways that maximize their own self-interests. Some citizens vote against school levies in order to save a few dollars in taxes, only to find that after a school levy fails, their property values fall, sometimes far more than the taxes they would have saved. So people do not always accurately assess their self-interests.

Meso- and Macro-Level Theories

Meso- and macro-level theories consider large units in the social world: organizations (such as General Motors or the Episcopal Church), institutions (such as education, religion, health care, politics, or economics), societies (such as Canada or Mexico), or global systems (such as the World Trade Organization or World Bank). For example, Hector lives in a modernizing country, Brazil, which is struggling to raise the standard of living of its people and compete in the world market. The decisions that are made by Hector's government at the national and international levels affect his life in a variety of ways. As Brazil industrializes, the nature of jobs and the modes of communication change. Local village cultures modify as the entire nation gains more uniformity of values, beliefs, and norms. Similarly, resources such as access to clean water may be allotted at the local level, but local communities need national and sometimes international support, as illustrated in the photo of tribal elders from Tanzania. We can begin to understand how the process of modernization influences Hector, this village in Tanzania, and other people around the globe by looking at two major macro-level approaches: the structural-functional and conflict perspectives.

The Tanzanian village elders in this photo continue to have authority to make local (micro-level) decisions about the traditional irrigation canals that are being improved in their village, but their expanded water supply is possible in part because of international financial support (meso- and macro-level decisions).

Structural-Functional Theory

The **structural-functional perspective**, also called **functional theory**, *assumes that all parts of the social structure (including groups, organizations, and institutions), the culture (values and beliefs), and social processes (e.g., social change or child rearing) work together to make the whole society run smoothly and harmoniously.* To understand the social world from this perspective, we must look at how the parts of society (structure) fit together and how each part contributes (functions) toward the maintenance of society. For instance, two functions of the family include reproducing children and teaching them to be members of society. These and other functions help perpetuate society, for without reproducing and teaching new members to fit in, societies would collapse.

Émile Durkheim (1858–1917) was a key social scientist in developing functionalism. He theorized that society is made up of necessary parts that fit together into a working whole. Durkheim felt that individuals conform to the rules of societies because of a collective conscience—the shared beliefs in the values of a group (Durkheim 1947). People grow up sharing the same values, beliefs, and rules of behavior as those around them. Gradually, individuals internalize these shared beliefs and rules. A person's behavior is, in a sense, governed from within because it feels right and proper to behave in accordance with what is expected. As such, the functionalist perspective of Durkheim and subsequent theorists places emphasis on social consensus, which gives rise to stable and predictable patterns of order in society. Because people need groups for survival, they adhere to the group's rules so that they fit in. This means that most societies run in an orderly manner, with most individuals fitting into their positions in society.

A Masai family works together as a unit, and in so doing, they enhance the stability and continuity of their entire society.

Functions can be manifest or latent. **Manifest functions** are *the planned outcomes of interactions, social organizations, or institutions.* The function of the microwave oven, for instance, has been to allow people to prepare meals quickly and easily, facilitating life in overworked and stressed modern families. **Latent functions** are *unplanned or unintended consequences of actions or of social structures* (Merton 1938, [1942] 1973). The unplanned consequences of the microwave oven were the creation of a host of new jobs and stimulation of the economy as people wrote new cookbooks and as businesses were formed to produce microwavable cookware and prepared foods for the microwave.

Dysfunctions are *those actions that undermine the stability or equilibrium of society* (Merton 1938). By allowing people to cook meals without using a convection oven, the microwave oven has contributed to some young people having no idea how to cook, thus making them highly dependent on expensive technology and processed foods, and in some cases adding to problems of obesity.

Although the microwave oven and fast-food restaurants have had many benefits for a society in a hurry, one dysfunction is the deterioration of health—especially due to obesity.

Some behaviors may be functional for an individual and dysfunctional for society. From a functionalist perspective, it is important to examine the possible functional and dysfunctional aspects of life in society in order to maintain harmony and balance in society as a whole.

To summarize the structural-functional perspective, the following points are key:

- It examines the macro-level organizations and patterns in society.
- It focuses on what holds societies together and enhances social continuity.
- It considers the consequences or "functions" of each major part in society.
- It focuses on the way the structure (groups, organizations, institutions), the culture, and social processes work together to make society function smoothly.
- It considers manifest functions (which are planned), latent functions (which are unplanned or secondary), and dysfunctions (which undermine stability).

Critique of the Structural-Functional Perspective. Some ideas put forth by functional theorists are so abstract that they are difficult to test with data. Moreover, functionalism does not explain social changes in society, such as conflict and revolution. As we try to understand the many societal upheavals in the world, from suicide bombings in the Middle East to the democracy and economic privatization movements in China, it is clear that dramatic social change is possible. The functionalist assumption is that if a system is running smoothly, it must be working well because it is free from conflict. It assumes that conflict is harmful, even though we know that stability may come about because of ruthless dictators suppressing the population. In short, stability is not always good for the people.

Feminist sociologists argue that functionalism supports the *status quo* (the way things currently are). If the family or economic system of society seems to be functioning smoothly, it does not mean that these systems are fair and equitable or that women and minorities are content with their roles in them. A paradigm that assumes so is making false assumptions, according to feminist theorists. Feminists and others reject the implicit idea of functionalism—that orderly society is necessarily positive. The point is that a stable system is not the same thing as a healthy system.

Functionalism has had a profound impact on social science analysis. Still, functionalism in the 21st century fails to explain many contemporary social situations, according to proponents of a rival macro-level perspective, conflict theory.

Thinking Sociologically

Are the existing social patterns in a society necessarily desirable? Is dramatic change necessarily dysfunctional as suggested by functional theory?

Conflict Theory

Conflict theory contends that *conflict is inevitable in any group or society.* To support this view, conflict theorists advance the following key ideas:

- Conflict and the potential for conflict underlie all social relations.
- Groups of people look out for their self-interest and try to obtain resources and make sure they are distributed primarily to members of their own group.
- Social change is desirable, particularly changes that bring about a greater degree of social equality.
- The existing social order reflects powerful people imposing their values and beliefs on the weak.

Conflict theorists claim that inequality and injustice are the source of the conflicts that permeate society. Because resources and power are distributed unequally in society, some members have more money, goods, and prestige than others. The rich protect their positions by using the power they have accumulated to keep those less fortunate in their places. From the perspective of poor people such as Hector, it seems the rich get all the breaks. Because most of us want more of the resources in society (money, good jobs, nice houses, and cars), conflict erupts between the haves and the have-nots. Therefore, conflict can sometimes bring about a change in the society.

Modern conflict theory has its origins in the works of Karl Marx (1818–1883), a German social philosopher who lived in England during the height of 19th-century industrial expansion. He recognized the plight of exploited underclass workers in the new industrial states of Europe and viewed the ruling elites and the wealthy industrial owners as exploiters of the working class. Marx wrote about the new working class crowded in urban slums, working long hours every day, not earning enough money for decent housing and food, and living and working in conditions that were appalling. Few of the protections enjoyed by workers today—such as retirement benefits, health coverage, sick leave, the 40-hour workweek, and restrictions against child labor—existed in Marx's time.

Capitalism emerged as the dominant economic system in Europe. *Capitalism* is an economic system in which (a) the equipment (machinery) and property (factory and land) for producing goods are owned privately by wealthy individuals, who have the right to use these resources however they want, and (b) the market system (supply and demand) determines the distribution of resources and the levels of income (including wages, rents, and profits). Although there are various forms of capitalism, the core principles involve private ownership of industries and nonintervention by government (Heilbroner and Milberg 2012).

Marx believed that two classes, the capitalists (also referred to as the bourgeoisie or "haves"), who owned the **means of production** *(property, machinery, and cash owned by capitalists)*, and the workers (also referred to as the proletariat or "have-nots") would continue to live in conflict until the workers shared more equally in the profits of their labor. The more workers came to understand their plight, the more awareness they would have of the unfairness of the situation. Eventually, Marx believed that workers would rise up and overthrow capitalism, forming a new, classless society. Collective ownership—shared ownership of the means of production—would be the new economic order (Marx and Engels [1848] 1969).

The idea of the *bourgeoisie* (the capitalist exploiters who own the factories) and the *proletariat* (the exploited workers who sell their labor) has carried over into analysis of modern-day conflicts between labor and management, between women's and men's interests, and between warring factions within countries such as Sudan in Africa and Muslim religious sects in the Middle East and North Africa. From a conflict perspective, Hector in Brazil and millions like him in other countries are part of the reserve labor force—a cheap labor pool that can be called on when labor is needed and disregarded when demand is low, thus meeting the changing labor needs of industry and capitalism. This pattern results in permanent economic insecurity and poverty for Hector and those like him.

Many branches of the conflict perspective have grown from the original ideas of Marx. Here, we mention three contributions to conflict theory, those of the American sociologists Harriet Martineau, W. E. B. Du Bois, and Ralf Dahrendorf. As you can see, social conflict has been a major focus of sociological investigation for more than a century.

Harriet Martineau (1802–1876), generally considered the first female sociologist, wrote several books that contributed to our understanding of modern sociological research methods and provided a critique of America's failure to live up to its democratic principles, especially as they related to women (Martineau 1838, [1837] 1962). In her work, published before Karl Marx's *Communist Manifesto* (with Friedrich Engels [1848] 1969), she points out that social life is guided by general laws and that these are influenced by population dynamics and what is happening in the natural physical environment. Her work represents the foundation for current feminist and conflict theories.

Another early American conflict theorist was W. E. B. Du Bois, the first African American to receive a doctorate from Harvard University. Du Bois felt that sociology should be active in bettering society, that although research should be scientifically rigorous and fair-minded, the ultimate goal of sociological work was social improvement—not just human insight. He saw the conflict between the haves and have-nots as being based largely on race in the United States, not just social class.

Du Bois not only wrote on these issues but also acted on them (Du Bois [1899] 1967). He was one of the cofounders of the National Association for the Advancement of Colored People (NAACP). He stressed the need for minority ethnic groups to become advocates for their rights, to create conflict—to object loudly when those in power do something to disadvantage minorities—and to change the society toward greater equality and participation. He was—and continues to be—an inspiration to many sociologists who believe that their findings should have real applications and should be used to create a more humane social world (Mills 1956). He was well ahead of his time in recognizing the conflicting nature of American society and the way privilege and self-interest blinded people to the inequities. He really is a part of the third tradition discussed above, an early public/applied sociologist.

A half-century later, Ralf Dahrendorf argued that society is always in the process of change and affected by forces that bring about change (Dahrendorf 1959). Dahrendorf refined Marx's ideas in several ways. First, he pointed out that the overthrow of capitalism that Marx had predicted had not come about because of changes in conditions for workers (employee organizations, unions). Instead, a middle class developed, some workers became part owners of companies, stockholders dispersed the concentration of wealth, and a higher standard of living was achieved for workers. Second, he proposed that class conflict occurs between the haves and the have-nots, and the have-nots develop consciousness of their situation and feel that change is possible. *Interest groups*, such as the members of Hector's *favela*, share a common situation or interests, including a desire for sanitation, running water, electricity, and a higher standard of living. From within such interest groups, *conflict groups* arise to fight for changes. There is always potential for conflict when those without power realize their common position and form interest groups. How much change or violence is brought about depends on how organized those groups become.

Dahrendorf's major contribution is the recognition that conflict over resources results not just in a conflict between the proletariat and the bourgeoisie but in a multitude of divisions including old people versus young people, rich versus poor, one region of the country versus another, Christians versus non-Christians, and so forth. This acknowledges multiple rifts in the society based on interest groups.

Whereas Marx emphasized the divisive nature of conflict, other theorists have offered a modified theory. The American theorist Lewis Coser took a very different approach to conflict from that of Marx, arguing that it can strengthen societies and the organizations within them (Coser 1956). According to Coser, problems in a society or group lead to complaints or conflicts—a warning message to the group that all is not well. Resolution of the conflicts shows that the group is adaptable in meeting the needs of its

Harriet Martineau (left) published a critique of America's failure to live up to its democratic principles 11 years before Karl Marx's most famous work, but she was not taken seriously as a scholar for more than a century because she was female—the first feminist theorist. Karl Marx (center) was a social analyst who is often identified as the founder of conflict theory. W. E. B. Du Bois (right) continued the development of conflict theory and was among the first to apply that theory to American society, especially to issues of race and ethnicity.

members, thereby creating greater loyalty to the group. Thus, conflict provides the message of what is not working to meet people's needs, and the system adapts to the needs for change because of the conflict (Coser 1956; Simmel 1955).

Critique of the Conflict Perspective. First, many conflict theorists focus on the macro-level analysis and lose sight of the individuals involved in conflict situations, such as Hector and his family. Second, empirical research to test conflict theory is limited. The conflict perspective often paints a picture with rather broad brushstrokes. Research to test the picture involves interpretations of broad spans of history and is more difficult to claim as scientific. Third, conflict theorists tend to focus on social stress, power dynamics, and disharmony. Conflict theory is not very effective in explaining social cohesion and cooperation. Fourth, many theorists are not convinced that self-interest is the ultimate motivator of virtually all human behavior or that altruism and cooperation are uncommon.

The notion that men and women can be seen as interest groups, each looking out for its own self-interests, has resulted in one particular version of conflict theory—feminist theory.

Thinking Sociologically

Imagine you are a legislator. You have to decide whether to cut funding for a senior citizens program or slash a scholarship program for college students. You want to be reelected, and you know that approximately 90% of senior citizens are registered to vote and most actually do vote. You also know that less than half of college-age people are likely to vote. These constituencies are about the same size. What would you do, and how would you justify your decision? How does this example illustrate conflict theory?

Feminist Sociological Theory

Feminist theory *critiques the hierarchical power structures, which feminists argue treat women and other minorities unequally* (Cancian 1992; Collins 2000). Feminists argue that sociology has been dominated by a male perspective and that the male perspective does not give a complete view of the social world. Much of feminist theory, then, has foundations in the conflict perspective. Women are viewed as disadvantaged by the hierarchical way in which society is arranged, whereas men experience privilege because of those arrangements. Men become an interest group intent on preserving their privileges.

Some branches of feminist theory, however, are not based on Marx's writings. Instead, their ideas come from interaction perspectives, emphasizing the way gender cues and symbols shape the nature of much human interaction. Thus, feminist theory moves from meso- and macro-level analysis (e.g., looking at national and global situations that give privileges to men) to micro-level analysis (e.g., the inequality between husbands and wives in marriage). In particular, feminist theory points to the importance of gender as a variable influencing social life (Hesse-Biber and Leavy 2007; Lorber 2009).

Feminists contend that there is a disparity between what actually goes on in women's lives and many accounts by social scientists of the social relations between males and females. Men's explanations of gender relations often have not presented women's lives in a way that is meaningful for women themselves. The ideas, work opportunities, and life experiences of women of color are even less understood by traditional sociology (Collins 2000). Thus, until recently many studies and writing about women had been far removed from women's own experiences.

In general, feminists point out, women's experiences in social relations involve interdependence with others, whereas males have been taught to be competitive and individualistic in sports, business competition, and many other social arenas. Males learn early in their lives that vulnerability must be avoided so that one is not exploited by others. This, according to feminist theorists, is one influence on the way men think about society. For example, rational choice theory maintains that each individual is out to protect self-interests and to make choices that benefit the self. This theory is based on a male view of society. Men are also more likely to view hierarchical social arrangements as normal, which contributes to their difficulty in recognizing how patriarchal our society actually is. Also, some feminists claim that we are blind to the fact that gender roles are socially created, not biologically determined. As a result of these differences in experience and in socialization, women's views on issues of justice, morality, and society lend a different interpretation to society (Brettell and Sargent 2001; Kramer 2010) and can present a more inclusive view of the world (Burn 2005; Lengermann and Niebrugge-Brantley 1990).

Many people are considered secondary citizens because of any one of many factors, and it is the interplay of these factors that interested Patricia Hill Collins. An important contemporary scholar, she examined the discrimination and oppression people face because of their race, class, gender, sexuality, or nationality, all of which are interconnected. For example, black women are often restricted in their opportunities because of others' definitions of who and what they should be. In response, people who are disprivileged due to one or more social traits often create their own self-definitions and self-images. The idea of multiple identities

Patricia Hill Collins is an innovative feminist scholar who has challenged sociologists to look at the ways race, social class, gender, and sexuality can work alone or in combination to provide privilege or disprivilege to certain citizens—sometimes without the awareness of the persons involved.

Michelle Obama has a law degree from an Ivy League university, has had a successful legal career, and also calls herself the "Mom-in-Chief." She is unapologetic about believing that men and women should be treated equally and about being called feminist.

(such as race, class, and gender) being intertwined and affecting individuals' life chances is a particularly powerful concept in sociology (Collins 2000, 2005).

It is interesting that many women today will begin a sentence with the disclaimer "I am not a feminist, but . . ." Perhaps this is because some feminists have had a rather strident style and often focused on men as the cause of problems. Not all feminists are strident or focus on men as oppressors. Indeed, many men call themselves feminists, for a feminist is someone who believes that men and women should be given equal standing and equal opportunities in society. Feminists have opened the door to understanding how social structures can bind and inhibit the freedom of both men and women. They also recognize that males have generally had more privileges than females in societies around the world. To study sociological questions, feminist methodology puts emphasis on methods that stress "role-taking" with respondents—that is, understanding the world from the female or male respondents' point of view.

Critique of the Feminist Sociological Perspective. Feminists are not the only group with concerns about being fairly and accurately represented in theory and research. Race and ethnic groups and social class groups are also affected. Thus, some theorists argue that theory should represent the relationship between race, class, and gender. When trying to understand minority women in minimum-wage jobs or the factors affecting homelessness, these relationships can provide a more complete view.

Thinking Sociologically

Consider the issue of homelessness in cities around the world. How could each of the theories discussed in this chapter be used to help us understand the problem of homelessness?

Multilevel Analysis: Max Weber's Contributions

Max Weber (1864–1920), a German-born social scientist, has had a lasting effect on sociology and other social sciences. Weber (pronounced *Veber*) cannot be pigeonholed easily into one of the theoretical categories or one level of analysis, for his contributions include both micro- and macro-level analyses. His emphasis on *Verstehen* (meaning deep empathetic understanding) gives him a place in micro-level theory, and his discussions of Karl Marx and of bureaucracies give him a place in meso- and macro-level theory (Weber 1946).

Verstehen stems from the interpretations or meanings individuals give to parts of their social worlds, to their subjective interpretations, or to understanding of the social world. Following Weber's footsteps, sociologists try to understand both people's behaviors and the meanings that people attach to their behaviors and their experiences.

The goal-oriented, efficient new organizational form called bureaucracy was the focus of much of Weber's writing at the meso level. This organizational form was based on rationality rather than long-standing tradition. In other words, decisions were based on what would best accomplish the organization's goals, not individual benefit. Hiring and promotion on the basis of individual merit (getting the most qualified person rather than hiring a friend or relative) is one example of this rational decision making. This is a principle we take for granted now, but it was not always so. The entire society becomes transformed through a change in how individuals make decisions on behalf of a bureaucratic organization.

Opportunities for jobs were changed, the culture became more geared to merit as a basis for decisions, and organizational life became more governed by rules and routines. All this came from a redefinition of appropriate ways to make decisions. Weber's conceptualizations of society at the meso level have laid the groundwork for a theoretical understanding of modern organizations.

Weber also attempted to understand macro-level processes. For instance, in his famous book *The Protestant Ethic and the Spirit of Capitalism* (Weber [1904–1905] 1958), he asked how capitalists understood the world around them. His work was influenced by Marx's writings, but where Marx focused on economic conditions as the key factor shaping history and power relations, Weber argued that Marx's focus was too narrow. He felt that politics, economics, religion, psychology, and people's ideas are interdependent—affecting each other. In short, Weber thought that the society was more complex than Karl Marx's core notion that two groups—the haves and the have-nots—are in conflict over economic resources.

Thinking Sociologically

To what extent are human beings free agents who can create their own social world and come up with their own ideas about how to live their lives? To what extent are our lives determined or influenced by the social systems around us and by our positions of power or powerlessness in the economic and political system?

Using Different Theoretical Perspectives

Each of the theoretical perspectives described in this chapter begins from a set of assumptions about humans. Each makes a contribution to our understanding, but each has limitations or blind spots, such as not taking into account the other levels of analysis (Ritzer 2011). Figure 2.3 provides a summary of cooperative versus competitive perspectives to illustrate how the theories differ.

It is important to understand that there are several different theoretical perspectives to help explain society. None of these is right or wrong. Rather, a particular theory may be more or less useful when studying some level of analysis or aspect of society. It is also important to learn how each major theoretical perspective can be used to provide a framework and viewpoint to guide research. The strength of a theory depends on its ability to explain and predict behavior accurately. Each theoretical perspective focuses on a different aspect of society and level of analysis and gives us a different lens through which to view our social world. The social world model helps us picture the whole system and determine which theory or synthesis of theories best suits our needs in analyzing a specific social process or structure.

	Macro analysis	**Micro analysis**
Humans viewed as cooperative (people interact with others on the basis of shared meanings and common symbols)	***Structural-Functional Theory***	***Symbolic Interactionism Theory***
Humans viewed as competitive (behavior governed by self-interest)	***Conflict Theory*** (group interests)	***Rational Choice Theory*** (individual interests)

Figure 2.3 Cooperative Versus Competitive Perspectives

So far, we have focused on what sociology is and how sociologists know what they know. The rest of the book examines what our social world is like. The next chapter explores how you can understand your culture and society at various levels in our social world.

What Have We Learned?

The opening question in "Think About It" asked, "How do you know?" In this chapter, we have outlined the process of research that describes how sociologists and other social scientists "know." The next question asks, "Why is evidence important?" Our simple answer is that it is better to base social policies on evidence (scientifically collected facts and data) than on our untested assumptions or biased opinions. We also asked, "How do sociologists gather dependable facts?" The process of planning and carrying out a scientific study is outlined in the beginning of this chapter and provides a partial answer to this question. Finally, "How can theories help us understand social forces affecting our lives?"

What makes a discipline scientific is not the subject matter, but how we conduct our research and what we consider valid evidence. The core features of a science are (1) commitment to empirically validated evidence, facts, and information that are confirmed through systematic processes of testing using the five senses; (2) an effort to disprove whatever it is we think is true, allowing us to be convinced by the evidence rather than by our preconceived ideas; (3) absolute integrity and objectivity in reporting and in conducting research; and (4) continual openness to having our findings reexamined and new interpretations proposed. It is the fourth feature that causes us to be open to criticism and alternative interpretations. To have credible findings, we always consider the possibility that we have overlooked alternative explanations of the data and alternative ways to view the problem. This is one of the hardest principles to grasp, but it is one of the most important in reaching the truth. Science—including social science—is not facts to be memorized. Science is a process that is made possible by a social exchange of ideas, a clash of opinions, and a continual search for truth. Knowledge in the sciences is created by vigorous debate. Rather than just memorizing the concepts in this book to take a test, we hope you will engage in the creation of knowledge by entering into these debates.

Theories serve as lenses to help us make sense of the data that we gather using various research strategies. However, the data themselves can be used to test the theories, so there is an ongoing reciprocal relationship between theory (the lens for making sense of the data) and the research (the evidence used to test the theories). The most important ideas in this chapter are what sociology considers data or evidence and how sociology uses methods to be a science. These ideas form the framework for the content of sociology.

Key Points

- Sociology is a science that studies society, and therefore it is essential to understand what is—and what is not—considered credible evidence; for a scientist, this means that ideas must be tested empirically, that is, scientifically. (See pp. 33–35.)
- As a science, sociology uses eight systematic steps to gather data and test theories about the social world. (See pp. 35–46.)
- In most cases, planning a research study requires that we identify causes (independent variables) and effects (dependent variables) and that we make sure the correlations of variables are not spurious; the simultaneous occurrence of two variables can be accidental or noncausal. (See pp. 36–38.)
- Major methods for gathering data in sociology include surveys (e.g., interviews and questionnaires), observation studies (direct observation of a natural setting), controlled experiments, and analysis of existing sources (through secondary sources or through content analyses). (See pp. 37–41.)
- Use of multiple methods—triangulation—increases confidence in the findings. (See p. 41.)
- Scientific confidence in results also requires representative samples, usually drawn randomly. (See pp. 41–44.)
- Responsible research also requires sensitivity to the ethics of research—ensuring that gathering scientific data does no one harm. (See pp. 45–46.)
- Attempts to understand society have existed for at least two and a half millennia, but gathering of scientific evidence to test hypotheses and validate claims is a rather modern idea. (See pp. 46–50.)
- Theories are especially important to science because they raise questions for research, and they explain the

relationships between facts. Sociology has four primary, overriding theoretical perspectives or paradigms: symbolic interaction theory, rational choice theory, structural-functional theory, and conflict theory. Other perspectives, such as feminist theory, serve as correctives to the main paradigms. Most of these theories are more applicable at the micro to meso level or at the meso to macro level. (See pp. 50–61.)

- Public sociologists fall under a large umbrella that includes all sociologists, including applied sociologists, who strive to better understand how society operates and to make practical use of their sociological findings.

Discussion Questions

1. Why do research questions have to be asked in a precise way? Give an example of a precise research question. How does it make it possible for you to test and measure your topic?
2. If you were to conduct a study to measure student satisfaction with a particular academic department on campus, what research method(s) would you use? Why? How would the method(s) you select vary according to (a) the size of the department and (b) the type of information you sought?
3. As stated in this chapter, one of the core features of a science is "continual openness to having our findings reexamined and new interpretations proposed." Describe a time when you changed your mind due to new information. Was it difficult for you to change your mind? Why or why not?
4. Why is the ability to be open to new ideas and interpretations so vital to the scientific perspective? Do you think you could carry this aspect of the scientific process out successfully—no matter the topic? Why or why not?
5. If you were to examine the relationship between the government and the economy in the United States today, which of the four major theoretical perspectives outlined in the chapter would be most helpful? Why?
6. Imagine you would like to conduct a sociological study of the students with whom you attended the fourth grade, to determine what key factors influenced their academic achievements. Which of the four major theoretical perspectives would you employ in your study? Why?

Contributing to Our Social World: What Can We Do?

At the Local Level

- *Local service organizations* are found in every community and work to provide for the unmet needs of community members: housing, legal aid, medical care, elder care, and so on. United Way works with most local service organizations and may be able to let you know which ones need help in your area. Going to idealist.org is also a great way to find volunteer opportunities in your area. Volunteer to work with an organization in its applied needs assessment research, and practice the sociological principles and research methods described in this chapter. If your college or university has a service-learning office, it will offer connections to many service opportunities, sometimes linked to specific fields of study. Many colleges and universities also offer academic service learning (ASL) credit in which course assignments include such community work under the supervision of the instructor.

At the State/Meso Level

- *State agencies* often have ongoing projects to gather data for more accurate information about the state and the needs of its citizens. Go to www.nationalservice.gov/about/contact/statecommission.asp and click on the name of a state service commission to find volunteer opportunities through your state government.

At the National and Global Levels

- *The U.S. Bureau of the Census* is best known for its decennial (every 10 years) enumeration of the population, but its work continues each year as it prepares special reports, population estimates, and regular publications (including *Current Population Reports*). Visit the Census Bureau's website at www.census.gov, and explore the valuable and extensive quantitative data and other information available. Visit your local Census Bureau office or click on www.census.gov/hrd/www/jobs/student.html to find volunteer and other opportunities for students at the Census.

Visit the Student Study Site at **www.sagepub.com/ballantine4e** to access additional study tools, including eFlashcards, web quizzes, video resources, audio resources, web resources, SAGE journal articles, recommended readings, and more.

PART II Social Structure, Processes, and Control

Whether we are building a house or a society, the process is parallel. Picture a house. First there is the wood frame, then the walls and roof. This provides the framework or structure. Within that structure, activities or processes take place—electricity to turn on lights and appliances, water to wash in and drink, and people to carry out these processes. If something goes wrong in the house, we take steps to control the damage and repair it.

Our social world is constructed in a similar way: Social structure is the framework of society with its groups and organizations, and social processes are the dynamic activities of this society. This section begins with a discussion of the structure of society, followed by the processes of culture and socialization through which individuals are taught cultural rules—how to function and live effectively within their society's structure. Although socialization takes place primarily at the micro level, we will explore its implications at the meso and macro levels as well.

If we break the social structure into parts, such as the wood frame, walls, and roof of a house, it is the groups and organizations (including bureaucracies) that make up the social structure. To work smoothly, these organizations depend on people's loyalty so that they do what society and its groups need to survive. However, smooth functioning does not always happen. Things break down. This means that those in control of societies try to control disruptions and deviant individuals in order to maintain control and smooth functioning.

As we explore the next few chapters, we will continue to examine social life at the micro, meso, and macro levels, for each of us as individuals is profoundly shaped by social processes and structures at larger and more abstract levels, all the way to the global level.

CHAPTER

3

Society and Culture

Hardware and Software of Our Social World

Depending on what resources are available where we live and what is considered usable and edible, we put something out to eat. It might be a juicy hamburger, dog meat, or bugs. What we consider food is influenced by the structure of society, including the organization of food production, distribution, and technology, and by the culture—the ideas about what is edible. In two of these photos, families from different continents gather around the things they would typically eat, while three others prepare their meals.

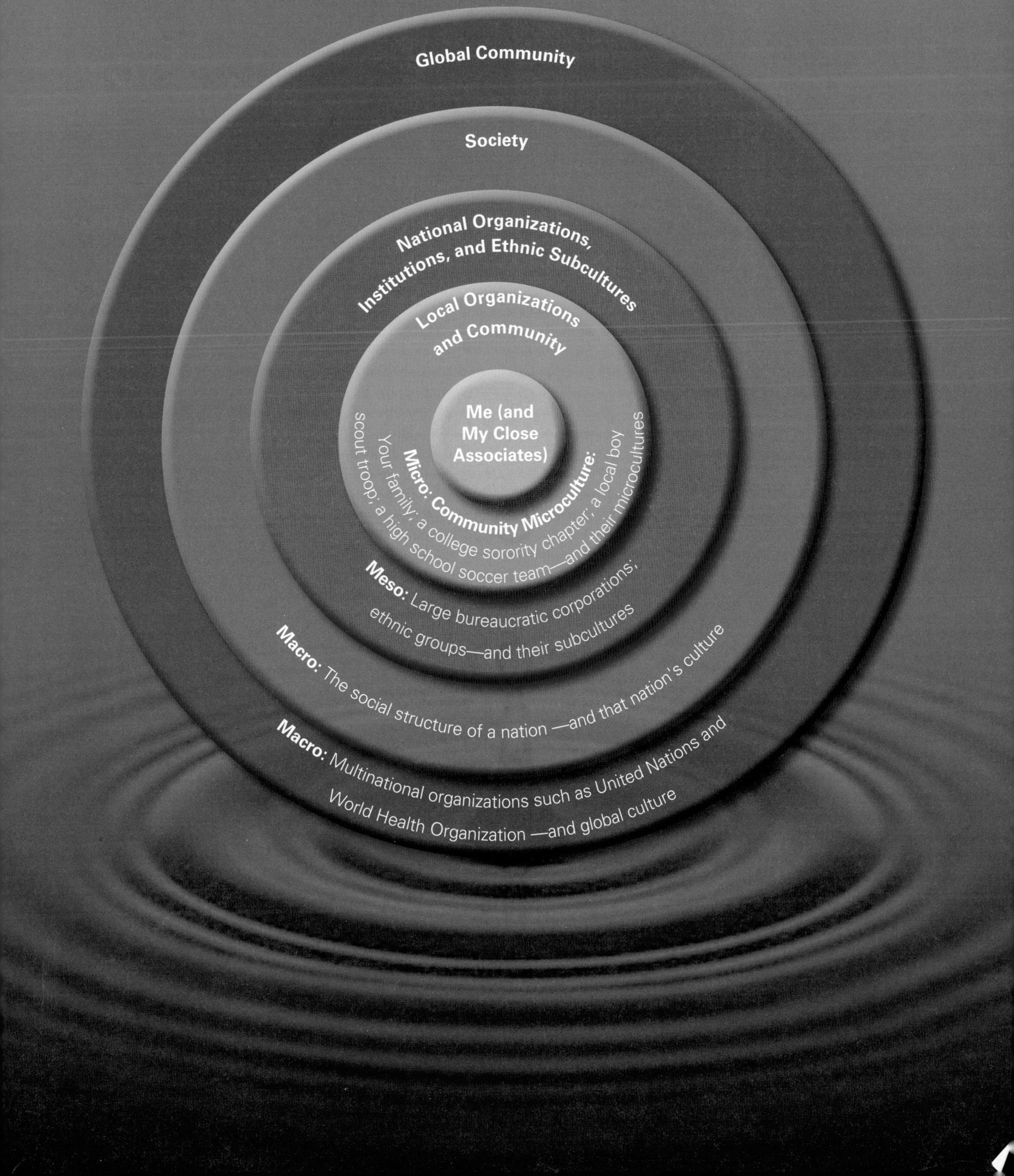

Global Community
Society
National Organizations, Institutions, and Ethnic Subcultures
Local Organizations and Community
Me (and My Close Associates)
Micro: Community Microculture: Your family; a college sorority chapter; a local boy scout troop; a high school soccer team—and their microcultures
Meso: Large bureaucratic corporations; ethnic groups—and their subcultures
Macro: The social structure of a nation —and that nation's culture
Macro: Multinational organizations such as United Nations and World Health Organization —and global culture

Think About It	
Micro: Me (and My Inner Circle)	Could you be human without culture?
Micro: Local Community	How do microcultures—your fraternity or athletic team—influence you?
Meso: National Institutions; Complex Organizations; Ethnic Groups	How do subcultures (such as your ethnic group) and countercultures (such as paramilitary hate groups) shape the character of your nation and influence your own life?
Macro: National Society	How do your nation's social structures and culture influence who you are and how you dress, eat, work, and live your life?
Macro: Global Community	Why do people live so differently in various parts of the world, and how can those differences be relevant to your own people?

What's coming in this chapter?

All animals eat to survive, but what they eat differs tremendously. Two of the photos in the chapter opening show the results when researchers asked families to buy food supplies for a week. They then took pictures of families with their weekly diets laid out. The differences in these foods and what each family paid to eat give us an insight into differences in one aspect common to all cultures around the world—food.

Mrs. Ukita, the mom in the Ukita family, rises early to prepare a breakfast of miso soup and a raw egg on rice. The father and two daughters eat quickly and rush out to catch their early morning trains to work and school in Kodaira City, Japan. The mother cares for the house, does the shopping, and prepares a typical evening meal of fish, vegetables, and rice for the family.

The Ahmed family lives in a large apartment building in Cairo, Egypt. The 12 members of the extended family include the women who shop for and cook the food—vegetables, including peppers, greens, potatoes, squash, tomatoes, garlic, spices, and rice, along with pita bread and often fish or meat. The adult men work in shops in one of the many bazaars, while the school-age children attend school, then help with the chores.

The nine members of the Ayme family live in Tingo, Ecuador, high in the Andes mountains, where the main occupation of Indian families is herding and growing potatoes and other crops suited to the high altitude and cool climate. Their diet consists of foods that are readily available in the market: plantains, potatoes, onions, carrots, and grains.

In the Breidjing refugee camp in Chad, many Sudanese refugees eat what relief agencies can get to them—and that food source is not always reliable. Typical for the Aboubakar family, a mother and five children, is rice or some other grain, oil for cooking, occasionally some root plants or squash that keep longer than fresh fruits and vegetables, dried legumes, and a few spices. The girls and women go into the desert to fetch firewood for cooking and to get water from whatever source has water at the time. This is a dangerous trip as they may be attacked and raped or even killed outside the camps.

The Walker family from Norfolk, Virginia, grabs dinner at a fast-food restaurant on their way to basketball practice and an evening meeting. Because of their busy schedules and individual activities, they cannot always find time to cook and eat together.

In Sicily, Italy, the Manzo family—mother, father, and three young boys—enjoy fresh bread from the baker for breakfast and often have pasta with sauce, vegetables, and fish or meat for dinner. Typically, the father works in the family orchard, while the mother takes care of the house, and the boys go to school, helping with chores after school.

Although most diets include some form of grain and starch, locally available fruits and vegetables, and perhaps meat or fish, broad variations in food consumption exist even within one society. Yet all of these differences have something in common: Each represents a society that has a unique culture that includes what people eat. Food is only one aspect of our way of life and what is necessary for survival. Ask yourself why you sleep on a bed, brush your teeth, or listen to music with friends. Our way of life is called culture.

Culture refers to *the way of life shared by a group of people—the knowledge, beliefs, values, rules or laws, language, customs, symbols, and material products (such as food, houses, and transportation) within a society that help meet human needs.* Culture provides guidelines for living. Learning our culture puts our social world in an understandable framework, providing a tool kit we can use to help construct the meaning of our world (Bruner 1996; Nagel 1994). We compare culture to *software* because it is the human ideas and input that make the society work. Otherwise, society would just be structures, like the framework of a house.

A **society** refers to *an organized and interdependent group of individuals who live together in a specific geographic area; who interact more with each other than they do with outsiders; who cooperate for the attainment of common goals; and who share a common culture over time.* Each society includes key parts called institutions—such as family, education, religion, politics, economics, and health—that meet basic human needs. This structure that makes up society is what we refer to here as the *hardware*. The way people think and behave in any society is largely prescribed by its shared culture, which is learned, transmitted, and reshaped from generation to generation. All activities in the society, whether educating young members, preparing and eating dinner, selecting leaders for the group, finding a mate, or negotiating with other societies, are guided by cultural rules and expectations. In each society, culture provides the social rules for how individuals carry out necessary tasks.

While culture provides the "software" for the way people live, society represents the "hardware"—the structure that gives organization and stability to group life. Society—organized groups of people—and culture—their way of life—are interdependent. The two are not the same thing, but they cannot exist without each other, just as computer hardware and software are each useless without the other.

This chapter explores the ideas of society and culture and discusses how they relate to each other. We will look at the following: what society is and how it is organized, how it influences and is influenced by culture, what culture is, how and why culture develops, and the components that make up culture, cultural theories, and policy issues. The first part of the chapter focuses on the hardware: society. After reading this chapter, we will have a better idea of how we as individuals fit into society and learn our culture.

Two of the photos on the opening page of this chapter show families from Egypt and Germany gathered around a typical week's food supply. Members of the Aboubakar family of Sudan gather here in front of their tent with a week's worth of food. Note the differences between the foods of these family groups.

Society: The Hardware

Families, groups of friends, neighborhoods or communities, and workplace or school groups—all provide the structure of society. Just as the computer hardware provides the framework within which the software operates, society provides the framework for culture.

All societies have geographical boundaries or borders and individuals who live together in families and communities and who share a culture. The structures that make up society include the interdependent positions we hold (as parents, workers), the groups to which we belong (family, work group, and clubs), and the institutions in which we participate. This "hardware" (structure) of our social world provides the framework for "software" (culture) to function.

Societies differ because they exist in different places with unique resources—mountains, coastal areas, jungles. Societies change over time with new technology and leadership. Although human societies have become more complex, especially in recent human history, people have been hunters and gatherers for 99% of human existence. A few groups remain hunter-gatherers today. As Table 3.1 on page 69 illustrates, if all human history were to be compressed into the lifetime of an 80-year-old person, humans would have started cultivating crops and herding animals for their food supply only a few months ago. Note the incredible rate of change that has occurred just in the past two centuries.

Thinking Sociologically

What major changes took place in your grandparents' lifetimes that affect the way you and your family live today? You may want to look at the timeline inside the cover of this book. It will provide some ideas.

Societies are organized in particular patterns, patterns that are shaped by a range of factors, including the way people procure food, the availability of resources, contact with other societies, and cultural beliefs. For example, people can change from herding to farming only if they have the knowledge, skills, and desire to do so and only in environments that will support agriculture. As societies develop, changes take place in the social structures and relationships between

Table 3.1 **One Million Years of Human History Compressed Into One 80-Year Lifetime**

Year	*Age*	*Event*
2.5 million years ago	Birth	*Homo habilis* is born—the first ancestor to make/use tools and have culture; evidence of sharing food, congregating, and probably sharing housing
2 million years ago	2 years old	*Homo erectus* shows early evidence of family structures; findings of longer life spans and three generations alive simultaneously
15,000 years ago	79 years old	Six months ago: North America settled by early humans, hunters and gatherers
11,000 years ago	79 years old	Five months ago: In the Middle East, the first agricultural communities, indicating food cultivation
10,000 years ago	79 years old	Twenty weeks ago: the last ice age is over; humans spread more widely over the planet
5,000 years ago	79 years old	Ten weeks ago: humans began to cast and use metals and built the pyramids
2,000 years ago	79 years old	Seven weeks ago: beginning of the Common Era (under the Holy Roman Empire)
220 years ago	79 years old	Two and a half weeks ago: the United States began a new experiment with democracy
100 years ago	79 years old	Yesterday morning: the airplane was invented
30 years ago	79 years old	Yesterday afternoon: humans first set foot on the moon; after dinner, we broke the DNA (genetic) code

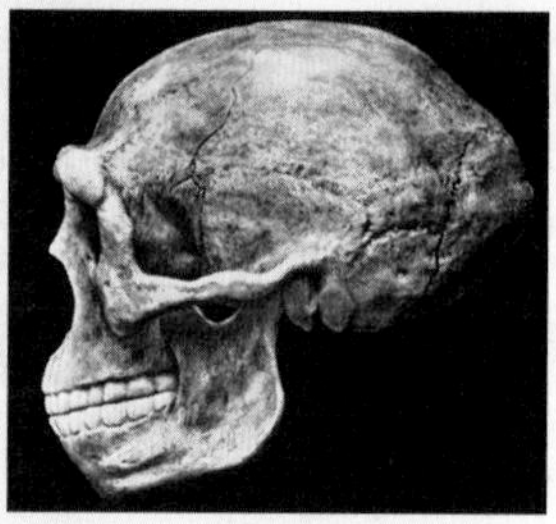

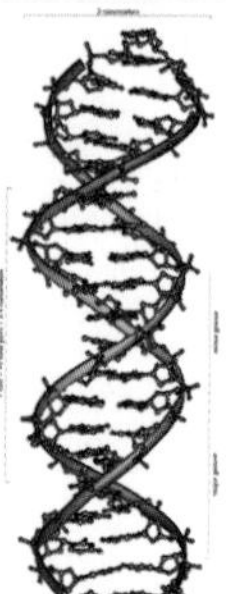

Increasingly in the United States, where both parents work, dinner is a fast-food takeout or ready-to-cook packaged meal—a quick dash for nourishment to assuage hunger in front of the TV rather than a communal event.

The Tuareg live a simple traditional life in the Sahara Desert in the Sahel region of Niger (Africa), and their social structure has few social positions except those defined by gender.

people that characterize each type of society. For example, in industrialized societies, relationships between people typically must become more formal because people must interact with strangers and not just relatives. It is important to note that not all societies go through all stages. Some are jolted into the future by political events or changes in the global system, and some resist pressures to become modernized and continue to live in simpler social systems.

Evolution of Societies

The Saharan desert life for the Tuareg tribe is pretty much as it has been for centuries. In simple traditional societies, individuals are assigned to comparatively few social positions or statuses. Today, however, few societies are isolated from global impact. Even the Tuareg are called on to escort adventurous tourists through the desert for a currency unknown to them and unneeded until recently.

In such traditional societies, men teach their sons everything they need to know, for all men do much the same jobs, depending on where they live—hunting, fishing, or farming and protecting the community from danger. Likewise, girls learn their jobs from their mothers—such as child care, fetching water, food preparation, farming, weaving, and perhaps house building. In contrast, in more complex societies, such as industrial or "modern" societies, thousands of interdependent job statuses are based on complex divisions of labor with designated tasks. An interesting question that has intrigued sociologists is how traditional societies such as the Tuareg change into new types of societies that are more complex, less personal, more technologically dependent, and more bureaucratic.

Émile Durkheim ([1893] 1947), an early French sociologist, pictured a continuum between simple and complex societies. He described simple premodern societies as held together by **mechanical solidarity**—*cohesion and integration based on the similarity of individuals in the group, including beliefs, values, and emotional ties between members of the group*. Furthermore, the division of labor is based largely on male/female distinctions and age groupings. Members of premodern societies tend to think the same way on important matters, and everyone fulfills his or her expected social position. This provides the glue that holds the society together. The entire society may involve only a few hundred people, with no meso-level institutions, organizations, or subcultures. Prior to the emergence of nation-states, there was no macro level either—only tribal groupings.

According to Durkheim ([1893] 1947), as societies transformed, they became more complex through increasingly complex divisions of labor and changes in the ways people carried out necessary tasks for survival. **Organic solidarity** refers to *cohesion and integration based on differences of individuals in the group so that they are interdependent*. The society has a substantial division of labor, with each member playing a highly specialized role in the society and each person being dependent on others due to interdependent, interrelated tasks. The society has cohesion regardless of whether people have common values and shared outlooks. Prior to the factory system, for example, individual cobblers made shoes to order. With the Industrial Revolution, factories took over the process, with many individuals carrying out interdependent tasks. The division of labor is critical because it leads to new forms of social cohesion (glue) based on interdependence, not on emotional ties. Gradual changes from mechanical (traditional) to organic (modern) society also involve harnessing new forms of energy and finding more efficient ways to use them (Nolan and Lenski 2008). For example, the use of steam engines and coal for fuel triggered the Industrial Revolution, leading to the development of industrial societies.

Also, as societies changed, they added more large organizations and institutions that reached individuals and families as never before. The meso level—institutions and large bureaucratic organizations—became more influential. Still, as recently as 200 years ago, even large societies had little global interdependence, and life for the typical citizen was influenced mostly by events at the micro and meso levels. Keep in mind that it was just over 200 years ago when American colonies selected representatives to form a loosely federated government that came to be called the United States. As communication and transportation around the world developed and expanded, the global level grew.

As you read about each of the following types of societies, from the simplest to the most complex, notice the presence of these variables: (a) division of labor, (b) interdependence of people's positions, (c) increasingly advanced technologies, and (d) new forms and uses of energy. Although none of these variables alone is *sufficient* to trigger evolution to a new type of society, they may all be *necessary* for a transition to occur.

According to Durkheim, then, in traditional societies with mechanical solidarity, interpersonal interaction and community life at the micro level were the most important aspects of social life. Meso- and macro-level societies developed as a result of changes toward more organic solidarity. As societies become more complex, meso- and macro-level institutions become more important and have more profound impacts on the lives of individuals.

A mother in Côte d'Ivoire (West Africa), carrying her load on her head, returns to the village with her daughter after gathering wood. Carrying wood and water is typically women's work. In this hunter-gatherer society, the primary social cohesion is mechanical solidarity.

Hunter-Gatherer Societies

In the Kalahari Desert of southwestern Africa live hunter-gatherers known as the !Kung. (The ! is pronounced with a click of the tongue.) The !Kung live a nomadic life, moving from one place to another as food supplies become available or are used up. As a result, they carry very few personal possessions and live in temporary huts, settling around water holes for a few months at a time. Settlements are small, rarely more than 20 to 50 people, for food supplies are not plentiful enough to support large, permanent populations (Lee 1984). !Kung women gather edible plants and nuts, while !Kung men hunt. Beyond division of labor by gender and age, however, there are few differences in roles or status.

Life is organized around kinship ties and reciprocity—that is, mutual assistance—for the well-being of the whole community. When a large animal is killed, people gather from a wide area to share in the bounty, and great care is taken to ensure that the meat is distributed fairly. Resources are shared among the people, but sharing is regulated by a complex system of mutual obligations. A visitor who eats food at another's hearth is expected to repay that hospitality in the future.

The !Kung are a typical **hunter-gatherer society**, in which *people rely on the vegetation and animals occurring naturally in their habitat to sustain life.* People make their clothing, shelter, and tools from available materials or obtain goods through trade with other nearby groups. People migrate seasonally to new food sources. Population size remains small as the numbers of births and deaths in the society are balanced.

From the beginning of human experience until recently, hunting and gathering (or foraging) were the sole means of sustaining life. Other types of societies emerged only recently; yet today, only a handful of societies still rely on hunting and gathering (Nolan and Lenski 2008). The hunter-gatherer lifestyle is becoming extinct. For example, much of the wild game on which the !Kung subsisted has been overhunted or is now protected on game preserves. The governments of South Africa and Botswana have attempted to settle such groups on reservations, and contacts with modern government have forever changed the way of life of the !Kung and other hunter-gatherer societies.

Herding and Horticultural Societies

The Masai inhabit the grasslands of Kenya and Tanzania, depending on their herds for survival. Their cattle and goats provide meat, milk, blood (which they drink), and hides. A seminomadic herding society, the Masai move camp to find grazing land for their animals and set up semipermanent shelters for the few months they will remain in one area. Settlements consist of huts constructed in a circle with a perimeter fence surrounding the compound. At the more permanent settlements, the Masai grow short-term crops to supplement their diet. The Masai are under some pressure to become agriculturalists, however, as the government of Kenya—a relatively new macro-level influence in their lives—now restricts their territory and herding practices that encroach on wild-animal refuges. Tourism also greatly influences their economy.

Herding societies *have food-producing strategies based on domestication of animals, whose care is the central focus of their activities.* Domesticating animals has replaced hunting them. In addition to providing food and other products, cattle, sheep, goats, pigs, horses, and camels represent forms of wealth that result in more social prestige for members of the group.

Horticultural societies are those in which *the food-producing strategy is based on domestication of plants, using digging sticks and wooden hoes to cultivate small gardens.* They may also keep domesticated animals, but they focus on primitive agriculture or gardening. They cultivate tree crops, such as date palms or bananas, and plant garden plots, such as yams, beans, taro, squash, or corn. This is more efficient than gathering wild vegetables and fruits. Both herding and horticultural societies differ from hunter-gatherer societies in that they make their living by cultivating food and have some control over its production (Ward and Edelstein 2009).

The ability to control food sources was a major turning point in human history. Societies became more settled and stored surpluses of food, which led to increases in population size. A community could contain as many as 3,000 individuals. More people, surplus food, and greater accumulation of possessions encouraged the development of private property and created new status differences between individuals and families. Forms of social inequality became even more pronounced in agricultural societies.

Masai men in Kenya herd their cattle, leading them to water or better grazing. The strategy of domesticating cattle rather than hunting game has been a survival strategy for the Masai, but it has also affected the culture in many other ways.

The end of the horticultural stage saw advances in irrigation systems, in the fertilization of land, and in crop rotation. The transition to herding and horticulture occurred as early as 14,500 years ago in Egypt, 10,000 years ago in Melanesia, and 9,000 to 7,000 years ago in the Middle East Fertile Crescent and many parts of Asia, and was characterized by more permanent settlements, landownership, human modification of the natural environment, higher population density (cities), changes in diets to more vegetables and cereals, and power hierarchies. However, the technological breakthrough that moved many societies from the horticultural to the agricultural stage was the plow, introduced more than 6,000 years ago. It marked the beginning of the agricultural revolution in Europe, the Middle East, and other parts of the world, and it brought about massive changes in social structures in many societies.

Agricultural Societies

Pedro and Lydia Ramirez, their four young children, and Lydia's parents live as an extended family in a small farming village in Nicaragua. They rise early, and while Pedro heads for the fields to do some work before breakfast, Lydia prepares his breakfast and lunch and sees that their eldest son is up and ready to go to school, while Lydia's mother looks after the younger children. After school, the boy also helps in the fields. Most of the land in the area is owned by a large company that grows coffee, but the Ramirezes are fortunate to have a small garden plot where they grow some vegetables for themselves. At harvest time, all hands help, including young children. The family receives cash for the crops they have grown, minus the rent for the land. The land is plowed with the help of strong animals such as horses and oxen, and fertilizers are used. Little irrigation is attempted, although the garden plots may be watered by hand in the dry season.

The Ramirezes' way of life is typical of life in an agricultural society. Like horticulturalists, an **agricultural society** *relies primarily on raising crops for food and makes use of technological advances such as the plow, irrigation, draft animals, and fertilization to continuously cultivate the same land.* Technological advances allow for intensive and continuous cultivation of the same land, thus permitting permanent settlements and greater food surpluses. Through time, as increasingly sophisticated agricultural technology resulted in surplus food, the size of population centers increased to as much as a million or more. Agricultural societies are more efficient in utilizing energy than foraging societies. The plow circulates nutrients better than a digging stick, and when an animal is used to pull the plow, strength beyond that of a person is marshaled.

As surpluses accumulated, land in some societies became concentrated in the hands of a few individuals. Wealthy landowners built armies and expanded their empires. During these periods, fighting for and controlling land took precedence over technological advance. War was prevalent, and societies were divided increasingly into rich and poor classes. Those who held the land and wealth could control the labor sources and acquire serfs or slaves. Thus, the feudal system was born. Serfs (the peasant class) were forced to work the land for their survival. Food surpluses also allowed some individuals to leave the land and to trade goods or services in exchange for food. For the first time, social inequality became extensive enough to divide society into social classes. At this point, religion, political power, a standing army, and other meso-level institutions and organizations came to be independent of the family. The meso level became well established.

As technology advanced, goods were manufactured in cities. Peasants moved from farming communities, where the land could not support the large population, to rapidly growing urban areas, where the demand for labor was great. It was not until the mid-1700s in England that the next major transformation of society took place, resulting largely from technological advances and additional harnessing of energy.

The invention of the plow was essential for agricultural societies to develop, and in the early period of agriculture, these were pushed by people and then pulled by animals. The harnessing of energy was taken to another level when gasoline engines could pull the plow, dig deeper, and cultivate thousands of acres. This represents the beginning of industrialization. Modern machinery such as this harvester has pushed farming into the new level of productivity.

Industrial Societies

The Industrial Revolution involved the harnessing of steam power and the manufacture of gasoline engines, permitting machines to replace human and animal power; a tractor can plow far more land in a week than a horse, and an electric pump can irrigate more acres than an ox-driven pump. As a result of the new technologies, raw mineral products such as ores, raw plant products such as rubber, and raw animal products such as hides could be transformed into mass-produced consumer goods. The Industrial Revolution brought about enormous changes in products and social structures.

Industrial societies *rely primarily on mechanized production for subsistence resulting in greater division of labor based on expertise.* Economic resources were distributed more widely among individuals in industrial societies, but inequities between owners and laborers persisted. Wage earning gradually replaced slavery and serfdom, and highly skilled workers earned higher wages, leading to the rise of a middle class. Farmworkers moved from rural areas to cities to find work in factories, which produced consumer goods such as cars and washing machines. Cities came to be populated by millions of people.

Family and kinship patterns at the micro level also changed. Agricultural societies need large, land-based, extended family units to do the work of farming (recall how the Ramirez parents, grandparents, and children in Nicaragua all help out at harvest time), but industrial societies need individuals with specific skills, ability to move to where the jobs are, and smaller families to support. Family roles have changed. For example, children are an asset in agricultural societies and begin farmwork at an early age. However, from a purely economic perspective, children become a liability in an industrial society because they contribute less to the finances of the family and ultimately compete with adults for jobs.

Meso- and macro-level dimensions of social life expand in industrializing societies and become more influential in the lives of individuals. National institutions and multinational organizations develop. Today, for example, global organizations such as the World Bank, the World Court, the United Nations, and the World Health Organization address social problems and sometimes even make decisions that change national boundaries or national policies. Medical organizations such as Doctors Without Borders work cross-nationally;

corporations such as Nike and Gap become multinational; and voluntary associations such as Amnesty International lobby for human rights around the globe.

Perhaps the most notable characteristic of the industrial age is the rapid rate of change compared with other stages of societal development. The beginning of industrialization in Europe was gradual, based on years of population movement, urbanization, technological development, and other factors of modernization. Today, however, societal change occurs so rapidly that societies at all levels of development are being drawn together into a new age—the postindustrial era.

Postindustrial or Information Societies

The difference between India and the United States is "night and day"—literally. As Keith and Jeanne finished chapters for this book, they were sent to India in the evening and returned typeset by morning, a feat made possible by the time differences. Technology, the efficiency of overnight delivery, and the lower cost of production have led many publishing companies to turn to businesses halfway around the world for much of the book production process. As India and other developing countries increase their trained, skilled labor force, they are being called on by national and multinational companies to carry out global manufacturing processes. India has some of the world's best technical training institutes and the most modern **technology**—*the practical application of tools, skills, and knowledge to meet human needs and extend human abilities*. Although many people in India live in poverty, a relatively new middle class is rapidly emerging in major business centers around the country.

After World War II, starting in the 1950s, the transition from industrial to postindustrial society began in the United States, Western Europe (especially Germany), and Japan. This shift was characterized by movement from human labor to automated production and from a predominance of manufacturing jobs to a growth in service jobs, such as computer operators, bankers, scientists, teachers, public relations workers, stockbrokers, and salespeople. More than two thirds of all jobs in the United States now reside in organizations that produce and transmit information, thus the reference to an "Information Age." Daniel Bell (1973) describes this transformation of work, information, and communication as "the third technological revolution" after industrialization based on steam (which he calls the first technological revolution) and the invention of electricity (the second technological revolution). According to Bell, the third technological revolution was the development of the computer, which has led to this postindustrial era or Information Age.

Postindustrial societies are *those that have moved from human labor and manufacturing to automated production and service jobs, largely processing information*. For example, postindustrial societies require workers with high levels of technical and professional education, such as those in India. Those without technical education are less likely to find rewarding employment in the technological revolution. This results in new class lines being drawn, based in part on skills and education in new technologies.

India now has some of the best technological training in the world, and due to phenomenal advances in communication and transportation, production of products can now occur anywhere in the world. This photo is of an assembly line for the Mahindra Reva Electric Vehicle—a car with a very low carbon footprint to reduce damage to the environment.

This Buddhist monk uses modern technology, including a laptop that can connect him with colleagues on the other side of the globe. In a postindustrial or information society, even rather traditional positions can be affected.

Inequalities in access to education and technology will create or perpetuate social inequalities. For example, one fifth of adults in the United States do not use the Internet, and 18% have no Internet access. That is 20 million households. One half of these nonusers are age 65 or older, and 56% have only a high school education (Sachoff 2008).

However, among teens and young adults from 12 to 29, 93% go online, compared to 74% of adults 18 and over. Only 38% of those age 65 or older use the Internet (Pew Internet and American Life Project 2010).

Note the decline in use of the Internet with end of work years and among older generations, who had less—or no—access to computers when they were growing up. The number of older generations online has been growing steadily, and they are engaging in more varied activities, such as shopping, looking for health information, and making travel reservations online (Jones and Fox 2009). Among computer users, 76% of adult females and 80% of adult males are active. Among English-speaking Hispanics, 68% use computers, compared to 80% of whites and 71% of blacks. Computer usage grows as household incomes and education increase, with more than 90% of households earning above $50,000 using computers (Pew Internet and American Life Project 2012). To examine these issues more fully, examine Table 3.2 in the next "Engaging Sociology" feature and test the data in your community.

Engaging Sociology

Demographics of Internet Users

Table 3.2 shows the percentage of each group of American adults who use the Internet, according to a February 2012 survey of the Pew Internet and American Life Project. For instance, 79% of women use the Internet.

Table 3.2 Percentage of American Adults Who Use the Internet, by Group

	Percentage Who Use the Internet
All Adults	80
Men	81
Women	79
Race/Ethnicity	
White, non-Hispanic	83
Black, non-Hispanic	71
Hispanic (English- and Spanish-speaking)	71
Age	
18–29	94
30–49	88
50–64	79
65+	48
Household Income	
Less than $30,000/yr.	65
$30,000–$49,999	85
$50,000–$74,999	94
$75,000+	98
Educational Attainment	
No high school diploma	45
High school grad	73
Some college	91
College +	97

Source: The Pew Research Center's Internet and American Life Project's February Tracking Survey conducted January 20–February 19, 2012. *N* = 2,253 adults age 18 and older, including 901 interviews conducted by cell phone. Interviews were conducted in both English and Spanish.

Challenges:

Interview 10 people you know to find out about their Internet use, keeping records on the gender, age, ethnicity, educational attainment, and income bracket of each. Then compare your figures with those in Table 3.2. Are they similar? If not, what are possible geographic or other social factors that might cause your figures to be different from those in this national survey?

Postindustrial societies rely on new sources of power such as atomic, thermal, wind, and solar energy and new uses of computer automation, such as computer-controlled robots, which eliminate the need for human labor other than highly skilled technicians. In an age of global climate change, there is also a lot of concern about technologies that reduce pollution, as the photo of the hybrid bus illustrates. The core issue in a postindustrial society is this: The control of information and the ability to develop technologies or provide services have become more important than the control of money or capital.

Values of 21st-century postindustrial societies favor scientific and creative approaches to problem solving, research, and development, along with attitudes that support the globalization of world economies. Satellites, cell phones, fiber optics, and, especially, the Internet are further transforming postindustrial societies of the Information Age, linking people from societies around the world.

In a study of postmodern communities, sociologist Richard Florida links creativity to the local cultural climate and to economic prosperity. His research has important applied dimensions and is useful to policymakers in local communities. As his research in the "Sociologists in Action" on page 78 makes clear, the organization of society and the means of providing the necessities of life have a profound impact on values, beliefs, lifestyle, and other aspects of culture.

Hybrid buses have been adopted in some cities and in national parks because of the effects of pollution on the globe and its occupants.

Thinking Sociologically

What are likely to be the growth areas for jobs in your community and society? What competencies and skills will be essential in the future for you to find employment and be successful on the job?

What will the future bring? Futurologists predict new trends based on current activities, predictions of new advances and technologies, and inventions on the horizon. Among the many ideas for the future, technological advances dominate the field. Predictions include the use of cell phones connecting the poorest corners of the globe with the rest of the world. One billion mobile phone users are predicted for China by 2020, with 80% of the population having phones. Alternative energy sources from wind and solar power will become essential, and plug-in hybrids, natural gas, and electric batteries may replace gasoline motors. One million hydrogen-fueled cars are predicted for the United States by the year 2035, and far more for Europe and Japan. Gas may be on the way out (*News of Future* 2012). Rechargeable batteries that will run for 40 hours without recharging will run most home appliances by 2030. Those who are paralyzed will find help from brain-computer interfaces, giving them the ability to control their environments. Many advances will occur in space travel, and medical advances will result in stem cell breakthroughs that can develop into various types of body tissue (Future for All 2008; National Institutes of Health 2012). These are just a few of the many predictions that will affect societies and alter some human interactions. The point is that rapid change is inevitable, and the future looks exciting.

In much of this book, we focus on complex, multilevel societies, for this is the type of system in which most of us reading this book now live. Much of this book also focuses on social interaction and social structures, including interpersonal networking, the growth of bureaucratic structures, social inequality within the structure, and the core institutions necessary to meet the needs of individuals and society. In short, "hardware"—society—is the focus of many subsequent chapters. The remainder of this chapter will focus primarily on the social "software" that complements the hardware of our society.

Culture: The Software

I sleep on a bed. Perhaps you sleep on a tatami mat or animal skins. I brush my teeth with a toothbrush and toothpaste. Perhaps you chew on a special stick to clean your teeth. I speak English, along with 500 million English speakers for whom it is their native or first language (Answers.com 2012). You may speak one of the many other languages in the world, as do more than 1 billion Chinese speakers (mostly Mandarin); 474 million Hindustani speakers in just India, and many others around the world; and 700 million

Sociologists in Action—Richard Florida

Creativity, Community, and Applied Sociology

Like the transformations of societies from the hunter-gatherer to the horticultural stage or from the agricultural to the industrial stage, our own current transformation seems to have created a good deal of "cultural wobble" within society. How does one identify the elements or the defining features of a new age while the transformation is still in progress? This was one of the questions that intrigued sociologist Richard Florida, who studied U.S. communities.

Professor Florida (2002, 2012a) combined several methods. First, he traveled around the country to communities that were especially prosperous and seemed to be on the cutting edge of change in U.S. society. In these communities, he did both individual interviews and focus-group interviews. Focus-group interviews are semistructured group interviews with seven or eight people where ideas can be generated from the group by asking open-ended questions. Professor Florida recorded the discussion and analyzed the transcript of the discussion. The collected data helped Professor Florida identify the factors that caused people to choose the place where they decided to live. His informants discussed quality of life and the way they make decisions. As certain themes and patterns emerged, he tested the ideas by comparing statistical data for regions that were vibrant, had growing economies, and seemed to be integrated into the emerging information economy. He used another method to compare communities and regions of the country—analyzing already existing archival data collected by various U.S. government agencies, especially the U.S. Bureau of Labor Statistics and the U.S. Census Bureau.

Florida argues that the economy of the 21st century is largely driven by creativity, and creative people often decide where to live based on certain features of the society. Currently, more than one third of the jobs in the United States—and almost all the extremely well-paid professional positions—require creative thinking. These include not just the creative arts but scientific research, computer and mathematical occupations, education and library science positions, and many media, legal, and managerial careers. People in this "creative class" are given an enormous amount of autonomy in their work; they have problems to solve and the freedom to figure out how to do so. Florida found that modern businesses flourish when they hire highly creative people. Thus, growing businesses tend to seek out places where creative people locate.

Through his research, Florida identified regions and urban areas that are especially attractive to the creative class. Florida's research led him to collaborate with Gary Gates, a scholar who was doing research on communities that are open and hospitable to gays and lesbians. Gates and Florida were amazed to find that their lists were nearly identical. Florida found that creative people thrive on diversity—ethnic, gender, religious, and otherwise—for when creative people are around others who think differently, it tends to spawn new avenues of thinking and problem solving. Tolerance of difference and even the enjoyment of individual idiosyncrasies are hallmarks of thriving communities.

Florida is now very much in demand as a consultant to mayors and urban-planning teams, and his books have become required reading for city council members. Some elected officials have decided that fostering an environment conducive to creativity that attracts creative people leads to prosperity because business will follow. Key elements for creative communities are local music and art festivals, the presence of organic food grocery stores, legislation that encourages interesting mom-and-pop stores (and keeps out large "box stores" that crush such small and unique endeavors), encouragement of quaint and locally owned bookstores and distinctive coffee shops, provisions for bike and walking paths throughout the town, and ordinances that establish an environment of tolerance for people who are "different."

Note: Richard Florida heads the Martin Prosperity Institute at the Rotman School of Management at the University of Toronto. He also runs a private creative class institute. He earned his bachelor's degree from Rutgers University and his doctorate in urban planning from Columbia University.

Spanish speakers in 23 countries in which Spanish is the official language (*New York Times Almanac* 2011). English is the top Internet language around the world with 536.9 million users, Chinese 444.9 million, Spanish 153.3 million, and Japanese 99.1 million. Many other languages are also used on the Internet (Internet World Stats 2010).

I like meat and veggies. Perhaps you like tofu and grasshoppers. I wear jeans and a T-shirt. Perhaps you wear a sari or burqa. In the United States, proper greetings include a handshake, a wave, or saying "Hello" or "Hi." The greeting ceremony in Japan includes bowing, with the depth of the bow defined by the relative status of each individual. The proper greeting behavior in many European countries calls for men as well as women to kiss acquaintances on both cheeks.

The point of these examples is to show that the culture—the ideas and "things" that are passed on from one generation to the next in a society, including their knowledge, beliefs, values, rules and laws, language, customs, symbols, and material products—varies greatly as we travel across the globe. Each social unit of cooperating and interdependent people, whether at the micro, meso, or macro level, develops a unique way of life. This culture provides guidelines for the actions and interaction of individuals and groups within society. The cultural guidelines that people follow when they greet another person are examples.

As you can see, the sociological definition of culture refers to far more than "high culture"—such as fine art, classical music, opera, literature, ballet, and theater—and also far more than "popular culture"—such as reality TV, professional wrestling, YouTube, and other mass entertainment. In fact, much of pop culture has been shaped by technology, as is illustrated in the "Engaging Sociology on page 80." The sociological definition of culture includes both high culture and pop culture and has a much broader meaning besides.

In Japan the person who is younger and of lower status must bow more deeply.

All people share a culture with others in their society. There may be different views within and between cultures about what rules and behaviors are the most important, but no one could survive without culture, for without culture, there would be no guidelines or rules of behavior. Societies would be chaotic masses of individuals. Culture provides the rules, routines, patterns, and expectations for carrying out daily rituals and interactions. Within a society, the process of learning how to act is called socialization (discussed in detail in Chapter 4). From birth, we learn the patterns of behavior approved in our society.

Culture evolves over time and is adaptive. What is normal, proper, and good behavior in hunter-gatherer societies, where cooperation and communal loyalty are critical to the hunt, differs from appropriate behavior in the Information Age, where individualism and competition are encouraged and enhance one's position and well-being.

The creation of culture is ongoing and cumulative. Individuals and societies continually build on existing culture to adapt to new challenges and opportunities. The behaviors, values, and institutions that seem natural to you are actually shaped by your culture. Culture is so much a part of life that you may not even notice behaviors that outsiders find unusual or even abhorrent. You may not think about touching someone on the head, putting a baby in a crib, or picking up food with your left hand, but in some other cultures, such acts may be defined as inappropriate or morally wrong.

The transmission of culture is the feature that most separates humans from other animals. Some societies of higher primates have shared cultures but do not systematically enculturate (teach a way of life to) the next generation. Primate cultures focus on behaviors relating to obtaining food, use of territory, and social status. Human cultures have significantly more content and are mediated by language. Humans are the only mammals with cultures that enable them to adapt to and even modify their environments so that they can survive on the equator, in the Arctic, or even beyond the planet.

Thinking Sociologically

Try playing a game of cards with four people in which each player thinks a different suit is trump (a trump is a rule whereby any card from the trump suit wins over any card from a different suit). In this game, one person believes hearts is trump, another assumes spades is trump, and so forth. What would happen? How would the result be similar to a society with no common culture?

Engaging Sociology

Pop Culture and Technology

How surprising to think that digital telephones, high-speed lines for computers, digitized print media, and the World Wide Web have all occurred within about the past half-century, many within the last 20 years. Vinyl records, dial telephones, and VHS tapes have been surpassed by CDs, high-speed cell phones, and DVDs. Slim laptops, iPads, and handheld computers have replaced bulky desktop computers. The following timeline shows the rapid advances of the Internet and World Wide Web in recent years; the point of this timeline is to illustrate the rapid advance of technology and the place it holds in our lives. Technology is now a primary conveyor of culture, especially pop culture.

An Internet and World Wide Web Timeline

1844: The telegraph constitutes a data network forerunner.

1866: Transoceanic telegraph service begins.

1876: The telephone is introduced.

1915: The first transcontinental phone call is made.

1946: Electronic Numerical Integrator and Computer (ENIAC), the first general-purpose computer, is developed for military purposes.

1951: UNIVersal Automatic Computer (UNIVAC) becomes the first civilian computer.

1962: The first communications satellite and the first digital phone networks are introduced.

1965: A highly usable computer language, Beginner's All-Purpose Symbolic Instruction Code (BASIC), is developed.

1971: Microprocessors are developed, making possible personal computer (PC) technology.

1972: The first video game, *Pong,* is introduced. E-mail is developed on the Advanced Research Projects Agency Network (ARPANET) for military use.

1977: The first fiber-optic network is created.

1978: Cellular phone service begins.

1982: The National Science Foundation sponsors a high-speed communications network, leading to the Internet.

1984: Apple Macintosh introduces the first PC with graphics.

1991: The Internet opens to commercial uses, HyperText Markup Language (HTML) is developed, and the World Wide Web is finally launched.

1993: The first point-and-click web browser, Mosaic, is introduced.

1995: Digital cellular phones are introduced. The first online auction house, eBay, is launched.

1996: Google makes its debut.

2000: Cookies technology allows for information profiles to be created, enabling data mining.

2001: Instant messaging services expand to allow exchanges between different service providers.

2002: Broadband technology is developed in South Korea.

2004: Mark Zuckerberg begins Facebook while a student at Harvard University.

2005: YouTube is created by PayPal employees Chad Hurley, Steve Chen, and Jawed Karim.

Continuing: The Internet continues to produce online versions of all media forms and communication websites, some of which have been created since this book was published.

The continuing rapid advances in technology have paralleled the development of shared pop culture in the United States and around the world, culture that is accessible to everyone, not just the elite. Music groups from other continents have gained audiences in the United States, with musical groups becoming instant success stories through YouTube. Webcasting allows for access to audio and video presentations on demand, and streaming allows people around the world to listen to broadcasts on the Internet. The spread of pop culture—music, mass art, fashion, books, you name it—has been made possible by advances in technology. "There is no turning back the clock once an innovation is introduced that makes communication more rapid, cheap, and broadly accessible" (Danesi 2008:21).

Engaging with Sociology

1. Identify four of the historic innovations that particularly interest you. What are some ways in which your life is

different today because of those four introductions to our popular culture?

2. Identify three positive and three negative ways these rapid changes are likely to affect the less technologically developed parts of the world.

3. Are technology and the spread of pop culture bringing the world closer together, or are these innovations more likely to cause tensions as societies attempt to protect their citizens against e-fraud, pornography, misuse of technology, and change of the local culture?

Ethnocentrism and Cultural Relativity

As scientists, sociologists must rely on careful use of the scientific method to understand behavior. The scientific method calls for objectivity—the practice of considering observed behavior independently of one's own beliefs and values. The study of social behavior thus requires both sensitivity to a wide variety of human social patterns and a perspective that reduces bias. This is more difficult than it sounds because sociologists themselves are products of society and culture. All of us are raised in a particular culture that we view as normal or natural. Yet not every culture views the same things as "normal."

The Arapesh of New Guinea, a traditional and stable society, encourage premarital sex according to famous anthropologist Margaret Mead. It is a way for a girl to prove her fertility, which makes her more attractive as a potential marriage partner (Mead [1935] 1963). Any babies born out of wedlock are simply absorbed into the girl's extended family. The baby's care, support, belonging, and lineage are not major issues for the Arapesh. The babies are simply accepted and welcomed as new members of the mother's family because the structure is able to absorb them. For the Arapesh and for the Bontoc of the Philippines, sexual behavior outside marriage is not a moral issue. Mead's findings have been questioned, but the fact that societies have many different views on premarital sex and pregnancy remains (Library of Congress 2010).

From studies of 154 societies documented in the *Human Relations Area Files,* a source of comparative information on many traditional societies around the world, scientists have found that about 42% of the 154 included societies encourage premarital sex, whereas 29% forbid such behavior and punish those who disobey this rule (Ford 1970). The remainder fall in between. As you can see, social values, beliefs, and behaviors can vary dramatically from one society to the next. These differences can be threatening and even offensive because most people judge others according to their own perspectives, experiences, and values.

The tendency to view one's own group and its cultural expectations as right, proper, and superior to others is called **ethnocentrism**—"ethno" for ethnic group and "centrism" for centered on. If you were brought up in a society that forbids premarital or extramarital sex, for instance, you might judge the Arapesh—or many Americans—to be immoral. In a few Muslim societies, people who violate this taboo may be severely punished or even executed, because premarital sex is seen as an offense against the faith and the family and as a weakening of social bonds. It threatens the lineage and inheritance systems. In turn, the Arapesh would find rules of abstinence to be strange and even wrong.

This Japanese family might think that eating with a fork or spoon or that sitting on a chair for dinner is quite strange. The children have been well socialized into their culture to know that polite eating involves competent use of chopsticks and kneeling on pillows.

Societies instill some degree of ethnocentrism in their members because ethnocentric beliefs hold groups together and help members feel that they belong to the group. Ethnocentrism promotes loyalty, unity, high morale, and conformity to the rules of society. Fighting for one's country, for instance, requires some degree of belief in the rightness of one's own society and its causes. Ethnocentric attitudes also help protect societies from rapid, disintegrating change.

If most people in a society did not believe in the rules and values of their own culture, the result could be widespread dissent, deviance, or crime.

Ethnocentrism can take many forms (see, for example, how you react to Map 3.1). Unfortunately, ethnocentrism often leads to misunderstandings between people of different cultures. In addition, the same ethnocentric attitudes that strengthen ties between some people may encourage hostility, racism, war, and genocide against others—even others within the society—who are different. Virtually all societies tend to "demonize" their adversary—in movies, the news, and political speeches—especially when a conflict is most intense. Dehumanizing another group with labels makes it easier to torture or kill its members or to perform acts of discrimination and brutality against them. We see this in the current conflicts in Afghanistan, in which both sides in the conflict feel hatred for each other. However, as we become a part of a global social world, it becomes increasingly important to accept those who are "different." Bigotry and attitudes of superiority do not enhance cross-national cooperation and trade—which is what the increasing movement toward global village and globalization entail.

Ethnocentrism can lead to misunderstandings between members of different cultures. Often people from one culture have pictures in their minds of what "others" are like. This affects the way people treat each other, sometimes with negative consequences.

American businesspeople who go to Japan try to negotiate deals and sign contracts. The Japanese way of doing business, however, takes time. It involves getting to know the other party by socializing over drinks in the evening. It is important not to rush the deal. To the Japanese, the Americans seem pushy, too concerned about contract

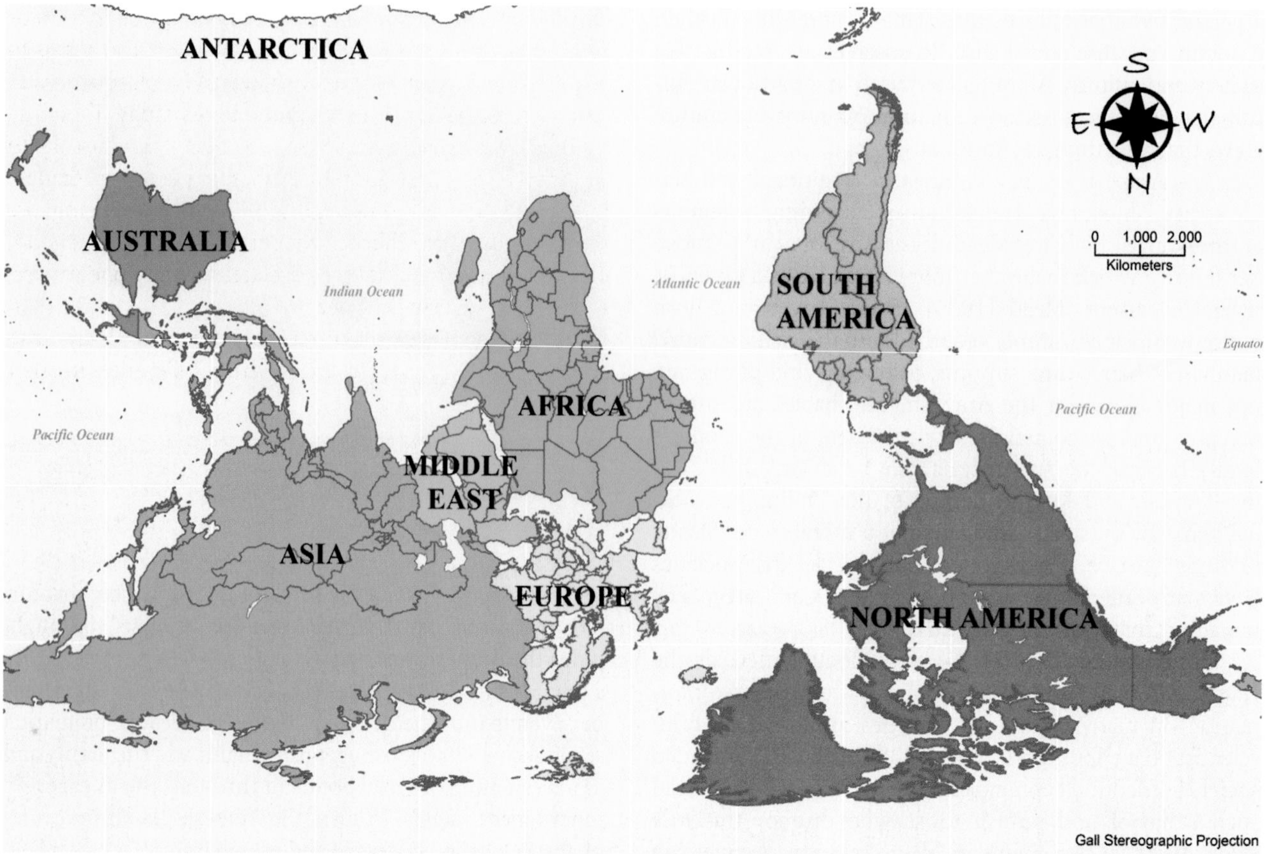

Map 3.1 "Southside Up" Global Map

Source: Map by Anna Versluis.

Note: This map illustrates geographic ethnocentrism. Americans tend to assume it is natural that north should always be "on top." The fact that this map of the world is upside-down, where south is "up," seems incorrect or disturbing, yet it illustrates an ethnocentric view of the world. Most people think of their countries or regions as occupying a more central and larger part of the world.

details rather than trust, and in too much of a hurry. Many an international business arrangement has fallen through because of such cultural misunderstandings.

U.S. foreign relations illustrate how ethnocentrism can produce hostility. Many U.S. citizens are surprised to learn that the United States—a great democracy, world power, and disseminator of food, medicine, and technological assistance to developing nations—is despised in many countries. One cause is the political dominance of the United States and the threat it poses to other people's way of life (Hertsgaard 2003). U.S. citizens are regarded by some as thinking ethnocentrically and only about their own welfare as their country exploits weaker nations. U.S. tourists are sometimes seen as loudmouthed ignoramuses whose ethnocentric attitudes prevent them from seeing value in other cultures or from learning other languages.

Anti-U.S. demonstrations in South America, the Middle East, and Asia have brought this reality to life through television. Indeed, politicians in several Latin American and European countries have run for office on platforms aimed at reducing U.S. influence. Thus, U.S. ethnocentrism may foster anti-American ethnocentrism among people from other countries. Note that even referring to citizens of the United States as "Americans"—as though people from Canada, Mexico, and South America do not really count as Americans—is seen as ethnocentric by many people from these other countries. *America* and the *United States* are not the same thing, but many people in the United States, including some presidents, fail to make the distinction, much to the dismay of other North and South Americans. If you visit Mexico, people might ask you where you are from. Say "America," and they will say they are from America too. Say North America, and Mexicans will say "From Canada or the United States?" We assume we are the main countries with claim to these names. Not all ethnocentrism is hostile; some of it is just a reaction to the strange ways of other cultures. An example is making judgments about what is proper food to eat and what is just not edible. While food is necessary for survival, there are widespread cultural differences in what people eat. Some of the New Guinea tribes savor grasshoppers; Europeans and Russians relish raw fish eggs (caviar); Eskimo children find seal eyeballs a treat; some Indonesians eat dog; and some Nigerians prize termites. Whether it is from another time period or another society, variations in food can be shocking to us.

In contrast to ethnocentrism, **cultural relativism** *requires setting aside cultural and personal beliefs and prejudices to understand another group or society through the eyes of members of that community using its own standards.* Instead of judging cultural practices and social behavior as good or bad according to one's own cultural practices, the goal is to be impartial in learning the purposes and consequences of practices and behaviors of the group under study. That does not mean we have to accept others' practices—just try to understand why they exist. Just as we may have preferences for certain software programs to do word processing, we can recognize that other software programs are quite good, may have some features that are better than the one we use, and are ingeniously designed.

Yet being tolerant and understanding is not always easy, and even for the most objective observer, differences in other

In the United States, dogs are family members and are highly cherished, with dog care becoming a growth industry. In Nanking, China, dogs are valued more as a culinary delicacy and a good source of protein. If you feel a twinge of disgust, that is part of the ethnocentrism we may experience as our perspectives conflict with those elsewhere in the world.

cultures can be difficult to understand. The idea of being "on time," which is so much a part of the cultures of the United States, Canada, Japan, and parts of Europe, is a rather bizarre concept in many societies. Among many Native American people, such as the Dineh (Apache and Navajo), it is ludicrous for people to let a timepiece that one wears on one's arm or a cell phone in one's pocket—pieces of machinery—govern the way one constructs and lives life. The Dineh orientation to time—that one should do things according to the natural rhythm of the body and not according to an artificial electronic mechanism—is difficult for many North Americans to grasp. Misunderstandings occur when those of European heritage think that "Indians are always late" and jump to the erroneous conclusion that "Indians" are undependable. Native Americans, on the other hand, think whites are neurotic about letting some instrument control them (Basso 1979; Farrer 1996; Hall 1959, 1983).

Whether it is from another time period or another society, variations in food can be shocking to us, making it hard to understand other people and other times, as the next "Sociology Around the World" illustrates. Cultural relativism requires that we shrug our shoulders and say, "Well, they are getting vitamins, proteins, and other nutrients, and it seems to work for them."

Cultural relativism does not require that social scientists accept or agree with all the beliefs and behaviors of the societies or groups they study. Certain behaviors, such as infanticide, cannibalism, headhunting, slavery, female genital mutilation (removal of the clitoris), forced marriage, terrorism, or genocide, may be regarded as unacceptable by almost all societies. Yet it is still important to try to understand those practices in the social and cultural contexts in which they occur so that abuses of human rights can be challenged. Many social scientists take strong stands against violations of human rights, environmental destruction, and other social policies. They base their judgments on the concept of universal human rights and the potential for harm to human beings and to the world community. Yet note that most Western democracies are adaptations to systems that thrive on values of extreme individualism, differentiation of job positions, and competition, consistent with a very complex society. Not all leaders of other societies agree that these values produce the type of life they wish for their people.

Thinking Sociologically

Small, tightly knit societies with no meso or macro level often stress cooperation, conformity, and personal sacrifice for the sake of the community. Complex societies with established meso- and macro-level linkages are more frequently individualistic, stressing personal uniqueness, individual creativity, and critical thinking. Why might this be so?

The following "Sociology Around the World" illustrates the differences in diets that sound unattractive to us today, certainly not what we think of as "normal." Some of the foods we find disgusting in other cultures or from past times may be healthier than our present diets, but ethnocentrism may prevent us from seeing this.

The Components of Culture: Things and Thoughts

Things and thoughts make up much of our culture. **Material culture** *includes all the objects we can see or touch including the artifacts of a group of people.* **Nonmaterial culture** includes *our thoughts, language, feelings, beliefs, values, and attitudes that make up much of our culture.* Together they provide the guidelines for our lives.

Material Culture: The Artifacts of Life

Material culture includes all the human-made objects we can see or touch, all the artifacts of a group of people—their grindstones for grinding cassava root, microwave ovens for cooking, bricks of mud or clay for building shelters, hides or woven cloth for making clothing, books or computers for conveying information, tools for reshaping their environments, vessels for carrying and sharing food, and weapons for dominating and subduing others.

Some material culture is from the local community; it is of micro-level origin. The kinds of materials with which homes are constructed and the materials used for clothing often reflect the geography and resources of the local area. Houses are an especially good example of material culture, since they both result from local ideas of what a "home" looks like and shape the interactions and attitudes of people in the society. Likewise, types of jewelry, pottery, musical instruments, or clothing reflect tastes that emerge at the micro and meso levels of family, community, and subculture. At a more macro level, national and international corporations interested in making profits work hard to establish trends in fashion and style that may cross continents and oceans.

Material culture in many ways drives the globalization process. Many of our clothes are now made in Asia or Central American countries. Our shoes may well have been produced in the Philippines. The oil used to make the plastic water bottles and devices in our kitchens

Sociology Around the World

The Paleo Diet

Early humans lived off the land and what they could hunt. Their culture centered on obtaining food by foraging and hunting in their environments, mostly small lean animals and birds and nuts and berries. The diet provided lean protein, polyunsaturated fats, monounsaturated fats, fiber, vitamins, minerals, antioxidants, and other important nutrients. Today, 10,000 years later, our modern diets and lifestyles are quite different even though our genome has remained pretty much the same. Many of these differences in diet that are causing diseases today began recently, after World War II when fast food became popular. The mass processing of foods for efficiency and low cost altered basic nutritional characteristics of ancestral diets. Because our bodies have not evolved to keep up with the changes in processed foods, our bodies are vulnerable to chronic diseases of Western civilization such as obesity, hypertension, diabetes, and atherosclerotic cardiovascular disease—all major causes of poor health and death today. Thus, today's culture including what we eat and our lifestyles do not meet the needs of our Paleolithic bodies. The following is an example of foods eaten by early humans.

Early Humans' Salad Bar

This is the menu of the early hominids, who lived in the savannas of eastern and southern Africa from roughly 1.5 million to 5 million years ago. Everything was served raw. Cooking with fire had not been discovered.

Main course: Nuts, birds' eggs, roots, tubers, beans, leaves, gum, sap, greens, insects, worms, grubs, termites, and seasonal berries and fruits (90% of the diet).

Raw meat appetizer tray: Gathered delicacies include small mammals, birds, reptiles, fish, shellfish, slow game, dead or dying animals, and infants of species such as antelope, pig, giraffe, or baboon when available. Bone marrow or the contents of animal heads and stomachs are delicious additions to this menu. Season with honey, rock salt, or puree of worms and insects (10% of the diet).

Ancestral Potluck Dinner

The first members of our own genus, *Homo erectus,* used these recipes from about 100,000 to 1.5 million years ago in the tropical and temperate zones of Africa and Eurasia. New technologies in fire making, advanced scavenging, and simple hunting as well as social advances in cooperation, sharing, and the gender division of labor provided some very tasty and nourishing meals for our ancestors.

Main courses: A stew or soup made with vegetables, bird bones, roots, nuts, and foods from the salad bar main course and raw meat appetizer tray, plus other gathered foods as available. Add leftovers and herbal seasonings (80% of the diet).

Outdoor barbecue: Sizzling deer haunch, roasted rabbit, shellfish, wild boar, ox, or cattle ribs (20% of the diet).

Sources: Cordain et al. 2005; Eaton, Konner, and Cordain 2010; O'Keefe and Cordain 2004; Ward 1996.

likely came from the Middle East. Even food is imported year-round from around the planet. That romantic diamond engagement ring—a symbol that represents the most intimate tie—may well be imported from a South African mine using low-paid or even slave labor. Our cars are assembled from parts produced on nearly every continent. Moreover, we spend many hours in front of a piece of material culture—our computers—surfing the World Wide Web. Material culture is not just for local homebodies.

Thinking Sociologically

Think of examples of material culture that you use daily: stove, automobile, cell phone, computer, refrigerator, clock, money, and so forth. How do these material objects influence your way of life and the way you interact with others? How would your behavior be different if these material objects, say iPhones or cars, did not exist?

Photo Essay

Houses as Part of a Society's Material Culture

Homes are good examples of material culture. Their construction is influenced not only by local materials but also by ideas of what a home is. Homes shape the context in which family members interact, so they can influence the nonmaterial culture. Indeed, in some cases, homes become status symbols that are far larger than the family needs; the family uses the home to make a prestige statement about its socioeconomic standing.

Nonmaterial Culture: Beliefs, Values, Rules, and Language

Saluting the flag, saying a blessing before meals to express gratitude for abundance in one's life, flashing someone an obscene gesture, and a football coach signaling the defense what defensive formation to run for the next play are all symbolic acts. In the case of the salute and the prayer, the acts undergird a belief about the nation or about a higher spiritual presence. In each case something is communicated, yet each of these acts refers to something deeper than any material object.

Nonmaterial culture refers to *the thoughts, language, feelings, beliefs, values, and attitudes that make up much of our culture.* They are the invisible and intangible parts of culture; they are of equal or even greater importance than material culture for they involve society's rules of behavior, ideas, and beliefs that shape how people interact with others and with their environment. Although we cannot touch the nonmaterial components of our culture, they pervade our life and are instrumental in determining how we think, feel, and behave. Nonmaterial culture is complex, comprising four main elements: values, beliefs, norms or rules, and language.

Coaches and players use hand signals to cue each other into an upcoming play or to convey what defense or offense to set up—an example of nonverbal communication.

Values are *shared judgments about what is desirable or undesirable, right or wrong, good or bad. They express the basic ideals of any group of people.* In industrial and postindustrial societies, for instance, a good education is highly valued. That you are in college shows you have certain values toward learning and education. Gunnar Myrdal (1964), a Swedish sociologist and observer of U.S. culture, referred to the U.S. value system as the "American creed." Values become a creed when they are so much a part of the way of life that they acquire the power of religious doctrine. We tend to take our core values for granted, including freedom, equality, individualism, democracy, free enterprise, efficiency, progress, achievement, and material comfort (Macionis 2010; Williams 1970).

At the macro level, conflicts may arise between groups in society because of differing value systems. For example, there are major differences between the values of various Native American groups and the dominant culture—whether that dominant culture is in North, Central, or South America (Lake 1990; Sharp 1991). Consider the story in the "Sociology Around the World" on page 88 about Rigoberta Menchú Tum and the experiences of Native American populations living in Guatemala.

The conflict in values between Native Americans and the national cultures of Canada, the United States, and many Latin American countries has had serious consequences. Cooperation is a cultural value that has been passed on through generations of Native Americans in both North and South America. This is because group survival has always depended on group cooperation in the hunt, in war, and in daily life. The value of cooperation can place native children at a disadvantage in North American schools that emphasize competition. Native American and Canadian First Nation children experience more success in classrooms that stress cooperation and sociability over competition and individuality (Lake 1990; Mehan 1992).

Another Native American value is the appreciation of and respect for nature. Conservation of resources and protection of the natural environment—Mother Earth—have always been important because of people's dependence on nature for survival. Today, we witness disputes between native tribes and the governments of Canada, the United States, Mexico, Guatemala, Brazil, and other countries over the raw resources found on native reservations. While many other North and South Americans also value cooperation and respect for the environment, these values do not govern decision making in most communities (Brown 2001; Marger 2012). The values honored by governments and

Sociology Around the World

Life and Death in a Guatemalan Village

In her four decades of life, Rigoberta Menchú Tum experienced the closeness of family and cooperation in village life. These values are very important in Chimel, the Guatemalan hamlet where she lives. She also experienced great pain and suffering with the loss of her family and community. A Quiche Indian, Menchú became famous throughout the world in 1992, when she received the Nobel Peace Prize for her work to improve conditions for Indian peoples.

Guatemalans of Spanish origin hold the reins of power and have used Indians almost as slaves. Some of the natives were cut off from food, water, and other necessities, but people in her hamlet helped support each other and taught children survival techniques. Most people had no schooling. Menchú's work life in the sugarcane fields began at age 5. At 14, she traveled to the city to work as a domestic servant. While there, she learned Spanish, which helped her be more effective in defending the rights of the indigenous population in Guatemala. Her political coming of age occurred at age 16, when she witnessed her brother's assassination by a group trying to expel her people from their native lands.

Her father started a group to fight the repression of the indigenous and poor, and at 20, Menchú joined the movement, Comité de Unidad Campesina (CUC, meaning "Peasant Unity Committee"), which the government claimed was communist inspired. Her father was murdered during a military assault, and her mother was tortured and killed. Menchú moved to Mexico with many other exiles to continue their nonviolent fight for rights and democracy.

The values of the native population represented by Menchú focus on respect for and a profound spiritual relationship with the environment, equality of all people, freedom from economic oppression, the dignity of her culture, and the benefits of cooperation over competition. The landowners tended to stress freedom of people to pursue their individual self-interests (even if inequality resulted), the value of competition, and the right to own property and to do whatever one desired to exploit that property for economic gain. Individual property rights were thought to be more important than preservation of indigenous cultures. Economic growth and profits were held in higher regard than religious connectedness to the earth.

The values of the native population and those of the landowners are in conflict. Only time will tell if the work of Indian activists such as Rigoberta Menchú Tum and her family will make a difference in the lives of this indigenous population.

corporations are those held by the people with power, prestige, and wealth.

Thinking Sociologically

The experiences of Rigoberta Menchú Tum are only one example of clashes between dominant and less powerful groups within a single nation. What are some other ways that differences in cultural values between dominant and native peoples can cause major problems?

Beliefs are *ideas we hold about life, about the way society works, and about where we fit into the world.* They are expressed as specific statements that we hold to be true. Many Hindus, for example, believe that fulfilling behavioral expectations of one's own social caste will be rewarded in one's next birth, or incarnation. In the next life, good people will be born into a higher social status. In contrast, some Christians believe that one's fate in the afterlife depends on whether one believes in certain ideas—for instance, that Jesus Christ is one's personal savior. Beliefs come from traditions established over time, from sacred scriptures, from experiences people have had, and from lessons given by parents and teachers or other individuals in authority. Beliefs influence the choices we make. Beliefs tend to be based on values, which are broader and more abstract notions of something desirable. One value might be that the environment is worth preserving, but a belief might be that humans have caused global warming. Another value might be eternal life, but a belief might be that this occurs through reincarnation and eventually nirvana.

Values and beliefs, as elements of nonmaterial culture, are expressed in two forms: an ideal culture and a real culture. **Ideal culture** consists of *practices, beliefs, and values that are regarded as most desirable in society and are consciously taught to children*. Not everyone, however, follows the approved cultural patterns, even though they may say they do. **Real culture** refers to *the way things in society are actually done*. For the most part, we hardly question these practices and beliefs that we see around us. Rather like animals that have always lived in a rain forest and cannot imagine a treeless desert, we often fail to notice how our culture helps us make sense of things. Because of this, we do not recognize the gap between what we tell ourselves and what we actually do.

For example, the ideal in many societies is to ban extramarital sex. Sex outside marriage can raise questions of paternity (who is the father) and inheritance (who is in line to inherit wealth), besides leading to spousal jealousy and family conflict. In the United States, about one fourth of all married men and one in seven married women report that they have had at least one extramarital affair (National Opinion Research Center 2010; Newman and Grauerholz 2002). While in ideal culture we claim that we believe in marital fidelity and this is at the core of family morality, actual behavior or real culture is frequently different.

Norms are *rules of behavior shared by members of a society and rooted in the value system*. All of our rather routine behaviors—from saying "Hi" to people we meet to obeying traffic signs—are examples. Norms range from religious warnings such as "Thou shalt not kill" to the expectation in many societies that young people will complete their high school education. Sometimes the origins of particular norms are quite clear. Few people wonder, for instance, why there is a norm to stop and look both ways at a stop sign. Other norms, such as the rule in many societies that women should wear skirts but men should not, have been passed on through the generations and have become unconsciously accepted patterns and a part of tradition. Sometimes we may not know how norms originated or even be aware of norms until they are violated.

Norms are generally classified into three categories—folkways, mores, and laws—based largely on how important the norms are in the society and people's response to the breach of those norms. *Folkways* are customs or desirable behaviors, but they are not strictly enforced: Some examples are responding appropriately and politely when introduced to someone, speaking quietly in a library, not scratching your genitals in public, using proper table manners, and covering your mouth when you cough. Violation of these norms causes people to think you are weird or even uncouth but not necessarily immoral or criminal.

Mores are norms that most members observe because they have great moral significance in a society. Conforming to mores is a matter of right and wrong, and violations of many mores are treated very seriously. The person who deviates from mores is considered immoral or bordering on criminal. Being honest, not cheating on exams, and being faithful in a marriage are all mores. The following box provides examples of violations of folkways and mores.

Norms and Violations of Norms

Folkways: Conventional Polite Behaviors
Violations viewed as "weird":

- Swearing in house of worship
- Wearing blue jeans to the prom
- Using poor table manners
- Picking one's nose in public

Mores: Morally Significant Behaviors
Violations viewed as "immoral":

- Lying or being unfaithful to a spouse
- Buying cigarettes or liquor for young teens
- Having sex with a professor as a way to increase one's grade
- Parking in handicap spaces when one is in good physical condition

Taboos are the strongest form of mores. They concern actions considered unthinkable or unspeakable in the culture. For example, most societies have taboos that forbid incest (sexual relations with a close relative) and prohibit defacing or eating a human corpse. Taboos are most common and numerous in societies that do not have centralized governments to establish formal laws and to maintain jails.

Taboos and other moral codes are of the utmost importance to a group because they provide guidelines for what is right and wrong. Yet behaviors that are taboo in one situation may be acceptable at another time and place. The incest taboo is an example found in all cultures, yet the application of the incest taboo varies greatly across cultures (Brown 1991). In medieval Europe, if a man and a woman were within 7 degrees of relatedness and wanted to marry, the marriage could be denied by the priest as incestuous. (Your first cousin is a third degree of relatedness from you.) On the other hand, the Balinese permit twins to marry because it is believed they have already been intimately bonded together in the womb (Leslie and Korman 1989). In some African and Native American societies, one cannot marry a sibling but might be expected to marry a first cousin. As Table 3.3 on page 90 illustrates, the definition of what is and what is not incest varies even from state to state in the United States.

Table 3.3 **Incest Taboos in the United States: States That Allow First-Cousin Marriage**

Alabama	Connecticut	Hawaii	New Mexico	South Carolina
Alaska	District of Columbia	Maryland	New York	Tennessee
California	Florida	Massachusetts	North Carolina	Vermont
Colorado	Georgia	New Jersey	Rhode Island	Virginia

States that allow it only under certain conditions such as marriage after a certain age or inability to bear children: Arizona, Illinois, Indiana, Maine, Utah, and Wisconsin.

Marriage of half cousins: Kansas, Maine, Montana, Nebraska, Nevada, and Oklahoma.

Marriage of adopted cousins: Louisiana, Mississippi, Oregon, and West Virginia.

States that do not allow first-cousin marriage: Fifteen other U.S. states disallow marriages to first cousins within the state: Arkansas, Delaware, Idaho, Iowa, Kentucky, Michigan, Minnesota, Missouri, New Hampshire, North Dakota, Ohio, Pennsylvania, South Dakota, Washington, and Wyoming.

Historically, in the United States, incest laws forbid in-law marriages far more than first-cousin marriages.

Source: National Conference of State Legislatures 2012.

Laws are *norms that have been formally encoded by those holding political power in society*, such as laws against stealing property or killing another person. The violator of a law is likely to be perceived not just as a weird or an immoral person but also as a criminal who deserves formal punishment. Many mores are passed into law, and some folkways are also made into law. Formal punishments are imposed. Spitting on the sidewalk is not a behavior that has high levels of moral contempt, yet it is illegal in some cities, resulting in fines to punish violators. Furthermore, behaviors may be folkways in one situation and mores in another. For example, nudity or various stages of near nudity may be only mildly questionable in some social settings (the beach or certain fraternity parties) but would be quite offensive in others (a four-star restaurant or a house of worship) and against the law in still other situations, incurring a penalty or sanction.

Sanctions *reinforce norms through rewards and penalties.* **Formal sanctions** *are rewards or punishments conferred by recognized officials to enforce the most important norms.* Fines for parking illegally, lowered grades on an assignment for plagiarism, or expulsion for bringing drugs or weapons to school are formal negative sanctions your school might impose. Honors and awards are formal positive sanctions. **Informal sanctions** are *unofficial rewards or punishments such as smiles, frowns, or ignoring unacceptable behaviors.* A private word of praise by your professor after class about how well you did on your exam would be an informal positive sanction; gossip or ostracism by other students because of the clothes you are wearing would be an informal negative sanction. Sanctions vary with the importance of the norm and can range from a parent frowning at a child who fails to use proper table

Nudity may be considered a violation of law, mores, or folkways, or it may simply be accepted as normal, as in the case of this nude beach.

manners to a prison term or death sentence. Similarly, when we obey norms, we are rewarded with jokes and pats on the back that indicate solidarity with others. Most often, adherence to norms is ingrained so deeply that our reward is simply "fitting in." Folkways and many mores are enforced through informal sanctions, yet sometimes penalties for deviant behavior can be severe.

Norms concerning sexual behaviors are often very strong and carry powerful sanctions; sometimes they are even imposed by national governments. A woman who becomes pregnant outside marriage in societies that strongly condemn nonmarital sex is likely to be ostracized and her child labeled illegitimate. Such children may be stigmatized for life, living as outcasts in poverty on the streets, begging for food. This was the case in Vietnam during the French colonial period and during the U.S.-Vietnam War, when many biracial children were excluded from participation in society. "Half-breed" children bore the stigma, fueled by nationalism and xenophobia (fear or contempt for strangers), because the children were reminders of the country's colonial and wartime past. Biracial children are still suffering discrimination in Vietnam (DiversityInc 2008; Nguyen 2005).

When a society faces change, especially from war, rapid urbanization, industrialization, and modernization, traditional norms that have worked for the society for centuries are challenged. In the past few decades, examples have been seen in many Islamic countries where modernization has been met with a resurgence of religious fundamentalism. A case in point is Iran. The rapid modernization and social changes that took place in the post–World War II era were met by a backlash from religious fundamentalists. Strict Muslim laws and swift, often severe punishments were meted out to offenders. Radio music and drinking of alcoholic beverages were banned, and women were required to again wear the veil, as in previous times. Afghanistan and other Muslim nations are currently struggling with the conflicts between traditional religious and cultural values and those related to pressures from the social environment—in this case Western nations—for change and modernization.

At the global level, there are newly emerging norms to deal with some areas of technology, such as fraud and theft on the Internet and the World Wide Web. Without norms, there are no guidelines for interactions between individuals and groups. E-mail has been in existence for civilians only since 1994, thus allowing social scientists to watch the emergence of norms in this new social environment.

Communication is often mediated and enhanced through nonverbal indicators such as tone of voice, inflection, facial expressions, or other gestures that communicate emotion. In an e-mail, the words are just words without context. To establish norms, many Listservs now have rules for polite communication to avoid "flaming" someone—insulting someone with insensitive words by a faceless person. The development of emoticons (such as smileys) adds combinations of characters that represent the emotional context of the message. Norms of Internet communication are still emerging, and you probably have experienced times when messages have been misunderstood because the norms of communication are ambiguous.

Thinking Sociologically

One of the problems of Internet communication has been that many norms of civil discourse are ignored, and new norms emerge. What do you see as the current rules for Internet and Twitter communication? When dealing with conflict, how do these norms differ from verbal norms of communication?

Language is *the foundation of every culture. It conveys verbal and nonverbal messages among members of society.* The minidrama between infant and adult is played out every day around the world as millions of infants learn the language of the adults who care for them. In the process, they acquire an important part of culture. Although many animals can communicate with a limited repertoire of sounds, the ability to speak a language is unique to humans.

Human infants have the potential for developing language because the human voice box, tongue, and brain make speech biologically possible. In their early months, babies make many sounds—squealing, growling, "raspberries," cooing, and tongue clicks. These become more recognizable as syllables in the second six months of life (Oller 2006). At about 1 year of age, most infants begin to pronounce recognizable words in the language of their culture. The baby soon learns that some of those sounds elicit enthusiastic responses from the adult caretakers, reinforcing their use.

Transport a baby from France to the Arapesh tribe in New Guinea and another baby from New Guinea to France, and each will learn to speak the language and adhere to the culture in which it is brought up. The reason is that language, like other components of culture, is learned. Language conveys verbal and nonverbal messages among members of society. Simply put, without language there would be little, if any, culture. Through the use of language, members of a culture can pass on essential knowledge to children and can share ideas with other members of their society. Work can be organized; the society can build on its experiences and plan its future. Through language, members express their ideas, values, beliefs, and knowledge, a key ingredient in the ability of humans to sustain social life.

Language takes three primary forms: spoken (as shown in the baby examples), written, and nonverbal. There are an estimated 5,000 languages spoken in the world. The most common ones are Chinese (with 845 million speakers), Spanish (329 million speakers), English (328 million), Hindu-Urdu (242 million), and Arabic (221 million) (Infoplease 2012; TopTenz.net 2011).

Written language enables humans to store ideas for future generations, accelerating the accumulation of ideas on which to build. It also makes possible communication over distances. Members of a society learn to read these shared symbols, some of which are displayed in Figure 3.1.

Nonverbal language consists of gestures, facial expressions, and body postures. This mode of communication may carry as much as 90% of the meaning of a message (Samovar and Porter 2003). Every culture uses nonverbal language to communicate, and just like verbal language, those cues may differ widely among cultures.

福
Поздравляю!
Θεος
לחם שר בא
-십 시요
العربية
राम

Figure 3.1 Societies Use Various Symbols to Communicate Their Written Language

The power to communicate nonverbally is illustrated in American Sign Language, designed for the hearing challenged and the mute. Complex ideas can be transmitted without vocalizing a word. Indeed, one can argue that the deaf have a distinctive culture of their own rooted in large part in the unique sign language that serves them. In addition, technology has aided communication among the hearing impaired through text messaging.

Misinterpretation of nonverbal signals can occur between male and female microcultures in Western societies. Consider the meanings in a nod of the head: When women nod their heads in response to a person who is talking, they often are encouraging the speaker to continue, signaling that they are listening and that they want the speaker to carry on with the clarification and explanation. It does not signal agreement. When men nod their heads when another person is speaking, they typically assume that the message is "I agree with what you are saying." This can lead to awkward, confusing, and even embarrassing miscues when men and women talk to one another, with the man mistakenly confident that the woman agrees with his ideas (Stringer 2006).

Thinking Sociologically

Explain a situation of miscommunication between you and a member of the other sex. What nonverbal messages were involved, and what happened?

Historically, communication was largely direct verbal communication or nonverbal cues that we interpreted, but in this digital age, social media has created a rather new phenomenon. This is discussed in the next "Sociology in Our Social World."

Language development is extremely important to becoming fully human, and it happens very rapidly from about the first year of life. Still, babies learn to communicate in a variety of other ways. Note how these infants communicate emotions nonverbally. What does each of them seem to be communicating?

Sociology in Our Social World

How We Communicate in the E-World

Current forms of social media present us with new options for communicating in spoken and written language. Around the world cell phones and Internet connections have changed once isolated villages into connected communities with friends and relatives in other places. Now they are but a Skype call away. The means of connecting are diverse, but serve the purpose of bringing together once separated people.

From sending a quick message to sharing one's life events and photos, social media provide a wide range of interactions. Consider the findings from a survey of a micro-sociology class at Hanover College in Indiana. It turned up the following forms of social media in use by students: e-mail, Draw (app), Facebook, Flickr, Instagram, LinkedIn, Pinterest, Skype, Spotify, StumbleUpon, texting, Twitter, Tumblr, and YouTube, among others.

The face-paced life we lead includes fast-paced interaction. Tweets with their 140-character limit include lots of shortcuts for on-the-move communication. A new vocabulary has emerged to cope with little time and space. Some examples from the students include:

SINS = sorry I'm not sorry	BTW= by the way
YOLO = you only live once	IOUE= I owe you
FOSHO = for sure	@ = friend
Aight = all right	# = hashtag
IDK = I don't know	ATM = at the moment
OMG = oh my God	BBN = big blue nation
B/K = because	

What do these new forms of communication mean for our interactions, and what are the pros and cons of reducing face-to-face interactions? Students pointed out the following:

Pros of Social Media

- It is a communication revolution allowing us to keep in contact with friends and acquaintances from around the world.
- It allows us to meet new friends with similar interests.
- It allows for the sharing of ideas and the ability to spend time with friends who are far away.
- It enhances strong relationships through ongoing communication.
- It fosters frequent and quick communication (even though it is less personal).
- It contributes to more informality in interrupted communication and relationships.
- It is inexpensive compared to other media.
- It allows individuals to develop different electronic and face-to-face communication styles and identities.
- It allows people share to their lives with a larger range of people.
- It allows for sharing in seconds—including photos, where one is, and where to meet.

Cons of Social Media

- Interpersonal skills may decline as a generation loses the ability to make "small talk."
- Face-to-face conversations are awkward for some who are dependent on social media as a screen.
- Texting limits conversations because communication is brief and abbreviated.
- Many in the younger generation have lost command of formal or proper communication.
- Personal interactions are often needed because incoming communications are given priority over the person who is present.
- Romantic breakups become complicated because an "ex" may stalk a person via constant texts or Facebook.
- Writing letters becomes a lost art.
- Relationships seem "valid and legit" only if they are posted on Facebook.
- People know every detail of each other's lives.
- It is difficult to stay connected without the latest technology.

Although these comments present a mixed picture, social media is changing the face of interpersonal communication. The question is how this might change our interactions and perhaps the society itself.

Thinking Sociologically

How has social media changed your life? That of your parents and grandparents? Do you think this is for the better or worse?

Language also plays a critical role in perception and in thought organization. The *linguistic relativity theory* posits that the people who speak a specific language make interpretations of their reality—they notice certain things and may fail to notice certain other things (Sapir 1929, 1949; Whorf 1956). "A person's 'picture of the universe' or 'view of the world' differs as a function of the particular language or languages that person knows" (Kodish 2003:384). For example, in some Native American cultures where life is dependent on the elements, there are a number of words for snow, each giving members of the group a description that could mean life or death—wet snow, dry snow, heavy snow, melting snow. Children in each different culture will learn about the world within the framework provided by their language.

White and black as colors have symbolic meaning—with phrases like "blackballed from the club" or "black sheep of the family" indicating negative judgment associated with blackness. Research shows that teams wearing black are called for more fouls than teams wearing white, which raises questions about how pervasive this association is in what we see.

To use another example, in the English language people tend to associate certain colors with certain qualities in a way that may add to the problem of racist attitudes (Levinson 2000). The definition of the word *black* includes "dismal," "boding ill," "hostile," "harmful," "inexcusable," "without goodness," "evil," "wicked," "disgrace," and "without moral light." The word *white*, on the other hand, is defined as "honest," "dependable," "morally pure," "innocent," and "without malice" (*Webster's Unabridged English Dictionary,* 1989). If the linguistic relativity thesis is correct, it is more than a coincidence that bad things are associated with the *black sheep* of the family, the *blacklist*, or *Black Tuesday* (when the U.S. stock market dropped dramatically and crashed in 1929).

This association of blackness with negative images and meanings is not true of all languages. The societies that have negative images for *black* and positive images for *white* are the same societies that associate negative qualities with people of darker skin. The use of *white* as a synonym for *good* or *innocent*—as in reference to a "white noise machine" or a "white lie"—may contribute to a cultural climate that devalues people of color. In essence, the language may influence our perception of color in a manner that contributes to racism. Interestingly, there is empirical evidence supporting this claim of color symbolism. Athletic teams that wear black uniforms have more penalties called on them than teams with lighter colored uniforms (Frank and Gilovich 1988).

Scientists continue to debate the extent to which language can influence thought, but most agree that while language may contribute to certain ways of thinking, it does not totally determine human thinking (Casasanto 2008; Gumperz and Levinson 1996; Lin 2010). Although the linguistic relativity theory is controversial and aspects have been misinterpreted, the idea of language, culture, consciousness, and behavior affecting each other is influential when studying the role of language.

In addition to influencing how we see our world, consider how language affects the planning of our day. Many nonindustrial peoples in Asia, Africa, Australia, and South and North America do not keep time in the kinds of exact units used in the industrial world—seconds, minutes, and hours. The smallest units might be sunrise, morning, midday, late afternoon, dusk, and night (Hall 1983). Meeting someone for an appointment requires great patience, for there are no words for what we call seconds, minutes, or even hours. Think about how this would change your life and the pace of everything around you. If you showed up at a predesignated location, your friend might appear three hours later but would be on time because the unit of time would include a four- or five-hour time period. In such a culture, one would eat when food is prepared or when one is hungry. One gets up when one is rested. Time-based words cause most of us to organize our days in particular ways and even to become irritated with others who do not adhere to these expectations (Bertman 1998).

When grouped together, material and nonmaterial components form cultural patterns. People's lives are organized around these patterns. For example, family life includes patterns of courtship, marriage, child rearing, and care of the elderly. Table 3.4 illustrates some of the more prominent material and nonmaterial cultural components involved in one aspect of Western society—sport.

We have seen that material artifacts and nonmaterial beliefs, values, norms, and language are the basic components of culture. Next, we explore the theoretical explanations for culture.

Thinking Sociologically

The words *bachelor* and *spinster* are supposedly synonymous terms, referring to unmarried adult males and females, respectively. Generate a list of adjectives that describe each of these words and that you frequently hear associated with them (e.g., *eligible, swinging, old, unattractive*). Are the associated words positive or negative in each case? How are these related to the position of the unmarried in societies?

Society, Culture, and Our Social World

Whether their people are eating termite eggs, fish eggs, or chicken eggs, societies always have a culture, and culture is always linked to a society. Culture provides guidelines for behaviors and actions at each level of society, from the global system to the individual family. The social world model at the beginning of the chapter, with its concentric circles, represents the micro to macro levels of society. Smaller social units such as a school operate within larger social units such as the community, which is also part of a region of the country. What takes place in each of these units is determined by the culture. There is a social unit—a structural "hardware"—and a culture or "software" at each level.

Microcultures: Micro-Level Analysis

Micro-level analysis focuses on social interactions in small-groups. To apply this idea to culture, we look at **microcultures**, *groups or organizations that affect only a small segment of one's life or influence a limited period of one's life*, such as membership in a Girl Scout troop, a boarding school, or prayer group (Gordon 1970). Other classic examples from sociology include a street gang, a college sorority, or a business office.

Hospitals are communities of people with a microculture. People in different-colored uniforms scurry around carrying out their designated tasks, part of the division of labor in the organization, each having symbolic significance indicating positions at the hospital. Hospital workers interact among themselves to attain goals of patient care. They have a common in-group vocabulary, a shared set of values, a hierarchy of positions with roles and behaviors for each position, and a guiding system of regulations for the organization—all of which shape interactions during the hours when each member works in the hospital. Yet the hospital microculture may have little relevance to the rest of the employees' everyday lives. Microcultures may survive over time, with individuals coming in as workers and patients and going out from the group, but in a complex society, no one lives his or her entire life within a microculture. The values, rules, and specialized language used by the hospital staff continue as one shift ends and other medical personnel enter and sustain that microculture.

Table 3.4 **Material and Nonmaterial Cultural Patterns in Sport**

Material objects	Balls: football, soccer ball, tennis ball, volleyball
Nonmaterial cultural components	Competition and fair play
Beliefs	Sports are healthy, create community around the sport. They express core American ideals of competition, work ethic, and the meritorious prevailing.
Values	One should support one's sports team—it is the best—and one should admire athletes.
Rules	Referees uphold the rules. Fans, players, and coaches sometimes challenge the refs' decisions, but are expected to engage in fair play.
Language or symbols	Each team has certain plays that it communicates by language or symbols. Supporters of teams use mascots, colors, and chants to cheer the team on.

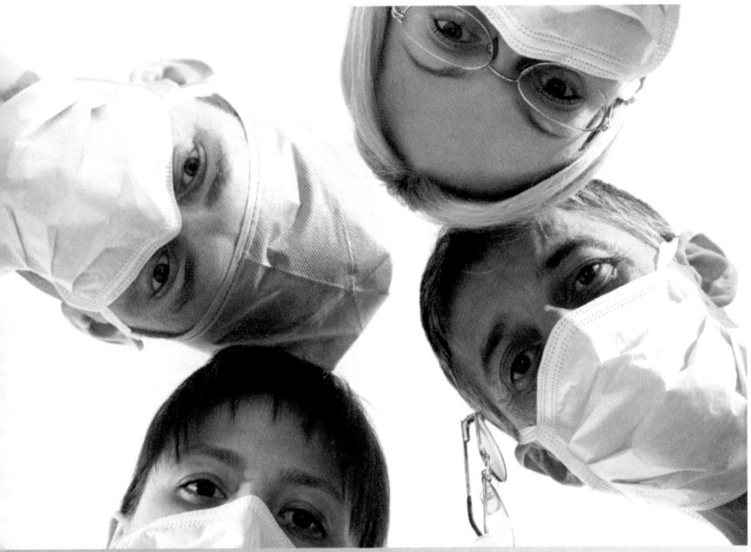

When these people work together in a hospital, they share a common culture: shared terminology, rules of interaction, and values regarding objectifying human body parts so that they are not sexualized. However, the hospital microculture only affects a part of each day and each week for the hospital personnel.

Every organization, club, and association is a social group and therefore must have a culture, a microculture, with its own set of rules and expectations. Schools develop their own unique cultures and traditions; as students graduate and move out of that microculture, others move into it. Many microcultures exist for a limited period of time or for a special purpose. A summer camp microculture may develop but exists only for that summer. The following summer, a very different culture may evolve because of new counselors and campers. A girls' softball team may develop its own cheers, jokes, insider slang, and values regarding competition or what it means to be a good sport, but next year, the girls may be realigned into different teams, and the transitory culture of the previous year changes. In contrast to microcultures, subcultures continue across a person's life span.

Subcultures and Countercultures: Meso-Level Analysis

A **subculture** is *the culture of a meso-level subcommunity that distinguishes itself from the dominant culture of the larger society. A subculture is smaller than the nation but, unlike a microculture, is large enough to support people throughout the life span.* A subculture is in some ways unique to that group yet at the same time shares the culture of the dominant society (Arnold 1970; Gordon 1970). Many ethnic groups within the larger society have their own subculture with their own sets of conventions and expectations. For example, picture a person who is African Canadian, Chinese Canadian, or Hispanic Canadian, living within an ethnic community that provides food, worship, and many other resources. Despite unique cultural traits, that person is still a good Canadian citizen, living within the national laws, norms, and way of life. It is just that this person's life has guidelines from the subculture in addition to the dominant culture of the society.

Because the social unit, such as the ethnic groups mentioned above, plays a more continuous role in the lifespan of group members than a summer camp or a sorority (microcultures), we analyze subcultures at the meso level. (Table 3.5 illustrates the connection between the social unit at each level and the type of culture at that level.)

Note that many of the categories into which we group people are not subcultures. For example, redheads, left-handed people, tall people, individuals who read *Wired* magazine, people who are single, visitors to Chicago, and DVD watchers do not make up subcultures because they do not interact as social units or share a common way of life. A motorcycle gang, a college fraternity, and a summer camp are also not subcultures because they affect only a segment of one's life (Gordon 1970; Yablonski 1959). A subculture, by contrast, pervasively influences a person throughout life.

In the United States, subcultures include ethnic groups, such as Mexican American and Korean American; exclusive religious groups, such as the Orthodox Jews in New York

Table 3.5 **Level of Social Units and of Culture**

Social Unit (People who interact and feel they belong)	*Culture (The way of life of that social unit)*
Dyads; small groups; local community	Microculture
Ethnic community or social class community	Subculture
National society	Culture of a nation
Global system	Global culture

City; and social class groups, including the exclusive subculture of the elite upper class on the East and West Coasts of the United States. The superwealthy have networks, exclusive clubs, and the Social Register, which lists the names and phone numbers of the elite so they can maintain contact with one another. They have a culture of opulence that differs from middle-class culture, and this culture is part of their experience throughout their lives.

Another example is Hasidic Jews, who adhere to the same laws as other Americans but follow additional rules specific to their religion. Clothing and hairstyles follow strict rules; men wear beards and temple locks (*payos*), and married women wear wigs. Their religious holidays are different from those of the dominant Christian culture. Hasidic Jews observe dietary restrictions, such as avoiding pork and shellfish, and they observe the Sabbath from sunset Friday to sunset Saturday. Hasidic Jews are members of a subculture in the larger society of which they are citizens. In today's world, this is a global subculture maintained through websites of, by, and for Hasidic Jews. Again, one can live one's entire life under the influence of the values and rules of the subculture, and this is certainly true of the Hasidic Jews.

Many societies have subcultures that are based on ethnicity or religion or other historical characteristics, but broad-based subcultures with extensive social networks can emerge in other ways as well. Perhaps the most fascinating is the deaf subculture in the United States, which is explained in the "Sociology in Our Social World" on page 98 by a scholar eminently qualified to discuss it.

A give-and-take exists between subcultures and the dominant culture, with each contributing to and influencing the other. Hispanic Americans have brought many foods to American cuisine, for example, including tacos, burritos, and salsa.

Subcultural practices can cause tensions with the dominant group, which has the power to determine cultural expectations in society. In direct conflict with the law, a very small faction of Mormons in the United States believe in and practice polygamy. Having more than one wife (polygyny) violates federal laws and state laws in Utah, where many of them live, but some hold onto the old teachings of the founder Joseph Smith and cling to this practice as sanctioned by God. When conflict with the larger culture becomes serious and laws of the dominant society are violated, a different type of culture emerges. A **counterculture** is *a group with expectations and values that contrast sharply with the dominant values of a particular society* (Yinger 1960).

One type of counterculture is represented by the Old Order Amish of Pennsylvania and Ohio. The Amish drive horse-drawn buggies and seldom use electricity or modern machines. They reject many mainstream notions of success and replace them with their own work values and goals. Conflicts between federal and state laws and Amish religious beliefs have produced compromises by the Amish on issues of educating children, using farm machinery, and transportation. The Old Order Amish prefer to educate their children in their own communities, insisting that their children not go beyond an eighth-grade education in the public school curriculum. They also do not use automobiles or conventional tractors. The Amish are pacifists and will not serve as soldiers in the national military.

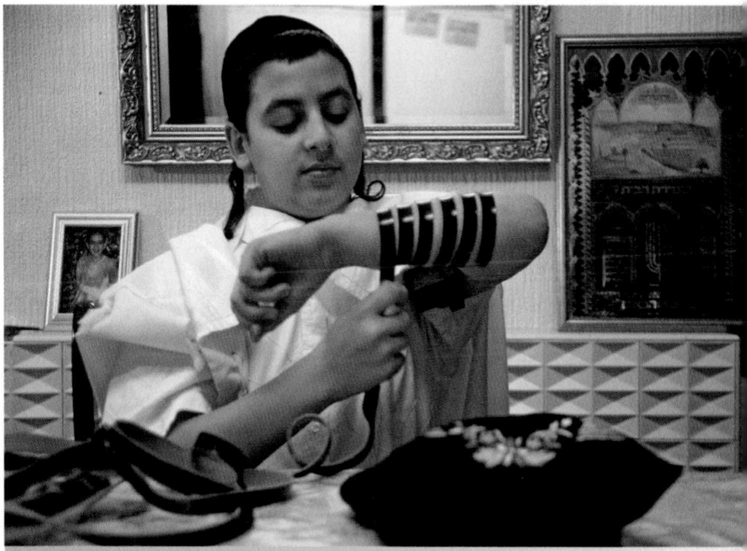

A young Orthodox Jewish boy prepares to pray according to Jewish law by wrapping the leather strap of his tefillin *around his arm and a* tallit *(prayer shawl) around his shoulders. He is part of a subgroup of the larger society, the Jewish faith community. This community will affect his values throughout life—from infancy to death. It is a subculture.*

A counterculture, such as the Amish, rejects important aspects of the mainstream or dominant culture like technology and consumerism, replacing it with biblical principles calling for a simple lifestyle.

Sociology in Our Social World

Deaf Subculture in the United States

by Thomas P. Horejes

The deaf subculture possesses its own language, norms, and social networks that are unique to the deaf. American Sign Language (ASL) has its own conversational rules and social norms such as mandatory eye gaze, appropriate facial expressions, and proper ways to interject ideas. Like other subcultures, the deaf subculture celebrates its own arts and entertainment, including Deaf View/Image Art (De'VIA), deaf poetry (ASL Slam), deaf music (Signmark), deaf theater (National Theatre of the Deaf and Deaf West Theatre), and deaf cinema (WorlDeaf Cinema Festival).The arts and entertainment of the deaf subculture are often expressed visually through perspectives, experiences, and/or metaphors only understood by those who are fluent in ASL and a part of the deaf subculture. For example, *"true biz have VP? GA to SK no more? PAH!"* would probably get a chuckle from someone who is immersed in the deaf subculture. Additionally, there are social gatherings and events by associations within the deaf subculture that host annual conferences and tournaments ranging from the Deaf World Softball Championships, to the National Black Deaf Advocates, to the Rainbow Alliance of the Deaf (an LGBT organization).

As with other subcultures, there is a deaf history and heritage that is passed on from generation to generation (e.g., Abbé Charles-Michel de l'Épée/Laurent Clerc's influence on sign language in deaf education in the 18th century and the 1990 "Deaf President Now" protest, which gave Gallaudet University its first deaf president after 124 years).

For many of the 5%–10% of deaf children who are born to deaf parents, they are immediately enculturated into their own deaf subculture. In contrast, a large majority (90%–95%) of deaf children (including myself, born to hearing parents) start with an identity from the larger world (hearing society). As we progress throughout life, however, our identities become negotiated as we become more aware of a subculture—a deaf subculture that each of us has embraced quite differently. Some reject the deaf subculture in favor of total immersion into hearing society while others navigate in the deaf subculture, but in different ways. In addition to those born deaf, there are many individuals who become deaf later in life whether it is due to age, illness, or even prolonged exposure to loud sounds.

Regardless of how one becomes deaf, there are those who integrate into the hearing society and deaf subculture simultaneously. Both become parts of their identity with a mixture of beliefs, values, rules, and language. These individuals may rely on technology (hearing aids or cochlear implants), will communicate with hearing individuals via spoken/written English or through an ASL interpreter, and express willingness to work in the workplace dominated by hearing members of the hearing society. At the same time, they attend deaf-based events and will socialize with the deaf community.

Other deaf individuals become fully immersed into the deaf subculture or what they call the deaf "world." They may attempt to be a part of a counterculture departing from the hearing culture by rejecting any values and beliefs possessed by the hearing society such as assistive-listening devices, speech therapy, and not placing their deaf child into hearing schools. These people typically attend only deaf plays, read about deaf history, take on jobs where communication is through sign language, and forbid any voiced English in favor of equal "access" in all aspects their daily activities. There are numerous people who become situated on the margins and/or the borderlands between the hearing world and the deaf subculture. They do not seem fully welcome in either social space. These people neither fully understand ASL to be able to "access" the deaf subculture nor are able to fully communicate via spoken English to "access" the hearing world.

The criteria for what constitutes a deaf subculture and who are its members remain fluid, as is the case with any vibrant culture. Members *within* the deaf subculture are highly diverse including people who are of color, range in socioeconomic status, have multiple disabilities, are members of the LGBT (lesbian, gay, bisexual, and transgender) community, practice different religions, and belong to different cultural groups.

In addition, deaf people possess varying decibel levels of hearing and because of that do not share the same history and experiences *within* the deaf subculture. Therefore, deaf people continually navigate their way through the hearing society, the deaf subculture, and the deaf counterculture in diverse ways.

It is very possible to navigate through these social landscapes in different phases of one's life. For example, some deaf people may immerse themselves into the counterculture at one time in their lives after being isolated from the dominant culture. Others come from a strong deaf culture and deaf "world" (those whose entire family is deaf) and are later immersed into the hearing world with peers from a different culture. Still others grow up being the only deaf person in a family, not having learned any sign language, and enroll in Gallaudet University—a university known for its strong deaf subculture and counterculture.

One common denominator in shaping deaf identity and deaf subculture is language: the incorporation or lack of sign language in the deaf individual's life. Each individual's perception and acceptance or rejection of ASL largely determines her or his place as a deaf individual and where that individual fits into society and the deaf subculture.

****

Thomas P. Horejes received his PhD at Arizona State University in justice studies and teaches sociology at Gallaudet University, the world's only university with programs and services specifically designed to accommodate students who are deaf or hard of hearing. He is author of a forthcoming book, *Social Constructions of Deafness: Examining Deaf Languacultures in Education,* by Gallaudet University Press.

Other types of countercultures seek to withdraw from society, to operate outside its economic and legal systems, or even to bring about the downfall of the larger society. Examples are survivalist groups such as racist militia and skinheads, who reject the principles of democratic pluralism.

Countercultures of all types have existed throughout history. The "Old Believers" of 17th-century Russia committed group suicide rather than submit to the authority of the czar of Russia on matters of faith and lifestyle (Crummey 1970). There are now Russian Old Believer communities in Oregon, northern Alberta, and the Kenai Peninsula of Alaska. Some of their villages are so isolated that they are virtually inaccessible by car, and visitors are greeted with "No Trespassing" signs. The Ranters—a group that arose in 16th-century England, with its strict Puritan attitudes toward sensuality and sex—flaunted their opposition to those attitudes by running naked through the streets and having sex in village squares (Ellens 1971; Hill 1991).

Some countercultures continue over time and can sustain members throughout their life cycle—such as the Amish. Like subcultures they operate at the meso level but reject mainstream culture. However, many countercultural groups, such as punk rock groups or violent and deviant teenage gangs, are short-lived or are relevant to people only at a certain age—operating only at the micro level.

Members of countercultures do not necessarily reject all the dominant culture, and in some cases, parts of their culture may eventually come to be accepted by the dominant culture. For example, a counterculture in Ohio in the mid-1800s established a communal living utopian society

There are now a number of Old Believer communities in the Kenai Peninsula of Alaska, such as this Church of St. Nicholas. Some of these Old Believer sects are so isolationist that they are accessible almost entirely by horse or by foot, and they have large "Keep Out" signs as one approaches the community. Commitment to the beliefs of the in-group is intense in this Russian Orthodox sect.

and a very alternative college—the first college in the world to be both racially integrated and coeducational. The idea of men and women attending the same college was unacceptable in the larger society, and no one thought whites and blacks could be in the same college classrooms. This college—Oberlin College—started a radical idea in 1833, but it has now become mainstream. Most colleges are coeducational (there are only three all-male colleges that are not either Jewish religious schools or military academies), and racial segregation has become unacceptable. Thus, the countercultural ideas of this college from 1833 are now mainstream and absorbed into the larger society.

Countercultures are not necessarily bad for society. According to conflict theory, which was introduced in Chapter 2, the existence of counterculture groups is clear evidence that there are contradictions or tensions within a society that need to be addressed. Countercultures often challenge the unfair treatment of groups in society that do not hold power and sometimes develop into social organizations or protest groups. Extremist religious and political groups, whether Christian, Islamic, Hindu, or any other, may best be understood as countercultures against Western or global influences that they perceive as threatening to their way of life. Figure 3.2 illustrates the types of cultures in the social world and the relationship between countercultures and their national culture. Countercultures, as depicted, view themselves and are viewed by others as "fringe" groups—partial outsiders within a nation.

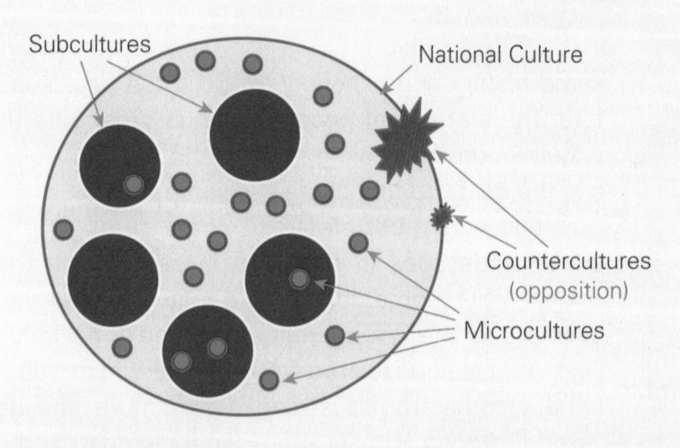

Figure 3.2 Cultures at Various Levels in the Social World

Thinking Sociologically

Describe a counterculture group whose goals are at odds with those of the dominant culture. Do you see any evidence to show that the group is influencing behavioral expectations and values in the larger society? What effect, if any, do countercultures have on your life?

National and Global Culture: Macro-Level Analysis

Canada is a national society, geographically bounded by the mainland United States to the south, the Pacific Ocean and Alaska to the west, the Atlantic Ocean to the east, and the Arctic to the north. The government in Ottawa passes laws that regulate activities in all provinces (which are similar to states or prefectures), and each province passes its own laws on regional matters. These geographic boundaries and political structures make up the national society of Canada.

National Society and Culture

The **national society** is *a population of people, usually living within a specified geographic area, who are connected by common ideas, cooperate for the attainment of common goals, and are subject to a particular political authority*. Within the nation, there may be smaller groups, such as ethnic, regional, or tribal subcultures, made up of people who identify closely with each other. Most nations have a **national culture** of *common values and beliefs that tie citizens of a nation together.* The national culture affects the everyday lives of most citizens. For example, within some countries of Africa and the Middle East that became self-governing nations during the 20th century by breaking their colonial ties, local ethnic or religious loyalties are much stronger than any sense of national culture. In fact, subcultural differences divide many nations. Consider the loyalties of Shiites, Sunnis, and Kurds in Iraq to their subcultures, where the national culture struggles for influence over its citizens through laws, traditions, and military force.

In colonial America, people thought of themselves as Virginians or Rhode Islanders rather than as U.S. citizens. Even during the "War Between the States" of the 1860s, the battalions were organized by states and often carried their state banners into battle. The fact that some Southern states still call it the War Between the States rather than the Civil War communicates the struggle over whether to recognize the nation or states as the primary social unit of loyalty and identity. People in the United States today are increasingly likely to think of themselves as U.S. citizens (rather than as Iowans or Floridians), yet the national culture determines only a few of the specific guidelines for everyday life. Nonetheless, the sense of nation has grown stronger in most industrialized societies over the past century, and the primary identity is likely to be "United States" or "Canadian" citizen.

Global Society and Culture

Several centuries ago, it would have been impossible to discuss a global culture, but with expanding travel, economic interdependence of different countries, international political linkages, global environmental concerns, and technology allowing for communication throughout the world, people now interact across continents in seconds. **Globalization** refers to *the process by which the entire world is becoming a single interdependent sociocultural entity, more uniform, more integrated, and more interdependent* (Pieterse 2004; Robertson 1997; Stutz and Warf 2005). Globalization is a process of increased connectedness, uniformity, and interdependency across the planet (Eitzen and Zinn 2006).

Western political and economic structures dominate in the development of this global society, largely as a result of the domination of Western (Europe and the United States) worldviews and Western control over resources. For example, the very idea of governing a geographic region with a bureaucratic structure known as a nation-state is a fairly new notion. Formerly, many small bands and tribal groupings dominated areas of the globe. However, with globalization, nation-states now exist in every region of the world.

Global culture includes *behavioral standards, symbols, values, and material objects that have become common across the globe.* Global beliefs are unspoken, unquestioned, internal assumptions we hold (International Beliefs and Values Institute 2012). We need to understand global culture to engage in human rights issues, global education, conflict resolution, sustainability, and religious and cultural understanding. For example, beliefs that monogamy is normal; that marriage should be based on romantic love; that people have a right to life, liberty, and the pursuit of happiness; that people should be free to choose their leaders; that women should have rights such as voting; that wildlife and fragile environments should be protected; and that everyone should have a cell phone and television set are spreading across the globe (Leslie and Korman 1989; Newman and Grauerholz 2002).

During the 20th century, the idea of the primacy of individual rights, civil liberties, and human rights spread around the world, creating conflicts within nations that traditionally lack democratic institutions and processes. Backlashes against these and other Western ideas also can be seen in the acts of groups that have embraced terrorism (Eitzen and Zinn 2006; Misztal and Shupe 1998; Turner 1991a, 1991b). This has resulted in Western societies scapegoating, or blaming, certain groups for economic and social crises (Morey and Yaqin 2011; "Muslims and Multicultural Backlash" 2011).

Still, these trends are aspects of the emerging global culture. Even 100 years ago, notions of global cooperation and competition would have seemed quite bizarre (Lechner and Boli 2005). However, in nations all over the globe, people who travel by plane know they must stand in line, purchase a ticket, negotiate airport security, squeeze their bodies into confined spaces, and stay seated in the airplane until they are told they can get up (Lechner and Boli 2005). Regardless of nationality, we know how to behave in any airport in the world.

There are many simple norms or beliefs about how to behave in public that are now becoming increasingly global—like staying seated in an airplane or waiting in line to be served at a bank or post office.

Nations are accepted as primary units of social control, and use of coercion is perfectly normal if it is done by the government. We compete in Olympic Games as citizens of nations, and the winners stand on the platform while their anthems are played. Across the globe, the idea of nations seems "normal," yet only a few centuries ago, the notion of nationhood would have seemed very strange (Lechner and Boli 2005).

As the world community becomes more interdependent and addresses issues that can only be dealt with at the global level (such as global warming, pirates from Somalia and other countries, massive human rights violations as in the Syrian revolution or Sudan war, international terrorism, and global financial crises), the idea of a common "software" of beliefs, social rules, and common interests takes on importance. Common ideas for making decisions allow for shared solutions to conflicts that previously would have resulted in war and massive killing of people. Global culture at the macro level affects our individual lives, and its influence will only increase.

However, global culture is not the only pattern that is new. Today, we are seeing a counterculture at the global level. Stateless terrorist networks such as al-Shabaab, al-Qaeda, and the Taliban reject the values of international organizations such as the World Court, the Geneva Convention, and other international systems designed to resolve disputes. Terrorists do not recognize the sovereignty of nations and do not acknowledge many values of respect for life or for civil discourse. This counterculture at the global level is a more serious threat than those at the micro and meso levels (see the discussion of terrorism in Chapter 13).

Thinking Sociologically

Make a list of social units of which you are a part. Place these groups into categories of microculture, subculture, national culture, and global culture. Consider which of them affects only a portion of your day or week (such as your place of work) or only a very limited time in your entire life span. Consider which groups are smaller than the nation but will likely influence you over much of your life. To what cross-national (global) groups do you belong? Do you belong to fewer groups at the national culture and global culture levels? If so, why do you suppose that is the case?

Theories of Culture

Cultural Theory at the Micro Level

To understand our interactions with family and friends, we turn to the micro level of analysis. Although external forces at the national and global macro levels shape us in many ways, that is not the whole story as we see when we examine the symbolic interaction approach to culture.

Symbolic Interaction Theory

How amazing it is that babies learn to share the ideas and meanings of complex cultures with others in those cultures. **Symbolic interaction theory** *considers how we learn to share the meanings of symbols, whether material or nonmaterial.* Culture is about symbols, such as rings, flags, and words that stand for or represent something. A ring means love and commitment. A flag represents national identity and is intended to evoke patriotism and love for one's country. A phrase such as *middle class* conjures up images and expectations of what the phrase means, and we share this meaning with others in our group. Together in our groups and societies, we define what is real, normal, and good.

Symbolic interaction theory maintains that our humanness comes from the impact we have on each other through these shared understandings of symbols that humans have created. When people create symbols, such as a new greeting ("Give me five") or a symbolic shield for a fraternity or sorority, symbols come to have an existence and importance for the group. In Step 1 the symbol is created. Who designed the Star of David and gave it meaning as a symbol of the Jewish people? Who initiated the sign of the cross for Catholics to use before prayer? Who designed the fraternity's or sorority's shield? Who determined that an eagle should symbolize the United States? Most people do not know the answers to these questions, but they do know what the symbol stands for. They share with others the meaning of a particular object. In Step 2, the symbol is objectified, assuming a reality independent of the creator. In fact, people may feel intense loyalty to the symbol itself. An entire history of a people may be recalled and a set of values rekindled when the symbol such as a national flag is displayed. In Step 3, the group has internalized the symbol. This may be the case whether the symbol is part of a material culture or a nonmaterial gesture. Members of a culture absorb the ideas or symbols of the larger culture—which were originally created by some individual or small group (Berger and Luckmann 1966).

Symbolic interaction theory pictures humans as consciously and deliberately creating their personal and collective histories. The theory emphasizes the part that verbal and nonverbal language and gestures play in the shared symbols of individuals and the smooth operation of society. More than any other theory in the social sciences, symbolic interaction stresses the active decision-making role of individuals—the ability of individuals to do more than conform to the larger forces of the society.

Many of our definitions of what is "normal" are shaped by what others around us define as "normal" or "good." The **social construction of reality** *is the process by which individuals and groups shape reality through social interaction.* One illustration of this is the notion of what is beautiful or ugly. In the late 18th and early 19th centuries, in Europe and the United States, beaches were considered eyesores since there was nothing there but crushed stone and dangerous water. A beach was not viewed as a place to relax in a beautiful environment. Likewise, when early travelers to the West encountered the Rocky Mountains, with soaring granite rising to snow-capped peaks, the idea was that these were incredibly ugly wounds in the earth's surface. The summits were anything but appealing. Still, over time, some individuals began to redefine these crests as breathtakingly beautiful. We now see both as beautiful, but the social construction of scenery has not always been so (Lofgren 1999, 2010).

This notion that individuals shape culture and that culture influences individuals is at the core of the symbolic interaction theory. Other social theories tend to focus at the meso and macro levels.

In the late 1700s and early 1800s, these beach and mountain views would have been considered eyesores—too ugly to enjoy. The social construction of reality—the definition of what is beautiful in our culture—has changed dramatically over the past two centuries.

Thinking Sociologically

Recall some of the local "insider" symbols that you used as a preteen, such as friendship bracelets, best-friend necklaces, matching outfits, and secret handshakes. Some individual started each idea, and it spread rapidly from one school to another and from one community to another. How are the three steps in the creation of symbols illustrated by a symbol you and your friends used or now use?

Cultural Theories at the Meso and Macro Levels

How can we explain such diverse world practices as eating termites and worshipping cows? Why have some societies allowed men to have four wives, whereas others—such as the Shakers—prohibited sex between men and women entirely? Why do some groups worship their ancestors, while others have many gods, and yet others believe in a single divine being? How can societies adapt to extremes of climate and geographical terrain—hot, cold, dry, wet, mountainous, and flat? Humankind has evolved practices so diverse that it would be hard to find a practice that has not been adopted in some society at some time in history.

To explain these cultural differences, we will examine two already familiar perspectives that have made important contributions to understanding culture at the meso and macro levels: structural-functional and conflict theories.

Structural-Functional Theory

Structural-functional theorists ask why members of an ethnic subculture or a society engage in certain practices. To answer, structural-functionalists look at how those practices contribute to the survival or social solidarity of the group or society as a whole. An example is the reverence for cattle in India. The "sacred cow" is protected, treated with respect, and not slaughtered for food. The reasons relate to India's ancient development into an agricultural society that required sacrifices (Harris 1989). Cattle were needed to pull plows and to provide a source of milk and dried dung for fuel. Cows gained religious significance because of their importance for the survival of early agricultural communities. They must, therefore, be protected from hungry people for the long-term survival of the group. Protecting cows was functional; that is, the practice served a purpose for society.

Functionalists view societies as composed of interdependent parts, each fulfilling certain necessary functions or purposes for the total society (Radcliffe-Brown

1935). Shared norms, values, and beliefs, for instance, serve the function of holding a social group together. At a global macro level, functionalists see the world moving in the direction of having a common culture, potentially reducing "we" versus "they" thinking and promoting unity across boundaries. Synthesis of cultures and even the loss of some cultures are viewed as a natural result of globalization.

Although most cultural practices serve positive functions for the maintenance and stability of society, some practices, such as slavery, may be functional for those in power (those using child labor) but dysfunctional for minority groups or individual members of society. The fact that some societies are weak or have died out suggests that their way of life may not have been functional in the long run. Consider the case of Haiti, a country weakened in part because all the forests have been cut down to provide firewood. The resulting erosion is making the land unusable for growing crops. Thus, some of the population has been starving (Diamond 2005). Add to the existing poverty and hunger the devastation brought about by the January 12, 2010, earthquake that damaged or destroyed most buildings. The country and its people must rely on external support and donations from other countries to survive and rebuild.

The functionalist perspective has been criticized because it fails to consider how much dysfunction a society has, how much conflict a society can tolerate, and how much unity is necessary for a society to survive. Some critics argue that functional theory overemphasizes the need for consensus and integration among different parts of society, thus ignoring conflicts that may point to problems in societies (Dahrendorf 1959).

Conflict theorists believe that society is composed of groups, each acting to meet its own self-interests, and those groups struggle to make their own cultural values supreme in the society. The conflict in Egypt in 2012 over who won a presidential election and where the country is headed in the future is one recent example.

Conflict Theory

Some communities in the United States have absorbed large numbers of immigrants from Mexico—some legal and some illegal. The influx of people who speak another language and whose cultural values are a bit different from those already in the community causes wariness of the newcomers. For one thing, residents fear that their religious beliefs and certain social ideas will no longer be the predominant ones in the community. They may not be able to prevent immigrants being issued green cards by the federal government, but they still do not want their own way of life challenged. They will do all they can to stop illegal immigrants from gaining access to U.S. citizenship. Some European countries are seeing prejudice against immigrants because of the immigrants' high birthrate, large influx, and different way of life that some residents feel threatens their future.

Another example of cultural conflict occurs between two movements—the "Tea Party movement" that wants less government, fewer restrictions on corporations and how the affluent use their resources, and more independence for people to use their resources however they see fit. Those on the other side of the divide—the "Occupy Wall Street movement"—want more restraints on the wealthy who they believe manipulate the system and undermine the 99% of the population who do not have such privileges. The latter want government protections for the environment and for the vulnerable among the citizenry. They therefore are demanding more services—like universal health coverage as a right of being a citizen. The Tea Party movement is related to the Libertarian Party, whose founder Ayn Rand claimed that competition, individualism, and survival of the fittest produced the best societies and that compassion was an evil force that fostered "softness" and social decay. The Occupy movement is more in line with Roosevelt's New Deal based on an extensive safety net and on President Johnson's Great Society and War on Poverty. Both movements affirm some long-standing American values but would take the country in very different directions.

Whereas functionalists assume consensus exists because all people in society have learned the same cultural values, rules, and expectations, conflict theorists do not view culture as having this uniting effect. Conflict theorists describe societies as composed of groups—class, ethnic, religious, and political groups at the meso level—vying for power. Each group protects its own self-interests and struggles to make its own cultural ways dominant in the society. Instead of consensus, the dominant groups may impose their cultural beliefs on minorities and other subcultural groups, thus laying the groundwork for conflict. Conflict theorists identify tension between meso and macro levels, whereas functionalists tend to focus on harmony and smooth integration between those levels.

Actually, conflict may contribute to a smoother-running society in the long run. The German sociologist Georg Simmel (1955) believed that some conflict could serve a positive purpose by alerting societal leaders to problem areas that need attention. The Republican primary to select a presidential candidate for the U.S. elections in 2012 witnessed candidates throwing mud at opponents, pointing out what they felt were problems in the U.S. system that needed fixing.

Conflict theorists argue that the people with privilege and power in society manipulate institutions such as religion and education. In this way, average people learn the values, beliefs, and norms of the privileged group and accept the dominant group's beliefs, self-interests, power, and advantage. The needs of the privileged are likely to be met, and their status will be secured. For instance, schools that serve lower-class children usually teach obedience to authority, punctuality, and respect for superiors—behaviors that make for good laborers. The children of the affluent, meanwhile, are more likely to attend schools stressing divergent thinking, creativity, and leadership, attributes that prepare them to occupy the most professional, prestigious, and highly rewarded positions in the society. Conflict theorists point to this control of the education process by those with privilege as part of the overall pattern by which the society benefits the rich.

Conflict theory can also help us understand global dynamics. Many poor nations feel that the global system protects the self-interests of the richest nations and that those rich nations impose their own culture, including their ideas about economics, politics, and religion, on the less affluent. Some scholars believe there is great richness in local customs that is lost when homogenized by cultural domination of the powerful nations (Ritzer 2007).

Conflict theory is useful for analyzing the relationships between societies (at a macro level) and between subcultures (at a meso level) within complex societies. It also helps illuminate tensions in a society when local (micro-level) cultural values clash with national (macro-level) trends. Conflict theory is not as successful, however, in explaining simple, well-integrated societies in which change is slow to come about and cooperation is an organizing principle.

The Fit Between Hardware and Software

Computer software cannot work with incompatible machines. Some documents cannot be easily transferred to another piece of hardware, although sometimes a transfer can be accomplished with significant modification in the formatting of the document. The same is true with the hardware of society and the software of culture. For instance, consider the size of families: The value (software) of having a large extended family, typical in agricultural societies, does not work well in the structure (hardware) of industrial and postindustrial societies that are mostly urban and crowded. Children in urban settings are generally a liability compared to those who work on the farm in agricultural societies. In short, there are limits to what can be transferred from one type of society to another, and the change of "formatting" may mean the new beliefs transferred to a different social setting are barely recognizable.

This local community has a farmers' market, and these organic farmers are helping mobilize the citizens against a state law that would authorize concentrated animal feeding operations—an approach to providing food that these people see as a violation of local cultural values. Here, we see the connection between the micro-level activities at a farmers' market and the state- and national-level policies on agriculture.

Attempts to transport U.S.-style "software" (culture)—individualism, capitalism, freedom of religion, and democracy—to other parts of the world illustrate that these ideas are not always successful in other settings. The hardware of other societies may be able to handle more than one type of software or set of beliefs, but there are limits to the adaptability. Thus, we should not be surprised when our ideas are transformed into something quite different when they are imported to another social system. If we are to understand the world in which we live and if we want to improve it, we must first fully understand other societies and cultures.

Thinking Sociologically

Some anthropologists argue that *team sports*, groups playing each other in coordinated competition, were learned by Europeans from certain Native American groups. Yet team sports are now a core component of American society. What does a team sport communicate or teach citizens that is consistent with the larger society? What lessons are learned in team sports that might be relevant to life in the business world?

Because there is such variation between societies and cultures in what they see as *normal*, how do any of us ever adjust to our society's expectations? The answer is addressed in the next chapter. Each society relies on the process of socialization to teach the culture to its members. Human life is a lifelong process of socialization to learn social and cultural expectations. The next chapter discusses the ways in which we learn our culture and become members of society.

What Have We Learned?

Individuals and small groups cannot live without the support of a larger society, the hardware of the social world. Without the software—culture—there could be no society, for there would be no norms to guide our interactions with others in society. Humans are inherently social and learn their culture from others. Furthermore, as society has evolved into more complex and multileveled social systems, humans have learned to live in and negotiate conflicts between multiple cultures, including those at micro (microcultures), meso (subcultures), and macro (global cultures) levels. Life in an Information Age society demands adaptability to different sociocultural contexts and tolerance of different cultures and subcultures. This is a challenge to a species that has always had tendencies toward ethnocentrism.

Key Points

- Society consists of individuals who live together in a specific geographic area, interact with each other more than with outsiders, cooperate to attain goals, and share a common culture over time. Each society has a culture, ideas, and "things" that are passed on from one generation to the next; the culture has both material and nonmaterial components. (See pp. 68–71.)
- Societies evolve from very simple societies to more complex ones, from the simple hunter-gatherer society to the information societies of the postindustrial world. (See pp. 71–77.)
- The study of culture requires that we try to avoid ethnocentrism (judging other cultures by the standards of our culture), taking a stance of cultural relativity instead so that the culture can be understood from the standpoint of those inside it. (See pp. 81–84.)
- Just as social units exist at various levels of our social world, from small groups to global systems, cultures exist within different levels of the social system—microcultures, subcultures, national cultures, and global cultures. Some social units at the micro or meso level stand in opposition to the dominant national culture, and they are called countercultures. (See pp. 95–102.)
- Various theories offer different lenses for understanding culture. While symbolic interaction illuminates the way humans bring meaning to events (thus generating culture), the functionalist and conflict paradigms examine cultural harmony/seamless fit and conflict between cultures, respectively. (See pp. 102–105.)
- The metaphor of hardware (society's structure) and software (culture) describes the interdependent relationship of society and culture, and as with computers, there must be some compatibility between the structure of a society and the culture. If there is none, either the cultural elements that are transported into another society will be rejected, or the culture will be "reformatted" to fit the society. (See pp. 105–106.)

Discussion Questions

1. Think about the evolution of societies described in this chapter. In which type of society (hunter-gatherer, herding, horticultural, agricultural, industrial, postindustrial) would you prefer to live? Why? In which would you be most likely to be (a) economically successful and (b) content? Why?
2. This chapter points out that material culture now, in many ways, "drives the globalization process." Look around at what your classmates are wearing and carrying and come up with some examples that support that point.
3. Think of a subculture to which you belong. What are the norms, values, and material artifacts that distinguish members of your subculture from those who do not belong to it?
4. Every classroom has norms of behavior. Some are mores, and some are folkways. Describe two of each in a typical classroom at your school. How are both enforced? How do you help enforce these norms?
5. Are you part of a counterculture? Why or why not? In what ways might a counterculture benefit a society?

Contributing to Our Social World: What Can We Do?

At the Local and National Levels

- *Ethnic group* organizations and clubs focus on the interests of specific ethnic groups: Arabic Americans, Chinese Americans, Italian Americans, Polish Americans, and so on. You may have one or more on your own campus. Contact one of these groups (of your own background or, even more interesting, of a background that differs from your own). Arrange to attend one of the group's meetings, and learn about the activities in which its members are involved. To find an ethnic association on campus, call your campus activities office. To find one in your local area, try Googling the name of the ethnic group, "club," and the name of your town or city.
- *Immigrant aid groups* are ethnically oriented organizations that assist recent immigrants in dealing with adjustment to American life, especially those from Mexico and other Spanish-speaking countries, Arabic-speaking countries of the Middle East, and East and South Asian countries such as China, Vietnam, the Philippines, Korea, and India. Contact one of these groups, and explore the possibility of volunteering or serving as an intern. You should be able to determine if one is in your area by Googling the name of your town or city, the name of the ethnic group, and "immigrant aid group."

At the Global Level

- *The United Nations Permanent Forum on Indigenous Issues* assists indigenous people around the world in facing threats to their cultures, languages, and basic rights as the process of globalization accelerates. We have experienced this in North America in relation to Native American and Inuit populations, but it is occurring throughout the world. Visit the forum's website at http://social.un.org/index/IndigenousPeoples.aspx, and contact the forum about the possibility of volunteering.
- *Cultural Survival (www.cs.org)* is an example of a leading nongovernmental organization (NGO) engaged in similar, action-oriented programs. The organization partners with indigenous people to secure rights, promote respect, ensure their participation, and assure rights to land. Another organization that works for the rights of indigenous peoples and acts as a representative for them and unrecognized nations is UNPO (Unrepresented Nations and Peoples Organization). You can learn more about UNPO at www.unpo.org.

Visit the Student Study Site at **www.sagepub.com/ballantine4e** to access additional study tools, including eFlashcards, web quizzes, video resources, audio resources, web resources, SAGE journal articles, recommended readings, and more.

CHAPTER 4

Socialization

Becoming Human and Humane

Whether at the micro, meso, or macro level, our close associates and various organizations teach us how to be human and humane in our society. Skills are taught, as well as values such as loyalty and caregiving.

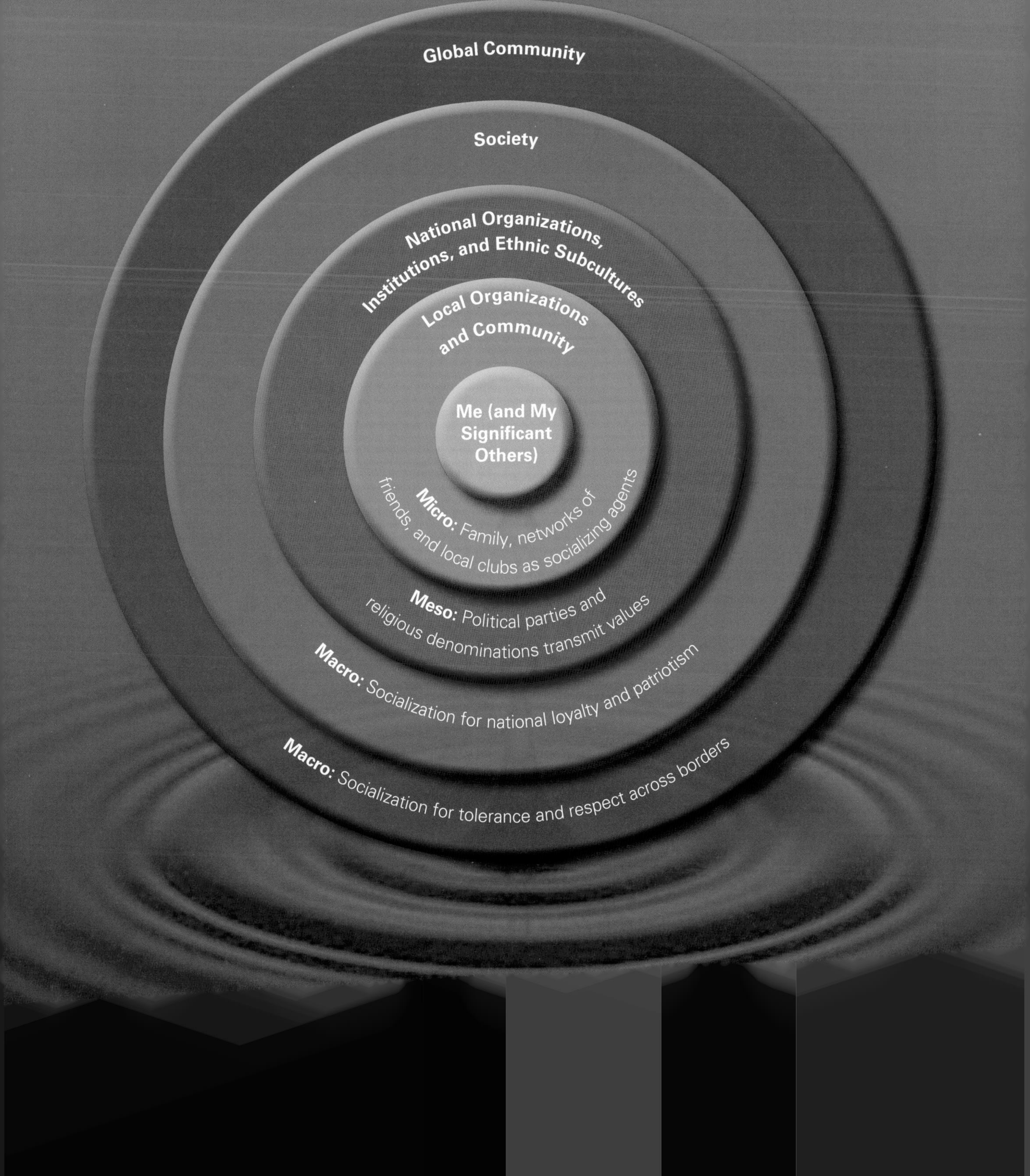
Global Community
Society
National Organizations, Institutions, and Ethnic Subcultures
Local Organizations and Community
Me (and My Significant Others)
Micro: Family, networks of friends, and local clubs as socializing agents
Meso: Political parties and religious denominations transmit values
Macro: Socialization for national loyalty and patriotism
Macro: Socialization for tolerance and respect across borders

Think About It	
Micro: Self and Inner Circle	What does it mean to have a "self"? How would you be different if you had been raised in complete isolation from other people?
Micro: Local Community	How have your local religious congregation and schools shaped who you are?
Meso: National Institutions; Complex Organizations; Ethnic Groups	How do various subcultures or organizations of which you are a member (your political party, your religious affiliation) influence your position in the social world?
Macro: National Society	What would you be like if you were raised in a different country? How does your sense of national identity influence the way you see things?
Macro: Global Community	How might globalization or other macro-level events such as the terrorist attack of 9/11 impact you and your sense of self?

What's coming in this chapter?

Phoebe Prince was a 15-year-old immigrant from Ireland. She and her family had recently settled in South Hadley, Massachusetts, and she enrolled in the high school. Unfortunately, she made a mistake! She dated a popular senior on the football team. This was not acceptable to a clique of girls who had it out for Phoebe. These "mean girls" sent her threatening text messages, threw things at her, called her "Irish slut" and "whore" on social networking sites such as Facebook and Twitter, and engaged in other bullying behaviors. Other students and even faculty who were aware of the bullying did nothing. After months of enduring this treatment, the "mean girls" threw a can at her—and she went home and hung herself (Crime Library 2012).

Phoebe's story and stories of hundreds of other bullied and abused children point to a problem in the process of socialization, both what the victim is experiencing and what the perpetrators are doing. In this chapter we will examine the process of socialization, how it involves development of our "self," and what can happen when socialization goes wrong.

Socialization is *the lifelong process of learning to become a member of the social world, beginning at birth and continuing until death.* It is a major part of what the family, education, religion, and other institutions do to prepare individuals to be members of their social world. In Phoebe's case, she had a negative socialization experience from peers, resulting in a damaged self-concept.

From the day they are born, infants are interactive, ready to be socialized into members of the social world. As they cry, coo, or smile, they gradually learn that their behaviors elicit responses from other humans. This exchange of messages—this **interaction**—is *the basic building block of socialization.* Out of this process of interaction, a child learns its culture and becomes a member of society. This process of interaction shapes the infant into a human being with a social self—perceptions we have of who we are.

Three main elements provide the framework for socialization: human biological potential, culture, and individual experiences. Babies enter this world unsocialized, totally dependent on others to meet their needs, and completely lacking in social awareness and an understanding of the rules of their society. Despite this complete vulnerability, they have the potential to learn the language, norms, values, and skills needed in their society. They gradually learn who they are and what is expected of them. Socialization is necessary not only for the survival of the individual but also for the survival of society and its groups. The process continues in various forms throughout our lives as we enter and exit various positions—from school to work to retirement to death.

In this chapter, we will explore the nature of socialization and how individuals become socialized. We consider why socialization is important. We also look at development of the self, socialization through the life cycle, who or what socializes us, macro-level issues in the socialization process, and a policy example illustrating socialization. First, we briefly examine an ongoing debate: Which is more influential in determining who we are—our genes (nature) or our socialization into the social world (nurture)?

Nature *Versus* Nurture—or *Both* Working Together?

What is it that most makes us who we are? Is it our biological makeup or the family and community in which we are raised that guides our behavior and the development of our self? One side of the contemporary debate regarding nature versus nurture seeks to explain the development of the self and human social behaviors—violence, crime, academic performance, mate selection, economic success, gender roles, and other behaviors too numerous to mention here—by examining biological or genetic factors (Harris 2009; Winkler 1991). Sociologists call this sociobiology, and psychologists refer to it as evolutionary psychology. The theory claims that our human genetic makeup wires us for social behaviors (Wilson et al. 1978).

The idea is that we perpetuate our own biological family and the human species through our social behaviors. Human groups develop power structures, are territorial, and protect their kin. A mother ignoring her own safety to help a child, soldiers dying in battle for their comrades and countries, communities feeling hostility toward outsiders or foreigners, and people defending property lines against intrusion by neighbors are all examples of behaviors that sociobiologists claim are rooted in the genetic makeup of the species. Sociobiologists would say that these behaviors continue because they result in an increased chance of survival of the species as a whole (Lerner 1992; Lumsden and Wilson 1981; Wilson 1980, 1987).

Most sociologists believe that sociobiology and evolutionary psychology explanations have flaws. Sociobiology is a *reductionist* theory; that is, it often reduces complex social behaviors to single inherited traits such as an altruism gene, an aggression gene, or any other behavioral gene. However, evidence for such inherited traits is lacking. Sociologists point to the fact that there are great variations in the way members of different societies and groups behave. People born in one culture and raised in another adopt social behaviors common to the culture in which they are raised (Gould 1997), not based on inherited traits. If specific social behavior is genetic, then it should be present regardless of the culture in which humans are raised. The key is that what makes humans unique is not our biological heritage but our ability to learn the ways of our culture through socialization.

Most sociologists recognize that individuals are influenced by biology, which limits the range of human responses and creates certain needs and drives, but they believe that nurture is far more important in shaping human social behavior through the socialization process. Some sociologists propose theories that consider both nature and nurture. Alice Rossi, former president of the American Sociological Association, has argued that we need to build both biological and social theories—or biosocial theories—into explanations of social processes such as parenting. In the 21st century, a few sociologists are developing an approach called evolutionary sociology, which takes seriously the way our genetic makeup—including a remarkable capacity for language—shapes our range of behaviors. However, it is also very clear from biological research that living organisms are often modified by their environments and the behaviors of others around them—with even genetic structure changing due to social interaction and experiences (Lopreato 2001; Machalek and Martin 2010).

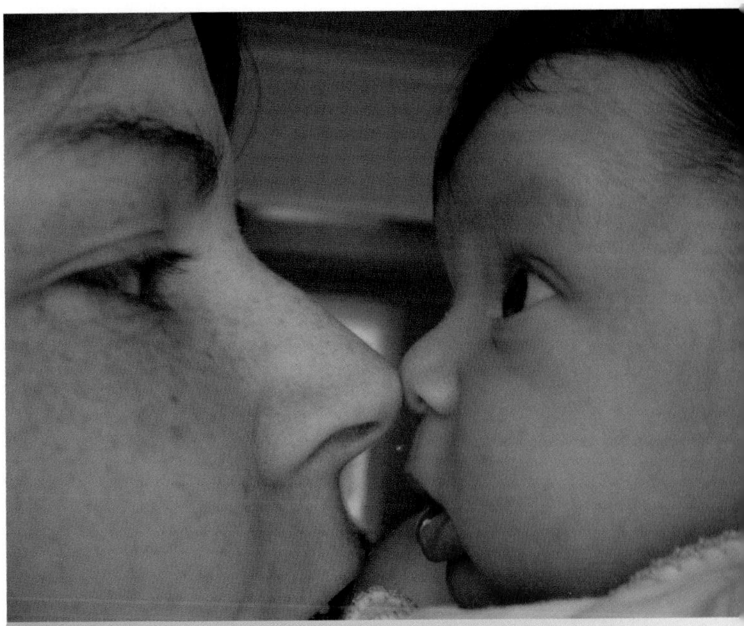

Babies interact intensively with their parents, observing and absorbing everything around them and learning what kinds of sounds or actions elicit response from the adults. Socialization starts at the beginning of life.

In short, biology influences human behavior, but human action and interaction can also modify biological traits. For example, the nutritional history of grandparents can affect the metabolism of their grandchildren, and what grandparents ate was largely shaped by cultural ideas about food (BBC's *Science and Nature* 2009; Freese, Powell, and Steelman 1999; Rossi 1984). What we eat today and whether we share food with the less privileged in our society are shaped by our cultural values. The point is that *socialization* is key in the process of "becoming human and becoming humane."

The Importance of Socialization

If you have lived on a farm, watched animals in the wild, or seen television nature shows, you probably have noticed that many animal young become independent shortly after birth. Horses are on their feet in a matter of hours, and by the time turtles hatch from eggs, their parents are long gone. Many species in the animal kingdom do not require contact with adults to survive because their behaviors are inborn and instinctual. Generally speaking, the more intelligent the species, the longer the period of gestation and of nutritional and social dependence on the mother and family. Humans clearly take the longest time to socialize their young. Even among primates, human infants have the longest gestation and dependency period, generally 6 to 8 years. Chimpanzees, very similar to humans in their DNA, take only 12 to 28 months. Table 4.1 compares human infants and other primate babies. This extended dependency period for humans—what some have referred to as the *long childhood*—allows each human being time to learn the complexities of culture. This suggests that biology and social processes work together.

Normal human development involves learning to sit, crawl, stand, walk, think, talk, and participate in social interactions. Ideally, the long period of dependence allows children the opportunity to learn necessary skills, knowledge, and social roles through affectionate and tolerant interaction with people who care about them. Yet what happens if children are deprived of adequate care or even human contact? The following section illustrates the importance of socialization by showing the effect of deprivation and isolation on normal socialization.

Isolated and Abused Children

What would children be like if they grew up without human contact? Among the most striking examples are cases of severely abused and neglected children whose parents kept them isolated in cellars or attics for years without providing even minimal attention and nurturing. When these isolated children were discovered, typically they suffered from profound developmental disorders that endured throughout their lives (Curtiss 1977; Davis 1947). Most experienced great difficulty in adjusting to their social world's complex rules of interaction, which are normally learned from infancy onward.

In case studies comparing two girls, Anna and Isabelle, who experienced extreme isolation in early childhood, Kingsley Davis found that even minimal human contact made some difference in their socialization (Davis 1947). Both "illegitimate" girls were kept locked up by relatives who wanted to keep their existence a secret. Both were discovered at about age 6 and moved to institutions where they received intensive training. Yet the cases were different in one significant respect: Prior to her discovery by those outside her immediate family, Anna experienced virtually no human contact. She saw other individuals only when they left food for her. Isabelle lived in a darkened room with her deaf-mute mother, who provided some human contact. Anna could not sit, walk, or talk and learned little in the special school in which she was placed. When she died from jaundice at age 11, she had learned the language and skills of a 2- or 3-year-old. Isabelle, on the other hand, did progress. She learned to talk and played with her peers. After 2 years, she reached an intellectual level approaching normal for her age but remained about 2 years behind her classmates in skill and competency levels (Davis 1940, 1947).

Less extreme than the cases of isolation but equally illustrative are the cases of children who come from war-torn countries, live in orphanages, or are neglected or

Table 4.1 **Dependence on Adults Among the Primates**

Primate Form	*Pregnancy Period*	*Period of Absolute Nutritional Dependency on Mother or Mother-Surrogate*	*Nursing Period*	*Social Independence*
Human	266 days	1 year or more	1–2 years	6–8 years
Ape: chimpanzee	235 days	3–6 months	2–3 months	12–28 months
Monkey: rhesus	166 days	1–3 weeks	2–4 weeks	2–4 months
Lemur	111–145 days	1–3 days	2–14 days	2–3 weeks

Note: Lemurs and monkeys, among the less complex members of the primate order, depend on adults for food for a much shorter time than do apes and humans. The period of dependence affords human infants time to absorb the extensive knowledge important to the survival of the species.

abused. Although not totally isolated, these children also experience problems and disruptions in the socialization process. Consider the case of child soldiers. A recent video, *Invisible Children*, went viral on YouTube, showing the plight of these children kidnapped by Joseph Kony's Lord's Resistance Army into a world of drugs, sex, and violence (Terra Networks 2013). Some of the children are killed, some "disappear," and most will have a difficult time integrating back into society although there are organizations trying to help them. These children's situations have been referred to as abusive, violent, and dead-end environments that are socially toxic because of their harmful developmental consequences for children.

What is the message? These cases illustrate the devastating effects on socialization of isolation, neglect, and abuse early in life. Less extreme but also damaging are the physical, mental, and sexual abuse and neglect suffered by many children around the world. Humans need more from their environments than food and shelter. They need positive contact, a sense of belonging, affection, safety, and someone to teach them knowledge and skills. This is children's socialization into the world, through which they develop a self. Before we examine the development of the self in depth, however, we consider the complexity of socialization in the multilevel (micro, meso, and macro) social world.

Intense interaction by infants and their caregiver, usually a parent, occurs in all cultures and is essential to becoming a part of the society and to becoming fully human. This African father shares a tender moment with his son.

Socialization and the Social World

Ram, a first grader from India, had been in school in Iowa for only a couple of weeks. The teacher was giving the first test. Ram did not know much about what a test meant, but he rather liked school, and the red-haired girl next to him, Elyse, had become a friend. He was catching on to reading a bit faster than she, but she was better at the number exercises. They often helped each other learn while the teacher was busy with a small group in the front of the class.

The teacher gave each child the test, and Ram saw that it had to do with numbers. He began to do what the teacher had instructed the children to do with the worksheet, but after a while, he became confused. He leaned over to look at the page Elyse was working on. She hid her sheet from him, an unexpected response. The teacher looked up and asked what was going on. Elyse said that Ram was "cheating." Ram was not quite sure what that meant, but it did not sound good. The teacher's scolding of Ram left him baffled, confused, and entirely humiliated.

This incident was Ram's first lesson in the individualism and competitiveness that govern Western-style schools. He was being socialized into a new set of values. In his parents' culture, competitiveness was discouraged, and individualism was equated with selfishness and rejection of community. Athletic events were designed to end in a tie so that no one would feel rejected. Indeed, a well-socialized person would rather lose in a competition than cause others to feel bad because they lost.

Like Ram, each of us learns the values and beliefs of our culture. In Ram's case, he moved from one cultural group to another and had to adjust to more than one culture within his social world.

Sociologists are interested in how individuals become members of their society and learn the norms of the culture to which they belong. Through the socialization process, individuals learn what is expected in their society. At the micro level, most parents teach children proper behaviors to be successful in life, and peers influence children to "fit in" and have fun. In fact, the process of socialization in groups allows the self to develop as individuals learn to interact with others in their culture. Interaction theory, focusing on the micro level, forms the basis of this chapter, as you will see.

Examples of the socialization process at the meso level include religious denominations teaching their versions of the Truth and educational systems teaching the knowledge and skills necessary for functioning in society. At the nationwide, macro level, television ads encourage viewers to be more masculine or feminine, buy products that will make them better and happier people, and join the military. From interactions with our significant others to dealing with government bureaucracy, most activities are part of the socialization experience that teaches us how to function in our society. Keep in mind that socialization is a lifelong process. Even your grandparents are learning how to live at their stage of life.

The social world model at the start of the chapter illustrates the levels of analysis in the social world. The process of socialization takes place at each level, linking the parts. Small micro-level groups include families, **peer groups** *whose members are roughly equal in some status within the society, such as the same age or the same occupation*, and voluntary groups such as the Girl Scouts. Examples of meso-level institutions are religious denominations and political parties, while an important macro-level unit is the federal government. All these have a stake in how we are socialized because they all need trained and loyal group members to survive. Organizations need citizens who have been socialized to devote the time, energy, and resources that these groups need to survive and meet their goals. For example, volunteer and charitable organizations cannot thrive unless people are willing to volunteer their energy, time, skills, and money. Lack of adequate socialization means social organizations will not receive the support they need to thrive, and it increases the likelihood of individuals becoming misfits or social deviants.

Most perspectives on socialization focus on the micro level, as we shall see when we explore the development of the self. This is because socialization takes place in each individual. Meso- and macro-level theories add to our understanding of how socialization prepares individuals for their roles in the larger social world. For example, structural-functionalist perspectives of socialization tend to see education in Global North societies reinforcing individualism and an achievement ethic, which are fundamental for the way the capitalist system works. Families often organize holidays around patriotic themes, such as a national independence day, or around religious celebrations. These activities are believed to strengthen family members' commitment to the nation and to buttress the moral values emphasized in churches, temples, and mosques. All these values are compatible with preparing individuals to support national political and economic systems.

Socialization can also be understood from the conflict perspective, with the linkages between various parts of the social world based on competition with or even direct opposition to another part. Socialization into a nation's military forces, for example, stresses patriotism and ethnocentrism, sometimes generating conflict and hostility toward other groups and countries. Demands from organizations for our resources (time, money, and energy devoted to the Little League, the Rotary Club, and library associations) may leave little to give to our religious communities or even our families, setting up a conflict. Each organization and unit competes to gain our loyalty in order to claim some of our resources.

At the meso level, the purposes and values of organizations or institutions are sometimes in direct conflict with other parts of the social system. Businesses and educational institutions try to socialize their workers and students to be serious, hardworking, sober, and conscientious, with lifestyles focused on achievement and the future. In contrast, many fraternal organizations and barrooms favor lifestyles that celebrate drinking, sex, and living for the moment. This creates conflicting values in the socialization process, because groups at the micro level sometimes instill values that are central at the meso level—discipline, a strong sober work ethic, and willingness to delay pleasures until a later time.

Conflict can occur in the global community as well. For example, religious groups often socialize their members to identify with humanity as a whole ("the family of God"). However, in some cases, nations do not want their citizens socialized to identify with those beyond their borders. They may seek to persuade Christians to kill other Christians or Jews or Muslims who are defined as "the enemy," as in the case of Nazi Germany's efforts to exterminate Jews during World War II in Europe. If religion teaches that all people are "brothers and sisters" and if religious people object to killing, the nation may have trouble mobilizing its people to arms when the leaders call for war.

Conflict theorists believe that those who have power and privilege use socialization to manipulate individuals to support the power structure and the self-interests of the elite. Those who have power and privilege are in the best position to get what they need, and they also have significant influence on the socialization of others through schools and political institutions. Although they may not realize it, most individuals have little power to control and decide their futures. For example, parents decide how they would like to raise their children and what values they want to instill in their children, but as soon as the school enters into socialization, parents must share the socialization process. One reason why some parents choose to home-school their children is to control external influences on the socialization process.

Each theoretical explanation has merit for explaining some situations. Whether we stress harmony in the socialization process or conflict rooted in power differences, the development of a sense of self through the process of socialization is an ongoing, lifelong process. Having considered the multiple levels of analysis and the issues that make socialization complicated, let us focus specifically on the micro level: Where does the development of self originate?

Thinking Sociologically

Although the socialization process occurs primarily at the micro level, it is influenced by events at each level of analysis shown in the social world model. Give examples of family, community, subcultural, national, or global events that might influence how you were socialized or how you would socialize your child.

Development of the Self: Micro-Level Analysis

A baby is born with the potential to develop a self, but that self can evolve in many directions. Think of a baby you have observed; what is influencing that baby from birth? Can you see how those influences contribute to the developing self? The main product of the socialization process is *the self*. Fundamentally, **self** refers to *the perceptions we have of who we are*. Throughout the socialization process, our self develops, largely from the way others respond to us—praising us, disciplining us, ignoring us. The development of the self allows individuals to interact with other people and to learn to function at each level of the social world.

Humans are not born with a sense of self. It develops gradually, beginning in infancy and continuing throughout adulthood. Selfhood emerges through interaction with others. Individual biology, culture, and social experiences all play a part in shaping the self. The hereditary blueprint each person brings into the world provides broad biological outlines, including particular physical attributes, temperament, and a maturational schedule. Each person is also born into a family that lives within a particular culture, illustrating that nature is shaped by nurture. This hereditary blueprint, in interaction with family and culture, helps create each unique person, different from any other person yet sharing the types of interactions by which the self is formed.

Most sociologists, although not all (Irvine 2004), believe that we humans are distinct from other animals in our ability to develop a self and to be aware of ourselves as individuals or objects. Consider how we refer to ourselves in the first person—*I* am hungry, *I* feel foolish, *I* am having fun, and *I* am good at basketball. We have a conception of who we are, how we relate to others, and how we differ from and are separate from others in our abilities and limitations. We have an awareness of the characteristics, values, feelings, and attitudes that give us our unique sense of self (James [1890] 1934; Mead [1934] 1962).

Thinking Sociologically

Who are some of the people who have been most significant in shaping your *self*? How have their actions and responses helped shape your self-concept as musically talented, athletic, intelligent, kind, assertive, clumsy, or any of the other hundreds of traits that might make up your self?

The Looking-Glass Self and Role-Taking

Ty: "Hi! What's up?" (Ty has had his eye on this girl in his class, so he approaches her before class.)

Valerie: "Nothin' much."

Ty: "So what do you think of our sociology class?"

Valerie: "It's OK." (She turns around, spots a friend, and walks away.) "Hey Julie, did you get your soc assignment done?"

Ty is left to reflect on how to interpret Valerie's response. Take this common interaction and apply it to interactions you have had. First you approach someone and open a conversation (or someone approaches you); second, the person takes you up on the conversation—or not; third, you evaluate the individual's response and modify your behavior based on your interpretation. These steps make up the *looking-glass self*, and they are repeated many times each day. We now explore these seemingly simple interactions that are key in developing our *self* and in our socialization process.

The looking-glass self idea is part of symbolic interaction theory, and offers important insights into how individuals develop the self. Two of the major scholars in this approach were Charles H. Cooley ([1909] 1983) and George Herbert Mead ([1934] 1962). Cooley believed that the self is a social product, shaped by interactions with others from the time of birth. He likened interaction processes to looking in a mirror wherein each person reflects an image of the other.

> Each to each a looking-glass
>
> Reflects the other that doth pass. (Cooley [1909] 1983:184)

For Cooley, the **looking-glass self** is *a reflective process that develops the self based on our interpretations and on our internalization of the reactions of others* (Cooley [1909] 1983). In this process, Cooley believed that there are three principal elements, shown in Figure 4.1: (1) We imagine how we appear to others, (2) others judge our appearance and respond to

Our sense of self is often shaped by how others see us and what is reflected back to us by the interactions of others. Cooley called this process, operating somewhat like a mirror, the "looking-glass self."

us, and (3) we react to that feedback. We experience feelings such as pride or shame based on this imagined judgment and respond based on our interpretation. Moreover, throughout this process, we actively try to manipulate other people's view of us to serve our needs and interests. This is one of the many ways we learn to be boys or girls—the image that is reflected back to us lets us know whether we have behaved in ways that are socially acceptable according to gender expectations. The issue of gender socialization in particular will be discussed in Chapter 9. Of course, this does not mean our interpretation of the other person's response is correct, but our interpretation does determine how we respond.

Our self is influenced by the many "others" with whom we interact, and each of our interpretations of their reactions feeds into our self-concept. Recall that the isolated children failed to develop this sense of self precisely because they lacked interaction with others. The next "Sociology in Our Social World" illustrates the looking-glass self process for African American males. This situation experienced by Brent Staples vividly illustrates the impact of others on us.

Thinking Sociologically

First, read the Sociology in Our Social World feature on the next page. Brent Staples goes out of his way to reassure others that he is harmless. What might be some other responses to this experience of having others assume one is dangerous and untrustworthy? How might one's sense of self be influenced by these responses of others? How are the looking-glass self and role-taking at work in this scenario?

Taking the looking-glass self idea a step further, Mead explained *that individuals take others into account by imagining themselves in the position of that other, a process called* **role-taking**. When children play mommy and daddy, doctor and patient, or firefighter, they are imagining themselves in another's shoes. Role-taking allows humans to view themselves from the standpoint of others. This requires mentally stepping out of our own experience to imagine how others experience and view the social world. Through role-taking, we begin to see who we are from the standpoint of others. In short, role-taking allows humans to view themselves as objects, as though they were looking at themselves through the eyes of another person.

Mead also argued that role-taking is possible because humans have a unique ability to use and respond to symbols (Mead [1934] 1962). **Symbols**, first described in Chapter 2, *are actions or objects that represent something else and therefore have meaning beyond their own existence.* Language and gestures are examples, for they carry specific meaning for members of a culture. Symbols such as language allow us

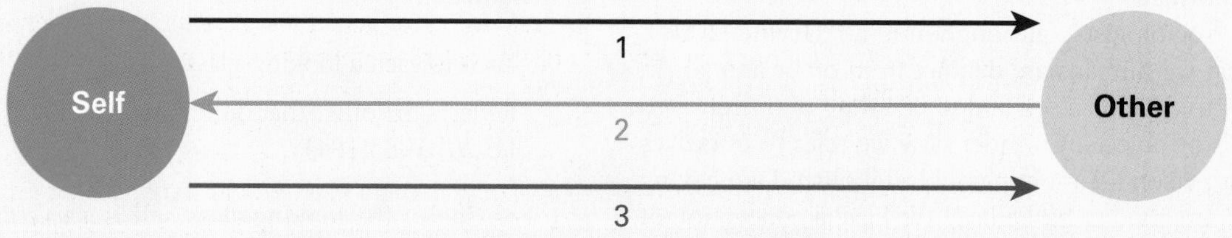

1. We imagine how we want to appear to others.
2. Others make judgments and respond.
3. We experience feelings and react based on our interpretations.

Figure 4.1 The Looking-Glass Process of Self-Development

Sociology in Our Social World

Black Men and Public Space

By Brent Staples

Many stereotypes—rigid images of members of a particular group—surround the young African American male in the United States. How these images influence these young men and their social world is the subject of this feature. Think about the human cost of stereotypes and their effect on the socialization process as you read the following essay. If your sense of self is profoundly influenced by the ways others respond to you, how might the identity of a young African American boy be affected by public images of black males?

My first victim was a woman—white, well dressed, probably in her early-twenties. I came upon her late one evening on a deserted street in Hyde Park, a relatively affluent neighborhood in an otherwise mean, impoverished section of Chicago. As I swung onto the avenue behind her, she cast back a worried glance. To her, the youngish black man—broad, six-feet two-inches tall, with a beard and billowing hair, both hands shoved into the pockets of a bulky military jacket—seemed menacingly close. After a few more quick glimpses, she picked up her pace and was running in earnest. Within seconds, she disappeared into a cross street.

That was more than a decade ago. I was 22 years old, a graduate student newly arrived at the University of Chicago. It was in the echo of that terrified woman's footfalls that I first began to know the unwieldy inheritance I'd come into. . . . It was clear that she thought herself the quarry of a mugger, a rapist, or worse. Suffering a bout of insomnia, however, I was stalking sleep, not defenseless wayfarers. . . . I was surprised, embarrassed, and dismayed all at once. Her flight . . . made it clear that I was indistinguishable from the muggers who occasionally seeped into the area from the surrounding ghetto. That first encounter, and those that followed, signified that a vast, unnerving gulf lay between night-time pedestrians—particularly women—and me. And I soon gathered that being perceived as dangerous is a hazard in itself. I only needed to turn a corner into a dicey situation, or crowd some frightened, armed person in a foyer somewhere, or make an errant move after being pulled over by a policeman. Where fear and weapons meet—and they often do in urban America—there is always the possibility of death.

In that first year, my first away from my hometown, I was to become thoroughly familiar with the language of fear. At dark, shadowy intersections, I could cross in front of a car stopped at a traffic light and elicit the thunk, thunk, thunk, thunk of the driver—black, white, male, or female—hammering down the door locks. On less-traveled streets after dark, I grew accustomed to but never comfortable with people crossing to the other side of the street rather than pass me. Then there was the standard unpleasantness with policemen, doormen, bouncers, cabdrivers, and those whose business it is to screen out troublesome individuals before there is any nastiness.

After dark, on the warren-like streets of Brooklyn where I live, I often see women who fear the worst from me. They seem to have set their faces on neutral, and with their purse straps strung across their chests bandolier style, they forge ahead as though bracing themselves against being tackled. I understand, of course, that . . . women are particularly vulnerable to street violence, and young black males are drastically overrepresented among the perpetrators of that violence. Yet these truths are no solace against the kind of alienation that comes of being ever the suspect. . . .

Over the years, I learned to smother the rage I felt at so often being taken for a criminal. Not to do so would surely have led to madness. I now take precautions to make myself less threatening. I move about with care, particularly late in the evening. I give a wide berth to nervous people on the subway platforms during the wee hours. . . . I have been calm and extremely congenial on those rare occasions when I've been pulled over by the police.

On late-evening constitutionals, I employ what have proved to be excellent tension-reducing measures: I whistle melodies from Beethoven and Vivaldi and the more popular classical composers. Even steely New Yorkers hunching toward nighttime destinations seem to relax, and occasionally they even join in the tune. Virtually everybody seems to sense that a mugger wouldn't be warbling bright, sunny selections from Vivaldi's Four Seasons. It is my equivalent of the cowbell that hikers wear when they know they are in bear country.

Source: Staples, Brent. 2001. "Black Men and Public Space." Pp. 244–46 in *The Production of Reality,* edited by Jodi O'Brien and Peter Kollock. Thousand Oaks, CA: Pine Forge Press.

to give names to objects in the environment and to infuse those objects with meanings. Once the person learns to symbolically recognize objects in the environment, the self can be seen as one of those objects. In the most rudimentary sense, this starts with possessing a name that allows us to see our self as separate from other objects. Note that the connection of symbol and object is arbitrary, such as the name LeBron James and a specific human being. When we say that name, most listeners would immediately think of the same person: an extraordinary athlete who largely turned around the fortunes of the Miami Heat professional basketball team to win the NBA championship.

Using symbols such as language is unique to humans. In the process of symbolic interaction, we take the actions of others and ourselves into account. Individuals may blame, encourage, praise, punish, or reward themselves. An example would be a basketball player missing the basket because the shot was poorly executed and thinking, "*What did I do to miss that shot? I'm better than that!*" Reflexive behavior, being able to look at oneself and one's behaviors as though from the outside looking in, includes the simple act of taking mental notes or mentally talking to one's self.

Parts of the Self

According to the symbolic interaction perspective, the self is composed of two distinct but related parts—dynamic parts in interplay with one another (Mead [1934] 1962). The most basic element of the self is what George Herbert Mead refers to as the **I**, *the spontaneous, unpredictable, impulsive, and largely unorganized aspect of the self.* These spontaneous, undirected impulses of the *I* initiate or give propulsion to behavior without considering the possible social consequences. We can see this at work in the "I want it now" behavior of a newborn baby or even a toddler. Cookie Monster on the children's television program *Sesame Street* illustrates the *I* in every child, gobbling cookies at every chance and insisting on more *now*.

The *I* continues as part of the self throughout life, tempered by the social expectations that surround individuals. In stages, humans become increasingly influenced by interactions with others who instill society's rules. Children develop the ability to see the self as others see them (role-taking) and critique the behavior of the *I*. Mead called this reflective capacity of the self the *Me*. The **Me** is *the part of the self that has learned the rules of society through interaction and role-taking, and it controls the I and its desires.* Just as the *I* initiates the act, the *Me* gives direction to the act. In a sense, the *Me* channels the impulsive *I* in an acceptable manner according to societal rules and restraints, yet meets the needs of the *I* as best it can. When we stop ourselves just before saying something and think to ourselves, "*I'd better not say that,*" it is our *Me* monitoring and controlling the *I*. Notice that the *Me* requires the ability to take the role of the other, to anticipate the other's reaction.

Cookie Monster can be understood as a symbol of Mead's concept of the I—the spontaneous, impulsive aspect of the self that seeks only to meet one's own immediate needs and desires.

Stages in the Development of the Self

The process of developing a social self occurs gradually and in stages. Mead identified three critical stages—(1) the imitation stage, (2) the play stage, and (3) the game stage—each of which requires the unique human ability to engage in role-taking. In the **imitation stage**, *children under 3 years old are preparing for role-taking by observing others and imitating their behaviors, sounds, and gestures.* The **play stage** involves *a child, usually from 3 to 5, having the ability to see things (role-take) from the perspective of one person at a time; simple role-taking or play-acting.* Listen to children who are 3 to 5 years old play together. You will notice that they spend most of their time telling each other what to do. One of them will say something like, "You be the mommy, and José can be the daddy, and Julie, you be the dog. Now you say 'Good morning, Dear,' and I'll say, 'How did you sleep?' and Julie, you scratch at the door like you want to go out." They will talk about their little skit for 15 minutes and then enact it, with the actual enactment taking perhaps 1 minute. Small children mimic or imitate role-taking based on what they have seen as they learn and practice future roles.

A child who is playing mommy or daddy with a doll is playing at *taking the role* of parent. The child is directing activity toward the doll in a manner imitative of how the

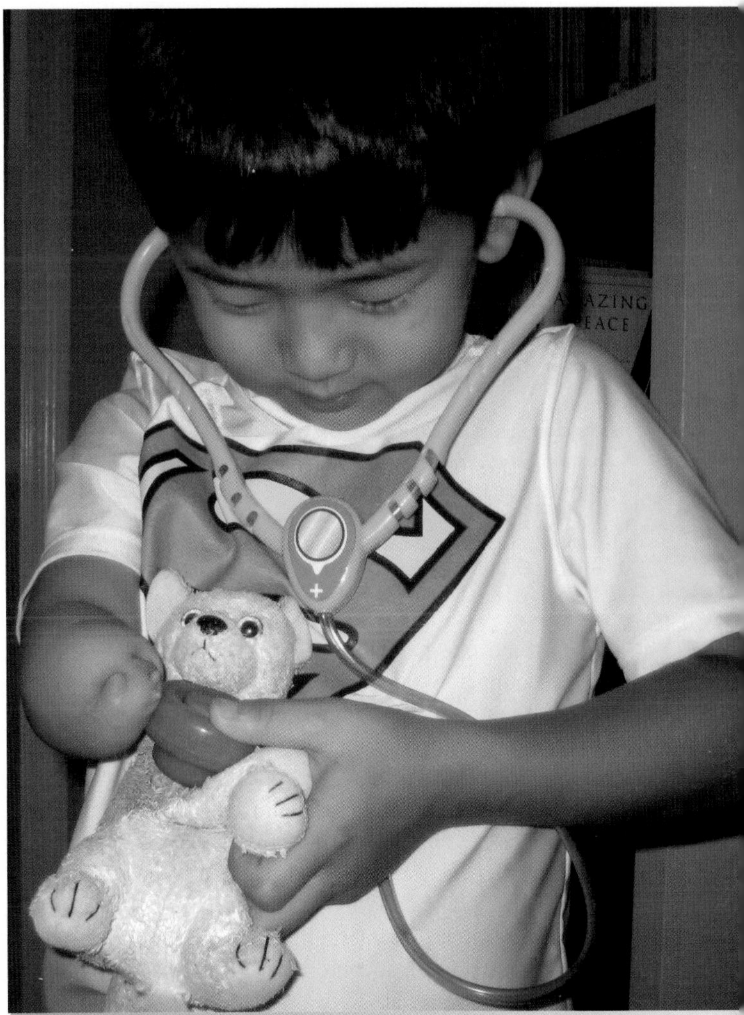

By imitating roles he has seen, this child is learning both adult roles and empathy with others. This kind of role enactment is an important prerequisite to the more complex interaction of playing a game with others.

parents direct activity toward the child. The child often does not know what to do when playing the role of a parent "going off to work" because children can play only roles they have seen or are familiar with. They do not know what the absent parent does at work when not in their presence. The point is that this "play" is actually extremely important "work" for children. They need to observe and imitate the relationships between roles, and they do this by observation and imitation (Handel, Cahill, and Elkin 2007).

Society and its rules are initially represented by **significant others**—*parents, guardians, relatives, siblings, or important individuals whose primary and sustained interactions are especially influential.* That is why much of the play stage involves role-taking based on these significant people in the child's life. The child does not yet understand the complex relations and multiple role players in the social world outside the immediate family. Children may have a sense of how their parents see them, but children are not yet able to comprehend how they are seen by the larger social world. Lack of role-taking ability is apparent when children say inappropriate things such as "Why are you so fat?"

The **game stage** *in the process of developing a social self is when a child develops the ability to take the role of multiple others concurrently and conform to societal expectations.* The child goes beyond the significant other such as the parent to value the opinion of all peers or expectations of the community.

Have you ever watched a team of young children play T-ball (a pre–Little League baseball game in which the children hit the ball from an upright rubber device that holds the ball), or have you observed a soccer league made up of 6-year-olds? If so, you have seen Mead's point illustrated vividly. In soccer (or football), 5- or 6-year-old children will not play their positions despite constant urging and cajoling by coaches. They all run after the ball, with little sense of their interdependent positions. Likewise, a child in a game of T-ball may pick up a ball that has been hit, turn to the coach, and say, "Now what do I do with it?" Most still do not quite grasp throwing it to first base, and the first-base player may actually have left the base to run for the ball. It can be hilarious for everyone except the coach, as a hit that goes 7 feet turns into a home run because everyone is scrambling for the ball.

Prior to the game stage, the vision of the whole process is not possible. When children enter the game stage at about age 7 or 8, they will be developmentally able to play the roles of various positions and enjoy a complex game. Each child learns what is expected and the interdependence of roles because he or she is then able to respond to the expectations of several people simultaneously (Hewitt 2007; Meltzer 1978). This allows the individual to coordinate his or her activity with others.

In moving from the play stage to the game stage, children's worlds expand from family and day care to neighborhood playmates, school, and other organizations. *This process gradually builds up a composite of societal expectations that the child learns from family, peers, and other organizations*, what Mead refers to as the **generalized other**. The child learns to internalize the expectations of society—the generalized other—over and above the expectations of any "significant others." Behavior comes to be governed by abstract rules ("no running outside of the baseline" or "no touching the soccer ball with your hands unless you are the goalie") rather than guidance from and emotional ties to a "significant other." Children become capable of moving into new social situations such as school, organized sports, and (eventually) the workplace to function with others in both routine and novel interactions. Individuals are active in shaping their social contexts, the self, and the choices they make about the future.

An illustration of internalizing the generalized other into one's conception of self is the common human experience of feeling embarrassed. Making an inappropriate remark at a party or having another call undue attention to one's appearance can cause embarrassment. Feeling embarrassed may

Very young children who play soccer do not understand the role requirements of games. They all—including the goalie—want to chase after the ball. Learning to play positions is a critical step in socialization, for it requires a higher level of role-taking than children can do at the play stage.

occur when one has violated a social norm and is taking into account how others view that behavior. According to this role-taking view, we see ourselves as objects from the standpoint of others, and we judge ourselves accordingly. Very young children, however, do not feel embarrassment when they do things such as soiling their pants or making inappropriate comments because they have not incorporated the generalized other. They have not yet learned the perspective of others. The capacity to feel embarrassed is not only an indicator of having internalized the generalized other but also a uniquely human outcome of our role-taking ability (Hewitt 2007; Koschate-Reis 2009).

As we grow, we identify with new in-groups such as a neighborhood, a college sorority, or the military. We learn new ideas and expand our understanding. Some individuals ultimately come to think of themselves as part of the global human community. Thus, for many individuals, the social world expands through socialization. However, some individuals never develop this expanded worldview, remaining narrowly confined and drawing lines between themselves and others who are different. Such narrow boundaries often result in prejudice against others.

Thinking Sociologically

Who are you? Write down 15 or 20 roles or attributes that describe who you are. How many of these items are characteristics associated with the *Me*—nouns such as *son, mother, student,* and *employee*? Which of the items are traits or attributes—adjectives such as *shy, sensitive, lonely, selfish,* and *vulnerable*? How do you think each of these was learned or incorporated into your conception of your self?

The Self and Connections to the Meso Level

In the preceding "Thinking Sociologically" exercise, we asked you to think about how you see yourself and what words you might use to portray yourself. If you were describing yourself for a group of people you did not know, we suspect that you would use mostly nouns or adjectives describing a status or a social position within the society: *student, employee, athlete, violinist, daughter, sister, Canadian, Lutheran,* and so forth. To a large extent, our sense of who we are is rooted in social positions that are part of organizations and institutions in the society (Kuhn 1964; Stryker 1980). This is a key point made by what is referred to as the Iowa School of symbolic interaction: Selfhood is relatively stable because we develop a core self—a stable inner sense of who we are regardless of the immediate setting in which we find ourselves. This core often centers on the most important social positions we hold in the larger structure of society. You may think of yourself as politically or religiously conservative or liberal, and that may influence the way you conduct yourself in a wide range of situations and social settings. It may shape your sexual behavior, the honesty with which you conduct business with others, and whether you are willing to cheat on an exam—even though you may not be around other people of your moral or political persuasion at the time (Kuhn 1964; Stryker 1980, 2000; Stryker and Stratham 1985; Turner 2003).

The Chicago School of symbolic interactionism emphasizes the role of the *I* and focuses on individuals' involvement in their own development and their agency in creating their world. The Iowa School places somewhat more emphasis on the *Me*—on the role of others and the external social environment in shaping us (Carrothers and Benson 2003).

Socialization Throughout the Life Cycle

The naming ceremony begins with an introduction of the 6-week-old baby, followed by the rituals surrounding the naming and welcoming of the newcomer into his tribe in Nigeria, Africa. By 6 weeks, the baby is considered likely to survive and thus given a name and incorporated into the group. Markers such as the naming ceremony point to movement from one stage to the next in the socialization process: birth, naming ceremonies or christenings, starting school at age 5 or 6, officially joining a church or temple at early puberty, obtaining a driver's license at about age 16, becoming eligible for military draft, being able to vote at age 18 and drink alcohol at age 21, and retiring from the

Death rituals differ depending on the culture and religion of the group. In India (top left), this body is being cremated by the holy Ganges River to release the soul from earthly existence. The closest relative lights the funeral pyre. The photo at the top right shows the Muslim tradition of washing and wrapping the dead before burial in Najaf, Iraq. At bottom left, a U.S. Honor Guard carries a casket with the remains of U.S. Air Force personnel at Arlington National Cemetery. A celestial burial master (bottom right) feeds the body of a dead Tibetan to the vultures in northwest China's Qinghai province. In Tibetan regions, the practice is known as jhator, *which literally means "giving alms to the birds," as people believe in rebirth and there is no need to preserve the body.*

One divorcée of three years told the authors, "There are many things to commend the single life, but I still have not adjusted to eating alone and cooking for myself. Worse than that are Sunday afternoons. That is the loneliest time."

Sometimes, resocialization refers to individuals' attempts to adjust to new statuses and roles, such as widowhood. In other cases, individuals are forced into resocialization to correct or reform behaviors that are defined as undesirable or deviant. Prison rehabilitation programs provide one example. However, research suggests that the difficulty in resocializing prisoners is rooted in the nature of the prison environment itself. Prisons are often coercive and violent environments, which may not provide the social supports necessary for bringing about change in a person's attitudes and behaviors.

Although resocialization is the goal of self-help groups such as Alcoholics Anonymous, Gamblers Anonymous, Parents Anonymous, drug rehabilitation groups, and weight loss groups, relapse is a common problem among participants. The same is true among former inmates who were supposedly resocialized by the criminal justice system. These groups and organizations aim to substitute new behaviors and norms for old undesirable ones, but the process of undoing socialization and achieving resocialization is difficult. Some public sociologists work on trying to understand why former inmates are at such high risk of repeating a crime and what might make the resocialization "stick," as is shown in the next "Sociologists in Action" feature (page 124). David Kirk used lessons from the aftermath of Katrina to solve a puzzle and make policy recommendations.

There are multiple individuals, groups, and institutions involved in the socialization process. These socialization forces are referred to as agents of socialization.

Sociologists in Action— David S. Kirk

Using Evidence-Based Research to Inform Public Policy: Resocialization Lessons From Hurricane Katrina

I have spent much of my professional career using the tools of sociology to examine the myriad consequences of criminal justice policies in the United States. Part of my focus has been on the influence of communities in the process of reintegrating ex-prisoners back into society. Research reveals that on leaving incarceration ex-prisoners tend to be geographically concentrated in a relatively small number of neighborhoods within metropolitan areas; they often return to the very same neighborhoods where they got into trouble with the law in the past, and fall into the same habits and routines that got them into trouble in the first place.

If criminal behavior is influenced by the types of neighborhoods we live in, as we become *socialized* and learn how to become a member of that social world, then it would seem counterproductive to prisoner reintegration for ex-offenders to return to the same locales where they got into trouble with the law in the past. The hope for ex-prisoners is that they will become *resocialized*, shedding their criminal identity as they learn the norms, behaviors, and routines of law-abiding citizens. Back in their old haunts, they find themselves surrounded by the socializing agents that helped lead them to criminal behavior in the first place. Thus, it is not surprising that large proportions of ex-prisoners end up back in prison within just three years.

These well-known facts about crime and justice in the United States serve as the backdrop of my research on prisoner reentry, the process of leaving prison and returning to the community. The tragedy of Hurricane Katrina, which devastated the gulf coasts of Louisiana and Mississippi in August 2005, afforded me a unique opportunity to examine what would happen if ex-prisoners did not return home to their old neighborhoods upon exiting prison as they typically do. Katrina provided a natural experiment for investigating the importance of residential change because it forced some people to move who otherwise would not have. It occurred to me that residential change may serve as a catalyst for sustained behavioral change by providing an opportunity for individuals to separate from the former contexts and associates that facilitated their prior criminal behavior. A fresh location enhanced resocialization efforts.

As I had hypothesized, prisoners exiting incarceration following Hurricane Katrina were much less likely to reside in the New Orleans neighborhoods where they resided prior to incarceration. Among those who did return to the same parish (a parish is the equivalent of a county) where they resided prior to incarceration, 26% were reincarcerated within one year of release from prison. By comparison, only 11% of offenders who moved to a new parish faced reincarceration one year after leaving prison. Based on these results, I concluded that separating individuals from their former residential environment reduces their likelihood of recidivism. Moving allows an individual to separate from the peers and routine activities that contributed to his or her criminal behavior in the past.

One critical component of disseminating information about scientific discoveries is to communicate the implications of the research. For instance, in many states, prisoners released on parole are legally required to return to their county of last residence, contributing to a return to old neighborhoods. So, parole policies, while designed to enhance public safety, may in fact undermine it. One implication of my research that I have discussed with key policy makers is that removing the institutional barriers to residential change may enhance public safety by reducing the likelihood of repeat offending. Additionally, providing incentives for individuals to move to new neighborhoods, such as public housing vouchers, may benefit public safety. Thus, in my experience, redesigning public policies is part of a methodical process that involves good science, communication of results, and further testing in a real-world environment.

* * * * * * *

David S. Kirk, PhD, is associate professor in the Department of Sociology and a faculty research associate of the Population Research Center at the University of Texas at Austin. This excerpt is adapted from Korgen, White, and White's *Sociologists in Action: Sociology, Social Change, and Social Justice* (Sage 2013).

Agents of Socialization: The Micro-Meso Connection

Agents of socialization are *the transmitters of culture—the people, organizations, and institutions that help us define our identity and teach us how to thrive in our social world.* Agents are the mechanism by which the self learns the values, beliefs, and behaviors of the culture. Agents of socialization help new members find their place, just as they prepare older members for new responsibilities in society. At the micro level, one's family, the peer group, and local groups and organizations help people know what is expected. At the meso level, formal sources of learning—education, religion, politics, economics, health—and other informal sources of learning such as the media and books are all agents that contribute to socialization. They transmit information to children and to adults throughout people's lives.

Thinking Sociologically

As you read this section, make a list of the socializing agents discussed in these pages. Indicate two or three central messages each agent of socialization tries to instill in people. Consider which agents are micro, meso, and macro agents. Are there different kinds of messages at each level? Do any of them conflict? If so, why, and what are the problems that are caused?

In early childhood, the family acts as the primary agent of socialization, passing on messages about respect for property and for authority, and the value of love and loyalty (Handel et al. 2007). Peer groups are also important, especially during the teenage years. Some writers even argue that the peer group is most important in the socialization process of children and teens (Aseltine 1995; Harris 2009). Each agent has its own functions or purposes and is important at different stages of the life cycle, but meso-level institutions play a more active role as one matures. For example, schools and religious bodies become more involved in socialization as children become 6 years old and older compared with when they were preschool age. For us, the authors of this book, other members of the American Sociological Association serve as "significant others" and shape our sense of appropriate behavior for sociologists and professors.

The "Sociology in Our Social World" on page 126 discusses how we know about socialization in schools by exploring an important and widely cited research project.

The primary socialization unit for young children is the family, but as they become teenagers, peers become increasingly important as a reference group, shaping their norms, values, and attitudes.

Note what kinds of data are viewed as legitimate evidence for understanding gender socialization.

Thinking Sociologically

First, read the gender socialization essay on page 125. Recall your own playground days or watch a sibling, a relative, or another child on the playground. What do your observations tell you about the role of play in gender socialization?

Lessons from one agent of socialization generally complement those from other agents. Parents work at home to support what school and religion teach. However, at times, agents provide conflicting lessons. For example, family and faith communities often give teens messages that conflict with those of peer groups regarding sexual activity and drug use. This is an example of mixed messages given by formal and informal agents.

Formal agents of socialization are *official or legal agents (e.g., families, schools, teachers, religious training) whose purpose it is to socialize the individual into the values, beliefs, and behaviors of the culture.* For example, a primary goal of families is to teach children to speak and to learn proper behavior. In addition, schoolteachers educate by giving formal instruction, and religious training provides moral instruction. (These formal agents of socialization will be discussed in Chapters 10–12.)

Sociology in Our Social World

Gender Socialization in American Public Schools

Pause for a moment as you pass a schoolyard, and observe the children at play. Children's behavior on the school playground translates into a powerful agent of gender socialization in a world that is very complex. Consider the evidence reported in the ethnographic study of Barrie Thorne (1993), recounted in her award-winning book *Gender Play*.

Many people assume that gender differences are natural and that we are "born that way." In contrast, Thorne provides evidence that gender differences are social constructions, influenced by the setting, the players involved in the situation, and the control people have over the situation. She is suggesting that we need to look at well-known everyday patterns from a fresh point of view. As an astute observer and researcher, Thorne suspected that girls and boys have complex relations that play out in the classroom and schoolyard. She chose the playground as the focus of her observation of the separate worlds of girls and boys (Thorne 1993). Through systematic participant observation, she found that children and adults play an active role in defining and shaping gender expectations through the collective practices of forming lines, choosing seats, teasing, gossiping, and participating in selected activities.

Thorne used two schools for her research—one in a small California city and another in a Midwest suburb. She entered the world of the children, sometimes sitting apart on the playground taking notes, sometimes participating in their activities such as eating and talking in the lunchroom. In each setting, she recorded her observations and experiences. For example, she noted what children call themselves and how they think of themselves. She was intrigued by the reference to the "opposite sex"—a term that stresses difference and opposition rather than similarity and the sense of "we." Thorne was struck by the active meaning construction involved as the children gained a notion of "normal" gender behavior. The real focus of her work is in taking seriously how children themselves make sense of sex differences.

Previous studies concluded that boys tend to interact in larger, more age-heterogeneous groups and in more rough-and-tumble play and physical fighting. Thorne also found that boys' play involves a much larger portion of the playground, and their play space was generally farther from the building, making them less subject to monitoring and sanctioning. Boys not only used roughly 90% of the playground, they would also often run "sneak invasions" into the girls' space to take things belonging to the girls. Many boys felt that they had a right to the geographical space that was occupied by girls. Girls played close to the buildings in much smaller areas and rarely ventured into the boys' area.

Girls' play tended to be characterized by cooperation and taking turns. They had more intense and exclusive friendships, which took shape around keeping and telling secrets, shifting alliances, and indirect ways of expressing disagreement. Instead of direct commands, girls more often used words such as "let's" or "we gotta." However, Thorne found that these notions of "separate girls' and boys' worlds" used in most previous studies miss the subtleties of race, class, and other factors in the situation.

In follow-up research, Valerie Ann Moore examined children at a summer day camp (Moore 2001). Like Thorne, she watched the children play and interact with one another, and found that children also use play to construct the meaning of race and age. All the boys in the camp showed their age by defying the adults' rules, which unified them across racial and age boundaries. The girls at the camp, on the other hand, were much more likely to separate by age and race when interacting with other campers. Narratives of romance were likely to break the physical boundaries among older campers (Moore 2001). These romances, however, emphasize gender differences. The camp counselors reinforced this difference by constantly creating and maintaining gender boundaries to prohibit romances from forming between the teens.

The major contribution of these two studies is to alert us to the complexity of the gender socialization process, helping us see the extent to which children are active agents creating their own definitions of social relations, not just short automatons who enact adult notions of what gender means.

Informal agents of socialization are *unofficial forces that shape values, beliefs, and behaviors in which socialization is not the express purpose.* Examples include the media, books, advertising, and the Internet. They bring us continuous messages even though their primary purpose is not socialization but entertainment or selling products. Children watch countless advertisements on television, many with messages about what is good and fun to eat and how to be more attractive, more appealing, smarter, and a better person through the consumption of products. This bombardment is a particularly influential part of socialization at young ages.

Japanese fathers and their sons eat lunch during a festival. While mothers are the key agents of socialization in Japan, fathers also have a role, especially during special events in the life of the child.

Thinking Sociologically

What confusion might be created for children when the formal and informal agents of socialization provide different messages about values or acceptable behaviors? Is this contradiction something that parents should be concerned about? Why or why not?

Micro-Level Socialization

Perhaps the most important formal agent of socialization is the family, and we usually experience this agent at the micro level—through the impact of our own parents and siblings. One way in which families teach children what is right and wrong is through rewards and punishments, called *sanctions*. Children who lie to their parents may receive a verbal reprimand or a slap on the hand, be sent to their rooms, have "time out," or receive a severe spanking, depending on differences in child-rearing practices in different families. These are examples of negative sanctions. Conversely, children may be rewarded for good behavior with a smile, praise, a cookie, or a special event. These are examples of positive sanctions. The number and types of sanctions dispensed in the family shape the socialization process, including development of the self and the perceptions we have of who we are and even whether we are good and clever or bad and stupid. Note that family influence varies from one culture to another.

In Japan, the mother is a key agent in the process of turning a newborn into a member of the group, passing on the strong group standards and expectations of family, neighbors, community, and society through the use of language and emotion. The child learns the importance of depending on the group and therefore fears being cast out. The need to belong creates pressure to conform to expectations, and the use of threats and the fear of shame help socialize children into Japanese ways (Hendry 1987; Holloway 2001).

Nonconformity is a source of shame in Japan. The resulting ridicule is a powerful means of social control. In some cases, the outcast is physically punished by peers. Thus, to bring shame on oneself or the family is behavior to be avoided. In the most extreme cases, young people have committed suicide because they did not conform to group expectations and felt profoundly ashamed as a result. The interaction of family and formal education in Japan is explored in more detail in the next "Sociology Around the World" (page 128).

Thinking Sociologically

First, read the Sociology Around the World feature on the next page. How did agents of socialization influence who you are today, and how did your experience differ from that of Japanese children described in the essay?

In the United States, most parents value friendliness, cooperation, orientation toward achievement, social competence, responsibility, and independence as qualities their children should learn, in contrast to the values of conformity and fitting into the group espoused in Japan. However, subcultural values and socialization practices may differ within the diverse groups in the U.S. population. Conceptions of what makes a "good person" or a "good citizen" and different goals of socialization bring about differences in the process of socialization around the world.

Sociology Around the World

Socialization in Japan: The Family and Early Schooling

By Wendy Ng

Each of our families prepares us through the socialization process for the culture we are entering. How families carry out this process differs around the world, just as the cultures for which they are preparing their children differ. Here we consider meso-level family and early schooling in Japanese socialization.

The family is one of the most important socializing influences in Japan. The basis of the family unit in Japan is called the *ie* (pronounced ee-ay). Traditionally, it is made up of blood relatives who reside in the same household, as well as their ancestors and the descendants not yet born. Thus, family in Japan goes beyond those who belong to the immediate nuclear grouping and includes a broader array of individuals. Compared with the past, the modern *ie* in Japan relies more on the nuclear and living extended family and serves as the major reference group that socializes individuals within the family. Thus, family members within the *ie* are responsible for teaching individuals their family roles, values, and norms within the culture.

A unique feature of interdependence that is found within the family structure is that of *amae* (ah-may), which roughly translated means passive love but is often referred to as an emotional bond usually held between mother and child. Through this relationship, children are socialized to understand that they are an important part of the family, and they also learn that parents are to be respected and obeyed as the adults within the family. Although this appears hierarchical, the emotional bond of *amae* sets up a relationship of interdependency between child and parent for their lifetime. As children grow into adulthood, they will take care of their parents in the way that they were taken care of as children. This bond of loyalty between parent and child within the family structure is translated into other social structures outside the family. For example, in a business organization, there is a similar expectation of group loyalty.

In terms of early childhood socialization, Japanese children learn the distinction between two related, yet distinct, concepts: *uchi* (inside) and *soto* (outside). These concepts apply to material distinctions of clean and unclean spaces. In behavior, this means taking one's shoes off outside the house because the inside is clean and the outside is unclean. In Japanese households, the bathroom has similar clean and unclean designations. The bath is "clean" and the toilet, used to dispose of bodily wastes, is "unclean." Thus, one would never wear the same shoes or slippers in the toilet room and the room for bathing because that would be mixing unclean and clean elements.

Within the family, immediate members are "insiders" and other people are "outsiders." Children learn that the family is a safe and secure environment where the emphasis is on harmony among the various family members. Interactions between individuals stress cooperation, and interpersonal disputes are avoided. If a disagreement happens, children are taught to apologize to one another. Reciprocity is yet another behavior that is emphasized within the family. Children are taught to put themselves in the role of the other person and to think of the consequences of their behavior before acting out. This type of role behavior suggests that harmony between and among family members is important and sets the foundation for the child's educational socialization.

Whereas the family serves as the central socializing force when children are very young, as they grow the educational system continues to socialize children through group interaction and learning. When children enter kindergarten they become familiar with participating in a social group with peers. The Japanese kindergarten system emphasizes group equality among children and thus socializes children to be loyal to their classmates and group. Other children now form their new *uchi* or "inside" associations and friendships. The emphasis on group over individual identities is accomplished through wearing identical uniforms or smocks, having similar educational tools for all students, and having children take turns in different duties in the classroom. For example, the responsibility of passing out paper in the classroom, or food at lunchtime, is rotated among all the children in the classroom. Thus, cooperation and group participation becomes an important defining feature of kindergarten socialization.

At first glance, the emphasis on equality among individuals in the kindergarten classroom setting might seem to conflict with the emphasis on hierarchical authority present in much of Japanese society. In fact, the emphasis on group socializing helps to encourage a sense of belonging and group identity that works well within hierarchical authority structures. By learning these behaviors at a young age, the children learn that they are individuals within a larger group, and that their actions reflect not only on themselves but also on their family, school, or whatever social group they belong to as adults.

* * * * * * *

Dr. Wendy Ng is chair of the Department of Sociology at San Jose State University. She has written about Asian cultures, among other things.

In addition, the number of children in a family and the placement of each child in the family can influence the unique socialization experience of the child. In large families, parents typically have less time with each additional child. Where the child falls in the hierarchy of siblings can also influence the development of the self. In fact, birth order is a strong predictor of social attitudes—perhaps more so than race, class, or gender—according to some studies, and firstborns are typically the highest achievers (Benokraitis 2008; "First Born Children" 2008; Freese et al. 1999: Paulhus, Trapnell, and Chen 1999). Younger children may be socialized by older siblings as much as by parents, and older siblings often serve as models that younger children want to emulate.

Meso-Level Socialization

At the meso level there are several agents at work in socializing people into specific cultural values and to the roles they must learn to fulfil. Education and religion are two obvious influences—both being institutions with primary responsibility for socialization. We will discuss those in more detail in Chapters 11 and 12, and here we will illustrate meso-level socialization influences with a focus on social class and the media.

Social Class

Our education level, our occupation, the house we live in, what we choose to do in our leisure time, the foods we eat, and our religious and political beliefs are just a few aspects of our lives that are affected by socialization. Applying what we know from sociological research, the evidence strongly suggests that socialization varies by **social class**, or *the wealth, power, and prestige rankings that individuals hold in society* (Pearce 2009). Meso-level patterns of distribution of resources—based on the quality of education in one's state or the economic opportunities created by state and national policies—affect who we become, as we see below.

Upper-middle-class and middle-class parents in the United States usually have above-average education and managerial or professional jobs. They tend to pass on to their children the skills and values necessary to succeed in the subculture of their social class. Subcultures, you will recall, operate at the meso level of the social system. Autonomy, creativity, self-direction (the ability to make decisions and take initiative), responsibility, curiosity, and consideration of others are especially important for middle-class success and are part of middle-class subculture (Kohn 1989). If the child misbehaves, for example, middle-class parents typically analyze the child's reasons for misbehaving, and punishment is related to these reasons. Sanctions often involve instilling guilt and denying privileges.

A Japanese mother helps her son at Heian Shinto Shrine during Shichi-go-san Matsuri, also called the Seven-Five-Three Festival, a celebration with prayers of long life for children aged 3 to 7.

Working-class parents using meso-level family patterns tend to pass on to children their cultural values of respect for authority and conformity to rules, lessons that will be useful if the children also have blue-collar jobs (Kohn 1989). Immediate punishment with no questions asked if a rule is violated functions to prepare children for positions in which obedience to rules is important to success. They are expected to be neat, clean, well-mannered, honest, and obedient students (MacLeod 2008). Socialization experiences for boys and girls are often different, following traditional gender-role expectations of the working class subculture. Moreover, these differences in behavior across social classes and parenting styles are apparent cross-culturally as well (Leung, Lau, and Lam 1998).

What conclusions can we draw from these studies? Members of each class are socializing their children to be successful in their social class and to meet expectations for adults of that class. Schools, like families, participate in this process. Although the extent to which schools create or limit opportunities for class mobility is debated, what is clear is that children's social class position on entering school has an effect on the socialization experiences they

This parents pass on a love for the piano to his young son. Because of the social class of this father, his son is likely to receive many messages about creativity, curiosity, and self-direction.

have in school (Ballantine and Hammack 2012). Families and schools socialize children to adapt to the settings in which they grow up and are likely to live.

Social class, however, is only one of many influencing agents. As we saw in *Black Men and Public Space*, race and ethnicity are very important factors in socialization, as is gender. Gender socialization will be discussed in more detail in Chapter 9, but we note here that race, class, and gender act as structural constraints on some members of the population. People from different social classes, ethnic and racial groups, and genders receive different messages about who they are and how they should behave. Therefore, it is important to recognize the interplay of these variables in people's lives.

Electronic Media

Television and computers are important informal agents of socialization at the meso level. They are intermediate-sized social units—larger than a local community, but smaller than a nation. They impact both nation-states and global agencies at the macro level by shaping public attitudes, and they affect family notions of what is normal or not normal at the micro level. In developed countries, there is scarcely a home without a television set, and over 75% of homes have computers and Internet access (WebSiteOptimization.com 2010).

Researchers have collected nearly five decades of information on how television has become a way of life in homes. By the time an average child in the United States reaches age 18, he or she will have spent more time watching television than doing any other single activity besides sleeping. On average, children between ages 8 and 18 spend 3 hours a day watching television, 1 hour and 11 minutes watching videos or DVDs, 1 hour and 44 minutes with audio media, 1 hour using computers, and 49 minutes playing video games, with a total media exposure in a typical day of 8 hours and 33 minutes. The next "Engaging Sociology" feature shows the total media exposure of children by several variables. Examine this issue in more depth by answering the questions following Tables 4.2 and 4.3.

The moguls of the mass media—a meso-level social system—are able to influence socialization within the most intimate of environments. "Children [in the United States] use computers at very young ages—21 percent of children 2 years and younger, 58 percent of 3- to 4-year-olds, and 77 percent of 5- to 6-year-olds"; seventy-four percent of the U.S. population uses the Internet (Internet World Statistics 2009; National Science Foundation 2005).

A serious concern related to socialization centers on the messages children receive from television and computer games, along with the behavioral effects of these messages. There is ample evidence that children are affected in negative ways by excessive television viewing, especially television violence, but a direct causal link between television viewing and behavior is difficult to establish (National Science Foundation 2005). Researchers know, however, that parents who play an active role in helping children understand the content of television shows can have a powerful effect on mitigating television's negative impacts and enhancing the positive aspects of television shows. The television-viewing habits of parents—length of viewing time, types of shows watched, times of day—can also influence how their children respond to television.

Perhaps the most important aspect of television and computers is something that we do not fully understand but that has frightening potential. For the first time in human history, we have powerful agents of socialization in the home from a child's birth onward. Time spent watching television or playing computer games means less time spent engaging in interaction with caregivers and peers. Intimate family bonds formed of affection and meaningful interaction are being altered by the dominant presence of electronic media in the home. In addition, those who control the flood of mass media messages received by children

Engaging Sociology

Media Exposure and Socialization

Examine Tables 4.2 and 4.3 and respond to the questions below.

Table 4.2 Total Media Exposure (Average Hours per Day)

Age	8–10 years old	7:51
	11–14 years old	11:53
	15–18 years old	11:23
Gender	Boys	11:12
	Girls	10:17
Race	White	8:36
	Black	12:59
	Hispanic	13:00
Parent education	High school or less	11:26
	Some college	11:30
	College graduate	10:00

Table 4.3 Average Amount of Time per Day Spent With Each Medium (8- to 18-Year-Olds)

Medium	*1999*	*2009*
Television	3:47	4:29
Music/audio	1:48	2:31
Computer	:27	1:29
Video games	:26	1:13
Print	:43	:38
Movies	:18	:25
Total media exposure	7:29	10:45
Multitasking proportion	16%	29%

Sociological Data Analysis:

1. Considering the data in Tables 4.2 and 4.3, how would you describe television watching and other media-engaged patterns among different groups?
2. Are the trends in media exposure over the first decade of the 21st century a matter of concern? Why or why not?
3. How might media time affect other aspects of socialization of children?
4. What might be the social consequences of ethnic minorities (blacks and Hispanics), and those children whose parents do not have a college education, having so much higher media exposure each day than whites and those who are more highly educated?
5. Do your conclusions cause any concerns about your society? Why or why not?

Source: Kaiser Family Foundation 2010; Rideout, Foehr, and Roberts 2010.

Children receive many messages from television and computer games, and these may influence attitudes toward life. The question of how much behavior is influenced is complex and still receiving attention by researchers.

may have interests and concerns that are very much at odds with those of parents.

We can conclude that a significant part of the informal socialization process occurs with the assistance of electronic equipment that shares the home with parents and siblings and that commands a significant portion of a child's time and attention. The next "Sociology in Our Social World" compares formal socialization in schools with informal socialization through television and the Internet. Which of the three agents of socialization compared in Table 4.4 do you think has the strongest impact on today's young generation? Do any of the values or life-perspectives of schools, television, and internet contradict one another? Do they contradict the values or norms instilled by families that you know?

With globalization, global knowledge and understanding also become important parts of school curricula and media coverage; we move next to a discussion of some of the national and global processes that influence socialization.

Elderly people learn how to use computers in Shanghai, China. Keeping up with the rapid pace of change—especially in technology—is sometimes a challenge for older citizens. Their grandchildren may know more than they do about technology.

Thinking Sociologically

What agents of socialization in addition to family, social class, and electronic media are important in teaching us our roles, norms, values, and beliefs? What is the impact, for example, of friendship networks or peer groups?

Socialization and Macro-Level Issues

Sense of Self Versus the "Other": Diverse Global Societies

Immigration patterns and ethnic conflicts around the world have resulted in a fairly new phenomenon: transnationalism. **Transnationalism** is *the process by which immigrants create multinational social relations that link together their original societies with their new locations. This means that an individual or a family has national loyalty to more than one country* (Levitt 2001, 2007; Levitt and Waters 2006). Often, it occurs after migration of war refugees, when one's roots lie in the country of origin and one's close family members may continue to live there.

Consider transnational children raised in war-torn countries. In the Palestinian territories, especially Gaza, and in Israeli settlements along the border, children grow up with fear and hatred, major influences on their socialization. Some war refugees spend childhoods in refugee camps and may never return to their native countries. For people experiencing transnationalism, there are conflicting messages about culturally appropriate behaviors and the obligations of loyalty to family and nation. Events of a national or global nature directly impact how an individual is socialized—with some of the socializing influences being from outside one's country of residence.

However, one need not migrate to another country to experience global pressures. The Internet and cell phones

Sociology in Our Social World

Formal and Informal Agents of Socialization: A Comparison of Schooling, Television, and the Internet

By Alan McEvoy and Laurie McCloud

Schooling, television, and the Internet share a basic characteristic: All are purveyors of messages to young people. Despite this similarity, however, there are also many differences. Schools are formal agents of socialization with the expressed purpose of socializing the young. Television and the Internet are informal agents of socialization because their goals are entertaining, selling products, and increasing consumerism. Socialization is a secondary result, as shown in Table 4.4.

Table 4.4 Schools, Television, and Internet: Formal and Informal Agents of Socialization

	Schools	*Television*	*Internet*
Location	Schooling is formal and bureaucratic; it takes place in specially designed buildings.	TV viewing generally takes place in the informal setting of one's home.	The majority of Internet users have home access, but others use the Internet in institutional settings such as work and school.
Rules	Acquisition of information requires obeying certain rules (e.g., no eating, no talking, no running around).	There are often no rules for watching TV, although parents may put limits on how much time can be spent viewing or what shows can be watched.	There are no rules for Internet viewing, except those imposed by parents. Listserv applications and blogs sometimes develop and impose their own rules of civility. The issue of rules for civil use is an emerging one in this new medium, especially with e-mail.
Structure of content	School is structured around a sequential, age-appropriate curriculum that intends to inform and to build on skills.	TV has no structured curriculum but a random content (channel surfing), which is usually designed to entertain. Watching TV requires no special skills.	The Internet has random content, and it can be user provided, which means a large variety of information and opinions is represented. Users need access and some skills.
Voluntary/involuntary	Students are a captive audience, required to attend school for specified periods (usually 8 a.m.–3 p.m., excluding weekends and certain holidays).	Watching TV is voluntary. Programs are available 24 hours per day throughout the year.	Internet use is voluntary. Websites are available 24 hours a day throughout the year.

(Continued)

Table 4.4 **(Continued)**

	Schools	*Television*	*Internet*
Power relations	There is a power imbalance between teachers and students; students have a role imposed on them and have little control over the requirements of that role. Students do not directly control the flow of information from teachers.	There are no role requirements imposed on the viewer from the TV. The viewer has power to control the flow of information with the on/off switch and choice of channels.	Many websites are interactive or have user content. Most users passively view content. Users can close web browsers and change pages at will.
Commercial content	Schools do not provide information to students for commercial purposes (no profit motive).	TV messages are generally provided to viewers for commercial purposes (excepting public TV).	Commercial website messages are generally provided to viewers to generate profit.
Groups	Students are grouped in classes by age or ability, and groups of students (15 to 30) together receive instruction.	Viewers watch TV individually or in small groups, and millions may receive the same message.	Internet users typically are individuals, though they may be communicating with people geographically very distant from themselves.
Interaction	Face-to-face interaction defines the relationship between students and teachers and among students, as each takes the other into account throughout the interaction. Face-to-face interaction allows for mutual influence.	Vicarious interaction with an electronic image (rather than a live person) defines the relationship between viewers and media personalities. Viewers are not able to interact directly with the millions of other people receiving the same messages, hence no mutual influence.	Websites vary in the ability to interact with the content provider. No face-to-face interaction occurs. Some sites allow users to post comments or edit content. Many sites allow only passive viewing of shared information.
Influence	Influence of schooling starts when the child begins school (about age 5).	The influence of TV begins in infancy when children become new members of the family, and the impact of TV is significant even before a child has entered school.	Many individuals are introduced to the Internet at a young age, and the web appears to have a growing influence throughout the life course.

have increasingly created a sense of connectedness to other parts of the world and an awareness of global interdependencies (Brier 2004; Roach 2004). Some commentators have even suggested that the Internet is a threat to the nation-state as it allows individuals to develop friendships, loyalties, and norms that are not in the interests of the state (Drori 2006). Ideas of social justice or progress may be shaped not just by the government that rules the country but by international human rights organizations and ideas that are obtained from media that cross borders, such as the World Wide Web. In recent uprisings in some Middle Eastern and North African countries, social networking kept movement participants in touch with others in the uprisings and with outside media and supporters. So socialization can include agents that are beyond the local community and beyond the national boundaries.

Access to international information and friendships across borders and boundaries are increasingly possible as more people have access to the Internet. Map 4.1 on Internet use around the world illustrates not only variability of access but also how widespread this access is becoming. One interesting question is how access or lack of access will influence the strength of "we" versus "they" feelings, insofar as sense of self is connected to belonging to a group—to a sense of "we."

At a time when people lived in isolated rural communities and did not interact with those unlike themselves, there was little price to pay for being bigoted or chauvinistic toward those who were different. However, we now live in a global village where we or our businesses will likely interact with very different people in a competitive environment. If we hold people in low regard because they are unlike us or because we think they are destined for hell, there may be a high cost for this animosity toward those who are not like us. Among other problems, terrorism is fermented when people feel alienated. Therefore, training in cultural sensitivity toward those "others" has become an economic and a political issue.

The reality is that children in the 21st century are being socialized to live in a globalized world. Increasingly, children around the world are learning multiple languages to enhance their ability to communicate with others. Some college campuses require experiences abroad as part of the standard curriculum because faculty members and administrators feel that a global perspective is essential in our world today and part of a college education. Global sensitivity and tolerance of those who were once considered "alien" has become a core element of our day (Robertson 1992; Schaeffer 2003; Snarr and Snarr 2008).

Map 4.1 Internet Users per 100 People

Source: World Bank.

Sometimes, global events can cause a different turn—away from tolerance and toward defensive isolation. When 19 young men from Saudi Arabia and other Middle Eastern countries crashed planes into the World Trade Center in New York City and into the Pentagon in Washington, DC, the United States was shocked and became mobilized to defend itself and its borders. The messages within schools and from the government suddenly took a more patriotic turn. So this event and other terrorist acts, clearly tragedies rooted in global political conflicts, can intensify the boundaries between people and loyalty to the nation-state. Global forces are themselves complex and do not always result in more tolerance.

Indeed, the only thing that we can predict with considerable certainty is that in this age of sharing a small planet, the socialization of our citizens will be influenced by events at the macro level, whether national or global.

Policy and Practice

Should preschoolers living in poverty be socialized in day care settings? Should adolescents work while going to school? Should new parents be required to take child-rearing classes? How should job-training programs be structured? How can communities use the talents and knowledge of retirees? Can the death process be made easier for the dying person and the family? Should we place emphasis in high school and college on in-group loyalty and patriotism or on developing a sense of global citizenship mobilized around common human issues? These are all policy questions—issues of how to establish governing principles that will enhance our common life.

These policy questions rely on an understanding of socialization—how we learn our beliefs and our positions in society. For example, making decisions about how to provide positive early-childhood education experiences at a time when young children are learning the ways of their culture depends on understanding the socialization they receive at home and at school. The quality of child care we provide for young children will affect not only how effective our future workforce is but also whether the children turn out to be productive citizens or a drain on society.

Some sociologists do research to provide policy makers with accurate data and interpretations of the data so that they can make wise decisions. Others are more activist, working in the field as public sociologists and trying to solve social problems through private foundations, consulting firms, or state agencies.

Now that we have some understanding of the process of socialization, we look next at the process of interaction and how individuals become members of small groups, networks, and large complex organizations.

What Have We Learned?

Human beings are not born to be noble savages or depraved beasts. As a species, we are remarkable in how many aspects of our lives are shaped by learning—by socialization. Human socialization is pervasive, extensive, and lifelong. We cannot understand what it means to be human without comprehending the impact of a specific culture on us, the influence of our close associates, and the complex interplay of pressures at the micro, meso, and macro levels. Indeed, without social interaction, there would not even be a self. We humans are, in our most essential natures, social beings. The purpose of this chapter has been to open our eyes to the ways in which we become the individuals we are. We move now to a discussion of how we use our socialization in interactions with groups and organizations.

Key Points

- Human beings come with their own biological makeup, but most of what makes us uniquely human we learn from our culture and society—our socialization. Humans who live in isolation from others do not receive the socialization necessary to be part of culture and are sometimes barely human. (See pp. 112–115.)
- The self consists of the interaction of the *I*—the basic impulsive human with drives, needs, and feelings—and the *Me*—the reflective self one develops by role-taking to see how others might see one. (See pp. 115–118.) The self is profoundly shaped by others, but it also has agency—it is an initiator of action and a maker of meaning. (See p. 120.)
- The self develops through stages, from mimicking others (the play stage) to more intellectually sophisticated abilities to role-take and to see how various roles complement each other (the game stage). (See 118–120.)

- Although the self is somewhat flexible in adjusting to different settings and circumstances, there is also a core self that is part of meso-level organizations and institutions in which the self participates. (See p. 120.)
- The self is modified as it moves through life stages, and some of those stages require major resocialization—shedding old roles and taking on new ones as one enters new statuses in life. (See pp. 120–124.)
- A number of agents of socialization are at work in each of our lives, communicating messages that are relevant at the micro, meso, or macro level of social life. At the meso level, for example, we may receive different messages about what it means to be a "good" person depending on our ethnic, religious, or social-class subculture. (See pp. 125–132.)
- Some of these messages may be in conflict with each other, as when global messages about tolerance for those who are different conflict with a nation's desire to have absolute loyalty and a sense of superiority. (See pp. 132–136.)

Discussion Questions

1. Cooley's idea of the "looking-glass self" helps us understand how our perceptions of how other people view us can influence how we view ourselves. How has your sense of your ability to succeed in college been influenced by the feedback you have processed from those around you (particularly teachers, peers, and family members)?
2. Socialization occurs throughout the life cycle. Into what role have you been socialized most recently? Who were the primary agents of this socialization process? Did you find the process relatively easy or difficult? Why?
3. Sociological studies have shown that middle-class and working-class parents tend to socialize their children differently. Explain the differences and describe how they relate to how you were socialized by your family of origin.
4. How has your socialization been influenced by television and video games? Do you think the extent to which these informal agents of socialization influence children these days has a positive impact or a negative impact on our society? Why?
5. If you were asked to create a government policy to promote positive socialization experiences that would strengthen our society, what might you propose? Why?

Contributing to Our Social World: What Can We Do?

At the Local Levels

In every community, numerous opportunities exist for volunteer work helping children from economically and otherwise disadvantaged backgrounds to succeed in school. Opportunities to help disadvantaged children succeed in school include:

- *Tutoring or mentoring in the local schools.* Contact an education faculty member for information.
- *Volunteering in Head Start centers for poor preschool children.* See the association's website at www.nhsa.org.
- *Helping in a local Boys and Girls Club* that provides socialization experiences for children through their teens. You can find a club near you by going to www.bgca.org/whoweare/Pages/FindaClub.aspx.
- *Taking service learning course credits.* Locate the service learning office at your college or university to learn about service learning programs on your campus that help disadvantaged children.

At the National and Global Levels

Literacy is a vital component of socialization, yet remains an unmet need in many parts of the world, especially in the less-developed countries of Africa and Asia.

- *World Education* provides training and technical assistance in nonformal education in economically disadvantaged communities worldwide. Go to the organization's website at www.worlded.org to learn about its wide variety of projects and volunteer/work opportunities.
- *CARE International* (www.care-international.org) and *Save the Children* (www.savethechildren.org) provide funding for families to send children to school and to receive specialized training.
- *Free the Children* (www.freethechildren.com), an organization that empowers young people to help other young people, has built more than 650 schools and schoolrooms for children in various parts of the world.
- *UNESCO (the United Nations Educational, Scientific and Cultural Organization)* promotes literacy around the world in many ways. Learn more about its efforts at www.unesco.org/new/en/education. Opportunities exist for fund-raising, internships, and eventually jobs with these organizations.

WWW Visit the Student Study Site at **www.sagepub.com/ballantine4e** to access additional study tools, including eFlashcards, web quizzes, video resources, audio resources, web resources, SAGE journal articles, recommended readings, and more.

CHAPTER

5 Interaction, Groups, and Organizations

Connections That Work

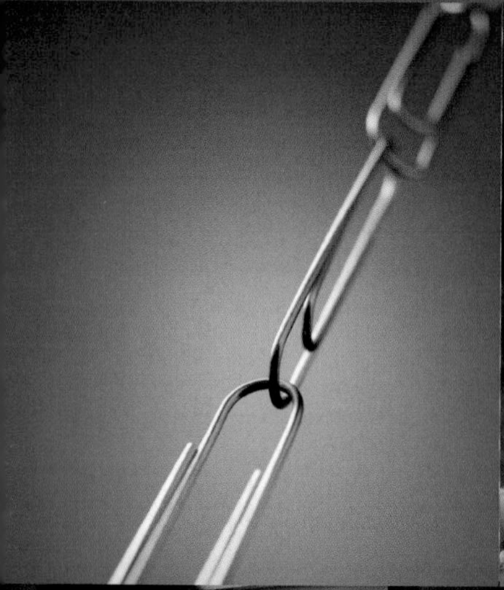

Human interaction results in connections—networks—that make life more fulfilling and our economic efforts more productive. These connections are critical in our social world—from small micro groups to large bureaucratic organizations.

Global Community
Society
National Organizations, Institutions, and Ethnic Subcultures
Local Organizations and Community
Me (and My Network of Close Friends)
Micro: Networks in organizations—alumni, civic groups
Meso: Ethnic organizations, political parties, religious denominations
Macro: Connections between citizens of a nation
Macro: Global networks; United Nations; international courts; transnational corporations

Think About It	
Micro: Self and Inner Circle	Are you likely to meet your perfect mate over the Internet?
Micro: Local Community	How does interaction with family and friends affect who you are and what you believe?
Meso: National Institutions; Complex Organizations; Ethnic Groups	Is bureaucratic red tape necessary and inevitable?
Macro: National Society	How do national trends—such as the spread of fast-food chains and "box stores"—influence your quality of life?
Macro: Global Community	How do networks across the globe affect you, your education, and your work?

What's coming in this chapter?

Peaceful demonstrators who gathered to protest the 2009 election in Iran were confronted with massive police forces. They were forced to disperse, many were beaten and arrested, and some were killed. Although the government imposed a news blackout and a crackdown on communications, demonstrators used their cell phones, blogs, Twitter, and Facebook to send pictures and video footage documenting the events around the world. Some have referred to this as the "Twitter Revolution." This cyber-inspiration has spread to protesters in other countries such as Tunisia, Yemen, Egypt, Oman, Bahrain, and Libya. Cyberspace links people around the world in seconds in ways that few governments can stop (Stone and Cohen 2009). There is no need to wait for the mail or even talk on the phone. The information superhighway is opening new communication routes and allowing individuals with common interests instantly to engage in networking.

No longer are paper and pencil the media of academics. Most universities are now requiring students to have laptops or access to computers on campus. The colleges now provide Wi-Fi Internet access, thus expanding modes of teaching, learning, and communicating.

Only a few decades ago, we read about cyberspace in science fiction novels written by authors with a little science background and a lot of imagination. Indeed, the word *cyberspace* was coined in 1984 by the science fiction writer William Gibson (Brasher 2004). The implications of the rapidly expanding links in cyberspace are staggering. We cannot even anticipate some of them because change is so rapid. For entertainment, we can talk with friends on Listservs or with people we have "met" through cyber social groups. Some of these acquaintances have never left their own country, which may be on the other side of the planet. All of this takes place in the comfort of our homes. Face-to-face communication may occur only on cameras attached to our computers and iPads.

Universities now communicate with students and employees by computer. You may be able to register for a class by "talking" to the computer. Computers track your registration and grades, and they may even send you letters about your status. They also monitor employee productivity. For doing certain types of research, library books are becoming secondary to the World Wide Web.

Jeanne, one of the coauthors of this book, took a leave of absence in the mid-1980s to do some research in Japan. A benefit of that leave was that she escaped the distractions of ringing phones and she could concentrate. Fax was almost unknown, and e-mail hardly existed for the civilian population. In 2007, she took a leave of absence to teach on Semester at Sea. Even in the middle of the ocean, she was in instant contact with her office, publisher, and family over the international Internet superhighway. She could insert earphones into her laptop computer and have a Skype conversation by voice or pick up a mobile phone and call her family or coauthor. What a change in 25 years! Technology is creating a smaller world where time zones are the only thing separating our communication, but it also may be making the world more impersonal because there is less need to meet face-to-face.

Even dating is changing. One of our students recently reported that she was ecstatic about having met the perfect man—over the Internet. She expressed reservations about meeting her perfect man in person because it might change this "perfect" relationship. Dating services have sprung up to introduce people via the Internet, and people put pictures and biographical webpages on the Internet. Whether cyberspace is limiting face-to-face contacts is a subject of much debate, but individuals do interact, whether through cyberspace or face-to-face, and form networks linking them to the social world.

The purpose of Chapter 5 is to lay the groundwork for understanding how we fit into the structure of our social world—exploring the link between the individual and the social structure. The process starts when we are born and continues with group activities as we join playgroups, preschool, and kindergarten groups. It broadens as we become members of larger organizations and bureaucracies within universities, workplaces, national political parties, and national and international religious organizations. First, we consider how networks and connections link individuals and groups to different levels of analysis. Then, we focus on micro-level interactions, meso-level groups, and meso- and macro-level organizations and bureaucracies. Finally, we consider macro-level national and global networks.

Networks and Connections in Our Social World

Try imagining yourself at the center of a web, such as a spider's web. Attach the threads that spread from the center first to family members and close friends, on out in the web to peers, then to friends of friends. Some thread connections are close and direct. Others are more distant but connect more and more people in an ever-expanding web. Now imagine trying to send a folder to someone you do not know. A researcher actually tried this experiment to discover how people are networked and how far removed citizens are from one another within the United States.

Perhaps you have heard it said that every American is only 6 steps (or degrees removed) from any other person in the country. This assertion is rooted in a study with evidence to support it. Stanley Milgram and his associates studied social networks by selecting several target people in different cities (Korte and Milgram 1970; Milgram 1967; Travers and Milgram 1969). Then, they identified "starting persons" in cities more than 1,000 miles away. Each starting person was given a folder with instructions and the target person's name, address, and occupation, as well as a few other facts. The starting person was instructed to pass the folder to someone he or she knew on a first-name basis who lived closer to or might have more direct networks with the target person than the starting person had. Although many folders never arrived at their destinations, one third did. The researchers were interested in how many steps were involved in the delivery of the folders that did arrive. The number of links in the chain to complete delivery ranged from 2 to 10, with most having 5 to 7 intermediaries. This is the source of the reference to "6 degrees of separation."

Networks are a bit like a spider's web—with many intersections and connective links.

More recently, research by scientists at Facebook and the University of Milan showed that the average number of acquaintances separating any two people in the world is now 4.74; in the United States the separation was only 4.37 people. The research was based on more than one tenth of the world's population (Markoff and Sengupta 2011). Clearly, networks are powerful linkages and create a truly small world.

Our **social networks**, then, refer to *individuals linked together by one or more social relationships, connecting us to the larger society.* We use our social network to get jobs or favors, often from people who are not very far removed from us in the web. Networks begin with micro-level contacts and exchanges between individuals in private interactions and expand to small groups, then to large (even global) organizations (Granovetter 2007; Tolbert and Hall 2008). The stronger people's networks are, the more influential they can be in a person's life. However, types of networks differ. For example, women's networks both for getting jobs and promotions and for succeeding in careers are broader (more extensive) than men's but also weaker than men's in helping with promotions. This is because men's networks are more "instrumental," that is, focused on the task at hand (Rothbard and Brett 2000). The web in Figure 5.1 illustrates that individuals are linked to other people, groups, organizations, and nations in the social world through networks.

Although network links can be casual and personal rather than based on official positions and channels, they place a person within the larger social structure, and it is from these networks that group ties emerge. People in networks talk to each other about common interests. This communication process creates linkages between clusters of people. For example, cyber networks on the Internet bring together people with common interests.

At the *micro level*, you develop close friends in college—bonds that may continue for the rest of your life. You introduce your friends from theater to your roommate's friends from the soccer team, and the network expands. These acquaintances from the soccer team may have useful information about which professors to avoid, how to make contacts to study abroad, and how to get a job in your field. Food cooperatives, self-help groups such as Alcoholics Anonymous and Weight Watchers, and computer user groups are examples of networks that connect individuals with common interests.

When you graduate from your university, you will be part of the university's alumni association, and this may become important to you for social contacts, business connections, or help with settling in a new location. When people refer to the Old Boy network, they are talking about contacts made through general association with people such as alumni. Men have used networks quite successfully in the past, and networks of working women—New Girl networks—are expanding rapidly. One of the reasons for the persistent inequality in our society is that members of certain groups may not have access to these privilege-enhancing networks.

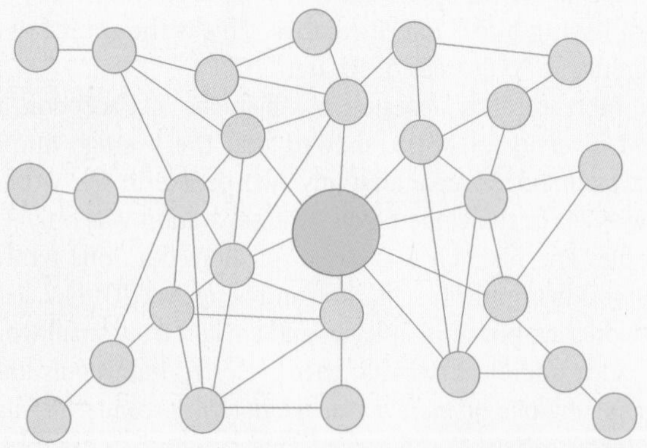

The golden circle represents an individual—perhaps you—and the blue dots represent your friends and acquaintances. Your network looks a bit like a web but is less complete in terms of every point connected to the adjacent point, since some of your friends do not know each other.

Figure 5.1 Networks: A Web of Connections

Thinking Sociologically

Map your social network web. What advantages do you get from your network? What economic or other benefits might your connections have for you?

Network links create new types of organizational forms at the *meso level*, such as those in the opening example of demonstrations and cyberspace. These networks cross societal, racial, ethnic, religious, and other lines that otherwise divide people. Networks also link groups at different levels of analysis. In fact, you are linked through networks to (1) micro-level local civic, sports, and religious organizations; (2) meso-level formal, complex organizations such as a political party or national fraternity and ethnic or social class subcultures; (3) the macro-level nation of which you are a citizen and to which you have formal obligations (such as the requirement that you go to war as a draftee if the government so decides); and (4) global entities such as the United Nations that use some of your donated resources or taxes to help impoverished people, tsunami victims, and earthquake survivors elsewhere in the world. These networks may open opportunities, but they also may create obligations that limit your freedom to make your own choices. As we move from micro-level interactions to larger meso- and macro-level organizations, interactions tend to become more formal. Formal organizations will be explored in the latter half of this chapter.

By linking individuals to people around the globe, Internet users have redefined networking through the creation of blogs, chat rooms, message boards, Listservs, newsgroups, and dozens of websites devoted to online networking ("Five Rules" 2005). Websites such as LinkedIn, Ecademy, Xing, and Plaxo offer business and professional networking, whereas other sites such as Myspace and Facebook focus on personal and social networking. There is even an international journal, *Social Networks,* that publishes interdisciplinary studies about the structure and impact of social networks and sites.

Some people find their partners using the Internet. Sites attract different users: Zoosk, Match.com, eHarmony, and OurTime.com. Consider the illustration from eHarmony on the next page. Together, these websites are revolutionizing the way people make friends, acquire information, and go about their daily lives.

Probably the most famous networking site is Facebook, and it became even more well known with the recent film

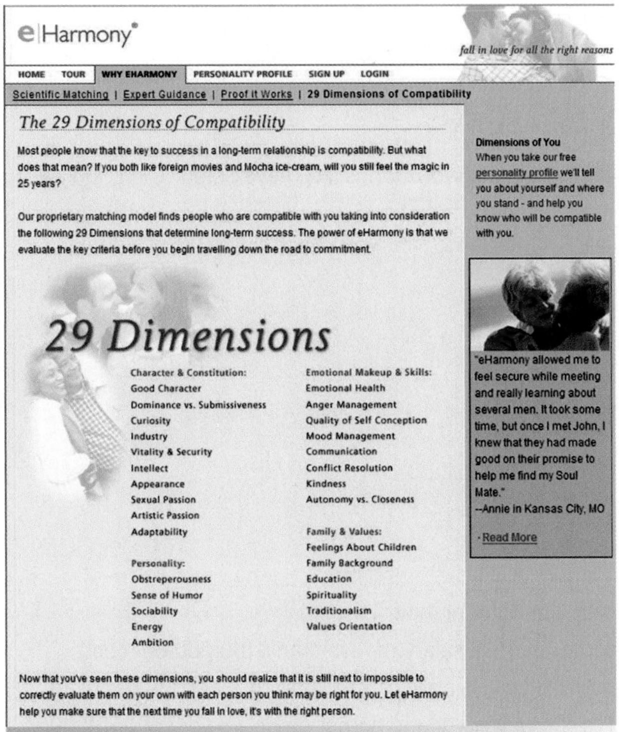

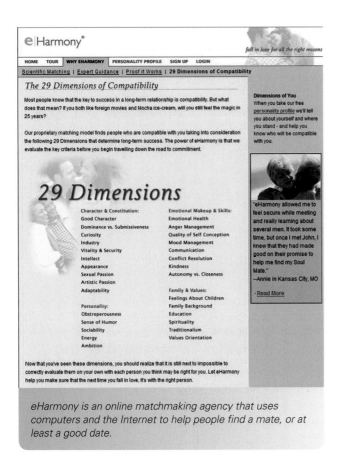

eHarmony is an online matchmaking agency that uses computers and the Internet to help people find a mate, or at least a good date.

about its founder, *The Social Network*. With members from all ages and places, Facebook truly does link the world. This social networking utility connects friends and friends of friends and people with common interests. There are more than 901 million active users around the world, with 1 in 7.7 people in the world having a Facebook account and 125 billion "friendships." The time logged per month on this single system exceeds 700 billion minutes. Users share blogs, news, web links, notes, photos, and more. Over 70% of users are outside of the home base, the United States, and Facebook is translated into 70 languages. Thirty-nine percent of business owners planned to market on Facebook in 2012. Some analysts argue that Facebook is changing the way we interact and connect with people (Bullas 2012; Facebook.com 2011).

Thinking Sociologically

Compare the way you communicate with your friends and the way your parents or grandparents communicate with their friends. Are there differences, and what are the advantages and disadvantages of each? Does one method result in closer relationships than another?

Like many other social networking sites, Facebook allows users to post a profile and pictures, create and join groups, and link to the profiles of "friends"—often a mixture of friends, colleagues, relatives, and acquaintances of varying levels and from various periods of life. Users can view the profiles of anyone within 4 degrees of separation—friends of friends of friends of friends—and search the network for people with the same friends, location, hometown, occupation, schools attended, interests, hobbies, or taste in movies, books, or television shows. In many cases, users link to dozens of friends and can access thousands of profiles around the world without reaching beyond the friends-of-friends level of connectivity. Once members are friends, they can view each other's "status," or read short messages declaring a user's location, recent activities, or personal thoughts. Benefits include getting to know acquaintances' movie preferences, music taste, and even contact information without having to have a face-to-face conversation. One downside is that some critics believe that social networking sites may provide a means for predators such as pedophiles to solicit sex from minors (Bahney 2009). As a way of examining your own networks, try the exercise in the next "Engaging Sociology" feature on page 144.

An even more recent development is the rapidly increasing popularity of Twitter, a microblogging website that allows users to post 140-character messages ("tweets") using their personal computer or the text messaging function on their mobile phone. Messages are mostly conversational (37.6%) and "pointless babble" (40%), but they also pass along news as well as self-promotion, and have been used by protesters to mobilize reform movements in oppressive countries (Infographics 2012). Interestingly, users have played a crucial role in developing Twitter, including inventing "hashtags" that indicate the subject of the tweet and allowing others to search for all tweets on the same topic (Johnson 2009).

The irony, of course, is that electronic technology has changed interactions by making them both more intimate and accessible—and less so. We can network through Facebook, and we can keep in touch constantly through text messaging. However, this means that people spend more time interacting with a piece of technology and less time interacting face-to-face. How ironic it is to see people at adjacent desks or offices, or with friends down the hall in the dorm, talking on cell phones or texting other friends. Sometimes those in physical proximity are ignored. Likewise, distance learning courses are in one sense less intimate—the instructor and the student may never meet face-to-face. Yet through Internet contact, the students may have more access to the ideas and the personal counsel of a professor than they would if they were in a large lecture class. We are only beginning to understand the implications of this technology on human interaction and on interpersonal skills.

Engaging Sociology

Networking via Facebook

If you are on Facebook, go to your Facebook account and note the number of friends you have listed. Then, look at them carefully to see if you can answer the following questions:

1. What is the age range of the friends on your list?
2. What is the gender composition of your list?
3. How many of each of the following racial or ethic groups are on your list:
   ____ African Americans
   ____ Whites of predominantly European heritage
   ____ Hispanics
   ____ Asians
   ____ Other (mixed)
4. What is the socioeconomic status of your friends?
   ____ Blue collar (families in which the primary wage earner works for an hourly wage)
   ____ Middle class (families in which the primary wage earner earns a salary of less than $100,000 per year)
   ____ Professional (families in which the primary wage earner earns a salary of $100,000 to $500,000 per year)
   ____ Highly affluent corporate executive (families in which the primary wage earner earns a salary of $500,000 to $10 million)
   ____ Upper class (families in which much of the family wealth is inherited and annual income is in the multimillions)

* * * * * * *

Engaging with sociological data:

- Now look at the data you have collected. What have you learned about your own networks?
- How much socioeconomic, age, and ethnic diversity do the data reveal about your networks?

Thinking Sociologically

How do Facebook and Twitter shape your interactions with friends?

The Process of Interaction: Connections at the Micro Level

Each morning as you rouse yourself and prepare for the challenges ahead, you consider what the day might bring, what activities and obligations are on your calendar, and who you will talk to. As you lift your limp, listless body from a horizontal to an upright position and blood begins coursing through your veins, thoughts of the day's events begin to penetrate your semiconscious state. A cup of caffeine, cold water on the face, and a mouth-freshening brush bring you to the next stage of awareness. You evaluate what is in store for you, what roles you will play during the day, and with whom you are likely to interact.

Should you wear the ragged but comfy jeans and T-shirt? Perhaps that will not work today, since there is that class trip to the courthouse. Something a bit less casual is in order. Then, you are meeting with your English professor to discuss the last essay you wrote. What approach should you take? You could act insulted that she failed to think of you as a future J. K. Rowling or Suzanne Collins. Maybe a meek, mild "Please tell me what I did wrong, I tried so hard" approach would work. She seems a nice, sympathetic sort. After class, there is a group of students who chat in the hall. It would be nice to meet them. What strategy should you use? Try to enter the conversation? Tell a joke? Make small talk? Talk to the students individually so you can get to know each before engaging the whole group? Each of these responses is a strategy for interaction, and each might elicit different reactions.

The Elements of Social Interaction

"Let's have a drink!" Such a simple comment might have many different meanings. We could imagine two children playing together, men going to a bar after work, a couple of friends getting together to celebrate an event, fraternity brothers at a party, or a couple on a date. In all these cases, *social interaction* consists of two or more individuals purposefully relating to each other.

"Having a drink," like all *interaction*, involves action on the part of two or more individuals, is directed toward a goal that people hope to achieve, and takes place in a social context that includes cultural norms and rules governing the situation, the setting, and other factors shaping the way people perceive the circumstances. The action, goal, and social context help us interpret the meaning of statements such as "Let's have a drink."

The norms governing the particular social context tell us what is right and proper behavior. Recall from Chapter 3 that norms are rules that guide human interactions. People assume that others will share their interpretation of a situation. These shared assumptions about proper behavior provide the cues for your own behavior that become a part of your social self. You look for cues to proper behavior and rehearse in your mind your actions and reactions. In the "Let's have a drink" scenario, you assume that the purpose of the interaction is understood. What dress, mannerisms, speech, and actions you consider appropriate depend on expectations from your socialization and past experience in similar situations, for in modern societies, a range of behaviors and responses is possible in any social situation (Parsons 1951b).

Although most people assume that talking, or *verbal communication*, is the primary means of communication between individuals, words themselves are actually only a part of the message. In most contexts, they make up less than 50% of the communication, and only 35% of the emotional content of the message (Birdwhistell 1970). **Nonverbal communication**—*interactions without words using facial expressions, the head, eye contact, body posture, gestures, touch, walk, status symbols, and personal space*—makes up the rest, estimated to be between 50% and 70% of all communication (Cherry 2012; Givens 2012). These important elements of communication are learned through socialization as we grow up. Although one may master another written and verbal language, it is much more difficult to learn the nonverbal language. People who travel to a country other than their own often use gestures to be understood. Like spoken language, nonverbal gestures vary from culture to culture, as illustrated in the photos on the next page. Communicating with others in one's own language can be difficult enough. Add to this the complication of individuals with different language, cultural expectations, and personalities using different nonverbal messages, and misunderstandings are likely. Nonverbal messages are the hardest part of another language to master because they are specific to a culture and learned through socialization.

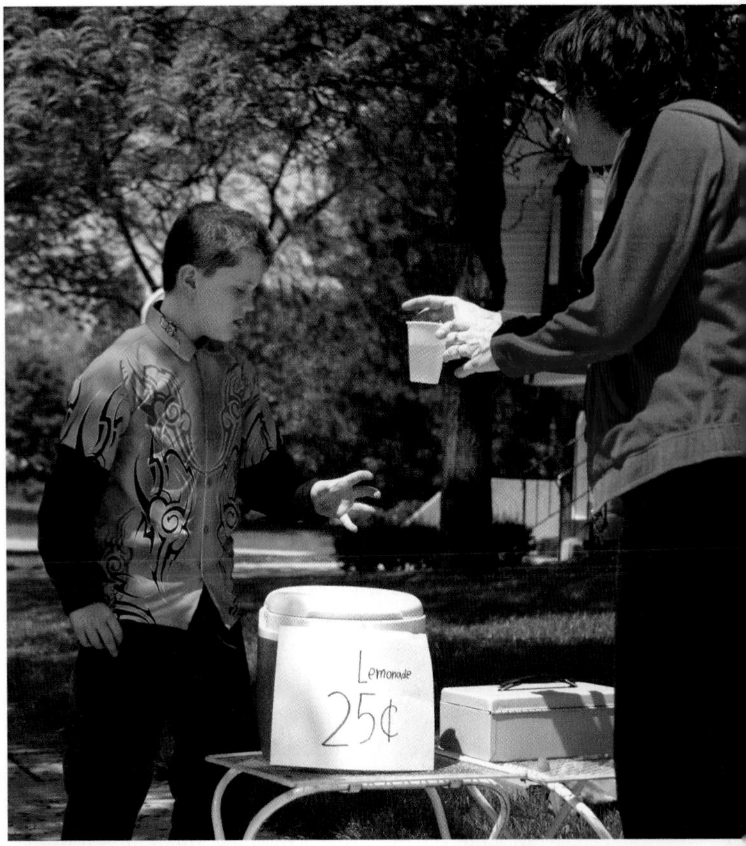

The same words, "Let's have a drink," may have very different meanings in different social interaction contexts. Humans must learn not only the language but also how to read interactional settings.

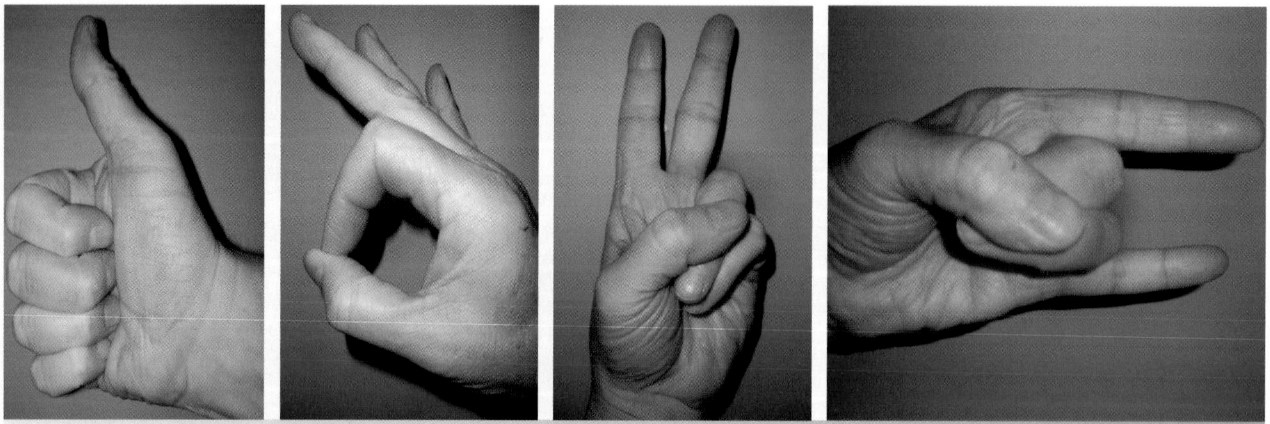

Gestures are symbolic forms of interaction. However, these gestures can have entirely different meanings in different cultures. A friendly gesture in one culture may be obscene in the next.

Consider the following example: You are about to wrap up a major business deal. You are pleased with the results of your negotiations, so you give your hosts the thumb-and-finger A-OK sign. In Brazil, you have just grossly insulted your hosts—it is the equivalent of giving them "the finger." In Japan, you have asked for a small bribe. In the south of France, you have indicated the deal is worthless. Although your spoken Portuguese, Japanese, or French may have been splendid, your nonverbal language did not cut the deal. Intercultural understanding is more than being polite and knowing the language.

Another example of nonverbal language involves personal space. Most people have experienced social situations, such as parties, where someone gets too close. One person backs away, the other moves in again, and the first backs away again—into a corner or a table with nowhere else to go. Perhaps the person approaching was aggressive or rude, but it is also possible that the person held different cultural norms or expectations in relation to personal space.

The amount of personal space an individual needs to be comfortable or proper varies with the cultural setting, gender, status, and social context of the interaction. Individuals from Arab countries are comfortable at very close range. However, people from Scandinavia or the United States need a great deal of personal space. Consider the following four categories of social distance and social space based on a study of U.S. middle-class people. Each category applies to particular types of activity (Hall and Hall 1992):

1. *Intimate distance:* from zero distance (touching, embracing, kissing) to 18 inches. Children may play together in such close proximity, and adults and children may maintain this distance, but between adults, this intimate contact is reserved for private and affectionate relationships.

2. *Personal distance:* from 18 inches to 4 feet. This is the public distance for most friends and for informal interactions with acquaintances.

3. *Social distance:* from 4 feet to 12 feet. This is the distance for impersonal business relations, such as a job interview or class discussions between students and a professor. This distance implies a more formal interaction or a significant difference in the status of the two people.

4. *Public distance:* 12 feet and beyond. This is the distance most public figures use for addressing others, especially in formal settings and in situations in which the speaker has a very high status.

Personal space also communicates one's position in relation to others. The higher the position, the greater the control of space. In social situations, individuals with higher positions spread out, prop their feet up, put their arms out, and use more sweeping gestures. Women and men differ with regard to personal space and other forms of nonverbal language. For instance, women are more sensitive to subtle cues such as status differences and the use of personal space (Henley, Hamilton, and Thorne 2000; Knapp and Hall 1997).

Sociologists study interactions, including verbal and nonverbal communication, to explain this very basic link between humans and the group. The following theoretical perspectives focus on the micro level of analysis in attempting to explain interactions.

Thinking Sociologically

What are some complications that you or your friends have had in interactions involving cross-cultural contacts or male-female miscommunication? What might help clarify communication in these cases?

In North America, friends interact at a close distance—1.5 to 4 feet—as in the top photo. A more formal setting calls for a distance of 4 to 12 feet, and that space can feel cold and intimidating. What is the message at the meeting in the lower photo?

When a respected person speaks in a public setting, listeners are expected to keep themselves at a greater distance.

Theoretical Perspectives on the Interaction Process

How many people do you interact with each day, and what happens in each of these interactions? You probably have not given the question much thought or analysis, but that process is exactly what fascinates interaction theorists. Why do two people interact in the first place? What determines whether the interaction will continue or stop? How do two people know how to behave and what to say around each other? What other processes are taking place as they "talk" to each other? Why do people interact differently with different people? What governs the way they make sense of messages and how they respond to them? These questions interest sociologists because they address the basic interaction processes that result in group formations that range in size from dyads (two people) to large organizations. The following section explores theories that attempt to provide explanations for interactions.

Symbolic Interaction Theory

Symbolic interaction theory focuses on how individuals interpret situations, such as "Let's have a drink," and how this, in turn, affects their actions. Symbolic interactionism is based on the idea that our humanness derives from the mutual impact we have upon each other. Humans act toward things on the basis of the meanings those things have for them. The meanings are derived by individuals as they interact with others. Hence, humans are above all symbol-creating and symbol-modifying creatures, for symbols have meaning beyond their own fleeting existence. Symbols are the key to understanding human life, for we go about the task of fitting our actions together because of shared perceptions or shared meanings. Meaning is not inherent in the events of life; it is created by individuals and communicated among them. Through our mental manipulation of symbols and interpretation of meaning, we *define situations* and determine how we should act in a given situation or how we should make sense of it (Charon 2010; Hewitt and Shulman 2011).

In the first Obama-Romney debate before the 2012 presidential election, Mitt Romney said on his first day in office he would have extensive meetings with Democrats to seek common ground. President Obama responded, "First of all, I think Governor Romney is going to have a busy first day, because he is also going to repeal ObamaCare, which is not going to be popular with Democrats." If you were sitting with Republicans when that comment was made, it may have been interpreted as "snarky" or snide, but a group of Democrats may well have hooted at what they interpreted as humor directed at Romney's naiveté about the office of President. Who you were near would change how this comment was interpreted—a humorous quip or an insulting condescension.

Symbolic interactionists see humans as active agents who consciously, deliberately, and directly fashion their personal and collective histories. These theorists emphasize the part that language and gestures play in the formation of the mind, the self, and society. More than any other theory in the social sciences, symbolic interactionism stresses the agency—the active decision-making role—of humans within their societies (Charon 2010; Hewitt and Schulman 2011).

In ambiguous situations, humans look to others to see how they have made sense of the situation or interaction taking place—is it frightening, funny, annoying, boring, or inspiring? If someone behaves in a manner that is unconventional—that is weird or strange—it could be cause for alarm or humor or disgust. Once one person defines the situation and acts, especially if that person is highly regarded or very self-confident, others will very often accept that response as "normal." This is how social interaction is involved in the social construction of reality—the social process of defining what is true or real or valid (Berger and Luckmann 1966; Hewitt and Shulman 2011; O'Brien 2011).

One approach to interaction analysis is called *dramaturgy*. Dramaturgy theorists analyze life as a play or drama on a stage, with scripts and props and scenes to be played. The play we put on creates an impression for our audience. In everyday life, individuals learn new lines to add to their scripts through the socialization process, including influence from family, friends, films, and television. They perform these scripts for social audiences to maintain certain images, much like the actors in a play.

Consider the following familiar example: Every day in high schools around the world, teenagers go on stage—in the classroom or the hallway with friends and peers and with adult authorities who may later be giving grades or writing letters of reference. The props these students use include their style of clothing; a backpack with books, paper, pen, and laptop; and a smile or a "cool" look. The set is the classroom, the cafeteria, and perhaps the athletic field. The script is shaped by the actors: Teachers may establish an authoritarian relationship, classmates engage in competition for grades, or peers seek social status among companions. The actors include hundreds of teens struggling with issues of identity, changing bodies, and attempts to avoid humiliation. Each individual works to assert and maintain an image through behavior, clothing, language, and friends.

As individuals perform according to society's script for the situation, they take into consideration how their actions will influence others. By carefully managing the impression they wish the acquaintance to receive—a process called *impression management*—people hope to create an impression that works to their advantage. In other words, the actors are trying to manipulate how others see them, especially as it relates to others' opinion of them.

Most of the time, we engage in front-stage behavior, the behavior safest with casual acquaintances because it is scripted and acted for the public and it presents a definition of self we hope others will accept as the "real me." A poor or unacceptable performance will be embarrassing both for us and for our audience. People develop strategies to cover up their weaknesses or failures, such as laughing at a joke even though they do not understand it.

Each part or character an individual plays, and each audience, requires a different script. For example, interacting with peers at a bar differs from meeting a professor in her office. We learn to avoid those performance activities that are likely to result in humiliation or failure or that contradict the image we have worked to create. At home or with close friends with whom we are more intimate, we engage in "backstage behavior," letting our feelings show and behaving in ways that might be unacceptable for other audiences (Goffman 1967, [1959] 2001). Dramaturgical analysis can be a useful approach to broadening our understanding of interactions.

Thinking Sociologically

Describe some ways in which your life feels like a dramatic production. Identify front-stage and backstage behaviors.

Rational Choice Theory

Rational choice or exchange theorists look at a different aspect of interaction—why relationships continue, considering the rewards and costs of interaction for the individual. They argue that the choices we make are guided by reason.

If the benefits of the interaction are high and if the costs are low, the interaction will be valued and sustained. Every interaction involves calculations of self-interest, expectations of reciprocity (a mutual exchange of favors), and decisions to act in ways that have current or eventual payoff for the individual (Smelser 1992).

Reciprocity is a key concept for rational choice theorists. The idea is that if a relationship is imbalanced over a period of time, it will become unsatisfying. As theorists from this perspective see human interaction, each person tends to keep a mental ledger of who "owes" whom. If I have done you a favor, you owe me one. If you have helped me in some way, I have an obligation to you. If I then fail to comply or even do something that hurts you, you will likely view it as a breach in the relationship and have negative feelings toward me. Moreover, if there is an imbalance in what we each bring to the relationship, one person may have more power in the relationship.

In the study of families, scholars use the "principle of least interest," which states that the person with the least interest in the relationship has the most power. The person with the least interest is the person who brings more resources (financial, physical, social, personal) to the relationship and receives less. That person could easily leave. The person who offers less to the relationship or who has fewer assets is more dependent on the relationship. This person is likely to give in when there is a disagreement, so the person with less interest gets her or his way. Lack of reciprocity can be important for how relationships develop. It is this idea that particularly interests rational choice theorists.

Sometimes a person may engage in a behavior where there is little likelihood of reciprocity from the other person—as in cases where the behavior is altruistic or self-giving. Rational choice theorists would argue that there is still a benefit. It might be enhanced feelings of self-worth, recognition from others, hope for a place in heaven, or just the expectation of indirect reciprocity. This latter notion is that the person I help might not help me, but if I am in a similar situation, I could hope for and expect someone to come to my assistance (Gouldner 1960; Turner 2003).

Social Status: Individuals' Link to Groups

A social **status** is *a social position in society. We interact with others and they react to us based in part on the statuses we hold.* We interact differently when in the daughter status with our parents, in a student status with our professor, or in friend status with our peers. Each individual holds many statuses, and this combination held by any individual is called a *status set:* for instance, daughter, mother, worker, teammate, student.

Each individual's unique status set is the product of family relationships and groups that the individual joins (a university or club) or into which she or he is born (an ethnic group or gender). Many statuses change with each new stage of life, such as student, work, marital, or parenthood status. Statuses at each stage of life and the interactions that result from those statuses form each person's unique social world.

Statuses affect the type of interactions individuals have. In some interactions (as with classmates), people are equals. In other situations, individuals have interchanges with people who hold superior or inferior statuses. If you are promoted to supervisor, your interaction with former peers and subordinates will change. Consider the possible interactions shown in Figure 5.2, in which the first relationship is between equals and the others are between those with unequal statuses.

With a friend, these status relationships are constantly being negotiated and bargained: "I'll do what you want tonight, but tomorrow I choose." By contrast, when individuals are in dominant or subordinate positions, power or deference affects their interactions. Studies of interaction between males and females find that gender, power, and hierarchical relationships are important in determining interaction patterns. The more powerful person, such as one who has more wealth or privilege, can interrupt in a conversation with his or her partner and show less deference in the interaction (Kim et al. 2007; Reid and Ng 2006; Wood 2008).

People have no control over certain statuses they hold. These **ascribed statuses** are *often assigned at birth and do not change during an individual's lifetime.* Some examples are gender and race or ethnicity. Ascribed statuses are assigned to a person without regard for personal desires, talents, or choices. In some societies, one's caste or the social position into which one is born (e.g., a slave) is an ascribed status because it is usually impossible to change.

Achieved status, on the other hand, is *chosen or earned by the decisions one makes and sometimes by personal ability.* Attaining a higher education, for example, improves an

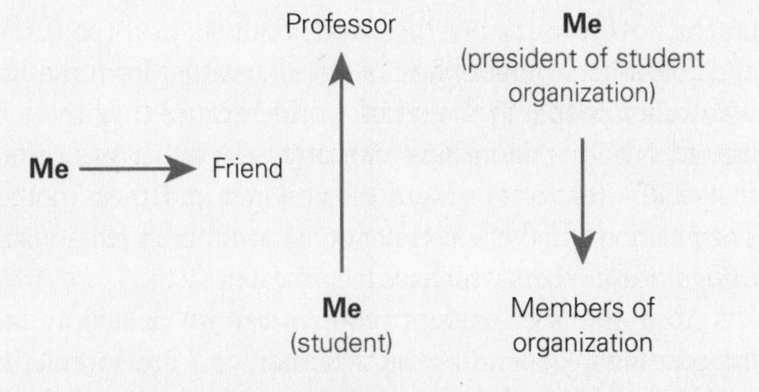

Figure 5.2 Types of Status Relationships Experienced by You

individual's occupational opportunities and thus his or her achieved status. Being a guitarist in a band is an achieved status and so is being a prisoner in jail, for both are earned positions based on the person's own decisions and actions.

At a particular time in life or under certain circumstances, one of an individual's statuses may become most important and take precedence over others, called a **master status**. Whether it is an occupation, parental status, or something else, it dominates and shapes much of an individual's life, activities, self-concept, and position in the community for a period of time. For a person who is very ill, for instance, that illness may occupy a master status, needing constant attention from doctors, influencing social relationships, and determining what that person can do in family, work, or community activities.

Thinking Sociologically

What are your statuses? Which ones are ascribed, and which are achieved statuses? Do you have a master status? How do these statuses affect the way you interact with others in your network of relationships?

The Relationship Between Status and Role

Every status (position) in your network includes certain behaviors and obligations as you carry out the **roles**, *the expected behaviors, rights, obligations, responsibilities, and privileges assigned to a social status.* Roles are the dynamic, action part of statuses in a society. They define how each individual in an interaction is expected to act (Linton 1937). The roles of an individual holding the status of "college student" include behaviors and obligations such as attending classes, studying, taking tests, writing papers, and interacting with professors and other students. Individuals enter most statuses with some knowledge of how to carry out the roles dictated by their culture. Through the process of socialization, individuals learn roles by observing others, watching television and films, reading, and being taught how to carry out the status. Both statuses (positions) and roles (behavioral obligations of the status) form the link with other people in the social world because they must be carried out in relationships with others. A father has certain obligations (or roles) toward his children and their mother. The position of father exists not on its own but in relationship to significant others who have reciprocal ties.

Your status of student requires certain behaviors and expectations, depending on whether you are interacting with a dean, a professor, an adviser, a classmate, or a prospective employer. This is because the role expectations of the status of student vary as one interacts with specific people in other statuses. In Figure 5.3, the student is the subject, and the others are those with whom the student interacts in the status of student.

Within a group, individuals may hold both formal and informal statuses. One illustration is the formal status of high school students, each of whom plays a number of informal roles in cliques that are not part of the formal school structure. A student may be known as a jock, a nerd, a loner, a goth, a clown, a prep, an outcast, or the life of the party. Each of these roles takes place in a status relationship with others: teacher-student, peer-peer, coach-athlete. The connections between statuses, roles, and environment are illustrated in Table 5.1.

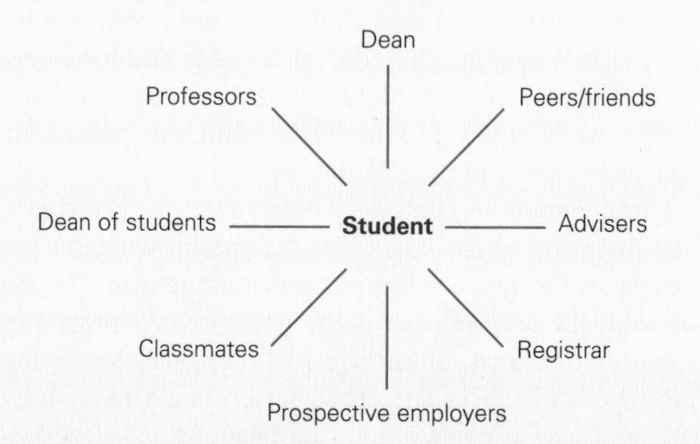

Figure 5.3 Connections Students Have With Reciprocal Status Holders

Table 5.1 The Relationship Between Statuses and Roles

Status (position in structure)	*Role (behavior, rights, obligations)*
Student	***Formal***
	Study, attend class, turn in assignments
	Informal
	Be a jock, clown, cut-up; abuse alcohol on weekends
Parent	***Formal***
	Provide financial support, child care
	Informal
	Be a playmate, lead family activities
Employee	***Formal***
	Work responsibilities: punctuality, doing one's tasks
	Informal
	Befriend coworkers, join lunch group, represent company in bowling league

Photo Essay

Work Status and Roles Around the World

Positions people carry out in different cultures depend on tasks important in that culture. Upper left: The two women from Ghana carry yams, a staple food, from the fields. Upper right: police officer begins his local beat. Middle left: Men in Ghana have the traditional male role of hand-stamping designs onto cloth. Middle right, these Asian women fulfill their roles as entrepreneurs at the market located on the water. Lower left: Men in China use traditional methods to keep the roads open. Lower right: Fishermen in India pull in a catch for their livelihood.

Social networks may be based on ascribed characteristics, such as age, race, ethnicity, and gender, or on achieved status, such as education, occupation, or common interests. These links, in turn, form the basis for social interactions and group structures (Hall 2002). However, at times, individuals cannot carry out their roles as others expect them to, creating role strain or conflict.

Role Strain and Role Conflict

Most people have faced times in their lives when they simply could not carry out all the obligations of a status, such as student—write two papers, study adequately for two exams, complete the portfolio for the studio art class, finish the reading assignments for five classes, and memorize lines for the oral interpretation class, all in the same week. Every status carries role expectations, the way the status is supposed to be carried out according to generally accepted societal or group norms. Yet in these cases, individuals face **role strain**, the *tension between roles within one of the statuses*. Role strain causes the individual to be pulled in many directions by various obligations of the single status, as in the example regarding the status of "student." Another such strain is often experienced by first-time fathers as they attempt to reconcile their role expectations of fathering with ideas held by their wives.

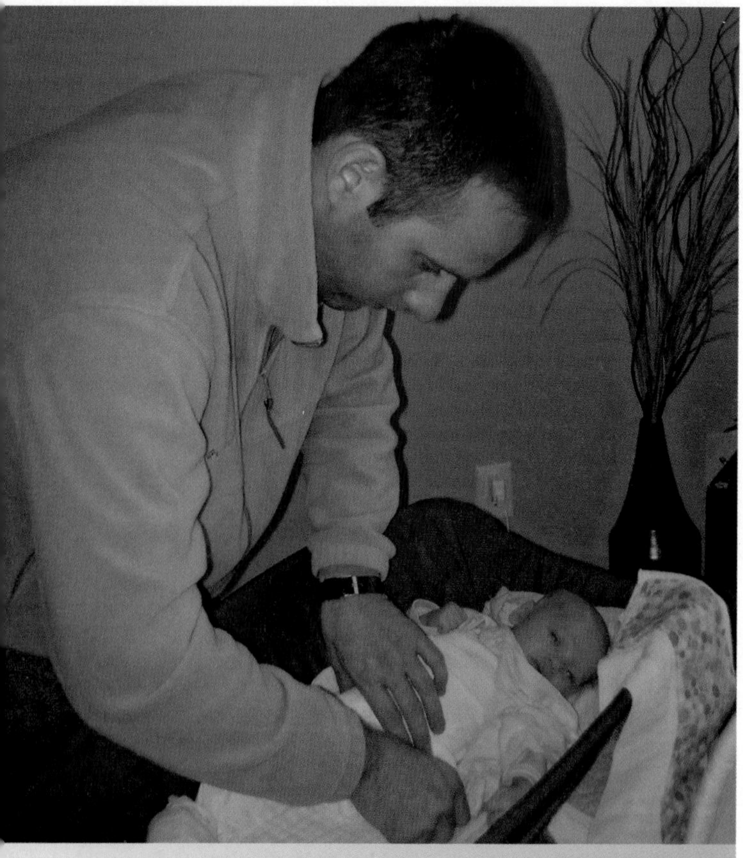

Parenting roles often need to be negotiated. In some traditional families in the past, the status had more explicit role expectations, and fathers were rarely expected to change diapers.

To resolve role strain, individuals cope in one of several ways: pass the problem off lightly (and thus not do well in classes); consider the dilemma humorous; become highly focused and pull a couple of all-nighters to get everything done; or become stressed, tense, fretful, and immobilized because of the strain. Most often, individuals set priorities based on their values and make decisions accordingly: "I'll work hard in the class for my major and let another one slide."

Role conflict refers to *conflict between the roles of two or more social statuses*. It differs from role strain in that conflict is *between* the roles of two or more statuses. The conflict can come from within an individual or be imposed from outside. College athletes face role conflicts from competing demands on their time (Adler and Adler 1991, 2004). They must complete their studies on time, attend practices and be prepared for games, perhaps attend meetings of a Greek house to which they belong, and get home for a little brother's birthday. Similarly, a student may be going to school, holding down a part-time job to help make ends meet, and raising a family. If the student's child gets sick, the status of parent comes into conflict with that of student and worker. In the case of role conflict, the person may choose—or be informed by others—which status is the master status. Figure 5.4 illustrates the difference between role conflict and role strain.

Statuses and the accompanying roles come and go. You will not always be a student, and someday you may be a parent and hold a professional job. Certainly, you will retire from your job. For instance, as people grow older, they disengage from some earlier statuses in groups and engage in new and different statuses and roles.

Our statuses connect us and make us integral parts of meso- and macro-level organizations. Our place within the social world, then, is guaranteed, even obligatory, because of statuses we hold—within small groups (family and peers), in larger groups and organizations (school and work organizations), in institutions (political parties or religious denominations), and ultimately as citizens of the society and the world (workers in global corporations). Each of these statuses connects us to a group setting.

Thinking Sociologically

Using Figure 5.4, fill in the statuses you hold in your social world and the roles you perform in these statuses. Then, list three examples of role conflicts and three examples of role strains that you experience.

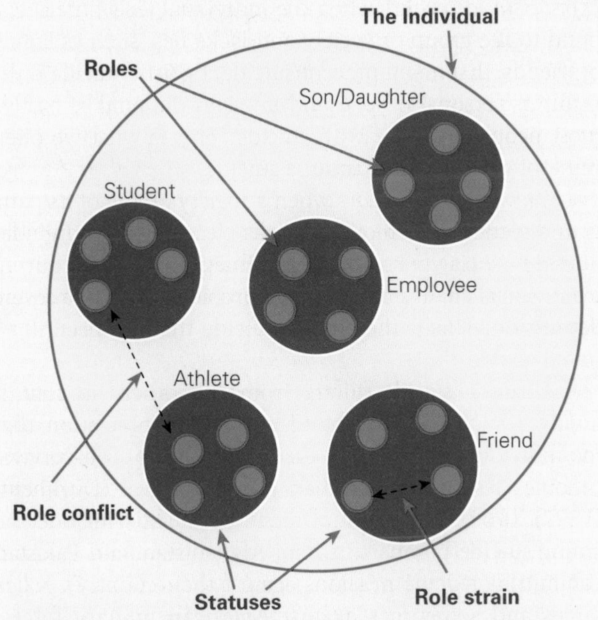

Figure 5.4 Role Strain and Role Conflict

Note: Each individual has many statuses: a status set. Each status has many roles: a role set. A conflict between two roles of the same status is a role strain. A conflict between the roles of two different statuses is a role conflict.

Groups in Our Social World: The Micro-Meso Connection

Groups refer to *units involving two or more people who interact with each other because of shared common interests, goals, experiences, and needs* (Drafke 2008). As we have seen throughout the early chapters of this book, humans are social beings. Few of us can survive without others; we constantly interact with the family we are born into, our socialization occurs in groups, and we depend on the group for survival. Groups are necessary for protection, to obtain food, to manufacture goods, and to get jobs done. Groups meet our social needs for belonging and acceptance, support us throughout our lives, and place restrictions on us. Groups can be small, intimate environments—micro-level interactions such as a group of friends—or they can become quite large as they morph into meso-level organizations. In any case, it is through our group memberships that the micro and meso levels are connected.

The members of a group feel they belong to the group and are seen by others as thinking, feeling, and behaving with a common goal. Members consider each other's behavior and engage in structured interaction patterns. Groups have defined memberships and ways to take in new members. They also have rules that guide the behavior of members. In this section, we look at several questions: What are groups, and how do they vary? How is interaction carried out in small groups? What is the importance of groups for individuals?

Not all collections of individuals are groups, however. For instance, your family is a group, but people shopping at a mall or waiting for a bus are not a group because they do not regularly interact or acknowledge shared common interests.

Groups form through a series of succeeding steps. Consider people forming a soccer team: The first step is initial interaction. If membership is rewarding and meets individuals' needs, the individuals will attempt to maintain the benefits the group provides (Mills 1984). A group of people interacts to form this team. In the second step, a collective goal emerges. For example, team members may work together to plan practice and game schedules, buy uniforms, and advertise the games. Groups establish their own goals and pursue them, trying to be free from external controls or constraints. In the third and final step, the group attempts to expand its collective goals by building on the former steps and by pursuing new goals. For example, the team may reach out to new players, to coaches, and to supporters for funding.

The Importance of Groups for the Individual

Groups are essential parts of human life (micro level) and of organizational structures (meso and macro levels). They establish our place in the social world, providing us with support and a sense of belonging. Few individuals can survive without groups. This becomes clear when we consider two problems: anomie and suicide.

Anomie and Suicide

Who commits suicide? Did you know that the answer to this is closely related to an individual's group affiliations? With the rapid changes and continued breakdown of institutional structures in Afghanistan as rival warlords vie for power over territory and in Libya as religious and political groups vie for power, horrific problems abound. Civil disorder, conflicts for power, suicide bombings, murder of police officers, and looting are frequent occurrences. Social controls (police and military forces) are strained, and leaders struggle to cope with the chaos. The result of this breakdown in norms is **anomie**, *the state of normlessness that occurs when the rules for behavior in society break down under extreme stress from rapid social change or conflict* (Merton 1938).

Suicide seems like an individual act, committed because of personal problems. However, the early sociologist Émile Durkheim took a unique approach to this problem. In his volume, *Suicide* (Durkheim [1897] 1964), he discussed the social factors contributing to suicide. Using existing statistical data to determine suicide rates in European populations, Durkheim looked at variables such as sex, age, religion, nationality, and the season in which the suicide was committed. His findings were surprising to many, and they demonstrate that individual problems cannot be understood without also understanding the group context in which they occur.

Durkheim found that Protestants committed suicide more often than Catholics, urban folks more often than people living in small communities, people in highly developed and complex societies more frequently than those in simple societies, and people who lived alone more than those situated in families. The key variable linking these findings was the degree to which an individual was integrated into a group, that is, the degree of social bond with others. During war, for instance, people generally felt a sense of common cause and belonging to their country. Thus, suicide rates were greater during peacetime because the social climate offered less cause for feeling that bond.

Jorge Parra was disabled in a General Motors plant in Colombia, South America, and subsequently fired. He and more than a dozen other injured workers protested for more than a year outside the U.S. Embassy in Colombia about being fired for a disability that occurred on the job and for lack of disability compensation. In the fall of 2012, some of the men went on a hunger strike and sewed their mouths closed so they could ingest only liquids. They have bonded with each other and have supportive families. Jorge decided he would fast until death, if necessary, to support the cause. As of January 2013 he had gone almost 70 days without food. The willingness to die voluntarily as part of solidarity with a group is called altruistic suicide.

Durkheim described three distinct types of suicide. *Egoistic suicide* occurs when the individual feels little social bond to the group or society and lacks ties, such as family or friends, that might prevent suicide. Egoistic suicide is the result of personal despair and involves the kind of motive most people associate with suicide. This is what we often think of when we hear about a suicide.

Anomic suicide occurs when a society or one of its parts is in disorder or turmoil and lacks clear norms and guidelines for social behavior. This situation is likely during major social change or economic problems such as a severe depression. This is the type of suicide that has been illustrated above.

Altruistic suicide differs from the others in that it involves such a strong bond and group obligation that the individual is willing to die for the group. Self-survival becomes less important than group survival (Durkheim [1897] 1964). Examples of altruistic suicide include the young suicide bombers in Iraq, Afghanistan, and Pakistan committing suicide missions against their country's police forces and sometimes against American military forces, which they have defined as invading forces. These suicides usually occur in societies or religious groups that have very clear norms and high levels of consensus about values arising from their religious or political commitments.

Many sociologists have studied suicide, and while not all studies support Durkheim's original findings, they do support the general finding that suicide rates are strongly influenced by social and psychological factors that can operate at the meso or macro level. Suicide is not a purely individualistic decision (Hall 2002; Nolan, Triplett, and McDonough 2010; Pescosolido and Georgianna 1989).

No individual is an island. The importance of groups and social influence from various levels in the system is an underlying theme of this text. Groups are essential to human life, but to understand them more fully, we must understand the various kinds of groups in which humans participate.

Types of Groups

Each of us belongs to several types of groups. Some groups provide intimacy and close relationships, whereas others do not. Some are required affiliations, and others are voluntary. Some provide personal satisfaction, and others are obligatory or necessary for survival. The following discussion points out several types of groups and the reasons why individuals belong to them.

Primary groups are characterized by cooperation among close, intimate, long-term relationships—the most micro level. Your family members and best friends, school classmates, and close work associates are all of primary importance in your everyday life. Primary groups provide a sense of belonging and shared identity. Group members care about you, and you care about the other group members, creating a sense of loyalty. Approval and disapproval from the primary group influence the activities you choose to pursue. Belonging to the group is the main reason for membership. The group is of intrinsic value—enjoyed for its own sake—rather than for some utilitarian value such as making money.

For individuals, primary groups provide an anchor point in society. You were born into a primary group—your family. You hold many statuses and play a variety of roles in primary relationships—those of spouse, parent, child, sibling, relative, close friend, and so on. You meet with other members face-to-face or keep in touch on a regular basis and know a great deal about their lives. What makes them happy or angry? What are sensitive issues? In primary groups you share values, say what you think, let down your hair, dress as you like, and share your concerns and emotions, your successes and failures (Goffman 1967, [1959] 2001). Charles H. Cooley ([1909] 1983), who first discussed the term *primary group*, saw these relationships as the source of close human feelings and emotions—love, cooperation, and concern.

Secondary groups are *those with formal, impersonal, and businesslike relationships, often temporary, and based on a specific limited purpose or goal.* In the modern world, people cannot always live under the protective wing of primary group relationships. Secondary groups are usually large and task oriented because they have a specific purpose to achieve and focus on accomplishing a goal. As children grow, they move from the security and acceptance of primary groups—the home and neighborhood peer group—to a secondary group—the large school classroom, where each child is one of many students vying for the teacher's approval and competing for rewards. Similarly, the job world requires formal relations and procedures: applications, interviews, contracts. Employment is based on specific skills, training, and job knowledge, and there may be a trial period. In Western cultures, we assume that people should be hired not because of personal friendship or nepotism but rather for their competence to carry out the role expectations in the position.

Because each individual in a secondary group carries out a specialized task, communication between members is often specialized as well. Contacts with doctors, store clerks, and even professors are generally formal and impersonal parts of organizational life. Sometimes associations with secondary groups are long lasting, sometimes of short duration—as in the courses you are taking this term. Secondary groups operate at the meso and macro levels of our social world, but they affect individuals at the micro level.

As societies modernize, they evolve from small towns and close, primary relationships to predominantly urban areas with more formal, secondary relationships. In the postindustrial world, as family members are scattered across countries and around the world, secondary relationships have come to play ever greater roles in people's lives. Large work organizations may provide day care, health clinics, financial planning, courses to upgrade skills, and sports leagues.

In the top photo, members of a Chinese family enjoy one another's company as they play a game of mah-jongg. In the lower photo, these teens enjoy being with friends at a cookout at the beach. In both cases, the interpersonal connections are valued for intrinsic reasons—not for some utilitarian gain.

Small micro-level and large macro-level groups often occur together. Behind most successful secondary groups are primary groups. Consider the small work group within a large organization that eats together or goes out for a beer on Friday afternoons. These relationships help individuals feel a part of the larger organization, just as residents of large urban areas have small groups of neighborhood friends.

Megachurches began in the 1950s, and some have more than 10,000 members. In fact, the largest church in

Even Buddhist nuns, who spend much of their lives devoted to private meditation, need the support and solidarity of a group.

the world (Yoido Full Gospel Church in South Korea) has nearly 850,000 members. About half of the megachurches are nondenominational Protestant, and the rest are related to evangelical or Pentecostal groups. The focus of programming is on creating small support groups (primary groups) within the huge congregation (PBS 2012; Sargeant 2000; Thumma and Travis 2007). In a formal setting such as a university or corporation, primary groups can play a major role in making people feel they belong. For instance, many students live with roommates at the university, study with a small group, go out on Friday nights with friends, and regularly have meals with close friends. Table 5.2 summarizes some of the dimensions of primary and secondary groups.

Problems in primary groups can affect performance in secondary groups. Consider the problems of a student who has an argument with a significant other or roommate, or experiences a failure of his or her family support system due to divorce or other problems. Self-concepts and social skills diminish during times of family stress and affect group relationships in other parts of one's life (Drafke 2008).

Thinking Sociologically

In the past, raising children was considered a family task, done by the primary family group. Today, many children are in child care settings, often run by secondary groups. What differences do you see between the experiences a child receives in a family and those received in child care? What might be the advantages and disadvantages of each? Can a secondary group provide care comparable with that provided by a family? Can the secondary group provide better care than do abusive families?

Reference groups are *composed of members who act as role models and establish standards against which members measure their conduct.* Individuals look to reference groups to set guidelines for behavior and decision making. The term is often used to refer to models in one's chosen career field. Students in premed, nursing, computer science, business, or sociology programs watch the behavior patterns of those who have become successful professionals in their chosen career. When people make the transition from student to professional, they adopt clothing, time schedules, salary expectations, and other characteristics from reference groups. Professional organizations such as the American Bar Association or the American Sociological Association set standards for behavior and achievements.

However, it is possible to be an attorney or an athlete and not aspire to be like others in the group if they are unethical or abuse substances such as steroids. Instead, a person might be shaped by the values of a church group or a political group with which he or she identifies. Not every group one belongs to is a reference group. It must provide a standard by which you evaluate your behavior for it to be a reference group. For example, ethnic groups provide some adolescents with strong

Table 5.2 **Primary and Secondary Group Characteristics**

	Primary Group	*Secondary Group*
Quality of relationships	Personal orientation	Goal orientation
Duration of relationships	Usually long-term	Variable, often short-term
Breadth of activities	Broad, usually involving many activities	Narrow, usually involving few largely goal-directed activities
Subjective perception of relationships	As an end in itself (friendship, belonging)	As a means to an end (to accomplish a task, earn money)
Typical examples	Families, close friendships	Coworkers, political organizations

reference group standards by which to judge themselves. The stronger the ethnic pride and identification, the more some teens may separate themselves from contact with members of other ethnic groups (Schaefer and Kunz 2007). This can be functional or dysfunctional for the teens, as shown in the next section on in-groups and out-groups.

An **in-group** is *one to which an individual feels a sense of loyalty and belonging*. It also may serve as a reference group, since any group may fit into more than one category of group. An **out-group** is *one to which an individual does not belong, but more than that, it is a group that is often in competition or in opposition to an in-group.*

Membership in an in-group may be based on sex, race, ethnic group, social class, religion, political affiliation, the school one attends, an interest group such as the fraternity or sorority one joins, or the area where one lives. People tend to judge others according to their own in-group identity. Members of the in-group—for example, supporters of a high school team—often feel hostility toward or reject out-group members—boosters of the rival team. The perceived outside threat or hostility is often exaggerated, but it does help create the in-group members' feelings of solidarity.

Unfortunately, these feelings of hostility can result in prejudice and ethnocentrism, overlooking the individual differences of group members. Teen groups or gangs such as the Bloods and the Crips are examples of in-groups and out-groups in action, as are the ethnic and religious conflicts between Sunni and Shiite Muslims in Iraq. In each case, the group loyalty is enhanced by hostility toward the out-group, resulting in gang conflicts and war.

Thinking Sociologically

What are some examples of your own group affiliations: Primary groups? Secondary groups? Peer groups? Reference groups? In-groups and out-groups?

Organizations and Bureaucracies: The Meso-Macro Connection

Our days are filled with activities that involve us with complex organizations: from the doctor's appointment to college classes; from the political rally for the issue we are supporting to worship in our church, temple, or mosque; from paying state sales tax for our toothpaste to buying a sandwich at a fast-food franchise. Figure 5.5 on page 158 shows the institutions of

Bloods gang members in Los Angeles use their in-group hand signal to identify one another.

society, each made up of thousands of organizations (medical organizations, educational organizations, religious groups, economic corporations, political movements, the government itself) and each following the cultural norms of the society. We have statuses and roles in each group, and these link us to networks and the larger social world.

How did these organizational forms develop? Let us consider briefly the transformations of organizations into their modern forms and the characteristics of meso-level organizations today.

Modern Organizations and Their Evolution

Empires around the world have risen and fallen since the dawn of civilization. Some economic, political, and religious systems have flourished. Others such as monarchies and fascism have withered. We cannot understand our social world at any historical or modern time without comprehending the organizational structures and processes present at that time. Recall from Chapter 3 the discussion of types of societies, from hunter-gatherer to postindustrial. Each type of society entails different organizational structures, from early cities and feudal manors to craft guilds, heavy industries, and web-based companies today (Blau 1956; Nolan and Lenski 2010).

The development of modern organizations and bureaucracies began with industrialization in the 1700s, and they had become the dominant form of industrial organizations by the 1800s. What Max Weber called **rationalization of social life**—*the attempt to maximize efficiency by creating rules and procedures focused solely on accomplishing goals*—was thought to be the best way to run organizations (Weber

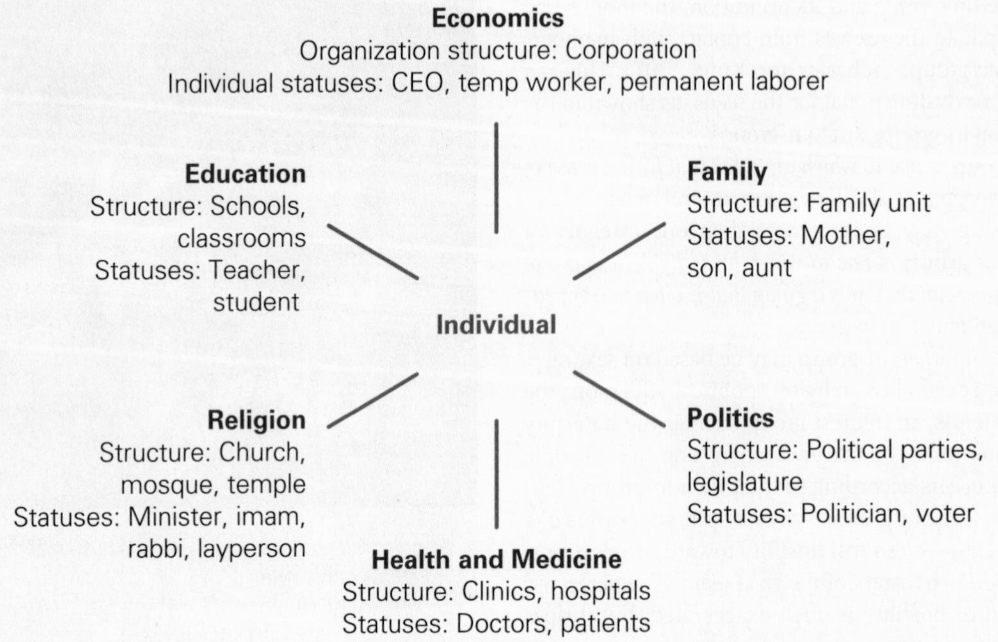

Figure 5.5 Our Social World: Institutions, Organizations, and Individual Status

1947). People were expected to behave in purposeful, coordinated ways to advance organizational efficiency. No longer were decisions made by tradition, custom, or the whim of a despot. Instead, trained leaders planned policies to achieve organizational efficiency. Tasks became more specialized, and some manual jobs were taken over by machines.

Standardization of products allowed for greater productivity, precision, and speed. **Formal organizations** (also called modern "rational" organizations) are composed of *complex secondary groups deliberately formed to pursue and achieve certain goals.* They are called "formal organizations" because of the written charters, constitutions, bylaws, and procedures that govern them. The Red Cross, the National Basketball Association (NBA), the Republican Party, and your university are all formal organizations. Another example of a formal organization is found in the fast-food empires springing up around the world. The next "Sociology Around the World" describes the trend toward the "McDonaldization of society"— Ritzer's pop culture term for rationalization in organizations.

Bureaucracies are *specific types of very large formal organizations that have the purpose of maximizing efficiency.* They are characterized by formal relations between participants, clearly laid-out procedures and rules, and pursuit of stated goals. Bureaucratization evolved as the most efficient way of producing products economically for mass markets (Ritzer 2013).

As societies became dominated by large organizations, fewer people worked the family farm or owned a cottage industry in their homes, and the number of small shopkeepers diminished. Today, some countries are organizational societies in which a majority of the members work in large organizations rather than being self-employed. Many other societies around the world are moving in this direction.

Societies making the transition between traditional and modern organizational structures often have a blend of the two, and in many industrializing countries, traditional organizational systems mix with newer forms (Nolan and Lenski 2010). Bribery, corruption, and favoritism govern some nations as they move toward modern bureaucracies. In these countries, people in government jobs are promoted based on their connections or their family tree, not on the basis of the individual's competence as assessed by formal training, examinations, or criteria derived from the needs of the position and the organization.

Postindustrial societies feature high dependence on technology and information sharing. Few people in such societies live and work on farms. In the United States today, only 1.1 million people claim farming as their main occupation, and only 2% live on farms ("How Many Farm Workers?" 2012; U.S. Environmental Protection Agency 2009). About 16% of the U.S. population lives in a rural area (Chiotakis 2011). This is compared with 15% in farm-related occupations in 1950 and 63.7% in 1850 (*Europa World Year Book* 2005; Wright 2007). The number of farms decreased from 5,648,000 in 1950 to 2,201,000 in 2010, while the average size of farms grew from 213 to 418 acres as agribusiness bought up small family farms (U.S. Census Bureau 2012h).

Sociology Around the World

The McDonaldization of Society

The process of rationalization described by Max Weber—the attempt to reach maximum bureaucratic efficiency—comes in a new modern version, expanded and streamlined, as exemplified by the fast-food restaurant business and the chain "box" stores found around the world. Efficient, rational, predictable sameness is sweeping the world—from diet centers such as Weight Watchers to NutriSystem to 7-Eleven and from Walmart to Gap clothing stores with their look-alike layouts. Most major world cities feature McDonald's or Kentucky Fried Chicken in the traditional main plazas or train stations for the flustered foreigners and curious native consumers.

The McDonaldization of society, as George Ritzer (2013) calls it, refers to several trends: First, *efficiency* is maximized by the sameness—same store plans, same mass-produced items, same procedures. Second is *predictability*, the knowledge that each hamburger or piece of chicken will be the same, leaving nothing to chance. Third, everything is *calculated* so that the organization can ensure that everything fits a standard—every burger is cooked the same number of seconds on each side. Fourth, there is *increased control* over employees and customers so there are fewer variables to consider—including substitution of technology for human labor as a way to ensure predictability and efficiency.

What is the result of this efficient, predictable, planned, automated new world? According to Ritzer, the world is becoming more dehumanized, and the efficiency is taking over individual creativity and human interactions. The mom-and-pop grocery, bed and breakfasts, and local craft or clothing shops are rapidly becoming a thing of the past, giving way to the McClones like In-N-Out Burger. This process of the McDonaldization of society, meaning principles of efficiency and rationalization exemplified by fast-food chains, is coming to dominate more and more sectors of our social world (Ritzer 2013). While there are aspects of this predictability that we all like, there is also a loss of the uniqueness and local flavor that individual entrepreneurs bring to a community.

To try to re-create this culture, Ritzer suggests, there is a movement toward "Starbuckization." Starbucks is unique because of its aesthetic contribution. Starbucks makes customers feel like they are purchasing a cultural product along with their coffee. This culture, however, is as controlled as any other McDonaldized endeavor, making Starbucks as much a McClone as its predecessors.

McDonaldization is so widespread and influential that many modern universities are McDonaldized. A large lecture hall is a very efficient way of teaching sociology or biology to many students at once. Similarly, distance learning, PowerPoint presentations, multiple-choice exams, and a limited choice of textbooks for professors increase the predictability of course offerings. Grade point averages and credit hours completed are very calculated ways to view students. Moreover, universities control students by deciding what courses are offered, when they are offered, and what professors will teach them.

Thinking Sociologically

Can anything be done to protect the non-McClone, individually owned "mom-and-pop" stores, or are they destined to be eliminated by the McCompetition?

Some organizations provide us with work necessary for survival. Others are forced on us—prisons, mental hospitals, military draft systems, even education up until a certain age. Still others are organizations we believe in and voluntarily join—scouts, environmental protest groups, sports leagues (Etzioni 1975). Membership in voluntary organizations is higher in the United States than in many other countries, yet in recent years, membership in voluntary organizations has dropped and even living with another person has declined, a factor discussed in the next "Sociology in Our Social World" (Johnson and Johnson 2006). Some analysts argue that new types of affiliations and interactions, including the Internet, are replacing some older affiliations.

Sociology in Our Social World

"Going Solo"

Given how utterly social humans are—more like dogs in packs than like cats—something surprising is happening! A huge number of adults in the United States and around the world are living alone—some by choice and some because of circumstances such as divorce or death of a spouse. Does this mean that the pundits are correct, that more people are becoming isolated due to lack of face-to-face communication that results from social isolation? Sociologist Eric Klinenberg asks these very questions in his book, *Going Solo: The Extraordinary Rise and Surprising Appeal of Living Alone* (New York: Penguin, 2012).

In 2001, Robert Putnam wrote a book called *Bowling Alone* in which he pointed out the decline in group activities. He argued that people who once participated in group activities were turning inward and not joining organized groups. This appeared to be an indication of breakdown in community in the United States. He speculated that this trend was due to disillusion with institutions and the increasing use of television and computers, staying home, and watching TV or surfing the Net. Yet newer studies are suggesting that people are forming different types of groups and affiliations.

Flash back to 1950 when 22% of adults in the United States were single. That is 4 million people who lived alone, or 9% of all households. If we fast-forward to 2012, 50% of adults were single. That translates to 31 million people, one in every seven individuals living alone, and 28% of households only having one person. These figures are quite low compared to Britain, Germany, France, Japan, and other Global North countries where even more people are single. Yet in some countries like Saudi Arabia living alone is rare. So why the tremendous increase in living solo, especially in Global North countries?

Once living alone seemed isolating with fewer opportunities for social life. However, today with social media, entertainment spots such as bars and restaurants, and cultural venues such as theater or arts events, classes, and sports catering to singles of all ages, there is actually more opportunity for the singles' social life than for couples. Also, singles have more time because of fewer family obligations. This is especially true in urban areas where social networks and friendship groups form "urban tribes." Active online networks also enhance social life for some singles, according to a Pew Research Center study (Hampton et al. 2012). Heavy Internet users have large and diverse social networks (PBS 2012).

Privileged classes use resources to buy privacy, personal space, freedom to make decisions and travel, personal control over resources and how time is spent, and self-realization. For young adults of middle-class background, being able to afford an apartment or a house may represent success. Older U.S citizens, often widowed, generally do not wish to date or remarry or to live with a child. Single seniors also tend to have many friends and keep busy with volunteer and group activities.

Because most people will live alone at some time, there are more opportunities to make this a good experience. For some, single friends are replacing spouses and workplace contacts, and activities are replacing domestic life. In some ways community may be declining, but even more it may be taking on new forms.

Thinking Sociologically

Make a list of your activities in a typical day. Which of these activities are, and which are not, associated with large (meso-level) formal organizations?

Modern Organizations and Modern Life

Organizations and modern life are almost synonymous. Live in one, and you belong to the other. Think about the many organizations that regularly affect your life: the legal system that passes laws, your college, your workplace, and voluntary organizations to which you belong. Human interactions take place in modern organizations, and modern organizations require human interaction to meet their needs. Some organizations, such as the local chapter of the Rotary Club or a chapter of a sorority, function at the micro level. Everyone is in a face-to-face relationship with every other member of the organization. However, those local chapters are part of a nationwide meso-level organization. At the macro level, the federal government is a complex modern organization that influences the lives of every citizen and organization. Meanwhile, transnational corporations and entities such as the United Nations are global in their reach.

These young people come together for the voluntary civic action of cleaning up the community—part of a local service project.

The hospital setting is an example of a modern organization that not only is governed by formal rules and impersonal relations but also increasingly involves extensive communication via computers.

Characteristics of Bureaucracy

To get a driver's license, pay school fees, or buy tickets for a popular concert or game, you may have to stand in a long line or fill out a form online. Finally, after waiting in line, you discover that you have forgotten your Social Security number, or they do not take a credit card. The rules and red tape are irksome. Yet what is the alternative? Some institutions have adopted telephone and online registration or ticket purchases, but even with this automated system, problems can occur.

If you have been to a Caribbean, African, Asian, or Middle Eastern market, you know that the bartering system is used to settle on a mutually agreeable price for goods. This system is more personal and involves intense interaction between the seller and the buyer, but it also takes more time and is less efficient. Bartering can be frustrating to the uninitiated visitor accustomed to the relative efficiency and predictability of bureaucracy, going to a store, selecting a product, and paying a set price. As societies transition, they tend to adopt bureaucratic forms of organization.

At the beginning of the 20th century, Max Weber (1864–1920) looked for the reasons behind the massive changes taking place that were causing the transition from traditional society to bureaucratic, capitalist society. He wanted to understand why the rate of change was more rapid in some parts of Europe than in others and why bureaucracy came to dominate the forms of organization in some countries. Whereas traditional society looked to the past for guidance, bureaucratic industrial society required a new form of thinking and behavior, a change in attitude toward rationality. Weber observed that leadership in business and government was moving from traditional forms with powerful families and charismatic leaders toward the more efficient and less personal bureaucracy.

Weber's concept of the *ideal-type bureaucracy* refers to the dominant and essential characteristics of organizations that are designed for reliability and efficiency (Weber 1947). The term describes not a good or perfect organization but merely an organization with a particular set of traits. Any particular bureaucracy is unlikely to have all the characteristics in the ideal type, but the degree of bureaucratization is measured by how closely an organization resembles the core characteristics of the ideal type. The following shows Weber's ideal-type bureaucracy with examples related to schools:

1. *Division of labor based on technical competence:* Administrators lead but do not teach, and instructors teach only in areas of their certification; staff are assigned positions for which their credentials make them most qualified, and recruitment and promotion are governed by formal policies.

2. *Administrative hierarchy:* There is a specified chain of command and designated channels of communication, from school board to superintendent to principal to teacher.

3. *Formal rules and regulations:* Written procedures and rules—perhaps published in an administrative manual—spell out systemwide requirements, including discipline practices, testing procedures, curricula, sick days for teachers, penalties for student tardiness, field trip policies, and other matters.

4. *Impersonal relationships:* Formal relationships tend to prevail between teachers and students and between teachers and administrative staff (superintendents, principals, counselors); written records and formal communication provide a paper trail for all decisions.

5. *Emphasis on rationality and efficiency to reach goals:* Established processes are used, based on the best interests of the school. Efficiency is defined in terms of the lowest overall cost to the organization in reaching a goal, not in terms of personal consequences.

6. *Provision of lifelong careers:* Employees may spend their entire careers working for the same organization, working their way up the hierarchy through promotions.

Although the list of characteristics makes bureaucracies sound formal and rigid, informal structures allow organizational members to deviate from rules both to meet the goals of the organization more efficiently and to humanize an otherwise uncaring and sterile workplace. The *informal structure* includes the unwritten norms and the interpersonal networks that people use within an organization to carry out roles. Likewise, although bylaws, constitutions, or contracts spell out the way things are supposed to be done, people often develop unwritten shortcuts to accomplish goals. The U.S. Postal Service has rules specifying that letter carriers are not supposed to walk across people's lawns, yet if they did not find shortcuts, it would take much longer for mail to be delivered.

Informal norms are not always compatible with those of the formal organization. Consider the following example from a famous classical study. In the Western Electric plant near Chicago, the study found that new workers were quickly socialized to do "a fair day's work," and those who did more or less than the established norm—what the work group thought was fair—were considered "rate busters" or "chiselers" and experienced pressure from the group to conform. These informal mechanisms gave informal groups of workers a degree of power in the organization (Roethlisberger and Dickson 1939).

Thinking Sociologically

How closely does each of Weber's characteristics of ideal-type bureaucracy describe your college or your work setting? Is your college highly bureaucratized, with many rules and regulations? Are decisions based on efficiency and cost-effectiveness, educational quality, or both? To what extent is your work setting characterized by hierarchy, and formal rules governing your work time? To what extent is it shaped by informal relationships?

Individuals in Bureaucracies

Lynndie England, a young woman from a small town in West Virginia, joined the military looking for opportunity and adventure. Instead, she became a victim and a scapegoat. The bureaucracy was the U.S. military; the setting was the Abu Ghraib prison in Iraq; the group pressure was to conform and fit in under stressful conditions by "going along with the guards," who were abusing and humiliating the prisoners (Zimbardo 2004). Caring and humane military officers may allow abuse of prisoners or order bombing strikes even though they know that some innocent people will be killed or maimed. In the military command in a war, a cold, impersonal cost-benefit analysis takes priority. In bureaucracies, self-preservation is the core value, and rational choice is often effective in explaining interactions in these contexts.

Humans can be moral, altruistic, and self-sacrificing for the good of others, but nations and other extremely large organizations (such as corporations or government) are inherently driven by a cost-benefit ratio. As one moves toward larger and more impersonal bureaucracies, the nature of interaction often changes.

Doctors, lawyers, engineers, and professors are considered to be *professionals* because they have particular attributes: advanced education, knowledge and competency in a field, high levels of autonomy to make decisions based on their expertise, a strong commitment to their field, a service orientation and commitment to the needs of the client, standards and regulations set by the profession, and a sense of intrinsic satisfaction from the work (rather than motivation rooted mainly in external rewards, such as salary). Professionals also claim authority, power, and control in their work area because of their mastery or expertise in a field (Tolbert and Hall 2008). Professionals within bureaucracies may face conflicting loyalties to their profession and to the bureaucratic organization in which they are employed. A scientist hired by a tobacco company faced a dilemma when his research findings did not support the company position that nicotine is not addictive. They wanted him to falsify his research, which would be a violation of professional ethics. Should he be a whistle-blower and publicly challenge the organization? Several professionals have done so but lost their jobs as a result.

Bureaucracy, some argue, can be the number-one enemy of professionalism, for it reduces autonomy. First, bureaucrats insist that authority rests in the person who holds an organizational status or title in the hierarchy rather than the person with the most expertise. Second, bureaucrats tend to reward people with external rewards such as bonuses rather than internal motivations. Third, bureaucrats focus on the needs of the organization as primary rather than on the needs of the client or professional. The potential clash between professionals and bureaucracy raises key concerns as universities, hospitals, and other large organizations are governed increasingly by bureaucratic principles (Roberts and Donahue 2000). Alienation among professionals occurs when they are highly regulated rather than when they have some decision-making authority and are granted some autonomy (Tolbert and Hall 2008). For example, high-tech companies that depend on engineering designers find that hierarchical structures undermine productivity, whereas factors such as intrinsic satisfaction, flexible hours, and relaxed work environments are central to creative productivity (Florida 2002, 2012b; Friedman 2005).

Women and minorities in bureaucracies may come up against barriers that keep them from reaching high levels of management. The result is that individuals from these groups are found disproportionately in midlevel positions with little authority and less pay than others with similar skills and credentials (Arulampalam, Booth, and Bryan 2007). When employees have little chance of promotion, they have less ambition and loyalty to the organization (Kanter 1977).

Despite this problem, research indicates that women executives bring valuable alternative perspectives to organizational leadership. They share information readily, give employees greater autonomy, and stress interconnectedness between parts of the organization, resulting in a more democratic type of leadership (Kramer 2010). The more women in an organization's senior positions, the more likely newcomers are to find support.

The interaction of people who see things differently because of religious beliefs, ethnic backgrounds, and gender experiences increases productivity in many organizations. Having a wide range of perspectives can lead to better problem solving (Florida 2004; Molotch 2003). Because diversity actually increases productivity and problem solving, the barriers to promotion have been irrational and dysfunctional to organizations.

Women in many countries have low-paid, dead-end jobs that make them feel uninvolved and unconnected. Such jobs result in alienation, but these women need the work and have little choice but to accept them.

Problems in Bureaucracies

Bureaucratic inefficiency and red tape are legendary and have been the theme of many classic novels, from Charles Dickens's *Bleak House*, which describes the legal system in England in the 1800s, to George Orwell's *1984*, which depicts a sterile, controlled environment. Yet bureaucracies are likely to stay, for they are the most efficient form of modern organization yet devised. Nonetheless, several individual and organizational problems created by bureaucratic structures are important to understand.

Alienation, feeling uninvolved, uncommitted, unappreciated, and unconnected to the group or the society, occurs when workers are assigned routine, boring tasks or dead-end jobs with no possibility of advancement. Marx believed that alienation is a structural feature of capitalism, with serious consequences: Workers lose their sense of purpose and seem to become dehumanized and objectified in their work, creating a product that they often do not see completed and for which they do not get the profits (Marx [1844] 1964).

Dissatisfaction comes from low pay and poor benefits; routine, repetitive, and fragmented tasks; lack of challenge and autonomy, leading to boredom; and poor working conditions. Workers who see possibilities for advancement put more energy into the organization, but those stuck in their positions are less involved and put more energy into activities outside the workplace (Kanter 1977).

Thinking Sociologically

How might participation in decision making, increased autonomy for workers, and stockholder shares in the company enhance commitment and productivity in your place of work? What might be some risks or downsides to such worker input and freedom?

Oligarchy, the concentration of power in the hands of a small group, is a common occurrence in organizations. In the early 1900s, Robert Michels, a French sociologist, wrote about the *iron law of oligarchy*, the idea that power becomes concentrated in the hands of a small group of leaders in political, business, voluntary, or other organizations. Initially, organizational needs, more than the motivation for power, cause these few stable leaders to emerge. As organizations grow, a division of labor emerges so that only a few leaders have access to information, resources, and the overall picture. This, in turn, causes leaders who enjoy their elite positions of power to become entrenched (Michels [1911] 1967). Yet recent events in the Middle East and North Africa illustrate that concentrated authority is being challenged. Likewise, in the United States, Wall Street high rollers felt immune from interference in their insulated world, but the public demanded the reinstatement of regulations to limit their power and make them accountable to someone for their actions.

Goal displacement occurs when the original motives or goals of the organization are displaced by new, secondary goals. Organizations are formed to meet specific goals. Religious organizations are established to worship a deity and serve humanity on behalf of that deity, schools are founded to educate children, and social work agencies are organized to serve the needs of citizens who seem to have fallen between the cracks. Yet, over time, the original goals may be met or become less important as other motivations and interests emerge (Merton 1938; Whyte 1956).

Parkinson's law, which states that in a bureaucracy work expands to fill the time and space available for its completion, is an example of inefficiency (Parkinson 1957). If we build a new room on our house, we are likely to fill it with "stuff." If classes are canceled for a day, our free day gets filled up with other activities. If we have two tests to study for, each takes half a day, but if we have one, it takes most of the day. Despite the expansion of space or time, we still do not seem to have enough time or room. Organizations work similarly. Parkinson's point is that organizations grow automatically, sometimes beyond efficiency or effectiveness.

Alternative organization structures are usually less hierarchical and include workplace democracy, employee participation in decision making, and employee ownership plans; they have been developed to deal with some of the problems discussed previously. Employee-owned companies are owned in part or in full by employees, who are given or can buy shares. Profit sharing and stock incentives for employees are generally part of the deal. If the company does well, all workers benefit. Studies show that this increases production and improves dedication, but the decision-making process is slower. However, the idea is that employees have a stake in their company and the job they do (Blasi, Kruse, and Bernstein 2003).

Democratic-collective organizations rely on cooperation, place authority and decision making in the collective group, and use personal appeals to ensure that everyone participates in problem solving. Rules, hierarchy, and status distinctions are minimized, and hiring is often based on shared values and friendships (Deming 2000). Members believe these organizations are more humane, and workers feel connected to the purpose and the product. The hope is that these new forms of organization—nonbureaucratic forms—may actually be a more effective way to organize postindustrial corporations. Google and some dot-com companies follow these models.

Although we may fantasize about escaping from the rat race or about isolating ourselves on an island, groups and bureaucracies are a part of modern life that few can escape.

Thinking Sociologically

In what areas of your college or workplace do you see goal displacement? That is, where do you see decisions being driven by goals other than the original purpose of the organization?

National and Global Networks: The Macro Level

In one sense, learning to understand people who are unlike us, to network with people who have different cultures, and to make allowances for alternative ideas about society and human behavior have become core competencies in our globalizing social world. Increasingly, colleges have study-abroad programs, jobs open up abroad for teaching English as a second language, and corporations seek employees who are multilingual and culturally competent in diverse settings. One young college graduate with a sociology degree found that she could use her sociology skills in leading groups of college-age students in international travel experiences. She explains this use of sociology in the next "Sociologists in Action."

Sociologists in Action—Elise Roberts

Using Sociology in International Travel and Intercultural Education

By Elise Roberts

After graduating from college with a bachelor's degree in sociology, I left the country to backpack through Mexico and Central America. My studies helped me to be more objective and aware as I experienced other societies. My international travel helped me examine my own societal assumptions and further understand how society creates so much of one's experience and view of the world. Eventually, I found a job leading groups of teenagers on alternative-education trips abroad. I was excited to get the job, but I was soon to learn that leading groups of teenagers in other countries is actually very hard work.

What struck me on meeting my first group was that I had very few students who initially understood this sociological perspective that I took for granted and that was so helpful in dealing with others. At times, my students would make fun of the way things were done in other countries, calling them "weird" or "stupid." They would mock the local traditions, until we discussed comparable traditions in American culture. These students were not mean or unintelligent. In fact, they loved the places we were seeing and the people we were meeting. They just thought everything was factually, officially weird. They had been socialized to understand their own society's ways as "right" and "normal." They were fully absorbed in the U.S. society, and they had never questioned it before.

It was rewarding to apply concepts from my textbooks in the real world. My coleaders and I learned to have fun while encouraging our students to become more socially conscious and analytical about their travel experience. We sent the groups out on scavenger hunts, and they would inevitably come back proudly announcing what they had paid for a rickshaw ride—only to learn that they had paid 10 times the local price. We would use this experience to talk about the role of foreigners, the assumptions that the local population made due to our skin color, and the culture of bartering. They had to learn to understand "odd" gestures, like pointing with the lips or side-to-side nodding. We would use these experiences to discuss nonverbal communication and gestures that we take for granted in U.S. culture.

We would encourage our novice travelers to interact with the people around them, which helped them understand the struggles facing immigrants and non-English speakers in the United States. We would force them to have conversations while standing toe-to-toe with each other, and they would finish with backaches from leaning away from one another. We would not allow them to explain their behavior with "because it's creepy to stand so close together," even though this was the consensus. "Why do you feel uncomfortable?" we would ask. "Why is this weird?" The answer has to do with social constructions of what is "normal" in any society.

Of course, while traveling internationally, one is surrounded by various other sociological issues, such as different racial or ethnic conflicts, gender roles, or class hierarchies, and learning about these issues was a part of our program as well. Without realizing it, many group conversations and meetings began to remind me of some of my favorite undergraduate sociology classes. "Study sociology!" I would say, plugging my major to the most interested students.

I have always thought that travel was an incredibly useful means not only to learn about the society and culture one is visiting but also to learn much about oneself and one's home society. For teenagers who otherwise might never step back to think about the role of being a foreigner or the traditions and social patterns they take for granted, it is even more important. Traveling abroad on my own and leading programs abroad were such extremely rich and rewarding experiences not only due to the cross-cultural exchanges and the intense personal examination that I saw in my students but also because it was fascinating and rewarding to be able to use my sociology degree every day on my job.

* * * * * * *

Elise Roberts graduated from Macalester College with a major in sociology. Her post-college travels took her through Central America, the South Pacific, and many parts of Asia. She recently graduated from Columbia University with a master's degree in international social work and is a regional organizer for Witness for Peace.

With modern communication and transportation systems and the ability to transfer ideas and money with a touch of the keyboard, global networks are superseding national boundaries. Multinational corporations now employ citizens from around the world and can make their own rules because there is no oversight body. National systems and international organizations, from the United Nations to the World Bank to multinational corporations, are typically governed through rational bureaucratic systems.

Technology has some interesting implications for human interaction. E-mail, texting, tweeting, webpages, chat rooms, and blogs have made it possible for people around the world to talk with each other, exchange ideas, and even develop friendships. Although authoritarian governments and dictators in the world try, they can no longer keep the citizenry from knowing what people outside their countries think. In China, as fast as officials censor information on the World Wide Web, computer experts find ways around the restrictions. Egyptian officials tried to block satellite communication and restrict access to the information highway during the January–February 2011 revolution. Despite these efforts by some nations to limit access, the process of change is occurring so rapidly that we cannot know what technology will mean for the global world. It is almost certain that the processes of interaction across national lines will continue despite some efforts to curb communication. The World Wide Web was not invented until 1989, and e-mail has been available to most citizens—even in the affluent countries—only since the early 1990s (Brasher 2004). (See the timeline at front of book for further examples.) Countries are still struggling with what this means for change.

Within nations, people with common interests, be it organic food, animal rights, or peace, can contact one another. Hate groups also set up webpages and mobilize others with their view of the world, and terrorists use the Internet to communicate with terrorist cells around the world. Clearly, the ability to communicate around the globe is transforming the world and our nations in ways that affect local communities and private individuals. Indeed, the Internet has become a major outlet for sellers and a source for consumers. A wide range of products can be obtained through Internet orders from websites that have no geographical home base. In some cases, there are no actual warehouses or manufacturing plants, and there might not be a home office. Some businesses are global and exist in the Ethernet, not in any specific nation (Ritzer 2007). This reality makes one rethink national and global loyalties and realities.

From the discussion of rationalization and the McDonaldization of society in the previous section, we see some consequences: Family loyalties are considered less important than the needs of the corporation. Feelings are subordinated to thought processes. Efficiency and calculability are highly prized in the social system. However, as these Western notions of how public life should operate are exported to other countries, a severe backlash has occurred. In many Middle Eastern Islamic countries, for example, these values clash with Muslim loyalties and priorities. The result has been high levels of anger at the United States and Western Europe. Many scholars believe that Middle Eastern anger at the United States is based not on opposition to freedom and democracy, as our politicians sometimes say, but on what some Middle Easterners see as the crass greed and impersonal organizational structures we try to import into their micro-, meso-, and macro-level worlds. They feel that their very culture is threatened (Ritzer 2007). Radical fundamentalist movements—groups that are fueled by religious beliefs and socioeconomic stressors and that cope by rejecting all ambiguity and seeing the world in absolutes—are mostly antimodernization movements turned militant (Antoun 2008; Marty and Appleby 2004). They have emerged in Christian, Jewish, Islamic, Sikh, and other groups, largely as a response to a perceived crisis (Armstrong 2000). Some aspects of global terrorism and international conflict are based on the way the Western world organizes its social life and exports it to other parts of the world. These conflicts, in turn, have resulted in mobilization of the military in the United States. The consequence is that members of your own family might be serving abroad even as you read these pages.

Thinking Sociologically

How do you think global interaction will be transformed through Internet technology? How will individual connections between people be affected by macro-level changes in our social world?

Policy Issues: Women and Globalization

Women in many parts of the world are viewed as second-class citizens, the most economically, politically, and socially marginalized people on the planet, caught in expectations of religion, patriarchy, and roles needed to sustain life (Schneider and Silverman 2006). They account for 70% of the world's population living in absolute poverty (Global Fund for Women 2012). To help their children survive, women do whatever their situation allows to make money: street selling, low-paying factory assembly line

Around the world, two thirds of the poorest adults are women, even though women produce more than two thirds of the food supplies in the world. A Laotian woman works in the field (top), and an Indian woman transports goods to the market (bottom).

Because women are often more vulnerable and have historically been exploited, global organizations like United Nations Women and microfinance groups like the Grameen Bank and FINCA have provided loans and other supports for women to begin their own business enterprises. When women are assisted, it usually has a marked improvement on the circumstances of children.

work, piecework (i.e., sewing clothing in their homes), prostitution and sex work, and domestic service. Women also produce 80% to 90% of the food crops in sub-Saharan Africa, and almost 50% in the world (Food and Agriculture Organization of the United Nations 2010–2011). They run households, and are often the main support for children in poor countries. Yet, due to the "feminization of poverty," two out of three poor adults are women (Enloe 2006). Causes of and policies to address the many problems facing women are found at each level of analysis and will be discussed throughout the book.

One macro-level organization with policies to help raise the status of women through development is the United Nations. Each decade since the 1960s, this global organization has set forth plans to improve conditions for women. Early plans to help poor countries were driven by the interests of capitalist countries in the developed world. This left powerless women out of the equation and planning. Women suffered more under some of these plans because their positions and responsibilities did not change. Conditions got worse as development money went to large corporations with the idea that profits would trickle down to the local level, an idea that did not materialize in most countries. Today organizations concerned with women's status advocate more tools, ownership or control of land, and a larger role in agriculture, estimating that this could boost food production by 20% to 30% (Boulding and Dye 2002; Global Fund for Women 2012).

The United Nations has sponsored conferences on the status of women. In July 2010, the organization launched a new division, UN Women, headed by former Chilean president Michelle Bachelet. The UN Division for the Advancement of Women and UN Women initiated policies to help educate local women in health, nutrition, basic first aid, and business methods.

A *World Development Report* (2012) outlines four priorities for improving the conditions for women: "1. Reducing excess female mortality and closing education gaps; 2. Improving access to economic opportunities for women; 3. Increasing women's voice and agency in the household and society; and 4. Limiting the reproduction of gender inequality across generations." Many projects have been spawned, including micro-lending organizations (Grameen Bank, SEWA, FINCA, CARE), allowing individuals and groups of women to borrow money to start cooperatives and other small-business ventures. These organizations can have very beneficial effects if they are used wisely by policy makers who care about the people involved. In the next few chapters, we will learn about some of the factors that cause some individuals and countries to be poorer than others.

Our networks play a major role in setting out norms and controlling our behaviors, usually resulting in our conformity to the social expectations of those in our network. This, of course, contributes to the stability of the entire social system because deviation can threaten the existence of "normal" patterns, as we see in the next chapter.

What Have We Learned?

Each of us has a network of people and groups that surrounds us. The scope of our networks has broadened with the increased complexity of societies and includes the global social world. Indeed, it is easy not to recognize how far our networks reach, even to the global level. Although some of our social experiences are informal (unstructured), we are also profoundly affected by another phenomenon of the past three centuries—highly structured bureaucracies. As a result of both, the intimate experiences of our personal lives are far more extensively linked to meso- and macro-level events and to people and places on the other side of the globe than was true for our parents' generation. If we hope to understand our lives, we must understand this broad context. Although it may have been possible to live without global connections and bureaucratic systems several centuries ago, these networks are intricately woven into our lifestyles and our economic systems today. The question is whether we control these networks or they control us.

Key Points

- People in the modern world are connected through one acquaintance to another in a chain of links, referred to as networks. (See pp. 141–142.)
- Increasingly, our electronic technology is creating networks that span the globe, but this same impersonal technology is used to enhance friendship networks and even to meet a romantic life partner. (See pp. 142–144.)
- Interpersonal interactions at the micro level are affected by unspoken assumptions that are understood due to context, by nonverbal communication, and by the symbolism of space between people. (See pp. 144–149.)
- Many of our behaviors are shaped by the statuses (social positions) we hold and the roles (expectations associated with a status) we play. However, our multiple-status occupancy can create role conflicts (between the roles of two statuses) and role strains (between the role expectations of a single status). (See pp. 149–153.)
- When the norms of behavior are unclear, we may experience anomie (normlessness), and this ambiguity compromises our sense of belonging and is linked to the reasons for individuals performing one of the most personal of acts—suicide. (See pp. 153–154.)
- Various types of groups affect our behavior—from primary and secondary groups to peer groups and reference groups. (See pp. 154–157.)
- At the meso level, we find that formal organizations in the contemporary modern world are ruled by rational calculation of the organization's goals rather than by tradition or emotional ties. These modern formal organizations expand, are governed by impersonal formal rules, and stress efficiency and rational decision making. They have come to be called bureaucracies. (See pp. 157–161.)
- Bureaucracies often create certain problems for individuals, and they may actually make them inefficient or destructive. (See pp. 161–164.)
- While bureaucratization emerged at the meso level as the defining element of the modern world, it is also found at the national and global levels, where people do not know each other on a face-to-face basis. (See pp. 164–166.)
- Some scholars think that this impersonal mode of organizing social life—so common in the West for several centuries now—is a critical factor in anti-American and anti-Western resistance movements. (See p.166)

Discussion Questions

1. Think about your social network. How useful might it be in helping you get a job (or a better job) once you graduate from college? Why?
2. During a typical day, when, respectively, do you engage in front- and backstage behavior? Why? With whom do you engage in each? Why?
3. Have you ever experienced role strain because of your status as a student? Explain why or why not. If so, how did/do you cope with it?
4. Most college students, particularly those with family, work, and/or sports team obligations, deal with role conflict. Describe a time when you dealt with a conflict between the roles you carry out and what you did about it. How might colleges and universities diminish role conflict among students?
5. To what primary and secondary groups do you belong? How does your involvement (or lack thereof) in primary groups on your campus impact your feelings of attachment to your school?
6. Would you rather live in a bureaucratic society or in a society without bureaucratic forms of organizations? Why? How does the informal structure at your college or university impact how the school functions? Does it do more to help or hurt students? Why?

Contributing to Our Social World: What Can We Do?

At the Local Level

- *Tutoring and mentoring* programs help students struggling with their studies. Contact the Student Affairs Office and arrange to observe and/or volunteer in a program. Helping students build *social capital*, which includes their knowledge of ways to obtain the help they need, can increase their chances of success.
- In many metropolitan areas, *low*-wage workers not represented by unions have come together to form *workers' centers*, often with the aid of local clergy. Workers' centers help these workers, many of whom are not being protected by current labor laws, organize and develop the social capital to obtain better wages, benefits, and workplace dignity. For a list of workers' centers, go to www.iwj.org/worker-center-network/locations.

At the Organizational or Institutional Level

- The social capital theory can also be applied to meso-level community organizations: *community organizations* that work to build power and implement social change, such as *IAF* (the Industrial Areas Foundation at www.industrialareasfoundation.org), *Gamaliel* (www.gamaliel.org), and *PICO National Network* (www.piconetwork.org), provide their members with social capital. Find an organization affiliated with one of these organizations near you.
- *Unions* also develop social capital for their members. Although far fewer Americans are unionized today than in past decades, membership in a union can make a significant improvement in the economic prospects of workers. For some workers, this can make the difference between living in poverty and obtaining a living wage. At 2.1 million members, the *Service Employees International Union (SEIU)* is the fastest-growing union in North America. Internships with unions like SEIU are a great way to learn about organizing social capital.
- *The Anti-Defamation League* (www.adl.org), *the American-Arab Anti-Discrimination Committee* (www.adc.org), *and the National Association for the Advancement of Colored People* (www.naacp.org) are examples of organizations that defend the rights of minority groups. These organizations often use volunteers or interns and can provide you with the opportunity to learn about the extent to which social contacts and networks play a role in managing social conflict.

At the National or Global Level

- Well-run *microfinance organizations* can help poor people, particularly women, gain social capital and economic independence. Three well-known and respected groups are *CRS* (Catholic Relief Services at http://crs.org/microfinance/), *FINCA* (www.finca.org), and *Kiva* (www.kiva.org). Check out their websites to learn how you can support their efforts.

WWW

Visit the Student Study Site at **www.sagepub.com/ballantine4e** to access additional study tools, including eFlashcards, web quizzes, video resources, audio resources, web resources, SAGE journal articles, recommended readings, and more.

CHAPTER 6

Deviance and Social Control

Sickos, Weirdos, Freaks, and Folks Like Us

Deviants are often thought of as perverts and rule breakers without consciences. We often contrast them to people like us, but the reality is that the line between deviants and conformists is frequently vague, and we may be surprised to learn that often the "deviants are us."

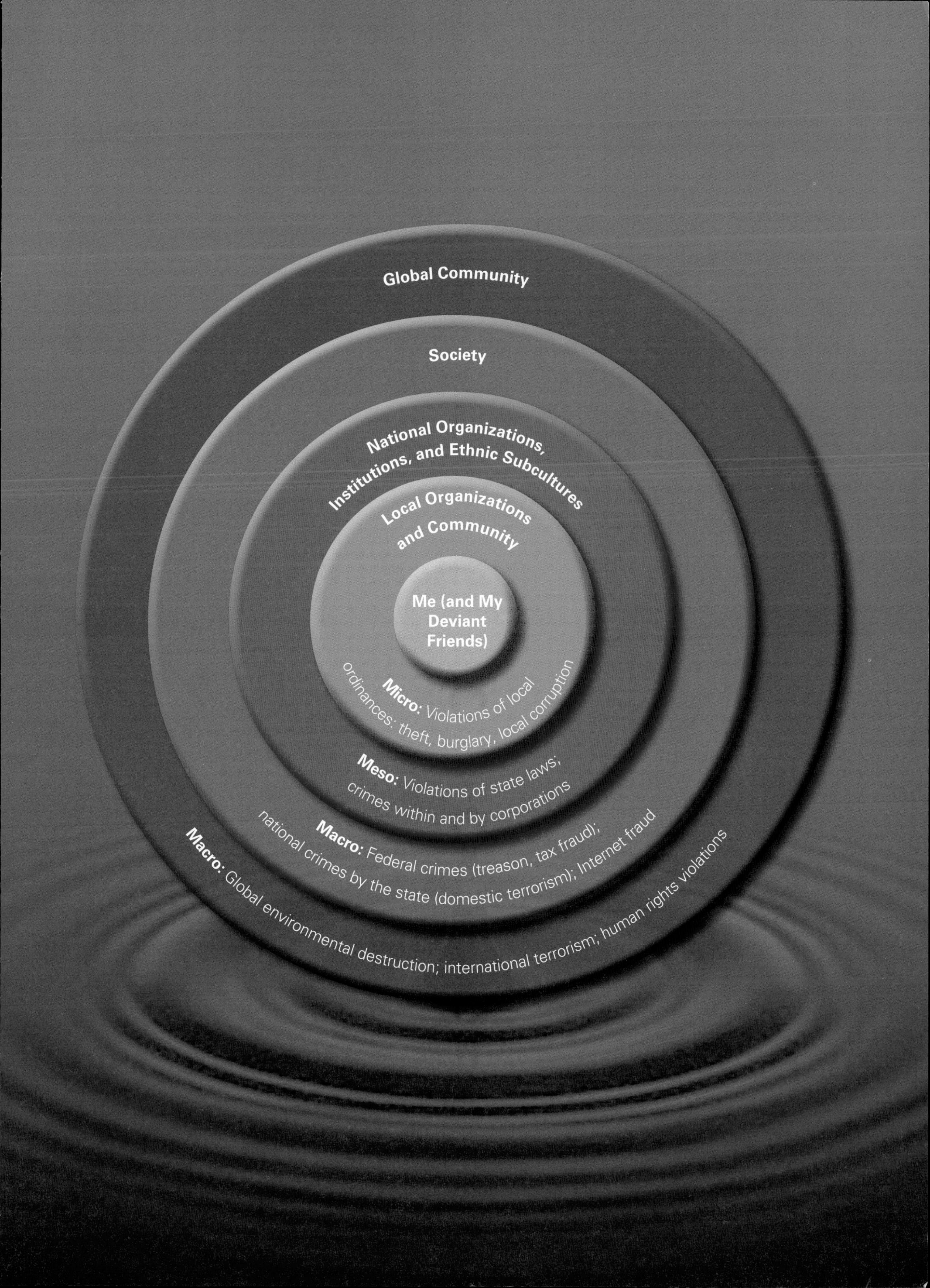

Global Community
Society
National Organizations, Institutions, and Ethnic Subcultures
Local Organizations and Community
Me (and My Deviant Friends)
Micro: Violations of local ordinances: theft, burglary, local corruption
Meso: Violations of state laws; crimes within and by corporations
Macro: Federal crimes (treason, tax fraud); national crimes by the state (domestic terrorism); Internet fraud
Macro: Global environmental destruction; international terrorism; human rights violations

Think About It	
Micro: Me (and My Friends)	Are you deviant? Who says so?
Micro: Local Community	Why do some people in your community become deviant while others do not?
Meso: National Institutions; Complex Organizations; Ethnic Groups	What are the implications of organized crime or occupational crime for large bureaucratic organizations?
Macro: National Society	What are the costs—and the benefits—of deviance for the nation?
Macro: Global Community	How can a global perspective on crime enhance our understanding of international and national criminal activities?

What's coming in this chapter?

Wafa grew up as other girls do, but she was destined to make world headlines on January 27, 2002—as the first female suicide bomber in the Palestinian-Israeli conflict. She was the age of most university students reading this book, but she never had an opportunity to attend college. Her task was to smuggle explosives across the Israeli border for the intended bomber, her brother. Instead, she blew up herself and an Israeli soldier. She was declared a martyr, a *sahida*, by the al-Aqsa Martyrs Brigade, and they took credit for the attack. Her act was given approval by the group's political leadership, opening the way for other women to follow. Why did this happen? What motivated her to commit suicide and take another life in the process? Was she driven by ideology to participate in the Palestinian-Israeli struggle? Were there social and structural factors that affected her decision? Most important, was she deviant in carrying out this act, and according to whom?

Wafa Idris grew up in Palestine. She was married at a young age but did not produce children. Because this leaves a woman with little role to play in Palestinian society, her husband divorced her and remarried. She had no future, for who would want a barren, divorced woman in a society that values women for their purity and their childbearing ability? She was a burden to her family. Her way out of an impossible and desperate situation was to commit suicide, bringing honor and wealth to her family and redeeming herself in the process. Other women who followed Wafa have similar stories: Most shared an inability to control their own lives in the patriarchal (male-controlled) society (Handwerk 2004; Victor 2003).

Ironically, terrorist cells in Palestine saw this as an opportunity to recruit other women. Some signed up for suicide missions because they believed in the cause of a free Palestine, but most who joined the cause were vulnerable, broken, with no way out of untenable situations, and they felt they had nothing to lose. This was a way not only to escape the problems in their lives but also to bring honor to their families in the process. It is not a measure of equality that women, too, commit suicide bombings. This development results from a structure of inequality, according to Barbara Victor (2003), who analyzed the lives of these women.

Our question is this: Are these women deviant criminal terrorists, hapless victims of terrorist groups, mentally ill "crazies," powerless and invisible victims in a patriarchal society, or martyrs who should be honored for their acts? Who says so? Each of these views is held by someone interested in this situation. From this opening example, we can begin to see several complexities that arise when considering deviance, and some of these ideas may encourage new ways of looking at what is deviant. In this chapter, we will consider who is deviant, under what circumstances, and in whose eyes. We will find that most people around the world conform to the social norms of their societies most of the time, and we will explore why some turn to deviance.

Occasionally most of us violate a norm, and depending on its importance and on the severity of the violation, the violator may or may not be seen as deviant. Wearing strange clothes may be seen as amusing and nonconformist once in a while, but it is labeled deviant if it becomes a regular occurrence. At the same time, a number of people adorning themselves with tattoos and rings to be distinctive and individualistic may result in widespread adoption of these behaviors, so that they become accepted rather than deviant.

In this chapter, we discuss **deviance**—*the violation of social norms*—and the social control mechanisms that keep most people from becoming deviant. We also explore crime, the forms of deviance that bring formal penalties like fines, jail, or prison sentences, imposed by societies' legal systems. The content of this chapter may challenge some of your deeply held assumptions about human behavior and defy some conceptions about deviance. In fact, it may convince you that we are all deviant at some times and in some places. The self-test in the next "Engaging Sociology" illustrates this point. Try taking it to see whether you have committed a deviant act.

What Is Deviance?

Deviance refers to the violation of society's norms, which then evokes negative reactions from others. The definition is somewhat imprecise because of the constantly changing ideas and laws about what acts are considered deviant. Some acts are deviant in most societies most of the time: murder, assault, robbery, and rape. **Crimes** are *those deviant actions for which there are severe formal penalties imposed by the government.* Occasionally, deviant acts may be overlooked or even viewed as understandable, as in the case of looting by citizens following Hurricane Katrina along the Gulf Coast in August 2005. Killing innocent people, looting, and burning houses during a civil or tribal war, as occurred in Syria in 2011 and 2012, also may seem reasonable to those committing the atrocities. Bad behavior can often be rationalized.

Other acts of deviance are considered serious offenses in one society but are tolerated in another. Examples include prostitution, premarital or extramarital sex, gambling, corruption, and bribery. Even within a single society, different groups may define deviance and conformity quite differently. The state legislature may officially define alcohol consumption by 19-year-olds as deviant, but on a Saturday night at the fraternity party, the 19-year-old "brother" who does not drink may be viewed as deviant by his peers. What do these cases tell us about what deviance is?

Deviance is socially constructed. This means that members of groups in societies define what is deviant. Consider the phenomenon of today's young people getting tattoos, studs, and rings anywhere on the body they can place them. Is this deviant? It depends on who is judging. Are tattoos, studs, and rings symbols of independence, rebellion, or a "cool" and unique look? What is deviant changes over time and in different places: When The Beatles started the long hair rage in the 1960s, this was deviant behavior to many. Today, we pay no special attention to men with long hair.

Engaging Sociology

Who Is Deviant?

Please jot down your answers to the following self-test questions. There is no need to share your responses with others.

Have you ever engaged in any of the following acts?

- ☐ 1. stolen anything, even if its value was under $10
- ☐ 2. used an illegal drug
- ☐ 3. misused a prescription drug
- ☐ 4. run away from home prior to age 18
- ☐ 5. used tobacco prior to age 18
- ☐ 6. drunk alcohol prior to age 21
- ☐ 7. engaged in a fist fight
- ☐ 8. carried a knife or gun
- ☐ 9. used a car without the owner's permission
- ☐ 10. driven a car after drinking alcohol
- ☐ 11. (boys) forced a girl to have sexual relations against her will
- ☐ 12. offered sex for money
- ☐ 13. damaged property worth more than $10
- ☐ 14. been truant from school
- ☐ 15. arrived home after your curfew
- ☐ 16. been disrespectful to someone in authority
- ☐ 17. accepted or transported property that you had reason to believe might be stolen
- ☐ 18. taken a towel from a hotel room after renting the room for a night

All of the above are delinquent acts (violations of legal standards), and most young people are guilty of at least one infraction. However, few teenagers are given the label of delinquent. If you have answered yes to any of the preceding questions, you have committed a crime in many states. Your penalty or sanction for the infraction could range from a stiff fine to several years in prison—if you got caught!

Questions:

1. Do you think of yourself as being deviant? Why or why not?
2. Are deviants only those who get caught? For instance, if someone steals your car but avoids being caught, is he or she deviant?
3. Who is considered deviant—and by whom?

Lady Gaga accepts MTV's Video of the Year award wearing an outfit made entirely of raw meat. Is this normal or deviant? Why would she do this?

Thinking Sociologically

What if many people begin to adopt a "deviant" behavior? Is it a sign of independence or deviance? Does it indicate conformity to a group? Do such "deviant" acts then become a symbol of conformity? Give examples.

Some acts are deviant at one time and place and not at others. Stem cell research had been viewed as unacceptable and a violation of U.S. law because of ethical concerns about using or destroying human cells. However, that policy changed with the change of president and administrations. In many other countries, there are no moral restrictions on stem cell research, and scientists are proceeding with such research.

An individual's status or group may be defined as deviant. Some individuals have a higher likelihood of being labeled deviant because of the group into which they were born, such as a particular ethnic group, or because of a distinguishing mark or characteristic, such as a deformity. Others may escape being considered deviant because of their dominant status in society. The higher one's status, the less likely that one will be suspected of violating norms and the less likely that any violations will be characterized as "criminal." Who would suspect that a respectable white-collar husband and father is embezzling funds from his company?

Even the looting that happened following Hurricane Katrina was addressed differently when it was done by whites than when it was done by African Americans (Huddy and Feldman 2006; Thompson 2009). An image of a looter in New Orleans appears in the upper center of this chapter's photo essay on the opposite page. The media showed photos of black "looters" who "stole food," but the same media described whites who "broke into grocery stores" in search of food as "resourceful." Likewise, gays and lesbians are often said to be deviant and accused of flaunting their sexuality. Heterosexuals are rarely accused of "flaunting" their sexuality, regardless of how overtly flirtatious or underdressed they may be. So one's group membership or ascribed traits may make a difference in whether or not one is defined as deviant.

Deviance represents a breakdown in norms. However, according to structural-functional theory, it can be problematic or functional for society. Deviance serves vital functions by setting examples of what is considered unacceptable behavior, providing guidelines for behavior that is necessary to maintain social order, and bonding people together through their common rejection of the deviant behavior. Deviance is also functional because it provides jobs for those who deal with deviants—police, judges, social workers, and so forth (Gans 2007). Furthermore, deviance can signal problems in society that need to be addressed and can therefore stimulate positive change. Sometimes deviant individuals break the model of conventional thinking, thereby opening society to new and creative paths of thinking. Scientists, inventors, and artists have often been rejected in their time but have been honored later for accomplishments that positively affected society. Famous artist Vincent van Gogh, for example, lived in poverty and mental turmoil during his life because many people did not recognize his genius, but he became recognized as a renowned painter after his death. His paintings now sell for millions of dollars.

Our task in this chapter is to understand what deviance is, what causes it, and where it fits in the social world. We look at theoretical perspectives that help explain deviance, how some deviant acts become crimes, and what policies might be effective in controlling or reducing crime.

Photo Essay

Social Construction of Deviance

Are any of these people deviant? Why or why not? How does your answer reflect the "social construction" of deviance?

Some sociologists point out that crime can be "functional" because it creates jobs for people such as those above and it unifies society against the nonconformists.

Misconceptions About Deviance

Many common beliefs about deviance are, in fact, misperceptions. Using scientifically collected data, the sociologist helps dispel false beliefs, as shown in the examples given below.

Popular belief: Some acts are inherently deviant. Fact: Deviance is relative to the time, place, and status of the individual. At some place or time, almost any behavior you can mention has been defined as deviant, just as most acts have been legal or even expected behaviors in other times and places. For example, homosexual liaisons were normal for men in ancient Greece and have been acceptable in various societies throughout time. Deviance is not inherent in certain behaviors but is defined by people and their governments (Erikson 1987, [1966] 2005).

Those in power have great influence over what is defined as deviant and can often determine punishments for those from different statuses. Some individuals are defined as deviant because they do not fit into the dominant system of values and norms. They may be seen as disruptive, a liability, or a threat to the system.

Famous individuals remembered in history books were often considered deviant in their time. In the Middle Ages, for example, anyone who questioned the concept of a flat earth at the center of the universe (with a sun and stars circling it) was considered a deviant and a religious heretic. In the early 17th century, Galileo, following Copernicus's lead, wrote a treatise based on empirical observations that upheld the concept of the earth revolving around the sun. He was tried by the Inquisition, a Roman Catholic Church court, in Rome and condemned for heresy because of his theory.

Definitions of deviance also vary depending on the social situation or context in which the behavior occurs (McCaghy et al. 2006). If we take the same behavior and place it in a different social context, perceptions of whether the behavior is deviant may well change. In Greece, Spain, and other Mediterranean countries, the clothing norms on beaches are very different from those in most of North America. Topless sunbathing by women and nudity on beaches for men is not at all uncommon, even on beaches designated as family beaches. Along the banks of the Rhine River men stroll and sunbathe in their birthday suits. On other beaches, the norms may be different. Even within a few feet of the beach on the Greek islands and in northern Spain, women will sunbathe topless, lying only 10 feet from the boardwalk where concessionaires sell beverages, snacks, and tourist items. If these women become thirsty, they cover up, walk the 15 feet to purchase a cola, and return to their beach blankets, where they again remove their tops. To walk onto the boardwalk topless would be highly deviant, yet to be topless on the sand next to the walk is acceptable.

Thinking Sociologically

Would there be any problems in a multicultural society if everyone conformed and no one ever deviated from social standards?

Likewise, drunken behavior during spring break or at Mardi Gras in New Orleans may be acceptable, but getting drunk while sipping champagne at a wedding reception would be a cause for disgust. The same behavior can be conventional or deviant depending on where it occurs. Even behaviors about which there is much agreement, such as murder and rape, can be justified by the perpetrators during times of war, in feuds, or after conquests.

Popular belief: We readily recognize those who are deviant. Fact: Most of us deviate from some norm at some time or the other, as you saw when completing the questionnaire on deviance. (See the opening "Engaging Sociology.") However, most behaviors that violate a norm are never socially recognized as deviant. Only about one third of all crime that is reported to the police in the United States ever leads to an arrest. This means that two thirds is never officially handled through the formal, legal structure, and the perpetrators escape being labeled deviant.

Popular belief: Deviants purposely and knowingly break the law. Fact: Although it is a popular notion that those who engage in deviant behavior make a conscious choice to do so, much deviance is driven by emotion, encouraged by friends, or caused by disagreements over norms (as in the case of whether marijuana use should be decriminalized), or is the result of conditions in the immediate situation (as in the case of teens spontaneously engaging in a behavior in response to boredom or a struggle for prestige among peers; McCaghy et al. 2006).

Popular belief: Deviance occurs because there is a dishonest, selfish element to human nature. Fact: While surveys show that many of us believe this, most people who commit deviant acts do not attribute their own deviance to basic dishonesty or other negative personality factors. These misperceptions imply that most deviant individuals know when they are being deviant. Yet there is little empirical evidence to support these beliefs, as the research reported in this chapter shows. Deviant individuals are often engaging in behaviors that they think their reference group would approve.

Thinking Sociologically

Think of examples in your life that illustrate the relative nature of deviance. For instance, are some of your behaviors deviant in one setting but not in another, or were they deviant when you were younger but not deviant now?

Medical marijuana patient Kay Mitchell, age 82, of Sonoma, joined more than 1,000 people protesting outside the California state capitol to rally for state-approved and licensed medical marijuana dispensaries in California, which are supposed to serve mostly terminally ill patients suffering from cancer, AIDS, and other ailments. The U.S. administration had announced that it would no longer prosecute those using marijuana for legal medical purposes, but recently U.S. Attorney General Eric Holder announced a crackdown on the burgeoning marijuana business.

Crime: Deviance That Violates the Law

It is rather easy for a Wall Street tycoon to commit illegal acts—*if* he or she does not get caught. Sometimes illegal acts committed by those in high positions are punished, as in the case of Bernie Madoff. In 2008 his economic Ponzi scheme cheated many individuals and organizations out of their savings. Madoff is now doing time in prison for his deviant acts. *Crime,* introduced above, refers to deviant actions for which there are severe formal penalties imposed by the government. Laws reflect opinions of what is considered right and wrong or good and bad at a particular time and place in a society. Like all other norms, laws change over time, reflecting changing public opinion based on social conditions or specific events. Still, there are formal sanctions—punishments—that the government imposes for violation of laws, and the social disapproval associated with these deviant acts results in the perpetrator being identified as "criminal."

At the end of the 1920s, 42 of the 48 U.S. states had laws forbidding interracial marriage (Coontz 2005; see

Map 6.1). Legislatures in half of these states removed those restrictions by the 1960s, but the rest of these laws became unconstitutional only after a U.S. Supreme Court ruling in 1967. Today, this legal bar on interracial marriage has been eliminated completely, illustrating that most laws change to reflect the times and sentiments of the majority of people. *When members of society are in general agreement about the seriousness of deviant acts, these are referred to as* **consensus crimes** (Brym and Lie 2007; Goodman and Brenner 2002). Predatory crimes (premeditated murder, forcible rape, and kidnapping for ransom) are consensus crimes that are considered wrong in and of themselves in most nations.

In contrast, **conflict crimes** *occur when public opinion about the seriousness of these crimes is divided, based on people's differing social class, status, and interests* (Hagan 1993, 1994). Examples include laws concerning public disorder, chemical (drug and alcohol) offenses, prostitution, gambling, property offenses, and political disenfranchisement (denying voting rights only to some citizens—females, particular ethnic groups, or those without property). Public opinion about the seriousness of these crimes is often divided, based on people's different social class, status, and interests. The severity of societal response also varies, with high disagreement over the harmfulness of conflict crimes. Consensus or conflict about whether the behavior is harmful has implications for the punishment or support experienced by the person who is accused.

Crimes are often thought to be the most threatening forms of deviance, but it is important to recognize that they are still just one type of deviant behavior. We will discuss crime further at a later point in this chapter. Be aware that as we discuss theories in the next section, the theories explain a range of deviant acts, including (but not limited to) crimes.

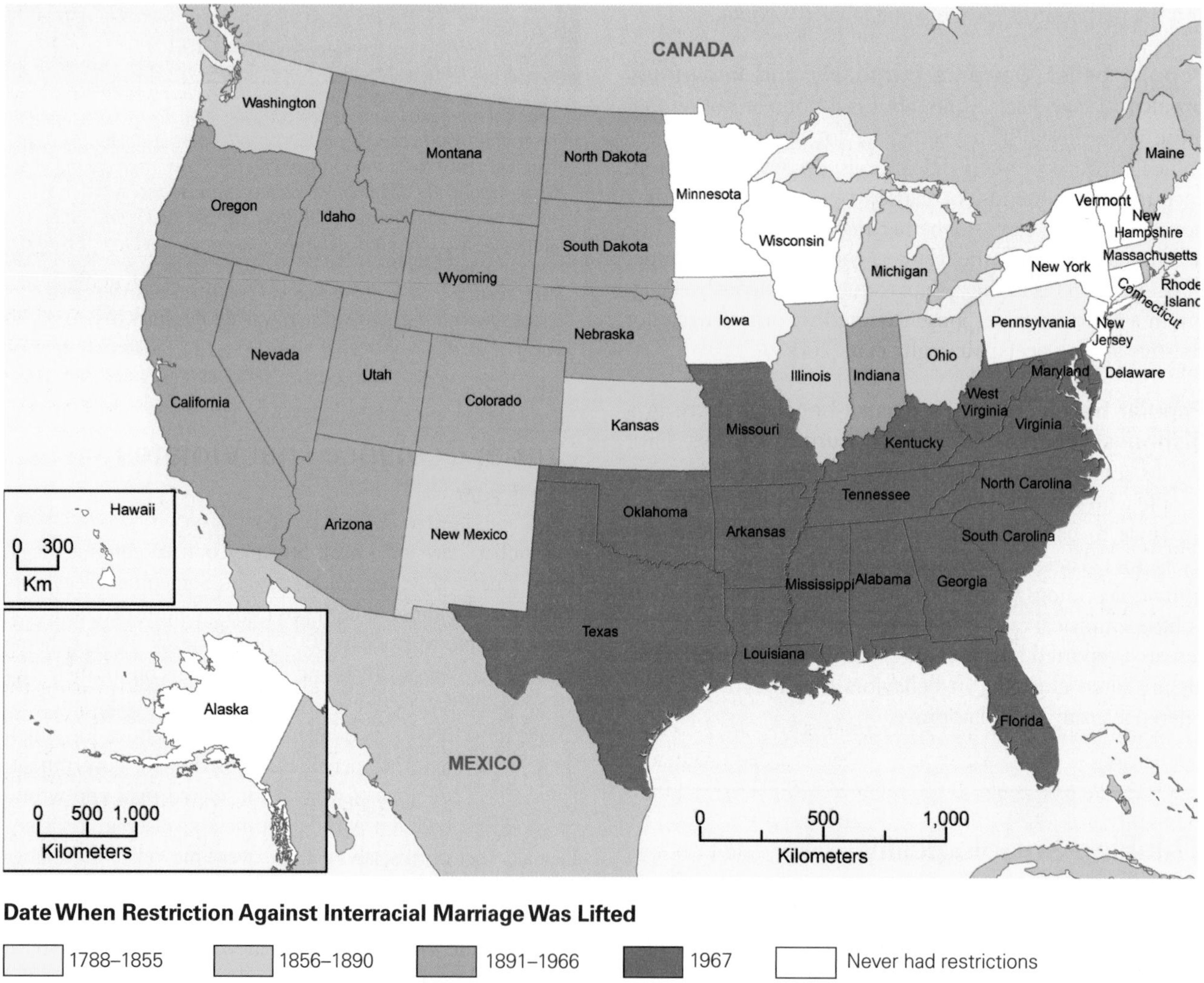

Map 6.1 Historical Restrictions on Interracial Marriage in the United States.

Source: Wallenstein (2002:253–254). Map by Anna Versluis.

What Causes Deviant Behavior? Theoretical Perspectives

Helena is a delinquent. Her father deserted the family when Helena was 10, and before that, he had abused Helena and her mother. Her mother has all she can cope with; she is just trying to survive financially and keep her three children in line. Helena gets little attention and little support or encouragement in her school activities. Her grades have fallen steadily. As a young teen, she sought attention from boys, and in the process, she became pregnant. Now, the only kids who have anything to do with her are others who have been in trouble; her friends are other young people who have also been labeled delinquent. Helena's schoolmates, teachers, and mother see her as a delinquent troublemaker, and it would be hard for Helena to change their views and her status.

How did this happen? Was Helena born with a biological propensity toward deviance? Does she have psychological problems? Is the problem in her social environment? Helena's situation is, of course, only one unique case. Sociologists cannot generalize from Helena to other cases, but they do know from their studies that there are thousands of teens with problems like Helena's. Below we consider some theories of deviance that help explain cases like Helena.

Throughout history, people have proposed explanations for why some members of society "turn bad"—from biological explanations of imbalances in hormones and claims of innate personality defects to social conditions within individual families or in the larger social structure. Biological and psychological approaches focus on personality disorders or abnormalities in the body or psyche of individuals, but they generally do not consider the social context in which deviance occurs.

Sociologists attempt to study questions of deviance scientifically. They examine why certain acts are defined as deviant, why some people engage in deviant behavior, and how other people in the society react to deviance. Sociologists place emphasis on understanding the interactions, social structure, and social processes that lead to deviant behavior, rather than on individual characteristics. They consider the socialization process and interpersonal relationships, group and social class differences, cultural and subcultural norms, and power structures that influence individuals to conform to or deviate from societal expectations. Theoretical explanations about why people are deviant are important because the interpretations influence social policy decisions about what to do with deviants.

In the United States, until 1968, this couple would have been violating the law in roughly half of the states, and their family would be "illegitimate." Interracial marriages were illegal until the Supreme Court decided otherwise. Change in definitions of what is illegal has been common in the past 50 years.

This section explores several approaches to understanding deviance. Some theories explain particular types of crime better than others (say, theft as opposed to sexual assault), and some illuminate micro-, meso-, or macro-level processes better than others. Taken together these theories help us understand a wide range of deviant and criminal behaviors.

Micro-Level Explanations of Deviance

No one is born deviant. Individuals learn to be law-abiding citizens or to be deviant through the process of socialization. Thus, behavior is acquired during the processes of interaction and socialization as individuals develop their social relationships. Why do some people learn to become deviant and others learn to follow the norms of society? Rational choice and symbolic interaction theories focus primarily on micro-level issues, as discussed next.

Rational Choice Approaches to Deviance

The basic idea behind *rational choice theory* is that when individuals make decisions, they calculate the costs and benefits to themselves. They consider the balance between pleasure and pain. Those who use *rational choice theory* focus on the cost-benefit analysis of one's choices about deviance or conformity. Social control to prevent deviance comes from shifting the balance toward more pain and fewer benefits for those who deviate from norms—jail time, fines, community service, embarrassment, a public record of deviance. However, some members of society find crime to be to their advantage within their situations and opportunities, the product of a conscious, rational, and calculated decision made after weighing the costs and benefits of alternatives. Often they choose lives of crime after failure in school or work or seeing others succeed in crime.

Rational choice theorists believe that punishment—imposing high "costs" for criminal behavior, such as fines, imprisonment, or even the death penalty—is the way to dissuade criminals from choosing the path of crime. When the cost outweighs the potential benefit and opportunities are restricted, it deters people from thinking that crime is a "rational" choice (Earls and Reiss 1994; Winslow and Zhang 2008). Even just changing the perception of the cost-benefit balance can be important in lowering the crime rate. Criminals make decisions based on the situational constraints and opportunities in their lives (Schmalleger 2013).

Social Control Theory. One of sociology's central concepts is social control—why people obey norms (Gibbs 1989; Hagan 2011). A specific rational choice application, control theory focuses on why most people conform most of the time and do not commit deviant acts. If human beings were truly free to do whatever they wanted, they would likely commit more deviant acts. Yet to live near others and with others requires individuals to control their behaviors based on social norms and sanctions—in short, social control.

Rational choice theories hold that people weigh the possible negative consequences of deviant behavior against its benefits, and if the benefits outweigh the costs, then violating official rules or expectations may be worth it. This would suggest that the cost must be increased to deter deviance. This little boy is weighing the costs and benefits of taking cookies, and the benefits are looking pretty sweet!

A perpetual question in sociology is the following: How is social order possible in the context of rapidly changing society? A very general answer is that social control results from social norms that promote order and predictability in the social world. When people fail to adhere to these norms, or when the norms are unclear, the stability and continuance of the entire social system may be threatened.

Control theory contends that people are bonded to others by four powerful factors:

1. *Attachment* to other people who respect the values and rules of the society. Individuals do not want to be rejected by those to whom they are close or whom they admire.
2. *Commitment* to conventional activities (such as school and jobs) that they do not want to jeopardize.
3. *Involvement* in activities that keep them so busy with conventional roles and expectations that they do not have time for mischief.
4. *Belief* in the social rules of their culture, which they accept because of their childhood socialization and indoctrination into those conventional beliefs.

Should these variables be weakened, there is an increased possibility that the person could commit deviant acts (Hirschi [1969] 2002).

Two primary factors shape our tendency to conform. The first is internal controls, those voices within us that tell us when a behavior is acceptable or unacceptable, right or wrong. The second is external controls—society's formal or informal controls against deviant behavior. Informal external controls include smiles, frowns, hugs, and ridicule from close acquaintances (Gottfredson and Hirschi 1990). Formal external controls come from the legal system through the police, judges, juries, and social workers. In both cases, the cost-benefit ratio shifts, making either conformity or deviance a rational choice. The basic idea in rational choice approaches is that when individuals make decisions, they calculate the costs and benefits to themselves. Humans seek to maximize pleasure (benefit) and minimize pain (costs), and the decision regarding whether to conform or deviate from social norms is determined by the individual's assessment and rational decision of the pleasure-pain ratio from his or her mental calculations in a given situation. Social control comes from shifting the balance toward more pain and fewer benefits for those who deviate from norms.

Positive sanctions reward those behaviors approved by society. This is the reason why schools have honor ceremonies, companies reward their top salespeople, and communities recognize civic leadership with "Citizen of the Year" awards. All these actions enhance the rewards for conventional behavior. Negative sanctions (or punishments) increase the cost to those who have deviated from the norm. They range from fines for traffic violations to prison sentences for serious crimes and even death for acts considered most dangerous to society.

Thinking Sociologically

Think of a time when you committed a deviant act or avoided doing so despite a tempting opportunity. What factors influenced whether you conformed to societal norms or committed a deviant act?

Symbolic Interaction Approaches to Deviance

How a group influences an individual's social construction of reality is the focus of another approach, based in symbolic interaction theory. The core issue is how people define reality and how they are influenced by the society in constructing who they are and what is acceptable behavior in society. One approach emphasizes that people learn to commit delinquent acts through their social relationships with peers and family members. Another stresses that if they adopt a deviant lifestyle that is stigmatized by others, including law enforcement, they come to be *labeled* deviant after committing a deviant act. Because symbolic interaction theorists stress variables other than pure self-interest—like getting rich quick—they are less inclined to think that increasing the penalties or changing the costs will change behavior and reduce deviance. The first symbolic interaction approach is differential association, focusing on how individuals learn deviant behavior.

Differential Association Theory. If someone offered you some heroin, what would determine whether you took it? First, would you define sticking a needle in your arm and injecting heroin as a good way to spend your afternoon? Second, do you typically hang around with others who engage in this type of behavior and define it as "the thing to do"? Third, would you know the routine—how to cook the heroin to extract the liquid—if you had never seen it done? You likely would not know the proper technique for how to prepare the drug or how to inject it. Why? It depends on whether you have associated with drug users and whether your family and friends define drug use as acceptable or deviant.

Differential association refers to two processes that can result in individuals learning to engage in crime. First is association with others who share criminal values and commit crimes, which results in learning how to carry out a criminal act (Sutherland, Cressey, and Luckenbil 1992). Second, learning deviant behaviors from associations with others also results in reinforcement of criminal behavior (Akers 1992, 1998; Burgess and Akers 1966; Lee, Akers, and Borg 2004).

Differential association theory focuses on the process of learning deviance from family, peers, fellow employees, political organizations, neighborhood groups such as gangs, and other groups in one's surroundings (Akers 1992; Akers et al. 1979; Sutherland et al. 1992). This theory is a symbolic interaction approach because the emphasis is on how others shape one's definition of what is normal and acceptable. Helena, for example, came to be surrounded by people who made dropping out of school and other delinquent acts seem normal. If her close friends and siblings were sexually active as teens, her teen pregnancy might not be remarkable and might even be a source of some prestige with her group of peers.

According to differential association theory, the possibility of becoming deviant depends on four factors related

Spending time and money shooting drugs is a way of life for some young people. Yet most teens would not know the technique for preparing and injecting illegal drugs, nor would they have learned from associates that this is a fun or acceptable way to spend one's time.

to associating with a deviant group: the *duration* of time spent with the group, the *intensity* of interaction, the *frequency* of interaction, and the *priority* of the group in one's friendship network (Sutherland et al. 1992). If deviant behavior exists in people's social circles and if the individual is exposed to deviance regularly and frequently (duration and intensity), especially if he or she is in close association with a group that accepts criminal behavior, the individual is more likely to learn deviant ways. Furthermore, individuals learn motives, drives, rationalizations, and attitudes, and they develop techniques that influence behavior and cause them to commit deviant acts.

Some theorists contend that lower-class life constitutes a distinctive subculture in which delinquent behavior patterns are transmitted through socialization. The values, beliefs, norms, and practices that have evolved in lower-class communities over time can often lead to violation of laws. These values and norms have been defined by those in power as deviant. Just as upper-class youth seem to be expected and destined to succeed, lower-class youth may learn other behaviors that those with privilege have defined as delinquent and criminal (Bettie 2003; Chambliss 1973). For some inner-city youth, the local norms are to be tough and disrespectful of authority, to live for today, to seek excitement, and to be "cool"—these are survival techniques.

Elijah Anderson's (2000) book, *Code of the Street*, describes two types of groups that coexist in poor neighborhoods: "decent people" and "street people." The code of the street often involves norms that are opposed to those of mainstream society, yet many children are socialized in areas where this code provides the dominant norms. "Street-oriented people" hang around with peers on streets and adopt a certain look with their clothes and jewelry—an image expected by the group. Peers become more important than society's social control agents. "Decent families" accept mainstream values and often find support systems in church communities or other organizations. It is the lower-status street youth who are more likely to be suspected, watched, and caught for deviant behavior than higher-status youth. Thus, the reported delinquency rates may be higher for this group even if the incidence of violence is not greater (Anderson 2000).

Today, we know that members of all social classes commit crimes, and no socioeconomic class has a monopoly on violence, graft, corruption, or dishonesty. However, *labeling* explains why some individuals and groups are more likely to be caught and punished for deviance.

Labeling Theory. It was a tragic loss of life, caused by labeling. In 2011, Tyler Clementi jumped to his death from the George Washington Bridge in New York. His roommate at Rutgers University had videotaped Clementi kissing another man, and put the videotape on the web. The jury accused the roommate of a hate crime and cyberbullying for which he could receive up to 10 years in jail (Zernike 2012). Why did Tyler commit suicide? Labeling theory is one possible explanation; the videotape labeled him as gay, opening him to humiliation.

Labeling theory is *a symbolic interaction approach that focuses on how people define deviants—what or who is or is not "normal"—and society's response to unacceptable behaviors, labeling as deviant those who violate society's norms.* Labels (such as "juvenile delinquent") are symbols that have meanings that affect an individual's self-concept and the way others see the individual. The basic assumption underlying labeling theory is that no behavior or individual is intrinsically deviant. Behavior is deviant because individuals in society label it deviant. The basic social process of labeling someone is as follows: Members of a society create deviance by defining certain behaviors as deviant—smoking pot, wearing long hair, holding hands in public, or whatever is seen as inappropriate at a particular time and place. They then react to the deviance by rejecting the deviant person or by imposing penalties.

Labeling theorists define two stages in the process of becoming a deviant. **Primary deviance** is a *violation of a norm that may be an isolated act or an initial act of rule breaking, such as a young teenager shoplifting something on a dare by friends.* Most people commit acts of primary deviance. However, many of us avoid being labeled "deviant" as a result of these primary acts. Remember how you marked the deviant behavior test that you took at the beginning of this chapter? If you have engaged in deviant acts, you were probably not labeled deviant for the offense. If you had been labeled, you might not be in college or taking this class, but be cooling your heels in jail or juvenile detention.

If an individual continues to violate a norm and begins to take on a deviant identity because of being labeled deviant, this is referred to as **secondary deviance**. Secondary deviance becomes publicly recognized, and the individual is identified as deviant, beginning a deviant career. If a teenager like Helena in the opening example is caught, her act becomes known, perhaps publicized in the newspaper. She may spend time in a juvenile detention center, and parents of other teens may not want their children associating with her. Employers and store managers may refuse to hire her. Soon, there are few options open to her because others expect her to be delinquent. The teen may continue performing the deviant acts and associating with delinquent acquaintances, in part because few other options are available within the expectations of community members. Society's reaction, then, is what defines a deviant person and may limit options for that person to change the label (Lemert 1951, 1972).

The process of labeling individuals and behaviors takes place at each level of analysis, from individual to society. If community or societal norms define a behavior as deviant, individuals are likely to believe it is deviant. Sanctions against juvenile delinquents can have the effect of reinforcing the deviant behavior by (a) increasing alienation from the social world, (b) forcing increased interaction with deviant peers, and

Shoplifting is often done by young people who have not been arrested for anything—a form of primary deviance.

(c) motivating juvenile delinquents to positively value and identify with the deviant status (Kaplan and Johnson 1991).

Self-fulfilling prophecy *occurs when a belief or a prediction becomes a reality, in part because of the prediction.* Individuals may come to see themselves as deviant because of harassment, ridicule, rejection by friends and family, and negative sanctions. For example, James is 8 years old and already sees himself as a failure because his parents, teachers, and peers tell him he is "dumb." In keeping with the idea of self-fulfilling prophecy, James accepts the label and acts accordingly. Unless someone—such as an insightful teacher—steps in to give him another image of himself, the label is unlikely to change.

Thinking Sociologically

What labels do you carry, and how do they affect your self-concept and behavior?

Another explanation of why certain individuals and groups are labeled deviant has to do with their status and power in society—a concern of conflict theory. Those who are on the fringes, away from power and nonparticipants in the mainstream, are more likely to be labeled deviants—the poor, minorities, members of new religious movements, or those who in some way do not fit into the dominant system. Because the powerful have the influence to define what is acceptable, they protect themselves from being defined as deviants. People from different subcultures, social classes, or religious groups may be accorded deviant labels.

A study by Chambliss (1973) illustrates the process of labeling in communities and groups. Perhaps during your high school years you witnessed situations similar to that described in his study. Chambliss looked at the behavior of two small peer groups of boys and at the reactions of community members to their behavior. The Saints, boys from "good" families, were some of the most delinquent boys at Hannibal High School. Although the Saints were constantly occupied with truancy, drinking, wild driving, petty theft, and vandalism, none were officially arrested for any misdeed during the two-year study, partly because they had cars and could go out of town for their pranks. The Roughnecks were constantly in trouble with the police and community residents, even though their rate of delinquency was about equal to that of the Saints. Chambliss found that poor kids—like the Roughnecks—may be involved in deviant behavior because the dominant cultural goals seem distant and unattainable. On the other hand, rich kids—like the Saints—indulge in delinquent activities to cope with boredom, to rebel, or to seek visibility among peers.

What was the cause of the disparity between these two groups? Community members, the police, and teachers alike labeled the boys based on their perceptions of the boys' family backgrounds and social class. The Saints came from stable, white, upper-middle-class families; were active in school affairs; and were precollege students who everyone expected would become professionals. The general community feeling was that the Roughnecks would amount to nothing. They carried around a label that was hard to change, and that label was realized. The Saints almost all became professionals, whereas none of the Roughnecks did. Two Roughnecks ended up in prison, two became coaches, and little is known of the others. For these groups of boys, the prophecy became self-fulfilling (Chambliss 1973). The belief that the Roughnecks would "amount to nothing" came true because that was what was expected by the community; their opportunities were affected by their labels, and the boys came to expect nothing for themselves.

Labels are powerful and can *stigmatize* an individual—branding the person as disgraceful or reprehensible as in the case of Tyler Clementi. This process can be extended to a number of issues, including fatness, as the next "Sociology in Our Social World" illustrates.

Sociology in Our Social World

Stigmatizing Fatness

By Leslie Elrod

The United States is now the fattest country in the world. "American society has become 'obesogenic,' characterized by environments that promote increased food intake, nonhealthful food, and physical inactivity . . . One in seven low-income preschool children is obese" (Centers for Disease Control and Prevention [CDC] 2009). The CDC has found that more than 60% of American adults are classified as overweight or obese, and 25% of children are classified as obese. Deviation from the idealized image of physical thinness allows others to judge and condemn nonconforming individuals, resulting in embarrassment, severe isolation, or alienation. According to Cooley's (1902, [1909] 1983) theory of the looking-glass self, because we tend to define ourselves by others' attitudes toward us and our interaction with others, the individuals who are obese may suffer lower self-esteem and have negative self-images, thus creating heightened levels of psychological distress. When a physical attribute is assigned social significance, violators of this norm are likely to endure negative labeling because of perceived physical imperfections. The obese, labeled as self-indulgent, gluttonous, lazy, sloppy, and mean, experience social condemnation. Obese women tend to experience greater discrimination than obese men.

Women are taught that their physical appearance is a valuable commodity, in both the public and private spheres. Ascertaining the degree to which they fit the media models of female perfection, women attempt to adapt their appearance to reach this standard of beauty. Holding up an image of female perfection, such as slenderness, daintiness, or being demure, the media insinuate that women themselves somehow fall short of that perfection. This is exemplified in print ads, magazines, television programming, and movies as well as merchandising directed toward females of all ages. The "feminine failing" not only jeopardizes women's happiness but also challenges their femininity. The appearance discrepancy is based on the fact that over the course of the past century, as real women grew heavier, models and "beautiful" women were portrayed as increasingly thinner. An example of the change in media imagery is that of the White Rock mineral girl, portrayed as 5 feet 4 inches tall and 140 pounds in 1950. More recently, she is 5 feet 10 inches tall, weighing 110 pounds (Phipher 1994).

While much of the research on women's obsession with weight assumes that all women and girls are affected by the culture of thinness, there is some evidence to suggest that not all women are affected equally. Obesity rates are highest among minorities, the poor, and the disenfranchised. Yet Powell and Kahn (1995) have noted that "few black women seem to have eating disorders . . . and less emphasis [is placed] on eating and weight in general among black college students compared to white students" (p. 190). When compared to black females, white women are under significantly greater social pressure to be thin. Hesse-Biber and Nagy (2007) find that eating disorders, an outcome of dissatisfaction with one's body, are no longer confined to upper-class white females, indicating that the effects of body mass on self-esteem may be changing.

This is not to suggest that people of color are not concerned about body image; rather, it suggests that the messages disseminated through the majority culture are mediated in various ways through the experiences and expectations that are associated with distinct social classes. Moreover, since media portrayals are still predominantly white, whether through the use of white models or those with white features—thin lips, thin hips, straight hair, and light complexion—there is less pressure on minorities to relate and compare themselves to the given images because these images do not represent their reference groups.

Because the obese are victims of prejudice and discrimination resulting from social norm violation, they are less likely than their nonobese counterparts to be involved in various organizational and social activities for fear of social rejection. Olson, Schumaker, and Yawn (1994) found that weight-based embarrassment was indicated as a reason that obese people shied away from social obligations. Several clinical studies have documented that obese women even delay seeking medical care and participating in preventative medical techniques.

Some obese people reject the stigmatizing "fat identity," using a variety of coping mechanisms such as avoidance of others who stigmatize them or coping through immersion in supportive subcultures. Those who suffer from low self-esteem may actively seek out activities and relationships that have the capacity to improve their self-esteem. While not all obese persons experience and internalize fat stigmatization, a statistically significant number of overweight and obese juveniles do indicate poor body image and diminished self-esteem. Many experts suggest that individuals should take a proactive approach by seeking medical or psychological help, joining support groups, and dealing with the problem if it is impairing their activities.

* * * * * * *

Leslie Elrod is an assistant professor of sociology at University of Cincinnati Raymond Walters College. Two of her specialties are studies of obesity and of teaching.

Thinking Sociologically

In addition to body weight, what other physical characteristics affect one's self-perception or cause one to be labeled as different or even deviant by others?

Why are some behaviors defined as deviant? Again, when a majority of individuals agree that an act is a violation of norms, it is labeled deviant. In other cases, powerful members of society who hold powerful positions can label certain behaviors as deviant. While labeling theory is mostly based on symbolic interactionism (a micro-level theory), labeling theorists also point to the role of macro-level social forces—social inequality or lack of access to power—in determining whether people are labeled or whether they can avoid being labeled as deviant. Thus, labeling theory is also sometimes used by conflict theorists. When members of the dominant group in society see certain behaviors as potentially threatening or disruptive to the society or to their privileged statuses, the group in power reinforces its position by creating an impossible situation for minority group members. The minority's nonacceptance of the rules becomes deviant. For instance, dissidents opposed to government restrictions or human rights violations against their groups in China, Myanmar (Burma), and other countries have been thrown in jail because their protests were labeled deviant by those in power.

Thinking Sociologically

You have a friend who is getting into drugs. From what you know about the above theories, what might be the reason why this is happening, and what, if anything, could you do for your friend?

Meso- and Macro-Level Explanations of Deviance

While micro-level interactions can result in becoming deviant and being labeled deviant, many sociologists believe that meso- and macro-level analysis creates greater understanding of the societal factors leading to deviance. Meso-level analysis focuses on ethnic subcultures, organizations, and institutions. Macro-level analysis focuses on national and global social systems.

Structural-Functional Approaches to Deviance

We look first at structural-functional theories of deviance, those with the longest history in sociology. They include two themes: (1) anomie, the breakdown of the norms guiding behavior, which leads to social disorganization, and (2) the strain created by the difference between definitions of success (goals) in a society and the means available to achieve those goals.

Anomie and Social Disorganization. Villagers from industrializing countries in Africa, Asia, and Latin America were pushed off marginally productive rural lands and were pulled by the lure of the city: to seek better lives and means for survival. They flocked to population centers with industrial opportunities, excitement, and a chance to change their lives, but when they arrived, they were often disappointed. Poor, unskilled, and homeless, they moved into crowded apartments or shantytowns of temporary shacks and tried to adjust to the new style of life, which often included unemployment.

Many industrializing countries face structural changes as their economies move from agricultural to industrial or service economies. Young men in particular leave behind strong bonds and a common value system that exists in the countryside and results in less deviance. In cities, individuals melt into the crowd and live anonymously. Old village norms that have provided the guidelines for proper behavior crumble, sometimes without clear expectations emerging to take their places. The lack of clear norms in the rapidly changing urban environment leads to high levels of social disorganization and deviant behavior.

Sociologists use the term **anomie**, or *the state of normlessness that occurs when rules for behavior in society break down under extreme stress from rapid social change or conflict* (see also Chapter 5). When norms are absent or conflicting, deviance increases, as the previous example illustrates. Émile Durkheim (1858–1917) first described this normlessness as a condition of weak, conflicting, or absent norms and values that arises when societies are disorganized. This situation is typical in rapidly urbanizing, industrializing societies; at times of sudden prosperity or depression; during rapid technological change; during a war; or when a government is overthrown. Anomie affects urban areas first but may eventually affect the whole society. Macro-level events, such as economic recessions or wars, show how important social solidarity is to an individual's core sense of values.

This general idea of anomie led a group of Chicago sociologists to study the social conditions of that city that are correlated with deviance. The Chicago School, as the research team is known, linked life in transitional slum areas to the high incidence of crime. Certain neighborhoods or zones in the Chicago area—generally inner-city transitional zones with recent settlers—have always had high delinquency rates, regardless of the group that occupied the area. Low economic status, ethnic heterogeneity, residential mobility, family disruption, and competing value systems (because of the constant transitions) led to community disorganization. Although new immigrant groups have replaced the older groups over time, the delinquency rate has remained high because each generation of newcomers experienced anomie (Shaw and McKay 1929). The high in-migration and out-migration in these communities in itself explains the lack of stability in primary families. Peer group norms became influential, and models of nondeviant behavior were scarce for many teenagers and adults (Anderson 2000).

Yemeni army soldiers try to stop antigovernment protesters demanding the resignation of the autocratic Yemeni president, Ali Abdullah Saleh. In response the president ordered a crackdown on Arab Spring protesters, and at least 120 people were killed in just one city in Yemen.

Strain Theory. Lakisha is not a stellar student. Although she works hard, she has the intellectual ability, and her parents punish her when she brings home poor grades, she has problems achieving in the middle-class school environment. Many of her neighborhood peers have dropped out of school, joined gangs, or become pregnant. Those young people who have chosen to try to succeed in school are teased by other kids as "acting white." Lakisha's goals are to do well in high school and go to a good college to become a social worker or teacher, but the way to achieve the goal (the means to get there) is difficult to find. Below we describe several goals-means options available to Lakisha and other young people.

Strain theory—a specific theory within the structural-functional framework—examines the breakdown of norms caused by the lack of shared, achievable goals and the lack of socially approved means to achieve those goals (Merton 1938). Most people in a society share similar values and goals, but those with poor education and few resources have less opportunity to achieve shared goals than others. When legitimate routes to success are cut off, frustration and anger can result, and deviant methods may be used to achieve goals. Strain theory focuses on the contradictions and tensions between the shared values and goals of a society on the one hand and the opportunity structures of the society on the other.

Strain theory (Merton 1968) suggests that the gap between an individual's or a society's *goals* and the legitimate ways of attaining those goals—*the means*—can lead to strain in the society. Individuals may agree with the society's *goals* for success (say, financial affluence) but may not be able to achieve them using the socially acceptable means of achieving that success. The strain that is created can lead to deviance. Merton (1968) uses U.S. society as an example because it places a heavy emphasis on success, measured by wealth and social standing. He outlines five ways by which individuals adapt to the strain. Figure 6.1 shows these five types and their relationship to goals and means. To illustrate these, we trace the choices of the lower-class student described above who realizes the value of an education and knows it is necessary to get ahead, but has problems financing her education and competing in the middle-class-dominated school setting.

1. *Conformity* means embracing the society's definition of success and adhering to the established and approved means of achieving success. The student works hard despite the academic and financial obstacles, trying to do well in school to achieve success and a good job placement. She uses legitimate, approved means—education and hard work—to reach goals that the society views as worthy.

2. *Innovation* refers to the use of illicit means to reach approved goals. Our student uses illegitimate means to achieve her education goals. She may cheat on exams or get papers from Internet sources. Success in school is all that matters, not how she gets there.

3. *Ritualism* involves strict adherence to the culturally prescribed rules, even though individuals give up on the goals they hoped to achieve. The student may give up the idea of getting good grades and graduating from college but, as a matter of pride and self-image, continues to try hard and to take classes. She conforms to expectations, for example, but with no sense of purpose. She just does what she is told.

4. *Retreatism* refers to giving up on both the goals and the means. The student either bides her time, not doing well, or drops out, giving up on future job goals. She abandons or retreats from the goals of a professional position in society and the means to get there. She may even turn to a different lifestyle—for example, becoming a user of drugs and alcohol—as part of the retreat.

5. *Rebellion* entails rejecting the socially approved ideas of success and the means of attaining that success. It replaces those with alternative definitions of success and alternative strategies for attaining the new goals. Rebelling against the dominant cultural goals and means, the student may join a radical political group or a commune, intent on developing new ideas of how society should be organized and what a "truly educated" person should be.

Deviant behavior results from retreatism, rebellion, and innovation. According to Merton (1968), the reasons why individuals resort to these behaviors lie in the social conditions that provide access to success, not in their individual biological or psychological makeup.

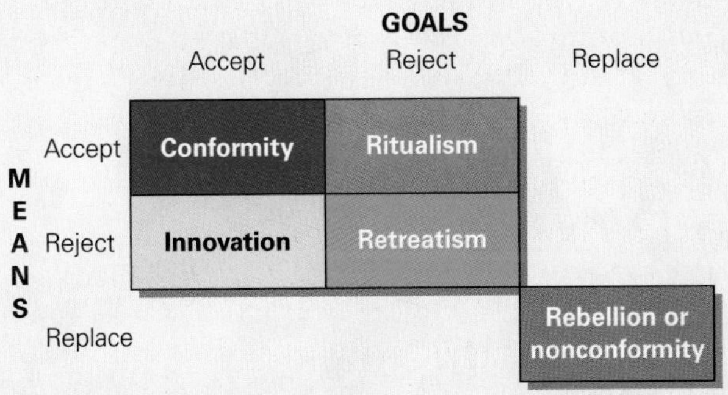

Figure 6.1 Merton's Strain Theory

The structural-functional approaches to deviance focus on what happens if deviance disrupts the ongoing social order. They explore what causes deviance, how to prevent disruptions, how to keep change slow and nondisruptive, and how deviance can be useful to the ongoing society. However, anomie and strain theories fail to account for class conflicts, inequities, and poverty, which conflict theorists argue cause deviance.

Conflict Theory of Deviance

The Syrian protests to overthrow the dictatorial government of President Bashar al-Assad began on March 15, 2011. In 2011 and 2012, thousands of citizens held peaceful protests against the autocratic regime. The strong and well-organized military of Syria has killed over 10,000 civilians in bloody attacks, especially in pockets of resistance, arguing that the unarmed protesters were rebels, terrorists, and enemies of the state. As government troops killed civilians, many soldiers turned to the rebel side, refusing to kill fellow Syrians. They were not convinced that their fellow citizens were dangerous deviants. President Assad and his ethnic group allies used power, but was it in the service of the society as a whole or to protect their own self-interests? (*The New York Times* 2013). In 2011 in Libya, North Africa, thousands of citizens revolted against the regime of the leader, Moammar Gadhafi, because of what they felt was an oppressive and corrupt ruling elite. Many educated young people joined the rebel ranks, and many were killed in the uprising. From 2002 to the present, antiwar protests have been held in many major cities around the world against the wars in Iraq and Afghanistan. Are these various protesters deviants and criminals, or are they brave heroes? The response depends on who answers the question.

Conflict theorists assume that conflict between groups is inevitable. Because many societies today are heterogeneous groupings of people, the differences in goals, resources,

People hold signs during a Tea Party protest in Freedom Plaza in Washington, DC. One protester's sign calls the president "Parasite in Chief." The Tea Party has taken a strident oppositional position to stop governmental growth and any possible increase in taxes. This event coincided with the day that American citizens are required to file their national income tax.

norms, and values between interest groups and groups in power often cause conflict. Conflict theory focuses on a meso- and macro-level analysis of deviance, looking at deviance as the result of social inequality or of the struggle between groups for power.

For conflict theorists, deviance is often seen as related to social class status, interest groups, or cultural conflict between the dominant group and ethnic, religious, political, regional, or gender groups. Wealthy and powerful elites want to maintain their control and their high positions (Domhoff 2009). They have the power to pass laws and define what is deviant, sometimes by effectively eliminating the opposition groups. The greater the cultural difference between the dominant group and other groups in society, the greater the possibility of conflict. This is because minority groups and subcultures challenge the norms of the dominant groups and threaten the consensus in a society (Huizinga, Loeber, and Thornberry 1994).

Some conflict theorists blame capitalist systems for the unjust administration of law and unequal distribution of resources, arguing that the ruling class uses the legal system to further the capitalist enterprise (Quinney 2002). The dominant or ruling class defines deviance, applies laws to protect its interests, represses any conflict or protest, and, in effect, may force those in subordinate classes to carry out actions that it has defined as deviant. These actions are necessary to survive when legitimate avenues to resources are restricted by the affluent. We see this in the case of the Syrian rebel fighters. This situation, in turn, supports the ideology that works against the subordinate classes.

Activities that threaten the interests and well-being of the wealthy capitalist class and those in power become defined as deviant. By subordinating certain groups and then defining them as deviant or criminal, the dominant group consolidates its powerful position. Because the dominant class is usually of one ethnic group and those of other races or ethnicities tend to be in the subordinate class, conflict often has racial and ethnic implications as well as social class dimensions. The fact that for the same offenses, subordinate class or race members are arrested and prosecuted more often than dominant class or race members is provided as evidence by conflict theorists to support this contention (Quinney 2002). When people feel they are not treated fairly by the society, they have less loyalty to the society and to its rules. This may result in activities considered deviant by those in power.

To reduce deviance and crime, conflict theorists believe that we must change the structure of society. For instance, laws in many countries claim to support equal and fair treatment for all, but when one looks at the law in action, another picture emerges. Recall the example of the Saints and Roughnecks; the students from powerful families and higher social classes received favored treatment. Unequal treatment of groups that differ from the dominant group—the poor, laboring class and racial or ethnic minorities in particular—is rooted in the legal, political, and occupational structures of societies.

If the structure of society were changed and there were no dominant groups exploiting the subordinate groups, would crime disappear? To answer this, we can look to patterns of crime in societies that have attempted to develop a communist, classless structure. The rate of crime in China and Cuba, for instance, is lower than in many Western democracies, in part because of the less dramatic inequality and the strict social controls on behavior (Nationmaster 2010). On the other hand, deviance is still present in noncapitalist societies. So although capitalistic inequality contributes to deviance, it is only one of the many variables at work.

Feminist Theory. The goal of most feminist theorists is to understand and improve women's status, including their treatment by men and those in power. Feminists argue that traditional theories do not give an adequate picture or understanding of women's situations. Although there are several branches of feminist theory, most see the macro-level causes of abuses suffered by women as rooted in the capitalist patriarchal system. Feminist theorists look for explanations for violence against women and the secondary status of most women in gender relations and social structures. They include the following ideas: (a) women are faced with a division of labor resulting from their sex, (b) the separation between public (work) and private (home) spheres of social activity create a "we" versus "they" thinking between men and women, and (c) socialization of children into gender-specific adult roles has implications for how males and females perceive and relate to each other.

One result of women's status is that they are often victims of crime. The type of victimization varies around the globe, from sex trafficking to rape (Bales 2012; Bales and Trodd 2008). Women are less often in a position to commit crimes. In fact, deviant acts by women have traditionally fallen into the categories of shoplifting, credit card or welfare fraud, writing bad checks (in developed societies), prostitution, and, in some countries, adultery or inappropriate attire. Many Western feminist theorists contend that until women around the world are on an equal footing with men, crimes against women and definitions of various behaviors of women as deviant are likely to continue.

Consider the case of intimate partner violence, including rape. Until recent years, there have been few serious consequences for the offenders in many countries (especially during times of anomie or war), and women often were blamed or blamed themselves for "letting it happen" (Boy and Kulczycki 2008). In some cultures, women fear reporting violence and may blame themselves for the beating or rape. Unfortunately, from recent data collected by the United Nations, we know that up to 59% of women will experience violence in their lifetime in some countries, many on a regular basis. For example, in Zambia, the rate of beatings, rape, and other violence is 59%, in Australia and Mozambique 48%, and in China and Hong Kong, 12% (United Nations 2010). Data also show that 16% to 52% of married women in the Middle East were assaulted in one year, compared with 1.3% in Europe and 12% North America (United Nations 2010). The next "Sociology Around the World" feature on page 190 illustrates this pattern.

Feminist theorists argue that we learn our gender roles, part of which is men learning to be aggressive. Women's status in society results in their being treated as sex objects—to be used for men's pleasure. Women's race and class identification become relevant in the exploitation of poor, ethnically distinct women from developing countries for human trafficking.

One thing is certain: Women who have been victimized need help from their family and loved ones to feel in control again, but some are unjustly blamed for the rape (McEvoy and Brookings 2008). Keep in mind that each cultural practice evolved for a reason in each society. The meaning of these standards needs to be understood through the eyes of that culture so that we can effectively deal with human rights abuses. Our values make it difficult to understand the reason for certain practices in different cultures.

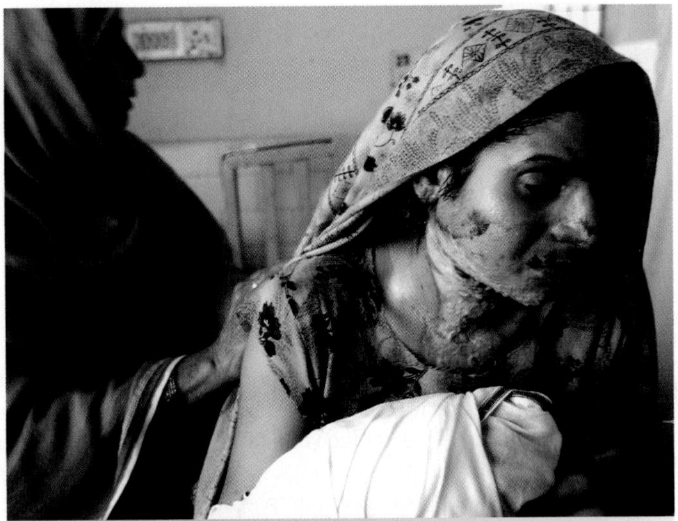

Ishrat Abdullah sits in her hospital bed showing the burns inflicted to over 30% of her body after her husband threw sulfuric acid over her during a domestic dispute. Such abuse is the concern of feminist scholars who see women as disproportionately the victims.

According to feminist theory, women's work in the private sphere—including housework, child care, and sexual satisfaction of their husbands—is undervalued, as are the women who carry out these roles. In some societies, women are the property of their husbands, with men's strength and physical force the ultimate means of control over women. Some branches of feminist theory argue that men exploit women's labor power and sexuality to continue their dominance. The system is reproduced through new generations that are socialized to maintain the patriarchy and to view inequality between the sexes as "normal" and "natural." Women who deviate from the cultural expectations of "normal" behavior are condemned.

No one theory of why deviance occurs can explain all the forms of deviance. Some theories consider the micro-level processes that shape one's values and self-identity. These approaches examine why certain behaviors and certain individuals are defined as deviant, and they explore the consequences of being labeled deviant. Meso- and macro-level theories attempt to explain the structural factors at the community, national, or even the global level that result in deviance being more common among certain groups, in certain areas, or at certain times. Thus, depending on the level of analysis of the questions sociologists wish to study (micro, meso, or macro), they select the theory that best fits the data they find.

In the following sections, we explore in more detail the micro-meso-macro connections as they apply to one manifestation of deviance—crime. This illustrates how the sociological imagination can be applied to deviance at each level in the social system.

Sociology Around the World

Blaming the Victim: Extreme Cases

Every woman fears being raped—being forced into having sex against her will. In most countries, rape is considered a deviant behavior on the part of the perpetrator—a crime punishable by imprisonment. The woman is provided medical help and counseling, yet only a small percentage of estimated rapes are reported. In a few countries or regions in countries, the legal system is based on strict interpretations of religious books by those who practice fundamentalist interpretations of the religion, in an attempt to guard against loss of a woman's virtue, shame, and illegitimate children. Some would also argue that these laws maintain patriarchal control. Recent rape laws proposed in Afghanistan would have permitted marital rape; stones were thrown at protesting women. Cases in other countries show the contentious nature of this issue. Although the following examples are rare, they show the extremes to which communities can go to protect the "virtue" of women and the family. In the first case, excerpted from *The New York Times*, a woman was blamed for sex outside marriage even though she had been raped.

> The evidence of guilt was there for all to see—a newborn baby in the arms of its mother, a village woman named Zafran Bibi. Her crime: She had been raped. Her sentence: death by stoning. Now, Ms. Zafran, who is about 26, is in solitary confinement in a death row cell in Kohat, a nearby town. The only visitor she is allowed is her baby daughter, now a 1-year-old being cared for by a prison nurse. In photographs, Ms. Zafran is a tall woman with striking green eyes—a peasant woman of the hot and barren hills of Pakistan's North-West Frontier country . . .
>
> Thumping a fat, red statute book, the white-bearded judge who convicted her—Anwar Ali Khan—said he had simply followed the letter of the Koran-based law, known as *hudood*, that mandates punishments. "The illegitimate child is not disowned by her and therefore is proof of *zina*," he said, referring to laws that forbid any sexual contact outside marriage. Furthermore, he said, in accusing her brother-in-law of raping her, Ms. Zafran had confessed to her crime.
>
> "The lady stated before this court that, yes, she had committed sexual intercourse, but with the brother of her husband," Judge Khan said. "This left no option to the court but to impose the highest penalty." Although legal fine points do exist, little distinction is made in court between forced and consensual sex. These strict interpretations of the law are practiced only in very traditional areas.
>
> When *hudood* was enacted 23 years ago, the laws were formally described as measures to ban "all forms of adultery, whether the offense is committed with or without the consent of the parties," but it is almost always the women who are punished, whatever the facts (Mydans 2002:A3). Zafran Bibi appealed the decision and was subsequently released from prison. Women's rights groups and the international community protested the charge; this may have helped the court to find her "not guilty," and she was released by the Federal Sharia Act in Pakistan. She still fears, however, that she will be the victim of violence because she became a public figure through the publicity her case received and because the individuals who opposed her acquittal know where she lives and what she looks like.

In another case, covered extensively by American and European news, a young Pakistani woman, Mukhtar Mai, was ordered to be raped as punishment for her brother who was seen with a woman from another, more powerful tribe. In 2004, Pakistani governments (mostly those of small towns and villages) ordered about 400 rapes as punishment for both sexual and nonsexual offenses. Higher-policing groups do occasionally arrest the rapists in these cases for sexual violation, but this is not uniform. For Mai, 6 of her 14 rapists have been charged with rape, and Mai has asked that the men not be acquitted (BBC News 2005). However, on April 21, 2011, 5 of the 6 alleged rapists were freed by the courts, and Mai says she fears for her life (Taseer 2011).

In Saudi Arabia, a young woman victim was abducted at knifepoint, gang raped for being seen with a man who had blackmailed the woman and her family, then beaten by her brother for disgracing the family, and sentenced by the court to 90 lashes for being seen with the man who was blackmailing them and who may have lured her into the trap ("Gang-Rape Victim Faces Lashes" 2007).

Thinking Sociologically

Meso- and macro-level social forces can be even more powerful than micro-level forces in explaining deviance. What might be the factors that contribute to deviance at the meso and macro levels? Pick a recent example of deviance from your newspaper or a television show. Which sociological theories help explain this deviance?

Every 3.2 seconds	1 property crime
Every 4.8 seconds	1 larceny, theft
Every 14.5 seconds	1 burglary
Every 26.8 seconds	1 motor vehicle theft
Every 22.2 seconds	1 violent crime
Every 36.6 seconds	1 aggravated assault
Every 1.2 minutes	1 robbery
Every 5.8 minutes	1 forcible rape
Every 30.9 minutes	1 murder

Figure 6.2 2009 Crime Clock

Source: U.S. Department of Justice (2010).

Crime and Individuals: Micro-Level Analysis

Crime, as introduced at the beginning of this chapter, is deviance that (if one is caught) involves severe formal penalties imposed by the government. A criminal justice system or court becomes involved in reinforcing conformity.

Crimes that affect the individual or primary group seem most threatening to us and receive the most attention in the press and from politicians. Yet these micro-level crimes are only a portion of the total crime picture and, except for hate crimes, are not the most dysfunctional or dangerous crimes. In the United States, more than 2,800 acts are listed as federal crimes. These acts fall into several types of crime, some of which are discussed below. First, we consider how crime rates are measured.

How Much Crime Is There?

How do sociologists and law enforcement officials know how much crime occurs? Not all crime is reported to the police, and when crime is reported, the methods of collecting data may differ. Each country has methods of keeping crime records. For instance, the official record of crime in the United States is found in the U.S. Federal Bureau of Investigation's *Uniform Crime Reports* (UCR). The FBI relies on information submitted voluntarily by law enforcement agencies and divides crimes into two categories: Type I and Type II offenses. Type I offenses, also known as *FBI index crimes*, include murder, forcible rape, robbery, aggravated assault, burglary, larceny theft, motor vehicle theft, and arson. Type II offenses include fraud, simple assault, vandalism, driving under the influence of alcohol or drugs, and running away from home. In fact, there are hundreds of Type II crimes. Figure 6.2 summarizes UCR records on Type I offenses.

To examine trends in crime, criminologists calculate a rate of crime, usually per 100,000 individuals. Recent data indicate that the rate of violent crime in the United States has dropped since the mid-1990s (see Table 6.1). In 1985, there were 558 violent crimes per 100,000 residents; in 1995, that number was 684.5; by 2005, the number had dropped to 2011, 386.3, 429.4. There were a total of 1,203,564 violent crimes in the United States in 2011, down 5.3% from 2008 and 7.5% below 2000 levels. Aggravated assault accounted for 61.2% and

Table 6.1 Index of Violent Crime, United States

Year	*Violent Crime Rate (per 100,000 residents)*
1985	556.6
1990	731.8
1995	684.5
2000	506.5
2005	469.0
2006	473.5
2007	466.9
2008	454.5
2009	429.4
2010	403.6.
2011	386.3

Source: UCR Crime Statistics (2011), www.fbi.gov/about-us/cjis/ucr/crime-in-the-u.s/2011/crime-in-the-u.s.-2011

robbery 31% of crimes (U.S. Department of Justice 2011). Crime records also show that black men were 6 times as likely to be homicide victims as white men (Stout 2009).

Although the UCR data provide a picture of how much crime gets reported to the police and leads to arrest, the FBI does not provide information on how much crime there is in the United States. Sometimes a crime that is reported to the police does not lead to an arrest, or an arrest is made but the case is never prosecuted in court, or a prosecutor will initiate prosecution but the case never comes to trial. Instead, in a majority of cases it is plea-bargained—a suspect agrees to plead guilty in exchange for being given a lesser charge, perhaps because the suspect feels guilt, because the person does not have the resources to fight the charges with a good attorney, or because the suspect is willing to exchange information for a lighter sentence. The reduction in the number of cases at each level of the criminal justice system is just one of the problems of attempting to determine accurate crime rates.

Changes in the UCR to eliminate some of its problems have led to a new measurement, the *National Incident-Based Reporting System* (NIBRS). In this measure, the reporting is incident driven, meaning that the FBI gathers not only information on the crime but also more detailed information on victim and offender characteristics and other, more detailed categories. Reports include the type of offense, whether a weapon was used, the location, whether drugs were a factor, and any motivations related to race, religion, or gender. This system provides more detailed and accurate crime statistics.

Another technique to assess crime rates is by carrying out self-reporting surveys—asking individuals what criminal acts they have committed. Criminal participation surveys typically focus on adolescents and their involvement in delinquency. Yet another way to assess crime rates is through victimization surveys—surveys that ask people how much crime they have experienced. The most extensively gathered victimization survey in the United States is the National Crime Victimization Survey, conducted by the Bureau of Justice Statistics. According to these records, the tendency to report crime to the police varies by the type of crime, with violent victimizations having the highest reporting rate. The victimization survey corroborates the findings of the Index of Crime, showing that violent crime rates have declined since the early 1990s.

How crime is measured affects what and how much crime is reported. Although differences in crime reports are often difficult to reconcile, each measurement instrument provides a different portion of the total picture of crime. By using several data-gathering techniques (triangulation), a more accurate picture of crime begins to emerge. Most of the crimes that concern average citizens of countries around the world are violent crimes committed by individuals or small groups. The following are some examples of types of micro-level crimes.

Thinking Sociologically

Imagine that you work for the Bureau of Justice Statistics as many sociologists do. Congress asks you to predict how many FBI agents will be needed to deal with different types of crime. How would you go about determining this, and what databases might you use?

Types of Crime

Crimes range from petty theft of a candy bar to a fist fight in a bar to rape and murder. The following outlines several major types of crime as designated by the FBI.

Predatory or Street Crimes

Crimes committed against individuals or property are called *predatory crimes* by law enforcement agencies and are considered the most serious crimes by public opinion. In the United States, the UCR lists eight serious predatory index crimes used to track crime rates: acts against people (murder, robbery, assault, and rape) and against property (burglary, arson, theft, and auto theft).

Citizens of the United States are increasingly afraid of violent predatory crime, especially by strangers. Many citizens feel they cannot trust others. Some keep guns. Others, especially women, African Americans, older Americans, and low-income individuals, are afraid to go out near their homes at night. Because one's property and bodily safety are at stake, the public fixates on these crimes as the most feared and serious. However, the total violent crime victimization rate declined by 4% in 2011 compared to 13% in 2010 and 4% in 2009, indicating an overall drop in violent crime rates (FBI 2012; Truman 2011). Below we discuss crimes committed by individuals—but stay tuned because most criminologists feel there are more serious crimes to be discussed under meso- and macro-level deviance.

Crimes Without Victims

Acts committed by or between individual consenting adults are known as **victimless** or **public order crimes**.

Depending on the laws of countries, these can include prostitution, homosexual acts, gambling, smoking marijuana and using drugs, drunkenness, and some forms of white-collar crime. The participants involved do not consider themselves to be victims, but the offense is mostly an affront to someone else's morals. While these acts are illegal and affirm the values of those who have power, they may be tolerated (the police look the other way) as long as they do not become highly visible. Some prostitution is overlooked in major cities of the world, but if it becomes visible or is seen as a public nuisance, authorities crack down, and it is controlled. Even though these acts are called victimless, there is controversy over whether individuals are victims even when consenting to the act and whether others such as family members are victims dealing with the consequences of the illegal activities.

A man lights up a marijuana pipe in Holland's Cannabis Castle, which provides some of the most potent strains of the herbal drug. Smoking pot is legal in the Netherlands. The Dutch think that because there is no victim, there should be no prohibition on the behavior.

Thinking Sociologically

Can a person be victimized by drugs even if he willingly uses them? Many prostitutes only consent to sex acts because poverty leaves them with few other options and because, like many women without resources, they are vulnerable to domination by men. Are they victims, or are these crimes without victims? Why?

Societies respond to victimless crimes such as using and selling drugs with a variety of policies, from execution in Iran and hanging in Malaysia to legalization in Holland. Long prison terms in the United States mean that 3 out of every 10 prison cells are now reserved for the user, the addict, and the drug seller—yet the problem has not diminished (Goode 2012). Proposals to legalize drugs, gambling, prostitution, and other victimless crimes meet with strong opinions both for and against. Although in many countries current policies and programs toward drugs are not working to reduce use and crime connected with use of drugs, the consequences of alternative proposals are also uncertain.

Hate Crimes

Ethnic violence around the world results in hate crimes in societies, between ethnic groups, in communities, at workplaces, and on college campuses. **Hate crimes** are *criminal offenses committed against a person, property, or a group that are motivated by the offender's bias against a religious, ethnic, or racial group; a national origin; a gender; or a sexual orientation*. Recall the example of Tyler Clementi who committed suicide after a hate crime against him in the discussion of labeling theory. In 2011, there were a reported 1,018 active hate groups in the United States (Southern Poverty Law Center 2011). The FBI reported 7,789 hate crimes and 8,336 victims in 2009. Most hate crimes are directed against property and involve destruction, damage, or vandalism; others involve direct intimidation. In 2009, 3,199 hate crimes were categorized as racial bias, 1,303 religious bias, 1,223 sexual orientation bias, 777 ethnicity/nationality bias, and 96 disability bias (U.S. Census Bureau 2012b).

Research suggests that most hate crimes are spontaneous incidents, often a case of the victim being in the wrong place at the wrong time. Consider the case of Matthew Shepard, the gay college student who was robbed, tied to a fence post, beaten, and left to die in the cold Wyoming night. Nearly 18% of hate crimes are against those with different sexual orientations. Victims often form supportive in-groups to protect themselves from others who create a "culture of hate" (Levin and McDevitt 2003).

Hate crimes are often vicious and brutal because the perpetrators feel rage against the victim as a representative of a group they despise. The crimes are committed by individuals or small vigilante groups. Emotionally based

In Munich, Germany, advocates of a hate-free world express their support for the LGBT community in the Christopher Street Day parade, an annual European celebration held in cities across Europe for the rights of LGBT people. Others (right) express their sentiment that Matthew Shepard, a gay student who was beaten and left to die in a Wyoming hate crime, was a deviant who had no moral standing and, seemingly, no right to live.

crimes upholding moral codes may threaten a person's own behavior as the most vociferous protesters may be hiding guilt. The targets are usually individuals who happen to have certain traits or are part of a particular community. In the case of some white supremacy movements, philosophical, political, and even religious principles guide their group beliefs (Blee 2008).

The examples above represent only three of the many types of micro-level crimes, characterized by individual or small-group actions. We now turn to crime in organizations and institutions. Not only is crime rooted in complex organizations at the meso level, but crimes themselves are committed within or by organizations.

Crime and Organizations: Meso-Level Analysis

Understanding criminal behavior is especially important if we wish to understand complex modern societies. First, as societies modernize, there is an almost universal tendency for crime rates to increase dramatically due to the anomie that new migrants and the poor experience in urban areas where old norms are no longer relevant (Merton 1938). Second, as societies become modernized and urban, they become more reliant on formal or bureaucratic mechanisms of control rather than small community pressures and conformity—in other words, development of a criminal justice system at the meso level of society.

Crimes Involving Organizations and Institutions

Jeanne, one of the authors of this book, recently got a call from a fraud office at an online retailer saying that her credit card had been compromised. Someone had ordered online items from Bloomingdale's, Coach, and DSW (Designer Shoe Warehouse). How did the retailer catch it? "Unusual behavior on the account." The problem is that only a few cases are identified, and only a few members of organized crime syndicates get caught. Some crimes are committed by highly organized, hierarchically structured syndicates that are formed for the purpose of achieving their economic objectives in any way possible—credit card fraud and identity theft being major crimes.

A high-profile area of fraud is the medical system. Health care costs and insurance premiums have been rising at alarming rates, and one of the contributing factors is fraud in Medicaid and Medicare. Medicare fraud is estimated at up to $80 billion a year, with 20% of every Medicare dollar going to fraud (PolitiFact.com 2009). For example, in South Florida, criminals open storefronts claiming to sell medical equipment; often these are located in dying strip malls, and the offices for the equipment are usually closed. Once the criminals have sent in false claims for Medicare payments, sometimes amounting to millions of dollars, they close the storefronts and move on so that they cannot be traced.

The federal government has had a small number of investigators who are hardly a match for the fast-moving get-rich-quick con artists. However, the government has recently added a number of investigators, resulting in rapid charges of fraud against 91 medical professionals in October 2012, accounting for $430 million in false billing (Reuters 2012). Fraud prosecutions are up 71% from 2005, and up 85% in 2011 compared to 2010. Savings from fraud will mean money put back into the health care system (Kennedy 2011).

This is but one example of crimes involving organizations. Some crimes are committed by highly organized, hierarchically structured syndicates that are formed for the purpose of achieving their economic objectives in any way possible. These groups intentionally flout the law. On the other hand, some crimes are committed by legitimate corporations. Their crimes are very serious, but the public image of such organizations is not criminal so they are not always suspected or caught. We will look first at organized criminal organizations and then at crimes committed by people within their legitimate occupations and organizations.

Films like The Godfather *romanticize and "domesticate" organized crime, creating a false image in the minds of the public about how dangerous this form of crime can really be.*

Organized Crime

Organized crime refers to *ongoing criminal enterprises by an organized group whose ultimate purpose is economic gain through illegitimate means* (Siegel 2009). Organized criminals use business enterprises for illegal profit. Sometimes they engage in violence and corruption to gain and maintain power and profit. Our image of this type of crime is sometimes glamorized, coming from stereotypes in films such as *No Country for Old Men, The Godfather, Goodfellas, Gangs of New York, The Sopranos,* and many others. On television, *The Sopranos* is the ultimate media "mob" depiction. Despite the alluring view of these idealized stories, organized crime is a serious problem in many countries. It is essentially a counterculture with a hierarchical structure, from the boss down to the underlings. The organization relies on power, control, fear, violence, and corruption. This type of crime is a particular problem when societies experience anomie and social controls break down.

Marginalized ethnic groups that face discrimination may become involved in a quest to get ahead through organized crime. Early in U.S. history, Italians were especially prominent in organized crime, but today, many groups are involved. Organized crime around the world has gained strong footholds in countries in transition (Siegel and Nelen 2008). For example, in Russia, the transition from a socialist economy to a market economy has provided many opportunities for criminal activity. The *Mafiya* is estimated to be 100,000 people strong, and some estimate that the members control 70% to 80% of all private business and 40% of Russia's wealth (Lindberg and Markovic n.d.; Schmalleger 2013). Organized crime usually takes one of three forms: (1) the sale of illegal goods and services, including gambling, loan sharking, trafficking in drugs and people, selling stolen goods, and prostitution; (2) infiltrating legitimate businesses and unions through threat and intimidation and using bankruptcy and fraud to exploit and devastate a legitimate company; and (3) racketeering—the extortion of funds in exchange for protection (i.e., not being hurt). Activities such as a casino or trash collection service often appear to be legitimate endeavors on the surface but may be cover operations for highly organized illegal crime rings.

Although the exact cost of organized crime in the United States is impossible to determine, estimates of the annual gross income of organized crime activity range from $50 billion—more than 1% of the gross national product—to $90 billion per year (CNBC 2010; "Organized Crime" 2011; Siegel 2009). Internationally, money laundering alone is estimated at 2% to 5% of the world's gross domestic product (Bjelopera and Finklea 2012).

Transnational organized crime takes place across national boundaries, using sophisticated electronic communications and transportation technologies. Experts identify several major crime clans in the world: (a) Hong Kong–based triads, (b) South American cocaine cartels, (c) Italian mafia, (d) Japanese *yakuza*, (e) Russian *Mafiya*, and (f) West African crime groups. Each operates across borders. Organized crime is responsible for thousands of deaths every year through drug traffic and murders, and it contributes to the climate of violence in many cities (Siegel 2009).

The value of the global illicit drug market is estimated at more than $320 billion at the retail level (based on retail prices). The largest market is cannabis, followed by cocaine, opiates, and other markets such as methamphetamine, amphetamine, and ecstasy (Smith Drug War Chronicle 2009). Many people survive the drug trade, from the poppy farmers in Afghanistan who grow more than 90% of the world's poppies to street drug dealers. In 2011, the acreage devoted to growing poppies was the highest ever, especially in southern and western Afghanistan (Afghanistan Opium Survey 2011; "Global Opium Production" 2011). The Taliban are protecting the crops that bring in more than $4 billion in profit, 10% of which goes to support their operations (Shah and Rubin 2012). This problem is not likely to end soon because the farmers are in debt to the Taliban and are therefore forced to continue growing poppies. The Taliban profit from the sales by more than $100 million per year, which helps keep them in power. Thus, Westerners who use opium drugs help in financially sustaining this group (National Public Radio 2008).

Add other types of crimes (transporting migrants, selling human organs, trafficking in women and children for the sex industry, drug sales, and sales of weapons and nuclear material), and the estimates of profits for international crime cartels are from $650 billion to more than $1.5 trillion a year ("Transnational Crime in the Developing World" 2011).

Occupational Crime

Although the Madoff financial scandal became public knowledge in December 2008, the details unfolded over the next several months. Bernard (Bernie) Madoff, former chair of the NASDAQ stock exchange, had developed a Ponzi scheme that is probably the largest investment fraud Wall Street has ever seen. The scheme defrauded and wrecked thousands of investors, public pension funds, charitable foundations, and universities of billions of dollars, with more than $65 billion missing from investor accounts. Named after Charles Ponzi, the first to be caught (in 1919), Ponzi schemes involve promises of large returns on investments, paying old investors with money from new investors. Money is shifted between investors ("The Madoff Case" 2009).

A violation of the law committed by an individual or a group in the course of a legitimate, respected occupation or financial activity is called *white-collar or occupational crime* (Coleman 2006; Hagan 2011). Occupational crime can be committed by individuals from virtually any social class, and it can occur at any organizational level. However, most often this refers to white-collar crimes. In the United States, these are "estimated to be ten times greater than all the annual losses from all the crimes reported to the police" (Coleman 2006:43). Antitrust violations cost $250 billion. Tax fraud costs $150 billion, and health care industry fraud costs $100 billion. Employee theft adds 2% to the retail purchase price of the products we buy (Coleman 2006).

Occupational crime receives less attention than violent crimes because it is less visible, does not always cause obvious physical injury to identifiable people, and is frequently committed by people in positions of substantial authority and prestige. Reports of violent crimes that appear on the television news each night attract more attention. Yet occupational crime is far more costly in currency, health, and lives. Victims of financial scams who have lost their life savings are well aware of this.

In addition to occupational crimes such as embezzlement, pilfering, bribery, tax evasion, price fixing, obstruction of justice, and various forms of fraud, computer crime is adding to the losses of businesses and government. Identity theft, embezzlement, international illegal transfers of money, illegal stock trades, sales of illegal or inferior products, creation of computer viruses, computer hacking—this list is long and will become longer. "As technology advances, it facilitates new forms of behavior . . . new and as yet unimaginable opportunities for criminals positioned to take advantage of technology and the power such technology will afford" (Schmalleger 2006:473).

Sociologists divide occupational crimes into four major categories: (1) against the company, (2) against employees, (3) against customers, and (4) against the general public or other organizations (Hagan 2011).

Crimes against the company include pilfering (using company resources such as the photocopy machine for personal business) and employee theft ("borrowing company property," taking from the till, and embezzlement). Most employees are otherwise upstanding citizens, but those who commit occupational crimes say they do so for several reasons. First, they feel little or no loyalty to the organization, especially if it is large and impersonal. It is like stealing from nobody, they say. Second, workers feel exploited and resentful toward the company. Stealing is getting back at the company. Third, the theft is seen as a "fringe benefit" or "informal compensation" that they deserve. Making personal long-distance calls on company phones or taking paper and pens are examples. Fourth, workers may steal because of the challenge. It makes the job more interesting if they can get away with it. It is important to note that these people do not see themselves as criminals, especially compared with "street" criminals (Altheide et al. 1978).

The next three types of corporate crime are often done on behalf of the company, and the victims are employees or members of the larger society. *Crimes against employees* refer to corporate neglect of worker safety. In the United States, the Occupational Safety and Health Act was passed in 1970 to help enforce regulations to protect workers, but there are still many problems. Government agencies estimate that the death rate each year from job-related illness and injuries is fivefold the number of deaths from street crimes. For example, one out of every five cancer cases has been traced to pollutants in workplaces, and many of these cases were preventable (Simon 2006). Government regulation has decreased fatalities in the workplace, down 22% since 2006, and nonfatal injuries are 3.5 cases per 100 workers, the lowest since 2003 (U.S. Bureau of Labor Statistics 2011).

Neglect of worker safety is a particularly serious problem in many developing or peripheral countries trying to attract multinational corporations with low taxes, cheap labor, and few regulations. Neglect of worker safety is related to environments where profits are expected by investors and benefits outweigh the costs (which illustrates rational choice theory).

Strain theory points out that the goals of corporations are to make the greatest short-term profits, and the method to do that is to cut expenses. In fact, it is illegal for a U.S. corporation to do anything contrary to the interests of the stockholders. Thus, to install expensive safety equipment cuts those profits, and many employers are concerned with the bottom line, not the long-term consequences. Government regulatory agencies responsible for reducing environmental hazards and workplace dangers do not have sufficient staff to police companies for adherence to laws. Internationally, there is little oversight. Multinational corporations generally look for the cheapest labor costs and fewest environmental regulations, and governments of poor countries try to attract foreign corporations to keep the poor populace employed regardless of the personal illnesses and environmental or workplace consequences.

Crimes against customers involve acts victimizing patrons, such as selling dangerous foods or unsafe products, consumer fraud, deceptive advertising, and price-fixing (i.e., setting prices in collusion with another producer). The purpose of advertising is to convince customers, by whatever means, to buy the product—appealing to their vanity, sexual interests, or desire to keep up with their neighbors. Sometimes these techniques cross the line between honesty and deception. The result can be customers purchasing products that are defective and even dangerous—all with the full knowledge of company officials.

Crimes against the public include acts by companies that negatively affect large groups of people. One example is hospitals or medical offices that overbill Medicare (discussed above), which costs U.S. taxpayers an estimated $80 billion a year. The FBI (2006a) estimates that 3% to 10% of the total health care expenditures, both public and private, are fraudulent.

Surreptitiously dumping pollutants into landfills, streams, or the air is another crime against the public. Proper disposal of contaminants can be costly and time-consuming for a company, but shortcuts can cause long-term effects for the public (Coleman 2006). Pollutants from industrial wastes have caused high rates of miscarriages, birth defects, and diseases among residents. These cases demonstrate how lethal crimes against the public can be.

After reviewing the evidence, Coleman (2006) draws the conclusion that white-collar crime committed by company executives is by far our most serious crime problem. The economic cost of white-collar crime is vastly greater than the economic cost of street crime. White-collar criminals kill considerably more people than all violent street criminals put together (Coleman 2006).

Thinking Sociologically

Why are meso-level crimes (occupational/white-collar crimes) considered more dangerous and more costly to the public than micro-level crimes? Why do they get so much less attention?

Some beaches in the United States, even in beautiful resort communities, have been closed due to unsafe water, and in some communities, children cannot play outside during the warm months due to risk of injury to their lungs. The U.S. Environmental Protection Agency has documented many cases in which industries violate pollution control laws, and it is the citizenry who suffer. This illustrates corporate crimes against citizens, but it is still not considered a "major" crime in the FBI index of crimes or by most journalists.

National and Global Crime: Macro-Level Analysis

National boundaries are blurring as people migrate around the globe and corporations have no loyalty to any boundaries. Crime syndicates are international as goods and people are moved surreptitiously across borders. Terrorist organizations, too, have no boundaries. Let us now explore crime at the national and global macro level.

Terrorism is *the planned use of random, unlawful (or illegal) violence or threat of violence against civilians to create (or raise) fear and intimidate citizens in order to advance the terrorist group's political or ideological goals* (U.S. Department of Defense 2011).

Add to that international terrorism practiced in one or more foreign countries, and terrorism becomes a worldwide problem. According to the U.S. State Department, the number of international terrorist attacks in 2010 was up 5% from 2009 with 11,500 attacks in 72 nations and more than 13,200 deaths (National Center for Victims of Crime 2011).

Detainees sit in a holding area at the naval base in Guantánamo Bay, Cuba, in the "temporary" detention facility. The Obama administration planned to shut down the facility in 2010, but legal complications have made this more difficult than President Obama anticipated. Although the number of detainees dropped from 245 in January 2009 to 172 in March 2011, those remaining are complicated legal cases (Guardian 2011; White House 2011). In several U.S. Supreme Court rulings (2006 and 2008), the verdict was that the rights of these people have been violated by the U.S. administration (Global Security 2009).

Table 6.2 Types of Terrorist Groups

Nationalist	Irish Republican Army, Basque Fatherland and Liberty, Kurdistan Workers' Party
Religious	Al-Qaeda, Hamas, Hezbollah, Aum Shinrikyo (Japan)
State sponsored	Hezbollah (backed by Iran), Abu Nidal Organization (Syria, Libya), Japanese Red Army (Libya)
Left wing	Red Brigades (Italy), Baader-Meinhof Gang (Germany), Japanese Red Army
Right wing	Neo-Nazis, skinheads, white supremacists
Anarchist	Some contemporary antiglobalization groups

Source: Schmalleger (2006:347).

Terrorist groups can be religious, state sponsored, left wing or right wing, or nationalist. Table 6.2 shows the major types of terrorist groups (Schmalleger 2006:347).

Crime is a national and global issue, as illustrated by *state organized crime.* Overlooked by the public and by social scientists, this form of crime includes acts defined by law as criminal but committed by state or government officials. For example, a government might be complicit in smuggling, assassination, or torture, acting as an accessory to national or international crime, which is then justified in terms of "national defense." Government offices may also violate laws that restrict or limit government activities such as eavesdropping. In some countries, political prisoners are held for long periods without charges, without access to lawyers, and without trials, or they are tortured, violating both national and international laws. An example is the Guantánamo Bay detainees held in Cuba by the United States. U.S. torture of enemy combatants during the Bush administration raised questions of legality, both nationally and internationally, and holding enemy combatants raises legal questions as well. Although countries may violate their own laws, it is difficult to prosecute when the guilty party is the government.

Bribery and corruption are the way of life in many governments, businesses, and police forces. The percentage of citizens who said that they had paid a bribe to obtain services is as high as 79% in Nigeria, 72% in Cambodia, and 71% in Albania. The institutions perceived to be most affected by corruption globally include political parties, the police, the judiciary and legislatures, and business (Global Corruption Barometer 2010/2011, Transparency International 2012). Map 6.2 shows an index of the perception of public sector corruption (from 1 to 10) in various countries around the world.

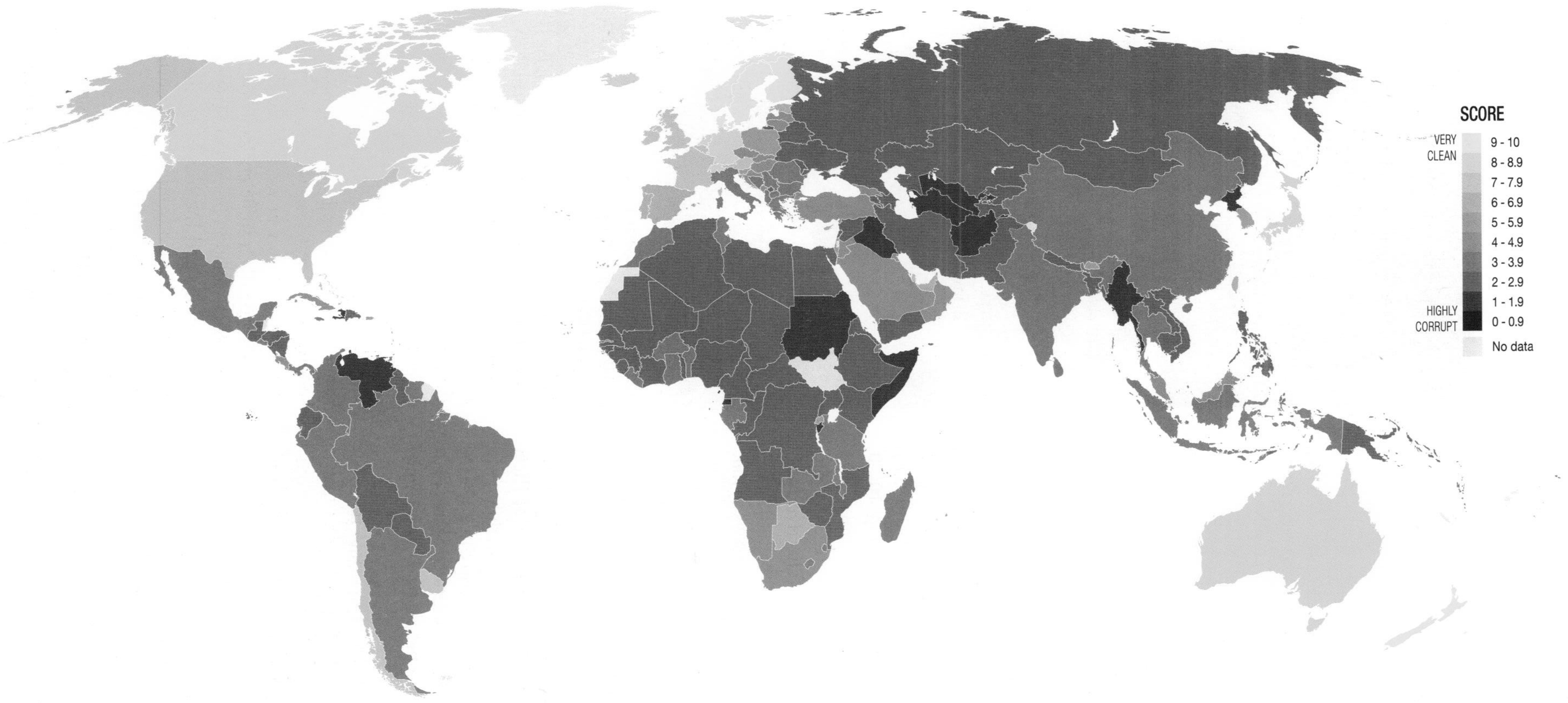

Map 6.2 Corruptions Percentage Index 2011

Source: Reprinted from CPI 2011. Copyright CPI 2011 Transparency International: the global coalition against corruption. Used with permission. For more information visit http://www.transparency.org.

Thinking Sociologically

Sometimes government officials and even heads of state are the perpetrators of crimes. Is there a difference if a crime is committed by an official and justified as necessary for national defense? Why or why not? Is it ever justified for a military or an intelligence agency to violate its own country's laws?

Japanese vending machines carry a wide range of products that are not freely available in the United States—such as pornographic magazines. However, young people do not purchase these products that are not meant for them, for they know the neighbors are watching and to do so would bring shame and embarrassment on them and on their families.

Cross-National Comparison of Crimes

The vending machine was on the corner near the Ballantines' house in Japan. The usual cola, candy, and sundries were displayed, along with cigarettes, beer, whiskey, sake, and pornographic magazines. Out of curiosity, Jeanne and her family watched to see who purchased what from the machines, and not once did they see teenagers sneaking the beer, cigarettes, or porn. It turns out that the Ballantines were not the only ones watching! The neighbors also kept an eye on who did what—the neighborhood watch being an effective form of social control in Japan. Because of the **stigma**—*disapproval attached to disobeying the expected norms so that a person is discredited as less than normal*—teens understand the limits, and vigilant neighbors help keep the overall amount of deviance low. The neighborhood watch sends a signal that deviant behavior is unacceptable and provides social control of behaviors of those who might be tempted to commit crimes.

Japan and the United States are both modern, urban, industrial countries, but their crime rates and the way they deal with deviant behavior and crimes are quite different. Japan had 637 murders for 127.1 million people in 2009 (5 for every 1 million people), whereas the United States had 12,658 murders for 307.2 million people or 41 per 1 million people (see Table 6.3).

How can these extreme differences in crime rates be explained? Researchers look at cultural differences: Japan's low violent crime rate is due in part to Japan's homogeneous society—inequality between citizens is not great; success is not as focused on material possessions and consumption; and there is loyalty to a historic tradition of cooperation that provides a sense of moral order, a network of group relations, strong commitment to social norms, and respect for law and order (Westermann and Burfeind 1991). The example of vending machines in Japan illustrates this idea. In addition, guns are outlawed.

Although Japan's crime rate is roughly one third the rate of crime in the United States, it is not attained through harsher penalties. The Japanese government actually spends far less of its gross national product on the police, courts, and prisons, and the police in Japan want to be thought of as kind and caring rather than strict in their enforcement of the law. For many crimes in Japan, the offender may simply be asked to write a letter of apology. This is frequently a sufficient sanction to deter the person from further violation of the law. The humiliation of writing an apology and the fear of shame and embarrassing one's family are strong enough to curb deviant behavior (Lazare 2004).

When looking for explanations of crime, criminologists consider the causes of economic inequality in different countries. If minority status prevents certain individuals and groups from fitting into the dominant society and getting ahead, this helps explain the higher levels of deviance among the disfranchised groups. The overall health of a country's economy—as measured by job opportunities, unemployment, and inflation—also affects the crime rate. When a country has a great income differential between members, the crime rates rise. Research shows that the incidence of homicide is higher in countries with greater income inequality.

Although comparing cross-national data on crime is difficult because there are variations in the definitions of crime and the measurements used, comparisons do give us insight into what types of crimes are committed, under what circumstances, and how often. Two sources of international data are Interpol (the International Criminal Police Organization) and the United Nations. Although these organizations collect and present data, they have no way to check the accuracy of the data they receive from countries.

Table 6.3 in the next "Engaging Sociology" on page 202 provides information on crimes in selected countries. Differences are due in part to the much higher disparity in income between the rich and the poor and the heterogeneity of populations. The size of the country is also provided since that is relevant to the comparison.

Global Crimes

Increasingly, crimes are global in nature. Some crimes are committed by transnational conglomerates and may involve organized crime and the smuggling of illegal goods and humans. Other crimes are committed by countries that violate international laws, treaties, and agreements. Consider international agreements regarding protection of the environment, which some countries and transnational corporations ignore when these agreements act against their own self-interests. Yet these violations of agreements may affect the entire global ecological system. The international community has the capacity to try people, organizations, and countries for violation of human rights or international laws, but the process is difficult and politically charged.

Some scholars use the world systems theory, arguing that the cause of global crime lies in the global economy, the inequalities between countries, and the competition between countries for resources and wealth. As a result of the capitalist mode of production, an unequal relationship has arisen between core nations (the developed, wealthy nations in the Global North) and periphery nations (the Global South). Core nations often take unfair advantage of peripheral nations. Peripheral nations, in turn, must find ways to survive in this global system, and they sometime turn to illegal methods—such as violating global environmental standards—to achieve their goals (Chase-Dunn and Anderson 2006). Some nations with many resources are semiperiphery nations. Benefiting from extensive trade, they are less vulnerable than the poorest nations. Map 6.3 on page 203 helps you see where some of these core, peripheral, and semiperipheral nations are located.

The U.S. "War on Drugs" has meant that the United States has pressured Mexico to crack down on drug use and trafficking. This has made drugs more scarce and drug trafficking a major source of income. Thus, a policy in another country impacts the lives of Mexican citizens. Crime and criminalization of behavior is clearly global in a way that it was not a century ago.

As you look at this map, note that the developed or affluent countries are almost all located in the Northern Hemisphere. Although some poor countries are north of the equator, the pattern is obvious. To avoid some misleading implications of the words *developed* and *developing*, many scholars now prefer the term *Global South* to refer to less affluent nations. If you see or hear the phrase Global South,

Engaging Sociology

Crime Comparison

The frequency of crimes varies across countries and is influenced by many variables. Examine Table 6.3 and then answer the questions below.

Table 6.3 **Crime Incidents in Selected Countries**

Country	*Murders*	*Rapes*	*Assaults*	*Burglaries*	*Auto Thefts*	*Population size (in millions)*
Australia	302	15,630	141,124	436,865	139,094	21.3
Canada	489	24,049	233,517	23,065	160,268	33.5
Chile	235	1,250	53,133	13,375	n.a.	16.6
Denmark	58	497	9,796	1,297	32,203	5.5
Finland	148	579	27,820	370,993	16,391	5.3
France	1,051	8,458	106,484	1,885	301,539	64.1
Germany	960	7,499	116,912	n.a.	83,063	82.3
Italy	746	2,336	29,068	n.a.	243,890	58.1
Japan	637	2,260	43,229	3,027	309,638	127.1
New Zealand	45	861	30,177	65,675	21,992	4.2
United Kingdom	850	8,593	450,865	836,027	338,796	61.1
United States	12,658	89,110	2,238,480	2,099,700	1,147,300	307.2

Source: Interpol 2007; World Factbook 2010.

n.a. = not available

Interpreting quantitative data:

1. Take the population (in millions) and divide it by the number of crimes in a given category (e.g., murders). If you do that for each country for a particular type of crime, you can see the ratio of crimes per person in the population.
2. Which countries have especially striking crime rates, either high or low?
3. What can you tell about countries from studying their crime rates?
4. Do any particular rates stand out?
5. Why and how might you explain those rates?

this map should help you see why it refers to developing or poor countries.

The forms of global corruption are too extensive to catalog here, so we will settle for an illustration of one of the newest manifestations of global crime against people and property: computer crimes. Internet deviance or cyberspace crime is growing faster than a cybergeek can move a mouse. This new world of crime ranges from online identity theft and gambling to cybersex and pornography, to hate sites and stalking, to hacking into government and military files, and to use by terrorists. WikiLeaks, a group that disseminates secret or sensitive government information over the Internet, has been controversial because some feel it is doing a service to citizens and others feel it is endangering people such as secret agents whose names may appear in the files (Thio 2008).

Even legitimate businesses such as Google, Yahoo, or eBay can unwittingly support crime by connecting people to illegal operations. The Internet Crime Complaint Center received 25,000 reports per month in 2010. Most common

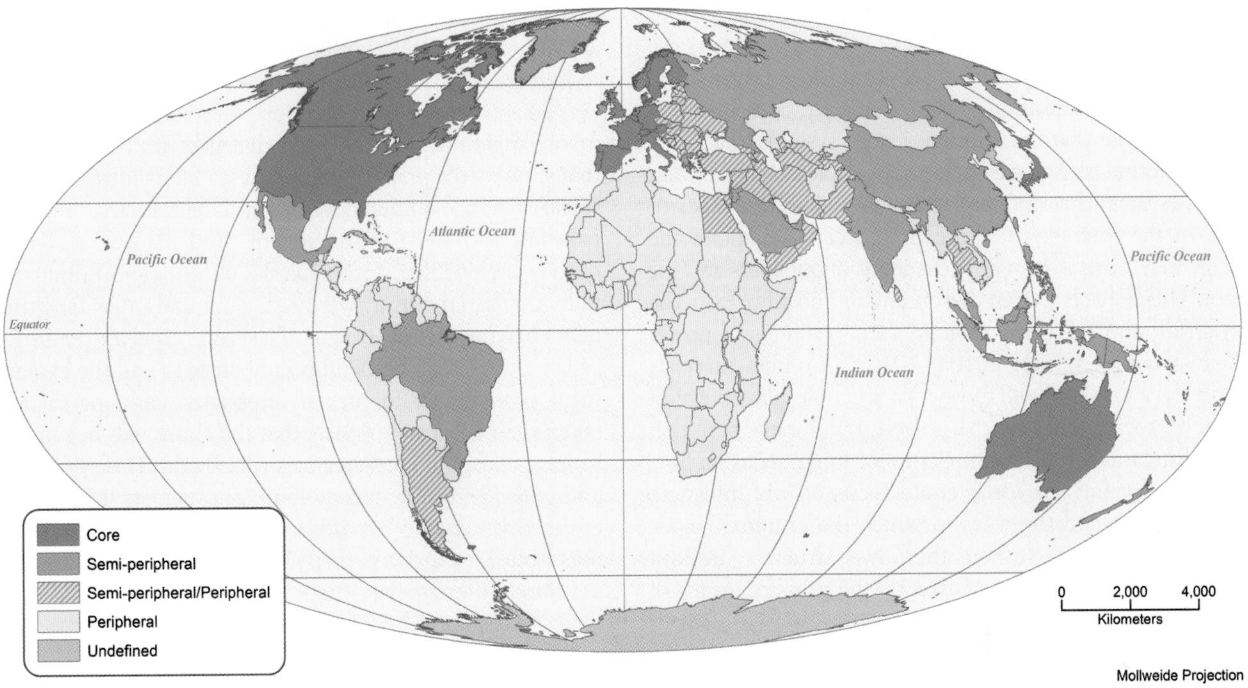

Map 6.3 Core, Semiperipheral, and Peripheral Countries of the World

Source: Map by Anna Versluis.
Note: Some countries are left undefined (in gray).

were Internet nondelivery of payment or merchandise scams (27.6% of complaints), related scams (13.2%), identity theft (9.8%), and computer crimes (9.1%) (FBI 2011b).

Drug trafficking is one of the most common forms of scam. For example, people purchase prescription drugs that are contaminated or diluted and can be life threatening, find recipes for making illegal methamphetamines, or purchase body-building or date rape drugs (gamma-hydroxybutyric acid [GHB]). Other crimes have also become easier to commit: The FBI reported a growing rate of child pornography, up 40% since 2006 to 9,000 cases. In 2009, 2,315 suspects were indicted (FBI 2011a).

One policy difficulty is that law enforcement gets gridlocked in both national and international jurisdictional confusion. As many as five different federal U.S. agencies can be involved in preventing financial fraud on the Internet, not to mention the state and local agencies that might play a role. If the fraud involves international cybercrime, the customs services and other branches of governments also may enter the investigation. The resulting confusion and lack of clear authority regarding who should prosecute can play into the hands of lawbreakers. Few local authorities feel that identity theft is within their jurisdiction, but government officials may not have the personnel or the interest to pursue these cases (Sager et al. 2006).

Controlling Crime: Social Policy Considerations

Someone commits a crime, gets caught, has a trial or plea bargain, and goes to jail or prison if found guilty. It sounds straightforward, but it is far from that. Most governments pass laws and make policies to keep deviance from disrupting the smooth functioning of society. This section discusses the mechanisms used by societies to control the amount of deviance and punish deviants.

Dealing With Crime: The Criminal Justice Process

When people are afraid to walk the streets because they might be assaulted and when a significant number of individuals are dropping out of society and taking up deviant lifestyles, deviance becomes a topic of great concern. Every society has a process for dealing with crime and criminals. Sometimes the ground rules and processes of justice respect human rights and represent blind justice, meaning that all people are treated equally, but often they are not.

Structural-functionalists see the justice system as important to maintaining order in society. Some conflict theorists argue that the criminal justice system depicts the threat of crime as a threat from poor people and minorities, which creates fear of victimization in members of society. It is in the interests of those in power to maintain the image that crime is primarily the work of outsiders and the poor. This deflects citizen discontent and hostility from the powerful, and helps them retain their positions of power (Reiman and Leighton 2010a, 2010b). Conflict theorists point out that there will always be a certain percentage of crime in society because the powerful will make sure that something is labeled deviant. So policy might focus on how to deter deviant acts, or it could focus on the injustices of the system and the ways in which the criminal justice system protects and sustains the power structure. In both cases, prisons and jails are currently the primary means of controlling individual criminal behavior.

Prisons and Jails

There is money to be made by locking up prisoners. Farming prisoners out to the private sector, often in other states, costs less than a state running its own prisons, according to advocates for privatization. Private prisons save on labor costs by not paying the high benefits that states must pay to employees. With competition, private prisons must please the states they serve. Therefore some argue that these prisons are safer and provide better living conditions and rehabilitation of prisoners than state-run facilities can provide.

Those against privatization argue that incarcerating (imprisoning) people for profit is a bad idea, morally and financially. They point out that costs per prisoner often rise after the initial contract with the state, and some states must incarcerate a certain number of people due to contracts with private prisons, thereby manipulating the criminal justice system. People in poverty may lose access to family members if prisoners are sent out of state. These are but a few of the arguments for and against private prisons, but they provide a taste of the controversies surrounding our high prison population (Current.com 2012; Michael n.d.).

Whether in public or private prisons, protecting the public from offenders often means locking up criminals, a form of *total institution* that completely controls the prisoners' lives and regulates all their activities. Goffman (1961) describes inmates' lives as being drastically changed through the processes of *degradation*, which marks the individual as deviant, and *mortification*, which breaks down the individual's original self as the inmate experiences resocialization (Irwin 1985; Irwin and Owen 2007). The inmate is allowed no personal property. There is little communication, and verbal abuse of inmates by guards is common. Heterosexual activity is prohibited, uniforms and standard buzz cuts are required, and the inmates' schedules are totally controlled.

Social systems that develop within the prison often involve rigid roles, norms, and privileges. In a famous study that simulated a prison situation, researchers illustrated the social organization that develops and the roles that individuals play within the prison system. Students were assigned roles as prisoners or prison guards. Within a short time, the individuals in the study were acting out their roles. The students playing the role of "guard" became cruel and sadistic, causing the researcher, Philip Zimbardo, to end the experiment prematurely to prevent problems. Participants had taken their roles so seriously that the abuse was beginning to have alarming consequences (Zimbardo, Haney, Banks, and Jaffe 1973). The recent abuse of prisoners in Iraq and at the Guantánamo Bay prison in Cuba parallels the findings from Zimbardo's earlier (2009) study of the roles that develop in these social situations.

Time in jails or prisons is often the formal sanctions applied to enforce the rules passed by legitimate officials. This woman is consulting with her lawyer about her options.

Jails in local communities have been called catchall asylums for poor people. Most people in jails are there for their "rabble existence"—including petty hustlers, derelicts, junkies, "crazies," and outlaws—but they are mostly disorganized and economically marginal members of society (Irwin 1985; Irwin and Owen 2007). Jails in Europe and the United States house disproportionate numbers of immigrants (especially those with non-European features and skin tones), young men, and members of the poorest class of the citizenry. Local jails hold 3 in 10 (2,266,800) people in the U.S. criminal justice system today. Another 7 in 10 (4,887,900) are under adult correctional authorities, including probation and parole (Glaze 2011).

In December 2010, 1,612,395 prisoners were being held in U.S. federal and state prisons (Guerino, Harrison, and Sabol 2011). Whites comprised 38.8% of the incarcerated population, yet their percentage of the U.S. population is about 63.7%. African Americans make up more than 34% of all inmates but only about 12.6% of the total population, and Hispanics make up 20% of all inmates and about 16.3% of the total population. More African American males are in prison today than were slaves in 1850; in many cases the guilt of these men is doubtful (Alexander 2011; Day 2011; Humes, Jones, and Ramirez 2011; Sabol, West, and Cooper 2009). Among women, African Americans were 2.9 times as likely to be incarcerated as whites, and Hispanic women were 1.5 times as likely to spend time in prison (Sentencing Project 2012).

Conflict theorists believe that these figures are strong evidence that jails and prisons are mostly about controlling or "managing" the minorities and poor people, not about public safety. African American males, for example, are 6 times more likely to be incarcerated than white men, with more than 10% having been in prison or jail for 25 to 39 years (Fathi 2009; Sentencing Project 2012; West and Sabol 2008). This is in spite of the fact that many scholars do not think that, when white-collar crimes are included, blacks commit more crimes than whites (Farley 2010). The makeup of U.S. prisons is presented in Table 6.4.

Overall, the number of incarcerated individuals in state and federal prisons decreased by 5,575 inmates between 2009 and 2010, after a substantial rise for a decade. The reasons for the recent decrease in incarceration rates in the United States is that more inmates are on parole due to overcrowding and fewer lockups for minor offenses. Still, the "War on Drugs" keeps the prison population high compared with that in any other Global North country, and accounts for the highest number of causes for imprisonment (Alexander 2011; Guerino, Harrison, and Sabol 2011). In fact, the 2010 U.S. incarceration rate of 731 per 100,000 people is the highest in the world (Sentencing Project 2012). Nearly half (47%) of people held in state prisons in 2009 were convicted of nonviolent offenses—mostly related to drugs or public order crimes. People convicted of drug offenses were 51% of federal prison inmates, but had only been 25% of inmates in 2002.

The increase in inmates in the United States, especially for drug-related crimes, has meant more jails being built at taxpayers' expense and more people being hired to work for the state in the legal system. All of this is despite the fact that crime rates have been falling for two decades.

Thinking Sociologically

From what you have learned so far in this chapter, why are the people who get sent to jail disproportionately young, poor immigrants, or racial and ethnic minorities?

The Purposes of Prisons

People are sent to prison for a variety of reasons, and the purpose of imprisoning people makes a difference in how prisoners are treated. So why do we, unlike people in many societies, lock people up for long periods?

From the functional perspective, prisons serve several purposes for society: (1) the desire for revenge or retribution, (2) removing dangerous people from society, (3) deterring would-be deviants, and (4) rehabilitating through counseling, education, and work training programs inside prisons (Johnson 2002). However, in prison, inmates are exposed to more criminal and antisocial behavior, so rehabilitation and deterrence goals are often undermined by

Table 6.4 **Characteristics of People in Prison**

	Makeup of U.S. prison population	*Makeup of U.S. population*	*Ratio of the population 30–34 years old in prison*	*Chance of spending time in prison during lifetime*
Black	38%	12.4%	1:10	32%
Hispanic	22%	14.1%	1:26	17%
White	32%	68%	1:61	6%

Source: Sentencing Project 2012.

the nature of prisons. According to a recent Bureau of Justice Statistics report, roughly 5% of prison inmates are sexually assaulted by other prisoners or prison guards, and 12% of youth in juvenile detention facilities are victims, often in gang rapes ("New Federal Report" 2010). This ongoing problem of assault, rape, and threat of violence in prison so brutalizes inmates that it becomes difficult for them to reenter society as well-adjusted citizens ready to conform to the conventional society that they feel also has brutalized them (Hensley, Koscheski, and Tewksbury 2005). Many prisoners suffer from mental health problems and have difficulty reintegrating into society (Fathi 2009; Liptak 2008).

Compared to the rates in other countries, the U.S. incarceration rate is much higher. With less than 5% of the world's population, one quarter of the world's prison population is in the United States. The median rate in all countries in the world is 125 per 100,000 citizens, one-sixth the rate in the United States. One reason is that the United States incarcerates people for lesser crimes and longer periods than most other countries (Liptak 2008). Table 6.5 compares the rates of incarceration in 11 countries.

Thinking Sociologically

From what you have read above, how does the U.S. criminal justice system compare with other countries? Why are rates of incarceration so much higher?

Table 6.5 **2011 World Comparative Rates of Incarceration (per 100,000 People)**

Top 11 Countries	
United States	716
Rwanda	595
Russia	568
Brazil	253
Spain	159
Australia	133
France	96
Germany	85
Sweden	78
Denmark	74
India	32

Source: Walmsey, Roy. 2011. *World Prison Population List*, 9th ed. International Centre for Prison Studies. Retrieved January 20, 2013 (http://www.idcr.org.uk/wp-content/uploads/2010/09/WPPL-9-22.pdf).

The disturbing reality is that despite the high rates of incarceration in the United States, **recidivism rates**—*the likelihood that someone who is arrested, convicted, and imprisoned will later be a repeat offender*—are also very high. More than half of all men who do time in prison will be confined again for a crime. This means that as a specific deterrent or for rehabilitation, imprisonment does not work very well (Quinney 2002; Siegel 2009). What options does government have? In the following sections, we discuss the death penalty and other alternatives to prisons.

The Death Penalty

Crimes of murder, assault, robbery, and rape usually receive severe penalties because citizens consider them the most dangerous. The most controversial (and irreversible) method of control is for the state to put the person to death. The most common argument for using the death penalty, more formally known as capital punishment, is to deter people from crime. The idea is that not only will the person who has committed the crime be punished, but also others will be deterred from committing such a crime because they know that the death penalty is a possibility for them too.

Sixty-one percent of the American public favors a punishment other than the death penalty for homicide and other severe crimes, and 88% of criminal justice experts feel the death penalty does not deter murder (Alarcon and Mitchell 2011; Radelet and Lacock 2009). In addition, the cost to execute any one of the 3,199 death row criminals in the United States is often many times higher than the cost would be for life imprisonment because of the trials, appeals, and other expenses. Despite this, 37 states still have death penalty clauses for at least some crimes. Why is this severe penalty by which the state is authorized to take someone's life still utilized?

While U.S. states with the death penalty assume that those contemplating crimes will be deterred, studies on the deterrent effects of capital punishment do not support this assumption. Fewer than 25% of prison inmates believe that the death penalty would have deterred them from a violent crime (Steele and Wilcox 2003). Inmates who had committed three or more violent crimes indicated that their crimes were not planned, that they "just happened," that "things went wrong," and that they were not thinking about the possible penalty when committing their crimes (Wilcox and Steele 2003). Murder is also more likely to happen in states with the death penalty. In fact, the 20 states with the highest murder rates in 2008 all had the death penalty (Death Penalty Information Center 2012). This is not very good evidence that this penalty has been a deterrent. However, it does serve as retribution or punishment for a crime (Hood 2002).

Only 17 states forbid executions, with Connecticut being the most recent in April 2012. A study in California shows that over $4 billion has been spent on 13 executions there since 1978, a cost of $308 million per execution. This is a much greater cost than life imprisonment due to the costs of pretrial and trial, various appeals processes (some of which are mandated by law to avoid mistakes), and the costs of special death row incarceration requirements (Alarcon and Mitchell 2011). Because of cost, overcrowding of prisons, and other reasons, the number of executions in the United States per year has been going down, from 52 in 2009 to 43 in 2011 (Death Penalty Information Center 2012).

Most developed countries do not use the death penalty, and in 2007 the United Nations passed a resolution calling on all nations to abolish it as "cruel and unusual punishment" (Amnesty International 2012; UN News Center 2010). However, as you can see from Map 6.4, the United States is one of the 20 countries that utilize the death penalty out of 198 where records are available (Amnesty International 2012). Only China and Yemen officially recorded more executions in 2010 than the United States (World Coalition 2012). The death penalty, also called capital punishment, is most commonly legal in Asia, the Middle East, and parts of Africa, typically in totalitarian states. There are approximately 18,750 people in the world under death sentences today, with 676 executed in 2011, not counting China and Iran. China leads the world with thousands of deaths, and Iran has an unknown number of executions. Countries use four main methods of execution: beheading, hanging, lethal injection, and shooting. In a few cases crimes are punished by stoning the guilty person to death. Overall, fewer countries are using the death penalty, but those few that do have been increasing the number of executions. Most are in the Middle East: Iraq, Iran, Saudi Arabia, and Yemen where uprisings have been common (Amnesty International 2012).

Thinking Sociologically

How can you explain the higher murder rates in U.S. states that have the death penalty?

Is the death penalty fairly administered? There is evidence that the death penalty is deeply influenced by race and class status of the prisoner. In most U.S. states with capital punishment, a disproportionate number of minority and lower-class individuals are put to death. Of those

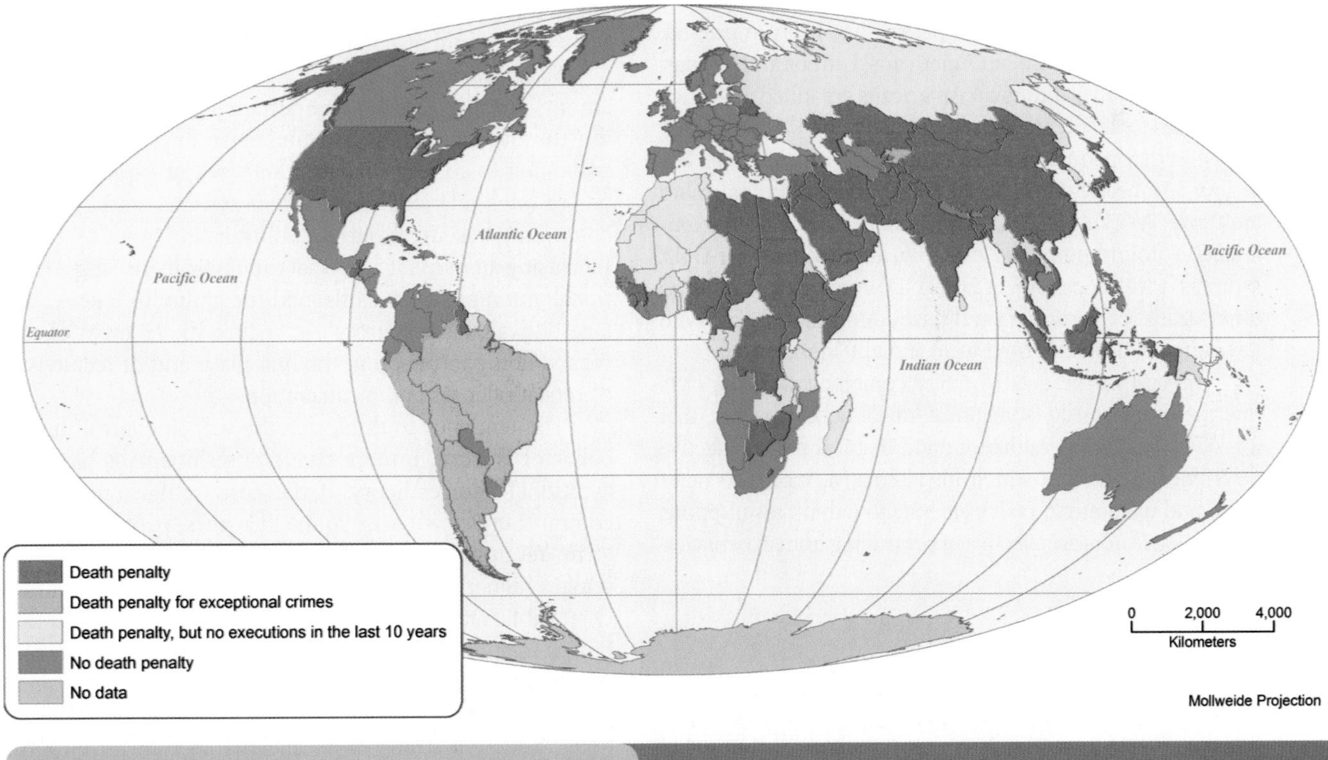

Map 6.4 Global Status of the Death Penalty in 2011

Source: Amnesty International. Map by Anna Versluis.

Prisoners awaiting the death penalty are held in a separate isolation unit known as "death row." More than 70% of the members of the United Nations have abolished the death penalty, including all of the European nations. More than 90% of all executions in 2010 occurred in six countries: China, Iran, Saudi Arabia, the United States, and Yemen (Amnesty International 2011).

executed since 1976, 56% have been white, 34% black, and 8% Hispanic. Yet the percentage of blacks in the total population is less than 13%. Furthermore, the death penalty is usually imposed if a white person has been murdered. Homicides in which African Americans, Latinos and Latinas, Native Americans, and Asian Americans are killed are much less likely to result in a death penalty for the murderer, implying that people in society view their loss of life as less serious (Amnesty International 2006). In addition, mistakes are made. As of early 2012, 289 prisoners have been exonerated, or found not guilty due to further evidence or DNA samples (Innocence Project 2012). DNA tests are acquitting other death row prisoners and have found that people who have already been executed were actually innocent.

The cost of the death penalty combined with the facts that the death penalty sometimes kills innocent people, that it is often racially discriminatory, and that it is not an effective deterrent has led to a search for alternative means to deter crime and has spurred policy analysts to rethink assumptions about what factors are effective in controlling human behavior.

Alternative Forms of Social Control

Imagine growing up in a poor community with no money to experience life or culture outside of your immediate surroundings. Your role models, sources of acceptance and success, and belonging are all based in your peer group. Without access to or knowledge of other opportunities, you are likely to follow the same path as those around you. Now consider a high school that has opened in your school district, one that requires hard work, long hours, and a guarantee of going on to college. Many students are applying, and selection is based on lottery, but it could be your way out of the ghetto. This scenario is playing out in poor neighborhoods around the United States, and many students are able to develop their talents, skills, social networks, and cultural knowledge. Such opportunities may well incline you and your friends to avoid getting into trouble and to want to conform to social expectations. Opportunity may be the road to success. However, the number of available schools is only a fraction of what is needed.

Based on the assumptions that most criminal behavior is learned through socialization, that criminals can be resocialized, and that tax dollars can be saved, several sociological theories of crime suggest early community intervention to reduce crime rates. Some of these ideas include high-quality schools, to prevent young people from entering the criminal justice system in the first place and methods of treatment other than brutalizing incarceration for those who do find themselves in trouble with the law. The goals are to provide alternative routes to success for those living in poverty, reduce the number of individuals who go to prison, and cut the number who are rearrested after being released—the recidivism rate. Improving the social capital of potential offenders is one approach.

Social capital refers to social networks within and among groups, access to important resources, and sharing the norms, values, and understandings that facilitate belonging to society (Flavin 2004). Social capital encompasses one's relationships, support systems, and access to community resources (Jarrett, Sullivan, and Watkins 2005). Increasing an individual's social capital by increasing educational attainment, job skills, and the ability to take advantage of available resources can reduce the chances of that person going to prison in the first place and of recidivism, or repeat offenses and incarceration.

The tendency to think that the way to control human behavior is through more severe punishments is based on a rational choice theory. If the cost is high enough for committing deviant acts, so the idea goes, people will conform. Yet despite severe punishments, crime rates generally remain higher in the United States than in other countries. One public sociologist, Susan Guarino-Ghezzi, found that hostile relations between young delinquents and police officers had developed into a cycle that simply made for more crime. She explains in the next "Sociologists in Action" how a different strategy was effective in transforming the dynamic that led to crime.

Sociologists in Action—Susan Guarino-Ghezzi

Police and Delinquent Youth: Changing Stereotypes and Making Peace

In the 1990s, I conducted research in Boston on two groups of people—police and gang-involved male juvenile offenders held at the Massachusetts Department of Youth Services (DYS). I was interested in how each group defined encounters with one another. Police and juveniles were each frustrated by the relentless violence and record homicide rate, and they blamed one another for the situation. Within both groups were subcultures that reinforced fallacies and stereotypes. These misunderstandings were perceived as "real" and locked each group into routine, ritualized behaviors, guaranteeing that they would clash.

My goal was to uncover these patterns, expose misleading stereotypes, and use these new understandings to change behaviors on both sides. Previous research I had conducted with others revealed that the youths who were the most alienated from police had the most frequent encounters with them (Guarino-Ghezzi and Carr 1996; Guarino-Ghezzi and Kimball 1996). Negative encounters with police were at the center of their lives, and I came to realize that while the offenders claimed to hate police, they actually looked forward to negative confrontations as opportunities to reinforce peer bonds.

At the same time, I learned that police painted ex–juvenile offenders with the same brush. If a juvenile offender returned to the community after a long program of rehabilitation, regardless of his or her willingness to reform, the individual was still a juvenile offender as far as the police were concerned. If a juvenile offender became a victim of crime, the police showed less sympathy than if the juvenile were a law-abiding victim.

I contacted the deputy superintendent of the experimental neighborhood policing district in Boston and shared my concerns. Together, with some other police officers, we established a program called "Make Peace With Police" (MPWP), which arranged communications sessions, role-plays, and other nonconfrontational encounters between police and gang-involved juveniles. As executive director, I oversaw 41 group meetings run by MPWP facilitators on a weekly basis. These sessions helped us to understand the sources of hostility on both sides, but more importantly, they helped to create useful dialogue between juveniles and police.

A key finding of the MPWP project was that without sincere efforts to establish relationships, juveniles lacking positive social bonds learn to define police negatively from their social environments. While some of the most defiant and hostile-seeming youths were biased against police based on their peer subcultures, our sessions became turning points for developing positive relationships.

Police told us that they were surprised to learn that young gang members were really "just kids." An officer who arrived at a session feeling tough and somewhat angry at the youths quickly attached to a youth during the session who was visibly upset when mentioning a death in his family. The officer offered to help the youth find a job when he was released from the DYS facility. When asked what made him change, the officer explained that he had no idea how young and vulnerable the youths were because he'd never looked beyond the "street tough" exteriors that were so common among groups of youths in high-crime communities.

Another officer received a surprise one weekend when a youth he had met in the detention facility recognized him in his cruiser and went out of his way to initiate a pleasant conversation. It was especially fulfilling because the boy was one of a small number who refused to even speak to police in his first MPWP session. The communication sessions provided a necessary "bridge" for redefining social norms.

* * * * * * *

Note: This excerpt is adapted from Korgen and White's Engaged Sociologist: Connecting the Classroom to the Community *(Sage 2013). Susan Guarino-Ghezzi is a professor of sociology and criminology at Stonehill College. She is the former director of research of the Massachusetts Department of Youth Services, and is a frequent consultant on juvenile crime.*

Deterrence is complex. It is influenced by dozens of variables, including the cultural values and meanings attached to specific behaviors. Not many people think that the apology technique used in Japan would work as a deterrent to crimes in other countries. On the other hand, there is a wide range of options available for dealing with crime other than harsh (and expensive) punishments. Seeing how crime is controlled in other countries may challenge assumptions in one's own country, causing authorities to come up with creative new solutions that do work. For example, many criminologists argue that the United States should concentrate on the serious criminals and reduce the number of minor offenders in jails by providing less expensive and longer-impact alternatives to prison time. They also suggest a number of alternatives to sending minor offenders to jails and prisons, such as community service, work release, and educational training programs.

Thinking Sociologically

Do you think changing the "cost-benefit" ratio so that the costs of crime to the criminal are higher will deter crime, or are other policies or methods more effective in enticing non-violent offenders to be responsible, contributing members of society? Why?

Prison reforms, rehabilitation, training programs, shock probation, work release, halfway houses, and other alternative programs are intended to integrate less serious offenders into the community in a productive way and help them regain social capital. If we can integrate the potential criminal into the community, reduce discrimination, and teach at-risk youth acceptable behavior patterns, we may reduce crime and gain productive citizens.

If ex-prisoners can turn to alternative behaviors other than crime, if they have educational or job skills, and if they have families to return to, they are less likely to commit further crimes. Therefore, some state penal systems provide education, from basic skills to college courses, and allow conjugal and family stays to help keep families together. Evidence shows that prison education programs reduce recidivism rates dramatically. Approximately 1 in 100 U.S. citizens are in prison (*Science Daily* 2011). The three-year recidivism rate (those returning to prison within three years of release) is estimated at between 43.3% and 51.8%. Yet research studies show that education and job opportunities reduce that rate: Earning a GED (high school equivalency) cuts recidivism to less than 50%; an associate's degree reduces recidivism to only 13.7%; a bachelor's degree to 5.6%, and a master's degree to 0% recidivism (Pew Center on the States 2011).

Other programs included shock probation (releasing first-time offenders early in the hope that the shock of prison life would deter them), community service to help develop citizenship and pay restitution for the offense, and day treatment and halfway houses to help inmates readjust to community life and find jobs. The programs can relieve overcrowded prisons and save money by reducing the cost of incarceration. There is some evidence that they reduce recidivism as well.

Work release programs build social capital by placing primarily nonviolent offenders in positions to earn wages and help support their families rather than accumulate debt while in prison. They also provide work experience and keep offenders away from hardened criminals in prison, thus helping reintegrate the offender into the community. A key to the success of such programs is adequate supervision. Transmitters are often used to track offenders and protect concerned community members (Urban Institute 2004).

Restitution puts the offender in the position of "making it right" with the victim. The offender renders money or service to the victim or community under supervised parole to compensate the victim. This is a positive way of teaching juvenile offenders lessons in responsibility without imprisoning and exposing them to more criminal behavior. Restitution is less costly than long incarceration, and victims are often satisfied with this type of program. The likelihood of repeated offense at a later time is also lower in restitution programs than for those who are sent to prison.

Thinking Sociologically

Considering what you have read, how has this affected some of your ideas about deviance, crime, and the criminal justice system?

At the beginning of the chapter, we said that some of the material presented in this chapter might surprise you, some commonly held assumptions about deviance might be challenged, and a different way of looking at deviance might emerge. Lack of respect for law and for social conventions is often tied to severe social inequality. Those without resources have fewer reasons to be committed to the existing system of rules and regulations, and they are more likely to become desperate for resources that they cannot access "by the rules." The next section deals with inequality, and the next chapter focuses on socioeconomic differences.

What Have We Learned?

Perhaps the answers to some of the chapter's opening questions—What is deviance? Why do people become deviant? and What should we do about deviance?—have now taken on new dimensions. Deviance as defined by society, communities, and even religion or subcultural groups has many possible explanations, and there are multiple interpretations about how it should be handled. Deviance and crime are issues for any society, for unless most of the people obey the rules most of the time, there can be real threats to stability, safety, and a sense of fairness, undermining the social structure. The criminal justice system tends to be a conservative force in society because of its focus on ensuring social conformity.

To make the society run more smoothly, we must understand why deviance and crime happen. Good policy must be based on accurate information and careful analysis of the information. We must also understand that deviance and conformity operate at various levels in the social world: micro, meso, and macro. In addition, it is important to understand that there may be positive aspects of deviance for any society, from uniting society against deviants to providing creative new ways to solve problems.

One of the dominant characteristics of modern society is social inequality, and as we have seen, inequality is often an issue in criminal activity. Indeed, many of our social problems are rooted in issues of inequality. Extreme inequality may even be a threat to the deeper values and dreams of a society, especially one that stresses individualism and achievement. In the following three chapters, we look at three types of inequality: socioeconomic, ethnic or racial, and gender-based inequity.

Key Points

- Deviance—the violation of social norms, including those that are formal laws—is a complex behavior that has both positive and negative consequences for individuals and for society. (See pp. 173–176.)
- Deviance is often misunderstood because of simplistic and popular misconceptions. (See pp. 176–177.)
- Many theories try to explain deviance—rational choice and social control; and symbolic interaction's anomie and labeling theories at the micro level; along with macro-level structural explanations: structural functional theory's differential association and strain theory; and conflict and feminist theory. (See pp. 179–190.)
- Many of the formal organizations concerned with crime (such as the FBI and the media) focus on crimes involving individuals—predatory crimes, crimes without victims, and hate crimes—but the focus on these crimes may blind us to crimes that actually are more harmful and more costly. (See pp. 191–194.)
- At the meso level, organized and occupational crimes may cost billions of dollars and pose a great risk to thousands of lives. Occupational crime may be against the company, employees, customers, or the public. (See pp. 195–197.)
- At the macro level, national governments sometimes commit state-organized crimes, sometimes in violation of their own laws or in violation of international laws. These crimes may be directed against their own citizens (usually the minorities) or people from other countries. (See pp. 198–202.)
- Also at the macro level, some crimes are facilitated by global networks and by global inequities of power and wealth. (See pp. 202–204.)
- Controlling crime has generated many policy debates, from the use of prisons to the death penalty and even to alternative approaches to the control of deviance. (See pp. 204–211.)

Discussion Questions

1. List five acts that were once considered deviant but are now considered courageous. Have you ever committed a deviant act because you believed it was the moral thing to do? If yes, please explain why. If not, in what sort of situation might you consider carrying out a deviant act because you thought it was the right thing to do?
2. Have you ever been labeled deviant? Why or why not? How does your social class, level of education, gender, race or ethnicity, and nation of origin impact the chances you will be considered deviant in the United States?
3. Which of the following theories of deviance described in the chapter—rational choice, differential association, labeling theory, anomie and social disorganization, strain theory, and conflict theory—best explain the increase in cheating among college students? Why?
4. Why is occupational crime not given as much attention as violent crime? What are some examples of occupational crimes that hurt millions of Americans every day? What would you suggest policy makers do to curb these crimes?
5. How do conflict theorists explain the demographic makeup of prisoners in the U.S. prison system? Do you agree with their explanation? Why or why not?
6. How can social capital help keep people out of prison and help former prisoners avoid returning to prison? How will your social capital help you conform (or not) to the norms of society?

Contributing to Our Social World: What Can We Do?

At the Local Level

- *LGBT groups* support students who are lesbian, gay, bisexual, and/or transgender. The Consortium of Higher Education LGBT Resource Professionals, a national organization of college and university groups, maintains a website at www.lgbtcampus.org. Regardless of your own sexual identity/orientation, consider contacting your campus LGBT group, attending meetings, and participating in its support and public education activities.
- *Boys and Girls Clubs* provide local programs and services to promote healthy development by instilling a sense of competence, usefulness, belonging, and influence in young people. Organizations for youth like Boys and Girls Clubs need interns and volunteers to provide role models for youth. Consider volunteering to help children with homework or activities. You can find a club near you by going to www.bgca.org/whoweare/Pages/FindaClub.aspx.

At the Organizational or Institutional Level

- The extensive and rapidly growing *criminal justice system* in the United States focuses on crime prevention, law enforcement, corrections, and rehabilitation. Identify the aspect of the system that interests you most and, using faculty and community contacts, select an appropriate organization for volunteer work, an internship, or a job.
- *Criminal courts* play a central role in the administration of criminal justice, and trials are often open to the public. Attending a trial and/or contacting a judge or magistrate could provide a good introduction to the court system and some of the people who work within it.
- *Crime prevention programs* are designed to reduce crime. Information can be found at the National Crime Prevention Council at www.ncpc.org/programs. In order to obtain a better understanding as to what types of crime prevention programs are most effective, go to the Center for the Study and Prevention of Violence's (CSPV) Blueprints for Violence Prevention website at www.colorado.edu/cspv/blueprints.

At the National and Global Levels

- *The Polaris Project:* This organization works to reduce global trafficking in women and children (www.polarisproject.org). Volunteers participate in letter-writing campaigns, support antitrafficking legislation, and conduct research on the problem.

Visit the Student Study Site at **www.sagepub.com/ballantine4e** to access additional study tools, including eFlashcards, web quizzes, video resources, audio resources, web resources, SAGE journal articles, recommended readings, and more.

PART III Inequality

Why are you affluent, while others in your sociology class are poor—or vice versa? Why do some people rise to the top of society with wealth, power, and prestige at their fingertips, and others languish near the bottom? Does ethnicity, race, or gender affect your position in society? These are the underlying questions in the next three chapters that focus on inequality, the process of stratification through which some people "make it" and others do not. At the very bottom of the human hierarchy are those starving and diseased world citizens who have no hope of survival for either themselves or their families. This compares with bankers, corporate executives, and some world politicians or royalty who have billions of dollars at their disposal.

Social inequality is one of the most important processes in modern societies, and the implications extend from the individual all the way to global social networks. Sometimes, the inequality is based on socioeconomic status, but the basis of differential treatment is often found in other characteristics: race, ethnicity, gender, sexual orientation, religion, or age. These differences often result in strong feelings like "we" versus "they" thinking. One factor runs throughout these patterns of inequality: They have implications for social interaction at the micro, meso, and macro levels of analysis. In this section, we do not try to cover all forms of inequality; rather, we illustrate the patterns by exploring issues of social class, race or ethnicity, and gender.

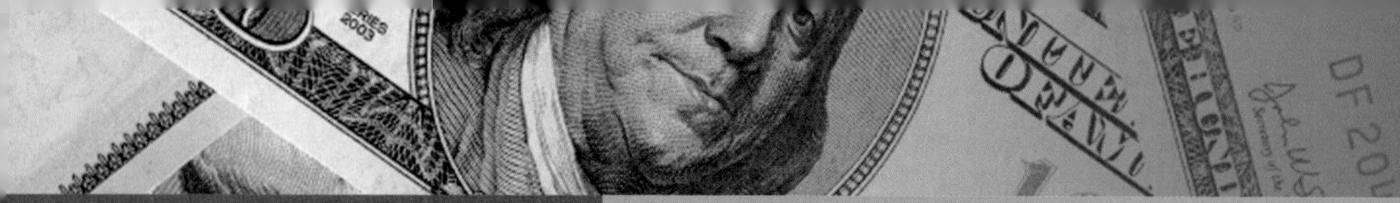

CHAPTER

7

Stratification

Rich and Famous—or Rags and Famine?

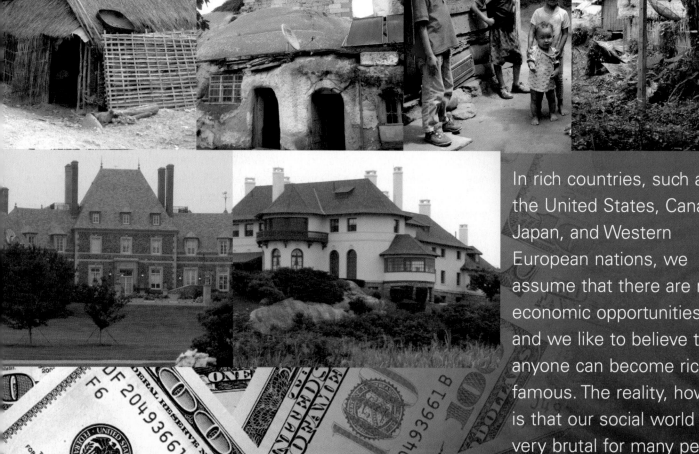

In rich countries, such as the United States, Canada, Japan, and Western European nations, we assume that there are many economic opportunities, and we like to believe that anyone can become rich and famous. The reality, however, is that our social world is very brutal for many people, and what they experience is rags and famine.

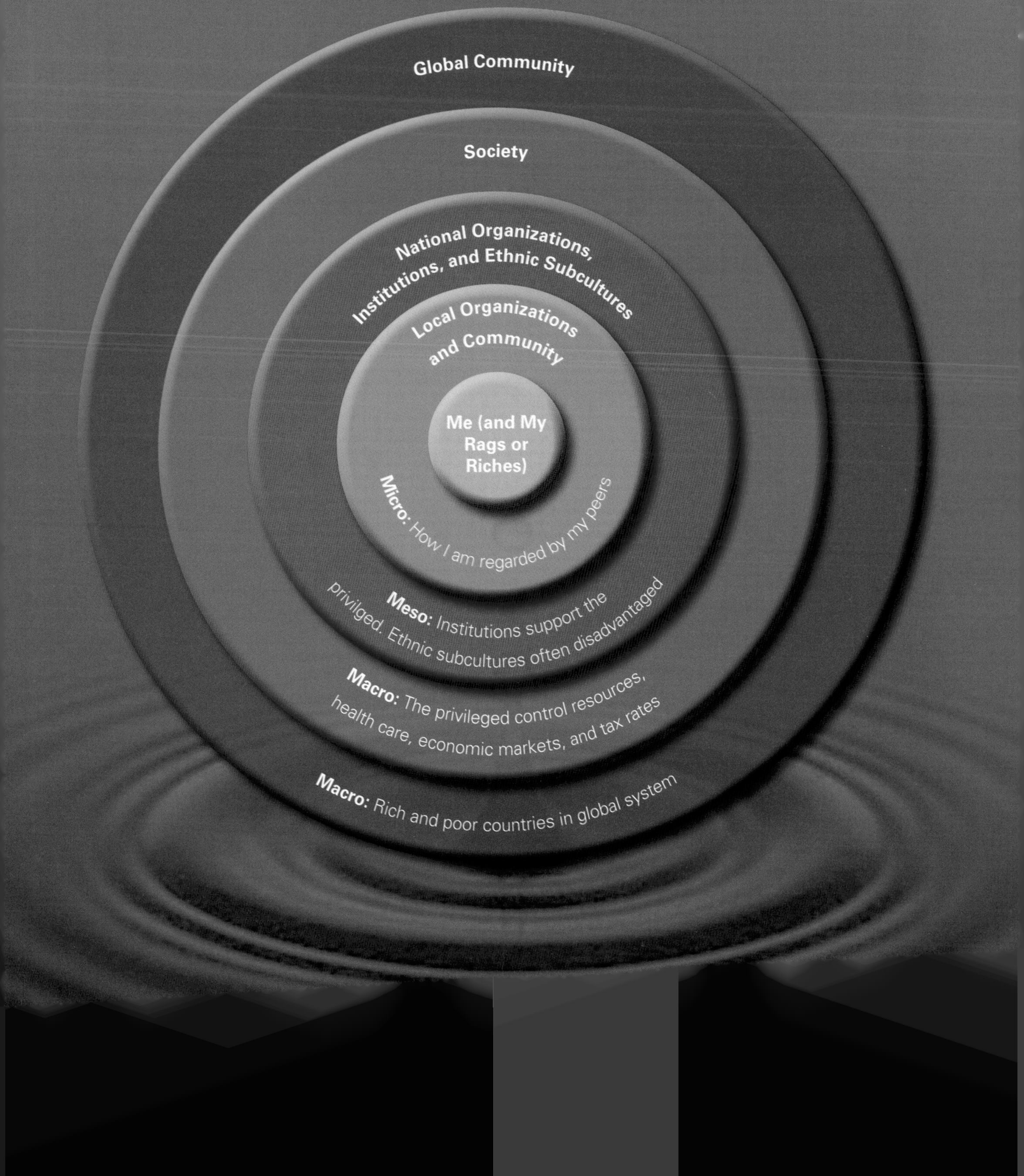

Global Community
Society
National Organizations, Institutions, and Ethnic Subcultures
Local Organizations and Community
Me (and My Rags or Riches)
Micro: How I am regarded by my peers
Meso: Institutions support the privilged. Ethnic subcultures often disadvantaged
Macro: The privileged control resources, health care, economic markets, and tax rates
Macro: Rich and poor countries in global system

Think About It	
Micro: Me (and My Inner Circle)	Why do you buy what you buy, believe what you believe, and live where you live?
Micro: Local Community	Why are some people in your community rich and others poor?
Meso: National Institutions; Complex Organizations; Ethnic Groups	How do institutions—such as education, the family, religion, health, and the economy—help keep people in the class they were born into?
Macro: National Society	Why are some nations affluent and others impoverished?
Macro: Global Community	How does the fact that we live in a global environment affect you and your social position?

What's coming in this chapter?

The Importance of Social Stratification
Theoretical Explanations of Stratification
Individuals' Social Status: The Micro Level
Social Mobility: The Micro-Meso Connection
Major Stratification Systems: Macro-Level Analysis
Poverty: Determinants and Social Policy

Pomp and circumstance surrounded the January 19, 2012, royal wedding of Prince of Wales William (heir to the British throne) and Catherine (Kate) Middleton, Duchess of Cambridge. All eyes in Britain and many eyes around the world were glued to TVs or lined the royal route to the palace. Few commoners will experience this lifestyle.

Prince William and the Duchess of Cambridge, Kate Middleton, were married in 2011 in Westminster Abbey with all the trappings of British royalty. They are in line to inherit the throne of England.

Not just anyone can belong to a royal family. One must be born as royalty or marry into it. Members of royal families such as Prince William and Prince Harry of Britain grow up in a world of the privileged: wealth, prestige, and access to power—or so it appears. Their lifestyles include formal receptions, horse races, polo games, royal hunts, state visits, and other social and state functions. The family has several elegant residences at its disposal. However, like most royalty, William, Harry, and now Kate Middleton also live within the confines of their elite status, with its strict expectations and limitations. They cannot show up for a beer at the local pub or associate freely with commoners, and their family problems or casual antics are subject matter for front pages of tabloids, as seen in antics of Pippa Middleton (Kate's sister) in a trip to Paris with friends that thrilled the paparazzi and dismayed the royal household. In today's world, some royalty are figureheads with little political power; others—such as the Ashanti chiefs in West Africa, King Bhumibol Adulyadej of Thailand, and Emperor Akihito in Japan—have great influence in state affairs.

In Newport, Rhode Island, spacious mansions are nestled along the coast, with tall-masted sailboats at the docks. These are the summer homes of the U.S. aristocracy. These individuals do not hold royal titles, but their positions allow for a life of comfort similar to that of royalty. Members of this class have an elegant social life, engage in elite sports such as fencing and polo, patronize the arts, and are influential behind the scenes in business and politics.

Hidden from the public eye in each country are people with no known names and no swank addresses; some have no address at all. We catch glimpses of their plight through vivid media portrayals of refugees in Darfur, Sudan; impoverished victims of natural disasters such as Hurricane Katrina in 2005 along the U.S. Gulf of Mexico coast; and famines occurring as you read this in Niger's Sahel desert, in Somalia, and in other poor countries. The earthquake and tsunami in Japan in March 2011 affected people from all socioeconomic levels, but many common people lived in more vulnerable areas. That quake measured 9.0 on the Richter scale triggering 10-meter-high waves that left 16,447 people dead and 4,666 missing (Diep 2011; Vervaeck and Daniell 2011).

Newport, Rhode Island, has long been one of the most affluent cities in North America, a community where mansions and yachts line the sea coast. The vessel on the right, docked in Newport, Rhode Island, is the largest privately owned yacht in the world.

Many of those worst affected by disasters are the poor, many of whom live in squalor. Economic hard times have pushed some of them from their rural homes to cities in hopes of finding jobs. However, with few jobs for unskilled and semiskilled workers in today's postindustrial service economies, many of the poor are left homeless. They live in abandoned buildings or sleep in unlocked autos, on park benches, under bridges, on beaches, or anywhere they can stretch out and hope not to be attacked or harassed. Beggars stake out spots on city sidewalks, hoping citizens and tourists will give them a handout. In the United States, cities such as Houston, Los Angeles, Washington, DC, and New York try to cope with the homeless by setting up sanitary facilities and temporary shelters, especially in bad weather; cities rely on religious and civic organizations such as churches and the Salvation Army to run soup kitchens.

In some areas of the world, such as sub-Saharan Africa and parts of India, the situation is much more desperate, and many families are starving. At daybreak, a cattle cart traverses the city of Kolkata (Calcutta), India, picking up bodies of diseased and starved homeless people who have died on the streets during the night. Mother Teresa, who won the Nobel Peace Prize for her work with those in dire poverty, established a home in India where these people could die with dignity. She also founded an orphanage for children who would otherwise wander the streets begging or lie on the sidewalk dying. These efforts are noble but only a drop in the world bucket of misery.

Survival, just maintaining life, is a daily struggle for the 40% of the world's population who live on 5% of the global income. Of the 1.9 billion children in the world, 2.2 million mostly from Global South countries die every year (6,000 a day) from malnutrition, diseases related to unsafe water, poor sanitation, and inadequate health care. One in 6, or 1.1 billion people, do not have access to safe drinking water (Blue Planet Network 2010; Gillis and Dugger 2011). Approximately 2.2 million children die annually because they are not immunized (United Nations Development Programme 2007). With progress toward meeting United Nations Millennium Goals, as of 2010 immunization programs had reduced deaths among children 5 and under by 28% (United Nations 2011). According to a 2012 report on urban children, 1 in 3 city dwellers lives in a slum, but that ratio is as high as 6 in 10 in Africa (UN News Center 2012). These urban children grow up in poverty, with lack of electricity, clean water, education, sanitation, health care, or adequate food. They die of preventable diseases. Those children in urban poverty often live on the streets and join criminal gangs for survival. These humans are at the bottom of the stratification hierarchy.

These examples raise the following question: Why do some people live like royalty and others live in desperate poverty? Most of us live between these extremes. We study and work hard for what we have, but we also live comfortably, knowing that starvation is not pounding at our door. This chapter discusses (a) why stratification is important, (b) why people are rich or poor (stratification systems), (c) the importance and consequences of social rankings for individuals, (d) whether one can change social class positions (social mobility), (e) characteristics of major stratification systems, (f) poverty and social policies to address problems, and (g) the global digital divide between rich and poor countries.

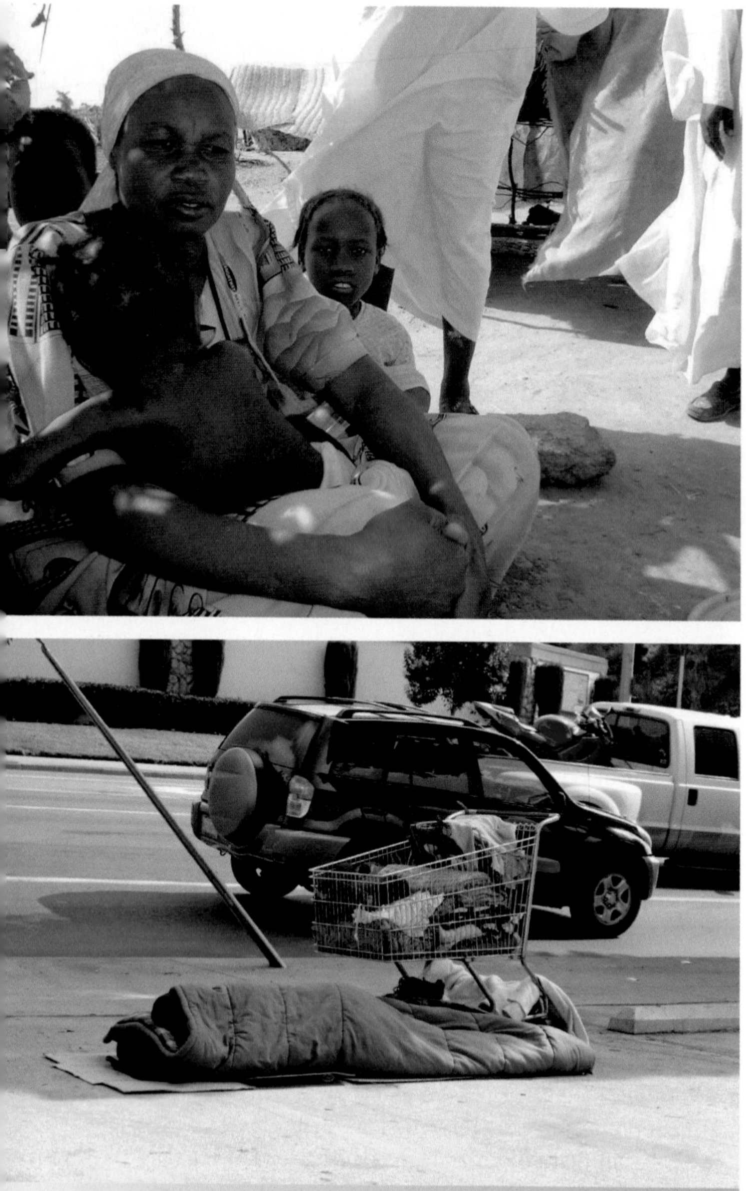

Poor people around the world find shelter wherever they can. A woman and her children displaced by war sit beneath a temporary shelter at a refugee camp in South Darfur. Even in affluent North America, some people are homeless and spend nights on sidewalks, in parks, or in homeless shelters.

The Importance of Social Stratification

Consider your own social ranking in your community and society. You were born into a family that holds a position in society—upper, middle, or lower class. The position of your family influences the neighborhood in which you live and where you shop, go to school, and attend religious services. Most likely, you and your family carry out the tasks of daily living in your community with others of similar position. Your position in the stratification system affects the opportunities available to you and the choices you make in life. Note the social world model at the beginning of the chapter provides a visual image of the social world and socioeconomic stratification. The stratification process affects everything from individuals' social rankings at the micro level of analysis to positions of countries in the global system at the macro level.

Social stratification refers to *how individuals and groups are layered and ranked in society according to how many valued resources they possess.* Stratification is an ongoing process of sorting people into different levels of access to resources, with the sorting determined and legitimated by cultural beliefs about why the inequality is justifiable. This chapter focuses on socioeconomic stratification, and subsequent chapters examine ethnic and gender stratification.

Three main assumptions underlie the concept of stratification: (1) People are divided into ranked categories; (2) there is an unequal distribution of things people want and need, meaning that some members of society possess more valued resources and others possess less; and (3) each society determines what it considers to be valued resources. In an agricultural society, members are ranked according to how much land or how many animals they own. In an industrial society, occupational position and income are two of the criteria for ranking. Most Japanese associate old age with wisdom, honor, and high rank, whereas Americans admire and offer high status to many people for their youthful vigor and beauty, such as sports or pop culture status.

What members of each society value and the criteria they use to rank other members depend on events in the society's history, its geographic location, its level of development in the world, the society's political philosophy, and the decisions of those in power. Powerful individuals are more likely to get the best positions, the most desirable mates, and the greatest opportunities. They may have power because of birth status, personality characteristics, age, physical attractiveness, education, intelligence, wealth, race, family background, occupation, religion, or ethnic group—whatever the basis for power is in that particular society. Those with power have advantages that perpetuate their power, and they try to hold onto those advantages through laws, customs, power, or ideologies.

Micro-Level Prestige and Influence

Remember how some of your peers on the playground were given more respect than others? Their high regard may have come from belonging to a prestigious family, having a dynamic or domineering personality, or owning symbols that distinguished them—"cool" clothing or shoes, a desirable bicycle, expensive toys, or a fancy car. This is stratification at its beginning stage.

Property, power, and prestige are accorded to those individuals who have cultural capital (knowledge and access to important information in the society) and social capital (networks with others who have influence). Individual qualities such as leadership, personality, sense of humor, self-confidence, quick-wittedness, physical attractiveness, or ascribed characteristics—such as the most powerful gender or ethnic group—influence cultural and social capital.

Meso-Level Access to Resources

Our individual status is shaped by our access to resources available through meso-level organizations and institutions. Our status is learned and reinforced in the family through the socialization process. We learn grammar and manners that affect our success in school, for example. Educational organizations treat children differently according to their social status, and our religious affiliation is likely to reflect our social status. Political systems, including laws, courts, and police, reinforce the stratification system. Access to health care often depends on one's position in the stratification system. Our position and connections in organizations have a profound impact on how we experience life and how we interact with other individuals and groups.

Look at all those forks and knives. Some people know what to do with each of them! Knowing which fork or knife to use for each course of a meal could influence someone's acceptance into elite society or chances of success on a job interview for certain kinds of jobs.

Macro-Level Factors Influencing Stratification

The economic system, which includes the occupational structure, level of technology, and distribution of wealth in a society, is often the basis for stratification (see Map 7.1 on page 220). Haiti, located on the island of Hispanola in the Caribbean, is the poorest country in the Western Hemisphere and one of the poorest countries in the world, with little technology, few resources, ineffective government, and an occupational structure based largely on subsistence farming. Even its forest resources are almost gone as desperately poor people cut down the last trees for firewood and shelters, leaving the land to erode (Diamond 2005). The economy is collapsing, resulting in many already poor people still more destitute and on the lowest rungs of the world's stratification system. Adding to the economic woes in Haiti, people faced further misery brought about by the 2010 earthquake and floods; people were driven from what meager shelters they had, and in addition faced a cholera epidemic. The economic position and geographic location of nations such as Haiti affect the opportunities available to individuals in those societies. There are currently no opportunities for Haitians to get ahead. Thus, macro-level factors can shape the opportunity structure and distribution of resources available to individuals.

Even the sports one plays—such as polo—are greatly influenced by social class and convey different kinds of social and cultural capital. Polo clearly requires a good deal of economic capital in order to play.

One problem for Haiti is that it has few of the resources that many other countries in the global system take for granted—a strong educational system, well-paying jobs in a vibrant economy, productive land, an ample supply of water, money to pay workers, access to the most efficient and powerful technology, and resources wanted by the world community. Almost all societies stratify members, and societies themselves are stratified in the world system,

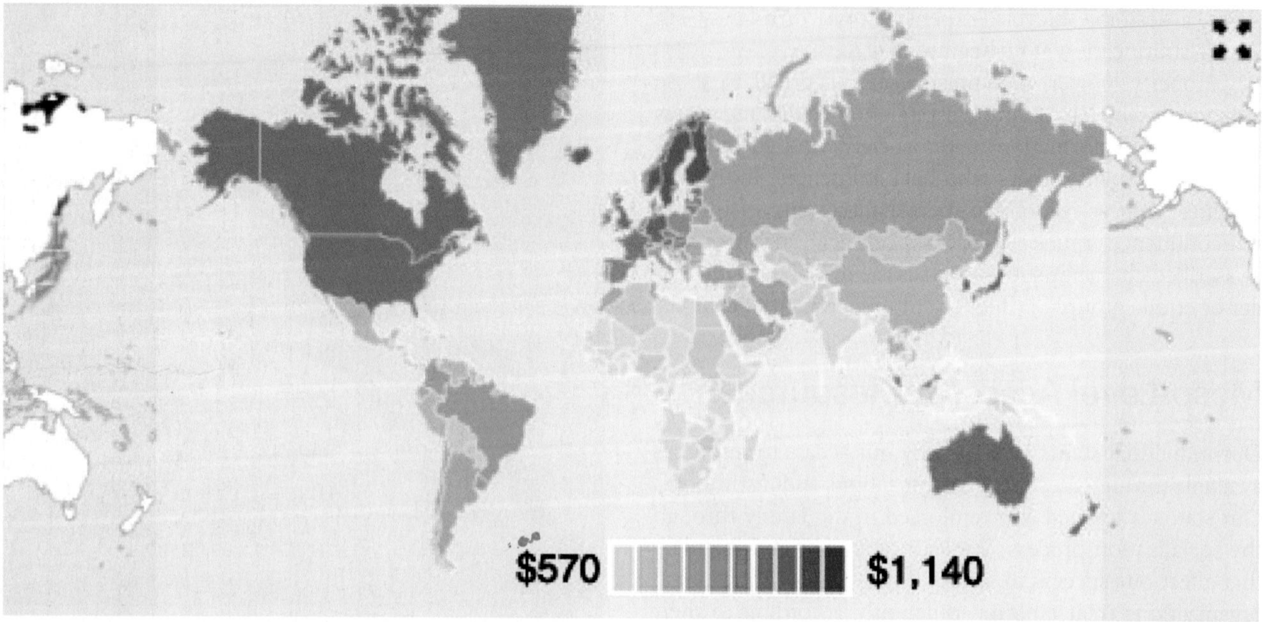

Map 7.1 Gross National Income per Capita in 2011

Source: World Bank. http://data.worldbank.org/indicator/NY.GNP.PCAP.PP.CD/countries?display=map

so each individual and nation experiences the world in unique ways related to its position. Stratification is one of the most powerful forces that we experience, but we are seldom conscious of how it works or how pervasive it is in our lives. This is the driving question sociologists ask when developing theories of stratification: How does it work?

Thinking Sociologically

Place yourself in the center of the social world model. Working outward from micro-level interactions toward the meso-level institutions and the macro-level global stratification system, indicate what has influenced where you fall in the stratification system.

Theoretical Explanations of Stratification

As we traverse the world we see continuous examples of rich and poor, those who have more resources than they need and those who do not have enough to survive. Why is the distribution of resources so uneven? Is that normal, inevitable, just? Most of us have opinions about these issues. Sociologists also have developed explanations—theories that help explain stratification. Recall that theories provide a framework for asking questions to be studied. Just as your interpretation of a question may differ from your friends' ideas, sociologists have developed different explanations for stratification and tested these with research data. These explanations of social rankings range from individual micro-level to national and global macro-level theories.

Micro-Level Theory

Our now familiar theories that relate to the micro level help us again, this time to understand differences between individuals on the stratification hierarchy.

Symbolic Interaction Theory

Most of us have been at a social gathering, perhaps at a swank country club or in a local bar, where we felt out of place. Each social group has norms that members learn through the socialization process. These norms are recognized within that group and can make clueless outsiders feel like space aliens. People learn what is expected in their groups—family, peer group, social class—through interaction with others. For instance, children are rewarded or punished for behaviors appropriate or inappropriate to their social position. This process transmits and perpetuates our positions in the social stratification system. Learning our social position means learning values, speech patterns, consumption habits, appropriate group memberships (including religious affiliation), and even our self-concept. It also provides us with the cultural capital we carry into our social positions.

Cultural capital refers to *knowledge, skills, language mastery, style of dress, and values that provide a person with access to a particular status in society.* Schools place children into courses and academic groups, influenced in part by the labels children receive due to their cultural capital. Home environments develop cultural capital of children. Some home environments teach children to obey rules and authority, and to repair houses and cars. Other families teach children by expanding vocabularies; developing good grammar; experiencing concerts, art, and theater; visiting historical sites; providing reading materials; and modeling engagement with reading. The higher-class parents tend to stress thinking skills as opposed to simply learning to obey authority figures. The result of this learning at home is that all children attain cultural capital, but children from the middle and upper classes or higher castes are more likely to get the best education, setting them up to be future leaders with better life chances. In this way, children's home experiences and education help reproduce the social class systems, that is, perpetuate the family's social class position in society (Ballantine and Hammack 2012).

Symbols often represent social positions. Clothing, for example, sets up some people as special and privileged. Young people wear expensive designer jeans that low-income people cannot afford. Drinking wine rather than beer, driving a Jaguar rather than a less expensive set of wheels, and living in a home that has six or eight bedrooms and is 5,000-plus square feet is an expression of *conspicuous consumption*—displaying goods in a way that others will notice and that will presumably earn the owner respect (Veblen 1902). Thus, purchased products become symbols that are intended to define the person as someone of high status.

In most of the Global North, one symbol of middle-class "decency" is the right to bathe and do one's grooming in privacy. Indeed, most young people in the United States expect to have their own bedrooms and expect no interruptions when sprucing up for the day. Homeless people in the United States do not have this luxury, and in India, bathing on the streets is not uncommon. So even privacy is a symbol of affluence.

A core idea in symbolic interaction theory is that reality is constructed, that as we figure out what our circumstances mean, we are constructing the reality we live. This

In India, many people must bathe every day in public in whatever water supply they can find. Even many people with homes would not have their own water supply. Privacy for one's grooming is a symbol of privilege for the affluent.

idea is explored in further depth in the next "Sociology in Our Social World" on page 222.

Rational Choice Theory

Rational choice theorists focus on individuals and the way they make decisions regarding their own self-interest. From this view, people are always making decisions based on their perception of costs and benefits. Some people evaluate potential benefits with a view to the long-term. They are willing to endure short-term expense or "pain" if the long-term gains are substantial. In order to take this view, one needs a sense of *delayed gratification*—delaying rewards or benefits until a later time. People who are willing or in a position to do this—living austerely now in order to experience prosperity later—may be more likely to have upward mobility and to experience greater affluence at a later time. While your friend from high school may have a job and drive a nicer car than you can afford, you may be building debts and living in a drab dormitory in hopes of a better future. Thus, rational choice theorists would focus on how our personal choices influence our place in the social system. The idea is that one's socioeconomic position is shaped largely by individual decisions.

In high school, many college prep students make decisions to become involved in athletic programs, the Spanish

Sociology in Our Social World

Understanding Urban Homeless People

Homeless people may find themselves sleeping under bridges or in parks, vacant lots, cars, or unused subway tunnels. Although many people look down on the homeless, most have held respectable jobs and had housing in the past. Bad economic times have left these citizens without jobs and with few opportunities. On any given night, there are an estimated 664,000 homeless people (Interagency Council on Homelessness 2009). Housing and Urban Development (HUD) officials measure overall homelessness via funding applications for housing services and state that even this number is a large underestimation of the total number of people who experience homelessness (HUD 2008).

In trying to make sense of homelessness, researchers identified key variables that distinguished different types of homelessness, and uncovered a wide range of causes, circumstances, and coping methods. Snow and Anderson (1993) have studied the microculture of street people, how they lend each other support and help each other make sense of their circumstances. They point to many forces at work on the homeless, from global economic trends to the way their families relate to them.

One question is how homeless people affirm a positive sense of self in this humiliating situation. After all, to be a person of worth in American society is to (1) own some property, (2) have someone who cares about you enough to take you in if you are really desperate, and (3) occupy a significant status in society by earning some money and having a career or position deserving of respect. The homeless not only lack all these, but their master status—"homeless person"—is one that elicits disrespect. "Dignity and worth are not primarily individual characteristics, but instead flow from the roles we play," write the authors (Snow and Anderson 1993:9). To be homeless, then, is far more than to be without a residence or shelter. It is to be without a place to restore one's dignity. So how did the homeless studied by Snow and Anderson (1993) cope?

This research showed a number of coping strategies. Sometimes, the homeless people explained away their circumstances as temporary "bad luck" or part of a normal cycle in which they just happened to be on the down end for a short period of time. Others would distance themselves from the role of homelessness, pointing out that they were "different" from other homeless people, "didn't really belong," and did not really deserve to be seen as homeless at all. Some people coped by fictive storytelling, pointing to pronounced achievements in the past (often fictionalized or embellished) or creating stories of their phenomenal accomplishments when they finally do get on their feet. By affirming another identity in the past or the future, their self-esteem was salvaged. However, perhaps the most surprising strategy to preserve self-worth was to embrace the role of being homeless with pride—to boast about how one was the best at being a survivor, the best at being a friend to the homeless, or the best at rejecting shallow values of materialism in our commercial society. They could thus affirm themselves for coping skills, for caring qualities, or for deep spirituality. They had defined reality in a way that allowed them to see themselves in a positive light. They had changed the social construction of reality, at least among themselves.

Club, leadership roles in the National Honor Society, or the junior prom committee because they want to list those involvements on college applications. They commit effort now—sometimes in activities that they care little about—in hopes of having a payoff in scholarships or even just admission to the college of their choice. Those same students become discouraged with classmates who will not help with the prom decorations or with building the junior class float. However, for young people whose parents have never gone to college, spending time at the local pool hall or bowling alley where they might meet people who could help them get a job in the local factory, spending time decorating a float makes no sense. Thus, the way one evaluates costs and benefits may actually be influenced by the social position one already holds. Interaction theories help us understand how individuals learn and live their positions in society. Next, we consider theories that examine the larger social structures, processes, and forces that affect stratification and inequality: structural-functional and various forms of conflict theory.

Meso- and Macro-Level Theories

Structural-Functional Theory

Structural-functionalists (sometimes simply called functionalists) view stratification within societies as an inevitable—and generally a necessary—part of the social world. The stratification system provides each individual a place or position in the social world and motivates individuals to carry out their roles. Societies survive by having an organized system into which each individual is born, where each is raised, and where each contributes some part to the maintenance of the society.

The basic elements of the structural-functional theory of stratification were explained by Kingsley Davis and Wilbert Moore (1945), and their work still provides the main ideas of the theory today. Focusing on stratification by considering different occupations and how they are rewarded, Davis and Moore argue the following:

1. *Value of positions*: Positions in society are neither equally valued nor equally pleasant to perform. Some positions—such as physicians—are more highly technical and valued because people feel they are very important to society and the public is dependent on this expertise. Therefore, societies must motivate talented individuals to prepare for and occupy the most important and difficult positions, such as being physicians.

2. *Preparation requires talent, time, and money*: To motivate talented individuals to make the sacrifices necessary to prepare for and assume difficult positions such as becoming a physician, differential rewards of income, prestige, power, or other valued goods must be offered. Thus, a doctor receives high income, prestige, and power as incentives.

3. *Unequal distribution of rewards*: The differences in rewards, such as pay for most valued positions, lead, in turn, to the unequal distribution of resources for occupations in society. Some people get richer. Therefore, stratification is inevitable. The unequal distribution of status and wealth in society motivates individuals to fill necessary positions—such as willingness to undertake the stress of being chief executive officer of a corporation in a highly competitive field.

In the mid-20th century, functional theory provided sociologists with a valuable framework for studying stratification, but things do change (Tumin 1953). In the 21st century, new criteria such as controlling information and access to information systems have become important for determining wealth and status, making scientists and technicians a new class of elites. The society also experiences conflict over distribution of resources that functionalism does not fully explain.

Conflict Theory

When interpreting status differences between groups, conflict theorists see stratification as the outcome of struggles for dominance and scarce resources, with some individuals in society taking advantage of others. Individuals and groups act in their own self-interest by trying to exploit others, leading inevitably to a struggle between those who have advantages and want to keep them and those who want a larger share of the pie.

Conflict theory developed in a time of massive economic transformation. With the end of the feudal system, economic displacement of peasants, and the rise of urban factories as major employers, a tremendous gap between the rich and the poor evolved. This prompted theorists to ask several basic questions related to stratification: (a) How do societies produce necessities—food, clothing, and shelter? (b) How are relationships between rich and poor people shaped by this process? and (c) How do people become alienated in their routine, dull jobs in which they have little involvement and no investment in the end product?

Karl Marx (1818–1883), considered the father of conflict theory, lived during this time of industrial transformation. Marx described four possible ways to distribute wealth, according to (1) what each person needs, (2) what each person wants, (3) what each person earns, or (4) what each person can take. It was this fourth way, Marx believed, that was dominant in competitive capitalist societies (Cuzzort and King 2002; Marx and Engels 1955).

Marx viewed the stratification structure as composed of two major economically based social classes: the *haves* and the *have-nots*. The *haves* consisted of the capitalist bourgeoisie, whereas the *have-nots* were made up of the working-class proletariat. Individuals in the same social class had similar lifestyles, shared ideologies, and held common outlooks on social life. The struggle over resources between haves and have-nots is the cause of conflict (Hurst 2013).

The haves control what Marx called the means of production—money, materials, and factories—the valued resources in society (Marx [1844] 1964). The haves dominate because the lower-class have-nots cannot accumulate enough money and power to change their positions. The norms and values of the haves dominate the society because of their power and ability to make the distribution of resources seem "fair" and justified. Laws, religious beliefs, educational systems, political structures and policies, and police or military forces ensure continued control by the haves. This keeps the have-nots from understanding their own self-interests and is why working-class people often support politicians whose policies really favor the rich 1%. The haves muddy the waters so those without privilege do not really assess costs and benefits accurately.

The unorganized lower-class have-nots can be exploited as long as they do not develop a *class consciousness*—a shared awareness of their poor status. Marx contended that, with the help of intellectuals who believed in the injustice of the exploited poor, the working class would develop a class consciousness, rise up, and overthrow the haves, culminating in a classless society in which wealth would be more equally shared (Marx and Engels 1955).

Thinking Sociologically

How can conflict theory help us understand the uprisings, led primarily by youth, in Egypt, Libya, Syria, and other Middle Eastern and North African countries? Can it help us understand the Occupy Wall Street protests? Explain.

Unlike the structural-functionalists, then, conflict theorists maintain that money and other rewards are not necessarily given to those in the most important positions in the society. Can we argue that a rock star or baseball player is more necessary for the survival of society than a teacher or police officer? Yet the pay differential is tremendous.

Not all the predictions of Karl Marx have come true. No truly classless societies have developed, in part because those in power protect their positions, perpetuating class distinctions. However, some developments have moved toward more sharing of wealth. Labor unions arose to unite and represent the working classes and put them in a more powerful position vis-à-vis the capitalists; managerial and technical positions emerged to create a large middle class; some companies moved to employee ownership; and workers gained legal protection from government legislative bodies in most industrial countries (Dahrendorf 1959).

Even societies that claim to be classless, such as China, have privileged classes and poor peasants. In recent years, the Chinese government has allowed more private ownership of shops, businesses, and other entrepreneurial efforts, motivating many Chinese citizens to work long hours at their private businesses to "get ahead." The only classless societies are a few small hunter-gatherer groups that have no extra resources that would allow some members to accumulate wealth.

Some theorists criticize Marx for his focus on only the economic system, pointing out that noneconomic factors enter into the stratification struggle as well. Max Weber (1864–1920), an influential theorist, amended Marx's theory by considering other elements in addition to economic forces. He agreed with Marx that group conflict is inevitable, that economics is one of the key factors in stratification systems, and that those in power try to perpetuate their positions. However, he added two other influential factors that he argued determine stratification in modern industrial societies: power and prestige. We consider these "three *Ps*"—property, power, and prestige—later in this chapter.

Selena Gomez was one of the Glamour *Women of the Year in 2012. Although she is just 20 and has little education, she is paid millions of dollars each year to entertain the public with acting and singing. Meanwhile the public school teacher (right) would take 30 years of teaching hundreds of children to read before her total cumulative income for her entire career would add up to $1 million.*

Recent theorists suggest that using the three *P*s, we can identify five classes—capitalists, managers, small business owners or the petty bourgeoisie, workers, and the underclass—rather than just the haves and have-nots. *Capitalists* own the means of production, and they purchase and control the labor of others. *Managers* sell their labor to capitalists and manage the labor of others for the capitalists. The *petty bourgeoisie*, such as small shop or business owners, own some means of production but control little of the labor of others; nevertheless, they have modest prestige, power, and property (Sernau 2010). *Workers* sell their labor to capitalists and are low in all three *P*s. Finally, the *underclass* has virtually no property, power, or prestige.

In the modern world, as businesses become international and managerial occupations continue to grow, conflict theorists argue that workers are still exploited but in different ways. Owners and chief executive officers (CEOs) get more income than many analysts feel is warranted by their responsibilities—for example, the CEO of Oracle received $84.5 million, of Boston Scientific $33.4 million, and of Occidental Petroleum $31.4 million in 2009 (Barr and Goldman 2010).

In 2011, the chief executives of the 500 biggest companies in the United States got a collective pay raise of 16% last year (2011), to $5.2 billion. The total averages out to $10.5 million apiece. Value from stock options and vested stock awards accounted for 61%. The average stock gain was $3.2 million, up from $2.7 million in 2011. Combined salary and bonuses were up an average of 8% to $3.5 million. The average CEO pay in the area of drugs and biotechnology is $18.3 million, though the top people in hotels, restaurants, and leisure do not do badly at $14.4 million (DeCarlo 2012). The argument for these enviable compensation packages is that it takes top dollar to get and keep the top executives. These figures contrast with average U.S. workers' raise of 3%—well below the CEO 16%. The Obama administration's pay czar is publishing names and salaries of the 25 most highly paid executives in a number of companies, including many of those that received help from the bailout—Citigroup, Bank of America, American International Group (AIG), Graduate Management Admission Council (GMAC), and others (Dealbook 2009).

Many people argue that better-educated and -skilled people get more income than is warranted by the differential in education. Moreover, the labor that produces our clothes, cell phones, digital cameras, televisions, and other products is increasingly provided by impoverished people around the world working for low wages at multinational corporations (Bonacich and Wilson 2005). Apple products are a recent case in point when they came into the news for poor factory conditions and pay in China. In rich countries, service providers receive low wages at fast-food chains and box stores such as Walmart (Ehrenreich 2001, 2005). One controversial question is whether multinational corporations are bringing opportunity to poor countries through manufacturing jobs, or exploiting them by paying low wages and allowing poor conditions, as many conflict theorists contend (Wallerstein 2004).

Thinking Sociologically

Do multinational corporations bring opportunity, or do they exploit people in order to make profits for stockholders? What reasoning and evidence support your position?

The Evolutionary Theory of Stratification: A Synthesis

Evolutionary theory borrows assumptions from both structural-functional and conflict theories in an attempt to determine how scarce resources are distributed and how that distribution results in stratification (Lenski 1966; Nolan and Lenski 2008). The basic ideas are as follows: (a) To survive, people must cooperate; (b) despite this, conflicts of interest occur over important decisions that benefit one individual or group over another; (c) valued items such as money and status are always in demand and in short supply; (d) there is likely to be a struggle over these scarce goods; and (e) customs or traditions in a society often prevail over rational criteria in determining distribution of scarce resources. After the minimum survival needs of both individuals and the society are met, power determines who gets the surplus: prestige, luxury living, the best health care, and so forth. Lenski (1966; Nolan and Lenski 2008) believes that privileges (including wealth) flow from having power, and prestige usually results from having access to both power and privilege (Hurst 2006).

Lenski (1966; Nolan and Lenski 2008) tested his theory by studying societies at different levels of technological development, ranging from simple to complex. He found that the degree of inequality increases with technology until it reaches the advanced industrial stage. For instance, in subsistence-level hunter-gatherer societies, little surplus is available, and everyone's needs are met to the extent possible. As surplus accumulates in agrarian societies, those who acquire power also control surpluses, and they use this to benefit their friends and relations. However, even if laws are made by those in power, the powerful must share some of the wealth or fear being overthrown. Interestingly, when societies finally reach the advanced industrial stage, there is less inequality. This happens because people in various social classes enjoy greater political participation and because more resources are available to be shared in the society.

Lenski's theory explains many different types of societies by synthesizing elements of both structural-functional and conflict theory (Lenski 1966; Nolan and Lenski 2008). For instance, evolutionary theory takes into consideration an idea shared by the structural-functionalists and rational choice theorists—that talented individuals need to be motivated to make sacrifices. This produces motivated, competent, and well-educated people in the most important social statuses. The theory also recognizes exploitation leading to inequality, a factor that conflict theorists find in capitalist systems of stratification. The reality is that while some inequality may be useful in highly complex societies, extraordinary amounts of inequality may undermine motivation and productivity. Upward mobility may seem so impossible that the most talented people do not necessarily get the most demanding and responsible jobs. So Nolan and Lenski conclude that the size of the inequality gaps in a society does matter (Nolan and Lenski 2008).

The amount of inequality differs in societies, according to evolutionary theorists, because of different levels of technological development. Industrialization brings surplus wealth, a division of labor, advanced technology, and interdependence among members of a society. No longer can one individual control all the important knowledge, skills, or capital resources. Therefore, this should eliminate the extreme gap between haves and have-nots because resources would normally be more evenly distributed.

The symbolic interaction, structural-functional, conflict, and evolutionary theories provide different explanations for understanding stratification in modern societies. These theories are the basis for micro- to macro-level discussions of stratification. Our next step is to look at some factors that influence an individual's position in a stratification system and the ability to change that position.

Thinking Sociologically

Why is the income gap currently increasing in the United States? How might conflict and functional theories each explain this pattern? What are some factors that determine your own position in the stratification system?

Individuals' Social Status: The Micro Level

You are among the world's elite. Less than 6.7% of the world's population has a college degree ("6.7% of World Has a College Degree" 2010). However, that number is expanding rapidly as countries such as China provide higher education opportunities to more students to support their growing economies. In 2010, 31 million Chinese students were enrolled in higher education, surpassing the U.S. enrollment, with an enrollment rate of 27%, an increase of 35% since 2005 (People's Daily Online 2011). Although China has more than 4,000 colleges and universities, the demand for a college education far exceeds the opportunity. Therefore, many Chinese college students are studying abroad, adding to their opportunities and enhancing China's knowledge of the world. In fact, Chinese students make up the largest number of international students studying in the United States. There were nearly 160,000 Chinese students in the United States in 2012, a 23% increase since 2009. Of these, 56,976 are undergraduates. Chinese make up more than 21% of the international students in the United States. In fact, some California institutions of higher education are turning away U.S. students for Chinese students who can pay money much needed by the colleges in a state with budget problems (Huffington Post 2012; Wong 2012).

Yet being able to afford the time and money for college is a luxury with little relevance to those struggling to survive each day. It is beyond the financial or personal resources of almost 95% of people in the world. Considered in this global perspective, college students learn professional skills

In terms of the global population, anyone who attends college is privileged, and anyone who has a college degree is extremely advantaged.

and have advantages that billions of other world citizens will never know or even imagine. Does that give you a new respect for the opportunities you have?

In the United States, access to higher education is greater than in many other countries because there are more levels of entry—including technical colleges, community colleges, large state universities, and private four-year colleges. However, with limited government help, most students must have financial resources to help cover tuition and the cost of living. Many students do not realize that the prestige of the college they choose makes a difference in their future opportunities. Those students born into wealth can afford better preparation for entrance exams as well as tutors or courses to increase SAT (Scholastic Aptitude and Reasoning Test) scores. They often attend private preparatory schools and gain acceptance to prestigious colleges that open opportunities not available to those attending the typical state university or nonelite colleges (Persell 2005).

Ascribed characteristics, such as gender, can also affect one's chances for success in life. Embedded gender stratification systems may make it difficult for women to rise in the occupational hierarchy. Many Japanese women, for example, earn college degrees but leave employment after getting married and having children (GlobeWomen 2013). However, the number of unmarried working women in Japan increased by 5% over 10 years, while married women's participation decreased by 3% during that time ("Japanese Women Face Difficulties" 2007). Furthermore, Japanese women hold only 2% of all corporate board seats, and few are on boards of directors (GlobeWomen's Business Network 2006). Issues of gender stratification will be examined in more depth in Chapter 9, but they intersect with socioeconomic class and must be viewed as part of a larger pattern resulting in inequality in the social world.

Individual Life Chances

Life chances refer to *one's opportunities, depending on both achieved and ascribed status in society*. That you are in college, probably have health insurance and access to health care, and are likely to live into your late 70s or 80s are factors directly related to your life chances. Let us consider several examples of how placement in organizations at the meso level affects individual experiences and has global ramifications.

Education

Although education is valued by most individuals, the cost of books, clothing, shoes, transportation, child care, and time taken from income-producing work may be an insurmountable barrier to attendance from grade school through college. Economically disadvantaged students in most countries are more likely to attend less prestigious and less expensive institutions if they attend high school or university at all. Globally speaking, girls are particularly disadvantaged (Lewis and Lockheed 2006).

For some people living in poverty, the standard of wealth is ownership of a single horse. The boys above travel to their village in Afghanistan, where they must work every day rather than going to school.

One's level of education affects many aspects of life, including political, religious, and marital attitudes and behavior. Generally speaking, the higher the education level, the more active individuals are in political life, the more mainstream or conventional their religious affiliation, the more likely they are to marry into a family with both economic and social capital, the more stable the marriage, and the more likely they are to have good health.

Health, Social Conditions, and Life Expectancy

Pictures on the news of children starving and dying dramatically illustrate global inequalities. The poorest countries in the world are in sub-Saharan Africa, where most individuals eat poorly, are susceptible to diseases, have great stress in their daily lives just trying to survive, and die at young ages compared with the developed world.

If you have a sore throat, you go to see your doctor. Yet many people in the world will never see a doctor. Access to health care requires doctors and medical facilities, money for transportation and treatment, access to child care, and released time from other tasks to get to a medical facility. The poor sometimes do not have these luxuries. In contrast, the affluent eat better food, are less exposed to polluted water and unhygienic conditions, are able to pay for medical care and drugs when they do have ailing health, and live twice as long. Even causes of death illustrate the differences between people at different places in the stratification hierarchy. For example, in the poor Global South, shorter life expectancies and deaths, especially among children, are due to controllable infectious diseases such as cholera, AIDS, typhoid, tuberculosis, and other respiratory ailments. In contrast, in affluent countries, heart disease, stroke, and lung cancer are the most common causes of death, and most deaths are of people above the age of 65. In recent years improvements in immunizations, mosquito nets to prevent malaria, better sanitation and water quality, access to medicines, better nutrition, and female literacy have extended life expectancy; for children under 5 there has been a 25% decline in deaths from 101 per 1,000 to 73 per 1,000 (U.S. Census Bureau, Population Division, International Programs Center 2011; World Bank 2010). So whether considered locally or globally, access to health care resources makes a difference in life chances. To an extent, the chance to have a long and healthy life is a privilege of the elite. Again, globally speaking, if you are reading this book as part of a college course, you are part of the elite.

The impact of social conditions on life expectancy is especially evident if we compare cross-national data. Countries with the shortest life expectancy at birth illustrate the pattern. These countries lack adequate health care, immunizations, and sanitation; have crises of war and displacement of population resulting in refugees; and experience illnesses, epidemics, and famine. Even a drought has more tragic impact when no other aid resources are available to help families cope. By studying Table 7.1 in the next "Engaging Sociology" feature, you can compare life expectancy with two other measures of life quality for the poorest and richest countries: the gross national product (GNP) per capita income—the average amount of money each person has per year—and the infant mortality rates (death rates for babies). Note that average life expectancy in poor countries is as low as 32 years, income is as low as $200 a year (many of the people in these populations are subsistence farmers), and infant mortality is as high as 180.2 deaths (estimated) in the first year of life for every 1,000 births and as low as

Engaging Sociology

Comparative Perspectives on Income, Life Expectancy, and Mortality

Analyzing the meaning of data can provide an understanding of the health and well-being of citizens around the world. A country's basic statistics including life expectancy, per capita gross national product, and infant mortality tell researchers a great deal about its economic health and vitality.

1. What questions do the data in Table 7.1 raise regarding differences in mortality and life expectancy rates around the world?
2. Considering what you know from this and previous chapters and from Table 7.1, what do you think are some differences in the lives of citizens in the richest and poorest countries?

Table 7.1 Life Expectancy, Per Capita Income, and Infant Mortality for Selected Poor and Rich Countries

Poor Countries	*Life Expectancy (in years)*	*Infant Mortality (deaths per 1,000 births)*	*Per Capita GNP ($)*	*Rich Countries*	*Life Expectancy (in years)*	*Infant Mortality (deaths per 1,000 births)*	*Per Capita GNP ($)*
Chad	48.7	93.6	1,900	**Singapore**	83.8	2.7	60,500
Afghanistan	49.7	121.6	1,000	**Hong Kong**	82.1	2.9	49,800
Zimbabwe	50.8	28.2	500	**Australia**	81.9	4.6	40,800
Somalia	50.8	103.7	600	**France**	81.5	3.7	35,600
Mozambique	52.0	76.9	1,100	**Canada**	81.5*	4.9*	41,100
Nigeria	52.0	74.3	800	**Sweden**	82.2	2.7	40,900
Zambia	52.6	64.6	1,600	**Switzerland**	81.2	4.0	43,900
Mali	53.0	109	1,100	**Iceland**	81.0	3.2	38,500
Niger	53.8	110.0	800	**New Zealand**	80.7	4.7	28,000
Ethiopia	56.6	75.3	1,100	**United Kingdom**	80.2	4.6	36,600
Liberia	57.4	72.4	500	**United States**	78.5**	6.0**	49,000

Source: World Factbook 2012a and 2012c for life expectancy and infant mortality; *World Factbook* 2012b for per capita income.

Note: Infant mortality is per 1,000 live births.

*Canada is 12th in life expectancy and 41st in infant mortality rates.

**United States is 50th in life expectancy and 49th in infant mortality rates.

2.8 in some Global North countries (Geocommons 2009; World Factbook 2012a, 2012b, 2012c). Numbers for the richest countries are dramatically different.

The United States has much larger gaps between rich and poor people than most other wealthy countries, resulting in higher poverty rates (more people at the bottom rungs of the stratification ladder). This is, in turn, reflected in health statistics, with infant mortality rates at six deaths in the first year of life per 1,000 births (World Factbook 2012c). The world average infant mortality rate is 49.4 deaths per 1,000 live births (World Population Prospects 2010). More than 25,000 children under 5 years old die each day on average; that is 1 child every three to five seconds, 17 to 18 every minute, and approximately 9 million per year (Shah 2009a). This evidence supports the assertion that health, illness, and death rates are closely tied to socioeconomic stratification, including class, race, and gender.

People living in poverty around the world often get health care at clinics or emergency rooms, if they have access to care, where they wait for hours to see a health care provider as shown in this mother-child health clinic in Kisumu, Kenya.

Thinking Sociologically

What factors at the micro, meso, and macro levels affect your life expectancy and that of your family members?

Individual Lifestyles

Your individual **lifestyle** includes *your attitudes, values, beliefs, behavior patterns, and other aspects of your place in the world, shaped by socialization.* As individuals grow up, the behaviors and attitudes consistent with their culture and their family's status in society become internalized through the process of socialization. Lifestyle is not a simple matter of having money. Acquiring money—say, by winning a lottery—cannot buy a completely new lifestyle (Bourdieu and Passeron 1977). This is because values and behaviors are ingrained in our self-concept from childhood. A person may gain material possessions, but that does not mean she has the lifestyle of the upper-class rich and famous. Even the way one dresses is often a statement about one's social class, and some people dress up for special occasions to have a "status holiday"—to pretend they are rich and famous for a night. Consider some examples of factors related to your individual lifestyle: attitudes toward achievement, political involvement, and religious membership.

Clothing not only covers our bodies but also acts as a symbol of our social status and reflects our lifestyles. This couple is either from a very affluent family or enjoying a night where they pretend to be rich.

Attitudes Toward Achievement

Attitudes toward achievement differ by social status and are generally closely correlated with life chances. Motivation to get ahead and beliefs about what you can achieve are in part products of our upbringing and the opportunities we see as available to us. These attitudes differ greatly depending on the opportunity structure around us, including what our families and friends see as possible and desirable. Then, consider the situation of children from poor countries and poor families. Their primary concern may be to help put food on the family's table. Even attitudes toward primary and secondary education reflect the luxury and inaccessibility that schooling is for some children. In Global North countries, opportunity is available for most children to attend school at least through high school and often beyond. However, some students do not learn to value achievement in school due to difficulty in school, peer pressures, lack of support from family members, poor self-concepts, poor role models, poor schools and teaching, language differences, cultural differences, and many other factors (Ballantine and Hammack 2012).

Family Life and Child-Rearing Patterns

Attitudes toward achievement are not the only things that differ between socioeconomic groups. Child-rearing patterns are also affected by social class and serve to reinforce one's social position in society. When you were growing up, were your afterschool hours, weekends, and summers filled with adult-organized activities (e.g., formal lessons, youth sports, camps)? In contrast, were you pretty much free to play on your own, watch TV, or hang out with friends or extended family? A family's social class location shapes the daily rhythms of family life (Lareau 2003). Middle-class parents engage in the "concerted cultivation" of their kids. They schedule their kids in multiple activities, engage in more elaborate verbal communication with them, and intervene on their behalf with school and other authorities. Working-class parents, other than providing daily essentials, tend to be more hands-off, an approach that researcher Annette Lareau (2003) labeled the "accomplishment of natural growth" (p. 238). These kids engage in more casual, unstructured play rather than having their time dominated by adult-organized activities, have fewer linguistic opportunities, and lack intervention of parents with school and other authorities to a greater degree than middle-class kids. When children in the United States from the lower and working class *are* disciplined, their parents tend to use more physical punishment than middle-class parents, who use guilt, reasoning, time-outs, and other nonphysical sanctions to control children's behavior. These differences may have implications for one's assumptions about how authority is exercised and whether it is acceptable to challenge authority figures.

While there are advantages and disadvantages of each pattern, these differences matter because they lead to the "transmission of differential advantages to children" (Lareau 2003:5). Middle-class children are enabled to navigate the educational and, later, occupational worlds more successfully than are working-class children, thus influencing the social class destinations of each group (Lashbrook 2009).

In addition, in many countries, higher social class correlates with later marriage and lower divorce rates. Members of lower classes tend to marry earlier and have more children. Because of tensions from life stresses including money problems, they often have less stable marriages and more instances of divorce and single parenthood.

Religious Membership

Religious affiliation also correlates with social status variables of education, occupation, and income. For instance, in the United States, upper-class citizens are found disproportionately in Episcopalian, Unitarian, and Jewish religious groups, whereas lower-class citizens are attracted to Nazarene, Southern Baptist, Jehovah's Witness, and other holiness and fundamentalist sects. Although there are exceptions, each religious group attracts members predominantly from one social class, as will be illustrated in Chapter 12 on religion (Roberts and Yamane 2012).

Political Behavior

What political preferences we hold and how we vote are also affected by several key variables: our orientation on issues of public policy, our assessment of the performance of government, and our evaluation of personal traits of the candidates. In addition, one's party identification and general ideological dispositions affect voting, and are in turn affected by social factors such as race, religion, region of the country, social class, gender, marital status, and age (Interuniversity Consortium for Political and Social Research 2011).

Around the world, upper-middle classes are most supportive of elite or procapitalist agendas because these agendas support their way of life; lower and working-class members are least supportive (Wright 2000). Generally, the lower the social class, the more likely people are to vote for liberal parties, and the higher the social status, the more likely people are to be conservative on economic issues—consistent with protecting their wealth (Domhoff 2005; Kerbo 2008).

In the United States, members of the lower class tend be liberal on economic issues, favoring government intervention to improve economic conditions. However, those with lower levels of education and income vote conservatively on many social issues relating to minorities and civil liberties (e.g., rights for homosexuals, gay marriage, and abortion (Gilbert 2011; Kerbo 2008). In the 2012 election, many voters had to make choices about economic policies they liked and whether those policies were more important than their preferences on some of the social issues.

Status Inconsistency

The reality is that some people experience high status on one trait, especially a trait that is achieved through education and hard work, but may experience low standing in another area. For example, a professor may have high prestige but low income. Max Weber called this unevenness in one's social standing *status inconsistency.* Individuals who experience such status inconsistency, especially if they are treated as if their lowest ascribed status is the most important one, are likely to be very liberal and to experience discontent with the current system (Weber 1946).

People tend to associate with others like themselves, perpetuating and reinforcing lifestyles. In fact, people often avoid contact with others whose lifestyles are outside their familiar and comfortable patterns. This desire for familiarity also means that most people remain in the same social class because they have learned the "subculture," and it is comfortable and familiar.

Life chances and lifestyles are deeply shaped by the type of stratification system that is prevalent in the nation. Life experiences such as hunger, unnecessary early death of family members, or pain of seeing one's child denied opportunities are all experienced at the micro level, but their causes are usually rooted in events and actions at other levels of the social world. This brings us to our next question: Can an individual change positions in a stratification system?

Thinking Sociologically

Describe your own lifestyle and life chances. How do these relate to your socialization experience and your family's position in the stratification system? What difference do they make in your life?

Social Mobility: The Micro-Meso Connection

The LeBron Jameses and Peyton Mannings of the world make millions of dollars—at least for the duration of their playing careers. For professionals in the world of sport, each hoop, goal, or touchdown throw is worth thousands of dollars. These riches give hope to those in rags that if they "play hard" on their local hoops, they too may be on the field or court making millions. The problem is that the chances of making it big are so small that such hopes are some of the cruelest hoaxes faced by young African Americans and others in the lower or working class. Therefore, it is a false promise to think of sports as the road to opportunity as chances of success or even of moving up through them are very limited (Dufur and Feinberg 2007; Edwards 2000).

Those few minority athletes who do "make it big" and become models for young people experience "stacking," holding certain limited positions in a sport. When retired from playing, few black athletes rise in the administrative hierarchy of the sports of football and baseball, although basketball has a better record of hiring black coaches and managers. Thus, when young people put their hopes and energies into developing their muscles and physical skills, they may lose the possibility of moving up in the social class system, which requires developing their minds and technical skills. Even those young players who make it into the National Basketball Association or other major leagues may have done so by leaving college after a single year. This thwarts their postathletic career opportunities. The whole idea of changing one's social position up or down in the stratification system is called social mobility.

This young street basketball player slam-dunks his ball in a milk-crate hoop as he dreams of glory on the courts. Despite grand dreams by young minorities, few experience dramatic social mobility through sports.

Social mobility refers to *the extent of individual movement up or down in the class system, changing one's social position in society—especially relative to one's parents* (Gilbert 2011). What is the likelihood that your status will be different from that of your parents over your lifetime? Will you start a successful business? Marry into wealth? Win the lottery? Experience downward mobility due to loss of a job, illness, or inability to complete your education? What factors at different levels of analysis might influence your chances of mobility? These are some of the questions addressed in this section and the next.

The four issues that dominate the analysis of mobility are (1) types of social mobility, (2) methods of measuring social mobility, (3) factors that affect social mobility, and (4) whether there is a "land of opportunity" for those wishing to improve their lot in life.

Types of Social Mobility

Mobility can be up, down, or sideways, as described below. *Intergenerational mobility* refers to change in class status compared with one's parents, usually resulting from education and occupational attainment. If you are the first to go to college in your family and you become an engineer, this would represent intergenerational mobility. The amount of intergenerational mobility—that is, the number of children who move up or down in the social structure compared to where their parents are—measures the degree to which a society has an open class system. The more movement there is between classes, meaning that you could move up or down in comparison with your parents in the stratification system, the more open the class system is. This type of movement is not possible in many societies. If you change positions at the same level in the stratification system (say, a postal service job to a police position), it is called *horizontal mobility*.

Intragenerational mobility (not to be confused with *intergenerational mobility*) refers to a change in position within a single individual's life. For instance, if you begin your career as a teacher's aide and end it as a school superintendent, that is upward intragenerational mobility. However, mobility is not always up. *Vertical mobility* refers to movement up or down in the hierarchy and sometimes involves changing social classes. You may start your career as a waitress, go to college part-time, get a degree in engineering, and get a more prestigious and higher-paying job, resulting in upward mobility. Alternatively, in the current economic situation you could lose a job and take one at a lower status, a reality for many. In the global economic downturn, people at all levels of the occupational structure are experiencing layoffs and downward intragenerational mobility because they often have problems finding new positions at comparable levels and pay.

How Much Mobility Is There? Measures of Social Mobility

Can one move up in the class system? One traditional method of measuring mobility is to compare fathers with sons and, in more recent research, with daughters. Surveys ask men about their occupations and those of their fathers or sons. Table 7.2 reflects data collected from questions asked of U.S. fathers about their sons' and daughters' mobility.

Table 7.2 **Outflow From Father's Occupation to Son's or Daughter's Occupation**

	Son's Occupation (in Percent) in Blue Daughter's Occupation (in Percent) in Red					
	Upper–White Collar	*Lower–White Collar*	*Upper Manual*	*Lower Manual*	*Farm*	*Total*
Father's Occupation						
Upper–White Collar	42	31	12	15	1	100
	54	33	9	3	*	
Lower–White Collar	34	33	13	19	1	100
	49	34	11	6	*	
Upper Manual	20	20	29	29	2	100
	35	37	18	8	1	
Lower Manual	20	22	20	36	12	100
	32	39	19	9	1	
Farm	16	18	19	35	3	100
	34	28	22	14	2	
Total (*N* = 3,398)	27	25	19	27	1	100
	27	25	19	27	3	

Source: Gilbert 2011:131, 135.

Note: Rows but not columns add to 100%. For example, read across the row that begins with "Lower Manual" on the far left to trace the sons of fathers who held unskilled "Lower Manual" jobs. While 20% rose to "Upper–White Collar" (professional or managerial) positions, the largest group (36%) followed their fathers into unskilled "Lower Manual" jobs.

Several conclusions can be derived from this table:

1. There is a high level of occupational inheritance—sons following fathers into jobs at the very same occupational level.
2. The higher the father's occupation level, the better the son's chances for occupational achievement.
3. There is also considerable movement up and down the occupational ladder from one generation to the next.
4. Sons are more likely to move up than down.
5. Daughters are even more likely to move up than sons.

Thinking Sociologically

Indicate where your father falls in the occupational categories in Table 7.2. Compare this with your intended occupation and likely social class position in a few years. What can you conclude about your chances for mobility?

Determining the mobility of women is more difficult because they often have lower-level positions, and their mothers may not have worked full-time, but a conclusion that can be drawn is that both women's and men's occupational attainment is powerfully influenced by class origins.

Factors Affecting an Individual's Mobility

Why are some people successful at moving up the ladder, while others lag behind? Mobility is driven by many factors, from your family's background to global economic variables. One's chances to move up depend on micro-level factors—one's family "cultural capital," socialization, personal characteristics, and education—and macro-level factors—the occupational structure and economic status of countries, population changes, the numbers of people vying for similar positions, discrimination based on gender or ethnicity, and the global economic situation.

The study of mobility is complicated because these key variables are interrelated. The macro-level forces (such as the economic vitality and occupational structure in a country) are related to meso-level factors (such as access to education and type of economy) and micro-level factors (socialization and family background; Blau and Duncan 1967). An individual's background accounts for nearly half of the factors affecting what job one gets (Jencks 1979). Consider a few of the variables that can make a difference in your chances for mobility.

Family Background, Socialization, and Education

Our family background socializes us into certain behavior patterns, language usage, and occupational expectations (Sernau 2010). Consider language. Parents in professional families use three times as many different words at home as parents in low-income families. By the time the children of professional families are 3 years old, they have a vocabulary of about 1,100 words and typically use 297 different words per hour. Children in working-class families have a 700-word vocabulary and use 217 words per hour, while children from low-income families have 500 words accessible to them and use 149 per hour. These numbers represent a gap in the range of words they hear at home (Hart and Risley 2003).

Thinking Sociologically

How might differences in one's vocabulary affect one's success in school? How might an expanded vocabulary affect one's opportunities in life and impress a potential employer?

College is one expectation, if not requirement, for upward mobility in the Global North countries. Although not all those with a college degree are successful in finding a job and moving up the success ladder, few in Global North countries have a chance to be successful without a two- or four-year college degree (Lareau 2003). College education is the most important factor for high-income status, and the rewards of college degrees have increased. Those with degrees become richer than those without, largely because of new types of jobs in the computer information age.

The demand is now for specialists who work with ideas, knowledge, and technology rather than manufacturing (Florida 2002; Hurst 2013). We can see from Table 7.3 that most students in the United States with high ability from high-status families go to college, while high-ability students from low-status families go to college much less

Table 7.3 **College Attendance by Social Class and Cognitive Ability (Percent in College)**

Cognitive Ability Quartile	*Family Socioeconomic Status Quartile*			
	Top	*Third*	*Second*	*Lowest*
Top	83	74	63	51
Second	69	51	42	33
Third	57	40	24	23
Lowest	35	20	13	13
Total (*N* = 11,995)	69	48	33	24

Source: Gilbert 2011:149.

often (83% vs. 51%). Note that a student with top cognitive ability but from the lowest-income families is less likely to enroll in college than someone from the third quartile of cognitive ability but the top socioeconomic quartile of society (51% vs. 57%)

When we look at actual college degrees, the pattern is more extreme, with diplomas going disproportionately to students in the top-status groups (50%), compared with only 10% of students from the bottom half of income levels. If American society were truly a **meritocracy**, *positions would be allocated in a social group or an organization according to their abilities and credentials*, as in level of education attained. One would expect cognitive ability to be the most important variable (Gilbert 2011). Despite claims that the United States is a meritocracy, these data raise doubts about that assertion.

Even when a young person is admitted to a college or university, she or he may be at a disadvantage in the classroom and alienated from past social ties. The culture of college is the culture of the well-educated upper-middle class, and everything from values to knowledge base to sense of humor may be different and uncomfortable (Dews and Law 1995). This alienation is explored in more detail in the next "Engaging Sociology."

Many poor people lack education and skills such as interviewing for jobs and getting recommendations needed to get or change jobs in the postindustrial occupational structure (Ehrenreich 2001, 2005; MacLeod 2008). Isolated from social networks in organizations, they lack contacts, or social capital, to help in the job search. The type of education system one attends also affects mobility. In Germany, Britain, France, and some other European countries, children are "streamed" (tracked) into either college preparatory courses or more general curricula, and the rest of their occupational experience usually reflects this early placement decision in school. In the United States, educational opportunities remain more open to those who can afford them—at least this is what is supposed to happen.

Economic Vitality and Shifting Jobs

The economic vitality of a country affects the chances for individual mobility, since there will be fewer positions at the top if the economy is stagnant. As agricultural work is decreasing and technology jobs are increasing in most areas of the world, these changes in the composition and structure of jobs affect individual opportunity (Hurst 2013). Thus, macro-level factors such as a country's

These men hold very different positions in society; one can offer his family more cultural capital that can be spent in influential positions and can provide more opportunities because of his education, family background, and networks with others in positions of influence. One of the two has a law degree.

Engaging Sociology

First-Generation College Students: Issues of Cultural and Social Capital

Socioeconomic classes develop subcultures that can be quite different from each other, and when one changes subcultures, it can be confusing and alienating. College campuses provide an example. Generally they are dominated by middle-class cultures. Young people from blue-collar backgrounds and those who are first-generation college students often find themselves in a world as alien to them as visiting another country. Students whose parents went to college are more likely to have "cultural or social capital" that helps them adjust and helps them understand their professors who are generally part of the middle-class culture. Answer the following survey questions. How might your own cultural or social capital cause you to feel at home or alienated, privileged or disprivileged, hopeful or despairing?

A. Which of the following experiences were part of your childhood?

- Had a library of books (at least 50 adult books) at your childhood home
- Had a subscription to a newspaper that was delivered to the home
- Had news magazine subscriptions that came to the home (*Time, Newsweek, The Economist*)
- Listened to music as a family, including classical or instrumental music such as harp or flute
- Traveled to at least 20 other states or to at least 5 other countries
- Took regular trips to the library
- Took regular trips to museums
- Attended movies
- Attended plays (theater productions)
- Attended concerts
- Played a musical instrument
- Took dance lessons
- Listened to National Public Radio (NPR)
- Watched PBS (Public Broadcasting Service) on television

B. Which of the following *relationships* were part of your childhood?

- My parents knew at least two influential people in my community on a first-name basis—such as the mayor, members of the city council, the superintendent of schools, members of the school board, the local county sheriff, the chief of police, the prosecuting attorney, the governor, or the district's representative to Congress.
- The regional leader of my religious group—church, temple, or mosque—knew and respected my family.
- My parents knew on a first-name basis at least three chief executive officers (CEOs) of corporations.
- When I entered new situations in high school, it was likely that my parents were known by the coaches, music directors, summer camp counselors/directors, or other authority figures who were "running the show."

(Continued)

(Continued)

- When I came to college, one or more professors and administrators at the college knew my parents, a sibling, or another family member.
- I have often interacted directly and effectively (in a nonadversarial way) with authority figures.

Engaging with Sociology:

1. If you experienced many of the items in #1 at home, you had fairly high cultural capital. If you marked most of the items in #2, you had a lot of social capital. If you did not, you may find the culture of a college campus to be alien and even confusing.
2. Which of the following makes a first-generation college student feel most alienated at your college and even within this sociology course: ***economic*** **capital** (money), ***social*** **capital** (networks with those who have resources), or ***cultural*** **capital** (knowledge of important aspects of the culture)? Why?

Survey constructed in part using ideas from Morris and Grimes 1997.

Some colleges have rather "blue collar" cultures, but most tend to be middle class or above. The environment can be quite alienating— "clilly" in more ways than one—to first generation students who do not have social and cultural capital that fits their new environment.

economy and its place in the global system shape employment chances of individuals. The global economic downturn that started in 2008 illustrates the vulnerability of both macro-level nations whose banks and companies are failing and micro-level individuals living in those nations who are losing jobs.

How possible is upward social mobility? Have recent generations found it harder to move to a higher social class than previous generations entering the workforce? There are a lot of data on the socioeconomic standing and income levels of Americans, but this gives little indication of how people move through their careers and become better off financially. Four scholars tried to remedy this missing link using survey data collected over nearly two decades. Two groups of young men, beginning as teenagers but from different decades, provided the participants for a *longitudinal study* (Morris et al. 2001). Gathering data from the same people over a period of time allows researchers to see how their lives develop and change. Morris et al. (2001) found several patterns about the structure of employment and how some young men negotiated the transition successfully:

- Changing jobs early in one's career (a) helps one find a position that is best suited for one's training, talents, and personal traits and (b) enhances one's prospects for greater income. However, this is only true for those with a good deal of education who are entering positions in the middle class or higher. Those with less education did not have the same positive effect from job switching early on.
- The pattern of a man's income is established, and his biggest gains are made relatively early in his career.
- After searching for the "best career and employment fit," stability in the job greatly enhances overall income and upward mobility over the life path. In short, changing employers beyond the first six or eight years seldom increases social mobility. Early job change followed by long tenures was the pattern best suited to upward mobility.
- Upward mobility has been more difficult for the younger generation of men, in large part because of instability in the job market and in corporations.
- Parents' socioeconomic level is a major predictor of the paths toward affluence or poverty. Those who have little social capital (networks) have less upward mobility, and this is even more true of the younger cohort.
- The society seems to be polarizing between rich and poor, and stagnating for all groups. Wage growth is becoming more difficult for all groups, but the American dream of mobility is not a positive dream for those most in need.

Poverty on the Hopi reservation in Arizona makes this town seem like it could be part of the Global South. The poverty is largely due to lack of resources, much of the Hopi land having been taken away by the federal government in the 19th century.

The authors conclude that there is a growing "stickiness" in low-wage, high-turnover jobs in the service industries that make it harder to ever "make it in the United States." This is due not to personality traits but to the structure of the service industry: There is a lack of stable positions, career training, or career ladders in these service positions, and this has created a lower-end labor market with few paths to mobility (Morris et al. 2001).

Population Trends

The U.S. nationwide baby boom that occurred following World War II resulted in a flood of job applicants and downward intergenerational mobility for the many who could not find work comparable with their social class at birth. In contrast, the smaller group following the baby boomer generation had fewer competitors for entry-level jobs. Baby boomers hold many of the executive and leadership positions today, so promotion has been hard for the next cohort. As baby boomers retire, opportunities will open up, and mobility should increase. The *fertility rates*, or number of children born at a given time, influence the number of people who will be looking for jobs.

Gender and Ethnicity

Many women and ethnic minority groups, locked in a cycle of poverty, dependence, and debt, have little chance of changing their status. Women in the U.S. workforce, for instance, are more likely than men to be in dead-end clerical

Table 7.4 **Median Annual Earnings by Race/Ethnicity and Sex**

Race/Gender	*Earnings*	*Wage Ratio*
White men	$44,200	100.0%
White women	35,578	80.4
Black men	32,916	74.4
Black women	30,784	69.6
Hispanic men	29,120	65.9
Hispanic women	26,416	59.7
Gender wage gap		81.2%
All men	$42,848	
All women	$34,788	

Source: U.S. Department of Labor (2011).

and service positions with no opportunity for advancement. In the past three decades, the wage gap between women and men has generally narrowed, and women who are employed full-time now earn 80% of what men earn, compared to 60% in 1980 (Fitzpatrick 2010; U.S. Department of Labor 2011). African American women make 69.6% of white men's earnings for comparable jobs (Fitzpatrick 2010). Table 7.4 shows the earnings for white males and the percentage of those earnings for other gender and ethnic groups.

Special circumstances such as war have often allowed women and others who were denied access to good jobs to get a "foot in the door" and have actually enhanced their upward mobility. A recent factor affecting career success of women is that more females than males are earning college degrees (Center for American Progress 2009).

Some people experience *privilege* (e.g., in the United States, white, European-born, native-speaking males who are in the middle class or higher), whereas some experience *disprivilege* due to socioeconomic status, ethnicity, gender, or a combination of these.

The Interdependent Global Market and International Events

If the Chinese or Japanese stock markets hiccup, it sends ripples through world markets. If high-tech industries in Japan or Europe falter, North American companies in Silicon Valley, California, may go out of business, costing many professionals their lucrative positions. In ways such as these, the interdependent global economies affect national and local economies, and that in turn affects individual families.

Whether individuals move from "rags to riches" is not determined solely by their personal ambition and work ethic. Mobility for the individual, a micro-level event, is linked to a variety of events at other levels of the social world, and one cannot assume that the unemployed individual is just lazy or incompetent.

Thinking Sociologically

Can you identify family members or friends who have lost jobs because of economic slowdowns at the meso or macro level or who have gotten jobs because of economic booms and opening opportunities? What changes have occurred in their mobility and social class?

Is There a "Land of Opportunity"? Cross-Cultural Mobility

Television shows bombard us with images of rich bachelors and the desirability of marrying a millionaire to improve one's status in life. By playing a game of trivia or being challenged on an island on a TV show, we too might "strike it rich." Another possibility is that we might win the lottery by buying a ticket at our local grocery. In reality, these quick fixes and easy get-rich-fast plans are seldom realized, and the chances of us profiting are slim indeed.

The question for this section concerns your realistic chances for mobility: Do you have a better chance to improve your status in England, Japan, the United States, or some other country? The answer is not simple. If there is a land of opportunity where individuals can be assured of improving their economic and social position, it is not easy to identify, as many variables affect the opportunity structure. Countless immigrants have sought better opportunities in new locations. Perhaps your parents or ancestors did just this. The reality of the "land of opportunity" depends on the historical period and current economic conditions, social events, and political attitudes toward foreigners when the immigrants came, their personal skills, and their ability to blend into the new society. With the recession of 2008–2009, unemployment in many countries around the world was higher, and fewer migrants found work in new countries. In the United States, not only were there fewer migrants entering from Latin America, but there was some reverse migration as disappointed workers returned to their countries of origin because of the weak economy, deportation threats, and dangers of crossing the border. According to the Pew Hispanic Center, Mexican immigration has fallen for the first time in four decades, with the number of immigrants declining and some previous immigrants returning to Mexico (Pilkington 2012).

During economic growth periods, many immigrants have found great opportunities for mobility in the United States and Europe. Early industrial tycoons in railroads, automobiles, steel, and other industries are examples of success stories. Fortunes have been made in the high-tech industries of China, India, and other countries, and in energy resources in Russia. The number of millionaires and billionaires in the world is increasing dramatically, yet this is still a very small percentage of the world's population. In 2010, there were an estimated 1,011 billionaires globally. The richest man was Carlos Slim Helú with $73 billion from América Móvil, a telecom company. Close behind was Bill Gates with $67 billion from Microsoft, and Warren Buffet with $53.5 billion from Berkshire Hathaway (Forbes 2012). China is the dramatic success story, reaching an estimated 260 billionaires in 2009, including many women, doubling the number in one year. At current growth rates, it will soon top the list of countries with the most billionaires (France 24 International News 2009; Spero News 2009). Such wealth eludes most people, especially immigrants, who must work multiple low-paying jobs just to feed their families and stay out of poverty.

Opportunities for upward mobility have changed significantly with globalization. Many manufacturing jobs in the global economy have moved from the Global North to the Global South to take advantage of cheap labor. This has reduced the number of unskilled and low-skilled jobs available in Global North countries. Multinational corporations look for the cheapest sources of labor in the Global South with low taxes, no labor unions, few regulations, and many workers needing jobs. This has drained away low-skilled jobs from the United States, making it even more essential to have advanced educational credentials (such as a diploma, a college degree, or a master's degree).

Why the changes in the job structure? First, there are fewer demands for manufacturing jobs. Service-producing jobs requiring higher education are expanding. Second, the increase in international trade results in demand for high-tech products from the United States, but it also means fewer manufacturing products, thus reducing manufacturing jobs. New technologies and automation leave low-skilled workers in Global North countries without jobs. The minimum-wage and low-wage jobs are all that is available to lower-skilled workers, and labor unions have less influence on the wages and working conditions of remaining manufacturing workers today (Gilbert 2011). High-tech positions are good news for those with college degrees and technical skills, but the replacement of laboring positions with service jobs in fast-food and box store chains (e.g., Walmart, Meijer, Home Depot, Lowe's) means a severe loss of genuine opportunity for living wages.

Although the new multinational industries springing up in Global South countries such as Malaysia, Thailand, and the Philippines provide opportunities for mobility to those of modest origins, much of the upward mobility in the world is taking place among those who come from small, highly educated families with individualistic achievement-oriented values and people who see education as a route to upward mobility (Featherman and Hauser 1978; Rothman 2005). They are positioned to take advantage of the changing occupational structure and high-tech jobs. As the gap between rich and poor individuals and countries widens, more individuals in the United States begin to move down rather than up in the stratification system.

Thinking Sociologically

What social factors in your society limit or enhance the likelihood of upward social mobility for you and your generation? Explain.

Major Stratification Systems: Macro-Level Analysis

Mansa works on a plantation in Mozambique. He tries in vain to pay off the debts left by his father's family. However hard he and his wife and children work, they will always be in debt because they cannot pay the total amount due for their hut or food from the owner's store. Basically, they are slaves—they do not have control over their own labor. They were born into this status, and there they will stay.

Imagine being born into a society in which you have no choices or options in life because of your family background, age, sex, and ethnic group. You cannot select an occupation that interests you, cannot choose your mate, and cannot live in the part of town you choose. You see wealthy aristocrats parading their advantages and realize that this will never be possible for you. You can never own land or receive the education of your choice.

This situation is reality for millions of people in the world—they are born this way and will spend their lives in this plight. In **ascribed stratification systems**, *characteristics beyond the control of the individual—such as family background, age, sex, and race—determine one's position in society.* In contrast, **achieved stratification systems** *allow individuals to earn positions through their ability, efforts, and choices.* In an open class system, it is possible to achieve a higher ranking by working hard, obtaining education, gaining power, or doing other things that are highly valued in that culture.

Ascribed Status: Caste and Estate Systems

Caste systems are *the most rigid ascribed stratification systems. Individuals are born into a status, which they retain*

The futures of these Aboriginal boys in Australia are determined by their ethnic group and family of birth, making it unlikely that they will ever experience much affluence in Australian society.

throughout life. That status is deeply embedded in religious, political, and economic norms and institutions. Individuals born into caste systems have predetermined occupational positions, marriage partners, residences, social associations, and prestige levels. A person's caste is easily recognized through clothing, speech patterns, family name and identity, skin color, or other distinguishing characteristics. From their earliest years, individuals learn their place in society through the process of socialization. To behave counter to caste prescriptions would be to go against religion and social custom and to risk not fitting into society. That can be a death sentence in some societies.

Religious ideas dictate that one's status after death (in Christian denominations) or one's next *reincarnation* or rebirth (in the Hindu tradition) also might be in jeopardy. Stability in Hindu societies is maintained in part by the belief that people can be reborn into a higher status in the next life if they fulfill expectations in their ascribed position in this life. Thus, believers in both religions work hard with the hope of attaining a better life after death or in the next reincarnation. The institution of religion works together with the family, education, and economic and political institutions to shape (and sometimes reduce) both expectations and aspirations and to keep people in their prescribed places in caste systems.

The clearest example of a caste system is found in India. The Hindu religion holds that individuals are born into one of four *varnas*, broad caste positions, or into a fifth group below the caste system, the *outcaste* group. The first and highest varna, called *Brahmans*, originally was made up of priests and scholars but now includes many leaders in society. The second varna, *Kshatriyas* or *Rajputs*, includes the original prince and warrior varna and now embraces much of the army and civil service. The *Vaishyas*, or merchants, are the third varna. The fourth varna, the *Sudras*, includes peasants, artisans, and laborers. The final layer, below the caste system, the outcastes encompass profoundly oppressed and broken people—"a people put aside"—referred to as untouchables, outcastes, *Chandalas* (a Hindu term), and *Dalits* (the name preferred by many "untouchables" themselves). Although the Indian Constitution of 1950 granted full social status to these citizens, and a law passed in 1955 made discrimination against them punishable, deeply rooted traditions are difficult to change. Caste distinctions are still very prevalent, especially in rural areas, as seen in the discussion in "Sociology Around the World."

Estate systems are characterized by the concentration of economic and political power in the hands of a small minority of political-military elite, with the peasantry tied to the land (Rothman 2005). Estate systems are based on ownership of land, the position one is born into, or military strength. An individual's rank and legal rights are clearly spelled out, and arranged marriages and religion bolster the system. During the Middle Ages, knights defended the realms and the religion of the nobles. Behind every knight in shining armor were peasants, sweating in the fields and paying for the knights' food, armor, and campaigns. For farming the land owned by the nobility, peasants received protection against invading armies and enough of the produce to survive. Their life was often miserable. If the yield of crops was poor, they ate little. In a good year, they might save enough to buy a small parcel of land. A very few were able to become independent in this fashion.

Estate systems existed in ancient Egypt, the Incan and Mayan civilizations, Europe, China, and Japan. Today, similar systems exist in some Central and South American, Asian, and African countries on large banana, coffee, and sugar plantations, as exemplified in the description of Mansa's life in Mozambique. Over time, development of a mercantile economy resulted in modifications in the early estate systems, and now peasants often work on the land in exchange for the right to live there and receive a portion of the produce.

Sociology Around the World

The Outcastes of India

The Dalits—sometimes called "untouchables"—are the most impoverished people in India and some of the most impoverished in the world. These are Dalit children, attending a school that is so poor that they do not have books, pencils, chairs, or desks.

The village south of Chennai (Madras) in the state of Tamil Nadu was on an isolated dirt road, 1 kilometer from the nearest town. It consisted of a group of mud and stick huts with banana leaf–thatched roofs. As our group of students arrived, the Dalit villagers lined the streets to greet us—and stare. Many had never seen Westerners. They played drums and danced for us and threw flower petals at our feet in traditional welcome.

Through our translator, we learned something of their way of life. The adults work in the fields long hours each day, plowing and planting with primitive implements, earning about 8 cents from the landowner, often not enough to pay for their daily bowl of rice. Occasionally, they catch a frog or bird to supplement their meal. In the morning, they drink rice gruel, and in the evening, they eat a bowl of rice with some spices. Women and children walk more than a kilometer to the water well—but the water is polluted during the dry season. There are no privies but the fields. As a result of poor sanitation, inadequate diet, and lack of health care, many people become ill and die from health problems that are easily cured in Western societies. For instance, lack of vitamin A, found in many fruits and vegetables to which they have little access, causes blindness in many village residents. Although the children have the right to go to the school in the closest village, many cannot do so because they have no transportation, shoes, or money for paper, pencils, and books. Also, the families need them to work in the fields alongside their parents or help care for younger siblings just to survive.

Many taboos rooted in tradition separate the Dalit from other Indians. For instance, they are forbidden to draw water from the village well, enter the village temple, or eat from dishes that might be used later by people of higher castes. The latter prohibition eliminates most dining at public establishments. About 95% are landless and earn a living below subsistence level.

Dalits who question these practices have been attacked and their houses burned. In one instance, 20 houses were burned on the birthday of Dr. B. R. Ambedkar, a leader of the Dalit rights movement. Official records distributed by the Human Rights Education Movement of India state that every hour, two Dalits are assaulted, three Dalit women are raped, two Dalits are murdered, and two Dalit houses are burned (Dalit Liberation Education Trust 1995; Thiagaraj 2007; Wilson 1993). Violence is used to control Dalits who try to uplift themselves and thus create threats to the social status and dominance of higher caste groups (Karthikeyan 2011). This group on the bottom rung of the stratification system has a long fight ahead to gain the rights that many of us take for granted.

A few Dalits have migrated to cities, where they blend in, and some of them have become educated and are now leading the fight for the rights and respect guaranteed by law. Recently, unions and interest groups have been representing the Dalit, and some members turn to religious and political groups that are more sympathetic to their plight, such as Buddhists, Christians, or Communists.

One social activist, Henry Thiagaraj, has committed his life to improving conditions for the Dalits. Thiagaraj works on the micro, meso, and macro levels. On the micro level, he suggests that those in power form Dalit youth and women *sangams* (activist groups) and organize the people who live in Dalit slums. At the meso level, Thiagaraj and other Dalit activists work to initiate micro lending to the Dalits and improve their education and labor training. On the macro level, Thiagaraj works with nongovernmental organizations to increase support for Dalit interests. He also works to improve media coverage of the Dalits to raise awareness of their experiences. Thiagaraj's (2007) book, *Human Rights From the Dalits' Perspective*, provides an outstanding retrospective of how India has addressed caste discrimination since the 1980s.

Thinking Sociologically

In much of the Global North, individualism is so highly valued that ascribed systems of stratification are rejected. What values—both positive and negative—might support ascribed systems? Why might those values make your society's system seem unacceptable and even offensive to people in other nonindustrial societies?

Achieved Status: Social Class Systems

Class stratification systems *allow individuals to earn positions through their ability, efforts, and choices.* Members of the same social class have similar income, wealth, and economic position, and they share styles of life, levels of education, cultural beliefs, and patterns of social interaction. In a class system our life circumstances and social respect are based in large measure on what we achieve in our lives. Most of us are members of class-based stratification systems, and we take advantage of opportunities available to our social class. Our families, rich or poor, educated or unskilled, provide us with an initial social ranking and socialization experience. We tend to feel a kinship and sense of belonging with those in the same social class—our neighborhood and work group, our peers and friends. We think alike, share interests, and probably look up to the same people as a reference group. Our social class position is based on the three main factors determining positions in the stratification system: (1) property, (2) prestige, and (3) power.

This is the trio—the three *Ps*—that, according to Max Weber, determines where individuals rank in relation to each other (Weber 1946, 1947). By *property* (wealth), Weber refers to owning or controlling the means of production. *Power*, the ability to control others, includes not only the means of production but also the position one holds. *Prestige* involves the esteem and recognition one receives, based on wealth, position, or accomplishments. Table 7.5 gives examples of households in the upper and lower social classes by illustrating the variables that determine a person's standing in the three areas of the stratification system.

Although these three dimensions of stratification are often found together, this is not always so. Recall the idea of *status inconsistency*: An individual can have a great deal of prestige yet not command much wealth (Weber 1946). Consider winners of the prestigious Nobel Peace Prize such as Wangari Maathai, a Kenyan environmentalist who won the prize for starting a movement to plant trees and for her political activism; Rigoberta Menchú Tum of Guatemala (see "Sociology Around the World" on page 88 in Chapter 3); or Betty Williams and Mairead Corrigan of Northern Ireland,

Table 7.5 Basic Dimensions of Social Stratification

	Property Variables	*Prestige Variables*	*Power Variables (Political-Legal)*
	Income Wealth Occupation Education Family stability	Occupational prestige Respect in community Consumption Participation in group life Evaluations of race, religion, and ethnicity	Political participation Political attitudes Legislation and governmental benefits Distribution of justice
Households in the upper social class	Affluence: economic security and power, control over material and human investment Income from work but mostly from property	More integrated personalities, more consistent attitudes, and greater psychic fulfillment due to deference, valued associations, and consumption	Power to determine public policy and its implementation by the state, thus giving control over the nature and distribution of social values
Households in the lower social class	Destitution: worthlessness on economic markets	Unintegrated personalities, inconsistent attitudes, sense of isolation and despair; sleazy social interaction	Political powerlessness, lack of legal recourse or rights, socially induced apathy

Source: Rossides (1997:15).

Note: Contains examples of values in the top and bottom classes within each dimension and examples of subdimensions. For expository purposes, religious and ethnic or racial rankings are omitted.

founders of the Community of Peace People to find a peaceful end to their country's problems. None of them was rich, but each made contributions to the world that gained them universal prestige. Likewise, some people gain enormous wealth through crime or gambling, but this wealth may not be accompanied by respect or prestige.

Compared with systems based on ascribed status, achieved status systems maintain that everyone is born with common legal status; everyone is equal before the law. In principle, all individuals can own property and choose their own occupations. However, in practice, most class systems pass privilege or poverty from one generation to the next. Individual upward or downward mobility is more difficult than the ideology invites people to believe.

The Property Factor

One's income, property, and total assets comprise one's **wealth**. These lie at the heart of class differences. The contrast of the splendor of Newport aristocrats and British royalty with the daily struggle for survival of those in poverty is an example of the differences extreme wealth or lack thereof creates. Another example is shown in the income distribution in the United States by quintiles (see Table 7.6). Note that there has been minimal movement between the groups over the years, and what little change has occurred has been toward the richest having even more of the assets in the United States. In 2012, the median household income in the United States was $50,020, 7.8% less than it was when the economic downturn began in December 2007 (Safdar 2012). However, the 2010 poverty rate was 15.1% of the population, up from 12.5% of the population in 2007 (DeNavas-Walt, Proctor, and Smith 2009; World Hunger Education Service 2012b). Of children under 18, 22% live in poverty (DeNavas-Walt, Proctor, and Smith 2011). In addition, as of 2011, 16.3% of U.S. citizens had no health insurance (Christie 2011).

Some analysts see the middle class in the United States today as dividing the haves and the have-nots with few actually in the "middle." The median household incomes dropped 2.3% between 2009 and 2010. The highest quintile (richest 20%) controls 84% of the wealth in the United States, and the richest 400 families have the same net worth as the bottom 50%. One in 6 households is now in poverty, and there is an increase in numbers at both extremes of the income scale (Harris 2011).

Table 7.6 **Share of Household Income in Quintiles**

	1980	*1990*	*2000*	*2010*
Lowest quintile	4.2	3.8	3.6	3.3
Second quintile	10.2	9.6	8.9	8.5
Third quintile	16.8	15.9	14.9	14.6
Fourth quintile	24.7	24.0	23.0	23.4
Highest quintile	44.1	46.6	49.8	50.2

Source: DeNavas-Walt, Proctor, and Smith (2011); Johnson (2011); U.S. Census Bureau (2009b).

Note: The lowest quintile has an income under $20,000 a year; the highest has an income over $100,066 a year. Each quintile has 23.7 million households.

The Power Factor

Power refers to the ability of a person or group to realize its own will in groups, even against the resistance of others. Positions of power are gained through family inheritance, family connections, political appointments, education, hard work, friendship networks, and sometimes force. Two theories dominate the explanations of power—power elite and pluralist theories.

As discussed earlier, the conflict theorists' view is that those who hold power are those who control the economic capital and the means of production in society (Ashley and Orenstein 2009). Consistent with Marx, many recent conflict theorists have focused on a **power elite** in which power is held by top leaders in corporations, politics, and the military. These interlocking elites make major decisions guiding nations (Domhoff 2001, 2005; Mills 1956). These people interact with each other and have an unspoken agreement to protect their positions and ensure that their power is not threatened. Each tends to protect the power of the other. The idea is that those who are not in this interlocking elite group do not hold real power and have little chance of breaking into the inner circles (Dye 2002).

Pluralist theorists argue that power is not held exclusively by an elite group but is shared among many power centers, each of which has its own self-interests to protect (Ritzer and Goodman 2004). Well-financed special interest groups (e.g., insurance industry, dairy and cattle farmers, or truckers' trade unions) and professional associations (e.g., the American Medical Association) have considerable power through collective action. From the pluralist perspective, officials who hold political power are vulnerable to pressure from influential interest groups, and each interest group competes for power with others. Creating and maintaining this power through networks and pressure on legislators is the job of lobbyists. For example, in the U.S. debate over health care legislation, interest groups from the medical community, insurance lobbies, and citizens' groups wield their power to influence the outcome, but, because these major interests conflict and no one group has the most power, a permanent health care resolution is hard to reach. The core idea of pluralist theorists, then, is that many centers of power create at least some checks and balances on those in elite positions.

The Prestige Factor

Prestige refers to *the esteem, recognition, and respect one receives, based on wealth, position, or accomplishments.* An

Power elite theorists believe that most power is held by the leaders in corporations, politics, and the military. These interlocking elites call the shots within a country and control the resources.

individual's prestige ranking is closely correlated with the value system of society. Chances of being granted high prestige improve if one's patterns of behavior, occupation, and lifestyle match those that are valued in the society. Among high-ranked occupations across nations are scientists, physicians, military officers, lawyers, and college professors. Table 7.7 shows occupational prestige rankings from a recent Harris poll in the United States (Harris Interactive 2009).

Note the correlation between recent events such as 9/11 and the increased rankings of occupations in which people have been portrayed as "heroes" in the United States. For example, 62% of the U.S. population sees firefighters as having "very great prestige," even though their incomes do not reflect this. Being a hero, obtaining material possessions, or increasing one's educational level can boost prestige but in itself cannot change class standing.

Thinking Sociologically

Describe your own wealth, power, and prestige in society. Does your family have one factor but not others? What difference does each of the factors make in your life? What part would you like these factors to play in your future, and what might you do to achieve your goal?

Table 7.7 Prestige Rankings of 20 Professions and Occupations

Occupations (Base: All Adults)	*Very Great Prestige*	*Hardly Any Prestige at All*
Firefighter	62%	5%
Scientist	57	7
Doctor	56	3
Nurse	54	4
Military officer	51	4
Teacher	51	10
Police officer	44	7
Priest/minister/clergyman	41	10
Engineer	39	5
Farmer	36	14
Architect	29	10
Member of Congress	28	22
Business executive	23	26
Athlete	21	19
Journalist	17	22
Union leader	17	30
Entertainer	19	25
Banker	16	18
Accountant	11	19
Real Estate Agent/Broker	5	30

Source: Harris Interactive 2009.

Social Classes in the United States

Imagine that you are a politician and the hot topic is how to help the middle class. Flash back to the most recent U.S. presidential campaign, and everyone was talking about the middle class. Did you ever hear the politicians define what they meant? You probably did not, because the broader and more inclusive the definition, the more useful it was to politicians who were trying to appeal to a range of voters. For social scientists, the term *middle class* has been defined in several ways: Sociologists often focus on occupations that are considered middle class, those that require extensive education and training and are compensated with a salary rather than an hourly wage. These include teachers, nurses, insurance agents, accountants, managers, and many other midlevel jobs, and are estimated to be about 45% of the population. Economists define *middle class* as those around 50% of the income distribution, families with incomes from $35,000 to $100,000. *Middle class* is also self-defined by individuals responding to polls. Researchers ask people to what class they belong; about 45% say middle class (matching the sociologists' estimate), and 45% say working class (Gilbert 2011).

In the current U.S. economic structure, there is slight movement to the upper class and somewhat more movement to the lower class. As noted previously, the U.S. system allows for mobility within the middle class, but there is little movement at the very top and very bottom of the social ladder. People in the top rung often use their power and wealth to insulate themselves and protect their elite status, and the bottom group is isolated because of vicious cycles of poverty that are hard to break. Figure 7.1 illustrates the social class structure in the United States.

How we identify ourselves expresses our feelings about our placement in the stratification system and also our class "culture." Classes have distinctive values, beliefs, and attitudes toward education, religion, politics, and what makes a good life in general. Often, what we define as "normal" is actually what is affirmed by others in our socioeconomic status. A number of scholars have written about the cultural shock they experienced when moving from their blue-collar experiences as children to becoming professors. The shift in culture was like entering a new country. Even the differences in vocabulary usage, discussed earlier in this chapter, represent part of the cultural difference (Hart and Risley 2003).

Since the 1970s, wealth has become increasingly concentrated in the hands of the richest 1% of households. The income gap between the top 5% and bottom 40% of the U.S. population is increasing, and the number of full-time workers in poverty is rising. There has been no reduction in poverty since the 1970s, and in fact it has grown in recent years, yet the proportion of families exceeding $100,000 in annual income continues to grow (Gilbert 2011).

Wages and salaries of the middle classes have declined since the 1980s whereas those of the upper classes have risen. Reasons for middle-class decline include downsizing and layoffs of workers, global shifts in production, technological innovations that displace laborers, competition, trade deficits between countries, and deregulation. All these are macro-level economic forces that mean lower incomes for middle-class workers. The wealthiest 1% earned 21.5% of income gains in the last economic expansion, resulting in two thirds of income gains going to the top 1%—hence the phrases "the 1%" and "the 99%" from the Occupy Wall Street movement (Feller and Stone 2009). Changes in class groups are largely due to changes in the occupational structure and transformations in the global economy. The upward movement among the few who have received huge gains in earning power is causing wages and earnings to become more unequal.

Upper-middle-class families typically have high income, high education, high occupational level (in terms of prestige and other satisfactions), and high participation in political life and voluntary associations. Families enjoy

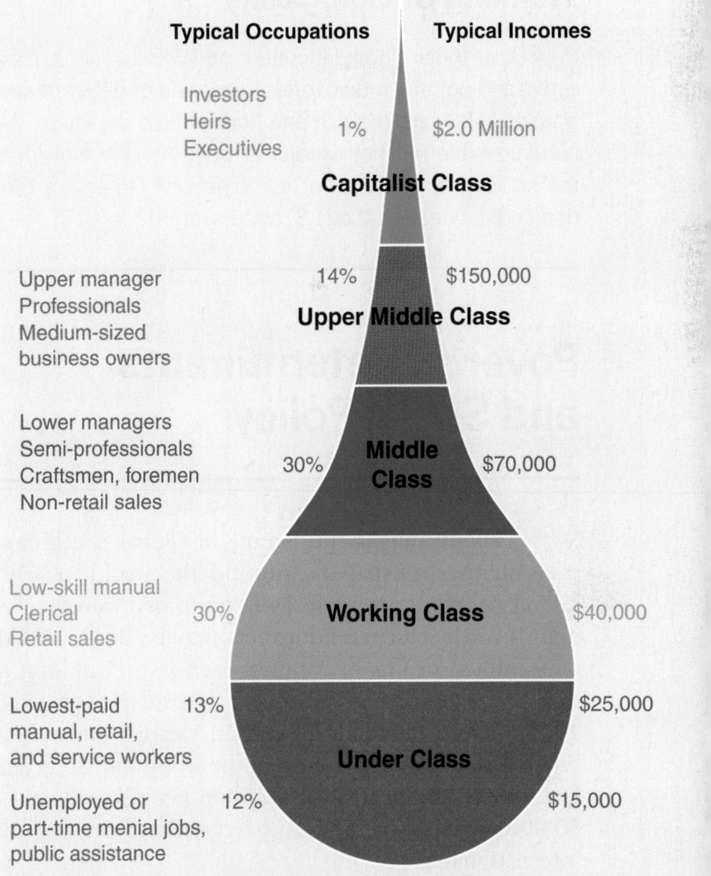

Figure 7.1 Gilbert-Kahl Model of Social Class

Source: Gilbert 2011:14.

a stable life, stressing companionship, privacy, pleasant surroundings in safe neighborhoods, property ownership, and stimulating associations. They stress internalization of moral standards of right and wrong, taking responsibility for their own actions, learning to make their own decisions, and training their children for future leadership positions.

The *middle to lower middle class* includes small businesspeople and farmers, semiprofessionals (teachers, local elected officials, social workers, nurses, police officers, firefighters); middle-management personnel, both private and public; and sales and clerical workers in comfortable office settings. Families in this class are relatively stable. They participate in community life, and although they are less active in political life than the upper classes, they are more politically involved than those in classes below them. Children are raised to work hard and obey authority. Therefore, child-rearing patterns more often involve swift physical punishment for misbehavior than talk and reasoning, which is typical of the upper middle class.

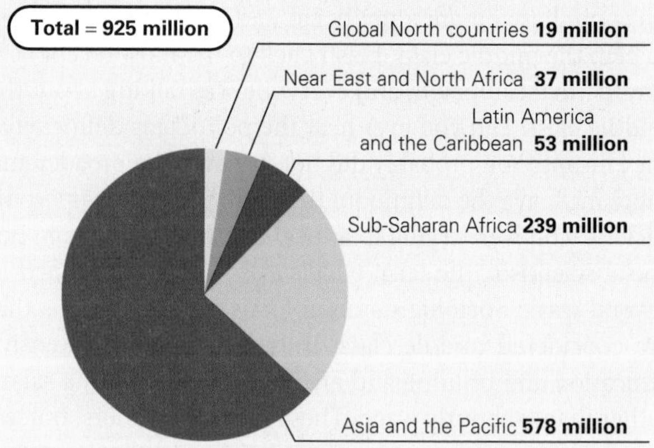

Figure 7.2 Distribution of Hunger in the World

Source: World Hunger Education Service 2011.

Thinking Sociologically

How does today's popular culture on TV and in films, magazines, and popular music reflect interests of different social classes? How are the rich and poor people depicted? Who is responsible for their wealth or poverty—the individuals, the society, or some other combination? Do any of these depictions question the U.S. class system?

Poverty: Determinants and Social Policy

Stories about hunger and famine in Global South countries fill the newspapers. Around the world, nearly 1 billion people, or roughly 14%, go to bed hungry every night (World Hunger Education Service 2011). Of the 10.9 million deaths of children each year, 5 million are directly related to malnutrition (World Hunger Facts 2009). These numbers have risen steadily since 1995. Figure 7.2 shows where most of the world hunger occurs. One third of all deaths—18 million people each year or 50,000 per day—are due to poverty-related causes (Vivat International 2012).

One hardly expects to see hunger in rich countries, yet 17.2 million U.S. households, or 14.5% of households (1 in 7), did not have enough food and were skipping meals during the 2010 year, the highest ever recorded in the United States (Coleman-Jensen et al. 2011). Demand at food pantries was up 20%, and the Supplemental Nutrition Assistance Program (SNAP) served a record 35 million recipients in 2010 (World Hunger Education Service 2012a). Twenty-five percent of Americans are afraid they will not be able to afford food at some point in the next year (Casteel 2011). With downturns in employment, low wages, and reduced aid to poor families, hunger and poor health in the United States are likely to continue.

Most people living in poverty have no property-based income and no permanent or stable work, only casual or intermittent earnings in the labor market. They often depend on help from government agencies or private organizations to survive. In short, they have personal troubles in large part because they have been unable to establish linkages and networks in the meso- and macro-level organizations of our social world. They have no collective power and, thus, little representation of their interests and needs in the political system.

Thinking Sociologically

Explain how your family's ability to provide food for its members at the micro level is largely dependent upon its connectedness to the meso and macro levels of society.

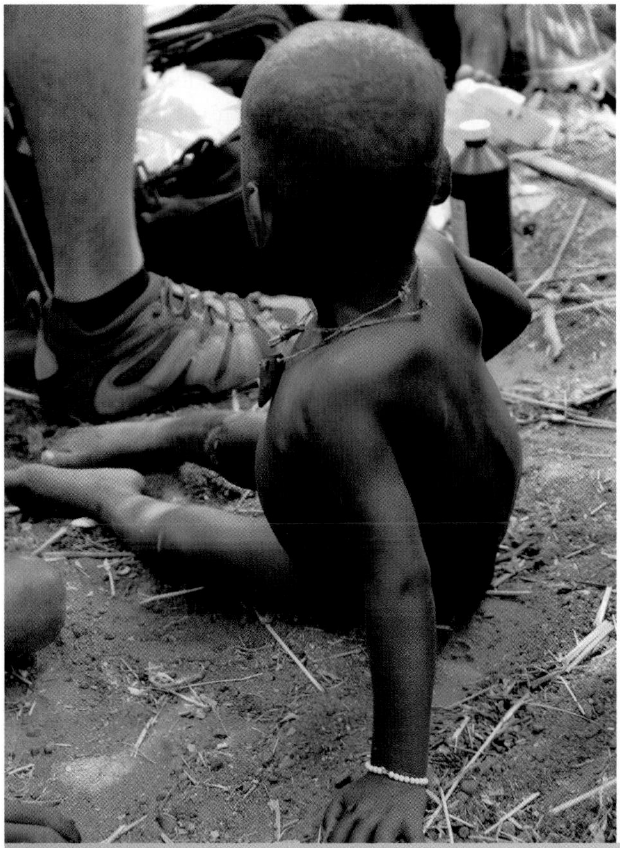

This little boy sits at the feet of an aid worker. How much power do you imagine this boy's parents have to make sure their child's needs are met? This boy and his family have personal troubles because the meso and macro systems of his society have failed to work effectively for individual families. Compare his circumstances to those of the little girl with her cell phone and riding in a limousine.

Sociologists recognize two basic types of poverty: (1) absolute poverty and (2) relative poverty. **Absolute poverty**, not having resources to meet basic needs, means no prestige, no access to power, no accumulated wealth, and insufficient means to survive. Whereas absolute poverty in the United States is quite limited, the Dalits of India, described earlier in "Sociology Around the World" (*The Outcastes of India*), provide an example of absolute poverty. Some die of diseases that might be easily cured in other people because the bodies of those in absolute poverty are weakened by chronic and persistent hunger and almost total lack of medical attention.

Relative poverty *occurs when one's income falls below the poverty line, resulting in an inadequate standard of living relative to others in the individual's country.* In most industrial countries, relative poverty means shortened life expectancy, higher infant mortality, and poorer health, but not many people die of starvation or easily curable diseases, such as influenza.

The *feminization of poverty* refers to the trend in which single females, increasingly younger and with children, make up a growing proportion of those in poverty. Vicki's situation provides one such example. After her parents divorced, she quit high school to take odd jobs to help her mother pay the bills. At 18, she was pregnant, and the baby's father was out of the picture, so Vicki lived on government aid because without a high school degree, she could not get a job that paid enough to support herself and her baby and certainly not enough to pay for health insurance. She eventually could not pay her rent and lived out of her car, which did not run because she lacked the money to repair it. Her life spiraled out of control, and her daughter has now been placed in foster care.

We do not like to admit that this can happen in affluent North American and European countries, and we try to blame the victim (why did Vicki drop out of high school, get pregnant, and not have an abortion?). Still, people do what they must to survive. This problem is heightened as many middle-class women are pushed into poverty through divorce. Some of them have sacrificed their own careers for husbands and family so their earning power is reduced, yet

While these men may look impoverished by North American standards, they are relatively well off in comparison to many urban neighbors in India, for they own a method of transportation that can earn a cash income, providing food and shelter for their families. Their poverty is not absolute.

many divorced women are unable to collect child support from the fathers. The numbers in poverty are highest in and around large central cities such as Paris, France; Mexico City, Mexico; São Paulo, Brazil; and Caracas, Venezuela. In the United States, numbers are highest in cities such as New York, Chicago, Detroit, Cleveland, and Los Angeles, where the percentage of poor African American families headed by females reaches close to 50% in some cities. Girls who grow up in female-headed households or foster homes, without a stable family model, are more likely to become single teen mothers and to live in poverty, causing disruption in their schooling and setting limits on their employment possibilities and marital opportunities.

Conflict theorists argue that poor women, especially women of color, in capitalistic economic systems are used as a reserve labor force that can be called on when labor is needed and dismissed when not needed (Aguirre and Baker 2007; Ehrenreich 2001). They are an easily exploited group.

Those in poverty live under constant stress that can cause mental or physical breakdowns and alienation from the social system. Some turn to alcohol or drugs to escape the pressure and failure or to crime to get money to pay the bills. Poor physical and mental health, inadequate nutrition, high mortality rates, obesity, low self-esteem, feelings of hopelessness, daily struggle to survive, and dependence on others are a few of the individual consequences of poverty within our social world. In addition, costs to the larger society are great:

- The loss of talents and abilities that these people could contribute.
- Expenditure of tax dollars to address their needs or to regulate their lives with social workers and police.
- The contradictions of their lives with cultural values: The United States claims that all citizens "are created equal" and are worthy of respect, yet not all can "make it" in U.S. society.

Welfare programs in affluent countries are only one of a number of kinds of government assistance programs. In the United States, such programs are often thought of as unearned giveaways for the poor. However, there are massive programs of government support for people at all levels of the social system: tax breaks for wealthy business owners, farmers, oil companies, and financial institutions; universal health care provided in most affluent countries; university students paying little or nothing to attend college in some countries. Support is clearly not just for the poor. The question is whether affluence and prosperity are viewed as collectively created and shared rather than as individual achievements. Ignoring the importance of either individual responsibility and initiative or how social systems collectively produce affluence (or poverty) is a mistake. Both are at work.

Thinking Sociologically

Are tax breaks and bailouts for business owners and wealthy companies "unearned giveaways"? Are programs that help the poor "unearned giveaways"? What is the difference?

For most societies, poverty means loss of labor, a drain on other members in society to support the poor, and extensive health care and crime prevention systems. Those working with people in poverty generally argue that the elimination of poverty takes money and requires choices by policy makers to *do* something about poverty but could save societies in the long run. Some argue that poverty will never be eliminated because poor people are needed in society. Consider the position put forth in the next "Sociology in Our Social World."

Solutions to Poverty: Some Policy Considerations

Government programs in the United States and other countries are designed to help individuals through difficult times, especially during economic downturns. The

Sociology in Our Social World

The Functions of Poverty

Surely wealthy countries such as the United States have the means to eliminate poverty if they choose to do so. Its persistence invites debate. Some sociologists argue that poverty serves certain purposes or *functions* for society, and these make it difficult to address the problem directly and systematically (Gans 1971, 1995). Some people actually benefit from having poor people kept poor. Consider the following points:

1. The fact that some people are in poverty provides us with a convenient scapegoat—someone to blame for individual and societal problems. We have individuals to blame for poverty—the poor individuals themselves—and can ignore meso- and macro-level causes of poverty that would be expensive to resolve.
2. Having poor people creates many jobs for those who are not poor, including "helping" professions such as social workers, as well as law enforcement jobs such as police, judges, and prison workers.
3. The poor provide an easily available group of laborers to do work, and they serve as surplus workers to hire for undesirable jobs.
4. The poor serve to reinforce and legitimate our own lives and institutions. Their existence allows the rest of us to feel superior to someone, enhancing our self-esteem.
5. Their violation of mainstream values helps remind us of those values, thereby constantly reaffirming the values among the affluent.

This perspective can be extended to poverty on the global scale.

1. Just as poor U.S. laborers can be hired for undesirable jobs, the global poor work at very low wages to provide consumers in wealthy nations with low-cost goods.
2. The gifted and talented individuals in poor societies often migrate to wealthier nations, creating a brain drain that removes human capital from poor states and increases it in wealthy states.
3. The poor of the world are blamed for macro-level social problems such as overpopulation and terrorism. As with our local poor, their existence allows us to overlook the macro-level causes of poverty.

From this perspective, the poor serve a role in the structure of society. Therefore, some groups of people, be it individuals or nations, will always be at the bottom of the stratification ladder.

Source: Herbert Gans 1971, 1995.

stated goal of most public and private poverty reduction and welfare programs is to change factors that perpetuate poverty, but this requires money, jobs, and remodeling our social institutions. Some policy makers suggest attacking the problem of poverty institution by institution, offering incentives for family stability, for students to finish high school, and for job training. Have welfare reform plans worked to "end welfare as we know it" as policy makers claim? Many major research universities are trying to answer this very question—in poverty research centers at universities in Wisconsin, Chicago, Michigan, Washington, Missouri, Oregon, Kentucky, and Illinois. Data collected on social problems such as poverty, drug problems, and welfare affect governmental decisions about how to deal most effectively with problems.

Welfare, Workfare, and Other Aid Programs

Most Global North countries provide assistance to citizens who need help when unemployed, sick, or elderly. The United States established the Great Society programs of the 1960s and 1970s, many of which were successful in reducing poverty by attacking the root causes. Some of these still exist. For example, the Women, Infants, and Children Program (WIC) provides nutritional help, and Head Start provides early childhood education. Both programs have received high grades for helping poor women and children, but funding to some of these programs has been cut back due to other funding priorities, and as a result, their effectiveness has diminished (which is likely to lead to questioning of their effectiveness). Other programs—Aid to Families With Dependent Children, Medicaid, Medicare, food stamps—helped many who had short-term problems but were criticized as creating dependence of families on aid (Blank 2002; Haskins 2006).

Britain, France, the United States, and other countries have instituted work-incentive programs such as *workfare* that encourage or require recipients of aid to work or attend job training in order to qualify for food stamps. In the United States, able-bodied unemployed or underemployed adults must work 20 to 30 hours a week, be receiving on-the-job training, or be getting education in basic skills or college work to qualify for assistance for up to five years. Since 1996, when welfare reform was legislated, the number of people on welfare has dropped 57% in the United States. Child poverty rates also initially dropped, although they are still high compared with those of other countries (MacDougal 2005). Since the recession began, the success story of workfare has been less compelling as a solution.

Work-incentive program advocates argue that many welfare recipients would work if provided support and motivation. In addition to micro-level incentives such as child care and work training, success in helping people out of poverty depends on meso-level economic conditions: Are there jobs available at living wages? Are taxpayers, many of whom are attracted to politicians who cut taxes, willing to provide money for social programs to help the "invisible" poor out of poverty as well as provide subsidies for other groups, including farmers? Ironically, government institutions such as prisons actually absorb public funds that could go to poverty reduction, yet crime itself is often a result of people in poverty feeling that they have no other options for survival.

Social workers and others working with people in poverty have seen increases in the number of people needing workfare, food stamps, food pantries and food kitchens, temporary shelter, and other stopgaps for those without basic needs being met. Since the recession of 2007 began, caseloads of welfare workers have increased over 10%, by more than 4.6 million households (Johnson 2012). Some policy makers argue for a new federal initiative that would put jobless individuals to work in public service employment, a plan that would help the communities and those needing assistance (Johnson, Rynell, and Young 2012). The American Recovery and Reinvestment Act and the American Graduation Initiative recommended that policy makers prioritize two-year associate degrees at community college in order to increase the number of adults who have better job skills and credentials (Carnevale 2012).

One problem with poverty reduction has to do with the fact that race, class, and gender often intersect, causing some people to be in a double or triple bind relative to poverty. Many policy analysts do consider this and do not look at how poverty reduction may require attention to different issues when another variable such as gender is at work. Thus, public sociologists sometimes contribute to policy formation. One example is Mary Gatta, who uses her sociological training to create policy and programs that help working-poor mothers gain education and skills training, as is described in the next "Sociologists in Action."

Thinking Sociologically

Recalling what you have learned about poverty, how would you develop a plan to attack the problem of poverty within your community or country taking into account factors at the different levels—micro, meso, and macro? Are the root causes a matter of job training, family values, breaking the cycle, welfare support, or something else?

National and Global Digital Divide: Macro-Level Stratification

Mamadou from Niger and Eric from Ghana answer their cell phones to the sound of chimes from London's Big Ben clock tower and a Bob Marley song. One speaks in Kanuri and French and the other in Twi to friends thousands of miles away. They are the future generation of elites from the Global South, fluent in the languages of several countries, adept in computer software, and at the forefront in their countries in digital technology. Many of their fellow citizens in Niger and Ghana in Africa are not so fortunate. They live subsistence lives and have little contact with the digital world swirling overhead through satellite connections. This represents the *digital divide*, the gap between those with access to information technology and those without it. The lines of the divide are drawn by the position of the country in the world, socioeconomic status, minority group membership, and urban versus rural residence (Mehra, Merkel, and Bishop 2004).

The world economic and political institutions are increasingly based on producing and transmitting information through digital technology. Few tools are more important in this process than the computer, Internet, cell phones, and iPods. In nearly every salaried and professional position, computer knowledge and ability to navigate the Internet are critical employment skills. Individuals with insufficient access to computers and lack of technical skills

Sociologists in Action— Mary Gatta

Poor Women, Work, and School—Help to Accomplish It All!

by Mary Gatta

Gender, race, class, age, and educational levels, among other variables, alter the effectiveness of public policies. Yet public officials and policy makers are not often trained to understand the effects of such variables. Working-poor women face a dual challenge: How will they survive economically in the present, and, then, how will they attain the skills that will enable them to be more marketable in the future? Women, and in particular single, working-poor mothers, face a system of structural barriers—child care, elder care, irregular work hours, and transportation inequities—that make it hard for them to gain education in traditional classroom settings.

Using a sociological framework, Dr. Mary Gatta examines how workforce development policies are formulated and implemented in order to understand why so many such policies have not succeeded in helping poor working women. With data gathered from posing as a client at workforce development centers, Gatta can see that working-poor women are caught in a system in which they are not only unable to support themselves, but also unable to acquire human capital resources to attain self-sufficiency via the traditional mechanisms of education and skills training.

Gatta helps create social policy and programs that take into account the effects of variables such as race and gender on marginalized groups. Specifically, Gatta has helped create and implement workforce development programs that provide access to education and skills training for single, working-poor mothers in ways that attend to their work and family needs. She has crafted programs that are flexible so that women can receive their education without compromising their family or work responsibilities.

To address education and work issues, Gatta has overseen a new and rapidly expanding system of training single working mothers via the Internet and conducts research on workplace flexibility for low-wage workers in a variety of professions. Her work enables single mothers to obtain better jobs and become more active participants in U.S. society by providing them with flexible educational alternatives. The Internet is available around the clock, so women can fit education into their lives, as opposed to fitting their lives into educational structures. In addition, these programs provide computers for the women and their children, helping bridge the digital divide.

Gatta's background in sociology helps her educate policy makers on the gender effects of policy. Her book, *Not Just Getting By: The New Era of Flexible Workforce Development* (2005), coauthored with Kevin McCabe, is an excellent example of her ability to use sociology for the public good. Gatta's use of sociological training in her work helps policy makers do their jobs more effectively and ensures that gender is taken into account at the policy table.

* * * * * * *

Mary Gatta is now Senior Scholar at Wider Opportunities for Women, a national organization based in Washington, DC. This excerpt is adapted from Korgen and White's *Engaged Sociologist: Connecting the Classroom to the Community* (Sage 2013).

face barriers to many professions and opportunities. Because computer skills are important for personal success, this is an important micro-level issue. The digital divide is breaking down for some young and elite members of developing societies such as Mamadou and Eric, but many individuals and Global South countries have insufficient technology and educated citizens to participate in this new economy (Drori 2006; Nakamura 2004). Still, the number of Internet users around the globe increased from 250 million in 2000 to 2 billion in 2011. In fact, as 2013 approached, nearly 35% of the world's population had Internet usage (Internet World Stats 2013; Renick 2011). As Table 7.8 on page 252 makes clear, this varies greatly by region of the world.

Researchers have laid out three tiers in the digital divide, based on the following: (1) personal computers per 100 in the population, (2) Internet users per 100 in the population, and (3) Internet bandwidth per person. Using these standards, all developed countries plus some additional countries in the Caribbean, Eastern Europe, and the Middle East are Tier 1—the places with most access. The second tier includes Brazil, Russia, China, and some smaller countries in South America. African nations

In Laos where many people live in grass houses such as this one (top), there is no reliable electricity or other support systems for Internet technology. Few people in such communities even know about the resources available through the World Wide Web. That contrasts with homes like the bottom one, where computers are seen as necessary equipment and are taken for granted.

Table 7.8 Internet Users in the World: Distribution by Regions 2013

World Regions	*Internet Penetration (% Population)*	*% Total Global Internet Users*
Africa	15.6	7.0
Asia	27.5	44.8
Europe	63.2	21.5
Middle East	40.2	3.7
North America	78.6	11.4
Latin America/ Caribbean	42,9	10.6
Oceania/Australia	67.6	1.0
WORLD TOTAL	**34.3**	**100.0%**

Source: Internet World Stats 2013.

account for the majority of members in the lowest tier, reflecting disadvantage of the continent in lack of computers, computer use, and bandwidth ("The International Digital Divide" 2011).

On the other hand, cell phone users around the world rose from 500 million in 2000 to nearly 6 billion (Read 2011). The rapid increase is fueled by the boom of mobile cellular telephone subscriptions in Global South countries, resulting in a total global user rate of 87% (Renick 2011).

South Korea is the most wired country in the world. The United States is in the top tier as well, but many poor people in the United States do not have access to computers or mentors to teach them how to use computers. This digital divide is beginning to close with active efforts by schools and libraries to provide accessibility. According to a recent sociological study, "black and Latino youth use media more than ever, outpacing white and Asian youth, but there's a big difference in how they use media," creating challenges for bridging the digital divide (National Public Radio 2011). African American youth are on the cutting edge of Twitter and other social media. Blacks and Latinos are as likely to be on Facebook as other groups, and use their mobile devices to listen to music, play games, and do social networking. However, the African American and Latino kids are less likely to be the ones on the cutting edge of technology, using it for creating and designing digital content. Some kids use technology to interact with friends, and others use it for interest-based reasons such as knowledge and hobbies (National Public Radio 2011).

English is the language for 536.6 million Internet users (although it is the second language for many users). Chinese is the next most popular language on the Internet as can be seen in Table 7.9 (Internet World Stats 2010).

A problem facing many nations is that most websites and e-mail services use English, many computer keyboards

Table 7.9 **Most Used Languages on the Internet**

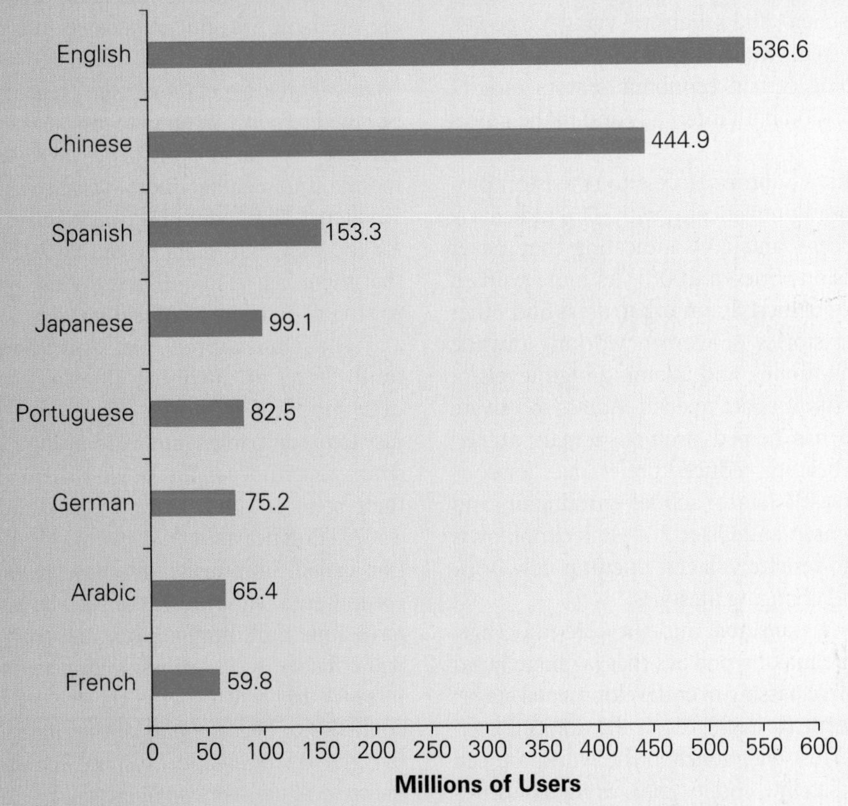

Source: Internet World Stats 2010.

are designed with a Western alphabet, and some of the digital systems in computers are established on the basis of English symbols and logic—a fact that many of us may not think about as we use the system (Drori 2006). For people who are struggling for the very survival of their culture, the dominance of English may feel like a threat, one more example of Western dominance. So where there is resistance to the use of computers and the Internet, it is more than a matter of finances or technology. There may be cultural objections as well.

Policy decisions at the international level affect the status of the Global South. The United Nations, the International Monetary Fund, and other international organizations have pressured countries to develop their Internet capacities. Indeed, this is sometimes used as a criterion for ranking countries in terms of their "level of modernization" (Drori 2006). Countries that have not been able to get "in the game" of Internet technology cannot keep pace with a rapidly evolving global economy.

Digital technology is an example of one important force changing the micro- to macro-level global stratification system—a spectrum of people and countries from the rich and elite to the poor and desperate.

Thinking Sociologically

What evidence of the digital divide do you see in your family, community, nation, and world? For instance, can your grandparents program their DVD player? Do they know how to work a cell phone or navigate the Internet? Could they create their own Facebook page if asked to do so?

The Global "Digital Divide" and Social Policy

Bengaluru (Bangalore) is home to India's booming digital industries, and provides an example of India's successful competition in the global high-tech market. Yet many villages and cities in India illustrate the contrasts between the caste system and the emerging class system. In traditional rural agricultural areas, change is extremely slow despite laws forbidding differential treatment of outcastes and mandating change. In urban industrial areas, new opportunities are changing the traditional caste structures, as competition for wealth and power is increasing with the changes in economic, political, and other institutional structures. The higher castes were the first to receive the education and lifestyles that create industrial leaders. Now, shopkeepers, wealthy peasants, teachers, and others are vying for power. Within the world system, India is generally economically poor but is developing certain economic sectors rapidly. Thus, India is in transition both internally and in the global world system.

In India and other countries, access to television programming has increased dramatically, with 45% indicating they always have access, and 20% indicating they never have access to television (Friesen 2008). As more women are exposed to images of lifestyles in urban areas and other countries—including stories of women working outside the home, controlling money, and attaining high levels of education—new possibilities are opened. Access to private cable television also has helped promote female autonomy, decreased wife beating, reduced preferences for sons over daughters, increased female school enrollment, and decreased fertility (Jensen and Oster 2007). Technology is bringing the world to remote villages, opening new horizons and options, and changing lifestyles.

As poor countries transition into the electronic age, some such as India are making policies that facilitate rapid modernization. They are passing over developmental stages that rich countries went through. As an illustration, consider the telephone. Most telephones in the world are cell phones, many using satellite connections. Some countries never did get completely wired for landlines, thus eliminating one phase of phone technology. With the satellite technology now in place, some computer and Internet options are available without expensive intermediate steps (Drori 2006). Cell phones that originated for the business elite have become a personal item. Use in poor countries has boomed, giving people access to health care and other services. By the end of 2011, there were almost 6 billion mobile phone subscribers—and the world's population is 7 billion. Cell phone subscriptions have grown 45% annually for the past four years (Whitney 2012). The point here is that there is a global digital divide, but that divide is narrowing in some areas of technology.

The One Laptop per Child foundation is helping fund efforts to distribute efficient small laptops for children around the world. Linux and Novatium, to name just two companies, are developing $100 computers, and some governments are buying them in large numbers for their schools (One Laptop per Child 2011; Rubenstein 2007). Engineers in India, working through an organization called Simputer Trust, have been designing a simple computer (a "simputer") that will be less expensive and will have more multilingual capacities than the PC. Such efforts will enhance access of poor countries to the computer and Internet and will provide the means for children in poor countries to become part of the digital age in the competitive global stratification system. Technology has the potential to level the world playing field.

We leave this discussion of stratification systems, including class systems, with a partial answer to the question posed in the beginning of this chapter: Why are some people rich and others poor? In the next two chapters, we expand the discussion to include other variables in stratification systems—race, ethnicity, and gender. By the end of these chapters, the answer to the opening question—why some are rich—should be even clearer. Socioeconomic status is important as a measure in any society, but it is not the sole basis for stratification. In the next chapter, we look at the role of race and ethnicity in social inequality.

What Have We Learned?

Perhaps your understanding of why you are rich or poor—and what effect your socioeconomic status has on what you buy, what you believe, and where you live—has taken on new dimensions. Perhaps you have gained some insight into what factors affect your ability to move up in the social class system. The issue of social stratification calls into question the widely held belief in the fairness of our economic system. By studying this issue, we better understand why some individuals are able to experience prestige (respect) and to control power and wealth at the micro, meso, and macro levels of the social system, while others have little access to those resources. Few social forces affect your personal life at the micro level as much as stratification. That includes the decisions you make about what you wish to do with your life or who you might marry. Indeed, stratification influenced the fact that you are reading this book.

Key Points

- Stratification—the layering or ranking of people within society—is one of the most important factors shaping the life chances of individuals. This ranking is influenced by micro, meso, and macro forces and resources. (See pp. 216–218.)
- Various theories of stratification disagree on whether inequality is functional or destructive to society and its members. The evolutionary perspective suggests ways stratification can be positive, but much of the inequality currently experienced creates problems for individuals and societies. (See pp. 218–226.)
- For individuals, personal respect (prestige) is experienced as highly personal, but it is influenced by the way the social system works at the meso and macro levels—from access to education and the problems created by gender and ethnic discrimination to population trends and the vitality of the global economy. (See pp. 226–231.)
- People without adequate connections to the meso and macro levels are likely to experience less power, wealth, and prestige. (See pp. 232–239.)
- Some macro systems stress ascribed status (assigned to one, often at birth, without consideration of one's individual choices, talents, or intelligence). Other systems purport to be open and based on achieved status (depending on one's contributions to the society and one's personal abilities and decisions). Unlike the caste system, the class system tends to stress achieved status, although it does not always perform openly. (See pp. 239–242.)
- The elements of stratification are complex, with property, power, and prestige influencing the system of inequality and one's standing. (See pp. 242–246.)
- Poverty itself is a difficult problem, one that can be costly to a society as a whole. Various solutions at the micro, meso, and macro levels have had mixed results, partially because it is in the interests of those with privilege to have an underclass to do the unpleasant jobs. (See pp. 246–250.)
- Technology is both a contributor and a possible remedy to inequality, as the digital divide creates problems for the poor, but electronic innovations may create new opportunities in the social structure for networking and connections to the meso and macro levels—even for those in the Global South, the poor regions of the world. (See pp. 250–254.)

Discussion Questions

1. Were you surprised to learn that so many of the world's children live in poverty, with 40% of the global population trying to survive on 5% of the word's income? Explain. What sociological theory best explains this fact? Support your answer.
2. Were you raised more by the "concerted cultivation" or "accomplishment of natural growth" parenting approach? How has this upbringing influenced your success in school and your willingness to challenge authority figures?
3. What is the social status of most of the people with whom you hang out? Why do you think you tend to associate with people from this social status?
4. Describe factors at the (a) micro, (b) meso, and (c) macro levels that impact your ability to move up the social class ladder.
5. How do the forces that have led to the shrinking of the middle class impact your chance of becoming (or remaining) a member of the (a) middle, (b) upper-middle, or (c) upper class after you graduate from college?
6. How can bridging the global digital divide lead to a decrease in inequality across the world? How does your ready access (or lack of access) to a computer and the Internet impact *your* life chances?

Contributing to Our Social World: What Can We Do?

At the Local Level

- *Volunteer to serve a meal* at an area soup kitchen. Your campus activities office should be able to help you find one in your area and even connect you with a group on campus that regularly volunteers at one.
- *Tip service people in cash.* Housekeepers in hotels and motels, maids, meal servers at restaurants, and food delivery employees may depend on tips to survive. In order to make it more likely that they receive the tips intended for them, be sure to tip in cash, rather than using a credit card.

At the Organizational or Institutional Level

- *Habitat for Humanity* pairs volunteers with current and prospective home owners in repairing or constructing housing for little or no cost. Habitat projects are under way or planned for many communities in the United

States and around the world. See the organization's website at www.habitat.org for more details and to see if you can volunteer for a project in your area.

- *AmeriCorps:* Founded in the early 1990s, AmeriCorps includes a variety of programs from intensive residential programs to part-time volunteer opportunities in communities across the United States. For more information, go to the organization's website at www.americorps.gov.

At the National and Global Levels

- *The Peace Corps* involves a serious, long-term commitment, but most who have done it agree that it is well worth the time and energy. The Peace Corps is an independent agency of the U.S. government, founded in 1961. Volunteers work in foreign countries throughout the world, helping local people improve their economic conditions, health, and education. The Peace Corps website (www.peacecorps.gov) provides information on the history of the organization, volunteer opportunities, and reports of former and present volunteers.
- *Grameen Bank* (www.grameen-info.org or www.grameenfoundation.org), a microcredit organization, was started in Bangladesh by Professor Muhammad Yunus, winner of the 2006 Nobel Peace Prize. It makes small business loans to people who live in impoverished regions of the world and who have no collateral for a loan. Consider doing a local fund-raiser with friends for the Grameen Bank or other microcredit organizations, such as FINCA (www.finca.org), KIVA (www.kiva.org), and CARE International (www.care-international.org).
- *Free the Children* is a youth-focused organization whose international programs help free people across the globe from the cycle of poverty by providing clean water, schools, health care, and sanitation. You can learn more about this organization and how you can join its efforts at www.freethechildren.com.

Visit the Student Study Site at **www.sagepub.com/ballantine4e** to access additional study tools, including eFlashcards, web quizzes, video resources, audio resources, web resources, SAGE journal articles, recommended readings, and more.

CHAPTER 8

Race and Ethnic Group Stratification

Beyond "We" and "They"

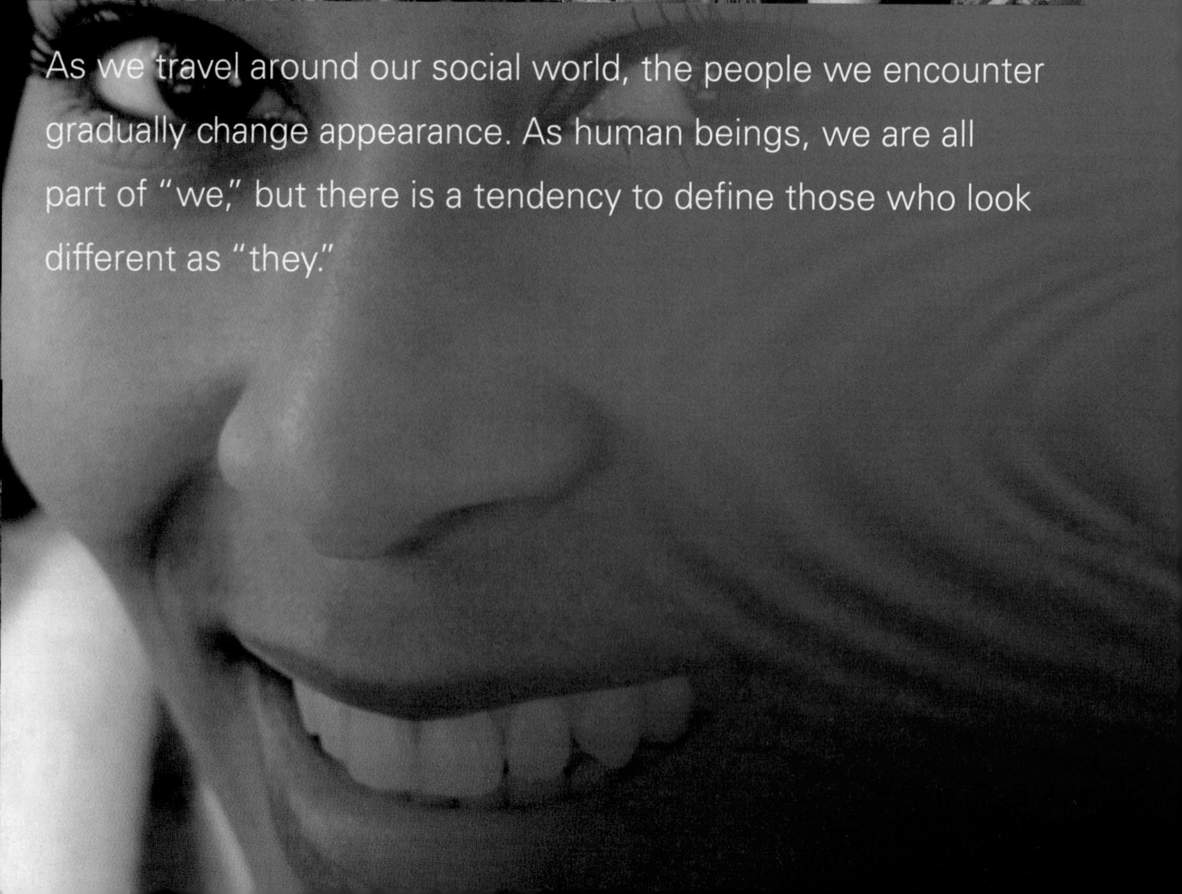

As we travel around our social world, the people we encounter gradually change appearance. As human beings, we are all part of "we," but there is a tendency to define those who look different as "they."

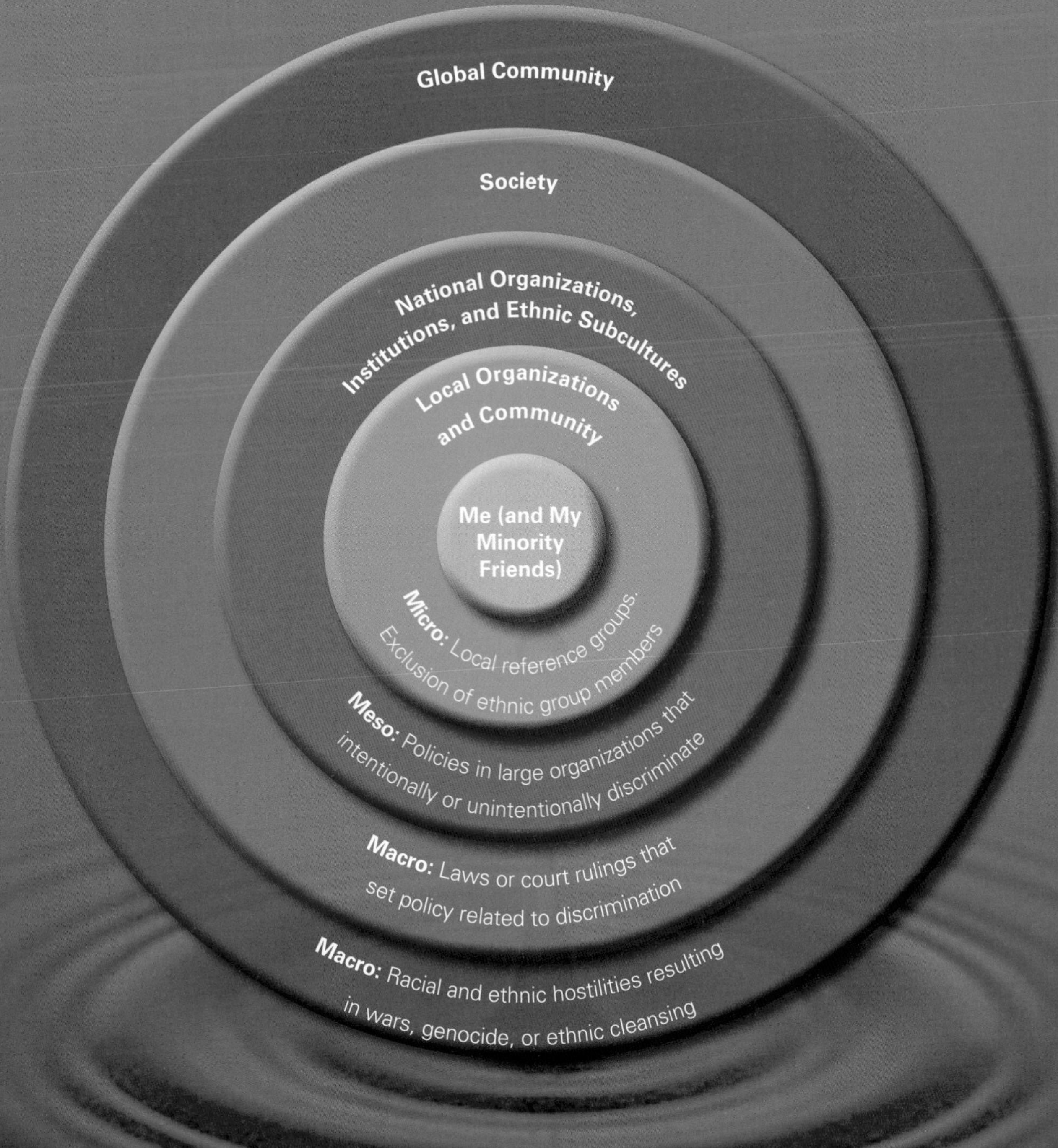
Global Community
Society
National Organizations, Institutions, and Ethnic Subcultures
Local Organizations and Community
Me (and My Minority Friends)
Micro: Local reference groups: Exclusion of ethnic group members
Meso: Policies in large organizations that intentionally or unintentionally discriminate
Macro: Laws or court rulings that set policy related to discrimination
Macro: Racial and ethnic hostilities resulting in wars, genocide, or ethnic cleansing

Think About It	
Micro: Me (and My Minority Friends)	Why do you look different from those around you? What relevance do these differences have for your life?
Micro: Local Community	Why do people in the local community categorize "others" into racial or ethnic groups?
Meso: National Institutions; Complex Organizations; Ethnic Groups	How might education, religion, politics, economics, and health experiences differ depending on your ethnicity?
Macro: National Society	Why are minority group members in most countries economically poorer than dominant group members?
Macro: Global Community	In what ways might ethnicity or race shape international negotiations and global problem solving? What can you do to make the world a better place for all people?

What's coming in this chapter?

> The unnamed adult female was brought to the UK by an organised gang with the intention of removing her organs and selling them to those desperate for a transplant.
>
> It is unclear whether the plot was uncovered before the organ removal took place, but campaigners said it was the first such case they had seen in Britain.
>
> It is understood the case is now the subject of a police investigation, but represents a sinister development in the already disturbing trade in human trafficking [and sale of organs] . . . (Evans 2012)

According to the World Health Organisation as many as 7,000 kidneys are illegally obtained by traffickers each year around the world.

While there is a market for organs such as hearts, lungs and livers, kidneys are the most sought after organs because one can be removed from a patient under proper medical conditions without any ill effects.

The United Nations estimates that 2.4 million people around the world were victims of human trafficking in 2012 alone; that's 1.8 people per 1,000 inhabitants in the world, and 3 per 1,000 in Asia and the Pacific ("Human Trafficking" 2012). Of these, 80% were in sexual services and mostly women and girls, but new markets in human body parts are growing. Human trafficking is lucrative—a $32 billion market (Lederer 2012). Thousands of women and children are smuggled into the United States and European countries each year as sex and domestic slaves or locked away in sweatshops (Bales 2012). In fact, the global market for child trafficking is over $12 billion a year with more than 1.2 million child victims (Stop Child Trafficking Now 2012).

In Calcutta's red-light district, more than 7,000 women and girls work as prostitutes. Only one group has a lower standing: their children. Zana Briski first began photographing prostitutes in Calcutta in 1998. Living in the brothels for months at a time, she quickly developed a relationship with many of the kids who, often terrorized and abused, were drawn to the rare human companionship she offered. Because the children were fascinated by her camera, Zana taught photography to the children of prostitutes. Learn more about her organization, Kids with Destiny, at www.kids-with-cameras.org.

It may surprise you to know that *slavery*—an individual or a family bound in servitude as the property of a person or household, bought and sold, and forced to work—is alive and flourishing around the world (Free the Slaves 2013). An estimated 27 million people, mostly women and children from poor families in poor countries, are slaves, auctioned off or lured into slavery each year by kidnap gangs, pimps, and cross-border syndicates. As a global phenomenon, human trafficking in slaves from places such as Ukraine, Myanmar (Burma), Laos, Nepal, and the Philippines, mostly for the commercial sex industry, is so profitable that criminal businesspeople invest in involuntary brothels much as they would in a mining operation (Bales 2007, 2012; Bales and Trodd 2008).

Around the stadiums of international events such as the Olympics, major soccer matches, and the Super Bowl, cheap hotels and brothels buy and sell child prostitutes (Elam 2011). Young foreign girls are brought in from other countries—chosen to be sex slaves because they are exotic and free from AIDS and because they cannot escape due to insufficient money and knowledge of the language of the country to which they are exported. Sometimes, poor families sell their daughters for the promise of high wages and perhaps money sent home. As a result, girls as young as 6 are held captive as prostitutes or as domestic workers. Child labor, a problem in many parts of the world, requires poor young children to do heavy labor for long hours in agriculture as well as brick-making, match-making, and carpet factories. Although they earn little, their income helps families pay debts.

Much of the cacao (used to make chocolate) and of the coffee that we buy (except for Fair Trade Certified products) supports slavery. More than 40% of the world's cacao beans are grown in Ivory Coast, West Africa. Boys and girls as young as 7 are kidnapped or sold, smuggled from neighboring countries, and sold to plantation owners. Young girls and boys work up to 80 hours a week in cacao plantations, but are not paid (Nall 2012). They are given a choice of unpaid hard labor (with beatings for any disobedience) or death by starvation or shooting (Bales 2000, 2012). Very little chocolate is produced *without* slave labor.

Debt bondage is another form of modern-day slavery. Extremely poor families—often people with differences in appearance or culture from those with power—work in exchange for housing and meager food. Severe debt, passing from generation to generation, may also result when farmers borrow money because they face drought or need cash to keep their families from starving. The only collateral they have on the loan is themselves—put up for bondage until they can pay off the loan. No one but the wealthy landowner keeps accounting records, which results in there being no accountability. The poor families may find themselves enslaved. The lack of credit available to marginal people contributes to slavery. Because those in slavery have little voice and no rights, the world community hears little

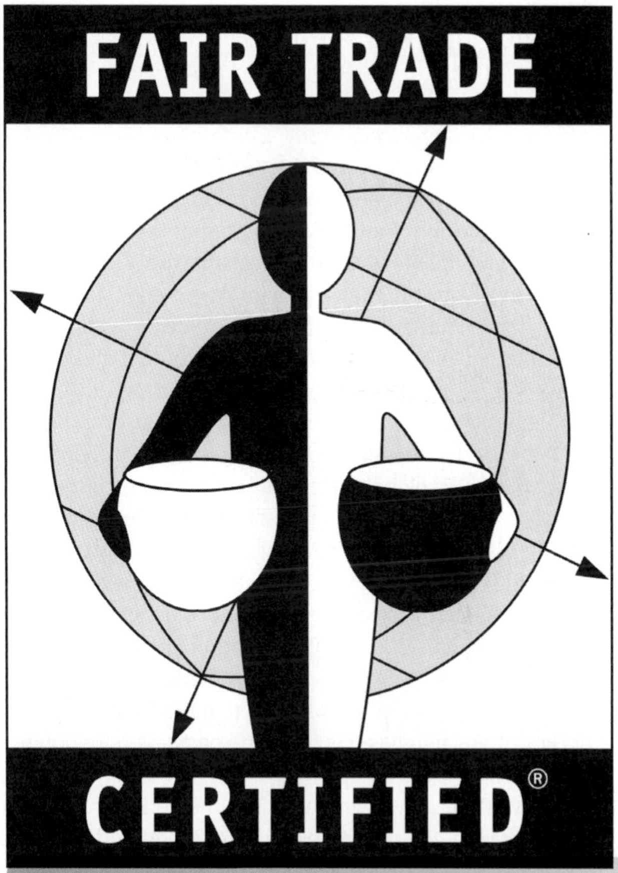

The Fair Trade Certified symbol signifies that products such as coffee, tea, and chocolate (made from cacao) meet sustainable development goals, help support family farmers at fair prices, and are not produced by slave labor.

Much of the work on cacao plantations is done by child slaves smuggled from poor countries. Fair trade requires respect for the dignity and autonomy of the workers. The photo at the right shows children working at a coffee plantation in Panama. This plantation does not have fair trade practices.

Sociologists in Action— By Kevin Bales | Stopping Slavery in the 21st Century

In the following excerpt from "Confronting Slavery With the Tools of Sociology," Kevin Bales describes how he has used his sociological training to draw attention to and work to combat modern slavery, living the life of a public sociologist.

Becoming an abolitionist sociologist crept up on me. The first tiny prodding was a leaflet I picked up at an outdoor event in London. The front of the leaflet read "There are Millions of Slaves in the World Today." I was a university professor, and I confess to an unpleasant mixture of pride and hubris in my reaction to the bold title of the leaflet. Having been involved in human rights for many years, I thought, "How could this be true if I don't know about it already?"

Something began to itch in my mind . . . what if? What if there were millions of people in slavery? What if almost all of us, governments, human rights groups, the media, the public, were simply unaware? Millions of hidden slaves seemed unlikely, but my nagging thought was that if there were millions of people in slavery, then finding them was the job of a social researcher. If there weren't millions of slaves, this type of literature needed debunking.

I pulled in students to help dig and sift through information, and paid one researcher to look further afield. As a faint picture of global slavery began to emerge, I came to understand why this issue was invisible. Slavery was hidden under a thick blanket of ignorance, concealed by the common assumption that it was extinct. With slavery illegal in every country, criminal slaveholders kept their activities hidden.

As I built up a picture of slavery, every new set of facts generated new questions. I began to realize that a large-scale research project was needed and I went in search of modern slavery, traveling to India, Pakistan, Thailand, Mauritania, and Brazil—often going undercover as I studied slave-based businesses in each country. The result was the book, *Disposable People: New Slavery in the Global Economy* (1999, 2004, 2012).

Some years later, I was able to build a database of slave prices over time that showed that slaves had been high-ticket capital purchase items in the past (even though occasional gluts caused prices to dip) and are normally low cost disposable inputs today.

In 2000, I, with three others, helped found Free the Slaves, the American sister-organization of Anti-Slavery International, the world's oldest (1787) and original human rights group. Free the Slaves works with local partners to liberate slaves around the world and change the systems that allow slavery to exist. In addition to addressing the crime of enslavement, this work often involves confronting gender inequality, racism, ethnic and religious discrimination, and the negative outcomes of global economic growth. We have learned that freedom and empowerment are viral, and that freed slaves will stop at nothing to stay free and help others to liberty.

Not every part of liberation and reintegration requires sociological training, but it would be very hard to be successful without it. Without carefully constructed longitudinal surveys of villages in slavery we could never have demonstrated the "freedom dividend," the powerful and positive economic change that comes to whole communities when slavery is abolished. Without training in the empathetic understanding of a social researcher we could never have developed the "slavery lens," a way of seeing this hidden crime, that the US government now requires of all its foreign aid program workers. Without learning about the complex interplay of culture, society, economics, politics, and social vulnerability, we would never be able to build the unique methodologies of liberation tailored to specific and culturally rooted forms of slavery. And there is nothing like the ugly reality of a crime like slavery to push young sociologists to do their best work—using solid social science to change the world.

* * * * * * *

Kevin Bales is a sociologist and professor of contemporary slavery at the Wilberforce Institute for the Study of Slavery and Emancipation (WISE) at the University of Hull, and cofounder of Free the Slaves in Washington. This excerpt is taken from White, White, and Korgen's *Sociologists in Action: Race, Class, and Gender* (Sage 2013).

about this tragedy (Bales 2007). A recent successful international movement in impoverished areas provides women very small loans—called *microcredit*—to help them start small businesses and move out of desperate poverty and slavery. We will read more about this in future chapters.

In the slavery of the 19th century, slaves were expensive, and there was at least some economic incentive to care about their health and survival so that they could be productive workers. In the new slavery, humans are cheap and replaceable. There is little concern about working them to death, especially if they are located in remote cacao or coffee plantations. By current dollars, a slave in the southern United States would have cost as much as $40,000, but contemporary slaves are cheap. They can be procured from poor countries for an average of $90 (Bales 2012). The cost is $40 in Mali for a young male and $1,000 in Thailand for an HIV-free female (Free the Slaves 2013). Those slaves worldwide produce an estimated $1.4 billion in produce and profits for their owners each year. Employers can legally exploit and abuse them with long hours and without legal interference because the slaves owe money.

Just as the issue of slavery mobilized people to start abolition movements in the first half of the 19th century, it is a cause for action by some public sociologists. The sociologist most at the forefront of the current movement to abolish slavery is featured in the "Sociologists in Action" on page 262.

Thinking Sociologically

Poor people around the world often lose control over their lives. What situations can lead to this condition, and what are the consequences for these people?

What is the significance of slavery for our discussion of race and ethnic group stratification? What all these human bondage situations have in common is that poor minority group members are victimized. Because many slaves are members of ethnic, racial, religious, tribal, gender, age, caste, or other minority groups with no cultural capital; are generally very poor; and have obvious physical or cultural distinctions from the people who exploit them, they are at a distinct disadvantage in the stratification system. Although all humans have the same basic characteristics and needs, few people have a choice about being born into a minority group, and it is difficult to change that minority status. Visible barriers include physical appearance, names, dress, language, and other distinguishing characteristics. Historical conditions and conflicts rooted in religious, social, political, and historical events set the stage for dominant or minority status, and people are socialized into their dominant or subservient group.

Minority- or dominant-group status affects most aspects of people's experiences and stratification position in the social world. These include status in the community, socialization experience, residence, opportunities for success in education and occupation, the religious group to which they belong, and the health care they receive. In fact, it is impossible to separate minority status from position in the stratification system (Aguirre and Turner 2011; Farley 2010; Rothenberg 2010).

In this chapter, we explore the characteristics of race and ethnic groups that lead to differential placement in stratification systems, including problems at the micro, meso, and macro levels—prejudice, racism, and discrimination. The next chapter considers ascribed status based on gender. The topics in this chapter and the next continue the discussion of stratification: who is singled out for differential treatment, why they are singled out, the consequences for both the individuals and the society, and some actions or policies that deal with differential treatment.

What Characterizes Racial and Ethnic Groups?

Migration, war and conquest, trade, and intermarriage have left virtually every geographical area of the world populated by groups of people with varying ethnicities. In this section, we consider the characteristics that set groups apart, especially groups that fall at the lower end of the stratification system.

Minority Groups

Several factors characterize **minority groups** and their relations with dominant groups in society (Dworkin and Dworkin 1999). **Minority groups**

1. can be distinguished from the group that holds power by factors that make them different—physical appearance, dress, language, or religion;
2. are excluded or denied full participation at the meso level of society in economic, political, educational, religious, health, and recreational institutions;
3. have less access to power and resources within the nation and are evaluated less favorably based on their characteristics as minority group members;
4. are stereotyped, ridiculed, condemned, or otherwise defamed, allowing dominant group members to justify and not feel guilty about unequal and poor treatment; and
5. develop collective identities to insulate themselves from the unaccepting world; this in turn perpetuates their group identity by creating ethnic or racial enclaves, intragroup marriages, and segregated group institutions such as religious congregations.

Thinking Sociologically

Based on the preceding list of minority group characteristics, explain how some people might be affected at the micro family level, the meso institutional level, or the macro level of society, depending on their membership in dominant or minority groups.

Because minority status changes with time and ideology, the minority group may be the dominant group in a different time or society. Throughout England's history, wars and assassinations changed the ruling group from Catholic to Protestant and back several times. In Iraq, Shiite Muslims are dominant in numbers and now also in power, but they were a minority under Saddam Hussein's Sunni rule.

Dominant groups are not always the numerical majority. In the case of South Africa, possession of advanced European weapons placed the native African Bantu population under the rule of a small percentage of white British and Dutch descendants in what became a complex system of planned discrimination called *apartheid.* Until recently, each major group—white, Asian, colored, and black—had its own living area, and members carried identification cards showing the "race" to which they belonged. In this case, racial classification and privilege were defined by the laws of the dominant group.

The Concept of Race

Racial minority is one of the two types of minority groups most common in the social world. The other is ethnic groups. A **race** is *a group identified by a society because of certain biologically inherited physical characteristics that cause members of the group to receive differential treatment.* However, in practice, it is impossible to accurately identify racial types. Most attempts at racial classifications have been based on combinations of appearance, such as skin color and shade, stature, facial features, hair color and texture, head form, nose shape, eye color and shape, height, and blood or gene type. Our discussion of race focuses on three issues: (1) origins of the concept of race, (2) the social construction of race, and (3) the significance of race versus class.

Origins of the Concept of Race

In the 18th and 19th centuries, scientists attempted to divide humans into four major groupings—Mongoloid, Caucasoid, Negroid, and Australoid—and then into more than 30 racial subcategories. In reality, few individuals fit clearly into any of these types. The next "Sociology in Our Social World" on page 266 provides insight into the origins of racial categories that have had a major impact on history and form the basis for many conflicts today.

From their earliest origins, thought to be in Ethiopia, East Africa, about 200,000 years ago, *Homo sapiens* slowly spread around the globe, south through Africa, north to Europe, and across Asia. Original migration patterns of early humans over thousands of years are shown in Map 8.1. As the map shows, many scholars believe that humans crossed Asia and the Bering Straits to North America around 20,000 BCE and continued to populate North and South America (Diamond 1999). Some other recent research has caused some geographers to believe that the migration followed the same path, but perhaps physical adaptations of isolated groups to their environments originally resulted in some differences in physical appearance—skin color, stature, hair type—but mixing of peoples over the centuries has left few if any genetically isolated people, only gradations as one moves around the world. Thus, the way societies choose to define race has come about largely through what is culturally convenient for the dominant group.

The United Nations, concerned about racial conflicts and discrimination based on scientifically inaccurate beliefs, issued a "Statement on Race" prepared by a group of eminent scientists from around the world (United Nations Educational, Scientific and Cultural Organization 1951). This and similar statements by scientific groups point out the harmful effects of racist arguments, doctrines, and policies. The conclusion of the UN document upheld that (a) all people are born free and equal both in dignity and in rights, (b) prejudice retards personal development, (c) conflicts (based on race) cost nations money and resources, and (d) racism foments international conflict. Racist doctrines lack any scientific basis, as all people belong to the same species and have descended from the same origin. In summary, problems arising from race relations are social, not biological, in origin; differential treatments of groups based on "race" falsely claim a scientific basis for classifying humans. Biologically speaking, a "race" exists in any life form when two groups cannot interbreed, and if they do, the offspring are infertile or sterile. This is not true of any group of human beings. So what is the problem?

Thinking Sociologically

On what bases do you classify people into groupings? How do you describe someone to another person? Do you use racial terms only for people of color? Why? Are people who are white "just normal"? If so, what does that say?

Social Construction of Race: Symbolic Interaction Analysis

Why are sociologists concerned about a concept that has little scientific accuracy and is ill defined? The answer is its social significance. The social reality is that people are defined or define themselves as belonging to a group based in part on physical appearance. As individuals try to make meaning of the social world, they may learn from others that some traits—eye or nose shape, hair texture, or skin color—are distinguishing traits that make people different. Jean Piaget, the famous cognitive psychologist, described the human tendency to classify objects as one of

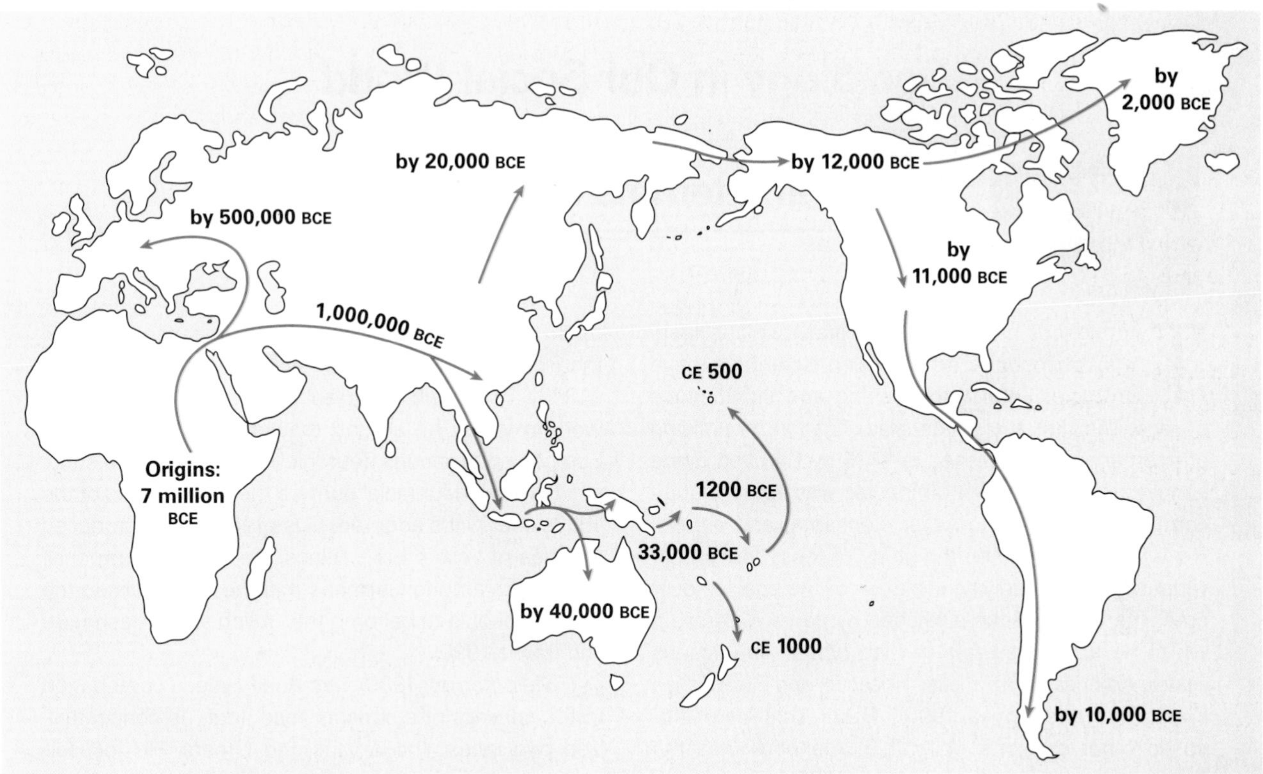

Map 8.1 The Spread of Humans Around the World

Source: Phys.Org 2009.

This map shows the historical spread of humans around the globe and the approximate time periods of the movements.

our most basic cognitive tools (Piaget and Inhelder [1955] 1999). This inclination has often been linked to the classifying of "racial" groups. Once in place, racial categories provide individuals with an identity based on ancestry—"my kind of people have these traits."

Symbolic interaction theory contends that if people believe something is real, it may become real in its consequences. It does not matter whether scientists say that attempts to classify people into races are inaccurate and that the word is biologically meaningless. People on the streets of your hometown think *they* know what the word *race* means. People do look different as we traverse the globe, partly because migration throughout history has resulted in interbreeding. That people *think* there are differences based on appearance has consequences. As a *social concept*, race has not only referred to physical features and inherited genes but has carried over to presumed psychological and moral characteristics, thus justifying discriminatory treatment. The following examples illustrate the complex problems in trying to classify people into "races."

With the enactment of "apartheid laws" in 1948, the white government in South Africa institutionalized differential laws based on its definitions of racial groups and specified the privileges and restrictions allotted to each group (Marger 2012). Bantu populations (the native Africans) and Coloreds (those of mixed blood) were restricted to separate living areas and types of work. Asians—descendants of immigrants from India and other Asian countries—received higher salaries than the Bantu groups but less than whites, while whites of European descent, primarily Dutch and English, had the highest living standard and best residential locations. Under the apartheid system, race was determined by tracing ancestry back for 14 generations. A single ancestor who was not Dutch or English might have caused an individual to be considered "Colored" rather than white. The "one drop of blood" rule made people a minority if they had any ancestry from another group. Physical features mattered little. Individuals carried a card indicating their race based on genealogy. Although this system began to break down in the 1990s due to international pressure and under the leadership of the first black president (Nelson Mandela, elected in 1994), vestiges of these notions of "reality" will take generations to change.

By contrast, in Brazil an individual's race is based on physical features—skin tone, hair texture, facial features,

Sociology in Our Social World

Historical Attempts to Define Race

Throughout history, political and religious leaders, philosophers, and even scientists have struggled with the meaning and significance of race. The first systematic classification of all living phenomena was published in 1735 by Carl von Linné (Linnaeus). His hierarchy of species was actually quite complex, including monkeys, elephants, and angels. His work was based on the study of fossil remains of various species, implying evolution of the species over time. Then, in 1758, he published *Systema Naturae*, in which he suggested four human types: Americanus (Native Americans), Asiaticus, Africanus, and Europeanus (Cashmore and Troyna 1990). Other scientists proposed other divisions. Johann Blumenbach was the first to use the word *race* in his 1775 classification system: Caucasian, Mongolian, Ethiopian, American, and Malay.

By the 19th century, race began to take on a biological meaning and to signify inherent physical qualities in humans (Goldberg 1990). From there, it was a short step to theorizing about inherent inequalities between races. For instance, Joseph Arthur—also known as Comte de Gobineau (1816–1882)—questioned why once great societies had declined and fallen. He argued that each race has specific characteristics, and he attributed the demise of societies to the inequality of races. His book *Essay on Inequality of the Human Races*, published in 1853–1855, earned him the title "father of modern racism."

A major event in theories of race was the publication of Charles Darwin's *The Origin of Species* ([1858] 1909). Among his many ideas was that human races *might* represent the stages or branches of a tree of evolution. This idea implied that those groups of humans who were biologically best suited to the environment would survive. He argued that "natural selection," or "survival of the fittest," was true of all races in the human species, not of individuals within a species. From Darwin's ideas emerged the concepts of *survival of the fittest* and *ever-improving races.*

These two late-19th-century concepts were taken out of context and became the foundation for a number of theories of superior races. For instance, in 1899, the Brit-turned-German Houston Stewart Chamberlain ([1899] 1911) published an aristocratic, anti-Semitic work in which he argued that northern and western European populations, Teutonic in particular, were superior. He argued for racial purity, a theme the Nazis of the 1930s and 1940s adopted. Gustaf Kossinna introduced the idea of *Volk* in his writings, claiming a commonality of traits among Germans that, he felt, qualified the German people to become the "ruling elite" (Cashmore and Troyna 1990).

Mein Kampf (1939) was Adolf Hitler's contribution to the concept of a superior race. In it, he conceptualized two races, the Aryans and Others. He focused attention on several groups, in particular the Jews, which he claimed caused the economic and social problems of Germany.

What followed in the name of German purity was the extermination of millions of Jews, Poles, Catholics, Gypsies, homosexuals, and other groups and individuals who were deemed "less human" or who opposed the Nazis. The extent to which Hitler succeeded exemplifies what can happen when one group needs to feel superior to others, blames other groups for its shortcomings, and has the power to act against those minorities. More recent attempts to classify groups have been based not on external characteristics but on blood or gene type, even though blood types and genomes do not always correlate with other traits.

As applied to mammals, the term *race* has biological significance only when it refers to closely inbred groups in which all family lines are alike—as in pure breeds of domesticated animals. These conditions are never realized in humans and are impossible in large populations of any species (Witzig 1996). Many groups have been mislabeled "races" when the differences are actually cultural. Jews, Poles, Irish, and Italians have all erroneously been called "races." In short, when it comes to humans, scientists do not agree about whether race is a biological reality at all.

eye color, and so forth—rather than on the "one drop of blood" rule as in South Africa. Brothers and sisters who have the same parents and ancestors may be classified as belonging to different races. The idea of race is based on starkly contrasting criteria in Brazil and South Africa, illustrating the arbitrary nature of racial classification attempts (Kottak 2010).

Before civil rights laws were passed in the United States in the 1960s, a number of states had laws that spelled out differential treatment for racial groups. These were commonly referred to as Jim Crow laws. States in the South passed laws defining who was African American or Native American. In many cases, it was difficult to determine to which category an individual belonged. For instance, African Americans in Georgia were defined as people with any ascertainable trace of "Negro" blood in their veins. In Missouri, 1/8 or more "Negro" blood was the standard, whereas in Louisiana, 1/32 Negro blood defined one as black. Differential treatment was spelled out in other states as well. In Texas, for example, the father's race determined the race of the child. In Vermont, newborn babies of racially mixed parentage were listed as "Mixed" on the birth certificate. In West Virginia, a newborn was classified as "black" if either parent was considered black. Until the latter half of the 20th century, several U.S. states still attempted to classify the race of newborns by the percentage of black blood or parentage (Lopez 1996). Federal law now prohibits discrimination on the basis of "racial" classifications, and most state laws that are explicitly racial have been challenged and dropped.

This house in the Chicago slums is not atypical of the quality of homes in segregated America in the 1940s.

The Significance of Race Versus Class

From the time of slavery in the Americas until the 21st century, *race* has been the determining factor in social stratification and opportunity for people of African descent in the United States, the Caribbean, and Brazil. Whether this is changing in the 21st century is a question that has occupied sociologists, politicians, educators, and other scientists in recent years. Some scholars argue that race is the primary cause of different placement in the stratification system, whereas others insist that race and social class are both at work, with socioeconomic factors (social class) more important than race.

Influential sociologist William Julius Wilson believes that the racial oppression that characterized the African American experience throughout the 19th century was caused first by slavery and then by a lingering caste structure that severely restricted upward mobility. However, the breakdown of the plantation economy and the rise of industrialism created more opportunities for African Americans to participate in the economy (Wilson 1978, 1993a, 1993b).

Wilson argues that after World War II, an African American class structure developed with characteristics similar to those of the white class structure. Occupation and income took on ever greater significance in social position, especially for the African American middle class. However, as black middle-class professionals moved up in the stratification structure, lower-class African American ghetto residents became more isolated and less mobile. Limited unskilled job opportunities for the lower class have resulted in poverty and stagnation so severe that some families are almost outside of the functioning economic system. Wilson (1978, 1984, 1993a) calls this group the *underclass*.

Some researchers assert that the United States cannot escape poverty because well-paid, unskilled jobs requiring few skills and little education are disappearing from the economy and because the poor are concentrated in segregated urban areas (Massey 2007; Massey and Denton 1998). Poorly educated African American teenagers and young adults see their job prospects limited to the low-wage sector (e.g., work at fast-food joints at minimum wage), and they experience record levels of unemployment. Movement out of poverty becomes almost impossible (Farley 2010; Wilson 1996).

When Wilson did his research in the 1980s and '90s, his point was illustrated by the fact that more than 2 in 5 African Americans were middle-class, compared with 1 in 20 in 1940. On the other hand, many adults in inner-city ghetto neighborhoods are not employed in a typical week. Thus, children in these neighborhoods may grow up without ever seeing someone go to work (Wilson 1996). The new global economic system is a contributing factor

Table 8.1 **Race/Ethnicity and Family Income**

	White	*Black*	*Hispanic*	*United States*
Median family annual income	$57,861	$32,584	$38,039	$49,777*
Percentage under $15,000	11.4	23.5	16.5	13
Percentage above $100,000	21.4	9.3	11.7	20.1

Source: U.S. Census Bureau (2012g).

Note: Figures are for 2009.

* Median family annual income down from $52,301 in 2000.

as unskilled jobs go abroad to cheaper labor (Friedman 2008; Massey 2007). Without addressing these structural causes of poverty, we cannot expect to reduce the number of people in the underclass—whether they are white, black, or another minority.

The situation for the black middle class has deteriorated since the economic crisis that began in 2007 with job loss and downward mobility. Comparing 2004 with 2009 figures, the median net worth of white households went from $134,280 to $97,860. For African Americans, the numbers dropped from $13,450 to $2,170. Thus, for every white person's dollar, blacks had 2 cents. By 2009, the black unemployment rate was 16.2%, and only 56% of black men over 20 were working. Many people lost their homes, but that involved 4.5% of whites and 8% of blacks (Washington 2011).

With these dismal figures in mind, a big debate among scholars surrounds the following question: Has race declined in significance and class become more important in determining placement in the stratification system? Tests of Wilson's thesis present us with mixed results (Jencks 1992). For instance, 84.2% of African Americans over 25 are high school graduates or more compared to 87.2% of whites, suggesting they have fairly comparable qualifications for employment. However, this equity stops at the high school level; 30.3% of whites are college graduates, compared with 19.8% of blacks (U.S. Census Bureau 2012f). More importantly, African Americans earn less than whites in the same occupational categories. As Tables 8.1 and 8.2 make clear, income levels for African Americans, Hispanics, and whites are not even close to being equal. Unemployment and poverty affect a higher percentage of black families than white ones. Yet economics alone does not seem a complete answer to who is in the underclass.

Although racial bias has decreased at the micro (interpersonal) level, it is still a significant determinant in the lives of African Americans, especially those in the lower class. The data are complex, but we can conclude that for upwardly mobile African Americans, class may be more important than race. Still, the interplay of race, class, and gender is complex, and contributes to class status; yet physical traits such as skin color cannot be dismissed (Farley 2010).

Table 8.2 **Income (in Dollars) by Education Level and Race/Ethnicity**

Education	*White*	*Black*	*Hispanic*
Not a high school graduate	$21,590	18,123	21,310
High school graduate	32,126	27,265	27,020
Some college, no degree	33,298	28,570	29,610
College graduate	59,866	46,527	48,081
Master's degree	72,125	58,311	74,122
Professional degree	127,968	104,656	81,968

Source: U.S. Census Bureau 2011c, 2011d, 2011e.

Thinking Sociologically

Considering the data and discussion above about race versus class as contributors to a person's status, what do you think is more important? Why?

Ethnic Groups

The second major type of minority group—the **ethnic group**—is *based on cultural factors: language, religion, dress, foods, customs, beliefs, values, norms, a shared group identity or feeling, and sometimes loyalty to a homeland, monarch, or religious leader.* Members are grouped together because they share a common cultural heritage, often connected with a national or geographical identity. Some social scientists prefer to call racial groups "ethnic groups" because the term *ethnic* encompasses most minorities, avoiding problems

Ethnic enclaves have a strong sense of local community, holding festivals from the old country and developing networks in the new country. Such areas, called "ghettos," are not necessarily impoverished. This photo depicts a street in San Francisco's Chinatown.

with the term *race*, and the ideas often go together (Aguirre and Turner 2011).

Visits to ethnic enclaves in large cities around the world give a picture of ethnicity. Little Italy, Chinatown, Greek Town, and Polish neighborhoods may have non-English street signs and newspapers, ethnic restaurants, culture-specific houses of worship, and clothing styles that reflect the ethnic subculture. Occasionally, ethnic groups share power in pluralistic societies, but most often they hold a minority status with little power.

How is ethnicity constructed or defined? Many very different ethnic groups have been combined in government categories, such as censuses conducted by countries, yet they speak different languages and often have very different religions. For example, in North America, native ethnic group members often do not view themselves as "Indian" or "Native American." Instead, they use 600 independent tribal nation names to define themselves, including the *Ojiba* (Chippewa), the *Dineh* (Navajo), the *Lakota* (Sioux), and many others. Likewise, in the U.S. census, Koreans, Filipinos, Chinese, Japanese, and Malaysians come from very different cultures but are identified as *Asian Americans*. People from Brazil, Mexico, and Cuba are grouped together in a category called *Hispanics* or *Latinos*. When federal funds for social services were made available to Asian Americans or American Indians, these diverse people began to think of themselves as part of a larger grouping for political purposes (Esperitu 1992). The federal government essentially created an ethnic group by naming and providing funding to that group. If people wanted services (health care, legal rights, and so forth), they had to become a part of a particular group—such as "Asian Americans." This process of merging many ethnic groups into one broader category—called *panethnicity*—emphasizes that ethnic identity is itself socially shaped and created.

Biracial and Multiracial Populations: Immigration, Intermarriage, and Personal Identification

Our racial and ethnic identities are becoming more complex as migration around the world brings new immigrants to distant shores in search of safety and a new start in life. Keep in mind that our racial and ethnic identities come largely from external labels placed on us by governments and our associates, but reinforced by our own self-identification. The important point is this: *Race is a social construct that can change with conditions in a country.*

Many European countries are now host to immigrants from their former colonies, making them multiracial. France hosts many North and West Africans, and Great Britain hosts large populations from Africa, India, and Pakistan. The resulting mix of peoples has blurred racial lines and created many multiracial individuals. The patterns illustrated in Map 8.1 illustrate that "push" factors drive people from some countries and pull them to other countries. The most common push-pull factors today are job opportunities, the desire for security, individual liberties, and availability of medical and educational opportunities. The target countries of migrants are most often in North America, Australia, or Western Europe, and the highest emigration rates are from Africa, Eastern Europe, Central Asia, and South and Central America.

The United States was once considered a biracial country, black and white (which, of course, disregarded the Native American population). However, the nation currently accepts more new immigrants than any other country (700,000 per year) and has the second highest rate of immigration (behind Canada) in terms of immigrants per 1,000 residents (Farley 2010). Immigration into the United States from every continent has led to a more diverse population, with 12% of the U.S. population (36.7 million residents) born elsewhere and 11% (33 million) having at least one foreign-born parent (UPI.com 2010). With new immigration, increasing rates of intermarriage, and many more individuals claiming multiracial identification, the picture is much more complex today, and the color lines have been redrawn (DaCosta 2007; Lee and Bean 2004, 2007). One in 40 individuals claims multiracial status today, and estimates are that 1 in 5 will do so by 2050 (Lee and Bean 2004). For the first time in 2008, the United States elected a biracial president, although the application of the "one drop of blood" rule in the United States has caused many people to refer to President Obama as "black."

Census data are used in countries to determine many characteristics of populations. In the United States, questions about race and ethnic classification have changed with each 10-year study. The important point is that government-determined categories thereafter define the racial and ethnic composition of a country. In the 2000 census, citizens were for the first time given the option of picking more than one racial category. By 2009, 5.2 million people checked multiracial on the U.S. Census survey (Nagai 2010; Schaefer 2012; Yen 2009).

Latinos, sometimes called Hispanics, made up 16.3% (50.5 million) of the total U.S. population in 2010 (308.7 million; Perez 2011). Hispanics accounted for 56% of the nation's growth since the 2000 census (Pew Hispanic Center 2011). Among Latinos, Mexicans made up roughly 65%, Puerto Ricans 9%, Cubans 3.5%, Salvadorians 3.2%, Dominicans 2.7%, and others 15.4% (National Council of La Raza 2011). Blacks follow Latinos with 12.6% of the population. Non-Hispanic whites make up 63.7% (196.8 million), Asians 4.8%, and Native Americans/Native Alaskans 0.9% of the total U.S. population (Day 2011; Humes, Jones, and Ramirez 2011). Figure 8.1 illustrates the ethnic group distribution and projections for the future for the United States.

Arbitrary socially constructed classifications of people into groups are frequently used as justification for treating individuals differently despite the lack of scientific basis for such distinctions (Williams 1996). The legacy of "race" remains even in countries where discrimination based on race is illegal.

The question remains: Why is a multiracial baby with any African, Native American, or other minority heritage classified by the minority status, not as a member of the majority? After all, the child has 50% genetic makeup from each parent.

Thinking Sociologically

Identify one dominant and one minority group in your community or on campus. Where do that group's members fit into the stratification or prestige system of the local community? How are the life chances of individuals in these groups influenced by factors beyond their control?

Prejudice: Micro-Level Analysis

Have you ever found yourself in a situation in which you were viewed as different, strange, undesirable, or "less than human"? Perhaps you have felt the sting of rejection, not based on judgment of you as a person but solely because of the ethnic group into which you were born. Then again, you may have been insulated from this type of rejection if you grew up in a homogeneous community or in a privileged group; you may have even learned some negative

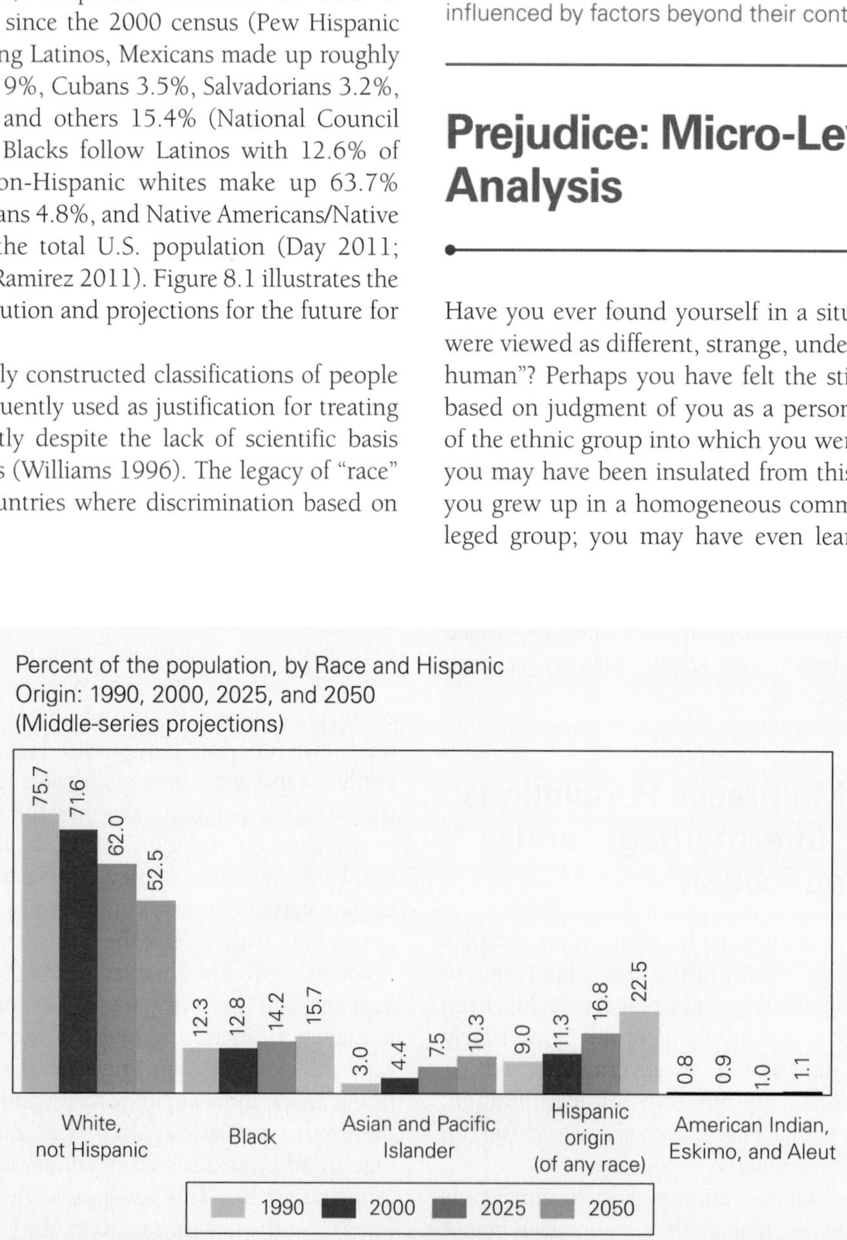

Figure 8.1 Percent of the Population, by Race and Hispanic Origin: 1990, 2000, 2025, and 2050

Source: U.S. Census Bureau.

Table 8.3 **Processes That Foster Racial and Ethnic Inequality**

Process	*Result*
Stratification	Minority status
Prejudice	Poor self-concept, negative relations with others
Discrimination	Poor jobs, income, education, housing
Racism	Systems that limit access to resources
Negative contact	Hostilities, war, conflict between groups

attitudes about those different from yourself. It is sobering to think that where and when in history you were born determine how you are treated, your life chances, and many of your experiences and attitudes.

Racial and ethnic minorities experience disproportionate prejudice and rejection. Several processes act to keep minority groups among the have-nots of society. Consider the factors in Table 8.3.

When minority groups are present within a society, prejudice influences dominant-minority group relations. **Prejudice** refers to *attitudes that prejudge a group, usually negatively and not based on facts.* Prejudiced individuals lump together people with certain characteristics as an undifferentiated group without considering individual differences. Although prejudice can refer to positive attitudes and exaggerations (as when patriots are prejudiced in thinking their society is superior), in this chapter, we refer to the negative aspects of prejudice. We also focus on the adverse effects brought on minority group members by prejudice. While prejudice can be stimulated by events such as conflicts at the institutional level and war at the societal level, attitudes are held by individuals and can be best understood as a micro-level phenomenon.

If prejudiced attitudes become actions, they are referred to as **discrimination**—*differential treatment and harmful actions against minorities.* These actions at the micro level might include refusal to sell someone a house because of the religion, race, or ethnicity of the buyer or employment practices that treat some candidates less well based on their minority status (Feagin and Feagin 2010). Discrimination, such as laws that deny opportunities or resources to members of a particular group, operates largely at the meso or macro level, discussed later in the chapter.

The Nature of Prejudice

Prejudice is an understandable response of humans to their social environment. To survive, every social group or unit—a sorority, a sports team, a civic club, or a nation—needs to mobilize the loyalty of its members. Each organization needs to convince people to voluntarily commit energy, skills, time, and resources so the organization can meet its needs. Furthermore, as people commit themselves to a group, they invest a portion of themselves and feel loyalty to the group.

Individual commitment to a group influences one's perception and loyalties, creating preference or even bias for the group. This commitment is often based on stressing distinctions from other groups and deep preference for one's own group. However, these loyalties may be dysfunctional for out-group members and the victims of prejudice.

One reason people hold prejudices is that it is easier to pigeonhole the vast amount of information and stimuli coming at us in today's complex societies, and to sort information into neat unquestioned categories, than to evaluate each piece of information separately for its accuracy. When prejudiced individuals use distorted, oversimplified, or exaggerated ideas to categorize a group of people and attribute personal qualities to them based on their dress, language, skin color, or other identifying features, it is called *stereotyping*. Stereotypes are not just generalizations; they are by definition misleading overgeneralizations that are prejudicial.

Stereotypes are passed down over generations through cultures. They are applied to all members of a group, regardless of individual differences, and used to justify prejudice, discrimination, and unequal distribution of power, wealth, and opportunities. Often, the result is unfair and inaccurate judgments about individuals who are members of the stereotyped groups. The problem is that both those stereotyping and those being stereotyped may come to believe the "pictures" in their heads and act accordingly.

Prejudice is difficult to change because it is rooted in traditions, cultural beliefs, and stereotypes of groups. Individuals grow up learning these ingrained beliefs, which often go unchallenged. These beliefs are also often used to rally in-group loyalty.

In wartime, the enemy may be the victim of racial slurs, or members of the enemy society may be depicted in films or other media as villains. During World War II, American films often showed negative stereotypes of Japanese and German people. These depictions likely reinforced the decision to intern more than 110,000 Japanese Americans, the majority of whom were U.S. citizens, in detention camps following the bombing of Pearl Harbor.

Similar issues and stereotypes have arisen for American citizens with Middle Eastern ancestry since the attacks on the New York World Trade Center on September 11, 2001. Note that there has been an increase in attacks on U.S. Muslims and the uproar over the plans to build a mosque for peace near the 9/11 site. Sociologist Saher Selod examines factors that have contributed to intensified bigotry toward Muslims in the next "Sociology in Our Social World."

Sociology in Our Social World

Anti-Muslim Sentiments in the United States

By Saher Selod

On September 11, 2001, the United States experienced the largest terrorist attack on U.S. soil. Four airplanes were hijacked by terrorists. Two of the airplanes were flown into the World Trade Center, causing the two buildings to collapse. Another airplane crashed into the Pentagon, and the fourth plane crashed due to a revolt by the passengers on board. The attacks claimed the lives of close to 3,000 Americans. The terrorists were Muslims from Saudi Arabia, United Arab Emirates, and Egypt. These horrific events changed the lives of all Americans, including Muslim Americans and immigrants.

A few sociologists studied the impact 9/11 had on Muslims living in the United States (Bakalian and Bozorgmehr 2009; Cainkar 2009; Peek 2011). Some of the findings reveal Muslims have become targets for antiterrorist laws and policies that were a part of a government-led campaign known as the "War on Terror" (Cainkar 2009). For example, a little over a month after the attacks, the USA PATRIOT Act (Uniting and Strengthening America by Providing Appropriate Tools Required to Intercept and Obstruct Terrorism Act) was signed into law. This 300-page document restricted the civil liberties of Muslims and any other American who could be connected to terrorism. The document loosely defined terrorism, justifying the surveillance of Muslims due to an inaccurate association of Islam with terrorism. As a result, mass deportations of Muslim immigrants for minor infractions of their visas were hidden from the public by the Patriot Act. There was also an increase in visitations of Muslims by the Federal Bureau of Investigation (FBI).

Another policy passed after 9/11 was the National Security Entry-Exit Registration System, initiated in September 2002 by the Immigration and Naturalization Services. This law required noncitizen men over the age of 16 from 25 countries (of which 24 were Muslim countries) to register with the government. Muslim men were forced to submit fingerprints and had their photos taken as if they were potential criminals. One of the consequences of these laws and policies is they created an environment where innocent people are treated as if they are guilty due to their shared religious identity with the perpetrators of the terrorist attacks. Since 9/11, over a thousand Muslims (mostly noncitizens) have been detained even though no connection to terrorism was determined. Furthermore these policies have encouraged the distrust of Muslims by their fellow citizens.

Muslims living in the United States have reported a rise in prejudice and discrimination. Lori Peek's study, *Behind the Backlash: Muslim Americans After 9/11,* highlights the backlash Muslims living in New York City and Colorado experienced in the few weeks after 9/11. Although it has been over 10 years since the terrorist attacks, anti-Muslim sentiments remain strong today. According to a Gallup report published in 2010, 43% of Americans admitted to feeling some prejudice toward Muslims, and 31% of Americans view Islam unfavorably (Gallup Center for Muslim Studies 2010). These rising anti-Muslim sentiments have had a direct impact on the everyday life of the Muslim population. Statistics compiled by the FBI reveal hate crimes against Muslims increased by almost 50% from 2009 to 2010. In August 2012, a mosque in Joplin, Missouri, was burned to the ground by an arsonist. As a consequence of government policies targeting Muslims and the perpetuation of stereotypes and myths that Muslims are a threat to national security and American cultural values, Muslims are living with a new racialized identity. Fortunately organizations such as the Council on American-Islamic Relations (CAIR) and the American Civil Liberties Union (ACLU) are heralding the fight against bigotry and discrimination against Muslims living in the United States.

* * * * * * *

Saher Selod is an assistant professor of sociology at Simmons College. Her areas of research are race and ethnicity and sociology of religion—especially the Muslim experience in the United States.

On December 7, 1941, Japan bombed Pearl Harbor in Hawaii, prompting President Franklin D. Roosevelt to sign an executive order designating the West Coast as a military zone from which "any or all persons may be excluded." Although not specified in the order, Japanese Americans were singled out for evacuation, and more than 110,000 were removed from many western states and sent to 10 relocation camps. Barber G. S. Hante points proudly to his bigoted sign against people with Japanese origin.

Explanations of Prejudice

We have all met them—people who express hostility toward others. They tell jokes about minorities, curse them, and even threaten action against them. Why do these individuals do this? The following theories have attempted to explain the prejudiced individual.

Frustration-aggression theory. In Greensboro, North Carolina, in 1978, a group of civil rights activists and African American adults and children listened as a guitarist sang freedom songs. A nine-car cavalcade of white Ku Klux Klan (KKK) and American Nazi Party members arrived. The intruders unloaded weapons from the backs of their cars, approached the rally, and opened fire for 88 seconds; then, they left as calmly as they had arrived. Four white men and a black woman were dead (Greensboro Justice Fund 2005). According to *frustration-aggression theory*, many of the perpetrators of this and other heinous acts feel angry and frustrated because they cannot achieve their work or other goals. They blame any vulnerable minority group—religious, ethnic, sexual orientation—and members of that group become targets of their anger. Frustration-aggression theory focuses largely on poorly adjusted people who express their frustration through aggressive attacks on others. Hate groups evolve from like-minded individuals, often because of prejudice and frustration (see Map 8.2 on page 274).

Scapegoating. When it is impossible to vent one's frustration on the real target—one's boss, teachers, the economic system—this frustration can take the form of aggressive action against minority group members, who are vulnerable because of their low status. They become the scapegoats. The word *scapegoat* comes from the Bible, Leviticus 16:5–22. Once a year, a goat (which was obviously innocent) was laden with parchments on which people had written their sins. The goat was then sent out to the desert to die. This was part of a ritual of purification, and the creature took the blame for others.

Scapegoating occurs when a minority group is blamed for the failures of others. It is difficult to look at oneself to seek reasons for failure but easy to transfer the blame for one's failure to others. Individuals who feel they are failures in their jobs or other aspects of their lives may blame minority groups. From within such a prejudiced mind-set, even violence toward the out-group becomes acceptable.

Consider the economic situation today. Jobs and promotions are harder for young adults to obtain than they were for the baby boom generation. The reason is largely demographic, but also a result of the changing economic system. The baby boom of the 1940s and 1950s resulted in a bulge in the population. There are many people in the workforce at the higher steps on the employment ladder, and it will be another few years before those baby boomers retire in large numbers. Given the economic downturn, potential retirees may further put off retirement, resulting in a good deal of frustration about the occupational stagnation. In fact, this frustration affected the U.S. presidential election rhetoric of 2012. It is easier—and safer—to blame others including minorities or affirmative action programs than to vent frustration at the next oldest segment of the population—one's grandparents—for having a large family or for working beyond age 65. Blacks, Hispanics, and other minorities become easy scapegoats.

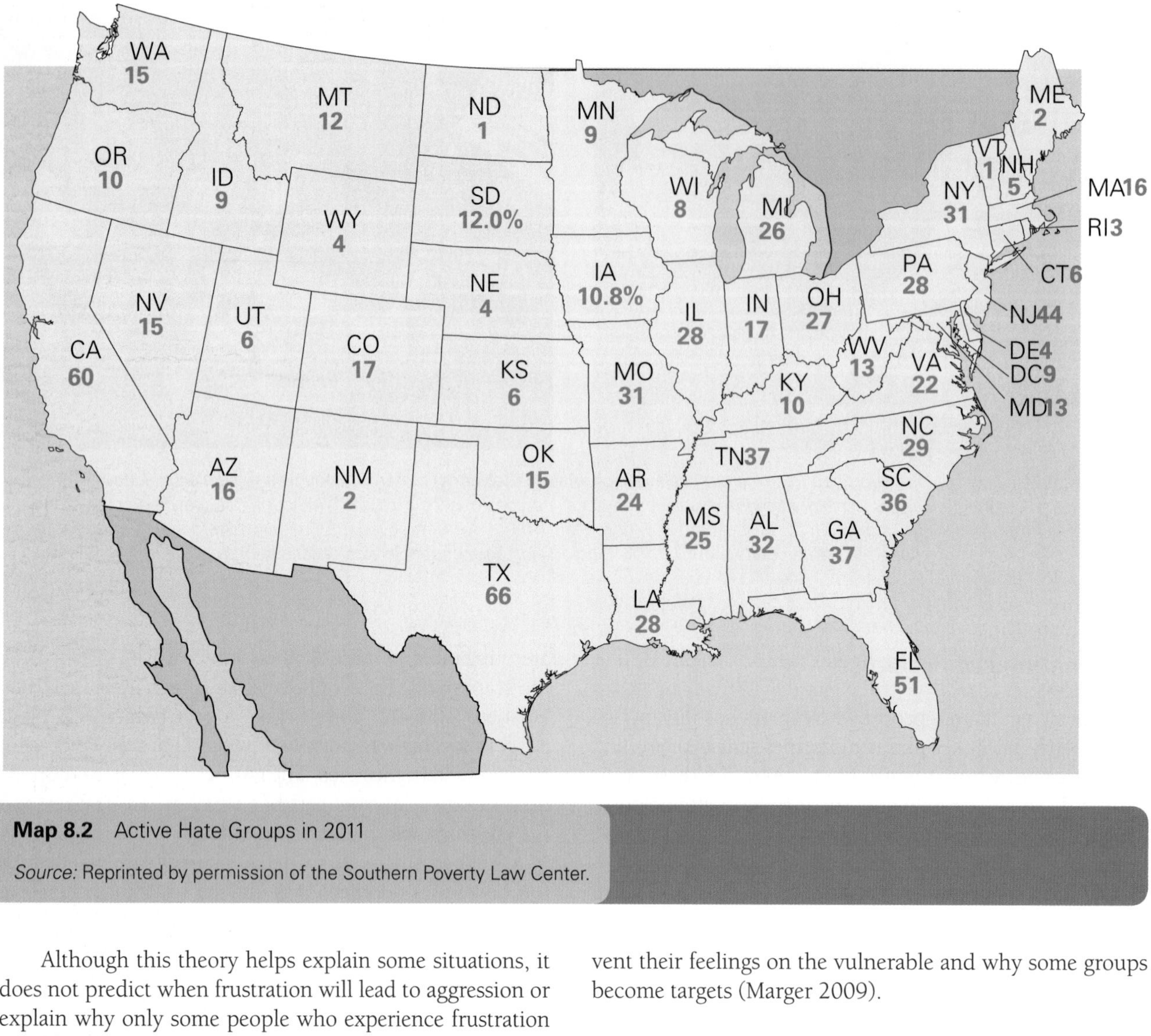

Map 8.2 Active Hate Groups in 2011

Source: Reprinted by permission of the Southern Poverty Law Center.

Although this theory helps explain some situations, it does not predict when frustration will lead to aggression or explain why only some people who experience frustration vent their feelings on the vulnerable and why some groups become targets (Marger 2009).

Klansmen in traditional white robes demonstrate in front of a courthouse in New York City in 1999. They are carrying a flag sewn together from parts of American and Confederate flags, a symbol of their blended loyalties.

Racial Bigotry and Its Forms

A bigot is someone who holds firmly and blindly to a particular idea, such as a stereotype. We see racial or ethnic bigotry at the micro level when minority group members are viewed as different and treated negatively. One form of bigotry is called *ideological bigotry*. It refers to ideas that attempt to *justify* less respectful treatment of people who are "different" by falsely portraying those ideas as science-based. It involves the belief that humans are divided into innately different groups, some of which are depicted as biologically inferior. People who hold these views see biological differences as the cause of most cultural and social differences. Remember Hitler's beliefs about the Jews and other groups? These illustrate bigotry based on ideological beliefs (Marger 2012). Hate groups in the United States, Europe, and many other countries justify themselves on the basis of ideological bigotry.

Another pattern of racial and ethnic bigotry at the micro level, called *symbolic bigotry,* is more subtle. In this case, individuals insist that they are not prejudiced or racist—that they are color-blind and committed to equality. At the same time, they oppose any social policies (such as scholarships specifically for minorities) that would reduce historically based disadvantage and make equality of opportunity possible (Farley 2010). People who display symbolic bigotry claim to reject the idea that race and racism are present but also fail to correct any problems that are created because racism is still embedded in our social system.

Symbolic bigotry allows discrimination that is hidden within the society's institutions to remain in place. Symbolic bigots reject ideological bigotry as blatant, crude, and ignorant, but fail to recognize that their actions may perpetuate inequalities at the institutional or meso level. (This will be discussed below.) Note that many people without social science training see racism as a micro-level issue—one involving *individual* bigotry—whereas most social scientists see the problem as occurring in meso-level organizations and macro-level policies or laws (Bonilla-Silva 2003).

Micro-level *racial bigotry* is found in either form discussed above and has psychological and social costs. For example, there is a waste of talent and energy, both for minorities and for those who justify and carry out discriminatory actions. In the 1990s, individual membership in white supremacy groups in Europe and North America grew, as did attacks on blacks, Jews, Muslims, immigrants, and those whose religious and cultural practices were different from those of the majority. For instance, in 2009 there were 1,211 anti-Semitic incidents in the United States involving vandalism, assaults, or threats directed at Jewish citizens or Jewish establishments (Anti-Defamation League 2010). This number increased to 1,239 in 2010 (Horn 2011). Unfortunately, until there are better economic opportunities for more people, bigotry is the likely consequence of economic competition for jobs (Farley 2010).

Although the social-psychological theories discussed above shed light on the most extreme cases of individual or small-group prejudice and racism, there is much these theories do not explain. They say little about the everyday hostility and reinforcement of prejudice that most of us experience or engage in, and they fail to deal with institutional discrimination.

A neo-Nazi protester makes a white power salute at the opening ceremony for the Holocaust Museum & Education Center in Skokie, Illinois, in 2009. The group chanted epitaphs expressing its hatred of Jews and other minority groups.

Discrimination: Meso-Level Analysis

DeBrun was a well-liked African American college student, actively involved in extracurricular activities. Like many college students, he enjoyed both alcohol consumption on weekends and the outrageous things that happened when people were inebriated. However, DeBrun's anger, normally kept in check, tended to surface when he was drunk. On one weekend some racial slurs were thrown around at a party, and when one of the perpetrators pushed DeBrun too far—including a sucker punch—DeBrun exploded in a fury of violence. No one died, but there were some serious injuries—the worst inflicted by the muscular DeBrun—and at one point a weapon was pulled. DeBrun was expelled from the university, and felony charges were leveled against him. Because there had been a weapon—one that did not belong to DeBrun but at one point ended up in his hand—the university president would not consider readmission. The local white prosecutor, who saw a powerfully built young black man who had tattoos and dreadlocks, assumed that this campus leader was a "thug" and insisted on the most severe felony charges and penalties. DeBrun, who had no previous encounters with law enforcement, ended up with a felony record and two years in prison. Because of both state and federal laws, the felony charges meant that he no longer qualified for any federal financial aid. As his family had very few resources, his hopes for a college degree were crushed. As a convicted felon, he would not be able to vote for the rest of his life, his future employment prospects were greatly diminished, and his family's hopes that he would be their first college graduate were crushed. The president of the college was not a bigot, but the professors who knew DeBrun well were convinced that neither his expulsion, nor his arrest, nor his conviction as a serious felony would have occurred had he been white.

This incident occurred during the 2011–2012 school year, so it is not ancient history. It represents a way that African Americans can experience a different United States of America than middle-class white males. The cause is not necessarily personal bigotry by people in power. **Discrimination**, *differential treatment and harmful actions against minorities,* can sometimes occur at individual and small-group levels, but is particularly problematic at the organizational and institutional levels—the meso level of analysis.

Discrimination is based on race, ethnicity, age, sex, sexual orientation, nationality, social class, religion, or whatever other category members of a society choose to make significant (Feagin and Feagin 2010).

Individual discrimination involves actions taken against a person or group by another, often because of minority group membership. It can take many forms, from avoiding contact by excluding individuals from one's club, neighborhood, or even country to physical violence against minorities, as seen in hate crime attacks on immigrant Americans, who are perceived to be taking jobs away from white Americans.

Racism is *any meso-level institutional arrangement that favors one racial group over another; this favoritism may result in intentional or unintentional consequences for minority groups* (Farley 2010). Racism is mostly embedded in institutions of society and often is supported by people who are not aware of the social consequence of their actions, as in the case of symbolic racism discussed above. So racism has nothing to do with being a nasty or mean-spirited person; it usually operates independently of racial bigotry (Bonilla-Silva 2003; Rothenberg 2011).

Racism, as sociologists use the concept, involves a normal or routine part of the way an organization operates that systemically disadvantages members of one group; the result is *institutional discrimination*. It can include intentional actions, such as laws restricting minorities, as well as unintentional actions, that have consequences restricting minorities. Institutional discrimination is built into organizations and cultural expectations in the social world. Even nonprejudiced people can participate in institutional racism quite unintentionally. For example, many schools place students in academic tracks based on standardized test results. Minority children end up disproportionately in lower tracks for a number of reasons (see Chapter 11). Thus, a policy that is meant to give all children an equal chance ends up legitimizing the channeling of many minority group students into the lower-achieving classroom groupings.

Jim Crow laws, passed in the late 1800s in the United States, and laws that barred Jews in Germany from living, working, or investing in certain places are examples of intentional discrimination embedded in organizations. By contrast, *unintentional discrimination* results from policies that have the unanticipated consequence of favoring one group and disadvantaging another. In this case there is discrimination "in fact" even if not in intent—entirely separated from personal ill will. It can be more damaging than that imposed by individuals at the micro level because it is often implemented by organizational officials who are not prejudiced and may not recognize the effects of their actions (Merton 1949). Still, those actions or policies can have sweeping consequences for minorities.

Unintentional discrimination usually occurs through one of two processes: (1) side-effect discrimination or (2) past-in-present discrimination (Feagin and Feagin 1986; Rydgren 2004). **Side-effect discrimination** refers to *practices in one institutional area that have a negative impact because they are linked to practices in another institutional area; because institutions are interdependent, discrimination in one results in unintentional discrimination in others.* Figure 8.2 illustrates this idea. Each institution uses information from the other institutions to make decisions. Thus, discrimination in the criminal justice system, which has in fact been well documented, may influence discrimination in the education or health care systems.

Consider the following examples of *side-effect discrimination*. The first is in the criminal justice and employment

Jim Crow laws in the southern states of the United States segregated many aspects of society, including which water fountain one could use.

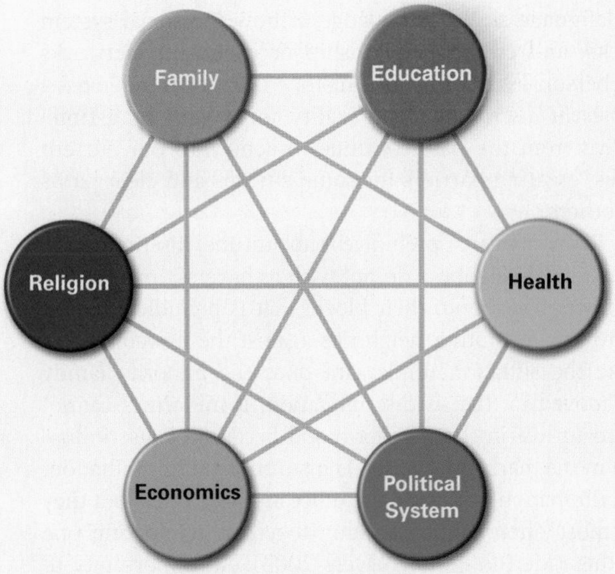

Each circle represents a different institution—family, education, religion, health, political-legal system, and economics. These meso-level systems are interdependent, using information or resources from the others. If discrimination occurs in one institution, the second institution may unintentionally borrow information or practices that results in discrimination. In this way, discrimination occurs at the meso level without awareness by individuals at the micro level.

Figure 8.2 Side-Effect Discrimination

systems. In an interview conducted by one of the authors, a probation officer in a moderate-size city in Ohio said that he had never seen an African American in his county get a not-guilty verdict and that he was not sure it was possible. He had known of cases in which minorities had pleaded guilty to a lesser charge even though they were innocent because they did not think they could receive a fair verdict in that city. When people apply for jobs, however, they are required to report the conviction on the application form. By using information about an applicant's criminal record, employers who clearly do not intend to discriminate end up doing so whether or not the individual was guilty. The side-effect discrimination is *unintentional discrimination*; the criminal justice system has reached an unjust verdict, and the potential employer is swayed unfairly.

A second example of side-effect discrimination shows that the Internet also plays a role in institutional discrimination and privilege. For example, in Alaska, 15.2% of the population is Native, but Natives hold only 5% of state jobs, and 27.3% of Native men and 16% of Native women are unemployed (AAANativeArts 2011; U.S. Census Bureau 2011a). Consider that the State of Alaska uses the Internet as its primary means of advertising and accepting applications for state jobs (State of Alaska 2006). Internet access is unavailable in the 164 predominantly Native villages in Alaska—a state so large and spread out that it is 2.2 times the size of Texas (Denali Commission 2001). Other options for application include requesting applications by mail, but a person must first know about the opening. The usefulness of this process is limited, however, by the reliability and speed of mail service to remote villages and the often short application periods for state jobs. State officials may not intentionally try to prevent Aleuts, Inupiats, Athabaskans, or other Alaska Natives from gaining access to state jobs, but the effect can be institutionalized discrimination. Here, Internet access plays a role in the participation of minorities in the social world (Nakamura 2004).

The point is that whites, especially affluent whites, benefit from privileges not available to low-income minorities. The privileged members may not purposely disadvantage others and may not be prejudiced, but the playing field is not level. The discrimination may be completely unintentional (Rothenberg 2011). Consider the following privileges that most of us who are part of the dominant group take for granted (McIntosh 2002:97–101):

> I can avoid spending time with people who mistrust people of my color.
>
> I can protect my children most of the time from people who might not like them.
>
> I can criticize our government and talk about how I fear its policies and behavior without being seen as a cultural "outsider" or not patriotic.
>
> I can easily buy posters, postcards, picture books, greeting cards, dolls, toys, and children's magazines featuring people of my race.
>
> I can arrange my activities so that I will never have to experience feelings of rejection owing to my race.

Now imagine *not* being able to take these and many other privileges for granted. What would your reaction be, and what could you do about it?

Thinking Sociologically

Imagine someone in your hometown who runs a business, and the business is hiring people. In order to make a decision about whom to hire, she uses information that has been provided by another institution or organization (say, the criminal justice system). How might some of that information be a source of unintended side-effect discrimination for a minority group member? How might the employer discriminate in hiring against a minority group person without realizing it?

Children play on the porch of their rustic home with no plumbing in the rural Alaska village of Akhiok, among the Aleutian Islands. Finding jobs through the Internet is not an option from this location.

Past-in-present discrimination refers to *practices from the past that may no longer be allowed but that continue to have consequences for people in the present* (Feagin and Feagin 1986; Verbeek and Penninx 2009).

Why do some minority groups do better than others? New immigrants to the United States from southern, central, and eastern Europe did better than African Americans, but why? Some explanations have focused on skin color and discrimination, yet Japanese and Chinese have fared well too. To address these questions, Stanley Lieberson (1980) did an extensive study and concluded that the new immigrants and blacks who were arriving in the U.S. North held similar aspirations for education and good jobs, but discrimination against blacks by employers, labor unions, realtors, and others was intense due to attitudes carried over from the slave period, a case of past-in-present discrimination. Immigrants were given better jobs and chances for mobility. Furthermore, Asians experienced less discrimination because their numbers were small and therefore less threatening, and they were viewed as less of a threat to white jobs, especially since many were in niche occupations that whites did not want. However, blacks flooded the job market in large numbers when they moved north and were marginalized as they became a threat to white jobs.

Another factor was the context of intergroup contact. Slaves and Native Americans were forced into contact with whites, whereas immigrants came voluntarily, usually for economic betterment. Voluntary immigrants perceived the economic conditions to be better because they chose to come. They started out with better economic prospects and more "cultural capital"—education, useful language skills, knowledge of how the social system works, and established kinship or friendship networks (Lieberson 1980). In short, historical patterns made *past-in-present discrimination* a reality for a very long time. Events from the past continue to echo into our current times, creating barriers for some citizens and clear paths for others.

Remember that prejudice is an attitude, discrimination an action. If neighbors do not wish to have minority group members move onto their block, that is prejudice. If they try to organize other neighbors against the newcomers or make the situation unpleasant once the minority family has moved in, that is discrimination. If minorities cannot afford to live in the neighborhood because of discrimination in the marketplace, that is institutional discrimination. Discrimination can cause prejudice and vice versa, but they are most often found working together, reinforcing one another (Merton 1949a; Myers 2003). An opportunity to clarify and to recognize interrelationships between some of these sociological terms can be explored in the next "Engaging Sociology" feature.

In the United States, things seem to have changed after 2008 when a biracial president was elected. Conservative commentators and many journalists are fond of saying that this means we entered a postracial society, that race has become irrelevant. While it is true that President Obama is the nation's first African American president, it is also true that no senator (out of 100) is black in 2012. We have also seen in Table 8.2 that college-educated African Americans earn significantly less than white college graduates. Whites with a professional degree earn about $117,787 per year, professional African Americans earn $101,376, and Hispanics with the same degree earn $82,627 (U.S. Census Bureau 2009a). In a poor economy, African Americans and other minorities continue to have higher unemployment than whites. Note also that on a typical Sunday morning, whites and blacks worship separately, with multiracial churches being rare (Emerson and Woo 2006; Marti 2005, 2009). As long as these and other differences divide the United States, it is hard to support the notion that it is a "postracial" society.

Thinking Sociologically

Think of some events in history that have an effect on particular groups today. Why might the events cause intergroup hostility or cooperation? How does discrimination, as discussed above, help us understand world conflicts, such as the intense hostility between Palestinians and Jews in Israel?

Engaging Sociology

Using Key Concepts and Relating Them to One Another

A lot of terms in this chapter have related to issues of prejudice, discrimination, and racism, and how they operate at micro and meso levels. Figure 8.3 indicates the levels at which each issue operates.

	Micro Level	Meso Level
Conscious and Intended	*Prejudice: Ideological Bigotry*	*Institutional Discrimination* (explicit)
Unconscious and Unintended	*Prejudice: Symbolic racism*	Indirect *Institutional Discrimination* *Side-effect discrimination* *Past-in-present discrimination*

Figure 8.3 Prejudice, Discrimination, and Levels of Analysis

Engaging With Sociology:

1. Define and provide an example of each term.
2. Identify which one or two cells represent "racism" as sociologists use the term.
3. Identify ways that each of these elements of intergroup conflict might foster the others.

Dominant and Minority Group Contact: Macro-Level Analysis

Economic hard times hit Germany in the 1930s, following that nation's defeat in World War I. To distract citizens from the nation's problems, a scapegoat was found—the Jewish population. The German states began restricting Jewish activities and investments. Gradually, the hate rhetoric intensified, but even then, most Jews had little idea about the fate that awaited them. Millions perished in gas chambers because the ruling Nazi party defined them as an undesirable *race* (although being Jewish is actually a religious or ethnic identification, not a biological category).

This and the following examples illustrate group contact. Consider, for instance, that Japan has a relatively homogeneous population, but the Burakumin (sometimes called the "invisible race") have been treated as outcasts in Japan. They make up 2% of the population, about 6 million people. Because their ancestors were relegated to performing work considered ritually unclean—butchering animals, tanning skins, digging graves, and handling corpses—they lived in isolated hamlets. Today, discrimination is officially against the law, but customs persist. Ostracized and kept within certain occupations and neighborhoods, the Burakumin rarely socialized with other Japanese. Today there is some intermarriage and blending into the larger society in cities, but the Burakumin remain a minority (International Humanist and Ethical Union 2009; Tofugu 2011).

One of the most horrific racial or ethnic policies was the Holocaust, the murder of 11 million people, including 6 million Jews, by the Nazi government in Germany under Adolf Hitler. This photo is horrible to view, but this is the consequence of bigotry that leads to genocide.

Mexico, Guatemala, and other Central American governments face protests by their Indian populations, descendants of the Aztecs, Maya, and Inca, who have distinguishing features and are generally relegated to servant positions. These native groups have been protesting against government policies and their poor conditions—usurping of their land, inability to own land, absentee land ownership, poor pay, and discrimination by the government (DePalma 1995). One result of discrimination against Central and South American native groups is that their numbers are diminishing and some groups, such as those in Tierra del Fuego, Chile, have died out.

These examples illustrate the contact between governments and minority groups. The Jews in Germany faced genocide; the Burakumin in Japan, segregation; and Native Americans, discrimination and forced relocation to new geographical areas. The form these relations take depends on the following:

1. Which group has more power
2. The needs of the dominant group for labor or other resources (such as land) that could be provided by the minority group, sometimes as slaves
3. The cultural norms of each group, including the level of tolerance of out-groups
4. The social histories of the groups, including their religious, political, racial, and ethnic differences
5. Physical and cultural identifiers that distinguish the groups
6. The times and circumstances (wars, economic strains, recessions)

Where power between groups in a society is unequal, the potential for differential treatment is always present. Yet some groups live in harmony whether their power is equal or not. The Pygmies of the Ituri rainforest have traded regularly with nearby local African settlements by leaving goods in an agreed-upon place in exchange for goods they need. There is often only minimal direct contact between these groups (Kitano, Aqbayani, and de Anda 2005; Kitano and Daniels 2001).

Whether totally accepting or prone to conflict, dominant-minority relations depend on the time, place, and circumstances. Figure 8.4 indicates the range of dominant-minority relationships and policies.

Genocide is *the systematic effort of one group, usually the dominant group, to destroy a minority group.* Christians were thrown to the lions in ancient Rome. Hitler sent Jews and other non-Aryan groups into concentration camps to be gassed. Iraqis used deadly chemical weapons against the Kurdish people in their own country. Members of the Serbian army massacred Bosnian civilians to rid towns of Bosnian Muslims, an action referred to as "ethnic cleansing" that is still used (Cushman and Mestrovic 1996; Evans 2010). From 1975 to 1979, 2 million Cambodians, almost 25% of the population, suffered genocide as a result of leaders instituting new political philosophies. In Rwanda, people of the Tutsi and Hutu tribes carried out mass killings against each other in the mid-1990s. In 2011, some politicians argued for intervention in the North African country of Libya because of the threat of genocide against civilians. Members of the international community intervened, but did so amid controversy. More recently, the Syrian dictator Bashir al-Assad and his military have killed many who defied his rule by demonstrating; most were Sunni Muslims, different from Assad's ruling group, the Alawites. Genocide has existed at many points in history, and it still exists today. These examples illustrate the lethal consequences of racism, one group systematically killing off another, often a minority, to gain control and power.

Subjugation refers to *the subordination of one group to another that holds power and authority.* Haiti and the Dominican Republic are two countries sharing the island of Hispaniola in the Caribbean. Because many Haitians are poor, they are lured by promises of jobs in the sugarcane fields of the Dominican Republic. However, they are forced to work long hours for little pay and are not allowed to leave until they have paid for housing and food, which may be impossible to do on their low wages.

Slavery is one form of subjugation that has existed throughout history. When the Roman Empire defeated other

Most Hostile to "Others" ⟷ **Most Accepting of "Others"**

Genocide	Subjugation	Population Transfer	Assimilation	Pluralism
Extermination of minorities	Oppression, slavery	Removal to new location	Cultural blending of groups	Groups share in legitimacy and power

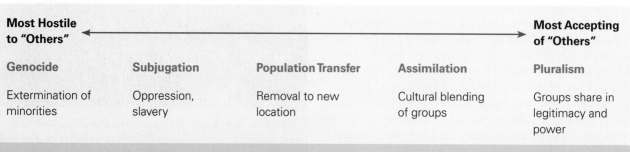

Figure 8.4 Types of Dominant-Minority Group Relations

lands, the captives became slaves. This included ancient Greeks, who also kept slaves at various times in their history. African tribes enslaved members of neighboring tribes, sometimes selling them to slave traders, and slavery has existed in Middle Eastern countries such as Saudi Arabia. As mentioned in the opening story for this chapter, slavery is flourishing in many parts of the world today (Bales 2000, 2007, 2012).

Segregation, a specific form of subjugation, keeps minorities powerless by formally separating them from the dominant group and depriving them of access to the dominant institutions. Jim Crow laws, instituted in the southern United States after the Civil War, legislated separation between groups—separate facilities, schools, and neighborhoods (Feagin and Feagin 2010; Massey and Denton 1998). Around the world, barrios, reservations, squatters' quarters, *favelas*, and even regions of a country (e.g., Tibet) are sometimes maintained by the dominant group, usually unofficially but sometimes officially, which serves to contain and isolate minorities in poor or overcrowded areas. In the United States the most vivid example was the Jim Crow segregation laws of the Deep South from about the 1890s until the 1960s (Alexander 2010).

These children in Sudan play outside their "home"—a tent at Andalus refugee camp. Some people have survived in refugee camps with almost no food and little water, but the alternative was to be killed in their homeland.

Domestic colonialism refers to exploitation of minority groups within a country (Blauner 1972; Kitano, Aqbayani, and de Anda 2005; Kitano and Daniels 2001). African Brazilians and Native Americans in the United States and Canada have been "domestically colonized groups"—managed and manipulated by members of the dominant group.

Population transfer refers to *the removal, often forced, of a minority group from a region or country.* Generally, the dominant group wants land, or resources, or political and economic power held by the minority. Due to the ongoing conflicts discussed above, an ongoing example of population transfer has been taking place in Darfur and South Sudan in Africa. Members of the population there must move from their villages or be burned out of their homes or get caught in the crossfire. Even in refugee camps women and children are subject to rape and other atrocities when they seek water or wood for fires outside of the camps. The Sudanese military forces and their subsidiaries have been forcing residents of the non-Arab parts of Sudan to leave their land; they have no place to go but refugee camps.

Other examples of *population transfers* are numerous: Native Americans in the United States were removed to reservations. The Cherokee people were forced to walk from Georgia and North Carolina to new lands west of the Mississippi—a "Trail of Tears" along which 40% of the people perished. During World War II, Japanese Americans were forcibly moved to "relocation centers" and had their land and property confiscated. Many Chinese were forced to flee from Vietnam on small boats in the 1970s. Homeless and even nationless people, they were dubbed "the boat people" by the press. In 1972, Idi Amin, dictator of Uganda, gave Asian Ugandans 36 hours to pack their bags and leave—even though it had been the homeland for many of them from birth—because they had great economic resources that he argued should belong to native Ugandans. Many Afghani people fled to Pakistan to escape oppression by the ruling Taliban and again—in 2001—to escape U.S. bombing. Today, civilians along the Pakistan-Afghanistan border still suffer displacement, and civilians from Syria are escaping the violent fighting and destruction by going to refugee camps in neighboring Turkey.

In 1988, people in horse-drawn covered wagons and on horseback reenacted the Trail of Tears, the 1,000-mile journey that the Cherokees traveled 150 years earlier.

The process by which immigrants create multinational social relations that link together their original societies with their new locations is called *transnationalism* (Basch, Schiller, and Blanc 1994). This involves people who fully participate in and have loyalty to two nations and cultures and often hold dual citizenship (Levitt 2007; Levitt and Waters 2006). An increasing number of naturalized U.S. citizens are also taxpaying members of their countries of origin, and they return often or send money to help families and neighbors with financial needs or immigration plans (Levitt 2001). Yet dual citizenship can create dilemmas of identity and sense of belonging.

Assimilation refers to *the social and cultural merging of minority and majority groups, a process by which minority members may lose most of their original identity but contribute to their new society. Interaction among racial and ethnic groups occurs in housing, schooling, employment, political circles, family groups, friendship, and social relationships* (Kitano, Aqbayani, and de Anda 2005; Kitano and Daniels 2001; Marger 2012). Assimilation is often a voluntary process in which a minority chooses to adopt the values, norms, and institutions of the dominant group.

The notion that we should be a "color blind" nation is really a call for assimilation, for the only way we cannot notice real differences between people is to obliterate the differences. This means that other people would have to give up their cultures and become like the dominant Euro American culture (Dalton 2012; Dyer 2012). It is for this reason that some minorities see assimilation policy as oppressive and an effort to destroy them.

Forced assimilation occurs when a minority group is compelled to suppress its identity. This happened in Spain around the time of World War II, when the Basque people were forbidden by the central government to speak or study the Basque language. For several centuries—ending only a few decades ago—the British government tried to stamp out the Welsh language from Wales. Assimilation is more likely to occur when the minority group is culturally similar to the dominant group. For instance, in the United States, the closer a group is to being white, English speaking, and Protestant, or what is referred to as WASP (white Anglo-Saxon Protestant), the faster its members will be assimilated into the society, adopting the culture and blending in biologically through intermarriage.

Pluralism *occurs when each ethnic or racial group in a country maintains its own culture and separate set of institutions but has recognized equity in the society.* For example, Switzerland has four dominant cultural language groups: French, German, Italian, and Romansh (or Rumantsch). These official languages are spoken in the government and taught in the schools. Laws are written in four languages. Each group respects the rights of the other groups to maintain a distinctive language and way of life. In Malaysia, three groups share power—Malays, Chinese, and Indians. Although the balance is not completely stable because Chinese and Indians hold more political and economic power than the native Malays, there is a desire to maintain a pluralistic society. While tensions do exist, both Switzerland and Malaysia represent examples of pluralist societies. Legal protection of smaller or less powerful groups is often necessary to have pluralism. In the United States, pluralism as a policy was first embraced by the nation's first president, George Washington, as explained in the next "Sociology in Our Social World."

Many individuals in the world face disruptions during their lifetimes that change their positions in society. The dominant-minority continuum illustrates the range of relations with dominant groups that can affect people's lives as transitions take place.

Thinking Sociologically

Think of examples from current news stories of positive and harmful intercultural contact. Where do your examples fit on the continuum from genocide to pluralism? What policies might address the issues raised in your examples?

The United States is becoming increasingly diverse and pluralistic. This billboard ad for McDonald's first appeared in August 2012 in St. Paul, Minnesota—an ad in the Hmong language.

Theoretical Explanations of Dominant-Minority Group Relations

Are humans innately cruel, inhumane, greedy, aggressive, territorial, or warlike? Some people think so, but the evidence is not very substantial. To understand prejudice in individuals or small groups, psychological and social-psychological theories are most relevant. To understand institutional discrimination, studying meso-level organizations is helpful, and to understand the pervasive nature

Sociology in Our Social World

Pluralism: A Long-Standing History in the United States

This Jewish synagogue, the oldest in the United States, proudly displays a letter from George Washington enshrining pluralism in the new nation's policies.

It is no mistake that the oldest Jewish synagogue in the United States is in Rhode Island, for separation of church and state and tolerance of other religious traditions was a founding principle of Rhode Island. After George Washington was elected president of the new nation, he received a letter from that early Jewish congregation in Newport, Rhode Island, asking about his policies of pluralism or multiculturalism (though those words had not been coined yet). In response in 1790, Touro Synagogue received a handwritten letter signed by President Washington (and now proudly on display at the synagogue) embracing an open and "liberal" policy to all American citizens, regardless of origins or religious affiliation. In this letter, George Washington affirmed a policy of pluralism from the very beginning of the country's existence as a nation. Passages from that letter follow.

> The Citizens of the United States of America have a right to applaud themselves for having given to mankind examples of an enlarged and liberal policy: a policy worthy of imitation. . . . It is now no more that toleration is spoken of, as if it was by the indulgence of one class of people, that another enjoyed the exercise of their inherent natural rights. For happily the Government of the United States, which gives to bigotry no sanction, to persecution no assistance, requires only that they who live under its protection should demean themselves as good citizens.
>
> . . . May the children of the Stock of Abraham, who dwell in this land, continue to merit and enjoy the good will of the other Inhabitants; while every one shall sit in safety under his own vine and fig tree, and there shall be none to make him afraid. May the father of all mercies scatter light and not darkness in our paths, and make us all in our several vocations useful here, and in his own due time and way everlastingly happy.
>
> —G. Washington

of prejudice and stereotypes over time in various societies, cultural explanations are useful. Although some aspects of macro-level theories relate to micro- and meso-level analysis, their major emphasis is on understanding the national and global systems of group relations.

Conflict Theory

In the 1840s, as the United States set out to build a railroad, large numbers of laborers immigrated from China to do the hard manual work. When the railroad was completed and competition for jobs became stiff, the once welcomed Chinese became targets of bitter prejudice, discrimination, and sometimes violence. Between 1850 and 1890, whites in California protested against Chinese, Japanese, and Chicano workers. Members of these minority groups banded together in towns or cities for protection, founding the Chinatowns we know today (Kitano, Aqbayani, and de Anda 2005; Kitano and Daniels 2001). Non-Chinese Asian groups suffered

Chinese men were invited and encouraged to come to North America to help build railroads. However, prejudice was extremely prevalent, especially once the railroads were completed and the immigrants began to settle into other jobs in the U.S. economy.

discrimination as well because the bigoted generalizations were applied to all Asians (Winders 2004).

Why does discrimination occur? Conflict theorists argue that creating a "lesser" group protects the dominant group's advantages. Because privileges and resources are usually limited, those who have them want to keep them. One strategy used by privileged people, according to conflict theory, is to perpetrate prejudice and discrimination against minority group members. A case in point is the *Gastarbeiter* (guest workers) in Germany and other western European countries, who immigrate from Eastern Europe, the Middle East, and Africa to fill positions in European economies. They are easily recognized because of cultural and physical differences and are therefore ready targets for prejudice and discrimination, especially in times of economic competition and slowing economies. This helps keep many of them in low-level positions. Today some European countries are considering laws to limit immigration, in part because of their weak economies.

Karl Marx argued that exploitation of the lower classes is built into capitalism because it benefits the ruling class. Unemployment creates a ready pool of labor to fill the marginal jobs, with the pool often made up of identifiable minority groups. This pool allows people to remain in their higher-level positions and prevents others from moving up in the stratification system and threatening their jobs.

Several theories stemming from conflict theory help explain minority relations. Two are discussed below. The first has to do with development of *hostilities between groups*, and the second involves *split labor markets*. Three critical factors contribute to animosity between groups, according to one conflict theorist (Noel 1968): First, if two groups of people can each be identified by their appearance, clothing, or language, then we-versus-they thinking and ethnocentrism may develop. However, this by itself does not mean there will be long-term hostility between the groups. Second, if the two groups conflict over scarce resources that both want, hostilities are very likely to arise. The resources might be the best land or cattle, the highest-paying jobs, access to the best schools for one's children, energy resources such as oil, or positions of prestige and power. If the third element is added to the mix—one group having much more power than the other—then intense dislike between the two groups and misrepresentation of each group by the other is fairly certain to occur.

What happens is that the group with more power uses that power to ensure that its members (and their offspring) get the most valued resources. However, because they do not want to see themselves as unfair and brutish people, they develop stereotypes and derogatory characterizations of "those other people" so that it seems reasonable and justified not to give "them" access to the valued resources. Discrimination (often at the macro level) comes first, and bigoted ideology comes later to justify the discrimination (Noel 1968). Thus, macro- and meso-level conflicts can lead to micro-level attitudes.

Split labor market theory, a branch of conflict theory, characterizes the labor market as having two main types of jobs. The primary market involves clean jobs, largely in supervisory roles, and provides high salaries and good advancement possibilities, whereas the secondary market involves undesirable, hard, and dirty work, compensated with low hourly wages and few benefits or career opportunities. Minorities, especially those from the urban underclass, are most likely to find dead-end jobs in the secondary market. For instance, when Mexicans work for little income picking crops as migrant laborers, they encounter negative stereotypes because they are poor and take jobs for low wages. Prejudice and discrimination build up against the new, cheaper workers, who threaten the next level of workers as the migrant workers seek to move up in the economic hierarchy. Thus, competition for lesser jobs pits minorities against each other and low-income whites against minorities. By encouraging division and focusing antagonism between worker groups, employers reduce threats to their dominance and get cheaper labor in the process. Workers do not organize against employers who use this dual system because they are distracted by the antagonisms that build up among themselves—hence, the *split labor market* (Bonacich 1972, 1976). This theory maintains that competition, prejudice, and ethnic animosity serve the interests of the powerful owners of capital because that atmosphere keeps the laboring classes from uniting. Note also that stereotypes are the consequence of hostility between groups—not the cause.

Conflict theory has also been used to illuminate issues of ethnic hostility on other continents, for this theory has wide application. Kichiro Iwamoto, who does sociological work on race relations issues in Africa and elsewhere, discusses the conflicts in Africa in the next "Sociology in Our Social World."

Conflict theory has taught us a great deal about racial and ethnic stratification. However, conflict theorists often focus on people with power quite intentionally oppressing others to protect their own self-interests. They depict the dominant group as made up of nasty, power-hungry people. As we have seen in the meso-level discussion of side-effect and past-in-present discrimination, privilege and disprivilege are often subtle and unconscious, which means they can continue even without ill will among those in the dominant group. Their privilege has been institutionalized. Conflict theorists sometimes miss this important point.

Sociology in Our Social World

Violence in Kenya

By Kichiro Iwamoto

In January 2008, violence gripped Kenya as rival political leaders representing different ethnic groups fought for control of the country in a contested election. Former Secretary General of the United Nations Kofi Annan said, while visiting western Kenya during the unrest, "What we saw was heart-wrenching. We saw houses burning, grandmothers and children being pushed out of their homes, and people suffering everywhere." He told the rival political leaders to resolve the political conflict as the violence was out of control in the country (UPI 2008).

At a small Assembly of God church in Kiambaa, Kenya, armed men trapped Kikuyu women, children, and elderly people inside, barricaded all the doors, and burned the building down, killing an estimated 50 people. The attackers were reported to be members of a rival tribe, the Kalenjin (Gettleman 2008). The scientific eye of sociology can identify the key variables in this complex, tragic event.

Political conflicts over power can incite age-old rivalries and erupt into genocide, systematic killing of "others." These ethnic differences between the tribal groups in Kenya generated prejudice and negative contact, with the Kalenjin and Kikuyu attacking each other. Tribalism leads to discrimination against other tribes that are viewed as economic and power rivals, "different," and often inferior, and then resentments result in reprisals. The violence is perpetuated in a vicious cycle of "we" versus "they" animosity.

What are some meso- and macro-level sociological factors that could be contributing to this massacre? As in most ethnic conflicts, economic and political factors contribute to a violent racial or ethnic event. In Kenya, the mob violence and social chaos may have been advantageous for those in high political positions as the "reign of terror" kept frightened people from protesting the controversial national election of December 2007. "President Mwai Kibaki's electoral victory, seen by the opposition as fraudulent, triggered days of ugly tribal violence," one report said (*Los Angeles Times* 2008). The tribal violence kept the population fragmented, weakening any opposition and challenge to the current political structure. The situation was also exacerbated by roads that are too dangerous to use so that help could not reach villages, tremendous food scarcity in many parts of the country, and many citizens struggling for survival rather than focusing on immediate political justice.

Some argue that the roots of these (Kenyan) conflicts are not tribal. "A *tribe* in Africa is a particular (social) identity construction created by colonial powers in an effort to more easily dominate the population. Ethnicity is a group of people who share a common identity, rituals, and most commonly, language. There are ethnic differences in Kenya, however constructed, but they are commonly trumped by kinship, class, labor, religion and even geographic identities" (Marcus 2008). Still, it is clear that the horrific violence is rooted in conflicts over scarce resources and defense of the self-interests of one group against another.

* * * * * * * *

Kichiro Iwamoto has taught for many years in the sociology/anthropology department at Santa Clara University in California's Silicon Valley.

Structural-Functional Theory

From the structural-functional perspective, maintaining a cheap pool of laborers who are in and out of work serves several purposes for society. Low-paying and undesirable jobs for which no special training is needed—busboys, janitors, nurse's aides, street sweepers, and fast-food service workers—are often filled by minority group members of societies, including immigrant populations seeking to improve their opportunities.

Not only does this cheap pool of labor function to provide a ready labor force for dirty work or menial unskilled jobs, these individuals also serve other functions for society. They make possible occupations that service the poor, such as social work, public health, criminology, and the justice and legal systems. They buy goods others do not want—day-old bread, old fruits and vegetables, secondhand clothes. They set examples for others of what not to be, and they allow others to feel good about giving to charity (Gans 1971, 1994).

Thomas Sowell (1994) contends that circumstances of the historical period and the situation into which one is born create the major differences in the social status of minority groups. He believes that minority individuals must work hard to make up for their disadvantages. His contentions are controversial in part because of the implication that institutional discrimination can be overcome by hard work. Conflict theorists counter his argument by saying that discrimination that reduces opportunities is built into institutions and organizations and must be dealt with through meso- and macro-level structural change. They argue that hard work is necessary but not sufficient for minorities to succeed.

Indian women (originally from the state of Rajasthan) inspect red chili peppers and other spices, a niche market to make a living in the United States and Canada.

Prejudice, discrimination, and institutional racism are dysfunctional for society, resulting in loss of human resources, costs to societies due to poverty and crime, hostilities between groups, and disrespect for those in power (Schaefer 2012).

Thinking Sociologically

What are some micro-, meso-, and macro-level factors that enhance the chances that minority persons can move up the social ladder to better jobs?

The Effects of Prejudice and Discrimination

Pictures of starving orphans from Sudan and Niger, and broken families from war-torn Bosnia and Syria, remind us of the human toll resulting from prejudice and discrimination. This section discusses the results of prejudice, racism, and discrimination for minority groups and for societies.

The Costs of Racism

Individual victims of racism suffer from the destruction of their lives, health, and property, especially in societies where racism leads to poverty, enslavement, conflict, or war. Poor self-concept and low self-esteem result from constant reminders of a devalued status in society.

Prejudice and discrimination result in costs to organizations and communities as well as to individuals. First, organizations and communities lose the talents of individuals who could be productive and contributing members. Because of poor education, substandard housing, and inferior medical care, these citizens cannot use their full potential to contribute to society. In 2010, 50.7 million or 16.7% of U.S. citizens did not have health insurance (Wolf 2010). The number of uninsured children is approximately 8 million and growing, or 10.4% of children in the United States (Children's Defense Fund 2011). Yet the U.S. health expenditures consume 17.6% of the country's gross domestic product (GDP), the highest expenditure in the world (U.S. Department of Health and Human Services 2011). The inequities in health care coverage are striking: 11.6% of whites (1 in 6) are without care, but the figure is 19.9% (1 in 5) for African Americans and 41.5% (more than 1 in 3) for Hispanics (Newport and Mendes 2009).

Second, government subsidies cost millions in the form of welfare, food stamps, and imprisonment, but they are made necessary in part by the lack of opportunities for minority individuals. Representation of ethnic groups in the U.S. political system can provide a voice for their concerns. Table 8.4 shows the representation of ethnic groups in Congress, but even this understates the lack of representation. In the entire history of the United States, the number of senators from minority ethnic groups is extremely small: African American: 6; Asian American: 5; Hispanic American: 6; Native American: 3 (U.S. Senate 2011).

Thinking Sociologically

How might lack of access to health care and insurance affect other aspects of a person's life (work, family life, education)?

Continued attempts to justify discrimination by stereotyping and labeling groups have cultural costs, too. There are many talented African American athletes who are stars on college and professional sports teams, but very few of them have been able to break into the ranks of coaches and managers (Eitzen and Sage 2003; Sage 2005). That said, there has been more opportunity in basketball than in other sports, where 14 of 30 National Basketball Association head coaches are black in a sport with 80% black players (Mahoney 2012). The number of African American and Mexican American actors and artists has increased, but the number of minority playwrights and screenwriters who can get their works produced or who have become directors remains limited.

Table 8.4 Representation in the U.S. Congress, 2011

	Native American	*Asian*	*Black*	*Hispanic*
Senate	0	1 (1%)	0	2 (2%)
House	1 (0.2%)	9 (2%)	44 (10%)	29 (6.7%)
% of Population	0.9%	4.8%	12.6%	16.3%

Source: Ethnic Majority 2010; Manning 2011.

Sudanese children wait in line to receive food in the Sudanese refugee camp of Narus. World Hunger reports 7.6 million childhood deaths in 2010 from malnutrition. That includes 1 in 8 children in sub-Saharan Africa and South Asia (World Hunger 2011).

African American musicians have found it much more difficult to earn royalties and therefore cannot compose full-time (Alexander 2003). Because these artists must create and perform their art "as a sideline," they are less able to contribute their talents to society. The rest of us in society are poorer for it.

Minority Reactions to Prejudice, Discrimination, and Racism

How have minority groups dealt with their status? Five different reactions are common: assimilation, acceptance, avoidance, aggression, and change-oriented actions directed at the social structure. The first four are micro-level responses; they do not address the meso- and macro-level issues.

Micro-Level Coping Strategies

Assimilation is an accommodation to prejudice and discrimination. Some minority group members attempt to *pass* or assimilate as members of the dominant group so as to avoid bigotry and discrimination. Although this option is not open to many because of their distinguishing physical characteristics, this strategy usually involves abandoning their own culture and turning their back on family roots and ties, a costly strategy in terms of self-esteem and sense of identity. People who select this coping strategy are forced to deny who they are as defined by their roots and to live their lives in constant anxiety, feeling as though they must hide something about themselves.

In the 1960s, popular items advertised in African American magazines included "whitening creams" or "skin bleaches." Some light-colored people with African ancestry would bleach their skin to pass as white. Skin-whitening creams can be found today on pharmacy shelves in many countries. Dissatisfaction with one's body can have an impact on one's self-concept. These creams are still popular in some Asian countries.

Passing—pretending to be a member of the privileged group when one is not fully a part of that community—also has been a common response of gays and lesbians who are afraid to come out. Homosexuals experience the costly impact on self-esteem and the constant fear that they may be discovered. Likewise, assimilated Jews have changed their religion and their names to be accepted. Despite the wrenching from their personal history, passing has allowed some individuals to become absorbed into the mainstream and to lose the stigma of being defined as a minority. To these people, this acceptance by the dominant group is worth the high cost.

Acceptance is another common reaction to minority status. Some minority groups have learned to live with their minority status with little overt challenge to the system. They may or may not hold deep-seated hostility, but they ultimately conclude that change in the society is not very likely, and acceptance may be the rational means to survive within the existing system.

There are many possible explanations for this seeming indifference. For example, religious beliefs allow poor Hindus in India to believe that if they accept their lot in life, they will be reincarnated in a higher life-form. If they rebel, they can expect to be reincarnated into a lower life-form. Their religion is a form of social control.

Unfortunately, many children are socialized to believe that they are inferior or superior because minority group members are expected by the dominant group to behave in certain ways and often live up to that expectation because of the self-fulfilling prophecy (Farley 2010). Evidence to support stereotypes is easily found in individual cases—"inferior" kids live in shabby houses, dress less well, speak a different dialect. At school and on the job, minority position is reaffirmed by these characteristics.

Avoidance means shunning all contact with the dominant group. This can involve an active and organized attempt to leave the culture or live separately as some political exiles have done. In the United States, Marcus Garvey organized a Back-to-Africa movement in the 1920s, encouraging blacks to give up on any hope of justice in American society and to return to Africa. Native Americans continually moved west in the 19th century—trying to or being forced to get away from the white Anglo settlers, who brought alcohol and deadly diseases. In some cases, withdrawal may mean dropping out of society as an individual—escaping by obliterating consciousness in drugs or alcohol. The escape from oppression and low self-concept is one reason why drug use is higher in minority ghettos and alcohol abuse is rampant on Native American reservations.

Avoidance that is not so destructive—more withdrawal and isolation—is also used by the Roma (sometimes called Gypsies—of which there are about a million in the United States) and by Native American groups that seek to preserve their cultures. Among some groups of isolated Apaches in New Mexico and Arizona, nearly half of the older population speaks no English and has no need or desire to learn it. They live according to old cultural ways in rather isolated desert climates. They have simply withdrawn from contact with the larger society (Farrer 2011).

Aggression resulting from anger and resentment over minority status and from subjugation may lead to retaliation or violence. Because the dominant group holds significant power, a direct route such as voting against the dominant group or defeating oppressors in war is not always possible. Indeed, direct confrontation can be very costly to those lacking political or economic power. Suicide bombers from Palestine, Iraq, and Afghanistan represent the many disaffected youth who are frustrated and angry over their situations, with no means to fight back, express their anger, or bring about change.

Aggression usually takes one of two forms, indirect aggression or displaced aggression. Indirect aggression includes biting assertiveness in the arts—literature, art, racial and ethnic humor, and music—and in job-related actions such as inefficiency and slowdowns by workers. Displaced aggression, on the other hand, involves hostilities directed toward individuals or groups other than the dominant group, as happens when youth gangs attack other ethnic gangs in nearby neighborhoods. They substitute aggression against the dominant group by acting against the other minority groups to protest against their frustrating circumstances and limited resources.

The four responses discussed thus far address the angst and humiliation that individual minorities feel. Each strategy allows an individual person to try to cope, but none addresses the structural causes of discrimination. The final strategy is *change-oriented action*. Minority groups in some countries embrace violent tactics as a means to bring about change—riots, insurrections, hijackings, and terrorist bombings aimed at the dominant group. Their hope is either to destroy the dominant power structure or to threaten the stability of the current macro-level system such that the group in power is willing to make some changes. Sometimes, minority reactions result in assimilation, but often, the goal is to create a pluralistic society in which cultures can be different yet have economic opportunities open to all. Minority groups pursue social change in the meso- and macro-level structures of society as discussed below.

Nonviolent Resistance: Institutional and Societal Policy for Change

Another technique for bringing about change at the meso and macro levels is nonviolent resistance by minority groups. The model for this technique comes from India, where, in the 1950s, Mahatma Gandhi led the struggle for independence from Britain. Although Britain clearly had superior weapons and armies, boycotts, sit-ins, and other forms of resistance eventually led to British withdrawal as the ruling colonial power. This strategy has been used successfully by workers and students to bring about change in many parts of the world.

In the United States, Martin Luther King Jr. followed in the nonviolent resistance tradition of India's Gandhi, who sought to change India's laws so that minorities could have equal opportunities within the society. King's strategy involved nonviolent popular protests, economic boycotts, and challenges to the current norms of the society. The National Association for the Advancement of Colored People (NAACP) sought to bring about legal changes through lawsuits that created new legal precedents supporting racial equality. Often, these lawsuits addressed side-effect discrimination—a meso-level problem. Many other associations for minorities—including the Anti-Defamation League (founded by Jews) and La Raza Unida (a Chicano organization)—also seek to address problems both within organizations and institutions (meso level) and in the nation as a whole (macro level). Like King, who had an undergraduate degree in sociology, many sociologists have used their training to address issues of discrimination and disprivilege through empowerment and change.

Mahatma Gandhi, leader of the Indian civil disobedience revolt, marched to the shore to collect salt, a clear violation of the law that he felt was inhumane and unjust. On the right is a woman lieutenant in his nonviolent resistance movement.

Some other minority individuals have used their sociology degrees in business, both to enhance their own competence in the business world and to help their ethnic communities. One example is the work of David Staddon, who writes about his applications of sociology in consulting, administration, and business. See the next "Sociologists in Action" on page 290.

The Occupy Wall Street movement (sometimes called "We Are the 99%") began on September 17, 2011, and has spread from New York to many cities around the world. The 99% minority (called a minority since they have less power and fewer resources than the top 1%) has protested against the lack of resource distribution in the United States, setting up encampments in city parks and marching against what they feel is inequity in the job and tax structure. One policy these individuals support is the "Robin Hood tax" on the financial sector that would affect mostly the rich who engage in massive transfer of funds. The profits would be used to address needs such as poor schools, climate change, and other issues facing the 99% (Robin Hood Tax 2012). Another policy the group supports is the Buffett Rule—named after investor and multibillionaire Warren Buffett who is one of the two wealthiest people in North America. He has proposed that a tax increase is needed for the society, only to be applied to those who earn more than $1 million in a given year. He came to this conclusion when he realized that he paid a lower tax than his secretary. The Occupy movement has latched on to his policy and advocates it.

On the opposite side of the political spectrum is the Tea Party Patriots, which focuses largely on smaller government and decreases in taxes for all—including the rich—because they feel that (1) this will stimulate the economy more and result in growth, and (2) they seek freedom for individuals to spend their resources however they please. So movements on both sides can use similar strategies to try to influence the direction of the society's policies (Tea Party Patriots 2012). Nonviolent resistance movements such as these illustrate efforts to bring about change.

Sociologists in Action—David Staddon

Native American Cultures and Applied Sociology

I have had several positions in Indian Country, beginning with the YMCA of Michigan's Native American Outreach Program. The program worked with every tribe in Michigan and included urban youth leadership development, family enhancement, and the preservation of traditional cultural values and behaviors. I left that position to attend graduate school at Central Michigan University where I eventually became director of the Native American Programs office. Since then I have worked with a number of indigenous nations, including the Saginaw Chippewa in Michigan and the Northern Arapaho in Wyoming. A person with sociological/intercultural skills can have a distinct advantage in the marketplace, especially considering the changing demographics in the United States. This is especially true where there are cultural intersections involved, and I experienced many of those working with Native nations.

One of the first challenges (of many) that I needed to overcome was the fact that 98% of all our casino customers in Wyoming were tribal members. That really did not help the Arapaho people since we were simply churning money through the local economy. We needed to diversify our customer base and bring in "outside" money. Many organizations currently talk about "reengineering their corporate culture" to be more friendly and accessible to minority groups. I was faced with the interesting challenge of creating an atmosphere where *non-Indians* felt safe, secure, and comfortable in our gaming environment, rather like "reverse engineering."

The situation was further complicated by the fact that I am from a different tribe than the Arapahos. Most people (including sociologists) have scant understanding of the intercultural differences between Indian tribes—an important factor in having a successful career in Indian Country. So I had to learn to deal with intersections between Arapaho-Ottawa-Mainstream-Male/female-Corporate values, outlooks, and behaviors. My challenge was to build a corporate culture that took all these factors into consideration and led to financial success of the business. So some of my first priorities were in image development and customer service.

Having spoken with many white folks in Riverton, I came away with the distinct view that many (if not all) of them felt that the casino was an unsafe place. I was told, "If I win money, I'll just get knocked in the head in the parking lot." We had to do many things to change the image, including designing a new logo for the casino and providing snazzy uniforms for all the staff. The logo was on everything, so we could unify the corporate image. I instituted customer service training and standards for interaction with customers, installed more lights in the parking lot, and started an escort service (not *that* kind!) where, upon request, our security staff would escort customers to their cars in the parking lot. I also took pictures of our security staff and developed some advertising materials emphasizing friendliness, safety, and security. I got active with the local chamber of commerce, establishing relationships with local business and opinion leaders.

By the time I left, we had experienced a complete turnaround with the business—both from a financial standpoint and from the standpoint of our customer base. Our customer base is now over 90% non-Native, and we were bringing millions of dollars into the local native community. Prior to this, the casino had only had 2 years of profitability out of 12 years in business.

A lot of other peripheral efforts went into developing the organization and improving its image. In short, we worked with "image-management" ideas from Goffman ([1959] 2001) and notions of how people define a situation—a central idea in symbolic interactionism. I was doing applied sociology to help this business venture work—a business venture that also helped a minority community.

My background in social sciences was vital in melding the cultural considerations that contributed to an organizational culture conducive to employee creativity, success, and enjoyment. My training and education in social science has had direct relevance for my various jobs. One interesting aspect of applied social science in business is the examination of corporate culture and its relationship to behavior, public image, policies, planning, and other organizational behavior. A liberal arts education is becoming increasingly important in the U.S. workplace, especially one that emphasizes cross-cultural understanding. For me, coupling this knowledge with my business skills was the key to success.

* * * * * * * * * *

David Staddon is a member of the Wikwemikong Band of Ottawa Indians, located on Manitoulin Island, Lake Huron, Georgian Bay, Southern Ontario. David has been working with "First Nation" governments most of his working life. With a bachelor's degree in sociology/social science and a master's in administration, he is well prepared to deal with Native issues. He now works with the St. Regis Mohawk Tribe near Massena, New York, as its director of public information.

Sometimes minority reactions result in assimilation, but often, the goal is to create a pluralistic society in which cultures can be different yet have economic opportunities open to all. This is the focus of many meso and macro level change movements.

Thinking Sociologically

The preceding discussion presents five types of responses by minorities to the experience of discrimination and rejection. Four of these are at the micro level, and one is at the meso and macro levels. Why do you suppose most of the coping strategies of minorities are at the micro level?

Policies Governing Minority and Dominant Group Relations

The dominant ethnic group in northern Sudan is Arabs—led by President Omar al-Bashir and his armies. In South Sudan, a new country, the citizens are dark-skinned Africans who have a very different culture. Until a tenuous peace was brokered by the United Nations, the southern Sudanese people were tortured and killed and their villages burned by the more powerful northern Sudanese. Two issues at stake are (1) cultural and ethnic differences and (2) oil reserves. Conflict over oil, which is located mostly near the border between the two countries, has made the peace plan and new country of South Sudan tenuous. While the hope was that the new border would separate warring factions, skirmishes continue to threaten the tenuous peace. In this case macro-level policies from the United Nations and world powers intervened to stop the atrocities, but this has not eliminated the meso-level causes of conflict—cultural differences and resources such as land and oil. Remember that conflict over resources is usually the cause of animosity between groups.

In the 1990s, residents fled from Albania, Bosnia, Cuba, Haiti, Rwanda, Zaire, and other nations to seek refuge from hostilities between groups. These conflicts are complex and represent different ethnic and religious groups fighting for power, land, and resources. For our purposes, the important point is that the refugees come from minority groups in the country, civilians caught in a conflict they cannot control.

War, famine, and economic dislocation force families to seek new locations where they can survive and perhaps improve their circumstances. About 17 countries have policies to host or accept refugees from war-torn countries as new citizens. Refugees who cannot return home may end up in a new country, perhaps on a new continent.

The degree of acceptance children and their families find in their newly adopted countries varies depending on the government's policies, the group's background, economic conditions in the host country, and whether the refugee group poses a threat to residents (Rumbaut and Portes 2001). Some formerly refugee-friendly countries are closing their doors to immigration because of the strain on their economy and threats of terrorism. In this section, we consider the policies that emerge as dominant and minority groups come into contact and interact.

Policies to Reduce Prejudice, Racism, and Discrimination

In the preceding pages, we considered some of the costs to individuals, groups, societies, and the global community inflicted by discriminatory behavior and policies. Discrimination's influence is widespread, from slavery and subjugation to unequal education and work opportunities, to legal and political arenas, and to every other part of the social world. If one accepts the premise that discrimination is destructive to both individuals and societies, then ways must be found to address the root problems effectively. However, finding solutions to ethnic tensions around the world leaves many experts baffled. Consider the ethnic strife in Bosnia and Croatia in Eastern Europe; conflicts between Palestinians and Israelis in the Middle East; conflicts between Shiites and Sunni Muslims in Iraq; tribal genocide in Kenya, Sudan, and Rwanda in Africa; and conflicts between religious groups in Northern Ireland. In places such as these, each new generation is socialized into the prejudice and antagonisms that perpetuate the animosity and violence. Social scientists and policy makers have made little progress in resolving conflicts that rest on century-old hostilities.

From our social world perspective, we know that no problem can be solved by working at only one level of analysis. A successful strategy must bring about change at every level of the social world—individual attitudes, organizational discrimination, cultural stereotypes, societal stratification systems, and national and international

There has been a great deal of controversy about the barbed and razor wire fence along the U.S. border with Mexico. Some people feel it is the only way to enforce immigration laws and to control the growth rate of the country. Others think that walls of this sort foster we-they thinking, are a waste of money, and do not lead to permanent solutions. Many Mexican Americans think such a wall is insulting to Mexican American people. Do you think such a wall is a step in the right direction or not, and why?

structures. However, most current strategies focus on only one level of analysis. Figure 8.5 shows some of the programs enacted to combat prejudice, racism, and discrimination at the individual, group, societal, and global levels.

Individual or Small-Group Solutions

Programs to address prejudice and stereotypes through human relations workshops, group encounters, and therapy can achieve goals with small numbers of people. For instance, African American and white children who are placed in interracial classrooms in schools are more likely to develop close interracial friendships (Ellison and Powers 1994). Also, the higher the people's education level, the more likely they are to respect and like others and to appreciate and enjoy differences. Education gives a broader, more universal outlook; reduces misconceptions and prejudices; shows that many issues do not have clear answers; encourages multicultural understanding; and focuses on individuals, not judging of groups.

Two groups with strong multicultural education programs are the Anti-Defamation League and the Southern Poverty Law Center's Teaching Tolerance program. Both groups provide schools and community organizations with literature, videos, and other materials aimed at combating intolerance and discrimination toward others.

However, these strategies do not address the social conditions underlying the problems because they reach only a few people. Thus, this approach alone achieves only limited results. It also does not begin to address dilemmas that are rooted in meso- and macro-level discrimination. Micro-level solutions are often blind to the structural causes of problems.

Group Contact

Many social scientists advocate organized group contact between dominant and minority group members to improve relations and break down stereotypes and fears. Although not all contact reduces prejudice, many studies have shown the benefits of structured contact. Some essential conditions for success are equal status of the participants, noncompetitive and nonthreatening contact, and projects or goals on which to cooperate (Farley 2010).

In a classic study of group contact, social psychologists Muzafer Sherif and Carolyn Sherif (1953) and their colleagues ran summer camps for boys of ages 11 and 12 and studied how groups were established and reestablished. On arrival, the boys were divided into two groups that

Types of Problems at Each Level	Types of Solutions or Programs at Each Level
Individual level: stereotypes and prejudice	Therapy, tolerance-education programs
Group level: negative group interaction	Positive contact, awareness by majority of their many privileges
Societal level: institutional discrimination	Education, media, legal-system revisions
Global level: deprivation of human rights	Human rights movements, international political pressures

Figure 8.5 Problems and Solutions

competed periodically. The more fierce the competition, the more hostile the two cabins of boys became toward each other. The experimenters tried several methods to resolve the conflicts and tensions:

1. *Appealing to higher values (be nice to your neighbors):* This proved of limited value.
2. *Talking with the natural leaders of the groups (compromises between group leaders):* The group leaders agreed, but their followers did not go along.
3. *Bringing the groups together in a pleasant situation (a mutually rewarding situation):* This did not reduce competition; if anything, it increased it.
4. *Introducing a superordinate goal that could be achieved only if everyone cooperated:* This technique worked. The boys were presented with a dilemma: The water system had broken, or a fire needed to be put out, and all were needed to solve the problem. The groups not only worked together, but their established stereotypes eventually began to fade away. Such a situation in a community might arise from efforts to get a candidate elected, a bill passed, or a neighborhood improved. At the global macro level, hostile countries sit together to solve issues.

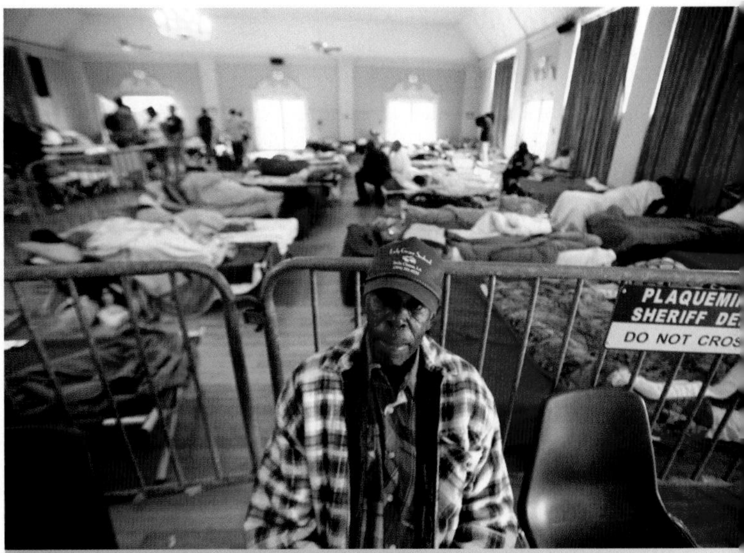

This Louisianan waits at a shelter as Hurricane Isaac bears down on the Louisiana coast in the summer of 2012. Minorities are more often living in vulnerable areas and therefore more often victimized. The solution proposed by some nongovernmental organizations (NGOs) is to address problems and suffering with volunteer work and donations. Others think the government should have a major role.

Programs involving group contact to improve conditions for minorities have been tried in many areas of social life, including integrated housing projects, job programs to promote minority hiring, and busing children to schools, to achieve a higher level of racial and socioeconomic integration. For instance, the Chicago Housing Authority opened a refurbished mixed-income housing experiment with resident participation in decision making. Although many predicted failure, the project thrived, with long waiting lists of families wanting to participate (McCormick 1992).

Positive group contact experiences can be effective in improving relations in groups at a micro level by breaking down stereotypes, but negative or ineffective group contact may also affect "the many cognitive, affective, situational and institutional barriers to positive contact" (Pettigrew and Tropp 2000:93). To solidify the positive gains, we must also address institutionalized inequalities, discussed below.

Institutional and Societal Strategies to Improve Group Relations

Sociologists contend that institutional and societal approaches to reduce discrimination get closer to the core of the problems and affect larger numbers of people than do micro-level strategies. For instance, voluntary advocacy organizations pursue political change through lobbying, watchdog monitoring, educational information dissemination, canvassing, protest marches, rallies, and boycotts (Minkoff 1995). Groups such as the NAACP and ACLU have filed lawsuits and lobbied legislators for changes in laws that they believed were discriminatory.

The Civil Rights Commission, Fair Employment Practices Commission, and Equal Employment Opportunity Commission are government organizations that protect rights and work toward equality for all citizens. These agencies oversee practices and hear complaints relating to racial, sexual, age, and other forms of discrimination. Legislation, too, can modify behaviors. Laws requiring equal treatment of minorities have resulted in increased tolerance of those who are "different" and have opened doors that previously were closed to minorities.

In the United States, executive action to end discrimination has been taken by a number of presidents. In 1948, Harry Truman moved to successfully end military segregation, and subsequent presidents have urged the passage of civil rights legislation and equal employment opportunity legislation. Affirmative action laws, first implemented during Lyndon Johnson's administration, have been used to fight pervasive institutional racism (Crosby 2004; Farley 2010).

Affirmative Action

One of the most contentious policies in the United States has been affirmative action. The following discussion addresses the goals and forms of the policy. As a societal policy for change, affirmative action actually involves three different policies:

Strict affirmative action, its simplest and original form, involves taking affirmative or positive steps to make sure that unintentional discrimination does not occur. It requires, for example, that an employer who receives federal monies must advertise a position widely and not just through internal or friendship networks. If the job requires an employee with a college education, then by federal law, employers must recruit through minority and women's colleges as well as state and private colleges in the region. If employers are hiring in the suburbs, they are obliged to contact unemployment agencies in poor and minority communities as well as those in the affluent neighborhoods. After taking these required extra steps, employers are expected to hire the most qualified candidate who applies, regardless of race, ethnicity, sex, religion, or other external characteristics. The focus is on providing opportunities for the best-qualified people. For many people, this is the meaning of affirmative action, and it is inconceivable that this could be characterized as reverse discrimination, for members of the dominant group will be hired if they are in fact the most qualified. These policies do not overcome the problem that qualified people who have been marginalized may be competent but do not have the traditional paper credentials that document their qualifications (Gallagher 2004).

A *quota system*, the second policy, is a requirement that employers *must* hire a certain percentage of minorities. For the most part, quotas are now unconstitutional. They apply only in cases where a court has found a company to have a substantial and sustained history of discrimination against minorities and where the employment position does not have many requirements (if the job entails sweeping floors and cleaning toilets, there would not be an expectation of a specific academic degree or a particular grade point average).

Preference policies are the third form, the one that has created the most controversy among opponents of corrective action. Preference policies are based on the concept of equity, the belief that sometimes people must be treated differently in order to treat them fairly. This policy was enacted to level the playing field, which was not rewarding highly competent people because of institutional racism.

The objectives of preference policies are to (a) eliminate qualifications that are not substantially related to the job but that unwittingly favor members of the dominant group and (b) foster achievement of objectives of the organization that are only possible through enhanced diversity. To overcome these inequalities and achieve certain objectives, employers and educational institutions take account of race or sex by making special efforts to hire and retain workers or accept students from groups that have been underrepresented. In many cases, these individuals bring qualifications others do not possess. Consider the following examples.

A goal of the medical community is to provide access to medical care for underserved populations. There is an extreme shortage of physicians on the Navajo reservation. Thus, a Navajo applicant for medical school might be accepted, even if her scores are slightly lower than those of another candidate's, because she speaks Navajo and understands the culture. One could argue that she is more qualified to be a physician on the reservation than someone who knows nothing about Navajo society but has a slightly higher grade point average or test score. Some argue that tests should not be the only measure to determine the merit of applicants.

Likewise, an African American police officer may have more credibility in a minority neighborhood and may be able to defuse a delicate conflict more effectively than a white officer who scored slightly higher on a paper-and-pencil placement test. Sometimes, being a member of a particular ethnic group can actually make one more qualified for a position.

A 1996 proposition in California to eliminate affirmative action programs in the state was passed in a statewide referendum. The result was that colleges in California are not allowed to offer preference to applicants based on race, but can give preference on the basis of state residency, athletic competency, musical skill, having had a parent graduate from the school, and many other factors. Many colleges and universities admit students because they need an outstanding point guard on the basketball team, an extraordinary soprano for the college choir, or a student from a distant state for geographic diversity. These students are shown preference by being admitted with lower test scores than some other applicants because they are "differently qualified." Many colleges also give preference to male students to achieve gender balance, even if more qualified females apply. The controversy about whether minority students should be given preference follows this same reasoning. Consider the following example.

A landmark case filed in a Detroit district court in 1997 alleged that the University of Michigan gave unlawful preference to minorities in undergraduate admissions and in law school admissions. In this controversial case, the court ruled that these undergraduate admissions were discriminatory because numbers rather than individualized judgments were used to make the admission determination (University of Michigan Documents Center 2003). Consider the next "Engaging Sociology" feature and decide whether you think the policy was fair and whether only race and ethnicity should have been deleted from the preferences allowed.

Engaging Sociology

Preference Policies at the University of Michigan

To enhance diversity on the campus—a practice that many argue makes a university a better learning environment and enhances the academic reputation of the school—many colleges have preference policies in admissions. However, the University of Michigan was sued by applicants who felt they were not admitted because others replaced them on the roster due to their racial or ethnic background.

The University of Michigan is a huge university where a numbering system is needed to handle the volume (tens of thousands) of applicants; the admissions staff cannot make a decision based on personal knowledge of each candidate. Thus, they give points for each quality they deem desirable in the student body. A maximum of 150 points is possible, and a score of 100 would pretty much ensure admission. The university feels that any combination of points accumulated according to the following formula will result in a highly qualified and diverse student body.

For academics, up to 110 points are possible:

- 80 points for grades (a particular grade point average in high school results in a set number of points; a 4.0 results in 80 points; a 2.8 results in 56 points)
- 12 points for standardized test scores (ACT or SAT)
- 10 points for the academic rigor of high school (so all students who go to tougher high schools earn points)
- 8 points for the difficulty of the curriculum (e.g., points for honors curriculum vs. keyboarding courses)

For especially desired qualities, including diversity, up to 40 points are possible for any combination of the following (but no more than 40 in this "desired qualities" category):

- Geographical distribution (10 for Michigan resident; an additional 6 for underrepresented Michigan county)
- Legacy—a relative has attended Michigan (4 points for a parent; 1 point for a grandparent or sibling)
- Quality of submitted essay (3 points)
- Personal achievement—a special accomplishment that was noteworthy (up to 5 points)
- Leadership and service (5 points each)
- Miscellaneous (only one of these can be used):
  __Socioeconomic disadvantage (20 points)
  __Racial or ethnic minority (20 points; disallowed by the court ruling)
  __Men in nursing (5 points)
  __Scholarship athlete (20 points)
  __Provost's discretion (20 points; usually the son or daughter of a large financial donor or of a politician)

In addition to ethnicity being given preference, athleticism, musical talent, having a relative who is an alum, or being the child of someone who is noteworthy to the university are also considered. Some schools also give points for being a military veteran. The legal challenge to this admissions system was based only on the racial and ethnic preference given to some candidates, not on the other items that are preferenced.

* * * * * * *

Engaging With Sociology:

1. Does this process seem reasonable as a way to get a diverse and highly talented incoming class of students? Why or why not?
2. Does it significantly advantage or disadvantage some students? Explain.
3. How would you design a fair system of admissions, and what other factors would you consider?

Predictions were that 25 years after the Michigan cases racial preferences would no longer be necessary to achieve the affirmative action goals. However, recently the Supreme Court has agreed to consider a case involving affirmative action at the University of Texas (*Fisher v. University of Texas*, No. 11-345). This case could end the practice of some public colleges and universities to consider race in admissions. As shown in California, doing away with preferences would most certainly reduce the number of minority students, especially African Americans and Latinos, in higher education (Liptak 2012; National Public Radio 2010).

The question remains: Should preferences be given to accomplish diversity? Some people feel that programs involving any sort of preference result in reverse discrimination. Others believe that such programs have encouraged employers, educational institutions, and government to look carefully at hiring policies and minority candidates and that many more competent minority group members are working in the public sector as a result of these policies.

Global Movements for Human Rights

A unique coalition of world nations has emerged from the terrorist attack of September 11, 2001. In this attack on the World Trade Center in New York City, a center housing national and international businesses and workers, citizens from 90 countries were killed when two hijacked commercial jetliners crashed into the towers. In addition to the worldwide condemnation of the attack, many countries' governments pledged to fight against terrorism. Yet why did such a heinous act occur? Many social scientists attempting to identify a cause point to the disparities between the rich and poor peoples of the world. The perpetrators likely felt that Muslims were treated as inconsequential players in the global world, and their values and way of life were threatened. They struck out to make a dramatic impact on the world community and the United States. The point is that global issues and ethnic conflicts in the social world are interrelated.

Some civil rights or human rights movements focus on international justice issues in other countries as their focal point. Amnesty International is one such movement, which has strong support at many college campuses.

The rights granted to citizens of any nation used to be considered the business of each sovereign nation, but after the Nazi Holocaust, German officers were tried at the Nuremberg Trials, and the United Nations passed the Universal Declaration of Human Rights. Since that time, many international organizations have been established, often under the auspices of the United Nations, to deal with health issues, world poverty and debt, trade, security, and many other issues affecting world citizens—the World Health Organization, the World Bank, the World Trade Organization, and numerous regional trade and security organizations.

The United Nations, several national governments (Britain, France, and Canada), and privately funded advocacy groups speak up for international human rights as a principle that transcends national boundaries. The most widely recognized private group is Amnesty International, a watchdog group that does lobbying on behalf of human rights and supports political prisoners and ethnic group spokespersons. When Amnesty International was awarded the Nobel Peace Prize in 1997, the group's visibility was dramatically increased. Even some activist sociologists have formed groups such as Sociologists Without Borders, or SSF (*Sociólogos Sin Fronteras*; www.sociologistswithoutborders.org), a transnational organization committed to the idea that "all people have equal rights to political and legal protections, to socioeconomic security, to self-determination, and to their personality."

Everyone can make a positive difference in the world, and one place to start is in our community (see "Contributing to Our Social World"). We can counter prejudice, discrimination, and socially embedded racism in our own groups by teaching children to see beyond "we" and "they" and by speaking out for fairness and against stereotypes and discrimination.

Socioeconomic inequality combined with racial and ethnic disprivilege results in problems for a society. However, a full understanding of inequality also requires insights into discrimination based on gender. In some ways, the most intriguing topic is the issues that arise when we look at the intersection and overlapping of race, class, and gender.

t Have We Learned?

n most countries
s? This and other
swered in part by
s have a tendency
and to treat those
an. The categories
can be based on physical appearance, cultural differences, religious differences, or anything the community or society defines as important. Once people notice differences with others, they are more inclined to hurt "them" or to harbor advantages for "us" if there is competition over resources that both groups want. Even within a nation, where people are supposedly all "us," there can be sharp differences and intense hostilities.

Key Points

- Although the concept of race has no real meaning biologically, race is a social construction because people *believe* it is real. (See pp. 260–263.)
- Minority group status—having less power and less access to resources—may occur because of racial status or because of ethnic (cultural) factors. (See pp. 263–270.)
- Prejudice operates at the micro level of society and is closest to people's own lives, but it has much less impact on minorities than discrimination. Symbolic racism has become a significant problem—the denial of overt prejudice but the rejection of any policies that might correct inequities. (See pp. 270–275.)
- At the meso level, institutional discrimination operates through two processes: side effect and past in present. These forms of discrimination are unintended and unconscious—operating quite separately from any prejudice of individuals in the society. (See pp. 275–279.)
- When very large ethnic groups or even nations collide, some people are typically displaced and find themselves in minority status. (See p. 281.)
- The policies of the dominant group may include genocide, subjugation, population transfer, assimilation, or pluralism. (See pp. 280–282.)
- The costs of racism to society are high, including loss of human talent and resources, and these costs make life more difficult for minority group members. (See pp. 286–287.)
- The coping devices used by minorities include five main strategies: assimilation, acceptance, avoidance, aggression, and organizing for societal change. Only one of these, organizing for societal change, addresses the meso- and macro-level causes. (See pp. 288–291.)
- Policies to address problems of prejudice and discrimination range from individual and small-group efforts at the micro level to institutional, societal, and even global social movements. (See pp. 291–294.)
- Affirmative action policies are one approach, but the broad term *affirmative action* includes three different sets of policies that are quite distinct and have different outcomes. (See pp. 294–296.)

Discussion Questions

1. Before you read this chapter, were you aware that slavery still exists throughout the world? If yes, describe how you learned about it and your reaction to this fact. If not, think about *how* your social privilege led to your learning about it for the first time in this course.
2. Have you ever experienced being stereotyped because of your race or ethnicity? Why or why not? How can racial stereotypes harm societies, as well as groups and individuals?
3. What is the difference between symbolic racism and ideological racism? Why is it so difficult to recognize and address symbolic racism in the United States today?
4. Give two examples, respectively, of both side-effect discrimination and past-in-present discrimination. How have they impacted you and your life chances? Why?
5. We know that efforts to reduce prejudice, racism, and discrimination must take place at all levels (micro, meso, and macro). Most organizations, though, must choose one level on which to focus their particular efforts. If you were going to start an organization to decrease racial or ethnic prejudice, would you focus on the micro, meso, or macro level? Why? Explain what your organization would do.
6. Do you agree with the Supreme Court ruling that upheld preferences for college applicants at the University of Michigan who were scholarship athletes or the sons or daughters of a large donor or a politician, but not for racial or ethnic minorities? Why or why not? How might each type of preference benefit (a) the university and (b) the larger society?

Contributing to Our Social World: What Can We Do?

At the Local Level

- *African American student associations, Arab American student associations, and Native American student associations* are all examples of student organizations dedicated to fighting bigotry and promoting understanding and the rights of racial minorities. Identify one of these groups on your campus and arrange to attend a meeting. If appropriate, volunteer to help with its work.

At the Organizational or Institutional Level

- *The Leadership Conference on Civil and Human Rights* is a national coalition dedicated to combating racism and its effects. It maintains a website that includes a directory of its membership of more than 200 organizations (www.civilrights.org). On its website you can find a "Take Action" link that will help you explore ways in which you can participate in its efforts.
- *Teaching Tolerance* (www.splcenter.org/center/tt/teach.jsp), a program of the Southern Poverty Law Center, has curriculum materials for teaching about diversity and a program for enhancing cross-ethnic cooperation and dialogue in schools. Check into internship opportunities in local primary and secondary schools, and explore ways in which the Teaching Tolerance approach can be incorporated into the curricula in your school district with local teachers and administrators.

At the National and Global Levels

- *Anti-Defamation League (ADL;* www.adl.org): The ADL acts to "stop the defamation of the Jewish people and to secure justice and fair treatment to all." The organization develops and implements educational programs on interfaith/intergroup understanding, scrutinizes and calls attention to hate groups, monitors hate speech on the Internet, and mobilizes communities to stand up to bigotry throughout the United States and abroad. Job listings, summer internships, and opportunities in Israel and other locations are listed on their website.
- *National Relief Charities* strives "to help Native American people improve the quality of their lives by providing opportunities for them to bring about positive changes in their communities." To do so, it partners with tribal and other groups on the ground in the tribal regions of the Plains and Midwest. You can find out how to support this group's work and the work of its partner organizations by going to www.nrcprograms.org/site/PageNavigator/index.
- *Cultural Survival and the UN Permanent Forum on Indigenous Issues* (www.cs.org and www.un.org/esa/socdev/unpfii) provide opportunities for combating racism globally. You should also consider purchasing only Fair Trade Certified (packages are clearly marked as such) coffee, and especially chocolate, and encouraging your school to sell Fair Trade Certified products. You can learn more about Fair Trade Certified products and issues by reading this article (www.nytimes.com/2012/09/28/business/media/green-mountain-coffee-begins-fair-trade-campaign-advertising.html) and looking at educational materials provided by the Fair Trade Resource Network (www.fairtraderesource.org).
- *Amnesty International* campaigns for internationally recognized human rights. It relies heavily on volunteers organized into chapters, many of them campus based. You can join the organization and learn how to participate in its action through its website at www.amnesty.org. Consider joining or starting one on your campus.

WWW Visit the Student Study Site at **www.sagepub.com/ballantine4e** to access additional study tools, including eFlashcards, web quizzes, video resources, audio resources, web resources, SAGE journal articles, recommended readings, and more.

CHAPTER

9

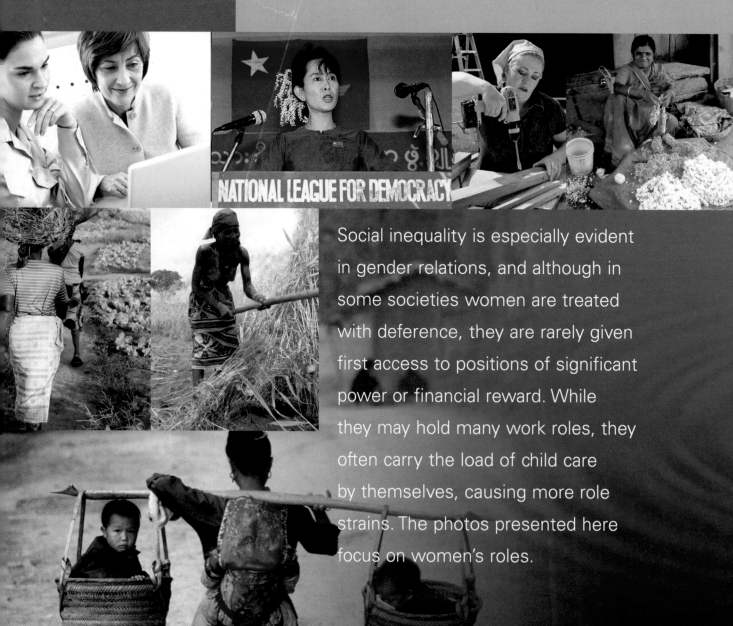

Gender Stratification

She/He—Who Goes First?

Social inequality is especially evident in gender relations, and although in some societies women are treated with deference, they are rarely given first access to positions of significant power or financial reward. While they may hold many work roles, they often carry the load of child care by themselves, causing more role strains. The photos presented here focus on women's roles.

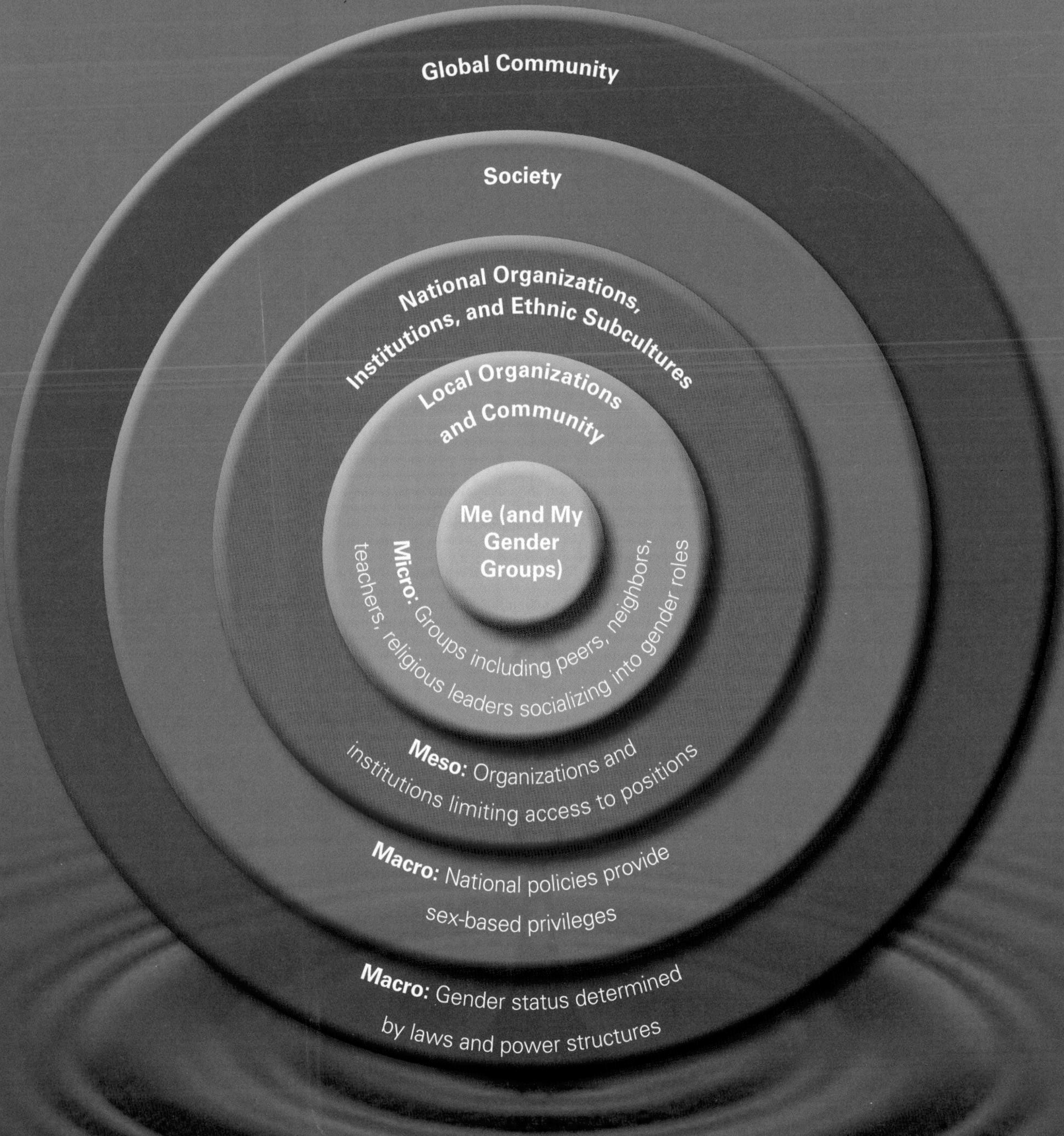
Global Community
Society
National Organizations, Institutions, and Ethnic Subcultures
Local Organizations and Community
Me (and My Gender Groups)
Micro: Groups including peers, neighbors, teachers, religious leaders socializing into gender roles
Meso: Organizations and institutions limiting access to positions
Macro: National policies provide sex-based privileges
Macro: Gender status determined by laws and power structures

Think About It	
Micro: Self and Inner Circle	How does being female or male affect your thoughts and behaviors?
Micro: Local Community	Why do some people face violence in their homes and communities because of their sexuality?
Meso: National Institutions; Complex Organizations; Ethnic Groups	Can anything be done in our organizations and institutions to make men and women more equal?
Macro: National Society	Why do women have second-class status in many societies?
Macro: Global Community	How is gender inequality an issue in this new age of globalization?

What's coming in this chapter?

As women around the world wake up to International Women's Day 2013, their lives are radically different, yet each woman holds the same basic goals: a trusting and happy relationship; healthy educated children with a fair chance in life; enough food on the table; self-respect; access to health care, and whatever individual desires are relevant in her society. Consider the following example from a Global North country that illustrates the problems women face in meeting basic goals:

> Jocelyn is now retired and is having trouble making ends meet. After training in nursing, including a master's degree, she married and dropped her career to raise her family. The marriage did not work out, and 15 years after her college training she found herself with no credit, two children, little job experience, and mounting expenses. She is a conscientious and hard worker, but with two children and meager child support from their father, she could not put much away for retirement. Nursing does not pay well in her town in the Midwest, but there had been few other career options for females in the early 1960s when she was getting her education.
>
> Moreover, she had worked a full-time job and done all the housework for 22 years. Two decades does not build a very large retirement annuity, and she had never been able to buy an adequate home on her income. If she had been a male with a master's degree, her lifetime earnings would have been nearly $1 million more in cumulative income (U.S. Census Bureau 2010c). Her life chances were clearly affected by the fact that she was a female.

Due to changes in gender roles and opportunities over the past 50 years, Jocelyn's granddaughter, Emma, will have a range of opportunities that were beyond consideration for her grandma. Ideas about sex, gender, and appropriate roles for women and men not only transform over time, but they also vary a great deal from one society to the next. Some practices of your own society may seem very strange to women and men in another society. Moreover, gender identities and roles are not stagnant; they change slowly over time, reflecting the economic, political, and social realities of the society. For instance, women in today's India seldom commit *sati* (suicide) on their husband's funeral pyre; however, before the practice of *sati* was outlawed, it was a common way to deal with widows who no longer had a social role or means of support (Ahmad 2009).

In this chapter, we will explore the concepts of sex, gender, and sexuality. We combine these issues with race and class for further understanding of the stratification system, or why people hold the positions they do in society. Although gender refers to a range of social behaviors, more emphasis will be on women's status and roles than men's as this is generally more relevant to our concern about stratification and minorities. At the micro level, we consider gender socialization or how girls learn to be women in their respective societies. At the meso and macro levels we consider gender stratification, or placement of women and men in the society's stratification system. A discussion of costs and consequences of gender stratification plus policy implications will end this chapter.

Sex, Gender, and the Stratification System

You name it, and some society has probably done it! Gender relations are no exception. Variations around the world show that most roles and identities are not biological but rather socially constructed. In Chapter 7, we discussed factors that stratify individuals into social groups (castes and classes), and in Chapter 8, we discussed the roles that race and ethnicity play in stratification. Add the concepts of sex and gender, and we have a more complex and complete picture of how class, race and ethnicity, and gender together influence the experiences that make us who we are and our positions in society. Consider the following examples from societies that illustrate some unusual human social constructions based on sex and gender. These examples show that gender roles are created by humans to meet the needs of their societies. We will then move to more familiar societies.

Men of the Wodaabe society in Niger, Africa, are nomadic cattle herders and traders who would be defined as effeminate by most Western standards because of their behavior patterns. The men are like birds, showing their colorful feathers to attract females. They take great care in doing their hair, applying makeup, and dressing to attract women. They also gossip with each other while sipping their tea. What are the women doing? They are cooking meals, caring for the children, cleaning, tending to the animals, planting small gardens, and preparing for the next move of this nomadic group (Beckwith 1993; Saharan Vibe 2007). These patterns have developed over time as a way for the group to meet its basic human needs and survive. The patterns determine the status and roles of each individual in society.

People in industrial societies might seem unacceptably aggressive and competitive to people of the Arapesh tribe in New Guinea, where gentleness and nonaggression are the rule for both women and men. Yet nearby, women of the Tchambuli people are assertive, businesslike, and the primary economic providers. Men of the Tchambuli exhibit expressive, nurturing, and gossipy behavior. The Mbuti and !Kung peoples of Africa value gender equality in their division of labor and treatment of women and men, and among the Agta of the Philippines, women do the hunting. In West African societies such as the Ashanti and Yoruba kingdoms, women control much of the market system (Dahlberg 1981; Mead [1935] 1963; Turnbull 1962). Each tradition has evolved over time to meet the basic human needs and to provide order to society. Each person knows what is expected.

Under the Taliban rule in Afghanistan at the turn of this century, women could not be seen in public without total body covering that meets strict requirements. Anyone not obeying could be stoned to death. Women could not hold public positions or work outside their homes. If they became ill, women could not be examined by a physician because all doctors are male. Instead, they have to describe their symptoms to a doctor through a screen (Makhmalbaf 2003).

Obligations of the youngest daughter in some Mexican households require that she forgo marriage, stay at home, and care for her parents as they age (Esquivel 2001). In China, women and men work in the factories and fields. Children are cared for in state-run child care settings and schools. Equality between the sexes is the goal, although many women claim that they serve in the public work arena in addition to doing a disproportionate amount of work in the private home setting.

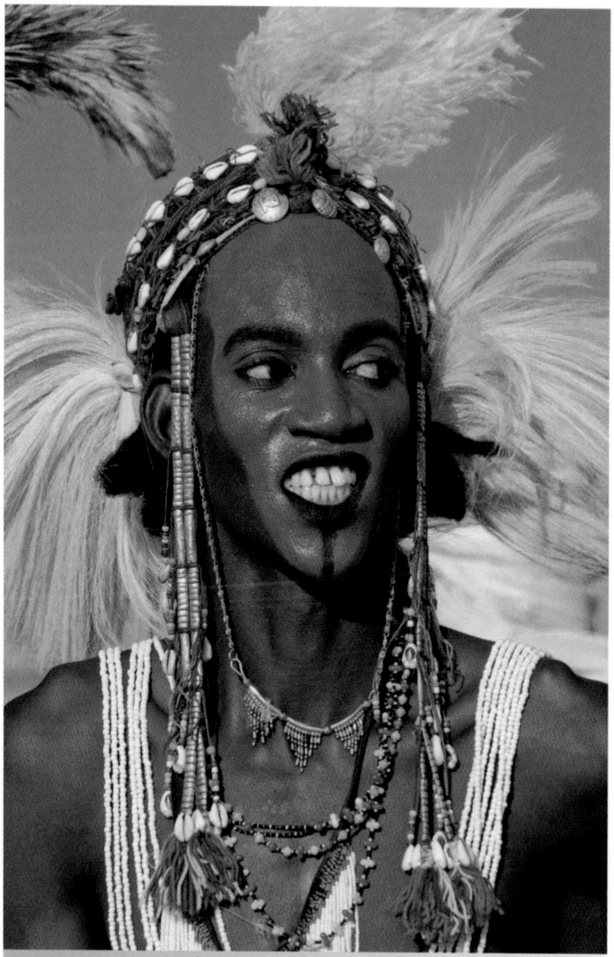

Wodaabe men in Niger (Africa) go to great pains with makeup, hair, and jewelry to ensure that they are highly attractive, a pattern that is thought by many people in North America to be associated with females.

Certain tasks must be carried out by individuals and organizations in each society for members to survive. Someone must be responsible for raising children, someone must provide people with the basic necessities (such as food, clothing, and shelter), someone needs to lead, someone must defend the society, and someone must help resolve conflicts. One's sex and age are often used to determine who holds what positions and who carries out what tasks. Each society develops its own way to meet all the needs, and this results in variations from one society to the next. The point is that gender roles and expectations are defined by tradition and power holders in each society. To defy these expectations can ostracize the individual; being out of line is a threat to the stable, established order—however that evolved.

Muslim girls in some parts of the world cover their faces when in public. The display of skin, even in a college classroom, would be immoral to many Muslims. However, in other Muslim countries such coverings would be unusual.

Thinking Sociologically

Why did groups in different corners of the globe develop such radically different ways of organizing their gender roles?

Sex

At birth, when doctors say, "It's a . . . ," they are referring to the distinguishing primary characteristics that determine sex—that is, the penis or vagina. **Sex** is *a biological term referring to ascribed genetic, anatomical, and hormonal differences between males and females.* Right? Partly. Sex is also "a determination made through the application of socially agreed upon biological criteria for classifying persons as females or males" (West and Zimmerman 1987:127). In other words, occasionally this binary male-female categorization by biological criteria is not clear. Occasionally, babies are born with ambiguous genitalia, not fitting the typical definitions of male or female (the *intersexed*). Up to five variations in sexes have been identified (Fausto-Sterling 2000). About 1.7% of babies are born with "anomalies of sex chromosomes, internal procreative organs, and external genitalia in a variety of combinations" (Fausto-Sterling 2000:50–54). In Global North countries, these babies often undergo surgeries to clarify their gender, with hormonal treatments and possible further surgery at adolescence (Chase 2000). Where medical interventions are not possible, people with sex anomalies may have special status, such as the transgendered *Hijras* (or *Aravanis*) in India. These special people are called on for special religious observances and other ceremonial occasions (Gannon 2009). Whether male, female, or intersexed, anatomical differences at birth and chromosomal typing before birth result in cultural attempts to clearly categorize sex. Still, the word *sex* when applied to a person refers largely to elements of one's anatomy.

In many societies, great lengths are taken to assign a sex to an infant. Why is this an issue? The reality is that sex constitutes a major organizing principle in most societies. Despite emphasis on "achieved status" in modern societies, society's expectations guiding roles and statuses are largely ascribed—determined by a person's sex. Our attraction to others is expressed by our sexuality and our sexual identity. Most people fall into the category of heterosexual (other sex), homosexual (same sex), bisexual (both sexes), or "varied." Our identities are defined by the cultural expectations held in most societies that a "normal" girl or boy will be sexually attracted to and eventually have sex with someone of the other sex (Lorber and Moore 2007). However, the point is that sex is not always a straightforward distinction and is as social as it is biological.

In adolescence, secondary characteristics further distinguish the sexes, with females developing breasts and hips and males developing body hair, muscle mass, and deep voices. Individuals are then expected to adopt the behaviors appropriate to their anatomical features as defined by their society. In addition to the physical sex differences between males and females, a few other physical conditions are commonly believed to be sex linked, such as a prevalence of color blindness, baldness, learning disabilities, autism, and hemophilia in males. Yet some traits that members of society commonly link to sex are actually learned through socialization. There is little evidence, for instance, that emotions, personality traits, or ability to fulfill most social statuses are determined by inborn physical sex differences.

Although the terms *sex*, *gender*, and *sexuality* are often used interchangeably, it is useful to understand the technical difference. A person's sex—male, female, or other—is a basis for stratification around the globe, used in every society to assign positions and roles to individuals. However, what is defined as normal behavior for a male, a female, or an intersexed person in one society could get one killed in another.

Gender

Gender refers to *a society's notions of masculinity and femininity—socially constructed meanings associated with being male or female—and how individuals construct their identity in terms of gender within these constraints. Gender identity* is how individuals form their identity using the categories of sex and gender, then negotiating the constraints they entail. The examples at the beginning of this section illustrate some differences in how cultures are structured around gender.

These gender meanings profoundly influence the statuses we hold within the social structure and our placement in the stratification system (Rothenberg 2010). Individuals are expected to fulfill positions appropriate for their sex category. Statuses are positions within the structures of society, and roles are expected behaviors within those statuses. **Gender roles**, then, are those commonly assigned tasks or expected behaviors linked to an individual's sex-determined statuses (Lips 2010). Members of each society learn the structural guidelines and positions expected of males and females (West and Zimmerman 1987). Our positions, which affect access to power and resources, are embedded in institutions at the meso level with culture defining what is right and wrong. The point is that there is not some global absolute truth governing gender or gender roles. While both vary across cultures, gender is a learned cultural idea, while gender roles are part of the structural system of the society.

Sexuality

Sexuality refers *to culturally shaped meanings both of sexual acts and of how we experience our own bodies—especially in relation to the bodies of others.* Strange as it may seem, sexuality is *socially constructed.* A sex act is a "social enterprise," with cultural norms defining what is normal and acceptable in each society, how we should feel, and hidden assumptions about what the act means (Steele 2005). Even what we find attractive is culturally defined. For a period, in China, men found tiny feet a sexual turn-on—hence, the bound feet of women. In some cultures, legs are the attraction, and in others, men are fascinated by breasts. In the United States and elsewhere, pornography is a moneymaker because of the way it stimulates people, yet as the next "Sociology in Our Social World" on page 306 indicates, the stimulation itself is variable by gender.

Consider the ideal male body as depicted in popular magazines in contemporary Western cultures: "over 6 feet tall, 180 to 200 pounds, muscular, agile, with straight white teeth, a washboard stomach, six-pack abs, long legs, a full head of hair, a large penis (discreetly shown by a bulge), broad shoulders and chest, strong muscular back, clean shaven, healthy, and slightly tanned if White, or a lightish brown if Black or Hispanic" (Lorber and Moore 2011:89–90). We grow up learning what is appealing.

The struggles that individuals have with their sexual identity are especially compelling in studies of *transgender*—when intersexed individuals do not fit clearly into female or male sex classifications (Kinsey Institute for Research in Sex, Gender, and Reproduction 2012; Leeder 2004). Transgender refers to "identification as someone who is challenging, questioning, or changing gender from that assigned at birth to a chosen gender—male-to-female, female-to-male, transitioning between genders, or gender 'queer' (challenging gender norms)" (Lorber and Moore 2007:6). Transgendered individuals are of interest to sociologists because of their ambiguous life—living on the boundaries. Due to the pressure to fit in, most transgendered people change themselves, sometimes through surgery, to fit into their chosen gender. They may "pass" as one sex or engage in social interaction as both men and women.

In summary, although the terms *sex*, *gender*, and *sexuality* are often used interchangeably, they do have distinct meanings. The distinctions between these terms are not always as clear-cut as the definitions would imply. One can be a masculine heterosexual female, a masculine homosexual male, or any of a number of possible combinations. Individuals continually negotiate the meanings attached to gender and sexuality, and when they are doing so they are *doing gender*, a process discussed later in this chapter ("Doing Gender" 2011; West and Zimmerman 1987).

Sex, Gender, and Sexuality: The Micro Level

"It's a boy!" brings varying cultural responses. In many Western countries, that exclamation results in blue blankets, toys associated with males (footballs, soccer balls, and trucks), roughhousing, and gender socialization messages. In some Asian societies, boys are sources for great rejoicing, whereas girls may be seen as a burden. In China and India, *female infanticide* (killing of newborn girl babies) is sometimes practiced in rural areas, in part because of the cost to poor families of raising a girl and the diminished value of girls. In China, the male preference system has been exacerbated by the government's edict that most couples may have only one child. Exceptions are made in rural areas and for minorities.

Sociology in Our Social World

Sexuality and Pornography: What Turns You On?

By Michael Norris

Sexuality and arousal are complex and vary between men and women. Pornography is often used to titillate the viewers sexually, and it has become big business. Consider the fact that adult videos generate more revenue than Hollywood box office cinema; more people visit porn sites on the Internet than they do prominent news sites; 70% of those who visit porn sites admit doing so at work; and college students have more legal access to pornography than to alcohol. So despite objections to the "thingification" of women (or of men) in pornography, it is widely used. Still, there are some seldom understood variations in how people respond to pornographic videos.

Meredith Chivers and her colleagues were interested in gender differences in reaction to sexual videos (Chivers, Seto, and Blanchard 2007). The researchers found that for women, sexual activity itself was arousing, whereas men tended to be influenced more by the gender of the actors in the videos. Women were aroused by sexual activity regardless of the gender of the participants and even when the actors were nonhuman primates. Women can apparently be genitally aroused just by cues of sexual activity. On the other hand, heterosexual men were aroused by videos of nude women engaged in nonsexual activities such as exercise. By contrast videos of nude males were no more arousing to heterosexual women than videos of the Himalayan mountain range (Newman 2008).

Chivers and her colleagues also discovered gender differences in biological arousal and subjective awareness of that arousal. Men were immediately aware of their physiological arousal while women were often not. This gender difference has been verified in previous research, which suggests that biological reactions precede subjective awareness of arousal in women, but not in men. Biological arousal may happen in women without any self-reported arousal at all.

This research adds to a growing body of literature suggesting greater flexibility of women's sexuality in terms of sexual identity, same-sex attraction, and same-sex behavior. Women's greater sexual flexibility may result from a tendency to identify with both male and female targets of sexual activity and greater same-sex emotional attachments than men.

This study also helps explain the fact that for heterosexuals viewing mainstream, commercially available pornography, watching two women having sex is more socially acceptable than watching two men having sex. A popular cultural belief, reinforced by comedians, is that men particularly enjoy "lesbian action" in adult videos. Research suggests that this is not the case. In fact, the adult video industry may include these vignettes because it stimulates women, and this may help sell the product. Sexuality is complex and involves both biological reactions and socially constructed definitions of sexuality.

Note: Michael Norris is a professor at Wright State University, where he teaches and does research in sociology and criminal justice.

At the micro level we trace stages in an individual's life as a female or male: early childhood socialization, school and community activities and experiences, adult statuses and roles of females and males, language patterns, and so on through the life cycle. Beginning at birth, each individual passes through many stages. At each, there are messages that reinforce appropriate gender behavior in that society. Although gender socialization differs in each society, proper roles are established by the culture and learned from birth. These gender expectations are inculcated into children by parents, siblings, grandparents, neighbors, peers, and even day care providers. If we fail to respond to the expectations of these significant people in our lives, we may experience negative sanctions: teasing, isolation and exclusion, harsh words, and stigma. To avoid these informal sanctions, children usually learn to conform, at least in their public behavior.

The lifelong process of gender socialization continues once we reach *school age* and we become more involved in activities separate from our parents. Other people in the community—teachers, religious leaders, coaches—also begin to influence us. We are grouped by sex in many of these social settings, and we come to think of ourselves as like *this* group and unlike *that* group: boys versus girls, we versus they. Even if our parents are not highly traditional in their gender expectations, we still experience many influences from peers, school and other sources at the micro level to conform to traditional gender notions.

With adulthood, the differential treatment and stratification of the sexes take new forms. Men traditionally have more networks and statuses, as well as greater access to resources outside the home. This has resulted in many women around the world having less power, because they depend more on husbands or fathers for resources. Even spousal abuse is related to imbalance of power in relationships. Lack of connections to the larger social system makes it difficult for women to remove themselves from abusive relationships.

The subtitle of this chapter asks, "Who goes first?" When it comes to the question of who walks through a door first, the answer is that in many Western societies, *she* does—or at least, formal etiquette would suggest this is proper. The strong man steps back and defers to the weaker female, graciously holding the door for her (Walum 1974). Yet when it comes to who walks through the metaphorical door to the professions, it is the man who goes first. Women are served first at restaurants and at other micro-level settings, but this seems little compensation for the fact that doors are often closed to them at the meso and macro levels of society.

Because daughters are a financial liability in some countries—such as India and China—there is a long-standing preference for sons. This results in extended families in which there are far more boys than girls due to sex-selective abortion and female infanticide.

Language can be powerful in shaping the behavior and perceptions of people, as discussed in the chapter on

Some women today are in major leadership positions, including 11 serving in the presidency of their nations in 2012. India's President Pratibha Patil (left) is the first woman to hold the post in her country, and she won the election with about twice the votes of the opposition candidate. Cristina Fernández de Kirchner was reelected president of Argentina in 2011, also with a landslide victory. Ellen Johnson Sirleaf is president of Liberia and the first elected female head of state in Africa. She is serving her second term as president and was one of the co-winners of the Nobel Prize for Peace in 2011.

culture. Women often end sentences with tag questions, a pattern that involves ending a declarative statement with a short tag that turns it into a question: "That was a good idea, don't you think?" This pattern may cause male business colleagues to think women are insecure or uncertain about themselves. The women themselves may view it as an invitation to collaboration and dialogue. Yet a perception of insecurity may prevent a woman from getting the job or the promotion. On the flip side, when women stop using these "softening" devices, they may be perceived by men as strident, harsh, or "bitchy" (Wood and Reich 2006; Sandberg 2013). Another aspect of men and women's language usage is that women tend to use more words related to psychological and social processes, while men prefer more discussion of objects and impersonal topics (Newman, Groom, Handelman, and Pennebaker 2008).

Other aspects of language may also be important. The same adverb or adjective, when preceded by a male or female pronoun, can take on very different meanings. When one says, "He's easy" or "He's loose," it does not generally mean the same thing as when someone says, "She's easy" or "She's loose." Likewise, there are words such as *slut* or *bitch* for women for which there are no equivalents for men. There is no female equivalent for *cuckold*, the term describing a man whose wife is making a fool of him by having an affair. Why is that? To use another example, the word *spinster* is supposed to be the female synonym for *bachelor*, yet it has very different connotations. Even the more newly coined *bachelorette* is not usually used to describe a highly appealing, perhaps lifelong role. What might be the implications of these differences?

Those who invoke the biological argument that women's options are limited by pregnancy, childbirth, or breast-feeding from participating in public affairs and politics ignore the fact that in most societies, these biological roles are time limited and that women play a variety of social roles in addition to keeping the home and hearth. They also ignore those societies in which males are deeply involved in nonaggressive and nurturing activities such as child rearing.

Thinking Sociologically

Some people always write *he* first when writing "he and she." Others sometimes put *she* first. Does language influence how we view gender roles, or does it just describe what exists? Explain.

Sex, Gender, and Sexuality: The Meso Level

Carrying out family roles, educating the young, providing health care, teaching principles of faith, providing for support through economic institutions, and participating in decision making or government signify passage into adulthood. By whatever age is defined as being an "adult" in a society, members are expected to assume leadership roles and responsibilities in the institutions of family, education, religion, politics and economics, health care, and the military. Our roles often differ depending on our gender, which determines our placements and many of our experiences in the social world (Brettell and Sargent 2008).

In most societies, sex and age stipulate when and how we experience *rites of passage*—rituals and ceremonies in institutions that mark a change of status in the family and community—the meso levels of society. These rites include any ceremonies or recognitions that admit one to adult duties and privileges. Rites of passage are institutionalized in various ways: religious rituals such as the Jewish male bar mitzvah or the female bat mitzvah ceremonies; education celebrations such as graduation ceremonies, which often involve caps and gowns of gender-specific colors or place females on one side of the room and males on the other; and different ages at which men and women are permitted to marry in many states.

Other institutions also segregate us by sex. Traditional Greek Orthodox Christian churches and Orthodox Jewish synagogues, for example, do not have families seated together. Men sit on one side of the sanctuary and women on the other. Many institutions, including religious, political, and economic organizations, have historically allowed only males to have leadership roles. Only men are to teach the scriptures to the young among traditional Jews, but few men are Sunday school teachers in contemporary Christian congregations.

Women's reduced access to power in micro-level settings has a lot to do with their lack of power and status in meso-level organizations and institutions. This is why gender roles are important. This is also a reason why policy makers concerned about gender equality have focused so much on inclusion of women in social institutions.

Empowerment of Women

Thirty village women gather regularly to discuss issues of health, crops, their herds, the predicted rains, goals for their children, and how to make ends meet. They are from a subsistence farming village in southern Niger on the edge of the Sahara desert. Recently, a micro-credit organization was established with a small grant of $1,500 from abroad. With training from CARE International, an international non-governmental organization (NGO), the women selected a board of directors to oversee the loans. Groups of five or six women have joined together to explain their projects to the board and request small loans. Each woman is responsible for paying back a small amount on the loan each week once the project is established and bringing in money.

Typical microcredit participants are women with several children, living at or below poverty, and sharing shelter with other families. With loans, women can make and sell items and build businesses to feed, clothe, and educate children (Foundation for Women 2012). A loan of between $20 and $50 from the micro-credit organization is a tremendous sum considering that for many of these women, it is equivalent to six months' earnings. Strong social norms are instituted to encourage repayment. Women who repay their loans promptly often decide who is eligible for future loans. Participation in the program encourages women and grants them economic and social capital otherwise unavailable to them.

With the new possibilities for their lives, they have big plans: For instance, one group plans to buy a press to make peanut oil, a staple for cooking in the region. Currently, people pay a great deal for oil imported from Nigeria. Another group will buy baby lambs, fatten them, and sell them for future festivals at a great profit. Yet another group plans to set up a small bakery. Women are also discussing the possibility of making local craft products to sell to foreign fair-trade organizations such as Ten Thousand Villages (a fair-trade organization that markets products made by villagers and returns the profits back to the villagers).

Some economists and social policy makers claim that grassroots organizations such as microcredits may be the way out of poverty for millions of poor families and that women are motivated to be small entrepreneurs to help support their families and buy education and health care for their children. Indeed, in 2006, Muhammad Yunus, who founded Grameen Bank—a microcredit lender for the very poor—received the Nobel Prize for Peace.

Microcredit lenders build significant economic and social capital for their participants, but critics suggest that there is an under-researched downside to micro lending. As they see it, despite its success, the solution is a micro-level attempt to address a macro-level problem. Macro economists such as Linda Mayoux (2002, 2008) question whether or not the program will address the gender inequalities in the developing nations it targets. Moreover, such loans may shift relations between husbands and wives, leaving men in a less powerful position within marriages. Most economists agree that micro lending works best alongside macro-level initiatives seeking to address national economic problems.

Thinking Sociologically

How might women's lack of positions of authority in organizations and institutions—the meso level of society—influence females' roles at the micro level? How might it influence their involvements at the macro level?

Microcredit banks have provided places for public sociologists to be involved in a variety of ways. For example, the next "Sociologists in Action" on page 310 feature describes how one class of undergraduate students got involved in trying to raise money and awareness of how meso-level organizations—banks—can impact people at the micro level.

Sex, Gender, and Sexuality: The Macro Level

People around the world engage in going to school, driving a car, and working, but in some parts of the world, schooling, driving, and working are forbidden for women. A 14-year-old Pakistani girl was shot and severely wounded for both going to school and speaking out for other girls to have that opportunity (Mehsud 2012). The Taliban are against girls going to school. When we turn to the national and global level, we again witness inequality between the sexes that is quite separate from any form of personal prejudice or animosity toward women. Patterns of social action that are embedded in the entire social system may influence women and men, providing unrecognized privileges or disadvantages (McIntosh 1992). This is called *institutionalized privilege* or *disprivilege*.

In hunter-gatherer and agricultural societies, women increase their power relative to men as they age and as people gain respect for their wisdom. Especially within a clan or a household, women become masters over their domains. Men move from active roles outside the home to passive roles after retirement, whereas women often do the opposite.

The winds of change are influencing the roles of women in many parts of the world, as is seen in governing structures. Although women are still denied the right to vote in a few countries, voting is a universal right for most. In the United States, women have voted for a little more than 90 years, following the passage of the Nineteenth Amendment

Sociologists in Action— Donna Yang, Christian Agurto, Michelle Benavides, Brianne Glogowski, Deziree Martinez, and Michele Van Hook

Sociology Students Engage With Microfinance

Students at William Paterson University describe their participation in a microcredit organization and how they used the sociological tools they gained in their Principles of Sociology course. They educated their classmates about Kiva, a microfinance project designed to aid women and diminish poverty globally, and raised money for the organization's efforts.

Kiva is an international microfinance organization dedicated to helping ordinary people across the globe become lenders to beginning entrepreneurs. After enrolling in an introductory sociology course, we collaborated to complete a group assignment that was designed to utilize various sociological concepts. We sought not only to raise money toward a Kiva loan, but—more importantly—to generate awareness about microfinance's ability to empower women and help fight poverty. The website, www.Kiva.org, is designed to facilitate partnerships between everyday people willing to give and low-income entrepreneurs seeking financial services. Kiva loans typically range from $25 to $3,000, and are temporarily financed by Kiva users who have browsed the profiles of potential entrepreneurs uploaded on the website.

Although gender inequality was central to our Kiva project, we used many other key sociological ideas. The purpose of the assignment was to promote the application of two important ideas from sociology, using a sociological eye and promoting social activism. Utilizing our collective sociological eye, we were able to look beneath the surface of society and recognize patterns of inequality intersecting along both class and gender lines. We realized that social stratification has created hierarchies through which women are marginalized economically, politically, and socially. Microfinance programs such as Kiva seek to mitigate this unequal access to wealth by creating greater accessibility for low-income individuals, mostly women, to financial services. In this way, they help to redistribute the accessibility of wealth across a wider spectrum of social classes. As a group, we felt passionate about Kiva because of its commitment to improve society by providing more equal lending opportunities.

We raised more than $150 toward a group loan for the communal bank "Mujeres Progresistas" (Progressive Women) in Cuenca, Ecuador. This bank is composed of 11 women, and our specific loan was distributed to 2 women—both mothers of four seeking loans to help finance their personal businesses in order to help support their families. Maria Huerta will use this second loan to invest in buying chickens and chicken feed to begin running a chicken farm. Maria Suqui will be using the loan to help establish a snack shop through which she hopes to earn enough money to eventually own a home.

In order to promote awareness about our project and Kiva's initiatives, we also created informational pamphlets and distributed them to students on our college campus. The pamphlets explained microfinance, how Kiva utilizes this process of lending to help low-income individuals around the globe, and how students can get involved. Additionally, we presented our project to peers enrolled in our Principles of Sociology class in hopes of inspiring other peer members to join Kiva's efforts. This project helped us realize the importance of sociology, its applicability within everyday life, and our obligation to act as socially conscious individuals in order to help promote greater social justice.

* * * * * * *

Note: This excerpt is adapted from Korgen and White's *Engaged Sociologist: Connecting the Classroom to the Community* (Sage 2013).

in 1920 prohibiting voter discrimination on the basis of sex. Yet in the entire history of the United States, only 45 women have served in the U.S. Senate, and a total of 297 in Congress since the first woman was elected in 1917. As of 2013, the number is at an all-time high, with 20 of the 100 senators being women. With 78 women serving in the House there are now 98 women in Congress—18.3% of all national representatives. Only four states (Delaware, Iowa, Mississippi, and Vermont) have never sent a woman to a Congressional seat (Center for American Women and Politics 2013).

The United States is far behind many other countries in women's representation in governing bodies. In fact, the global average for women in national parliaments is 18.4%, so the United States is slightly below the average in female representation. The nation with the highest percentage of women in the national parliament or congress is Rwanda (sub-Saharan Africa) with 56.3% women—one of only two countries to reach or surpass 50%. Canada is tied for 50th among nations, and the United States ranked 96th in 2012—tied with Morocco and Venezuela and well below Global North countries like Sweden (#4), Spain (#20), and Germany (#25), and trailing Global South countries like Afghanistan (#39) and Iraq (#47) (Inter-Parliamentary Union 2012). Because 23 women were elected to serve in the 113th Congress, representation by women in the United States should move up to 88th in ranking.

Several factors have been especially effective in increasing women's positions in national parliaments in Africa: the existence of a matriarchal culture (where women may have increased authority and power in decision making), political systems that stress proportional representation, and the adoption of gender quotas for government positions (Yoon 2004, 2008, 2011a, 2011b). Yet democratization of governmental systems is sometimes linked to a *decrease* in representation by women, a sad reality for those committed to establishing democracy around the world (Yoon 2001, 2005). Globally, women's access to power and prestige is highly variable, with African and northern European countries having a position of leadership when it comes to gender equity in government (see Table 9.1). As you study Table 9.1, note that researchers find that the needs and interests of women are not fully represented unless a critical mass is reached, and that critical mass is usually about 35% (Yoon 2011b).

Cross-cultural analyses confirm that gender roles either evolve over centuries or are transformed by sweeping reform laws such as voting rights. The fact that women in China generally work outside the home whereas women

Men and women are segregated in many social settings, including rituals of various sorts. At this Lubavitch (Hasidic Jewish) wedding ceremony, a partition separates the women from the men.

Table 9.1 **Women in National Parliaments (selected countries), 2012**

Rank	*Country*	*Lower/Single House: % Women*	*Upper House/ Senate: % Women*
1	Rwanda	56.3	38.5
2	Andorra	50.0	—
3	Cuba	45.2	—
4	Sweden	44.7	—
5	Seychelles	43.8	—
6	Finland	42.5	—
7	South Africa	42.3	32.1
8	Netherlands	40.7	36.0
9	Nicaragua	40.2	
10	Iceland	39.7	—
11	Norway	39.6	—
12	Mozambique	39.2	—
18	Spain	36.0	—
22	Germany	32.9	—
25	New Zealand	32.2	—
36	Afghanistan	27.7	27.5
40	Mexico	26.2	22.7
42	Iraq	25.2	—
45	Australia	24.7	38.2
46	Canada	24.7	37.9
62	United Kingdom	22.3	21.9
71	China	21.3	—
84	France	18.9	21.9
96	United States of America	16.9	17.0
97	Turkmenistan	16.8	—

Source: Inter-Parliamentary Union (IPU) 2012, www.ipu.org. Reprinted with permission of the Inter-Parliamentary Union (IPU).

Note: To examine the involvement of women in other countries or to see even more recent figures, go to www.ipu.org/wmn-e/classif.htm.

Thinking Sociologically

What factors might affect the ranking of countries in Table 9.1 of the number of women involved in government? What factors might explain why the United States and Canada rank so poorly in representation of women in their governments?

in some Muslim societies hardly venture from their homes is due to differences in cultural norms about gender roles that are dictated by governments or tradition and learned through the socialization process.

Gender Socialization: Micro- and Meso-Level Analyses

"Sugar and spice and everything nice—that's what little girls are made of. Snips and snails and puppy dog tails—that's what little boys are made of." As the verse implies, different views of little girls and little boys start at birth, based on gender and stereotypes about what is biologically natural. Behavioral expectations stem from cultural beliefs about the nature of men and women, and these expectations guide socialization from the earliest ages and in intimate primary group settings.

Socialization into gender is the process by which people learn the cultural norms, attitudes, and behaviors appropriate to their gender. That is, they learn how to think and act as boys or girls, women or men. Socialization reinforces the "proper" gender behaviors and punishes the improper behaviors. This process, in turn, reinforces *gender stereotypes*. In many societies, traits of gentleness, passivity, and dependence are associated with femininity, whereas boldness, aggression, strength, and independence are identified with masculinity. For instance, in most Western societies, aggression in women is considered unfeminine, if not inappropriate or disturbing (Sandberg 2013). Likewise, the gentle, unassertive male is often looked on with scorn or pity, stigmatized as a "wimp." Gender stereotypes in the United States are less rigid than in the past, but they are still a big part of popular culture and provide guidelines for parents, especially for boys' behavior. Girls' norms of femininity have expanded more than norms of masculinity, and more girls have aspirations for law and medical school than boys have for nursing. Girls have more flexibility in sports they choose and in tomboy toys they can play with ("Gender Stereotypes" 2011). Expectations related to these stereotypes are rigid in many societies (Pollack 1999).

From infancy, messages are sent to children and to visitors so that no one is likely to mistake the sex of the child.

Stages in Gender Socialization

Bounce that rough-and-tumble baby boy and cuddle that precious, delicate little girl. Thus begins gender socialization, starting at birth and taking place through a series of life stages, discussed in Chapter 4 on socialization. Examples from infancy and childhood show how socialization into gender roles takes place.

Infancy

Learning how to carry out gender roles begins at birth. Parents in the United States describe their newborn daughters as soft, delicate, fine featured, little, pretty, cute, awkward, and resembling their mothers. They depict their sons as strong, firm, alert, and well coordinated (Lindsey 2011; Rubin 1974). Clothing, room decor, and toys also reflect notions of gender. In Spain, parents and grandparents dress babies and their carriages in pink or blue depending on gender, proudly showing off the little ones to friends as they promenade in the evenings. Although gender stereotypes have declined in recent years, they continue to affect the way we handle and treat male and female infants (Karraker 1995).

Childhood

Once they are out of infancy, research shows that many boys are encouraged to be more independent and exploratory, whereas girls are protected from situations that might prove harmful. More pressure is put on boys to behave in "gender-appropriate" ways (Kramer 2010). Boys are socialized into "the boy code" that provides rigid guidelines (see the next "Sociology in Our Social World" feature). Cross-cultural studies show boys often get more attention than girls because of their behavior, with an emphasis on achievement, autonomy, and aggression for boys (Kimmel and Messner 2009).

Sociology in Our Social World

The Boy Code

Boys and girls begin to conform to gender expectations once they are old enough to understand that their sex is rather permanent, that boys are not capable of becoming "mommies." They become even more conscious of adhering to norms of others in their gender category.

The Old Boy network in American society favors adult men over women through a system of networks. This system actually starts with "the boy code," the rules about boys' proper behavior. Young boys learn "the code" from parents, siblings, peers, teachers, and society in general. They are praised for adhering to the code and punished for violating its dictates. William Pollack writes that boys learn several stereotyped behavior models exemplifying the boy code (Pollack 1999):

1. "The sturdy oak": Men should be stoic, stable, and independent; a man never shows weakness.
2. "Give 'em hell": From athletic coaches and movie heroes, the consistent theme is extreme daring, bravado, and attraction to violence.
3. "The 'big wheel'": Men and boys should achieve status, dominance, and power; they should avoid shame, wear the mask of coolness, and act as though everything is under control.
4. "No sissy stuff": Boys are discouraged from expressing feelings or urges perceived as feminine—dependence, warmth, empathy.

The boy code is ingrained in society; by 5 or 6 years of age, boys are less likely than girls to express hurt or distress. They have learned to be ashamed of showing feelings and of being weak. This gender straitjacket, according to Pollack, causes boys to conceal feelings in order to fit in and be accepted and loved (Pollack 1999). As a result, some boys, especially in adolescence, become silent, covering any vulnerability and masking their true feelings. This affects boys' relationships, performance in school, and ability to connect with others. It also causes young males to put on what Jackson Katz calls the "tough guise," when young men and boys emphasize aggression and violence to display masculinity (Katz 2006). Moreover, if fathers emphasize competition and toughness, their sons are much more likely to become bullies and are likely to have few deep friendships, especially in the later teen years (Kindlon and Thompson 2000; Way 2011).

Pollack suggests that we can help boys reconnect to nongendered norms by

1. giving some undivided attention each day just listening to boys;
2. encouraging a range of emotions;
3. avoiding language that taunts, teases, or shames;
4. looking behind the veneer of "coolness" for signs of problems;
5. expressing love and empathy;

(Continued)

(Continued)

6. dispelling the "sturdy oak" image; and
7. advocating a broad, inclusive model of masculinity (Pollack 1999).

With the women's movement and shifts in gender expectations have come new patterns of male behavior. Some men are forming more supportive and less competitive relationships with other men, and there are likely to be continued changes in and broadening of "appropriate" behavior for men (Kimmel and Messner 2009; Way 2011). Kindlon and Thompson found that although boys are innately as capable of expressing emotion as girls, they learn to suppress emotions (Kindlon and Thompson 2000). The one legitimate emotion boys can express is anger. This inability to share inner feelings, these scholars found, has serious repercussions for psychological well-being and for healthy relationships. Niobe Way found a more complex pattern. Just as many girls resist the mainstream culture's messages of passivity and obsession with appearance as core to being female, many boys are also a part of a resistance movement (Way 2011). They have quite intimate relationships with male friends—sharing emotions, vulnerabilities, and secrets—especially during childhood and early adolescence. Sadly, Way found that while most boys in her sample deeply valued intimate same-sex friendships, those ties weakened considerably by late adolescence, and many boys struggled privately with the loss. The important finding in Way's study was that boys do not just accept the boy code blindly. Many resist aspects of that code and try to resist the culture's definitions of masculinity.

Thinking Sociologically

What evidence do you see of the boy code when you observe your friends and relatives? What is the impact of the boy code? Is there a similar code for girls?

Stereotypes for girls in a majority of societies label feminine behaviors as soft, nonaggressive, and noncompetitive. Consider that boys act out their aggressive feelings, but girls are socialized to be nice, nurturing, and not aggressive. In a study about how schoolgirls express aggression, Simmons (2002) finds that girls express "relational aggression"—that is, aggression that affects girls' social contacts indirectly through rumors, name-calling, giggling, ignoring, backbiting, exclusion, and manipulation of victims. Friendship and needing to belong are the weapons—rather than sticks and stones. This form of bullying is subtle and hard to detect, but it can have long-lasting effects on girls (Girls Health 2009; Simmons 2002). Names for children also reflect stereotypes about gender. Boys are more often given strong, hard names that end in consonants. The top 10 boys' names include Jacob, Mason, William, Jayden, Noah, Michael, Ethan, Alexander, Aiden, and Daniel. Girls are more likely to be given soft pretty names with vowel endings such as most of the top 10: Sophia, Isabella, Emma, Olivia, Ava, Emily, Abigail, Madison, Mia, and Chloe (Social Security Online 2010).

Alternatively, girls may be given feminized versions of boys' names—Roberta, Jessica, Josephine, Nicole, Michelle, or Donna. Sometimes boys' names are given to girls without first feminizing them. Names such as Lynn, Stacey, Tracey, Faye, Dana, Jody, Lindsay, Robin, Carmen, Kelly, Kim, Beverly, Ashley, Carol, Shannon, and Leslie used to be names exclusively for men, but within a decade or two after they were applied to girls, parents stopped using them for boys (Kean 2007). So a common name for males may for a time be given to either sex, but then, it is given primarily to girls. The pattern rarely goes the other direction. Once feminized, the names seem to have become tainted and unacceptable for boys (Lieberson, Dumais, and Bauman 2000).

In the early childhood years, children become aware of their own gender identity. As they reach school age, they learn that their sex is permanent, and they begin to categorize behaviors that are appropriate for their sex. As children are rewarded for performing proper gender roles, these roles are reinforced. That reinforcement solidifies gender roles, setting the stage for gender-related interactions, behaviors, and choices in later life.

One example of gender roles and *doing gender* is illustrated in the following "Sociology in Our Social World." Note that this is one example of how gender socialization affects our attitudes toward everyday events that we take for granted.

Sociology in Our Social World

Gender and Food

By Jacqueline Bergdahl

Behavior is generally considered *gendered* when it differs for men versus women. Driving is gendered—men operate motor vehicles differently than women. Men are more likely to drive at night and after drinking, to tailgate more, and to speed more; therefore they are more likely to die in car crashes than women.

Food is also gendered. In food preparation, women are more likely than men to be the primary food preparer in households, while there are more male professional chefs than female ones. Women are more likely to bake than men, and men are more likely to grill than women. Food practices are shaped by gender, even though we prefer to think that what and how we eat are due to personal preferences, rather than larger social forces.

Some food items are considered to have a gender. Meat, potatoes, and coffee are foods that many people consider to be masculine, while yogurt and fruit are feminine, and chicken and oranges are gender neutral (Rappoport 2003). McPhail, Beagan, and Chapman (2012) asked subjects to sort the pictures of food items into men's foods and women's foods. Salad, fish, couscous, and stir-fry were generally considered women's foods while pizza, hotdogs, macaroni and cheese, pot roast, and bacon cheeseburgers were considered men's foods.

Food preferences are also gendered. Salads are considered food for women, while men require red meat. Women are said to eat daintily and men heartily. Part of these differences could be argued to be biological, as men generally require more calories to maintain their greater muscle mass than women, but generally these expectations about who eats what have more to do with cultural gender constructions than the physicality of our bodies.

In the study by McPhail et al. (2012), food was considered women's food when it was colorful, delicate, in smaller portions, lighter, or healthier. Part of the attribution of foods to women had to do with weight control. Women were perceived as needing to be more concerned with maintaining or losing weight. Men were thought to prefer both heartier fare and larger portions—little worrying about controlling their food intake or weight. Most of the women expressed concern about eating healthily and watching their weight, although there were a few men who also expressed these concerns.

Women were more adventurous than men when it came to food choices, while ease of preparation and consumption were felt to be the primary considerations for men. Men were also found to be less concerned about their health, more reluctant to eat vegetables, and more likely to prefer spicy foods. Most participants in the study considered meat, and particularly red meat, to be men's food.

Some foods were less gendered. Fish was generally considered women's food as it was healthy and light, but many considered fish to be men's food because more men than women like to catch and eat their own fish. Sushi was seen by some as women's food because of its appearance but as men's food by others because it contained raw fish. Despite all these clearly gendered ideas about food, all of McPhail et al.'s (2012) subjects denied that their eating was gendered. All identified their food preferences as a matter of individual choice, not the result of social patterns or forces.

Why is it important to understand that food is gendered? It allows us to see that our behavior is under the influence of larger structural forces. We may recognize the influence generally (in this case by being willing to sort food photographs into piles according to gender), but we prefer to view our own behavior as simply a matter of choice. Until we acknowledge the effects of gender in all spheres, it will be difficult to eradicate gender inequality. Thinking about how food is gendered is a way of seeing the effects of gender in our lives and would make interesting dinner conversation.

* * * * * * *

Jacqueline Bergdahl is associate professor of sociology at Wright State University. She studies food, gender, and obesity among other topics.

Meso-Level Agents of Gender Socialization

Clues to proper gender roles surround children in materials produced by corporations (books, toys, games), in mass media images, in educational settings, and in religious organizations and beliefs. In Chapter 4 on socialization, we learned about agents of socialization. Those agents play a major role in teaching children proper gender roles. The following examples demonstrate how organizations and institutions in our society teach and reinforce gender assumptions and roles.

Corporations

Corporations have produced materials that help socialize children into proper conduct. Publishers, for example, produce many books that present images of expected gender behavior. The language and pictures in preschool picture books, elementary children's books, and school textbooks are steeped in gender role messages, reflecting society's expectations and stereotypes. In a classic study of award-winning children's books from the United States that have sold more than 3 million copies, Weitzman made several observations: (a) Males appear more often in stories as central characters; (b) activities of male and female characters in books differ, with boys playing active roles and girls being passive or simply helping brothers, fathers, or husbands; and (c) adult women are pictured as more passive and dependent, whereas males are depicted as carrying out a range of activities and jobs (Weitzman et al. 1972).

While some studies as recently as the early 2000s indicated modest expansion in the roles book characters play, they confirm a continuing pattern of gender role segregation in children's books (Anderson and Hamilton 2005; Diekman and Murmen 2004). Whether Peter Rabbit, Curious George the Monkey, or Babar the Elephant, the male animal characters in children's books outnumber females; studies of children's books showed that males of any species most often were portrayed as adventurous, brave, competent, clever, and fun, whereas female counterparts have been depicted as incompetent, fearful, and dependent on others.

However, the most recent analysis of winners in the prestigious Caldecott children's book prize indicate that the winning authors practically reverse the roles of women and men, reflecting gender images contrary to older books. Women are engaged in many gender-neutral activities (Houlis 2011). This does not mean all new children's books are gender neutral, but there is at least a new acceptability of gender-neutral books. Still, the tens of thousands of older, classic books in public and school libraries mean that a parent or child picking a book off the shelf is still likely to select a book that has stereotypical views of boys and girls.

Producers of toys and games also contribute to traditional messages about gender. Store-bought toys fill rooms in homes of children in the Western world, and it is usually quite clear which are boys' rooms and which are girls' rooms. Each toy or game prepares children for future gender roles. Choices ranging from college major and occupational choice to activities that depend on visual-spatial and mathematical abilities appear to be affected by these early choices and childhood learning experiences (Tavris and Wade 1984).

Girls and boys quickly pick up messages—from parents, other children, and the media—about what kinds of toys are appropriate for someone of their sex. Many toys, like Barbie dolls and construction toys, have very explicit gender messages.

Boys' rooms are filled with sports equipment, army toys, building and technical toys, and cars and trucks. Girls' rooms have fewer toys, and most are related to dolls and domestic roles. Boys have more experience manipulating blocks, Tinkertoys, LEGO bricks, and Erector Sets—toys paralleling masculinized activities outside the home in the public domain, from constructing and building trades to military roles and sports. Girls prepare for domestic roles with toys relating to domestic activities. Barbie dolls stress physical appearance, consumerism, and glamour. Only a few Barbies are in occupational roles. In contrast, the Ken dolls that Mattel designed to match Barbie (and later discontinued) were often doctors or other professionals. This supports the prevailing stereotype that girls play with Barbies and boys with trucks. Toy stores are generally divided into distinct boys' and girls' sections, shaping parents' and children's choices, and girls' and boys' future skills and interests (Williams 2006). Each toy or game prepares children through anticipatory socialization for future gender roles. Toys that require building, manipulating, and technical skills provide experiences for later life.

It is Friday night at the game store; groups of adolescent males gather to play games. Their two favorites are the card game *Magic: The Gathering* (MTG or Magic) and the online game *World of Warcraft* (WoW). WoW is played with many online players, and the individual players can sit in front of their computers alone, interacting only online. Popular video games that attract primarily boys include *Grand Theft Auto: Vice City* (adventure), *Halo 2* (action), *Gran Turismo 3: A-Spec* (driving), and *Madden NFL* (sports). The bottom line is that gender portrayals are unequal and the few females presented are in stereotypical roles—supporting, needing rescue, or sexually alluring. Research shows that adolescents identify with these characters, often as role models (Mou and Peng 2009). Girls are generally missing or peripheral to the play.

Thinking Sociologically

Why are video and role-playing games primarily a boy thing? Where are the girls? What effect might girls' and boys' different activities have on their futures?

Mass Media

Have you ever noticed the media coverage of female celebrities who have made poor choices? The men who get into trouble are slapped on the hand. "Boys will be boys," after all. However, actresses such as Lindsay Lohan, Britney Spears, and Miley Cyrus experience intense curiosity, scrutiny, and even hostility. Is this because of their class, their gender, or their nontraditional roles and nonconforming behavior? Whatever variables affect the reactions to these women, they are subjects of mass media frenzy.

Mass media comes in many forms—magazines, ads, films, music videos, Internet sites—and is a major agent of socialization into gender roles. Young men and women, desiring to fit in, are influenced by messages from the media. For instance, the epidemic of steroid use among boys in attempts to stimulate muscle growth results from desire to be successful in sports and have an appealing body image. One issue that is media driven for girls is an obsession with thinness (Dixon 2011). A study of more than 2,000 10- to 14-year-old girls found that almost 30% were trying to lose weight and 10.5% had an eating disorder (McVey, Tweed, and Blackmore 2004). Dieting among girls, driven in part by ads, is a health concern in the United States and some other countries (Taub and McLorg 2010). Yet manufacturers advertise food products with promises to remake teens into more attractive people.

Some recent action films include adventurous and competent girls and women, helping counter images of sexy

At the left is the display for Barbie dolls in a Toys "R" Us store in Louisville, Kentucky. Mattel's Barbie dolls have been criticized for their extremely traditional and highly sexualized images of young women. The boy at the right looks at toys marketed for boys, and the message he receives is very different.

and helpless females. The *Hunger Games* heroine, Katniss Everdeen, has become a brave idol for teenage girls; Mattel has even made a Barbie version of the heroine. *The Girl with the Dragon Tattoo* and other films in that series present an extremely clever and unique heroine in Lisbeth. *Crouching Tiger, Hidden Dragon* heroine Yu Shu Lien is a noble and gracious martial arts expert. *Hanna* is about a young girl defending herself and her father. Hermione in *Harry Potter* is intelligent and creative. Éowyn, a noblewoman in *Lord of the Rings: The Return of the King*, dresses as a soldier and kills the evil Nazgûl. Queen of Naboo and Senator Amidala in *Star Wars* and Lyra Belacqua in *The Golden Compass* are strong, brave, and intelligent (as well as beautiful). Maggie Fitzgerald, boxer in *Million Dollar Baby*, is a gutsy and determined female fighter. Lara Croft in *Tomb Raider* holds her own against evil. Despite the above examples, highly competent females are seen less frequently than men.

Television is another powerful socializing agent. "Children in the U.S. watch an average of 3 to 4 hours of television a day. By the time of high school graduation they will have spent more time watching television than they have in the classroom" ("Children and Watching TV" 2011:1). Time watching TV reduces activities such as reading, school work, playing, exercise, family interaction, and social development. In addition, watching hours of TV is correlated with getting lower school grades, reading fewer books, exercising less, and being overweight. TV ads feature junk foods, fast foods, and toys, and have common themes of violence, sexuality, race and gender stereotypes, and drug and alcohol abuse ("Children and Watching TV" 2011). These behaviors also contribute to the growing obesity epidemic in the United States (Randerson 2008).

Television presents a simple, stereotyped view of life, from advertisements to situation comedies to soap operas. Women in soap operas and ads, especially those working outside the home, are often depicted as having problems in carrying out their role responsibilities (Boston Women's Health Book Collective 2006). Even the extraordinary powers of superheroes on Saturday morning television depict the female characters as having gender-stereotyped skills such as superintuition. Notice the next time you are in a video game room that the fighting characters are typically male and often in armor. When fighting women do appear, they are usually clad in skin-revealing bikini-style attire—odd clothing in which to do battle!

Films and television series in the United States seldom feature average-size or older women (although a greater variety of ages and body types is seen in British Broadcasting Company and other British productions such as the recent film *The Best Exotic Marigold Hotel* featuring older stars). Most U.S. films feature stars who are attractive and thin, presenting an often unattainable model for young women, making many feel inadequate and feeding the diet frenzy (Taub and McLorg 2010). In U.S. media, women who are quite large are almost entirely depicted as comic figures in U.S. television. However, women who suffer health issues such as diabetes and heart disease because of obesity are not a joke.

How do social scientists know that television affects gender role socialization? Studies have shown that the more television children watch, the more gender stereotypes they hold. From cartoons to advertisements, television in many countries provides enticing images of a world in which youth is glorified, age is scorned, and female and male roles are stereotyped and/or made unattainable (Kilbourne 2000; Witt 2000). However, research has also found that these media images have a much greater impact on White girls than on African American teens (Milkie 1999).

Thinking Sociologically

Think of recent mass media examples that you have seen. How do they depict women and men? How might these meso-level depictions affect young men and women individually at the micro level?

Educational Systems

Girls and boys often have very different experiences in school. As noted in the examples below, education systems are socialization agents of children through classroom, lunchroom, and playground activities; students' popularity and recognition; sports and Title IX programs; and teachers' attitudes and expectations. For example, boys are encouraged to join competitive team sports and girls to support them (Gilligan 1982; Kramer 2010). Some argue that this simulates hierarchical adult roles of boss/secretary and physician/nurse. Furthermore, the team sports that boys (more than girls) play teach them strategic thinking—a critical skill that involves anticipating the moves of the opponent and countering with one's own strategy. This is a very useful skill in the business world and is not explicitly taught in other places in the school curriculum. Girls' games rarely teach this skill.

Children's separate experiences in grade school and middle school reinforce boundaries of "us" and "them" in classroom seating and activities, in the lunchroom, and in playground activities, as girls and boys are seated, lined up, and given assignments by sex (Sadker and Sadker 2005). Those who go outside the boundaries, especially boys, are ridiculed by peers and sometimes teachers, reinforcing stereotypes and separate gender role socialization (Sadker and Sadker 2005; Thorne 1993).

Boys act out and receive more attention in school classrooms than girls do, even though it may be negative

Olsen twins Mary-Kate and Ashley (left) pose together in front of their new star on the Walk of Fame in Hollywood. Like most glamour stars, they must conform to the image of very thin, shapely femininity. By contrast, an older not-particularly-thin actor, Stephanie Cole, plays the leading role in the BBC series Waiting for God*—a comedy about people in an assisted living nursing home. Few roles—except comic relief—are available for older and heavier women in U.S. media.*

attention. Boys are called on more often to do physical chores such as erasing the boards and emptying the trash. Teachers reward girls for being passive and obedient. Boys begin at young ages to work and play together as teams. Girls also join team sports, but their play more frequently involves one-on-one activities. In contrast to girls, boys learn the skills of competition, negotiating, bargaining, aggressive pursuit of a goal, and strategic thinking.

Part of the issue of male-female inequality in schools is tied to the issue of *popularity*, which it seems has less to do with being liked than with being known and visible. If everyone knows a person's name, she or he is popular (Eder, Evans, and Parker 1995). At the middle school level, there are more ways by which boys can become known. Boys who charm peers and adults, are smooth talkers, and hang out in the popular set are cool (Adler and Adler 1998; Milner 2006). In sports, even when there are both boys' and girls' basketball teams, many spectators come to the boys' contests and very few to the girls' games. Thus, few people know the female athletes by name. In fact, a far more visible position is cheerleader—standing on the sidelines cheering for the boys—because those girls are at least seen (Eder et al. 1995; Milner 2006).

High schools are breeding grounds for status consciousness. Which lunch table one sits at, with whom one goes to the prom, who holds the popular positions (such as cheerleader and football player), and what clothing one wears are all status-enhancing activities and symbols needed to be cool (Milner 2006). Girls are visible or known because of their physical appearance, a major standard of popularity and esteem (Eder et al. 1995). The bottom line is that there are far more visible positions for boys than for girls in middle and high school, allowing them to be recognized and become leaders.

Title IX of the U.S. Education Amendments of 1972 was a major legislative attempt to level the educational and sports playing field. Passed in order to bar gender discrimination in schools receiving federal funds, this legislation mandates equal opportunity for participation in school-sponsored programs (Lindsey 2011). The law has reduced or eliminated blatant discrimination in areas ranging from admissions and health care to counseling and housing, sex-segregated programs, financial aid, dress codes, and other areas that were of concern. However, the biggest impact of Title IX legislation has been in athletics.

Partly aided by Title IX, the number of women's athletic programs and scholarship opportunities grew in the late 1990s, but it has slowed since 2000 and still lags behind men's levels. From 1995 to 2005, the number of women in college sports at 738 National Collegiate Athletic Association (NCAA) schools surveyed grew from 26,000 to 205,492, while the number of men was 291,797 (Rosen 2007). Some men's sports have been cut back, but others have grown, resulting in a steady number of opportunities for men in sports. One third of high school women participate in sports compared with 45% of males. Overall, 79% of the public supports Title IX and what it has accomplished (Women's Sports Foundation 2005).

High school and college athletics are much less reliable paths for women to become known on campus since so few people come to the games. Even this college game with a winning team has sparse attendance (top photo). By contrast, women in very sexy outfits are highly visible and can even become local celebrities when they perform as cheerleaders in front of 80,000 fans at men's sporting events (bottom photo).

Religious Organizations

Religious organizations serve as agents of socialization by defining, reinforcing, and perpetuating gender role stereotypes and cultural beliefs. Religious teachings provide explanations of proper male/female roles. Although the specific teachings vary, the three major monotheistic religions that affirm that there is only one God—Christianity, Islam, and Judaism—are traditionally patriarchal, stressing separate female and male spheres (Kramer 2010). The following are examples of some of these traditional role expectations and the status of women in various religions.

Some interpretations of the Adam and Eve creation story in the Hebrew Bible (the Old Testament in the Christian Bible) state that because man was created first, men are superior. Because Eve, created from the rib of man, was a sinner, her sins keep women forever in an inferior, second-class position. For these reasons, in some branches of these religions, women are restricted in their roles within the family and religious organizations. They cannot be priests in Catholic churches and cannot vote on business matters in some religious organizations. However, recent work by feminist scholars is challenging the notion of patriarchy in Judaic and Christian history, pointing out that women may have played a much broader role in religious development than currently recognized (Hunter College Women's Studies Collective 2005). Even *Yahweh*—the name for God in the Hebrew Bible—had both male and female connotations, and when God was referred to as a source of wisdom, feminine pronouns and references were used (Borg 1994). Increasingly, denominations are granting women greater roles in the religious hierarchies, ministries, and priesthood.

Women in Judaism lived for 4,000 years in a patriarchal system where men read, taught, and legislated while women followed (Lindsey 2011). Today, three of the five main branches of Judaism allow women equal participation, illustrating that religious practices do change over time. However, Hasidic and Orthodox Jews have a division of labor between men and women following old laws, with designated gender roles for the home and religious life.

Some Christian teachings have treated women as second-class citizens, even in the eyes of God. For this reason, some Christian denominations have excluded women from a variety of leadership roles and told them they must be subservient to their husbands. Other Christians point to the admonition by Saint Paul that theologically speaking, "There is no such thing as . . . male and female, for you are all one in Christ Jesus." This suggests that women and men are not spiritually different (Galatians 3:28).

Traditional Hindu religion painted women as seductresses, strongly erotic, and a threat to male spirituality and asceticism. To protect men from this threat, women were kept totally covered in thick garments and veils and seen only by men in their immediate families. Today, Hinduism comes in many forms, most of which honor the woman's domestic sphere of life—as mothers, wives, and homemakers—while accepting women in public roles (Lindsey 2011).

Traditional Islamic beliefs also portrayed female sexuality as dangerous to men, although many women in Islamic societies today are full participants in the public and private sphere. The Quran (also spelled Qur'an or Koran), the Muslim sacred scripture, includes a statement that men are superior to women because of the qualities God has given men. Hammurabi's Code, written in the Middle East between 2067 and 2025 BCE, is the earliest recorded legal system. The laws about women's status were written to distinguish between decent women, belonging to one man, and indecent or public women. Some aspects of these traditional beliefs have carried over to present times. Sharia law, strict Islamic law, adopted in several countries and among some groups, has been used to punish women accused of violating its rules. Recent cases include a woman in Nigeria who had a child out of wedlock and another woman in Pakistan who was a rape victim. Both women were sentenced to death by stoning, but their sentences have not been carried out because of protests from within and outside the countries. Some Muslim women in Britain have tried to get an Islamic divorce, but a Sharia council must approve. Women who are in forced marriages and who are abused have little recourse as Sharia councils grant few of these divorces (Proudman 2012). These women suffer social humiliation, degradation, and potential death, but they also demonstrate the severe penalties for violating the social expectations, lessons for others who might stray from the laws (Mydans 2002).

Women in fundamentalist Muslim societies such as Algeria, Iran, Syria, and Saudi Arabia are separated from men (except for fathers and brothers) in work and worship. They generally remain covered. *Purdah*, which means curtain, refers to practices of seclusion and separate worlds for women and men in Islamic cultures. Screens in households and veils in public enforce female modesty and prevent men from seeing women where this is dictated (Ward and Edelstein 2009). Today, some women argue that the veil they wear is for modesty, for cosmetic purposes, or to protect them from the stares of men. Others claim that the veil is a symbol of oppression and subservience, showing that women must keep themselves in submissive positions. In Turkey, a secular Muslim society, schools, universities, and public institutions such as courtrooms, state hospitals, and Parliament have long forbidden religious representation, including the wearing of scarves. However, recent debates in Turkey under the leadership of a more conservative president have challenged the rulings forbidding scarves in schools, and the president has declared it legal for women to choose whether to wear scarves (Gusten 2012; Knickmeyer 2008). France has the largest Muslim minority in Western Europe, 5 million or 10% of the French population. France banned head scarves from state schools in 2004, and banned full facial coverings in April 2011 (Reuters 2011). The debate in Turkey, France, and other countries over wearing of head scarves or burqas continues.

Religious laws often provide the justifications to keep women servile, and public shaming and threat of severe punishments reinforce the laws. Meso-level religious systems influence how different societies interpret proper gender roles and how sometimes these belief systems change with new interpretations of scriptures. (Further discussion of the complex relationship between religion and gender appears in Chapter 12.)

From family and education to media and religion, meso-level agents of socialization reinforce "appropriate" gender roles in each society.

Thinking Sociologically

What are some of the books, toys, games, television shows, school experiences, religious teachings, and peer interactions that have influenced your gender role socialization? In what ways did they do so?

Gender Stratification: Meso- and Macro-Level Processes

When women are not able to work long hours and therefore cannot advance within a company; when women are primarily in the secretarial staff without advancement paths; when there is a lack of women in senior political offices in a country, we see elements of the glass ceiling. "The *glass ceiling* keeps women from reaching the highest levels of corporate and public responsibility, and the 'sticky floor' keeps the vast majority of the world's women stuck in low-paid jobs" (Hunter College Women's Studies Collective 2005:393).

The phrase *glass ceiling* generally applies to processes that limit progress to the highest job or status positions because of invisible barriers that bar promotion within an organization. Although the woman or minority member may have superior skills or experience, she or he is passed over due to race, ethnicity, sex, or other factors. The reason this is a big deal is loss of talent, unfair discrimination, and the impact on salaries. Although there are high-profile women as chief executive officers and in government leadership positions in the United States, women earn only about 80 cents to every dollar earned by men (Berman 2010; U.S. Bureau of Labor Statistics 2012).

Men, on the other hand, face the "glass escalator," especially in traditionally female occupations. Even if they do not seek to climb in the organizational hierarchy, occupational social forces push them up the job ladder to the higher echelons (Wingfield 2009). One analysis found that women around the world do more than half of the work (when home and family maintenance is included), they receive 10% of the world's income, and they own 1% of the world's means of production (Global Citizen Corps 2010). They make up more than 40% of the world's paid workforce but hold only about 20% of the managerial jobs, and for those, they are often compensated at lower pay than their male counterparts. Only 5% of the top corporate jobs are held by women. However, companies with women in leadership positions do realize high profits (CNNMoney.com 2010; Hunter College Women's Studies Collective 2005). The next "Engaging Sociology" provides an exercise to think about how our ideas may subtly maintain the glass ceiling.

Although public school teachers are disproportionally women and although serving in the classroom is the normal channel for working into high administrative posts, principals and superintendents with higher pay and more authority are disproportionally men. This is an example of a gendered organization.

Women and Men at Work: Gendered Organizations

"How can I do it all—marriage, children, education, career, social life?" This is a question that women in college classes ask. They already anticipate a delicate balancing act. Work has been central to the definition of masculinity in U.S. society, and for the past half-century women have been joining the workforce in ever greater numbers (Kramer 2010). Today, women outnumber men in the workforce, with 800,000 more women than men on payrolls in January 2010, according to the U.S. Department of Labor. Figure 9.1 on page 324 shows how men's and women's incomes vary in the United States for several career fields. The same pattern is true in a number of Global North countries, in part because of changes in workforce needs (20-First 2010).

Working is necessary for many women, especially single mothers, to support their families, and many women with career education and goals want to work. Among countries of the Global North, Sweden has the highest percentage of women in the labor force at more than 8 out of 10 women participating. Yet even in Sweden, with its parental leave and other family-friendly policies, women feel pressures of work and family responsibilities (Eshleman and Bulcroft 2010). Dual-career marriages raise questions about child rearing, power relations, and other factors in juggling work and family.

Every workplace has gendered relationships: ratios of female to male workers, gender reflected in subordinate-supervisor positions, and distribution of positions between men and women. This, in turn, affects our experiences in the workplace. Consider the example of mothers who are breastfeeding their babies. Must they quit their jobs or alter their family schedules if the workplace does not provide a space for breastfeeding? Some workplaces accommodate family needs, but others do not. Many women have multiple responsibilities: They try to support their families financially and in other ways, by being good mothers and by being responsible employees or employers. Men do not face the same issues because most corporations in the United States assume the average worker is male.

Research shows that workers are more satisfied when the sex composition of their work group and the distribution of men and women in power are balanced (Britton 2000). Feminists propose ideas to minimize gender differences in

Engaging Sociology

Masculinity and Femininity in Your Social World

1. Mark each characteristic with an *M* or an *F* depending on whether you think it is generally defined by society as a masculine or a feminine characteristic.

____ achiever
____ aggressive
____ analytical
____ caring
____ confident
____ dynamic
____ deferential (defers to others; yields with courtesy)
____ devious
____ intuitive
____ loving
____ manipulative
____ nurturing
____ organized
____ passive
____ a planner
____ powerful
____ sensitive
____ strong
____ relationship-oriented (makes decisions based on how others will *feel*)
____ rule oriented (makes decisions based on *abstract procedural rules*)

2. Next, mark an *X* just to the right of 10 characteristics that you think are the essential qualities for a leadership position in a complex organization (business, government, etc.). You might want to ask 20 of your acquaintances to do this and then add up the scores for "masculinity," "femininity," and "leadership trait."
3. Do you (and your acquaintances) tend to view leadership as having the same traits as those marked "masculine" or "feminine"? What are the implications of this for the "glass ceiling"?
4. How might correlations between the traits of leadership and gender notions help explain the data on income in Table 9.2?

Table 9.2 **U.S. Income by Education Level and Sex (in Dollars)**

Education	*Men*	*Women*
Not a high school graduate	24,831	14,521
High school graduate	36,753	24,329
College graduate (bachelor's)	72,868	44,078
Master's degree	88,450	54,517
Doctorate	116,574	70,898
Professional degree	147,518	87,723

Source: U.S. Census Bureau 2011c, 2001d, 2011e.

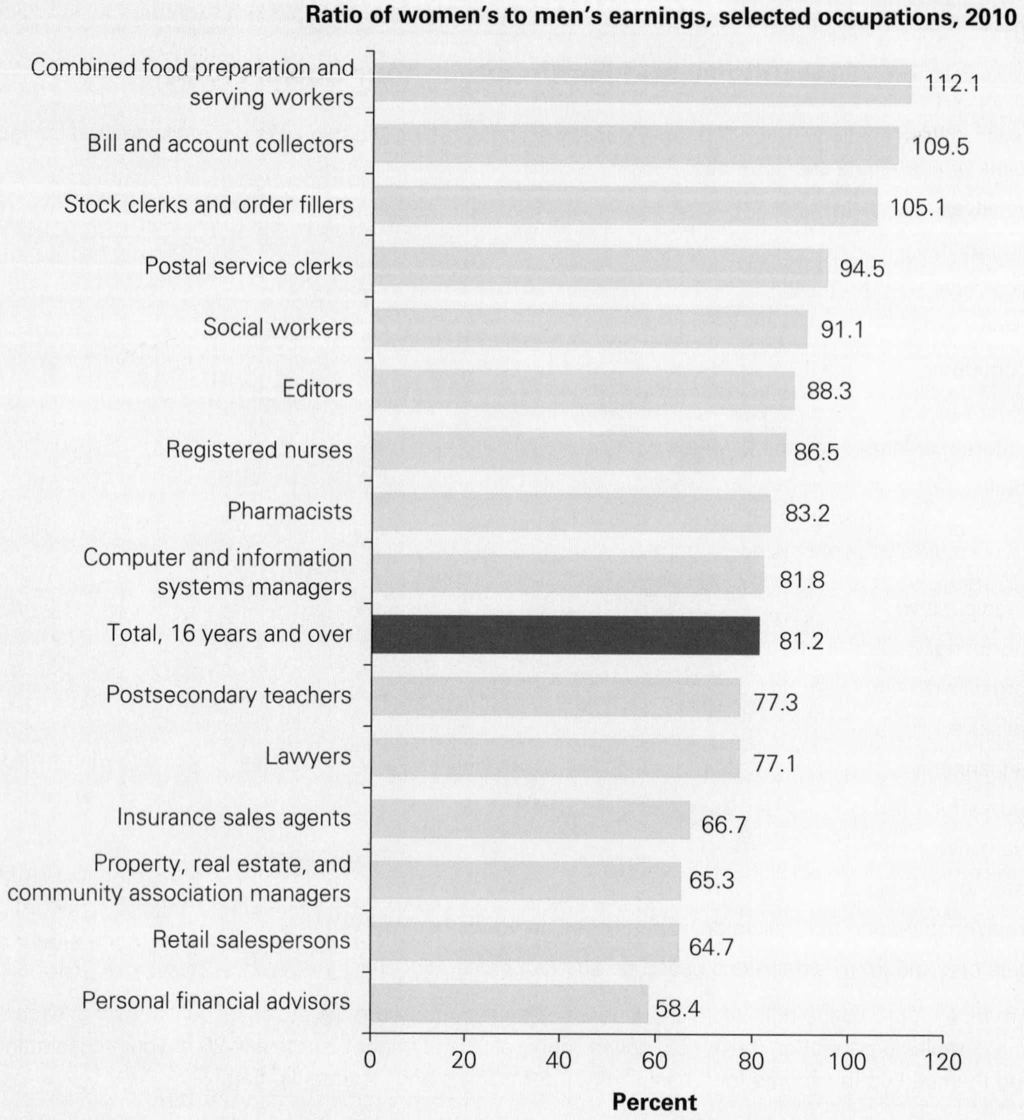

Figure 9.1 Ratio of Women's to Men's Earnings for Selected Occupations, 2010

Source: Thompson 2011.

organizations—that is, to "degender" organizations so that all members have equal opportunities (Britton 2000).

Thinking Sociologically

If corporate structures were reversed so that women structured and organized the workplace, how might the workplace environment change?

Institutionalized Gender Discrimination

Gender stratification at the meso level—like race and ethnic stratification—can occur quite independently of any overt prejudice or ill will by others. It becomes part of the social system, and we are not even conscious of it, especially if we are one of the privileged members of society. *When discrimination is built into organizations and cultural expectations and includes both intentional actions and unintentional actions or structures that have consequences that restrict minorities,* it is called **institutional discrimination**.

You may recall from the previous chapter that **side-effect discrimination** involves *practices in one institutional area that have a negative impact because they are linked to practices in another institutional area; because institutions are interdependent, discrimination in one results in unintentional discrimination in others.* For example, if roles of women in family life are determined by rigid gender expectations, as research shows, then women find it more difficult to devote themselves to gaining job promotions. In addition, as long as little girls learn through socialization to use their voices and to hold their bodies and to gesture in ways that communicate deference, employers assume a lack of the self-confidence necessary for major leadership roles. If women are paid less despite the same levels of education (see Table 9.2 on page 323), they are less likely to have access to the best health care or to be able to afford a $40,000 down payment for a house, unless they are married. This makes women dependent on men in a way that most men are not dependent on women.

A factor affecting differences in incomes is the type of academic degrees that men and women receive (e.g., engineering rather than education). However, even when these differences are factored in, men still make considerably more on average than women with identical levels of experience and training.

Past-in-present discrimination refers to *practices from the past that may no longer be allowed but that continue to affect people today.* For example, at an appliance industry in the Midwest investigated by one of the authors, there is a sequence of jobs one must hold to be promoted up the line to foreman. This requirement ensures that the foreman understands the many aspects of the production at the plant. One of the jobs involves working in a room with heavy equipment that cuts through and bends metal sheets. The machine is extremely powerful and could easily cut off a leg or hand if the operator is not careful. Because of the danger, the engineers designed the equipment so it would not operate unless three levers were activated at the same time. One lever was triggered by stepping on a pedal on the floor. The other two required reaching out with one's hands so that one's body was extended. When one was spread-eagled to activate all three levers, there was no way one could possibly have a part of one's body near the blades. It was brilliant engineering.

There was one unanticipated problem: The hand-activated levers were 5 feet, 10 inches off the ground and 5 feet apart. Few women had the height and arm span to run this machine, and therefore, no women had yet made it through the sequence of positions to the higher-paying position of foreman. The equipment cost millions of dollars, so it was not likely to be replaced. Neither the engineers who designed the machine nor the upper-level managers who established the sequence of jobs to become foreman had deliberately tried to exclude women. Indeed, they were perplexed when they looked at their employee figures and saw so few women moving up through the ranks. The cause of women's disadvantage was not mean-spirited men but features of the system that had unintended consequences resulting in past-in-present discrimination. The barriers women face, then, are not just matters of socialization or other micro-level social processes. The nature of sexism is often subtle yet pervasive in the society, operating at the meso and macro levels as institutional discrimination.

Little girls learn to use their voices and hold their bodies and gesture in ways that communicate deference. This little girl does not look very powerful or confident. When women tilt their heads—either forward or to one side—they also look like they lack confidence, and this hurts their chances of promotion in the corporate world.

Men often get defensive and angry when people talk about sexism in society because they feel they are being attacked or asked to correct injustices of the past. However, the empirical reality is that the playing field is not level for men and women. Most men—like your second author—do not do anything to intentionally harm women, and they may not feel prejudiced toward women, but sexism operates so that men are given privileges they never asked for and may not even recognize.

Gender Differences in Internet Use

Consider gender differences in Internet use. Internet-related gender stratification exhibits itself not just in terms of *whether* a person uses the Internet but also in terms of *how* a person uses the Internet. Even within industrialized countries such as the United States, women tend to use mostly the e-mail services, with the intent of keeping up with family and friends (Shade 2004). Women's use focuses on personal growth, maintaining a social group, getting information about products and brands, and sites offering anonymity not available on Facebook and Twitter. A recent Nielsen study shows that 75.8% of women who are online use social networking sites compared to 69.7% of men. Globally, women account for 47.9% of visitors to social-networking sites, and spend 30% more time on social networking sites than men (ComScore 2010; Morrison 2010).

For men, the Internet is used to gather information and to exchange ideas, knowledge of events in the world, job skills, awareness of job openings, networks that extend beyond national borders, and facts relevant to professional activities. Thus, "women are using the Internet to reinforce their private lives and men are using the Internet for engaging in the public sphere" (Shade 2004:63). The difference also reflects differences in the professional positions men and women hold. For men, the Internet is enhancing their careers. This is less true for women.

The difference in Internet use by women as a percentage of all users varies significantly by development levels of countries: Women are roughly 45% of the Internet users in Sweden and Denmark, 46% in Mexico, 49% in South Africa and Thailand each, a bit more than 40% in Israel, about 30% in China, 17% in Senegal, and 14% in Ethiopia. In the Arab world, women account for only 4% of the online population (Drori 2006).

In some countries, there is a huge gender digital divide. In others, nearly as many women as men use computers. However, research shows that women tend to use computers in different ways. These women in Iraq are learning computer skills.

In Chapter 7, we explored global differences in Internet usage and found that the largest variance was based on the wealth of the country and access to technology. The same principle holds for women's usage in the Global North and South. African countries may have only a small percent of the population online, but in none of the African countries cited by Drori do women have more than 15% of that tiny share (Drori 2006). So of the women in most African countries, fewer than 7 out of 10,000 had used the Internet in 2006; however, that number is growing rapidly. Clearly, the majority of African women are "out of the digital loop." Yet competency in use of the Internet has become an extremely important resource in the contemporary global economy. Lack of access and savvy use is a handicap.

The story is different in the United States, where women have recently caught up with or outpaced their male peers. The direction of U.S. usage parallels that of other Global North countries and may predict the future in other countries (Madden and Zickuhr 2011).

Thinking Sociologically

Ask several people from different generations and different genders how they use computer technology and the Internet and how they learned these skills. What do you conclude about differences between women and men?

Gender Stratification: Micro- to Macro-Level Theories

In recent years, some biologists and psychologists have considered whether there are innate differences in the makeup of women and men. For instance, males produce more testosterone, a hormone found to be correlated with aggression. Research shows that in many situations, males tend to be more aggressive and concerned with dominance, whether the behavior is biologically programmed or learned or both. Other traits, such as nurturance, empathy, and altruism, show no clear gender difference (Fausto-Sterling 1992; Sapolsky 2011).

Although biological and psychological factors are part of the difference between females and males, our focus here is on the major contribution that *social factors* make in the social statuses of males and females in human society. This section explores social theories that explain gender differences.

Symbolic Interaction Theory: Micro-Level Analysis

Traditional notions of gender are hard to change. Confusion over proper masculine and feminine roles creates anxiety and even anomie in a society. People want guidelines. Thus, it is easier to adhere to traditional notions of gender that are reinforced by religious or political dogmas, making those ideas appear sacred, absolute, and beyond human change. Absolute answers are comforting to those who find change disconcerting. Others believe the male prerogatives and privileges of the past were established by men to protect their rights. Any change in concepts of gender or of roles assigned to males and females will be hard to bring about precisely because they are rooted in the meaning system and status and power structures present in the social world—that is, they are socially created and constructed.

Symbolic interactionists look at gender as socially constructed. Sex is the biological reality of different "plumbing" in our bodies, and interactionists are interested in how those physical differences come to be symbols, resulting in different social rights and rewards. This chapter's discussions of micro-level social processes have pointed out that the meaning assigned to one's sex is connected to notions of masculinity and femininity. The symbolic interaction perspective has been forceful in insisting that notions of proper gender behavior are not intrinsically related to a person's sex. The bottom line is that gender is a socially created or constructed idea.

Symbolic interaction—more than any other theory—stresses the idea of *human agency*—the notion that humans not only are influenced by the society in which they live but also actively help create it (Charon 2010; Hewitt and Shulman 2011). In a study of elementary children in classrooms and especially on playgrounds, Barrie Thorne (1993) found that while teachers influenced the children, the children themselves were active participants in creating the student culture that guided their play. As children played with one another, Thorne noticed the ways in which they created words, nicknames, distinctions between one another, and new forms of interaction. This is a very important point: Humans do not just passively adopt cultural notions about gender; they *do gender*. They create it as they behave and interact with others in ways that define "normal" male or female conduct (West and Zimmerman 1987). "Doing gender" is an everyday, recurring, and routine occurrence. It is a constant ongoing process that defines each situation, takes place in organizations and between individuals, and becomes part of institutional arrangements. Social movements such as civil rights and the women's movement challenge these arrangements and can bring about change. Understanding the process of doing gender helps us understand why we think and act as we do.

Some cultures suggest that women are helpless and need the door held for them, and women's stylish attire—such as many forms of shoes and dresses—actually does make them more vulnerable and helpless in certain situations. In these decisions and behaviors, men and women are "doing gender." Does this give men more power?

When children are in an ambiguous situation, they may spontaneously define their sex as the most relevant trait about themselves or others. Indeed, even when children act as if gender matters, they are helping make it a reality for those around them. This process helps make the notion of gender more concrete and real to the other children. As the next child adopts the "definition of reality" from the first, acting as if sex is more important than hair color or eye color, it makes gender the most prominent characteristic in the mind of the next child. Yet each child, in a sense, could choose to ignore gender and decide that something else is more important. This is part of human agency—the freedom to define reality differently from others. The same principle applies to adults. When a person "chooses" to recognize gender as a critical distinction between two individuals or two groups, that person is "doing gender." We *do gender* all the time, every day. In fact, we cannot avoid it! It is present in our interactions, and we are conscious that we will be judged by others. That judgment could be harsh if we go outside accepted boundaries of gender behavior. Thus, little girls and boys learn to do their appropriate gender roles (Hewitt and Shulman 2011; O'Brien 2011; Schoepflin 2011).

Through interaction, people do gender, and although this process begins at a micro level, it has implications all the way to the global level. The next section explores meso- and macro-level forces that shape gender and stratification based on sex.

Thinking Sociologically

How do you *do gender*? How did you learn these patterns of behavior? Are they automatic responses, or do you think about "who opens the door" and other gender behaviors?

Structural-Functional and Conflict Theories: Meso- and Macro-Level Analyses

Structural-Functional Theory

From the structural-functional perspective, each sex has a role to play in the interdependent groups and institutions of society. Some early theorists argued that men and women carry out different roles and are, of necessity, unequal because of the needs of societies and practices that have developed since early human history. Social relationships and practices that have proven successful in the survival of a group are likely to continue and be reinforced by society's norms, laws, and religious beliefs. Thus, relationships between women and men that are believed to support survival are maintained. In traditional hunter-gatherer, horticultural, and pastoral societies, for instance, the division of labor is based on sex and age. Social roles are clearly laid out, indicating who performs which everyday survival tasks. The females often take on the primary tasks of child care, gardening, food preparation, and other duties near the home. Men do tasks that require movements farther from home, such as hunting, fishing, or herding.

As societies industrialize, roles and relationships change due to structural changes in society. Durkheim ([1893] 1947) described a gradual move from traditional societies held together by *mechanical solidarity* (the glue based on shared beliefs, values, and traditions) to modern societies that hold together due to *organic solidarity* (social coherence based on division of labor, with each member playing a highly specialized role). According to early functionalists, gender division of labor exists in modern societies because it is efficient and useful to have different-but-complementary male and female roles. They believed this accomplishes essential tasks and maintains societal stability (Lindsey 2011).

More recent structural-functional theorists describe society as an integrated system of roles that work together to carry out the necessary tasks in society. In the traditional family, the father works, the mom stays at home, and they have two children. The female plays the expressive role through childbearing, nursing, and caring for family members in the home. The male carries out the instrumental role by working outside the home to support the family (Parsons and Bales 1953). Although this pattern was relevant during the industrial revolution and again after World War II, when men returned to take jobs women had held during the war, it characterized only 23% of U.S. families in 2011. More children are being raised by single moms than married couples (Aulette 2010; Coontz 2011).

In reality, gender segregation has seldom been total because in most cultures, women's work has combined their labor in the public sphere—that is, outside the home—with their work in the private sphere—inside the home (Lopez-Garza 2002). Poor minority women in countries around the world must often work in low-paying service jobs in the public sphere and carry the major burden for roles in the private sphere. Gender analysis through a structural-functional perspective stresses efficiencies that are believed to be gained by the structural-functional view of specialization of tasks (Waite and Gallagher 2000).

Conflict Theory

Conflict theorists view males as the haves—controlling the majority of power positions and most wealth—and females as the have-nots. Women have less access to power and have historically depended on males for survival. This is the case even though they raise the next generation of workers and consumers, provide unpaid domestic labor, often grow much of the food, and assure a pool of available, cheap labor during times of crisis, such as war. By keeping women in subordinate roles, males control the means of production and protect their privileged status.

A classical conflict explanation of gender stratification is found in the writings of Karl Marx's colleague, Friedrich Engels ([1884] 1942). In traditional societies, where size and strength were essential for survival, men were often dominant, but women's roles were respected as important and necessary to the survival of the group. Men hunted, engaged in warfare, and protected women. Over time, male physical control was transformed into control by ideology, by the dominant belief system itself. Capitalism strengthened male dominance by making more wealth available to men and their sons. Women became dependent on men, and their roles were transformed into "taking care of the home" (Engels [1884] 1942).

Ideologies based on traditional beliefs and values have continued to be used to justify the social structure of male domination and subjugation of women. It is in the interest of the dominant group, in this case men, to maintain a position of privilege. Conflict theorists believe it unlikely that those in power by virtue of sex, race, class, or political or religious ideology will voluntarily give up their positions as long as they are benefiting from them. By keeping women in traditional gender roles, men maintain control over institutions and resources (Collins 1971).

Feminist Theory

Feminist theorists agree with Marx and Engels that gender stratification is based on power struggles, not biology. On the other hand, some feminist theorists argue that Marx and Engels failed to include a key variable in women's oppression: patriarchy. Patriarchy involves a few men dominating and holding authority over all others, including women, children, and the less powerful men (Arrighi 2000; Lindsey 2011). According to feminist theory, women will continue to be oppressed by men until patriarchy is eliminated.

A distinguishing characteristic of most feminist theory is that it actively advocates a change in the social order, whereas many other theories we have discussed try only to explain the social world (Anderson 2006; Lorber 1998). There is a range of feminist theories. However, all feminist theories argue for bringing about a new and equal ordering of gender relationships to eliminate the patriarchy and sexism of current gender-stratification systems (Kramer 2010).

Feminist theorists try to understand the causes of women's lower status and seek ways to change the systems to provide more opportunities, to improve the standard of living, and to give women control over their bodies and reproduction. Feminist theorists also feel that little change will occur until group consciousness is raised so that women understand the system that limits their options and do not blame themselves for their situations (Sapiro 2003).

As societies become technologically advanced and need an educated workforce, women of all social classes and ethnic groups around the world are likely to gain more equal roles. Women are entering institutions of higher education in record numbers, and evidence indicates they are needed in the world economic system and the changing labor force of most countries. Societies in which women are not integrated into the economic system generally lag behind other countries. Feminist theorists examine these global and national patterns, but they also note the role of patriarchy in interpersonal situations—such as domestic violence.

Violence against women perpetuates gender stratification, as is evident in the intimate environment of many homes. Because men have more power in the larger society, they often have more resources within the household as well (an example of side-effect discrimination). Women are often dependent on the man of the house for his resources, meaning they must yield on many decisions. Power differences in the meso- and macro-level social systems also contribute to power differentials and vulnerability of women in micro-level settings. In addition, women have fewer options when considering whether to leave an abusive relationship. Although there are risks of staying in an abusive relationship, many factors enter into a woman's decision to stay or leave (Scott, London, and Myers 2002). The following "Sociology in Our Social World" discusses one form of violence around the world that is perpetuated predominantly against women: rape.

By contrast to the clothing and gestures that create vulnerability in women, men are encouraged to use gestures that communicate strength and self-assurance, and their clothing and shoes allow them to defend themselves or flee danger.

Men who play cards, games, or sports together or who join men-only clubs or golf courses develop networks that enhance their power and their ability to "close deals." When women are not part of the same networks, they are denied the same insider privileges. Many conflict theorists would argue that this is purposeful, whereas others point to it as a reality even if it is not intentional, like past-in-present discrimination.

Sociology in Our Social World

Rape and the Victims of Rape

For many women around the world, rape is the most feared act of violence and the ultimate humiliation. Rape is a sexual act but closely tied to macho behavior. Often it is a power play to intimidate, hurt, and dominate women. As an act of war, rape humiliates the enemies who cannot protect their women ("Male Dominance Causes Rape" 2008; Sanday and Goodenough 1990). Some societies are largely free from rape whereas others are prone toward rape. What is the difference? When a society is relatively tolerant of interpersonal violence, holds beliefs in male dominance, and strongly incorporates ways to separate women and men, rape is more common ("Male Dominance Causes Rape" 2008; Sanday and Goodenough 1990). Rape is also more common when gender roles and identities are changing and norms about interaction between women and men are unclear.

An alarming problem is rape on college campuses in the United States. What does this say about the United States, where 1 in 4–5 college women will be raped or survive a rape attempt during her college years (Burn 2011; One in Four, Inc. n.d.)? That is 1 every 21 hours. Ninety percent occur under the influence of alcohol.

Eighteen percent of women in the United States have survived a complete or an attempted rape—22 million women. In the United States, someone is sexually assaulted or raped every two minutes, averaging more than 2,000 rapes daily. Annually, there are 169,370 female, 15,020 male, and a total of 272,350 rapes or sexual assaults (Truman 2011). The U.S. Justice Department estimates that only 26% of rapes and attempted rapes are reported (Anti-Violence Resource Guide 2012; National Center for Injury Prevention and Control 2011).

The fallout from rape and attempted rape is that victims "often experience anxiety, guilt, nervousness, phobias, substance abuse, sleep disturbances, depression, alienation, sexual dysfunction, aggression, and distrust of others." Physical disorders are also common, including sexually transmitted diseases (Anti-Violence Resource Guide 2012). All of this indicates that rape and sexual assault really do intimidate a significant portion of the population, making the targeted group feel vulnerable and less confident. The net result means a reduction of power, as pointed out by feminist theory.

Women report being sexually assaulted whereas few males define their behavior as assault. This discrepancy points to the stereotypes and misunderstandings that can occur because of different beliefs and attitudes. Rape causes deep and lasting problems for women victims as well as for men accused of rape because of "misreading" women's signals. Some college men define gang rape as a form of male bonding. To them, it is no big deal. The woman is just the object and instrument. Her identity is immaterial (Martin and Hummer 1989; Sanday and Goodenough 1990).

Men who hold more traditional gender roles view rape very differently than women and less traditional men. The former tend to attribute more responsibility to the female victim of a rape, believe sex rather than power is the motivation for rape, and look less favorably on women who have been raped. In a strange twist of logic, one study showed that some men actually believe that women want to be forced into having involuntary sex (Szymanski et al. 1993). Researchers have found that societies with widespread gender stratification report more gendered violence (Palmer 1989; Sanday 1996, 2007).

Many citizens and politicians see rape as an individualized, personal act, whereas social scientists tend to see it as a structural problem that stems from negative stereotypes of women, subservient positions of women in society, and patriarchal systems of power. A number of sociologists and anthropologists believe that rape will not be substantially reduced unless our macho definitions of masculinity are changed (McEvoy and Brookings 2008).

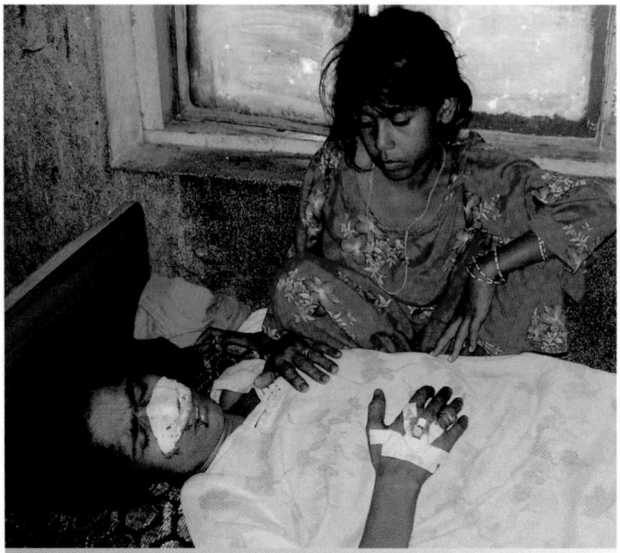

When women have less power at the meso level, they may also be more vulnerable at home. This girl attends to her injured mother at a hospital in Hyderabad, Pakistan, after the woman's husband chopped off her nose with an axe and broke all her teeth. According to the Pakistan Institute of Medical Sciences, more than 90% of married women report being severely abused when husbands are dissatisfied with their cooking or cleaning or when the women give birth to a girl instead of a boy or are unable to bear a child at all.

In summary, feminist analysis finds gender patterns embedded in social institutions of family, education, religion, politics, economics, and health care. If the societal system is patriarchal, ruled by men, the interdependent institutions are likely to reflect and support this system. Feminist theory helps us understand how patriarchy at the meso and macro levels can influence patriarchy at the micro level and vice versa.

Thinking Sociologically

Why do women and men stay in abusive relationships? If these behaviors are hurtful or destructive, what might be done to change the situation, or what policies might be enacted to address the problems?

The Interaction of Class, Race, and Gender

Zouina is Algerian, but she was born in France to her immigrant parents. She lived with them in a poor immigrant suburb of Paris until she was forced to return to Algeria for an arranged marriage to a man who already had one wife. That marriage ended, and she returned to her "home" in France. Since she returned to France, Zouina has been working wherever she can find work. The high unemployment and social and ethnic discrimination, especially against foreign women, makes life difficult (as shown in the film *The Perfumed Garden*; Benguigui 2000). An estimated 70,000 forced (and illegal) polygamous marriages occurred in 2006 in the immigrant communities of France (Levy 2008).

The situation is complex. Muslim women from Tunisia, Morocco, and Algeria living in crowded slum communities outside Paris face discrimination in the workplace and community (Lazaridis 2011). Expected to be both good Muslim women and good family coproviders—which necessitates working in French society—they face ridicule when they wear their *hijabs* (coverings) to school or to work. However, they encounter derision in their community if they do not wear them. They are caught between two cultures, and may be the scapegoats for frustrated young men who cannot find work.

Because of high unemployment in the immigrant communities, many youth roam around the streets. Gang rapes by North African youth against young women have been on the rise in France and elsewhere abroad. These rapes mean that North African women are faced with rejection and disdain in France, in the immigrant community, and in their original African communities. With the conflicting messages due to their ethnic differences (race), their poor status (class), and their gender, these women attempt to construct their identities under grueling circumstances (Killian 2006).

Feminist theory seeks explanations for the conditions women face. One current trend in feminist interpretation, illustrated in the previous example, is to view the social world as an intersection of class, race, and gender (Anderson and Collins 2006). In this way, one can look at the variety of ways by which many common citizens are controlled by those who have a monopoly on power and privilege.

The reality is that some women are quite privileged and wealthy. Not all women live in poverty. However, even privileged women often have less power than their husbands or other men in their lives. It is also true that some women in the world are privileged because of their race or ethnicity (Rothenberg 2010). In many respects, they have more in common with men of their own ethnicity or race than they do with women of less esteemed groups, and they may choose to identify with those statuses that enhance their privilege.

Still, many women are not a part of the privileged classes. In the United States, income for men and women varies significantly depending on ethnicity, and this means that minority women are even more disprivileged. However, even when ethnicity is held constant, women get paid less than men (see Table 9.3 on page 332).

Table 9.3 **Median Earnings of Workers by Race, Sex, and Percent of Men's Earnings by Women, 2011**

Race and Ethnicity	*Male*	*Female*	*Women's % of Men's Earnings*
Asian American	$49,296	$39,624	80.4
White	44,512	36,348	81.7
African American	32,292	30,680	95.0
Hispanic or Latino	30,004	26,780	89.2

Source: U.S. Department of Labor 2012.

These examples illustrate that race, class, and gender have crosscutting lines that may affect one's status in the society. Sexual orientation, age, nationality, and other factors also have the effect of either diminishing or increasing minority status of specific women, and theorists are paying increasing attention to these intersections (Rothenberg 2010). Chapter 8 discussed the fact that race and class lines may be either crosscutting or parallel. In the case of gender, there are always crosscutting lines with race and social class. However, gender always affects one's prestige and privilege within that class or ethnic group. Thus, to get a full picture, these three variables—race, class, and gender—need to be considered simultaneously.

Thinking Sociologically

What are some other ways by which race, class, and gender inequality have intersected in your community so that some people receive more privilege or disprivilege?

Putting these characteristics together suggests that women are indeed a "minority group," subject to stereotypes, prejudice, and discrimination. Women of color can face the triple status determinants of being poor (class) women (gender) of color (race/ethnicity). They may be at risk to their lives when they are first born (see photo) and later in life (see the next "Sociology Around the World").

Gender, Homosexuality, and Minority Status

We have already learned that sex, gender, and sexuality are not binary (male-female) concepts but embrace a broader combination of masculine, feminine, heterosexual, homosexual, and other variations. This range is normal in human sexuality. It is societal expectations developed over time that impose categories on human sexuality.

Homosexuality has always existed. It has been accepted and even required at some times and places and rejected or outlawed in others. In some cases, homosexuals and transgendered individuals have been placed in a separate sexual category with special roles. For example, the *Hijras* in India and some other areas in South Asia are usually physiological males who have feminine gender identity. Many live in *Hijra* communities and have designated roles in Indian festivals and celebrations.

Some societies ignore the existence of homosexuality, and a few consider it a psychological illness or form of depraved immorality. A very few even consider this form of sexuality a crime (as in some Muslim societies today and in most states in the United States during much of the 20th century). In a recent global controversy in Uganda, Africa, the parliament proposed a bill to outlaw homosexuality and even put homosexuals to death. This move was fueled in part by an American evangelist who is accused of fomenting antigay hysteria that resulted in persecution, arrest, torture, and even murder of homosexuals in Uganda. Human rights outcries kept the bill from passing in 2009, but in 2012 the bill was reintroduced (Goodstein 2012). In each case around the world, the government or dominant religious group determines the status of homosexuals. The reality is that deviation from a society's gender norms, such as attraction to a member of the same sex, may cause one to experience minority status.

Homophobia—intense fear and hatred of homosexuality and homosexuals, whether male or female—is highly correlated with and perhaps a cause of people holding traditional notions of gender and gender roles (Shaw and Lee 2005). The issue of homophobia focuses on prejudice held and transmitted by individuals, and it therefore operates only at the micro level.

Some homosexuals deviate from traditional notions of masculinity and femininity and therefore from significant norms of many societies. This may result in hostile reactions and stigma from the dominant group. Indeed, homosexual epitaphs are often used to reinforce gender conformity and to intimidate anyone who would dare to be different from the norm. Because in most societies women are economically dependent on men, their status in society is typically based on their relationship with men. Therefore, lesbians—women who are attracted to other women—go against norms of societies and are in some instances perceived as dangerous, unnatural, or a threat to men's power (Burn 2011; Ward and Edelstein 2009). One researcher describes her daily struggles dealing with a society that does not fully accept who she

Sociology Around the World

Dowry and Death: Some Dangers of Marriage

Dowry is a longstanding tradition in India, Bangladesh, Pakistan, and Sri Lanka, though it has been the practice in many lands. It involves "payment from the bride's family to the groom and groom's family at the time of marriage" and includes the money, goods, and estate or property that a woman brings her husband in marriage (Srinivasan and Lee 2004:1108). When a son is married, the son's family receives a dowry. Though once a practice of the wealthy, it is now most common in poorer families where sons are often more "valuable" than daughters because they can bring a dowry, and a dowry can amount to the equivalent of a year's salary. The idea of dowry is one of reciprocity; that is, the wife's family is also contributing something to the well-being of the younger generation. The bride receives her inheritance at the time of the wedding rather than at the time of death of her parents.

Although dowry payments were prohibited in India by the Dowry Prohibition Act in 1961, this traditional practice is still widespread (Bradley, Tomalin, and Subramaniam 2009). The problem is that misunderstandings surrounding dowry agreements and payments can result in a form of dowry death called bride burning. These marriages are typically arranged between families and generally do not involve consent or love. It is a business deal. When the business deal fails or results in disagreement, the bride may be found soaked in kerosene or other flammable liquid and burned to death, usually in the kitchen. Authorities often rule these bride burnings as suicides. The husband can then seek another bride and another dowry (Ward and Edelstein 2009). In 2010, 8,391 dowry death cases were reported across India; that is one bride burned to death every 90 minutes, and that number is on the rise (Bedi 2012). Hundreds of cases are estimated to go unreported. Although police receive many calls, there are very few convictions for the crime.

Women's groups in South Asia have formed to protest against both dowries and the problems they bring, especially to poor young women who have no power or options. Some women's shelters and burn wards in hospitals have been established. The Dowry Project, established in 1995, does research on the practice, especially the link between violence and death, or bride burning. However, traditions are strong and poverty great; bride burnings are likely to continue until the penalties make it unprofitable.

is and that puts individuals in boxes with labels, even when those boxes do not fit the individual (Lucal 1999). Likewise, many gay men violate norms of machoism, which sometimes include boasting about women who have been sexually "conquered."

Heterosexism is the notion that the society reinforces heterosexuality and marginalizes anyone who does not conform to this norm. Heterosexism focuses on social processes that define homosexuality as deviant and legitimize heterosexuality as the only normal lifestyle (Oswald 2000, 2001). In short, heterosexism operates often at the meso and macro levels of society, through privileges such as rights to health care and jobs granted to people who are heterosexual and denied to those who are not.

In the mass media inclusion of gay characters, the following have been among the top 10 ranked films: *A Single Man* (2009), *Milk* (2008), *Shelter* (2007), *Brokeback Mountain* (2005), and *Latter Days* (2003), plus television features such as *Ellen* and *Will and Grace* (Ayers 2010). In addition there are many well-known gay news commentators and show hosts, which illustrates popular culture's change in acceptance of homosexuals. Gallup polls reveal that U.S. public acceptance of gays passed 50% in 2010, and those calling homosexuality "morally wrong" dropped to 43%. Fifty-eight percent felt relations between consenting adults should be legal (Saad 2010). Over 90% of the U.S. population now supports equal opportunity for homosexuals on the job (Johnson 2005). Despite these indications of greater openness in attitudes, in 2010 it was still legal in 29 states to fire someone based on his or her sexuality (Topix.com 2010).

The movement among gays, lesbians, bisexuals, and transsexuals for equal rights and recognition is not just a North American or European phenomenon. These Nepalese transsexuals are among hundreds from across the country who gathered in Kathmandu, the capital, to demand official recognition and political representation in Nepal. This is a global movement.

Thinking Sociologically

The concept of *homophobia* focuses on micro-level processes, whereas the notion of *heterosexism* is most relevant at the meso and macro level. Which of these concepts reveals the most about issues faced by the lesbian and gay community? Why?

Still, homosexuality—especially same-sex marriage—was a hot topic in the elections of 2012. Views on both extremes were presented, and this social issue seemed to split the country between the religious right and the liberal left. In several states bans on same-sex marriage have been passed, yet the public opinion is inching toward more acceptance. Most states have "Defense of Marriage Acts" or constitutional amendments prohibiting same-sex marriage (Hamilton 2012; National Conference of State Legislatures 2012). This has spawned debates about family life and whether homosexuals should be allowed to marry, to adopt or have children, or to have the same rights as heterosexuals. In short, many institutions including family, economics and work, politics, religion, and health care have been influenced by this debate over sexuality and gender. Note how meso-level institutions control personal relationships—even trying to restrain who one is to love deeply.

The point here is not to argue for or against same-sex marriage but to note that homosexuals do not have many of the rights that heterosexuals have, a discrepancy based on sexual preferences. Heterosexuals in the United States have a variety of rights—ranging from insurance coverage and inheritance rights for lifelong partners to jointly acquired property, hospital visitation rights as family, rights to claim the body of a deceased partner, and rights to have the deceased prepared for burial or cremation. The U.S. federal government confers 1,138 rights on heterosexuals that they normally take for granted, but often, these rights do not extend to same-sex partners in a long-term committed relationship. Most states also bestow more than 200 specific rights to persons who "marry," but because most states do not allow same-sex marriages, homosexuals do not have these same rights (U.S. General Accounting Office 2004). In Canada and many European countries, citizens do have a right to same-sex marriage, and this has reduced the number of discrepancies in the rights of homosexuals and heterosexuals.

Costs and Consequences of Gender Stratification

In rapidly changing modern societies, role confusion abounds. Men hesitate to offer help to women, wondering if gallantry will be appreciated or scorned. Women are torn between traditional family roles on the one hand, and working to support the family and fulfilling career goals on the other. As illustrated in the following examples, sex- and gender-based stratification limits individual development and causes problems in education, health, work, and other parts of the social world.

Psychological and Social Consequences: Micro-Level Implications

For both women and men, rigid gender stereotypes can be very constraining. Individuals who hold highly sex-typed attitudes feel compelled to behave in stereotypic ways, ways that are consistent with the pictures they have in their heads of proper gender behavior (Kramer 2010). However, individuals who do not identify rigidly with masculine or feminine gender types tend to have a broad acceptable repertoire of behaviors and know how to cope with changing situations (Cheng 2005). They are more flexible in thoughts and behavior, score higher on intelligence tests, have greater spatial ability, and have higher levels of creativity. Because they allow themselves a wider range of behaviors, they have more varied abilities and experiences and become more tolerant of others' behaviors. High masculinity in males sets up rigid standards for male behavior and has been correlated with anxiety, guilt, and neuroses, whereas less rigid masculine expectations are associated with emotional stability, sensitivity, warmth, and enthusiasm. Rigid stereotypes and resulting sexism affect everyone and can curtail our activities, behaviors, and perspectives.

Results of Gender Role Expectations

Women in many societies are expected to be beautiful, youthful, and sexually interesting and interested, while at the same time preparing the food, caring for the children, keeping a clean and orderly home, sometimes bringing in money to help support the family, and being competent and successful in their careers. Multiple, sometimes contradictory, expectations for women can cause stress and even serious psychological problems. The resulting strain contributes to depression and certain health problems such as headaches, nervousness, and insomnia (Wood 2008).

Gender expectations also affect women's self-concepts and body images. Beautiful images jump out at us from billboards, magazine covers, and TV and movie screens. Some of these images are unattainable by most women because they have been created through surgeries and eating disorders—and even by the use of airbrushing on photographs. Disorders, including anorexia and bulimia nervosa, relate to societal expectations of the ideal woman's appearance (Taub and McLorg 2010).

Studies suggest that about 1 in 200 American women suffers from anorexia, and 2 to 3 in 100 from bulimia ("Eating Disorder Statistics" 2008). Eating disorders occur most frequently in females between 12 and 18 years of age, caused by distortions in body image that are brought on by what the women, especially white middle- and upper-middle-class women, see as societal images of beauty, often images created in magazines that are unattainable in real life (ANRED 2007; Kilbourne 1999; Taub and McLorg 2010).

In fact, an increasing number of eating disorders now occur among women over 30 and even into their 60s, often triggered by a life-changing event such as divorce, unemployment, menopause, or loss of a parent or a child leaving home. Pressure to look good as one ages is exacerbated by young-looking celebrities (Campbell 2010).

Thinking Sociologically

If females are encouraged to spend money, energy, and attention on how they look to ensure that they are physically appealing to others, how might this affect their view of themselves, their health, their use of time, and their access to positions of power?

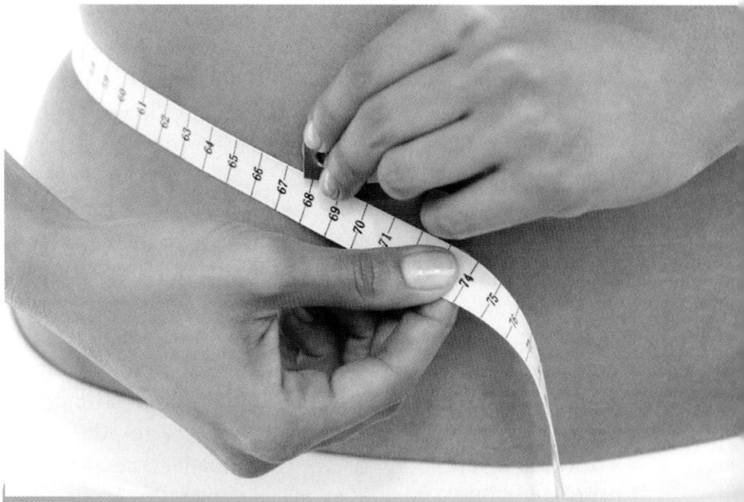

The beauty-image obsession in North America is far more of an issue with white Anglos than African Americans or Latinas, but especially with young white women it results in disorders relative to eating. Obsessed with thinness, some young women consider a small salad a complete dinner.

Men also suffer psychological consequences of stereotyping, from eating disorders (perhaps 10% of men) to fitness magazines that picture the "perfect" male body and advertise exercise equipment and steroids ("Eating Disorder Statistics" 2008). In addition, men die earlier than women, in part due to environmental, psychological, and social factors. Problems in Global North countries such as heart disease, stroke, cirrhosis, cancers, accidents, and suicides are linked in part to the role expectations that males should appear tough, objective, ambitious, unsentimental, and unemotional—traits that require men to assume great responsibility and suppress their feelings (Leit, Gray, and Pope 2002).

Societal Costs: Meso- and Macro-Level Implications

Gender stratification creates costs for societies around the world in a number of ways. *Poor education achievement* of female children leads to the loss of human talents and resources of half the population. This is a serious loss for societies. *Social divisiveness*—we-they thinking based on sex—can create alienation, if not hostility, and this can result in aggression. Discrimination and violence against women, whether physical or emotional, has consequences for all institutions in a society.

Consider how the ratio of women to men in an occupational field affects the prestige of the occupation. As more men enter predominantly female fields such as nursing and library science, the fields gain higher occupational prestige, and salaries tend to increase. It seems that men take their gender privilege with them when they enter female professions (Kramer 2010). However, the evidence indicates that as women enter male professions such as law, the status tends to become lower, making women's chances of improving their position in the stratification system limited.

Gender stratification has often meant loss of the talents and brainpower of women, and that is a serious loss to all societies, including modern postindustrial societies, because human capital—the resources of the human population—is central to social prosperity in societal systems. Yet resistance to expanding women's public sphere and professional roles is often strong. For example, Japanese women make up close to 50% of the workforce, but only 10.1% hold managerial positions (Fackler 2007). A poll of major Japanese corporations found that most want to use women's talents as women are well educated, but in fact only a small number (5.4%) of lower-level management positions in companies were held by women (Gaijinpot 2010). Although their education levels are generally high, Japanese and Korean women earn wages that are only about 66% of their male counterparts' wages, the largest wage gap among Global North countries (Japan Institute for Labour Policy and Training 2009; Kumlin 2006). Breaking through the glass ceiling continues to be not only a barrier for individual women but also a challenge for entire societies that could benefit from abilities never fully maximized.

Changing Gender Stratification and Social Policy

Good social policy needs to be informed by social science research. Some public feminist sociologists, for example, have focused on women's issues in North America, working in shelters for battered women, in rape response centers, and with other agencies addressing the needs of girls and women.

Another policy issue is more global and has to do with multinational corporations that create a dilemma for women: Is it better for a woman to have a poor-paying job and poor working conditions, or no job? On the one hand, few wage-paying jobs are available in some areas, and most of these positions in manufacturing and assembly positions that do become available are for women. Yet women in factories in the Global South face dangerous conditions and low pay. Sweatshops exist because poor women and sometimes men have few other job options to support their families and because people in rich countries want to buy the cheap products that perpetuate the multinational corporate system. For example, over 1 million Mexicans work in *maquiladoras* (foreign-owned manufacturing and assembly plants) in Mexican border towns.

The maquiladoras are owned by U.S., European, and Japanese conglomerates, and hire primarily unskilled young women who work for as little as 50 cents an hour; skilled workers may get $1 to $2 an hour. The employees produce electronic equipment, clothing, plastics, furniture, appliances, and auto parts, most of which are shipped to the United States (Rosenberg 2012). The hours worked per week range from 50 to 75, with some maquiladoras paying $40–$50 for a 60-hour week. Women and children often make less than men ("Misery of the Maquiladoras" 2011). However, a North American Free Trade Agreement (NAFTA) report compares Chinese and Mexican wages, finding that Chinese manufacturing wages are even less than Mexican workers receive (NAFTA 2011). Why the difference in reporting of wages? In part this is because different agendas are at stake in the reporting, and therefore different wages are reported. Whatever the truth, workers are not paid a living wage in most maquiladoras and in other multinational corporations in the Global South.

In El Salvador, women employees of the Taiwanese maquiladora, Mandarin, work shifts of 12 to 21 hours during which they are seldom allowed bathroom breaks. They are paid about 18 cents per shirt, which is later sold for $20. Mandarin makes clothes for the Gap, J.Crew, and Eddie Bauer. In Haiti, women sewing clothing at Disney's contract plants are paid 6 cents for every $19.99 *101 Dalmatians* outfit they sew. They make 33 cents an hour. Meanwhile, according to critics, Disney makes record profits and could easily pay workers a living wage for less than one half of 1% of the sales price of one outfit. In Vietnam, 90% of Nike's workers are females between the ages of 15 and 28. Nike's labor costs for a pair of basketball shoes (which retail for $149.50) are $1.50, 1% of the retail price (Burn 2011).

One result of low wages and poor working conditions is exploitation of women in other parts of the world. Another is loss of income for workers in the United States, including men. Manufacturers within the United States are starting to hire after the recession, but the wages they are offering are $10 to $15 an hour less than before the economic recession (Kelber 2012). So the "race to the bottom" by multinationals (seeking the lowest price for labor) is affecting earnings of men and women in the United States. We really live in an interconnected world.

What can be done about the abusive treatment of women workers around the world? This is a tough issue: Governments have passed legislation to protect workers, but governments also want the jobs that multinational corporations bring and therefore do little to enforce regulations. International labor standards are also difficult to enforce because multinational corporations are so large and located in many different parts of the world. Trade unions have had little success attracting workers to join because companies squash their recruiting efforts immediately.

One way activist groups protest for fair wages and conditions for workers is to adopt practices that have worked for other groups facing discrimination in the past. Consider the following possibilities used by these groups to bring about change: holding nonviolent protests—sit-down strikes and walkouts—to protest unequal and unfair treatment; working together in support groups to help children, neighborhoods, and communities; encouraging companies to help the communities in which they are located; using the Internet to carry the message to others; carrying out boycotts against companies that mistreat employees; using the arts, storytellers, and teachers to express frustration, educate others, and create strategies for resistance; and building on traditions of community and religious activism (Collins 2000). Most of these strategies require organized movements, but such efforts face the possibility of antagonizing the companies so that they move to other countries. It is a delicate balance.

Women in Thailand produce shoes at extremely low rates. These jobs are better than no employment at all, but before pressures from Western societies changed their cultures, most people were able to feed their families on farms in small villages. Changes in the entire world system have made that form of life no longer feasible, but working for multinational corporations also keeps these women impoverished.

Thinking Sociologically

Take a look at the clothing in your closet and your drawers. Figure out where it was made either by reading the labels or by looking up the companies' factories on the Internet. Would you be willing to pay more for that clothing so that other people could have better conditions? What about your friends? Should you be concerned about these workers' lives, or do you think you have no obligation to consider them?

At women's conferences around the world, policy makers debate the means to create solutions to women's problems. Most UN member countries have at least fledgling women's movements fighting for the improved status of women and their families. The movements attempt to change laws that result in discrimination, poverty, abuse, and low levels of education and occupational status. Although the goals of eliminating differential treatment of women, especially minority women, are jointly affirmed by most women's groups, the means to improve conditions for women are debated between women's groups. For instance, some advocates work within existing institutions to bring about equal rights. Others push for the complete overhauling of existing systems to bring about a new order that would ignore sex as a variable in assigning power. Whether any of these efforts will change women's individual lives and the lives of their children is unknown.

We would be too optimistic to predict that grassroots efforts or boycotts against those who are enjoying the fruits of poor women's labor will change the system. The best hope may lie in increased opportunities for women as countries modernize, and in efforts of countries that strive to enforce labor laws and improve conditions and wages for workers. One example is the Better Factories Movement in Cambodia (Kampuchea) that works to address worker problems. These efforts will work only if a number of countries join in, if they maintain a competitive labor market, and if buyers support products made in countries with fair labor practices (Better Factories 2012).

Inequality based on class, race, ethnicity, and gender is taking place at all levels of analysis and is often entrenched at the meso level within institutions. Major institutions include family, education, religion, politics, economics, and medicine. In complex societies, there are other necessary institutions including health care, science and technology, sport, and the military. We turn now to a discussion of institutions in our social world.

What Have We Learned?

In the beginning of this chapter, we asked how being born female or male affects our lives. Because sex is a primary variable on which societies are structured and stratification takes place, being born female or male affects our public and private sphere activities, our health, our ability to practice religion or participate in political life, our opportunities for education, and just about everything we do. As sociologists with a focus on empirical ways of knowing and scientific methods, we focus on what we can study objectively. Other disciplines, such as philosophy and theology, may articulate what "ought" to be. Public sociologists sometimes move from an analysis of empirical data to questions of how to improve the quality of people's lives by suggesting solutions. Likewise, policy recommendations are those that take what is known about gender relations and offer plans for changing and improving the society. Gender inequality clearly exists. What should be done to alleviate the problems is a matter of debate.

Key Points

- Whereas sex is biological, notions of gender identity and gender roles are socially constructed and learned, and vary across cultures. (See pp. 302–305.)
- Notions of gender are first taught at the micro setting—in the intimacy of the home—but they are reinforced at the meso and macro levels. (See pp. 305–309.)
- While "she" may go first in micro-level social encounters (served first in a restaurant or the first to enter a doorway), "he" goes first in meso and macro settings—with the doors open wider for men to enter leadership positions in organizations and institutions. (See pp. 309–321.)
- Greater access to resources at the meso level makes it easier to have entrée to macro-level positions, but it also influences the respect one receives in micro settings. (See pp. 321–326.)
- Much of the gender stratification today is unconscious and unintended—not caused by angry or bigoted men who purposefully oppress women. Inequality is rooted in institutionalized privilege and disprivilege. (See pp. 322–325.)
- Various social theories shed different light on the issues of sex roles and inequality. (See pp. 326–332.)
- For modern postindustrial societies, there is a high cost for treating women like a minority group—individually for the people who experience it and for the society, which loses the intelligence, skills, and commitment of highly competent people. (See pp. 334–337.)

Discussion Questions

1. Describe some of the ways socializing agents (e.g., family, peers, the media, religion, teachers) encouraged you to conform to traditional gender norms. Do you think you will encourage (or have you encouraged) your own children to conform to traditional gender norms? Why or why not?
2. Give two examples of side-effect gender discrimination that leads to economic inequality between men and women.
3. How does gender socialization influence who runs for office and for whom we vote? How are female politicians treated by the media, compared to male politicians? How has that impacted your own perception of female politicians?
4. How does gender discrimination harm society? What could be done on your campus to improve the status of women? How might you join these efforts?
5. What are your career goals? Do they follow traditional gender roles? Why or why not? How has your gender socialization impacted your career plans?
6. More women than men are now in college. How do you think this fact will impact gender roles on campus and in the larger society?

Contributing to Our Social World: What Can We Do?

At the Local Level

- *To combat gender discrimination on your campus*, schedule an interview with the director or other staff members of the human resources or affirmative action offices on your campus to learn about your school's policies regarding gender discrimination. What procedures exist for hiring? Do women and men receive the same salaries, wages, and benefits for equal work? Explore the possibility of your working as a volunteer or an intern in the office, specifically in the area of gender equity.

At the Organizational and National Levels

- *The National Organization for Women (NOW)* is the world's leading advocate for gender equity. It deals with issues such as abortion and reproductive rights, legislative outreach, economic justice, ending sex discrimination, and promoting diversity. Several internship programs are listed on the organization's website, www.now.org, along with contact information, state and regional affiliates, and "NOW on Campus" links.
- *Sociologists for Women in Society (SWS)*, an organization that "works to improve women's lives through advancing and supporting feminist sociological research, activism and scholars," provides many resources for students. SWS provides students with scholarships, opportunities to be mentored, and an award to recognize students who improve the lives of women through activism.

At the Global Level

- *MADRE*, an international women's rights organization, works primarily in less developed countries. You can find numerous opportunities for working on issues of justice, human rights, education, and health on its website at www.madre.org.
- *Equality Now*, an international nongovernmental organization, provides many venues for those interested in promoting equality for women and curbing gender violence and discrimination. You can find more about this organization at www.equalitynow.org.
- *The United Nations Inter-Agency Network on Women and Gender Equality* works on relevant global issues, including violence against women and women's working conditions. Its WomenWatch website at www.un.org/womenwatch contains news, information, and ideas for contributing to the worldwide campaign for women's rights.

Visit the Student Study Site at **www.sagepub.com/ballantine4e** to access additional study tools, including eFlashcards, web quizzes, video resources, audio resources, web resources, SAGE journal articles, recommended readings, and more.

PART IV Institutions

Picture a house, a structure in which you live. Within that house there are the action and activities that bring the house to life—the processes. Flip a switch, and the lights go on because the house is well wired. Adjust the thermostat, and the room becomes more comfortable as the structural features of furnace or air-conditioning systems operate. If the structural components of the plumbing and water heating systems work, you can take a hot shower when you turn the knob. These actions taken within the structure make the house livable. If something breaks down, you need to get it fixed so that everything works smoothly.

Institutions, too, provide a *structure* for society, which is a framework that promotes stability. *Processes* are the action dimension within institutions—the activities that take place. They include the interactions between people, decision making, and other actions in society. These processes are often dynamic and can lead to significant change within the structure—like a decision about whether new homeowners should remodel their kitchen. Institutions are meso-level structures because they are larger in scope than the face-to-face social interactions of the micro level, yet they are smaller than the nation or the global system.

Institutions such as family, education, religion, politics, economics, and health care include certain patterns and expectations that differ in each society. They are interdependent and mutually supportive, just as the plumbing, heating system, and electricity in a house work together to make a home functional. However, a breakdown in one institution or conflict over limited resources between institutions affects the whole society, just as a malfunction in the electrical system may shut the furnace off and cool down the water heater.

The Importance of Institutions

Institutions are not anything concrete that you can see, hear, or smell. The concept of *institutions* is a way of describing and understanding how society works. For example, the institution of family meets certain needs that are found in almost all societies. Family as an institution refers to the behavior of thousands of people, which—taken as a whole—form a social structure. Think of your own family. It has unique ways of interacting and raising children, but it is part of a community with many families. Those many families, in turn, are part of a national set of patterned behaviors we call "the family." This pattern meets the basic needs of the society for producing and socializing new members and providing an emotionally supportive environment.

Institutions do not dictate exactly how you will carry out the roles within your family. However, they do specify certain needs families will meet and statuses (husband, wife, child) that will relate to each other in certain mutually caring ways and filling certain seminegotiable roles. An institution provides a blueprint (much like a local builder needs a blueprint to build a house), and in your local version of the institution you may make a few modifications to the plans to meet your micro-level needs. Still, through this society-encompassing structure and interlocking set of statuses, the basic needs for individuals at the micro level and for society at the macro level are met.

Institutions, then, are *organized, patterned, and enduring sets of social structures that provide guidelines for behavior and help each society meet its basic survival needs.* While institutions operate mostly at the meso level, they also act to integrate micro and macro levels of society. Let us look more deeply at this definition.

1. *Organized, patterned, and enduring sets of social structures* mean that institutions are not the bricks and mortar of buildings but refer to a complex set of groups or organizations, statuses within those groups, and norms of conduct that guide people's behavior. These structures ensure socialization of children, education of the young, sense of meaning in life, companionship, and the economic unit to obtain needed goods (food, clothing, automobiles, iPods, cell phones) for the members of the society. If this patterned behavior were missing, these needs might not be addressed. At the local level, we may go to a neighborhood school, or we may attend worship at a congregation we favor. These are local organizations—local franchises, if you will—of a much more encompassing structure (education and religion) that provides guidelines for education or addresses issues of meaning of life for an enormous number of people. The Catholic Church in your town, for example, is a local "franchise" of an organization that is transnational in scope and global in its concerns.

2. *Guidelines for behavior* help people know how to conduct themselves to obtain basic needs. Individuals and local "franchises" actually carry out the institutional guidelines in each culture; the exact ways the guidelines are carried out vary by locality. In local "franchises" of the political system, people know how to govern and how to solve problems at the local level because of larger norms and patterns provided by the political institution. Individual men and women operate a local hospital or clinic (a local "franchise" of the medical institution) because a national blueprint of how to provide health care informs local expectations and decisions. The specific activities of a local school, likewise, are influenced by the guidelines and purposes of the larger notions of "formal education" in a given nation.

3. *Meeting basic survival needs* is a core component of institutions because societies must meet needs of their members; otherwise the members die, or the society collapses. Institutions, then, are the structures that support social life in a large bureaucratized society. Common to all industrialized societies are family, education, religion, economics, politics, and health. These institutions are discussed in the following chapters.

4. *Integrating micro and macro levels of society* is critical because one of the collective needs of society is coherence and stability—including some integration between the various levels of society. Institutions help provide that integration for the entire social system. They

do this by meeting needs at the local franchise level (food at the grocery, education at the local school, health care at the local clinic) at the same time they coordinate national and global organizations and patterns.

Again, if all this sounds terribly abstract, that is because institutions *are* abstractions. You cannot touch institutions, yet they are as real as air, love, or happiness. In fact, in the modern world institutions are as necessary to life as is air, and they help provide love and happiness that make life worth living.

The Development of Modern Institutions

If we go all the way back to early hunter-gatherer societies, there were no meso or macro levels to their social experience. People lived their lives in one or two villages, and while a spouse might come from another village or one might move to a spouse's clan, there was no national or state governance, and certainly no awareness of a global social system. In those simple times, family and community provided whatever education was needed, produced and distributed goods, paid homage to a god or gods, and solved conflicts and disputes through a system of familial (often patriarchal) power distribution. One social unit such as the family served multiple functions.

As societies have become more complex and differentiated, not only multiple levels of the social system but also various new institutions have emerged. Sociology textbooks in the 1950s identified only "five basic institutions": family, economic systems, political systems, religion, and education (formal public education only having been created in the mid-19th century). These five institutions were believed to be the core structures that met the essential needs of individuals and societies in an orderly way.

Soon thereafter, *medicine* moved from the family and small-town doctors to be recognized as an institution. Medicine had become bureaucratized in hospitals, medical labs, professional organizations, and other complex structures that provided health care. *Science* is also now something more than flying kites in thunderstorms in one's backyard. It is a complex system that provides training, funding, research institutes, peer review, and professional associations to support empirical research. New information is the lifeblood of an information-based or postindustrial society. Science, discussed in Chapter 16, is now an essential institution. Although it is arguable whether sports are an essential component for social viability, sports have clearly become highly structured in the past 50 years, and many sociologists consider sports an institution. The mass media and military also fall into the category of institutions in more advanced countries. There are gray areas as to whether or not something is considered an institution, but the questions to ask are (a) whether the structure meets basic needs of the society for survival, (b) whether it has become a complex organization providing routinized structures and guidelines for society, and (c) whether it is national or even global in its scope, while also having pervasive local (micro) impact.

The Interconnections Between Institutions

The global economic crisis that began in 2008 illustrates the forces that bring about changes through interconnections between institutions. As described by "the sociological imagination," our individual problems such as loss of a job are tied to the macro-level changes in the economy. So the family is affected, and citizens expect the government to intervene and fix the problem when we enter an economic recession. Religious congregations have experienced increased demands at their food banks, soup kitchens, and thrift shops run for low-income people, yet religious contributions from religious congregants are more difficult to make in tough economic times. Schools also suffer from lack of income following the economic downturn.

Interconnections between meso-level institutions are a common refrain in this book. As you read these chapters, notice that change in one institution affects others. Sociologists studying the legal system, the

Table I.1 The Impact of Institutions at Each Level of Analysis

	Family	*Education*	*Economic Systems*	*Political Systems*	*Religion*	*Medicine*
Macro (National and global social systems and trends)	Kinship and marriage structures, such as monogamy versus polygamy; global trends in family such as choice of partners rather than arranged marriages	National education system; United Nations Girls' Education Initiative	Spread of capitalism around the world; World Bank; International Monetary Fund; World Trade Organization	National government; United Nations; World Court; G8 (most powerful eight nations in the world)	Global faith-based movements and structures: National Council of Churches; World Council of Churches; World Islamic Council; World Jewish Congress	National health care system; World Health Organization; transnational pandemics
Meso (Institutions, complex organizations, ethnic subcultures, state/provincial systems)	The middle-class family; the Hispanic family; the Jewish family	State/provincial department of education; American Federation of Teachers*	State/provincial offices of economic development; United Auto Workers*	State/provincial governments; national political parties; each state or province's supreme court	National denominations/movements: United Methodist Church; American Reform Judaism	HMOs; Minnesota Nurses Association; American Medical Association
Micro (Local "franchises" of institutions)	Your family; local parenting group; local Parents Without Partners; county family counseling clinic	Your teacher; local neighborhood school; local school board	Local businesses; local chamber of commerce; local labor union chapter	Neighborhood crime watch program; local city or county council	Your local religious study group or congregation	Your doctor and nurse; local clinic; local hospital

* These organizations are national in scope and membership, but they are considered meso level here because they are complex organizations *within* the nation.

mass media, medicine, science, sports, or the military as an institution would raise similar questions and would want to know how it influences the micro, meso, and macro levels of a society. We begin with the family—an institution that is an intimate part of our lives and often called the "most basic" institution of society.

Thinking Sociologically

From Table I.1, see if you can place other institutions (mass media, science, sports, the military) in the framework.

AND FOR
HANGE

CHAPTER 10

Family

Partner Taking, People Making, and Contract Breaking

Appearing in rich variety, the family is often referred to as the "most basic" institution. In this social relationship, we take partners and "make people"—both biologically and socially speaking. In the modern world, these intimate "basic" unions often experience conflict, violence, and contract breaking as well.

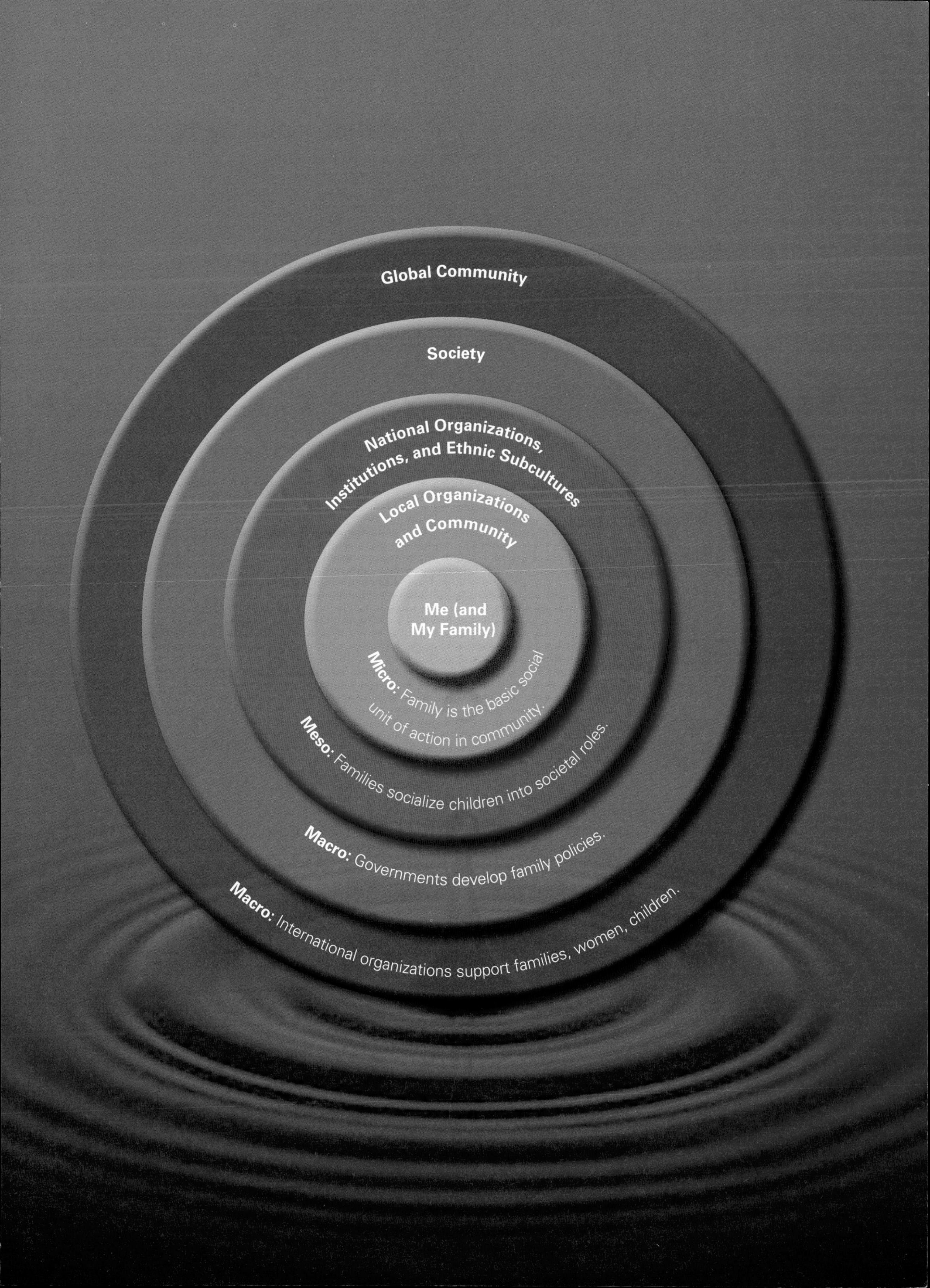

Global Community
Society
National Organizations, Institutions, and Ethnic Subcultures
Local Organizations and Community
Me (and My Family)
Micro: Family is the basic social unit of action in community.
Meso: Families socialize children into societal roles.
Macro: Governments develop family policies.
Macro: International organizations support families, women, children.

Think About It	
Micro: Self and Inner Circle	Why is family important to you?
Micro: Local Community	How do people find life partners?
Meso: National Institutions; Complex Organizations; Ethnic Groups	Why is family seen as the core or basic institution of society?
Macro: National Society	What, if anything, should be done by government to strengthen families?
Macro: Global Community	Why are families around the world so different?

What's coming in this chapter?

A Guatemalan family in a rural village prepares for the day's chores. Maria fixes the breakfast as Miguel cares for the animals. The children fix their lunches of tortillas, beans, rice, and banana to take to school. When they return home they will help with the farm chores. They live together with their extended family, several generations of blood relatives living side-by-side.

In recent decades, the definition of family has broadened. No longer is it necessarily limited to heterosexual couples. These gay men are parents to this baby.

It is morning in Sweden. Anders and Karin Karlsson are rushing to get to their offices on time. The children, a 12-year-old son and an 8-year-old daughter, are being hurried out the door to school. All will return in the evening after a full day of activities and join together for the evening meal. In this dual-career family, common in many postindustrial societies, both parents are working professionals.

The gossip at the African village water well this day is about the rich local merchant, Abdul, who has just taken his fourth and last wife. She is a young, beautiful girl of 15 from a neighboring village. She is expected to help with household chores and bear children for his already extensive family unit. Several of the women at the well live in affluent households where the husband has more than one wife.

Tom and Henry recently adopted Ty into their family. The couple share custody of the 5-year-old boy. Ty's two fathers attend his school events and teach him what all parents are expected to teach their children. Adoption by same-sex couples is legal in only 16 U.S. states and the District of Columbia ("Gay Adoption Nationwide" 2011). However, both political candidates in the 2012 U.S. presidential campaign supported a policy allowing gay couples to adopt children (Cronkite 2012). Dora, a single mom, lives next door with her two children. She bundles them off to school before heading to her job. After school, she has an arrangement with other neighbors to care for the children until she gets home.

What do the very different scenes described at the outset of this chapter have in common? Each describes a family, yet there is controversy about what constitutes a family. Those groupings that are officially recognized as families tend to receive hundreds of privileges and rights, such as health insurance and inheritance rights (Degenova, Stinnett, and Stinnett 2011). In this chapter, we will discuss characteristics of families, theoretical perspectives on family, family dynamics, family as an institution, family issues, and policies regarding marriage and family dissolution.

Families come in many shapes, sizes, and color combinations. We begin our exploration of this institution with a discussion of what *is* family.

What Is a Family?

Who defines what constitutes a family: individuals, the government, or religious groups? Is a family just Ma, Pa, and the kids? Let us consider several definitions. The U.S. Census Bureau says "two or more people (one of whom is the householder) related by birth, marriage, or adoption and residing together; all such people (including other related family members) are considered as members of the family" (U.S. Census Bureau 2012a). Thus, a family in the United States might be composed of siblings, cousins, a grandparent and grandchild, or other groupings. Some sociologists define family more broadly, such as "two or more individuals who maintain an intimate relationship that they expect will last indefinitely—or in the case of parent and child, until the child reaches adulthood—and who usually live under the same roof and pool their incomes and household labor" (Cherlin 2010:14). This definition would include same-sex couples and many cohabiting heterosexuals as families. Some religious groups define family as a mother, a father, and their children, whereas others include several spouses and even parents and siblings living under the same roof.

How do you define the ideal family? Answering the questions in "Engaging Sociology" on page 350 will indicate the complexity of this question.

The family is often referred to as the most basic institution of any society. First, it is the place where we learn many of the norms for functioning in the larger society. Second, most of us spend our lives in the security of a family. People are born and raised in families, and many will die in a family setting. Through good and bad, sickness and health, most families provide for our needs, both physical and psychological. Therefore, families meet our primary, our most basic, needs. Third, major life events—marriages, births, graduations, promotions, anniversaries, religious ceremonies, holidays, funerals—take place within the family context and are celebrated with family members. In short, family is where we invest the most emotional energy

This Romanian family does not have much money, but the children learn many survival skills, and the most basic needs of the children, physical and psychological, are met.

Engaging Sociology

The Ideal Family

What is "the ideal family"? Does it have one adult woman and one adult man? One child or many? Grandparents living with the family? A same-sex couple? First, complete the following survey. Then ask a friend or relative to answer the questions below.

1. How many adults should the ideal family contain? ________________
2. How many children should the ideal family contain? ________________
3. What should be the sex composition of the adults in an ideal family? (check all that apply)
   a. One female and one male
   b. Male-male or female-female
   c. Several males and several females
   d. Other (write in) ____________

(Continued)

(Continued)

4. What should be the sexes of the child(ren) in the ideal family? ______________________________

5. Who should select the marriage partner? (check all that apply)
   a. The partners should select each other.
   b. The parents or close relatives should select the partner.
   c. A matchmaker should arrange the marriage.
   d. Other ______________________________

6. What is the ideal number of generations living in the same household?
   a. One generation: partners and no children
   b. Two generations: partners and children
   c. Three or more generations: partners, children, grandparents, and great-grandparents
   d. Other ______________________________

7. Where should the couple live?
   a. By themselves
   b. With parents
   c. With brothers or sisters
   d. With as many relatives as possible

8. What should the sexual arrangements be? (check all that apply)
   a. Partners have sex only with each other.
   b. Partners can have sex outside of marriage if it is not "disruptive" to the relationship.
   c. Partners are allowed to have sex with all other consenting adults.
   d. Male partners can have sex outside marriage.
   e. Female partners can have sex outside marriage.
   f. Other ______________________________

9. Which person(s) in the ideal family should work to help support the family?
   a. Both partners
   b. Male only
   c. Female only
   d. Both, but the mother only after children are in school
   e. Both, but the mother only after children graduate from high school
   f. All family members including children
   g. Other ______________________________

10. Should the couple have sex before marriage if they wish? Yes ___ No ___ Other___________

11. Should physically disabled aging parents
    a. Be cared for in a child's home?
    b. Be placed in a nursing care facility?
    c. Other ______________________________

Why do you hold these particular views of "the ideal family"? Are your answers different from those of your friend or relative? Why might others in your society have answered differently?

Note that all of these options can be found in some societies.

No other institution can fulfill the functions of the family, but the family can fulfill many functions of other institutions. On the left, a family works together as an economic team to produce food. On the right, a family in the United States prays together before lunch.

and spend much of our leisure time. Fourth, the family is capable of satisfying a range of social needs—belonging to a group, economic support, education or training, raising children, religious socialization, resolution of conflicts, and so forth. One cannot conceive of the economic system providing emotional support for each individual or the political system providing socialization and personalized care for each child. Family carries out these functions (Benokraitis 2012).

The family is the place where we confirm our partnerships as adults, and it is where we *make people*—not just biologically, but socially. In the family, we take an organism that has the potential to be fully human, and we mold this tiny bit of humanity into a caring, compassionate, productive person.

Thinking Sociologically

What purposes does your family serve for its members? What role does each member play in the family? Why might this be important for the larger society?

In most Global North societies, individuals are born and raised in the **family of orientation**, *the family into which we are born*. This family consists of parent(s) and possibly sibling(s); individuals are born and raised in this family, receive early socialization, and learn the language, norms, core values, attitudes, and behaviors of the community and society. A **family of procreation** is *the family we create ourselves*. We find a life mate and/or have children. The transmission of values, beliefs, and attitudes from our family of orientation to our family of procreation preserves and stabilizes the family system. Because family involves emotional investment, we have strong feelings about what form it should take.

Whether we consider families at micro, meso, or macro levels, sociological theories can help us understand the role of families in the social world.

Theoretical Perspectives on Family

Consider the case of Felice, a young mother locked into a marriage that provides her with little satisfaction. For the first year of marriage, Felice tried to please her husband, Tad, but gradually he seemed to drift further away. He began to spend evenings out. Sometimes, he came home drunk and yelled or hit her. Felice became pregnant shortly after their marriage and had to quit her job. This increased the financial pressure on Tad, and they fell behind in paying the bills.

Then came the baby. They were both ecstatic at first, but Tad soon reverted to his old patterns. Felice felt trapped. She was afraid and embarrassed to go to her parents. They had warned her against marrying so young without finishing school, but she was in love and had gone against their wishes. She and Tad had moved away from their hometown, so she was out of touch with her old support network and had few friends in her new neighborhood. Her religious beliefs told her she should try to stick it out, suggesting that the trouble was partly her fault for not being a "good enough wife." Lacking a job or skills to get one, she could not live on her own with a baby. She thought of marriage counseling, but Tad refused to consider this and did not seem interested in trying to work out the problems. He had his reasons for behaving the way he did, including feeling overburdened with the pressure of caring for two dependents. The web of this relationship seems difficult to untangle, but sociological theories provide us with some tools to analyze such family dynamics.

Micro-Level Theories of Family and the Meso-Level Connection

Symbolic Interaction Theory

Symbolic interaction theory can help us understand Felice's situation by explaining how individuals learn their particular behavior patterns and ways of thinking. Our relationship roles are developed through socialization and interaction with others. Felice, for example, developed certain expectations and patterns of behavior by modeling her experiences on her family of orientation (the family into which she was born), observing others, and developing expectations from her initial interactions with Tad. Tad developed a different set of expectations for his role of husband, modeled after his father's behavior. His father had visited bars after work, had affairs with other women, and expected "his woman" to be at home and to accept this without question. Two related concepts in symbolic interaction theory are the *social construction of reality* and the *definition of a situation*. What we define as real or as normal is shaped by what significant others around us accept as ordinary or acceptable. Our ideas about family, like anything else, are socially shaped by our experiences and our significant others. Children who grow up in homes where adults argue or hit one another or shout at one another with sarcastic put-downs may come to think of this behavior as typical or a normal part of family life. They simply have known no other type of interaction. Thus, without seeing other options, they may create a similar pattern of family interaction in their own families of procreation (the families they create). Interaction with others, according to this theoretical model, is based on people's shared meanings. Concepts such as *family*, *wife*, and *parenting* carry meaning to you and your siblings but may mean something very different to the person sitting beside you in class or to a potential mate.

Thinking Sociologically

Concepts such as *family, wife,* and *parenting* carry meaning to you and your siblings but may mean something very different to the person sitting beside you in class or to a potential mate. Ask several people you know to explain the words *husband, wife,* and *parenting* and what these words mean to them.

One of the great challenges of newlyweds is meshing their ideas about division of labor, family holidays, discipline of children, spousal relations, and economic necessities, along with their assumptions about being in a committed relationship. A new couple socially constructs a new relationship, blending the models of life partnership from their own childhood homes or creating an entirely new model as they jointly define their relationship. Furthermore, the meaning of one's identity and

Introduction of a baby to a household changes the interpersonal dynamics, the topics of conversation, the amount of sleep people are able to get, the sense of responsibility for the future, relationships to the larger community (including schools), and many other aspects of social life.

one's obligations to others change dramatically when one becomes a parent. The mother and father have to work out what this means for each of them, for their interactions with each other, and for their interactions with the child. This brings us back to a central premise of symbolic interaction: Humans are active agents who create their social structure through interaction. We not only learn family patterns; we *do family* just as we *do gender* in the sense that we create roles and relationships and pass them on to others as "normal."

Our individual identities and family patterns are shaped by institutional arrangements at the meso level; for example, corporations, religious bodies, legal systems, and other government entities define the roles of "wife" and "husband." Each U.S. state actually spells out in its legal codes the duties of husbands and wives. Those who do not fulfill these duties may be in "neglect of duty." These family roles are embedded in the larger structure in ways that many people do not realize.

Rational Choice Theory

Rational choice theory can also shed light on Felice's situation, helping us understand why people seek close relationships and why they stay in abusive relationships. As discussed in Chapter 2, rational choice theory asserts that individuals evaluate the costs and rewards of engaging in interaction. We look for satisfaction of our needs—emotional, sexual, and economic—through interaction. Patterns in the family are reinforced to the extent that exchanges are beneficial to members. When the costs outweigh the rewards, the relationship is unlikely to continue. Women in abusive relationships weigh the costs of suffering abuse against the rewards of having social legitimacy, income, social and religious acceptance, a home, and companionship. Many factors enter into the complex balance of the exchange. Indeed, costs and benefits of various choices are often established by meso-level organizations and institutions: insurance programs, health care options, and legal regulations that make partnering decisions easy or difficult.

According to rational choice theorists, even the mate selection process is shaped by a calculation of exchange. People estimate their own assets—physical, intellectual, social, and economic—and try to find the "best deal" they can make, with attention to finding someone with at least the level of resources they possess, even if those assets are in different areas. Marrying someone with more assets gives the other person more power and forces one to put up with things that equal partners would not tolerate. Cost/benefit, according to this view, affects the forming of the relationship and the power and influence in the relationship.

Thinking Sociologically

What situations can you identify within your family when cost/benefit calculations seemed to drive decisions? When is reciprocity the norm in family relationships?

Meso- and Macro-Level Theories of the Family

Structural-Functional Theory

Structural-functional theory points out the common purposes of family institutions in every society. Despite great variations in family forms, most human family systems satisfy similar needs, or functions, for their members and for society. Although the families described at the beginning of this chapter vary greatly, their members have a number of common needs and problems. For instance, they all must secure food and shelter, raise children, and care for dependents.

Why do all societies have families? One answer is that families fulfill certain purposes, or functions, for societies that enhance survival of individuals and societies. Traditionally, there have been at least six ways the family has helped stabilize the society, according to structural-functional theory:

Sexual Regulation. Physically speaking, any adult human could engage in sex with any other human. However, in practice, no society allows total sexual freedom. Every society

This woman in New Guinea became more attractive to men as a potential wife after she had proven her fertility by having a child.

Photo Essay

Family Interactions

Families vary a great deal from one culture to another, but if the members of a family work well together, they provide support, a sense of identity, and feelings of belonging and caring.

attempts to regulate the sexual behavior of its members in accordance with its own particular values. This is most often accomplished through marriage. Regulation ensures that this strong biological drive is satisfied in an orderly way that does not create ongoing disruption, conflict, or jealousy. Certain people are "taken" and "off limits" (Ward and Edelstein 2009).

Reproduction and Replacement. Societies need children to replace members who die, leave, or are incapacitated. Reproduction is controlled to keep family lineage and inheritance clear. Parent and caretaker roles are clearly defined and reinforced in many societies by ceremonies: baby showers, birth announcements, christenings, and naming ceremonies that welcome the child as a member of the family. In some places, such as New Guinea, procreation is so important that a young girl who has had children is more desirable because she has established her fertility.

Socialization. The family is the main training ground for children. In our families, we begin to learn values and norms, proper behavior, roles, and language. Later socialization in most societies is carried out by schools, religious organizations, and other institutions, but the family remains the most important initial socializing agent to prepare us for roles in society. Much of the socialization is done by parents, but siblings, grandparents, and other relatives are important to socialization as well.

Emotional Support and Protection. Families are the main source of love and belonging in many societies, giving us a sense of identity, security, protection, and safety from harm. The family is one place where people may experience unqualified acceptance and feelings of being cherished. Problems of children in youth shelters and incidents of family violence and neglect are reminders that this function is not always successfully provided in families. Still, the family is the environment most capable of meeting this need if all is working well.

Status Assignment. Our family of orientation is the most important determinant of our social status, life chances, and lifestyles. It strongly affects our educational opportunities, access to health care, religious and political affiliations, and values. In fact, in societies with caste systems, the ascribed position at birth is generally the position at death. Although in class societies individuals may achieve new social statuses, our birth positions and the early years of socialization have a strong impact throughout life on who and what we are.

Economic Support. Historically, the family was a unit of production—running a farm, a bakery, or a cobbler shop. Although this function is still predominant in many societies, the economic function carried out in individual families has pretty much disappeared in most Global North families. However, the family remains an economic unit of consumption. Who paid for your clothing, food, and other needs as you were growing up? Who helps many of you pay your college tuition and expenses? Taxing agencies, advertising and commercial enterprises, workplaces, and other social organizations also treat the family as the primary economic unit.

Functional theorists ask about the consequences of what takes place in the family for other parts of the society. They are likely to recognize ways that the micro-level processes of the family (e.g., socialization of Japanese children to be cooperative and members of groups and of U.S. children to be competitive and individualistic) are compatible with structural needs of society at the meso and macro levels (e.g., in the United States, the need for motivated workers who thrive on competition). Each part of the system, according to functionalists, works with other parts to create a functioning society.

Changing Family Functions. In some societies, the family is the primary unit for bearing and educating children, practicing religion, structuring leisure time activities, caring for the sick and aged, and even conducting politics. However, as societies modernize, many of these functions are transferred to other institutions.

As societies change, so do family systems. The sociohistorical perspective of family tells us that changes in intimate relationships—sexuality, marriage, and family patterns—have occurred over the centuries. Major transitions from

Siblings often provide some of the emotional support and part of the socialization for younger siblings. This is especially true in the poor Global South, where mothers often must work or carry water for the family from distant water sources. This sister cares for her younger sister in Soweto, South Africa.

agricultural to industrial to postindustrial societal systems change all the institutions within those societies. The institution of family in agricultural societies is often large and self-sufficient, with families producing their own food and providing their own shelter; this is not the case in contemporary urban societies.

Industrialization and urbanization typical in 18th- and 19th-century Europe and the United States created a distinct change in roles. The wife and child became dependent on the husband who "brought home the bread." The family members became consumers rather than independent and self-supporting coworkers on a farm. This male breadwinner notion of family has become uncommon in the Global South (Coontz 2005). In addition to evolving roles, other changes in society have brought shifts to the family. Improved technology, for example, brought medical advances, new knowledge and skills to be passed on in schools, recreation outside the family unit organized according to age groups, and improved transportation.

In Kimukunda village in southern Uganda, orphaned siblings between the ages of 4 and 8 return from working as daily laborers on a nearby farm. Their parents died of AIDS, and they are now cared for by their 60-year-old grandmother, Teddy Nakawoeisi. Together they struggle to fulfill the functions of a family.

As many families moved to urban areas, the economic function has been transferred to the factory, store, and office. Social prestige is increasingly centered on a family member rather than the family surname. Socialization is increasingly done in schools, and in some cases teachers have become substitute parents. They do a great deal of the preparation of the child for the larger world. The traditional protection and care function has been partially replaced by police, reform schools, unemployment compensation, social security, health care systems (e.g., Medicare and Medicaid), and other types of services provided by the state. Little League baseball, industrial bowling teams, aerobic exercise groups, television, and computer games have replaced the family as the source of leisure activities and recreation. Although many would argue that the family still remains the center of caring and affection and is the only recognized place for producing children, one does not have to look far to discover that these two functions are also increasingly found outside the boundaries of the traditional family unit.

These changes have made the family's functions more specialized, though family remains a critical institution in society. Most families still function to provide stable structures to carry out early childhood socialization and to sustain love, trust, affection, acceptance, and an escape from the impersonal world.

Thinking Sociologically

Does reduction of traditional family functions mean a decline in the importance of family or merely an adaptation of the family to changes in society? Is the modern family—based largely on emotional bonds rather than structural interdependency—a healthier system, or is it more fragile?

Conflict Theory

Conflict theorists study both individual family situations and broad societal family patterns. They argue that conflict in families is natural and inevitable. It results from the struggle for power and control in the family unit and in the society at large. As long as there is an unequal allocation of resources, conflict will arise.

Family conflicts take many forms. For instance, conflicts occur over allocation of resources, a struggle that may be rooted in conflict between men and women in the society: Who makes decisions, who gets money for clothes or a car, who does the dishes? On the macro level, family systems are a source of inequality in the general society, sustaining class inequalities by passing on wealth, income, and education opportunities for their own members or perpetuating disadvantages such as poverty and lack of cultural capital.

Yet some conflict theorists argue that conflict within the family can be important because it forces constant negotiation among individual family members and may bring about change that can strengthen the unit as a whole. Believing that conflict is both natural and inevitable, these theorists focus on root causes of conflict and how to deal with the discord. For conflict theorists, there is no assumption of a harmonious family. The social world is characterized more by tension and power plays than by social accord.

Feminist Theory

The feminist approach is based on sociological studies done on, by, and for women. Because women often occupy very different places in society than men, feminist theorists argue the need for a feminist perspective to understand family dynamics. Feminist scholars begin by placing women at the center, not to suggest their superiority but to spotlight them as subjects of inquiry and as active agents in the working of society. The biases rooted in male assumptions are uncovered and examined (Eshleman and Bulcroft 2010).

One micro-level branch of feminist theory, the interpretive approach, considers women within their social contexts—the interpersonal relations and everyday reality facing women as they interact with other family members. It does not ignore economic, political, social, and historical factors but focuses on the ways women construct their reality, their opportunities, and their place in the family and community. According to feminist theorists, this results in a more realistic view of family and women's lives than many other theories provide. Applying this feminist approach to understand Felice's situation, for example, the theorists would consider the way she views her social context and the way she assesses her support systems.

Many branches of feminist theory have roots in conflict theory. These theorists argue that patterns of patriarchy and dominance lead to inequalities for women. One of the earliest conflict theorists, Friedrich Engels (Karl Marx's close associate), argued that the family was the chief source of female oppression and that until basic resources were reallocated within the family, women would continue to be oppressed. However, he said that as women become aware of their collective interests and oppression, they will insist on a redistribution of power, money, and jobs (Engels [1884] 1942).

One vivid example of how women and men can be viewed as groups with competing interests is through a feminist analysis of domestic violence. In the United States, one in four (25%) women has experienced domestic violence in her lifetime. With an estimated 1 to 3 million women assaulted by an intimate partner each year, there is an incident of domestic violence every 25 seconds in the United States. A total of 85% of the victims of those acts of domestic violence are women (Domestic Violence Resource Center 2012). Boys who witness domestic violence are more than twice as likely to abuse their own wives later in life. Thirty-five percent of female murder victims were murdered by a spouse or boyfriend, with three women and one man killed each day by a spouse or intimate partner (Domestic Violence Resource Center 2012; U.S. Federal Bureau of Investigation 2009).

Domestic violence is a major issue in many families in the United States, with an average of three women and one man actually killed each day by a spouse or partner.

In most Global North societies, men are under pressure to be successful. When they are not, home may be the place where they vent their frustrations. When socialization results in a hypermasculine sense of identity, and this is combined with emotional dependency on a female, it is a lethal combination. Cultural messages tell men that they are to be in charge, but knowing that they are emotionally and sometimes economically dependent on their wives may result in violence to regain control.

Women are most severely exploited in societies that treat them as property and in which the family is a key political unit for power and status. Where men are the heads of families and women are dependent, women may be treated as less than equal both within the family and in the labor market. A woman's role is clearly prescribed. Consider the practice of *sati* in India. The widow was expected to (or was forced to) throw herself on her husband's funeral pyre because there was no structural place for her in the family after her husband's death. Although outlawed now, the practice lingers in some areas of India.

In some societies such as the Masai of East Africa and in some communities in Brazil, it is accepted that a husband can beat his wife if he is dissatisfied with her cooking, housekeeping, or child care, or for violating gender expectations (Rani, Bonu, and Diop-Sidibe 2004). In some cultural situations, the woman's life is valuable only as it relates to her economic value, production of sons, and the needs of men. Changes in the patriarchal family structure, education and employment opportunities for women, and child care availability can lead to greater freedom of choice, equality, and autonomy for women, according to feminist theorists (Shaw and Lee 2005).

Family Dynamics: Micro-Level Processes

The Agabi family belongs to the Hausa tribe of West Africa. They share a family compound composed of huts or houses for each family unit of one wife and her young children, plus one building for greeting guests, one for cooking, one for the older children, and one for washing. The compound is surrounded by an enclosure. Each member of the family carries out certain tasks: food preparation, washing, child care, farming, herding—whatever is needed for the well-being of the group. Wives live with their husbands' families. Should there be a divorce, the children generally belong to the husband's household because in this tribe the family lineage is patrilineal through the father's side.

The eldest male is the leader and makes decisions for the group. When a child is born, the eldest male within the family presides over a ceremony to name and welcome the child into the group. When the child reaches marrying age, the eldest male plays a major role in choosing a suitable mate. On his death, the power he has held passes to his eldest son, and his property is inherited by his sons.

However, the eldest Agabi son has moved away from the extended family to the city, where he works in a factory to support himself. He lives in a small room with several other migrants. He has met a girl from another tribe and may marry her, but he will have to do so without his family's blessing. He will probably have a small family because of money and space constraints in the city. His lifestyle and even values have already altered considerably. The global trend toward the Global North model of industrialization and urbanization is altering cultures around the world and changing family life.

Families can be studied at each level of analysis: as interdependent micro-level social units with Mom, Dad, and the kids; as meso-level institutions that can be seen as economic units; and as part of the macro-level social system. Many individual family issues that seem very intimate and personal are actually affected by norms and forces at other levels (such as migration, urbanization, and economic conditions). Likewise, decisions of individuals at the micro level affect meso- and macro-level social structures (such as size of families). Individual families are, in essence, local franchises of a larger social phenomenon.

Thinking Sociologically

What kinds of changes in families would you anticipate as societies change from agricultural to industrial to information technology economies and as individuals move from rural to urban areas? What changes has your family undergone over several generations?

Mate Selection: How Do New Families Start?

At the most micro level, two people get together to begin a new family unit. In 2011 the world population passed 7 billion people, but it is highly unlikely that your significant other was or will be randomly selected from the entire global population. Even in Global North societies, where we think individuals have free choice of marriage partners, mate selection is seldom an entirely free choice. Indeed, mate selection is highly limited by geographical proximity, ethnicity, age, social class, and a host of other variables. As we shall see, micro- and macro-level forces influence each other in a process as personal as mate selection.

Norms Governing Choice of Marriage Partners: Societal Rules and Intimate Choices

A number of cultural rules—meso- and macro-level expectations—govern the choice of a mate in any society. Most are unwritten societal norms. They vary from culture to culture, but in every society we learn them from an early age. One of the cultural rules is **exogamy**, *norms governing the choice of a mate that require individuals to marry outside of their own immediate group*. The most universal form of exogamy is the *incest taboo*, including restrictions against father-daughter, mother-son, and brother-sister marriages. Some countries, including about half the U.S. states, forbid first cousins to marry (see Table 3.3 on page 90). Others, such as some African groups and many Syrian villages, encourage first-cousin marriages to solidify family ties and property holdings. Some societies require village exogamy (marriage outside the village) because it bonds together villages and reduces the likelihood of armed conflict between neighboring groups.

Reasons given for exogamy range from recognition of the negative biological results of inbreeding to necessity for families to make ties with outside groups for survival. One clear issue is that rights to sexual access can cause jealousy that rips a social unit apart. If father and son became jealous about who was sleeping with the wife/mother/sister, relationships would be destroyed and parental authority sabotaged. Likewise, if the father was always going to the daughter for sexual satisfaction, the mother and daughter bond would be severely threatened (Williams, Sawyer, and Wahlstrom 2013). No society can allow this to happen to its family system. Any society that has failed to have an incest taboo self-destructed long ago.

On the other hand, *norms of* **endogamy** *require individuals to marry inside certain human boundaries, whatever the societal members see as protecting the homogeneity of the group.* The purpose is to encourage group bonding and solidarity, and to help minority groups survive in societies with different cultures. Endogamous norms may require individuals to select mates of the same race, religion, social class, ethnic background, or clan (Williams et al. 2013). For example, strictly endogamous religious groups include the Armenian Iranians, Orthodox Jews, Old Order Amish, Jehovah's Witnesses, and the Parsis of India. The result is less biologically diversified groups, but protection of the minority identity (Belding 2004). Whether marriages are arranged or entered into freely, both endogamy and exogamy limit the number of possible mates. In addition to marrying within a group, most people choose a mate with similar social characteristics—age, place of residence, educational background, political philosophy, moral values, and psychological traits—a practice called *homogamy*.

Going outside the expected and accepted group in mate selection can make things tough for newlyweds who need family and community support. Few take this risk. For instance, in the United States, close to 90% marry people with similar religious values (Williams et al. 2013). About 80% to 90% of Protestants marry other Protestants, and 64% to 85% of Catholics marry within their religious faith. For Jews, the figure has been as high as 90% but has dropped in recent decades to as low as 50% for some Jews, depending on the type of Judaism (Newman 2009). In Canada, only one person in five marries across religious boundaries (British Columbia Ministry of Labour & Citizens' Services 2006). However, with increased tolerance for differences, cross-denominational marriage is more likely today than a century ago.

Interracial marriages also challenge norms of endogamy, yet the practice is becoming more common with every passing year. In African nations, men from India often take African wives; in Latin America, Amerindians and Europeans mixed to form Mestizo populations; in the Middle East and North Africa, trading routes brought mixing of populations; and in Japan, 20% of the men are married to non-Japanese women, mostly from Asia. Of interracial marriages in the United States, 14.5% involve a spouse from a different race or ethnic group (Inniss 2010). Also, one in five has a close relative in a mixed-race marriage, and one half of the dating population has dated someone of a different race. The most common pattern is a white American married to someone from a different ethnic or racial group. However, among Hispanics, one in four is married to someone of another Latin ethnicity (e.g., a Mexican American marrying a Cuban American). Among Hispanics, Puerto Ricans are the most likely to marry a non-Hispanic, with 21% of marriages being exogamous. Among Mexicans and Cuban Americans, roughly 12% marry non-Hispanics—usually whites. Black-white marriages usually involve black men and white women with nearly 15% percent of black men and a bit less than 7% of black women in mixed-race marriages (Carroll 2010). By contrast, Asian American women are more likely to marry exogamously than Asian American men, and there is an overall pattern of 40% marrying whites (Carroll 2010; Lee and Edmonston 2005).

Each group may have different definitions of where the exogamy boundary is. For Orthodox Hasidic Jews, marriage to a Reform Jew is exogamy—strictly forbidden. For the Amish, the marriage of a Hostetler Amish woman to a Beachy Amish man is beyond consideration. Marriage of a Hopi to a Navajo has also been frowned on as marriage to an "Other"—even though many Anglos would think of this as an endogamous marriage of two Native Americans.

So cultural norms of societies limit individual decisions about micro-level matters such as choice of a spouse, and they do so in a way that most individuals do not even recognize. Exogamy and endogamy norms and expectations generally restrict the range of potential marriage partners, even though some of these norms are weakening. Still, the question remains: How do we settle on a life partner?

Finding a Mate

In most societies, mate selection is achieved through arranged marriages, free-choice unions, or some combination of the two. In either case, selection is shaped by cultural rules of the society.

Arranged marriages *involve a pattern of mate selection in which someone other than the couple—elder males, parents, a matchmaker—selects the marital partners.* This method of mate selection is most common in traditional, often patriarchal, societies. Some examples follow.

For many traditional girls in Muslim societies, marriage is a matter of necessity, for her support comes from the family system. Economic arrangements and political alliances between family groups are solidified through marriage. Daughters are valuable commodities in negotiations to secure these ties between families (Burn 2011). Beauty, youth, talent, and pleasant disposition bring a high price and a good match. Should the young people like each other, it is icing on the

Japanese weddings are very formal and colorful events, and in many cases they still involve the parental selection of spouse, often with the help of a matchmaker.

cake. Daughters must trust that the male elders in their families will make the best possible matches for them. Most often, the men hold the power in this vital decision.

Seated front and center with the bride and groom at many Japanese weddings is the matchmaker, the person responsible for bringing the relationship into being. After both families agree to the arrangement, the couple meets over tea several times to decide whether the match suits them. Today, about 30% of marriages in Japan are still arranged this way, the rest being called "love marriages" (About.com 2013).

Where arranged marriages are the norm, love has a special meaning. The man and woman may never have set eyes on each other before the wedding day, but respect and affection generally grow over time as the husband and wife live together. People from societies with arranged marriages are assured a mate and have difficulty comprehending marriage systems based on love, romance, and courtship—factors that they believe to be insufficient grounds for a lifelong relationship. They wonder why anyone would want to place themselves in a marriage market, with all the uncertainty and rejection. Such whimsical and unsystematic methods would not work in many societies, where the structure of life is built around family systems.

Free-choice marriage involves *a pattern of mate selection in which the partners select each other based primarily on romance and love.* Sonnets, symphonies, rock songs, poems, and plays have been written to honor love and the psychological and physiological pain and pleasure that the mating game brings. However impractical romance may seem, marriage choice based on *romantic love*, the idea that each person has the right to choose a partner with minimal interference from others, is becoming prevalent as societies around the world become more Westernized, women gain more rights and freedoms, and families exert less control over their children's choice of mates (Eshleman and Bulcroft 2010). Industrial and postindustrial societies tend to value love and individualism and tend to have high marriage rates, low fertility rates, and high divorce rates.

Free-choice mate selection is found in most wealthy Global North societies where individualism is emphasized over community interests. Couples in the United States tend to put more emphasis on romantic love and the process of attracting a mate than most other societies. For example, 86% of U.S. college students say they would not marry without love, the figure being higher for men than for women. The old adages about women "hooking a man" and men being "snagged or caught" are challenged by data that suggest men are more likely than women to prefer marriage over the single status for life. In a recent U.S. survey, 66% of men agreed that "it is better to get married" compared with 51% of women (Eshleman and Bulcroft 2010).

The Internet facilitates romance and mate selection in many modern societies, helping people of all ages enter into relationships and find compatible mates. There is no shortage of Internet mate shoppers who spend more than $900 million a year on online dating. The Internet facilitates what those in arranged marriage systems find bewildering about free-choice systems—how do you meet possible mates? Many of the e-dating services claim that their profiles and processes are based on social science research. The burgeoning business in e-romance introduces people with common interests, backgrounds, ages, and other variables. Several popular sites are Match.com, PerfectMatch.com, Chemistry.com, and eHarmony.com (Consumer Rankings 2012). For example, according to eHarmony, each day approximately 15,000 individuals fill out their extensive 258-question questionnaire to create a personality profile that the company claims is a "scientifically proven" compatibility-matching system. More than 33 million users from 150 countries hope for one or more matches from the system. If the reported average of 236 members who marry every day is an indication, many would-be mates are finding their partners (eHarmony 2012). In addition to those above, many specialized services have sprung up based on race, religion, sexual orientation, and other interests such as GoodGenes.com and ConservativeDates.com.

Thinking Sociologically

Is e-dating a modern-day form of the matchmaker? Is it replacing other forms of finding a mate? Why or why not?

Starting with the assumption that eligible people are most likely to meet and be attracted to others who have similar values and backgrounds, sociologists have developed various mate selection theories, several of which view dating as a three-stage process (see Figure 10.1).

1. *Stimulus:* We meet someone to whom we are attracted by appearance, voice, dress, similar ethnic background, sense of humor, or other factors. Something serves as a stimulus that makes us take notice. Of course, sometimes the stimulus is simply knowing the other person is interested in us.
2. *Value comparison:* As we learn about the other's values, we are more likely to find that person compatible if she or he affirms our own beliefs and values toward life, politics, religion, and roles of men and women in society and marriage. If values are not compatible, the person does not pass through our filter. We look elsewhere.
3. *Roles and needs stage:* Another filter comes when the couple explores roles of companion, parent, housekeeper, and lover. This might involve looking for common needs, interests, and favored activities. If roles and needs are not complementary to one's own, desire for a permanent relationship wanes.

The mate selection process varies somewhat from person to person, but social scientists believe that a sequential series of decisions, in a pattern such as that described earlier, is often part of the process (Eshleman and Bulcroft 2010; Murstein 1987).

The notion of mate selection described above is sometimes referred to as a filter theory. It is as though you were filtering specs of gold: The first filter holds out the large stones, the second filter holds back pebbles, and the third filter stops sand, but the flakes of gold come through. Each stage in the mate selection process involves filtering some people out of the process (Eshleman and Bulcroft 2010; Murstein 1987). For you there may be other filter factors as well—such as religious similarities or common ethnicity.

Thinking Sociologically

Conduct a small survey of dating and married couples you know. Ask them about how they became involved in their relationship and their process of deciding to get together or marry. How do their comments mesh with the three-stage process described above?

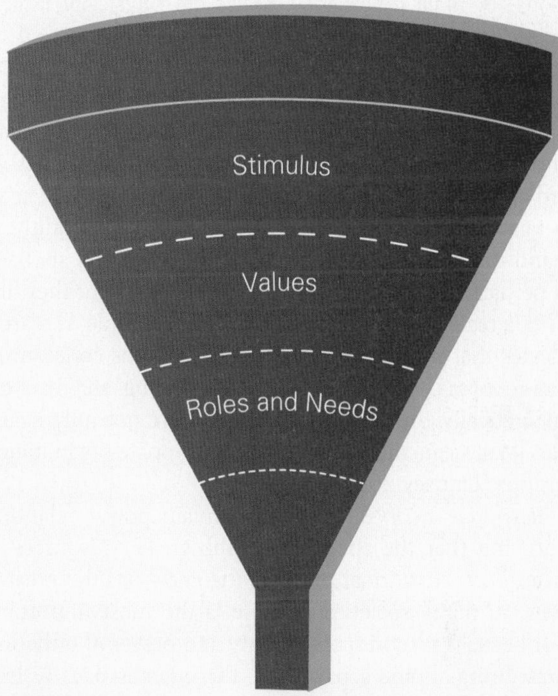

Figure 10.1 Mate Selection "Filtering"
The notion of mate selection described above is sometime referred to as a filter theory. It is as though you were filtering specs of gold, and the first filter holds out the large stones, the second filter holds back pebbles, the third filter stops sand, but the flakes of gold come through. Each stage in the mate selection process involves filtering some people out of the process. For you there may be other filter factors as well—such as religious similarities or common ethnicity.

Who Holds the Power? Authority in Marriage

Power relations, another micro-level issue shaped by cultural norms at the macro level, affect the interactions and decision making in individual families. Two areas that have received particular sociological attention are decision making in marriage and work roles.

Decision Making in Marriage

Cultural traditions establish the power base in society and family: patriarchy, matriarchy, or egalitarianism. The most typical authority pattern in the world is patriarchy, or male authority. Matriarchy, female authority, is rare. Even where the lineage is traced through the mother's line, males generally dominate decision making. Some analysts have suggested reasons for male dominance: Males are physically larger, they are free from childbearing, and they are not tied to one place by homemaking and agricultural responsibilities. However, social scientists find no evidence that there are any inherent intellectual or personality foundations for male authority as opposed to female authority (Kramer 2010; Ward and Edelstein 2009).

Egalitarian family patterns—in which power, authority, and decision making are shared between the spouses and perhaps with the children—are emerging, but they are not yet a reality in most households. For example, research indicates that in many U.S. families, decisions concerning vacation plans, car purchases, and housing are reached democratically. Still, most U.S. families are not fully egalitarian. Males generally have a disproportionate say in major decisions (Lindsey 2011).

Resource theory attempts to explain power relations by arguing that the spouse with the greater resources—education, occupational prestige, income—has the greater power. In many societies, income is the most important factor because it represents identity and power. If only one spouse brings home a paycheck, the other is usually less powerful (Tichenor 1999). In families where the wife is a professional, other factors in addition to income such as persuasion and egalitarian values may enter into the power dynamic (Lindsey 2011). Regardless of who has greater resources, men in two-earner couples tend to have more say in financial matters and less responsibility for children and household tasks.

Men are increasingly sharing the household tasks such as cooking and cleaning.

Who Does the Housework?

The *second shift,* a term coined by Hochschild (1989), refers to the housework and child care that employed women do after their first-shift jobs. Studies indicate that women work doing household activities (2.6 hours per day and 18 hours per week) whereas men work 2 hours per day. Men spend more time doing leisure activities. On an average day in 2011, 83% of women and 66% of men spent some time doing housework (U.S. Bureau of Labor Statistics 2012). The "Engaging Sociology" shows the breakdown in hours spent by men and women at various household activities.

Employment schedules also affect the amount of time each spouse contributes to household tasks. Husbands who are at home during hours when their wives are working tend to take on more tasks. Employment, education, and earnings give women more respect and independence and a power base for a more equitable division of labor across tasks (Cherlin 2010; Kramer 2010). Recent research also clearly shows a narrowing of the gap in time spent by men and women on household tasks, though such factors as presence and the ages of children, how many years the mother has worked outside the home, and socioeconomic status of the family influence how involved men are and how much real "free time" each experiences. When women do have free time, it is much more likely to be interrupted than is true for men (Kan, Sullivan, and Gershuny 2011; Mattingly and Sayer 2006; Saxbe, Repetti, and Graesch 2011).

Interestingly, husbands who do an equitable share of the household chores actually report higher levels of satisfaction with the marriage, and the couple is less likely to divorce (Lorillard 2011). The success or failure of a marriage depends in large part on patterns that develop early in the marriage for dealing with the everyday situations including power relationships and division of labor.

While many women in the world are economically dependent on men, men are often dependent on women emotionally, for they are less likely to have same-sex friends with whom they share feelings and vulnerabilities. Men bond with one another, but they seldom develop truly intimate ties that provide support in hard times. So women are not entirely without power even where they are dependent. It is just that their power frequently takes a different form (and results in fewer privileges; Newman 2009).

Engaging Sociology

Household Tasks by Gender

In many households, household talks are highly gendered. As recently as the 1980s, wives and daughters spent two or three times as much time as fathers and sons in household tasks such as cleaning and laundry and yard work. However, the tides have been shifting, and while they are not entirely equal, they are more balanced.

Sociological Data Analysis:

1. What is the division of labor (by gender) for household maintenance in your family?
2. How did it evolve?
3. Is it considered fair by all participants?
4. How does it compare to the data in Figure 10.2?

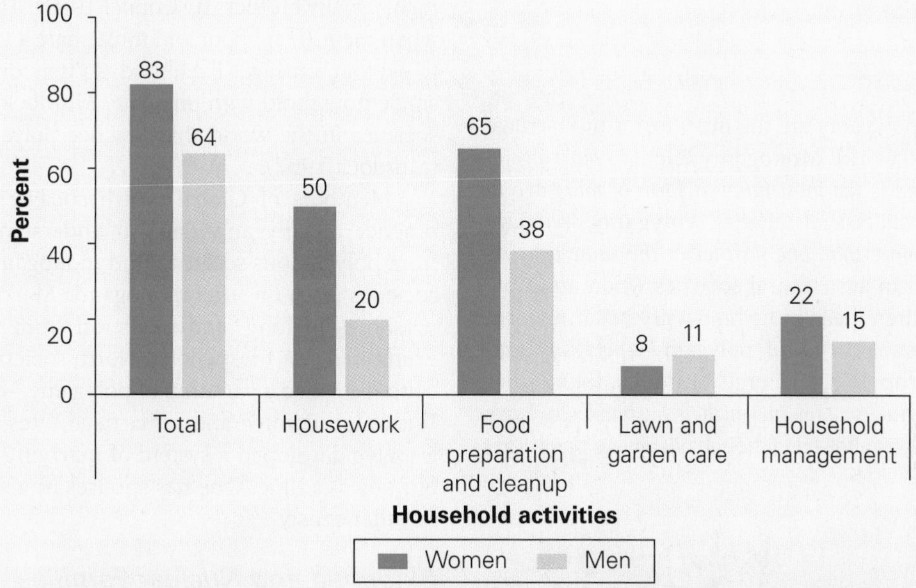

Figure 10.2 Percentage of Men and Woman Who Engage in Some Type of Household Tasks Each Day

Source: Bureau of Labor Statistics (2011).

The Family as an Institution: Meso-Level Analysis

We experience family life at a very personal level, but if we consider common elements of all families, we have the family as an institution at the meso level of society. In this section, we look at the structure and parts of family as an institution, and the family and its relationship to other institutions. Some of the changes in the family have resulted from—or caused—changes in other institutions.

The Structure and Parts of Family as an Institution

Although the family is an institution in the larger social system, it does vary in interesting ways from one society to another. One example is how many mates one should have. Some societies believe that several wives provide more hands to do the work and establish useful political and economic alliances between family groups. They bring more children into the family unit and provide multiple family members for emotional and physical support and satisfaction. On the other hand, having one spouse per adult probably meets most individuals' social and emotional needs very effectively, is less costly, and eliminates the possibility of conflict or jealousy among spouses. It is also easier to relocate a one-spouse family to urban areas, a necessity for many families in industrial and postindustrial societies. Let us examine the issue of adult partners in a family. Institutions lay out the general framework for families in any society and include types of marriages, extended and nuclear families, and other structural models of families. Individual families are local expressions of a larger system of families that make up the institution of family in a society.

Types of Marriages

Monogamy and polygamy are the main forms of marriage found around the world. **Monogamy** refers to *marriage of two individuals and is the most familiar form of marriage in industrial and postindustrial societies.* **Polygamy**, *marriage of one person to more than one partner at the same time,* is most often found in agricultural societies where multiple spouses and children mean more help with the farm work. There are two main forms of polygamy—*polygyny* and *polyandry*. Anthropologist George Murdock found that **polygyny**, *a marital system in which a husband can have more than one wife,* was allowed (although not always practiced) in 709 of the 849 societies he cataloged in his classic *Ethnographic Atlas*. Only 16% (136 societies) were exclusively monogamous (Barash 2002). Polygyny is limited because it is expensive to maintain a large family, brides must be bought at high prices in some societies, and there are religious and political pressures plus a global movement toward monogamy. Because the numbers of men and women are usually fairly balanced in a society, there are seldom enough extra women to go around. Polygyny does increase at times of war when the number of men is reduced due to war casualties.

This polyandrous family poses for a photo in front of their tent in northwest China. Fraternal polyandry means that brothers share a common wife. When children are born, they call the oldest brother father and all other brothers uncle, regardless of who the biological father is. China's marriage law does not officially permit polyandry.

Polyandry, *a marital system in which a wife has more than one husband,* is practiced in less than 1% of the world's societies. Among the Todas of Southern India, for example, brothers can share a wife (O'Connel 1993). The Marquesas Islanders allow wives to have more than one husband. A Tibetan practice originating in the country's system of land ownership and inheritance allows a woman to marry several men, usually brothers (O'Connel 1993). This often happens when the men are poor and must share a single plot of land to eke out a meager livelihood, so they decide to remain a single household with one wife. Murdock found only four societies in the world that practice polyandrous marriage (Murdock 1967).

Members of Global North societies often find the practice of polygamy hard to understand, just as those from polygamous societies find monogamy strange. Some societies insist on strict monogamy: Marriage to one other person is lifelong, and deviation from that standard is prohibited. Yet most Global North societies practice what could be called a variation of polygamy—*serial monogamy*. With high divorce and remarriage rates, Western societies have developed a system of marrying several spouses, but one at a time. One has spouses in a series rather than simultaneously.

Extended and Nuclear Families

The typical "Ma, Pa, and kids" monogamous model that is familiar in many industrialized parts of the world is not as typical as it appears. From a worldwide perspective, it is only one of several structural models of family.

Extended families include *two or more adult generations that share tasks and living quarters.* This may include brothers, sisters, aunts, uncles, cousins, and grandparents. In most extended family systems, the eldest male is the authority figure. This is a common pattern around the world, especially in agricultural societies. Some ethnic groups in the United States, such as Mexican Americans and some Asian Americans, live in extended monogamous families with several generations under one roof. This is financially practical and helps group members maintain their traditions and identity by remaining somewhat isolated from Anglo society.

As societies become more industrialized and fewer individuals and families engage in agriculture, the **nuclear family**, *consisting of two parents and their children—or any two of the three*—becomes more common. This worldwide trend toward nuclear family occurs because more individuals live in urban areas where smaller families are more practical, mate selection is based on love, couples establish independent households after marriage, marriage is less of an economic arrangement between families, fewer marriages take place between relatives such as cousins, and equality between the sexes increases (Burn 2011; Goode 1970).

No matter what form the family manifests itself in a society, the family as an institution is interdependent at the meso level with each of the other major institutions. For example, if the health care institution is unaffordable or not functioning well, families may not get the care they need to prevent serious illness. If the economy goes into a recession and jobs are not available, families experience stress, abuse rates increase, and marriages are more likely to become unstable. When husbands lose jobs, it often makes their primary role in the family ambiguous, causing sense of failure by the husband and stress in the relationship. In single-parent families in which the mother is the custodial parent, the loss of her job can be financially devastating. In worst-case scenarios, families who lose their incomes may become homeless.

In many societies, the family is still the primary unit of economic production. These family members in Myanmar are selling the goods they produced as a family.

Thinking Sociologically

Under what social circumstances would an extended family be helpful? Under what circumstances would it be a burden? What are the strengths and weaknesses of nuclear families?

The Economic Institution and the Family

The family is the primary economic unit of consumption, so what happens when economic times are rough? In the past several years much of the world economy has been troubled, resulting in employment instability and uncertainty, economic strain, and even poverty causing strained family relations. Low-income families, especially single-parent families headed by women, are particularly hard-hit and often have to struggle for survival. In some cases, families are so financially devastated that they are homeless, which is difficult, especially for children.

Poverty and Families in the United States

The poverty threshold for a family of four was $23,050 in 2012, and for a single person was $11,170 (HHS Poverty Guidelines 2012). In 2010, 15.1% of all persons in the United States lived below the poverty line (U.S. Census Bureau 2008a). Single-woman heads of household were the hardest hit group with 31.6% living in poverty. By contrast, 6.2% of married couples had incomes below the poverty line. The average family has gotten poorer in the past 10 years as the median household income fell over 7% since 2000 (Cauchon and Hansen 2011). Table 10.1 shows the percentage of individuals and families in poverty.

Table 10.1 **Poverty Status of U.S. Families by Family Type in 2011**

Poverty Status and Family Type	*Total Percentage Below Poverty Level*
Total (all) families	11.8% (9.5 million)
Married-couple families	6.2% (3.7 million)
Single female householder	31.2% (4.9 million)
Single male householder	16.1% (0.9 million)

Source: U.S. Census Bureau 2012f.

The *feminization of poverty*, discussed in earlier chapters, is a global problem. It occurs where single motherhood is widespread and where there are few policies to reduce poverty, especially for this group (Williams et al. 2013). Single mothers, whether in capitalist or socialist countries, have some common experiences, including dual roles as workers and mothers, lower earnings than men, irregular paternal support payments, and underrepresentation in policy-making bodies. What differs around the world are governmental policies that help mothers with child support, child care, health care, maternity leave, and family allowances. Single mothers are as prevalent in Sweden as in the United States, but U.S. single mothers are many times more likely to be poor because of fewer support systems from the state (Winkler 2002). For single teens, early motherhood, lack of education, and insufficient income lead to a multiproblem family pattern.

One cause of single-parent families has been divorce. However, the change in birthrates in which more children are born to single women is also a factor. Table 10.2 shows the shift in 30 years from about 18% to 41% of babies born outside of marriage.

Another reason for the increase in single-parent households among African American women is that there are 47.6% males compared to 52.4% females out of 37 million (Bowman 2010). This difference is due in large part to high mortality and incarceration rates of African American males. The difference in marriage by age group shows that 87% of African American women 55 years of age and older have been married at some time in their lives. By contrast, 70.5% of African American women between 25 and 29 are not married (Stanley 2011). Although African Americans value family, many poor men cannot fulfill the economic role of husband and father because the number of jobs available to less educated men is decreasing (MacLeod 2008; Madyun and Lee 2010; Wilson 1987). Some argue that a culture of poverty, a set of attitudes and values including a sense of hopelessness and passivity, low aspirations, feelings of powerlessness and inferiority, and present-time orientation (concern only for the present and not planning for the future), is passed from one generation to the next (Lewis 1961, 1986). However, many sociological researchers support the argument that poverty itself causes the values and attitudes that develop as survival mechanisms in poor communities (MacLeod 2008). In a field study of an African American ghetto community, Carol Stack found some creative adaptations to unhealthy environmental conditions. Relatives and intimate friends shared money, child care, food, and housing to meet each other's needs in times of crisis. In this example, the notion of family is expanded to include a network of people who provide mutual care. On the flip side, when someone does succeed in escaping the slum, close friends and relatives lean on the person for support and contacts, and the person can get drawn back

This young woman sits at the wheel of her car with all of her possessions inside as her children, Jordain (3) and Jomari (2), sit in the back seat. They are hoping to be admitted to a homeless shelter in Fort Lauderdale, Florida. The homeless population is larger now than it was in the 1980s, with the main increase being children who spend their nights moving from shelter to shelter. Most urban shelters require that a family must leave the site by 6:30 a.m. These are not conditions that make for effective parenting.

Table 10.2 Percentage of Births to Unmarried and Married Women: United States

Year	Births to Unmarried Women (%)	Births to Married Women (%)
2009	41.0	59.0
2000	33.2	66.8
1995	32.2	67.8
1990	28.0	72.0
1985	22.0	78.0
1980	18.4	81.6

Source: DeParle and Tavernise (2012).

into the impoverished networks. So the same networks can be both supportive and entrapping (Stack 1998).

Dual-Worker Families

A different kind of economic influence can be seen in dual-career marriages. Two incomes may relieve economic strain on a household, but family life in dual-worker families may be quite complicated. Browse through the checkout-line magazine racks next time you are in a grocery store. Note the number of articles offering advice on how to cope with stress and overload or how to budget time, cook meals in minutes, rise to the top, and "make it" together. Stress, role conflict, and work overload are common, but most couples are aware of these strains and have chosen to combine marriage, sometimes children, and the intense involvement required by a career.

With the stress found in juggling the competing home-work responsibilities, some women and men are finding that work provides a haven from their hectic, sometimes unrewarding home life. Women are tending to spend more time at work, but men are not spending more time at home to balance the equation (Hochschild 1997; Schneider and Waite 2005).

In many Global North societies, government and industry support dual-career families with various family-friendly policies: readily available child care facilities, parenting leaves for childbirth and illness, and flexible work hours or telecommuting (working from one's home). These policies allow families to combine both work and family lives with some time for leisure thrown in. Some public sociologists focus on family policy issues, trying to help policy makers and individual families know what really does contribute to healthy families and marriages, as indicated in the "Sociologists in Action" feature on page 368.

The United States has been slower than many other Global North countries to adopt family-friendly policies. The U.S. government passed the Family and Medical Leave Act in 1993, allowing for 12 weeks of unpaid leave for the birth of a baby or care of a newborn, foster care or adoption, serious health issues in the immediate family, or serious medical conditions of the employee (U.S. Office of Personnel Management 2007). However, many corporations in the United States have been slow to respond to dual-career family needs. Company-sponsored day care and paternity leave are still rare. A few businesses are experimenting with family-friendly policies such as flex-time (allowing individuals to schedule their own work hours within certain time frames) and job sharing (allowing individuals to split a job, with one family member working in the morning and the other in the afternoon).

When both parents have full-time jobs, one solution to the stress is to hire other people to do some of the familial jobs, including care of children. Many people who use child care feel it has been very good for the children, and studies confirm this—depending on the quality of the care individual or agency.

Family is a diverse and complex social institution. It interacts with other institutions and in some ways reinforces them. Families prepare the next generation. They pray together and talk as families about what happens after death. They provide care of disabled, infirm, or sick members. As a basic institution, the family plays a role in the vitality of the entire nation. So it should not be surprising that at the macro level, many national and global policy decisions concern how to strengthen the family institution.

Thinking Sociologically

What are the challenges facing dual-career families? What might alleviate the stress?

National and Global Family Issues: Macro-Level Analysis

An effective way to explore macro-level issues pertaining to families is to explore policy matters that affect the family

Sociologist in Action
W. Bradford Wilcox

Strategies for Successful Marriages

Juggling work, child rearing, and housework can take a toll on a marriage. When parents have to work more than they would like, other responsibilities become harder to manage, tensions can mount, and divorce becomes more likely. Sociologist Bradford Wilcox directs the National Marriage Project, "a nonpartisan, nonsectarian, and interdisciplinary initiative" designed to "provide research and analysis on the health of marriage in America, to analyze the social and cultural forces shaping contemporary marriage, and to identify strategies to increase marital quality and stability" (National Marriage Project 2012).

Every year, Wilcox helps create a *State of Our Union* research report about marriages in the United States. The report, a joint effort by the National Marriage Project and the Institute for American Values, examines the social and cultural forces impacting marriages. In doing so, it provides data that policy makers can use to support families and increase marital happiness and stability.

The *2011 State of Our Union* report indicates the need for more part-time work opportunities for parents, particularly mothers. The findings in the report reveal that over half (58%) of all married mothers (compared to 20% of married fathers) would like to work just part-time. Mothers who work more than they prefer are more likely to divorce than those who work the same or less than their ideal number of hours per week.

It is important, though, that fathers, as well as mothers, have time to contribute to housework and child care. Both are happier and less likely to divorce when housework "(e.g., cleaning, cooking, taking out the garbage) and childcare are 'shared equally'" (National Marriage Project 2012:22). This sharing of domestic responsibilities requires flexible hours for full-time workers, as well as part-time work opportunities.

These work policy issues affect all aspects of family life, including happiness in the bedroom. As noted in the *State of Our Union* report, "women are more likely to report that they are sexually satisfied when . . . they share housework with their husbands. What happens outside of the bedroom seems to matter a great deal in predicting how happy husbands and wives are with what happens in the bedroom" (Wilcox and Marquardt 2011:36). These findings are particularly important when combined with those that reveal that for *both* mothers and fathers, sexual satisfaction is a key predictor of marital happiness and stability. Fortunately, public sociologists like Wilcox are making these connections and helping policy makers understand them, as well.

* * * * * * *

W. Bradford Wilcox is the director of the National Marriage Project at the University of Virginia, an associate professor of sociology at the University of Virginia, and a member of the James Madison Society at Princeton University.

or that are intended to strengthen families. After exploring issues of national concern—cohabitation, homosexual relationships, and divorce—we look at some global trends in marriage and family life.

Cohabitation

Cohabitation—living together in a sexual relationship without marriage—is a significant macro-level trend in many countries that has implications for national family laws, tax laws, work benefits, and other macro-level issues. In European and North American countries, cohabitation has become the norm for many groups. For example, in the United States, the number of "unmarried households" reported by the Census has been rising dramatically for several decades. "Unmarried couples, both single [same sex] and opposite sex, living together rose from 7.1 million in 2009 to more than 8.1 million in 2010" (Kreider 2010b). There was an unusually large 13% increase (868,000 couples) in cohabiting couples between 2009 and 2010, in large part influenced by the economic downturn (Jayson 2011; Kreider 2010b). The overall trend in the number of "unmarried households" has been a dramatic rise for several decades. Two thirds of couples married in the past decade lived together for an average of two years before marriage (Jay 2012; Kreider and Elliott 2009).

Is cohabitation replacing dating? Some argue that a newly emerging pattern for some young adults between 25 and 34 is serial cohabitation (Lichter, Turner, and Sassler 2010). As Figure 10.3 shows, the increases in cohabiting households (same-sex and different-sex couples) in the United States over 50 years are dramatic. Still, at any given point in time, only about 9% of the population in the United States is cohabiting (Benokraitis 2012; Lamanna and Riedmann 2010).

Thinking Sociologically

Why do couples decide to cohabitate? Is it usually with expectation of marriage, or is something else at work? Ask some friends or family members who are cohabiting their reasons and compile a list of motivations.

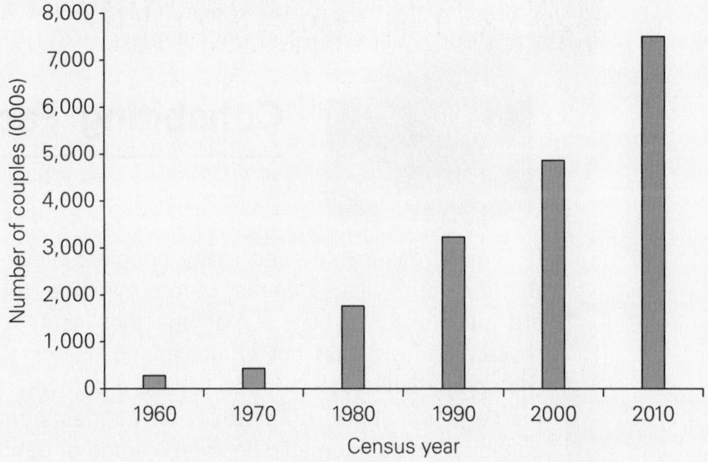

Figure 10.3 Cohabiting Households in the United States, 1960–2010

Source: Fitch, Goeken, and Ruggles 2005; Kreider 2010b.

Countries in Europe with the highest percentage of cohabiting couples between the ages of 20 and 34 include Denmark (28.6%), Estonia (23.5%), Finland (28.3%), France (21.3%), Netherlands (21.9%), Norway (22.7%), and the United Kingdom (22.2%; OECD Family Database 2010). Latin American and Caribbean surveys have indicated that more than one in four women between the ages of 15 and 49 are in relationships they call consensual unions, living together without official sanction. Such women typically have far less legal protection than European women during or after such unions.

Marriage versus cohabitation rates and reasons vary significantly by ethnicity. For whites in the United States, cohabitation is often a precursor to marriage. For African Americans, it may be an alternative to marriage. Financial problems encourage cohabitation in African American families because many African American men avoid marriage if they do not think they can support a family and fulfill the breadwinner role. Although childbearing increases the chance of marriage, it is a much stronger impetus for white than for black cohabiters.

We might assume that cohabiting would allow couples to make more realistic decisions about entering permanent relationships. However, some studies have shown that this is not always the case. When couples have different objectives for cohabiting, or have not discussed the future of the relationship before moving in together, problems may arise, and divorce may result as indicated in the "Sociology in Our Social World on page 370."

Thinking Sociologically

For about four decades, cohabitation by a couple was linked to greater likelihood of divorce, and explanations of that difference were offered. (See the "Sociology in Our Social World" feature.) In very recent years this pattern has changed. What hypotheses can you generate to explain the shift in outcomes for cohabitation?

Same-Sex Relationships and Civil Unions

A hotly debated macro-level policy matter concerning the family is the official status of homosexual couples. Policy decisions affect rights and benefits for partners, but there is intense disagreement over whether this issue is about human rights or about divinely determined rights and wrongs.

In the United States, the Defense of Marriage Act grants married couples 1,138 federal rights not available to unmarried partners (U.S. General Accounting Office 2004). As same-sex relationships become more widely

Sociology in Our Social World

Cohabiting: Facts and Fiction

It seems reasonable—and many people believe—that if a couple lives together before marriage, they are more likely to have a marriage that lasts. Yet, research shows that not all cohabiting unions are the same. While cohabitation can be a pathway to marriage for some, other research suggests that cohabitation has primarily become a stage of dating instead of an inevitable path to marriage (Sassler and Miller 2011).

Many cohabiting couples never marry. It is more common for a cohabiting couple to have a child together than it is for them to marry (Cherlin 2010). However, some cohabiting couples do choose to marry. Those who had not talked about the possibility of marriage before moving in together are more likely to divorce than couples who did not cohabit prior to marriage (Stanley and Rhoades 2009).

The association between cohabitation before marriage and higher risk of divorce for some couples has intrigued researchers. Linda Waite and Maggie Gallagher (2000) point out that marriage has many benefits. Married people have better physical and mental health, have more frequent and more satisfying sex, and are substantially better off financially by the time of retirement than single people (they have more than double the money invested per person). Interestingly, the same benefits do not accrue to people who cohabit.

Much of this is because marriage links two people together in a way that makes them responsible to each other. If one smokes or drinks excessively, the partner has the right to complain about it—to essentially nag that person into better health patterns—because one partner's health has a direct impact on the other's and vice versa. Likewise, if one partner likes to spend money freely on vacations, the more frugal person is likely to restrain these spending habits. This is acceptable because their financial futures are closely intertwined. As each person restrains the habits of the other, the couple is likely to end up with more savings. At the end of their careers, the couple is likely to have more money put away for retirement. Also, people tend to be more adjusted when they have unqualified and unambiguous emotional support from another person whose life is inextricably tied to their own.

The cohabiting relationship is not grounded in a bargain created by a marriage contract, and this may change the relationship. This is especially true for couples who live together without intending to marry or having discussed marriage. These cohabiters are more likely to keep their finances separate and their options open. Moreover, they do not feel as if they have the right to nag the other person about health habits or finances. Their bond is emotional, but their actions toward one another do not always show that they see their futures as being intertwined. Thus, many of the advantages that come with marriage are lost. Yet inertia may lead them into marriage. When a cohabiting couple does marry, a partner may be shocked to find the other person beginning to nag her or to restrain his spending habits. The relationship is quite different, and partners are irritated by the changed behavior. So cohabitation does not always tell us what life with this other person will be like, if the intent to marry was not present from the outset (Stanley and Rhoades 2009; Waite and Gallagher 2000).

Still, the strong relationship between cohabiting and likelihood of divorce that existed for several decades has declined dramatically in the past decade or so, with recent research indicating that the gap in divorce rates between cohabiters and those who did not live together prior to marriage has nearly evaporated. The one exception is high divorce rates for "serial cohabiters" who have many partners before finally marrying (Cohen and Manning 2010; Manning, Longmore, and Giordano 2007). Note also that this decline in the connection between cohabitation and likelihood of divorce has happened at precisely the time when the divorce rates are dropping significantly—as we will see below.

acknowledged in the Global North, many gay and lesbian couples are living together openly as families. Denmark was the first country to recognize same-sex unions in 1989, granting legal rights to couples. In 2001, the Netherlands was the first country to allow same-sex marriages. Ten other countries now allow same-sex marriages, including Canada. However, some other countries have threatened punishment for openly gay individuals, and Uganda almost passed a bill authorizing the death penalty for homosexuals. It was deterred by international condemnation, but that bill recently was reintroduced for consideration (Goodstein 2012; Martin and Thompkins 2009).

The 2010 U.S. Census reports approximately 594,000 same-sex couple households in the United States, or about 1% of all couple households (U.S. Census Bureau 2011f). Most scholars acknowledge that this is probably an underreporting because of the stigma of reporting that one is gay or lesbian. One out of every nine unmarried cohabiting couples is gay or lesbian, and one quarter of gay couples are raising children (Benokraitis 2012; James 2011).

On the other hand, as of the fall of 2012, eight states and Washington, DC, have legalized same-sex marriage. These include Massachusetts, Connecticut, Iowa, Vermont, New Hampshire, New York, Washington, and Maryland (National Conference of States Legislatures 2012). Some states have passed this through the legislatures, and in other cases it has been a ruling by a court that the ban is discriminatory and denies people equal rights. Court or legislative actions legalizing same-sex marriages have also been made in Hawaii, Alaska, and Maine, but a state referendum by voters has overruled the decision. The battle between court rulings and votes by the populace has raged for almost a decade, but as of the fall of 2012 the courts had ruled that the proposition banning same-sex marriage (passed in 2008) violates the equal protection provisions of the U.S. Constitution. Six other states also legalize same-sex relationships through "civil unions"—contracts that grant state-level spousal rights to same-sex couples (Boston Globe 2012; National Conference of State Legislatures 2012). More than half of the states have amended their state constitutions so that marriage is limited to one man and one woman, and most do not recognize same-sex marriages or civil unions contracted in other states (The Gay Law Report 2011). Map 10.1 on page 372 indicates states that allow or recognize same-sex marriage and those that have legal or constitutional bans against it (National Conference of State Legislatures 2012).

Statutory provision means that the legislature has passed laws making same-sex marriage illegal (or legal). These are much easier to change than a constitutional amendment. Judicial provisions mean that the courts have ruled that any laws barring same-sex marriage are a violation of rights and therefore such marriage is legal.

One reason many people in the *lesbigay* community are so intent on having same-sex marriage is that same-sex partnerships or civil unions are "insufficiently institutionalized," making them somewhat less stable and creating ambiguity about their roles and rights (Cherlin 1978; Stewart 2007). They argue that if we actually believe that stable relationships and families make for a healthier and more stable society, then families with same-sex adults need public recognition.

Those who favor gay and lesbian marriages claim that supportive lifelong relationships are good for individuals and good for society. They see the fact that homosexuals want stable socially sanctioned relationships as an encouraging sign about how important the family is to society and how homosexuals want to fit in. Moreover, because many societies offer tax benefits, insurance coverage, and other privileges to married couples, the denial of marriage on the basis of one's gender attraction is seen as discriminatory and may be costly to partners who are denied rights, and to societies that must care for the needs of the uninsured or unemployed.

Those opposed argue that marriage has been a function of the church, temple, and mosque for centuries. None of the religious traditions have historically recognized gay

In the backyard of their home in Beverly Hills, comedian Ellen DeGeneres, left, and Portia de Rossi got married during one of the short windows when same-sex marriage was legal in California.

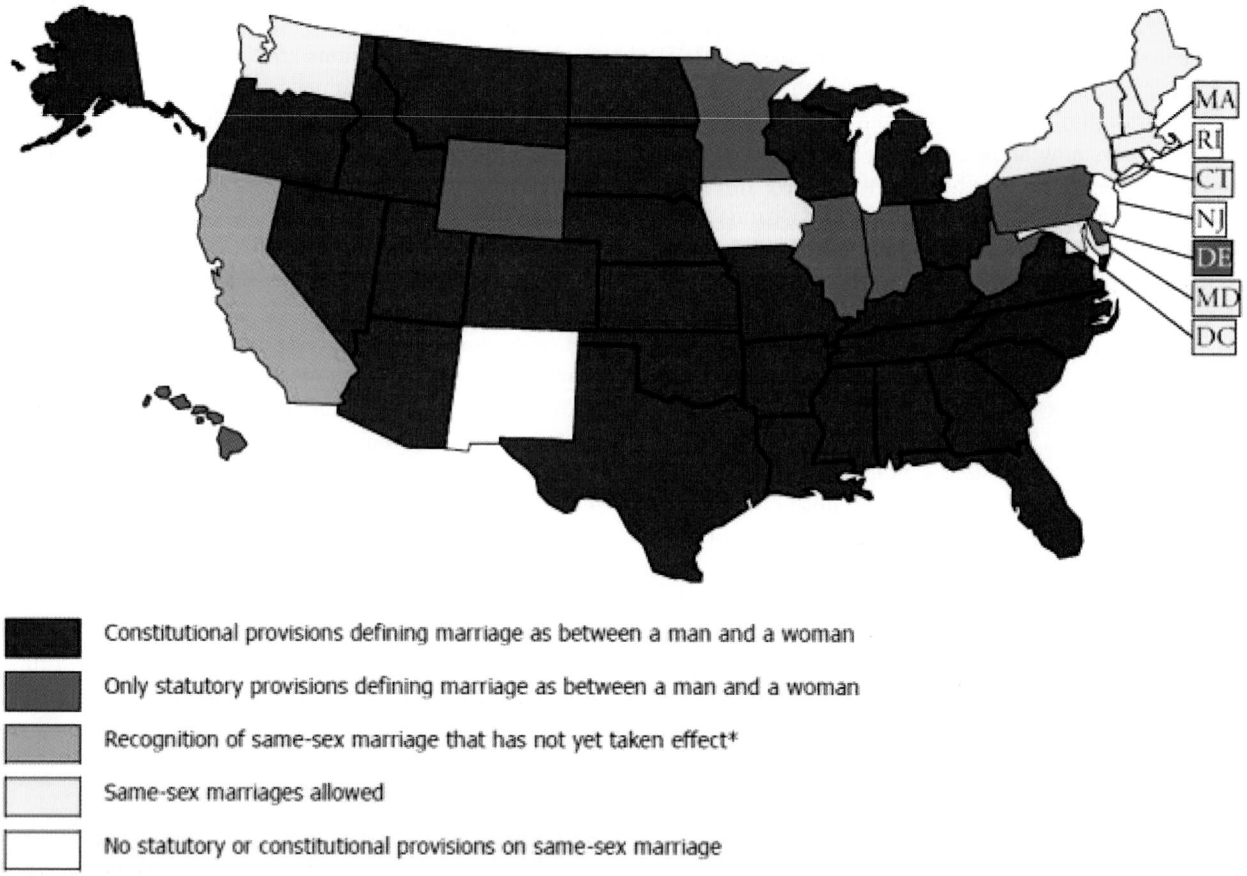

Map 10.1 State Defense of Marriage Acts and Same-Sex Marriage Laws

Note: Constitutional provisions mean that same-sex marriage is now barred by the state constitution.

relationships as legitimate (although a few are doing so now). Some opponents appeal to biology with the assertion that marriage is a legitimate way to propagate the species. Because homosexual unions do not serve this purpose, they do not serve the society, according to the opponents of same-sex marriage. However, many same-sex couples are providing homes for children, their own or adopted.

Divorce: Contract Breaking

Is the family breaking down? Is it relevant in today's world? Although most cultures extol the virtues of family life, the reality is that not all partnerships work. Support is not forthcoming for the partner, trust is violated, abuse is present, and relationships deteriorate. So we cannot discuss family life without also recognizing the often painful side of family life that results in contract breaking.

Some commentators view divorce rates as evidence that the family is deteriorating. They see enormous problems created by divorce. There are costs to adults who suffer guilt and failure, to children from divided homes, and to the society that does not have the stabilizing force of intact lifelong partnerships. For example, many children around the world are raised without both natural parents present; nearly half of all U.S. children today live at least part of their lives in single-parent families. About 9% of households in the United States are headed by single parents, that is, 12.9 million. If we consider only households with children, just over 67% of children under 18 years live with two married parents, 29.5% in single-parent households, and roughly 4% are in other arrangements (U.S. Census Bureau 2011b). Considering single-parent families by ethnicity in 2010, 66% of African American children live in single-parent households, 52% of American Indians, 16% of Asian and Pacific Islander,

41% of Hispanic or Latino, and 24% of white children (Kids Count Data Center 2010).

Others argue that marriage is not so much breaking down as adapting to a different kind of social system. They claim that the family of the 1950s would be ill suited to the societies we have today. Indeed, more people today express satisfaction with marriage than at any previous time period, and there are more golden (50-year) wedding anniversaries now than ever before (Kain 2005). Even late in the 19th century, the average length of a marriage was only 13 years—mostly because life expectancy was so short. "Til death do us part" was not such a long time then as it is today, when average life expectancy in Global North countries reaches into the 80s (Coontz 2005). There are many misconceptions about divorce in the 21st century as well, and the next "Sociology in Your Social World" addresses some of those.

Thinking Sociologically

Micro-level issues of divorce are often rooted in the personalities and relationships of the individuals involved. Talk with friends and families of those who have divorced about micro-level factors that contributed. Now, based on the previous discussion, make a list of meso-level factors (e.g., religious, economic, legal, educational) that contribute to or reduce divorce rates.

Sociology in Your Social World

Debunking Misconceptions About Divorce

By David Popenoe

Divorce Fallacy 1: Because people learn from their bad experiences, second marriages tend to be more successful than first marriages.

Fact: Although many people who divorce have successful subsequent marriages, the divorce rate of remarriages is in fact higher than that of first marriages.

Divorce Fallacy 2: Having a child together will help a couple improve their marital satisfaction and prevent a divorce.

Fact: Many studies have shown that the most stressful time in a marriage is after the first child is born. Couples who have a child together have a slightly decreased risk of divorce compared to couples without children, but the decreased risk is far less than it used to be.

Divorce Fallacy 3: When parents don't get along, children are better off if their parents divorce than if they stay together.

Fact: A recent large-scale, long-term study suggests that while parents' marital unhappiness and discord have a broad negative impact on virtually every dimension of their children's well-being, so does going through a divorce. It was only the children in very high-conflict homes who benefited from a divorce. In lower-conflict marriages that end in divorce—as many as two thirds of divorces—the situation of the children was made much worse following a divorce. Therefore, except in high-conflict marriages it is better for the children if their parents stay together and work out their problems than if they divorce.

Divorce Fallacy 4: Being very unhappy at certain points in a marriage is a good sign that the marriage will eventually end in divorce.

Fact: All marriages have their ups and downs. Recent research using a large national sample found that 86 percent of people who were unhappy in their marriages but stayed with the marriage indicated five years later that they were happy. Indeed, three fifths of the formerly unhappily married couples rated their marriages as either "very happy" or "quite happy."

Divorce Fallacy 5: It is usually men who initiate divorce proceedings.

Fact: Two thirds of all divorces are initiated by women.

David Popenoe 2002.

A security guard checks people for weapons before they board Miami-Dade County's Family Division Circuit Court bus, which was dubbed "The Divorce Bus." More than two dozen uncontested divorce cases were heard in fewer than 45 minutes. This does seem to give new meaning to the idea of divorce made convenient.

Macro-level social issues also contribute to divorce. These in turn result in micro-level individual family problems. When U.S. divorce laws became more lenient in the 1970s, there was a boomlet of divorces, stimulated by the increasing number of women who entered the labor force and changed family dynamics. As the U.S. family adapted to the new reality of women's changing roles, one adaptation was to pool income from both spouses. In addition, many couples wait longer to marry. Because dual-income families are generally more educated, they have economic stability and more marriage stability.

Divorce rates for most groups have been dropping since 1996 (Cherlin 2010; Clarkson 2011). Currently, macro-level factors such as the poor housing market and slow economy prohibit couples from divorcing because they cannot afford the expenses of two homes and child support (Divorce Rate 2011). The divorce rate has dropped from 15.9 per 1,000 citizens each year in 1980 to 3.6 in 2010. Despite this, the United States still has one of the highest rates of divorce in Global North countries (Centers for Disease Control and Prevention/National Center for Health Statistics 2012b).

If we grant that not everyone will be able to sustain a nurturing marriage for 50 years, and if we acknowledge that people do change over time, what would be an acceptable divorce rate for our society—5% of all marriages, 20%, or 30%? This is difficult for governments to decide, but many people feel that the current rate (3.6 per 1,000 people each year) is too high (Centers for Disease Control and Prevention/National Center for Health Statistics 2012b; Religious Tolerance 2009a). When people say that more than half of today's marriages will end in divorce, they are pointing out that with upward divorce trends, by the time people now in their 20s reach their 70s, the rate of people who have experienced divorce could be 50% to 55%. However, it is also possible that such predictions will not come true. We know that social predictions can change as people and societies alter their behaviors and their policies. In the past two decades, the divorce rate in the United States has been dropping. From the 1960s to the 1980s there was a very dramatic increase in divorce rates, but recently, the divorce rate has been moving in a downward direction (Coontz 2005; U.S. Census Bureau 2012d).

A major cause of divorce is family violence that can result from problems in the family's environment, such as unemployment. Domestic abuse takes many forms: emotional abuse, denial and blame, intimidation, coercion or threats, use of power, isolation, using children as pawns, and economic abuse—including withholding of funds (Mayo Clinic 2011; Straus, Gelles, and Steinmetz 2006).

Children are sometimes the unwitting victims of abuse—beaten, bullied, abused, raped, targeted by predators, and neglected—and this is one factor in marital dissolution. The stress on the family when violence is present means the family is not fulfilling its functions of security and belonging. Mothers may sometimes endure the pain themselves, especially if they feel they are trapped with no alternatives, but the same woman may take action when it is her child who suffers. No wonder families experiencing domestic abuse often end up in a divorce.

Another reason for the dramatic increase in the U.S. divorce rate after the 1970s was a policy change: no-fault divorce laws. For centuries in the United States, one had to prove that the other party was in breach of contract. Marriage was a lifelong contract that could only be severed by one party having violated the terms of the contract. Each state spelled out those acts that were so odious that they justified ending such a sacred vow. Even then, if both parties had done something wrong (he was an adulterer, but she did not clean the house and was therefore in "neglect of duty"), the judge was obligated to rule that because they both violated the contract, the divorce would be denied. This resulted in ugly and contested divorces and in people being forced to live together in unloving, non-nurturing relationships.

In 1970, the state of California was the first to initiate no-fault divorce wherein a couple could end a marriage without proving that the other person was in breach of contract. A bilateral no-fault divorce (sometimes called *dissolution*) requires both parties to agree that they want out of the marriage. If they agree to the terms of settlement (child custody, child visitation rights, split in property, and so forth), the marriage can be dissolved (Gilchrist 2003). A second form, unilateral no-fault divorce, allows one person to insist that the marriage features irreconcilable differences—the two do not have to agree. Many women feel this arrangement protects vulnerable women from staying in an unloving or abusive relationship. They do not have to give up everything to get him to sign the agreement.

All this makes divorce in the United States much easier to obtain than in previous years. However, some ask if divorces are being sought for the slightest offense. Some critics believe that this ease has led to a *divorce culture*—a society in which people assume that marriages are fragile rather than assuming that marriages are for life (a *marriage culture*). Keep in mind, however, that the divorce rate has been dropping in the United States since its high in the 1980s.

Thinking Sociologically

Is divorce really a problem, or is it a solution to a worse problem? Does divorce have lasting consequences for the spouses and children? What evidence supports your position?

Divorce and Its Social Consequences

The highest rates of divorce in the world are among young couples. Marriages that occur at later ages have lower divorce rates. In the United States, the highest rates are for women in their teens and men between 20 and 24. The rate of divorce has leveled off and even dropped since the U.S. high mark in 1981 (as shown in Table 10.3). In Canada, roughly 40% of first marriages end in divorce, with around 70,000 divorces in the country in a given year. The peak in Canada was also in the 1980s (CBC News 2010).

Table 10.3 **U.S. Divorce Rate Trends**

Year	*Divorces per 1,000 Population*
1950	2.6
1960	2.2
1970	3.5
1980	5.2
1981	5.3 (Highest rate)
1950	4.7
2000	4.1
2010	3.6

Source: Centers for Disease Control and Prevention/National Center for Health Statistics (2012a).

The emotional aspects of divorce are for many the most difficult. Divorce is often seen as a failure, rejection, or even punishment. Moreover, a divorce often involves a splitting with family and many close friends; with one's church, mosque, or synagogue; and from other social contexts in which one is known as part of a couple (Amato 2000). No wonder divorce is so wrenching. Unlike simple societies, most modern ones have no ready mechanism for absorbing people back into stable social units such as clans.

Adjustment to divorced status varies by gender: Men typically have a harder time emotionally adjusting to singlehood or divorce than women. Divorced men must often leave not only their wives but also their children, and whereas many women have support networks, fewer men have developed or sustained friendships outside marriage. Finances, on the other hand, are a bigger problem for divorced women than for men, especially since women are more likely to have custody of the children. Many divorced and widowed women fall into poverty during the first five years of being single. In fact, at least 28% of divorced women with children found themselves living below the poverty line in 2009, with a 52% drop in their income. That is 2.83 times more poverty than mothers who are married (Newman 2009; Reason 2011).

Support from the noncustodial parent can help relieve the poverty, yet one quarter of custodial parents receive no help at all. Of the remaining 75%, 70.8% receive some or all of what is owed, with 41.2% of those receiving full child support (U.S. Census Bureau 2011b).

There are other costs for children, 1 million of whom experience their parents' divorce each year in the United States. These children's lives are often turned upside down: Many children move to new houses and locations, leave one parent and friends, and must make adjustments to new schools and to reduced resources. Adjustment depends on the age of the children and the manner in which the parents handle the divorce. Children in families with high levels of marital conflict may be better off long-term if parents divorce (Booth and Amato 2001; Sobolewski and Amato 2007). If the children are torn between two feuding parents or if they are the focus of a bitter custody battle, they may suffer substantial scars. Many studies indicate that divorce lowers the well-being of children in the short-term, affecting school achievement, peer relationships, and behavior. However, more important may be the long-term or lasting effects on their achievement and quality of life as these children become adults (Amato and Sobolewski 2001). The studies offer quite variable findings on this. One study that followed children of divorce for 15 years showed that through adolescence and into adulthood, many children continue to feel anxious and have fears, anger, and guilt (Wallerstein and Blakeslee 2004). Adults whose parents divorced when they were children may experience depression, lower

Men often find emotional adjustment to divorce especially difficult since they often leave the children and they have fewer intimate friendships outside of marriage.

levels of life satisfaction, lower marital quality and stability, more frequent divorce, poorer relationships with parents, poorer physical health, and lower educational attainment, income, and occupational prestige (Eshleman and Bulcroft 2010). Other studies suggest that later in life, individuals whose parents divorced during their childhood have a higher probability of teen marriage, divorce, peer problems, depression, delinquency, truancy, and other behavior problems (Newman 2009). Often the impacts depend on the age of the person at the time of the divorce (Niolon 2010). A summary of typical impacts on children at various ages is presented in Table 10.4.

On the other hand, some studies find that children who are well adjusted at the outset have an easier time with divorce, especially if they can remain in their home and in their familiar school, with both parents part of their lives, and if they maintain their friendship networks. Grandparents, too, can provide stability during these traumatic times.

Thinking Sociologically

Would making it harder to get a divorce create stronger and healthier families? Would it create more stable but less healthy and nurturing families? If you were making divorce policies, what would you do? What are the positive and negative aspects of your policy?

Table 10.4 **Effects of Parental Divorce on Children of Varying Ages**

Age at Time of Divorce	*Initial Reactions*	*Later Reactions (2 to 10 years)*
Preschool (2.5 to 6 years)	Blame themselves for the divorce. Fear abandonment by remaining parent. Experience confusion and fantasize about parental reconciliation. Difficulty expressing feelings. Boys and girls have different kinds of problems as a result of the divorce—boys with achievement and girls with relationships.	Fewer memories of family conflicts. Closer to custodial parent and a competent stepparent. Sometimes anger at an unavailable noncustodial parent.
Elementary School (7 to 12 years)	Tend to express feelings of sadness, fear, and anger. Less likely to blame themselves, but experience divided loyalties. Able to utilize support from outside sources.	Special difficulties adapting to remarriage and stepparenting. Challenge family rules and regulations. Rejection of authority with lines like "You're not my real father/mother" during conflict. Decreased academic performance. Problems with peer relationships.
Adolescence (13 to 18 years)	Difficulty coping with sadness, anger, or shame. May disengage from the family in order to examine own values.	Feelings similar to the 7 to 12 group but trouble expressing them. May fear long-term relationships with others with adjustment difficulties that include truancy, delinquency, and running away.

Source: Nolin 2010.

Marriage, Divorce, and Social Policies

Family systems around the world are changing in similar ways, pushed by industrialization and urbanization, by migration to new countries or refugee status, by changing kinship and occupational structures, and by many other influences from outside the family. The most striking changes include free choice of spouse, more equal status for women, equal rights in divorce, neolocal residency (when partners in a married couple live separate from either set of parents), bilateral kinship systems (tracing lineage through both parents), and pressures for individual equality (McKie and Callan 2012). However, countermovements in some parts of the world call for strengthening of marriage through modesty of women, separation of the sexes (in both public and private spheres), and rejection of some Global North trends such as high divorce rates.

Global forces, such as ethnic holocausts that create refugees, can strain and destroy families. This is a scene of refugees at a camp in the Central African Republic.

Global Family Patterns and Policies

National policies can limit families' access to birth control and knowledge about family planning, as in the cases of governments that prohibit birth control in attempts to increase declining populations. These policies in turn affect the economic circumstances of people who have no choice but to raise large families. One result is more single-parent families created by out-of-wedlock births. In addition, as individuals and couples around the world make decisions such as choosing a spouse based on love, rejecting multiple wives, or establishing a more egalitarian family, the collective impact may rock the foundations of the larger society. Because governments make policies that influence families, the interaction between policy makers and social scientists can lead to laws based on better information and more comprehensive analysis of possible consequences. This is part of the contribution of public sociology—providing accurate information and analysis for wise public policy decisions.

Government policies can affect the size of nuclear families. One of the most vivid examples is the one-child policy in China.

Family life, which seems so personal and intimate, is actually linked to global patterns. Global aid is activated when drought, famine, or another disaster affects communities and a country is not able to provide for families. In such cases, international organizations such as the United Nations, Doctors Without Borders, Oxfam, and the Red Cross mobilize to support families in crises. Support varies from feeding starving children to opposing the slavery that occurs when parents are reduced to selling their children to survive. International crises can lead to war, perhaps removing the main breadwinner from the family or taking the life of a son or daughter who was drafted to fight. Homes and cultivated fields may be destroyed and the families forced into refugee status.

Do marriage and divorce rates indicate that the family is in crisis? To answer this question, we need information on current patterns, historical trend lines, and patterns in various parts of the world. The next "Sociology Around the World" provides cross-cultural data on marriage and divorce ratios.

We have been talking about an international trend (divorce rates) regarding an institution (the family) and the impact it has on individual family members. Processes at

Sociology Around the World

Cross-Cultural Differences in Family Dissolution

Is the institution of the family breaking down around the world? Perhaps this is the wrong question. We may, instead, need to consider how the family copes with changing national and global demands. Family conflict and disorganization occur when members of the family unit do not or cannot carry out roles expected of them by spouses, other family members, the community, or the society. This may be due to voluntary departure (divorce, separation, desertion), involuntary problems (illness or other catastrophe), a crisis caused by external events (war or deteriorating economic conditions), or failure to communicate role expectations and needs. Many of these role failures are a direct consequence of societal changes due to globalization. Once again, the social world model helps us understand macro-level trends and patterns that affect us in micro-level contexts.

Divorce is still very limited in some parts of the world, and it may be an option for only one gender. In some Arab countries, only the husband has had the right to declare "I divorce thee" in front of a witness on three separate occasions, after which the divorce is complete. The wife returns, sometimes in disgrace, to her family of orientation, while the husband generally keeps the children in the patriarchal family and is free to take another wife. Only recently is divorce initiated by the wife coming to be accepted in some countries, although the grounds for divorce by women may be restricted (Khazaleh 2009). Despite a seemingly easy process for men to divorce, the rate remains rather low in many Global South countries because family ties and allegiances are severely strained when divorces take place. Thus, informal pressures and cultural attitudes restrain tendencies to divorce.

Still, when family turmoil and conflict are too great to resolve or when the will to save the family disappears, the legal, civil, and religious ties of marriage may be broken. The methods for dissolving marriage ties vary, but most countries have some form of divorce. Table 10.5 compares marriage and divorce rates in selected industrial countries. Notice that while the divorce rate in countries such as the United States is quite high, the marriage rate is also high.

Table 10.5 **Marriage and Divorce Rates in Selected Countries, 1980–2008**

	Marriages per 1,000 Persons in Population				*Divorces per 1,000 Persons in Population*			
Country	*1980*	*1990*	*2000*	*2008*	*1980*	*1990*	*2000*	*2008*
USA	15.9	14.9	12.5	10.6	7.9	7.2	6.2	5.2
Canada	11.5	10.0	7.5	6.4	3.7	4.2	3.1	n.a.
Japan	9.8	8.4	9.2	n.a.	1.8	1.8	3.1	n.a.
Denmark	8.0	9.1	10.8	10.3	4.1	4.0	4.0	4.1
France	9.7	7.7	7.9	6.6	2.4	2.8	3.0	n.a.
Germany	X	8.2	7.6	6.9	X	2.5	3.5	3.5
Ireland	10.9	8.3	7.6	n.a.	n.a.	n.a.	1.0	n.a.
Italy	8.7	8.2	7.3	6.3	0.3	0.7	1.0	1.3
Netherlands	9.6	9.4	8.2	6.7	2.7	2.8	3.2	2.9
Spain	9.4	8.5	7.9	6.2	n.a.	0.9	1.4	3.5
Sweden	7.1	7.4	7.0	8.3	3.7	3.5	3.8	3.5
United Kingdom	11.6	10.0	8.0	n.a.	4.1	4.1	4.0	n.a.

Source: U.S. Census Bureau 2012c, Table 1335.

Note: n.a. = not available; X = country was two nations at that time.

the macro and meso levels affect the micro level of society, and decisions at the micro level (i.e., to dissolve a marriage) affect the community and the nation. The various levels of the social world are indeed interrelated in complex ways. Within each nation, patterns and trends in families affect the countries' policies as shown in the next section on U.S. policies.

National Family Patterns and Policies in the United States

Obtaining a divorce in the United States is relatively easy compared with the process in many other countries. All 50 U.S. states have no-fault provisions based on "irreconcilable differences" or "irreconcilable breakdown of the marriage" (Benokraitis 2012). The conservative U.S. organization Council on the American Family has argued that the family is being challenged by many forces that weaken the family structure and purpose (Council on the American Family n.d.). Some conservative groups argue that the United States should go back to fault divorce to make it less easy to end a marriage in what they consider this "divorce culture." They argue that many couples enter marriages assuming that the marriage will probably not last. An assumption of impermanence is no way to begin a marriage, they believe, insisting that profamily policies promote stability and are a precursor to healthy relationships (Hunter College Women's Studies Collective 2005). Other scholars think that making the divorce process more restrictive would leave many women in highly vulnerable positions in relationships with abusive men, and while such a strategy may create more marriages that stay together, it would not necessarily create healthy ones. Healthy marriages are what help the society, not unhappy ones, say the defenders of no-fault divorce.

A social policy proposal related to healthy marriages aims to change the marriage contract itself. With the innovative covenant marriage laws implemented in Louisiana (1997), Arizona (1998), and Arkansas (2002), and with 20 other states considering the laws, people can choose whether they want a standard marriage or an "upgraded" covenant marriage. If they opt for covenant marriage, they make a lifelong commitment to marriage. Premarital counseling is required before the wedding, and a year of counseling is necessary before a fault divorce is permitted. Thus, the availability of no-fault divorce is restricted by longer requirements of counseling (Leon 2009; Nock, Sanchez, and Wright 2008; Witte and Ellison 2005). Contracts mean marriages are less easily dissolved.

One aspect of covenant marriage is that couples must choose which kind of contract they want—which critics think makes marriage a consumer choice, rather like choosing toothpaste.

Because legislatures make policies that influence family decisions such as fertility rates, the interaction between policy makers and social scientists can lead to laws based on better information and more comprehensive analysis of possible consequences. This is part of the public contribution of public sociology—providing accurate information and analysis for wise public policy.

Thinking Sociologically

Would it strengthen marriages to remove all no-fault divorce laws and return to a fault divorce where one member of the couple must prove that the other person is in breach of contract? Why or why not?

The family is a powerful socializing agent and the first social experience of most human beings. As children grow up and branch out from the embrace of the family, the social environments they experience first are usually the local school and a religious institution. These provide lifelong training for participation in society. It is to the institution of education that we turn next.

What Have We Learned?

Despite those who lament the weakening of the family, the institution of family is here to stay. Its form may alter as it responds and adapts to societal and global changes, and other institutions will continue to take on functions formerly reserved for the family. Still, the family is an institution crucial to societal survival, and whatever the future holds, the family will adapt in response to changes in other parts of the social world. It is an institution that is sometimes vulnerable and needs support, but it is also a resilient institution—the way we partner and "make people" in any society.

Our happiest and saddest experiences are integrally intertwined with family. Family provides the foundation, the group through which individuals' needs are met. Societies depend on families as the unit through which to funnel services. It is the political, economic, health, educational, religious, and sexual base for most people. These are some of the reasons family is important to us.

Key Points

- Families are diverse entities at the micro level, having a wide range of configurations, but families also collectively serve as a core structure of society—institutions—at the meso and macro levels. (See p. 348.)
- The family is sometimes called the most basic unit of society, for it is a core unit of social pairing into groups (partner taking), a primary unit of procreation and socialization (people making), and so important that when it comes unglued (contract breaking), the whole social system may be threatened. (See pp. 349–351.)
- Various theories—rational choice, symbolic interactionism, functionalism, conflict theory, and feminist theory—illuminate different aspects of family and help us understand conflicts, stressors, and functions of families. (See pp. 351–358.)
- At the micro level, people come together in partner-taking pairs, but the rules of partner taking (exogamy/endogamy, free choice/arranged marriage, polygamy/monogamy) are meso level. (See pp. 358–361.)
- Power within a partnership—including distribution of tasks and authority—is assigned through intimate processes that are again largely controlled by rules imposed from another level in the social system. (See pp. 361–368.)
- At the macro level, nations and even global organizations try to establish policies that strengthen families. Issues that are of concern to some analysts include cohabitation patterns that seem a threat to family, same-sex households (including same-sex marriage), and contract breaking (divorce). (See pp. 368–379.)

Discussion Questions

1. What do you believe is the ideal makeup of a family? Why? How does your description relate to the functions the family performs in society?
2. Which of the main theoretical perspectives discussed in this chapter (functionalist, conflict, and feminist) is most useful when examining the families with which you are familiar? Why?
3. A majority of Americans and a strong majority of young Americans (those below 30) now support same-sex marriages. What are some cultural and structural changes that have led to this increase in support for marriage equality over the past decade?
4. Does (or did) your family expect you to marry someone of a particular (a) race or ethnicity, (b) social class, (c) education background, or (d) religion? Why or why not? How do you think endogamous norms impact (a) individual marriages and (b) society?
5. How does your family's income influence the (a) amount and (b) quality of the time family members spend together? How might (a) more or (b) less money influence your family members' relationships with one another? Why?
6. Do you think it is a good idea to give people the choice to have a "covenant marriage"? Why or why not? If yes, would you consider supporting an effort to make marriage licenses more expensive for those who do not opt for "covenant marriages"? Why or why not?

Contributing to Our Social World: What Can We Do?

At the Local Level

- *Support groups for married or partnered students* respond to the needs of an ever-increasing number of undergraduate students living on or near campus with spouses, partners, and children. If your campus has a support group, arrange to attend a meeting and work with members to help them meet the challenges associated with their family situation. If such a group does not exist, consider forming one.
- Is there *day care available on your campus*? Day care on campus can be invaluable for parents. If there is, look at the cost and availability of care for the children of faculty, staff, and students. If there is not a day care, look at the possibilities of creating, funding, and staffing one. How might it benefit the college or university, as well as the families it will serve?

At the Organizational or Institutional Level

- *Support groups for multigeneration households* provide an important opportunity to support this growing population. Approximately one in five households contains more than one generation of adults. *House builders* have begun to change how they design some houses in order to meet the needs of such households. Contact your local *Habitat for Humanity* chapter (www.habitat.org) and ask if you can help the organization create more homes suitable for multigeneration households. You can find some ideas for such homes at http://articles.chicagotribune.com/2012-09-10/special/chi-primetime-multigen-091412_1_bedroom-floor-plan-designs.

At the National and Global Levels

- *Influencing marriage policies* is another way for sociology students to make a difference in our social world. Select a family-related issue about which you feel strongly—pro or con (for example, covenant marriage, no-fault divorce options, or same-sex marriage policies). Find out about the laws of the United States or your state regarding the issue. Next, identify your members in the U.S. House of Representatives (www.house.gov), the U.S. Senate (www.senate.gov), and/or your state legislature (www.ncsl.org/about-us/ncslservice/state-legislative-websites-directory.aspx). Contact those people via letter or e-mail, stating your views.
- *Voices* is a multi-issue advocacy group for children with member organizations across the nation. The organization strives to improve the lives of children and their families, particularly those most at risk. You can learn about the issues on which this group is working and join its efforts, if you would like to do so, by going to its website at www.voices.org.
- *Hofstra University* maintains a resource site on international family law at http://people.hofstra.edu/lisa_a_spar/intlfam/intlfam.htm where you can learn more about the field.

WWW Visit the Student Study Site at **www.sagepub.com/ballantine4e** to access additional study tools, including eFlashcards, web quizzes, video resources, audio resources, web resources, SAGE journal articles, recommended readings, and more.

CHAPTER 11

Education

What Are We Learning?

In schools, students are learning a lot besides the three *Rs*, and sociologists have learned a great deal about what and how they are learning. Even the settings in which learning occurs tell us something about what and how students learn and the place of education within societies.

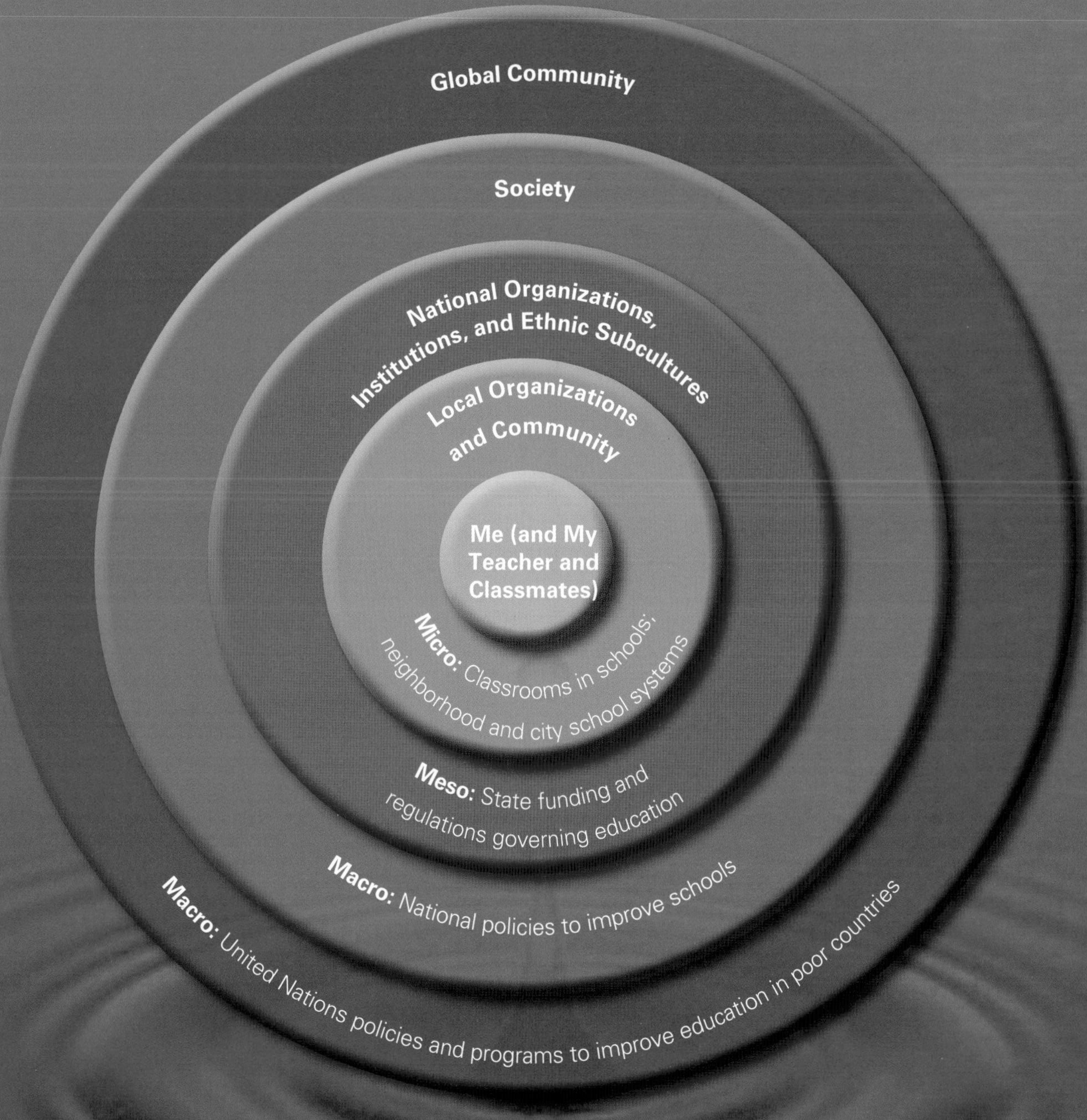
Global Community
Society
National Organizations, Institutions, and Ethnic Subcultures
Local Organizations and Community
Me (and My Teacher and Classmates)
Micro: Classrooms in schools; neighborhood and city school systems
Meso: State funding and regulations governing education
Macro: National policies to improve schools
Macro: United Nations policies and programs to improve education in poor countries

Think About It	
Micro: Self and Inner Circle	What did you personally learn—both formally and informally—in school?
Micro: Local Community	How do role expectations of people in a local school—student, teacher, principal—affect the learning that occurs in that school?
Meso: National Institutions; Complex Organizations; Ethnic Groups	Do families help or hurt children's school achievement? Explain.
Macro: National Society	How is education changing in your nation?
Macro: Global Community	Why is education a major concern around the world?

What's coming in this chapter?

State of the World's Education: An Overview
The Ins and Outs of Local Schools: Micro-Level Interactions in Educational Organizations
After the School Bell Rings: Meso-Level Analysis of Educational Organizations
Education, Society, and the Road to Opportunity: The Macro Level
Educational and Social Policy Issues

Tomás is a failure. At 9 years of age, he cannot read, write, or get along with his peers, and out of frustration, he sometimes misbehaves. He has been a failure since he was 3, but his failure started earlier than that. His parents have told Tomás over and over that he will not amount to anything if he does not shape up. His teachers have noticed that he is slow to learn and has few friends. So two strikes against him are the judgments of his parents and his teachers. The third strike is Tomás's own acceptance of the label "failure." He has little evidence to contradict their judgment. Tomás is an at-risk child, identified as having characteristics inclining him toward failure in school and society. Probably, he will not amount to anything, and he may even get in trouble with the law *unless* caring people intervene, encouraging him to realize his abilities.

Tomás goes to school in Toronto (Ontario), Canada, but he could live in any country. Although successful children develop a positive self-concept that helps them deal with disappointments and failures, the Tomáses internalize failures. Successful children negotiate the rules and regulations of school, and school provides them with necessary skills for future occupations. Tomás carries a label with him that will shape his life because, next to home, schools play the biggest role in affecting children's self-concepts and attitudes toward achievement. What factors could change the educational outcomes for students such as Tomás?

At least Tomás is in the education system. *Schooling*—learning skills such as reading and math in a building via systematic instruction by a trained professional—is a luxury some children will never know. On the other hand, in most urban areas around the world and in affluent countries, formal education is necessary for success—and for survival. Education of the masses in a school setting is a modern concept that became necessary when literacy and math skills became essential to many jobs (even if just to read instructions for operating machinery). Literacy is also necessary for democratic governments, where informed citizenry elect officials and vote on public policies.

In this chapter, we will explore the state of the world's education, micro-level interactions in educational organizations, what happens in schools after the school bell rings, education at the macro level, whether education is the road to opportunity, and educational social policy issues.

State of the World's Education: An Overview

Every society educates its children. In most societies, national education systems are created for this task.

Global macro-level organizations concerned with education also contribute. For the past 50 years, UNESCO (the United Nations Educational, Scientific and Cultural Organization) has become the "global center for discussion and implementation of educational ideas and organization models" (Boli 2002:307). It provides teacher training, curricular guidance, and textbook sources, and it gathers international statistics on educational achievement. Many countries have adopted UNESCO standards, including the organizational model of 6 years of primary school, typically for students from ages 6 to 12; 2 to 3 years of middle school or junior high school; and 4 years of high school (UNESCO Institute for Statistics 2012).

What is considered essential knowledge to be taught in schools is based largely on a country's level of development, its cultural values and political ideology, and guidelines from international standards. Leaders believe that a literate population is necessary for economic development and expansion, a thriving political system, and the well-being of the citizenry. "Education has become a global social process that both reflects and helps create the global society that is under formation" (Boli 2002:312). In the world today, an estimated 793 million adults cannot read or write. Two thirds are women, and most are concentrated in three regions—the Arab states, South and West Asia, and sub-Saharan Africa (Index Mundi 2012h; World Factbook 2012c, 2012g)—and have no experience with technology. The result is that they cannot participate in the global economy, unemployment is far higher, and poverty is a fact of life for many. If a woman stays in school just one additional year, her earnings can increase by 10% to 20% over a lifetime, and her children are more likely to survive (Bokova and Bush 2012). In poor Global South countries in Southeast Asia and sub-Saharan Africa, the literacy rate (those who have basic reading skills) is between 50% and 64% (UNESCO Institute for Statistics 2010a). Several countries have literacy rates of between 99.8% and 100% for both men and women: Finland, Georgia, Greenland, Luxembourg, Cuba, Estonia, and Poland (Index Mundi 2012h). Countries with the lowest literacy rates are mostly in sub-Saharan Africa: Burkina Faso (23.6%), Mali (24%), Chad (25.7%), Niger (28.7%), and Guinea (29.5%; Infoplease 2011). (See Map 11.1 on page 386.)

Overcrowding in classrooms is not uncommon in poor countries, such as in this somewhat affluent school in South Africa (top) and in this Darfur refugee camp school (bottom). Note that the students are primarily boys—the situation in many Global South countries.

As mass education spreads around the world, communication, transportation, and globalization also continue to make countries more interdependent and more accessible to each other. This globalization also means that Global North countries influence the levels and types of education worldwide. The national education curriculum of many poor countries is similar to models of mass education used in Global North countries (Chabbott and Ramirez 2000; McEneaney and Meyer 2000). Mathematics, for instance, is taught universally, and science has been taught in most schools since World War II. A world culture model of education shows that there are similarities between many nations' education systems (Griffiths and Knezevic 2009). Whether this trend toward similar curricula can meet the needs of individuals in all countries is a matter of debate.

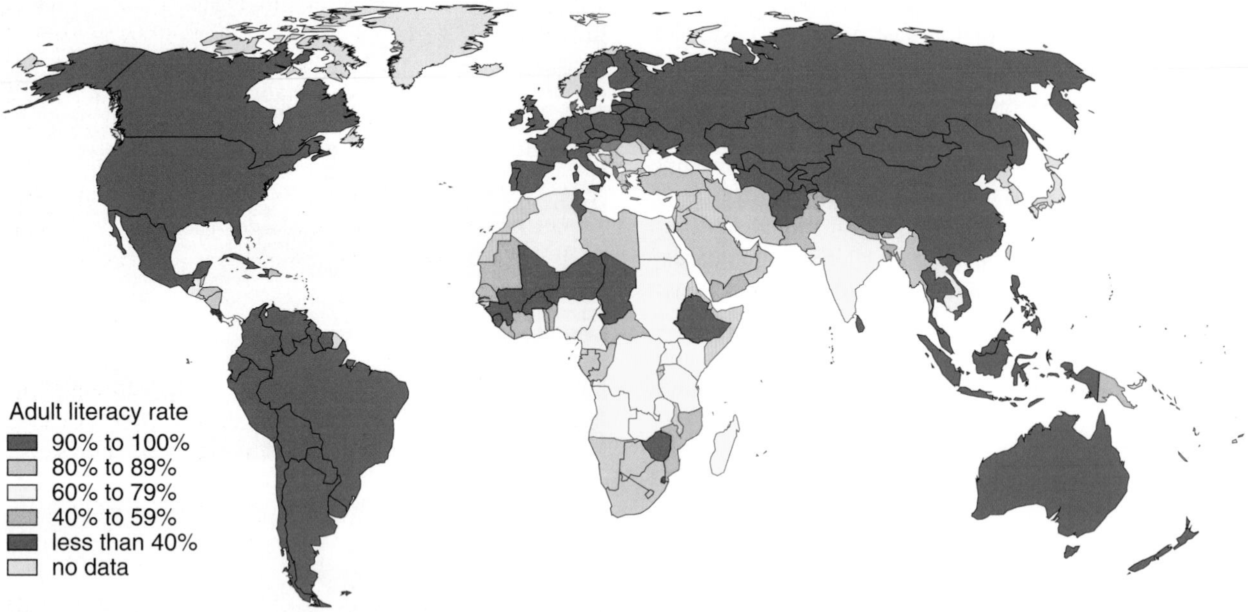

Map 11.1 Adult Literacy Rates by Country

Source: Huebler, Friedrich. 2012. "Adult and Youth Literacy in 2010." *International Education Statistics*, May 31. Retrieved January 27, 2013 (http://huebler.blogspot.com/2012/05/literacy.html).

Education can be studied through several different lenses or perspectives. The next section provides a summary of how various theories attempt to understand and explain education in society.

While Ethiopia shares the commitment to mass education of all young people, its resources are very meager, as we can see from this photo of a crowded impoverished school in an Ethiopian village. Children have no texts, pencils, or paper.

The Ins and Outs of Local Schools: Micro-Level Interactions in Educational Organizations

The process of education takes place at the micro level in the classrooms and corridors and on the playgrounds of local schools, with key players who enact the everyday drama of teaching and learning. You probably recall an important learning experience you had in which someone helped you master a skill—a scout leader, grandmother, choir director, coach, religious leader, neighbor, or teacher. You know how important one-on-one mentoring can be to the learning process, how education often is an intimate exchange between two people. Education has the power to change the way people think about the world, influence their sense of competency, and affect their self-esteem and personal outlooks on self and society. First, let us review two micro-level theories, and then consider some typical in-school interactions.

Micro-Level Theories: Individuals Within Schools

Symbolic Interaction Perspective and the Classroom

The symbolic interaction theory focuses on how people interact based on the meaning they have assigned to various traits, behaviors, or symbols (such as clothing). Children actively create distinctions among individuals and groups, becoming agents in determining the social reality in which they live. Popularity, a major issue for many children, especially in middle school years, is mostly a function of being noticed and liked and having everyone know who you are. Students may increase their popularity by being attractive, representing the school in an athletic contest, or being seen in a leadership position. The difficulty is that there are few such positions, leading to a competition in which some individuals are going to be losers. In the United States, the losers are more likely to be children from families that cannot afford to purchase popular clothing or other status symbols or send their children to sports training or camps. Winners have access to material and symbolic resources that give them high visibility. They are given special privileges in the school and are more likely to develop leadership skills and to feel good about themselves—forms of social and cultural capital.

Classrooms are like small societies of peers that reflect the interaction patterns and problems of the larger world (Durkheim 1956). That includes students learning to fit into the larger world. Research findings indicate that girls around the world have more struggles with self-esteem and gender inequality than do boys, especially in middle schools (American Association of University Women

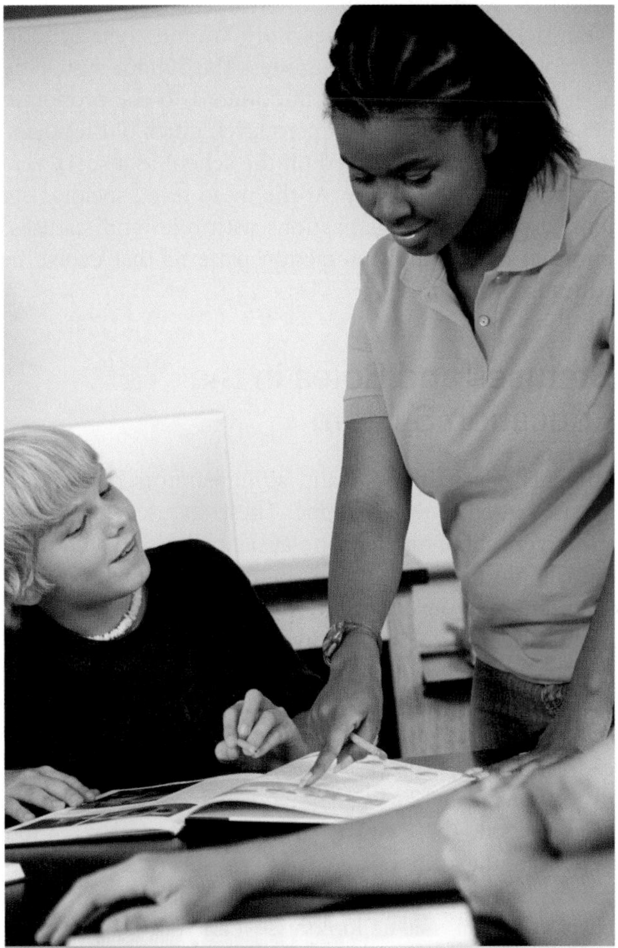

Small group and interpersonal interactions occur continuously in local schools—such as this tutorial between a young student and a college student involved in a "service learning" project.

Males have many ways of becoming known and respected. Male athletic competitions draw bigger crowds than female athletics, and one can become a local celebrity based on one's skill on the field or court.

Educational Foundation 2001; Vijayakumar 2012). One's sense of self—an intensely personal experience—is shaped by the micro interactions of the school. Thus, for young people from 6 to 18 years of age, the extensive time spent in school means that the status of student has an enormous impact on how individuals see themselves. The image that is reflected back to someone—as student or as teacher, for example—can begin to mold one's sense of competence, intelligence, and likability.

The larger school organization creates a structure that influences how individuals make sense of their reality and interact with others. Some symbolic interaction theorists, including those representing the Iowa School, emphasize the link between the self and meso-level positions or statuses (Stryker 2000). Official school positions—such as president of the student council or senior class president or varsity team member—become important elements of one's *self*.

Thinking Sociologically

How do you think teachers affect the sense of self of students? How do you think students affect the sense of self, the confidence, and the achievement goals of each other and of teachers?

Rational Choice Theory and Educational Settings

Rational choice theory focuses on the cost-benefit analysis that individuals undertake in virtually everything they do. What are the costs—in terms of money, relationships, self-esteem, or other factors—and what are the benefits? If benefits outweigh costs, the individual is likely to continue the rewarding activities, but if costs outweigh benefits, the individual is likely to seek other courses of action.

How might weighing costs and benefits influence decisions about education? Students who consider dropping out of school go through some analysis of costs to themselves—for example, a decision may be shaped by battered self-esteem in schools. Similarly, teachers make rational choices about staying in the teaching profession. In recent years in the United States, approximately 85% of all teachers stayed in the same school, 7.6% moved to new schools, and 8% left teaching (Keigher and Cross 2010). Rational choice theorists explain teacher retention or attrition by looking at perceived costs, such as poor salary given one's educational attainment; lack of respect from parents, students, and administrators; 12- to 14-hour days for 9 months of the year; and lack of professionalism in treatment of teachers. Teachers compare these costs with the benefits of teaching—the feeling of making a contribution to society and helping children; getting time off in the summer; and enjoying many aspects of teaching, coaching, or directing. The costs today are seen by many teachers as higher than they used to be for professionals in teaching, causing them to leave the profession.

Thinking Sociologically

Think of a teacher you know or have observed. What seem to be the costs and benefits of the various roles teachers fulfill? Do you think that most teacher behavior is shaped by this kind of rational choice calculation?

Schools are important organizations in local communities, a source of pride and a unifying symbol of identity. Local communities rally around their school. Moreover, in many communities, the school system is a large employer with real importance to the economic vitality of the area. At the micro level, much of the sociological analysis has focused on the school as a social setting within a community. At the meso level, sociologists look at schools as organizations with roles and statuses, informal norms, and interaction patterns that evolve in educational settings.

Statuses and Roles in the Education System

Students, teachers, staff, and administrators hold major statuses in education systems. These statuses are part of the larger school organization at the meso level, and individuals are temporary occupants of the statuses during their tenure in the organization. The roles associated with each status in educational organizations bring both obligations and inherent problems. When the status holders agree on expected behaviors (role expectations), schools function smoothly. When they do not agree, conflicts can arise as was the case in the Chicago teachers' strike in September 2012. Teachers and their union were concerned about the evaluation, promotion, and retention policies of the school system. After a week, the union and the city of Chicago settled their dispute, and everyone was back to school. Let us look at several statuses and their accompanying roles in schools.

Students and the Peer Culture of Schools

In a private Rwandan secondary school students crowd onto benches. They are quiet, respectful, and very hardworking. They know that they are in a privileged position, and many students are lined up to take their place on the bench should they not carry out their roles, work hard, and succeed. Although they have no written texts, students write down the lectures in their notebooks and memorize the material. In some countries such as Rwanda, going to high school is a privilege. In others such as the United States, it is a necessary part of life that many students resist.

The status and roles of girls and boys differ in schools. Consider the example of minority students in majority white high schools: Boys gain recognition through athletics, participation in urban "hip-hop star," and playing down negative stereotypes. Girls do not have access to most of these strategies for social status, and thus have fewer opportunities for social integration (Holland 2012).

While many experts acknowledge that girls and boys have different experiences in school, a recent debate in Britain and the United States focuses on whether boys and girls should be taught in separate classrooms. Those who argue for separate classrooms, especially in the middle school years, point out the different interests, opportunities for involvement and recognition, and learning styles of girls and boys at these early-adolescent ages. Others argue that equality requires mixed-gender classes. Some parochial schools have long been single sex, and now public school districts are experimenting with single-sex classes. Research such as that presented in the "Sociology in Our Social World" on page 390 discusses the concerns that have been raised about gender differences in U.S. schools (Weil 2008).

Another gender issue is sexual harassment in schools. In Grades 7 to 12 in 2010–2011, 48% of students experienced some form of sexual harassment and reported negative effects. Abuse was verbal, physical, and electronic, with over 30% experiencing harassment through electronic media such as Twitter and Facebook. Girls reported more harassment than boys: in person 52% to 35%, and electronic 36% to 24%. However few report it (Hill and Kearl 2011; Munsey 2012). Compared with boys, girls experience "hostile hallways" in more physically and psychologically harmful ways, and students who identified themselves as gay, lesbian, bisexual, or transgendered experienced high levels of bullying and assaults as well (American Association of University Women Educational Foundation 2001; Gay, Lesbian, and Straight Education Network 2006). Mental Health America concludes that this is a major mental health issue in the United States:

> While trying to deal with all the challenges of being a teenager, gay/lesbian/bisexual/transgender (GLBT) teens additionally have to deal with harassment, threats, and violence directed at them on a daily basis. They hear anti-gay slurs such as "homo," "faggot," and "sissy" about 26 times a day or once every 14 minutes. Even more troubling, a study found that 31% of gay youth had been threatened or injured at school in the last year alone. (Mental Health America 2011)

In Rwandan secondary schools, as many as 45 students may be in a classroom with little more than wooden benches and tables.

In summary, parents, teachers, and administrators need to be aware of the problem and help children know what is and what isn't appropriate.

Teachers: The Front Line

Teachers in the classroom occupy the front line in implementing the goals of the school, the community, and the society. Teachers are those role partners who serve as gatekeepers, controlling the flow of students, activities, resources, and privileges. One scholar estimated that teachers have more than a thousand interchanges a day in their roles as classroom managers (Jackson 1968).

As primary socializers and role models for students, they are expected to support and encourage students and at the same time judge their performance—giving grades and recommendations as part of the selection and allocation functions of education. This creates role strain, which can interfere with the task of teaching and contribute to teacher burnout. U.S. teachers are held accountable for students' progress as measured on standardized tests, as well as being tested for their own competency as measured in tests to determine their knowledge and skills (Dworkin and Tobe 2012).

Sociology in Our Social World

Where the Boys Are—and Where Are the Boys?

The Fragile Girl, The War Against Boys, Failing at Fairness, How America's Schools Cheat Girls, and *At Colleges, Women Are Leaving Men in the Dust*—these are just a few titles of articles in a debate about whether girls or boys have the biggest advantage or disadvantage in schools. For many years, concern focused on the factors that inhibited minorities' educational attainment in school. Recently, some authors are turning the tables and focusing their concern on gender.

Statistics indicate that the state of educational achievement varies greatly by sex, age, race or ethnicity, and socioeconomic status. Why is this so? Among the many reasons for the differences, researchers point out the incredible gains made by women and the fact that women tend to study more. In the United States, African American, Hispanic, and low-income males lag behind all other groups, including females from their own ethnic group. Asians and Pacific Islanders have a higher high school completion rate (96.6%) than whites (96.2%), blacks (90.1%), Hispanics (82.3%), and Native Americans (86.4%). The gap has been narrowing in recent years (Stillwell 2010).

"More than 60% of the people in prison are now racial and ethnic minorities. For Black males in their 30s, 1 in every 10 is in prison or jail on any given day," further reducing their chances for education, good jobs, and a stable family life (Sentencing Project 2012b). The reasons are many, but the bottom line is that these young men feel disconnected from a society that helps women with children but ignores the vulnerabilities of men (Mincy 2006). They often feel alienated from their society. The following figures provide a partial picture:

- An estimated 2 million to 3 million youth between the ages of 16 and 24 are without postsecondary education and are disconnected—neither in school nor employed (Mincy 2006).
- Black teens have not witnessed education as a path to better jobs for their parents, siblings, and neighbors: In January 2011 unemployment for African Americans aged 20 or older was 14.6% compared to an 8.4% unemployment rate for whites of the same age (Allegretto, Amerikaner, and Pitts 2011).
- A review of college attendance statistics shows that women are attending and graduating at a higher rate than men, and black men are at the bottom of the graduation rates. Table 11.1 compares these groups.

Table 11.1 **College Attendance Rates and Graduation Rates**

Race	*College Attendance Rate %*
White, non-Hispanic	72
Hispanic	64
Black	56
Males	66
Females	72

Source: U.S. Department of Education, National Center for Education Statistics. (2012). *The Condition of Education 2011* (NCES 2012-045), Indicator 45. Retrieved January 27, 2013 (http://nces.ed.gov/fastfacts/display.asp?id=40).

One result of lower high school graduation rates and disillusion with education among males is that higher education is experiencing "feminization." Women have surpassed men in college completion with a 61% completion rate in 6 years, while males had a 56% rate of completion (National Center for Education Statistics 2012b; Pollard 2011). Men, regardless of race or class, get lower grades, take more time to graduate, and are less likely to get a bachelor's degree (Lewin 2006). However, men from the highest-income group attend college at a slightly higher rate than women in that group, and men from low-income families—disproportionately African American and Hispanic in composition—are the most underrepresented in higher education.

The gender gap in college admissions favors females, and by 2020 is predicted to be 58.6% women and 41.4% men (Hennigan 2012). This trend has been most pronounced among low-income white, Hispanic, and African American males. The imbalance is of such concern to college admissions officers that some colleges are turning away more qualified females in favor of males (Britz 2006). Some colleges are even adding activities such as football to attract more male students ("Colleges' Gender Gap" 2010). What is the big deal? The issue is the changing job market and who will have the training to get the jobs. As more high-tech and white-collar workers are needed, those without higher education lose. That means that women are moving into jobs requiring college education.

Some researchers argue that the gender gap is not nearly as significant as the differences for race, ethnicity, and social class. Furthermore, men still dominate math and science fields, where jobs pay more money and result in more power. Data indicate that although women do not score as high as men on achievement tests in math and science, women hold higher educational aspirations, are more likely to enroll in college, and receive more of the undergraduate diplomas. Also, women have surpassed men in the number of doctoral degrees received in the United States (Jaschik 2010).

Despite successes in Global North countries, girls and women face serious educational problems in many Global South countries, and women in Global North countries are still at a disadvantage in hiring for high-paid jobs and equal wages. The concern about boys is a relatively new twist in the equity issue. Ultimately, educators hope to create an education system that equally benefits all groups.

In Japan, where education is considered extremely important for training future generations, teachers are treated with great respect and honor. They receive salaries competitive with those in industry and professions such as law and medicine (Ballantine and Hammack 2012). In Europe, many high schools are organizationally like universities. Teachers think of themselves as akin to professors. In contrast, studies in Australia and the United States show teachers feel they are unappreciated (Saha and Dworkin 2006). In the United States, secondary teachers think of themselves as more like middle school teachers than like university professors (Legters 2001). The organizational context of the teachers' work is a key source of problems. Overcoming poor social standing and lack of respect for teaching requires better recruiting, training, and upgrading the status of teachers (Ingersoll and Merrill 2012).

Most professionals have some sense of calling and commitment and are motivated not just by money but by a sense of contribution to society, prestige, and pride in belonging to the profession. Two key features of being a professional are autonomy on the job and self-regulation by the profession. Incentives from the macro-level federal government in the form of pay increases were proposed by the Obama administration, along with other incentives to improve the quality of teaching. Yet when government regulates standards for teachers, the quality might actually decrease as teachers—faced with a lack of respect as professionals and a lack of control over their work—opt instead for other occupations. This has the potential to leave schools with less capable and less committed instructors.

Thinking Sociologically

Who should enforce high teacher standards—the federal, state, or local government? Teacher unions? Community interest groups? Who should decide what these standards are?

Administrators: The Managers of the School System

Key administrators—superintendents, assistant superintendents, principals and assistant principals, and headmasters and headmistresses—hold the top positions in the educational hierarchy of local schools. They are responsible for a long list of tasks: issuing budget reports; engaging in staff negotiations; hiring, firing, and training staff members; meeting with parents; carrying out routine approval of projects; managing public relations; preparing reports for boards of directors, local education councils, legislative bodies, and national agencies; keeping up with new regulations; making recommendations regarding the staff; and

Photo Essay

Student and Teacher Roles

Students and teachers in schools play a variety of roles and often are identified by labels. What labels might apply to the teachers and students in these photos, and what were some of the labels applied to students and teachers in your high school?

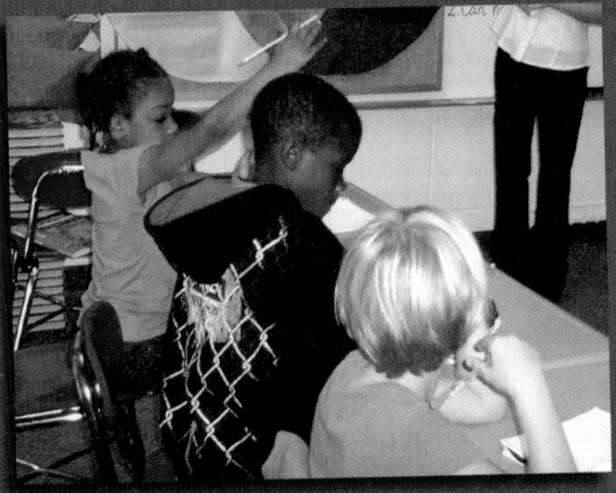

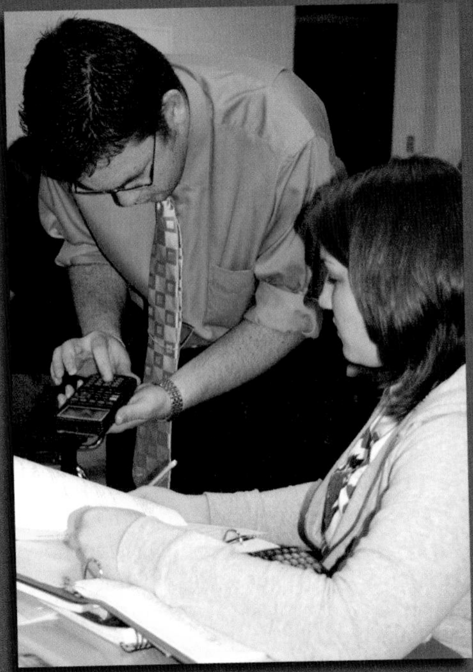

many other tasks. Status holders in schools follow many rules and norms, some written and some not. The informal system is as important a part of the educational organization as formal rules, as we will see.

The Informal System: What Really Happens Inside a School?

It is the first day of class, and the professor asks a question. Should you respond or let someone else answer? If you respond, the professor might be impressed, but the other students might think you are showing off or currying favor. What if you answer incorrectly and sound foolish?

The informal system of schooling includes the unspoken, unwritten, and implicit norms of behavior that we learn, whether in kindergarten or in college. These norms may be created or enforced by teachers or by the student peer culture. The informal system does not appear in written goal statements or course syllabi but nevertheless influences our experiences in school in important ways. Dimensions of the informal system include the hidden curriculum, the educational climate, the value climate, power dynamics, and coping strategies in the classroom.

The *hidden curriculum* refers to the implicit "rules of the game" that students learn in school (Snyder 1971). It includes everything that is not explicitly taught, such as unstated social and academic norms. Students have to learn and respond to these to be socially accepted and to succeed in the education system (Snyder 1971).

Children worldwide begin learning what is expected of them in preschool and kindergarten, providing the basis for schooling in the society (Neuman 2005). For example, one scholar describes early-school socialization as "academic boot camp" (Gracey 1967). Kindergarten teachers teach children to follow rules, to cooperate with each other, and to accept the teacher as the boss who gives orders and controls how time is spent. All this is part of what young children learn, lessons instilled in students even though it is not yet the formal curriculum of reading, writing, and arithmetic. These less formal messages form the hidden curriculum, an alternative set of "three *Rs*"—rules, routines, and regulations. Sometimes being tardy has a bigger impact on grades than whether one has actually learned the material—as some children can face failure for being late more than five times even if they score 90% on the exams.

According to functional theorists, it is through the hidden curriculum that students learn the expectations, behaviors, and values necessary to succeed in school and society. For conflict theorists, the hidden curriculum is a social and economic agenda that maintains class differences. More is expected of elites, and they are given greater responsibility and opportunities for problem solving that result in higher achievement (Brookover and Erickson 1975). Many working-class schools stress order and discipline, teaching students to obey rules and accept their lot as responsible, punctual workers (Willis 1979).

Four-year-old preschoolers recite the Pledge of Allegiance. Developing patriotism is part of the implicit and informal curriculum of schools—and sometimes part of the formal curriculum.

Schools have a formal structure and a culture that affect the classroom. Note the arrangement of desks and the norm of raising a hand before a student may speak. This may seem "normal" to many Americans, but it is far from the universal pattern in schools in North America or around the globe. The formal system is only part of the classroom environment, for every school and classroom also has an informal culture.

The Educational Climate of Schools

Schools can be comfortable and stimulating or cold and unfriendly places. Some have an atmosphere of excitement about learning, with artwork and posters on the walls and excited noises coming from classrooms. Other schools have rules and warnings posted everywhere and hall guards, and uniformed students walk in columns and sit up straight in neat rows. These are aspects of school climate, a general social environment that characterizes a group, organization, or community such as a school (Brookover, Erickson, and McEvoy 1996).

School architecture, classroom layouts, teacher expectations, and student groupings by age and ability—all affect the educational and cultural climate of the school. Schools also have ceremonies and rituals that contribute to the climate—logos, symbols, athletic events, pep rallies, and awards ceremonies. In addition to the physical features in the school, classroom climates for students are influenced by the teachers' use of discipline and encouragement, the organization of tasks and opportunities for student interaction, and the grouping and seating arrangements. These nuances can create an atmosphere that celebrates or stifles student achievement (Ballantine and Hammack 2012).

The friendships students make depend in part on how schools and classrooms are organized. Some schools track students on the basis of their tested ability in certain subjects, thus fostering the development of friendship groups within those tracks. Tracking systems also tend to create and maintain racial, ethnic, and social class segregation (Lucas and Berends 2002; Oakes 2005), whereas educational desegregation can integrate minority and immigrant students (Van Houtte and Stevens 2009).

Teachers' responses to class, ethnicity or race, and gender differences create climates that have subtle but profound impacts on students' experiences and learning. Studies indicate that teachers give boys more attention. For example, they call on them more often and give them instructions for accomplishing tasks independently. In contrast, teachers more often do the tasks *for* the girls in the class (Sadker and Sadker 1995; Spade 2004).

Another study found that teachers unconsciously tend to groom white girls for academic attainment while encouraging African American girls to emphasize social relationships over academic work. White boys are groomed for high attainment and high-status social roles, while African American boys are trained for social conformity and are carefully monitored and controlled in the classroom (Grant 2004).

Low achievement is linked to low expectations, and bias is subtle. Do students have equal access to materials and technology? Are all students active and influential participants in the learning process? Goals of equitable teaching and learning are challenged in increasingly diverse classrooms with immigrant students from linguistically and culturally diverse backgrounds. "Different" students tend to end up in lower-ability groups, guaranteeing their poorer achievement (Oakes 2005; Rubin 2008). The result is that students' and teachers' perceptions of themselves and the learning environment help shape the school climate and influence achievement. Table 11.2 illustrates teacher expectations. Note that all of these are social variables that impact learning in the classroom.

Value Climate of Schools

> Dear Teacher, I would like to introduce you to my son, Wind-Wolf. He is probably what you would consider a typical Indian kid. He was born and raised on the reservation. He has black hair, dark brown eyes, and an olive complexion, and, like so many Indian children his age, he is shy and quiet in the classroom. He is 5 years old, in kindergarten, and I can't understand why you have already labeled him a "slow learner." He has already been through quite an education compared with his peers in Western society. He was bonded to his mother and to the Mother Earth in a traditional native childbirth ceremony. And he has been continuously cared for by his mother, father, sisters, cousins, aunts, uncles, grandparents, and extended tribal family since this ceremony. . . .
>
> Wind-Wolf was strapped (in his baby basket like a turtle shell) snugly with a deliberate restriction on his arms and legs. Although Western society may argue this hinders motor-skill development and abstract reasoning, we believe it forces the child to first develop his intuitive faculties, rational intellect, symbolic thinking, and five senses. Wind-Wolf was with his mother constantly, closely bonded physically, as she carried him on her back or held him while breast-feeding. She carried him everywhere she went, and every night he slept with both parents. Because of this, Wind-Wolf's educational setting was not only a "secure" environment, but it was also very colorful, complicated, sensitive, and diverse.
>
> As he grew older, Wind-Wolf began to crawl out of the baby basket, develop his motor skills, and explore the world around him. When frightened or sleepy, he could always return to the basket, as a turtle withdraws into its shell. Such an inward journey allows one to reflect in privacy on what he has learned and to carry the new knowledge deeply into the unconscious and the soul. Shapes, sizes, colors, texture, sound, smell, feeling, taste, and the learning process are therefore functionally integrated—the physical and spiritual, matter and energy, and conscious and unconscious, individual and social.
>
> It takes a long time to absorb and reflect on these kinds of experiences, so maybe that is why you think my Indian child is a slow learner. His aunts and grandmothers taught him to count and to know his numbers

while they sorted materials for making abstract designs in native baskets. And he was taught to learn mathematics by counting the sticks we use in our traditional native hand game. So he may be slow in grasping the methods and tools you use in your classroom, ones quite familiar to his white peers, but I hope you will be patient with him. It takes time to adjust to a new cultural system and learn new things. He is not culturally "disadvantaged," but he is culturally different. (Lake 1990:48–53)

This letter expresses the frustration of a father who sees his son being labeled and not given a chance by the school system—mostly because he grew up with a different set of values from those in the dominant culture. Schools reinforce a set of values, affirming some behaviors and relationships and ignoring or belittling others. This can be hard for children who come from cultures with values different from those of the dominant culture.

The value climate of a school also includes students' motivations, aspirations, and achievements. Why is achievement significantly higher in some schools than in others? How much influence do the values and outlooks of peers, parents, and teachers have on students? Sociologists know that a student's home is influential in determining educational motivation. Recall the opening case of Tomás,

Table 11.2 **Teacher Expectations**

Teachers are influenced by the same stereotypes as others, and those mistaken perceptions can lead to lower expectations for some children. The following factors can sometimes create lower expectations for certain groups of students.

Sex	Boys and girls are sometimes the recipients of low academic expectations because of beliefs about boys' maturation and gender assumptions about girls' mathematics skills.
Socioeconomic status	Low expectations are typically held for children from families with low income and education levels, low-status jobs, and an undesirable neighborhood residence.
Race and ethnic identifiers	Teachers are less likely to expect African American, Hispanic, and Native American students to succeed. They are also less likely to expect African American and Hispanic students to attend college. In contrast, school personnel often have high expectations for Asian American students.
The location of the school	Rural and inner-city schools often have lower expectations than suburban schools. This sometimes evolves into a negative "can't do anything" climate.
Appearance and neatness	Lower expectations are associated with clothes and grooming that are out of style, made of cheaper material, not branded, or purchased at thrift or discount stores. Poor handwriting and other sloppiness in presentation can also create assumptions about the intellectual abilities of students.
Oral language patterns	Nonstandard English grammar and vocabulary is a basis for holding lower expectations for students.
The halo effect	There is a tendency to label a student's current achievement based on past performance evaluations of the child. Therefore, blind grading—evaluation of student work without knowledge of who wrote the material until after it is graded—is important.
The seating position	Lower expectations are typically transmitted to students who sit on the sides and in the back of a classroom.
Student behavior	Students with nonacademic behaviors that are inappropriate by middle-class standards also tend to receive lower academic expectations from teachers.
Tracking or grouping	Students in lower academic tracks are presumed to have been placed there for a good reason (i.e., they have limited capacities and can never be expected to learn critical knowledge and skills), yet in some cases, placements may have been arbitrary or incorrect.

Source: Adapted from *Creating Effective Schools: An In-Service Program for Enhancing School Learning Climate and Achievement* by Wilbur B. Brookover, Fritz J. Erickson, and Alan W. McEvoy. Copyright © 1997, 1982, Wilbur B. Brookover, Fritz J. Erickson, and Alan W. McEvoy. Published by Learning Publications, Inc.

who received only negative comments and little encouragement at home and school. Parents' backgrounds and current social class location provide the basis for child rearing and transmission of class values. These influence the child's motivation and academic achievement (Roksa and Potter 2011).

Cultural context such as the neighborhood racial, ethnic, and class composition also affects the value climate, including educational decisions like whether to go to college. Disadvantaged neighborhoods are culturally mixed with many value systems, and though students may say they plan to go to college, that value is often not realized (Harding 2011). By contrast, researchers have found that classrooms integrated along ethnic or class lines frequently raise the level of motivation and achievement for members of minority groups (Lucas and Berends 2002). Also, students who are expected to do very well generally rise to meet these expectations (Downey and Pribesh 2004; Morris 2005).

Students perform less well if they feel their school success is futile or hopeless or if they think that the teachers do not believe in them or are obsessed with discipline. If teachers have negative expectations, students are likely to have lower aspirations and achievement levels. This is why teacher morale is so important (Rosenthal and Jacobson 1968). Others' expectations of students can become a self-fulfilling prophecy, affecting how children feel about their abilities. This, in turn, affects students' motivation to achieve and ultimately their life chances.

Knowing what we know about the importance of value climate, a group of researchers undertook to raise the value climate and expectations of teachers and students in a group of Chicago public schools. They based their plan on three goals for creating an effective academic learning climate: (1) Schools need to be safe and orderly with no violence or disruptions, (2) schools need to be organized so that they become true academic learning communities with no ability groupings that result in large numbers of failures, and (3) schools need to be clear on what students will learn at each level in math, science, social studies, language, and technical skills such as computer literacy.

Although eliminating ability grouping (tracking) is controversial in some school districts, in Chicago, the school achievement levels rose significantly with this plan (Brookover et al. 1996). Following up on the Chicago reform plan discussed above is Renaissance 2010, a movement to create 100 new small schools in neighborhoods across the city to relieve crowding, increase students' feelings of belonging, and bring in new leadership (Ayers and Klonsky 2006; Chicago Public Schools 2011; Duncan 2006). These are only two of many plans to improve school achievement levels and influence the value climate in schools. Plans need to take into consideration the educational and value climates of schools in order to be successful. Whether throughout the school or in a particular classroom, the atmosphere that pervades the learning environment and expectations has an impact on students' educational achievement.

Thinking Sociologically

How might schools unintentionally misunderstand Wind-Wolf and other minority children in ways that have negative consequences for the children's success?

Power Dynamics and Coping Strategies in the Classroom

For teachers, getting students to obey or cooperate or take responsibility is challenging. For students, winning some control from teachers or freedom from supervision is often a goal. Both students and teachers develop strategies to cope with pressures and difficult situations. Student coping strategies range from complete compliance to outright rebellion. For instance, college students set priorities for studying various subjects, deciding which test is most important and figuring out where to cut corners. Do the following five strategies sound familiar? They are taken in part from Merton's (1938) strain theory of deviance (see Chapter 6) and represent strategies students use to cope with school pressures:

- *Conformity:* acceptance of goals and means—doing the schoolwork expected
- *Innovation:* finding alternative or unapproved methods to achieve conventional goals—cheating or plagiarizing to pass a course or to win an academic contest
- *Retreatism:* rejection of goals and means—rebelling against school establishment by not conforming or cooperating
- *Ritualism:* indifference toward goals—"getting by" through following rules but not learning anything
- *Rejection with replacement:* rejection of goals and means in favor of another strategy—being a discipline problem or dropping out of school to pursue other activities (Hammersley and Turner 1980; Merton 1968)

Teachers try to elicit cooperation and participation from students by creating a cost-benefits ratio that favors compliance. Manipulating the classroom is one effective means of control: putting students at tables or in a circle, breaking up groups of chattering friends, or leading a discussion while standing beside the most disruptive child.

Thinking Sociologically

What examples of the informal system can you see in the courses you are currently taking? How do these norms and strategies affect your learning experience?

After the School Bell Rings: Meso-Level Analysis of Educational Organizations

Schools can be like mazes, with passages to negotiate, hallways lined with pictures and lockers, and classrooms that set the scene for the education process. Schools are mazes in a much larger sense as well. They involve complex interwoven social systems at the meso level—the state agencies above the local community that affect a school's operations. At this level, we encounter the formal organization of the school system in a more bureaucratized form.

Classrooms are loaded with power dynamics, and as this photo shows, it is very clear who is in charge of the classroom.

Formal Education Systems

Formal education came into being in the Western world in 16th-century Europe. Schools were seen as a way for Catholics to indoctrinate people into religious faith and for Lutherans to teach people to read so that they could interpret the Bible for themselves. The first compulsory education was in a Lutheran monastery in Germany in 1619. By the 19th century, schooling was seen as necessary to teach the European lower classes better agricultural methods, skills for the rapidly growing number of factory jobs, national loyalty, and obedience to authorities (Gatto 2003).

After 1900, national state school systems were common in Europe and its colonial outposts and former colonial empires. These systems shared many common organizational structures, curricula, and methods, as nations borrowed ideas from other countries. The Prussian model, with strict discipline and ties to the military, became popular in Europe in the 1800s, for example, and the two-track system of education that developed—one for the rich and one for the poor—was debated worldwide.

Thus, formal education systems came into being when other social institutions required new roles, skills, and knowledge that parents could not teach. Knowledge needed by the young became too complex to be taught informally in families through example, moral lessons, and stories. Industrializing societies required workers with reading and math skills, and eventually, they would need electronic technology skills. Schooling that formerly served only the elite gradually became available to the masses, and some societies began to require schooling for basic literacy (usually third-grade level). Schools emerged as major formal organizations and eventually developed extensive bureaucracies. The postwar period from 1950 to 1970 brought about a rapid rise in education worldwide, with worldwide enrollment in primary schooling jumping from 36% to 84% and secondary enrollments going from 13% to 36% (Boli 2002). Figure 11.1 on page 398 shows trends since 1970, with worldwide primary schooling up to 90% by 2009 and secondary schooling reaching 68% (UNESCO 2012).

Sometimes, differing goals for education systems lead to conflict. What need, for example, does a subsistence farmer in Nigeria or Kenya have for Latin? Yet Latin was often imposed as part of the standard curriculum in colonialized nations. Many countries have revised curricula based on the goals and needs of agriculturally based economies.

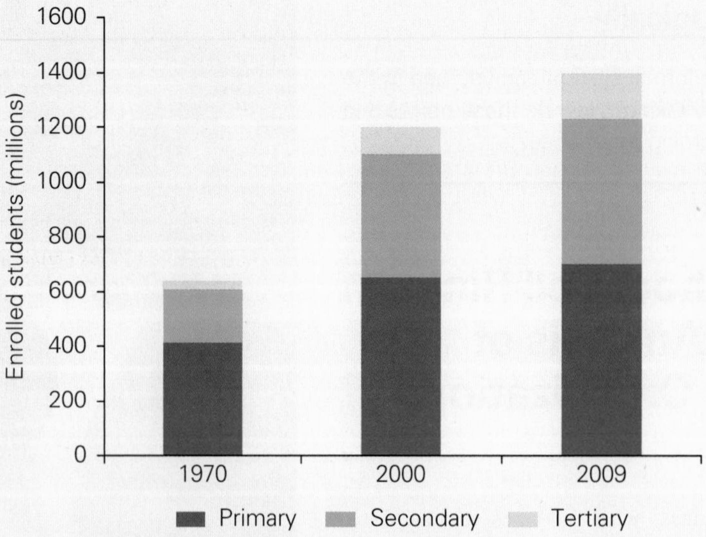

Figure 11.1 Number of Students (in Millions) Worldwide Enrolled in School From Primary to Tertiary Education, 1970, 2000, and 2009

Source: United Nations Educational, Scientific and Cultural Organization. 2012. *World Atlas of Gender Equality in Education* (p. 9). Retrieved January 27, 2013 (http://www.uis.unesco.org/Education/Documents/unesco-world-atlas-gender-education-2012.pdf).

The Bureaucratic School Structure

The meso-level formal bureaucratic atmosphere that permeates many schools arose because it was cost-effective, efficient, and productive. Bureaucracy provided a way to document and process masses of students coming from different backgrounds. Recall Weber's (1947) bureaucratic model of groups and organizations, discussed in Chapter 5:

1. Schools have a division of labor among administrators, teachers, students, and support personnel. The roles associated with the statuses are part of the school structure. Individual teachers or students hold these roles for a limited time and are replaced by others coming into the system.
2. The administrative hierarchy incorporates a chain of command and channels of communication.
3. Specific rules and procedures in a school cover everything from course content to discipline in the classroom and use of the schoolyard.
4. Personal relationships are downplayed in favor of formalized relations among members of the system, such as placement on the basis of tests and grading.
5. Rationality governs the operations of the organization; people are hired and fired on the basis of their qualifications and how well they do their jobs.

One result of bureaucracy is that some children are not helped with personal problems or learning difficulties (Kozol 2006; Sizer 1984; Waters 2012). Impersonal rules can lock people into rigid behavior patterns, leading to apathy and alienation. In schools, these feelings cause passivity among students, which in turn frustrates teachers. Children like Tomás in the opening example do not fit into neat cubbyholes that bureaucratic structures invariably create. These children view school not as a privilege but as a requirement imposed by an adult world. Caught between the demands of an impersonal bureaucracy and goals for their students, teachers cannot always give every child the personal help she or he needs. Thus, we see that organizational requirements of education systems at a meso level can influence the personal student-teacher relationship at the micro level. This is another example of how the social world model helps us understand human behavior in organizations.

The bottom line is that formal bureaucratic structures can thwart the goals of an education system. Even colleges and universities face controversies over control of decision making and direction of programs. For instance, the funding of the university from business and government grants requires many professors to concentrate on research. In so doing, it takes time away from other functions of the university, such as teaching (Gamson 1998).

These chairs represent the bureaucracy or hierarchy of the school, with every student facing the teacher as though she or he is the only student who is expected to speak and is worthy of undivided attention. Look through other photos in this chapter, especially the photos from Global South countries. Do you notice any differences in the arrangement of students that suggest differences in relationships in the school?

Education and the Social Institution of Family

Interconnections between meso-level institutions are a common refrain in this book. There are many interconnections between the institutions of family and education. When children enter kindergarten or primary school, they bring their prior experience, including socialization experiences and cultural capital from a parent or parents, brothers, sisters, and other relatives (Jaeger 2011). Family background, according to many sociologists, is the single most important influence on children's school achievement (Jencks 1972). For example, children who grow up in father-absent homes have lower high school graduation and college attendance rates, score lower on standardized tests, and are more likely to use drugs (Barajas 2011). Children succeed in large part because of what their parent(s) do to support them in their educations (Jaeger 2011; Schneider and Coleman 1993).

Most families stress the importance of education, but they do so in different ways. Middle-class parents in the Global North tend to manage their children's education, visiting schools and teachers, having educational materials in the home, and holding high expectations for their children's achievement. In these families, children learn the values of hard work, good grades, and deferred gratification for reaching future goals.

Involvement of parents from lower socioeconomic status and from immigrant families can motivate children and have a significant impact on children's educational outcomes, yet these parents tend to look to schools as the authority (Cheung and Pomerantz 2012; Domina 2005). They are less involved in their children's schooling, leaving decisions to the school. Unfortunately, children who must make educational decisions on their own are more likely to do poorly or drop out of school (Jaeger 2011). Much of the disadvantage experienced by children from immigrant families, however, is rooted in poverty.

Shifts in the other institutions— such as family and the economy—can impact educational achievement as well. Changes in family and work structures put parents under more stress. For example, busy single parents often have little time to help their children with schoolwork. People who work 60- or 70-hour weeks also find that their time for being attentive to their children's learning is limited.

Thinking Sociologically

How do religion, health, politics, economics, and other meso-level institutions influence education and vice versa? Provide some examples of links between schools and other social institutions.

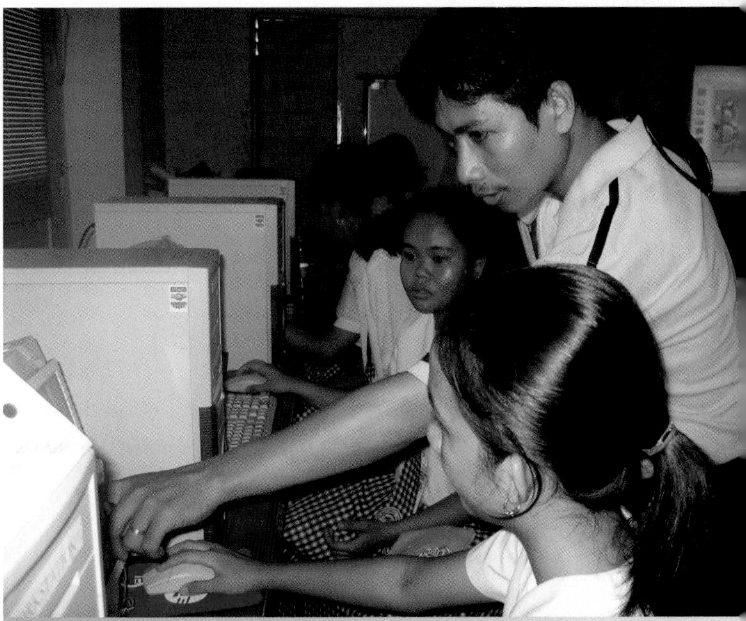

Computer skills are increasingly essential in societies and schools, yet some children come from families that do not have access to computers. Children who have computers at home have a significant advantage. These students are receiving help from their teacher in the Philippines.

Educational Decision Making at the Meso Level

Who should have the power to make decisions about what children learn? In relatively homogeneous countries such as Japan and Sweden, centralized goal setting and school decisions are possible. Educational decision making typically causes little controversy. Centralized national ministries of education are also common in Latin American, Asian, and African countries, where educational standards and funding are controlled by the national government. In contrast, heterogeneous societies such as Canada, Israel, and the United States include many different racial, ethnic, regional, and religious subcultures, each with its own needs and interests. Teachers, administrators, school boards, parents, and interest groups all claim the right to influence the curriculum. Consider the following influences from micro and macro levels on the meso-level organization.

Local-Level Influences

At the U.S. local community level, curricular conflicts occur routinely over the selection of reading material and sex education courses, as well as over any content that is thought to contain obscenity, sex, nudity, political or economic bias, profanity, slang or nonstandard English, racism or racial hatred, and antireligious or presumed anti-American sentiment. For example, Tucson, Arizona, suspended its Mexican American studies program and banned a number of books related to the program because they were thought by some parents to "promote resentment toward a race or class of people" (Delfattore 2004; Goodman and Gonzalez 2012). Another example comes from Family Friendly Libraries, an online grassroots interest group that started in Virginia and argues that the popular *Harry Potter* books should be banned from school libraries. The members of this group believe the series promotes the religion of witchcraft (DeMitchell and Carney 2005).

Banned books in the past have included *The Wonderful Wizard of Oz, Rumpelstiltskin, Anne Frank: The Diary of a Young Girl, Madame Bovary, The Grapes of Wrath, Adventures of Huckleberry Finn,* Shakespeare's *Hamlet*, Chaucer's *The Miller's Tale,* and Aristophanes's *Lysistrata* (Ballantine and Hammack 2012). Table 11.3 shows the most frequently challenged books in 2011. Frequently challenged classics in literature include *The Great Gatsby* by F. Scott Fitzgerald, *The Catcher in the Rye* by J. D. Salinger, *The Grapes of Wrath* by John Steinbeck, *To Kill a Mockingbird* by Harper Lee, and *The Color Purple* by Alice Walker (American Library Association 2013).

Decisions about sex education curricula are equally fraught with controversy. The number of sexually active teens in the United States has not changed much since 1991; about one third of high school students indicate that they are sexually active. The exception is a decrease among African American students where those sexually active have declined in number from 59% in 1991 to 41% in 2011

Table 11.3 The 10 Most Challenged Books of 2011

	Title	Reason for Banning
1.	*ttyl; ttfn; 18r, g8r* (series), by Lauren Myracle	Offensive language; religious viewpoint; sexually explicit; unsuited to age group.
2.	*The Color of Earth* (series), by Kim Dong Hwa	Nudity; sex education; sexually explicit; unsuited to age group.
3.	*The Hunger Games* (trilogy), by Suzanne Collins	Anti-ethnic; antifamily; insensitivity; offensive language; occult/satanic; violence.
4.	*My Mom's Having a Baby! A Kid's Month-by-Month Guide to Pregnancy*, by Dori Hillestad Butler	Nudity; sex education; sexually explicit; unsuited to age group.
5.	*The Absolutely True Diary of a Part-Time Indian*, by Sherman Alexie	Offensive language; racism; religious viewpoint; sexually explicit; unsuited to age group.
6.	*Alice* (series), by Phyllis Reynolds Naylor	Nudity; offensive language; religious viewpoint.
7.	*Brave New World*, by Aldous Huxley	Insensitivity; nudity; racism; religious viewpoint; sexually explicit.
8.	*What My Mother Doesn't Know*, by Sonya Sones	Nudity; offensive language; sexually explicit.
9.	*Gossip Girl* (series), by Cecily Von Ziegesar	Drugs; offensive language; sexually explicit.
10.	*To Kill a Mockingbird*, by Harper Lee	Offensive language; racism.

Source: American Library Association 2013.

(Child Trends Data Bank 2012). Most sexually active teens (86% of women and 93% of men) have used at least one method of birth control (Guttmacher Institute 2012a).

A growing number of large city school districts, concerned with teen pregnancy and sexually transmitted disease, including AIDS, now provide teens with sex education, information about contraception, counseling, and sometimes condoms. Many who oppose sex education in schools claim that these programs encourage premarital sex rather than abstinence and teach teens how to have sex. Critics also believe that sex education should be left to families and religious institutions.

National-Level Influences

Whether or not the national government should control education is a question in all societies. Because the U.S. Constitution leaves education in the hands of each state, the involvement of the federal government has been more limited than in most countries. Yet the federal government wields enormous influence through its power to make federal funds available for special programs, such as mathematics and science, reading, or special education. The government may withhold funds from schools that are not in compliance with federal laws and the U.S. Constitution. For example, the federal government, courts, and public opinion forced all-male military academies to become coeducational, despite the schools' resistance to such change. School changes as a result of the Civil Rights Act and the Americans with Disabilities Act are other examples of federal government influence on local schools through the enforcement of federal laws. Schools have accommodated people with various disabilities—people who in the past would have been left out of the system. With their classroom experiences and working with other teachers and children, the differently abled can participate fully in society. However, as the "Sociology in Our Social World" on page 402 shows, this process is not always smooth.

Policy decisions by federal lawmakers influence what and how children learn. This changes with each administration, based on liberal or conservative responses to calls for school reform. Reports evaluating reforms have variously called for strengthening high school graduation requirements, raising college entrance requirements, emphasizing basic skills, requiring a longer school day and school year, improving the training and status of teachers, holding educators responsible for students' performance, providing the funds necessary to improve the education system, and holding families accountable for children's achievement.

Since 1965 and the establishment of the U.S. Department of Education, each president has put his mark on the U.S. education system. President George W. Bush's controversial No Child Left Behind (NCLB) initiative was a prime example. It tied school performance to federal funds and required annual competency testing of students. Under this program, schools were required to administer achievement tests for accountability—tests that focus on math and reading. Schools failing to meet guidelines were penalized. The result was that 70% of schools reduced instructional time in other subject areas (Center for Education Policy 2006; Ginicola and Saccoccio 2008). So even in the decentralized United States, where only 1 out of 14 education dollars comes from the federal government, the macro-level policies have an impact on what happens in the intimate environment of classrooms.

Critics argued that NCLB ignored much of what educators and social scientists know from research about teaching and learning. It overemphasized testing, penalized schools with lots of low-income students, demoralized and deprofessionalized teachers, and failed to provide adequate funding for the mandates (Bracey 2005; Hallett and Meanwell 2012; Karen 2005).

President Obama and his education secretary, Arne Duncan, changed the NCLB plan by funding parts of the law that were left unfunded, allowing states to opt out of certain parts of the program, establishing funding for new initiatives as part of the "Race to the Top" agenda to improve schools, adding new assessment measures of student learning, providing some alternatives to the high-stakes testing, stressing rewards for high-performing teachers, and nationalizing some of the standards that were previously in the hands of states. They placed new emphasis on "zero to five" education by expanding Head Start funding for preschoolers, and they are trying to increase parental involvement. Still, critics charge that the Obama administration continued with many of the NCLB policies that caused problems in the previous administration, especially the use of high-stakes testing and centralized control ("Plan for Lifetime Success Through Education" 2008). Note that recent presidents from both major political parties have supported an expansion of national rather than local control of school curriculum.

Thinking Sociologically

The discussion above shows that educational needs at the micro (individual) level, the meso (institutional or ethnic group) level, and the macro (national) level can be very different. This raises the question of who makes decisions and whether individual needs or societal needs take precedence.

Macro-level political and economic trends outside a country can have a significant impact on the education system as well. External influences include international relations, globalization, and new technologies and knowledge. In the United States, for example, the terrorist attacks on the World Trade Center and Pentagon on September 11, 2001, reshaped school curricula overnight, as schools added units on terrorism, American values, and Islam.

Sociology in Our Social World

Disability and Inequality

By Robert M. Pellerin

Living with a visual disability for over 40 years has provided me with lived experience. I have also been doing research on experiences of others with disabilities as part of my PhD research. My results show that having a disability puts people at a disadvantage in education, employment, attitudes of others toward those with disabilities, and personal relationships. Technologies for those with disabilities have advanced, legislation has been introduced and sometimes passed, and advocacy for rights abound, but I still have to remind others, including professionals, that due to my visual impairment some methods of communication, such as print media, do not work. Additionally, most of the technology from which those with visual impairment could benefit is unaffordable, and most mainstream companies do not include features that would make products disability-friendly. The bottom line is that many of us are ready, willing, and able to be productive citizens, but we are often precluded from positions because of our disabilities and difficulty obtaining accommodation.

Disability in America has undergone a significant transition since the late 1800s. Most of those who have helped bring disability to the forefront have been American veterans who were wounded in war and notable figures like Helen Keller who influenced societal perceptions of disability. They have helped define disabilities as being a relative disadvantage instead of a tragedy. Historically, disability has been synonymous with an inability to engage in employment. During the 1800s and early 1900s, people deemed unfit were often warehoused in asylums or institutions and placed in residential schools where they were provided with less-than-adequate instruction. For several decades in the early 20th century some countries—including the United States—sterilized people with disabilities. However, advocates campaigned during the late 1960s to change such laws and to close asylums for the disabled.

Media portrayals have contributed to false stereotypes that promoted both false beliefs and lowered goal attainment for people with disabilities. Examples of images fostered by the media include miracle cures for people who become religious; foolish tales about superhuman hearing and "face feeling"; stories of blind or visually impaired males who are depicted as wise sages; and images of disabled women who are depicted as pure, vulnerable, and in need of rescue.

The most well-known legislation seeking to end exclusion and increase participation in areas of education and employment are the Rehabilitation Act of 1973 and the Americans with Disabilities Act (ADA) of 1990. The 1973 regulations apply federally; the ADA applies to the states and public accessibility (that is, access to jobs, public services, and telecommunications). Despite this legislation, approximately 70% of people with disabilities do not participate in the workforce. Unfortunately, people with disabilities are at higher risk for engaging in drug and alcohol use, sexual promiscuity, higher levels of abuse, and suicidal ideation than other groups.

Prior to the 1970s, people with disabilities were excluded from public education. Due to advocacy and legislation, today approximately 75% of school-aged students with disabilities attend public school. Legislation regarding full inclusion has not proven as useful as planned, although exposure to students with disabilities has increased comfort levels of teachers and nondisabled peers. Recent deficiencies in providing equal education include lack of adequate technology and skills needed in college or in vocational or social settings.

Regarding employment, historically people with disabilities have gone from being evaluated on the same standards as nondisabled individuals to being assessed according to how well they know themselves, their accommodation needs, and their job qualifications. Despite legislation, courts have generally ruled in favor of employers in discrimination suits. Some social scientists advocate for improving the social capital or human capital of those with disabilities as a way to increase the level of workforce participation. Many employers believe the candidate is responsible for ensuring employment is attained, while some potential employers continue to believe people with disabilities are too difficult to hire and accommodate despite their academic achievement. Employees with disabilities, including myself, concur with recommendations such as improving social and human capital, educating employers about the benefits of hiring people with disabilities, and dispelling misconceptions and negative stereotypes.

The discrimination and inequality experienced by many with disabilities results in a decreased sense of health and well-being and increased feelings of isolation. The tragedy here is that people with disabilities, despite their efforts, continue to meet with virtual hoops posed by court decisions, changes in education, and negative labeling. I believe that until society views people as having abilities and strengths as opposed to disabilities, stigma will predominate, and society will be deprived of talents and qualities from which all can benefit.

* * * * * * *

Robert Pellerin was granted a PhD in arts and sciences from Union Institute and University. His research has been on employment barriers for people with visual disabilities, and he is currently a clinician doing marriage and family therapy in California.

Education, Society, and the Road to Opportunity: The Macro Level

In Dalton, Georgia, Latinos make up over half the school-age population. In the school that researcher Hector Tobar visited there, 80% of the student body was Hispanic. The town has been unable to recruit bilingual teachers to this rural community, so the community sends the teachers to Mexico to learn Spanish. The principal at the elementary school admits that it is expensive, but the people in Dalton think it is important for their children to be bilingual and for everyone to be educated. The teachers do instruction in both English and Spanish. Dalton spends more than $7,400 per student, and it funds its schools entirely through income from the town's carpet factories (more than 100 of them) where most of the parents work. The cofounder of the Georgia Project, which assists new immigrants in their adjustment, believes that "the factories need the workers, and the workers come with families . . . Without good schools for the workers' children, the county would leave itself wide open to a whole host of social problems down the road. Giving Dalton's Mexican kids a decent education was the sensible thing to do, 'pure self-interest'" (Diggs 2011:59–60).

Other states have not been so accommodating—or pragmatic—with Mexican immigrants. In 2000, voters in Arizona approved the most restrictive English-only education law in the country, and since that time non-English-speakers in Arizona public schools have been part of an English-only program, with no Spanish spoken in school.

The idea behind the No Child Left Behind policy is that the society must make resources available so that all children can learn and can have a chance to make a contribution to society. This little girl is getting tutoring in the use of a computer in a government-supported program.

Mexican students start behind and stay behind according to teachers (Diggs 2011).

Educational decisions made by states and national governments affect individual families and their kids and the communities, states, and national economic and education systems. Let us look at some implications of education for societies. This section focuses on the role of education in the stratification system. Although it has implications regarding individual families' chances to succeed, the reality is that education is deeply interwoven into the macro-level inequalities of the society.

Why Societies Have Education Systems: Macro-Level Theories

In a rural Indian village in Uttar Pradesh, children gather in a lean-to shelter for their morning lessons before going to the fields to help with the animals. The average number of years of schooling of adults in India is 5.1 years. However, enrollment in primary school today has increased dramatically, close to 80% of boys (UNESCO 2010). However, in some rural areas of India and other Global South countries, little more than basic literacy is considered necessary or possible, especially for girls. Basic literacy is a goal for all citizens in most countries, but it is sometimes limited to urban areas in the Global South where basic academic skills (literacy, mathematics, and science) are essential to find employment. Mass education was not even a goal until the 1900s (Benavot, Meyer, and Kamens 1991). It was only then that it became clear that a literate citizenry is necessary for economic development and informed political participation. Even today, transportation to schools can be an issue, with children in Myanmar crowding on to a gondola and youngsters in school buses in India having four passengers per small bench.

These children, who live near Inle Lake in Myanmar (Burma), take the only available mode of transportation to get to school, a gondola school bus.

Wherever it takes place and whatever the content, education gives individuals the information and skills that their society regards as important and prepares them to live and work in their societies. Education plays a major role in providing children with skills for their adult lives—but how education takes place varies across societies. Village children in many Global South countries around the world go to the community school, tablets in hand, but when the family needs help in the fields or with child care, older children often stay at home. Even though attending several years of school is mandated by law in most countries, not all people become literate. Learning survival skills—how to grow crops, care for the home, treat diseases, and make clothing—takes most of an individual's available time and energy. These essential skills come before formal schooling.

Functionalist Perspective on the Purposes of Education

Functional theorists argue that formal and informal education serve certain crucial purposes in society, especially as societies modernize. The functions of education as a social institution are outlined in Figure 11.2. Note that some functions are planned and formalized (manifest functions), whereas others are unintended and unorganized—the informal results of the education process (latent functions).

Manifest Functions (intended; formalized)

- Socialize children to be productive members of society.
- Select and train individuals for positions in society.
- Promote social participation, change, and innovation.
- Enhance personal independence and social development.

Latent Functions (unintended; informal)

- Confine and supervise underage citizens.
- Weaken parental controls over youths.
- Provide opportunities for peer cultures to develop.
- Provide contexts for the development of friendships and mate selection.

Figure 11.2 Key Functions of Education

Latent functions of schooling are often just as important to the society as manifest functions. For example, schools give parents release time from child care responsibilities so that they can perform other roles. Schools also keep children off the streets until they can be absorbed into productive roles in society. They provide young people with a place to congregate and interact among themselves, fostering a "youth culture" of music, fashion, slang, dances, dating, and cliques or gangs. At the ages when social relationships are being established, schools are the central meeting place for the young—a kind of mate selection market. Education also weakens parental control over youths, helps them begin the move toward independence, and provides experience in large, impersonal secondary groups.

In the functionalist view, the structure and processes within the educational institution remain stable only if basic functions are met. When social functions are not met adequately, an education system becomes ripe for change. Government proposals for education reforms are stimulated by new knowledge and technologies and by indications of poor outcomes, such as falling behind in international test comparisons or experiencing high unemployment due in part to an undertrained labor force.

Education provides hope in this refugee camp in the Central African Republic. The adults created this school for children, even though families often lack food. They view education as a functional necessity for the future of their children.

Socialization: Teaching Children to Be Productive Members of Society. Societies use education to pass on essential information of a culture—especially the values, skills, and knowledge necessary for survival. Sometimes this process occurs in formal classrooms and other times in informal places. In West African villages, children may have several years of formal education in a village school, but they learn what is right and wrong, values, and future roles informally by observing their elders and by "playing" at the tasks they will soon undertake for survival. The girls help pound cassava root for the evening meal, while the boys build model boats and practice negotiating the waves and casting nets. In less prosperous countries, formal education beyond basic literacy is reserved mainly for the elite—the sons and daughters of the rulers and the wealthy.

In all postindustrial Global North societies, however, elders and family members cannot teach all the skills necessary for survival. Formal schooling emerged as a meso-level institution to meet the needs of macro-level industrial and postindustrial societies, furnishing the specialized training required by rapidly growing and changing technology. Schools also teach students culture beyond what families in heterogeneous societies can provide. Diverse groups must learn common rules that maintain the social order, for example (Brint, Contreras, and Matthews 2001).

Selecting and Training Individuals for Positions in Society. Students take standardized tests, receive grades at the end of the term or the year, and ask teachers to write recommendation letters. These activities are part of the selection process prevalent in competitive societies with formal education systems. Individuals accumulate credentials—grade point averages, standardized test scores, and degrees—that determine the colleges or job opportunities available to them, the fields of study or occupations they can pursue, and ultimately their positions in society. In some societies, education systems enact this social function through tracking, ability grouping, grade promotion and retention, high-stakes and minimum-competency testing, and pullout programs that contribute to job training, such as vocational education and service learning.

Thus, education outfits people for making a living in their society and contributing to the economy. Individual, family, community, state, and national income and standard of living are linked to education of the citizens. For example, Map 11.2 in the next "Engaging Sociology" indicates the distribution of college degrees in the United States (see page 406).

Promoting Change and Innovation. In multicultural societies such as Israel, France, and England, citizens expect schools to help assimilate immigrants by teaching them the language and customs, along with strategies for reducing intergroup tensions. In Israel, for example, many recent Jewish immigrants from Africa and Russia work hard to master Hebrew and to move successfully through the Israeli education system. In most societies, providing educational opportunity to all groups is a challenge, but effective social participation and readiness for change require it.

Institutions of higher education are expected to generate new knowledge, technology, and ideas and produce students with up-to-date skills and knowledge to lead industry and

Engaging Sociology

Consequences of High or Low Numbers of Bachelor's Degrees

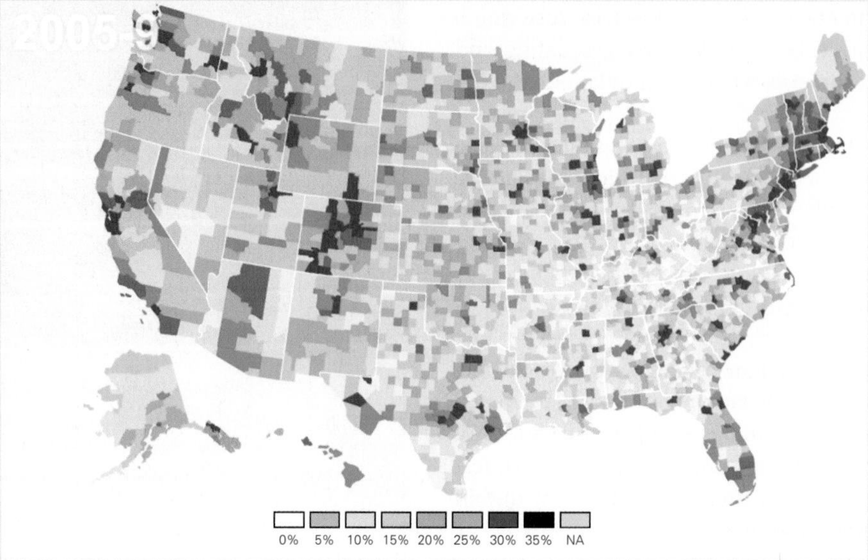

Map 11.2 Percentage of the U.S. Population Holding a Bachelor's Degree or Higher by State

Source: Ogunwole, Drewery, and Rios-Vargas 2012.

Engaging With Sociological Data:

1. How does your state rank?
2. How might the economy of a state be affected when an especially low percentage of the population has a college degree?
3. What kinds of businesses, industries, or professionals are more likely to locate in a state with a very high percentage of its population having a college education?
4. How might the politics, the health care system, or science be influenced by the high or low levels of education within the state?
5. Look at the states that have especially high or especially low levels of the population with college degrees. What might be some causes for these high or low rates of college graduation? Provide some results. Check the statistics on your state or province.
6. What else can we learn or do you notice? What questions does this map raise?

other key institutions in society. In our high-tech age, critical thinking and analytical skills are more essential for problem solving than rote memorization, and this fact is reflected in curriculum change. Thus, the curriculum changes to meet the changing needs of people in new social circumstances. Familiarity with technological equipment—computers, Internet resources, electronic library searches, and so forth—becomes a critical survival skill. Lack of training in these areas by some members of the population fosters further division of social classes and reduced chances for social mobility.

India has top-ranked technology institutes, and the highly skilled graduates are employed by multinational companies around the world. Companies in Europe and the United States also send information to India for processing and receive it back the next morning because of the time difference. Well-trained, efficient engineers and computer experts working in India for lower wages than workers in many highly developed countries have become an essential part of the global economy (Friedman 2005).

Enhancing Personal and Social Development. Do you remember your first day of elementary school? For many it marks a transition between the intimate world of the family and an impersonal school world that emphasized discipline, knowledge and skills, responsibility, and obedience. In school, children learn that they are no longer accepted unconditionally as they typically were in their families. Rather, they must meet certain expectations and compete for attention and rewards.

In school, children are taught educational and social skills and ethical conduct that will enable them to function in society. For example, in addition to the three *R*s, they learn to get along with others, resolve disputes, stay in line, follow directions, obey the rules, take turns, be kind to others, be neat, tell the truth, listen, plan ahead, work hard, meet deadlines, and so on. Children worldwide begin learning what schools expect of them in preschool and kindergarten, providing the basis for schooling in the society (Neuman 2005). In the functionalist view, the prosocial values and social competencies learned in academic boot camp are necessary for social cohesion and social order (Gracey 1967).

Conflict Perspectives on Stratification and Education

Fortunate students around the world receive elite educations, but many others do not. Critics of functionalism emphasize the role of education in social stratification and competition between groups. They focus on the impact education or lack thereof has on children's life chances and unequal opportunity in society. In part, this disparity is because of class, race, and gender differences between children.

Consider the following example of social stratification in education: Attendance at an elite school is a means of attaining high social status. Graduates of British "public" schools (similar to U.S. private or preparatory schools), American preparatory (prep) schools, private high schools, and international schools in countries around the world attend the best universities and become leaders of government, business, and the military. Elite preparatory (prep) schools in England, Japan, the United States, and many other countries traditionally have been the training ground for the sons and daughters of the elite.

Schoolgirls in Kenya wait for classes to begin. Children like this, whose parents can afford to send them to school, will likely grow up with enough education to have better economic prospects. Conflict theorists point out ways that inequality is deeply embedded in schooling and how it fosters even more inequality.

Because elite schools are very expensive and highly selective, affluent members of society have the most access to them and thereby learn class privilege and advantage (Howard and Gaztambide-Fernandez 2010; Persell and Cookson 1985; Wade 2012). Elite schools perpetuate elevated prestige and "reproduce social class" (Khan 2011). Many leaders of former colonized countries have had the opportunity to study abroad, perpetuating Global North influence in Global South countries. Those not born into positions of advantage have very limited chances to participate in elite education and leadership positions.

According to conflict theory, when elites of society protect their educational advantages, the result is **reproduction of class**—*the socioeconomic positions of one generation passing on to the next.* This process takes place in part through the socialization of young people into adult work roles and compliance with the modern economic and political institutions and their needs. Schools teach students from lower socioeconomic positions to obey authority and accept the dominant ideology that justifies social inequality. If citizens believe that those with the best educations and jobs in their society personally earned them, they are not motivated to change the system. By promoting the legitimacy of the system, schools serve the interests of the privileged (Bowles and Gintis 2002; Collins 2004).

At a macro level, conflict theorists see institutions, including education, as tools of powerful affluent groups to ensure that their self-interests are met. Educational opportunities are manipulated in ways that keep the sons and daughters of the haves in positions of privilege, while lower-class children are prepared for less prestigious and less rewarding positions in society. If schools do not provide equal educational opportunities for all children in a society, as conflict theorists contend, then students cannot compete equally in the job market.

The cultural values and social norms of the dominant group, such as ideas of etiquette, proper ways of speaking and writing, and notions of deference to superiors, are transmitted to all social classes and legitimated through formal schooling. Other definitions of reality from other ethnic or socioeconomic groups are marginalized. Studies comparing working-class schools with upper-middle-class schools and private schools with public schools support this view, revealing structural differences in the ways schools are organized that reinforce class differences, especially among the poorest children (Kozol 2005, 2012). According to conflict theorists, this process enhances power and confirms the privileges of the dominant group. The education system is not equally beneficial to all or even to the majority of citizens in society. In addition, private schools sometimes become sanctuaries for those who do not want race- and class-integrated schools, perpetuating religious, economic, and racial segregation.

Some children from non-elite families have access to choice and voucher plans allowing students and parents to choose their schools. Critics of choice and voucher plans fear that public schools might be left with the least capable students and teachers, further stratifying an already troubled system. This issue was at the root of the Chicago teachers' union strike in September 2012 that closed down the schools for more than a week (Chubb and Moe 1990; Tareen and Keyser 2012).

Zimbabwe once had one of the best education systems in Africa, but after a severe economic crisis in the country, educational conditions have declined rapidly. Still, some children are privileged over other children, who do not get any education. This system that provides education only for the privileged protects the interests of the elite.

Having explored some lenses through which sociologists analyze education systems, we now focus on the classrooms, corridors, local schools, and key players where the everyday drama of teaching and learning plays out.

Thinking Sociologically

Consider the community in which you went to high school. Do you think the education there enhances upward social mobility and serves all students and the community, or does it mostly serve the affluent, reproducing social class and training people to fulfill positions at the same level as their parents?

Can Schools Bring About Equality in Societies?

Equal opportunity exists when all people have an equal chance of achieving high socioeconomic status in society regardless of their class, ethnicity, race, or gender (Riordan 2004). James Coleman describes the meaning and goals of equal educational opportunity:

- To provide a common curriculum for all children regardless of background
- To provide that children from diverse backgrounds attend the same school
- To provide equality within a given locality (Coleman 1968, 1975, 1990)

In the United States, equal opportunity means that children are provided with equal facilities, financing, and access to school programs. Schools in poor neighborhoods or in rural villages in the United States and around the world, however, often lack the basics—safe buildings, school supplies and books, and funds to operate. Lower-class minority students who live in these areas fall disproportionately to the bottom of the educational hierarchy. Many children face what seem to be insurmountable barriers to educational success: increasing numbers of children living in poverty, lack of health care and immunizations, school absence due to illness or homelessness, or dropouts to help the family (Kozol 2012). These conditions at home and in neighborhoods affect children's achievement in school and test scores (Boger and Orfield 2009; Coleman 1990). Integration of schools, often achieved by busing students to other schools and magnet school programs, became the controversial methods of providing equal opportunity. However, many scholars agree that schools alone cannot create equal opportunity (Jencks 1972). Today, busing and other methods to desegregate schools such as magnet schools and choice plans are in place.

Who Gets Ahead and Why? The Role of Education in Stratification

Education is supposed to be a **meritocracy**, *a social group or organization in which people are allocated to positions according to their abilities and credentials, as in level of education attained.* This, of course, is consistent with the principles of a meritocratic social system where the most qualified person is promoted and decisions are impersonal and based on "credentials" (Charles et al. 2007). Still, in societies around the world, we see evidence that middle-class and elite children, especially boys in the Global South, receive more and better education than equally qualified poor children. Children do not attend school on an equal footing, and in many cases, meritocracy does not exist. Why is Tomás "unlucky" while others succeed? Explanations go beyond a focus on the children's abilities to the analyses of background factors, the ethnic groups, the placements of their families in the stratification system, and the role of their country in the world system. Conflict theorists, in particular, maintain that education creates and perpetuates inequality. The haves hold the power to make sure that institutions, including schools, serve their own needs and protect their access to privileges (Sadovnik 2007). Elite parents have social and cultural capital—language skills, knowledge of how the social system works, and networks—to ensure that their children succeed (Kao 2004).

A country's level of education is a key indicator of quality of life and placement in the global social world. Industrialized countries want to trade with poor countries, which provide natural resources and new pools of workers and consumers. Education helps enable poorer countries and their citizens to participate and compete in global markets. As a consequence, international organizations such as the United Nations and transnational business communities have become more involved in educational development, especially in programs for training workers in technology.

Sources of Inequality

Three sources of inequality in schools—testing, tracking, and funding—illustrate how schools reproduce and perpetuate social stratification. They also give clues as to what might be done to minimize the repetitious pattern of poverty.

Assessing Student Achievement: Testing. Testing is one means of placing students in schools according to their achievement and merit and of determining progress being made. Yet many scholars including sociologists of education argue that standardized test questions, the vocabulary employed, and testing situations disadvantage lower-class, minority, and immigrant students, resulting in lower scores, thus relegating these students to lower tracks in the education system. In addition, in the case of IQ tests, scientists know that intelligence is complex and that paper-and-pencil tests measure only selected types of intelligence (Gardner 1987, 1999; M. Smith 2008). Scholars also question whether the tests have hidden biases based on socioeconomic backgrounds. Higher-class students with better schooling and enriched backgrounds do better on achievement tests, even if they have not gained as much knowledge. Nonetheless, testing is the means used to evaluate student achievement locally, nationally, and internationally. Table 11.4 in the "Engaging Sociology" on page 410 shows differences in ACT (American College Test) and SAT (Scholastic Assessment Test) scores depending on sex, race, and ethnic group. Answer the questions that are posed as you engage with the sociological data.

Governments compare their students' educational test scores on the International Assessment of Educational Progress and the International Association for the Evaluation of Educational Achievement (IEA) with other countries' scores to determine how their students and education systems are performing. These are tests of children around the world in literacy, mathematics, science, civic education, and foreign language.

On one such international education score comparison, the 2009 PISA international test, U.S. students ranked 30 in math, 23 in sciences, and 17 in reading. Researchers point out that the United States is much more heterogeneous than most countries, and that if U.S. schools were equal the scores would be higher. As it stands, many schools in the United States can compete with the best in the world, but others cannot (Berliner 2001; Hassard 2012).

Educational inequality among countries results in differences in achievement. For example, some countries rank higher in math and science, but the same countries do not always rank high in reading. East Asian countries routinely score high in math and science achievement. Many educators believe that gleaning ideas and adapting methods from other successful systems will help improve scores, but in fact, cultural context determines what will be successful, and not all methods work in all countries (Houlihan 2005; Zhao 2005).

Student Tracking. How easy it is to judge children on their appearance, names, addresses, language usage, and test scores; yet these judgments by school administrators, counselors, and teachers affect children for a lifetime. Tracking (sometimes called *streaming*) places students in ability groups, presumably to allow educators to address students' individual learning needs. Many sociologists of education have argued against tracking, pointing out that it contributes

Engaging Sociology

Test Score Variations by Gender and Ethnicity

Evaluate your testing experiences and compare them to those of other groups:

Table 11.4 **ACT and SAT Scores by Sex and Race/Ethnicity**

ACT Scores: 2010	*Average*	*SAT Scores: 2011*	*Average*
Composite, total scores	21	SAT Writing, all students	489
Male	21.2	Male	482
Female	20.9	Female	496
White	22.3	White	516
African American	16.9	Black/African American	417
American Indian/Alaska Native	19.0	American Indian/Alaska Native	465
Hispanic	18.6	Hispanic	444
Asian American/Pacific Islander	23.4	Asian/Pacific Islanders	528
SAT Scores: 2011	*Average*	SAT Math, all students	514
SAT Critical Reading, all students	497	Male	531
Male	500	Female	500
Female	495	White	535
White	528	Black/African American	427
Black/African American	428	Hispanic	463
Hispanic	451	Asian/Pacific Islander	595
Asian/Pacific Islanders	517	American Indian/Alaska Native	488
American Indian/Alaska Native	484		

Source: National Center for Education Statistics (2011, 2012a).

Sociological Data Analysis:

1. Were your scores an accurate measure of your ability or achievement? Why or why not?
2. What other factors such as your gender or ethnicity enter in?
3. Have your scores affected your life chances? Are there ways in which you have been privileged or disprivileged in the testing process?
4. What might be some causes of the variation in test scores between groups or categories of students?

to the stratification process that perpetuates inequality. Research finds that levels at which students are tracked correlate with factors such as the child's background and ethnic group, language skills, appearance, and other socioeconomic variables (Rosenbaum 1999; Wells and Oakes 1996). In other words, track placement is not always a measure of a student's ability. It can be arbitrary, based on teachers' impressions or questionable test results. Even language differences between teachers and students can affect placement. Over time, differences in children's achievement become reinforced. Students from lower social classes and minority groups are clustered in the lower tracks and complete fewer years and lower levels of school (Lucas and Berends 2002; Oakes et al. 1997). School failure in early adolescence leads to other problems later on that affect employment and socioeconomic status (Chen and Kaplan 2003).

Still, other research indicates that students do better in school when working in groups based on their achievement levels. In comparing Massachusetts middle schools that track students with those that have "detracked" students, researchers found that schools that track in math courses have more advanced math students than those that do not (Loveless 2009). The bottom line is that if a school district does track students, it should find ways to eliminate possible race or gender bias, and students should be tracked in each subject independently, not in a single track for all subjects.

Some school districts have accomplished both integration and tracking by establishing magnet schools. These plans draw students from around the districts to learning centers of excellence focused on science, the arts, and other subject areas. The Obama administration funded a number of STEM (science, technology, engineering, and math) high schools to attract students to the science fields.

The magnet school concept has only been partially successful in desegregating schools. Most children bused have been black, and many parents sent their children to the closest school regardless of the program offered. Yet magnet schools have made desegregation palatable. Many districts struggle to understand how to integrate schools and improve student achievements. Some proposed solutions include magnet schools such as those discussed earlier, charter schools, and publicly owned schools.

Tracking also takes place in postsecondary educational settings. Some community and technical colleges have been forming partnerships with industries to educate students for specific available jobs, tracking some students into specific occupations. Even President Obama pushed these partnerships as mutually beneficial (CASE 2012). While this is useful to students in securing a job, critics argue that it is minorities and students from low-income families who are directed toward these programs. The jobs often do not have many options for promotion into higher-paying positions.

Thinking Sociologically

Were you tracked in any subjects? What effect, if any, did this have on you? What effect did tracking have on friends of yours? How might tracking shape friendship networks?

School Funding. The amount of money available to fund schools and the sources providing it affect the types of programs offered, an important issue for nations that must compete in the global social and economic system. Money for education comes, in some societies, from central governments and, in others, from a combination of federal, state, and local government and private sources, such as tuition, religious denominations, and philanthropies. In Uganda, for example, the government runs the schools, but most of the funding comes from tuition paid by each student or by the student's family.

Whatever the source, schools sometimes face budget crises and must trim staff and programs. In the United States, unequal public school spending results from reliance on local property taxes. States fund about 48% of elementary and secondary school budgets from income taxes, corporate taxes, sales taxes, and fees. Local districts provide about 44%, mostly from property taxes. About 8% comes from the federal government (*Education Week* 2011).

Spending is closely related to the racial and class composition of schools and to student achievement levels. Schools in low-income communities are particularly disadvantaged by smaller tax bases and fewer local resources (Condron and Roscigno 2003). Wealthier districts, on the other hand, can afford better education for their children because more money is collected from property taxes. Higher-class students have advantages not available in poor districts (*Education Week* 2011; Kozol 1991, 2005). Controversies over equitable school funding in the United States have reached the courtroom in a number of states, but overall, the United States spends less money per student on education than most other Global North nations.

"The Little Red School Bus," sponsored by the nonprofit Christian Appalachian Project, helps residents in rural Kentucky prepare for high school equivalency certificates and a better chance of finding a job. This may be the only chance for an education these people will experience.

This computer class is held at a formerly failing inner-city British school, transformed by new management and increased governmental funding. Many students come from situations that present educational challenges: having refugee status, living in temporary shelters, or being from non-English-speaking homes. However, the school is highly successful and has become a "government beacon school" in Britain.

Thinking Sociologically

Educational needs at the micro (individual) level, the meso (institutional or ethnic group) level, and the macro (national) level can be very different. This raises the question of who makes decisions and whether individual needs or societal needs take precedence. Where do you think the primary authority for decision making should be—local, state, or national level? Why?

In addition to the structural features of schools as organizations, education is interconnected with national and global forces in interesting and complex ways. We turn next to the issue of social policy affecting education.

Educational and Social Policy Issues

In the 21st century, school systems around the world face dramatic changes. The need for technological training of citizenry, increased demand for access to high school and higher education, changes in the student composition of the classroom, and accountability and testing of students and teachers are but a few of the many issues facing schools. Because education reflects societal politics and problems, policies swing from conservative to liberal and back again, depending on who is in power and what their agenda is for change.

Recently in the United States, the issues of accountability, standardized testing, and teaching basic skills have been at the forefront of educational policy, but movements toward individualization of education and developing the whole child are reappearing (ASCD 2013; The Whole Child 2012). Although the past century brought some improvement in equality in education, much remains to be done to level the playing field (King 2006). The greatest barrier to equal education in the 21st century, both within and between countries, may prove to be socioeconomic, with many minorities represented in lower classes. Sociologists of education contribute to the policy discussions in their roles as researchers, consultants, policy analysts, and public sociologists.

Educational Policies in the United States

What path should nations take to improve their education systems? In the United States there is constant debate about fair and equitable funding policies, about the best methods of teaching children, about accountability, and about many other issues. At the core of these issues lies the question of *who* should make decisions about education. Should the centralized leadership of the federal government be dominant so that there is some coherence and consistency in educational policy across states? Should states that provide the majority of funding for schools determine educational policies? Should local districts have most power since they know the local situation and needs?

Today, despite numerous U.S. government policies and reports, the data on school success show a worsening picture. There are 27 million functionally illiterate U.S. citizens, with many 17-year-olds unable to write well or solve mathematical problems and lacking the basic skills needed to enter business and the military. Although the high school graduation rate had increased from 2001 to 2010, there were still 1,550 high schools in the United States in which 60% of students did not graduate on time (Layton 2012).

Although the federal government pays only about 8% of school funding, federal policies have a major impact on local school decisions. We have already discussed President Obama's administration's modifications of the No Child Left Behind program and his "Race to the Top" initiative for schools. The Obama plan also called for placing new emphasis on "zero to five" (preschool) education.

Changes are also in store for higher education where some propose that community college education should be free. Also, tuition may be waived for those who become long-term teachers, and tax credits may be given for community service and college tuition. What both Presidents Bush and Obama have in common is increased centralization of power in the federal government, establishing standards of learning.

Early-childhood education has been touted as providing the start that many children need to be successful in school, as discussed later. Compensatory education helps narrow the opportunity gap. Evaluations of the Head Start program in the United States, designed for 3- to 5-year-olds from disadvantaged backgrounds, show that it increases the likelihood that enrolled children stay in school, receive preventive health care, avoid later remedial classes, and do not become juvenile delinquents. Comparing early-childhood education programs, research in China, India, Brazil, Canada, and Europe demonstrates similar findings. Yet in the United States less than half of the eligible children take part in the program due to fluctuations in support as political administrations change.

Occasionally private policy makers initiate school programs that provide models for other schools. One example is public sociologist Geoffrey Canada who has had success with implementing programs for poor children in Harlem, from preschool to high school, as discussed in the next "Sociologists in Action" feature on page 414.

Global Policy Issues in Education

Most societies view the education and training of young people as an economic investment in the future. Countries with capitalist economic systems are more likely to have an education system that stresses individualism and competition, pitting students against one another for the best

Two young girls use the computers in a classroom during a Head Start program. The Head Start program introduces reading and writing to children who are about to enter elementary school. It is one federal effort in the United States to provide support to children from poor neighborhoods and families.

Sociologists in Action—Geoffrey Canada

Harlem Children's Zone

The United States is "the land of opportunity," but not for residents of Harlem, according to Geoffrey Canada. In Harlem, the goal is to avoid being beaten, shot, or raped. Geoffrey Canada has an ambitious agenda—to break the cycle of poverty and have all young people in the Harlem Children's Zone graduate from college. Sometimes policy agendas are forwarded by citizens who have knowledge, organizational skills, and a saleable idea to raise funds. Canada's life experience prepared him to work as a social activist and educator. He grew up in the South Bronx, was raised by a single mom, and then had a lucky break. He moved to the suburbs with his grandparents and from there received a college degree from Bowdoin College and a master's from the Harvard Graduate School of Education.

Having been given an opportunity for education, he is now giving back to the community. As president and CEO of the Harlem Children's Zone in New York, he works with students to increase high school and college graduation rates. The Harlem Children's Zone started out as a 24-block area of Harlem but has grown to 97 blocks due to its success. In the 97-block neighborhood, his center follows the academic careers of youth, providing social, medical, and educational services that are free to the 10,000 children who live in the Zone. He has built his own charter school, the Promise Academy, with 1,200 students in Grades K through 10, soon to be through 12th grade. Tuition to the school is free, and admission is done by lottery. For those who do not win the school's admissions lottery, Harlem Children's Zone still provides services to everyone in the Zone, including parenting classes, preschool language classes, school preparation classes, and SAT tutoring.

The Promise Academy has long days and a short summer vacation, a dress code, and strict discipline. The student-teacher ratio is 6 to 1. For students who work hard and achieve, there are rewards. Canada is not apologetic about "buying" the students' cooperation. Some get free trips to Disneyland for good grades, and others get paid for good high school grades.

The Zone is not cheap to run, but Canada points out that the costs of a child ending up in the criminal justice system are much greater, for if a child fails, the community and society have also failed. Therefore, he believes that the investment is sound. The program costs $76 million a year, or $5,000 per child. Much of the funding comes from the business community and Wall Street. That may sound like a lot of money, but the national average in 2006 was more than $9,000 per student, and the average expenditure per student for the state of New York was nearly $15,000 (U.S. Census Bureau 2008b). To test the effectiveness of the school and program, a Harvard economics professor studied the data from tests of achievement and other academic indicators. He found that the Promise Academic elementary school had closed the gap in math and reading between its students and students in white or mixed schools, and outperformed many of the comparison schools. Those middle school students who started at the Promise Academy were behind, but they caught up with students in comparison schools. According to the evaluator, the results were "stunning."

The project has been called "one of the biggest social experiments of our time" (Tough 2008; see also Harlem Children's Zone 2009). Because of the proven success of the Harlem Children's Zone, U.S. President Obama has taken notice and plans to replicate the model in 20 other cities across the nation.

* * * * * * *

Note: Geoffrey Canada received his undergraduate degree from Bowdoin College and his master's in education from Harvard. He has written several books and articles, including *Reaching Up for Manhood: Transforming the Lives of Boys in America* (1998).

grades and the best opportunities. The elites often ensure that their own children get a very different education than the children of the laboring class. Socialist and traditional economic systems often encourage cooperation and collaboration among students, with the collective needs of society viewed as more important than those of individuals. The social and economic values of the society are reflected in approaches to learning and in motivation of students (Rankin and Aytaç 2006).

Other studies compare the curricula of nations and changes in those curricula to determine how similar and different they are. Findings generally support a convergence of curricular themes across nations, reflecting the interdependence of nations. However, many researchers question whether that convergence is good for all people in all societies, especially students from peripheral Global South countries.

Political and economic trends outside a country can also have an impact on the education system within the country. Examples of external influences include technological trends, new inventions, and new knowledge. Even an event such as the terrorist attacks on the World Trade Center and the Pentagon on September 11, 2001, shapes the school curricula, as schools give greater weight to patriotism. In addition to loyalty, however, schools often need to teach people to accept those who are different from themselves—that is, to reduce prejudice.

Education of Girls Around the Globe

"One of the silent killers attacking the developing world is the lack of quality basic education for large numbers of the poorest children in the world's poorest countries—particularly girls" (Sperling 2005:213). In 2011, 55% of out-of-school children were girls, and two-thirds of illiterate adults were women (Global Campaign for Education 2011). Another 150 million dropped out of primary school. About 47% of children in sub-Saharan Africa are not in school, and 54% of those children are girls (EFA Global Monitoring Report 2009). Of the 793 million illiterate adults worldwide, 64% were women, and female literacy rate in the world is 79.2% compared to 88.3% for men. The lowest literacy rates are in sub-Saharan Africa (World Factbook 2012c, 2012g).

An important factor in access to education is where one lives. In Niger, for instance, only 12% of the girls in rural areas are in primary school compared with 83% in the capital city, Niamey. In refugee camps in Africa, only 6% of children receive any secondary education due to hardships from lack of teachers, the impact of AIDS, and orphaned status. Even when children do receive some primary education, the quality is such that many children leave school without basic skills (UNESCO 2005). For example, in just two refugee camps in Djibouti, Africa, 29,000 children do not go to school because there are no classrooms or teachers, and no toilets or exercise books (AlertNet 2012).

The availability of clean drinking water is a major issue in the Global South. Because women and girls must spend as much as six hours a day carrying water home (26% of a woman's day in Africa), the daughters are needed to care for children. When wells were built and usable water became more accessible, the school attendance of girls immediately increased by 11% because of better sanitation and local access to water. Indeed, research by WaterAid estimates that in the Global South, 443 million school days are lost each year due to water-related issues and diseases (Foundation Source Access 2013; WaterAid 2013).

What is clear is that when girls are educated, the consequences are great: "What is striking is the breadth of benefits derived from educating girls—not only economic benefits in terms of higher wages, greater agricultural

The Central Asia Institute is a nonprofit organization that builds schools in Afghanistan and Pakistan, an initiative that has been especially important for girls who had previously been low priority for learning to read and write. These girls work together in a Central Asia Institute school funded mostly by donors in the United States—another example of the global links across the globe.

Recent controversy in France has focused on Islamic girls and women wearing the traditional head covering (hijab) to schools—including a school fair where hula hoops are played. French officials thought the distinctive dress was a contributor to the "we" versus "they" polarization between Muslims and non-Muslims. Many scholars insist that societies work better when there is diversity and tolerance of diversity rather than sameness and conformity.

Because women in the Global South must carry water as much as six hours a day for their families, the lack of a local well affects school attendance for girls. The daughters are often needed to either fetch the water or stay home with young children while the mother totes the filled water jugs.

In Namibia, as elsewhere around the world, education is increasingly necessary as the economy is globalized and skills in literacy and numeracy become critical to survival and hopes of prosperity.

productivity, and faster economic growth, but also health benefits" (Sperling 2006:274). More educated girls and women tend to be healthier; have lower fertility rates and lower maternal, infant, and child mortality; provide greater protection against HIV/AIDS; have increased labor force participation and earnings; provide better health care and education to their children; lift households out of poverty; and have greater ability to pass on these benefits to the next generation (World Bank 2012a).

Marrying at a young age and sex without contraception are dramatically reduced when girls are in school and learn about AIDS. Girls in Uganda are only one-third as likely to be HIV-positive if they have had some secondary education (Sperling 2005). In China, better-educated citizens hold more egalitarian gender attitudes, and in Turkey, gender inequalities in education are lessened in metropolitan areas and in less patriarchal families (Rankin and Aytaç 2006; Shu 2004). In Taiwan, the education of girls is raising the standards of living for their families (Jao and McKeever 2006).

Thinking Sociologically

How might education be important to children in a rural agricultural area? How might education in a local community or refugee camp be affected by global events, such as a war or a worldwide economic recession?

The Future of Education in the Global System

The search for the perfect model of education is never ending. School systems around the world are under pressure to meet the diverse needs of both the societies as a whole and their individual citizens. A major concern in Global North countries in the Information Age is this: What will become of those students who do not complete enough education to fit into the technological and economic needs in the 21st century? In these countries, high school used to prepare most young people for a job and marriage. By the 1990s in the Global North, high school was preparation for college, which was itself necessary to find a decent job in the globalizing world. Although the value of going into debt to receive a college education is debated today, most studies show that those with college degrees receive much higher salaries and lifelong earnings (McArdle 2012). In the United States, educators, corporations, wealthy individuals, and philanthropies—concerned that minority groups are falling behind—support special programs to reduce the technological divide between the haves and the have-nots, the latter composed of poor and minority families (Attewell 2001).

The role of technology in the future of education is expanding, and the technological cyber gap may be closing in some parts of the world. However, there are differences in the implementation of new innovations and ways computers are used. Global South countries will need to invest in Internet bandwidth and other technologies to allow citizens to close the gap, and this is slowly being achieved as fiber-optic cable is laid various places around the world (*Science Daily* 2011a). Electronic textbooks and materials have potential to give both the affluent Global North and the poor Global South immediate access to new knowledge and ideas that can continually be updated through e-textbooks. Some predict that e-texts will replace most paper texts within five years in Global South countries (TechWench 2010).

Video games are used by corporations, the government, and the military to educate. Advocates argue, "They let people participate in the world. They let players . . . *inhabit* roles that are otherwise inaccessible to them" (Shaffer et al. 2005:105). Much learning will take place without walls, clocks, or age segregation as students study via distance learning and through digital technology on their own time. Classrooms of the future will incorporate technological innovations and use information networks.

One form of technology that is having a major impact on the future is the Internet. The next "Sociology Around the World" (page 418) discusses application of the Internet and other computer technologies to higher education.

Computer and Internet skills are essential to success in college and most jobs in this globalized social world. Many courses, even degrees, can now be done online.

Thinking Sociologically

First, read about distance education on the previous page. How might distance learning in higher education affect segments of the population—the poor, the working class, the middle class—differently? What implications does it have for equal access to education for ethnic groups? People of color? Men and women? In what ways would it be beneficial, and in what ways might it cause new problems?

The link between school completion and work, or what is referred to as the *school-to-work transition*, is clearly defined and planned by public policy in most European countries and Russia. Schools offer postsecondary options such as vocational school and associate degrees to prepare young people for available skilled positions, and the numbers of needed engineers, doctors, or dentists determine the educational slots available in these fields (Kerckhoff 2001). However, these options are poorly defined in other countries, especially the United States. The mismatch between jobs available and over-educated students seeking work results in dissatisfaction (Brooks and Waters 2010; Levinson 2010). This problem has been accentuated by the current job crisis in the United States.

In the process of governments developing their educational policies, we again see the interconnections of our social world. Curricula respond to global events and international markets and are also shaped by micro-level effectiveness or ineffectiveness of teachers and students in individual classrooms. The macro-level concerns and the micro-level processes come together in education, with the ultimate objective of preparing individuals in each classroom to meet the needs of the community, the state, the nation, and the world.

Sociology Around the World

Distance Education: Breaking Access Barriers?

By Amy J. Orr

Technology has had a tremendous impact on education. Computers are used in a variety of ways in classrooms around the world for both the consumption and the production of knowledge. The Internet, as well as programs such as WebCT and Blackboard, has made the distribution of education around the world much more feasible. Today, thousands of individuals worldwide can obtain a college degree while sitting in front of their computers.

According to the U.S. Department of Education (2004–05), distance learning is defined as "an option for earning course credit at off-campus locations via cable television, Internet, satellite classes, videotapes, correspondence courses, or other means." In 2008, about two thirds (66%) of postsecondary institutions in the United States offered distance education courses, and the number continues to increase. Around the world, distance education is available in both Global North and Global South countries (National Center for Education Statistics 2006).

One of the primary purposes of distance learning is to increase access by learners who might not ordinarily be able to obtain a traditional postsecondary education. For example, distance education courses are often heavily used by nontraditional students who wish to continue their education but face barriers such as family or employment. Questions arise, however, regarding the level of accessibility that is truly provided to underrepresented groups throughout the United States and the world. Does distance education provide new opportunities for these groups to attain postsecondary education? Or are new barriers created due to the increasing use of technology to deliver a college curriculum?

In an attempt to address these questions, a study of California's higher education system finds that distance education can increase students' access to college and efficiency of gaining an education (Chapman 2010). The National Postsecondary Education Cooperative (NPEC) concluded that (1) distance education increases overall access to postsecondary education, (2) a "digital divide" still remains for some groups, such as blacks and Hispanics, (3) a "dearth of germane information, literacy barriers, and limited diversity of content are significant barriers to getting lower income users online," and (4) low-income students are less likely than those with higher incomes to have opportunities to gain the skills required to use the technology (NPEC 2004).

Similar issues arise on a global level. Access to technology differs significantly by nation. Like disadvantaged students in the United States, individuals in the least developed nations may face literacy barriers or find the curriculum irrelevant. An additional concern arises with regard to diversity of cultural contexts and perspectives. Numerous studies report cross-cultural differences in student learning styles as well as diverse preferences for teaching approaches. For example, Weisenberg and Stacey (2005), on reviewing a number of cross-cultural studies, note that Asian students are accustomed to individualized learning techniques and tend to prefer "teacher-centered" teaching styles. Online pedagogies tend to emphasize collaborative learning and "student-centered" techniques. Because distance learning rests on the technological foundations of Western culture, minority cultures around the world may be further marginalized, as the dominant pedagogies may not be responsive to their cultural uniqueness (Smith and Ayers 2006).

Overall, distance education presents a dilemma with regard to the accessibility of postsecondary education. Although it provides unprecedented opportunities to expand access to education, distance education also runs the risk of creating new divides.

* * * * * * *

Amy Orr received her PhD in sociology from the University of Notre Dame. Her primary area of research is educational inequality, including race, class, and gender differences. She is the George A. Westcott III Distinguished Professor in Sociology at Linfield College.

Education is one of the first institutions after the family that a child encounters, and like the family, it is primarily concerned with the process of socialization of the populace. Another institution that is deeply concerned with socialization and the inculcation of values into young people is religion. Both religion and education tend to address issues of "what" and "why," but whereas education tends to focus on answers that have to do with knowledge—causality and the relationship between facts—religion tends to address questions of ultimate meaning in life. We turn in the next chapter to a sociological perspective on religion.

What Have We Learned?

Education systems are typically viewed as the means to reduce inequality, the source of upward mobility, the way to improve the economy, and the path for reduction of prejudice in societies. However, institutions such as education also have a vested interest in stability. Schools foster patriotism and loyalty toward the political system, families support schools and education, and education is expected to support the economic vitality of the nation. Institutions and organizations are driven by interest in their own survival, and risk-taking behaviors on behalf of change are not necessarily ones that foster survival. Taking risks may threaten those who have power, privilege, and influence. It should not be surprising, therefore, that education does more to enhance stability than to create change. Still, those who seek to improve the society see tremendous potential in education as an agent of change if its influence can be harnessed. It works largely with young minds in the socialization process—carrying out what powerful policy makers feel is important.

Key Points

- Education is one of the primary institutions of society, focusing on the socialization of children and adults into their cultures so that they become contributing members. (See pp. 384–386.)
- At the micro level, various statuses and roles interact within a school, and classrooms develop their own cultures that may or may not enhance learning. (See pp. 386–393.)
- What we learn in schools goes far beyond the formal curriculum. Sometimes these implicit messages support the education system, but sometimes they sabotage the formal and intended messages. (See pp. 393–397.)
- At the micro level, social theory is attentive to interaction in classrooms and local schools, using concepts of symbolic interaction or cost-benefit analysis to understand the climate of learning. (See pp. 387–393.)
- At the meso level, education can be understood as a formal organization that works toward certain goals (bureaucracy) but that has many of the dysfunctions of other bureaucracies. (See pp. 397–403.)
- At the macro level, national governments often try to see that their national needs are met by shaping educational policy, and their actions often create tension with those administrators and teachers at the meso and micro levels who do the actual work of teaching. (See pp. 403–404.)
- Macro-level theories focus on how education supports the social system (functionalism) or on how education serves the interests of the "haves" and reproduces social inequality (conflict theory). (See pp. 404–411.)
- Educating is also a global concern, with a variety of questions about how to help economic development in the Global South without imposing Western models that are incompatible with the cultures of other countries. (See pp. 411–417.)

Discussion Questions

1. Why is a good system of education important for a democracy? How can gaining a sociological perspective help people become more effective participants in a democratic society?
2. Who were the most popular kids in your high school? What made them popular? How did the reasons for their popularity vary based on their gender?
3. How do functionalist and conflict theorists describe the "hidden curriculum" in schools? What description best matches your own school experience? Why?
4. Do you think there should be ability grouping (tracking) in schools? Why or why not? How has tracking (or an absence of tracking) in your schools impacted your education and sense of yourself as a student? How does ability grouping in schools impact society?

5. This chapter describes several ways social class influences educational success. How has your family of origin's social class influenced your educational achievement? How did it influence your selection of a college to attend?

6. How do schools "reproduce and perpetuate social stratification"? If you had the power and desire to use the school system to reduce inequality, what policies would you implement? What do you think the chances are of your policies actually being put into place? Why?

Contributing to Our Social World: What Can We Do?

At the Local Level

- Some colleges and universities have established programs called *FIGs (First-Year Interest Groups)* to assist first-year students as they adjust to college and help them form a community with other students. Learn more about FIGs at schools such as the University of Wisconsin (http://figs.wisc.edu/), the University of Washington (http://fyp.washington.edu/figs/), or the University of Missouri (http://reslife.missouri.edu/fig/). If your school does not have this program, try to initiate one.
- Every college and university provides opportunities for students to *tutor and mentor other students*. Ask the chair of your department how you can help!

At the Organizational or Institutional Level

- Most primary schools welcome *reading and math tutors*, volunteers and service learning students who can read to young students and tutor them in reading and math. Contact a faculty member on your campus who specializes in early-childhood education and investigate the opportunities for such volunteer work.
- *Volunteers of America* (www.voa.org) chapters organize to provide low-income and homeless children with school supplies and backpacks every year through "Operation Backpack." You can learn more about the program and how to locate your local VOA chapter at the VOA website or by Googling "VOA and operation backpack" and the name of your state.

At the National and Global Levels

- *Teach for America* (http://www.teachforamerica.org/), a national organization, modeled along the lines of AmeriCorps and Peace Corps, places recent college graduates in short-term (approximately two-year) assignments teaching in economically disadvantaged neighborhood schools. "Teach for America is the national corps of outstanding recent college graduates and professionals of all academic majors and career interests who commit 2 years to teach in urban and rural public schools and become leaders in the effort to expand educational opportunity. . . . [Its] mission is to build the movement to eliminate educational inequity by enlisting our nation's most promising future leaders in the effort."
- *Teaching abroad* provides an opportunity to make a difference in the lives of children. Consider teaching English abroad through one of many organizations that sponsor teachers. Visit www.globaltesol.com, www.teachabroad.com, www.jetprogramme.org, and related websites.

WWW Visit the Student Study Site at www.sagepub.com/ballantine4e to access additional study tools, including eFlashcards, web quizzes, video resources, audio resources, web resources, SAGE journal articles, recommended readings, and more.

CHAPTER 12

Religion

The Meaning of Sacred Meaning

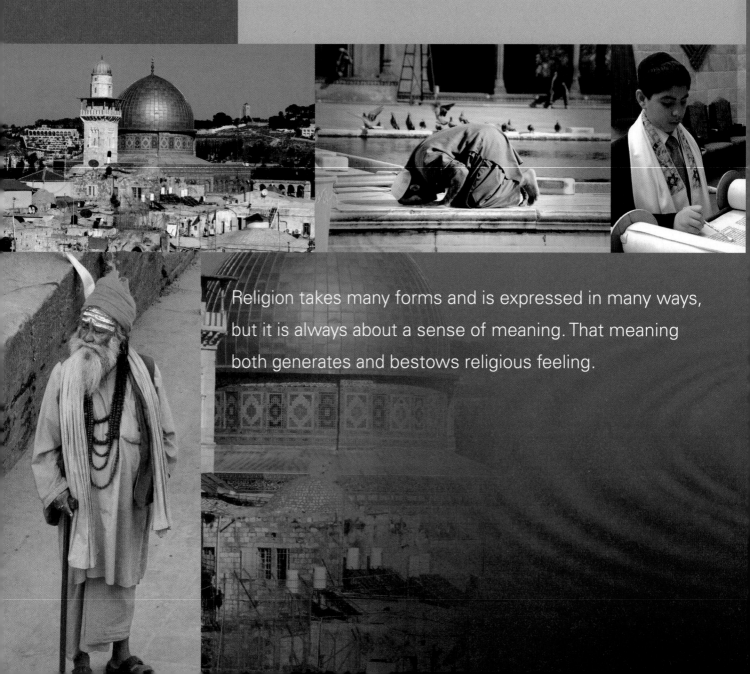

Religion takes many forms and is expressed in many ways, but it is always about a sense of meaning. That meaning both generates and bestows religious feeling.

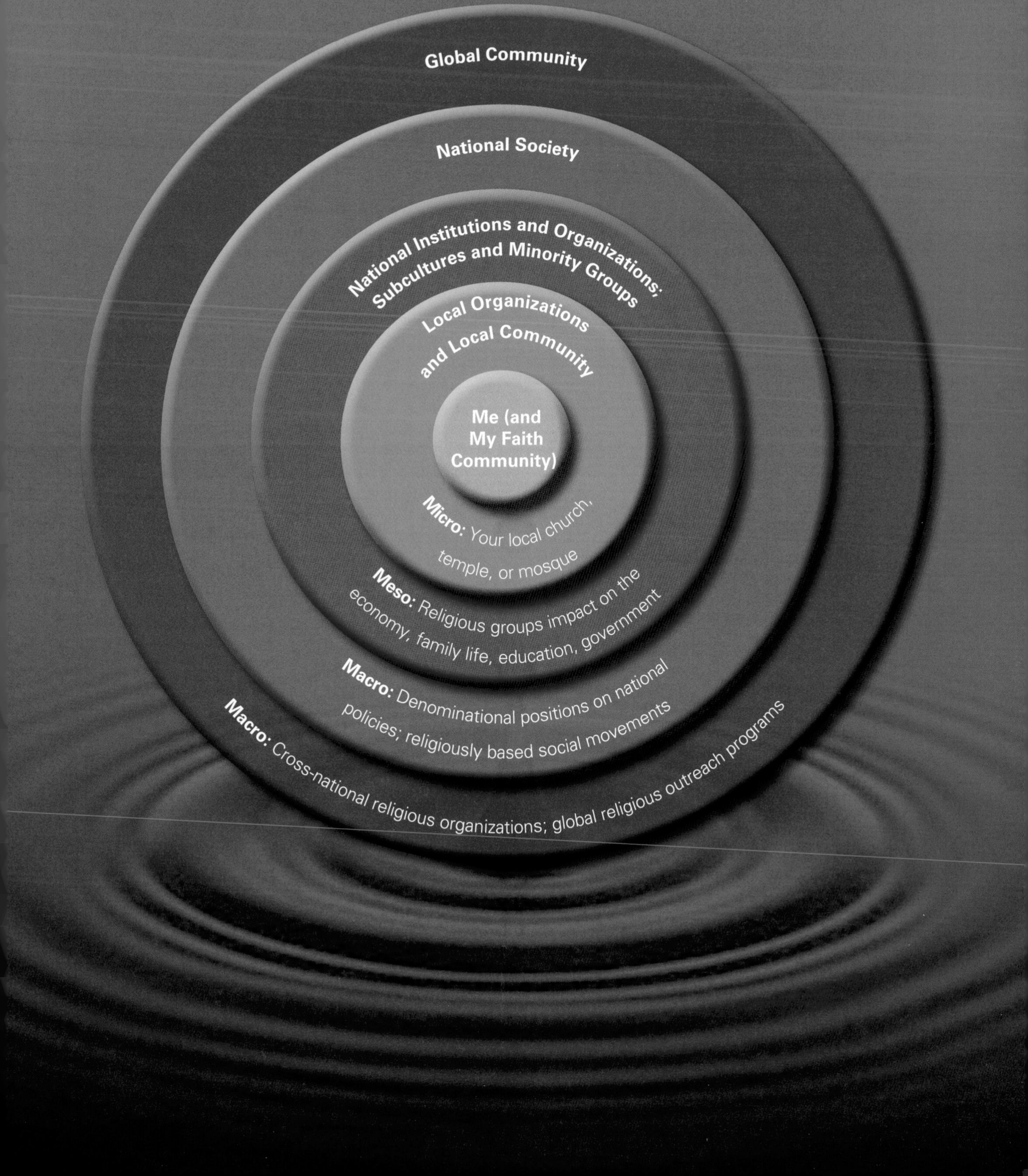

Global Community
National Society
National Institutions and Organizations; Subcultures and Minority Groups
Local Organizations and Local Community
Me (and My Faith Community)
Micro: Your local church, temple, or mosque
Meso: Religious groups impact on the economy, family life, education, government
Macro: Denominational positions on national policies; religiously based social movements
Macro: Cross-national religious organizations; global religious outreach programs

Think About It	
Micro: Me (and My Inner Circle)	How did you become committed to a faith and a church, temple, or mosque, or not become so?
Micro: Local Community	How does your religious congregation interact with the local community?
Meso: National Institutions; Complex Organizations; Ethnic Groups	How does the institutionalization of a religion help it survive?
Macro: National Society	How do religions provide solidarity or conflict within your country?
Macro: Global Community	How do religions help solve world problems (war, poverty, hunger, disease, bigotry) or contribute to them?

What's coming in this chapter?

Abu Salmaan, a Muslim father and shopkeeper in Syria, prays frequently in keeping with the commands of the holy book of his faith. Like his neighbors, when the call to prayer is heard, he comes to the village square, faces Mecca, and prostates himself, with his head to the ground, to honor God and to pray for peace. Doing this five times a day is a constant reminder of his ultimate loyalty to God, whom he calls Allah. As part of the larger Abrahamic religious tradition (which includes Judaism, Christianity, and Islam), he believes in one God and accepts the Hebrew Bible and the authority of Jeremiah, Isaiah, Amos, and Jesus as prophets. He believes that God also revealed Truth through another voice—that of Muhammad. He is devoted, worshipping daily, cherishing his family as directed by his scriptures, giving generously to charities, and making business decisions based on the moral standards of a God-loving Muslim.

Trevor Weaver is a Presbyterian living in Louisville, Kentucky. He attends worship and prays to God in church and during emergencies, when he feels helpless. Trevor had undertaken theological studies at a church-related college, and he has a strong knowledge of the scriptures. When he makes daily decisions, he thinks about the ethical implications of his behavior as "a member of the larger family of God." He opposes prayer in schools because this would make some children feel ostracized. He values diversity and acceptance of other traditions, and he believes each person needs to "work out his own theology." He thinks of himself as a person of faith, but his evangelical neighbor thinks he is a fallen soul.

Tuneq, knowledgeable Netsilik Eskimo hunter that he is, apologizes to the soul of the seal he has just killed. He shares the meat and blubber with his fellow hunters, and he makes sure that every part of the seal is used or consumed—skin, bones, eyes, tendons, brain, and muscles. If he fails to honor the seal by using every morsel or if he violates a rule of hunting etiquette, an invisible vapor will come from his body and sink through the ice, snow, and water. This vapor will collect in the hair of Nuliajuk, goddess of the sea. In revenge, she will call the sea mammals to her so the people living on the ice above will starve. Inuit religion provides rules that help enforce an essential ecological ethic among these arctic hunters to preserve the delicate natural balance.

Before going to bed, Nandi Nwankwo from Nigeria sets out a bowl of milk and some food for the ancestors who, he believes, are present outside the family's dwelling at night. Respected ancestors protect family members, but they are also a powerful and even frightening force in guiding social behavior. Children are told that they must behave or the ancestors will punish them.

These are but a few examples from the world's many and varied religious systems. What they have in common is that each system provides directions for appropriate and expected behaviors and serves as a form of social control for individuals within that society. Whether ancestors, gods, one God, prophets, or elders are watching over us, the sanctions that encourage conformity are strong. Indeed, they are made *sacred*, a realm of existence different from mundane everyday life. Religion, according to Andrew M. Greeley, the well-known Catholic priest and sociologist, pervades the lives of people of faith (Greeley 1989). It cannot be separated from the rest of the social world. Members of societies believe so strongly in their religions that conquests and wars throughout history have been based on spreading or defending the faith.

Sociologists are interested in these relationships—in the way social relationships and structures affect religion and in the consequences of religion for individuals and for society as a whole. In this chapter, we explore religion as a complex social phenomenon, one that is interrelated with other processes and institutions of society. We investigate what religion does for individuals, how individuals become religious, how religion and modern societies interact, and what religious policies have to say about homosexuality, abortion, and other social issues.

What Does Religion Do for Us?

We began this chapter by looking at examples of daily experiences in which religion and society have enormous power over people. What do people have to gain from religious practices, beliefs, and organizations? In short, they may find that religion meets some very basic needs.

Human questions about the meaning of life, the finality of death, or whether injustice and cruelty will ever be ended cannot normally be answered by science or by everyday experience. Religion helps explain the meaning of life, death, suffering, injustice, and events beyond our control. As sociologist Émile Durkheim pointed out, humans generally view such questions as belonging to a realm of existence different from the mundane or profane world of our everyday experience (Durkheim [1915] 2002). He called this separate dimension the *sacred realm.* This sacred realm elicits feelings of awe, reverence, and even fear. It is viewed as being above normal inquiry and doubt. Religious guidelines, beliefs, and values dictate "rights and wrongs," provide answers to the big questions of life, and instill moral codes and ideas about the world in members of each society or subculture. For that reason, religions are extremely important in controlling everyday behavior (Ammerman 2009; Durkheim [1915] 2002).

Thus, religion is more than a set of beliefs about the supernatural. It often *sacralizes* (makes sacred and unquestionable) the culture in which we live, the class or caste position to which we belong, the attitudes we hold toward other people, and the morals to which we adhere. Religion is a part of our lifestyle, our gender roles, and our place in society. We are often willing to defend it with our lives. Around the world, many different people believe quite as strongly as we do that they have found the Truth—the ultimate answers—in their religions. They, too, are willing to die for their faith, which they are convinced is "the only way."

Note the various wars between Hindus and Muslims in India, between Catholics and Protestants in Northern Ireland, or between the two Muslim sects of Sunni and Shiite in several Muslim countries. Although the root causes of these wars are political and economic, religious differences help polarize we-versus-they sentiments. Such conflicts are never exclusively about religion, but religion can convince the members of each group that God is on their side. Religion is an integral part of most societies and is important in helping individuals define reality and determine what is worth living or dying for.

Thinking Sociologically

Consider your own religious tradition. Which of the purposes or functions of religion mentioned above does your religious faith address? If you are not part of a faith community or do not hold religious beliefs, are there other beliefs or groups that fulfill these functions for you?

Components of Religion

Religion normally involves at least three components: (1) a faith or worldview that provides a sense of meaning and purpose in life (which we will call the *meaning system*), (2) a set of interpersonal relationships and friendship networks (which we will call the *belonging system*), and (3) a stable pattern of roles, statuses, and organizational practices (which we will call the *structural system*; Roberts and Yamane 2012).

Meaning System

The *meaning system* of a religion includes the ideas and symbols it uses to provide a sense of purpose in life and to help explain why suffering, injustice, and evil exist. It provides a big picture to explain events that would otherwise seem chaotic and irrational. For example, although the loss of a family member through death may be painful, many people find comfort and hope and a larger perspective on life in the idea of life after death. Most religious people find that a deep love of God (or gods) gives purpose and deep satisfaction to life (discussed later in this chapter).

Because each culture has different problems to solve, the precise needs reflected in the meaning system vary. Hence, different societies have developed different ways of answering questions and meeting needs. In agricultural societies, the problems revolve around growing crops and securing the elements necessary for crops—water, sunlight, and good soil. Meaning systems often reflect these concerns. Among the Zuni of New Mexico and the Hopi of Arizona, water for crops is a critical concern. These Native American people typically grow corn in a climate that averages roughly 10

At this temple in Japan, people write their hopes and wishes on strips of paper, attaching them to ropes and trees as a form of prayer. When their life circumstances seem out of control, people will often appeal to a nonempirical or supernatural source for help, and this provides hope and some sense of meaningful action.

Buddhist monks pray at Bayon Temple in Angkor Thom, Cambodia. Their religious system gives them a sense of meaning and purpose in life, but also provides social ties.

inches of rain per year, so it is not surprising that the central focus of the dances and the supernatural beings—*kachinas*—is to bring rain. In many societies, the death rate is so high that high fertility has been necessary to perpetuate the group. Thus, fertility goddesses take on great significance. In other societies, strong armies and brave soldiers have been essential to preserve the group from invading forces; hence, gods or rituals of war have been popular. Over time, the meaning systems of religion have reflected the needs of the societies in which the religion is practiced.

Belonging System

Belonging systems are profoundly important in most religious groups. Many people remain members of religious groups not so much because they accept the meaning system of the group but because that is where their belonging system—their friendship and kinship network—is found. Their religious group is a type of extended family. In fact, church membership increases as people get older and move through the family life cycle of marriage, childbearing, and child rearing, though the increase is slowing in some denominations (Cline 2008; Religious Tolerance 2006). A prayer group may be the one area in their lives in which people can be truly open about their personal pain and feel safe to expose their vulnerabilities. Irrespective of the meaning system, a person's sense of identity may be very much tied up with being a Buddhist, a Christian, a Muslim, or a follower of some other religion (Kosmin and Keysar 2009; Smith and Denton 2005; Smith and Snell 2009).

The religious groups that have grown the fastest in recent years are those that have devised ways to strengthen the sense of belonging and to foster friendship networks within the group, including emphasis on endogamy—marrying within one's group. If a person is a member of a small group in which interpersonal ties grow strong—a church bridge club, a Quran study group, or even a working committee—he or she is likely to feel a stronger commitment to the entire organization. In short, the belonging system refers to the interpersonal networks and emotional ties that develop among adherents of a particular faith.

Structural System

A religion involves a group of people who share a common meaning system. However, if each person interprets the beliefs in his or her own way and if each attaches his or her own meanings to the symbols, the meaning system becomes so individualized that *sacralization* of common values can no longer occur. Therefore, some system of control and screening of new revelations must be developed. Religious leaders in designated statuses must have the authority to interpret the theology and define the essentials of the faith. The group also needs methods of designating leaders, of raising funds to support their programs, and of ensuring continuation of the group. To teach the next generation the meaning system, members need to develop a formal structure to determine the content and form of their educational materials, and then they must produce and distribute them. In short, if the religion is to survive past the death of a charismatic leader, it must undergo institutionalization. In other words, a *structural system* of established statuses, norms, ways to access resources, and routine procedures for addressing problems must be set up.

Religious institutions embrace several interrelated components: (a) the meaning system, mostly operating at the micro level; (b) the belonging system, critical at the micro level but also part of various meso-level organizations; (c) and the structural system, which tends to have its major impact at the meso and macro levels. These may reinforce one another and work in harmony toward common goals, or there may be conflict between them. When change occurs, it usually occurs because of disruption in one of the systems.

Because religion is one institution in the larger society, it is interdependent and interrelated with the political, economic, family, education, health, and technology systems. Changes in any one of these areas can bring change to religion, and changes in religion can bring changes to other institutions of society. Consider the furor in parts of the United States over the teaching of intelligent design as part of the science curriculum in public schools. The conflict is reverberating in congregations, schools, legislative chambers, courts, and scientific communities.

Although some people dislike the idea of organized religion, the fact remains that a group cannot survive in the modern world unless it undergoes *routinization of charisma*. That is, the religious organization must develop established roles, statuses, groups, and routine procedures for making decisions and obtaining resources (Weber 1947).

At the local level, too, a formal religious structure develops, with committees doing specific tasks, such as overseeing worship, maintaining the building, recruiting religious educators, and raising funds. These committees report to an administrative board that works closely with the clergy (the ordained ministers) and has much of the final responsibility for the life and continued existence of the congregation. The roles, statuses, and committees make up the structural system. The structure is every bit as important as the meaning system if the group is to thrive.

Furthermore, like any other formal organization in society, meso-level religious structures consist of individuals and committees doing specialized tasks. Contemporary Christian denominations in the United States, for example, may have national commissions on global outreach, evangelism, worship, world peace, social justice, and so forth. In addition, bishops, presbyters, or other leaders provide guidelines for the work of several hundred pastors who lead their own congregations. Religious organizations are, among other things, bureaucracies. The formal organization may be caught up in some of the dysfunctions that can plague any organization: goal displacement, the iron law of oligarchy, alienation, and other problems discussed in Chapter 5.

Just as any organization needs data on its effectiveness, religious organizations collect information to help inform policy. The "Sociologists in Action" feature on page 430 describes the work of a sociologist who does research within such a denominational structure.

Thinking Sociologically

Think about the meaning, belonging, and structural systems of a religion with which you are familiar. How do these elements influence and how are they influenced by the larger social world, from individual to national and global systems?

Becoming Part of a Faith Community: Micro-Level Analysis

We are not born religious, although we may be born into a religious group. We learn our religious beliefs through socialization, just as we learn our language, customs, norms, and values. Our family usually determines the religious environment in which we grow up, whether it is an all-pervasive message or a one-day-a-week aspect of socialization. We start imitating religious practices such as prayer before we understand these practices intellectually. Then, as we encounter the unexplainable events of life, religion is there to provide meaning. Gradually, religion becomes an ingrained part of many people's lives.

It is unlikely that we will adopt a religious belief that falls outside the religions of our society. For instance, if we are born in India, we will be raised in and around the Hindu, Muslim, or Sikh faiths. In most Arab countries, we will become Muslim; in South American countries, Catholic; and in many Southeast Asian countries, Buddhist. However, even if we had been born into the family next door, our religion and politics might be different. Indeed,

Sociologists in Action—C. Kirk Hadaway

Research for Religious Organizations

By C. Kirk Hadaway

My interest in research on and for religious institutions began when I worked with my graduate school mentor on a grant studying the growth and decline of denominations. I explored demographic change and church growth, denominational switching, and the impact of new church development on the growth of established denominations.

I am a church research officer, a position that entails everything from mundane gathering of statistics to serious social research. Our office of six persons collects membership, attendance, and giving data from all United Church of Christ (UCC) churches and analyzes those data. We do surveys among our churches, pastors, staff, and lay leaders on a wide variety of topics (issues related to congregational health, leadership, use of denominational resources, beliefs and attitudes, and so forth). I also conduct research on the state of religion/churches in modern society and on social trends that might impact our churches. This research is written up in reports and published in books that give advice to our churches and pastors. I speak to clergy groups regularly on related topics. My clients get an interpretation of data based on broader, sociologically grounded understanding of the religious trends.

I have studied church trends (patterns of growth and decline) using data from local congregations and studies of religious participation and religious marginality. Also, I have conducted large-scale surveys with pastors from several denominations as key informants. It is particularly gratifying to see theories confirmed with real data on real churches.

The least rewarding facets of my job are grunt work (providing routine information) and other aspects of life in a bureaucracy (forms to fill out, committee meetings, staff retreats, performance evaluations, and having one's work ignored due to other agendas).

The most rewarding aspect of my work is the ability to help church leaders see their situation from a different perspective and use that perspective and information to make a positive difference in their work.

* * * * * * *

Note: Dr. C. Kirk Hadaway received his PhD in sociology from the University of Massachusetts Amherst. He has worked for various boards and agencies of the Southern Baptist Convention, has been director of research at the United Church of Christ, and is currently director of research for the Episcopal Church.

although our religious affiliation may seem normal and typical to us, no religion has a majority of the people of this world as its adherents, and we may in fact be part of a rather small minority religious group when we think in terms of the global population. Table 12.1 shows this explicitly.

Learning the meaning system of a religious group is both a formal and an informal process. In some cultures, religious faith pervades everyday life. For the Amish, farming without machines or the use of electricity is part of their Christian teachings, which affect their total lifestyle. Formal teaching in most religions takes place primarily in the temple, church, or mosque. The formal teaching may take the form of Bar or Bat Mitzvah classes, Sunday school, or parochial school. Informal religious teaching occurs when we observe others "practicing what they preach."

One church or temple member may be committed to the meaning system, another to the belonging system through strong friendship networks, and a third to the structural system, making large financial donations to a congregation even though he rarely attends services. In most cases, however, commitment to one of these systems will reinforce commitment to the others. They usually go together (see Figure 12.1).

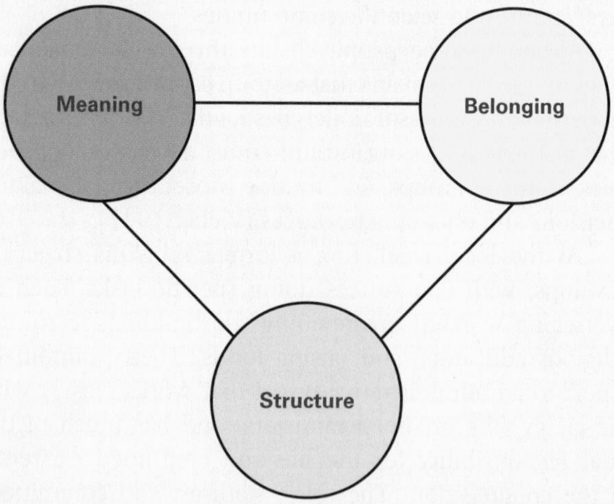

Figure 12.1 The Three Components of Religion

Note: Religious commitment can involve any one or more of these dimensions of religion.

Table 12.1 **Religious Membership Around the Globe**

Religion	*Membership (in Millions)*	*Percentage of World Population*
Christian (Total)	2,280.6	33.0
Roman Catholic	1,150.7	16.7
Independent	419.8	6.1
Protestant	370.7	5.4
Orthodox	270.2	3.9
Anglican	86.1	1.2
Unaffiliated	119.0	1.7
Muslim	1,553.2	22.5
Hindu	942.9	13.6
Nonreligious	659.8	9.6
Buddhist	462.6	6.7
Chinese Folk Religion	454.4	6.6
Atheist	137.6	2.0
Sikh	23.7	0.3
Jewish	14.8	0.2
Spiritist	13.7	0.2
Taoist	8.4	0.1
Baha'i	7.3	0.1
Confucianist	6.5	0.1
Jain	5.3	0.1
Shintoist	2.8	a
Zoroastrian	0.2	a

Source: Barrett, Johnson, and Crossing. 2011. "2010 Annual Megacensus of Religion." *Time Almanac 2011.* Reprinted with permission from *Encyclopedia Britannica Almanac* 2011 Copyright © 2011 by Encyclopedia Britannica, Inc.

Note: Numbers add up to more than the total world population because many people identify themselves with more than one religious tradition. Thus, the percentages will also add up to more than 100%. Percentages are rounded.

a = Less than 0.05%.

Kwanzaa, which means "first fruits of the harvest" in Kiswahili, was initiated in 1966 by Maulana Karenga. It is an African American celebration of the traditional African values of family, community responsibility, and self-improvement. This family celebrates Kwanzaa, which runs from December 26 to January 1. Such rituals create in children a sense of sacredness about certain values and outlooks on life.

The Bat Mitzvah, shown here, is an initiation ceremony into the faith for Jewish girls.

Most people do not belong to a religious group because they accept its belief system. Rather, they come to believe because they want to belong and are socialized to feel they are an integral part of the group (Greeley 1972; Roberts and Yamane 2012). People generally accept the explanation of death, injustice, and suffering provided by the religious group. They feel comfortable sharing similar feelings and beliefs.

Research on people who switch religious affiliations or join new religious movements (NRMs) indicates that loyalty to a friendship network usually comes first, followed by commitment to the meaning and structural systems. In many cases, accepting a new meaning system is the final stage rather than the initial stage of change (Roberts and Yamane 2012).

There is more fluidity in religious membership now than at any time of our history. Historically, most people remained part of the same religious group for a lifetime. A Pew Forum study found that 28% of Americans have left the faith in which they were raised, and 44% of Americans will change their religious affiliation in their lifetime, just as a very high percentage will change their place of residence, their jobs, and even their spouses (Pew Forum on Religion and Public Life 2012b). To illustrate, 62% of Americans age

70 and older are Protestant, but only 43% of those age 18 to 29 are, and younger Americans are more likely to say they are not affiliated with any particular religion. In fact, the increase in interreligious marriages is a factor in the religious switching, as 37% of current marriages involve spouses with different religious affiliations (Pew Forum on Religion and Public Life 2012b). Change is becoming part of the norm in North America, particularly since World War II, and this is affecting religious affiliation as well. Still, the change is likely to be to a new branch of the same religion rather than to an entirely different religious tradition, and when it does involve a more major shift, it is usually because of the increased diversity of our society enabling us to know people from other faith traditions.

Because changing religious groups occurs most often through change of friendship networks, religious groups frequently try to control the boundaries and protect their members from outside influences. The Amish in the United States have done this by living in their own communities and attempting to limit schooling of their children by outside authorities. To help perpetuate religious beliefs and practices, most religious groups encourage endogamy, marrying within the group. For example, Orthodox Jews have food taboos and food preparation requirements that limit the likelihood that they will share a meal with "outsiders."

Religious groups also try to socialize members to make sacrifices of time, energy, and financial resources on behalf of their faith. If one has sacrificed and has devoted one's resources and energy for a cause, one is likely to feel a commitment to the organization—the structural system (Kanter 2005; Sherkat and Ellison 1999). Many young men in the Church of Jesus Christ of Latter-Day Saints (Mormons) devote 2 years of their lives to being missionaries, and young women devote 1 to 1½ years. They must save money in advance to support themselves. This sacrifice of other opportunities and investment of time, energy, and resources in the church creates an intense commitment to the organization. Few of them later feel that they have wasted those years or that the investment was unwise.

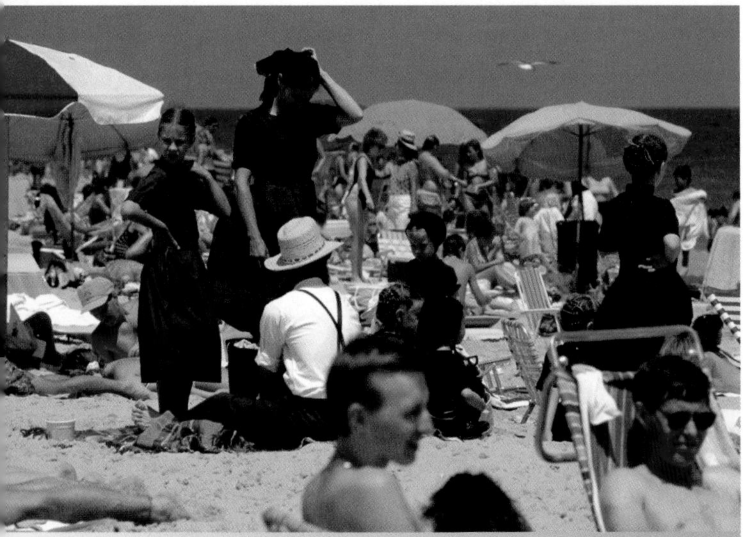

An Amish family enjoys a trip to the beach. The faith of the Amish influences every aspect of their lives, including their beach attire.

The survival of a religious group depends in part on how committed its members are and whether they share freely of their financial and time resources. Most religious groups try, therefore, to socialize their members into commitment to the meaning system, the belonging system, and the structural system of their religion.

Thinking Sociologically

How did you or individuals you know become committed to a faith tradition? Did you think about the process as it occurred?

Symbols and the Creation of Meaning: A Symbolic Interactionist Perspective

Dina is appalled as she looks around the Laundromat. The *gaje* (the term Gypsies use to refer to non-Gypsies) just do not seem to understand cleanliness. These middle-class North American neighbors of hers are very concerned about whether their clothes are *melalo*—dirty with dirt. In contrast, they pay no attention to whether they are *marime*—defiled or polluted in a spiritual sense. She watches in disgust as a woman not only places the clothing of men, women, and children in a single washing machine but also includes clothing from the upper and lower halves of the body together. No respectable Gypsy would allow such mixing, and if it did occur, the cloth could be used only as rags. The laws of spiritual purity make clear that the lower half of the body is defiled. Anything that comes in contact with the body below the waist or that touches the floor becomes *marime* and can never again be considered *wuzho*—truly "clean." Food that touches the floor becomes filthy and inedible.

Ideally, a Gypsy woman would have separate washtubs for men's upper-body clothing, men's lower-body clothing, women's upper-body clothing, women's lower-body clothing, and children's clothing. Gypsies know too well that the spirit of Mamioro brings illness to homes that are *marime*. The lack of spiritual cleanliness of non-Gypsies causes Gypsies to minimize their contact with these *gaje*, to avoid sitting on a chair used by a *gaje*, and generally to recoil at the thought of assimilation into the larger culture (Sutherland 1986; Sway 1988). How we make sense of the world takes place through meaning systems, as illustrated in the above example. For the Gypsies, things have meaning in ways that differ from the ideas that are prominent in the larger society, and the different meanings result in different behaviors and sometimes distancing from "outsiders."

Symbolic interaction theory focuses on how we make sense of the meaning of things and how we construct our worlds. In an ambiguous situation, we seek help from others: Is the situation funny, scary, bizarre, normal, or mysterious? Think about how you feel attracted to, or perhaps put off by, someone who wears a cross or another religious symbol, such as a yarmulke, worn by Orthodox Jewish men to cover the crown of the head, or a head scarf, worn by Muslim women. Symbols affect micro-level interaction—the way we feel about people and whether we are inclined to form a relationship. Note that a Muslim woman may wear a head scarf, and while she finds it a reassuring reminder of her family's long tradition, others may view it as a symbol of women's oppression or even find it a cause for hatred of the "other."

It is the meaning system that most interests symbolic interactionists—the worldview or conceptual framework by which people make sense of life and cope with suffering and injustice. Religious meaning systems are made up of three elements: myths, rituals, and symbols.

Myths are *stories, true or not, that transmit values and embody ideas about life and the world.* When sociologists of religion use the word *myth*, they are not implying that the story is untrue. A myth may relate historical incidents that actually occurred, it may involve fictional events, or it may communicate abstract ideas, such as reincarnation. Regardless of the literal truth or fiction of these stories, myths transmit values and a particular outlook on life. If a story, such as the exodus from Egypt by ancient Hebrew people, elicits some sense of sacredness, communicates certain attitudes and values, and helps make sense of life, then it is a myth. The Netsilik Eskimo myth of the sea goddess Nuliajuk (explained in the third story that opened this chapter) reinforces and makes sacred the value of conservation in an environment of scarce resources. It provides messages for appropriate behavior in that group. Thus, whether a myth is factual or not is irrelevant. Myths are always "true" in some deeper metaphorical sense. Stories that are not true—in some deeper sense—are simply not "myths."

Rituals are *ceremonies or repetitive practices, often to invoke a sense of awe of the sacred and to make certain ideas sacred.* The ceremonies may include music, dancing, kneeling, praying, chanting, storytelling, and other symbolic acts. A number of religions, such as Islam, emphasize devotion to orthopraxy (conformity of behavior) more than orthodoxy (conformity to beliefs or doctrine; Preston 1988; Tipton 1990). Praying five times a day while facing Mecca, mandated for the Islamic faithful, is an example of orthopraxy.

A Romanian Gypsy woman uses different tubs to wash upper- and lower-body clothing and men's and women's apparel separately so that they will not become spiritually defiled.

The yarmulke (skullcap or kippah*) has been worn by Jewish men since roughly the 2nd century CE. It symbolizes respect for and fear of God and serves to remind the wearer of the need for humility: There is always some distance between himself and God. These caps are also a sign of belonging and commitment to the Jewish community.*

Often, rituals involve an enactment of myths. In some Christian churches, the symbolic cleansing of the soul is enacted by actually immersing people in water during baptism. Likewise, Christians frequently reenact the last supper of Jesus (Communion or Eucharist) as they accept their role as modern disciples. Among the Navajo, rituals enacted by a medicine man may last as long as 5 days. An appropriate myth is told, and sand paintings, music, and dramatics lend power and unique reality to the myths.

Muslims pray to God (whom they call Allah) five times a day, removing their shoes and prostrating themselves as they face Mecca. This is an important ritual, and it illustrates that orthopraxy is central for Muslims. Personal devotion, which is expressed in actions, is emphasized in Islam.

The group environment of the ritual is important. Ethereal music, communal chants, and group actions such as kneeling or taking off one's shoes when entering the shrine or mosque create an aura of separation from the everyday world and a mood of awe so that the beliefs seem eternal and beyond question. They become sacralized. Rituals also make ample use of symbols, discussed in Chapters 2 and 4.

A **symbol** is an *object or an action that represents something else and therefore has meaning beyond its own existence; flags and wedding rings are examples.* Because religion deals with a transcendent realm, a realm that cannot be experienced or proven with the five senses, sacred symbols are a central part of religion. They have a powerful emotional impact on the faithful and reinforce the sacredness of myths.

Sacred symbols are in some ways comparable to computer chips in that they both store an enormous amount of information and can deliver that information with powerful immediacy (Leach 1979). Seeing a cross can flood a Christian's consciousness with a whole series of images, events, and powerful emotions concerning Jesus and his disciples. Tasting the bitter herb during a Jewish Seder service may likewise elicit memories of the story of slavery in Egypt, recall the escape under the leadership of Moses, and send a moral message to the celebrant to work for freedom and justice in the world today. The mezuzah, a plaque consecrating a house, fixed to the doorpost of a Jewish home, is a symbol reminding the occupants of their commitment to obey God's commandments and reaffirming God's commitment to them as a people. Because symbols are often heavily laden with emotion and can elicit strong feelings, they are used extensively in rituals to represent myths.

Myths, rituals, and symbols are usually interrelated and interdependent (see Figure 12.2). Together, they form the meaning system—a set of ideas about life or about the cosmos that seem uniquely realistic and compelling. They reinforce rules of appropriate behavior and even political and economic systems by making them sacred. They can also control social relationships between different groups. The Gypsy revulsion at the filthy *marime* practices of middle-class Americans, like the Kosher rules for food preparation among the Jews, creates boundaries between "us" and "them" that nearly eliminate prospects of marriage or even of close friendships outside the religious community. Some scholars think that these rituals and symbolic meanings

Removal of shoes before entering a mosque is an expression of respect for the sacred among Muslims. Hundreds of Iraqi Shiite Muslim pilgrims have arrived to pray at this mosque in northern Baghdad.

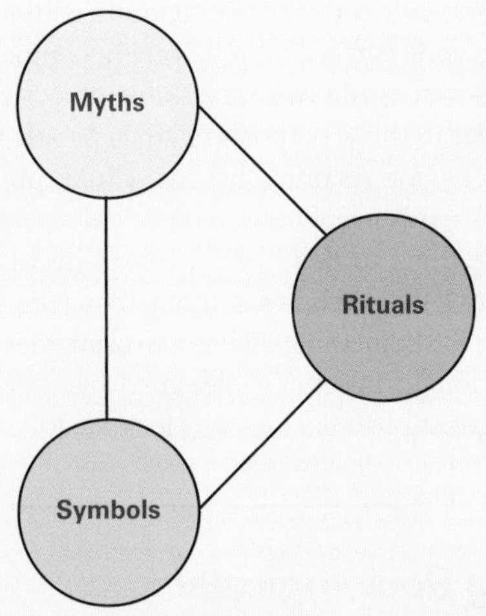

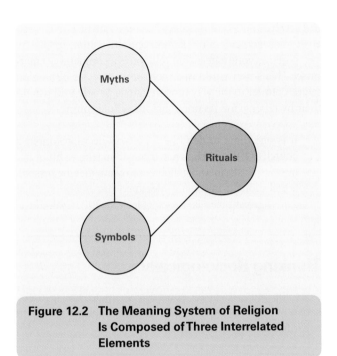

Figure 12.2 The Meaning System of Religion Is Composed of Three Interrelated Elements

Clan totems are part of the cultural and religious tradition of native peoples in northwestern North America, from Oregon to Alaska, and totem poles are used to tell stories. This photo from St. John's United Methodist Church in Anchorage, Alaska, is interesting because it blends local cultural and religious symbols (totem images carved in the wood) with a Christian symbol (the Cross) and includes them in a Christian sanctuary. This totem pole tells the Easter story using Tsimshian symbols.

are the key reason why Gypsies and Jews have survived for millennia as distinct groups without being assimilated or absorbed into dominant cultures. The symbols and meanings have created barriers that prevent the obliteration of their cultures.

When symbolic interactionists study religion, they tend to focus on how symbols influence people's perception of reality and on the role rituals and myths play in defining what is "really real" for people. Symbolic interactionists stress that humans are always trying to create, determine, and interpret the meaning of events. Clearly, no other institution focuses as explicitly on determining the meaning of life and its events as religion.

Thinking Sociologically

In a tradition with which you are familiar, how do symbols and sacred stories reinforce a particular view of the world or a particular set of values and social norms?

Seeking Eternal Benefits: A Rational Choice Perspective

People with religious freedom make rational choices to belong to a religious group or change to another religion after weighing the costs (financial contributions, time involved) and benefits (eternal salvation, a belonging system, and a meaning system) of belonging (Finke and Stark 2005). Rational choice theory is based on an economic model of human behavior. The basic idea is that the process people use to make decisions is at work in religious choices: What are the benefits, and what are the costs? Do the benefits outweigh the costs? The benefits, of course, are nonmaterial when it comes to religious choices—a feeling that life has meaning, confidence in an afterlife, a sense of communion with God, and so forth. This approach views churchgoers as consumers who are out to meet their needs or obtain a "product." It depicts churches as entrepreneurial establishments, or "franchises," in a competitive market, with "entrepreneurs" (ministers) as leaders. Competition for members leads churches to "market" their religion to consumers. Converts, and religious people generally, are thus regarded as active and rational agents pursuing self-interests, and growing churches are those that meet

This advertisement ran in the Daily Sundial, *the paper at California State University, Northridge (CSUN). The church is located only a few miles from the university and hoped to catch, with its student-friendly service (and its targeted marketing), the interest of CSUN students.*

"consumer demand" (Finke and Stark 2005; Jelen 2002). Religious groups produce religious "commodities" (rituals, meaning systems, a sense of belonging, symbols, and so forth) to meet the "demands" of consumers (Christiano, Swatos, and Kivisto 2008).

Rational choice theorists believe that aggressive religious entrepreneurs who seek to produce religious products that appeal to a target audience will reap the benefits of a large congregation. Churches, temples, and mosques are competitive enterprises, and each must make investments of effort, time, and resources to attract and keep potential buyers. There are many religious entrepreneurs seeking to increase their flocks. The challenge is for the various groups to beat the competition by meeting the demand of the current marketplace (Finke and Stark 2005).

For instance, when the United States separated church from state so that most individuals were not automatically members of a state religion, organized religions had to offer a product that would sell to consumers. Indeed, some scholars argue that where religion is an ascribed identity (adopted based on one's family of birth or the country's official religion), it is likely to be much less vigorous than in places where there is a competitive religious marketplace and religion is an achieved identity chosen freely from many options (Finke and Stark 2005; Iannaccone and Bainbridge 2010).

Rational choice theorists believe that when more religious groups compete for the hearts and minds of members, concern about spiritual matters is invigorated, and commitment is heightened. Religious pluralism and spiritual diversity increase the rates of religious activity as each group seeks its market share and as more individual needs are met in the society (Finke and Stark 2005; Iannaccone and Bainbridge 2010).

Not everyone agrees that religion is a competitive enterprise. This strictly utilitarian economic analysis of religion seems counter to the way most religious people understand their own behavior. As one religious scholar put it,

> It is one thing to describe a person's decision to join a church *as if* the person were trying to maximize his or her benefits; it is something different to claim that the person's *actual* thought in joining measured his or her potential gains against potential losses. (McGuire 2002:298–99)

Thinking Sociologically

Does the rational choice approach seem to you to make sense of religious behavior? Is religious behavior similar to self-interested economic behavior?

Religion and Modern Life: Meso-Level Analysis

The Yaqui youth was very ill. He had been bitten by a rattlesnake in the hot Arizona desert just outside his village. Although there was a medical clinic staffed by nurses and a visiting doctor, the family decided to use traditional Yaqui medicine, a blend of Native American rituals and what is referred to as *pagan Catholicism.* The medicine man broke eggs, mixed curative potions, and chanted incantations over the sick boy. These familiar rituals gave comfort to the family waiting anxiously for signs of the boy's recovery. After the boy had received the medicine man's treatment, he went to the medical clinic as well. He recovered, and the people believed that what led to the recovery was adherence to their traditional method of healing. The interaction of traditional religious practices and modern health care institutions illustrates these interconnections at the meso level.

In this section, we explore other types of religious organizations and how religion as an institution interacts with other institutions.

Types of Religious Organizations

The unique history of religious organizations in the United States has led one observer to describe America as the "denominational society" (Greeley 1972). Although religious establishments existed in the American colonies, the

United States as a nation is religiously diverse in two senses: multiple religious groups living side-by-side with no single faith tradition being dominant, and church and state given their own autonomous realms by the U.S. Constitution (Stark and Finke 2000).

Denominations and Denominationalism

In the United States and most other western countries, local congregations are part of a larger centralized organizations. These *centralized coordinating bodies or associations that link local congregations with a similar history and theology* are called **denominations**. In the long history of human society, denominationalism is a unique and rather recent way of organizing religion (Ammerman 2006). For most of human history religion has been characterized by an undifferentiated religious worldview, so that individuals experienced the world and life in such a way that religion was diffused through all of life. Under these conditions, religion and the rest of life are seamless and undifferentiated (Bellah 1970).

Over time, religion gradually became distinct from other social institutions, in particular the political or governmental structures. The result is that specifically religious organizations arise. Initially, a single religious organization dominated a particular geographic area, so that for several centuries the Roman Catholic Church was the dominant religious group in Europe. Eventually, however, the religious sphere itself came to be diverse as various regional movements arose, some of them within Catholicism (the Dominicans, the Jesuits, and so forth). The Reformation Era (1517–1648), however, launched Protestantism and brought about the emergence of different Christian groups that were distinct in beliefs and organization. Most of them were splinter groups from Catholicism, such as the Lutherans (Gorski 2000).

Although this spawned some religious pluralism, each religious group attempted to become the official and government-approved church in its territory. Conflict rather than peaceful coexistence came to characterize Europe, and many people were forced out of their own countries because of their faith.

Some of those driven out of Europe for religious reasons were followers of the Calvinist Puritan movement who were seeking to reform the Church of England. They ended up founding the New England colonies and creating religious establishments of their own. Four of the colonies (Rhode Island, Delaware, New Jersey, and Pennsylvania) were religiously very diverse and had no state-sponsored church. As a result, no single religious group established dominance or control in North America. This led to necessary peaceful coexistence: religious pluralism and official separation of church and state.

Freedom of religion and prohibition of a state-endorsed church are key conditions for denominationalism. When scholars have referred to the United States as "the denominational society," they mean a society that is characterized by religious congregations united into denominations that are presumed equal under the law and that generally treat other bodies with an attitude of mutual respect (Greeley 1972). As a consequence of this organizational pattern of religious pluralism, there are hundreds of denominations in America (Mead, Hill, and Atwood 2005). Indeed, the *Handbook of Denominations in the United States* lists 31 Baptist denominations and 17 denominations in the Calvinist/Reformed tradition alone (Mead et al. 2005). This denominationalism has also become a global phenomenon; the *World Christian Encyclopedia* reports 33,830 denominations within Christianity worldwide (Barrett, Kurian, and Johnson 2001; Roberts and Yamane 2012).

Yaqui dancers, who blend Christian and indigenous beliefs, appeal to the supernatural for healing.

Although diversity within Protestantism was a key force for denominationalism, it has become fully incorporated by all major religious groups in the United States. Some scholars have even identified Jewish "denominationalism" in reference to the four branches of Judaism—Orthodox, Conservative, Reform, and Reconstructionist (Lazerwitz et al. 1998). The Nation of Islam and American Society of Muslims are distinctively American Islamic denominations (though the former is often viewed negatively by traditional Muslims). If this pattern continues, we might eventually see

There were 10 Lutheran denominations in the United States as of 2010, and most of the splits were based on immigration and ethnicity patterns rather than race or doctrinal differences. This congregation, St Pedro's, began as a Danish congregation, but is now affiliated with the largest of the Lutheran groups, the Evangelical Lutheran Church in America. The ELCA is the largest because of a series of consolidations. So denominationalism is characterized by fission (splits) and by fusion (mergers).

Sunni and Shiite Islamic organizations develop as distinctive Islamic denominations. Buddhism and Hinduism also have different branches or schools, though like Islam they were brought to America in large numbers only recently, so time will tell whether there will be an evolution of those branches into recognizable denominations.

Denominational Structures and the Micro-Meso Connection

Denominations have organizational structures, but they are not all alike. Three types of denominational structures prevail: congregational, episcopal, and presbyterian (Ammerman 2006; DiMaggio and Powell 1983; Roberts and Yamane 2012). Note that these are *not* the same as churches by those names, but rather the organizational structure (or "polity") of a number of churches.

In a *congregational* polity or structure, the authority of the local congregation is supreme. For example, the thousands of Baptist and United Church of Christ congregations in the United States hire and fire their own ministers, control their own finances, own their own property, decide whether to ordain women, and make other decisions about the congregation (Ammerman 1990, 2009).

The *episcopal*—also called "hierarchical"— pattern of governance places ultimate authority over local churches in the centralized hands of bishops (the word *episcopal* means "governed by bishops"). Each of the Roman Catholic Church's nearly 20,000 U.S. congregations (or "parishes") are geographically defined. They are clustered into a "diocese," which is under the authority of the local bishop and, ultimately, under the authority of the Bishop of Rome—the Pope. In an episcopal structure, a bishop and his or her executive staff decides who will be the priest or minister of the local church. A committee of the local congregation may be consulted, but the bishop has the final say. Christian churches that have some form of episcopal organization include Anglican, Episcopalian, Eastern Orthodox, Methodist, African Methodist Episcopal, AME Zion, and *some* Lutherans. So, the local United Methodist church building in your community is actually *owned* by the larger denomination and is only maintained by the local congregation, and a bishop decides who will be the minister.

Presbyterian polity, quite simply, is a middle ground between episcopal (with a bishop having tremendous power—actually *owning* the buildings the congregation worships in) and congregational (where the congregation has total authority). In presbyterian polity, authority is shared so that neither a single local congregation nor the hierarchy can trump the other. The Presbyterian Church is the best example of this compromise position. Presbyterian structure usually involves a local board in a congregation that can make decisions—called Sessions. There are also organizations composed of groups of congregations at regional and national levels that, in order of regional to national, are typically called Presbyteries, Synods, and then the National Assembly. Almost all Reformed churches use this approach: Dutch Reformed, Swiss Reformed, and the Presbyterian Church, which is an offshoot of the Scottish Reformed tradition. Table 12.2 provides some examples of which churches tend to follow which polity.

Denominational structure either places authority in the hands of a hierarchy or grants that power locally. Still, local congregations in the United States tend to have a significant measure of autonomy to do their own thing. This is because congregational churches have had a very long and pervasive influence on the United States. Even Roman Catholic and Episcopal churches in the United States tend to have more local congregational autonomy than in Europe, meaning that traditions in a country may influence the relationship between the local congregation and the meso-level denomination (Ammerman 2006; Warner 1993, 2005).

There is a great deal of variation between Catholic parishes in the United States, and the dissimilarities are often influenced by region of the county and the other congregations in the area. If there are lots of churches with congregational and presbyterian structures in the community (what we called the group's "social environment" in Chapter 1), the members of Catholic parishes begin to expect more control and influence. This is evident in how local dioceses and congregations implement—or

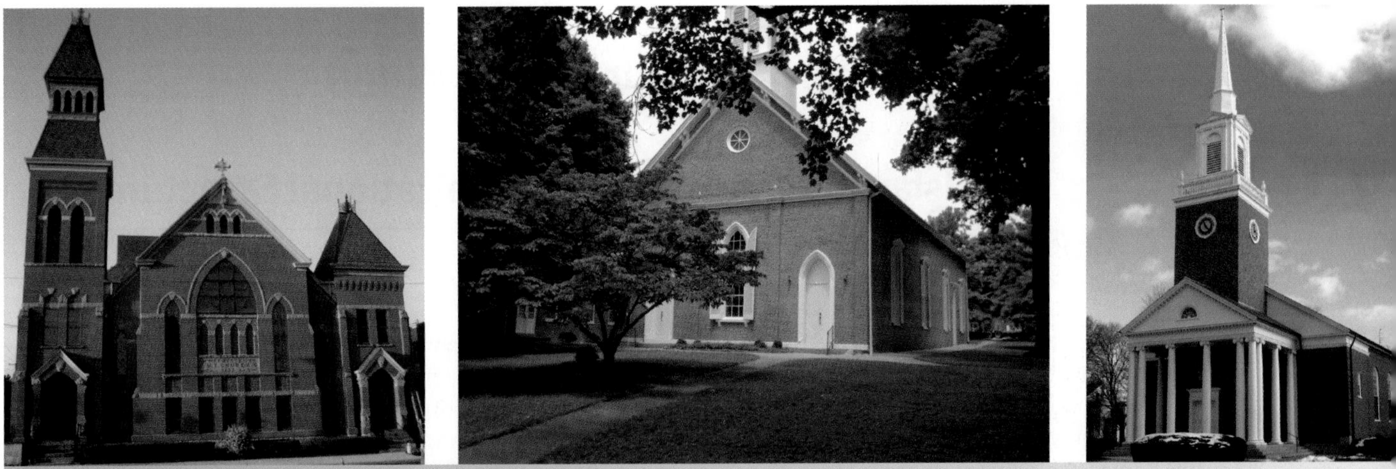

One cannot tell by looking at these buildings, but the organizational structure and who owns them is quite different. The Methodist church on the left is episcopal in structure; the center photo is a Presbyterian church with a presbyterian organization, and the one on the right is a Congregational church with congregational structure.

Table 12.2 **Polity or Organizational Structures of Selected Churches**

Congregational Polity	*Episcopal Polity*	*Presbyterian Polity*
United Church of Christ (Congregationalists)	Roman Catholic Church	Reformed Churches
National Baptist	Episcopal Church	Dutch Reformed
Southern Baptist	Anglican Church	Swiss Reformed
Christian Church (Disciples of Christ)	United Methodist	French Reformed
Churches of Christ	African Methodist Episcopal	Church of Scotland
Unitarian Universalists	Evangelical Lutheran	Presbyterian Church USA

choose not to implement—policies passed down from the church hierarchy (Gillis 1999; Warner 2005; Yamane and MacMillen 2006). In addition, many Catholic congregations expect to have some input into the appointment of a priest to their church—something that would be unthinkable in Italy or Spain.

Both denominations and congregations from all religious traditions are susceptible to influence from the larger social system. Hence, they have a tendency to become like each other (Ammerman 2006). Scholars recognize a tendency for organizations to morph into similar forms (DiMaggio and Powell 1983). The point is that while denominational structure or polity strongly affects the structure of a local congregation and how it works, the social environment can also cause a certain amount of adaptation.

Although the idea of a congregational authority emerged from the study of Christianity, this organizational form is not limited to the Christian tradition. Further, the tendency to assimilate to the pattern in the social environment happens to religious groups as much as it does to individuals, as shown in the "Sociology in Our Social World" on page 438.

Nondenominational Meso-Level Structures

Although the United States is still a "denominational" society—in which a multiplicity of religious traditions are seen as legitimate—there are some significant developments in American religious life suggesting that denominations are not the full meso-level picture.

By all accounts, one of the most dynamic sectors of both the American and the global religious scenes is evangelical Christianity (Freston 2007). In the United States, individuals belonging to evangelical traditions now constitute over half of all Protestants (Pew Forum on Religion and Public Life 2012b). Most scholars recognize that evangelicalism is a movement, not a denomination or even a collection of denominations. It is, in fact, a *transdenominational movement*. This transdenominational evangelicalism, however, is built around networks and organizations, including seminaries like the Moody Bible Institute, publications like *Christianity Today*, various evangelical Christian colleges, and a few conservative denominations. The evangelical movement has also influenced a number of the mainline

Sociology in Our Social World

Islam, Mosques, and Organizational Structure

Most mosques in the United States are relatively new, with 87% having been founded since 1970 and 62% of those since 1980. The number of mosques is up 74% since 2000. At the turn of the century, there were 1,209 mosques in the United States, and by 2010 there were 2,106 (Grossman 2012a).

Christian congregations tend to be somewhat autonomous entities: supported by members but linked organizationally to a denomination. According to the Islamic scholar Ihsan Bagby, "Most of the world's mosques are simply a place to pray. . . . A Muslim cannot be a member of a particular mosque" because mosques belong to God, not to the people (Bagby 2003:115). The role of the imam—the minister—is simply to lead prayers five times a day and to run the services on the Sabbath, including delivery of a sermon. Unlike many Christian and Jewish leaders in the United States, the imam does not run an organization and does not need formal training at a seminary. In some countries, mosques are government supported, so imams had to make major changes in how they operate when they started congregations in North America. Because they could not depend on government funding, Islamic mosques needed to adapt to the congregational model: recruiting members who were loyal to a particular local mosque and would support it. They also began to put more emphasis on religious education (which had been managed largely by extended families in the "old country"), religious holidays are celebrated at the mosque rather than with families, and life cycle celebrations (births and marriages) became events for the congregation. This is a major change in the role of the mosque and the imam for many Muslims.

Bagby reports that there are two main categories of mosques: (1) those attended primarily by African Americans and (2) those attended primarily by immigrants. African American mosques represent only 27% of the total number of mosques, and they are in some important ways different in organizational structure from those attended by immigrants (28% of the remaining American Muslims being from South Asia, 15% being Arab, and 30% having a mixed background). So even the makeup of mosques is unlike anything most Americans might expect. Only 28% of American mosques depend on an imam as the final authority, whereas the majority are led by an executive committee or board of directors (called the *majlis*). More important, 93% of African American mosques are led by an imam, compared with only 38% of immigrant-attended mosques.

About 33% of all mosques in the United States have a paid, full-time imam, and 16% of those imams need to hold a second job. In comparison, 89% of other congregations (Christian and Jewish) have paid ministers. Only 13% of imams have a master's degree in theology, which is the standard expected for most mainstream Christian and Jewish clergy. So despite having exceptionally high levels of adherents in management and the professions, with exceptionally high incomes, and having 58% of adherents with college degrees, Islamic mosques are less bureaucratized, with less emphasis on professional credentials, membership roles, or denominational connections. It is likely that mosques will begin to assimilate to the religious organizational pattern of the larger society.

denominations, but evangelicalism in the United States is not primarily about a single denomination or about starting a new denomination (Kosmin and Keysar 2009).

The nondenominational nature of the movement is partially because an increasing number of Americans choose not to identify their religion according to a denominational label; they are "just Christians" or "spiritual but not religious." Roughly one out of six congregations in the United States is nondenominational (Chaves 2004). These Christians have the youngest age composition, so the growth of this group in the future is likely (Kosmin and Keysar 2009).

The result is the rise of meso-level religious, special-purpose groups that operate alongside denominations, crossing boundaries and providing for joint efforts between various groups (Wuthnow 1988). The 20th century has

The issue of abortion cuts across many denominational lines, uniting evangelicals and sometimes bringing Catholics and evangelical Protestants together. This Grave of the Unborn along a street in a midwestern community is an ongoing protest against a policy that rallies those who oppose abortion.

seen special-purpose groups with religious origins arise to address public issues that concern people of faith: war and peace, abortion legislation, world hunger, civil rights, changes in gender roles, abortion, family stability, and homosexuality. The Full Gospel Business Men's Fellowship, the Christian Legal Society, the Fellowship of Christian Athletes, Christian Voice, Sojourners, and Witness for Peace are only a few examples of special-purpose groups for which religion is closely connected to social and political issues. These are meso-level organizations that operate between and across denominations, but they are not denominations themselves. They are sometimes called *paradenominational groups*.

Thinking Sociologically

Why are meso-level organizations so important to the particularly vibrant religiosity of the United States? Does the competition between denominations fill more needs? Does it cause more commitment to one's own religious outlook when others nearby are offering alterative views of life, death, and the meaning of it all?

New Religious Movements (NRMs) or Cults

New religious movements, or NRMs, are *innovative religious groups that may become established new religions if they survive for several generations*. They are splinter groups that arise to meet specific needs that people have not met through traditional religious organizations. Unlike sects, NRMs that endure become a new religion rather than a denomination of an existing faith. *Cult* was once the common term for this kind of movement, but the media and the public have so completely misused the word that its meaning has become unclear and often negative. The term *cult*, as sociologists have historically used it, is simply descriptive, not judging the group as good, bad, or kooky. Most sociologists of religion now prefer to use the term *NRM* to describe these religious forms (Christiano et al. 2008).

NRMs either are imported into a country as immigrants enter from other lands or are founded on a new revelation (or insight) by a charismatic leader. They are usually out of the mainstream religious system, at least in their early days. Christianity, Buddhism, and Islam all began as NRMs or cults. The estimated number of NRMs in North America at the turn of the century was between 1,500 and 2,000 (Melton 1993; Nichols, Mather, and Schmidt 2006). There could be 10,000 more NRMs in Africa and an undetermined but large number in Asia (Hadden 2006; Religious Worlds 2007).

An NRM is often started by a charismatic leader, someone who claims to have received a new insight, often directly from God. For example, Reverend Sun Myung Moon founded an NRM called the Unification Church, the members of which are often referred to as *Moonies*. While claiming to be a part of Christianity, the Unification Church has its own additional scripture to complement the Bible, and Reverend Moon has a standing equal to Jesus—an idea offensive to most Christian groups.

Some sensational NRMs have ended in tragedy: Reverend Jim Jones led his devoted followers to a retreat in Guyana, South America, and ultimately to their suicides in the belief that heaven was awaiting them (Lacayo 1993; Wright 1995). A group suicide also occurred in 1997 in California by a band called Heaven's Gate, whose members thought supernatural beings were coming to take them away in a flying saucer (Wessinger 2000).

Most new religious groups are not dangerous to members. Furthermore, most religious groups that are now accepted and established were stigmatized as weird or evil when they started. Early Christians were characterized by Romans as dangerous cannibals, and in the early decades of the 20th century in the United States, Roman Catholics were depicted in the media as dangerous, immoral, and anti-American (Bromley and Shupe 1981). When we encounter media reports about NRMs, we should listen to and read these with a good dose of skepticism and recognize that not all cults are like the sensational ones.

NRMs tend to be hard to study because the members feel they might be persecuted for their faith and beliefs. Witchcraft (or Wicca) is one example of a religion that has been forced to remain secretive, and the next "Sociology in Our Social World" explores the strategies of one sociologist to examine this interesting religious community.

Sociology in Our Social World

Witchcraft in the United States

Wiccans participate in a lunar ritual in Illinois.

In *A Community of Witches: Contemporary Neo-Paganism and Witchcraft in the United States*, Helen Berger applies sociological analysis to conduct a fascinating study of contemporary Wicca (Berger 1999). She did participant observation in a newly formed coven in New England. A coven is a small congregation of witches, usually having no more than 10 or 12 members. It took considerable effort to establish trust with the members, but this method of gathering data allowed her to experience firsthand the close-knit support group and the actual behaviors and interactions within the group. A national organization provided her with a wealth of printed material produced by Neo-Pagans and allowed her entry to several national Neo-Pagan festivals, where she observed the rituals. She also did in-depth, open-ended interviews with 40 members from a number of covens. By using a variety of methods, Berger was able to gain in-depth information, but she was also able to get an idea of whether her experiences were generalizable to all parts of the country.

Although Berger found Wicca to be a rather healthy and vibrant movement, she also found that it experiences some of the same dilemmas as any other religious congregation. Wicca is feminist, believing in a goddess and emphasizing gender equality. It also celebrates the spiritual unity of humans with nature and therefore has a strong ecology ethic. The religion encourages an intuitive approach to decision making (rather than using logic) and celebrates the senses. This sensuousness embraces sexuality, fertility, and being at one with the universe.

Berger finds that Wicca is a product of the globalized world, for the religion involves bits and pieces selected from religions around the world. It has spread with modern technology, including Internet communication, desktop publishing, and fax machines. Furthermore, it is a religion about self-fulfillment, in keeping with a contemporary emphasis on self-awareness and self-transformation. Wicca is a fast-growing religion, especially among women (Religious Tolerance 2006).

In a more recent book, *Teenage Witches*, Berger worked with an Australian scholar, Douglas Ezzy, to explore the expansion of witchcraft among teenagers in the English-speaking world (Berger and Ezzy 2007). The book is based on interviews that Berger and Ezzy did with 90 young people in the United States, United Kingdom, and Australia (30 from each country). Young people, even more than the generation before them, are attracted by the emphasis on self-transformation. Many of the past generation found their politics, particularly their belief in environmentalism and gender equity, mirrored in Wicca. Unlike the past generation, the new generation of witches is more likely to practice alone—that is, outside the covens. These individuals learn about the religion through books and magazines and online. They may interact with others on websites, through blogs, or in Wiccan chat rooms, but they remain solitary practitioners.

With the increase in the number of teenagers becoming interested in supernatural ideas from Harry Potter to the *Twilight* series, witches are in part a product of the growth of positive media representations of magic and supernaturalism. The expansion in Wiccan covens may be one result of this shift in media depictions. However, Berger and Ezzy found that many more young people search online for information about witchcraft or read books about it than actually become witches. Although the media may stimulate interest, media do not cause young people to join. Those who do become witches tend to find that the religion speaks to their personal needs. They are more likely to already have had an interest in the occult and to have felt themselves to be different from their peers. The influx of young people has the potential to significantly change the face of the religion, particularly because so few of them seek coven training and have the traditional ideas and practices passed on to them.

Thinking Sociologically

What factors might cause the birth and success of NRMs?

Religion and Other Social Institutions

In traditional societies, religion is not separated from other social institutions, as the Yaqui religious practice was separate from the clinic, but is an integral part of people's social world. In complex societies, on the other hand, religion denotes a distinctive group or organization. The dominant religion(s) in any complex society generally supports the political system and ideology of the dominant group. It is closely related to the economic system, is linked to the education system, and legitimates the family system through sacred rites of passage for marriage, birth, and death. Even the health system, as shown in the Yaqui example, is closely linked to religious beliefs about the healing process, disease, and death.

Religion not only supports other institutions but may also experience support or pressure from these other institutions. The Catholic Church has faced increasing criticism from international organizations, political movements, governments, religious groups, and educational institutions for its ban on birth control. Due to rapid population growth, especially in poor Catholic nations, many interested parties are putting pressure on the Catholic Church to ease its strict birth control ban in these countries. The Church cannot ignore these pressures, for they will undermine its legitimacy if they are not addressed or countered. Even if the Church does not change, it must expend considerable effort to defend its position in order to keep from losing credibility in the eyes of members and nonmembers alike. Some Catholic clergy and a number of lay members have defected over the positions of the Church. Let us consider the relationship between religion and three other social institutions: family, politics, and economics.

Religion and Family

Everyone was dressed in colorful finery to welcome the baby into the religious community. The naming ceremony in this Nigerian village takes place when the baby reaches 6 weeks and is considered a viable human being, healthy enough to live. After the ceremony, the bonds of religious community are solidified with food, music, and dancing.

Our parents provide our first contact with religion. They may say prayers, attend worship services, and talk about proper behavior as defined by their religious group. Religious congregations make marriages sacred through ceremonies. Mother's Day, Father's Day, and Grandparents' Day are recognized by many religions and societies, thereby honoring and legitimating parenting. Many of the sacred ceremonies in religion are family affairs: births, christenings or naming of new members, marriages, and funerals. Jews, Muslims, and Latter-Day Saints (Mormons) are especially known for their many ceremonies and gatherings designed specifically for family units, and their moral codes place a high value on family loyalty and responsibility.

Religiosity, a person's degree of religious involvement, is positively associated with moral beliefs and behavior in youth and influences interaction with children and support of spouses in marriages. Some religious groups, such as conservative Protestants and fundamentalist groups of other religions, are involved in child rearing, producing parenting manuals to guide families. Some of these manuals have created controversy because of their emphasis on hierarchical and authority-centered parenting models (Grille 2005). Tensions can arise between family and religion over social control. Among the Amish, if the bishop orders a member of the church to be shunned, the family must comply and must refuse to speak to or associate with that person. If the family does not comply, it will be ostracized by the other members of the community. This sometimes leads to intense tension as the church tries to direct communication patterns and interactions within a family (Clarke 2007; Hostetler 1993).

The New Right and other conservative organizations sometimes argue that if society could reinstate the family and the religious values of the past, today's societal problems would be reduced. They believe that if parents would spend more time instilling proper values in their children, things would be better. However, working parents today often spend more time with their children than parents did in past times. Stereotypes of the families and the religious values of the "good old days" come from a small segment of the total population: those upper-middle-class families in which only one parent had to work (Coontz 1997, 2005). Today, many of the problems and pressures facing families occur at different levels of analysis and are out of the control of the family or the local religious group. However, religiously affiliated organizations and social movements may also attempt to transform or strengthen other institutions. The conservative Christian organization, Focus on the Family, which has a syndicated newspaper column, radio programs, books, DVDs, and a monthly magazine produced by its founder James Dobson, is one example of an effort to strengthen families by restoring the traditional model of family life. Although religion cannot solve all family problems, most religions encourage a stable family life.

Religion and Politics: Theocracies and Civil Religion

Jan, a Swede, belongs to a state religion: Lutheranism. He was raised a Lutheran and does not really think about the possibility of other religious beliefs, although there is a growing Pentecostal movement in Sweden. The Nwankwo family, mentioned in the chapter opening, practices an ancient tribal religion, also with no thought that another religious belief might have something better to offer. Most of us are raised in a particular belief system from childhood and adhere to that religion because it is part of the custom and tradition most familiar to us. We seldom question our "choice."

In a pure **theocracy**, *or rule by God, religious leaders rule society in accordance with God's presumed wishes.* Iran is one example where religion clearly has a privileged position. In other countries, religion is used as a tool of the state to manipulate the citizenry and to maintain social control. A state religion, on the other hand, has some autonomy but receives support from tax money. Sweden, Britain, and Italy are examples. Some countries, such as the former Soviet Union, outlawed religion altogether so that nothing competed with loyalty to the nation. The continuum in Figure 12.3 shows the possible relationships between church and state.

Countries with diverse religious groups experience multiple pressures on their political systems: religious voting blocs, conflicts over definitions of public morality, and lobbying efforts for policies that have moral implications—abortion, euthanasia, rights for homosexuals, care of the poor, war and peace, and so forth. Sometimes, religious groups form the basis for political parties. Even in the United States, which professes separation between church and state matters, religious groups influence policies such as prayer in school, selection of textbooks and reading matter, and abortion. In some countries, religious groups strongly oppose the government and seek to undermine the authority and power of political leaders. In Nazi

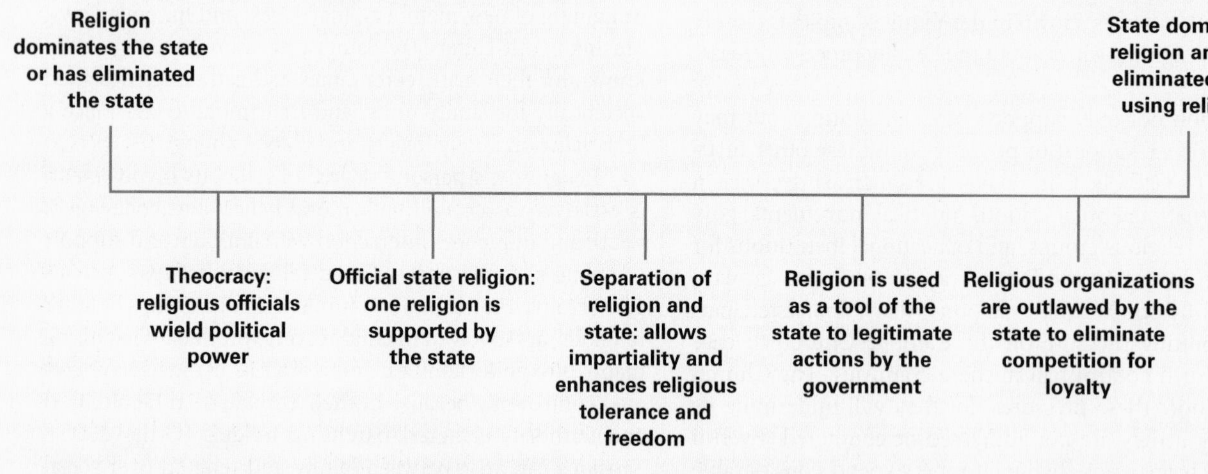

Figure 12.3 Links Between Religion and the State

Iran's supreme leader, Ayatollah Ali Khamenei, speaks to ethnic Arabs during a visit to Dehlavieh in the southern oil province of Khuzestan. Religious leaders in Iran have advocated theocracy in that country—a national government operated on the principles of the Quran.

Germany, some church leaders formulated the Barmen Declaration in opposition to Hitler. Many Christian groups in South Africa opposed apartheid. In some parts of Latin America, church leaders work for human rights and more equitable distribution of land and resources. Although religion often reinforces the power of the state, it may also be a source of conflict and tension on issues regarding morality, justice, and legitimate authority. Indeed, depending on the organizational structures, religion can provide a source of authority that offers a real challenge to the power of the state when that government has become oppressive, as shown in the next "Sociology Around the World" on page 444.

In simple homogeneous societies, religion serves as a kind of glue, making sacred the existing social system by offering it supernatural legitimacy. In complex and heterogeneous societies, on the other hand, no single religion can provide the core values of the culture. In such circumstances, an alternative form of religion called civil religion frequently evolves. **Civil religion** *refers to the cultural beliefs, practices, and symbols that relate a nation to the ultimate conditions of its existence* (Yamane 2007). The beliefs, symbols, and rituals serve to create a sacredness about the nation and what that nation stands for (Wimberly and Swatos 1998). Although civil religion lacks the structural system of organized religion, it is often supported by various types of patriotic groups. These small voluntary associations develop intense belonging systems, and civil religion also tends to strengthen the sense of belonging of all citizens as members of that society (Bellah 1992; Roberts and Yamane 2012).

Civil religion blends reverence for the nation with more traditional symbols of faith. Pictured is the chapel at Punchbowl, the Pacific cemetery for U.S. military personnel, located in Hawaii. Note that two U.S. flags are inside the altar area and are more prominent than two of the three religious symbols that also adorn the chancel: the Christian Cross, the Jewish Star of David, and the Buddhist Wheel of Dharma.

Rituals of civil religion include saying the Pledge of Allegiance, saluting the flag, and singing the national anthem. For example, American civil religion is not explicitly Christian, for it must appeal to those who are non-Christian as well, but it involves reference to God in many areas of civilian life and a legitimation of the political system. It attempts to give the nation and the government supernatural blessing and authority (Bellah 1970). It also calls the nation to a higher standard of justice and may be used by change agents such as Martin Luther King Jr. to make social change more acceptable and compelling.

In Ireland, part of the intense conflict between Protestants and Catholics is over civil religion. Protestants and Catholics

Sociology Around the World

Transnational Religion: The Catholic Church and Political Systems

The Roman Catholic Church was one of the first complex organizations to be truly transnational, external to any one nation and including representation from many countries. Many religious organizations are contained within a single nation. This type of religious association is not linked to congregations or a denomination in other countries (Roberts and Yamane 2012).

The Catholic Church is an international body that must be sympathetic to the circumstances of people in many nations, for its membership and its organizational reach span the globe. It cannot align itself with the economic and political interests of one nation or set of nations without risking the alienation of tens of millions of members in another part of the world.

Multinational religious organizations such as the Catholic Church can have a real impact on the social and economic policies within a nation, sometimes protecting the welfare of the people against a tyrannical state. In Poland during the 1970s and 1980s, the citizenry often felt colonized by a foreign power—the Soviet Union. The communist government in Poland was extremely unpopular, and the people had no real way to make the government more responsive to their needs. In 1983, only 3% of Poles who were surveyed felt that the government-dominant political hierarchy represented the interests of the Polish people. In contrast, 60% identified the Catholic Church and the Pope as protecting Polish interests (Tamney 1992).

The Catholic Church became a major power broker in negotiations between unions and the government in Poland (Tamney 1992). Catholic bishops sometimes took on a role akin to union leaders and, in so doing, became major players in the political future of the country. Because those bishops were ultimately responsible to the Pope and had a source of support external to the nation, they experienced a good deal of independence from the communist party that was in power. Clergy supported by a church financed with tax dollars would not have had the same freedom to challenge the government. The global nature of the Catholic Church influenced the role bishops could play in the Polish situation.

Transnationalism can influence the power of religious officials in our complex global environment. It provides an external source of authority that may be seen by citizens as superseding the political authority. In many single-nation religious denominations, the primary function of churches is to support the political power of the particular state or affirm an ethnic or national identity (Turner 1991b). Poland is an especially intriguing case in that a single religion tended to be identified with national pride and culture but that religion was global in its power base. That combination provided an exceptionally strong base for challenging governmental policies that were not in the interests of the citizens (Tamney 1992).

Being a religion that crosses national boundaries can also be a source of suspicion in some circumstances. Roman Catholics were traditionally suspected of lacking national loyalty in the United States. They were derisively called "papists" in the first half of the 20th century. Likewise, Jews have often been accused of maintaining dangerous, subversive ties because of their international networks with others who share their faith. The fact that a religion is more inclusive than just national boundaries can have benefits as well as risks for individuals and the state. This is true of any religious tradition.

not only come from different economic strata and different ethnic backgrounds but also have different visions for the future of the country and different ideas about what gives the country its special place in history. Although civil religion is supposed to unite a country, in Ireland and other divided countries, civil religion can itself be a point of intense conflict (McGuire 2002; Yamane 2007). The problem is that there is a difference in the image of what the nation stands for and where it is headed. In the United States the Tea Party and the Occupy Wall Street movement have sharply contrasting images of the meaning and the future of the nation.

Thinking Sociologically

How does civil religion manifest itself in your country? Give specific examples.

Religion and the Economy: The Protestant Ethic and Capitalism

Why do most of us study hard, work hard, and strive to get ahead? Why are we sacrificing time and money now—taking this and other college courses—when we might spend that money on an impressive new car? Our answers probably have something to do with our moral attitudes about work, about those who lack ambition, and about the proper way to live. Max Weber saw a relationship between the economic system, particularly capitalism, and ideas about work and sacrifice. He gathered information by studying many documents, including the diaries of Calvinists (a branch of Protestantism), sermons and religious teachings, and other historical papers. The following is his argument in a nutshell (Weber [1904–1905] 1958).

Noting that the areas of Europe where the Calvinists had strong followings were the same areas where capitalism grew the fastest, Weber argued that four elements in the Calvinist Protestant faith created the moral and value system necessary for the growth of capitalism: predestination, a calling, self-denial, and individualism.

1. *Predestination* meant that one's destiny was predetermined. Nothing anyone could do would change what was to happen. Because God was presumed to be perfect, he was not influenced by human deeds or prayer. Those people who were chosen by God were referred to as the *elect* and were assumed to be a small group. Therefore, people looked for signs of their status—salvation or damnation. High social status was sometimes viewed as a sign of being among the elect, so motivation was high to succeed in *this* life.
2. The *calling* referred to the concept of doing God's work. Each person was put on Earth to serve God, and each had a task to do in God's service. One could be called by God to any occupation, so the key was to work very hard and with the right attitude. Because work was a way to serve God, laziness or lack of ambition came to be viewed as a sin. These ideas helped create a society in which people's self-worth and their evaluation of others were tied to a work ethic. The Protestants became workaholics.
3. *Self-denial* involved living a simple life. If one had a good deal of money, one did not spend it on a lavish home, expensive clothing, or various forms of entertainment. Such consumption would be offensive to God. Therefore, if people worked hard and began to accumulate resources, they simply saved them or invested them in a business. This self-denial was tied to an idea that we now call *delayed gratification*, postponing the satisfaction of one's present wants and desires in exchange for a future reward. The reward they sought was in the afterlife. Because Calvinists believed in predestination, they did not expect to earn salvation, but they believed that they could demonstrate to themselves and others that they were among the elect.
4. *Individualism* meant that each individual faced his or her destiny alone before God. Previous Christian theology had emphasized group salvation, the idea that an entire community would be saved or damned together. The stark individualism of Calvinistic theology stressed that each individual was on his or her own before God. Likewise, in the economic system that was emerging, individuals were on their own. The person who thrived was an individualist who planned wisely and charted his or her own course. Religious individualism and economic individualism reinforced one another (Weber [1904–1905] 1958).

The Protestant ethic that resulted from these elements stressed hard work, simple living, and rational decision making by daring individualists. Businesspeople and laborers spent long hours working at their calling, and the profits were reinvested for new equipment or expansion of the company. Individualism allowed people to pursue their own course of action and not to feel guilty for doing so. This combination was ideal for the growth of capitalism. Religion led to major changes in cultural values, which, in turn, transformed the economic system. Weber saw both the religious and the economic systems as dynamic, interrelated, and ever-changing (Weber [1904–1905] 1958).

Gradually, the capitalistic system, stimulated by the Protestant ethic, spread to other countries and to other religious groups. Many of the attitudes about work and delayed gratification no longer have supernatural focus, but they are part of the larger cultural value system nonetheless. They influence our feelings about people who are not industrious and our ideas about why some people are poor. In fact, some religious groups see individuals as responsible for their own fate, believing that the poor and jobless got themselves into their circumstances and should solve their own problems rather than depend on government aid (Davidson 2008). This view was expressed by Mitt Romney in the 2012 presidential election and is shared by a number of Americans (Brooks 2012; Rubin 2012).

Weber recognized that other factors also had to be present for capitalism to develop, but he believed that the particular set of moral values and attitudes that Calvinism instilled in the people was critical. Whereas

Marx argued that religion kept workers in their places and allowed the capitalists to exploit the system and maintain their elite positions, Weber focused on the change brought about in the economic system as a result of religious beliefs and values.

Religion interacts with the economy in other ways as well. For one thing, religion is big business. In the United States, more than 222,000 religious organizations receive donations, mostly from individual members. Of the total estimated charitable contributions, 32% go to religious organizations, a total of $95.88 billion in 2011. Yet this figure showed a slight decline, probably due to declining membership in mainline Protestant denominations and the poor economy (Center on Philanthropy 2012). In most countries, religions (a) employ clergy and other people who serve the church, (b) own land and property, and (c) generate millions through collections and fund-raising. Some of this money goes to the upkeep of the building, some to charitable activities, and some to investments. Religious ventures continue to expand into many areas, from shopping centers to homes and apartment buildings for the elderly. In the United States, televangelism and megachurches (congregations with upwards of 10,000 members) are multimillion-dollar industries with sophisticated marketing strategies. The televangelism industry, for example, involves the sale of books and tapes; donations of hundreds of millions of dollars by listeners; the establishment of colleges, hospitals, and amusement parks; and the provision of jobs in a wide variety of technical electronic areas. These megachurches become corporations and use information from the corporate world to ensure success.

In the high-tech South Barrington, Illinois, Willow Creek Community Church, images of the pastor can be seen projected on several televisions during a worship service. Megachurches, which sometimes draw 20,000 to 30,000 worshippers on a weekend, offer high-entertainment worship and a range of other services. These churches are run—and marketed—like a business.

There are other ways in which religion and economic institutions are linked. When large religious organizations take a moral stand on poverty, they may influence the economy. Moreover, when the economy is especially bad, certain kinds of religious movements are more likely to be spawned: Millenarian movements, which expect the end of the world soon, almost always occur when economic prospects are bleak (Roberts and Yamane 2012).

Although religion today may not have the power to transform the economy or other social institutions, each institution does affect others. Society also shapes the kind of organization and the relationship to other institutions that the religious group adopts, as discussed in the next section.

Thinking Sociologically

Religion is influenced not only by other institutions in society but also by the media. What messages from the media (movies, TV, music) reflect the state of religion in society?

Religion in Society: Macro-Level Analysis

As an integral part of society, religion meets the needs of individuals and of the social structure. In this section, we explore functionalist and conflict theories as we consider some functions of religion in society, the role of religion in supporting stratification systems, and various conflicts within societies and in the global system.

The Contribution of Religion to Society: A Functionalist Perspective

Regardless of their personal belief or disbelief in the supernatural, sociologists of religion acknowledge that religion has important social consequences. Functionalists contend that religion has positive consequences—helping people answer questions about the meaning of life and providing part of the glue that helps hold a society together. Let us look at some of the social functions of religion, keeping in mind that the role of religion varies depending on the structure of the society and the time period.

Social Cohesion

Religion helps individuals feel a sense of belonging and unity with others, a common sense of purpose with those who share the same beliefs. It serves to hold any social unit together and gives the members a sense of camaraderie. Durkheim's widely cited study of suicide stresses the importance of belonging to a group (Durkheim [1897] 1964). Research shows that religious homogeneity and a high rate of congregational membership in a community are associated with lower rates of suicide. This lower suicide rate among the highly religious appears to hold in Muslim societies as well as in the United States (Ellison, Burr, and McCall 1997; Lotfi, Ayar, and Shams 2012). Thus, religion serves society well as long as religious views are consistent with other values of society (Bainbridge and Stark 1981). If there are competing religions, cohesion may be reduced and the religions may even be a source of conflict and hatred. Societies with competing religions often develop a civil religion—a theology of the nation—that serves to bless the nation and to enhance conformity and loyalty.

Legitimating Social Values and Norms

The values and norms of a culture must not be seen as random or arbitrary if they are to be followed by members of the society. Religion often sacralizes social norms—grounds them in a supernatural reality or a divine command that makes them larger than life. Whether those norms have to do with care for the vulnerable, the demand to work for peace and justice, the immorality of extramarital sex, the sacredness of a monogamous heterosexual marriage, or proper roles for men and women, the foundations of morality from scripture create feelings of absoluteness. This lends stability to society: Agreement on social control of deviant behavior is easier, and the society needs to rely less on coercion and force to get citizens to follow social norms. The absoluteness of the norms also makes it more difficult to change them as the society evolves. This inflexibility is precisely what pleases religious conservatives and distresses theological liberals, the latter often seeking new ways to interpret the old norms.

Of course, what people say they believe and how they behave are not always compatible, as the "Sociology in Our Social World" on page 448 makes clear.

Social Change

Depending on the time and place, religion can work for or against social change. Some religions fight to maintain the status quo or return to simpler times. This is true of many fundamentalist religions—whether they are branches of

Sociology in Our Social World

Red Sex, Blue Sex

Even sex has political-religious guidelines and implications. The reactions at the 2008 Republican convention to the pregnancy of vice presidential candidate Sarah Palin's unmarried evangelical 17-year-old daughter were far from what some people might have expected. One delegate said, "I think it's great that she instilled in her daughter the values to have the child and not to sneak off someplace and have an abortion." Another added, "Even though young children are making that decision to become pregnant, they've also decided to take responsibility for their actions and . . . get married and raise this child" (Talbot 2008:1).

For social liberals in the U.S. "blue states," sex education is key. They are not particularly bothered by teens having sex before marriage but would regard a teenage daughter's pregnancy as devastating news. On the other hand, social conservatives in the "red states" generally advocate abstinence-only education and denounce sex before marriage. However, they are relatively unruffled when a teenager does become pregnant, as long as she does not choose to have an abortion.

From a national survey of 3,400 teens from 13 to 17 years old and from a government study of adolescent sexual behavior, the authors of the **National Longitudinal Study of Adolescent Health** conclude that "religion is a good indicator of attitudes toward sex, but a poor one of sexual behavior, and that this gap is especially wide among teenagers who identify themselves as evangelical" (Regnerus 2007; Sessions 2012). The vast majority of white evangelical adolescents (74%) say that they believe in abstaining from sex before marriage. (Only half of mainline Protestants and a quarter of Jews say that they believe in abstinence.) Moreover, among the major religious groups, evangelical virgins are the least likely to anticipate that sex will be pleasurable and the most likely to believe that having sex will cause their partners to lose respect for them. Yet the adolescent health research indicated that evangelical teenagers are more sexually active than Mormons, mainline Protestants, and Jews. On average, white evangelical Protestants make their "sexual debut" shortly after turning 16; 80% of unmarried evangelicals are having sex, and 30% of their pregnancies end in abortion (Regnerus 2007; Sessions 2012; Shriver 2007). It is interesting to note that states with comprehensive sex education programs in schools have half the teen birth rates as those in the evangelical south that ban sex education in schools (Sessions 2012). Some sociologists argue that teens used to get married at earlier ages, but now wait to marry until they are economically secure, demanding that evangelical young people remain sexless during their young adulthood. This may not be realistic.

Another key difference between evangelical and other teens is that "evangelical protestant teenagers are significantly less likely than other groups to use contraception. This could be because evangelicals are also among the most likely to believe that using contraception will send the message that they are looking for sex" and that condoms will not really protect them from pregnancy or venereal disease (Talbot 2008:1).

The disconnect between the ideals of one's faith and actual behavior is obvious when we examine the outcomes of abstinence-pledge movements. Roughly 2½ million people have taken a pledge to remain celibate until marriage, usually under the auspices of religiously based movements such as True Love Waits or the Silver Ring Thing. However, more than half of those who take such pledges end up having sex before marriage, usually not with their future spouse. While those who take the pledge tend to delay their first sexual intercourse for 18 months longer than nonpledgers and have fewer partners, communities with high rates of pledging also have very high rates of sexually transmitted diseases (STDs). This could be because fewer people in these communities use condoms when they break the pledge (Regnerus 2007; Talbot 2008).

The main point is that sexual attitudes and behaviors can be linked to our religious affiliations but perhaps not in the ways we expect.

that Americans report high levels of attendance at religious worship services, but as you can see, there are significant geographical variations. Attendance at weekly worship is shown in Figure 12.5.

The question of what it means to be "religious" is discussed in the next "Engaging Sociology."

Table 12.4b Leading Religious Indicators (in Percent)

Belief in God	92[a]
Member of a church, temple, or mosque	63[b]
Say they attend worship services regularly	43[c]
Religion *very important* in life	55[a]
Prays daily	58[d]
High confidence in organized religion	44[e]

Sources:

a. Newport (2012e).

b. Newport (2009).

c. Newport (2010).

d. Pew Forum on Religion and Public Life (2009).

e. Saad (2012).

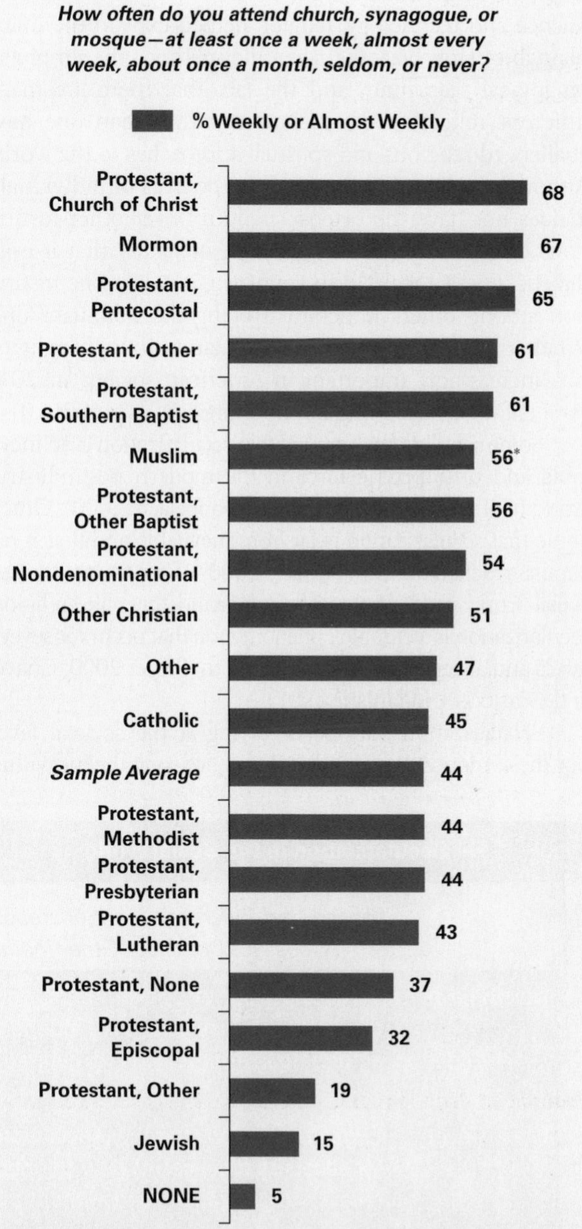

Figure 12.5 Mosque Attendance/Church/ Synagogue

Source: Bukhari (2003); Newport (2006).

Note: Data on Muslims come from a difference source and from an earlier date (Bukhari 2003).

Engaging Sociology

Determining What It Means to Be "Religious"

- Study the list of items in Table 12.4a. Do issues such as belief in God, church membership, or frequency of attendance seem like a good measure of one's religiousness? Why might the answers to those questions be indicating something other than the depth of one's religious faith?
- Look at the variability of attendance indicated in Figure 12.5. Given the fact that attendance varies so much by religious group, does that mean that members of some groups are less religious, or does that mean that attendance is not a very good measure of religiosity for some groups?
- Is asking whether religion is very important in one's life, whether religion answers problems in life, or how much confidence one has in religious organizations a good indicator of religiosity? What might be some misleading dimensions of using these as measures of "religiosity"?
- Some scholars have argued that how religious beliefs actually affect one's behavior is a good indicator of religiosity. So in studying Islam, Judaism, or some forms of Christianity, the measure has been how much one gives to charitable causes—including the church but also including help given to those less fortunate. Is this an accurate way to understand levels of religious influence in the society? Why or why not?

Religion and Secularization: Micro-, Meso-, and Macro-Level Discord

Secularization refers to *the diminishing influence and role of religion in everyday life*. Instead of religion being the dominant institution, it is but one of many. Secularization involves a movement away from supernatural and sacred interpretations of the world and toward decisions based on empirical evidence and logic. Before the advent of modern science and technology, religion helped explain the unexplainable. However, the scientific method, the emphasis on logical reasoning, and the fact that there are many different religious interpretations rather than one have challenged religious and spiritual approaches to the world. Although religion is still strong in the lives of individuals, it does not have the extensive control over other institutions of education, health, politics, or family that it once did. In most Global North countries, it is just one institution among others rather than being the dominant one. Whereas in 1957 69% of the population thought religion was increasingly important in American society, in 2010 70% felt it was declining in importance (Newport 2010).

Some scholars have argued that secularization is an inevitable and unstoppable force in the modern postindustrial world (Gorski and Altinordu 2008; Dobbelaere 2000). Others argue that secularization is far from inevitable and that it has almost reached its limit (Stark 2000; Warner 1993). Our social world model helps us understand that, like religion, secularization is a complex phenomenon that occurs at several levels and affects each society differently (Beyer 2000; Chaves and Gorski 2001; Yamane 1997).

Secularization may be occurring at the societal level, but the evidence suggests that this is not so at the individual level in North America (Bellah et al. 1996; Chaves and Gorski 2001). According to a 2011 Gallup poll, 92% of Americans believe in God or a universal spirit, although other research has found that 12% to 15% of Americans do not identify with any specific religious tradition (Newport 2012e; Pew Forum on Religion and Public Life 2012a, 2012b). Still, 63% claim membership in a local congregation, and 55% say religion is very important in their lives (Newport 2009). Religion remains a strong influence in Canadian life as well as indicated above. When religious faith guides people's everyday lives—their conduct on the job, their political choices, their sexual behavior, or their attitudes toward race relations—then secularization at the micro level is weak, and religious influence is strong. Faith still matters to many people.

Within church-related organizations (Baptist hospitals, Presbyterian colleges, Jewish social service foundations), the decisions about how to deliver services or who will be hired or fired are based on systematic policies designed for organizational efficiency. In other words, meso-level secularization is present even within many religious organizations. Likewise, policies in the society at large are made with little discussion of the theological implications, decisions being based on human rights arguments rather than on what is sinful, again suggesting that society has become secular at the macro level (Chaves 1993; Roberts and Yamane 2012; Yamane 1997). Debates about prayer in schools, court decisions about "one nation under God" in the Pledge of Allegiance to the flag, and the involvement of religious leaders in political issues suggest that societal-level secularization is a point of controversy in the United States. Still, few will deny that the bureaucratic structures of the United States and virtually every other postindustrial nation are thoroughly secularized. Macro, meso, and micro levels of secularization do not seem to be in harmony, as illustrated in Table 12.5.

Table 12.5 **Secularization in the Social World**

	Institutional Differentiation (Separation of Religion So It Does Not Dominate Other Institutions)	*Decision Making*
Macro Level	In the larger society, government, education, and the economic institutions are independent and autonomous from religious organizations.	Decision making about social policies uses logic, empirical data, and cost/benefit analysis rather than scripture, theological arguments, or proclamations of religious authorities.
Meso Level	*Organizations* look to other social associations for accepted practices of how to operate, not to religious organizations and authorities.	Decision making about an organization's policies is based on analyses of possible consequences, rather than on scripture, theological arguments, or proclamations of religious authorities.
Micro Level	*Individuals* emphasize being "spiritual rather than religious," formulate their own meaning system or theology, and may believe that spirituality has little to do with other aspects of their lives.	Decision making about life decisions is based on individual self-interest without concern for the teachings of the religious group or the clergy.

Source: Roberts (2004).

Photo Essay

Secularization and Faith in Context

Religious faith is very strong at the micro level in American society, but public policy and the operation of organizations and institutions such as the government and public schools are secularized—based on principles of pluralism, rational deliberation rather than doctrine, and scientific evidence rather than scripture or dogma. Protests arise—such as "See You at the Pole" prayers around the American flag (the symbol of the nation); this sign about the Ten Commandments in Kentucky, where the courts had ruled that the Ten Commandments were not to be posted in the city hall or the courthouse; and crèche scenes displayed on public properties, amid controversies and conflicting court rulings on whether this constitutes endorsement of one religious tradition.

Despite the process of secularization in some parts of the world, the sense of awe before the holy remains strong for many people. This enormous Buddha at the Yungang Buddhist Caves at Wuzhou Mountain in China was built out of a sense of the sacredness of Buddha, and it then became a source of veneration for subsequent generations.

In short, most sociologists of religion believe that religion continues to be a particularly powerful force at the individual level and that it has some influence in the larger culture (at the meso and macro levels). There is a macro-level trend toward secularization in most Global North societies, but the trend is neither inevitable nor uniform across societies (Roberts and Yamane 2012; Sommerville 2002).

At the global level, no particular theological authority has the power to define reality or determine policies, religious authority structures are minimal, and secularization is well established. Perhaps, this is one reason why conservatives of nearly every religious faith are leery of global processes and global organizations, such as the United Nations. Our global organizations are governed by rational-legal (secular) authority, not religious doctrines.

Thinking Sociologically

What might be the results if a society is secularized at the meso and macro levels but not at the micro level? Is this a problem? Does it create problems in decision making and social coherence? Is separation of church and state with government policies based on secular calculations of the interests of the nation still a good idea? Why or why not?

Religion: Contributor to War or Peace?

Can religion bring peace to the world? Most religious systems advocate living in harmony with other humans and with nature, yet peace is not the reality. Although the meaning systems of all the Abrahamic religions—Christianity, Judaism, and Islam—embrace a world of peace and justice, the structural system does not always reward those who pay attention to the meaning system, as we see in cases of racism and sexism. Christian denominations often foster nationalistic loyalty—with displays of the flag and even pledges of allegiance to the flag during worship. This endorsement of national pride can actually foster we-versus-they thinking and can undermine peace. Congregations that take peace activities seriously may decline in membership and financial stability, whereas those that stir up chauvinistic sentiments attract large numbers. So the structural system may actually undermine the message of the meaning system because growth and financial vitality are major concerns for many local church leaders. Despite the rhetoric, fiscal concerns can actually trump claims to worship the "Prince of Peace."

Still, there is movement toward interfaith and transnational cooperation. Christian, Islamic, Jewish, and other world faiths sponsor a variety of programs aimed at health care, hunger relief, and easing of suffering caused by natural disasters. Prior to the 1700s, remarkably few efforts had been made to reach out to people in other cultures. Moreover, from 1700 until well into the 20th century, outreach programs were aimed almost exclusively at trying to convert the "heathens," those with belief systems that differed.

Liberal theologies suggest that God may speak to people through a variety of channels, including the revelations of other religious traditions. While religious leaders may feel that their beliefs provide the fullest and most complete expression of God's Truth, they recognize that other beliefs also provide paths to Truth. Many global religious programs today are ecumenical and aimed at humanitarian relief rather than proselytizing.

Members of fundamentalist groups—whether they are Orthodox Jews, traditional Muslims, or born-again Christians—generally believe in a literal interpretation of their holy books and a personal experience with Allah or God. They usually believe that they have the only Truth, which they must defend. Some even try to spread "the true Word" by force. This generates ethnocentrism and sometimes hatred, causing people to fight and die to defend their belief systems and way of life. Fundamentalist religious groups use strategies to attempt to preserve their distinctive identity as a people or group (Marty and Appleby 1991, 2004). They seldom believe in pluralism or tolerance of other beliefs but rather believe that they are the only true religion. Consequently, they resist and defend themselves against modernism, which threatens their beliefs and way of life (Ebaugh 2005; Stern 2003; Wessinger 2000). Thus, religious groups may engage in violent acts against others.

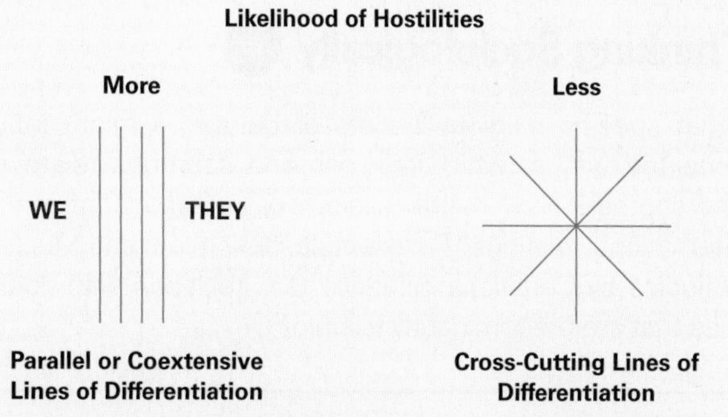

Figure 12.6 Lines of Differentiation Between "We" and "They"

Note: Imagine that each line represents a division in society between groups based on religion, ethnicity, political party, economic status, language spoken, skin color, or other factors. Parallel lines of differentiation divide people in each conflict along the same lines. *Crosscutting lines* cut the differences, so that people who were part of "they" in a previous antagonism become part of "we" in the present discord. This lessens the likelihood of deep and permanent hostilities within a social unit.

Conflict between religious groups is especially intense if ethnic, economic, and religious differences are present. Consider Ireland, where the main landowners (the wealthy) are Protestants who are of Scottish descent. The laborers (lower income) are predominantly native Irish in ethnicity and are Roman Catholic. So the lines of "we" and "they" are virtually the same on social class, ethnicity, and religion, and therefore are identical on political party affiliation. Hatred between Protestants and Catholics is exacerbated by the lack of crosscutting loyalties or friendships (McGuire 2002). The frustrations of groups not in power lead to ethnocentrism and sometimes hatred against others. Those in power similarly develop stereotypes about those unlike themselves, whose ideology and values are different. Crosscutting social cleavages reduce social hostilities, as Figure 12.6 illustrates. When one is in a group—say, a political party—that has people of different religions, different ethnicities, and different socioeconomic class, it becomes much less likely that one will vilify people from those other groups. They no longer—as a category—can be seen as uniformly evil or as the enemy. This is what is meant by crosscutting divisions.

Religion has the greatest potential for reducing hatred between groups when the groups share some type of common identification. If the conflict is over ethnicity and economics, a common religious heritage can lessen the likelihood of violent confrontation. If more people were in political parties or in social clubs (like Kiwanis Club or local American Legion Post) with Muslims, then they would not be vilified as they were by the September 2012 controversial YouTube video desecrating Muhammad and Islam. Some religious groups (including Christian, Jewish, and Muslim) have joined together in peaceful enterprises such as attempts to ban nuclear weapons or to address global poverty or climate change. These common purposes provide for cooperation and collaboration, thus lessening animosity and we-versus-they thinking.

The core reason why some countries are secular may be found in their history. The conflicts in Europe between religious groups were very brutal, beginning with the bloodletting in the Hundred Years' War. From that time, "religion was the sixteenth century word for nationalism" (Wallerstein 2005:125). The intense religious in-group loyalties led to a willingness to kill those who were Other. The horrific religious conflicts in European societies did not reach closure until the Enlightenment. At this time, tolerance of other religions became dominant, as did a primary foundation for determining national policy (Dobbelaere 1981, 2000; Lambert 2000).

As we have seen, the disconnect between micro and macro levels—religious passion at the micro level and secular domination at the macro level—has resulted in severe tensions around the world (Wallerstein 2005). For instance, in the United States, the movement is toward increasing religiosity at the micro level and increasing secularism—with its openness to diversity—at the macro level.

The rise of religious fundamentalism around the world in the 20th and 21st centuries, whether Islamic, Buddhist, Hasidic Jewish, evangelical Christian, or Malaysian Dukway, appears to be a local reaction against global modernization (Salzman 2008). Rapid global change has resulted in anomie as people confront change—fear of obliteration of their own culture and religious beliefs, the increasing secularization of society as the supernatural realm shrinks, the threat to the material self-interests of religious organizations, and fear of interdependence among the powerful nations of the Western world. All these threats have strengthened fundamentalism, which is a reaction to global secularization.

Thinking Sociologically

What specific religious beliefs or behaviors might influence the way in which religions and countries relate to one another? How might religious organizations influence international relations? For example, how might anti-Muslim prejudice by Christians influence U.S. relations with countries that are predominantly Islamic?

Religion, Technology, and the World Wide Web

Technology and the Internet affect not only nations but also religions. From television broadcasts of megachurch services to Muslim chat rooms using technology to communicate, religious messages travel in new ways.

Prior to the wide distribution of religious texts to people who were not ordained ministers, the hierarchies of Christendom controlled what was disseminated as Truth. The common (and typically illiterate) member of the local church did not have any basis for challenging the Pope or other church leaders. Those leaders were the authority. However, Martin Luther used the printed word in many powerful ways. He and other reformers claimed that the Bible alone was the ultimate source of Truth and religious authority. The church leaders were to be believed only insofar as they were faithful to the scriptures. Luther himself used the printed word to spread his version of Christian Truth, and he did so with a vengeance. He not only wrote more than the other dissenters; he outpublished the entire legion of Vatican defenders. He published in the common languages of the people rather than in Latin, and the Protestant Reformation was launched. It is doubtful whether this could have happened without the printing press. The printing press had similar revolutionary effects within Judaism (Brasher 2004).

Today, television and multimedia worship have enhanced the marketing of religion, including the modification of the product to meet "consumer" demand (Ebaugh 2005; Roberts and Yamane 2012; Sargeant 2000). The Internet is the most recent technology with enormous impacts. There are more than a million religion websites, and they cover an extraordinarily wide range of religious beliefs and practices (Brasher 2004). Even conservative Christians such as Jerry Falwell, who dubbed the Internet an evil Tower of Babel, have used it to spread their message. The panic over whether the turn of the millennium (Y2K) would result in massive crashes in computers around the world was related to the "end of the world" prophecies by some conservative Christians (Brasher 2004). The computer, in short, was to be the medium to bring an end to life in this world.

The medium of the Internet is fast paced and oriented to the now. Technology is often outdated in a few years if not in a few months, and the past hardly seems a source of authority or of Truth. Yet traditional religious communities often excel in maintaining and propagating memories of past events that give meaning to life or that define notions of sacredness and Truth as the world around them changes rapidly. It is too early to tell for sure what impacts these most recent technologies might have on religions around the world, but one thing is clear: The Internet allows instant access to information about religions that otherwise might be obscure or nonexistent for many people. Note that the immediacy of access to the deceptive YouTube video on Islam in 2012 led to riots in many Islamic countries. This would not happen without the immediacy of communication technology.

Social Policy: The Homosexuality Debates

Gays in the church, ordination of gay ministers, and same-sex marriage in churches make for heated debate over church policy and threaten to split some denominations. Most established religious groups assume the normality of heterosexuality, but public opinion is shifting. A recent study found that 61% of Americans define households with two women raising a child as a "family." Only 38% of the population was rigidly exclusionist regarding same-sex relationships never being recognized as legitimate (Powell et al. 2010). So the public, especially the younger generation, is increasingly willing to grant gay and lesbian households a status as legitimate families.

Marriage is sanctified by religious ceremony in all major religious groups, but recently, some religious bodies have recognized the possibility of officially sanctioned weddings for gays and lesbians. In the Christian tradition, there are six passages in scripture that condemn homosexual relationships, only one of which condemns lesbian relationships (Genesis 19:1–28; Leviticus 18:22, 20:13; Romans 1:26–27; I Corinthians 6:9; I Timothy 1:10). Opposition to homosexuality is especially high among religious fundamentalists. In recent years, there have been strident conflicts in the Presbyterian (U.S.) and United Methodist denominations, but in the most conservative denominations, few questions are even raised about homosexuality because the rightness of absolute heterosexuality is taken for granted.

Liberals in the churches tend to see this issue as one of prejudice against people for a characteristic that is immutable. They assume that homosexuality is an inborn trait. Conservatives argue that homosexuality is a choice that has moral implications, and see homosexuality as a behavior that is acquired through socialization. Therefore, acceptance of homosexuality will likely increase the numbers of people who engage in this lifestyle, conservatives believe. Conservatives see liberal notions about homosexuality and gender roles as a threat to society, family, and the moral social order. Liberals typically see no moral issue and no threat to society when sexuality is expressed within a committed relationship. The real moral issue for them is bigotry—lack of tolerance for other lifestyles. Thus, conservatives and liberals have socially constructed the meaning of morality differently.

Some mainstream denominations have developed policies supportive of lesbian, gay, and bisexual persons in local churches: More Light (Presbyterian), Open and Affirming (United Church of Christ and Christian Church), Reconciled in Christ (Lutheran), and Reconciling Congregations (Methodist). These designations apply to about 300 congregations that wish to be known as "gay and lesbian friendly" (Phoenix Declaration 2012). A new denomination, Universal Fellowship of Metropolitan Community Churches (UFMCC), affirms homosexuality as a legitimate lifestyle for Christians (Rodriguez and Ouellette 2000). It also has more than 172 local churches in 37 countries (Metropolitan Community Churches 2012). One study conducted on a UFMCC congregation in New York found that homosexuals affiliated with this church have exceptionally positive personal adjustment. They are more likely to have an integrated self-concept as both a gay person and a religious person (Rodriguez and Ouellette 2000). At the same time, some religious people who are homosexual and members of traditional congregations struggle with their sense of self-concept. Yet more American adults (54%) are finding gay or lesbian relationships morally acceptable, and that carries over to acceptance of gay church members, gay marriage, gays in the military, and gay clergy (Saad 2012).

In the 2012 elections, many states had referenda and state constitutional amendment proposals on the ballot. In Minnesota, for example, the church leaders were deeply divided. Some denominations, like the United Church of Christ—took an official stand against limiting marriage to heterosexuals. In one rally of clergy opposed to the amendment—and therefore supporting same-sex marriage—there were more than 100 ministers from a wide range of denominations present (Kane 2012).

Even within denominations there are major splits on this issue. The governing document for the United Methodist church says that "homosexuality is incompatible with Christian teaching." This belief has been used to prevent same-sex marriages and ordination of gay and lesbian clergy. After the church's national legislative body voted to keep that line in church policy, the west coast regional organization issued a statement of "Gospel Obedience" that in keeping with Christian faith the west coast Methodist church would act as though that policy "does not exist." Thus, same-sex marriage is affirmed by Methodists in at least one region of the country (Western Jurisdictional Conference 2012). Methodists in southern states, in particular, are outraged by this stand.

One of the most controversial issues in several mainline denominations is over ordination of homosexuals as ministers. A Gallup poll shows an overall shift toward acceptance of homosexual clergy by Americans: Whereas only 36% approved in 1977, 56% approved by 2004, and the number is increasing (Gallup 2004; Gallup and Lindsay 1999; Saad 2012). Still, most denominations do not knowingly ordain homosexuals as ministers and do not allow their ministers to perform marriages or "holy unions" of two gay men or two lesbian women. If ministers do so, they may be defrocked. In one denomination, the Episcopalian Church in the United States, the election in 2003 of the gay clergyman Gene Robinson as bishop created a breach in the international Anglican community, as African churches cut off ties with the Episcopalians in the United States. In the summer of 2008, the Presbyterian Church (U.S.) also officially voted to change its rules and to approve ordination of gay and lesbian pastors. The decision is highly controversial, but the policy shift has been building for many years (Helfand 2008).

Thinking Sociologically

Are the core issues in same-sex marriage and ordination of homosexual clergy ones of the right of religious communities to decide their own values, or is this a broader civic issue of individual rights? How can this conflict in the definition of the problem be resolved?

Some ministers continue to perform marriage ceremonies as a protest against a policy they think is immoral. They may take a "don't ask, don't tell" position with their bishops. One retired minister estimated that even in his very conservative midwestern state, there are roughly 50 homosexual holy unions performed by Methodist pastors each year. He stated,

> Back in the 1950s, ministers could lose their ordination and ministerial privileges if they married someone in a church wedding who had been divorced. Performing a marriage of someone who had been divorced was a serious offense in the Methodist church—and in most other Protestant churches, too. If a divorced person wanted to marry a second time, a civil wedding was supposedly the only option. Many of us in the pastorate thought that the policy was inhumane. These were people whom we pastored. They had made a mistake in a previous selection of a

spouse and wanted to start again. Many clergy secretly went against formal policy of the church, but we did not tell our bishops. By the 1960s, if the church purged all of us who had done this, the Methodist church would have lost more than half of its ministers. In another 20 years, the same thing will be true with holy unions. If you have two people in your congregation who really care for each other and want to ritually affirm their lifelong commitment, how can we not honor that commitment and caring? I think it is a matter of time before this will become widely accepted. (Roberts and Yamane 2012:289)

In our social world, religious organizations influence society, and the larger society influences religious groups. Moreover, attitudes in a local community or a region of the country influence attitudes within a congregation, irrespective of the positions of the official denomination (Koch and Curry 2000). Two catalysts are creating tension for change in religious organizations: (1) the emphasis on the equality of all people before God in Christian theology and (2) an impetus in the larger society that legitimates people in leadership roles based on competence and commitment rather than on traits beyond their control (skin color, gender, or sexual orientation).

Thus, the policy issues for all religious communities are (1) whether a homosexual person can ever have the spiritual qualities to lead a congregation as its minister; (2) whether that faith community should or should not endorse and permit same-sex marriages in its churches, mosques, or temples; and (3) whether faith groups should be involved in government policy regarding the right of the state to grant marriage licenses to homosexuals or licenses for a civil union—a secular equivalent to the marriage contract that would allow more than 1,000 rights and privileges that heterosexuals enjoy. One proposed solution is that because marriage has historically been "owned" by religious communities, the state could grant licenses for civil unions (not marriages) for both homosexuals and heterosexuals. Faith communities alone would decide whether they acknowledge a couple as married. The notion that the state should have any say in the matter of marriage began only with Martin Luther, who insisted that marriage was not a sacrament. These highly contested areas of public policy continue to be contentious.

Thinking Sociologically

How is hostility toward homosexuals similar to and different from sexism and racism? Does religion play a role in heterosexism and homophobia? Why or why not?

Religion deals with issues of meaning and, like education, it serves as a core socialization agent in the society. It provides socialization of members of society on important values, which sometimes makes cooperation more possible within a society. However, conflict cannot always be overcome by appeals to values, and sometimes the issues between individuals and groups come down to matters of power and access to resources. In the next chapter, we try to penetrate power and privilege and to understand how penetrating into our lives power and privilege can be. We turn now to the institutions of politics and economics.

What Have We Learned?

Religion is a powerful force in the lives of people around the world. It typically elicits passions and deep loyalties, and in so doing, it can stimulate people to great acts of self-sacrificing charity, or it can elicit horrible atrocities and intergroup bigotries. People's religious affiliation is strongly related to their nationality, ethnic and racial group, and lifestyle. Religion is the one institution in most societies that consistently professes a desire for peace and goodwill, yet there may be inconsistencies between what people say and what they do. Religion can provide us with the hope that the world's problems may be dealt with in humanitarian ways.

Religion provides a sense of meaning in life regarding the big questions, and that is why religious symbols come to have sacred meaning. They address our spiritual life and our sense of purpose. Humans in the modern world, however, are not just spiritual. They live in states with massive governmental bureaucracies that hold power and resolve conflicts, and they participate in economic systems that produce and distribute the goods and services needed for survival. The next institutions we will examine are politics and economics—how power relations are negotiated at each level in the social world.

Key Points

- Religion makes our most important values sacred, operating through three interconnected systems: (1) a meaning system, (2) a belonging system, and (3) a structural system. (See pp. 424–425.)
- We become committed through these three systems, by our attachment to a reference group that becomes a belonging system, by making investments in the organization (the structural system), and by holding as real the system of ideas (the meaning system). (See pp. 425–427.)
- At the micro level, symbolic interaction theory illuminates how the meaning system works, with an interaction of myths, rituals, and symbols coming to define reality and making the values and the meaning system sacred. Rational choice theory focuses on the costs and benefits that influence the decisions individuals make about religious commitments, but it also examines how religious organizations go about seeking a "market share" in the competition for members. (See pp. 427–434.)
- At the meso level, religious communities usually have a mutually supportive relationship with other institutions—the family, the political system, and the economy. Religious organizations themselves can evolve into one of several types of structures (or even bureaucracies): ecclesia, denomination, sect, or new religious movement (NRM). (See pp. 434–446.)
- At the macro level of analysis, functionalists maintain that religions can serve as a kind of glue to help solidify the country and can meet the basic needs of the populace. In contrast, conflict theorists focus on the ways in which religion reinforces conflicts and inequalities in society, whether socioeconomic, racial, or gender. (See pp. 446–453.)
- In the United States and Canada, secularization is dominant at the meso and macro levels but does not seem to be happening much at the micro level. This is the source of tension in societies. (See pp. 453–460.)
- At the global level, religion can be involved in issues of war and peace (sometimes unwittingly undermining peace) and is currently experiencing interface with the world of technology and the World Wide Web. (See pp. 456–460.)
- Finally, homosexuality, same-sex marriage, and ordination of gay or lesbian clergy are examples of religious policy issues causing considerable controversy. (See pp. 462–464.)

Discussion Questions

1. What are some ways that religion and government are interdependent and interrelated in the United States?
2. If you are a person of faith and affiliated with a religious community, how did you become so? If you are not, why is that so? How did your family members and peers influence your views toward religion?
3. What motivates you to work hard and try to succeed professionally? Think about how Weber perceived the relationship between the capitalist economic system and thoughts about sacrifice and work. Does it relate to your answer to the first part of this question? Why or why not?
4. Do you think religion is more of a unifying or divisive force in (a) the United States and (b) the world today? Why? Do you have many friends from different religious groups? Why or why not?
5. What do you think might happen to society if religions did not exist? Why? How would an absence of religion impact you personally?

Contributing to Our Social World: What Can We Do?

At the Local Level

- *Campus religious foundations or ministries:* Most colleges and universities, including many of those not affiliated with a religion, have religious groups on campus. If you are not already a member and would like to join such an organization on your campus, contact a student representative or faculty sponsor, attend a meeting, and become involved. Most of these organizations participate in various types of outreach work, including volunteering for soup kitchens, food pantries, or thrift stores for the poor. If you attend a religiously affiliated college or university, you will find many and varied ministries to choose from.

At the Organizational or Institutional Level

- *College-based religious organizations.* Many religious campus organizations such as the Newman Foundation (Roman Catholic; http://newmanfnd.org), InterVarsity (Christian; www.intervarsity.org), Muslim Students Association (MSA; http://msanational.org), and Hillel Foundation (Jewish; www.hillel.org) are branches of larger organizations. You can find out more about them and how to start or join a chapter by going to their websites.

- *American Atheists* (www.atheists.org) provides similar services to atheists. According to its website, "Now in its fourth decade, American Atheists is dedicated to working for the civil rights of Atheists, promoting separation of state and church, and providing information about Atheism." Volunteers assist in this work through contributions, research, and legal support.

At the National and Global Levels

Several religious groups are committed to working for justice and peace at the national and global levels.

- *Tikkun Community* (www.tikkun.org) is an interreligious organization, started by the Jewish community, to "mend, repair, and transform the world." It is an "international community of people of many faiths calling for social justice and political freedom."
- *The American Friends Service Committee* (www.afsc.org), a Quaker organization, "includes people of various faiths who are committed to social justice, peace, and humanitarian service."
- *Catholic Relief Services* (www.crs.org) "carries out the commitment of the Bishops of the United States to assist the poor and vulnerable" in over 100 countries.
- *Lutheran World Relief* (www.lwr.org) "extends the hand of Christian love to people overcoming poverty and injustice in 50 countries."

These and similar faith-based organizations sponsor many relief and peace projects around the world. You can find out more by going to their websites.

WWW

Visit the Student Study Site at **www.sagepub.com/ballantine4e** to access additional study tools, including eFlashcards, web quizzes, video resources, audio resources, web resources, SAGE journal articles, recommended readings, and more.

CHAPTER 13

Politics and Economics

Penetrating Power and Privilege

Power and privilege penetrate every aspect of our lives. The chapter subtitle has a double meaning, however, for sociology helps us penetrate the sources and the consequences of power and privilege—both political and economic.

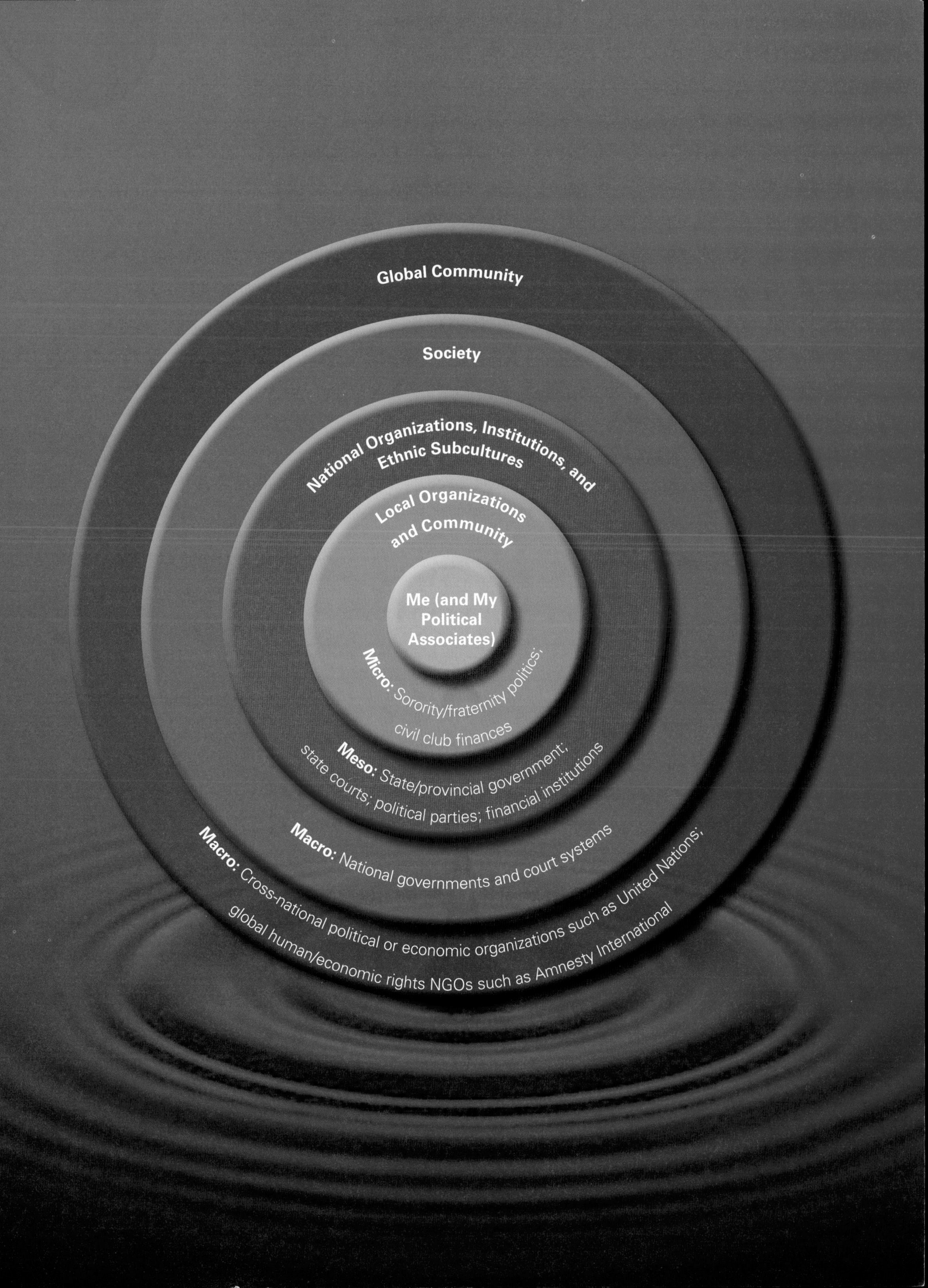

Global Community
Society
National Organizations, Institutions, and Ethnic Subcultures
Local Organizations and Community
Me (and My Political Associates)
Micro: Sorority/fraternity politics; civil club finances
Meso: State/provincial government; state courts; political parties; financial institutions
Macro: National governments and court systems
Macro: Cross-national political or economic organizations such as United Nations; global human/economic rights NGOs such as Amnesty International

Think About It	
Micro: Me (and My Political and Economic Life)	How do political power and economic power penetrate my own life, even in the privacy of my home?
Micro: Local Community	How do people in my local community exercise power in constructive or destructive ways?
Meso: National Institutions; Complex Organizations; Ethnic Groups	How does the political institution interact with the economic institution?
Macro: National Society	Why does economic instability threaten a government?
Macro: Global Community	Why do struggles over power and privilege often evolve into war and terrorism?

What's coming in this chapter?

Imagine that a nuclear disaster has struck. The mortality rate is stunning. The survivors gather together for human support and collectively attempt to meet their basic survival needs. They come from varying backgrounds and have diverse skills. Before the disaster, some—the stockbroker and the business executive, for instance—earned more money and held higher social status than the others, but that is in the past. Faced with the new and unfamiliar situation, different skills are more immediately important for survival.

Politics is about power and about mobilizing support to lead. The 2012 presidential primaries generated a lot of interest as these two candidates—Mitt Romney (left) and Barack Obama (right)—battled for the most powerful political office on the planet: the U.S. presidency.

Where should this group begin? Think about the options. Some sort of organization seems essential, a structure that will help the group meet its needs. Food, shelter, and medical care are paramount. Those with experience in agriculture, building trades, and health care are likely to take leadership roles to provide these initial necessities. As time goes on, the need for clear norms and rules emerges. These survivors decide that all members must work—must contribute their share of effort to the collective survival. At first, these norms are unwritten, but gradually some norms and rules are declared more important than others and are recorded, with sanctions (penalties) attached for noncompliance. Committees are formed to deal with group concerns, and a semblance of a judicial system emerges. One person is appointed to coordinate work shifts and others to oversee emerging aspects of this small society's life. This scenario could play out in many ways.

What is happening? A social structure is evolving. Not everyone in the group will agree with the structure, and some people will propose alternatives. Whose ideas are adopted? Leadership roles may fall to the physically strongest, or perhaps the most persuasive, or those with the most skills and knowledge for survival. Those who are most competent at organizing may become the leaders, but that outcome is by no means assured.

Political systems that have developed and have been refined over centuries probably went through similar processes under less immediately dire circumstances. However, in our world of power and privilege, a war, an invading power, or revolutionary overthrow of an unstable government can change the form of a political system overnight, necessitating rapid reorganization. The daily news brings stories of governments overthrown by military leaders in coups, with new governments emerging to fill the gap, as has been happening in the Middle East and some African countries.

The opening scenario and the political activity in our modern society share a common element—power. The concept of power is critical to understanding many aspects of our social world. Our primary focus in this chapter is on the political and economic dimensions of society, since both political and economic systems enforce the distribution of power in a society. Political systems involve the power relationships between individuals and the larger social institutions. Economic systems produce and distribute goods and services. Not everyone gets an equal share, thus giving some citizens privileges that others do not have.

In this chapter, we will consider the nature of power, politics, and economics at each level in our social world; theoretical perspectives on power and privilege; individuals and power; political systems and the distribution of power and privilege through political and economic institutions; and national and global systems of governance, including international conflicts, war, and terrorism. Because the topic of economics has been explored in many chapters of this book, such as chapters on inequality, more emphasis will be given to political systems and their relation to economic systems.

Thinking Sociologically

A nuclear disaster has killed all but a few people. How would you construct a social system from scratch? What are the issues that would need to be resolved if one were to build a system from scratch?

What Is Power?

Power is an age-old theme in many great scholarly discussions. Social philosophers since Plato, Aristotle, and Socrates have addressed the issue of political systems and power. Machiavelli, an early 16th-century Italian political philosopher, is perhaps best known for his observation that "the ends justify the means." His understanding of how power was exercised in the 15th, 16th, and 17th centuries significantly influenced how monarchs used the powers of the state (the means) to obtain wealth, new territories, and trade dominance (the ends).

The most common definition of power used in social sciences today comes from Max Weber, who saw **power** as *the ability of a person or group to realize its own will in group action, even against resistance of others who disagree* (Weber 1947).

Building on Weber's idea of power, we can identify various *power arenas*. First, the nation-state (national government) attempts to control the behavior of individuals through (a) *physical control* (police force) or *outright coercion* (threats and actual violence), (b) *symbolic control* such as intimidation or manipulation of people, and (c) *rules of conduct* that channel behavior toward desired patterns, such as workplace rules. For instance, the dictator and military in Syria have used torture, rapes, and death to intimidate dissidents and families, representing physical force as a mechanism of power. The opposition has also used force, but does not have the same degree of power.

Second, Weber's definition explains power as the ability to influence social life. Wherever people interact or participate in activities or organizations, power is a consequence (Olsen 1970). Therefore, individuals who have an understanding of interorganizational dynamics and can manipulate organization members are likely to have more power than others in organizational settings.

Third, there is a perspective that focuses on a traditional Marxist approach to class structures, arguing that the control of economic resources and production allows the ruling class to keep ruling (Therborn 1976). This points to the tight link between the institutions of politics and economics. Capitalism, for example, refers to a system in which workers help produce wealth, but that wealth is then seized by owners. Workers only own their labor, which they sell (Glasberg and Shannon 2011). People who control economic resources also protect their self-interests by controlling political processes through ideology, economic constraints, and physical coercion or political resources.

In one of many recent examples from both the Global North and the Global South, the African leader of Zimbabwe, Robert Mugabe, used all these methods, especially rigged elections and violence, to intimidate the population and opponents—to control political processes and hold onto power. In the United States, Marxists interpret those with power and privilege as using media in their self-interest to convince the public that they will eventually also be super-rich. Therefore, the inequalities seem fair to the public, and the members of the middle and working classes are convinced that further tax breaks and advantages to the wealthy are—in the long run—in their own self-interest. Power is found in all parts of the social world and is an element of every social situation (Domhoff 2005; Kettl 1993). So how does power work at each level?

Thinking Sociologically

How do you, your family members, your boss, or your professors use power? Why does each of these people have power?

Power and Privilege in the Social World

Power can be found at the most micro levels of interaction, from individuals to family groups. In family life, husband-wife relations often involve negotiation and sometimes involve conflict over how to run a household and spend money. Interactions between parents and children also involve power issues as parents socialize their children. Indeed, the controversy over whether spanking is an effective discipline or an abusive imposition of pain is a question of how parents use their power to teach their children and control their behavior.

At the meso level, power operates in cities, counties, and states and provinces. Governments make decisions about which corporations receive tax breaks to locate their plants within the region. They pass laws that regulate everything from how long one's grass can be before a fine is imposed to how public schools will be funded. State and provincial governments in Global North democracies can also control the way people live and make their living. Therefore, people have an interest in influencing governments by selecting their leaders, contributing to political campaigns, and helping elect the people who support their views. Interest groups such as ethnic or minority groups and national organizations and bureaucracies also wield power and try to influence the political process at the meso level.

Individuals can work to elect the party—and the candidates—that they think will make their lives better and improve conditions in the world. They work at the micro level to influence the meso and macro systems.

At the macro level, international organizations such as the United Nations and World Bank; nongovernmental organizations (NGOs) such as Doctors Without Borders; and military, political, and economic alliances such as the North Atlantic Treaty Organization (NATO) are parts of the global system of power. Thus, power processes pervade the micro, meso, and macro levels. Locally organized groups can force change that influences politics at the local, state/provincial, national, or global levels. In many states, local groups have organized to oppose laws that support free trade—insisting that free trade undermines fair trade because free trade places all the power in the hands of corporations whose focus is profits, not fairness.

Provincial or state laws shape what can and cannot be done at the local level. These laws may either limit or enhance the ability of citizens to protest or express their views, by limiting where and when protests can occur.

Laws at the national and global levels influence state, provincial, or county politics and policies. Global treaties, for example, affect national autonomy. This challenge to national autonomy is the main reason the United States is one of only two countries in the world that has refused to sign the international Convention on the Rights of the Child or the Universal Declaration of Human Rights (UNICEF 2005).

Power can be studied in political organizations such as local, state, or federal governments; in political parties such as Republican or Democrat; and in other types of organizations such as the auto and banking industries. Power can also be understood in terms of the allocation of economic resources in a society and what factors influence patterns of resource distribution. Both economic and political systems are important in the sociologist's consideration of power distribution in any society. Let us first consider the theoretical lenses that help us understand power and politics.

Theoretical Perspectives on Power and Privilege

Do you and I have any real decision-making power? Can our voices or votes make a difference, or do leaders hold all the power? Many sociologists and political scientists have studied these questions and found several answers to who holds power and the relationship between the rulers and the ruled.

Among the common theoretical perspectives on power are our familiar ones: interaction, rational choice, structural-functional, and conflict theories. *Interaction theorists* focus on symbols and constructions of reality that allow some people to assume power. A core concern is the legitimacy of power, or whether power is accepted by those who are ruled. *Rational choice* theorists emphasize that people calculate their own self-interests and make choices—including political choices—based on benefits to themselves and avoiding inconveniences or costs. Much analysis of voting behavior has to do with how people vote to advance themselves, but also how they sometimes fail to understand what policies would really be advantageous to them.

Focusing on the macro level, *structural-functionalists* believe that citizens legitimize political systems by supporting them through their votes or traditions. They do this because political systems serve important functions, or purposes, in society. They establish and coordinate societal goals—for example, promoting stability, providing law and order, carrying out societal goals, engaging in relations with other countries, providing protection, and meeting social needs. *Conflict theorists* believe that the state protects the privileged position of a few, allowing them to consolidate power and wealth and to perpetuate inequalities that keep them in power. This power elite theory stems from conflict theory's contention that power is concentrated in the hands of the elite, and the masses have little power.

Thinking Sociologically

How does each of the above theories help you understand the political system and power in your country?

Micro- and Meso-Level Perspectives: Legitimacy of Power

Interaction theorists focus on symbols and constructions of reality that allow some people to assume power. For symbolic interactionists, a central question is how loyalty to the power of the state is created—a loyalty that is so strong that citizens are willing to die for the state in a war. In the founding years of the United States, loyalty tended to be mostly to individual states. Even as late as the Civil War, northern battalions fought under the flag of their own state rather than that of the United States. The Federalist Party, which stressed centralized government in early U.S. history, faded from the scene. The Democratic-Republican Party, which evolved into the current Democratic Party, had downplayed the power of the federal government. This has changed. Today, the Democratic Party generally supports a larger role for the federal government than its rival, although Republican President George W. Bush expanded federal powers substantially.

Most people in the United States now tend to think of themselves as U.S. citizens more than Virginians, Pennsylvanians, or Oregonians, and they are willing to defend the whole country. National symbols such as anthems and flags help create loyalty to nations. The treatment of flags is an interesting issue that illustrates the social construction of meaning around national symbols. The "Sociology in Our Social World" on page 472 explores this issue.

Thinking Sociologically

First, read "The Flag, Symbolism, and Patriotism" essay on page 472. Is wearing a shirt or sweater with the U.S. stars and stripes in some sort of artistic design an act of desecration of the flag or a statement of patriotism? Does flying a Confederate flag symbolize disrespect for the national U.S. flag? Why or why not?

Socialization of individuals at the micro level generally instills a strong sense of the legitimacy and authority of the reigning government in a particular society. This includes loyalty to a flag or a monarch that represents the nation, as illustrated above. Individuals learn their political and economic attitudes, values, and behaviors—their political socialization—from family, schools, the media, and their nation. For example, any nation's leaders provide much of the information for newspapers and other media and can spin that information to suit their needs and manage the perceptions of the public. Governments also play a role in what is taught in schools, including a nation's worldview on capitalism or socialism or other political economic systems (Glasberg and Shannon 2011).

Social Constructions of Politics: Legitimacy, Authority, and Power

Max Weber distinguished between legitimate and illegitimate power. *Power that people consider legitimate* is **authority**, and is recognized as rightful by those subject to it (Weber 1946). Governments are given legitimate power when citizens acknowledge that the government has the right to exercise power over them. This is measured by two factors: (1) whether the state can govern without the use or threat of forceful coercion and (2) the degree to which challenges to state authority are processed through normal channels such as the legal system (Jackman 1993). Citizens of Western societies recognize elected officials and laws made by elected bodies as legitimate authority. They adhere to a judge's rulings because they recognize that court decrees are legitimate. In contrast, illegitimate power,

Sociology in Our Social World

The Flag, Symbolism, and Patriotism

Flags have become pervasive symbols of nations, creating a national identity (Billig 1995). In some countries, loyalty to the nation is taught with daily pledges to the flag at work or school. National loyalty becomes sacred, and that sacredness is embedded in the flag as a symbol of patriotism. Indeed, the nation is *reified*—that is, it becomes a concrete material reality—through this symbol. Émile Durkheim maintained that one's national group elicits loyalty and, thereby, becomes sacred. He believed that sacredness actually is a form of respect for that which transcends the individual, including the state (Durkheim 1947).

In the United States, the flag and its construction illustrate key ideas in symbolic interaction theory. For many decades after the nation was founded, U.S. citizens had more loyalty to their state than to a federal government, but in the aftermath of the Civil War, a sense of nation began to gel (Answers.com 2011). The stars and stripes each have specific meaning related to states and the nation.

Symbolic interactionists sometimes speak of how a symbol is created, gains a life separate from the original creator, and then comes to be an important part of the life of individuals (Berger and Luckmann 1966). In the case of the U.S. flag, the symbol was created by Betsy Ross in the summer of 1776, it came to have a life of its own separate from its creator when the official arrangement of stars was established by Presidential Order in 1912, and it gradually came to be incorporated into the lives of Americans as a meaningful symbol of "us" (Independence Hall Association 2010). In places such as Britain and India, a national flag does not have the same symbolic power and internal resonance as a national symbol. This is not because those countries are less loyal to the nation or less proud of their heritage. It is that other symbols, such as royal status, work just as well.

Care of the U.S. flag is an interesting example of symbolism and respect for that symbol. Flag etiquette instructions make it clear that flying a flag that is faded, soiled, or dirty is considered an offense to the flag. We are told to either burn or bury a damaged flag as a way to honor and respect it.

Some propose a constitutional amendment prohibiting burning of the U.S. flag to prevent protesters from using the flag as a protest statement against certain American policies. Because protests show disrespect, some patriots have a visceral reaction of outrage. As recently as June 2006, the Senate came within one vote of sending the flag burning amendment to the individual states for ratification (CNN.com 2006). Supporters want flag burners punished and disrespect for the flag outlawed. For many, the flag is dear and symbolizes all that is good about the United States (Billig 1995).

Those who oppose this amendment feel that only tyrannical countries limit freedom of speech. They feel that the principle of free speech, central to democracy, must be allowed even if a sacred symbol is at stake. Indeed, opponents of the amendment think passing such a law would be a desecration of what that flag stands for. The two sides have each attached different meanings to what is considered desecration of the national symbol. In the meantime, if you have a tattered or fading flag, burning it is the way you honor that flag—as long as you do so in private!

Other aspects of the U.S. Flag Code, which specifies what is considered official respect for or desecration of the flag, are interesting precisely because many people violate this code while they believe themselves to be displaying their patriotism (Sons of Union Veterans of the Civil War 2010).

1. The flag should *never* be used for advertising in any manner whatsoever. It should not be embroidered on cushions, handkerchiefs, or scarves, or reproduced on paper napkins, carryout bags, wrappers, or anything else that will soon be thrown away.
2. No *part* of the flag—depictions of stars and stripes that are in any form other than that approved for the flag design itself—should ever be used as a costume, a clothing item, or an athletic uniform.
3. Displaying a flag after dark should not be done unless it is illuminated, and it should not be left out when it is raining.

4. The flag should never be represented flat or horizontally (as many marching bands do). It should *always* be aloft and free.

5. The flag should under no circumstances be used as a ceiling covering. (U.S. Flag Code 2008)

According to the standards established by U.S. military representatives and congressional action, any of these forms of display may be considered a desecration of the flag, yet the meaning that common people give to these acts is quite different. Symbolic interactionists are interested in the meaning people give to actions and how symbols themselves inform behavior.

This man no doubt feels he is expressing his patriotism, yet technically he is violating the U.S. Flag Code and "desecrating" the American flag. During the Vietnam War, protesters risked attack for dressing this way, which was viewed as disrespect for the flag and the country.

or coercion, includes living under force of a military regime or being kidnapped or imprisoned without charge (see Figure 13.1). These distinctions between legitimate and illegitimate power are important to our understanding of how leaders or political institutions establish the right to lead. To Weber, illegitimate power is sustained by brute force or coercion. Authority is granted by the people who are subject to the power, which means that no coercion is needed (Weber 1946).

Force + Consent = Power

Force < Consent = Legitimate Power (authority)

Force > Consent = Illegitimate Power (e.g., dictatorship)

Figure 13.1 Weber's Formula Regarding Power

How Do Leaders Gain Legitimate Power?

In constitutional democracies, those with power do not have the right to hold people against their will, to take their property, to demand they make unauthorized payments, or to kill them to protect others. Yet, even in democracies, certain people in power have the right to carry out such duties against people who are determined to be threats to society. Consider the interrogations of military detainees (considered terrorist suspects) held by the United States, or the drone attacks in sovereign countries such as Pakistan. How do leaders get these rights? To establish legitimate power or authority, leaders generally gain their positions in one of three ways:

1. *Traditional authority* is passed on through the generations, usually within a family line, so that positions are inherited. Tribal leaders in African societies pass their titles and power to their sons. Japanese and many European royal lines pass from generation to generation. Usually called a monarchy, this has been the most common form of leadership throughout history. Authority is seen as "normal" for a family or a person because of tradition. It has always been done that way, so no one challenges it. When authority is granted based on tradition, authority rests with the position rather than the person. The authority is easily transferred to another heir of that status.

2. *Charismatic authority* is power held by an individual resulting from a claim of extraordinary, even divine, personal characteristics. Charismatic leaders often emerge at times of change when strong, new leadership is needed. Some vivid examples of charismatic religious leaders include Jesus, Muhammad, and the founder of the Mormon Church, Joseph Smith. Charismatic political leaders include Mao Zedong in China and Mahatma Gandhi in India. Both

Prince William and Kate Middleton are in line eventually to inherit the throne of England as King and Queen, and their positions have legitimacy because the citizenry of England consent to the system. The authority of the throne is traditional.

Aung San Suu Kyi, opposition leader in Burma (Myanmar), spent 15 years under house arrest after the government was taken over by the strict authoritarian military junta. While she was in prison she won the Nobel Prize for Peace. She has been released from house arrest to participate in the changing political situation in Burma, and her party has recently won 40 of 45 elected seats in the government.

men led their countries to independence and had respect from citizens that bordered on "awe." Some women have also been recognized as charismatic leaders, such as Burma's (Myanmar) Aung San Suu Kyi, pro-democracy activist, widely recognized prisoner of conscience, leader of the National League for Democracy of Burma, and winner of many awards including the Nobel Peace Prize in 1991.

Other leaders such as Adolf Hitler, leader of Nazi Germany, and Jim Jones, leader of the Jonestown cult that urged its members toward mass suicide, were charismatic but led their followers to negative ends. The key point is that for charismatic leaders, unlike traditional authority leaders, the right to lead rests with the person, not the position. Followers believe power is rooted in the personality of a dynamic individual. This is an inherently change-oriented and unstable form of leadership because authority resides in a single person. The most common pattern is that, as stability reemerges, power will become institutionalized—rooted in stable routine patterns of the organization. Charismatic leaders are effective during transitional periods but are often replaced by rational-legal leaders once affairs of state become stable.

3. *Rational-legal authority* is the most typical in modern nation-states. Leaders have the expertise to carry out the duties of their positions, and the leadership structure is usually bureaucratic and rule bound. Individuals are granted authority because they have proper training or have proven their merit. This is the form of authority most familiar to individuals living in democracies. The rational-legal form of authority often seems entirely irrational and an invitation to chaos to people in tradition-oriented societies. It is important that authority in this system is divided between the position (which establishes criteria and credentials for the position) and the person (who has achieved those credentials for the position).

Each of these three types of authority is a "legitimate" exercise of power because the people being governed give their consent, at least implicitly, to the leaders (Weber 1947, 1958). However, on occasion, leaders overstep their legitimate bounds and rule by force. Some of these rulers, such as Bashar al-Assad in Syria, are challenged and overthrown.

Self-Interest as a Path to Legitimacy

In the United States, legitimacy to govern is often rooted in ideology—in the dreams and self-image of the nation. However, in contemporary democratic politics, there is often, and perhaps increasingly, explicit reference to self-interests of voters. This reflects the *rational choice perspective* that humans tend to vote for their own self-interests and benefit, regardless of whether the actions of government would be fair to all citizens. Both U.S. Republican and Democratic parties draw support based on self-interests.

Both parties try to convince the public that their own policies will serve the self-interests of each voter. Democrats tend to argue that their government policies benefit citizens directly. For example, the democratic appeals from Vice

President Joe Biden tend to be very clear and forceful in support of the self-interests of the working and middle classes.

Republicans stress that less government and more tax breaks to those with wealth create a greater stimulus to the economy than anything the government can do (though the immediate affect is beneficial to the wealthy), but will have long-term benefits for the entire populace. Again, the appeal is to self-interests. Ronald Reagan appealed to self-interest when he asked in his campaign for the presidency: "Are you better off now than you were four years ago when this administration took office" (Shirley 2012)? This explicit appeal is one path to legitimacy of power, and it is the explanation favored by rational choice theorists.

An issue that interests many theorists is that many people do not understand their own self-interests. This is especially true in the world of politics with propaganda on various sides of any issue and with the complexity of social policies. The result is that people may vote for people who support policies that would actually harm them. To make it even more complex, some people vote based on values—right to life or protection of the environment, for example—because they think it is the right thing to do. The policy may not be in the person's self-interests—unless the person is considering long-term noneconomic interests, such as a desire to please God and to have a good place in the afterlife.

Macro-Level Perspectives: Who Rules?

Pluralist Theory

Pluralist theory holds that power is distributed among various groups so that no one group rules. According to pluralists, it is primarily through interest groups that you and I influence decision-making processes. Our interests are represented by groups such as unions or environmental organizations that act to keep power from being concentrated in the hands of an elite few (Dahl 1961; Dye and Zeigler 1983). One current example of an interest group in the United States is the Tea Party, which is discussed in the next "Sociology in Our Social World" on page 476.

Politics involves negotiation and compromise between competing groups. Interest groups can veto policies that conflict with their own interests by mobilizing large numbers against certain legislative or executive actions. Witness the efforts to influence health care reform in the United States and to reform government and industry practices. Greenpeace, Common Cause, Earth First!, Bread for the World, the Christian Coalition of America, Focus on the Family, the Family Research Council, various labor unions, and other consumer, environmental, religious, and political action groups have had impacts on policy decisions. According to pluralists, shared power is found in each person's ability to join groups and influence policy decisions and outcomes.

Pluralist theorists see value in having many sources of power in a society, so that no one group can dominate. For workers, this usually means uniting to have a strong voice through unions. Here we see several hundred autoworkers and their supporters stage a protest against poor working conditions and violation of labor practices by their company.

National or international nongovernmental organizations (NGOs) can have a major impact on global issues and policy making, as exemplified by the Grameen Bank and other microcredit organizations (Yunus and Jolis 1999). NGOs exert influence on power holders because of the numbers they represent, the money they control, the issues they address, and the effectiveness of their spokespeople or lobbyists. Sometimes they form coalitions around issues of concern such as the environment, human rights, health care, and women's and children's issues. An example is opposition to the USA Patriot Act by Libertarians on the far right and the American Civil Liberties Union on the far left. Although the groups differ on many issues, their opposition to infringements of civil liberties and individualism brought them together to contest many aspects of the Patriot Act, which was intended to fight terrorism, but also limits freedoms.

According to pluralists, multiple power centers offer the best chance to maintain democratic forms of government because no one group dominates, and many citizens are involved. Although an interest group may dominate decision making on a specific issue, no one group dictates all policy.

Another major theory counters the pluralists, arguing that the real power centers at the national level are controlled by an elite few and that most individuals like you and me have little power.

Elite Theory

Power elite theorists believe it is inevitable that a small group of elite will rule societies. They argue that this is the nature

Sociology in Our Social World

Interest Groups in Politics: The Tea Party

According to pluralist theorists, interest groups influence the decision-making process, though ideally no one group has complete power. The Tea Party movement in the United States began as a small group of disaffected individuals opposed to government expansion and higher taxes. With big wins in the 2010 congressional election, it has become a major determinant of Republican Party politics. Its accomplishments include electing a number of new members to the U.S. Congress, resulting in the House of Representatives being controlled by the fiscally conservative wing of the Republican Party, and the Senate Republicans being strongly influenced by this group voting in a bloc so as to not offend those in this movement (Skocpol and Williamson 2012).

The Tea Party is the latest Republican interest group to shape the political landscape. In the 1960s, "T Parties" were right-wing, antitax advocates. The current iteration is a grassroots revolt with a similar philosophy. In addition to the U.S. House and Senate, Tea Party members have also won approximately 700 seats in state legislatures around the country. Their impact moved the Republican platform to the right, and focused debates in Congress on the national debt and reducing the size of the federal government (Martin and Meckler 2012; Tanenhaus 2012).

Though sometimes short on specific proposals, they rely on ideas from conservative think tanks like the Heritage Foundation and the Cato Institute. A book by two cofounders of the Tea Party, Jenny Beth Martin and Mark Meckler, sets forth a "forty-year plan for America's future." The plan presents an overall philosophy and states that "when the creativity, ingenuity, and genius of the American people are unleashed, wonderful things happen" (Martin and Meckler 2012).

The Young Guns, the new leadership in the Republican-controlled house, practice a new mode of governance—confrontational politics representing ideological goals. This made compromise with the president and Democrats nearly impossible, especially over the debt limit. Under this leadership, Republicans recruited many highly ideological and uncompromising conservative candidates to run for offices in the 2010 and 2012 elections and then supported their candidacies. In addition to electing fiscal conservatives, the goal was to encourage disaffection with the Washington establishment and reduce support for big government programs including health care and social programs (Mann and Ornstein 2012; Ryan, Cantor, and McCarthy 2010).

The new era of no-compromise politics resulted in stalemates on many issues. Perhaps the 2012 presidential election results will change this dynamic. Some pundits, including Sarah Palin, warn of a growing schism between the elites among conservatives and the rest of the right-wing base. In the 2012 election, President Obama's campaign played to this schism by stressing that tax-cut policies have mostly benefited the wealthy and may result in reduction of services for the middle class.

Citizens join such a movement because of a common core of concerns—a central one being the staggeringly large national debt—over \$16 trillion—the interest of which consumed nearly \$230 billion of the annual federal budget in 2011 (U.S. Debt Clock 2012; U.S. Government Accountability Office 2012). The second driving concern of the movement is lower taxes, with the idea that lower taxes will allow those who have more resources to spend them on new businesses and expand the economy.

Rational choice theorists contend that people support programs serving their own interests. The citizens who join the movement, therefore, might fit into *at least* one of four categories: (1) those who see government programs as expensive to themselves and as benefitting those who contribute least to society, (2) those who are quite affluent and would benefit most from tax cuts, (3) those who have aspirations and expectations of attaining such wealth in the future, and (4) those who believe that the current system has not addressed their own needs.

Symbolic interactionists tend to focus on another social reality—the way people socially construct what a good and fair society looks like. Tea Party advocates are less likely to see a good society as one that stresses collective well-being and community enhancement, and more likely to want society to maximize individualism and personal autonomy. However, it is more complex than this in that some members of the Tea Party are concerned about how a huge national debt can undermine an entire economy and entire society. After all, each citizen in the United States owes well over \$12,000—just on the interest alone. This issue in particular is one that the society simply must address, and the Tea Party is determined to keep it center stage (Tanenhaus 2012).

of individuals and society and that pluralists are imagining a world that does not exist. Individuals have limited power through interest groups, but real power is held by the power elite (Domhoff 2005, 2008; Dye 2002; Mills 1956). They wield power through their institutional roles and make decisions about war, peace, the economy, wages, taxes, justice, education, welfare, and health issues—all of which have serious impact on citizens. These powerful elites attempt to maintain, perpetuate, and even strengthen their rule. Robert Michels, a well-known political philosopher, believed that elite rule is inevitable. He described this pattern of elite domination as the *iron law of oligarchy*. In democratic and totalitarian societies alike, leaders have influence over who is elected to succeed them and to whom they give political favors. This influence eventually leads those in elite positions to abuse their power (Michels [1911] 1967).

The social philosopher Vilfredo Pareto expanded on this idea of abuse of power, pointing out that abuse would cause a counter group to challenge the elite for power. Eventually, as the latter group gains power, its members become corrupt as well, and the cycle—a circulation of the elite—continues. Corruption in many countries illustrates this pattern. Consider the long-lasting regimes in the Middle East and North Africa that have amassed power and money over many years and are now being challenged by members of their public who no longer tolerate corruption, abuses, and the poverty into which many are relegated (Pareto [1911] 1955).

C. Wright Mills points out another angle, that there is an invisible but interlocking power elite in U.S. society, consisting of leaders in military, business, and political spheres, wielding their power from behind the scenes. They make the key political, economic, and social decisions for the nation. This group manipulates what the public hears (Mills 1956). At the turn of the century, the top U.S. elite included 7,314 people from these three spheres (Dye 2002). For example, in the business sphere, the top corporations control more than half of the nation's industrial assets, transportation, communication, and utilities. They also manage two thirds of the insurance assets. These corporations are controlled by 4,500 presidents and directors. According to the power elite theory, the U.S. upper class provides a cohesive economic-political power structure that represents upper-class interests (Domhoff 2005, 2008).

Private preparatory schools are one example of how elite status is transmitted to the next generation (Howard 2007; Persell and Cookson 1985). Many of those who hold top positions on national committees and boards or in the foreign policy-making agencies of national government attended the same private preparatory schools and Ivy League colleges—Brown, Columbia, Cornell, Harvard, University of Pennsylvania, Dartmouth, Princeton, and Yale.

Domhoff analyzed the power elite in domestic and foreign policy decision making and found that the elite have the strongest impact on national policy decisions because they run large corporations and financial institutions. Their common characteristics promote a network of connections, or "higher circles," and constitute a pool of potential appointees to top government positions. Key government officials come from industry, finance, law, and universities. They are linked with an international elite that helps shape the world economy. According to this theory, Congress ultimately has minimal power. The elected representatives accede to the power elite. Elite theorists believe that government seldom regulates business. Instead, business co-opts politicians to support its interests by providing financial support needed to run political election campaigns (Domhoff 2008).

Pluralist theorists, however, disagree, believing that one reason we have big government is that a very powerful government serves as a balance to the enormous power of the corporate world. Big business and big government are safety checks against tyranny—and each is convinced that the other is too big. Thus, although middle-level white-collar workers make decisions in specialized areas of interest, their decisions have much less influence on our lives than those made at the macro level by the few at the top.

Thinking Sociologically

Is your national society controlled by pluralist interest groups or a power elite? Can individuals influence the power elite? What evidence supports your view?

Micro-Level Analysis: Individuals, Power, and Participation

Karin signed up for every credit card available in the United States. She would max out one card and move on to the next, always paying just enough to keep the debt collectors from the door—until the day it all came crashing down on her. By then she was $53,000 in debt. She had transferred money from one no-interest card to another to avoid paying the interest. Then the monetary crisis of late 2008 hit, and soon banks were in such serious trouble that they had to tighten policies. Loans were hard to get, credit card companies became more selective, and when she could not pay the minimum due, Karin's interest rate jumped to 26%. She had little choice but to declare bankruptcy, even though it would devastate her credit rating for at least seven years. The bankruptcy provision is governed by laws passed by her government and administered by the courts. Little does Karin know that credit cards did not even exist until the 1950s, but the trajectory of her life for the next few years will be shaped by the innovations of an entrepreneur, by global economic forces, and by legislative and judicial political systems that define her options.

Whether you have health insurance or are subject to a military draft depends in part on the political and economic decisions made by the government in power. Political systems influence our personal lives in myriad ways, some of which are readily apparent: health and safety regulations, taxation, military draft, regulations on food and drugs that people buy, and even whether the gallon of gas pumped into one's car is really a full gallon. In this section, we explore the impact individuals have on the government and the variables that influence participation in political and economic policy-making processes. A key issue at the micro level is decisions by individuals to vote or otherwise participate in the political system. This private decision is, in turn, affected by where those individuals fall in the stratification system of society, not just by personal choices.

Participation in Democratic Processes

Citizens in democratic countries have the power to vote. Most countries, even dictatorships, have some form of citizen participation. In only a handful of countries are there no elections. Sociologists ask many questions about voting patterns, such as what influences voting and why some individuals do not participate in the political process at all. Social scientists want to know how participation affects (and is affected by) the individual's perception of his or her power in relationship to the state. The next "Sociologists in Action" feature discusses the world of a political sociologist as he considers the voting patterns of red, blue, and purple states in the United States.

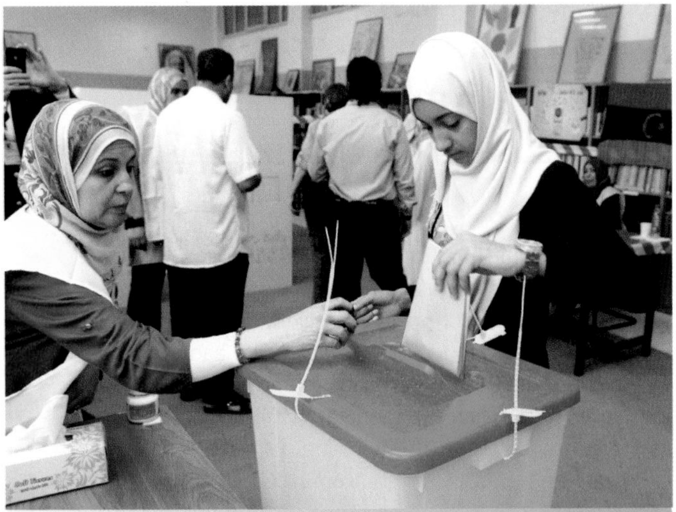

A woman in Libya casts her ballot during the 2012 national Congress elections. The elections were considered a crucial step for Libya, but they occurred amid fears of violence. Voting is viewed as a wonderful privilege and a source of hope in this setting, but it is also an act of courage.

Ideology and Attitudes About Politics and Economics

Political ideology refers to how people think about power. Let us consider several ways that our beliefs and attitudes affect our political ideas:

First, what do we believe about the power of the individual versus the power of the state? If we believe that individuals are motivated by selfish considerations and desire for power, we may feel as the 17th-century English philosopher Thomas Hobbes did: Humans need to be controlled, and order must be imposed by an all-powerful sovereign. This is more important than individual freedom and liberty. On the other hand, we might believe, as did John Locke, another 17th-century political philosopher, that human nature is perfectible and rational, that we are not born selfish but earn selfishness through experience with others. Humans, Locke argued, should have their needs and interests met, and among these needs are liberty, ability to sustain life, and ownership of property. He felt that the people should decide who governs them. Thus, we can see that support for democracy is influenced by one's core assumptions about what it means to be human.

Second, do we believe in equal distribution of resources—wealth, property, and income—or do we think that those who are most able or have inherited high status should receive more of the wealth? Some social scientists, politicians, and voters think that individuals have different abilities and are therefore entitled to different rewards. Some people are successful, and some are not. (Recall the structural-functional theory discussion in the stratification chapter about the inevitability of inequality.) Others think government should facilitate more equal distribution of resources simply because all persons are equally deserving of human dignity—food, shelter, education, and health care. Conflict theorists tend to support this view.

In the United States, for example, Republicans (and others on "the right") tend to believe that individuals and local communities should take more responsibility for education, health care, welfare, child care, and other areas of common public concern, feeling that this protects rights to local control and prevents creation of a powerful bureaucracy. This would reserve the right for each community to make its own decisions about what citizens receive which benefits. Democrats (and those on "the left") are more likely to argue for the federal government's social responsibility to the people. For instance, Democrats have been concerned that leaving policies such as school integration to local communities would perpetuate inequality and discriminatory patterns

Sociologists in Action—Ruy Teixeira

The Future of Red, Blue, and Purple America

Presidential elections are exciting times in the political arena. Prominent among those studying elections is Ruy Teixeira, a sociologist and specialist in political demography and geography.

Teixeira conducts research that considers the U.S. political scene with its red and blue states and, particularly, "purple" or swing states. He convened a group of researchers to consider social changes that affected the American political landscape. Each researcher focused on a specific aspect of the political scene. Teixeira focused particularly on the purple or swing states.

When Barack Obama was first elected in the 2008 election, new issues were shaping voter behavior. Seven dominant themes that affected the political landscape in 2008 emerged from the work of these researchers:

1. The structure of American suburbs and changes in urban living patterns more generally
2. Geographic clustering—the idea that people are increasingly likely to live near, and vote like, those who look, act, and think just like them (Cushing and Bishop 2008)
3. Race and immigration factors, including changes in the numbers and voting patterns of blacks, Hispanics, and Asians
4. Class structure changes, especially the decline of the white working class and the rise of the mass upper middle class
5. American family modifications, including the decline in the number of married couple households with children and the rise in the proportion of singles
6. Cultural issues that make the nation both more secular and more religious, resulting in more polarization
7. Aging of the baby boomers, the largest generation in American history, and the rise of the Millennials (Teixeira 2008)

With major social shifts in class structure since World War II in education levels (more high school graduates and more college-educated citizens), types of occupations (more white-collar jobs), and income levels, plus these demographic trends, the themes mentioned above, and geographic movements, new political alignments have emerged (Teixeira 2012a). Thus, five major trends influenced the 2012 presidential election:

1. Minority voters increased their share of the voting population from 26% in 2008 to 28% in 2012.
2. Minority voters maintained their overwhelming support for Obama.
3. The gender gap got even bigger; Obama carried women 55% to 44%, but lost men 45% to 52%.
4. Professionals continued their strong support for Democrats.
5. Young voters (the Millennials) turned out again in droves for the Democrats, comprising 19% of the electorate, up from 18% in 2008 (Teixeira 2012b).

(See Map 13.1 on the following page for the political breakdown of states in the 2012 presidential election.)

The political strength and orientations of various groups has shifted over the past several decades, resulting in deadlock on each side of the political spectrum. However, Teixeira and other researchers believe that this deadlock is likely to ease by the 2016 elections. Growth in Hispanic and Asian groups, shifts of the population not only to different regions of the country but also to suburbs and just beyond the suburbs, changing family structures and shifting women's roles, aging of baby boomers, and the high levels of political engagement by Millennials who generally value diversity combine to suggest major changes by the 2016 election.

Teixeira predicts that "culture wars"—the polarization and clashes between segments of society over differences in values—will not be as important in the future. Issues such as how to help nontraditional families, improve education,

(Continued)

(Continued)

and provide health care will be shared concerns that unite people. Therefore, he predicts that the polarization that has divided some communities will not last.

Teixeira has found that sociology provides exceptionally useful theory and methods to help understand our political world.

* * * * * * *

Ruy Teixeira is a senior fellow at the Century Foundation and the Center for American Progress, and a fellow at the Brookings Institution. Being a fellow means employment as a scholar to carry out research that meets the goals of the organization or *think tank*.

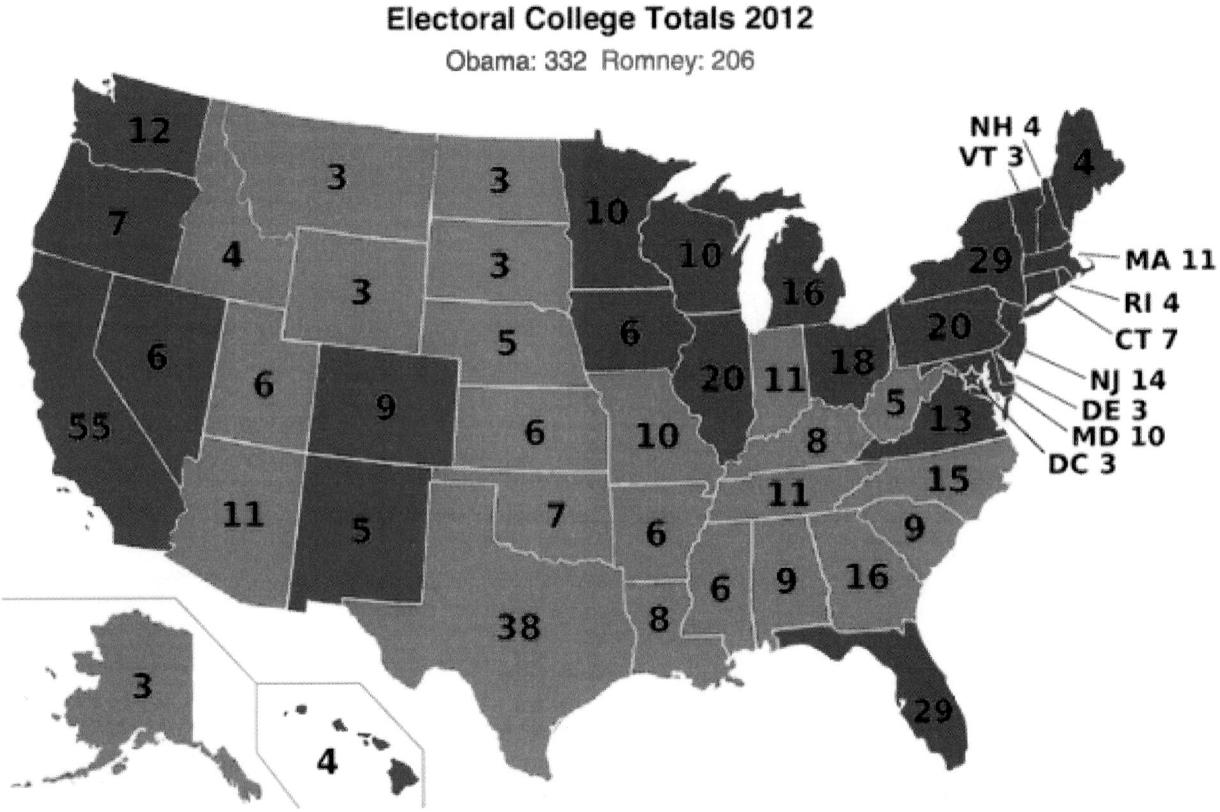

Map 13.1 States That Voted Republican (Romney/Ryan) or Democratic (Obama/Biden) in the U.S. Presidential Election of 2012

Note: The numbers indicate electoral votes a state gets.

Source: www.latinospost.com/articles/6570/20121107/latest-presidential-election-2012-map-obama-beats.htm.

in some communities. National government involvement, they feel, protects the rights of all citizens. Republicans argue that less government allows more individual freedom and also stimulates the innovation as individuals seek to solve problems and make money by doing so. The ongoing debates about the national welfare system and health care policies in the United States reflect these different philosophies. Both parties support government spending and national laws; the question is for what: Military? Social programs? Education? Health care? Abortion? Prisons?

Third, do we believe that change is desirable? Generally, these views fall into two camps: change as a potential threat to stability versus policy change to benefit the general population or segments of the population. Views on change affect how people vote.

Voters in many countries are influenced by issues such as the environment or immigration rather than traditional party ideology. Party affiliation based on ideology is becoming relatively weak in the United States, and an increasing number of people are identifying themselves as Independents rather than Democrats or Republicans, either because they do not want to commit themselves to one ideology or because they are more interested in specific issues than in an overriding philosophy of government.

Thinking Sociologically

How might your decision about how to vote (a micro-level decision) be affected by the above ideology and attitudes about politics and economics? How might these make a difference at the state/provincial, national, or global level?

Levels of Participation in Politics

A key right of most adult citizens in participatory democracies in the world is to elect their leaders. This right in some countries is an obligation, with penalties for those who do not participate. Voting provides shared citizens' power. However, in dictatorships citizens do not have the right to determine their leadership; rather it is determined by tyrannical power or birthright (Glasberg and Shannon 2011).

The majority of people in the world are uninvolved in the political process because there are few opportunities for them to be meaningfully involved (especially in nondemocratic countries). They feel that involvement can have little relevance for them (apathy) or that they cannot affect the process and are disaffected by the scandals or corruption in politics (alienation from a system that does not value them). People in higher-income jobs are more likely to vote because of more skills for analyzing policy and making decisions and more insight into what serves their self-interests (Glasberg and Shannon 2011). Structural factors also influence voting. The 2012 debates over voter registration in the United States are a case in point, with some states combing their voter lists for ineligible voters or making registration and voting difficult for some citizens, usually the elderly, minorities, and people in poverty.

Political decisions may affect people directly, and they may be drawn unwittingly into the political arena. Peasants making a subsistence living may be forced off the land and into refugee camps by wars over issues that have little relevance to them. Their children may be drafted and taken away to fight and be killed in these battles. Religious or ideological factions may force them to help pay for conflicts in which they see no purpose or have no stake. In recent years, such situations have drawn the uninvolved into politics in Guatemala, Uganda, Cambodia (Kampuchea), Haiti, Rwanda, Somalia, India, Iraq, Lebanon, Gaza, Afghanistan, the Middle East, North Africa, and Darfur (Sudan).

In representative systems, citizens are encouraged to have a voice, although their levels of involvement vary greatly. While some remain uninvolved, some vote in most elections but otherwise do not participate in politics. Others have contact with government representatives only when they have issues of personal concern. Still others are involved in local politics, actively working on issues or local elections that are of concern to them. The most involved engage in both local and national political campaigns. In some countries voting is mandatory, and even inmates in prison are expected to vote (Alexander 2010).

Political participation is affected by election laws, including those that enfranchise people, that stress voting as a requirement of citizenship, and that structure elections to facilitate representation by historically underrepresented groups. In some countries, voting is an obligation of citizenship, and voter turnout is above 90%. For example, in Argentina, Australia, Brazil, Chile, and Congo, it is a violation of the law not to vote (World Factbook 2011). Fines, community service, and even jail time are penalties for not voting. Elections are held over many days to ensure that people can get to the polls. Some other countries also make sure that ethnic minorities and women have a voice by structuring elections to ensure broad representation. The "Sociology Around the World" on page 484 examines the reasons that an African country—the war-torn nation of Rwanda—emerged early in the 21st century with the highest percentage of women in government of any nation in the world.

In the United States, voter turnout in presidential elections had dropped from 63% of registered voters in 1960 to 47.3% in 2000. However, in the 2008 presidential election turnout was 62%, and in 2012 the initial reports indicated a 57.5% turnout (Lederman 2012; United States Election Project 2012). Further, some people only voted on local issues and did not cast a vote on the presidential race. As a result, with Obama winning 50% of the votes cast (roughly half of the 57.5% who bothered to show up at the polls), just under 29% of the eligible voters really voted for the president. An even smaller percentage voted for Governor Romney. The result seems like a small mandate for the leadership of a country that calls itself a democracy. Still, presidential-year elections do have a higher turnout than "off-year" elections, and the numbers have generally been higher in the 21st century than in the three decades from 1970 to 2000 (Information Please Almanac 2008b; Lederman 2012; McDonald 2009). Higher African

Sociology Around the World

Women and Political Change in Postgenocide Rwanda

By Melanie Hughes

In 2003, Rwanda became the new global leader in women's political representation. In 2011, women were elected to 56% of the seats in Rwanda's Chamber of Deputies, plus the speaker's chair and cabinet positions, making it the most gender balanced of any national legislature in the history of the world (McCrummen 2008; Paxton and Hughes 2007; see also Table 9.1). For the first time since 1988, a country outside of Scandinavia garnered the top spot in women's political representation, and for the first time in history, the position was held by an African country. From just 10 years earlier, the number of women serving in Rwanda's parliament almost tripled.

Many were particularly surprised about Rwanda's women's involvement, given the country's recent history of economic upheaval and civil war. The instability culminated in 1994, when during a span of 100 days, an estimated 800,000 Rwandans died at the hands of their countrymen and -women in a horrific ethnic genocide. So, how did Rwanda bounce back within a decade to lead the world in women's political representation?

At the micro level, research suggests that the behavior of individual women during and after the Rwandan genocide generated support for their empowerment (Hughes 2004). During the civil war, women served on the front lines with men, led military actions, and worked as mediators to help end the insurgency. After conflict subsided, women played key roles in the reconstruction effort (UNIFEM 2002). Interviews with Rwandans suggest that the burdens taken on by women during this period generated both the political will and the public support necessary to advance women in politics (Mutamba 2005).

Important changes also occurred at the meso level. Immediately after the killing subsided, women's associations, both new and old, began to step into the void (Longman 2005). Women's organizations took action early on to shape the new state. For example, in 1994, an organization of women's associations drafted a document addressing Rwanda's postconflict problems and suggesting how women could foster reconciliation (Powley 2003). Building up to the adoption of the new constitution in 2003, women's organizations served as a bridge, taking suggestions from women at the grassroots level into meetings with the transitional government.

Women at all levels were supported by international organizations and foreign aid. Rwanda's economic troubles meant that dependence on international funding was unavoidable, and women were well situated to take advantage of foreign monies. The empowerment of women, especially in the Global South, was on the agenda of the United Nations and other global bodies. Therefore, many international organizations helped advance the idea that women's incorporation into political decision-making positions was essential for sustainable peace (Hughes 2004).

Action by individual women, native women's associations, and international organizations all helped encourage the transitional government to adopt female-friendly political institutions. Women's councils and women-only elections were established to guarantee female representation down to the grassroots level. In addition, the new constitution mandated that women fill 30% of all policy-making posts in Rwanda.

Rwanda today has a democratically elected government, but with a fairly authoritarian leader. However, since the election in 2003, women have still been able to revise inheritance laws, pass a law banning discrimination against women, and strengthen rape laws (Longman 2005). Rwanda has come a long way toward giving women a political voice.

* * * * * * *

Melanie M. Hughes is assistant professor of sociology at the University of Pittsburgh. She is coauthor of *Women, Politics, and Power: A Global Perspective* (Sage Publications), now in its second edition.

American and Latino participation has been especially important to the increase (Sherwood 2012; Short 2009).

In off-year elections—when many Senators, congressional representatives, and state governors are elected—the turnout hovers in the low 40s or even below. This means that if 40% of the eligible population votes and it is a very close election, only slightly more than 20% of the citizenry has supported the new officeholder. Figure 13.2 indicates voter turnout since 1990.

Participation in elections in the United States is the second lowest of the Global North democracies, as indicated in Table 13.1. This means that citizens are not exercising their right to vote. The unusually high number of "inactives" is not an encouraging sign for the vitality of a democracy. Still, there was a resurgence of interest in politics among those under 30 years old during the 2008 presidential campaign as discussed in the "Sociology in Our Social World" on page 484 with the primary elections for nomination of candidates and the November election itself yielding record-breaking turnouts. Of course the fact that Barack Obama is very charismatic, appealed to young voters in 2008 with very intentional strategies using the latest technologies, and is the first African American ever to be on the ballot for a major party made the presidential election an unusual draw for young people and for minorities.

Although election turnouts mean that about 29% of the total citizenry actively supported President Obama, the outcome has consequences for the direction of the country. In 2012, the Obama family celebrated the reelection of the president.

Table 13.1 **Average Voter Participation Over 60 Years (All Elections)**

Country	*Voter Participation % (All Elections for 60 Years)*	*Most Recent Parliamentary Election*
Italy	92.5	80.5
Iceland	89.5	85.1
New Zealand	86.2	74.2
South Africa	85.5	77.3
Austria	85.1	81.7
Netherlands	84.8	75.4
Australia	84.4	93.2
Denmark	83.6	86.6
Sweden	83.3	84.6
Germany	80.6	70.8
United Kingdom	74.9	65.8
Argentina	70.6	79.4
Japan	69.0	69.3
Canada	68.4	61.4
France	67.3	60.0
Bolivia	61.4	94.5
USA	48.3	41.6
Mexico	48.1	62.5
Brazil	47.9	81.9

Source: International Institute for Democracy and Electoral Assistance 2008.

*The figures are averages of voter participation for all elections over a 60-year period. Note that enfranchisement of women and various ethnic minorities changed in some countries during that time, so these should be viewed as very crude overall indicators of voting patterns.

Note: To see the voting participation figures for 172 countries in the world, go to http://www.idea.int/vt/.

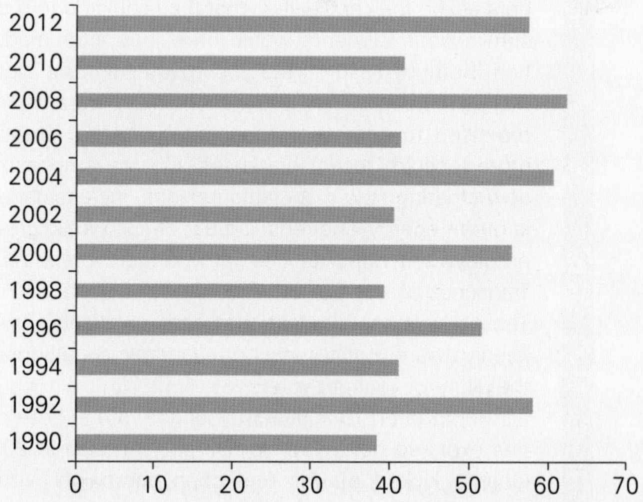

Figure 13.2 Voter Turnout in the United States: 1990-2012 (by percentage of eligible voters)

Source: United States Election Project 2012

Sociology in Our Social World

The 2012 Presidential Election and the Youth Vote

By Jeremiah Castle

The 2012 U.S. presidential election was a close race between incumbent Barack Obama and challenger Mitt Romney. The election saw the creation or evolution of several trends that impact younger voters. Recognizing that the 18–29 age group was a key part of Obama's coalition in 2008, both campaigns attempted to reach out to this key constituency in debates and advertisements. Social media again played an important role, as the campaigns used platforms like Facebook and Twitter to keep followers updated on news and appearances. Together, these trends suggest that both parties are increasingly realizing the impact of younger voters.

Throughout the campaign both candidates stressed how their policies would improve life for recent graduates. For example, youth-specific issues played an important role in the second presidential debate. During the debate, which was conducted in a "town hall" format where undecided voters asked the candidates questions, a 20-year old college student asked the candidates what they could do to make sure college students would have jobs after graduation. Romney assured the young voter that he would maintain the Pell Grant and student loan programs, and promised to improve the economy, thereby creating more jobs for recent graduates. Obama emphasized how creating new manufacturing jobs, increasing jobs in green energy, and reducing the deficit would create employment opportunities for younger voters ("Full Transcript of the Second Presidential Debate" 2012). Their responses suggest that both candidates were keenly aware of the impact of economic conditions on the plight of younger voters.

In an effort to appeal to younger voters, both parties explored new ways to use social media in 2012. Obama kicked off his reelection campaign with a video posted on YouTube (Cillizza 2011; "It Begins With Us" 2012). Throughout the campaign, both Obama (@BarackObama) and Romney (@MittRomney) used Twitter accounts to spread news, advocate policies, and keep supporters energized over the course of the campaign. In an effort to attract new followers, the Obama campaign used Facebook to hold drawings for dinner with the president, while the Romney team offered an opportunity to accompany him for a day on the campaign trail (Felix 2012). Facebook also served as a nonpartisan platform to increase civic engagement among users, including offering a tool for users to find their polling places and encouraging them to announce that they voted via a status update on Election Day.

While both campaigns used social media, data suggest that the Obama campaign was able to reach a wider audience. For example, as of November 6, 2012, Obama's Facebook page had 32 million likes, while Romney's page had just 12 million. Obama's advantage appeared to be even greater on Twitter: As of November 6, 2012, Obama had over 22 million followers, while Romney had just 1.7 million followers. Certainly not all of those who like the page are citizens or can vote in the U.S. election, but it still suggests that Obama had a major advantage in the breadth of his social media following.

Obama also had the advantage among youth voters at the polls. Early exit polls confirmed that, while Obama's advantage among younger voters was not as large as it was in 2008, it remained substantial. In 2012, 60% of voters ages 18–29 supported Obama (down from 66% of younger voters in 2008), while 36% supported Romney. Exit polls also show that younger voters represented about 19% of the total electorate, up roughly a point from 2008 (Kingkade 2012). One study showed that if the votes of those under 30 were not counted, Romney would have won the crucial battleground states of Ohio, Florida, Virginia, and Pennsylvania, thereby giving him the presidency ("At Least 80 Electoral Votes Depended on Youth" 2012). This finding leaves little doubt that younger voters had a significant impact on the outcome of the election.

The pattern of (slightly) increasing turnout from younger voters led experts, including Rock the Vote president Heather Smith, to speculate that higher youth turnout is due to differing norms between the Millennial generation (the current youth generation, born between the 1980s and 2000s) and Generation X (those born between the 1960s and 1980s; Robillard 2012).

However, it remains to be seen whether this trend will continue in the future. Given that Obama is prohibited from seeking another term by the Constitution, both the Republicans and the Democrats will be seeking new potential presidential candidates over the coming years. Certainly one criterion that will be used to evaluate candidates will be their appeal to younger voters. While nothing is certain, current evidence suggests that younger voters will continue to play an important role in national politics in the coming years.

* * * * * * *

Jeremiah Castle earned a minor in sociology in college and is now a PhD candidate in political science at the University of Notre Dame.

Thinking Sociologically

How important do you think voting blocs were in the 2008 and 2012 U.S. presidential election—the youth vote, women, African Americans, the religious right?

Meso-Level Analysis: Distributions of Power and Privilege Within a Nation

A village within the Bantu society of southern Africa has lost its chief. Bantu societies provide for heirs to take on leadership when a leader dies. However, there is no male heir to the position, so a female from the same lineage is appointed. This woman must assume the legal and social roles of a male husband, father, and chief by acting as a male and taking a "wife." The wife is assigned male sexual partners, who become the biological fathers of her children. This provides heirs for the lineage, but the female "husband" is their social father because she has socially become a male. This pattern has been common practice in many southern Bantu societies and among many other populations in four separate geographic areas of Africa. Anthropologists interpret this as a means of maintaining public positions of dominance and power in the hands of males in a particular family and community (O'Brien 1977). Ruling groups in society, in this case a meso-level tribal society under the jurisdiction of a nation-state, have mechanisms for ensuring a smooth transition of power to keep the controlling structure functioning.

Meso-level political institutions include state or provincial governments, national political parties, and large formal organizations within the nation. Equally important is that meso-level political institutions influence and are influenced by other institutions: family, education, religion, health care, and economics.

Among the Bantu of southern Africa, if a chief dies it is possible for a woman within the family lineage to succeed him, but she must take a "wife" and fulfill the leadership role normally established for males.

What Purposes Do Political and Economic Institutions Serve?

Most of us have had an argument over ownership of property, have been in an accident, have met people who needed help to survive, or have been concerned about wars raging around the world. The political institution addresses these issues and serves a variety of other purposes, or *functions*, in societies. The economic institution includes the statuses, groups, and processes that ensure the production of goods and services that people in the society need to survive and to thrive.

For most people, interaction with the government begins with a record of their birth and ends with a record of their death. In between, the government is the institutional structure that provides security, looks out for the needs of citizens, establishes standards for education, and represent the country in interaction with other countries and international bodies—though not all governments successfully carry out these tasks.

We have learned in earlier chapters that each institution has purposes or functions it serves. Just as family, education, medicine, and religion meet certain societal needs, so do the political and economic systems. The following six activities are typical purposes (functions) of meso-level political and economic institutions. They set the stage for power and privilege carried out at the macro level in national and international arenas.

1. *To maintain social control:* We expect to live in safety, to live according to certain "rules," to be employed in meaningful work, and to participate in other activities prescribed or protected by law. Ideally, governments help clarify expectations and customs and implement laws that express societal values. However, in some cases, governments rule with an iron hand and people live in fear because of the social control imposed by government. This has been the case in Afghanistan under the Taliban, when leaders used armed militia to terrorize the country by imprisoning, torturing, and killing suspected dissenters to make sure the population did the Taliban's bidding.

2. *To serve as an arbiter in disputes:* When disputes arise over property or the actions of another individual or group, a judicial branch of government can intervene. In some systems, such as tribal groups mentioned above, a council of elders or powerful individuals performs judicial functions. In other cases, elected or appointed judges have the right to hear disputes, make judgments, and carry out punishment for infractions.

3. *To protect citizens of the group:* Governments are responsible for protecting citizens from takeover by external powers or disruption from internal sources. However, they are not always successful. Cities are often violent, gangs roam the streets, terrorists threaten lives, minority groups receive unfair treatment, and governments lose territory or even control of their countries to external forces. While former Venezuelan President Hugo Chávez nationalized some of the nation's oil and other industries to prevent foreign interests from controlling the country's resources, Mexico's former President Felipe Calderón fought a difficult war against drug cartels (Herman and Peterson 2006; Hispanic-Americans.com 2011).

4. *To represent the group in relations with other groups or societies:* Individuals cannot negotiate agreements with foreign neighbors. Official representatives deal with other officials to negotiate arms and trade agreements, protect the world's airways, determine fishing rights, and establish military bases in foreign lands, among other agreements. The four functions listed thus far are rather clearly political in nature; the last two are areas of contention between political and economic realms.

5. *To make plans for the future of the group:* As individuals, we have little direct impact on the direction our society takes, but the official governmental body—be it elected, appointed, or imposed through force—shares responsibility with economic institutions for planning in the society. In some socialist societies, this planning dictates what each individual will contribute to the nation: how many engineers, teachers, or nurses they need. They then train people according to these projections. In other societies, power is much less direct. In capitalist systems, for instance, supply and demand are assumed to regulate the system, and there is less governmental planning—especially in economic matters—than in socialist societies. The question of who plans for the future is often a source of stress between the political and economic institutions: Are the planners elected politicians or private entrepreneurs?

A Pakistani child points his gun toy at an effigy representing the United States during a protest in Karachi during a pro-Taliban demonstration of about 2,000 people. Sometimes animosities toward a feared "other," such as the United States, are so strong that people will support even oppressive authoritarian regimes.

6. *To provide for the needs of their citizens:* Governments differ greatly in the degree to which they attempt to meet

the material needs of citizens. Some provide for most of the health and welfare needs of citizens, whereas others tend to leave this largely to individuals, families, local community agencies, and other institutions such as religion. Not everyone agrees that providing needs is an inherent responsibility of the state. Their idea is that the economy will produce higher-quality goods and in the right proportions for the population if the government gets out of the way and lets individuals make the decisions based on what is in their self-interests. The debates over a health care system and welfare system in the United States point to the conflicts over who should be responsible—the state or private individuals. Should such services be coordinated by the government or left to "the invisible hand" of market forces?

The ways in which governments carry out these six functions are largely determined by their philosophies of power and political structures. Political and economic institutions, such as family and religious institutions, come in many forms. In essence, these variations in political institutions reflect variations in human ideas of power. The point is that functionalists focus on the positive role of each institution in the lives of people and for the stability of society.

Thinking Sociologically

In an era of terrorist threats, how do you think the "protecting the safety of the citizens" function has affected the ability of governments to meet their other functions?

Meso- and Macro-Level Systems of Power and Privilege

While *politics* refers to the social institution that determines and exercises power relations in society, *economics* is the social institution that deals with production and distribution of goods and services. These two institutions overlap in part because to have power means one has access to resources. Both politics and economics focus on questions related directly to the concept of power and power relationships between individuals, organizations, nation-states, and societies. How goods are distributed to the members of society—a major function of economics—is often determined by who has power.

Getting elected to positions of power requires significant financial resources, so being in political position means cultivating relationships with leaders in the economic system. Thus, there is a reciprocal relationship between economics and politics. In many countries, the government is the largest employer, purchaser of goods, controller of exports and imports, and regulator of industry and of interest rates. In the United States, many government regulatory agencies, such as the Food and Drug Administration, Department of Agriculture, and Justice Department, watch over the economic sector to protect consumers.

Government officials have a vested interest in the well-being of the economy, for should the economy fail, the state is likely to fail as well. Recessions, depressions, and high rates of inflation put severe strains on governments that need stable economies to run properly. When problems occur, government officials are inclined to increase their roles in the economic sector. Witness the volatile money markets since 2008 and measures such as bailouts taken by governments to stabilize the economy.

In September 2008, the Dow Jones index dropped an unprecedented 777 points in a single day and fell another 782 points a week later. The New York Stock Exchange, usually bustling, was nearly empty, and President Bush and Congress immediately began to look for "stimulus packages" to keep the economy from going into a deep recession. As Obama became president in 2009, turning the economy around became one of the key challenges of his presidency. The problem of a dramatic drop in financial markets is a loss of confidence so that no one invests, lending institutions are not able to loan money easily, business stagnates, unemployment rates skyrocket, and the entire government may be held responsible for lack of economic vitality. When a country goes into a recession, the party in power is often held responsible and will not likely be reelected if the recovery takes too long. Economic recessions can destroy the careers of politicians but can also create such dissatisfaction that the entire government may be at risk of an uprising from citizens.

Dennis Blair, then director of U.S. national intelligence, said in February 2009 that the global economic crisis is the most serious national security issue facing the nation (Miller 2009). He pointed out that in the past, countries have been able to export more goods to work their way out of a recession, but that is not possible when the economic slump is global. The result could be unstable governments, waves of refugees crossing national borders, and a "backlash against American efforts to create free markets" (Miller 2009). The economic crisis could mean that governments cannot meet their defense obligations or provide the services necessary to their citizens. Therefore Blair called the extreme economic downturn a "bigger threat than Al Qaeda terrorists" (Haniffa 2009). Recession in countries around the world influences other countries because of trade and international markets. A vivid example in 2012 was the instability of the Greek economy, which has created fear in the rest of the European Union that this one economy might undermine the rest of the countries in that union.

A stable economic system is essential to political stability, and extreme fluctuations in the economy are frightening to those in power. On the day the Dow Jones index dropped dramatically, the New York Stock Exchange, usually bustling with activity, was nearly empty.

Types of Political Systems

The major political systems in the world range from fascist totalitarianism to democracy. However, each culture puts its own imprint on the system it uses, making for tremendous variation in actual practice. Two broad approaches are discussed below to illustrate the point.

Authoritarian Political Systems. The government of Saudi Arabia is a hereditary monarchy based on traditional leadership. **Authoritarian political systems** such as this *are controlled by absolute monarchs or dictators who allow limited or no participation of the population in government and control much of what happens in the lives of individuals.* They often have the backing of the military to keep them in power. Authoritarian regimes have been common forms of government in the world. Some are helpful to citizens—benevolent dictators—but most control and discourage dissent. The Castro brothers—Fidel and more recently Raúl—have maintained absolute control of Cuba since 1959, and while they are despised by many Cuban immigrants in the United States and subject to U.S. government embargos, they are admired by many Cubans as ruling in the best interests of the people, even if autocratically.

A **totalitarian government** is *any form of government that almost totally controls people's lives.* Totalitarian states are often based on a specific political ideology and run by a single ruling group or party, referred to as an *oligarchy*. Russia under Joseph Stalin, Germany under Adolf Hitler, and Libya under Moammar Gadhafi are examples. (The next "Sociology Around the World" provides an example of one totalitarian regime.) The state typically controls the workplace, education, the media, and other aspects of life. All actions revolve around state-established objectives. Dissent and opposition are discouraged or forcefully eliminated as we have seen in Iran in recent years with violent crackdowns on demonstrators. Interrogation by secret

The Castro brothers, Fidel and his younger brother Raúl, overthrew a dictatorship in Cuba in 1959, one that was supportive of the wealthy. Although the leadership of the Castros has been more supportive of the common laborer, it is still very much a dictatorship.

Sociology Around the World

The Khmer Rouge Revolution: A Totalitarian Regime

These skulls are the remains of people massacred by the Khmer Rouge government in the Killing Fields in Cambodia (also called Kampuchea).

When the Khmer Rouge faction took over the government of Cambodia in 1978, it abolished private property, relocated urban dwellers to rural areas, seized personal property, classified some people as peasants, workers, or soldiers—and killed the rest. The group's most amazing feat was the total evacuation of the capital city, Phnom Penh. This was done to remove urban civilization and isolate Cambodia from other political influences, such as democracy.

This complete social and economic revolution under the leadership of Pol Pot was planned in Paris by a small group of intellectual revolutionaries. They believed that it would allow Kampuchea, their former name for the country, to rebuild from scratch, eliminating all capitalism, private property, and Western culture and influence.

After urban dwellers were resettled in rural camps, the totalitarian regime tried to break down the family system by prohibiting contact between members, including sexual relations between husbands and wives. Many people, including defeated soldiers, bureaucrats, royalty, businesspeople, intellectuals with opposing views, Muslims, and Buddhist monks were slaughtered for minor offenses—hence the term *the killing fields* to describe the execution sites. The death toll is estimated at more than 1.25 million. However, the Cambodian Genocide Program has uncovered meticulous records kept by Khmer Rouge leaders, and combined with evidence from mass graves, these data may double that number (Crossette 1996; Mydans 2009).

Famine followed the killings, causing many Cambodians to flee their land, traveling by night and hiding by day to reach refugee camps across the border in Thailand. Today, the economy in Cambodia is growing, especially in the areas of garment work and tourism. Thousands of tourists visit the ancient temples of Angkor Wat and the Killing Fields each year. Despite economic growth, more than 57% of the citizens work in agriculture, 16% in industry, and 17% in the service sector (World Factbook 2012f).

The economy in Cambodia mostly provides sweatshop employment; much of the sweat labor is for sports and college clothing. Young women making Dallas Cowboys jackets work 60-hour weeks, sewing 10 hours a day, 6 days a week, to earn $100 per month. Other sweatshops pay 29 cents an hour, often requiring overtime to meet quotas. More than 300,000 Cambodians, mostly young women, work in sweatshops (Fainaru-Wada and Gubar 2012). To keep their jobs, they must often work overtime, up to 80 hours a week, with no extra pay (Sine 2002). While these may seem like cruel conditions, some who are knowledgeable about Cambodia argue that these jobs are coveted by many because they are far better than other options (Kristof 2009).

Cambodia has never been a country at peace, and that seems to be true today. Violence still exists. The Human Rights Center reports chaos, corruption, poverty, and a reign of terror in Cambodia, as the military kills and extorts money from citizens. Killings, violence, and intimidation have surrounded elections, though the parliamentary elections of 2012 had somewhat fewer problems than in the past (Loy 2012).

police, imprisonment, and torture are used to quiet dissenters. Terror is used as a tactic to deal with both internal and external dissent, but when it is used by the state to control the citizenry or to terrorize those of another nation, it is called *state terrorism*.

Throughout history, most people have lived under authoritarian or totalitarian systems. Under certain conditions, totalitarian regimes can turn into democratic ones, and of course, democratically elected leaders can become self-proclaimed dictators, as was the case of a number of elected leaders who changed the constitutions to allow for them to run again (Venezuela, Zimbabwe, and Russia are examples).

Democratic Systems. In contrast to totalitarian regimes, democratic systems are characterized by accountability of the government to the citizens and a large degree of control by individuals over their own lives. Democracies always have at least two political parties that compete in elections for power and that generally accept the outcome of elections. Mechanisms for the smooth transfer of power are laid out in a constitution or another legal document. "Ideal-type" democracies share the following characteristics, although few democracies fit this description exactly:

1. *Citizens participate in selecting the government:* There are free elections with anonymous ballots cast, widespread suffrage (voting rights), and competition between members of different parties running for offices. Those who govern do so by the consent of the majority, but the political minorities have rights, representation, and responsibilities.

Within a democracy, individuals have a variety of ways in which they can influence the government such as voting, working for political parties, and protesting policies. Such individual voices are greatly enhanced if one has constitutional guarantees of freedom of speech. In this photo protesters in front of the U.S. White House in Washington, DC, try to get the attention of President Obama regarding the policies affecting women's rights in Iran.

2. *Civil liberties are guaranteed:* These usually include freedom of association, freedom of the press, freedom of speech, and freedom of religion. Such individual rights ensure dissent, and dissent creates more ideas about how to solve problems. These freedoms are therefore essential for a democracy to thrive.

3. *Government powers are limited by constitution:* The government can intrude only into certain areas of individuals' lives. Criminal procedures and police power are clearly defined, thus prohibiting harassment or terrorism by the police. The judicial system helps maintain a balance of power. These limits have caused recent dissent in several areas of U.S. law, with debates over Hispanics being asked for citizenship papers when stopped by police—something that is not done to most other people.

4. *Governmental structure and process are spelled out:* Generally, some officials are elected whereas others are appointed, but all are accountable to the citizens. Representatives are given authority to pass laws, approve budgets, and hold the executive officer accountable for activities.

5. *Written documents such as constitutions are the basis for the development of legal systems:* The constitutions describe activities in which the government must—or must not—engage. Constitutions can provide some protection against tyrants and arbitrary actions by government. The two main forms of democratic constitutional government are the parliamentary and presidential systems. In typical parliamentary governments, the head of state is often a monarch, and the head of government is a prime minister, chancellor, or premier. These are two different people. Belgium, Canada, Denmark, the United Kingdom, Japan, the Netherlands, Norway, and Sweden have this model. Examples of presidential governments include France, Italy, the United States, and Germany. The presidents in these countries tend to have more autonomy than the heads of parliamentary governments.

Proportional representation means that each party is given a number of seats corresponding to the percentage of votes it received in the election. In "winner-takes-all" systems, the individual with more than 50% of the votes gets the seat. In the United States, the winner-takes-all system has come under attack because the winner of the presidential popular vote can lose the electoral vote to an opponent who wins several of the most populous states by narrow margins. This actually happened in a presidential election in the United States: Al Gore received the most votes for president in 2000, but because all but two states (Maine and

The British system of government is a democracy and parliamentary in form. This is the opening ceremony in 2012 for the Parliament. Note the pomp and circumstance that are used to create a sense of awe for power and authority.

Nebraska) had a winner-takes-all system for electing the Electoral College, George W. Bush became the next president, as elected by the Electoral College. Defenders of this system of choosing the president argue that this protects the voice of each state, even if each individual voice is not given the same weight.

Constitutional governments may have from two to a dozen or more parties, as has been the case in Switzerland. Most have four or five viable ones. In European countries, typical parties include Social Democrats, Christian Democrats, Communists, Liberals, and other parties specific to local or state issues, such as green parties.

Technology and Democracy

In the modern world, there are new challenges and issues that face democracies. Electronic technology—the Internet and other telecommunications technologies—can be a boon to democracy, an opportunity for people around the world to gain information necessary to be an informed electorate, or a burden that hinders thoughtful debate and civic engagement in ideas, these being essential ingredients of a functioning democracy (Barber 2006). For example, the 2012 election for U.S. president had unlimited political contributions that funded negative campaign ads. These ads were often deceptive and required good analytical skills to avoid being manipulated by them.

The Internet, fax machines, camcorders, and other telecommunications devices have been major instruments for indigenous people, linking them to the outside world and combating oppressive governments. On the other hand, blogs, talk shows, webpages, and Internet discussions are often known more for sound bites and polemical attacks on opponents than for reasoned debates in which opposing sides express views. The key contribution that these technologies bring is speed. However, speed is not necessarily good for democracy, which takes thought, patience, and consideration. Both representative democracy and direct democracy are speed-averse, requiring time and patience to implement laws (Barber 2006).

Representative democracy involves citizens electing officials periodically and then letting them make the decisions. In a direct democracy, the voters make major policy decisions, and citizens work in communities to govern their social life, develop civic trust, and create social capital. This, of course, requires a literate and well-informed electorate, which does not always exist.

Rapid communication can help individuals stay in touch with their representatives in a representative democracy. However, we must be aware of the pros and cons of various technologies for democratic decision making. Several features of technology can produce contradictory outcomes:

1. Speed and the need for careful deliberation in democratic process;
2. The tendency of digital media to reduce everything to simplistic binary opposites, as though only two choices are possible;
3. The tendency to isolate individuals behind their own keyboards and monitors, so that collaborative skills may wane;
4. Pictorial images that sensationalize issues so that decisions are based on emotional responses more than reasoned deliberation;
5. Immoderate, impulsive rhetoric—divisive attacks by people who know little or nothing about the history of the problem (as often happens on blogs and talk shows);
6. The tendency for the Internet (and many other media) to be primarily about commerce—creating a consumer mentality rather than a place for debate and problem solving; and
7. A confounding of information (with which we are sometimes overloaded) with wisdom, which is solely needed (Barber 2006).

Social policy consideration—careful deliberative reflection—is necessary if we are to have technology benefit and not undermine democratic systems.

Thinking Sociologically

How can the seven issues of technology be problems for representative democracy? Which are benefits? What effect do they have on direct participatory democracy?

Types of Economic Systems

As societies become industrialized, one of two basic economic systems evolves: a planned system or a market system. Planned or centralized systems involve state-based planning and control of property, whereas market systems stress individual planning and private ownership of property, with much less governmental coordination or oversight. These basic types vary depending on the peculiarities of the country and its economy. For instance, China has a highly centralized planned economy with strict government control, yet some private property and incentive plans exist, and these are expanding. The United States is a market system, yet the government puts many limitations on business enterprises and regulates the flow and value of money. Distinctions between the two major types rest on the degree of centralized planning and the ownership of property. In each type of system, decisions must be made concerning which goods to produce (and in what quantity), what to do in the event of shortages or surpluses, and how to distribute goods. Who has power to make these decisions helps determine what type of system it is.

Market Systems/Capitalism. *These are economic systems driven by the balance of supply and demand, allowing free competition to reward the efficient and the innovative with profits; they stress individual planning and private ownership of property.* The goal of capitalism is profit, made through free competition between competitors for the available markets. It assumes that the laws of supply and demand will allow some to profit, while others fail. Needed goods will be made, and the best product for the price will win out over the others. No planning is needed by any oversight group because the invisible hand of the market will ensure sufficient quality control, production, and distribution of goods. This system also rewards innovative entrepreneurs who take risks and solve problems in new ways, resulting in potential growth and prosperity.

The goal of capitalist manufacturers is to bring in more money than they pay out to produce goods and services. Because workers are a production cost, getting the maximum labor output for the minimum wage is beneficial to capitalists. Thus, for example, multinational corporations look for the cheapest world sources of labor with the fewest restrictions on employment and operations. Marx predicted that there would be victims in such a system—those whom the system exploited. This potential for exploitation leads most governments to exercise some control over manufacturing and the market, although the degree of control varies widely.

Capitalism was closest to its pure form during the Industrial Revolution, when some entrepreneurs gained control of the capital and resources to manipulate those who needed work and became laborers. Using available labor and mechanical innovations, these entrepreneurs built industries. Craftspeople such as cobblers could not compete with the efficiency of the new machine-run shops, and many were forced to become laborers in new industries to survive.

Marx predicted that capitalism would cause citizens to split into two main classes: the *bourgeoisie*, capitalists who own the means of production (the "haves"), and the *proletariat*, those who sell their labor to capitalists (the "have-nots"). He argued that institutions such as education, politics, laws, and religion would evolve to preserve the privileges of the elite.

Religious ideology often stresses hard work and deference to authority, allowing entrepreneurs to increase profits that benefit the owners. Furthermore, members of the economic and political elite usually encourage patriotism to distract the less privileged from their conflicts with the elite. According to Marx, the elite want the masses to draw the line between "us" and "them" based on national loyalty, not based on lines of economic self-interests (Gellner and Breuilly 2009). So in Marxist thought, even patriotism is a tool of the elite to control the workers. However, Marx believed that ultimately the workers would realize their plight, develop political awareness or consciousness, and rebel against their conditions. They would overthrow the "haves" and bring about a new and more egalitarian order.

The revolutions that Marx predicted have not occurred in most countries. Labor unions have protected workers from the severe exploitation that Marx witnessed in the early stages of industrialization in England, and capitalist governments have created and expanded a wide array of measures to protect citizens, including social security systems, unemployment compensation, disability programs, welfare systems, and health care systems. Therefore, workers have not been discontent to the point of revolt, but they have expressed frustrations through union walkouts and strikes followed by compromises between workers and capitalist owners.

Some contend that the largest multinational corporations in the world have such enormous power that they own the corporate global network (Upbin 2011). Systems theorists in Switzerland discovered a core of 147 dominant firms (mostly banks and investment companies) at the center of multinational corporations that together control 40% of the world's corporate wealth. Looking at a total of 737 corporations in this same group of multinational corporations, they control 80% of corporate wealth. These figures are out of 37 million companies and investors and 43,060 transnational corporations in the world, each with interlocking networks. Although some analysts question aspects of the theorists' model, the interconnections and the global control of wealth by a small number of the multinational corporations are accepted (Upbin 2011). The top corporate owners in terms of wealth—listed in order of most financial holdings—are as follows:

- Barclays
- Capital Group Companies Inc.
- FMR Corporation
- AXA
- State Street Corporation
- JPMorgan Chase & Co.
- Legal and General Group
- Vanguard Group Inc.
- UBS AG
- Merrill Lynch & Co. Inc.
- Wellington Management Company
- Deutsche Bank
- Franklin Resources
- Credit Suisse Group
- Walton Enterprises LLC (holding company for Walmart heirs)
- Bank of New York Mellon Corporation
- Natixis
- Goldman Sachs Group Inc.
- T. Rowe Price Group Inc.
- Legg Mason Inc.

Most of these are banking and investment firms (Upbin 2011).

A few elite businesspeople control many top companies through a system of interlocking directorates, giving them enormous power (Domhoff 2005, 2008; Rothenberg 2006). If people running the corporations pursue their own interests, as some corporate heads seemed to do even after they received millions in "federal rescue money" in 2008 and 2009, the nation and the populace may be in trouble.

Efforts by the government to control aspects of corporations and the markets encourages a close relationship between U.S. corporations and the government's decision-making apparatus. Business interests often argue that government intervention in markets or regulation of commerce discourages competition, encourages mergers, and causes concentration of wealth and power in fewer and fewer hands. Thus, they argue that it is in the best interests of corporate decision makers to have influence in politics and government. According to power elite theorists, they do!

Barclays Bank owns more corporate stock than any other investment firm in the world.

Thinking Sociologically

Should we be worried that freedom of the press—and therefore democracy—is threatened when a few corporations own a very large number of the nation's radio stations and newspapers? Why or why not?

One of the major criticisms of pure capitalism is that profit is the only value that drives the system. Human dignity and well-being, environmental protection, rights of ethnic groups, and other social issues are important only as they affect profits. This leaves some people deeply dissatisfied with capitalism.

Planned (or Centralized) Systems. Planned systems are *economic systems that attempt to limit private ownership of property and have the government do planning of production and distribution.* They deemphasize private control of property and economic autonomy and have the government do economic planning. Matters of production and labor are, in theory, governed with the "communal" good in mind. There is deep suspicion of the exploitation that can occur when individuals all pursue their own self-interests. Those who hold to this philosophy believe that the market system also results in oligarchy—a system run by the financial elite in the pursuit of their own self-interests. According to Marxist analysis, when the ideal state is achieved, motivating incentives for individuals such as earning more money are not needed. Each individual contributes to the general welfare of the community or society in exchange for benefits from the system, including food, shelter, employment, schooling, health care, and cultural events. The state oversees the total economy. Monotonous, tedious jobs are shared voluntarily by all. The idea is that this frees individuals to concentrate on the humanistic and culturally important aspects of life. Values other than profits can be protected and affirmed. China, Cuba, and about 24 nations in Africa, Asia, and Latin America have planned economies with industry controlled by the state (Freedom House 2002).

In reality, however, no system is a perfect planned state with the complete elimination of private property

The Chinese and Vietnamese systems have been highly centralized economies in which the government has done the planning. In recent years, both China and Vietnam *have permitted more initiatives by entrepreneurs, rewarding those who would take a risk in the market. This photo is of a bustling street in Ho Chi Minh City, Vietnam.*

or differences in privilege. China, based on a planned and government-controlled system, made rapid progress in tackling hunger, illiteracy, drug addiction, and other problems by using its strong central government to establish five-year economic development plans. Today, however, the government is experimenting with new economic plans, including limited private entrepreneurship, more imported goods, and trade and development agreements with other countries. Much of China has moved beyond the survival level and can experiment with modifications to the economic system. China has not, however, granted much political freedom to its citizenry.

One key criticism of planned systems is that placing both economic power and political power in the hands of the same people can lead to control by a few leaders, resulting in tyranny. Multiple power centers in government, the business world, and the military can balance each other and help protect against dictatorships and tyranny (Heilbroner and Milberg 2012).

Mixed Economies. Some systems are mixed economies, sometimes called "welfare states" or "democratic socialism" because they try to balance societal needs and individual freedoms. **Democratic socialism**, for example, refers to *collective or group planning of the development of the society, but within a democratic political system.* Private profit is less important than in capitalism, and the good of the whole is paramount. Planning may include goals of creating equality, protecting the environment, or supporting families, but individuals' rights to pursue their own self-interests are also allowed within certain parameters. The system seeks checks and balances so that both political and economic decision makers are accountable to the public. Several countries, including Sweden, the United Kingdom, Norway, Austria, Canada, France, and Australia, have incorporated some democratic socialist ideas into their governmental policies, especially in public services. Many Western European democracies redistribute income through progressive tax plans that tax according to people's ability to pay. The government uses this tax money to nationalize education, health plans and medical care, pensions, maternity leaves, and sometimes housing for its citizens. Although much of the industry is privately run, the government provides regulations for the industry and assesses high taxes to pay for government programs. Typically, public service industries such as transportation, communications, and power companies are government controlled.

When U.S. President Obama was elected, he was faced with a huge economic crisis that was extremely complex, but most analysts believe that a major cause had been deregulation of banks and the system of loans for home mortgages and businesses. The president—like his Republican predecessor, George W. Bush—pushed a massive stimulus plan through Congress, this one for $787 billion (Espo 2009). The problem was lack of regulation of the economy, and the solution was massive support for corporations and businesses, actions that some consider socialist. Democratic socialism in the United States includes Social Security, Medicaid, Medicare, farm subsidies, federal unemployment insurance, a national parks system that ensures open natural spaces, the idea of public schools to educate the citizenry, policies that limit pollution and protect the environment that all the citizens share, and thousands of other programs that most Americans affirm and rely on. So despite hostility to the term *socialism*, any government program that "bails out" the economy (such as rescuing a failing bank) or that "protects consumers" is a mixed economy that includes some socialist policies.

Economic systems that attempt to balance market and planned economies are relatively recent experiments in governance, and they remain an idealized vision that has yet to be fully implemented or understood. In some ways, democratic socialist states outproduce capitalist ones, and in some ways, they can seem cumbersome ways to run a complex society. The bottom line in evaluating which system works best comes down to value priorities: individualism and economic growth for companies versus values such as equality, distribution of wealth, and protection of the environment.

Many theorists believe that democratic socialism is what Karl Marx really had in mind, not the bureaucratic system that evolved in the Soviet Union, China, and elsewhere. Marx, after all, felt that the worst of all governments was *state capitalism*—a system in which the state controlled the economy. His early writings, in particular, put much more emphasis on decentralization and even a withering away of the government (Marx [1844] 1963). Few social democrats today think that the government will ever wither away, but they think that the public, not just the elite, should have input into economic as well as governmental decisions and planning. The market system (capitalism) and the planned systems (socialism and communism) both have their advocates, but each system also has its shortcomings. The mixed-economy systems combine some elements of both major systems. The question, then, is whether there is an economic system that can avoid the dangers of each.

More than two centuries ago, it was widely believed, perhaps rightly at that time, that democracy could not work. The notion of self-governance by the citizenry was discredited as a pipe dream. Yet this experiment in self-governance is continuing, despite some flaws and problems. In a speech to the British House of Commons in 1947, then Prime Minister Winston Churchill said that "democracy is the worst form of government, except for all those other forms that have been tried" (Churchill 2009). Some economists and social philosophers have argued that if the people can plan for self-governance, they certainly should be able to plan for economic development in a way that does not put economic power solely in the hands of a political elite.

The institutions of politics and economics cannot be separated. In the 21st century, new political and economic relationships will emerge as each institution influences the other. Both institutions ultimately have a close connection to power and privilege.

Macro-Level Analysis: National and Global Systems of Governance and Power

Power and the Nation-State

A *nation-state* is a political, geographical, and cultural unit with recognizable boundaries and a system of government. Boundaries of nation-states have been established through wars, conquests, negotiations, and treaties. These boundaries change as disputes over territory are resolved by force or negotiation. For example, Russia and the country of Georgia had a conflict in 2008 over whether two breakaway provinces of Georgia—Ossetia and Abkhazia—belonged within the national boundaries of Georgia.

There are officially 196 nation-states in the world today, 193 of which are represented in the United Nations (Worldometers 2012). This number is increasing as new independent nation-states continue to develop in Europe, Asia, Africa, and other parts of the world. One of the newest countries is South Sudan, which broke away from Sudan in Africa and declared independence in 2011.

Within each nation-state, power is exerted by the systems that govern people through leaders, laws, courts, tax structure, the military, and the economic system. Different forms of power dominate at different times in history and in different geographical settings.

The notions of the nation-state and of nationalism are so completely internalized as realities that we do not stop to think of them as social constructions of reality, created by people to meet group needs. In historical terms, nationalism is a rather recent or modern concept, emerging only after the nation-state (Gellner 1983, 1993; Gellner and Breuilly 2009). Medieval Europe, for example, knew no nation-states. One scholar writes that

> throughout the Middle Ages, the mass of inhabitants living in what is now known as France or England did not think of themselves as "French" or "English." They had little conception of a territorial nation (a "country") to which they owed an allegiance stronger than life itself. (Billig 1995:21)

Some argue that the nation-state has "no precedent in history" prior to the 16th century and perhaps considerably later than that (Giddens 1987:166). This raises an interesting question: Why did nation-states emerge in Europe and then spread throughout the rest of the world? This puzzle of modern history has to do with the change to rational organizational structures (Billig 1995). It is noteworthy that today every square foot of the Earth's land space is thought to be under the ownership of a nation-state. Yet, even today, a sense of nationalism or patriotism linking one's personal identity to the welfare of a nation is a foreign idea to many. People have loyalty to their region, their ethnic or tribal group, their religious group, or their local community, but a sense of being Pakistani, Kenyan, or Afghani is weak at best. Yet, in places such as the United States, having a passionate sense of national loyalty for which one would die is so taken for granted that anyone lacking this loyalty is suspect or deviant. Note the earlier discussion of the role of the flag. The nation is largely an imagined reality, something that exists because we choose to believe that it exists (Anderson 2006; McCrone 1998). Indeed, for some people, belonging to the nation has become a substitute for religious faith or belonging to local ethnic groups (Theroux 2012).

Revolutions and Rebellions

From the 1980s to the present, significant social and political changes have taken place throughout the world. The Berlin

Another nonviolent revolution has been the Zapatista movement in southern Mexico (Chiapas). Here we see Zapatista commanders holding a Mexican flag as they attend a mass rally in Mexico City's main square. They are calling for indigenous rights, including clean water and schooling through sixth grade for their children. The Zapatistas wear masks to avoid identification and persecution by the government, despite the fact that they are nonviolent. They are in communication with other human rights movements around the globe.

Revolutions can be violent overthrow of governments or nonviolent events such as this Burmese monk protest that was violently suppressed by the government in Myanmar, formerly Burma. Courageous acts like this did lead to change, and Aung San Suu Kyi, depicted in the photo on page 476, is now a member of the government in Myanmar.

Wall was dismantled, leading to unification of East and West Germany. The Baltic states of Estonia, Latvia, and Lithuania became independent. In Eastern Europe, political and social orders established since World War II underwent radical change. When the Soviet Union and Yugoslavia broke apart, national boundaries were redrawn. Internal strife resulted from ethnic divisions formerly kept under check by the strong centralized governments in these areas. In addition, 2011–2012 was the time of the "Arab Spring," during which many dictators in the Middle East fell from power.

Were these changes around the world revolutions? **Revolution** refers to *social and political transformations of a nation that result when states fail to fulfill their expected responsibilities* (Skocpol 1979). Revolutions can be violent, and generally result in altered distributions of power in the society. Revolutions typically occur when the government does not respond to citizens' needs and when leadership emerges to challenge the existing regime. News from around the world frequently reports on nation-states that have been challenged by opposition groups attempting to overthrow the regimes. This is the case in Syria and other Middle Eastern nations. Today revolutions are enhanced by new technologies, as is discussed in the next "Sociology Around the World."

The Meso-Macro Political Connection

State or provincial governments and national political parties are meso-level organizations that operate beyond the local community, but they are less encompassing in their influence than national or federal governments or global systems. Still, decisions at the state or provincial government level can have major influences in political processes at the national level. We have already seen some of these debates elsewhere in this book in discussions of state and federal policies on same-sex versus strictly heterosexual marriage. There were likewise controversies in 2012 when some state governors refused the federal funds for expanding Medicaid to cover more poor residents. Here we look at another issue: the recent controversies about how to nominate and elect a president within the United States. Although the focus is on the U.S. political system, this discussion should be seen as illustrative of the tensions and peculiarities of the meso-macro link in any complex political system.

In some U.S. states, each political party runs its own caucuses (face-to-face meetings of voters in homes, schools, and other buildings) to discuss policy and to carry out public votes. In caucus states, the political party funds and operates the process of selecting delegates who will nominate the presidential candidate. In contrast, other states have primary elections run by the state government. However, even states that use a primary are not all the same. On the Democratic side, states distribute their delegates

Sociology Around the World

Social Media and Political Protests

By Jeremiah Castle

Recent events confirm that social media is playing a significant role in modern political protests. For example, social media has helped maintain news coverage of events going on inside Syria since the civil war began there in 2011. After the Syrian government attempted to restrict nonstate reporters following the outbreak of protests, members of the rebel groups and bystanders tweeted and uploaded YouTube videos of the government-led violence going on there (Mackey 2011). These videos helped bolster support for the rebels both inside Syria and in some parts of the broader international community.

There are a number of potential benefits to social media, the most obvious of which is a nearly limitless audience. Social media websites like Facebook, Twitter, and YouTube make it possible for networks of people with similar opinions to connect across great distances. Social media and text messaging can help large groups of people coordinate actions quickly, and the greater anonymity of the Internet can facilitate communication of political ideologies that might otherwise go unshared (Woods 2011). However, critics point out that social media–based networks are often not as "deep" as more traditional networks like those that provided a foundation for the civil rights movement in the United States (Gladwell 2010).

Crackdowns on protesters in Iran and other countries have provided support for growing fears that governments will use social media to identify and silence dissidents (Howard 2011; Morozov 2009). However, the events in Syria are part of a growing pattern that suggests protesters are willing to face the potential costs in order to enjoy the immense organizational benefits of social media. In 2009, protesters in Moldova used Twitter, Facebook, and text messages to mobilize opposition to the Communist Party's recent election wins (Barry 2009). A few months later, citizens and reporters in Iran used social media to keep more traditional media outlets informed of events going on there following the disputed 2009 elections (Landler and Stelter 2009). Protesters used YouTube to distribute videos of police beating crowds, raiding Tehran University, and shooting women in the streets, causing concerns among the media due to the graphic nature of the videos and the difficulty in verifying their authenticity (Stelter 2009). In 2011, Twitter, Facebook, and YouTube all played a role in the protests that ended Egyptian President Hosni Mubarak's tenure in office. A Facebook group titled "We are all Khaled Said," dedicated to the memory of an Alexandrian man beaten to death by police, had over 1.8 million subscribers (Preston 2011). In the fall of 2012, citizens of the Philippines protested a new law that might allow social media users to be prosecuted for libel by replacing their Facebook profile pictures with black silhouettes and making blank posts (Whaley 2012). Widening Internet access, faster connection speeds, and improvements in strategy provide reasons to believe that social media will play an increasing role in the future of political protest.

Interestingly, new evidence suggests that social media can also cause protests in a more direct fashion. Social media has dramatically expanded the marketplace of ideas, and now anyone with a keyboard, phone, or camera can distribute his or her thoughts to a worldwide audience. In one recent case, an American filmmaker who published an anti-Islamic film on YouTube helped spark a series of protests in numerous Muslim countries, including Egypt, Syria, Libya, and Sudan (Mackey and Stack 2012). After an attack on the U.S. Embassy in Libya killed Ambassador J. Christopher Stevens and several others, some Libyans even used social media to tweet pictures apologizing for the behavior of their fellow nationals (Mackey 2012). This tragic incident serves as a reminder that, with the democratization of ideas brought by social media, one person's actions have the potential to affect the lives of others around the world.

* * * * * * *

Jeremiah Castle is a graduate student working on a PhD in political science at Notre Dame University. He minored in sociology in college.

based on the proportion of the vote won by a candidate in that state. If a candidate wins 40% of the vote, she wins 40% of the delegates. On the Republican side, the delegate selection in 20 states is based on the proportion of the vote for each candidate, whereas in 20 other states it is a winner-takes-all system. In such elections, even if one candidate wins by only a half of a percentage point, he or she wins all the delegates for that state. Still others have a formula by which some delegates are elected in the primary based on proportion of the statewide vote, while others are chosen based on who wins each congressional district. See Table 13.2 for caucus and primary states. (The processes for each state—whether winner-takes-all or proportional—are listed in a table at www.sagepub.com/ballantine4e.)

In some states, only members of the party can vote. In other states, citizens who are registered as Independents can vote in either the Republican or the Democratic primary election and help select the party's candidate. In other states, Democrats and Republicans can cross over and vote in the primary for the other party (see Table 13.2). What are the implications of having different rules in different states about crossover party voting?

Eleven states have split primaries, so the Democratic and Republican primaries are not on the same day: Hawaii, Idaho, Kansas, Maine, Montana, Nebraska, New Mexico, South Carolina, Washington, West Virginia, and Wyoming. New Hampshire even has in its state constitution a clause that the state *must* have the first presidential primary.

Table 13.2 Meso-Level Presidential Nomination Variations in the United States

States With Caucuses Rather Than Primaries	*"Open"*	*Semiclosed*
Controlled by the political parties rather than the state	Allowing citizens to cross over to vote in the other party's election	Allowing Independents to vote in the other party's election
Alaska, Maine, Nevada, Colorado, Minnesota, North Dakota, Iowa, Washington, Kansas, Nebraska, Wyoming	Alabama, Minnesota, Tennessee, Arkansas, Mississippi, Vermont, Idaho, Missouri, Virginia, Indiana, North Dakota, Washington, Missouri, South Carolina, Wisconsin	Alaska, Illinois, New Hampshire, California, Iowa, Ohio, Georgia, Massachusetts, Rhode Island
	* * * * *	
Texas has both a primary and a caucus.	Open in the Democratic but closed in the Republican processes: Montana, Utah, West Virginia	Semiclosed in the Democratic but closed in the Republican processes: Kansas

Sources: BBC News (2008), Bowen (2008), Center for Voting and Democracy (2008), The Green Papers (2008a, 2008b), National Archives and Records Administration (2008), *The New York Times* (2008), Project Vote Smart (2008), State of Delaware (2008), Voting and Democracy Research Center (2008).

Thinking Sociologically

Is it acceptable that some states never get any say in the nomination of candidates because the process is completed before they vote? Should one state be able to write into its constitution that it must have the first primary election, or should this be a decision that is somehow made at the national level? Who has the authority to tell a state it cannot put a regulation about having the first presidential primary in its constitution?

This means that some state governments decide when the primaries will be held, while elsewhere the selection of nominees is "owned" by the political parties. With a contentious U.S. election held in 2008, several controversial questions were raised. Can a political party tell a state when to have its elections and then punish that state if it does not obey by refusing to seat its delegates at the party convention? This is exactly what happened in Michigan and Florida in 2008. However, it gets even more complicated. In Florida, a Republican-dominated legislature moved the date of the primary election. The Democrats from that state were outvoted in the state legislature, but they still lost the right to represent their state at the convention where a presidential candidate is nominated. Can a state legislature—a meso-level political entity—tell a national political party—also a meso-level political entity—how to run its nomination process? The answers to these questions are not clear, yet they can have profound effects on who becomes the next president of the most powerful nation on Earth.

Finally, in two states—Montana and Nebraska—the Republican primary is a "beauty contest" with no binding outcome. The results are purely advisory, and the delegates from that state are free to ignore the outcome of the election. The delegates are selected by the party insiders in that state, not by the voters. The Democratic Party has only recently passed a national policy banning this kind of primary. On the other hand, the Democratic Party has 915 "superdelegates"—party insiders who have not been elected by the populace and who may commit their votes to anyone they please. So both parties allow delegates to vote who are not representing any constituency that elected them. What are the implications for a democracy?

Even selection of the Electoral College, which actually decides who will be president after the general election, is not uniform in policy across the states. Two states—Nebraska and Maine—have proportional distribution of electors, and all the others have winner-takes-all. If one additional state with large numbers of electors were to shift to proportional distribution of electors, it could change the outcome of our national elections for a long time to come.

Thinking Sociologically

Should there be consistency between the states in the way the Electoral College is selected? Should state elections all be proportional, or should they all be winner-takes-all?

Because the Constitution grants considerable autonomy to states to make these decisions, how does the nation ever get consistency? At the state (meso) level, legislatures are very protective of their right to make their own decisions. Yet governance of the nation and the nation's relationships with the global community may be at stake. The point is this: Meso-level political power can shape power at the macro level, which then influences policies relevant to individual lives. The three levels are intimately linked. The next "Engaging Sociology" raises questions about where authority for decisions resides at each level in the social system.

Global Interdependencies: Cooperation and Conflicts

Dependency theorists and world systems theorists point out the inequality between rich core countries and developing peripheral countries that are dependent on the core countries. The more dependent a country is, the more inequality is likely to exist between that country and core countries. The physical quality of life for citizens in dependent countries is also likely to be poor. For example, permitting a foreign company to mine resources in a Global South country may produce a short-term gain in employment for the country and may make some leaders wealthy, but when the exhaustible resources are gone, the dependent country is often left with its natural resources destroyed and an even poorer economy (Wallerstein 1979, 1991).

Young democracies are emerging in peripheral countries in Eastern Europe, East Asia, Africa, and Latin America. In several Central and Latin American countries

Engaging Sociology

Political Decisions: Social Processes at the Micro, Meso, and Macro Levels

Imagine that your state legislature is considering a change in the presidential election process. Your Electoral College state representatives would be selected according to the percentage of the popular vote in your state going to each candidate (Republican, Democratic, Libertarian, and Green Party). (*Note*: Currently, almost all states distribute their electors on a winner-takes-all basis.)

1. Identify two possible micro-level consequences of this policy change. (For example, how might it affect an individual's decision to vote or how the local board of elections does its job?)
2. Identify three consequences at the macro level. (For example, how might the change affect how presidential candidates spend their resources and time, how might Congress respond to such an initiative, and so forth?)
3. How does this illustrate the influence of meso-level organizations on micro and macro levels of the social system? For example, is it a problem for a *national* democracy when the delegate selection system is so complete a variable at the meso level, or does this make elections even more democratic because states can make their own autonomous decisions? Explain your answer.
4. Which system—winner-takes-all or percentage of the popular vote—would produce the fairest outcome? Why?

formerly ruled by civilian and military dictatorships, democratic governments are taking hold, and elected officials are gaining power. Despite the movement toward political liberalization, democracy, and market-oriented reforms in countries such as Chile, Mexico, Nigeria, Poland, Senegal, Thailand, and Turkey, not all these societies are ready to adopt democratic forms of governance (Diamond 1992, 2009). The most affluent countries in the Global North have democracies, but there is some question about how to create a democratic system in poor countries with different cultural values and systems (Etounga-Manguelle 2000). What are the chances that the United States or another powerful nation-state will be successful in attempts to create democracies elsewhere? The odds are probably not good, according to a number of political analysts. Foreign powers can do little to alter the social structure and cultural traditions of other societies, and as indicated, these structures are key to the successful development of democracy. If the imposed system is premature or incompatible with the society's level of development and other institutional structures, authoritarian dictatorship rather than democracy may emerge as the traditional authority structure breaks down. Some scholars believe certain preconditions are necessary for the emergence of democracy:

- High levels of economic well-being
- The absence of extreme inequalities in wealth and income
- Social pluralism, including a particularly strong and autonomous middle class
- A market-oriented economy
- Influence in the world system of democratic states
- A culture that is relatively tolerant of diversity and can accommodate compromise
- A functioning and impartial media that will hold the government accountable
- A literate population (80% or more) that is informed about issues
- A written constitution with guarantees of free speech and freedom of assembly (Bottomore 1979; Inglehart 1997)

Thinking Sociologically

Why might some analysts believe that Iraq or Afghanistan—where the United States has attempted to set up democracies—may not be ready for a successful democratic government? Can you describe societies with which you are familiar that are—or are not—ready for democratic government?

Socioeconomic development strengthens democracy by contributing to social stability (Diamond 1992). Promoting democracy means offering moral, political, financial, and diplomatic support to efforts to replace authoritarian regimes (Diamond 1992, 2003). Thus, an outside power can help establish the structures necessary to support democracy but is seldom successful trying to impose those structures. If countries in the Global North want more democracies around the world, an important strategy is to support economic development in less affluent countries. Again, politics and economics are intertwined.

Some Global South countries see discussions of democracy as a ploy—a cover-up used by dominant affluent nations for advancing their wealth. For example, the Global North nations have combined to form a coalition of nations calling itself the Group of Eight (or the G8—the United States, Japan, Germany, Canada, France, Great Britain, Italy, and Russia). The G8 uses its collective power to regulate global economic policies to ensure stability (and thereby ensure that its members' interests are secure). The G8 has the power to control world markets through the World Trade Organization, the World Bank, and the International Monetary Fund (Brecher, Costello, and Smith 2012; Kaiser Family Foundation 2010). Global South nations have responded to the G8 with an organization of poor countries that they called the G77. They are attempting to create collective unity so they will have some power to determine their own destinies (Brecher, Costello, and Smith 2012; Eitzen and Zinn 2012; Hearn 2012). Map 13.2 shows where the G8 and G77 nations are located.

Political systems can face threats from internal sources such as disaffected citizens, the military, and interest groups vying for power, or they can be challenged by external sources such as other nations wanting land or resources or by coalitions of nations demanding change. This is the situation for North Korea and Iran as coalitions of nations demand that they drop their nuclear enrichment programs. Sometimes these power struggles erupt into violence. The following section discusses how war, terrorism, and rebellion challenge existing systems.

Violence on the Global Level

Once upon a time, gallant knights in shining armor went forth to battle with good luck tokens from their ladies and the cause of their religion or their monarch to spur them on. They seldom died in these battles, and the daily life of the society went on as usual. In contrast, since the invention of modern weaponry, no one has been safe from death and destruction in war. Weapons can destroy whole civilizations. A malfunctioning computer, a miscalculation, a deranged person, a misunderstanding between hostile factions, or a terrorist attack could kill millions of people.

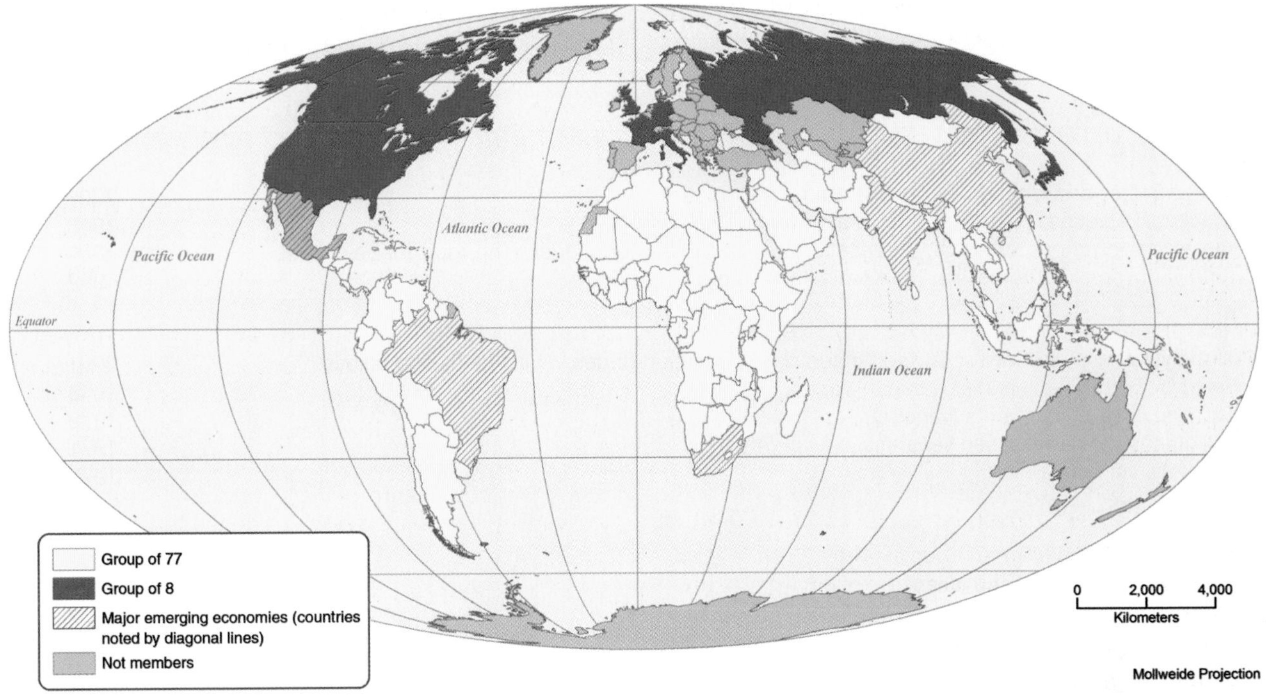

Map 13.2 Countries of the Group of 8, Major Emerging Economies, and Countries of the Group of 77

Source: www.g77.org. Map by Anna Versluis.

Palestinian schoolchildren take cover under their desks in their classroom during an emergency drill. This exercise to prepare for war is stimulated by the government's fear of attacks by neighboring enemies. Children in North America today seldom live with such anxieties.

War is *armed conflict occurring within, between, or among societies or groups. It is sometimes called "organized mass violence"* (Nolan 2002:1803). War is a frequent but not inevitable condition of human existence. Many countries are now engaged in wars that are debilitating and detrimental to their economies and morale. Some of these wars (between India and Pakistan, in the Sudan, between Palestine and Israel, and between rival factions in the Congo) have lasted for years. Others have been short and decisive, such as the "Desert Storm" war with Iraq. In 2010 there were 24 active armed conflicts, 4 fewer than in 2009 (Ploughshares 2011). Table 13.3 on page 502 lists ongoing world conflicts as of 2010. Some of the most recent conflicts in Libya, Egypt, and Syria are not listed.

Why Do Nations Go to War?

Leaders use moral, religious, or political ideology to legitimize war, although the cause may be conflicts over economic resources or ethnic tensions. Wars have been waged to support religions through crusades and jihads; to liberate a country from domination by a foreign power; to protect borders, resources, and cultural customs; and to capture resources, including slaves, land, and oil. War can also distract citizens from other problems in their country, and it may therefore be used by politicians intent on staying in power. On the other hand, there are cultures where war is virtually unknown. Groups, often isolated, live in

Table 13.3 Significant Ongoing Armed Conflicts, 2010

Main Warring Parties	*Year Began*[1]
Middle East	
United States and United Kingdom vs. Iraq	2003
Israel vs. Palestine	1948
Yemen: government forces vs. the rebel group Shabab al-Moumineen (The Youthful Believers)	2004
Turkey: government forces vs. the Kurdistan Workers' Party (PKK)	1999
Asia	
Afghanistan: United States, United Kingdom, and coalition forces vs. al-Qaeda and Taliban	2001
India vs. Kashmiri separatist groups/Pakistan	1948
India vs. Assam insurgents (various)	1979
Philippines vs. Mindanaoan separatists (MILF/ASG)	1971
Sri Lanka vs. Tamil Eelam[2]	1978
Africa	
Algeria vs. Armed Islamic Group (GIA)	1991
Somalia vs. rival clans and Islamist groups	1991
Sudan vs. Darfur rebel groups	2003
Uganda vs. Lord's Resistance Army (LRA)	1986
Europe	
Russia vs. Chechen separatists	1994
Latin America	
Colombia vs. National Liberation Army (ELN)	1978
Colombia vs. Revolutionary Armed Forces of Colombia (FARC)	1978
Colombia vs. United Self-Defense Forces of Colombia (AUC)	1990

Sources: Project Ploughshares (www.ploughshares.ca) and Information Please Database (2009).

Note: As of October 2009.

1. Where multiple parties and long-standing but sporadic conflict are concerned, date of first combat deaths is given.

2. 2002 cease-fire collapsed in 2006.

peace and cooperation, with little competition for land and resources. The bottom line is that war is a product of societies and their leaders, created by societies, and learned in societies.

Two familiar sociological theories attempt to explain the social factors that can lead to war. Functional theorists think underlying social problems cause disruptions to the system, including war, terrorism, and revolution. If all parts of the system were working effectively, they contend these problems would not occur. Agents of social control and a smooth-running system would prevent disruptions. However, some functionalists also argue that war brings a population together behind a cause, resulting in social solidarity.

Conflict theorists see war, terrorism, and revolution as the outcome of oppression by the ruling elite and an attempt to overthrow that oppression. Many businesses profit from wars because their manufacturing power is put to full use. In fact, more money is spent on war than on prevention of disease, illiteracy, hunger, and other human problems. Citizens from the lower classes and racial minorities join the military, fight, and die in disproportionate numbers. They are more likely to join the military as an avenue to employment and job training. They join as enlistees who serve on the front lines and are more at risk.

Some nations are more war prone than others, and one cannot tell simply by paying attention to the rhetoric about war and peace. U.S. politicians give much vocal support to peace, but the country has been at war 193 of the 233 years since the colonies declared independence. Indeed, during the entire 20th century, there were only 6 years when the United States was not engaged in some sort of military action around the world (Brandon 2005; Noguera and Cohen 2006).

The conclusion is that war is not a natural or biological necessity. It is in large part a result of leaderships' decisions. Some sociologists believe that war—like incest, slavery, and cannibalism (which at times were thought to be instinctual but have come to be understood as aberrations)—can be "unlearned," though not all agree (Stoessinger 1993).

How Can Nations Avoid War?

Deterrence is one approach to discourage and perhaps avoid war. Some government officials argue that if a nation is militarily strong, no one will dare attack it, the country will be secure, and leaders can "negotiate from strength." Believers in this approach argue that nations should become superior to others or maintain a balance with other militaristic nations. However, evidence from ongoing statistical analyses of militarization concludes that deterrence has not been effective in reducing the chance of war. The more militarized a country becomes, the more likely the country is to enter into war. Continual buildup of weapons increases mistrust and raises the potential for misunderstandings, mistakes, or disaster. Furthermore, military personnel often have a vested interest in war—that is, what the military is trained to do and what proves its competence. Business interests and economies may also profit from supporting war.

Deterrence is extremely expensive. As countries develop their military power, the spiral toward bigger, more sophisticated, and expensive technological weaponry such as nuclear weapons in North Korea and Iran continues. Figure 13.3 shows military spending around the world, giving rise to what is often called the military-industrial complex. The question is whether *brinkmanship*, expending money and pushing the potential for conflict to the brink, works to deter others. The question has been applied to many international conflicts, including North Korea.

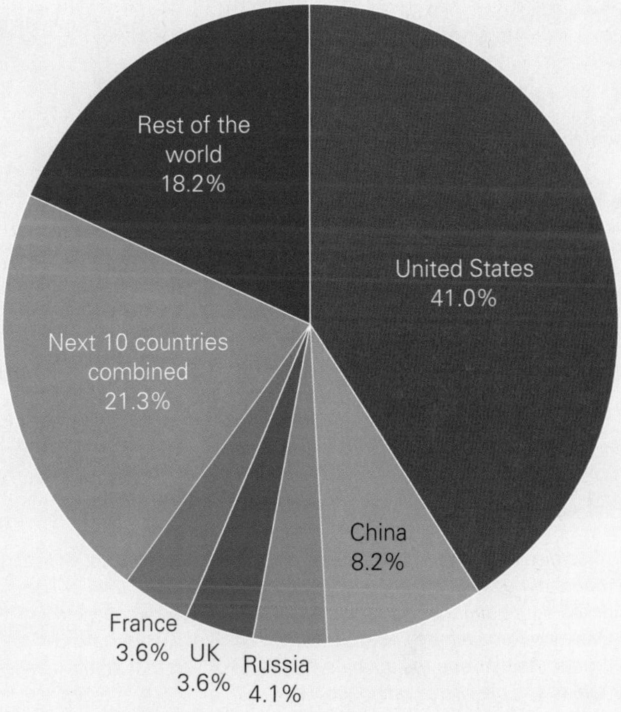

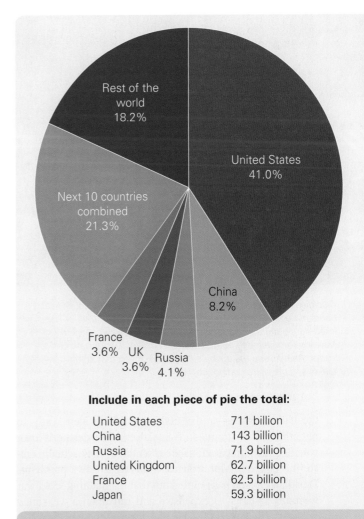

Include in each piece of pie the total:

United States	711 billion
China	143 billion
Russia	71.9 billion
United Kingdom	62.7 billion
France	62.5 billion
Japan	59.3 billion

Figure 13.3 U.S. Military Spending Versus the World, 2011 (in Billions of U.S. Dollars and Percentage of Total Global)

Source: Global Issues 2012. Reprinted with permission.

Two classic experiments (Deutsch and Krauss 1960; Deutsch and Lewicki 1970) that have been replicated numerous times consider the many possible strategies leading up to brinkmanship and how to reduce threats. The results indicate that parties with similar power or wealth usually do not lock themselves into positions they cannot reverse, especially if they will continue to have interaction with their opponents. Brinkmanship is a high-risk strategy.

World military expenditures in 2011 were $1.7 trillion and rising (Shah 2012). The United States accounts for 41% of world military spending, China 8.2%, and Russia 4.1% (Shah 2012). In 2010, the United States spent an estimated $675 billion not counting nuclear weapons at $23 billion a year, an increase in its military budget of $47 billion (Shah 2011; Stockholm International Peace Research Institute 2010).

Military expenditures are outpacing the GDP (gross domestic product) of world countries, the equivalent of $236 for each person in the world (Shah 2012). This is usually at the expense of social programs such as education and health care (Hinton 2010). Spending for weapons widens the gap between rich and poor countries and diverts money from social causes at home and abroad (Ayers 2006; Isaacs 2011). Still, many people feel that protection of the citizenry is the government's most essential responsibility, and brinkmanship is the way to achieve security.

Negotiation is the second approach to avoiding war and resolving conflicts by discussion to reach agreement. For example, diplomacy and treaties have set limits on nuclear weapons and their use. Due to negotiations, stockpiles of U.S. weapons have been reduced in one year (2010) from 10,000 long- and short-range nuclear weapons—enough to annihilate the human race many times over—to 5,113 intact warheads and 2,468 deployed warheads in (Isaacs 2011; Stockholm International Peace Research Institute Yearbook 2010). There are an estimated 31,000 nuclear warheads deployed or in the stockpiles of eight nations—China, France, United Kingdom, India, Israel, Pakistan, Russia, and

A soldier, just back from Iraq after finishing his service, looks at boots of nearly 2,000 U.S. soldiers and thousands of Iraqi civilians killed during the Iraq war. The display was at a military park in Newark, New Jersey. Those who have served in wartime know better than anyone the agonies and costs of war that statistical tables and pie charts cannot convey.

International Solidarity Movement (ISM) activists join Palestinians in a protest against the construction of the Israeli security wall near a West Bank town. Dozens of people from many nations have put their own bodies on the line to prevent bulldozing of Palestinian homes and construction of the wall. American Rachel Corrie, a member of the ISM, was run over and killed by an Israeli bulldozer on March 16, 2003, when she tried to stop it from destroying a family's home.

the United States—and 4,600 are on high alert ready to be launched in minutes (Ware 2008). The debate is over whether such preparations are essential or they actually create the possibility for violence as a way to solve problems. President Obama has pointed out that maintaining "cold war weapons systems" is expensive and can drain a weakened economy (Zeleny 2009). He and former Russian President Medvedev signed a nuclear arms reduction agreement that was approved by the U.S. Senate and Russia's Duma (Baker and Bilefsky 2010; Nuclear Threat Initiative 2010).

In the 1990s, the superpowers made major efforts to move into a new peaceful era. Peace talks were held in the Middle East, Cambodia, Rwanda, the former Yugoslavia and Bosnia, Ireland, and other countries threatened by tensions and war. Leaders of the United Nations were often involved in diplomatic attempts to resolve conflicts. The inherent problem, however, is that more positive negotiation means a partial win—and a partial loss—for each side. Each gives a little, and each gets a little. Both sides tend to want a win/lose resolution—with the other side losing. Commitment to a win/lose perspective can lead to a lose/lose situation with neither side really winning.

Some citizens are not satisfied to leave peacekeeping efforts to their government leaders. Strong grassroots peace movements in Europe, the Middle East, the United States, South Africa, and other countries are aimed at lessening tensions and conflicts around the world. The widespread demonstrations in many European and U.S. cities by people opposed to the wars in Iraq and Afghanistan are examples.

Many peace groups sponsor educational programs and museum displays. The horrors depicted in the Hiroshima Peace Memorial Museum in Japan; the Killing Fields in Cambodia; the Holocaust Memorial Museum in Washington, DC; the Anne Frank Museum in Amsterdam, the Netherlands; the Rwanda Genocide Museum; and the Korean War and Vietnam Veterans Memorials in Washington, DC, all help sensitize the public and politicians to the effects of war. Interestingly, most war memorials in the United States glorify the wars and lionize the heroes who fought in them. In Europe, many memorials stress the pathos and agony of war. However, the Vietnam Veterans Memorial sends a message about the sorrows of war. Peace advocates and veterans of the war often stand and weep together in front of that memorial.

Scholars draw several conclusions from studies of war in the past century: (a) No nation that began a major war in the 20th century emerged a clear winner; (b) in the nuclear age, war between nuclear powers could be suicidal; and (c) a victor's peace plan is seldom lasting. Those peace settlements that are negotiated on the basis of equality are much more permanent and durable. War is often stimulated by inequitable distribution of resources. Therefore, peace that is lasting also requires attention to at least semi-equitable distribution of resources, illustrating that economics are also at the heart of war and peace issues.

In the long run, people around the world would seem to benefit from peace, yet many leaders and citizens hold bitter hatred against their neighbors. Obviously, this is not a climate for peace. As long as there is discrimination, hunger, and poverty in the world, the roots of violence are present. The world is a complex interdependent system. When the linkages between peoples are based on ideologies that stress we/they polarities and power differentials that alienate people, then war, terrorism, and violence will not disappear from the globe.

The Vietnam Veterans Memorial Wall in Washington, DC, is more like many European war memorials than most U.S. war memorials. It expresses and elicits a sense of the anguish of war—loss, pain, suffering. This man mourns the loss of a close friend and comrade as he leans into the wall of names of those killed in the Vietnam War.

Terrorism

"Geronimo! Bin Laden, mastermind of 9/11, is dead!" was the headline on May 2, 2011. For the 10 years since September 11, 2001, the search had been on. That was when three commercial airplanes became the missiles of terrorists, two crashing into the Twin Towers of the World Trade Center in New York City and one into the Pentagon in Washington, DC, killing more than 3,025 people from 68 nations and injuring countless others. This was an act of terrorists. Why did they do it?

Terrorism refers to *the planned use of random, unlawful (or illegal) violence or threat of violence against civilians to create (or raise) fear and intimidate citizens in order to advance the terrorist group's political or ideological goals* (U.S. Department of Defense 2012). Terrorism usually refers to acts of violence by private nonstate groups to advance revolutionary political goals, but *state terrorism* also proliferates—government use of terror to control people. Terrorists are found at all points on the political continuum: anarchists, nationalists, religious fundamentalists, and members of ethnic groups. There were 11,604 terrorist attacks in 72 countries in 2010, resulting in 49,901 victims and 13,186 deaths. This is a 5% rise in attacks over the previous year, but a drop in deaths (U.S. Department of State 2011).

What makes terrorism effective? Terrorists strike randomly and change tactics so that governments have no clear or effective way of dealing with them. This unpredictability causes public confidence in the ability of government to protect citizens and deal with crises to waver. Terrorists seldom attack targets in oligarchic or dictatorial societies because these countries ignore their demands despite the risk to innocent civilians and hostages' lives (Frey 2004).

Why do terrorists commit hostile acts? We cannot address terrorism if we do not understand its root causes. In our anger against terrorists, we sometimes fail to look at why they commit these atrocities. Who are the terrorists, and what have they to gain? Without understanding the underlying causes of terrorism, we can do little to prevent it.

Few terrorists act alone. They are members of groups that are highly committed to an ideology or a cause—religious, political, or both. One person's terrorist may be someone else's freedom fighter—it is in the eye of the beholder. Terrorists are willing to die to support their group's cause. Class, ethnic, racial, or religious alienation often lies at the roots of terrorism. The ideology of terrorist groups stresses "*we* versus *they*" perceptions of the world, with *they* being "evil." Those committing terrorist acts often feel that they are the victims of more powerful forces, and sometimes, they see their only weapon to fight back as the ultimate sacrifice—their lives. Some feel their situation is so bad that they have nothing to lose.

Founders of terrorist groups are often charismatic and preach a message that appeals to followers. Osama bin Laden was one such leader of the terrorist network al-Qaeda. His death in May 2011 by U.S. commandos has altered the command structure and maybe even the organization itself. Yet al-Qaeda is still considered the biggest threat to the United States and other nations (U.S. Department of Defense 2011).

Ahmad is a 20-year-old terrorist. All his life, his family has been on the move, forced to work for others for hardly a living wage, and controlled by rules made up by other people—ones that he feels are hostile to his group. When he was very young, his family's home was taken away, and the residents of his town scattered to other locations. He began to resent those who he thought had dislocated his family, put neighbors in jail, and separated him from friends and relatives. Ahmad sees little future for himself or his people, little hope for education or a career of his choosing. He feels that he has nothing to lose by joining a resistance organization to fight for what he sees as justice. Its members keep their identities secret. They are not powerful enough to mount an army to fight, so they rely on terrorist tactics against those they see as oppressors.

Security officers in Bulgaria look at a damaged bus carrying Israeli tourists after it was hit by a bomb explosion in 2012. This was identified as an act of terrorism against Israel.

Ahmad puts the "greater good" of his religious and political beliefs and his group above his individual well-being. When he agrees to commit a terrorist act, he truly believes it is right and is the only way he can retaliate and bring attention to the suffering of his people. If killed, he knows he will be praised and become a martyr within his group. His family may even receive compensation for his death.

Continued frustration by those who are alienated is illustrated by ongoing current events: militants setting off bombs in London, Madrid, Pakistan, and Mumbai, India; suicide bombers in Iraq; and terrorist attacks by Palestinian suicide bombers in Israel. These are but a few examples of terrorist incidents in a long string of violent, sophisticated, and bloody acts. Those who are attacked feel that they are the real victims and have done nothing to deserve the brutality.

Religious and political beliefs are usually at the root of what leads terrorists to commit violent acts. Timothy McVeigh and Terry Nichols were charged with bombing the Alfred P. Murrah Federal Building in Oklahoma City, Oklahoma. Research on their backgrounds shows connections to paramilitary, antigovernment militia groups, many of which opposed government intervention in the private lives of Americans. These patriot groups are antigovernment (despite their fanatic pro-Americanism) and white supremacist. Most patriot paramilitary groups consider themselves to be devoutly Christian, and they believe that their acts are justified by their religion and their "good intentions." They are scattered throughout the United States as shown in Map 8.2.

Structural explanations help predict when conditions are right for terrorism. Terrorism and war are unlikely to exist unless there is conflict and strife within and between societal systems. Ahmad learned his attitudes, hatreds, and stereotypes from his family, his friends, charismatic leaders, and media such as the Internet. These beliefs were reinforced by his leaders, religious beliefs, and schools. However, their origin was anger and economic despair.

Conflict theory explanations of terrorism lie in the unequal distribution of world resources and the oppression of groups in the social world. Wealthy countries such as Germany, Japan, and the United States control resources and capital and have considerable economic influence and power over peripheral nations. Citizens of poor countries work for multinational corporations, often for very low wages, and the profits are returned to wealthy countries, helping perpetuate their elite status. The result is that the rich get richer, and the poor get poorer. This inequity results in feelings of alienation, hostilities, and sometimes terrorism against the more powerful country. The attack on the New York City World Trade Center was carried out in part to terrorize and punish the United States.

Reactions to terrorism range from demands for immediate retaliation to frustration with the lack of power and control to fight a "hidden" enemy. People disagree over whether governments should negotiate with the terrorists and try to understand their demands or hold firm by not negotiating or giving in to such coercion. Terrorism, then, is the means by which the powerless can attempt to receive attention to their cause and gain some power in the global system, even if it involves hijackings, bombings, suicides, kidnappings, and political assassinations. Terrorists feel they are justified in their actions. The victims of these acts are understandably outraged.

Democracy comes in many forms and structures. If you want to live in a society where you have a voice, get involved in the political system and stay well informed about the policies that your government is considering or has recently enacted. Healthy political systems need diverse voices and critics—regardless of what party is currently in power—to create vibrant societies that represent the citizens. The following chapter focuses on the institution of health care (an anatomy of medicine for a sociological perspective) and explores the interaction of medicine with other institutions—such as the economy and the political system.

What Have We Learned?

The most direct source of power is the political system, with the ability to influence decisions about how society is run. The most direct source of privilege is the economic system, and these two institutions are highly interlinked. There is no one right way to organize a political or an economic system, for each approach has shortcomings. However, some systems do a better job of distributing power and privilege, ensuring accountability, and providing checks on abuses of power.

Key Points

- The study of political and economic processes and systems involves penetrating power—in the sense that we try to penetrate the meanings and consequences of power and that power penetrates every aspect of our lives. Power involves ability to realize one's will, despite resistance. (See pp. 468–469.)
- Power and economics penetrate our intimate (micro-level) lives, our (meso-level) organizations and institutions, and our (macro-level) national and global structures and policies. (See pp. 469–470.)
- Leadership facilitates getting things done in any social group. It can be accomplished through raw power (coercion) or through authority (granted by the populace). Different types of leadership invest authority in the person, the position, or both. (See pp. 473–474.)
- Various theories illuminate different aspects of political power and view the nation's policy-making processes very differently—as dominance of the power elite or as pluralistic centers of power. (See pp. 470–477.)
- At the micro level, a key issue is each citizen's decision to vote or participate in politics. These decisions are not just individual choices but are shaped by culture and structures of the society. (See pp. 477–485.)
- At the meso level, the political institution (when it functions well) works to resolve conflicts and to address social needs within the political system, and this may be done with authoritarian or democratic structures. Within nations, meso-level policies can also have major implications for national power distribution. (See pp. 485–495.)
- The economic system ensures production and distribution of goods in the society, and the type of economy in a society determines who has the power to plan for the future and who has access to resources. (See pp. 485–487.)
- At the macro level, nation-states have emerged only in the past four or five centuries as part of modernity. (See pp. 495–499.)
- At the global level, issues of power, access to resources, alienation, and ideology shape economic policies, war, terrorism, and the prospects for lives of peace and prosperity for citizens around the planet. (See pp. 499–506.)

Discussion Questions

1. As you were growing up, did your parents encourage you to try to influence your local community or society? Why or why not? Was their perspective on power more like the pluralist or elite theoretical perspective? Why? How have their views about power influenced your own?
2. Is your family of origin part of what G. William Domhoff refers to as the "power elite"? What makes you think so? Are you a member of the power elite? Why or why not? If you are not, what do you think your chances are of becoming a member of the power elite? Why?
3. Do you think that large corporations have undue influence over the U.S. government? Why or why not?
4. If you had the choice, would you rather live in a society with a planned/centralized economic system or a market/capitalist economic system? Why?
5. How do conflict theorists explain terrorism? Do you agree? Why or why not? How would you suggest the U.S. government try to stem terrorism? What theoretical perspective do you think is most helpful in terms of understanding and dealing with terrorism? Why?

Contributing to Our Social World: What Can We Do?

At the Local Level

- Consider getting involved in the *student government* on your campus. Most students do not know the power they have on their own campus. Organized students can make a major impact. If you would like to see something changed on your campus, establish relationships with key administrators and organize other students. Consider running for a leadership position in a student club or the student government association. Doing so will help you learn how to gain and use power (the ability to act) and learn the basic principles of the democratic process.
- *Model legislature or Model UN programs* may be found on most campuses, and are usually administered through the department of political science. Consider joining yours, and gain valuable knowledge and skills in debating and governing.
- *Arrange a campus visit by a local political candidate or officeholder.* If this can be done through a sociology club, it would be especially appropriate to have the visitor discuss the political system as a social institution.

At the Organizational or Institutional Level

- *Government internships.* Consider doing an internship in your *state/provincial legislature* (www.ncsl.org/legislative-staff.aspx?tabs=856,33,816) *or in Congress* (www.senate.gov/reference/Index/Employment.htm *and* www.house.gov/content/educate/internships.php) with a state/provincial legislator, the governor's office (Google "governor's office," "internship," and the name of your state), or a court judge (Google "court judge," the name of your district, and "internship").
- *Special-interest parties.* Become involved in a special-interest political group such as the Green Party (www.gp.org), the Libertarians (www.lp.org), the Socialist Party (www.sp-usa.org), the Tea Party (www.teaparty.org), Occupy Together (www.occupytogether.org), or any number of others.

At the National and Global Levels

- *Internships at the White House or one of the executive offices, such as the Department of State, Agriculture, or Commerce.* You can learn about the White House internship program and how to apply at www.whitehouse.gov/about/internships. Google the name of a cabinet office to obtain contact information for the other executive offices.
- Several agencies of the *United Nations* hire interns. The general contact for relevant information is www.un.org/Depts/OHRM/sds/internsh.

WWW Visit the Student Study Site at **www.sagepub.com/ballantine4e** to access additional study tools, including eFlashcards, web quizzes, video resources, audio resources, web resources, SAGE journal articles, recommended readings, and more.

CHAPTER 14

Medicine

An Anatomy of Health and Illness

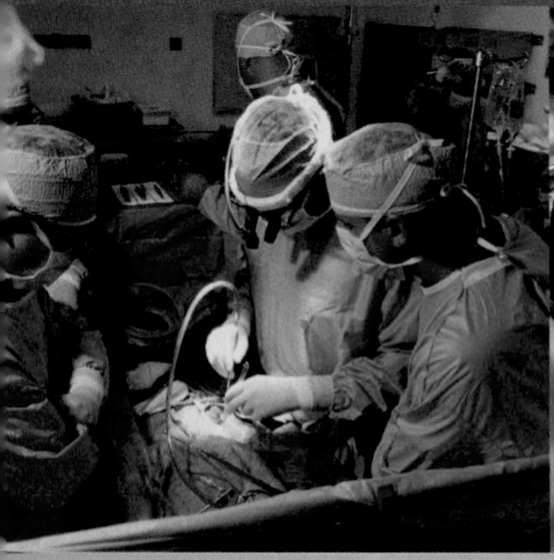
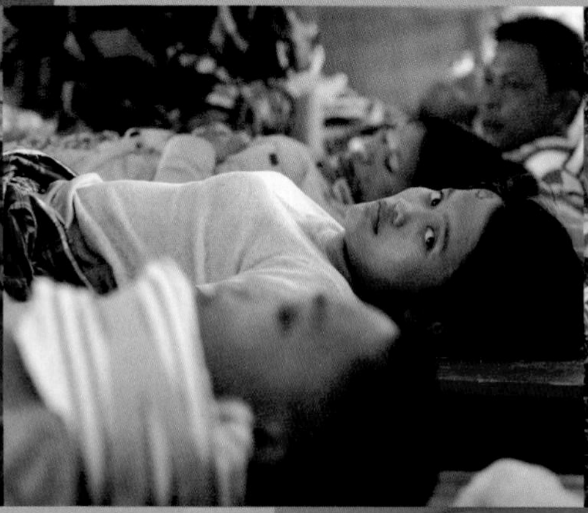

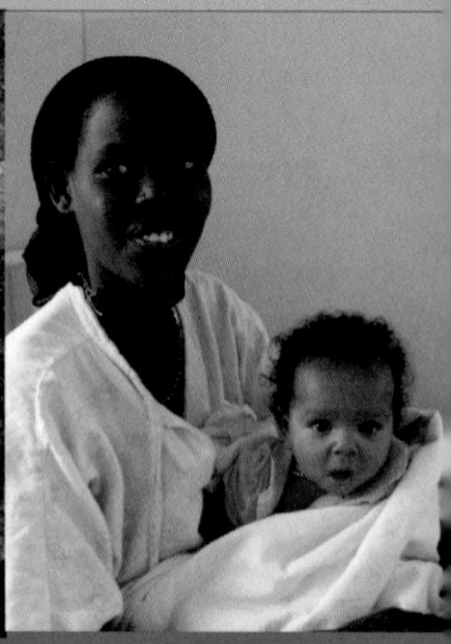

Health and illness are social matters, influenced by social interactions, affected by complex organizations intended to provide health care, and shaped by social policies at national and global levels. A true anatomy of health and illness involves comprehension of the social parts of medicine.

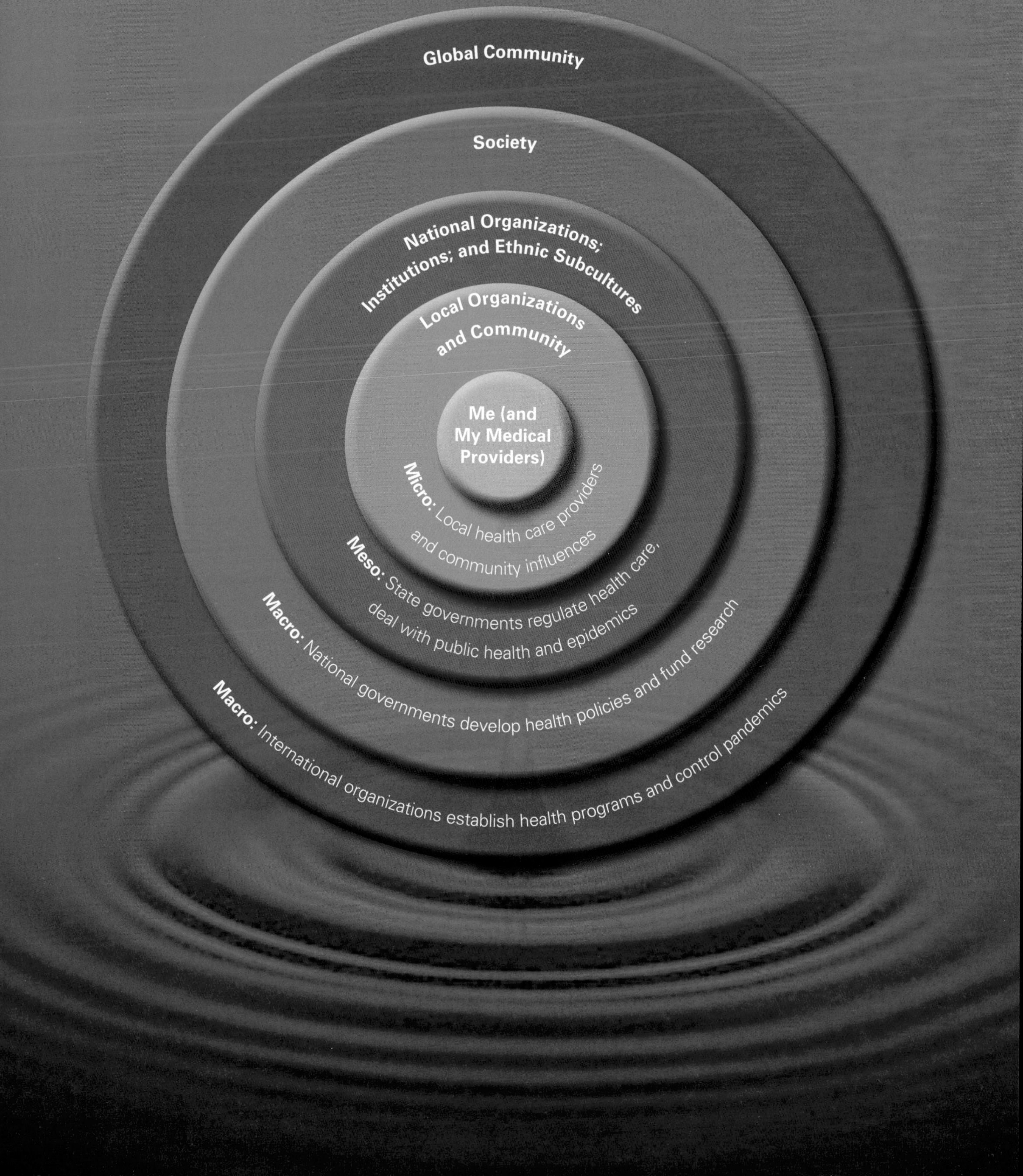

Global Community
Society
National Organizations; Institutions; and Ethnic Subcultures
Local Organizations and Community
Me (and My Medical Providers)
Micro: Local health care providers and community influences
Meso: State governments regulate health care, deal with public health and epidemics
Macro: National governments develop health policies and fund research
Macro: International organizations establish health programs and control pandemics

Think About It	
Micro: Me (and My Inner Circle)	What does it mean for you to be sick or healthy? Why is this a social status and not just an individual concern?
Micro: Local Community	How does the health or illness of community members affect the functioning of you and your local community?
Meso: National Institutions; Complex Organizations; Ethnic Groups	What type of health care system keeps people healthiest?
Macro: National Society	What are costs to the nation of having a national health care system, and what are the costs of not having one?
Macro: Global Community	What are variations in health care around the world?

What's coming in this chapter?

Terri Schiavo died March 31, 2005, after making headlines for months. Though unconscious and in a vegetative state, the controversy surrounding her removal from life support kept the nation's attention. Politicians entered the debate, and then President Bush signed an order to keep her alive. Her husband argued that she would not have wanted to go on in her current state and that it would be a kindness to let her die. However, her parents and court rulings argued to keep her alive through the feeding and oxygen tubes. The case is significant because it raises issues of when and how a person should die—and who has the right to decide. Technology allows us to keep people alive, even in vegetative states so that the patient cannot make the choice. Some people prefer to die rather than live in that condition and have the family's resources depleted. Who has the right to decide? The lines are often unclear.

Another euthanasia case involved Debbie, a 20-year-old woman in Portland, Oregon, lying in pain and dying from ovarian cancer. She had not eaten or slept for two days and was struggling for air. Her words to the physician were, "Let's get this over with." In this case of medical futility, in which treatment "fails to end total dependence on intensive medical care," the physician relieved her suffering with a syringe of morphine sulfate. She began breathing normally and shortly thereafter died as a result of the physician-assisted suicide. These two cases and others like them raise great controversy in medical, legal, and religious communities. One thing is clear: Very personal decisions about health, illness, and death are not just personal. They may be governed or overruled by state or even federal laws.

Allowing individuals to choose death to relieve the irreversible suffering of an incurable disease and allowing physicians to hasten the death of terminally ill patients are actions accepted by proponents of active or voluntary euthanasia (sometimes called "the good death"). This involves aiding the dying individual by prescribing or administering a lethal dose of drugs to patients who

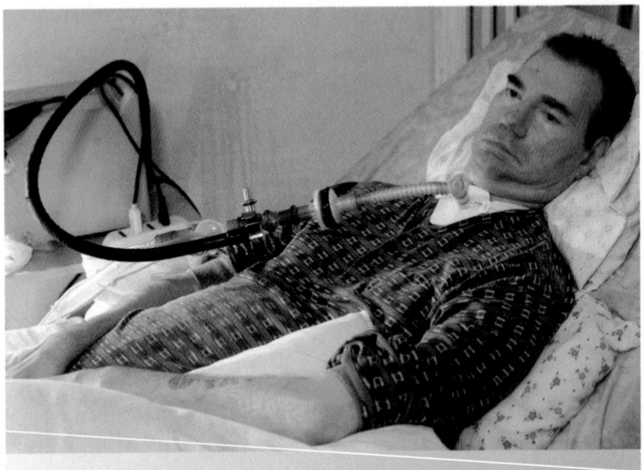

Piergiorgio Welby, vice president of Coscioni Association for Freedom of Scientific Research, awaited a court's ruling on the fate of a paralyzed, terminally ill Italian man who wants doctors to take him off life support so he can die. Welby suffers from advanced muscular dystrophy and is confined to a bed, attached to a respirator. He is lucid and speaks via a computer that interprets his eye movements. He has appeared on Italian news programs asking to be allowed to "find peace for my tortured and shattered body."

request it, usually under legally controlled conditions. A number of European countries and several U.S. states allow competent, terminally ill adults the legal right to obtain a prescription for a lethal dose of medication to be self-administered (Death with Dignity 2012; Hyde n.d.). Most deaths of terminally ill individuals are planned and sometimes hastened by medical interventions (American Psychological Association 2008). In addition, anyone can sign a living will or "Right to Die" form and "Do Not Resuscitate" form requesting that no extraordinary efforts be made to help keep one alive when death would naturally occur (passive euthanasia). However, opponents see aiding death as a sin or even as murder.

Those who favor euthanasia argue that (a) physicians should be able to create comfortable environments for death to occur, (b) terminally ill individuals have a right—without interference by the state—to determine how they die and to make the decision to die, (c) legal safeguards are available to prevent abuse of physician-assisted suicide, (d) high rates of self-induced suicide already exist among terminally ill patients, (e) a majority of the public favors legalization of physician-assisted suicides, and (f) extending life with no hope of recovery is costly to families as well as to the medical care system.

Those opposed to euthanasia argue that (a) physicians are responsible to sustain life and relieve suffering; (b) medical measures are available to relieve pain, so few have to suffer; (c) religious beliefs affirm the sanctity of life, which means supporting life at every turn; (d) terminally ill individuals who request to die are often acting out of depression, or they may feel pressured to accept a facilitated death to save the family's resources; and (e) a terminally ill patient's acceptance of active euthanasia may make suicide a more acceptable option for those people who are depressed, disabled, elderly, or retarded (Weiss and Lonnquist 2012).

Some countries and states have passed laws legalizing and controlling euthanasia. Euthanasia is legal—but with very strict regulations—in the Netherlands, Belgium, Albania, Luxembourg, Switzerland, and Japan. In the United States, euthanasia is legal in Oregon, Washington, and Montana. In 2011, the number of Deaths with Dignity in Oregon was 71, a slow increase since 1998 when euthanasia was legalized. From that starting time until 2010, a total of 525 euthanasia cases occurred in Oregon. Note the demographics of those opting for Death with Dignity: Almost all deaths were whites with college degrees, and more than half were in hospice care (Oregon Public Health Division 2012). The courts require that two or more doctors must agree that the patient has six or fewer months to live, and the patient must also ask to die at three different times, the last time in writing, before doctors can act on the request. Doctors have to wait for 15 days before complying with the patient's wishes (Oregon's Euthanasia Law 2010).

The cost of dying differs tremendously, from nothing in many poor Global South countries with no health care for the dying and no burial restrictions, to $50 billion paid by Medicare for patients in the last two months of life—with as much as 30% of expenditures being "unnecessary" (CBS News 2010; Krieger 2012). On average, the last week of life in the United States costs $2,917, though for those patients who have had end-of-life discussions with their doctors, the average cost is $1,876 because fewer medical interventions take place (Zhang et al. 2009). About 30% of the budget for the U.S. government's Medicare program goes toward the final year of life (Neurological Correlates 2008). In less than 12 years, the number of people who are sick, old, and frail will double, and the Medicare system will be under great pressure to cover expenses at the current rate due to increased medical costs and increasing numbers of people living longer (Appleby 2006).

Whereas in the past people died from heart attacks and bad infections, today people who are afflicted with these problems can be kept alive. Policy analysts point out that cost for elder care could be reduced and quality of care improved by providing more in-home services to allow people to die at home rather than in an intensive care unit of a hospital. In a public survey of attitudes toward end-of-life issues, 48% of respondents thought it was sensible to weigh the costs of keeping a person alive as long as possible, versus 40% who argued that a person should be kept alive as long as possible regardless of cost (Appleby 2006).

Dying is not something that just happens. How we die, where we die, who is with us when we die, and whether we have a choice about when to die are decisions bound in cultural values, beliefs, and laws. Death and its various issues are but one aspect of the interrelationship between our physical condition and our social system. This chapter illustrates that events surrounding health, illness, and death are social events governed by rules of the social world. In this chapter, we will consider why health is a social issue, and we will examine theoretical perspectives on health and illness, the status and roles of sick people, modern health care systems, and health care policy issues at the national and global levels.

Why Is Health a Social Issue?

In the West African country of Nigeria, dogmatic religious leaders in the northern part of the country have refused to allow international medical teams to immunize children against polio, resulting in an outbreak of this crippling disease that had almost been eradicated elsewhere. The religious leaders had little trust in the motives of

Western medical teams. When the epidemic broke out, however, and children began dying, some leaders relented and allowed the immunization programs to take place. Since 1989, a worldwide campaign to eradicate polio has reduced victims from 350,000 across 125 countries to fewer than 2,000, mostly in 4 countries: India, Pakistan, Afghanistan, and Nigeria. In Nigeria, where average life expectancy is 52, polio is spreading in the northern states and has been reintroduced and is spreading in at least 12 African countries thought to be polio free (Cooke 2012; World Factbook 2013g). This illustration of health at the global level points out how individual decisions have an effect on health of a community and nation, and shows the importance of medical organizations and their efforts to control world pandemics such as polio, AIDS, SARS, bird flu, swine flu (H1N1), and other illnesses.

Outbreaks of illness and death also occur within countries due to food poisoning, environmental problems such as leaks of toxic chemicals, or contamination of medicines. In the fall of 2012, cases of a rare type of meningitis cropped up in many U.S. states. The common factor was a batch of contaminated drugs from a compounding pharmacy, used to treat a form of back pain. About 14,000 people received the steroid shots with a fungal contamination that led to the deaths of more than 15 people (Edney 2012).

Let us explore some of the factors that affect health, illness, and death in the world. **Health** is *a state of physical, mental, and social well-being, or the absence of disease.* **Illness**, or *lack of health*, affects the way we perform our individual responsibilities in the social world. Like any key social issue, effective health care affects how individuals and groups carry out their lives at the micro, meso, and macro levels.

Health at the Micro Level

Sociologists are concerned with how our state of health affects our individual ability to carry out social responsibilities. Everyday lives are shaped by our own state of health or illness and that of our loved ones and close associates. If a roommate, significant other, or child is ill, it affects our lives in a number of ways. It alters our schedules, takes time as we deal with the illness, causes us to worry, and costs us in terms of medical care and lost work time. If a parent is dying of cancer or a child has epilepsy, our lives are influenced in profound and disruptive ways.

In many societies, communities are responsible for providing adequate health care, sanitation, and clean drinking water to citizens—services that affect the health of citizens. The health of citizens also affects community activities. A serious outbreak of influenza in the public schools may force schools to close for several days, causing repercussions in workplaces throughout the community as parents struggle to deal with child care issues. Thus, health status affects other institutions in the community, from family to schools to the workplace.

Health at the Meso Level

The institution of health care provides for the physical, mental, and social well-being of citizens. This includes prevention, diagnosis, and treatment of illness and regulation of the dispensing of medicine. The health care institution works in conjunction with families, education, religion, politics, and economics. What happens in the system of health care affects every part of the social world, as shown in the example of assisted suicide. The economic well-being of individuals in a society relates to health care access and who can pay. This often determines who lives, who dies, who is healthy, and who is not. Education about health care influences health and life expectancy. Well-educated citizens are more likely to develop health-enhancing lifestyles. Families attempt to prevent illness and care for sick individuals and often have responsibility to care for the ill and ailing. Political systems determine standards for health care and regulate medicinal drugs. Religious organizations establish support systems and health services, sometimes offer faith-healing alternatives to supplement the established medical system, and offer solace in times of illness and death. At the meso level, institutions are interconnected.

Institutions such as schools interact with health care systems in a variety of ways. The Chinese school toilet facility shown here indicates a different standard of sanitation and health than what many of us are accustomed to seeing.

Health at the Macro Level

Each society has a vested interest in the health of its citizenry because the general state of health affects the quality of life of the people and the state of the economy. Imagine the society in which citizens had "permission" to be sick frequently. How would that society continue to function? Societies have social policies that influence the way medicine is organized and health services are delivered. Beliefs about who is ill with what kinds of illness and for how long vary by society.

Consider the case of the now-dissolved Soviet Union. After the Soviet victory over Czarist Russia in 1917, the new revolutionary government was faced with an underdeveloped nation that essentially still produced its food with human-powered plows and simple hoes. The task of leading the country out of the 16th century and into the 20th was formidable. It called for a total effort from the nation's workforce. Confronted with a severe shortage of labor, the new government determined that absenteeism at work, regardless of excuse, had to be kept very low. Accordingly, the government instituted rules that required workers to obtain a certificate allowing them to be absent from work because of illness (Weiss and Lonnquist 2012). These certificates could be obtained only from government clinics, and each clinic could issue a limited number of permits. In some cases, physicians were actively encouraged to compete with one another to see how few certificates they could issue. Thus, absence due to illness was controlled, and the human resources needed for rebuilding the nation were augmented. The macro-level needs were met at the expense of hardship for individuals.

Global health focuses on several issues, including possible pandemics of highly contagious diseases, which have become worldwide threats as global travel increases. A *pandemic* is a disease that is prevalent throughout an entire country and may infect a continent or reach around the world. The global nature of the pandemic AIDS is illustrated in Map 14.1 on page 516. To control such diseases requires cooperation across national boundaries by organizations such as the United Nations. For instance, smallpox remained a serious global threat from the Middle Ages until the mid-20th century. The World Health Organization of the United Nations eliminated the disease completely in the 1960s. River blindness afflicted thousands of West Africans but has been eradicated due to international cooperation. Funding by organizations such as the Bill and Melinda Gates Foundation provides for research, treatment, and eradication of killer diseases such as malaria, AIDS, and tuberculosis. However, the threat of bioterrorism has raised the specter of other diseases such as smallpox and polio reappearing.

Illness may seem like an individual problem, but as shown in the above examples, it is far more than that. It is a national and global issue. This chapter examines health care at each level of analysis, from individual behaviors and decisions, to religious, political, and economic aspects, to the effect of stratification and ethnic status on the quality of health care one receives. Keep the social world model in mind as you read about health, illness, and medical care.

A Guatemalan child infected with HIV marches outside the site where an AIDS conference was being held in Guatemala City. Hundreds of people from different countries marched to bring attention to the problems of poor medical assistance and lack of government attention for the infected people.

Thinking Sociologically

Why do pandemic diseases that affect a local community require international attention and solutions?

Theoretical Perspectives on Health and Illness

In the analysis of institutions, each major paradigm or perspective in sociology offers a lens for understanding different aspects of the institution; health and illness in a given society and within the global system are no exceptions. Let us consider those major theoretical perspectives as they relate to health and illness.

Map 14.1 Estimated Percentage of Adults Living With HIV in 2009
Source: **Index Mundi 2012f; www.indexmundi.com/map/?v=32.**

Micro-Level Theoretical Perspectives

Unruly schoolchildren were once considered ill mannered or ill behaved. Now, they are often labeled as hyperkinetic or having attention deficit disorder, suffering from conditions that can be controlled by appropriate medication. Those with learning disabilities were labeled dumb or lazy. Now we know better, thanks to medical science. Heavy gamblers, alcoholics, and drug abusers are now defined as addicts needing medical or psychological help rather than as people lacking self-discipline. How conditions are labeled can result in social stigma of varying degrees and lead to different policies to treat problems.

The Symbolic Interaction Perspective and Labeling Theory

To symbolic interactionists, illness is whatever is given that label by powerful individuals in society, such as doctors. In recent years, the definition of illness in many Global North societies has expanded to encompass substance abuse and some forms of deviant behavior, giving physicians even more power and authority over broad areas of social life. Illness used to be viewed as a physical condition—germs, viruses, bacteria—causing the body to malfunction. Through the labeling process, behaviors that were once seen as criminal or "bad" are now defined as illnesses.

Medicalization and Labeling. **Medicalization** refers to *the shift in handling of some forms of deviance as well as some normal human functions (such as pregnancy and childbirth) from the familial, legal, or religious arenas to the health care system.* In some cases, the shift is away from the issue of individual self-control and toward medical diagnosis and treatment. Consider addictive behaviors such as alcoholism and drug abuse. There is considerable debate about how we define alcoholism because this influences the interpretation of the problem, the physician's role in treatment, whether we hold the patient to blame for the problem, and how it will be treated (Cockerham 2012). Symbolic interactionists emphasize the social definitions or labels such as *alcoholic* or *drug addict* and examine the effect such labels have on the life of the individual. Consider that medical conditions can be treated, and less stigma may be attached to these illnesses if they are not labeled as moral degeneracy (Conrad 2007). On the other hand, labeling the alcoholic as sick creates another type of stigma that may never be erased, and seeing alcoholism as a medical condition takes away individual responsibility, putting control in the hands of the health care system. The next "Sociology in Our Social World" explores the issue of policy toward alcoholism.

Sociology in Our Social World

Alcoholism, Medicalization, and Policy

Perhaps you know someone who struggles with an alcohol problem. A hotly contested debate in the medical, sociological, and psychological fields is how to define *alcoholism*, for that definition affects everything from treatment procedures to who has responsibility for rehabilitation. Is the alcoholic to be held individually responsible, or is this a condition beyond the individual's control? The idea that alcoholism is a disease, for instance, was first proposed in the 1930s by two reformed drinkers and later given scientific support (Jellinek 1960). In the aftermath of social and political debates, key professional groups officially labeled alcoholism a disease. The debate continues: The Alcoholics Anonymous approach to alcoholism treatment is to involve laypeople in groups, helping each other in a spiritually oriented manner. The "medicalization of alcoholism" calls for treatment by professionals—psychiatrists, psychologists, hospitals, and clinics. These two approaches are seen by some as complementing each other, and by others as conflicting (Conrad 2007; Roisen 2012).

Through the process of medicalization of alcoholism, it was added to the list of behaviors that were formerly considered morally reprehensible—bad, something sinners did, or a result of individual weakness—but are now considered medical problems over which the individual has little control (Conrad and Schneider 1992; Martin 2006; Roisen 2012). The individual became "sick" rather than "bad." Alcoholism was being defined as a medical problem with medical solutions. Detoxification clinics use medical interventions and drugs to treat alcoholics. In the process, the medical definition of alcoholism came to include three dimensions: biophysical, psychological, and social.

Alcoholism is a primary, chronic disease with genetic, psycho-social, and environmental factors influencing its development and manifestations. The disease is often progressive and fatal. It is characterized by impaired control over drinking, preoccupation with the drug alcohol, use of alcohol despite adverse consequences, and distortions in thinking, mostly denial. Each of these symptoms may be continuous or periodic (Meyer 1996:163).

The medical view of alcoholism has several implications: Unless there is intervention, alcoholics suffer physical and emotional breakdown and an early death. Those who are vulnerable are characterized by

1. having a physiological predisposition in the way their bodies process alcohol;
2. taking up drinking and thus becoming ill;
3. drinking resulting in consumption of ever greater amounts with increasingly severe consequences;
4. drinking that results in distinctive disability, including the loss of ability to choose when it comes to alcohol consumption; and
5. progressing through a predictable sequence of stages, independent of individual characteristics (Schoeman 1991).

The label alcoholic *has a number of implications, including the fact that the stigma associated with the term may prevent some people from seeking help. This is one reason many alcohol treatment centers have recast alcoholism as a disease, hoping that the redefinition would remove stigma. Other problems arise when the issue is medicalized.*

(Continued)

(Continued)

Many health care professionals, however, are reluctant to treat alcohol as a problem drug (Meyer 1996). Some argue that the disease concept is the wrong approach—that what is really at stake is "heavy drinking" as a way of life. Rather than treating a "disease," they feel that professionals should be concerned with approaches that will change the way in which individuals organize their behaviors. These researchers and practitioners argue that heavy drinkers can become nondrinkers or moderate drinkers and can control their drinking. Some critical sociological theorists see medicalization as one more form of social control. By labeling alcoholism as a medical disease, the medical profession becomes an agent of social control for the state (Conrad and Schneider 1992). Changing the alcoholic by altering perceptions, routines, attitudes, and habits of behavior gives the individual responsibility in a context of supportive family or friends, economic opportunities, and alternative role models.

A third possibility exists—that there is truth in both models based on individual differences. Treatment programs can be found based on both of these models, and the debate about the best approach continues. Recent approaches to alcoholism often combine medical and social-behavioral treatments, some of which have been illustrated in the TV show *Intervention* (A&E 2012; Roisen 2012). Key in approaches to alcoholism is to help alcoholics recognize that they need help.

Thinking Sociologically

Many of us have a friend or relative who consciously or unconsciously struggles with alcohol problems. Do you see that person being labeled by others? Is the problem a lack of self-discipline or a physical illness needing medical treatment? What might you do to help the person?

Social critics argue that once conditions are medicalized, they come to be controlled and exploited by powerful experts. Yet some "problems" may not be problems at all. For example, as a result of movements to "demedicalize" some behaviors, homosexuality has been removed from the American Psychiatric Association's list of mental disorders.

Clearly, modern societies have gone overboard in medicalizing behaviors. However, some scholars see medicalization of health issues positively because identifying the issues as medical in nature lessens the stigma. The issues can then be more effectively addressed.

Having some sense of the issues raised by the symbolic interactionists in the examples above, we turn now to how the experience of illness or health at the micro level is shaped by forces at the meso and macro levels in our social world.

Meso- and Macro-Level Theoretical Perspectives

The institution of health care in Western culture differs dramatically from that of many other cultures around the world. Consider the conflicting ideas of illness between the Hmong culture in the United States, made up of immigrants from Vietnamese hill tribes, and the U.S. medical community. In *The Spirit Catches You and You Fall Down*, Anne Fadiman describes the contrasts between how an immigrant Hmong family views an epileptic child and how the hospital in the family's U.S. community sees the situation. When the parents take their child for treatment of her epileptic seizures, everything from the concepts of what causes the problem, to the cures, to communication about the disease is problematic. The medical staff treat the epileptic seizures with Western medical techniques, whereas the Hmong family attributes the seizures to spirits (Fadiman 1997). Concepts of health and disease vary greatly in different ethnic groups. Theories and cross-cultural knowledge help understand this and other cultural differences in approaches to health care.

The Functionalist Perspective

Functional theorists focus primarily on the macro level of the health care system. Studies of suicide, carried out by the early French sociologist Émile Durkheim (discussed in Chapter 5), illustrate that social conditions and events in the larger society and people's group affiliations affected inclinations to commit suicide. Other studies have linked illnesses such as heart disease, kidney failure, stroke, mental illness, and infant mortality to macro-level processes and trends in societies. For example, economic recessions cause social stress and disruption in lifestyles, which can activate mental problems. These, in turn, can result in health problems.

According to functionalists, social norms define what counts as illness and how to treat it. The purpose of the health care system in society is to maintain the social structure and a harmonious balance between individuals and institutions in society. Illness is potentially disruptive to the balanced social world. The sick role is sometimes considered a deviant one because it "robs" the society of normal role functioning. As we saw in the Soviet example, if too many people claim the sick role at the same time, the tasks necessary to maintain the society cannot be performed. The primary task, or function, of the medical profession is to control illness and prevent individuals from being unable to perform their social roles.

Functionalists like Talcott Parsons also see positive value in the hierarchical structure of the medical profession and in the power of the physician over the patient. He felt that this led to better care for patients with the "experts" in charge, but that view is not shared by all as we will see below.

Despite the harmonious view of functionalists, ambivalence does exist in the doctor-patient relationship. Physicians hold power over patients in the doctor-patient relationship, and patients may have contradictory expectations for their treatment (Starr 1982). We turn to conflict theory for a different perspective on the health care system.

One way to combat diarrhea diseases in India is through provision of safe drinking water and sanitary facilities by the government. This is a primary concern of the World Health Organization. However, the World Bank and International Monetary Fund have been pushing for privatization of water, meaning that water would be clean but not affordable for many.

Thinking Sociologically

What duties and responsibilities do you relinquish when you occupy a sick role? Which ones do you continue during your illness?

The Conflict Perspective

Poverty, unemployment, low wages, malnutrition, and a host of other economic conditions affect people's access and ability to compete for health care and medicines in many countries. Differential access is a key theme in conflict theorists' approach to health issues. Consider the case of Nkosi, a 4-year-old boy in a rural Ghanaian village. He came down with an infection due to polluted water, causing diarrhea and vomiting. Nkosi was already weakened by malnutrition and parasites, and by the time his family got help, dehydration was so extensive that he died, one of millions of similar casualties. Why was health care not available?

Nkosi had less access to medical treatment, immunizations, antibiotics, vitamins, and a balanced diet than children in the Global North countries or even in urban areas of the Global South. Children in poor countries around the world suffer from malnutrition and chronic disease before succumbing to pneumonia or other infections, which are normally curable diseases. The explosion in new "emerging infectious diseases" such as AIDS, Brazilian purpuric fever, new strains of Ebola, various insect- and bird-transported diseases such as SARS and bird flu, and swine flu (H1N1) add to the problems faced by health care workers in the Global South (Farmer 1999). Dr. Paul Farmer, a U.S. infectious disease specialist and anthropologist, set up an organization, Partners in Health, with the goal of conquering diseases among the world's poor (Kidder 2004). With life expectancy (average length of life) as low as 35 years in some drought-ridden and war-torn countries, the challenge is formidable.

In the world system of rich and poor countries, individuals suffer different illnesses depending on the level of development of their society and their position in it. Poor people in poor countries die from ailments that are curable infectious diseases in rich countries. Conflict theorists point out the disparities between citizens of rich versus poor countries. Consider the case of one of the poorest world countries: Swaziland in sub-Saharan Africa. The country's population of 1.4 million people is weakened from poor nutrition and hunger because their land has been ravaged by drought; many people in Swaziland die of treatable diseases (United Nations 2009). However, the real killer is

AIDS. About 26% of the country's population is infected with HIV/AIDS (Doctors without Borders 2012). In 2011, the numbers were estimated to be 173,617 adults and 21,780 children. Among pregnant women, the number of HIV infections reported by health facilities is 12,156, or about 41% (UNAIDS 2012b). The result is that life expectancy at birth in Swaziland was approximately 49 years in 2011 (World Factbook 2013h). The number of AIDS orphans is growing rapidly. Children orphaned in the Global South are concerned with trying to survive on the little food available and to raise their younger siblings. International aid organizations provide most of the meager food they consume.

Many governments officially proclaim that health care is a basic right of all citizens, although many do not have the means to meet the health needs of citizens. One country that has revolutionized its health care system under the revolutionary government of Hugo Chávez is Venezuela. With oil revenues and tax dollars, the government has built clinics called *Mission Barrio Adentro* to serve those living in urban and rural poverty. Before the Chávez government revolutionized the health delivery system, many poor people had no access to care. Today, each clinic serves a community for free. In the four-tiered system, Tier 1 provides basic care; Tier 2 has some beds, does small surgeries, and treats asthma and similar illnesses; Tier 3 includes small hospitals that accept referrals from the clinics for medical tests such as MRIs and X-rays; and Tier 4 is a hospital for surgeries and other procedures (Witness for Peace 2008). One result of these changes has been that the infant mortality rate has been cut in half, and life expectancy has risen. However, many poor countries do not have oil or other natural resources as Venezuela does to help pay for health care. Cuba has also developed a system to reach all its citizens, as explained in the next "Sociology Around the World."

At the global level, multinational companies that build plants in the poor Global South provide examples of the profit motive's influence on health conditions. These businesses are looking for large profit margins and cost-cutting opportunities, so they may seek countries where health and safety standards are lower than those in the Global North, which has more stringent health regulations. Although many multinational companies provide health clinics for workers, lower safety standards can lead to long-term illnesses, eye problems, lung disease, and other debilitating health problems. Moreover, multinational pharmaceutical companies have resisted generic drugs or inexpensive vaccines that are crucial to combating disease in the Global South. Poor countries are places to save money in manufacturing labor costs and raw materials but are not places to provide services because people there can afford little and provide little profit. A few countries such as India are developing their own cheaper versions of drugs for AIDS and other diseases, bypassing international pharmaceutical companies.

As we said above, Talcott Parsons's functional model of the sick status stresses the physician's need for total authority over the patient in order to meet the needs of clients (Parsons 1975). Some conflict theorists argue that physicians seek this power so that they can decide who they will treat. Some physicians prefer not to locate in poor or rural areas or countries, to treat elderly patients, or to spend time on those with AIDS. The most lucrative positions with the most prestige are generally located in major global urban areas and at well-known clinics, treating people who can pay for private care. This leads some conflict theorists to discuss the doctor-patient relationship as an association in which the doctor exercises control, and loyalty of the doctor to the patient depends in part on the social status of the patient (White 2002).

The point that should be clear is that poverty—whether in the Global North or the Global South—has major impacts on quality of life and health care of the citizens. In the United States, individuals who have poor health care or who lack the resources for health insurance are affected in many ways, as the "Engaging Sociology" on page 522 illustrates.

Feminist Theory

For feminist theorists, gender is a key variable that affects health and illness. Feminist theorists argue that the patriarchal control of women carries over to health care systems and reinforces dependence, submission, and definitions of what is illness for women. Women in the Global North are profitable for the health care system because they are seen more often and have more expensive procedures (White 2002). For example, cesarean section surgery to remove the newborn from the womb tops 31% of births in the United States. Some of these are necessary, but others may be for convenience or to avoid lawsuits (Weiss 2010). According to feminist theorists, controlling women's reproductive health and defining women's normal biological experiences as medical problems are issues rooted in Western society's class interests and in maintaining patriarchal authority. However, in some countries, women are important and respected healers and doctors. One illustration is Gujarat, India, where women medical practitioners hold significant positions of leadership and autonomy in the medical establishment, giving women power and a voice in their health care (Mavalankar et al. 2009).

Feminist theorists contend that women have been kept in inferior social positions through much of history because powerful members of society said that their bodies limited them. This is especially true in Global North societies. For instance, drugs to control depression keep women in the situations that caused the depression in the first place. Also, menopause has sometimes been treated as an illness rather than a normal life transition. Some feminists argue that women are defined by doctors and others in the

Sociology Around the World

Health Care: Cuba's Pride

One thing all Cubans were promised under the Communist regime of Fidel Castro was access to good health care, which he viewed as a basic right of all people. When Cuba had trading partners and support from the former Soviet Union and allied nations in Europe's eastern bloc, its system was considered a model, especially for a Global South country. Now, the country has lost external support due to the collapse of the Soviet system. Cuba has fallen on hard economic times primarily because of the U.S.-imposed embargo on goods going to Cuba, with the health care system being one victim. Shortages of drugs, diagnostic equipment, and medical supplies have forced Cuba's well-trained doctors to be creative. They use herbal remedies, hypnosis, and acupuncture in place of needed supplies and equipment.

The health care system may well have the best doctor-patient ratio in the world—1 doctor to every 170 inhabitants (Plant 2007). Hospitals and clinics are spread throughout the country. Infant mortality in 2011 at 4.8 (deaths per 1,000 live births in the first year) and life expectancy rates (78 in 2011) are comparable with those of most Global North developed countries (World Factbook 2013d). However, because of economic hardships and lack of medicine and equipment that could easily control some illnesses and diseases, some experts fear these numbers will begin to slip. Cuba experienced a typhoid fever and tuberculosis outbreak in the early 1990s, even though these diseases were once almost nonexistent in the country. Water contamination in Cuba is increasing. These problems illustrate the interrelationship between health, economic resources, and global links between countries.

Health statistics have a human face; diary entries of a recent visitor to Cuba tell of the impact that economic sanctions have on the health of ordinary citizens:

> I visited Dr. Barbara, a young family doctor, in her neighborhood *consultorio* in Havana, Cuba. Her waiting room was full of young mothers holding plump and healthy babies, sitting against a wall covered with a hand-painted wall mural. A portrait of Fidel Castro (Cuba's former head of government) hung next to a painted caricature of Mickey Mouse on the wall behind her desk. Her eyes bright, her long hair bouncing against her shoulders, she said she was very proud to be a Cuban physician and to care for a patient community of 200 families.
>
> However, she added with a pause, sometimes she felt helpless to provide the care that her patients needed. She explained that diagnostic tests were often missed or delayed because of shortages of X-ray film or replacement parts for equipment. Blood work was limited by lack of reagents needed in the labs. Her prescription choices were restricted to the medicines available at the time, a situation that she found very frustrating when her patient had multiple medical problems that dictated the use of one medicine rather than another. Prozac and other state-of-the-art antidepressants were unheard of, and only a few drugs for treating depressive and anxiety disorders were available. Many anticancer medicines were difficult or impossible to get. She said that people were dying sooner than necessary because of these scarcities (Lemkau 2006).

medical profession by their reproductive organs and life cycle (White 2002). One result is that more women than men are patients because their normal life cycles have been defined as medical problems.

Women's risks of maternal death from pregnancy and childbirth complications are much greater in the Global South than in the Global North. In the least developed countries of the Global South, the risk of dying in pregnancy or childbirth is 1 in 16, whereas in the Global North, 1 in 4,100 die. The United Nations Millennium Development Goals have a target of 2015 to reduce maternal mortality by three quarters. The good news is that the rate of maternal deaths in sub-Saharan Africa dropped 41% in the 20 years from 1990 to 2010, to 500 deaths per 100,000 live births (WHO, UNICEF, UNFPA, and World Bank 2012). However, the opposite is true in South Africa where the number of women dying in childbirth quadrupled over 20 years. The high rate of HIV affects the maternal death rate there (Smith 2011).

Engaging Sociology

Decisions About Health Care When Living in Poverty

Look at the following list of basic needs. Most of us provide these for our families through our jobs. Now imagine that you and your family are faced with a major financial crisis, and you simply cannot meet all your needs. Which of the items listed below would you give up? If that was still not sufficient to make ends meet, what decisions would you make to balance the budget?

- Health care and health insurance
- A car or other reliable transportation
- Food for the family
- Decent shelter
- Clothing—especially adequate for cold weather and perhaps appropriate for the breadwinner's occupation
- Housing in a safe neighborhood
- Access to good schools for the family's children
- Other essentials . . .

Many people choose to postpone or sacrifice health care insurance or doctors' visits. Identify how poor health care might affect your income and at least three of the items above.

1. ______________________________
2. ______________________________
3. ______________________________

Now consider items you chose to eliminate other than health care. How might those decisions have a long-term impact on other aspects of your quality of life—*including* the health of family members?

1. ______________________________
2. ______________________________
3. ______________________________

Also in Global South countries, girls are often married at a young age, and having children at a very young age can cause major health problems. The probability that a 15-year-old female will die from complications of pregnancy and childbirth is the highest in Niger, Africa (1 in 7), and lowest in Ireland (1 in 48,000; UN Population Fund 2007). One of the most socially difficult problems for young girls who are married and give birth at a young age is *obstetric fistula*, a childbirth injury in which tissue is torn between the vaginal wall and the bladder or rectum. This causes ulcerations, incontinence, and infections (Burn 2011). More than 2 million young women are affected, and they are often ostracized and abandoned. Several international organizations carry out the simple operation to repair the damaged area and return these young girls' lives.

To regain control of women's health, some feminists have formed health organizations concerned with reproductive health: midwifery, natural childbirth, home deliveries, and menopause. With increasing numbers of women physicians, attitudes toward women's health and communication practices between women and physicians are changing.

Each theory illuminates a different set of issues in health, illness, and health care as an institution. Each also has blind spots. It is appropriate to now examine health and illness at a micro level, so we turn to the sick role and being sick as we experience them individually.

The Status and Roles of the Sick Person: Micro-Level Analysis

What constitutes sick behavior rests on the signs, symptoms, and circumstances defined by one's social group rather than on a set of universally recognized bodily malfunctions. Cultural definitions combined with physical symptoms help us understand illness (Weiss and Lonnquist 2012). A poor Central American woman, asked if she has been sick, illustrates this point by commenting that she wished she knew what it meant to be sick. Sometimes she felt so bad she thought she could curl up and die, but she kept going because the kids needed her, and she lacked money to spend on a doctor. She did not have time to be sick. She asks, "How does one know when someone is sick?" Some of us can go to bed almost any time with any illness, but many of the world's people cannot be sick, not even when they need to be (Koos 1954).

To this woman, being sick was not just a physical condition or how she felt or any physical symptoms she displayed. From a cultural perspective, she had responsibilities that could not be ignored, little access to health care, and no money to buy medicine or care. So who defines the poor woman above as sick? She herself? Her friends and family? Her employer? A health care professional? What is necessary before we can say, from the sociological point of view, that someone is sick?

Illness, or being sick, is a complex matter resulting from changes in the body. Try comparing illness to an iceberg: We do not see the whole iceberg. Similarly, most illness lies under the surface and may never come to public attention unless it forces the person to alter routines or fail in carrying out responsibilities. Generally, physical disorders can be identified, and a health professional can relieve pain or discomfort and return individuals to a healthy state.

However, for the sociologist, the view of illness as only a physical disorder is too limited. A society's definitions influence who is considered sick and under what conditions. Illness, then, is in part socially constructed. The health establishment, schools, and workplaces acknowledge illness only if certain society-defined conditions are present.

Surveys of health in populations around the world indicate that few people are totally free from some degree of physical disorder. Yet the presence of such disorders does not mean that individuals will seek treatment or that the illness will be recognized and treated. Both individual (micro) and structural (meso or macro) factors are important in health care decisions and treatment. The political and economic environment, access to the health care system that provides services, and the predisposition by an individual to seek medical care all enter into health care decisions.

Thinking Sociologically

The Central American woman felt like she could "curl up and die," but she survived. Was she sick? Would you be sick if you felt the way she did? Why might your definition of your situation be different from hers?

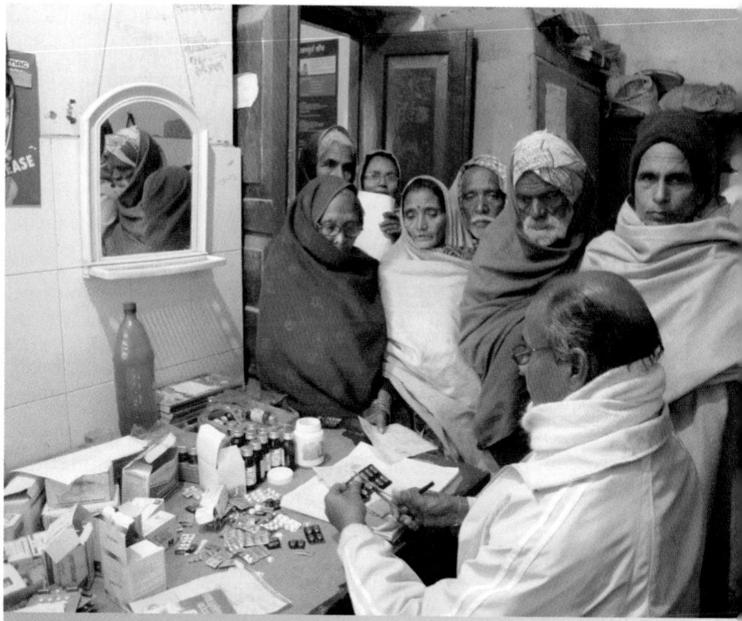

Being sick is more than a physical problem of fever, aches and pains, loss of energy, and other symptoms. Being sick changes relationships, how other people spend their time, and how other people respond to the sick person, including lowered expectations of what that person can do and taking on a new role. The experience of being sick differs across countries. This primary health care center in rural India does not have a pharmacist. A filing clerk doubles up as a pharmacist.

The Sick Role

Think of all the social relationships, engagements, and responsibilities that are affected when you are sick. You miss class, have to cancel other engagements, avoid your friends so that you do not infect them with your germs, and cannot carry out your usual responsibilities. Most people are sympathetic for a couple of days, but then, they expect you to get back to your usual routines and responsibilities. Let us consider this "role" of being sick.

Those who are ill occupy a special position or status in society—the **sick role** (Parsons 1975). They are deviant in that they are not carrying out their role expectations. Other members must pick up those responsibilities. Unlike other deviance, however, the sick role is not punished but is tolerated as long as the sick individual cooperates and acts to overcome illness, returning as soon as possible to fulfill his or her usual social roles. That can be difficult for people facing chronic illness who are both governed by and consumers of medicine, as seen in the model below (Varul 2010).

In an early contribution to the sociology of health, Parsons (1951a) presented a functional theoretical model of the "sick role," outlining four interrelated behavioral expectations—two rights and two obligations:

Right 1: The sick person has the right to be excused from normal social responsibility as needed to be restored to normal functioning in the society. For example, sick students expect to receive permission to miss class or to make up a missed exam.

Right 2: The sickness is not the individual's fault. The sick person did not mean to deviate from normal social expectations and cannot become well by self-decision or by willing it so.

Obligation 1: The sick person should define being sick as undesirable. To avoid the accusation of laziness or malingering, the sick person must not prolong illness unnecessarily to avoid social obligations.

Obligation 2: Those in the sick status are expected to seek technically competent help and cooperate in getting well. In Western countries, the help is most often a medical doctor.

Parsons describes the physicians' roles as complementing the "sick role"—to restore routine behavior and "orderliness" in patients. The models presented by Parsons are clearly related to functionalist thought. They focus on integrating all aspects of medical care into a working social system (Parsons 1951a).

One problem is that some individuals might like being excused from tasks and allowed to deviate from social responsibility (such as taking tests or doing an arduous task). Certainly, being sick can be a less demanding lifestyle than going to work or school or taking care of a family. The sick role can also legitimize failure by providing a ready excuse for poor performance at some task (Cole and Lejeune 1972). People who believe they are permanently unable to fulfill their normal social roles may be motivated to define themselves as sick. Yet an excess of sick people could be disruptive to the social fabric, so it is necessary to develop means to control who enters the sick status, as did the Soviet regime, and to guard against misuse of illness as an excuse for avoiding social responsibility.

Individuals make choices about their own health and lifestyles—decisions about leisure time activities; exercise; the amount and type of food they consume; use of alcohol, drugs, and tobacco; and sexual behavior. All these choices affect health. Any of these taken to extremes can result in illness. Health and lifestyle choices are influenced by socialization patterns, family backgrounds, peers, jobs, and cultural expectations.

Eating patterns are a concern for U.S. public health officials. Both children and adults fall into the couch potato syndrome of a sedentary life as flab accumulates into excess weight, a recipe for certain illnesses. Fast food has become a convenient timesaver and a recipe for gaining weight. Health care workers have developed education campaigns to change eating patterns, and schools are removing pop machines from cafeterias and improving nutrition content of school meals. New York City's Mayor Michael Bloomberg has put forth several initiatives to address the obesity epidemic and related illnesses such as heart disease and diabetes. He sought a ban from the city health department, which was approved, controlling the size of soft drinks. Supersize soft drinks over 16 ounces sold at fast-food establishments and other outlets are banned and likely to bring attention to the calorie sources that are causing health problems (Goldman and Stanford 2012). Another concern is the millions of people with negative body images that result in health problems as some men and women abuse their bodies with excessive and unhealthy eating and behavior patterns, such as extreme diets and steroid use.

Many people in industrialized societies, especially in the United States, are extremely overweight, a serious health hazard that brings with it many risks. This is a concern to the society as a whole because it means lowered productivity and increased health care costs.

Thinking Sociologically

Do you feel that eating unhealthy food and becoming obese (for example, those depicted in the film *Super Size Me*) are serious problems related to the health of a nation? Should this be an individual matter of choice, or a national problem because of resulting health care costs? Do changes in eating patterns need to be made, and if so, what would you recommend to policy makers?

Determining who is sick goes beyond physical symptoms and feelings of discomfort. Symptoms such as distress, anxiety, or perceived seriousness of the symptoms often result in seeking health care. Individuals may postpone health action or not seek health care because of lack of availability and affordability or because they deny the existence of the ailment.

Social Factors in Illness and Health

An American Peace Corps volunteer in a South American village could not understand the resigned attitude of the mother, Mónica, as she held her dying baby. He offered to help Mónica get the baby to the clinic 15 miles away, but she seemed resigned to its death. The expectations that shaped Mónica's behavior were learned in her cultural setting. Three of her seven children had died. In this rural Global South setting, as many as half of the babies born will die in infancy because of curable illness, poor sanitation, lack of clean water, and lack of health care and medicine. People come to accept infant deaths, often easily preventable, as normal. Many children are not even named until their parents determine that they are likely to live.

Individual beliefs, experiences, and decisions about health and illness may be deeply rooted in the meso- and macro-level structural factors that shape the availability of medicines and health services as well as in the factors that shape one's lifestyle and attitudes toward health care. Consider some of the social dimensions that affect our individual health.

Cultural Belief Systems and Health. Western scientific medicine centers on physicians who use medical technology to heal those who are sick and return them to society as contributing members. In non-Western parts of the world, quite different healing approaches are used, often combined with Western medical procedures. In North

Gerardo Queupukura, a renowned shaman of the Mapuche tribe in Chile, attends to the line of patients and looks at the urine samples to determine the patients' health status. The medicine man holds consultations twice a week.

Africa, for example, members of the Azande tribe believe in a spiritual system of healing centered on the activities of the local shaman. Illness occurs, they believe, when an offended individual arranges for a "sickness pellet" to be placed in the body of the offender. Through spiritual ceremonies, the sorcerer sees that the pellet is withdrawn from the body and restores the person to health.

Some Hispanic cultures practice a unique, ancient, and complex system of healing known as *curanderismo*. The origins are found in indigenous herbal medicine, indigenous religious belief systems, witchcraft, and Spanish Catholicism. Good health and a strong body are viewed as God's blessing for the faithful. Illness comes either when one has sinned or as a message from God to help the person learn to be good. The relationship between the *curandero*, or healer, and the patient is close, relying on psychological and spiritual as well as physical treatments. Many Hispanics combine Western medicine and *curanderismo*. For "non-Hispanic illnesses," the physician is the healer of choice. However, for culture-specific conditions such as *susto* (characterized by extreme fright), the *curandero* may be consulted because many believe that such conditions are impervious to even the highest technology of the scientific physician (Weiss and Lonnquist 2012). The role of the *curandero* combines elements of a psychologist and a healer.

Definitions of who is considered mentally ill and who is put away for their own and society's protection vary greatly across societies. Consider the case of Manuel, a schizophrenic who "goes crazy" when the moon is full (the concept of lunacy) and is put in a Nicaraguan mental hospital during that time. Otherwise, he lives a relatively normal life with his parents. In another culture, he might be put in long-term hospital care or given drugs to control the condition. His mental instability might even be given a different definition (Fernando 2002). Pain is a universal experience, yet how it is perceived, experienced, and reacted to varies by cultural background, ethnic group membership, genetic and gender differences, psychological differences, and socialization experience (Addictionblog.org 2011; Galanti 2008). For example, Asian patients rarely ask for pain medication, but patients from Mediterranean cultures readily ask for help to relieve the slightest pain. Why is there a difference? In a classic U.S. hospital-based study of reactions to pain, researchers observed that patients' responses fell into two main categories: stoic and emotive. Patients with Jewish and Italian cultural backgrounds responded to pain emotionally, while patients of Yankee background were stoic and tried to bravely endure pain. Those of Irish descent denied pain altogether. Although the Jewish American and Italian American patients exhibited similar reactions to pain, their reasons for these reactions were different. The Jewish American patients took a long-term view toward pain. They were concerned about its meaning for their future, and their reactions did not subside when pain-relieving drugs were administered. The Italian American patients, on the other hand, were mainly concerned with the pain itself, and drugs both relieved the pain and their complaints (Lasch 2002; Thomas and Rose 1991; Zborowski 1952).

Other studies have linked expressive, emotive responses to Hispanic, Middle Eastern, and Mediterranean patients, while stoic patients were more often from Northern European and Asian backgrounds (D'Arcy 2009; Galanti 2008). Decisions we make and experiences we have are directly related to our socialization, culture, and definition of reality.

Social Predictors in Individual Health and Illness. Individual micro-level variables such as age, gender, ethnicity, economic factors, social status, and urban or rural residence are important in determining patterns of health and illness as well. For example, age affects health in several ways. People 65 years or older are increasing in number in the United States due to the baby boomer cohort reaching 65. These individuals need medical intervention and hospitalization more often than any other age group, and their numbers are increasing with aggravated illnesses such as diabetes and hypertension, advances in technology and more testing, and more awareness of medical issues (Cherry, Lucas, and Decker 2010). Medicare covers this group and accounts for 20% of the national health expenditures. The baby boomers also receive more preventative care than other age groups. Of the approximately 40 million citizens 65 years and older, 24.2% had 10 or more visits per year to doctor offices, emergency departments, and home visits (compared to 18.2% for those 55 to 64 years), and 36.7% had 4 to 9 visits (Centers for Disease Control and Prevention/National Center for Health Statistics/Office of Analysis and Epidemiology 2012). Figure 14.1 shows the number of visits by females and males to physicians.

Gender patterns are clear, too: In Global North cultures, women report more health problems than do men. They use more physician services on a regular basis and receive more preventive and reproductive care, take more medications, and are more likely to be hospitalized (Weiss and Lonnquist 2012). In contrast, men use emergency services more.

Ethnic groups, meso-level groups, affect the micro level through socialization of individuals into health behaviors and experiences. Recall the cases of Hispanic *curanderismo*, the Hmong concepts of illness, and different experiences of pain discussed earlier. Socialization into possible health care options ranges from modern medical practitioners to alternative medical practitioners (from traditional folk healers to modern chiropractors who are not part of the medical establishment), nonmedical professions (e.g., social workers and clergy), lay advisers, and self-care (Pescosolido 1992).

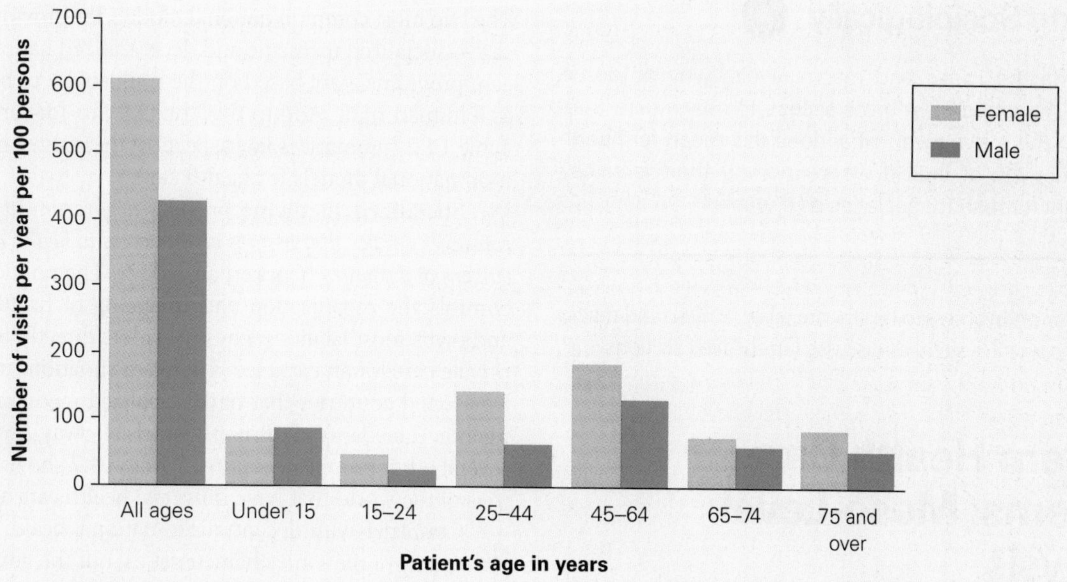

Figure 14.1 Number of Visits per Year to Physicians by U.S. Women and Men

As we saw in Chapter 8, racial privilege and disprivilege are often rooted in discrimination in organizations and are often not a result of individual prejudice. In the United States, African Americans are less likely to have regular health care providers and more likely to use hospital emergency rooms and health clinics than the majority of the population. Health care is less available in inner cities and rural areas, where there are concentrations of minority residents. Minority women are less likely to receive prenatal care than other women, and the infant mortality gap between whites, African Americans, and other minorities in the United States (i.e., the number of live-born infants who die in their first year per 1,000 births) is shown in Table 14.1 (MacDorman and Mathews 2011). The high infant-mortality rate of the United States compared with rates in other affluent countries is due largely to social class differentials between whites and minorities and differential access to health care in the United States. African Americans also have higher rates of cancers and shorter survival times than whites at all stages of cancer diagnosis (American Cancer Society 2006; Ries et al. 2000).

Table 14.1 **Infant Deaths per 1,000 Live Births by Race of Mother (in the United States)**

Race or Ethnic Origin	*Number per 1,000*
All racial/ethnic groups	6.75
Black	13.3
Puerto Rican	7.7
American Indian/Alaskan	9.2
White	5.6
Hispanic	5.5
Asian American	4.8

Source: MacDorman and Mathews (2011).

Social status affects health because wealthier individuals are more likely to seek professional help early for physical or psychological distress, partly because they can afford treatment. However, contact with physicians is highest among the lowest income categories (7.6 doctor visits per year compared with an average of 6 for the entire population; Weiss and Lonnquist 2012). Lower-income citizens' perceptions of necessary health consultation often involve response to crises. The "working poor" who do not qualify for Medicaid but cannot afford private insurance or medical care delay care (Weiss and Lonnquist 2012). Roughly one in four adults in the United States lacked health care in 2010, and one in five did not receive the needed health-related services because they could not afford to visit a doctor (Centers for Disease Control and Prevention 2012; Schiller et al. 2012). Without universal access to health care, income affects health status.

Thinking Sociologically

Considering the meso and macro levels, why do some people in the world have more access to health care than others? At the micro level, what does this mean for health and productivity of individuals supporting their families? What might it mean for societies as a whole?

Differences in access to health care relate to meso and macro levels of the social system, as discussed in the next sections.

Modern Health Care Systems: Meso-Level Analysis

At one time, health care was largely an issue addressed in homes by families. Today, in wealthy countries, health care has become institutionalized. The bustling hospital, the efficient nurses and nurses' aides, and the technically proficient physicians have replaced home care, visiting doctors, folk remedies, and homes as the setting for births, deaths, and many health issues in between. Much of the treatment of diseases depends on research that is funded by governments or foundations, and health delivery is performed by organizations that are bureaucratized corporations. This section explores the institution of medicine: organization of health care systems, hospitals as complex organizations, and changes of professional status for physicians.

The Organization of Health Care Systems

Citizens' access to health care depends on several factors: the cultural values concerning the government's role in providing health care, whether health care is seen as a human right for all citizens or a privilege for those who can pay, the amount and source of funding to provide health care, and the type of health care available. Societies around the world struggle with issues of cost, quality and access to care, and medical technology. In the Global North, these struggles result from aging populations with more health needs and smaller numbers of citizens in the taxpaying working population to support health care programs. Nations in the Global South struggle with problems that result in high death rates from curable diseases and from epidemics. Nations develop health care philosophies and systems based on population needs and their ability to address them.

Types of National Health Care Systems

The two most common national models for providing health care—socialized medicine and decentralized national health care programs—are based on the philosophy of health care as a human right. Add to that the U.S. fee-for-service plan. Table 14.2 summarizes key aspects of these three most common national models for health care.

Socialized medicine *provides a government-supported consumer service that assures equal access to health care for all citizens of a country* (Cockerham 2012). The political system controls the organization and financing of health services and owns most facilities, pays providers directly, and allows private care for an extra fee. There are variations in systems. Developed countries that have socialized medicine systems include Canada, Great Britain, Israel, Norway, Sweden, and several other European countries. Map 14.2 shows the countries of the world that have universal health care as of 2012.

Countries with decentralized national health programs have many of the same characteristics, but the government's role is different. The government has less direct control over health care and acts to regulate the system, but not operate it (Cockerham 2012). Countries with decentralized systems include France, Germany, Japan, and the Netherlands. The United States, unique among Global North countries, has **fee-for-service health care**, in which *doctors and hospitals are paid for each service they perform, and decide the prices charged for every service.* They typically can order as many tests as they feel necessary, and they make lots of money by deciding the prices. In the United States, this system is financed by not only a mix of private and public purchasers but also government-run Medicare and Medicaid programs for poor and elderly that are closer to socialized medicine plans.

Thinking Sociologically

Do profit motive and competition create higher quality in a service field such as health care, as they seem to in manufacturing organizations? Why or why not? What are some positive and some negative consequences of a competitive system with the "winners" rewarded by higher profits?

Most governments in Europe decided to support health care as a human right for all citizens and put these systems into place in the late 1800s and early 1900s. Their motivations were to develop healthier populations, to strengthen their military forces and their economic systems, and to reduce the possibility of revolution by the poor and working classes by providing for basic health care needs. By providing health insurance and protection for the injured or unemployed, financial security in case of illness was increased.

Table 14.2 **Types of Health Care Delivery Systems Around the World**

Role of Government	Fee-for-Service	Socialized Medicine	Decentralized National Health
Regulation	Limited	Direct	Indirect
Payment to providers	Limited	Direct	Indirect
Ownership of facilities	Private and public	Private and public	Private and public
Public access	Not guaranteed	Guaranteed	Guaranteed
Private care	Dominant	Limited	Limited

Source: Cockerham (2012).

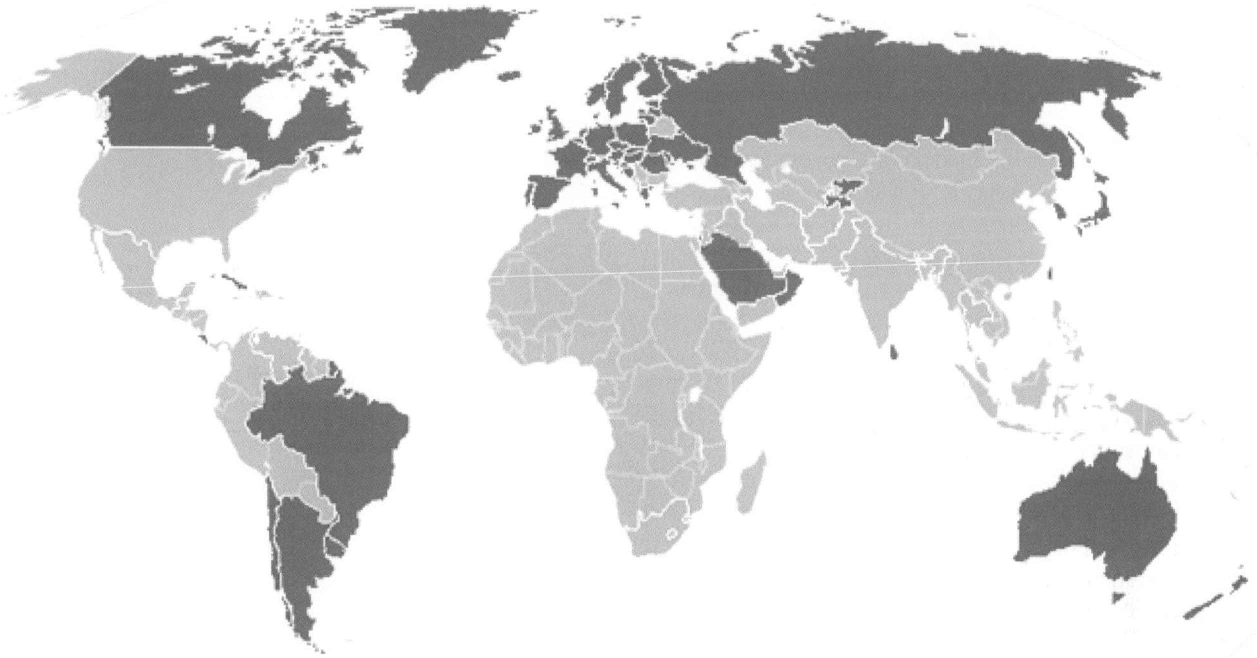

Map 14.2 Countries That Provide Universal Health Care

Source: Fisher, Max. 2012. "Here's a Map of the Countries That Provide Universal Health Care (America's Still Not on It)." *The Atlantic*, June 28. Retrieved February 6, 2013 (http://www.theatlantic.com/international/archive/2012/06/heres-a-map-of-the-countries-that-provide-universal-health-care-americas-still-not-on-it/259153/).

This is the philosophy of the health care system in Canada, described in the "Sociology Around the World" on page 530.

Thinking Sociologically

Based on the "Sociology Around the World" feature on health care in Canada compared to the United States, what do you conclude about pros and cons of these two approaches to health care?

Health care systems in poor countries are often based on previous colonial models. However, most countries struggle to provide for basic health care needs, to ensure access to health care for citizens living in rural areas, and to deal with costly diseases such as AIDS. Because of the lack of physicians, especially in rural areas, most countries in the Global South rely on a combination of Western scientific practices and indigenous medical practices using herbs and other local remedies. Trained midwives deliver babies, and health education workers travel to villages to teach about the spread of diseases such as AIDS, sometimes making condoms available. In Ugandan villages, where a

Sociology Around the World

Comparing Health Care Systems: The Canadian Model

Two principles underlie Canada's system: All Canadians should have the right to health care, and financial barriers to care should be eliminated. After World War II, the Canadian government established a group of health insurance plans ("socialized insurance") that provided universal health insurance to improve the health of all Canadians. The costs are shared by federal and provincial governments with 70% paid by public funds and 30% by copayments, insurance, and other funding. The government, in consultation with medical professionals, sets prices for services (Schabloski 2008).

Infant mortality and life expectancy are two key measures of a country's health status. Comparing these major indicators in Canada and the United States, Canada has lower infant mortality (4.9 deaths per 1,000 live births in Canada vs. over 6 in the United States in 2011; the European Union's rate is 4.49). Canada also has higher life expectancy—81.5 years in Canada compared to 78.5 years in the United States (World Factbook 2013a; World Factbook 2013j). Canada pays for its health care system—taxes in Canada are 10% to 15% higher than those in the United States—but total cost per capita (per person) is 33% less for health care. In other words, the overall cost to consumers means higher taxes but lower costs overall. Canada spent 11.3% of its gross domestic product (GDP) in 2011 on health expenditures, while the United States committed 17.4% of its GDP (*Huffington Post* 2012a).

Comparing Canada and the United States with 16 developed countries, the United States spent the most per capita ($7,960) in 2011. Norway is second in cost per citizen at $5,352, and Canada is only about half as expensive at $4,478 (see Table 14.3).

Table 14.3 **Health Expenditures in the Most Expensive Countries and Life Expectancy Outcomes**

	Annual Cost Per Citizen	*% of Gross Domestic Product*	*Average Life Expectancy*
Denmark	$4,438	11.5%	79.0 years
Canada	$4,478	11.3%	81.5 years
Netherlands	$4,914	12.0%	80.6 years
Switzerland	$5,344	11.6%	82.3 years
Norway	$5,352	9.6%	81.0 years
United States	$7,960	17.4%	78.5 years

Source: Huffington Post. 2012a. "10 Countries Spending the Most on Health Care: 24/7 Wall St." Retrieved February 2, 2013 (www.huffingtonpost.com/2012/03/29/healthcare-spending-countries_n_1388306.html).

Note: Switzerland has the closest health care system to the newly passed U.S. Patient Protection and Affordable Care Act.

Problems of care denied because of lack of insurance, discrimination, and geographic maldistribution—major issues in the U.S. system—have been largely solved (Reid 2009). In a comparison of access in the U.S. and Canadian systems, 13% of Americans are unable to get needed care, many for financial reasons. In Canada, 3.7% cannot get care, almost none for financial reasons (American Academy of Pediatrics 2008; Bolduan 2009; HealthReform.gov 2010; Hiebert-White 2010).

In addition, controls by insurance companies result in hospital stays in the United States that are 20% to 40% shorter than in most other countries for similar procedures. Some attribute this to the profit motive, which undermines attention to services and to client needs as foremost. Yet, in Canada, waiting periods for nonessential procedures are longer, and tests such as MRIs are given less often. However, individuals can sometimes pay for private care—as U.S. citizens do—for more rapid care.

Fewer people in the United States report being satisfied with their health system than in Canada. Concern in the United States about government control and interference with private enterprise has helped keep the U.S. system in private hands. Other concerns raised about the Canadian system have to do with access to some types of care, substantial waiting periods for nonessential surgeries and to see a primary physician, and rationing of care for some procedures (Cockerham 2012). No system is perfect, including the Canadian one. The issue of how to provide better and affordable care to citizenry is shaping key political debates and was a central issue in the 2012 presidential election in the United States.

high percentage of the adult working population has been infected with or died from AIDS, social workers visit regularly to be sure orphaned children are getting enough to eat and are sowing crops necessary for their survival.

Global health organizations serve many poor countries, primarily with immunizations and humanitarian aid during wars or epidemics. The World Health Organization and other international organizations help provide immunizations and treatment for epidemics, but not for ongoing health needs. For example, Kenya in East Africa has a rapidly growing population, 85% of which lives in rural areas. Kenya has a socialized health care system based on the British model, with a national health service that employs doctors and owns hospitals. However, these services are available primarily in the largest cities of Nairobi and Mombasa. In fact, 80% to 85% of the health care budget goes to these urban areas. Rural areas are served by only 10% of the doctors in the national health system, and citizens in remote areas rely on folk healers and herbalists for care (Cockerham 2012). Recently, some African nations, including Kenya and Rwanda, are experimenting with locally trained health care workers that go door to door to provide medicines and assess health care needs. Emergency needs for dislocated populations or in war-torn nations are provided by the Red Cross, Doctors without Borders, and other international aid organizations.

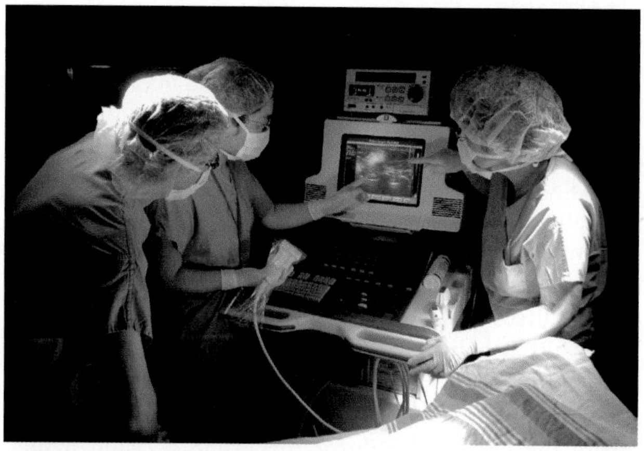

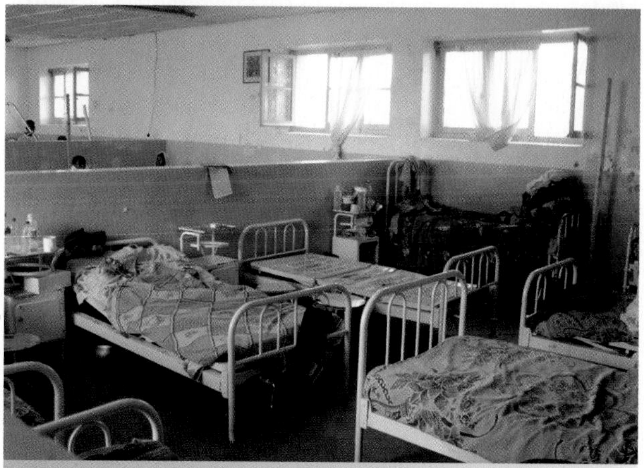

High-tech medical equipment is expensive (top), but in places such as Ethiopia (bottom), hospitals have few resources, and physicians must use whatever limited technology is available.

Hospitals as Complex Organizations

Hospitals are *places for the care and treatment of the sick and injured, providing centralized medical knowledge and technology for treatment of illnesses and accidents.* The Industrial Revolution in Western Europe and the United States caused population shifts to urban areas. These shifts, in turn, precipitated new and threatening environmental and health conditions due to crowding and lack of sanitation. Rational, systematic approaches to health care replaced individual folk remedies. In the late 1800s, there was an explosive growth in the number of hospitals, many of which were sponsored by religious organizations. The focus of these early hospitals was on segregating the destitute and terminally ill, who might be contagious and were likely to die. At this time, most hospitals were still small, but improvements in medical knowledge and competency were changing the old system.

The status of the hospital shifted dramatically in the early 1900s due to advances in medical science. Trained staff, sterile conditions, and more advanced techniques and technology changed hospitals from being the last resort of the urban poor and the dying to places of healing for all classes. Small community hospitals were an essential element of town life. As hospital care has become more available, the structure of hospitals also changed.

The post–World War II period produced huge growth in health care facilities and numbers of employees in the health care system. Medicines and vaccines controlled many infectious diseases that had formerly killed and disabled individuals. This period also saw the growth and funding of medical schools and large medical facilities that provided not only patient care but also education and research. Thus began the dominance of the hospital in providing medical care. Today, many hospitals are centers of medical knowledge and technology, housing not only patients and surgical units but also laboratories and diagnostic centers, specialty clinics, and rehabilitation centers.

Although medical health systems differ across societies, hospitals exhibit many characteristics similar to other large, bureaucratic organizations: hierarchical structures, rules and regulations, statuses (doctors, nurses) based on competency and training, hiring and promotion based on merit, and contracts for work performed. Primary-care physicians and other gatekeepers control client access to hospitals.

Historically, U.S. hospitals were designed for the convenience of physicians. However, today two rather independent bureaucracies function within modern large-scale hospital organizations. Physicians dominate the medical operations, while lay administrators operate the everyday functioning.

Health care systems are major employers in most affluent nations. In the United States, for instance, more than 14 million people are employed in a variety of the 5,754 hospitals (American Hospital Association 2012). They hold jobs as nurses, hospital administrators, pharmacists, physical therapists, physician's assistants, and imaging specialists (those who work with X-rays), and the number of employees is growing. Nurses are the largest group of health care workers, with licensed registered nurses (2,737,400) and licensed practical nurses (752,300) accounting for nearly six nurses per physician (Bureau of Labor Statistics 2012a, 2012b). In the hospital, the nurse manages the patient care team under the authority of the physician, who is the prime decision maker. Under the nurse's authority in this hierarchical structure come increasing numbers of ancillary personnel.

As hospitals and other medical facilities in the United States are increasingly owned and operated by for-profit corporations, the overwhelming power of the professional or medical line is giving way to powerful corporate management—the lay or administrative line. Physicians have become the customers of the hospital, buying space and time to carry out their functions. Sometimes, the physician's orders contradict those of the administrative line, especially with regard to medical decisions versus cost-saving decisions.

Thinking Sociologically

Who controls the medical facilities in your community? What structure do they have, and what roles predominate? Do you see evidence of hospitals' corporate structures being geared to efficiency and profit? What effect, if any, might changes have on service and commitment to clients?

Changing Professional Status of Employees in the Health Care System

Special features distinguish the hospital from other large-scale organizations or bureaucracies. The division of labor in the hospital is extensive and more highly specialized than other formal organizations. The hospital has a hierarchical pecking order based on prestige and power, and hospitals depend on the cooperation of highly skilled people whose work must be coordinated. Not only are patterns of authority rigidly followed, but the clothing and symbols peculiar to particular positions are recognizable and serve as status badges. The physicians, at the top of the stratification ladder, exercise the most power and receive the highest financial and prestige rewards. Signs of their superior status include wearing long white coats or not wearing special uniforms at all.

The physician's position is changing in modern societies. Physicians rank among the most respected professionals in most societies. Although trust and prestige seem to decline each year for all professions, physicians continue to command great respect, based on an assumption that they have special esoteric knowledge and humanitarian intent (Starr 1982; Weiss and Lonnquist 2012).

The widespread acceptance of physician authority is relatively recent. Before the 19th century, too little medical knowledge was established, and too few means of practice were successful to command such recognition. Physicians gained status from the discovery that some diseases were caused by bacteria and could be treated with antiseptics, from the introduction of anesthesia, and from the idea that specially trained people could treat illnesses. Coupled with scientific advances and more sophisticated diagnostic tools, these beliefs began to elevate the status of physicians and scientific medicine (Pescosolido and Boyer 2010).

The transformation of physicians to a position of professional recognition in the United States came when some 250 physicians meeting in Philadelphia in May 1847 established the American Medical Association (AMA). This umbrella organization became the means to gain legitimacy and power over health care practice (Cockerham 2012). The predominantly female health care areas such as midwifery and other holistic approaches such as osteopathy, chiropractic medicine, and homeopathy were delegitimized by the powerful new AMA. Only one approach was granted credibility: **allopathy**, *medical treatment supported by the American Medical Association and most Western medicine, involving remedies that are based on directly countering a patient's symptoms with drugs or surgery*.

Physicians entering practice in the United States today are faced with several major challenges. First, health care is now a system shaped by the purchasers of care and the competition for profits where it was once run by doctors who knew their patients and were committed to the Hippocratic oath of healing. Second, there has simultaneously been a decline in the public's trust of physicians, with greater willingness to question them and even outright distrust by some people. Third, an emphasis on specialization and subspecialization has arisen where previously there had been prestige and rewards in primary care (family doctors). Fourth, outpatient care in homes and doctors' offices is once again becoming more common, where the middle part of the 20th century saw an emphasis on hospitalization. Finally, there is a demand by payers (especially insurance companies) for detailed accounts of medical decision making, fixed prepayment rates established by insurers, and less willingness to pay doctors based solely on their decisions about patients' needs (Cockerham 2012; Vanderminden and Potter 2010).

Photo Essay

Clothing and Status in the Hospital

Note the difference in how each of these people dresses. The outfits they wear are not insignificant, for they distinguish status, authority, and rights to certain prerogatives within the hospital or clinic.

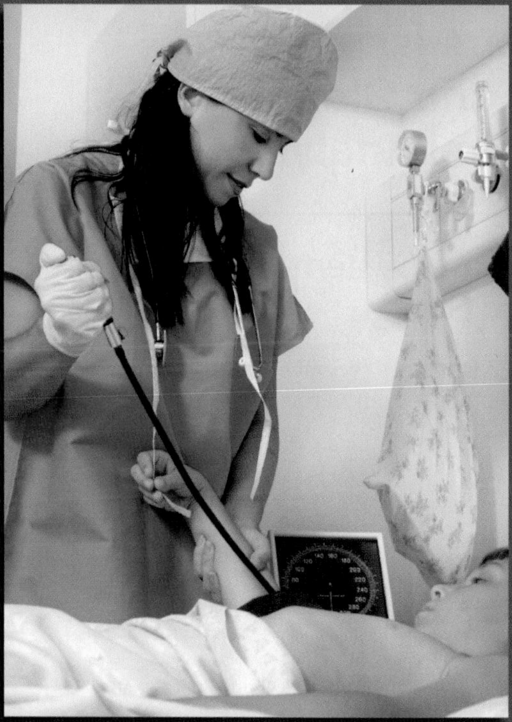

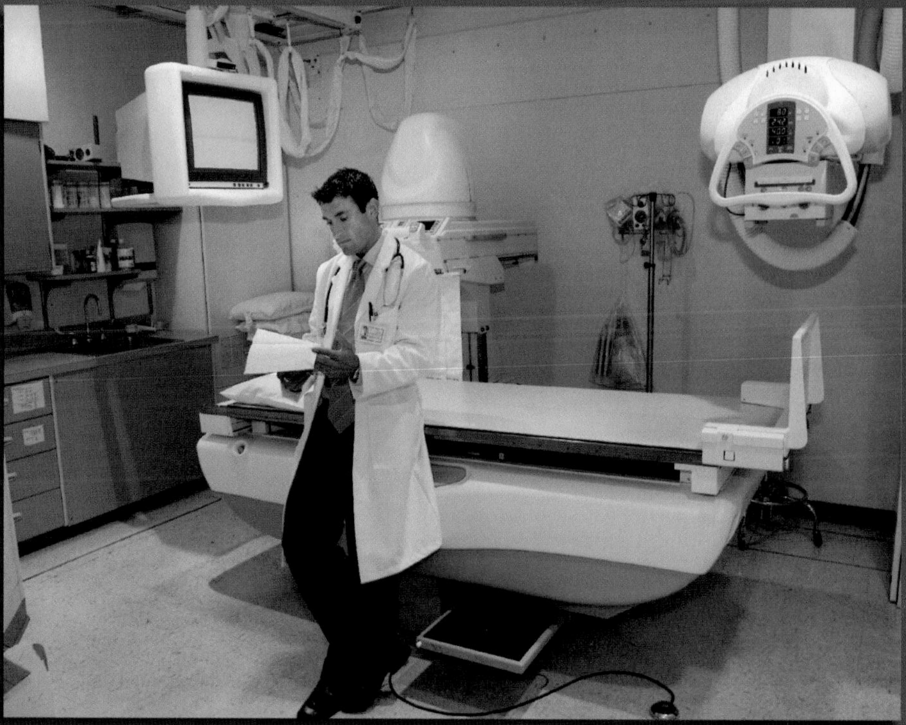

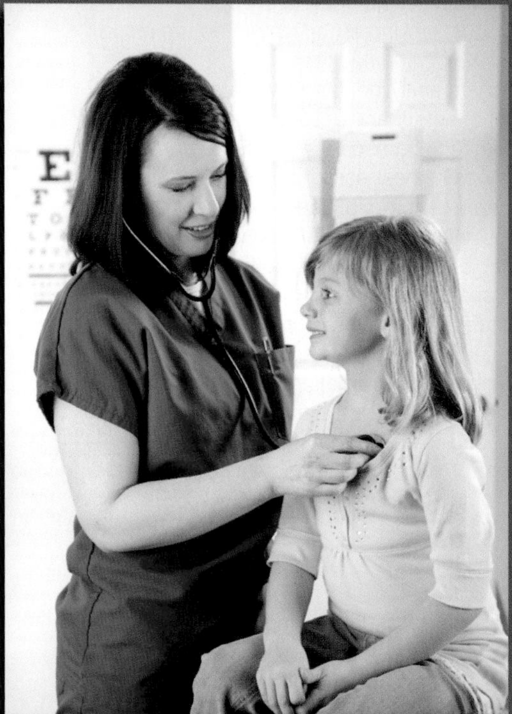

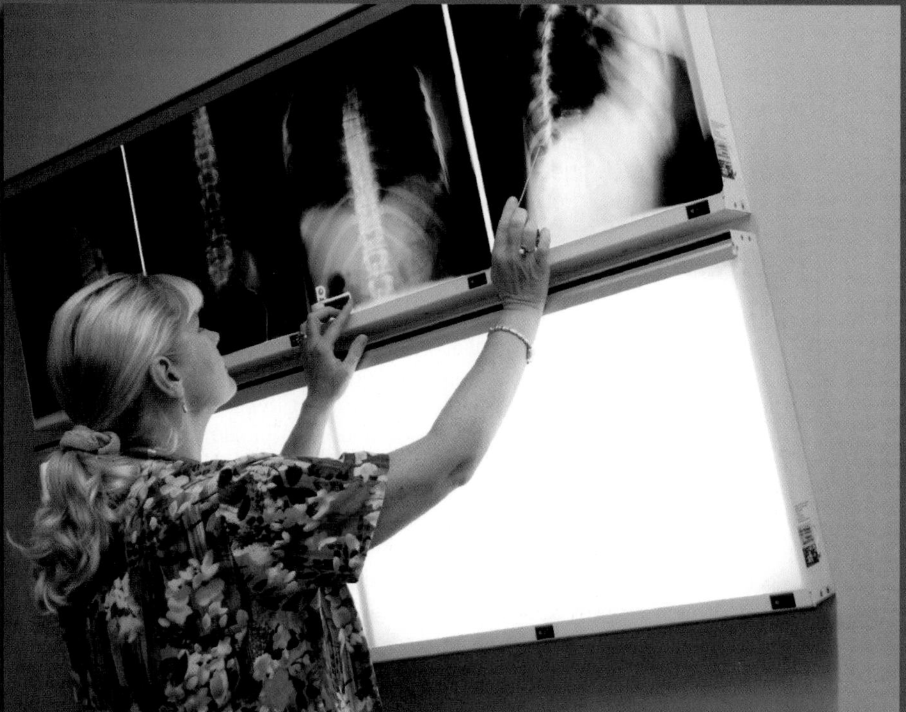

Deprofessionalization *is the process though which a professional occupation loses autonomy, respect, and service orientation because the professionals come to be controlled by nonprofessionals and outside forces—financial concerns, government regulation, technological changes, and administrators or management.* Many physicians now work for managed care systems, so their own autonomy is limited by the bureaucrats for whom they work (Pescosolido and Boyer 2010). Moreover, bureaucratization of hospitals and controls by insurance companies on doctors' decisions have reduced the autonomy of physicians to make decisions they think are best for the patient, another element of deprofessionalization. They lose much of their authority as the possessors of distinctive knowledge the others lack, and their respect drops. Nurses face similar issues that can cause burnout, as discussed in the following "Sociologists in Action."

We have explored issues of health care at the micro level (the role of sick people) and at the meso level (organization of health care and hospitals as complex organizations). We now move on to macro-level policy issues at national and global levels.

Thinking Sociologically

Doctors have been depicted in many television shows over the past five decades. How might these depictions affect people's expectations of doctors and hospitals? How might TV images of doctor and nurse roles influence our expectations of medical work in a hospital?

Health Care Issues at National and Global Levels: Macro-Level Analysis

The Health Care System in the United States

The United States has the best system—and the worst. It is one of the best in the world in terms of quality medical

Sociologists in Action—James Anderson: The Case of Nurse Burnout

With a shortage of trained nurses in the health care industry and a growing elderly population living in long-term care facilities, the United States does not need to lose nurses to burnout. This problem of nurse burnout in retirement communities is what Dr. James G. Anderson and his former doctoral student, Dr. Kathleen Abrahamson, set out to study.

Burnout refers to feeling unappreciated, feeling not respected, having low status, lacking autonomy to do the job, and being unsupported by the establishments for which these nurses work.

To learn about the experiences of nurses in long-term care facilities, the researchers analyzed interview data from the Partners in Caregiving study, funded by the National Institute on Aging. A finding that affects many of us is that for nurses, conflict with patients and their families was a leading cause of dissatisfaction and burnout (Abrahamson et al. 2009). Even what might appear to be minor issues such as patients' laundry became irritants. Burnout was highest early in the nurse's career cycle, then leveled off but did not go away. The finding that initial episodes of conflict have a strong influence on nursing staff burnout highlights the importance of interpersonal conflict within nursing homes on both individual and institutional outcomes.

In addition to sampling nursing staff, the researchers used computer simulations to incorporate multiple variables into the equation for burnout, and to predict the major causes of burnout. The use of computer simulation modeling allowed the investigators to assess the cumulative effects of conflict between staff and families on staff burnout and test strategies that could be used to reduce the harmful effects of conflict.

Dr. Anderson has a background in engineering that has trained him to use quantitative modeling (structural equation modeling and computer simulation) to test hypotheses on social processes and social structural influences on behaviors. Modeling allows for consideration of multiple equations and variables, and to ask "what if" questions, posing scenarios to be tested. In other research, he has looked at the acceptance of information technology in health care settings, including physicians' willingness to use electronic record-keeping technology (Anderson and Aydin 2005).

* * * * * * *

Dr. James G. Anderson received engineering degrees and a PhD in sociology and education at Johns Hopkins University in Baltimore. He is a professor of medical sociology and health communication. Dr. Kathleen Abrahamson, an RN with her PhD from Purdue, is currently an assistant professor in the Department of Public Health at Western Kentucky University.

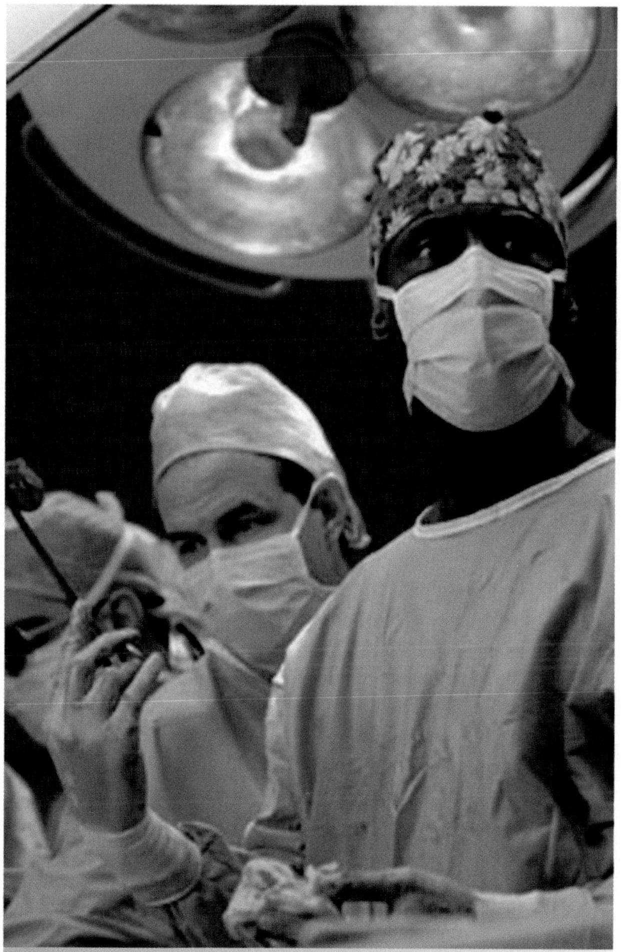

Television shows such as Grey's Anatomy *depict doctors as highly autonomous and respected professionals. Although there is some truth to this, physicians especially in the United States are increasingly working in bureaucratic settings in which the bureaucracy governs many of their decisions, causing deprofessionalization.*

care, trained practitioners, facilities, and advanced medical technology. People from around the world seek training and care in the United States. It is also the worst system: It requires the highest cost per capita in the world to provide care (discussed in more detail later), does not provide equal access to citizens, is inefficient, has competing interests, and is fragmented. Some of these issues are being addressed as the Patient Protection and Affordable Health Care Act (sometimes nicknamed Obamacare) is phased in.

Eloise knew something was seriously wrong when she lost her appetite, vomited when she ate more than a few bites, and lost her usually abundant energy. Without health insurance and fearing to lose her job if she missed work to sit in the outpatient waiting room of the hospital to see a doctor, she tried home remedies and hoped the symptoms would go away. When she finally did go to the hospital, she was in serious condition. Eloise spent a few days in intensive care and is now on treatments, but without income from her job, she cannot pay the bills for herself and her child. This is but one case in which health care is only available to those who can pay, and they get quick treatment.

Similar medical emergencies occur across the United States for more than 50.7 million people who lack medical insurance (DeNavas-Walt, Proctor, and Smith 2012). Because of cases like Eloise, some critics claim that the U.S. health care system is a social problem. It developed without specific direction and responded to demands piecemeal, allowing practitioners, medical facilities, and insurance and drug companies to establish themselves and then protect their self-interests, sometimes at the expense of citizens. In a discussion of the development of the U.S. health care system (see next "Sociology in Our Social World" on page 536), Paul Starr uses historical analysis to determine key elements in its transformation.

Health Care Advances

Medical research into gene therapy, understanding of the human genome, and research into new drug and technological therapies make research one of the most rapidly advancing medical fields. New therapies will help people live longer, more comfortable and productive lives—*if* they can afford the care. As science moves rapidly, ethical questions about the use of fetal tissue in experiments and treatments, cloning, prolonging life, and other issues challenge ethicists and lawmakers (Mike 2003).

In addition to advances in medical science, there have been achievements in public health and education that prolong lives: motor vehicle safety, safer workplaces, control of infectious diseases, decline in heart problems, healthier foods, healthier mothers and babies, family planning, clean drinking water, and education of citizens about the dangers of tobacco and other substances as health hazards.

Problems in the U.S. Health Care System

The fragmented way in which the U.S. health care system has developed has led to two major problems: lack of universal access to health care and constantly escalating health care costs along with a sizeable uninsured population, resulting in lack of health care security (LeBow 2004; Oberlander 2002; Pescosolido and Boyer 2010).

Access to Health Care. No matter how advanced technical-medical skills may be, they are of little use to society if they are not available to those who need them. In the United States, services are not necessarily distributed according to the needs of the people (Quesnal-Vallee and Jenkins 2010).

First, there is a maldistribution of services. The shortage of physicians in rural areas in the United States and many other countries is particularly serious. Only 9% of physicians practice in rural areas, but 20% of the population live

Sociology in Our Social World

The Social Transformation of American Medicine

In his Pulitzer Prize–winning book, Paul Starr (1982) uses historical documents to analyze the development of medicine in America from the 1700s to the 1980s. The research was a massive undertaking. Starr consulted books, journals, historical documents and accounts of medical practice, government reports, public health documents and records of specific diseases, hospital records, medical cost reports, medical school histories and catalogs, information on medical organizations, biographies and autobiographies, and other documents that shed light on the history and development of medicine in the United States. By doing content analysis on each historical period—that is, systematically studying the written materials available about medicine—he pieced together a picture of the themes and trends at different time periods. Starr used many sociological concepts and theories throughout his research to give his analysis depth.

His book represents two long movements: (1) the rise of medical profession sovereignty and (2) the transformation of medicine into an industry with the expansion of corporate influence and state control. Starr examines a number of issues about the institution of medicine. Why, for example, did Americans change from being wary of medicine to being devoted to it? Doctors who were previously deeply divided became united—and prosperous. Why was that? Hospitals, medical schools, clinics, and other medical organizations assumed forms in the United States that were unlike those institutions in other countries, an intriguing difference. In the process, hospitals became the central institutions in medical care while public health became marginalized, unlike other places in the world. Similarly, there is no national health insurance in the United States, and commercial indemnity insurance now dominates the private health insurance market. In an interesting twist, some physicians are now taking part in the creation of corporate health care systems, a new development. Why did systems evolve the way they did? Medicine is now a business as well as a cultural phenomenon in the United States, and Starr's investigation helps us understand that reality.

During the early years of U.S. history, the medical profession was not yet established. Many doctors were educated people who had no coursework in the sciences, and hospitals were places where people went to die, not to be healed. With the advent of modern medicine—sanitation and sterilization, understanding of disease, medicines, and vaccines—medicine grew in stature, and people turned to doctors and hospitals for their medical needs. Starr documents the changing trends in medicine and ends with a discussion of recent problems with insurance systems and the debates between private insurance, medical systems, and public programs. Concerns today center on privatization of health care, hospital and physician services, insurance, and containment of costs.

By using historical analysis, Starr was able to give both an overview of trends and a detailed account of medicine throughout U.S. history. Only such a long-term perspective could help us deeply understand many of the issues regarding medical care, the status of physicians, and the institutionalization of medicine.

there. About 7,500 primary care physicians are needed in underserved areas, rural and urban. Medicare gives a bonus to physicians in underserved areas, yet there is little indication that this problem will be solved soon, though the Patient Protection and Affordable Care Act offers additional incentives to physicians in poorly served areas (Kavilanz 2010).

Some free-enterprise advocates contend that an oversupply of physicians will lead to a trickle-down to rural areas, but data analysis shows that this is not occurring. The expectation that family or primary-care physicians would gravitate to rural areas is not occurring either. The United States has followed the lead of some other countries that cover physician education costs in exchange for a commitment to work in poor or rural areas for a set time period. Called the National Health Service Corps (NHSC), this strategy encourages better distribution of health services.

More than 10,000 corps practitioners serve 10.5 million people regardless of ability to pay (NHSC 2011). The downside is that this brings less experienced and nonpermanent physicians to poor and rural locations.

Within cities, physicians are concentrated in certain neighborhoods—and outside other neighborhoods. As a hospital's service area becomes increasingly populated by poorer residents, the facility faces a higher demand for free care. Closure and relocation to more profitable areas are particularly common among for-profit hospitals, and poor minority populations suffer.

Another aspect of maldistribution is the lack of family physicians. Many physicians choose to enter one of more than 30 specialty areas in medicine. The reward system of medicine in terms of prestige, income, and lifestyle makes specialty practice more appealing than general medicine. Moreover, most specialists are found in urban areas. The result of lack of access in rural areas and urban poor areas, especially for the poor and uninsured, is less frequent care, fewer regular physician visits and procedures, and a higher chance of serious costly illness and of dying in a hospital once they do get admitted.

Even the distribution of doctors across states is significant, meaning that people in some states have more access than those in other states. Massachusetts has the most "active patient care doctors" per 100,000 residents with 314; Mississippi has the fewest with 159. Look at Map 14.3 on page 538 to see the variation. Given the discussion above, how might where you live affect your health care?

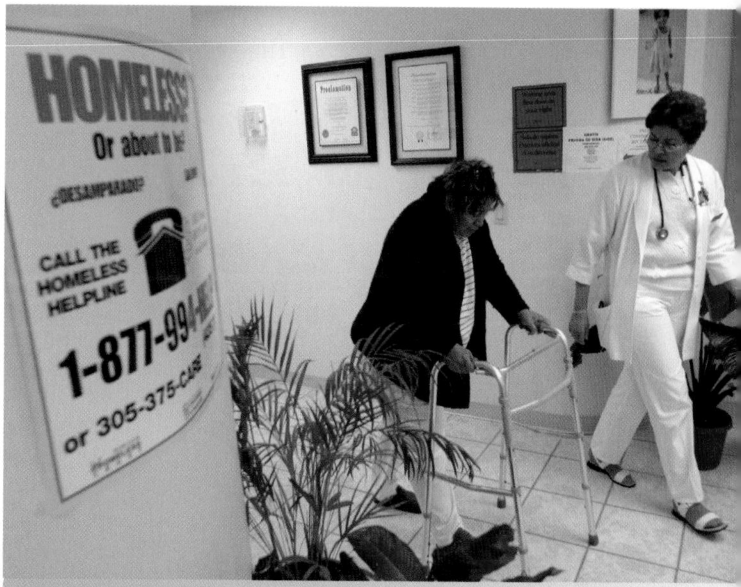

Dr. Nilda Soto, director of the Open Door Health Center in Homestead, Florida, walks with a patient along a hallway. The Open Door Health Center is a free health clinic that assists the uninsured poor. Those who serve the poor often do so with very poor financial compensation for their training. In other countries, governments generally do not expect health care to be provided by altruistic people. Insurance helps pay for medical care in developed countries.

Health Care Cost and Funding. Perhaps the most serious problem for health care systems and consumers in the United States, however, is the escalating cost of health care. Since 1947, expenditures for health care in the United States (now at 16% of the gross national product) have increased more rapidly than expenditures for other areas of the economy, and the United States spends twice as much per year on health care as other countries. For example, Switzerland spends 10.9% of the gross domestic product and Canada 9.7% (National Coalition on Health Care 2008). About 30% of health care costs in the United States go to administration, an unusually high figure compared to other Global North countries (Reinhardt 2008). Table 14.4 shows the increases in costs of health care over time in the United States.

Thinking Sociologically

Develop several hypotheses to explain why health care costs are rising rapidly, focusing on the United States. How would you test these hypotheses? What factors might cause lower costs per capita for health care in other countries?

Table 14.4 **National Health Expenditures: United States**

Year	*In Billion Dollars*	*Percentage of Gross Domestic Product*	*Yearly Amount per Capita (in Dollars)*
1960	126.9	5.1	1,141
1970	173.2	7.1	1,341
1980	1,247.2	8.9	1,051
1990	1,699.5	12.2	2,689
2000	1,309.4	13.3	4,670
2009	2,500.0	17.6	8,086

Source: Centers for Medical and Medicaid Services 2012.

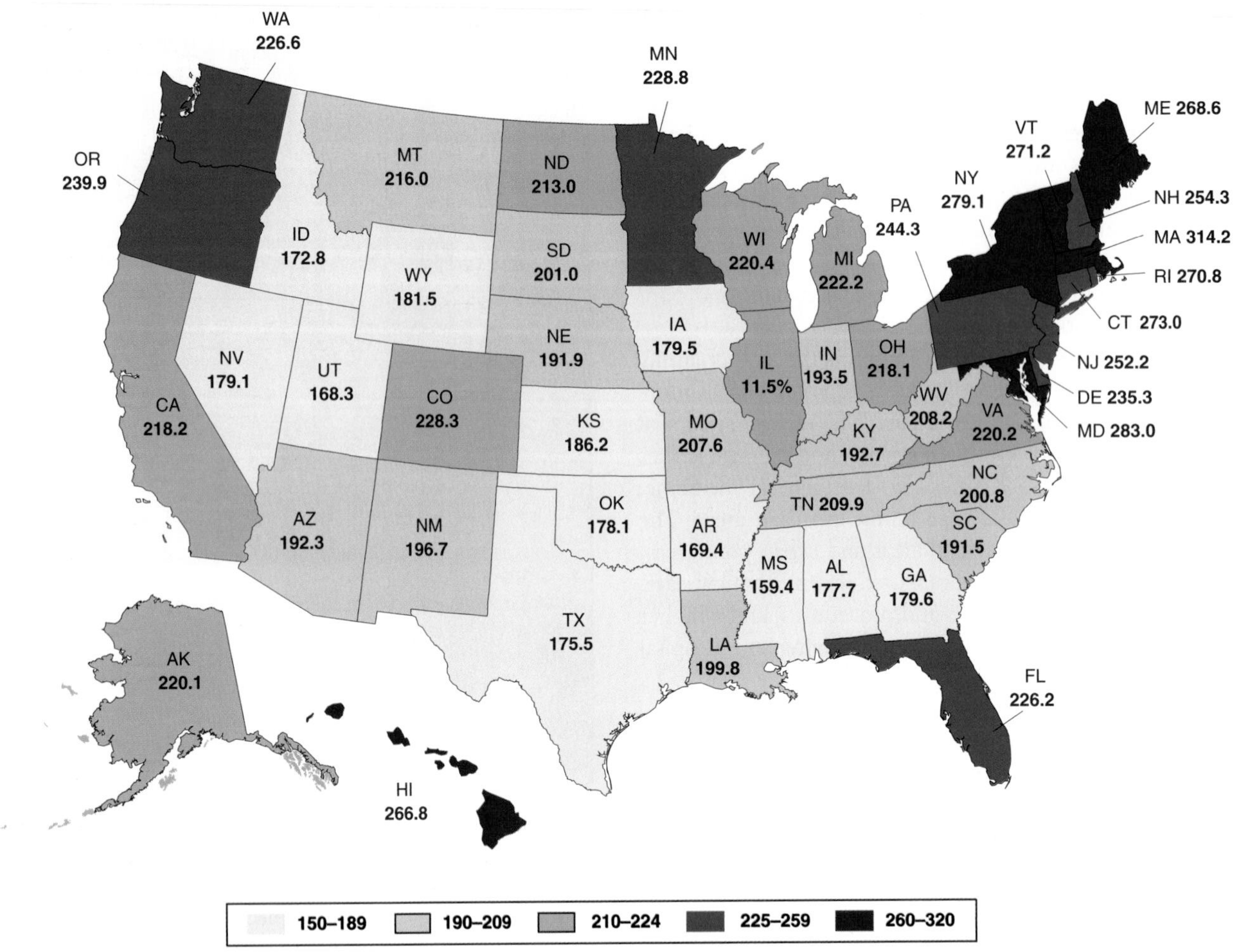

Map 14.3 Active Physicians per 100,000 Population

Source: Center for Workforce Studies. 2011.

The United States has been the only developed country in the world that did not have a national health insurance program providing health care coverage for all citizens. Most countries have a single-payer (government-run) system. A proposal for a modified universal coverage plan was upheld by the U.S. Supreme Court in 2012, but is still a contentious issue because of philosophical differences between politicians and some opposition from private insurance companies, physicians, and drug companies. The medical profession fought against the first proposed government medical insurance programs—Medicare and Medicaid (Marmor 1999). The programs passed mainly because they allowed physicians to retain their autonomy and to control their financial rewards. Prior to 2009 attempts to nationalize health care in the United States failed or stalled in large part due to lobbying and public influence ads by insurance and drug companies. The AMA and many insurance companies, in contrast, supported the Patient Protection and Affordable Care Act in 2009.

Managed health care plans developed quickly to fill the gap after the 1994 national health plan failed to pass in Congress (Pescosolido and Boyer 2010). Today about 61% of insured patients are in managed health care plans. Health care companies control costs by limiting visits to specific physicians in their network, requiring referrals for specialists, and demanding preauthorization for hospital stays. Each insured individual is guaranteed care in exchange for a monthly sum paid by the employer and employee.

Managed care tries to integrate two goals—efficiency and high quality. The two means to carry this out are financing and health care delivery. Evidence indicates that managed health care plans are making profits. Still, fear that every citizen will have to buy health insurance drives some opposition to the plan, even though those in need will receive financial help to comply. There have also been strong media campaigns against the plan by those whose self-interests are threatened. As a result, by 2012 surveys showed that 22.6% of the U.S. public approved or strongly approved of the 2010 health care reform law, while 62% disapproved or strongly disapproved (American Panel Survey 2012). Interestingly, specific aspects of the program—assured coverage even with a preexisting medical condition and young people being covered by parental insurance until their mid-20s—are extremely popular.

As health care costs rise, employers providing health care to their workers are shifting more of the cost to employees by charging higher deductibles, using mail-order and generic prescription programs, and increasing patient co-pays. Employees paid an average of $2,764 in 2012, a 40% increase from 2007. The combined cost for employees and companies was 5.9%, or $11,664 per person (Young 2012). The problem is that these strategies cannot keep up with the rising costs. These recent developments in administration and cost containment have helped control but not reduced costs because of increased demand for care, rising numbers of baby boomer senior citizens who need more health care, and expensive new technologies.

Managed care has its critics who argue that for-profit corporations do not belong in the business of health care because health is a human right. Costs of for-profit care are high and rising, leading to demands for a national health plan that would provide universal coverage at less expense, such as the plan the Clinton administration hoped to develop and the plan the Obama administration proposed and passed in 2009.

Almost all other Global North countries have national health care systems that cover all citizens, financed by citizens paying higher taxes for the coverage. However, the cost structure for administration is much less, saving money for individuals and the state. Michael Moore's 2007 documentary film, *Sicko*, and recent books and articles compare health care systems; they look at the high profitability of the U.S. health care industries (including insurance companies, drug manufacturers, and some practitioners) to the free universal health care offered at lower overall cost in countries such as Canada, United Kingdom, and France (PBS Newshour 2009; Reid 2009). Table 14.5 shows sources of funding for U.S. health care.

Controversies such as extending health benefits to domestic partners—unmarried cohabiting heterosexual and homosexual couples—have further clouded the issues of insurance coverage. However, some city and state government employees do receive partner benefits.

Table 14.5 **National Health Expenditures by Type 2009 (in Trillions of Dollars)**

Total national health expenditures	$2.49 trillion
Annual percentage change	4.0% higher
Percentage of gross domestic product	17.6%
Private expenditures	$1,403.1 trillion
Public expenditures	$1,083.2 trillion

Source: U.S. Census Bureau (2012f).

Thinking Sociologically

What are the benefits of the U.S. managed health care systems? What are the benefits of national health care systems? What are the problems with each? What is your solution to the health care problems faced by the United States?

Health Care Security and the Patient Protection and Affordable Care Act. The biggest criticism of the U.S. system has been the lack of health insurance for millions, making health security unattainable. If those who have insurance through their employer lose their job or if they have a preexisting condition, health care is unattainable. Many of these individuals receive funding from taxpayer dollars for visits to the emergency room. According to a Commonwealth Fund poll, more than one out of four Americans, or between 48 and 50 million people below 65 years of age, were uninsured at some point in 2011, in part due to loss of jobs (Morgan 2012). The estimated uninsured population at any given time since 2007 ranged from 19% to 25% of the population (Hiebert-White 2010; Schiller et al. 2012). With the passage of the 2010 health care bill, many of these uninsured will be covered by or before 2014, and those individuals with preexisting conditions cannot be denied coverage (White House 2013).

Currently, for clients who cannot pay in the pay-for-service system of health care, options are limited: public hospitals (which are few in number), county and state facilities, and free clinics. Paying for health care was the number-one economic concern of 50% of U.S. citizens in 2008, and many uninsured citizens delayed health care (National Coalition on Health Care 2008). By the time the uninsured sought help, the situation was often an emergency. Yet who pays in this situation? Public hospitals have relied on tax dollars from all taxpaying citizens to foot the bill for those who did not have insurance or cash. Emergency room visits are expensive and the number of visits is accelerated because

Union members and health care workers demonstrate for national health care and Medicaid. This demonstration in New York City was stimulated by federal cuts in Medicaid that left many people without health care.

Table 14.6 **Health Insurance: Type of Coverage for Persons Below 65 Years of Age**

Insurance Type	*Total U.S.*	*White*	*Black*	*Hispanic*
Private (%)	71.7	79.3	57.0	46.6
Medicaid	9.4	6.3	19.3	12.5
Other Public	2.1	1.9	3.7	1.0
Uninsured	16.8	10.4	16.0	30.7

Source: Centers for Disease Control and Prevention (2009); Kaiser Commission on Medicaid and the Uninsured (2011).

the poor have no other option. In addition, health care costs for the poor are often higher because treatment has been delayed and the condition has deteriorated. The new health care system is intended to alleviate such problems.

Of the people in the United States with no insurance in 2010, 9.8% were children below 18 years; 27.2% of young adults from 18 to 24 years of age and 28.4% of those 25 to 34 years old had no insurance. After that people qualify for Medicare. A disproportionate number have been unmarried women, often with children, or members of ethnic groups. For example, 30.7% of Hispanics and 20.8% of African Americans have no health insurance (U.S. Census Bureau 2010 and 2011). During recessions, the number of uninsured grows because families and individuals cannot afford insurance premiums. Even in the best of times, roughly 6% of people applying for coverage have been refused (HealthReform.gov 2010), and roughly an equal number are charged significantly higher rates if they have preexisting medical conditions. Insurance companies have been able to deny medical claims to reduce their costs if they deem a procedure unnecessary. This policy will change under the Patient Protection and Affordable Care Act. Still, there will likely be unexpected consequences of the new program that no one has foreseen, for that happens with virtually all social policies, regardless of how well intended.

Barriers to health care and lack of health insurance have kept many from using services, even with the payments of Medicare and Medicaid. Table 14.6 shows the differences and disparities in health insurance coverage between groups in the United States. Note the numbers of uninsured, lowest for white citizens at 12.5%, and the number of privately insured, highest for whites at 79.3%.

Medicare and Medicaid—services for the growing percentage of citizens 65 years and older (estimated to be one in five by 2050) and for the poor—were legislated without cost limits. Whatever the medical profession charged was what the government paid. Since the original legislation, Congress has had some success in regulating and limiting charges and the length of hospital stays, but "creative billing" has thwarted government attempts to control the costs of the services. Thus, efforts to reform the system and control costs continue. This manipulation of the government system—with higher costs resulting—is part of the reason some critics have opposed the Patient Protection and Affordable Care Act.

Policy Issues and Social Reforms in the U.S. System

We return to this question: Is medical care a right or a privilege? Some argue that it is a human right that cannot be bought and sold to the highest bidder or richest segments of society. Others argue that it is a privilege, a commodity to be purchased in a free market and that competition will both improve quality and reduce costs. The human rights argument provides the model for most of the Global North, whereas the market-driven system has been the main model in the United States for all but the elderly and poor, who qualify for some government insurance. The new U.S. model combines elements of both the human right to health care and a market-driven system.

Some recent attempts in the United States to insure more citizens have been carried out at the state level, with some states reaching close to 90% coverage rates. Depending on the success of federal health care reform, states may continue to be the ones actually achieving reform (Pescosolido and Boyer 2010).

A significant problem for state and federal governments and for individuals is the high cost of drug prescriptions. The pharmaceutical industry does not cap costs in the United States as it does in many other countries, as required by governments, partly due to what the industry argues are research costs connected with developing new drugs. For this reason also, only brand-label drugs can be sold in the United States for a certain period before similar but cheaper generic drugs can be sold. Many individuals and even states have turned to Canada, Mexico, and other countries for cheaper drugs to control costs. However, the U.S. administration has upheld bans on purchases outside the United States, pointing out possible problems with quality control.

The passage of a comprehensive reform plan in the United States in 2010 resulted in a compromise package that accomplished some goals of the Obama administration for meeting health care needs, compromised some, and left some needs unmet.

Change is inevitable. The new health care plan of the United States tries to address three main challenges: (1) what to do about the rising uninsured population; (2) how to control costs, especially in a managed care system; and (3) what the physician-client relationship will be under new structures of health care (Pescosolido and Boyer 2010). These provisions are being implemented gradually and should be in place by 2014, unless political winds shift and parts of the legislation are repealed.

Health Care Around the Globe

During a yearlong sabbatical in England, the Ballantine family was signed up with a local surgeon, as the British call family physicians. Their sore throats, upset tummies, and bruised feet were taken to the doctor at no direct cost. The school referred their daughter to the hospital eye clinic for glasses at no cost. Their son was diagnosed and treated for "glandular fever" (mononucleosis), again at no cost. In Great Britain, all citizens have access to treatment by family physicians and dentists, to the dispensing of prescribed drugs, to eye care, and to community nursing and health visitor services. Universal health care is covered by taxes, and as noted above at a cost much less than the U.S. cost for health care.

The demographic makeup, value systems, and financial status of each country will have an effect on how health care is delivered. Global North societies, with a high proportion of elderly and a low proportion of young people, have very different needs from those of Global South societies with many dependent children. In societies with many elders, special care for chronic illness is more necessary, whereas societies with many children must deal with childhood illnesses.

One global health issue is the maldistribution of physicians, which is illustrated in Map 14.4 in the next "Engaging Sociology" on page 542. The countries with the most doctors—the highest number of physicians per 1,000 people—are Greece (6.2), Belarus (5.2), Austria (4.9), Georgia (4.8), Norway (4.2), and Switzerland (4.1). The United States has 2.4 doctors per 1,000 people, and Canada has 2.0. The lowest numbers are in Global South countries such as Colombia, Ghana, and Mauritania with 0.1 physician per 1,000 people, and Afghanistan and Cambodia with 0.2 physician per 1,000 people (World Bank 2012b). Most of these are located in urban areas. The World Health Organization recommends at least 1 physician for every 600 citizens by 2015. In some Global South countries, local rural residents are trained both in emergency medicine and to recognize illnesses. In Rwanda, for example, health care workers make house calls to inquire about diseases and provide the required treatment (PBS *NOW* 2009), referring those with serious illnesses to regional hospitals.

Each society organizes its health care system in ways congruous with its culture. Although societies have developed different ways of dealing with illness, Western scientific medicine is spreading throughout the world. Ideas about health and medicine are moving in more than one direction and each country has a different system, but they all face similar problems as they search for ways to contain costs, provide high-quality and effective care, enhance access to that care for all citizens, manage care for disabilities and chronic illnesses, and find treatments for infectious diseases (Pescosolido and Boyer 2010).

Some of the ideas from other parts of the world are now influencing Western approaches to health and illness, as the following example from China illustrates. China mixes traditional with Western medicine.

The People's Republic of China: Medicine in a Communist State

Little was known outside China about China's health care system until the 1970s, when visitors, including health observers, were welcomed by the government. When the "bamboo curtain" that isolated China was raised in 1971, the outside world learned that, despite a background of poverty, a primary network of health services had been established. Still, health care delivery faced problems because the country was so large and the population so spread out. The political leaders were determined to bring industrialization and a modern lifestyle to the country in a very short time. Privatization of some aspects of the social system eliminated some government and communal support for primary health care. This put severe pressures on all of China's institutions.

Jeanne, one of your coauthors, met Xi (pronounced "She") on a train in China. He was returning to his village after completing a medical training course that covered first aid treatment, immunizations, and recognition of serious symptoms. He was one of more than a million barefoot doctors or *countryside doctors*—paramedics

Engaging Sociology

Access to Health Care for Rich and Poor

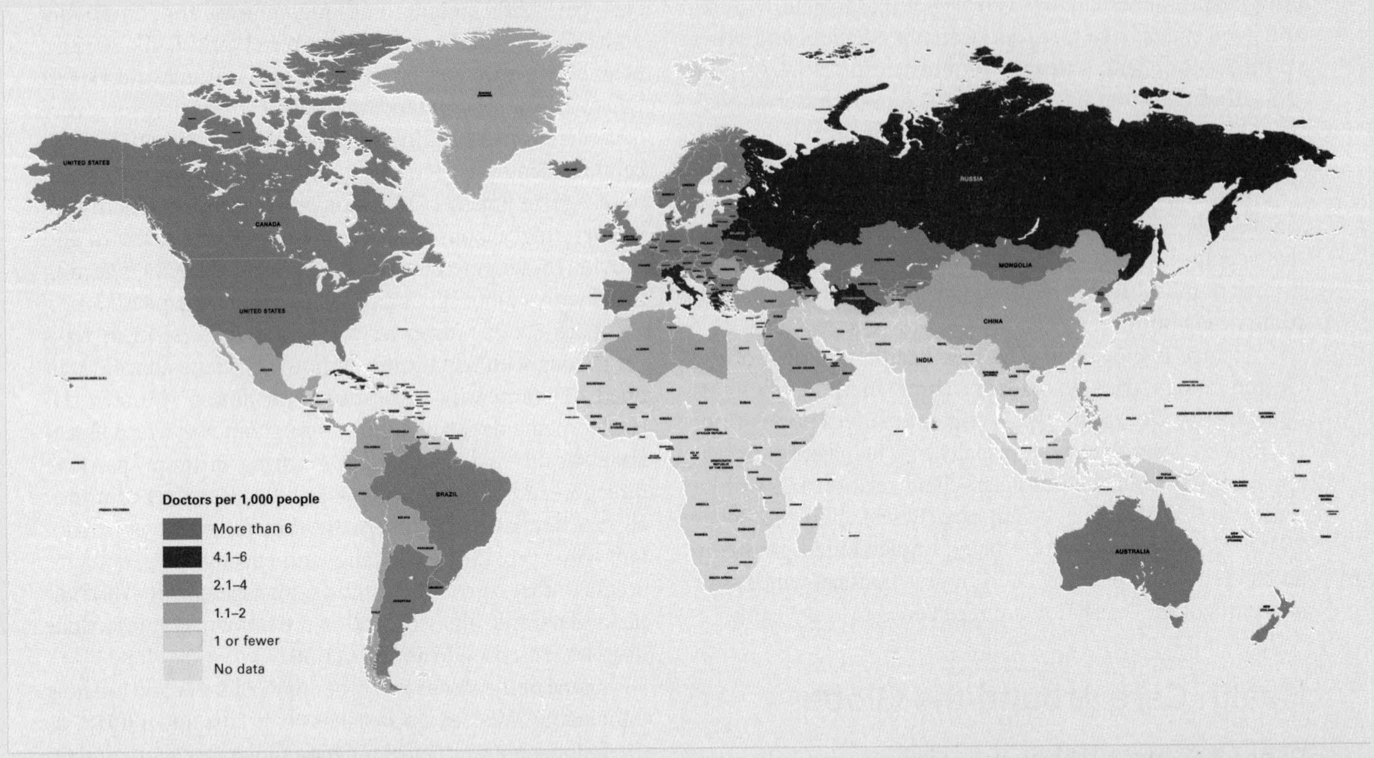

Map 14.4 Number of Physicians per 1,000 People

Source: NationMaster.com 2013.

Engaging With Sociology. Study the map on physicians per 1,000 people. Then, answer the following questions:

1. How do you think the Global South and rural scarcity of physicians will affect health care of individuals?
2. How might a surplus of physicians influence health care?
3. How could a nation increase the number of qualified medical workers and people who have access to health care?
4. How might health care differ depending on where one lives in the United States?

trained in basic medicine to provide health care for rural residents in China's villages. The program was very successful in curbing infectious diseases. In fact, the program has provided a model for reaching out into the countryside for several Global South countries, including Kenya and Rwanda.

Barefoot doctors were generally local peasants selected by fellow members of their agricultural communes. Many continued to work on the farm but, after some training, took responsibility for preventive medicine and some aspects of primary care in the local neighborhood. If they passed an exam they could become a village doctor, licensed to carry out additional medical procedures. Their income was determined in the same manner as other agricultural workers. The barefoot doctor was generally the only medical practitioner that many of the 800 million people living in rural China ever saw. From a sociological perspective, a positive feature of these practitioners was their within-culture socialization. Given the homogeneity of peasant neighborhoods, the barefoot doctor had little difficulty understanding the local culture and their resistance to certain procedures. This program to spread health care to all areas of China began in 1951.

Today this program that provided a model for poor countries has all but collapsed—beginning in the late 1970s with the privatization of agriculture, private enterprises, and rapid growth in China. No longer were there collective farms with groups of people to finance the barefoot doctors. The government was also unwilling to train them. This left many villages with no primary care or immunization programs. Diseases that many thought had been eradicated began to resurface. Since most of the doctors in China are located in urban areas and regional hospitals, many people in rural areas had to depend on home remedies (Casella 2009). A remaining element of the rural medicine program is the Lifeline Express train in Xinjiang Province; it travels the countryside providing cataract eye surgery for residents. Also, the remaining village doctors often support themselves with money from medical drugs they sell (Hays 2011). Recently, the central government has allocated funds to increase basic coverage in regional areas and improve hospitals, and it has a goal of insuring 90% of the population (Wang 2009). The doctor-to-patient ratio is now 1 to 950, but most doctors are concentrated in cities. Further, many of those being trained as physicians in China are now practicing in African nations where the wages and social standing are higher (Hays 2011).

Once introduced, Western-style medicine expanded rapidly in China. Beginning in 1978, the number of traditional Chinese medical personnel increased slightly, but the number of medical personnel with training in Western medicine increased significantly. Today, some clinics for preventive care, birth control, and first aid are found in rural areas, and the very sick go to regional hospitals. Many health care workers now blend Western medicine practices with traditional Chinese approaches. Increasingly, doctors are trained in both.

Chinese medical practices are also influencing medicine around the world. Consider the example of acupuncture, an ancient Chinese method for treating certain physical problems and relieving pain. It is part of a healing system that understands health and the human body in relation to nature. The body seeks a balance between itself and the world around it. When imbalance occurs, disease results. Thus, part of the goal of Chinese medicine is to restore internal balance to the body.

Acupuncture, along with related treatments, is based on the idea that the body has 700 points that ease and control pain and stimulate body functions. The process of inserting fine sharp needles into selected points related to affected organs in the body is essentially painless, and doctors have even done operations without chemical anesthesia using acupuncture to block pain. The procedures are widely practiced in Asia and are gaining popularity in many Western countries.

Although acupuncture has been practiced for more than 5,000 years in China, only in the 1970s, when relations with China improved, did this treatment become known and practiced in the West. Many doctors in the Global North reject the practice as unscientific and ineffective, and some regulating agencies have put limits on its practice. However, many patients feel otherwise. California (among other states) licenses the estimated 15,000 qualified acupuncture practitioners in the state (China.org 2009). An increasing number of acupuncture pain clinics are opening around the world, and about 6.5% of U.S. citizens have used acupuncture clinics. Some insurance companies also cover the costs of acupuncture, and the World Health Organization recognizes more than 40 conditions that can be effectively treated by acupuncture (Weiss and Lonnquist 2012). This is an example of diffusion of medical knowledge throughout the world that brings new practices to all countries.

The Chinese health care system does face problems. In rural areas, many people practice traditional folk medicine, and diseases, poor sanitation, pollution, ignorance, and smoking result in lowered life expectancy. In urban areas air pollution and other urban environmental issues cause health problems (Watts 2012). One major factor affecting Chinese health is that China accounts for about 30% of the world's tobacco consumption, with more than

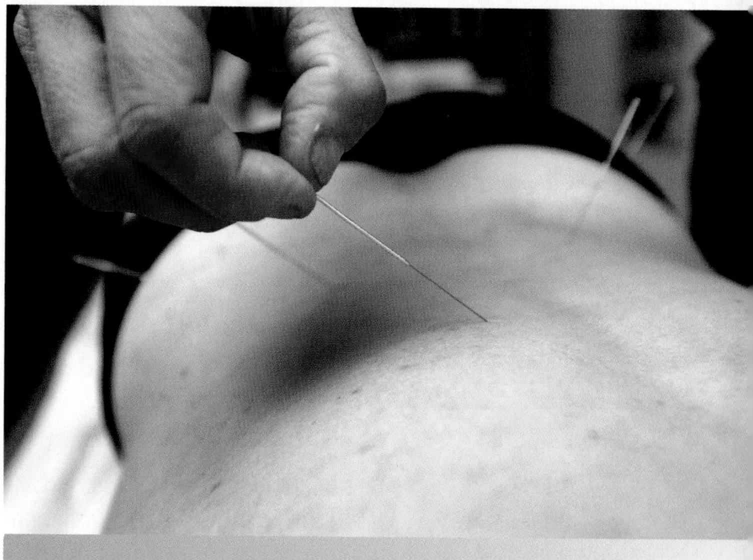

This acupuncturist is inserting needles on the back of his patient. This is an ancient and highly respected medical technique in China, and it has gained adherents in the United States and other Western countries.

300 million smokers—about 31% of the population—and 740 million people exposed to secondhand smoke. China is the world's largest tobacco producer and consumer—with over 1.31 trillion cigarettes consumed per year. Smoking-related illnesses result in 1 million deaths yearly (ChinaDaily.com 2012). This is not surprising since smoking causes 90% of lung cancer deaths worldwide (Ong et al. 2007). Government motivation and efforts to control smoking have been uneven because the government receives needed money from foreign tobacco sales.

Today, China's health care system is financed by the central government, patient fees, and health insurance. Health care expenditures amount to more than 4.6% of the gross domestic product (Index Mundi 2012c). The average life expectancy in China is now 73.8 years—up from 44.6 years in 1955 (United Nations Department of Economic and Social Affairs/Population Division 2011). Most significant for the rest of the world is the impact Chinese traditional medical techniques and remedies are having around the world.

Health care systems around the world illustrate the impact of national and global political and economic factors on the health care available to citizens. The political systems of countries and their economic status influence the philosophy toward health care and the money each country puts into health care. International policies such as embargoes between countries influence availability of health care *within* countries. International organizations, such as the World Health Organization, focus on epidemics and pandemics throughout the world.

Many people around the world engage in tobacco use, a serious health hazard that brings many risks. This is also a concern to the society as a whole because it means lowered productivity and increased health care costs for all.

Thinking Sociologically

What are some positive features of the Chinese approach to health care? What are some drawbacks of the Chinese approach? How is it similar to and how is it different from the Cuban and Canadian models discussed earlier in the chapter?

Globalization of Medical Problems

A dramatic worldwide health problem illustrating the interconnectedness between countries is the international sale of body parts. In some countries, people at the bottom of the stratification system are so desperately poor that they sell their body parts to help their families survive. For example, mothers and fathers in some poor slums of Mumbai and other cities in India and Pakistan sell their kidneys for money to pay for housing, food, education for their children, and dowries for their daughters to marry. In the process, their health often deteriorates, and when the money is gone, life is even more difficult. Although laws were passed in India in 1994 banning the sale of human organs, few violators are caught and punished ("Body Parts for Sale" 2008; "Cruellest Cut" 2009; Kumar 2001). As of 2008, the only nation where the sale of body organs was legal was Iran ("Body Parts for Sale" 2008). Recently, sales of skin, bones, tissue, and dental implants from fresh corpses have been growing, with a center of such activity in the Ukraine. However, the United States is the biggest supplier and market, with 2 million products bought each year. These body parts allow people to see with cornea transplants, to walk with recycled tendons, and to receive other repairs (Wilson et al. 2012).

Wealthy individuals usually benefit from these body parts since they are expensive. The transplant trade attracts medical tourists from Europe, who visit impoverished countries in Latin America and Asia for transplants and other "cheap" treatments. This is a dramatic illustration of world stratification of health care, effects of government policies, the differences in health attitudes, and behavior between rich and poor.

The illegal market in body parts is spreading to many countries. For example, a global mafia in human body parts is spreading. Estimates are that in the next 12 months, 5,000 humans will sell a kidney on the illegal market. U.S. citizens have gone to Nicaragua and Peru for transplants, and organs are available from former Soviet Republics including Azerbaijan, Belarus, and Moldova (Van Conoley 2012).

Even officials in coroners' offices have been apprehended harvesting body parts without consent of family members, often making a profit from the sales (Mashberg

2002). Reports from Nigeria indicate that mortuary and cemetery workers are selling body parts at markets (Ananova 2001), and a survey of low-income students in the United Kingdom found that one in four would sell a kidney to help pay for their education (Ananova 2002). This issue emphasizes the global differences between rich and poor people and countries. Where there is a need and a market for goods, those in need will step in to fill the gap, and many sick individuals will pay handsomely for body parts.

The status of a nation's health and medical care is often measured by key international markers—decrease in infant mortality and increase in life expectancy. The *infant mortality rate* for each country is a good indicator of the availability of and access to prenatal care and care for infants, and *life expectancy* rates reflect the overall health conditions in a country. The global infant mortality and life expectancy statistics appeared in Table 7.1 on page 228. The lowest national rate for infant mortality is 1.7 per 1,000 live births and the highest is 121.6. Life expectancy rates have an equally wide span—from 32.6 in Swaziland to more than 89 in Monaco.

Note the different causes of death in affluent/Global North versus poor/Global South countries in Table 14.7 on page 546. In the past, people in the Global North died of heart attacks and bad infections. Today, cancer is the leading cause of death (World Health Organization 2009), but many can be kept alive, even cured, extending life expectancy into the 80s. Yet infectious diseases are major killers in the Global South, reducing life expectancy in some poor countries to 40 years or less.

Globalization and the Mobility of Disease

In December 2007, a man boarded an international flight bound for the United States. The passengers and crew did not know that he was carrying a deadly strain of tuberculosis, one that is very difficult to treat with current medicines. The Centers for Disease Control and Prevention knew he carried the strain, tracked him down, and brought him in for testing. They needed to know if he was contagious. If so, they would need to contact all people on the flight and start preventative measures to reduce the possibility of a pandemic. The media picked up this story, and it blanketed the front pages of newspapers for several days, showing the concern about uncontrollable diseases spreading around the globe.

When the West Nile virus—a deadly mosquito-borne disease—was first discovered in New York City, it killed seven people before any action could be taken. Within a year, it had spread to 12 states, and within two years, it was found not only in mosquitoes but also in 60 species of birds and a dozen different types of mammals (Wilson 2006). Although health officials acted rapidly to stem the spread of this disease and others such as H1N1, pandemics are a constant threat.

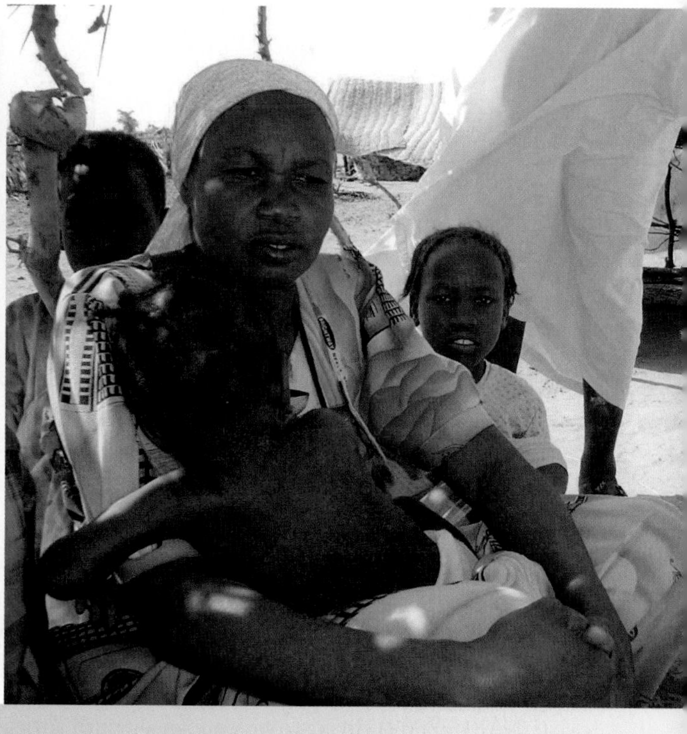

These two women are of similar age, both in their 30s. Health facilities make an enormous difference in one's life chances, one's health, and how one ages. The woman on the left lives in North America; the woman on the right raises a family in Senegal, West Africa.

Table 14.7 **Leading Causes of Death**

Poor Countries' Deaths (in Percentage)		*Affluent Countries' Deaths (in Percentage)*	
Lower respiratory infections	11.3	Coronary heart disease	15.6
Diarrheal diseases	8.2	Stroke/cerebrovascular disease	8.7
HIV/AIDS (leading cause of death for women)	7.8	Tracheal/bronchial/lung cancers	5.9
Coronary heart disease	6.1	Alzheimer and other dementias	4.1
Malaria	5.2	Lower respiratory infections	3.8
Stroke/cerebrovascular diseases	4.9	Chronic obstructive pulmonary disease	3.5
Tuberculosis	4.3	Colon and rectal cancers	3.3
Prematurity, low birth weight	3.2	Diabetes mellitus	2.6
Birth asphyxia and birth trauma	2.9	Hypertensive heart disease	2.3
Neonatal infections	2.6	Breast cancer	1.9

Source: World Health Organization (2011).

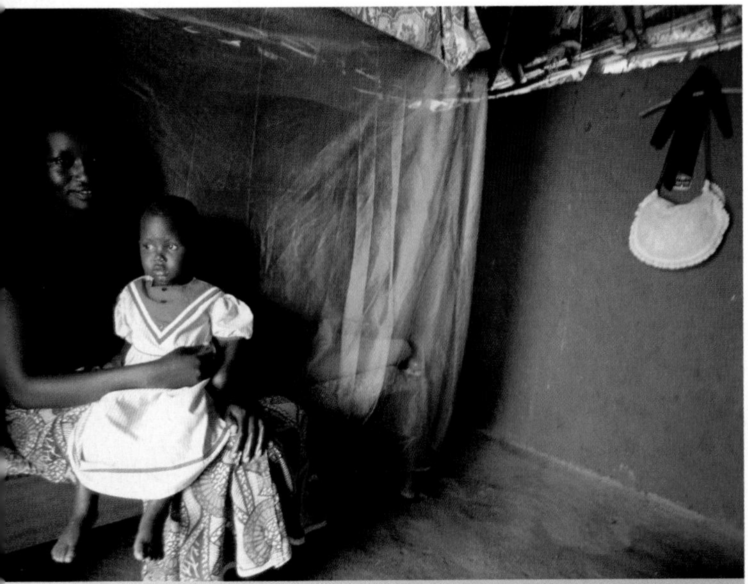

This woman has just acquired new bed nets, which her family members will use to protect themselves from malaria-causing mosquitoes. Often, people are bitten and infected while they sleep.

In 2010, the HIV/AIDS pandemic took the lives of 1.53 million people in sub-Saharan Africa alone, and an additional 1.8 million people in the region became newly infected with HIV (Avert 2010; UNAIDS 2009). Sixty-eight percent of the 33.3 million people living with HIV today are in sub-Saharan Africa. Two million people in the world died of AIDS in 2008, and there are an estimated 16.6 million AIDS orphans in Africa. Women have 50% of the cases (UNAIDS 2009). In just one country—South Africa—the HIV-infected population grew to 18.8% of the total population, with 5.5 million people infected and 320,000 dead in 2008 (Avert 2010). Local traditions contribute to the spread of AIDS. For example, men travel to urban areas for work and contract AIDS from prostitutes. When they return, they infect their wives. A major problem is the lack of resources for contraception and medications.

The issue of mobility of global health is not limited to diseases and their treatment. Use of tobacco is a major health issue, with perhaps a trillion "sticks" per year—mostly American and Chinese made—being sold to and smuggled into countries around the world. More than 303 billion cigarettes were bought in the United States, most from three leading companies with Philip Morris topping the manufacturers (Centers for Disease Control and Prevention 2012).

The world is highly connected, and diseases anywhere in the world can quickly spread to other continents, overpowering the medical communities' ability to diagnose, isolate, and treat diseases. Because both people and infection are highly mobile today, the problem is global. Global change and interconnectedness facilitate the spread of diseases and require countries and world organizations working together to attack health problems.

The density and mobility of the world's population (discussed in Chapter 15) affects human health. For example, use of land and space determines the number of rodents and insects, the water supplies, and the direct contact people have with one another. Currently, about half of the world's people live in urban areas and many in slums surrounding major cities. Problems such as open sewers, inadequate sanitation, lack of electricity, and polluted water pervade these slums. Most infections spread more readily where there is a population of at least 150,000, although more than 1 million is even more favorable for infectious germs by increasing the chances that the germs will find hosts that are not already immune (Wilson 2006). Our globe has increasing numbers of cities that exceed 1 million people.

Other factors that help the spread of disease are the growing numbers of locations with shared circulated air (airplanes, domed stadiums, air-conditioned office buildings and hotels), especially because most diseases travel by direct contact with other infected people. A World Health Organization study indicates that of the infections leading to death, 65% are due to person-to-person contact. Another 22% come from food, water, or soil contamination; 13% are transmitted by insects; and just 0.3% are acquired directly from animals (bird flu, rabies, etc.; Wilson 2006). Because people are moving around the globe for business and tourism much more today than in the past, they are exposed to more people in more environments. More than 5,000 airports now host international travelers, and more than 1 million people travel across international borders each day, counting only commercial airline travel (Wilson 2006). Examples of contagious diseases spread by world travelers include SARS, bird flu, tuberculosis, H1N1, and HIV/AIDS.

Indigenous Medicine: Traditional and Modern Medical Practices

In India, an ancient Hindu approach to medical care focuses on the link between mind and body. It suggests that health can be achieved if there is an adequate balance between the two and that balance can be brought about through meditation and medication, a combination of Western medicines and appropriate relaxation and exercise. Such beliefs are consistent with the overall pattern of Indian culture and religion.

In a rural Mexican–Native American village in Arizona, a gravely ill young boy named Yas is being treated by the shaman of the village for a rattlesnake bite. Prayers are chanted by all present as the shaman pours a mixture of herbs and other ingredients over Yas's head. After this procedure, Yas is taken to a local health care clinic for additional Western-style treatment.

An elderly Nicaraguan woman, Lucia, comes to a rural clinic with the complaint of "sadness in my body and fear in my chest." Is this a heart problem? Arthritis? Some other sickness? Knowing the cultural context of the woman's description, the doctor determines her problem. After checking her physical condition, he finds that her complaint is symptomatic not of a heart attack, but rather of missing her children, who have all left to work in foreign countries. For a modest fee based on her income, and with limited access to psychological care, she has found what help she could.

In an African village in Ghana, the local shaman, Kofa, grows his own herbal garden, which produces many of the medicinal plants that he uses for treatment, using recipes passed down through the generations. There are herbal mixtures for infection, impotence, infertility, asthma, stomach ailments, and numerous other problems. Using

This sign in a rural area of Ethiopia is an effort to educate local people about the dangers of AIDS and methods to protect oneself.

combinations of traditional and Western treatments, he gains legitimacy. He points out that the herbal medicines he uses are very effective and, in fact, form the basic substances of many Western medicines. Down the road from this shaman, patients can seek treatment from Amma, the priestess, in exchange for a small contribution. The closest role in Western medicine to Amma's services would be a psychologist or psychiatrist. Her visitors include the lovesick, the lonely, the hypochondriacs, and the bereaved. She sings, chants, prescribes potions (mixtures of herbs, often sedatives), and gives advice.

People around the world rely on a variety of medical models and practitioners to meet their needs. As migrations

Depicted here is the process of creating traditional medicines, from start to finish, in Ethiopia. First, the plants are cultivated or picked from wild herbs. Then the medicine is extracted from the plants. This is sold in the equivalent of pharmacies or prescribed by traditional healers.

occur, practices spread. Western medicine has borrowed from folk medicine traditions; tested many of the traditional herbal remedies; incorporated acupuncture, pressure point, and massage therapies; and used other procedures adopted from traditional medicine. *Allopathy* (medicine based on remedies that simply reverse one's symptoms) retains dominance over alternative medical practices—homeopathy, chiropractic, acupuncture, and other types of medical practices that Global North medical practitioners sometimes label as quackery. Yet folk medicines in many societies, often combined with Global North medicine, effectively treat people's illnesses in their social contexts. Medicine itself has become globally informed, delivered with awareness of local social settings.

One result of the spread of medical ideas around the world is the complementary and alternative medicine (CAM) movement in the United States and other Global North countries. CAM includes health care systems, practices, and products that are used to complement conventional medicine or as alternative medicine used in place of conventional medicine. CAM therapies include acupuncture and chiropractic, natural products, special diets, and megavitamin therapy (GoodTherapy.org 2012). Of interest to sociologists is the spread of practices, along with who accepts alternative practices and who resists them.

In a major survey of U.S. health practices, 38% (4 in 10) of adults and 12% of children said they use some form of CAM for health reasons. The profile of CAM users looks like this: more women than men, those with higher education, those who have been hospitalized, and former smokers. About 12% of the study population sought care from a CAM practitioner such as an acupuncturist or a chiropractor (Barnes, Bloom, and Nahin 2008; National Institutes of Health 2007).

Pressures for change in the health care system come from consumers, health care financing, and competition to keep medical practices profitable. As the population ages and people live longer, as patients look for alternative ways to deal with chronic illness, and as alternative health providers set up shop, more doctors are adding aspects of holistic medicine and CAM to meet consumer demands (Winnick 2006). The medical establishment has incorporated some of these practices, especially if scientific study finds them effective, but others lie outside accepted Western medicine at this time. The most prevalent CAM practices that have been imported to Western countries from traditional medical practices are acupuncture, Ayurveda, biofeedback, chelation therapy, chiropractic care, deep breathing exercises, diet-based therapies, energy healing therapy, folk medicine, guided imagery, homeopathic treatment, hypnosis, massage, meditation, megavitamin therapy, natural products, neuropathy, prayer for health reasons, progressive relaxation, Qigong, Reiki, Tai Chi, and Yoga. Figure 14.2 shows the percentages using the 10 most common CAM practices.

Because of the uneven distribution of health care, doctors, and medicines around the world, many preventable and curable diseases go untreated. When the average life expectancy in countries is in the 30s, we know that medical help is not available for common medical problems. For example, dehydration from diarrhea caused by water-borne diseases such as cholera, blindness caused by vitamin A deficiency, malaria caused by infected mosquitoes, and other preventable diseases are unnecessary afflictions in today's world. Yet many nations in the Global South have few physicians per capita (United Nations Development Programme 2005). Folk remedies are the only health care most of these citizens have.

As long as there is inequality in countries of our social world, adequate health care is unlikely to reach all people and all countries equally. In spite of increasingly sophisticated medical technology and medicines, availability, cost, distribution, and policies of governments are the determinants of who receives health care around the world.

Thinking Sociologically

We live in a global world, yet our most immediate experiences are local. What are benefits you and your family might receive if international agencies resolve health problems in Africa, Asia, and South America?

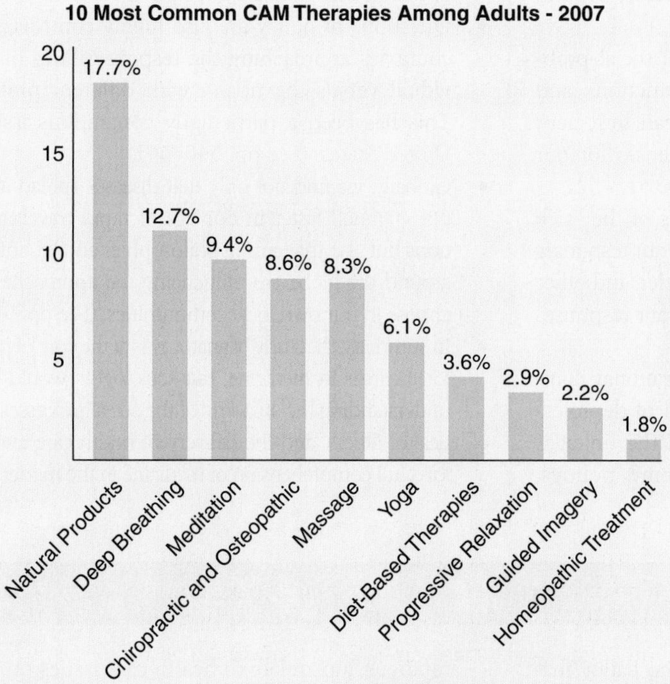

Therapies with significant increases between 2002 and 2007 are

	2002	2007
Deep breathing	11.6%	12.7%
Meditation	7.6%	9.4%
Massage	5.0%	8.3%
Yoga	5.1%	6.1%

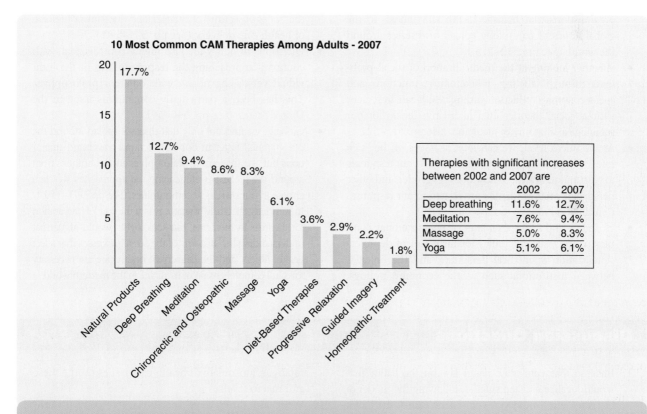

Figure 14.2 The 10 Most Common CAM Therapies Among Adults

Source: **National Institute of Health (2008).**

Our social institutions—from family, education, and religion to politics, economics, and health—maintain stability in societies. However, the world in which we live is a dynamic one. In the final two chapters, we turn to an examination of how change occurs. First, we examine two forces that have changed exponentially in the past two centuries—population patterns and urbanization. We close with an examination of social change in its many manifestations.

What Have We Learned?

When you are sick and when you are diagnosed and cared for, the norms that allow you to be sick and the expectations of you in the sick role may differ from the expectations placed on others around the world. Although health is a private, personal concern, it is also a public concern, delivered through organizations dispensing health care and government practices determining access and funding of health care. Distant from your daily life but important to your well-being are the global health organizations that concern themselves with global epidemics. In addition, whether you have insurance or money to pay doctors depends in part on the economic conditions in society and the global marketplace of health care delivery.

Key Points

- Sociology looks at the anatomy of medicine by examining the social implications of health and illness—from the micro level of individuals coping with illness to the meso level of institutional interactions and complex organizations that manage health and illness, to the global issues of controlling spread of diseases around the world. (See pp. 512–515.)
- Whether looking at the medicalization of social problems through labeling or examining functions and socioeconomic conflicts regarding health care in society, various social theories offer alternative lenses for our sociological anatomy of medicine. (See pp. 515–522.)
- At the micro level, we can look at issues of the "sick role," how social and cultural factors affect our responses to pain and ill health, or how our age, gender, and other personal aspects of identity are related to our responses to health and illness. (See pp. 522–528.)
- Hospitals and other elements of organizational complexity, the issues of professionalism and of deprofessionalization of medical personnel, and the linkages between institutions such as the economy, politics, education, and family are all aspects of health care at the meso level. (See pp. 528–534.)
- The national level is often linked to access to health care, the cost as a proportion of the nation's resources, the issues of security of citizens, and questions of reform of health care delivery. (See pp. 534–540.)
- Questions of policy are also highly controversial, with countries approaching the responsibilities of the individual versus the nation with different philosophies. This has been a particularly contentious issue in the United States. (See pp. 540–541.)
- Globally, we find not only that diseases spread around the planet much faster in our age of rapid travel and migrations but also that curing philosophies and techniques from around the globe are influencing the approaches we each choose in our own local communities. (See pp. 541–549.)
- In summary, the study of anatomy is at the core of preparation for a career in medicine, but sociologists would argue that understanding the anatomy of the social processes that affect health, illness, and the delivery of health care are necessary for a full comprehension of medicine in the modern world.

Discussion Questions

1. Imagine that your state has a law on the ballot that would legalize assisted suicide, following the model of Oregon's law. Would you vote for or against the ballot question? Why? Would the conditions necessary for the legality of assisted suicide described in Oregon's law influence your vote? Why or why not? Why do you think most of those who participated in the Death with Dignity program in Oregon were whites with college degrees?
2. Think of the last time you or someone close to you was seriously ill. What were the repercussions of the illness on the micro level? How did these repercussions relate to health care issues on the meso and macro levels?
3. What are three ways social class impacts health? Describe how social class has impacted your health and the health of your family members.
4. Do you think health care is a human right? Why or why not? How can inequality in health care negatively impact a society?
5. Are you in favor of a ban on supersize, sugary soft drinks, as part of an overall effort to curb obesity? Why or why not? If you were a policy maker, how might you try to address the obesity epidemic?

Contributing to Our Social World: What Can We Do?

At the Local Level

- You can learn about *health issues related to college* at www.cdc.gov/Features/CollegeHealth.
- *Obesity in America* (www.obesityinamerica.org) provides information on a wide range of resources related to studies on eating behavior, many of which are directly applicable to problems faced by students.
- Can you find *healthy food on campus*? If your school does not offer enough healthy options, start a petition and present it to your campus administrators asking them to address this issue. An article that describes some schools' attempts to go healthy—and, in some cases, "green"—can be found at www.hercampus.com/health/10-healthiest-college-dining-halls-america?page=2.

At the Organizational or Institutional Level

- *Free or low-cost clinics.* Most communities provide health screening and other services to uninsured individuals and families. The U.S. Department of Health and Human Services has a locator website at http://findahealthcenter.hrsa.gov/Search_HCC.aspx that searches for free clinics by state and city. Most have volunteer and internship opportunities that afford interesting and valuable experiences, especially if you are considering a career in a health care field.

At the National and Global Levels

- *The Joint United Nations Program on HIV/AIDS* (www.unaids.org/en) works throughout the globe to fight the pandemic. If you are interested in learning more about and possibly raising funds for this effort, go to www.unaids.org/en.
- *World Vision* (www.worldvision.org) helps children, their families, and their communities in an effort to combat malnutrition, AIDS, and other health- and poverty-related problems across the world. The organization's Hope Child program lists several suggestions for getting involved, including sponsorship of a child.
- *AVERT*, an international AIDS charity, provides material to educate yourself and your classmates about AIDS on the organization's website at www.avert.org/worldaid.htm.

Visit the Student Study Site at **www.sagepub.com/ballantine4e** to access additional study tools, including eFlashcards, web quizzes, video resources, audio resources, web resources, SAGE journal articles, recommended readings, and more.

PART V Social Dynamics

Social structures such as institutions—family, education, religion, health, politics, and economics—tend to resist change. Yet this entire book shows that societies are dynamic and changing. Institutions and organizations come alive with processes that are fluid and vibrant. Globalization itself, a major theme in this book, is a process bringing transformation to our social world. We do not live in the same sort of world our grandparents inhabited. The macro- and meso-level dimensions of the world have become increasingly powerful, which is exactly why we need a sociological imagination to understand how the events in our own micro worlds are influenced by the larger society.

This section looks at some of those dynamic, fluid, and vibrant processes—population changes, urbanization, expansion of technology, social movements, and more. When we are in periods of rapid change, understanding how that change occurs and what processes are involved is key to influencing change. For example, from global climate change to terrorism and from new digital technologies to immigrants in our communities, we need to understand what the actual facts are regarding causes and consequences before we can respond constructively. We live in exciting and challenging times, and we will thrive best if we understand the micro-, meso-, and macro-level dimensions of change in our lives and the linkages between parts of our social world. We turn next to population dynamics and urbanization.

CHAPTER 15

Population and Urbanization

Living on Spaceship Earth

The human population is limited to this one moderate-sized sphere on which it depends for survival. The question is whether human groups can cooperate with each other and use the resources of the planet responsibly. The challenges of controlling population size, migration patterns, and the spread of disease add to the need for global cooperation. In the meantime, humans are concentrated in dense urban areas. As the night shot in the background of this page illustrates, bright lights beam from urban centers in Europe but from fewer places in Africa, illustrating the differences in both population density and level of development.

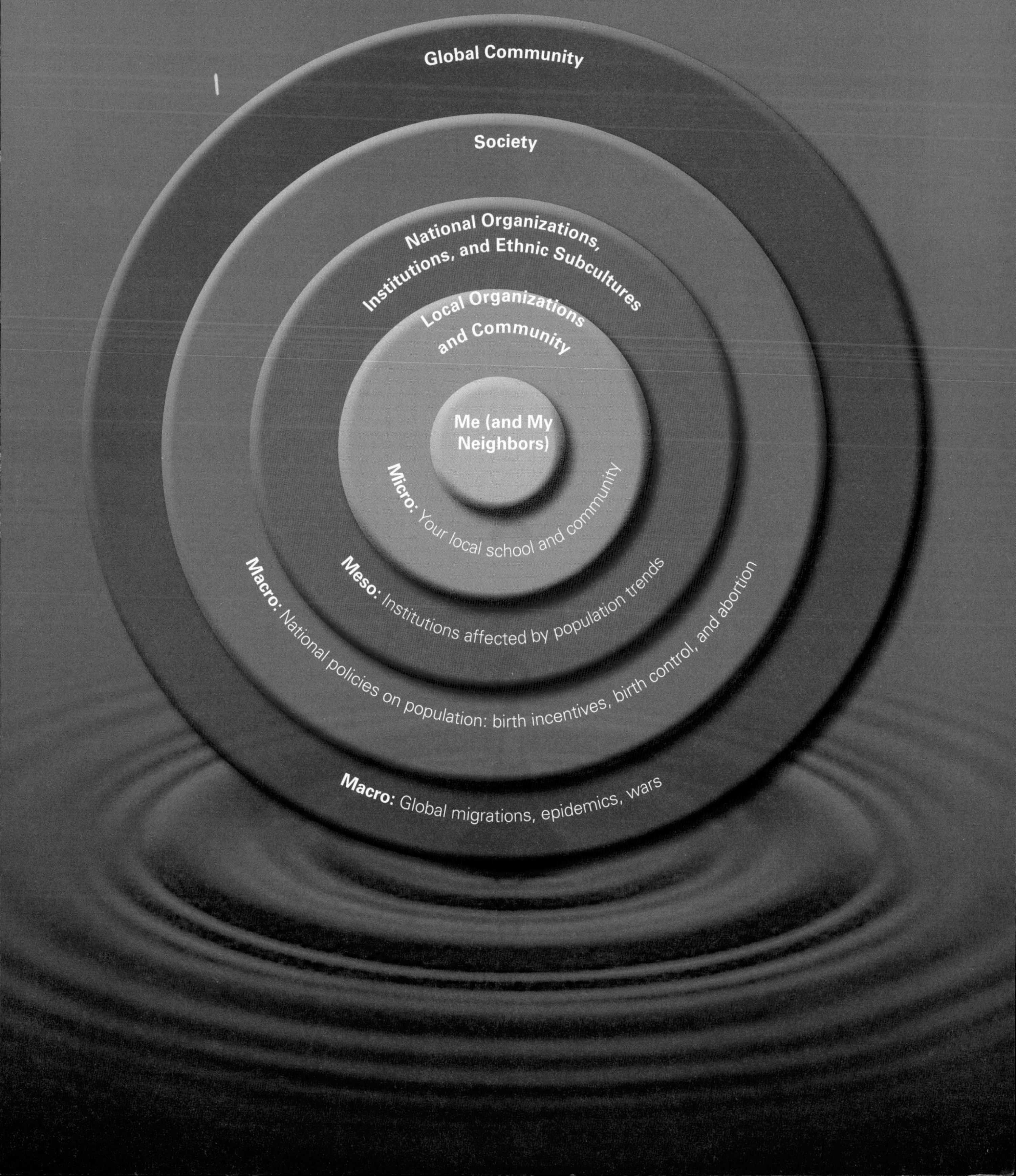
Global Community
Society
National Organizations, Institutions, and Ethnic Subcultures
Local Organizations and Community
Me (and My Neighbors)
Micro: Your local school and community
Meso: Institutions affected by population trends
Macro: National policies on population: birth incentives, birth control, and abortion
Macro: Global migrations, epidemics, wars

Think About It	
Micro: Self and Inner Circle	What factors affected the size of your family?
Micro: Local Community	What characterizes the population composition of your hometown? Where do you fit into that composition?
Meso: National Institutions; Complex Organizations; Ethnic Groups	Why do people move from rural areas to urban areas? What problems does this pattern of movement create?
Macro: National Society	How might immigration affect the makeup of a nation, and what effect could this have on a nation's policies?
Macro: Global Community	How do global issues relating to urbanization, the environment, and technology affect your family and your local community?

What's coming in this chapter?

- Macro-Level Patterns in World Population Growth
- Meso-Level Institutional Influences on Population Change
- Micro-Level Population Patterns
- Urbanization: Movement From Rural to Urban Areas
- Cities as Micro-Level Living Environments
- How Did Cities Evolve? Meso-Level Organizational Structures
- Urban Problems, the Environment, and Social Policy: Macro-Level Perspectives

When Sally Ride, the first U.S. woman in space, looked down at the earth, she saw a beautiful green and blue spherical object drifting through space. She described the view at night when parts of the sphere glow with lights while other parts are dark. In 2012 Ride died of pancreatic cancer. Her mission in life was to share part of that awesome experience with young people, especially girls, and encourage them to explore sciences.

That relatively small planet that Ride viewed from afar is home to earthlings. The controlling inhabitants of the planet are humans, just over 7 billion of them and increasing by 211,090 people daily ("Is Overpopulation a World Threat?" 2011; World Population Clock 2012). The topic of this chapter is the life, death, spread, and distribution of those humans living on spaceship earth (Diamond 2005).

Since the emergence of *Homo sapiens* in East Africa, human populations have grown in uneven surges and declines due to births, deaths, and migrations. The World Population Clock (see Table 15.1) illustrates the current state of the human population.

The world's human population grew sporadically over the millennia, so the explosion of human beings on the planet in the past two and a half centuries is stunning. If we collapsed all human history into one 24-hour day, the time period since 1750 would consume 1 minute. Yet 25% of all humans have lived during this 1-minute time period. In the 200 years between 1750 and 1950, the world's population mushroomed from 800 million to 2.5 billion. On October 12, 1999, the global population reached 6 billion. It has now expanded to more than 7 billion with most growth in the poorest countries (Population Reference Bureau 2012d; World Population Clock 2012). This means that the world is growing each year by the number of people in the country of Germany, Philippines, or Vietnam. Every minute in 2012, for example, 267 children were born and 107 people died around the world, resulting in a net increase of 160 people per minute (Population Reference

Table 15.1 **Population Clock, 2012 (in Thousands)**

	World	*Global South (Less Developed)*	*Global North (More Developed)*
Population	7,057,075	5,814,057	1,234,018
Births per day	385	347	38
Births per year	140,542	126,618	13,924
Deaths per day	154	121	33
Deaths per year	56,238	44,046	12,192
Infant deaths per day	15.8	15.6	0.2
Natural annual increase	84,304	82,572	81,185

Source: Population Reference Bureau (2012c).

Bureau 2012a). Between 2000 and 2050, virtually all the world's growth will occur in Africa, Asia, and Latin America. Overcrowded cities such as Calcutta, Dhaka, Jakarta, and Manila, all in Asia, are at extreme risk of impacts from climate change such as flooding (YubaNet.com 2011).

Let us start by focusing on one area of our world, Kenya in East Africa. We begin here partly because East Africa, where Kenya and Tanzania are located, was home to spaceship earth's earliest human inhabitants. Scientists believe that bones found in the dry Olduvai Gorge area are the oldest remains of *Homo sapiens* ever found. We also focus here because today Kenya is making human history for another reason. With a population of 43 million people, and a growth rate of 2.44% annually, Kenya has one of the most rapidly growing populations on earth (World Factbook 2013f). Kenya is made up of many tribal groups of people. With different religions and value systems, the people have clashed in power struggles in recent years. Still, there are several themes that pervade most Kenyan subcultures, as illustrated by the following example.

Changes in the environment and in the global economy make it difficult for this Kenyan family to provide for itself. Some of these children and their cousins may find it necessary to move to urban centers, a worldwide migration trend. Much of the socialization they received in villages will not be relevant to their adult urban lives.

Wengari, like Kenyan girls of most tribal affiliations, married in her teens. She has been socialized to believe that her main purpose in life is to bear children, to help with the farming, and to care for parents in their old age. Children are seen as an asset in Kenya. Religious beliefs and cultural value systems encourage large families. However, the population of Kenya is 45.2% dependent: people under 15 or over 65, who rely on working-age citizens to support them (World Factbook 2013f). The working-age population is becoming scarce and cannot continue to feed the growing population. Add to that severe droughts in parts of the country—droughts that are killing animal herds and preventing growth of crops. These facts, however, have little meaning to young women like Wengari, who have been socialized to conform to the female role within their society.

By contrast, far to the north—in many of the industrialized, urbanized countries of Europe—birthrates are below population replacement levels, meaning population size eventually will begin to drop. The natural growth rate in Germany is 0.21%, in France 0.5%, and in the United Kingdom 0.56%. Hungary, Latvia, the Czech Republic, and many other countries in Eastern Europe are losing population. This is compared to Zimbabwe in Africa with a growth rate of 4.31% (Index Mundi 2012d).

While Asia's share of the world population may continue to hover around 60% through the next century, Europe's portion has declined sharply and is likely to drop even more during the 21st century. Africa and Latin America each will gain part of Europe's portion. By 2100, Africa is expected to capture the greatest share. Countries growing by less than 1% annually include Japan, Australia, New Zealand, Russia, and much of Europe (Population Reference Bureau 2013b). In industrialized societies, children in the middle class and above are dependent until they leave home. Typical European young people often wait until their late 20s or even 30s to start a family, postponing children until their education is complete and a job is in hand. Many limit their family size because societal values such as educating children support small families. It is difficult to house large families in small urban apartments where the majority of the population lives. Workers must support and feed their families on earned wages rather than through farming. Both mother and father often work, and unlike many children in the Global South, most children born in Europe will survive to old age. Life expectancy, the average age at death, is 63.07 years in Kenya (World Factbook 2013f). In some European countries, it is older than 81 years.

On yet another continent, China, the country with the largest population in the world (1.34 billion people), had the greatest drop in population growth in the late 20th century due to strict governmental family planning practices (World Factbook 2013c). India, the second-largest country, has a population growth rate (increase in a country's population during a specified period of time) of 1.31% a year, just over replacement level (World Factbook 2013e).

Although some countries have birthrates below population replacement levels, the world's population continues to grow because of the skyrocketing growth rate in other countries and because of *population momentum* caused by the large number of individuals of childbearing age having children. Even though birthrates per couple drop, the number of women of childbearing age is still very high, resulting in continued growth in population size. Unfortunately, most

Hanoi, Vietnam, is a crowded Asian city. The overcrowding in some cities means that governments have a difficult time providing the infrastructure and services needed for the growing urban population.

of the countries with the highest growth rates are in the Global South, where there are fewer resources to support the additional population.

What we have been discussing is called **demography**, *the study of human populations*. When demographers speak of **populations**, they mean *all permanent societies, states, communities, adherents of a common religious faith, racial or ethnic groups, kinship or clan groups, professions, and other identifiable categories of people*. The size, geographical location, and spatial movement of the population; its concentration in certain geographical areas, including urban areas; and changing characteristics of the population are important elements in the study of demography. With growing populations and limited farmland to support the population, hungry people move to cities in hopes of finding jobs. This *pattern of movement from rural areas to cities* is called **urbanization**. The second half of this chapter will consider the evolution, growth, and development of populated areas, including movements from rural areas to cities, the organization of micro-level urban life, the relationship between individuals and the city, and some problems facing cities.

The previous chapters have been organized by moving from micro- to macro-level analysis. Because demographic work has focused on societies and global trends, we will reverse the order in the first section and discuss macro-level patterns in world population growth first, followed by meso-level institutional influences on population, and micro-level factors affecting population patterns.

Thinking Sociologically

Do you have a choice in how many children you have? What factors go into your decision? How might your decision differ if you were in a different country? Should global patterns—which include food shortages and climate change—be a consideration in the size of your family and your neighbors' families? Why or why not?

Macro-Level Patterns in World Population Growth

Early humans roamed the plains of Africa for thousands of years, their survival and growth depending on the environment in which they lived. They mastered fire and tools, then domesticated animals and invented agriculture, and with these skills slowly increased control over the environment, allowing their numbers to expand. This evolution in the growth patterns of human populations is worth closer examination.

Patterns of Population Growth Over Time

Members of the small band of early *Homo sapiens* who inhabited the Olduvai Gorge moved gradually, haltingly, from this habitat into what are now other parts of Africa, Asia, and Europe. The process took thousands of years. At times, births outnumbered deaths and populations grew, but at other times, plagues, famines, droughts, and wars decimated populations. From the beginning of human existence, estimated from perhaps 1 million years ago until modern times, the number of births and deaths balanced each other over the centuries (Diamond 2005). The large population we see today results from population evolution that consisted of three phases:

1. Humans, because of their thinking ability, competed satisfactorily in the animal kingdom to obtain the basic necessities for survival of the species.
2. With the agricultural revolution that occurred about 10,000 years ago and the resulting food surplus, mortality rates declined, and the population grew as more infants survived and people lived longer.
3. The biggest increase came with the Industrial Revolution, beginning about 300 years ago. Improved medical knowledge and sanitation helped bring the death rate down.

When industrialization made its debut, it not only brought the social and economic changes in societies, discussed in Chapter 3 (e.g., machines replacing human labor and mass production using resources in new ways), but it also augmented urbanization of societies. The population explosion began with industrialization in Europe and spread to widely scattered areas of the globe. With trade and migrations came the diffusion of ideas and better medical care, influencing population growth rates in all parts of the world by keeping people alive longer. Figures 15.1 and 15.2 show population growth throughout history. The worldwide *rate* of population growth reached its peak in the 1960s. Although it has dropped to a current rate of about 1.1% per year, the population will continue to increase until large baby booms level off, resulting in the world population doubling every 61 years (World Factbook 2013k).

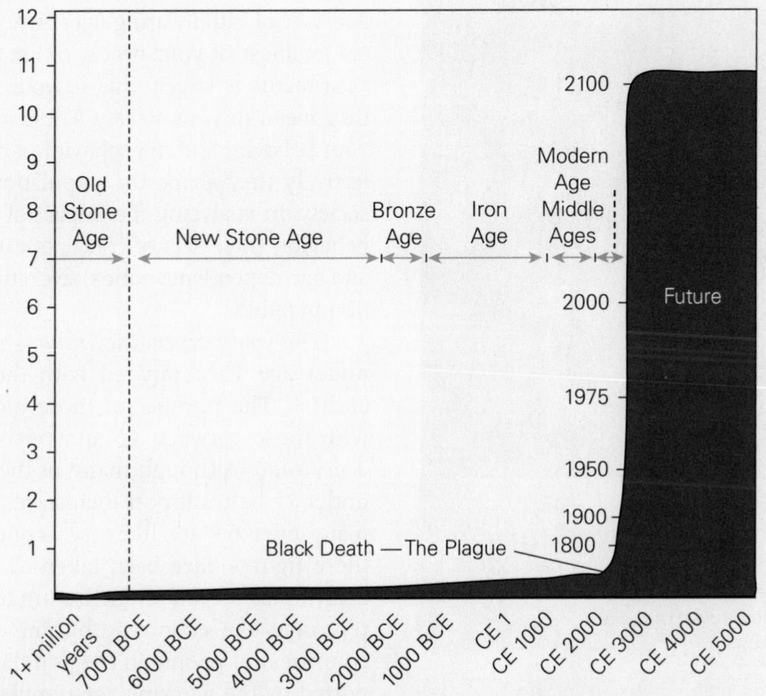

Figure 15.1 The Exponential World Population Growth From About 8000 BCE to 21st Century

Source: Abu-Lughod (2001:50).

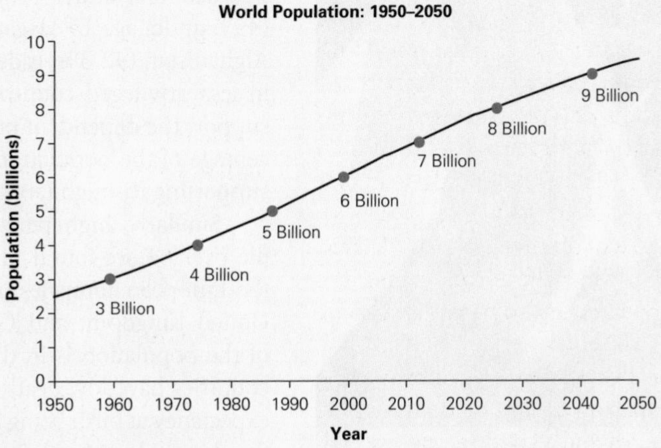

Figure 15.2 World Population Growth Rate, 1950–2050

Source: United Nations, Department of Economic and Social Affairs, Population Division (2012b).

Predictors of Population Growth

In some villages in sub-Saharan and East African countries, children are forced to fend for themselves. With large percentages of the working-age population dead (or dying) from AIDS, orphaned children take care of their younger siblings. In some villages in Uganda, for instance, social workers visit periodically to bring limited food for survival and see that children are planting crops. These children must learn survival skills and gender roles at a very young age. They have little chance to experience a childhood typical in other places or to receive an education (Avert 2009).

AIDS has a horrific impact on individuals at the micro level, on families and communities at the meso level, and on entire societies at the macro level. Joseph Mwila comforts his younger brother Aaron in Chilonga in Zambia, with their sister Joanna behind. This is what remains of the family after both parents died of AIDS.

A Palestinian boy carrying the Palestinian flag demonstrates against evictions of families from their houses. With half of the Palestinian population under age 15, younger Palestinians are taking active roles in politics, and many are responsible for helping to support their families.

Think for a moment about the impact that your age and sex have on your position in society and your activities. Are you of childbearing age? Are you dependent on others for most of your needs, or are you supporting others? Your status is largely due to your age and sex, and what they mean in your society. These matters greatly influence your behavior and the behavior of others like you, and collectively they shape the population patterns of an entire society. In analyzing the impact of age and sex on human behavior, three sets of concepts can be very useful: youth and age dependency ratios, sex ratios, and age-sex population pyramids.

The *youth dependency ratio* is the number of children under age 15 compared with the number between 15 and 64. The number of those older than 64 compared with those between 15 and 64 is called the *age dependency ratio*. Although many of the world's young people under 15 help support themselves and their families, and many over 64 are likewise economically independent, these figures have been taken as the general ages when individuals are not contributing to the labor force. They represent the economic burden (especially in wealthy countries) of people in the population who must be supported by the working-age population. The **dependency ratio**, then, is *the ratio of those in both the young and aged groups compared with the number of people in the productive age groups between 15 and 64 years old.*

In several resource-poor countries nearly half of the population is under 15 years of age. These include Niger (49% under age 15), Uganda (49.9%), Congo (44.4%), and Afghanistan (42.3%; Index Mundi 2012b). Working adults in less privileged countries have a tremendous burden to support the dependent population, especially if a high percentage of the population is urban and not able to be self-supporting through farming.

Similarly, high percentages of older dependent people over 64 are found in most Global North countries. In the European countries of Norway, Sweden, Denmark, the United Kingdom, and Germany, between 15% and 20% of the population is in the age group 65 and older. These countries have low death rates, resulting in the average life expectancy at birth being as high as 83.6 years for women in Sweden (Index Mundi 2013; World Factbook 2013i). Using fertility and death rates to make projections based on current patterns, Josef Wöss predicts that from 2010 to 2050 the dependency ratio will increase by 92% (Wöss 2012).

The percentage of dependent elderly people is growing, especially in affluent countries. Consider the case of Japan, which faces the problem of its "graying" or aging population. In 2011, 21.5% of its population was 65 or older, and the average life expectancy was over 82 years. The Japanese population is graying nearly twice as fast as the population in many other nations, in large part because the birthrate is low, 8.7 births per 1,000 in the population; with a death rate of 9.1 per 1,000, there is a negative growth rate of −0.1% per year (Pearce 2010; Trading Economics 2012). There simply are not enough replacement workers to support the aging population. Japan provides a glimpse into the future for other rapidly aging societies, including Germany, the United States, and China (see Figure 15.3 for a vivid depiction of the expected transformation in one century).

The *sex ratio* refers to the ratio of males to females in the population. For instance, the more females, especially females in the fertile years, the more potential there is for population growth. The sex ratio also determines the supply of eligible spouses. Marriage patterns are affected by economic cycles, wars in which the proportion of males to females may decrease, and migrations that generally take males from one area and add them to another. **Population pyramids** *are pyramid-shaped diagrams that illustrate sex ratios and dependency ratios* (see Figure 15.4 on page 564).

The graphic presentation of the age and sex distribution of a population tells us a great deal about that population. The structures are called pyramids because that is the shape they took until several decades ago. By looking up and down the pyramid, we can see the proportion of population at each age level. Looking to the right and left of the centerline tells us the balance of males to females at each age. The bottom line shows us the total population at each age.

The first pyramid shows populations that have fairly low birth- and death rates, typical of Global North countries. The second pyramid illustrates populations with high birthrates and large dependent youth populations, typical of Global South countries. The world population has been getting both younger (the Global South) *and* older (the Global North), resulting in large numbers of people dependent on the working-age population between 15 and 65 years of age.

As Global South nations have more and more children, they are creating more potential parents in later years, adding momentum to the world's population growth. Today young children survive their early years, whereas in the past they might have died of disease and malnutrition. Fewer deaths of infants and children, which can be credited to immunizations and disease control, result in lower mortality rates, younger populations, and higher potential numbers of births in the future.

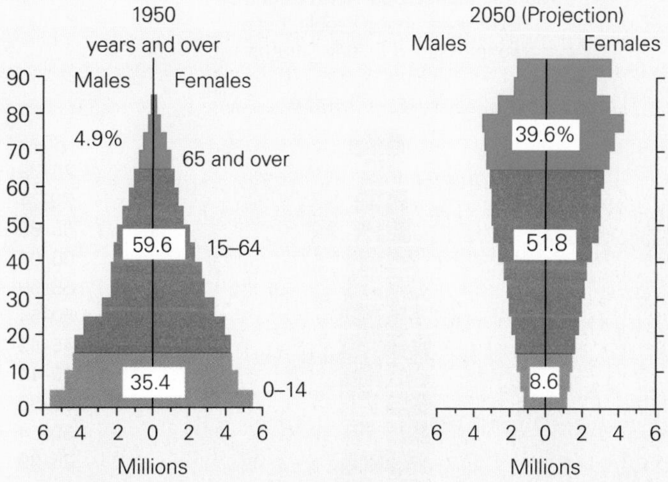

Japan's percentage of population over 65 is growing faster than that of any other nation, and in one century will have become transformed.

Figure 15.3 Japan Grows Old

Source: Statistical Handbook of Japan (2010).

Japan is an aging society, with life expectancy exceeding 81 years and 21.5% of the population over age 65. Ninety-two-year-old Toshi Uechi practices a traditional Japanese dance in Okinawa. An active lifestyle and a Spartan diet have helped make Okinawa the home of an exceptionally high percentage of centenarians (those over 100 years).

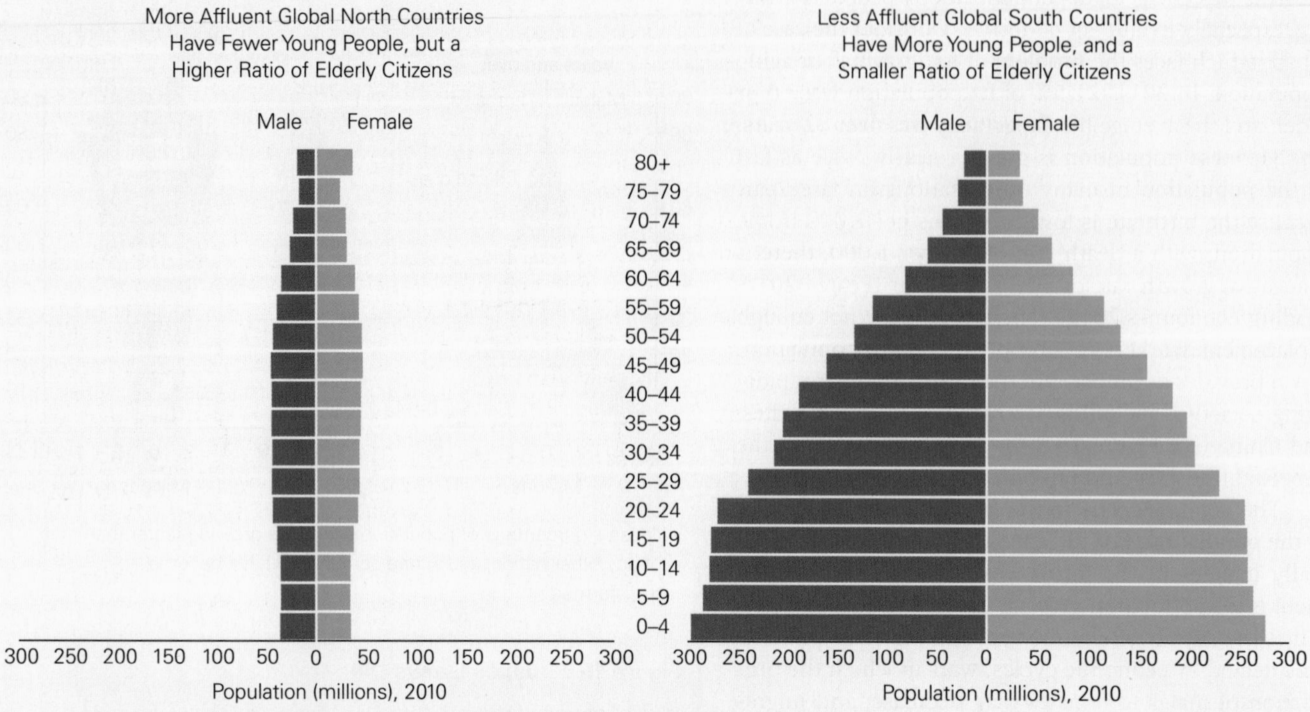

Figure 15.4 Population Pyramids, by Level of Affluence, 2010

Source: Bremner et al. (2009). Reprinted with permission.

Thinking Sociologically

Consider your own country's population pyramid. You can find it at www.census.gov. What can you tell about your country's level of development by studying the population pyramid? How might societies differ if they have a young versus old population?

Population Patterns: Theoretical Explanations

Interest in population size and growth began with the earliest historical writings. Scriptures such as the Quran and the Bible have supported population growth to increase the ranks of the faithful. Of course, population expansion made sense at the time these holy tracts were written. Government leaders throughout the ages have adopted various philosophies about the best size of populations. The ancient Greek philosopher Plato argued that the city-state should have 5,040 citizens and that measures should be taken to increase or decrease the population to bring it in line with this figure (Plato [350 BCE] 1960). However, the first significant scholarly analysis that addressed global population issues came from Thomas Malthus (1766–1834), an English clergyman and social philosopher.

Malthus's Theory of Population

In his "Essay on the Principle of Population," Malthus argued that humans are driven to reproduce and will multiply without limits if no checks are imposed (Malthus [1798] 1926). An unchecked population increases geometrically: 2 parents could have 4 children, 16 grandchildren, 64 great-grandchildren, and so forth—and that is simply with a continuous average family size of 4 children. Because the means of subsistence (food) increases at best only arithmetically or lineally (5, 10, 15, 20, 25), the end result is a food shortage and possible famine.

Malthus recognized several positive checks on populations, factors that would keep populations from excessive growth—wars, disease epidemics, and food shortages leading to famine (a drastic, wide-reaching shortage of food). Malthus held strong political views based in part on his population theory. He suggested preventive checks on rapid population growth, primarily in the form of delayed marriage and practice of sexual abstinence until one could afford a family. Contraception technology was crude and often unrealistic in his day, and therefore he did not present it as an option for population control.

Looking at the world today, we see examples of these population checks. War decimated the populations of several countries during the world wars and has taken its toll on other countries in Eastern Europe, Africa, and the Middle East since then. The AIDS virus, SARS, Ebola, and bird flu have raised fears of new plagues (epidemics of often fatal diseases). Waterborne diseases such as cholera and typhus strike after floods, and the floods themselves are often caused by environmental destruction resulting from too many humans in a geographic area. Food shortages necessitating food aid due to impending famines were found in many countries in 2010, including North Korea, Afghanistan, Congo, Burundi, Eritrea, Sudan, Angola, Chad, Liberia, Zimbabwe, Bangladesh, Ethiopia, and Somalia (World Famine Timeline 2011). Countries in the horn of Africa received massive relief efforts, but too little and too late to save thousands who died of starvation. Famines are caused in part by erosion and stripping the earth of natural protections such as forests and grasslands by people in need of more land to grow food and graze animals and of more firewood to cook. Today, economic factors are also affecting populations as imported cheap food is driving local farmers out of business in some areas, resulting in food shortages and farmers with no income.

Malthus predicted that if left unchecked, population increases would result in massive famine and disease. Actress/activist Mia Farrow took this photo of food distribution in famine-plagued Sudan, Africa.

People in Haiti were so desperate for resources that they stripped the hillsides bare, which then created other environmental problems, including erosion of soil, mudslides, and lack of habitat for animals and birds.

Four main criticisms have been raised about Malthus's theory. First, Malthus did not anticipate the role capitalism would play in population dynamics, exploiting raw materials and laborers and encouraging excessive consumption patterns in wealthy industrial nations. In fact, having large families made sense to many, who believed having more children provided more workers and more economic security (Robbins 2011). Second, Malthus's idea that food production would grow arithmetically and could not keep up with population growth must be modified in light of current agricultural techniques that increase yields, at least in some parts of the world. Third, Malthus saw abstinence from sex, even among the married, as the main method of preventing births and did not recognize the potential for contraception. Fourth, poverty has not always proven to be an inevitable result of population growth.

Two neo-Malthusians, scientists who accept much of his theory but make modifications based on current realities, are Garrett Hardin and Paul Ehrlich. Hardin, a biologist, argues that individuals' personal goals are not always consistent with societal goals and needs related to population growth. An individual may decide to have many children, but this could be detrimental to the whole society. If people act solely on their own and have many children, societal tragedy may well ensue (Hardin 1968).

Ehrlich adds to the formula of "too many people and too little food." The additional problem of a "dying planet" is caused by environmental damage. To hold on to economic gains, population must be checked, and to check population,

Scarcity of freshwater and other resources threatens survival. Women walk long distances to find water, as in these two water sources near Alem Ketema in Ethiopia. In the 19th century, Thomas Malthus predicted shortages of food and water due to population increases.

family planning is necessary (Ehrlich and Ehrlich 1990). Ehrlich's ideas can be summed up as follows:

> America and other rich nations have a clear choice today. They can continue to ignore the population problem and their own massive contributions to it. Then they will be trapped in a downward spiral that may well lead to the end of civilization in a few decades. More frequent droughts, more damaged crops and famines, more dying forests, more smog, more international conflicts, more epidemics . . . will mark our course. (Ehrlich and Ehrlich 1990:23)

The neo-Malthusians favor contraception rather than simple reliance on the moral restraint that Malthus proposed. They also acknowledge that much of the environmental damage is caused by corporate pollution and excessive consumption habits in affluent areas such as the United States, Canada, and Europe (Weeks 2012).

The bottom line is that Malthus went too far in arguing for *environmental determinism*, the idea that we can do little about the environment as it controls our lives. He could not anticipate the social and technological changes that would allow humans to increase population and production of food and other needs. However, his warnings still have merit and should be heeded as we try to balance consumption and production with population growth and development (Bell 2012).

Thinking Sociologically

What are contemporary examples of Malthus's checks on population growth—war, disease, famine? Are family planning and contraception sufficient to solve the problem of global overpopulation by humans? Can you think of other alternatives?

Demographic Transition: Explaining Population Growth and Expansion

Why should a change in the economic structure such as industrialization and movement from rural agricultural areas to urban cities have an impact on population size? One explanation is found in the **demographic transition theory**, *which compares countries' stages of economic development with trends in birth and death rates. It is used to determine how changes in economic structure and movement from agricultural areas to urban areas can have an impact on population size.*

Three stages of development are identified in this theory:

Stage 1: These populations have high birth- and death rates that tend to balance each other over time. Births may outpace deaths until some disaster diminishes the increase. This has been the pattern for most of human history.

Stage 2: Populations still have high birthrates, but death rates decline (i.e., more people live longer) because of improvements in health care and sanitation, establishment of public health programs, disease control and immunizations, and food availability and distribution. This imbalance between continuing high births and declining deaths means that the population growth rate is very high.

Stage 3: Populations level off at the bottom of the chart with low birthrates and low death rates. Most industrial and postindustrial societies are in this stage. Population growth rates in these countries are very low because Global North urban nuclear families are small.

These stages are illustrated in Figure 15.5.

Demographic transition theory helps explain the developmental stage and population trends in countries around the world, but it does not consider some important factors that affect the size of populations:

1. People's age at marriage determines how many childbearing years they have (late marriage means fewer years until menopause).
2. Contraceptive availability determines whether families can control their number of children.
3. A country's resources and land may determine how much population a country can support.
4. The economic structure of a country, religious beliefs, and political philosophies affect attitudes toward birth control and family size.
5. Economic expansion rates influence a country's need for labor.

Not all societies go through the same time frame in transition from one stage to another. For example, demographic transition occurred rapidly in Europe, where notions of modernization, urbanization, and progress evolved naturally from the cultural values. People generally married later, and the value of having children varied with resources available. In addition, many deadly diseases that at one time kept population growth in check were under control.

Critics argue that there is a built-in assumption that modernization in the second and third stages will result in rational choices about family size. Yet unless women gain status by having smaller families, they are likely to continue to have large families (Robbins 2011). However, economic development generally results in a decline in the birthrate. The process of modernization that parallels economic development puts pressure on extended families to break apart into smaller nuclear family units, especially as families move to crowded urban areas. Urban families tend to have fewer children because children are a liability and cannot help support the family. Economic development, modernization, and urbanization did not occur together in all parts of the world, so the outcome of the three-stage transition has not always occurred as predicted in the theory.

The *wealth flow theory* suggests that two strategies are operating in couples' personal decisions about their family size. When wealth flows from children to parents—that is, when children are an asset working on the family farm or laboring—parents have larger families. When wealth flows from parents to children, families are likely to have fewer children (Caldwell 1982). To raise a child born in 2008 to 18 years in the United States, for instance, costs an average of more than $222,360 (Belkin 2011).

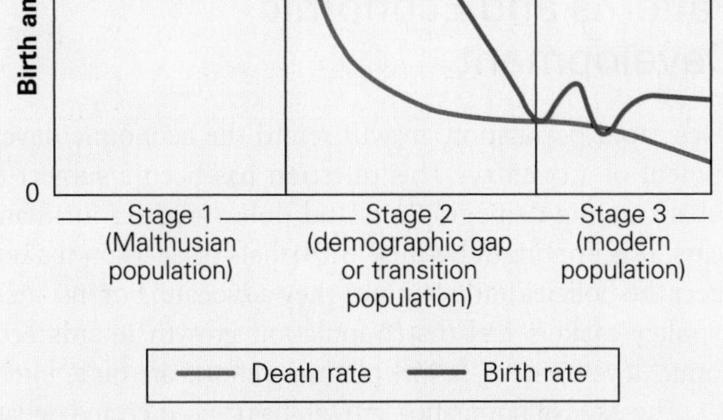

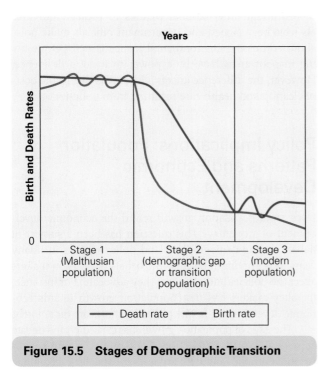

Figure 15.5 Stages of Demographic Transition

Conflict Theorists' Explanations of Population Growth

Karl Marx and Friedrich Engels did not agree with Malthus's idea that population growth outstrips food and resources because of people's fertility rates, resulting in poverty. They felt that social and structural factors built into the economic system were the cause of poverty. Capitalist structures resulted in wealth for the capitalists and created overpopulation and poverty for those at the periphery of the system. Workers were expendable, kept in competition for low wages, used when needed, and let go when unprofitable to capitalists. In short, for conflict theorists, inequitable distribution and control of resources are at the heart of the problem.

Socialist societies, Marx argued, could absorb the growth in population so the problem of overpopulation would not exist. In a classless society, all would be able to find jobs, and the system would expand to include everyone. Engels asserted that population growth in socialist societies could be controlled by the central government. This regulation is, in fact, what is happening in most present-day socialist countries through such methods as strict family planning and liberal abortion policies.

Environmental racism and justice are directly related to the social status differences of groups in society. People of color are 2 to 3 times more likely to live in communities with hazardous waste problems. It has become a pressing issue in many neighborhoods, especially poor minority areas where housing has knowingly been built on contaminated land (Bell 2012; United Church of Christ 2007).

Overpopulation presents a challenge to food and water resources, and large populations damage the environment and provide little ecological recovery time. The top photo shows pollution of a stream in Yunnan, China. The bottom photo pictures a billboard in Shanghai advertising China's "One Child Only" policy.

Toxic dumps and burns, hazardous waste sites, landfills on which people must live because of lack of space, and dumping waste in indigenous "First Nations" lands and abandoned chemical plants and mines occur not only in poor countries but also in poor areas of Global North countries. Regulations in the United States to prevent housing being built on contaminated land are controversial because they require testing and delay development. Conflict between haves and have-nots is clear in such an issue.

From these problems has come the *environmental justice movement*. Prominent on the agenda of many environmental groups is concern about contamination near poor, often minority neighborhoods. Race and social class often go together when justice is of concern, and that is true of environmental issues as well. Consider these examples: In Los Angeles, minority schools are located in areas with high levels of airborne toxins; in Missouri, industrial-scale hog farms are located in counties with low income; in Massachusetts, communities with high proportions of low-income minorities are 10 times more likely to experience chemical releases from industries than high-income communities. Other quality of life indicators like poor-quality drinking water and noise pollution from highways are common in low-income and minority neighborhoods (Bell 2012). One award-winning study in Chicago focused on efforts to have a more eco-friendly or "green" city by doing more recycling. However, there were substantial problems of pollution, disease risk, and other costs to the neighborhoods where this recycling was done. It is sobering to realize that environmentally friendly policies have often been implemented at a cost to those who have the fewest resources—people living in poverty and minorities (Pellow 2002).

Although international treaties to protect individuals have been signed and government officials make noise about addressing environmental justice issues, people living in poor areas have little power to make a difference. However, the difference affects all humans due to the costs of cleanup and health care resulting from pollution.

Policy Implications: Population Patterns and Economic Development

Does rapid population growth retard the economic development of a country? This question has been a subject of debate among demographers and policy makers for many years. It is important because the beliefs of decision makers affect the policies and solutions they advocate. For instance, if policy makers feel that population growth retards economic development, family planning efforts are more likely.

The issue of population growth has caused heated debate at several World Population Conferences. Some socialist and Catholic countries argue that capitalistic economic exploitation and political control, not population growth, cause poverty in Global South countries. They point out that multinational companies and foreign countries exploit poor countries' resources, sometimes with payoffs to government officials. This leaves poor people with no gains. High population growth contributes to global problems and policy challenges; countries cannot adjust quickly enough to provide the infrastructure (housing, health care, sanitation, education) for so many additional people. The largest impact of high fertility and resulting additional people is in five areas: food security and distribution of food sources; contribution of humans to climate change; ability of governments to reduce poverty; demographic shifts that affect populations such as urbanization and population aging; and health and maternal and child mortality. Government programs such as reproductive education and accessible contraception to reduce fertility but retain reproductive choice can help, but local traditions need to be considered for programs to be acceptable (World Economic Forum 2012). Also important to limiting population growth is providing opportunities for citizens, especially women, to obtain education and jobs.

In an urban area in Cambodia (Kampuchea), residents crowd onto this truck, a common form of transportation. With a high fertility rate and migration from rural to urban areas, crowded transportation is common.

Meso-Level Institutional Influences on Population Change

Populations change in (1) size (overall number of people), (2) composition (the makeup of the population, including sex ratio, age distribution, and religious or ethnic representation in the population), and (3) distribution (density or concentration in various portions of the land). The key demographic processes that cause change are **fertility** *(the birthrate)*, **mortality** *(the death rate)*, and **migration** *(movement of people from one place to another)*. Populations change when births and deaths are not evenly balanced or when significant numbers of people move from one area to another. Migration does not change the size or composition of the world as a whole, but can affect size or makeup in a local micro-level or national macro-level population. The most unpredictable yet controllable population factor in the world or in a nation is fertility.

Factors Affecting Fertility Rates

Jeanne, one of the coauthors of this book, was riding in the back of a "mammy wagon," a common means of transport in West Africa. Crowded in with the chickens and pigs and people, she did not expect the conversation that ensued. The man in his late 20s asked if she was married and for how long. Jeanne responded, "Yes, for three years." The man continued, "How many children do you have?" Jeanne answered, "None." The man commented, "Oh, I'm sorry!" Jeanne replied, "No, don't be sorry. We planned it that way!" This man had been married for 10 years to a woman 3 years younger than him and had eight children. The ninth was on the way. In answer to his pointed questions, Jeanne explained that she was not being cruel to her husband and that birth control was what prevented children, and no, it did not make sex less enjoyable. He expressed surprise that limiting the number of children was possible and rather liked the idea. He jumped at the suggestion that he visit the family planning clinic in the city. With his meager income, he and his wife were finding it hard to feed all the little mouths. The point is that knowledge of and access to family planning options are not always available.

Demographers consider micro-, meso-, and macro-level factors in attempting to understand fertility rates around the world. We know that individuals' personal decisions are key. People deciding to marry, couples' decisions to use contraception, their ideas about the acceptability of abortion, and whether they choose to remain childless can have an impact on national and global rates of population change. So choices at the micro level do make a difference at the macro level.

Economic Factors

Overpopulation is complex, related to poverty, the status of women, and exploitation of resources and labor by wealthy individuals and countries. These are just some factors that contribute to overpopulation. Note the cyclical nature of the problem—overpopulation leads to poverty, which leads to overpopulation. The relationship between poverty and population reduction is very complex, which makes agreement about a solution difficult.

Fertility also fluctuates with what is happening in meso-level institutions such as economic, political, and family systems. During depressions, for example, the rate of fertility tends to drop. However, macro-level structural factors also affect fertility: (a) level of economic prosperity within the nation, (b) the government's commitment to providing tax incentives or controlling contraception, (c) changes in norms and values about sexuality within a society, and (d) health care factors, including the availability of food and water.

We know that one of the most significant distinguishing characteristics between the rich Global North and the poor Global South countries is their fertility rates. The worldwide fertility rate has fallen in every major world region, but some still remain very high. Thirty-three Global South countries in sub-Saharan Africa and 14 in Asia have especially low incomes, high economic vulnerability, and poor indicators such as low life expectancy at birth and low levels of education. Yet these countries are growing at the fastest rate in the world—2.4% per year. The average number of children per woman in sub-Saharan Africa is 5.1, which is high, but that number has actually dropped since 1950, when the average was 6.7. In the Global North, the number of children per woman fell to 1.3 in many countries, although government subsidies for child care and tax relief for having children have kept the rate at about 2.0 in France, Norway, and some other countries (Population Reference Bureau 2012a). Figure 15.6 compares population increases in the Global North regions of the world with the poor Global South regions.

Extremely dense populations are often found in poverty-stricken areas. This slum in Kolkata (Calcutta), India, houses many rural migrants who are the lucky ones, having found a spot in the overpopulated sliver of land by a highway where they put up a shelter with whatever materials are available. Others sleep on sidewalks and highway medians.

Thinking Sociologically

What does Figure 15.6 (Comparison of Population Growth) tell you about changing patterns of population growth in different regions?

Women's fertile years are roughly from 15 to 44. One woman dies every minute in pregnancy or birth—that is 10 million women over a generation. Most of these live in Global South countries (United Nations Population Fund 2009). With care, these women would not be at such risk.

The key point is that various meso-level organizations, institutions, and government programs do affect fertility rates.

Government Influence

Some governments provide incentives to parents to have more children, whereas others discourage high fertility. Thus, meso- and macro-level social policies shape decisions of families at the micro level. Government *pronatalist policies* (those that encourage fertility) or *antinatalist policies* (those that discourage fertility) take several forms: (1) manipulating contraceptive availability; (2) promoting change in factors that affect fertility such as the status of women, education, and degree of economic development; (3) using propaganda for or against having children; (4) creating incentives (maternity leaves, benefits, and tax breaks) or penalties (such as fines); and (5) passing laws governing age of marriage, size of family, contraception, and abortion.

Antinatalist policies arise out of concern over available resources and differences in birthrates among population subgroups. Singapore, a country in Asia located off the Malay peninsula, consists of one main island and many smaller islands. It is one of the most crowded places on earth, with 18,645 people per square mile. This is compared with 84 in the United States, 9 in Canada, and 836 in Japan (Information Please Database 2007). The entire population of Singapore is urban, and 90% live in the capital city. The country has little unemployment and one of the highest per capita incomes in Asia. However, it depends on imports from other countries for most of its raw materials and food.

Some years ago, the central government in Singapore started an aggressive antinatalist plan. Birth control was

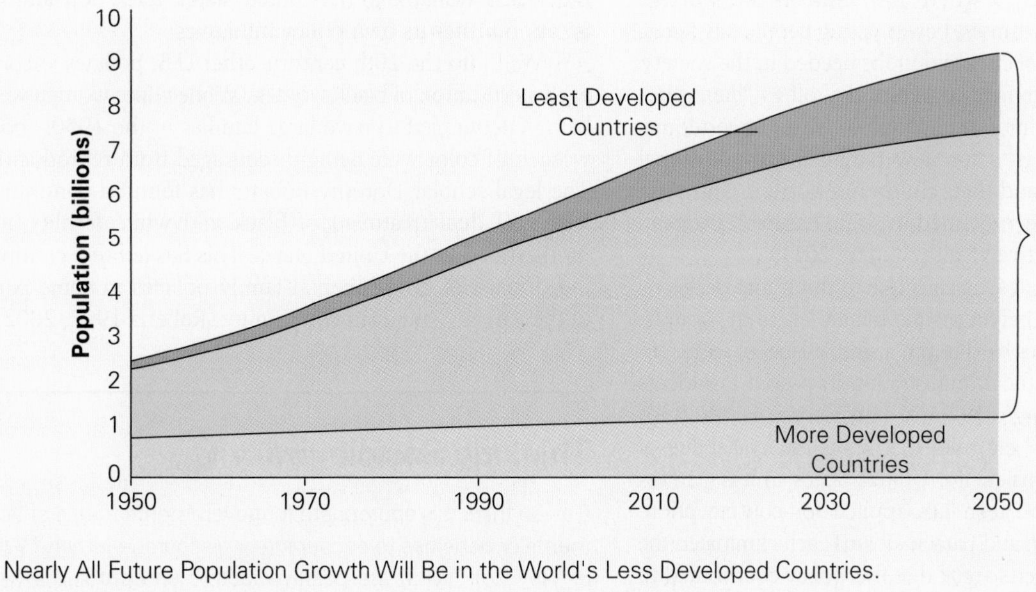

Figure 15.6 Comparison of Regions of Greatest Population Growth from 1950 to 2050.

Source: Population Reference Bureau 2012a

made available, and residents of Singapore who had more than one or two children were penalized with less health care, smaller housing, and higher costs for services such as education. Singapore now claims one of the lowest natural increase rates (the birthrate minus the death rate) in Southeast Asia, at 0.8% a year, just behind China. Singapore's governmental policies have controlled the natural increase rate.

China's antinatalist policy has been in effect since 1962. The government discourages traditional preferences for early marriage, large families, and many sons by using group pressure, privileges for small families, and easy availability of birth control and abortion. The government has reduced the fertility rate to 1.55 children per family, down from 1.6 in 2010. The government plan is to keep the rate at or below 1.8, the replacement level. An estimated 400 million births were averted due to the one-child policy (Johnson 2012). Unfortunately, there are side effects to such a stringent policy among a people who value male children. There has been an increase in selective abortions by couples hoping to have sons, and there are instances of female infanticide—killing of female infants when they are born—so that families can try for a male child. Recent challenges to the one-child policy come from two levels: (1) the micro level where individual women have been forced to have abortions, sometimes late in pregnancy, and (2) the macro level as Chinese society ages and birthrates are low, resulting in a shortage of young people to support the increasingly aging society (Zakaria 2012).

A condom mascot offers leaflets to teenagers in Bangkok, Thailand, during a promotional campaign to educate Thai youths on how to use condoms. The issue is partially related to birth control and partially to HIV/AIDS prevention. This is an antinatalist effort to lower the fertility rate.

Examples of pronatalist government policies can be seen in Eastern Europe where governments are worried about the drop in birthrates. Fewer young people pay taxes, and mass migration occurs to do jobs needed in the society. Incentives include giving workers a day off to "have sex"; free summer camps for young couples—without condoms; cars and monetary gifts for new parents; and additional benefits for parents and their children. Abortions and even birth control have been banned in some Eastern European countries (Reproductive Health Matters 2011).

In the United States, citizens like to think that decisions about fertility are entirely a private matter left to the couple. Indeed, it is sometimes hard to pin a simple label of antinatalist or pronatalist on the administration in power. Presidents Ronald Reagan, George W. Bush, and George H. W. Bush each implemented a "gag rule" that limits the availability of birth control for teens in the United States unless parents are informed that the teen has applied for contraception. Presidents Bill Clinton and Barack Obama each eliminated the gag policy. Many experts argue that this policy contributed to the increased teen pregnancy rates in the United States. Others argue that it is a parent's responsibility, not the government's, to deal with such matters. The Bush administration also blocked U.S. funding to international family planning groups that, among their services, offer abortion and abortion counseling, and he proposed a 19% cut in international family planning contributions ("Overseas Population Spending Threatened" 2006). The Obama administration reversed this abortion-funding policy, allowing international family planning clinics and the United Nations Population Fund to receive $610 million in U.S. funding for maternal health care and contraception, even if they provide counseling on abortion (CNN Politics 2009). This funding, according to the Guttmacher Institute, will have major effects on the world's population:

- 31.6 million women and couples receive contraceptive services and supplies;
- 9.4 million unintended pregnancies, including 4.1 unplanned births, are averted;
- 4 million induced abortions are averted (3 million of them unsafe);
- 22,000 maternal deaths are averted;
- 2.8 million fewer healthy years of life are lost among women; and
- 96,000 fewer children lose their mothers (Guttmacher Institute 2012b).

Both limits to contraceptive availability and prohibitions on abortion are pronatalist because they increase fertility. While promoting births may not be the intention of those who oppose birth control and abortion, the policy has the latent consequence of population increases. Other governmental policies that might encourage larger families, such as family tax breaks or access to day care centers, are much less available in the United States. Each new administration brings its own policy initiatives.

Well into the 20th century, other U.S. policies encouraged sterilization of black women. While white women were being encouraged to have large families in the 1950s, poor women of color were being discouraged from reproducing. The legal scholar Dorothy Roberts has found a continuing legacy of dual treatment of black and white fertility and motherhood in the United States. This has led to a continuing distrust of governmental family policies in some parts of the African American community (Roberts 1997, 2002).

Thinking Sociologically

Do you think it is appropriate for governments to use enticements or penalties to encourage or discourage fertility? Why or why not? What are positive factors and problems with different policies mentioned above?

Religious and Cultural Norms

Religion is a primary shaper of morality and values in most societies. Norms and customs of a society or subculture also influence fertility. In some cultures, pronatalist norms support a woman having a child before she is married so she can prove her fertility. In other societies, a woman can be stoned to death for having a child or even sex out of wedlock.

Some religious groups oppose any intervention, such as birth control or abortion, in the natural processes of conception and birth. Roman Catholicism, for example, teaches that large families are a blessing from God and that birth control is a sin. The Roman Catholic Church officially advocates the rhythm method to regulate conception, a less reliable method in lessening birthrates than contraception technology. However, a great many Catholics in the Western world are not following these teachings and are little different from their neighbors in use of contraception (Rodricks 2012). Nonreligious cultural customs affect fertility as well. Couples may be pressured to delay marriage until they are in their late 20s or even 30s when they are economically secure. In Ireland, the mean age at first marriage for men was 33.8 and for women 31.7 years (Taylor 2011). Although Ireland is a predominantly Catholic country, delayed marriage helps keep the birthrate down. Another custom that affects fertility in some polygamous societies is sexual abstinence after birth of a child, usually during the lactating (breast-feeding) period. The mother and child often go to live with the mother's family, an absence that lasts anywhere from 1 to 5 years.

Education

Women with secondary schooling have smaller families—substantially smaller than the families of women lacking that level of education. In other words, the higher women's status in society—as measured by education level and job opportunities—the lower their fertility (Population Reference Bureau 2013a). If a country wants to control population growth, raising the status of women is key. Figure 15.7 shows the relationship between education and family size in five Global South countries (Population Reference Bureau 2012b). Note in the figure that the higher the education level, the lower the fertility rate and population growth. So, again, education and reduction of poverty are major variables contributing to moderation.

Studies repeatedly show that investing in education of girls and women raises every index of a country's progress toward economic growth and development. An estimated 101 million children are out of school, and more than half are girls (UNICEF 2011). Of the world's population over 15 years, 83.7% are literate—that is, can read and write. Of males 88.3% and of females 79.2% are literate. At this point more than two thirds of the world's illiterate adults are found in just eight countries (Bangladesh, China, Egypt, Ethiopia, India, Indonesia, Nigeria, and Pakistan), and of

In Indonesia, Nur Azizah binti Hanafiah, 22, receives a caning, having been found by a citizen having illegal sex with her boyfriend at her house. This Aceh region of Indonesia has practiced Islamic Sharia law since 2001. In some societies, she would have been stoned to death for having premarital sex.

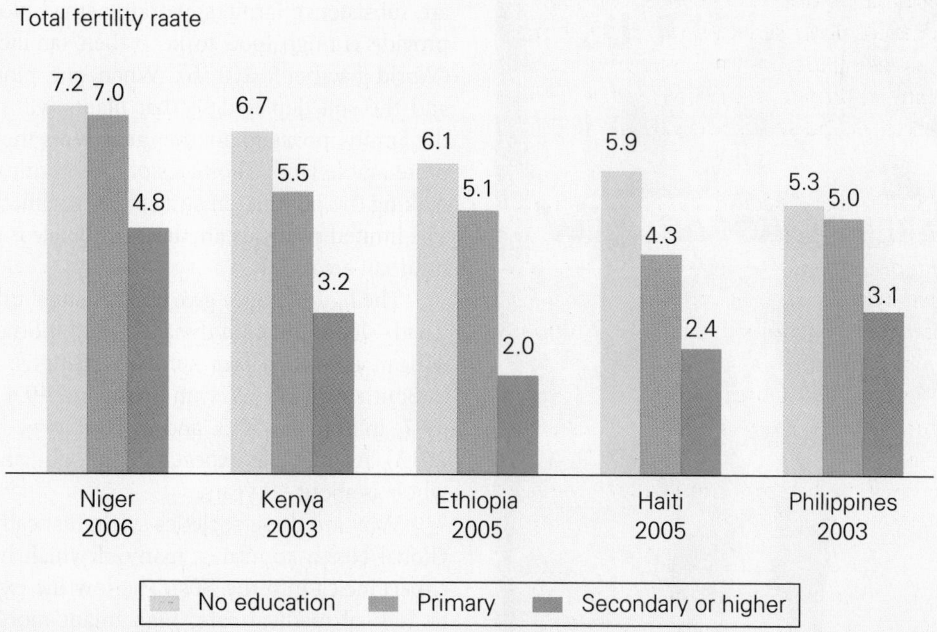

Figure 15.7 Women's Education and Family Size in Selected Countries, 2000s

Source: Population Reference Bureau (2012b).

the illiterate in those countries, women comprise two thirds of the total (Index Mundi 2012h). Although the gender gap in literacy has narrowed, it persists in sub-Saharan Africa, some Arab states, and South and West Asia.

Availability of contraception may determine a woman's ability to control the number of children she has. Family planning programs and contraceptive use have increased in much of the world. However, availability and use in sub-Saharan Africa remains low. Global use of modern contraception was 57% in 2012, but 222 million Global South women who would like to control family size are not using contraception because of limited access, fear of side effects, cultural or religious opposition, and gender-based barriers (World Health Organization 2012). The consequence is 76 million unplanned births a year (Medical News Today 2009).

As seen above, many factors affect fertility rates. Lower population growth means less pressure on governments to provide emergency services for booming populations and more attention to services such as schools, health care, and jobs. Most population experts encourage governments and other meso-level institutions in fast-growing countries to act aggressively to control population size. There are consequences of population fluctuations in affluent parts of the world as well as poor parts. The impact of the baby boom in the United States illustrates this, as discussed in the next "Sociology in Our Social World" on page 573.

AIDS is a huge problem in Africa. This roadside billboard in Kitwe, Zambia, is part of a campaign for education to help control the pandemic.

Thinking Sociologically

After reading "Sociology in Our Social World," discuss what impact the baby boom and baby boomlet have had on your opportunities for education and a career. How will retirement of baby boomers affect your opportunities?

Factors Affecting Mortality Rates

Life expectancy refers to *the average number of years a person in a particular society can expect to live.* It indicates the overall health conditions in a country. In affluent countries, medicines cure many of the diseases that cause death in the Global South. For example, polluted water spreads diseases as seen in the cholera epidemics in Cuba, Ghana, and Haiti in 2012. Note that the life expectancy in Haiti is 62.5 years. That means that the average Haitian has about 62.5 years to live (Index Mundi 2012e). Imagine living in Chad, Africa, where the life expectancy at birth is 48.7 years and the average number of children for each mother is 4.9. Of every 1,000 babies born alive, 93.6 will die within the first year (World Factbook 2013b). At 24, life is half over. Over 72% of men and women live in rural areas where most are subsistence farmers, working small plots that may not provide enough food to keep their families from starving (World Factbook 2013b). When one plot is overfarmed and the soil depleted so that plants will no longer grow, the family moves to another and clears the land, depleting more arable land. Shortages of food result in malnutrition, making the population susceptible to illnesses and disease. The limited medical care that is available is mostly available in urban areas.

The figures above give us substantial information about Chad—its population dynamics and mortality. Some other African countries face similar situations: life expectancy in South Africa is 49.4, in Swaziland 49.4, in Afghanistan 49.7, in Somalia 50.8, and in Zimbabwe 51.8 (Infoplease 2013). Average life expectancy for sub-Saharan Africa as a whole is about 49 years.

Why are these societies so dramatically different from Global North countries, many of which have average life expectancies into the 80s? The low life expectancy is due to lack of medical care, high infant mortality, epidemics such as AIDS, wars and civil strife, corrupt governments, droughts and famine, malnutrition, and resulting susceptibility to diseases. Table 15.2 on page 574 shows the infant mortality rate around the world, meaning the number of infant deaths (children under 1 year) per 1,000 births. This is a key indicator of a country's overall well-being.

Sociology in Our Social World

The Significance of the Baby Boom

At the end of World War II, the birthrate shot up temporarily in most countries involved in the war, as many young people who had been forced to delay marriage made up for lost time. The postwar economy was growing, people were employed in relatively well-paying positions, and the norms supported large families. While this baby boom lasted only about 3 years after World War II in Britain, it lasted 17 years in the United States, from 1946 to 1963.

The baby boom phenomenon has had many impacts. During the late 1960s, school boards and contractors were busy building schools to educate the growing number of children. By the 1980s, student numbers declined, and towns were consolidating schools and closing buildings. When the baby boomers entered the job market starting in the mid-1960s, there were great numbers of applicants for jobs, and employers could pay less. The supply was so great they were assured that someone would take the job.

Two decades later, it was much easier for young people to find jobs because there were fewer of them in that age range looking for starting-level positions. However, that generation is finding it hard to get promotions because the baby boomers have dominated so many of the high-level positions. In addition, trends in marketing and advertising have, for years, been dictated by the baby boomer generation because they are such a large segment of the consumer public.

By the 1960s, people's views of the ideal family size and the proper age for marriage changed. The zero population growth movements and environmental concerns slowed the rate of growth. The period from the late 1960s to early 1970s has been referred to as a "baby bust" or the "birth dearth." (This fluctuation resulted in a population structure that did not look very much like a pyramid, as shown in Figure 15.8 on page 581.)

In the mid-1970s and into the 1980s, when the baby boom generation started having babies, there was another baby boom—or "baby boomlet"—but it was much smaller because the baby boomers had smaller families. The result is that population growth in many developed countries has remained below the replacement level, or the number of births or migrants a location needs to maintain its population. Currently, growth in the overall size of populations in the Global North is due largely to immigration. Otherwise, many populations would be declining more significantly.

The 1950s was the era of the baby boom.

Population growth and change also trigger cultural and social change. Each generation—Silent and "Greatest" generations, Boomers, Gen X, and Millennials—faces new and different political environments, ethnic group changes, and societal changes (Pew Research Center 2011). Gen Xers (or the children of the baby boomers) now look at careers as transient, and they often move from job to job to advance instead of working up the internal labor market of one firm or organization. Similarly, Generation Xers are experiencing "delayed adulthood" (Furstenberg 2003). Unlike their parents, who saw having a family as the major rite of passage for growing up, Gen Xers spend more time attaining education and delay partnering and parenting until they achieve fiscal security. These are two strategies societies have made to adapt to population shifts. The point is that extreme fluctuations in fertility rates can affect societies in a number of ways.

Table 15.2 Infant Mortality Rates Around the World

Region	*Infant Mortality Rate*[a]
World	41
More affluent (Global North) countries	5
Less affluent (Global South) countries	49
Least affluent (the very poor Global South)	72
Africa	67
North America	6
Latin America	20
Asia	37
Europe	5

Source: Population Reference Bureau (2012d).

a. The infant mortality rate indicates deaths of children under 1 year per 1,000 births.

Migration and Mobility: Why and Where People Move

Most of us have moved one or more times in our lives, a process called **migration**, *the movement of people from one place to another*. Perhaps, we have moved to a larger house down the block, maybe to another area for a job opportunity or school, or even to another country altogether. The process of changing one's place of residence is called *geographic mobility*. Over the history of the human race, people have migrated to the far reaches of the globe. Because of adaptability to climatic and geographic barriers, humans have dispersed to more areas of the globe than any other species. Even inhospitable locations such as the Arctic North and the South Pole have human settlements.

The *push-pull* model points out that some people are pushed from their original locations by wars, plagues, famine, political or religious conflicts, economic crises, or other factors and pulled to new locations by economic opportunities or political and religious tolerance. Most people do not leave a location unless they have been forced out or they have a viable alternative in the new location. They weigh the benefits of moving versus the costs (Weeks 2012). Migration is often initiated at the micro level: a lucrative job offer in another location requires a move, the family dwelling becomes too small, a relative needs help, or a family member's health requires a different climate. If an opportunity is present, the individual or family may move. However, if the risks are high, if the information about migration is scarce, or if negative factors such as leaving family behind are present, individuals may decide not to move. For rational choice theorists, assessment of costs and benefits by individuals are the driving forces in migration.

Although the decision to move is often a personal or family one, it is also influenced by the sociocultural environment. History is replete with examples of large groups of people who left an area because of aspirations to improve their life chances, hopes of retaining a way of life, or expulsion by political, economic, or religious forces. Chinese railroad workers came to the United States for economic reasons. Amish and Mennonite settlers from Europe sought religious freedom and preservation of their way of life. The Amish, a group originating in Germany, left Germany *en masse*, and the members of this group now live entirely in North America. Italian immigration to the United States took place in a collective manner. When a family left Italy, it would usually move to a U.S. city where a relative or a previous acquaintance lived. Thus, residents of entire apartment buildings in the North End of Boston were from the same extended family, or entire city blocks of people came from the same town or region of southern Italy (Gans 1962). Also, former colonial powers have numerous immigrants from colonized countries. This has helped make many European cities, such as London and Paris, the multicultural environments they are today.

Those living at the receiving end have not always been welcoming, and in fact have often tried to isolate the newcomers in ghettos, preventing them from moving into neighborhoods. Job opportunities are sometimes limited, especially in difficult economic times when competition for jobs is greatest (Foner 2005). Immigration laws in the United States, for example, reflect the nation's attitudes toward immigrants at different time periods. The Chinese Exclusion Act of 1882 ended Chinese immigration; the "National Origin System" in 1921 targeted southern Europeans and reduced immigration from Greece and Italy; the Immigration and Naturalization Act of 1965 and the Immigration Reform and Control Act of 1986 aimed to keep out less skilled and illegal immigrants but facilitated entry of skilled workers and relatives of U.S. residents (Schaefer 2012). Current stalemates in the U.S. Congress over immigration reform show the contentious nature of policies related to immigration, especially illegal immigrants crossing borders.

Social science studies of the impact of immigration counter some of the negative stereotypes, pointing out the net economic gain for countries. Yet some U.S. states and European cities are burdened with newcomers who are not yet self-sufficient. California Proposition 187, for example, illustrated anger against illegal immigration. Known as "Save Our State" (SOS), this bill denied education, welfare, and nonemergency health care to illegal immigrants (Shin and Havrilla 2008). These policies often make life difficult for immigrants, even if they do have official papers.

Migrations can be international, from one country to another, or internal, within a single nation. Moves from rural farm communities to urban areas are a common internal migration pattern found around the world. For people who depend on the land, drought and other adverse environmental conditions force movement. International moves are often influenced by political unrest or discrimination against a group of people. Nazi persecutions of the Jewish population are one example.

International Migration

More than 3.1% of the world's population is "on the go" each year. That is 214 million international migrants, or 1 out of every 33 persons in the world. Half are women. These migrants change the size and characteristics of populations around the world, from those being expanded to those being left behind (International Organization for Migration 2012).

From 1995 to 2000, 2.6 million migrants left the Global South for Global North countries, and more than half of them entered the United States or Canada. An entirely new phenomenon—previously unknown in human history—is also occurring: Cyber-migration is a process by which the Internet creates global Internet connections across physical and cultural borders, allowing for new opportunities for migration (http://cybermigration.com).

International migration is especially common where political turmoil, wars, famines, or natural disasters ravage a country. *Refugees*, those "who flee in search of refuge in times of war, political oppression, or religious persecution," numbered 43.7 million, half of them children. This is a 15-year high (UNHCR 2012). The ongoing crises in Syria and South Sudan will add significantly to the numbers. Roughly 27.5 million citizens are also *internally displaced*, forcibly relocated within their own countries by violent conflict or environmental disaster. Countries with the most refugees were Afghanistan and Iraq, accounting for 45% of all refugees under United Nations responsibility (Koleth 2012).

The tsunamis in Indonesia and Japan, the hurricanes that hit Haiti and New Orleans and the Gulf coastal areas, and the flooding that affected farms and towns along the Mississippi River are examples of natural disaster displacement. People from war-torn Darfur, in Sudan, Africa, seek refuge in neighboring Chad. The list of international population movements due to internal crises and natural disasters is extensive and constantly changing. These are not just irrelevant events occurring elsewhere in the world. They involve human beings who are seeking a place to live and may end up as your neighbors. Each migrant has a unique story.

This ship containing more than 300 immigrants from Eritrea, East Africa, was spotted by an Italian customs police helicopter. Every year, thousands of illegal immigrants departing from the Mediterranean coasts of Africa try to reach Europe through Sicily. The voyage is dangerous, and many immigrants are found dead on the Sicilian shoreline, but the desire for a better future keeps the masses coming.

Mohammed from Senegal traverses the streets of Verona, Italy, during the day selling children's books and trying to make enough to live on, hoping he might have some money left to send back to his family. Mohammed speaks five languages and has a high school education, but opportunities in his homeland are limited, and he is an illegal immigrant in Italy. Most Global North countries are desirable destinations for those seeking economic opportunities. European countries, especially those that formerly had colonies, have large populations of immigrants from North Africa and the Middle East. These immigrants often face great peril in their attempts to seek a better life, and many find themselves in crowded, unsanitary housing conditions with little economic opportunity once they arrive in European cities.

Economic opportunities and the demand for cheap labor have brought many guest workers from the Global

South to European nations and the Persian Gulf states, where foreign workers make up the majority of the labor force. Women, who make up a growing proportion of those seeking economic opportunities, total 50% of legal immigrants to the United States, or 18.9 million. Over one quarter of these women came from Mexico (Immigration Policy Center 2010). This high percentage has to do with the demand for specific types of work. For example, women and children often enter countries illegally due to human trafficking.

Prior to 1914, when World War I began, it was not standard practice for nations to require a passport to enter a country (Friedman 2005). Because most people could not afford intercontinental travel, controlling the flow of people was not an issue. The United States has had a more restrictive stance than Canada or most European countries regarding immigration (Farley 2010). Still, the number of foreign-born people in the United States was 39.9 million (or 12.9%), an increase of 4% over one year (Center for American Progress Immigration Team 2012; Passel and Cohn 2012). This number is expected to rise to 48 million by 2025, resulting in 14% of the U.S. population being foreign-born (Morello and Keating 2009). Forty-four percent were naturalized citizens, 24% were legal permanent residents, and 29% were unauthorized migrants (Center for American Progress Immigration Team 2012).

About 11.5 million illegal migrants now live in the United States, an increase of one third since 2000. They make up 5.2% of the U.S. labor force, but only 3.7% of the nation's population (Center for American Progress Immigration Team 2012; CNN 2012). Some people are so desperate to cross over to the United States that they risk everything. Although numbers have dropped from 253 in 2009–2010 to 179 in 2011–2012, still 150 to 250 migrants die each year trying to cross the desert to the U.S. border (No More Deaths 2012).

Luis is an illegal immigrant. His story in the next "Sociology Around the World," illustrates the hardships that migrants will endure to seek a better life for themselves and their families. To these migrants a better life awaits *if* they can reach it.

Thinking Sociologically

First, read the essay on the Entering the United States on page 577. What are reasons that Luis and others risk their lives, pay all their money, and know there is a likelihood of being deported or not getting a job? How can this be explained by conflict, symbolic interaction, and rational choice theories?

Two factors curb migrations: (1) restrictive immigration laws of receiving countries and (2) economic recessions. During recessions, many countries restrict immigration by passing strict immigration quotas, even for political refugees from war-torn countries. In fact, the number of immigrants to the United States has dropped with the economic downturn by 14%, or 1.7 million people between 2007 and 2009, according to some estimates (Jacoby 2009).

Since the terrorist attacks of September 11, 2001, the idea that the U.S. borders are porous has been highly divisive as the U.S. Congress and state legislatures struggle to find appropriate immigration policies. The lack of agreement stems from conflicts over how the country feels about immigrants. Some favor the diversity and new ideas brought by skilled, highly educated immigrants, as well as the labor brought by low-skilled immigrants, who work at jobs not filled by U.S. citizens. Conflicts focus on who the migrants are, their religions, economic impact of immigrants, settlement patterns, whether immigrants bring crime, political loyalties of immigrants, moral values, and work habits. Research finds that, for the most part, immigrants are industrious, innovative, and hardworking. They pay taxes and contribute to their communities. In 2009 there were 4.31 legal migrants to the United States per 1,000 population (Migration Information Source 2011). However, 9/11 affected attitudes about immigration, with a 20% increase in U.S. citizens favoring policies restricting immigration. One such policy, for example, is the fence along a length of the Mexican-U.S. border (Inhofe 2008). Another is an increase in border patrols. While the Obama administration has pushed for immigration reform in Congress, this is a controversial topic on which agreement is hard to reach (Migration Information Source 2011).

Many laws protect the rights of immigrant workers and their families to education and health care. Most immigrants are of working age and will account for three quarters of the labor force increase between 2010 and 2020 (Kochhar 2012); they will account for almost all of the population increase within 5 to 25 years (Population Reference Bureau 2012e).

The debate about immigration in the United States and other countries is intense, and the solutions will not be easy. The Obama administration in the United States has proposed changes that have yet to be enacted into law by Congress, but the new policy is unlikely to be as restrictive as many against immigration would like as indicated by the change to allow children of undocumented migrants to stay in the United States if they are under 30 years old, are in school or working, and have been in the United States continuously for the past 5 years.

Internal Migration in the United States

The rate of internal migration in the United States is high compared with that in most places in the world. Patterns of migration have primarily involved individual "pull" to economic opportunities and better housing. Almost half report

Sociology Around the World

Entering the United States From South of the Border

Nancy Brown Diggs

In March, when Luis and his group of 60 made the journey (across the Arizona desert), temperatures can range as high as the nineties during the day and plunge to freezing at night. The group was told that they would be walking in the desert for about six hours, and to be sure to bring food and water for that time. They were to carry nothing else, in order not to slow down their travel. As often happens, not long after their start, their guide claimed that in order to avoid the Immigration and Naturalization Service they would take a longer way—a march through the desert that would end up lasting a hellish two and a half days, almost all the way without food or water. It was so hot during the day that when they chanced upon water tanks for animals, they rushed to gulp down the green and slimy water—at least most did.

Along the path, the travelers skirted the remains of one man who hadn't made it. Having been instructed to bring nothing but the clothes on their backs, they were not able to bury him.

At night in the desert cold, without extra clothing or blankets, Luis and his companions huddled together for warmth. In order not to be spotted, they were told to wear dark clothes and no white hats. Smoking and whistling were also forbidden. At last they came to a highway to be crossed, where they would wait until late at night when there was no traffic at all. When a car stopped on the road, the guide warned everyone not to move and to keep their eyes closed so the light wouldn't reflect off the whites.

When all was dark and quiet, the guide called another coyote, who came in about a half-hour with two vans. The sound of a helicopter caused everyone to push and shove in a vain attempt to squeeze 60 people into the two vehicles. Some had to remain behind, including Luis, who waited anxiously for the coyotes to return. Fortunately, there was a big incentive: Luis and his companions had not yet paid them.

At the next step of the journey, the immigrants were loaded into a truck trailer that was "incredibly hot," with no water, let alone air conditioning. After traveling some 400 miles, they eventually arrived in the Los Angeles area where they were able to buy plenty of food and drinks. After spending the night in a safe house, Luis and his group met their new American coyote who sent them off in different directions. Luis took a bus to Las Vegas where his uncle lived.

From: Nancy Brown Diggs, *Hidden in the Heartland* (2011).

housing as the main reason for their relocation: A better apartment or house, owning rather than renting, cheaper housing, and a better neighborhood with less crime are primary reasons for moving. Table 15.3 on page 578 provides reasons for moving that fall into several categories.

During different historical periods, movement directions have varied. For many years, rural residents in the United States moved to higher-income urban areas. Until the 1950s, people moved out of the southern states and into northern states, especially north central states. Then the pattern reversed, and the flow started south and west. Movement since the 1960s has been toward the Sunbelt, especially to California, Arizona, Texas, and Florida. Movement to the Pacific Coast and even Alaska has also increased due to economic opportunities in these locations.

One major form of internal migration is **urbanization**—*the process by which an increasing percentage of the population moves from rural areas to more densely populated cities.* For people who are seeking economic opportunity, excitement, and anonymity, they are "pulled" to cities. The urbanization process involves a change of lifestyle for individuals that results from living in cities. This process is so important that the second half of this chapter is devoted to analysis of urbanization of the population across the globe.

Although decisions about family size and migration are individual ones, they are influenced by what happens at the meso and macro levels as we see in the next section.

Table 15.3 **Reasons for Moving by Type of Move, 2009 (in Percentages)**

		Type of Mobility		
Reasons for Mobility	*All Movers*	*Intracounty*	*Intercounty*	*From Abroad*
Family-related reasons	**26.3**	**26.5**	**26.6**	**19.9**
Change in marital status	5.4	5.5	5.4	2.9
To establish own household	9.5	11.6	5.4	2.6
Other family reasons	11.5	9.5	15.8	14.4
Housing reasons	**45.9**	**57.2**	**24.3**	**5.7**
Wanted to own home	5.5	6.6	3.6	0.2
New/better house/ apartment	14.5	18.6	6.5	2.5
Cheaper housing	11.1	13.9	5.8	0.4
Work-related reasons	**17.9**	**8.9**	**35.5**	**48.5**
New job/job transfer	8.7	2.1	22.0	28.1
To look for work/lost job	2.7	1.0	5.4	15.8
Closer to work/easier commute	5.0	5.0	5.6	1.0
Retired	0.4	0.2	0.8	0.9
Other job-related reasons	0	6	0.8	
Other reasons (college, health, climate, natural disaster)	**9.8**	**7.5**	**13.6**	**25.9**

Source: U.S. Census Bureau (2011f).

Thinking Sociologically

What are the benefits and costs for individuals and governments of extensive internal migration? What are the advantages and disadvantages of having large numbers of internal immigrants?

Micro-Level Population Patterns

You might get the impression that population studies are mostly about other places and problems that do not affect your country. However, understanding demography can be extremely important for comprehending social processes very close to your everyday life. While most Global North countries do not have massive famines or population explosions, population fluctuations influence them in many ways. Consider the life choice decisions you as an individual will be making regarding education, employment, and retirement.

In 1969, Keith, one of the coauthors of this book, lived in Boston, and his wife taught in a suburban school system there. The elementary school where she taught had four first-grade classrooms, with 28 children per room—112 first graders in the school. By the next year, the decline in the fertility rate 6 years earlier was being felt, and the number of first graders declined. Within 4 years, the number of first graders in her school was reduced to 40, with two classrooms and only 20 students per class. Some school systems lost half of their student population in a few years. One year, first-grade teachers were losing their jobs or having to move to another grade, and the next year, it was second-grade teachers who were scrambling. The third year, third-grade teachers were in oversupply, and so forth. With low demand, these were not times for college students to be pursuing teaching careers. A personal decision was being influenced by population trends—and this pattern continues.

We have already mentioned the impact of the baby boom (the high fertility rates from 1946 to about 1963) and the following baby bust (the drop in fertility for more than a decade following the baby boom). The impact on the population is graphically represented in the population pyramid of the United States (see Figures 15.8 and 15.9). As we can see, the U.S. population no longer looks anything like a pyramid, yet from it we can tell a great deal about job prospects, retirement security, career decisions, and deviance rates, to name only a few of the outcomes. As that bulge for the baby boomer group moves into the senior citizens' category, it is likely to have a real impact on the society.

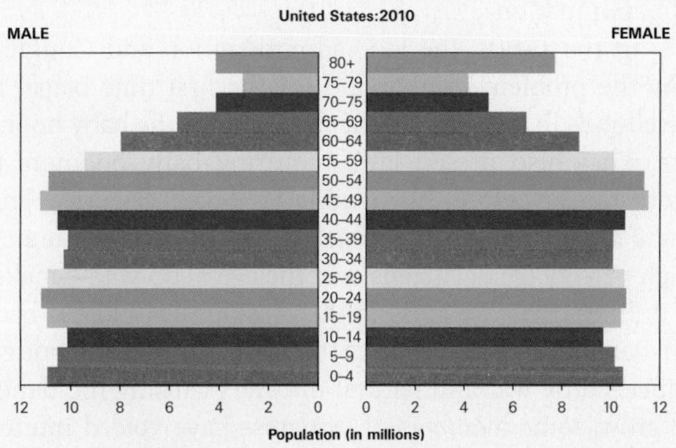

Figure 15.8 United States, 2010

Source: Nationmaster (2011).

Thinking Sociologically

Why do population experts predict the population pyramid will look like Figure 15.9 by 2050? What factors in society might lead to this? What kinds of problems do you think this sort of configuration might cause?

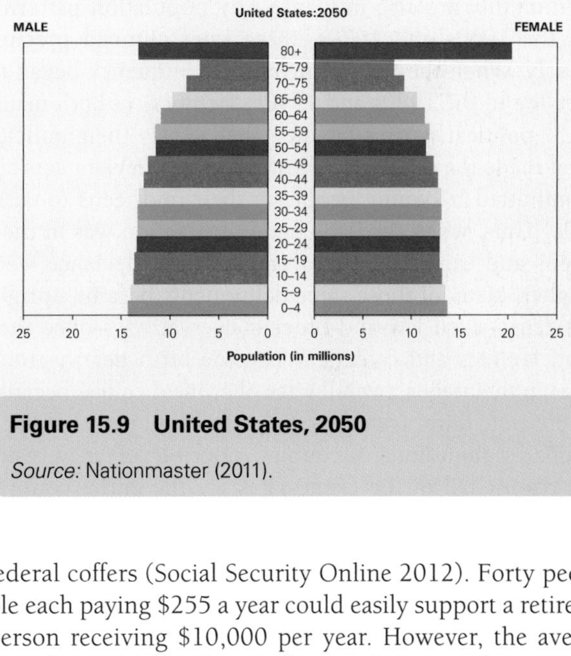

Figure 15.9 United States, 2050

Source: Nationmaster (2011).

The decision about your career choice is a deeply personal decision, but population trends also shape that decision. For example, if a business that produces baby products expands its production shortly after a dip in fertility rates, the timing of the business expansion may cause severe financial hardships or even bankruptcy for the company. Smart businesspeople pay a great deal of attention to characteristics of the population. That same information might be relevant to an individual deciding on a career. For example, this is an incredibly good time for students who enjoy working with older people (gerontology) or in the medical field to think about a career in gerontology or health care.

Retirement is another topic for which population patterns are critical. Most countries in the Global North are struggling with how young working people are going to support the nonworking aging populations. The number of working people contributing to pensions compared with retirees who depend on support is changing dramatically. Systems in many countries are in trouble because of low birthrates and increasing numbers of nonworking elderly people.

When Social Security was established in the United States in the 1930s, life expectancy from birth was 58 for men and 62 for women (Social Security Administration 2013). The number of people in the age-dependent categories of under 15 and over 65 was low. For each person who received Social Security in 1945, 42 paid into the federal coffers (Social Security Online 2012). Forty people each paying $255 a year could easily support a retired person receiving $10,000 per year. However, the average life expectancy has shifted, and the age-dependent population has increased. Currently in the United States, 13.5% of the population is over the age of 65, as opposed to 4% in the 1930s (World Factbook 2013j). Moreover, predictions are that by 2035, 20% of the population will be over 65. As the baby boomers are beginning to collect Social Security, the people born during the birth dearth are increasingly the ones in their prime earning years, but there are far fewer of them paying into the system. Even by 2010, there were roughly three beneficiaries for each person covered by Social Security (Social Security Online 2012). When commentators and politicians say Social Security is in trouble, therefore, they are not generally saying it has been mismanaged. They are pointing to problems created by changes in the composition of the U.S. population.

In the 1980s, the U.S. administration and Congress saw the problem coming and for the first time began to save funds in a Social Security account for the baby boomers. They also passed laws requiring baby boomers to work longer before they qualify for Social Security. That there are so many baby boomers—and that an extremely high percentage of citizens over the age of 65 vote—makes it unlikely that Congress or the president would cut back on benefits to this group. Still, with the federal budget squeezed by war and natural disasters causing the deficit to grow, some members of Congress have voiced interest in "borrowing" from the Social Security reserves. Members of the younger generations will be the ones to pay if insufficient funds are available for the baby boomers, and their future pensions may be in jeopardy. The aging population and need for funds could have a profound influence on your own family budget and retirement.

Rates of deviance and juvenile delinquency in a local community are also influenced by population patterns. In the 1960s and 1970s, these rates climbed precipitously. When the rates of juvenile delinquency began to decline in the 1980s and 1990s, members of both major U.S. political parties claimed that it was their policies that made the difference. However, most deviant acts are committed by young people in their mid-teens to early 20s. Thus, when the baby boom generation was in their teens and early 20s, the overall rates of deviance were higher. Many of those same delinquents became upright citizens—even law-and-order conservatives—once they had families and careers. When the birth dearth group was in their teens, overall rates of crime dropped because there were fewer teenagers. So private and personal decisions by thousands of couples (micro level) may result in rise or fall of the crime rates for the entire country 15 years later.

Because population trends will shape your life, understanding those trends can help you use that knowledge to your advantage. To illustrate the power of demographic trends on individual decisions, the next "Engaging Sociology" provides an exercise in problem solving using information from population pyramids of U.S. cities.

Thinking Sociologically

Have you thought about economic security after retirement? What plans can you make now for this long period of life after work? Why is this planning important?

In Mumbai (Bombay) many children have no choice but to sleep on the streets each night.

Urbanization: Movement From Rural to Urban Areas

Mumbai (Bombay), India; Caracas, Venezuela; Lagos, Nigeria; Shanghai, China; and New York City, United States—all are bustling megacities (cities with more than 10 million people) with traffic congestion and people rushing to their destinations. Carts, bicycles, and taxis weave in and out of traffic jams. The local spices and other aromas

Engaging Sociology

Population Pyramids and Predicting Community Needs and Services

Study these three population pyramid graphs. Based on what you see, answer the following questions:

1. Which community would be likely to have the lowest crime rate? Explain.
2. Which would be likely to have the most cultural amenities (theaters, art galleries, concert halls, and so forth)? Explain.
3. Imagine you were an entrepreneur planning on starting a business in one of these communities.
   a. Name three businesses that you think would be likely to succeed in each community. Explain.
   b. Name one business that you think would be unlikely to succeed in each community. Explain.

Norfolk, Virginia

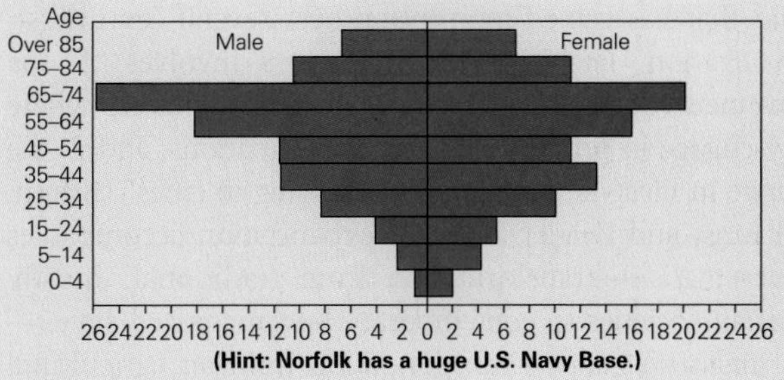

(Hint: Norfolk has a huge U.S. Navy Base.)

Bloomington, Indiana

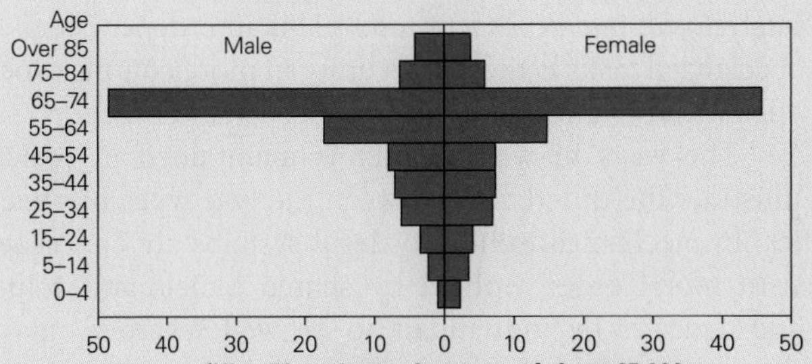

(Hint: Bloomington is a town of about 65,000 and is the home of Indiana University, a large Big Ten university.)

Naples, Florida

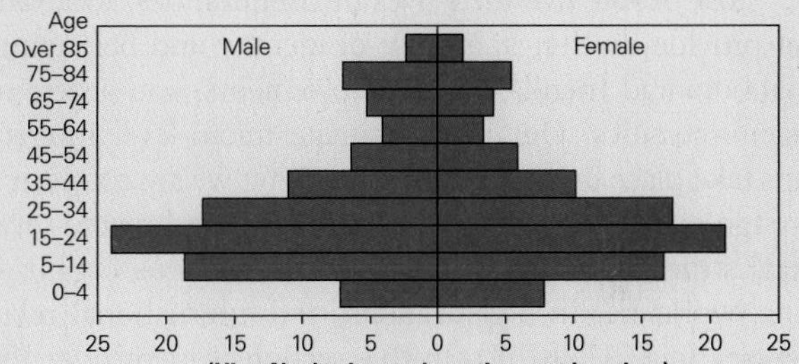

(Hint: Naples is a major retirement location.)

scent the air. Sidewalk merchants display vegetables and fruits unique to the country. Beggars and the homeless, often migrants from rural areas, dot the sidewalks, while merchants sell colorful wares. Cities are vibrant places with diversity and contributions of a variety of ethnic traditions coming together. The amazing sights, sounds, smells, tastes, and cultural activities—from art and theater, to music and nightclubs—mean there is always excitement. There is also the draw of possible exciting and high-paying jobs. These options and opportunities lure people to cities.

For people who are seeking economic opportunity, excitement, and anonymity, they are "pulled" to cities. Migration is most often from rural areas to urban cities. The urbanization process involves a change of lifestyle for individuals that results from living in cities (Brunn, Williams, and Zeigler 2003). The problem is that the poor, who come to cities to find opportunities, often live with no running water, electricity, or sewage disposal and lack basic services, including health care and education. They set up makeshift shelters of any materials available. Some live on the streets.

Countries and cities have little money to provide needed services to the migrants, and migrants often lack the skills needed for success in urban areas. Yet the world continues to become more urbanized as small farms in rural areas cannot support the growing populations.

The second half of this chapter is a continuation of the discussion of demographic patterns. However, we will return here to the pattern used in previous chapters of discussing micro-level analysis first, followed by meso- and macro-level analyses. First, how do urban environments affect us as individuals?

These megacities around the world are part of a global trend that has gained momentum over several centuries—urbanization. The urbanization process involves "1. the movement of people from rural to urban places, where they engage in primarily non-rural occupations, and 2. the change in lifestyle that results from living in cities" (Brunn, Williams, and Zeigler 2003:5). Urbanization accompanies *modernization*—transformation from traditional, mostly agrarian societies to contemporary bureaucratized states—and *industrialization*—transformation from an agricultural base and handmade goods to manufacturing industries. We explore urbanization in this section as a very specific demographic trend that has major social implications for how people live and interact. The next "Engaging Sociology" feature – on page 583 – invites you to explore some consequences of major urbanization trends in the world (Brunn, Hays-Mitchell, and Zeigler 2011).

Most people live their lives in communities: locations that provide dwellings, a sense of identity and belonging, neighbors and friends, social involvements, and access to basic necessities. Our most intimate micro-level interactions take place in these communities. Yet we are connected through our communities to larger meso- and macro-level social structures, such as political and religious organizations, world health organizations, and international relief agencies (e.g., UNICEF). In this section, we consider the development of communities—from rural areas and small towns to urban areas such as megacities.

Cities as Micro-Level Living Environments

In the 17th and 18th centuries, when Europe was undergoing dramatic changes, small, charming villages contrasted sharply with the rapidly growing urban centers. Ferdinand Tönnies (1855–1936) described these two extreme types on a continuum from **Gemeinschaft**, a German word indicating *a small traditional community*, to **Gesellschaft**, meaning *a large, impersonal urban area.* He saw social life as an evolution from family units to rural villages, towns, cities, nations, and finally cosmopolitan urban life (Tönnies [1887] 1963). Family, friendship, relations to the land, common values, traditions, and experiences are key elements of Gemeinschaft. Gesellschaft, a product of urban industrial society, is characterized by formal relations, contracts, laws, and economies built on money. People in urban areas do not necessarily know one another or share common values. They tend to be employees of bureaucratic organizations, and they tend to be more isolated as individuals rather than members of a collectivity.

A number of other theorists living in the Europe of the 19th century suggested similar contrasts. Émile Durkheim (1858–1917) described the social bonds that held society together and the changes that arose from industrialization and urbanization. **Mechanical solidarity**, introduced in Chapter 3, was his term *for the glue that holds a society together through shared beliefs, values, and traditions typical of rural areas and simple societies.* In mechanical solidarity, social bonds were formed by homogeneity of thought.

Think of any large business in which each employee has a specific task to perform in the division of labor. Similarly, the social glue that holds modern industrial and postindustrial societies and people together is **organic solidarity**, *the social coherence (glue) based on a division of labor with each member playing a highly specialized role in the society and each person being dependent on others due to interrelated, interdependent tasks.* This interdependence of specialized tasks is the key to unity in more complex societies with organic solidarity (see also Chapter 3).

The ways in which order is maintained in society illustrate the differences between the two types of societies. In mechanical solidarity, legal systems are concerned with moral order, upheld by shared beliefs and values and a desire by individuals to be well regarded in the community. Organic solidarity stresses making amends for a wrongdoing by paying fines or spending time in jail (Durkheim [1893] 1947). So even the notion of how to maintain social order varies as this transformation in the society occurs.

For most of human history, humans lived in small population centers. Rural areas dominated. *Rural sociology*, which refers to the study of social life in nonmetropolitan areas, considers patterns and behaviors among people at a distance from population centers. In the United States, **rural areas** *have fewer than 1,000 people per square mile.* According to the 2010 U.S. census, this constituted 19.3% (59,492,276 people) of the U.S. population (U.S. Census Bureau 2012c). Some rural residents are in farming or agribusiness and are concerned with the economics of farm production, ranching, and mining. Others live in resort towns or cater to tourists. Popular rural destinations are mountain areas, the Ozarks, coastal regions, and some midwestern areas in Nebraska, Kansas, and surrounding states.

Engaging Sociology

World Urbanization Trends

World Urbanization Prospects are reports published by the United Nations Population Division. They provide valuable data on past, present, and future urbanization trends in regions and subregions of the world. They also provide data on individual cities and urban areas. Consider the impact of major migration trends on the environment, friends and relatives left behind, dual-career families, maintaining one's culture, the impact of new cultural ideas spreading, and many more impacts. The major findings of the most recent edition follow in Figures 15.10–12.

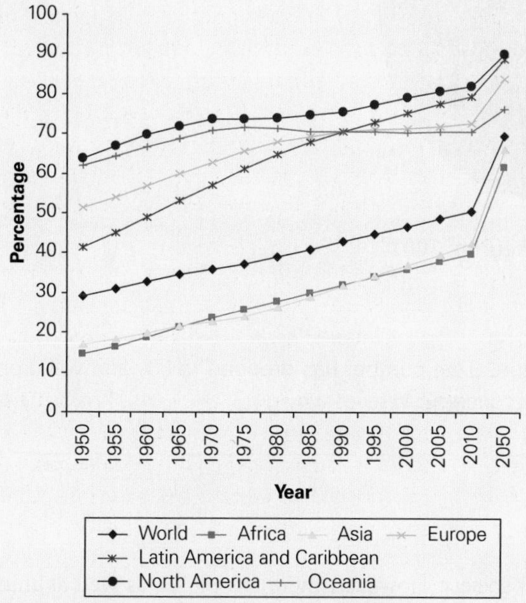

Figure 15.10 Percentage of Population Residing in Urban Areas

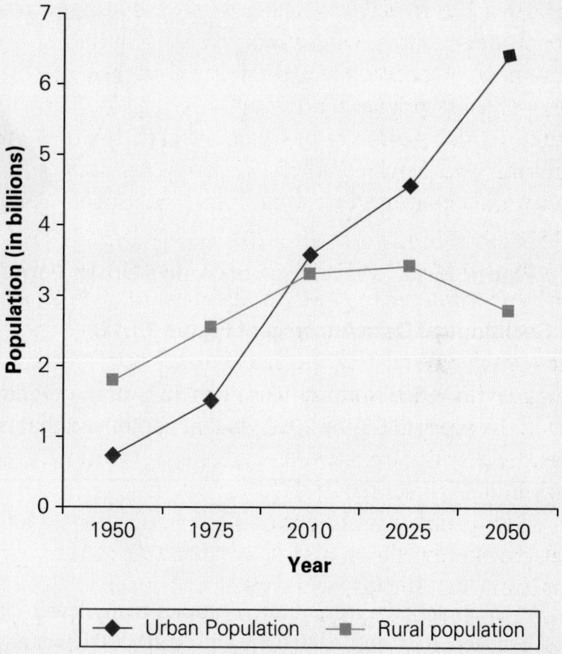

Figure 15.11 Urban and Rural Population of the World, 1950–2050

Sociological Data Analysis of Figure 15.10:

- What do you learn from these graphs about world urbanization trends? Which continents seem to be urbanizing most rapidly?
- How might these trends affect people moving to urban areas?
- What might be some effects on global climate change, the possibilities of globally transmitted diseases, political stability or instability, or the global economy?
- How might the global trend toward urbanization affect your own life?

Sociological Data Analysis of Figure 15.11:

- When the size of the rural population declines, how might it affect the culture of a nation?
- Identify two positive and two negative consequences of this urbanization trend for a nation.

(Continued)

(Continued)

Sociological Data Analysis of Figure 15.11:

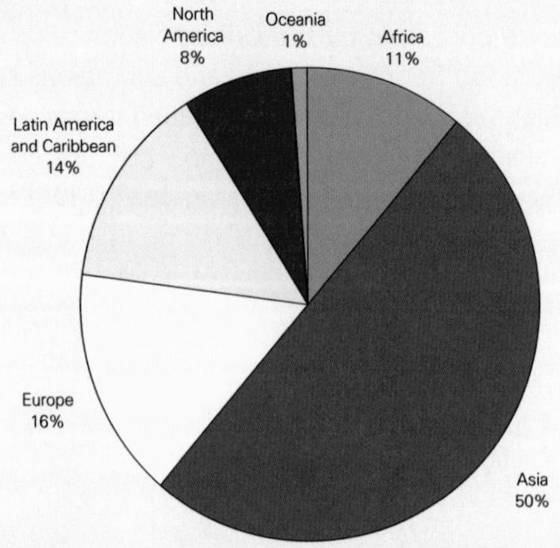

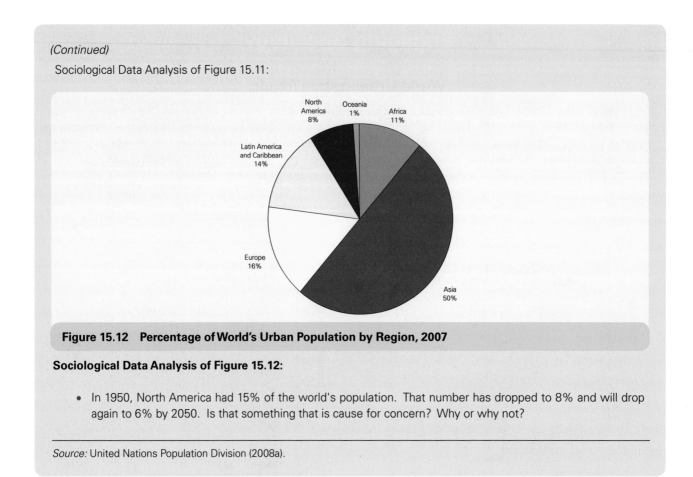

Figure 15.12 Percentage of World's Urban Population by Region, 2007

Sociological Data Analysis of Figure 15.12:

- In 1950, North America had 15% of the world's population. That number has dropped to 8% and will drop again to 6% by 2050. Is that something that is cause for concern? Why or why not?

Source: United Nations Population Division (2008a).

As the years pass, agriculture occupies many fewer citizens. Between 2010 and 2020 there will be 20,000 fewer agricultural workers (Occupational Outlook Handbook 2012). A rural exodus has been under way, with movement to cities that have more economic opportunities and better health care and education. Rural areas face problems just as cities do: environmental degradation from overfarming, overuse of water resources, toxic dumps, and poverty due to reductions in economic opportunities and selling of family farms.

Major population shifts from rural to urban areas came with industrialization in Europe and North America, followed by the same process in other areas of the world. As urbanization continues to sweep the world, many rural areas are disappearing, and those that remain are taking on aspects of metropolitan life as they move away from mechanical and toward organic solidarity. Even the remotest villages are influenced by urban and global concerns. For instance, decisions about what crops to grow are often tied to demand elsewhere in the country or the world. Poor farmers in South America and Afghanistan make more money growing poppies for drug suppliers in big cities than from food crops to feed the local population, making them food dependent (Scribd 2012).

The early interpretations of urbanization, especially by European sociologists, were made through a rather pessimistic lens. The trend was seen largely as a decline of civil society. However, there are pluses as well as minuses in quality of life as people inhabit more densely populated areas. Many city planners have worked to make cities more habitable and "green."

Life in the City

On warm evenings, the residents come out of their oppressive apartments to sit on the front steps. Children play ball in the street or splash in front of open fire hydrants. Neighbors chat about work and politics and other things neighbors share. Across the interstate highway, the professional couple is having cocktails with friends from work in their renovated, air-conditioned Victorian home. In a nearby suburb, families are returning from sports practices, mowing their lawns, and preparing dinner. Political, economic, and cultural factors help shape these different scenarios in the inner city and its surrounding area, as described by urban residential patterns and suburbanization.

Urban Residential Patterns

Neighborhoods are identifiable areas within the larger metropolitan area. Four characteristics help define neighborhoods:

Many urban areas now have urban planners who work to make cities beautiful, aesthetically pleasing, and recreation-friendly. This scene in New York City is possible because planners had the foresight to put in several sizeable parks.

While life in urban areas of North America is typically individualistic and bureaucratic, life in small towns, such as Bhaktapur, Nepal (top), and a Tibetan village (bottom) is more communal and personal, but one has much less privacy.

1. A neighborhood can meet most of the needs of residents: food, schools, faith communities.
2. Neighborhoods are "natural areas"; that is, to a great degree, residents are homogeneous with respect to income, interests, ethnicity or race, and other shared characteristics.
3. There is substantial social interaction among the residents of a neighborhood.
4. There is symbolic commitment, the feeling of belonging to a meaningful sociogeographic area.

Some neighborhoods in cities, especially in ethnic immigrant concentrations, are close-knit. This is especially true when members of extended families live in the same area and provide support for one another (Guest and Stamm 1993; Logan and Spitze 1994). In major cities around the world, ethnic enclaves offer security, familiarity, and protection. For new migrants to cities, neighborhoods provide gradual adaptation to the strange new society and the dominant group. Immigrant groups often attempt to re-create their former, more intimate village-type settings within their urban neighborhood (Gans 1962). Ethnic communities can provide job opportunities and gradual acculturation into language and customs.

Supportive ethnic enclaves are also found in African American inner-city neighborhoods of predominantly single mothers and children. Carol Stack found that women created support networks—sustaining each other through sharing of child care and resources (Stack 1998). However, in some low-income tenement areas, little interaction has been found because of high turnover of residents and fear of violence (Renzetti 2003).

Homogeneous middle-class city and suburban dwellers often have an active neighborhood life as well. A *suburb* is a municipality located outside the political boundaries of a city, but adjacent to the city or to its other suburbs. Generally suburbs form a band around a city, and have lower density than the city. The suburbs end where open space or farmland becomes dominant. *Suburban* can refer to a way of life. The variables that create a sense of community are complex, and generalizations that apply to all types of communities are difficult to make. Over half of the U.S. population lives in suburbs (Friedman 2007).

City dwellers become accustomed to the fast pace of life, the danger of stepping off the curb to cross the street, the crowds jostling and pushing them along as they rush to work, the impersonal attitudes of clerks, and the impatience with inconveniences. The thrill of city life outweighs the problems for many residents, who are sentimentally attached to the unique nature of life in cities. Let us look at some of the variables that affect how people experience city life.

Human Relationships in Cities

Sociologist Georg Simmel was concerned with the experience of urban life, with what it does to people's thoughts and behavior. He argued that two factors—the intensity and stimulation of city life and the economic effects on urban relations—cause people to have different attitudes, beliefs, and values from those in rural areas (Simmel [1902–1917] 1950). City dwellers have no choice but to be somewhat insensitive, to avoid intense relationships, and to keep social relationships superficial to protect their privacy. However, he did not feel this was necessarily negative. Cities free people from the social constraints of close relationships in small towns. Erving Goffman called behaviors of urban dwellers *civil inattention*, elaborate modes of pretending that we do not look, make eye contact, bump into others, pay attention, or listen to what others are doing. Residents show an awareness of others without being conspicuous, threatening, or overly friendly. To visitors or strangers to city life, these behaviors seem callous and cold. However, they offer anonymity and freedom in a crowded environment (Goffman [1959] 2001).

Sociologist Louis Wirth also contended that because urban residents live in heterogeneous, high-density areas, they develop coping mechanisms for dealing with the situation. They become sophisticated, removed from others to insulate themselves from too many personal claims and expectations of others. The depersonalization that results from lower commitment to a common community "goal" also leads to a higher tolerance for nonconformity in cities, resulting in more individual freedom—and as a result a higher level of deviance (Wirth 1964).

Despite the sometimes impersonal environment of cities, local neighborhoods in urban areas often have a sense of community and local traditions. Here we see people playing chess at Washington Square in New York City. This is enough of a community event that it attracts interested spectators.

Urban sociologist Claude Fischer argues that urbanism shapes social life rather than leaving residents as alienated individuals in a sea of traffic, noise, and pollution. City life strengthens social groups, promotes diverse subcultures, and encourages intimate social circles. These urban groups share similar activities or traits. The larger numbers of people make it possible for individuals with similar interests—from ethnic subcultures to gay communities to artist groups—to draw together as clubs, organizations, or neighborhoods. These little social worlds "touch but do not interpenetrate" (Fischer 1984:37). As long as there are enough members of a group, each can maintain its own identity. When different groups come in contact with each other, the result may be positive sharing of cultures, or it may be conflict, causing members to associate all the more closely with their own group. Gangs fall into this latter category. So rather than creating isolated individuals who interact defensively with others, urban life may create choices about lifestyle and enhance a different kind of community base, intensifying the interactions.

Despite these benefits of urban life in countries where cities have substantial resources to provide services, urbanization can have very different consequences, especially in poor regions of the world. Rapidly growing cities in impoverished countries often face challenges to provide services—shelter, water, electricity, sanitation, schools, health care—for the increasing numbers of residents.

Thinking Sociologically

What do you see as the most important impact(s) on individuals or groups living in urban areas?

How Did Cities Evolve? Meso-Level Organizational Structures

Human settlements have gone through massive transitions over the past 100,000 years, from small agricultural settlements to bustling crowded metropolises with millions of people. The first step in the development of urban life came when those living nomadic lives became more settled. Archeological evidence indicates that the earliest settlements were in the Middle East and North Africa, most probably in Oman about 125,000 years ago, as human nomads followed rivers into Arabia to Wadi Aybut in Dhofar (Global Arab Network 2010). Other early settlements have been excavated in Ethiopia, Morocco, United Arab Emirates, South Africa,

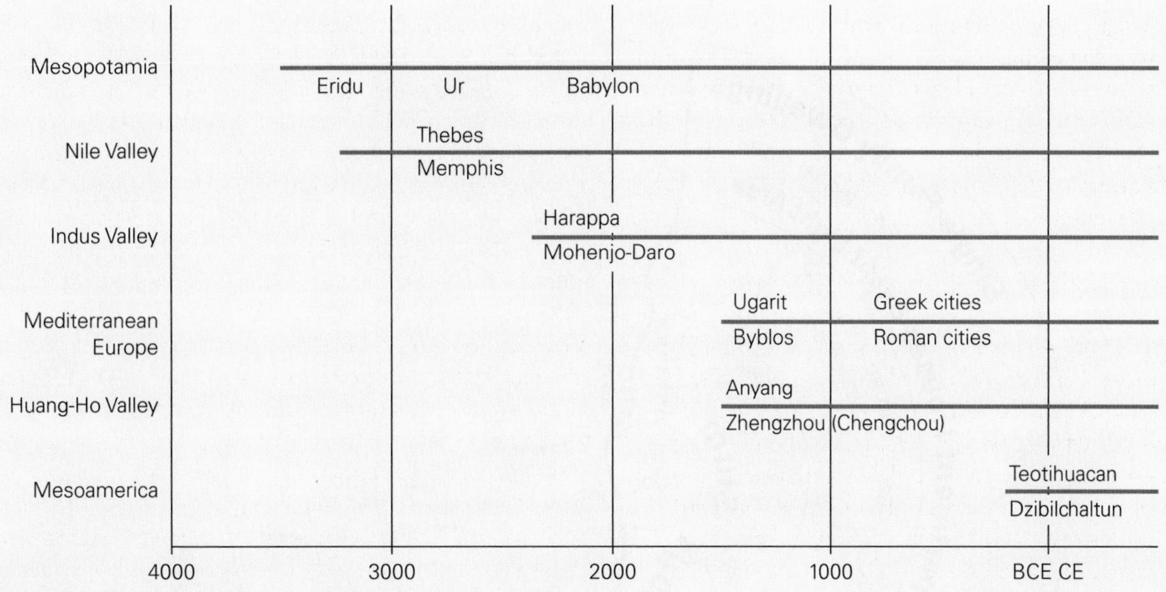

Figure 15.13 Cities in Antiquity

Source: Sjoberg (1965:56–57).

Pakistan, and Israel. Starting about 10,000 years ago with the advent of agriculture, domestication of animals, and the shift from food gathering to food production, small groups established permanent settlements. Among the first was Eridu in Iraq, a settlement of some 25 permanent compounds with a population of up to 200 in each compound and a grain storage facility in the center (see Figure 15.13). The people grew wheat and barley and domesticated dogs, goats, and sheep.

These settlements were not cities as we think of them today, however, because they had different cultural and economic structures, and there was little division of labor. Everyone shared roles, worked the land to support the population, and banded together for protection. Cities, in contrast, are large permanent settlements with nonagricultural specialists, a literate elite, and surplus food to support the social classes that are not involved in food production. They have been the source of intense fascination for many social science theorists.

Theories of Urban Development

Among the first sociologists in the United States were urban scholars, dubbed the Chicago School, who studied problems in the city of Chicago. Their studies of urban ecology focused on the patterns of land use and residential distribution of people in urban areas. These theorists pictured the city's growth pattern as a series of circles. Moving out from the center, each circle was dominated by a particular type of activity and residential pattern, from central city ghettoes and rooming houses to working-class apartments and bungalows, to middle-class housing, to upper-class suburbs (Park, Burgess, and McKenzie [1925] 1967). See Figure 15.14 on page 588 for an illustration of this pattern.

Urban ecologists further refined the Chicago School's original ideas by exploring social, economic, political, and technological systems of cities' spatial patterns (Abu-Lughod 1991). Several processes constantly take place in urban areas: residential segregation; invasion by a new ethnic, religious, or socioeconomic group; and succession by that group. These processes are part of dynamic city life (Berry and Kasarda 1977).

Racial and ethnic segregation is a continuing and troubling issue in many urban areas of the United States. Despite some reductions in racism in the nation, American cities—especially northern cities—have high levels of residential segregation. This segregation affects individual networking, school composition, and access to community resources. The next "Engaging Sociology" on page 589 examines the likelihood that someone of a given race will have contacts in his or her neighborhood that cross racial lines. This figure is based on one city—Chicago, Illinois—but you can easily check the residential patterns in your city by going to www.censusscope.org/segregation.html.

In the past three decades, very new and different theories of urban development have emerged, spurred in part by the decay, riots, and disturbances in cities around the world that dramatized inequalities and prompted sociologists to find new explanations for urban problems. The idea is that urban space is both socially defined and in scarce supply. Therefore, political-economic conflict will arise over how space gets allocated and by whom. Any effective solution to urban problems must address inequalities between groups and allocations of resources in urban areas (Castells 1977; Harvey 1973).

Some conflict theorists see growing city problems as a result of domination by elites, creating poverty and

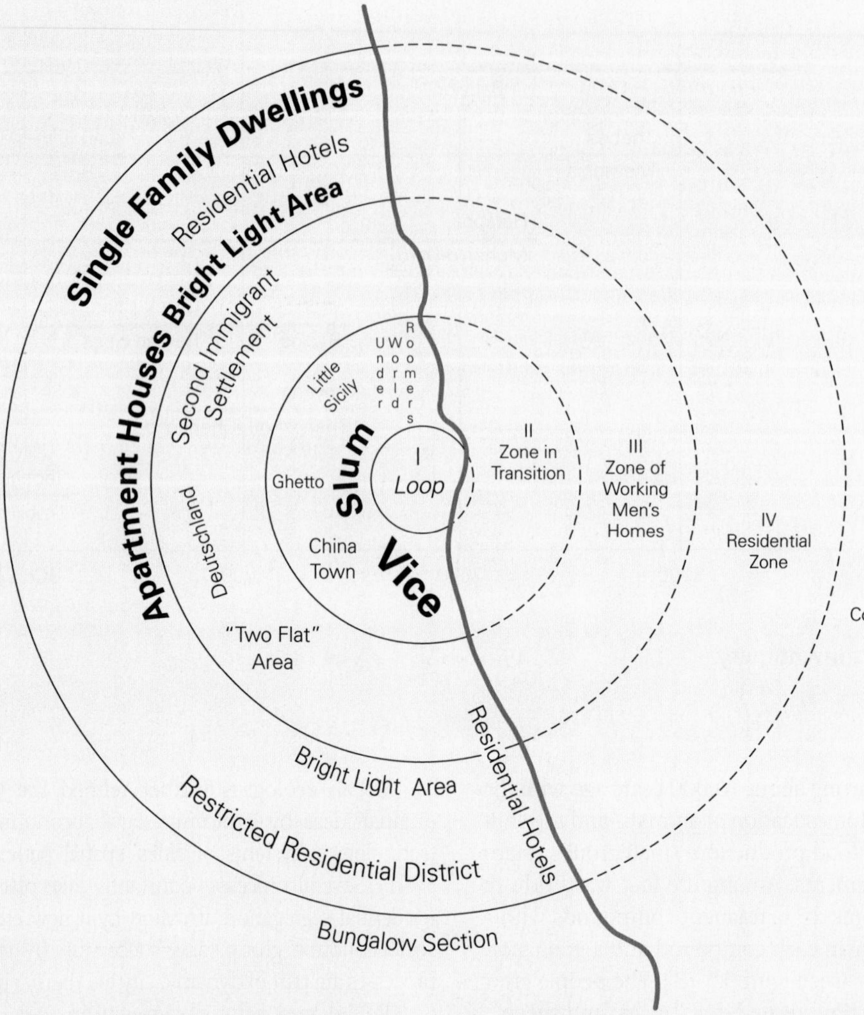

Figure 15.14 Burgess's Theory of City Growth

Source: Park et al. ([1925] 1967:55).

Note: The Chicago School envisioned urban growth as a series of concentric circles, with ethnicity, class, residential patterns, and types of activity evolving with each ring removed from the central city.

exploitation of the poor (Flanagan 2001; Gottdiener and Hutchison 2006). Cities produce profits for those who buy and sell property and for investors and politicians who redevelop urban areas. Sometimes, poor urban residents are displaced in the process (Hannigan 1998). In short, conflict theorists see urbanization and modernization as a cause of poverty among city residents around the world.

Types of Cities

Although organizational structures of cities have changed and evolved over time, in the following section, we will focus on industrial and several variants of postindustrial cities.

Industrial Cities

The onset of industrialization in 17th- and 18th-century Europe started the trend toward urbanized nations, countries in which more than half of the population lives in urban areas. Rural peasants migrated to the cities in search of opportunities and to escape the tedium and poverty of agricultural existence and shortage of available farmland. Often, this resulted in a rapid influx of migrants and an unplanned urbanization process. Cities served the rapidly advancing industrial sector, but crowded conditions, poor sanitation, polluted water supplies, and poor working conditions all contributed to the misery of poor urban residents and to their short life expectancy compared with those living in the countryside. Urban systems became over-

Engaging Sociology

Residential Segregation and Cross-Race Contact

Unless there is complete integration, the racial composition of neighborhoods where most whites live differs from the composition of neighborhoods lived in by ethnic minorities. To examine this, the Census Bureau calculates exposure indices—the average racial composition of neighborhoods experienced by members of each group. The bar graph in Figure 15.15 illustrates typical contact of most residents with members of their own and other races in a metropolitan area. In this graph, the first five columns represent the average racial composition of the neighborhood of a person of a given race. The rightmost column shows the racial composition of the metropolitan area as a whole. Study the line graphs and answer the following questions.

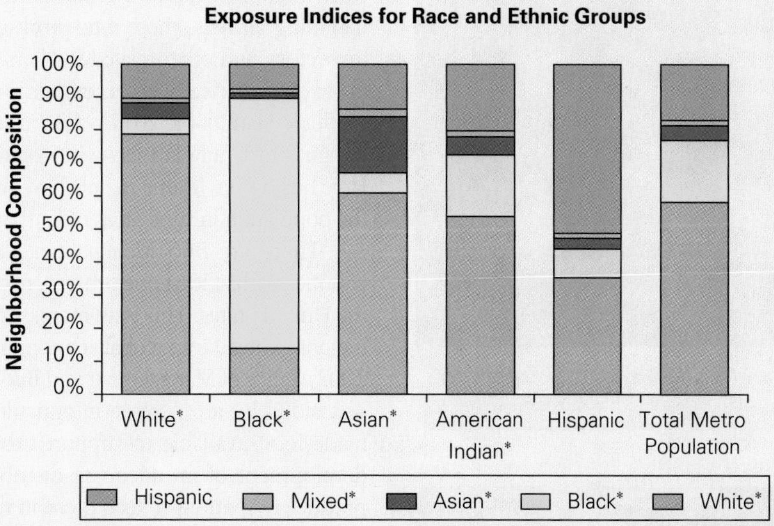

Figure 15.15 Exposure Indices for Race and Ethnic Groups: Chicago

Interpreting Sociological Data

1. How likely are whites to experience diversity in their neighborhoods compared with the diversity of the city as a whole?
2. Which group experiences the most diversity and is likely to have opportunity to encounter groups unlike itself?
3. Which groups experience the most segregation?
4. What might be some results of living in neighborhoods that are homogeneous? Which group might experience more negative consequences because of the homogeneity? Why?
5. Go to www.censusscope.org/segregation.html and enter a city near you to see how exposure rates fare for various groups in that city. What do you conclude?

Source: Residential Segregation and Cross-Race Contact: Chicago, Illinois. www.censusscope.org/segregation.html.

whelmed by the large numbers of migrants, and conditions became as desperate as those the people had tried to escape in the rural areas. Today, Global North countries are more than 75% urban, and Global South countries are on average 40% urban. By 2030, this imbalance will be even greater.

Industrial cities became primarily commercial centers motivated by competition, a characteristic that differentiated them from preindustrial cities. The advent of power-driven machinery and the new capitalist factory system transformed and replaced the former craft and cottage industries and guild structures (Abu-Lughod 1991). Roads, waterways, and railroads made travel and communication between towns and cities easier and faster. Cities became fast-paced as mechanical vehicles took to the streets.

By 1850, profound changes began taking place in many European countries and in the United States. A shift from predominantly rural to urban living was under way. In about 1870, Great Britain became the first truly urban nation with more than 50% of the population in urban areas. Economically changing conditions in the British Isles were conducive to urbanization and industrialization. Parliament had passed "reorganization of land acts" that pushed many rural citizens from the countryside to cities. In addition, raw materials were available from colonies; new technology was rapidly advancing manufacturing techniques; and the banking facilities, credit, stock, and other financing for industry were falling into place (Benevolo 1995; Mumford 1961).

Despite the many jobs created, one of the downsides of industrialized cities is phenomenal pollution.

While these men may look impoverished by North American standards, they are relatively well-off in comparison to many urban neighbors in India, for they own a method of transportation that can earn a cash income, providing food and shelter for their families. For them, this is life in a postindustrial city.

Residential population patterns in the United States are illustrative. About 90% of the U.S. population lived on farms in the 1790s. By 1900, 41% of the labor force worked in agriculture. Today, agricultural workers hold only about 757,900 jobs, including farmers, those who work with animals, agricultural inspectors, and other related workers. This number is continuing to drop as fewer workers engage in agriculture (Occupational Outlook Handbook 2012). Agribusiness conglomerates have bought out family farmers who could not compete with these large businesses. Young people have moved from farms, leaving the population in rural areas older than that in urban areas.

There are 366 *Metropolitan Statistical Areas*—adjacent counties with at least one urban core of 50,000 population—in the United States. This is an increase from 33 in 1940 as many regions evolved into global economic centers (Federal Register 2002; Office of Management and Budget 2010). Urban growth was aided by an increase in agricultural productivity, which made food available to support urban dwellers, and by the development of an adequate distribution system to get the produce to markets to feed those in urban areas.

With the advent of public transportation in the late 1800s, people in many countries began to escape crowded city conditions by moving out into emerging suburbs. Private automobiles and telephones aided movement to the suburbs. Road systems were developed to accommodate the growing numbers of autos, and more businesses and services relocated to suburban areas.

Since the 1990s, the U.S. Census has shown that some rural areas are once again gaining population. This is especially the case in recreation areas, where urban residents relocate to exurbs (rural areas within commuting distance of city jobs), and retired people look for new locations with clean air, space, interpersonal civility, and a slower pace than the city (Johnson and Fuguitt 2000).

Postindustrial Cities

Postindustrial cities have a high percentage of employees in the service sector—business headquarters, government and intergovernmental organizations, research and development, tourism, finance, health, education, and telecommunications (Bell [1976] 1999). They are found in the most technologically advanced, wealthy nations. Washington, DC, fits most of these characteristics, as does La Défense, an urban center on the outskirts of Paris, built as a commercial, service, and information exchange center to serve France.

Postindustrial cities are closely tied to the economic structures of capitalism, with global production systems and instant exchanges of information (Abu-Lughod 2001; Friedman 2005). In the transformation from industrial to postindustrial economies, from manufacturing to service economies, some people get left behind. There are often severe income disparities between those trained for the new economies and those with less training and in lower-level positions. Cities such as Bengaluru (Bangalore), India, illustrate the disparities between high-tech industries and poor agricultural peasants in the surrounding areas. These high-tech centers attract business from around the world. This book would have been produced in the United States a few years ago, but with the competitive publication market, publishers find it economically prudent to outsource and save on costs.

Some urban areas are carefully planned. *New towns*, for example, are cities built in previously undeveloped areas as economically self-sufficient entities with all the needed urban amenities. Urban planners believed that these cities could relieve the congestion of urban areas, provide new economic bases and residences near jobs, and solve many problems faced by older cities. Some new towns have been success stories: Columbia, Maryland; Brasília, Brazil (the relatively new capital); Canberra, Australia. However, planning has proven difficult as cities around the world have experienced influxes of poor migrants who squat (set up shelter) in any location available—abandoned buildings, cemetery mausoleums, hillsides surrounding cities. The next "Sociology Around the World" on page 594 discusses archeological research indicating that large planned cities existed in North America before white Europeans even knew the continent existed.

As people move to the suburbs, manufacturing firms, services, commerce, and retail trade follow. Although there have been criticisms of suburbs, suburbanites continue to move to suburbs and they are thriving (Clapson 2003; Gans 1982). Yet movement of economic activities formerly located in cities removes an economic base of cities. These internal migrations lock cities and suburbs into competition over jobs and tax revenues. When this happens, farmland and open lands disappear; quality of construction is often shoddy because builders want to make big profits by using cheap materials; energy and water demands increase, often straining public utilities; and sprawl leads to vast, crowded freeway systems. Such a suburbanization of industry took place between 1970 and 1990, as many industries relocated out of central city areas, looking for favorable tax rates.

Suburbs are increasingly facing problems of poverty as low-income city residents relocate to suburbs. Recently foreclosure on houses has been a particular problem for those who made the move. Poverty in suburban areas increased from 11% in 1980 to 15% in 2000—and climbing. Even government programs such as Hope VI (relocation of urban poor to areas outside of the city) have increased poverty in suburbs while gentrification has reduced poverty levels in cities (Sink and Ceh 2011).

In some urban areas, neatly manicured lawns and freshly painted exteriors reflect new directions away from either suburbanization or deterioration of inner-city neighborhoods. The process of **gentrification** refers to *members of the middle and upper classes, mostly young white professionals, buying and renovating rundown properties in central-city locations and displacing poor residents*. The process begins when affluent urban residents leave their stylish homes and move to suburbs. Poorer residents are left behind to rent once-fashionable homes from absentee owners. Later, affluent professionals buy the rundown homes at bargain rates, renovate them, and live in these newly gentrified areas (Feagin 1983). However, recent research indicates that minority householders, especially those with at least a high school degree, do not all leave. They make up, on average, 33% of the gentrified neighborhoods compared with 20% college-educated whites. More middle-class minorities, such as Hispanics, also move to gentrified neighborhoods. The bottom line is that all residents tend to do better economically as income and housing prices increase in gentrified areas, and these become more ethnically diverse neighborhoods as well (McKinnish, Walsh, and White 2008). In recent years, these neighborhoods, which are often adjacent to the central business districts, have become "fashionable" residential areas. Georgetown in Washington, DC, and German Village in Columbus, Ohio, are examples. Beautiful classic old homes have become affordable to young upper-middle-class professionals and remain within reach of middle-class minorities who decide that they want ready access to the occupational and cultural opportunities of the city. Walkability—ability to walk to most "hot spots" in the city and dispense with owning a car—has become a primary standard for many young urbanites (Palmer 2012). This gentrification brings consumers, leadership, and a tax base to the city.

For those low-income people who move because of rising costs, many are pushed into less attractive parts of town with fewer services and recreational areas, and often pay higher rents for less adequate housing. Alternative housing for displaced residents may be difficult to find, contributing to problems of homelessness. Conflict theorists view gentrification and other urban developments that favor the wealthy and displace or exclude the poor to be exploitation by real estate capitalists. In contrast, others argue that wealthy residents who choose the lifestyle of the city over suburbia are helping support viable, livable cities.

Thinking Sociologically

What are some positive and negative aspects of gentrification for individuals and cities? Explain.

Sociology Around the World

City Planning in Prehistoric Central America: Teotihuacan

Teotihuacan was a Mesoamerican city (between the American continents) created by a society that had no metal tools, had not invented the wheel, and had no pack animals. At its height, Teotihuacan covered 8 square miles (20 square kilometers), which made it larger than imperial Rome. Its central religious monument, the Temple of the Sun, was as broad at its base as the great pyramid of Cheops in Egypt. Its population may have reached 100,000.

Strategically located astride a valley that was the gateway to the lowlands of Mexico, Teotihuacan flourished for 500 years as a great urban commercial center. Yet it was more than that. It was the mecca of the New World, a religious and cultural capital that probably housed pilgrims from as far away as Guatemala. Perhaps most startling, Teotihuacan was a totally planned city. Its two great pyramids, its citadel, its hundred lesser religious structures, and its 4,000 other dwellings were laid out according to an exact design. Streets (and many of its buildings) were organized on a perfect grid aligned with the city center. Even the shape of the river that divided the city was changed to fit the grid pattern.

Planning for the construction of Teotihuacan's major temples must have been an incredible undertaking. The Temple of the Sun, for instance, rises to a height of 215 feet and has a base of 725 square feet. These dimensions mean that it took about 1 million tons of sunbaked mud bricks to build the temple. When the Spaniards conquered Mexico in the 16th century, they were amazed to find Teotihuacan's ruined temples. Local inhabitants claimed that the temples had been built by giants. They showed the Spaniards the bones of giant elephants (which had lived there in prehistoric times) to prove their point.

Small buildings as well as large ones were cleverly conceived in Teotihuacan. Houses were apparently planned for maximum space and privacy. Apartments were constructed around central patios, with each patio designed to give dwellers light and air, as well as an efficient drainage system. In a Teotihuacan housing complex, a person could indeed have lived in relative comfort (Jordan-Bychkov and Domoch 1998).

Megacities

As we look at Earth from space, some areas glow. These urban areas of 10 million or more residents, called megacities, dot the globe. In the 1950s, New York City was the only place in the world that had 10 million people. At that time, there were 75 cities in the world with 1 to 5 million residents, mostly in the Global North. Table 15.4 shows the rapid change in this pattern with the 10 largest population centers in 2000 and 2011.

As the world becomes more congested and cities continue to attract residents, cities start to merge or to become continuous urban areas without rural areas between them. Those who have driven from Boston to Washington, DC, an area sometimes called BosWash, know the meaning of *megalopolis*, a spatial merging of two or more cities along major transportation corridors (Brunn, Hays-Mitchell, and Zeigler 2011).

Table 15.4 **The 10 Largest Population Centers (Population in Millions)**

2000 Rank	Urban Center	Population	2011 Rank	Urban Center	Population	2025 Projected Rank	Urban Center	Population
1	Tokyo, Japan	34,450	1	Tokyo, Japan	37,200	1	Tokyo, Japan	38,700
2	Mexico City, Mexico	18,066	2	Delhi, India	22,700	2	Delhi, India	32,900
3	New York/Newark, USA	17,846	3	Mexico City, Mexico	20,400	3	Shanghai, China	28,400
4	São Paulo, Brazil	17,099	4	New York/Newark, USA	20,400	4	Mumbai (Bombay), India	26,600
5	Mumbai (Bombay), India	16,086	5	Shanghai, China	20,200	5	Mexico City, Mexico	24,600
6	Kolkata (Calcutta), India	13,058	6	São Paulo, Brazil	19,900	6	New York/ Newark, USA	23,600
7	Shanghai, China	12,887	7	Mumbai (Bombay), India	19,700	7	São Paulo, Brazil	23,200
8	Buenos Aires, Argentina	12,583	8	Beijing, China	15,600	8	Dhaka, Bangladesh	22,900
9	Delhi, India	12,441	9	Dhaka, Bangladesh	15,400	9	Beijing, China	22,600
10	Los Angeles, USA	11,814	10	Kolkata (Calcutta), India	14,400	10	Karachi, Pakistan	20,200

Source: United Nations, Department of Economic and Social Affairs, Population Division (2012a).

Thinking Sociologically

As you compare the three columns in Table 15.4 with the largest cities in 2000, 2011, and projected 2025, what conclusions can you draw about population movements and changes in regions of the world?

Global City Variations

Many people around the globe live in cities with long, often glorious histories. Some live in relatively new suburbs surrounding central cities, and others live in new urban areas, recently planned and constructed. Cities' spatial arrangements vary by their histories, as the following examples illustrate.

An *indigenous* community is a group of people that originates and lives in an area or environment. Kabul, Afghanistan, is an example of a traditional, indigenous city in the Global South. Kabul dates back to between 500 and 300 BCE, and it became the capital of Afghanistan in 1776. In the old section, bazaars and flat-roofed houses crowd the narrow winding streets, which were designed for foot and cart traffic. The newer sections have wide, tree-lined streets. Land use is mixed, with small businesses and residences sharing the same dwellings. Indigenous cities usually predate European cities. In many indigenous cities, certain occupational types occupy distinctive areas. The centers of indigenous cities generally include a market or bazaar, monuments, government buildings, and a religious mosque, church, or temple. Some of the elite live in the heart of these cities, whereas the poor live on the periphery of the city or on the city streets, a pattern vastly different from affluent North America. Global South countries often have dual cities such as Delhi and New Delhi, India, and Abidjan, Ivory Coast, in which a modern Westernized colonial central city is located next to a traditional indigenous city.

From cities built on ancient foundations to new urban centers, cities are a main organizational structure in modern life. How do these urban areas develop? This leads us to a discussion of macro-level issues.

The hills surrounding Caracas, the capital of Venezuela, are densely packed with migrants from rural areas looking for opportunities in the urban area. Many of these areas lack the most basic services.

Urban Problems, the Environment, and Social Policy: Macro-Level Perspectives

The mountains rise from the sea, dotted with pastel-colored shanties. On the drive from the port city of La Guaira up into the mountains to the capital city of Caracas, Venezuela, one sees settlements nestled into the hillsides. The poor, who have come from throughout the country to find opportunities in the capital, make shelters in the hills surrounding Caracas, often living with no running water, electricity, or sewage disposal. The laundry list of urban problems is overwhelming: excessive size and overcrowding; shortages of services, education, and health care; slums and squatters; traffic congestion; unemployment; and effects of global restructuring, including loss of agricultural land, environmental degradation, and resettlement of immigrants and refugees (Brunn, Williams, and Zeigler 2003). This section considers several of the many problems facing urban areas such as Caracas.

Rural Migrants and Overcrowding

Barriadas surround the outskirts of Caracas, a situation in many cities where migrants find any available space within or around the city to squat. For example, in Cairo, Egypt, a huge, sprawling graveyard full of large mausoleums, the City of the Dead, has become home to thousands of families transplanted from rural areas. Cities in India such as Chennai (the former colonial name was Madras), Mumbai (Bombay), and Kolkata (Calcutta) have thousands of homeless migrants living on the sidewalks, on highway medians, and in river channels that flood during the rainy season.

Overcrowding exists in cities throughout the world but causes special problems in the Global South, where rural residents seek opportunities in urban areas. Squatters with hopes for a better future set up shacks of any material available—tin, cardboard, leaves, mud, and sticks—in settlements known as *barriadas* in Spanish, *shantytowns* in English, *bidonvilles* in French, *favelas* in Portuguese-speaking Brazil, and *bustees* in India. The majority of migrants to the city are young. They are pulled to the city in hopes of finding jobs and often have been pushed from the rural areas because of limited land on which to farm.

In the past three decades, the urban populations in Africa, Asia, and Latin America have begun to grow rapidly, and as Map 15.1 shows, many of the largest cities in the world are now in the Global South. Rural-to-urban migration and development of megacities dominate the economic and political considerations in many countries. The newcomers spill out into the countryside, engulfing towns along the way. Figure 15.16 shows the population living in urban and rural areas by more or less developed regions of the world, indicating trends from 1950 to 2007 and making projections through 2030 (United Nations, Department of Economic and Social Affairs, Population Division 2012c).

Countries have little time or money to prepare infrastructures and provide services for the rapidly increasing numbers of urban residents. Technological development, job opportunities, and basic services have not kept up with the large migrations of would-be laborers. Providing services such as water, electricity, sanitation, schools, transportation, and health services to these people has become a major problem—even impossible for some poor governments. Health and disease, especially contagious diseases, cause deadly epidemics due to the lack of services and poor sanitary conditions. The "Sociology in Our Social World" on page 596 describes one plague that ravaged much of Europe.

Lack of adequate housing is a worldwide problem. It is not helped by high birthrates and lower death rates in resource-poor countries, which cause population increases that are greater than the rate of economic growth or the capacity of society to absorb the migrants into urban areas. Because residents of the squatter settlements hold traditional rural values, adaptation to urban bureaucracy and overcrowding becomes even more difficult, resulting in *anomie* (normlessness) and exacerbating urban problems. Planning and social policy have failed poor migrants in rapidly growing slums of many world cities.

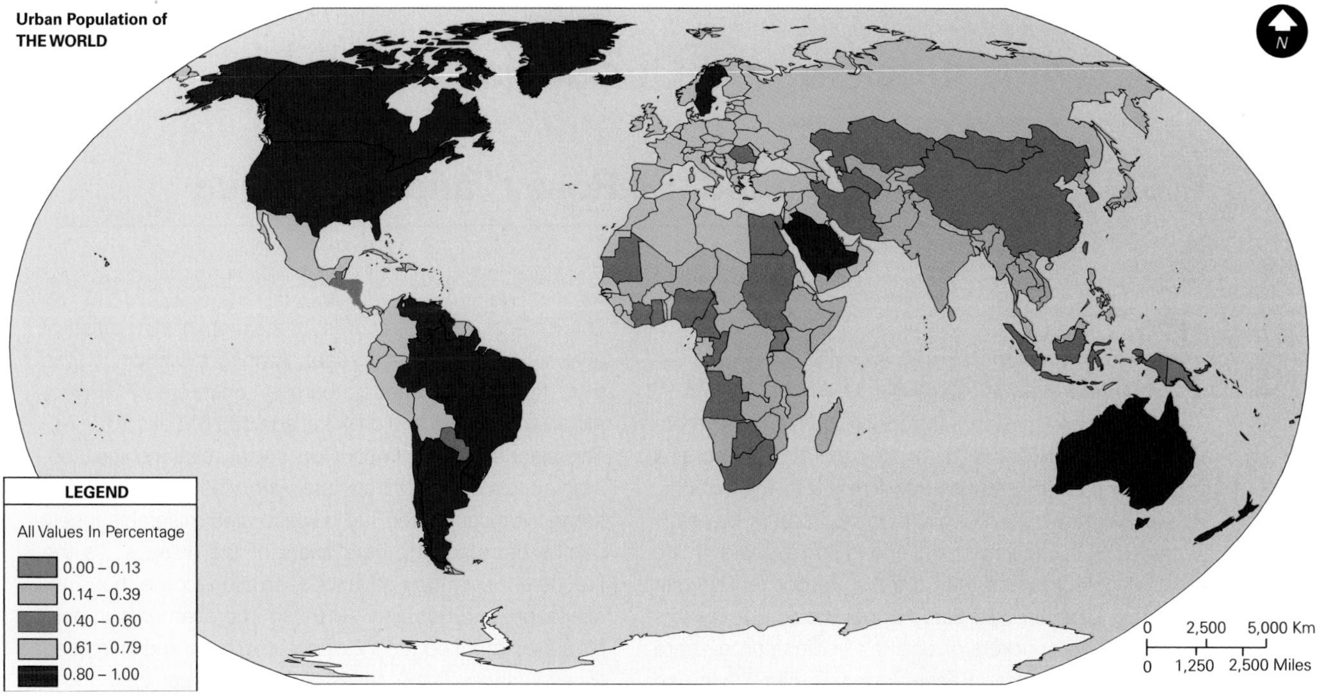

Map 15.1 Percent Urban Population by Country in 2006

Source: World Bank. Map by Anna Versluis.

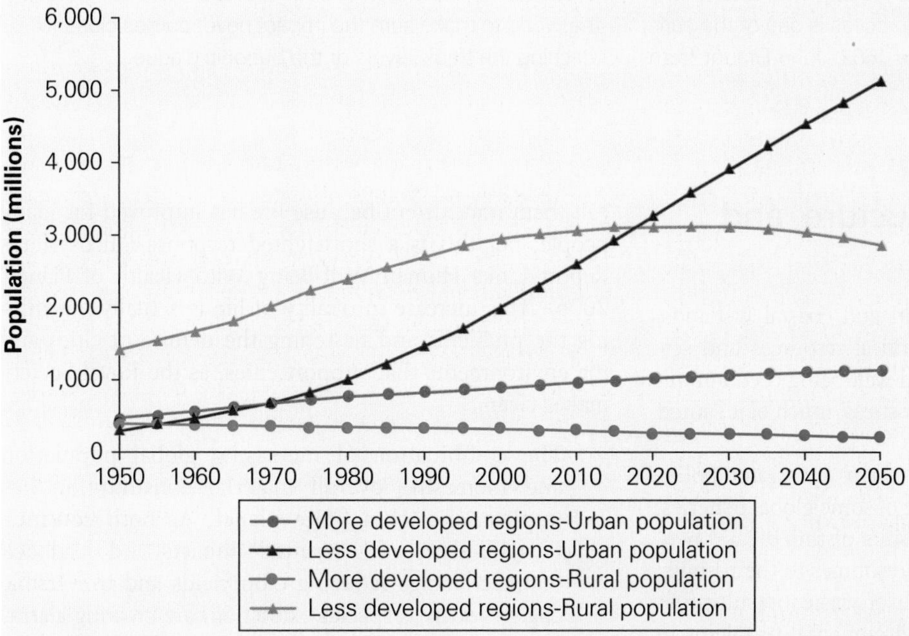

Figure 15.16 Urban and Rural Populations, 1950–2030

Source: United Nations Population Division 2012.

Sociology in Our Social World

"Ring Around the Rosey" and the Plague

Ring around the Rosey, Pockets full of posies, Ashes, Ashes, We all fall down!

Remember this nursery school rhyme? You probably did not understand the meaning of the rhyme as a child. Some interpretations say it refers to the bubonic plague, which ravaged England and Europe in the early to mid-1600s, leaving dead and dying people in its wake. People infected with the plague got red circular sores that smelled very bad. People would put flowers (posies) in their pockets or on their bodies somewhere to cover up the smell. Because people were dying so rapidly, it was difficult to keep up with burials, and the dead were burned to reduce the spread of the disease (ashes, ashes). So many people were sick and dying that "we all fall down." Although there are variations on this story, it is probably true that the rhyme was related to a major plague in London (Snopes.com 2007).

From 1603 to 1849, the clergy had the task of recording the deaths, the burials, and the cause of deaths that occurred. These were circulated weekly, with a summary put out before Christmas. This process is one of the earliest records of vital statistics. In 1662, John Graunt from London analyzed the records for the first known statistical analysis of demographic data. Among his findings was that "for every 100 people born in London, only 16 were still alive at age 36 and only 3 at age 66" (Weeks 2012:73). The plague had an impact on social relationships, too. Many citizens avoided anyone who was a stranger, and some who contracted the disease died miserable lonely deaths because of others' fears of the disease. As the Industrial Revolution advanced, so did income, housing, sanitation, and nutrition. All these improvements in people's lives reduced the incidence of plague and increased life expectancy. Today, cases of the plague can be found in several places, including India and the rural southwestern United States. Antibiotics are effective treatment for people who have access to them, but many poor people cannot afford expensive medications from affluent countries.

Modern plagues, such as avian influenza (bird flu) and severe acute respiratory syndrome (SARS), have claimed hundreds of lives this decade, but both have significantly smaller impact than the bubonic plague. The World Health Organization is monitoring bird flu and SARS throughout the world to make sure the impact never comes close to reaching the tragic levels of the bubonic plague.

Environment, Infrastructure, and Urban Ecosystems

Ecosystems—streams, rivers, inland and coastal wetlands, grasslands, and forests—provide critical resources and services that sustain human health and well-being (EcoSummit 2012). Yet our ecosystems are under stress, much of it caused by human activity.

Extinction of species, lack of water and water pollution, resource exploitation, collapse of some global fisheries, and new diseases are the likely results of this breakdown. Urbanization by 2050 will stretch resources to their limits. Cities will have no way to dispose of wastes, resulting in epidemics. We cannot address environmental problems in detail here, but humans are contributing to the problems that are killing people now and will kill many in the future. The problems are exacerbated by an increase in natural disasters (e.g., hurricanes), which scientists believe to be a result of climate change. We can ignore the problems or call them nonexistent because life has improved for many people, but this is a shortsighted response ("Ecosystems Report Links Human Well-Being With Health of Planet" 2006). This increase in quality of life is actually magnifying the problems and hastening the demise of cities and the environments that support cities, as the Royal Society makes clear:

> The combination of increasing global population and increasing overall material consumption has implications for a finite planet. As both continue to rise, signs of unwanted impacts and feedback (climate change reducing crop yields and irreversible changes such as species extinction) are growing alarmingly . . . Demographic change is driven by economic development, social and cultural factors as well as environmental change. (Royal Society 2012)

Additional infrastructure problems threaten to immobilize cities in the Global South. Traffic congestion and pollution are so intense in some cities that the slow movement of people and goods reduces productivity, jobs, health, and vital services. Pollution of the streets and air are chronic problems, especially with expansion of automobile use around the world. Older cities face deteriorating infrastructures, with water, gas, and sewage lines in need of replacement. Even in affluent cities like Tokyo and London, many people are forced to wear face masks in July and August due to pollution. In Global South countries, concern for these problems has brought some action and relief, but in impoverished countries where survival issues are pressing, environmental contamination is a low priority. Thus, the worst air pollution is now found in major cities in the Global South, such as Mexico City; São Paulo, Brazil; and several Chinese cities, including Beijing, host to the 2008 Olympics.

Water, an essential resource for survival, illustrates the complex urban ecosystem. Cities pipe in millions of gallons of water each day from lakes, rivers, or reservoirs, sometimes located at a distance from the city. Through a complex network of pipes, the water is connected to each establishment. After use—cooking, cleaning, showering, disposing of wastes—the water is discarded and becomes an output. Some of the water is used in products or for industrial uses and some is stored, but most wastewater—about 95%—is piped out to sewer plants, rivers, or other disposal sites. Water is but one example of the complex urban ecosystem with its interdependent parts (Galbraith 2012).

The encouraging conclusion is that many scientists and governments are working to find sustainable solutions for ecosystems. The negative side is that these cost money and in difficult economic times there is little interest in supporting the future. Yet to improve the ecosystem experts argue for a number of actions that are needed "yesterday": rebalance consumption between Global North and South; stabilize population growth, especially in Global South countries; bring those in absolute poverty out of this condition; develop plans for urban growth; provide access to reproductive health and family planning; and adopt plans to reduce human consumption (Royal Society 2012).

To understand the urban ecosystem, its growth, and its decay, we must understand that there are pressures on the city from both external sources and internal dynamics, as illustrated in the next topic.

Poverty in the World's Cities

Poor people are often invisible. Around the world, they are tucked away in enclaves most affluent people do not see. Until something brings attention to the poor, leaders and most of the citizenry can ignore them. Invisibility of urban poverty results because these residents have little power to make their problems public and little energy beyond that needed for survival. Earlier chapters addressed reasons for poverty and the groups who fall disproportionately into poverty. Urban residential patterns generally reflect the same patterns of poverty.

The *permanent underclass* refers to the poor worldwide, people who do not have education or skills to become part of the local or world economy. Children leave school at young ages to help support their families, reducing their opportunities to get out of poverty. However, modernizing economies have little need for unskilled labor.

The *feminization of poverty* refers to the increase of women and their children in the ranks of the impoverished. This is a growing problem in rich and poor countries. The increasing numbers of teenage mothers who have little education, are unemployed, and have few prospects to get out of poverty result in their disproportionate representation among the homeless. (The "Sociology in Our Social World" feature on page 222 examined the circumstances and coping strategies of homeless people.) One cause of feminization of poverty is divorces, which may leave women with small children and poor job prospects. Single-parent homes with a woman as the breadwinner are far more likely than other types of households to be in economic trouble, with poor housing, lack of education, and scant job opportunities.

In some cities, residents are working collectively for survival and improvement in their conditions. In Harlem, New York, some residents live in cooperatives and rental buildings that they manage, taken over after landlords abandoned the buildings. The "community household model" in which residents control their own housing may provide a new method of organization and leadership by tenants and community activists (Leavitt and Saegert 1990).

Crime and Delinquency in the City

Social disruption and crime are not intrinsic to cities. One can walk through many areas of Toronto, London, or Paris at night with little likelihood of problems. Traditional African cities had very low crime rates, but today, they are much less safe because of high numbers of new migrants. When people are transient, when they move frequently, they are more likely to experience *anomie*, to have less commitment to community norms, and to lack a sense of commitment to the norms and the well-being of the local community. Add to that the desperate situation of the very poor, and you have a recipe for crime.

In the United States, crime rates in cities of 1 million or more have been dropping up to 5% in four years; cities of 500,000 have seen drops of 5.6%, and smaller cities drops of 6.9%. Why is this happening in a period of recession when many people are hurting financially? Criminologists are somewhat baffled, but suggest that tighter security, more electronic surveillance and alarms, and change in city demographics with movement of more prosperous citizens into urban areas could improve neighborhood quality and safety (Newcombe 2012). Demographics also affect crime rates, with periods when a higher proportion of the populations are teenagers, since teens and 20-year-olds account for higher rates of crime than 40-, 50-, and 60-year-olds. The aging of our population may be bringing the overall crime rates down.

As young people move from rural to urban life, juvenile delinquency becomes a problem. In rural communities and tribal cultures, strict norms govern behavior, but in urban areas, cohesiveness of families and ties with tribal groups are lessened. When education, economic security, and social services increase, conformity again becomes a norm for these newcomers, replacing the anomie of the transition.

A key message from the study of urbanization is that people's lives are influenced by the environment in which they live. Public sociologists can play a role in improving the conditions of urban areas, as described in the next "Sociologists in Action."

Sociologists in Action—Jay Weinstein

Improving Quality of Life by Transforming Community Structure

As is true of many urban centers, Detroit, Michigan, has its share of distressed neighborhoods. Dr. Jay Weinstein has been director of an interdisciplinary team attempting to bring about economic, social, and physical restructuring of some of these areas. By developing long-term relationships in several urban neighborhoods, the team has had success working with residents and others to improve conditions. Weinstein calls this approach *relationship brokering*—bringing people together to share perspectives and to clear up misperceptions between residents, local officials, service providers, and police. These efforts have helped empower residents to take action and improve their neighborhoods.

A major project along these lines, which began in 1990, is in the Detroit suburb of Taylor. For decades, residents of Taylor and the surrounding Down River area were painfully aware of the problems of their neighborhood, known by uncomplimentary names such as "Crack Ridge," "Hooker Heaven," and "Sin City." With about 7,500 people packed into an area of one-half square mile, most residents were living in rental units controlled by the U.S. Department of Housing and Urban Development Section 8 program (subsidized private housing). An influential local newspaper published a series of articles showing that the neighborhood had earned the labels applied to it. The articles inspired local and federal political leaders to demand action. Weinstein and his colleagues were awarded a research grant by the City of Taylor Department of Community Development. The purposes of the work were to assess the problems and to make recommendations to improve the community. The fact-finding stage revealed that the residents of the neighborhood were not the main perpetrators. Instead, the area had been under siege by nonresidents who came and went, drifted from apartment to apartment, or illegally occupying residences after threatening to harm the rightful owners.

The research team recommended a plan for a thorough physical, economic, social, and political reconstruction of the neighborhood. Fortunately, city and federal officials accepted the recommendations of the sociological team and set out on a 10-year program of implementation. Working with residents of the neighborhood and other citizens of the city, Taylor's mayor, city council, Department of Human Resources, police department, and many others tackled the problem, with Weinstein and his colleagues' help.

Today, the neighborhood has a new name (The Villages of Taylor), a new human services center, a new residential owner (a private nonprofit corporation established by the city), and many new or redesigned buildings. The population density has been reduced by more than 20%, and all this without one person being displaced against his or her will, other than drug dealers. The average median income of Taylor is now higher than the national average. After receiving national attention, Taylor was called "a model for the nation" by the secretary of Housing and Urban Development. Many communities have looked at Taylor's plans for redevelopment. For Weinstein, sociological theory is at the root of his neighborhood work. He tries to identify the "definitions of reality" held by the residents and then helps residents examine those definitions, a symbolic interaction approach. Only by understanding their definitions can residents begin to act to change the situation.

In his work, Weinstein uses a multiple-methods approach: surveys, participant observation, census data, and other large data sets. Using a variety of approaches in combination brings him closer to the elusive truths of social life.

* * * * * * *

Dr. Jay Weinstein, a professor emeritus at Eastern Michigan University, specializes in urban sociology, demography, and social change. He received his doctorate from the University of Illinois at Urbana-Champaign and has been doing private consulting for more than 20 years, with contracts from international and local governments and nonprofit organizations. His studies have included analysis of demographic trends and changes in India, Albania, Bulgaria, and Jamaica.

Cities and the World Economy

Major economic restructuring is changing the fate of cities around the world, for better and for worse. Some cities are becoming international centers of finance, and others are losing their manufacturing base and therefore jobs. For example, the United States was the major economic, political, and military power until the 1970s. That is when the rebuilding of economies in Western Europe and Japan began to impact U.S. economic dominance.

International financial markets became powerful players in the world economy, and the institutional arrangements set up after World War II that favored the United States began breaking down; the United States as a nation was no longer the dominant economic power in the world. Multinational corporations and banks became major competitors, and cities with educated workforces and supportive infrastructure hosted major multinationals. The rise of China and the indebtedness of the United States to Japan and China again reduced the U.S. role in the world economy. International firms are surpassing national systems in their economic power. One major consequence of globalization is that the United States receives less tax income from former U.S. companies (Sassen 2012).

Today some contend that economic, political, and technical forces are the main driving forces of economies, not mass production such as manufacturing. Service industries including banks and technological firms began in the 1980s and command great earnings, weak unions, and both low-wage jobs and high-income jobs. This includes more part-time and temporary jobs as companies try to remain flexible in the worldwide markets. How does this affect cities? First, cities house major growth sectors with either very low- or very high-paying jobs; second, there is an increase in small service operations to serve the big companies; third, the reduction of manufacturing in cities tends to be greatest in large cities such as New York and Los Angeles (Sassen 2012).

Urban Planners and Social Policy in the Global Social World

Try planning an ideal city. First, list everything you need to consider such as how big the city should be. Now think of organization: Who will handle what? Keep in mind services, maintenance, financing, and leadership. Ideal city planning would be quite a task. The problem is that most urban planners do not have the luxury of starting from scratch. They must work with decaying areas, being cognizant of the meaningful landmarks and treasured sites. Planners may also have to undo hasty or inadequate planning from previous actions. Among other things, they attempt to maximize technical efficiency such as getting water from Point A to Point B.

Planners must meet needs for housing, sanitation, education, food distribution, jobs, family life, and recreation. Planning efforts need to take into consideration what will happen to various groups, including the poor, elderly, women, children, and homeless populations.

In the urban Global South, many homeless people must bathe every day in public in whatever water supply they can find. Here in Kolkata (Calcutta), India, even some people with homes do not have their own water supply and have to use fire hydrants on the streets, as this family is doing.

Although cities have many problems, they are exciting bustling places to live or to visit. Some of the liveliness of urban neighborhoods is depicted in this street scene in Bhaktapur, Nepal.

In the early 21st century, a number of global trends affect urban planning (Brunn, Hays-Mitchell, and Zeigler 2011).

1. The process of urbanization—people migrating to cities—will continue, exacerbating the already difficult situation of providing services for many of the world's crowded urban areas.

2. Information and transportation technologies allow people in any part of the globe to be in contact. However, this may also reduce the feelings of belonging to a specific place, thus reducing commitment to work on city problems and conform to urban expectations.

3. International boundaries will diminish in importance as the flow of information, goods, services, labor, and capital increasingly ignores national boundaries. For example, migration of Asians to cities around the world will continue and will have an impact on these cities.

4. Economies will increasingly rely on brainwork, including invention of new technologies, rather than on the brawn work of older manufacturing. Thus, the gap between haves and have-nots is likely to continue.

5. Conflicts between cultural and political groups, including religious and political extremists, will continue to affect urban life.

6. *McDonaldization*—creation of a consumer world dominated by major Western food, music, fashion, and entertainment—will continue, even as we see an increasing diversity of people within Western nations and communities (Ritzer 2013b).

Awareness of these trends can help urban planners in their efforts to design cities to meet the needs of the future (Friedman 2006).

In the past, men were designers of cities, but women also experience them. Some analysts believe that women have unique needs in the city that differ from men's in political, economic social, and educational fields. If this is not taken into account, urban spaces can disadvantage women and make them more vulnerable. By 2030 more than two thirds of the world's population will live in urban areas, and with this growth will come more poverty around the periphery of large cities. Key gender issues include informal settlements on the outskirts of cities, availability of water and sanitation, living arrangements, livelihoods (how to make ends meet), employment, and transportation. For example, women often have little access to affordable land and ownership, factors that affect women trying to make due for their families but living in urban poverty. Related issues include health and safety. Women often have to travel long distances by foot or public transport to access needs, and this is often not safe. Gender-specific sanitation needs of women are also problematic—not well located and with no privacy. Most of these problems require sensitivity on the part of planners to specific needs of women, often as heads of households (UN Habitat 2012).

Spaces that have been designed with women in mind emphasize opportunities for participation, involvement in community development, and leisure activities such as informal places for meeting (Hayden and Baron 2007). In the United Kingdom, social science research has informed urban development and renewal with women as consultants (UNESCO 2009). Unfortunately, profit is often the motivation in planning models, and few planning efforts consider cities in a holistic fashion. Urban planners in socialist countries with centralized national plans for urban areas may find it easier to consider the needs of all residents.

Millions of people live satisfying lives in cities, but for others, life is misery. Whether the economic base and urban planners can keep up with the demands for even basic services in the Global South remains to be seen. This is especially true in areas of the world where population is outstripping the amount of land available, and people are flocking to cities for survival. This basic population pattern—urbanization—has consequences at the most global levels and at the most micro levels of human life. Our social world model—which looks at the connections of micro, meso, and macro levels of the social system—makes us cognizant of the consequences of decisions made by millions of individuals and families. It also makes us mindful of the consequences for individuals and for cities of global trends and forces.

Many factors including population dynamics and urbanization create change in a society. Some factors contributing to social dynamics push for innovation and change in a particular direction, and other factors retard change. The next chapter examines the larger picture of social transformation and change in our complex and multileveled social world.

What Have We Learned?

Population trends, including migration resulting in urbanization, provide a dynamic force for change in societies. Whether one is interested in understanding social problems, social policy, or factors that may affect one's own career, demographic processes are critical forces. We ignore them at our peril—as individuals and as a society. Family businesses can be destroyed, retirement plans obliterated, and the health of communities sabotaged by population factors if they are overlooked. If they are considered, however, they can enhance planning that leads to prosperity and enjoyment of our communities. Urban living creates problems, but it can have enormous benefits as well. Urbanization is but a single example of a population trend.

Key Points

- Population analysis (called demography) looks at the composition, distribution, and size of a population as the society is affected by variables of fertility, mortality, and migration. (See pp. 558–560.)
- The planetwide increase in the human population's fertility is stunning. Implications for adequate resources to support life are illustrated in the population pyramids. (See pp. 561–564.)
- Various theories explain causes of the rapid growth, ranging from medical technology to cultural factors. (See pp. 564–566.)
- Many institutions affect and are affected by fertility and mortality rates at the meso level—political policies, religious beliefs, economic factors, education, and health care. (See pp. 569–573.)
- Migration is also an important issue for the society—whether the migration is international or internal—for it can change the size, distribution, and composition of a nation's citizenry. (See pp. 574–577.)
- Population patterns can also affect individual decisions at the micro level, from career choices to business decisions to programs that will affect retirement possibilities. (See pp. 578–580.)
- A major element of population migration has been urbanization. As populations become more densely concentrated, this creates a series of opportunities and problems for meeting human needs. (See pp. 580–582.)
- At the micro level, human relationships are affected by having widespread or dense population concentration. In urban areas, social relations may be less closely knit. On the negative side, this creates anomie and alienation. On the positive side, it provides more choices for people about their social relationships and lifestyles. (See pp. 582–586.)
- Cities themselves are extremely complex meso-level social settings that vary in size and operations. (See pp. 585–593.)
- At the macro level, urban environments must be understood as ecosystems that have dense poverty and homelessness, major pollution issues, and higher crime rates. These are the focus of urban planners, who try to use sociological knowledge to plan for a better future. (See pp. 596–601.)

Discussion Questions

1. Why is it important for policy makers to understand the demographic trends in their nation? Why should *you* be interested in such knowledge? How might it impact your understanding of and positions on issues related to (a) immigration, (b) education, (c) health care, and (d) social security legislation?
2. How many children (if any) do you think you would (ideally) like to have? Why? What might make this (ideal) number change?
3. What are some examples of (a) pronatalist and (b) antinatalist policies? Do you approve of such policies? Why or why not? How might your perspective differ depending on the demographics of your particular nation?
4. How is the social status of girls and women related to a society's ability to control population growth? If you were a male leader in the government of an overcrowded nation, why and how might you use this information to promote gender equality in your country? How might your ideas be perceived differently if you were a man or a woman?
5. What are some of the major reasons people leave their country of origin and move to another? Have you ever done so? Why? If not, under what circumstances would you be willing to leave the country in which you were born and move to another?
6. When was the last time you practiced what Erving Goffman described as "civil inattention"? Why did you do so? What do you think would have happened if you did not do so?

Contributing to Our Social World: What Can We Do?

At the Local Level

- The *U.S. Census Bureau* is always at work collecting, analyzing, and disseminating demographic information. It is a great source of data, ranging from information on your block to the whole nation. Invite a representative to your campus to discuss the bureau's activities. You can check internship and job opportunities with the census at www.census.gov/hrd/www/jobs/student.html.
- Check out your *local department of urban planning, urban and regional development, or community development* by Googling those terms and the name of your town, county, or province. Invite a representative to your campus or visit the department's offices. Discuss how population information is used in planning and service delivery contexts. Consider an internship with one of the organizations you find in your area.

At the Organizational or Institutional Level

- *The Population Association of America (PAA)* "is a non-profit, scientific, professional organization that promotes research on population issues," according to its website. At www.populationassociation.org, you can find information on demographic issues and ways to get involved in efforts to promote legislation promoted by the PAA.

At the National and Global Levels

- The *Population Reference Bureau* (www.prb.org/About.aspx) "informs people around the world about population, health, and the environment, and empowers them to use that information to advance the well-being of current and future generations."
- *Planned Parenthood* (www.plannedparenthood.org) promotes family planning education and outreach programs throughout the United States. Planned Parenthood International (www.ippf.org) works in 180 nations. The organizations use volunteers and interns, as well as providing long-term employment opportunities.
- *The Population Council* (www.popcouncil.org) promotes family planning in order to reduce poverty, create healthier populations and communities, empower women, and improve lives across the globe. You can find fact sheets and other information at the organization's website. You can also look for possible job and internship opportunities at www.popcouncil.org/employment/index.asp.

WWW Visit the Student Study Site at **www.sagepub.com/ballantine4e** to access additional study tools, including eFlashcards, web quizzes, video resources, audio resources, web resources, SAGE journal articles, recommended readings, and more.

CHAPTER 16

The Process of Change

Can We Make a Difference?

Individuals are profoundly influenced by the macro structures around them, but people are also capable of creating change, especially if they band together with others and approach change in an organized way. Social movements such as those depicted in the photos above are one powerful way to bring about change.

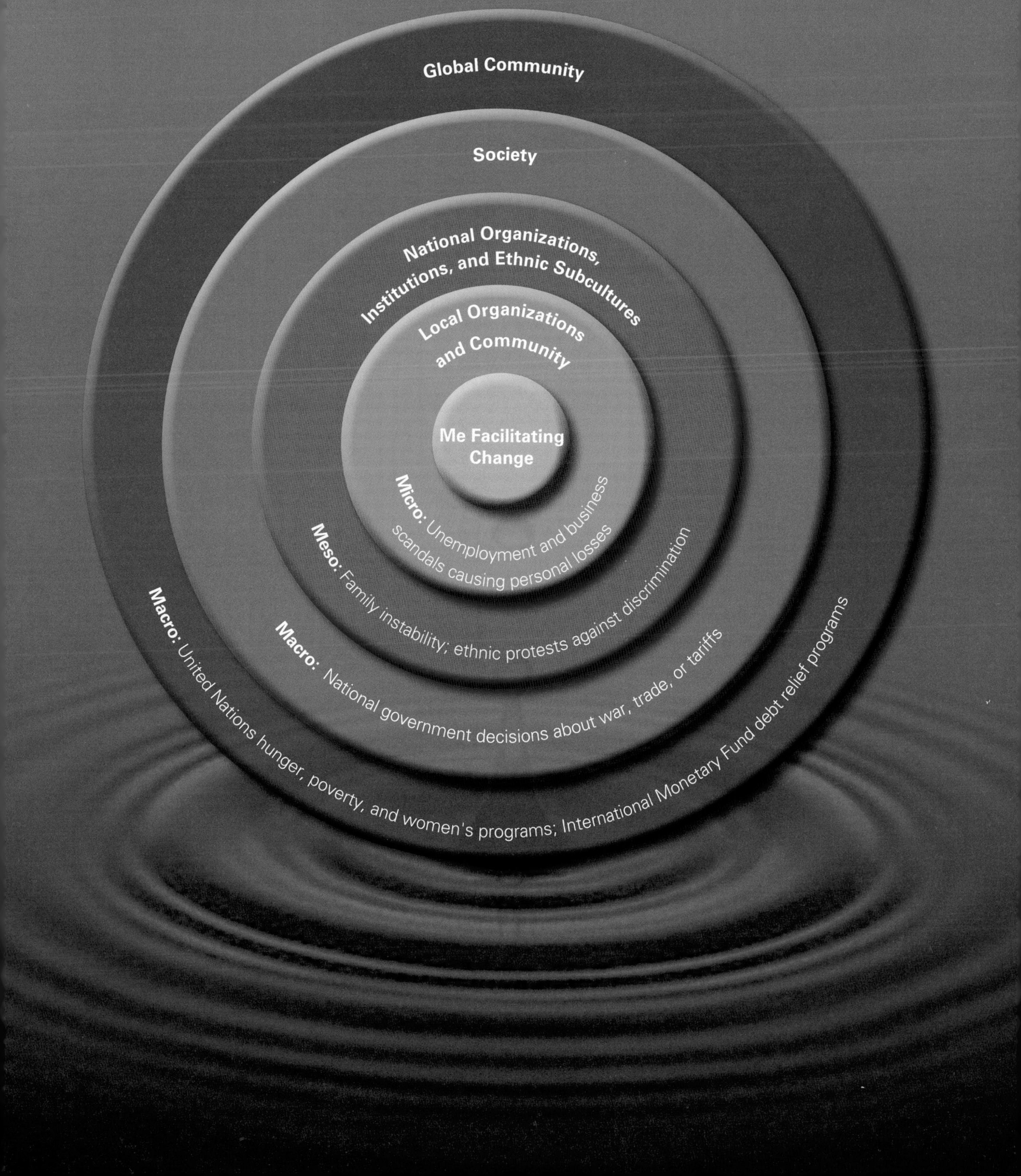

Global Community
Society
National Organizations, Institutions, and Ethnic Subcultures
Local Organizations and Community
Me Facilitating Change
Micro: Unemployment and business scandals causing personal losses
Meso: Family instability; ethnic protests against discrimination
Macro: National government decisions about war, trade, or tariffs
Macro: United Nations hunger, poverty, and women's programs; International Monetary Fund debt relief programs

Think About It	
Micro: Self and Inner Circle	Can you as an individual bring about change in the world?
Micro: Local Community	What do you think needs to change in your community?
Meso: National Institutions; Complex Organizations; Ethnic Groups	What about your community (organizational or ethnic factors) influences the possibility and type of social change?
Macro: National Society	How does training and support from national governments for technological innovation affect the process of change in your country?
Macro: Global Community	How do global changes—such as climate change—impact people and societies at each level?

What's coming in this chapter?

Our planet is in peril—according to evidence from the Asian subcontinent to the Arctic and from Africa to the Americas (Tollefson 2012; United Nations Climate Change Conference 2009). A major part of the problem is the waste humans create. Wet, dry, smelly, and sometimes recyclable—garbage is a problem, and we are running out of space to dispose of our refuse. We dump it in the ocean and see garbage surfacing on beaches and killing fish (Heyes 2012). We bury it in landfills, and the surrounding land becomes toxic. We sort and recycle it, creating other problems, such as where to dispose of recycled materials (Bell 2012). Perhaps your community or campus has separate bins for glass, cans, paper, and garbage. Recycling is a relatively new movement in response to the urgent pleas from environmentalists about our garbage and trash that pollute water sources, cause areas of the oceans to die, and deplete renewable resources.

Recycling, salvaging items that can be reused, is part of a social reform movement—the environmental movement. However, few issues have simple solutions. The dumping and recycling have to take place somewhere. Many of the recycling plants and trash dumps are located in areas where poor people and minorities live. Some have referred to this as *environmental racism*, in which ethnic minorities are put at risk by the diseases and pollutants that recycling entails (Bell 2012; Pellow 2002). This illustrates the complexity of global problems: While individuals and small groups may help solve problems at the micro level, others may be created. At the micro level, each of us can do our part in the environmental movement to save the planet through responsible personal actions. At the meso level, the environmental movement can help local and regional governments enact policies and plans to reduce the garbage problem. At the macro level, world leaders need to find responsible ways to dispose of environmental wastes. Yet the solution to this

Dumping garbage in the ocean clearly has consequences, as we can see from this shot of a beach area near Borneo.

macro-level issue of protecting the earth's resources may have micro-level implications for local minority families. Our social world is, indeed, complex and interdependent.

Turn on the morning or evening news, and there are lessons about other aspects of our changing social world. We see headlines about medical advances and cures for disease; biological breakthroughs in cloning and the DNA code; terrorist bombings in Afghanistan, Israel, Iraq, Pakistan, Chechnya, and other parts of the world; famine in drought-afflicted sub-Saharan Africa; disasters such as earthquakes, hurricanes, tsunamis, and floods; and social activists calling for boycotts of chocolate, coffee, Walmart, oil companies, or other multinational corporations. Some events seem far away and hard to imagine: thousands killed by a tidal wave in India, hundreds swept away by mud from an erupting volcano in Colombia, a massive oil spill in the Gulf of Mexico, or a rise in terrorism reflecting divisions in world economic, political, and religious ideologies. Some of these are natural events, but most are the result of human actions.

Social change is *variations or alterations over time in the structure, culture (including norms and values), and behavior patterns of a society*. Some change is controllable, and some is out of our hands, but change *is* inevitable and ubiquitous. Change can be rapid, caused by some disruption to the existing system, or it can be gradual and evolutionary. Very often, change at one level in the social world occurs because of change at another level. Micro, meso, and macro levels of society often work together in the change process but are sometimes out of sync.

In this chapter, we explore the process of change, the causes of change, and some strategies for bringing about desired change. We consider the complexity of change in our social world, explanations and theories of social change, the role of collective behavior in bringing about change, planned change in organizations, and macro-level social movements, technology, and environmental actions as they affect and are affected by change.

Our social world model is based on the assumption that change, whether evolutionary or revolutionary, is inevitable and ever present in the social world. The impetus for change may begin at the micro, meso, or macro level of analysis. Studies of the change process are not complete, however, until the level under study is understood in relation to other levels in the model, for each level affects the others in multiple ways.

Thinking Sociologically

In what ways do you take actions to lessen your impact on the environment? Might your activities be linked to improving conditions for the planet or worsening conditions for ethnic minorities on the planet?

The Complexity of Change in Our Social World

The Yir Yoront, a group of Australian aborigines, have long believed that if their own ancestors did not do something, then they must not do it. It would be wrong and might cause evil to befall the group (Sharp 1990). Obviously, these are not a people who favor change or innovation. In contrast, *progress* is a positive word in much of Australia and in other countries where change is seen as normal, even desirable. The traditions, cultural beliefs of a society, and internal and external pressures all affect the degree and rate of change in society (Berman 2011).

Change at the Individual Level: Micro-Level Analysis

One of the nation's top entrepreneurs, Microsoft's Bill Gates, combines intelligence, business acumen, and philanthropy, qualities that appeal to American individualism. Gates has the power to influence others because of his fame, wealth, and personal charisma. He is able to bring about change in organizations through his ability to motivate people and set wheels in motion. Many people have persuasive power to influence decision making, but it is not always based on charisma. For some, it is due to expertise, wealth, privileged position, access to information, or the ability to use coercive force. Any of us, if we feel strongly about an issue, can rally others and bring about change in society. Each individual in society has the potential to be a change agent.

Most organizations—schools, businesses, volunteer associations—use one or more of the following strategies to persuade individuals to accept change: They appeal to individuals' values, they use persuasion by presenting hard data and logic, they convince individuals that the existing benefits of change outweigh the costs, they remove uncooperative individuals from the organization ("addition by subtraction"), they provide rewards or sanctions for acceptance of change to alter the cost-benefit ratio, or they compel individuals to change by an order from authority figures. Thus, individuals are active agents who initiate and bring about change.

Change at the Institutional Level: Meso-Level Analysis

The terrorist attacks of September 11, 2001, which killed 3,025 innocent people from 68 nations, resulted in repercussions in many U.S. institutions. Local, state, and national governments responded by putting in place measures to deter any further attacks and to seek out and punish the guilty parties. Religious services had high attendance in the weeks

Mother Teresa, a nun who devoted her life to helping the destitute and dying in India, established the orphanage shown here in Kolkata (Calcutta) (left). In the other photo, Bill Gates (right) holds a child who is receiving a trial malaria vaccine at a medical research center in Mozambique. Gates, who supports many health initiatives, announced a grant of $168 million to fight malaria, a disease that kills more than 1 million people a year, 90% of them children in Africa (Gates 2013). Sometimes, social change occurs because of individual initiatives.

following 9/11 as religious leaders and U.S. citizens tried to make sense of the brutal attacks. Some families lost loved ones. Other families were soon separated as the military and the National Guard were called into action. Security measures were stepped up at airports and other transportation centers. These institutions at the meso level—government, religion, the family, the military—guided the response to the attacks.

Terrorism refers to the *planned use of random, unlawful (or illegal) violence or threat of violence against civilians to create (or raise) fear and intimidate citizens in order to advance the terrorist group's political or ideological goals* (U.S. Department of Defense 2012). This usually refers to acts of violence by private nonstate groups.

Contemporary terrorism is a meso-level phenomenon, even though it has both personal and global ramifications. Think of the additional hassles we must endure when flying—all in reaction to terrorist threats. Most modern terrorist organizations are not nations. They are ethnic, political, ideological, or religious subgroups that have elicited passionate loyalty from followers—even to the point of suicide on behalf of the group and its ideology.

Terrorism also has consequences for economies and other institutions. Not only do terrorist acts destabilize economies, but they change the kinds of jobs that are available. Consider the new jobs created in airport and seaport security. In addition to new jobs in security, investors hesitate to invest their money if they think the economy will be negatively affected by security threats, and this lack of investment can spawn a recession. Economic and political disruptions or ripple effects are a core motivating factor for terrorists. Furthermore, after 9/11, health care professionals began to make plans for biological and chemical terrorist attacks, changing the way monies are allocated in the health care industry (O'Toole and Henderson 2006). Thus, terrorism is a concern of the medical institution as well.

Change at the National and Global Levels: Macro-Level Analysis

To understand why terrorism occurs around the world, we must look at some of the driving forces. Although the picture is complex, one key factor is the unequal distribution of world resources. This has inspired deep anger toward affluent countries among the poor countries, which believe that the rich are using their power to maintain the inequities and to spread their political and religious philosophies. High-income countries consume over $22,000 billion in resources (World Resources Institute 2007). That amounts to 76.6% of the world's resources for 20% of the world's people. The world's middle-income countries, with 60% of the world's people, consume 21.9% of the world's resources, and the world's poorest people consume 1.5% of resources (Shah 2009b). U.S. citizens make up less than 5% of the total world population, yet the United States accounts for roughly 33% of the consumed resources in the world and 25% of the world's energy resources (Shah 2009b; World Resources Institute 2007). The average U.S. citizen consumes six times more energy than the world average (U.S. Department of Energy 2006). This seems grossly unfair to people who can barely feed their families and who have limited electricity, water, and sanitation and minimal shelter for their children. The World Wildlife Fund's 2012 report "The Living Planet" includes the top polluting countries—Qatar, Kuwait, the United Arab Emirates, Denmark, Belgium, and the United States—and the gap in pollution rates is increasing.

In fact, the world is using 50% more resources than what can be sustainably produced. Furthermore, wealthy countries have considerable economic influence over the nations of the Global South because poor countries are dependent on the affluent countries for income, employment, and loans. Citizens of poor countries may work for multinational corporations, often for very low wages. However, the profits are returned to the wealthy countries, helping perpetuate the gross inequity in the distribution of resources. Whether or not we think it is justified, this inequity leads to hostilities and sometimes terrorism as a means of striking out against more powerful countries.

The 9/11 attack was partially motivated by Middle Easterners who were intensely pro-Palestinian and anti-Israeli. Of the hijackers, 15 of the 19 were originally from Saudi Arabia; none were actually Iraqi, and none actually lived in Palestine, but they sympathized with those who had been displaced by the establishment of Israel. From the terrorist perspective, the attack on the New York City World Trade Center was an attempt to strike out at the United States.

The events of September 11 changed the United States as a nation and the core issues, priorities, spending, and values of the Bush presidency. George W. Bush's administration proposed, and Congress approved, a Patriot Act that channeled resources into heightened security and military preparedness. The provisions of the bill also greatly restricted civil liberties and allowed the government to snoop into the private lives of citizens in ways that had never before been tolerated, from monitoring the home telephone connections

People at the local (micro) level will often try to influence policies at the meso level. At this local community event, people lobby their neighbors on a state referendum in an upcoming election.

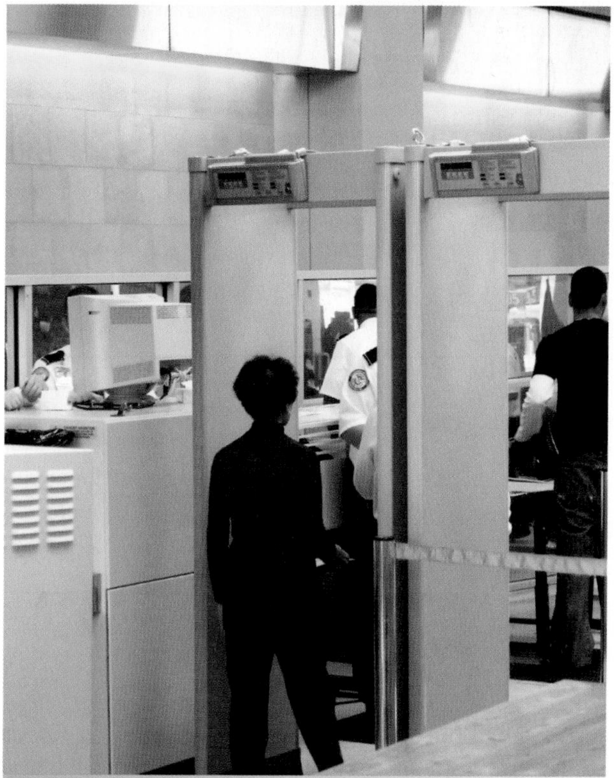

Only a decade ago family members could walk to the airplane arrival or departure gate to meet or send off a family member or friend. The terrorist attacks of 9/11 changed that, with extensive security checks that can take an hour to get through.

Terrorist tactics try to intimidate the citizens and governments so they will change their policies. In this photo, we see the memorial site for the 9/11 terrorist attack on the Twin Towers in New York, with the names of those who died engraved in stone around the waterfall memorial.

of Americans to scrutinizing the books they checked out of the library. Fear for their security led many U.S. citizens to welcome the efforts to prevent further attacks, although the root causes of terrorism were not addressed.

Thinking Sociologically

How has terrorism affected institutions and countries with which you are familiar? Has your life been changed by threats of terrorism?

Societal-Level Change

Take a look at the impact of humans on the global environment and the constant change we are bringing to our planet. To illustrate the increasingly complex and biologically interdependent social world, consider that pollution of the environment by any one country now threatens other countries. Carcinogens, acid rain, and other airborne chemicals carry across national boundaries (Brecher, Costello, and Smith 2012). People in the United States comprise less than 5% of the world's population but emit 25% of the heat-trapping gases (Lindsay 2006). In 2010, the U.S. emitted about 90 million tons of pollution into the atmosphere. While high in comparison with many other countries, it represents a drop of air pollutants by 67% since the 1980s despite increases in vehicle miles traveled, energy consumption, and population growth (Environmental Protection Agency 2011). However, that downward trend may have been reversing since 2010 ("Global Warming and Climate Change" 2013). Pollutants affect the air that surrounds the entire planet, destroying the ozone that protects us from the intense sun rays and warming the planet in ways that could threaten all of us.

In the past century, scientists claim, the earth's surface has warmed by 1 degree. That does not sound like much until one considers that during the last ice age, the earth's surface was only 7 degrees cooler than it is today. Small variations can make a huge difference, and we do not know what the consequences might be if the earth's surface temperature increases by another 2 or 3 degrees. Currently, massive blocks of sea ice are melting each year at a rate that equals the size of Maryland and Delaware combined (Cousteau 2008; Lindsay 2006). It is alarming to visit the glaciers on the South Island of New Zealand (closest to Antarctica) and realize that they are melting so fast that they have receded by as much as 10 or 12 miles in just a couple of decades. In the Northern Hemisphere, Greenland is home to many glaciers. Warming recently caused the Petermann glacier to calve an iceberg twice the size of Manhattan (BBC News 2012).

In a warmer world, there is less snowfall, resulting in smaller mountain icecaps and, thus, a smaller spring runoff of crucial freshwater. In fact, 80% of the world's population today lives in areas with shortages of water for human use (Environment 911 2012). While some of the environmental change may be rooted in natural causes, the preponderance

Due to the well-documented phenomenon of global climate change, polar bears are only one of a many species that are endangered because of a disappearing habitat. This is an issue that no one nation can address on its own.

of evidence suggests that human activity—the way we consume and the way we live our lives—is the primary cause (Gore 2012). Even if humans were not a significant cause, global climate change would have consequences that mandate change in many aspects of our lives.

Thinking Sociologically

What do you think happens when people do not have enough water in their current location to survive? What happens when they try to move into someone else's territory to gain access to needed resources?

Obviously, this is a global issue with implications for nations to work together for change. Yet some nations resist change because they feel controls will impede progress. The Kyoto Protocol on global warming requires commitment by nations to curb carbon dioxide and other emissions, but U.S. President Bush rejected it because it "does not make economic sense" (Lindsay 2006:310–11). As of September 2011, 192 countries and the European Commission had approved the treaty. The exceptions are the United States, Afghanistan, the Vatican, and the newly formed country of South Sudan (United Nations 2012). The Obama administration has indicated support for dramatic efforts to curb climate change and global warming, but passage of a bill in Congress is still pending. Fixing the environmental issues will be expensive, it may hinder the economy and slow the rate of growth, and it may even contribute to continuation of the recession. Because recessions are terrifying for any elected politician who aims to keep the public happy, change is not easy. Still, most of the world's nations have signed the Kyoto Protocol, and there is continuing pressure on the United States to sign. Because nations are still the most powerful units for allocating resources and for setting policy, changes in national policies that address the issues of a shared environment are of critical importance. The two big quandaries are (1) the costs and benefits to various nations of participating in a solution and (2) the question of time—will nations respond before it is too late to make a difference? Currently, most of the cost of pollution is accruing to impoverished countries, while rich nations benefit from the status quo. International treaties could change that.

Global Systems and Change

As the world becomes increasingly interconnected and interdependent, the impetus for change comes from global organizations, national and international organizations and governments, and multinational corporations. New and

Environmental destruction and global climate change are problems that necessitate cooperation among nations. Air pollution around China's Three Gorges Dam reduces visibility and creates health hazards.

shifting alliances between international organizations and countries link together nations, form international liaisons, and create changing economic and political systems. The following international alliances between countries, for example, are based primarily on economic ties:

- SADC: Southern African Development Community
- NAFTA: North American Free Trade Agreement
- CAFTA-DR: Dominican Republic–Central America Free Trade Agreement
- WIPO: World Intellectual Property Organization
- G8: Group of Eight—the most affluent and most powerful countries in the world
- OPEC: Organization of the Petroleum Exporting Countries
- APEC: Asia-Pacific Economic Cooperation
- EU: European Union

Consider NAFTA, which was initiated in 1993 to establish a free trade area between Canada, the United States, and Mexico in order to facilitate trade in the region. Promoters, including many global corporations, promised that the agreement would create thousands of new high-wage jobs, raise living standards in each of the countries, improve environmental conditions, and transform Mexico from a poor developing country into a booming new market.

Opponents (including labor unions, environmental organizations, consumer groups, and religious communities) argued the opposite—that NATFA would reduce wages; destroy jobs, especially in the United States; undermine democratic policy making in North America by giving corporations a free rein; and threaten health, the environment, and food safety (U.S. Trade Representative 2012).

Analyses of the agreement show mixed results. There is some indication that tariffs are down and U.S. exports have increased. The treaty countries trade $2.7 billion daily, and trade tripled between 1993 and 2011, from $288 billion to $1 trillion (U.S. Trade Representative 2012). NAFTA has been more effective in increasing trade in agricultural commodities than nonagricultural products. Some analysts argue that there is improvement in the areas of environmental protection and labor rights, but many others argue that these have declined. The truth is hard to determine, but there are probably both gains and losses (Amadeo 2009).

In the above discussion of changes at different levels of analysis, the principle is that change at one level leads to change in other levels, as it has done in the global cases of terrorism, climate change, and NAFTA. Changes at the macro level affect individuals, just as change at the micro level has repercussions at the meso and macro levels.

Social Change: Process and Theories

The Process of Social Change

Something always triggers a social change. The impetus may come from within the organization, a source of change known as *strain*. Sometimes, it comes from outside the organization, what sociologists call *stress*. Let us consider two examples of strain: (1) conflicting goals and (2) different belief systems within the organization.

Conflicting goals are seen in the case of the platinum mining industry and its union workers. In the Lonmin South African platinum mines (providing materials for catalytic converters and jewelry), 44 workers died in August 2012 during strikes demanding pay hikes. Individual miners work in difficult, dangerous conditions to try to meet their basic needs for food and shelter for their families. Sometimes they must live at the mines away from their families for many months, but when jobs are scarce one does what one must. Company goals focus on the bottom line, being profitable in a competitive environment. The company argues that it cannot afford to raise wages and still be competitive (Herskovitz 2012). This conflict and others like it demonstrate how the needs of the workers can be at odds with those of the company.

Contrasting belief systems (political, religious, economic, and social) within a society can also have a major effect on the type and rate of change. For example, some religious groups oppose stem cell research, which uses the cells of fetuses, most of which were created in test tubes. Others within the same congregation believe this research will alleviate the suffering of loved ones and save lives. Although both sides believe they are pro-life, the internal strain in the religious group emanates from events and forces in science, medicine, and other institutions (Religious Tolerance 2010).

Stresses, those pressures for change that come from the organization's external environment, can be traced to several sources: the natural environment and natural disasters, population dynamics, actions of leaders, new technologies, changes in other institutions, and major historical events.

The natural environment can bring about either slow or dramatic change in a society. Natural disasters such as floods, hurricanes, tsunamis, heavy snows, earthquakes, volcanic eruptions, mudslides, tornadoes, and other sudden events are not planned occurrences, but they can have dramatic consequences. Disease epidemics are often unpredictable, such as the cholera outbreaks in Zimbabwe that in 2008–2009 killed over 4,000 people and the one in Haiti that has killed thousands since 2011 and resulted in more than 110,000 cases in 2012 (Nichols 2012; Rusere 2009). Natural disasters are so important that the sociology of disasters has become a specialty field within the discipline, as indicated by one of the classic sociological studies of disasters, reported in the next "Sociology in Our Social World."

Natural disasters—floods, hurricanes, tornadoes, earthquakes, volcanic eruptions—can be the cause of major social changes in a community. As shown in this photo from a community on Lake Pontchartrain near New Orleans, Hurricane Katrina took its toll on Mississippi and Louisiana.

Sociology in Our Social World

Disasters and Their Aftermath

A series of small villages were settled along a mountain creek in West Virginia known as Buffalo Creek. This was mining country, and at the top of the creek, a coal company had poured more than 1 million tons of wastewater and coal waste into a company-created basin. The restraining embankment of shale, clay, slag, and low-quality coal that created the reservoir was referred to by the coal company as an "impoundment," but the people themselves referred to it as a "dam."

Whatever one called it, this restraining wall was weakened by heavy rains in the winter of 1972, and on February 26, it broke, setting forth a massive flood of black sludge and oily, slag-filled wastewater down the valley toward the homes of 5,000 residents in the mountain villages. The first village hit was not just crushed; it disappeared entirely. This meant that the villages farther down the creek bed had not just filthy water coming at them but the remains of homes, churches, stores, vehicles, and bodies. By the time the water subsided, the flood had taken with it almost everything in its path.

Newspapers reported the economic loss and the staggering death toll, but lawyers, psychologists, and sociologists were interested in the human cost to survivors—costs to their sense of self, their mental and emotional well-being, and their family and friendship ties. Here was a community that had had an extraordinarily close-knit social network, where crime was virtually nonexistent, divorces were extraordinary, chemical abuse and mental problems were far below the national norms, and neighborhoods were like extended families. Yet the community had been ripped apart by the flood. Time had not healed the social and emotional wounds, even years after the flood: Few marriages remained intact, problems of deviance and delinquency were rife, and more than 90% of the people interviewed were judged to be in need of psychological counseling.

The federal government's response to the flood in Buffalo Creek dealt mostly with the immediate needs for survival. Thus, mobile homes were brought in, and emergency food was provided, but people were placed in these shelters without taking into account their existing ties with family members, friends, and neighbors. Thus, people found themselves surrounded by strangers at a time when they desperately needed support and when they also had few interpersonal resources to forge new relationships.

The mental health symptoms tied to individual trauma include psychic numbness (feeling mentally blank and emotionally limp), constant anxiety about death, guilt at having survived when so many members of one's family had not, guilt for not having saved people who were seen being swept down the river, loss of the "furniture of self" (the symbols of one's life that might include one's home, family heirlooms, photographs of loved ones, and other artifacts that connect one to others and to a personal history), and loss of trust in the order of the universe or a loving God, who people believed was in control of life's events.

The "collective trauma" was more important to understand than the individual trauma: "People find it difficult to recover from the effects of individual trauma so long as the community around them remains in shreds" (Erikson 1976:155). The collective trauma included five dimensions:

1. *Disorientation:* Erikson found that many persons were so socially displaced that they could hardly orient themselves in time and space, even two or three years after the flood.
2. *Loss of morale and morality:* Following the flood, people were more likely to commit deviant acts and to think they were surrounded by immoral people.
3. *Loss of connection:* Marriages began to disintegrate, and people lost their sense of connection to others. "Members of a family find that intimacy and gentleness are hard to sustain in an emotional atmosphere as dry as this one," reports Erikson (1976:221).
4. *Illness and identity:* People seemed to feel that the land was polluted and untrustworthy, with some people being afraid to till the soil lest they find a body part of a family member or a

(Continued)

(Continued)

neighbor buried there. Because the land was polluted, many people felt their own bodies were polluted, too.

5. *Loss of a sense of safety:* People slept in their clothes and boots, and whenever it rained, many residents would run to the creek every hour to check on the water levels.

This disaster at Buffalo Creek indicates how much of our personal mental health rests in the health of the larger community. It helps us understand how anomie (normlessness) can create anxiety and disorientation. Most of all, it helps us understand that natural disasters and human catastrophes, such as the September 11 terrorist attacks, devastating storms such as Hurricane Katrina, and the daily killings in Iraq, can have pervasive effects on individuals and communities. Although Erikson has been a leading figure in outlining what steps to take after a disaster, his work is not always considered when larger policies are made.

Work on collective trauma forces us to be aware of the extent to which we depend on a larger community to regain our footing when a disaster disrupts our lives. We humans are, indeed, profoundly social beings. Changes that disrupt our social ties can have severe and wide-ranging consequences.

Thinking Sociologically

What lessons can we take from Erikson's findings to shed light on recent natural disasters with which you are familiar?

Epidemics such as the H1N1 flu and SARS (severe acute respiratory syndrome) have brought about change in the World Health Organization, global medical reporting systems, and response networks. For instance, the Global Public Health Intelligence Network scans Internet communications for rumors and reports of suspicious diseases. This way, health organizations from the local to global levels can act quickly to contain the spread of deadly epidemics.

Less rapid natural changes also can have incremental but dramatic effects. For example, most scientists predict that the climatic changes resulting from the greenhouse effect are warming our atmosphere due to a buildup of carbon dioxide or other gases (Environmental Protection Agency 2012). These scientists are convinced that climate change is a human-generated problem that, at worst, is a threat to our survival and, at best, will increase the cost of living in ways that drastically change the lifestyle of ordinary people (Environmental Defense Fund 2012). While there is nearly total agreement among scientists that global climate change is occurring, the point of debate is how much of it is caused by humans.

Population dynamics—birth- and death rates, size of populations, age distribution, and migration patterns—can be important contributors to external stress on organizations. Where populations are growing at extremely rapid rates, strains on government systems result in an inability to meet the basic needs of the people. Values and beliefs regarding childbearing, knowledge of birth control, and the position of women in society are some of the crucial social variables in addressing the ability to meet needs. Immigration due to political upheavals or motivated by

These Ugandan refugees have survived without their parents and must now cope with life as best they can. They were forced to flee from their homes or they would have been killed.

anticipated economic opportunities creates stress on the societies that receive the newcomers as they attempt to meet the immigrants' needs. For example, many refugees from the conflicts in the Darfur region in Sudan are fleeing to camps in the nearby country of Chad. Map 16.1 shows the global hot spots for refugees entering other countries.

Leaders influence change through their policy decisions or the social movements they help generate. India's Mohandas K. (Mahatma) Gandhi taught the modern world nonviolent methods of bringing about change in political systems. The policies of Charles Taylor, former military dictator of Liberia, created long-term war and resulted in thousands of deaths. President Robert Mugabe of Zimbabwe locked his country in a downward spiral of economic turmoil and disease, killing thousands. These leaders' actions created internal strains in their own countries and external stressors resulting in change in the international community.

Technology also influences societal change. William F. Ogburn compiled a list of 150 social changes in the United States that resulted from the invention of the radio, such as instant access to information (Ogburn 1933). Other lists could be compiled for cell phones, automobiles, television, computers, and new technologies such as iPhones. Some of these changes give rise to secondary changes. For example, automobile use led to paved highways, complex systems of traffic patterns and rules, and gasoline stations. The next "Sociology in Our Social World" explores several issues involving the automobile and change.

New arrivals at Al Salam camp, in Sudan's Darfur region, make temporary shelters out of household goods they were able to carry with them. A U.S. Agency for International Development (USAID)–supported program at this site is helping register more than 10,000 people who were displaced by violence in their home regions. Migration is a major factor in social change, and in cases like this, it is associated with great suffering and hardship.

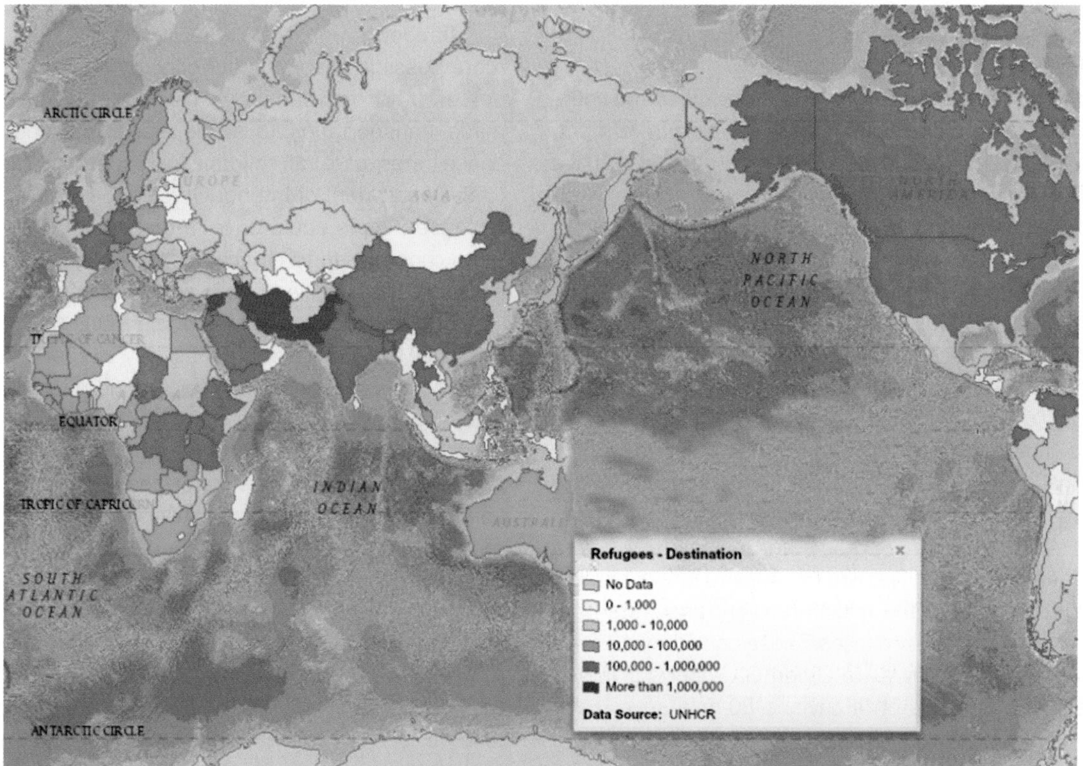

Map 16.1 Countries Receiving Refugees, Asylum Seekers, and Internally Displaced People

Sociology in Our Social World

Technology and Change: The Automobile

Only a century ago, a newfangled novelty was spreading quickly from urban areas to the countryside: the automobile. At the turn of the 20th century, this strange horseless carriage was often referred to in rural areas as the "devil wagon." The introduction of this self-propelled vehicle was controversial, and in the 1890s and early 1900s, some cities and counties had rules forbidding motorized vehicles. In Vermont, a walking escort had to precede the car by an eighth of a mile with a red warning flag, and in Iowa, motorists were required to telephone ahead to a town they planned to drive through to warn the community lest their horses be alarmed (Berger 1979; Clymer 1953; Glasscock 1937; Morris 1949). In most rural areas, motorists were expected to pull their cars to a stop or even to shut down the motor when a horse-drawn buggy came near. "Pig and chicken legal clauses" meant the automobile driver was liable for any injury that occurred when passing an animal near the road, even if the injury was due to the animal running away (Scott-Montagu 1904).

Automobiles were restricted to cities for nearly a decade after their invention because roads were inadequate outside of the urban areas and they often slid off muddy roads into ditches. These conditions had not deterred horses. In 1915, Owen G. Roberts invented a seatbelt because on a daylong 80-mile drive westward from Columbus, Ohio, Mary Roberts was knocked unconscious when the rough roads caused her head to smack the roof of the car. Paving of roads became a necessity for automobile travel and, of course, made automobile travel much faster and more common. The expansion was stunning. Roughly 85,000 motored vehicles were in use in America in 1911. By 1930, the number was nearly 10 million, and in 2007 the estimated number of registered passenger vehicles was 254.4 million (Berger 1979; Tilley 2009).

Forms of entertainment began to change when people were able to be more mobile. As the Model T made cars affordable, families no longer had only each other for socializing, and entertainment became available virtually any night of the week (Berger 1979; McKelvie 1926). Thus, dependence on family was lessened, possibly weakening familial bonds and oversight (Berger 1979). Even courting was substantially changed, as individuals could go farther afield to find a possible life partner, couples could go more places on dates, and two people could find more privacy.

Transportation that made traversing distances more possible changed how people related to a number of other institutions as well. Motorized buses made transportation to schools possible, and attendance rates of rural children increased substantially (U.S. Department of Interior Office of Education 1930). Because people could drive farther to churches, they often chose to go to city churches, where the preachers were more skilled public speakers and the music was of higher quality. Some people found that a country drive was a more interesting way to spend Sunday mornings, and preachers often condemned cars for leading people away from church (Berger 1979). Many country churches consolidated or closed. Still, once pastors could afford cars, rural people received new services such as pastoral calls (Wilson 1924). The automobile was also a boon to the mental health of isolated farm women, allowing them to visit with neighbors (Berger 1979; McNall and McNall 1983).

As people could live in less congested areas but still get to work in a reasonable amount of time via an automobile or public transport, the suburbs began to develop around major cities. No longer did people locate homes close to shopping, schools, and places of worship. Still, a dispersed population needs to use more gasoline, thereby creating pollution. As the wealthy moved to expensive suburbs and paid higher taxes to support outstanding schools, socioeconomic and ethnic stratification between communities increased.

When Owen G. Roberts built one of the first automobiles in Ohio and established a large automobile dealership, it was not his intent to heighten segregation, to create funding problems for poor inner-city areas, or to pollute the environment. Yet, these are some of the *unintended consequences* of the spread of the automobile. It sometimes takes decades before we can identify the consequences of the technologies we develop and adopt.

Thinking Sociologically

What might be some long-term social consequences for our individual lives and societies of the expanded use of the computer, cell phones and iPhones, the microwave oven, and cars that can navigate themselves and warn us of hazards around us?

The diffusion or spread of technology throughout the world is likely to be uneven, especially in the early stages of the new technology. For example, computer technology has advanced rapidly, but those advances began in corporate boardrooms, military bases, and university laboratories. Policies of governing bodies—such as funding for school computers—determine the rate of public access. Thus, only gradually are computers reaching the world's citizenry through schools, libraries, and eventually private homes.

Major historical events—wars, economic crises, assassinations, political scandals, and catastrophes—can change the course of world events. For instance, the triggering event that actually started World War I was the assassination of Archduke Franz Ferdinand of the Austro-Hungarian Empire. This assassination resulted in the German invasion of several other countries and the beginning of the war. So a micro-level act, the murder of an individual, had global ramifications. Clearly, internal strains and external stressors give impetus to the processes of change. The question is "How do these processes take place?"

Theories of Social Change

Social scientists seek to explain the causes and consequences of social change, sometimes in the hope that change can be controlled or guided. Theories of change often reflect the events and belief systems of particular historical time periods. For example, conflict theory developed during periods of change in Europe. It gained adherents in the United States during the 1960s, when intense conflict over issues of race and ethnic relations, the morality of the Vietnam War, and changes in social values peaked. Theories that focused on social harmony were of little help.

The major social change theories can be categorized as micro-level (symbolic interaction and rational choice theories) or meso- and macro-level (evolutionary, functional, conflict, and world systems theories). As we review these theories, many of them will be familiar to you from previous chapters. However, in this case they are related to the process of change.

Micro-Level Theories of Change

Symbolic Interactionism. According to symbolic interaction theory, human beings are always trying to make sense of the things they experience, figure out what an event or interaction means, and determine what action is required of them. Humans construct meanings that agree with or diverge from what others around them think. This capacity to define one's situation, such as concluding that one is oppressed, even though others have accepted the circumstances as normal, can be a powerful impetus to change. It can be the starting point of social movements, cultural changes, and revolutions.

Some sociologists believe that individuals are always at the core of any social trends or movements, even if those movements are national or global (Blumer 1986; Giddens 1986; Simmel [1902–1917] 1950). After all, it is individuals who act, make decisions, and take action. There are a number of leaders, for example, who have changed the world—for better or worse—including Adolf Hitler and Mahatma Gandhi. Neither corporations, nor nations, nor bureaucracies make decisions—people do. The way in which an individual defines the reality he or she is experiencing makes a huge difference in how she or he will respond to it.

Social institutions and structures are always subject to maverick individuals "thinking outside the box" and changing how others see things. Individual actions can cause riots, social movements, planned change in organizations, and a host of other outcomes that have the potential to transform society. That people may construct reality in new ways can be a serious threat to the status quo, and those who want to protect the status quo try to ensure that people will see the world the same way they do. If change feels threatening to some members who have a vested interest in the current arrangements, those individuals who advocate change may face resistance. Consider the current state of the world, in which some nations are making rapid technological advances and others are resisting modernization as a threat to their religious cultures and way of life.

Leaders often provide opportunities for group members to participate in suggesting, planning, and implementing change in order to help create acceptance and positive attitudes toward change. This collaborative process is often used when a firm or a public agency is planning a major project, such as the development of a shopping mall or a waste disposal site, and cooperation and support by other parts of the community become essential. Symbolic interactionists would see this as an effort to build a consensus about what the social changes mean and to implement change in a way that is not perceived as threatening to the members.

Rational Choice. To rational choice theorists, behaviors are largely driven by individuals seeking rewards and limiting costs. Because of this, most individuals engage in those activities that bring positive rewards and try to avoid actions that can have negative outcomes. A group seeking change can attempt to set up a situation in which the desired behavior is rewarded with positive sanctions and undesirable behavior receives negative sanctions.. The typology presented in Figure 16.1 shows the relationship between behaviors and sanctions.

Bringing about change may not require a change in costs or rewards. It may be sufficient simply to change people's perception of the advantages and disadvantages of certain actions. Sometimes, people are not aware of all the rewards, or they have failed to accurately assess the costs of an action. For example, few citizens in the United States realize all the financial, health, and legal benefits of marriage. To change the marriage rates, we may not need more benefits to encourage marriage. We may do just as well to change the population's appraisal of the benefits already available.

Meso- and Macro-Level Theories of Change

Social Evolutionary Theories. Social evolutionary theories at the macro level assume that societies change slowly from simple to more complex forms. Early unilinear theories maintained that all societies moved through the same steps and that advancement or progress was desirable and would lead to a better society. These theories came to prominence during the Industrial Revolution, when European social scientists sought to interpret the differences between their own societies and the "primitive societies" of other continents. Europe was being stimulated by travel, exposure to new cultures, and a spawning of new philosophies, a period called the Enlightenment. Europeans witnessed the development of mines, railroads, cities, educational systems, and industries, which they defined as "progress" or "civilization." World travelers reported that other peoples and societies did not seem to have these developments. These reports provided the empirical evidence that early sociologist Auguste Comte used in proposing his theory of unilinear development from simple to complex societies. Unilinear theories came to legitimate colonial expansion and exploitation of other people and lands that were seen as "inferior."

In a more recent version of evolutionary theory, Patrick Nolan and Gerhard Lenski discuss five stages through which societies progress: hunter-gatherer, horticultural, agrarian, industrial, and postindustrial (Nolan and Lenski 2010; see also Chapter 3). This does not mean that some stages are "better" than others; it means that this is the typical pattern of change resulting from new technologies and more efficient harnessing of energy. Despite their claim that this theory does not judge some stages as "better," the authors do use the term *progress*. This word refers to greater technological sophistication rather than to moral superiority. Still, in terms of technology, they do think the later stages are more advanced.

		Sanction	
		Formal	**Informal**
Behavior	**Positive**	Bonuses, advances, fringe benefits, recognition	Praise, smile, pat on the back
	Negative	Demotion, loss of salary	Ridicule, exclusion, talk behind back

Figure 16.1 Relationship Between Behaviors and Sanctions

Photo Essay

Transportation Systems and Change

The efficiency and speed of modes of transportation for goods and people vary around the world, often reflecting the level of development of the region or country. "Premodern" modes of transportation cause less pollution and sometimes move more easily through congested streets than gas- or diesel-operated motors. Sometimes, technological progress has a high cost, and resistance to that "progress" may make sense.

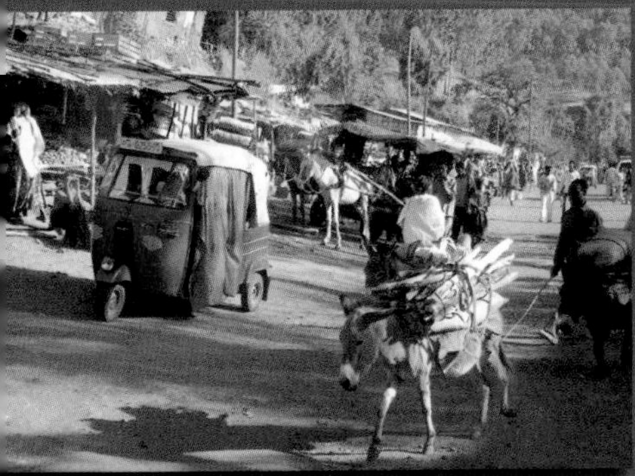

Many modern cases do not fit this pattern because they skip steps or are selective about what aspects of technology they wish to adopt. Countries such as India and China are largely agricultural but are importing and developing the latest technology that allows them to skip over developmental steps. Most African countries will not see landlines for phones, but instead will have cell phones even in remote areas. Furthermore, advocates of some religious, social, and political ideologies question the assumption that "material progress" (which is what technology fosters) is desirable.

Even the phrase *developing countries* has been controversial with some scholars because it might imply that all societies are moving toward the type of social system characterized by the affluent or "developed" societies. Many now use the term *Global South* because poor countries are disproportionately located south of the 20th parallel north, whereas affluent nations are typically situated north of that latitude. Note that the term is a metaphor for all poor countries. Some prosperous countries are in the Global South and some poor ones in the Global North, but the term is meant to avoid an assumption of inevitable evolution toward Western cultures.

Contemporary evolutionary theories are multilinear, acknowledging that change takes place in multiple ways and not just in a straight line. The rapid spread of ideas and technologies means that societies today may move quickly from simple to complex, creating modern states. Consider the mass of contradictions in the Middle East today. Due to the world demand for their oil, several countries in this region now have among the highest per capita incomes (average income for each individual) in the world. In 2012, Qatar had an income of $102,800 for each individual, while the average for the United States was $49,800 (World Factbook 2012a). The urban elite in these countries have access to modern conveniences such as the latest technology, jets, and cell phones. Yet other Middle Eastern people still live traditional lives as nomads or herders in small villages or earn their living from the desert. Not all segments of society change at the same rate, making categorization of some societies difficult. A single nation may be divided into both postindustrial and pastoral.

Functionalist Theories. Functional theorists assume that societies are basically stable systems held together by the shared norms and values of their members. The interdependent parts work together to make the society function smoothly. A change in one part of the society affects all the other parts, each changing in turn until the system resumes a state of equilibrium. Change can come from external or internal sources, from stresses in contact with other societies or from strains within.

Slow, nondisruptive change occurs as societies become more complex, but any change may be seen as threatening to the equilibrium of a system. Rapid change is seen as especially dysfunctional or disruptive. Because sudden, disruptive change is difficult to explain using functional theory and because any major change is viewed with some suspicion, some sociologists have turned to conflict theories to help explain change, especially rapid or violent changes.

Conflict Theories. Conflict theorists assume that societies are dynamic and that change and conflict are inevitable. According to Karl Marx, socioeconomic class conflict is the major source of tension leading to change in any society. Karl Marx and Friedrich Engels predicted that the antagonistic relationship they saw developing between the workers (proletariat) and the owners of the production systems (bourgeoisie) in 19th-century England would lead to social revolution. From this, they believed a new world order would emerge in which the workers themselves would own the means of production. Thus, conflict between the owners and the workers would be the central factor driving social change (Marx and Engels [1848] 1969).

Other conflict theorists study variables such as gender, religion, politics, and ethnic and interest group problems in their analyses, feeling that these factors can also be the grounds for oppression and "we" versus "they" differences (Dahrendorf 1959). Some see conflict as useful for society because it forces societies to adapt to new conditions and leads to healthy change (Coser 1956). Conflicts over slavery and over gender inequality are examples of problems that cause stresses and strains, eventually resulting in an improved society. The recent conflict over health care in the United States is also likely to lead to a better system.

World Systems Theory of Global Change. World systems theorists focus on the historical development of the whole world and how that development has influenced individual countries today. Capitalist economies first appeared about 1500. Since then, except for a few isolated tribal groupings, almost all societies have been at least indirectly influenced by dominant capitalist world economic and political systems (Wallerstein 1974).

This theory divides the world system into three main parts: the core, semiperipheral areas, and peripheral areas (see Figure 16.2). Core countries include most Western European states, Australia and New Zealand, Japan, Canada, the United States, and a few others (Wallerstein 1974). Historically, they have controlled global decision making, received the largest share of the profits from the world economic system, and dominated the peripheral areas politically, economically, and culturally by controlling the flow of technology and capital into and out of those countries. Peripheral countries, most of which are in Africa, Asia, and South America, provide cheap labor and raw materials for the core countries' needs.

The semiperipheral countries are in an intermediate position, trading with both the core and the peripheral countries. The Baltic regions of Eastern Europe, Brazil, Argentina, South Africa, India, the Philippines, Iran, and Mexico are among the semiperipheral areas. Because most semiperipheral countries are industrializing, they serve as areas to which core-country businesses and multinational corporations can move for continued growth, often in partnerships, as semiperipheral states aspire to join the core countries. The core and semiperipheral countries process raw materials, often taken from peripheral countries for little return, and may sell the final products back to the peripheral countries. The semiperipheral countries and the peripheral countries need the trade and the resources of the core countries, but they are also at a severe disadvantage in competition and are exploited by those at the core, resulting in an uneasy relationship.

These basic relationships between countries have endured since the 1700s. However, South Korea, Thailand, Taiwan, India, and China may challenge the existing relationships with their rapidly expanding economies (Friedman 2005). Furthermore, since the 1960s, production processes have modified the relationships between the regions of the world. Changes in technology and in international global institutions have allowed corporations to break their production processes into smaller segments. These segments are then scattered over the world to take advantage of the lower manufacturing costs in the periphery. This process creates commodity chains—worldwide networks of labor resources and production processes that create a product. Each piece of the chain can be located in a core, semiperipheral, or peripheral country. Because manufacturing processes are often performed in semiperipheral countries, their share of the world's manufacturing and trade production has risen sharply. In contrast, the distribution of profits from multinational corporations still benefits the core countries.

Core countries have been a major force in the development of global institutions, such as the International Monetary Fund (IMF), that facilitate and attempt to control international capital flow. By increasing the frameworks for debt restructuring for peripheral countries, the IMF attempts to restore sustainability and growth to countries that default on their loans. At least 30 countries have restructured their debt under IMF guidelines (IMF 2003).

However, the IMF leaves countries little economic autonomy. The restructuring plans control what countries do even within their own national boundaries, creating debt dependencies on core countries that most poorer countries can never overcome. For example, the IMF has demanded and instituted freezes on salaries and minimum wages in countries such as Greece, Brazil, and Argentina. It has mandated the opening of borders to imports and has unintentionally undermined the economies of some very poor countries. The problem has been one of insisting on the application of economic theories that work in affluent countries but not always in poor ones (The Dollars and Sense Collective 2012; Gibler 2012; Rothkopf 2012; Stiglitz 2012).

In this typical situation, these South African miners are all black and work for low wages, whereas the supervisors and managers are white. These gold miners from poor peripheral countries are part of a multinational corporation and the larger world economic system, with stockholders from the core capitalist world system.

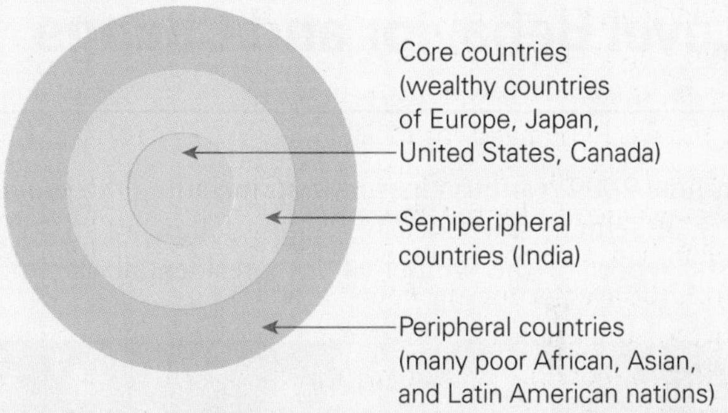

Figure 16.2 World Systems Theory

In one sense, world systems theory is a conflict theory that is global in nature, with core countries exploiting the poor countries. As we might expect from conflict theory, some groups of noncore countries have increased their collective power by forming alliances such as OPEC (Organization of the Petroleum Exporting Countries), OAS (Organization of African States), and SEATO (Southeast Asia Treaty Organization). These alliances present challenges to the historically core countries of the world system because of their combined economic and political power. For example, the price we pay at the gas pump reflects the power of OPEC to set prices.

When we understand international treaties and alliances as part of larger issues of conflict over resources and economic self-interests, the animosity of noncore countries toward core countries such as the United States begins to make sense. Likewise, the mistrust of the United States toward countries that seem to be getting U.S. jobs is not entirely unfounded. The problem is an extraordinarily complex system that always leaves the most vulnerable more at risk and the wealthiest even richer.

Sometimes behavior that results in change is unplanned, even spontaneous, as described in the following section.

Thinking Sociologically

Where is your clothing made? Did a multinational corporation have it assembled in the Global South? Who benefits from companies buying cheap labor from the Global South: You? The workers? Governments? The companies that manufacture the products? Who, if anyone, is hurt?

Collective Behavior: Micro-Level Behavior and Change

In June 2009, various cities in Iran, including the capital city of Tehran, saw extensive rioting following an "official" report of the winner of the presidential election.

Suspicion of fraudulent vote counts that reelected an unpopular Iranian president—Mahmoud Ahmadinejad—resulted in extensive rioting, as well as more peaceful protests.

Although Iran's president has limited power, the position remains the highest public office decided by a popular vote. Supporters of the reform candidate, Mir Hossein Mousavi, convinced that there had been extensive voter fraud, vented their anger with both peaceful and violent expressions of contempt for the process. Iranian police and military officers responded with arrests and counterviolence, attempting to control the situation and stop the protests. While not everyone was disheartened by the election, this eruption of anger illustrates the unpredictable nature of collective behavior.

Collective behavior refers to *actions that are spontaneous, unstructured, and disorganized and that may violate norms; this behavior arises when people are trying to cope with stressful situations and unclear or uncertain conditions* (Goode 1992; Smelser 1963, 1988). Collective behavior falls into two main types: crowd behavior and mass behavior. It often starts as a response to an event or a stimulus. It could begin with a shooting or beating, a speech, a sports event, or a rumor. The key is that as individuals try to make sense of the situations they are in and respond based on their perceptions, collective social actions emerge.

Crowd behaviors—mobs, panics, riots, and demonstrations—are all forms of collective behavior in which a crowd acts, at least temporarily, as a unified group (LeBon [1895] 1960). Crowds are often made up of individuals who see themselves as supporting a just cause. Because the protesters are in such a large group, they may not feel bound by the normal social controls—either internal (normal moral standards) or external (fear of police sanctions).

Mass behavior occurs when individual people communicate or respond in a similar manner to ambiguous or uncertain situations, often based on common information from the news or on the Internet. Examples include public opinion, rumors, fads, and fashions. Unlike social movements, these forms of collective behavior generally lack a hierarchy of authority and clear leadership, a division of labor, and a sense of group action.

Theories of Collective Behavior

Social scientists studying group and crowd dynamics find that most members of crowds are respectable, law-abiding citizens, but faced with specific situations, they act out (Berk 1974; Ritzer 2013a; Turner and Killian 1993). Several explanations of individual involvement dominate the modern collective behavior literature.

Based on principles of rational choice theory, *the minimax strategy* suggests that individuals try to minimize their losses or costs and maximize their benefits (Berk 1974). People are more likely to engage in behavior if they feel the rewards outweigh the costs. Individuals may become involved in a riot if they feel the outcome—drawing attention to their plight, the possibility of improving conditions, solidarity with neighbors and friends, looting goods—will be more rewarding than the status quo or the possible negative sanctions.

Emergent norm theory points out that individuals in crowds have different emotions and attitudes guiding their behaviors than if they act alone (Turner and Killian 1993). The theory addresses the unusual situations, involving the breakdown of norms, in which most collective behavior takes place. Unusual situations may call for the development of new norms and even new definitions of what is acceptable behavior. The implication of this theory is that in ambiguous situations, people look to others for clues about what is happening or what is acceptable, and norms emerge in ambiguous contexts that may be considered inappropriate in other contexts. This really is the most widely used approach to understanding collective behavior (Ritzer 2013a).

Imagine that you were in a situation at an athletic event where someone in the crowd with a very loud voice began to taunt a referee or a player from the visiting team. Initially some people around you laughed, but as the initiator began to chant an insult, your friends and others around you began to join in. Chances are good that in the camaraderie of the moment, you followed suit and joined the cheer—even if it was very disrespectful. Normally you would not make such an insulting remark to someone's face, but the pattern of behavior emerged, and you joined the crowd. This would be an example of emergent norm affecting an entire crowd.

Value-added theory (sometimes called structural-strain theory) describes the conditions for crowd behavior and social movements. Key elements are necessary for collective behavior, with each new variable adding to the total situation until conditions are sufficient for individuals to begin to act in common. At this point, collective behavior emerges (Smelser 1963). These are the six factors identified that can result in collective behavior:

1. *Structural conduciveness:* Existing problems create a climate that is ripe for change (e.g., the tensions between religious and ethnic groups in Iraq).
2. *Structural strain:* The social structure is not meeting the needs and expectations of the citizens, which creates widespread dissatisfaction with the status quo—the current arrangements (e.g., the Iraqi government is unable to control violence and provide basic services).
3. *Spread of a generalized belief:* Common beliefs about the cause, effect, and solution of the problem evolve, develop, and spread (e.g., U.S. troops begin to leave; militias are killing the members of other groups).

Crowds can stimulate change in a society, but they can also become unruly and unpredictable. Government officials spend a good deal of money and time equipping and training officers to control angry and radicalized members of crowds.

4. *Precipitating factor:* A dramatic event or incident occurs to incite people to action (e.g., groups of men from different religious groups are kidnapped, bound, and shot).
5. *Mobilization for action:* Leaders emerge and set out a path of action, or an emergent norm develops that stimulates common action (e.g., citizens gather to protest the killings and angry spokespersons enrage the crowd).
6. *Social controls are weak:* If the police, the military, or strong political or religious leaders are unable to counter the mobilization, a social movement or other crowd behavior (e.g., a riot or a mob) is likely to develop. Some analysts have argued that protests in Iraq evolved into a full-scale civil war because of a lack of a trained police force.

When all six factors are present, some sort of collective behavior will emerge. Those interested in controlling crowds that are volatile must intervene in one or more of these conditions (Kendall 2004; Smelser 1963).

On the southern outskirts of Basra in Iraq, British soldiers monitor a checkpoint leading into the city, checking people for weapons. A young Iraqi girl experiences the tense and hostile realities of war. This kind of military presence is often scary for residents and is very dangerous work for soldiers. This is an example of the precariousness of maintaining social control in volatile situations.

Thinking Sociologically

Think of an example of crowd behavior or a social movement, preferably one in which you have been involved. Try to identify each of the six factors from Smelser's theory as they operated in your example.

Types of Collective Behavior

Collective behavior ranges from spontaneous violent mobs to temporary fads and fashions. Figure 16.3 shows the range of actions.

Mobs are *emotional crowds that engage in violence against a specific target. Examples include lynchings, killings, and hate crimes.* Near the end of the U.S. Civil War, self-appointed vigilante groups roamed the countryside in the South looking for army deserters, torturing and killing both those who harbored deserters and the deserters themselves. There were no courts and no laws, just "justice" in the eyes of the vigilantes. The members of these groups constituted mobs. The film *Cold Mountain* depicts these scenes vividly. Unless deterred, mobs often damage or destroy their target.

Riots—*an outbreak of illegal violence against random or shifting targets committed by crowds expressing frustration or anger against people, property, or groups in power*—begin when certain conditions occur. Often, a sense of frustration or deprivation sets the stage for a riot—hunger, poverty, poor housing, lack of jobs, discrimination, poor education, or an unresponsive or unfair judicial system. If the conditions for collective behavior are present, many types of incidents can be the precipitating factor setting off a riot. For example, in late 2010 as a response to the rumor that Nepalese United Nations soldiers brought the cholera epidemic from Nepal, frustrated Haitian citizens rioted, wounding a number of UN peacekeeping troops. The distinction between riots and mobs is illustrated in Figure 16.4.

Panic *occurs when a large number of individuals become fearful or try to flee threatening situations that are beyond their control, sometimes putting their lives in danger*. Panic can occur in a crowd situation, such as a restaurant or theater in which someone yells "Fire," or it can occur following rumors or information spread by the media. Panic started by rumors set off the run on the stock market in October 1929. A large number of actions by individuals caused the stock market crash in the United States, with repercussions around the world. In 2008, the collapse of the global investment banking and securities trader Bear Stearns & Co. resulted in turmoil in the financial markets. Only with radical intervention by the federal government was the immediate panic abated. Panics can result in collapse of an organization, destruction, or even death as a result of the group action.

Rumors are *forms of mass behavior in which unsupported or unproven reports about a problem, an issue, or a concern circulate widely throughout the public.* Rumors may spread only in a local area, but with electronic means available, rumors are spreading more widely and rapidly. Without authoritative information, ambiguous situations can produce faulty information on which decisions are made and actions are based. *Urban legends*, one example of widely

Spontaneous and often violent					**Less spontaneous and seldom violent**
	Crowd behavior			**Mass behavior**	
Mob	Riot	Panic	Rumor	Fad	Fashion

Figure 16.3 Types of Collective Behavior

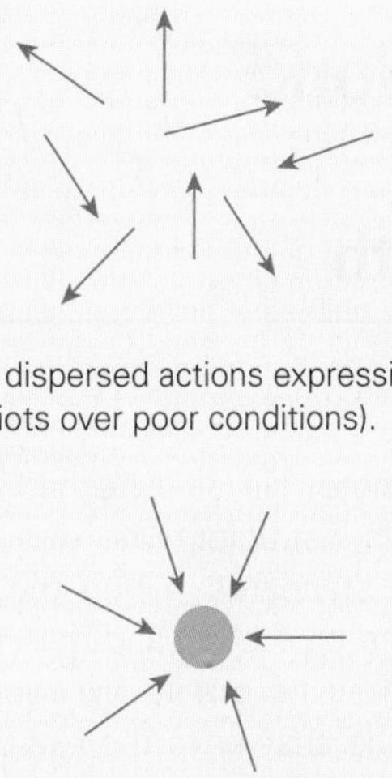

Riots involve dispersed actions expressing frustration (e.g., urban riots over poor conditions).
Mobs involve a group collectively focusing their action on a single individual or location (e.g., a lynch mob).

Figure 16.4 The Difference Between Riots and Mobs

spread but unverified messages, are unsubstantiated stories that sound plausible and become widely circulated. The people telling these stories usually believe them (Mikkelson and Mikkelson 2012). The next "Sociology in Our Social World" on page 626 provides an example. Go to www.snopes.com/college/college.asp for some additional entertaining urban legends about professors, exam scams, embarrassments, and other college pranks.

Fads are *temporary behaviors, activities, or material objects that spread rapidly and are copied enthusiastically by large numbers of people*. Body modification, especially tattooing, appeals mostly to young people of all social classes. Tattoo artists emblazon IDs, secret society and organization emblems, fraternity symbols, and decorations to order on all parts of the customers' bodies. Body modification has taken place for centuries, but it goes through fads (University of Pennsylvania 2010). Sometimes, fads become institutionalized—that is, they gain a permanent place in the culture. Other fads die out, replaced by the next hot item.

Fashions refer to *a style of appearance and behavior that is temporarily favored by a large number of people*. Clothing styles, music genres, color schemes in home decor, types of automobiles, and architectural designs are examples. Fashions typically last longer than fads but sometimes survive only a season, as can be seen in the clothing industry. Music styles such as "hardcore techno," "acid," "alternative hip-hop," and "UK 2-step garage" were popular among some groups as the previous edition of this book was being written, but two years later as we finished the fourth edition, the fads were "dub step," "indie," "electropop," "screamo," and "Latin pop." These styles will probably be passé by the time you read this, replaced by new fads emerging in mass behavior.

Each of these forms of collective behavior involves micro-level individual actions that cumulatively become collective responses to certain circumstances. However, ripples are felt in other levels of the social world. Insofar as these various types of collective activity upset the standard routines of society and the accepted norms, they can unsettle the entire social system and cause lasting change.

The separation of each of the forms of change into levels is somewhat artificial, of course, for individuals are also acting in organizations and in national social movements. However, when we move to meso- and macro-level analyses, the established structures and processes of society become increasingly important. Much of the change at these levels is planned change.

Fashions are established largely at fashion shows, where designers introduce new clothing styles. Fashions cannot occur unless there is a very high level of affluence, where people can afford to throw away perfectly good clothing for something more stylish. For many people in the Global South, it is a gift just to have clean, warm clothing, and the very existence of such displays of consumerism is both amazing and appealing—or sometimes appalling.

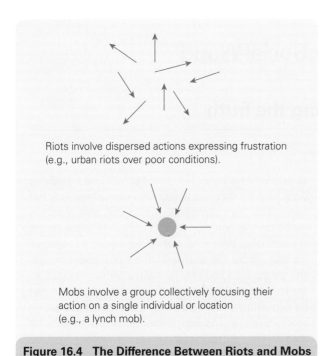

Sociology in Our Social World

Exam Stories: Testing the Truth

College exams are quickly approaching, so it is a good time to take a look at the latest chapter in the tome of teacher-student legend and rumors.

The first one was reported from Calgary, Alberta, by a civil engineering student at the University of Manitoba. This tale says a professor announced an open-book final examination in which the students could "use anything they are able to carry into the exam room." One innovative undergraduate, it is reported, carried in a graduate student who wrote his exam for him.

Another legend came from North Carolina. Supposedly, on the day before the final exam, the professor left his office unattended, with the door open and the examinations left sitting on his desk. A student who came by to ask a question found the room empty and quickly left with one of the exams. However, the professor had printed the exact number of exams that he needed, and the next morning, he counted them again before going to the classroom. Discovering that he was one short, he suspected that it had been stolen, so he trimmed a half-inch from the bottom of the remaining exams. When the exam papers were turned in, the student whose paper was longer than the others' received a failing grade.

A student procrastinated on writing a paper. Twenty-four hours before the paper was due, he went to the university library and found an old paper on the topic. He copied it and turned it in. A few weeks later, the professor returned the papers, and he stopped by the student's desk. He supposedly said to the student, "Twenty-five years ago, when I wrote this paper, it got a B. I always thought it deserved an A." There was an A on the cover, but the professor added, "Try anything like this again, and I'll have you thrown out of school."

Another college legend goes like this: Jack, a less than industrious student, was taking an examination with two blue books, a pen, and a question that had him baffled. Being naturally bright, even if lazy, he solved the problem in the following way. In one of the blue books, he wrote a letter to his mother, telling her that he had finished his exam early but was waiting for a friend to finish and was taking the opportunity to write her a note. He said he had been studying very hard for this instructor, who was a nice guy but had pretty high standards. When the time was up, he handed in one blue book and quickly left with the unused one. When he got to his room, he opened his text, wrote the answer to the exam question, and mailed the blue book to his mother. When the instructor found the letter, he called Jack, who explained that he had written in two blue books and must have gotten them mixed up. The examination essay must be in the mail on the way to Boston where his mother lived, he explained. He offered to call his mother and have her send the envelope back as soon as she got it. He did, she did, and the blue book was returned, with the inner envelope postmarked the day of the test and the outer envelope postmarked Boston.

Finally, in an introductory chemistry class, two guys were taking chemistry, and they had done well on all the quizzes, so that by the last week of class they each had a solid A. These friends were so confident going into the final that for the weekend just before the exam they decided to drive some distance to party at another college. However, after a very good time and hangovers on Monday, they overslept and did not make it back to campus until late on Monday—the day of the exam. They found the professor and told him they missed the final because they had been away, had had a flat tire on the way back to campus, and were without a spare. The professor thought this over and agreed that they could make up the final on the following day. So the two studied intensely that night and went in the next day for the exam. The professor placed them in separate rooms and handed each of them a test booklet and told them to begin. The first problem was simple and was worth 5 points. It looked like it was going to be an easy exam, and they were both relieved. They did the first problem and then turned the page. The next question was "Which tire? (95 points)."

Campus legends such as these help reduce the strain of college life and spread the reputations of legendary professors. Furthermore, they keep alive hopes of someday outfoxing the professors—or the students, depending on which side you are on.

Source: www.snopes.com.

Planned Change in Organizations: Meso-Level Change

The board of trustees of a small liberal arts college has witnessed recent drops in student enrollments that could cause the college to go out of business, but the college has a long tradition of fine education and devoted alumni. How does the college continue to serve future students and current alumni? The problem is how to plan change to keep the college solvent.

A company manufactures silicon chips for computers. Recently, the market has been flooded with inexpensive chips, primarily from Asia, where they are made more cheaply than this North American firm can possibly make them. Does the company succumb to the competition, figure out ways to meet it, or diversify its products? What steps should be taken to facilitate the change? Many companies in Silicon Valley, California, face exactly this challenge.

A Native American nation within the United States faces unemployment among its people due in large measure to discrimination by Anglos in the local community. Should the elders focus their energies and resources on electing sympathetic politicians, boycotting racist businesses, filing lawsuits, becoming entrepreneurs as a nation so they can hire their own people, or beginning a local radio station so they will have a communication network for a social movement? What is the best strategy to help this proud nation recover from centuries of disadvantage?

All these are real problems faced by real organizations. Anywhere we turn, organizations face questions involving change, questions that arise because of internal strains and external stresses. How organizational leaders and applied sociologists deal with change will determine the survival and well-being of the organizations.

How Organizations Plan for Change

When working for an organization, you will engage in the process of planning for change. Some organizations spend time and money writing long-range strategic plans and doing self-studies to determine areas for ongoing change. Sometimes, change is desired, and sometimes, it is forced on the organization by stresses from society, more powerful organizations, or individuals (Kanter 1983, 2001a, 2001b; Olsen 1968). Moreover, a problem solved in one area can create unanticipated problems someplace else.

Planned change such as strategic planning is the dream of every organizational leader. It involves deliberate, structured attempts, guided by stated goals, to alter the status quo of the social unit (Bennis, Benne, and Chin 1985; Ferhansyed 2008). There are several important considerations when we think about planned change: How can we identify what needs to be changed? How can we plan or manage the change process successfully? What kind of systems adapt well to change? Here, we briefly touch on the topic and outline three approaches advocated by experts to plan change. Keep in mind the levels of analysis as you read about change models. Some public sociologists devote their careers to combining research and advocacy of change, as illustrated in the "Sociologists in Action" feature on page 628.

Models for Planning Organizational Change

Change models fall into two main categories: (1) closed-system models, which deal with the internal dynamics of the organization, and (2) open-system models (such as our social world model), which consider the organization and its environment. Let us sample a couple of these models.

Closed-system models, often called classical or mechanistic models, focus on the internal dynamics of the organization. The goal of change using closed models is to move the organization closer to the ideal of bureaucratic efficiency and effectiveness. An example is time and motion studies, which analyze how much time it takes a worker to do a certain task and how it can be accomplished more efficiently. Each step in McDonald's process of getting a hamburger to the customer has been planned and timed for the greatest efficiency (Ritzer 2013b). In some closed-system models, change is legislated by the top executives and filters down to the workers.

By contrast, the organizational development approach claims that participants in the organization should be involved in decision making leading to change. The leadership is more democratic and supportive of workers, and the atmosphere is transparent—open, honest, and accountable to workers and investors. This model emphasizes that change comes about through adjusting workers' values, beliefs, and attitudes regarding new demands on the organization. Many variations on this theme have evolved, with current efforts including team building and change of the organizational culture to improve worker morale. Closed-system models tend to focus on group change that occurs from within the organization.

Open-system models combine both internal processes and the external environment. The latter provides the organization with inputs (workers and raw materials) and feedback (acceptability of the product or result). In turn, the organization has outputs (products) that affect the larger society. There are several implications of this model: (1) Change is an ever-present and ongoing process, (2) all parts of the organization and its immediate environment are linked, and (3) change in one part has an effect on the other parts. The model in Figure 16.5 on page 628 illustrates the open system.

Sociologists in Action— Stephen Steele | **Local Community Research Center**

Stephen Steele started using sociology to help a business he was working for solve a problem and bring about needed change. He has been in the business of helping organizations solve problems with sociological knowledge ever since.

"If someone has knowledge and fails to use it, that is a terrible waste," comments Steele. The idea of being involved in social betterment and making a difference were the guiding principles that led Steele to a life of sociological research. In 1978, he used his research skills to help set up a Community Research Center at the local community college. The goals of the nonprofit center were to help community organizations solve their problems, train students to use research skills, help bring about needed change, and provide a service to all. In 1982, he became its director, a position he still holds.

Many students have developed sophisticated analytical and research skills by working on projects in the community, and the center has supported itself by contracting its high-quality, low-cost research services to community organizations. Although the range of the center's research is broad, the main foci have been community change, economic development, and county government issues. For instance, Steele's company, Applied Data Associates, received a federal grant to evaluate an antidrug project and another to evaluate ways to increase the active involvement of Hispanic Americans in community civic organizations.

The interaction between theory and research is crucial in his work. Consider the four basic sociological theories: He looks for systems of interaction (functionalism), for power centers (conflict), for interaction patterns and definitions of reality within corporate cultures (symbolic interactionism), and for the costs and benefits of various choices (rational choice).

Steele likens applied sociology to being a "social plumber"—there is a specific problem, so he uses his tools to fix it. He finds being a social plumber rewarding and exciting, using sociological knowledge and tools to change groups, organizations, and environments and in the process improving the quality of life for people.

* * * * * * *

Stephen Steele received his bachelor's and master's degrees from Eastern Michigan University and his doctorate from Catholic University of America. He teaches sociology at Ann Arundel Community College in Maryland and runs his own research center. His students gain practical experience working in the center.

Thinking Sociologically

Using the model in Figure 16.5, fill in the parts as they relate to your college or university. For example, inputs might include students, federal student aid grants, new knowledge, and technology.

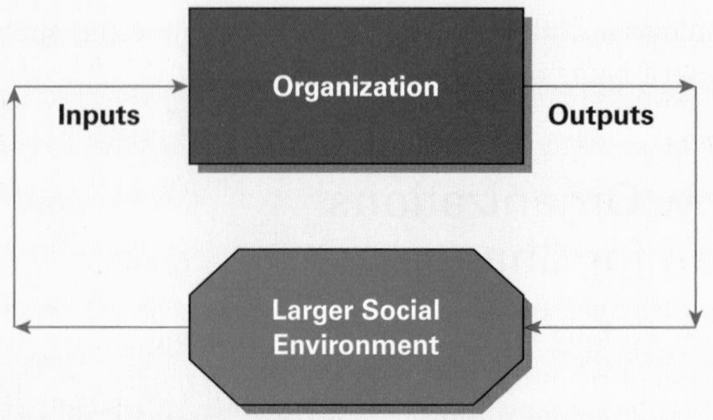

Figure 16.5 Open Systems Model

The Process of Planned Change

A huge issue in the Global South is the availability of clean drinking water. Nongovernmental organizations (NGOs) plan ways to improve the lives of individuals in many parts of the world. For example, in parts of Africa, women must spend as much as 6 hours a day carrying water to their homes. Because daughters are needed to care for the younger siblings while the mother is away, many girls are unable to attend school. This, in turn, has implications for the continuation of poverty. Further, if estimates are correct that 443 million school days are lost each year due to water-related diseases, the crisis of continuing poverty is aggravated (WaterAid 2008).

Clean water is essential for life and for health, but more than 884 million people live without access to safe water and 2.6 billion people live without sanitation. This affects the quality of their lives and results in more than 4,000 children dying every day from diarrheal diseases (WaterAid 2012).

With global climate change, the glaciers on top of mountains such as Mount Kenya are melting. Although that mountain peak has been snow covered for more than 10,000 years, the glaciers are expected to be completely gone in perhaps 20 years (Cousteau 2008). When the snow at the mountain top disappears, the water supply for hundreds of thousands of people and animals will disappear (Barnett, Adam, and Lettenmaier 2005; Struck 2007). One British NGO that is bringing about change in this area is WaterAid, launched in 1981. It has grown to become an international NGO that focuses entirely on water and sanitation issues, including hygiene. Communities in poor countries in Zambia and Sri Lanka were the first to receive support, with projects following in Ethiopia, Tanzania, Uganda, Sierra Leone, Ghana, Kenya, Bangladesh, Nepal, India, Gambia, Nigeria, Mozambique, Zambia, Madagascar, and Malawi. Now communities throughout the world are assisted in developing the most appropriate technologies for clean water, given the geographical features and resources of their areas.

WaterAid helped more than 1.6 million people with safe water and sanitation in 2010–2011, and 15.9 million people in the poorest parts of the world gain access to one of the most fundamental of human requirements—safe water (WaterAid 2012). In 2006, the organization was voted Britain's most admired charity. It all started with a group of people and their vision, some organizational skills, and a passionate commitment to improving the quality of life for people. Some other organizations also working on this issue have employed the skills of sociologists, who use their understanding of social processes that exacerbate or can lessen this problem. This is illustrated by the work of Ruth Meinzen-Dick, which is described in the "Sociologists in Action" on page 630.

This example shows one of the many types of organizations that both changes within itself to meet new conditions and brings about change in the world—thereby adding to our understanding of change. The process of planned change is like a puzzle with a number of pieces that differ for each organization but must fit together for the smooth operation of the organization. The goal of most organizations is to remain balanced and avoid threats or conflict. Slow, planned reform of the system is generally perceived by organizations and countries as a desirable way to bring about change. Unplanned change can be disruptive to the system.

Development projects go through stages just as change does. The United Nations Millennium Goals set benchmarks to be reached in addressing water and sanitation, poverty, famine, illiteracy, and disease around the world, and living standards in most countries have been rising for several decades. However, a United Nations report argues that advances cannot continue and in fact may be reversed if social inequalities and environmental deterioration, such as water pollution, continue to intensify (UN Human Development Report 2011). The Millennium Project is now becoming the Sustainability Project, with emphasis on controlling environmental degradation through planned change (McMichael 2012). A big problem with this initiative lies in "the global land grab" (McMichael 2012). China and Middle Eastern countries, followed by many others, and investors from these countries are buying up land in Africa, South and Southeast Asia, South America, and Central Asia, mostly to ensure their countries' food security in the future. This does not bode well for environmental protection.

At the societal and global macro levels, change is often stimulated by individuals and events outside the chambers of power, and there is much less control over how the change evolves. We turn next to an exploration of change at the macro level.

Social Movements: Macro-Level Change

Beijing, China, hosted the prestigious summer 2008 Olympics, athletic games that promote peace and goodwill around the globe. The Olympic torch traversed the globe to prepare for and celebrate the event. However, its journey and the opening of the games were far from peaceful and full of goodwill. Protests about Chinese human rights and autonomy for Tibet (now a part of China) dogged the torch, and major political leaders refused to attend the opening ceremonies. A social movement was spurred by an uprising in Tibet, a region that was an independent country until the 1950s. The issues—human rights violations by China and autonomy for Tibet—sparked off protests and demonstrations around the world. Will this social movement bring about change in the status of Tibetans or in human rights in China? Worldwide attention may aid the cause of those in Tibet seeking improved life conditions, or it may not. However, those people who raised these issues at the games in China were hoping to change more important, life-and-death policies for the people. The point is that a social movement tries to bring about change. Let us explore several questions: What is a social movement? What brings it about? What might be the results?

What Is a Social Movement?

From human rights and women's rights to animal rights and environmental protection, individuals seek ways to express their concerns and frustrations. **Social movements** are *consciously organized attempts outside of established institutions to enhance or resist change through group action.*

Sociologists in Action—Ruth Meinzen-Dick
Natural Resource Management in Developing Countries

What does a sociologist have to say about natural resource management? This is a question Ruth Meinzen-Dick has often been asked during her career. For 22 years, she has been showing the importance of understanding how farmers are organized and relate to government and other organizations as part of her work at the International Food Policy Research Institute (IFPRI), part of a larger network of international agricultural research organizations.

Her interest came from growing up in a dry part of India, where water was critical. She returned to India to study how small-scale irrigation systems were operated and found that farmers' organizations played an important role, even though the systems were formally under government management. Other students and faculty from different fields at Cornell University were finding similar patterns of farmer-managed irrigation systems in other parts of the world, so Meinzen-Dick was able to be part of a larger effort to understand the human side of water management. This was not just an academic exercise, as the Cornell program advised USAID. Even while still in graduate school, Meinzen-Dick had a consultancy with the World Bank to review the extent of farmer participation in their irrigation programs.

During her work at IFPRI, Meinzen-Dick has been able to continue studying what brings people together to manage water systems in developing countries and to compare this with the factors that encourage collective action for managing forests, rangelands, and other natural resources. This has involved field research in countries such as India, Pakistan, Zimbabwe, Kenya, and Uganda. She has been able to bring all this together by coordinating an international network on Collective Action and Property Rights (CAPRi), which helps people working on different aspects of agricultural research and natural resource management in developing countries to understand that the social institutions of property rights and collective action play a major role in shaping how people use and share resources. Working with these institutions requires a combination of qualitative and quantitative research methods to understand how people in different societies relate to each other and to their natural resources. The CAPRi program, therefore, provides training to researchers and practitioners on collective action, property rights, and research strategies.

Much of Meinzen-Dick's professional life has involved working across disciplines. This has also been deeply satisfying when people from other backgrounds see the relevance of social institutions or when principles from other disciplines offer new insights into familiar problems. It has been especially important for her to communicate the findings of sociological research clearly to nonsociologists. Institutional economics and a strong background in quantitative analysis have been especially helpful for her in communicating with her colleagues—mostly economists. She says, "It is exhilarating when the research team achieves changes in government policies or development programs such as allowing farmers to have more voice in water management."

* * * * * * *

Ruth Meinzen-Dick received her master's and PhD degrees in development sociology at Cornell University, with minors in agricultural economics and international agriculture.

Movements focus on a common interest of members, such as abortion policy. They have an organization, a leader, and one or more goals that aim to correct some perceived wrongs existing in society or even around the globe. Social movements are most often found in industrial or postindustrial societies although they can occur any place groups of people have a concern or frustration. Generally such movements are made up of diverse groups, each advocating for its own goals and interests.

Social movements entail large groups of people—usually without political power and influence—that decide to promote or resist social change. Table 16.1 illustrates how social movements differ from other forms of collective behavior. The problems leading to social movements often result from the way resources—human rights, jobs, income, housing, money for education and health care, and power—are distributed. In turn, countermovements—social movements against the goals of the original movement—may develop, representing other opinions (McCarthy and Zald 1977).

Many individuals join social movements to change the world or their part of the world and affect the direction of history. In fact, social movements have been successful in doing just that. Consider the movements around the world that have protected lands, forests, rivers, and oceans, seeking environmental protection for the people whose survival depends on those natural resources. For example, the Chipko movement (meaning "embrace") in a number of areas in India has been fighting the logging of forests by commercial industries.

Villagers, mostly women who depend on the forests, use Gandhi-style nonviolent methods to oppose the deforestation. These women have set an example for environmentalists in many parts of the world who wished to save trees (Scribd 2011). Another example is a movement by local peasants in Bihar, India, who fought efforts by government officials to control their fishing rights in the Ganges River. Those controls would have limited their livelihoods, but the citizens stood up against the power of the state.

Protesters hold signs outside the White House in Washington, DC, during a demonstration organized by Amnesty International. The group was calling on China to respect human rights, using the Olympic Games in Beijing as an occasion to pressure China by damaging its international reputation.

Stages of Social Movements

Why do people become involved in social movements such as PETA (People for the Ethical Treatment of Animals), pro-choice or pro-life movements, or political demonstrations against policies such as war? Social movements begin because of cultural conflicts in society and because people who want to create—or resist—social change come together. Movements take the time and energy of individual volunteers, and these human resources must be focused as the movement evolves.

In the first stage, the purpose of the movement is set. Long-standing problems or very recent events may create dissatisfaction and discontent in the general public or a part of the public. This discontent can galvanize people through a single event.

Sociologists have identified several conditions that give rise to the *preliminary stage*:

a) Individuals must share some basic values and ideals. They often occupy similar social statuses or positions and share concerns.

b) Social movements need to have a "preexisting communication network" that allows alienated or dissatisfied people to share their discontent (Farley 2010). Several recent political movements, such as MoveOn.org and Crossroads GPS, were carried out primarily on the Internet.

c) A strain and a precipitating event galvanize people around the issue. Effective leadership emerges—leaders who can mobilize people, organize the movement, and garner resources to fund the movement.

d) The people in the movement develop a sense of efficacy, a sense that they actually can be successful and change the system. Sometimes, as in the case of the civil rights movement, a sense of confidence in success comes from a religious conviction that God will not let the movement fail (Farley 2010). The *second step* in the development of a movement is

Table 16.1 **Social Movements and Other Forms of Collective Behavior: Similarities and Differences**

Similarities	***Differences***	
	Social Movements	*Other Forms of Collective Behavior*
Participants engage in unconventional behavior that defies social norms and expectations.	Organized	Disorganized
Such participation is strongly influenced by other participants' behavior.	Deliberate	Unplanned
Such participation relieves strain or tension in society, the community, or organizations.	Long-lasting	Brief

Source: Monnier (2010).

popularization, in which individuals coalesce their efforts, define their goals and strategies, develop recruitment tactics, and identify leaders. The social movement enters the public arena. The leaders present the social problems and solutions as seen by the members of the social movement. Now the social movement enters the institutionalized stage, becoming a formal organization. This organized effort generates the resources and members for the social change efforts.

In some movements, the *final stage* is fragmentation and demise. The group may or may not have achieved its goals, but fragmentation breaks apart the organization because the resources may be exhausted, the leadership may be inept or may have lost legitimacy, or the leaders may be co-opted by powerful mainline organizations. In this latter case, radical renewal movements may arise among those still strongly committed to the original cause (Mauss 1975).

Consider the case of the women's movement. Concerned women began sharing their basic values and ideals through coffee klatches and writings. The women became linked into "preexisting communication networks" such as serving on state Commissions on the Status of Women (Ferree and Merrill 2000). The refusal of the Equal Employment Opportunity Commission to consider women's rights as equal to those of racial minorities became the strain and precipitating event that led women to form the National Organization for Women (NOW), a group that continues to fight for women's rights today (Freeman 1975). The Equal Rights Amendment (ERA) provided a major issue around which women's groups rallied. Many women spent a tremendous amount of time and effort to have the ERA ratified by the necessary number of states. Spokespersons emerged, and fund-raiser events provided resources. For a long time, the advocates were convinced that the campaign would be successful. However, when the realization of failure came, an era in the women's movement ended. Some women's organizations fragmented and faded from the scene, while others revised their goals and strategies and moved on to new efforts to attain women's empowerment. In 2009 President Obama signed the Lilly Ledbetter Fair Pay Restoration Act, accomplishing one of the goals of the women's movements. However, a major issue that is reenergizing women's groups today is the challenge to women's health rights (National Women's Law Center 2012).

Social movements sometimes focus on regional or even organizational modification, but typically, their focus is on national or global issues. For example, Amnesty International's primary interest is human rights violations by nations, and the organization publishes information on violations around the world. Thus, another way to classify social movements is by their purpose or goals.

Types of Social Movements

Stonewall is a gay, lesbian, and bisexual rights movement that began when patrons of a gay bar fought back against a police raid in New York in 1969. After that incident, the concern about gay rights erupted from a small number of activists into a widespread movement for rights and acceptance. Stonewall now has gone global, with chapters in other countries and continents.

Proactive social movements advocate moving forward with a new initiative—proposing something that did not exist before. One example would be the gay rights movement, which promotes change in a new direction for the society. The 2010 lifting of the ban on openly gay and lesbian soldiers in the military and marriage rights in some states are examples of recent victories for the gay rights movement.

Reactive social movements resist change, reacting against something that exists or against new trends or new social policies—like same-sex marriage initiatives. James Dobson's Focus on the Family and other conservative religious associations have organized lobbying efforts and rallies against the acceptance of homosexuality or giving gay couples equal status to heterosexual married couples (although this is not the organization's only concern). The reactive movement had success in the 1990s with the Defense of Marriage Act that allowed states not to honor same-sex marriages that were contracted in another state.

Note that liberals and conservatives can be involved in reactive movement. When businesses want to build a corporation or plant in an area that will wipe out a native forest or destroy a historic area, liberals can be at the forefront of fighting "progress." Whether proactive or reactive, there are five main types of social movements:

Expressive movements *take place in groups, but they focus on changing individuals and saving people from corrupt lifestyles.* Many expressive movements are religious, such as the born-again Christian movements, Zen Buddhism, Scientology, the Christian Science Church, and Transcendental Meditation. Expressive movements also include secular psychotherapy movements and self-help or self-actualization groups.

Social reform movements *seek to change some specific dimension of society, usually involving legislative policy modification or appeals to the courts.* Movement members generally support the society as a whole but think things could be better if attention were given to environmental protection, women's rights, same-sex marriage, "just and fair" globalization, reducing the national debt, or abortion policy.

These movements are not interested in disrupting the functioning of the entire society: They have one issue they think needs reform. For example, many individuals with disabilities are given little attention, hope, or opportunity to get ahead and are institutionalized or left to languish. However, social reform movements have advocated for legislation to promote the rights of the differently abled. One such movement is Special Olympics International, begun by Eunice Kennedy Shriver in 1968 to give those with intellectual disabilities an opportunity to excel in sports. Over 3 million athletes from 150 countries now participate in these games (www.specialolympics.org). The summer 2012 Paralympic Games were held in London, featuring athletes with physical, mental, and sensorial disabilities. The events brought attention to the movement and issues faced by those with disabilities. Of particular interest were the advances the movement has helped to stimulate in physical adaptations for amputees (Disabled World 2012).

The Sojourners Community, another example of a social reform movement, was started in the early 1970s by highly committed theology students at Trinity Evangelical Divinity School in Deerfield, Illinois. Their group was theologically evangelical and conservative Christian, but wanted their faith to engage the social crisis that surrounded them, including civil rights, poverty, and the Vietnam War. They began a newspaper that eventually became known as *Sojourners* magazine. They advocate for a consistent pro-life policy (antiabortion, antiwar, and anti–death penalty). Their widely known and charismatic leader, Jim Wallis, writes and speaks around the country, arguing that on matters of faith and social policy, "the right gets it wrong and the left doesn't get it" (Wallis 2005, 2013). They have been a voice critical of social stands of the evangelical community to which they belong, but they are also highly critical of many on the political "left." They advocate for policies they believe stem from the compassion and love of the Christian message, and they are also unapologetic about their traditional stance on the core of the faith.

Revolutionary movements *attempt to transform society, to bring about total change in society by overthrowing existing power structures and replacing them with new ones. These movements often resort to violent means to achieve their goals, as has been the case with many revolutions throughout history.* When we read in the paper that there has been a coup, we are learning about a revolutionary movement that has ousted the government in power. Recently there was an attempted coup d'état in Ecuador that killed four people, but did not succeed in overthrowing the government in power (Carroll 2010). Although it was not violent, Nelson Mandela's African National Congress succeeded in taking power in South Africa in 1994, rewriting the constitution, and purging the apartheid social system, which had oppressed four fifths of the South African population.

Resistance or regressive movements *try to protect an existing system, protect part of that system, or return to what a system had been by overthrowing current laws and practices. They see societal change as a threat to values or practices and wish to maintain the status quo or return to a former status by reversing the change process* (Eitzen and Zinn 2012; Inglehart and Baker 2001). The Taliban religious movement in Afghanistan was a regressive movement against modernization, especially against the Western pattern of giving freedom and autonomy to women. The movement was successful in gaining power in the 1990s, imposing a harsh brand of Islamic law in the sections of Afghanistan under its control. The Taliban insists that its version of Islam is pure in that it follows a literal understanding of the Muslim holy book. This means that someone believed to have committed adultery should be stoned to death; the hands or arms of thieves should be amputated; and women who deviate from the Taliban interpretation of Muslim law should be mutilated, publically beaten, and sometimes executed (Antonowicz 2002).

Many environmental and peace groups use nonviolent protest, legislative means, and appeals to the public or to the courts to accomplish their desired goals. This is a silent protest on the beach in Santa Monica, California, where protesters set up crosses to represent all of the deaths of U.S. soldiers in Iraq. It is a reform movement.

Global transnational movements *are mobilized groups that take place across societies as international organizations seek change in the status of women, child labor, rights of indigenous peoples, environmental degradation, global warming, disease pandemics, and other issues that affect the global community.* An example is Free the Slaves, a global antislavery organization started by sociologist Kevin Bales. This organization has researched and written about the plight of millions of indentured people, the 27 million slaves in the world "forced to work without pay, under threat of violence and unable to walk away" (Bales 2007; Bales, Trodd, and Williamson 2009; Bales and Soodalter 2010; Free the Slaves 2013).

An example of a transnational or global protest against a multinational corporation is the autoworkers' conflict with General Motors in Colombia. A group of 68 autoworkers at a GM assembly plant outside of Bogotá formed a protest movement in May 2011. The issue was that a number of workers were fired when they could no longer perform their jobs due to severe workplace injuries, including severe impairments to backs and rotator cuffs. Some of the workers will never be able to work again. Medical records were changed to read "injuries unrelated to occupation" and a labor inspector who authorized the firings is now in jail, but compensation was still not forthcoming. After 15 months of protests, 13 protesters began a hunger strike, 8 of them sewing their mouths shut. International supporters began solidarity actions to put pressure on the GM to enter into negotiations, and American supporters were sending money, writing letters, and even engaging in fasting or hunger strikes themselves (Witness for Peace 2012). This is a local issue in Colombia that has mobilized people in other parts of the world.

Figure 16.6 summarizes the types of movements and the focus of each, from the micro to the macro level.

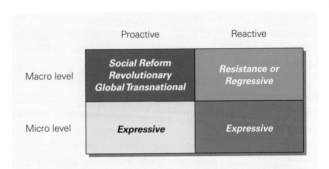

	Proactive	Reactive
Macro level	***Social Reform Revolutionary Global Transnational***	***Resistance or Regressive***
Micro level	***Expressive***	***Expressive***

Figure 16.6 Types of Movements

Thinking Sociologically

Consider a social movement with which you are familiar. What type of movement is it, and what was or is it trying to accomplish?

These are three of the men who were so desperate they went on a hunger strike—even sewing their lips together—outside the U.S. Embassy in Bogotá, Columbia. A nonprofit organization learned of the protest involving General Motors firing the injured men, apparently without disability compensation, and it became an issue in the United States.

Nelson Mandela, voting for the first time in South Africa in 1994, participated in the first democratic election open to all races after segregation was abolished. A political prisoner for 26 years, Mandela was held by the apartheid-based government as a dangerous revolutionary for his beliefs in racial equality. He was elected president of his country in this election and was later a corecipient of the Nobel Peace Prize for his work for democracy and equality. His nonviolent movement provided a model for nonviolent revolutionary change, but it did so with the help of pressures from other countries and movements that advocated for racial justice.

Globalization and Social Movements

Social movements are about people trying to improve their situations within their societies. They are intriguing because they provide compelling evidence that humans make choices and are capable of countering macro- and meso-level forces. As Eitzen and Zinn put it,

> Powerful social structures constrain what we do, but they can never control (us) entirely. Human beings are not passive actors. . . . Individuals acting alone, or with others, can shape, resist, challenge, and sometimes change the social structures that impinge on them. These actions constitute *human agency.* (Eitzen and Zinn 2012:269)

Since World War II, power in the global system has been dominated by a group of industrial giants calling themselves the Group of 8 (or the "G8"). These nations control world markets and regulate economic and trading policies (International Encyclopedia of the Social Sciences 2008). Included among these elites are the dominant three (Japan, representing the East; Germany, representing central Europe; and the United States, representing the American continents) and five other important but less dominating powers (Canada, France, Great Britain, Italy, and now Russia). The G8 are the core countries that have the most power in the World Trade Organization, the World Bank, the IMF, and other regulatory agencies that preside over the global economy. These agencies have often required that poor countries adhere to their demands or lose the right to loans and other support. These policies imposed from above (through the World Bank and IMF) have often been disastrous for poor countries, causing situations in which a debt burden is created that can never be paid off. The IMF (2013) points out that the loans are the only way poor countries can meet the UN Millennium Development Goals, but critics argue that the loans make poor countries dependent on wealthy countries and that the loans should be forgiven. They argue that if these were individuals rather than countries, we would call them indentured servants or slaves (Brecher, Costello, and Smith 2012; Weller and Hersh 2006). This creates nations where hopelessness would seem to reign supreme, yet social movements are arising in precisely these places and are often joining forces across national boundaries (Eitzen and Zinn 2012; Ferree 2012; Muchhala 2012). Even some groups within the G8 nations—labor unions, college student groups, and religious bodies concerned about social justice—are joining the movements.

Global South nations, calling themselves the G77, are now uniting, rather like a labor union seeking collective unity among workers, in attempts to gain some power and determine their own destinies by challenging what they experience as the tyranny of the G8 (Brecher, Costello, and Smith 2012; Hayden 2006). Map 13.2 on page 501 displays the location of G8 and G77 countries. At the 2009 climate change talks in Copenhagen, Denmark, Global South countries joined together to demand that Global North countries do more to alleviate environmental problems since "they started them" with industrialization.

In the competition to find cheaper labor for higher profits, there is a "race to the bottom," as communities must lower standards or else lose jobs to some other part of the world that is even more impoverished. Globalization as it now exists—with corporate profits as the ruling principle of most decision making—has lessened environmental standards, consumer protection, national sovereignty and local control of decisions, and safety protections for workers. When jobs move elsewhere, the people who had come to depend on those jobs are devastated and often thrust into poverty and homelessness, and the country loses tax revenue.

Although workers risk losing jobs by participating in protests for higher wages and better working conditions, one result of globalization has been a rise in countermovements. "Globalization from below" refers to the efforts by common people in small groups and protest movements to fight back (della Porta, Andretta, Mosca, and Reiter 2006; Eitzen and Zinn 2012). Rather than globalization being controlled solely by the pursuit of profits, these countermovements seek to protect workers, to defend the environment, and to combat the bone-crunching poverty that plagues so much of the Global South. The argument goes like this:

> It is the activity of people—going to work, paying taxes, buying products, obeying government officials,

Five hundred protesters sitting on the ground are confronted by riot police during a World Trade Organization conference in Seattle, with demonstrators mostly from the G8 countries. The protesters oppose policies that they feel are harmful to common citizens—Global North or Global South—and seek a "globalization from below" transnational movement.

> staying off private property—that continually re-creates the power of the powerful. . . . [The system, for all its power and resources, is dependent on common people to do the basic jobs that keep the society running.] This dependency gives people a potential power over the society—but one that can be realized only if they are prepared to reverse their acquiescence. . . . Social movements can be understood as the collective withdrawal of consent to established institutions. (Brecher, Costello, and Smith 2012:279)

The movement against globalization can be understood as withdrawing consent for such globalization (Brecher, Costello, and Smith 2012). There are thousands of small resistance actions against what are sometimes perceived to be the oppressive policies of G8 transnational corporations (Hearn 2012). They involve micro-level actions to bring change at the macro level. Consider the following examples:

> Under heavy pressure from the World Bank, the Bolivian government sold off the public water system of its third-largest city, Cochabamba, to a subsidiary of the San Francisco–based Bechtel Corporation, which promptly doubled the price of water for people's homes. Early in 2000, the people of Cochabamba rebelled, shutting down the city with general strikes and blockades. The government declared a state of siege, and a young protester was shot and killed. Word spread all over the world from the remote Bolivian highlands via the Internet. Hundreds of e-mail messages poured into Bechtel from all over the world, demanding that it leave Cochabamba. In the midst of local and global protests, the Bolivian government, which had said that Bechtel must not leave, suddenly reversed itself and signed an accord accepting every demand of the protesters. (Brecher, Costello, and Smith 2012:284)
>
> * * * * *
>
> Concerned groups in Europe, Japan, and the U.S. found that global corporations were increasingly fostering growth of sweatshops in the Global South. They pressured companies like The Gap and Nike to establish acceptable labor and human rights conditions in their factories around the world. Their efforts gradually grew into an anti-sweatshop movement with strong labor and religious support and tens of thousands of active participants. In the U.S., college students took up the anti-sweatshop cause on hundreds of campuses, ultimately holding sit-ins on many campuses to force their college stores to ban the use of college logos on products not produced under acceptable labor conditions. (Brecher, Costello, and Smith 2012:275)

Many concerned citizens in the Global North now buy Fair Trade Certified goods such as coffee, cocoa, and fruits. This is an effort by individuals to support globalization from below—a different model of how to change the world.

Many activists believe that actions by individuals and small groups—globalization from below—can have a real impact on global problems. Consider how effective you think the actions taken by individuals and local groups can be by thinking about the issues in the next "Engaging Sociology."

In summary, some social change is planned by organizations, some is initiated by groups that are outside the organizational structure (social movements), and some is unplanned and spontaneous (collective behavior). The most important point, however, is that actions taken by individuals

Engaging Sociology

Micro to Macro: Change From the Bottom Up

The idea of globalization "from the bottom up" suggests that the actions of a lot of people at the micro or local level can have a significant impact on how things develop at the most macro level of the social world we inhabit. Think about that process and what forces can enhance or retard that kind of change:

1. Are you familiar with cases in which "globalization from below" has made a difference in local, national, or international events? If so, what are those?
2. Identify three structural challenges that might make it hard for people at the micro level to change the national and global forces that interfere with the quality of their lives.
3. Identify three reasons to be optimistic about why change from the bottom up can be successful.
4. To examine a specific example of a group that approaches globalization from below, do an Internet search of the Zapatistas or of their leader, Subcomandante Marcos. What are the pros and the cons of this movement? Do the Zapatistas have any chance of bringing change to the poor, disfranchised people of southern Mexico?

affect the larger social world, sometimes even having global ramifications. Likewise, national and international changes and social movements influence the lives of individuals.

Technology, Environment, and Change

At the edge of the town of Bhopal, India, looms a subsidiary plant of the American-based Union Carbide Corporation. The plant provides work for many of the town's inhabitants. However, on December 3, 1984, things did not go as normal. A storage tank from the plant, filled with the toxic chemical liquid methyl isocyanate, overheated and turned to gas, which began to escape through a pressure relief valve. The gas formed a cloud and drifted away from the plant. By the time the sirens were sounded, it was too late for many people. The deadly gas had done its devastating work: More than 3,000 were dead and thousands ill, many with permanent injuries from the effects of the gas. Put in perspective, the number of casualties was about equal to the number in the terrorist attack on the Twin Towers of New York City on September 11, 2001.

Global protests often focus on the actions of Western multinational corporations. Women demonstrators, including the Bhopal gas victims in India, hold a "Wanted" poster of former Union Carbide Chairman Warren Anderson, arguing that he should be tried for criminal negligence at the plant, causing the deaths of more than 3,000 people and injuries of tens of thousands in Bhopal, India.

This example illustrates change at multiple levels of analysis. We see a global multinational company (Union Carbide) in a society (India) that welcomed the jobs for its citizens. A community within that larger society benefited from the jobs until many residents were killed or disabled, leaving shattered families and devastated individual lives. The accident also spawned a number of forms of collective behavior. The immediate aftermath of the accident at Bhopal included panic, as people tried to flee the deadly gas. Later, it resulted in several social movements as activists from India and other countries demanded accountability and safety measures. The courts finally rendered a decision in 2010—after 25 years—about the legal ramifications of the leak. The disaster also brought about planned change in the way Union Carbide does business and protects workers and citizens.

Technology refers to *the practical application of tools, skills, and knowledge to meet human needs and extend human abilities.* Technology and environment cannot be separated, as we see from the Bhopal tragedy. The raw products that fuel technology come from the environment, the wastes return to the environment, and technological mistakes affect the environment. This section discusses briefly the development and process of technology, the relationship between technology and the environment, and the implications for change at each level of analysis.

Throughout human history, there have been major transition periods when changes in the material culture brought about revolutions in human social structures and cultures (Toffler and Toffler 1980). For example, the agricultural revolution resulted in the use of the plow to till the soil, establishing new social arrangements and eventually resulting in food surpluses that allowed cities to flourish. With the Industrial Revolution came machines powered by steam and petrol, resulting in mass production, population increases, urbanization, the division of labor in manufacturing, social stratification, and the socialist and capitalist political-economic systems. Today, postindustrial technology, based on the microchip, is fueling the spread of information, communication, and transportation on a global level, and even to explore outer space and analyze, store, and retrieve masses of information in seconds. However, each wave of innovation initially affects only a portion of the world, leaving other people and countries behind and creating divisions between the Global North and the Global South.

Sociologist William Ogburn has argued that change is brought about through three processes: discovery, invention, and diffusion. *Discovery* is a new way of seeing reality.

The material objects or ideas have been present, but they are seen in a new light when the need arises or conditions are conducive to the discovery. It is usually accomplished by an individual or a small group, a micro-level activity (Ogburn [1922] 1938, 1961, 1964).

Invention refers to combining existing parts, materials, or ideas to form new ones. There was no light bulb or combustion engine lying in the forest waiting to be discovered. Human ingenuity was required to put together something that had not previously existed. Technological innovations often result from research and the expansion of science, increasingly generated at the meso level of the social system.

Diffusion is the spread of an invention or discovery from one place to another. The spread of ideas such as capitalism, democracy, and religious beliefs has brought about changes in human relationships around the world. Likewise, the spread of various types of music, film technology, telephone systems, and computer hardware and software across the globe has had important ramifications for global interconnectedness. Diffusion often involves expansion of ideas across the globe, but it also requires individuals to adopt ideas at the micro level.

Technology and Science

Science is *the systematic process of producing human knowledge; it uses empirical research methods to discover facts and test theories*. The question "How do we know what we know?" is often answered: "It's science." Whether social, biological, or physical, science provides a systematic way to approach the world and its mysteries. It uses empirical research methods to discover facts and test theories. Technology applies scientific knowledge to solve problems. Early human technology was largely the result of trial and error, not based on scientific knowledge or principles. Humans did not understand why boats floated or fires burned. Since the Industrial Revolution, many inventors and capitalists have seen science and technology as routes to human betterment and happiness. Science has become a major social institution in industrial and postindustrial societies, providing the bases of information and knowledge for sophisticated technology.

Scientists have developed technologies to ease the looming energy crisis and ward off climate change. Solar panels on this restaurant in Portugal reduce dependence on other sources of energy.

Indeed, one of the major transformations in modern society is the result of science becoming an institution. Prior to the 18th century, science was an avocation. People like Benjamin Franklin experimented in their backyards with whatever spare cash they had to satisfy their own curiosity.

Science in the contemporary world is both a structure and a social process. Institutionalization means creation of the organized, patterned, and enduring sets of social structures that provide guidelines for behavior and help the society meet its needs. Modern science involves mobilizing financial resources and employing the most highly trained people (which, in turn, requires the development of educational institutions). Innovation resulting in change will be very slow until a society has institutionalized science—providing extensive training and paying some people simply to do research. Specialization in science speeds up the rates of discovery. A researcher focuses on one area and gets much more in-depth understanding. Effective methods of communication across the globe mean that we do not need to wait several years for a research manuscript to cross the ocean and to be translated into another language. Competition in science means that researchers move quickly on their findings. Delaying findings may mean that the slowpoke does not get a permanent position, called tenure, at his or her university, promotion in the research laboratory, or awards for innovation.

We would not have automobiles, planes, missiles, space stations, computers, the Internet, and many of our modern conveniences without the institutionalization of science and without scientific application (technology). Science is big business, funded by industry and political leaders. University researchers and some government-funded science institutes engage in *basic research* designed to discover new knowledge, often on topics that receive funding. Industry and some governmental agencies such as the military and the Department of Agriculture employ scientists to do *applied research* and to discover practical uses for existing knowledge.

Scientific knowledge is usually cumulative, with each study adding to the existing body of research. However, radical new ideas can result in scientific revolutions (Kuhn 1970). Galileo's finding that the earth revolves around the Sun and Darwin's theory of evolution are two examples of radical new ideas that changed history. More recently, cumulative scientific knowledge has resulted in energy-efficient engines that power cars and computer technology that has revolutionized communication.

Thinking Sociologically

Imagine what your life would have been like before computers, e-mail, and the Internet. What would be different? (Note that you are imagining the world from only 10 to 20 years ago.) Ask your parents or grandparents what this past world was like.

Technology and Change

The G8 has yearly meetings to regulate global economic policy and markets. The group's power enables those eight countries to dominate technology by controlling raw products such as oil. In the process, they profoundly influence which countries will be rich or poor. Although some politicians like to tell us they believe in a free market economy, uninhibited by governmental interference, they actually intervene regularly in the global market.

New technological developments can be a force not only for world integration but also for economic and political disintegration (Schaeffer 2003). For example, research and development (R&D) is an important measure of investment in the future. For many years the biggest investors have been the European Union, the United States, and Japan. However, since 2002, China has increased its R&D while the top research countries reduced their share. In fact, in 2002 Global North countries provided 83% of the research and development, but today the European Union, the United States, and China each provide 20% of the world's researchers, with Japan at 10% and Russia at 7% (UNESCO Institute for Statistics 2010b).

The technological revolution in communications has resulted in fiber-optic cable and wireless microwave cell phones and satellite technologies that make it easier to communicate with people around the world. We now live in a global village, a great boon for those fortunate enough to have the education and means to take advantage of it (Drori 2006; Howard and Jones 2004; Salzman and Matathia 2000).

However, the changes in technology do not always have a positive effect on less affluent countries. For example, by substituting fiber-optic cable for old technologies, the demand for copper, used for more than 100 years to carry electrical impulses for telephones and telegraphs, has bottomed out. Countries such as Zambia and Chile, which depended on the copper trade, have seen major negative impacts on their economies. New developments resulting in artificial sweeteners reduced the demand for sugar, the major source of income for the 50 million people who work

Thomas Edison had more than 1,000 patented inventions, including the light bulb, recorded sound, and movies, but perhaps his most influential invention was the research lab—in which people were paid to invent and to conduct research—at Menlo Park in New Jersey. This was the seminal step in the institutionalization of science.

Technology has had some unexpected consequences, including a staggering increase in the amount of trash generated. Illustrated here is trash from the fast-food industry in Egypt. The volume of trash has created problems of disposal and pollution control.

in the beet and cane sugar industries around the globe. As new technologies bring substantial benefits to many in the world, those benefits actually harm people in other parts of the interconnected world. Changes in technology and the economy have forced many individuals to leave their native villages in search of paid labor positions in urban factories and the tourism industry, disrupting family lives.

Rapid technological change has affected generational relationships as well. It is not uncommon for younger generations to have more technological competence than their elders, and this sometimes creates a generational digital divide in competencies regarding use of computers, cell phones, and other electronic devices. In some settings, younger people are looked to for their expertise, whereas in the past, the elders were the source of knowledge and wisdom. Often the older members of a business or group feel devalued and demoralized late in their careers because those with technical competence view the older members as "outdated has-beens." Even networks and forms of entertainment such as the Wii-U and Nintendo 3DS further the social distance between generations. With the changes brought about by technology come changes in the nonmaterial culture—values, political ideologies, and human relationships. Clearly, technology can have a variety of social impacts—both positive and negative.

In the opening questions, we asked whether you as an individual can make a difference. In closing, we present in the final "Engaging Sociology" a plan you can follow to make a difference.

Thinking Sociologically

First, read "Engaging Sociology: Making a Difference." Then use the steps to plan how you would bring about a change that would make a difference in your community, in your country, or in the world. Go to "Contributing to Our Social World: What Can We Do?" at the end of this and other chapters to find ways in which you could be actively involved in bettering society.

Engaging Sociology

Making a Difference

If you want to bring about social change, consider the following steps used by public/applied sociologists: Because bringing about change requires cooperation, working in a group context is often essential. Flexibility, openness to new ideas, and willingness to entertain alternative suggestions are also key factors in successful change. The following steps provide a useful strategy for planning change:

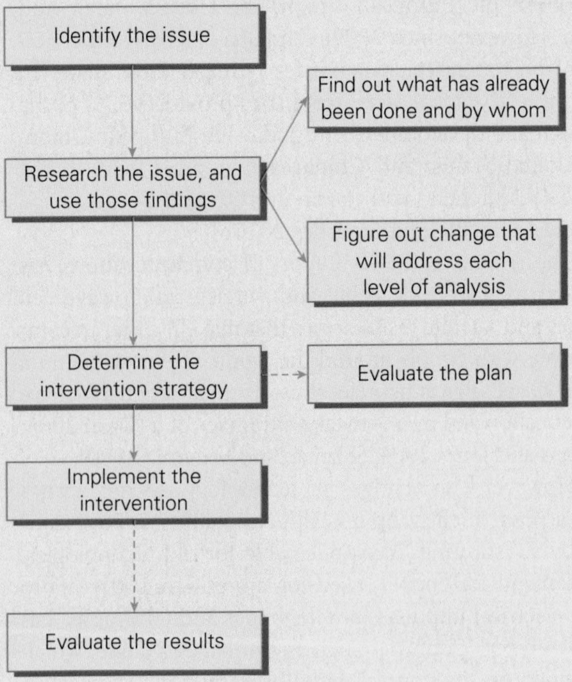

1. *Identify the issue:* Be specific and focus on what is to be changed. Without clear focus, your target for change can get muddied or lost in the attempt.
2. *Research the issue and use those findings:* Learn as much as you can about the situation or problem to be changed. Use informants, interviews, written materials, observation, existing data (such as U.S. Census Bureau statistics), or anything that helps you understand the issues. That will enable you to find the most effective strategies to bring about change.
3. *Find out what has already been done and by whom:* Other individuals or groups may be working on the same issue. Be sure you know what intervention has already taken place. This can also help determine whether attempts at change have been tried, what has been successful, and whether further change is needed.

4. *Change must take into account each level of analysis:* When planning a strategy, you may focus on one level of analysis, but be sure to consider what interventions are needed at other levels to make the change effective or to anticipate the effects of change on other levels.
5. *Determine the intervention strategy:* Map out the intervention and the steps to carry it out. Identify resources needed, and plan each step in detail.
6. *Evaluate the plan:* Get feedback on the plan from those involved in the issue and from unbiased colleagues. If possible, involve those who will be affected by the intervention in the planning and evaluation of the change. When feasible, test the intervention plan before implementing it.
7. *Implement the intervention:* Put the plan into effect, watching for any unintended consequences. Ask for regular feedback from those affected by the change.
8. *Evaluate the results:* Assess what is working, what is not, and how the constituents that experience the change are reacting. Sociological knowledge and skills should help guide this process.

What Have We Learned?

Can you change the world? The underlying message of this chapter and the text is that the choices we make facilitate change at each level in our social world. Understanding sociology provides the knowledge and tools to make informed decisions and allows us to work with groups to make a difference. One of the founders of sociology, Émile Durkheim, argued that sociology is not worth a single hour's work if it does not help change the world to be a better place (Durkheim [1893] 1947).

As you face individual challenges to bring about change in your social world, keep in mind this message: Change at one level affects all other levels. Sociology as a discipline is focused on gathering accurate information about the society in which we live. But sociologists as citizens often use their knowledge to advocate for changes that they think will make a better society, and applied sociologists help organizations bring about change. We hope that through his book and your course you have gained important insights that will help you contribute to the dialogue about how to make our social world a better, more humane place.

Key Points

- Social change—variation or alteration over time in behavior patterns, culture, or structure in a society—typically involves change at one level of the social system that ripples through the other levels, micro, meso, and macro. (See pp. 608–612.)
- Strains within an organization or group can induce change, as can stress that is imposed from the outside environment. (See pp. 612–617.)
- Sociological theories—whether micro or macro—offer explanations for the causes of change. (See pp. 617–622.)
- At the micro level, change is often initiated through collective behavior, which can take several forms: crowds, mobs, riots, rumors, fads, and fashions. (See pp. 622–626.)
- At the meso level, change in organizations is often managed through a planned process. (See pp. 626–629.)
- Social movements often provide impetus for change at the macro level. Social changes can be induced at the micro level, but they have implications even at the global level. (See pp. 629–637.)
- Science and technology can also stimulate change, but science has its greatest impact for change when it is institutionalized. (See pp. 637–639.)
- Social structures constrain what we do, but individuals, especially when acting in concert with others, can challenge, resist, and change the social systems that constrain them. We can change our society through *human agency*. (See pp. 639–642)

Discussion Questions

1. How old were you on September 11, 2001? How did the terrorist attacks that day affect you and your perspective on terrorism? How do you think the 9/11 attacks impacted people in different ways depending on their age?
2. What is the latest technological device you or your family has acquired? How has it changed your life? What are the (a) intended and (b) unintended consequences of your having it?
3. Every organization must adapt to change. Describe how an organization to which you belong coped with change. Was the adaptation successful? Why or why not? What was your role? Did you feel as though you had some influence over the adaptation strategy? Why or why not?
4. Were you aware that the United States gives far less than the 0.7% of gross national product the United Nations has requested of nations, in order to achieve the UN Millennium Development Goals to decrease poverty, illiteracy, famine, and disease? Why do you think most Americans believe the nation contributes more? Do you think it would be in the self-interest of the United States to contribute more? Why or why not?
5. What sociological theory best explains what has happened in many Arab countries that gave rise to the "Arab Spring" and its aftermath? Why? How might you use this theory to explain what happened—and what might happen in the future—in this region?

Contributing to Our Social World: What Can We Do?

At the Local Level

- *Campuswide movements:* A wide range of social issues, including international peace, environmental issues, human rights, and specific student concerns such as campus safety and the rising cost of higher education, may have movements represented on your campus. Consider participating in such activities. If you feel strongly about an issue for which no movement exists, consider organizing one with a few like-minded students. You can find tools to create a campus movement at www.campusactivism.org/index.php, www.campusactivism.org/displayresource-471.htm, and www.thetaskforce.org/reports_and_research/campus_manual.
- Many *community movements* bring about change at the local level, sometimes with national and even international effects. Check with your professors, service learning and campus activities offices, and chambers of commerce to find these.

At the Organizational or Institutional Level

- *Invite a movement leader to campus.* Consider inviting movement leaders to your campus for a lecture, or organize a conference that features several experts in a particular field. Environment, civil rights, and modern slavery are topics that have wide appeal. Professors who teach classes that cover these issues will be able to help you find a good speaker. Work with your sociology club or student government to provide funding for the speaker.
- *Volunteer Match* seeks to connect individuals with movements of interest to them. Its website (www.volunteermatch.org) has suggestions for getting involved in your local area.

At the National and Global Levels

- *The Jubilee Movement* promotes international debt forgiveness for the world's poorest countries—a solution that the U.S. government has embraced in principle and for whose implementation it has appropriated billions of dollars in funding. A major obstacle to improvement in living conditions in the less developed countries is the enormous amount of money they owe to the World Bank and International Monetary Fund, as well as governments in the industrialized nations for past-due, development-oriented loans. Named for the principle offered in the Hebrew scriptures that creditors are to cancel all debt owed to them every jubilee year (once every 49 years), the organization sponsors legislative programs, research work, and educational outreach activities throughout the world. The website of Jubilee USA (www.jubileeusa.org/about-us) provides information on ways in which you can get involved, and includes information about international debt, activities, and the history of the movement.

WWW Visit the Student Study Site at **www.sagepub.com/ballantine4e** to access additional study tools, including eFlashcards, web quizzes, video resources, audio resources, web resources, SAGE journal articles, recommended readings, and more.

References

AAANativeArts. 2011. "Facts About Alaskan Natives." Retrieved April 19, 2011 (www.aaanativearts.com/alaskan-natives/index.html).

About.com. 2013. "Getting Married in Japan." Retrieved January 24, 2013 (http://japanese.about.com/library/weekly/aa080999.htm).

Abrahamson, K., J. G. Anderson, M. Anderson, J. Suitor, and K. Pillemer. 2009. "The Cumulative Influence of Conflict on Nursing Home Staff: A Computer Simulation Approach." *Research in Gerontological Nursing.* Retrieved January 15, 2010 (www.geronurseresearch.com/advanced.asp).

Abu-Lughod, Janet L. 1991. *Changing Cities: Urban Sociology.* New York: HarperCollins.

Abu-Lughod, Janet L. 2001. *New York, Chicago, Los Angeles: America's Global Cities.* Minneapolis: University of Minnesota Press.

Addictionblog.org. 2011. "Why Do People Have Different Pain Tolerances?" July 2. Retrieved July 17, 2012 (http://drug.addication blog.org/why-do-people-have-different-pain-tolerances/).

Adler, Patricia A. and Peter Adler. 1991. *Backboards and Blackboards: College Athletes and Role Engulfment.* New York: Columbia University Press.

Adler, Patricia A. and Peter Adler. 1998. *Peer Power: Preadolescent Culture and Identity*. New Brunswick, NJ: Rutgers University Press.

Adler, Patricia A. and Peter Adler. 2004. "The Gloried Self." pp. 117–26 in *Inside Social Life,* 4th ed., edited by Spencer E. Cahill. Los Angeles: Roxbury.

A&E. 2012. *Intervention.* Retrieved July 16, 2012 (www.aetv.com).

Afghanistan Opium Survey. 2011. Retrieved April 13, 2012 (www.unodc.org/documents/crop-monitoring/Afghanistan/Executive_Summary_2011_web.pdf).

Aguirre, Adalberto and David V. Baker. 2007. *Structured Inequality in the United States,* 2nd ed. Englewood Cliffs, NJ: Prentice Hall.

Aguirre, Adalberto, Jr., and Jonathan H. Turner. 2011. *American Ethnicity: The Dynamics and Consequences of Discrimination,* 7th ed. Boston: McGraw-Hill.

Ahmad, Nehaluddin. 2009. "Sati Tradition—Widow Burning in India: A Socio-legal Examination." *Web Journal of Current Legal Issues,* 2 WEB JCLI. Retrieved April 7, 2011 (http://webjcli.ncl.ac.uk-/2009/issue2/almad2/html).

Akers, Ronald. 1992. *Deviant Behavior: A Social Learning Approach,* 3rd ed. Belmont, CA: Wadsworth.

Akers, Ronald. 1998. *Social Learning and Social Structure: A General Theory of Crime and Deviance.* Boston: Northeastern University Press.

Akers, Ronald L., Marvin D. Krohn, Lonn Lanza-Kaduce, and Marcia Radosevich. 1979. "Social Learning and Deviant Behavior." *American Sociological Review* 44(August):635–54.

Alarcon, Arthur L. and Paula M. Mitchell. 2011. "Executing the Will of the Voters? A Roadmap to Mend or End the California Legislature's Multi-Billion Dollar Death Penalty Debacle." *Loyola of Los Angeles Law Review* 44(June):S41.

Alatas, Syed Farid. 2006. "Ibn Khaldun and Contemporary Sociology." *International Sociology* 21(6):782–95.

AlertNet. 2012. "World Refugee Day 2012—Refugee Camps in Eastern Africa Are Overflowing and Underfunded." June 20. Retrieved September 14, 2012 (www.trust.org/alertnet/news/world-refugee-day-2012-refugee-camps-in-eastern-africa-are-overflowing-and-underfunded-lwf-dadaab-camp-manager/).

Alexander, Michelle. 2010. *The New Jim Crow: Mass Incarceration in the Age of Color Blindness*. New York: The New Press.

Alexander, Michelle. 2011. "More Black Men Are in Prison Today Than Were Enslaved in 1850." October 10. Retrieved April 15, 2012 (www.huffingtonpost.com/2011/10/12/michelle-alexander-more-Black-men-are-in-prison-today-than-were-enslaved-in-1850_n_1007368.html).

Alexander, Victoria D. 2003. *Sociology of the Arts: Exploring Fine and Popular Forms.* Malden, MA: Blackwell.

Allegretto, Sylvia, Ary Amerikaner, and Steven Pitts. 2011. "Black Employment and Unemployment: Teen Employment Population Ratios by Race." Chart 14, p. 14. *Work in the Black Community*, February 4. University of California at Berkeley Labor Center. (Retrieved April 17, 2011 (http://laborcenter.berkeley.edu/blackworkers/monthly/bwreport_2011-02-04_27.pdf).

Altheide, David, Patricia A. Adler, Peter Adler, and Duane Altheide. 1978. "The Social Meanings of Employee Theft." P. 90 in *Crime at the Top,* edited by John M. Johnson and Jack D. Douglas. Philadelphia: Lippincott.

Amadeo, Kimberley. 2009. "NAFTA Pros and Cons." Retrieved December 20, 2009 (http://useconomy.about.com/b/2008/04/24/nafta-pros-and-cons.htm).

Amato, Paul R. 2000. "The Consequences of Divorce for Adults and Children." *Journal of Marriage and the Family* 62(November):1269–87.

Amato, Paul R. and Juliana M. Sobolewski. 2001. "The Effects of Divorce and Marital Discord on Adult Children's Psychological Well-Being." *American Sociological Review* 63(December):697–713.

American Academy of Pediatrics. 2008. "Fact Sheet: Children's Health Insurance." Retrieved January 9, 2010 (www.aap.org/research/factsheet.pdf).

American Association of University Women Educational Foundation. 2001. "Hostile Hallways: Bullying, Teasing, and Sexual Harassment in School." Retrieved April 17, 2010 (www.aauw.org/research/upload/hostilehallways.pdf).

American Cancer Society. 2006. *Cancer Facts and Figures for African Americans 2005–2006.* Atlanta, GA: Author.

American Hospital Association. 2012. "Health Forum." Retrieved July 17, 2012 (www.ahadataviewer.com/).

American Library Association. 2013. "Banned and Challenged Classics." Retrieved January 28, 2013 (www.ala.org/advocacy/banned/frequentlychallenged/challengedclassics).

American Panel Survey. 2012. "Notes on Public Attitudes Toward Health Care Reform and the Supreme Court." Weidenbaum Center on the Economy, Government, and Public Policy, June 25. Retrieved August 1, 2012 (http://wc.wustl.edu).

American Psychological Association. 2008. "Report From: Working Group on Assisted Suicide and End-of-Life Decisions." Retrieved August 16, 2008 (www.apa.org/pi/aseol/introduction.html).

American Sociological Association. 2006. "'What Can I Do with a Bachelor's Degree in Sociology?' A National Survey of Seniors Majoring in Sociology." Washington DC: American Sociological Association Research and Development Department.

American Sociological Association. 2009. *21st Century Careers With an Undergraduate Degree in Sociology.* Washington, DC: Author.

American Sociological Association Task Force on Institutionalizing Public Sociologies. 2005. *Public Sociology and the Roots of American Sociology: Re-Establishing our Connection to the Public.* Washington, DC: Author.

Ammerman, Nancy. 1990. *Baptist Battles: Social Change and Religious Conflict in the Southern Baptist Convention.* New Brunswick, NJ: Rutgers University Press.

Ammerman, Nancy. 2006. "Denominationalism/Congregationalism." Pp. 353–72 in *Handbook of Religion and Social Institutions*, edited by Helen Rose Ebaugh. New York: Springer.

Ammerman, Nancy. 2009. "Congregations: Local, Social, and Religious." Pp. 562–80 in *Oxford Handbook of the Sociology of Religion*, edited by Peter Clarke. New York, Oxford: Oxford University Press.

Amnesty International. 2006. "Facts and Figures on the Death Penalty." Retrieved August 8, 2006 (http://web.amnesty.org/pages/deathpenalty-facts-eng, http://web.amnesty.org/pages/deathpenaltycountries-eng).

Amnesty International. 2011. "Death Penalty in 2010." Retrieved July 7, 2011 (www.amnesty.org/en/news-and-updates/report/death-penalty-2010-executing-countries-left-isolated-after-decade-progress).

Amnesty International. 2012. "Death Penalty 2011: Alarming Levels of Executions in the Few Countries That Kill." March 27. Retrieved April 16, 2012 (www.amnesty.org/en/news/deasth-penalty-2011-alarming-level-executions-few-countries--kill-2012-03-27).

Ananova. 2001. "Death Workers Sell Body Parts for Extra Christmas Cash." Retrieved December 4, 2005 (www.ananova.com/news/sm_465113.html).

Ananova. 2002. "Students Willing to Sell Body Parts to Fund Education." April 8. Retrieved August 26, 2006 (www.ananova.com).

Anderson, Benedict. 2006. *Imagined Communities: Reflections on the Origin and Spread of Nationalism,* Rev. ed. London: Verso. Anderson, David A. and Mykol Hamilton. 2005. "Gender Role Stereotyping of Parents in Children's Picture Books: The Invisible Father." *Sex Roles: A Journal of Research* 52(3/4):145.

Anderson, Elijah. 2000. *Code of the Street: Decency, Violence, and the Moral Life of the Inner City.* New York: Norton.

Anderson, James G. and Carolyn E. Aydin. 2005. *Evaluating the Organizational Impact of Health Care Information Systems.* New York: Springer.

Anderson, Margaret and Patricia Hill Collins. 2006. *Race Class and Gender: An Anthology*, 6th ed. Belmont: Wadsworth.

ANRED (Anorexia Nervosa and Related Eating Disorders, Inc.). 2007. "Statistics: How Many People Have Eating Disorders?" Retrieved April 17, 2010 (www.anred.com).

Answers.com. 2011. "Flag." Retrieved December 21, 2001 (http://www.answers.com/flag&r=67).

Answers.com. 2012. "How Many English Native Speakers Are There in the World?" Retrieved March 7, 2012 (http://wiki.answers.com/Q/How_many_English_native_speakers_are_there_in_the_world).

Anti-Defamation League. 2010. "ADL Audit: 1,211 Anti-Semitic Incidents Across the Country in 2009." Retrieved April 7, 2011 (www.adl.org/PresRele/ASUS_12/5814_12.htm).

Anti-Violence Resource Guide. 2012. "Facts About Violence." *Feminist.com.* Retrieved May 26, 2012 (www.feminist.com/antiviolence/facts.html).

Antonowicz, Anton. 2002. "Zarmina's Story." *Daily Mirror,* June 19. Retrieved February 7, 2013 (www.freerepublic.com/focus/news/702415/posts).

Antoun, Richard T. 2008. *Understanding Fundamentalism: Christian, Islamic, and Jewish Movements,* 2nd ed. Walnut Creek, CA: AltaMira.

Appleby, Julie. 2006. "Debate Surrounds End-of-Life Health Care Costs." *USA Today,* October 18. Retrieved April 4, 2008 (www.usatoday.com/money/industries/heaslth/2006-10-18-end-of-life-costs_x.htm).

Armstrong, Karen. 2000. *The Battle for God.* New York: Knopf.

Arnold, David O., ed. 1970. *The Sociology of Subcultures.* Berkeley, CA: Glendessary.

Arrighi, Barbara A. 2000. *Understanding Inequality: The Intersection of Race, Ethnicity, Class, and Gender.* Lanham, MD: Rowman & Littlefield.

Arulampalam, Wiji, Alison L. Booth, and Mark L. Bryan. 2007. "Is There a Glass Ceiling Over Europe? Exploring the Gender Pay gap Across the Wages Distribution." *Industrial and Labor Relations Review* 60(1):163–86.

ASCD. 2013. "The Whole Child Initiative." Retrieved February 8, 2013 (www.ascd.org/whole-child.aspx).

Aseltine, Robert H., Jr. 1995. "A Reconsideration of Parental and Peer Influences on Adolescent Deviance." *Journal of Health and Social Behavior* 36(2):103–21.

Ashley, David and David Michael Orenstein. 2009. *Sociological Theory,* 7th ed. Boston: Allyn & Bacon.

"At Least 80 Electoral Votes Depended on Youth." 2012. Center for Information & Research on Civic Learning and Engagement. Retrieved November 1, 2012 (www.civicyouth.org/at-least-80-electoral-votes-depended-on-youth/).

Attewell, Paul. 2001. "The First and Second Digital Divides." *Sociology of Education* 74(3):252–59.

Aulette, Judy Root. 2010. *Changing American Families.* Boston: Allyn & Bacon.

Avert. 2009. "Worldwide HIV and AIDS Statistics: Regional Statistics for HIV and AIDS, End of 2008." Retrieved April 13, 2010 (www.avert.org/worldstats.htm).

Avert. 2010. "Global HIV and AIDS Estimates, End of 2009." Retrieved May 14, 2011 (www.avert.org/worldstats.htm).

Ayers, Dennis. 2010. "Top 50 Favorite Gay Films!" *Afterelton,* September 20. Retrieved May 27, 2012 (www.afterelton.com/movies/2010/9/favorite-gay-films?page=0%20).

Ayers, William, 2006. "Hearts and Minds: Military Recruitment and the High School Battlefield." *Phi Delta Kappan* 87(8):594–99.

Ayers, William and Michael Klonsky. 2006. "Chicago's Renaissance 2010: The Small Schools Movement Meets the Ownership Society." *Phi Delta Kappan* (February):453–56.

Bagby, Ihsan. 2003. "Imams and Mosque Organization in the United States: A Study of Mosque Leadership and Organizational Structure in American Mosques." Pp. 113–34 in *Muslims in the United States*, edited by Philippa Strum and Danielle Tarantolo. Washington, DC: Woodrow Wilson International Center for Scholars.

Bahney, Anna. 2009. "Don't Talk to Invisible Strangers." *New York Times*, March 9. Retrieved August 13, 2009 (www.nytimes.com/2006/03/09/fashion/thursdaystyles/09parents.html).

Bainbridge, William S. and Rodney Stark. 1981. "Suicide, Homicide, and Religion: Durkheim Reassessed." *Annual Review of the Social Sciences of Religion* 5:33–56.

Baker, Peter and Dan Bilefsky. 2010. "Russia and U.S. Sign Nuclear Arms Reduction Pact." *The New York Times*, April 8. Retrieved July 14, 2012 (www.nytimes.com/2010/04/09/world/europe/09prexy.html).

Bales, Kevin. 1999. *Disposable People: New Slavery in the Global Economy*, Updated ed. Berkeley: University of California Press.

Bales, Kevin. 2000. *New Slavery: A Reference Handbook*, 2nd ed. Santa Barbara, CA: ABC-CLIO.

Bales, Kevin. 2004. *Disposable People: New Slavery in the Global Economy*, 2nd ed. Berkeley: University of California Press.

Bales, Kevin. 2007. *Ending Slavery: How We Free Today's Slaves*. Berkeley: University of California Press.

Bales, Kevin. 2012. *Disposable People: New Slavery in the Global Economy*, 3rd ed. Berkeley: University of California Press.

Bales, Kevin. 2013. "Confronting Slavery With the Tools of Sociology." In *Sociologists in Action: Race, Class, and Gender*, edited by Shelley White, Jonathan White, and Kathleen Odell Korgen. Thousand Oaks, CA: Sage.

Bales, Kevin and Ron Soodalter. 2010. *The Slave Next Door: Human Trafficking and Slavery in America Today*. Berkeley: University of California Press.

Bales, Kevin, Zoe Trodd, and Alex Kent Williamson. 2009. *Modern Slavery: The Secret World of 27 Million People*. Oxford, UK: Oneworld Press.

Bales, Kevin and Zoe Trodd. 2008. *To Plead Our Own Cause: Personal Stories by Today's Slaves*. Ithaca, NY: Cornell University Press.

Bakalian, Anny and Medhi Bozorgmehr. 2009. *Backlash 9/11: Middle Eastern and Muslim Americans Respond*. Berkeley: University of California Press.

Ballantine, Jeanne H. and Floyd M. Hammack. 2012. *The Sociology of Education: A Systematic Analysis*, 7th ed. Upper Saddle River, NJ: Prentice Hall.

Barajas, Mark S. 2011. "Academic Achievement of Children in Single Parent Homes: A Critical Review." *The Hilltop Review* 5(1): Article 4. Retrieved September 13, 2012 (http://scholarworks.wmich.edu/hilltopreview/vol5/iss1/4).

Barash, David. 2002. "Evolution, Males, and Violence." *The Chronicle Review* (May 24):B7.

Barber, Benjamin R. 2006. "The Uncertainty of Digital Politics: Democracy's Relationship with Information Technology." Pp. 61–69 in *Globalization: The Transformation of Social Worlds*, edited by D. Stanley Eitzen and Maxine Baca Zinn. Belmont, CA: Wadsworth.

Barber, Bonnie L., Jacquelynne S. Eccles, and Margaret R. Stone. 2001. "Whatever Happened to the Jock, the Brain, and the Princes? Young Adult Pathways Linked to Adolescent Activity Involvement and Social Identity." *Journal of Adolescent Research* 16(5):429–55.

Barnes, P. M., B. Bloom, and R. Nahin. 2008. "Complimentary and Alternative Medicine Use Among Adults and Children: US 2007." *CDC National Health Statistics Report* 12(December).

Barnett, T. P., J. C. Adam, and D. P. Lettenmaier. 2005. "Potential Impacts of a Warming Climate on Water Availability in Snow-Dominated Regions." *Nature* 438(November 17):303–309.

Barr, Colin and David Goldman. 2010 "20 Highest Paid CEOs." April 6. Retrieved March 11, 2011 (http://money.cnn.com/galleries/2010/news/1004/gallery.top_ceo_pay/).

Barrett, David B., Todd M. Johnson, and Peter F. Crossing. 2011. "2010 Annual Megacensus of Religion." *Time Almanac*. Chicago: Encyclopedia Britannica, Inc.

Barrett, David, George Kurian, and Todd Johnson, eds. 2001. *World Christian Encyclopedia*, 2 vols. New York: Oxford University Press.

Barry, Ellen. 2009. "Protests in Moldova Explode, With Help of Twitter." *New York Times*, April 8: A1. Retrieved October 6, 2012 (www.nytimes.com).

Basch, Linda, Nina Glick Schiller, and Cristina Szanton Blanc. 1994. *Nations Unbounded: Transnational Projects, Postcolonial Predicaments, and Deterritorialized Nation-State*. Amsterdam: Gordon and Breach.

Basso, Keith H. 1979. *Portraits of the Whiteman: Linguistic Play and Cultural Symbols Among the Western Apache*. Cambridge, UK: Cambridge University Press.

BBC News. 2005. "Mukhtar Mai—History of a Rape Case." Retrieved July 13, 2008 (http://news.bbc.co.uk/2/hi/south_asia/4620065.stm).

BBC News. 2008. "U.S. Elections Map: State by State Guide." Retrieved February 8, 2013 (http://news.bbc.co.uk/2/hi/in_depth/629/629/7223461.stm).

BBC News. 2012. "Iceberg Breaks Off From Greenland's Petermann Glacier." July 19. Retrieved February 8, 2013 (www.bbc.co.uk/news/world-europe-18896770).

BBC's Science and Nature. 2009 "The Ghost in Your Genes." Retrieved November 12, 2009 (www.bbc.co.uk/sn/tvradio/programmes/horizon/ghostgenes.shtml).

Beckwith, Carol. 1983. "Niger's Wodaabe: People of the Taboo." *National Geographic* 164(4):483–509.

Beckwith, Carol. 1993. *Nomads of Niger*. New York: Harry N. Abrams.

Bedi, Rahul. 2012. "Indian Dowry Deaths on the Rise." *The Telegraph*, February 27. Retrieved May 26, 2012 (www.telegrlaph.co.uk/news/worldnews/asia/india/9108642/Indian-dowry-deaths-on-the-rise.html).

Belding, Theodore C. 2004. "Nobility and Stupidity: Modeling the Evolution of Class Endogamy." Retrieved August 7, 2008 (http://arxiv.org/abs/nlin.AO/0405048).

Belkin, Lisa. 2011. "The Cost of Raising a Child." *New York Times*, July 27.

Bell, Daniel. 1973. *The Coming of Post-Industrial Society: A Venture in Social Forecasting*. New York: Basic Books.

Bell, Daniel. [1976] 1999. *The Coming of Post-Industrial Society: A Venture in Social Forecasting*, Special anniversary edition. New York: Basic Books.

Bell, Michael Mayerfeld. 2012. *An Invitation to Environmental Sociology*, 4th ed. Thousand Oaks, CA: Sage/Pine Forge.

Bellah, Robert N. 1970. "Civil Religion in America." Pp. 168–215 in *Beyond Belief: Essays on Religion in a Post-Traditionalist World*. New York: Harper & Row.

Bellah, Robert N. 1992. *The Broken Covenant: American Civil Religion in Time of Trial.* Chicago: University of Chicago Press.

Bellah, Robert N., Richard Madsen, William M. Sullivan, Ann Swindler, and Steven M. Tipton. 1996. *Habits of the Heart: Individualism and Commitment in American Life,* Updated ed. Berkeley: University of California Press.

Benavot, Aaron, John Meyer, and David Kamens. 1991. "Knowledge for the Masses: World Models and National Curricula: 1920–1986." *American Sociological Review* 56(1):85–100.

Benevolo, Leonardo. 1995. *The European City.* Cambridge, MA: Blackwell.

Benguigui, Yamina. 2000. *The Perfumed Garden.* Brooklyn, NY: First Run Icarus Films.

Bennis, Warren G., Kenneth D. Benne, and Robert Chin. 1985. *The Planning of Change,* 4th ed. New York: Holt, Rinehart Winston.

Benokraitis, Nijole V. 2008. *Marriages and Families: Changes, Choices, and Constraints,* 6th ed. Englewood Cliffs, NJ: Prentice Hall.

Benokraitis, Nijole V. 2012. *Marriages and Families: Changes, Choices, and Constraints—2010 Census Update*, 7th ed. Englewood Cliffs, NJ: Prentice Hall.

Berger, Helen A. and Douglas Ezzy. 2007. *Teenage Witches: Magical Youth and the Search for the Self.* New Brunswick, NJ: Rutgers University Press.

Berger, Michael L. 1979. *The Devil Wagon in God's Country: The Automobile and Social Change in Rural America, 1893–1929.* Hamden, CT: Archon.

Berger, Peter L. and Thomas Luckmann. 1966. *The Social Construction of Reality.* Garden City, NY: Doubleday.

Berk, Richard A. 1974. *Collective Behavior.* Dubuque, IA: Brown.

Berliner, David. 2001. *Our Schools vs. Theirs: Averages That Hide the True Extremes.* Center for Education Research, Analysis, and Innovation, January 28. Retrieved September 14, 2012 (http://nepc.colorado.edu/files/cerai-o1-02.htm).

Berman, Bruce J. 2011. "Of Magic, Invisible Hands and Elfs: How Not to Study Ethnicity in Africa." Presented at the ECAS4, Uppsala, Sweden, June 14–18.

Berman, Carol. 2010. "Glass Ceiling Is Still Solid." March 15. Retrieved May 25, 2012 (http://jobs.aol.com/articles/2010/03/15/glass-ceiling-is-still-solid-especially-if-you-have-an-mba/).

Berry, Brian J. L. and John Kasarda. 1977. *Contemporary Urban Ecology.* New York: Macmillan.

Bertman, Stephen. 1998. *Hyperculture: The Human Cost of Speed.* Westport, CT: Praeger.

Better Factories. 2012. *Better Factories Cambodia Newsletter* 9(March). Retrieved May 28, 2012 (www.betterfactories.org/content/documents/1/Newsletter%20No.%2019_Eng.pdf.

Bettie, Julie. 2003. *Women Without Class: Girls, Race, and Identity.* Berkeley: University of California Press.

Beyer, Peter. 2000. "Secularization From the Perspective of Globalization." Pp. 81–93 in *The Secularization Debate,* edited by William H. Swatos, Jr. and Daniel V. A. Olson. Lanham, MD: Rowman & Littlefield.

Bibby, Reginald W. 2002. *Restless Gods: The Renaissance of Religion in Canada.* Toronto, Canada: Stoddard.

Billig, Michael. 1995. *Banal Nationalism.* Thousand Oaks, CA: Sage.

Birdwhistell, Raymond L. 1970. *Kinesics and Context: Essays on Body Motion Communication.* Philadelphia: University of Pennsylvania Press.

Bjelopera, Jerome P. and Kristin M. Finklea. 2012. "Organized Crime: An Evolving Challenge for U.S. Law Enforcement." Congressional Research Service. Retrieved April 13, 2012 (www.fas.org/sgp/crs/misc/R41547.pdf).

Blank, Rebecca M. 2002. "Evaluating Welfare Reform in the United States." *Journal of Economic Literature* 40(4):1105–166.

Blasi, Joseph, Douglas Kruse, and Aaron Bernstein. 2003. *In the Company of Owners.* New York: Basic Books.

Blau, Peter M. 1956. *Bureaucracy in Modern Society.* New York: Random House.

Blau, Peter M. 1964. *Exchange and Power in Social Life.* New York: John Wiley.

Blau, Peter and Otis Dudley Duncan. 1967. *The American Occupational Structure.* New York: John Wiley.

Blauner, Robert. 1972. *Racial Oppression in America.* New York: Harper & Row.

Blee, Kathleen M. 2008. "White Supremacy as Extreme Deviance." Pp. 108–17 in *Extreme Deviance,* edited by Erich Goode and D. Angus Vail. Thousand Oaks, CA: Pine Forge.

Blue Planet Network. 2010. "The Facts About the Global Drinking Water Crisis." Retrieved May 14, 2012 (http://blueplanetnetwork.org/water/facts).

Blumer, Herbert. 1969. *Symbolic Interactionism: Perspective and Method.* Englewood Cliffs, NJ: Prentice Hall.

Blumer, Herbert. 1986. *Symbolic Interactionism: Perspective and Method.* Berkeley: University of California Press.

"Body Parts for Sale." 2008. *Science and Society,* May 6. ABC News. Retrieved January 11, 2010 (blogs.abcnews.com/scienceandsociety/2008/05/body-parts-for.html).

Boger, John Charles and Gary Orfield. 2009. *School Resegregation: Must the South Turn Back?* University of North Carolina Press.

Bokova, Irina and Laura Bush. 2012. "Literacy Is Key to Unlocking the Cycle of Poverty." *Houston Chronicle,* September 7. Retrieved January 28, 2013 (www.chron.com/opinion/outlook/article/Literacy-is-key-to-unlocking-the-cycle-of-poverty-3848564.php).

Bolduan, Kate 2009. "The Plight of Young Uninsured Americans." CNN Politics.com, March 7. Retrieved January 10, 2010 (www.cnn.com/2009/POLITICS/03/07/young.uninsured/index.html).

Boli, John. 2002. "Globalization." Pp. 307–13 in *Education and Sociology: An Encyclopedia,* edited by David L. Levinson, Peter W. Cookson, Jr., and Alan R. Sadovnik. New York: RoutledgeFalmer.

Bonacich, Edna. 1972. "A Theory of Ethnic Antagonism: The Split Labor Market." *American Sociological Review* 37(October):547–59.

Bonacich, Edna. 1976. "Advanced Capitalism and Black-White Race Relations in the United States: A Split Labor Market Interpretation." *American Sociological Review* 41(February):34–51.

Bonacich, Edna and Jake B. Wilson. 2005. "Hoisted by Its Own Petard: Organizing Wal-Mart's Logistics Workers." *New Labor Forum* 14:67–75.

Bonilla-Silva, Eduardo. 2003. *Racism Without Racists: Color-Blind Racism and the Persistence of Racial Inequality in the United States.* Berkeley: University of California Press.

Booth, Alan and Paul R. Amato. 2001. "Parental Predivorce Relations and Offspring Postdivorce Well-Being." *Journal of Marriage and the Family* 63(February):197–212.

Borg, Marcus J. 1994. *Meeting Jesus Again for the First Time.* San Francisco: Harper San Francisco.

Boston Globe. 2012 "Where the States Stand on Gay Marriage." June 10. Retrieved June 10, 2012 (www.boston.com/business/articles/2012/06/10/where_the_states_stand_on_gay_marriage/.

Boston Women's Health Book Collective. 2006. *Our Bodies, Ourselves: Menopause*. New York: Touchstone.

Bottomore, Tom. 1979. *Political Sociology.* New York: Harper & Row.

Boulding, Elise with Jennifer Dye. 2002. "Women and Development." In *Introducing Global Issues,* 2nd ed., edited by Michael T. Snarr and D. Neil Snarr. Boulder, CO: Lynne Rienner.

Bourdieu, P. and J. C. Passeron. 1977. *Reproduction in Education, Society and Culture.* London: Sage.

Bowen, Debra. 2008. "History Behind California's Primary Election System." Retrieved March 21, 2008 (www.sos.ca.gov/elections/elections_decline.htm).

Bowles, Samuel and Herbert Gintis. 1976. *Schooling in Capitalist America.* New York: Basic Books.

Bowles, Samuel and Herbert Gintis. 2002. "Schooling in Capitalist America Revisited." *Sociology of Education* 75(1):1–18.

Bowman, Bobbi. 2010. "A Portrait to Black America on the Eve of the 2010 Census." *The Root,* February 10. Retrieved June 5, 2012 (www.theroot.com/views/portrait-black-america-eve-2010-census).

Boy, Angie and Andrzej Kulczycki. 2008. "What We Know About Intimate Partner Violence in the Middle East and North Africa." *Violence Against Women* 14(1):53–70.

Bracey, Gerald W. 2005. "The 15th Bracey Report on the Condition of Public Education." *Phi Delta Kappan* (October):138–53.

Bradley, Tamsin, Emma Tomalin, and Mangala Subramaniam. 2009. *Dowry: Bridging the Gap Between Theory and Practice.* London: Zed Books.

Brandon, Emily. 2012. "65-and-Older Population Soars." *US News Money,* January 9. Retrieved March 31, 2012 (http://money.usnews.com/money/retirement/articles/2012/01/09/65-and-older-population-soars).

Brandon, Mark E. 2005. "War and American Constitutional Order." In *The Constitution in Wartime: Beyond Alarmism and Complacency,* edited by Mark Tushner. Durham, NC: Duke University Press.

Brasher, Brenda E. 2004. *Give Me That On-Line Religion.* New Brunswick, NJ: Rutgers University Press.

Brecher, Jeremy, Tim Costello, and Brendan Smith. 2012. "Globalization and Social Movements." Pp. 272–90 in *Globalization: The Transformation of Social Worlds,* 3rd ed., edited by D. Stanley Eitzen and Maxine Baca Zinn. Belmont, CA: Wadsworth.

Bremner, Jason, Carl Haub, Marlene Lee, Mark Mather, and Eric Zuehlke. 2009. "World Population Highlights." *Population Bulletin* 64(3):3. Population Reference Bureau. Retrieved January 10, 2010 (www.prb.org/pdf09/64.3highlights.pdf).

Brettell, Caroline B. and Carolyn F. Sargent. 2001. *Gender in Cross-Cultural Perspective,* 3rd ed. Englewood Cliffs, NJ: Prentice Hall.

Brettell, Caroline B. and Carolyn F. Sargent. 2008. *Gender in Cross-Cultural Perspective,* 5th ed. Englewood Cliffs, NJ: Prentice Hall.

Brier, Noah Rubin. 2004. "Coming of Age." *American Demographics* 26(9):16.

Brint, Steven, Mary F. Contreras, and Michael T. Matthews. 2001. "Socialization Messages in Primary Schools: An Organizational Analysis." *Sociology of Education* 74(July):157–80.

British Columbia Ministry of Labour & Citizens' Services. 2006. *B.C. Stats Infoline* 6(40). October 6. Retrieved April 17, 2010 (www.bcstats.gov.bc.ca/releases/info2006/in0647.pdf).

Britton, Dana M. 2000. "The Epistemology of the Gendered Organization." *Gender and Society* 14(3):418–34.

Britz, Jennifer Delahunty. 2006. "Are Today's Girls Too Successful?" *Dayton Daily News* (March 31):A7.

Bromley, David G. and Anson D. Shupe, Jr. 1981. *Strange Gods: The Great American Cult Scare.* Boston: Beacon.

Brookover, Wilbur B. and Edsel L. Erickson. 1975. *Sociology of Education.* Homewood, IL: Dorsey.

Brookover, Wilbur B., Edsel L. Erickson, and Alan McEvoy. 1996. *Creating Effective Schools: An In-Service Program.* Holmes Beach, FL: Learning Publications.

Brooks, David. 2012. "Thurston Howell Romney." *New York Times,* September 17. Retrieved September 18, 2012 (www.nytimes.com/2012/09/18/opinion/brooks-thurston-howell-romney.html?_r=0).

Brooks, Rachel and Johanna Waters. 2010. "Student Mobility as a Response to Labour Market Congestion." Presented at International Sociological Association meetings in Sweden, July.

Broom, Leonard and Philip Selznick. 1963. *Sociology: A Text With Adapted Readings,* 3rd ed. New York: Harper & Row.

Brown, Dee. 2001. *Bury My Heart at Wounded Knee: An Indian History of the American West,* 30th anniversary ed. New York: Holt.

Brown, Donald E. 1991. *Human Universals.* Philadelphia: Temple University Press.

Bruner, Jerome. 1996. *The Culture of Education.* Cambridge, MA: Harvard University Press.

Brunn, Stanley D., Maureen Hays-Mitchell, and Donald J. Zeigler. 2011. *Cities of the World: World Regional Urban Development,* 4th ed. Lanham, MD: Rowman and Littlefield.

Brunn, Stanley D., Jack F. Williams, and Donald J. Zeigler. 2003. *Cities of the World: World Regional Urban Development,* 3rd ed. Lanham, MD: Rowman & Littlefield.

Brym, Robert J. and John Lie. 2007. *Sociology: Your Compass for a New World,* 3rd ed. Belmont, CA: Wadsworth.

Buechler, Steven. 2008. "What Is Critical About Sociology?" *Teaching Sociology* 36(4):318–30.

Bukhari, Zahid H. 2003. "Demography, Identity, Space: Defining American Muslims." Pp. 7–18 in *Muslims in the United States,* edited by Philippa Strum and Danielle Tarantolo. Washington DC: Woodrow Wilson International Center for Scholars.

Bullas, Jeff. 2012. "20 Interesting Facts, Figures and Statistics Revealed by Facebook." Jeffbullas.com. Retrieved September 25, 2012 (www.jeffbullas.com/2012/04/30/20-interesting-facts-figures-and-statistics-revealed-by-facebook/).

Burawoy, Michael. 2005. "For Public Sociology." *American Sociological Review* 56(2):4–28.

Bureau of Labor Statistics. 2012a. "Licensed Practical and Licensed Vocational Nurses." *Occupational Outlook Handbook,* March 29. Retrieved February 6, 2013 (http://www.bls.gov/ooh/healthcare/licensed-practical-and-licensed-vocational-nurses.htm).

Bureau of Labor Statistics. 2012b. "Registered Nurses." *Occupational Outlook Handbook,* March 29. Retrieved February 6, 2013 (http://www.bls.gov/ooh/healthcare/registered-nurses.htm).

Burgess, Robert and Ronald L. Akers. 1966. "A Differential Association-Reinforcement Theory of Criminal Behavior." *Social Problems* 14:363–83.

Burn, Shawn Meghan. 2011. *Women Across Cultures: A Global Perspective,* 3rd ed. New York: McGraw-Hill.

Cainkar, Louise A. 2009. *Homeland Insecurity: The Arab American and Muslim American Experience After 9/11.* New York: Russell Sage Foundation.

Caldwell, John C. 1982. *Theory of Fertility Decline.* New York: Academic Press.

Calhoun, Craig, ed. 2007. *Sociology in America: A History.* Chicago: University of Chicago Press.

Campbell, Denis. 2010. "The New Anorexics: Big Increase in Eating Disorders Among Women over 30." *The Guardian*, October 8. Retrieved May 27, 2012 (www.guardian.co.uk/society/2010/oct/08/new-anorexics-women-over-30).

Campbell, Ernest Q. and Thomas F. Pettigrew. 1959. *Christians in Racial Crisis.* Washington, DC: Public Affairs Press.

Canadian Health Care. 2007. "Introduction." Retrieved May 14, 2011 (www.canadian-healthcare.org/).

Cancian, Francesca M. 1992. "Feminist Science: Methodologies That Challenge Inequality." *Gender and Society* 6(4):623–42.

Carnevale, Anthony P. 2012. "Postsecondary Education and Training As We Know It Is Not Enough." Urban Institute. Retrieved May 17, 2012 (www.urban.org/issues/reducing-poverty-economic-distress.cfm).

Carroll, Lizz. 2010. "Interracial Marriage: Which Groups Are More Likely to Wed?" *DiversityInc*, May 27. Retrieved April 10, 2011 (www.diversityinc.com/article/7719/Interracial-Marriage-Which-Groups-Are-More-Likely-to-Wed/).

Carroll, Rory. 2010. "Ecuador Declares State of Emergency as Country Thrown Into Chaos." September 30. Retrieved December 2, 2010 (www.guardian.co.uk/world/2010/sep/30/equador-chaos-police-rafael-correa).

Carrothers, Robert M. and Denzel E. Benson. 2003. "Symbolic Interactionism in Introductory Textbooks: Coverage and Pedagogical Implications." *Teaching Sociology* 31(2):162–81.

Casasanto, Daniel. 2008. "Who's Afraid of the Big Bad Whorf? Crosslinguistic Differences in Temporal Language and Thought." *Language Learning* 58(1):63–79.

CASE. 2012. "Community College and Business Partnerships Take Root." February 14. *Community College Advancement News* 1(8).

Casella, Alexander. 2009. "Rural China Misses 'Barefoot Doctors.'" *Asia Times*, January 16. Retrieved January 10, 2010 (www.atimes.com/atimes/China/KA16Ad04.html).

Cashmore, Ellis and Barry Troyna. 1990. *Introduction to Race Relations.* London: Routledge.

Casteel, Chris. 2011. "New Survey on Hunger In America Measures Problems, Perceptions." March 11. Retrieved March 18, 2011 (http://newsok.com/new-survey-on-hunger-in-america-measures-problems-perceptions.article/3547666).

Castells, Manuel. 1977. *The Urban Question: A Marxist Approach.* Cambridge, MA: MIT Press.

Castiello, Umberto, Cristina Becchio, Stefania Zoia, Cristian Nelini, Luisa Sartori, Laura Blason, Giuseppina D'Ottavio, Maria Bulgheroni, and Vittorio Gallese. 2010. "Wired to Be Social: The Ontogeny of Human Interaction." *PLoS ONE* 5(10). Retrieved October 19, 2010 (www.plosone.org/article/info%3Adoi%2F10.1371%2Fjournal.pone.0013199).

Cauchon, Dennis and Barbara Hansen. 2011. "Typical U.S. Family Got Poorer During the Past 10 Years." *USA Today*, September 13. Retrieved June 5, 2012 (www.usatoday.com/news/nation/story/. . ./census. . ./1).

CBS News. 2010. "The Cost of Dying." *60 Minutes*, December 3. Retrieved July 16, 2012 (www.cbsnews.com/2100-18560_162-5711689.html?tag=contentMain;contentBody).

CBC News. 2010. "Four in 10 First Marriages End in Divorce." October 4. Retrieved June 27, 2012 (www.cbc.ca/news/canada/story/2010/10/04/vanier-study004.html).

Center for American Progress. 2009. "Wage Gap by the Numbers." January 6. Retrieved November 11, 2009 (www.americanprogress.org/issues/2009/01/wage_gap_numbers.html).

Center for American Progress Immigration Team. 2012. "The Facts on Immigration Today." July 6. Retrieved July 30, 2012 (www.americanprogress.org/issues/2012/07/immigration_facts.html).

Center for American Women and Politics. 2013. "Historical Information About Women in Congress." Retrieved January 19, 2013 (http://www.cawp.rutgers.edu/fast_facts/levels_of_office/Congress-HistoricalInfo.php).

Center for Education Policy. 2006. *Survey on Hours Spent on Subjects.* Menlo Park, CA: SRI International.

Center for Voting and Democracy. 2008. "Understanding Super Tuesday: State Rules on February 5 and Lessons for Reform." Retrieved March 21, 2008 (www.fairvote.org/?page=27&pressmode=showspecific&showarticle=185).

Center for Workforce Studies. 2011. *2011 State Physician Workforce Data Release*, March. "Figure 1. Active Physicians per 100,000 Population by Degree Type, 2009" (p. 2). Association of American Medical Colleges. Retrieved February 4, 2013 (https://www.aamc.org/download/181238/data/state_databook_update.pdf).

Center on Philanthropy. 2012. "Has America's Charitable Giving Climbed Out of Its Great Recession-Fueled Trough?" June 19. Retrieved September 19, 2012 (www.philanthropy.iupui.edu/news/article/has-americas-charitable-giving=climbed-out-of-its-great=recession-fueled-trough).

Centers for Disease Control and Prevention. 2009. "Lack of Health Insurance and Type of Coverage." Retrieved February 6, 2013 (http://www.cdc.gov/nchs/data/nhis/earlyrelease/200906_01.pdf).

Centers for Disease Control and Prevention. 2009. "National Health Interview Survey." Retrieved January 10, 2010 (www.cdc.gov/nchs/data/nhis/earlyrelease/200906_01.pdf).

Centers for Disease Control and Prevention. 2009. "Overweight and Obesity." July 27–29. Retrieved November 4, 2009 (www.cdc.gov/obesity/index.html).

Centers for Disease Control and Prevention. 2011a. "Births, Marriages, Divorces, and Deaths: Provisional Data for 2009." *National Vital Statistics Report 2009* 58(25).

Centers for Disease Control and Prevention. 2011b. "National Marriage and Divorce Rate Trends." Retrieved June 5, 2012 (www.cdc.gov/nchs/nvss/marriage_divorce_tables.htm).

Centers for Disease Control. 2011c. "U.S. Divorce Rate .68% for 2009." *National Vital Statistics Report*, February 7. Retrieved April 12, 2011 (http://familylaw.typepad.com/stats/2011/02/us-divorce-rate-068-for-2009-table-of-state-totals.html).

Centers for Disease Control and Prevention. 2012. "Economic Facts About U.S. Tobacco Production and Use." Retrieved August 3, 2012 (www.cdc.gov/tobacco/data_statistics/fact_sheets/economics/econ_facts/).

Centers for Disease Control and Prevention. 2012. "National Ambulatory Medical Care Survey: 2009." Retrieved October 15, 2012 (http://www.cdc.gov/nchs/fastats/docvisit.htm).

Centers for Disease Control and Prevention/National Center for Health Statistics. 2012a. "National Vital Statistics System: Marriages and Divorces." Retrieved January 24, 2013 (http://www.cdc.gov/nchs/mardiv.htm).

Centers for Disease Control and Prevention/National Center for Health Statistics. 2012b. "National Vital Statistics System: National Marriage and Divorce Rate Trends: Provisional Number of Divorces and Annulments and Rate: United States, 2000–2010." Retrieved January 24, 2013 (www.cdc.gov/nchs/nvss/marriage_divorce_tables.htm).

Centers for Disease Control and Prevention/National Center for Health Statistics/Office of Analysis and Epidemiology. 2012. "Health, United States, 2011." Retrieved February 2, 2013 (http://www.cdc.gov/nchs/hus.htm).

Centers for Medical and Medicaid Services. 2012. *Health Care Indicators.* Baltimore, MD: Office of the Actuary, Office of National Health Statistics.

Chabbott, Colette and Francisco O. Ramirez. 2000. "Development and Education." Pp. 163–87 in *Handbook of Sociology of Education,* edited by Maureen T. Hallinan. New York: Kluwer Academic/Plenum.

Chalfant, H. Paul and Charles W. Peck. 1983. "Religious Affiliation, Religiosity, and Racial Prejudice: A New Look at Old Relationships." *Review of Religious Research* 25(December):155–61.

Chamberlain, Houston Stewart. [1899] 1911. *The Foundations of the Nineteenth Century,* translated by John Lees. London, New York: John Lane.

Chambliss, William J. 1973. "The Saints and the Roughnecks." *Society* 11(December):24–31.

Chapman, Paige. 2010. "Report Calles for Distance Learning to Improve Higher Education Access and Efficiency in California." *The Chronicle of Higher Education,* October 29. Retrieved April 17, 2011 (http://chronicle.com/blogs/wiredcampus/distance-learning-can-improve-higher-education-access-and-efficiency-in-california/27978).

Charles, Camille Z., Vincent J. Roscigno, and Kimberly C. Torres. 2007. "Racial Inequality and College Attendance: The Mediating Role of Parental Investments." *Social Science Research* 36(1):329–52.

Charon, Joel. 2010. *Symbolic Interactionism: An Introduction, and Interpretation, an Integration,* 10th ed. Englewood Cliffs, NJ: Prentice Hall.

Chase, Cheryl. 2000. "Genital Surgery on Children Below the Age of Consent: Intersex Genital Mutilation." In *Psychological Perspectives on Human Sexuality,* edited by L. Szuchman and F. Muscarella. New York: Wiley.

Chase-Dunn, Christopher and E. N. Anderson. 2006. *The Historical Evolution of World-Systems.* New York: Palgrave Macmillan.

Chaves, Mark. 1993. "Denominations as Dual Structures: An Organizational Analysis." *Sociology of Religion* 54(20):147–69.

Chaves, Mark. 1999. *Ordaining Women: Culture and Conflict in Religious Organizations.* Cambridge, MA: Harvard University Press.

Chaves, Mark. 2004. *Congregations in America.* Cambridge, MA: Harvard University Press.

Chaves, Mark and Philip S. Gorski. 2001. "Religious Pluralism and Religious Participation." *Annual Review of Sociology* 27:261–81.

Chen, Zeng-Yin and Howard B. Kaplan. 2003. "School Failure in Early Adolescence and Status Attainment in Middle Adulthood: A Longitudinal Study." *Sociology of Education* 76(2):110–27.

Cheng, Cecilia. 2005. "Processes Underlying Gender-Role Flexibility: Do Androgynous Individuals Know More or Know How to Cope?" *Journal of Personality* 73(3):645–73.

Cherlin, Andrew. 1978. "Remarriage as an Incomplete Institution." *American Journal of Sociology* 84(3):634–50.

Cherlin, Andrew J. 2010. *The Marriage-Go-Round: The State of Marriage and the Family in America Today.* New York: Random House.

Cherry, Donald, Christine Lucas, and Sandra L. Decker. 2010. "Population Aging and the Use of Office-Based Physician Services." National Center for Health Statistics. *NCHS Data Brief* 41(August). Retrieved July 17, 2012 (www.cdc.nchs.gov/data/databriefs/db41.pdf).

Cherry, Kendra. 2012. "Understanding Body Language." *About.com Psychology.* Retrieved September 25, 2012 (http://psychology.about.com/od/nonverbalcommunication/ss/understanding-body-language.htm).

Cheung, Cecilia Sin-Sze and Eva M. Pomerantz. 2012. "Why Does Parents' Involvement Enhance Children's Achievement? The Role of Parent-Oriented Motivation." August. *Journal of Educational Psychology* 14(3):820–32.

Chicago Public Schools. 2011. "Renaissance 2010." Retrieved September 13, 2012 (www.cps.edu/PROGRAMS/DISTRICINITIATIVES/Pages/Renaissance 2010.aspx).

Child Trends Data Bank. 2012. "Sexually Active Teens." Retrieved September 13, 2012 (www.childtrendsdatabank.org/?q=node/315).

"Children and Watching TV." 2011. *American Academy of Child and Adolescent Psychiatry* 54(December). Retrieved May 24, 2012 (www.aacap.org/cs/root/facts_for_families/children_and_watching_tv).

Children's Defense Fund. 2011. "Number and Percentage of Uninsured Children in Each State." Retrieved April 7, 2011 (www.childrensdefense.org/policy-priorities/childrens-health/uninsured-children/uninsured-children-state.html).

ChinaDaily.com. 2012. "Tobacco Consumption Rises Amid Economic Slowdown." July 19. Retrieved August 2, 2012 (www.chinadaily.com.cn/business/2012-07-19/content_15598994.htm).

China.org. 2009. "Acupuncture, Herbal Medicine Become More Popular in U.S." Retrieved January 10, 2010 (www.china.org.cn/health/2009-06/25/content_18009726.htm).

Chiotakis, Steve. 2011. "U.S. Census: Only 16% Live in Rural America." *American Public Media,* July 28. Retrieved September 26, 2012 (www.marketplace.org/topics/business/us-census-only-16-live-rural-america).

Chivers, M. L., M. C. Seto, and R. R. Blanchard. 2007. "Gender and Sexual Orientation Differences in Sexual Response to Sexual Activities Versus Gender of Actors in Sexual Films." *Journal of Personality and Social Psychology* 93(6):1108–1121.

Christiano, Kevin J., William H. Swatos, Jr., and Peter Kivisto. 2008. *Sociology of Religion: Contemporary Developments,* Rev. ed. Walnut Creek, CA: AltaMira.

Christie, Les. 2011. "Number of People without Health Insurance Climbs." *CNN Money,* September 13. Retrieved May 16, 2012 (http://money.cnn.com/2011/09/13/news/economy/census_bureau_health_insurance/index.htm).

Chubb, John E. and Terry M. Moe. 1990. *Politics, Markets, and America's Schools.* Washington, DC: Brookings Institution.

Churchill, Winston. 2009. *Churchill by Himself: The Definitive Collection of Quotations,* edited by Richard Langworth. Jackson, TN: Public Affairs.

Cillizza, Chris. 2011. "Facebook, President Obama, and the Youth Vote in 2012." *The Washington Post,* April 20. Retrieved November 1, 2012 (www.washingtonpost.com/blogs/the-fix/post/facebook-president-obama-and-the-youth-vote-in-2012/2011/04/20/AF9zCwCE_blog.html).

Clapson, Mark. 2003. *Suburban Century: Social Change and Urban Growth in England and the USA.* Oxford and New York: Berg Publishers.

Clark, Warren and Grant Schellenberg. 2008. "Who's Religious?" *Statistics Canada.* Retrieved January 30, 2013 (http://www.statcan.gc.ca/pub/11-008-x/2006001/9181-eng.htm#half).

Clarke, Anne. 2007. "Amish Traditions—Shunning." *EzineArticles.com,* June 12. Retrieved December 13, 2009 (http://enzinearticles.com/?Amish-Traditions-Shunning&id=603322).

Clarkson, Lamar. 2011. "Divorce Rates Falling, Report Finds." *CNN Living,* May 19. Retrieved June 6, 2012 (http://articles.cnn.com/2011-05-19/living/divorce.rates.drop_1_divorce-rate-divorce-laws-marriage?_s=PM:LIVING).

Clausen, John A. 1986. *The Life Course: A Sociological Perspective.* Englewood Cliffs, NJ: Prentice Hall.

Cline, Michael E. 2008. "Comparison of Potential Demographic Influences on Church Membership of Two United Methodist Congregations in San Antonio, Texas." Pp. 237–49 in *Applied Demography in the 21st Century,* edited by Steve H. Murdock and David A. Swanson. Netherlands: Springer.

Clymer, Floyd. 1953. *Those Wonderful Old Automobiles.* New York: Bonanza.

CNBC. 2010. "Mob Money: An American Greed." July 7. Retrieved February 8, 2013 (www.cnbc.com/id/37593299/mob_money).

CNN. 2012. "Facts on Immigration in the United States." June 15. Retrieved July 30, 2012 (http://news.blogs.cnn.com/2012/06/15/facts-on-immigration-in-the-united-states/).

CNN.com. 2006. "Flag-Burning Amendment Fails by a Vote." June 28. Retrieved August 16, 2008 (www.cnn.com/2006/POLITICS/06/27/flag.burning).

CNNMoney.com. 2010. "Fortune 500: Women CEOs." Retrieved January 20, 2013 (http://money.cnn.com/magazines/fortune/fortune500/2010/womenceos/).

CNN Politics. 2009. "Obama Reverses Abortion-Funding Policy." Retrieved July 25, 2011 (http://articles.cnn.com/2009-01-23/politics/obama.abortion_1_abortion-counseling-family-planning-family-planning?_s=PM:POLITICS).

Cockerham, William C. 2012. *Medical Sociology,* 12th ed. Englewood Cliffs, NJ: Prentice Hall.

Cohen, Jessica and Wendy D. Manning. 2010 "The Relationship Context of Premarital Serial Cohabitation." *Social Science Research* 39(September):766–76.

Cole, Stephen and Robert Lejeune. 1972. "Illness and the Legitimation of Failure." *American Sociological Review* 37(3):347–56.

Coleman, James S. 1968. "The Concept of Equality of Educational Opportunity." *Harvard Education Review* 38(Winter):7–22.

Coleman, James S. 1975. "What Is Meant By 'An Equal Educational Opportunity'?" *Oxford Review of Education* 1(1):27–29.

Coleman, James. 1990. *Equality and Achievement in Education.* Boulder, CO: Westview.

Coleman, James William. 2006. *The Criminal Elite: Understanding White Collar Crime,* 6th ed. New York: Worth.

Coleman-Jensen, Alisha, Mark Nord, Margaret Andrews, and Steven Carlson. 2011. "Household Food Security in the United States in 2010." ERR-125, U.S. Department of Agriculture, Economic Research Service, September. Retrieved May 17, 2012 (www.cbpp.org/cms/index.cfm?fa=view&id=2226).

"Colleges' Gender Gap." 2010. *Los Angeles Times,* January 25. Retrieved September 12, 2012 (http://articles.latimes.com/2010/jan/25/opinion/la-ed-gender25-2010jan25).

Collins, Patricia Hill. 2000. *Black Feminist Thought: Knowledge, Consciousness, and the Politics of Empowerment,* 2nd ed. New York: Routledge.

Collins, Patricia Hill. 2005. *Black Sexual Politics: African Americans, Gender and the New Racism.* New York: Routledge.

Collins, Randall. 1971. "A Conflict Theory of Sexual Stratification." *Social Problems* 19(Summer):2–21.

Collins, Randall. 2004. "Conflict Theory of Educational Stratification." *American Sociological Review* 36:47–54.

ComScore. 2010. "Social Networking Sites Reach a Higher Percentage of Women Than Men Worldwide." July 28. Retrieved May 25, 2012 (www.comscore.com/Press_Events/Press_Releases/2010/7/Social_Networking_Sites_REach_a -Higher_Percentage_of_Women_than_Men_).

Condron, Dennis J. and Vincent J. Roscigno. 2003. "Disparities Within: Unequal Spending and Achievement in an Urban School District." *Sociology of Education* 76(January):18–36.

Conrad, Peter. 2007. *The Medicalization of Society: On the Transformation of Human Conditions Into Treatable Disorders.* Baltimore, MD: Johns Hopkins University Press.

Conrad, Peter and Joseph Schneider. 1992. *Deviance and Medicalization: From Badness to Sickness.* Philadelphia: Temple University Press.

Consumer Rankings. 2012. "The 5 Best Dating Sites of 2012." June 2. Retrieved June 3, 2012 (www.consumer-rankings.com/dating/).

Cook, Karen S., Jodi O'Brien, and Peter Kollock. 1990. "Exchange Theory: A Blueprint for Structure and Process." Pp. 158–81 in *Frontiers of Social Theory: The New Syntheses,* edited by George Ritzer. New York: Columbia University Press.

Cooke, Jennifer G. 2012. "Polio in Nigeria: The Race to Eradication." Center for Strategic and International Studies, February 10. Retrieved July 16, 2012 (http://csis.org/publication/polio-nigeria).

Cooley, Charles Horton. 1902. *Human Nature and the Social Order.* New York: Scribner.

Cooley, Charles Horton. [1909] 1983. *Social Organization: A Study of the Larger Mind.* New York: Schocken Books.

Coontz, Stephanie. 1997. *The Way We Really Are: Coming to Terms With America's Changing Families.* New York: Basic Books.

Coontz, Stephanie. 2005. *Marriage, a History: From Obedience to Intimacy, or How Love Conquered Marriage.* New York: Viking.

Coontz, Stephanie. 2011a. "On Marriage." January 4. Retrieved February 25, 2012 (www.youtube.com/watch?v=gwtb7jz8G4k).

Coontz, Stephanie. 2011b. "What Is the 'Traditional American Family'? Interview with Stephanie Coontz." *The Mother Company,* November 22. Retrieved May 25, 2012 (www.themotherco.com/2011/1/what-is-the-traditional-family/).

Cordain, L., S. B. Eaton, A. Sabastian, N. Mann, S. Lindeberg, B. A. Watkins, J. H. O'Keefe, and J. Brand-Miller. 2005. "Origins and Evolution of the Western Diet: Health Implications for the 21st Century." *American Journal of Clinical Nutrition* 82(August): 483–84.

Coser, Lewis A. 1956. *The Functions of Social Conflict.* New York: Free Press.

Council on the American Family. N.d. "Marriage and Families." Retrieved June 6, 2012 (http://caf-usa.org/).

Cousteau, Jacques-Yves. 2008. "The Great Ocean Adventure." Lecture at Hanover College, January 15.

Creswell, John W. 2009. *Research Design: Qualitative, Quantitative, and Mixed Methods Approaches,* 3rd ed. Thousand Oaks, CA: Sage.

Crime Library. 2012. "Worst Cases of Bullying." Retrieved October 5, 2012 (www.gtrutv.com/library/crime/photogallery/worst-cases-of-bullying.html?curPhoto=3).

Cronkite, Walt. 2012. "Romney Says He's 'Fine' With Gay Couples Adopting Children." *CBS News,* May 10. Retrieved June 3, 2012 (www

.cbsnews.com/8301-503544_162-57432292-503544/romney-says-hes-fine-with-gay-couples-adopting-children/).

Crosby, Faye J. 2004. *Affirmative Action Is Dead; Long Live Affirmative Action.* New Haven, CT: Yale University Press.

Crossette, Barbara. 1996. "Angkor Emerges From the Jungle." *The New York Times*, January 28. Retrieved September 9, 2008 (http://query.nytimes.com/gst/fullpage.html?res=9500e0d91139f93ba15752c0a960958260&sec=travel&spon=&pagewanted=1).

"Cruellest Cut—Pakistan's Kidney Mafia." 2009. Retrieved January 11, 2010 (www.youtube.com/watch?v=vi7A_jK64qc).

Crummey, Robert O. 1970. *The Old Believers and the World of Antichrist: The Vyg Community and the Russian State, 1694–1855.* Madison: University of Wisconsin Press.

Current.com. 2012. "The War Room With Jennifer Granholm: The Pros and Cons of Private Prisons." February 21. Retrieved October 7, 2012 (http://current.com/shows/the-pros-and-cons-of-private-prisons).

Curtiss, S. 1977. *Genie: A Psycholinguistic Study of a Modern-Day "Wild Child."* New York: Academic Press.

Cushing, Bill and Robert G. Bishop. 2008. *The Big Sort: Why the Clustering of Like-Minded America Is Tearing Us Apart.* Boston: Houghton Mifflin Harcourt.

Cushman, Thomas and Stjepan G. Mestrovic. 1996. *This Time We Knew: Western Responses to Genocide in Bosnia.* New York: New York University Press.

Cuzzort, R. P. and Edith W. King. 2002. *Social Thought Into the Twenty-First Century,* 6th ed. Belmont, CA: Wadsworth.

DaCosta, Kimberly McClain. 2007. *Making Multiracials: State, Family, and Market in the Redrawing of the Color Line.* Stanford, CA: Stanford University Press.

Dahl, Robert A. 1961. *Who Governs?* New Haven, CT: Yale University Press.

Dahlberg, Frances. 1981. *Woman the Gatherer.* New Haven, CT: Yale University Press.

Dahrendorf, Ralf. 1959. *Class and Class Conflict in Industrial Societies.* Palo Alto, CA: Stanford University Press.

Dalit Liberation Education Trust. 1995. *10th Anniversary Newsletter* (May). Madras: Human Rights Education Movement of India.

Dalton, Harlon. 2012. "Failing to See." Pp. 15–18 in *White Privilege,* edited by Paula S. Rothenberg. New York: Worth.

Danesi, Marcel. 2008. *Popular Culture.* Lanham, MD: Rowman & Littlefield.

D'Arcy, Yvonne. 2009. "The Effect of Culture on Pain." *Nursing Made Incredibly Easy!* 7(3):5–7.

Darr, Kurt. 2007. "Assistance in Dying: Part II. Assisted Suicide in the U.S." *Hospital Topics* 85(2):31–36.

Darwin, Charles. [1858] 1909. *The Origin of Species.* New York: P. F. Collier.

Data360. 2012. "U.S. Life Expectancy Rates." Retrieved March 31, 2012 (http://www.data360.org/dsg.aspx?Data_Set_Group_Id=195).

Davidson, James D. 2008. "Religious Stratification: Its Origins, Persistence, and Consequences" *Sociology of Religionsocrel.oxfordjournals.org Sociology of Religion* 69(4):371–95.

Davis, Kingsley. 1940. "Extreme Social Isolation of a Child." *American Journal of Sociology* 45:554–65.

Davis, Kingsley. 1947. "A Final Note on a Case of Extreme Isolation." *American Journal of Sociology* 52:432–37.

Davis, Kingsley and Wilbert Moore. 1945. "Some Principles of Stratification." *American Sociological Review* 10(April):242–45.

Day, Jennifer Cheeseman. 2011. U.S. "Population Profile of the U.S.: Percentage of the Population, by Race and Hispanic Origin." Census Bureau, Population Division Retrieved April 19, 2011 (http://www.census.gov/population/www/pop-profile/natproj.html).

Dealbook. 2009. "Pay Czar Said to Plan to Disclose Top Salaries." Retrieved January 20, 2013 (www.dealbook.nytimes.com/2009/09/17/pay-czar-seen-disclosing-top-executive-salaries/).

Death Penalty Information Center. 2012. "Facts about the Death Penalty." April 13. Retrieved April 16, 2012 (www.deathpenaltyinfo.org/documents/FactSheet.pdf).

Death with Dignity. 2012. "Physicians' Frequently Asked Questions." Death with Dignity National Center. Retrieved July 16, 2012 (www.deathwithdignity.org/resources/physiciansquestions).

DeCarlo, Scott. 2012. "CEO Pay." *Forbes.com*, April 4. Retrieved May 14, 2012 (www.forbes.com/forbes/2012/0423/ceo-compensation-12-company-earnings-highest-gravity-defying-pay.html).

DeGenova, Mary Kay, Nick Stinnett, and Nancy Stinnett. 2011. *Intimate Relationships, Marriages, and Families,* 8th ed. New York: McGraw-Hill.

Delfattore, Joan. 2004. "Romeo and Juliet Were Just Good Friends." Pp. 177–83 in *Schools and Society,* 2nd ed., edited by Jeanne H. Ballantine and Joan Z. Spade. Belmont, CA: Wadsworth.

Della Porta, Donatella, Massimillano Andretta, Lorenzo Mosca, and Herbert Reiter. 2006. *Globalization From Below: Transnational Activists and Protest Networks.* Minneapolis: University of Minnesota Press.

DeMartini, Joseph R. 1982. "Basic and Applied Sociological Work: Divergence, Convergence, or Peaceful Coexistence?" *Journal of Applied Behavioral Science* 18(2):205–206.

Deming, W. E. 2000. *Out of the Crisis.* Cambridge, MA: MIT Press.

DeMitchell, Todd A. and John J. Carney. 2005. "Harry Potter and the Public School Library." *Phi Delta Kappan* (October):159–65.

Denali Commission. 2001. "Telecommunications Inventory Survey." Retrieved June 29, 2006 (www.commonwealth.north.org/transcripts/denalicom.html).

DeNavas-Walt, Carmen, Bernadette D. Proctor, and Jessica C. Smith. 2010. "Income, Poverty, and Health Insurance Coverage in the United States: 2009." U.S. Census Bureau, Report P60-238, Table B-2, pp. 62–67. Retrieved January 23, 2013 (http://www.census.gov/prod/2010pubs/p60-238.pdf).

DeNavas-Walt, Carmen, Bernadette D. Proctor, and Jessica C. Smith. 2011. "Income, Poverty, and Health Insurance Coverage in the United States: 2010." Retrieved January 28, 2013 (http://www.census.gov/prod/2011pubs/p60-239.pdf).

DeNavas-Walt, Carmen, Bernadette D. Proctor, and Jessica C. Smith. 2012. "Income, Poverty, and Health Insurance Coverage in the United States: 2011." U.S. Census Bureau Current Population Reports, September. Retrieved February 6, 2013 (http://www.census.gov/prod/2012pubs/p60-243.pdf).

DePalma, Anthony. 1995. "Racism? Mexico's in Denial." *The New York Times*, June 11, p. E4.

DeParle, Jason and Sabrina Tavernise. 2012. " For Women Under 30, Most Births Occur Outside Marriage." *The New York Times*, February 17. Retrieved June 5, 2012 (www.nytimes.com/2012/02/18/us/for-women-under-30-most-births-occur-outside-marriage.html?pagewanted=all).

Deutsch, M. and R. M. Krauss. 1960. "The Effect of Threat on Interpersonal Bargaining." *Journal of Abnormal and Social Psychology* 61:181–89.

Deutsch, Morton and Roy J. Lewicki. 1970. "'Locking-In' Effects During a Game of Chicken." *Journal of Conflict Resolution* 14(3):367–78.

Dews, C. L. Barney and Carolyn Leste Law, eds. 1995. *This Fine Place So Far From Home: Voices of Academics From the Working Class.* Philadelphia: Temple University Press.

Diamond, Jared. 2005. *Collapse: How Societies Choose to Fail or Succeed.* New York: Viking.

Diamond, Larry. 1992. "Introduction: Civil Society and the Struggle for Democracy." Pp. 1–28 in *The Democratic Revolution: Struggles for Freedom and Pluralism in the Developing World,* edited by Larry Diamond. New York: Freedom House.

Diamond, Larry. 2003. "Universal Democracy?" *Policy Review* (June/July). Retrieved August 28, 2008 (www.hoover.org/publications/poicyreview/3448571.html).

Diamond, Larry. 2009. *The Spirit of Democracy: The Struggle to Build Free Societies Throughout the World.* New York: Times Books/Henry Holt & Co.

Diekman, Amanda B. and Sarah K. Murmen. 2004. "Learning to Be Little Women and Little Men: The Inequitable Gender Equality of Nonsexist Children's Literature." *Sex Roles: A Journal of Research* 50(5/6):373.

Diep, Francie. 2011. "Fast Facts About the Japan Earthquake and Tsunami." *Scientific American,* March 14. Retrieved May 13, 2012 (www.scientificamerican.com/article.cfm?if=fast-facts-japan).

Diggs, Nancy Brown. 2011. *Hidden in the Heartland.* East Lansing: Michigan State University Press.

DiMaggio, Paul and Walter Powell. 1983. "The Iron Cage Revisited: Institutional Isomorphism and Collective Rationality in Organizational Fields." *American Sociological Review* 48:147–60.

Disabled World. 2012. "2012 London Summer Paralympic Games." Retrieved September 9, 2012 (www.disabled-world.com/sports/paralympics/2012/).

DiversityInc. 2008. "Belonging Nowhere: The Biracial Children of Vietnam Veterans." October 13. Retrieved October 16, 2009 (diversityinc.com/content/1757/article/4574).

Divorce Rate. 2011. "Divorce Updates and Divorce Rate in 2011." Retrieved June 6, 2012 (http://divorcerate2011.com/divorce-updates).

Dixon, Patrick. 2011. "Steroid Use." *Global Change.* Retrieved May 23, 2012 (www.globalchange.com/steroids.htm).

Dobbelaere, Karel. 1981. *Secularization: A Multidimensional Concept.* Beverly Hills, CA: Sage.

Dobbelaere, Karel. 2000. "Toward an Integrated Perspective of the Processes Related to the Descriptive Concept of Secularization." Pp. 21–39 in *The Secularization Debate,* edited by William H. Swatos, Jr. and Daniel V. A. Olson. Lanham, MD: Rowman & Littlefield.

Doctors without Borders. 2012. "Swaziland: Community Takes Part in HIV Treatment." February 13. Retrieved July 16, 2012 (http://doctorswithout borers.org/news/article.cfm?id=5763&cat=video&ref-tag-index).

"Doing Gender." 2011. *Creative Sociology.* August 10. Retrieved May (http://creativesociology.blogspot.com/2011/08/doing-gender.html).

The Dollars and Sense Collective. 2012. Pp. 81–91 in *Globalization: The Transformation of Social Worlds,* 3rd ed., edited by D. Stanley Eitzen and Maxine Baca Zinn. Belmont, CA: Wadsworth.

Domestic Violence Resource Center. 2012. "Domestic Violence Statistics." Retrieved June 21, 2012 (www.dvrc-or.org/domestic/violence/resources/C61).

Domhoff, G. William. 2005. "The Class-Domination Theory of Power." *Who Rules America,* 6th ed. Retrieved May 16, 2012 (www2.ucsc.edu/whorulesamerica/power/class_domination.html).

Domhoff, G. William. 2008. "Who Rules America.net: Power, Politics, and Social Change." Retrieved March 24, 2008 (http://sociology.ucsc.edu/whoruleeesamerica).

Domhoff, G. William. 2009. *Who Rules America: Challenges to Corporate and Class Dominance.* Upper Saddle River, NJ: Prentice Hall.

Domina, Thurston. 2005. "Leveling the Home Advantage: Assessing the Effectiveness of Parental Involvement in Elementary School." *Sociology of Education* 78(3):233–49.

Dotzler, Robert J. and Ross Koppel. 1999. "What Sociologists Do and Where They Do It—The NSF Survey on Sociologists' Work Activities and Work Places." *Sociological Practice: A Journal of Clinical and Applied Sociology* 1(1):71–83.

Downey, Douglas B. and Shana Pribesh. 2004. "When Race Matters: Teachers' Evaluations of Students' Classroom Behavior." *Sociology of Education* 77(4):267–82.

Drafke, Michael. 2008. *The Human Side of Organizations.* Englewood Cliffs, NJ: Prentice Hall.

Drori, Gili S. 2006. *Global E-Litism: Digital Technology, Social Inequality, and Transnationality.* New York: Worth.

Du Bois, W. E. B. [1899] 1967. *The Philadelphia Negro: A Social Study.* New York: Schocken.

Dufur, Mikaela J. and Seth L. Feinberg. 2007. "Artificially Restricted Labor Markets and Worker Dignity in Professional Football." *Journal of Contemporary Ethnography* 36(5):505–36.

Duncan, Arne. 2006. "Chicago's Renaissance 2010: Building on School Reform in the Age of Accountability." *Phi Delta Kappan* (February):457–58.

Durkheim, Émile. [1893] 1947. *The Division of Labor in Society,* translated by George Simpson. New York: Free Press.

Durkheim, Émile. [1897] 1964. *Suicide.* Glencoe, IL: Free Press.

Durkheim, Émile. [1915] 2002. In *Classical Sociological Theory,* edited by Craig Calhoun. Malden, MA: Blackwell.

Durkheim, Émile. 1947. *Elementary Forms of Religious Life.* Glencoe, IL: Free Press.

Durkheim, Émile. 1956. *Education and Society.* Translated by Sherwood D. Fox. Glencoe, IL: Free Press.

Dworkin, Anthony Gary and Rosalind J. Dworkin. 1999. *The Minority Report: An Introduction to Racial, Ethnic, and Gender Relations,* 3rd ed. Fort Worth, TX: Harcourt Brace.

Dworkin, Anthony Gary and Pamela F. Tobe. 2012. "Teacher Burnout in Light of School Safety, Student Misbehavior, and Changing Accountability Standards." Pp. 199–211 in *Schools and Society: A Sociological Approach to Education,* edited by Jeanne H. Ballantine and Joan Z. Spade. Thousand Oaks, CA: Sage Pine Forge.

Dye, Thomas, R. 2002. *Who's Running America? The Clinton Years.* Upper Saddle River, NJ: Prentice Hall.

Dye, Thomas and Harmon Zeigler. 1983. *The Irony of Democracy.* North Scituate, MA: Duxbury Press.

Dyer, Richard. 2012. "The Matter of Whiteness." Pp. 9–14 in *White Privilege,* edited by Paula S. Rothenberg. New York: Worth.

Earls, Felton M. and Albert J. Reiss. 1994. *Breaking the Cycle: Predicting and Preventing Crime.* Washington, DC: National Institute of Justice.

"Eating Disorder Statistics." 2008. South Carolina Department of Mental Health. Retrieved May 27, 2012 (www.state.sc.us/dmh/anorexia/statistics/htm).

Eaton, S. B., M. J. Konner, and L. Cordain. 2010. "Diet-Dependent Acid Load, Paleolithic (Corrected) Nutrition, and Evolutionary Health Promotion." *American Journal of Clinical Nutrition* 91 (February):295–97.

Ebaugh, Helen Rose Fuchs. 2005. *Handbook of Religion and Social Institutions.* New York: Springer.

Eckert, Penelope. 1989. *Jocks and Burnouts: Social Categories and Identity in High School.* New York: Teacher's College Press.

EcoSummit 2012. "Ecological Sustainability: Restoring the Planet's Ecosystem Services." *Fourth International Ecosummit.* www.ecosummit2012.org/ (Retrieved July 31, 2012)

"Ecosystems Report Links Human Well-Being With Health of Planet." 2006. *Popline* 28(January/February):1.

Eder, Donna, Catherine Colleen Evans, and Stephen Parker. 1995. *School Talk: Gender and Adolescent Culture.* New Brunswick, NJ: Rutgers University Press.

Edney, Anna. 2012. "Meningitis Risk Spreads to 14,000 People Given Back-Pain Shot." Bloomberg News, October 12. Retrieved October 12, 2012 (www.sfgae.com/business/bloomberg/article/Meningitis-Risk-Spreads-to-14,000-People-Given-3941544.php).

Education Week. 2011. "School Finance." June 20. Retrieved September 14, 2012 (www.edweek.org/ew/issues/school-finance/).

Edwards, Harry. 2000. "Crisis of the Black Athlete on the Eve of the 21st Century." *Society* 37(3):9–13.

EFA Global Monitoring Report. 2009. "Overcoming Inequality: Why Governance Matters." Retrieved September 15, 2012 (http://unesdoc.unesco.org/images/0017/001776/177683e.pdf).

eHarmony. 2012. "Information." Retrieved February 9, 2013 (http://advice.eharmony.com/information).

Ehrenreich, Barbara. 2001. *Nickel and Dimed: On (Not) Getting By in America.* New York: Henry Holt.

Ehrenreich, Barbara. 2005. *Bait and Switch: The (Futile) Pursuit of the American Dream.* New York: Henry Holt.

Ehrlich, Paul and Ann Ehrlich. 1990. *The Population Explosion.* New York: Simon and Schuster.

Eitzen, D. Stanley and George H. Sage. 2003. *Sociology of North American Sport.* Boston: McGraw-Hill.

Eitzen, D. Stanley and Maxine Baca Zinn, eds. 2006. *Globalization: The Transformation of Social Worlds.* Belmont, CA: Wadsworth.

Eitzen, D. Stanley and Maxine Baca Zinn. 2012. "Changing Global Structures: Resistance and Social Movements." Pp. 269–71 in *Globalization: The Transformation of Social Worlds*, 3rd ed., edited by D. Stanley Eitzen and Maxine Baca Zinn. Belmont, CA: Wadsworth.

Eitzen, D. Stanley and Maxine Baca Zinn. N.d. "Commonsense Sayings." *Sociological Conceptual Tools Room.* Retrieved February 9, 2013 (www.angelfire.com/or/sociologyshop/CONCEPTTOOLS.html#css).

Elam, Jerome. 2011. "Pedophiles and Pimps Score at Large Sporting Events Like Super Bowl XLVI." *The Washington Times,* January 17. Retrieved January 21, 2013 (http://communities.washingtontimes.com/neighborhood/heart-without-compromise-children-and-children-wit/2012/jan/17/pedophiles-and-pimps-score-large-sporting-events-s/).

Ellens, G. F. S. 1971. "The Ranting Ranters: Reflections on a Ranting Counter-Culture." *Church History* 40(March):91–107.

Ellison, Christopher G., J. A. Burr, and P. L. McCall. 1997. "Religious Homogeneity and Metropolitan Suicide Rates." *Social Forces* 76(1):273–99.

Ellison, Christopher G. and Daniel A. Powers. 1994. "The Contact Hypothesis and Racial Attitudes Among Black Americans." *Social Science Quarterly* 75(2):385–400.

Emerson, Michael O., with Rodney Woo. 2006. *People of the Dream: Multiracial Congregations in the United States.* Princeton, NJ: Princeton University Press.

Engels, Friedrich. [1884] 1942. *The Origin of the Family, Private Property, and the State.* New York: International Publishing.

Enloe, Cynthia. 2006. "Daughters and Generals in the Politics of the Globalized Sneaker." In *Beyond Borders: Thinking Critically About Global Issues,* edited by Paula S. Rothenberg. New York: Worth.

Environment 911. 2012. "Causes of Water Shortages." Retrieved February 8, 2013 (www.environment911.org/221.Causes_of_Water_Shortages).

Environmental Defense Fund. 2012. "Climate: Facts, Dangers and What You Can Do." Retrieved September 8, 2012 (www.edf.org/climate-facts-dangers-and-what-climatechange&gclid).

Environmental Protection Agency. 2004. "Terms of Environment." Retrieved (www.epa.gov/OCEPAterms/gterms.html).

Environmental Protection Agency. 2011. "Air Quality Trends." Retrieved September 7, 2012 (www.epa.gov/airtrends/aqtrends.html).

Environmental Protection Agency. 2012. "Greenhouse Gas Emissions." Retrieved February 8, 2013 (www.epa.gov/climatechange/ghgemissions/).

Erikson, Erik H. 1950. *Childhood and Society.* New York: Norton.

Erikson, Kai T. 1976. *Everything in Its Path: Destruction of Community in the Buffalo Creek Flood.* New York: Simon & Schuster.

Erikson, Kai T. 1987. "Notes on the Sociology of Deviance." pp. 9–21 in *Deviance: The Interactionist Perspective,* 5th ed., edited by Earl Rubington and Martin S. Weinberg. New York: Macmillan.

Erikson, Kai T. [1966] 2005. *Wayward Puritans: A Study in the Sociology of Deviance.* Boston: Pearson Education.

Eshleman, J. Ross and Richard A. Bulcroft. 2006. *The Family,* 11th ed. Boston: Allyn & Bacon.

Eshleman, J. Ross and Richard A. Bulcroft. 2010. *The Family,* 12th ed. Boston: Allyn & Bacon.

Esperitu, Yen Le. 1992. *Asian American Panethnicity: Bridging Institutions and Identities.* Philadelphia: Temple University Press.

Espo, David. 2009. "$797 Billion Stimulus Plan Ok'd in Victory for Obama." *Los Angeles Daily News,* February 14. Retrieved February 24, 2009 (www.dailynews.com/search/ci_11703066).

Esquivel, Laura. 2001. *Like Water for Chocolate.* New York: Anchor.

Ethnic Majority. 2010. "African, Hispanic (Latino), and Asian American members of Congress." Retrieved April 22, 2011 (www.ethnicmajority.com/congress.htm).

Etounga-Manguelle, Daniel. 2000. "Does Africa Need a Cultural Adjustment Program?" Pp. 65–77 in *Culture Matters: How Values Shape Human Progress,* edited by Lawrence E. Harrison and Samuel P. Huntington. New York: Basic Books.

Etzioni, Amitai. 1975. *A Comparative Analysis of Complex Organizations.* New York: Free Press.

Europa World Year Book. 2005. London: Europa.

Evans, Martin. 2012. "First Case of People Trafficking for Organs Uncovered in UK." *The Telegraph,* April 25. Retrieved January 19, 2013 (http://www.telegraph.co.uk/news/uknews/crime/9227137/First-case-of-people-trafficking-for-organs-uncovered-in-UK.html).

Evans, Tom. 2010. "Bosnian Leader: 'Ethnic Cleansing' Continues 15 Years After War." *CNN World,* March 1. Retrieved May 6, 2012 (http://articles.cnn.com/2010-03-01/world/bosnia.herzegovina_1_ethnic-cleansing-serb-bosnian-leader?_s=PM:WORLD).

Evon, Dan. 2012. "Laura Dekker Completes Round-the-World Journey." Retrieved February 23, 2012 (www.inquisitr.com/184540/laura-dekker-completes-round-the-world-journey-video/).

Facebook.com. 2011. "Facebook Facts." Retrieved March 6, 2011 (www.facebook.com/press/info/php?statistics).

Fackler, Martin. 2007. "Career Women in Japan Find a Blocked Path." *The New York Times,* August 6. Retrieved November 8, 2009 (www.nytimes.com/2007/08/06/world/asia/06equal.html).

Fadiman, Anne. 1997. *The Spirit Catches You and You Fall Down.* New York: Noonday.

Fainaru-Wada, Mark and Justine Gubar. 2012. "The Unseen Faces of Sports Apparel." ESPN, January 9. Retrieved July 12, 2012 (http://espn.go.com/espn/otl/story/id/7435424/dallas=cowboys-dip=sports-apparel-business-comes-allegations-sweatshop-labor).

Farley, John E. 2010. *Majority-Minority Relations,* 6th ed. Englewood Cliffs, NJ: Prentice Hall.

Farmer, Paul. 1999. *Infections and Inequalities: The Modern Plagues.* Berkeley: University of California Press.

Farrer, Claire R. 1996. *Thunder Rides a Black Horse: Mescalero Apaches and the Mythic Present,* 2nd ed. Prospect Heights, IL: Waveland.

Farrer, Claire R. 2011. *Thunder Rides a Black Horse: Mescalero Apaches and the Mythic Present,* 3rd ed. Long Grove, IL: Waveland.

Fathi, David C. 2009. "Prison Nation." Human Rights Watch, April 9. Retrieved April 15, 2009 (www.hrw.org/en/news/2009/04/09/prison-nation).

Fausto-Sterling, Anne. 1992. *Myths of Gender: Biological Theories About Women and Men,* 2nd ed. New York: Basic Books.

Fausto-Sterling, Anne. 2000. "The Five Sexes, Revisited." *Sciences* 40(July/August):118.

Federal Bureau of Investigation. 2006a. "2006 Financial Crime Report." Retrieved February 8, 2008 (www.fbi.gov/publications/financial/fcs_report2006/financial_crime_2006.htm).

Federal Bureau of Investigation. 2009. "Crime in the United States: Expanded Homicide Data." Retrieved June 3, 2012 (www2.fbi.gov/ucr/cius2009/offenses/expanded_information/homicide.html).

Federal Bureau of Investigation. 2011a. "Child Pornography Prosecutions Soaring." February 5. Retrieved April 14, 2012 (http://rapecrisiscenter.org/sanfrancisco02053011.html).

Federal Bureau of Investigation. 2011b. "FBI 2010 Cybercrime Statistics." February 27. Retrieved April 14, 2012 (http://scamfraudalert.net/2011/02/27/fbi-2010-cybercrime-statistics/).

Federal Bureau of Investigation. 2012. "Crime Rates Are Down." *Uniform Crime Report,* June 11. Retrieved October 6, 2012 (www.fbi.gov/news/stories/2012/june/crimes_061112/crimes_061112).

Feagin, Joe R., 1983. *The Urban Real Estate Game: Playing Monopoly with Real Money.* Englewood Cliffs, NJ: Prentice Hall.

Feagin, Joe R. and Clairece Booher Feagin. 1986. *Discrimination American Style: Institutional Racism and Sexism.* Malabar, FL: Krieger.

Feagin, Joe R. and Clairece Booher Feagin. 2010. *Racial and Ethnic Relations,* 9th ed. Englewood Cliffs, NJ: Prentice Hall.

Featherman, David L. and Robert Hauser. 1978. *Opportunity and Change.* New York: Academic Press.

Federal Register. 2002. *Office of the Federal Register, National Archives and Records* 67.

Felix, Samantha. 2012. "Side by Side: How Obama and Romney's Social Media Battle Stacks Up." *Business Insider*, September 23. Retrieved November 1, 2012 (www.businessinsider.com/winner-of-the-obamaromney-social-media-campaign-2012-9?op=1).

Feller, Avi and Chad Stone. 2009. "Top 1% of Americans Reaped Two-Thirds of Income Gains in Last Economic Expansion." Center on Budget and Policy Priorities, September 9. Retrieved January 7, 2010 (www.cbpp.org/cms/index.cfm?fa=view&id=2908).

Ferhansyed. 2008. "Fundamental Terminology of Planned Change." Retrieved December 21, 2009 (http://organizationdevelopment.wordpress.com/2008/08/10/fundamental-terminology-of-organization-development).

Fernando, Suman. 2002. *Mental Health, Race and Culture,* 2nd ed. New York: Palgrave.

Ferree, Myra Marx. 2012. "Globalization and Feminism: Opportunities and Obstacles for Activism in a Global Arena." Pp. 291–320 in *Globalization: The Transformation of Social Worlds,* 3rd ed., edited by D. Stanley Eitzen and Maxine Baca Zinn. Belmont, CA: Wadsworth.

Ferree, Myra Marx and David A. Merrill. 2000. "Hot Movements, Cold Cognition: Thinking About Social Movements in Gendered Frames." *Contemporary Sociology: A Journal of Reviews* 12:626–48.

Fine, Gary Alan. 1990. "Symbolic Interactionism in the Post-Blumerian Age." Pp. 117–57 in *Frontiers of Social Theory: The New Synthesis,* edited by George Ritzer. New York: Columbia University Press.

Finke, Roger and Rodney Stark. 2005. *The Churching of America, 1776–1990: Winners and Losers in Our Religious Economy*, 2nd ed. New Brunswick, NJ: Rutgers University Press.

"First Born Children." 2008. Retrieved June 29, 2008 (http://social.jrank.org/pages/261/Firstborn-children.html).

Fischer, Claude S. 1984. *The Urban Experience,* 2nd ed. San Diego, CA: Harcourt Brace Jovanovich.

Fish, Virginia Kemp. 1986. "The Hull House Circle: Women's Friendships and Achievements." Pp. 185–227 in *Gender, Ideology, and Action: Historical Perspectives on Women's Public Lives*, edited by Janet Sharistanian. Westport, CT: Greenwood.

Fisher, Max. 2012. "Here's a Map of the Countries That Provide Universal Health Care (America's Still Not on It)." *The Atlantic,* June 28. Retrieved February 6, 2013 (http://www.theatlantic.com/international/archive/2012/06/heres-a-map-of-the-countries-that-provide-universal-health-care-americas-still-not-on-it/259153/).

Fitch, Catherine, Ron Goeken, and Steven Ruggles. 2005. "The Rise of Cohabitation in the United States: New Historical Estimates." Retrieved July 14, 2011 (http://www.hist.umn.edu/~ruggles/cohab-revised2.pdf).

Fitzpatrick, Laura. 2010. "Why Do Women Still Earn Less Than Men?" *Time,* April 20. Retrieved March 18, 2011 (www.time.com/time/nation/article/0,8599,1983185,00.html).

"Five Rules for Online Networking." 2005. CNN, April 1. Retrieved July 25, 2006 (www.cnn.com/2005/US/Careers/03/31/online.networking).

Flanagan, William G. 2001. *Urban Sociology: Images and Structure,* 4th ed. Boston: Allyn & Bacon.

Flavin, Jeanne. 2004. "Employment, Counseling, Housing Assistance . . . and Aunt Yolanda? How Strengthening Families' Social Capital Can Reduce Recidivism." *Fordham Urban Law Journal* 3(2):209–16.

Florida, Richard. 2002. *The Rise of the Creative Class.* New York: Basic Books.

Florida, Richard. 2004. *Cities and the Creative Class.* New York: Routledge.

Florida, Richard. 2012a. "Creative Class Group." March 2. Retrieved March 5, 2012 (www.creativeclass.com/richard_florida).

Florida, Richard. 2012b. "The Joys of Urban Tech." *The Wall Street Journal,* August 31. Retrieved September 25, 2012 (www.creativeclass.com/rfcgdb/articles/WSJ%20The%20Joys%20of%20Urban%20Tech.pdf).

Foner, Nancy. 2005. *In a New Land: A Comparative View of Immigration.* New York: New York University Press.

Food and Agriculture Organization of the United Nations, Jacques Diouf. 2010–2011. *Women—Key to Food Security.* Retrieved October 1, 2012 (www.fao.org/docrep/014/am719e/am719e00.pdf).

Forbes. 2012. "The World's Billionaires." May 5. Retrieved May 16, 2012 (http://www.forbes.com/billionaires/).

Ford, Clennan S. 1970. *Human Relations Area Files: 1949–1969—A Twenty Year Report.* New Haven, CT: Human Relations Area Files.

Foundation Source Access. 2013. "Children and WaterAid." Retrieved February 9, 2013 (http://access.foundationsource.com/project/children-and-wateraid).

Foundation for Women. 2012. "Eliminating Global Poverty through Microcredit." Retrieved May 21, 2012 (www.foundationforwomen.org/).

France 24 International News. 2009. "Increase in Number of Billionaires Despite Credit Crisis." October 13. Retrieved November 11, 2009 (www.france24.com/en/20091013-global-crisis-china-billionaires-economy-asia-wealthy-rich-list).

Frank, Mark G. and Thomas Gilovich. 1988. "The Dark Side of Self- and Social Perception: Black Uniforms and Aggression in Professional Sports." *Journal of Personality and Social Psychology* 54(1):74–85.

Freedom House. 2002. *Freedom in the World 2001–2002.* New York: Author.

Freeman, Jo. 1975. *The Politics of Women's Liberation: A Case Study of an Emerging Social Movement and Its Relation to the Policy Process.* New York: McKay.

Freese, J., B. Powell, and L. C. Steelman. 1999. *Rebel Without a Cause or Effect: Birth Order and Social Attitudes.* Washington, DC: American Sociological Association.

Free the Slaves. 2013. "Our Mission." Retrieved January 19, 2013 (www.freetheslaves.net).

Freston, Paul. 2007. "Evangelicalism and Fundamentalism: The Politics of Global Popular Protestantism." Pp. 205–26 in *Sage Handbook of the Sociology of Religion*, edited by James Beckford and N. J. Demerath III. Thousand Oaks, CA: Sage.

Freud, Sigmund. [1923] 1960. *The Ego and the Id.* New York: Norton.

Frey, Bruno S. 2004. *Dealing With Terrorism: Stick or Carrot?* Cheltenham, UK: Edward Elgar.

Friedman, Judith J. 2007. "Suburbs: Urban, Rural and Community Sociology." *Blackwell Encyclopedia of Sociology Online.* Retrieved July 30, 2012 (www.sociologyencyclopedia.com/public/tocnode?id=g978140512433125_ss1_298).

Friedman, Thomas L. 2005. *The World Is Flat: A Brief History of the Twenty-First Century.* New York: Farrar, Straus, & Giroux.

Friedman, Thomas L. 2006. "Opening Scene: The World Is Ten Years Old." pp. 21–29 in *Globalization: The Transformation of Social Worlds,* edited by D. Stanley Eitzen and Maxine Baca Zinn. Belmont, CA: Wadsworth.

Friedman, Thomas L. 2008. *Hot, Flat and Crowded: Why We Need a Green Revolution—and How It Can Renew America.* New York: Farrar, Straus & Giroux.

Friesen, Kenneth. 2008. "Globalization on the Ground in India." *All Academic.* Retrieved May 18, 2012 (http://citation.allacademic.com/meta/p_mla_apa_research_citation/5/0/0/1/2/pages500122/p500122-23.php).

"Full Transcript of the Second Presidential Debate." 2012. *New York Times*, October 16. Retrieved November 1, 2012 (www.nytimes.com/2012/10/16/us/politics/transcript-of-the-second-presidential-debate-in-hempstead-ny.html?pagewanted=all&_r=0).

Furstenberg, F. F. 2003. "Growing Up in American Society: Income, Opportunities, and Outcomes." Pp. 211–33 in *Social Dynamics of the Life Course: Transitions, Institutions, and Interrelations,* edited by W. R. Heinz and V. W. Marshall. New York: A. deGruyter.

Future for All. 2008. "Future Technology and Society." Retrieved January 14, 2008 (www.futureforall.org).

Gaijinpot 2010. "Japanese Women Stand Low on the Corporate Ladder." August 30. Retrieved May 27, 2012 (http://injapan.gaijinpot.com/work-tips/2010/08/30/japanese-women-stand-low-on-the-corporate-ladder/).

Galanti, Geri-Ann. 2008. *Caring for Patients From Different Cultures,* 4th ed. Philadelphia: University Pennsylvania Press.

Galbraith, Kate. 2012. "Taking the Ick Factor Out of Recycled Water." *The New York Times*, July 25. Retrieved July 31, 2012 (www.nytimes.com/2012/07/26/business/global/26iht-green26.html).

Gallagher, Charles. 2004. "Transforming Racial Identity Through Affirmative Action." Pp. 153–70 in *Race and Ethnicity: Across Time, Space and Discipline,* edited by Rodney D. Coates. Leiden, Holland: Brill.

Gallup 2004. "Women in the Clergy: Perception and Reality." March 30. Retrieved September 20, 2012 (www.gallup.com/poll/11146/women-cleregy-perception-reality.aspx).

Gallup. 2009. "Muslim Americans: A National Portrait." The Muslim West Facts Project. Retrieved September 24, 2012 (www.gallup.com/strategicconsulting/153572/REPORT-Muslim-Americans-National-Portrait.aspx).

Gallup. 2011. "More Than 9 in 10 Americans Continue to Believe in God." June 3. Retrieved July 14, 2011 (www.gallup.com/poll/147887/americans-continue-believe-god.aspx).

Gallup. 2013. "Religion." Retrieved January 30, 2013 (http://www.gallup.com/poll/1690/religion.aspx).

Gallup, George, Jr., and D. Michael Lindsay. 1999. *Surveying the Religious Landscape: Trends in U.S. Beliefs.* Harrisburg, PA: Morehouse.

"Gang-Rape Victim Faces Lashes." 2007. Retrieved November 4, 2009 (www.news.com.au/story/0,23599,21332543-2,00.html).

Gannon, Shane Patrick. 2009. *Translating the Hijra: The Symbolic Reconstruction of the British Empire in India.* PhD thesis, University of Alberta.

Gans, Herbert J. 1962. *The Urban Villagers: Group and Class in the Life of Italian-Americans.* New York: Free Press.

Gans, Herbert J. 1971. "The Uses of Poverty: The Poor Pay All." *Social Policy* 2(2):20–24.

Gans, Herbert. 1982. *The Levittowners: Ways of Life and Politics in a New Suburban Community*. New York: Columbia University Press.

Gans, Herbert J. 1994. "Positive Functions of the Undeserving Poor: Uses of the Underclass in America." *Politics and Society* 22(3):269–83.

Gans, Herbert J. 1995. *The War Against the Poor.* New York: Basic Books.

Gans, Herbert J. 2007. "No, Poverty Has Not Disappeared." Reprinted in *Sociological Footprints,* edited by Leonard Cargan and Jeanne Ballantine. Belmont, CA: Wadsworth.

Gardner, Howard. 1987. "The Theory of Multiple Intelligences." *Annual Dyslexia* 37:19–35.

Gardner, Howard. 1999. *Intelligence Reframed: Multiple Intelligences for the 21st Century.* New York: Basic Books.

Gates, Bill. 2013. "Annual Letter." Retrieved February 5, 2013 (www.gatesfoundation.org/annualletter).

Gatta, Mary L. and Kevin McCabe. 2005. *Not Just Getting By: The New Era of Flexible Workforce Development.* Lanham, MD: Lexington Books.

Gatto, John Taylow. 2003. *The Prussian Connection.* New York: The Odysseus Group.

"Gay Adoption Nationwide." 2011. *AZ Living*, May 2. Retrieved June 3, 2012 (www.azcentral.com/news/azliving/articles/2011/05/02/20110502gay-dads-adoption-facts-resources.html).

The Gay Law Report. 2011. "Gay Facts and Statistics in 2011." January 3. Retrieved April 12, 2011 (http://www.gaylawreport.com/gay-facts-statistics-2011/).

Gay, Lesbian, and Straight Education Network (GLSEN). 2006. "GLESEN's 2005 National School Climate Survey Sheds New Light on Experiences of Lesbian, Gay, Bisexual and Transgendered (LGBT) Students." Retrieved August 8, 2008 (www.glsen.org/cgi-bin/iowa/all/library/record/1927.html).

"Gender Stereotypes Easing More for Girls than Boys." 2011. *USA Today.* Retrieved May 21, 2012 (www.usatoday.com/news/health/wellness/teen-ya/story/2011/05/Gender-stereotypes-easing-more-for-girls-than-boys/46886846/1).

Geocommons. 2009. "Infant Mortality Rates, World by Country, 2009." Retrieved February 9, 2013 (http://finder.geocommons.com/overlays/11932).

Gettleman, Jeffery. 2008. "Mob Sets Kenya Church on Fire, Killing Dozens." *The New York Times*, January 2. Retrieved June 3, 2008 (www.nytimes.com/2008/01/02/world/africa/02kenya.html?pagewanted=1&ref=africa).

Inniss, Janis Prince. 2010. "A Closer Look at Interracial Marriage Statistics." *Everyday Sociology*, August 2. Retrieved April 10, 2011 (nortonbooks.typepad.com/everydaysociology/2010/08/a-closer-look-at-interracial-marriage-statistics.html).

Gellner, Ernest. 1983. *Culture, Identity, and Politics.* Cambridge, UK: Cambridge University Press.

Gellner, Ernest. 1993. "Nationalism." Pp. 409–11 in *Blackwell Dictionary of Twentieth Century Thought,* edited by William Outhwaite and Tom Bottomore. Oxford, UK: Basil Blackwell.

Gellner, Ernest and John Breuilly. 2009. *Nations and Nationalism,* 2nd ed. Ithaca, NY: Cornell University Press.

Gibler, John. 2012. "Mexico's Ghost Towns." Pp. 68–72 in *Globalization: The Transformation of Social Worlds*, 3rd ed., edited by D. Stanley Eitzen and Maxine Baca Zinn. Belmont, CA: Wadsworth.

Giddens, Anthony. 1986. *The Constitution of Society.* Berkeley: University of California Press.

Gilbert, Dennis. 2011. *The American Class Structure in an Age of Growing Inequality*, 8th ed. Thousand Oaks, CA: Sage.

Gilchrist, John. 2003. *Anderson's Ohio Family Law.* Cincinnati, OH: Anderson.

Gilligan, Carol. 1982. *In a Different Voice: Psychological Theory and Women's Development.* Cambridge, MA: Harvard University Press.

Gillis, Chester. 1999. *Roman Catholicism in America.* New York: Columbia University Press.

Gillis, Justin and Celia A Dugger. 2011. "U.N. Forecasts 10.1 Billion People by Century's End." *The New York Times,* May 3. Retrieved June 5, 2012 (www.nytimes.com/2011/05/04/world/04population.html).

Ginicola, Misty M. and Christina Saccoccio. 2008. "Good Intentions, Unintended Consequences: The Impact of NCLB on Children's Mental Health." *Emotional and Behavioral Disorders in Youth* (Spring):27–35.

Girls Health. 2009. "Bullying." *Girlshealth.gov*. Retrieved May 21, 2012 (www.girlshealth.gov/bullying/).

Givens, David B. 2012. "Nonverbal Communication." *Center for Nonverbal Studies*. Retrieved September 25, 2012 (http://center-for-nonverba-studies.org/nvcom.htm).

Gladwell, Malcolm. 2010. "Small Change: Why the Revolution Will Not Be Tweeted." *The New Yorker*, October 4. Retrieved October 9, 2012 (http://www.newyorker.com).

Glasberg, Davita Silfen and Deric Shannon. 2011. *Political Sociology: Oppression, Resistance, and the State.* Thousand Oaks, CA: Sage.

Glasscock, C. B. 1937. *The Gasoline Age: The Story of the Men Who Made It.* Indianapolis, IN: Bobbs-Merrill.

Glaze, Lauren E. 2011. "Correctional Populations in the U.S. 2010." December 15. Retrieved April 15, 2012 (http://bjs.ojp.usdoj.gov/index.cfm?ty=tp&tid=13).

Global Arab Network. 2010. "British Archaeologist: 125,000 Years Ago First Human Settlement Began in Oman." April 9. Retrieved July 30, 2012 (www.english.globalarabnetwork.com/201004095443/Cu5000-years-ago-first-human-settlement-began-in-oman.html).

Global Campaign for Education. 2011. "100th Anniversary of International Women's Day." Retrieved April 17, 2011 (www.campaignforeducation.org/en/news/gces-news).

Global Citizen Corps. 2010. "Women's Rights." December 6. Retrieved April 8, 2011 (www.globalcitizencorps.org/groups/issue-human-rights/14178).

Global Fund for Women. 2012. "Status of Women Fact Sheet." Retrieved October 1, 2012 (www.globalfundforwomen.org/impact/media-center/fact-sheets/status-of-women-fact-sheet).

Global Issues. 2012. "World Military Spending." Retrieved July 27, 2012 (www.globalissues.org/print/article/75#WorldMilitarySpending).

"Global Opium Production." 2011. *The Economist*, June 24. Retrieved April 13, 2012 (www.economist.com/node/16432922).

Global Security. 2009. "Guantanamo Bay Detainees." Retrieved April 14, 2012 (www.globalsecurity.org/military/facility/guantanamo-bay_detainees.htm).

"Global Warming and Climate Change." 2013. *The New York Times,* January 8. Retrieved February 5, 2013 (http://topics.nytimes.com/top/news/science/topics/globalwarming/index.html).

Globe Women. 2013. "WEXPO: Women's Online Marketplace." Retrieved January 23, 2013 (http://www.wexpo.biz/).

Globe Women's Business Network. 2006. "Corporate Women Directors International." Retrieved August 21, 2006 (www.globewomen.com).

Goffman, Erving. [1959] 2001. *Presentation of Self in Everyday Life.* New York: Harmondsworth, UK: Penguin.

Goffman, Erving. 1961. *Asylums: Essays on the Social Situation of Mental Patients and Other Inmates.* New York: Anchor.

Goffman, Erving. 1967. *Interaction Ritual.* New York: Anchor.

Goldberg, David Theo, ed. 1990. *Anatomy of Racism.* Minneapolis: University of Minnesota Press.

Goldman, Henry and Duane D. Stanford. 2012. "MYC Mayor Bloomberg Seeks Ban on Super-Size Soft Drinks." *Bloomberg News*, May 31. Retrieved July 17, 2012 (www.bloomberg.com/news/2012-05-31/nyc-mayor-bloomberg-seeks-ban-on-super-size-soft-drinks.html).

Goode, William J. 1970. *World Revolution and Family Patterns.* New York: Free Press.

Goode, Erich. 1992. *Collective Behavior.* New York: Harcourt Brace Jovanovich.

Goode, Erich. 2012. *Drugs in American Society,* 8th ed. Boston: McGraw-Hill.

Goodman, Marc D. and Susan W. Brenner. 2002. "The Emerging Consensus on Criminal Conduct in Cyberspace." *International Journal of Law and Information Technology* 10(2):139–223.

Goodman, Amy and Juan Gonzalez. 2012. "Debating Tucson School District's Book Ban after Suspension of Mexican American Studies Program." *Democracy Now*, January 18. Retrieved January 28, 2013 (www.democracynow.org/2012/1/18/debating_tucson_school_district_book_ban).

Goodstein, Laurie. 2012. "Ugandan Gay Rights Group Sues U.S. Evangelist." *The New York Times*, March 14. Retrieved May 27, 2012 (www.nytimes.com/2012/03/15/us/ugandan-gay-rights-group-sues-scott-lively-an-american-evangelist.html).

GoodTherapy.org. 2012. "Complementary and Alternative Medicine (CAM)." Retrieved August 3, 2012 (www.goodtherapy.org/complementary-alternative-medicine.html).

Gordon, Milton. 1970. "The Subsociety and the Subculture." Pp. 150–63 in *The Sociology of Subcultures,* edited by David O. Arnold. Berkeley, CA: Glendessary.

Gore, Al. 2012. "Global Warming Is Real." *EarthSky,* April 30. Retrieved September 7, 2012 (http://earthsky.org/human-world/al-gore-at-hampshire-college-global-warming-is-real).

Gorski, Phillip S. 2000. "Historicizing the Secularization Debate: Church, State, and Society in Late Medieval and Early Modern Europe, ca 1300 to 1700." *Social Forces*(February):138–67.

Gorski, Philip and Ates Altinordu. 2008. "After Secularization." *Annual Review of Sociology* 34:55–85.

Gottdiener, Mark and Ray Hutchison. 2006. *The New Urban Sociology*, 3rd ed. Boston: McGraw-Hill.

Gottfredson, Michael R. and Travis Hirschi. 1990. *A General Theory of Crime.* Palo Alto, CA: Stanford University Press.

Gottlieb, Lori. 2006. "How Do I Love Thee?" *The Atlantic,* March. Retrieved February 9, 2013 (http://www.theatlantic.com/magazine/archive/2006/03/how-do-i-love-thee/304602/).

Gould, Stephen J. 1997. *The Mismeasure of Man.* New York: Norton.

Gouldner, Alvin W. 1960. "The Norm of Reciprocity: A Preliminary Statement." *American Sociological Review* 25(2):161–78.

Gracey, Harry L. 1967. "Learning the Student Role: Kindergarten as Academic Boot Camp." Pp. 215–26 in *Readings in Introductory Sociology,* 3rd ed., edited by Dennis Wrong and Harry L. Gracey. New York: Macmillan.

Grandpa Junior. 2006. "If You Were Born Before 1945." Retrieved July 20, 2006 (www.grandpajunior.com/1945.shtml).

Granovetter, Mark. 2007. "Introduction for the French Reader." *Sociologica* 1(Suppl.):1–10.

Grant, Linda. 2004. "Everyday Schooling and the Elaboration of Race-Gender Stratification." Pp. 296–308 in *Schools and Society: A Sociological Approach to Education,* 2nd ed., edited by Jeanne H. Ballantine and Joan Z. Spade. Belmont, CA: Wadsworth.

Greeley, Andrew M. 1972. *The Denominational Society.* Glenview, IL: Scott, Foresman.

Greeley, Andrew M. 1989. *Religious Change in America.* Cambridge, MA: Harvard University Press.

The Green Papers. 2008a. "Presidential Primaries, Caucuses, and Conventions." Retrieved March 21, 2008 (www.thegreenpapers.com/P08/CO-R.phtml).

The Green Papers. 2008b. "Presidential Primaries 2008: Republican Delegate Selection and Voter Eligibility." Retrieved March 21, 2008 (www.thegreenpapers.com/P08/R-DSVE.phtml?sort=a).

Greensboro Justice Fund. 2005. "Courage From the Past." *GJF Newsletter* (17, Summer):1.

Griffiths, Tom G. and Lisa Knezevic. 2009. "World-Systems Analysis in Comparative Education: An Alternative to Cosmopolitanism." *Current Issues in Comparative Education* 12(1):66–75.

Grille, Robin. 2005. "Religious Extremism: A Parenting Style." In *Parenting for a Peaceful World.* Longueville Media.

Grossman, Cathy Lynn. 2012a. "Number of U.S. Mosques Up 74% Since 2000." *USA Today,* February 29. Retrieved June 7, 2012 (www.usatoday.com/news/religion/story/2012-02-29/islamic-worship-growth-us/53298792/1).

Grossman, Cathy Lynn. 2012b. "Survey Finds 19% Without Religious Affiliation." *USA Today,* February 29. Retrieved September 20, 2012 (www.usatoday.com/news/religion/story/2012-07-19/no-religion-affiliation/56344976/1).

Guardian. 2011. "Guantanamo Bay Detainees Full List." January 11. Retrieved April 14, 2012 (www.guardian.co.uk/world/. . ./guantanamo-bay-detainees-full-list).

Guarino-Ghezzi, Susan. 2013. *The Engaged Sociologist: Connecting the Classroom to the Community*. Thousand Oaks, CA: Sage.

Guarino-Ghezzi, S. and Carr, B. 1996. "Juvenile Offenders Versus the Police: A Community Dilemma." *Caribbean Journal of Criminology and Social Psychology* 1(2):24–43.

Guarino-Ghezzi, S. and Kimball, L. 1996, April. *Transitioning Youth From Secure Treatment to the Community.* Boston, MA: Department of Youth Services.

Guerino, Paul, Paige M. Harrison, and William J. Sabol. 2011. "Prisoners in 2010 (Revised)." December 15. Retrieved April 15, 2012 (http://bjs.ojp.usdoj.gov/index.cfm?ty=tp&tid=13).

Guest, Avery M. and Keith R. Stamm. 1993. "Paths of Community Integration." *Sociological Quarterly* 34(4):581–95.

Gumperz, John J. and Stephen C. Levinson, eds. 1996. *Rethinking Linguistic Relativity.* Cambridge, UK: Cambridge University Press.

Gusten, Susanne. 2012. "New Twists and Turns in Turkey's Head-Scarf Debate." *The New York Times,* February 1. Retrieved May 25, 2012 (www.nytimes.com/2012/02/02/world/middleeast/new-twists-and-turns-in-turkeys-head-scarf-debate.html?pagewanted=all).

Guttmacher Institute. 2012a. "Contraceptive Use in the United States." July. Retrieved September 13, 2012 (www.guttmacher.org/pubs/fb_contr_use.html).

Guttmacher Institute. 2012b. "Just the Numbers: The Impact of U.S. International Family Planning Assistance." April 27. Retrieved July 28, 2012 (www.guttmacher.org/media/inthenews/2012/04/27/index.html).

Hadden, Jeffrey K. 2006. "New Religious Movements." Retrieved August 14, 2008 (www.hirr.hartsem.edu/denom/new_religious_movements.html).

Hagan, Frank E. 2011. *Introduction to Criminology,* 7th ed. Thousand Oaks, CA: Sage.

Hagan, John L. 1993. "The Social Embeddedness of Crime and Unemployment." *Criminology* 31:465–91.

Hagan, John L. 1994. *Crime and Disrepute.* Thousand Oaks, CA: Pine Forge.

Hall, Edward T. 1959. *The Silent Language*. New York: Doubleday.

Hall, Edward T. 1983. *The Dance of Life*. Garden City, NY: Anchor Books/Doubleday.

Hall, Edward T. and Mildred Reed Hall. 1992. *An Anthropology of Everyday Life*. New York: Doubleday.

Hall, Richard H. 2002. *Organizations: Structures, Processes, and Outcomes*, 7th ed. Englewood Cliffs, NJ: Prentice Hall.

Hallett, Tim and Emily Meanwell. 2012. "Sociologists Explore the Changing Meaning of 'No Child Left Behind.'" Presented at American Sociological Association meetings, Denver, CO, August 18.

Hamilton, Rebecca. 2012. "Factbox: Which States Allow Same-Sex Marriage?" *Reuters*, February 13. Retrieved May 27, 2012 (www.reuters.com/article/2012/02/13/us-usa-gaymarriage-states-idUSTRE81C1YH2020213).

Hammersley, Martyn and Glenn Turner. 1980. "Conformist Pupils." In *Pupil Strategies: Explorations in the Sociology of the School*, edited by Peter Woods. London: Croom Helm.

Hampton, Keith, Lauren Sessions Goulet, Cameron Marlow, and Lee Rainie. 2012. "Why Most Facebook Users Get More Than They Give." Pew Internet and American Life Project, February 3. Retrieved January 10, 2013 (www.pewinternet.org/Reports/2012/Facebook-users.aspx).

Handel, Gerald, Spencer Cahill, and Frederick Elkin. 2007. *Children and Society: The Sociology of Children and Childhood Socialization*. New York: Oxford University Press.

Handwerk, Brian. 2004. "Female Suicide Bombers: Dying to Kill." *National Geographic News*, December 13. Retrieved July 5, 2008 (http://news.nationalgeographic.com/news/2004/12/1213_041213_tv_suicide_bombers.html).

Haniffa, Aziz. 2009. "Financial Crisis Bigger Than Al Qaeda, Says U.S. Intelligence Czar." *Rediff India Abroad*. February 13. Retrieved March 17, 2009 (www.rediff.com/money/2009/feb/15bcrisis-financial-crisis-bigger-threat-than-al-qaeda-says-us-intel-chief.htm).

Hannigan, John. 1998. *Fantasy City: Pleasure and Profit in the Postmodern Metropolis*. London: Routledge.

Hansen, Randall and Katharine Hansen. 2003. "What Do Employers Really Want? Top Skills and Values Employers Seek From Job-Seekers" (Quintessential Careers). Retrieved June 23, 2008 (www.quintcareers.com/job_skills_values.html).

Hardin, Garrett. 1968. "The Tragedy of the Commons." *Science* 162(3859):1243–48.

Harding, David J. 2011. "Rethinking the Cultural Context of Schooling Decisions in Disadvantaged Neighborhoods: From Deviant Subculture to Cultural Heterogeneity." *Sociology of Education* 84 (October):322–39.

Harlem Children's Zone. 2009. "The HCZ Project." Retrieved January 28, 2013 (www.hcz.org/about-us/the-hcz-project).

Harris, Judith Rich. 2009. *The Nurture Assumption: Why Children Turn Out the Way They Do*, Revised and updated edition. New York: Free Press.

Harris, Marvin. 1989. *Cows, Pigs, War, and Witches: The Riddles of Culture*. New York: Random House.

Harris, Paul. 2011. "The Decline and Fall of the American Middle Class." September 13. Retrieved May 17, 2012 (www.guardian.co.uk/commentisfree/cifamerica/2011/sep/13/american-middle-class-poverty).

Harris Interactive. 2009. "Most Prestigious Occupations: Firefighters, Scientists Top List: Prestige of 23 Professions and Occupations." *Marketing Charts*. Retrieved May 17, 2012 (www.marketingcharts.com/topics/behavior-marketing/most-prestigious-occupations-firefighters-scientist-top-list-10045/harris-interactive).

Hart, Betty and Todd R. Risley. 2003. "The Early Catastrophe: The 30 Million Word Gap by Age 3." *American Educator* 27(1):4–9.

Harvey, David. 1973. *Social Justice and the City*. London: Edward Arnold.

Haskins, Ron. 2006. *Work Over Welfare: The Inside Story of the 1996 Welfare Reform Law*. Washington, DC: Brookings Institution Press.

Hassard, Jack. 2012. "In Math and Science, Have American Students Fallen Behind?" *The Art of Teaching Science*. Retrieved September 14, 2012 (www.artofteachingscience.org/2012/07/29/obamas-personal-view-teaching-conflict-u-s-department-education/).

Hayden, Dolores and Patricia Baron. 2007. "Urban Planning and Women's Needs." *Journal of Planning Education and Research* 26(3):370.

Hayden, Tom. 2006. "Seeking a New Capitalism in Chiapas." pp. 348–54 in *Globalization: The Transformation of Social Worlds*, edited by D. Stanley Eitzen and Maxine Baca Zinn. Belmont, CA: Wadsworth.

Hays, Jeffrey. 2011. "China's Barefoot Doctors: What Happened?" CR Studies, August 5. Retrieved August 2, 2012 (www.wengewang.org/read.php?tid=30852).

HealthReform.gov. 2010. "Coverage Denied: How the Current Health Insurance System Leaves Millions Behind." Retrieved January 10, 2010 (www.healthreform.gov/reports/denied_coverage/index.html).

Hearn, Kelly. 2012. "Big Oil Wreaks Havoc in the Amazon, but Communities Are Fighting Back." Pp. 313–16 in *Globalization: The Transformation of Social Worlds*, 3rd ed., edited by D. Stanley Eitzen and Maxine Baca Zinn. Belmont, CA: Wadsworth.

Heilbroner, Robert L. and William Milberg. 2007. *The Making of Economic Society*, 12th ed. Englewood Cliffs, NJ: Prentice Hall.

Heilbroner, Robert L. and William Milberg. 2012. *The Making of Economic Society*. Upper Saddle River, NJ: Pearson.

Helfand, Duke. 2008. "Presbyterian Leaders OK Gay Clergy." *Los Angeles Times*, June 28. Retrieved August 18, 2008 (www.latimes.com/news/local/la-me-ordain28-2008jun28,0,7679148.story).

Hendry, Joy. 1987. *Becoming Japanese: The World of the Preschool Child*. Honolulu: University of Hawaii Press.

Henley, Nancy, Mykol Hamilton, and Barrie Thorne. 2000. "Womanspeak and Manspeak: Sex Differences in Communication, Verbal and Nonverbal." Pp. 111–15 in *Sociological Footprints*, edited by Leonard Cargan and Jeanne Ballantine. Belmont, CA: Wadsworth.

Hennigan, Ashley. 2012. "Missing Men: Addressing the College Gender Gap." *Higher Ed Live*. Retrieved September 12, 2012 (http://higheredlive.com/missing-men/).

Hensley, Christopher, M. Koscheski, and Richard Tewksbury. 2005. "Examining the Characteristics of Male Sexual Assault Targets in a Southern Maximum-Security Prison." *Journal of Interpersonal Violence* 20(6):667–79.

Herman, Edward S. and David Peterson. 2006. "The Threat of Global State Terrorism: Retail vs. Wholesale Terror." Pp. 252–57 in *Globalization: The Transformation of Social Worlds*, edited by D. Stanley Eitzen and Maxine Baca Zinn. Belmont, CA: Wadsworth.

Herskovitz, Jon. 2012. "Militant South African Union Tells Lonmin to Pay Up." Reuters, September 7. Retrieved September 8,

2012 (www.reuters.com/article/2012/09/07/us-safrica-mines-id USBRE8860U820120907).

Hertsgaard, Mark. 2003. *The Eagle's Shadow: Why America Fascinates and Infuriates the World.* New York: Picador.

Hesse-Biber, Sharlene Nagy. 2007. *The Cult of Thinness,* 2nd ed. New York: Oxford University Press.

Hesse-Biber, Sharlene Nagy, and Patricia Lina Leavy. 2007. *Feminist Research Practice: A Primer.* Thousand Oaks, CA: Sage.

Hewitt, John P. 2007. *Self and Society: A Symbolic Interactionism Social Psychology,* 10th ed. Boston: Allyn & Bacon.

Hewitt, John P and David Shulman. 2011. *Self and Society: A Symbolic Interactionist Approach to Social Psychology*, 11th ed. Englewood Cliffs, NJ: Prentice Hall.

Heyes, J. D. 2012. "Plastic Waste Garbage Floating in Pacific Ocean Has Increased 100-Fold." *NaturalNews.com,* May 15. Retrieved September 7, 2012 (www.naturalnews.com/035866_garbage_floating_Pacific_Ocean.html).

HHS Poverty Guidelines. 2012. "2012 Poverty Guidelines for the 48 Contiguous States and the District of Columbia." Retrieved June 5, 2012 (http://aspe.hhs.gov/poverty/12poverty.shtml).

Hiebert-White, Jane. 2010. "Uninsured Expected to Rise to 52 Million by 2010." *Health Affairs,* June 2. Retrieved January 10, 2010 (http://healthaffairs.org/blog/2009/06/02/52-million-uninsured-americans-by-2010/).

Hill, Catherine and Holly Kearl. 2011. "Crossing the Line: Sexual Harassment at School." Washington, DC: AAUW. November. Retrieved September 20, 2012 (www.aauw.org/learn/research/upload/CrossingTheLine.pdf).

Hill, Christopher. 1991. *The World Turned Upside Down: Radical Ideas During the English Revolution.* New York: Penguin.

Hinton, Christopher. 2010."Global Military Spending to Outpace GDP Growth in 2010." *Market Watch*, June 18. Retrieved May 10, 2011 (www.marketwatch.com/story/worlds-militaries-see-another-budget-busting-year-2010-06-18).

Hispanic-Americans.com. 2011. "Mexico Leader Likens Drug Battle to Fight Against French." May 6. Retrieved May 9, 2011 (http://hispanic-americans.com/blog/mexiconews/mexican-leader-likens-drug-battle-to-fight-against-french.aspx).

Hochschild, Arlie. 1989. *The Second Shift: Working Parents and the Revolution at Home.* New York: Viking.

Hochschild, Arlie. 1997. *The Time Bind: When Work Becomes Home and Home Becomes Work.* New York: Metropolitan Books.

Holland, Megan M. 2012. "Only Here for the Day: The Social Integration of Minority Students at a Majority White High School." *Sociology of Education* 85(April):101–20.

Holloway, Susan. 2001. "Mothers of Japanese Preschoolers." *GSE Term Paper* 8(1). University of California, Berkeley. Retrieved April 17, 2010 (http://gse.berkeley.edu/admin/publications/termpaper/fall01/fall01/html).

Homans, George C. 1974. *Social Behavior: Its Elementary Forms.* New York: Harcourt, Brace Jovanovich.

Hood, Roger. 2002. *The Death Penalty: A World-Wide Perspective,* 3rd ed. Oxford, UK: Clarendon Press.

Horn, Jordana. 2011. "US Sees Slight Increase in Anti-Semitic Incidents." *The Jerusalem Post,* October 4. Retrieved February 9, 2013 (www.jpost.com/JewishWorld/JewishFeatures/Article.aspx?id=240522).

Hostetler, John A. 1993. *Amish Society,* 4th ed. Baltimore: John Hopkins University Press.

Houlihan, G. Thomas. 2005. "The Importance of International Benchmarking for U.S. Educational Leaders." *Phi Delta Kappan* (November):217–18.

Houlis, Anna Marie. 2011. "Gender Stereotypes in Picture Books Are Blamed for Affecting Children." June 13. Retrieved May 23, 2012 (http://annamariehoulis.wordpress.com/2011/06/13/gender-stereotypes-in-picture-books-are-blamed-for-affecting-children/).

Housing and Urban Development. 2008. "HUD Reports Drop in the Number of Chronically Homeless Persons" (News Release No. 08–113). Retrieved August 23, 2008 (www.hud.gov/news).

Howard, Adam. 2007. *Learning Privilege: Lessons of Power and Identity in Affluent Schooling.* New York: Taylor & Francis.

Howard, Adam and Ruben Gaztambide-Fernandez, eds. 2010. *Educating Elites: Class Privilege and Educational Advantage*. Lanham, MD: Rowman and Littlefield.

Howard, Philip. 2011. "The Upside Downside of Social Media." *Reuters,* August 23. Retrieved October 3, 2012 (http://blogs.reuters.com).

Howard, Philip N. and Steve Jones, eds. 2004. *Society On-Line: The Internet in Context.* Thousand Oaks, CA: Sage.

Hozien, Muhammad. N.d. "Ibn Khaldun: His Life and Work." Retrieved May 7, 2009 (www.muslimphilosophy.com/ik/klf.htm).

Huddy, Leonie and Stanley Feldman. 2006. "Worlds Apart: Blacks and Whites React to Hurricane Katrina." *Du Bois Review* 3(1):97–113. Retrieved July 7, 2011 (http://journals.cambridge.org/action/displayAbstract?fromPage=online&aid=462978).

Huebler, Friedrich. 2008. "International Education Statistics." Retrieved December 6, 2009 (http://huebler.blogspot.com/2008/11/ptr.html).

Huebler, Friedrich. 2012. "Adult and Youth Literacy in 2010." *International Education Statistics,* May 31. Retrieved January 27, 2013 (http://huebler.blogspot.com/2012/05/literacy.html)

Huffington Post. 2012a. "10 Countries Spending the Most on Health Care: 24/7 Wall St." March 29. Retrieved August 1, 2012 (www.huffingtonpost.com/2012/03/29/healthcare-spending-countries_n_1388306.html#s825346&title=1_United_States).

Huffington Post. 2012b. "Shaken By USC Shooting, Chinese Students Still Seek US Colleges." June 4. Retrieved June 4, 2012 (www.huffingtonpost.com/2012/04/12/shaken-by-usc-shooting-ch_n_1420171.html).

Hughes, Melanie M. 2004. "Armed Conflict, International Linkages, and Women's Parliamentary Representation in Developing Nations." Master's thesis, Department of Sociology, Ohio State University.

Huizinga, David, Rolf Loeber, and Terence P. Thornberry. 1994. "Urban Delinquency and Substance Abuse: Initial Findings." OJJDP Research Summary. Washington, DC: Government Printing Office.

Human Development Report 2009. "Old Age Dependency Ratio." Retrieved May 13, 2011 (http://hdrstats.undp.org/en/indicators/147.html).

"Human Trafficking: Trafficking by the Numbers." 2012. WGBH, October 8. Retrieved October 8, 2012 (www.wgbh.org/articles/Human-Trafficking-Trafficking-by-the-numbers-285).

Humes, Karen R., Nicholas A. Jones, and Roberto R. Ramirez. 2011. "2010 Census Briefs: Overview of Race and Hispanic Origins: 2010." March, p. 1. Retrieved April 7, 2011 (http://www.census.gov/prod/cen2010/briefs/c2010br-02.pdf).

Hunter College Women's Studies Collective. 2005. *Women's Realities, Women's Choices: An Introduction to Women's Studies,* 3rd ed. New York: Oxford University Press.

Hurst, Charles E. 2006. *Social Inequality: Forms, Causes and Consequences*, 6th ed. Boston: Allyn & Bacon.

Hurst, Charles E. 2013. *Social Inequality: Forms, Causes, and Consequences*, 8th ed. Pearson.

Hyde, Christopher. N.d. "Why Should California Pass a Law That Protects Aid in Dying for Terminally-Ill Patients Who Are Suffering at the End of Their Lives?" Retrieved July 16, 2012 (www.compassinandchoicesnca.org/pdf/88530_Hyde,Christopher.pdf).

Iannaccone, Laurence and William S. Bainbridge. 2010. "Economics of Religion." Pp. 461–75 in *The Routledge Companion to the Study of Religion*, 2nd ed., edited by John Hinnells. New York: Routledge.

Immigration Policy Center. 2010. "Immigrant Women in the United States: A Portrait of Demographic Diversity." Retrieved May 15, 2011 (www.immigrationpolicy.org/just-facts/immigrant-women-in-the-united-states-portrait-demographic-diversity).

Independence Hall Association. 2010. "Betsy Ross and the American Flag." Retrieved December 21, 2011 (http://www.ushistory.org/betsy/flagtale.html).

Index Mundi 2012a. "Angola Demographics Profile 2012." Retrieved October 12, 2012 (www.indexmundi.com/angola/demographics_profile.html).

Index Mundi. 2012b. "Countries." Retrieved February 7, 2013 (http://www.indexmundi.com/factbook/countries).

Index Mundi. 2012c. "Country Comparison: Health Expenditures." January 1. Retrieved February 4, 2013 (www.indexmundi.com/g/raspx?v=2225).

Index Mundi. 2012d. "Country Comparison: Population Growth Rate." Retrieved July 27, 2012 (www.indexmundi.com/g/r.aspx?v=24).

Index Mundi 2012e. "Haiti Demographics Profile 2012." Retrieved October 12, 2012 (www.indexmundi.com/haiti/demographics_profile.html).

Index Mundi. 2012f. "HIV/AIDS Adult Prevalence Rate—World." Retrieved August 26, 2012 (www.indexmundi.com/map/?v=32).

Index Mundi 2012g. "World Demographic Profile 2012." Retrieved July 29, 2012 (www.indexmundi.com/world/demographics_profile.html).

Index Mundi. 2012h. "World Literacy." Retrieved January 28, 2013 (www.indexmundi.com/world/literacy.html).

Index Mundi. 2013. "Sweden Life Expectancy at Birth" (2012 est.). Retrieved February 7, 2013 (http://www.indexmundi.com/sweden/life_expectancy_at_birth.html).

Infographics. 2012. "What's Happening? Twitter Facts and Figures." Retrieved September 25, 2012 (www.infographicsarchive.com/social-media/twitter-facts-and-figures/).

Infoplease. 2011. "Lowest Literacy Rates." Retrieved January 28, 2013 (www.infoplease.com/world/countries/lowest-literacy-rates.html).

Infoplease. 2012. "Most Widely Spoken Languages in the World." Retrieved September 30, 2012 (www.Infoplease.com/ipa/A0775272.html).

Infoplease. 2013. "Lowest Life Expectancy, 2012." Retrieved February 4, 2013 (www.infoplease.com/world/countries/lowest-life-expectancy.html).

Information Please Almanac. 2008. "Languages." Retrieved January 20, 2008 (www.infoplease.com/ipa/A0775272.html).

Information Please Database. 2007. "Population Density per Square Mile of Countries." Retrieved February 7, 2013 (http://www.infoplease.com/ipa/A0934666.html).

Information Please Database. 2009. "National Voter Turnout in Federal Elections: 1960–2008." Retrieved March 17, 2009 (www.infoplease.com/ipa/A0781453.html).

Ingersoll, Richard M. and Elizabeth Merrill. 2012. "The Status of Teaching as a Profession." In *Schools and Society: A Sociological Approach to Education*, edited by Jeanne H. Ballantine and Joan Z. Spade. Thousand Oaks, CA: Sage Pine Forge.

Inglehart, Ronald. 1997. *Modernization and Postmodernization: Cultural, Economic, and Political Change in 43 Societies*. Princeton, NJ: Princeton University Press.

Inglehart, Ronald and Wayne E. Baker. 2001. "Modernization's Challenge to Traditional Values: Who's Afraid of Ronald McDonald?" *The Futurist* 35(2):16–22.

Inhofe, James M. 2008. "Senate Republicans Introduce Package of Immigration Enforcement Bills." Retrieved April 9, 2008 (www.imhofe.senate.gov/public/index.cfm?FuseAction=PresRoom.PressReleases&Co).

Innocence Project. 2012. "289 Exonerated." April 16. Retrieved April 16, 2012 (www.innocenceproject.org/).

Interagency Council on Homelessness. 2009. "HUD Awards $1.4 Billion in Grants to Homeless Programs." Retrieved January 7, 2010 (www.ich.gov).

International Beliefs and Values Institute. 2012. "Mission." Staunton, VA: Mary Baldwin College. Retrieved March 23, 2012 (www.ibavi.org).

"The International Digital Divide." 2011. *Science Daily*, February 8. Retrieved May 18, 2012 (www.sciencedaily.com/releases/2011/02/110208121345.htm).

International Encyclopedia of the Social Sciences. 2008. Retrieved December 21, 2009 (www.encyclopedia.com/doc/1G2-3045300884.html).

International Humanist and Ethical Union. 2009. "Untouchability in Japan: Discrimination Against Burakumin." August 21. Retrieved December 4, 2009 (www.iheu.org/untouchability-japan-discrimination-against-burakumin).

International Institute for Democracy and Electoral Assistance. 2008. "Turnout in the World—Country by Country Performance." Retrieved April 17, 2010 (www.idea.int/vt/survey/voter_turnout_pop2.cfm).

International Monetary Fund. 2003. "Proposal for a Sovereign Debt Restructuring Mechanism: A Factsheet." Retrieved September 29, 2006 (www.imf.org/external/np/exr/facts/sdrm.htm).

International Monetary Fund. 2013. "Debt Relief Under the Heavily Indebted Poor Countries (HIPC) Initiative." January 10. Retrieved February 7, 2013 (http://www.imf.org/external/np/exr/facts/hipc.htm).

International Organization for Migration. 2012. "Global Estimates and Trends." Retrieved July 30, 2012 (www.iom.int/jahia/Jahia/about-migration/facts -and-figures/lang/en).

Internet World Statistics. 2009. "U.S. Internet Usage and Broadband Usage Report." June. Retrieved October 21, 2009 (www.internetworldstats.com/am/us.htm).

Internet World Stats. 2010. "Internet World Users by Language." Retrieved May 18, 2012 (www.internetworldstats.com/stats7.htm).

Internet World Stats. 2013. "Usage and Population Stats." Retrieved January 23, 2012 (www.internetworldstats.com/list2.htm).

Inter-Parliamentary Union. 2012. "Women in National Parliaments." Retrieved January 21, 2013 (www.ipu.org/wmn-e/classif.htm).

Interpol. 2007. "Interpol News." Retrieved July 27, 2009 (http://www.interpol.int/Public/News/news2009.asp).

Interuniversity Consortium for Political and Social Research. 2011. "Voting Behavior: The 2008 Election." Retrieved May 16, 2012 (http://www.icpsr.umich.edu/icpsrweb/SETUPS2008/voting.jsp).

Irvine, Leslie. 2004. *If You Tame Me: Understanding Our Connection With Animals.* Philadelphia: Temple University Press.

Irwin, John. 1985. *The Jail: Managing the Underclass in American Society.* Berkeley: University of California Press.

Irwin, John. 2005. *The Warehouse Prison: Disposal of the New Dangerous Class.* Los Angeles: Roxbury.

Irwin, John and Barbara Owen. 2007. *The Warehouse Prison: Disposal of the New Dangerous Class.* New York: Oxford University Press.

Isaacs, John. 2011. "Current U.S. and Russian Nuclear Weapons Stockpiles." Retrieved December 21, 2011 (http://armscontrolcenter.org/policy/nuclearweapons/articles/031009_current_nuclear_weapons_stockpiles/).

"Is Overpopulation a World Threat?" 2011. Helium. Retrieved July 28, 2011 (www.helium.com/debates/166036-is-overpopulation-a-world-threat/side_by_side).

"It Begins With Us." 2011. YouTube. Retrieved November 1, 2012 (www.youtube.com/watch?v=f-VZLvVF1FQ).

Jackman, Robert W. 1993. *Power Without Force: The Political Capacity of Nation-States.* Ann Arbor: University of Michigan Press.

Jackson, Philip W. 1968. *Life in Classrooms.* New York: Holt, Rinehart & Winston.

Jacoby, Jeff. 2009. "A Bad Sign Illegal Immigrants Are Leaving." Center for Immigration Studies. September 6. Retrieved April 17, 2010 (www.boston.com/. . ./2009/. . ./a_bad_sign_illegal_immigrants_are_leaving).

Jaeger, Mads Meier. 2011. "Does Cultural Capital Really Affect Academic Achievement? New Evidence from Combined Sibling and Panel Data." *Sociology of Education* 84(October):281–98.

James, Susan Donaldson. 2011. "Census 2010: One-quarter of Gay Couples Raising Children." *ABC News,* June 23. Retrieved June 5, 2012 (http://abcnews.go.com/Health/sex-couples-census-data-trickles-quarter-raising-children/story?id=13850332).

James, William. [1890] 1934. *The Principles of Psychology.* Mineola, NY: Dover.

Jao, Jui-Chang and Matthew McKeever. 2006. "Ethnic Inequalities and Educational Attainment in Taiwan." *Sociology of Education* 79(2):131–52.

Japan Institute for Labour Policy and Training. 2009. "The Gender Gap in the Japanese Labor Market." February 26. Retrieved November 8, 2009 (www.ikjeld.com/en/news/91/the-gender-gap-in-the-labor-market).

"Japanese Women Face Difficulties Balancing Work and Family Life." 2007. *Japan for Sustainability*. October 1. Retrieved April 7, 2011 (www.japanfs.org/en/pages/026799).

Jarrett, R. L., P. J. Sullivan, and N. D. Watkins. 2005. "Developing Social Capital Through Participation in Organized Youth Programs: Qualitative Insights From Three Programs." *Journal of Community Psychology* 33(1):41–55.

Jaschik, Scott. 2010. "Women Lead in Doctorates." September 14. *Inside Higher Ed.* Retrieved January 28, 2013 (www.insidehighered.com/news/2010/09/14/doctorates).

Jay, Meg. 2012. "The Downside of Cohabiting before Marriage." *The New York Times Sunday Review,* April 14. Retrieved June 5, 2012 (www.nytimes.com/2012/04/15/opinion/sunday/the-downside-of-cohabiting-before-marriage.html?pagewanted=all).

Jayson, Sharon. 2011. "Cohabitation Numbers Jump 13%, Linked to Job Losses." *USA Today.* Retrieved June 5, 2012 (www.usatoday.com/news/nation/census/2010-09-24-cohabitation24ONLINE_ST_N.htm).

Jelen, Ted, ed. 2002 *Sacred Markets, Sacred Canopies: Essays on Religious Markets and Religious Pluralism*: New York: Rowman & Littlefield.

Jellinek, E. M. 1960. *The Disease Concept of Alcoholism.* New Haven, CT: Hillhouse.

Jencks, Christopher. 1972. *Inequality: A Reassessment of the Effects of Family and Schooling in America.* New York: Basic Books.

Jencks, Christopher, ed. 1979. *Who Gets Ahead? The Determinants of Economic Success in America.* New York: Harper & Row.

Jencks, Christopher. 1992. *Rethinking Social Policy: Race, Poverty, and the Underclass.* Cambridge, MA: Harvard University Press.

Jensen, Robert, and Emily Oster. 2007. *The Power of TV: Cable Television and Women's Status in India* (NBER Working Paper No. 13305). Cambridge, MA: National Bureau of Economic Research.

Johnson, Ben. 2012. "Chinese Officials: One-Child Policy Has Helped Prevent 400 Million Births." July 27. Retrieved July 28, 2012 (www.lifesitenews.com/news/chinese-officials-one-child-policy-has-prevented-400-million-births).

Johnson, Clifford M., Amy Rynell, and Melissa Young. 2012. "Publicly Funded Jobs: An Essential Strategy for Reducing Poverty and Economic Distress Throughout the Business Cycle." Urban Institute. Retrieved May 17, 2012 (www.urban.org/issues/reducing-poverty-economic-distress.cfm).

Johnson, David. 2011. "Income Gap: Is It Widening?" U.S. Census Bureau, September 15. Retrieved May 17, 2012 (http://blogs.census.gov/2011/09/15/income-gap-is-it-widening/).

Johnson, David W. and Frank P. Johnson. 2006. *Joining Together: Group Theory and Group Skills,* 9th ed. Boston: Allyn & Bacon.

Johnson, Kenneth M. and Glenn V. Fuguitt. 2000. "Continuity and Change in Rural Migration Patterns, 1950–1995." *Rural Sociology* 65(1):27–49.

Johnson, Nicholas. 2012. "Laboratories of Underfunding? State Financing for Antipoverty Programs." Urban Institute. Retrieved May 17, 2012 (www.urban.org/issues/reducing-poverty-economic-distress.cfm).

Johnson, Paul. 2005. "Majority of Americans Believe Homosexuality Should Not Be Illegal, Support Partner Rights: Gallup Poll." Retrieved August 22, 2006 (www.sodomylaws.org/usa/usnews141.htm).

Johnson, Robert. 2002. *Hard Time: Understanding and Reforming the Prison.* Belmont, CA: Wadsworth/Thompson Learning.

Johnson, Steven. 2009. "How Twitter Will Change the Way We Live (in 140 Characters or Less)." *Time,* June 15, pp. 32–37.

Jones, Sydney and Susannah Fox. 2009. "Generations Online in 2009." Pew Internet and American Life Project, January 28. Retrieved June 25, 2011 (www.pewinternet.org/Reports/2009/Generations-Online-in-2009.aspx).

Jordan-Bychkov, Terry G., and Mono Domoch. 1998. *The Human Mosaic,* 8th ed. New York: Freeman.

Kain, Edward. 2005. "Family Change and the Life Course: Cohorts and Social Change in the Year 2050." Paper presented at the annual meetings of the Southern Sociological Society, Charlotte, NC.

Kaiser Commission on Medicaid and the Uninsured. 2011. "The Uninsured: A Primer." Retrieved February 2, 2013 (http://www.kff.org/UNINSURED/UPLOAD/7451-07.PDF).

Kaiser Family Foundation. 2005. "Generation M: Media in the Lives of 8 to 18 Year-Olds—Report." Retrieved July 20, 2006 (www.kff.org/entmedia/7251.cfm).

Kaiser Family Foundation. 2010. "G8 leaders to Discuss Economic Policy, Developing World, Maternal and Child Health, Haitian Rebuilding." June 25. Retrieved July 13, 2012 (http://globalhealth.Kff.org/Daily-Reports/2010/June/25/GH-062510-G8-G20-Summits.aspx).

Kan, Man Yee, Oriel Sullivan, and Jonathan Gershuny. 2011. "Gender Convergence in Domestic Work: Discerning the Effects of Interactional and Institutional Barriers from Large-Scale Data" *Sociology* 45(2):234–51.

Kane, Maggie. 2012. "Minnesota Clergy Unite Against Marriage Amendment." *Southwest Journal*, June 7. Retrieved September 26, 2012 (www.swjournal.com/index.php?&story=18542&page=152&category=63).

Kanter, Rosabeth Moss. 1977. *Men and Women of the Corporation.* New York: Basic Books.

Kanter, Rosabeth Moss. 1983. *The Change Masters: Innovation for Productivity in the American Corporation.* New York: Simon & Schuster.

Kanter, Rosabeth Moss. 2001a. "Creating the Culture for Innovation." In *Leading for Innovation: Managing for Results,* edited by Frances Hesselbein, Marshall Goldsmith, and Iain Somerville. San Francisco: Jossey-Bass.

Kanter, Rosabeth Moss. 2001b. "From Spare Change to Real Change: The Social Sector as Beta Site for Business Innovation." *Harvard Business Review on Innovation* 77(3):122–33.

Kanter, Rosabeth Moss. 2005. *Commitment and Community.* Cambridge, MA: Harvard University Press.

Kao, Grace. 2004. "Social Capital and Its Relevance to Minority and Immigrant Populations." *Sociology of Education* 77:172–76.

Kaplan, Howard B. and Robert J. Johnson. 1991. "Negative Social Sanctions and Juvenile Delinquency: Effects of Labeling in a Model of Deviant Behavior." *Social Science Quarterly* 72(1):117.

Karen, David. 2005. "No Child Left Behind? Sociology Ignored!" *Sociology of Education* 78(2):165–82.

Karraker, Katherine Hildebrant. 1995. "Parent's Gender-Stereotyped Perceptions of Newborns: The Eye of the Beholder Revisited." *Sex Roles* 33(9/10):687–701.

Karthikeyan, D. 2011. "Dalits Pay the Price for Their Political Assertion." *The Hindu: Tamil Nadu,* February 18, p. 1.

Katz, Jackson. 2006. *The Macho Paradox: Why Some Men Hurt Women and How All Men Can Help.* Naperville, IL: Sourcebooks.

Kavilanz, Parija. 2010. "Doctor-Starved: America's Heartland in Crisis." CNN Money, March 28. Retrieved July 17, 2012 (http://money.cnn.com/2010/03/26/news/economy/health_care_rural_care_country_doctors/index.htm).

Kean, Sam. 2007. "What's in a Name?" *The New York Times,* October 28. Retrieved May 21, 2012 (www.nytimes.com/2007/10/28/magazine/28wwln-idealab-t.html).

Keigher, Ashley and Freddie Cross. 2010. "Teacher Attrition and Mobility." School and Staffing Survey. IES. NCES. Retrieved April 17, 2011 (http://nces.ed.gov/pubs2010/2010353.pdf).

Kelber, Harry. 2012. "Manufacturers Are Hiring Workers in America, But Offer a Sharp Drop in Wages and Benefits." *The Labor Educator,* January 2. Retrieved May 28, 2012 (www.laboreducator.org/It120102.htm).

Kendall, Diane. 2004. *Sociology in Our Times: The Essentials,* 4th ed. Belmont, CA: Wadsworth.

Kennedy, Kelly. 2011. "Health Care Fraud Prosecutions on Pace to Rise 85%." *USA Today,* August 29. Retrieved April 13, 2012 (www.usatoday.com/news/washington/story/2011-08-29/Health-care-fraud-prosecutions-on-pace-to-rise-85/50180282/1).

Kerbo, Harold R. 2008. *Social Stratification and Inequality,* 7th ed. Boston: McGraw-Hill.

Kerckhoff, Alan C. 2001. "Education and Social Stratification Processes in Comparative Perspective." *Sociology of Education* (Extra Issue: Currents of Thought: Sociology of Education at the Dawn of the 21st Century):3–18.

Kettl, Donald F. 1993. *Sharing Power: Public Governance and Private Markets.* Washington, DC: Brookings.

Khazaleh Lorenz. 2009. "Internet Fatwas Cautiously Support Divorce Among Women" *CULCOM,* October 29. Retrieved January 4, 2010 (www.culcom.uio.no/english/news/2009/bogstad.html).

Khan, Shamus Rahman. 2011. *Privilege: The Making of an Adolescent Elite at St. Paul's School.* Princeton, NJ: Princeton University Press.

Kidder, Tracy. 2004. *Mountains Beyond Mountains.* New York: Random House.

Kids Count Data Center. 2010. "Children in Single-Parent Families by Race-2010." *The Annie E. Casey Foundation.* Retrieved June 6, 2012 (http://datacenter.kidscount.org/data/acrosstates/Rankings.aspx?ind=107).

Kilbourne, Jean. 1999. *Deadly Persuasion: Why Women and Girls Must Fight the Additive Power of Advertising.* New York: Free Press.

Kilbourne, Jean. 2000. *Killing Us Softly, III* (Video). Northampton, MA: Media Education Foundation.

Killian, Caitlin. 2006. *North African Women in France: Gender, Culture, and Identity.* Palo Alto, CA: Stanford University Press.

Kim, Min-Sun, Katsuya Tasaki, In-Duk Kim, and Hye-ryeon Lee. 2007. "The Influence of Social Status on Communication Predispositions Focusing on Independent and Interdependent Self-Construals." *Journal of Asian Pacific Communication* 17(2):303–329.

Kimmel, Michael S. and Michael A. Messner. 2009. *Men's Lives,* 8th ed. Boston: Allyn & Bacon.

Kindlon, Dan and Michael Thompson. 2000. *Raising Cain: Protecting the Emotional Life of Boys.* New York: Ballantine Books.

King, Edith W. 2006. *Meeting the Challenges of Teaching in an Era of Terrorism.* Belmont, CA: Thomson.

Kingkade, Tyler. 2012. "Youth Vote 2012 Turnout: Exit Polls Show Greater Share of Electorate Than in 2008." *Huffington Post,* November 7. Retrieved November 8, 2012 (www.huffingtonpost.com/2012/11/07/youth-vote-2012-turnout-exit-polls_n_2086092.html).

Kinsey Institute for Research in Sex, Gender, and Reproduction. 2012. Retrieved May 20, 2012 (www.kinseyinstitute.org).

Kitano, Harry H., Pauline Aqbayani, and Diane de Anda. 2005. *Race Relations,* 6th edition. Englewood Cliffs, NJ: Prentice Hall.

Kitano, Harry H. L. and Roger Daniels. 2001. *Asian Americans: Emerging Minorities,* 3rd ed. New York: Pearson.

Klinenberg, Eric. 2012. *Going Solo: The Extraordinary Rise and Surprising Appeal of Living Alone.* New York: Penguin.

Knapp, Mark L. and Judith A. Hall. 1997. *Nonverbal Communication in Human Interaction,* 4th ed. Fort Worth: Harcourt Brace.

Knickmeyer, Ellen. 2008. "Turkey's Gul Signs Head Scarf Measure." February 23. Retrieved April 17, 2010 (www.washingtonpost.com/>world).

Koch, Jerome R. and Evans W. Curry. 2000. "Social Context and the Presbyterian Gay/Lesbian Debate: Testing Open Systems Theory." *Review of Religious Research* 42(2):206–214.

Kochhar, Rakesh. 2012. "Labor Force Growth Slows, Hispanic Share Grows." Pew Research Social and Demographic Trends, February 13. Retrieved February 6, 2013 (www.pewsocialtrends.org/2012/02/13/labor-force-growth-slows-hispanic-growth-grows-2/).

Kodish, Bruce I. 2003. "What We Do With Language—What It Does With Us." *ETC: A Review of General Semantics* 60:383–95.

Kohlberg, Lawrence. 1971. "From Is to Ought." Pp. 151–284 in *Cognitive Development and Epistemology,* edited by T. Mischel. New York: Academic Press.

Kohn, Melvin. 1989. *Class and Conformity: A Study of Values,* 2nd ed. Chicago: University of Chicago Press.

Koleth, Elsa. 2012. "Asylum Seekers: An Update: Briefing Paper No. 1/2012." NSW Parliamentary Library. Retrieved July 30, 2012 (www.parliament.nsw.gov.au/prod/parment/publications.OD189A/SFile/Asylum%20seekers%20Final%20March%20202012.pdf).

Koos, Earl. 1954. *The Health of Regionville.* New York: Columbia University Press.

Korgen, Kathleen Odell and Jonathan M. White. 2013. *The Engaged Sociologist: Connecting the Classroom to the Community,* 3rd ed. Thousand Oaks, CA: Sage.

Korgen, Kathleen Odell, Jonathan M. White, and Shelley K. White. 2013. *Sociologists in Action: Sociology, Social Change, and Social Justice,* 2nd ed. Thousand Oaks, CA: Sage.

Korte, Charles and Stanley Milgram. 1970. "Acquaintance Networks Between Racial Groups." *Journal of Personality and Social Psychology* 15:101–108.

Koschate-Reis, Miriam. 2009. "The Social Psychology of Embarrassment." Research project at the School of Psychology, University of St. Andrews. Retrieved March 31, 2012 (http://sites.google.com/site/embarrassmentproject/home).

Kosmin, Barry and Ariela Keysar. 2009. *American Religious Identification Survey (ARIS 2008) Summary Report.* March. Hartford, CT: Trinity College.

Kottak, Conrad Phillip. 2010. *Prime-Time Society: An Anthropological Analysis of Television and Culture,* Updated edition. Walnut Creek, CA: Left Coast Press.

Kozol, Jonathan. 1991. *Savage Inequalities: Children in America's Schools.* New York: Crown.

Kozol, Jonathan. 2005. "Confections of Apartheid: A Stick-and-Carrot Pedagogy for the Children of Our Inner-City Poor." *Phi Delta Kappan* (December):265–75.

Kozol, Jonathan. 2006. *The Shame of the Nation: The Restoration of Apartheid Schooling in America.* New York: Crown.

Kozol, Jonathan. 2012. *Fire in the Ashes: Twenty-five Years Among the Poorest Children in America.* New York: Random House Crown Publishing Group.

Kramer, Laura. 2010. *The Sociology of Gender: A Brief Introduction,* 3rd ed. New York: Oxford University Press.

Kreider, Rose M. 2010a. "Estimates of Cohabiting Couples ASEC 2009 and 2010" (Table 1). U.S. Census Bureau, Current Population Survey, September 15. Retrieved October 14, 2012 (www.census.gov/population/www/socdemo/Inc-Opp-sex-2009-to-2010.pdf).

Kreider, Rose M. 2010b. "Increase in Opposite-Sex Cohabiting Couples From 2009 to 2010 in the Annual Social and Economic Supplement to the Current Population Survey." U.S. Census Bureau, September 15. Retrieved April 11, 2011 (www.census.gov/population/www/socdemo/Inc-Opp-sex-2009-to-2010.pdf).

Kreider, Rose. 2010c. "Working Paper on the Change in Cohabiting Couples from 2009 to 2010." Retrieved July 14, 2011 (http://www.census.gov/population/www/socdemo/Inc-Opp-sex-2009-to-2010.pdf).

Kreider, Rose M. and Diana B. Elliott. 2009. "America's Families and Living Arrangements: 2007." U.S. Census Bureau *Current Population Reports,* P20-561. Retrieved January 24, 2013 (http://www.census.gov/prod/2009pubs/p20-561.pdf).

Krieger, Lisa M. 2012. "The Cost of Dying: It's Hard to Reject Care Even as Costs Soar." *San Jose Mercury Sun.* Retrieved July 16, 2012 (www.mercurynews.com/health/ci_19898736).

Kristof, Nicholas D. 2009. "Where Sweatshops Are a Dream." *The New York Times,* January 14. Retrieved May 9, 2011 (www.nytimes.com/2009/01/15/opinion/15kristof.html).

Kristof, Nicholas and Sheryl WuDunn. 2009 *Half the Sky: Turning Oppression Into Opportunity for Women Worldwide.* New York: Alfred A. Knopf.

Kübler-Ross, Elizabeth. 1997. *Death, the Final Stage of Growth,* Rev. ed. New York: Scribner.

Kuhn, Manford. 1964. "Major Trends in Symbolic Interaction Theory in the Past Twenty-Five Years." *Sociological Quarterly* 5:61–84.

Kuhn, Thomas. 1970. *The Structure of Scientific Revolutions,* 2nd ed. Chicago: University of Chicago Press.

Kumar, Sanjay. 2001. "Despite Ban, Organs Still Sold in India." *Reuters Health,* March 9. Retrieved September 20, 2006 (www.geocities.com/somewherereal/bodyparts.html).

Kumlin, Johanna. 2006. "The Sex Wage Gap in Japan and Sweden: The Role of Human Capital, Workplace Sex Composition, and Family Responsibility." *European Sociological Review* (advance access published online on December 18). Retrieved April 17, 2010 (http://esr.oxfordjournals.org/cgi/content/abstract/23/2/203).

Lacayo, Richard. 1993. "Cult of Death." *Time* (March 15):36.

Lake, Robert. 1990. "An Indian Father's Plea." *Teacher Magazine* 2 (September):48–53.

Lamanna, Mary Ann and Agnes Riedmann. 2010. *Marriages and Families: Making Choices Throughout the Life Cycle,* 10th ed. Belmont, CA: Wadsworth.

Lambert, Yves. 2000. "Religion in Modernity as a New Axial Age: Secularization or New Religious Forms?" Pp. 95–125 in *The Secularization Debate,* edited by William H. Swatos, Jr. and Daniel V. A. Olson. Lanham, MD: Rowman & Littlefield.

Landau, Elizabeth. 2009. "Life Expectancy Could Be Topic in Health Care Debate." June 11. Retrieved April 17, 2010 (www.cnn.com/2009/HEALTH/06/. . ./life.expectancy.health.care).

Landler, Mark and Brian Stelter. 2009. "Washington Taps Into a Potent New Force in Diplomacy." *New York Times,* June 17, p. A12. Retrieved December 22, 2009 (www.nytimes.com).

Lareau, Annette. 2003. *Unequal Childhoods: Class, Race, and Family Life.* Berkeley: University of California Press.

Lasch, Kathryn E. 2002 "Culture and Pain." Pain: Clinical Updates, December. *International Association for the Study of Pain* X(5):1–9.

Lashbrook, Jeffrey. 2009. "Social Class Differences in Family Life." P. 224 in *Our Social World,* 2nd ed., edited by Jeanne H. Ballantine and Keith A. Roberts. Thousand Oaks, CA: Sage.

Layton, Lyndsey. 2012. "High School Graduation Rate Rises in U.S." *The Washington Post,* March 18. Retrieved September 19, 2012 (www.washingtonpost.com/local/education/high-school-graduation-rate-rises-in-us/2012/03/16/gIQAxZ9rLS_story.html).

Lazare, Aaron. 2004. *On Apology.* New York: Oxford University Press.

Lazaridis, Gabriella. 2011. *Security, Insecurity and Migration in Europe*. Farnham, UK: Ashgate Publishing, Ltd.

Lazerwitz, Bernard, J. Alan Winter, Arnold Dashefsky, and Ephraim Tabory. 1998. *Jewish Choices: American Jewish Denominationalism*. Albany: SUNY Press.

Leach, Edmund R. 1979. "Ritualization in Man in Relation to Conceptual and Social Development." Pp. 333–37 in *Reader in Comparative Religion*, 3rd ed., edited by William A. Lessa and Evon Z. Vogt. New York: Harper & Row.

Leavitt, Jacqueline and Susan Saegert. 1990. *From Abandonment to Hope: Community-Households in Harlem* (Columbia History of Urban Life). New York: Columbia University Press.

LeBon, Gustave. [1895] 1960. *The Crowd: A Study of the Popular Mind*. New York: Viking.

LeBow, Bob. 2004. *Health Care Meltdown: Confronting the Myths and Fixing Our Failing System*. Chambersburg, PA: Alan C. Hood.

Lechner, Frank J. and John Boli. 2005. *World Culture: Origins and Consequences*. Malden, MA: Blackwell.

Lederer, Edith M. 2012. "Human Trafficking Victims: 2.4 Million People Across the Globe Are Trafficked for Labor, Sex." *Huff Post World*, April 3. Retrieved January 21, 2013 (www.huffingtonpost .com/2012/04/03/human-trafficking-victims_n_1401673.html).

Lederman, Josh. 2012. "Voter Turnout Shaping Up to Be Lower Than 2008." *Huffington Post*, November 7. Retrieved November 11, 2012 (http://www.huffingtonpost.com/2012/11/07/voter-turnout_n_2088810.html).

Lee, B. C. and J. L. Werth. 2000. *Observations on the First Year of Oregon's Death With Dignity Act*. Washington, DC: American Psychological Association.

Lee, Gang, Ronald L. Akers, and Marian J. Borg. 2004. "Social Learning and Structural Factors in Adolescent Substance Use." *Western Criminology Review* 5(1):17.

Lee, Jennifer and Frank D. Bean. 2004. "America's Changing Color Lines: Immigration, Race/Ethnicity, and Multiracial Identification." *Annual Review of Sociology* 30(August):222–42.

Lee, Jennifer and Frank D. Bean. 2007. "Redrawing the Color Line?" *City and Community* 6(1):49–62.

Lemert, Edwin M. 1951. *Social Pathology*. New York: McGraw-Hill.

Lee, Richard B. 1984. *The Dobe!Kung*. New York: Holt, Rinehart & Winston.

Lee, Sharon M., and Barry Edmonston. 2005. "New Marriages, New Families: U.S. Racial and Hispanic Intermarriage." *Population Bulletin* 60(2). Retrieved August 7, 2008 (www.prb.org/pdf05/60.2NewMarriages.pdf).

Leeder, Elaine J. 2004. *The Family in Global Perspective: A Gendered Journey*. Thousand Oaks, CA: Sage.

Legters, Nettie E. 2001. "Teachers as Workers in the World System." Pp. 417–26 in *Schools and Society: A Sociological Approach to Education*, edited by Jeanne H. Ballantine and Joan Z. Spade. Belmont, CA: Wadsworth.

Lehman, Edward C., Jr. 1985. *Women Clergy: Breaking Through Gender Barriers*. New Brunswick, NJ: Transaction.

Leit, R. A., J. J. Gray, and H. G. Pope. 2002. "The Media's Representation of the Ideal Male Body." *International Journal of Eating Disorders* (doi.wiley.com).

Lemert, Edwin M. 1972. *Human Deviance, Social Problems, and Social Control*, 2nd ed. Englewood Cliffs, NJ: Prentice Hall.

Lemkau, Jeanne Parr. 2006. "Fences, Volcanoes, and Embargoes." Unpublished manuscript.

Lengermann, Patricia M., and Jill Niebrugge-Brantley. 1990. "Feminist Sociological Theory: The Near-Future Prospects." Pp. 316–44 in *Frontiers of Social Theory: The New Synthesis*, edited by George Ritzer. New York: Columbia University Press.

Lenski, Gerhard E. 1966. *Human Societies*. New York: McGraw-Hill.

Leon, Kim. 2009. "Covenant Marriage: What Is It and Does It Work?" *MissouriFamilies.org*. Retrieved June 6, 2012 (http://missourifamilies.org/features/divorcearticles/divorcefeature23.htm).

Lerner, Richard M. 1992. "Sociobiology and Human Development: Arguments and Evidence." *Human Development* 35(1):12–51.

Leslie, Gerald R. and Sheila K. Korman. 1989. *The Family in Social Context*, 7th ed. New York: Oxford University Press.

Leung, K., S. Lau, and W. L. Lam. 1998. *Parenting Styles and Academic Achievement: A Cross-Cultural Study*. Detroit, MI: Wayne State University Press.

Levin, Jack and Jack McDevitt. 2003. *Hate Crimes Revisited: America's War on Those Who Are Different*. Boulder, CO: Westview.

Levinson, David L. 2010. "Grand Solution or Grab Bag?" *The American Prospect* (November):14–17. Retrieved February 9, 2013 (www .prospect.org).

Levinson, Stephen C. 2000. "Yeli Dnye and the Theory of Basic Color Terms." *Journal of Linguistic Anthropology* 1:3–55.

Levitt, Peggy. 2001. *The Transnational Villagers*. Berkeley: University of California Press.

Levitt, Peggy. 2007. *God Needs No Passport: Immigrants and the Changing American Religious Landscape*. New York: New Press.

Levitt, Peggy, and Mary Waters, eds. 2006. *The Changing Face of Home: The Transnational Lives of the Second Generation*. Russell Sage Foundation. Retrieved June 27, 2011 (www.russellsage.org/publications/changing-face-home).

Levy, Audrey. 2008. "No to Forced Marriages!" *France Diplomatie*. Retrieved April 17, 2010 (www.diplomatie.gouv.fr/. . .no. . ./seen-from-france_4737.html).

Lewin, Tamar. 2006. "At Colleges, Women Are Leaving Men in the Dust." *The New York Times*, July 9, pp. A1, 18.

Lewis, Maureen A. and Marlaine E. Lockheed. 2006. *Inexcusable Absence: Why 60 Million Girls Still Aren't in School and What to Do About It*. Washington, DC: Center for Global Development.

Lewis, Oscar. 1961. *The Children of Sánchez: Autobiography of a Mexican Family*. New York: Random House.

Lewis, Oscar. 1986. *La Vida: A Puerto Rican Family in the Culture of Poverty*. New York: Irvington.

Library of Congress 2010. "Margaret Mead: Human Nature and the Power of Culture." July 27. Retrieved March 7, 2012 (www.loc .gov/exhibits/mead/field-sepik.html).

Lichter, Daniel T., Richard N. Turner, and Sharon Sassler. 2010. "Marriage and Family in the New Millenium: Papers in Honor of Steven L. Nock." *Social Science Research* 39(5):754–65. Retrieved April 11, 2011 (doi:10.1016/j.ssresearch.2009.11.002).

Lieberson, Stanley. 1980. *A Piece of the Pie: Blacks and White Immigrants Since 1880*. Berkeley: University of California Press.

Lieberson, Stanley, Susan Dumais, and Shyon Bauman. 2000. "The Instability of Androgynous Names: The Symbolic Maintenance of Gender Boundaries." *American Journal of Sociology* 105(5):1249–87.

Lin, June. 2010. "What Are the Main Criticisms of Whorf's Theory of Linguistic Determinism and Relativity?" August 3. Retrieved March 21, 2012 (www.quora.com/What-are-the-main-criticisms-of-Whorfs-theory-of-linguistic-determinism-and-relativity).

Lincoln, Erik and Laurence Mamiya. 1990. *The Black Church in the African American Experience*. Durham, NC: Duke University Press.

Lindberg, Richard and Vesna Markovic. N.d. "Organized Crime Outlook in the New Russia: Russia Is Paying the Price of a Market Economy in Blood." Retrieved January 4, 2001 (www.search-international.com/Articles/crime/russiacrime.htm).

Lindow, Megan. June 20, 2009. "South Africa's Rape Crisis: 1 in 4 Men Say They've Done It." *Time/World*. Retrieved February 27, 2012 (www.time.com/time/world/article/0,8599,1906000,00.html).

Lindsay, James M. 2006. "Global Warming Heats Up." Pp. 307–13 in *Globalization: The Transformation of Social Worlds*, edited by D. Stanley Eitzen and Maxine Baca Zinn. Belmont, CA: Wadsworth.

Lindsey, Linda L. 2011. *Gender Roles: A Sociological Perspective*, 5th ed. Englewood Cliffs, NJ: Prentice Hall.

Linton, Ralph. 1937. *The Study of Man*. New York: D. Appleton-Century.

Lips, Hilary M. 2010. *Sex and Gender: An Introduction*, 9th ed. Boston: McGraw-Hill.

Liptak, Adam. 2008. "U.S. Prison Population Dwarfs that of Other Nations." April 23. *The New York Times*. Retrieved April 15, 2012 (www.nytimes.com/2008/04/23/world/americas/23iht-23prisons.12253738.html).

Liptak, Adam. 2012. "Justices Take Up Race as a Factor in College Entry." *The New York Times*, February 21. Retrieved May 12, 2012 (www.nytimes.com/2012/02/22/us/justices-to-hear-case-on-affirmative-action-in-higher-education.html?pagewanted=all).

Liptak, Adam and Maria Newman. 2005. "*New York Times* Reporter Jailed for Keeping Source Secret." July 6. Retrieved March 3, 2012 (www.nytimes.com/2005/07/06/po9litics/06cnd-leak.html?pagewanted=all).

Lofgren, Orvar. 1999. *On Holiday: A History of Vacationing*. Berkeley: University of California Press.

Lofgren, Orvar. 2010. "The Global Beach." Pp. 37–55 in *Tourists and Tourism*, 2nd ed., edited by Sharon Bohn Gmelch. Long Grove, IL: Waveland Press.

Loftsdottir, Kristin. 2004. "When Nomads Lose Cattle: Wodaabe Negotiations of Ethnicity." *African Sociological Review* 8(2):55–76.

Logan, John R. and Glenna D. Spitze. 1994. "Family Neighbors." *American Journal of Sociology* 100(2):453–76.

Longman, Timothy. 2005. "Rwanda: Achieving Equality or Serving an Authoritarian State?" Pp. 133–150 in *Women in African Parliaments*, edited by Gretchen Bauer and Hannah Britton. Boulder, CO: Lynne Reinner.

Lopez, Ian F. Haney. 1996. *White by Law*. New York: New York University Press.

Lopez-Garza, Marta. 2002. "Convergence of the Public and Private Spheres: Women in the Informal Economy." *Race, Gender, and Class* 9(3):175–92.

Lopreato, Joseph. 2001. "Sociobiological Theorizing: Evolutionary Sociology." Pp. 405–33 in *Handbook of Sociological Theory*. Secaucus, NJ: Springer.

Lorber, Judith. 1998. "Reinventing the Sexes: The Biomedical Construction of Femininity and Masculinity." *Contemporary Society* 27(5):498–99.

Lorber, Judith. 2009. *Gender Inequality: Feminist Theories and Politics*. New York: Oxford University Press.

Lorber, Judith. and Lisa Jean Moore. 2007. *Gendered Bodies*. Los Angeles, CA: Roxbury.

Lorber, Judith and Lisa Jean Moore. 2011. *Gendered Bodies: Feminist Perspectives*, 2nd ed. New York: Oxford University Press.

Lorillard, Didi. 2011. "What's Going on With the Venerable State of Marriage?" *GoLocal Lifestyle*. Retrieved June 4, 2012 (www.golocalprov.com/lifestyle/modern-manners-etiquette-sharing-household-chores/).

Los Angeles Times. 2008. "Kenyans Recall the Screams of the Dying in Burning Church." January 3. Retrieved June 3, 2008 (http://articles.latimes.com/2008/jan/03/world/fg-church3).

Lotfi Yaser, Ali Ayar, and Simin Shams. 2012. "The Relation Between Religious Practice and Committing Suicide: Common and Suicidal People in Darehshahr, Iran." *Procedia—Social and Behavioral Sciences* July 16–18(50):1051–60.

Loveless, Tom. 2009. "Tracking and Detracking: High Achievers in Massachusetts Middle Schools." Thomas B. Fordham Institute. Retrieved April 17, 2010 (http://edexcellence.net/. . ./news_tracking-and-detracking-high-achievers-in-massachusetts-middle-schools).

Loy, Irwin. 2012. "Observers: Cambodian Vote Improved but Problems Remain." *Voice of America*. Retrieved July 25, 2012 (www.voanews.com/content/observers-cambodian-elections-improved-but-problems-remain/1146999.html).

Lucal, Betsy. 1999. "Building Boxes and Policing Boundaries: (De) constructing Intersexuality, Transgender and Bisexuality." *Sociology Compass*. Retrieved April 8, 2011 (www.blackwell-compass.com/subject/sociology/article_view?article_id=soco_tr_bpl100).

Lucas, Samuel R. and Mark Berends. 2002. "Sociodemographic Diversity, Correlated Achievement, and De Facto Tracking." *Sociology of Education* 75(4):328–48.

Lumsden, Charles J. and Edward O. Wilson. 1981. *Genes, Mind, and Culture: The Coevolutionary Process*. Cambridge, MA: Harvard University Press.

Luscombe, Belinda. 2010. "Marriage: What's It Good For?" *Time* 176(November 29):48–56.

MacDorman, Marian F. and T. J. Mathews. 2011. "Understanding Racial and Ethnic Disparities in U.S. Infant Mortality Rates." Centers for Disease Control and Prevention, National Center for Health Statistics: Data Brief #74. Retrieved August 28, 2012 (www.cdc.gov/nchs/data/databriefs/db74.pdf).

MacDougal, Gary. 2005. *Make a Difference: A Spectacular Breakthrough in the Fight Against Poverty*. New York: St. Martin's Press.

Machalek, Richard, and Michael W. Martin. 2010. "Evolution, Biology, and Society: A Conversation for the 21st Century Classroom." *Teaching Sociology* 38(1):35–45.

Macionis, John. 2010. *Sociology*, 13th ed. Upper Saddle River, NJ: Prentice Hall.

Mackey, Robert. 2011, April 23. "Social Media Accounts of the Protests in Syria." The Lede Weblog, *New York Times*. Retrieved October 3, 2012 (thelede.blogs.nytimes.com).

Mackey, Robert. 2012. "Update on Rage Over Anti-Islam Film." The Lede Weblog, *New York Times*, September 12. Retrieved October 2, 2012 (thelede.blogs.nytimes.com).

Mackey, Robert and Liam Stack. 2012. "Obscure Film Mocking Muslim Prophet Sparks Anti-U.S. Protests in Egypt and Libya." The Lede Weblog, *New York Times*, September 11. Retrieved October 2, 2012 (thelede.blogs.nytimes.com).

MacLeod, Jay. 1995. *Ain't No Makin' It: Aspirations and Attainment in a Low-Income Neighborhood*. Boulder, CO: Westview.

MacLeod, Jay. 2008. *Ain't No Makin' It: Aspirations and Attainment in a Low-Income Neighborhood*, 3rd ed. Boulder, CO: Westview.

Madden, Mary and Kathryn Zickuhr. 2011. "65% of Online Adults Use Social Networking Sites." *Pew Internet*. Retrieved May 25, 2012 (http://pewinternet.org/Reports/2011/Social-Networking-Sites.aspx).

"The Madoff Case: A Timeline." 2009. *The Wall Street Journal,* March 12. Retrieved November 5, 2009 (http://online.wsj.com/article/SB112966954231272304.html?mod=googlenews.wsj).

Madyun, Na'im and Moo Sung Lee. 2010. "The Influence of Female-Headed Households on Black Achievement." *Urban Education* 45(4):424–47.

Mahoney, Brian. 2012. "NBA 'Set The Tone' with Black Coaches." *Athletic Business Daily* E-News, April 27. Retrieved May 10, 2012 (http://athleticbusiness.com/articles/lexisnexis.aspx?Inarticleid=1654581846&Intopicid=136030023).

Makhmalbaf, Mohsen, producer. 2003. *Kandahar: The Sun Behind the Moon* (Film).

"Male Dominance Causes Rape." 2008. *Journal of Feminist Insight*, December 8. Retrieved April 8, 2011 (http://journaloffeministinsight.blogspot.com/2008/12/male-dominance-causes-rape.html).

Malthus, Thomas R. [1798] 1926. *First Essay on Population 1798.* London: Macmillan.

Mann, Thomas E. and Norman J. Ornstein. 2012. *It's Even Worse Than It Looks: How the American Constitutional System Collided With the New Politics of Extremism*. New York: Basic Books.

Manning, Jennifer E. 2011. "Membership of the 112th Congress: A Profile." Congressional Research Service Report to Congress. Retrieved April 22, 2011 (www.senate.gov/reference/resources/pdf/R41647.pdf).

Manning, Wendy D., Monica A. Longmore, and Peggy C. Giordano. 2007. "The Changing Institution of Marriage: Adolescents' Expectations to Cohabit and to Marry." *Journal of Marriage and Family* 69(August):559–75.

Marcus, Richard R. 2008. "Kenya's Conflict Isn't 'Tribal.'" *Los Angeles Times*, January 24. Retrieved June 3, 2008 (www.latimes.com/news/opinion/la-oew-marcus24jan24,0,4231203.story).

Marger, Martin N. 2009. *Race and Ethnic Relations: American and Global Perspectives,* 8th ed. Belmont, CA: Wadsworth/Cengage Learning.

Marger, Martin N. 2012. *Race and Ethnic Relations: American and Global Perspectives*, 9th ed. Belmont, CA: Wadsworth.

Markoff, John and Somini Sengupta. 2011. "Separating You and Me? 4.74 Degrees." *The New York Times,* November 21. Retrieved September 25, 2012 (www.nytimes.com/2011/11/22/technolgoy/between-you-and-me-4-74-degrees.html).

Marmor, Theodore R. 1999. *The Politics of Medicare,* 2nd ed. Hawthorne, NY: Aldine de Gruyter.

Marti, Geraldo. 2009. "Affinity, Identity, and Transcendence: The Experience of Religious Racial Integration in Diverse Congregations" *Journal for the Scientific Study of Religion* 48(March):54–96.

Martin, Jenny Beth and Mark Meckler. 2012. *Tea Party Patriots: The Second American Revolution*. New York: Henry Holt and Company.

Martin, Michel and Gwen Thompkins. 2009. "Proposed Uganda Law: If You See a Homosexual, Call The Police." National Public Radio: "Tell Me More," December 18. Retrieved April 12, 2011 (www.npr.org/templates/story/story.php?storyId=121605525).

Martin, Patricia Yancey and Robert A. Hummer. 1989. "Fraternities and Rape on Campus." *Gender and Society* 3(4):457–73.

Martin, Scott C. 2006. *From Temperance to Alcoholism in America.* Baltimore: Johns Hopkins University Press.

Martineau, Harriet. [1837] 1962. *Society in America.* Garden City, NY: Doubleday.

Martineau, Harriet. 1838. *How to Observe Manners and Morals.* London: Charles Knight & Co.

Marty, Martin E., and R. Scott Appleby, eds. 1991. *Fundamentalism Observed.* Chicago: University of Chicago Press.

Marty, Martin E. and R. Scott Appleby, eds. 2004. *Accounting for Fundamentalism: The Dynamic Character of Movements.* Chicago: University of Chicago Press.

Marx, Karl. [1844] 1963. "Contribution to the Critique of Hegel's Philosophy of Right." Pp. 43–59 in *Karl Marx: Early Writings,* translated and edited by T. B. Bottomore. New York: McGraw-Hill.

Marx, Karl. [1844] 1964. *The Economic and Philosophical Manuscripts of 1844.* New York: International Publishers.

Marx, Karl and Friedrich Engels. [1848] 1969. *The Communist Manifesto.* Baltimore: Penguin.

Marx, Karl and Friedrich Engels. 1955. *Selected Work in Two Volumes.* Moscow: Foreign Language Publishing House.

Mashberg, Tom. 2002. "Med Examiner's Office Has Secret Body-Parts Deal." *Boston Herald* (May 20):1.

Mason-Schrock, Douglas. 1996. "Transsexual's Narrative Construction of the 'True Self.'" *Social Psychology Quarterly* 59(3):176–92.

Massey, Douglas S. 2007. *Categorically Unequal: The American Stratification System.* New York: Russell Sage.

Massey, Douglas S. and Nancy A. Denton. 1998. *American Apartheid: Segregation and the Making of the Underclass.* Cambridge, MA: Harvard University Press.

Masters, William H. and Virginia Johnson. 1966. *Human Sexual Response.* Boston: Little, Brown.

Masters, William H. and Virginia Johnson. 1970. *Human Sexual Inadequacy.* Boston: Little, Brown.

Mathews, T. J. and Marian F. MacDorman. 2008. "Infant Mortality Statistics From the 2005 Period Linked Birth/Infant Death Data Set." *National Vital Statistics Reports* 27(2). Retrieved January 23, 2010 (www.cdc.gov/nchs/data/nvsr/nvsr57/nvsr57_02.pdf).

Mattingly, Marybeth and Liana C. Sayer. 2006. "Under Pressure: Trends and Gender Differences in the Relationship Between Free Time and Feeling Rushed." *Journal of Marriage and Family* 68(1):205–21.

Mauksch, Hans. 1993. "Teaching of Applied Sociology: Opportunities and Obstacles." Pp. 1–7 in *Teaching Applied Sociology: A Resource Book,* edited by C. Howery. Washington, DC: American Sociological Association Teaching Resources Center.

Mauss, Armand. 1975. *Social Problems as Social Movements.* Philadelphia: Lippincott.

Mavalankar, Dileep V., Kranti S. Vora, K. V. Ramani, Parvathy Raman, Bharati Sharma, and Mudita Upadhyaya. 2009. "Maternal Health in Gujarat, India: A Case Study." *Journal of Health, Population, and Nutrition* 27(April):235–48.

Mayo Clinic. 2011. "Domestic Violence Toward Women: Recognize the Patterns and Seek Help." Retrieved January 21, 2013 (www.mayoclinic.com/health/domestic-violence/WO00044).

Mayoux, Linda. 2002. "Women's Empowerment or Feminisation of Debt? Towards a New Agenda in African Microfinance." Report at the One World Action Conference in London, March 21–22.

Mayoux, Linda, ed. 2008. *Sustainable Learning for Women's Empowerment: Ways Forward in Micro-Finance.* Warwickshire, UK: ITDG Publishing.

McAdam, Doug. 1999. *Political Process and the Development of Black Insurgency, 1930–1970,* 2nd ed. Chicago: University of Chicago Press.

McAdam, Doug. 2003. "Beyond Structural Analysis: Toward a More Dynamic Understanding of Social Movements." Pp. 281-198 in *Social Movements and Networks: Relational Approaches to Collective Action*, edited by Mario Diani and Doug McAdam. New York: Oxford University Press.

McArdle, Megan 2012. "The College Bubble: Is College a Lousy Investment?" *Newsweek*, September 17, pp. 22–26.

McCaghy, Charles H., Timothy A. Capron, J. D. Jamieson, and Sandra Harley Carey. 2006. *Deviant Behavior: Crime, Conflict, and Interest Groups,* 7th ed. Boston: Allyn & Bacon.

McCarthy, John D. and Mayer N. Zald. 1977. "Resource Mobilization and Social Movements: A Partial Theory." *American Journal of Sociology* 82(6):1212–41.

McConnell, E. D. and E. Delgado-Romero. 2004. "Latinos, Panethnicity, and Census 2000: Reality or Methodological Construction." Retrieved February 24, 2008 (www.allacademic.com/meta/p109991_index.html).

McCormick, John. 1992. "A Housing Program That Actually Works." *Newsweek*, June 22, pp. 61.

McCrone, David. 1998. *The Sociology of Nationalism.* London: Routledge.

McCrummen, Stephanie. 2008. "Women Run the Show in a Recovering Rwanda." *The Washington Post*, October 27. Retrieved May 6, 2011 (www.washingtonpost.com/wp-dyn/content/article/2008/10/26/AR2008102602197.html).

McDonald, Michael. 2009. "2008 General Election Turnout Rates." Retrieved July 11, 2009 (http://elections.gmu.edu/Turnout_2008G.html).

McEneaney, Elizabeth H. and John W. Meyer. 2000. "The Content of the Curriculum: An Institutionalist Perspective." Pp. 189–211 in *Handbook of the Sociology of Education,* edited by Maureen T. Hallinan. New York: Kluwer Academic/Plenum.

McEvoy, Alan W. and Jeff B. Brookings. 2008. *If She Is Raped: A Guidebook for the Men in Her Life,* 4th ed., abridged. Tampa, FL: Teal Ribbon Books.

McGuire, Meredith. 2002. *Religion: The Social Context,* 5th ed. Belmont, CA: Wadsworth.

McIntosh, Peggy. 1992. "White Privilege and Male Privilege: A Personal Account of Coming to See Correspondences through Work in Women's Studies." Pp. 70–81 in *Race, Class, and Gender: An Anthology*, edited by Margaret A. Anderson and Patricia Hill Collins. Belmont, CA: Wadsworth.

McIntosh, Peggy. 2002. "White Privilege: Unpacking the Invisible Knapsack." Pp. 97–101 in *White Privilege: Essential Readings on the Other Side of Racism*, edited by Paula S. Rothenberg. New York: Worth.

McKelvie, Samuel R. 1926. "What the Movies Meant to the Farmer." *Annals of the American Academy of Political and Social Science* 128(November):131.

McKie, Linda and Samantha Callan. 2012. *Understanding Families: A Global Introduction*. Thousand Oaks: Sage.

McKinnish, Terra, Randall Walsh, and Kirk White. 2008. "Who Gentrifies Low Income Neighborhoods?" Retrieved April 17, 2010 (papers.ssrn.com/so13/papers.cfm?abstract_id=1139352).

McLeod, Jay. 2009. *Ain't No Makin' It: Aspirations and Attainment in a Low-Income Neighborhood,* 3rd ed. Boulder, CO: Westview.

McMichael, Philip. 2012. *Development and Social Change: A Global Perspective*. Los Angeles: Sage.

McNall, Scott G. and Sally Allen McNall. 1983. *Plains Families: Exploring Sociology Through Social History.* New York: St. Martin's Press.

McPhail, Deborah, Brenda Beagan, and Gwen E. Chapman. 2012. "'I Don't Want to Be Sexist But . . .' Denying and Re-Inscribing Gender Through Food." *Food, Culture & Society* 15(3):473–89.

McVey, G., S. Tweed, and E. Blackmore. 2004. "Dieting Among Preadolescent and Young Adolescent Females." *CMAJ* (May 11): 1559–61. Retrieved May 23, 2012 (www.ncbi.nlm.nih.gov/pubmed/15136549).

Mead, Frank, Samuel Hill, and Craig Atwood, eds. 2005. *Handbook of Denominations in the United States*, 12th ed. Nashville, TN: Abingdon Press.

Mead, George Herbert. [1934] 1962. *Mind, Self, and Society.* Chicago: University of Chicago Press.

Mead, Margaret. [1935] 1963. *Sex and Temperament in Three Primitive Societies.* New York: William Morrow.

Medical News Today. 2009. "Women's Health." September 4. Retrieved January 6, 2010 (www.medicalnewstoday.com/articles/162997.php).

Mehan, Hugh. 1992. "Understanding Inequality in Schools: The Contribution of Interpretive Studies." *Sociology of Education* 65(1):1–20.

Mehra, Bharat, Cecelia Merkel, and Ann P. Bishop. 2004. "The Internet for Empowerment of Minority and Marginalized Users." *New Media and Society* 6:781–802.

Mehsud, Saud. 2012. "Pakistani Girl Shot by Taliban Defied Threats for Years." *Reuters,* October 10. Retrieved October 11, 2012 (www.reuters.com/article/2012/10/10/us-pakistan-girl-family-idUSBRE8990T720121010).

Melton, J. Gordon. 1993. "Another Look at New Religions." *Annals of the American Academy of Political and Social Science* (May): 97–112.

Meltzer, B. 1978. "Mead's Social Psychology." Pp. 15–27 in *Symbolic Interactionism: A Reader in Social Psychology,* 3rd ed., edited by J. Manis and B. Meltzer. Boston: Allyn & Bacon.

Meltzer, Bernard N., John W. Petras, and Larry T. Reynolds. 1975. *Symbolic Interactionism: Genesis, Varieties and Criticism.* London: Routledge & Kegan Paul.

Mental Health America. 2011. "Bullying in Schools: Harassment Puts Gay Youth at Risk." Retrieved April 17, 2011 (www.nmha.org/index.cfm?objectid=CA866DCF-1372-4D20-C8EB26EEB30B9982).

Merton, Robert K. 1938. "Social Structure and Anomie." *American Sociological Review* 3(October):672–82.

Merton, Robert K. [1942] 1973. *The Sociology of Science: Theoretical and Empirical Investigations.* Chicago: University of Chicago Press.

Merton, Robert K. 1949. "Discrimination and the American Creed." Pp. 99–126 in *Discrimination and American Welfare,* edited by Robert M. MacIver. New York: Harper.

Merton, Robert K. 1968. *Social Theory and Social Structure,* 2nd ed. New York: Free Press.

Metropolitan Community Churches. 2008. "Churches." Retrieved March 1, 2008 (www.mccchurch.org/AM/Template.cfm?Section=Find_an_MCC).

Metropolitan Community Churches. 2011. "Beliefs." Retrieved April 8, 2011 (http://www.blackwell-compass.com/subject/sociology/article_view?article_id=soco_tr_bpl100).

Metropolitan Community Churches. 2012. "Our Churches." Retrieved January 30, 2013 (http://mccchurch.org/ourchurches).

Meyer, R. 1996. "The Disease Called Addiction: Emerging Evidence in a Two Hundred Year Debate." *The Lancet* 347(8995):162–66.

Michael, John. N.d. "Pros and Cons of Private Prisons." Retrieved February 9, 2012 (www.ehow.com/info_8110862_pros-cons-private-prisons.html).

Michels, Robert. [1911] 1967. *Political Parties.* New York: Free Press.

Migration Information Source. 2011. Retrieved May 15, 2011 (www.migrationinformation.org/Resources/unitedstates.cfm).

Mike, Valerie. 2003. "Evidence and the Future of Medicine." *Evaluation and the Health Professions* 26(2):127–52.

Mikkelson, Barbara and David P. Mikkelson. 2012. "Urban Legends." Retrieved January 1, 2012 (www.snopes.com/college/college.asp).

Milgram, Stanley. 1967. "The Small World Problem." *Psychology Today* 1:61–67.

Milkie, Melissa. 1999. "Social Comparisons, Reflected Appraisals, and Mass Media. The Impact of Pervasive Beauty Images on Black and White Girl's Self Concept." *Social Psychology Quarterly* 62(2):190–210.

Miller, Greg. 2009. "Global Economic Crisis Called Biggest U.S. Security Threat." *Los Angeles Times.* Retrieved February 13, 2009 (http://articles.latimes.com/2009/feb/13/nation/na-security-threat13).

Mills, C. Wright. 1956. *The Power Elite.* New York: Oxford University Press.

Mills, C. Wright. 1959. *The Sociological Imagination.* New York: Oxford University Press.

Mills, Theodore M. 1984. *The Sociology of Small Groups,* 2nd ed. Englewood Cliffs, NJ: Prentice Hall.

Milner, Murray. 2006. *Freaks, Geeks, and Cool Kids: American Teenagers, Schools, and the Culture of Consumption.* London: Routledge.

Mincy, Ronald B. 2006. *Black Males Left Behind.* Washington, DC: Urban Institute Press.

Minkoff, Debra C. 1995. *Organizing for Equality.* New Brunswick, NJ: Rutgers University Press.

"Misery of the Maquiladoras." 2011. *Socialist Worker,* November 18. Retrieved May 27, 2012 (http://socialistworker.org/2011/11/18/misery-of-the-maquiladoras).

Misztal, Bronislaw and Anson D. Shupe. 1998. *Fundamentalism and Globalization: Fundamentalist Movements at the Twilight of the Twentieth Century.* Westport, CT: Praeger.

Molotch, Harvey. 2003. *Where Stuff Comes From: How Toasters, Toilets, Cars, Computers, and Many Other Things Come to Be as They Are.* London: Routledge.

Monnier, Christine 2010. "Social Movements." Global Sociology. Retrieved September 9, 2012 (https://globalsociology.pbworks.com/w/page/14711254/Social%20Movements).

Moore, Valerie Ann. 2001. "Doing Racialized and Gendered Age to Organize Peer Relations: Observing Kids in Summer Camp." *Gender and Society* 15(6):835–58.

Morello, Carol, and Dan Keating. 2009. "Number of Foreign-Born U.S. Residents Drops." September 22. Retrieved January 5, 2010 (www.washingtonpost.com/wp-dyn/content/article/2009/09/21/AR2009092103251.html).

Morey, Peter and Amina Yaqin. 2011. *Framing Muslims: Stereotyping and Representation After 9/11.* Cambridge, MA: Harvard University Press.

Morgan, David. 2012. "One in Four Americans Without Health Coverage." Reuters, April 19. Retrieved August 1, 2012 (www.reuters.com/article/2012/04/19/us-usa-healthcare-insurance-idUSBRE83117420120419).

Morris, Edward W. 2005. "From 'Middle Class' to 'Trailer Trash': Teachers' Perceptions of White Students in a Predominately Minority School." *Sociology of Education* 78(2):99–121.

Morris, Joan M. and Michael D. Grimes. 1997. *Caught in the Middle: Contradictions in the Lives of Sociologists From Working Class Backgrounds.* Westport, CT: Praeger.

Morris, Lloyd R. 1949. *Not So Long Ago.* New York: Random House.

Morris, Martina, Mark Stephen Handcock, Marc A. Scott, and Annette D. Bernhardt. 2001. *Divergent Paths: Economic Mobility in the New American Labor Market.* New York: Russell Sage.

Morrison, Maureen. 2010. "New Data Shed Light on Women's Internet Usage." *Ad Age,* August 3. Retrieved May 25, 2012 (http://adage.com/article/adagestat/data-research-women-s-internet-usage/145224/).

Morozov, Evgeny. 2009. "How Dictators Watch Us on the Web." *Prospect.* Retrieved October 9, 2012 (http://www.prospectmagazine.co.uk/magazine/how-dictators-watch-us-on-the-web/).

Mou, Yi and Wei Peng. 2009. "Gender and Racial Stereotypes in Popular Video Games." IGI Global OnDemand.

Muchhala, Bhumika. 2012. "Students Against Sweat Shops." Pp. 303–12 in *Globalization: The Transformation of Social Worlds,* 3rd ed., edited by D. Stanley Eitzen and Maxine Baca Zinn. Belmont, CA: Wadsworth.

Mumford, Lewis. 1961. *The City in History: Its Origins, Transformations, and Prospects.* New York: Harcourt, Brace, & World.

Munsey, Christopher. 2012. "Hostile Hallways." *American Psychological Association: Monitor on Psychology* 43(February):58.

Murdock, George Peter. 1967. *Ethnographic Atlas.* Pittsburgh: University of Pittsburgh Press.

Murstein, Bernard I. 1987. "A Clarification and Extension of the SVR Theory of Dyadic Pairing." *Journal of Marriage and the Family* 49(November):929–33.

"Muslims and Multicultural Backlash." 2011, July. Retrieved March 23, 2012 (http://harvardpress.typepad.com/hup_publicity/2011/07/framing-muslims-morey-yaqin.html).

Mutamba, John. 2005. "Strategies for Increasing Women's Participation in Government." Expert Group Meeting on Democratic Governance in Africa, Nairobi, Kenya, December 6–8.

Mydans, Seth. 2002. "In Pakistan, Rape Victims Are the 'Criminals.'" *The New York Times,* May 17, p. A3.

Mydans, Seth. 2009. "For Khmer Rouge Guard, It Was Kill or Be Killed." March 1. Retrieved July 11, 2009 (www.nytimes.com/2009/03/01/world/asia/01iht-guard.1.20501994.html).

Myers, John P. 2003. *Dominant-Minority Relations in America: Linking Personal History With the Convergence in the New World.* Boston: Allyn & Bacon.

Myrdal, Gunnar. 1964. *An American Dilemma.* New York: McGraw-Hill.

Nagai, Tyrone. 2010. "Multiracial Identity and the U.S. Census." *ProQuest Discovery Guides,* January (pp. 10–13). Retrieved January 21, 2013 (www.csa.com/discoveryguides/census/review.pdf).

Nagel, Joane. 1994. "Constructing Ethnicity: Creating and Recreating Ethnic Identity and Culture." *Social Problems* 41(1):152–76.

Nakamura, Lisa. 2004. "Interrogating the Digital Divide: The Political Economy of Race and Commerce in the New Media." Pp. 71–83 in *Society On-Line: The Internet in Context,* edited by Philip N. Howard and Steve Jones. Thousand Oaks, CA: Sage.

Nall, Jeff. 2012. "Combating Slavery in Coffee and Chocolate Production." *Toward Freedom,* January 5. Retrieved May 1, 2012 (http://www.towardfreedom.com/labor/2673-combating-slavery-in-coffee-and-chocolate-production).

Nancy Brown Diggs. 2011. *Hidden in the Heartland*. East Lansing, MI: Michigan State University Press.

National Alliance to End Homelessness. 2012. "The State of Homelessness in America 2012." Retrieved July 31, 2012 (www.endhomelessness.org/content/asrticle/detail/4361/).

National Archives and Records Administration. 2008. "What Is the Electoral College?" Retrieved March 21, 2008 (www.archives.gov/federal-register/electoral-college/about.html).

National Center for Education Statistics. 2006. "Revenues and Expenditures for Public Elementary and Secondary Education" (Table 1). National Center for Education Statistics. Retrieved April 17, 2011 (http://nces.ed.gov/ccd/pubs/npefs03/tables.asp).

National Center for Education Statistics. 2011. "ACT Score Averages and Standard Deviations, by Sex and Race/Ethnicity, and Percentage of ACT Test Takers, by Selected Composite Score Ranges and Planned Fields of Study: Selected Years, 1995 through 2010" (Table 155). *Digest of Education Statistics.* Retrieved September 14, 2012 (http://nces.ed.gov/programs/digest/d10/tables/dt10_155.asp).

National Center for Education Statistics. 2012a. "Higher Education: Gaps in Assess and Persistence Study." Indicator 24: College Entrance Exams. Retrieved September 14, 2012 (http://nces.ed.gov/pubs2012/2012046/chapter 4_8.asp).

National Center for Education Statistics. 2012b. "Postsecondary Graduation Rates." Retrieved September 12, 2012 (http://nces.ed.gov/programs/coe/indicator_pgr.asp).

National Center for Health Statistics. 2011. *Health, United States, 2007: With Chartbook on Trends in the Health of Americans.* Hyattsville, MD: Author.

National Center for Injury Prevention and Control. 2011. "The National Intimate Partner and Sexual Violence Survey: 2010." Atlanta, GA: Centers for Disease Control and Prevention, November. Retrieved May 29, 2012 (www.cdc.gov/ViolencePrevention/pdf/NISVS_Executive_Summary-a.pdf).

National Center for Victims of Crime. 2011. "Terrorism." August 25. Retrieved April 13, 2012 (www.ncvc.org/ncvc/main.aspx?dbName=DocumentViewer&DocumentID=47702).

National Coalition on Health Care. 2008. "Health Insurance Cost." Retrieved April 17, 2010 (www.nchc.org OR www.whitehouse2.org/. . ./305-facts-from-the-national-coalition-on-health-care).

National Conference of State Legislatures. 2012. "Defining Marriage: Defense of Marriage Acts and Same-Sex Marriage Laws." Retrieved June 10, 2012 (www.ncsl.org/issues-research/human-services/same-sex-marriage-overview.aspx).

National Conference of State Legislatures. 2012 "State Laws Regarding Marriages Between First Cousins." Retrieved June 20, 2012 (www.ncsl.org/issues-research/human-services/state-laws-regarding-marriages-between-first-cousi.aspx).

National Council of La Raza. 2011. "Who Makes Up the U.S. Hispanic Population?" Retrieved January 21, 2013 (www.nclr.org/index.php/about_us/faqs/most_frequently_asked_questions_about_hispanics_in_the_us/).

National Geographic Society. December 8, 2011. "7 Billion." Retrieved February 25, 2012 (http://itunes.apple.com/us/aoo/7-billion/id473524096?mt=8).

National Health Service Corps. 2011. "Mission and History." U.S. Department of Health and Human Services." Retrieved July 17, 2012 (http://nhsc.hrsa.gov/corpsexperience/aboutus/missionhistory/index.html).

National Institutes of Health. 2007. "The Use of Complementary and Alternative Medicine in the United States." Retrieved April 4, 2008 (http://nccam.nih.gov/news/camsurvey_fs1.htm).

National Institutes of Health. 2008. "10 Most Common CAM Therapies Among Adults." Retrieved February 9, 2013 (http://nccam.nih.gov/sites/nccam.nih.gov/files/news/camstats/2007/72_dpi_CHARTS/chart4.htm).

National Institutes of Health. 2012. "Stem Cell Information: Stem Cell Basics." February 13. Retrieved March 7, 2012 (http://stemcells.nih.gov/info/basics/basics4.asp).

National Marriage Project. 2012. "About the National Marriage Project: Mission." Retrieved October 9, 2012 (http://nationalmarriageproject.org/about/).

National Opinion Research Center. 2010. "More Than 60% of Marriages Break Up Because of Adultery." Retrieved February 28, 2011 (www.norc.uchicago.edu/).

National Postsecondary Education Cooperative. 2004. "How Does Technology Affect Access in Postsecondary Education? What Do We Really Know?" (NPEC 2004–831), prepared by Ronald A. Phipps for NPEC Working Group on Access-Technology. Washington, DC.

National Public Radio. 2008. "Poppy Growing in Afghanistan." *Morning Edition*, February 9.

National Public Radio. 2010. "Affirmative Action: How Far Have We Come?" *All Things Considered*, August 15. Retrieved May 12, 2012 (www.npr.org/templates/story/story.php?storyId=129216337).

National Public Radio. 2011. "Closing Digital Divide." June 29. Retrieved May 18, 2012 (www.npr.org/2011/06/29/137499299/closing-digital-divide-expanding-digital-literacy).

National Science Foundation. 2005. *Children, TV, Computers and More Media: New Research Shows Pluses, Minuses.* Retrieved July 20, 2006 (www.eurekalert.org/pub_releases/2005-02/nsf-ctc021005.php).

National Vital Statistics System, Centers for Disease Control and Prevention. 2011. "National Marriage and Divorce Rate Trends." Retrieved April 12, 2011 (www.cdc.gov/nchs/nvss/marriage_divorce_tables.htm).

National Women's Law Center. 2012. "Health Care and Reproductive Rights." July 5. Retrieved July 9, 2012 (www.nwlc.org/repro).

Nationmaster. 2010. "Crime Stats: China vs. Cuba." Retrieved July 5, 2011 (www.nationmaster.com/compare/China/Cuba/Crime).

Nationmaster. 2011. "United States Population Pyramids." Retrieved May 19, 2011 (www.nationmaster.com/country/us/Age_distribution).

NationMaster.com. 2012. "Physicians Per 1,000 People." Retrieved August 30, 2012 (http://www.nationmaster.com/graph/hea_phy_per_1000_peo-physicians-per-1-000-people).

Neuman, Michelle J. 2005. "Global Early Care and Education: Challenges, Responses, and Lessons." *Phi Delta Kappan* (November):188–92.

Neurological Correlates. 2008. "The 30% on Medicare Spent of Last-Year-of-Life Care: Let's Not Forget We're Humans." Retrieved January 8, 2010 (neurologicalcorrelates.com/wordpress/2008/03/12/about-30-of-medicare-is-spent-on-end-of-life-care-what-should-we-do-about-it).

Newcombe, Tod. 2012. "Urban Areas Defy Crime Trends." *Governing the State and Localities*, August. Retrieved July 31, 2012 (www.governing.com/columns/urban-notebook/urban-areas-defy-crime-trends.html).

"New Federal Report: Sexual Abuse Plagues U.S. Prisons and Jails." 2010. *Just Detention,* August 26. Retrieved March 8, 2011 (www.businesswire.com/).

Newman, Andy. 2008. "What Women Want (Maybe)." *The New York Times*, June 12):E6.

Newman, David. 2009. *Families: A Sociological Perspective*. New York: McGraw-Hill.

Newman, David M. and Liz Grauerholz. 2002. *Sociology of Families,* 2nd ed. Thousand Oaks, CA: Pine Forge.

Newman, Matthew L., Carla J. Groom, Lori D. Handelman, and James W. Pennebaker. 2008. "Gender Differences in Language Use: An Analysis of 14,000 Text Samples." *Discourse Process* 45:211–36.

Newport, Frank. 2006. "Mormons, Evangelical Protestants, Baptists Top Church Attendance List." Gallup. Retrieved April 17, 2010 (www.gallup.com/. . ./mormons-evangelical-protestants-baptists-top-church-attendance-list.aspx).

Newport, Frank. 2009. "This Christmas, 78% of Americans Identify as Christian." Gallup, December 24. Retrieved September 26, 2012 (www.gallup.com/poll/124793/This-Christmas-78-Americans-Identify-Christian.aspx).

Newport, Frank. 2010. "American's Church Attendance Inches Up in 2010." Gallup, June 25. Retrieved September 20, 2012 (www.gallup.com/poll/141044/americans-church-attendance-inches-2010.aspx).

Newport, Frank. 2012a. "Nearly One in Five Americans Would Not Vote for a Mormon Presidential Candidate." Gallup, June 21. Retrieved September 24, 2012 (www.gallup.com/video/155270/Nearly-One-Five-Americans-Not-Vote-Mormon-Candidate.aspx).

Newport, Frank. 2012b. "The Highly Religious Choose Romney, the Less Religious, Obama." Gallup. Retrieved September 24, 2012 (www.gallup.com/video/154112/Highly-Religious-Choose-Romney-Less-Religious-Obama.aspx).

Newport, Frank. 2012c. "In U.S., 46% Hold Creationist View of Human Origins." Gallup, June 1. Retrieved September 24, 2012 (www.gallup.com/poll/155003/Hold-Creationist-View-Human-Origins.aspx).

Newport, Frank. 2012d. "Hispanic Catholics Pro-Obama; Non-Hispanic Catholics Pro Romney." Gallup, May 1. Retrieved September 24, 2012 (www.gallup.com/poll/154424/ Hispanic-Catholics-Pro-Obama-Non-Hispanic-Catholics-Pro Romney.aspx).

Newport, Frank. 2012e. "More Than Nine in Ten Americans Continue to Believe in God." Gallup. Retrieved September 26, 2012 (www.gallup.com/poll/147887/americans-continue-believe-god.aspx).

Newport, Frank and Elizabeth Mendes. 2009. "About One in Six U.S. Adults Are Without Health Insurance." Gallup, July 22. Retrieved April 7, 2011 (http://www.gallup.com/poll/121820/one-six-adults-without-health-insurance.aspx).

The New York Times. 2008. "Primary Calendar: Democratic Nominating Contests." Retrieved March 30, 2008 (http://politics.nytimes.com/election-guide/2008/primaries/democraticprimaries/index.html).

The New York Times. 2013. "Syria—Uprising and Civil War." Retrieved January 20, 2013 (http://topics.nytimes.com/top/news/international/countriesandterritories/syria/index.html?8qa).

New York Times Almanac. 2011. "Major Languages of the World." New York: Penguin Reference, p. 505.

News of Future. 2012. "1 Million Hydrogen-Fueled Cars in U.S." Retrieved March 7, 2012 (www.newsoffuture.com/million_hydrogen_fueled_cars_in_us_future_energy.html).

Nichols, Larry A., George A. Mather, and Alvin J. Schmidt. *2006 Encyclopedic Dictionary of Cults, Sects, and World Religions*, Revised and updated ed. Grand Rapids, MI: Zondervan.

Nichols, Michelle. 2012 "U.N. Says Haiti Struggling to Cope With Cholera as Aid Withdrawn." *Chicago Tribune,* August 31. Retrieved September 10, 2012 (http://articles.chicagotribune.com/2012-08-31/news/sns-rt-us-haiti-unbre87u1b5-20120831_1_cholera-cases-cholera-outbreak-cholera-epidemic).

Nightingale Alliance. 2007. "Fast Facts." Retrieved January 20, 2008 (www.nightingalealliance.org/cgi-bin/home.pl?section=3).

Niolon, Richard. 2010. "Children of Divorce and Adjustment." *Psych-Page,* September 19. Retrieved June 26, 2012 (www.psychpage.com/family/childrenadjust.html).

Nock, Steven L., Laura Ann Sanchez, and James D. Wright. 2008. *Covenant Marriage: The Movement to Reclaim Tradition in America.* New Brunswick, NJ: Rutgers University Press.

Noel, Donald. 1968. "A Theory of the Origin of Ethnic Stratification." *Social Problems* 16(Fall):157–72.

Noguera, Pedro, and Robby Cohen. 2006. "Patriotism and Accountability: The Role of Educators in the War on Terrorism." *Phi Delta Kappan* 87(8):573–78.

Nolan, Cathal J. 2002. "Terrorism." Pp. 1648–49 and "War" in *The Greenwood Encyclopedia of International Relations.* London: Greenwood.

Nolan, Patrick and Gerhard Lenski. 2008. *Human Societies.* Boulder, CO: Paradigm.

Nolan, Patrick and Gerhard Lenski. 2010. *Human Societies: An Introduction to Macrosociology,* 11th ed. Boulder, CO: Paradigm.

Nolan, Patrick D., Jennifer Triplett, and Shannon McDonough. 2010. "Sociology's Suicide: A Forensic Autopsy." *The American Sociologist* 41:292–305.

No More Deaths. 2012. "Deaths on AZ Border Since October 1, 2011." Retrieved July 30, 2012 (www.nomoredeaths.org/Information/deaths.html).

North American Free Trade Agreement. 2011. "Mexico Is Taking Back Manufacturing Work." *Bloomberg News.* Retrieved May 27, 2012 (www.teamnafta.com/index.php/Latest/2011-Labor-and-Wage-Report-for-Mexico.html).

Noss, David S. and John B. Noss. 1990. *A History of the World's Religions.* New York: Macmillan.

Nuclear Threat Initiative. 2010. "Obama's Nuclear Nonproliferation and Disarmament Agenda: Building Steam or Losing Traction." January 15. Retrieved April 10, 2010 (www.nti.org/e_research/e3_obama_administration_agenda.html).

Oakes, Jeannie. 2005. *Keeping Track: How Schools Structure Inequality*, 2nd ed. New Haven, CT: Yale University Press.

Oakes, Jeannie, Amy Stuart Wells, Makeba Jones, and Amanda Datnow. 1997. "Detracking: The Social Construction of Ability, Cultural Politics, and Resistance to Reform." *Teacher's College Record* 98(3):482–510.

Oberlander, Jonathan. 2002. "The U.S. Health Care System: On a Road to Nowhere?" *Canadian Medical Association Journal* 167(2):163–69.

O'Brien, Denise. 1977. "Female Husbands in Southern Bantu Societies." In *Sexual Stratification: A Cross-Cultural View,* edited by Alice Schlegel. New York: Columbia University Press

O'Brien, Jody. 2011. *The Production of Reality,* 5th ed. Thousand Oaks, CA: Sage

O'Connel, Sanjida. 1993 "Meet My Two Husbands." *Guardian,* March 4, Sec. 2, p. 12.

Occupational Outlook Handbook. 2012. "Agricultural Workers." *Bureau of Labor Statistics.* Retrieved July 30, 2012 (www.bls.gov/ooh/farming-fishing-and forestry/agricultural-workers.html).

OECD Family Database. 2010. "Cohabitation Rate and Prevalence of Other Forms of Partnership." Retrieved June 5, 2012 (www.oecd.org/dataoecd/52/27/41920080/pdf).

Office of Management and Budget. 2010. "Table of United States Metropolitan Statistical Areas." U.S. Census Bureau, March 29. Retrieved July 30, 2012 ().

Ogburn, William F. [1922] 1938. *Social Change, With Respect to Culture and Original Nature.* New York: Viking.

Ogburn, William F. 1933. *Recent Social Trends.* New York: McGraw-Hill.

Ogburn, William F. 1961. "The Hypothesis of Cultural Lag." Pp. 1270–73 in *Theories of Society: Foundations of Modern Sociological Theory,* Vol. 2, edited by Talcott Parsons, Edward Shils, Kaspar D. Naegele, and Jesse R. Pitts. New York: Free Press.

Ogburn, William F. 1964. In *On Culture and Social Change: Selected Papers,* edited by Otis Dudley Duncan. Chicago: University of Chicago Press.

Ogunwole, Stella U., Malcolm P. Drewery, Jr., and Merarys Rios-Vargas. 2012. "The Population with a Bachelor's Degree or Higher by Race and Hispanic Origin: 2006–2010." American Community Survey Briefs, U.S. Census, May. Retrieved February 10, 2013 (http://www.census.gov/prod/2012pubs/acsbr10-19.pdf).

O'Keefe, J. H., and L. Cordain. 2004. "Cardiovascular Disease Resulting From a Diet and Lifestyle at Odds With Our Paleolithic Genome: How to Become a 21st-Century Hunter-Gatherer." *Mayo Clinic Proc.* 79(May):703–704, 707.

Oller, Kimbrough. 2006. "Development and Evolution in Human Vocal Communication." *Biological Theory* 1(4):349–51.

Olsen, Marvin E. 1968. *The Process of Social Organization.* New York: Holt, Rinehart, & Winston.

Olsen, Marvin E. 1970. "Power as a Social Process." Pp. 2–10 in *Power in Societies,* edited by Marvin Olsen. New York: Macmillan.

Olson, C. L., H. D. Schumaker, and B. P. Yawn. 1994. "Overweight Women Delay Medical Care." *Archives of Family Medicine* 3(10).

One in Four, Inc. N.d. Retrieved November 6, 2009 (www.oneinfourusa.org).

One Laptop per Child. 2011. Retrieved March 18, 2011 (http://laptop.org/en/vision/).

Ong, Michael, Elisa K. Tong, Quan Gan, Teh-wei Hu, Yuan Jiang, Yan Yang, and Yi Nan. 2007. "360 Million Smokers in China and High Prevalence of Smoking Among Physicians." *American Journal of Preventative Medicine,* August 8. Retrieved April 17, 2010 (www.news-medical.net/news/2007/08/08/28574.aspx).

Oregon Public Health Division. 2012. "Table 1: Characteristics of End-of-Life Care of 596 DWDA Patients Who Have Died From Ingesting a Lethal Dose of Medication as of February 29, 2012, by Year, Oregon, 1998–2011." Retrieved July 16, 2012 (http://www.compassionoforegon.org/wp-content/uploads/2010/08/year14-tbl-11.pdf).

Oregon's Euthanasia Law. 2010. "Law Library." Retrieved January 11, 2010 (http://law.jrank.org/pages/6602/Euthanasia-Oregon-s-Euthanasia-law.html).

"Organized Crime." 2011. Retrieved August 6, 2011 (http://law.jrank.org/pages/11951/Organized-Crime.html).

Oswald, Ramona Faith. 2000. "A Member of the Wedding? Heterosexism and Family Ritual." *Journal of Social and Personal Relationships* 17(June):349–68.

Oswald, Ramona Faith. 2001. "Religion, Family, and Ritual: The Production of Gay, Lesbian, and Transgendered Outsiders-Within." *Review of Religious Research* 43(December):39–50.

O'Toole, Tara and Donald A. Henderson. 2006. "A Clear and Present Danger: Confronting the Threat of Bioterrorism." Pp. 239–45 in *Globalization: The Transformation of Social Worlds,* edited by D. Stanley Eitzen and Maxine Baca Zinn. Belmont, CA: Wadsworth.

"Overseas Population Spending Threatened." 2006. *Popline* 29 (March/April):1.

Palmer, Craig. 1989. "Is Rape a Cultural Universal? A Re-examination of the Ethnographic Data." *Ethnology* 28(Jan):1–16.

Palmer, Kim. 2012. "Young Home Buyers Seek 'Walkability.'" *Minneapolis Star Tribune,* August 6. Retrieved Aug. 10, 2012 (www.startribune.com/lifestyle/homegarden/164822116.html?refer=y).

Papalia, Diane E., Sally Wendkos Olds, and Ruth Duskin Feldman. 2006. *A Child's World: Infancy Through Adolescence,* 10th ed. Boston: McGraw-Hill.

Pareto, Vilfredo. [1911] 1955. "Mathematical Economics." In *Encyclopedie des Sciences Mathematique.* New York: Macmillan.

Park, Robert Ezra, Ernest W. Burgess, and Roderick D. McKenzie. [1925] 1967. *The City.* Chicago: University of Chicago Press.

Parkinson, C. Northcote. 1957. *Parkinson's Law.* Boston: Houghton Mifflin.

Parsons, Talcott. 1951a. *The Social System.* New York: Free Press.

Parsons, Talcott. 1951b. *Toward a General Theory of Action.* New York: Harper & Row.

Parsons, Talcott. 1975. "The Sick Role and Role of the Physician Reconsidered." *Milbank Memorial Fund Quarterly* 53(3):257–78.

Parsons, Talcott, and Robert F. Bales. 1953. *Family, Socialization, and Interaction Process.* Glencoe, IL: Free Press.

Passel, Jeffrey and D'Vera Cohn. 2012. "U.S. Foreign-Born Population: How Much Change From 2009 to 2010?" Pew Research Center, January 9. Retrieved July 30, 2012 (www.pewhispanic.org/2012/01/09/u-s-foreign-born-population-how-much-change-from-2009-to-2010/).

Paulhus, D. L., P. D. Trapnell, and D. Chen. 1999. *Birth Order Effects on Personality and Achievement Within Families.* Malden, MA: Blackwell.

Paxton, Pamela and Tess Pearce. 2009. "How Does Social Class Affect Socialization Within The Family?" Exploring Social Science Research, April 24. Retrieved March 1, 2011 (http://ibssblog.wordpress.com/2009/04/24/how-dues-social-class-affect-socialisation-within-the-family/).

Paxton, Pamela and Melanie M. Hughes. 2007. *Women, Politics, and Power: A Global Perspective.* Thousand Oaks, CA: Pine Forge.

PBS. 2012. "World's Biggest Congregation" *Religion and Ethics Newsweekly,* August 10. Retrieved October 3, 2012 (www.pbs.org/wnet/religionandethics/episodes/january-27-2012/worlds-biggest-congregation/10162/).

PBS Newshour. 2009. "Comparing International Health Care Systems." October 6. Retrieved January 25, 2010 (www.pbs.org/newshour/globalhealth/july-dec09/insurance_1006.html).

PBS NOW. 2009. "Africa: House Calls and Health Care." December 18.

Pearce, Fred. 2010. "As Longevity Grows, The World Might Become a Better Place." *Washington Post,* May 25. Retrieved July 28, 2011 (www.washingtonpost.com/wp-dyn/content/article/2010/05/24/AR2010052402607.html).

Peek, Lori. 2011. *Behind the Backlash: Muslim Americans After 9/11.* Philadelphia: Temple University Press.

Pellow, David Naguib. 2002. *Garbage Wars: The Struggle for Environmental Justice in Chicago.* Cambridge: MIT Press.

People's Daily Online. 2011. March 11. Retrieved May 15, 2012 (http://english.peopledaily.com.cn/90001/98649/7315789.html).

Perez, Miguel. 2011. "The Latino Backlash Is Coming Sooner Than Republicans Expected." April 6. Retrieved April 7, 2011 (http://www.paragoulddailypress.com/articles/2011/04/06/opinion/doc4d9ba4c6c2ef4312670875.txt).

Persell, Caroline Hodges. 2005. "Race, Education, and Inequality." pp. 286–24 in *Blackwell Companion to Social Inequalities,* edited by M. Romero and E. Margolis. Oxford, UK: Blackwell.

Persell, Caroline Hodges and Peter W. Cookson, Jr. 1985. "Chartering and Bartering: Elite Education and Social Reproduction." *Social Problems* 33(2):114–29.

Pescosolido, Bernice A., 1992. "Beyond Rational Choice: The Social Dynamics of How People Seek Help." *American Journal of Sociology* 97(4):1113.

Pescosolido, Bernice A. and Carol A. Boyer. 2010. "The American Health Care System: Beginning the 21st Century With High Risk, Major Challenges, And Great Opportunities." Pp. 391–411 in *The New Blackwell Companion to Medical Sociology,* edited by William C. Cockerham. Malden, MA: Wiley-Blackwell.

Pescosolido, Bernice A. and Sharon Georgianna. 1989. "Durkheim, Suicide, and Religion: Toward a Network Theory of Suicide." *American Sociological Review* 54(February):33–48.

Pettigrew, Thomas F. and Linda R. Tropp. 2000. "Does Intergroup Contact Reduce Prejudice? Recent Meta-Analytic Findings." Pp. 93–114 in *Reducing Prejudice and Discrimination,* edited by Stuart Oskamp. London: Psychology Press, Taylor and Francis Group.

Pew Center on the States. 2011. "State of Recidivism: The Revolving Door of American Prisons." The Per Charitable Trusts, April 3, p. 2. Retrieved April 16, 2012 (www.percenteronthestates.org/initiatives_detail.aspx?initiativeID).

Pew Forum on Religion and Public Life. 2008. "U.S. Religious Landscape Survey, 2008." Retrieved March 2, 2008 (http://religions.pewforum.org/pdf/report-religious-landscape-study-full.pdf).

Pew Forum on Religion and Pubic Life. 2009. "Most Latino Evangelicals Pray Every Day." June 11. Retrieved September 26, 2012 (www.pewforum.org/Frequency-of-Prayer/Most-Latino-Evangelicals-Pray-Every-Day.aspx).

Pew Forum on Religion and Public Life. 2012a. "'Nones' on the Rise: One-in-Five Adults Have No Religious Affiliation." Retrieved October 10, 2012 (www.pewforum.org/uploadedFiles/Topics/Religious_Affiliation/Unaffiliated/NonesOnTheRise-full.pdf October 9).

Pew Forum on Religion and Public Life. 2012b. "U.S. Religious Landscape Survey." September 18. Retrieved September 18, 2012 (http://religions.pewforum.org/reports).

Pew Hispanic Center. 2011. "Hispanics Account for 56% of Nation's Growth in Past Decade." Retrieved April 7, 2011 (http://pewhispanic.org/).

Pew Internet and American Life Project. 2010. "Change in Internet Access by Age Group, 2000–2009." February 3. Retrieved February 27, 2011 (www.pewinternet.org/Infographics/2010/Internet-access-by-age-group-over-time.aspx).

Pew Internet and American Life Project. 2012. "Demographics of Internet Users." Retrieved March 5, 2012 (http://www.pewinternet.org/Static-Pages/trend-Data/Whos-Online.aspx).

Pew Research Center. 2010. "The Decline of Marriage and Rise of New Families." *Pew Social & Demographic Trends,* November 18. Retrieved March 8, 2012 (www.pewsocialtrends.org/2010/11/18/the-decline-of-marriage-and-rise-of-new-families/).

Pew Research Center. 2011. "The Generation Gap and the 2012 Election." November 3. Retrieved July 29, 2012 (www.people-press.org/2011/11/03/section-1-how-generations-have-changed/).

Phipher, Mary. 1994. *Reviving Ophelia: Saving the Selves of Adolescent Girls.* New York: Ballantine Books.

Phoenix Declaration. 2012. "A New Declaration for a New Decade." Retrieved September 20, 2012 (www.nolongersilent.org/Phoenix-Declaration-2012.html).

Phys.Org. 2009. "Humans Spread Out of Africa Later." Retrieved October 9, 2012 (http://phys.org/news171286860.html).

Piaget, Jean. 1989. *The Child's Conception of the World.* Savage, MD: Littlefield, Adams Quality Paperbacks.

Piaget, Jean, and Barbel Inhelder. [1955] 1999. *Growth of Logical Thinking.* London: Routledge & Kegan Paul.

Pickard, Ruth, and Daryl Poole. 2007. "The Study of Society and the Practice of Sociology." Previously unpublished essay.

Pieterse, Jan Nederveen. 2004. *Globalization and Culture.* Lanham, MD: Rowman & Littlefield.

Pilkington, Ed. 2012. "Mexican Immigration Falls for First Time in 4 Decades." The Guardian April 23. Retrieved May 16, 2012 (www.guardian.co.uk/world/2012/apr/23/illegal-immigrants-mexico-us-economy).

"Plan for Lifetime Success Through Education." 2008. Retrieved April 17, 2010 (www.barackobama.com/pdf/issues/Prek-12Education FactSheet.pdf; www.americanthinker.com/2008/. . ./obamas_national_public_educati.html).

Plant, Hanna. 2007. "The Challenges of Health Care in Cuba." Retrieved January 8, 2010 (www.global-politics.co.uk/issue9/hanna).

Plato. [ca. 350 BCE] 1960. *The Laws.* New York: Dutton.

Ploughshares. 2011. "Armed Conflicts Report." Retrieved July 13, 2012 (www.ploughshares.ca/content/armed-conflicts-report-0).

PolitiFact.com. 2009. "Coburn Says 20% of Every Medicare Dollar Goes to Fraud." Retrieved April 13, 2012 (www.politifact.com/truth-o-meter/statements/2009/aug/27/tom-coburn/coburn-says-20-percent-of-every-medicare-dollar-goes-to-fraud).

Pollack, William. 1999. *Real Boys: Rescuing Our Sons From the Myths of Boyhood.* New York: Owl Books.

Pollard, Kelvin. 2011. "The Gender Gap in College Enrollment and Graduation." *Population Reference Bureau.* Retrieved September 12, 2012 (www.prb.org/Articles/2011/gender-gap-in-education.aspx).

Popenoe, David. 2002. "Debunking Divorce Myths." *National Marriage Project.* New Brunswick, NJ: Rutgers. Retrieved November 30, 2009 (health.discovery.com/centers/loverelationships/articles/divorce.html).

Population Reference Bureau. 2010a. "World Population Clock." Retrieved May 13, 2011 (www.prb.org/Articles/2010/worldpopulationclock2010.aspx).

Population Reference Bureau. 2010b. "World Population Data Sheet." Retrieved July 27, 2011 (www.prb.org/pdf10/10wpds_eng.pdf).

Population Reference Bureau. 2011a. "Human Population: Women." Retrieved December 22, 2011 (www.prb.org/Educators/TeachersGuides/HumanPopulation/Women.aspx).

Population Reference Bureau. 2012a. "Fact Sheet: World Population Trends 2012." Retrieved August 25, 2012 (www.prb.org/Publications/Datasheets/2012/world-population-data-sheet/fact-sheet-world-population.aspx).

Population Reference Bureau. 2012b. "Human Population: Women." Retrieved August 25, 2012 (www.prb.org/educators/teachers guides/humanpopulation/women.aspx).

Population Reference Bureau. 2012c. "Population Reference Bureau's Population Clock." Retrieved August 23, 2012 (www.prb.org/Publications/Datasheets/2012/world-population-data-sheet/population-clock.aspx).

Population Reference Bureau. 2012d. "World Population Data Sheet." Retrieved August 25, 2012 (www.prb.org/pdf12/2012-population-data-sheet_eng.pdf).

Population Reference Bureau. 2013a. "Total Fertility Rate, 2012." Retrieved February 7, 2013 (http://www.prb.org/DataFinder/Topic/Rankings.aspx?ind=17).

Population Reference Bureau. 2013b. "World Population Growth, 1950–2050: Exponential Growth." Retrieved February 5, 2013 (www.prb.org/Educators/TeachersGuides/HumanPopulation/PopulationGrowth.aspx).

Powell, Andrea D. and Arnold S. Kahn. 1995. "Racial Differences in Women's Desires to Be Thin." *International Journal of Eating Disorders* 17(2):191–95.

Powell, Brian, Catherine Bolzendahl, Claudia Geist, and Lala Carr Steelman. 2010. *Counted Out: Same-Sex Relations and Americans' Definitions of Family.* New York: Russell Sage Foundation.

Powley, Elizabeth. 2003. "Strengthening Governance: The Role of Women in Rwanda's Transition." In *Women Waging Peace,* edited by S. N. Anderlini. Washington, DC: Hunt Alternatives Fund.

Preston, David L. 1988. *The Social Organization of Zen Practice: Constructing Transcultural Reality.* Cambridge, UK: Cambridge University Press.

Preston, Jennifer. 2011. "The Year in Media: Social Media and Egypt's Revolution." Media Decoder Weblog, *New York Times,* December 21. Retrieved October 6, 2012 (http://mediade coder.blogs.nytimes.com).

Project Vote Smart. 2008. "State Presidential Primary and Caucus Dates." Retrieved April 17, 2010 (www.votesmart.org/election_president_state_primary_dates.php).

Proudman, Charlotte Rachael. 2012 "Sex and Sharia: Muslim Women Punished for Failed Marriages." *The Independent,* April 2. Retrieved May 24, 2012 (http://blogs.independent .co.uk/2012/04/02/sex-and-sharia-muslim-women-punished-for-failed-marriages/).

Putnam, Robert. 2001. *Bowling Alone: The Collapse and Revival of American Community.* New York: Simon & Schuster.

Pyle, Ralph E. 2006. "Trends in Religious Stratification: Have Religious Group Socioeconomic Distinctions Declined in Recent Decades?" *Sociology of Religion* 67(Spring):61–79.

Quesnal-Vallee and Jenkins. 2010. "Social Policies and Health Inequalities." Pp. 455–83 in *The New Blackwell Companion to Medical Sociology,* edited by William C. Cockerham. Malden, MA: Wiley/Blackwell.

Quinney, Richard. 2002. *Critique of Legal Order: Crime Control in Capitalist Society.* New Brunswick, NJ: Transaction.

Radcliffe-Brown, A. R. 1935. "On the Concept of Functional in Social Science." *American Anthropologist* 37(3):394–402.

Radelet, Michael L. and Traci L. Lacock. 2009. "Do Executions Lower Homicide Rates? The Views of Leading Criminologists." *The Journal of Criminal Laws and Criminology* 99(2).

Randerson, James. 2008. "Cutting TV Time Makes Children Healthier, Says U.S. Study." *The Guardian,* March 4.

Rani, M., S. Bonu, and N. Diop-Sidibe. 2004. "An Empirical Investigation of Attitudes Towards Wife-beating Among Men and Women in Seven Sub-Saharan African Countries." *African Journal of Reproductive Health* 8(3):116–36.

Rankin, Bruce H. and Is¸ik A. Aytaç. 2006. "Gender Inequality in Schooling: The Case of Turkey." *Sociology of Education* 79(1):25–43.

Ranu, Manju, Sekhur Bonu, and Nafissalon Diop-Sidibe. 2004. "An Empirical Investigation of Attitudes Towards Wife-Beating Among Men and Women in Seven Sub-Saharan African Countries." *African Journal of Reproductive Health.* Women's Health and Action Research Centre. Retrieved June 3, 2012 (www.jstor.org/discover/10.2307/3583398?uid=3739840&uid=2129&uid=2&uid=70&uid=4&uid=3739256&sid=56228966303).

Rappoport, Leon. 2003. *How We Eat: Appetite, Culture and the Psychology of Food.* Toronto, Ontario, Canada: ECW Press.

Read, Kristen. 2011. "Number of Internet Users Worldwide Climbs to 2 Billion." UN International Telecommunications Union, January 28. Retrieved March 18, 2011 (http://graphicartsmag .com/news/2011/01/number-of=internet-users-worldwide).

Reason. 2011. "In-Depth Study: After Divorce, 44% of Women Fell Into Poverty." *Family Research Council,* May 31. Retrieved June 6, 2012 (http://primacyofreason.blogspot.com/2011/05/in-depth-study-after-divorce-44-of_31.html).

Regnerus, Mark D. 2007. *Forbidden Fruit: Sex and Religion in the Lives of American Teenagers.* New York: Oxford University Press.

Reid, T. R. 2009. *The Healing of America: A Global Quest for Better, Cheaper and Fairer Health Care.* New York: Penguin Press.

Reid, Scott A. and Sik Hung Ng. 2006. "The Dynamics of Intragroup Differentiation in an Intergroup Social Context." *Human Communication Research* 32:504–525.

Reiman, Jeffrey and Paul Leighton. 2010a. *The Rich Get Richer and the Poor Get Prison: Ideology, Class, and Criminal Justice,* 9th ed. Boston: Pearson.

Reiman, Jeffrey and Paul Leighton. 2010b. *The Rich Get Richer and the Poor Get Prison: A Reader.* Boston: Allyn & Bacon.

Reinhardt, Uwe E. 2008. "Why Does U.S. Health Care Cost So Much? (Part II: Indefensible Administrative Costs)." *New York Times,* November 21. Retrieved August 28, 2012 (http://economix .blogs.nytimes.com/2008/11/21/why-does-us-health-care-cost-so-much-part-ii-indefensible-administrative-costs/).

Religious Congregations and Membership Study. 2010. "2010 U.S. Religion Census." Retrieved September 25, 2012 (www .rcms2010.org/compare.php).

Religious Tolerance. 2006. "Trends Among Christians in the U.S." Retrieved December 13, 2009 (www.religioustolerance.org/chr_tren.htm).

Religious Tolerance. 2009a. "U.S. Divorce Rates for Various Faith Groups, Age Groups, and Geographic Areas." Retrieved April 17, 2010 (www.religious tolerance.org/chr_dira.htm).

Religious Tolerance. 2010. "Stem Cell Research: All Viewpoints." Retrieved September 8, 2012 (www.religioustolerance.org/res_stem.htm).

Religious Tolerance. 2012. "The Status of Women, Currently and Throughout History." Retrieved November 30, 2012 (http://www.religioustolerance.org/women.htm).

Religious Worlds. 2007. "New Religious Movements." Retrieved August 14, 2008 (www.religiousworlds.com/newreligions.html).

Renick, Oliver. 2011. "Disconnected: 70 Percent of World Doesn't Have Internet, Despite Rising Phone Usage." *Laptop*, October 31. Retrieved May 18, 2012 (http://blog.laptopmag.com/disconnected-70-percent-of-world-doesn%E2%80%99t-have-internet-despite-rising-phone-usage).

Renzetti, Claire. 2003. "Urban Violence Against Women." *Speech*, September 30, Dayton, OH: Wright State University.

Reproductive Health Matters. 2011. "Pro-Natalist Policies in Eastern Europe Hit Young Women Hard." August 19. Retrieved July 28, 2012 (www.rhmjournal.org.uk/news.php?newsID=952).

Residents of Hull House. [ca. 1895] 1970. *Hull House Maps and Papers*. New York: Arno.

Reuters. 2011. "France Starts Ban on Full-Face Veil, Factbox on Veils In Europe." Reuters, April 11. Retrieved May 25, 2012 (http://blogs.reuters.com/faithworld/2011/04/11/france-starts-ban-on-full-face-veil-factbox-on-veils-in-europe/).

Reuters. 2012. "91 Are Charged With Fraud, Billing Millions to Medicare." *The New York Times*, October 4. Retrieved October 6, 2012 (www.nytimes.com/2012/10/05/business/medicare-fraud-charged-against-91.html).

Richardson, John. 2010. "Workfare Program Makes Welfare Work." October 18. Retrieved May 17, 2012 (www.onlinesentinel.com/news/workfare-programmakes-welfare-work_2010-10-17.html).

Rideout, Victoria J., Ulla G. Foehr, and Donald F. Roberts. 2010. "Generation M2: Media in the Lives of 8- To 18-Year-Olds." A Kaiser Family Foundation Study, January. Retrieved March 2, 2011 (www.kff.org/entmedia/upload/8010.pdf).

Riehl, Carolyn. 2001. "Bridges to the Future: Contributions of Qualitative Research to the Sociology of Education." *Sociology of Education* (Extra Issue):115–34.

Ries, L. A. G., M. P. Eisner, C. L. Kossary, B. F. Hankey, B. A. Miller, and B. K. Edwards, eds. 2000. *SEER Cancer Statistics Review, 1973–1997*. Bethesda, MD: National Cancer Institute.

Riley, Charles. 2011. "One California Budget Fix: Abolish Death Row." CNN Money, June 20. Retrieved April 16, 2012 (http://money.cnn.com/2011/06/20/news/economy/california_death-penalty/index.htm).

Riordan, Cornelius. 2004. *Equality and Achievement: An Introduction to the Sociology of Education*. Upper Saddle River, NJ: Prentice Hall.

Ritzer, George. 2007. *The Globalization of Nothing*, 5th ed. Thousand Oaks, CA: Pine Forge.

Ritzer, George. 2011. *The Globalization of Nothing*. Thousand Oaks, CA: Pine Forge.

Ritzer, George. 2013a. *Introduction to Sociology*. Thousand Oaks, CA: Sage.

Ritzer, George. 2013b. *The McDonaldization of Society*, 20th anniversary edition. Thousand Oaks, CA: Sage.

Ritzer, George and Douglas J. Goodman. 2004. *Sociological Theory*, 6th ed. New York: McGraw-Hill.

Roach, Ronald. 2004. "Survey Reveals 10 Biggest Trends in Internet Use." *Black Issues in Higher Education*, October 21.

Robbins, Mandy. 1998. "A Different Voice: A Different View." *Review of Religious Research* 40(1):75–80.

Robbins, Richard H. 2011 *Global Problems and the Culture of Capitalism*, 5th ed. Upper Saddle River NJ: Prentice Hall.

Roberts, Dorothy. 1997. *Killing the Black Body: Race, Reproduction, and the Meaning of Liberty*. New York: Pantheon.

Roberts, Dorothy. 2002. *Shattered Bonds: The Color of Child Welfare*. New York: Basic Books.

Roberts, Judith C. and Keith A. Roberts. 2008. "Deep Reading, Cost/Benefit, and the Construction of Meaning: Enhancing Reading Comprehension and Deep Learning in Sociology Courses." *Teaching Sociology* 36(April):125–40.

Roberts, Keith A. 2003. *Interviews With Ohio Residents in Communities Considering Tax Levies*. Unpublished manuscript.

Roberts, Keith A. and Karen A. Donahue. 2000. "Professing Professionalism: Bureaucratization and Deprofessionalization in the Academy," *Sociological Focus* 33(4):365–83.

Roberts, Keith A. and David Yamane. 2012 *Religion in Sociological Perspective*, 5th ed. Thousand Oaks, CA: SAGE/Pine Forge Press.

Robertson, Roland. 1992. *Globalization: Social Theory and Global Culture*. London: Sage.

Robertson, Roland. 1997. "Social Theory, Cultural Relativity and the Problem of Globality." Pp. 69–90 in *Culture, Globalization and the World System*, edited by Anthony King. Minneapolis: University of Minnesota Press.

Robillard, Kevin. 2012. "Study: Youth Vote Was Decisive." *Politico*, November 7. Retrieved November 1, 2012 (www.politico.com/news/stories/1112/83510.html).

The Robinhood Tax. 2010. Retrieved February 10, 2013 (http://robinhoodtax.org/).

Robinson, Bruce. 2007. "Physician Assisted Suicide." *Religious Tolerance*, June 2. Retrieved October 20, 2009 (www.religioustolerance.org/euth_us2htm).

Rodricks, Dan. 2012. "Catholics, Contraception and the Heretic Faithful." *The Baltimore Sun*, February 8. Retrieved Feb. 5, 2013 (http://articles.baltimoresun.com/2012-02-08/news/bs-ed-rodricks-catholics-20120208_1_cafeteria-catholics-church-leaders-protest-catholic-identity).

Rodriguez, Eric M. and S. C. Ouellette. 2000. "Gay and Lesbian Christians: Homosexual and Religious Identity Integration in the Members of a Gay-Positive Church." *Journal for the Scientific Study of Religion* 39(3):333–47.

Roethlisberger, Fritz J. and William J. Dickson. 1939. *Management and the Worker*. Cambridge, MA: Harvard University Press.

Roisen, Ron. 2012. "Mrs. Marty Mann and the Early Medicalization of Alcoholism." *The Atlantic*, February 22. Retrieved July 16, 2012 (www.theatlantic.com/health/archive/2012/02/mrs-marty-mann-and-the-early-medicalization-of-alcoholism/252286/).

Roksa, Josipa and Daniel Potter. 2011. "Parenting and Academic Achievement: Intergenerational Transmission of Educational Advantage." *Sociology of Education* 84(October):299–321.

Roof, Wade Clark. 1999. *Spiritual Marketplace: Baby Boomers and the Remaking of American Religion*. Princeton, NJ: Princeton University Press.

Rosen, Karen. 2007. "Women Still Lag in College Sports." June 6. Retrieved March 7, 2008 (www.oxfordpress.com/sports/content/shared/sports/stories/2007/WOMEN_SPORTS_0606_COX.html).

Rosenbaum, James E. 1999. "If Tracking Is Bad, Is Detracking Better? A Study of a Detracked High School." *American Schools* (Winter):24–47.

Rosenberg, Matt. 2012. "Maquiladoras in Mexico: Export Assembly Plants for the United States." *About.com Geography*. Retrieved May 28, 2012 (http://geography.about.com/od/urbaneconomicgeography/a/maquiladoras.htm).

Rosenthal, Robert and Lenore Jacobson. 1968. *Pygmalion in the Classroom*. New York: Holt, Rinehart & Winston.

Rossi, Alice S. 1984. "Gender and Parenthood." *American Sociological Review* 49(February):1–19.

Rossides, Daniel W. 1997. *Social Stratification: The Interplay of Class, Race, and Gender.* Englewood Cliffs, NJ: Prentice Hall.

Rothbard, Nancy P. and Jeanne M. Brett. 2000. "Promote Equal Opportunity by Recognizing Gender Differences in the Experience of Work and Family." In *The Blackwell Handbook of Principles of Organizational Behavior,* edited by Edwin A. Locke. Malden, MA: Blackwell.

Rothenberg, Paula S. 2006. *Beyond Borders: Thinking Critically About Global Issues.* New York: Worth.

Rothenberg, Paula S. 2010. *Race, Class, and Gender in the United States: An Integrated Study,* 8th ed. New York: Worth.

Rothenberg, Paula S. 2011. *White Privilege: Essential Readings on the Other Side of Racism,* 3rd ed. New York: Worth Publishers.

Rothkopf, David. 2012. "Two Septembers." Pp. 100–103 in *Globalization: The Transformation of Social Worlds*, 3rd ed., edited by D. Stanley Eitzen and Maxine Baca Zinn. Belmont, CA: Wadsworth.

Rothman, Robert A. 2005. *Inequality and Stratification: Race, Class, and Gender,* 5th ed. Englewood Cliffs, NJ: Prentice Hall.

The Royal Society. 2012. *People and the Planet.* April. Retrieved July 31, 2012 (royalsociety.org/uploadedFiles/Royal_Society_Content/policy/projects/people-planet/2012-04-25-PeoplePlanet.pdf).

Rubenstein, Grace. 2007. "Computers for Peace: The $100 Laptop." Retrieved April 21, 2009 (www.edutopia.org/computers-peace).

Rubin, Beth C. 2008. "Detracking in Context: How Local Constructions of Ability Complicate Equity-Geared Reform." *Teachers College Record* 110(3):646–99.

Rubin, Jeffrey Z. 1974. "The Eye of the Beholder: Parents' Views on Sex of Newborns." *American Journal of Orthopsychiatry* 44(4):512–19.

Rubin, Richard. 2012. "Romney's 47% Comments Distance Him from Bush-Era Republicans." *San Francisco Chronicle,* September 18. Retrieved September 24, 2012 (www.sfgate.com/business/bloomberg/article/Romney-s-47-Comments-Distance-Him-From-3875115.php).

Rumbaut, Ruben G. and Alejandro Portes. 2001. *Ethnicities: Children of Immigrants in America.* Los Angeles: University of California Press.

Rusere, Patience. 2009. "Rainy Season Brings New Cholera Outbreaks in Zimbabwe, Five Deaths Reported." *Voice of America News,* November 16. Retrieved December 20, 2009 (www1.voanews.com/zimbabwe/news/a-13-56-74-2009-11-16-voa48-70422597.html).

Ryan, Paul, Eric Cantor, and Kevin McCarthy. 2010. *Young Guns: A New Generation of Conservative Leaders.* New York: Simon and Schuster.

Rydgren, Jens. 2004. "Mechanisms of Exclusion: Ethnic Discrimination in the Swedish Labour Market." *Journal of Ethnic and Migration Studies* 30(4):687–716.

Saad, Lydia. 2010. "Americans' Acceptance of Gay Relations Crosses 50% Threshold." Gallup Politics, May 25. Retrieved May 27, 2012 (www.gallup.com/poll/135764/americans-acceptance-gay-relations-crosses-threshold.aspx).

Saad, Lydia. 2012. "U.S. Confidence in Organized Religion at Low Point." *Gallup Politics,* July 12. Retrieved September 20, 2012 (www.gallup.com/poll/155690/confidence-organized-religion-low-point.aspx).

Sabol, William J., Heather C. West, and Matthew Cooper. 2009. "Prisoners in 2008." *Bureau of Justice Statistics Bulletin.* U.S. Department of Justice, December. Retrieved December 20, 2009 (bjs.ojp.usdoj.gov/content/pub/pdf/p08.pdf).

Sachoff, Mike. 2008. "18% of U.S. Households Have No Internet Access." WebProNews.com, May. Retrieved February 27, 2011 (http://www.webpronews.com/18-of-us-households-have-no-internet-access-2008-05).

Sadker, Myra and David Sadker. 2005. *Teachers, Schools, and Society,* 7th ed. New York: McGraw-Hill.

Sadovnik, Alan R. 2007. *Sociology of Education: A Critical Reader.* New York: Routledge.

Safdar, Khadeeja. 2012. "Median Income Falling, Even as More Find Jobs." *The Huffington Post,* March 7. Retrieved May 16, 2012 (www.huffingtonpost.com/2012/03/07/media-income-2011_n_1324859.html).

Sage, George H. 2005. "Racial Inequality and Sport." Pp. 266–75 in *Sport in Contemporary Society,* 7th ed., edited by Stanley D. Eitzen. Boulder, CO: Paradigm.

Sager, Ira, Ben Elgin, Peter Elstrom, Faith Keenan, and Pallavi Gogoi. 2006. "The Underground Web." Pp. 261–70 in *Globalization: The Transformation of Social Worlds,* edited by D. Stanley Eitzen and Maxine Baca Zinn. Belmont, CA: Wadsworth.

Saha, Lawrence and A. Gary Dworkin. 2006. "Educational Attainment and Job Status: The Role of Status Inconsistency on Occupational Burnout." Paper presented at the International Sociological Association, July 23–29, Durban, South Africa.

Saharan Vibe. 2007. "Wodaabe Beauty Ceremony." February 19. Retrieved November 6, 2009 (saharanvibe.blogspot.com/2007/02/wodaabe-beauty-ceremony.html).

Salzman, Marian and Ira Matathia. 2000. "Lifestyles of the Next Millennium: 65 Forecasts." Pp. 466–71 in *Sociological Footprints,* edited by Leonard Cargan and Jeanne Ballantine. Belmont, CA: Wadsworth.

Salzman, Michael B. 2008. "Globalization, Religious Fundamentalism and the Need for Meaning." *International Journal of Intercultural Relations* 32(July):318–27.

Samovar, Larry A. and Richard E. Porter. 2003. *Intercultural Communication.* Belmont, CA: Wadsworth.

Sanday, Peggy Reeves. 1996. *A Woman Scorned: Acquaintance Rape on Trial.* Berkeley: University of California Press.

Sanday, Peggy Reeves. 2007. *Fraternity Gang Rape: Sex, Brotherhood, and Privilege on Campus.* New York: New York University Press.

Sanday, Peggy and Ruth Gallagher Goodenough, eds. 1990. *Beyond the Second Sex.* Philadelphia: University of Pennsylvania Press.

Sandberg, Sheryl. 2013. *Lean In: Women, Work, and the Will to Lead.* New York: Alfred A. Knopf.

Sapir, Edward. 1929. "The Status of Linguistics as a Science." *Language* 5:207–214.

Sapir, Edward. 1949. In *Selected Writings of Edward Sapir in Language, Culture, and Personality,* edited by David G. Mandelbaum. Berkeley: University of California Press.

Sapiro, Virginia. 2003. *Women in American Society: An Introduction to Women's Studies,* 5th ed. Mountain View, CA: Mayfield.

Sapolsky, Robert. 2011. "The Trouble With Testosterone." In *The Kaleidoscope of Gender,* 3rd ed., edited by Joan Z. Spade and Catherine G. Valentine. Thousand Oaks: Pine Forge.

Sargeant, Kimon Howland. 2000. *Seeker Churches: Promoting Traditional Religion in a Nontraditional Way.* New Brunswick, NJ: Rutgers University Press.

Sassen, Saskia. 2012. *Cities in a World Economy*, 4th ed. Thousand Oaks, CA: Sage.

Sassler, Sharon and Amanda J. Miller. 2011. "Waiting to Be Asked: Gender, Power, and Relationship Progression Among Cohabiting Couples." *Journal of Family Issues* 32(April):482–506.

Saxbe, Darby E., Rena L Repetti, and Anthony P. Graesch. 2011. "Time Spent in Housework and Leisure: Links With Parents' Physiological Recovery From Work." *Journal of Family Psychology* 25(April):271–81.

Scarce, Rik. 1999. "Good Faith, Bad Ethics: When Scholars Go the Distance and Scholarly Associations Do Not." *Law and Social Inquiry* 24(4):977–86.

Schabloski, Alyssa Kim. 2008. *Health Care Systems Around the World.* Insure the Uninsured Project, p. 3. Retrieved February 3, 2013 (www.itup.org/Reports/Fresh%20Thinking/Health_Care_Systems_Around_World.pdf).

Schaefer, Richard T. 2007. *Racial and Ethnic Groups*, 11th ed. Upper Saddle River, NJ: Prentice Hall.

Schaefer, Richard T. 2012. *Racial and Ethnic Groups,* 13th ed. Upper Saddle River, NJ: Prentice Hall.

Schaefer, Richard T. and Jenifer Kunz. 2007. *Racial and Ethnic Groups.* Upper Saddle River, NJ: Pearson/Prentice Hall.

Schaeffer, Robert K. 2003. *Understanding Globalization: The Social Consequences of Political, Economic, and Environmental Change,* 2nd ed. Lanham, MD: Rowman & Littlefield.

Schiller J. S., J. W. Lucas, B. W. Ward, and J. A. Peregoy. 2010. "Summary Health Statistics for U.S. Adults: National Health Interview Survey, 2010." *National Center for Health Statistics—Vital Health Statistics* 10(252). Retrieved August 28, 2012 (www.cdc.gov/nchs/data/series/sr_10/sr10_252.pdf).

Schmalleger, Frank. 2006. *Criminology Today: An Integrative Introduction,* 4th ed. Upper Saddle River, NJ: Prentice Hall.

Schmalleger, Frank. 2013. *Criminology Today: An Integrative Introduction,* 12th ed. Upper Saddle River, NJ: Prentice Hall.

Schoeman, Ferdinand. 1991. "Book Review: Heavy Drinking: The Myth of Alcoholism as a Disease." *The Philosophical Review* 100(3):493–98.

Schneider, Barbara and James S. Coleman. 1993. *Parents, Their Children, and Schools.* Boulder, CO: Westview.

Schneider, Linda and Arnold Silverman. 2006. *Global Sociology,* 4th ed. Boston: McGraw-Hill.

Schneider, Barbara and Linda J. Waite. 2005. *Being Together, Working Apart: Dual-Career Families and the Work-Life Balance.* Cambridge University Press.

Schoepflin, Todd. 2011. "Doing Gender." *Creative Sociology,* August 10. Retrieved May 25, 2012 (http://creativesociology.blogspot.com/2011/08/doing-gender.html).

Science Daily. 2011a. "The International Digital Divide." February 8. Retrieved September 14, 2012 (www.sciencedaily.com/releases/2011/02/110208121345.htm).

Science Daily. 2011b. "Prison Education Programs Reduce Inmate Prison Return Rate, Study Shows." October 4. Retrieved April 16, 2012 (www.sciencedaily.com/releases/2011/10/111004180121.htm).

Scott, Ellen K., Andrew S. London, and Nancy A. Myers. 2002. "Dangerous Dependencies: The Intersection of Welfare Reform and Domestic Violence." *Gender and Society* 16(6):878–97.

Scott-Montagu, John. 1904. "Automobile Legislation: A Criticism and Review." *North American Review* 179(573):168–77.

Scribd. 2011. "Chipko Movement." Retrieved January 1, 2012 (www.scribd.com/doc/27513230/Chipko-Movement).

Scribd. 2012. "Afghanistan in Transition: Illicit Drugs and Afghanistan." May. Retrieved July 30, 2012 (www.scribd.com/doc/93907735/Illicit-Drugs-Afghanistan-Key-Trends).

Sentencing Project. 2012a. "Facts About Prisons and Prisoners." Retrieved May 30, 2012 (www.sentencingproject.org/doc/publications/publications/inc_factsAboutPrisons_jan2012.pdf).

Sentencing Project. 2012b. "Rate of Incarceration per 100,000, by Gender and Race, 2010." Retrieved September 12, 2012 (www.sentencingproject.org/template/page.cfm?id=122).

Sernau, Scott. 2010. *Social Inequality in a Global Age.* Thousand Oaks, CA: SAGE/Pine Forge Press.

Sessions, David. 2012. "Evangelicals Struggle to Address Premarital Sex and Abortion." *The Daily Beast,* July 13. Retrieved September 20, 2012 (www.thedailybeast.com/articles/2012/07/13/evangelicals-struggle-to-address-premarital-sex-and-abortion.html).

Shade, Leslie Regan. 2004. "Bending Gender Into the Net: Feminizing Content, Corporate Interests, and Research Strategy." Pp. 57–70 in *Society On-Line: The Internet in Context,* edited by Philip N. Howard and Steve Jones. Thousand Oaks, CA: Sage.

Shah, Anup. 2009a. "Today, Over 25,000 Children Died Around the World." March 22. Retrieved November 10, 2009 (www.globalissues.org/article/715/today-over-25000-children-died-around-the-world).

Shah, Anup. 2009b. "World Military Spending." Retrieved December 17, 2009 (www.globalissues.org/article/75/world-military-spending).

Shaffer, David Williamson, Kurt R. Squire, Richard Haverson, and James P. Gee. 2005. "Video Games and the Future of Learning." *Phi Delta Kappan* (October):95–112.

Shah, Anup. 2011. "World Military Spending." Retrieved December 21, 2011 (www.globalissues.org/article/75/world-military-spending).

Shah, Anup. 2012. "World Military Spending: Expenditures in 2011." Retrieved February 10, 2013 (www.globalissues.org/print/article/75=WorldMilitarySpending).

Shah, Taimoor and Alissa J. Rubin. 2012. "In Poppy War, Taliban Aim to Protect a Cash Crop." *The New York Times,* April 12. Retrieved April 14, 2012 (www.nytimes.com/2012/04/12/world/asia/taliban-poppy-war-targets-tractors-and -police.html).

Sharp, Henry S. 1991. "Memory, Meaning, and Imaginary Time: The Construction of Knowledge in White and Chipewayan Cultures." *Ethnohistory* 38(2):149–73.

Sharp, Lauriston. 1990. "Steel Axes for Stone-Age Australians." Pp. 410–24 in *Conformity and Conflict,* 7th ed., edited by James P. Spradley and David W. McCurdy. Glenview, IL: Scott Foresman.

Shaw, Clifford R. and Henry D. McKay. 1929. *Delinquency Areas.* Chicago: University of Chicago Press.

Shaw, Susan M. and Janet Lee. 2005. *Women's Voices, Feminist Visions: Classic and Contemporary Readings,* 3rd ed. Boston: McGraw-Hill.

Sherif, Muzafer and Carolyn Sherif. 1953. *Groups in Harmony and Tension.* New York: Harper & Row.

Sherkat, Darren E. and Christopher G. Ellison. 1999. "Recent Developments and Current Controversies in the Sociology of Religion." *Annual Review of Sociology* 25:363–94.

Sherwood, I-Hsien. 2012. "Latest Presidential Election 2012 Map." *Latinos Post.* Retrieved November 12, 2012 (www.latinospost.com/articles/6570/20121107/latest-presidential-election-2012-map-obama-beats.htm).

Shin, Jean H. and Karina J. Havrilla. 2008. "Proposition 187." In *Encyclopedia of Race, Ethnicity, and Society,* edited by Richard T. Shaefer. Retrieved February 6, 2013 (http://knowledge.sagepub.com/view/ethnicity/n439.xml).

Shirley, Craig. 2012. "Better Off Circa 2012." *Politico,* September 5. Retrieved October 11, 2012 (www.politico.com/news/stories/0912/80719.html).

Short, Katherine. 2009. "Voter Participation Rate, 2008." Retrieved April 17, 2010 (www.askquestions.org/details.php?id=21094).

Shriver, Eunice Kennedy. 2007. *Add Health Study.* Washington, DC: National Institute of Child Health and Human Development. Retrieved December 24, 2009 (www.nichd.nih.gov/health/topics/add_health_study.cfm).

Shu, Xiaoling. 2004. "Education and Gender Egalitarianism: The Case of China." *Sociology of Education* 77(4):311–36.

Siegel, Dina and Hans Nelen, eds. 2008. "Organized Crime: Culture, Markets, and Policies." *Series: Studies in Organized Crime* 7. New York: Springer.

Siegel, Larry J. 2009. *Criminology: Theories, Patterns, and Typologies,* 10th ed. Belmont, CA: Thomson/Wadsworth.

Simmel, Georg. [1902–1917] 1950. *The Sociology of Georg Simmel,* translated by Kurt Wolff. Glencoe, IL: Free Press.

Simmel, Georg. 1955. *Conflict and the Web of Group Affiliation*, translated by Kurt H. Wolff. New York: Free Press.

Simmons, Rachel. 2002. *Odd Girl Out: The Hidden Culture of Aggression in Girls.* Orlando, FL: Harcourt.

Simon, David R. 2006. *Elite Deviance,* 8th ed. Boston: Allyn & Bacon.

Sine, Richard. 2002. "Garment Workers Say Gap Aided in Cambodian Strife." Retrieved September 2, 2008 (http://laborcenter.berkeley.edu/press/sfchronicle_dec02.shtml).

Sink, Todd and Brian Ceh 2011. "Relocation of the Urban Poor in Chicago: HOPE VI Policy Outcomes." *GeoForum* 42(January):71–82.

SIPRI Military Expenditure Database. 2012. Retrieved July 13, 2012 (http:milexdata.sipri.org).

"6.7% of World Has a College Degree." 2010. Retrieved March 11, 2011 (www.huffingtonpost.com/2010/05/19/percent-of-world-with-col_n_581807.html).

Sizer, Theodore R. 1984. *Horace's Compromise: The Dilemma of the American High School.* Boston: Houghton Mifflin.

Sjoberg, Gideon. 1965. "The Origin and Evolution of Cities." *Scientific American* 213(September):56–57.

Skocpol, Theda. 1979. *States and Social Revolutions: A Comparative Analysis of France, Russia, and China.* Cambridge, UK: Cambridge University Press.

Skocpol, Theda and Vanessa Williamson. 2012. *The Tea Party and the Remaking of Republican Conservatism.* New York: Oxford University Press.

Smelser, Neil J. 1963. *Theory of Collective Behavior.* New York: Free Press.

Smelser, Neil J. 1988. "Social Structure." Pp. 103–29 in *Handbook of Sociology,* edited by Neil J. Smelser. Newbury Park, CA: Sage.

Smelser, Neil J. 1992. "The Rational Choice Perspective: A Theoretical Assessment." *Rationality and Society* 4:381–410.

Smith, Alex Duval. 2011. "South Africa's Maternal Mortality Rate Increases Fourfold." *The Guardian*, August 12. Retrieved July 17, 2012 (www.guardian.co.uk/global-development/2011/aug/12/south-africa-maternal-mortality-health).

Smith, Christian and Robert Faris. 2005. "Socioeconomic Inequality in the American Religious System: An Update and Assessment." *Journal for the Scientific Study of Religion* 44(1):95–104.

Smith, Christian and Melinda Lundquist Denton. 2005. *Soul Searching: The Religious and Spiritual Lives of American Teenagers.* New York: Oxford University Press.

Smith, Christian, with P. Snell. 2009. *Souls in Transition: The Religious and Spiritual Lives of Emerging Adults.* New York: Oxford University Press.

Smith, Daniel R. and David F. Ayers. 2006. "Culturally Responsive Pedagogy and Online Learning: Implications for the Globalized Community College." *Community College Journal of Research and Practice* 30.

Smith, Mark K. 2008. "Howard Gardner and Multiple Intelligences." *The Encyclopedia of Informal Education.* Retrieved April 17, 2011 (http://www.infed.org/thinkers/gardner.htm).

Smith Drug War Chronicle. 2009. "Prohibition: UN Drug Chief Says Black Market Drug Profits Propped Up Global Banking System Last Year." Retrieved November 4, 2009 (http://stopthedrugwar.org/chronicle/570/costa_UNODC_drug_trade_banks).

Snarr, Michael T. and D. Neil Snarr. 2008. *Introducing Global Issues,* 4th ed. Boulder, CO: Lynne Rienner Publishers

Snopes.com. 2007. "Ring Around the Rosie." Retrieved July 31, 2012 (www.snopes.com/language/literary/rosie.asp).

Snow, David A. and L. Anderson. 1993. *Down on Their Luck: A Study of Homeless Street People.* Berkeley: University of California Press.

Snyder, Denson R. 1971. *The Hidden Curriculum.* New York: Alfred A. Knopf.

Sobolewski, Juliana M. and Paul R. Amato. 2007. "Parents' Discord and Divorce, Parent-Child Relationships, and Subjective Well-Being in Early Adulthood: Is Feeling Close to Two Parents Always Better Than Feeling Close to One?" *Social Forces* 85(March):1105–124.

Social Security Administration. 2013. "Social Security History." Retrieved February 6, 2013 (www.ssa.gov/history/lifeexpect.html).

Social Security Online. 2010. "Isabella Reigns as New Queen of Baby Names: Takes Top Spot on Social Security's Most Popular Baby Names List." May 7. Retrieved April 7, 2011 (http://www.ssa.gov/pressoffice/pr/baby-names2009-pr.htm).

Social Security Online. 2012. "History." Retrieved February 6, 2013 (www.prb.org/DataFinder/Topic/Rankings.aspx?ind=17).

Sommerville, C. John. 2002. "Stark's Age of Faith Argument and the Secularization of Things: A Commentary." *Review of Religious Research* (Fall):361–72.

Sons of Union Veterans of the Civil War. 2010. "The United States' Flag Code." Retrieved December 212, 2011 (http://suvcw.org/flag.htm).

Southern Poverty Law Center. 2013. "Active Hate Groups." Retrieved January 20, 2013 (www.splcenter.org/get-informed/hate-map).

Sowell, Thomas. 1994. *Race and Culture: A World View.* New York: Basic Books.

Spade, Joan Z. 2004. "Gender in Education in the United States." Pp. 287–95 in *Schools and Society: A Sociological Approach to Education,* 2nd ed., edited by Jeanne H. Ballantine and Joan Z. Spade. Belmont, CA: Wadsworth.

Sperling, Gene B. 2005. "The Case for Universal Basic Education for the World's Poorest Boys and Girls." *Phi Delta Kappan* (November): 213–16.

Sperling, Gene B. 2006. "What Works in Girls' Education." PBS Wide Angle. Retrieved July 11, 2009 (www.pbs.org/wnet/wideangle/episodes/time-for-school-series/essay-what-works-in-girls-education/274).

Spero News. 2009. "China: Good News From Beijing, the Number of Billionaires Is Rising, So Is the Economy." October 13. Retrieved November 11, 2009 (www.speronews.com/a/20830/china—good-news-from-beijing-the-number-of-billionaires-is-rising-so-is-the-economy).

Srinivasan, Padma and Gary R. Lee. 2004. "The Dowry System in Northern India: Women's Attitudes and Social Change." *Journal of Marriage and Family* 66:1108–17.

Stack, Carol B. 1998. *All Our Kin: Strategies for Survival in a Black Community* (Reissued). New York: Harper & Row.

Stanley, Angela. 2011. "Black, Female and Single." *The New York Times Sunday Review,* December 10. Retrieved June 5, 2012 (www.nytimes.com/2011/12/11/opinion/sunday/black-and-female-the-marriage-question.html?pagewanted=all).

Stanley, Scott M. and Galena K. Rhoades. 2009. "Marriages at Risk: Relationship Formation and Opportunities for Relationship Education." Pp. 21–44 in *What Works in Relationship Education,* edited by Harry Benson and Samantha Callan. Doha, Qatar: Doha International Institute for Family Studies and Development.

Staples, Brent. 2001. "Black Men and Public Space." Pp. 244–46 in *The Production of Reality,* edited by Jodi O'Brien and Peter Kollock. Thousand Oaks, CA: Pine Forge Press.

Stark, Rodney. 2000. "Secularization, R.P.I." Pp. 41–66 in *The Secularization Debate,* edited by William H. Swatos, Jr., and Daniel V. A. Olson. Lanham, MD: Rowman & Littlefield.

Stark, Rodney and Roger Finke. 2000. *Acts of Faith: Explaining the Human Side of Religion*. Berkeley: University of California Press.

Starr, Paul D. 1982. *The Social Transformation of American Medicine.* New York: Basic Books.

State of Alaska. 2006. "Workplace Alaska: How to Apply." Retrieved July 5, 2006 (http://notes3.state.ak.us/WA/MainEntry.nsf/WebData/HTMLHow+to+Apply/?open).

State of Delaware. 2008. "Presidential Primary Election." Retrieved March 21, 2008 (http://elections.delaware.gov/information/elections/presidential_2008.shtml).

Statistical Handbook of Japan. 2010. "Population." Retrieved May 13, 2011 (www.stat.go.jp/english/data/handbook/c02cont.htm#cha2_2).

Steele, Tracey L. 2005. *Sex, Self, and Society: The Social Context of Sexuality.* Belmont, CA: Thomson Wadsworth.

Steele, Tracey and Norma Wilcox. 2003. "A View From the Inside: The Role of Redemption, Deterrence, and Masculinity on Inmate Support for the Death Penalty." *Crime and Delinquency* 49(2):285–313.

Stelter, Brian. 2009. "In Coverage of Iran, Amateurs Take the Lead." Mediadecoder Weblog, *New York Times,* June 17. Retrieved December 22, 2009 (http://mediadecoder.blogs.nytimes.com).

Stern, Jessica. 2003. *Terror in the Name of God: Why Religious Militants Kill.* New York: HarperCollins.

Stewart, Susan D. 2007. *Brave New Stepfamilies: Diverse Paths Toward Stepfamily Living.* Thousand Oaks, CA: Sage.

Stiglitz, Joseph E. 2012. "A Real Cure for the Global Economic Crackup." Pp. 104–109 in *Globalization: The Transformation of Social Worlds*, 3rd ed., edited by D. Stanley Eitzen and Maxine Baca Zinn. Belmont, CA: Wadsworth.

Stillwell, Robert. 2010. "Public School Graduates and Dropouts From the Common Core of Data: School Year 2007–08." Retrieved July 14, 2011 (nces.ed.gov/pubs2010/2010341.pdf).

Stockholm International Peace Research Institute. 2010. "World Military Expenditures Increase Despite Financial Crisis." June 2. Retrieved May 10, 2011 (www.sipri.org/media/pressreleases/2010/100602yearbooklaunch).

Stoessinger, John. 1993. *Why Nations Go to War.* New York: St. Martin's Press.

Stone, Brad and Noam Cohen. 2009. "Social Networks Spread Defiance Online." *The New York Times,* June 16. Retrieved June 30, 2009 (www.nytimes.com/2009/06/16/world/middleeast/16media.html?_r=1&ref=world).

Stop Child Trafficking Now. 2012. "Child Trafficking Statistics." Retrieved May 1, 2012 (http://sctnow.org/contentpages.aspx?parentnavigationid=5827-4e7a-bde1-f61690fa44a8).

Stout, David. 2009. "Violent Crime Fell in 2008, F.B.I. Report Says." *The New York Times*, September 14. Retrieved November 4, 2009 (www.nytimes.com/2009/09/15/us/15crime.html).

Straus, Murray and Richard J. Gelles. 1990. *Physical Violence in American Families.* New Brunswick, NJ: Transaction.

Straus, Murray A., Richard J. Gelles, and Suzanne K. Steinmetz. 2006. *Behind Closed Doors: Violence in the American Family.* New Brunswick, NJ: Transaction.

Stringer, Donna M. 2006. "Let Me Count the Ways: African American/European American Marriages." Pp. 170–76 in *Intercultural Communication: A Reader,* edited by Larry A. Samovar, Richard E. Porter, and Edwin R. McDaniel. Belmont, CA: Wadsworth.

Struck, Doug. 2007. "Warming Will Exacerbate Global Water Conflicts." *Washington Post,* August 20. Retrieved August 21, 2008 (www.washingtonpost.com/wp-dyn/content/article/2007/08/19/AR2007081900967.html).

Stryker, Sheldon. 1980. *Symbolic Interactionism: A Social Structural Version.* Menlo Park, CA: Benjamin Cummings.

Stryker, Sheldon. 2000. "Identity Competition: Key to Differential Social Involvement." Pp. 21–40 in *Identity, Self, and Social Movements,* edited by Sheldon Styker, Timothy Owens, and Robert White. Minneapolis: University of Minnesota Press.

Stryker, Sheldon and Anne Stratham. 1985. "Symbolic Interaction and Role Theory." Pp. 311–78 in *Handbook of Social Psychology,* edited by Gardiner Lindsey and Eliot Aronson. New York: Random House.

Stutz, Fredrick P. and Barney Warf. 2005. *The World Economy.* Upper Saddle River, NJ: Prentice Hall.

Sutherland, Anne. 1986. *Gypsies: The Hidden Americans.* Prospect Heights, IL: Waveland.

Sutherland, Edwin H., Donald R. Cressey, and David Luckenbil. 1992. *Criminology.* Dix Hills, NY: General Hall.

Sway, Marlene. 1988. *Familiar Strangers: Gypsy Life in America.* Urbana: University of Illinois Press.

Sweet, Stephen. 2001. *College and Society: An Introduction to the Sociological Imagination.* Boston: Allyn & Bacon.

Szymanski, Linda A., Ann Sloan Devlin, Joan C. Chrisler, and Stuart A. Vyse. 1993. "Gender Role and Attitude Toward Rape in Male and Female College Students." *Sex Roles* 29:37–55.

Talbot, Margaret. 2008. "Red Sex, Blue Sex." *The New Yorker,* November 3. Retrieved December 24, 2009 (www.newyorker.com/reporting/2008/11/03/081103fa_fact_talbot).

Tamney, Joseph B. 1992. *The Resilience of Christianity in the Modern World.* Albany: State University of New York Press.

Tanenhaus, Sam. 2012. "History vs. the Tea Party." *The New York Times*, January 14. Retrieved July 15, 2012 (www.nytimes.com/2012/01/15/sunday-review/gop-history-vs-the-tea-party.html?pagewanted=all).

Tareen, Sophia and Jason Keyser. 2012. "Chicago Teachers Strike: No Deal Reached Yet, Talks Continue on Day 5." *Huffington Post,* September 14. Retrieved September 14, 2012 (www.huffingtonpost.com/2012/09/14/chicago-teachers-strike-n_0_n_1883626.html).

Taseer, Shehrbano. 2011. "True Survivor." *The Daily Beast*, May 1. Retrieved April 12, 2012 (www.thedailybeast.com/newsweek/2011/05/01/true-survivor.html).

Taub, Diane E. and Penelope A. McLorg. 2010. "Influences of Gender Socialization and Athletic Involvement on the Occurrence of Eating Disorders." Pp. 73–82 in *Sociological Footprints: Introductory Readings in Sociology*, 11th ed., edited by Leonard Cargan and Jeanne H. Ballantine. Belmont, CA: Wadsworth Cengage Learning.

Tavris, Carol and Carol Wade. 1984. *The Longest War,* 2nd ed. San Diego, CA: Harcourt Brace Jovanovich.

Taylor, Charlie. 2011. "Average Marriage Age Continues to Rise." *The Irish Times*, September 17. Retrieved July 28, 2012 (www.irishtimes.com/newspaper/ireland/2011/0917/1224304266172.html).

Tea Party Patriots. 2012. "About Tea Party Patriots." Retrieved June 13, 2012 (http://www.teapartypatriots.org/about/?gclid=CLyk15G6y7ACFcIUKgod00KPXw).

TechWench. 2010. "Physical Books to Be Overshadowed by E-Books Within 5 Years." October 19. Retrieved April 17, 2011 (www.techwench.com/physical-books-to-be-overshadowed-by-e-books-within-5-years/).

"Teen Ends Globe-Circling Voyage in St Maarten." 2012. *USA Today,* January 21. Retrieved February 23, 2012 (www.usatoday.com/news/world/story/2012-01-21/teen-sails-globe/52723684/1).

Terra Networks. 2013. *Kony 2012 Viral Campaign Sheds Light on Ugandan Violence.* Retrieved March 30, 2012 (http://en.terra.com/latin-in-america/news/kony_2012_viral_campaign_sheds_light_on_ugandan_violence/hof18171/ECID=US_ENGLISH_terrausa_SEMSearch_Kony).

Teixeira, Ruy. 2008. "The Decline of the White Working Class and the Rise of a Mass Upper Middle Class." Brookings Institution. Retrieved June 27, 2008 (www.brookings.edu/experts.aspx).

Teixeira, Ruy. 2012a. *America's New Swing Region: Changing Politics and Demographics in the Mountain West.* Washington DC: The Brookings Institution.

Teixeira, Ruy. 2012b. "The Emerging Democratic Majority Turns 10." *The Atlantic,* November. Retrieved November 10, 2012 (www.theatlantic.com/politics/archive/2012/11/the-emerging-democratic-majority-turns-10).

Therborn, Goran. 1976. "What Does the Ruling Class Do When It Rules?" *Insurgent Sociologist* 6:3–16.

Theroux, David J. 2012. "Secular Theocracy: The Foundations and Folly of Modern Tyranny." *The Independent Institute,* January 11. Retrieved July 13, 2012 (www.independent.org/newsroom/article.asp?id=3206).

Thiagaraj, Henry. 2006. *Minority and Human Rights From the Dalits' Perspective.* Chennai, India: Oneworld Educational Trust.

Thomas, V. J. and F. D. Rose. 1991. "Ethnic Differences in the Experience of Pain." *Social Science and Medicine* 32(9):1063–1066.

Thompson, A. C. 2009. "Katrina's Hidden Race War." *The Nation,* January 5. Retrieved July 7, 2011 (www.thenation.com/article/katrinas-hidden-race-war).

Thompson, Derek. 2011. "How Women in the Workforce Are Changing America." *The Atlantic,* March 9. Retrieved June 9, 2012 (www.theatlantic.com/business/archive/2011/03/how-women-in-the-workforce-are-changing-america/72235/).

Thorne, Barrie. 1993. *Gender Play: Girls and Boys in School.* New Brunswick, NJ: Rutgers University Press.

Thumma, Scott and Dave Travis. 2007. *Beyond Megachurch Myths: What We Can Learn From America's Largest Churches.* Hoboken, NJ: Jossey-Bass.

Tichenor, Veronica Jaris. 1999. "Status and Income as Gendered Resources: The Case of Marital Power." *Journal of Marriage and the Family* 61(August):638–50.

Tilley, Michael. 2009. "Power Shift? Proponents Again Push for Natural Gas-Powered Vehicles." Retrieved January 17, 2011 (www.thecitywire.com/index.php?q=node/5479).

Tipton, Steven M. 1990. "The Social Organization of Zen Practice: Constructing Transcultural Reality." *American Journal of Sociology* 96(2):488–90.

Toffler, Alvin and Heidi Toffler. 1980. *The Third Wave.* New York: Morrow.

Tofugu. 2011. "The Burakumin: Japan's Invisible Race." November 18. Retrieved May 6, 2012 (www.tofugu.com/2011/11/18/the-burakumin-japans-invisible-race/).

Tolbert, Pamela S. and Richard H. Hall. 2008. *Organizations: Structures, Processes, and Outcomes,* 10th ed. Upper Saddle River, NJ: Prentice Hall.

Tollefson, Jeff. 2012. "Heatwaves Blamed on Global Warming." *Nature.* Retrieved September 7, 2012 (www.nature.com/news/heatwaves-blamed-on-global-warming-1.11130).

Tönnies, Ferdinand. [1887] 1963. *Community and Society.* New York: Harper & Row.

Topix.com. 2010. "Fired for Being Gay? It's Legal in 29 States." Retrieved July 10, 2011 (www.topix.com/forum/state/de/TP9N5JVK30FRS3NLO).

TopTenz.net. 2011. "Top 10 Most Spoken Languages." March 29. Retrieved September 30, 2012 (www.toptenz.net/top-10-most-spoken-languages.php).

Tough, Paul. 2008. *Whatever It Takes: Geoffrey Canada's Quest to Change Harlem and America.* Boston: Houghton Mifflin Harcourt.

Trading Economics. 2012. "Age Dependency Ratio (% of Working-age Population) in Japan." Retrieved July 28, 2012 (www.tradingeconomics.com/japan/age-dependency-ratio-percent-of-working-age-population-wb-data.html).

"Transnational Crime in the Developing World." 2011. Cited in "The 12 Most Profitable International Crimes." Retrieved April 13, 2012 (http://247wallst.com/2011/02/10/the-12-most-profitable-international-crimes/).

Transparency International. 2012. "Global Corruption Barometer 2010/11." Retrieved October 6, 2012 (http://gcb.transparency.org/gcb201011/infographic/).

Travers, Jeffrey and Stanley Milgram. 1969. "An Experimental Study ot the Small World Problem." *Sociometry* 32:425–43.

Truman, Jennifer L. 2011a. "Criminal Victimization, 2010." National Crime Victimization Survey, U.S. Department of Justice, September. Retrieved May 26, 2012 (www.bjs.gov/content/pub/pdf/cv10.pdf).

Truman, Jennifer L. 2011b. "Rate of Total Violent Crime Victimization Declined by 13% in 2010." U.S. Bureau of Justice Statistics, September 15. Retrieved April 13, 2012 (www.bjs.ojp.usdoj.gov/index.cfm?ty=pbdetail&iid=2224).

Tumin, Melvin M. 1953. "Some Principles of Social Stratification: A Critical Analysis." *American Sociological Review* 18(August):387–94.

Turnbull, Colin M. 1962. *The Forest People.* New York: Simon & Schuster.

Turner, Bryan S. 1991a. "Politics and Culture in Islamic Globalism." Pp. 161–81 in *Religion and Global Order,* edited by Roland Robertson and William R. Garrett. New York: Paragon.

Turner, Bryan S. 1991b. *Religion and Social Theory.* London: Sage.

Turner, Jonathan H. 2003. *The Structure of Sociological Theory,* 7th ed. Belmont, CA: Wadsworth.

Turner, Ralph H. and Lewis M. Killian. 1993. "The Field of Collective Behavior." Pp. 5–20 in *Collective Behavior and Social Movements,* edited by Russell L. Curtis, Jr. and Benigno E. Aguirre. Boston: Allyn & Bacon.

20-first. 2010. "It's Official at Last: Women Outnumber Men in US Workforce." Retrieved May 25, 2012 (www.20-first.com/1317-0-its-official-at-last-women-outnumber-men-in-us-workforce.html).

UNAIDS. 2009. "AIDS Epidemic Update." November. Retrieved January 11, 2010 (www.avert.org/worldstats.htm).

UNAIDS. 2012a. "AIDS Dependency Crisis: Sourcing African Solutions." Retrieved August 3, 2012 (www.unaids.org/en/media/contentassets/documents/unaidspublication/2012/JC2286_Sourcing-African-Solutions_en.pdf).

UNAIDS. 2012b. "Swaziland Country Report on Monitoring the Political Declaration on HIV and AIDS." March. Retrieved July 16, 2012 (www.unaids.org/en/dataanalysis/monitoringcountry progress/progressreports/2012countries/ce_SZ_Narrative_Report[1].pdf).

UNESCAP. 2007. "Gender Inequality Continues—at Great Cost." The Economic and Social Survey for Asia and the Pacific 2007. Retrieved April 9, 2010 (www.unescap.org/survey2007/backgrounder/gender_inequality.asp).

UNESCO. 2005. *Education for All Global Monitoring Report 2005: The Quality Imperative.* Paris: Author.

UNESCO. 2009. "Women and Accessibility in Town Centers: Open Sesame Project, UK." Retrieved January 6, 2010 (www.unesco.org/most/westeu23.htm).

UNESCO. 2010. "Education (All Levels) Profile—India." Institute of Statistics. Retrieved September 13, 2012 (http://stats.uis.unesco.org/unesco/TableViewer/document.aspx).

UNESCO Institute for Statistics. 2010a. "Adult and Youth Literacy: Global Trends in Gender Parity." *UIS Fact Sheet* 3(September). Retrieved September 14, 2012 (www.uis.unesco.org/FactSheets/Documents/Fact_Sheet_2010_Lit_EN.pdf).

UNESCO Institute for Statistics. 2010b. "World Science Report 2010." November 17. Retrieved December 2, 2010 (www.uis.unesco.org/ev_en.php?ID=8167_201&ID2=DO_TOPIC).

UNESCO Institute for Statistics. 2012. "Primary School Curricula on Reading and Mathematics in Developing Countries." *Technical Paper* 8. Retrieved January 28, 2013 (www.uis.unesco.org/Education/. . .tp8-education-curriculum-reading-math-2012-en3.pdf).

UN Habitat. 2012. "Issues and Trends." United Nations Human Settlements Programme. Retrieved July 31, 2012 (www.scribd.com/doc/99074172/Gender-and-Urban-Planning).

UNHCR. 2012. "UNHCR Report Shows Highest Number of Refugees in 15 Years." June 19. Retrieved July 30, 2012 (www.euronews.com/2012/06/19/unhrc-report-shows-highest-number-of-refugees-in-15-yeasrs/).

UN Human Development Report. 2011. "Sustainability and Equity: A Better Future for All." Retrieved September 9, 2012 (http://hdr.undp.org/en/reports/global/hdr2011/).

UNICEF. 2005. "Convention on the Rights of the Child." Retrieved July 23, 2012 (www.unicef.org/crc/index_30229.html).

UNICEF. 2011. "Basic Education and Gender Equality: Equal Access to Education." Retrieved July 29, 2012 (www.unicef.org/education/index_access.html).

UNIFEM. 2002. "Report of the Learning Oriented Assessment of Gender Mainstreaming and Women's Empowerment Strategies in Rwanda." Retrieved April 7, 2008 (www.unifem.org/attachments/products/rwanda_assessment_report_eng.pdf).

Uniform Crime Reports. 2009. "Hate Crime Statistics." Retrieved February 10, 2013 (www2.fbi.gov/ucr/hc2009/index.html).

United Church of Christ. 2007. "Toxic Waste and Race at Twenty: 1987–2007." Environmental Justice/Environmental Racism. Retrieved April 22, 2009 (www.ejnet.org/ej).

United Nations. 2007. *The Millennium Development Goals Report 2007.* Retrieved January 23, 2013 (www.un.org/millenniumgoals/pdf/mdg2007.pdf).

United Nations. 2009. "World Food Program: Swaziland." November. Retrieved April 13, 2010 (www.wfp.org/countries/swaziland).

United Nations. 2010. "Violence Against Women." Ch. 6 in *The World's Women: Trends and Statistics.* Retrieved April 11, 2012 (http://unstats.un.org/unsd/demographic/products/Worldswomen/WW2010%20Report_by%20chapter(pdf)/Vnce%20against%20women.pdf).

United Nations. 2011. *The Millennium Development Goals Report 2011.* Retrieved January 23, 2013 (www.un.org/millenniumgoals/11_MDG%20Report_EN.pdf).

United Nations. 2012. "Status of Ratification of the Kyoto Protocol." United Nations Framework Convention on Climate Change. Retrieved September 7, 2012 (http://unfccc.int/kyoto_protocol/status_of_ratification/items/).

United Nations Climate Change Conference. 2009. Retrieved December 22, 2009 (http://en.cop15.dk/about+cop15).

United Nations, Department of Economic and Social Affairs, Population Division. 2011. *World Population Prospects: The 2010 Revision. Vol. 1: Comprehensive Tables.* "Table A30. Life Expectancy at Birth by Major Area, Region and Country: Estimates and Projections, 1950–2050." Retrieved February 4, 2013 (http://books.google.com/books?idf=ghTtZ89QOt4C&pg=PA6=life%20expectancy%20in%20China%20in%201955%2040.8%20years&f=false).

United Nations, Department of Economic and Social Affairs, Population Division. 2012a. "Data on Cities and Urban Agglomerations." *World Urbanization Prospects: The 2011 Revision.* Retrieved December 22, 2012 (http://esa.un.org/unpd/wup/CD-ROM/Urban-Agglomerations.htm).

United Nations, Department of Economic and Social Affairs, Population Division. 2012b. "Total, Urban and Rural Populations by Major Area" (Table 7). *World Urbanization Prospects: The 2011 Revision.* Retrieved October 13, 2012 (http://esa.un.org/unup/pdf/WUP2011_Highlights.pdf).

United Nations, Department of Economic and Social Affairs, Population Division. 2012c. "Urban and Rural Populations by Development Group, 1959–2050" (Figure 1). P. 3 in *World Urbanization Prospects: The 2011 Revision.* Retrieved February 7, 2013 (http://esa.un.org/unup/pdf/WUP2011_Highlights.pdf).

United Nations Development Programme. 2005. "Human Development Indicators." *Human Development Report.* Retrieved April 17, 2010 (http://hdr.undp.org/en/reports/global/hdr2005).

United Nations Educational, Scientific and Cultural Organization. 1951. *Statement on Race.* Retrieved January 22, 2013 (http://unesdoc.unesco.org/images/0017/001789/178908eb.pdf).

United Nations Population Fund. 2007. "Maternal Mortality Figures." *State of the World.* Retrieved April 17, 2010 (unic.un.org/imucms/LegacyDish.aspx?loc=11&pg=795).

United Nations Population Fund. 2009. "Because Everyone Counts: Giving Birth Should Not Be a Matter of Life and Death." Retrieved February 7, 2013 (www.unfpa.org/webdav/site/global/shared/safemotherhood/docs/maternalhealth_factsheet_en.pdf).

University of Michigan Documents Center. 2003. "Documents in the News—1997/2003: Affirmative Action in College Admissions." Retrieved April 17, 2010 (www.lib.umich.edu/files/libraries/govdocs/pdf/affirm/pdf).

University of Pennsylvania. 2010. "Body Modification." Retrieved November 18, 2010 (penn.museum/sites/body_modification/bodmodpierce.shtml).

UN News Center. 2010. "Senior UN Official Cites Evidence of Growing Support for Abolishing Death Penalty." February 24. Retrieved March 8, 2011 (www.un.org/apps/news/story.asp?NewsID=33877&Cr=death+penalty&Cr1=).

UN News Center. 2012. "Millions of Children in Cities Face Poverty and Exclusion." *The State of the World's Children 2012*, February 28. Retrieved May 14, 2012 (www/im/prg/apps/news/story.asp?NewsID=41395&Cr=children&Cr1).

Upbin, Bruce. 2011. "The 147 Companies That Control Everything." *Forbes*, October 22. Retrieved July 13, 2012 (www.forbes.com/sites/bruceupbin/2011/10/22/the-147-companies-that-control-everything/).

UPI.com. 2010. "12 Percent in U.S. Foreign Born." October 19. Retrieved May 5, 2012 (www.upi.com/Top_News/US/2010/10/19/12-percent-in-US-foreign-born/UPI-87261287522622/).

Urban Institute. 2004. "Family Support, Substance Abuse Help, and Work Release Programs Are Essential as Ex-Prisoners Restart Lives in Baltimore." Retrieved April 17, 2010 (www.urban.org/url.cfm?ID=900688).

U.S. Bureau of Labor Statistics. 2008. "Marriage and Divorce Rates by Country: 1980–2008." Retrieved June 6, 2012 (www.census.gov/compendia/statab/2011/tables/11s1335.pdf).

U.S. Bureau of Labor Statistics. 2011. "Injuries, Illnesses, and Fatalities." Retrieved April 13, 2012 (www.bls.gov/iif/).

U.S. Bureau of Labor Statistics. 2012. "American Time Use Survey Summary" (2011 Results). Retrieved January 24, 2013 (http://www.bls.gov/news.release/atus.nr0.htm).

U.S. Bureau of Labor Statistics. 2012. "Women's Earnings as a Percent of Men's in 2010." January 10. Retrieved May 25, 2012 (www.bls.gov/opub/ted/2012/ted_20120110.htm).

U.S. Census Bureau. 2005. "Housing Vacancies and Housing Ownership." *Annual Statistics 2005*. Retrieved September 15, 2006 (www.census.gov/hhes/www/housing/hvs/annual05/ann05def.html).

U.S. Census Bureau. 2007. "America's Families and Living Arrangements: 2007." Retrieved February 21, 2009 (http://www.census.gov/prod/2009pubs/p20-561.pdf).

U.S. Census Bureau. 2008a. "Number of Poor Families." Retrieved April 17, 2010 (www.census.gov/Press-Release/www/. . ./012528.html).

U.S. Census Bureau. 2008b. *Public Education Finances: 2006*. Retrieved January 7, 2010 (www2.census.gov/govs/school/06f33pub.pdf).

U.S. Census Bureau. 2009a. "American Factfinder." Retrieved April 17, 2010 (http://factfinder.census.gov/servlet/SAFFPopulation).

U.S. Census Bureau. 2009b. "Historical Income Tables—Households." Retrieved April 26, 2009 (www.census.gov/hhes/www/income/histinc/h02AR.html).

U.S. Census Bureau. 2010a. "Housing Vacancies and Housing Ownership." *Annual Statistics 2005*. Retrieved September 15, 2006 (www.census.gov/hhes/www/housing/hvs/annual05/ann05def.html).

U.S. Census Bureau. 2010b. "Income, Poverty, and Health Insurance Coverage in the United States, 2010." Report P60, n. 238, Table B-2, pp. 68–73.

U.S. Census Bureau. 2010c. "Mean Earnings by Level of Highest Degree (Dollars)." Statistical Abstracts Table 227. Retrieved April 13, 2010 (www.census.gov/compendia/statab/cats/health_nutrition.html).

U.S. Census Bureau. 2010d. "Weighted Average Poverty Thresholds 2008." September. Retrieved November 28, 2009 (www.irp.wisc.edu/faqs/faq1.htm).

U.S. Census Bureau. 2010 and 2011. "Table 8. People Without Health Insurance Coverage by Selected Characteristics: 2009 and 2010." Current Population Survey, Annual Social and Economic Supplements. Retrieved February 6, 2013 (http://www.census.gov/hhes/www/hlthins/data/incpovhlth/2010/table8.pdf).

U.S. Census Bureau. 2011a. "Alaska QuickFacts." quickfacts.census.gov/qfd/states/02000.html (Retrieved April 7, 2011)

U.S. Census Bureau. 2011b. "Custodial Parents Becoming Less Likely to Received Full Amount of Child Support, Census Bureau reports." December 7. Retrieved June 6, 2012 (www.census.gov/newsroom/releases/archives/children/cb11-206.html).

U.S. Census Bureau. 2011c. "Educational Attainment by Selected Characteristics: 2009" (Table 227). Retrieved April 15, 2011 (www.census.gov/compendia/statab/2011/tables/11s0227.pdf).

U.S. Census Bureau. 2011d. "Income (in Dollars) by Educational Level and Race/Ethnicity" (Table 228). Retrieved April 19, 2011 (http://www.census.gov/compendia/statab/2011/tables/11s0228.pdf).

U.S. Census Bureau. 2011e. "Mean Earnings by Highest Degree Earned: 2008" (Table 228). Statistical Abstract of the United States. Retrieved April 23, 2011 (www.census.gov/compendia/statab/2011/tables/11s0228.pdf).

U.S. Census Bureau. 2011f. "Movers by Type of Move and Reason for Moving: 2009." Retrieved May 19, 2011 (www.census.gov/compendia/statab/2011/tables/11s0031.pdf).

U.S. Census Bureau. 2011g. "Same-Sex Couple Households." *American Community Survey Briefs*, September. Retrieved June 5, 2012 (www.census.gov/prod/2011pubs/acsbr10-03.pdf).

U.S. Census Bureau. 2012a. "Current Population Survey—Definitions." Retrieved January 24, 2013 (http://www.census.gov/cps/about/cpsdef.html).

U.S. Census Bureau. 2012b. "Hate Crime Statistics, 2009." U.S. Department of Justice, FBI, p. 205. Retrieved October 6, 2012 (www.census.gov/compendia/statab/2012/tables/12s0322.pdf).

U.S. Census Bureau. 2012c. "How Many People Reside in Urban or Rural Areas for the 2010 Census? What Percentage of the U.S. Population Is Urban or Rural?" Retrieved February 7, 2013 (www.census.gov/geo/www/ua/uafaq.html).

U.S. Census Bureau. 2012d. "Marriage and Divorce Rates by Country: 1980–2008." *Statistical Abstract of the United States,* Table 1335. Retrieved June 28, 2012] (www.census.gov/compendia/statab/2012/tables/12s1336.pdf).

U.S. Census Bureau. 2012e. "Marriages and Divorces: 1990 to 2009." Table 133. Retrieved October 10, 2012 (www.census.gov/compendia/statab/2012/tables/12s0133.pdf).

U.S. Census Bureau. 2012f. "National Health Expenditures." Retrieved August 28, 2012 (www.census.gov/compendia/statab/cats/health_nutrition/health_expenditures.html).

U.S. Census Bureau. 2012g. "Poverty Status of Families, by Type of Family, Presence of Related Children, Race, and Hispanic Origin: 1959 to 2011." Retrieved October 11, 2012 (www.census.gov/hhes/www/poverty/data/historical/hstpov4.xls).

U.S. Census Bureau. 2012h. "Table 8: People Without Health Insurance Coverage by Selected Characteristics: 2009–2010." Retrieved August 1, 2012 (www.census.gov/hhes/www/hlthins/data/incpovhlth/2010/table8.pdf).

U.S. Census Bureau. 2012i. "Table 157: People Without Health Insurance for the Entire Year by Selected Characteristics." *The 2012 Statistical Abstract National Data Book.* Retrieved July 17, 2012 (www.census.gov/compendia/statab/casts/health_nutrition/health_insurance.html).

U.S. Census Bureau. 2012j. Table 229: "Educational Attainment by Race and Hispanic Origin." Retrieved May 5, 2012 (www.census.gov/compendia/statab/2012/tables/12s0229.pdf).

U.S. Census Bureau. 2012k. Table 690: "Money Income of Households: Percentage Distribution by Income Level, Race, and Hispanic Origin, in Constant (2009) Dollars." Retrieved May 5, 2012 (www.census.gov/compendia/statab/2012/tables/12s0691).

U.S. Census Bureau. 2012l. Table 824: "Farms—Number and Acreage: 1990 to 2010." Retrieved September 26, 2012 (www.census.gov/compendia/statab/2012/tables/12s0824.pdf).

U.S. Census Bureau. 2012m. "World Population: 1950–2050." Retrieved October 13, 2012 (www.census.gov/population/international/data/idb/worldpopgraph.php).

U.S. Census Bureau, Population Division, International Programs Center. 2011. "International Data Base." Retrieved August 6, 2011 (www.census.gov/ipo/www/idbnew.html).

U.S. Debt Clock. 2012. Retrieved September 27, 2012 (http://www.usdebtclock.org/).

U.S. Department of Defense. 2011. *Dictionary of Military and Associated Terms,* January 31. Retrieved January 19, 2013 (http://ra.defense.gov/documents/rtm/jp1_02.pdf).

U.S. Department of Defense. 2012. "Department of Defense Antiterrorism Program Memo: Instruction No. 2000.12." March 1. Retrieved July 28, 2012 (www.dtic.mil/whs/directives/corres/pdf/200012p.pdf).

U.S. Department of Education. 2004–05. "Integrated Postsecondary Education Data System: Glossary." Retrieved July 10, 2009 (http://nces.ed.gov/ipeds/glossary/?charindex=D).

U.S. Department of Energy. 2006. "Energy Consumption: Energy Kids Page." Retrieved November 8, 2006 (www.eia.doe.gov/kids/energyfacts/saving/efficiency/savingenergysecondary.html).

U.S. Department of Health and Human Services. 2011. "NHE Fact Sheet." Retrieved April 7, 2011 (www.cms.gov/NationalHealthExpendData/25_NHE_Fact_Sheet.asp).

U.S. Department of Interior Office of Education. 1930. *Availability of Public School Education in Rural Communities* (Bulletin No. 34, edited by Walter H. Gaummitz). Washington, DC: Government Printing Office.

U.S. Department of Justice. 2009. "Crime in the U.S.: Violent Crime." Federal Bureau of Investigation. Retrieved April 12, 2012 (www2.fbi.gov/ucr/cius2009/offenses/violent_crime/index.html).

U.S. Department of Justice. 2010. "Crime Clock Statistics." *Crime in the United States, 2009.* Retrieved July 7, 2011 (http://www2.fbi.gov/ucr/cius2009/about/crime_clock.html).

U.S. Department of Labor. 2011. "Highlights of Women's Earnings in 2010." *Report 1031.* Retrieved June 5, 2012 (www.bls.gov/cps/cpswom2010.pdf).

U.S. Department of Labor. 2012. "Usual Weekly Earnings of Wage and Salary Workers." Bureau of Labor Statistics News Release, April 17. Retrieved June 10, 2012 (www.bls.gov/news.release/pdf/wkyeng.pdf).

U.S. Department of State. 2011. *Country Reports on Terrorism 2010.* Retrieved July 14, 2012 (www.state.gov/documents/organization/170479.pdf).

United States Election Project. 2012. "Turnout 1980–2012." Retrieved November 12, 2012 (http://elections.gmu.edu/voter_turnout.htm).

U.S. Environmental Protection Agency. 2009. "Ag101: Demographics." Retrieved March 30, 2010 (www.epa.gov/oecaagct/ag101/demographics/html).

U.S. Flag Code. 2008. "U.S. Flag Code (4 US Code 1)." Retrieved August 28, 2008 (http://suvcw.org/flag.htm).

U.S. General Accounting Office. 2004. "Defense of Marriage Act: Update to Prior Report." GAO-04-353R, January 23. Retrieved June 30, 2012 (http://www.gao.gov/products/GAO-04-353R).

U.S. Government Accountability Office. 2012. "Budget and Federal Debt." Retrieved September 27, 2012 (www.gao.gov/special.pubs/longterm/debt/budgetdebt.html#affectbudget).

U.S. Senate. 2011. "Ethnic Diversity in the Senate." Retrieved April 22, 2011 (www.senate.gov/artandhistory/history/common/briefing/minority_senators.htm).

U.S. Trade Representative. 2012. "Joint Stats From 2012 NAFTA Commission Meeting." Retrieved September 8, 2012 (www.ustr.gov/).

Van Conoley, R. 2012. "The Illegal Sale of Human Body Parts for Profit—Part 1." *Sanity and Sense,* April 1. Retrieved August 2, 2012 (Sanityandsense.com/2012/04/01/the-illegal-sale-of-human-body-parts-for-profit-part-1/).

Vanderminden, Jennifer and Sharyn J. Potter. 2010. "Challenges to the Doctor-Patient Relationship in the 21st Century." In *The New Blackwell Companion to Medical Sociology,* edited by William C. Cockerham. Malden, MA: Wiley/Blackwell.

Van Houtte, Mieke and Peter A. Stevens. 2009. "School Ethnic Composition and Students Integration Outside and Inside Schools in Belgium." *Sociology of Education* 82(July):217–39.

Varul, Matthias Zick. 2010. "Talcott Parsons, the Sick Role and Chronic Illness." *Body Society* 16(2):72–94.

Veblen, Thorstein. 1902. *The Theory of the Leisure Class: An Economic Study of Institutions.* New York: Macmillan.

Verbeek, Stjin and Rinus Penninx. 2009. "Employment Equity Policies in Work Organisations." Pp. 69–94 in *Equal Opportunity and Ethnic Inequality in European Labour Markets: Discrimination, Gender, and Policies of Diversity*, edited by Karen Kraal, Judith Roosblad, and John Wrench. Amsterdam: University of Amsterdam Press.

Vervaeck, Armand and James Daniell. 2011. "Japan Tohoku Tsunami and Earthquake: The Death Toll Is Climbing Again." Earthquake Report, August 15. Retrieved May 13, 2012 (Httlp://earthquake-report.com/2011/08/04/japan-tsunami-following-up-the-aftermath-part-16-june/).

Victor, Barbara. 2003. *Army of Roses: Inside the World of Palestinian Women Suicide Bombers.* Emmaus, PA: Rodale Books.

Vijayakumar, Gowri. 2012. "Girls and Education: A Global Approach." May 20. Retrieved January 28, 2013 (www.socwomen.org/web/images/stories/resources/fact_sheets/fact_2_2012-girlseducation.pdf).

Vivat International. 2012. "Poverty." Retrieved January 23, 2013 (vivatinternational.org/our-work/poverty-eradication/).

Voting and Democracy Research Center. 2008. "Primaries: Open and Closed." Retrieved March 21, 2008 (www.fairvote.org/?page=1801).

Wade, Lisa. 2012. "The New Elite: Attributing Privilege and Class vs. Merit." *Sociological Images: Inspiring Sociological Imaginations Everywhere*, June 21. Retrieved September 14, 2012 (http://thesocietypages.org/socimages/2012/06/21/the-new-elite-attributing-privilege-to-class-vs-merit/).

Waite, Linda J. and Maggie Gallagher. 2000. *The Case for Marriage: Why Married People Are Happier, Healthier, and Better Off Financially.* New York: Doubleday.

Wallerstein, Immanuel. 1974. *The Modern World System.* New York: Academic Press.

Wallerstein, Immanuel. 1979. *The Capitalist World Economy.* London: Cambridge University Press.

Wallerstein, Immanuel. 1991. *Geopolitics and Geoculture: Essays on the Changing World-System.* Cambridge, MA: Cambridge University Press.

Wallerstein, Immanuel. 2004. *World Systems Analysis: An Introduction.* Durham, NC: Duke University Press.

Wallerstein, Immanuel. 2005. "Render Unto Caesar? The Dilemmas of a Multicultural World." *Sociology of Religion* 66(2):121–33.

Wallerstein, Judith. 1996. *Surviving the Breakup: How Children and Parents Cope With Divorce.* New York: Basic Books.

Wallerstein, Judith S. and Sarah Blakeslee. 1996. *The Good Marriage: How and Why Love Lasts.* New York: Warner Books.

Wallerstein, Judith S. and Sarah Blakeslee. 2004. *Second Chances: Men, Women and Children a Decade After Divorce,* 15th ed. Boston: Houghton Mifflin.

Wallis, Jim. 2005. *God's Politics: Why the Right Gets It Wrong and the Left Doesn't Get It.* New York: HarperCollins.

Wallis, Jim. 2013. *On God's Side: What Religion Forgets and Politics Hasn't Learned About Serving the Common Good.* Grand Rapids, MI: Brazos Press.

Walmsey, Roy. 2011. *World Prison Population List,* 9th ed. International Centre for Prison Studies. Retrieved January 20, 2013 (http://www.idcr.org.uk/wp-content/uploads/2010/09/WPPL-9-22.pdf).

Walum, Laurel Richardson. 1974. "The Changing Door Ceremony: Some Notes on the Operation of Sex Roles in Everyday Life." *Urban Life and Culture* 2(4):506–515.

Wang, Tina. 2009. "China Health Care Markets." *Forbes,* January 22. Retrieved January 10, 2010 (www.forbes.com/2009/01/22/china-health-care-markets-econ-cx_twdd_0122markets04.html).

Ward, Martha C. and Monica Edelstein. 2009. *A World Full of Women,* 5th ed. Boston: Allyn & Bacon.

Ware, Alyn. 2008. "Nuclear Stockpiles" (Project of the Nuclear Age Peace Foundation). Retrieved September 3, 2008 (www.nuclearfiles.org/menu/key-issues/nuclear-weapons/basics/nuclear-stockpiles.htm).

Warner, R. Stephen. 1993. "Work in Progress Toward a New Paradigm for the Sociological Study of Religion in the United States." *American Journal of Sociology* 98(5):1044–1093.

Warner, R. Stephen. 2005. *A Church of Our Own: Disestablishment and Diversity in American Religion.* New Brunswick, NJ: Rutgers University Press.

Washington, Jesse. 2011. "The Disappearing Black Middle Class." *Chicago Sun Times,* July 10. Retrieved May 4, 2012 (www.suntimes.com/news/nation/6397110-418/the-disappearing-black-middle-class.html).

WaterAid. 2008. "WaterAid's Key Facts and Statistics." Retrieved February 25, 2008 (www.wateraid.org/international/what_we_do/statistics/default.asp).

WaterAid. 2012. "Annual Review 2010/11." Retrieved September 9, 2012 (www.wateraid.org/uk/about_us/annual_report/default.asp).

WaterAid. 2013. "Precipitation for Education." Retrieved February 10, 2013 (www.wateraid.org/other/Print.asp).

Waters, Tony. 2012. *Schooling, Childhood, and Bureaucracy: Bureaucratizing the Child.* Basingstoke, England: Palgrave Macmillan.

Watts, Jonathan. 2012. "Air Pollution Could Become China's Biggest Health Threat, Expert Warns." *The Guardian,* March 16. Retrieved August 2, 2012 (www.guardian.co.uk/environment/2012/mar/16/air-pollution-biggest-threat-china).

Way, Niobe. 2011 *Deep Secrets: Boys' Friendships and the Crisis of Connection.* Cambridge, MA: Harvard University Press.

Weaver, Janelle. 2010. "Social Life Starts in the Womb." *ScienceShot,* October 12. Retrieved October 19, 2010 (http://news.sciencemag.org/sciencenow/2010/10/scienceshot-social-life-starts-in.html?rss=1&utm_source=twitterfeed&utm_medium=twitter).

Weber, Max. [1904–1905] 1958. *The Protestant Ethic and the Spirit of Capitalism,* translated by Talcott Parsons. New York: Scribner.

Weber, Max. 1946. *From Max Weber: Essays in Sociology*, translated and edited by Hans H. Gerth and C. Wright Mills. New York: Oxford University Press.

Weber, Max. 1947. *The Theory of Social and Economic Organization*, translated and edited by A. M. Henderson and Talcott Parsons. New York: Oxford University Press.

WebSiteOptimization.com. 2010. "U.S. Broadband Penetration Jumps to 45.2%—U.S. Internet Access Nearly 75%." April 13. Retrieved March 1, 2011 (www.websiteoptimization.com/bw/0403/).

Webster's Unabridged English Dictionary. 1989. New York: Gramercy Books.

Weeks, John R. 1999. *Population: An Introduction to Concepts and Issues,* 7th ed. Belmont, CA: Wadsworth.

Weeks, John R. 2012. *Population: An Introduction to Concepts and Issues,* 11th ed. Belmont, CA: Wadsworth.

Weil, Elizabeth. 2008. "Teaching to the Testosterone." *The New York Times Magazine*, March 2, p. 38.

Weisenberg, Faye and Elizabeth Stacey. 2005. "Reflections on Teaching and Learning Online: Quality Program Design, Delivery, and Support Issues From a Cross-Global Perspective." *Distance Education,* 26(3).

Weiss, Gregory L. and Lynne E. Lonnquist. 2012. *The Sociology of Health, Healing, and Illness,* 7th ed. Englewood Cliffs, NJ: Prentice Hall.

Weiss, Robin Elise. 2010. "Pregnancy and Childbirth." Retrieved January 9, 2010 (pregnancy.about.com/od/cesareansections/ss/cesarian.htm).

Weitzman, Lenore J., Deborah Eifler, Elizabeth Hokada, and Catherine Ross. 1972. "Sex-Role Socialization in Picture Books for Preschool Children." *American Journal of Sociology* 77(May):1125–50.

Weller, Christian E. and Adam Hersh. 2006. "Free Markets and Poverty." Pp. 69–73 in *Globalization: The Transformation of Social Worlds,* edited by D. Stanley Eitzen and Maxine Baca Zinn. Belmont, CA: Wadsworth.

Wells, Amy Stuart and Jeannie Oakes. 1996. "Potential Pitfalls of Systemic Reform: Early Lessons From Research on Detracking." *Sociology of Education* 69(Extra Issue):135–43.

Wessinger, Catherine. 2000. *How the Millennium Comes Violently: From Jonestown to Heaven's Gate.* New York: Seven Bridges.

West, Candace and Don H. Zimmerman. 1987. "Doing Gender." *Gender and Society* 1(2):125–51.

West, Heather C. and William J. Sabol. 2008 "Prisoners in 2007." Bureau of Justice Statistics Bulletin. U.S. Department of Justice. Retrieved December 23, 2008 (www.ojp.usdoj.gov/bjs/pub/pdf/p07.pdf).

Westermann, Ted D. and James W. Burfeind. 1991. *Crime and Justice in Two Societies: Japan and the United States.* Pacific Grove, CA: Brooks/Cole.

Western Jurisdictional Conference. 2012. "Passed: A Statement of Gospel Obedience." Western Jurisdictional Conference of the United Methodist Church, July 20. Retrieved September 26, 2012 (www.pnwumc.org/gc2012/passed-a-statement-of-gospel-obedience/).

Whaley, Floyd. 2012. "New Internet Law in Philippines Takes Effect, Raising Fears." *New York Times*, October 3. Retrieved October 6, 2012 (http://www.nytimes.com).

White House. 2011. "Fact Sheet: New Actions on Guantanamo and Detainee Policy." March 7. Retrieved April 14, 2012 (www.whitehouse.gov/sites/default/files/Fact_Sheet_--_Guantanamo_and_Detainee_Policies.pdf).

White House. 2013. "Health Reform in Action." Retrieved February 2, 2013 (www.whitehouse.gov/issues/health-care).

White, Kevin. 2002. *An Introduction to the Sociology of Health and Illness.* London: Sage.

White, Shelley, Jonathan White, and Kathleen Odell Korgen. 2013. *Sociologists in Action: Race, Class, and Gender.* Thousand Oaks, CA: Sage.

Whitney, Lance. 2012. "2011 Ends with Almost 6 Billion Mobile Phone Subscriptions." CNET News. Retrieved May 18, 2012 (http://news.cnet.com/8301-1023_3-57352095-93/2011-ends-with-almost-6-billion-mobile-phone-subscriptions/).

WHO, UNICEF, UNFPA, and World Bank. 2012. "Trends in Maternal Mortality: 1990–2010." Work Health Organization. Retrieved July 17, 2012 (http://africa.unfpa.org/public/pid/10773).

The Whole Child. 2012. "Award-Winning Programs Demonstrate Excellence in Summer Learning." August 30. Retrieved September 14, 2012 (www.wholechildeducation.org/blog/award-winning-programs-demonstrate-excellence-in-summer-learning).

Whorf, Benjamin Lee. 1956. *Language, Thought, and Reality.* New York: John Wiley.

Whyte, William H. 1956. *The Organization Man.* New York: Simon and Schuster.

Wilcox, Norma and Tracey Steele. 2003. "Just the Facts: A Descriptive Analysis of Inmate Attitudes Toward Capital Punishment." *The Prison Journal* 83(4):464–82.

Wilcox. W. Bradford and Elizabeth Marquardt. 2011. *2011 State of Our Unions.* Retrieved October 9, 2012 (http://stateofourunions.org/2011/SOOU2011.pdf).

Williams, Brian K., Stacey C. Sawyer, and Carl M. Wahlstrom. 2013. *Marriages, Families, and Intimate Relationships,* 3rd ed. Boston: Allyn & Bacon.

Williams, Christine L. 2006. *Inside Toyland: Working, Shopping, and Social Inequality.* Berkeley: University of California Press.

Williams, Robin Murphy, Jr. 1970. *American Society: A Sociological Interpretation,* 3rd ed. New York: Alfred Knopf.

Willis, Paul. 1979. *Learning to Labor: How Working Class Kids Get Working Class Jobs.* Aldershot, Hampshire, England: Saxon House.

Wilson, Edward O. 1980. *Sociobiology.* Cambridge, MA: Belknap.

Wilson, Edward O. 1987. *The Coevolution of Biology and Culture.* Cambridge, MA: Harvard University Press.

Wilson, Edward O., Michael S. Gregory, Anita Silvers, and Diane Sutch. 1978. "What Is Sociobiology?" *Society* 15(6):1–12.

Wilson, K. 1993. *Dialectics of Consciousness: Problems of Development, the Indian Reality.* Madras: Oneworld Educational Trust.

Wilson, Kate, Vlad Lavrov, Martina Keller, Thomas Jajer, and Gerard Ryle. 2012. "Skin, Bones and Tissue for Sale: How the Dead Are Being Used for Grisly Trade in Human Body Parts." *Daily Mail,* July 17. Retrieved August 2, 2012 (www.dailymail.co.uk/news/article-2175006/Skin-bones-tissue-sale-How-dead-used-grisly-trade-human-body-parts.html).

Wilson, Mary E. 2006. "Infectious Concerns: Modern Factors in the Spread of Disease." Pp. 313–19 in *Globalization: The Transformation of Social Worlds,* edited by D. Stanley Eitzen and Maxine Baca Zinn. Belmont, CA: Wadsworth.

Wilson, Warren H. 1924. "What the Automobile Has Done to and for the Country Church." *Annals of the American Academy of Political and Social Science* 116(November):85–86.

Wilson, William Julius. 1978. *The Declining Significance of Race: Blacks and Changing American Institutions.* Chicago: University of Chicago Press.

Wilson, William Julius. 1984. "The Black Underclass." *The Wilson Quarterly* (Spring):88–89.

Wilson, William Julius. 1993a. *The Ghetto Underclass: Social Science Perspectives.* Newbury Park, CA: Sage.

Wilson, William Julius. 1993b. "The New Urban Poverty and the Problem of Race." *The Tanner Lecture on Human Values,* October 22 (printed in *Michigan Quarterly Review,* 247–73).

Wilson, William Julius. 1996. *When Work Disappears.* New York: Alfred A. Knopf.

Wimberly, Ronald C. and William H Swatos, Jr. 1998. "Civil Religion." Pp. 94–96 in *Encyclopedia of Religion and Society,* edited by William H. Swatos, Jr. Altamira Press.

Winders, Bill. 2004. "Changing Racial Inequality: The Rise and Fall of Systems of Racial Inequality in the U.S." Paper presented at the Annual Meeting of the American Sociological Association, San Francisco.

Wingfield, Adia Harvey. 2009. "Racializing the Glass Escalator: Reconsidering Men's Experiences With Women's Work." *Gender and Society* 23(5):5–26.

Winkler, Celia. 2002. *Single Mothers and the State: The Politics of Care in Sweden and the United States.* London: Rowman and Littlefield.

Winkler, Karen J. 1991. "Revisiting the Nature vs. Nurture Debate: Historian Looks Anew at Influence of Biology on Behavior." *Chronicle of Higher Education,* May 22, pp. A5, A8.

Winnick, Terri A. 2006. "Medical Doctors and Complementary and Alternative Medicine: The Context of Holistic Practice." *Health: An Interdisciplinary Journal for the Social Study of Health, Illness and Medicine* 10(2):149–73.

Winslow, Robert W. and Sheldon X. Zhang. 2008. *Criminology: A Global Perspective.* Upper Saddle River, NJ: Pearson Prentice Hall.

Wirth, Louis. 1964. "Urbanism as a Way of Life." *American Journal of Sociology* 44(1):1–24.

Witness for Peace. 2008. Venezuelan Delegation on Health Care, March (Personal communication; interviews with members of the delegation).

Witness for Peace. 2012. "Mediation With GM Fails, Workers Re-Start Hunger Strike." September 3. Retrieved October 14, 2012 (http://witnessforpeace.org/).

Witt, Susan D. 2000. "The Influence of Television on Children's Gender Role Socialization." *Childhood Education* 76. Retrieved May 24, 2012 (www.eric.ed.gov/ERICWebPortal/recordDetail?accno=EJ610307).

Witte, John Jr. and Eliza Ellison. 2005. *Covenant Marriage in Comparative Perspective.* Grand Rapids, MI: Wm. B. Eerdmans.

Witzig, Ritchie. 1996. "The Medicalization of Race: Scientific Legitimation of a Flawed Social Construct." *Annals of Internal Medicine: American College of Physicians* 125(8):675–76.

Wolf, Richard. 2010. "Number of uninsured Americans Rises to 50.7 Million." *USA Today,* September 17. Retrieved April 7, 2011 (www.usatoday.com/news/nation/2010-09-17-uninsured17_ST_N.htm).

Women's Sports Foundation. 2005. "Women's Sports: Title IX Q and A" (May). Retrieved April 17, 2010 (www.womenssportsfoundation.org/. . ./Title-IX/. . ./Briefing-Paper-Five).

Wong, Adrienne. 2012. "Chinese Applications to U.S. Schools Skyrocket." *NBC Nightly News.* Retrieved May 15, 2012 (http://behindthewall.msnbc.msn.com/_news/2012/01/11/9679479-chinese-applicatons-to-us-schools-skyrocket?lite).

Wood, Julia T. 2008. *Gendered Lives: Communication, Gender, and Culture,* 8th ed. Belmont, CA: Wadsworth.

Wood, Julia T. and Nina M. Reich. 2006. "Gendered Communication Styles." Pp. 177–86 in *Intercultural Communication,* 11th ed., edited by Larry A. Samovar, Richard E. Porter, and Edwin R. McDaniel. Belmont, CA: Wadsworth.

Woodberry, Robert D. and Christian S. Smith. 1998. "Fundamentalism et al: Conservative Protestants in America." *Annual Review of Sociology* 24:25–26.

Woods, Andrew K. 2011. "These Revolutions Are Not All Twitter (Op-Ed)." *New York Times*, February 1. Retrieved October 6, 2012 (http://www.nytimes.com).

World Bank. 2010. "Child Mortality in Developing Countries Has Declined by 25% Since 1990." September 8. Retrieved May 15, 2012 (http://data.worldbank.org/news/developing-countries-child-mortality-declines).

World Bank. 2012a. "Girls' Education: Learning for All." Retrieved September 14, 2012 (http://web.worldbank.org/WBSITE/EXTERNAL/TOPICS/EXTEDUCATION/o,,contentMDK:20298916~menuPK:617572~pagePK:148956~piPK:216618~theSitePK:282386,00.html).

World Bank. 2012b. "Physicians (per 1,000 People)." Retrieved August 2, 2012 (Data.worldbank.org/indicator/SH.MED.PHYS.ZS).

World Coalition. 2012. "World Database." World Coalition Against the Death Penalty. Retrieved May 29, 2012 (http://www.worldcoalition.org/worldwide-database.html).

World Development Report. 2012. *World Development Report: Gender Equality and Development*. World Bank. Retrieved October 1, 2012 (http://go.worldbank.org/6R2KGVEXPO).

World Economic Forum. 2012. "Seven Billion and Growing: A 21st-Century Perspective on Population." Retrieved July 28, 2012 (http://reports.weforum.org/global-agenda-council-2012/councils/population-growth/).

World Factbook. 2010. "Country Comparison: Population." Central Intelligence Agency. Retrieved February 1, 2010 (www.cia.gov/library/publications/the-world-factbook/rankorder/2119rank.html).

World Factbook. 2011. "Field Listing: Suffrage." Retrieved May 6, 2011 (www.cia.gov/library/publications/the-world-factbook/fields/2123.html).

World Factbook. 2012a. "Country Comparison: GDP Per Capita." Retrieved February 9, 2013 (https://www.cia.gov/library/publications/the-world-factbook/rankorder/2004rank.html).

World Factbook 2012b. "Country Comparison: Life Expectancy at Birth." Retrieved August 30, 2012 (www.cia.gov/library/publications/the-world-factbook/rankorder/2102rank.html).

World Factbook. 2012c. "Field Listing: Literacy." Retrieved January 28, 2013 (https://www.cia.gov/library/publications/the-world-factbook/fields/2103.html).

World Factbook. 2012d. "GDP Per Capita." Retrieved August 30, 2012 (www.cia.gov/library/publications/the-world-factbook/rankorder/2004rank.html).

World Factbook. 2012e. "Infant Mortality Rate." Retrieved August 30, 2012 (www.cia.gov/library/publications/the-world-factbook/rankorder/2091rank.html).

World Factbook. 2012f. "Labor Force—by Occupation." Retrieved July 12, 2012 (www.cia.gov/library/publications/the-world-factbook/fields/2048.html).

World Factbook. 2012g. "World Statistics: Literacy." February 8. Retrieved February 26, 2012 (http://cia.gov/library/publications/the-world-factbook/geos/countrytemplate_xx.html).

World Factbook. 2013a. "Canada." Retrieved February 6, 2013 (https://www.cia.gov/library/publications/the-world-factbook/geos/ca.html).

World Factbook. 2013b. "Chad." Retrieved February 7, 2013 (https://www.cia.gov/library/publications/the-world-factbook/geos/cd.html).

World Factbook. 2013c. "China." Retrieved February 7, 2013 (https://www.cia.gov/library/publications/the-world-factbook/geos/ch.html).

World Factbook. 2013d. "Cuba." Retrieved February 6, 2013 (https://www.cia.gov/library/publications/the-world-factbook/geos/cu.html).

World Factbook. 2013e. "India." Retrieved February 7, 2013 (https://www.cia.gov/library/publications/the-world-factbook/geos/in.html).

World Factbook. 2013f. "Kenya." Retrieved February 7, 2013 (https://www.cia.gov/library/publications/the-world-factbook/geos/ke.html).

World Factbook. 2013g. "Nigeria." Retrieved February 6, 2013 (https://www.cia.gov/library/publications/the-world-factbook/geos/ni.html).

World Factbook. 2013h. "Swaziland." Retrieved February 6, 2013 (https://www.cia.gov/library/publications/the-world-factbook/geos/wz.html).

World Factbook. 2013i. "Sweden." Retrieved February 7, 2013 (https://www.cia.gov/library/publications/the-world-factbook/geos/sw.html).

World Factbook. 2013j. "United States." Retrieved February 6, 2013 (https://www.cia.gov/library/publications/the-world-factbook/geos/us.html).

World Factbook. 2013k. "World." Retrieved February 7, 2013 (https://www.cia.gov/library/publications/the-world-factbook/geos/xx.html).

World Famine Timeline. 2011. "World Disasters: Famine Timeline in 21st Century." Retrieved May 13, 2011 (www.mapreport.com/subtopics/d/0.html#2010).

World Health Organization. 2009. Retrieved April 17, 2010 (apps.who.int/whosis/database/core/WHO2009–12–27–151422.csv).

World Health Organization. 2011. "The Top 10 Causes of Death." Retrieved August 29, 2012 (www.who.int/mediacentre/factsheets/fs310/en/index.html).

World Health Organization. 2012. "Family Planning: Fact Sheet No. 351." July. Retrieved July 29, 2012 (www.who.int/mediacentre/factsheets/fs351/en/index.html).

World Hunger. 2011. "World Child Hunger Facts." December 18. Retrieved May 10, 2012 (www.worldhunger.org/articles/Learn/child_hunger_facts.htm).

World Hunger Education Service. 2011. "World Hunger and Poverty Facts and Statistics." Retrieved April 12, 2011 (www.worldhunger.org/articles/Learn/world%20hunger%20facts%202002.htm#).

World Hunger Education Service. 2012a. "Hunger in America: 2012 United States Hunger and Poverty Facts." Retrieved May 17, 2012 (www.worldhunger.org/articles/Learn/us_hunger_facts.htm).

World Hunger Education Service. 2012b. "World Hunger and Poverty Facts and Statistics." Retrieved May 16, 2012 (www.worldhunger.org/articles/Learn/world%20hunger%20facts%20202002.htm).

World Hunger Facts. 2009. Retrieved November 11, 2009 (www.worldhunger.org/articles/Learn/world%20hunger%20facts%202002.htm).

Worldometers: World Statistics Updated in Real Time. 2012. "United Nations Member States." Retrieved July 13, 2012 (www.worldometers.info/united-nations/).

World Population Clock. 2012. "World POPclock Projections." July 26. Retrieved July 27, 2012 (www.census.gov/population/popclock world.html).

World Resources Institute. 2007. "Ask Earth Trends: How Much of the World's Resource Consumption Occurs in Rich Countries?" *EarthTrends*. Retrieved April 14, 2008 (http://earthtrends.wri.org/updates/node/236).

WorldWideLearn. 2007. "Guide to College Majors in Sociology." Retrieved June 23, 2008 (www.worldwidelearn.com/online-education-guide/social-science/sociology-major.htm).

World Wildlife Fund. 2012. "The Living Planet Report." Retrieved September 7, 2012 (www.panda.org/lpr).

Wöss, Josef. 2012. "Tackling the Ageing Challenge: The Labour Market as a Key Determinant." Retrieved August 25, 2012 (www.esip.org/files/RT2_Josef%20W%C3%B6ss.pdf).

Wright, Erik Olin. 2000. *Class Counts: Comparative Studies in Class Analysis,* Student ed. Cambridge, MA: Cambridge University Press.

Wright, John W., ed. 2007. *The New York Times Almanac 2008*. New York: Penguin Reference.

Wright, Stuart A. 1995. *Armageddon in Waco: Critical Perspectives on the Branch Davidian Conflict*. Chicago: University of Chicago Press.

Wuthnow, Robert. 1988. *The Restructuring of American Religion: Society and Faith Since World War II*. Princeton, NJ: Princeton University Press

Yablonski, Lewis. 1959. "The Gang as a Near-Group." *Social Problems* 7(Fall):108–117.

Yamane, David. 1997. "Secularization on Trial: In Defense of a Neosecularization Paradigm." *Journal for the Scientific Study of Religion* 36(1):109–122.

Yamane, David. 2007. "Civil Religion." Pp. 506–507 in *The Blackwell Encyclopedia of Sociology*, Vol. II, edited by George Ritzer. Oxford: Blackwell.

Yamane, David and Sarah MacMillen. 2006. *Real Stories of Christian Initiation: Lessons for and from the RCIA*. Collegeville, MN: Liturgical Press.

Yen, Hope. 2009. "Multiracial Americans Become Fastest-Growing U.S. Group." *The Huffington Post,* May 28. Retrieved May 5, 2012 (www.huffingtonpost.com/2009/05/29/multiraction-americans-bec_n_208989.htlm).

Yinger, J. Milton. 1960. "Contraculture and Subculture." *American Sociological Review* 25(October):625–35.

Yoon, Mi Yung. 2001. "Democratization and Women's Legislative Representation in Sub-Saharan Africa." *Democratization* 8(2):169–90.

Yoon, Mi Yung. 2004. "Explaining Women's Legislative Representation in Sub-Saharan Africa." *Legislative Studies Quarterly* 29(3):447–68.

Yoon, Mi Yung. 2005. "Sub-Saharan Africa." Chapter 7 in *Sharing Power: Women, Parliament, Democracy,* edited by Manon Tremblay and Yvonne Galligan. Aldershot, UK: Ashgate.

Yoon, Mi Yung. 2008. "Special Seats for Women in the National Legislature: The Case of Tanzania." *Africa Today* 55(Fall): 61–85.

Yoon, Mi Yung. 2011a. "More Women in the Tanzanian Legislature: Do Numbers Matter?" *Journal of Contemporary African Studies* 29(January):83–98.

Yoon, Mi Yung. 2011b. "Factors Hindering 'Larger' Representation of Women in Parliament: The Case of Seychelles." *Commonwealth and Comparative Politics* 49(February):98–114.

Young, Jeffrey. 2012. "Health Insurance Costs More, Covers Less, Survey Says." *The Huffington Post*, March 3. Retrieved August 1, 2012 (www.huffingtonpost.com/2012/03/08/health-insurance-costs-n-1327861.html).

youthxchange. 2007. "Women's Literacy." (youthxchange.net/utils/download.asp?filename…pdf).

YubaNet.com. 2011. "World's Fastest Growing Populations…" October 26. Retrieved July 27, 2012 (http:/yubanet.com/world/World-39-s-fastest-growing-populations-increasingly-vulnerable-to-impacts-of-climate-change.php).

Yunus, Muhammad and Alan Jolis. 1999. *Banker to the Poor: Micro-Lending and the Battle Against World Poverty*. New York: Public Affairs.

Zakaria, Fareed. 2012. "Could China's One-Child Policy Change?" Retrieved July 28, 2012 (www.cnn.com/WORLD/fareed.zakaria.qa/archive/index.html).

Zborowski, Mark. 1952. "Cultural Components in Response to Pain." Journal of Social Issues 8(4):16–30.

Zeleny, Jeff. 2009. "Obama Vows, 'We Will Rebuild' and 'Recover'." New York Times. February 25. Retrieved February 25, 2009 (www.nytimes.com/2009/02/25/us/politics/25obama.html?scp=1&sq=obama%20vows%20we%20will%20rebuild&st=cse).

Zernike, Kate. 2012. "Former Rutgers Student Found Guilty of Hate Crimes." March 17. Retrieved April 16, 2012 (www.bostonglobe.com/news/nation/2012/03/16/defendent-rutgers-spying-case-guilty-hate-crimes/7KF8AAexk3gih01WS4W09/story/html)

Zhang, Baohui, Alexi A. Wright, Haiden A. Huskamp, Matthew E. Nilsson, Matthew L. Maciejewski, Craig C. Earle, Susan D. Block, Paul K. Maciejewski, and Holly Prigerson. 2009. "Health Care Costs in the Last Week of Life." *Archives of Internal Medicine.* 16(5):480–488.

Zhao, Yong. 2005. "Increasing Math and Science Achievement: The Best and Worst of the East and West." *Phi Delta Kappan* (November):219–22.

Zimbardo, Philip C. 2004. "Power Turns Good Soldiers Into 'Bad Apples.'" *Boston Globe* (May 9). Retrieved July 5, 2008 (www.boston.com/news/globe/editorial_opinion/oped/articles/2004/05/09/power_turns_good_soldiers_into_bad_apples).

Zimbardo, Philip C., Craig Haney, Curtis Banks, and David Jaffe. 1973. "The Mind Is a Formidable Jailer: A Pirandellian Prison." *The New York Times* (April 8):38–60.

Zull, James E. 2002. *The Art of Changing the Brain: Enriching the Practice of Teaching by Exploring the Biology of Learning*. Sterling, VA: Stylus.

Credits

Image, "How Do We Know?" features. © iStockphoto .com.

Image, "What Have We Learned?" features. © iStockphoto.com.

Image, "Sociology Around the World" features. © iStockphoto.com.

Image, "Sociology in Your Social World" features. © iStockphoto.com.

Chapter 1

Photo 1.1 CO, page 2. © iStockphoto.com

Photo 1.2 CO, page 2. © Mansir Petrie

Photo 1.3 CO, page 2. © iStockphoto.com/Juan Collado

Photo 1.4 CO, page 2. © iStockphoto.com/Judy Foldetta

Photo 1.1, page 4. © Keith Roberts

Photo 1.2, page 5. © Peter Turnley/Corbis

Photo 1.3, page 6. © Keith Roberts

Photo 1.4, page 8. © PhotoStock-Israel/Alamy

Photo 1.5, page 9. © Dan Lundberg/Wikipedia

Photo 1.6, page 10. © iStockphoto.com/Jessica Liu

Photo 1.7, page 11. © Image Source/Corbis

Photo 1.8, page 11. © iStockphoto.com/Pascal Genes

Photo 1.9, page 12. Photo courtesy of Hanover College

Photo 1.10, page 14. © Thinkstock

Photo 1.11, page 18. Image courtesy Central Asia Institute

Photo 1.12, page 19. © WOLFGANG KUMM/DPA/ Landov

Photo 1.13, page 20. © Peter Turnley/CORBIS

Photo 1.14, page 23. © Benjamin J. Myers/Corbis

Photo 1.15, page 25. © iStockphoto.com/Sylvie Fourgeot

Chapter 2

Photo 2.1 CO, page 30. © iStockphoto.com/ Vicktor Pryymachuk

Photo 2.2 CO, page 30. © iStockphoto.com

Photo 2.3 CO, page 30. © iStockphoto.com/mikeuk

Photo 2.4 CO, page 30. © iStockphoto.com/Laurence Gough

Photo 2.5 CO, page 30. © James McDivitt, Gemini 4, NASA

Photo 2.1, page 32. © Sean Sprague/The Image Works

Photo 2.2, page 33. © iStockphoto.com/Monte Wilson

Photo 2.3, page 34. © Jared Embree

Photo 2.4, page 36. © Keith Roberts

Photo 2.5, page 37. © Digital Vision/Christopher Robbins/Thinkstock

Photo 2.6, page 37. © Keith Roberts

Photo 2.7, page 39. © Jeanne Ballantine

Photo 2.8, page 39. © Ed Quinn/Corbis

Photo 2.9, page 40. © Keith Roberts

Photo 2.10, page 42. © istockphoto.com/ David H. Lewis

Photo 2.11, page 41. N/A

Photo 2.12, page 48. © Charles Marville/ The Bridgeman Art Library/Getty Images

Photo 2.13, page 47. © Jean-Pierre Houël/Wikipedia

Photo 2.14, page 51. © istockphoto.com/andipantz

Photo 2.15, page 53. © Keith Roberts

Photo 2.16, page 54. © istockphoto.com

Photo 2.17, page 55. N/A

Photo 2.18, page 55. © Jeanne Ballantine

Photo 2.19, page 56. © Karen Porter

Photo 2.20, page 58. © Photodisc/ Digital Vision/ Thinkstock

Photo 2.21a, page 58. N/A

Photo 2.21b, page 58. © Bettmann/CORBIS

Photo 2.21c, page 58. © Bettmann/CORBIS

Photo 2.22, page 60. © Courtesy of the American Sociological Association

Photo 2.23, page 60. © SAUL LOEB/Getty Images

Chapter 3

Photo CO 3.1, page 66. © Jared Embree

Photo CO 3.2, page 66. © Peter Menzel/menzelphoto .com

Photo CO 3.3, page 66. © Peter Menzel/menzelphoto .com

Photo CO 3.4, page 66. © Jared Embree

Photo CO 3.5, page 66. © Lawrence Manning / Corbis

Photo 3.1, page 69. © Peter Menzel/menzelphoto.com

Photo 3.2, page 71. © Canstock

Photo 3.3, page 71. © Keith Roberts

Photo 3.4, page 72. © Olivier Martel/Corbis

Photo 3.5, page 73. © istockphoto.com/Britta Kasholm-Tengve

Photo 3.6, page 74. © Ben Penner

Photo 3.7, page 74. © Keith Roberts

Photo 3.8, page 75. © JAGADEESH NV/EPA /Landov

Photo 3.9, page 75. © iStockphoto,com/Richard Stamper

Photo 3.10, page 77. © Keith Roberts

Photo 3.11, page 79. © Digital Vision/Thinkstock

Photo 3.12, page 80. N/A

Photo 3.13, page 81. © Lifesize/Thinkstock

Photo 3.14, page 81. © istockphoto.com/Paige Falk

Photo 3.15, page 83. © Elise Roberts

Photo Essay 3.1, page 86. © Keith Roberts

Photo Essay 3.2, page 86. © Keith Roberts

Photo Essay 3.3, page 86. © Jared Embree

Photo Essay 3.4, page 86. © Keith Roberts

Photo Essay 3.5, page 86. © Jared Embree

Photo Essay 3.6, page 86. © Elise Roberts

Photo 3.16, page 83. © Comstock/Thinkstock

Photo 3.17, page 87. © istockphoto.com/ Andrew Leve

Photo 3.18, page 90. © www.istockphoto.com

Photo 3.19, page 92. © Sarah Jolly

Photo 3.20, page 92. N/A

Photo 3.21, page 92. © Courtesy of Hanover College

Photo 3.22, page 94. © iStockphoto.com/ Vasiliy Koval

Photo 3.23, page 96. © Andy Aitchison/Corbis

Photo 3.24, page 97. © iStockphoto.com /Diane Diederich

Photo 3.25, page 97. © Keith Roberts

Photo 3.26, page 99. © Thinkstock

Photo 3.27, page 101. N/A

Photo 3.28, page 103. N/A

Photo 3.29, page 103. © Daniel Berehulak/ Getty

Photo 3.30, page 104. © Jeanne Ballantine

Chapter 4

Photo 4.1 CO, page 108. © Yang Liu/Corbis

Photo 4.2 CO, page 108. © Yang Liu/Corbis

Photo 4.3 CO, page 108. © Ariel Skelley

Photo 4.4 CO, page 108. © iStockphoto.com/ Sean Locke

Photo 4.5 CO, page 108. Image courtesy Central Asia Institute

Photo 4.1, page 111. © iStockphoto.com/Ben German

Photo 4.2, page 113. © iStockphoto.com/Peeter Viisimaa

Photo 4.3, page 116. © Keith Roberts

Photo 4.4, page 118. © Bill Pierce/Getty Images

Photo 4.5, page 119. © Keith Roberts

Photo 4.6, page 120. © iStockphoto.com/Christopher Knittel

Photo 4.7, page 121. © Digital Vision/Thinkstock

Photo 4.8, page 122. © ZUMA Wire Service/Alamy

Photo 4.9a, page 123. © istockphoto.com/Carsten Brandt

Photo 4.9b, page 123. © Jehad Nga/Corbis

Photo 4.9c, page 123. © iStockphoto.com/Alan Eisen

Photo 4.9d, page 123. © ZHAO ZP/EPA /Landov
Photo 4.10, page 123. © Comstock/Jupiterimages/ Thinkstock
Photo 4.11, page 123. © Everett Kennedy Brown/epa/ Corbis
Photo 4.12, page 123. © Tibor Bognar/Corbis
Photo 4.13, page 125. © Digital Vision/Jeff Randall/ Thinkstock
Photo 4.14, page 127. © Brand X Pictures/ Thinkstock
Photo 4.15, page 128. © Ryan Pyle/Corbis

Chapter 5

Photo 5.1 CO, page 138. © BananaStock/Thinkstock
Photo 5.2 CO, page 138. © iStockphoto.com/ Aaron Kohr
Photo 5.3 CO, page 138. © iStockphoto.com/Sean Locke
Photo 5.4 CO, page 138. © Tim Pannell/Corbis
Photo 5.5 CO, page 138. © iStockphoto.com
Photo 5.1, page 140. © Keith Roberts
Photo 5.2, page 141. N/A
Photo 5.3, page 143. N/A
Photo 5.4, page 145. © iStockphoto.com /Jim Jurica
Photo 5.5, page 145. © iStockphoto.com /Jacob Wackerhausen
Photo 5.6a, page 146. © iStockphoto.com /Mark Coffey
Photo 5.6b, page 146. © Michael Westhoff/ iStockphoto.com
Photo 5.6c, page 146. © iStockphoto.com/Julie Deshaies
Photo 5.6d, page 146. © iStockphoto.com
Photo 5.7a, page 146. © iStockphoto.com/Stephanie Phillips
Photo 5.7b, page 146. © istockphoto.com/ Sean Locke
Photo 5.8, page 146. © Jim Winstead
Photo Essay 5.1, page 151. © Jeanne Ballantine
Photo Essay 5.2, page 151. © Bruno Morandi/Corbis
Photo Essay 5.3, page 151. © Jeanne Ballantine
Photo Essay 5.4, page 151. © Jeanne Ballantine
Photo Essay 5.5, page 151. © Kate Ballantine
Photo Essay 5.6, page 151. © iStockphoto.com/ Frances Twitty
Photo 5.9, page 146. © iStockphoto.com/Nancy Louie
Photo 5.10, page 147. N/A
Photo 5.11a, page 147. © Jeanne Ballantine
Photo 5.11b, page 147. © Thinkstock
Photo 5.12, page 147. © Elise Roberts
Photo 5.13, page 151. © Steve Starr/Corbis
Photo 5.14, page 151. © iStockphoto.com/Sean Locke
Photo 5.15, page 151. © Tim Pannell/Corbis
Photo 5.16, page 152. © USAID
Photo 5.17, page 153. © Elise Roberts
Photo 5.18a, page 155. © Clay Ballantine
Photo 5.18b, page 155. © Clay Ballantine
Photo 5.19, page 156. © FAO/Giulio Napolitano

Chapter 6

Photo 6.1 CO, page 170. © Mark Goddard/ iStockphoto.com
Photo 6.2 CO, page 170. © Thinkstock/Ryan McVay
Photo 6.3 CO, page 170. © Stephanie Phillips/ iStockphoto.com
Photo 6.4 CO, page 170. © Carson Ganci/Design Pics/Corbis
Photo 6.5 CO, page 170. © Jose Fuste Raga/Corbis
Photo 6.1, page 174. © EdStock/istock
Photo Essay 6.1, page 175. © Jose Fuste Raga/Corbis
Photo Essay 6.2, page 175. © iStockphoto.com/ Jennifer Matthews
Photo Essay 6.3, page 175. © iStockphoto.com/Eva Serrabassa
Photo Essay 6.4, page 175. © Keith Roberts
Photo Essay 6.5, page 175. N/A
Photo 6.2, page 175. © iStockphoto.com/ Jerry Koch
Photo 6.3, page 177. N/A
Photo 6.4, page 176. © Kim Kulish/Corbis
Photo 6.5, page 176. © Jupiterimages/ Pixland/ Thinkstock
Photo 6.6, page 177. © Keith Roberts
Photo 6.7, page 176. © www.istockphoto.com
Photo 6.8, page 176. © Polka Dot/Jupiterimages/ Thinkstock
Photo 6.9, page 177. © Ta'izz, Yemen/ Corbis
Photo 6.10, page 179. © MICHAEL REYNOLDS/ epa/Corbis
Photo 6.11, page 180. N/A
Photo 6.12, page 181. © AP Images
Photo 6.13a, page 183. © blueskybcn/ istock
Photo 6.13b, page © Adam Mastoon/CORBIS
Photo 6.14, page © Moviestore collection Ltd / Alamy
Photo 6.15, page 186. © iStockphoto.com/ Ryan Tacay
Photo 6.16, page 188. © Ron Sachs/CNP/Corbis
Photo 6.17, page 193. © Jupiterimages/ Thinkstock
Photo 6.18, page © DANIEL AGUILAR/Reuters / Landov
Photo 6.19, page 194. © Comstock/ Thinkstock
Photo 6.20, page 194. © istockphoto.com/ Slobo Mitic

Chapter 7

Photo 7.1 CO, page 214. © Keith Roberts
Photo 7.2 CO, page 214. © Keith Roberts
Photo 7.3 CO, page 214. © Jeanne Ballantine
Photo 7.4 CO, page 214. © Jeanne Ballantine
Photo 7.5 CO, page 214. © iStockphoto.com/Juan Collado
Photo 7.6 CO, page 214. © Elise Roberts
Photo 7.7 CO, page 214. © iStockphoto.com/Skip O'Donnell
Photo 7.1, page 215. © epa european pressphoto agency b.v. / Alamy
Photo 7.2a, page 217. © Keith Roberts
Photo 7.2b, page 217. © Keith Roberts
Photo 7.3a, page 217. © USAID
Photo 7.3b, page 217. © iStockphoto.com/Thania Navarro
Photo 7.4, page 218. © iStockphoto.com/Thomas Hottner
Photo 7.5, page 218. © istockphoto.com/Tomaz Levstek
Photo 7.6, page 219. © Jeanne Ballantine
Photo 7.7a, page 219. © istockphoto.com/ GYI NSEA
Photo 7.7b, page 219. © Paul Almasy/CORBIS
Photo 7.8, page 221. © Keith Roberts
Photo 7.9, page 224. © USAID
Photo 7.10, page 224. © Wendy Stone/CORBIS
Photo 7.11, page 225. © Chris Clinton/Thinkstock
Photo 7.12, page 226. © www.istockphoto.com/ Fernando Caceres
Photo 7.13a, page 227. © Jeanne Ballantine
Photo 7.13b, page 227. © Keith Roberts
Photo 7.14, page 229. © Keith Roberts
Photo 7.15, page 229. © Keith Roberts
Photo 7.16, page 231. © Elise Roberts
Photo 7.17, page 234. © Keith Roberts
Photo 7.18a, page 234. © istockphoto.com/ peeterv
Photo 7.18b, page 236. © istockphoto.com/Pgiam
Photo 7.18c, page © istockphoto.com/ M
Photo 7.19a, page 237. © istockphoto.com
Photo 7.19b, page 239. © Emma Rian/zefa/Corbis
Photo 7.20, page 240. © Jeanne Ballantine
Photo 7.21a, page 241. © Elise Roberts
Photo 7.21b, page © Keith Roberts

Chapter 8

Photo 8.1 CO, page 258. © iStockphoto.com
Photo 8.2 CO, page 258. © Jeanne Ballantine
Photo 8.3 CO, page 258. © Jeanne Ballantine
Photo 8.4 CO, page 258. © Robert A. Sabo/Getty Images
Photo 8.5 CO, page 258. © Jiang Dao Hua/ iStockphoto.com
Photo 8.6 CO, page 258. © Elise Roberts
Photo 8.1, page 260. © Zana Briski and Kids with Cameras. Used with permission from "Kids with Cameras."
Photo 8.2, page N/A
Photo 8.3, page 261. © Sophie Elbaz/Sygma/Corbis
Photo 8.4, page 261. © Bettmann/CORBIS
Photo 8.5, page 267. © istockphoto.com /Jerry Moorman
Photo 8.6a, page 269. © Library of Congress/ Photographer Ansel Adams
Photo 8.6b, page 270. © Bettmann/Corbis
Photo 8.7, page 273. © Andrew Holbrooke/Corbis
Photo 8.8, page 273. © Scott Olson/Getty Images
Photo 8.9, page 274. © Bettmann/CORBIS
Photo 8.10, page 275. © Phil Schermeister/CORBIS
Photo 8.11, page 276. N/A
Photo 8.12, page 278. © MOHAMED NURELDIN ABDALLAH/Reuters/Landov
Photo 8.13, page 279. © Ed Lallo/Time Life Pictures/ Getty Images
Photo 8.14, page 281. © Keith Roberts
Photo 8.15, page 281. © Keith Roberts
Photo 8.16, page 282. © Josef Scaylea/CORBIS
Photo 8.17, page 283. © istockphoto.com/ brytta
Photo 8.18, page 284. © William Campbell/Sygma/Corbis
Photo 8.19, page 286. © Bettmann/CORBIS
Photo 8.20, page 287. © istockphoto.com
Photo 8.21, page 289. © SEAN GARDNER/Reuters / Landov
Photo 8.22, page 292. © TOUHIG SION/CORBIS SYGMA

Chapter 9

Photo 9.1 CO, page 300. © Kazuyoshi Nomachi/Corbis
Photo 9.2 CO, page 300. © iStockphoto.com/Zsolt Nyulaszi
Photo 9.3 CO, page 300. © Mansir Petrie
Photo 9.4 CO, page 300. © Mansir Petrie
Photo 9.5 CO, page 300. © iStockphoto.com/Jo Ann Snover
Photo 9.6 CO, page 300. © Jeanne Ballantine
Photo 9.7 CO, page 300. © David Van Der Veen/epa/ Corbis
Photo 9.1, page 303. © Atlantide Phototravel/Corbis
Photo 9.2, page 304. © Thomas Strange/iStockphoto .com
Photo 9.3, page 307. © Kate Ballantine
Photo 9.4a, page 307. © www.Istockphoto.com/GYI NSEA
Photo 9.4b, page 307. © www.Istockphoto.com/GYI NSEA
Photo 9.4c, page 307. © Rebecca Blackwell/ AP Images
Photo 9.5, page 308. © Marc Asnin/ Corbis
Photo 9.6, page 310. © www.Istockphoto.com/Zsolt Nyulaszi
Photo 9.7, page 311. © Jostein Hauge/iStockphoto.com
Photo 9.8, page 312. © Keith Roberts
Photo 9.9a, page 313. © Keith Roberts
Photo 9.9b, page © Keith Roberts
Photo 9.10a, page 316. © www.Istockphoto.com/ GYI NSEA
Photo 9.10b, page © Daily Mail/Rex / Alamy
Photo 9.11a, page 317. Photo by Joe Robbins; courtesy of Hanover College
Photo 9.11b, page 317. © Wesley Hitt/ Getty Images
Photo 9.12, page 317. © istockphoto.com/Aldo Murillo
Photo 9.13, page 319. © iStockphoto.com/ Pathathai Chungyam
Photo 9.14, page 319. © USAID
Photo 9.15, page 320. © Trinette Reed/Brand X/Corbis
Photo 9.16, page 320. © istock.com/ kali9
Photo 9.17, page 322. © Jeanne Ballantine
Photo 9.18, page 325. © Nadeem Khawer/epa/Corbis
Photo 9.19, page 326. © Narendra Shrestha /epa/ Corbis
Photo 9.20, page 327. © goodshot/thinkstock
Photo 9.21, page 329. © UNESCO, photo by Dominique Rogers

Chapter 10

Photo 10.1 CO, page 346. © Akram Saleh/Reuters/ Corbis
Photo 10.2 CO, page 346. © iStockphoto.com/
Photo 10.3 CO, page 346. © iStockphoto.com/Radu Razvan
Photo 10.4 CO, page 346. © iStockphoto.com/Nancy Louie
Photo 10.5 CO, page 346. © SAUL LOEB/AFP/Getty Images
Photo 10.6 CO, page 346. © iStockphoto.com/Fred Palmieri
Photo 10.1, page 348. © Elena Korenbaum
Photo 10.2, page 349. © Kate Ballantine
Photo 10.3a, page 351. © Kate Ballantine
Photo 10.3b, page 351. © istockphoto.com/ Glenda Powers
Photo 10.4, page 351. © Kate Ballantine
Photo 10.5, page 352. © Wolfgang Kaehler/CORBIS
Photo Essay 10.1, page 354. © Kate Ballantine
Photo Essay 10.2, page 354. © iStockphoto.com/ Jelani Memory
Photo Essay 10.3, page 354. © Kate Ballantine
Photo Essay 10.4, page 354. © iStockphoto.com/Jaren Wicklund
Photo Essay 10.5, page 354. © Kate Ballantine
Photo 10.6, page 352. © Carla Howery
Photo 10.7, page 352. © Andualem Sisay
Photo 10.8, page 353. © Photodisc/ Barbara Penoyar/ Thinkstock
Photo 10.9, page 353. © istock.com/GYI NSEA
Photo 10.10, page 353. © Comstock/ JupiterImages/ Thinkstock
Photo 10.11, page 353. © China Photos/Getty Images
Photo 10.12, page 355. © Elise Roberts
Photo 10.13, page 356. © JOE SKIPPER/Reuters / Landov
Photo 10.14, page 357. © Comstock/ Jupiterimages/ Thinkstock
Photo 10.15, page 360. © Mark Savage/Corbis
Photo 10.16, page 362. © David Adame/Getty Images
Photo 10.17, page 364. © Hemera/Thinkstock
Photo 10.18, page 365. © iStockphoto.com/ NI QIN
Photo 10.19, page 366. © Mansir Petrie
Photo 10.20, page 367. © Thinkstock

Chapter 11

Photo 11.1 CO, page 382. © iStockphoto.com
Photo 11.2 CO, page 382. © Jared Embree
Photo 11.3 CO, page 382. Photo courtesy of Hanover College
Photo 11.4 CO, page 382. © Jeanne Ballantine
Photo 11.5 CO, page 382. © Elise Roberts
Photo 11.1a, page 385. © Father Celse Hakuziyaremye
Photo 11.1b, page 385. © Father Celse Hakuziyaremye
Photo 11.2, page © Jared Embree
Photo 11.3, page 386. © Jupiterimages/Thinkstock
Photo 11.4, page 387. © iStockphoto.com/Brandon Laufenberg
Photo 11.5, page 387. © Jeanne Ballantine
Photo 11.6, page 389. © Thinkstockphotos.com/ Jupiterimages
Photo Essay 11.1, page 392. © iStockphoto.com/ Bonnie Jacobs
Photo Essay 11.2, page 392. © Keith Roberts
Photo Essay 11.3, page 392. N/A
Photo Essay 11.4, page 392. © iStockphoto.com/ Charles Silvey
Photo Essay 11.5, page 392. © Keith Dannemiller/ D70s/Corbis
Photo Essay 11.6, page 392. © USAID
Photo 11.7, page 390. © Najlah Feanny/Corbis
Photo 11.8, page 391. © Keith Roberts
Photo 11.9, page 392. © iStockphoto.com/Bonnie Jacobs
Photo 11.10, page 392. © Keith Roberts
Photo 11.11, page 393. © USAID
Photo 11.12, page 391. N/A
Photo 11.13, page 392. © Najlah Feanny/ Corbis
Photo 11.14, page 393. © Elise Roberts
Photo 11.15, page 393. © miafarrow.org
Photo 11.16, page 397. © Karen Kasmauski/Corbis
Photo 11.17, page 399. © Gideon Mendel/Corbis
Photo 11.18, page 399. © Karen Kasmauski/Corbis
Photo 11.19, page 402. © Gideon Mendel/Corbis
Photo 11.20, page 403. © Najlah Feanny/Corbis
Photo 11.21, page 404. © Central Asia Institute
Photo 11.22, page 405. © Alain Nogues/Corbis
Photo 11.23, page 407. © Lynn Johnson/ Corbis
Photo 11.24, page 408. © Anthony Bannister/Corbis
Photo 11.25, page 411. Courtesy of Hanover College

Chapter 12

Photo 12.1 CO, page 422. © iStockphoto.com/Steven Allen
Photo 12.2 CO, page 422. © iStockphoto.com/Nancy Louie
Photo 12.3 CO, page 422. © iStockphoto.com
Photo 12.4 CO, page 422. © Elise Roberts
Photo 12.1, page 426. © Jeanne Ballantine
Photo 12.2, page 426. © Christophe Boisvieux/Corbis
Photo 12.3, page 429. © Creatas/ Thinkstock
Photo 12.4, page 429. © istockphoto.com/ Graham Graham
Photo 12.5, page 430. © Kevin Fleming/Corbis
Photo 12.6, page 431. © Peter Turnley/CORBIS
Photo 12.7, page 431. © iStockphoto.com/Matthias Wassermann
Photo 12.8, page 432. © Antoine Gyori/CORBIS SYGMA
Photo 12.9, page 432. © AHMAD AL-RUBAYE/AFP/ Getty Images
Photo 12.10, page 433. © Keith Roberts
Photo 12.11, page 434. Used with permission from the First Presbyterian Church of Granada Hills.
Photo 12.12, page 435. Ken Matesich, photographer. Courtesy of the Arizona State Museum and the University of Arizona.
Photo 12.13, page 436. © Keith Roberts
Photo 12.14a, page 437. © Keith Roberts
Photo 12.14b, page 437. © Keith Roberts
Photo 12.14c, page 437. © Keith Roberts
Photo 12.15, page 439. © Keith Roberts
Photo 12.16, page 440. © Scott Olson/ Getty Images
Photo 12.17, page 443. © AFP/Getty
Photo 12.18, page 443. © Keith Roberts
Photo 12.19, page 443. © JOHN GRESS/Reuters/ Corbis
Photo 12.20, page 449. © Virginia Caudill
Photo 12.21, page 452. © Keith Roberts
Photo 12.22a, page 454. © Brand X Pictures/ Thinkstock
Photo 12.22b, page 457. © Keith Roberts
Photo 12.22c, page 457. © www.istockphoto.com/ Marcin Pawinski
Photo 12.23, page 457. © Elise Roberts

Chapter 13

Photo 13.1 CO, page 466. © Mark Poprocki
Photo 13.2 CO, page 466. © iStockphoto.com/ Ann Steer
Photo 13.3 CO, page 466. © iStockphoto.com/Tony Tremblay

Photo 13.4 CO, page 466. © USAID
Photo 13.5 CO, page 466. © Keith Roberts
Photo 13.1, page 468. © Pablo Martinez Monsivais/ Corbis
Photo 13.2, page 470. © Digital Vision/ Thinkstock
Photo 13.3, page 473. © Canstock Photo
Photo 13.4, page 474. © istock.com/ EdStock2
Photo 13.5, page 474. OpenMyanmar Photo Project
Photo 13.6, page 475. © istock.com/GYI NSEA
Photo 13.7, page 478. © epa european pressphoto agency b.v. / Alamy
Photo 13.8, page 483. © Ralf-Finn Hestoft/ Corbis
Photo 13.9, page 485. © Ernst Haas/Ernst Haas/Getty Images
Photo 13.10, page 486. © REUTERS/Beawiharta
Photo 13.11, page 488. © Mario Tama/Getty Images
Photo 13.12, page 488. © PRENSA LATINA/Reuters / Landov
Photo 13.13, page 489. © Ernst Haas/Ernst Haas/ Getty Images
Photo 13.14, page 490. © Elise Roberts
Photo 13.15, page 491. © POOL/Reuters /Landov
Photo 13.16, page 493. © istock.com/ Linda Steward
Photo 13.17, page 494. © Keith Roberts
Photo 13.18, page 496. © JORGE UZON/AFP/Getty Images
Photo 13.19, page 496. © AFP/AFP/Getty Images
Photo 13.20, page 501. © AHMAD GHARABLI/AFP/ Getty Images
Photo 13.21, page 504. © Mia Song/Star Ledger/Corbis
Photo 13.22, page 504. © Mahmoud Shanti/ Corbis
Photo 13.23, page 505. © Ursillo Catherine/ Getty
Photo 13.24, page 506. © NIKOLAY DONCHEV/ Corbis

Chapter 14

Photo 14.1 CO, page 510. © iStockphoto.com/ Andreej Tokarski
Photo 14.2 CO, page 510. © Tony Arruza/CORBIS
Photo 14.3 CO, page 510. © Luis Enrique Ascui/ Reuters/Corbis
Photo 14.4 CO, page 510. © iStockphoto.com/ Matthew Rambo
Photo 14.5 CO, page 510. © Jared Embree
Photo 14.1, page 512. © Claudio Peri/ Corbis
Photo 14.2, page 514. © Kate Ballantine
Photo 14.3, page 515. © Reuters/CORBIS
Photo 14.4, page 517. © istockphoto.com/ Suzanne Toro
Photo 14.5, page 519. © World Health Organization 2006
Photo 14.6, page 523. © The Washington Post/Getty Images
Photo 14.7, page 524. © istockphoto.com/ Luis Pedrosa
Photo 14.8, page 525 . © Erwin Patzelt/dpa/Corbis
Photo 14.9a, page 531. © iStockphoto.com/ David Elfstrom
Photo 14.9b, page 531. © Jared Embree
Photo 14.10a, page 531. © iStockphoto.com/Leah-Anne Thompson
Photo 14.10b, page 531. © iStockphoto.com/Sean Locke
Photo 14.10c, page 533. © iStockphoto.com/Rich Legg
Photo 14.10d, page 533. © iStockphoto.com/Joseph Abbot
Photo 14.11, page 533. © 2006 CNET Networks, Inc
Photo 14.12, page 533. © Ed Kashi/CORBIS
Photo 14.13, page 533. © Najlah Feanny/CORBIS SABA
Photo 14.14, page 533. © iStockphoto.com/Havard Saebo
Photo 14.15, page 535. © istockphoto.com/ Rasmus Jurkatam
Photo 14.16a, page 537. © Noriko Coop
Photo 14.16b, page 537. © USAID Dakar, Senegal
Photo 14.17, page 540. © USAID
Photo 14.18, page 543. © Jared Embree
Photo 14.19a, page 544. © 2006 World Health Organization. All Rights Reserved
Photo 14.19b, page 544. © 2006 World Health Organization. All Rights Reserved
Photo 14.19c, page 544. © 2006 World Health Organization. All Rights Reserved

Chapter 15

Photo 15.1 CO, page 554. © NASA
Photo 15.2 CO, page 554. © NASA
Photo 15.1, page 557. © USAID
Photo 15.2, page 558. © Elise Roberts
Photo 15.3, page 560. © Gideon Mendel/CORBIS
Photo 15.4, page 561. © AHMAD GHARABLI/ Getty Images
Photo 15.5, page 563. © Reuters/CORBIS
Photo 15.6, page 563. © Alain Keler/Sygma/Corbis
Photo 15.7, page 564. Morel/ Associated Press
Photo 15.8a, page 566. © 2006 World Health Organization
Photo 15.8b, page 567. © 2006 World Health Organization
Photo 15.9a, page 568. © Kate Ballantine
Photo 15.9b, page 569. © Wolfgang Kaehler/CORBIS
Photo 15.10, page 571. © www.downtheroad.org
Photo 15.11, page 572. © Jeanne Ballantine
Photo 15.12, page 573. © PORNCHAI KITTIWONGSAKUL/AFP/Getty Images
Photo 15.13, page 575. © Nani Afrida/epa/Corbis
Photo 15.14, page 580. © Louise Gubb/CORBIS SABA
Photo 15.15, page 585. © Ted Streshinsky/CORBIS
Photo 15.16, page 585. © Mimi Mollica/Corbis
Photo 15.17, page 586. © Louie Psihoyos/CORBIS
Photo 15.18, page 580. © Keith Roberts
Photo 15.19a, page 580. © Keith Roberts
Photo 15.19b, page 580. © Kate Ballantine
Photo 15.20, page 580. © Michael S. Yamashita/ CORBIS
Photo 15.21, page 593. © iStockphoto.com
Photo 15.22, page 594. © Jeanne Ballantine
Photo 15.23, page 594. © Michael Wassmer/Wikipedia
Photo 15.24, page 596. © iStockphoto.com/ Loic Bernard
Photo 15.25, page 598. © Elise Roberts
Photo 15.26, page 599. © Elise Roberts

Chapter 16

Photo 16.1 CO, page 604. © iStockphoto.com/Bart Sadowski
Photo 16.2 CO, page 604. © Brave New Films
Photo 16.3 CO, page 604. © Christopher J. Morris/ CORBIS
Photo 16.1, page 606. © Stockbyte/ Thinkstock
Photo 16.2a, page 608. © Jeanne Ballantine
Photo 16.2b, page 608. © Jon Hrusa/epa/Corbis
Photo 16.3, page 609. © Keith Roberts
Photo 16.4, page 609. © Keith Roberts
Photo 16.5, page 610. Photo by Luigi Novi/Wikipedia
Photo 16.6, page 610. © istockphoto.com/ Erlend Kvalsvik
Photo 16.7, page 611. © Jeanne Ballantine
Photo 16.8, page 612. © istockphoto.com/ParkerDeen
Photo 16.9, page 614. © USAID
Photo 16.10, page 615. © USAID
Photo 16.11, page 616. © Keith Roberts
Photo Essay 16.1, page 619. © Jeanne Ballantine
Photo Essay 16.2, page 619. © Keith Roberts
Photo Essay 16.3, page 619. © Keith Roberts
Photo Essay 16.4, page 619. © Keith Roberts
Photo Essay 16.5, page 619. © Keith Roberts
Photo Essay 16.6, page 619. © Keith Roberts
Photo Essay 16.7, page 619. © Keith Roberts
Photo Essay 16.8, page 619. © Keith Roberts
Photo Essay 16.9, page 619. © Keith Roberts
Photo Essay 16.10, page 619. © Getty Images
Photo 16.12, page 621. © Gideon Mendel/Corbis
Photo 16.13, page 622. © Corbis
Photo 16.14, page 623. © iStockphoto.com/Xuan Busto
Photo 16.15, page 624. © TONY KARUMBA/ Getty Images
Photo 16.16, page 625. © Thinkstock
Photo 16.17, page 631. © Nicholas Kamm/AFP/Getty Images
Photo 16.18, page 633. © istockphoto.com/ bgwalker
Photo 16.19, page 634. Witness for Peace
Photo 16.20, page 634. © WALTER DHLADHLA/ AFP/Getty Images
Photo 16.21, page 635. © Christopher J. Morris/ CORBIS
Photo 16.22, page 637. © TEKEE TANWAR/AFP/ Getty Images
Photo 16.23, page 638. © Jeanne Ballantine
Photo 16.24, page 639. © Keith Roberts
Photo 16.25, page 639. © Jeanne Ballantine

Glossary

Absolute poverty. Not having resources to meet basic needs, 247

Achieved status. Social status that is chosen or earned by decisions one makes and sometimes by personal ability, 149

Achieved stratification systems. Societal systems that allow individuals to earn positions through their ability, efforts, and choices, 239

Agents of socialization are the transmitters of culture—the people, organizations, and institutions that help us define our identity and teach us how to thrive in our social world, 125

Agricultural societies. Societies that rely primarily on raising crops for food and make use of technological advances such as the plow, irrigation, animals, and fertilization to continuously cultivate the same land, 73

Allopathy. Medical treatment supported by the American Medical Association and most Western medicine, involving remedies that are based on directly countering a patient's symptoms, 532

Anomie. The state of normlessness that occurs when rules for behavior in society break down under extreme stress from rapid social change or conflict, 153

Applied sociology. Applying sociological knowledge and research skills to address organizational needs or problems in government, education, health care settings, social service agencies, and business organizations; often the client determines the research questions, 49

Arranged marriages. A pattern of mate selection in which someone other than the couple—elder males, parents, a matchmaker—selects the marital partners, 359

Ascribed statuses. Social statuses that are often assigned at birth and that do not change during an individual's lifetime; gender, race, or ethnic status group are examples, 147

Ascribed stratification system. A societal system in which characteristics beyond the control of the individual—such as family background, age, sex, and race—determine one's position in society, 239

Assimilation. The structural and cultural merging of minority and majority groups in society, 281

Authoritarian political systems are controlled by absolute monarchs or dictators who allow limited or no participation of the population in government and control much of what happens in the lives of individual, 478

Authority. Power that people consider legitimate, 473

Beliefs. Ideas about life, the way society works, and where one fits in, 88

Bureaucracies. Specific types of large formal organizations that have the purpose of maximizing efficiency; they are characterized by formal relations between participants, clearly laid-out procedures and rules, and pursuit of shared goals, 158

Cause-and-effect relationships. Occur when there is a relationship between variables so that one variable stimulates a change in another, 38

Civil religion refers to the cultural beliefs, practices, and symbols that relate a nation to the ultimate conditions of its existence, 443

Collective behavior. Actions that are spontaneous, unstructured, and disorganized and that may violate norms; this behavior arises when people are trying to cope with stressful situations and unclear or uncertain conditions, 622

Conflict crimes occur when public opinion about the seriousness of these crimes is divided, based on people's differing social class, status, and interests, 178

Conflict theory. Theory that focuses on societal groups competing for scarce resources, 57

Consensus crimes are those where members of society are in general agreement about the seriousness of deviant acts, 178

Content analysis. Entails the systematic categorizing and recording of information from written or recorded sources—printed materials, videos, radio broadcasts, or artworks, 41

Control group. In a controlled experiment, the group in which the subjects are not exposed to the variable the experiment wants to test, 40

Controlled experiments. Experiments in which all variables except the one being studied are controlled so researchers can study the effects of the variable under study, 40

Controls. Steps used by researchers to eliminate all variables except those related to the hypothesis—especially those variables that might be spurious, 38

Correlation. relationship between variables SUCH AS POVERTY AND LOW LEVELS OF EDUCATION, WITH change in one variable is associated with change in another, 38

Counterculture. Groups with expectations and values that contrast sharply with the dominant values of a particular society, 97

Crime. Deviant actions for which there are severe formal penalties imposed by the government, 173

Cultural capital refers to knowledge, skills, language mastery, style of dress, and values that provide a person with access to a particular status in society, 223

Cultural relativism requires setting aside cultural and personal beliefs and prejudices to understand another group or society through the eyes of members of that community using its own standards, 83

Culture. The way of life shared by a group of people—the knowledge, beliefs, values, rules or laws, language, customs, symbols, and material products within a society that help meet human needs, 68

Democratic socialism. Collective or group planning of the development of society, but within a democratic political system; the good of the whole is paramount, 494

Democratic systems are political forms characterized by accountability of the government to the citizens and a large degree of control by individuals over their own lives, 490

Demographic transition theory. Compares countries' stages of economic development with trends in birth and death rates; used to determine how changes in economic structure and movement from agricultural areas to urban areas can have an impact on population size, 564

Demography. The study of human populations, 558

Denominations. Centralized coordinating bodies or associations that link local congregations with a similar history and theology, 435

Dependency ratio. The ratio of those in both the young and aged groups compared with the number of people in the productive age groups between 15 and 64 years old, 560

Dependent variable. The variable in a cause-and-effect relationship that is affected by and comes after the independent variable in time sequence, 38

Deprofessionalization is the process though which a professional occupation loses autonomy, respect, and service orientation because the professionals come to be controlled by nonprofessionals and outside forces—financial concerns, government regulation, technological changes, and administrators or management, 532

Deviance. The violation of social norms, 173

Discrimination. Differential treatment and harmful actions against minorities, 271

Dysfunctions. Actions that undermine the stability or equilibrium of society, 56

Empirical knowledge involves use of the five senses to gather facts that have been objectively (without opinion or bias) observed and carefully measured. This is done so that the reality of what is being measured should be the same for all the people who observe it, 33

Endogamy. Norms that require individuals to marry inside certain human boundaries, whatever the societal members see as protecting the homogeneity of the group, 359

Environment. The setting in which the social unit operates, including everything that influences the social unit, such as its physical surroundings and technological innovations, 20

Ethnic group. A group within the human species that is based on cultural factors: language, religion, dress, foods, customs, beliefs, values, norms, a shared group identity or feeling, and sometimes loyalty to a homeland, monarch, or religious leader, 268

Ethnocentrism. The tendency to view one's own group and its cultural expectations as right, proper, and superior to others, 81

Evidence. Facts and information that are confirmed through systematic processes of testing, using the five senses, 24

Existing sources. Materials that already exist but are being employed in a new way or analyzed to understand a different research question, 40

Exogamy. Norms governing the choice of a mate that require individuals to marry outside of their own immediate group, 358

Experimental group. In a controlled experiment, the group in which people are exposed to the variable being studied to test its effect, 40

Expressive movements. Group phenomena that focus on changing individuals and saving people from corrupt lifestyles; religious movements, secular psychotherapy movements, and self-help or self-actualization groups are examples, 632

Extended family include two or more adult generations that share tasks and living quarters. This may include brothers, sisters, aunts, uncles, cousins, and grandparents, 364

Fads are temporary behaviors, activities, or material objects that spread rapidly and are copied enthusiastically by large numbers of people, 625

Family of orientation the family into which we are born, 351

Family of procreation is the family we create ourselves, 351

Fashions are a style of appearance and behavior that is temporarily favored by a large number of people, 625

Fee-for-service health care. Doctors and hospitals are paid for each service they perform and decide the prices charged for every service, 528

Feminist theory. Critiques the hierarchical power structures, which feminists argue treat women and other minorities unequally, 59

Fertility. Demographic processes referring to the birth rate, 567

Formal agents of socialization are official or legal agents (e.g .families, school, teachers, religious training) whose purpose it is to socialize the individual into the values, beliefs, and behaviors of the culture, 125

Formal organizations. Modern rational organizations comprised of complex secondary groups deliberately formed to pursue and achieve certain goals, 158

Formal sanctions. Rewards or punishments conferred by recognized officials to enforce the most important norms, 90

Free-choice marriage. A pattern of mate selection in which the partners select each other based primarily on romance and love, 360

Functional theory assumes that all parts of the social structure (including groups, organizations, and institutions), the culture (values and beliefs), and social processes (social change or child rearing) work together to make the whole society run smoothly and harmoniously, 55

Game stage. Stage in the process of developing a social self when a child develops the ability to take the role of multiple others concurrently (norms, values, and expectations of the generalized other) and conform to societal expectations, 119

Gemeinschaft. German term meaning "small traditional community," 582

Gender refers to a society's notions of masculinity and femininity—socially constructed meanings associated with being male or female—and how individuals construct their identity in terms of gender within these constraints, 305

Gender roles are those commonly assigned tasks or expected behaviors linked to an individual's sex-determined statuses, 305

Generalized other. A composite of societal expectations that a child learns from family, peers, and other organizations, 119

Genocide. The systematic effort of one group, usually the dominant group, to destroy a minority group, 280

Gentrification. Refers to members of the middle and upper class, mostly young white professionals, buying and renovating rundown properties in central-city locations, and displacing poor residents, 591

Gesellschaft. German term meaning "large impersonal urban areas," 582

Global culture. Behavioral standards, symbols, values, and material objects that have become common across the globe, 101

Global transnational movements are mobilized groups that take place across societies as international organizations seek change in the status of women, child labor, rights of indigenous peoples, environmental degradation, global warming, disease pandemics, and other issues that affect the global community, 633

Globalization is the process by which the entire world is becoming a single interdependent sociocultural entity, more uniform, more integrated, and more interdependent, 101

Groups. Units involving two or more people who interact with each other because of shared common interests, goals, experiences, and needs, 153

Hate crimes. Criminal offenses committed against a person, property, or group that are motivated by the offender's bias against a religious, ethnic, or racial group; national origin; gender; or sexual orientation, 193

Health. A state of physical, mental, and social well-being or the absence of disease, 514

Herding society. Society in which the food-producing strategy is based on the society's domestication of animals, whose care is the central focus of their activities, 73

Horticultural societies. Societies in which the food-producing strategy is based on domestication of plants, using digging sticks and wooden hoes to cultivate small gardens, 73

Hospitals. Organizations for the care and treatment of the sick and injured, providing centralized medical knowledge and technology for treatment of patients, 531

Hunter-gatherer society. A society in which people rely on the vegetation and animals occurring naturally in their habitat to sustain life, 72

Hypothesis is an educated guess about how variables are related to each other, including causal relationships; the speculations do not yet have supporting data, 36

I. The spontaneous, unpredictable, impulsive, and largely unorganized aspect of the self, 118

Ideal culture consists of practices, beliefs, and values that are regarded as most desirable in society and are consciously taught to children, 89

Illness. Lack of health, 514

Imitation stage. A period when children under 3 years old are preparing for role-taking by observing others and imitating their behaviors, sounds, and gestures, 118

An **independent variable** is the variable in a cause-and-effect relationship that comes first in a time sequence and causes a change in another variable, 38

Industrial societies rely primarily on mechanized production for subsistence, resulting in greater division of labor based on expertise, 74

Informal agents of socialization. Unofficial forces that shape values, beliefs, and behaviors in which socialization is not the express purpose; examples are the media, books, advertising, and the Internet, 127

Informal sanctions. Unofficial rewards or punishments such as smiles, frowns, or ignoring unacceptable behaviors, 90

In-group. A group to which an individual feels a sense of loyalty and belonging; it also may serve as a reference group, 157

Institutions. Social units in societies through which organized social activities take place that provide the rules, roles, and relationships set up to meet human needs and direct and control human behavior. They provide the setting for activities essential to human and societal survival, 342

Interaction. The exchange of verbal and nonverbal messages, 110

Labeling theory. Symbolic interaction view that labels people carry affect their own and others' perceptions, directing behavior to conformity or deviance, 182

Language. Conveys verbal and nonverbal messages among members of society; the foundation of every culture, 91

Latent functions are unplanned or unintended consequences of actions or of social structures, 56

Levels of analysis. Social groups from the largest to the smallest, 16

Life expectancy. The average number of years a person in a particular society can expect to live, 572

Lifestyle. Includes attitudes, values, beliefs, behavior patterns, and other aspects of one's place in the world, shaped by socialization, 229

Looking-glass self. A reflective process that develops our *self* based on our interpretations and internalization of the reactions of others to us, 115

Macro-level analysis. Analysis of the largest social units in the social world, including entire nations, global forces, and international social trends, 22

Manifest functions are *the planned outcomes of interactions, social organizations, or institutions*, 56

Market systems/capitalism. An economic system driven by the balance of supply and demand, allowing free competition to reward the efficient and innovators with profits; stresses individual planning and private ownership of property, 492

Master status. An individual's social status that becomes most important and takes precedence over other statuses, 150

Material culture. Includes all the objects we can see or touch; all the artifacts of a group of people, 84

Me. The part of the self that has learned the rules of society through interaction and role-taking, and it controls the *I* and its desires, 118

Means of production. Karl Marx's concept of property, machinery, and cash owned by capitalists, 57

Mechanical solidarity is social cohesion and integration based on the similarity of individuals in the group, including shared beliefs, values, and emotional ties between members of the group, 71

Medicalization refers to the shift in handling of some forms of deviance as well as some normal human functions (such as pregnancy and childbirth) from the familial, legal, or religious arenas to the health care system, 516

Meritocracy. A social group or organization in which people are allocated to positions according to their abilities and credentials, as in level of education attained, 233

Meso-level analysis. Analysis of intermediate-size social units, smaller than the nation but large enough to encompass more than the local community or region, 22

Microculture. The culture of a group or an organization that affects only a small segment of one's life or influences a limited period of one's life, 96

Micro-level analysis. Analysis with a focus on individual or small group interaction in specific situations, 21

Migration. In terms of demographic processes, refers to the movement of people from one place to another, 567

Minority groups. Groups in a population that differ from others in some characteristicsand are therefore subject to less power,fewer privileges, anddiscrimination, 265

Mobs. Emotional crowds that engage in violence against a specific target; lynchings, killings, and hate crimes are examples, 624

Monogamy. The most familiar form of marriage in industrial and postindustrial societies; refers to marriage of two individuals, 364

Mortality. In terms of demographic processes, refers to the death rate, 567

Myths are stories, true or not, that transmit values and embody ideas about life and the world, 431

National culture refers to common values and beliefs that tie citizens of a nation together, 100

National society is a population of people, usually living within a specified geographic area, who are connected by common ideas, cooperate for the attainment of common goals, and are subject to a particular political authority, 100

New religious movements (NRMs). Innovative religious groups that may become established new religions if they survive for several generations, 439

Nonmaterial culture. The thoughts, language, feelings, beliefs, values, and attitudes that make up much of our culture, 84

Nonverbal communication. Interactions without words using facial expressions, the head, eye contact, body posture, gestures, touch, walk, status symbols, and personal space, 145

Norms. Rules of behavior shared by members of a society and rooted in the value system, 89

Objectivity entails steps taken to ensure that ones's personal opinions or values do not bias or contaminate data collection or analysis, 34

Observational studies (also called field methods). (also called field methods) involve systematic, planned observation and recording of interactions or human behavior in natural settings, 40

Organic solidarity. Émile Durkheim's term for social coherence (glue) based on division of labor, with each member playing a highly specialized role in the society and each person being dependent on others due to interrelated, interdependent tasks, 71

Organized crime. Ongoing criminal enterprises by an organized group whose ultimate purpose is economic gain through illegitimate means, 195

Out-group. A group to which an individual does not belong and a group that is often in competition with or in opposition to an in-group, 157

Panic. Occurs when a large number of individuals become fearful or try to flee threatening situations that are beyond their control, sometimes putting their lives in danger, 624

Past-in-present discrimination refers to practices from the past that may no longer be allowed but that continue to have consequences for people in the present, 278

Peer group. A group of people who are roughly equal in some status within the society, such as the same age or the same occupation, 114

Planned or centralized systems. An economic system that attempts to limit private ownership of property and have the government do planning of production and distribution, 492

Play stage involves a child, usually between 3 and 5, having the ability to see things (role-take) from the perspective of one person at a time; simple role-taking or play-acting, 118

Pluralism occurs when each ethnic or racial group in a country maintains its own culture and separate set of institutions but has recognized equity in the society, 282

Polyandry, a marital system in which a wife has more than one husband, 364

Polygamy, refers to marriage of one person to more than one partner at the same time, 364

Polygyny, a marital system in which a husband can have more than one wife, 364

Population transfer. The removal, often forced, of a minority group from a region or country, 281

Populations. Permanent societies, states, communities, adherents of a common religious faith, racial or ethnic groups, kinship or clan groups, professions, and other identifiable categories of people, 558

Postindustrial societies. Societies that have moved from human labor and manufacturing to automated production and service jobs, largely processing information, 75

Power. Ability of a person or group to realize its own will in groups, even against the resistance of others, 243

Power elite. Power held by top leaders in corporations, politics and military; this interlocking elite makes major decisions guiding the nation, 243

Predatory crimes are those crimes committed against individuals or property and are considered by the public to be the most serious crimes, 192

Prejudice. Attitudes that prejudge a group, usually negatively and not based on facts, 271

Prestige refers to the esteem, recognition, and respect one receives, based on wealth, position, or accomplishments, 243

Primary deviance. A violation of a norm that may be an isolated act, or an initial act of rule breaking, 182

Primary groups. Groups characterized by close, intimate, long-term contacts, cooperation, and relationships, 154

Public sociologists strive to better understand how society operates and to make practical use of their sociological findings, 49

Race refers to a group identified by a society because of certain biologically inherited physical characteristics that cause members of the group to receive differential treatment, 264

Racism is any meso-level institutional arrangement that favors one racial group over another; this favoritism may result in intentional or unintentional consequences for minority groups, 276

Rational choice (exchange) theory. A theory that focuses on humans as fundamentally concerned with self-interests, making rational decisions based on weighing costs and rewards of the projected outcome, 53

Rationalization of social life is the attempt to maximize efficiency by creating rules and procedures focused solely on accomplishing goals, 157

Real culture. The way things in society are actually done, 89

Recidivism rates. The likelihood that someone who is arrested, convicted, and imprisoned will later be a repeat offender, 205

Reference groups. Groups comprised of members who act as role models and establish standards against which members evaluate their conduct, 156

Relative poverty. Occurs when one's income falls below the poverty line, resulting in an inadequate standard of living relative to others in the individual's country, 247

Reproduction of class refers to the socioeconomic positions of one generation passing on to the next, 407

Resistance or regressive movements try to protect an existing system, protect part of that system, or return to what a system had been by overthrowing current laws and practices. They see societal change as a threat to values or practices and wish to maintain the status quo or return to a former status by reversing the change process, 633

Resocialization. The process of shedding one or more positions and taking on others; it involves learning new norms, behaviors, and values suitable to the newly acquired status, 122

Revolution. Social and political transformations of a nation that result when states fail to fulfill their expected responsibilities, 496

Revolutionary movements. Attempt to transform society to bring about a total change in society by overthrowing existing power structures and replacing them with new ones; these movements often resort to violent means to achieve goals, 633

Riots are outbreaks of illegal violence against random or shifting targets committed by crowds expressing frustration or anger against people, property, or groups in power, 624

Rituals are ceremonies or repetitive practices, often to invoke a sense of awe of the sacred and to make certain ideas sacred, 431

Role conflict. Conflict between the roles of two or more social statuses, 152

Role strain. Tension between roles within one of the social statuses, 150

Role-taking. The process by which individuals take others into account by imagining themselves in the position of the other, 116

Roles. The expected behaviors, rights, obligations, responsibilities, and privileges assigned to a social status, 150

Rumors. Forms of mass behavior in which unsupported or unproven reports about a problem, issue, or concern circulate widely throughout the public, 624

Rural areas. Areas having fewer than 1,000 people per square mile, 582

Sample is a small group of systematically chosen people in survey research who represent a much larger group, 41

Sanctions. Rewards and penalties that reinforce norms, 90

Science. The systematic process of producing human knowledge; it uses empirical research methods to discover facts and test theories, 638

Secondary analysis uses existing data, information that has already been collected in other studies—including data banks such as the national census, 40

Secondary deviance. Occurs when an individual continues to violate a norm and begins to take on a deviant identity *because* of being labeled as deviant, 182

Secondary groups. Groups characterized by formal, impersonal, and businesslike relationships; often temporary, based on a specific limited purpose or goal, 155

Secularization. The diminishing influence and role of religion in everyday life; involves a movement away from supernatural and sacred interpretations of the world and toward decisions based on empirical evidence and logic, 454

Self. Refers to the perceptions we have of who we are, 115

Self-fulfilling prophecy refers to a belief or a prediction becomes a reality, in part because of the prediction, 183

Sex. A biological term referring to ascribed genetic, anatomical, and hormonal differences between males and females, 304

Sexuality refers to culturally shaped meanings both of sexual acts and of how we experience our own bodies--especially in relation to the bodies of others, 305

Sick role. The role or position in society occupied by the ill; the sick role is not punished but is tolerated as long as the sick individual cooperates and acts to overcome illness, returning as soon as possible to fulfill his or her usual social roles, 523

Side-effect discrimination refers to practices in one institutional area that have a negative impact because they are linked to practices in another institutional area; because institutions are interdependent, discrimination in one results in unintentional discrimination in others, 276

Significant others. Parents, guardians, relatives, siblings, or important individuals whose primary and sustained interactions with the individual are especially influential, 117

Social change. Variations or alterations over time in the behavior patterns, culture (including norms and values), and structure of society, 607

Social class. The wealth, power, and prestige rankings that individuals hold in society; a large group with similar rankings, 129

Social construction of reality. The process by which individuals and groups shape reality through social interaction, 102

Social institutions. Organized, patterned, and enduring sets of social structures that provide guidelines for behavior and help each society meet its basic survival needs, 19

Social mobility refers the extent of individual movement up or down in the class system, changing one's social position in society—especially relative to one's parents, 231

Social movements. Consciously organized attempts outside of established institutional mechanisms to enhance or resist change through group action, 630

Social networks refer to individuals linked together by one or more social relationships, connecting us to the larger society. 141

Social processes. Take place through actions of people in institutions and other social units or structures, 20

Social reform movements seek to change some specific dimension of society, usually involving legislative policy modification or appeals to the courts, 632

Social stratification. How individuals and groups are layered or ranked in society according to how many valued resources they possess, 220

Social structure. The stable patterns of interactions, statuses, roles, and institutions that provide stability for the society and bring order to individuals' lives, 18

Social units. Interconnected parts of the social world ranging from small groups to societies, 18

Social world model. The levels of analysis in our social surroundings as an interconnected series of small groups, organizations, institutions, and societies, 16

Socialization is the lifelong process of learning to become a member of the social world, beginning at birth and continuing until death, 110

Socialized medicine provides a government-supported consumer service that assures equal access to health care for all citizens of a country, 528

Society. An organized and interdependent group of individuals who live together in a specific geographical area and who interact more with each other than they do with outsiders; they cooperate for the attainment of common goals and share a common culture over time, 69

Sociological imagination. The recognition of the complex and interactive relationship between micro-level individual experiences and macro-level public issues, 10

Sociology. The scientific study of social life, social change, and the social causes and consequences of human behavior, 6

Spurious relationships occur when there is no causal relationship between the independent and dependent variables, but they vary together, often due to a third variable affecting both of them, 38

Status is a social position in society, 149

Stigma is disapproval attached to disobeying the expected norms so that a person is discredited as less than normal, 199

Structural-functional perspective (See functional theory)

Subculture. The culture of a meso-level subcommunity that distinguishes itself from the dominant culture of the larger society, 96

Subjugation. The subordination of one group to another that holds power and authority, 280

Survey method. Research method used by sociologists who want to gather information directly from a number of people regarding how they think or feel or what they do; two common survey forms are the interview and the questionnaire, 37

Symbolic interaction theory. Sees humans as active agents who create shared meanings of symbols and events and then interact on the basis of those meanings, 51

Symbols are actions or objects that represent something else and therefore have meaning beyond their own existence. Flags and wedding rings are examples, 51

Technology. The practical application of tools, skills, and knowledge to meet human needs and extend human abilities, 75

Terrorism is the planned use of random, unlawful (or illegal) violence of threat of violence against civilians to create (or raise) fear and intimidate citizens in order to advance the terrorist group's political or ideological goal, 198

Theocracy. Religion in which religious leaders rule society in accordance with God's presumed wishes, 442

Theoretical perspective. The broadest theories in sociology; overall approaches to understanding the social world and social problems; such basic views of society guide sociologists' ideas and research, 51

Theories are statements or explanations regarding how and why two or more facts are related to each other and the connections between these facts, 35

Total institution. A place that cuts people off from the rest of society and totally controls their lives in the process of resocialization; examples are prisons and boot camps, 122

Totalitarian government. Form of government that almost totally controls people's lives, 488

Transnationalism is the process by which immigrants create multinational social relations that link together their original societies with their new locations; this usually entails national loyalty to more than one country, 132

Triangulation is the utilization of two or more methods of data collection to enhance the amount of data for analysis and the accuracy of the findings, 41

Urbanization is the pattern of movement from rural areas to cities, 558

Values. Nonmaterial shared judgments about what is desirable or undesirable, right or wrong, good or bad; they express the basic ideals of any culture, 87

Variables. Concepts (ideas) that can vary in frequency of occurrence from one time, place, or person to another, 36

Victimless crimes (public order crimes). Acts committed by or between consenting adults, 192

War. Armed conflict occurring within, between, or among societies or groups, 501

Wealth. One's income, property, and total assets, 243

White-collar (or occupational) crime is the violation of law by an individual or group in the course of a legitimate, respected occupation or financial activity, 196

Index

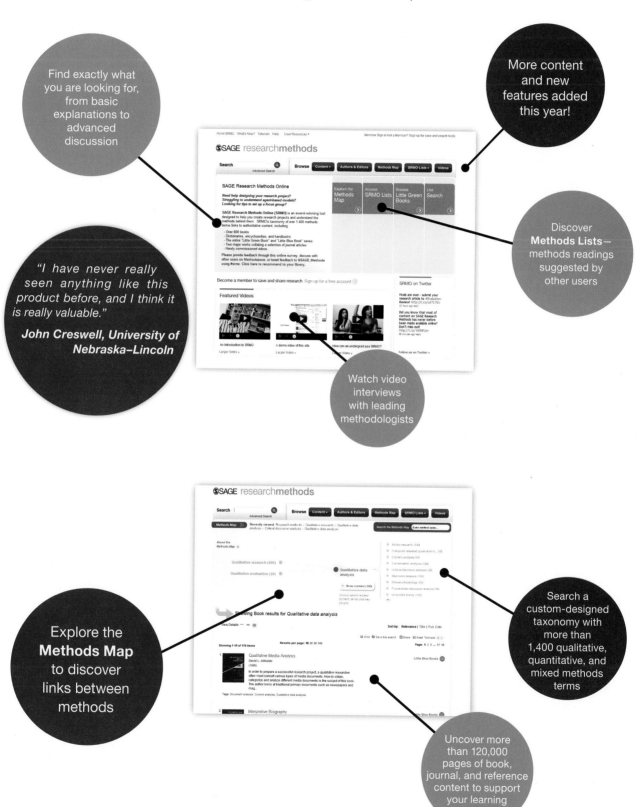